LEABHARLANN CHONTAE

A TO Z
OF SPORT

Also by Trevor Montague

A to Z of Everything

A TO Z

OF SPORT

The Compendium of
Sporting Knowledge

TREVOR MONTAGUE

LITTLE, BROWN

A *Little, Brown* Book

First published in Great Britain in 2004 by Little, Brown

Copyright © 2004 Trevor Montague

The moral right of the author has been asserted.

A CIP catalogue record for this book is available
from the British Library.

ISBN 0 316 72645 1 (hardback with jacket)
ISBN 0 316 72946 9 (laminated with board)

Typeset by M Rules
Printed and bound in Great Britain by
The Bath Press, Bath

Little, Brown
An imprint of
Time Warner Book Group UK
Brettenham House
Lancaster Place
London WC2E 7EN
www.twbg.co.uk

Contents

C
O
N
T
E
N
T
S

ABOUT THE AUTHOR

Trevor Montague is the founder of the British Quiz Association and widely acknowledged as one of the leading general knowledge experts in Great Britain. But less well known is Trevor's passion for sport – both watching and playing it.

A useful sportsman in several spheres he competed for many years for his local athletics club in Crawley and had the versatility to run 100 metres in 11 seconds and 1500 metres in under four minutes, and just for good measure he was the regular Southern League club shot putter and hurdler too. In fact, Trevor has the distinction of having competed in every track and field event for his club.

Despite his enthusiasm, Trevor was only ever a rank-and-file athlete but the popularity of the BBC's *Superstars* series in the late 1970s spawned a new type of athletic event in which he was able to thrive. This type of competition favoured a jack of all trades with good fitness levels, and Trevor's ability to chin the bar 60 times in one minute, complete five basketball lay-ups in 20 seconds, run a sub-two-minute 800 metres, clean and jerk 100kg, or adapt to skill sports such as table tennis and archery, won him the Crawley Sportsman of the Year title in 1981 and 1982, and for the next ten years he mopped up titles in gyms all over England. He came out of retirement to compete in the Zest Peugeot National Fitness Challenge in 2000 at which, in an original field of more than 10,000, Trevor managed to row two kilometres in 6 minutes 36 seconds, cycle five kilometres on a lifecycle in 3 minutes 35 seconds, run a mile in 4 minutes 41 seconds and bench-press at least 100kg ten times to gain the bronze medal.

Trevor, at the age of 50, is now getting to grips with a new sport of cycling and, thanks to a Pete Read training schedule, he managed to gain a first place in an open race in April 2004, ride a 10-mile time trial in 22 minutes 30 seconds and win the Crawley Wheelers All-Members Cup for 2004.

Introduction

For many years I have pounded the streets, pumped iron, punched inanimate objects, dragged tyres along, climbed ropes, watched my diet, hopped, skipped, jumped, stretched, twisted and tumbled, all in the vain hope of reaching that state of athletic nirvana where all goals have been achieved and the world takes note of my unrivalled athletic prowess.

In reality it has been a hopeless task, since for every Phil Taylor there are a hundred 'arrer' throwers like myself whose simple ambition is to hit the treble twenty with three consecutive darts; for every Ronnie O'Sullivan there are a thousand snooker players striving to make that elusive 50 break; and for every Tiger Woods there are countless golfers who eulogise over that sunny day when they were cheated out of a sub-par round by having to abort on the third hole due to a lack of golf balls! To coin a phrase: 'Many are called, but few are chosen.'

But what is the fascination of sport? Why do some 20,000 apparently normal, well-adjusted people go stir-crazy each April and feel compelled to break loose and run 26 miles through the streets of London, and why do millions of spectators line the streets of France every July to catch a fleeting glimpse of a cyclist's coloured jersey? To corrupt a famous observation of Karl Marx: sport is undoubtedly the opium of the people. It is a common language throughout the world and unites – and occasionally divides – nations, cities and households alike.

What underlies this fascination is passion. The late, great Liverpool manager Bill Shankly perhaps captured this feeling definitively in a Sunday newspaper article in 1981 when he stated that 'Some people think football is a matter of life and death. I don't like that attitude. I can assure them it is much more serious than that.'

My goal now is to do justice to our – participants and spectators – fascination with and passion for sport

The point of the *A to Z of Sport* is to encapsulate in a single volume a comprehensive coverage of as many different sports as I could possibly justify without resorting to the macabre and ridiculous and thus provide the ultimate sporting companion.

Although I have included quite a lot of minority sports there were some I have omitted until they become better established or prove they are more than just local oddities. Gurning, bog-snorkelling (both prone and on bicycle), cheese-rolling, welly throwing, shin-kicking and conkers are examples of sporting activities I deemed inappropriate for this first volume but I am prepared to be persuaded for subsequent editions.

The format is consistent throughout the book – that is to say, obscure sports will have an introductory page only; minority sports will have some statistical information following the introduction; and more popular sports will additionally include biographies of leading protagonists. I have adhered to my principle of trying not to include superfluous information, and to this end my biographies are by and large statistical records rather than subjective appraisals.

Result sections are as fully up-to-date as they could be at the time of going to press (Graeme Souness's replacement of Sir Bobby Robson as manager of Newcastle United FC being the last item included for those interested in such things), although I have isolated all the results from the 2004 Olympics and given the Games its own section at the front of the book.

Biographical information of sporting stars who remain active are generally qualified by giving a date as to their efficacy but in other instances can be inferred. Sometimes it will be useful to check the sporting chronology for 2003 and 2004 to get a wider perspective of things – for instance, Shane Warne and Muttiah Muralitharan have both held the record for Test wickets this year so it would perhaps be more useful to check the dates in the chronology section. Similarly, Yelena Isinbayeva broke the pole vault world record several times this summer by the almost obligatory centimetre and the dates are given in this section.

This is the first *A to Z of Sport*. I hope you are entertained and edified by it. I have endeavoured to give it a global feel, but it is the nature of some sports that they are dominated by a particular nation. Since this is a book published in Britain there may be a preponderance of British data, especially in the Athens 2004 report – I hope this is understandable and acceptable.

Finally, and most importantly, although I have done my utmost to achieve 100 per cent accuracy, with a project of this magnitude covering such a wide range of sports, it seems unavoidable that mistakes will be made, for which I apologise. I would be delighted to have these pointed out to ensure that future editions are as correct as can be. If you wish to do so, or wish to suggest new ideas for the book, please write to me c/o Time Warner Book Group UK.

Trevor Montague
September 2004

ACKNOWLEDGEMENTS

I would like to thank the following people for their help in the production of this work:

Mark Bytheway ensured I wouldn't get caught by a sucker-punch in the boxing ring and was also one of the two assistant referees on the football field. Dag Griffiths coxed much of the rowing section in superb style and Mark Kerr tackled many of the rugby union biographies without flinching. Eric Kilby played an absolute blinder on the football field and also drove the motor sports section home before changing into silks to help out in the stables. Eric would have to be my nomination for man of the match. Mel Kinsey was my quarterback on American football and ensured the baseball section had no curve-balls. Trevor Parry raked the bunkers and helped out on the back nine of the golf course. Geoff Thomas played with a remarkably straight bat in attacking the cricket biographies – a world-class all-rounder and captain's dream. Mention should be made that former Sussex and England fast bowler John Snow fielded at third man. (I should add that John was adamant he was not worthy of inclusion in the final team for biography selection but fortunately I was captain so overruled him.) Tim Westcott was the other assistant referee on the football field and also ensured no high sticking on the ice-hockey rink. John Wilson patrolled the touch-line magnificently in the rugby league section.

Special thanks to Ruth Benjamin for helping me with the pre-submission proofreading and generally availing herself freely to further the cause. I must also thank my old training partner, former international decathlete Phil Lewis, for being a sporting inspiration to me and more importantly for arranging the photocopying of the proofs. Another source of inspiration was the redoubtable Jeremy Beadle MBE, who introduced me to some sporting cognoscenti and lent support generally.

My all-star domestiques include Gavin Fuller, Ann Kelly, Anita Oxley, Ritchie Venner and Neil White.

Finally, a huge thank you to June for supplying the halftime oranges.

ABBREVIATIONS: COUNTRIES

The names of countries and territories are abbreviated as follows:

ALG	Algeria	INA	Indonesia
AND	Andorra	IND	India
ARG	Argentina	IOP	Individual Olympic Participant
ARM	Armenia	IRE	All-Ireland
AUS	Australia	IRI	Islamic Republic of Iran
AUT	Austria	IRL	Republic of Ireland
AZE	Azerbaijan	IRN	Iran
BAH	Bahamas	ISL	Iceland
BDI	Burundi	ISR	Israel
BEL	Belgium	ITA	Italy
BER	Bermuda	JAM	Jamaica
BLR	Belarus	JPN	Japan
BOH	Bohemia	KAZ	Kazakhstan
BRA	Brazil	KEN	Kenya
BUL	Bulgaria	KGZ	Kyrgyzstan
BWI	British West Indies	KOR	Republic of Korea (South Korea)
CAN	Canada	KSA	(Kingdom of) Saudi Arabia
CEY	Ceylon	KUW	Kuwait
CHI	Chile	LAT	Latvia
CHN	People's Republic of China	LIE	Liechtenstein
CIS	Confederation of Independent States	LTU	Lithuania
	(previously Soviet Union)	LUX	Luxembourg
CIV	Ivory Coast	MAR	Morocco
CMR	Cameroon	MAS	Malaysia
COL	Colombia	MDA	Moldova
CRC	Costa Rica	MEX	Mexico
CRO	Croatia	MGL	Mongolia
CUB	Cuba	MLI	Mali
CYP	Cyprus	MLT	Malta
CZE	Czech Republic	MON	Monaco
DEN	Denmark	MOZ	Mozambique
DJI	Djibouti	NAM	Namibia
DMA	Dominica	NED	Netherlands
DOM	Dominican Republic	NGR	Nigeria
ECU	Ecuador	NIR	Northern Ireland
EGY	Egypt	NOR	Norway
ENG	England	NRH	Northern Rhodesia
ERI	Eritrea	NZL	New Zealand
ESP	Spain	PAK	Pakistan
EST	Estonia	PAN	Panama
ETH	Ethiopia	PAR	Paraguay
FIJ	Fiji	PER	Peru
FIN	Finland	PHI	Philippines
FRA	France	POL	Poland
FRG	Federal Republic of Germany (West Germany)	POR	Portugal
		PRK	People's Republic of Korea (North Korea)
GBR	Great Britain & Northern Ireland (Great Britain & Ireland until 1922)	PUR	Puerto Rico
		QAT	Qatar
GDR	German Democratic Republic (East Germany)	RHO	Rhodesia
		ROM	Romania
GEO	Georgia	RSA	Republic of South Africa
GER	Germany	RUS	Russia/Russian Federation
GHA	Ghana	SAF	South Africa (before June 1961)
GRE	Greece	SAM	Western Samoa
GRN	Grenada	SCG	Serbia & Montenegro
GUA	Guatemala	SCO	Scotland
GUY	Guyana	SEN	Senegal
HAI	Haiti	SKN	St Kitts & Nevis
HKG	Hong Kong	SLO	Slovenia
HUN	Hungary	SMR	San Marino

SOM	Somalia	TUN	Tunisia
SRI	Sri Lanka	TUR	Turkey
SUI	Switzerland	UKR	Ukraine
SUR	Surinam	URS	Soviet Union
SVK	Slovakia	URU	Uruguay
SWE	Sweden	USA	United States of
SWZ	Swaziland		America
SYR	Syria	UZB	Uzbekistan
TAN	Tanzania	VEN	Venezuela
TCH	Czechoslovakia	WAL	Wales
THA	Thailand	YUG	Yugoslavia
TJK	Tajikistan	ZAI	Zaire
TPE	Chinese Taipei	ZAM	Zambia
TRI	Trinidad & Tobago	ZIM	Zimbabwe

FAMOUS PEOPLE

AUTHOR'S NOTE

Note on metric/imperial units
Metric weights and measures are standard throughout this book. However, imperial units of measurement are employed in the rules or laws of some sports (especially those based principally in the United States). In such cases, measurements are given in imperial units with the metric equivalent in parentheses.
   The laws of a few sports (e.g. association football) specify metric units of measurement that are exact conversions of previous imperial measurements still in common use, particularly in Great Britain. In these cases only, metric units are cited with their imperial equivalents in parentheses.

Note on German Olympic teams
Please note that competitors from East and West Germany took part in the Olympic Games as a unified German team between 1948 and 1964.

THE ATHENS OLYMPICS

(The XXVIII Olympiad in Athens 13–29 August 2004)

The Opening Ceremony of the 2004 Summer Olympics was held on 13 August 2004 at the Olympic Stadium, Maroussi, Athens, Greece. Seventy-two thousand spectators attended the event, and 11,099 athletes from 202 countries were eligible to participate in the parade.

A 28-second countdown paced by the sounds of an amplified heartbeat led into the fireworks and theatre depicting thousands of years of Greek history, Eros the god of love hovering above throughout the spectacular pageant. The countdown itself signified the 28 Olympiads since the inaugural Modern Games. This is a little confusing since there have been only 25 Summer Olympic events since the 1896 Games (26 if you count the interim games of 1906 held in Athens as a decennial anniversary), the 1916, 1940 and 1944 Games having been cancelled due to war. However, the word 'Olympiad' in this context means the four-year period between proposed Games.

Tradition was broken by necessity when St Lucia was given the honour of being the first nation into the stadium. In the past, the Greek nation has always led the opening parade and the host nation completed (as indeed did the Greeks in 2004). That St Lucia entered first is explained by the use of the Greek alphabet to spell the countries' names.

Dutchman DJ Tiësto provided the music, becoming the first disc jockey ever to spin music live during an Olympic parade. Icelandic singer Björk performed the song 'Oceania' immediately after the Parade of Nations ended. Dignitaries attending the opening included President George Bush Sr, Tony Blair, Crown Prince Haakon of Norway and Crown Prince Fredrik of Denmark.

International Olympic Committee President Jacques Rogge delivered a speech before handing over to Greek president Costis Stephanopoulos, who declared the Games officially open.

The Opening Ceremony culminated with the end of the torch relay, a tradition begun when Berlin hosted the games in 1936. Nikos Galis, considered to be the greatest Greek basketball player of all time, entered the stadium first and passed the torch, in sequential order, to Greek football legend Mimis Domazos, 1992 Olympic 100m hurdles champion Paraskevi Patoulidou, 1996 and 2000 Olympic weightlifting champion Akakios Kakhiasvillis, and 1996 Olympic gymnastics champion Ioannis Melissanidis. The torch was finally passed to the 1996 Olympic boardsailing champion Nikolaos Kaklamanakis, who lit a giant torch-shaped cauldron that would burn for the duration of the Olympics. In 2004 the torch

relay, which began at Olympia, visited every continent for the first time.

The first gold medal of the Games was won by China's Li Du in the women's 10m air rifle competition but before this we were reminded of the inevitable cloud of controversy hanging over all modern sporting competitions when the host countries' two leading sprinters, Ekaterini Thanou and Konstantinos Kenteris, failed to turn up for random dope testing and were immediately withdrawn from the Games.

The first British medal was a silver won by Peter Waterfield and Leon Taylor in the synchronised diving. The first gold medal won by Great Britain is a little more complex. The Yngling sailing crew were so comfortably ahead of the field that they won the competition with a day to spare, although *officially* the first gold medal winner in completed competition was thought to be Chris Hoy in the 1km cycling time-trial. However, Bettina Hoy of Germany was adjudged to have walked through the start twice during the show jumping phase of the three-day event and was penalised sufficiently to give Leslie Law the gold – three days after the original result.

British athletes were concerned in many of the judging controversies; Alison Williamson made the archery semi-final after her opponent was deemed to have shot out of turn in the quarterfinal match. Helen Reeves was originally placed fourth in the women's K1 slalom and the picture of her glimpsing the result board during a BBC interview to find she was actually in bronze medal position due to a retrospective penalty awarded against Peggy Dickens of France was one of the moments of the Games. Conversely, James Goddard was initially awarded the bronze medal on the disqualification of Aaron Peirsol for an illegal turn during the swimming 200m backstroke final but was then stood down to fourth following an appeal from the American camp. Amazingly, Campbell Walsh was then promoted from bronze to silver in the men's K1 slalom following a retrospective penalty awarded against Fabien Lefevre of France. Pippa Funnell won a bronze as a result of Bettina Hoy's misfortune which cost the German rider two gold medals.

Perhaps the biggest travesty of justice was in the men's all-round gymnastics competition when it was found that the bronze-medallist Yang Tae-Young had inadvertently been docked a tenth of a point in error and should have been awarded the gold. The gymnastic judges hardly covered themselves in glory when they succumbed to 'people power' during the men's high bar competition where they upgraded Alexei Nemov's score following a ten-minute protest by the spectators.

Fortunately this incident did not affect the medal positions.

On a more positive note there were some outstanding performances. From a British perspective swimmer Stephen Parry's unexpected bronze medal in the 200m butterfly lifted the whole team. Parry had only sneaked into the last 16 by five hundredths of a second and then in the semi-final miraculously posted the fastest time to gain lane four in the final. David Davies smashed the British record for 1500m freestyle by 12 seconds and finished only two seconds behind Grant Hackett, the greatest distance swimmer of all time. Cyclist Bradley Wiggins gained three medals of different colours and his gold medal ride against Brad McGee in the 4000m pursuit was a reversal of fortune for the Australian, who had caught Wiggins at the world championships during their last encounter. Ben Ainslie ended the first day of the sailing Finn class in 19th place having been disqualified in race two for a technical infringement but dominated thereafter for a comfortable gold. The two outstanding British performances were Kelly Holmes' incredible 800m/1500m double and Matthew Pinsent's fourth consecutive rowing gold medal, which was won after a manic finish to the coxless fours. Special mention must be made of Amir Khan, the lone British boxer to attend the Games. The 17-year-old captured the hearts of the British nation with his mature boxing and his outstanding ability. He gained a silver medal, losing narrowly in the final to an amateur boxing legend, but a star was most definitely born. (The Val Barker Trophy for the most outstanding boxer of the Games was awarded to Bakhtiyar Artayev of Kazakhstan.)

From a general perspective Kathrin Boron of Germany emulated Matthew Pinsent's feat of four consecutive rowing gold medals but even this was eclipsed by fellow German Birgit Fischer, who won her eighth canoeing gold medal since she started her quest at Moscow in 1980. Jana Pittman of Australia finished only fifth in the final of the women's 400m hurdles in a modest, for her, 53.92 seconds but when one considers she had keyhole surgery on her knee less than three weeks before the final it was a meritorious accomplishment. Cian O'Connor rode Waterford Crystal to Ireland's only medal, and a gold at that, in the show jumping competition – a bitter-sweet moment as it was Britain's Nick Skelton who led into the final round. The climax of the men's shot put competition highlighted the intensity and burning desire of competitors to succeed at Olympic level when American Adam Nelson lost the gold medal on an inferior second-best put despite having the two longest throws in the competition (adjudged marginal fouls). His frustration was for all to see when he hurled the shot out towards 22m in the final round only to again foul the ground outside the circle. He refused to leave the circle until he could see the evidence of the foul and appeared oblivious to his error. The undoubted star of the Games though has to be American swimmer Michael Phelps, who won six gold and two bronze medals in his eight swimming races (although he didn't actually swim in the final of the 4 × 100 medley relay, giving up his place to team-mate Ian Crocker).

The last gold medal was won by Stefano Baldini of Italy in a dramatic men's marathon that was marred by the impeding of the race leader, Vanderlei de Lima of Brazil, by a protester at the same 22-mile point that witnessed the sad demise of British athlete Paula Radcliffe during the women's race. De Lima strode on gloriously having lost 15 seconds of his 30-second lead and ultimately won the bronze medal. He was awarded the Baron de Coubertin medal for his sportsmanship.

The closing ceremony took place on 29 August with Kelly Holmes carrying the flag for Great Britain.

Final Medals Table

	Country	Gold	Silver	Bronze	Total		Country	Gold	Silver	Bronze	Total
1	United States	35	39	29	103	22	Turkey	3	3	4	10
2	China	32	17	14	63	23	Poland	3	2	5	10
3	Russia	27	27	38	92	24	New Zealand	3	2	0	5
4	Australia	17	16	16	49	25	Thailand	3	1	4	8
5	Japan	16	9	12	37	26	Belarus	2	6	7	15
6	Germany	14	16	18	48	27	Austria	2	4	1	7
7	France	11	9	13	33	28	Ethiopia	2	3	2	7
8	Italy	10	11	11	32	29	Iran	2	2	2	6
9	South Korea	9	12	9	30	29	Slovakia	2	2	2	6
10	Great Britain	9	9	12	30	31	Taiwan	2	2	1	5
11	Cuba	9	7	11	27	32	Georgia	2	2	0	4
12	Ukraine	9	5	9	23	33	Bulgaria	2	1	9	12
13	Hungary	8	6	3	17	34	Jamaica	2	1	2	5
14	Romania	8	5	6	19	34	Uzbekistan	2	1	2	5
15	Greece	6	6	4	16	36	Morocco	2	1	0	3
16	Norway	5	0	1	6	37	Denmark	2	0	6	8
17	Netherlands	4	9	9	22	38	Argentina	2	0	4	6
18	Brazil	4	3	3	10	39	Chile	2	0	1	3
19	Sweden	4	1	2	7	40	Kazakhstan	1	4	3	8
20	Spain	3	11	5	19	41	Kenya	1	4	2	7
21	Canada	3	6	3	12	42	Czech Republic	1	3	4	8

	Country	Gold	Silver	Bronze	Total
43	South Africa	1	3	2	6
44	Croatia	1	2	2	5
45	Lithuania	1	2	0	3
46	Egypt	1	1	3	5
46	Switzerland	1	1	3	5
48	Indonesia	1	1	2	4
49	Zimbabwe	1	1	1	3
50	Azerbaijan	1	0	4	5
51	Belgium	1	0	2	3
52	Bahamas	1	0	1	2
52	Israel	1	0	1	2
54	Cameroon	1	0	0	1
54	Dominican Republic	1	0	0	1
54	Ireland	1	0	0	1
54	United Arab Emirates	1	0	0	1
58	North Korea	0	4	1	5
59	Latvia	0	4	0	4
60	Mexico	0	3	1	4

	Country	Gold	Silver	Bronze	Total
61	Portugal	0	2	1	3
62	Finland	0	2	0	2
62	Serbia and Montenegro	0	2	0	2
64	Slovenia	0	1	3	4
65	Estonia	0	1	2	3
66	Hong Kong	0	1	0	1
66	India	0	1	0	1
66	Paraguay	0	1	0	1
69	Nigeria	0	0	2	2
69	Venezuela	0	0	2	2
71	Colombia	0	0	1	1
71	Eritrea	0	0	1	1
71	Mongolia	0	0	1	1
71	Syrian Arab Republic	0	0	1	1
71	Trinidad and Tobago	0	0	1	1

The United States finished top of the medals table for the third-consecutive Summer Olympics, but the emergence of China in second place with 32 golds, its best-ever placing, augurs well for the nation in Beijing in four years time.

Six nations won golds for the first time: Chile, Dominican Republic, Georgia, Israel, Taiwan and United Arab Emirates.

Two nations won medals for the first time: Paraguay and Eritrea. Serbia and Montenegro was formerly called Yugoslavia so does not count as they won medals under their former name.

Australia, with 16 golds in Sydney, became the first nation to increase its gold medal tally four years after hosting the Summer Games. They also had the distinction of placing second after the Bahamas in winning the most medals per capita; approximately one for every 400,000 head of population. The Bahamas gained one for every 146,000. Bottom of this particular table was India with one medal for its 1.027 billion population, although Pakistan did not win a single medal.

In all, 75 of the 202 competing nations won at least one medal. In Sydney, 80 won medals.

THE ATHENS OLYMPICS

Medal Winners

(WR = World Record; OR = Olympic Record)

	Gold	Silver	Bronze
Archery			
MEN			
70m individual	Marco Galiazzo (ITA)	Hiroshi Yamamoto (JPN)	Tim Cuddihy (AUS)
70m team	South Korea (Im Dong-Hyun, Yong Ho Jang, Kyung Mo Park)	Taiwan (Szu Yuan Chen, Ming Huang Liu, Cheng Pang Wang)	Ukraine (Dmytro Hrachov, Viktor Ruban, Oleksandr Serdyuk)
WOMEN			
70m individual	Sung Hyun Park (KOR)	Sung Jin Lee (KOR)	Alison Williamson (GBR)
70m team	South Korea (Sung Jin Lee, Sung Hyun Park, Yun Mi-Jin)	China (Ying He, Sang Lin, Juanjuan Zhang)	Taiwan (Li Ju Chen, Hui Ju Wu, Shu Chi Yuan)

	Gold	Silver	Bronze
Athletics			
MEN			
100m	Justin Gatlin (USA) 9.85	Francis Obikwelu (POR) 9.86	Maurice Greene (USA) 9.87
200m	Shawn Crawford (USA) 19.79	Bernard Williams (USA) 20.01	Justin Gatlin (USA) 20.03
400m	Jeremy Wariner (USA) 44.00	Otis Harris (USA) 44.16	Derrick Brew (USA) 44.42
800m	Yuriy Borzakovskiy (RUS) 1:44.45	Mbulaeni Mulaudzi (RSA) 1:44.61	Wilson Kipketer (DEN) 1:44.65
1500m	Hicham El Guerrouj (MAR) 3:34.18	Bernard Lagat (KEN) 3:34.30	Rui Silva (POR) 3:34.68
5000m	Hicham El Guerrouj (MAR) 13:14.39	Kenenisa Bekele (ETH) 13:14.59	Eliud Kipchoge (KEN) 13:15.10
10,000m	Kenenisa Bekele (ETH) 27:05.10 (OR)	Sileshi Sihine (ETH) 27:09.39	Zersenay Tadesse (ERI) 27:22.57
Marathon	Stefano Baldini (ITA) 2:10.55	Mebrahtom Keflezighi (USA) 2:11.29	Vanderlei de Lima (BRA) 2:12.11
110m hurdles	Xiang Liu (CHN) 12.91 (equals WR)	Terrence Trammell (USA) 13.18	Anier Garcia (CUB) 13.20
400m hurdles	Felix Sanchez (DOM) 47.63	Danny McFarlane (JAM) 48.11	Naman Keita (FRA) 48.26
3000m steeplechase	Ezekiel Kemboi (KEN) 8:05.81	Brimin Kipruto (KEN) 8:06.11	Paul Kipsiele Koech (KEN) 8:06.64
4 × 100m relay	Great Britain 38.07 (Jason Gardener, Darren Campbell, Marlon Devonish, Mark Lewis-Francis)	United States 38.08 (Shawn Crawford, Justin Gatlin, Coby Miller, Maurice Greene)	Nigeria 38.23 (Olusoji Fasuba, Uchenna Emedolu, Aaron Egbele, Deji Aliu)
4 × 400m relay	United States 2:55.91 (Otis Harris, Derrick Brew, Jeremy Wariner, Darold Williamson)	Australia 3:00.60 (John Steffensen, Mark Ormrod, Patrick Dwyer, Clinton Hill)	Nigeria 3:00.90 (James Godday, Musa Audu, Saul Weigopwa, Enefiok Udo Obong)
20km walk	Ivano Brugnetti (ITA) 1:19:40	Francisco Javier Fernandez (ESP) 1:19:45	Nathan Deakes (AUS) 1:20:02

	Gold	**Silver**	**Bronze**
50km walk	Robert Korzeniowski (POL) 3:38:46	Denis Nizhegorodov (RUS) 3:42:50	Aleksey Voyevodin (RUS) 3:43:34
High Jump	Stefan Holm (SWE) 2.36	Matt Hemmingway (USA) 2.34	Jaroslav Baba (CZE) 2.34
Long Jump	Dwight Phillips (USA) 8.59	John Moffitt (USA) 8.47	Joan Lino Martinez (ESP) 8.32
Pole Vault	Timothy Mack (USA) 5.95	Toby Stevenson (USA) 5.90	Giuseppe Gibilisco (ITA) 5.85
Triple Jump	Christian Olsson (SWE) 17.79	Marian Oprea (ROM) 17.55	Danila Burkenya (RUS) 17.48
Shot Put	Yuriy Bilonog (UKR) 21.16	Adam Nelson (USA) 21.16	Joachim Olsen (DEN) 21.07
Discus*	Virgilijus Alekna (LIT) 69.89	Zoltan Kovago (HUN) 67.04	Aleksander Tammert (EST) 66.66
Hammer**	Koji Murofushi (JPN) 82.91	Ivan Tikhon (BLR) 79.81	Esref Apak (TUR) 79.51
Javelin	Andreas Thorkildsen (NOR) 86.50	Vadims Vasilevskis (LAT) 84.95	Sergey Makarov (RUS) 84.84
Decathlon	Roman Sebrle (CZE) 8893	Bryan Clay (USA) 8820	Dmitriy Karpov (KAZ) 8725
	100m: (10.85secs, 894pts)	100m: (10.44secs, 989pts)	100m: (10.50secs, 975pts)
	Long Jump: (7.84m, 1020pts)	Long Jump: (7.96m, 1050pts)	Long Jump: (7.81m, 1012pts)
	Shot Put: (16.36m, 873pts)	Shot Put: (15.23m, 804pts)	Shot Put: (15.93m, 847pts)
	High Jump: (2.12m, 915pts)	High Jump: (2.06m, 859pts)	High Jump: (2.09m, 887pts)
	400m: (48.36secs, 892pts)	400m: (49.19secs, 852pts)	400m: (46.81secs, 968pts)
	110m Hurdles: (14.05secs, 968pts)	110m Hurdles: (14.13secs, 958pts)	110m Hurdles: (13.97secs, 978pts)
	Discus: (48.72m, 844pts)	Discus: (50.11m, 873pts)	Discus: (51.65m, 905pts)
	Pole Vault: 5.00m, 910pts)	Pole Vault: 4.90m, 880pts)	Pole Vault: 4.60m, 790pts)
	Javelin: (70.52m, 897pts)	Javelin: (69.71m, 885pts)	Javelin: (55.54m, 671pts)
	1500m: (4:40.00, 680pts)	1500m: (4:41.70, 670pts)	1500m: (4:38.10, 692pts)

*Robert Fazekas of Hungary won the discus final (70.93 OR) but was disqualified for subsequently trying to tamper with a sample during a dope test.
**Adrian Annus of Hungary won the hammer final (83.19) but was disqualified for refusing to take a second drug test despite passing the first.

WOMEN

100m	Yuliya Nesterenko (BLR) 10.93	Lauryn Williams (USA) 10.96	Veronica Campbell (JAM) 10.97
200m	Veronica Campbell (JAM) 22.05	Allyson Felix (USA) 22.18	Debbie Ferguson (BAH) 22.30
400m	Tonique Williams-Darling (BAH) 49.41	Ana Guevara (MEX) 49.56	Natalya Antyukh (RUS) 49.89
800m	Kelly Holmes (GBR) 1:56.38	Hasna Benhassi (MOR) 1:56.43	Jolanda Ceplak (SLO) 1:56.43
1500m	Kelly Holmes (GBR) 3:57.90	Tatyana Tomashova (RUS) 3:58.12	Maria Cioncan (ROM) 3:58.39
5000m	Meseret Defar (ETH) 14:45.65	Isabella Ochichi (KEN) 14:48.19	Tirunesh Dibaba (ETH) 14:51.83
10,000m	Huina Xing (CHN) 30:24.36	Ejegayehu Dibaba (ETH) 30:24.98	Derartu Tulu (ETH) 30:26.42
Marathon	Mizuki Noguchi (JPN) 2:26.20	Catherine Ndereba (KEN) 2:26.32	Deena Kastor (USA) 2:27.20
100m hurdles	Joanna Hayes (USA) 12.37	Olena Krasovska (UKR) 12.45	Melissa Morrison (USA) 12.56
400m hurdles	Fani Halkia (GRE) 52.82	Ionela Tirlea-Manolache (ROM) 53.38	Tetiana Tereshchuk-Antipova (UKR) 53.44
4 × 100m relay	Jamaica 41.73 (Tanya Lawrence, Sherone Simpson, Aleen Bailey, Veronica Campbell)	Russia 42.27 (Olga Fyodorova, Yuliya Tabakova, Irina Khabarova, Larisa Kruglova)	France 42.54 (Veronique Mang, Muriel Hurtis, Sylviane Felix, Christine Arron)
4 × 400m relay	United States 3:19.01 (DeeDee Trotter, Monique Henderson, Sanya Richards, Monique Hennagan)	Russia 3:20.16 (Olesya Krasnomovets, Natalya Nazarova, Olesya Zykina, Natalya Antyukh)	Jamaica 3:22.00 (Novlene Williams, Michelle Burgher, Nadia Davy, Sandie Richards)
20km walk	Athanasia Tsoumeleka (GRE) 1:29.12	Olimpiada Ivanova (RUS) 1:29.16	Jane Saville (AUS) 1:29.25
High Jump	Yelena Slesarenko (RUS) 2.06	Hestrie Cloete (RSA) 2.02	Viktoriya Styopina (UKR) 2.02
Long Jump	Tatyana Lebedeva (RUS) 7.07	Irina Simagina (RUS) 7.05	Tatyana Kotova (RUS) 7.05
Pole Vault	Yelena Isinbayeva (RUS) 4.91 WR	Svetlana Feofanova (RUS) 4.75	Anna Rogowska (POL) 4.70
Triple Jump	Francoise Mbango Etone (CAM) 15.30	Hrysopiyi Devetzi (GRE) 15.25	Tatyana Lebedeva (RUS) 15.14
Shot Put*	Yumileidi Cumba (CUB) 19.59	Nadine Kleinert (GER) 19.55	Svetlana Krivelyova (RUS) 19.49
Discus	Natalya Sadova (RUS) 67.02	Anastasia Kelesidou (GRE) 66.68	Irina Yatchenko (BLR) 66.17
Hammer	Olga Kuzenkova (RUS) 75.02 (OR)	Yipsi Moreno (CUB) 73.36	Yunaika Crawford (CUB) 73.16
Javelin	Osleidys Menendez (CUB) 71.53 (OR)	Steffi Nerius (GER) 65.82	Mirela Manjani (GRE) 64.29
Heptathlon	Carolina Kluft (SWE) 6952	Austra Skujyte (LIT) 6435	Kelly Sotherton (GBR) 6424
	100m hurdles: (13.21secs, 1093pts)	100m hurdles: (14.03secs, 974pts)	100m hurdles: (13.44secs, 1059pts)
	High Jump: (1.91m, 1119pts)	High Jump: (1.76m, 928pts)	High Jump: (1.85m, 1041pts)
	Shot: (14.77m, 845pts)	Shot: (16.40m, 955pts)	Shot: (13.29m, 747pts)
	200m: (23.27secs, 1052pts)	200m: (24.82secs, 903pts)	200m: (23.57secs, 1022pts)
	Long Jump: (6.78m, 1099pts)	Long Jump: (6.30m, 943pts)	Long Jump: (6.51m, 1010pts)
	Javelin: (48.89m, 839pts)	Javelin: (49.58m, 852pts)	Javelin: (37.19m, 613pts)
	800m: (2:14.15, 905pts)	800m: (2:15.92, 880pts)	800m: (2:12.27, 932pts)

*Irina Korzhanenko (RUS) 21.06 won the women's shot put but was subsequently disqualified after failing a drugs test.

Badminton

Men's Singles	Taufik Hidayat (INA)	Shon Seung Mo (KOR)	Soni Dwi Kuncoro (INA)
Men's Doubles	Kim Dong Moon/Ha Tae Kwon (KOR)	Lee Dong Soo/Yoo Yung Sung (KOR)	Eng Hian/Flandy Limpele (INA)
Women's Singles	Zhang Ning(CHN)	Mia Audina (NED)	Zhou Mi (CHN)
Women's Doubles	Zhang Jiewen/Yang Wei (CHN)	Huang Sui/Gao Ling (CHN)	Ra Kyung Min/Lee Kyung Won (KOR)

	Gold	Silver	Bronze
Mixed Doubles	Zhang Jun/Gao Ling (CHN)	Nathan Robertson/Gail Emms (GBR)	Jens Eriksen/Mette Schjoldager (DEN)

Baseball

	Gold	Silver	Bronze
Team Men	Cuba	Australia	Japan

Basketball

	Gold	Silver	Bronze
Team Men	Argentina (beat Italy 84-69 in gold medal match)	Italy	United States (beat Lithuania 104-96 in bronze medal match)
Team Women	United States (beat Australia 74-63 in gold medal match)	Australia	Russia (beat Brazil 71-62 in bronze medal match)

Boxing

	Gold	Silver	Bronze
under 48kg	Yan Bhartelemy Varela (CUB) (pts 21-16)	Atagun Yalcinkaya (TUR)	Sergey Kazakov (RUS) Shiming Zou (CHN)
48-51kg	Yuriorkis Gamboa Toledano (CUB) (pts 38-23)	Jerome Thomas (FRA)	Rustamhodza Rahimov (GER) Fuad Aslanov (AZE)
51-54kg	Guillermo Rigondeaux Ortiz (CUB) (pts 22-13)	Worapoj Petchkoom (THA)	Bahodirjon Sooltonov (UZB) Aghasi Mammadov(AZE)
54-57kg	Alexei Tichtchenko (RUS) (pts 39-17)	Song Guk Kim (PRK)	Vitali Tajbert (GER) Seok Hwan Jo (KOR)
57-60kg	Mario Cesar Kindelan Mesa (CUB) (pts 30-22)	Amir Khan (GBR)	Serik Yeleuov (KAZ) Murat Khrachev (RUS)
60-64kg	Manus Boonjumnong (THA) (pts 17-11)	Yudel Johnson Cedeno (CUB)	Boris Georgiev (BUL) Ionut Gheorghe (ROM)
64-69kg	Bakhtiyar Artayev (KAZ) (pts 36-26)	Lorenzo Aragon Armenteros (CUB)	Jung Joo Kim (KOR) Oleg Saitov (RUS)
69-75kg	Gaydarbek Gaydarbekov (RUS) (pts 28-18)	Gennadiy Golovkin (KAZ)	Andre Dirrell (USA) Suriya Prasathinphimai (THA)
75-81kg	Andre Ward (USA) (pts 20-13)	Magomed Aripgadjiev (BLR)	Utkirbek Haydarov (UZB) Ahmed Ismail (EGY)
81-91kg	Odlanier Solis Fonte (CUB) (pts 22-13)	Viktar Zuyev (BLR)	Naser Al Shami (SYR) Mohamed Elsayed (EGY)
over 91kg	Alexander Povetkin (RUS) w/o	Mohamed Aly (EGY) (unable to fight in final)	Roberto Cammarelle (ITA) Michel Lopez Nunez (CUB)

Canoeing

Flatwater and Slalom

MEN

	Gold	Silver	Bronze
K1 500m	Adam van Koeverden (CAN) 1:37.919	Nathan Baggaley (AUS) 1:38.467	Ian Wynne (GBR) 1:38.547
K1 1000m	Eirik Veraas Larsen (NOR) 3:25.897	Ben Fouhy (NZL) 3:27.413	Adam van Koeverden (CAN) 3:28.218
K2 500m	Germany 1:27.040 Ronald Rauhe/Tim Wieskoetter	Australia 1:27.920 Clint Robinson/Nathan Baggaley	Belarus 1:27.996 Raman Piatrushenka/Vadzim Makhneu
K2 1000m	Sweden 3:18.420 Markus Oscarsson/Henrik Nilsson	Italy 3:19.484 Antonio Rossi/Benjamino Bonomi	Norway 3:19.528 Eirik Veraas Larsen/Nils Olav Fjeldheim
K4 1000m	Hungary 2:56.919 Zoltan Kammerer/Botond Storcz/ Akos Vereckei/Gabor Horvath	Germany 2:58.659 Andreas Ihle/Mark Zabel/Bjoern Bach/Stefan Ulm	Slovakia 2:59.314 Richard Riszdorfer/Michal Riszdorfer/Erik Vlcek/Juraj Baca
C1 500m	Andreas Dittmer (GER) 1:46.383	David Cal (ESP) 1:46.723	Maxim Opalev (RUS) 1:47.767
C1 1000m	David Cal (ESP) 3:46.201	Andreas Dittmer (GER) 3:46.721	Attila Vajda (HUN) 3:49.025
C2 500m	China 1:40.278 Guanliang Meng/Wenjun Yang	Cuba 1:40.350 Ibrahim Rojas Blanco/Ledis Frank Balceiro Pajon	Russia 1:40.442 Alexander Kostoglod/Alexander Kovalev
C2 1000m	Germany 3:41.802 Christian Gille/Tomasz Wylenzek	Russia 3:42.990 Alexander Kostoglod/Alexander Kovalev	Hungary 3:43.106 Gyorgy Kozmann/Gyorgy Kolonics
K1 Slalom	Benoit Peschier (FRA) 187.96	Campbell Walsh (GBR) 190.17	Fabien Lefevre (FRA) 190.99
C1 Slalom	Tony Estanguet (FRA) 189.16	Michal Martikan (SVK) 189.28	Stefan Pfannmoeller (GER) 191.56
C2 Slalom	Slovakia 207.16 Pavel Hochschorner/Peter Hochschorner	Germany 210.98 Marcus Becker/Stefan Henze	Czech Republic 212.86 Jaroslav Volf/Ondrej Stepanek

WOMEN

	Gold	Silver	Bronze
K1 500m	Natasa Janics (HUN) 1:47.741	Josefa Idem (ITA) 1:49.729	Caroline Brunet (CAN) 1:50.601
K2 500m	Hungary 1:38.101 Katalin Kovacs/Natasa Janics	Germany 1:39.533 Birgit Fischer/Carolin Leonhardt	Poland 1:40.077 Aneta Pastuszka/Beata Sokolowska Kulesza

	Gold	Silver	Bronze
K4 500m	Germany 1:34.340 (Birgit Fischer, Maike Nollen, Katrin Wagner, Carolin Leonhardt)	Hungary 1:34.536 (Katalin Kovacs, Szilvia Szabo, Erzsebet Viski, Kinga Bota)	Ukraine 1:36.192 (Inna Osypenko, Tetyana Semykina, Hanna Balabanova, Olena Cherevatova)
K1 Slalom	Elena Kaliska (SVK) 210.03	Rebecca Giddens (USA) 214.62	Helen Reeves (GBR) 218.77

Cycling
Road
Men

	Gold	Silver	Bronze
Individual Time Trial (48k 3 laps)	Tyler Hamilton (USA) 57:31.74	Viateslav Ekimov (RUS) 57:50.58	Bobby Julich (USA) 57:58.19
Individual Road Race	Paolo Bettini (ITA) 5:41.44	Sergio Paulinho (POR) 5:41.45	Axel Merckx (BEL) 5:41.52

Women

	Gold	Silver	Bronze
Individual Time Trial	Leontien Zijlaard-van Moorsel (NED) 31:11.53	Deirdre Demet-Barry (USA) 31:35.62	Karin Thuerig (SUI) 31:54.89
Individual Road Race	Sara Carrigan (AUS) 3:24.24	Judith Arndt (GER) 3:24.31	Olga Slyusareva (RUS) 3:25.03

Track
Men

	Gold	Silver	Bronze
1km Individual Time Trial	Chris Hoy (GBR) 1:00.711 (OR)	Arnaud Tournant (FRA) 1:00.896	Stefan Nimke (GER) 1:01.186
Sprint	Ryan Bayley (AUS)	Theo Bos (NED)	Rene Wolff (GER)
4000m Individual Pursuit	Bradley Wiggins (GBR)	Brad McGee (AUS)	Sergi Escobar (ESP)
Team Pursuit	Australia (3:56.342 WR in qualifying) (Graeme Brown, Brett Lancaster, Brad McGee, Luke Roberts)	Great Britain (3:59.866 BR in qualifying) (Steve Cummings, Rob Hayles, Paul Manning, Bradley Wiggins) (Chris Newton and Bryan Steel awarded silver medals for early rounds)	Spain (Carlos Castano, Sergi Escobar, Asier Maeztu, Carlos Torrent)
Points Race	Mikhail Ignatyev (RUS) 93	Joan Llaneras (ESP) 82	Guido Fulst (GER) 79
Madison	Graeme Brown/Stuart O'Grady (AUS) 22	Franco Marvulli/Bruno Risi (SUI) 15	Rob Hayles/Bradley Wiggins (GBR) 12
Keirin	Ryan Bayley (AUS)	Jose Escuredo (ESP)	Shane Kelly (AUS)
Team Sprint	Germany (Jens Fiedler, Stefan Nimke, Rene Wolff)	Japan (Toshiaki Fushimi, Masaki Inoue, Tomohiro Nagatsuka)	France (Mickael Bourgain, Laurent Gane, Arnaud Tournant)

Women

	Gold	Silver	Bronze
500m Individual Time Trial	Ann Meares (AUS) 33.952 (WR)	Yonghua Jiang (CHN) 34.112	Natallia Tsylinskaya (BLR) 34.167
Sprint	Lori-Ann Muenzer (CAN)	Tamilla Abassova (RUS)	Anna Meares (AUS)
3000m Individual Pursuit	Sarah Ulmer (NZL)	Katie Mactier (AUS)	Leontien Zijlaard-van Moorsel (NED)
Points Race	Olga Slyusareva (RUS) 20	Belem Guerrero Mendez (MEX) 14	Maria Luisa Calle Williams (COL) 12

Mountain Biking

	Gold	Silver	Bronze
Cross-country Men	Julien Absalon (FRA) 2:15.02	Jose Antonio Hermida (ESP) 2:16.02	Bart Brentjens (NED) 2:17.05
Cross-country Women	Gunn-Rita Dahle (NOR) 1:56.51	Marie-Helene Premont (CAN) 1:57.50	Sabine Spitz (GER) 1:59.21

Diving
Men

	Gold	Silver	Bronze
10m Platform	Jia Hu (CHN) 540.78	Mathew Helm (AUS) 521.22	Liang Tian (CHN) 520.62
3m Springboard	Bo Peng (CHN) 531.21	Alexandre Despatie (CAN) 501.24	Dmitri Sautin (RUS) 496.89
Synchronised:10m Platform	Liang Tian/Jinghui Yang (CHN) 383.88	Peter Waterfield/Leon Taylor (GBR) 371.52	Mathew Helm/Robert Newbery (AUS) 366.84
Synchronised: 3m Springboard	Nikolaos Siranidis/Thomas Bimis (GRE) 353.34	Andreas Weis/Tobias Schellenberg (GER) 350.01	Robert Newbery/Steven Barnett (AUS) 349.59

Women

	Gold	Silver	Bronze
10m Platform	Chantelle Newbery (AUS) 590.31	Lishi Lao (CHN) 576.30	Loudy Tourky (AUS) 561.66
3m Springboard	Jingjing Guo (CHN) 390.09	Minxia Wu (CHN) 371.61	Yulia Pakhalina (RUS) 373.20
Synchronised:10m Platform	Lishi Lao/Ting Li (CHN) 352.14	Natalia Goncharova/Yulia Koltunova (RUS) 340.92	Blythe Hartley/Emilie Heymans (CAN) 327.78
Synchronised: 3m Springboard	Minxia Wu/Jingjing Guo (CHN) 336.90	Vera Ilyana/Yulia Pakhalina (RUS) 330.84	Irene Lashko/Chantelle Newbery (AUS) 309.30

	Gold	Silver	Bronze
Equestrian			
Individual Dressage	Anky van Grunsven (NED) SALINERO 79.278	Ulla Salzgeber (GER) RUSTY 78.833	Beatriz Ferrer-Salat (ESP) BEAUVALAIS 76.667
Team Dressage	Germany Ulla Salzgeber, RUSTY, Martin Schaudt, WELTALL, Hubertus Schmidt, WANSUELA SUERTE, Heike Kemmer, BONAPARTE	Spain Beatriz Ferrer-Salat, BEAUVALAIS, Rafael Soto, INVASOR, Juan Antonio Jimenez, GUIZO, Ignacio Rambla, OLEAJE	United States Deborah McDonald, BRENTINA, Robert Dover, KENNEDY, Guenter Seidel, ARAGON, Lisa Wilcox, RELEVANT 5
Individual Show Jumping	Cian O'Connor (IRE) Waterford Crystal 4	Rodrigo Pessoa (BRA) Baloubet Du Rouet 8	Chris Kappler (USA) Royal Kaliber 8
Team Show Jumping	Germany Ludger Beerbaum, GOLDFEVER, Marco Kutscher, MONTENDER, Otto Becker, CENTO, Christian Ahlmann, COSTER	United States Chris Kappler, ROYAL KALIBER, Beezie Madden, AUTHENTIC, McLain Ward, SAPPHIRE, Peter Wylde, FEIN CERA	Sweden Peder Fredericson, MAGIC BENGTSSON, Rolf-Goran Bengtsson, MAC KINLEY, Peter Eriksson, CARDENTO, Malin Baryard, BUTTERFLY FLIP
Individual Three-Day Eventing*	Leslie Law (GBR) SHEAR L' EAU 44.40	Kimberly Severson (USA) WINSOME ADANTE 45.20	Pippa Funnell (GBR) PRIMMORE'S PRIDE 46.60
Team Three-Day Eventing*	France Nicolas Touzaint, GALAN DE SAUVAGERE, Jean Teulere, ESPOIR DE LA MARE, Didier Courreges, DEBAT D'ESTRUVAL, Cedric Lyard, FINE MERVEILLE, Arnaud Boiteau, EXPO DU MOULIN	Great Britain Philippa Funnell, PRIMMORE'S PRIDE, Leslie Law, SHEAR L' EAU, Mary King, KING SOLOMON III, Jeanette Brakewell, OVER TO YOU, William Fox-Pitt, TAMARILLO	United States Kimberly Severson, WINSOME ADANTE, Amy Tryon, POGGIO II, Darren Chiacchia, WINDFALL 2, John Williams, CARRICK, Julie Richards, JACOB TWO TWO

*Bettina Hoy (GER) RINGWOOD COCKATOO was originally awarded the gold medal but was penalised for cantering through the start twice during the show jumping phase. The German team was also originally awarded gold but the deduction of Hoy's marks put them out of the medals.

	Gold	Silver	Bronze
Fencing			
MEN			
Individual Foil	Brice Guyart (FRA)	Salvatore Sanzo (ITA)	Andrea Cassara (ITA)
Team Foil	Italy (Simone Vanni, Salvatore Sanzo, Andrea Cassara)	China (Hanxiong Wu, Haibin Wang, Zhaozhi Dong, Chong Ye)	Russia (Renal Ganeev, Rouslan Nassiboulline, Youri Moltchan, Viatcheslav Pozdniakov)
Individual Épée	Marcel Fischer (SUI)	Lei Wang (CHN)	Pavel Kolobkov (RUS)
Team Épée	France (Hugues Obry, Eric Boisse, Fabrice Jeannet, Jerome Jeannet)	Hungary (Gabor Boczko, Ivan Kovacs, Geza Imre, Krisztian Kulcsar)	Germany (Daniel Strigel, Sven Schmid, Joerg Fiedler)
Individual Sabre	Aldo Montana (ITA)	Zsolt Nemcsik (HUN)	Vladislav Tretiak (UKR)
Team Sabre	France (Gael Touya, Julien Pillet, Damien Touya)	Italy (Gianpiero Pastore, Aldo Montano, Luigi Tarantino)	Russia (A. Diatchenko, S. Charikov, S. Pozdniakov, A. Yakimenko)
WOMEN			
Individual Foil	Valentina Vezzali (ITA)	Giovanna Trillini (ITA)	Sylwia Gruchala (POL)
Individual Épée	Timea Nagy (HUN)	Laura Flessel-Colovic (FRA)	Maureen Nisima (FRA)
Team Épée	Russia (O. Ermakova, A. Sivkova, T. Logounova, K. Aznavourian)	Germany (Imke Duplitzer, Claudia Bokel, Britta Heidemann)	France (M. Nisima, H. K. Picot, L. Flessel-Colovic, S. Daninthe)
Individual Sabre	Mariel Zagunis (USA)	Xue Tan (CHN)	Sada Jacobson (USA)
Football			
Team Men	Argentina (beat Paraguay 1-0 in final)	Paraguay	Italy (beat Iraq 1-0 in bronze medal match)
Team Women	United States (beat Brazil 2-1 aet in final)	Brazil	Germany (beat Sweden 1-0 in bronze medal match)
Gymnastics			
Artistic			
MEN			
Individual All-Around	Paul Hamm (USA) 57.823	Dae Eun Kim (KOR) 57.811	Yang Tae-Young (KOR) 57.774
Horizontal Bar (High Bar)	Igor Cassina (ITA) 9.812	Paul Hamm (USA) 9.812	Isao Yoneda (JPN) 9.787
Parallel Bars	Valeri Goncharov (UKR) 9.787	Hiroyuki Tomita (JPN) 9.775	Xiaopeng Li (CHN) 9.762
Vault	Gervasio Deferr (ESP) 9.737	Evgeni Sapronenko (LAT) 9.706	Marian Dragulescu (ROM) 9.612
Pommel Horse	Haibin Teng (CHN) 9.837	Marius Urzica (ROM) 9.825	Takehiro Kashima (JPN) 9.787

	Gold	**Silver**	**Bronze**
Rings	Dimosthenis Tampakos (GRE) 9.862	Jordan Jovtchev (BUL) 9.850	Yuri Chechi (ITA) 9.812
Floor Exercise	Kyle Shewfelt (CAN) 9.787	Marian Dragulescu (ROM) 9.787	Jordan Jovtchev (BUL) 9.775
Team	Japan 173.821	United States 172.933	Romania 172.384
	(Takehiro Kashima, Hisashi Mizutori, Daisuke Nakano, Hiroyuki Tomita, Naoya Tsukahara, Isao Yoneda)	(Jason Gatson, Morgan Hamm, Paul Hamm, Brett Mcclure, Blaine Wilson, Guard Young)	(Marian Dragulescu, Ilie Daniel Popescu, Dan Nicolae Potra, Razvan Dorin Selariu, Ioan Silviu Suciu, Marius Daniel Urzica)

WOMEN

	Gold	**Silver**	**Bronze**
All-Around	Carly Patterson (USA) 38.387	Svetlana Khorkina (RUS) 38.211	Nan Zhang (CHN) 38.049
Asymmetric (uneven) Bars	Emilie Lepennec (FRA) 9.687	Terin Humphrey (USA) 9.662	Courtney Kupets (USA) 9.637
Balance Beam	Catalina Ponor (ROM) 9.787	Carly Patterson (USA) 9.775	Alexandra Eremia (ROM) 9.700
Vault	Monica Rosu (ROM) 9.656	Annia Hatch (USA) 9.481	Anna Pavlova (RUS) 9.475
Floor Exercise	Catalina Ponor (ROM) 9.750	Nicoleta Daniela Sofronie (ROM) 9.562	Patricia Moreno (ESP) 9.487
Team	Romania 114.283	United States 113.584	Russia 113.235
	(Oana Ban, Alexandra Georgiana Eremia, Catalina Ponor, Monica Rosu, Nicoleta Daniela Sofronie, Silvia Stroescu)	(Mohini Bhardwaj, Annia Hatch, Terin Humphrey, Courtney Kupets, Courtney Mccool, Carly Patterson)	(Liudmila Ezhova, Svetlana Khorkina, Maria Krioutchkova, Anna Pavlova, Elena Zamolod-chikova, Natalia Ziganchina)
Rhythmic (ball, hoop and ribbon)			
Individual All-Around	Alina Kabaeva (RUS) 108.400	Irina Tchachina (RUS) 107.325	Anna Bessonova (UKR) 106.700
Team	Russia 51.100	Italy 49.450	Bulgaria 48.600
	(Olesia Beluguina, Olga Glatskikh, Tatiana Kurbakova, Natalia Lavrova, Elena Murzina, Elena Posevina)	(Elisa Blanchi, Fabrizia D'Ottavio, Marinella Falca, Daniela Masseroni, Elisa Santoni, Laura Vernizzi)	(Zhaneta Ilieva, Eleonora Kezhova, Zornitsa Marinova, Kristina Ranguelova, Galina Tancheva, Vladislava Tancheva)

Handball

	Gold	**Silver**	**Bronze**
Team Men	Croatia (beat Germany 26-24 in final)	Germany	Russia (beat Hungary 28-26 in bronze medal match)
Team Women	Denmark (beat Korea 38-36 in final)	Korea	Ukraine (beat France 21-18 in bronze medal match)

Hockey

	Gold	**Silver**	**Bronze**
Team Men	Australia (beat Netherlands 2-1 in final)	Netherlands	Germany (beat Spain 4-3 in bronze medal match)
Team Women	Germany (beat Holland 2-1 in final)	Netherlands	Argentina (beat China 1-0 in bronze medal match)

Judo

MEN

	Gold	**Silver**	**Bronze**
Extra Lightweight (60kg/132lb)	Tadahiro Nomura (JPN)	Nestor Kerghiani (GEO)	Min Ho Choi (KOR) Khashbaatar Tsagaanbaatar (MGL)
Half Lightweight (66kg/145.5lb)	Masato Uchishiba (JPN)	Jozef Krnac (SVK)	Georgi Georgiev (BUL) Yordanis Arencibia (CUB)
Lightweight (73kg/164lb)	Won Hee Lee (KOR)	Vitaliy Makarov (RUS)	Leandro Guilheiro (BRA) James Pedro (USA)
Half Middleweight (81kg/178.5lb)	Ilias Iliadis (GRE)	Roman Gontyuk (UKR)	Dmitri Nossov (RUS) Flavio Canto (BRA)
Middleweight (90kg/198.5lb)	Zurab Zviadauri (GEO)	Hiroshi Izumi (JPN)	Mark Huizinga (NED) Khasanbi Taov (RUS)
Half Heavyweight (100kg/220lb)	Ihar Makarau (BLR)	Sung Ho Jang (KOR)	Michael Jurack (GER) Ariel Zeevi (ISR)
Heavyweight (Over 100kg/220lb)	Keiji Suzuki (JPN)	Tamerlan Tmenov (RUS)	Dennis Van Der Geest (NED) Indrek Pertelson (EST)

WOMEN

	Gold	**Silver**	**Bronze**
Extra Lightweight (48 kg/106lb)	Ryoko Tamura-Tani (JPN)	Frederique Jossinet (FRA)	Feng Gao (CHN) Julia Matijass (GER)
Half Lightweight (52 kg/114lb)	Dongmei Xian (CHN)	Yuki Yokosawa (JPN)	Amarilys Savon (CUB) Ilse Heylen (BEL)
Lightweight (57 kg/125.7lb)	Yvonne Boenisch (GER)	Sun Hui Kye (KOR)	Deborah Gravenstijn (NED) Yurisleidy Lupetey (CUB)
Half Middleweight (63kg/138.6lb)	Ayumi Tanimoto (JPN)	Claudia Heill (AUT)	Urska Zolnir (SLO) Driulys Gonzalez (CUB)

	Gold	Silver	Bronze
Middleweight (70 kg/154.5lb)	Masae Ueno (JPN)	Edith Bosch (NED)	Dongya Qin (CHN) Annett Boehm (GER)
Half Heavyweight (78 kg/172lb)	Noriko Anno (JPN)	Xia Liu (CHN)	Lucia Morico (ITA) Yurisel Laborde (CUB)
Heavyweight (Over 78 kg/172lb)	Maki Tsukada (JPN)	Dayma Beltran (CUB)	Fuming Sun (CHN) Tea Donguzashvili (RUS)

Modern Pentathlon

	Gold	Silver	Bronze
Individual Men	Andrey Moiseev (RUS) 5480 Shooting: (175, 1036pts) Fencing: (22v-9d, 1000pts) Swimming: (01:58.90, 1376pts) Riding: (67.79, 1032pts) Running: (09:51.90, 1036pts)	Andrejus Zadneprovskis (LIT) 5428 Shooting: (172, 1000pts) Fencing: (19v-12d, 916pts) Swimming: (02:04.30, 1308pts) Riding: (77.00, 1088pts) Running: (09:35.50, 1116pts)	Libor Capalini (CZE) 5392 Shooting: (179, 1084pts) Fencing: (14v-17d, 776pts) Swimming: (02:02.00, 1336pts) Riding: (71.74, 1116pts) Running: (09:40.70, 1080pts)
Individual Women	Zsuzsanna Voros (HUN) 5448 Shooting: (182, 1120pts) Fencing: (19v-12d, 916pts) Swimming: (02:15.60, 1296pts) Riding: (82.57, 1124pts) Running: (11:22.00, 992pts)	Jelena Rublevska (LAT) 5380 Shooting: (171, 988pts) Fencing: (23v-8d, 1028pts) Swimming: (02:27.00, 1160pts) Riding: (71.04, 1116pts) Running: (10:58.00, 1088pts)	Georgina Harland (GBR) 5344 Shooting: (156, 808pts) Fencing: (16v-15d, 832pts) Swimming: (02:14.60, 1308pts) Riding: (71.40, 1144pts) Running: (10:17.30, 1252pts)

Rowing

MEN

	Gold	Silver	Bronze
Single Sculls	Olaf Tufte (NOR) 6:49.30	Jueri Jaanson (EST) 6:51.42	Ivo Yanakiev (BUL) 6:52.80
Lightweight Double Sculls	Poland 6:20.93 Tomasz Kucharski/Robert Sycz	France 6:21.46 Frederic Dufour/ Pascal Touron	Greece 6:23.23 Vasileios Polymeros/Nikolaos Skiathitis
Double Sculls	France 6:29.00 Sebastien Vielledent/Adrien Hardy	Slovenia 6:31.72 Luka Spik/Iztok Cop	Italy 6:32.93 Rossano Galtarossa/A. Sartori
Quadruple Sculls	Russia 5:56.85 (Nikolai Spinev, Igor Kravtsov, Alekseij Svirin, Sergej Fedorovtsev)	Czech Republic 5:57.43 (David Kopriva, Tomas Karas, Jakub Hanak, David Jirka)	Ukraine 5:58.87 (Sergij Grin, Sergij Bilushchenko, Oleg Lykov, Leonid Shaposhnikov)
Pair Oar (coxless)	Australia 6:30.76 Drew Ginn/James Tomkins	Croatia 6:32.64 Sinisa Skelin/Niksa Skelin	South Africa 6:33.40 Donovan Cech/R. Clemente
Lightweight Four Oar (coxless)	Denmark 6:01.39 (Thor Kristensen, Thomas Ebert, Stephan Moelvig, Eskild Ebbesen)	Australia 6:02.79 (Glen Loftus, Anthony Edwards, Ben Cureton, Simon Burgess)	Italy 6:03.74 (Lorenzo Bertini, Catello Amarante, Salvatore Amitrano, Bruno Mascarenhas)
Four Oar (coxless)	Great Britain 6:06.98 (Steve Williams, James Cracknell, Ed Coode, Matthew Pinsent)	Canada 6:07.06 (Cameron Baerg, Thomas Herschmiller, Jake Wetzel, Barney Williams)	Italy 6:10.41 (Lorenzo Porzio, Dario Dentale, Luca Agamennoni, Raffaello Leonardo)
Eight-Oar	United States 5:42.48 (Jason Read, Wyatt Allen, Chris Ahrens, Joseph Hansen, Matt Deakin, Dan Beery, Beau Hoopman, Bryan Volpenhein, Pete Cipollone)	Netherlands 5:43.75 (Matthijs Vellenga, Gijs Vermeulen, Jan-Willem Gabriels, Daniel Mensch, Geert Jan Derksen, Gerritjan Eggenkamp, Diederik Simon, Michiel Bartman, Chun Wei Cheung)	Australia 5:45.38 (Stefan Szczurowski, Stuart Reside, Stuart Welch, James Stewart, Geoff Stewart, Boden Hanson, Mike McKay, Steve Stewart, Michael Toon)

WOMEN

	Gold	Silver	Bronze
Single Sculls	Katrin Rutschow-Stomporowski (GER) 7:18.12	Ekaterina Karsten (BLR) 7:22.04	Rumyana Neykova (BUL) 7:23.10
Lightweight Double Sculls	Romania 6:56.05 Constanta Burcica/Angela Alupei	Germany 6:57.33 Daniela Reimer/Claudia Blasberg	Netherlands 6:58.54 Kirsten van Der Kolk/Marit van Eupen
Double Sculls	New Zealand 7:01.79 Georgina and Caroline Evers-Swindell	Germany 7:02.78 Peggy Waleska/Britta Oppelt	Great Britain 7:07.58 Sarah Winckless/Elise Laverick
Quadruple Sculls	Germany 6:29.29 (Kathrin Boron, Meike Evers, Manuela Lutze, Kerstin El Qalqili)	Great Britain 6:31.26 Alison Mowbray, Debbie Flood, (Frances Houghton, Rebecca Romero)	Australia 6:34.73 (Dana Faletic, Rebecca Sattin, Amber Bradley, Kerry Hore)
Pair Oar (coxless)	Romania 7:06.55 Georgeta Damian/Viorica Susanu	Great Britain 7:08.66 Katherine Grainger/Cath Bishop	Belarus 7:09.86 Yuliya Bichyk/Natallia Helakh
Eight-Oar	Romania 6:17.70 (Rodica Florea, Viorica Susanu, Aurica Barascu, Ioana Papuc, Liliana Gafencu, Elisabeta Lipa, Georgeta Damian, Doina Ignat, Elena Georgescu)	United States 6:19.56 (Kate Johnson, Samantha Magee, Megan Dirkmaat, Alison Cox, Caryn Davies, Laurel Korholz, Anna Mickelson, Lianne Nelson, Mary Whipple)	Netherlands 6:19.85 (Froukje Wegman, Marlies Smulders, Nienke Hommes, Hurnet Dekkers, Annemarieke van Rumpt, Annemiek de Haan, Sarah Siegelaar, Helen Tanger, Ester Workel)

THE ATHENS OLYMPICS

	Gold	Silver	Bronze

Sailing
MEN

	Gold	Silver	Bronze
Windsurfer – Mistral	Gal Fridman (ISR) 42	Nikolaos Kaklamanakis (GRE) 52	Nick Dempsey (GBR) 53
Single-handed Dinghy – Finn	Ben Ainslie (GBR) 38.0	Rafael Trujillo (ESP) 51.0	Mateusz Kusznierewicz (POL) 53.0
Double-handed Dinghy – 470	Paul Foerster/Kevin Burnham (USA) 71.0	Nick Rogers/Joe Glanfield (GBR) 74.0	Kazuto Seki/Kenjiro Todoroki (JAP) 90.0
Keelboat – Star	Torben Grael/Marcelo Ferreira (BRA) 42.0	Ross Macdonald/Mike Wolfs (CAN) 51.2	Xavier Rohart/Pascal Rambeau (FRA) 54.0

WOMEN

	Gold	Silver	Bronze
Windsurfer – Mistral	Faustine Merret (FRA) 31	Jian Yin (CHN) 33	Alessandra Sensini (ITA) 34
Single-handed Dinghy – Europe	Siren Sundby (NOR) 47.0	Lenka Smidova (CZE) 65.0	Signe Livbjerg (DEN) 74.0
Double-handed Dinghy – 470	Greece 38.0 Sofia Bekatorou/Aimilia Tsoulfa	Spain 62.0 Natalia Via Dufresne/Sandra Azon	Sweden 63.0 Therese Torgersson/Vendela Zachrisson
Keelboat – Yngling	Great Britain 39.0 (Shirley Robertson, Sarah Webb, Sarah Ayton)	Ukraine 50.0 (Ruslana Taran, Ganna Kalinina, Svitlana Matevusheva)	Denmark 54.0 (Dorte Jensen, Helle Jespersen, Christina Otzen)

Open (men and women)

	Gold	Silver	Bronze
Single-handed Dinghy – Laser	Robert Scheidt (BRA) 55.0	Andreas Geritzer (AUT) 68.0	Vasilij Zbogar (SLO) 76.0
Double-handed Dinghy – 49er	Iker Martinez/Xavier Fernandez (ESP) 67.0	Rodion Luka/George Leonchuk (UKR) 72.0	Chris Draper/Simon Hiscocks (GBR) 77.0
Multihull – Tornado	Austria 34.0 Roman Hagara/Hans Peter Steinacher	United States 45.0 John Lovell/Charlie Ogletree	Argentina 54.0 Santiago Lange/Carlos Espinola

Shooting
MEN

	Gold	Silver	Bronze
50m rifle 3 positions (60 shots)	Zhanbo Jia (CHN) 1264.5	Michael Anti (USA) 1263.1	Christian Planer (AUT) 1262.8
50m rifle prone (60 shots)	Matthew Emmons (USA) 703.30	Christian Lusch (GER) 702.20	Sergei Martynov (BLR) 701.60
10m air rifle (60 shots)	Qinan Zhu (CHN) 702.7	Jie Li (CHN) 701.3	Jozef Gonci (SVK) 697.4
50m pistol (60 shots)	Mikhail Nestruev (RUS) 663.3	Jong Oh Jin (KOR) 661.5	Jong Su Kim (PRK) 657.7
25m rapid fire pistol (60 shots)	Ralf Schumann (GER) 694.9	Sergei Poliakov (RUS) 692.7	Sergei Alifirenko (RUS) 692.3
10m air pistol (60 shots)	Yifu Wang (CHN) 690.0	Mikhail Nestruev (RUS) 689.8	Vladimir Isakov (RUS) 684.3
10m running target (60 shots)	Manfred Kurzer (GER) 682.4	Alexander Blinov (RUS) 678.0	Dimitri Lykin (RUS) 677.1
Trap (125 targets)	Alexei Alipov (RUS) 149	Giovanni Pellielo (ITA) 146	Adam Vella (AUS) 145
Double trap (150 targets)	Ahmed Almaktoum (UAE) 189	Rajyavardhan Rathore (IND) 179	Zheng Wang (CHN) 178
Skeet (125 targets)	Andrea Benelli (ITA) 149	Marko Kemppainen (FIN) 149	Juan Miguel Rodriguez (CUB) 147

WOMEN

	Gold	Silver	Bronze
50m rifle 3 positions (60 shots)	Lioubov Galkina (RUS) 688.40	Valentina Turisini (ITA) 685.90	Chengyi Wang (CHN) 685.40
10m air rifle (40 shots)	Li Du (CHN) 502.0	Lioubov Galkina (RUS) 501.5	Katerina Kurkova (CZE) 501.1
25m pistol (30 + 30 shots)	Maria Grozdeva (BUL) 688.2	Lenka Hykova (CZE) 687.8	Irada Ashumova (AZE) 687.3
10m air pistol (40 shots)	Olena Kostevych (UKR) 483.3	Jasna Sekaric (S&M) 483.3	Maria Grozdeva (BUL) 482.3
Trap (75 targets)	Suzanne Balogh (AUS) 88	Maria Quintanal (ESP) 84	Bo Na Lee (KOR) 83
Double trap (120 targets)	Kimberly Rhode (USA) 146	Bo Na Lee (KOR) 145	E. Gao (CHN) 142
Skeet	Diana Igaly (HUN) 97	Ning Wei (CHN) 93	Zemfira Meftakhetdinova (AZE) 93

Softball

	Gold	Silver	Bronze
Team Women	United States	Australia	Japan

Swimming
MEN

	Gold	Silver	Bronze
50m Freestyle	Gary Hall (USA) 21.93	Duje Draganja (CRO) 21.94	Roland Mark Schoeman (RSA) 22.02

	Gold	Silver	Bronze
100m Freestyle	Pieter van den Hoogenband (NED) 48.17	Roland Mark Schoeman (RSA) 48.23	Ian Thorpe (AUS) 48.56
200m Freestyle	Ian Thorpe (AUS) 1:44.71	Pieter van den Hoogenband (NED) 1:45.23	Michael Phelps (USA) 1:45.32
400m Freestyle	Ian Thorpe (AUS) 3:43.10	Grant Hackett (AUS) 3:43.36	Klete Keller (USA) 3:44.11
1500m Freestyle	Grant Hackett (AUS) 14:43.40 (OR)	Larsen Jensen (USA) 14:45.29	David Davies (GBR) 14:45.95
100m Backstroke	Aaron Peirsol (USA) 54.06	Markus Rogan (AUT) 54.35	Tomomi Morita (JPN) 54.36
200m Backstroke	Aaron Peirsol (USA) 1:54.95 (OR)	Markus Rogan (AUT) 1:57.35	Razvan Florea (ROM) 1:57.56
100m Breaststroke	Kosuke Kitajima (JPN) 1:00.08	Brendan Hansen (USA) 1:00.25	Hugues Duboscq (FRA) 1:00.88
200m Breaststroke	Kosuke Kitajima (JPN) 2:09.44	Daniel Gyurta (HUN) 2:10.80	Brendan Hansen (USA) 2:10.87
100m Butterfly	Michael Phelps (USA) 51.25 (OR)	Ian Crocker (USA) 51.29	Andriy Serdinov (UKR) 51.36
200m Butterfly	Michael Phelps (USA) 1:54.04	Takashi Yamamoto (JPN) 1:54.56	Stephen Parry (GBR) 1:55.52
200m Individual Medley	Michael Phelps (USA) 1:57.14 (OR)	Ryan Lochte (USA) 1:58.78	George Bovell (TRI) 1:58.80
400m Individual Medley	Michael Phelps (USA) 4:08.26 (WR)	Erik Vendt (USA) 4:11.81	Laszlo Cseh (HUN) 4:12.15
4 × 100m Freestyle Relay	South Africa 3:13.17 (WR) (Roland Mark Schoeman, Lyndon Ferns, Darian Townsend, Ryk Neethling)	Netherlands 3:14.36 (Johan Kenkhuis, Mitja Zastrow, Klaas-Erik Zwering, Pieter van den Hoogenband)	United States 3:14.62 (Ian Crocker, Michael Phelps, Neil Walker, Jason Lezak)
4 × 200m Freestyle Relay*	United States 7:07.33 (Michael Phelps, Ryan Lochte, Peter Vanderkaay, Klete Keller)	Australia 7:07.46 (Grant Hackett, Michael Klim, Nicholas Sprenger, Ian Thorpe)	Italy 7:11.83 (Emiliano Brembilla, Massimiliano Rosolino, Simone Cercato, Filippo Magnini)
4 × 100m Medley Relay**	United States 3:30.68 (WR) (Aaron Peirsol, Brendan Hansen, Ian Crocker, Jason Lezak)	Germany 3:33.62 (Steffen Driesen, Jens Kruppa, Thomas Rupprath, Lars Conrad)	Japan 3:35.22 (Tomomi Morita, Kosuke Kitajima, Takashi Yamamoto, Yoshihiro Okumura)

*Phelps awarded gold for swimming in heats
**Peirsol 53.45 backstroke leg world record

WOMEN

50m Freestyle	Inge de Bruijn (NED) 24.58	Malia Metella (FRA) 24.89	Lisbeth Lenton (AUS) 24.91
100m Freestyle	Jodie Henry (AUS) 53.84	Inge De Bruijn (NED) 54.16	Natalie Coughlin (USA) 54.40
200m Freestyle	Camelia Potec (ROM) 1:58.03	Federica Pellegrini (ITA) 1:58.22	Solenne Figues (FRA) 1:58.45
400m Freestyle	Laure Manaudou (FRA) 4:05.34	Otylia Jedrzejczak (POL) 4:05.84	Kaitlin Sandeno (USA) 4:06.19
800m Freestyle	Ai Shibata (JPN) 8:24.54	Laure Manaudou (FRA) 8:24.96	Diana Munz (USA) 8:26.61
100m Backstroke	Natalie Coughlin (USA) 1:00.37	Kirsty Coventry (ZIM) 1:00.50	Laure Manaudou (FRA) 1:00.88
200m Backstroke	Kirsty Coventry (ZIM) 2:09.19	Stanislava Komarova (RUS) 2:09.72	Reiko Nakamura (JAP) 2:09.88 Antje Buschschulte (GER) 2:09.88
100m Breaststroke	Xuejuan Luo (CHN) 1:06.64	Brooke Hanson (AUS) 1:07.15	Leisel Jones (AUS) 1:07.16
200m Breaststroke	Amanda Beard (USA) 2:23.37 (OR)	Leisel Jones (AUS) 2:23.60	Anne Poleska (GER) 2:25.82
100m Butterfly	Petria Thomas (Aus) 57.72	Otylia Jedrzejczak (Pol) 57.84	Inge de Bruijn (Ned) 57.99
200m Butterfly	Otylia Jedrzejczak (POL) 2:06.05	Petria Thomas (AUS) 2:06.36	Yuko Nakanishi (JPN) 2:08.04
200m Individual Medley	Yana Klochkova (UKR) 2:11.14	Amanda Beard (USA) 2:11.70	Kirsty Coventry (ZIM) 2:12.72
400m Individual Medley	Yana Klochkova (UKR) 4:34:83	Kaitlin Sandeno (USA) 4:34:95	Georgina Bardach (ARG) 4:37:51
4 × 100m Freestyle Relay	Australia 3:35:94 (WR) (Alice Mills, Lisbeth Lenton, Petria Thomas, Jodie Henry)	United States 3:36:39 (Kara Lynn Joyce, Natalie Coughlin, Amanda Weir, Jenny Thompson)	Netherlands 3:37:59 (Chantal Groot, Inge Dekker, Marleen Veldhuis, Inge de Bruijn)
4 × 200m Freestyle Relay	USA 7:53.42 (WR) (Natalie Coughlin, Carly Piper, Dana Vollmer, Kaitlin Sandeno)	China 7:55.97 (Yingwen Zhu, Yanwei Xu, Yu Yang, Jiaying Pang)	Germany 7:57.35 (Franziska van Almsick, Petra Dallmann, Antje Buschschulte, Hannah Stockbauer)
4 × 100m Medley Relay	Australia 3:57.32 (WR) (Giaan Rooney, Leisel Jones, Petria Thomas, Jodie Henry)	United States 3:59.12 (Natalie Coughlin, Amanda Beard, Jenny Thompson, Kara Lynn Joyce)	Germany 4:00.72 (Antje Buschschulte, Sarah Poewe, Franziska van Almsick, Daniela Gotz)

Synchronised Swimming

Duet Women	Anastasia Davydova/Anastasia Ermakova (RUS) 99.934	Miya Tachibana/Miho Takeda (JPN) 98.417	Alison Bartosik/Anna Kozlova (USA) 96.918
Team Women	Russia 99.501 (Elena Azarova, Olga Brusnikina, Anastasia Davydova, Anastasia Ermakova, Elvira Khasyanova, Maria Kiseleva, Olga Novolshchenova, Anna Shorina)	Japan 98.501 (Michiyo Fujimaru, Saho Harada, Kanako Kitao, Emiko Suzuki, Miya Tachibana, Miho Takeda, Juri Tatsumi, Yoko Yoneda)	United States 97.418 (Alison Bartosik, Tamara Crow, Rebecca Jasontek, Anna Kozlova, Sara Lowe, Lauren McFall, Stephanie Nesbitt, Kendra Zanotto)

Table Tennis

Men's Singles	Seung Min Ryu (KOR)	Wang Hao (CHN)	Wang Liqin (CHN)
Men's Doubles	Qi Chen/Lin Ma (CHN)	Lai Chak Ko/Ching Li (HK)	Michael Maze/Finn Tugwell (DEN)
Women's Singles	Yining Zhang (CHN)	Hyang-Mi Kim (PRK)	Kyung-Ah Kim (KOR)
Women's Doubles	Wang Nan/Zhang Yining (CHN)	Eun Sil Lee/Eun Mi Seok (KOR)	Yue Guo/Jianfeng Niu (CHN)

THE ATHENS OLYMPICS

	Gold	Silver	Bronze
Taekwondo			
MEN			
Under 58kg	Mu Yen Chu (TAI)	Oscar Francisco Salazar Blanco (MEX)	Tamer Bayoumi (EGY)
58-68kg	Hadi Saei Bonehkohal (IRN)	Chih Hsiung Huang (TAI)	Myeong Seob Song (KOR)
68-80kg	Steven Lopez (USA)	Bahri Tanrikulu (TUR)	Yossef Karami (IRN)
Over 80kg	Dae Sung Moon (KOR)	Alexandros Nikolaidis (GRE)	Pascal Gentil (FRA)
WOMEN			
Under 49kg	Shih Hsin Chen (TAI)	Yanelis Yuliet Labrada Diaz (CUB)	Yaowapa Boorapolchai (THA)
49-57kg	Ji Won Jang (KOR)	Nia Abdallah (USA)	Iridia Salazar Blanco (MEX)
57-67kg	Wei Luo (CHN)	Elisavet Mystakidou (GRE)	Kyung Sun Hwang (KOR)
Over 67kg	Zhong Chen (CHN)	Myriam Baverel (FRA)	Adriana Carmona (VEN)
Tennis			
Men's Singles	Nicolas Massu (CHI)	Mardy Fish (USA)	Fernando Gonzales (CHI)
Men's Doubles	Fernando Gonzales/Nicolas Massu (CHI)	Nicolas Kiefer/Rainer Schuettler (GER)	Mario Ancic/Ivan Ljubicic (CRO)
Women's Singles	Justine Henin-Hardenne (BEL)	Amelie Mauresmo (FRA)	Alicia Molik (AUS)
Women's Doubles	Ting Li/Tian Tian Sun (CHN)	Conchita Martinez/Virginia Ruano Pascual (ESP)	Paola Suarez/Patricia Tarabini (ARG)
Trampolining			
Individual Men	Yuri Nikitin (UKR) 41.50	Alexander Moskalenko (RUS) 41.20	Henrik Stehlik (GER) 40.80
Individual Women	Anna Dogonadze (GER) 39.60	Karen Cockburn (CAN) 39.20	Shanshan Huang (CHN) 39.00
Triathlon			
Individual Men	Hamish Carter (NZL) 1:51.07 (Swim: 18:19, Cycle 1:00:44, Run 32:04)	Bevan Docherty (NZL) 1:51.15 (Swim: 18:13, Cycle 1:00:51, Run 32:11)	Sven Riederer (SUI) 1:51.33 (Swim: 18:17, Cycle 1:00:45, Run 32:31)
Individual Women	Katie Allen (AUT) 2:04.43 (Swim: 20:38, Cycle 1:09:52, Run 34:13)	Loretta Harrop (AUS) 2:04.50 (Swim: 18:37, Cycle 1:09:05, Run 37:08)	Susan Williams (USA) 2:05.08 (Swim: 19:02, Cycle 1:08:58, Run 37:08)
Volleyball			
INDOOR			
Team Men	Brazil	Italy	Russia
Team Women	China	Russia	Cuba
BEACH			
Team Men	Brazil (Ricardo/Emanuel)	Spain (Bosma/Herrera)	Switzerland (Heuscher/Kobel)
Team Women	United States (Walsh/May)	Brazil (Behar/Shelda)	United States (McPeak/Youngs)
Water Polo			
Team Men	Hungary (beat Serbia & Montenego 8-7 in final)	Serbia & Montenegro	Russia (beat Greece 6-5 in bronze medal match)
Team Women	Italy (beat Greece 10-9 in gold medal match)	Greece	United States (beat Australia 6-5 in bronze medal match)
Weightlifting			
MEN			
under 56kg	Halil Mutlu (TUR) 295 (135 + 160)	Meijin Wu (CHN) 287.5 (130 + 157.5)	Sedat Artuc (TUR) 280 (125 + 155)
56-62kg	Zhiyong Shi (CHN) 325 (152.5 OR + 172.5)	Maosheng Le (CHN) 312.5 (140 + 172.5)	Israel Jose Rubio (VEN) 295 (132.5 + 162.5)
62-69kg	Guozheng Zhang (CHN) 347.5 (160 + 187.5)	Bae Young Lee (KOR) 342.5 (152.5 + 190)	Nikolay Petchalov (CRO) 337.5 (150 + 187.5)
69-77kg	Taner Sagir (TUR) 375 OR (172.5 OR + 202.5)	Sergey Filimonov (KAZ) 372.5 (172.5 + 200)	Oleg Perepetchenov (RUS) 365 (170 + 195)
77-85kg	George Asanidze (GEO) 382.5 (177.5 + 205)	Andrei Rybakou (BLR) 380 (180 + 200)	Pyrros Dimas (GRE) 377.5 (175 + 202.5)
85-94kg	Milen Dobrev (BUL) 407.5 (187.5 + 220)	Khadjimourad Akkaev (RUS) 405 (185 + 220)	Eduard Tjukin (RUS) 397.5 (182.5 + 215)
94-105kg	Dmitry Berestov (RUS) 425 (195 + 230)	Igor Razoronov (UKR) 420 (190 + 230)	Gleb Pisarevskiy (RUS) 415 (190 + 225)
over 105kg	Hossein Reza Zadeh (IRA) 472.5 (210 + 262.5)	Viktors Scerbatihs (LAT) 455 (205 + 250)	Velichko Cholakov (BUL) 447.5 (207.5 + 240)

Leonidas Sampanis of Greece was originally placed third in the 56-62kg class but was later disqualified for failing a drug test.
Ferenc Gyurkovics of Hungary was originally placed second in the 94-105kg class but was later disqualified for failing a drug test.
Note: The weights in parenthesis are for the two disciplines of the event, the first being the snatch and the second the clean & jerk.

Gold	Silver	Bronze
Women		
under 48kg	Nurcan Taylan (TUR) 210 WR (97.5 WR + 112.5)	Zhuo Li (CHN) 205 (92.5 + 112.5)	Aree Wiratthaworn (THA) 200 (85 + 115)
48-53kg	Udomporn Polsak (THA) 222.5 (97.5 + 125)	Raema Lisa Rumbewas (INA) 210 (95 + 115)	Mabel Mosquera (COL) 197.5 (87.5 + 110)
53-58kg	Yanqing Chen (CHN) 237.5 OR (107.5 OR + 130)	Song Hui Ri (PRK) 232.5 (102.5 + 130)	Wandee Kameaim (THA) 230 (102.5 + 130)
58-63kg	Nataliya Skakun (UKR) 242.5 (107.5 + 135 OR)	Hanna Batsiushka (BLR) 242.5 (115 WR + 127.5)	Tatsiana Stukalava (BLR) 222.5 (100 + 122.5)
63-69kg	Chunhong Liu (CHN) 275(122.5 WR + 152.5 WR)	Eszter Krutzler (HUN) 262.5 (117.5 + 145)	Zarema Kasaeva (RUS) 262.5 (117.5 + 145)
69-75kg	Pawina Thongsuk (THA) 272.5 (122.5 + 150 OR)	Natalia Zabolotnaia (RUS) 272.5 (125 WR + 147.5)	Valentina Popova (RUS) 265 (120 + 145)
over 75kg	Gonghong Tang (CHN) 305 (122.5 + 182.5 WR)	Mi Ran Jang (KOR) 302.5 (130 + 172.5)	Agata Wrobel (POL) 290 (130 + 160)

Wrestling

Graeco-roman

	Gold	Silver	Bronze
under 55kg	Istvan Majoros (HUN)	Gueidar Mamedaliev (RUS)	Artiom Kiouregkian (GRE)
55-60kg	Ji Hyun Jung (KOR)	Roberto Monzon Gonzalez (CUB)	Armen Nazarian (BUL)
60-66kg	Farid Mansurov (AZE)	Seref Eroglu (TUR)	Mikhitar Manukyan (KAZ)
66-74kg	Alexandr Dokturishivili (UZB)	Marko Yli-Hannuksela (FIN)	Varteres Samourgachev (RUS)
74-84kg	Alexei Michine (RUS)	Ara Abrahamian (SWE)	Viachaslau Makaranka (BLR)
84-96kg	Karam Ibrahim (EGY)	Ramaz Nozadze (GEO)	Mehmet Ozal (TUR)
96-120kg	Khasan Baroev (RUS)	Georgiy Tsurtsumia (KAZ)	Rulon Gardner (USA)

Freestyle

MEN

	Gold	Silver	Bronze
under 55kg	Mavlet Batirov (RUS)	Stephen Abas (USA)	Chikara Tanabe (JPN)
55-60kg	Yandro Miguel Quintana (CUB)	Masuod Jokar (IRN)	Kenji Inoue (JPN)s
60-66kg	Elbrus Tedeyev (UKR)	Jamill Kelly (USA)	Makhach Murtazaliev (RUS)
66-74kg	Buvaysa Saytiev (RUS)	Gennadiy Laliyev (KAZ)	Ivan Fundora (CUB)
74-84kg	Cael Sanderson (USA)	Eui Jae Moon (KOR)	Sazhid Sazhidov (RUS)
84-96kg	Khadjimourat Gatsalov (RUS)	Magomed Ibragimov (UZB)	Alireza Heidari (IRN)
96-120kg	Artur Taymazov (UZB)	Alireza Rezaei (IRN)	Aydin Polatci (TUR)

WOMEN

	Gold	Silver	Bronze
under 48kg	Ireni Merleni (UKR)	Chiharu Icho (JPN)	Patricia Miranda (USA)
48-55kg	Saori Yoshida (JPN)	Tonya Verbeek (CAN)	Anna Gomis (FRA)
55-63kg	Kaori Icho (JPN)	Sara McMann (USA)	Lise Legrand (FRA)
63-72kg	Xu Wang (CHN)	Gouzel Maniourova (RUS)	Kyoko Hamaguchi (JPN)

THE ATHENS OLYMPICS

British Medal Winners

GOLD		**Sailing**	
Athletics		Women's Yngling	
Women's 800m		Shirley Robertson	21.08.04
Kelly Holmes	23.08.04	Sarah Webb	21.08.04
Women's 1500m		Sarah Ayton	21.08.04
Kelly Holmes	28.08.04	Men's Finn	
Men's 4 × 100m relay		Ben Ainslie	21.08.04
Jason Gardener	28.08.04		
Darren Campbell	28.08.04	**SILVER**	
Marlon Devonish	28.08.04	**Badminton**	
Mark Lewis-Francis	28.08.04	Mixed doubles	
Cycling Track		Gail Emms	19.08.04
Men's 1 km time trial		Nathan Robertson	19.08.04
Chris Hoy	20.08.04	**Boxing**	
Men's individual pursuit		Men's 57-60kg	
Bradley Wiggins	21.08.04	Amir Khan	29.08.04
Equestrian Eventing		**Canoe/Kayak Slalom**	
Mixed individual		Men's K-1	
Leslie Law	18.08.04	Campbell Walsh	20.08.04
Rowing		**Cycling Track**	
Men's four		Men's team pursuit 4000m	
Steve Williams	21.08.04	Steve Cummings	23.08.04
James Cracknell	21.08.04	Rob Hayles	23.08.04
Ed Coode	21.08.04	Paul Manning	23.08.04
Matthew Pinsent	21.08.04	Bradley Wiggins	23.08.04
		Chris Newton	23.08.04
		Bryan Steel	23.08.04

Diving
Men's synchronised 10m
Peter Waterfield	14.08.04
Leon Taylor	14.08.04

Equestrian Eventing
Mixed team
Jeanette Brakewell	18.08.04
William Fox-Pitt	18.08.04
Philippa Funnell	18.08.04
Mary King	18.08.04
Leslie Law	18.08.04

Rowing
Women's coxless pair
Katherine Grainger	21.08.04
Cath Bishop	21.08.04

Women's coxless quad sculls
Alison Mowbray	22.08.04
Debbie Flood	22.08.04
Frances Houghton	22.08.04
Rebecca Romero	22.08.04

Sailing
Men's 470
Nick Rogers	21.08.04
Joe Glanfield	21.08.04

BRONZE

Archery
Women's individual (70m)
Alison Williamson	18.08.04

Athletics
Women's heptathlon
Kelly Sotherton	21.08.04

Canoe/Kayak Flatwater
Men's K-1 500m
Ian Wynne	28.08.04

Canoe/Kayak Slalom
Women's K-1
Helen Reeves	18.08.04

Cycling Track
Men's Madison
Rob Hayles	25.08.04
Bradley Wiggins	25.08.04

Equestrian Eventing
Mixed individual
Philippa Funnell	18.08.04

Modern Pentathlon
Women's individual
Georgina Harland	27.08.04

Rowing
Women's double sculls
Sarah Winckless	21.08.04
Elise Laverick	21.08.04

Sailing
Mixed 49er
Chris Draper	26.08.04
Simon Hiscocks	26.08.04

Men's Windsurfing Mistral
Nick Dempsey	25.08.04

Swimming
Men's 200m butterfly
Stephen Parry	17.08.04

Men's 1500m free
David Davies	21.08.04

Olympic Games General Information

Flag

Designed by Baron de Coubertin after the Stockholm Olympics of 1912 at which athletes from every continent competed for the first time. It has five interlocking rings of blue, yellow, black, green and red, on a white background. The rings represent the continents, Asia, Africa, Europe, Australasia and the Americas. The colours were chosen because at least one can be found on every flag of the participating country. It was first paraded at the seventh Olympiad in Antwerp.

Flame

Dutch architect Jan Wils had included a tower in his design for the Olympic stadium for the 1928 Amsterdam Olympics and came up with the idea of having a fire burn throughout as in the Ancient Olympics of 776BC. The Olympic flame commemorates the theft of fire from the Greek god Zeus by Prometheus. On 28 July 1928 an employee of the electricity board lit the first Olympic fire in this so-called Marathontower, known as the 'KLM's ashtray' by the locals. The idea caught on and for the Berlin Games of 1936 German sports official and sports scientist Carl Diem conceived the idea of an Olympic torch relay. More than 3000 runners carried the torch from Olympia to Berlin. German track and field athlete Fritz Schilgen was the last to carry the torch, igniting the cauldron in the stadium. The torch relay thus became part of the Olympic Games. Although the Winter Games of 1936 also included a cauldron of fire it was not until the 1952 Oslo Games that the corresponding torch relay was inaugurated. The flame for the Summer Olympics is always ignited in Olympia but on several occasions for the Winter Games it has been ignited elsewhere. In 1952, 1960 and 1994 the flame was ignited in Morgedal, Norway, in the fireplace of Sondre Norheim, who pioneered the sport of skiing. In 1956 the relay began in Rome but all other Winter Games have begun the torch relay at Olympia several months before the commencement of the Games. The torch is lit at Olympia by use of parabolic mirrors that deflect the sun's rays.

Here follows a list of all the final torchbearers who lit the Olympic flames in the host country's stadia.

1936	Berlin	Fritz Schilgen (German track and field athlete)
1948	London	John Mark (British track and field athlete)
1952	Helsinki	Hannes Kolehmainen and Paavo Nurmi (Finnish distance runners)
1952	Oslo	Eigil Nansen (the grandson of polar explorer Fridtjof Nansen)
1956	Melbourne	Ron Clarke (Australian distance runner), Hans Wilke (Swedish rider who lit the flame in Stockholm for equestrian events)
1956	Cortina	Guido Caroli (Italian speed skater)
1960	Rome	Giancarlo Peris (Italian-born track athlete of Greek descent)
1960	Squaw Valley	Ken Henry (American speed skating champion)
1964	Tokyo	Yoshinori Sakai (student born 6 August 1945, the day the Atomic bomb was dropped on Hiroshima)
1964	Innsbruck	Joseph Rieder and Paul Aste (alpine skiers)

1968	Mexico City	Norma Enriqueta Basilio de Sotelo (Mexican hurdler and first woman to light the flame)
1968	Grenoble	Alain Calmat (French figure skater)
1972	Munich	Gunter Zahn (German middle distance runner)
1972	Sapporo	Hideki Takada (Japanese speed skater)
1976	Montreal	Sandra Henderson and Stephane Prefontaine (Canadian track and field athletes)
1976	Innsbruck	Josef Feistmantl (Austrian luge athlete) and Christl Haas (Austrian skier)
1980	Moscow	Sergei Belov (Soviet basketball player)
1980	Lake Placid	Charles Kerr (psychiatrist elected by the other torch bearers)
1984	Los Angeles	Rafer Johnson (American decathlete)
1984	Sarajevo	Sandra Dubravcic (Yugoslavian figure skater)
1988	Seoul	Chong Son-Man, Kim Won-Tak, Sohn Mi-Chong (Korean teacher and two students)
1988	Calgary	Robyn Perry (12-year-old figure skating enthusiast)
1992	Barcelona	Antonio Rebello (a Paralympic archer lit the flame with an arrow)
1992	Albertville	Michel Platini (French footballer) and Francois-Cyrille Grange (eight-year-old schoolboy)
1994	Lillehammer	Crown Prince Haakon of Norway (son of King Harald V and Queen Sonia)
1996	Atlanta	Muhammad Ali (American heavyweight boxer)
1998	Nagano	Midori Ito (Japanese figure skater)
2000	Sydney	Cathy Freeman (Australian 400m runner)
2002	Salt Lake City	Mike Eruzione (American ice hockey player)
2004	Athens	Nikolaos Kaklamanakis (Greek boardsailing champion)

Mascots

The idea for identifying mascots to Olympic Games began at the 1968 Winter Olympics in Grenoble. Schuss the skier was an unofficial mascot though and official mascots commenced in the 1972 Games.

1972	Munich	Waldi the dachshund the first official mascot of the Summer Olympic Games
1976	Innsbruck	Schneemann the snowman the first official mascot of the Winter Olympic Games
1976	Montreal	Amik the beaver Amik is native American for beaver, a symbol of hard work
1980	Lake Placid	Roni the raccoon Roni always appeared in various sporting poses on merchandise
1980	Moscow	Misha the Russian bear (full name Mikhail Potapych Toptygin) there was also a mascot for the sailing at Tallinn, a seal named 'Vigri'
1984	Sarajevo	Vucko the little wolf mascot was chosen by a national newspaper poll
1984	Los Angeles	Sam the eagle national symbol of the United States was chosen by Walt Disney Productions
1988	Calgary	Hidy and Howdy the polar bears (the first dual mascots) the names derive from friendly colloquial greetings
1988	Seoul	Hodori the tiger (friendly tiger of Korean folklore) there was also a seldom seen female mascot called Hosuni
1992	Albertville	Magique the snow imp replaced an earlier mascot 'Chamois', a mountain goat
1992	Barcelona	Cobi the dog there were in fact a team of mascots but Cobi was undoubtedly the top dog
1994	Lillehammer	Haakon and Kristin two children from Norwegian folklore
1996	Atlanta	Izzy an abstract figure whose name apparently derives from people asking 'whatizit?'
1998	Nagano	Sukki, Nokki, Lekki and Tsukki the snow owls replaced an earlier mascot 'Snowple' the weasel
2000	Sydney	Ollie (Olympic) the kookaburra, Syd (Sydney) the platypus, and Millie (Millennium) the echidna chosen to represent air, water and earth, the ancient elements
2002	Salt Lake City	Powder a snowshoe hare, Copper a coyote and Coal a black bear chosen to represent the Olympic Motto: Faster, Higher, Stronger
2004	Athens	Athena and Apollo (aka Phoebus) represented in doll forms brother and sister gods of wisdom, war and light

THE ATHENS OLYMPICS

Medals

Olympic medals must be at least 60 millimetres (2.36 inches) in diameter and three millimetres thick. The gold medals are actually made of silver, gilded with a minimum of six grams (about 1/4 ounce) of pure gold. On the medals awarded between 1928 and 2002 the goddess Nike was seated, holding an ear of corn in one hand and a wreath in the other, while the second element of the main side was the exterior of an arena that resembled the Colosseum. For the Athens 2004 Games the main side of the medals depict Nike flying in the interior of Panathinaikon Stadium where the Olympic Games were revived in 1896. The main side of the medals also includes the sport in which the athlete won it. There are three elements on the second side of the medals: the eternal flame; the opening lines of Pindar's Eighth Olympic Ode composed in 460BC to honour the victory of Alkimedon of Aegina in wrestling; and the Athens 2004 Olympic Games emblem.

The tradition of awarding a gold medal to the champion, a silver medal for second place, and a bronze medal for third place didn't begin until 1908. In 1896 only the top two finishers were awarded medals, a silver for the winner and a bronze for second. They also received crowns – one of olive branches for the winner and a laurel crown for the second. In 1900 and 1904, the Games were attached to the Paris Exhibition and the St Louis Worlds Fair respectively and were not very successful. The protocol laid down by the IOC is as follows. The medal ceremony takes place as soon after the event as possible. The gold medal winner stands in the middle of the podium with the second on the right and the third on the left. After the names of the winners are announced the medals are presented by either the IOC president or an IOC member. Then, as the national anthem of the gold medallist plays, the flags of the medallists' countries are raised on flagpoles, with the flag of the winner in the middle.

Motto   *Citius, Altius, Fortius* (Faster, Higher, Stronger). Taken by Baron de Coubertin from a speech given by his close friend Dominican priest, Henri Didon.

Opened by

Date	Venue	
1896	Athens	King George I of Greece
1900	Paris	No official opening
1904	St Louis	President of Louisiana Purchase Exposition David Francis
1908	London	King Edward VII of Great Britain
1912	Stockholm	King Gustav V of Sweden
1920	Antwerp	King Albert I of the Belgians
1924	Paris	French President Gaston Doumergue
1924	Chamonix	French Physical Education Minister Gaston Vidal
1928	Amsterdam	HRH Prince Hendrik of Mecklenburg-Schwerin
1928	St Moritz	President of the Swiss Confederation Edmund Schulthess
1932	Los Angeles	United States Vice-President Charles Curtis
1932	Lake Placid	Governor of New York Franklin Delano Roosevelt
1936	Berlin	German Chancellor Adolf Hitler
1936	Garmisch	German Chancellor Adolf Hitler
1948	London	King George VI of Great Britain
1948	St Moritz	President of the Swiss Confederation Enrico Celio
1952	Helsinki	Finnish President Juho Paasikivi
1952	Oslo	Princess Ragnhild of Norway
1956	Melbourne	HRH Prince Philip, the Duke of Edinburgh
1956	Cortina	Italian President Giovanni Gronchi
1960	Rome	Italian President Giovanni Gronchi
1960	Squaw Valley	United States Vice-President Richard Nixon
1964	Tokyo	Japanese Emperor Hirohito
1964	Innsbruck	Austrian President Adolf Scharf
1968	Mexico City	Mexican President Gustavo Diaz Ordaz
1968	Grenoble	French President Charles De Gaulle
1972	Munich	West German President Gustave Heinemann
1972	Sapporo	Japanese Emperor Hirohito
1976	Montreal	Queen Elizabeth II of Great Britain (and Head of the Commonwealth)
1976	Innsbruck	Austrian President Rudolf Kirchschlager
1980	Moscow	Soviet President Leonid Brezhnev
1980	Lake Placid	United States Vice-President Walter Mondale
1984	Los Angeles	United States President Ronald Reagan
1984	Sarajevo	Yugoslavian President Mika Spiljak
1988	Seoul	South Korean President Roh Tae Woo
1988	Calgary	Governor-General of Canada Jeanne Sauvé
1992	Barcelona	King Juan Carlos I of Spain
1992	Albertville	French President François Mitterrand
1994	Lillehammer	King Harald V of Norway
1996	Atlanta	United States President William Clinton
1998	Nagano	Japanese Emperor Akihito
2000	Sydney	Governor-General of Australia Sir William Deane
2002	Salt Lake City	United States President George W. Bush
2004	Athens	Greek President Costis Stephanopoulos

Participants

		Opened	Closed	Male/Female Split	Total athletes	Number of countries
1896	Athens	6-Apr	15-Apr	241 - 0	241	14
1900	Paris	14-May	28-Oct	975 - 22	997	24
1904	St Louis	1-Jul	23-Nov	645 - 6	651	12

		Opened	Closed	Male/Female Split	Total athletes	Number of countries
1908	London	27-Apr	31-Oct	1971 - 37	2008	22
1912	Stockholm	5-May	27-Jul	2359 - 48	2407	28
1920	Antwerp	20-Apr	12-Sep	2561 - 65	2626	29
1924	Paris	4-May	27-Jul	2954 - 135	3089	44
1928	Amsterdam	17-May	12-Aug	2606 - 277	2883	46
1932	Los Angeles	30-Jul	14-Aug	1206 - 126	1332	37
1936	Berlin	1-Aug	16-Aug	3632 - 331	3963	49
1948	London	29-Jul	14-Aug	3714 - 390	4104	59
1952	Helsinki	19-Jul	3-Aug	4436 - 519	4955	69
1956	Melbourne	22-Nov	8-Dec	2938 - 376	3314	72
1960	Rome	25-Aug	11-Sep	4727 - 611	5338	83
1964	Tokyo	10-Oct	24-Oct	4473 - 678	5151	93
1968	Mexico City	12-Oct	27-Oct	4735 - 781	5516	112
1972	Munich	26-Aug	11-Sep	6075 - 1059	7134	121
1976	Montreal	17-Jul	1-Aug	4824 - 1260	6084	92
1980	Moscow	19-Jul	3-Aug	4064 - 1115	5179	80
1984	Los Angeles	28-Jul	12-Aug	5263 - 1566	6829	140
1988	Seoul	17-Sep	2-Oct	6197 - 2194	8391	159
1992	Barcelona	25-Jul	9-Aug	6652 - 2704	9356	169
1996	Atlanta	19-Jul	4-Aug	6806 - 3512	10,318	197
2000	Sydney	15-Sep	1-Oct	6582 - 4069	10,651	199
2004	Athens	13-Aug	29-Aug	not yet available	11,099	202

THE ATHENS OLYMPICS

ADVENTURE RACING

The fledgling sport of adventure racing originated in New Zealand in the 1970s. Kiwi Steve Gurney was an early pioneer and became one of the most accomplished of all competitors.

The term 'adventure race' is a generic one as each course and structure of events differs considerably, but typically an adventure race includes both individuals and teams who are required to trek up mountains on foot or bicycle and then run, ski, cycle, or abseil down. Without having time to draw breath the contestants may then be required to swim or paddle across water before having to exhaust themselves by running or riding horses across a finishing line.

Adventure racing, also referred to as 'multi-sports', was a logical extension of established endurance sports such as the Iditarod Classic Dog Sled Race. This event began in 1973 in the Alaskan wilderness over an official distance of 1049 miles (1688km) (Alaska being the 49th state) and the first winning musher was Dick Wilmarth in a time of 20 days 49mins 41secs. In 2002 Martin Buser covered the course in 8 days 22hrs 46mins. The course was amended in 2003 and Robert Sorlie's winning time of 9 days 15 hrs 47mins has become the new benchmark for the extended course of over 1100 miles (1770km). The famous Coast to Coast race began in New Zealand in 1980 and by now adventure races had began to have more of a structure.

A French reporter, Gérard Fusil, is often thought to be the inspiration behind the popularising of adventure racing. While reporting on some of the top endurance events, such as the Paris–Dakar Rally and the Marathon de Sables, he dreamt of a sport where mixed-gender groups would have to work as teams to overcome harsh, uninviting terrain. The Raid Gauloises was the fruit of this dream. The first Raid was held in New Zealand in 1989 and consisted of 130 participants trekking 35km before rafting 221km, horse riding and running 60km before finally canoeing across rapids and climbing rocks. Twenty-six teams started of which sixteen completed the course. The Eco-Challenge, first held in Salt Lake City, Utah, in 1995, popularised the sport further and it has now become one of the fastest-growing sports in the world with team budgets in excess of £50,000 for some events.

Typically, but not necessarily, teams consist of four members made up of both genders. The team always work together and the team to cross the line in the shortest period of time wins the race. The race course is generally in remote wilderness areas and the length of races ranges from eight hours to 36 hours and even to multi-day races. In a 36-hour race teams may be expected to cover 100 miles (160km) outracing the night without sleep. A multi-day event may be up to 250 miles (402km) covered over five days with only one hour of sleep per night. Maps are provided and skilful course management is essential.

Canada has a very active series and typical events are called Urban, Enduro, Night Enduro, Overnight and Urban Overnight, descriptive of the terrain and length of race. Other North American events include the Beast of the East, Colorado Bend Rattlesnake, Red River Gorge 12-Hour, Gold Rush Paddle Adventure, Southern Traverse and the Odyssey Sapphire Sprint. Because of the considerable stresses involved in adventure racing the events have a very low number of finishers; the average is less than 50 per cent.

AIR RACING

The world's first air meet was held at Reims, France, in August 1909. Prizes were offered for the highest altitude achieved, the longest flight, most passengers carried, and the fastest one-, two-, and three-lap flights over a 10km course. Glenn H. Curtiss of the US won the two biggest prizes, the James Gordon Bennett Trophy for the fastest two laps and the Prix de la Vitesse for the fastest three laps. Curtiss, who had earlier built and raced bicycles and motorcycles, used the $5000 Bennett Trophy prize money to establish his own aircraft company.

Apart from their competitive aspects, these meetings were important in the development of aircraft design, and the sport soon became a shop window for manufacturers to advertise their wares. The first US air meet took place less than a year later at Los Angeles, where Curtiss set a world record of 55mph (85kph) for a plane carrying one passenger. In October 1910, a second international air meet was sponsored by the Aero Club of America at Belmont Park in Elmont, New York.

Among the other important trophies offered during the early years of aviation were the Michelin Cup, for the longest flight between sunrise and sundown of a single day (the first competition was won by Orville Wright in 1908), the London *Daily Mail* prize for the first flight over the English Channel, won by Louis Blériot of France in 1909, and the William Randolph Hearst Prize of $50,000, offered in 1911 for the first pilot who could fly across the continent in 30 days or less. The prize inspired the first transcontinental flight, by Cal Rodgers, but he didn't get the money because the flight – which included 19 crashes – took him 49 days!

The 1912 Bennett Trophy winner, France's Jules Vedrines, was the first flier to average more than 100mph (161kph). Bennett Trophy racing was suspended in 1914 because of World War I, but a final race was held in 1920, when the French retired the trophy permanently by winning for the third straight time.

Several other major trophies and prizes were established almost as soon as World War I ended. Among them was another London *Daily Mail* prize, of £10,000, for the first non-stop flight between England and America, which was claimed by two British military pilots in 1919.

Also in 1919, a New York hotel owner offered a $25,000 prize for a solo, non-stop flight from New York to France. This ultimately led to one of the most famous flights in history: Charles A. Lindbergh claimed the prize on 21 May 1927 when he flew from Long Island, New York, to Paris, in a Ryan monoplane, *The Spirit of St Louis*, in a time of 33½hrs.

Jacques Schneider, the son of a French arms manufacturer, was infected with the flying bug around 1910 and became one of the officials in the French government responsible for the development of aviation. Schneider decided that since so much of the earth was covered with water, and major cities were located on ocean shores or along rivers, aircraft should develop the ability to land on water, either on pontoons (seaplanes) or on hulled fuselages (flying boats). In order to move aviation in this direction he created an international competition – the Coupe d'Aviation Maritime Jacques Schneider, better known as the Schneider Cup. The rules of the Schneider competition reflected his intent, although in a sometimes bizarre way. Aeroplanes were to float on the water for six hours and prove their seaworthiness by travelling a distance of about 550yds (504m) on water. Twice during the flight portion, planes had to land on (or 'come in contact with') the water, the wording of which stipulation gave rise to a bouncing manoeuvre. If the pontoons took on water, the planes had to continue their flight carrying the added weight. The rules called for the trophy to go permanently to the country that won three consecutive competitions; each competition was to be held in and managed by the country currently holding the trophy.

Two contests were held before World War I – in 1913 and 1914 – both off the coast of Monaco. The planes raced in these years were land planes fitted with clumsy pontoons haphazardly attached to the underside of the fuselage. The Frenchman Maurice Prevost, who won the first race in a Deperdussin, was the only pilot to finish, his pontoons heavy with water by the time he crossed the line. The following year, Tom Sopwith and Harry Hawker brought to the race a Tabloid plane equipped with pontoons and piloted by Howard Pixton. Pixton's bounce won the race for the British, though the French were quick to point out that the Tabloid used a French-built Gnome engine and that Pixton's bounce manoeuvre was the deciding factor in his nearly halving the previous year's time.

The race was suspended during the war and resumed in 1919 at Bournemouth near the Isle of Wight, England. The 1927, 1929, and 1931 races (now officially held every two years) were won by the British, who thus captured permanent possession of the trophy. The planes that won were all Supermarines – the S5, S6, and S6B, respectively – designed by Mitchell and equipped with 'R' engines developed by Sir Henry Royce of Rolls-Royce, and capable of delivering 1500hp. The last Schneider Cup race was held on 13 September 1931, at Lee-on-Solent, England.

The 1930s were a golden age for aviation and pilots such as American Wiley Post, with his distinctive black patch over one eye, were to the fore. The barnstorming Post flew a Lockheed Vega called *Winnie Mae*. Other great aviators of the era included Roscoe Turner and Speed Holman, who was killed in 1931 while stunting in Omaha.

The most famous British air race took place on 8 September 1922 at Croydon, England, when the first King's Cup Race was held. The winner was Captain F.L. Barnard in a De Havilland DH4A. The most famous British aerodrome is at Biggin Hill, Kent, where air racing took place until 1981.

After World War II the popularity of air racing declined but in 1964 the Reno, Nevada, National Championships began (now held biannually) and in 1969 a system of Formula One racing began in the United States.

In closed-circuit air racing, the course is marked by six pylons, about 30ft (9m) high, and placed so a pilot can see at least the next two pylons from any point along the course. There are two straights. The length of the course varies with the type of plane being raced, from 2-3 miles (3.2-4.8km) for Formula Vee planes up to 9-10 miles (14.5-16km) for planes in the Unlimited class. In Formula One racing, the course is usually 3 miles (4.8km) in length and each straight is 1 mile (1.6km) long. The number of planes in a race is generally limited to eight. If more than eight planes are entered, they may compete in preliminary heats, with the top finishers in each heat advancing to the finals. In some events, qualifying laps are used to determine the finalists. Each plane flies two laps and the average speed for the second lap is used for qualifying.

There are two types of starts. An air start is similar to the start of a motor race: the planes get into the air, line up in formation behind a pace plane, and follow the pace plane to the starting line. Just beyond the starting line, the pace plane pulls up and the race is on. In a racehorse start, the planes line up in a takeoff grid on the runway. Positions in the grid are usually determined by qualifying times. At the drop of a flag, the pilots take off and head for the course. Timing begins when the first plane crosses the start line.

A race is made up of a predetermined number of laps. In major Formula One races there are usually eight laps, for a total of 24 miles (38.6km). A plane must pass outside the pylon when cornering. Travelling inside or over the top of a pylon is a violation that usually results in a time penalty. Altitude must range from 25ft to 500ft (7.6m to 152.4m), although a pilot may fly higher for reasons of safety. During an emergency, which is signalled by a yellow flag from the officials, the lead plane must climb to at least 300ft (91.4). The other planes must follow to that altitude and remain there until the emergency has passed. The aircraft must keep a safe distance apart during the race. A pilot attempting to pass is responsible for ensuring the safety of the manoeuvre. However, a pilot being passed must stay on course, without attempting to impede the other plane. The plane that crosses the finish line first, after completion of the required number of laps, is the winner, provided no penalties were incurred during the race.

There are four classes of racing in the United States: AT6/SNJ, Biplanes, Formula One, and Unlimited. Specifications for a class prescribe design and structural standards, the type of engine used, and the allowable power. Each plane is inspected before a race to ensure that it meets specifications.

A
I
R

R
A
C
I
N
G

American Football

The game of rugby was undoubtedly a major influence in the development of American football but the true roots of the game were established in the American colleges. In 1820 a group of students at Princeton began playing a game known as 'ballown'. Initially fists were used to advance the ball into the goal but gradually it became permissible to use feet. Following the introduction of a round rubber ball in the 1850s, the freshman and sophomore classes at Harvard competed in a football-type game, played on the first Monday of each school year. This event became known as 'Bloody Monday', because of the ferocity of the tackles.

The first formal football organisation in the United States was established in 1862 by Gerritt Smith Miller, a 17-year-old student; the Oneida Football Club of Boston, Massachusetts, which from 1862 to 1865 was never beaten or scored against. In 1867 the Princeton Rules were drafted and these called for teams to be composed of 25 players. At the same time Rutgers College (New Brunswick, New Jersey) issued a set of rules and the football itself was patented for the first time. On 6 November 1869 the two colleges met and Rutgers won by a score of six goals to four, and thus was played what has become known as the very first intercollegiate football game, albeit using many of the rules of English soccer-style football. In 1873 representatives from Columbia, Rutgers, Princeton and Yale met in New York City to formulate the first intercollegiate football rules, with running the ball and throwing it now allowed. The number of players on each side was also reduced to 15. The first game under these rules was between Harvard and Yale, at New Haven, Connecticut, in 1875, with Harvard winning by four goals and four tries (touchdowns) to none. In 1880, Walter Camp, the coach at Yale and leader of the Intercollegiate Football Association's (IFA) rules committee, reduced the number of players in a team to 11, standardised the length of the playing field to 110 yards (100m) (reduced to 100 yards (91.4m) in 1912), and substituted scrimmage for the scrummage, or scrum. In scrummage the ball was put between the two opposing interlocked packs of forwards but in the new scrimmage the ball was put in the possession of one team, with one of its members, the snapback (now called the centre), putting the ball into play with his foot, without interference, to a player described as the quarterback. In 1882 Camp introduced the system of downs, initially allowing three attempts to advance the ball 5yds (4.6m), but this was changed to 10yds (9.14m) in 1906. The fourth down was added in 1912. The new rule gave rise to the practice of marking the field with horizontal lines 5yds apart, thus giving the sport its nickname of gridiron. Tackling below the waist had been introduced in 1888. Professional football was first played in 1895, after the demise of the IFA, and in 1920 the American Professional Football Association was formed (renamed the National Football League (NFL) in 1922).

At the end of each NFL season, the champions from the National and American conferences meet in the Super Bowl to determine a national champion, and, in effect, a world champion. In January 1967, the Green Bay Packers won the first Super Bowl, beating the Kansas City Chiefs 35-10 in front of 61,946 fans at the Los Angeles Coliseum, and from then on the Super Bowl became the biggest annual one-day sports event in the United States. By 2004, the sport of American football had organised leagues throughout the world and its popularity attracted vast television viewing figures.

General Information

abbreviations: common

AFC – American Football Conference	OL – offensive line
DB – defensive back	P – punter
DL – defensive line	PK – place kicker
LB – line backer	QB – quarterback
MVP – Most Valuable Player	RB – running back
NFC – National Football Conference	TD – touchdown
NFL – National Football League	WR – wide receiver

AFC teams and home stadiums

Baltimore Ravens – M & T Bank Stadium, Baltimore, Maryland
Buffalo Bills – Ralph Wilson Stadium, Buffalo, New York
Cincinnati Bengals – Paul Brown Stadium, Cincinnati, Ohio
Cleveland Browns – Cleveland Browns Stadium, Cleveland, Ohio
Denver Broncos – Invesco Field at Mile High Stadium, Denver, Colorado
Houston Texans – Reliant Stadium, Houston, Texas
Indianapolis Colts – RCA Dome, Indianapolis, Indiana
Jacksonville Jaguars – Alltel Stadium, Jacksonville, Florida
Kansas City Chiefs – Arrowhead Stadium, Kansas City, Missouri

Miami Dolphins – Pro Player Stadium, Miami, Florida
New England Patriots – Gillette Stadium, Foxborough, Massachusetts
New York Jets – Giants Stadium, East Rutherford, New Jersey
Oakland Raiders – Network Associates Coliseum, Oakland, California
Pittsburgh Steelers – Heinz Field, Pittsburgh, Pennsylvania
San Diego Chargers – Qualcom Stadium, California
Tennessee Titans – The Coliseum, Nashville, Tennessee

All-America teams
Instigated in 1889 by Caspar Whitney and constituting a fantasy team of the best players of the year. From 1897 Walter Camp published his All-America team in *Collier's Weekly*. After his death in 1925, Grantland Rice picked the teams until 1947.

ball: dimensions
The prolate spheroid-shaped ball consists of a leather case covering a rubber bladder inflated to the pressure of between 12½lb (86kPa) and 13½lb (93kPa). Its long axis measures between 10⅞ins (27.6cm) and 11⅜ins (29cm), its short circumference measures between 20¾ins (52.7cm) and 21¼ins (54cm), its weight is between 14oz (400g) and 15oz (425g).

Bowl Championship Series
Prior to the 1998 regular football season, the FedEx Orange, Nokia Sugar, Rose and Tostitos Fiesta Bowls joined with the Atlantic Coast, Big East, Big 12, Big Ten, Pacific-10 and Southeastern conferences and the University of Notre Dame to form the Bowl Championship Series (BCS). The BCS was established to determine the national champion for college football while maintaining and enhancing the bowl system, which has provided significant support to college football for nearly a century.

bowls: details
Apart from those listed here, with results, there are many other bowls, including the Alamo (San Antonio, Texas), Gator (Jacksonville, Florida), Peach (Atlanta, Georgia) and Sun (El Paso, Texas).

Cotton Bowl: details
The Cotton Bowl is a United States college football game played annually since 1937 in Dallas, Texas. For 40 years the champion of the Southwest Conference played as the home team. When the conference folded in 1996, the bowl lost much of its stature. It now matches teams from the Big 12 Conference and Southeastern Conference. The Cotton Bowl is also the name of the home ground of the SMU (Southern Methodist University) Mustangs. The stadium was opened in 1932 and is situated on the State Fair Grounds, Dallas, Texas.

field: dimensions
Playing area is 300ft (91.4m) long and 160ft (48.8m) wide. The end zones and goal posts are used to score points. There are lines across the field numbered from 50 to 10 from mid-field. The lines are only used to determine the distance of the teams from the end zone. Latitudinal lines every 5yds (4.6m) mark the pitch and at each end of the playing area is an end zone measuring 10yds (9.1m) across. In the centre of each end zone stand goal posts 20ft (6.1m) high, with a crossbar 10ft (3m) high and with the uprights on either side 23ft 4ins (7.1m) apart.

forward pass: year approved
In 1906 the forward pass was approved following a campaign by John Heisman, for whom college football's most prized individual trophy was later named.

fouls and penalties
Penalties may be the loss of 5, 10, or 15 yards, or half the distance to the goal line; loss of down (for a foul by the offensive team); automatic first down against the defence; the award of the ball to the opponent at the place of a foul; and disqualifications.

Heisman Memorial Trophy: details
Annual award given to outstanding college football players in the United States. It is named after the college coach and DAC (Downtown Athletic Club, New York City) Director of Athletics, John W. Heisman, and was first presented in 1935.

kickoff to start play
The receiving team gets ready to receive the ball after the opposing team begins play by kicking the ball upfield from its 35-yard line. A player on the receiving team catches the ball and starts to run towards the opponent's end zone, with the help of team-mates. Meanwhile, the team that began play tries to tackle the ball-carrier before he gains too much distance. The play is stopped when the ball-carrier has at least a knee down on the ground. The specialist teams take care of this phase of the game. Both special teams exit the field and the receiving team is now replaced by the offence as they now have the ball, and the kicking team by the defence, as they are now protecting.

NFC teams and home stadiums
Arizona Cardinals – new stadium in Glendale, Arizona, to open in 2006
Atlanta Falcons – Georgia Dome, Atlanta, Georgia
Carolina Panthers – Ericsson Stadium, Charlotte, North Carolina
Chicago Bears – Soldier Field II Stadium, Chicago, Illinois
Dallas Cowboys – Texas Stadium, Irving, Texas
Detroit Lions – Ford Field, Detroit, Michigan
Green Bay Packers – Lambeau Field, Green Bay, Wisconsin
Minnesota Vikings – Metrodome, Minneapolis, Minnesota
New Orleans Saints – Louisiana Superdome, New Orleans, Louisiana
New York Giants – Giants Stadium, East Rutherford, New Jersey

AMERICAN FOOTBALL

Philadelphia Eagles – Lincoln Financial Field, Philadelphia, Pennsylvania
San Francisco 49ers – Candlestick Park, San Francisco, California
Seattle Seahawks – Seahawks Stadium, Seattle, Washington
St Louis Rams – Edward Jones Dome, St Louis, Missouri
Tampa Bay Buccaneers – Raymond James Stadium, Tampa, Florida
Washington Redskins – FedEx Field, Washington DC

NFL Europe League: details
The NFL Europe League started life in 1991 as the World League of American Football. It was created by the NFL as a way to spread the popularity of American football worldwide. The original World League consisted of ten teams: six in the United States (Birmingham Fire, Sacramento Surge, Raleigh-Durham Skyhawks, New York/New Jersey Knights, Orlando Thunder and San Antonio Riders), one in Canada (Montreal Machine) and three in Europe (London Monarchs, Frankfurt Galaxy and Barcelona Dragons). The league was suspended after the 1992 season and the decision was made to restructure the league, making it European-only. The league returned in 1995 with the three original European teams and three new teams: Amsterdam Admirals, Rhein Fire (based in Düsseldorf) and Scottish Claymores (based in Edinburgh). The London Monarchs were renamed the England Monarchs in 1997.

officials
In the NFL each game is controlled by seven officials: a referee, umpire, head linesman, field judge, back judge, line judge and side judge.

Orange Bowl: details
The Orange Bowl is an intersectional United States college game played annually since 1935 at the Orange Bowl Stadium, Miami, Florida.

professional game: first
Played in Latrobe, Pennsylvania, 31 August 1895, Latrobe YMCA beating Jeannette Athletic Club 12-0.

Rose Bowl
Played on New Year's Day in Pasadena, California, between the Western Conference (Big Ten) and Pacific-10 Conference champions. First game was played in 1902 between the University of Michigan and Stanford University, with Michigan convincing 49-0 winners. The second game was not played until 1916. The Rose Bowl Stadium was built in 1923.

rules and tactics: general
The aim of the sport is to score more points than your opponent by the end of the game. The duration of the game is 60 minutes, divided into four quarters of 15 minutes. Usually a game lasts for between two and four hours because the clock is stopped during time-outs. Although a team consists of 11-a-side on the pitch at any one time, the squad of players these 11 are chosen from is very much larger. The squads are formed by very specialised players.
Every play starts the same way. A player of the offence (centre) hands the ball between the legs to the quarterback, or QB (captain of the offence). The QB has the option to hand the ball to the RB (running back) or to pass to a WR (wide receiver). The offensive line has the responsibility to protect the QB or to help the RB to run through the defence. The defensive backs protect the field against long passes and are the last barriers. They must be fast to keep up with receivers and strong to tackle them. The linebackers stop the running backs and defend against short passes. The special team includes a place kicker, who tries to place the ball between the goal posts by kicking it, and a punter, who kicks the ball as far upfield as possible. Offensive teams usually comprise a quarterback, a fullback, two halfbacks, seven linemen, a centre, two guards, two tackles and two ends. A typical defensive unit has two tackles and two ends, who play on the line, as well as three linebackers, two cornerbacks and two safeties. At the end of the first and third quarters the teams exchange ends. Each half begins with a kickoff, which also initiates play after every score except a safety.

rules played
Harvard Rules

scoring methods
Points can be scored by touchdown (6 points), where a player places the ball in the opponent's end zone; field goal (3 points), where the ball is kicked through the opponent's goal posts; safety (2 points), when an opponent is tackled in his own end zone; conversion or point after touchdown (1 or 2 points), where the ball is kicked over the crossbar of the goal post for 1 point (the usual ploy), or by running or passing the ball over the goal line from 2yds (1.8m) for 2 points.

Sugar Bowl: details
Conceived in 1927 by Colonel James Thomson and Fred Digby and played at the Louisiana Superdome, New Orleans, Louisiana, since 1976, when it was transferred from Tulane University Stadium. The first-ever game had taken place in 1935, with Tulane beating Temple 20-14. The champion team of the Southeastern Conference usually plays in what is an invitational event.

Super Bowl
Championship game of the National Football League, played annually in January by the winners of the league's American Football Conference and National Football Conference.

touchdown: explanation
To score a touchdown it is necessary to advance the ball across the opponent's goal line. In advancing the ball a team may run with it or pass it forwards or sideways, but the team must gain 10yds (9.14m) in four plays or lose possession. To gain ten yards at once is very rare, so the gain of ground

is accomplished step by step. A team has four attempts (downs) to cover the ten yards. If the team gains at least ten yards in four downs then it can continue on its advance. If it fails then the team must surrender possession of the ball. On the last down a team can punt the ball upfield which loses the play but ensures the opposition have possession in their own half. To give an example of the terminology, here is a possible scenario of the four downs. First down and ten (first try and ten yards to go); two-yard gain in the play. Second down and eight (second try and eight yards to go); four-yard gain in play. Third down and four (third try and four yards to go); four-yard loss. Fourth down and eight (fourth try and eight yards to go); six-yard gain. The team required eight yards but only managed six, so the team loses possession of the ball and becomes the defence. If the eight yards had been gained in the last down then mission would have been accomplished and a fresh first down and ten could begin, until the end zone is reached for score. The defending team can gain possession of the ball before the end of four downs by recovering a dropped ball (fumble) or by intercepting a pass.

Tournament of the Roses   Alternative name for the Rose Bowl
year of deaths   In 1905 there were reportedly 18 deaths in American college games.

Super Bowl

	Winners			**Runners-Up**
1967	Green Bay Packers	NFC	35-10	Kansas City Chiefs
1968	Green Bay Packers	NFC	33-14	Oakland Raiders
1969	New York Jets	AFC	16-7	Baltimore Colts
1970	Kansas City Chiefs	AFC	23-7	Minnesota Vikings
1971	Baltimore Colts	AFC	16-13	Dallas Cowboys
1972	Dallas Cowboys	NFC	24-3	Miami Dolphins
1973	Miami Dolphins	AFC	14-7	Washington Redskins
1974	Miami Dolphins	AFC	24-7	Minnesota Vikings
1975	Pittsburgh Steelers	AFC	16-6	Minnesota Vikings
1976	Pittsburgh Steelers	AFC	21-17	Dallas Cowboys
1977	Oakland Raiders	AFC	32-14	Minnesota Vikings
1978	Dallas Cowboys	NFC	27-10	Denver Broncos
1979	Pittsburgh Steelers	AFC	35-31	Dallas Cowboys
1980	Pittsburgh Steelers	AFC	31-19	Los Angeles Rams
1981	Oakland Raiders	AFC	27-10	Philadelphia Eagles
1982	San Francisco 49ers	NFC	26-21	Cincinnati Bengals
1983	Washington Redskins	NFC	27-17	Miami Dolphins
1984	Los Angeles Raiders	AFC	38-9	Washington Redskins
1985	San Francisco 49ers	NFC	38-16	Miami Dolphins
1986	Chicago Bears	NFC	46-10	New England Patriots
1987	New York Giants	NFC	39-20	Denver Broncos
1988	Washington Redskins	NFC	42-10	Denver Broncos
1989	San Francisco 49ers	NFC	20-16	Cincinnati Bengals
1990	San Francisco 49ers	NFC	55-10	Denver Broncos
1991	New York Giants	NFC	20-19	Buffalo Bills
1992	Washington Redskins	NFC	37-24	Buffalo Bills
1993	Dallas Cowboys	NFC	52-17	Buffalo Bills
1994	Dallas Cowboys	NFC	30-13	Buffalo Bills
1995	San Francisco 49ers	NFC	49-26	San Diego Chargers
1996	Dallas Cowboys	NFC	27-17	Pittsburgh Steelers
1997	Green Bay Packers	NFC	35-21	New England Patriots
1998	Denver Broncos	AFC	31-24	Green Bay Packers
1999	Denver Broncos	AFC	34-19	Atlanta Falcons
2000	St Louis Rams	NFC	23-16	Tennessee Titans
2001	Baltimore Ravens	AFC	34-7	New York Giants
2002	New England Patriots	AFC	20-17	St Louis Rams
2003	Tampa Bay Buccaneers	NFC	48-21	Oakland Raiders
2004	New England Patriots	AFC	32-29	Carolina Panthers

AMERICAN FOOTBALL

Cotton Bowl

	Winners		**Runners-Up**
1937	TCU Horned Frogs	16-6	Marquette Golden Eagles
1938	Rice Owls	28-14	Colorado Buffaloes
1939	St Mary's Gaels	20-13	Texas Tech Red Raiders
1940	Clemson Tigers	6-3	Boston College Eagles
1941	Texas A&M Aggies	13-12	Fordham Rams

1942	Alabama Crimson Tide	29-21	Texas A&M Aggies
1943	Texas Longhorns	14-7	Georgia Tech Yellow Jackets
1944	Texas Longhorns	7-7 (Tie)	Randolph Field
1945	Oklahoma A&M	34-0	TCU Horned Frogs
1946	Texas Longhorns	40-27	Missouri Tigers
1947	Arkansas Razorbacks	0-0	LSU Tigers
1948	SMU Mustangs	13-13	Penn State Nittany Lions
1949	SMU Mustangs	21-13	Oregon Ducks
1950	Rice Owls	27-13	North Carolina Tar Heels
1951	Tennessee Volunteers	20-14	Texas Longhorns
1952	Kentucky Wildcats	20-7	TCU Horned Frogs
1953	Texas Longhorns	16-0	Tennessee Volunteers
1954	Rice Owls	28-6	Alabama Crimson Tide
1955	Georgia Tech Yellow Jackets	14-6	Arkansas Razorbacks
1956	Ole Mississippi Rebels	14-13	TCU Horned Frogs
1957	TCU Horned Frogs	28-27	Syracuse Orangemen
1958	Navy Midshipmen	20-7	Rice Owls
1959	TCU Horned Frogs	0-0	Air Force Falcons
1960	Syracuse Orangemen	23-14	Texas Longhorns
1961	Duke Blue Devils	7-6	Arkansas Razorbacks
1962	Texas Longhorns	12-7	Ole Mississippi Rebels
1963	LSU Tigers	13-0	Texas Longhorns
1964	Texas Longhorns	28-6	Navy Midshipmen
1965	Arkansas Razorbacks	10-7	Nebraska Cornhuskers
1966 (Jan)	LSU Tigers	14-7	Arkansas Razorbacks
1966 (Dec)	Georgia Bulldogs	24-9	SMU Mustangs
1968	Texas A&M Aggies	20-16	Alabama Crimson Tide
1969	Texas Longhorns	36-13	Tennessee Volunteers
1970	Texas Longhorns	21-17	Notre Dame Fighting Irish
1971	Notre Dame Fighting Irish	24-11	Texas Longhorns
1972	Penn State Nittany Lions	30-6	Texas Longhorns
1973	Texas Longhorns	17-13	Alabama Crimson Tide
1974	Nebraska Cornhuskers	19-3	Texas Longhorns
1975	Penn State Nittany Lions	41-20	Baylor Bears
1976	Arkansas Razorbacks	31-10	Georgia Bulldogs
1977	Houston Cougars	30-21	Maryland Terrapins
1978	Notre Dame Fighting Irish	38-10	Texas Longhorns
1979	Notre Dame Fighting Irish	35-34	Houston Cougars
1980	Houston Cougars	17-14	Nebraska Cornhuskers
1981	Alabama Crimson Tide	30-2	Baylor Bears
1982	Texas Longhorns	14-12	Alabama Crimson Tide
1983	SMU Mustangs	7-3	Pittsburgh Panthers
1984	Georgia Bulldogs	10-9	Texas Longhorns
1985	Boston College Eagles	45-28	Houston Cougars
1986	Texas A&M Aggies	36-16	Auburn Tigers
1987	Ohio State Buckeyes	28-12	Texas A&M Aggies
1988	Texas A&M Aggies	35-10	Notre Dame Fighting Irish
1989	UCLA Bruins	17-3	Arkansas Razorbacks
1990	Tennessee Volunteers	31-27	Arkansas Razorbacks
1991	Miami Hurricanes	46-3	Texas Longhorns
1992	Florida State Seminoles	10-2	Texas A&M Aggies
1993	Notre Dame Fighting Irish	28-3	Texas A&M Aggies
1994	Notre Dame Fighting Irish	24-21	Texas A&M Aggies
1995	USC Trojans	55-14	Texas Tech Red Raiders
1996	Colorado Buffaloes	38-6	Oregon Ducks
1997	Brigham Young Cougars	19-15	Kansas State Wildcats
1998	UCLA Bruins	29-23	Texas A&M Aggies
1999	Texas Longhorns	38-11	Mississippi State Bulldogs
2000	Arkansas Razorbacks	27-6	Texas Longhorns
2001	Kansas State Wildcats	35-21	Tennessee Volunteers
2002	Oklahoma Sooners	10-3	Arkansas Razorbacks
2003	Texas Longhorns	35-20	LSU Tigers
2004	Ole Mississippi Rebels	31-28	Oklahoma State

Orange Bowl

	Winners		Runners-Up		Winners		Runners-Up
1935	Bucknell	26-0	Miami	1971	Nebraska	17-12	Louisiana State
1936	Catholic U.	20-19	Mississippi	1972	Nebraska	38-6	Alabama
1937	Duquesne	13-12	Mississippi State	1973	Nebraska	40-6	Notre Dame
1938	Auburn	6-0	Michigan State	1974	Penn State	16-9	Louisiana State
1939	Tennessee	17-0	Oklahoma	1975	Notre Dame	13-11	Alabama
1940	Georgia Tech	21-7	Missouri	1976	Oklahoma	14-6	Michigan
1941	Mississippi State	14-7	Georgetown	1977	Ohio State	27-10	Colorado
1942	Georgia	40-26	Texas Christian	1978	Arkansas	31-6	Oklahoma
1943	Alabama	37-21	Boston College	1979	Oklahoma	31-24	Nebraska
1944	Louisiana State	19-14	Texas A&M	1980	Oklahoma	24-7	Florida State
1945	Tulsa	26-12	Georgia Tech	1981	Oklahoma	18-17	Florida State
1946	Miami	13-6	Holy Cross	1982	Clemson	22-15	Nebraska
1947	Rice	8-0	Tennessee	1983	Nebraska	21-20	Louisiana State
1948	Georgia Tech	20-14	Kansas	1984	Miami	31-30	Nebraska
1949	Texas	41-28	Georgia	1985	Washington	28-17	Oklahoma
1950	Santa Clara	21-13	Kentucky	1986	Oklahoma	25-10	Penn State
1951	Clemson	15-14	Miami	1987	Oklahoma	42-8	Arkansas
1952	Georgia Tech	17-14	Baylor	1988	Miami	20-14	Oklahoma
1953	Alabama	61-6	Syracuse	1989	Miami	23-3	Nebraska
1954	Oklahoma	7-0	Maryland	1990	Notre Dame	21-6	Colorado
1955	Duke	34-7	Nebraska	1991	Colorado	10-9	Notre Dame
1956	Oklahoma	20-6	Maryland	1992	Miami	22-0	Nebraska
1957	Colorado	27-21	Clemson	1993	Florida State	27-14	Nebraska
1958	Oklahoma	48-21	Duke	1994	Florida State	18-16	Nebraska
1959	Oklahoma	21-6	Syracuse	1995	Nebraska	24-17	Miami
1960	Georgia	14-0	Missouri	1996 (Jan)	Florida State	31-26	Notre Dame
1961	Missouri	21-14	Navy	1996 (Dec)	Nebraska	41-21	Virginia Tech
1962	Louisiana State	25-7	Colorado	1998	Nebraska	42-17	Tennessee
1963	Alabama	17-0	Oklahoma	1999	Florida	31-10	Syracuse
1964	Nebraska	13-7	Auburn	2000	Michigan	35-34 (OT)	Alabama
1965	Texas	21-17	Alabama	2001	Oklahoma	13-2	Florida State
1966	Alabama	39-28	Nebraska	2002	Florida	56-23	Maryland
1967	Florida	27-12	Georgia Tech	2003	Southern		
1968	Oklahoma	26-24	Tennessee		California	38-17	Iowa
1969	Penn State	15-14	Kansas	2004	Miami	16-14	Florida State
1970	Penn State	10-3	Missouri				

Sugar Bowl

	Winners		Runners-Up		Winners		Runners-Up
1935	Tulane	20-14	Temple	1957	Baylor	13-7	Tennessee
1936	Texas Christian	3-2	LSU	1958	Mississippi	39-7	Texas
1937	Santa Clara	21-14	LSU	1959	LSU	7-0	Clemson
1938	Santa Clara	6-0	LSU	1960	Mississippi	21-0	LSU
1939	Texas Christian	15-7	Carnegie Tech	1961	Mississippi	14-6	Rice
1940	Texas A&M	14-13	Tulane	1962	Alabama	10-3	Arkansas
1941	Boston College	19-13	Tennessee	1963	Mississippi	17-13	Arkansas
1942	Fordham	2-0	Missouri	1964	Alabama	12-7	Mississippi
1943	Tennessee	14-7	Tulsa	1965	LSU	13-10	Syracuse
1944	Georgia Tech	20-18	Tulsa	1966	Missouri	20-18	Florida
1945	Duke	29-26	Alabama	1967	Alabama	34-7	Nebraska
1946	Oklahoma A&M	33-13	St Mary's,	1968	LSU	20-13	Wyoming
			California	1969	Arkansas	16-2	Georgia
1947	Georgia	20-10	North Carolina	1970	Mississippi	27-22	Arkansas
1948	Texas	27-7	Alabama	1971	Tennessee	34-13	Air Force
1949	Oklahoma	14-6	North Carolina	1972 (Jan)	Oklahoma	40-22	Auburn
1950	Oklahoma	35-0	LSU	1972 (Dec)	Oklahoma	14-0	Penn State
1951	Kentucky	13-7	Oklahoma	1973	Notre Dame	24-23	Alabama
1952	Maryland	28-13	Tennessee	1974	Nebraska	13-10	Florida
1953	Georgia Tech	24-7	Mississippi	1975	Alabama	13-6	Penn State
1954	Georgia Tech	42-19	West Virginia	1977	Pittsburgh	27-3	Georgia
1955	Navy	21-0	Mississippi	1978	Alabama	35-6	Ohio State
1956	Georgia Tech	7-0	Pittsburgh	1979	Alabama	14-7	Penn State

AMERICAN FOOTBALL

1980	Alabama	24-9	Arkansas		1993	Alabama	34-13	Miami
1981	Georgia	17-10	Notre Dame		1994	Florida	41-7	West Virginia
1982	Pittsburgh	24-20	Georgia		1995 (Jan)	Florida State	23-17	Florida
1983	Penn State	27-23	Georgia		1995 (Dec)	Virginia Tech	28-10	Texas
1984	Auburn	9-7	Michigan		1997	Florida	52-20	Florida State
1985	Nebraska	28-10	LSU		1998	Florida State	31-14	Ohio State
1986	Tennessee	35-7	Miami		1999	Ohio State	24-14	Texas A&M
1987	Nebraska	30-15	LSU		2000	Florida State	46-29	Virginia Tech
1988	Syracuse	16-16 (Tie)	Auburn		2001	Miami	37-20	Florida
1989	Florida State	13-7	Auburn		2002	LSU	47-34	Illinois
1990	Miami	33-25	Alabama		2003	Georgia	26-13	Florida State
1991	Tennessee	23-22	Virginia		2004	LSU	21-10	Oklahoma
1992	Notre Dame	39-28	Florida					

Rose Bowl

	Winners		Runners-Up			Winners		Runners-Up
1902	Michigan	49-0	Stanford		1960	Washington	44-8	Wisconsin
1916	Washington State	14-0	Brown		1961	Washington	17-7	Minnesota
1917	Oregon	14-0	Pennsylvania		1962	Minnesota	21-3	UCLA
1918	Mare Island	19-7	Camp Lewis		1963	Southern California	42-37	Wisconsin
1919	Great Lakes	17-0	Mare Island		1964	Illinois	17-7	Washington
1920	Harvard	7-6	Oregon		1965	Michigan	34-7	Oregon State
1921	California	28-0	Ohio State		1966	UCLA	14-12	Michigan State
1922	Washington & Jefferson	0-0 (Tie)	California		1967	Purdue	14-13	Southern California
1923	Southern California	14-3	Penn State		1968	Southern California	14-3	Indiana
1924	Navy	14-14 (Tie)	Washington		1969	Ohio State	27-16	Southern California
1925	Notre Dame	27-10	Stanford		1970	Southern California	10-3	Michigan
1926	Alabama	20-19	Washington		1971	Stanford	27-17	Ohio State
1927	Alabama	7-7 (Tie)	Stanford		1972	Stanford	13-12	Michigan
1928	Stanford	7-6	Pittsburgh		1973	Southern California	42-17	Ohio State
1929	Georgia Tech	8-7	California		1974	Ohio State	42-21	Southern California
1930	Southern California	47-14	Pittsburgh		1975	Southern California	18-17	Ohio State
1931	Alabama	24-10	Washington State		1976	UCLA	23-10	Ohio State
1932	Southern California	21-12	Tulane		1977	Southern California	14-6	Michigan
1933	Southern California	35-0	Pittsburgh		1978	Washington	27-20	Michigan
1934	Columbia	7-0	Stanford		1979	Southern California	17-10	Michigan
1935	Alabama	29-13	Stanford		1980	Southern California	17-16	Ohio State
1936	Stanford	7-0	Southern Methodist		1981	Michigan	23-6	Washington
1937	Pittsburgh	21-0	Washington		1982	Washington	28-0	Iowa
1938	California	13-0	Alabama		1983	UCLA	24-14	Michigan
1939	Southern California	7-3	Duke		1984	UCLA	45-9	Illinois
1940	Southern California	14-0	Tennessee		1985	Southern California	20-17	Ohio State
1941	Stanford	21-13	Nebraska		1986	UCLA	45-28	Iowa
1942	Oregon State	20-16	Duke		1987	Arizona State	22-15	Michigan
1943	Georgia	9-0	UCLA		1988	Michigan State	20-17	Southern California
1944	Southern California	29-0	Washington		1989	Michigan	22-14	Southern California
1945	Southern California	25-0	Tennessee		1990	Southern California	17-10	Michigan
1946	Alabama	34-14	Southern California		1991	Washington	46-34	Iowa
1947	Illinois	45-14	UCLA		1992	Washington	34-14	Michigan
1948	Michigan	49-0	Southern California		1993	Michigan	38-31	Washington
1949	Northwestern	20-14	California		1994	Wisconsin	21-16	UCLA
1950	Ohio State	17-14	California		1995	Penn State	38-20	Oregon
1951	Michigan	14-6	California		1996	Southern California	41-32	Northwestern
1952	Illinois	40-7	Stanford		1997	Ohio State	20-17	Arizona State
1953	Southern California	7-0	Wisconsin		1998	Michigan	21-16	Washington State
1954	Michigan State	28-20	UCLA		1999	Wisconsin	38-31	UCLA
1955	Ohio State	20-7	Southern California		2000	Wisconsin	17-9	Stanford
1956	Michigan State	17-14	UCLA		2001	Washington	34-24	Purdue
1957	Iowa	35-19	Oregon State		2002	Miami	37-14	Nebraska
1958	Ohio State	10-7	Oregon		2003	Oklahoma	34-14	Washington State
1959	Iowa	38-12	California		2004	Southern California	28-14	Michigan

Heisman Memorial Trophy Winners

	Winner	School	Position
1935	Jay Berwanger	Chicago	halfback
1936	Larry Kelley	Yale	end
1937	Clint Frank	Yale	halfback
1938	Davey O'Brien	Texas Christian	quarterback
1939	Nile Kinnick	Iowa	halfback
1940	Tom Harmon	Michigan	halfback
1941	Bruce Smith	Minnesota	halfback
1942	Frank Sinkwich	Georgia	halfback
1943	Angelo Bertelli	Notre Dame	quarterback
1944	Les Horvath	Ohio State	quarterback/halfback
1945	Felix Blanchard	Army	fullback
1946	Glenn Davis	Army	halfback
1947	Johnny Lujack	Notre Dame	quarterback
1948	Doak Walker	Southern Methodist	halfback
1949	Leon Hart	Notre Dame	end
1950	Vic Janowicz	Ohio State	halfback
1951	Dick Kazmaier	Princeton	halfback
1952	Billy Vessels	Oklahoma	halfback
1953	Johnny Lattner	Notre Dame	halfback
1954	Alan Ameche	Wisconsin	fullback
1955	Howard Cassady	Ohio State	halfback
1956	Paul Hornung	Notre Dame	quarterback
1957	John David Crow	Texas A&M	halfback
1958	Pete Dawkins	Army	halfback
1959	Billy Cannon	LSU	halfback
1960	Joe Bellino	Navy	halfback
1961	Ernie Davis	Syracuse	halfback
1962	Terry Baker	Oregon State	quarterback
1963	Roger Staubach	Navy	quarterback
1964	John Huarte	Notre Dame	quarterback
1965	Mike Garrett	Southern California	halfback
1966	Steve Spurrier	Florida	quarterback
1967	Gary Beban	UCLA	quarterback
1968	O.J. Simpson	Southern California	halfback
1969	Steve Owens	Oklahoma	halfback
1970	Jim Plunkett	Stanford	quarterback
1971	Pat Sullivan	Auburn	quarterback
1972	Johnny Rodgers	Nebraska	wide receiver
1973	John Cappelletti	Penn State	running back
1974	Archie Griffin	Ohio State	running back
1975	Archie Griffin	Ohio State	running back
1976	Tony Dorsett	Pittsburgh	running back
1977	Earl Campbell	Texas	running back
1978	Billy Sims	Oklahoma	running back
1979	Charles White	Southern California	running back
1980	George Rogers	South Carolina	running back
1981	Marcus Allen	Southern California	running back
1982	Herschel Walker	Georgia	running back
1983	Mike Rozier	Nebraska	running back
1984	Doug Flutie	Boston College	quarterback
1985	Bo Jackson	Auburn	running back
1986	Vinny Testaverde	Miami	quarterback
1987	Tim Brown	Notre Dame	wide receiver
1988	Barry Sanders	Oklahoma State	running back
1989	Andre Ware	Houston	quarterback
1990	Ty Detmer	Brigham Young	quarterback
1991	Desmond Howard	Michigan	wide receiver
1992	Gino Torretta	Miami	quarterback
1993	Charlie Ward	Florida State	quarterback
1994	Rashaan Salaam	Colorado	running back
1995	Eddie George	Ohio State	running back
1996	Danny Wuerffel	Florida	quarterback
1997	Charles Woodson	Michigan	cornerback
1998	Ricky Williams	Texas	tailback
1999	Ron Dayne	Wisconsin	tailback
2000	Chris Weinke	Florida State	quarterback
2001	Eric Crouch	Nebraska	quarterback

AMERICAN FOOTBALL

| 2002 | Carson Palmer | Southern California | quarterback |
| 2003 | Jason White | Oklahoma | quarterback |

NFL Europe League Winners (World Bowl)

1991	London Monarchs	21-0	Barcelona Dragons
1992	Sacramento Surge	21-17	Orlando Thunder
1995	Frankfurt Galaxy	26-22	Amsterdam Admirals
1996	Scottish Claymores	31-27	Frankfurt Galaxy
1997	Barcelona Dragons	38-24	Rhein Fire
1998	Rhein Fire	34-10	Frankfurt Galaxy
1999	Frankfurt Galaxy	38-24	Barcelona Dragons
2000	Rhein Fire	13-10	Scottish Claymores
2001	Berlin Thunder	24-17	Barcelona Dragons
2002	Berlin Thunder	26-20	Rhein Fire
2003	Frankfurt Galaxy	35-16	Rhein Fire
2004	Berlin Thunder	30-24	Frankfurt Galaxy

Biographies of Players, Coaches and Owners

Allen, Marcus   Born San Diego, California, 26 March 1960. Running back, Los Angeles Raiders, Kansas City Chiefs. Rookie of the Year in 1982, Allen became the first player in National Football League (NFL) history to rush for 10,000-plus yards and catch for 5000 more. He was MVP (Most Valuable Player) in Super Bowl XVIII and NFL MVP in 1985. He had career totals of 12,243yds rushing, 5411 receiving and 145 touchdowns. Elected to the Hall of Fame in 2003.

Anderson, Gary Allan   Born Durban, South Africa, 16 July 1959. Kicker, Pittsburgh Steelers, Philadelphia Eagles, San Francisco 49ers, Minnesota Vikings, Tennessee Titans. The all-time NFL point scoring record holder with 2302 up to the 2003 season. He holds the NFL record of 510 career field goals. In 1998 became the first NFL player to complete a season without missing a kick, converting 35 of 35 field goals and 59 of 59 extra points. His 308 regular season games is the most by any active player.

Baugh, Samuel A. ('Sammy')   Born Temple, Texas, 17 March 1914. Quarterback, Washington Redskins. The first quarterback to develop the passing game, 'Slingin" Sammy led the Redskins to their first world championship in 1937. In the days of all-round players he was also an accomplished punter. His best season was 1943 when he became the only player to lead the NFL in passing, punting and interceptions. Six times NFL passing leader. When he retired in 1952 he held most NFL passing records and a career completion average of 56.5 per cent. Elected to the Pro Football Hall of Fame in 1963.

Berry, Raymond   Born Corpus Christi, Texas, 27 February 1933. End, Baltimore Colts. Not a natural player, Berry made himself into one of the best receivers in the game. A favourite target for quarterback Johnny Unitas, it was Berry's ability to catch anything and everything that made him special. In 1958 his performance helped the Colts to their first NFL title. In the championship game he had 12 catches for 178yds and a touchdown. His 13-year career saw him make 631 receptions for 9278yds. He was elected to the Hall of Fame in 1973.

Blanda, George F.   Born Youngwood, Pennsylvania, 17 September 1927. Quarterback, kicker, Chicago Bears, Houston Oilers, Oakland Raiders. Blanda's 26-year career is the longest in pro football history. He began as a QB with the Bears, but his 46.7 completion percentage did not impress. An injury sidelined him for half of the 1954 season, after which he was used as a back-up QB and a kicker for the rest of his Chicago career. He announced his retirement in 1959; however the new Houston club, founded in 1960, tempted him back and that year he became their starting QB. He led the American Football League (AFL) in passing yardage and touchdown passes in 1961. The same year he was named as the league's Player of the Year. In 1967 he was traded to the Raiders, primarily as a kicker, and he became a legend to Raiders fans when in five weeks in the 1970 season he passed and kicked the Raiders to five victories to win the AFL Western division. Blanda was named AFL Player of the Year and the Associated Press Athlete of the Year. He finally announced his retirement in 1975, shortly before his 49th birthday. During his career he completed 1911 of 4007 passes for 26,920yds and 236 touchdowns, with 277 interceptions. He kicked 943 extra points and had 335 field goals for a then-record 2002 points. Elected to the Hall of Fame in 1981.

Bradshaw, Terry   Born Shreveport, Louisiana, 2 September 1948. Quarterback, Pittsburgh Steelers. The only quarterback to lead his side to four Super Bowl titles. A tough competitor, Bradshaw excelled in big games. He led the Steelers to their first Super Bowl in 1974 and repeated the feat the following year. His finest season was 1978 when he won the NFL Player of the Year, completing 207 of 368 passes for 2915yds and a league-leading 28 touchdowns. He was voted MVP, in the Super Bowl, throwing four touchdowns in the victory over Dallas Cowboys. The following year he was again Super Bowl MVP, passing for 309yds and two touchdowns. He retired in 1983 and was elected to the Hall of Fame in 1989.

Brown, James N.   Born St Simons Island, Georgia, 17 February 1936. Fullback, Cleveland Browns. Considered by many to be the greatest back of all time. He joined the Browns in 1957 and was named Rookie of the Year after gaining 942yds on 202 carries. During the next eight seasons Brown rushed for more than 1000yds seven times, falling short by just four yards in 1962. Led the league in rushing every season he played, except 1962 when he was second. While making a movie (*The Dirty Dozen*) in 1966, Brown announced he was retiring from football to concentrate on acting he was just 30 years of age. In his eight seasons he rushed 2359 times for 12,312yds. He also caught 262 passes for 2499yds and 20 touchdowns. Elected to the Hall of Fame in 1971.

Butkus, Richard M. (Dick)   Born Chicago, Illinois, 9 December 1942. Middle linebacker, Chicago Bears. The Chicago Bears have often had one player who symbolised the team. Dick Butkas was that player for nine seasons. At 1.9m and 111kg, Butkas was mobile enough to cover backs on pass patterns and to cover virtually the entire width of the field on running plays. A knee injury in 1970 slowed him somewhat, but he continued to star for the Bears until injury forced his retirement in 1973. During his career, he intercepted 22 passes, returning them for 166yds, and recovered 27 fumbles, including one for his only NFL touchdown. Elected to the Hall of Fame in 1979.

Clark, Earl H. ('Dutch')   Born Fowler, Colorado, 11 October 1906. Quarterback, Portsmouth Spartans, Detroit Lions. An outstanding college player, Clark joined the Spartans in 1930 and stayed with them for two seasons, being named All-Pro quarterback in both years. The club had problems paying his $140-a-game salary so he went to Colorado to coach. In 1933 the Portsmouth franchise moved to Detroit and he returned to the team. He was All-Pro quarterback for four seasons in a row, and he twice led the league in scoring, with 55 points in 1935 and 73 in 1936. In 1935 he led Detroit to the NFL championship, beating the New York Giants in the title game 26-7. He became player-coach in 1937 and retired from playing in 1938. Elected to the Hall of Fame in 1963. He died 5 August 1978.

Donovan, Arthur jnr (Art)   Born Bronx, New York, 5 June 1925. Defensive tackle, Baltimore Colts, New York Yanks, Dallas Texans. Joining the Colts in 1950, Donovan went with the team to New York and Dallas before the franchise returned to Baltimore in 1953. The 1.9m, 120kg defensive tackle was smart and quick, able both to rush the passer and move laterally to stop running plays. He anchored the defence in Baltimore's first championship team in 1958. Donovan retired in 1962. Elected to the Hall of Fame in 1968.

Graham, Otto   Born Waukegan, Illinois, 6 December 1921. Quarterback, Cleveland Browns. Joined the Browns in the new All American Football Conference, where he became a T-formation quarterback for the first time. Cleveland used Graham's passing ability and was the most successful team in pro football for the next decade. The Browns won all four AAFC championships, winning 52 games and losing only four. The AAFC folded in 1950 and the Browns joined the NFL. Most experts felt they would struggle against the stronger competition but, led by Graham, they won the NFL championship game that year, beating the Los Angeles Rams 30-28 with Graham throwing four touchdown passes. Four years later he passed for three and ran for three as the Browns beat the Detroit Lions 56-10 to land another title. Graham announced his retirement at the end of that season, but returned in 1955 to lead Cleveland to another championship, again beating the Rams in the final game. During his ten-year career he completed 1464 of 2626 attempts for 23,584yds and 174 touchdowns. He rushed 405 times for 882yds and 44

touchdowns. Elected to the Hall of Fame in 1965. He died 17 December 2003.

Grange, Harold ('Red')   Born Forksville, Pennsylvania, 13 June 1903. Halfback, Chicago Bears, New York Yankees. After a record-breaking college career at the University of Illinois, Grange signed a contract worth $100,000 with promoter Charles C. Pyle, who promised to deliver him to the Bears in time for the end of the 1925 season. The promoter arranged a barnstorming tour for the Bears, in which 400,000 fans paid to see 'The Galloping Ghost' run. His decision to play for money had made the difference between the pro game slowly going out of business and growing into the most popular and profitable sport in America. After the tour, Pyle founded the American Football League and Grange played with the New York Yankees. The AFL folded after one season and the Yankees were admitted to the NFL. Grange's knee was badly injured in a game against the Bears and he was never the same player again. After sitting out the 1928 season he joined the Bears in 1929 and played with them through 1934. No longer an outstanding runner, he was still a very good player and a genuine defensive star. Grange was named in the first official All-Pro team in 1931 and was an All-Pro again in 1932. In the 1933 championship game against the Portsmouth Spartans, Grange scored the only touchdown. In the 1934 championship game, with the Bears leading the New York Giants 23-21 in the dying seconds, Grange made a championship-winning tackle to prevent a lateral pass. In a post-season exhibition game in January 1935 he broke into the open on a 50-yard run, but was caught from behind by a lineman. He decided it was time to retire. Elected to the Hall of Fame in 1963. He died 28 January 1991.

Halas, George S.   Born Chicago, Illinois, 2 February 1895. End, coach, owner, Decatur Staleys, Chicago Bears. In 1920 the Decatur Staleys, with Halas as player/coach, joined the new American Professional Football Association. The team moved to Chicago in 1921. Halas and his partner bought the franchise in 1922 and renamed the team the Bears. At the annual league meeting in 1922, Halas suggested that the APFA should also be given a new name, the National Football League, and the other owners agreed. 'Papa Bear', as Halas became known, was associated with the team until his death in 1983. He won his first championship in 1921 and his last in 1963. He retired as a player in 1929, but came back to coach the team in 1933. Apart from the war years in which he served in the navy, and 1956-57, Halas coached the Bears every year until 1967. During his 40 seasons as the Bears' coach, Halas won 324 games, lost 151 and tied 31. The Bears won the NFL championship in 1921, 1933, 1934, 1937, 1940, 1946 and 1963. Elected to the Hall of Fame in 1963. He died 31 October 1983.

Harris, Franco   Born Fort Dix, New Jersey, 7 March 1950. Running back, Pittsburgh Steelers, Seattle Seahawks. When the great Steelers team of the seventies needed sure yardage, the players invariably turned to Franco Harris, from the time that the Steelers reached their first-ever title game in Harris's rookie season of 1972. Only the third man past the 10,000yds barrier, he was a Pro-Bowler for nine straight seasons, his six consecutive 1000yd rushing seasons was a long-time record, while he held or shared in 23 others at one time. His 'Immaculate Reception' from Terry Bradshaw's pass, with 22 seconds of the game remaining, running 42yds for

AMERICAN FOOTBALL

the winning touchdown against Oakland in the 1972 playoffs, became one of the most famous in NFL history. That one touchdown began the great Steelers years, which would produce four Super Bowl titles. A contract dispute after the 1983 season meant a sad end to Harris's Pittsburgh career. He played for one season in Seattle, but without success and retired at the end of the 1984 season. In a 13-year career he rushed 2949 times for 12,020yds with 91 touchdowns. Elected to the Hall of Fame in 1990.

Hirsch, Elroy   Born Wausau, Wisconsin, 17 June 1923. Halfback, end, Chicago Rockets (AAFC), Los Angeles Rams. The 'long bomb', a passing option beloved of fans, is a spectacularly difficult play to execute. It involves a receiver dashing downfield, taking an over-the-shoulder pass in mid-stride and attempting to carry it over for a touchdown. Yet 'Crazylegs' Hirsch did just that no less than nine times in 1951, averaging over 64yds per catch. That was undoubtedly his best season, ending with 17 of the Rams' 51 touchdowns, 66 receptions for 1495yds at an astonishing average of 22.7yds per catch. He retired at the end of the 1957 season with 387 career receptions and 7029yds. He was elected to the Hall of Fame in 1968. He died 28 January 2004.

Huff, Samuel (Sam)   Born Morgantown, West Virginia, 4 October 1934. Linebacker, New York Giants, Washington Redskins. Despite his small stature for the position, Huff was the game's most tenacious linebacker of the 1950s. He led the Giants defence and the team reached six NFL finals, though it won only one. His meetings with the game's leading running backs are the stuff of legend, but his defensive skills were such that he had 30 career interceptions. At the end of the 1963 season the Giants thought he was too old and traded him to the Washington Redskins. He played on for three and a half seasons before an ankle injury forced him to miss the last four games of the 1968 season, the first he had missed since he became a pro. He retired but came back in 1969 to help coach Vince Lombardi with the team. Lombardi's death in 1970 finally ended the career of 'The Hard Man'. Elected to the Hall of Fame in 1982.

Hutson, Donald (Don)   Born Pine Bluff, Arkansas, 31 January 1913. End, Green Bay Packers. There are only a handful of true innovators in any sport. In the history of American football, Don Hutson is one of them. He took hold of part of the game and turned it into an art form. He could glide past defenders with feints and shimmies, leap with almost balletic grace and cradle the ball in his safe hands. 'The Alabama Antelope' was the first true pass receiver. In the 1930s the game was played on the ground and passes were scorned by purists. Hutson's inventiveness in running patterns changed that concept for ever. He started his NFL career by running in his first-ever catch for a touchdown. His career statistics stood untouchable for decades. He had 488 career receptions for 7991yds. He retired in 1945, at which time he held 18 NFL records. In 1969 Hudson was named as the NFL's all-time end. Elected to the Hall of Fame in 1963. He died 26 June 1997.

Jones, David 'Deacon'   Born Eatonville, Florida, 9 December 1938. Defensive end, Los Angeles Rams, San Diego Chargers, Washington Redskins. Jones was among the first of the fast, tough, mobile defensive linemen. Noted for clean but hard-hitting play, he specialised in quarterback 'sacks', a term he

invented. In 1967, when he was at the peak of his career, he registered more sacks of his own (26) than entire teams of opponents did on the Rams QB (25). Despite his outstanding defence, he never played in a championship team. He retired in 1974 and was elected to the Hall of Fame in 1980.

Lambert, Jack   Born Mantua, Ohio, 8 July 1952. Linebacker, Pittsburgh Steelers. For ten years Lambert was an integral part of the 'Steel curtain', the defence of the great Pittsburgh team of the 1970s and early 1980s. A rough, tough brawler both on and off the field, he was a hero to the Pittsburgh fans, who saw him lead the Steelers defence to four Super Bowl victories. He was twice named NFL Defensive Player of the Year. Elected to the Hall of Fame in 1990.

Lane, Richard (Dick)   Born Austin, Texas, 16 April 1928. Cornerback, Los Angeles Rams, Chicago Cardinals, Detroit Lions. During his career the game changed, with quarterbacks throwing more passes. The changes played into Lane's hands as he perfected the new art of corner-backing. In his rookie season he grabbed an NFL-record 14 interceptions. He invented the 'neck-tie' tackle; instead of aiming at the knees, 'Night Train' thundered into his man high and hard. On occasion, such a tackle would send the unfortunate player, the ball and probably the helmet all flying in different directions. After six fruitless years in Chicago he was traded, at the age of 32, to Detroit. This proved to be the best part of his career, developing the role of cornerback as he went along, with unorthodox play. Only age put a stop to his dominance in 1965, at the age of 37. Elected to the Hall of Fame in 1974. He died 29 January 2002.

Lilly, Robert (Bob)   Born Olney, Texas, 26 July 1939. Defensive tackle, Dallas Cowboys. The first-ever draft pick for the Cowboys, he was also the first Cowboy to be enshrined in the Pro Football Hall of Fame. He was a local boy made good who would ensure the team remained at the top level for most of his career. After a heartbreaking last-second field goal defeat in Super Bowl V, 'Mr Cowboy' got his Super Bowl ring the following year, when his defence conceded just one field goal all day. Lilly missed only one game through injury in 14 seasons. He retired in 1975, the Cowboys retiring his number 74 the next year. Elected to the Hall of Fame in 1980.

Lombardi, Vincent   Born Brooklyn, New York, 11 June 1913. Coach, Green Bay Packers, Washington Redskins. Regarded as the greatest coach of all time – he never had a losing season – Lombardi led his Packers team to five NFL championships, including victory in the first two Super Bowls. His system of perfecting simple plays worked and his players worshipped him. He left the Packers after the second Super Bowl triumph to take over at Washington. After just one season he was taken ill with cancer and died at the age of 57. As a lasting tribute, the Super Bowl Trophy was named after him. Elected to the Hall of Fame in 1971. He died 3 September 1970.

Luckman, Sidney (Sid)   Born Brooklyn, New York, 21 November 1916. Quarterback, Chicago Bears. In his 12 seasons, Luckman led the Bears to four NFL championships. He was a master of the 'T-formation' invented by George Halas. In the 1940 championship game the Bears beat the Washington Redskins by a record 73-0. They repeated the victory a year later 37-9 against the New York Giants. Runners-up in 1942, they were champions again in 1943. This was

Luckman's best year; he threw seven touchdown passes in a game against the Giants. He also became the first man to throw for more than 400yds in a game. His final championship was in 1946, when he wrapped up the win with his first and only touchdown run of the season. His final season in 1947 saw him lead the NFL in touchdown passes, with 31. He retired in 1950 with a career total 14,686yds in 1744 attempts. Elected to the Hall of Fame in 1965. He died 5 July 1998.

Marino, Daniel (Dan) Born Pittsburgh, Pennsylvania, 15 September 1961. Quarterback, Miami Dolphins. If based on statistics alone, Dan Marino is the greatest quarterback ever to have played the game. Starting with three touchdown passes in his debut game in 1983, they continued to flow from then on. He was named Rookie of the Year and became the first rookie to start at quarterback in a Super Bowl. In 1984 he really burst to the forefront. He set single season records for touchdown passes (48), completions (362) and yards (5084), the only black spot being defeat in the 1985 Super Bowl by the San Francisco 49ers. Marino became the only quarterback to top the 60,000-yard passing mark. He was also the first to throw more than 400 touchdown passes. He has thrown more pass attempts and more completions than anyone else in the history of the game. He retired at the end of the 1999 season, holding 20 NFL records and a share of three others.

Montana, Joseph Clifford (Joe) Born New Eagle, Pennsylvania, 11 June 1956. Quarterback, San Francisco 49ers, Kansas City Chiefs. In a remarkable career, Montana led his teams to 31 fourth-quarter comeback wins, including a 92-yard drive in the closing stages of Super Bowl XXIII. This ability to bring teams back from the brink of defeat became known simply as 'Montana Magic'. He won the NFL passing titles in 1987 and 1989, passed for 300yds or more in a game 39 times, seven times over 400yds. He steered his team to the play-offs 11 times, winning nine divisional championships and four Super Bowls. He was named MVP in three of them. In 1994 Montana became only the fifth quarterback to pass for more than 40,000yds in a career. He retired in 1994 with career totals of 40,551yds passing, 5391 attempts, 273 passing touchdowns, 3409 completions. Elected to the Hall of Fame in 2000.

Nagurski, Bronko Born Rainy River, Ontario, Canada, 3 November 1908. Fullback, Chicago Bears. Bronko Nagurski was spotted by George Halas, joining the Bears in 1930, and soon powered the club back to the top. A backfield containing him and Red Grange could hardly be stopped. In the 1932 championship clincher against Portsmouth, Bronko showed another side to his talent. With fourth and goal, everyone thought another power play was coming, instead he tossed a short pass to Grange to win the title. The following year he repeated the feat to beat the New York Giants in the championship game. He scored himself in 1934 as the Bears recorded a hat-trick of titles. He decided to retire in 1937, but with the war taking its toll on players he returned in 1943 as a tackle, at the age of 35. As the old magic returned, he moved to fullback. Elected to the Hall of Fame in 1963. He died 7 January 1990.

Namath, Joseph (Joe) Born Beaver Falls, Pennsylvania, 31 May 1943. Quarterback, New York Jets, Los Angeles Rams. 'We will win Super Bowl III, I guarantee it', and the underdog Jets overcame large odds to do just that. With that one sentence

Joe Namath won the hearts of the nation. It was Namath's game, even though he did not throw a touchdown pass. He threw for over 3000yds in three of his first four seasons, including 1967 when he became the first player in NFL history to throw for over 4000yds. With film-star looks his life off the field was as much in the public eye as it was on. By 1972, however, his knees were starting to go and injuries cut down his appearances. In 1977 he was traded to the Rams but could not recover the glory days. He retired at the end of the season with 27,663yds from 3762 attempts, a completion rate of 50.1 per cent. Elected to the Hall of Fame in 1985.

Payton, Walter Perry Born Columbia, Mississippi, 25 July 1954. Running back, Chicago Bears. A first-round draft choice, Payton quickly established himself as a rushing superstar, and went on to rewrite the NFL record book. The records held at the time of his retirement included 16,726 total yards, 10 seasons with 1000 or more yards rushing, 275yds rushing in one game (against Minnesota in 1977), 77 games with more than 100yds rushing and 110 rushing touchdowns. An exceptionally durable player, he missed one game of his rookie season, then played in 186 consecutive games, only breaking the run late in his final season. He retired in 1987. Elected to the Hall of Fame in 1993. He died 1 November 1999.

Pihos, Peter Born Orlando, Florida, 22 October 1923. End, Philadelphia Eagles. An all-round player in the Eagles teams of the 1940s and 1950s, he caught the winning pass in the 1949 NFL championship game. He was the NFL receiving champion three years running, 1953 to 1955. Pihos retired in 1955 with 373 catches for 5619yds. Elected to the Hall of Fame in 1970.

Rice, Jerry Lee Born Crawford, Mississippi, 13 October 1962. Wide receiver, San Francisco 49ers, Oakland Raiders. With 14 NFL records, 12 Pro-Bowl invitations, and selection for the NFL's 75th Anniversary team, not only is Jerry Rice the greatest wide receiver ever to play in the NFL, but he is arguably the greatest player the game has ever seen. His records are too numerous to list, but include receptions, total receiving yards and total touchdowns, in a career which, in 2004, is still active. In 1998 he became the first player to achieve 17,000yds either rushing or receiving. His amazing resilience has seen him through 19 NFL seasons. At the end of 2003 he had a career record of 23,466yds on 1519 receptions and 194 touchdowns.

Riggins, John Born Seneca, Kansas, 4 August 1949. Running back, New York Jets, Washington Redskins. John 'The Diesel' Riggins based his running game on sheer power. A first-round draft pick, he soon became a mainstay of the Jets and in 1975 became the first Jet to rush for over 1000yds. He joined the Redskins as a free agent in 1976 and quickly established himself as a favourite with the fans in two more seasons with over 1000yds. His most famous game was Super Bowl XVII, when he had 166yds, scored the winning touchdown from 43yds and was named MVP. He sat out the whole 1980 season, but came back to play five more years, including a career-high 1347yds in 1983. He retired in 1985. Elected to the Hall of Fame in 1992.

Ringo, James (Jim) Born Orange, New Jersey, 21 November 1931. Centre, Green Bay Packers, Philadelphia Eagles. Though playing in the unheralded position of centre, Ringo was one of the main reasons Green Bay was such a great side in

AMERICAN FOOTBALL

the 1960s. He played on through the winning years despite injury and pain, but always gave a special effort for his team's sake. Between 1954 and 1967 he started 182 straight games. Elected to the Hall of Fame in 1981.

Sanders, Barry   Born Wichita, Kansas, 16 July 1968. Running back, Detroit Lions. The second-leading rusher of all-time with 15,269yds. Holds the all-time NFL record for consecutive 1000yd rushing seasons, with ten. Holds the NFL single-season record for most 100 yard rushing games and most consecutive 100 yard games, with 14 in 1997. He retired in 1998 with a career-record 109 touchdowns. Elected to the Hall of Fame in 2004.

Sayers, Gale Eugene   Born Wichita, Kansas, 30 May 1943. Halfback, Chicago Bears. In a career cruelly cut short by injuries, Sayers left a lasting impression on the game. In his rookie season of 1967 he scored six touchdowns in one game to equal the NFL record. He continued his electrifying form through 1968, but halfway through the 1969 season suffered the knee injury that would end his career just before the 1972 season. His four-and-a-half-year career saw totals of 9435 combined yards, 4956 rushing and 336 points scored. Elected to the Hall of Fame in 1977.

Shula, Donald (Don)   Born Grand River, Ohio, 4 January 1930. Head coach, Baltimore Colts, Miami Dolphins. Shula's record as head coach of the 1963 to 1969 Colts and the 1970 to 1995 Dolphins is unparalleled in NFL history. He completed his 33rd season in 1995 with a 347-173-6 record, the highest number of wins in NFL history. Along with George Halas he is the only NFL coach with over 300 victories. His teams reached the play-offs 20 times and he holds the record of having coached six Super Bowl teams, with two wins. In Super Bowl VII, the 1972 Dolphins completed their historic 17-0-0 campaign, the only perfect season in NFL history, with a 14-7 win over the Washington Redskins. In 1973 they beat the Minnesota Vikings in Super Bowl VIII to complete a two-season span in which they won 32 of 34 games. Elected to the Hall of Fame in 1997.

Simpson, Orenthal James (OJ)   Born San Francisco, California, 9 July 1947. Running back, Buffalo Bills, San Francisco 49ers. The 'Orange Juice' was the number one draft pick in 1969 and his 11-year career record proved the rave notices he received were justified. His best season was in 1973 when he became the first back in history to rush for over 2000yds. He led the league in rushing for four years and was three times named NFL Player of the Year. His career total includes 11,236 rushing yards, 2142 receiving yards on 203 receptions, 14,368 combined yards. He retired in 1979 and had a very successful acting career before his involvement in one of the most controversial murder enquiries in US history. Elected to the Hall of Fame in 1985.

Smith, Emmitt J.   Born Pensecola, Florida, 15 May 1969. Running back, Dallas Cowboys, Arizona Cardinals. The third-ranked rusher in NFL history, he has also won four NFL rushing records, three Super Bowl titles, league MVP in 1993 and MVP of Super Bowl XXVIII. The NFL rushing touchdown leader with 145. He reached 100 touchdowns in just 93 games, the fastest in history. Smith is the only player in NFL history with over 1400yds rushing in five straight seasons. At the end of the 2003 season he had 17,418 rushing yards.

Stabler, Kenneth (Ken)   Born Foley, Alabama, 25 December 1945. Quarterback, Oakland Raiders, Houston Oilers, New Orleans Saints, Regarded as the best left-handed quarterback of all time. He led the Raiders to four consecutive AFL championships, culminating in 1976 with victory in Super Bowl XI. As his arm faded, he was traded to the Oilers and then the Saints. He retired in 1984 with 3793 career passing attempts, and 2270 completions for 27,938yds.

Starr, Bart   Born Montgomery, Alabama, 9 January 1934. Quarterback, Green Bay Packers. As a seventeenth-round draft pick, Starr could not have imagined a 16-year career that would see him lead the Packers to five NFL titles and two Super Bowls (he was MVP in both games). He played in four Pro-Bowls and was NFL Player of the Year in 1966. A fringe player, he was spotted by new coach Vincent Lombardi and became starting QB for Green Bay in 1960. They lost to the Philadelphia Eagles that year, but won the title in 1961. It was the start of one of the most dominant eras in pro football, and Starr was at the centre of it. A second title followed in 1962 and a third in 1965. In 1967 he led the Packers to victory in Super Bowl I, repeating the feat in 1968. Though never a big-number passer (2433yds in 1962 his best), he was a master tactician and the brains behind the great Packers team of the 1960s. He retired in 1971 with career totals of 3149 passing attempts, 1808 completions and 24,718yds. Elected to the Hall of Fame in 1977.

Staubach, Roger   Born Cincinnati, Ohio, 5 February 1942. Quarterback, Dallas Cowboys. In the 1970s Staubach *was* the Dallas Cowboys. His touch was delicate, his leadership unquestioned, his impact devastating. After two seasons on the bench, Staubach became starting QB in 1971, leading the team to its first Super Bowl victory with a 24-3 win over the Miami Dolphins, Staubach was MVP. For nine seasons he made the difference at Dallas and the team declined in the 1980s without him. Known as 'The Artful Dodger', his never-say-die attitude often pulled the club round from the brink of defeat. He lost to Terry Bradshaw's Pittsburgh Steelers in Super Bowl X, but led Dallas to victory in XII against Denver. Super Bowl XIII is often considered the best ever. The Steelers, under Bradshaw, led 35-17 with two and a half minutes to go. Staubach threw a seven-yard TD pass, and led a nine-play drive for another touchdown. Dallas, though, failed to recover an on-side kick and lost 35-31. Saubach had just one more year in the NFL, retiring in 1979 with career totals of 2958 passing attempts, 1685 completions for 22,700yds. Elected to the Hall of Fame in 1985.

Stenarud, Jan   Born Fetsund, Norway, 26 November 1942. Place kicker, Kansas City Chiefs, Green Bay Packers, Minnesota Vikings. A Norwegian international ski-jumper, Stenarud discovered football at Montana State. His ability to kick soon saw him embark on a new career. His 19 seasons in the NFL left him with a career record of 373 field goals from 573 attempts. 580 of 600 extra-point attempts and a total of 1699 points. He retired in 1985 and was elected to the Hall of Fame in 1991.

Tarkenton, Fran   Born Richmond, Virginia, 3 February 1940. Quarterback, Minnesota Vikings, New York Giants. 'Fran the Scram' was how Tarkenton became known for his style of play, after he developed a running game when his receivers were not open. He rushed for 3674yds in a 19-year career, from QB, made 6467 pass attempts and connected with 3686 of them. His passing was always first class, with career figures of 47,003yds and 342 touchdowns, all NFL records at the time of his retirement in 1978. Elected to the Hall of Fame in 1986.

Thorpe, Jim   Born Prague, Oklahoma, 28 May 1888. Halfback, Canton Bulldogs, Cleveland Indians, Oorang Indians, Toledo Maroons, Rock Island Independents, New York Giants, Chicago Cardinals. Born into the Sac and Fox Native American tribe. He was given the name Wa-Tho-Huk, meaning 'Bright Path', an apt description for perhaps the greatest athlete ever. Winner of the Olympic pentathlon and decathlon gold medals at the 1912 Stockholm Games, only to have them taken away when it was discovered he had played semi-pro baseball for $2 a game. After 70 years of campaigning the medals were returned to his family in 1982, 29 years after his death. He played baseball in the major leagues for the New York Giants, appearing in the 1917 World Series. It was on the gridiron, however, that the legend grew. Thorpe played football with unmitigated savagery. Added to this he could pass, punt, block and kick, all with equal brilliance. He trailed his skills around several teams, but at the age of 40 drink and gambling took over and he retired in 1928. He was elected to the Hall of Fame in 1963. He died 28 March 1953.

Unitas, John (Johnny)   Born Pittsburgh, Pennsylvania, 7 May 1933. Quarterback, Baltimore Colts, San Diego Chargers. In 18 seasons and 211 games, Unitas set every passing record worth setting. Rejected by his hometown Steelers, he was rescued from semi-pro football to lead the Colts to victory in the 1958 NFL championship game against the New York Giants, in what is described as the most famous game in football history. An audience of millions watched spellbound as Unitas moved the Colts 66yds for a game-tying TD near the end of normal time. He was just 25 years old that day as he moved the Colts into the end zone for victory. It was the NFL's first sudden-death championship. The following year Unitas led the Colts to a second title. He also led them to three Super Bowls. However, injuries and a surprising lack of form on the greatest football stage of all, saw him perform well below his best. He had one season in San Diego before retiring in 1973. His career records were 5186 pass attempts, 2830 completions for 40,239yds and 290 touchdowns. Elected to the Hall of Fame in 1979. He died 11 September 2002.

Warfield, Paul   Born Warren, Ohio, 28 November 1942. Wide receiver, Cleveland Browns, Miami Dolphins, Memphis Southmen (World Football League). Matching great speed with safe hands, Warfield scored a touchdown with every fifth pass he caught. For 13 years he was the main deep threat in the league, averaging over 20yds per catch. After an unsuccessful spell in Miami he played ten games in the WFL for Memphis, but was rescued by his beloved Browns. He retired in 1977. Career records include 427 receptions for 8565yds and 85 touchdowns. Elected to the Hall of Fame in 1983.

AMERICAN FOOTBALL

ANGLING

Angling is the sport of fishing with a hook, line and bait. It is the biggest mass participation sport in the world and has millions of enthusiasts 'hooked'. Many sources record angling as being started by the Egyptians in 2000BC, however, the oldest fishhooks to have been found were made of bone and discovered in Czechoslovakia. These are believed to be 20,000 years old.

It is impossible to determine when fishing became a sport and not primarily a means of survival. In some parts of the world, fishing as a sport would be unthinkable even to this day. But at some point anglers began to use rods when fishing to 'give the fish a chance' and make fishing more of a challenge.

The rod enables the angler to extend his reach. The earliest rods were simple poles with lines attached. By the 18h century rods were becoming longer and were made of multiple sections of woods such as ash, hickory, lancewood, and greenheart. By the middle of the 19th century bamboo was the favoured material for making a rod. Many fine bamboo rods are still used to the present day, but they are outnumbered by those made of fibreglass and graphite.

The world freshwater championships (WFC) have been held since 1957 and the world fly fishing championships since 1981. In 1997 women began to take part in the WFC, when England's Wendy Locker won the women's individual championships and England also won the women's team competition. England maintained its dominance of women's angling by taking the team title in 1999, while Gillian Foy won the individual gold. Sandra Scotthorne, wife of Alan, has kept the tradition going by winning the last two championships in 2001 and 2003. By winning the 2003 world angling championships Alan and Sandra have gained a unique place in sporting history by becoming the only husband and wife to win world championships in the same sport in the same year.

The most fundamental difference between fly fishing and other styles of fishing is that a heavy line is used to cast a near weightless 'fly', rather than a near weightless line carrying heavier bait.

Other well-known anglers of today include Ian Heaps, Bob James, Ivan Marks, Bob Nudd, Martin Page, Des Taylor, Dave Thomas, Richard Walker and Chris Yates. Television presenters John Wilson and, more recently, Matt Hayes have also raised the profile of the sport with their professional tips.

The definitive book for the angler is Isaak Walton's *The Compleat Angler* (1653).

World Freshwater Champions

	Individual	Team		Individual	Team
1957	Mandelli (ITA)	Italy	1980	Wolf-Rudiger Kremkus (FRG)	West Germany
1958	Garroit (BEL)	Belgium	1981	Dave Thomas (ENG)	France
1959	Robert Tesse (FRA)	France	1982	Kevin Ashurst (ENG)	Holland
1960	Robert Tesse (FRA)	Belgium	1983	Wolf-Rudiger Kremkus (FRG)	Belgium
1961	Ramon Legogue (FRA)	East Germany	1984	Bobby Smithers (IRL)	Luxembourg
1962	Raimondo Tedasco (ITA)	Italy	1985	Dave Roper (ENG)	England
1963	William Lane (ENG)	France	1986	Lud Wever (NED)	Italy
1964	Joseph Fontanet (FRA)	France	1987	Clive Branson (WAL)	England
1965	Robert Tesse (FRA)	Romania	1988	Jean-Pierre Fourgeat (FRA)	England
1966	Henri Guiheneuf (FRA)	France	1989	Tom Pickering (ENG)	Wales
1967	Jacques Isenbaert (BEL)	Belgium	1990	Bob Nudd (ENG)	France
1968	Gunter Grebenstein (FRG)	France	1991	Bob Nudd (ENG)	England
1969	Robin Harris (ENG)	Holland	1992	David Wesson (AUS)	Italy
1970	Marcel Van den Eynde (BEL)	Belgium	1993	Mario Barros (POR)	Italy
1971	Dino Bassi (ITA)	Italy	1994	Bob Nudd (ENG)	England
1972	Hubert Levels (NED)	France	1995	Paul Jean (FRA)	France
1973	Pierre Michiels (BEL)	Belgium	1996	Alan Scotthorne (ENG)	Italy
1974	Aribert Richter (FRG)	France	1997	Alan Scotthorne (ENG)	Italy
1975	Ian Heaps (ENG)	France	1998	Alan Scotthorne (ENG)	England
1976	Dino Bassi (ITA)	Italy	1999	Bob Nudd (ENG)	Spain
1977	Jean Mainil (BEL)	Luxembourg	2000	Jacopo Falsinilta (ITA)	Italy
1978	Jean-Pierre Fourgeat (FRA)	France	2001	Umberto Ballabeni (ITA)	England
1979	Gerard Heulard (FRA)	France	2002	G. Blasco (ESP)	Spain
			2003	Alan Scotthorne (ENG)	Hungary

World Fly Fishing Champions

	Individual	Team		Individual	Team
1981	C. Wittkamp (NED)	Holland	1993	Russell Owens (WAL)	England
1982	Viktor Diez (ESP)	Italy	1994	Pascal Cognard (FRA)	Czech Republic
1983	S. Fernandez (ESP)	Italy	1995	Jeremy Herrmann (ENG)	England
1984	Tony Pawson (ENG)	Italy	1996	Perluigi Coccito (ITA)	Czech Republic
1985	Leslaw Frasik (POL)	Poland	1997	Pascal Cognard (FRA)	France
1986	Slivoj Svoboda (TCH)	Italy	1998	T. Starychfolta (CZE)	Czech Republic
1987	Brian Leadbetter (ENG)	England	1999	Ross Steward (AUS)	Australia
1988	John Pawson (ENG)	England	2000	Pascal Cognard (FRA)	France
1989	Wladislaw Trzebuinia (POL)	Poland	2001	Vladimir Sedivy (CZE)	France
1990	Franciszek Szajnik (POL)	Czechoslovakia	2002	Jerome Brossutti (FRA)	France
1991	Brian Leadbetter (ENG)	New Zealand	2003	Stefano Cotungo (ITA)	France
1992	Perluigi Coccito (ITA)	Italy			

British Freshwater Records

(as at 31 August 2004)

Barbel

Latin name	*Barbus barbus*
Maximum length	90cm
Life span	15-17 years
Principal natural food	Mayfly larvae, caddis-fly larvae, dragonfly larvae, pea mussel, gudgeon, worms and snails
Habitat	Rivers. Collecting at weirpools and waterfalls, feeding in the dark hours. In winter time they gather in deeper parts of the river and holes in banks.
Official British record	19lb 1oz (8.64kg) by Tony Gibson, Berkshire, 2001

Bleak

Latin name	*Alburnus alburnus*
Maximum length	23-25cm
Life span	6-8 years
Principal natural food	Daphnia, mayfly and fly pupae
Habitat	Living in shoals, it can be found in slow-moving water and prefers no vegetation in its area. Found usually in open water, near the surface. Moves to deeper water over winter.
Official British record	4oz 9dr (129.34g) by Dennis Flack, River Lark, Cambridgeshire, 1998

Bream

Latin name	*Abramis brama*
Maximum length	60-65cm
Life span	15-20 years
Principal natural food	Pea mussel, water slater, ram's horn snail, worms (tubiflex), fly larvae, daphnia and plant fragments
Habitat	Found mostly in slow-moving or still waters with a clay or muddy bottom. Older fish keep over a clean bottom when feeding, moving to shallows at night. Densely packs into shoals at winter.
Official British record	18lb 9oz (8.42kg) by Kerry Walker Bawburgh, Norfolk, 2001

Carp (variations are Common, Mirror, Leather, Linear, Wild, Grass)

Latin name	*Cyprinus carpio*
Maximum length	89cm
Life span	40+ years
Principal natural food	Water bugs, mayfly larvae, pond snail, cyclops, daphnia, water slater, fly larvae, caddis fly, worms, water spider and plant seeds
Habitat	Mainly nocturnal feeding, it prefers waters that are holding dense vegetation and muddy bottoms. Can be found all over a lake scanning the area for food.
Official British record	Carp 59lb 12oz (27.16kg) by Mark Toland, Conningbrook Lake, 2001
	Grass Carp 31lb (14.06kg) by Derek Smith, Church Lake, Horton, Berkshire, 1997

ANGLING

Chub

Latin name	*Leuciscus cephalus*
Maximum length	56-59cm
Life span	12 years
Principal natural food	Mayfly larvae, caddis-fly larvae, caddis fly, trout fry, fly larvae, worms and silkweed
Habitat	Rivers, mostly with strong undercurrents. The larger specimens are usually solitary with small chub shoaling near the surface. Feeds mostly in the dark hours. In general, migrates to deeper waters in winter time.
Official British record	8lb 10oz (3.91kg) by Peter Smith, River Tees, Blackwell, County Durham, 1994

Crucian Carp

Latin name	*Carassius carassius*
Maximum length	46cm
Life span	13-15 years
Principal natural food	Worms, caddis-fly larvae, freshwater shrimp, pond snail, daphnia, cyclops, pea mussel and fly larvae
Habitat	A hardy fish, it can survive in swampy overgrown waters that other fish cannot exist in. Feeding among weeds during the warm summer months. During winter, it hibernates almost buried in mud.
Official British record	4lb 9oz (2.01kg) by Martin Bowler, Summer Pit, Yateley, 16 May 2003

Dace

Latin name	*Leuciscus leuciscus*
Maximum length	30cm
Life span	10-12 years
Principal natural food	Worms, freshwater shrimp, plants and fly larvae
Habitat	Prefers cool running water and lakes.
Official British record	1lb 4oz 4dr (574.1g) by J.L. Gasson, Little Ouse, Thetford, 1960

Eel

Latin name	*Anguilla anguilla*
Maximum length	1m
Life span	25 years
Principal natural food	Worms, freshwater shrimp, freshwater fish eggs, pond snail, crayfish and fly larvae
Habitat	Almost all waters. Prefers feeding after dark.
Official British record	11lb 2oz (5.05kg) by Steve Terry, Kingfisher Lake, Ringwood, Hampshire, 1978

Gudgeon

Latin name	*Gobio gobio*
Maximum length	20cm
Life span	5-8 years
Principal natural food	Ostracods, caddis-fly larvae, fish eggs, worm and fly larvae
Habitat	Prefers fast running water over sand or gravel but also occurs in lakes. During summer it shoals up in shallow water and during winter finds the deep water.
Official British record	5oz (141.75g) by D.H. Hull, River Nadder, Sutton Mandeville, Wiltshire, 1990

Minnow

Latin name	*Phoxinus phoxinus*
Maximum length	12cm
Life span	6 years
Principal natural food	Caddis-fly larvae, freshwater shrimp, stone-fly and stone-fly larvae
Habitat	Upper reaches of rivers in cool running sandy or stony bottom. Very rare in lakes. Found in shoals of 100 or more.
Official British record	13.5 dr (23.92g) by J. Sawyer, Whitworth Lake, Spennymoor, 1998

Perch

Latin name	*Perca fluviatilis*
Maximum length	50cm
Life span	13 years
Principal natural food	Cyclops, fly larvae, mayfly larvae, freshwater shrimps, young crayfish, elvers, roach, bleak
Habitat	Still, slow and fast running water. Prefers dark, poorly lit bare bottom.
Official British record	5lb 9oz (2.55kg) by John Shayler at a private lake in Kent, 1985

Pike

Latin name	*Esox lucius*
Maximum length	1.27m
Life span	18-25 years
Principal natural food	Roach, bream, bleak, rudd, dace, perch, frogs, duckling and pike!
Habitat	Still or slow running water. Hiding in reeds or well-weeded areas. Larger pike in large lakes often stray into open deeper water.
Official British record	46lb 13oz (21.23kg) by Ray Lewis, Llandegfedd, Wales, 1992

Roach

Latin name	*Rutilus rutilus*
Maximum length	36cm
Life span	10-15 years
Principal natural food	Fly larvae, rotifers, freshwater shrimp, pond snail and water-weed
Habitat	Still or slow running water. Browsing for food on silt beds/weeds during the day and moving to shallow area at dusk. Winter roach gather in the deepest water.
Official British record	4lb 3oz (1.90kg) by Ray Clarke, Dorset Stour, 1990

Rudd

Latin name	*Scardinius erythrophthalmus*
Maximum length	40-45cm
Life span	12 years
Principal natural food	Pulmonate snail, mayfly larvae, caddis-fly larvae and fly larvae
Habitat	Warm lakes, and slow moving rivers. Feeding mainly on plant leaves (e.g. stonewort). Moves to deep water over winter.
Official British record	4lb 10oz (2.1kg) by Simon Parry, Freshwater Lake in Co. Armagh, 2001

Ruffe

Latin name	*Gymnocephalus cernua*
Maximum length	18cm
Life span	7-9 years
Principal natural food	Worms, mayfly larvae, freshwater shrimp, pea mussel, freshwater fish eggs and fly larvae
Habitat	Active feeding by day, it can be found on bare-bottomed lakes and lower reaches of rivers.
Official British record	5oz 4dr (148.83g) by R.J. Jenkins, West View Farm, Cumbria, 1980

Tench

Latin name	*Tinca tinca*
Maximum length	60-66cm
Life span	20 years
Principal natural food	Alder-fly larvae, fly larvae, pea mussel, worms and pond snails
Habitat	Still or very slow moving waters. Does well in soft-bottomed lakes with rich vegetation.
Official British record	14lb 7oz (6.55kg) by Gordon Beaven, private water, Hertfordshire, 1993

Zander

Latin name	*Stizostedion lucioperca*
Maximum length	1m
Life span	20 years
Principal natural food	Smelt, roach, perch, bleak
Habitat	Found mostly in the lower reaches of rivers in fast flowing open areas of water, away from pike. Hunting in packs.
Official British record	19lb 5oz (8.76kg) by Dave Lavender, fen water, Cambridgeshire, 1998

ANGLING

ARCHERY

Archery is one of the oldest arts still practised today. It probably dates to the New Stone Age (around 8000BC), although the earliest people known to have used the bow and arrow were the ancient Egyptians, who adopted it at least 5000 years ago for purposes of hunting and warfare.

In 1200BC, the Hittites' use of bows from light, fast chariots enabled them to become dreaded opponents in Middle Eastern battles. Their neighbours, the Assyrians, also used archery extensively, building bows from animal tendon, horn and wood. They gave the bow a new, recurved shape that was far more powerful and, being shorter, was more easily handled by an archer on horseback.

Chinese civil archery, introduced to Japan in the sixth century AD, had an overriding influence on later etiquette and techniques. One of Japan's martial arts was originally known as *kyujutsu* (the art of the bow) and is now known as *kyudo* (the way of the bow). Kyudo today continues to be taught in the traditionally prescribed manner. After certain ritual movements, the archer advances with deliberate steps to the shooting line and shoots at a target 36cm in diameter set in a bank of sand that is roofed over, from a distance of 28m. The bow is 2.21m long and made of laminated strips of bamboo and wood.

In Greek mythology, reference is often made to archers. In the Greco-Roman period, the bow began to be used more for personal exploits and hunting rather than in warfare. The Romans are said to have been second-rate archers as, until the fifth century AD, their bows were shot by drawing the string to the chest, instead of the longer draw to the face which gives the arrow far more accuracy. Their opponents often had far better skills. The Parthians, for instance, were horsemen who developed the skill of swivelling around in the saddle and could shoot backwards at full gallop.

For Native Americans, the bow was a means of both subsistence and existence, even before the days of English and later American colonisation. This was also the case – and still is in some countries – on the African continent.

The popularity of archery is reflected in the many ballads and folklore concerned with the subject, such as the stories of Robin Hood, the most famous and reputedly the greatest archer of them all. Recent evidence of a tunnel found in Nottingham Castle is fuelling the debate on whether Robin and his band of merry men may have in fact existed.

English literature too honours the longbow, for famous victories in the battles of Crécy, Agincourt and Poitiers.

Roger Ascham's *Toxophilus* (1545) popularised archery as a sport. The first known organised competition in archery was held at Finsbury, England, in 1583 and included 3000 participants. By the time of the Thirty Years War (1618-48), it was clear that the bow as a weapon belonged to the past, due to the introduction of gunpowder. Since then, archery has developed as a recreational sport.

The Royal Company of Archers, the monarch's bodyguard in Scotland, was founded in 1676. The Toxophilite Society was founded in 1780 and the Prince of Wales, later George IV, became its patron in 1787; it thus became the Royal Toxophilite Society. The Grand National Archery Society, the governing body of archery in the United Kingdom, was founded in 1841.

Archery became an Olympic sport for men in 1900 and remained so in 1904, 1908 and 1920, resuming its place in 1972. Women's archery was included in the 1904 and 1908 Olympics and then resumed in Munich alongside the men's events.

The Fédération Internationale de Tir à l'Arc (FITA), the world governing body of archery, was formed in 1931 by Belgium, France, Poland and Sweden. Great Britain joined in 1932 and the United States in 1933.

Since the formation of FITA, technological advances in toxophily equipment have been vast. The old yew longbows could shoot accurately to up to 300yds (274m) but the new composite, laminated plastic and fibreglass bows are accurate up to three times that distance. The drawing force of the bow has increased considerably and it is not unusual to see 50lb (23kg) bows, although their use requires some strengthening of the muscles of the lower arm. Stabilisers, torque flight compensators, counterweight rods and lens-free bow-sights have made the modern bow look like a highly technical piece of equipment but the truth is that the bowman is still all-important, especially when shooting outdoors.

In domestic competitions, rounds include York (72 arrows at 100yds (91m), 48 at 80 (73m), 24 at 60 (55m), for men), Albion (36 arrows each at 80, 60 and 50yds (73m, 55m and 46m), for men and women), Hereford (72 arrows at 80yds (73m), 48 at 60 (55m) and 24 at 50 (46m), for men and women), St George's (36 arrows each at 100, 80 and 60yds (91m, 73m and 55m), for men), Long Western (48 arrows each at 80 and 60yds (73 and 55m), for men and women), and Western (48 arrows each at 60 and 50yds (55 and 46m), for men and women).

FITA rounds consist of 36 arrows fired over 90, 70, 50 and 30m for men, and 70, 60, 50 and 30m for women.

The world championships were instituted in 1931 using FITA rounds but from 1987 the championships have been held on a knockout basis with scores not being accumulated over the various rounds. In 1999 the championships added the compound bow to the competition.

The format of the men's and women's individual competitions is the same and now consists of a ranking round followed by the FITA Olympics round. Both men's and women's competitions consist of a 70m individual and a 70m team event.

In the ranking round, archers shoot 72 arrows at a target 70m away in 12 ends (rounds) of six arrows each. A perfect score is 720. The same set of shots is used to seed teams for the team competitions.

The FITA Olympic round is divided into an elimination round and a finals round. The 64 competitors, seeded from the ranking round, advance to the elimination round, a single-elimination, head-to-head competition (seed no. 64 v seed no. 1, 63 v 2, etc). Six ends of three arrows – for a total of 18 – are shot at a target 70m away with a 40sec time limit per arrow. Winners of each match move on to the next round.

The finals round is held when the field has been narrowed down to eight archers, beginning with the quarter-finals. In the semi-final and final rounds, archers shoot four ends of three arrows each – for a total of 12 – with a 40sec time limit per arrow.

Each team consists of three archers. In all matches in the team event, each team shoots three ends of nine arrows each, with each archer on the team shooting one end. Each of the three archers is required to finish their end within three minutes.

Only one archer in the team shoots at a time. When the first archer finishes shooting his end, the second archer starts. The third archer follows the second. The arrows are scored and pulled after each team shoots nine arrows.

Losing semi-finalists shoot in the bronze medal match and the two winners shoot in the gold medal final. Archers shoot four ends of three arrows in all matches after the quarter-finals.

Ties are broken with 'sudden death' overtime. Each archer shoots one arrow and the highest score wins. If tied, a second arrow is shot for highest score. If still tied, a single closest-to-the-centre arrow determines the winner. Archers have 50 seconds to shoot each tie-breaking arrow.

The target, usually made of paper, has a diameter of 122cm. It is divided into five coloured rings and each ring is divided in half. The width of each colour zone is 12.2cm and the width of each scoring zone – half of a colour zone – is 6.1cm.

The inner colour zone is gold and the outer ring is white. The rings and their corresponding points values are as follows (from innermost to outermost):

Gold inner:	10 points
Gold outer:	9 points
Red inner:	8 points
Red outer:	7 points
Blue inner:	6 points
Blue outer:	5 points
Black inner:	4 points
Black outer:	3 points
White inner:	2 points
White outer:	1 point

If an arrow is touching two rings, the ring with the higher point score is counted. If an arrow becomes embedded in another arrow, the score of the first arrow is taken. If an arrow misses the target, no points are scored.

If an arrow rebounds from or passes through the target, the score is taken from the mark left by the arrow, providing it can be identified. The archer raises a flag after finishing an end to let the judges know an arrow has rebounded.

Archers may wear a few specific items of protection, such as finger protection, a glove on the bow hand and glasses, as long as they provide nothing that gives an advantage.

Archers may use their own bows and arrows, providing they conform to the specifications set out by competition officials. An arrow is considered a shot if it goes beyond the reach of the archer. If an arrow falls to the ground within reach, it may be shot again.

If an archer shoots an extra arrow, or shoots an arrow out of sequence or outside the time limit, the highest scoring arrow of that end is not counted. In team events, archers may be coached while on the shooting line.

The Olympic archery competition is considered part of the FITA's Recurve Division and thus competitors must use a bow that meets the standards of that group. The recurve bow must use a single string, attached between the ends of the bow, to propel the arrow. No system of pulleys, as employed in a compound bow, is allowed.

A single, mechanical sight is permitted, but no optical enhancements, such as lenses or prisms, may be used. Stabilisers are allowed on the bow as long as they do not touch anything but the bow, serve as a string guide, or impede other competitors. Fibreglass recurve bows today can launch aluminium or carbon-graphite arrows at speeds of about 240kph over the 70m distance.

Any type of arrow is allowed, provided the diameter of the shaft does not exceed 11mm. The arrows of each competitor must be marked on the shaft with the competitor's name or initials and all arrows used in the same end shall carry the same pattern and colours.

ARCHERY

Archery: Target World Champions

	Men	Team	Women	Team
1931	M. Sawicki (POL)	France	J. Kurkowska (POL)	——
1932	L. Reth (BEL)	Poland	J. Kurkowska (POL)	——
1933	D. McKenzie (USA)	Belgium	J. Kurkowska (POL)	Poland
1934	H. Kjellson (SWE)	Sweden	J. Kurkowska (POL)	Poland
1935	A van Kohlen (BEL)	Belgium	Ina Catani (SWE)	Great Britain
1936	E. Heilborn (SWE)	Czechoslovakia	J. Kurkowska (POL)	Poland
1937	G de Rons (BEL)	Poland	Ingo Simon (GBR)	Great Britain
1938	F. Hadas (TCH)	Czechoslovakia	N.-Weston Martyr (GBR)	Poland
1939	R. Beday (FRA)	France	J. Kurkowska (POL)	Poland
1946	E. T. Holbek (DEN)	Denmark	N. de Wharton Burr (GBR)	Great Britain
1947	H. Deutgen (SWE)	Czechoslovakia	J. Kurkowska (POL)	Denmark
1948	H. Deutgen (SWE)	Sweden	N. de Wharton Burr (GBR)	Czechoslovakia
1949	H. Deutgen (SWE)	Czechoslovakia	B. Waterhouse (GBR)	Great Britain
1950	H. Deutgen (SWE)	Denmark	Jean Lee (USA)	Finland
1952	S. Andersson (SWE)	Sweden	Jean Lee (USA)	USA
1953	B. Lundgren (SWE)	Sweden	Jean Richards (USA)	Finland
1955	N. Andersson (SWE)	Sweden	K. Wisniowska (POL)	Great Britain
1957	O. Smathers (USA)	USA	C. Meinhart (USA)	USA
1958	S. Thysell (SWE)	Finland	S. Johansson (SWE)	USA
1959	J. Caspers (USA)	USA	Ann Corby (USA)	USA
1961	J. Thornton (USA)	USA	N. Vonderheide (USA)	USA
1963	C. Sandlin (USA)	USA	V. Cook (USA)	USA
1965	M. Haikonen (FIN)	USA	M. Lindholm (FIN)	USA
1967	Ray Rogers (USA)	USA	M. Maczynska (POL)	Poland
1969	Hardy Ward (USA)	USA	D. Lidstone (CAN)	Soviet Union
1971	J. Williams(USA)	USA	E. Gapchenko (URS)	Poland
1973	V. Sidoruk (URS)	USA	Linda Myers (USA)	Soviet Union
1975	Darrell Pace (USA)	USA	Z. Rustamova (URS)	Soviet Union
1977	R. McKinney (USA)	USA	Luann Ryon (USA)	USA
1979	Darrell Pace (USA)	USA	Kim Jin-Ho (KOR)	Korea
1981	K. Laasonen (FIN)	USA	N. Butuzova (URS)	Soviet Union
1983	R. McKinney (USA)	USA	Kim Jin-Ho (KOR)	Korea
1985	R. McKinney (USA)	Korea	I. Soldatova (URS)	Soviet Union
1987	V. Yesheyev (URS)	W. Germany	Ma Xiaojun (CHN)	Soviet Union
1989	S. Zabrodskiy (URS)	USSR	Kim Soo-Nyung (KOR)	Korea
1991	S. Fairweather (AUS)	Korea	Kim Soo-Nyung (KOR)	Korea
1993	K. Park (KOR)	France	K. Hyo-Jung (KOR)	Korea
1995	Lee Kyung-Chul (KOR)	Korea	N. Valeeva (MDA)	Korea
1997	Kim Kyung-Ho (KOR)	Korea	Kim Du-Ri (KOR)	Korea
1999	Hong Sung-Chil (KOR)	Italy	Lee Eun-Kyung (KOR)	Italy
2001	J.K. Yeon (KOR)	Korea	S. H. Park (KOR)	China
2003	M. Frangilli (ITA)	Korea	Yun Mi-Jin (KOR)	Korea

42nd World Championships 2003 (New York)

Men's

Compound
1　Clint Freeman (AUS)
2　Dave Cousins (USA)
3　Braden Gellenthein (USA)
4　Jari Haavisto (FIN)

Compound Team
1　USA
2　Italy
3　Canada
4　Netherlands
5　Denmark
6　France
7　Sweden
8　Germany
9　Great Britain
10　Slovenia

Recurve
1　Michele Frangilli (ITA)
2　Im Dong-Hyun (KOR)
3　David Barnes (AUS)
4　Tim Cuddihy (AUS)

Recurve Team
1　South Korea
2　Sweden
3　Italy
4　India
5　USA
6　Netherlands
7　Chinese Taipei
8　Ukraine
9　Germany
10　Russia

Women's

Compound
1 Mary Zorn (USA)
2 Amber Dawson (USA)
3 Irma Luyting (NED)
4 Sandrine Vandionant (FRA)

Compound Team
1	USA	6	Mexico
2	France	7	Netherlands
3	Germany	8	Russia
4	Norway	9	Sweden
5	Australia	10	Finland

Recurve
1 Yun Mi-Jin (KOR)
2 Park Sung-Byung (KOR)
3 Lee Hyun-Jun (KOR)
3 Marg Galinovskaya (RUS)

Recurve Team
1	South Korea	6	India
2	Japan	7	China
3	Ukraine	8	Great Britain
4	France	9	Russia
5	Poland	10	Chinese Taipei

ARCHERY

ATHLETICS

The ancient Olympic Games commenced in 776BC in Olympia, Greece, and formed part of a religious festival. In those days the athletes competed as nature intended them to and the earliest games consisted of one solitary athletic event, a footrace the length of the stadium. Gradually other events were added: discus and javelin throws, long jump, boxing, wrestling, chariot racing and the pentathlon. The event, held every four years, became more a sporting event than a religious festival. Winners became folk-heroes and were feted throughout the land.

Following the subjugation of Greece by Rome the games were eventually abolished in AD393, although the individual disciplines flourished to varying degrees as pastimes and national sports on which to wager.

Baron Pierre de Coubertin, a French nobleman, reintroduced the Games in 1896 and the Olympics have grown in stature with the development of track and field athletics, the core event of any Olympic Games. In over 100 years of structured athletic pursuits the sport has changed relatively little: the Olympic motto,

Citius, Altius, Fortius (Faster, Higher, Stronger) was as true then as it is now. Humankind's pursuit of sporting excellence is as keen in the modern world as it was in the late 19th century.

Better training techniques, facilities, dietary control, evolution and coaching methods have ensured that the sport will always intrigue and surprise. At one time few thought a man such as Roger Bannister would break the four-minute mile, it was thought to be physiologically impossible. It was hard to imagine even recently that a female athlete like Paula Radcliffe would beat all the British men home in the London Marathon, as happened in 2003. For participants the sport is all about personal bests and personal goals, for fans it is all about the anticipation of superhuman performances.

The following section includes biographies of world stars past and present, alongside comprehensive results from Olympics, World, European and Commonwealth championships, world record holders, top ten all-time listings, and general information.

General Information

Amateur Athletic Association	Founded in 1880 from the Amateur Athletic Club of 1866.
Commonwealth Games: details	The Reverend Astley Cooper (1866-94) of Yorkshire, first mooted the idea in 1891. Between 1930 and 1954 they were called the British Empire Games; between 1954 and 1966 the British Empire and Commonwealth Games; between 1966 and 1974 the British Commonwealth Games; and from 1978 the Commonwealth Games.
decathlon: order of events	First day: 100m, long jump, shot, high jump, 400m; second day: 110m hurdles, discus, pole vault, javelin, 1500m
discus: weight and dimensions	Men's 2k; women's 1kg; circle: 2.5m
5000m: first under 13 minutes	Said Aouita (Morocco)
four-minute mile: first	Roger Bannister wearing No. 41 ran 3mins 59.4secs at Iffley Rd, Oxford, 6 May 1954. Harold Abraham was the chief time-keeper.
four-minute mile: second	John Landy (Australia) (3mins 57.9secs, 21 June 1954)
hammer: weight (men's)	16lb (7.26kg)
heptathlon: order of events	First day: 100m hurdles, high jump, shot, 200m; second day: long jump, javelin, 800m
high jump: first to 2m leap (woman)	Rosie Ackermann (German Democratic Republic (1977)
first to 6ft leap (man)	Marshall Jones Brooks (1876)
first to 6ft leap (woman)	Iolanda Balas (ROM) (1958)
first to 7ft (man)	Charles Dumas (USA) (1956)
100m: first (man) under 10 seconds	Jim Hines (USA) (1968)
100yds: first (man) under 10 seconds	J.P. Tennent (1868)
110m hurdles: first (man) under 13 seconds	Renaldo Nehemiah (USA) (1981)
hurdles: dimensions	Men's 110m: 3ft 6ins (106.7cm); women's 100m: 2ft 9ins (83.8cm). Men's 400m: 3ft (91.4cm), 35m between; women's 400m: 2ft 6ins (26.2cm), 35m between
javelin: weight and dimensions	Men's: 800g, minimum length 260cm; women's: 600g, minimum length 220cm
marathon: distance	26 miles 385 yards
marathon: origin	This was the distance run by Pheidippides to relay news of the Battle of Marathon (490BC) (an extra 385 yards was added in the 1908 Olympics so as to finish the race in front of the Royal Box).
mile: first man under 3 minutes 50 seconds	John Walker (New Zealand) (1975)

mile: first woman under 5 minutes	Diane Leather (Great Britain) (1954)
Olympics: Intercalated Games of 1906	After the disappointing games of 1900 and 1904, Baron de Coubertin decided to hold games in Athens every four years between Olympics. These games were cancelled after the 1906 event.
pentathlon: ancient	running, jumping, discus, javelin, wrestling
pentathlon: modern	riding, fencing, shooting, swimming, cross-country
pentathlon: women	200m, 100m hurdles, shot, high jump, long jump (800m and javelin added for heptathlon)
pole vault: first man over 6m	Sergey Bubka (Ukraine) (1985)
shot: dimensions	Men's 7.26kg; women's: 4kg. Circle: 2.134m.
steeplechase: waterjump	not jumped on first lap so seven times in all during a 3000m race.
World Championships: won first six	Sergey Bubka (Ukraine) won the first six World Championship pole vault events (1983, 1987, 1991, 1993 1995, 1997).
world record holders; became MPs	Chris Chataway (North Lewisham, Chichester), Sebastian Coe (Falmouth and Camborne) and Lord Burghley (Peterborough)
world records: five in a day	Jesse Owens (USA) (1935)
world records: not broken at Olympics	Only the Men's discus record has never been broken at an Olympic Games.

World Record Holders

(as at 6 September 2004)

Men

100m	Tim Montgomery (USA)	9.78	Paris, 14.09.2002
200m	Michael Johnson (USA)	19.32	Atlanta, 01.08.1996
300m	Michael Johnson (USA)	30.85	Pretoria, 24.03.2000
400m	Michael Johnson (USA)	43.18	Seville, 26.08.1999
800m	Wilson Kipketer (KEN)	1:41.11	Cologne, 24.08.1997
1000m	Noah Ngeny (KEN)	2:11.96	Rieti, 05.09.1999
1500m	Hicham El Guerrouj (MAR)	3:26.00	Rome, 14.07.1998
1 Mile	Hicham El Guerrouj (MAR)	3:43.13	Rome, 07.07.1999
2 Miles	Daniel Komen (KEN)	7:58.61	Hechtel, 19.07.1997
2000m	Hicham El Guerrouj (MAR)	4:44.79	Berlin, 07.09.1999
3000m	Daniel Komen (KEN)	7:20.67	Rieti, 01.09.1996
5000m	Kenenisa Bekele (ETH)	12:37.37	Hengelo, 31.05.2004
10,000m	Kenenisa Bekele (ETH)	26:20.31	Ostrava, 08.06.2004
20,000m	Arturo Barrios (MEX)	56:55.60	La Flèche, 30.03.1991
1 Hour	Arturo Barrios (MEX)	21,101m	La Flèche, 30.03.1991
Half Marathon	Paul Tergat (KEN)	59:17	Milan, 04.04.1998
25,000m (road)	Paul Kosgei (KEN)	1:12:45	Berlin, 08.05.2004
30,000m (road)	Takayuki Matsumiya (JPN)	1:28:36	Kumamoto, 16.02.2003
Marathon	Paul Tergat (KEN)	2:04:55	Berlin, 28.09.2003
3000m Steeplechase	Saif Saeed Shaheen (QAT)	7:53.63	Brussels, 03.09.2004
20km Walk	Jefferson Perez (ECU)	1:17:21	Paris, 23.08.2003
50km Walk	Denis Nizhegorodov (RUS)	3:35:29	Cheboksary, 13.06.2004
110m Hurdles	Colin Jackson (GBR)	12.91	Stuttgart, 20.08.1993
	Xiang Liu (CHN)	12.91	Athens, 27.08.2004
400m Hurdles	Kevin Young (USA)	46.78	Barcelona, 06.08.1992
4 × 100m	United States	37.40	Barcelona, 08.08.1992
4 × 200m	Santa Monica Track Club	1:18.68	Walnut, 17.04.1994
4 × 400m	United States	2:54.20	Uniondale, 22.07.1998
4 × 800m	Great Britain (P. Elliott, G. Cook, S. Cram, S. Coe)	7:03.89	London, 30.08.1982
4 × 1500m	Germany	14:38.80	Cologne, 17.08.1977
Pole Vault	Sergey Bubka (UKR)	6.14m	Sestriere, 31.07.1994
High Jump	Javier Sotomayor (CUB)	2.45m	Salamanca, 27.07.1993
Long Jump	Mike Powell (USA)	8.95m	Tokyo, 30.08.1991
Triple Jump	Jonathan Edwards (GBR)	18.29m	Göthenburg, 07.08.1995
Shot Put	Randy Barnes (USA)	23.12m	Westwood, 20.05.1990
Discus	Jürgen Schult (GDR)	74.08m	Neubrandenburg, 06.06.1986
Hammer	Yury Sedykh (URS)	86.74m	Stuttgart, 30.08.1986
Javelin	Jan Zelezny (CZE)	98.48m	Jena, 25.05.1996
Decathlon	Roman Sebrle (CZE)	9026	Götzis, 27.05.2001

Women

100m	Florence Griffith-Joyner (USA)	10.49	Indianapolis, 16.07.1988
200m	Florence Griffith-Joyner (USA)	21.34	Seoul, 29.09.1988

A
T
H
L
E
T
I
C
S

400m	Marita Koch (GDR)	47.6	Canberra, 06.10.1985
800m	Jarmila Kratochvilova (TCH)	1:53.28	Münich, 26.07.1983
1000m	Svetlana Masterkova (RUS)	2:28.98	Brussels, 23.08.1996
1500m	Qu Yunxia (CHN)	3:50.46	Beijing, 11.09.1993
2000m	Sonia O'Sullivan (IRL)	5:25.36	Edinburgh, 08.07.1994
1 Mile	Svetlana Masterkova (RUS)	4:12.56	Zurich, 14.08.1996
3000m	Wang Junxia (CHN)	8:06.11	Beijing, 13.09.1993
5000m	Elvan Abeylegasse (TUR)	14:24.68	Bergen, 11.06.2004
10,000m	Wang Junxia (CHN)	29:31.78	Beijing, 08.09.1993
20,000m	Tegla Loroupe (KEN)	1:05:26.06	Borgholzhausen, 03.09.2000
25,000m	Tegla Loroupe (KEN)	1:27:05.90	Mengerskirchen, 21.09.2002
3,000m s/chase	Gulnara Samitova (RUS)	9:08.33	Tula, 10.08.2003
1 Hour	Tegla Loroupe (KEN)	18,304m	Borgholzhausen, 07.08.1998
Half Marathon	Elana Meyer (RSA)	1:6:44	Tokyo, 15.01.1999
Marathon	Paula Radcliffe (GBR)	2:15:25	London, 13.04.2003
30,000m	Tegla Loroupe (KEN)	1:45:50	Warstein, 06.06.2003
10km Walk	Nadezhda Ryashkina (URS)	41:56:23	Seattle, 24.07.1990
20km Walk	Olimpiada Ivanova (URS)	1:24:50	Moscow, 04.03.2001
100m Hurdles	Yordanka Donkova (BUL)	12.21	Stara Zagora, 20.08.1988
400m Hurdles	Yuliya Pechonkina (RUS)	52.34	Tula, 08.08.2003
4 × 100m	East Germany	41.37	Canberra, 06.10.1985
4 × 200m	United States	1:27.46	Philadelphia, 29.04.2000
4 × 400m	Soviet Union	3:15.17	Seoul, 01.10.1988
4 × 800m	Soviet Union	7:50.17	Moscow, 05.08.1984
Pole Vault	Yelena Isinbayeva (RUS)	4.92m	Brussels, 03.09.2004
High Jump	Stefka Kostadinova (BUL)	2.09m	Rome, 30.08.1987
Long Jump	Galina Chistyakova (URS)	7.52m	Leningrad, 11.06.1988
Triple Jump	Inessa Kravets (UKR)	15.5m	Göthenburg, 10.08.1995
Shot Put	Natalya Lisovskaya (URS)	22.63m	Moscow, 07.06.1987
Discus	Gabriele Reinsch (GDR)	76.8m	Neubrandenburg, 09.07.1988
Hammer	Mihaela Melinte (ROM)	76.07m	Rüdlingen, 29.08.1999
Javelin (pre 1999)	Petra Felke (GER)	80m	1998 but now erased
Javelin (post 1999)	Osleidys Menendez (CUB)	71.54m	Réthymno, 01.07.2001
Heptathlon	Jackie Joyner-Kersee (USA)	7291	Seoul, 24.09.1988

NB: Marathon and half marathon records are officially 'world bests' rather than world records due to the non-standardisation of courses. Sergey Bubka (UKR) vaulted 6.15m indoors at Donetsk, 21 February 1993.

All-Time Track and Field Lists

(as at 6 September 2004)

(A at altitude; I = indoor)

Men

100m

9.78		Tim Montgomery (USA)	2002
9.79		Maurice Greene (USA)	1999
9.84		Donovan Bailey (CAN)	1996
9.84		Bruny Surin (CAN)	1999
9.85		Leroy Burrell (USA)	1994
9.85		Justin Gatlin (USA)	2004
9.86		Carl Lewis (USA)	1991
9.86		Frankie Fredericks (NAM)	1996
9.86		Ato Boldon (TRI)	1998
9.86		Francis Obikwelu (POR)	2004
9.87		Linford Christie (GBR)	1993
9.87	A	Obadele Thompson (BAR)	1998
9.87		Asafa Powell (JAM)	2004

200m

19.32		Michael Johnson (USA)	1996
19.68		Frankie Fredericks (NAM)	1996
19.72	A	Pietro Mennea (ITA)	1979
19.73		Mike Marsh (USA)	1992
19.75		Carl Lewis (USA)	1983
19.75		Joe DeLoach (USA)	1988
19.77		Ato Boldon (TRI)	1997
19.79		Shawn Crawford (USA)	2004
19.83	A	Tommie Smith (USA)	1968

Women

100m

10.49		Florence Griffith-Joyner (USA)	1988
10.65	A	Marion Jones (USA)	1998
10.73		Christine Arron (FRA)	1998
10.74		Merlene Ottey (JAM)	1996
10.76		Evelyn Ashford (USA)	1984
10.77		Irina Privalova (RUS)	1994
10.78	A	Dawn Sowell (USA)	1989
10.79		Li Xuemei (CHN)	1997
10.79		Inger Miller (USA)	1999
10.81		Marlies Gohr (GDR)	1983

200m

21.34		Florence Griffith-Joyner (USA)	1988
21.62	A	Marion Jones (USA)	1998
21.64		Merlene Ottey (JAM)	1991
21.71		Marita Koch (GDR)	1979
21.71		Heike Drechsler (GDR)	1986
21.72		Grace Jackson (JAM)	1988
21.72		Gwen Torrence (USA)	1992
21.74		Marlies Gohr (GDR)	1984
21.74		Silke Gladisch (GDR)	1987

19.84		Francis Obikwelu (NIG)	1999	21.75		Juliet Cuthbert (JAM)	1992
19.85		John Capel (USA)	2000				
19.85		Konstantin Kenteris (GRE)	2002				

400m

43.18		Michael Johnson (USA)	1999
43.29		Butch Reynolds (USA)	1988
43.50		Quincy Watts (USA)	1992
43.81		Danny Everett (USA)	1992
43.86	A	Lee Evans (USA)	1968
43.87		Steve Lewis (USA)	1988
43.97	A	Larry James (USA)	1968
44.00		Jeremy Wariner (USA)	2004
44.09		Alvin Harrison (USA)	1996
44.09		Jerome Young (USA)	1998

400m

47.60		Marita Koch (GDR)	1985
47.99		Jarmila Kratochvilova (TCH)	1983
48.25		Marie-Jose Perec (FRA)	1996
48.27		Olga Vladykina (URS)	1985
48.59		Tatiana Kocembova (TCH)	1983
48.63		Cathy Freeman (AUS)	1996
48.83		Valerie Brisco-Hooks (USA)	1984
48.89		Ana Guevara (MEX)	2003
49.05		Chandra Cheeseborough (USA)	1984
49.10		Falilat Ogunkoya (NGR)	1996
48.90		Olga Nazarova (URS) (hand-timed)	1988

800m

1:41.11	Wilson Kipketer (DEN)	1997
1:41.73	Sebastian Coe (GBR)	1981
1:41.77	Joaquim Cruz (BRA)	1984
1:42.28	Sammy Koskei (KEN)	1984
1:42.34	Wilfred Bungei (KEN)	2002
1:42.47	Yuri Borzakovsky (RUS)	2001
1:42.55	Andre Bucher (SUI)	2001
1:42.58	Vebjorn Rodal (NOR)	1996
1:42.60	Johnny Gray (USA)	1985
1:42.62	Patrick Ndururi (KEN)	1997

800m

1:53.28	Jarmila Kratochvilova (TCH)	1983
1:53.43	Nadezhda Olizarenko (URS)	1980
1:54.44	Ana Quirot (CUB)	1989
1:54.81	Olga Mineyeva (URS)	1980
1:54.94	Tatyana Kazankina (URS)	1976
1:55.05	Doina Melinte (ROM)	1982
1:55.19	Maria Mutola (MOZ)	1994
1:55.19	Jolanda Ceplak (SLO)	2002
1:55.26	Sigrun Wodars (GDR)	1987
1:55.32	Christine Wachtel (GDR)	1987

1000m

2:11.96	Noah Ngeny (KEN)	1999
2:12.18	Sebastian Coe (GBR)	1981
2:12.88	Steve Cram (GBR)	1985
2:13.56	Kennedy Kimwetich (KEN)	1999
2:13.73	Noureddine Morceli (ALG)	1993
2:13.96	Mehdi Baala (FRA)	2003
2:13.90	Rick Wohlhuter (USA)	1974
2:14.09	Joaquim Cruz (BRA)	1984
2:14.28	Japheth Kimutai (KEN)	2000
2:14.41	William Yampoy (KEN)	1999

1000m

2:28.98	Svetlana Masterkova (RUS)	1996
2:29.34	Maria Mutola (MOZ)	1995
2:30.60	Tatyana Providokhina (URS)	1978
2:30.67	Christine Wachtel (GDR)	1990
2:30.85	Martina Kampfert (GDR)	1980
2:31.50	Natalya Artyomova (URS)	1991
2:31.50	Maricica Puica (ROM)	1986
2:31.51	Sandra Gasser (SUI)	1989
2:31.60	Beate Liebech (GDR)	1980
2:31.65	Olga Dvirna (URS)	1982

1500m

3:26.00	Hicham El Guerrouj (MAR)	1998
3:26.34	Bernard Lagat (KEN)	2001
3:27.39	Noureddine Morceli (ALG)	1995
3:28.12	Noah Ngeny (KEN)	2000
3:28.95	Fermin Cacho (ESP)	1997
3:28.98	Mehdi Baala (FRA)	2003
3:29.18	Venuste Niyongabo (BDI)	1997
3:29.29	William Chirchir (KEN)	2001
3:29.46	Said Aouita (MAR)	1985
3:29.46	Daniel Komen (KEN)	1997

1500m

3:50.46	Qu Yunxia (CHN)	1993
3:50.98	Jiang Bo (CHN)	1997
3:51.34	Lang Yinglai (CHN)	1997
3:51.92	Wang Junxia (CHN)	1993
3:52.47	Tatyana Kazankina (URS)	1980
3:53.91	Yin Lili (CHN)	1997
3:53.96	Paula Ivan (ROM)	1988
3:53.97	Lan Lixin (CHN)	1997
3:54.23	Olga Dvirna (URS)	1982
3:54.52	Zhang Ling (CHN)	1997

1 Mile

3:43.13	Hicham El Guerrouj (MAR)	1999
3:43.40	Noah Ngeny (KEN)	1999
3:44.39	Noureddine Morceli (ALG)	1993
3:46.32	Steve Cram (GBR)	1985
3:46.38	Daniel Komen (KEN)	1997
3:46.70	Venuste Niyongabo (BDI)	1997
3:46.76	Said Aouita (MAR)	1987
3:47.28	Bernard Lagat (KEN)	2001
3:47.33	Sebastian Coe (GBR)	1981
3:47.65	Laban Rotich (KEN)	1997

1 Mile

4:12.56	Svetlana Masterkova (RUS)	1996
4:15.61	Paula Ivan (ROM)	1989
4:15.80	Natalya Artyomova (URS)	1984
4:16.71	Mary Decker Slaney (USA)	1985
4:17.25	Sonia O'Sullivan (IRL)	1994
4:17.33	Maricica Puica (ROM)	1985
4:17.57	Zola Budd (RSA)	1985
4:18.13	Doina Melinte (ROM)	1990
4:19.30	Gabriela Szabo (ROM)	1998
4:19.41	Kirsty McDermott/Wade (GBR)	1985

2000m

4:44.79	Hicham El Guerrouj (MAR)	1999
4:46.88	Ali Saidi-Sief (ALG)	2001
4:47.88	Noureddine Morceli (ALG)	1995
4:48.69	Venuste Niyongabo (BDI)	1995
4:48.74	John Kibowen (KEN)	1998
4:50.08	Noah Ngeny (KEN)	1999
4:50.81	Said Aouita (MAR)	1987

2000m
(# = split time in 3000m race)

5:25.36		Sonia O'Sullivan (IRL)	1994
5:26.93		Yvonne Murray (GBR)	1994
5:28.69		Maricica Puica (ROM)	1986
5:28.72		Tatyana Kazankina (URS)	1984
5:29.41	#	Wang Junxia (CHN)	1993
5:29.64		Tatyana Pozdnyakova (URS)	1984

A
T
H
L
E
T
I
C
S

4:51.30	Daniel Komen (KEN)	1998
4:51.39	Steve Cram (GBR)	1985
4:51.52	John Walker (NZL)	1976

3000m

7:20.67	Daniel Komen (KEN)	1996
7:23.09	Hicham El Guerrouj (MAR)	1999
7:25.02	Ali Saidi-Sief (ALG)	2000
7:25.09	Haile Gebrselassie (ETH)	1998
7:25.11	Noureddine Morceli (ALG)	1994
7:26.62	Mohammed Mourhit (BEL)	2000
7:27.18	Moses Kiptanui (KEN)	1995
7:27.59	Luke Kipkosgei (KEN)	1998
7:27.72	Eliud Kipchoge (KEN)	2004
7:27.75	Thomas Nyariki (KEN)	1996
7:28.41	Paul Bitok (KEN)	1996

5000m

12:39.36	Haile Gebrselassie (ETH)	1998
12:39.74	Daniel Komen (KEN)	1997
12:48.81	Stephen Cherono (KEN)	2003
12:49.28	Brahim Lahlafi (MAR)	2000
12:49.71	Mohammed Mourhit (BEL)	2000
12:49.87	Paul Tergat (KEN)	1997
12:50.24	Hicham El Guerrouj (MAR)	2003
12:50.80	Salah Hissou (MAR)	1996
12:50.86	Ali Saidi-Sief (ALG)	2000
12:52.26	Kenenisa Bekele (ETH)	2003

10,000m

26:22.75	Haile Gebrselassie (ETH)	1998
26:27.85	Paul Tergat (KEN)	1997
26:30.03	Nicholas Kemboi (KEN)	2003
26:36.26	Paul Koech (KEN)	1997
26:38.08	Salah Hissou (MAR)	1996
26:38.76	Abdullah Ahmad Hassan (QAT)	2003
26:49.38	Sammy Kipketer (KEN)	2002
26:49.57	Kenenisa Bekele (ETH)	2003
26:49.90	Assefa Mezgebu (ETH)	2002
26:50.20	Richard Limo (KEN)	2002

3000m Steeplechase

7:53.63	Saif Saeed Shaheen (QAT)	2004
7:55.28	Brahim Boulami (MAR)	2001
7:55.72	Bernard Barmasai (KEN)	1997
7:56.16	Moses Kiptanui (KEN)	1997
7:57.29	Reuben Kosgei (KEN)	2001
7:57.42	Paul Kipsiele Koech (KEN)	2003
7:59.08	Wilson Boit Kipketer (KEN)	1997
8:01.69	Misoi Kipkirui (KEN)	2001
8:02.49	Ezekiel Kemboi (KEN)	2003
8:03.41	Patrick Sang (KEN)	1997

note: Shaheen formerly known as Stephen Cherono (KEN)
07:53.17 Brahim Boulami (MAR) (disqualified) 2002

Half Marathon

59:17	Paul Tergat (KEN)	1998
(59:06 in 2000 to be ratified)		
59:20	Hendrik Ramaala (RSA)	2000
59:31	Patrick Ivuti (KEN)	2000
59:38	Faustin Baha (TAN)	2000
59:41	Haile Gebrselassie (ETH)	2002
59:43	António Pinto (POR)	1998
59:47	Moses Tanui (KEN)	1993
59:51	William Kiplagat (KEN)	2000
59:52	Fabián Roncero (ESP)	2001
59:53	Paul Rugut (KEN)	2002

Marathon

2:04:55	Paul Tergat (KEN)	2003
2:04:56	Sammy Korir (KEN)	2003
2:05:38	Khalid Khannouchi (USA)	2002

5:30.19	Zola Budd (GBR)	1986
5:30.92	Galina Zakharova (URS)	1984
5:32.70	Mary Decker (USA)	1984
5:32.83	Roberta Brunet (ITA)	1996

3000m

8:06.11	Wang Junxia (CHN)	1993
8:12.18	Qu Yunxia (CHN)	1993
8:16.50	Zhang Linli (CHN)	1993
8:19.78	Ma Liyan (CHN)	1993
8:21.42	Gabriela Szabo (ROM)	2002
8:21.64	Sonia O'Sullivan (IRL)	1994
8:21.84	Zhang Lirong (CHN)	1993
8:22.20	Paula Radcliffe (GBR)	2002
8:22.62	Tatyana Kazankina (URS)	1984
8:23.23	Edith Masai (KEN)	2002

5000m

14:24.68	Elvan Abeylegasse (TUR)	2004
14:28.09	Jiang Bo (CHN)	1997
14:29.32	Olga Yegorova (RUS)	2001
14:29.32	Berhane Adere (ETH)	2003
14:29.82	Dong Yanmei (CHN)	1997
14:30.88	Gete Wami (ETH)	2000
14:31.42	Paula Radcliffe (GBR)	2002
14:31.48	Gabriela Szabo (ROM)	1998
14:32.08	Zahra Ouaziz (MAR)	1998
14:32.33	Liu Shixiang (CHN)	1997

10,000m

29:31.78	Wang Junxia (CHN)	1993
30:01.09	Paula Radcliffe (GBR)	2002
30:04.18	Berhane Adere (ETH)	2003
30:07.15	Werknesh Kidane (ETH)	2003
30:07.20	Sun Yingjie (CHN)	2003
30:12.53	Lornah Kiplagat (NED)	2003
30:13.37	Zhong Huandi (CHN)	1993
30:13.74	Ingrid Kristiansen (NOR)	1986
30:17.49	Derartu Tulu (ETH)	2000
30:22.48	Gete Wami (ETH)	2000

3000m Steeplechase

9:08.33	Gulnara Samitova (RUS)	2003
9:16.51	Alesya Turova (BLR)	2002
9:22.29	Justyna Bak (POL)	2002
9:24.78	Lyubov Ivanova (RUS)	2003
9:30.70	Melissa Rollison (AUS)	2001
9:32.31	Yekaterina Volkova (RUS)	2003
9:33.12	Elodie Olivares (FRA)	2002
9:33.16	Cristina Iloc-Casandra (ROM)	2002
9:38.31	Melanie Schultz (GER)	2002
9:39.51	Irene Limika (KEN)	2001

Half Marathon

1:05.40	Paula Radcliffe (GBR) (not ratified)	2003
1:05.44	Susan Chepkemei (KEN) (not ratified)	2001
1:06:34	Lornah Kiplagat (KEN) (not ratified)	2001
1:06:40	Ingrid Kristiansen (NOR) (not ratified)	1987
1:06:43	Masako Chiba (JPN) (not ratified)	1997
1:06:44	Elana Meyer (RSA)	1999
1:06:47	Paula Radcliffe (GBR)	2001
1:06:49	Esther Wanjiru (KEN)	1999
1:07:03	Derartu Tulu (ETH) (not ratified)	2001
1:07:11	Liz McColgan (GBR)	1992

note: the 'not ratified' entries were run on slightly downhill courses

Marathon

2:15:25	Paula Radcliffe (GBR)	2003
2:18:47	Catherine Ndereba (KEN)	2001
2:19:39	Sun Yingjie (CHN)	2003

2:05:50	Evans Rutto (KEN)	2003
2:06:05	Ronaldo da Costa (BRA)	1998
2:06:14	Felix Limo (KEN)	2004
2:06:15	Titus Munji (KEN)	2003
2:06:16	Moses Tanui (KEN)	1999
2:06:16	Daniel Njenga (KEN)	2002
2:06:16	Toshinari Takaoka (JPN)	2002

2:19:46	Naoko Takahashi (JPN)	2001
2:20:43	Tegla Loroupe (KEN)	1999
2:20:43	Margaret Okayo (KEN)	2002
2:21:06	Ingrid Kristiansen (NOR)	1985
2:21:16	Deena Drossin/Kastor (USA)	2003
2:21:18	Mizuki Noguchi (JPN)	2003
2:21:21	Joan Benoit Samuelson (USA)	1985

110m Hurdles

12.91	Colin Jackson (GBR)	1993
12.91	Xiang Liu (CHN)	2004
12.92	Roger Kingdom (USA)	1989
12.92	Allen Johnson (USA)	1996
12.93	Renaldo Nehemiah (USA)	1981
12.94	Jack Pierce (USA)	1996
12.98	Mark Crear (USA)	1999
13.00	Tony Jarrett (GBR)	1993
13.00	Anier Garcia (CUB)	2000
13.01	Larry Wade (USA)	1999

100m Hurdles

12.21	Yordanka Donkova (BUL)	1988
12.25	Ginka Zagorcheva (BUL)	1987
12.26	Lyudmila Narozhilenko (RUS)	1992
12.33	Gail Devers (USA)	2000
12.36	Grazyna Rabsztyn (POL)	1980
12.37	Joanna Hayes (USA)	2004
12.39	Vera Komisova (URS)	1980
12.39	Natalya Grigoryeva (URS)	1991
12.42	Bettine Jahn (GDR)	1983
12.42	Anjanette Kirkland (USA)	2001

400m Hurdles

46.78	Kevin Young (USA)	1992
47.02	Edwin Moses (USA)	1983
47.03	Bryan Bronson (USA)	1998
47.10	Samuel Matete (ZAM)	1991
47.19	Andre Phillips (USA)	1988
47.23	Amadou Dia Ba (SEN)	1988
47.25	Felix Sanchez (DOM)	2003
47.37	Stephane Diagana (FRA)	1995
47.38	Danny Harris (USA)	1991
47.48	Harald Schmid (FRG)	1982

400m Hurdles

52.34	Yuliya Pechonkina (RUS)	2003
52.61	Kim Batten (USA)	1995
52.62	Tonja Buford (USA)	1995
52.74	Sally Gunnell (GBR)	1993
52.79	Sandra Farmer-Patrick (USA)	1993
52.82	Deon Hemmings (JAM)	1996
52.82	Fani Halkia (GRE)	2004
52.89	Daimi Pernia (CUB)	1999
52.90	Nezha Bidouane (MAR)	1999
52.94	Marina Stepanova (URS)	1986

4 × 100m Relay

37.40	United States	1992
37.69	Canada	1996
37.73	Great Britain	1999
37.79	France	1990
37.90	Brazil	2000
37.91	Nigeria	1999
38.00	Cuba	1992
38.02	Soviet Union	1987
38.12	Ghana	1997
38.17	Australia	1995

4 × 100m Relay
(X = run in race with men)

41.37		East Germany	1985
41.47		United States	1997
41.49		Russia	1993
41.73		Jamaica	2004
41.78		France	2003
41.91		Germany	1991
41.92		Bahamas	1999
41.94		Jamaica	1991
42.08	X	Bulgaria	1984
42.20		Soviet Union	1991
42.23		China	1997

4 × 400m Relay

2:54.20	United States	1998
2:56.60	Great Britain	1996
2:56.75	Jamaica	1997
2:58.00	Poland	1998
2:58.19	Bahamas	2001
2:58.54	Brazil	1999
2:58.68	Nigeria	2000
2:58.96	France	2003
2:59.13	Cuba	1992
2:59.63	Kenya	1992

4 × 400m Relay

3:15.17	Soviet Union	1988
3:15.51	United States	1988
3:15.92	East Germany	1984
3:18.38	Russia	1993
3:20.32	Czechoslavakia	1983
3:20.65	Jamaica	2001
3:20.92	Germany	1997
3:21.04	Nigeria	1996
3:21.21	Canada	1984
3:21.94	Ukraine	1986

20km Walk

1:17.21	Jefferson Perez (ECU)	2003
1:17:22	Francisco Fernández (ESP)	2002
1:17:23	Vladimir Stankin (RUS)	2004
1:17:46	Julio Martínez (GUA)	1999
1:17:46	Roman Rasskazov (RUS)	2000
1:17:56	Alejandro López (MEX)	1999
1:18:04	Bo Lingtang (CHN)	1994
1:18:05	Dmitriy Yesipchuk (RUS)	2001
1:18:06	Viktor Burayev (RUS)	2001
1:18:12	Artur Meleshkevich (BLR)	2001

20km Walk

1:24:50	Olimpiada Ivanova (RUS)	2001
1:25:18	Tatyana Gudkova (RUS)	2000
1:25:20	Olga Polyakova (RUS)	2000
1:25:29	Irina Stankina (RUS)	2000
1:25:59	Tamara Kovalenko (RUS)	2000
1:26:22	Yan Wang (CHN)	2001
1:26:22	Yelena Nikolayeva (RUS)	2003
1:26:23	Liping Wang (CHN)	2001
1:26:35	Hongyu Liu (CHN)	2001
1:26:50	Natalya Fedoskina (RUS)	2001

50km Walk

3:35:29	Denis Nizhegorodov (RUS)	2004
3:36:03	Robert Korzeniowski (POL)	2003
3:36:42	German Skurygin (RUS)	2003
3:37:26	Valeriy Spitsyn (RUS)	2000
3:37:41	Andrey Perlov (URS)	1989
3:37:46	Andreas Erm (GER)	2003
3:38:01	Aleksandr Voyevodin (RUS)	2003
3:38:17	Ronald Weigel (GDR)	1986
3:38:29	Vyacheslav Ivanenko (URS)	1988
3:38:43	Valent'n Massana (ESP)	1994

High Jump

2.45		Javier Sotomayor (CUB)	1993
2.42		Patrik Sjöberg (SWE)	1987
2.42		Carlo Thränhardt (FRG)	1988
2.41		Igor Paklin (URS)	1985
2.40		Rudolf Povamitsin (URS)	1985
2.40		Sorin Matei (ROM)	1990
2.40	I	Hollis Conway (USA)	1991
2.40		Charles Austin (USA)	1991
2.40		Vyacheslav Voronin (RUS)	2000
2.39		Zhu Jianhua (CHN)	1984
2.39	I	Dietmar Mögenburg (FRG)	1985
2.39	I	Ralf Sonn (GER)	1991

High Jump

2.09		Stefka Kostadinova (BUL)	1987
2.07		Lyudmila Andonova (BUL)	1984
2.07		Heike Henkel (GER)	1992
2.06		Kajsa Bergqvist (SWE)	2003
2.06		Hestrie Cloete (RSA)	2003
2.06		Yelena Slesarenko (RUS)	2004
2.05		Tamara Bykova (URS)	1984
2.05		Inga Babakova (UKR)	1995
2.04		Silvia Costa (CUB)	1989
2.04	I	Alina Astafei (GER)	1995
2.04		Hestrie Cloete (RSA)	1999
2.04		Venelina Veneva (BUL)	2001
2.04		Anna Chicherova (RUS)	2003

Pole Vault

6.15	I	Sergey Bubka (UKR)	1993
6.05		Maksim Tarasov (RUS)	1999
6.05		Dmitriy Markov (AUS)	2001
6.03		Okkert Brits (RSA)	1995
6.03		Jeff Hartwig (USA)	2000
6.02	I	Rodion Gataullin (URS)	1989
6.01		Igor Trandenkov (RUS)	1996
6.00		Tim Lobinger (GER)	1997
6.00	I	Jean Galfione (FRA)	1999
6.00	I	Danny Ecker (GER)	2001
6.00		Toby Stevenson (USA)	2004

Pole Vault

4.92		Yelena Isinbayeva (RUS)	2004
4.88		Svetlana Feofanova (RUS)	2004
4.83		Stacy Dragila (USA)	2004
4.77		Annika Becker (GER)	2002
4.72		Tatyana Polnova (RUS)	2003
4.72		Monika Pyrek (POL)	2004
4.70		Yvonne Buschbaum (GER)	2003
4.70		Anna Rogowska (POL)	2004
4.67		Kellie Suttle (USA)	2004
4.66	I	Christine Adams (GER)	2002

Long Jump

8.95		Mike Powell (USA)	1991
8.90	A	Bob Beamon (USA)	1968
8.87		Carl Lewis (USA)	1991
8.86	A	Robert Emmiyan (URS)	1987
8.74		Larry Myricks (USA)	1988
8.74	A	Erick Walder (USA)	1994
8.71		Iván Pedroso (CUB)	1995
8.63		Kar. Streete-Thompson (USA)	1994
8.60		James Beckford (JAM)	1997
8.59	I	Miguel Pate (USA)	2002
8.59		Dwight Phillips (USA)	2004

Long Jump

7.52		Galina Chistyakova (URS)	1988
7.49		Jackie Joyner-Kersee (USA)	1994
7.48		Heike Drechsler (GDR)	1988
7.43		Anisoara Stanciu (ROM)	1983
7.42		Tatyana Kotova (RUS)	2002
7.39		Yelena Belevskaya (URS)	1987
7.37		Inessa Kravets (UKR)	1992
7.31		Yelena Kokonova-Khlopotnova (URS)	1985
7.31		Marion Jones (USA)	1998
7.26	A	Maurren Maggi (BRA)	1999

Triple Jump

18.29		Jonathan Edwards (GBR)	1995
18.09		Kenny Harrison (USA)	1996
17.97		Willie Banks (USA)	1985
17.92		Khristo Markov (BUL)	1987
17.92		James Beckford (JAM)	1995
17.90		Vladimir Inozemtsev (URS)	1990
17.89	A	João Oliveira (BRA)	1975
17.87		Mike Conley (USA)	1987
17.86		Charlie Simpkins (USA)	1985
17.85		Yoelbi Quesada (CUB)	1997

Triple Jump

15.50		Inessa Kravets (UKR)	1995
15.36		Tatyana Lebedeva (RUS)	2004
15.30		Francoise Mbango Etone (CAM)	2004
15.29		Yamilé Aldama (CUB)	2003
15.25		Hrysopiyi Devetzi (GRE)	2004
15.20		Sarka Kasparkova (CZE)	1997
15.20		Tereza Marinova (BUL)	2000
15.18		Iva Prandzheva (BUL)	1995
15.16		Rodica Mateescu (ROM)	1997
15.16	I	Ashia Hansen (GBR)	1998

Shot Put

23.12		Randy Barnes (USA)	1990
23.06		Ulf Timmermann (GDR)	1988
22.91		Alessandro Andrei (ITA)	1987
22.86	A	Brian Oldfield (USA)	1975
22.75		Werner Günthör (SUI)	1988
22.67		Kevin Toth (USA)	2003
22.64		Udo Beyer (GOR)	1986
22.52		John Brenner (USA)	1987
22.51		Adam Nelson (USA)	2002
22.24		Sergey Smirnov (URS)	1986

Shot Put

22.63		Natalya Lisovskaya (URS)	1987
22.50	I	Helena Fibingerovà (TCH)	1977
22.45		Ilona Briesenick (CDR)	1980
22.19		Claudia Losch (FRG)	1987
21.89		Ivanka Khristova (BUL)	1976
21.86		Marianne Adam (GDR)	1979
21.76		Meisu Li (CHN)	1988
21.73		Natalya Akhrimenko (URS)	1988
21.69		Vita Pavlysh (UKR)	1998
21.66		Xinmei Sui (CHN)	1990

Discus

74.08	Jürgen Schult (GDR)	1986
73.88	Virgilius Alekna (LIT)	2000
71.86	Yuriy Dumchev (URS)	1983
71.70	Róbert Fazekas (HUN)	2002
71.50	Lars Riedel (GER)	1997
71.32	Ben Plucknett (USA)	1983
71.26	John Powell (USA)	1984
71.26	Ricky Bruch (SWE)	1984
71.26	Imrich Bugár (TCH)	1985
71.18	Art Burns (USA)	1983

Hammer

86.74	Yuriy Syedikh (URS)	1986
86.04	Sergey Litvinov (URS)	1986
84.86	Koji Murofushi (JPN)	2001
84.62	Igor Astapkovich (BLR)	1992
84.48	Igor Nikulin (URS)	1990
84.40	Jüri Tamm (URS)	1984
84.32	Ivan Tikhon (BLR)	2003
83.68	Tibor Gécsek (HUN)	1998
83.46	Andrey Abduvaliyev (URS)	1990
84.19	Adrian Annus (HUN)	2003

Javelin

98.48	Jan Zelezny (CZE)	1996
93.09	Aki Parviainen (FIN)	1999
92.61	Sergey Makarov (RUS)	2002
92.60	Raymond Hecht (GER)	1995
91.69	Kostas Gatsioúdis (GRE)	2000
91.46	Steve Backley (GBR)	1992
90.60	Seppo Räty (FIN)	1992
90.44	Boris Henry (GER)	1997
89.16	Tom Petranoff (USA)	1991
89.10	Patrik Bodén (SWE)	1990

Decathlon

9026	Roman Sebrle (CZE)	2001
8994	Tomás Dvorák (CZE)	1999
8891	Dan O'Brien (USA)	1992
8847	Daley Thompson (GBR)	1984
8832	Jürgen Hingsen (FRG)	1984
8820	Bryan Clay (USA)	2004
8815	Erki Nool (EST)	2001
8792	Uwe Freimuth (GDR)	1984
8784	Tom Pappas (USA)	2003
8762	Siegfried Wentz (FRG)	1983

Discus

76.80	Gabriele Reinsch (GDR)	1988
74.56	Zdenka Silhavá (TCH)	1984
74.56	Ilke Wyludda (GDR)	1989
74.08	Diana Gansky (GDR)	1987
73.84	Daniela Costian (ROM)	1988
73.36	Irina Meszynski (GDR)	1984
73.28	Galina Yermakova (URS)	1984
73.22	Tsvetanka Khristova (BUL)	1987
73.10	Gisela Beyer (GDR)	1984
72.92	Martina Hellmann (GDR)	1987

Hammer

76.07	Mihaela Melinte (ROM)	1999
75.68	Olga Kuzenkova (RUS)	2000
75.18	Yipsi Moreno (CUB)	2004
74.50	Manuela Montebrun (FRA)	2003
74.16	Irina Sekachova (UKR)	2004
73.16	Yunaika Crawford (CUB)	2004
72.71	Gulfiya Khanafeyeva (RUS)	2004
72.60	Kamila Skolimowska (POL)	2002
72.42	Zhang Wenxiu (CHN)	2004
72.36	Gu Yuan (CHN)	2004

Javelin
(since the 1999 changes in implement)

71.54	Osleidys Menéndez (CUB)	2001
69.48	Trine Hattestad (NOR)	2000
67.51	Miréla Manjani (GRE)	2000
67.20	Tatyana Shikolenko (RUS)	2000
66.91	Tanja Damaske (GER)	1999
66.80	Louise Currey (AUS)	2000
66.54	Sonia Bisset (CUB)	2001
65.76	Steffi Nerius (GER)	2000
65.71	Nikola Tomecková (CZE)	2001
65.30	Claudia Coslovich (ITA)	2000

Heptathlon

7291	Jackie Joyner-Kersee (USA)	1988
7007	Larisa Nikitina (URS)	1989
7001	Carolina Kluft (SWE)	2003
6985	Sabine Braun (GER)	1992
6946	Sabine John (GDR)	1984
6942	Ghada Shouaa (SYR)	1996
6935	Ramona Neubert (GDR)	1983
6861	Eunice Barber (FRA)	1999
6859	Natalya Shubenkova (URS)	1984
6858	Anke Behmer (GDR)	1988
6845	Irina Belova (RUS)	1992

A
T
H
L
E
T
I
C
S

Biographies

Abera, Gezahegne   Born Etya, Ethiopia, 23 April 1978 Marathon runner. Olympic champion in 2000 and world champion in 2001. He has won the Fukuoka Marathon, arguably the most challenging of all Japan's top marathons, three times but by a combined total of just five seconds. In fact, all of his six victories, out of 11 outings over the classic distance, have come in sprint finishes, including his 2001 World Championships win when he turned on the accelerator over the final 300 metres to beat Kenya's Simon Biwott by one second. He married fellow Ethiopian marathon runner Elfenesh Alemu in 2003.

Abrahams, Harold   Born Bedford, 15 December 1899. A sprinter and long jumper, he was a student at Cambridge when he qualified for the 1920 Olympics but was unplaced. In 1924, after receiving professional training, he qualified for the Olympics again and won gold in the 100m, equalling the Olympic record of 10.6secs, and silver in the 4 × 100m relay. Before the Olympics he set a new British record in the long jump (24ft 2¼ins) that stood for 33 years. He retired due to a leg injury in 1925 and spent the next forty years as an athletics journalist and commentator. He was awarded the CBE in 1957. Abrahams' story was told in the award-winning film Chariots of Fire. He died 14 January 1978 in Enfield.

Ackermann, Rosemarie   Born Rosemarie Witschas, Lohsa, Germany, 4 April 1952. High jumper, European champion 1974, Olympic champion 1976 and won silver in the 1978 European Championships. Having broken the world record on 8 September 1974 (1.96m) and again on 14 August 1977 (1.97m), she was the first woman to clear 2m (26 August 1977, in West Berlin). She retired after the 1980 Olympics.

Akabusi, Kriss   Born 28 November 1958. Lively and outgoing, warm and friendly, are adjectives that well describe the man whose howling laughter has captivated the nation. Despite his laid-back and easy approach, Kriss was undoubtedly a competitor of steel and determination. A 400m runner of the highest calibre, when he transferred his natural speed to the 400m hurdles he was a revelation. Hardly a master technician, Kriss would run as fast as possible between the obstacles and accommodate the leap over the obstacles the best way he could. In fact, by 1990 his technique was quite solid. In that year he won the European Championship gold over the 400m hurdles and broke David Hemery's long-standing British record to boot. He began his international career in 1983 as a member of the 4 × 400m relay squad and will probably always be remembered for helping Britain clinch the gold and beat the Americans in the World Championship 4 × 400m relay in Tokyo in 1991.

Akii-Bua, John   Born Kampala, Uganda, 3 December 1949. He began as a 110m hurdler but after failing to qualify for the 1968 and 1970 Commonwealth Games, he changed to 400m hurdles. Setting a new world record of 47.82secs, he took Olympic gold on 2 September 1972. Akii-Bua could not defend his Olympic title in 1976 due to the African boycott and political turmoil in Uganda curtailed his career.

Anton, Abel   Born Ojoel, Spain, 24 October 1962. Anton won the 10,000m at the 1987 European Cup, was European champion in 1994 and took bronze in the 5000m. He took up the marathon in 1996 and won the Berlin Marathon, the Korean Marathon, and was world champion in 1997.

Aouita, Said   Born Kenitra, Morocco, 2 November 1959. Said Aouita dominated middle-distance running in the 1980s. He took bronze at the 1983 World Championships at 1500m and gold in the 5000m at the 1984 Olympics. On 23 August 1985 in Berlin he set a new world record of 3mins 29.46secs in the 1500m. He then won gold at 5000m at the World Championships in 1987, also setting a world indoor record of 7mins 47.94secs at 3000m. He was also fast enough to win bronze in the 1988 Olympic 800m final. At the Bislett Games on 1 July 1989 he set a new world record of 7mins 29.45secs at 3000m, making him owner of six of the ten fastest times in athletics.

Ashford, Evelyn   Born Shreveport, Louisiana, 15 April 1957. Evelyn Ashford took part in five Olympic Games, winning gold in the 100m and 4 × 100m at the 1984 Olympics and setting a new world record of 10.76secs on 22 August 1984 in Zürich. She won silver in the 100m and gold in the 4 × 100m at the 1988 Olympics. At the Olympic Games in 1992 she won gold again in the 4 × 100m at the age of 35.

Austin, Charles   Born Bay City, Texas, 19 December 1967. High jumper. World champion at the 1991 championships, he also won gold at the 1996 Olympics. Austin's nickname was 'Snake'.

Babers, Alonzo   Born Montgomery, Alabama, 31 October 1961. 400m runner. Babers took gold in the 400m and 4 × 400m at the 1984 Olympics while a serving officer in the USAF.

Backley, Steve   Born Sidcup, Kent, 12 February 1969. He set a new javelin world record of 89.58m at Stockholm in 1990, extending this to 91.46m in New Zealand in 1992. Gold medallist at the Commonwealth Games and European champion in 1990, he retained both titles in 1994, keeping his European title again in 1998. Backley took bronze at the 1992 Olympics and silver in 1996 and 2000. He won Commonwealth gold in 2002 and was European champion for the fourth successive time. Steve Backley is one of the all-time British greats, although often thwarted for international honours by his arch-rival, Jan Zelezny. He was awarded the MBE in 1995 and the OBE in 2003.

Bailey, Donovan   Born Manchester, Jamaica, 16 December 1967. Moved to Canada in 1981 and now a Canadian citizen. Bailey won gold in the 100m at the 1996 Olympics, setting a new world record of 9.84secs in the process. He also won gold in the 4 × 100m. He then won gold in the 100m and 4 × 400m at the World Championships in 1995, retaining the 4 × 100m title at the 1997 World Championships and winning silver in the 100m.

Balas, Iolanda   Born Timisoara, Romania, 12 December 1936, Balas is the all-time great of high jumping. She broke her first world record on 14 July 1956 at 1.75m and improved it 13 times in the next eight years. Between 1956 and 1966, she won 140 competitions and in 1958 became the first woman to clear 6ft (1.83m). She won Olympic gold in 1960 and 1964 and was European champion in 1958 and 1962.

Banks, Willie   Born Trans Airforce Base, California, 11 March 1956. Willie set a world record of 58ft 11½ins (17.97m) in the triple jump at Indianapolis. He was also in the 1984 and 1988 United States Olympic teams. Banks started the now commonplace practice of encouraging the crowd to clap hands while speeding down the runway.

Bannister, Sir Roger   Born Harrow, Middlesex, 23 March 1929. A successful athlete from his teens, Bannister went up to Oxford in 1946 to study medicine. While there he researched the capacity of the body to endure sub four-minute mile running, which at the time was thought to be impossible. He proved this was not the case when he ran 3mins 59.4secs on 6 June 1954 at Iffley Road Stadium, Oxford, wearing the number 41 shirt and assisted by pacemakers Chris Brasher and Chris Chataway. He retired from athletics at the end of 1954. He was awarded the CBE in 1955 and knighted in 1975 for his services to medicine.

Barber, Eunice   Born Freetown, Sierra Leone, 17 November 1974. Barber became a French citizen in 1999 and was the world's greatest all-round athlete at this time, winning the heptathlon gold in the World Championships at Seville. Injury has dogged her progress since then but despite lack of training and competition she performed miraculously at the World Championships in Paris in 2003 and walked away with gold in the long jump.

Barmasai, Bernard   Born Keiyo, Kenya, 6 May 1974. Barmasai set a world record of 7mins 55.72secs in the 3000m steeplechase at Köln. He also won silver in the same event at the 1998 Commonwealth Games.

Batten, Kim   Born McRae, Georgia, 29 March 1969. Batten set a new world record of 52.61secs in the 400m hurdles as she took gold in the World Championships at Gothenburg on 8 August 1995. She won the silver medal at the 1996 Olympics and at the 1997 World Championships, she won bronze in the 400m hurdles and silver in the 4 × 400m relay.

Bayi, Filbert   Born Karatu, Tanganyika (now Tanzania), 23 June 1953. Bayi set a new 1500m world record of 3mins 32.16secs and took gold at the Commonweath Games in 1974. He gained a silver at the 1978 Commonwealth Games and showed his versatility by gaining a silver in the steeplechase at the 1980 Moscow Olympics.

Beamon, Bob   Born Jamaica, New York, 29 August 1946. Long jumper. Took gold at the 1968 Olympics and set a world record of 29ft 2½ ins (8.90m) that stood for 24 years. He was the first man to jump more than 28ft and 29ft. Beamon's leap was something of a freak as he had never shown the form required for such a jump in previous competitions. British champion Lynn Davies commented that Beamon's leap had 'destroyed' the event and it was the prime reason for Davies' retirement. Beamon himself was forced to retire through injury in 1969.

Bennett, Charles   Born Shapwick, Dorset, 1870. The first British athlete to win an Olympic gold medal, the 1500m in 1900. He also won gold in the 4 × 5000m and silver in the 4000m steeplechase. His 1500m was the fastest ever recorded at the time. He died in 1948.

Benoit-Samuelson, Joan   Born Cape Elizabeth, Maine, 16 May 1957. Marathon runner. She won the Boston Marathon in 1979 and again in 1983, setting a new world record of 2hrs 22mins 43secs. She then won the first women's marathon gold medal at the 1984 Olympics.

Beyer, Udo   Born Ebenshuttenstadt, East Germany, 9 August 1955. Shot putter. He won gold at the 1976 Olympics. He set a new world record of 22.15m at Gothenburg on 6 July 1978. He was European champion in 1978 and 1982 and won bronze at the 1980 Olympics.

Bikila, Abebe   Born Jato, Ethiopia, 7 August 1932. Marathon runner. Bikila was the first African to win an Olympic medal, taking gold in the marathon at the 1960 Olympics, also setting a new world record of 2hrs 15mins 16secs. He retained his title at the 1964 Olympics six weeks after surgery for appendicitis, with another world record of 2hrs 12mins 11secs. Bikila was paralysed in a road traffic accident in 1968 but it did not stop him competing in sport, winning Norwegian cross-country sledge competitions. He died 25 October 1973.

Black, Roger   Born Portsmouth, 31 March 1966. 400m runner. European and Commonwealth champion in 1986 and 1990, he also took gold in the 4 × 400m at the European Championships. Having won gold in the 4 × 400m relay and silver in the 400m at the 1991 World Championships, he took gold again at the 1994 European Championships for the 4 × 400m relay. Won silver in the 400m at the 1996 Olympics behind Michael Johnson.

Blankers-Koen, Fanny   Born Francina Elsje Koen, Baarn, Netherlands, 26 April 1918. A great all-round athlete who showed an initial aptitude for swimming but shifted her allegiance to track and field aged 16. Her father was a high-class shot-putter and discus thrower and her success made athletics the obvious mode for Fanny to express her sporting prowess. She made her Olympic debut in 1936, placing sixth in the high jump and fifth as the second-leg runner in the Dutch 4 × 100m team, in 1940. She competed in the 1948 Olympics and won gold in the 100m, 200m, 80m hurdles and 4 × 100m relay, the only woman to win four track gold medals at one Games. This could have been more but for the same restrictions, though somewhat relaxed, that prevented Babe Didrikson

winning more medals. Blankers-Koen set world records in the 100yds, 100m, 200m, 80m hurdles, high jump, long jump, pentathlon and 4 × 100m relay. She also won three European titles in 1946 and two in 1950. She died 25 January 2004.

Board, Lillian   Born Durban, South Africa, 13 December 1948. Board took silver for Great Britain in the 400m at the 1968 Olympics and won gold in the 1969 European Championships for the 800m and 4 × 400m relay, when the relay team also set a new world record. Board was awarded the MBE in 1970. A career and life full of promise was cut short by cancer and she died two weeks after her 22nd birthday, 26 December 1970, in Munich where an avenue near the Olympic Stadium carries her name.

Boldon, Ato   Born Port of Spain, Trinidad, 30 December 1973. In 1992, Boldon won both 100m and 200m in the World Junior Championships. He took bronze in the 1995 World Championships for the 100m and bronze for both 100m and 200m at the 1996 Olympics. He then won gold in the 200m at both the 1997 World Championships and the 1998 Commonwealth Games. At the 2000 Olympics he took silver in the 100m and bronze in the 200m. He was part of the relay team that took bronze in the 4 × 100m 2001 World Championships.

Borzov, Valery   Born Sambor, Ukraine, 20 October 1949. Sprinter. Did the 100m and 200m double at the 1971 European Championships and the 1972 Olympics, also taking silver in the 4 × 100m relay. At the 1976 Games he won bronze in the 4 × 100m. He is married to gymnast Lyudmila Tourischeva and is the Ukraine Minister of Youth and Sports.

Boston, Ralph   Born Laurel, Mississippi, 9 May 1939. Long jumper. Broke Jesse Owens' 25-year-old record on 12 August 1960 with a jump of 26ft 11¼ins (8.22m). He went on to break his world record four more times. Boston became the first man to leap 27ft in May 1961. He won gold at the 1960 Olympics, silver in 1964 and bronze in 1968.

Brasher, Chris   Born Georgetown, British Guiana, 21 August 1928. Middle distance runner and marathon organiser. Chris Brasher was one of the two pacemakers accompanying Roger Bannister on his successful attempt at the four-minute mile. He took gold in the 3000m steeplechase at the 1956 Olympics. After his track career he developed orienteering in the UK and became a sports journalist and outdoor clothing specialist. His introduction of the London Marathon in 1981 revolutionised marathon running. He died 28 February 2003.

Brisco-Hooks, Valerie   Born Greenwood, Mississippi, 6 July 1960. Sprinter. Became the first person to do the 200m and 400m double at the 1984 Olympics, also taking gold in the 4 × 400m relay. She also took silver in the 4 × 400m relay at the 1988 Olympics. She ran the 400m in 49.83secs, becoming the first American woman to break 50secs in the event, and in 1985 she set a world indoor record of 52.99secs.

Brumel, Valeriy   Born Tolbuzino, Siberia, 14 April 1942. High jumper. He took silver at the 1960 Olympics and gold in 1964, breaking his own world record six times between 1960 and 1965. His elite competing career came to an end in 1965 after a motorbike accident. He died 26 January 2003.

Bubka, Sergey   Born Voroshilougrad, Ukraine, 4 December 1963. Pole vaulter. Bubka totally dominated the event during his career, first winning gold at the World Championships in 1983, retaining the title at the next five championships. Boycotts and injury meant he won only one Olympic gold medal, in 1988. He was European champion in 1986 and broke the world record 17 times outdoors and 18 times indoors, becoming the first to clear 6m on 13 July 1985.

Budd, Zola   Born Bloemfontein, 1966. Although excelling at middle-distance running, Budd was unable to compete internationally due to the South African ban. She applied for, and was given, British citizenship and competed for Great Britain in the 1984 Olympics, where she finished a controversial seventh in the 3000m after clashing with crowd favourite Mary Decker-Slaney. Although originally disqualified she was reinstated when video evidence showed her to be blameless. She won the world cross-country championship in 1985 and 1986 and was European champion in 1985 at 5000m, with a new world record of 14mins 48.07secs. Budd was banned from the Commonwealth Games in 1986 and returned to South Africa in 1988.

Buder, Oliver-Sven   Born Erlabrunn, East Germany, 23 June 1966. Shot putter. If there was ever an athlete who could be described as the 'perennial bridesmaid', it would have to be Buder. At the European Championships on 29 August 1990, Buder won the silver medal with his fourth-round throw of 21.01m. In 1991, he finished fourth at the World Championships in Tokyo with a best throw of 20.10m. Buder won silver at both the 1997 and 1999 World Athletics Championships as well as the 1998 European Championships.

Burghley, Lord David (Marquess of Exeter)   Born Stamford, Lincs, 9 February 1905. Hurdler. Lord Burghley won gold in the 400m hurdles at the 1928 Olympics and silver in the 4 × 400m relay. He was a member of the IOC for 48 years and President of the IAAF for 30 years, as well as being on the organising committee of the 1948 Olympics. He died 22 October 1981. In 1927 he 'ran the Great Court' at Trinity College, Oxford, in the time it took the Trinity clock to toll 12 o'clock, a feat wrongly attributed to Harold Abrahams in the film *Chariots of Fire*. Lord Burghley became MP for Peterborough and Governor of Bermuda.

Burke, Thomas   Born Boston, Massachusetts, USA,15 January 1875. Sprinter who won gold in the 100m and 400m at the 1896 Olympics. He died 14 February 1929.

Burrell, Leroy   Born Philadelphia, 21 February 1967. Sprinter. He set a new world record of 1min 19.11secs in the 4 × 200m with the Santa Monica Track Club on 25 April 1992 and a new world record in the 100m in 1991. At the 1992 Olympics, Burrell won gold in the 4 × 100m, also setting a new record of 37.40secs, and took gold in the 4 × 100m at the 1993 World Championships. On 17 April 1994 his club again broke the 4 × 200m world record with 1min 18.68secs. He set a new world record of 9.85secs in the 100m at Lausanne later that year.

Cacho, Fermin   Born Agreda, Spain, 16 February 1969. Middle-distance runner. He won gold at the 1992 Olympics, a silver at the 1993 World Championships, silver at the 1996 Olympics, silver at the 1997 World Championships and bronze at the 1998 European Championships, all at 1500m. He was though constantly in the shadow of Noureddine Morceli.

Capes, Geoff   Born Holbeach, Lincs, 21 August 1949. Shot putter. Capes has made more international appearances than any other male in British athletics. He took gold at the 1974 and 1978 Commonwealth Games and bronze at the 1974 European Championships. Also a former holder of the World's Strongest Man title. He is now one of Britain's leading budgie breeders and exhibitors.

Carlos, John   Born Harlem, New York, 1945. Sprinter. Took bronze in the 200m at the 1968 Olympics and joined with gold medallist Tommie Smith in a civil rights protest on the victory podium. They raised their black-gloved fists to symbolise black power and unity, wearing only socks on their feet to symbolise poverty. The silver medallist, the Australian Peter Norman, participated in the protest by wearing an Olympic Project for Human Rights Badge. The OPHR had been started by black athletes in 1967. Carlos and Smith were afterwards suspended from the United States team and banned from the Olympic Village, while Norman was reprimanded.

Carr, Henry   Born Montgomery, Alabama, 27 November 1942. Sprinter. He set a world record at 200m of 20.4secs, then broke it twice more within the next four days, taking it down to 20.2secs. At the 1964 Olympics, he took gold in the 200m and 4 × 400m relay. Carr later became a pro American footballer.

Catherwood, Ethel   Born Hannah, North Dakota, 28 April 1908. High jumper. She broke the high jump world record in 1926, then took gold at the 1928 Olympics representing Canada, the first Games at which women were allowed to compete in athletics. Catherwood was known as the 'Saskatoon Lily'.

Chambers, Dwain   Born London, 5 April 1978. Sprinter. The 1998 Commonwealth champion at 4 × 100m, he also took bronze in the 100m and silver in the 4 × 100m at the 1999 World Championships. Chambers then won gold in the 100m and 4 × 100m at the 2002 European Championships.

Campbell, Darren   Born 12 September 1973, Manchester. Sprinter. Took bronze in the 4 × 100m at the 1997 World Championships. European champion at 100m in 1998, he won silver in the 200m at the 2000 Olympics. In 2002, Campbell took gold in the 4 × 100m at both the Commonwealth Games and the European Championships. With an unexpected 100m bronze at the 2003 World Championships.

Christie, Linford   Born 2 April 1960. Sprinter. Olympic 100m champion at the 1992 Games and 100m world champion in 1993, he also took silver in the 4 × 100m. At the European Championships, Christie took gold in the 100m and bronze in the 4 × 100m in 1986, won 100m gold and 4 × 100m silver in 1990 and was European champion at 100m in 1994.

Cierpinski, Waldemar   Born Neugattersleben, Germany, 3 August 1950. Marathon runner. He took gold at 1976 Olympics and retained his title in 1980, only the second athlete to successfully defend a marathon title.

Cochran Brothers   From a Mississippi farming family of ten children, Commodore (1902-69) and Leroy (1919-81) are the the only brothers to win Olympic gold medals. Commodore took gold in the 4 × 400m relay at the 1924 Olympics and Leroy won gold in the 400m hurdles and 4 × 400m relay in 1948.

Coe, Sebastian   Born 29 September 1956, Chiswick, London. Middle-distance runner. He set three world records within 41 days in 1979 for the

800m, 1 mile and 1500m. Having won gold in the 1500m and silver in the 800m at the 1980 Olympics, he retained the 1500m title at the 1984 Olympics and took the silver again at 800m. He was European champion at 800m in 1986 and silver medallist at 1500m, having won bronze at 800m in 1978 and silver in 1982. Coe was a British Member of Parliament 1992-97. Now elevated to the House of Lords, he is President of the AAA and a member of the IOC.

Conley, Mike Born Chicago, 5 October 1962. US athlete who won several national long jump titles but excelled as a triple jumper. Conley was world champion in 1993 and world record holder in triple jump.

Connolly, James Born Boston, Massachusetts, 28 November 1868. He became the first athlete to win an Olympic gold medal in the modern era, taking gold in the 1896 triple jump. He also won silver in the high jump and bronze in the long jump. Connolly won an Olympic silver medal at triple jump in 1900 and went on to become a journalist, war correspondent and novelist. He died 20 January 1957.

Cook, Kathy Born Kathy Smallwood, Winchester, Hampshire, 3 May 1960. Kathy is the fastest British woman in history. She won Olympic bronze in the 4 × 100m relay at the 1980 Olympics, and at the 1984 Games took bronze in the 400m and 4 × 100m relay. At the World Championships in 1983, she won silver in the 4 × 100m and bronze in the 200m. Has seven Commonwealth Games medals including three 4 × 100m golds won in 1978, 1982 and 1986. Kathy married 400 and 800m runner Gary Cook in the early 1980s. Her times for 100m (11.10secs in Rome, 5 September 1981), 200m (22.10secs in Los Angeles, 9 August 1984) and 400m (49.43secs in Los Angeles, 6 August 1984) remain British records.

Courtney, Tom Born Newark, New Jersey, 17 August 1933. Middle-distance runner. He took gold at 800m and 4 × 400m at the 1956 Olympics and set a world record of 1min 46.8secs in the 800m in 1957.

Cram, Steve Born 14 October 1960. Cram's many achievements include six gold medals at Commonwealth, European and World Championships and a silver medal at the Olympics. In 1977 he broke the UK aged-16 world record for 1500m (3mins 47.07secs); the following year he broke the aged-17 world record for the mile (3mins 57.04secs) and won the English Schools 1500m title, a feat he repeated in 1979. He placed eighth in the Moscow Olympics and in 1982 won a gold medal in the European Championships. In 1983 he won gold again at the European Cup and also gold at the inaugural World Championships, all at 1500m. He won silver at the 1984 Olympics and in 1985 broke world records at 1500m (3mins 29.67secs in Nice), 2000m (4mins 51.39secs in Budapest), and mile (3mins 46.32secs in Oslo) all within 19 days; the latter lasted almost nine years. Cram also won gold medals in the 800m and 1500m at the Commonwealth Games of 1986 and European gold at 1500m. In 1983 he was voted BBC Sports Personality of the Year and in 1986 he was awarded the MBE.

Davies, Lynn Born Nantymoel, South Wales, 20 May 1942. 'Lynn the Leap' was Britain's greatest-ever long jumper. He won the gold medal at the Tokyo Olympics in 1964, and was AAA champion five times outdoors and three times indoors. His British record of 8.23m stood for 34 years until Chris Tomlinson leapt 8.27m in 2002.

Decker-Slaney, Mary Born Mary Decker, Bunnvale, New Jersey, 4 August 1958. American middle-distance runner who has held seven separate American track and field records from the 800m to 10,000m. She won both 1500m and 3000m at the 1983 World Championships in Helsinki (known as the 'Decker Double'), but no Olympic medals. Her best chance was in 1984 when she was firm favourite but was accidentally tripped by Britain's Zola Budd.

Devers, Gail Born in Seattle, Washington, 19 November 1966. Devers won Olympic gold at 100m in 1992 and 1996, and was world champion at 100m (1993) and 100m hurdles (1993, 1995 and 1999). While those are impressive achievements, what made Devers's Olympic victory in particular all the more remarkable was that only 18 months earlier she had been so sickened by Graves' disease and a secondary skin condition that she could barely walk and feared that her feet would have to be amputated.

Didrikson, Mildred Ella Born Texas, 26 June 1911. Mildred 'Babe' Didrikson was undoubtedly the greatest all-round sportsperson of all time. Her parents, Ole and Hannah Didriksen, came from Norway (Mildred later changed the spelling of her last name). A precociously gifted child who excelled in every sport she was allowed to compete in, Mildred once hit five home runs in a single game of baseball; this earned her the name she was always to be known by, Babe (after Babe Ruth). After winning the national basketball championships, she was entered for the national athletics team championships and US Olympic trials held on 16 July 1932. The year before she had broken the world record for 80m hurdles (practising by jumping over hedges). Babe entered eight events and set world records in the javelin and the 80m hurdles, tying with Jean Shiley for a world record in the high jump. Babe also won the baseball throw, shot put and long jump, and her fourth place in the discus meant she won the national team championship on her own with 30 points from the second-placed Illinois Women's Athletics Club with 22. Didrikson wanted to enter at least six events at the 1932 Olympics but officialdom prevented her competing in more than three. She won javelin gold on the Sunday with her first throw, a new world record of 143ft 4ins (43.7m), but took no further part in the competition as she tore a cartilage in her right shoulder. On the Wednesday she won the 80m hurdles in a new world record of 11.7secs. Both she and her great rival Jean Shiley then broke their previous high jump world record with leaps of 5ft 5¼ins (1.66m) but failed at 5ft 6ins (1.68m). At the subsequent jump-off both cleared their new world record height but Didrikson was disqualified for 'diving'. Her western roll style had not yet been held as allowable, the scissors being the prescribed method of clearing the bar. Babe became the golden girl of the games but she breached her amateur status unwittingly soon after and was banned from subsequent participation.

In 1934, now known as Babe Didrikson Zaharias (following her marriage to professional wrestler George Zaharias), she became a professional golfer and soon dominated the sport like no other before or since. She won 17 tournaments in a row during the 1940s and in 1950 was instrumental in forming the Ladies' Professional Golf Association. Babe developed cancer in 1950 but after a remission period won the 1954 US Open by 12 strokes. This was to be a brief remission however and Babe died on 27 September 1956.

Dillard, Harrison Born Cleveland, Ohio, 8 July 1923. Harrison remains the only man to win Olympic gold medals in both sprints (100m in 1948) and hurdles (110m in 1952). He also won golds in the 4 × 100m relays in 1948 and 1952. Dillard won 82 straight races in 1947 and 1948. He was presented with his first set of running shoes by Jesse Owens. His nickname was 'Bones' because of his slim build.

Drechsler, Heike Born Heike Daute, 16 December 1964. East German before reunification in 1991, she set a world long jump record (7.45m) in 1986 and won long jump gold medals at the 1992 Olympics and the 1983 and 1993 World Championships. She also gained a silver medal in the long jump and bronze in both 100m and 200m sprints at the 1988 Olympics. She is still competing actively today and hoping to make the German team for the 2004 Olympics.

El Guerrouj, Hicham Born Berkane, Morocco, 14 September 1974. Currently the number one ranked 1500m runner in the world and the world record holder over both 1500m and 2000m, as well as being the mile record holder. Dominant since the mid-1990s, he was expected to win the 1500m Olympic title in 1996 but tripped on the heels of Noureddine Morceli at the start of the final lap and eventually finished last in the final.

Elliott, Herb Born Subiaco, Western Australia, 25 February 1938. Great Australian runner who was undefeated from 1958-60. He ran 17 sub four-minute miles, held three world records, won a gold medal in the 1500m at the 1960 Olympics, before retiring at the age of 22.

Elliott, Peter Born Yorkshire, 9 October 1962. The gritty middle-distance athlete emerged from the shadows of Steve Ovett and Seb Coe to become a world-class performer in his own right, winning silver at 1500m in the 1988 Olympics and following up with a gold medal at the Commonwealth Games two years later. Injury shortened his career at a time when he seemed destined for even greater things.

Evans, Lee Born Madera, California, 25 February 1947. The dominant quarter-miler in the world from 1966-72, his 400m world record set at the 1968 Olympics stood for 20 years. Evans' style of running was unique inasmuch as he could run four even-paced 11-second 100m splits during a 400m race.

Ewry, Ray Born Lafayette, Indiana, 14 October 1873. He won 10 gold medals (although two are not recognised by the IOC) over four consecutive Olympics (1900, 1904, 1906, 1908); all the events he won (the standing high jump, long jump and triple jump) were discontinued in 1912. His achievements are all the more astonishing as he spent his childhood confined to a wheelchair, suffering from polio. He died 29 September 1937.

Fixx, Jim Born 23 April 1932. Author who popularised the sport of running; his 1977 bestseller, *The Complete Book of Running*, is credited with helping start America's fitness revolution. He died of a heart attack while running, 20 July 1984.

Fosbury, Dick Born Portland, Oregon, 6 March 1947. Fosbury revolutionised the high jump with his back-first 'Fosbury Flop' technique, which he employed to win the gold medal at the 1968 Olympics.

Foster, Brendan Born 12 January 1948. Foster was a triple Olympian; fifth in the 1972 Munich 1500m, at the 1976 Montreal Olympics he won bronze in the 10,000m (Britain's only athletics medal) and placed fifth in the 5000m after setting an Olympic record of 13mins 20.3secs in his heat. Foster has a remarkable range of personal bests from 800m to the marathon, with the 3000m and two-mile marks being former world records – 1min 51.1secs (800m), 3mins 37.6secs (1500m), 3mins 55.9secs (mile), 7mins 35.2secs (3000m), 8mins 13.7secs (2 mile), 13mins 14.6 secs (5000m), 27mins 30.3secs (10,000m) and 2hrs 15mins 49secs (marathon). Since retiring he has become a successful athletics broadcaster.

Foster, Greg Born 4 August 1958. A three-time winner of the World Championship 110m hurdles (1983, 1987 and 1991), Foster also won silver in the 1984 Olympics and was world indoor champion in 1991.

Freeman, Cathy Born 16 February 1973. Australian Aborigine who lit the cauldron at the start of the 2000 Sydney Olympics and provided one of the Games' most memorable moments by winning gold in the 400m on her home soil. Twice world champion in the 400m (1997 and 1999), she also won silver in the 400m at the 1996 Olympics in Atlanta.

Griffith-Joyner, Florence Born Delores Florence Griffith, Los Angeles, 21 December 1959. At the United States Olympic trials in July 1988, Griffith-Joyner shattered the previous world record of 10.76secs in the 100m (although the first time was discounted because of the wind) four times in 48 hours with, respectively, 10.60, 10.49, 10.71 and 10.61secs. 'FloJo' earned the unofficial title of the world's fastest woman.

At the 1988 Olympics in Seoul, Griffith-Joyner confirmed her star status by winning three gold medals in the 100m, 200m and 4 × 100m relay and a silver medal in the 4 × 400m relay. She broke the 200m world record of 21.71secs twice, with 21.56secs in the semis and 21.34 in the final. She announced her retirement in February 1989 to concentrate on an acting and writing career. She was named as co-chairperson of the President's Council on Physical Fitness and Sports in 1993. She died of suffocation during an epileptic seizure, 21 September 1998.

Gunnell, Sally Born 29 July 1966. Gunnell was a good all-round athlete, specialising in the 100m hurdles before finding her place as a world-class 400m hurdler. Sally won all the major honours, including Olympic gold in 1992.

Hayes, Bob Born 20 December 1942. Hayes won a gold medal in the 100m at the 1964 Olympics and immediately joined Dallas Cowboys as a wide receiver. He won the Super Bowl with the Cowboys in 1972. He was convicted of drug trafficking in 1979 and served 18 months of a five-year sentence. He died 18 September 2002.

Hemery, David Born 18 July 1944. Hemery enthralled the British public in 1968 by running a storming race to win Olympic gold in the 400m hurdles at altitude in Mexico City.

Holmes, Kelly Born Pembury, Kent, 19 April 1970. Holmes played volleyball in the army and was a services judo champion before turning her attention to track and field. Her career has continually been blighted by injury ever since she left the army to concentrate full time on athletics. Between injuries, however, she has proved herself to be an excellent competitor and despite restricted training in 2003 managed a silver medal behind her great friend and training partner Maria Mutola at the World Championships in Paris.

Jackson, Colin   Born Cardiff, 18 February 1967. Jackson remains the world record holder at 110m hurdles (12.91secs, set in the final of the 1993 World Championships in Stuttgart) and is also European record holder at 4 × 100m. He won 44 successive hurdles victories between August 1993 and February 1995 and the only major title that eluded him was the Olympic title. Jackson became world indoor champion in 1999. He retired in 2003.

Jarrett, Tony   Born 13 August 1968. A sprint hurdler who, at his best, was able to match Colin Jackson and Jon Ridgeon as a world-class hurdler, Jarrett has struggled with injury and technical problems. Often disqualified through false-starting and never having achieved his potential, he would still be considered a giant of British athletics had he not been competing in the same era as Jackson. Jarrett was the Commonwealth 110m hurdles champion in 1998.

Jenner, Bruce   Born 28 October 1949. Jenner won the gold medal in the decathlon at the Montreal Olympics of 1976 and became something of a pin-up and glamour icon. He left athletics for a career in acting.

Johnson, Ben   Born 30 December 1961. Until he was disgraced and stripped of his Olympic gold medal for illegal drug use, the Jamaican-born Canadian sprinter had been the fastest man on earth. Johnson struggled for years to win the respect of the media, the sports establishment and his arch-rival, the flamboyant American track superstar Carl Lewis. After winning four gold medals at the 1984 Olympic Games, Lewis had been consistently beaten by Johnson. At the World Championships in Rome in the summer of 1987, the two men were pitted against each other in an event that *Sports Illustrated* rightly called the 'most compelling 100m dash in history'. Johnson achieved much more than a decisive first-place finish. He shattered the world record for the 100m, running it in 9.83secs.

'Big Ben', as Johnson was called because of his muscular physique, won the gold medal at the 1988 Games in Seoul, Korea, in spectacular fashion. Besting second-place finisher Lewis once again, he broke his own world record, running the 100m in 9.79secs. But within a matter of days, Johnson was stripped of both his medal and the world record when he tested positive for the use of steroids. His world record was revoked officially in 1989 for admitted steroid use; he returned drug free in 1991, but performed poorly. He was banned for life by the IAAF in 1993 for testing positive yet again.

Johnson, Michael   Born 13 September 1967. American super-athlete Johnson shattered the world record for 200m (19.32secs) and set an Olympic record in the 400m (43.49secs) to become the first man to win gold in both races in a single Olympic Games at Atlanta in 1996. He was also twice world champion at 200m (1991 and 1995) and four times world champion at 400m (1993, 1995, 1997 and 1999). He set a world record in 400m (43.18secs) at the 1999 World Championships in Seville. When he won the 400m in Sydney in 2000 he became the only man to win the event in two consecutive Olympics. Johnson retired in 2001 after dominating the 200m and 400m events like no one before him.

Johnson, Rafer   Born 18 August 1935. American athlete who won a silver medal in the 1956 Olympic decathlon and gold in 1960. He became a minor film actor and lit the Olympic Flame in Los Angeles (1984).

Jones, Marion   Born 12 October 1975. American sprinter who won three golds (100m, 200m, 4 × 100m) at the Sydney Games in 2000. Jones is a five-time world champion: 100m (1997 and 1999), 200m (2001) and 4 × 100m (1997 and 2001). A former college basketball star at North Carolina, she was voted Women's Athlete of the Year by *Track & Field News* in 1997, 1998 and 2000. She missed the 2003 World Championships as she was otherwise occupied giving birth to her son. Jones failed to qualify for the US team at 100m and 200m for the 2004 Olympics but won the long jump at the US trials.

Joyner-Kersee, Jackie   Born 3 March 1962. Jackie was twice world champion in both the long jump (1987 and 1991) and heptathlon (1987 and 1993). She won heptathlon gold medals at the 1988 and 1992 Olympics and long jump gold at the 1988 Games. She also won Olympic silver (1984) in the heptathlon and bronze (1992 and 1996) in the long jump. So dominant in her sport was she that she became the only woman to receive *The Sporting News* Man of the Year award!

Juantorena, Alberto   Born 21 November 1950. The great Cuban athlete won both 400m and 800m gold medals at the 1976 Olympics. He was noted for his slow starts over 400m but, like the great American Lee Evans before him, he could maintain an even pace for the whole race.

Keino, Kip   Born Kipsano, Kenya, 17 January 1940. Kipchoge Keino was one of the most versatile and popular track athletes of the 1960s and early 1970s. Competing adequately at the Tokyo Olympics, he burst into world class in 1965 by breaking the world records for 3000m (7min 39.6secs, Helsingborg, 27 August) and 5000m (13min 24.2secs, Auckland, 30 November). Keino won the 1968 Olympic gold medal for 1500m and four years later captured the 3000m steeplechase title.

Kipketer, Wilson   Born Kapsabat, Kenya, 12 December 1970. Kipketer was unable to run at the Atlanta Olympics because of a wrangle with the Kenya Athletic Federation over his switch of nationality to Danish. He was, however, the dominant 800m runner in the mid and late 1990s, and arguably the best of all time. He won three consecutive world titles in 1995, 1997 and 1999 but lost the gold to Nils Schumann at the Sydney Olympics after suffering a string of illnesses that destroyed his preparations.

Klüft, Carolina   Born Boras, Sweden, 2 February 1983. Klüft's mother was an international long jumper and her father a premier league footballer so it was perhaps inevitable that she would be a talented athlete. Her chosen event was the heptathlon and after becoming world junior champion in 2002 she beat her seniors at the World Athletics Championships in Paris in 2003, scoring a magnificent 7001 points. Despite the prestigious talents of Britain's Denise Lewis and France's Eunice Barber, it seems the young Swede is destined to become one of the greatest-ever all-round athletes.

Komen, Daniel   Born 17 May 1976. Kenyan athlete who set world records for 3000m, 2 miles and 5000m in the mid-1990s. His incredible time of 7mins 20.67secs for 3000m still stands today.

Kristiansen, Ingrid Born 21 March 1956. Norwegian distance runner who succeeded Grete Waitz as the leading marathon performer of her day. She won the London Marathon in 1984 and 1985 and was twice Boston Marathon winner (1986 and 1989) and also won the New York City Marathon in 1989, as well as being a former world record holder in the marathon.

Lewis, Carl Born 1 July 1961. Lewis won nine Olympic gold medals: four in 1984 (100m, 200m, 4 × 100m, long jump), two in 1988 (100m, long jump), two in 1992 (4 × 100m, long jump) and one in 1996 (long jump). He also has eight World Championship titles and nine medals in all. This record makes him possibly the greatest athlete of them all.

Lewis-Francis, Mark Born 4 September 1982. A precocious talent, winning world honours as a junior, Lewis-Francis has not made the expected transition to the top as a senior athlete but remains one of the world's great sprinters, capable of beating anyone on his day. His legal best 100m time of 10.04secs set in Paris on 5 July 2002 will be threatened in 2004.

McColgan, Liz Born Liz Lynch, 24 May 1964. Doughty Scottish distance runner who dominated her fields in the same way that Paula Radcliffe has done subsequently. Despite the lack of a finishing kick, she won gold medals at 10,000m in the 1986 and 1990 Commonwealth Games and the 1991 World Championships. McColgan remains an all-time great of British athletics.

Maduaka, Joice Born 30 September 1973. Currently Britain's top sprinter, Maduaka has personal bests of 11.24secs over 100m and 22.83secs at 200m.

Masterkova, Svetlana Born Arcinsk, Russia, 17 January 1968. One of the great middle-distance athletes of all time, she won the 800m and 1500m double at the 1996 Olympics and still holds world records for the 1000m and mile.

Mathias, Bob Born 17 November 1930. Mathias was the youngest winner of a decathlon gold medal when he succeeded in the 1948 Olympics aged 17. He also won the 1952 Olympic title to become the first superstar of the event. He retired aged 23 and became a film actor before serving in Congress between 1967 and 1975.

Miller, Inger Born Los Angeles, 12 June 1972. Inger, one of the world's leading sprinters, is the daughter of Lennox Miller (Jamaica), the Olympic silver medallist at 100m in 1968. They are the first-ever father-and-daughter Olympic medallists in athletics, Inger having won a 4 × 100m relay gold in Atlanta in 1996.

Mills, Billy Born Pine Ridge, South Dakota, 30 June 1938. Mills, an Oglala Sioux Indian whose given Native-American name is 'Loves His Country', was the upset winner of the 10,000m gold medal at the 1964 Olympics. His life was portrayed in the film *Running Free*.

Moorcroft, Dave Born 10 April 1953. A world-class 1500m runner, Moorcroft was unfortunate to be born in the same era as the likes of Steve Ovett and Sebastian Coe. He did manage a Commonwealth gold medal in 1978 but decided to move up distance soon after. On 7 July 1982 he became a world-beater himself when he smashed the 5000m world record by a clear eightsecs in Oslo. His time of 13mins 0.41secs was to stand for five years. He is currently the chief executive of UK Athletics.

Moses, Edwin Born USA, 31 August 1955. The world's greatest 400m hurdler of all time. Twice an Olympic gold medallist (1976 and 1984), politics prevented his appearance in Moscow in 1980.

Moses won an unprecedented unbroken series of 122 races (between 1977 and 1987) in his event, more than once setting the world record, which he held at 47.02secs. At the age of 48 he was talking of attempting a comeback to try and make the US Olympic squad.

Mutola, Maria de Lurdes Born Maputo, Mozambique, 27 October 1972. Mutola has been the dominant 800m runner from 1990 to the present day. She competed in Seoul and after finishing fifth at the Barcelona Olympics was unbeaten for three years and 42 races, her streak finally ending at the 1995 World Championships when she was disqualified for breaking from her lane too early at the start. She is the present Olympic and world champion.

Myerscough, Carl Born 21 October 1979. Myerscough came to prominence in 2003 by breaking Geoff Capes' long-standing British shot put record with a throw of 21.92m, an improvement of more than a metre from 2002.

Ngeny, Noah Born Kabenas, Kenya, 2 November 1978. Noah is the brother of Philipp Kibitok (best 800m time of 1min 43.55secs in 1996) but exceeded him in athletic prowess. Noah ran the fastest 1500m for a junior athlete in 1997 at Monaco but it was never ratified for record purposes as there were no doping controls implemented. He defeated the firm favourite El Guerrouj to win the Olympic 1500m title in 2000. With personal bests of 1min 44.49secs (800m), 3mins 28.12secs (1500m), 3mins 43.4secs (1 mile), 4mins 50.08secs (2000m) and 7mins 35.46secs (3000m), Noah has been one of the outstanding middle-distance athletes of the last decade. He is also the world record holder for the seldom-run 1000m, with a time of 2mins 11.96secs.

Noel-Baker, Philip John Born 1 November 1889. Having competed in the 1912 Olympics he captained the British Olympic track team in 1920 – winning silver at 1500m – and 1924. He was captain of the Olympic team in 1952. Noel-Baker was a lifelong pacifist and was Commandant of The Friends Ambulance Unit in World War I. A principal in the formation of the League of Nations and Member of Parliament for Coventry (1929-31) and Derby (1936-70), he later became Baron Noel-Baker of Derby. He was awarded the Nobel Peace Prize in 1959. Noel-Baker died in 1982.

Nurmi, Paavo Born Turku, Finland, 13 June 1897. Known as 'the Flying Finn', Nurmi won nine gold medals (six individual) in the 1920, 1924 and 1928 Olympics. Between 1921 and 1931 he broke 23 world outdoor records in events ranging from 1500m to 20,000m and held a stop-watch in his left hand during races. In the 1920 Olympics he won silver in the 5000m, following up with gold in the 10,000m and a further two golds for the individual and team cross-country. In 1924 he won five golds, in the 1500m, 5000m, 10,000m cross country, and 3000m and 10,000m team cross country. In 1928 he won gold in the 10,000m. Nurmi carried the Olympic torch into the stadium for the 1952 Games held in Helsinki. He died 2 October 1973.

O'Brien, Dan Born Portland, Oregon, 18 July 1966. O'Brien succeeded Daley Thompson as the world's greatest all-round athlete. The first American to dominate the sport since Bruce Jenner in the mid-1970s, he was odds-on favourite to take top honours at the 1992 Olympic Games in Barcelona. At the trial competition prior to the Games, however, O'Brien failed to qualify for the United States decathlon team, after botching his three chances to clear the bar in the pole vault. Determined to make up for that heartbreaking setback, he set the world record of 8891 points later that year. O'Brien won World Championship gold in 1991, 1993 and 1995. He also won Olympic gold in 1996 but injury prevented him from taking further part in the event.

O'Brien, Parry Born 28 January 1932. O'Brien revolutionised shot-putting with his 'O'Brien Shift' (aka 'O'Brien Glide') technique but was a prodigious athlete in his own right. In four consecutive Olympics (1952-64) he won two gold medals, a silver and a fourth place in the shot put.

Oerter, Al Born 19 September 1936. Oerter's four discus gold medals in consecutive Olympics from 1956-68 is an unmatched Olympic record in athletics and he is still competing at the highest level as a veteran athlete.

O'Sullivan, Sonia Born Cork, Ireland, 28 November 1969. Ireland's greatest-ever female athlete, at her very best she was invincible as a racer. Her finishing kick was a weapon that no other distance runner could compete with. If it were not for the controversial Chinese athletes of the 1990s (several of chief coach Ma Junren's athletes subsequently failed drug tests), Sonia would have secured several gold medals.

Ottey, Merlene Born Cold Spring, Jamaica, 10 May 1960. Ottey is still competing at world class at the age of 43. She has won 34 medals in major championships and from May 1989 to March 1991 she won 73 successive races. Her personal bests of 10.74secs for 100m and 21.64secs for 200m rank her as one of the greatest athletes in history. She was formerly married to Nat Page and now competes for Slovenia.

Ovett, Steve Born 9 October 1955. The Brighton-based athlete was a precocious schoolboy talent who excelled in long jump and sprint races. He made his breakthrough into world class after the 1976 Montreal Olympics and for the next six years he was to dominate the world of 800m and 1500m alongside his fierce rival Seb Coe. Although Ovett was originally more of a sprinter (a legend throughout the country when he applied himself) and Coe more of an endurance athlete, when they entered the senior ranks the roles were reversed. In the 1980 Moscow Olympics it was expected that Coe would win the 800m and the best Ovett could hope for was gold in the 1500m. Yet in a scintillating 800m Ovett ran the perfect race to defeat Coe. Possibly because of a lack of focus once he had achieved his goal, or possibly because Coe drew inspiration from defeat, the roles were reversed in the 1500m and Ovett had to be content with bronze. His thoroughbred style and finishing kick were legendary and his air-writing of the letters ILY (for I Love You) to his future wife after races was an indelible image.

Owens, Jesse Born James Cleveland Owens, Oakville, Alabama, 12 September 1913. Owens was one of the most remarkable athletes of all time. He broke five world records and equalled another in one afternoon at the Big Ten Championships (25 May 1935). In just 45 minutes he ran 9.4secs for the 100yds to equal the world record, leapt 26ft 8¼ins (8.13m) in the long jump, then ran 20.3secs in the 220yds and 22.6secs for the 200yds hurdles. He was also credited with world records for the 200m and 200m low hurdles. A year later, he upstaged Hitler by winning four golds (100m, 200m, 4 × 100m relay and long jump) at the 1936 Olympics in Berlin. Jesse turned professional straight after the Olympics and made money by racing horses. On one famous

occasion he raced Joe Louis, the world heavyweight boxing champion, and lost – but only because he tripped. He died of lung cancer, 31 March 1980.

Perec, Marie-José Born Basse-Terre, Guadeloupe, 1968. Sprinter who became the second woman (after Valerie Brisco-Hooks) to win the 200m and 400m events in the same Olympics (1996); her time in the 400m (48.25secs) set an Olympic record. She also won the 400m in the 1992 Games but mysteriously bowed out of the Sydney Games in 2000 due to injury and loss of form. Perec officially retired in 2004.

Peters, Mary Born Halewood, Lancashire, 6 July 1939. Peters was the darling of British sport after winning Olympic pentathlon gold in Munich at the age of 33. She was awarded the MBE in 1973 and CBE in 1990.

Powell, Mike Born 10 November 1963. On 30 August 1991 the longest-standing world record in track and field was shattered by the 27-year-old American long jumper. With a leap of 8.95m, Powell surpassed by 2ins (5cm) the mark set in the high altitude of Mexico City by Bob Beamon, who at the 1968 Olympics had soared almost 2ft (61cm) farther than any long jumper previously. Powell's record-setting leap was the culmination of a fierce rivalry between him and Carl Lewis, who had not lost a long-jump competition since February 1981.

Prefontaine, Steve Born Oregon, USA, 25 January 1951. The All-America distance runner was the first athlete to win the same event at the NCAA championships four years running (5000m, 1970-73). He finished fourth in the 5000m at the 1972 Munich Olympics and was the first athlete to endorse Nike running shoes. Known simply as 'Pre', he was killed in a car accident, 30 May 1975.

Radcliffe, Paula Born Northwich, Cheshire, 17 December 1973. Possibly the greatest distance runner the world has ever seen. Her lack of finishing pace always made her vulnerable in major championships but by sheer guts and determination Radcliffe has worked on her speed-endurance and strength and this, coupled with a step up in distance, has made her almost unbeatable over distances ranging from 10,000m to the marathon. She married international 1500m runner Gary Lough on 15 April 2000. She is the current marathon world record holder with a time faster than any British male athlete managed in the 2003 London Marathon. Radcliffe was the BBC Television Sports Personality of the Year in 2002. Her great aunt Charlotte Radcliffe won a swimming silver medal at the 1920 Olympics (4 × 100m freestyle).

Regis, John Born Lewisham, London, 13 October 1966. Regis emerged as a potent force on the international sprinting scene at the 1987 World Championships, where he won a bronze medal in the 200m. At the 1988 Olympics, he won a silver medal as a member of Great Britain's 4 × 100m relay team. Regis competed at the 1990 Commonwealth Games in Auckland, where he won the silver medal in the 200m, and then a gold medal as a member of England's 4 × 100m relay team.

Arguably the greatest achievement of Regis's career occurred later that year at the European Championships in Split. He won bronze in the 100m and then gold in hte 200m; followed by silver in the 4 × 100m relay and gold in the 4 × 400m. John's four medals were the most ever won by a male athlete at a single edition of the European Championships.

A
T
H
L
E
T
I
C
S

Reynolds, Butch Born Harry Reynolds, 8 June 1964. 'Butch' Reynolds held the world record in the 400m from 1988 to 1999 when it was finally broken by Michael Johnson. Banned for 2½ years for allegedly failing a drug test in 1990, he sued the IAAF and won a $27.4 million judgment in 1992, although the award was voided in 1994. Reynolds won a silver medal in the 400m and gold as member of the US 4 × 400m relay team at both the 1993 and 1995 World Championships.

Ryun, Jim Born Wichita, Sedgewick County, Kansas, USA, 29 April 1947. A precocious athlete, Jim Ryun was the first high school child to run a sub four-minute mile (3:55.3 in 1963). Ryun competed in three Olympics, 1964, 1968 (silver behind his great rival Kip Keino) and 1972. In July 1966 he set his first world record of 3:51.3 for the mile and the following year reduced it further to 3:51.1, a time which stood for eight years. Although Keino beat him to Olympic gold, Ryun was unbeatable in all other races but retired from the sport aged only 22! In 1971 he made a comeback and was an overwhelming favourite for the 1500m gold in Munich but fell 500m from the finish in his heat. Ryun is, in 2004, a US congressman for the state of Kansas.

Salazar, Alberto Born 7 August 1958. A top runner in the 5000m and 10,000m since 1977, Salazar turned to the road in 1980 and won his first marathon, the New York City, in 2hrs 9mins 41secs, a course record and the fastest marathon debut in history. The following year he won the New York race in 2hrs 8mins 13secs, a new world record, and in 1982 he surged ahead of Mexico's Rudolfo Gomez to finish the event in 2hrs 9mins 29secs. He won the 1982 Boston Marathon in 2hrs 8mins 51secs, a course record.

Sanderson, Tessa Born 14 March 1956. Tessa's much-vaunted rivalry with Fatima Whitbread ensured that Britain had the two top throwers in the world by 1985. She competed in five Olympics (1976-92). The pinnacle of Tessa's career came in the 1984 Olympic final when she won the gold medal against the odds. She was awarded the MBE in 1985.

Seagren, Bob Born USA, 17 October 1946. Seagren won a gold medal in the pole vault at the 1968 Olympics. He also broke the world outdoor record five times and became a World Superstars champion on retiring from competitive athletics.

Shorter, Frank Born Munich, Germany, 31 October 1947. Shorter won a gold medal in the marathon at the 1972 Olympics, becoming the first American to win the event in 64 years, ironically in the city of his birth.

Snell, Peter Born New Zealand, 17 December 1938. Snell won a gold medal in the 800m at the 1960 Olympics, and then won both the 800m and 1500m at the 1964 Games.

Sotomayor, Javier Born 13 October 1967. Great Cuban athlete who became the first man to clear 8ft (2.44m) in the high jump on 29 July 1989. He won a gold medal at the 1992 Olympics with a jump of 7ft 8ins (2.34m). He broke the world record with a leap of 8ft ½ins (2.45m) in 1993. He had a controversial drug suspension (for the recreational use of cocaine) reduced, which allowed him to participate in the 2000 Olympics. He won the silver medal in Sydney with a leap of 2.32m.

Szabo, Gabriela Born Bistrita, Romania, 14 November 1975. Szabo's finishing kick has usually been decisive over distances ranging from 1500m to 5000m and only Sonia O'Sullivan at her very best could finish a race faster. In 1998 she was the world's fastest at 1500m, 1 mile, 2000m, 3000m and 5000m. She is still competing today although injury meant her 2003 season was not quite as good as previous ones.

Thompson, Daley Born Francis Morgan Thompson, Notting Hill, London, 30 July 1958. The son of a Nigerian father and Scottish mother, Thompson is undoubtedly one of the world's finest-ever athletes, having dominated the decathlon from the late 1970s to the late 1980s. As a junior athlete he set a British record of 6685 points in 1974 and although the Crawley-based athlete only managed a lowly 18th position in the Montreal Olympics of 1976 his talent was self-evident. Daley could have represented Great Britain at several events from 100m up to 400m and was a fine pole-vaulter and the very best British long-jumper. In 1977 he won the European junior decathlon championship and the following year became Commonwealth champion in Edmonton, Canada. Daley was beaten at the European Championships but was not to lose another decathlon for nine years. In May 1980 he set a world record 8622 points and then won the first of his Olympic titles. In 1983 he won gold at the first World Athletics Championships and was also awarded the OBE.

In 1984 Daley won his second Olympic title in a fierce duel with the giant Jurgen Hingsen and although his points tally of 8797 was initially adjudged to be one point short of the world record, the scoring tables introduced in 1985 and implemented retrospectively showed the new adjusted total to be 8847 and a new record. In 1986 he won both the Commonwealth gold in Edinburgh and the European gold in Stuttgart. Injury now prevented Daley training effectively; he was beaten into fourth place in the 1987 World Championships and had the same result at the Seoul Olympics of 1988. He attempted to make the 1992 Olympic team but retired after the 100m sprint at the trials.

Thorpe, Jim Born James Francis Thorpe, 28 May 1888. Thorpe (birth name Wa-tho-huck, meaning 'bright path') was born a Sac-Fox Native American, his great-grandfather being Chief Black Hawk, who in 1832 led the Sac and Fox in the war that bears his name. Thorpe won both pentathlon and decathlon at the 1912 Olympics but was stripped of his medals a month later for playing semi-professional baseball prior to the Games. He had his medals restored on 13 October 1982. He married Iva Miller in 1913 (he later married Freeda Kirkpatrick in 1925 and Patricia Askew in 1945) and promply set out on a pro baseball and football career. He died 28 March 1953.

Torrence, Gwen Born 12 June 1965. Torrence won two gold medals at the 1992 Olympics in Barcelona, in the 200m and the 4 × 100m relay. In 1994 she ranked first in the world in both the 100m and 200m, and a year later she won the 100m in the World Championships. At one point she boasted the longest streak of indoor victories in recent memory, 49 races over a four-year period.

Tullett, Hayley Born Hayley Parry, Swansea, 17 February 1973. Hayley became a world-class athlete in 2003 when she broke fourminutes for 1500m (3mins 59.95secs) during the World Championships in Paris (31 August 2003). Her 800m personal best was also reduced to 2mins 0.49secs in Madrid (19 July 2003) and 2004 promises much. Hayley married pole-vaulter Ian Tullett in 1999.

Tyus, Wyomia Born 29 August 1945. Tyus was the first woman to win consecutive Olympic gold medals in the 100m (1964 and 1968).

Viren, Lasse Born Finland, 22 July 1949. Viren won gold medals at 5000m and 10,000m in the 1972 Munich Olympics and repeated this remarkable feat in the 1976 Games. Just for good measure, he added a fifth-place finish in the marathon. A truly professional athlete, Viren was often beaten in between the Olympics of 1972 and 1976 but this did not concern him. He peaked for the Games and seemed invincible when focused.

Waitz, Grete Born Norway, 1 October 1953. Waitz was nine-times winner of the New York City Marathon between 1978 and 1988. She also won a silver medal at the 1984 Olympics. She was famous for training intensively over shorter distances than was usual for the marathon event.

Wells, Allan Born Scotland, 3 May 1952. A remarkable athlete who started his career as a long-jumper, in the late 1970s Wells decided to turn his attention to the 100m and 200m sprints. He had immediate success. At the 1978 Commonwealth Games he came second to Don Quarrie in the 100m, but won the 200m in a wind-assisted time of 20.12secs. Between the Commonwealth Games and the 1980 Olympics, Wells secured his place at the pinnacle of men's sprinting and duly won the 100m gold medal in Moscow. At the 1982 Commonwealth Games he completed the double of 100m and 200m gold, although the 200m was shared by fellow Briton Mike McFarlane.

Whitbread, Fatima Born Stoke Newington, 3 March 1961. Fatima had a close rivalry with Britain's other great javelin thrower, Tessa Sanderson, and together with Petra Felke, they dominated world javelin throwing in the mid-1980s. Fatima won the European Championship gold medal in 1986 and followed up with the World Championship gold the following year, throwing 76.64m to defeat Felke. She had previously held the world record which Felke usurped. Fatima's glory years were preceded by some bitter disappointments, none more so than when she led the 1983 World Championships going into the final round only to see the great Finnish thrower, Tina Lillak, snatch the gold from her with the final throw of the competition. She was strong favourite to win the 1984 Olympics but managed only the bronze behind Sanderson. She was awarded the MBE in 1987.

White, Kelli Born Oakland, California, 1 April 1977. Kelli won the sprint double at the World Championships in 2003 but in winning the 100m and 200m she fell foul of the doping procedures and it is still not certain whether her feats will remain in the record books.

Zatopek, Emil Born Czechoslovakia, 19 September 1922. Zatopek won the 1948 Olympic gold medal at 10,000m. Four years later he won an unprecedented Olympic triple crown (5000m, 10,000m and marathon) at the 1952 Games in Helsinki. He died 22 November 2000.

Zelezny, Jan Born Mlada Boleslav, Czechoslovakia, 16 June 1966. Zelezny entered the 1988 Olympics as the javelin world record holder. He set an Olympic record in the qualifying round and led the final until the last thrower of the last round. Tapio Korjus of Finland, beat him by 16cm. At the 1992 Barcelona Olympics, Zelezny won the gold medal with his first throw of the final, breaking his own Olympic record by 3.76m. At 77kg, Zelezny was the lightest of the javelin competitors at the 1996 Atlanta Olympics but again took gold. In Sydney in 2000, Zelezny was again the lightest competitor, and again he set an Olympic record. Zelezny is the only javelin thrower in Olympic history to win three gold medals and four medals in total.

ATHLETICS

Olympic Games

(Note: Where times are not shown they were not recorded but estimated)

1896 Athens

Men's	Gold	Silver	Bronze
100m	Thomas Burke (USA) 12.0	Fritz Hofmann (GER) 12.2	Francis Lane (USA) 12.6
400m	Thomas Burke (USA) 54.2	Herbert Jamison (USA) 55.2	Charles Gmelin (GBR)
800m	Edwin Flack (AUS) 2:11.0	Nandor Dani (HUN) 2:11.8	Demitrios Golemis (GRE) 2:28.0
1500m	Edwin Flack (AUS) 4:33.2	Arthur Blake (USA) 4:34.0	Albin Lermusiaux (FRA) 4:37.0
Marathon	Spiridon Louis (GRE) 2:58:50	Charilaos Vasilakos (GRE) 3:06:03	Gyula Kellner (HUN) 3:06:35
110m Hurdles	Thomas Curtis (USA) 17.6	Grantley Goulding (GBR) 17.6	(only two competitors)
High Jump	Ellery Clark (USA) 1.81	James Connolly (USA) 1.65	——
		Robert Garrett (USA) 1.65	
Pole Vault	William Wells Hoyt (USA) 3.30	Albert Tyler (USA) 3.20	Evangelos Damaskos (GRE) 2.60
Long Jump	Ellery Clark (USA) 6.35	Robert Garrett (USA) 6.00	James Connolly (USA) 5.84
Triple Jump	James Connolly (USA) 13.71	Alexandre Tuffere (FRA) 12.70	Ioannis Persakis (GRE) 12.52
Shot Put	Robert Garrett (USA) 11.22	Miltiades Gouskos (GRE) 11.03	Georgios Papasideris (GRE) 10.36
Discus	Robert Garrett (USA) 29.15	Panagiotis Paraskevopoulos (GRE) 28.95	Sotirios Versis (GRE) 27.78

1900 Paris

Men's	Gold	Silver	Bronze
60m	Alvin Kraenzlein (USA) 7.0	Walter Tewksbury (USA) 7.1	Stanley Rowley (AUS) 7.3
100m	Frank Jarvis (USA) 11.0	Walter Tewksbury (USA) 11.1	Stanley Rowley (AUS) 11.2
200m	Walter Tewksbury (USA) 22.2	Norman Pritchard (GBR) 22.8	Stanley Rowley (AUS) 22.9
400m	Maxey Long (USA) 49.4	Willam Holland (USA) 49.6	Ernst Schulz (DEN)
800m	Alfred Tysoe (GBR) 2:01.2	John Cregan (USA) 2:03.0	David Hall (USA)

1500m	Charles Bennett (GBR) 4:06.2	Henri Deloge (FRA) 4:06.6	John Bray (USA) 4:07.2
Marathon	Michel Theato (FRA) 2:59:45	Emile Champion (FRA) 3:04:17	Ernst Fast (SWE) 3:37:14
110m Hurdles	Alvin Kraenzlein (USA) 15.4	John McLean (USA) 15.5	Fred Moloney (USA)
200m Hurdles	Alvin Kraenzlein (USA) 25.4	Norman Pritchard (GBR) 26.6	Walter Tewksbury (USA)
400m Hurdles	Walter Tewksbury (USA) 57.6	Henri Tauzin (FRA) 58.3	George Orton (CAN)
2500m Steeplechase	George Orton (CAN) 7:34.4	Sidney Robinson (GBR) 7:38.0	Jacques Chastanie (FRA)
4000m Steeplechase	John Rimmer (GBR) 12:58.4	Charles Bennett (GBR) 12:58.6	Sidney Robinson (GBR) 12:58.8
5000m Team	Great Britain/Australia 15:20.0	France	——
High Jump	Irving Baxter (USA) 1.90	Patrick Leahy (GBR-IRL) 1.78	Lajos Gonczy (HUN) 1.75
Pole Vault	Irving Baxter (USA) 3.30	Meredith Colkett (USA) 3.25	Carl-Albert Anderson (NOR) 3.20
Long Jump	Alvin Kraenzlein (USA) 7.18	Meyer Prinstein (USA) 7.17	Patrick Leahy (GBR-IRL) 6.95
Triple Jump	Meyer Prinstein (USA) 14.47	James Connolly (USA) 13.97	Lewis Sheldon (USA) 13.64
Shot Put	Richard Sheldon (USA) 14.10	Josiah McCracken (USA) 12.85	Robert Garrett (USA) 12.37
Discus	Rudolf Bauer (HUN) 36.04	Frantisek Janda-Suk (BOH) 35.25	Richard Sheldon (USA) 34.60
Hammer	John Flanagan (USA) 49.73	Truxtun Hare (USA) 49.13	Josiah McCracken (USA) 42.46
Standing High Jump	Ray Ewry (USA) 1.65	Irving Baxter (USA) 1.52	Lewis Sheldon (USA) 1.50
Standing Long Jump	Ray Ewry (USA) 3.21	Irving Baxter (USA) 3.135	Emile Torcheboeuf (FRA) 3.03
Standing Triple Jump	Ray Ewry (USA) 10.58	Irving Baxter (USA) 9.95	Robert Garrett (USA) 9.50
Tug of War	Sweden/Denmark	France	

1904 St Louis

Men's	Gold	Silver	Bronze
60m	Archie Hahn (USA) 7.0	William Hogenson (USA) 7.2	Fay Moulton (USA) 7.2
100m	Archie Hahn (USA) 11.0	Nathan Cartmell (USA) 11.2	William Hogenson (USA) 11.2
200m	Archie Hahn (USA) 21.6	Nathan Cartmell (USA) 21.9	William Hogenson (USA)
400m	Harry Hillman (USA) 49.2	Frank Waller (USA) 49.9	Herman Groman (USA) 50.0
800m	James Lightbody (USA) 1:56.0	Howard Valentine (USA) 1:56.3	Emil Breitkreutz (USA) 1:56.4
1500m	James Lightbody (USA) 4:05.4	Frank Verner (USA) 4:06.8	Lacey Hearn (USA)
Marathon	Thomas Hicks (USA) 3:28:53	Albert Corey (USA) 3:34:52	Arthur Newton (USA) 3:47:33
110m Hurdles	Fred Schule (USA) 16.0	Thaddeus Shideler (USA) 16.3	Lesley Ashburner (USA) 16.4
200m Hurdles	Harry Hillman (USA) 24.6	Frank Castleman (USA) 24.9	George Poage (USA)
400m Hurdles	Harry Hillman (USA) 53.0	Frank Waller (USA) 53.2	George Poage (USA)
3000m Steeplechase	James Lightbody (USA) 7:39.6	John Daly (IRL) 7:40.6	Arthur Newton (USA) 7:46.0
5000m Team	Great Britain	France	——
Standing High Jump	Raymond Ewry (USA) 1.60	Joseph Stadler (USA) 1.45	Lawson Robertson (USA) 1.45
High Jump	Samuel Jones (USA) 1.803	Garret Serviss (USA) 1.778	Paul Weinstein (GER) 1.778
Pole Vault	Charles Dvorak (USA) 3.505	Leroy Samse (USA) 3.43	Louis Wilkins (USA) 3.43
Long Jump	Meyer Prinstein (USA) 7.34	Daniel Frank (USA) 6.89	Robert Stangland (USA) 6.88
Triple Jump	Meyer Prinstein (USA) 14.35	Fred Englehardt (USA) 13.90	Robert Stangland (USA) 13.36
Shot Put	Ralph Rose (USA) 14.81	William Coe (USA) 14.40	Leon Feuerbach (USA) 13.37
Discus	Martin Sheridan (USA) 39.28	Ralph Rose (USA) 39.28	Nicolaos Georgantas (GRE) 37.68
Hammer	John Flanagan (USA) 51.23	John DeWltt (USA) 50.265	Ralph Rose (USA) 45.73
Decathlon	Thomas Kiely (GBR-IRL) 6036	Adam Gunn (USA) 5907	Truxton Hare (USA) 5813
Cross Country Team	New York AC 21:17.8	Chicago AA	——
Standing Long Jump	Raymond Ewry (USA) 3.476	Charles King (USA) 3.28	John Biller (USA) 3.26
Standing Triple Jump	Raymond Ewry (USA) 10.54	Charles King (USA) 10.16	Joseph Stadler (USA) 9.60
56lb Weight Throw	Etienne Desmarteau (CAN) 10.46	John Flanagan (USA) 10.16	James Mitchel (USA) 10.13
Tug of War	Milwaukee Athletic Club	St Louis Southwest Turnverein No 1	St Louis Southwest Turnverein No 2

1908 London

Men's	Gold	Silver	Bronze
100m	Reginald Walker (SAF) 10.8	James Rector (USA) 10.9	Robert Kerr (CAN) 11.0
200m	Robert Kerr (CAN) 22.6	Robert Cloughen (USA) 22.6	Nathaniel Cartmell (USA) 22.7
400m	Wyndham Halswelle (GBR) 50.0	(all other athletes withdrew or were disqualified)	
800m	Melvin Sheppard (USA) 1:52.8	Emilio Lunghi (ITA) 1:54.2	Hanna Braun (GER) 1:55.2
1500m	Melvin Sheppard (USA) 4:03.4	Harold Wilson (GBR) 4:03.6	Norman Hallows (GBR) 4:04.0
5 Miles	Emil Voigt (GBR) 25:11.2	Edward Owen (GBR) 25:24.0	John Svanberg (SWE) 25:37.2
Marathon	John Hayes (USA) 2:55:18	Charles Heferon (SAF) 2:56:06	Joseph Forshaw (USA) 2:57:10
110m Hurdles	Forrest Smithson (USA) 15.0	John Garrels (USA) 15.7	Arthur Shaw (USA)
400m Hurdles	Charles Bacon (USA) 55.0	Harry Hillman (USA) 55.3	Leonard Tremeer (GBR) 57.0
3500m Walk	George Larner (GBR) 14:55.0	Ernest Webb (GBR) 15:07.4	Harry Kerr (NZL) 15:43.4
10 Mile Walk	George Larner (GBR) 1:15:57	Ernest Webb (GBR) 1:17:31	Edward Spencer (GBR) 1:21:20
3000m Steeplechase	Arthur Russell (GBR) 10:47.8	Archie Robertson (GBR) 10:48.4	John Eisele (USA)
4 × 400m Relay	USA 3:29.4	Germany	Hungary
3 Miles Team	Great Britain 6	USA 19	France 32
High Jump	Harry Porter (USA) 1.90	Con Leahy (GBR-IRL) 1.88 Istvan Somodi (HUN) 1.88 Geo Andre (FRA) 1.88	——

Pole Vault	Edward Cooke (USA) 3.71	Alfred Gilbert (USA) 3.71	Ed Archibald (CAN) 3.58
			Charles Jacobs (USA) 3.58
			Bruno Söderström (SWE) 3.58
Long Jump	Francis Irons (USA) 7.48	Daniel Kelly (USA) 7.09	Calvin Bricker (CAN) 7.085
Triple Jump	Timothy Aheame (GBR-IRL) 14.91	J. Garfield MacDonald (CAN) 14.76	Edvard Larsen (NOR) 14.39
Shot Put	Ralph Rose (USA) 14.21	Dennis Horgan (GBR) 13.62	John Garrels (USA) 13.18
Discus	Martin Sheridan (USA) 40.89	Merritt Giffin (USA) 40.70	Marquis Horr (USA) 39.445
Hammer	John Flanagan (USA) 51.92	Matthew McGrath (USA) 51.18	Cornelius Walsh (USA) 48.51
Freestyle Javelin	Erik Lemming (SWE) 54.445	Michel Dorizas (GRE) 51.36	Arne Halse (NOR) 49.73
Javelin	Erik Lemming (SWE) 54.825	Arne Halse (NOR) 50.57	Otto Nisson (SWE) 47.10
Standing High Jump	Ray Ewry (USA) 1.575	Konstantin Tsiklitiras (GRE) 1.55	John Biller (USA) 1.55
Standing Long Jump	Ray Ewry (USA) 3.335	Konstantin Tsiklitiras (GRE) 3.23	Martin Sheridan (USA) 3.22
Discus Ancient Style	Martin Sheridan (USA) 38.00	Marquis Horr (USA) 37.32	Werner Jarvinen (FIN) 36.48
Tug of War	Great Britain	Great Britain	Great Britain

1912 Stockholm

Men's	Gold	Silver	Bronze
100m	Ralph Cook Craig (USA) 10.8	Alvah Meyer (USA) 10.9	Donald Lippincott (USA) 10.9
200m	Ralph Cook Craig (USA) 21.7	Donald Lippincott (USA) 21.8	William Applegarth (GBR) 22.0
400m	Charles Reidpath (USA) 48.2	Hanns Braun (GER) 48.3	Edward Lindberg (USA) 48.4
800m	James Edward Meredith (USA) 1:51.9	Melvin Sheppard (USA) 1:52.0	Ira Davenport (USA) 1:52.0
1500m	Arnold Jackson (GBR) 3:56.8	Abel Kiviat (USA) 3:56.9	Norman Taber (USA) 3:56.9
5000m	Johannes Kolehmainen (FIN) 14:36.6	Jean Bouin (FRA) 14:36.6	George Hutson (GBR) 15:07.6
10,000m	Johannes Kolehmainen (FIN) 31:20.8	Louis Tewanima (USA) 32:06.6	Albin Stenroos (FIN) 32:21.8
Marathon	Kenneth McArthur (SAF) 2:36:55	Christian Gitsham (SAF) 2:37:52	Gaston Strobino (USA) 2:38:42
110m Hurdles	Frederick Kelly (USA) 15.1	James Wendell (USA) 15.2	Martin Hawkins (USA) 15.3
4 × 100m Relay	Great Britain 42.4	Sweden 42.6	——
4 × 400m Relay	United States of America 3:16.6	France 3:20.7	Great Britain 3:23.2
10km Walk	George Goulding (CAN) 46:28.4	Ernest Webb (GBR) 46:50.4	Fernando Altimani (ITA) 47:37.6
High Jump	Alma Richards (USA) 1.93	Hans Liesche (GER) 1.91	George Horine (USA) 1.89
Pole Vault	Henry Babcock (USA) 3.95	Frank Nelson (USA) 3.85	William Happenny (CAN) 3.80
		Marcus Wright (USA) 3.85	Frank Murphy (USA) 3.80
Long Jump	Albert Gutterson (USA) 7.60	Calvin Bricker (CAN) 7.21	Georg Aberg (SWE) 7.18
Triple Jump	Gustaf Lindblom (SWE) 14.76	Georg Aberg (SWE) 14.51	Erik Almlof (SWE) 14.17
Shot Put	Patrick McDonald (USA) 15.34	Ralph Rose (USA) 15.25	Lawrence Whitney (USA) 13.93
Discus	Armas Taipale (FIN) 45.21	Richard Byrd (USA) 42.32	James Duncan (USA) 42.28
Hammer	Matthew McGrath (USA) 54.74	Duncan Gillis (CAN) 48.39	Clarence Childs (USA) 48.17
Javelin	Eric Lemming (SWE) 60.64	Juho Saaristo (FIN) 58.66	Mor Koczan (HUN) 55.50
Decathlon	James Thorpe (USA) 8412	Hugo Wieslander (SWE) 7724	Charles Lomberg (SWE) 7414
3000m Team	United States of America	Sweden	Great Britain
Cross Country Individual	Johannes Kolemainen (FIN) 45:11.6	Hjalmar Andersson (SWE) 45:44.8	John Eke (SWE) 46:37.6
Cross Country Team	Sweden	Finland	Great Britain
Pentathlon	James Thorpe (USA) no score recorded	Ferdinand Bie (NOR) no score recorded	James Donahue (USA) no score recorded
Standing Long Jump	Konstantin Tsiklitiras (GRE) 3.37	Platt Adams (USA) 3.36	Benjamin Adams (USA) 3.28
Standing High Jump	Platt Adams (USA) 1.63	Benjamin Adams (USA) 1.60	Konstantin Tsiklitiras (GRE) 1.55
Shot Put Both Hands	Ralph Rose (USA) 27.70 (15.23+12.47)	Patrick McDonald (USA) 27.53 (15.08+12.45)	Elmer Niklander (FIN) 27.14 (14.71+12.43)
Discus Both Hands	Armas Taipale (FIN) 82.86 (44.68+38.18)	Elmer Niklander (FIN) 77.96 (40.28+37.68)	Emil Magnusson (SWE) 77.37 (40.58+36.79)
Javelin Both Hands	Julius Saaristo (FIN) 109.42 (61.00+48.42)	Vaiino Siikaniemi (FIN) 101.13 (54.09+47.04)	Urho Peltonen (FIN) 100.24 (53.58+46.66)
Tug of War	Sweden	Great Britain	

1920 Antwerp

Men's	Gold	Silver	Bronze
100m	Charles Paddock (USA) 10.8	Morris Kirksey (USA) 10.8	Harry Edward (GBR) 11.0
200m	Allen Woodring (USA) 22.0	Charles Paddock (USA) 22.1	Harry Edward (GBR) 22.2
400m	Bevil Rudd (SAF) 49.6	Guy Butler (GBR) 49.9	Nils Engdahl (SWE) 50.0
800m	Albert Hill (GBR) 1.53.4	Earl Eby (USA) 1.53.6	Bevil Rudd (SAF) 1.54.0
1500m	Albert Hill (GBR) 4:01.8	Philip Noel-Baker (GBR) 4:02.4	Lawrence Shields (USA) 4:03.1
5000m	Joseph Guillemot (FRA) 14:55.6	Paavo Nurmi (FIN) 15:00.0	Erik Backman (SWE) 15:13.0
10,000m	Paavo Nurmi (FIN) 31:45.8	Joseph Gullemot (FRA) 31:47.2	James Wilson (GBR) 31:50.8
Marathon	Johannes Kolehmainen (FIN) 2:32:36	Juri Lossmann (EST) 2:32:49	Valerio Arri (ITA) 2:36:33
3000m Steeplechase	Percy Hodge (GBR) 10:00.4	Patrick Flynn (USA)	Ernesto Ambrosini (ITA)
110m Hurdles	Earl Thomson (CAN) 14.8	Harold Barron (USA) 15.1	Frederick Murray (USA) 15.2

ATHLETICS

400m Hurdles	Frank Loomis (USA) 54.0	John Norton (USA) 54.3	August Desch (USA) 54.5
3000m Walk	Ugo Frigerio (ITA) 13:14.2	George Parker (AUS) 13:20.6	Richard Frederick Remer (USA) 13:23.6
10,000m Walk	Ugo Frigerio (ITA) 48:06.2	Joseph Pearman (USA) 49:40.8	Charles Gunn (GBR) 49:44.4
4 × 100m Relay	United States of America 42.2	France 42.6	Sweden 42.9
4 × 400m Relay	Great Britain 3:22.2	South Africa 3:24.8	France 3:24.8
3000m Team	United States of America	Great Britain	Sweden
High Jump	Richmond Landon (USA) 1.93	Harold Muller (USA) 1.90	Bo Ekelund (SWE) 1.90
Pole Vault	Frank Foss (USA) 4.09	Henry Petersen (DEN) 3.70	Edwin Myers (USA) 3.60
Long Jump	William Petersson (SWE) 7.15	Carl Johnson (USA) 7.09	Erik Abrahamsson (SWE) 7.08
Triple Jump	Vilho Tuulos (FIN) 14.50	Folke Jansson (SWE) 14.48	Erik Almlof (SWE) 14.27
Shot Put	Ville Porhola (FIN) 14.81	Elmer Niklander (FIN) 14.15	Harry Liversedge (USA) 14.15
Discus	Elmer Niklander (FIN) 44.68	Armas Taipale (FIN) 44.19	Augustus Pope (USA) 42.13
Hammer	Patrick Ryan (USA) 52.87	Carl Johan Lind (SWE) 48.43	Basil Bennet (USA) 48.25
Javelin	Jonni Myyra (FIN) 65.78	Urho Peltonen (FIN) 63.50	Paavo Johansson (FIN) 63.09
Decathlon	Helge Lovland (NOR) 6803	Brutus Hamilton (USA) 6771	Bertil Ohlson (SWE) 6580
Cross Country Individual	Paavo Nurmi (FIN) 27:15.0	Erik Backman (SWE) 27:17.6	Heikki Limatainen (FIN) 27:37.4
Cross Country Team	Finland	Great Britain	Sweden
Pentathlon	Eero Lehtonen (FIN) 14	Everett Bradley (USA) 24	Hugo Lahtinen (FIN) 26
56lb Weight Throw	Patrick McDonald (USA) 11.26	Patrick Ryan (USA) 10.96	Carl Johan Lind (SWE) 10.25
Tug of War	Great Britain	Netherlands	Belgium

1924 Paris

Men's	Gold	Silver	Bronze
100m	Harold Abrahams (GBR) 10.6	Jackson Scholz (USA) 10.7	Arthur Porritt (NZL) 10.8
200m	Jackson Scholz (USA) 21.6	Charles Paddock (USA) 21.7	Eric Liddell (GBR) 21.9
400m	Eric Liddell (GBR) 47.6	Horatio Fitch (USA) 48.4	Guy Butler (GBR) 48.6
800m	Douglas Lowe (GBR) 1:52.4	Paul Martin (SUI) 1:52.6	Schuyler Enck (USA) 1:53.0
1500m	Paavo Nurmi (FIN) 3:53.6	Willy Scharer (SUI) 3:55.0	Henry Stallard (GBR) 3:55.6
5000m	Paavo Nurmi (FIN) 14:31.2	Ville Ritola (FIN) 14:31.4	Edvin Wide (SWE) 15:01.8
10,000m	Ville Ritola (FIN) 30:23.2	Edvin Wide (SWE) 30:55.2	Eero Berg (FIN) 31:43.0
Marathon	Albin Stenroos (FIN) 2:41:23	Romeo Bertini (ITA) 2:47:20	Clarence Demar (USA) 2:48:14
3000m Steeplechase	Ville Ritola (FIN) 9:33.6	Elias Katz (FIN) 9:44.0	Paul Bontemps (FRA) 9:45.2
110m Hurdles	Daniel Kinsey (USA) 15.0	Sydney Atkinson (SAF) 15.0	Sten Pettersson (SWE) 15.4
400m Hurdles	F Morgan Taylor (USA) 52.6	Erik Vilen (FIN) 53.8	Ivan Riley (USA) 54.2
4 × 100m Relay	United States of America 41.0	Great Britain 41.2	Netherlands 41.8
4 × 400m Relay	United States of America 3:16.0	Sweden 3:17.0	Great Britain 3:17.4
10,000m Walk	Ugo Frigerio (ITA) 47:49.0	Gordon Goodwin (GBR) 48:37.9	Cecil Charles McMaster (SAF) 49:08.0
High Jump	Harold Osborn (USA) 1.98	Leroy Brown (USA) 1.95	Pierre Lewden (FRA) 1.92
Pole Vault	Lee Barnes (USA) 3.95	Glenn Graham (USA) 3.95	James Brooker (USA) 3.90
Long Jump	William De Hart Hubbard (USA) 7.44	Edward Gourdin (USA) 7.27	Sverre Hansen (NOR) 7.26
Triple Jump	Anthony Winter (AUS) 15.52	Luis Brunetto (ARG) 15.42	Vilho Tuulos (FIN) 15.37
Shot Put	Clarence Houser (USA) 14.99	Glenn Hartranft (USA) 14.89	Ralph Hills (USA) 14.64
Discus	Clarence Houser (USA) 46.15	Vilho Nittymaa (FIN) 44.95	Thomas Lieb (USA) 44.83
Hammer	Frederick Tootell (USA) 53.29	Matthew McGrath (USA) 50.84	Malcolm Nokes (GBR) 48.87
Javelin	Jonni Myyra (FIN) 62.96	Gunna Lindstrom (SWE) 60.92	Eugene Oberst (USA) 58.35
Decathlon	Harold Osborn (USA) 7710.77	Emerson Norton (USA) 7350.89	Aleksander Klumberg (EST) 7329.36
3000m Team	Finland	Great Britain	United States of America
Cross Country Individual	Paavo Nurmi 32:54.8	Ville Ritola (FIN) 34:19.4	Earl Johnson (USA) 35:21.0
Cross Country Team	Finland	United States of America	France
Pentathlon	Eero Lehtonen (FIN)	Elemer Somfay (HUN)	Robert Legendre (USA)

1928 Amsterdam

Men's	Gold	Silver	Bronze
100m	Percy Williams (CAN) 10.8	Jack London (GBR) 10.8	Georg Lammers (GER) 10.9
200m	Percy Williams (CAN) 21.8	Walter Rangeley (GBR) 21.9	Helmut Kornig (GER) 21.9
400m	Raymond Barbuti (USA) 47.8	James Ball (CAN) 48.0	Joachim Buchner (GER) 48.2
800m	Douglas Lowe (GBR) 1:51.8	Erik Bylehn (SWE) 1:52.8	Hermann Engelhard (GER) 1:53.2
1500m	Harry Larva (FIN) 3:53.2	Jules Ladoumegue (FRA) 3:55.8	Eino Purje (FIN) 3:56.4
5000m	Ville Ritola (FIN) 14:38.0	Paavo Nurmi (FIN) 14:40.0	Edvin Wide (SWE) 14:41.2
10,000m	Paavo Nurmi (FIN) 30:18.8	Ville Ritola (FIN) 30:19.4	Edvin Wide (SWE) 31:00.8
Marathon	Mohamed El Quafi (FRA) 2:32:57	Miguel Plaza (CHI) 2:33:23	Martti Marttelin (FIN) 2:35:02
3000m Steeplechase	Toivo Loukola (FIN) 9:21.8	Paavo Nurmi (FIN) 9:31.2	Ove Andersen (FIN) 9:35.6
110m Hurdles	Sidney Atkinson (SAF) 14.8	Stephen Anderson (USA) 14.8	John Collier (USA) 14.9

400m Hurdles	David Burghley (GBR) 53.4	Frank Cuhel (USA) 53.6	F. Morgan Taylor (USA) 53.6
4 × 100m Relay	United States of America 41.0	Germany 41.2	Great Britain 41.8
4 × 400m Relay	United States of America 3:14.2	Germany 3:14.8	Canada 3:15.4
High Jump	Rober King (USA) 1.94	Benjamin Hedges (USA) 1.91	Claude Menard (FRA) 1.91
Pole Vault	Sabin Carr (USA) 4.20	William Drogenmueller (USA) 4.10	Charles McGinnis (USA) 3.95
Long Jump	Edward Hamm (USA) 7.73	Silvio Cator (HAI) 7.58	Alfred Bates (USA) 7.40
Triple Jump	Mikio Oda (JPN) 15.21	Levi Casey (USA) 15.17	Vilho Tuulos (FIN) 15.11
Shot Put	John Kuck (USA) 15.87	Hermann Brix (USA) 15.75	Emil Hirschfeld (GER) 15.72
Discus	Clarence Houser (USA) 47.32	Antero Kivi (FIN) 47.23	James Corson (USA) 47.10
Hammer	Patrick O'Callaghan (IRL) 51.39	Ossian Skold (SWE) 51.29	Edmund Black (USA) 49.03
Javelin	Erik Lundkvist (SWE) 66.60	Bela Szepes (HUN) 65.26	Olav Sunde (NOR) 63.97
Decathlon	Paavo Yrjola (FIN) 8053	Akilles Jarvinen (FIN) 7932	John Ken Doherty (USA) 7707

Women's	**Gold**	**Silver**	**Bronze**
100m	Elizabeth Robinson (USA) 12.2	Fanny Rosenfeld (CAN) 12.3	Ethel Smith (CAN) 12.3
800m	Lina Radke (GER) 2:16.8	Kinue Hitomi (JPN) 2:17.6	Inga Gentzel (SWE) 2:17.8
4 × 100m Relay	Canada 48.4	United States of America 48.8	Germany 49.0
High Jump	Ethel Catherwood (CAN) 1.59	Carolina Gisolf (NED) 1.56	Mildred Wiley (USA) 1.56
Discus	Halina Konopacka (POL) 39.62	Lillian Copeland (USA) 37.08	Ruth Svedberg (SWE) 35.92

1932 Los Angeles

Men's	**Gold**	**Silver**	**Bronze**
100m	Eddie Tolan (USA) 10.3	Ralph Metcalfe (USA) 10.3	Arthur Jonath (GER) 10.4
200m	Eddie Tolan (USA) 21.2	George Simpson (USA) 21.4	Ralph Metcalfe (USA) 21.5
400m	William Carr (USA) 46.2	Benjamin Eastman (USA) 46.4	Alexander Wilson (CAN) 47.4
800m	Thomas Hampson (GBR) 1:49.7	Alexander Wilson (CAN) 1:49.9	Philip Edwards (CAN) 1:51.5
1500m	Lugi Beccali (ITA) 3:51.2	John Cornes (GBR) 3:52.6	Philip Edwards (CAN) 3:52.8
5000m	Lauri Lehtinen (FIN) 14:30.4	Ralph Hill (USA) 14:30.4	Lauri Virtanen (FIN) 14:44.0
10,000m	Janusz Kusocinski (POL) 30:11.4	Volmari Iso-Hollo (FIN) 30:12.6	Lauri Virtanen (FIN) 30:35.0
Marathon	Juan Carlos Zabala (ARG) 2:31:36	Samuel Ferris (GBR) 2:31:55	Armas Toivonen (FIN) 2:32:12
3000m Steeplechase	Volmar Iso-Hollo (FIN) 10:33.4	Thomas Evenson (GBR) 10:46.0	Joseph McCluskey (USA) 10:46.2
110m Hurdles	George Saling (USA) 14.6	Percy Beard (USA) 14.7	Donald Finlay (GBR) 14.8
400m Hurdles	Robert Tisdall (IRL) 51.7	Glenn Hardin (USA) 51.9	F. Morgan Taylor (USA) 52.0
50km Walk	Thomas Green (GBR) 4:50:10	Janis Dalinsch (LAT) 4:57:20	Ugo Frigerio (ITA) 4:59:06
4 × 100m Relay	United States of America 40.0	Germany 40.9	Italy 41.2
4 × 400m Relay	United States of America 3:08.2	Great Britain 3:11.2	Canada 3:12.8
High Jump	Duncan McNaughton (CAN) 1.97	Robert Van Osdel (USA) 1.97	Simeon Toribio (PHI) 1.97
Pole Vault	William Miller (USA) 4.31	Shuhei Nishida (JPN) 4.30	George Jefferson (USA) 4.20
Long Jump	Edward Gordon (USA) 7.64	Charles Lambert Redd (USA) 7.60	Chuhei Nambu (JPN) 7.45
Triple Jump	Chuhei Nambu (JPN) 15.72	Erik Svensson (SWE) 15.32	Kenkichi Oshima (JPN) 15.12
Shot Put	Leo Sexton (USA) 16.00	Harlow Rothert (USA) 15.67	Frantisek Douda (TCH) 15.61
Discus	John Anderson (USA) 49.49	Henri Jean Laborde (USA) 48.47	Paul Winter (FRA) 47.85
Hammer	Patrick O'Callaghan (IRL) 53.92	Ville Porhola (FIN) 52.27	Peter Zaremba (USA) 50.33
Javelin	Matti Jarvinen (FIN) 72.71	Matti Sippala (FIN) 69.80	Eino Penttila (FIN) 68.70
Decathlon	James Aloysius Bausch (USA) 8462.23	Akilles Jarvinen (FIN) 8292.48	Wolrad Eberle (GER) 8030.80

Women's	**Gold**	**Silver**	**Bronze**
100m	Stanislawa Walasiewicz (POL) 11.9	Hilda Strike (CAN) 11.9	Wilhelmina von Bremen (USA) 12.0
80m Hurdles	Mildred Didriksen (USA) 11.7	Evelyne Hall (USA) 11.7	Majorie Clark (SAF) 11.8
4 × 100m Relay	United States of America 46.9	Canada 47.0	Great Britain 47.6
High Jump	Jean Shiley (USA) 1.66	Mildred Didriksen (USA) 1.66	Eva Dawes (CAN) 1.60
Discus	Lillian Copeland (USA) 40.58	Ruth Osburn (USA) 40.12	Jadwiga Wajsowna (POL) 38.74
Javelin	Mildred Didriksen (USA) 43.68	Ellen Braumuller (GER) 43.49	Tilly Fleischer (GER) 43.00

1936 Berlin

Men's	**Gold**	**Silver**	**Bronze**
100m	Jesse Owens (USA) 10.3	Ralph Metcalfe (USA) 10.4	Martinus Osendarp (NED) 10.5
200m	Jesse Owens (USA) 20.7	Matthew Robinson (USA) 21.1	Martinus Osendarp (NED) 21.3
400m	Archie Williams (USA) 46.5	Arthur Godfrey Brown (GBR) 46.7	James Lu Valle (USA) 46.8
800m	John Woodruff (USA) 1:52.9	Mario Lanzi (ITA) 1:53.3	Philip Edwards (CAN) 1:53.6
1500m	John Lovelock (NZL) 3:47.8	Glenn Cunningham (USA) 3:48.4	Lugi Beccali (ITA) 3:49.2
5000m	Gunnar Hockert (FIN) 14:22.2	Lauri Lehtinen (FIN) 14:25.8	Henry Jonsson (SWE) 14:29.0
10,000m	Ilmari Salminen (FIN) 30:15.4	Arvo Askola (FIN) 30:15.6	Volmari Iso-Hollo (FIN) 30:20.2
Marathon	Kitei Son (JPN) 2:29:19	Ernest Harper (GBR) 2:31:23	Shoryu Nan (JPN) 2:31:42
3000m Steeplechase	Volmari Iso-Hollo (FIN) 9:03.8	Kaarlo Tuominen (FIN) 9:06.8	Alfred Dompert (GER) 9:07.2
110m Hurdles	Forrest Towns (USA) 14.2	Donald Finlay (GBR) 14.4	Frederick Pollard (USA) 14.4
400m Hurdles	Glenn Hardin (USA) 52.4	John Loaring (CAN) 52.7	Miguel White (PHI) 52.8
50km Walk	Harold Whitlock (GBR) 4:30:41	Arthur T. Schwab (SUI) 4:32:09	Adalberts Bubenko (LAT) 4:32:42

4 × 100m Relay	United States of America 39.8	Italy 41.1	Germany 41.2
4 × 400m Relay	Great Britian 3:09.0	United States of America 3:11.0	Germany 3:11.8
High Jump	Cornelius Johnson (USA) 2.03	David Albritton (USA) 2.00	Delos Thurber (USA) 2.00
Pole Vault	Earle Meadows (USA) 4.35	Shuhei Nishida (JPN) 4.25	Sueo Oe (JPN) 4.25
Long Jump	Jesse Owens (USA) 8.06	Luz Long (GER) 7.87	Naoto Tajima (JPN) 7.74
Triple Jump	Naoto Tajima (JPN) 16.00	Masao Harada (JPN) 15.66	John Patrick Metcalfe (AUS) 15.50
Shot Put	Hans Woelke (GER) 16.20	Sulo Barlund (FIN) 16.12	Gerhard Stock (GER) 15.66
Discus	Kenneth Carpenter (USA) 50.48	Gordon Dunn (USA) 49.36	Giorgio Oberwegger (ITA) 49.23
Hammer	Karl Hein (GER) 56.49	Erwin Blask (GER) 55.04	Fred Warngard (SWE) 54.83
Javelin	Gerhard Stock (GER) 71.84	Yrjo Nikkanen (FIN) 70.77	Kalervo Tolvonen (FIN) 70.72
Decathlon	Glenn Morris (USA) 7900	Robert Clark (USA) 7601	Jack Parker (USA) 7275

Women's	Gold	Silver	Bronze
100m	Helen Stephens (USA) 11.5	Stanislawa Walasiewicz (POL) 11.7	Kathe Krauss (GER) 11.9
80m Hurdles	Trebisonda Valla (ITA) 11.7	Anni Steuer (GER) 11.7	Elizabeth Taylor (CAN) 11.7
4 × 100m Relay	United States of America 46.9	Great Britain 47.6	Canada 47.8
High Jump	Ibolya Csak (HUN) 1.60	Dorothy Odam (GBR) 1.60	Elfriede Kaun (GER) 1.60
Discus	Gisela Mauermayer (GER) 47.63	Jadwiga Wajsowna (POL) 46.22	Paula Mollenhauer (GER) 39.80
Javelin	Tilly Fleischer (GER) 45.18	Luise Kruger (GER) 43.29	Maria Kwasniewska (POL) 41.80

1948 London

Men's	Gold	Silver	Bronze
100m	Harrison Dillard (USA) 10.3	Barney Ewell (USA) 10.4	Lloyd LaBeach (PAN) 10.4
200m	Melvin Patton (USA) 21.1	Barney Ewell (USA) 21.1	Lloyd LaBeach (PAN) 21.2
400m	Arthur Wint (JAM) 46.2	Herbert McKenley (JAM) 46.4	Malvin Whitfield (USA) 46.9
800m	Malvin Whitfield (USA) 1:49.2	Arthur Wint (JAM) 1:49.5	Marcel Hansenne (FRA) 1:49.8
1500m	Henry Eriksson (SWE) 3:49.8	Lennart Strand (SWE) 3:50.4	Willem Slijkhuis (NED) 3:50.4
5000m	Gaston Reiff (BEL) 14:17.6	Emil Zatopek (TCH) 14:17.8	Willem Slijkhuis (NED) 14:26.8
10,000m	Emil Zatopek (TCH) 29:59.6	Alain Mimoun (FRA) 30:47.4	Bertil Albertsson (SWE) 30:53.6
Marathon	Delfo Cabrera (ARG) 2:34:51	Thomas Richards (GBR) 2:35:08	Etienne Gailly (BEL) 2:35:33
3000m Steeplechase	Thore Sjostrand (SWE) 9:04.6	Erik Elmsater (SWE) 9:08.2	Gote Hagstrom (SWE) 9:11.3
110m Hurdles	William Porter (USA) 13.9	Clyde Scott (USA) 14.1	Craig Dixon (USA) 14.1
400m Hurdles	Leroy Cochran (USA) 51.1	Duncan White (SRI) 51.8	Rune Larsson (SWE) 52.2
10km Walk	John Mikaelsson (SWE) 45:13.2	Ingemar Johansson (SWE) 45:43.8	Fritz Schwab (SUI) 46:00.2
50km Walk	John Ljunggren (SWE) 4:41:52	Godel Gaston (SWI) 4:48:17	T. Lloyd Johnson (GBR) 4:48:31
4 × 100m Relay	United States of America 40.6	Great Britain 41.3	Italy 41.5
4 × 400m Relay	United States of America 3:10.4	France 3:14.8	Sweden 3:16.0
High Jump	John Winter (AUS) 1.98	Bjorn Paulson (NOR) 1.95	George Stanich (USA) 1.95
Pole Vault	O. Guinn Smith (USA) 4.30	Erkki Kataja (FIN) 4.20	Robert Richards (USA) 4.20
Long Jump	Willie Steele (USA) 7.82	Theodore Bruce (AUS) 7.55	Herbert Douglas (USA) 7.54
Triple Jump	Arne Ahman (SWE) 15.40	George Avery (AUS) 15.36	Ruhi Sarialp (TUR) 15.02
Shot Put	Wilbur Thompson (USA) 17.12	James Delaney (USA) 16.68	James Fuchs (USA) 16.42
Discus	Adolfo Consolini (ITA) 52.78	Giuseppe Tosi (ITA) 51.78	Fortune Gordien (USA) 50.77
Hammer	Imre Nemeth (HUN) 56.07	Ivan Gubijan (YUG) 54.27	Robert Bennett (USA) 53.73
Javelin	Kai Tapio Rautavaara (FIN) 69.77	Steve Seymour (USA) 67.56	Jozsef Varszegi (HUN) 67.03
Decathlon	Robert Mathias (USA) 7139	Ignace Heinrich (FRA) 6974	Floyd Simmons (USA) 6950

Women's	Gold	Silver	Bronze
100m	Fanny Blankers-Koen (NED) 11.9	Dorothy Manley (GBR) 12.2	Shirley Strickland (AUS) 12.2
200m	Fanny Blankers-Koen (NED) 24.4	Audrey Williamson (GBR) 25.1	Audrey Patterson (USA) 25.2
80m Hurdles	Fanny Blankers-Koen (NED) 11.2	Maureen Gardner (GBR) 11.2	Shirley Strickland (AUS) 11.4
4 × 100m Relay	Netherlands 47.5	Australia 47.6	Canada 47.8
High Jump	Alice Coachman (USA) 1.68	Dorothy Tyler (GBR) 1.68	Micheline Ostermeyer (FRA) 1.61
Long Jump	Olga Gyarmati (HUN) 5.69	Noemi Simonetto de Portela (ARG) 5.60	Ann-Britt Leyman (SWE) 5.57
Shot Put	Micheline Ostermeyer (FRA) 13.75	Amelia Piccinini (ITA) 13.09	Ine Schaffer (AUT) 13.08
Discus	Micheline Ostermeyer (FRA) 41.92	Edera Cordila Gentile (ITA) 41.17	Jacqueline Mazeas (FRA) 40.47
Javelin	Herma Bauma (AUT) 45.57	Kaisa Parviainen (FIN) 43.79	Lily Carlstedt (DEN) 42.08

1952 Helsinki

Men's	Gold	Silver	Bronze
100m	Lindy Remigino (USA) 10.4	Herbert McKenley (JAM) 10.4	Emmanuel McDonald Bailey (TRI) 10.4
200m	Andrew Stanfield (USA) 20.7	W. Thane Baker (USA) 20.8	James Gathers (USA) 20.8
400m	V. George Rhoden (JAM) 45.9	Herbert McKenley (JAM) 45.9	Ollie Matson (USA) 46.8
800m	Malvin Whitfield (USA) 1:49.2	Arthur Wint (JAM) 1:49.7	Heinz Ulzheimer (GER) 1:49.8
1500m	Josef Barthel (LUX) 3:45.3	Robert McMillen (USA) 3:45.4	Werner Lueg (GER) 3:45.7
5000m	Emil Zatopek (TCH) 14:06.7	Alain Mimoun (FRA) 14:07.6	Herbert Schade (GER) 14:08.8
10,000m	Emil Zatopek (TCH) 29:17.0	Alain Mimoun (FRA) 29:32.8	Aleksandr Anufriev (URS) 29:48.2

	Gold	Silver	Bronze
Marathon	Emil Zatopek (TCH) 2:23:03	Reinaldo Gorno (ARG) 2:25:35	Gustaf Jansson (SWE) 2:26:07
3000m Steeplechase	Horace Ashenfelter (USA) 8:45.4	Vladimir Kazantsev (URS) 8:51.6	John Disley (GBR) 8:51.8
110m Hurdles	Harrison Dillard (USA) 13.7	Jack Davis (USA) 13.7	Arthur Barnard (USA) 14.1
400m Hurdles	Charles Moore (USA) 50.8	Yuri Lituyeu (URS) 51.3	John Holland (NZL) 52.2
10km Walk	John Mikaelsson (SWE) 45:02.8	Fritz Schwab (SUI) 45:41.0	Bruno Yunk (URS) 45:41.0
50km Walk	Giuseppe Dordoni (ITA) 4:28:7	Josef Dolezal (TCH) 4:30:17	Antal Roka (HUN) 4:31:27
4 × 100m Relay	United States of America 40.1	Soviet Union 40.3	Hungary 40.5
4 × 400m Relay	Jamaica 3:03.9	United States of America 3.04.2	Germany 3:06.6
High Jump	Walter Davis (USA) 2.04	Kenneth Wiesner (USA) 2.01	Jose Telles da Conceicao (BRA) 1.98
Pole Vault	Robert Richards (USA) 4.55	Donald Laz (USA) 4.50	Ragnar Lundberg (SWE) 4.40
Long Jump	Jerome Biffle (USA) 7.57	Meredith Gourdine (USA) 7.53	Odon Foldessy (HUN) 7.30
Triple Jump	Adhemar Ferreira da Silva (BRA) 16.22	Leonid Sherbakov (URS) 15.98	Arnoldo Devonish (VEN) 15.52
Shot Put	Parry O'Brien (USA) 17.41	Darrow Hooper (USA) 17.39	James Fuchs (USA) 17.06
Discus	Sim Iness (USA) 55.03	Adolfo Consolini (ITA) 53.78	James Dillon (USA) 53.28
Hammer	Jozsef Csermak (HUN) 60.34	Karl Storch (GER) 58.86	Imre Nemeth (HUN) 57.74
Javelin	Cyrus Young (USA) 73.78	William Miller (USA) 72.46	Toivo Hyytiainen (FIN) 71.89
Decathlon	Robert Mathias (USA) 7887	Milton Campbell (USA) 6975	Floyd Simmons (USA) 6788

Women's	Gold	Silver	Bronze
100m	Marjorie Jackson (AUS) 11.5	Daphne Hasenjager (SAF) 11.8	Shirley Strickland de la Hunty (AUS) 11.9
200m	Marjorie Jackson (AUS) 23.7	Bertha Brouwer (NED) 24.2	Nadezhda Khnykina (URS) 24.2
80m Hurdles	Shirley Strickland de la Hunty (AUS) 10.9	Maria Golubnichaya (URS) 11.2	Maria Sander (GER) 11.4
4 × 100m Relay	United States of America 45.9	Germany 45.9	Great Britain 46.2
High Jump	Esther Brand (SAF) 1.67	Sheila Lerwill (GBR) 1.65	Aleksandra Chudina (URS) 1.63
Long Jump	Yvette Williams (NZL) 6.24	Aleksandra Chudina (URS) 6.14	Shirley Cawley (GBR) 5.92
Shot Put	Galina Zybina (URS) 15.28	Marianne Werner (GER) 14.57	Klaudia Tochenova (URS) 14.50
Discus	Nina Romaschkova (URS) 51.42	Yelisaveta Bagryantseva (URS) 47.08	Nina Dumbadze (URS) 46.29
Javelin	Dana Zatopkova (TCH) 50.47	Aleksandra Chudina (URS) 50.01	Yelena Gorchakova (URS) 49.76

1956 Melbourne

Men's	Gold	Silver	Bronze
100m	Bobby Joe Morrow (USA) 10.5	W. Thane Baker (USA) 10.5	Hector Hogan (AUS) 10.6
200m	Bobby Joe Morrow (USA) 20.6	Andrew Stanfeld (USA) 20.7	W Thane Baker (USA) 20.9
400m	Charles Jenkins (USA) 46.7	Karl-Friedrich Haas (GER) 46.8	Voitto Hellsten (FIN) 47.0
800m	Tom Courtney (USA) 1:47.7	Derek Johnson (GBR) 1:47.8	Auden Boysen (NOR) 1:48.1
1500m	Ron Delany (IRL) 3:41.2	Klaus Richtzenhan (GDR) 3:42.0	John Landy (AUS) 3:42.0
5000m	Volodymyr Kuts (URS) 13:39.6	Gordon Pirie (GBR) 13:50.6	Derek Ibbotson (GBR) 13:54.4
10,000m	Volodymyr Kuts (URS) 28:45.6	Jozsef Kovacs (HUN) 28:52.4	Allan Lawrence (AUS) 28:53.6
Marathon	Alain Mimoun (FRA) 2:25:0	Franjo Mihalic (YUG) 2:26:32	Veikko Karvonen (FIN) 2:27:47
3000m Steeplechase	Chris Brasher (GBR) 8:41.2	Sandor Rozsnyoi (HUN) 8:43.6	Ernst Larsen (NOR) 8:44.0
110m Hurdles	Lee Calhoun (USA) 13.5	Jack Davis (USA) 13.5	Joel Shankle (USA) 14.1
400m Hurdles	Glenn Davis (USA) 50.1	Eddie Southern (USA) 50.8	Joshua Culbreath (USA) 51.6
20km Walk	Leonid Spirin (URS) 1:31:27	Antanas Mikenas (LIT) 1:32:03	Bruno Junk (URS) 1:32:12
50km Walk	Norman Read (NZL) 4:30:42	Yevgeny Maskinskov 4:32:57	John Ljunggren (SWE) 4:35:02
4 × 100m Relay	United States of America 39.5	Soviet Union 39.8	Germany 40.3
4 × 400m Relay	United States of America 3:04.8	Australia 3:06.2	Great Britain 3:07.2
High Jump	Charles Dumas (USA) 2.12	Charles Porter (AUS) 2.10	Igor Kashkarov (URS) 2.08
Pole Vault	Robert Richards (USA) 4.56	Robert Gutowski (USA) 4.53	Georgios Roubanis (GRE) 4.50
Long Jump	Gregory Bell (USA) 7.83	John Bennett (USA) 7.68	Jorma Valkama (FIN) 7.48
Triple Jump	Ademar Ferreira da Silva (BRA) 16.35	Vilhjalmur Einarsson (ISL) 16.26	Vitold Kreyer (URS) 16.02
Shot Put	Parry O'Brien (USA) 18.57	William Nieder (USA) 18.18	Jiri Skobla (TCH) 17.65
Discus	Al Oerter (USA) 56.36	Fortune Gordien (USA) 54.81	Desmond Koch (USA) 54.40
Hammer	Harold Connolly (USA) 63.19	Mikhail Krivonosov (URS) 63.03	Anatoly Samotsvetov (URS) 62.56
Javelin	Egil Danielsen (NOR) 85.71	Janusz Sidlo (POL) 79.98	Viktor Tsybulenko (URS) 79.50
Decathlon	Milton Campbell (USA) 7937	Rafer Johnson (USA) 7587	Vassily Kusnetsov (URS) 7465

Women's	Gold	Silver	Bronze
100m	Elizabeth Cuthbert (AUS) 11.5	Christa Stubnick (GDR) 11.7	Marlene Matthews (AUS) 11.7
200m	Elizabeth Cuthbert (AUS) 23.4	Christa Stubnick (GDR) 23.7	Marlene Matthews (AUS) 23.8
80m Hurdles	Shirley Strickland de la Hunty (AUS) 10.7	Gisela Kohler (GDR) 10.9	Norma Thrower (AUS) 11.0
4 × 100m Relay	Australia 44.6	Great Britain 44.7	United States of America 45.0
High Jump	Mildred McDaniel (USA) 1.76	Thelma Hopkins (GBR) 1.67	Maria Pissaryeva (URS) 1.67
Long Jump	Elzbieta Krzesinska (POL) 6.35	Willye White (USA) 6.09	Nadezhda Dvalischvili (URS) 6.07
Shot Put	Tamara Tyshkevich (URS) 16.59	Galina Zybina (URS) 16.53	Marlanne Werner (GDR) 15.61
Discus	Olga Fikotova (TCH) 53.69	Irina Beglyakova (URS) 52.54	Nina Ponomaryeva (URS) 52.02
Javelin	Inese Jaunzame (URS) 53.86	Marlene Ahrens (CHI) 50.38	Nadezhda Konyayeva (URS) 50.28

ATHLETICS

1960 Rome

Men's	Gold	Silver	Bronze
100m	Armin Hary (FRG) 10.32	David Sime (USA) 10.35	Peter Radford (GBR) 10.42
200m	Livio Berruti (ITA) 20.62	Lester Carney (USA) 20.69	Abdoulaye Seye (SEN) 20.83
400m	Otis Davis (USA) 44.9	Carl Kaufmann (GDR) 44.9	Malcolm Spence (RSA) 45.5
800m	Peter Snell (NZL) 1:46.3	Roger Moens (BEL) 1:46.5	George Kerr (JAM) 1:47.1
1500m	Herb Elliott (AUS) 3:35.6	Michel Jazy (FRA) 3:38.4	Istvan Rozsavolgyi (HUN) 3:39.2
5000m	Murray Halberg (NZL) 13:43.4	Hans Grodotzki (GDR) 13:44.6	Kazimierz Zimny (POL) 13:44.8
10,000m	Pyotr Bolotnikov (URS) 28:32.2	Hans Grodotzki (GDR) 28.37.2	David Power (AUS) 28:38.2
Marathon	Abebe Bikila (ETH) 2:15:16	Rhadi Ben Abdesselem (MAR) 2:15:42	Barry Magee (NZL) 2:17:18
3000m Steeplechase	Zdzislaw Krzyszkowiak (POL) 8:34.2	Nikolai Sokolov (URS) 8:36.4	Semyon Rzhischin (URS) 8:42.2
110m Hurdles	Lee Calhoun (USA) 13.98	Willie May (USA) 13.99	Haynes Jones (USA) 14.17
400m Hurdles	Glenn Davis (USA) 49.3	Cliff Cushman (USA) 49.6	Dick Howard (USA) 49.7
20km Walk	Volodymyr Golubnychy (URS) 1:34:07	Noel Freeman (AUS) 1:34:16	Stanley Vickers (GBR) 1:34:56
50km Walk	Don Thompson (GBR) 4:25:30	John Ljunggren (SWE) 4:25:47	Abdon Pamich (ITA) 4:27:55
4 × 100m Relay	Germany 39.5	Soviet Union 40.1	Great Britain 40.2
4 × 400m Relay	United States of America 3:02.2	Germany 3:02.2	West Indies Federation (BWI/JAM/BAR) 3:04.0
High Jump	Robert Shavlakadze (URS) 2.16	Valery Brumel (URS) 2.16	John Thomas (USA) 2.14
Pole Vault	Donald Bragg (USA) 4.70	Ronald Morris (USA) 4.60	Eeles Landstrom (FIN) 4.55
Long Jump	Ralph Boston (USA) 8.12	Bo Roberson (USA) 8.12	Igor Terovanesyan (URS) 8.04
Triple Jump	Jozef Schmidt (POL) 16.81	Vladimir Goryayev (URS) 16.63	Vitold Kreyer (URS) 16.43
Shot Put	William Nieder (USA) 19.68	W. Parry O'Brien (USA) 19.11	Dallas Long (USA) 19.01
Discus	Al Oerter (USA) 59.18	Rink Babka (USA) 58.02	Richard Cochran (USA) 57.16
Hammer	Vasily Rudenkov (URS) 67.10	Gyula Zsivotzky (HUN) 65.79	Tadeusz Rut (POL) 65.64
Javelin	Viktor Tsybulenko (URS) 84.64	Walter Kruger (GDR) 79.36	Gergely Kulcsar (HUN) 78.57
Decathlon	Rafer Johnson (USA) 8392	Yang Chuan-Kwang (TPE) 8334	Vassily Kuznetsov (URS) 7809

Women's	Gold	Silver	Bronze
100m	Wilma Rudolph (USA) 11.0	Dorothy Hyman (GBR) 11.3	Giuseppina Leone (ITA) 11.3
200m	Wilma Rudolph (USA) 24.0	Jutta Heine (GDR) 24.4	Dorothy Hyman (GBR) 24.7
800m	Lyudmyla Shevtsova (URS) 2:04.3	Brenda Jones (AUS) 2:04.4	Ursula Donath (GDR) 2:05.6
80m Hurdles	Iryna Press (URS) 10.8	Carole Quinton (GBR) 10.9	Gisela Birkemeyer (GER) 11.0
4 × 100m Relay	United States of America 44.5	Germany 44.8	Poland 45.0
High Jump	Iolanda Balas (ROM) 1.85	Jaroslawa Jozwiakowska (POL) 1.71	Dorothy Shirley (GBR) 1.71
Long Jump	Vira Krepkina (URS) 6.37	Elizbieta Krzesinska (POL) 6.27	Hildrun Claus (GDR) 6.21
Shot Put	Tamara Press (URS) 17.32	Johanna Luttge (GDR) 16.61	Earlene Brown (USA) 16.42
Discus	Nina Ponomaryeva (URS) 55.10	Tamara Press (URS) 52.59	Lia Manoliu (ROM) 52.36
Javelin	Elvira Ozolina (URS) 55.98	Dana Zatopkova (TCH) 53.78	Birute Kalediene (LTU) 53.45

1964 Tokyo

Men's	Gold	Silver	Bronze
100m	Robert Hayes (USA) 10.05	Enrique Figuerola Camue (CUB) 10.25	Harry Jerome (CAN) 10.27
200m	Henry Carr (USA) 20.36	Otis Paul Drayton (USA) 20.58	Edwin Roberts (TRI) 20.63
400m	Michael Larrabee (USA) 45.15	Wendell Mottley (TRI) 45.24	Andrzej Badenski (POL) 45.64
800m	Peter Snell (NZL) 1:45.1	William Crothers (CAN) 1:45.6	Wilson Kiprogut Chuma (KEN) 1:45.9
1500m	Peter Snell (NZL) 3:38.1	Josef Odlozil (TCH) 3:39.6	John Davies (NZL) 3:39.6
5000m	Robert Schul (USA) 13:48.8	Harald Norpoth (GDR) 13:49.6	William Dellinger (USA) 13:49.8
10,000m	William Mills (USA) 28:24.4	Mohamed Gammoudi (TUN) 28:24.8	Ron Clarke (AUS) 28:25.8
Marathon	Abebe Bikila (ETH) 2:12:11	Basil Heatley (GBR) 2:16:19	Kokichi Tsuburaya (JPN) 2:16:23
3000m Steeplechase	Gaston Roelants (BEL) 8:30.8	Maurice Herriot (GBR) 8:32.4	Ivan Bylyayev (URS) 8:33.8
110m Hurdles	Hayes Jones (USA) 13.67	Blaine Lindgren (USA) 13.74	Anatoly Mikhailov (URS) 13.78
400m Hurdles	Rex Cawley (USA) 49.6	John Cooper (GBR) 50.1	Salvatore Morale (ITA) 50.1
20km Walk	Ken Matthews (GBR) 1:29:34	Dieter Lindner (GDR) 1:31:13	Volodymyr Golubnychy (URS) 1:32:00
50km Walk	Abdon Pamich (ITA) 4:11:12	Paul Nihill (GBR) 4:11:31	Ingvar Petterson (SWE) 4:14:17
4 × 100m Relay	United States of America 39.06	Poland 39.36	France 39.36
4 × 400m Relay	United States of America 3:00.7	Great Britain 3:01.6	Trinidad 3:01.7
High Jump	Valery Brumel (URS) 2.18	John Thomas (USA) 2.18	John Rambo (USA) 2.16
Pole Vault	Frederick Hansen (USA) 5.10	Wolfgang Reinhardt (GDR) 5.05	Klaus Lehnertz (GDR) 5.00
Long Jump	Lynn Davies (GBR) 8.07	Ralph Boston (USA) 8.03	Igor Ter-Ovanesyan (URS) 7.99
Triple Jump	Josef Schmidt (POL) 16.85	Oleg Fyedoseyev (URS) 16.58	Viktor Kravchenko (URS) 16.57
Shot Put	Dallas Long (USA) 20.33	James Randel Matson (USA) 20.20	Vilmos Varju (HUN) 19.39
Discus	Al Oerter (USA) 61.00	Ludvik Danek (TCH) 60.52	David Weill (USA) 59.49
Hammer	Romuald Klim (URS) 69.74	Gyula Zsivotzky (HUN) 65.79	Ume Beyer (GDR) 68.09
Javelin	Pauli Nevala (FIN) 82.66	Gergely Kulcsar (HUN) 82.32	Janis Lusis (URS) 80.57
Decathlon	Willi Holdorf (GDR) 7887	Rein Aun (URS) 7842	Hans-Joachim Walde (GDR) 7809

Women's	Gold	Silver	Bronze
100m	Wyomia Tyus (USA) 11.49	Edith McGuire (USA) 11.62	Ewa Klobukowska (POL) 11.64
200m	Edith McGuire (USA) 23.05	Irena Kirszenstein (POL) 23.13	Marilyn Black (AUS) 23.18
400m	Elizabeth Cuthbert (AUS) 52.0	Ann Packer (GBR) 52.2	Judith Moore (AUS) 53.4
800m	Ann Packer (GBR) 2:01.1	Maryvonne Dupureur (FRA) 2:01.9	Ann Marise Chamberlain (NZL) 2:02.8
80m Hurdles	Karin Balzer (GDR) 10.54	Teresa Ciepla-Wieczorek (POL) 10.55	Pamela Kilborn (AUS) 10.56
4 × 100m Relay	Poland 43.69	United States of America 43.92	Great Britain 44.09
High Jump	Iolanda Balas (ROM) 1.90	Michele Brown (AUS) 1.80	Taisa Chenchyk (URS) 1.78
Long Jump	Mary Rand (GBR) 6.76	Irena Kirszenstein (POL) 6.60	Tatyana Schelkanova (URS) 6.42
Shot Put	Tamara Press (URS) 18.14	Renate Garisch-Culmberger (GDR) 17.61	Galina Zybina (URS) 17.45
Discus	Tamara Press (URS) 57.27	Ingrid Lotz (GDR) 57.21	Lia Manoliu (ROM) 56.97
Javelin	Mihaela Penes (ROM) 60.54	Marta Rudas (HUN) 58.27	Yelena Gorchakova (URS) 57.06
Pentathlon	Iryna Press (URS) 5246	Mary Rand (GBR) 5035	Galina Bystrova (URS) 4956

1968 Mexico City

Men's	Gold	Silver	Bronze
100m	James Hines (USA) 9.95	Lennox Miller (JAM) 10.04	Charles Greene (USA) 10.07
200m	Tommie Smith (USA) 19.83	Peter Norman (AUS) 20.06	John Carlos (USA) 20.10
400m	Lee Evans (USA) 43.86	G. Lawrence James (USA) 43.97	Ronald Freeman (USA) 44.41
800m	Ralph Doubell (AUS) 1:44.3	Wilson Kiprugut Chuma (KEN) 1:44.5	Thomas Farrell (USA) 1:45.4
1500m	Kip Keino (KEN) 3:34.9	Jim Ryun (USA) 3:37.8	Bodo Tummler (FRG) 3:39.0
5000m	Mohamed Gammoudi (TUN) 14:05.0	Kip Keino (KEN) 14:05.2	Naftali Temu (KEN) 14:06.4
10,000m	Naftali Temu (KEN) 29:27.4	Mamo Wolde (ETH) 29:28.0	Mohamed Gammoudi (TUN) 29:34.2
Marathon	Mamo Wolde (ETH) 2:20:26	Kenji Kimihara (JPN) 2:23:31	Michael Ryan (NZL) 2:23:45
3000m Steeplechase	Amos Biwott (KEN) 8:51.0	Benjamin Kogo (KEN) 8:51.6	George Young (USA) 8:51.8
110m Hurdles	Willie Davenport (USA) 13.33	Ervin Hall (USA) 13.42	Eddy Ottoz (ITA) 13.46
400m Hurdles	David Hemery (GBR) 48.12	Gerhard Hennige (FRG) 49.02	John Sherwood (GBR) 49.12
20km Walk	Volodymyr Holubnychy (URS) 1:33:58	Jose Pedraza Zuniga (MEX) 1:34:00	Mykola Smaha (URS) 1:34:03
50km Walk	Christoph Hohne (GDR) 4:20:13	Antal Kiss (HUN) 4:30:17	Larry Young (USA) 4:31:55
4 × 100m Relay	United States of America 38.24	Cuba 38.40	France 38.43
4 × 400m Relay	United States of America 2:56.2	Kenya 2:59.6	Federal Republic of Germany 3:00.5
High Jump	Dick Fosbury (USA) 2.24	Edward Caruthers (USA) 2.22	Valentin Gavrilov (URS) 2.20
Pole Vault	Bob Seagren (USA) 5.40	Claus Schiprowski (FRG) 5.40	Wolfgang Nordwig (GDR) 5.40
Long Jump	Bob Beamon (USA) 8.90	Klaus Beer (GDR) 8.19	Ralph Boston (USA) 8.16
Triple Jump	Viktor Saneyev (URS) 17.39	Nelson Prudencio (BRA) 17.27	Giuseppe Gentile (ITA) 17.22
Shot Put	James Randel Matson (USA) 20.54	George Woods (USA) 20.12	Eduard Gushchin (URS) 20.09
Discus	Al Oerter (USA) 64.78	Lothar Milde (GDR) 63.08	Ludvik Danek (TCH) 62.92
Hammer	Gyula Zsivotzky (HUN) 73.36	Romuald Klim (URS) 73.28	Lazar Lovasz (HUN) 69.78
Javelin	Janis Lusis (URS) 90.10	Jorma Kinnunen (FIN) 88.58	Gergely Kulcsar (HUN) 87.06
Decathlon	Bill Toomey (USA) 8193	Hans-Joachim Walde (FRG) 8111	Kurt Bendlin (FRG) 8064

Women's	Gold	Silver	Bronze
100m	Wyomia Tyus (USA) 11.08	Barbara Ferrell (USA) 11.15	Irena Szewinska (POL) 11.19
200m	Irina Szewinska (POL) 22.58	Raelene Boyle (AUS) 22.74	Jennifer Lamy (AUS) 22.88
400m	Colette Besson (FRA) 52.03	Lillian Board (GBR) 52.12	Natalya Pechenkina (URS) 52.25
800m	Madeleine Manning (USA) 2:00.9	Ileana Silai (ROM) 2:02.5	Maria Gommers (NED) 2:02.6
80m Hurdles	Maureen Caird (AUS) 10.39	Pamela Kilborn (USA) 10.46	Chi Cheng (TPE) 10.51
4 × 100m Relay	United States of America 42.80	Cuba 43.36	Russia 43.41
High Jump	Miloslava Rezkova (TCH) 1.82	Antonina Okorokova (URS) 1.80	Valentyna Kozyr (TCH) 1.80
Long Jump	Viorica Viscopoleanu (ROM) 6.78	Sheila Sherwood (GBR) 6.68	Tatyana Talisheva (URS) 6.66
Shot Put	Margitta Gummel (GDR) 19.61	Marita Lange (GDR) 18.78	Nadezhda Chizhova (HUN) 17.78
Discus	Lia Manoliu (ROM) 58.28	Liesel Westermann (FRG) 57.76	Jolan Kleiber (HUN) 54.90
Javelin	Angela Nemeth (HUN) 60.36	Mihaela Penes (ROM) 59.92	Eve Janko (AUT) 58.04
Pentathlon	Ingrid Becker (FRG) 5098	Liese Prokop (AUT) 4966	Annamaria Toth (HUN) 4959

1972 Munich

Men's	Gold	Silver	Bronze
100m	Valeriy Borzov (URS) 10.14	Robert Taylor (USA) 10.24	Lennox Miller (JAM) 10.33
200m	Valeriy Borzov (URS) 20.00	Larry Black (USA) 20.19	Pietro Mennea (ITA) 20.30
400m	Vincent Matthews (USA) 44.66	Wayne Collett (USA) 44.80	Julius Sang (KEN) 44.92
800m	Dave Wottle (USA) 1:45.9	Yevhen Arzhanov (URS) 1:45.9	Michael Boit (KEN) 1:46.0

ATHLETICS

	Gold	Silver	Bronze
1500m	Pekka Vasala (FIN) 3:36.3	Kip Keino (KEN) 3:36.8	Rod Dixon (NZL) 3:37.5
5000m	Lasse Viren (FIN) 13:26.4	Mohamed Gammoudi (TUN) 13:27.4	Ian Stewart (GBR) 13.27.6
10,000m	Lasse Viren (FIN) 27:38.4	Emiel Puttemans (BEL) 27:39.6	Miruts Yifter (ETH) 27:41.0
Marathon	Frank Shorter (USA) 2:12:20	Karel Lismont (BEL) 2:14:32	Mamo Wolde (ETH) 2:15:08
3000m Steeplechase	Kip Keino (KEN) 8:23.6	Benjamin Jipcho (KEN) 8:24.6	Tapio Kantanen (FIN) 8:24.8
110m Hurdles	Rodney Milburn (USA) 13.24	Guy Drut (FRA) 13.34	Thomas Hill (USA) 13.48
400m Hurdles	John Akii-Bua (UGA) 47.82	Ralph Mann (USA) 48.51	David Hemery (GBR) 48.52
20km Walk	Peter Frenkel (GDR) 1:26:42	Volodymyr Holubnychy (URS) 1:26:55	Hans-Georg Reimann (GDR) 1:27:17
50km Walk	Bernd Kannenberg (FRG) 3:56:12	Veniamin Soldatenko (URS) 3:58:24	Larry Young (USA) 4:00:46
4 × 100m Relay	United States of America 38.19	Soviet Union 38.50	Federal Republic of Germany 38.79
4 × 400m Relay	Kenya 2:59.8	Great Britain 3:00.5	France 3:00.7
High Jump	Juri Tarnak (URS) 2.23	Stefan Junge (GDR) 2.21	Dwight Stones (USA) 2.21
Pole Vault	Wolfgang Nordwig (GDR) 5.50	Robert Seagren (USA) 5.40	Jan Johnson (USA) 5.35
Long Jump	Randy Williams (USA) 8.24	Hans Baumgartner (FRG) 8.18	Arnie Robinson (USA) 8.03
Triple Jump	Viktor Saneyev (URS) 17.35	Jorg Drehmel (GDR) 17.31	Nelson Prudencio (BRA) 17.05
Shot Put	Wladyslaw Komar (POL) 21.18	George Woods (USA) 21.17	Hartmut Briesenick (GDR) 21.14
Discus	Ludvik Danek (TCH) 64.40	L. Jay Silvester (USA) 63.50	Bjorn Rickard Bruch (SWE) 63.40
Hammer	Anatoly Bondarchuk (URS) 75.50	Jochen Sachse (GDR) 74.96	Vasily Khmelevski (URS) 74.04
Javelin	Klaus Wolfermann (FRG) 90.48	Janis Lusis (URS) 90.48	William Schmidt (USA) 84.42
Decathlon	Mykola Avilov (URS) 8454	Leonid Lytvynenko (URS) 8035	Ryszard Katus (POL) 7984

Women's	Gold	Silver	Bronze
100m	Renate Stecher (GDR) 11.07	Raelene Boyle (AUS) 11.23	Silvia Chivas (CUB) 11.24
200m	Renate Stecher (GDR) 22.40	Raelene Boyle (AUS) 22.45	Irena Szewinska (POL) 22.74
400m	Monika Zehrt (GDR) 51.08	Rita Wilden (FRG) 51.21	Kathy Hammond (USA) 51.64
800m	Hildegard Falck (FRG) 1:58.6	Nijole Sabaite (URS) 1:58.7	Gunhild Hoffmeister (GDR) 1:59.2
1500m	Lydmila Bragina (URS) 4:01.4	Gunhild Hoffmeister (GDR) 4:02.8	Paola Cacchi (ITA) 4:02.9
100m Hurdles	Anneliese Ehrhardt (GDR) 12.59	Valeria Bufanu (ROM) 12.84	Karin Balzer (GDR) 12.90
4 × 100m Relay	Federal Republic of Germany 42.81	German Democratic Republic 42.95	Cuba 43.36
4 × 400m Relay	German Democratic Republic 3:23.00	United States of America 3:25.20	Federal Republic of Germany 3:26.5
High Jump	Ulrike Meyfarth (FRG) 1.92	Yordanka Blagoyeva (BUL) 1.88	Ilona Gusenbauer (AUT) 1.88
Long Jump	Heidemarie Rosendahl (FRG) 6.78	Diana Yorgova (BUL) 6.77	Eva Suranova (TCH) 6.67
Shot Put	Nadezhda Chizhova (URS) 21.03	Margitta Gummel (GDR) 20.22	Ivanka Hristova (BUL) 19.35
Discus	Faina Melnik (URS) 66.62	Argentina Menis (ROM) 65.06	Vassilka Stoyeva (BUL) 64.34
Javelin	Ruth Fuchs (GDR) 63.88	Jacqueline Toten (GDR) 62.54	Kathryn Schmidt (USA) 59.94
Pentathlon	Mary Peters (GBR) 4801	Heidemarie Rosendahl (FRG) 4791	Burglinde Pollak (GDR) 4768

1976 Montreal

Men's	Gold	Silver	Bronze
100m	Hasley Crawford (TRI) 10.06	Don Quarrie (JAM) 10.07	Valery Borzov (URS) 10.14
200m	Don Quarrie (JAM) 20.22	Millard Hampton (USA) 20.29	Dwayne Evans (USA) 20.43
400m	Alberto Juantorena (CUB) 44.26	Frederick Newhouse (USA) 44.40	Herman Frazier (USA) 44.95
800m	Alberto Juantorena (CUB) 1:43.50	Ivo van Damme (BEL) 1:43.86	Richard Wohlhuter (USA) 1:44.12
1500m	John Walker (NZL) 3:39.17	Ivo van Damme (BEL) 3:39.27	Paul Heinz Wellmann (FRG) 3:39.33
5000m	Lasse Viren (FIN) 13:24.76	Dick Quax (NZL) 13:25.16	Klaus-Peter Hildenbrand (FRG) 13:25.38
10,000m	Lasse Viren (FIN) 27:40.38	Carlos Lopes (POR) 27:45.17	Brendan Foster (GBR) 27:54.92
Marathon	Waldemar Cierpinski (GDR) 2:09:55	Frank Shorter (USA) 2:10:46	Karel Lismont (BEL) 2:11:12
3000m Steeplechase	Anders Garderud (SWE) 8:08.2	Bronislaw Malinowski (POL) 8:09.2	Frank Baumgartl (GDR) 8:10.4
110m Hurdles	Guy Drut (FRA) 13.30	Alejandro Ramirez (CUB) 13.38	Willie Davenport (USA) 13.40
400m Hurdles	Edwin Moses (USA) 47.63	Michael Shine (USA) 48.69	Yevgeny Gavrilenko (URS) 49.45
20km Walk	Daniel Bautista Rocha (MEX) 1:24:41	Hans-Georg Reimann (GDR) 1:25:14	Peter Frenkel (GDR) 1:25:29
4 × 100m Relay	United States of America 38.33	German Democratic Republic 38.66	Soviet Union 38.78
4 × 400m Relay	United States of America 2:58.65	Poland 3:01.43	Federal Republic of Germany 3:01.98
High Jump	Jacek Wszola (POL) 2.25	Greg Joy (CAN) 2.23	Dwight Stones (USA) 2.21
Pole Vault	Tadeusz Slusarski (POL) 5.50	Antti Kalliomaki (FIN) 5.50	David Roberts (USA) 5.50
Long Jump	Arnie Robinson (USA) 8.35	Randy Williams (USA) 8.11	Frank Wartenberg (GDR) 8.02
Triple Jump	Viktor Saneyev (URS) 17.29	James Butts (USA) 17.18	Joao Carlos de Oliveira (CUB) 16.81
Shot Put	Udo Beyer (GDR) 21.05	Yevgeny Mironov (URS) 21.03	Aleksandr Baryshnikov (URS) 21.00
Discus	Mac Wilkins (USA) 67.50	Wolfgang Schmidt (GDR) 68.22	John Powell (USA) 65.70
Hammer	Yuri Sedykh (URS) 77.52	Aleksei Spiridonov (URS) 76.08	Anatoly Bondarchuk (URS) 75.48
Javelin	Miklos Nemeth (HUN) 94.58	Hannu Siitonen (FIN) 87.92	Gheorghe Megelea (ROM) 87.16
Decathlon	Bruce Jenner (USA) 8618	Guido Kratschmer (FRG) 8411	Mykola Avilov (URS) 8369

Women's	Gold	Silver	Bronze
100m	Annegret Richter (FRG) 11.08	Renate Stecher (GDR) 11.13	Inge Helten (FRG) 11.17
200m	Barbel Eckert (GDR) 22.37	Annegret Richter (FRG) 22.39	Renate Stecher (GDR) 22.47
400m	Irena Szewinska (POL) 49.28	Christine Brehmer (GDR) 50.51	Ellen Streidt (GDR) 50.55
800m	Tatyana Kazankina (URS) 1:54.94	Nikolina Shtereva (BUL) 1:55.42	Elfi Zinn (GDR) 1:55.60

1500m	Tatyana Kazankina (URS) 4:05.48	Gunhild Hoffmeister (GDR) 4:06.02	Ulrike Klapezynski (GDR) 4:06.09
100m Hurdles	Johanna Schaller (GDR) 12.77	Tatyana Anisimova (URS) 12.78	Natalya Lebedeva (URS) 12.80
4 × 100m Relay	German Democratic Republic 42.55	Federal Republic of Germany 42.59	Soviet Union 43.09
4 × 400m Relay	German Democratic Republic 3:19.23	United States of America 3:22.81	Soviet Union 3:24.24
High Jump	Rosemarie Ackermann (GDR) 1.93	Sara Simeoni (ITA) 1.91	Yordanka Blagoyeva (BUL) 1.91
Long Jump	Angela Voigt (GDR) 6.72	Kathy McMillan (USA) 6.66	Lidiya Alfeyeva (URS) 6.60
Shot Put	Ivanka Hristova (BUL) 21.16	Nadezhda Chizhova (URS) 20.96	Helena Fibingerova (TCH) 20.67
Discus	Evelin Schlaak (BUL) 69.00	Maria Vergova (BUL) 67.30	Gabriele Hinzmann (GDR) 66.84
Javelin	Ruth Fuchs (GDR) 65.94	Marion Becker (FRG) 64.70	Kathryn Schmidt (USA) 63.96
Pentathlon	Siegrun Siegl (GDR) 4745	Christine Laser (GDR) 4745	Burglinde Pollak (GDR) 4740

1980 Moscow

Men's	Gold	Silver	Bronze
100m	Allan Wells (GBR) 10.25	Silvio Leonard (CUB) 10.25	Peter Petrov (URS) 10.39
200m	Pietro Mennea (ITA) 20.19	Allan Wells (GBR) 20.21	Don Quarrie (JAM) 20.29
400m	Viktor Markin (URS) 44.60	Richard Mitchell (AUS) 44.84	Frank Schaffer (GDR) 44.87
800m	Steve Ovett (GBR) 1:45.40	Sebastian Coe (GBR) 1:45.85	Nikolai Kirov (URS) 1:45.94
1500m	Sebastian Coe (GBR) 3:38.40	Jurgen Straub (GDR) 3:38.80	Steve Ovett (GBR) 3:38.99
5000m	Miruts Yifter (ETH) 13:20.91	Suleiman Nyambui (TAN) 13:21.60	Kaarlo Maaninka (FIN) 13:22.00
10,000m	Miruts Yifter (ETH) 27:42.69	Kaarlo Maaninka (FIN) 27:44.28	Mohammed Kedir (ETH) 27:44.64
Marathon	Waldemar Cierpinski (GDR) 2:11:03	Gerard Nijboer (NED) 2:11:20	Satymkul Dzhumanazarov (URS) 2:11:35
3000m Steeplechase	Bronislaw Malinowski (POL) 8:09.7	Filbert Bayi (TAN) 8:12.5	Eshetu Tura (ETH) 8:13.6
110m Hurdles	Thomas Munkelt (GDR) 13.29	Alejandro Ramirez (CUB) 13.40	Aleksandr Puchkov (URS) 13.44
400m Hurdles	Volker Beck (GDR) 48.70	Vasyl Arkhypenko (URS) 48.86	Gary Oakes (GBR) 49.11
20km Walk	Maurizio Damilano (ITA) 1:23:35	Pyotr Pochinchuk (URS) 1:24:45	Roland Wieser (GDR) 1:25:58
50km Walk	Hartwig Gauder (GDR) 3:49:24	Jorge Ribas (ESP) 3:51:25	Yevgeny Ivchenko (URS) 3:56:32
4 × 100m Relay	Soviet Union 38.26	Poland 38.33	France 38.53
4 × 400m Relay	Soviet Union 3:01.1	German Democratic Republic 3:01.3	Italy 3:04.3
High Jump	Gerd Wessig (GDR) 2.36	Jacek Wszola (POL) 2.31	Jorg Freimuth (GDR) 2.31
Pole Vault	Wladyslaw Kozakiewicz (POL) 5.78	Tadeuszw Slusarski (POL) 5.65	Konstantin Volkov (URS) 5.65
Long Jump	Lutz Dombrowski (GDR) 8.54	Frank Paschek (GDR) 8.21	Valery Pidluzhny (URS) 8.18
Triple Jump	Jaak Uudmae (URS) 17.35	Viktor Saneyev (URS) 17.24	Joao Carlos de Oliveira (BRA) 17.22
Shot Put	Volodymyr Kyselyov (URS) 21.35	Aleksandr Baryshnikov (URS) 21.08	Udo Beyer (GDR) 21.06
Discus	Viktor Rashchupkin (URS) 66.64	Imrich Bugar (TCH) 66.38	Luis Delis Fournier (CUB) 66.32
Hammer	Yuri Sedykh (URS) 81.80	Sergei Litvinov (URS) 80.64	Juri Tamm (URS) 78.96
Javelin	Dainis Kula (URS) 91.20	Aleksandr Makarov (URS) 89.64	Wolfgang Hanisch (GDR) 86.72
Decathlon	Daley Thompson (GBR) 8495	Yuri Kutsenko (URS) 8331	Sergei Zhelanov (URS) 8315

Women's	Gold	Silver	Bronze
100m	Lyudmila Kondratyeva (URS) 11.06	Marlies Gohr (GDR) 11.07	Ingrid Auerswald (GDR) 11.14
200m	Barbel Wockel (GDR) 22.03	Natalia Bochina (URS) 22.19	Merlene Ottey (JAM) 22.20
400m	Marita Koch (GDR) 48.88	Jarmila Kratochvilova (TCH) 49.46	Christina Lathan (GDR) 49.66
800m	Nadiya Olizarenko (URS) 1:53.43	Olga Mineyeva (URS) 1:54.81	Tatyana Providokhina (URS) 1:55.46
1500m	Tatyana Kazankina (URS) 3:56.6	Christine Wartenberg (GDR) 3:57.8	Nadiya Olizarenko (URS) 3:59.6
100m Hurdles	Vera Komisova (URS) 12.56	Johanna Klier (GDR) 12.63	Lucyna Langer (POL) 12.65
4 × 100m Relay	German Democratic Republic 41.60	Soviet Union 42.10	Great Britain 42.43
4 × 400m Relay	Soviet Union 3.20.2	German Democratic Republic 3.20.4	Great Britain 3.27.5
High Jump	Sara Simeoni (ITA) 1.97	Urszula Kielan (POL) 1.94	Jutta Kirst (GDR) 1.94
Long Jump	Tatyana Kolpakova (URS) 7.06	Brigitte Wujak (GDR) 7.04	Tatyana Skachko (URS) 7.01
Shot Put	Ilona Slupianek (GDR) 22.41	Svetlana Krachevskaya (URS) 21.42	Margitta Pufe (GDR) 21.20
Discus	Evelin Jahl (GDR) 69.96	Maria Petkova (BUL) 67.90	Tatyana Lesovaya (URS) 67.40
Javelin	Maria Ruenes (CUB) 68.40	Saida Gunba (URS) 67.76	Ute Hommola (GDR) 66.56
Pentathlon	Nadiya Tkachenko (URS) 5083	Olga Rukavishnikova (URS) 4937	Olga Kuragina (URS) 4875

1984 Los Angeles

Men's	Gold	Silver	Bronze
100m	Carl Lewis (USA) 9.99	Sam Graddy (USA) 10.19	Ben Johnson (CAN) 10.22
200m	Carl Lewis (USA) 19.80	Kirk Baptiste (USA) 19.96	Thomas Jefferson (USA) 20.26
400m	Alonzo Babers (USA) 44.27	Gabriel Tiacoh (CIV) 44.54	Antonio McKay (USA) 44.71
800m	Joaquim Cruz (BRA) 1:43.00	Sebastian Coe (GBR) 1:43.64	Earl Jones (USA) 1:43.83
1500m	Sebastian Coe (GBR) 3:32.53	Steve Cram (GBR) 3:33.40	Jose Abascal (ESP) 3:34.30
5000m	Said Aouita (MAR) 13:05.59	Markus Ryffel (SUI) 13:07.54	Antonio Leitao (POR) 13:09.20
10,000m	Alberto Cova (ITA) 27:47.54	Mike McLeod (GBR) 28:06.22	Mike Musyoki (KEN) 28:06.46
Marathon	Carlos Lopez (ESP) 2:09:21	John Treacy (IRL) 2:09:56	Charlie Spedding (GBR) 2:09:58
3000m Steeplechase	Julius Korir (KEN) 8:11.80	Joseph Mahmoud (FRA) 8:13.31	Brian Diemer (USA) 8:14.06
110m Hurdles	Roger Kingdom (USA) 13.20	Greg Foster (USA) 13.23	Arto Bryggare (FIN) 13.40
400m Hurdles	Edwin Moses (USA) 47.75	Danny Harris (USA) 48.13	Harald Schmid (FRG) 48.19

ATHLETICS

Event	Gold	Silver	Bronze
20km Walk	Ernesto Canto (MEX) 1:23:13	Raul Gonzales (MEX) 1:23:20	Maurizio Damilano (ITA) 1:23:26
50km Walk	Raul Gonzales (MEX) 3:47:26	Bo Gustafsson (SWE) 3:53:19	Sandro Bellucci (ITA) 3:53:45
4 × 100m Relay	United States of America 37.83	Jamaica 38.62	Canada 38.70
4 × 400m Relay	United States of America 2:57.91	Great Britain 2:59.13	Nigeria 2:59.32
High Jump	Dietmar Mogenburg (FRG) 2.35	Patrik Sjoberg (SWE) 2.33	Zha Jianhua (CHN) 2.31
Pole Vault	Pierre Quinon (FRA) 5.75	Mike Tully (USA) 5.65	Earl Bell (USA) 5.60 Thierry Vigneron (FRA) 5.60
Long Jump	Carl Lewis (USA) 8.54	Gary Honey (AUS) 8.24	Giovanni Evangelisti (ITA) 8.24
Triple Jump	Al Joyner (USA) 17.26	Mike Conley (USA) 17.18	Keith Connor (GBR) 16.87
Shot Put	Alessandro Andrei (ITA) 21.26	Michael Carter (USA) 21.09	Dave Laut (USA) 20.97
Discus	Rolf Dannenburg (FRG) 66.60	Mac Wilkins (USA) 66.30	John Powell (USA) 65.46
Hammer	Juha Tiainen (FIN) 78.08	Karl-Hans Riehm (FRG) 77.98	Klaus Ploghaus (FRG) 76.68
Javelin	Arto Harkonen (FIN) 86.76	Dave Ottley (GBR) 85.74	Kenth Eldebrink (SWE) 83.72
Decathlon	Daley Thompson (GBR) 8798	Jurgen Hingsen (FRG) 8673	Siegfried Wenz (FRG) 8412

Women's	**Gold**	**Silver**	**Bronze**
100m	Evelyn Ashford (USA) 10.97	Alice Brown (USA) 11.13	Merlene Ottey (JAM) 11.16
200m	Valerie Brisco-Hooks (USA) 21.81	Florence Griffith (USA) 22.04	Merlene Ottey (JAM) 22.09
400m	Valerie Brisco-Hooks (USA) 48.83	Chandra Cheeseborough (USA) 49.05	Kathy Cook (GBR) 49.42
800m	Doine Melinte (ROM) 1:57.60	Kim Gallagher (USA) 1:58.63	Fita Lovin (ROM) 1:58.83
1500m	Gabriella Dorio (ITA) 4:03.25	Doine Melinte (ROM) 4:03.76	Maricica Puica (ROM) 4:04.15
3000m	Maricica Puica (ROM) 8:35.96	Wendy Sly (GBR) 8:39.47	Lynn Williams (CAN) 8:42.14
Marathon	Joan Benoit (USA) 2:24:52	Grete Waitz (NOR) 2:26:18	Rosa Mota (POR) 2:26:57
100m Hurdles	Benita Fitzgerald-Brown (USA) 12.84	Shirley Strong (GBR) 12.88	Kim Turner (USA) 13.06 Michele Chardonnet (FRA) 13.06
400m Hurdles	Nawal El Moutawakil (MAR) 54.61	Judie Brown (USA) 55.20	Cristina Cojacaru (ROM) 55.41
4 × 100m Relay	United States of America 41.65	Canada 42.77	Great Britain 43.11
4 × 400m Relay	United States of America 3:18.29	Canada 3:21.21	Federal Republic of Germany 3:22.98
High Jump	Ulrike Meyfarth (FRG) 2.02	Sara Simeoni (ITA) 2.00	Joni Huntley (USA) 1.97
Long Jump	Anisoara Stanciu (ROM) 6.96	Vali Ionescu (ROM) 6.81	Sue Hearnshaw (GBR) 6.80
Shot Put	Claudia Losch (FRG) 20.48	Mihaela Loghin (ROM) 20.47	Gael Martin (AUS) 19.19
Discus	Ria Stalman (NED) 65.36	Leslie Deniz (USA) 64.86	Florenta Craciunescu (ROM) 63.64
Javelin	Tessa Sanderson (GBR) 69.56	Tina Lillak (FIN) 69.00	Fatima Whitbread (GBR) 67.14
Heptathlon	Glynis Nunn (AUS) 6390	Jackie Joyner (USA) 6385	Sabine Everts (FRG) 6363

1988 Seoul

Men's	**Gold**	**Silver**	**Bronze**
100m	Carl Lewis (USA) 9.92	Linford Christie (GBR) 9.97	Calvin Smith (USA) 9.99
200m	Joe Deloach (USA) 19.75	Carl Lewis (USA) 19.79	Robson da Silva (BRA) 20.04
400m	Steve Lewis (USA) 43.87	Harry Reynolds (USA) 43.93	Danny Everett (USA) 44.09
800m	Paul Ereng (KEN) 1:43.45	Joaquim Cruz (BRA) 1:43.90	Said Aouita (MAR) 1:44.06
1500m	Peter Rono (KEN) 3:35.95	Peter Elliott (GBR) 3:36.15	Jens-Peter Herold (GDR) 3:36.21
5000m	John Ngugi (KEN) 13:11.70	Dieter Baumann (FRG) 13:15.52	Hansjorg Kunze (GDR) 13:15.73
10,000m	Brahim Boutayeb (MAR) 27:21.46	Salvatore Antibo (ITA) 27:23.55	Kipkemboi Kimeli (KEN) 27:25.16
Marathon	Gelindo Bordin (ITA) 2:10:32	Douglas Wakiihuri (KEN) 2:10:47	Ahmed Saleh (DJI) 2:10:59
3000m Steeplechase	Julius Kariyuki (KEN) 8:05.51	Peter Koech (KEN) 8:06.79	Mark Rowland (GBR) 8:07.96
110m Hurdles	Roger Kingdom (USA) 12.98	Colin Jackson (GBR) 13.28	Tony Campbell (USA) 13.38
400m Hurdles	Andre Phillips (USA) 47.19	Amadou Dia Ba (SEN) 47.23	Edwin Moses (USA) 47.56
20km Walk	Jozef Fribilinec (TCH) 1:19:57	Ronald Weigel (GDR) 1:20:00	Maurizio Damilano (ITA) 1:20:14
50km Walk	Vyacheslav Ivanenko (URS) 3:38:29	Ronald Weigel (GDR) 3:38:56	Hartwig Gauder (GDR) 3:39:45
4 × 100m Relay	Soviet Union 38.19	Great Britain 38.28	France 38.40
4 × 400m Relay	United States of America 2:56.16	Jamaica 3:00.30	Federal Republic of Germany 3:00.56
High Jump	Gennadi Avdeyenko (URS) 2.38	Hollis Conway (USA) 2.36	Rudolf Povarnitsyn (URS) 2.36 Patrick Sjöberg (SWE) 2.36
Pole Vault	Sergey Bubka (URS) 5.90	Rodion Gataullin (URS) 5.85	Grigory Yegorov (URS) 5.80
Long Jump	Carl Lewis (USA) 8.72	Mike Powell (USA) 8.49	Larry Myricks (USA) 8.27
Triple Jump	Hristo Markov (BUL) 17.61	Igor Lapshin (URS) 17.52	Aleksander Kovalenko (URS) 17.42
Shot Put	Ulf Timmermann (GDR) 22.47	Randy Barnes (USA) 22.39	Werner Gunther (SUI) 21.99
Discus	Jurgen Schult (GDR) 68.82	Romas Ubartas (URS) 67.48	Rolf Danneberg (FRG) 67.38
Hammer	Sergey Litvinov (URS) 84.80	Yuri Sedykh (URS) 83.76	Juri Tamm (URS) 81.16
Javelin	Tapic Korjus (FIN) 84.28	Jan Zelezny (TCH) 84.12	Seppo Raaty (FIN) 83.26
Decathlon	Christian Schenk (GDR) 8488	Torsten Voss (GDR) 8399	Dave Steen (CAN) 8328

Women's	**Gold**	**Silver**	**Bronze**
100m	Florence Griffith-Joyner (USA) 10.54	Evelyn Ashford (USA) 10.83	Heike Drechsler (GDR) 10.85
200m	Florence Griffith-Joyner (USA) 21.34	Grace Jackson (JAM) 21.72	Heike Drechsler (GDR) 21.95

400m	Olga Brygina (URS) 48.65	Petra Muller (GDR) 49.45	Olaga Nazarova (URS) 49.90
800m	Sigrun Wodars (GDR) 1:56.10	Christine Wachtel (GDR) 1:56.64	Kim Gallagher (USA) 1:56.91
1500m	Paula Ivan (ROM) 3:53.96	Lailuta Baikauksite (URS) 4:00.24	Tatyana Samolenko (URS) 4:00.30
3000m	Tatyana Samolenko (URS) 8:26.53	Paula Ivan (ROM) 8:27.15	Yvonne Murray (GBR) 8:29.02
10,000m	Olga Bondarenko (URS) 31:05.21	Liz McColgan (GBR) 31:08.44	Yelena Zhupieva (URS) 31:19.81
Marathon	Rosa Mota (POR) 2:25:40	Lisa Martin (AUS) 2:25:53	Kathrin Dorre (GDR) 2:26:21
100m Hurdles	Yordanka Donkova (BUL) 12.38	Gloria Siebert (GDR) 12.61	Claudia Zackiewicz (FRG) 12.75
400m Hurdles	Debbie Flintoff-King (AUS) 53.17	Tatyana Ledovskaya (URS) 53.16	Ellen Fiedler (GDR) 53.63
4 × 100m Relay	United States 41.98	German Democratic Republic 42.09	Soviet Union 42.75
4 × 400m Relay	Soviet Union 3:15.18	United States of America 3:15.51	German Democratic Republic 3:18.29
High Jump	Louise Ritter (USA) 2.03	Stefka Kostadinova (BUL) 2.01	Tamara Bykova (URS) 1.99
Long Jump	Jackie Joyner-Kersee (USA) 7.40	Heike Drechsler (GDR) 7.22	Galina Chistyakova (URS) 7.11
Shot Put	Natalya Lissovskaya (URS) 22.24	Kathrin Neimke (GDR) 21.07	Li Meisu (CHN) 21.06
Discus	Martina Hellmann (GDR) 72.30	Diana Gansky (GDR) 71.88	Tzvetanka Hristova (BUL) 69.74
Javelin	Petra Felke (GDR) 74.68	Fatima Whitbread (GBR) 70.32	Beate Koch (GDR) 67.30
Heptathlon	Jackie Joyner-Kersee (USA) 7291	Sabine John (GDR) 6897	Anke Behmer (GDR) 6858

1992 Barcelona

Men's	Gold	Silver	Bronze
100m	Linford Christie (GBR) 9.96	Frankie Fredericks (NAM) 10.02	Dennis Mitchell (USA) 10.04
200m	Mike Marsh (USA) 20.01	Frankie Fredericks (NAM) 20.13	Michael Bates (USA) 20.38
400m	Quincy Watts (USA) 43.50	Steve Lewis (USA) 44.21	Samson Kitur (KEN) 44.24
800m	William Tanui (KEN) 1:43.66	Nixon Kiprotich (KEN) 1:43.70	Johnny Gray (USA) 1:43.97
1500m	Fermin Cacho (ESP) 3:40.12	Rachid El-Basir (MAR) 3:40.62	Mohamed Suleiman (QAT) 3:40.69
5000m	Dieter Baumann (GER) 13:12.52	Paul Bitok (KEN) 13:12.71	Fita Bayisa (ETH) 13:13.03
10,000m	Khalid Skah (MAR) 27:46.70	Richard Chelimo (KEN) 27:47.72	Addis Abebe (ETH) 28:00.72
Marathon	Young Cho Hwang (KOR) 2:13:23	Koichi Morishita (JPN) 2:13:45	Stephen Freigang (GER) 2:14:00
3000m Steeplechase	Matthew Birir (KEN) 8:08.84	Patrick Sang (KEN) 8:09.55	William Mutwol (KEN) 8:10.74
110m Hurdles	Mark McKoy (CAN) 13.12	Tony Dees (USA) 13.24	Jack Pierce (USA) 13.26
400m Hurdles	Kevin Young (USA) 46.78	Winthrop Graham (JAM) 47.66	Kriss Akabusi (GBR) 47.82
20km Walk	Daniel Plaza Montero (ESP) 1:21:45	Guillaume Leblanc (CAN) 1:22:25	Giovanni de Benedictis (ITA) 1:23:11
50km Walk	Andrei Perlov (CIS) 3:50:13	Carlos Mercenario (MEX) 3:52:09	Ronald Weigel (GER) 3:53:45
4 × 100m Relay	United States of America 37.40	Nigeria 37.98	Cuba 38.00
4 × 400m Relay	United States of America 2:55.74	Cuba 2:59.51	Great Britain 2:59.73
High Jump	Javier Sotomayor (CUB) 2.34	Patrik Sjöberg (SWE) 2.34	Artur Partyka (POL) 2.34 Hollis Conway (USA) 2.34 Tim Forsythe (AUS) 2.34
Pole Vault	Maxim Tarasov (CIS) 5.80	Igor Trandenkov (CIS) 5.80	Javier Garcia (ESP) 5.75
Long Jump	Carl Lewis (USA) 8.67	Mike Powell (USA) 8.64	Joe Greene (USA) 8.34
Triple Jump	Mike Conley (USA) 18.17	Charles Simpkins (USA) 17.60	Frank Rutherford (BAH) 17.36
Shot Put	Mike Stulce (USA) 21.70	James Doehring (USA) 20.96	Vyacheslav Lykho (CIS) 20.94
Discus	Romas Ubartas (LTU) 65.12	Jurgen Schult (GER) 64.94	Roberto Moya (CUB) 64.12
Hammer	Andrei Abduvalyev (CIS) 82.54	Igor Astapkovich (CIS) 81.96	Igor Nikulin (CIS) 81.38
Javelin	Jan Zelezny (CZE) 89.66	Seppo Raaty (FIN) 86.60	Steve Backley (GBR) 83.38
Decathlon	Robert Zmelik (CZE) 8611	Antonio Penalver (ESP) 8412	Dave Johnson (USA) 8309

Women's	Gold	Silver	Bronze
100m	Gail Devers (USA) 10.82	Juliet Cuthbert (JAM) 10.83	Irina Privalova (CIS) 10.84
200m	Gwen Torrence (USA) 21.81	Juliet Cuthbert (JAM) 22.02	Merlene Ottey (JAM) 22.09
400m	Marie-Jose Perec (FRA) 48.83	Olga Bryzgina (CIS) 49.05	Ximena Restrepo (COL) 49.64
800m	Ellen van Langen (NED) 1:55.54	Lilia Nurutdinova (CIS) 1:55.99	Ana Quirot (CUB) 1:56.80
1500m	Hassiba Boulmerka (ALG) 3:55.30	Ludmila Rogacheva (CIS) 3:56.91	Qu Yunxia (CHN) 3:57.08
3000m	Yelena Romanova (CIS) 8:46.04	Tatyana Dorovski (CIS) 8:46.85	Angela Chalmers (CAN) 8:47.22
10,000m	Deratu Tulu (ETH) 31:06.0	Elana Meyer (RSA) 31:11.7	Lynn Jennings (USA) 31:19.8
Marathon	Valentina Yegorova (CIS) 2:32:41	Yuko Arimori (JPN) 2:32:49	Lorraine Moller (NZL) 2:33:59
100m Hurdles	Paraskevi Patoulidou (GRE) 12.64	LaVonna Martin (USA) 12.69	Yordanka Donkova (BUL) 12.70
400m Hurdles	Sally Gunnell (GBR) 53.23	Sandra Farmer-Patrick (USA) 53.69	Janeene Vickers (USA) 54.31
10km Walk	Chen Yueling (CHN) 44.32	Yelena Nikolayeva (CIS) 44.33	Li Chunxiu (CHN) 44.41
4 × 100m Relay	United States of America 42.11	CIS 42.16	Nigeria 42.81
4 × 400m Relay	CIS 3:20.20	United States of America 3:20.92	Great Britain 3:24.23
High Jump	Heike Henkel (GER) 2.02	Galina Astafei (ROM) 2.00	Joamnet Quintero (CUB) 1.97
Long Jump	Heike Drechsler (GER) 7.14	Inessa Kravets (CIS) 7.12	Jackie Joyner-Kersee (USA) 7.07
Shot Put	Svetlana Krivelyova (CIS) 21.06	Huang Zhihong (CHN) 20.47	Kathrin Neimke (GER) 19.78
Discus	Maritza Marten (CUB) 70.06	Tzvetanka Hristova (BUL) 67.78	Daniela Costian (AUS) 66.24
Javelin	Silke Renk (GER) 68.34	Natalya Shikolenko (CIS) 68.26	Karen Forkel (GER) 66.86
Heptathlon	Jackie Joyner-Kersee (USA) 7044	Irina Belova (CIS) 6845	Sabine Braun (GER) 6649

ATHLETICS

1996 Atlanta

Men's	Gold	Silver	Bronze
100m	Donovan Bailey (CAN) 9.84	Frankie Fredericks (NAM) 9.89	Ato Boldon (TRI) 9.90
200m	Michael Johnson (USA) 19.32	Frankie Fredericks (NAM) 19.68	Ato Boldon (TRI) 19.80
400m	Michael Johnson (USA) 43.49	Roger Black (GBR) 44.41	Davis Kamoga (UGA) 44.53
800m	Vebjoern Rodal (NOR) 1:42.58	Hezekiel Sepeng (RSA) 1:42.74	Fred Onyancha (KEN) 1:42.79
1500m	Noureddine Morceli (ALG) 3:35.78	Fermin Cacho (ESP) 3:36.40	Stephen Kipkorir (KEN) 3:36.72
5000m	Vanuste Niyongabo (BDI) 13:07.96	Paul Bitok (KEN) 13:08.16	Khalid Boulami (MAR) 13:08.37
10,000m	Haile Gebrselassie (ETH) 27:07.34	Paul Tergat (KEN) 27:08.17	Salah Hissou (MAR) 27:24.67
Marathon	Josia Thugwane (RSA) 2:12:36	Bong-Ju Lee (KOR) 2:12:39	Eric Wainaina (KEN) 2:12:44
3000m Steeplechase	Joseph Keter (KEN) 8:07.12	Moses Kiptanui (KEN) 8:08.33	Alessandro Lambruschini (ITA) 8:11.28
110m Hurdles	Allen Johnson (USA) 12.95	Mark Crear (USA) 13.09	Florian Schwarthoff (GER) 13.17
400m Hurdles	Derrick Adkins (USA) 47.54	Samuel Matete (ZAM) 47.78	Calvin Davis (USA) 47.96
20km Walk	Jefferson Perez (ECU) 1:20:07	Ilya Markov (RUS) 1:20:16	Bernardo Segura (MEX) 1:20:23
50km Walk	Robert Korzeniowski (POL) 3:43:30	Mikhail Shchennikov (RUS) 3:43:46	Valentin Massana (ESP) 3:44:19
4 × 100m Relay	Canada 37.69	United States of America 38.05	Brazil 38.41
4 × 400m Relay	United States of America 2:55.99	Great Britain 2:56.60	Jamica 2:59.42
High Jump	Charles Austin (USA) 2.39	Artur Partyka (POL) 2.37	Steve Smith (GBR) 2.35
Pole Vault	Jean Galfione (FRA) 5.92	Igor Trandenkov (RUS) 5.92	Andrei Tivontchik (GER) 5.92
Long Jump	Carl Lewis (USA) 8.50	James Beckford (JAM) 8.29	Joe Greene (USA) 8.24
Triple Jump	Kenny Harrison (USA) 18.09	Jonathan Edwards (GBR) 17.88	Yoelbi Quesada (CUB) 17.44
Shot Put	Randy Barnes (USA) 21.62	John Godina (USA) 20.79	Oleksander Bagach (RUS) 20.75
Discus	Lars Riedel (GER) 69.40	Vladimir Dubrovshchik (BLR) 66.60	Vasiliy Kaptyukh (BLR) 65.80
Hammer	Balazs Kiss (HUN) 81.24	Lance Deal (USA) 81.12	Oleksiy Krykun (RUS) 80.02
Javelin	Jan Zelezny (CZE) 88.16	Steve Backley (GBR) 87:44	Seppo Raty (FIN) 86.98
Decathlon	Dan O'Brien (USA) 8824	Frank Busemann (GER) 8706	Thomas Dvorak (CZE) 8664

Women's	Gold	Silver	Bronze
100m	Gail Devers (USA) 10.94	Merlene Ottey (JAM) 10.94	Gwen Torrence (USA) 10.96
200m	Marie-José Perec (FRA) 22.12	Merlene Ottey (JAM) 22.24	Mary Onyali (NGR) 22.38
400m	Marie-José Perec (FRA) 48.25	Cathy Freeman (AUS) 48.63	Falilat Ogunkoya (NGR) 49.10
800m	Svetlana Masterkova (RUS) 1:57.73	Ana Quirot Fidelia (CUB) 1:58.11	Maria Mutola Lurdes (MOZ) 1:58.71
1500m	Svetlana Masterkova (RUS) 4:00.83	Gabriela Szabo (ROM) 4:01.54	Theresia Kiesl (AUT) 4:03.02
3000m	Wang Junxia (CHN) 14:59.88	Pauline Konga (KEN) 15:03.49	Roberta Brunet (ITA) 15:07.52
10,000m	Fernanda Ribeiro (POR) 31:01.63	Wang Junxia (CHN) 31:02.58	Gete Wami (ETH) 31:06.65
Marathon	Fatuma Roba (ETH) 2:26:05	Valentina Yegorova (RUS) 2:28:05	Yuko Arimori (JPN) 2:28:39
100m Hurdles	Ludmila Engquist (SWE) 12.58	Brigita Bukovec (SLO) 12.59	Patricia Girard-Leno (FRA) 12.65
400m Hurdles	Deon Hemmings (JAM) 52.82	Kim Batten (USA) 53.08	Tonja Buford-Bailey (USA) 53.22
10km Walk	Yelena Nikolayeva (RUS) 41:49	Elisabetta Perrone (ITA) 42:12	Wang Yan (CHN) 42:19
4 × 100m Relay	United States of America 41.95	Bahamas 42.14	Jamaica 42.24
4 × 400m Relay	United States of America 3:20.91	Nigeria 3:21.04	Germany 3:21.14
High Jump	Stefka Kostadinova (BUL) 2.05	Niki Bakogianni (GRE) 2.03	Inna Babakova (RUS) 2.01
Long Jump	Chioma Ajunwa (NGR) 7.12	Fiona May (ITA) 7.02	Jackie Joyner-Kersee (USA) 7.00
Triple Jump	Inessa Kravets (UKR) 15.33	Inna Lasovskaya (RUS) 14.98	Sarka Kasparkova (CZE) 14.98
Shot Put	Astrid Kumbernuss (GER) 20.56	Sui Xinmei (CHN) 19.88	Irina Khudorozhkina (RUS) 19.35
Discus	Ilke Wyludda (GER) 69.66	Natalya Sadova (RUS) 66.48	Ellina Zvereva (RUS) 65.64
Javelin	Heli Rantanen (FIN) 67.94	Louise McPhail (AUS) 65.54	Trine Hattestad (NOR) 64.98
Heptathlon	Ghada Shouaa (SYR) 6780	Natalya Sazanovich (BLR) 6563	Denise Lewis (GBR) 6489

2000 Sydney

Men's	Gold	Silver	Bronze
100m	M. Greene (USA) 9.87	A. Boldon (TRI) 9.99	O. Thompson (BAR) 10.04
200m	K. Kenteris (GRE) 20.09	D. Campbell (GBR) 20.14	A. Boldon (TRI) 20.20
400m	M. Johnson (USA) 43.84	A. Harrison (USA) 44.40	G. Haughton (JAM) 44.70
800m	N. Schumann (GDR) 1:45.08	W. Kipketer (DEN) 1:45.14	A.D. Said-Guerni (ALG) 1:45.16
1500m	N. Ngeny (KEN) 3:32.07	H. El Guerrouj (MOR) 3:32.32	B. Lagat (KEN) 3:32.44
5000m	M. Wolde (ETH) 13:35.49	A. Saidi-Sief (ALG) 13:36.20	B. Lahlafi (MOR) 13:36.47
10,000m	H. Gebrselassie (ETH) 27:18.20	P. Tergat (KEN) 27:18.29	A. Mezgebu (ETH) 27:19.75
Marathon	G. Abera (ETH) 2:10:11	E. Wainaina (KEN) 2:10:31	T. Tola (ETH) 2:11:10
3000m Steeplechase	R. Kosgei (KEN) 8:21.43	W. B. Kipketer (KEN) 8:21.77	A. Ezzine (MAR) 8:22.15
110m Hurdles	A. Garcia (CUB) 13.00	T. Trammell (USA) 13.16	M. Crear (USA) 13.22
400m Hurdles	A. Taylor (USA) 47.50	H.S. Somayli (SAU) 47.53	L. Herbert (RSA) 47.81
20km Walk	R. Korzeniowski (POL) 1:18:59	N. Hernandez (MEX) 1:19:03	V. Andreyev (RUS) 1:19:27
50km Walk	R. Korzeniowski (POL) 3:42:22	A. Fadejevs (LAT) 3:43:40	J. Sanchez (MEX) 3:44:36
4 × 100m Relay	United States of America 37.61	Brazil 37.90	Cuba 38.04
4 × 400m Relay	United States of America 2:56.35	Nigeria 2:58.68	Jamaica 2:58.78
High Jump	S. Kliugin (RUS) 2.35	J. Sotomayor (CUB) 2.32	A. Hammad (ALG) 2.32
Pole Vault	N. Hysong (USA) 5.90	L. Johnson (USA) 5.90	M. Tarasov (RUS) 5.90

Long Jump	I. Pedroso (CUB) 8.55	J. Taurima (AUS) 8.49	R. Schurenko (UKR) 8.31
Triple Jump	J. Edwards (GBR) 17.71	Y. Garcia (CUB) 17.47	D. Kasputin (RUS) 17.46
Shot Put	A. Harju (FIN) 21.29	A. Nelson (USA) 21.21	J. Godina (USA) 21.20
Discus	V. Alekna (LTU) 69.30	L. Riedel (GDR) 68.50	F. Kruger (RSA) 68.19
Hammer	S. Ziolkowski (POL) 80.02	N. Vizzoni (ITA) 79.64	I. Astapkovich (BEL) 79.17
Javelin	J. Zelezny (CZE) 90.17	S. Backley (GBR) 89.85	S. Makarov (RUS) 88.67
Decathlon	E. Nool (EST) 8641	R. Sebrle (CZE) 8606	C. Huffins (USA) 8595

Women's	Gold	Silver	Bronze
100m	M. Jones (USA) 10.75	E. Thanou (GRE) 11.12	T. Lawrence (JAM) 11.18
200m	M. Jones (USA) 21.84	P. Davis-Thompson (BAH) 22.27	S. Jayasinghe (SRI) 22.28
400m	C. Freeman (AUS) 49.11	L. Graham (JAM) 49.58	K. Merry (GBR) 49.72
800m	M. Mutola (MOZ) 1:56.15	S. Graf (AUS) 1:56.64	K. Holmes (GBR) 1:56.80
1500m	N. Merah-Benida (ALG) 4:05.10	V. Szekely (ROM) 4:05.15	G. Szabo (ROM) 4:05.27
5000m	G. Szabo (ROM) 14:40.79	S. O'Sullivan (IRL) 14:41.02	G. Wami (ETH) 14:42.23
10,000m	D. Tulu (ETH) 30:17.49	G. Wami (ETH) 30:22.48	F. Ribeiro (POR) 30:22.88
Marathon	N. Takahashi (JAP) 2:23:14	L. Simon (ROM) 2:23:22	J. Chepchumba (KEN) 2:24:45
100m Hurdles	O. Shishigina (KAZ) 12.65	G. Alozie (NIG) 12.68	M. Morrison (USA) 12.76
400m Hurdles	I. Privalova (RUS) 53.02	D. Hemmings (JAM)	N. Bidouane (MAR) 53.57
20km Walk	Wang Liping (CHN) 1:29:05	K. Plaetzer (NOR) 1:29:33	M. Vasco (ESP) 1:30:23
4 × 100m Relay	Bahamas 41.95	Jamaica 42.13	United States of America 42.20
4 × 400m Relay	United States of America 3:22.62	Jamaica 3:23.25	Russia 3:23.46
High Jump	Y. Yelesina (RUS) 2.01	H. Cloete (RSA) 2.01	K. Bergqvist (SWE) 1.99 O. Pantelimon (ROM) 1.99 note: joint gold medallists and joint bronze medallists
Pole Vault	S. Dragila (USA) 4.60	T. Grigorieva (AUS) 4.55	V. Flosadottir (ICL) 4.50
Long Jump	H. Drechsler (GDR) 6.99	F. May (ITA) 6.92	M. Jones (USA) 6.92
Triple Jump	T. Marinova (BUL) 15.20	T. Lebedeva (RUS) 15.00	O. Hovorova (UKR) 14.96
Shot Put	Y. Korolchik (BLR) 20.56	L. Peleshenko (RUS) 19.92	A. Kumbernuss (GDR) 19.62
Discus	E. Zvereva (BLR) 68.40	A. Kelesidou (GRE) 65.71	I. Yatchenko (BLR) 65.20
Hammer	K. Skolimowska (POL) 71.16	O. Kuzenkova (RUS) 69.77	K. Muenchow (GER) 69.28
Javelin	T. Hattestad (NOR) 68.91	M. Maniani-Tzelili (GRE) 67.51	O. Menendez (CUB) 66.18
Heptathlon	D. Lewis (GBR) 6584	Y. Prokhorova (RUS) 6531	N. Sazanovich (BLR) 6527

2004 Athens

Men's	Gold	Silver	Bronze
100m	Justin Gatlin (USA) 9.85	Francis Obikwelu (POR) 9.86	Maurice Greene (USA) 9.87
200m	Shawn Crawford (USA) 19.79	Bernard Williams (USA) 20.01	Justin Gatlin (USA) 20.03
400m	Jeremy Wariner (USA) 44.00	Otis Harris (USA) 44.16	Derrick Brew (USA) 44.42
800m	Yuriy Borzakovskiy (RUS) 1:44.45	Mbulaeni Mulaudzi (RSA) 1:44.61	Wilson Kipketer (DEN) 1:44.65
1500m	Hicham El Guerrouj (MAR) 3:34.18	Bernard Lagat (KEN) 3:34.30	Rui Silva (POR) 3:34.68
5000m	Hicham El Guerrouj (MAR) 13:14.39	Kenenisa Bekele (ETH) 13:14.59	Eliud Kipchoge (KEN) 13:15.10
10,000m	Kenenisa Bekele (ETH) 27:05.10 (OR)	Sileshi Sihine (ETH) 27:09.39	Zersenay Tadesse (ERI) 27:22.57
Marathon	Stefano Baldini (ITA) 2:10.55	Mebrahtom Keflezighi (USA) 2:11.29	Vanderlei de Lima (BRA) 2:12.11
110m hurdles	Xiang Liu (CHN) 12.91 (equals WR)	Terrence Trammell (USA) 13.18	Anier Garcia (CUB) 13.20
400m hurdles	Felix Sanchez (DOM) 47.63	Danny McFarlane (JAM) 48.11	Naman Keita (FRA) 48.26
3000m steeplechase	Ezekiel Kemboi (KEN) 8:05.81	Brimin Kipruto (KEN) 8:06.11	Paul Kipsiele Koech (KEN) 8:06.64
4 × 100m relay	Great Britain 38.07	United States 38.08	Nigeria 38.23
4 × 400m relay	United States 2:55.91	Australia 3:00.60	Nigeria 3:00.90
20km walk	Ivano Brugnetti (ITA) 1:19:40	Francisco Javier Fernandez (ESP) 1:19:45	Nathan Deakes (AUS) 1:20:02
50km walk	Robert Korzeniowski (POL) 3:38:46	Denis Nizhegorodov (RUS) 3:42:50	Aleksey Voyevodin (RUS) 3:43:34
High Jump	Stefan Holm (SWE) 2.36	Matt Hemmingway (USA) 2.34	Jaroslav Baba (CZE) 2.34
Long Jump	Dwight Phillips (USA) 8.59	John Moffitt (USA) 8.47	Joan Lino Martinez (ESP) 8.32
Pole Vault	Timothy Mack (USA) 5.95	Toby Stevenson (USA) 5.90	Giuseppe Gibilisco (ITA) 5.85
Triple Jump	Christian Olsson (SWE) 17.79	Marian Oprea (ROM) 17.55	Danila Burkenya (RUS) 17.48
Shot Put	Yuriy Bilonog (UKR) 21.16	Adam Nelson (USA) 21.16	Joachim Olsen (DEN) 21.07
Discus*	Virgilijus Alekna (LIT) 69.89	Zoltan Kovago (HUN) 67.04	Aleksander Tammert (EST) 66.66
Hammer**	Koji Murofushi (JPN) 82.91	Ivan Tikhon (BLR) 79.81	Esref Apak (TUR) 79.51
Javelin	Andreas Thorkildsen (NOR) 86.50	Vadims Vasilevskis (LAT) 4.95	Sergey Makarov (RUS) 84.84
Decathlon	Roman Sebrle (CZE) 8893	Bryan Clay (USA) 8820	Dmitriy Karpov (KAZ) 8725

*Robert Fazekas of Hungary won the discus final (70.93 OR) but was disqualified for subsequently trying to tamper with a sample during a dope test.
**Adrian Annus of Hungary won the hammer final (83.19) but was disqualified for refusing to take a second drug test despite passing the first.

Women's	Gold	Silver	Bronze
100m	Yuliya Nesterenko (BLR) 10.93	Lauryn Williams (USA) 10.96	Veronica Campbell (JAM) 10.97
200m	Veronica Campbell (JAM) 22.05	Allyson Felix (USA) 22.18	Debbie Ferguson (BAH) 22.30
400m	Tonique Williams-Darling (BAH) 49.41	Ana Guevara (MEX) 49.56	Natalya Antyukh (RUS) 49.89

800m	Kelly Holmes (GBR) 1:56.38	Hasna Benhassi (MOR) 1:56.43	Jolanda Ceplak (SLO) 1:56.43
1500m	Kelly Holmes (GBR) 3:57.90	Tatyana Tomashova (RUS) 3:58.12	Maria Cioncan (ROM) 3:58.39
5000m	Meseret Defar (ETH) 14:45.65	Isabella Ochichi (KEN) 14:48.19	Tirunesh Dibaba (ETH) 14:51.83
10,000m	Huina Xing (CHN) 30:24.36	Ejegayehu Dibaba (ETH) 30:24.98	Derartu Tulu (ETH) 30:26.42
Marathon	Mizuki Noguchi (JPN) 2:26.20	Catherine Ndereba (KEN) 2:26.32	Deena Kastor (USA) 2:27.20
100m hurdles	Joanna Hayes (USA) 12.37	Olena Krasovska (UKR) 12.45	Melissa Morrison (USA) 12.56
400m hurdles	Fani Halkia (GRE) 52.82	Ionela Tirlea-Manolache (ROM) 53.38	Tetiana Tereshchuk-Antipova (UKR) 53.44
4 × 100m relay	Jamaica 41.73	Russia 42.27	France 42.54
4 × 400m relay	United States 3:19.01	Russia 3:20.16	Jamaica 3:22.00
20km walk	Athanasia Tsoumeleka (GRE) 1:29.12	Olimpiada Ivanova (RUS) 1:29.16	Jane Saville (AUS) 1:29.25
High Jump	Yelena Slesarenko (RUS) 2.06	Hestrie Cloete (RSA) 2.02	Viktoriya Styopina (UKR) 2.02
Long Jump	Tatyana Lebedeva (RUS) 7.07	Irina Simagina (RUS) 7.05	Tatyana Kotova (RUS) 7.05
Pole Vault	Yelena Isinbayeva (RUS) 4.91 WR	Svetlana Feofanova (RUS) 4.75	Anna Rogowska (POL) 4.70
Triple Jump	Francoise Mbango Etone (CAM) 15.30	Hrysopiyi Devetzi (GRE) 15.25	Tatyana Lebedeva (RUS) 15.14
Shot Put*	Yumileidi Cumba (CUB) 19.59	Nadine Kleinert (GER) 19.55	Svetlana Krivelyova (RUS) 19.49
Discus	Natalya Sadova (RUS) 67.02	Anastasia Kelesidou (GRE) 66.68	Irina Yatchenko (BLR) 66.17
Hammer	Olga Kuzenkova (RUS) 75.02 (OR)	Yipsi Moreno (CUB) 73.36	Yunaika Crawford (CUB) 73.16
Javelin	Osleidys Menendez (CUB) 71.53 (OR)	Steffi Nerius (GER) 65.82	Mirela Manjani (GRE) 64.29
Heptathlon	Carolina Kluft (SWE) 6952	Austra Skujyte (LIT) 6435	Kelly Sotherton (GBR) 6424

*Irina Korzhanenko (RUS) 21.06 won the women's shot put but was subsequently disqualified after failing a drugs test.

World Athletics Championships

1983 Helsinki

Men's	Gold	Silver	Bronze
100m	Carl Lewis (USA) 10.07	Calvin Smith (USA) 10.21	Emmit King (USA) 10.24
200m	Calvin Smith (USA) 20.14	Elliott Quow (USA) 20.41	Pietro Mennea (ITA) 20.51
400m	Bert Cameron (JAM) 45.05	Michael Franks (USA) 45.22	Sunder Nix (USA) 45.24
800m	Willi Wulbeck (FRG) 1:43.65	Rob Druppers (NED) 1:44.20	Joaquim Cruz (BRA) 1:44.27
1500m	Steve Cram (GBR) 3:41.49	Steve Scott (USA) 3:41.87	Said Aouita (MAR) 3:42.02
5000m	Eamonn Coghlan (IRL) 13:28.53	Werner Schildhauer (GDR) 13:30.20	Martti Vainio (FIN) 13:30.34
10,000m	Alberto Cova (ITA) 28:01.04	Werner Schildhauer (GDR) 28:01.18	Hansjorg Kunze (GDR) 28:01.26
Marathon	Robert de Castella (AUS) 2:10:03	Kebede Balcha (ETH) 2:10:27	Waldemar Cierpinski (GDR) 2:10:37
3000m Steeplechase	Patriz Ilg (FRG) 8:15.06	Boguslaw Maminski (POL) 8:17.03	Colin Reitz (GBR) 8:17.75
110m Hurdles	Greg Foster (USA) 13.42	Arto Bryggare (FIN) 13.46	Willie Gault (USA) 13.48
400m Hurdles	Edwin Moses (USA) 47.50	Harald Schmid (FRG) 48.61	Aleksandr Kharlov (URS) 49.03
50km Walk	Ronald Weigel (GDR) 3:43:08	Jose Marn (ESP) 3:43:42	Sergey Yung (URS) 3:49:03
4 × 100m Relay	United States of America 37.86	Italy 38.37	Soviet Union 38.41
4 × 400m Relay	Soviet Union 3:00.79	Federal Republic of Germany 3:01.83	Great Britain 3:03.53
High Jump	Gennadiy Avdeyenko (URS) 2.32	Tyke Peacock (USA) 2.32	Jianhua Zhu (CHN) 2.29
Pole Vault	Sergey Bubka (URS) 5.70	Konstantin Volkov (URS) 5.60	Atanas Tarev (BUL) 5.60
Long Jump	Carl Lewis (USA) 8.55	Jason Grimes (USA) 8.29	Mike Conley (USA) 8.12
Triple Jump	Zdzislaw Hoffmann (POL) 17.42	Willie Banks (USA) 17.18	Ajayi Agbebaku (NGR) 17.18
Shot Put	Edward Sarul (POL) 21.39	Ulf Timmermann (GDR) 21.16	Remigius Machura (TCH) 20.98
Discus	Imrich Bugir (TCH) 67.72	Luis Delis (CUB) 67.36	Gejza Valent (TCH) 66.08
Hammer	Sergey Litvinov (URS) 82.68	Yuriy Sedykh (URS) 80.94	Zdzislaw Kwasny (POL) 79.42
Javelin	Detlef Michel (GDR) 89.48	Tom Petranoff (USA) 85.60	Dainis Kula (URS) 85.58
Decathlon	Daley Thompson (GBR) 8666	Jurgen Hingsen (FRG) 8561	Siegfried Wentz (FRG) 8478

Women's	Gold	Silver	Bronze
100m	Marlies Oelsner-Gohr (GDR) 10.97	Marita Koch (GDR) 11.02	Diane Williams (USA) 11.06
200m	Marita Koch (GDR) 22.13	Merlene Ottey (JAM) 22.19	Kathy Cook (GBR) 22.37
400m	Jarmila Kratochvilova (TCH) 47.99	Tatiana Kocembova (TCH) 48.59	Mariya Pinigina (URS) 49.19
800m	Jarmila Kratochvilova (TCH) 1:54.68	Lyubov Gurina (URS) 1:56.11	Yekaterina Podkopayeva (URS) 1:57.58
1500m	Mary Decker (USA) 4:00.90	Zamira Zaitseva (URS) 4:01.19	Yekaterina Podkopayeva (URS) 4:02.25
3000m	Mary Decker (USA) 8:34.62	Brigitte Kraus (FRG) 8:35.11	Tatyana Kazankina (URS) 8:35.13
Marathon	Grete Waitz (NOR) 2:28:09	Marianne Dickerson (USA) 2:31:09	Raisa Smekhnova (URS) 2:31:13
100m Hurdles	Bettine Jahn (GDR) 12.35	Kerstin Knabe (GDR) 12.42	Ginka Zagorcheva (BUL) 12.62
400m Hurdles	Yekaterina Fesenko (URS) 54.14	Anna Ambraziene (URS) 54.15	Ellen Fiedler (GDR) 54.55
4 × 100m Relay	German Democratic Republic 41.76	Great Britain 42.71	Jamaica 42.73

4 × 400m Relay	German Democratic Republic 3:19.73	Czechoslovakia 3:20.32	Soviet Union 3:21.16
High Jump	Tamara Bykova (URS) 2.01	Ulrike Meyfarth (FRG) 1.99	Louise Ritter (USA) 1.95
Long Jump	Heike Daute (GDR) 7.27	Anisoara Stanciu (ROM) 7.15	Carol Lewis (USA) 7.04
Triple Jump	Helena Fibingerova (TCH) 21.05	Helma Knorscheidt (GDR) 20.70	Ilona Slupianek (GDR) 20.56
Discus	Martina Opitz-Hellmann (GDR) 68.94	Galina Murashova (URS) 67.44	Maria Petkova (BUL) 66.44
Javelin	Tiina Lillak (FIN) 70.82	Fatima Whitbread (GBR) 69.14	Anna Verouli (GRE) 65.72
Heptathlon	Ramona Neubert (GDR) 6714	Sabine Paetz-John (GDR) 6662	Anke Vater (GDR) 6532

1987 Rome

Men's	Gold	Silver	Bronze
100m	Carl Lewis (USA) 9.93	Raymond Stewart (JAM) 10.08	Linford Christie (GBR) 10.14
200m	Calvin Smith (USA) 20.16	Gilles Queneherve (FRA) 20.16	John Regis (GBR) 20.18
400m	Thomas Schonlebe (GDR) 44.33	Innocent Egbunike (NGR) 44.56	Harry Reynolds (USA) 44.80
800m	Billy Konchellah (KEN) 1:43.06	Peter Elliott (GBR) 1:43.41	Jose Luiz Barbosa (BRA) 1:43.76
1500m	Abdi Bile (SOM) 3:36.80	Jose Luis Gonzalez (ESP) 3:38.03	Jim Spivey (USA) 3:38.82
5000m	Said Aouita (MAR) 13:26.44	Domingos Castro (POR) 13:27.59	Jack Buckner (GBR) 13:27.74
10,000m	Paul Kipkoech (KEN) 27:38.63	Francesco Panetta (ITA) 27:48.98	Hansjorg Kunze (GDR) 27:50.37
Marathon	Douglas Wakiihuri (KEN) 2:11:48	Ahmed Salah (DJI) 2:12:30	Gelindo Bordin (ITA) 2:12:40
3000m Steeplechase	Francesco Panetta (ITA) 8:08.57	Hagen Melzer (GDR) 8:10.32	William van Dijck (BEL) 8:12.18
110m Hurdles	Greg Foster (USA) 13.21	Jonathan Ridgeon (GBR) 13.29	Colin Jackson (GBR) 13.38
400m Hurdles	Edwin Moses (USA) 47.46	Danny Harris (USA) 47.48	Harald Schmid (FRG) 47.48
20km Walk	Maurizio Damilano (ITA) 1:20:45	Jozef Pribilinec (TCH) 1:21:07	Jose Marin (ESP) 1:21:24
50km Walk	Hartwig Gauder (GDR) 3:40:53	Ronald Weigel (GDR) 3:41:30	Vyacheslav Ivanenko (URS) 3:44:02
4 × 100m Relay	United States of America 37.90	Soviet Union 38.02	Jamaica 38.41
4 × 400m Relay	United States of America 2:57.29	Great Britain 2:58.86	Cuba 2:59.16
High Jump	Patrik Sjoberg (SWE) 2.38	Igor Paklin (URS) 2.38	Gennadiy Avdeyenko (URS) 2.38
Pole Vault	Sergey Bubka (URS) 5.85	Thierry Vigneron (FRA) 5.80	Radion Gataulllin (URS) 5.80
Long Jump	Carl Lewis (USA) 8.67	Robert Emmiyan (URS) 8.53	Larry Myricks (USA) 8.33
Triple Jump	Khristo Markov (BUL) 17.92	Mike Conley (USA) 17.67	Oleg Sakirkin (URS) 17.43
Shot Put	Werner Gunthor (SUI) 22.23	Alessandro Andrei (ITA) 21.88	John Brenner (USA) 21.75
Discus	Jurgen Schult (GDR) 68.74	John Powell (USA) 66.22	Luis Delis (CUB) 66.02
Hammer	Sergey Litvinov (URS) 83.06	Juri Tamm (URS) 80.84	Ralf Haber (GDR) 80.76
Javelin	Seppo Raty (FIN) 83.54	Viktor Yevsyukov (URS) 82.52	Jan Zelezny (TCH) 82.20
Decathlon	Torsten Voss (GDR) 8680	Siegfried Wentz (FRG) 8461	Pavel Tarnavetsky (URS) 8375

Women's	Gold	Silver	Bronze
100m	Silke Gladisch (GDR) 10.90	Heike Drechsler (GDR) 11.00	Merlene Ottey (JAM) 11.04
200m	Silke Gladisch (GDR) 21.74	Florence Griffith (USA) 21.96	Merlene Ottey (JAM) 22.06
400m	Olga Vladykina-Bryzgina § (URS) 49.38	Petra Muller (GDR) 49.94	Kirsten Emmelmann (GDR) 50.20
800m	Sigrun Wodars (GDR) 1:55.26	Christine Wachtel (GDR) 1:55.32	Lyubov Gurina (URS) 1:55.56
1500m	Tatyana Samolenko (URS) 3:58.56	Hildegard Korner (GDR) 3:58.67	Doina Melinte (ROM) 3:59.27
3000m	Tatyana Samolenko-Dorovskikh (URS) 8:38.73	Maricica Puica (ROM) 8:39.45	Ulrike Bruns (GDR) 8:40.30
10,000m	Ingrid Kristiansen (NOR) 31:05.85	Yelena Zhupiyeva (URS) 31:09.40	Kathrin Ullrich (GDR) 31:11.34
Marathon	Rosa Mota (POR) 2:25.17	Ivanova Zoya (URS) 2:32.38	Jocelyn Villeton (FRA) 2:32.53
100m Hurdles	Ginka Zagorcheva (BUL) 12.34	Gloria Uibel (GDR) 12.44	Cornelia Oschkenat (GDR) 12.46
400m Hurdles	Sabine Busch (GDR) 53.62	Debbie Flintoff-King (AUS) 54.19	Cornelia Ullrich (GDR) 54.31
10km Walk	Irina Strakhova (URS) 44.12	Kerry Saxby-Junna (AUS) 44.23	Hong Yan (CHN) 44.42
4 × 100m Relay	United States of America 41.58	German Democratic Republic 41.58	Soviet Union 42.33
4 × 400m Relay	German Democratic Republic 3:18.63	Soviet Union 3:19.50	United States of America 3:21.04
High Jump	Stefka Kostadinova (BUL) 2.09	Tamara Bykova (URS) 2.04	Susanne Beyer (GDR) 1.99
Long Jump	Jackie Joyner-Kersee (USA) 7.36	Yelena Belevskaya (URS) 7.14	Heike Drechsler (GDR) 7.13
Shot Put	Natalya Lisovskaya (URS) 21.24	Kathrin Neimke (GDR) 21.21	Ines Müller (GDR) 20.76
Discus	Martina Hellmann (GDR) 71.62	Diana Gansky (GDR) 70.12	Tsvetanka Khristova (BUL) 68.82
Javelin	Fatima Whitbread (GBR) 76.64	Petra Felke-Meier (GDR) 71.76	Beate Peters (FRG) 68.82
Heptathlon	Jackie Joyner-Kersee (USA) 7128	Larisa Nikitina (URS) 6564	Jane Frederick (USA) 6502

1991 Tokyo

Men's	Gold	Silver	Bronze
100m	Carl Lewis (USA) 9.86	Leroy Burrell (USA) 9.88	Dennis Mitchell (USA) 9.91
200m	Michael Johnson (USA) 20.01	Frankie Fredericks (NAM) 20.34	Atlee Mahorn (CAN) 20.49
400m	Antonio Pettigrew (USA) 44.57	Roger Black (GBR) 44.62	Danny Everett (USA) 44.63
800m	Billy Konchellah (KEN) 1:43.99	Jose Luiz Barbosa (BRA) 1:44.24	Mark Everett (USA) 1:44.67

A
T
H
L
E
T
I
C
S

	Gold	Silver	Bronze
1500m	Noureddine Morceli (ALG) 3:32.84	Wilfred Kirochi (KEN) 3:34.84	Hauke Fühlbrügge (GER) 3:35.28
5000m	Yobes Ondieki (KEN) 13:14.45	Fita Bayissa (ETH) 13:16.64	Brahim Boutayeb (MAR) 13:22.70
10,000m	Moses Tanui (KEN) 27:38.74	Richard Chelimo (KEN) 27:39.41	Khalid Skah (MAR) 27:41.74
Marathon	Hiromi Taniguchi (JPN) 2:14:57	Ahmed Salah (DJI) 2:15:26	Steve Spence (USA) 2:15:36
3000m Steeplechase	Moses Kiptanui (KEN) 8:12.59	Patrick Sang (KEN) 8:13.44	Azzedine Brahmi (ALG) 8:15.54
110m Hurdles	Greg Foster (USA) 13.06	Jack Pierce (USA) 13.06	Tony Jarrett (GBR) 13.25
400m Hurdles	Samuel Matete (ZAM) 47.64	Winthrop Graham (JAM) 47.74	Kriss Akabusi (GBR) 47.86
20km Walk	Maurizio Damilano (ITA) 1:19:37	Mikhail Schennikov (URS) 1:19:46	Yevgeny Misyulya (URS) 1:20:22
50km Walk	Aleksandr Potashov (URS) 3:53:09	Andrey Perlov (URS) 3:53:09	Hartwig Gauder (GER) 3:55:14
4 × 100m Relay	United States of America 37.50	France 37.87	Great Britain 38.09
4 × 400m Relay	Great Britain 2:57.53	United States of America 2:57.57	Jamaica 3:00.32
High Jump	Charles Austin (USA) 2.38	Javier Sotomayor (CUB) 2.36	Hollis Conway (USA) 2.36
Pole Vault	Sergey Bubka (URS) 5.95	Istvan Bagyula (HUN) 5.90	Maksim Tarasov (URS) 5.85
Long Jump	Mike Powell (USA) 8.95	Carl Lewis (USA) 8.91	Larry Myricks (USA) 8.42
Triple Jump	Kenny Harrison (USA) 17.78	Leonid Voloshin (URS) 17.75	Mike Conley (USA) 17.62
Shot Put	Werner Günthör (SUI) 21.67	Lars Arvid Nilsen (NOR) 20.75	Aleksandr Klimenko (URS) 20.34
Discus	Lars Riedel (GER) 66.20	Erik de Bruin (NED) 65.82	Attila Horvath (HUN) 65.32
Hammer	Yuri Sedykh (URS) 81.70	Igor Astapkovich (URS) 80.94	Heinz Weis (GER) 80.44
Javelin	Kimmo Kinnunen (FIN) 90.82	Seppo Rety (FIN) 88.12	Vladimir Sasimovich (URS) 87.08
Decathlon	Dan O'Brien (USA) 8812	Mike Smith (CAN) 8549	Christian Schenk (GER) 8394

Women's	Gold	Silver	Bronze
100m	Katrin Krabbe (GER) 10.99	Gwen Torrence (USA) 11.03	Merlene Ottey (JAM) 11.06
200m	Katrin Krabbe (GER) 22.09	Gwen Torrence (USA) 22.16	Merlene Ottey (JAM) 22.21
400m	Marie-José Perec (FRA) 49.13	Grit Breuer (GER) 49.42	Sandra Myers (ESP) 49.78
800m	Liliya Nurutdinova (URS) 1:57.50	Ana Fidelia Quirot (CUB) 1:57.55	Ella Kovacs (ROM) 1:57.58
1500m	Hassiba Boulmerka (ALG) 4:02.21	Tatyana Dorovskikh (URS) 4:02.58	Lyudmila Rogachova (URS) 4:02.72
10,000m	Liz McColgan (GBR) 31:14.31	Zhong Huandi (CHN) 31:35.1	Wang Xiuting (CHN) 31:36.0
Marathon	Wanda Panfil (POL) 2:29:53	Sachiko Yamashita (JPN) 2:29:57	Katrin Dörre (GER) 2:30:10
100m Hurdles	Ludmila Engquist (SWE) 12.59	Gail Devers (USA) 12.63	Natalya Grigoryeva (URS) 12.69
400m Hurdles	Tatyana Ledovskaya (URS) 53.11	Sally Gunnell (GBR) 53.16	Janeene Vickers (USA) 53.47
10km Walk	Alina Ivanova (URS) 42:57	Madelein Svensson (SWE) 43:13	Sari Essayah (FIN) 43:13
4 × 100m Relay	Jamaica 41.94	Soviet Union 42.2	Germany 42.33
4 × 400m Relay	Soviet Union 3:18.4	United States of America 3:20.2	Germany 3:21.2
High Jump	Heike Henkel (GER) 2.05	Yelena Yelesina (URS) 1.98	Inga Babakova (URS) 1.96
Long Jump	Jackie Joyner-Kersee (USA) 7.32	Heike Drechsler (GER) 7.29	Larisa Berezhnaya (URS) 7.11
Shot Put	Huang Zhihong (CHN) 20.85	Natalya Lisovskaya (URS) 20.29	Svetlana Krivelyova (URS) 20.16
Discus	Tsvetanka Khristova (BUL) 71.02	Ilke Wyludda (GER) 69.12	Larisa Mikhalchenko (URS) 68.26
Javelin	Demei Xu (CHN) 68.78	Petra Felke (GER) 68.68	Silke Renk (GER) 66.80
Heptathlon	Sabine Braun (GER) 6672	Liliana Nastase (ROM) 6493	Irina Belova (URS) 6448

1993 Stuttgart

Men's	Gold	Silver	Bronze
100m	Linford Christie (GBR) 9.87	Andre Cason (USA) 9.92	Dennis Mitchell (USA) 9.99
200m	Frankie Fredericks (NAM) 19.85	John Regis (GBR) 19.94	Carl Lewis (USA) 19.99
400m	Michael Johnson (USA) 43.65	Harry Reynolds (USA) 44.13	Samson Kitur (KEN) 44.54
800m	Paul Ruto (KEN) 1:44.71	Giuseppe d'Urso (ITA) 1:44.86	Billy Konchellah (KEN) 1:44.89
1500m	Noureddine Morceli (ALG) 3:34.24	Fermin Cacho (ESP) 3:35.56	Abdi Bile (SOM) 3:35.96
5000m	Ismael Kirui (KEN) 13:02.75	Haile Gebrselassie (ETH) 13:03.17	Fita Bayissa (ETH) 13:05.40
10,000m	Haile Gebrselassie (ETH) 27:46.02	Moses Tanui (KEN) 27:46.54	Richard Chelimo (KEN) 28:06.02
Marathon	Mark Plaatjes (USA) 2:13:57	Luketz Swartbooi (NAM) 2:14:11	Bert van Vlaanderen (NED) 2:15:12
3000m Steeplechase	Moses Kiptanui (KEN) 8:06.36	Patrick Sang (KEN) 8:07.53	Alessandro Lambruschini (ITA) 8:08.78
110m Hurdles	Colin Jackson (GBR) 12.91	Tony Jarrett (GBR) 13.00	Jack Pierce (USA) 13.06
400m Hurdles	Kevin Young (USA) 47.18	Samuel Matete (ZAM) 47.60	Winthrop Graham (JAM) 47.62
20km Walk	Valenti Massana (ESP) 1:22:31	Giovanni de Benedictis (ITA) 1:23:06	Daniel Plaza (ESP) 1:23:18
50km Walk	Jesus Angel Garcia (ESP) 3:41:41	Valentin Kononen (FIN) 3:42:02	Valeriy Spitsyn (RUS) 3:42:50
4 × 100m Relay	United States of America 37.48	Great Britain 37.77	Canada 37.83
4 × 400m Relay	United States of America 2:54.3	Kenya 2:59.8	Germany 3:00.0
High Jump	Javier Sotomayor (CUB) 2.40	Artur Partyka (POL) 2.37	Steve Smith (GBR) 2.37
Pole Vault	Sergey Bubka (UKR) 6.00	Grigoriy Yegorov (KAZ) 5.90	Maksim Tarasov (RUS) 5.80
Long Jump	Mike Powell (USA) 8.59	Stanislav Tarasenko (RUS) 8.16	Vitaliy Kirilenko (UKR) 8.15
Triple Jump	Mike Conley (USA) 17.86	Leonid Voloshin (RUS) 17.65	Jonathan Edwards (GBR) 17.44
Shot Put	Werner Günthör (SUI) 21.97	Randy Barnes (USA) 21.80	Aleksandr Bagach (UKR) 20.40
Discus	Lars Riedel (GER) 67.72	Dmitriy Shevchenko (RUS) 66.90	Jürgen Schult (GER) 66.12
Hammer	Andrey Abduvaliyev (TJK) 81.64	Igor Astapkovich (BLR) 79.88	Tibor Gzcsek (HUN) 79.54
Javelin	Jan Zelezny (CZE) 85.98	Kimmo Kinnunen (FIN) 84.78	Mick Hill (GBR) 82.96

	Gold	Silver	Bronze
Decathlon	Dan O'Brien (USA) 8817	Eduard Hemeleinen (BLR) 8724	Paul Meier (GER) 8548

Women's	Gold	Silver	Bronze
100m	Gail Devers (USA) 10.82	Merlene Ottey (JAM) 10.82	Gwen Torrence (USA) 10.89
200m	Merlene Ottey (JAM) 21.98	Gwen Torrence (USA) 22.00	Irina Privalova (RUS) 22.13
400m	Jearl Miles-Clark (USA) 49.82	Natasha Kaiser-Brown (USA) 50.17	Sandie Richards (JAM) 50.44
800m	Maria Mutola (MOZ) 1:55.43	Lyubov Gurina (RUS) 1:57.10	Ella Kovacs (ROM) 1:57.92
1500m	Liu Dong (CHN) 4:00.50	Sonia O'Sullivan (IRL) 4:03.48	Hassiba Boulmerka (ALG) 4:04.29
3000m	Yunxia Qu (CHN) 8:28.71	Linli Zhang (CHN) 8:29.25	Lirong Zhang (CHN) 8:31.95
10,000m	Junxia Wang (CHN) 30:49.30	Huandi Zhong (CHN) 31:12.55	Sally Barsosio (KEN) 31:15.38
Marathon	Junko Asari (JPN) 2:30:03	Maria Manuela Machado (POR) 2:30:54	Tomoe Abe (JPN) 2:31:01
100m Hurdles	Gail Devers (USA) 12.46	Marina Azyabina (RUS) 12.60	Lynda Tolbert (USA) 12.67
400m Hurdles	Sally Gunnell (GBR) 52.74	Sandra Farmer-Patrick (USA) 52.79	Margarita Ponomaryova (RUS) 53.48
10km Walk	Sari Essayah (FIN) 42:59	Ileana Salvador (ITA) 43:08	Encarna Granados (ESP) 43:21
4 × 100m Relay	Russia 41.49	United States of America 41.49	Jamaica 41.94
4 × 400m Relay	United States of America 3:16.71	Russia 3:18.38	Great Britain 3:23.41
High Jump	Ioamnet Quintero (CUB) 1.97	Silvia Costa (CUB) 1.97	Sigrid Kirchmann (AUT) 1.97
Long Jump	Heike Drechsler (GER) 7.11	Larisa Berezhnaya (UKR) 6.98	Renata Nielsen (DEN) 6.76
Triple Jump	Anna Biryukova (RUS) 15.09	Iolanda Chen (RUS) 14.70	Iva Prandzheva (BUL) 14.23
Shot Put	Zhihong Huang (CHN) 20.57	Svetlana Krivelyova (RUS) 19.97	Kathrin Neimke (GER) 19.71
Discus	Olga Burova (RUS) 67.40	Daniela Costian (AUS) 65.36	Chunfeng Min (CHN) 65.26
Javelin	Trine Hattestad (NOR) 69.18	Karen Forkel (GER) 65.80	Natalya Shikolenko (BLR) 65.64
Heptathlon	Jackie Joyner-Kersee (USA) 6837	Sabine Braun (GER) 6797	Svetlana Buraga (BLR) 6635

1995 Gothenburg

Men's	Gold	Silver	Bronze
100m	Donovan Bailey (CAN) 9.97	Bruny Surin (CAN) 10.03	Ato Boldon (TRI) 10.03
200m	Michael Johnson (USA) 19.79	Frankie Fredericks (NAM) 20.12	Jeff Williams (USA) 20.18
400m	Michael Johnson (USA) 43.39	Harry Reynolds (USA) 44.22	Gregory Haughton (JAM) 44.56
800m	Wilson Kipketer (DEN) 1:45.08	Arthémon Hatungimana (BDI) 1:45.64	Vebjørn Rodal (NOR) 1:45.68
1500m	Noureddine Morceli (ALG) 3:33.73	Hicham El Guerrouj (MAR) 3:35.28	Venuste Niyongabo (BDI) 3:35.56
5000m	Ismael Kirui (KEN) 13:16.77	Khalid Boulami (MAR) 13:17.15	Shem Kororia (KEN) 13:17.59
10,000m	Haile Gebrselassie (ETH) 27:12.95	Khalid Skah (MAR) 27:14.53	Paul Tergat (KEN) 27:14.70
Marathon	Martin Fiz (ESP) 2:11:41	Dionicio Cerin (MEX) 2:12:13	Luiz Antonio dos Santos (BRA) 2:12:49
3000m Steeplechase	Moses Kiptanui (KEN) 8:04.16	Christopher Koskei (KEN) 8:09.30	Saad Shaddad Al-Asmari (KSA) 8:12.95
110m Hurdles	Allen Johnson (USA) 13.00	Tony Jarrett (GBR) 13.04	Roger Kingdom (USA) 13.19
400m Hurdles	Derrick Adkins (USA) 47.98	Samuel Matete (ZAM) 48.03	Stephane Diagana (FRA) 48.14
20km Walk	Michele Didoni (ITA) 1:19:59	Valenti Massana (ESP) 1:20:23	Yevgeny Misyulya (BLR) 1:20:48
50km Walk	Valentin Kononen (FIN) 3:43:42	Giovanni Perricelli (ITA) 3:45:11	Robert Korzeniowski (POL) 3:45:57
4 × 100m Relay	Canada 38.31	Australia 38.50	Italy 39.07
4 × 400m Relay	United States of America 2:57.32	Jamaica 2:59.88	Nigeria 3:03.18
High Jump	Troy Kemp (BAH) 2.37	Javier Sotomayor (CUB) 2.37	Artur Partyka (POL) 2.35
Pole Vault	Sergey Bubka (UKR) 5.92	Maksim Tarasov (RUS) 5.86	Jean Galfione (FRA) 5.86
Long Jump	Ivan Pedroso (CUB) 8.70	James Beckford (JAM) 8.30	Mike Powell (USA) 8.29
Triple Jump	Jonathan Edwards (GBR) 18.29	Brian Wellman (BER) 17.62	Jerome Romain (DMA) 17.59
Shot Put	John Godina (USA) 21.47	Mika Halvari (FIN) 20.93	Randy Barnes (USA) 20.41
Discus	Lars Riedel (GER) 68.76	Vladimir Dubrovshchik (BLR) 65.98	Vasiliy Kaptyukh (BLR) 65.88
Hammer	Andrei Abduvaliyev (TJK) 81.56	Igor Astapkovich (BLR) 81.10	Tibor Gzcsek (HUN) 80.98
Javelin	Jan Zelezny (CZE) 89.58	Steve Backley (GBR) 86.30	Boris Henry (GER) 86.08
Decathlon	Dan O'Brien (USA) 8695	Eduard Hemeleinen (BLR) 8489	Mike Smith (CAN) 8419

Women's	Gold	Silver	Bronze
100m	Gwen Torrence (USA) 10.85	Merlene Ottey (JAM) 10.94	Irina Privalova (RUS) 10.96
200m	Merlene Ottey (JAM) 22.12	Irina Privalova (RUS) 22.12	Galina Malchugina (RUS) 22.37
400m	Marie-José Perec (FRA) 49.28	Pauline Davis (BAH) 49.96	Jearl Miles-Clark (USA) 50.00
800m	Ana Fidelia Quirot (CUB) 1:56.11	Letitia Vriesde (SUR) 1:56.68	Kelly Holmes (GBR) 1:56.95
1500m	Hassiba Boulmerka (ALG) 4:02.42	Kelly Holmes (GBR) 4:03.04	Carla Sacramento (POR) 4:03.79
5000m	Sonia O'Sullivan (IRL) 14:46.47	Fernanda Ribeiro (POR) 14:48.54	Zahra Quaziz (MAR) 14:53.77
10,000m	Fernanda Ribeiro (POR) 31:04.99	Derartu Tulu (ETH) 31:08.10	Tegla Loroupe (KEN) 31:17.66
Marathon	Maria Manuela Machado (POR) 2:25:39	Anuta Catuna (ROM) 2:26:25	Ornella Ferrara (ITA) 2:30:11
100m Hurdles	Gail Devers (USA) 12.68	Olga Shishigina (KAZ) 12.80	Yuliya Graudyn (RUS) 12.85
400m Hurdles	Kim Batten (USA) 52.61	Tonja Buford (USA) 52.62	Deon Hemmings (JAM) 53.48
10km Walk	Irina Stankina (RUS) 42:13	Elisabetta Perrone (ITA) 42:16	Yelena Nikolayeva (RUS) 42:20
4 × 100m Relay	United States of America 42.12	Jamaica 42.25	Germany 43.01
4 × 400m Relay	United States of America 3:22.39	Russia 3:23.98	Australia 3:25.88

A
T
H
L
E
T
I
C
S

High Jump	Stefka Kostadinova (BUL) 2.01	Alina Astafei (GER) 1.99	Inga Babakova (UKR) 1.99
Long Jump	Fiona May (ITA) 6.98	Niurka Montalvo (CUB) 6.86	Irina Mushailova (RUS) 6.83
Triple Jump	Inessa Kravets (UKR) 15.50	Iva Prandzheva (BUL) 15.18	Anna Biryukova (RUS) 15.08
Shot Put	Astrid Kumbernuss (GER) 21.22	Zhihong Huang (CHN) 20.04	Svetlana Mitkova (BUL) 19.56
Discus	Ellina Zvereva (BLR) 68.64	Ilke Wyludda (GER) 67.20	Olga Chernyavskaya (RUS) 66.86
Javelin	Natalya Shikolenko (BLR) 67.56	Felicia Tilea (ROM) 65.22	Mikaela Ingberg (FIN) 65.16
Heptathlon	Ghada Shouaa (SYR) 6651	Svetlana Moskalets (RUS) 6575	Rita Inincsi (HUN) 6522

1997 Athens

Men's	Gold	Silver	Bronze
100m	Maurice Greene (USA) 9.86	Donovan Bailey (CAN) 9.91	Tim Montgomery (USA) 9.94
200m	Ato Boldon (TRI) 20.04	Frankie Fredericks (NAM) 20.23	Claudinei Quirino da Silva (BRA) 20.26
400m	Michael Johnson (USA) 44.12	Davis Kamoga (UGA) 44.37	Tyree Washington (USA) 44.39
800m	Wilson Kipketer (DEN) 1:43.38	Norberto Tellez (CUB) 1:44.00	Rich Kenah (USA) 1:44.25
1500m	Hicham El Guerrouj (MAR) 3:35.83	Fermin Cacho (ESP) 3:36.63	Reyes Estevez (ESP) 3:37.26
5000m	Daniel Komen (KEN) 13:07.38	Khalid Boulami (MAR) 13:09.34	Tom Nyariki (KEN) 13:11.09
10,000m	Haile Gebrselassie (ETH) 27:24.58	Paul Tergat (KEN) 27:25.62	Salah Hissou (MAR) 27:28.67
Marathon	Abel Anton (ESP) 2:13:16	Martin Fiz (ESP) 2:13:21	Steve Moneghetti (AUS) 2:14:16
3000m Steeplechase	Wilson Kipketer (KEN) 8:05.84	Moses Kiptanui (KEN) 8:06.04	Bernard Barmasai (KEN) 8:06.04
110m Hurdles	Allen Johnson (USA) 12.93	Colin Jackson (GBR) 13.05	Igor Kovoc (SVK) 13.18
400m Hurdles	Stéphane Diagana (FRA) 47.70	Llewellyn Herbert (RSA) 47.86	Bryan Bronson (USA) 47.88
20km Walk	Daniel Garcia (MEX) 1:21:43	Mikhail Shchennikov (RUS) 1:21:53	Mikhail Khmelnitski (BLR) 1:22:01
50km Walk	Robert Korzeniowski (POL) 3:44:46	Jesus Angel Garcia (ESP) 3:44:59	Miguel Angel Rodriguez (MEX) 3:48:30
4 × 100m Relay	Canada 37.86	Nigeria 38.07	Great Britain 38.14
4 × 400m Relay	United States of America 2:56.47	Great Britain 2:56.65	Jamaica 2:56.75
High Jump	Javier Sotomayor (CUB) 2.37	Artur Partyka (POL) 2.35	Tim Forsyth (AUS) 2.35
Pole Vault	Sergey Bubka (UKR) 6.01	Maksim Tarasov (RUS) 5.96	Dean Starkey (USA) 5.91
Long Jump	Ivan Pedroso (CUB) 8.42	Erick Walder (USA) 8.38	Kirill Sosunov (RUS) 8.18
Triple Jump	Yoelbi Quesada (CUB) 17.85	Jonathan Edwards (GBR) 17.69	Aliecer Urrutia (CUB) 17.64
Shot Put	John Godina (USA) 21.44	Oliver-Sven Buder (GER) 21.24	C.J. Hunter (USA) 20.33
Discus	Lars Riedel (GER) 68.54	Virgilijus Alekna (LTU) 66.70	Jurgen Schult (GER) 66.14
Hammer	Heinz Weis (GER) 81.78	Andrey Skvaruk (UKR) 81.46	Vasiliy Sidorenko (RUS) 80.76
Javelin	Marius Corbett (RSA) 88.40	Steve Backley (GBR) 86.80	Kostas Gatsioudis (GRE) 86.64
Decathlon	Tomas Dvorak (CZE) 8837	Eduard Hemelainen (FIN) 8730	Frank Busemann (GER) 8652

Women's	Gold	Silver	Bronze
100m	Marion Jones (USA) 10.83	Zanna Pintusevich (UKR) 10.85	Sevatheda Fynes (BAH) 11.03
200m	Zanna Pintusevich (UKR) 22.32	Susanthika Jayasinghe (SRI) 22.39	Merlene Ottey (JAM) 22.40
400m	Cathy Freeman (AUS) 49.77	Sandie Richards (JAM) 49.79	Jearl Miles-Clark (USA) 49.90
800m	Ana Fidelia Quirot (CUB) 1:57.14	Yelena Afanasyeva (RUS) 1:57.56	Maria Mutola (MOZ) 1:57.59
1500m	Carla Sacramento (POR) 4:04.24	Regina Jacobs (USA) 4:04.63	Anita Weyermann (SUI) 4:04.70
5000m	Gabriela Szabo (ROM) 14:57.68	Roberta Brunet (ITA) 14:58.29	Fernanda Ribeiro (POR) 14:58.85
100m Hurdles	Ludmila Engquist (SWE) 12.50	Svetlana Dimitrova (BUL) 12.58	Michelle Freeman (JAM) 12.61
400m Hurdles	Nezha Bidouane (MAR) 52.97	Deon Hemmings (JAM) 53.09	Kim Batten (USA) 53.52
10km Walk	Annarita Sidoti (ITA) 42:55.49	Olga Kardopoltseva (BLR) 43:30.20	Valentina Tsybulskaya (BLR) 43:49.24
4 × 100m Relay	United States of America 41.47	Jamaica 42.10	France 42.21
4 × 400m Relay	Germany 3:20.92	United States of America 3:21.03	Jamaica 3:21.30
High Jump	Hanne Haugland (NOR) 1.99	Olga Kaliturina (RUS) 1.96	Inga Babakova (UKR) 1.96
Long Jump	Lyudmila Galkina (RUS) 7.05	Niki Xanthou (GRE) 6.94	Fiona May (ITA) 6.91
Triple Jump	Sarka Kasparkova (CZE) 15.20	Rodica Petrescu-Mateescu (ROM) 15.16	Yelena Govorova (UKR) 14.67
Shot Put	Astrid Kumbernuss (GER) 20.71	Vita Pavlysh (UKR) 20.66	Stephanie Storp (GER) 19.22
Discus	Beatrice Faumuina (NZL) 66.82	Ellina Zvereva (BLR) 65.90	Natalya Sadova (RUS) 65.14
Javelin	Trine Hattestad (NOR) 68.78	Joanna Stone (AUS) 68.64	Tanja Damaske (GER) 67.12
Heptathlon	Sabine Braun (GER) 6739	Denise Lewis (GBR) 6654	Remigija Nazaroviene (LTU) 6566

1999 Seville

Men's	Gold	Silver	Bronze
100m	Maurice Greene (USA) 9.80	Bruny Surin (CAN) 9.84	Dwain Chambers (GBR) 9.97
200m	Maurice Greene (USA) 19.90	C. Quirino da Silva (BRA) 20.00	Francis Obikwelu (NGR) 20.11
400m	Michael Johnson (USA) 43.18	C. Parrela Sanderlei (BRA) 44.29	Alejandro Cardenas (MEX) 44.31
800m	Wilson Kipketer (DEN) 1:43.30	Hezekiel Sepeng (RSA) 1:43.32	Djabir Sad-Guerni (ALG) 1:44.18
1500m	Hicham El Guerrouj (MAR) 3:27.65	Noah Ngeny (KEN) 3:28.73	Reyes Estevez (ESP) 3:30.57
5000m	Salah Hissou (MAR) 12:58.13	Benjamin Limo (KEN) 12:58.72	Mohammed Mourhit (BEL) 12:58.80

	Gold	Silver	Bronze
10,000m	Haile Gebrselassie (ETH) 27:57.27	Paul Tergat (KEN) 27:58.56	Assefa Mezgebu (ETH) 27:59.15
Marathon	Abel Anton (ESP) 2:13:36	Vincenzo Modica (ITA) 2:14:03	Nobuyuki Sato (JPN) 2:14:07
3000m Steeplechase	Christopher Koskei (KEN) 8:11.76	Wilson Kipketer (KEN) 8:12.09	Ali Ezzine (MAR) 8:12.73
110m Hurdles	Colin Jackson (GBR) 13.04	Anier Garcia (CUB) 13.07	Duane Ross (USA) 13.12
400m Hurdles	Fabrizio Mori (ITA) 47.72	Stéphane Diagana (FRA) 48.12	Marcel Schelbert (SUI) 48.13
20km Walk	Ilya Markov (RUS) 1:23:34	Jefferson Perez (ECU) 1:24:19	Daniel Garcia (MEX) 1:24:31
50km Walk	Ivano Brugnetti (ITA) 3:47:54	Nikolay Matyukhin (RUS) 3:48:18	Curt Clausen (USA) 3:50:55
4 × 100m Relay	United States of America 37.59	Great Britain 37.73	Nigeria 37.91
4 × 400m Relay	United States of America 2:56.45	Poland 2:58.91	Jamaica 2:59.34
High Jump	Vyacheslav Voronin (RUS) 2.37	Mark Boswell (CAN) 2.35	Martin Buss (GER) 2.32
Pole Vault	Maksim Tarasov (RUS) 6.02	Dmitri Markov (AUS) 5.90	Aleksandr Averbukh (ISR) 5.80
Long Jump	Ivan Pedroso (CUB) 8.56	Yago Lamela (ESP) 8.40	Gregor Cankar (SLO) 8.36
Triple Jump	Charles Friedek (GER) 17.59	Rostislav Dimitrov (BUL) 17.49	Jonathan Edwards (GBR) 17.48
Shot Put	C.J. Hunter (USA) 21.79	Oliver-Sven Buder (GER) 21.42	Aleksandr Bagach (UKR) 21.26
Discus	Anthony Washington (USA) 69.08	Jurgen Schult (GER) 68.18	Lars Riedel (GER) 68.09
Hammer	Karsten Kobs (GER) 80.24	Zsolt Nemeth (HUN) 79.05	Vladislav Piskunov (UKR) 79.03
Javelin	Aki Parviainen (FIN) 89.52	Kostas Gatsioudis (GRE) 89.18	Jan Zelezny (CZE) 87.67
Decathlon	Tomas Dvorak (CZE) 8744	Dean Macey (GBR) 8556	Chris Huffins (USA) 8547

Women's	Gold	Silver	Bronze
100m	Marion Jones (USA) 10.70	Inger Miller (USA) 10.79	Ekaterini Thanou (GRE) 10.84
200m	Inger Miller (USA) 21.77	Beverly McDonald (JAM) 22.22	Merlene Frazer (JAM) 22.26
400m	Cathy Freeman (AUS) 49.67	Anja Rucker (GER) 49.74	Lorraine Graham (JAM) 49.92
800m	Ludmila Formanova (CZE) 1:56.68	Maria Mutola (MOZ) 1:56.72	Svetlana Masterkova (RUS) 1:56.93
1500m	Svetlana Masterkova (RUS) 3:59.53	Regina Jacobs (USA) 4:00.35	Kutre Dulecha (ETH) 4:00.96
5000m	Gabriela Szabo (ROM) 14:41.82	Zahra Ouaziz (MAR) 14:43.15	Ayelech Worku (ETH) 14:44.22
10,000m	Gete Wami (ETH) 30:24.56	Paula Radcliffe (GBR) 30:27.13	Tegla Loroupe (KEN) 30:32.03
Marathon	Song-Ok Jong (PRK) 2:26:59	Ari Ichihashi (JPN) 2:27:02	Lidia Simon (ROM) 2:27:41
100m Hurdles	Gail Devers (USA) 12.37	Glory Alozie (NGR) 12.44	Ludmila Engquist (SWE) 12.47
400m Hurdles	Daimi Pernia (CUB) 52.89	Nezha Bidouane (MAR) 52.90	Deon Hemmings (JAM) 53.16
20km Walk	Hongyu Liu (CHN) 1:30:50	Yan Wang (CHN) 1:30:52	Kerry Saxby-Junna (AUS) 1:31:18
4 × 100m Relay	Bahamas 41.92	France 42.06	Jamaica 42.15
4 × 400m Relay	Russia 3:21.98	United States of America 3:22.09	Germany 3:22.43
High Jump	Inga Babakova (UKR) 1.99	Yelena Yelesina (RUS) 1.99	Svetlana Lapina (RUS) 1.99
Pole Vault	Stacy Dragila (USA) 4.60	Anzhela Balakhonova (UKR) 4.55	Tatiana Grigorieva (AUS) 4.45
Long Jump	Niurka Montalvo (ESP) 7.06	Fiona May (ITA) 6.94	Marion Jones (USA) 6.83
Triple Jump	Paraskevi Tsiamita (GRE) 14.88	Yamile Aldama (CUB) 14.61	Olga Vasdeki (GRE) 14.61
Shot Put	Astrid Kumbernuss (GER) 19.85	Nadine Kleinert (GER) 19.61	Svetlana Krivelyova (RUS) 19.43
Discus	Franka Dietzsch (GER) 68.14	Anastasia Kelesidou (GRE) 66.05	Nicoleta Grasu (ROM) 65.35
Hammer	Mihaela Melinte (ROM) 75.20	Olga Kuzenkova (RUS) 72.56	Lisa Misipeka (ASA) 66.06
Javelin	Mirela Manjani-Tzelili (GRE) 67.09	Tatyana Shikolenko (RUS) 66.37	Trine Hattestad (NOR) 66.06
Heptathlon	Eunice Barber (FRA) 6861	Denise Lewis (GBR) 6724	Ghada Shouaa (SYR) 6500

2001 Edmonton

Men's	Gold	Silver	Bronze
100m	Maurice Greene (USA) 9.82	Tim Montgomery (USA) 9.85	Bernard Williams (USA) 9.94
200m	Konstantinos Kenteris (GRE) 20.04	Christopher Williams (JAM) 20.20	Kim Collins (SKN) 20.20
400m	Avard Moncur (BAH) 44.64	Ingo Schulz (GER) 44.87	Gregory Haughton (JAM) 44.98
800m	Andre Bucher (SUI) 1:43.70	Wilfred Bungei (KEN) 1:44.55	Pawel Czapiewski (POL) 1:44.63
1500m	Hicham El Guerrouj (MAR) 3:30.68	Bernard Lagat (KEN) 3:31.10	Driss Maazouzi (FRA) 3:31.54
5000m	Richard Limo (KEN) 13:00.77	Million Wolde (ETH) 13:03.47	John Kibowen (KEN) 13:05.20
10,000m	Charles Kamathi (KEN) 27:53.25	Assefa Mezgebu (ETH) 27:53.97	Haile Gebrselassie (ETH) 27:54.41
Marathon	Gezahegne Abera (ETH) 2:12:42	Simon Biwott (KEN) 2:12:43	Stefano Baldini (ITA) 2:13:18
110m Hurdles	Allen Johnson (USA) 13.04	Anier Garcia (CUB) 13.07	Dudley Dorival (HAI) 13.25
400m Hurdles	Felix Sanchez (DOM) 47.49	Fabrizio Mori (ITA) 47.54	Dai Tamesue (JPN) 47.89
3000m Steeplechase	Reuben Kosgei (KEN) 8:15.16	Ali Ezzine (MAR) 8:16.21	Bernard Barmasai (KEN) 8:16.59
20km Walk	Roman Rasskazov (RUS) 1:20:31	Ilya Markov (RUS) 1:20:33	Viktor Burayev (RUS) 1:20:36
50km Walk	Robert Kozeniowski (POL) 3:42:08	Jesus Angel Garcia (ESP) 3:43:07	Edgar Hernandez (MEX) 3:46:12
4 × 100m Relay	United States of America 37.96	South Africa 38.47	Trinidad & Tobago 38.58
4 × 400m Relay	United States of America 2:57.54	Bahamas 2:58.19	Jamaica 2:58.39
High Jump	Martin Buss (GER) 2.36	Yaroslav Rybakov (RUS) 2.33	Vyacheslav Voronin (RUS) 2.33
Pole Vault	Dmitri Markov (AUS) 6.05	Aleksandr Averbukh (ISR) 5.85	Nick Hysong (USA) 5.85
Long Jump	Ivan Pedroso (CUB) 8.40	Savante Stringfellow (USA) 8.24	Carlos Calado (POR) 8.21
Triple Jump	Jonathan Edwards (GBR) 17.92	Christian Olsson (SWE) 17.47	Igor Spasovhodski (RUS) 17.44
Shot Put	John Godina (USA) 21.87	Adam Nelson (USA) 21.24	Arsi Harju (FIN) 20.93
Discus	Lars Riedel (GER) 69.72	Virgilijus Alekna (LTU) 69.40	Michael Mollenbeck (GER) 67.61
Hammer	Szymon Ziolkowski (POL) 83.38	Koji Murofushi (JPN) 82.92	Ilya Konovalov (RUS) 80.27
Javelin	Jan Zelezny (CZE) 92.80	Aki Parviainen (FIN) 91.31	Konstadinos Gatsioudis (GRE) 89.95
Decathlon	Thomas Dvorak (CZE) 8902	Erki Nool (EST) 8815	Dean Macey (GBR) 8603

ATHLETICS

Women's	Gold	Silver	Bronze
100m	Zhanna Pintusevich-Block (UKR) 10.82	Marion Jones (USA) 10.85	Ekaterini Thanou (GRE) 10.91
200m	Marion Jones (USA) 22.39	Debbie Ferguson (BAH) 22.52	Kelli White (USA) 22.56
400m	Amy Mbacke Thiam (SEN) 49.86	Lorraine Fenton (JAM) 49.88	Ana Guevara (MEX) 49.97
800m	Maria Mutola (MOZ) 1:57.17	Stephanie Graf (AUT) 1:57.20	Letitia Vriesde (SUR) 1:57.35
1500m	Gabriela Szabo (ROM) 4:00.57	Violeta Szekely (ROM) 4:01.70	Natalya Gorelova (RUS) 4:02.40
5000m	Olga Yegorova (RUS) 15:03.39	Marta Dominguez (ESP) 15:06.59	Ayelech Worku (ETH) 15:10.17
10,000m	Derartu Tulu (ETH) 31:48.81	Berhane Adere (ETH) 31:48.85	Gete Wami (ETH) 31:49.98
Marathon	Lidia Simon (ROM) 2:26:01	Reiko Tosa (JPN) 2:26:06	Svetlana Zakharova (RUS) 2:26:18
100m Hurdles	Anjanette Kirkland (USA) 12.42	Gail Devers (USA) 12.54	Olga Shishigina (KAZ) 12.58
400m Hurdles	Nezha Bidouane (MAR) 53.34	Yuliya Nosova (RUS) 54.27	Daimi Pernia (CUB) 54.51
20km Walk	Olimpiada Ivanova (RUS) 1:27:48	Valentina Tsybulskaya (BLR) 1:28:49	Elisabetta Perrone (ITA) 1:28:56
4 × 100m Relay	United States of America 41.71	Germany 42.32	France 42.39
4 × 400m Relay	Jamaica 3:20.65	Germany 3:21.97	Russia 3:24.92
High Jump	Hestrie Cloete (RSA) 2.00	Inha Babakova (UKR) 2.00	Kajsa Bergquist (SWE) 1.97
Pole Vault	Stacy Dragila (USA) 4.75	Svetlana Feofanova (RUS) 4.75	Monika Pyrek (POL) 4.55
Long Jump	Fiona May (ITA) 7.02	Tatiana Kotova (RUS) 7.01	Niurka Montalvo (ESP) 6.88
Triple Jump	Tatyana Lebedeva (RUS) 15.25	Francoise Mbango Etone (CMR) 14.60	Tereza Marinova (BUL) 14.58
Shot Put	Yanina Korolchik (BEL) 20.61	Nadine Kleinert-Schmitt (GER) 19.86	Vita Pavlysh (UKR) 19.41
Discus	Natalya Sadova (RUS) 68.57	Ellina Zvereva (BLR) 67.10	Nicoleta Grasu (ROM) 66.24
Hammer	Yipsi Moreno (CUB) 70.65	Olga Kuzenkova (RUS) 70.61	Bronwyn Eagles (AUS) 68.87
Javelin	Osleidys Menendez (CUB) 69.53	Mirela Manjani-Tzelili (GRE) 65.78	Sonia Bisset (CUB) 64.69
Heptathlon	Yelena Prokhorova (RUS) 6694	Natalya Sazanovich (BEL) 6539	Sheila Burrell (USA) 6472

2003 Paris

Men's	Gold	Silver	Bronze
100m	Kim Collins (SKN) 10.07	Darrel Brown (TRI) 10.08	Darren Campbell (GBR) 10.08
200m	John Capel (USA) 20.30	Darvis Patton (USA) 20.31	Shingo Suetsugu (JPN) 20.38
400m	Jerome Young (USA) 44.50	Tyree Washington (USA) 44.77	Marc Raquil (FRA) 44.79
800m	Djabir Said-Guerni (ALG) 1:44.81	Yuriy Borzakovskiy (RUS) 1:44.84	Mbulaeni Mulaudzi (RSA) 1:44.90
1500m	Hicham El Guerrouj (MAR) 3:31.77	Mehdi Baala (FRA) 3:32.31	Ivan Heshko (UKR) 3:33.17
5000m	Eliud Kipchoge (KEN) 12:52.79	Hicham El Guerrouj (MAR) 12:52.83	Kenenisa Bekele (ETH) 12:53.12
10,000m	Kenenisa Bekele (ETH) 26:49.57	Haile Gebrselassie (ETH) 26:50.77	Sileshi Sihine (ETH) 27:01.44
Marathon	Jaouad Gharib (MAR) 2:08:31	Julio Rey (ESP) 2:08:38	Stefano Baldini (ITA) 2:09:14
110m Hurdles	Allen Johnson (USA) 13.12	Terrence Trammell (USA) 13.20	Xiang Liu (CHN) 13.23
400m Hurdles	Felix Sanchez (DOM) 47.25	Joey Wood (USA) 48.18	Periklis Iakovakis (GRE) 48.24
3000m Steeplechase	Saif Saaeed Shaheen (QAT) 8:04.39	Ezekiel Kemboi (KEN) 8:05.11	Eliseo Martin (ESP) 8:09.09
20km Walk	Jefferson Perez (ECU) 1:17:21	Francisco J Fernandez (ESP) 1:18:00	Roman Rasskazov (RUS) 1:18:07
50km Walk	Robert Korzeniowski (POL) 3:36:03	German Skurygin (RUS) 3:36:42	Andreas Erm (GER) 3:37:46
4 × 100m Relay	United States of America 38.06	Brazil 38.26	Netherlands 38.87
4 × 400m Relay	United States of America 2:58.88	France 2:58.96	Jamaica 2:59.60
High Jump	Jacques Freitag (RSA) 2.35	Stefan Holm (SWE) 2.32	Mark Boswell (CAN) 2.32
Pole Vault	Giuseppe Gibilisco (ITA) 5.90	Okkert Brits (RSA) 5.85	Patrik Kristiansson (SWE) 5.85
Long Jump	Dwight Phillips (USA) 8.32	James Beckford (JAM) 8.28	Yago Lamela (ESP) 8.22
Triple Jump	Christian Olsson (SWE) 17.72	Yoandri Betanzos (CUB) 17.28	Leevan Sands (BAH) 17.26
Shot Put	Andrei Mikhnevich (BLR) 21.69	Adam Nelson (USA) 21.26	Yuriy Bilonog (UKR) 21.10
Discus	Virgilijus Alekna (LTU) 69.69	Róbert Fazekas (HUN) 69.01	Vasiliy Kaptyukh (BLR) 66.51
Hammer	Ivan Tikhon (BLR) 83.05	Adrián Annus (HUN) 80.36	Koji Murofushi (JPN) 80.12
Javelin	Sergey Makarov (RUS) 85.44	Andrus Varnik (EST) 85.17	Boris Henry (GER) 84.74
Decathlon	Tom Pappas (USA) 8750	Roman Sebrle (CZE) 8634	Dimitry Karpov (KAZ) 8374

Women's	Gold	Silver	Bronze
100m	Kelli White (USA) 10.85	Torri Edwards (USA) 10.93	Zhanna Block (UKR) 10.99
200m	Kelli White (USA) 22.05	Anastasiya Kapachinskaya (RUS) 22.38	Torri Edwards (USA) 22.47
400m	Ana Guevara (MEX) 48.89	Lorraine Fenton (JAM) 49.43	Amy Mbacke Thiam (SEN) 49.95
800m	Maria de Lourdes Mutola (MOZ) 1:59.89	Kelly Holmes (GBR) 2:00.18	Natalya Khrushchelyova (RUS) 2:00.29
1500m	Tatyana Tomashova (RUS) 3:58.52	Süreyya Ayhan (TUR) 3:59.04	Hayley Tullett (GBR) 3:59.95
5000m	Tirunesh Dibaba (ETH) 14:51.72	Marta Domínguez (ESP) 14:52.26	Edith Masai (KEN) 14:52.30
10,000m	Berhane Adere (ETH) 30:04.18	Werknesh Kidane (ETH) 30:07.15	Yingjie Sun (CHN) 30:07.20
Marathon	Catherine Ndereba (KEN) 2:23:55	Mizuki Noguchi (JPN) 2:24:14	Masako Chiba (JPN) 2:25:09
100m Hurdles	Perdita Felicien (CAN) 12.53	Brigitte Foster (JAM) 12.57	Miesha McKelvy (USA) 12.67
400m Hurdles	Jana Pittman (AUS) 53.22	Sandra Glover (USA) 53.65	Yuliya Pechonkina (RUS) 53.71
20km Walk	Yelena Nikolayeva (RUS) 1:26:52	Gillian O'Sullivan (IRL) 1:27:34	Valentina Tsybulskaya (BLR) 1:28:10
4 × 100m Relay	France 41.78	United States of America 41.83	Russia 42.66
4 × 400m Relay	United States of America 3:22.63	Russia 3:22.91	Jamaica 3:22.92
High Jump	Hestrie Cloete (RSA) 2.06	Marina Kuptsova (RUS) 2.00	Kajsa Bergqvist (SWE) 2.00
Pole Vault	Svetlana Feofanova (RUS) 4.75	Annika Becker (GER) 4.70	Yelena Isinbayeva (RUS) 4.65

Long Jump	Eunice Barber (FRA) 6.99	Tatyana Kotova (RUS) 6.74	Anju Bobby George (IND) 6.70
Triple Jump	Tatyana Lebedeva (RUS) 15.18	Francoise Mbango Etone (CMR) 15.05	Magdelín Martínez (ITA) 14.90
Shot Put	Svetlana Krivelyova (RUS) 20.63	Nadezhda Ostapchuk (BLR) 20.12	Vita Pavlysh (UKR) 20.08
Discus	Irina Yatchenko (BLR) 67.32	Anastasia Kelesídou (GRE) 67.14	Ekaterina Vóggoli (GRE) 66.73
Hammer	Yipsi Moreno (CUB) 73.33	Olga Kuzenkova (RUS) 71.71	Manuela Montebrun (FRA) 70.92
Javelin	Miréla Manjani (GRE) 66.52	Tatyana Shikolenko (RUS) 63.28	Steffi Nerius (GER) 62.70
Heptathlon	Carolina Klüft (SWE) 7001	Eunice Barber (FRA) 6755	Natalya Sazanovich (BLR) 6524

European Championships

1934 Turin

Men's	Gold	Silver	Bronze
100m	Christaan Berger (NED) 10.6	Erich Borchmeyer (GER) 10.7	Jozsef Sir (HUN) 10.7
200m	Christaan Berger (NED) 21.5	Jozsef Sir (HUN) 21.5	Martinus Osendarp (NED) 21.6
400m	Adolf Metzner (GER) 47.9	Pierre Skawinski (FRA) 48.0	Bertil von Wachenfeldt (SWE) 48.0
800m	Miklos Szabo (HUN) 1:52.0	Mario Lanzi (ITA) 1:52.0	Wolfgang Dessecker (GER) 1:52.2
1500m	Luigi Beccali (ITA) 3:54.6	Miklos Szabo (HUN) 3:55.2	Roger Normand (FRA) 3:57.0
5000m	Roger Rochard (FRA) 14:36.8	Janusz Kusocinski (POL) 14:41.2	Ilmari Salminen (FIN) 14:43.6
10,000m	Ilmari Salminen (FIN) 31:02.6	Arvo Askola (FIN) 31:03.2	Henry Nielsen (DEN) 31:27.4
Marathon	Armas Toivonen (FIN) 2:52:29	Thore Enochsson (SWE) 2:54:36	Aurelio Genghini (ITA) 2:55:03
110m Hurdles	Jozsef Kovacs (HUN) 14.8	Erwin Wegner (GER) 14.9	Holger Albrechtsen (NOR) 15.0
400m Hurdles	Hans Scheele (GER) 53.2	Akilles Jarvinen (FIN) 53.7	Christos Mantikas (GRE) 54.9
50km Walk	Janis Dahlinsch (LAT) 4:49:53	Arthur Schwab (SUI) 4:53:08	Ettore Rivolta (ITA) 4:54:05
4 × 100m Relay	Germany 41.0	Hungary 41.4	Netherlands 41.6
4 × 400m Relay	Germany 3:14.1	France 3:15.6	Sweden 3:16.6
High Jump	Kalevi Kotkas (FIN) 2.00	Birger Halvorsen (NOR) 1.97	Veikko Perasalo (FIN) 1.97
Pole Vault	Gustav Wegner (GER) 4.00	Bo Ljungberg (SWE) 4.00	John Lindroth (FIN) 3.90
Long Jump	Wilhelm Leichum (GER) 7.45	Otto Berg (NOR) 7.31	Luz Long (GER) 7.25
Triple Jump	Willem Peters (NED) 14.89	Eric Svensson (SWE) 14.83	Onni Rajasaari (FIN) 14.74
Shot Put	Arnold Viiding (EST) 15.19	Risto Kuntsi (FIN) 15.19	Frantisek Douda (TCH) 15.19
Discus	Harald Andersson (SWE) 50.38	Paul Winter (FRA) 47.09	Istvan Donogan (HUN) 45.91
Hammer	Ville Porhola (FIN) 50.34	Fernando Vandelli (ITA) 48.69	Gunnar Jansson (SWE) 47.85
Javelin	Matti Jarvinen (FIN) 76.66	Matti Sipala (FIN) 69.97	Gustav Sule (EST) 69.31
Decathlon	Hans-Heinrich Sievert (GER) 8013	Leif Dahlgren (SWE) 7770	Jerzy Plawcyk (POL) 7552

1938 Paris

Men's	Gold	Silver	Bronze
100m	Martinus Osendarp (NED) 10.5	Orazio Mariani (ITA) 10.6	Lennart Strandberg (SWE) 10.6
200m	Martinus Osendarp (NED) 21.2	Jakob Scheuring (NED) 21.6	Alan Pennington (GBR) 21.6
400m	Godfrey Brown (GBR) 47.4	Karl Baumgarten (NED) 48.2	Erich Linnhoff (GER) 48.8
800m	Rudolph Harbig (GER) 1:50.6	Jacques Leveque (FRA) 1:51.6	Mario Lanzi (ITA) 1:52.0
1500m	Sydney Wooderson (GBR) 3:53.6	Joseph Mostert (BEL) 3:54.5	Luigi Beccali (ITA) 3:55.2
5000m	Taisto Maki (FIN) 14:26.8	Henry Jonsson (SWE) 14:27.4	Kauko Pekuri (FIN) 14:29.2
10,000m	Ilmari Salminen (FIN) 30:52.4	Giuseppe Beviacqua (ITA) 30:53.2	Max Syring (GER) 30:57.8
Marathon	Vaino Muinonen (FIN) 2:37:29	Squire Yarrow (GBR) 2:39:03	Henry Palme (SWE) 2:42:14
3000m Steeplechase	Lars Larsson (SWE) 9:16.2	Ludwig Kaindl (SWE) 9:19.2	Alf Lindblad (SWE) 9:21.4
110m Hurdles	Donald Finlay (GBR) 14.3	Hakan Lidman (SWE) 14.5	Reindert Brasser (NED) 14.8
400m Hurdles	Prudent Joye (FRA) 53.1	Jozef Kovacs (HUN) 53.3	Kell Areskoug (SWE) 53.6
50km Walk	Harold Whitlock (GBR) 4:41:51	Herbert Dill (GER) 4:43:54	Edgar Buun (NOR) 4:44:35
4 × 100m Relay	Germany 40.9	Sweden 41.1	Great Britain 41.1
4 × 400m Relay	Germany 3:13.7	Great Britain 3:14.9	Sweden 3:17.3
High Jump	Kurt Lundqvist (SWE) 1.97	Kalevi Kotkas (FIN) 1.94	Lauri Kalima (FIN) 1.94
Pole Vault	Karl Sutter (GER) 4.05	Bo Ljungberg (SWE) 4.00	Pierre Ramadier (FRA) 4.00
Long Jump	Wilhelm Leichum (GER) 7.65	Arturo Maffei (ITA) 7.61	Luz Long (GER) 7.56
Triple Jump	Onni Rajasaari (FIN) 15.32	Jouko Noren (FIN) 14.95	Karl Kotratschek (GER) 14.73
Shot Put	Aleksander Kreek (EST) 15.83	Gerhard Stock (GER) 15.59	Hans Woellke (GER) 15.52
Discus	Willi Schroder (GER) 49.70	Giorgio Oberweger (ITA) 49.48	Gunnar Bergh (SWE) 48.72
Hammer	Karl Hein (GER) 58.77	Erwin Blask (GER) 57.34	Oscar Malmbrant (SWE) 51.23
Javelin	Matti Jarvinen (FIN) 76.87	Yrjo Nikkanen (FIN) 75.00	Jozsef Varszegi (HUN) 72.78
Decathlon	Olle Bexell (SWE) 7214	Witold Gerutto (POL) 7006	Josef Neumann (SUI) 6664

Women's	Gold	Silver	Bronze
100m	Stanislava Walasiewicz (POL) 11.9	Kathe Krauss (GER) 12.0	Fanny Blankers-Koen (NED) 12.0
200m	Stanislava Walasiewicz (POL) 23.8	Kathe Krauss (GER) 24.4	Fanny Blankers-Koen (NED) 24.9
80m Hurdles	Claudia Testoni (ITA) 11.6	Lisa Gelius (GER) 11.7	Catherine ter Braake (NED) 11.8

ATHLETICS

4 × 100m Relay	Germany 46.8	Poland 48.2	Italy 49.4
High Jump	Ibolya Csak (HUN) 1.64	Nelly van Balen-Blanken (NED) 1.64	Feodora Solms (GER) 1.64
Long Jump	Irmgard Praetz (GER) 5.88	Stanislava Walasiewicz (POL) 5.81	Gisela Voss (GER) 5.47
Javelin	Lisa Gelius (GER) 45.58	Susi Pastoors (GER) 44.14	Luise Kruger (GER) 42.49
Shot Put	Hermine Schroder (GER) 13.29	Gisela Mauermayer (GER) 13.27	Wanda Flakowicz (POL) 12.55
Discus	Gisela Mauermayer (GER) 44.80	Hildegard Sommer (GER) 40.95	Paula Mollenhauer (GER) 39.81

1946 Oslo

Men's	Gold	Silver	Bronze
100m	John Archer (GBR) 10.6	Haakon Tranberg (NOR) 10.7	Carlo Monti (ITA) 10.8
200m	Nikolai Karakulov (URS) 21.6	Haakon Tranberg (NOR) 21.7	Jiri David (TCH) 21.9
400m	Niels Holst-Sorensen (DEN) 47.9	Jacques Lunis (FRA) 48.3	Derek Pugh (GBR) 48.9
800m	Rune Gustafsson (SWE) 1:51.0	Niels Holst-Sorenson (DEN) 1:51.1	Marcel Hansenne (FRA) 1:51.2
1500m	Lennart Strand (SWE) 3:48.0	Henry Eriksson (SWE) 3:48.8	Erik Jurgensen (DEN) 3:52.8
5000m	Sydney Wooderson (GBR) 14:08.6	Willem Slijhuis (NED) 14:14.0	Evert Nyberg (SWE) 14:23.2
10,000m	Viljo Heino (FIN) 29:52.0	Helga Perala (FIN) 30:31.4	Andras Csaplar (HUN) 30:35.2
Marathon	Mikko Hietanen (FIN) 2:24:55	Vaino Muinonen (URS) 2:26:21	Jakov Punko (URS) 2:26:21
3000m Steeplechase	Raphael Pujason (FRA) 9:01.4	Eric Elmsater (SWE) 9:11.0	Tore Sjostrand (SWE) 9:14.0
110m Hurdles	Haken Lidman (SWE) 14.6	Hippolyte Braekman (BEL) 14.9	Vaino Suvivuo (FIN) 15.0
400m Hurdles	Bertil Storskrubb (FIN) 52.2	Sixten Larsson (SWE) 52.4	Rune Larsson (SWE) 52.5
10,000m Walk	John Mikaelsson (SWE) 46:05.2	Fritz Schwab (SUI) 47:03.6	Emile Maggi (FRA) 48:10.4
50km Walk	John Ljunggren (SWE) 4:38:20	Henry Forbes (GBR) 4:42:58	Charles Megnin (GBR) 4:57:04
4 × 100m Relay	Sweden 41.5	France 42.0	Czechoslovakia 42.2
4 × 400m Relay	France 3:14.4	Great Britain 3:14.5	Sweden 3:15.5
High Jump	Anton Bolinder (SWE) 1.99	Alan Paterson (GBR) 1.96	Nils Nicklen (FIN) 1.93
Pole Vault	Allan Lindberg (SWE) 4.17	Nikolai Osolin (URS) 4.10	Jan Bem (TCH) 4.10
Long Jump	Olle Laessker (SWE) 7.42	Lucien Graff (SUI) 7.40	Miroslav Rihosek (TCH) 7.29
Triple Jump	Valdemar Rautio (FIN) 15.17	Bertil Johnsson (SWE) 15.15	Arne Ahman (SWE) 14.96
Shot Put	Gunnar Huseby (ISL) 15.56	Dmitriy Goryanov (URS) 15.25	Yrjo Lehtila (FIN) 15.23
Discus	Adolfo Consolini (ITA) 53.23	Giuseppe Tosi (ITA) 50.39	Veikko Nyqvist (FIN) 48.14
Hammer	Bo Ericsson (SWE) 56.44	Erik Johansson (SWE) 53.54	Duncan Clark (GBR) 51.32
Javelin	Lennart Atterwall (SWE) 68.74	Yrjo Nikkanen (FIN) 67.50	Tapio Rautavaara (FIN) 66.40
Decathlon	Godtfred Holmvang (NOR) 6987	Sergey Kusnetzov (URS) 6930	Goran Waxberg (SWE) 6661

Women's	Gold	Silver	Bronze
100m	Yevgenia Setschenova (URS) 11.9	Winifred Jordan (GBR) 12.1	Claire Bresolles (FRA) 12.2
200m	Yevgenia Setschenova (URS) 25.4	Winifred Jordan (GBR) 12.1	Lea Caurla (FRA) 25.6
80m Hurdles	Fanny Blankers-Koen (NED) 11.8	Jelena Gokieli (URS) 11.9	Valentina Fokina (URS) 11.9
4 × 100m Relay	Netherlands 47.8	France 48.5	Soviet Union 48.7
High Jump	Anne-Marie Colchen (FRA) 1.60	Alexandra Chudina (URS) 1.57	Anne Iversen (DEN) 1.57
Long Jump	Gerda Koudys (NED) 5.67	Lidia Gaile (URS) 5.66	Valentina Vasiljeva (URS) 5.63
Javelin	Klaudia Mayutschaya (URS) 46.25	Ludmilla Anokina (URS) 45.84	Johanna Koning (NED) 43.24
Shot Put	Tatyana Sevryukova (URS) 14.16	Micheline Ostermeyer (FRA) 12.84	Amelia Piccinini (ITA) 12.21
Discus	Nina Dumbadse (URS) 44.52	Ans Niesink (NED) 40.46	Jadwiza Wajs (POL) 39.37

1950 Brussels

Men's	Gold	Silver	Bronze
100m	Etienne Bally (FRA) 10.7	Franco Leccese (ITA) 10.7	Vladimir Sucharev (URS) 10.7
200m	Brian Shenton (GBR) 21.5	Etienne Bally (FRA) 21.8	Jan Lammers (NED) 22.1
400m	Derek Pugh (GBR) 47.3	Jacques Lunis (FRA) 47.6	Lars-Erik Wolfbrandt (SWE) 47.9
800m	John Parlett (GBR) 1:50.5	Marcel Hansenne (FRA) 1:50.7	Roger Bannister (GBR) 1:50.7
1500m	Willem Slijhuis (NED) 3:47.2	Patrick El Mabrouk (FRA) 3:47.8	William Nankeville (GBR) 3:48.0
5000m	Emil Zatopek (TCH) 14:03.0	Alain Mimoun (FRA) 14:26.0	Gaston Reiff (BEL) 14:26.2
10,000m	Emil Zatopek (TCH) 29:12.0	Alain Mimoun (FRA) 30:21.0	Vaino Koskela (FIN) 30:30.8
Marathon	Jack Holden (GBR) 2:32:13	Veikko Karvonen (FIN) 2:32:45	Fedosiy Vanin (URS) 2:33:47
3000m Steeplechase	Jindrich Roudny (TCH) 9:05.4	Petar Segedin (YUG) 9:07.8	Erik Blomster (FIN) 9:08.8
110m Hurdles	Andre-Jacques Marie (FRA) 14.6	Ragnar Lundberg (SWE) 14.7	Peter Hildreth (GBR) 15.0
400m Hurdles	Armando Filiput (ITA) 51.9	Yuriy Lituyev (URS) 52.4	Harry Whittle (GBR) 52.7
10,000m Road Walk	Fritz Schwab (SUI) 46:01.8	Emile Maggi (FRA) 46:16.8	John Mikaelsson (SWE) 46:48.2
50km Walk	Giuseppe Dordoni (ITA) 4:40:43	John Ljunggren (SWE) 4:43:25	Verner Ljunggren (SWE) 4:49:28
4 × 100m Relay	Soviet Union 41.5	France 41.8	Sweden 41.9
4 × 400m Relay	Great Britain 3:10.2	Italy 3:11.0	Sweden 3:11.6
High Jump	Alan Paterson (GBR) 1.96	Arne Ahman (SWE) 1.93	Claude Benard (FRA) 1.93
Pole Vault	Ragnar Lundberg (SWE) 4.30	Valto Olenius (FIN) 4.25	Jukka Piironen (FIN) 4.25
Long Jump	Torfi Bryngeirsson (ISL) 7.32	Gerard Wessels (NED) 7.22	Jaroslav Fikejz (TCH) 7.20
Triple Jump	Leonid Tscherbakow (URS) 15.39	Valdemar Rautio (FIN) 14.96	Ruhi Sarialp (TUR) 14.53
Shot Put	Gunnar Huseby (ISL) 16.74	Angiolo Profeti (ITA) 15.16	Otto Grigalka (URS) 15.14

Discus	Adolfo Consolini (ITA) 53.75	Giuseppe Tosi (ITA) 52.31	Olavi Partanen (FIN) 48.69
Hammer	Sverre Strandli (NOR) 55.71	Teseo Taddia (ITA) 54.73	Jiri Dadak (TCH) 53.64
Javelin	Toivo Hyytiainen (FIN) 71.26	Per-Arne Berglund (SWE) 70.06	Ragnar Ericzon (SWE) 69.82
Decathlon	Ignace Heinrich (FRA) 7364	Orn Clausen (ISL) 7297	Kjell Tannander (SWE) 7175

Women's	Gold	Silver	Bronze
100m	Fanny Blankers-Koen (NED) 11.7	Yevgenia Setschenova (URS) 12.3	June Foulds (GBR) 12.4
200m	Fanny Blankers-Koen (NED) 24.0	Yevgenia Setschenova (URS) 24.8	Dorothy Hall (GBR) 25.0
80m Hurdles	Fanny Blankers-Koen (NED) 11.1	Maureen Dyson (GBR) 11.6	Micheline Ostermeyer (FRA) 11.7
4 × 100m Relay	Great Britain 47.4	Netherlands 47.4	Soviet Union 47.5
High Jump	Sheila Alexander (GBR) 1.63	Dorothy Tyler (GBR) 1.63	Galina Ganeker (URS) 1.63
Long Jump	Valentina Bogdanova (URS) 5.82	Wilhelmine Lust (NED) 5.63	Maire Osterdahl (FIN) 5.57
Javelin	Natalya Smirnizkaya (URS) 47.55	Herma Bauma (AUT) 43.87	Galina Sybina (URS) 42.75
Shot Put	Anna Andreyeva (URS) 14.32	Klaudya Totschenova (URS) 13.92	Micheline Ostermeyer (FRA) 13.37
Discus	Nina Dumbadze (URS) 48.03	Rimma Schumskaya (URS) 42.25	Edera Cordiale (ITA) 41.57
Pentathlon	Arlette Ben Hamo (FRA) 3544	Bertha Crowther (GBR) 3409	Olga Modrachova (TCH) 3412

1954 Bern

Men's	Gold	Silver	Bronze
100m	Heinz Futterer (FRG) 10.5	Rene Bonino (FRA) 10.6	George Ellis (GBR) 10.7
200m	Heinz Futterer (FRG) 20.9	Ardalion Ignatev (URS) 21.1	George Ellis (GBR) 21.2
400m	Ardalion Ignatev (URS) 46.6	Voitto Hellsten (FIN) 47.0	Zoltan Adamik (HUN) 47.6
800m	Lajos Szentgali (HUN) 1:47.1	Lucien de Muynck (BEL) 1:47.3	Auden Boysen (NOR) 1:47.4
1500m	Roger Bannister (GBR) 3:43.8	Gunnar Nielsen (DEN) 3:44.4	Stanislav Jungwirth (TCH) 3:45.4
5000m	Vladimir Kutz (URS) 13:56.6	Chris Chataway (GBR) 13:56.6	Emil Zatopek (TCH) 14:10.2
10,000m	Emil Zatopek (TCH) 28:58.0	Jozsef Kovacs (HUN) 29:25.8	Frank Sando (GBR) 29:27.6
Marathon	Veikko Karvonen (FIN) 2:24:51	Boris Grischayev (URS) 2:24:55	Iwan Filin (URS) 2:25:26
3000m Steeplechase	Sandor Rozsnyoi (HUN) 8:49.6	Olavi Rinteenpaa (FIN) 8:52.4	Ernst Larsen (DEN) 8:53.2
110m Hurdles	Yevgeniy Bulantschik (URS) 14.4	John Parker (GBR) 14.6	Berthold Steines (FRG) 14.7
400m Hurdles	Anatoly Yulin (URS) 50.5	Yuriy Lituyev (URS) 50.8	Sven-Oswald Mildh (FIN) 51.5
10km Walk	Josef Dolezal (TCH) 45:01.8	Anatoli Jegorow (URS) 45:53.0	Sergei Lobastow (URS) 45:53.0
50km Walk	Vladimir Ukhov (URS) 4:22:11	Josef Dolezal (TCH) 4:25:07	Antal Roka (HUN) 4:31:32
4 × 100m Relay	Hungary 40.6	Great Britain 40.8	Soviet Union 40.9
4 × 400m Relay	France 3:08.7	West Germany 3:08.8	Finland 3:11.5
High Jump	Bengt Nilsson (SWE) 2.02	Jiri Lansky (TCH) 1.98	Jaroslav Kovar (TCH) 1.96
Pole Vault	Eeles Landstrom (FIN) 4.40	Ragnar Lundberg (SWE) 4.40	Geoff Elliott (GBR) 4.30
			Jukka Piironen (FIN) 4.30
Long Jump	Odon Foldessy (HUN) 7.51	Zbigniew Iwanski (POL) 7.46	Ernest Wanko (FRA) 7.41
Triple Jump	Leonid Shcherbakov (URS) 15.90	Roger Norman (SWE) 15.17	Martin Rehak (TCH) 15.10
Shot Put	Jiri Skobla (TCH) 17.20	Otto Grigalka (URS) 16.69	Heino Heinaste (URS) 16.27
Discus	Adolfo Consolini (ITA) 53.44	Giuseppe Tosi (ITA) 52.34	Jozsef Szecsenyi (HUN) 51.58
Hammer	Mikhail Krivonosov (URS) 63.34	Sverre Strandli (NOR) 61.07	Jozsef Csermak (HUN) 59.72
Javelin	Janusz Sidlo (POL) 76.35	Vladimir Kuznetsov (URS) 74.61	Soini Nikkinen (FIN) 73.38
Decathlon	Vassiliy Kusnezov (URS) 7043	Torbjorn Lassenius (FIN) 6821	Heinz Oberbeck (FRG) 6733

Women's	Gold	Silver	Bronze
100m	Irina Turowa (URS) 11.8	Bertha van Duyne-Brouwer (NED) 11.9	Ann Pashley (GBR) 11.9
200m	Maria Itkina (URS) 24.3	Irina Turowa (URS) 24.4	Shirley Hampton (GBR) 24.4
800m	Nina Otkalenko (URS) 2:08.8	Diane Leather (GBR) 2:09.8	Lyudmila Lysenko (URS) 2:11.2
80m Hurdles	Maria Golubnitschaya (URS) 11.0	Anneliese Seonbuchner (FRG) 11.2	Pamela Seabourne (GBR) 11.3
4 × 100m Relay	Soviet Union 45.8	Federal Republic of Germany 46.3	Italy 46.6
High Jump	Thelma Hopkins (GBR) 1.67	Iolanda Balas (ROM) 1.65	Olga Modrachova (TCH) 1.63
Long Jump	Jean Desforges (GBR) 6.04	Alexandra Tschudina (URS) 5.93	Elzbieta Dunska (POL) 5.83
Javelin	Dana Zatopkova (TCH) 52.91	Virve Roolaid (URS) 49.94	Nadezhda Konyayeva (URS) 49.49
Shot Put	Galina Zybina (URS) 15.65	Mariya Kusnetsova (URS) 14.99	Tamara Tyshkevich (URS) 14.78
Discus	Nina Ponomareva (URS) 48.02	Irina Beglyakova (URS) 45.79	Galina Zybina (URS) 44.77
Pentathlon	Alexandra Chudina (URS) 4526	Maria Sander (FRG) 4485	Maria Sturm (FRG) 4357

1958 Stockholm

Men's	Gold	Silver	Bronze
100m	Armin Hary (FRG) 10.3	Manfred Germar (FRG) 10.4	Peter Radford (GBR) 10.4
200m	Manfred Germar (FRG) 21.0	David Segal (GBR) 21.3	Jocelyn Delecour (FRA) 21.3
400m	John Wrighton (GBR) 46.5	John Salisbury (GBR) 46.5	Karl-Friedrich Haas (FRG) 47.0
800m	Michael Rawson (GBR) 1:47.8	Auden Boysen (NOR) 1:47.9	Paul Schmidt (FRG) 1:47.9
1500m	Brian Hewson (GBR) 3:41.9	Dan Waern (SWE) 3:42.1	Ronnie Delany (IRL) 3:42.3
5000m	Zdzislaw Krzyszkowiak (POL) 13:53.4	Kazimierz Zimny (POL) 13.55.2	Gordon Pirie (GBR) 14:01.6

ATHLETICS

10,000m	Zdzislaw Krzyszkowiak (POL) 28:56.0	Jewgeni Zhukov (URS) 29:02:2	Nikolay Pudov (URS) 29:02:2
Marathon	Sergey Popov (URS) 2:15:17	Ivan Filin (URS) 2:20:51	Fred Norris (GBR) 2:21:15
3000m Steeplechase	Jerzy Chromik (POL) 8:38.2	Semyon Rzhishchin (URS) 8:38.8	Hans Huneke (FRG) 8:43.6
110m Hurdles	Martin Lauer (FRG) 13.7	Stanko Lorger (YUG) 14.1	Anatoly Mikhaylov (URS) 14.4
400m Hurdles	Yuriy Lituyev (URS) 51.1	Per-Ove Trollsas (SWE) 51.6	Bruno Galliker (SUI) 51.8
20km Walk	Stanley Vickers (GBR) 1:33:09	Leonid Spirin (URS) 1:35:04	Lennart Back (SWE) 1:35:22
50km Walk	Yevgeniy Maskinskov (URS) 4:17:15	Abdon Pamich (ITA) 4:18:00	Max Weber (GDR) 4:19:58
4 × 100m Relay	German Democratic Republic 40.2	Great Britain 40.4	Soviet Union 40.4
4 × 400m Relay	Great Britain 3:07.9	German Democratic Republic 3:08.2	Sweden 3:10.7
High Jump	Rickard Dahl (SWE) 2.12	Jiri Lansky (TCH) 2.10	Stig Pettersson (SWE) 2.10
Pole Vault	Eeles Landstrom (FIN) 4.50	Manfred Preussger (GDR) 4.50	Vladimir Bulatov (URS) 4.50
Long Jump	Igor Ter-Ovanesyan (URS) 7.81	Kazimierz Kropidlowski (POL) 7.67	Henryk Grabowski (POL) 7.51
Triple Jump	Josef Schmidt (POL) 16.43	Oleg Ryakhovskiy (URS) 16.02	Vilhjalmur Einarsson (ISL) 16.00
Shot Put	Arthur Rowe (GBR) 17.78	Viktor Lipsnis (URS) 17.47	Jiri Skobla (TCH) 17.12
Discus	Edmund Piatkowski (POL) 53.92	Todor Artarski (BUL) 53.82	Vladimir Trusenyov (URS) 53.74
Hammer	Tadeusz Rut (POL) 64.78	Mikhail Krivonosov (URS) 63.78	Gyula Zsivotzky (HUN) 63.68
Javelin	Janusz Sidlo (POL) 80.18	Egil Danielsen (NOR) 78.27	Gergely Kulcsar (HUN) 75.26
Decathlon	Vassiliy Kusnetsov (URS) 7865	Uno Palu (URS) 7448	Walter Meier (GDR) 7405

Women's	Gold	Silver	Bronze
100m	Heather Young (GBR) 11.7	Vera Krepkina (URS) 11.7	Christa Stübnick (GDR) 11.8
200m	Barbara Janiszewska (POL)	Hannelore Sadau (GDR) 24.3	Maria Itkina (URS) 24.3
400m	Marina Itkina (URS) 53.7	Yekaterina Parluk (URS) 54.8	Molly Hiscox (GBR) 55.7
800m	Yelizabeta Yermolayeva (URS) 2:06.3	Diane Leather (GBR) 2:06.6	Dzidra Levicka (URS) 2:06.6
80m Hurdles	Galina Bystrova (URS) 10.9	Zenta Kopp (FRG) 10.9	Gisela Birkemeyer (FRG) 11.0
4 × 100m Relay	Soviet Union 45.3	Great Britain 46.0	Poland 46.0
High Jump	Iolanda Balas (ROM) 1.77	Taissia Tschentschik (URS) 1.70	Dorothy Shirley (GBR) 1.67
Long Jump	Liesel Jakobi (FRG) 6.14	Valentina Litujeva (URS) 6.00	Nina Prochenko (URS) 5.99
Javelin	Dana Zatopkova (TCH) 56.02	Birute Zalogaitite (URS) 51.30	Jutta Neumann (FRG) 50.50
Shot Put	Marianne Werner (URS) 15.74	Tamara Tyshkevich (URS) 15.54	Tamara Press (URS) 15.53
Discus	Tamara Press (URS) 52.32	Stepanka Mertova (TCH) 52.19	Kriemhild Hausmann (FRG) 50.99
Pentathlon	Galina Bystrova (URS) 4733	Nina Vinogradova (URS) 4627	Edeltraud Eiberle (FRG) 4545

1962 Belgrade

Men's	Gold	Silver	Bronze
100m	Claude Piquemal (FRA) 10.4	Jocelyn Delecour (FRA) 10.4	Peter Gamper (FRG) 10.4
200m	Owe Jonssen (SWE) 20.7	Marian Foik (POL) 20.8	Sergio Ottolina (ITA) 20.8
400m	Robbie Brightwell (GBR) 45.9	Manfred Kinder (GDR) 46.1	Hans Joachim Reske (FRG) 46.4
800m	Manfred Matuschewski (GDR) 1:50.5	Valeriy Bulyshev (URS) 1:51.2	Paul Schmidt (FRG) 1:51.2
1500m	Michel Jazy (FRA) 3:40.9	Witold Baran (POL) 3:42.1	Tomas Salinger (TCH) 3:42.2
5000m	Bruce Tulloch (GBR) 14:00.6	Kazimierz Zimny (POL) 14:01.8	Pyotr Bolotnikov (URS) 14:02.6
10,000m	Pyotr Bolotnikov (URS) 28:54.0	Frederich Janke (GDR) 29:01.6	Roy Fowler (GBR) 29:02.0
Marathon	Brian Kilby (GBR) 2:23:19	Aurele Vanderdriesche (BEL) 2:24:02	Viktor Baykov (URS) 2:24:20
3000m Steeplechase	Gaston Roelants (BEL) 8:32.6	Zoltan Vamos (ROM) 8:37.6	Nikolai Sokolov (URS) 8:40.6
110m Hurdles	Anatoly Mikhailov (URS) 13.8	Giovanni Cornacchia (ITA) 14.0	Nikolay Berezutskiy (URS) 14.2
400m Hurdles	Salvatore Morale (ITA) 49.2	Jorg Neumann (FRG) 50.3	Helmut Janz (FRG) 50.5
20km Walk	Ken Matthews (GBR) 1:35:55	Hans-Georg Reimann (GDR) 1:36:14	Vladimir Golubnichiy (URS) 1:36:37
50km Walk	Abdon Pamich (ITA) 4:18:47	Grigori Panichkin (URS) 4:24:36	Don Thompson (GBR) 4:29:00
4 × 100m Relay	Federal Republic of Germany 39.5	Poland 39.5	Great Britain 39.8
4 × 400m Relay	Federal Republic of Germany 3:05.8	Great Britain 3:05.9	Switzerland 3:07.0
High Jump	Valeriy Brumel (URS) 2.21	Stig Pettersson (SWE) 2.13	Robert Shavlakadze (URS) 2.09
Pole Vault	Pentti Nikkola (FIN) 4.80	Rudolf Tomasek (TCH) 4.60	Kauko Nystrom (FIN) 4.60
Long Jump	Igor Ter-Ovanesyan (URS) 8.19	Rainer Stenius (FIN) 7.85	Pentti Eskola (FIN) 7.85
Triple Jump	Jozef Schmidt (POL) 16.55	Vladimir Goryayev (URS) 16.39	Oleg Fedoseyev (URS) 16.24
Shot Put	Vilmos Varju (HUN) 19.02	Viktor Lipsnis (URS) 18.38	Alfred Sosgornik (POL) 18.26
Discus	Vladimir Trusenyov (URS) 57.11	Kees Koch (NED) 55.96	Lother Milde (GDR) 55.47
Hammer	Gyula Zsivotzky (HUN) 69.64	Aleksey Baltovskiy (URS) 66.93	Yuriy Bakarinov (URS) 66.57
Javelin	Janis Lusis (URS) 82.04	Viktor Tsibulenko (URS) 77.92	Vladyslav Nikiciuk (POL) 77.66
Decathlon	Vasiliy Kusnetsov (URS) 8026	Werner von Moltke (FRG) 8022	Manfred Bock (FRG) 7835

Women's	Gold	Silver	Bronze
100m	Dorothy Hyman (GBR) 11.3	Jutta Heine (FRG) 11.3	Tereza Ciepla (POL) 11.4
200m	Jutta Heine (FRG) 23.5	Dorothy Hyman (GBR) 23.7	Barbara Sobotha (POL) 23.9
400m	Maria Itkina (URS) 53.4	Joy Grieveson (GBR) 53.9	Tilly van der Swaard (NED) 54.4
800m	Gerda Kraan (NED) 2:02.8	Waltraud Kaufmann (GDR) 2:05.0	Olga Cazy (HUN) 2:05.0
80m Hurdles	Tereza Ciepla (HUN) 10.6	Karin Balzer (GDR) 10.6	Maria Piatkowski (POL) 10.6

4 × 100m Relay	Poland 44.5	Federal Republic of Germany 44.6	Great Britain 44.9
High Jump	Iolanda Balas (ROM) 1.83	Olga Gere (YUG) 1.76	Linda Knowles (GBR) 1.73
Long Jump	Tatyana Shchelkanova (URS) 6.36	Elzabieta Krzesinska (POL) 6.22	Mary Rand (GBR) 6.22
Javelin	Elvira Ozolina (URS) 54.93	Maria Diaconescu (ROM) 52.10	Alevtina Shastitko (URS) 51.80
Shot Put	Tamara Press (URS) 18.55	Renate Garisch (GDR) 17.17	Galina Zybina (URS) 16.95
Discus	Tamara Press (URS) 56.91	Doris Muller (GDR) 56.30	Yolan Konchek (HUN) 52.82
Pentathlon	Galina Bystrova (URS) 4833	Denise Guenard (FRA) 4735	Helga Hoffmann (FRG) 4676

1966 Budapest

Men's	Gold	Silver	Bronze
100m	Wieslaw Maniak (POL) 10.5	Roger Bambuck (FRA) 10.5	Claude Piquemal (FRA) 10.5
200m	Roger Bambuck (FRA) 20.9	Marian Dudziak (POL) 21.0	Jean Claude Nallet (FRA) 21.0
400m	Stanislaw Gredzhinski (POL) 46.0	Andrzej Badenski (POL) 46.2	Manfred Kinder (FRG) 46.3
800m	Manfred Matuschewski (GDR) 1:45.9	Franz Josef Kemper (FRG) 1:46.0	Bodo Tummler (FRG) 1:46.3
1500m	Bodo Tummler (FRG) 3:41.9	Michel Jazy (FRA) 3:42.2	Harold Norporth (FRG) 3:42.4
5000m	Michel Jazy (FRA) 13:42.8	Harold Norporth (FRG) 13:44.0	Bernd Diessner (GDR) 13:47.8
10,000m	Jurgen Haase (GDR) 28:26.0	Lajos Macser (HUN) 28:27.0	Leonid Michienko (URSR) 28:32.2
Marathon	James Hogan (GBR) 2:20:05	Aurele Vandenriesche (BEL) 2:21:44	Gyula Toth (HUN) 2:22:02
3000m Steeplechase	Viktor Kudinskiy (URS) 8:26.6	Anatoliy Kuryan (URS) 8:28.0	Gaston Roelants (BEL) 8:28.0
110m Hurdles	Eddy Ottoz (ITA) 13.7	Henrich John (FRG) 14.0	Marcel Duriez (FRA) 14.0
400m Hurdles	Roberto Frinolli (ITA) 49.8	Gerd Lossdorfer (FRG) 50.3	Robert Poirier (FRA) 50.5
20km Walk	Dieter Lindner (GDR) 1:29:25	Vladimir Golubnichiy (URS) 1:30:06	Nikolay Smaga (URS) 1:30:18
50km Walk	Abdon Pamich (ITA) 4:18:42	Gennadiy Agapov (URS) 4:20:01	Aleksandr Shcherbina (URS) 4:20:47
4 × 100m Relay	France 39.4	Soviet Union 39.8	German Democratic Republic 39.8
4 × 400m Relay	Poland 3:04.5	Federal Republic of Germany 3:04.8	German Democratic Republic 3:05.7
High Jump	Jacques Madubost (FRA) 2.12	Robert Sainte-Rose (FRA) 2.12	Valeriy Skvorzov (URS) 2.09
Pole Vault	Wolfgang Nordwig (GDR) 5.10	Christos Papanicolaou (GRE) 5.05	Hervé d'Encausse (FRA) 5.00
Long Jump	Lynn Davies (GBR) 7.98	Igor Ter-Ovanesyan (URS) 7.88	Jean Cochard (FRA) 7.88
Triple Jump	Georgi Stojkowski (BUL) 16.67	Hans-Jurgen Ruckborn (GDR) 16.66	Henrik Kalocsai (HUN) 16.59
Shot Put	Vilmos Varju (HUN) 19.43	Nikolay Karasov (URS) 18.82	Wladyslaw Komar (POL) 18.68
Discus	Detlef Thorith (GDR) 57.42	Hartmut Losch (GDR) 57.34	Lothar Milde (GDR) 56.80
Hammer	Romuald Klim (URS) 70.02	Gyula Zsivotzky (HUN) 68.62	Uwe Beyer (FRG) 67.28
Javelin	Janis Lusis (URS) 84.48	Wladyslaw Nikiciuk (POL) 81.76	Gergely Kulcsar (HUN) 80.54
Decathlon	Werner von Moltke (FRG) 7740	Jorg Mattheis (FRG) 7614	Horst Beyer (FRG) 7562

Women's	Gold	Silver	Bronze
100m	Ewa Klobukowska (POL) 11.5	Irena Kirszenstein (POL) 11.5	Karin Frisch (FRG) 11.8
200m	Irena Kirszenstein (POL) 23.1	Ewa Klobukowska (POL) 23.4	Vyera Popkova (URS) 23.7
400m	Anna Smelkova (TCH) 52.9	Antonia Munkacsi (HUN) 53.9	Monique Noirot (FRA) 54.0
800m	Vera Nikolic (YUG) 2:02.8	Zsuzsa Szabo Nagy (HUN) 2:03.1	Antje Gleichfeld (FRG) 2:03.7
80m Hurdles	Karin Balzer (FRG) 10.7	Karin Frisch (FRG) 10.7	Elzbieta Bednarek (POL) 10.7
4 × 100m Relay	Poland 44.4	Federal Republic of Germany 44.4	Soviet Union 44.6
High Jump	Taisiya Chenchik (URS) 1.75	Lyudmila Komleva (URS) 1.73	Jaroslawa Bieda (POL) 1.71
Long Jump	Irena Kirszenstein (POL) 6.55	Diana Yorkova (BUL) 6.45	Helga Hoffmann (FRG) 6.38
Javelin	Marion Luttge Graefe (FRG) 58.74	Mihaela Penes (ROM) 56.94	Valentina Popova (URS) 56.70
Shot Put	Nadezhda Chizhova (URS) 17.22	Margitta Gummel (FRG) 17.05	Marita Lange (FRG) 16.96
Discus	Christine Spielberg (FRG) 57.76	Liesel Westermann (FRG) 57.38	Anita Hentschel (FRG) 56.80
Pentathlon	Valentina Tikhomirova (URS) 4787	Heidemarie Rosendahl (FRG) 4765	Ingeborg Hechsner (GDR) 4713

1969 Athens

Men's	Gold	Silver	Bronze
100m	Valeriy Borzov (URS) 10.4	Alain Sarteur (FRA) 10.4	Philippe Clerc (SUI) 10.5
200m	Philippe Clerc (SUI) 20.6	Herman Burde (GDR) 20.9	Zenon Nowosz (POL) 20.9
400m	Jan Werner (POL) 45.7	Jean Claude Nallet (FRA) 45.8	Stanislaw Grezhinski (POL) 45.8
800m	Dieter Fromm (GDR) 1:45.9	Jozef Plachy (POL) 1:46.2	Manfred Matuschewski (GDR) 1:46.8
1500m	John Whetton (GBR) 3:39.4	Francis Murphy (IRL) 3:39.5	Henryk Szordykowski (POL) 3:39.8
5000m	Ian Stewart (GBR) 13:44.8	Rasid Sarafundinov (URS) 13:45.8	Allan Blinston (GBR) 13:47.6
10,000m	Jurgen Haase (GDR) 28:41.6	Michael Tagg (GBR) 28:43.2	Nikolay Sviridov (URS) 28:45.8
Marathon	Ron Hill (GBR) 2:16:48	Gaston Roelants (BEL) 2:17:22	Jim Alder (GBR) 2:19:06
3000m Steeplechase	Michail Zhelev (BUL) 8:25.0	Aleksandr Morozov (URS) 8:25.6	Vladimir Dudin (URS) 8:26.6
110m Hurdles	Eddy Ottoz (ITA) 13.5	David Hemery (GBR) 13.7	Alan Pascoe (GBR) 13.9

ATHLETICS

400m Hurdles	Vyacheslav Skomorokhov (URS) 49.7	John Sherwood (GBR) 50.1	Andrew Todd (GBR) 50.3
20km Walk	Paul Nihill (GBR) 1:30:48	Leonida Karaiosifoglu (ROM) 1:31:06	Nikolayi Smaga (POL) 1:31:20
50km Walk	Christoph Hoene (GDR) 4:12:33	Peter Seltzer (GDR) 4:16:10	Benjamin Soldatenko (URS) 4:23:04
4 × 100m Relay	France 38.8	Soviet Union 39.3	Czechoslovakia 39.5
4 × 400m Relay	France 3:02.3	Soviet Union 3:03.0	Federal Republic of Germany 3:03.1
High Jump	Valentin Gavrilov (URS) 2.17	Reijo Vahala (FIN) 2.17	Erminio Azzaro (ITA) 2.17
Pole Vault	Wolfgang Nordwig (GDR) 5.30	Kjell Isaksson (SWE) 5.20	Aldo Righi (ITA) 5.10
Long Jump	Igor Ter-Ovanesyan (URS) 8.17	Lynn Davies (GBR) 8.07	Tonu Lepik (URS) 8.04
Triple Jump	Viktor Saneyev (URS) 17.34	Zoltan Cziffra (HUN) 16.85	Klaus Neumann (GDR) 16.68
Shot Put	Dieter Hofmann (GDR) 20.12	Hans Joachim Rothenberg (GDR) 20.05	Hans Peter Gies (GDR) 19.78
Discus	Harmut Losch (GDR) 61.82	Richy Bruch (SWE) 61.08	Lothar Milde (GDR) 59.34
Hammer	Anatoli Bondarchuk (URS) 74.68	Romuald Klim (URS) 72.74	Reinhard Theimer (GDR) 72.02
Javelin	Janis Lusis (URS) 91.52	Pauli Nevala (FIN) 89.58	Janusz Sildo (POL) 82.90
Decathlon	Joakim Kirst (GDR) 8041	Herbert Wessel (GDR) 7828	Viktor Chelnikov (URS) 7801

Women's	Gold	Silver	Bronze
100m	Petra Vogdt (GDR) 11.6	Vilma van der Berg (NED) 11.7	Anita Neal (GBR) 11.8
200m	Petra Vogdt (GDR) 23.2	Renate Meissner (GDR) 23.3	Valerie Peat (GBR) 23.3
400m	Nicole Duclos (FRA) 51.7	Colette Besson (FRA) 51.7	Maria Sykora (AUS) 53.0
800m	Lillian Board (GBR) 2:01.4	Anneliese Damm Olesen (DEN) 2:02.6	Vera Nikolic (YUG) 2:02.6
1500m	Jaroslava Jehlickova (TCH) 4:10.7	Maria Gommers (NED) 4:11.9	Paola Pighni (ITA) 4:12.2
100m Hurdles	Karin Balzer (GDR) 13.29	Barbel Pondzheva (GDR) 13.68	Teresa Nowak (POL) 13.77
4 × 100m Relay	German Democratic Republic 43.63	Federal Republic of Germany 44.09	Great Britain 44.39
4 × 400m Relay	Great Britain 3:30.8	France 3:30.8	Federal Republic of Germany 3:32.7
High Jump	Miroslawa Rezlova (TCH) 1.83	Antonina Lasareva (URS) 1.83	Maria Mracnova (TCH) 1.83
Long Jump	Miroslawa Sarna (POL) 6.49	Viorica Viscopoleanu (ROM) 6.45	Berit Berthelsen (NOR) 6.44
Javelin	Angela Nemeth Ranky (HUN) 59.76	Marta Vidos Paulanyi (HUN) 58.80	Valentina Evert (URS) 56.56
Shot Put	Nadezhda Chizhova (URS) 20.43	Margitta Gummel (GDR) 19.58	Marita Lange (GDR) 19.56
Discus	Tamara Danilova (URS) 59.28	Lyudmilla Muravyova (URS) 59.24	Karin Ilgren (GDR) 58.66
Pentathlon	Liese Prokop (AUT) 5030	Meta Antenen (SUI) 4793	Maria Chisiakova (URS) 4773

1971 Helsinki

Men's	Gold	Silver	Bronze
100m	Valeriy Borzov (URS) 10.26	Gerhard Wucherer (GDR) 10.48	Vasilis Papageorgopoulos (GRE) 10.56
200m	Valeriy Borzov (URS) 20.30	Franz Peter Hofmeister (FRG) 20.71	Jorg Pfeifer (GDR) 20.72
400m	David Jenkins (GBR) 45.45	Marcelo Fiasconaro (ITA) 45.49	Jan Werner (POL) 45.56
800m	Yevgeniy Arzhanov (URS) 1:45.6	Dieter Fromm (GDR) 1:46.0	Andrew Carter (GBR) 1:46.2
1500m	Francesco Arese (ITA) 3:38.4	Henryk Szordykowski (POL) 3:38.7	Brendan Foster (GBR) 3:39.2
5000m	Juha Vaatainen (FIN) 13:32.6	Jean Wadoux (FRA) 13:33.6	Harald Norporth (FRG) 13:33.8
10,000m	Juha Vaatainen (FIN) 27:52.8	Jurgen Haase (GDR) 27:53.4	Pachid Sharafetdinov (URS) 27:56.4
Marathon	Karel Lismont (BEL) 2:13:09	Trevor Wright (GBR) 2:14:00	Ron Hill (GBR) 2:14:35
3000m Steeplechase	Jean Paul Villain (FRA) 8:25.2	Dusan Moravcik (POL) 8:26.2	Pavel Sysoyev (URS) 8:26.4
110m Hurdles	Frank Siebek (GDR) 14.00	Alan Pascoe (GBR) 14.09	Lubomir Nadenicek (POL) 14.30
400m Hurdles	Jean Claude Nallet (FRA) 49.2	Christian Rudolph (GDR) 49.3	Dimitriy Stukalov (URS) 50.0
20km Walk	Nikolay Smaga (URS) 1:27:20	Gerhard Sperling (GDR) 1:27:29	Paul Nihill (GBR) 1:27:35
50km Walk	Veniamin Soldatenko (URS) 4:02:22	Christoph Hoene (GDR) 4:04:45	Peter Seltzer (GDR) 4:06:11
4 × 100m Relay	Czechoslovakia 39.3	Poland 39.7	Italy 39.8
4 × 400m Relay	Federal Republic of Germany 3:02.9	Poland 3:03.6	Italy 3:04.6
High Jump	Kestutis Sapka (URS) 2.20	Csaba Dosa (ROM) 2.20	Rustam Akhmetov (URS) 2.20
Pole Vault	Wolfgang Nodwig (GDR) 5.35	Kiel Isacsson (SWE) 5.30	Renato Dionisi (ITA) 5.30
Long Jump	Max Klauss (GDR) 7.92	Igor Ter-Ovanesyan (URS) 7.91	Stanislaw Szundrowicz (POL) 7.87
Triple Jump	Jorg Drehmel (GDR) 17.16	Viktor Saneyev (URS) 17.10	Carol Corbu (ROM) 16.87
Shot Put	Hartmut Briesenik (GDR) 21.08	Hans Joachim Rothenberg (GDR) 20.47	Wladyslaw Komar (POL) 20.04
Discus	Ludvik Danek (TCH) 63.90	Lothar Milde (GDR) 61.62	Geza Fejer (HUN) 61.54
Hammer	Uwe Beyer (FRG) 72.36	Reinhard Theimer (GDR) 71.80	Anatoliy Bondarchuk (URS) 71.40
Javelin	Janis Lusis (URS) 90.68	Janis Donins (URS) 85.30	Wolfgang Hanisch (GDR) 84.22
Decathlon	Joachim Kirst (GDR) 8196	Lennart Hedmark (SWE) 8038	Hans Joachim Walde (FRG) 7951

Women's	Gold	Silver	Bronze
100m	Renate Stecher (GDR) 11.4	Ingrid Mickler (FRG) 11.5	Efgard Schittenhelm (FRG) 11.5
200m	Renate Stecher (GDR) 22.7	Gyorgyi Balogh (HUN) 23.2	Irena Szewinska (POL) 23.3
400m	Helga Seidler (GDR) 52.1	Inge Bodding (FRG) 52.9	Ingelore Lohse (FRG) 52.9

800m	Vera Nikolic (YUG) 2:00.0	Pat Lowe (GBR) 2:01.7	Rosemary Stirling (GBR) 2:02.1
1500m	Karin Burneleit (GDR) 4:09.6	Gunhild Hoffmeister (GDR) 4:10.3	Elen Tittel (FRG) 4:10.4
100m Hurdles	Karin Balzer (GDR) 12.94	Annelie Ehrhardt (GDR) 12.96	Teresa Sukniewicz (POL) 13.21
4 × 100m Relay	Federal Republic of Germany 43.3	German Democratic Republic 43.6	Soviet Union 44.5
4 × 400m Relay	German Democratic Republic 3:29.3	Federal Republic of Germany 3:33.0	Soviet Union 3:34.1
High Jump	Ilona Gusenbauer (AUT) 1.87	Cornelia Popescu (ROM) 1.85	Barbara Inkpen (GBR) 1.85
Long Jump	Ingrid Mickler (FRG) 6.76	Meta Antenen (SUI) 6.73	Heide Rosendahl (FRG) 6.66
Javelin	Daniela Jaworska (POL) 61.00	Aneli Koloska (FRG) 59.40	Ruth Fuchs (GDR) 59.16
Shot Put	Nadezhda Chizhova (URS) 20.16	Marita Lange (GDR) 19.25	Margitta Gummel (GDR) 19.22
Discus	Faina Melnik (URS) 64.22	Liesel Westermann (FRG) 61.68	Lyudmila Muravyova (URS) 59.48
Pentathlon	Heidemarie Rosendahl (FRG) 5299	Burglinde Pollak (GDR) 5275	Margrit Herbst (GDR) 5179

1974 Rome

Men's	Gold	Silver	Bronze
100m	Valeriy Borzov (URS) 10.27	Pietro Mennea (ITA) 10.34	Klaus Dieter Bieler (FRG) 10.35
200m	Pietro Mennea (ITA) 20.60	Manfred Ommer (FRG) 20.76	Hans Jurgen Bombach (GDR) 20.83
400m	Karl Honz (FRG) 45.04	David Jenkins (GBR) 45.67	Bernd Herrmann (FRG) 45.78
800m	Luciano Susanj (YUG) 1:44.1	Steve Ovett (GBR) 1:45.8	Markku Taskinen (FIN) 1:45.9
1500m	Klaus Peter Justus (FRG) 3:40.6	Tom Hansen (DEN) 3:40.8	Tomas Wessinghage (FRG) 3:41.1
5000m	Brendan Foster (GBR) 13:17.2	Manfred Kuschmann (GDR) 13:24.0	Lasse Viren (FIN) 13:24.6
10,000m	Manfred Kuschmann (GDR) 28:25.8	Anthony Simmons (GBR) 28:25.8	Giuseppe Cindolo (ITA) 28:27.2
Marathon	Ian Thompson (GBR) 2:13:19	Eckhard Lasse (GDR) 2:14:57	Gaston Roelants (BEL) 2:16:30
3000m Steeplechase	Bronislaw Malinowski (POL) 8:15.0	Anders Garderud (SWE) 8:15.4	Michael Karst (FRG) 8:18.0
110m Hurdles	Guy Drut (FRA) 13.40	Miroslaw Wodzynski (POL) 13.67	Leszek Wodzynski (POL) 13.71
400m Hurdles	Alan Pascoe (GBR) 48.82	Jean Claude Nallet (FRA) 48.94	Yevgeniy Gavrilenko (URS) 49.32
20km Walk	Vladimir Golubnichiy (URS) 1:29:30	Bernd Kannenberg (FRG) 1:29:38	Roger Mills (GBR) 1:32:34
50km Walk	Christoph Hoene (GDR) 3:59:06	Otto Bartsch (URS) 4:02:39	Peter Selzer (GDR) 4:04:28
4 × 100m Relay	France 38.69	Italy 38.88	German Democratic Republic 38.99
4 × 400m Relay	Great Britain 3:03.3	Federal Republic of Germany 3:03.5	France 3:04.6
High Jump	Jesper Torring (DEN) 2.25	Kestutis Sapka (URS) 2.25	Vladimir Maly (TCH) 2.19
Pole Vault	Vladimir Kisyukin (URS) 5.35	Wladyslaw Kozakiewicz (POL) 5.35	Yuriy Isakov (URS) 5.30
Long Jump	Valeriy Podluzhniy (URS) 8.12	Nenad Stekic (YUG) 8.05	Yevgeniy Shubin (URS) 7.98
Triple Jump	Viktor Saneyev (URS) 17.23	Carol Corbu (ROM) 16.68	Andrzej Sontag (POL) 16.61
Shot Put	Hartmut Briesnick (GDR) 20.50	Ralf Reichenbach (FRG) 20.38	Geoff Capes (GBR) 20.21
Discus	Pentti Kahma (FIN) 63.62	Ludvik Danek (TCH) 62.76	Ricky Bruch (SWE) 64.00
Hammer	Aleksey Spiridonov (URS) 74.20	Jochen Sachse (GDR) 74.00	Reinhard Theimer (GDR) 71.62
Javelin	Hannu Siitonen (FIN) 89.58	Wolfgang Hanisch (GDR) 85.46	Terje Thorslund (NOR) 83.68
Decathlon	Ryszard Skowronek (POL) 8207	Yves Le Roy (FRA) 8146	Guido Kratschmer (FRG) 8132

Women's	Gold	Silver	Bronze
100m	Irena Szewinska (POL) 11.13	Renate Stecher (GDR) 11.23	Andrea Lynch (GBR) 11.28
200m	Irena Szewinska (POL) 22.51	Renate Stecher (GDR) 22.68	Mona Lisa Pursiainen (FIN) 23.17
400m	Riita Salin (FIN) 50.14	Ellen Streidt (GDR) 50.69	Rita Wilden (FRG) 50.88
800m	Liliana Tomova (BUL) 1:58.1	Gunhild Hoffmeister (GDR) 1:58.8	Mariana Suman (ROM) 1:59.8
1500m	Gunhild Hoffmeister (GDR) 4:02.30	Liliana Tomova (BUL) 4:05.00	Grete Andersen (NOR) 4:05.20
3000m	Nina Holmen (FIN) 8:55.2	Lyudmila Bragina (URS) 8:56.2	Joyce Smith (GBR) 8:57.4
100m Hurdles	Annelie Ehrhardt (GDR) 12.66	Annerose Friedler (GDR) 12.89	Teresa Nowak (POL) 12.91
4 × 100m Relay	German Democratic Republic 42.51	Federal Republic of Germany 42.75	Poland 43.48
4 × 400m Relay	German Democratic Republic 3:25.2	Finland 3:25.7	Soviet Union 3:26.1
High Jump	Rosemarie Witschas (GDR) 1.95	Milada Karbanova (TCH) 1.91	Sara Simeoni (ITA) 1.89
Long Jump	Ilona Brusenyak (HUN) 6.65	Eva Suranova (TCH) 6.65	Pirkko Helenius (FIN) 6.59
Javelin	Ruth Fuchs (GDR) 67.22	Jacqueline Todten (GDR) 62.10	Natasa Urbancic (YUG) 61.66
Shot Put	Nadezhda Chizhova (URS) 20.78	Marianne Adam (GDR) 20.43	Helena Fibingerova (TCH) 20.33
Discus	Faina Melnik (URS) 69.00	Argentina Menis (ROM) 64.62	Gabrielle Hinzmann (GDR) 62.50
Pentathlon	Nadezhda Tkachenko (URS) 4776	Burglinde Pollak (GDR) 4600	Sonya Spasovkhonskaya (URS) 4550

1978 Prague

Men's	Gold	Silver	Bronze
100m	Pietro Mennea (ITA) 10.27	Eugen Ray (GDR) 10.36	Vladimir Igatienko (URS) 10.37
200m	Pietro Mennea (ITA) 20.16	Olaf Prenzler (GDR) 20.61	Peter Muster (SUI) 20.64
400m	Franz Peter Hofmeister (FRG) 45.73	Karol Kolar (TCH) 45.77	Francois Demarthon (FRA) 45.97
800m	Olaf Beyer (GDR) 1:43.84	Steve Ovett (GBR) 1:44.09	Sebastian Coe (GBR) 1:44.76
1500m	Steve Ovett (GBR) 3:35.59	Eamon Coghlan (IRL) 3:36.75	David Moorcroft (GBR) 3:36.70
5000m	Venanzio Ortis (ITA) 13:28.57	Markus Ryffel (SUI) 13:28.66	——

ATHLETICS

	Gold	Silver	Bronze
		Aleksandr Fedotkin (URS) 13:28.66	
10,000m	Martti Vainio (FIN) 27:30.99	Venanzio Ortis (ITA) 27:31.48	Aleksandr Antipov (URS) 27:31.50
Marathon	Leonid Moseyev (URS) 2:11:57	Nikolae Penzin (URS) 2:11:59	Karel Lismont (BEL) 2:12:08
3000m Steeplechase	Bronislaw Malinowski (POL) 8:15.08	Patriz Ilg (FRG) 8:16.92	Ismo Tuokonen (FIN) 8:18.29
110m Hurdles	Thomas Munkelt (GDR) 13.54	Jan Pusty (POL) 13.55	Arto Bryggare (FIN) 13.56
400m Hurdles	Harald Schmid (FRG) 48.51	Dmitriy Stukalov (URS) 49.72	Vasiliy Arkhipenko (URS) 49.77
20km Walk	Ronald Wieser (GDR) 1:23:11	Pyotr Pochenchuk (URS) 1:23:43	Anatoly Solomin (URS) 1:24:11
50km Walk	Jorge Llopart (ESP) 3:53:30	Veniamin Soldatenko (URS) 3:55:12	Jan Ornoch (POL) 3:55:16
4 × 100m Relay	Poland 38.58	German Democratic Republic 38.78	Soviet Union 38.82
4 × 400m Relay	Federal Republic of Germany 3:02.03	Poland 3:03.62	Czechoslovakia 3:04.99
High Jump	Vladimir Yashkenko (URS) 2.30	Aleksandr Grigoreyev (URS) 2.28	Rolf Beilschmidt (GDR) 2.28
Pole Vault	Vladimir Trofimenko (URS) 5.55	Antti Kalliomaki (FIN) 5.50	Rauli Pudas (FIN) 5.45
Long Jump	Jacques Rousseau (FRA) 8.18	Nenad Stecic (YUG) 8.12	Vladimir Tsepelyov (URS) 8.01
Triple Jump	Milos Srejovic (YUG) 16.94	Viktor Saneyev (URS) 16.93	Anatoliy Piskulin (URS) 16.87
Shot Put	Udo Beyer (GDR) 21.08	Yevgeniy Mironov (URS) 20.87	Aleksandr Baryshnikov (URS) 20.68
Discus	Wolfgang Schmidt (GDR) 66.82	Markku Tuokko (FIN) 64.90	Imrich Bugar (TCH) 64.66
Hammer	Yuriy Sedykh (URS) 77.28	Roland Steuk (GDR) 77.24	Karl Hans Riehm (FRG) 77.02
Javelin	Michael Wessing (FRG) 89.12	Nikolay Grebniev (URS) 87.82	Wolfgang Hanisch (GDR) 87.66
Decathlon	Aleksandr Grebenyuk (URS) 8340	Daley Thompson (GBR) 8289	Siegfried Stark (GDR) 8208

Women's	Gold	Silver	Bronze
100m	Marlies Gohr (GDR) 11.13	Linda Haglund (SWE) 11.29	Ludmilla Maslakova (URS) 11.31
200m	Ludmilla Kondratieva (URS) 22.52	Marlies Gohr (GDR) 22.53	Carla Bodendorf (GDR) 22.64
400m	Marita Koch (GDR) 49.94	Christina Brehmer (GDR) 50.38	Irena Szewinska (POL) 50.40
800m	Tatyana Providokhina (URS) 1:55.80	Nadezhda Mushta (URS) 1:55.82	Zoya Rigel (URS) 1:56.57
1500m	Giana Romanova (URS) 3:59.8	Natalia Marasescu (ROM) 3:58.77	Totka Petrova (BUL) 4:00.15
3000m	Svetlana Ulmasova (URS) 8:33.16	Natalia Marasescu (ROM) 8:33.53	Grete Waitz (NOR) 8:34.33
100m Hurdles	Johanna Klier (GDR) 12.62	Tatyana Anisimova (URS) 12.67	Gudrun Berend (GDR) 12.73
400m Hurdles	Tatyana Zelentsova (URS) 54.89	Sylvia Holmann (FRG) 55.14	Karin Rossley (GDR) 55.36
4 × 100m Relay	Soviet Union 42.54	Great Britain 42.72	German Democratic Republic 43.07
4 × 400m Relay	German Democratic Republic 3:21.20	Soviet Union 3:22.53	Poland 3:26.76
High Jump	Sara Simeoni (ITA) 2.01	Rosemarie Ackermann (GDR) 1.99	Brigitte Holtzapfel (FRG) 1.95
Long Jump	Vilma Bardauskiene (URS) 6.88	Angela Voigt (GDR) 6.79	Jarmila Nygrynova (TCH) 6.69
Javelin	Ruth Fuchs (GDR) 69.16	Tessa Sanderson (GBR) 62.40	Ute Hommola (GDR) 62.32
Shot Put	Ilona Slupianek (GDR) 21.41	Helena Fibingerova (TCH) 20.86	Margitta Droese (GDR) 20.58
Discus	Evelin Jahl (GDR) 66.98	Margitta Droese (GDR) 64.04	Natalya Gorbacheva (URS) 63.58
Pentathlon	Margit Papp (HUN) 4655	Burglinde Pollak (GDR) 4600	Kristine Nitzsche (GDR) 4599

1982 Athens

Men's	Gold	Silver	Bronze
100m	Frank Emmelmann (GDR) 10.21	Pier Francesco Pavoni (ITA) 10.25	Marian Woronin (POL) 10.28
200m	Olaf Prentzler (GDR) 20.46	Cameron Sharp (GBR) 20.47	Frank Emmelmann (GDR) 20.60
400m	Hartmut Weber (FRG) 44.72	Andreas Knebel (GDR) 45.29	Viktor Markin (URS) 45.30
800m	Hans Peter Ferner (FRG) 1:46.33	Sebastian Coe (GBR) 1:46.68	Jorma Harkonen (FIN) 1:46.90
1500m	Steve Cram (GBR) 3:36.49	Nikolay Kirov (URS) 3:36.99	Jose Manuel Abascal (ESP) 3:37.04
5000m	Thomas Wessinghage (FRG) 13:28.90	Werner Schildhauer (GDR) 13:30.03	David Moorcroft (GBR) 13:30.42
10,000m	Alberto Cova (ITA) 27:41.03	Werner Schildhauer (GDR) 27:41.21	Martti Vainio (FIN) 27:42.51
Marathon	Gerard Nijboer (NED) 2:15:16	Armand Parmentier (BEL) 2:15:51	Karel Lismont (BEL) 2:16:04
3000m Steeplechase	Patriz Ilg (FRG) 8:18.52	Boguslaw Maminski (POL) 8:19.22	Domingo Ramon (ESP) 8:20.48
110m Hurdles	Thomas Munkelt (GDR) 13.41	Andrey Prokofyev (URS) 13.44	Arto Brygarre (FIN) 13.60
400m Hurdles	Harald Schmid (FRG) 47.48	Aleksandr Yatsevich (URS) 48.60	Uwe Ackermann (GDR) 48.64
20km Walk	Jose Marin (ESP) 1:23:43	Jozef Priblinec (TCH) 1:25:55	Pavol Blazek (TCH) 1:26:13
50km Walk	Reima Salonen (FIN) 3:55:29	Jose Marin (ESP) 3:59:18	Bo Gustafsson (SWE) 4:01:21
4 × 100m Relay	Soviet Union 38.60	German Democratic Republic 38.71	Federal Republic of Germany 38.71
4 × 400m Relay	Federal Republic of Germany 3:00.51	Great Britain 3:00.67	Soviet Union 3:00.79
High Jump	Dietmar Mogenburg (FRG) 2.30	Janusz Trzepizur (POL) 2.27	Gerd Nagel (FRG) 2.24
Pole Vault	Aleksandr Krupski (URS) 5.60	Vladimir Polyakov (URS) 5.60	Atanas Tarev (BUL) 5.60
Long Jump	Lutz Dombrowski (GDR) 8.41	Antonio Corgos (ESP) 8.19	Jan Leitner (TCH) 8.08
Triple Jump	Keith Connor (GBR) 17.29	Vasiliy Grishchenkov (URS) 17.15	Bela Bakosi (HUN) 17.04
Shot Put	Udo Beyer (GDR) 21.50	Janis Bojars (URS) 20.81	Remigius Machura (TCH) 20.59
Discus	Imrich Bugar (TCH) 66.64	Igor Duginyets (URS) 65.60	Wolfgang Warnemunde (GDR) 64.20
Hammer	Yuriy Sedykh (URS) 81.66	Igor Nikulin (URS) 79.44	Sergey Litvinov (URS) 78.66
Javelin	Uwe Hohn (GDR) 91.34	Heini Puuste (URS) 89.56	Detlef Michel (GDR) 89.32
Decathlon	Daley Thompson (GBR) 8743	Jurgen Hingsen (FRG) 8517	Siegfried Stark (GDR) 8433

Women's	Gold	Silver	Bronze
100m	Marlies Gohr (GDR) 11.01	Barbel Wockel (GDR) 11.20	Rose Aimee Baccoul (FRA) 11.29
200m	Barbel Wockel (GDR) 22.04	Kathy Smallwood (GBR) 22.13	Sabine Rieger (GDR) 22.51
400m	Marita Koch (GDR) 48.16	Jarmila Kratochvilova (TCH) 48.85	Tatiana Kocembova (TCH) 50.55
800m	Olga Mineyeva (URS) 1:55.41	Lyudmila Veselkova (URS) 1:55.96	Margrit Klinger (FRG) 1:57.22
1500m	Olga Dvirna (URS) 3:57.8	Zamira Zaytseva (URS) 3:58.82	Gabriella Dorio (ITA) 3:59.02
3000m	Svetlana Ulmasova (URS) 8:30.28	Maricica Puica (ROM) 8:33.33	Yelena Sipatova (URS) 8:34.06
Marathon	Rosa Mota (POR) 2:36:04	Laura Fogli (ITA) 2:36:29	Ingrid Kristiansen (NOR) 2:36:39
100m Hurdles	Lucyna Kalek (POL) 12.45	Yordanka Donkova (BUL) 12.54	Kerstin Knabe (GDR) 12.54
400m Hurdles	Ann Louise Skoglund (SWE) 54.58	Petra Pfaff (GDR) 54.90	Chantal Rega (FRA) 54.94
4 × 100m Relay	German Democratic Republic 42.19	Great Britain 42.66	France 42.68
4 × 400m Relay	German Democratic Republic 3:19.05	Czechoslovakia 3:22.17	Soviet Union 3:22.79
High Jump	Urlike Mayfarth (GDR) 2.02	Tamara Bykova (URS) 1.97	Sara Simeoni (ITA) 1.97
Long Jump	Vali Ionescu (ROM) 6.79	Anisoara Stanciu (ROM) 6.73	Yelena Ivanova (URS) 6.73
Javelin	Anna Verouli (GRE) 70.02	Antje Kempe (GDR) 67.94	Sofia Sakorafa (GRE) 67.04
Shot Put	Ilona Slupiamek (GDR) 21.59	Helena Fibengerova (TCH) 20.94	Nina Abashidze (URS) 20.82
Discus	Tsvetanka Khristova (BUL) 68.34	Mariya Vergova (BUL) 67.94	Galina Savinkova (URS) 67.82
Heptathlon	Ramona Neubert (GDR) 6664	Sabine Mobius (GDR) 6594	Sabine Everts (FRG) 6418

1986 Stuttgart

Men's	Gold	Silver	Bronze
100m	Linford Christie (GBR) 10.15	Steffen Bringmann (GDR) 10.20	Bruno Marie Rose (FRA) 10.21
200m	Vladimir Krylov (URS) 20.52	Jürgen Evers (FRG) 20.75	Andrey Fedoriv (URS) 20.84
400m	Roger Black (GBR) 44.59	Thomas Schonlebe (GDR) 44.63	Mattias Schering (GDR) 44.85
800m	Sebastian Coe (GBR) 1:44.50	Tom McKean (GBR) 1:44.61	Steve Cram (GBR) 1:44.88
1500m	Steve Cram (GBR) 3:41.09	Sebastian Coe (GBR) 3:41.67	Han Kulker (NED) 3:42.11
5000m	Jack Buckner (GBR) 13:10.15	Stefano Mei (ITA) 13:11.57	Tim Hutchings (GBR) 13:12.88
10,000m	Stefano Mei (ITA) 27:56.79	Alberto Cova (ITA) 27:57.93	Salvatore Antibo (ITA) 28:00.25
Marathon	Gelindo Bordin (ITA) 2:10:54	Orlando Pizzaloto (ITA) 2:10:57	Herbert Steffney (FRG) 2:11:41
3000m Steeplechase	Hagen Meltzer (GDR) 8:16.65	Francesco Panetta (ITA) 8:16.85	Patriz Ilg (FRG) 8:16.92
110m Hurdles	Stephane Caristan (FRA) 13.20	Arto Bryggare (FRA) 13.42	Carlos Sala (ESP) 13.50
400m Hurdles	Harald Schmid (FRG) 48.65	Aleksandr Vasileyev (URS) 48.76	Sven Nylander (SWE) 49.38
20km Walk	Jozef Pribilinec (TCH) 1:21:15	Maurizio Damilano (ITA) 1:21:17	Miguel Prieto (ESP) 1:21:36
50km Walk	Hartwig Gauder (GDR) 3:40:55	Vyascheslav Ivanchenko (URS) 3:41:54	Valeriy Suntsov (URS) 3:42:38
4 × 100m Relay	Soviet Union 38.29	German Democratic Republic 38.64	Great Britain 38.71
4 × 400m Relay	Great Britain 2:59.84	Federal Republic of Germany 3:00.17	Soviet Union 3:00.47
High Jump	Igor Paklin (URS) 2.34	Sergey Malchenko (URS) 2.31	Carlo Thranhardt (FRG) 2.31
Pole Vault	Sergey Bubka (URS) 5.85	Vasiliy Bubka (URS) 5.75	Philippe Collet (FRA) 5.75
Long Jump	Robert Emmiyan (URS) 8.41	Sergey Layevskiy (URS) 8.01	Giovanni Evangelisti (ITA) 7.92
Triple Jump	Khristo Markov (BUL) 17.66	Maris Bruzhiks (URS) 17.33	Oleg Protsenko (URS) 17.28
Shot Put	Werner Gunthor (SUI) 22.22	Ulf Timmermann (GDR) 21.84	Udo Beyer (GDR) 20.74
Discus	Romas Ubartas (URS) 67.08	Georgiy Kolnootchenko (URS) 67.02	Vaclavas Kidikas (URS) 66.32
Hammer	Yuriy Sedykh (URS) 86.74	Sergey Litvinov (URS) 85.74	Igor Nikulin (URS) 82.00
Javelin	Klaus Tafelmeier (FRG) 84.76	Detlef Michel (GDR) 81.90	Viktor Yevsyukov (URS) 81.80
Decathlon	Daley Thompson (GBR) 8811	Jurgen Hingsen (FRG) 8730	Siegfried Wentz (FRG) 8676

Women's	Gold	Silver	Bronze
100m	Marlies Gohr (GDR) 10.91	Anelia Nuneeva (BUL) 11.04	Nelli Cooman (NED) 11.08
200m	Heike Drechsler (GDR) 21.71	Marie Christine Cazier (FRA) 22.32	Silke Gladisch (GDR) 22.49
400m	Marita Koch (GDR) 48.22	Olga Vladykina (URS) 49.67	Petra Muller (GDR) 49.88
800m	Nadezhda Olizarenko (URS) 1:57.15	Sigrun Wodars (GDR) 1:57.42	Lyubov Gurina (URS) 1:57.73
1500m	Raviya Angletdinova (URS) 4:01.19	Tatiana Samolenko Dorovschin (URS) 4:02.36	Doina Melinte (ROM) 4:02.44
3000m	Olga Bodarenko (URS) 8:33.99	Maricica Puica (ROM) 8:35.92	Yvonne Murray (GBR) 8:37.15
10,000m	Ingrid Kristiansen (NOR) 30:23.25	Olga Bodarenko (URS) 30:57.21	Ulrike Bruns (GDR) 31:19.76
Marathon	Rosa Mota (POR) 2:28:38	Laura Fogli (ITA) 2:32:52	Yekaterina Khramamenko (URS) 2:34:18
100m Hurdles	Yordanka Donkova (BUL) 12.38	Cornelia Oschkenat (GDR) 12.55	Ginka Zagorcheva (BUL) 12.70
400m Hurdles	Marina Stepanova (URS) 53.32	Sabine Busch (GDR) 53.60	Cornelia Feuerbach (GDR) 54.13
10km Walk	Maria Cruz Diaz (ESP) 46.09	Ann Jansson (SWE) 46.13	Siw Ybanez (SWE) 46.19
4 × 100m Relay	German Democratic Republic 41.84	Bulgaria 42.68	Soviet Union 42.74
4 × 400m Relay	German Democratic Republic 3:16.87	Federal Republic of Germany 3:22.80	Poland 3:24.65
High Jump	Stefka Konstadinova (BUL) 2.00	Svetlana Issaeva (BUL) 1.93	Olga Turchak (URS) 1.93
Long Jump	Heike Drechsler (GDR) 7.27	Galina Chistyakova (URS) 7.09	Helga Radke (GDR) 6.89

Javelin	Fatima Whitbread (GBR) 76.32	Petra Felke (GDR) 72.52	Beate Peters (GDR) 68.04
Shot Put	Heidi Krieger (GDR) 21.10	Ines Muller (GDR) 20.81	Natalya Akhrimenko (URS) 20.54
Discus	Diana Sachse (GDR) 71.36	Tsvetanka Khristova (BUL) 69.52	Martina Hellmann (GDR) 68.26
Heptathlon	Anke Brehmer (GDR) 6717	Natalya Schubenkova (URS) 6645	Judy Simpson (GBR) 6623

1990 Split

Men's	Gold	Silver	Bronze
100m	Linford Christie (GBR) 10.00	Daniel Sangouma (FRA) 10.04	John Regis (GBR) 10.07
200m	John Regis (GBR) 20.11	Jean-Charles Troubal (FRA) 20.31	Linford Christie (GBR) 20.33
400m	Roger Black (GBR) 45.08	Thomas Schonlebe (GDR) 45.13	Jens Carlowitz (GDR) 45.27
800m	Tom McKean (GBR) 1:44.76	David Sharp (GBR) 1:45.59	Piotr Piekarski (POL) 1:45.76
1500m	Jens Peter Herold (GDR) 3:38.25	Gennaro di Napoli (ITA) 3:38.60	Mario Silva (POR) 3:38.73
5000m	Salvatore Antibo (ITA) 13:22.00	Gary Staines (GBR) 13:22.45	Slawomir Majusiak (POL) 13:22.92
10,000m	Salvatore Antibo (ITA) 27:41.27	Are Nakkim (NOR) 28:04.04	Stefano Mei (ITA) 28:04.46
Marathon	Gelindo Bordin (ITA) 2:14:02	Pier Giovanni Poli (ITA) 2:14:55	Dominique Chauvelier (FRA) 2:15:20
3000m Steeplechase	Francesco Panetta ITA) 8:12.66	Mark Rowland (GBR) 8:13.27	Alessandro Lambruschini (ITA) 8:15.82
110m Hurdles	Colin Jackson (GBR) 13.18	Tony Jarrett (GBR) 13.21	Dietmar Kozwewski (FRG) 13.50
400m Hurdles	Kriss Akabusi (GBR) 47.92	Sven Nylander (SWE) 48.43	Niklas Wallenlind (SWE) 48.52
20km Walk	Pavol Blazek (TCH) 1:22:05	Daniel Plaza (ESP) 1:22:22	Thierry Toutain (FRA) 1:23:22
50km Walk	Andrey Perlov (URS) 3:54:36	Bernt Gummelt (GDR) 3:56:33	Hartwig Gauder (GDR) 4:00:48
4 × 100m Relay	France 37.79	Great Britain 37.98	Italy 38.39
4 × 400m Relay	Great Britain 2:58.22	Federal Republic of Germany 3:00.64	German Democratic Republic 3:01.51
High Jump	Dragutin Topic (YUG) 2.34	Aleksey Yemelin (URS) 2.34	Georgi Dakov (BUL) 2.34
Pole Vault	Rodion Gataulin (URS) 5.85	Grigoriy Yegorev (URS) 5.75	Herman Fehringer (AUT) 5.75
Long Jump	Dietmar Haaf (FRG) 8.25	Angel Hernandez (ESP) 8.15	Franz Maas (NED) 8.09
Triple Jump	Leonid Voloshin (URS) 17.74	Khristo Markov (BUL) 17.43	Igor Lapshin (URS) 17.34
Shot Put	Ulf Timmermann (GDR) 21.32	Sven Buder (GDR) 21.01	Georg Andersen (NOR) 20.71
Discus	Jurgen Schult (GDR) 64.58	Erik de Bruin (NED) 64.46	Wolfgang Schmitz (FRG) 64.10
Hammer	Igor Astapkovich (URS) 84.14	Tibor Gecsec (HUN) 80.14	Igor Nikoulin (URS) 80.02
Javelin	Steve Backley (GBR) 87.30	Victor Zaitsev (URS) 83.30	Patrik Boden (SWE) 82.66
Decathlon	Christian Plaziat (FRA) 8574	Dezso Szabo (HUN) 8436	Christian Schenk (GDR) 8433

Women's	Gold	Silver	Bronze
100m	Katrin Krabbe (GDR) 10.89	Silke Moller (GDR) 11.10	Kerstin Behrendt (GDR) 11.17
200m	Katrin Krabbe (GDR) 21.95	Heike Drechsler (GDR) 22.19	Galina Malchugina (URS) 22.23
400m	Grit Breuer (GDR) 49.50	Petra Schersing (GDR) 50.51	Marie-José Perec (FRA) 50.84
800m	Sigrun Wodars (GDR) 1:55.87	Christine Wachtel (GDR) 1:56.11	Lilia Nurutdinova (URS) 1:57.39
1500m	Snezana Pajkic (YUG) 4:08.12	Ellen Kiessling (GDR) 4:08.67	Sandra Gasser (SUI) 4:08.89
3000m	Yvonne Murray (GBR) 8:43.06	Yelena Romanova (URS) 8:43.68	Roberta Brunet (ITA) 8:46.19
10,000m	Yelena Romanova (URS) 31:46.83	Kathrin Urlich (URS) 31:47.70	Annette Sergent (FRA) 31:51.68
Marathon	Rosa Mota (POR) 2:31:27	Valentina Yegorova (URS) 2:31:32	Maria Rebello (FRA) 2:35.51
100m Hurdles	Monique Ewanje Epee (FRA) 12.79	Gloria Siebert (GDR) 12.91	Lidiya Yurkova (URS) 12.92
400m Hurdles	Tatyana Ledovskaya (URS) 53.62	Anita Protti (SUI) 54.36	Monica Westen (SWE) 55.45
10km Walk	Annarita Sidoti (ITA) 44.00	Olga Kardopoltseva (URS) 44.06	Ileana Salvador (ITA) 44.38
4 × 100m Relay	German Democratic Republic 41.68	Federal Republic of Germany 43.09	Great Britain 43.32
4 × 400m Relay	German Democratic Republic 3:21.02	Soviet Union 3:23.34	Great Britain 3:24.78
High Jump	Heike Henkel (FRG) 1.99	Biljiana Petrovic (YUG) 1.96	Yelena Yelesina (URS) 1.96
Long Jump	Heike Drechsler (GDR) 7.30	Marieta Ilcu (ROM) 7.02	Helga Radtke (GDR) 6.94
Javelin	Paivi Alafrantti (FIN) 67.68	Karen Forkel (GDR) 67.56	Petra Felke (GDR) 66.56
Shot Put	Astrid Kumbernuss (GDR) 20.38	Natalya Lisovskaya (URS) 20.06	Kathrin Neimke (GDR) 19.96
Discus	Ilke Wyludda (GDR) 68.46	Olga Burova (URS) 66.72	Martina Hellmann (GDR) 66.66
Heptathlon	Sabine Braun (FRG) 6688	Heike Tischler (GDR) 6572	Peggy Beer (GDR) 6531

1994 Helsinki

Men's	Gold	Silver	Bronze
100m	Linford Christie (GBR) 10.14	Geir Moen (NOR) 10.20	Aleks Porkhomovskiy (RUS) 10.31
200m	Geir Moen (NOR) 20.30	Vladislav Dologodin (UKR) 20.47	Patrick Stevens (BEL) 20.68
400m	Duaine Ladejo (GBR) 45.09	Roger Black (GBR) 45.20	Matthias Rusterholz (SUI) 45.96
800m	Andrea Benvenuti (ITA) 1:46.12	Vebjørn Rodal (NOR) 1:46.53	Tomas de Teresa (ESP) 1:46.53
1500m	Fermain Cacho (ESP) 3:35.27	Isaac Viciosa (ESP) 3:36.01	Branko Zorko (CRO) 3:36.88
5000m	Dieter Baumann (GER) 13:36.93	Rob Denmark (GBR) 13:37.50	Abel Anton (ESP) 13:38.04
10,000m	Abel Anton (ESP) 28:06.03	Vincent Rousseau (BEL) 28:06.63	Stephane Franke (GER) 28:07.95

Marathon	Martin Fiz (ESP) 2:10:31	Diego Garcia (ESP) 2:10:46	Alberto Juzdado (ESP) 2:11:18
3000m Steeplechase	Alessandro Lambruschini (ITA) 8:22.40	Angelo Carosi (ITA) 8:23.53	William van Dijck (BEL) 8:24.86
110m Hurdles	Colin Jackson (GBR) 13.08	Florian Schwarthoff (GER) 13.16	Tony Jarrett (GBR) 13.23
400m Hurdles	Oleg Tverdokhleb (UKR) 48.06	Sven Nylander (SWE) 48.22	Stephane Diagana (FRA) 48.23
20km Walk	Mikhail Shchennikov (RUS) 1:18:45	Yevgeniy Misyula (BLR) 1:19:22	Valentin Massana (ESP) 1:20:33
50km Walk	Valeriy Spitsyn (RUS) 3:41:07	Thierry Toutain (FRA) 3:43:52	Giovanni Perricelli (ITA) 3:43:55
4 × 100m Relay	France 38.57	Ukraine 38.98	Italy 38.99
4 × 400m Relay	Great Britain 2:59.13	France 3:01.11	Russia 3:03.10
High Jump	Steinar Hoen (NOR) 2.35	Artur Partyka (POL) 2.33 Steve Smith (GBR) 2.33	—
Pole Vault	Rodion Gataullin (RUS) 6.00	Igor Trandenkov (RUS) 5.90	Jean Galfione (FRA) 5.85
Long Jump	Ivailo Mladenov (BUL) 8.09	Milan Gombala (CZE) 8.04	Kostas Koukodimos (GRE) 8.01
Triple Jump	Denis Kapustin (RUS) 17.62	Serge Halan (FRA) 17.55	Maria Bruzhiks (LAT) 17.20
Shot Put	Aleksandr Kilmenko (UKR) 20.78	Aleksandr Bagach (UKR) 20.34	Roman Virastyuk (UKR) 19.59
Discus	Vladimir Dubrovchik (BLR) 64.78	Dmitriy Shevchenko (RUS) 64.56	Jürgen Schult (GER) 64.18
Hammer	Vasiliy Sidorenko (RUS) 81.10	Igor Astapkovich (BLR) 80.40	Heinz Weis (GER) 78.48
Javelin	Steve Backley (GBR) 85.20	Seppo Raty (FIN) 82.90	Jan Zelezny (CZE) 82.58
Decathlon	Alain Blondel (FRA) 8453	Henrik Dagard (SWE) 8362	Lev Lobodin (UKR) 8201

Women's	Gold	Silver	Bronze
100m	Irina Privalova (RUS) 11.02	Zhanna Tarnopolskaya (UKR) 11.10	Melanie Paschke (GER) 11.28
200m	Irina Privalova (RUS) 22.32	Zhanna Tarnopolskaya (UKR) 22.77	Galina Malchugina (RUS) 22.90
400m	Marie-Jose Perec (FRA) 50.33	Svetlana Goncharenko (RUS) 51.24	Phylis Smith (GBR) 51.30
800m	Lyubov Gonna (RUS) 1:58.55	Natalya Dukhnova (BLR) 1:58.55	Lyudmila Rogachova (RUS) 1:58.69
1500m	Lyudmila Rogachova (RUS) 4:18.93	Kelly Holmes (GBR) 4:19.30	Yekaterina Podkopayeva (RUS) 4:19.37
3000m	Sonia O'Sullivan (IRL) 8:31.84	Yvonne Murray (GBR) 8:36.48	Gabriela Szabo (ROM) 8:40.08
10,000m	Fernanda Ribeiro (POR) 31:08.75	Conceicao Ferreira (POR) 31:32.82	Dana Nauer (SUI) 31:35.96
Marathon	Manuela Machado (POR) 2:29:54	Maria Curatolo (ITA) 2:30:33	Adriana Barbu (ROM) 2:30:55
100m Hurdles	Svetla Dimitrova (BUL) 12.72	Yuliya Graudyn (RUS) 12.93	Yordanka Donkova (BUL) 12.93
400m Hurdles	Sally Gunnell (GBR) 53.33	Silvia Rieger (GER) 54.68	Anna Knoroz (RUS) 54.68
10km Walk	Sari Essayah (FIN) 42.37	Annarita Sidoti (ITA) 42.43	Yelena Nikolayeva (RUS) 42.43
4 × 100m Relay	Germany 42.90	Russia 42.96	Bulgaria 43.00
4 × 400m Relay	France 3:22.34	Russia 3:24.06	Germany 3:24.10
High Jump	Brita Bilac (SLO) 2.00	Yelena Gulyayeva (RUS) 1.96	Noele Zilinskiene (LTU) 1.93
Long Jump	Heike Drechsler (GER) 7.14	Inessa Kravets (UKR) 6.99	Fiona May (ITA) 6.90
Triple Jump	Anna Biryukova (RUS) 14.89	Inna Lasovskaya (RUS) 14.85	Inessa Kravets (UKR) 14.67
Javelin	Trine Hattestad (NOR) 68.00	Karen Forkel (GER) 66.10	Felicia Tilea (ROM) 64.34
Shot Put	Viktoriya Pavlysh (UKR) 19.61	Astrid Kumbernuss (GER) 19.49	Svetla Mitkova (BUL) 19.49
Discus	Ilke Wyludda (GER) 68.72	Etlina Zvereva (BLR) 64.46	Mette Bergmann (NOR) 64.34
Heptathlon	Sabine Braun (GER) 6419	Rita Inansci (HUN) 6404	Urezula Wlodarczyk (POL) 6322

1998 Budapest

Men's	Gold	Silver	Bronze
100m	Darren Campbell (GBR) 10.04	Dwain Chambers (GBR) 10.10	C. Papadias (GRE) 10.17
200m	Doug Walker (GBR) 20.53	Doug Turner (GBR) 20.64	Julian Golding (GBR) 20.72
400m	Iwan Thomas (GBR) 44.52	Robert Mackowiak (POL) 45.04	Mark Richardson (GBR) 45.14
800m	Nils Schumann (GER) 1:44.89	André Bucher (SUI) 1:45.04	Lukas Vydra (CZE) 1:45.23
1500m	Reyes Estevez (ESP) 3:41.31	Rui Silva (POR) 3:41.84	Fermin Cacho (ESP) 3:42.13
5000m	Isaac Viciosa (ESP) 13:37.46	Manuel Pancorbo (ESP) 13:38.03	Mark Carroll (IRL) 13:38.15
10,000m	Antonio Pinto (POR) 27:48.62	Dieter Baumann (GER) 27:56.75	Stephane Franke (GER) 27:59.90
Marathon	Stefano Baldini (ITA) 2:12:01	Danilo Goffi (ITA) 2:12:11	Vincenzo Modica (ITA) 2:12:53
110m Hurdles	Colin Jackson (GBR) 13.02	Falk Balzer (GER) 13.12	Robin Korving (NED) 13.20
400m Hurdles	Pawel Januszewski (POL) 48.17	Ruslan Mashchenko (RUS) 48.25	Fabrizio Mori (ITA) 48.71
20km Walk	Ilya Markov (RUS) 1:21:10	Aigars Fadejevs (LAT) 1:21:25	Francisco Fernandez (ESP) 1:21:39
50km Walk	Robert Korzeniowski (POL) 3:43:51	Valentin Kononen (FIN) 3:44:29	Andrey Plotnikov (RUS) 3:45:53
4 × 100m Relay	Great Britain 38.52	France 38.87	Poland 38.98
4 × 400m Relay	Great Britain 2:58.68	Poland 2:58.88	Spain 3:02.47
High Jump	Atur Partyka (POL) 2.34	Dalton Grant (GBR) 2.34	Sergey Klyugin (RUS) 2.32
Pole Vault	Maksim Tarasov (RUS) 5.81	Tim Lobinger (GER) 5.81	Jean Galfione (FRA) 5.76
Long Jump	Kiril Sosunov (RUS) 8.28	Bogdan Tarus (ROM) 8.21	Petko Dacher (BUL) 8.06
Triple Jump	Jonathan Edwards (GBR) 17.99	Denis Kapustin (RUS) 17.45	R. Dimitrov (BUL) 17.26
Shot Put	Aleksandr Bagach (UKR) 21.17	Oliver Buder (GER) 20.98	Yuri Belonog (UKR) 20.92
Discus	Lars Riedel (GER) 67.07	Jurgen Schult (GER) 66.69	Virgilijus Alekna (LTU) 66.46
Hammer	Tibor Gecsek (HUN) 82.98	Balazs Kiss (HUN) 81.26	Karsten Kobs (GER) 80.13
Javelin	Steve Backley (GBR) 89.72	Mick Hill (GBR) 86.92	Raymond Hecht (GER) 86.63
Decathlon	Erki Nool (EST) 8667	E. Hamalainen (FIN) 8587	Lev Lobodin (RUS) 8571

Women's

Women's	Gold	Silver	Bronze
100m	Christine Arron (FRA) 10.73	Irina Privalova (RUS) 10.83	Ekaterini Thanou (GRE) 10.87
200m	Irina Privalova (RUS) 22.62	Zhanna Pintusevich (UKR) 22.74	Melanie Paschke (GER) 22.78
400m	Grit Breuer (GER) 49.93	Helena Fuchsova (CZE) 50.21	Olga Kotlyarova (RUS) 50.38
800m	Yelena Afanasyeva (RUS) 1:58.50	Malin Ewerlof (SWE) 1:59.61	Stephanie Graf (AUT) 2:00.11
1500m	Svetlana Masterkova (RUS) 4:11.91	Carla Sacramento (POR) 4:12.62	Anita Weyermann (SUI) 4:13.06
3000m	Sonia O'Sullivan (IRL) 15:06.50	Gabriela Szabo (ROM) 15:08.31	Marta Dominguez (ESP) 15:10.54
10,000m	Sonia O'Sullivan (IRL) 31:29.33	Fernanda Ribeiro (POR) 31:32.42	Lidia Simon (ROM) 31:32.64
Marathon	Manuela Machado (POR) 2:27:10	M. Biktagirova (RUS) 2:28:01	Maura Viceconte (ITA) 2:28:31
100m Hurdles	Svetla Dimitrova (BUL) 12.56	Brigita Bukovec (SLO) 12.65	Irina Korotya (RUS) 12.85
400m Hurdles	Ionela Tirlea (ROM) 53.37	Tatyana Tereshchuk (UKR) 54.07	Silvia Rieger (GER) 54.45
10km Walk	Annarita Sidoti (ITA) 42.49	Erica Alfridi (ITA) 42.54	Susana Feitor (POR) 42.55
4 × 100m Relay	France 42.59	Germany 42.68	Russia 42.73
4 × 400m Relay	Germany 3:23.03	Russia 3:23.56	Great Britain 3:25.66
High Jump	Monica Dinescu (ROM) 1.97	Donata Jancewicz (POL) 1.95	Alina Astafei (GER) 1.95
Pole Vault	Anzhela Balakhonova (UKR) 4.31	Rieger Humbert (GER) 4.31	Yvonne Buschbaum (GER) 4.31
Long Jump	Heike Drechsler (GER) 7.16	Fiona May (ITA) 7.11	Lyudmila Galkina (RUS) 7.06
Triple Jump	Olga Vasdeki (GRE) 14.55	Sarka Kasparkova (CZE) 14.53	Tereza Marinova (BUL) 14.50
Shot Put	Vita Pavlysh (UKR) 21.69	Irina Korzhanenko (RUS) 19.71	Yanina Korolchik (BLR) 19.23
Discus	Franka Dietzsch (GER) 67.49	Natalya Sadova (RUS) 66.94	Nicoleta Grasu (ROM) 65.94
Hammer	Mihaela Melinte (ROM) 71.17	Olga Kuzenkova (RUS) 69.28	Kirsten Muenchow (GER) 65.61
Javelin	Tanja Damaske (GER) 69.10	Tatyana Shikolenko (RUS) 66.92	Mikaela Ingberg (FIN) 64.92
Heptathlon	Denise Lewis (GBR) 6559	Urszula Wlodarczyk (POL) 6460	Natalya Sazanovich (BLR) 6410

2002 Munich

Men's

Men's	Gold	Silver	Bronze
100m	Dwain Chambers (GBR) 9.96	Francis Obikwelu (POR) 10.06	Darren Campbell (GBR) 10.15
200m	Konstantinos Kenteris (GRE) 19.85	Francis Obikwelu (POR) 20.21	Marlon Devonish (GBR) 20.24
400m	Ingo Schultz (GER) 45.14	David Canal (ESP) 45.24	Daniel Caines (GBR) 45.28
800m	Wilson Kipketer (DEN) 1:47.25	Andre Bucher (SUI) 1:47.43	Nils Schumann (GER) 1:47.60
1500m	Mehdi Baala (FRA) 3:45.25	Reyes Estevez (ESP) 3:45.25	Rui Silva (POR) 3:45.43
5000m	Alberto Garcia (ESP) 13:38.18	Ismail Sghyr (FRA) 13:39.81	Sergey Lebid (UKR) 13:40.00
10,000m	Jose Manuel Martinez (ESP) 27:47.65	Dieter Baumann (GER) 27:47.87	Jose Rios (ESP) 27:48.29
Marathon	Janne Holmen (FIN) 2:12:14	Pavel Loskutov (EST) 2:13:18	Julio Rey (ESP) 2:13:21
3000m Steeplechase	Antonio Jimenez (ESP) 8:24.34	Simon Vroemen (NED) 8:24.45	Luis Martin (ESP) 8:24.72
110m Hurdles	Colin Jackson (GBR) 13.11	Stanislavs Olijars (LAT) 13.22	Artur Kohutek (POL) 13.32
400m Hurdles	Stephane Diagana (FRA) 47.58	Jiri Muzik (CZE) 48.43	Pawel Januszewski (POL) 48.46
20km Walk	Francisco Fernandez (ESP) 1:18:37	Vladimir Andreyev (RUS) 1:19:56	Juan Molina (ESP) 1:20:36
50km Walk	Robert Korzeniowski (POL) 3:36:39	Aleksey Voyevodin (RUS) 3:40:16	Jose Garcia (ESP) 3:44:33
4 × 100m Relay	Great Britain 38.19	Ukraine 38.53	Poland 38.71
4 × 400m Relay	Great Britain 3:01.25	Russia 3:01.34	France 3:02.76
High Jump	Yaroslav Rybakov (RUS) 2.31	Stefan Holm (SWE) 2.29	Staffan Strand (SWE) 2.27
Pole Vault	Alex Averbukh (ISR) 5.85	Lars Borgeling (GER) 5.80	Tim Lobinger (GER) 5.80
Long Jump	Oleksiy Lukashevich (UKR) 8.08	Sinsa Ergotic (CRO) 8.00	Yago Lamela (ESP) 7.99
Triple Jump	Christian Olsson (SWE) 17.53	Charles Friedek (GER) 17.33	Jonathan Edwards (GBR) 17.32
Shot Put	Yuriy Belonog (UKR) 21.37	Joachim Olsen (DEN) 21.16	Ralf Bartels (GER) 20.58
Discus	Robert Fazekas (HUN) 68.83	Virgiiljus Alekna (LTU) 66.62	Michael Mollenbeck (GER) 66.37
Hammer	Adrian Annus (HUN) 81.17	Vladislav Piskunov (UKR) 80.39	Alexandros Papadimitriou (GRE) 80.21
Javelin	Steve Backley (GBR) 88.54	Sergey Makarov (RUS) 88.05	Boris Henry (GER) 85.33
Decathlon	Roman Sebrle (CZE) 8800	Erki Nool (EST) 8438	Lev Lobodin (RUS) 8390

Women's

Women's	Gold	Silver	Bronze
100m	Ekaterini Thanou (GRE) 11.10	Kim Gevaert (BEL) 11.22	Manuela Levorato (ITA) 11.23
200m	Muriel Hurtis (FRA) 22.43	Kim Gevaert (BEL) 22.53	Manuela Levorato (ITA) 22.75
400m	Olesya Zykina (RUS) 50.45	Grit Breuer (GER) 50.70	Lee McConnell (GBR) 51.02
800m	Jolanda Ceplak (SLO) 1:57.65	Mayte Martinez (ESP) 1:58.86	Kelly Holmes (GBR) 1:59.83
1500m	Sureyya Ayhan (TUR) 3:58.79	Gabriela Szabo (ROM) 3:58.81	Tatyana Tomashova (RUS) 4:01.28
5000m	Marta Dominguez (ESP) 15:14.76	Sonia O'Sullivan (IRL) 15:14.85	Yelena Zadorozhnaya (RUS) 15:15.22
10,000m	Paula Radcliffe (GBR) 30:01.09	Sonia O'Sullivan (IRL) 30:47.59	Lyudmila Biktasheva (RUS) 31:04.00
Marathon	Maria Guida (ITA) 2:26:05	Luminita Zaituc (GER) 2:26:58	Sonja Oberem (GER) 2:28:45
100m Hurdles	Glory Alozie (ESP) 12.73	Olena Krasovska (UKR) 12.88	Yana Kasova (BUL) 12.91
400m Hurdles	Ionela Tirlea (ROM) 54.95	Heike Meissner (GER) 55.89	Anna Olichwierczuk (POL) 56.18
20km Walk	Olimpiada Ivanova (RUS) 1:26:42	Yelena Nikolayeva (RUS) 1:28:20	Erica Alfridi (ITA) 1:28:33
4 × 100m Relay	France 42.46	Germany 42.54	Russia 43.11
4 × 400m Relay	Germany 3:25.10	Russia 3:25.59	Poland 3:26.15

High Jump	Kajsa Berqvist (SWE) 1.98	Marina Kuptsova (RUS) 1.92	Olga Kaliturina (RUS) 1.89
Pole Vault	Svetlana Feofanova (RUS) 4.60	Yelena Isinbayeva (RUS) 4.55	Yvonne Buschbaum (GER) 4.50
Long Jump	Tatyana Kotova (RUS) 6.85	Jade Johnson (GBR) 6.73	Tunde Vaszi (HUN) 6.73
Triple Jump	Ashia Hansen (GBR) 15.00	Heli Koivula (FIN) 14.83	Yelena Oleynikova (RUS) 14.54
Shot Put	Irina Korzhanenko (RUS) 20.64	Vita Pavlysh (UKR) 20.02	Svetlana Krivelova (RUS) 19.56
Discus	Ekaterini Vogoli (GRE) 64.31	Natalya Sadova (RUS) 64.12	Anastasia Kelesidou (GRE) 63.92
Hammer	Olga Kuzenkova (RUS) 72.94	Kamila Skolimowska (POL) 72.46	Manuela Montebrun (FRA) 72.04
Javelin	Mirela Manjani (GRE) 67.47	Steffi Nerius (GER) 64.09	Mikaela Ingberg (FIN) 63.50
Heptathlon	Caroline Kluft (SWE) 6542	Sabine Braun (GER) 6434	Natalya Sazanovich (BEL) 6341

Commonwealth Games

NOTE: Where times are not shown they were not recorded but estimated. Between 1958 and 1966 all measurements are imperial. Before 1958 and from 1970 onwards, all measurements are metric as they were originally recorded. Metric equivalents are given in brackets in 1958, 1962 and 1966.

1930 Hamilton

Men's	Gold	Silver	Bronze
100yds	Percy Williams (CAN) 9.9	Ernest Page (ENG) 10.2	John Fitzpatrick (CAN) 10.2
220yds	Stanley Englehart (ENG) 21.8	John Fitzpatrick (CAN)	William Walters (SAF)
440yds	Alex Wilson (CAN) 48.8	William Walters (SAF) 48.9	George Golding (AUS)
880yds	Thomas Hampson (ENG) 1:52.4	Reg Thomas (ENG) 1:56.4	Alex Wilson (CAN) 1:56.5
1 Mile	Reg Thomas (ENG) 4:14.0	William Whyte (AUS)	Jerry Cornes (ENG)
3 Miles	Stan Tomlin (ENG) 14:27.4	Alex Hillhouse (AUS) 14:27.6	Jack Winfield (ENG) 14:28.0
6 Miles	John Savidan (NZL) 30:49.6	Ernest Harper (ENG)	Tom Evenson (ENG)
Marathon	Duncan Wright (SCO) 2:43:43	Sam Ferris (ENG) 2:47:13	Johnny Miles (CAN) 2:48:23
2 Miles Steeplechase	George Bailey (ENG) 9:52.0	Alex Hillhouse (AUS)	Vernon Morgan (ENG)
120yds Hurdles	Lord Burghley (ENG) 14.6	Howard Davies (SAF) 14.7	Fred Gaby (ENG)
440yds Hurdles	Lord Burghley (ENG) 54.4	Roger Leigh-Wood (ENG) 55.9	Douglas Neame (ENG)
4 × 110yds Relay	Canada 42.2	England 42.7	South Africa
4 × 440yds Relay	England 3:19.4	Canada 3:19.8	South Africa
High Jump	Johannes Viljoen (SAF) 1.90	Colin Gordon (BGU) 1.88	William Stargratt (CAN) 1.85
Pole Vault	Victor Pickard (CAN) 3.73	Howard Ford (ENG) 3.73	Robert Stoddard (CAN) 3.66
Triple Jump	Gordon Smallacombe (CAN) 14.76	Reginald Revans (ENG) 14.29	Leonard Hutton (CAN) 13.90
Long Jump	Leonard Hutton (CAN) 7.20	Reginald Revans (ENG) 6.96	Johannes Viljoen (SAF) 6.86
Shot Put	Harry Hart (SAF) 14.58	Robert Howland (ENG) 13.46	Charles Herman (CAN) 12.98
Discus	Harry Hart (SAF) 41.43	Charlie Herman (CAN) 41.22	Abe Zvonkin (CAN) 41.18
Javelin	Stanley Lay (NZL) 63.13	Doral Pilling (CAN) 55.94	Harry Hart (SAF) 53.22
Hammer	Malcolm Nokes (ENG) 47.13	Bill Britton (IRE) 46.90	John Cameron (CAN) 44.46

1934 London

Men's	Gold	Silver	Bronze
100yds	Arthur Sweeney (ENG) 10.0	Martinus Theunisson (SAF) 10.0	Ian Young (SCO) 10.1
220yds	Arthur Sweeney (ENG) 21.9	Martinus Theunisson (SAF) 22.0	Walter Rangeley (ENG) 22.1
440yds	Godfrey Rampling (ENG) 48.0	Bill Roberts (ENG) 48.5	Crew Stoneley (ENG) 48.6
880yds	Phil Edwards (GUY) 1:54.2	Johannes Botha (SAF) 1:55.0	James Stothard (SCO) 1:55.1
1 Mile	Jack Lovelock (NZL) 4:12.8	Sydney Wooderson (ENG) 4:13.4	Jerry Cornes (ENG) 4:13.6
3 Miles	Walter Beavers (ENG) 14:32.6	Charles Allen (ENG) 14:37.8	Alex Burns (ENG) 14:45.4
6 Miles	Arthur Penny (ENG) 31:00.6	Robert Rankine (CAN) 31:01.6	Arthur Furze (ENG)
Marathon	Harold Webster (CAN) 2:40:36	Donald Robertson (SCO) 2:45:08	Duncan Wright (SCO) 2:56:20
2 Miles Steeplechase	Stanley Scarsbrook (ENG) 10:23.4	Tom Everson (ENG) 10:25.8	George Bailey (ENG)
120yds Hurdles	Don Finlay (ENG) 15.2	Jim Worrall (CAN) 15.5	Ashleigh Pilbrow (ENG) 15.7
440yds Hurdles	Alan Hunter (SCO) 55.2	Charles Reilly (AUS) 55.8	Ralph Brown (ENG) 56.0
4 × 110yds Relay	England 42.2	Canada 42.5	Scotland 43.0
4 × 440yds Relay	England 3:16.8	Canada 3:17.4	Scotland
High Jump	Edwin Thacker (SAF) 1.96	Joseph Haley (CAN) 1.90	James Michie (SCO) 1.90
Pole Vault	Sylvanus Apps (CAN) 3.81	Alfred Gilbert (CAN) 3.81	Fred Woodhouse (AUS) 3.73
Triple Jump	Jack Metcalfe (AUS) 15.63	Sam Richardson (CAN) 14.65	Harold Brainsbury (NZL) 14.62
Long Jump	Sam Richardson (CAN) 7.17	Johann Luckhoff (SAF) 7.10	Jack Metcalfe (AUS) 6.93
Shot Put	Harry Hart (SAF) 14.67	Robert Howland (ENG) 13.53	Kenneth Pridie (ENG) 13.43
Discus	Harry Hart (SAF) 41.53	Douglas Bell (ENG) 40.44	Bernard Prendergast (JAM) 40.24
Javelin	Bob Dixon (CAN) 60.02	Harry Hart (SAF) 58.28	Johann Luckhoff (SAF) 56.50
Hammer	Malcolm Nokes (ENG) 48.25	George Sutherland (CAN) 46.25	William McKenzie (SCO) 42.50

ATHLETICS

Women's	Gold	Silver	Bronze
100yds	Eileen Hiscock (ENG) 11.3	Hilda Strike (CAN) 11.5	Lilian Chalmers (ENG) 11.6
220yds	Eileen Hiscock (ENG) 25.0	Aileen Meagher (CAN) 25.4	Nellie Halstead (ENG) 25.6
880yds	Gladys Lunn (ENG) 2.19.4	Ida Jones (ENG) 2:21.0	Dorothy Butterfield (ENG) 2:21.4
80yds Hurdles	Marjorie Clark (SAF) 11.8	Betty Taylor (CAN) 11.9	Elsie Green (ENG) 12.2
110 × 220 × 110yds Relay	England 49.4	Canada 50.2	Rhodesia 52.0
220 × 110 × 220 × 110yds Relay	Canada 1:14.4	England	Scotland
High Jump	Marjorie Clark (SAF) 1.60	Eva Dawes (CAN) 1.57	Margaret Bell (CAN) 1.52
Long Jump	Phyllis Bartholomew (ENG) 5.47	Evelyn Goshawk (CAN) 5.41	Violet Webb (ENG) 5.23
Javelin	Gladys Lunn (ENG) 32.19	Edith Halstead (ENG) 30.94	Margaret Cox (ENG) 30.08

1938 Sydney

Men's	Gold	Silver	Bronze
100yds	Cyril Holmes (ENG) 9.7	John Mumford (AUS) 9.8	Edward Best (AUS) 9.8
220yds	Cyril Holmes (ENG) 21.2	John Mumford (AUS) 21.3	Edward Best (AUS) 21.4
440yds	Bill Roberts (ENG) 47.9	William Fritz (CAN) 47.9	Denis Shore (SAF) 48.1
880yds	Vernon Boot (NZL) 1:51.2	Frank Handley (ENG) 1:53.5	William Dale (CAN) 1:53.6
1 Mile	Jim Alford (WAL) 4:11.6	Gerald Backhouse (AUS) 4:12.2	Vernon Boot (NZL) 4:12.6
3 Miles	Cecil Matthews (NZL) 13:59.6	Peter Ward (ENG) 14:05.4	Bob Rankine (CAN) 14:24.0
6 Miles	Cecil Matthews (NZL) 30:14.5	Bob Rankine (CAN)	Wally Hayward (SAF)
Marathon	Johannes Coleman (SAF) 2:30:50	Albert Norris (ENG) 2:37:57	Jackie Gibson (SAF) 2:38:20
120yds Hurdles	Tom Lavery (SAF) 14.0	Larry O'Connor (CAN) 14.2	Sid Stenner (AUS) 14.4
440yds Hurdles	John Loaring (CAN) 52.9	John Park (AUS) 54.6	Alan McDougall (AUS) 55.2
4 × 110yds Relay	Canada 41.6	England 41.8	Australia 41.9
4 × 440yds Relay	Canada 3:16.9	England 3:19.5	New Zealand 3:22.5
High Jump	Edwin Thacker (SAF) 1.96	Robert Heffernan (AUS) 1.88	Douglas Shetliffe (AUS) 1.88
Pole Vault	Andries du Plessis (SAF) 4.11	Les Fletcher (AUS) 3.97	Stuart Frid (CAN) 3.88
Triple Jump	Jack Metcalfe (AUS) 15.63	Lloyd Miller (AUS) 15.41	Basil Dickinson (AUS) 15.28
Long Jump	Harold Brown (CAN) 7.43	James Panton (CAN) 7.25	Basil Dickinson (AUS) 7.15
Shot Put	Louis Fouche (SAF) 14.48	Eric Coy (CAN) 13.96	Francis Drew (AUS) 13.80
Discus	Eric Coy (CAN) 44.76	David Young (SCO) 43.05	George Sutherland (CAN) 41.47
Javelin	Jim Courtright (CAN) 62.81	Stanley Lay (NZL) 62.21	Jack Metcalfe (AUS) 55.53
Hammer	George Sutherland (CAN) 48.71	Keith Pardon (AUS) 45.13	James Leckie (NZL) 44.34

Women's	Gold	Silver	Bronze
100yds	Decima Norman (AUS) 11.1	Joyce Walker (AUS) 11.3	Jeanette Dolson (CAN) 11.4
220yds	Decima Norman (AUS) 24.7	Jean Cloeman (AUS) 25.1	Eileen Wearne (AUS) 25.3
80yds Hurdles	Barbara Burke (SAF) 11.7	Isabel Grant (AUS) 11.7	Rona Tong (NZL) 11.8
110 × 220 × 110yds Relay	Australia 49.1	Canada 49.9	England 51.3
220 × 110 × 110yds Relay	Australia 1:15.2	England 1:17.2	Canada 1:19.0
High Jump	Dorothy Odam (ENG) 1.60	Dora Gardner (ENG) 1.57	Elizabeth Forbes (NZL) 1.57
Long Jump	Decima Norman (AUS) 5.80	Ethel Raby (ENG) 5.66	Thelma Peake (AUS) 5.55
Javelin	Robina Higgins (CAN) 38.28	Antonia Robertson (SAF) 36.98	Gladys Lunn (ENG) 36.41

1950 Auckland

Men's	Gold	Silver	Bronze
100yds	John Treloar (AUS) 9.7	Bill de Gruchy (AUS) 9.8	Donald Pettie (CAN) 9.9
220yds	John Treloar (AUS) 21.5	David Johnson (AUS) 21.8	Donald Jowett (NZL) 21.8
440yds	Edwin Carr (AUS) 47.9	Les Lewis (ENG) 48.0	David Batten (NZL) 48.8
880yds	John Parlett (ENG) 1:53.1	Jack Hutchins (CAN) 1:53.4	William Parnell (CAN) 1:53.4
1 Mile	William Parnell (CAN) 4:11.0	Len Eyre (ENG) 4:11.8	Maurice Marshall (NZL) 4:13.2
3 Miles	Len Eyre (ENG) 14:23.6	Harold Nelson (NZL) 14:27.8	Anthony Chivers (ENG) 14:28.1
6 Miles	Harold Nelson (NZL) 30:29.6	Andrew Forbes (SCO) 30:31.9	Noel Taylor (NZL) 30:31.9
Marathon	Jack Holden (ENG) 2:32:57	Sydney Luyt (SAF) 2:37.02	James Clark (NZL) 2:39:26
120yds Hurdles	Peter Gardner (AUS) 14.3	Ray Weinberg (AUS) 14.4	Tom Lavery (SAF) 14.6
440yds Hurdles	Duncan White (CEY) 52.5	John Holland (NZL) 52.7	Geoff Goodacre (AUS) 53.1
4 × 110yds Relay	Australia 42.2	England 42.5	New Zealand 42.6
4 × 440yds Relay	Australia 3:17.8	England 3:19.3	New Zealand 3:20.0
High Jump	John Winter (AUS) 1.98	Joshua Majekodunmi (NGR) 1.95 Alan Paterson (SCO) 1.95	
Pole Vault	Tim Paterson (ENG) 3.97	Stan Egerton (CAN) 3.97	Peter Denton (AUS) 3.88
Triple Jump	Brian Oliver (AUS) 15.61	Leslie McKeand (AUS) 15.28	Ian Polmear (AUS) 14.67
Long Jump	Neville Price (SAF) 7.31	Bevan Hough (NZL) 7.20	David Dephoff (NZL) 7.08
Shot Put	Maitaika Tuicakau (FIJ) 14.64	Harold Moody (ENG) 13.92	Leo Roininen (CAN) 13.68
Discus	Ian Reed (AUS) 47.72	Mataika Tuicakau (FIJ) 43.96	Svein Sigfusson (CAN) 43.48
Javelin	Leo Robinson (CAN) 57.11	Luke Tunabuna (FIJ) 56.02	Doug Robinson (CAN) 55.60

Hammer	Duncan Clark (SCO) 49.94	Keith Pardon (AUS) 47.84	Herbert Baker (AUS) 45.62
Women's	**Gold**	**Silver**	**Bronze**
100yds	Marjorie Jackson (AUS) 10.8	Shirley Strickland (AUS) 11.0	Verna Johnston (AUS) 11.1
220yds	Marjorie Jackson (AUS) 24.3	Shirley Strickland (AUS) 24.5	Daphne Robb (SAF) 25.0
80yds Hurdles	Shirley Strickland (AUS) 11.6	June Schoch (NZL) 11.6	Joan Shackleton (NZL) 11.7
110 × 220 × 110yds Relay	Australia 47.9	England 48.7	Canada 50.0
220 × 110 × 110yds Relay	Australia 1:13.4	England 1:17.5	Canada
High Jump	Dorothy Tyler (ENG) 1.60	Bertha Crowther (ENG) 1.60	Noeline Swinton (NZL) 1.55
Long Jump	Yvette Williams (NZL) 5.91	Judith Canty (AUS) 5.77	Ruth Dowman (NZL) 5.74
Javelin	Charlotte MacGibbon (AUS) 38.84	Yvette Williams (NZL) 37.96	Cleo Rivette-Carnac (NZL) 34.43

1954 Vancouver

Men's	**Gold**	**Silver**	**Bronze**
100yds	Mike Agostini (TRI) 9.6	Don McFarlane (CAN) 9.7	Hec Hogan (AUS) 9.7
220yds	Donald Jowett (NZL) 21.5	Brian Shenton (ENG) 21.5	Ken Jones (WAL) 21.9
440yds	Kevan Gosper (AUS) 47.2	Donald Jowett (NZL) 47.4	Terry Tobacco (CAN) 47.8
880yds	Derek Johnson (ENG) 1:50.7	Brian Hewson (ENG) 1:51.2	Ian Boyd (ENG) 1:51.9
1 Mile	Roger Bannister (ENG) 3:58.8	John Landy (AUS) 3:59.6	Rich Ferguson (CAN) 4:04.6
3 Miles	Chris Chataway (ENG) 13:35.2	Fred Green (ENG) 13:37.2	Frank Sando (ENG) 13:37.4
6 Miles	Peter Driver (ENG) 29:09.04	Frank Sando (ENG) 29:10.0	Jim Peters (ENG) 29:20.0
Marathon	Joseph McGhee (SCO) 2:39:36	Jack Meckler (SAF) 2:40:57	Johannes Barnard (SAF) 2:51:50
120yds Hurdles	Keith Gardner (JAM) 14.2	Chris Higham (ENG) 14.9	Norman Williams (CAN) 14.9
440yds Hurdles	David Lean (AUS) 52.4	Harry Kane (ENG) 53.3	Bob Shaw (WAL) 53.3
4 × 110yds Relay	Canada 41.3	Nigeria 41.3	Australia 41.7
4 × 440yds Relay	England 3:11.2	Canada 3:11.6	Australia 3:16.0
High Jump	Emmanuel Ifeajuna (NGR) 2.03	Patrick Etolu (UGA) 1.99	Nafiu Osagie (NGR) 1.99
Pole Vault	Geoff Elliott (ENG) 4.26	Ron Miller (CAN) 4.20	Andries Burger (SAF) 4.13
Triple Jump	Ken Wilmshurst (ENG) 15.28	Peter Esiri (NGR) 15.25	Brian Oliver (AUS) 15.14
Long Jump	Ken Wilmshurst (ENG) 7.54	Karim Oluwu (NGR) 7.39	Sylvanus Williams (NGR) 7.22
Shot Put	John Savidge (ENG) 16.77	John Pavelich (CAN) 14.95	Stephanus du Plessis (SAF) 14.93
Discus	Stephanus du Plessis (SAF) 51.71	Roy Pella (CAN) 49.54	Mark Pharoah (ENG) 47.85
Javelin	James Archurch (AUS) 68.52	Muhammad Nawwaz (PAK) 68.09	Jalal Khan (PAK) 67.50
Hammer	Muhammad Iqbal (PAK) 55.38	Jakobus Dreyer (SAF) 54.75	Ewan Douglas (SCO) 52.80
Women's	**Gold**	**Silver**	**Bronze**
100yds	Marjorie Jackson (AUS) 10.7	Winsome Cripps (AUS) 10.8	Edna Maskell (ZAM) 10.8
220yds	Marjorie Jackson (AUS) 24.0	Winsome Cripps (AUS) 24.5	Shirley Hampton (ENG) 25.0
80yds Hurdles	Edna Maskell (NRH) 10.9	Gwendolyn Hobbins (CAN) 11.2	Jean Desforges (ENG) 11.2
4 × 110yds Relay	Australia 46.8	England 46.9	Canada 47.8
High Jump	Thelma Hopkins (NIR) 1.67	Dorothy Tyler (ENG) 1.60	Alice Whitty (CAN) 1.60
Long Jump	Yvette Williams (NZL) 6.08	Thelma Hopkins (NIR) 5.84	Jean Desforges (ENG) 5.84
Shot Put	Yvette Williams (NZL) 13.96	Jacqueline McDonald (CAN) 12.98	Magdalena Swanepoel (SAF) 12.81
Discus	Yvette Williams (NZL) 45.01	Suzanne Allday (ENG) 40.02	Marie Depree (CAN) 38.66
Javelin	Magdalena Swanepoel (SAF) 43.83	Pearl Fisher (NRH) 41.97	Shirley Couzens (CAN) 38.98

1958 Cardiff

Men's	**Gold**	**Silver**	**Bronze**
100yds	Keith Gardner (JAM) 9.4	Thomas Robinson (BAH) 9.5	Michael Agostini (CAN) 9.6
220yds	Thomas Robinson (BAH) 21.0	Keith Gardner (JAM) 21.0	Gordon Day (SAF) 21.1
440yds	Milkha Singh (IND) 46.6	Malcolm Spence (SAF) 46.9	Terry Tobacco (CAN) 47.0
880yds	Herb Elliott (AUS) 1:49.3	Brian Hewson (ENG) 1:49.5	Michael Rawson (ENG) 1:51.1
1 Mile	Herb Elliott (AUS) 3:59.0	Mervyn Lincoln (AUS) 4:01.9	Albert Thomas (AUS) 4:02.7
3 Miles	Murray Halberg (NZL) 13:15.0	Albert Thomas (AUS) 13:24.4	Neville Scot (NZL) 13:26.2
6 Miles	David Power (AUS) 28:47.8	John Merriman (WAL) 28:48.8	Arere Anentia (KEN) 28:51.2
Marathon	David Power (AUS) 2:22:46	Johannes Barnard (SAF) 2:22:57	Peter Wilkinson (ENG) 2:24:42
120yds Hurdles	Keith Gardner (JAM) 14.0	Jacobus Swart (SAF) 14.2	Ghulam Raziq (PAK) 14.3
440yds Hurdles	Gerhardus Potgieter (SAF) 49.7	David Lean (AUS) 50.6	Bartonjo Rotich (KEN) 51.7
4 × 110yds Relay	England 41.0	Nigeria 41.0	Australia 41.5
4 × 440yds Relay	South Africa 3:08.1	England 3:09.6	Jamaica 3:10.0
High Jump	Ernie Haisley (JAM) 6.9 (2.06)	Charles Porter (AUS) 6.8 (2.03)	Richard Kotei (GHA) 6.7 (2.00)
Pole Vault	Geoffrey Elliott (ENG) 13.8 (4.16)	Bob Reid (CAN) 13.8 (4.16)	Mervyn Richards (NZL) 13.8 (4.16)
Triple Jump	Ian Tomlinson (AUS) 51.7 (15.74)	Jack Smyth (CAN) 51.6 (15.69)	David Norris (NZL) 50.8 (15.45)
Long Jump	Paul Foreman (JAM) 24.6 (7.47)	Derrick Taylor (JAM) 24.6 (7.47)	Ramzan Ali (PAK) 24.0 (7.32)
Shot Put	Arthur Rowe (ENG) 57.8 (17.57)	Martyn Lucking (ENG) 54.2 (16.50)	Barry Donath (AUS) 51.1 (15.79)
Discus	Stephanus du Plessis (SAF) 183.6 (55.94)	Leslie Mills (NZL) 169.8 (51.73)	Gerald Carr (ENG) 169.4 (51.62)

A
T
H
L
E
T
I
C
S

Javelin	Colin Smith (ENG) 233.10 (71.29)	Jalal Khan (PAK) 232.4 (70.83)	Hans Moks (CAN) 231.0 (70.41)
Hammer	Michael Ellis (ENG) 206.4 (62.90)	Muhammad Iqbal (PAK) 202.5 (61.70)	Peter Allday (ENG) 188.11 (57.58)

Women's	Gold	Silver	Bronze
100yds	Marlene Matthews-Willard (AUS) 10.6	Heather Young (ENG) 10.6	Madeleline Weston (ENG) 10.7
220yds	Marlene Matthews-Willard (AUS) 23.6	Betty Cuthbert (AUS) 23.6	Heather Young (ENG) 23.9
80yds Hurdles	Norma Thrower (AUS) 10.7	Carole Quinton (ENG) 10.7	Gloria Cooke-Wigney (AUS) 10.9
4 × 110yds Relay	England 45.3	Australia 46.1	Canada 47.2
High Jump	Micheline Mason (AUS) 5.7 (1.70)	Mary Donaghy (NZL) 5.7 (1.70)	Helen Frith (AUS) 5.5 (1.65)
Long Jump	Sheila Hoskin (ENG) 19.9 (6.02)	Mary Bignal (ENG) 19.7 (5.97)	Beverley Watson (AUS) 19.7 (5.97)
Shot Put	Valerie Sloper (NZL) 51.0 (15.54)	Sue Allday (ENG) 47.5 (14.44)	Jacqueline Gelling (CAN) 46.1 (14.03)
Discus	Sue Allday (ENG) 150.8 (45.91)	Jennifer Thompson (NZL) 148.7 (45.29)	Valerie Sloper (NZL) 147.5 (44.94)
Javelin	Anna Pazera (AUS) 188.4 (57.41)	Magdalena Swanepoel (SAF) 159.10 (48.73)	Averil Williams (ENG) 153.5 (46.78)

1962 Perth

Men's	Gold	Silver	Bronze
100yds	Serafino Antao (KEN) 9.5	Tom Robinson (BAH) 9.6	Michael Cleary (AUS) 9.6
220yds	Serafino Antao (KEN) 21.1	Dave Jones (ENG) 21.5	Johann du Preez (RHO) 21.6
440yds	George Kerr (JAM) 46.7	Robbie Brightwell (ENG) 46.8	Amos Omolo (UGA) 46.8
880yds	Peter Snell (NZL) 1:47.6	George Kerr (JAM) 1:47.8	Anthony Blue (AUS) 1:49.0
1 Mile	Peter Snell (NZL) 4:04.06	John Davies (NZL) 4:05.1	Terence Sullivan (RHO) 4:06.6
3 Miles	Murray Halberg (NZL) 13:34.2	Ron Clarke (AUS) 13:36.0	Bruce Kidd (CAN) 13:36.4
6 Miles	Bruce Kidd (CAN) 28:26.6	David Power (AUS) 28:34.0	John Merriman (WAL) 28:40.8
Marathon	Brian Kilby (ENG) 2:21:17	David Power (AUS) 2:22:15	Rod Bonella (AUS) 2:24:07
3000m Steeplechase	Trevor Vincent (AUS) 8:43.4	Maurice Herriott (ENG) 8:45.0	Ron Blackney (AUS) 9:00.6
120yds Hurdles	Ghulam Raziq (PAK) 14.3	David Prince (AUS) 14.4	Laurence Taitt (ENG) 14.7
440yds Hurdles	Ken Roche (AUS) 51.5	Kimaru Songok (KEN) 51.9	Benson Ishiepai (UGA) 52.3
4 × 110yds Relay	England 40.6	Ghana 40.6	Wales 40.8
4 × 440yds Relay	Jamaica 3:10.2	England 3:11.2	Ghana 3:12.3
High Jump	Percy Hobson (AUS) 6.11 (2.11)	Charles Porter (AUS) 6.10 (2.08)	Anton Norris (BAR) 6.8 (2.03)
Pole Vault	Trevor Bickle (AUS) 14.9 (4.49)	Daniel Burger (RHO) 14.6 (4.42)	Ross Filshie (AUS) 14.6 (4.42)
Triple Jump	Ian Tomlinson (AUS) 53.2 (16.20)	John Baguley (AUS) 52.9 (16.08)	Fred Alsop (ENG) 52.7 (16.03)
Long Jump	Michael Ahey (GHA) 26.5 (8.05)	Dave Norris (NZL) 25.5 (7.74)	Wellesley Clayton (JAM) 25.4 (7.72)
Shot Put	Martyn Lucking (ENG) 59.4 (18.08)	Michael Lindsay (SCO) 59.3 (18.05)	Dave Steen (CAN) 58.9 (17.90)
Discus	Warwick Selvey (AUS) 185.4 (56.48)	Michael Lindsay (SCO) 172.6 (52.58)	John Sheldrick (ENG) 166.3 (50.67)
Javelin	Alf Mitchell (AUS) 256.3 (78.11)	Colin Smith (ENG) 255.8 (77.94)	Nick Birks (AUS) 246.3 (75.07)
Hammer	Howard Payne (ENG) 202.3 (61.65)	Richard Leffler (AUS) 196.3 (59.33)	Robert Brown (AUS) 189.1 (57.64)

Women's	Gold	Silver	Bronze
100yds	Dorothy Hyman (ENG) 11.2	Doreen Porter (NZL) 11.3	Brenda Cox (AUS) 11.4
220yds	Dorothy Hyman (ENG) 23.8	Joyce Bennett (AUS) 24.2	Margaret Burvill (AUS) 24.5
880yds	Dixie Willis (AUS) 2:03.7	Marise Chamberlain (NZL) 2:05.7	Joy Jordan (ENG) 2:05.9
80yds Hurdles	Pamela Kilborn (AUS) 10.9	Betty Moore (ENG) 11.3	Avis McIntosh (NZL) 11.4
4 × 110yds Relay	Australia 46.6	England 46.6	New Zealand 46.9
High Jump	Robyn Woodhouse (AUS) 5.10 (1.78)	Helen Frith (AUS) 5.8 (1.73)	Micheline Mason (AUS) 5.8 (1.73)
Long Jump	Pamela Kilborn (AUS) 20.7 (6.27)	Helen Frith (AUS) 20.6 (6.24)	Janet Knee (AUS) 20.1 (6.13)
Shot Put	Valerie Young (NZL) 49.11 (15.23)	Jean Roberts (AUS) 47.7 (14.52)	Suzanne Allday (ENG) 44.6 (13.56)
Discus	Valerie Young (NZL) 164.8 (50.20)	Rosslyn Williams (AUS) 153.1 (46.66)	Mary McDonald (AUS) 151.8 (46.23)
Javelin	Sue Platt (ENG) 164.10 (50.25)	Rosemary Morgan (ENG) 162.9 (49.62)	Anna Pazera (AUS) 159.8 (48.68)

1966 Kingston

Men's	Gold	Silver	Bronze
100yds	Harry Jerome (CAN) 9.4	Tom Robinson (BAH) 9.4	Edwin Roberts (TRI) 9.5
220yds	Stanley Allotey (GHA) 20.7	Edwin Roberts (TRI) 20.9	David Njoke (NGR) 21.0
440yds	Wendell Mottley (TRI) 45.0	Kent Bernard (TRI) 46.1	Don Domansky (CAN) 46.4
880yds	Noel Clough (AUS) 1:46.9	Wilson Kiprugut (KEN) 1:47.2	George Kerr (JAM) 1:47.2

1 Mile	Kip Keino (KEN) 3:55.3	Alan Simpson (ENG) 3:57.1	Ian Studd (NZL) 3:58.4
3 Miles	Kip Keino (KEN) 12:57.4	Ron Clarke (AUS) 12:59.2	Allan Rushmer (ENG) 13:08.6
6 Miles	Naftali Temu (KEN) 27:14.6	Ron Clarke (AUS) 27:39.4	Jim Alder (SCO) 28:15.4
Marathon	Jim Alder (SCO) 2:22:07	Bill Adcocks (ENG) 2:22:13	Mike Ryan (NZL) 2:27:59
3000m Steeplechase	Peter Welsh (NZL) 8:29.6	Kerry O'Brien (AUS) 8:32.4	Benjamin Kogo (KEN) 8:33.0
120yds Hurdles	David Hemery (ENG) 14.1	Mike Parker (ENG) 14.2	Ghulam Raziq (PAK) 14.3
440yds Hurdles	Ken Roche (AUS) 51.0	Kingsley Agbabokha (NGR) 51.5	Peter Warden (ENG) 51.5
20 Miles Walk	Ron Wallwork (ENG) 2:44:42	Ray Middleton (ENG) 2:45:19	Norman Read (NZL) 2:46:28
4 × 110yds Relay	Ghana 39.8	Jamaica 40.0	Australia 40.0
4 × 440yds Relay	Trinidad 3:02.8	Canada 3:04.9	England 3:06.5
High Jump	Lawrie Peckham (AUS) 6.10 (2.08)	Samuel Igun (NGR) 6.8 (2.03)	Anton Norris (BAR) 6.7 (2.00)
Pole Vault	Trevor Bickle (AUS) 15.9 (4.80)	Mike Bull (NIR) 15.6 (4.72)	Gerry Moro (CAN) 15.3 (4.65)
Triple Jump	Samuel Igun (NGR) 53.10 (16.40)	George Ogan (NGR) 52.9 (16.08)	Fred Alsop (ENG) 52.4 (15.96)
Long Jump	Lynn Davies (WAL) 26.3 (7.99)	John Morbey (BER) 25.11 (7.89)	Wes Clayton (JAM) 25.8 (7.83)
Shot Put	Dave Steen (CAN) 61.8 (18.79)	Les Mills (NZL) 60.3 (18.37)	George Puce (CAN) 56.3 (17.14)
Discus	Les Mills (NZL) 184.4 (56.18)	George Puce (CAN) 183.6 (55.94)	Robin Tait (NZL) 180.6 (55.02)
Javelin	John Fitzsimons (ENG) 261.9 (79.78)	Nick Birks (AUS) 249.10 (76.16)	Mohammed Nawaz (PAK) 229.5 (69.93)
Hammer	Howard Payne (ENG) 203.4 (61.98)	Praveen Kumar (IND) 197.3 (60.12)	Muhammad Iqbal (PAK) 195.5 (59.56)
Decathlon	Roy Williams (NZL) 7270	Clive Longe (WAL) 7123	Gerry Moro (CAN) 6983

Women's	**Gold**	**Silver**	**Bronze**
100yds	Dianne Burge (AUS) 10.6	Irene Piotrowski (CAN) 10.8	Jill Hall (ENG) 10.8
220yds	Dianne Burge (AUS) 23.8	Jennifer Lamy (AUS) 23.8	Irene Piotrowski (CAN) 23.9
440yds	Judy Pollock (AUS) 53.0	Deirdre Watkinson (ENG) 54.1	Una Morris (JAM) 54.2
880yds	Abigail Hoffman (CAN) 2:04.3	Judy Pollock (AUS) 2:04.5	Anne Smith (ENG) 2:05.0
80yds Hurdles	Pamela Kilborn (AUS) 10.9	Carmen Smith (JAM) 11.0	Jennifer Wingerson (CAN) 11.0
4 × 110yds Relay	Australia 45.3	England 45.6	Jamaica 45.6
High Jump	Michelle Brown (AUS) 5.8 (1.73)	Dorothy Shirley (ENG) 5.7 (1.70)	Robyn Woodhouse (AUS) 5.7 (1.70)
Long Jump	Mary Rand (ENG) 20.10 (6.36)	Sheila Parkin (ENG) 20.8 (6.30)	Violet Odogwu (NGR) 20.2 (6.15)
Shot Put	Valerie Young (NZL) 54.2 (16.50)	Mary Peters (NIR) 53.6 (16.30)	Nancy McCredie (CAN) 50.4 (15.34)
Discus	Valerie Young (NZL)163.4 (49.78)	Jean Roberts (AUS) 161.5 (49.20)	Carole Martin (CAN) 159.9 (48.69)
Javelin	Margaret Parker (AUS) 168.7 (51.38)	Anna Bocson (AUS) 156.10 (47.80)	Jay Dahlgren (CAN) 156.5 (47.68)

1970 Edinburgh

Men's	**Gold**	**Silver**	**Bronze**
100m	Don Quarrie (JAM) 10.2	Lennox Miller (JAM) 10.3	Hasley Crawford (TRI) 10.3
200m	Don Quarrie (JAM) 20.5	Ed Roberts (TRI) 20.6	Charles Asati (KEN) 20.7
400m	Charles Asati (KEN) 45.0	Ross Wilson (AUS) 45.6	Saimone Tamani (FIJ) 45.8
800m	Robert Ouko (KEN) 1:46.8	Benedict Cayenne (TRI) 1:47.4	Bill Smart (CAN) 1:47.4
1500m	Kip Keino (KEN) 3:36.6	Dick Quax (NZL) 3:38.1	Brendan Foster (ENG) 3:40.6
5000m	Ian Stewart (SCO) 13:22.8	Ian McCafferty (SCO) 13:23.4	Kip Keino (KEN) 13:27.6
10,000m	Lachie Stewart (SCO) 28:11.8	Ron Clarke (AUS) 28:13.4	Dick Taylor (ENG) 28:15.4
Marathon	Ron Hill (ENG) 2:09:28	Jim Alder (SCO) 2:12:04	Don Faircloth (ENG) 2:12:19
3000m Steeplechase	Tony Manning (AUS) 8:26.2	Ben Jipcho (KEN) 8:29.6	Amos Biwott (KEN) 8:30.8
110m Hurdles	David Hemery (ENG) 13.6	Mal Baird (AUS) 13.8	Godfrey Murray (JAM) 14.0
400m Hurdles	John Sherwood (ENG) 50.0	William Koskei (UGA) 50.1	Charles Yego (KEN) 50.1
20 Mile Walk	Noel Freeman (AUS) 2:33:33	Bob Gardiner (AUS) 2:35:55	Bill Sutherland (SCO) 2:37:24
4 × 100m Relay	Jamaica 39.4	Ghana 39.7	England 40.0
4 × 400m Relay	Kenya 3:03.6	Trinidad & Tobago 3:05.4	England 3:05.5
High Jump	Lawrie Peckham (AUS) 2.14	John Hawkins (CAN) 2.12	Cheikh Tidiane Faye (GAM) 2.10
Pole Vault	Mike Bull (NIR) 5.10	Allan Kane (CAN) 4.90	Bob Raftis (CAN) 4.90
Triple Jump	Phil May (AUS) 16.72	Mike McGrath (AUS) 16.41	Mohinder Singh (IND) 15.90
Long Jump	Lynn Davies (WAL) 8.06	Phil May (AUS) 7.94	Alan Lerwill (ENG) 7.94
Shot Put	Dave Steen (CAN) 19.21	Jeffrey Teale (ENG) 18.43	Les Mills (NZL) 18.40
Discus	George Puce (CAN) 59.02	Les Mills (NZL) 57.84	Bill Tancred (ENG) 56.68
Javelin	Dave Travis (ENG) 79.50	John McSorley (ENG) 76.74	John Fitzsimons (ENG) 73.20
Hammer	Howard Payne (ENG) 67.80	Bruce Fraser (ENG) 62.90	Barry Williams (ENG) 61.58
Decathlon	Geoff Smith (AUS) 7492	Peter Gabbett (ENG) 7469	Barry King (ENG) 7201

Women's	**Gold**	**Silver**	**Bronze**
100m	Raelene Boyle (AUS) 11.2	Alice Annum (GHA) 11.3	Marion Hoffman (AUS) 11.3
200m	Raelene Boyle (AUS) 22.7	Alice Annum (GHA) 22.8	Margaret Critchley (ENG) 23.1
400m	Marilyn Neufville (JAM) 51.0	Sandra Brown (AUS) 53.6	Judith Ayaa (UGA) 53.7
800m	Rosemary Stirling (SCO) 2:06.2	Pat Lowe (ENG) 2:06.2	Cheryl Peasley (AUS) 2:06.3
1500m	Rita Ridley (ENG) 4:18.2	Joan Page (ENG) 4:19.0	Thelma Flynn (CAN) 4:19.1

100m Hurdles	Pamela Kilborn (AUS) 13.2	Maureen Caird (AUS) 13.7	Christine Bell (ENG) 13.8
4 × 100m Relay	Australia 44.1	England 44.2	Canada 44.6
High Jump	Debbie Brill (CAN) 1.78	Ann Wilson (ENG) 1.70	Moira Walls (SCO) 1.70
Long Jump	Sheila Sherwood (ENG) 6.73	Ann Wilson (ENG) 6.50	Joan Hendry (CAN) 6.28
Shot Put	Mary Peters (NIR) 15.93	Barbara Poulsen (NZL) 15.87	Jean Roberts (AUS) 15.32
Discus	Rosemary Payne (SCO) 54.46	Jean Roberts (AUS) 51.02	Carole Martin (CAN) 48.42
Javelin	Petra Rivers (AUS) 52.00	Ann Farquhar (ENG) 50.82	Jay Dahlgren (CAN) 49.54
Pentathlon	Mary Peters (NIR) 5148	Ann Wilson (ENG) 5037	Jennifer Meldrum (CAN) 4736

1974 Auckland

Men's	Gold	Silver	Bronze
100m	Don Quarrie (JAM) 10.38	John Mwebi (KEN) 10.51	Ohene Karikari (GHA) 10.51
200m	Don Quarrie (JAM) 20.73	George Daniels (GHA) 20.97	Bevan Smith (NZL) 21.08
400m	Charles Asati (KEN) 46.04	Silver Ayoo (UGA) 46.07	Claver Kamanya (TAN) 46.16
800m	John Kipkurgat (KEN) 1:43.85	Mike Boit (KEN) 1:44.4	John Walker (NZL) 1:44.9
1500m	Filbert Bayi (TAN) 3:32.16	John Walker (NZL) 3:32.52	Ben Jipcho (KEN) 3:33.16
5000m	Ben Jipcho (KEN) 13:14.4	Brendan Foster (ENG) 13:14.6	Dave Black (ENG) 13:23.6
10,000m	Richard Tayler (NZL) 27:46.4	Dave Black (ENG) 27:48.6	Richard Juma (KEN) 27:57.0
Marathon	Ian Thompson (ENG) 2:09:12	Jack Foster (NZL) 2:11:19	Richard Mabuza (SWZ) 2:12:54
3000m Steeplechase	Ben Jipcho (KEN) 8:20.67	John Davies (WAL) 8:24.80	Evans Mogaka (KEN) 8:28.51
110m Hurdles	Fatwell Kimaiyo (KEN) 13.69	Berwyn Price (WAL) 13.84	Max Binnington (AUS) 13.88
400m Hurdles	Alan Pascoe (ENG) 48.83	Bruce Field (AUS) 49.32	William Koskei (KEN) 49.34
20 Mile Walk	John Warhurst (ENG) 2:35:23	Roy Thorpe (ENG) 2:39:03	Peter Fullager (AUS) 2:42:09
4 × 100m Relay	Australia 39.31	Ghana 39.61	Nigeria 39.70
4 × 400m Relay	Kenya 3:04.43	England 3:06.66	Uganda 3:07.45
High Jump	Gordon Windeyer (AUS) 2.16	Lawrie Peckham (AUS) 2.14	Claude Ferragne (CAN) 2.12
Pole Vault	Don Baird (AUS) 5.05	Mike Bull (NIR) 5.00	Brian Hooper (ENG) 5.00
Triple Jump	Joshua Owuso (GHA) 16.50	Mohinder Singh (IND) 16.44	Moise Pomaney (GHA) 16.23
Long Jump	Alan Lerwill (ENG) 7.94	Chris Commons (AUS) 7.92	Joshua Owuso (GHA) 7.75
Shot Put	Geoff Capes (ENG) 20.74	Mike Winch (ENG) 19.36	Bruce Pirnie (CAN) 18.68
Discus	Robin Tait (NZL) 63.08	Bill Tancred (ENG) 59.48	John Hillier (ENG) 57.22
Javelin	Charles Clover (ENG) 84.92	Dave Travis (ENG) 79.92	John Mayaka (KEN) 77.56
Hammer	Ian Chipchase (ENG) 69.56	Howard Payne (ENG) 68.02	Peter Farmer (AUS) 67.48
Decathlon	Mike Bull (NIR) 7417	Barry King (ENG) 7277	Robert Lethbridge (AUS) 7270

Women's	Gold	Silver	Bronze
100m	Raelene Boyle (AUS) 11.27	Andrea Lynch (ENG) 11.31	Denise Robertson (AUS) 11.50
200m	Raelene Boyle (AUS) 22.50	Denise Robertson (AUS) 22.73	Alice Annum (GHA) 22.90
400m	Yvonne Saunders (CAN) 51.67	Verona Bernard (ENG) 51.94	Charlene Rendina (AUS) 52.08
800m	Charlene Rendina (AUS) 2:01.1	Sue Haden (NZL) 2:02.0	Sabina Chebichi (KEN) 2:02.6
1500m	Glenda Reiser (CAN) 4:07.8	Joan Allison (ENG) 4:10.7	Thelma Wright (CAN) 4:12.3
100m Hurdles	Judy Vernon (ENG) 13.45	Gaye Dell (AUS) 13.54	Modupe Oshikoya (NGR) 13.69
4 × 100m Relay	Australia 43.51	England 44.30	Ghana 44.35
4 × 400m Relay	England 3:29.23	Australia 3:30.72	Canada 3:33.92
High Jump	Barbara Lawton (ENG) 1.84	Louise Hanna (CAN) 1.82	Brigitte Bittner (CAN) 1.80
Long Jump	Modupe Oshikoya (NGR) 6.46	Brenda Eisler (CAN) 6.38	Ruth Martin-Jones (WAL) 6.38
Shot Put	Jane Haist (CAN) 16.12	Valerie Young (NZL) 15.29	Jean Roberts (AUS) 15.24
Discus	Jane Haist (CAN) 55.52	Rosemary Payne (SCO) 53.94	Carol Martin (CAN) 53.16
Javelin	Petra Rivers (AUS) 55.48	Jenny Symon (AUS) 52.14	Sharon Corbett (ENG) 50.26
Pentathlon	Mary Peters (NIR) 4455	Modupe Oshikoya (NGR) 4423	Ann Wilson (ENG) 4236

1978 Edmonton

Men's	Gold	Silver	Bronze
100m	Don Quarrie (JAM) 10.03	Allan Wells (SCO) 10.07	Hasly Crawford (TRI) 10.09
200m	Allan Wells (SCO) 20.12	James Gilkes (GUY) 20.18	Colin Bradford (JAM) 20.43
400m	Rick Mitchell (AUS) 46.34	Joseph Coombs (TRI) 46.54	Glenn Bogue (CAN) 46.63
800m	Mike Boit (KEN) 1:46.4	Seymour Newman (JAM) 1:47.3	Peter Lemashon (KEN) 1:47.6
1500m	Dave Moorcroft (ENG) 3:35.5	Filbert Bayi (TAN) 3:35.6	John Robson (SCO) 3:35.6
5000m	Henry Rono (KEN) 13:23.0	Mike Musyoki (KEN) 13:29.9	Brendan Foster (ENG) 13:31.4
10,000m	Brendan Foster (ENG) 28:13.7	Mike Musyoki (KEN) 28:19.1	Mike McLeod (ENG) 28:34.3
Marathon	Gidamis Shahanga (TAN) 2:15:40	Jerome Drayton (CAN) 2:16:13	Paul Bannon (CAN) 2:16:52
3000m Steeplechase	Henry Rono (KEN) 8:26.5	James Munyala (KEN) 8:32.2	Kip Rono (KEN) 8:34.1
110m Hurdles	Berwyn Price (WAL) 13.70	Max Binnington (AUS) 13.73	Warren Parr (AUS) 13.73
400m Hurdles	Daniel Kimaiyo (KEN) 49.48	Garry Brown (AUS) 50.04	Alan Pascoe (ENG) 50.09
30km Walk	Ollie Flynn (ENG) 2:22:04	Willi Sawall (AUS) 2:22:59	Tim Erickson (AUS) 2:26:34
4 × 100m Relay	Scotland 39.24	Trinidad 39.29	Jamaica 39.33
4 × 400m Relay	Kenya 3:03.5	Jamaica 3:04.0	Australia 3:04.2
High Jump	Claude Ferragne (CAN) 2.20	Greg Joy (CAN) 2.18	Dean Bauck (CAN) 2.15
			Brian Burgess (SCO) 2.15

	Gold	Silver	Bronze
Pole Vault	Bruce Simpson (CAN) 5.10	Don Baird (AUS) 5.10	Brian Hooper (ENG) 5.00
Triple Jump	Keith Connor (ENG) 17.21	Ian Campbell (AUS) 16.93	Aston Moore (ENG) 16.69
Long Jump	Roy Mitchell (ENG) 8.06	Chris Commons (AUS) 8.04	Suresh Babu (IND) 7.94
Shot Put	Geoff Capes (ENG) 19.77	Bruno Pauletto (CAN) 19.33	Bishop Dolegiewicz (CAN) 18.45
Discus	Borys Chambul (CAN) 59.70	Brad Cooper (BAH) 57.30	Robert Gray (CAN) 55.48
Javelin	Phil Olsen (CAN) 84.00	Mike O'Rourke (NZL) 83.18	Peter Yates (ENG) 78.58
Hammer	Peter Farmer (AUS) 71.10	Scott Neilson (CAN) 69.92	Chris Black (SCO) 68.14
Decathlon	Daley Thompson (ENG) 8467	Peter Hadfield (AUS) 7623	Alan Drayton (ENG) 7484

Women's	Gold	Silver	Bronze
100m	Sonia Lannaman (ENG) 11.27	Raelene Boyle (AUS) 11.35	Denise Boyd (AUS) 11.37
200m	Denise Boyd (AUS) 22.82	Sonia Lannaman (ENG) 22.89	Colleen Beazley (AUS) 22.93
400m	Donna Hartley (ENG) 51.69	Verona Elder (ENG) 52.94	Bethanie Nail (AUS) 53.06
800m	Judy Peckham (AUS) 2:02.8	Tekla Chemabwai (KEN) 2:02.9	Jane Colebrook (ENG) 2:03.1
1500m	Mary Stewart (ENG) 4:06.34	Christine Benning (ENG) 4:07.53	Penny Werthner (CAN) 4:08.14
3000m	Paula Fudge (ENG) 9:13.0	Heather Thomson (NZL) 9:20.7	Ann Ford (ENG) 9:24.1
100m Hurdles	Lorna Boothe (ENG) 12.98	Shirley Strong (ENG) 13.08	Sharon Colyear (ENG) 13.17
4 × 100m Relay	England 43.70	Canada 44.26	Australia 44.78
4 × 400m Relay	England 3:27.2	Australia 3:28.7	Canada 3:35.8
High Jump	Katrina Gibbs (AUS) 1.93	Debbie Brill (CAN) 1.90	Julie White (CAN) 1.83
Long Jump	Sue Reeve (ENG) 6.59	Erica Hooker (AUS) 6.58	June Griffith (GUY) 6.52
Shot Put	Gael Mulhall (AUS) 17.31	Carmen Ionesco (CAN) 16.45	Judy Oakes (ENG) 16.14
Discus	Carmen Ionescu (CAN) 62.16	Gael Mulhall (AUS) 57.60	Lucette Moreau (CAN) 56.64
Javelin	Tessa Sanderson (ENG) 61.34	Alison Hayward (CAN) 54.52	Laurie Kern (CAN) 53.60
Pentathlon	Diane Konihowski (CAN) 4768	Sue Mapstone (ENG) 4222	Yvette Wray (ENG) 4211

1982 Brisbane

Men's	Gold	Silver	Bronze
100m	Allan Wells (SCO) 10.02	Ben Johnson (CAN) 10.05	Cameron Sharp (SCO) 10.07
200m	Allan Wells (SCO) 20.43	Cameron Sharp (SCO) 20.55	—
	Mike McFarlane (ENG) 20.43		
400m	Bert Cameron (JAM) 45.89	Rick Mitchell (AUS) 46.61	Gary Minihan (AUS) 46.68
800m	Peter Bourke (AUS) 1:45.18	James Maina Boi (KEN) 1:45.45	Chris McGeorge (ENG) 1:45.60
1500m	Steve Cram (ENG) 3:42.37	John Walker (NZL) 3:43.11	Mike Boit (KEN) 3:43.33
5000m	Dave Moorcroft (ENG) 13:33.00	Nick Rose (ENG) 13:35.97	Peter Koech (KEN) 13:36.95
10,000m	Gidamis Shahanga (TAN) 28:10.15	Zacharia Barie (TAN) 28:10.55	Julian Goater (ENG) 28:16.11
Marathon	Rob de Castella (AUS) 2:09:18	Juma Ikangaa (TAN) 2:09:30	Mike Grattan (ENG) 2:12:06
3000m Steeplechase	Julius Korir (KEN) 8:23.94	Graeme Fell (ENG) 8:26.64	Greg Duhaime (CAN) 8:29.14
110m Hurdles	Mark McKoy (CAN) 13.37	Mark Holton (ENG) 13.43	Don Wright (AUS) 13.58
400m Hurdles	Garry Brown (AUS) 49.37	Peter Rwamuhanda (UGA) 49.95	Greg Rolle (BAH) 50.50
30km Walk	Steve Barry (WAL) 2:10:16	Marcel Jobin (CAN) 2:12:24	Guillaume Leblanc (CAN) 2:14:56
4 × 100m Relay	Nigeria 39.15	Canada 39.30	Scotland 39.33
4 × 400m Relay	England 3:05.45	Australia 3:05.82	Kenya 3:06.33
High Jump	Milt Ottey (BAH) 2.31	Steve Wray (BAH) 2.31	Nick Saunders (BER) 2.19
Pole Vault	Ray Boyd (AUS) 5.20	Jeff Gutteridge (ENG) 5.20	Graham Eggleton (SCO) 5.20
Triple Jump	Keith Connor (ENG) 17.81	Ken Lorraway (AUS) 17.54	Aston Moore (ENG) 16.76
Long Jump	Gary Honey (AUS) 8.13	Steve Hanna (BAH) 7.79	Steve Walsh (NZL) 7.75
Shot Put	Bruno Pauletto (CAN) 19.55	Mike Winch (ENG) 18.25	Luby Chambul (CAN) 17.46
Discus	Brad Cooper (BAH) 64.04	Rob Gray (CAN) 60.66	Bishop Dolegiewicz (CAN) 60.34
Javelin	Mike O'Rourke (NZL) 89.48	Laslo Babits (CAN) 84.88	Zakayo Maalekwa (TAN) 80.22
Hammer	Bob Weir (ENG) 75.08	Martin Girvan (NIR) 73.62	Chris Black (SCO) 69.84
Decathlon	Daley Thompson (ENG) 8410	Dave Steen (CAN) 8004	Fidelis Obikwu (ENG) 7726

Women's	Gold	Silver	Bronze
100m	Angella Taylor (CAN) 11.00	Merlene Ottey (JAM) 11.03	Colleen Pekin (AUS) 11.24
200m	Merlene Ottey (JAM) 22.19	Kathy Smallwood (ENG) 22.21	Angella Taylor (CAN) 22.48
400m	Raelene Boyle (AUS) 51.26	Michelle Scutt (WAL) 51.97	Joslyn Hoyte-Smith (ENG) 52.53
800m	Kirsty McDermott (WAL) 2:01.31	Anne Clarkson (SCO) 2:01.52	Heather Barralet (AUS) 2:01.70
1500m	Christina Boxer (ENG) 4:08.28	Gillian Dainty (ENG) 4:10.80	Lorraine Moller (NZL) 4:12.67
3000m	Anne Audain (NZL) 8:45.53	Wendy Smith (ENG) 8:48.47	Lorraine Moller (NZL) 8:55.76
100m Hurdles	Shirley Strong (ENG) 12.78	Lorna Boothe (ENG) 12.90	Susan Kameli (CAN) 13.10
400m Hurdles	Debbie Flintoff (AUS) 55.89	Ruth Kyalisima (UGA) 57.10	Yvette Wray (ENG) 57.17
4 × 100m Relay	England 43.15	Canada 43.66	Jamaica 43.69
4 × 400m Relay	Canada 3:27.70	Australia 3:27.72	Scotland 3:32.92
High Jump	Debbie Brill (CAN) 1.88	Christine Stanton (AUS) 1.88	Barbara Simmonds (ENG) 1.83
Long Jump	Shonel Ferguson (BAH) 6.91	Robyn Strong (AUS) 6.88	Bev Kinch (ENG) 6.78
Shot Put	Judy Oakes (ENG) 17.92	Gael Mulhall (AUS) 17.68	Rosemarie Hauch (CAN) 16.71
Discus	Meg Ritchie (SCO) 62.98	Gael Mulhall (AUS) 58.64	Lynda Whiteley (ENG) 54.78
Javelin	Sue Howland (AUS) 64.46	Petra Rivers (AUS) 62.28	Fatima Whitebread (ENG) 58.86
Heptathlon	Glynis Nunn (AUS) 6282	Judy Livermore (ENG) 6214	Jill Ross (CAN) 5981

ATHLETICS

1986 Edinburgh

Men's	Gold	Silver	Bronze
100m	Ben Johnson (CAN) 10.07	Linford Christie (ENG) 10.28	Mike McFarlane (ENG) 10.35
200m	Atlee Mahorn (CAN) 20.31	Todd Bennett (ENG) 20.54	Ben Johnson (CAN) 20.64
400m	Roger Black (ENG) 45.57	Darren Clark (AUS) 45.98	Phil Brown (ENG) 46.80
800m	Steve Cram (ENG) 1:43.22	Tom McKean (SCO) 1:44.80	Peter Elliott (ENG) 1:45.42
1500m	Steve Cram (ENG) 3:50.87	John Gladwin (ENG) 3:52.17	David Campbell (ENG) 3:54.06
5000m	Steve Ovett (ENG) 13:24.11	Jack Buckner (ENG) 13:25.87	Tim Hutchins (ENG) 13:26.84
10,000m	Jon Solly (ENG) 27:57.42	Steve Binns (ENG) 27:58.01	Steve Jones (WAL) 28:02.48
Marathon	Rob de Castella (AUS) 2:10:15	Dave Edge (CAN) 2:11:08	Steve Moneghetti (AUS) 2:11:18
3000m Steeplechase	Graeme Fell (CAN) 8:24.29	Roger Hackney (WAL) 8:25.15	Colin Reitz (ENG) 8:26.14
110m Hurdles	Mark McKoy (CAN) 13.31	Colin Jackson (WAL) 13.42	Don Wright (AUS) 13.64
400m Hurdles	Phil Beattie (NIR) 49.60	Max Robertson (ENG) 49.77	John Graham (CAN) 50.25
30km Walk	Simon Baker (AUS) 2:07:47	Guillaume Leblanc (CAN) 2:08:38	Ian McCombie (ENG) 2:10:36
4 × 100m Relay	Canada 39.15	England 39.19	Scotland 40.41
4 × 400m Relay	England 3:07.19	Australia 3:07.81	Canada 3:08.69
High Jump	Milt Ottey (CAN) 2.30	Geoff Parsons (SCO) 2.28	Alain Metellus (CAN) 2.14
			Henderson Pierre (ENG) 2.14
Pole Vault	Andy Ashurst (ENG) 5.30	Bob Ferguson (CAN) 5.20	Neil Honey (AUS) 5.20
Triple Jump	John Herbert (ENG) 17.27	Mike Makin (ENG) 16.87	Peter Beames (AUS) 16.42
Long Jump	Gary Honey (AUS) 8.08	Fred Salle (ENG) 7.83	Kyle McDuffie (CAN) 7.79
Shot Put	Billy Cole (ENG) 18.16	Joe Quigley (AUS) 17.97	Stuart Gyngell (AUS) 17.70
Discus	Ray Lazdins (CAN) 58.86	Paul Nandapi (AUS) 57.74	Werner Reiterer (AUS) 57.34
Javelin	Dave Ottley (ENG) 80.62	Mick Hill (ENG) 78.56	Gavin Lovegrove (NZL) 76.22
Hammer	David Smith (ENG) 74.06	Martin Girvan (NIR) 70.48	Phil Spivey (AUS) 70.30
Decathlon	Daley Thompson (ENG) 8663	Dave Steen (CAN) 8173	Simon Poelman (NZL) 8015

Women's	Gold	Silver	Bronze
100m	Heather Oakes (ENG) 11.20	Paula Dunn (ENG) 11.21	Angella Issajenko (CAN) 11.21
200m	Angella Issajenko (CAN) 22.91	Kathy Cook (ENG) 23.18	Sandra Whittaker (SCO) 23.46
400m	Debbie Flintoff (AUS) 51.29	Jillian Richardson (CAN) 51.52	Kathy Cook (ENG) 51.88
800m	Kirsty Wade (WAL) 2:00.94	Diane Edwards (ENG) 2:01.12	Lorraine Baker (ENG) 2:01.79
1500m	Kirsty Wade (WAL) 4:10.91	Debbie Bowker (CAN) 4:11.94	Lynn Williams (CAN) 4:12.66
3000m	Lynn Williams (CAN) 8:54.29	Debbie Bowker (CAN) 8:54.83	Yvonne Murray (SCO) 8:55.32
10,000m	Liz Lynch (SCO) 31:41.42	Anne Audain (NZL) 31:53.31	Angela Tooby (WAL) 32:25.38
Marathon	Lisa Martin (AUS) 2:26:07	Lorraine Moller (NZL) 2:28:17	Odette Lapiere (CAN) 2:31:48
100m Hurdles	Sally Gunnell (ENG) 13.29	Wendy Jeal (ENG) 13.41	Glynis Nunn (AUS) 13.44
400m Hurdles	Debbie Flintoff (AUS) 54.94	Donalda Duprey (CAN) 56.55	Jenny Laurendet (AUS) 56.57
4 × 100m Relay	England 43.39	Canada 43.83	Wales 45.37
4 × 400m Relay	Canada 3.28.92	England 3:32.82	Australia 3:32.86
High Jump	Chris Stanton (AUS) 1.92	Sharon McPeake (NIR) 1.90	Janet Boyle (NIR) 1.90
Long Jump	Joyce Oladapo (ENG) 6.43	Mary Berkeley (ENG) 6.40	Robyn Lorraway (AUS) 6.35
Shot Put	Gael Martin (AUS) 19.00	Judy Oakes (ENG) 18.75	Myrtle Augee (ENG) 17.52
Discus	Gael Martin (AUS) 56.42	Venissa Head (WAL) 56.20	Karen Pugh (ENG) 54.72
Javelin	Tessa Sanderson (ENG) 69.80	Fatima Whitbread (ENG) 68.54	Sue Howland (AUS) 64.74
Heptathlon	Judy Simpson (ENG) 6282	Jane Flemming (AUS) 6278	Kim Hagger (ENG) 5823

1990 Auckland

Men's	Gold	Silver	Bronze
100m	Linford Christie (ENG) 9.93	Davidson Ezinwa (NGR) 10.05	Bruny Surin (CAN) 10.12
200m	Marcus Adam (ENG) 20.10	John Regis (ENG) 20.16	Ade Mafe (ENG) 20.26
400m	Darren Clark (AUS) 44.60	Samson Kitur (KEN) 44.88	Simon Kipkemboi (KEN) 44.93
800m	Sammy Tirop (KEN) 1:45.98	Nixon Kiprotich (KEN) 1:46.00	Matthew Yates (ENG) 1:46.62
1500m	Peter Elliott (ENG) 3:33.39	Wilfred Kirochi (KEN) 3:34.41	Peter O'Donoghue (NZL) 3:35.14
5000m	Andrew Lloyd (AUS) 13:24.86	John Ngugi (KEN) 13:24.94	Ian Hamer (WAL) 13:25.63
10,000m	Eamonn Martin (ENG) 28:08.57	Moses Tanui (KEN) 28:11.56	Paul Williams (CAN) 28:12.71
Marathon	Douglas Wakiihuri (KEN) 2:10:27	Steve Moneghetti (AUS) 2:10:34	Simon Robert Naali (TAN) 2:10:38
3000m Steeplechase	Julius Kariuki (KEN) 8:20.64	Joshua Kipkemboi (KEN) 8:24.26	Colin Walker (ENG) 8:26.50
110m Hurdles	Colin Jackson (WAL) 13.08	Tony Jarrett (ENG) 13.34	David Nelson (ENG) 13.54
400m Hurdles	Kriss Akabusi (ENG) 48.89	Gideon Yego (KEN) 49.25	John Graham (CAN) 50.24
30km Walk	Guillaume Leblanc (CAN) 2:08:28	Andrew Jachno (AUS) 2:09:09	Ian McCombie (ENG) 2:09:20
4 × 100m Relay	England 38.67	Nigeria 38.85	Jamaica 39.11
4 × 400m Relay	Kenya 3:02.48	Scotland 3:04.68	Jamaica 3:04.96
High Jump	Nick Saunders (BER) 2.36	Dalton Grant (ENG) 2.34	Milt Ottey (CAN) 2.23
			Geoff Parsons (SCO) 2.23
Pole Vault	Simon Arkell (AUS) 5.35	Ian Tullett (ENG) 5.25	Simon Poelman (NZL) 5.20
Triple Jump	Marios Hadjiandreou (CYP) 16.95	Jonathan Edwards (ENG) 16.93	Edrick Floreal (CAN) 16.89
Long Jump	Yusuf Alli (NGR) 8.39	David Culbert (AUS) 8.20	Festus Igbinoghene (NGR) 8.18

	Gold	Silver	Bronze
Shot Put	Simon Williams (ENG) 18.54	Adewale Olukoju (NGR) 18.48	Paul Edwards (WAL) 18.17
Discus	Adewale Olukoju (NGR) 62.62	Werner Reiterer (AUS) 61.56	Paul Nandapi (AUS) 59.94
Javelin	Steve Backley (ENG) 86.02	Mick Hill (ENG) 83.32	Gavin Lovegrove (NZL) 81.66
Hammer	Sean Carlin (AUS) 75.66	David Smith (ENG) 73.52	Angus Cooper (NZL) 71.26
Decathlon	Mike Smith (CAN) 8525	Simon Poelman (NZL) 8207	Eugene Gilkes (ENG) 7705

Women's	Gold	Silver	Bronze
100m	Merlene Ottey (JAM) 11.02	Kerry Johnson (AUS) 11.17	Pauline Davis (BAH) 11.20
200m	Merlene Ottey (JAM) 22.76	Kerry Johnson (AUS) 22.88	Pauline Davis (BAH) 23.15
400m	Fatima Yusuf (NGR) 51.08	Linda Keough (ENG) 51.63	Charity Opara (NGR) 52.01
800m	Diane Edwards (ENG) 2:00.25	Ann Williams (ENG) 2:00.40	Sharon Stewart (AUS) 2:00.87
1500m	Angela Chalmers (CAN) 4:08.41	Christina Cahill (Boxer) (ENG) 4:08.75	Beverley Nicholson (ENG) 4:09.00
3000m	Angela Chalmers (CAN) 8:38.38	Yvonne Murray (SCO) 8:39.46	Liz McColgan (SCO) 8:47.66
10,000m	Liz McColgan (SCO) 32:23.56	Jill Hunter (ENG) 32:33.21	Barbara Moore (NZL) 32:44.73
Marathon	Lisa Martin (AUS) 2:25:28	Tani Ruckle (AUS) 2:33:15	Angela Pain (ENG) 2:36:35
100m Hurdles	Kay Morley (WAL) 12.91	Sally Gunnell (ENG) 13.12	Lesley-Ann Skeete (ENG) 13.31
400m Hurdles	Sally Gunnell (ENG) 55.38	Debbie Flintoff-King (AUS) 56.00	Jenny Laurendet (AUS) 56.74
10km Walk	Kerry Saxby (AUS) 45:03	Anne Judkins (NZL) 47:03	Lisa Langford (ENG) 47:23
4 × 100m Relay	Australia 43.87	England 44.15	Nigeria 44.67
4 × 400m Relay	England 3:28.08	Australia 3:30.74	Canada 3:33.26
High Jump	Tania Murray (NZL) 1.88	Janet Boyle (NIR) 1.88	Tracy Phillips (NZL) 1.88
Long Jump	Jane Fleming (AUS) 6.78	Beatrice Utondu (NGR) 6.65	Fiona May (ENG) 6.55
Shot Put	Myrtle Augee (ENG) 18.48	Judy Oakes (ENG) 18.43	Yvonne Hanson-Nortey (ENG) 16.00
Discus	Lisa-Marie Vizaniari (AUS) 56.38	Jacqueline McKernan (NIR) 54.86	Astra Vitols (AUS) 53.84
Javelin	Tessa Sanderson (ENG) 65.72	Sue Howeland (AUS) 61.18	Kate Farrow (AUS) 58.98
Heptathlon	Jane Fleming (AUS) 6695	Sharon Jaklofsky-Smith (AUS) 6115	Judy Simpson (ENG) 6085

1994 Victoria

Men's	Gold	Silver	Bronze
100m	Linford Christie (ENG) 9.91	Michael Green (JAM) 10.05	Frankie Fredericks (NAM) 10.06
200m	Frankie Fredericks (NAM) 19.97	John Regis (ENG) 20.25	Daniel Effiong (NGR) 20.40
400m	Charles Gitonga (KEN) 45.00	Duaine Ladejo (ENG) 45.11	Sunday Bada (NGR) 45.45
800m	Patrick Konchellah (KEN) 1:45.18	Hezekiel Sepeng (RSA) 1:45.76	Savieri Ngidhi (ZIM) 1:46.06
1500m	Reubin Chesang (KEN) 3:36.70	Kevin Sullivan (CAN) 3:36.78	John Mayock (ENG) 3:37.22
5000m	Rob Denmark (ENG) 13:23.00	Philemon Hanneck (ZIM) 13:23.20	John Nuttall (ENG) 13:23.54
10,000m	Agutu Lameck (KEN) 28:38.22	Tendai Chimusasa (ZIM) 28:47.72	Fackson Nkandu (ZAM) 28:51.72
Marathon	Stephen Moneghetti (AUS) 2:11:49	Sean Quilty (AUS) 2:14:57	Mark Hudspith (ENG) 2:15:11
3000m Steeplechase	Johnstone Kipkoech (KEN) 8:14.72	Gedion Chirchir (KEN) 8:15.25	Graeme Fell (CAN) 8:23.28
110m Hurdles	Colin Jackson (WAL) 13.08	Tony Jarrett (ENG) 13.22	Paul Gray (WAL) 13.54
400m Hurdles	Samuel Matete (ZAM) 48.67	Gideon Biwoit (KEN) 49.43	Barnabas Kinyor (KEN) 49.40
30km Walk	Nicholas Ahern (AUS) 2:07:53	Tim Berrett (CAN) 2:08:22	Scott Nelson (NZL) 2:09:10
4 × 100m Relay	Canada 38.39	Australia 38.88	England 39.39
4 × 400m Relay	England 3:02.14	Jamaica 3:02.32	Trinidad & Tobago 3:02.78
High Jump	Timothy Forsyth (AUS) 2.32	Stephen Smith (ENG) 2.32	Geoffrey Parsons (SCO) 2.31
Pole Vault	Neil Winter (WAL) 5.40	Curtis Heywood (CAN) 5.30	James Miller (AUS) 5.30
Triple Jump	Julian Golley (ENG) 17.03	Jonathan Edwards (ENG) 17.00	Brian Wellman (BER) 17.00
Long Jump	Obinna Eregbu (NGR) 8.05	David Culbert (AUS) 8.00	Ian James (CAN) 7.93
Shot Put	Matthew Simson (ENG) 19.49	Courtney Ireland (NZL) 19.38	Chima Ugwu (NGR) 19.26
Discus	Werner Reiterer (AUS) 62.76	Adewale Olukoju (NGR) 62.46	Robert Weir (ENG) 60.86
Javelin	Steve Backley (ENG) 82.74	Mick Hill (ENG) 81.84	Gavin Lovegrove (NZL) 80.42
Hammer	Sean Carlin (AUS) 73.48	Paul Head (ENG) 70.18	Peter Vivian (ENG) 69.80
Decathlon	Mike Smith (CAN) 8326	Peter Winter (AUS) 8074	Simon Shirley (ENG) 7980

Women's	Gold	Silver	Bronze
100m	Mary Onyali (NGR) 11.06	Charity Opara Thompson (NGR) 11.22	Paula Thomas (ENG) 11.23
200m	Cathy Freeman (AUS) 22.25	Mary Onyali (NGR) 22.35	Melinda Gainsford (AUS) 22.68
400m	Cathy Freeman (AUS) 50.38	Fatima Yusuf (NGR) 50.53	Sandie Richards (JAM) 50.69
800m	Inez Turner (JAM) 2:01.74	Charmaine Crooks (CAN) 2:02.35	Gladys Wamuyu (KEN) 2:03.12
1500m	Kelly Holmes (ENG) 4:08.86	Paula Schnurr (CAN) 4:09.65	Gwen Griffiths (RSA) 4:10.16
5000m	Angela Chalmers (CAN) 8:32.17	Robyn Meagher (CAN) 8:45.59	Alison Wyeth (ENG) 8:47.98
10,000m	Yvonne Murray (SCO) 31:56.97	Elana Meyer (RSA) 32:06.02	Jane Omoro (KEN) 32:13.01
Marathon	Carole Rouillard (CAN) 2:30:41	Lizanne Bussieres (CAN) 2:31:07	Yvonne Danson (ENG) 2:32:24
100m Hurdles	Michelle Freeman (JAM) 13.12	Jacqueline Agyepong (ENG) 13.14	Samantha Farquharson (ENG) 13.38
400m Hurdles	Sally Gunnell (ENG) 54.51	Deon Hemmings (JAM) 55.11	Debbie-Ann Parris (JAM) 55.25
10km Walk	Kerry Saxby-Junna (AUS) 44:25	Anne Manning (AUS) 44:37	Janice McCaffrey (CAN) 44:54
4 × 100m Relay	Nigeria 42.99	Australia 43.43	England 43.46

ATHLETICS

4 × 400m Relay	England 3:27.06	Jamaica 3:27.63	Canada 3:32.52
High Jump	Alison Inverarity (AUS) 1.94	Charmaine Weavers (RSA) 1.94	Debora Marti (ENG) 1.91
Long Jump	Nicole Boegman (ENG) 6.82	Oluyinka Idowu (ENG) 6.73	Christy Opara-Thompson (NGR) 6.72
Shot Put	Judy Oakes (ENG) 18.16	Myrtle Augee (ENG) 17.64	Lisa Vizaniari (AUS) 16.61
Discus	Daniela Costian (AUS) 63.72	Beatrice Faumuina (NZL) 57.12	Lizette Etzebeth (RSA) 55.74
Javelin	Louise McPaul (AUS) 63.76	Kirsten Hellier (NZL) 60.40	Sharon Gibson (ENG) 58.20
Heptathlon	Denise Lewis (ENG) 6325	Jane Flemming (AUS) 6317	Catherine Bond-Mills (CAN) 6193

1998 Malaysia

Men's	Gold	Silver	Bronze
100m	Ato Boldon (TRI) 9.88	Frankie Fredericks (NAM) 9.96	Obadele Thompson (BAR) 10.00
200m	Julian Golding (ENG) 20.18	Christian Malcolm (WAL) 20.29	John Regis (ENG) 20.40
400m	Iwan Thomas (WAL) 44.52	Mark Richardson (ENG) 44.60	Sugath Thilakaratne (SRI) 44.64
800m	Japheth Kimutai (KEN) 1:43.82	Hezekiel Sepeng (RSA) 1:44.44	Johan Botha (RSA) 1:44.57
1500m	Laban Rotich (KEN) 3:39.49	John Mayock (ENG) 3:40.46	Anthony Whiteman (ENG) 3:40.70
5000m	Daniel Komen (KEN) 13:22.57	Thomas Nyariki (KEN) 13:28.09	Richard Limo (KEN) 13:37.42
10,000m	Simon Maina (KEN) 28:10.00	William Kalya (KEN) 29:01.68	Stephen Moneghetti (AUS) 29:02.76
Marathon	Thabiso Moqhali (LES) 2:19:15	Simon Basiligitwa (TAN) 2:19:42	Andea Geway Suja (TAN) 2:19:50
3000m Steeplechase	John Kosgei (KEN) 8:15.34	Bernard Barmasai (KEN) 8:15.37	Kikpurut Misoi (KEN) 8:18.24
110m Hurdles	Tony Jarrett (ENG) 13.47	Steve Brown (TRI) 13.48	Shaun Brownes (RSA) 13.53
400m Hurdles	Dinsdale Morgan (JAM) 48.28	Rohan Robinson (AUS) 48.99	Kenneth Harnden (ZIM) 49.06
20km Walk	Nicholas Ahern (AUS) 1:24:59	Arturo Huerta (CAN) 1:25:49	Nathan Deakes (AUS) 1:26:06
50km Walk	G. Saravanan (MAS) 4:10:05	Duane Cousins (AUS) 4:10:30	Dominic McGrath (AUS) 4:12:52
4 × 100m Relay	England 38.20	Canada 38.46	Australia 38.69
4 × 400m Relay	Jamaica 2:59.03	England 3:00.82	Wales 3:01.86
High Jump	Dalton Grant (ENG) 2.31	Benjamin Challenger (ENG) 2.28	Timothy Forsyth (AUS) 2.28
Pole Vault	Riaan Botha (RSA) 5.60	Paul Burgess (AUS) 5.50	Kersley Gardenne (MRI) 5.35
Long Jump	Peter Burge (AUS) 8.22	Jai Taurima (AUS) 8.22	Wendell Williams (TRI) 7.95
Triple Jump	Onochie Achike (ENG) 17.10	Andrew Owusu (GHA) 17.03	Remmy Kimutai Limo (KEN) 16.89
Shot Put	Burger Lambrechts (RSA) 20.01	Michalis Louca (CYP) 19.52	Shaun Pickering (WAL) 19.33
Discus	Robert Weir (ENG) 63.93	Frantz Kruger (RSA) 63.93	Jason Tunks (CAN) 62.22
Hammer	Stuart Rendell (AUS) 74.71	Michael Jones (ENG) 74.02	Chris Harmse (RSA) 72.83
Javelin	Marius Corbett (RSA) 88.75	Steve Backley (ENG) 87.38	Mick Hill (ENG) 83.80
Decathlon	Jagan Hames (AUS) 8490	Scott Ferrier (AUS) 8307	Michael Smith (CAN) 8143

Women's	Gold	Silver	Bronze
100m	Chandra Sturrup (BAH) 11.06	Philomena Mensah (CAN) 11.19	Tania van Heer (AUS) 11.29
200m	Nova Peris-Kneebone (AUS) 22.77	Juliet Campbell (JAM) 22.79	Lauren Hewitt (AUS) 22.83
400m	Sandie Richards (JAM) 50.17	Allison Curbishley (SCO) 50.71	Donna Fraser (ENG) 51.01
800m	Maria Mutola (MOZ) 1:57.60	Argentina Paulino (MOZ) 1:58.39	Diane Modahl (ENG) 1:58.81
1500m	Jackline Maranga (KEN) 4:05.27	Kelly Holmes (ENG) 4:06.10	Julia Sakara (ZIM) 4:07.82
5000m	Kate Anderson (AUS) 15:52.74	Andrea Whitcombe (ENG) 15:56.85	Samukeliso Moyo (ZIM) 15:57.57
10,000m	Esther Wanjiru (KEN) 33:40.13	Kylie Risk 33:42.11	Clare Fearnley (AUS) 33:52.13
Marathon	Heather Turland (AUS) 2:41:24	Lisa Dick (AUS) 2:41:48	Elizabeth Mongudhi (NAM) 2:43:28
100m Hurdles	Gillian Russell (JAM) 12.70	Sriani Kulawansha (SRI) 12.95	Katie Anderson (CAN) 13.04
400m Hurdles	Andrea Blackett (BAR) 53.91	Gowry Retchakan Hodge (ENG) 55.25	Karlene Houghton (CAN) 55.53
10km Walk	Jane Saville (AUS) 43:57	Kerry Saxby-Junna (AUS) 44:27	Lisa Kehler (ENG) 45:03
4 × 100m Relay	Australia 43.39	Jamaica 43.49	England 43.69
4 × 400m Relay	Australia 3:27.28	England 3:29.28	Canada 3:29.97
High Jump	Hestrie Storbeck (RSA) 1.91	Joanne Jennings (ENG) 1.91	Alison Inverarity (AUS) 1.88
Pole Vault	Emma George (AUS) 4.20	Elmarie Gerryts (RSA) 4.15	Trista Bernier (CAN) 4.15
Long Jump	Joanne Wise (ENG) 6.63	Jacqueline Edwards (BAH) 6.59	Nicole Boegman (AUS) 6.58
Triple Jump	Ashia Hansen (ENG) 14.32	Francoise Mbango (CMR) 13.95	Connie Henry (ENG) 13.94
Shot Put	Judy Oakes (ENG) 18.83	Myrtle Augee (ENG) 17.16	Johanna Abrahamse (RSA) 16.52
Discus	Beatrice Faumuina (NZL) 65.92	Lisa-Marie Vizaniari (AUS) 62.14	Alison Lever (AUS) 59.80
Hammer	Deborah Sosimenko (AUS) 66.56	Lorraine Shaw (ENG) 62.66	Caroline Wittrin (CAN) 61.67
Heptathlon	Denise Lewis (ENG) 6513	Jane Jamieson (AUS) 6354	Joanne Henry (NZL) 6096
Javelin	Louise McPaul (AUS) 66.96	Karen Martin (ENG) 57.82	Kirsty Morrison (ENG) 56.34

2002 Manchester

Men's	Gold	Silver	Bronze
100m	Kim Collins (SKN) 9.98	Uchenna Emedolu (NGR) 10.11	Pierre Browne (CAN) 10.12
200m	Frankie Fredericks (NAM) 20.06	Marlon Devonish (ENG) 20.19	Darren Campbell (ENG) 20.21
400m	Michael Blackwood (JAM) 45.07	Shane Niemi (CAN) 45.09	Avard Moncur (BAH) 45.12
800m	Mbulaeni Mulaudzi (RSA) 1:46.32	Joseph Mutua (KEN) 1:46.57	Kris McCarthy (AUS) 1:46.79
1500m	Mike East (ENG) 3:37.35	William Chirchir (KEN) 3:37.70	Youcef Abdi (AUS) 3:37.77
5000m	Sammy Kipketer (KEN) 13:13.51	Benjamin Limo (KEN) 13:13.57	Willy Kiptoo Kirui (KEN) 13:18.02
10,000m	Wilberforce Talel (KEN) 27:45.39	Paul Malakwen (KEN) 27:45.46	John Yuda (TAN) 27:45.78
Marathon	Francis Naali (TAN) 2:11:58	Joshua Chelanga (KEN) 2:12:44	Andrew Letherby (AUS) 2:13:23
3000m Steeplechase	Stephen Cherono (KEN) 8:19.41	Ezekiel Kemboi (KEN) 8:19.78	Abraham Cherono (KEN) 8:19.85
110m Hurdles	Shaun Bownes (RSA) 13.35	Colin Jackson (WAL) 13.39	Maurice Wignall (JAM) 13.62
400m Hurdles	Chris Rawlinson (ENG) 49.14	Matt Elias (WAL) 49.28	Ian Weakley (JAM) 49.69
20km Walk	Nathan Deakes (AUS) 1:25:35	Luke Adams (AUS) 1:26:03	David Kimutai (KEN) 1:28:20
50km Walk	Nathan Deakes (AUS) 3:52:40	Craig Barrett (NZL) 3:56:42	Tim Berrett (CAN) 4:04:25
4 × 100m Relay	England 38.62	Jamaica 38.62	Australia 38.87
4 × 400m Relay	England 3:00.40	Wales 3:00.41	Bahamas 3:01.35
High Jump	Mark Boswell (CAN) 2.28	Kwaku Boateng (CAN) 2.25	Ben Challenger (ENG) 2.25
Pole Vault	Okkert Brits (RSA) 5.75	Paul Burgess (AUS) 5.70	Dominic Johnson (LCA) 5.60
Long Jump	Nathan Morgan (ENG) 8.02	Gable Garenamotse (BOT) 7.91	Kareem Streete-Thompson (CAY) 7.89
Triple Jump	Jonathan Edwards (ENG) 17.86	Phillips Idowu (ENG) 17.68	Leevan Sands (BAH) 17.26
Shot Put	Justin Anlezark (AUS) 20.91	Janus Robberts (RSA) 19.97	Carl Myerscough (ENG) 19.91
Discus	Frantz Kruger (RSA) 66.39	Jason Tunks (CAN) 62.61	Robert Weir (ENG) 59.24
Hammer	Mick Jones (ENG) 72.55	Philip Jensen (NZL) 69.48	Paul Head (ENG) 68.60
Javelin	Steve Backley (ENG) 86.81	Scott Russell (CAN) 78.98	Nick Nieland (ENG) 78.63
Decathlon	Claston Bernard (JAM) 7830	Matt McEwen (AUS) 7685	Jamie Quarry (SCO) 7630

Women's	Gold	Silver	Bronze
100m	Debbie Ferguson (BAH) 10.91	Veronica Campbell (JAM) 11.00	Sevatheda Fynes (BAH) 11.07
200m	Debbie Ferguson (BAH) 22.20	Juliet Campbell (JAM) 22.54	Lauren Hewitt (AUS) 22.69
400m	Aliann Pompey (GUY) 51.63	Lee McConnell (SCO) 51.68	Sandie Richards (JAM) 51.79
800m	Maria Mutola (MOZ) 1:57.35	Diane Cummins (CAN) 1:58.82	Agnes Samaria (NAM) 1:59.15
1500m	Kelly Holmes (ENG) 4:05.99	Hayley Tullett (WAL) 4:07.52	Helen Pattinson (ENG) 4:07.62
5000m	Paula Radcliffe (ENG) 14:31.42	Edith Masai (KEN) 14:53.76	Ines Chenonges (KEN) 15:06.06
10,000m	Salina Kosgei (KEN) 31:27.83	Susan Chepkemei (KEN) 31:32.04	Susie Power (AUS) 31:32.20
Marathon	Kerryn McCann (AUS) 2:30:05	Krishna Stanton (AUS) 2:34:52	Jackie Gallagher (AUS) 2:36:37
100m Hurdles	Lacena Golding-Clark (JAM) 12.77	Vonette Dixon (JAM) 12.83	Angela Atede (NGR) 12.98
400m Hurdles	Jana Pittman (AUS) 54.40	Debbie-Ann Parris (JAM) 55.24	Karlene Haughton (CAN) 56.13
20km Walk	Jane Saville (AUS) 1:36:34	Lisa Kehler (ENG) 1:36:45	Yu Fang Yuan (MAS) 1:40:00
4 × 100m Relay	Bahamas 42.44	Jamaica 42.73	England 42.84
4 × 400m Relay	Australia 3:25.63	England 3:26.73	Nigeria 3:29.16
High Jump	Hestrie Cloete (RSA) 1.96	Susan Jones (ENG) 1.90	Nicole Forrester (CAN) 1.87
Pole Vault	Tatiana Grigorieva (AUS) 4.35	Kym Howe (AUS) 4.15	Bridgid Isworth (AUS) 4.10 Stephanie McCann (CAN) 4.10 Irie Hill (ENG) 4.10
Long Jump	Elva Goulbourne (JAM) 6.70	Jade Johnson (ENG) 6.58	Anju Bobby George (IND) 6.49
Triple Jump	Ashia Hansen (ENG) 14.86	Francoise Mbango (CMR) 14.82	Trecia Smith (JAM) 14.32
Shot Put	Vivian Chukwuemeka (NGR) 17.53	Valerie Adams (NZL) 17.45	Veronica Abrahamse (RSA) 16.77
Discus	Beatrice Faumuina (NZL) 60.83	Neelam Jaswant Singh (IND) 58.49	Shelley Newman (ENG) 58.13
Hammer	Lorraine Shaw (ENG) 66.83	Bronwyn Eagles (AUS) 65.24	Karyne Di Marco (AUS) 63.40
Javelin	Laverne Eve (BAH) 58.46	Cecilia McIntosh (AUS) 57.42	Kelly Morgan (ENG) 57.42
Heptathlon	Jane Jamieson (AUS) 6059	Kylie Wheeler (AUS) 5962	Margaret Simpson (GHA) 5906

ATHLETICS

AUSTRALIAN RULES FOOTBALL

It is a commonly held misconception about Australian Rules football that its origins are in Gaelic football. In fact, Australian football started as a variation on the various football games played in the English public schools during the 1850s. The two men who defined Australian football as a sport distinct from the English games were Thomas Wentworth Wills (1835-80) and H.C.A. Harrison (1836-1929).

Tom Wills was born in Gundagai, NSW, but was sent to England at the age of 14 where he attended Rugby School in the Midlands. Though not a brilliant scholar, he excelled at games. He became captain of football (obviously Rugby style) and was a champion cricketer, scoring 51 runs in a match against an All England XI and taking nine wickets for Kent against the Gentlemen of Sussex. He returned to Australia in 1856 and became well known there for his cricketing talents. But he was soon looking for a winter activity and this inspired him to discuss various ideas with friends and family.

The new game was devised by Wills, W.J. Hammersley, J.B. Thompson, and a relative of his, who was also a popular writer of the day, H.C.A. Harrison. The Melbourne Football Club was formed on 7 August 1858 – the year of the code's first recorded match between Scotch College and Melbourne Grammar School.

A few games of football were played in 1858 but it was not until 17 May 1859, that Tom Wills chaired the meeting of seven men who framed the first rules of Australian football. Four of the seven had experience of football at Britain's schools and universities. Divided on what the rules should be, they consulted copies of the rules of the English schools – Rugby, Eton, Winchester and Harrow. They framed a set of ten rules from their knowledge of the English games and their experience of the previous season. They wanted a game that was simpler than the complicated rugby and had less of the 'vigour and roughness' of rugby and other school games.

The game quickly blossomed. The Geelong Football Club was formed in 1859, and in 1866 an updated set of rules was put in place and competition started.

The Victorian Football League (VFL) was established in 1896 and the following year the League's first games were played among the foundation clubs – Carlton, Collingwood, Essendon, Fitzroy, Geelong, Melbourne, St Kilda and South Melbourne. In 1908, Richmond and University joined the competition. But after the 1914 season, University left the League. In 1925, Footscray (now the Western Bulldogs), Hawthorn and North Melbourne (now the Kangaroos) joined the VFL.

After operating with 12 Victorian suburban teams for over fifty years, the VFL expanded geographically in 1982 when South Melbourne became the Swans after moving to Sydney. The line-up of 12 clubs remained unchanged until 1987 when the league was enlarged to include the West Coast Eagles and the Brisbane Bears.

In 1990, the league became known as the Australian Football League (AFL).

By 1997, the competition comprised 16 clubs after Adelaide (in 1991), Fremantle (in 1995) and Port Adelaide (in 1997) joined, and foundation club Fitzroy merged with the Brisbane Bears to form the Brisbane Lions after the 1996 season.

The Grand Final, the equivalent of Britain's FA Cup, is played every year at the Melbourne Cricket Ground on the last Saturday in September. The record attendance of 121,696 was in 1970 and West Coast Eagles, in 1992, were the first team from outside Victoria to win.

Each team consists of 18 players with an extra four players on the interchange bench. These interchange players may come on and off at any stage through the match.

The ball is bounced in the centre of the ground to commence the game. The players then try to move the ball towards their goals by either handpassing – holding the ball in one hand and punching it with the other hand – or kicking it. If a player kicks the ball and another player, either his team-mate or an opponent, catches it (called a mark), then that player can stop play without fear of being tackled by the opposition. Players may run with the ball no more than 9.1m without bouncing it on the ground. Throwing the ball is illegal, and there is no offside rule.

A goal is scored when a player kicks the ball through the two taller upright posts. Six points is given for a goal. If the ball passes either side of the tall posts, a behind is registered for one point. The total score is the addition of goals and behinds. For example: 3 goals, 2 behinds = 20 points.

A game consists of four quarters of 20 minutes each. Time is added on when a goal is scored or a bounce up is conducted.

The game is played on an oval field with a greatest width of between 110m and 155m and a length of between 135m and 180m.

Two posts, called goal posts, with a minimum height of 6m are placed at each end of the playing surface at a distance of 6.4m apart. A further two posts, called behind posts, with a minimum height of 3m, are placed at a distance of 6.4m on each side of the goal posts so that a straight line can be drawn on the ground to join each post. To prevent injuries when running at high speeds, the goalposts are padded in accordance with AFL rules.

A football must be between 720mm and 730mm in length and 545mm to 555mm in width and be inflated between 62 and 76kpa.

Australian Football League Teams

Adelaide Crows

Joined league: 1991
Home venue: Football Park, Adelaide
Official colours: Navy blue guernsey, with red and gold hoops
Home venue dimensions: 180 metres x 145 metres
Premierships: 2

Brisbane Lions

Joined league: 1987
Home venue: The Gabba, Queensland
Official colours: Maroon guernsey, with gold 'V' and white trim
Home venue dimensions: 165 metres x 145 metres
Premierships: 2

Carlton Blues

Joined league: 1897
Home venue: Optus Oval, Victoria
Official colours: Navy blue guernsey with white monogram
Home venue dimensions: 152 metres x 139 metres
Premierships: 15

Collingwood Magpies

Joined league: 1897
Home venue: Melbourne Cricket Ground
Official colours: Vertical black and white striped guernsey
Home venue dimensions: 161 metres x 140 metres
Premierships: 14

Essendon Bombers

Joined league: 1897
Home venue: Melbourne Cricket Ground
Official colours: Black guernsey with red sash
Home venue dimensions: 161 metres x 140 metres
Premierships: 15

Fremantle Dockers

Joined league: 1995
Home venue: Subiaco, Western Australia
Official colours: Purple guernsey with green and red chest.
Panels separated by a white anchor
Home venue dimensions: 173 metres x 129 metres
Premierships: 0

Geelong Cats

Joined league: 1897
Home venue: Shell Stadium, Victoria
Official colours: Navy blue and white hooped guernsey
Home venue dimensions: 171 metres x 117 metres
Premierships: 6

Hawthorn Hawks

Joined league: 1925
Home venue: Telstra Dome, Victoria
Official colours: Vertical brown and gold striped guernsey
Home venue dimensions: 180 metres x 142 metres
Premierships: 9

Melbourne Demons

Joined league: 1897
Home venue: Melbourne Cricket Ground
Official colours: Navy blue guernsey with red yolk
Home venue dimensions: 161 metres x 140 metres
Premierships: 12

North Melbourne Kangaroos

Joined league: 1925
Home venue: Telstra Dome, Victoria
Official colours: Vertical royal blue and white striped guernsey
Home venue dimensions: 161 metres x 140 metres
Premierships: 2

Port Adelaide Power

Joined league: 1997
Home venue: Football Park, Adelaide
Official colours: blue, black and white guernsey
Home venue dimensions: 180 metres x 145 metres
Premierships: 0

Richmond Tigers

Joined league: 1908
Home venue: Melbourne Cricket Ground
Official colours: black guernsey with gold sash
Home venue dimensions: 161 metres x 140 metres
Premierships: 10

St Kilda Saints

Joined league: 1897
Home venue: Telstra Dome, Victoria
Official colours: Vertical red, white and black striped guernsey
Home venue dimensions: 180 metres x 142 metres
Premierships: 1

Sydney Swans

Joined league: 1897 (South Melbourne) 1982 (Sydney)
Home venue: Sydney Cricket Ground
Official colours: White guernsey with red yoke incorporating
Sydney Opera House insignia
Home venue dimensions: 153 metres x 137 metres
Premierships: 3

West Coast Eagles

Joined league: 1987
Home venue: WACA, Western Australia
Official colours: Royal blue guernsey with gold eagle wings
Home venue dimensions: 165 metres x 129 metres
Premierships: 2

Western Bulldogs

Joined league: 1925
Home venue: Telstra Dome, Victoria
Official colours: Royal blue guernsey with red and white bands
Home venue dimensions: 152 metres x 132 metres
Premierships: 1

AUSTRALIAN RULES FOOTBALL

The Grand Final

(Played at the Melbourne Cricket Ground except in 1945 when it was played at North Carlton)

1897	Essendon won on round robin from Geelong			1951	Geelong	81-70	Essendon
1898	Fitzroy	38-23	Essendon	1952	Geelong	86-40	Collingwood
1899	Fitzroy	27-26	South Melbourne	1953	Collingwood	77-65	Geelong
1900	Melbourne	34-30	Fitzroy	1954	Footscray	102-51	Melbourne
1901	Essendon	43-16	Collingwood	1955	Melbourne	64-36	Collingwood
1902	Collingwood	60-27	Essendon	1956	Melbourne	111-48	Collingwood
1903	Collingwood	33-29	Fitzroy	1957	Melbourne	116-55	Essendon
1904	Fitzroy	61-37	Carlton	1958	Collingwood	82-64	Melbourne
1905	Fitzroy	30-17	Collingwood	1959	Melbourne	115-78	Essendon
1906	Carlton	94-45	Fitzroy	1960	Melbourne	62-14	Collingwood
1907	Carlton	50-45	South Melbourne	1961	Hawthorn	93-51	Footscray
1908	Carlton	35-26	Essendon	1962	Essendon	90-58	Carlton
1909	South Melbourne	38-36	Carlton	1963	Geelong	109-60	Hawthorn
1910	Collingwood	61-47	Carlton	1964	Melbourne	64-60	Collingwood
1911	Essendon	41-35	Collingwood	1965	Essendon	105-70	St Kilda
1912	Essendon	47-33	South Melbourne	1966	St Kilda	74-73	Collingwood
1913	Fitzroy	55-43	St Kilda	1967	Richmond	114-105	Geelong
1914	Carlton	45-39	South Melbourne	1968	Carlton	56-53	Essendon
1915	Carlton	78-45	Collingwood	1969	Richmond	85-60	Carlton
1916	Fitzroy	85-56	Carlton	1970	Carlton	111-101	Collingwood
1917	Collingwood	74-39	Fitzroy	1971	Hawthorn	82-75	St Kilda
1918	South Melbourne	62-57	Collingwood	1972	Carlton	177-145	Richmond
1919	Collingwood	78-53	Richmond	1973	Richmond	116-86	Carlton
1920	Richmond	52-35	Collingwood	1974	Richmond	128-87	North Melbourne
1921	Richmond	36-32	Carlton	1975	North Melbourne	122-67	Hawthorn
1922	Fitzroy	79-68	Collingwood	1976	Hawthorn	100-70	North Melbourne
1923	Essendon	63-46	Fitzroy	1977	North Melbourne	151-124	Collingwood
1924	Essendon won on round robin from Richmond			1978	Hawthorn	121-103	North Melbourne
1925	Geelong	79-69	Collingwood	1979	Carlton	82-77	Collingwood
1926	Melbourne	119-72	Collingwood	1980	Richmond	159-78	Collingwood
1927	Collingwood	25-13	Richmond	1981	Carlton	92-72	Collingwood
1928	Collingwood	96-63	Richmond	1982	Carlton	103-85	Richmond
1929	Collingwood	79-50	Richmond	1983	Hawthorn	140-63	Essendon
1930	Collingwood	100-70	Geelong	1984	Essendon	105-81	Hawthorn
1931	Geelong	68-48	Richmond	1985	Essendon	170-92	Hawthorn
1932	Richmond	92-83	Carlton	1986	Hawthorn	110-70	Carlton
1933	South Melbourne	71-29	Richmond	1987	Carlton	104-73	Hawthorn
1934	Richmond	128-89	South Melbourne	1988	Hawthorn	152-56	Melbourne
1935	Collingwood	78-58	South Melbourne	1989	Hawthorn	144-138	Geelong
1936	Collingwood	89-76	South Melbourne	1990	Collingwood	89-41	Essendon
1937	Geelong	122-90	Collingwood	1991	Hawthorn	139-86	West Coast Eagles
1938	Carlton	100-85	Collingwood	1992	West Coast Eagles	113-85	Geelong
1939	Melbourne	148-95	Collingwood	1993	Essendon	133-89	Carlton
1940	Melbourne	107-68	Richmond	1994	West Coast	143-63	Geelong
1941	Melbourne	127-98	Essendon	1995	Carlton	141-80	Geelong
1942	Essendon	132-79	Richmond	1996	North Melbourne	131-88	Sydney
1943	Richmond	86-81	Essendon	1997	Adelaide	125-94	St Kilda
1944	Fitzroy	66-51	Richmond	1998	Adelaide	105-70	North Melbourne
1945	Carlton	103-75	South Melbourne	1999	North Melbourne	124-89	Carlton
1946	Essendon	150-87	Melbourne	2000	Essendon	135-75	North Melbourne
1947	Carlton	86-85	Essendon	2001	Brisbane Lions	108-82	Essendon
1948	Melbourne	89-50	Essendon	2002	Brisbane Lions	75-66	Collingwood
1949	Essendon	125-52	Carlton	2003	Brisbane Lions	134-84	Collingwood
1950	Essendon	92-54	North Melbourne				

BADMINTON

Badminton has a surprisingly long history given its relatively recent introduction to the Olympic scene. Its origins date back at least two thousand years to the game of battledore and shuttlecock played in ancient Greece, India and China, the battledore being a paddle and the shuttlecock a small feathered cork, now usually called a 'bird'. Also played for centuries by children in India, Thailand and Japan, this was a cooperative game in which the players worked together to keep the 'bird' in the air for as long as possible. A net was later added and the game had become a competitive sport called 'poona' by the 1860s, when British Army officers were playing it in India. Some of them brought equipment back to England and introduced the new sport there during the early 1870s.

The game was played at a lawn party held by the Duke of Beaufort at his country seat, Badminton, Gloucestershire, in 1873, and it became known as 'the Badminton game' among various guests who introduced it to other friends. Coincidentally, Gloucestershire is now the base for the International Badminton Federation.

The Bath Badminton Club, organised in 1877, developed the first written rules, and these have remained essentially the same ever since. In 1893, the Badminton Association of England was founded as the first national governing body and the first All-England Championship was held in 1899.

The Badminton Club of New York was organised in 1878, but it was primarily a social club. The Badminton Health Club of Boston, founded in 1908, devoted more time to the sport and its membership grew to more than 300 by 1925. But badminton did not become genuinely popular in the USA until the 1930s. In 1935, the American Badminton Association (ABA) was founded and it conducted the first national championship tournament on 1 April 1937.

The International Badminton Federation (IBF) was founded in 1934, its nine original members being Canada, Denmark, England, France, Ireland, Netherlands, New Zealand, Scotland and Wales. Membership of the Federation has since risen steadily, with a notable increase in new members after badminton's Olympic debut. Development in the sport continues and the current membership of 142 is expected to increase further. The first team world championship took place in 1949 and individual world championships are now held in odd-numbered years (beginning in 1977), team championships in even-numbered years. The leading team competitions are the Thomas Cup (men) and the Uber Cup (women).

Badminton became a Commonwealth Games sport in 1966 and was staged as a demonstration sport at the 1972 Olympics. It was added to the Olympic programme at Barcelona in 1992 with singles and doubles competition for men and women. The mixed doubles event was added in 1996. Badminton also became a Pan-American Games sport in 1995.

Badminton became a professional sport in the 1980s, when the IBF established the World Grand Prix Circuit. The US Open, which offers $200,000 in prize money, is the highest-paying tournament on the tour.

The court is 44ft (13.4m) long and 17ft (5.18m) wide for singles, 20ft (6.1m) wide for doubles. A net 5ft (1.52m) high stretches across the width of the court at its centre. The shuttle may be made from natural or synthetic fibres but must have 16 feathers protruding from the base. The tips of the feathers shall lie on a dome-shaped base with a diameter from 58mm to 68mm. The shuttle must weigh between 4.74g and 5.50g. Shuttles rarely last more than a few points in international games although a club player may use the same one for days. The frame of the racket should not exceed 680mm in overall length and 230mm in overall width. The stringed area should not exceed 280mm in overall length and 220mm in overall width. However, the strings may extend into an area which otherwise would be the throat, provided that the width of the extended stringed area does not exceed 35mm and that the overall length of the stringed area does not then exceed 330mm.

A match consists of the best of three games, unless otherwise arranged. In doubles and men's singles a game is won by the first side to score 15 points. In women's singles a game is won by the first side to score 11 points. If the score becomes 14-all (10-all in women's singles), the side which first scored 14 (10) exercises the choice to continue the game to 15 (11) points, i.e. not to 'set' the game; or to 'set' the game to 17 (13) points.

The side winning a game serves first in the next game.

Only the serving end can add a point to its score.

Players change ends at the end of each game and if a third game is played then ends are changed after 8 points (in a 15-point game) or 6 points (in an 11-point game).

The server and receiver stand within diagonally opposite service courts without touching the boundary lines of these service courts. In singles the server must serve from, and receive in, their respective right service courts when the server has not scored or has scored an even number of points in that game. The players serve from, and receive in, their respective left service courts when the server has scored an odd number of points in that game.

In doubles, at the start of a game, and each time a side gains the right to serve, the service is commenced from the right service court. Points may only be scored on service.

All-England Badminton Championships

Men's Singles

1900	Sidney H. Smith (ENG)	1958	Erland Kops (DEN)
1901	Captain H.W. Davies (ENG)	1959	Tan Joe Hok (INA)
1902	Ralph Watling (ENG)	1960	Erland Kops (DEN)
1903	Ralph Watling (ENG)	1961	Erland Kops (DEN)
1904	Henry Norman Marrett (ENG)	1962	Erland Kops (DEN)
1905	Henry Norman Marrett (ENG)	1963	Erland Kops (DEN)
1906	Norman Wood (ENG)	1964	Knud Aage Nielsen (DEN)
1907	Norman Wood (ENG)	1965	Erland Kops (DEN)
1908	Henry Norman Marrett (ENG)	1966	Tan Aik Huang (MAS)
1909	Frank Chesterton (ENG)	1967	Erland Kops (DEN)
1910	Frank Chesterton (ENG)	1968	Rudy Hartono (INA)
1911	Guy A. Sautter (ENG)	1969	Rudy Hartono (INA)
1912	Frank Chesterton (ENG)	1970	Rudy Hartono (INA)
1913	Guy A. Sautter (ENG)	1971	Rudy Hartono (INA)
1914	Guy A. Sautter (ENG)	1972	Rudy Hartono (INA)
1915-19 not held		1973	Rudy Hartono (INA)
1920	Sir George Alan Thomas (ENG)	1974	Rudy Hartono (INA)
1921	Sir George Alan Thomas (ENG)	1975	Svend Pri (DEN)
1922	Sir George Alan Thomas (ENG)	1976	Rudy Hartono (INA)
1923	Sir George Alan Thomas (ENG)	1977	Flemming Delfs (DEN)
1924	Gordon 'Curly' Mack (IRL)	1978	Liem Swie King (INA)
1925	Frank Devlin (IRL)	1979	Liem Swie King (INA)
1926	Frank Devlin (IRL)	1980	Prakash Padukone (IND)
1927	Frank Devlin (IRL)	1981	Liem Swie King (INA)
1928	Frank Devlin (IRL)	1982	Morten Frost (DEN)
1929	Frank Devlin (IRL)	1983	Luan Jin (CHN)
1930	Donald C. Hume (ENG)	1984	Morten Frost (DEN)
1931	Frank Devlin (IRL)	1985	Zhao Jianhua (CHN)
1932	Ralph C.F. Nichols (ENG)	1986	Morten Frost (DEN)
1933	R.M. White (ENG)	1987	Morten Frost (DEN)
1934	Ralph C.F. Nichols (ENG)	1988	Ib Frederiksen (DEN)
1935	R.M. White (ENG)	1989	Yang Yang (CHN)
1936	Ralph C.F. Nichols (ENG)	1990	Zhao Jianhua (CHN)
1937	Ralph C.F. Nichols (ENG)	1991	Ardy Wiranata (INA)
1938	Ralph C.F. Nichols (ENG)	1992	Liu Jun (CHN)
1939	Tage Madsen (DEN)	1993	Heryanto Arbi (INA)
1940-46 not held		1994	Heryanto Arbi (INA)
1947	Conny Jepsen (SWE)	1995	Poul Erik Høyer (DEN)
1948	Jørn Skaarup (DEN)	1996	Poul Erik Høyer (DEN)
1949	Dave G. Freemann (USA)	1997	Dong Jiong (CHN)
1950	Wong Peng Soon (MAS)	1998	Sun Jun (CHN)
1951	Wong Peng Soon (MAS)	1999	Peter Gade (DEN)
1952	Wong Peng Soon (MAS)	2000	Xia Xuanze (CHN)
1953	Eddy B. Choong (MAS)	2001	Pulella Gopichand (IND)
1954	Eddy B. Choong (MAS)	2002	Cheng Hong (CHN)
1955	Wong Peng Soon (MAS)	2003	Hafiz Hashim (MAS)
1956	Eddy B. Choong (MAS)	2004	Lin Dan (CHN)
1957	Eddy B. Choong (MAS)		

Women's Singles

1900	Ethel B. Thomson (ENG)	1915-19 not held	
1901	Ethel B. Thomson (ENG)	1920	Kitty McKane (ENG)
1902	Muriel Lucas (ENG)	1921	Kitty McKane (ENG)
1903	Ethel B. Thomson (ENG)	1922	Kitty McKane (ENG)
1904	Ethel B. Thomson (ENG)	1923	Lavinia C. Radeglia (ENG)
1905	Ethel B. Thomson (ENG)	1924	Kitty McKane (ENG)
1906	Ethel B. Thomson (ENG)	1925	Margaret Stocks (ENG)
1907	Ethel B. Thomson (ENG)	1926	F.G. Barrett (ENG)
1908	Ethel B. Thomson (ENG)	1927	F.G. Barrett (ENG)
1909	Ethel B. Thomson (ENG)	1928	Margaret Rivers Tragett (ENG)
1910	Ethel B. Thomson (ENG)	1929	F.G. Barrett (ENG)
1911	Margaret Larminie (ENG)	1930	F.G. Barrett (ENG)
1912	Margaret Rivers (Larminie) Tragett (ENG)	1931	F.G. Barrett (ENG)
1913	Lavinia C. Radeglia (ENG)	1932	Leoni Kingsbury (ENG)
1914	Lavinia C. Radeglia (ENG)	1933	Alice Woodroffe (ENG)

1934	Leoni Kingsbury (ENG)
1935	Betty Uber (ENG)
1936	Telma Kingsbury (ENG)
1937	Telma Kingsbury (ENG)
1938	Daphne Young (ENG)
1939	Dorothy Walton (CAN)
1940-46 not held	
1947	Marie Ussing (DEN)
1948	Kirsten Thorndahl (DEN)
1949	Aase Schiøtt Jacobsen (DEN)
1950	Tonny Ahm (DEN)
1951	Aase Schiøtt Jacobsen (DEN)
1952	Tonny Ahm (DEN)
1953	Marie Ussing (DEN)
1954	Judy Devlin (USA)
1955	Margaret Varner (USA)
1956	Margaret Varner (USA)
1957	Judy Devlin (USA)
1958	Judy Devlin (USA)
1959	Heather M. Ward (ENG)
1960	Judy Devlin (USA)
1961	Judy (Devlin) Hashman (USA)
1962	Judy Hashman (USA)
1963	Judy Hashman (USA)
1964	Judy Hashman (USA)
1965	Ursula Smith (ENG)
1966	Judy Hashman (USA)
1967	Judy Hashman (USA)
1968	Eva Twedberg (SWE)
1969	Hiroe Yuki (JPN)
1970	Etsuko Takenake (JPN)
1971	Eva Twedberg (SWE)
1972	N. Nakayama (JPN)

1973	Margaret Beck (ENG)
1974	Hiroe Yuki (JPN)
1975	Hiroe Yuki (JPN)
1976	Gillian Gilks (ENG)
1977	Hiroe Yuki (JPN)
1978	Gillian Gilks (ENG)
1979	Lene Køppen (DEN)
1980	Lene Køppen (DEN)
1981	Hwang Sun Ai (KOR)
1982	Zhang Ailing (CHN)
1983	Zhang Ailing (CHN)
1984	Li Lingwei (CHN)
1985	Han Aiping (CHN)
1986	Kim Yun-Ja (KOR)
1987	Kirsten Larsen (DEN)
1988	Gu Jiaming (CHN)
1989	Li Lingwei (CHN)
1990	Susi Susanti (INA)
1991	Susi Susanti (INA)
1992	Tang Jiuhong (CHN)
1993	Susi Susanti (INA)
1994	Susi Susanti (INA)
1995	Lim Xiao Qing (SWE)
1996	Bang Soo Hyun (KOR)
1997	Ye Zhaoying (CHN)
1998	Ye Zhaoying (CHN)
1999	Ye Zhaoying (CHN)
2000	Gong Zhichao (CHN)
2001	Gong Zhichao (CHN)
2002	Camilla Martin (DEN)
2003	Zhou Mi (CHN)
2004	Gong Ruina (CHN)

Men's Doubles

1899	D. Oakes/Stewart Massey (ENG)
1900	H.L. Mellersh/F.S. Collier (ENG)
1901	H.L. Mellersh/F.S. Collier (ENG)
1902	H.L. Mellersh/F.S. Collier (ENG)
1903	Stewart Marsden Massey/E.L. Huson (ENG)
1904	Albert Davis Prebble/Henry Norman Marrett (ENG)
1905	C.T.J. Barnes/Stewart Marsden Massey (ENG)
1906	Henry Norman Marrett/George Alan Thomas (ENG)
1907	Albert Davis Prebble/Norman Wood (ENG)
1908	Henry Norman Marrett/George Alan Thomas (ENG)
1909	Frank Chesterton/Albert Davis Prebble (ENG)
1910	Henry Norman Marrett/George Alan Thomas (ENG)
1911	P.D. Fitton/Ernest Edward Shedden Hawthorn (ENG)
1912	Henry Norman Marrett/George Alan Thomas (ENG)
1913	Frank Chesterton/George Alan Thomas (ENG)
1914	Frank Chesterton/George Alan Thomas (ENG)
1915-19 not held	
1920	A.F. Engelbach/R. Du Roveray (ENG)
1921	Sir George Alan Thomas/Frank Hodge (ENG)
1922	Guy A. Sautter (ENG)/Frank Devlin (IRL)
1923	Frank Devlin/Gordon 'Curly' Mack (IRL)
1924	Sir George Alan Thomas/Frank Hodge (ENG)
1925	Herbert Uber/A.K. Jones (ENG)
1926	Frank Devlin/Gordon 'Curly' Mack (IRL)
1927	Frank Devlin/Gordon 'Curly' Mack (IRL)
1928	Sir George Alan Thomas/Frank Hodge (ENG)
1929	Frank Devlin/Gordon 'Curly' Mack (IRL)
1930	Frank Devlin/Gordon 'Curly' Mack (IRL)
1931	Frank Devlin/Gordon 'Curly' Mack (IRL)
1932	Donald C. Hume/R.M. White (ENG)

1933	Donald C. Hume/R.M. White (ENG)
1934	Donald C. Hume/R.M. White (ENG)
1935	Donald C. Hume/R.M. White (ENG)
1936	L. Nichols/Ralph C.F. Nichols (ENG)
1937	L. Nichols/Ralph C.F. Nichols (ENG)
1938	L. Nichols/Ralph C.F. Nichols (ENG)
1939	T.H. Boyle/J.L. Rankin (IRL)
1940-46 not held	
1947	Tage Madsen/Poul Holm (DEN)
1948	Preben Dabelsteen/Børge Frederiksen (DEN)
1949	Ooi Teck Hock/Tech Seng Khoon (MAS)
1950	Jørn Skaarup/Preben Dabelsteen (DEN)
1951	David Ewe Choong/Eddy B. Choong (MAS)
1952	David Ewe Choong/Eddy B. Choong (MAS)
1953	David Ewe Choong/Eddy B. Choong (MAS)
1954	Ooi Teik Hock/Ong Poh Lim (MAS)
1955	Finn Kobberø/Jørgen Hammergaard Hansen (DEN)
1956	Finn Kobberø/Jørgen Hammergaard Hansen (DEN)
1957	J.C. Alston (USA)/'Johny' Heah (MAS)
1958	Erland Kops/Poul Erik Nielsen (DEN)
1959	Lim Say Hup/Teh Kew San (MAS)
1960	Finn Kobberø/Poul Erik Nielsen (DEN)
1961	Finn Kobberø/Jørgen Hammergaard Hansen (DEN)
1962	Finn Kobberø/Jørgen Hammergaard Hansen (DEN)
1963	Finn Kobberø/Jørgen Hammergaard Hansen (DEN)
1964	Finn Kobberø/Jørgen Hammergaard Hansen (DEN)
1965	Ng Boon Bee/Tan Yee Khan (MAS)
1966	Ng Boon Bee/Tan Yee Khan (MAS)
1967	Henning Borch/Erland Kops (DEN)
1968	Henning Borch/Erland Kops (DEN)

BADMINTON

1969	Henning Borch/Erland Kops (DEN)
1970	Tom Bacher/Poul Petersen (DEN)
1971	Ng Boon Bee/Punch Gunalan (MAS)
1972	Christian/Ade Chandra (INA)
1973	Christian/Wahjudi (INA)
1974	Tjun Tjun/Wahjudi (INA)
1975	Tjun Tjun/Wahjudi (INA)
1976	Bengt Frøman/Thomas Kihlstrøm (SWE)
1977	Tjun Tjun/Wahjudi (INA)
1978	Tjun Tjun/Wahjudi (INA)
1979	Tjun Tjun/Wahjudi (INA)
1980	Tjun Tjun/Wahjudi (INA)
1981	Rudy Heryanto/H. Kartono (INA)
1982	Razif Sidek/Jalani Sidek (MAS)
1983	Thomas Kihlstrøm/Stefan Karlsson (SWE)
1984	Rudy Heryanto/H. Kartono (INA)
1985	Kim Moon Soo/Park Joo Bong (KOR)
1986	Kim Moon Soo/Park Joo Bong (KOR)
1987	Li Yongbo/Tian Bingyi (CHN)
1988	Li Yongbo/Tian Bingyi (INA)
1989	Lee Sang Bok/Park Joo Bong (KOR)
1990	Kim Moon Soo/Park Joo Bong (KOR)
1991	Li Yongbo/Tian Bingyi (INA)
1992	Rudy Gunawan/Eddy Hartono (INA)
1993	Jon Holst-Christensen/Thomas Lund (DEN)
1994	Rudy Gunawan/Bambang Suprianto (INA)
1995	Rexy Mainaky/Ricky Subagja (INA)
1996	Rexy Mainaky/Ricky Subagja (INA)
1997	Ha Tae-Kwon/Kang Kyung-Min (KOR)
1998	Lee Dong Soo/Yoo Yong Sung (KOR)
1999	Tony Gunawan/Chandra Wijaya (INA)
2000	Ha Tae Kwon/Kim Dong-Moon (KOR)
2001	Tony Gunawan/Halim Heryanto (INA)
2002	Ha Tae-Kwon/Kim Dong-Moon (KOR)
2003	Sigit Budiarto/Candra Wijaya (INA)
2004	Jens Eriksen/Martin Hansen (DEN)

Women's Doubles

1899	Muriel Lucas/Graeme (ENG)
1900	Muriel Lucas/Graeme (ENG)
1901	St John/E. Moseley (ENG)
1902	Ethel B. Thomson/Muriel Lucas (ENG)
1903	M. Hardy/D.K. Douglas (ENG)
1904	Ethel B. Thomson/Muriel Lucas (ENG)
1905	Ethel B. Thomson/Muriel Lucas (ENG)
1906	Ethel B. Thomson/Muriel Lucas (ENG)
1907	G.L. Murray/Muriel Lucas (ENG)
1908	G.L. Murray/Muriel Lucas (ENG)
1909	G.L. Murray/Muriel Lucas (ENG)
1910	M.K. Bateman/Muriel Lucas (ENG)
1911	A. Gowenlock/D. Cundall (ENG)
1912	A. Gowenlock/D. Cundall (ENG)
1913	Hazel Hogarth/M.K. Bateman (ENG)
1914	Margaret Rivers (Larminie) Tragett/Eveline Grace Peterson (ENG)
1915-19 not held	
1920	Lavinia C. Radeglia/Violet Elton (ENG)
1921	Kitty McKane/Margaret McKane (ENG)
1922	Margaret Rivers Tragett/Hazel Hogarth (ENG)
1923	Margaret Rivers Tragett/Hazel Hogarth (ENG)
1924	Margaret (McKane) Stocks/Kitty McKane (ENG)
1925	Margaret Rivers Tragett Hazel Hogarth (ENG)
1926	A.M. Head/Violet Elton (ENG)
1927	Margaret Rivers Tragett/Hazel Hogarth (ENG)
1928	F.G. Barrett/Violet Elton (ENG)
1929	F.G. Barrett/Violet Elton (ENG)
1930	F.G. Barrett/Violet Elton (ENG)
1931	Marion Horsley/Betty Uber (ENG)
1932	F.G. Barrett/Leoni Kingsley (ENG)
1933	Thelma Kingsbury/Marjorie Bell (ENG)
1934	Marjorie Henderson/Thelma Kingsbury (ENG)
1935	Marjorie Henderson/Thelma Kingsbury (ENG)
1936	Marjorie Henderson/Thelma Kingsbury (ENG)
1937	Betty Uber/D. Doveton (ENG)
1938	Betty Uber/D. Doveton (ENG)
1939	Ruth Dalsgaard/Tonny Olsen (DEN)
1940-46 not held	
1947	Tonny (Olsen) Ahm/Kirsten Thorndahl (DEN)
1949	Betty Uber/Queenie Allen (ENG)
1950	Tonny Ahm/Kirsten Thorndahl (DEN)
1951	Tonny Ahm/Kirsten Thorndahl (DEN)
1952	Tonny Ahm/Aase Schiøtt Jacobsen (DEN)
1953	Iris Cooley/June White (ENG)
1954	Sue Devlin Judy Devlin (USA)
1955	Iris Cooley/June White (ENG)
1956	Sue Devlin Judy Devlin (USA)
1957	Anni Hammergaard Hansen/Kirsten Thorndahl (DEN)
1958	Margaret Varner (USA)/Heather M. Ward (ENG)
1959	Iris Rogers/June (White) Timperley (ENG)
1960	Sue Devlin/Judy Devlin (USA)
1961	Judy (Devlin) Hashman (USA)/Sue Peard (IRL)
1962	Judy Hashman (USA)/Tonny Holst-Christensen (DEN)
1963	Judy Hashman (USA)/Sue Peard (IRL)
1964	Karin Jørgensen/Ulla Rasmussen (DEN)
1965	Karin Jørgensen/Ulla (Rasmussen) Strand (DEN)
1966	Judy Hashman (USA)/Sue Peard (IRL)
1967	Imre Rietveld (NED)/Ulla Strand (DEN)
1968	Minarni/Koestijah (INA)
1969	Margaret Boxall/Sue (Pound) Whetnall (ENG)
1970	Margaret Boxall/Sue Whetnall (ENG)
1971	Noriko Takagi/Hiroe Yuki (JPN)
1972	Machiko Aizawa/Etsuko Takanaka (JPN)
1973	Machiko Aizawa/Etsuko Takanaka (JPN)
1974	Margaret Beck/Gillian Gilks (ENG)
1975	Machiko Aizawa/Etsuko Takanaka (JPN)
1976	Gillian Gilks/Sue Whetnall (ENG)
1977	Etsuko Toganoo/Emika Ueno (JPN)
1978	Atsuko Tokuda/Mikiko Takada (JPN)
1979	Verawaty Wiharig/Imalda Wigoeno (INA)
1980	Gillian Gilks/Nora (Gardner) Perry (ENG)
1981	Nora Perry/Jane Webster (ENG)
1982	Lin Yin/Wu Dixi (CHN)
1983	Xu Rong/Wu Jianqiu (CHN)
1984	Lin Yin/Wu Dixi (CHN)
1985	Han Aiping/Li Lingwei (CHN)
1986	Chung Myung-Hee/Hwang Hye-Young (KOR)
1987	Chung Myung-Hee/Hwang Hye-Young (KOR)
1988	Chung So-Young/Kim Yun-Ja (KOR)
1989	Chung Myung-Hee/Chung So-Young (KOR)
1990	Chung Myung-Hee/Hwang Hye-Young (KOR)
1991	Chung So-Young/Hwang Hye-Young (KOR)
1992	Lin Yanfan/Yao Fen (CHN)
1993	Chung So-Young/Gil Young-Ah (KOR)
1994	Chung So-Young/Gil Young-Ah (KOR)
1995	Gil Young-Ah/Jang Hye Ock (KOR)
1996	Ge Fei/Gu Jun (CHN)
1997	Ge Fei/Gu Jun (CHN)
1998	Ge Fei/Gu Jun (CHN)
1999	Chung Jae-Hee/Ra Kyung-Min (KOR)
2000	Ge Fei/Gu Jun (CHN)
2001	Gao Ling/Huang Sui (CHN)
2002	Gao Ling/Huang Sui (CHN)
2003	Gao Ling/Huang Sui (CHN)
2004	Gao Ling/Huang Sui (CHN)

Mixed Doubles

1899	D. Oakes/St John (ENG)
1900	D. Oakes/St John (ENG)
1901	F.S. Collier/E.M. Stawell-Brown (ENG)
1902	L.U. Ransford/E.M. Moseley (ENG)
1903	George Alan Thomas/Ethel B. Thomson (ENG)
1904	Henry Norman Marrett/Dorothea Katharine Douglas (ENG)
1905	Henry Norman Marrett/Hazel Hogarth (ENG)
1906	George Alan Thomas/Ethel B. Thomson (ENG)
1907	George Alan Thomas/G.L. Murray (ENG)
1908	Norman Wood/Muriel Lucas (ENG)
1909	Albert Davis Prebble/D. Boothby (ENG)
1910	Guy A. Sautter/Penelope Dora Cundall (ENG)
1911	George Alan Thomas/Margaret Larminie (ENG)
1912	E. Hawthorn/Hazel Hogarth (ENG)
1913	Guy A. Sautter/M.E. Mayston (ENG)
1914	George Alan Thomas/Hazel Hogarth (ENG)
1915-19	not held
1920	Sir George Alan Thomas/Hazel Hogarth (ENG)
1921	Sir George Alan Thomas/Hazel Hogarth (ENG)
1922	Sir George Alan Thomas/Hazel Hogarth (ENG)
1923	Gordon 'Curly' Mack (IRL)/Margaret Rivers Tragett (ENG)
1924	Frank Devlin (IRL)/Kitty McKane (ENG)
1925	Frank Devlin (IRL)/Kitty McKane (ENG)
1926	Frank Devlin (IRL)/E.G. Peterson (ENG)
1927	Frank Devlin (IRL)/E.G. Peterson (ENG)
1928	A.E. Harbot/Margaret Rivers Tragett (ENG)
1929	Frank Devlin (IRL)/R.J. Horsley (ENG)
1930	Herbert Uber/Betty Uber (ENG)
1931	Herbert Uber/Betty Uber (ENG)
1932	Herbert Uber/Betty Uber (ENG)
1933	Donald C. Hume/Betty Uber (ENG)
1934	Donald C. Hume/Betty Uber (ENG)
1935	Donald C. Hume/Betty Uber (ENG)
1936	Donald C. Hume/Betty Uber (ENG)
1937	I. Maconachie (IRL)/Thelma Kingsbury (ENG)
1938	R.M. White/Betty Uber (ENG)
1939	Ralph C.F. Nichols/B.M. Staples (ENG)
1940-46	not held
1947	Poul Holm/Tonny Ahm (DEN)
1948	Jørn Skaarup/Kirsten Thorndahl (DEN)
1949	Clinton Stephens/Mrs Stephens (USA)
1950	Poul Holm/Tonny Ahm (DEN)
1951	Poul Holm/Tonny Ahm (DEN)
1952	Poul Holm/Tonny Ahm (DEN)
1953	David Ewe Choong (MAS)/June White (ENG)
1954	John Best/Iris Cooley (ENG)
1955	Finn Kobberø/Kirsten Thorndahl (DEN)
1956	Tony Jordan/June Timperley (ENG)
1957	Finn Kobberø/Kirsten Thorndahl (DEN)
1958	Tony Jordan/E.J. Timperley (ENG)
1959	Poul Erik Nielsen/Inge Birgit Hansen (DEN)
1960	Finn Kobberø/Kirsten Granlund (DEN)
1961	Finn Kobberø/Kirsten Granlund (DEN)
1962	Finn Kobberø/Ulla Rasmussen (DEN)
1963	Finn Kobberø/Ulla Rasmussen (DEN)
1964	Tony Jordan/Jennifer Pritchard (ENG)
1965	Finn Kobberø/Ulla Strand (DEN)
1966	Finn Kobberø/Ulla Strand (DEN)
1967	Svend Pri/Ulla Strand (DEN)
1968	Tony Jordan/Sue Pound (ENG)
1969	Roger Mills/Gillian Perrin later Gilks (ENG)
1970	Per Walsøe/Pernille Mølgaard Hansen (DEN)
1971	Svend Pri/Ulla Strand (DEN)
1972	Svend Pri/Ulla Strand (DEN)
1973	Derek Talbot/Gillian Gilks (ENG)
1974	David Eddy/Sue Whetnall (ENG)
1975	Elliott C. Stuart/Nora Gardner (ENG)
1976	Derek Talbot/Gillian Gilks (ENG)
1977	Derek Talbot/Gillian Gilks (ENG)
1978	Mike Tredgett/Nora Perry (ENG)
1979	Christian/Wigoeno (INA)
1980	Mike Tredgett/Nora Perry (ENG)
1981	Mike Tredgett/Nora Perry (ENG)
1982	Martin Dew/Gillian Gilks (ENG)
1983	Thomas Kihlstrøm (SWE)/Nora Perry (ENG)
1984	Martin Dew/Gillian Gilks (ENG)
1985	Billy Gilliland (Scotland)/Nora Perry (ENG)
1986	Park Joo Bong/Chung Myung-Hee (KOR)
1987	Lee Deuk-Choon/Chung Myung-Hee (KOR)
1988	Wang Pengren/Shi Fangjing (CHN)
1989	Park Joo Bong/Chung Myung-Hee (KOR)
1990	Park Joo Bong/Chung Myung-Hee (KOR)
1991	Park Joo Bong/Chung Myung-Hee (KOR)
1992	Thomas Lund/Pernille Dupont (DEN)
1993	Jon Holst-Christensen/Grethe Mogensen (DEN)
1994	Nick Ponting/Joanne Wright (ENG)
1995	Thomas Lund/Marlene Thomsen (DEN)
1996	Park Joo Bong/Ra Kyung-Min (KOR)
1997	Ge Fei/Liu Yong (CHN)
1998	Kim Dong-Moon/Ra Kyung-Min (KOR)
1999	Simon Archer/Jo Goode (ENG)
2000	Kim Dong-Moon/Ra Kyung-Min (KOR)
2001	Zhang Jun /Gao Ling, (CHN)
2002	Kim Dong-Moon/Ra Kyung-Min (KOR)
2003	Zhang Jun /Gao Ling, (CHN)
2004	Kim Dong-Moon/Ra Kyung-Min (KOR)

B
A
D
M
I
N
T
O
N

Thomas Cup

1949	Malaysia	8-1	Denmark	Preston	1984	Indonesia	3-2	China	Kuala Lumpur
1952	Malaysia	7-2	USA	Singapore	1986	China	3-2	Indonesia	Jakarta
1955	Malaysia	8-1	Denmark	Singapore	1988	China	4-1	Malaysia	Kuala Lumpur
1958	Indonesia	6-3	Malaysia	Singapore	1990	China	4-1	Malaysia	Tokyo
1961	Indonesia	6-3	Thailand	Jakarta	1992	Malaysia	3-2	Indonesia	Kuala Lumpur
1964	Indonesia	5-4	Denmark	Tokyo	1994	Indonesia	3-0	Malaysia	Jakarta
1967	Malaysia	6-3	Indonesia	Jakarta	1996	Indonesia	5-0	Denmark	Hong Kong
1970	Indonesia	7-2	Malaysia	Kuala Lumpur	1998	Indonesia	3-2	Malaysia	Hong Kong
1973	Indonesia	8-1	Denmark	Jakarta	2000	Indonesia	3-0	China	Kuala Lumpur
1976	Indonesia	9-0	Malaysia	Bangkok	2002	Indonesia	3-2	Malaysia	Guang Zhou
1979	Indonesia	9-0	Denmark	Jakarta	2004	China	3-1	Denmark	Jakarta
1982	China	5-4	Indonesia	London					

Note: The first tournament was held at the Queen's Hall in Preston in February 1949. Sir George Thomas, founder president of the IBF, donated the Thomas Cup trophy.

Uber Cup

1957	USA	6-1	Denmark	St Annes	1986	China	3-2	Indonesia	Jakarta
1960	USA	5-2	Denmark	Philadelphia	1988	China	5-0	South Korea	Kuala Lumpur
1963	USA	4-3	England	Wilmington	1990	China	3-2	South Korea	Tokyo
1966	Japan	5-2	USA	Wellington	1992	China	3-2	South Korea	Kuala Lumpur
1969	Japan	6-1	Indonesia	Tokyo	1994	Indonesia	3-2	China	Jakarta
1972	Japan	6-1	Indonesia	Tokyo	1996	Indonesia	4-1	China	Hong Kong
1975	Indonesia	5-2	Japan	Jakarta	1998	China	4-1	Indonesia	Hong Kong
1978	Japan	5-2	Indonesia	Auckland	2000	China	3-0	Denmark	Kuala Lumpur
1981	Japan	6-3	Indonesia	Tokyo	2002	China	3-1	Korea	Guang Zhou
1984	China	5-0	England	Kuala Lumpur	2004	China	3-1	Korea	Jakarta

Note: The first Uber Cup competition was held at Lytham St Annes in Lancashire, England, in 1957. The Uber Cup trophy was donated by Mrs H.S. Uber.

Olympic Games

Men's singles

	Gold		**Silver**
1992	Allan Budi Kusuma (INA)	15-12 18-13	Ardy Wiranata (INA)
1996	Polu-Erik Høyer-Larsen (DEN)	15-12 15-10	Dong Jiong (CHN)
2000	Ji Xinpeng (CHN)	15-4 15-13	Hendrawan (INA)

Women's Singles

1992	Susi Susanti (INA)	5-11 11-5 11-3	Bang Soo-Hyun (KOR)
1996	Bang Soo-Hyun (KOR)	11-6 11-7	Mia Audina (INA)
2000	Gong Zhichao (CHN)	13-10 11-3	Camilla Martin (DEN)

Men's Doubles

1992	Kim Moon-Soo/Park Joo-Bong (KOR)	15-11 15-7	Eddy Hartono/Rudy Gunawan (INA)
1996	Rexy Mainaky/Ricky Subagja (INA)	5-15 15-13 15-12	Cheah Soon Kit/Yap Yim Hock (MAS)
2000	Tony Gunawan/Candra Wijaya (INA)	15-10 9-15 15-7	Lee Dong-Soo/Yoo Yong-Sung (KOR)

Women's Doubles

1992	Hwang Hye-Young/Chung So-Young (KOR)	18-16 12-15 15-13	Guan Weizhen /Nong Qunhua (CHN)
1996	Ge Fei/Gu Jun (CHN)	7-15 15-4 15-8	Gil Young-Ah/Jang Hye-Ock (KOR)
2000	Ge Fei/Gu Jun (CHN)	15-5 15-5	Huang Nanyan/Yang Wei (CHN)

Mixed Doubles

1996	Kim Dong-Moon/Gil Young-Ah (KOR)	13-15 15-4 15-12	Park Joo-Bong/Ra Kyung-Min (KOR)
2000	Zhang Jun/Gao Ling (CHN)	11-15 15-13 15-11	Tri Kushanjanto/Minarti Timur (INA)

Badminton World Championships

1977 Malmo

	Gold		**Silver**
Men's singles	Flemming Delfs (DEN)	15-5 15-6	Svend Pri (DEN)
Women's singles	Lene Koppen (DEN)	12-9 12-11	Gillian Gilks (ENG)
Men's doubles	Tjun Tjun/Johan Wahjudi (INA)	15-6 15-4	Ade Chandra/Christian Hadinata (INA)
Women's doubles	Etsuko Toganoo/Erniko Ueno (JPN)	15-10 15-11	van Beusekom/Ridder (NED)
Mixed doubles	Steen Skovgaard/Lene Koppen (DEN)	15-12 18-17	Derek Talbot/Gillian Gilks (ENG)

1980 Jakarta

Men's singles	Rudy Hartono (INA)	15-9 15-9	Liem Swie King (INA)
Women's singles	Verawaty Wiharjo (INA)	11-1 11-3	Ivana Lie (INA)
Men's doubles	Ade Chandra/Christian Hadinata (INA)	5-15 15-5 15-7	Kartono/Heryanto (INA)
Women's doubles	Nora Perry/Jane Webster (ENG)	15-12 15-9	Imelda Wiguno/Verawaty (INA)
Mixed doubles	Christian Hadinata/Imelda Wiguno (INA)	15-12 15-4	Mike Tredgett/Nora Perry (ENG)

1983 Copenhagen

Men's singles	Icuk Sugiarto (INA)	15-8 12-15 17-16	Liem Swie King (INA)
Women's singles	Li Lingwei (CHN)	11-8 6-11 11-7	Han Aiping (CHN)
Men's doubles	Steen Fladberg/Jasper Helledie (DEN)	15-10 15-10	Mike Tredgett/Martin Dew ENG)
Women's doubles	Lin Ying/Wu Dixi (CHN)	15-4 15-12	Nora Perry/Jane Webster (ENG)
Mixed doubles	Thomas Kihlstrøm (SWE)/ Nora Perry (ENG)	15-1 15-11	Steen Fladberg/Pia Nielsen (DEN)

1985 Calgary

Men's singles	Han Jian (CHN)	14-18 15-10 15-8	Morten Frost Hansen (DEN)
Women's singles	Han Aiping (CHN)	6-11 12-11 11-2	Wu Jianqin (CHN)
Men's doubles	Park Joo Bong/Kim Moon Soo (KOR)	5-15 15-7 15-9	Li Yongbo/Tian Bingyi (CHN)
Women's doubles	Han Aiping/Li Lingwei (CHN)	15-9 14-18 15-9	Lin Ying/Wu Dixi (CHN)
Mixed doubles	Park Joo Bong/Yoo Sang Hee (KOR)	15-10 12-15 15-12	Stefan Karlsson/ Maria Bengtsson (SWE)

1987 Beijing

Men's singles	Yang Yang (CHN)	15-2 13-15 15-12	Morten Frost Hansen (DEN)
Women's singles	Han Aiping (CHN)	10-12 11-4 11-7	Li Lingwei (CHN)
Men's doubles	Li Yongbo/Tian Bingyi (CHN)	15-2 8-15 15-9	Jalani Sidek/Razif Sidek (MAS)
Women's doubles	Lin Ying/Guan Weizhen (CHN)	15-7 15-8	Han Aiping/Li Lingwei (CHN)
Mixed doubles	Wang Pengren/Shi Fangjing (CHN)	15-8 15-7	Lee DeukChoon/ Chung Myung-Hee (KOR)

1989 Jakarta

Men's singles	Yang Yang (CHN)	15-10 2-15 15-5	Ardy Wiranata (INA)
Women's singles	Li Lingwei (CHN)	11-6 12-9	Huang Hua (CHN)
Men's doubles	Li Yongbo/Tian Bingyi (CHN)	15-3 15-12	Chen Kang/Chen Hongyong (CHN)
Women's doubles	Lin Ying/Guan Weizhen (CHN)	15-1 15-7	Chung Myung-Hee/ Hwang HyeYoung (KOR)
Mixed doubles	Park Joo Bong/ Chung Myung-Hee (KOR)	15-9 15-9	Eddy Hartono/Verawaty Fajrin (INA)

1991 Copenhagen

Men's singles	Zhao Jianhua (CHN)	18-13 15-4	Alan Budi Kusuma (INA)
Women's singles	Tang Jiuhong (CHN)	11-6 11-1	Sarwendah Kusumawardhani (INA)
Men's doubles	Park Joo Bong/Kim Moon Soo (KOR)	15-4 15-6	Jon Holst-Christensen/T. Lund (DEN)
Women's doubles	Nong Qunhua/Guan Weizhen (CHN)	15-7 15-4	Christine Magnusson/ Maria Bengtsson (SWE)
Mixed doubles	Park Joo Bong/Chung Myung-Hee (KOR)	15-5 15-17 15-9	Thomas Lund/Pernille Dupont (DEN)

1993 Birmingham

Men's singles	Joko Suprianto (INA)	15-15 15-11	Hermawan Susanto (INA)
Women's singles	Susi Susanti (INA)	7-11 11-9 11-3	Bang Soo Hyun (KOR)
Men's doubles	Gunawan/Ricky Subagja (INA)	15-11 15-3	Cheah Soon Kit/Soo Beng Kiang (MAS)
Women's doubles	Nong Qunhua/Zhou Lei (CHN)	15-5 15-10	Chen Ying/Wu Yuhong (CHN)
Mixed doubles	T. Lund (DEN)/	10-15 15-6 15-12	J.H.Christensen/
	Catrine Bengtsson (SWE)		Grete Mogensen (DEN)

1995 Lausanne

Men's singles	Hariyanto Arbi (INA)	15-11 15-8	Park Sung Woo (KOR)
Women's singles	Ye Zhaoying (CHN)	11-7 11-0	Han Jingna (CHN)
Men's doubles	Rexy Mainaky/Ricky Subagja (INA)	15-5 15-2	J.H.Christensen/Thomas Lund (DEN)
Women's doubles	Gil Young Ah/Jang Hye Ock (KOR)	3-15 15-11 15-10	Finarsih/Lili Tampi (INA)
Mixed doubles	Thomas Lund/Marlene Thomsen (DEN)	15-2 15-6	Jens Eriksen/Helene Kirkegaard (DEN)

1997 Glasgow

Men's singles	Peter Rasmussen (DEN)	16-17 18-13 15-10	Sun Jun (CHN)
Women's singles	Ye Zhaoying (CHN)	12-11 11-8	Gong Zhichao (CHN)
Men's doubles	Candra Wijaya/Sigit Budiarto (INA)	8-15 18-17 15-7	Cheah Soon Kit/Yap Kim Hock (MAS)
Women's doubles	Ge Fei/Gu Jun (CHN)	15-1 15-8	Qin Yiyuan/Tang Yongshu (CHN)
Mixed doubles	Liu Yong/Ge Fei (CHN)	15-5 16-17 15-4	Jens Eriksen/Marlene Thomsen (DEN)

1999 Brondby

Men's singles	Sun Jun (CHN)	15-6 15-13	Fung Permadi (TPE)
Women's singles	Camilla Martin (DEN)	11-6 6-11 11-10	Dai Yun (CHN)
Men's doubles	Kim Dong Moon/Ha Tae Kwon (KOR)	15-5 15-5	Lee Dong Soo/Yoo Yung Sung (KOR)
Women's doubles	Ge Fei/Gu Jun (CHN)	15-4 15-5	Ra Kyung Min/Chung Jae Hee (KOR)
Mixed doubles	Kim Dong Moon/Ra Kyung Min (KOR)	15-10 15-13	Simon Archer/Joanne Goode (ENG)

2001 Seville

Men's singles	Hendrawan (INA)	15-6 17-16	Peter Gade Christensen (DEN)
Women's singles	Gong Ruina (CHN)	11-9 11-4	Zhou Mi (CHN)
Men's doubles	Halim Haryanto/Tony Gunawan (INA)	15-0 15-13	Kim Dong Moon/Ha Tae Kwon (KOR)
Women's doubles	Huang Sui/Gao Ling (CHN)	15-11 17-15	Zhang Jiewen/Wei Yili (CHN)
Mixed doubles	Zhang Jun/Gao Ling (CHN)	15-10 12-15 17-16	Kim Dong-Moon/Ra Kyung-Min (KOR)

2003 Birmingham

Men's singles	Xia Xuanze (CHN)	15-6 13-15 15-6	Wong Choon Hann (MAS)
Women's singles	Zhang Ning (CHN)	11-6 11-3	Gong Ruina (CHN)
Men's doubles	Lars Paaske/Jonas Rasmussen (DEN)	15-7 13-15 15-13	Sigit Budiarto/Candra Wijaya (INA)
Women's doubles	Huang Sui/Gao Ling (CHN)	15-8 15-11	Zhao Tingting/Wei Yili (CHN)
Mixed doubles	Kim Dong Moon/Ra Kyung Min (KOR)	15-7 15-8	Zhang Jun/Gao Ling (CHN)

Commonwealth Games Gold Medallists

Men's Singles

1966 T.A. Huang (MAS)	1986 S. Baddeley (ENG)
1970 J. Paulson (CAN)	1990 R. Sidek (MAS)
1974 P. Gunalan (MAS)	1994 R. Sidek (MAS)
1978 P. Prakash (IND)	1998 Choong Hann Wong (MAS)
1982 S. Modi (IND)	2002 M.H. Hashim (MAS)

Men's Doubles

1966 A.H. Tan/C.H. Yew (MAS)	1986 W. Gilliland/D. Travers SCO
1970 B.B. Ng/P. Gunalan (MAS)	1990 J. Sidek/R. Sidek (MAS)
1974 D. Talbot/E. Stuart (ENG)	1994 S.K. Cheah/B.K. Soo (MAS)
1978 R. Stevens/M. Tredgett (ENG)	1998 W.W. Lee/T.F. Choong (MAS)
1982 R. Sidek/B. Ong (MAS)	2002 C.E. Chew/C.M. Chan (MAS)

Women's Singles

1966 A.M. Bairstow (ENG)
1970 M. Beck (ENG)
1974 G. Gilks (ENG)
1978 S. Ng (MAS)
1982 H. Troke (ENG)

1986 H. Troke (ENG)
1990 F. Smith (ENG)
1994 L. Campbell (AUS)
1998 K. Morgan (WAL)
2002 Li Li (SIN)

Women's Doubles

1966 H.J. Horton/U.H. Smith (ENG)
1970 M. Boxall/S. Whetnall (ENG)
1974 M. Beck/G. Gilks (ENG)
1978 N. Perry/A. Statt (ENG)
1982 C. Backhouse/J. Falardeau (CAN)

1986 G. Clarke/G. Gowers (ENG)
1990 F. Smith/S. Sankey (ENG)
1994 J. Wright/J. Muggeridge (ENG)
1998 D. Kellogg/J. Goode (ENG)
2002 P. S. Lim/L.P. Ang (MAS)

Mixed Doubles

1966 R.J. Mills/A.M. Bairstow (ENG)
1970 D. Talbot/M. Boxall (ENG)
1974 D. Talbot/G. Gilks (ENG)
1978 M. Tredgett/N. Perry (ENG)
1982 M. Dew/K. Chapman (ENG)

1986 M. Scandolera/A. Tuckey (AUS)
1990 C. Chan/A. Chan (HKG)
1994 C. Hunt/G. Clark (ENG)
1998 S. Archer/J. Goode (ENG)
2002 S. Archer/J. Goode (ENG)

BADMINTON

BANDY

The game of bandy originated in England in the early 18th century and was the precursor of the modern game of ice hockey. In fact it is a cross between field hockey, ice hockey and soccer. It is played by teams of 11 players on a rink 120yds (110m) by 70yds (65m) over two halves of 45 minutes each. A low barrier (6ins/15cm) is placed along the side of the rink to stop the ball from rolling out of play. The goals are in the same position as in soccer, but smaller, being 7ft (2.1m) tall and 11ft (3.5m) wide. The orange-coloured ball is approximately 3ins (7cm) in diameter. All players move around on skates but only the ten outfield players use the curved-bladed sticks (bandies); the goalkeeper uses his hands and body to make saves. Play begins from the centre circle and is called a 'stroke-off'. The ball can be controlled by any part of the body but only passed via the bandy-stick. Unlike ice hockey, play is not allowed behind the goals. Goals are scored by shooting the ball between the goalposts. Teams consist of 14 players per side but only 11 may be on the ice at any one time. Offsides and penalties are awarded as in soccer.

The game is now dominated by northern European teams and since the inception of the World Championships in 1957, Russia and Sweden have dominated.

BASEBALL

For years, Abner Doubleday, a bewhiskered American Civil War general, was held to be the inventor of baseball but after extensive research he was discredited, although he did contribute a good deal to the game from 1839 onwards and in 1936 the National Baseball Hall of Fame and Museum was established in his home town of Cooperstown, New York. Egyptian tomb carvings more than 5000 years old show bat and ball contests. The Moors learnt such games from Arab tribes who had seen the Egyptians at play, and brought them to France and Spain in around the 11th century.

The term 'baseball' dates from 1744, when the British developed a variation that was described in *A Little Pretty Pocket-Book*, a children's book published that year. The pitcher attempted to throw the ball past a bat-holder to hit a stool. More wooden stools were added and these became known as bases. In time a child's game evolved called feeder, or rounders, in which players ran around wooden posts stuck in the ground. English colonists brought rounders to New England, where it became known as baseball or goalball. The 1834 American publication, *The Book of Sports*, shows baseposts laid out in the form of a diamond. Alexander Cartwright, a New York fireman and surveyor, set down the formal rules and field layout in 1845.

A National Association of Professional Baseball Players was formed in 1871 and became the National League of Professional Baseball Clubs in 1876. A rival American League, comprising cities outside the National League, was established in 1901 and since 1903 the winning teams of each league have played a post-season championship known as the World Series. Although there were black players in integrated teams in the early days of organised baseball, by 1889 segregation was complete and the Negro Leagues had been formed, separate from the white leagues. The colour bar was lifted in 1947, when Jackie Robinson signed for the Brooklyn Dodgers and the leagues became totally integrated.

In 1969 the National and American Leagues were reorganised into eastern and western divisions, with a central division added in 1993. Until 1969 the pennant (or championship) winners were the team with the best winning percentage but since then the divisional leaders, plus a wild-card from 1995 onwards, have played a League Championship Series to decide who wins the pennant. The wild-card is awarded to the second-placed team with the highest winning percentage. They play the best of the three divisional leaders. The two pennant winners then play the World Series at the conclusion of the season, which runs from April to October. In 2004, baseball is widely played throughout the world and has major leagues in Japan and Latin America. It remains the national sport of the USA.

General Information

American League: team details

Anaheim Angels (formerly Los Angeles Angels/California Angels) – founded 1961 and play at Edison International Field, Anaheim, California

Baltimore Orioles (formerly St Louis Browns, founded 1885) – founded 1953 and play at Oriole Park at Camden Yards, Baltimore, Maryland

Boston Red Sox (formerly Boston Pilgrims, founded 1901) – founded 1907 and play at Fenway Park, Boston, Massachusetts

Chicago White Sox – founded 1900 and play at U.S. Cellular Field, Chicago, Illinois

Cleveland Indians – founded 1901 and play at Jacobs Field, Cleveland, Ohio

Detroit Tigers – founded 1901 and play at Comerica Park, Detroit, Michigan

Kansas City Royals – founded 1969 and play at Kauffman Stadium, Kansas City, Missouri

Minnesota Twins – founded 1960 from the Washington Senators and play at Hubert H. Humphrey Metrodome, Minneapolis, Minnesota

New York Yankees – founded 1903 and play at Yankee Stadium, Bronx, New York

Oakland Athletics (A's) – founded 1901 as the Philadelphia A's and became the Kansas City A's in 1954 and the Oakland A's in 1968. They play at the Network Associates Coliseum, Oakland, California

Seattle Mariners – founded 1977 and play at Safeco Field, Seattle, Washington

Tampa Bay Devil Rays – founded 1998 and play at Tropicana Field, St Petersburg, Florida

Texas Rangers (formerly Washington Senators, founded 1960 – following the transfer of Calvin Griffith's Franchise to Minnesota) founded 1971 and play at Ameriquest Field in Arlington, Texas

Toronto Blue Jays – founded 1976 and play at SkyDome, Toronto, Canada

designated hitter	From 1973 the American League allowed the pitcher not to bat; a designated hitter (DH) was substituted who could bat at any position, even though the pitcher was invariably at number nine.
night game: first	The first AL night game was played at Shibe Park, Philadelphia, in 1939, the Athletics losing to Cleveland 8-3.
ball: size, weight and composition	The ball must have a circumference between 9ins (23cm) and 9¾ins (25cm) and weigh between 5oz (142g) and 5¼oz (149g). A cork sphere is covered by a layer of black rubber, with a layer of red rubber over this. This is then wound with 121yds (111m) of blue-grey wool yarn, and 45yds (41m) of white wool which brings the circumference to 8¾ins (22.2cm). Another 53yds (48.5m) of blue-grey yarn are then added to increase the circumference to 8⅞ins (22.5cm) and weight to 3⁷⁄₁₆oz (97g). Next, about 150yds (137m) of fine cotton yarn are added to bring the weight to 4⅝oz (130g). A coat of rubber cement is now applied and a tanned cow-hide cover lined with rubber cement is hand-stitched on to the ball. There are exactly 216 stitches applied to hold the cover in place. Finally the ball is placed in a rolling machine while slightly damp to flatten the stitches on the surface and make it uniform.
bases: dimensions of	Bases are 15ins (38cm) square, 3ins (7.6cm) thick and made of high-quality bonded polyester padding with a tough vinyl cover. They are 90ft (27.4m) apart.
bat: dimensions	Maximum length of 42ins (107cm), maximum thickness of 2¾ins (7cm), no weight restriction but 30-35oz (849-991g) is the norm in the modern game, although the likes of Lou Gehrig, Babe Ruth and Jimmy Foxx used big-nosed 36-43oz (1019-1217g) bats. They are constructed of northern white ash timber between 40 and 50 years old.
black player: first to play in major league	Moses Fleetwood Walker – a catcher for Toledo (then a major league team) between 1883 and 1889. Walker's brother, Welday Wilberforce Walker, was one of a dozen or more black players who followed him into the major league before pressure from several white players (most notably Cap Anson) led to the raising of the colour bar in 1887. This barrier stood for 60 years and was not broken until Jackie Robinson joined the Brooklyn Dodgers in 1947.
Black Sox Scandal	Eight members of the Chicago White Sox were accused of accepting bribes to throw the 1919 World Series. Although subsequently found not guilty, the players were suspended for life from the 1921 season onwards.
Black Sox Scandal: judge	Kenesaw Mountain Landis
Cartwright Rules	In 1845 Alexander J. Cartwright, an amateur New York City baseball player, drafted the first rules for the game.
commissioner: first	Kenesaw Mountain Landis
Continental League: inaugurated	27 July 1959
earned run average (ERA)	A pitcher's ERA is calculated by dividing (a) the number of runs given up to opponents, with unearned runs (resulting from bases on balls, fielding errors and the like) deducted, by (b) the number of innings pitched dividing by nine. Thus, a pitcher who gives up five earned runs in 18 innings pitched will have an ERA of 2.50 per full game equivalent (it's a bit artificial, since pitchers don't throw complete nine-inning games any more). An ERA under 3.50 is good; under 3.00 is excellent.
fielding positions	Apart from the pitcher and catcher (known as the battery) and the three basemen, there are four other fielders. Shortstop, positioned behind and between second and third base in the infield, acts as a connection between the three outfielders and the infielders and also backs up the second baseman in covering the base. The three outfielders are right, left and centre field. Right field is positioned between first and second base, left field is between second and third base, and centre field is usually behind the second baseman and between the other two outfielders. The outfielders are responsible for fielding long hits and getting an opponent out by catching fly balls, i.e. a ball that is hit high into the air, or by throwing a ball to a baseman before the runner makes base. The centre fielder has the most ground to cover and must be quick, agile and have a strong arm.
general strike: first	In 1972 baseball had its first general strike, which lasted for 13 days, causing the cancellation of 86 regular-season games and delaying the divisional play-offs and World Series by ten days.
Hall of Fame	Founded in 1936 in Cooperstown, New York
home plate: dimensions of	Home plates are five-sided. The flat front faces the pitcher and the sharp tip points towards the catcher. The point is a 90 degree angle, fitting it into the junction of the foul lines at the plate. It is 17ins (43cm) wide and 23ins (58cm) from front to rear. Home plates are flush-to-the-ground 4ins (10cm) vinyl slabs weighing about 20lb (9kg) that are spiked into the turf.
Japanese Leagues	Top teams in the Japanese Baseball League include Yomiuri Giants, Yakult Swallows, Nippon Ham Fighters, Hanshin Tigers, Orix BlueWave, Fukuoka Daiei, Hawks, Kintetsu Buffaloes, Chunichi Dragons, Seibu Lions, Yokohama Bay Stars, Hiroshima Toyo Carp and Chiba Lotte Marines.
Little League: details	Conceived by Carl Stotz and Bert and George Bebble in 1946. It began with a three-team league in Williamsport, Pennsylvania, now the site of Little

League headquarters and the Museum Hall of Excellence. By the early 1960s the Little League consisted of more than 33,000 teams and 6000 leagues in 26 countries. Since the 1970s, girls have also been eligible to play in Little League.

longest major league game
On 1 May 1920 at Boston Braves Field, the Brooklyn Dodgers played the Boston Braves. The game ended as a draw after the nine innings, with both teams scoring a run in their sixth innings. Ultimately, 26 innings were played and the game ended with a 1-1 tie being declared. The two starting pitchers, Leon Cadore of the Dodgers and Joe Oeschger of the Braves, threw almost the equivalent of three full games in one day!

longest winning sequence
The Cincinnati Reds made history by becoming the first professional baseball club but also by running up the longest winning sequence of 81 consecutive games (unofficially, counting exhibitions, perhaps in excess of 130). They were finally beaten by Brooklyn Atlantics, 8-7, in 11 innings, 14 June 1870.

National League: team details
Arizona Diamondbacks – founded 1998 and play at Bank One Ballpark, Phoenix, Arizona
Atlanta Braves (formerly Boston Braves, founded 1876, then Milwaukee Braves in 1953) – founded 1966 and play at Turner Field, Atlanta, Georgia
Chicago Cubs (formerly Chicago White Stockings, founded 1876) – became Cubs in 1907 and play at Wrigley Field, Chicago, Illinois
Cincinnati Red Stockings – founded 1869 and play at the Great American Ball Park, Cincinnati, Ohio
Colorado Rockies – founded 1993 and play at Coors Field, Denver, Colorado
Florida Marlins – founded 1993 and play at Pro Player Stadium, Miami, Florida
Houston Astros (formerly Houston Colt .45s founded 1962) – became Astros in 1965 and play at Minute Maid Park, Houston, Texas
Los Angeles Dodgers (formerly Brooklyn Dodgers founded 1890) – founded 1958 and play at Dodger Stadium
Milwaukee Brewers – founded 1970 from the Seattle Pilots Franchise and play at Miller Park, Milwaukee, Wisconsin
Montreal Expos – founded 1969 and play at the Olympic Stadium, Montreal, Canada
New York Mets – founded 1961 and play at Shea Stadium, Flushing, New York
Philadelphia Phillies – founded 1883 and play at Citizens Bank Park, Philadelphia, Pennsylvania
Pittsburgh Pirates – founded 1887 as the Pittsburgh Alleghenies, before adopting present name in 1889. The Pirates play at PNC Park, Pittsburgh, Pennsylvania
St Louis Cardinals – founded 1876 as the St Louis Brown Stockings and became the St Louis Perfectos 1899, before adopting their present name in 1900. The Cardinals play at Busch Stadium, St Louis, Missouri
San Diego Padres – founded 1969 and play at PETCO Park, San Diego, California
San Francisco Giants (formerly New York Gothams, founded 1883, and became New York Giants in 1885) – moved to San Francisco in 1958 and play at SBC Park, San Francisco, California

nicknames of famous teams
Cincinnati Reds (1970s) – Big Red Machine; St Louis Cardinals (1930s) – Gas House Gang; New York Yankees (generally) – The Bronx Bombers; Philadelphia Phillies (1950 team) – The Whiz Kids; Brooklyn Dodgers (1940s and 1950s) – Brooklyn Bums; Anaheim Angels (generally) – The Halos

oldest existing ballpark
Fenway Park, Boston, has hosted major league baseball since 1912.

oldest existing sports team
The Philadelphia Phillies are the oldest continuous, one-name, one-city team in any professional sport.

pitcher's plate
Also called the rubber, the plate is 24ins (61cm) long and four-sided with each face 6ins (15cm) wide. The plate is hollow inside and is reinforced with aluminium tubing. The four sides may be rotated to the surface position for extended wear.

playing area
Diamond

rules codified by
Alexander Joy Cartwright in 1845

rules of the game
Baseball is played on a shell-shaped field with a 90ft (27.4m) square, or diamond, marked at the apex. A base is set at each corner of the diamond; going anti-clockwise, they are first base, second base, third base and home plate. The bases are marked by small, heavy canvas pillows attached to the ground. The area within the square is called the infield; territory beyond the bases but between the two foul lines, which run along the sides of the field, is designated the outfield.

Two teams of nine players each take turns as the batting (offensive) team and the fielding (defensive) team. The aim of the batting team is to score runs. A run is scored when a player makes one complete circuit of the three bases and returns to home plate safely. The offensive team sends players to bat in a consecutive, pre-arranged order. Seven of the nine players on the fielding team take their positions in the infield and outfield; the other two, the

B
A
S
E
B
A
L
L

pitcher and the catcher, form the battery. While awaiting a pitch, the catcher crouches behind and within stepping distance of home plate without impeding the batter. The pitcher stands 60ft 6ins (18.4m) away in the centre of the infield.

The batter stands at home plate and attempts to hit the baseball, thrown by the opposition's pitcher. Batters are only required to hit pitches that fall in the strike zone, an imaginary window over home plate that extends from the batter's knees up to the shoulders. A pitcher must be very skilled to place the ball within the strike zone yet still elude the bat. Pitches that fall outside the strike zone are called balls. Four balls allow the batter to walk to first base. Strikes occur in any of three circumstances, i.e. the batter swings at the ball and misses, the batter declines to swing at a ball pitched in the strike zone, the batter hits the ball into foul territory. A batter is allowed three strikes and on the third strike is out, losing turn at bat.

A batter is safe at base if, after hitting the ball, he reaches the base before the defenders can field the ball and throw it to that base. If the fielder gets the ball to the player guarding the base before the runner gets there, the runner is out. A single is a hit enabling the batter to reach first base safely. A double puts the latter on second base and a triple on third base. A home run is scored when the batter hits the ball far enough, often over the field's fence, to complete a full circuit before the ball can be successfully fielded. If the batter hits a home run when the bases are loaded, i.e. there are runners on the three bases, then all four runners advance to home plate and four runs are scored, a grand slam.

An inning is over when the offensive team accumulates three outs; they then become the defensive team until the other team also accumulates three outs. A game consists of nine innings. If the score is tied after that, extra innings are played until one team wins. The home team always bats last, so if they are ahead after the away team has completed a ninth turn at bat, the game ends.

Ruth, George Herman: nickname	'Babe' and 'The Sultan of Swat'
umpires	Four umpires run a game, positioned near the home plate and the three bases.
World Series: first night game played	In 1971

Biographies of Players and Administrators

Aaron, Henry Louis ('Hank')   Born Mobile, Alabama, 5 February 1934. Outfielder, Milwaukee (Atlanta) Braves, Milwaukee Brewers. The all-time home run leader with a career total of 755. Beginning in the Negro Leagues, with the Indianapolis Clowns, Aaron joined the Boston Braves organisation at the age of 18. He made his major league debut in 1954. Hitting only 13 homers in his first full season, he then averaged 34 for the next 22 seasons. In addition to his home run total, he established 12 other major league records, including 6856 total bases. He appeared in 24 All-Star games and twice won the National League batting title. In 1957 Aaron was the National League MVP (Most Valuable Player) and his three home runs helped the underdog Braves beat the New York Yankees in the World Series. Aaron retired in 1976 with a lifetime batting average of .305. He was elected to the Hall of Fame in 1982

Alexander, Grover Cleveland   Born Elba, Nebraska, 26 February 1887. Pitcher, Philadelphia Phillies, Chicago Cubs, St Louis Cardinals. 'Ol' Pete' Alexander overcame epilepsy, alcoholism and harrowing combat in World War I to become one of the greatest pitchers in baseball history. No other National League pitcher has surpassed his marks of 373 wins and 90 shut-outs. He is remembered in baseball folklore for his performance in game seven of the 1926 World Series against the New York Yankees. Despite having pitched a complete game the day before (and enjoyed a drink to celebrate), he entered the game at the bottom of the seventh inning with the Cardinals holding a 3-2 lead. With the bases loaded he struck out Tony Lazzeri to end

the inning. He then shut out the Yankees in the eighth and ninth innings, allowing only a walk (to Babe Ruth, who was thrown out stealing, to end the series), saving the first World Series title in franchise history. Alexander retired in 1930 with a career ERA (earned run average) of 2.56. He was elected to the Hall of Fame in 1938. He died 4 November 1950.

Bench, Johnny Lee   Born Oklahoma City, Oklahoma, 7 December 1947. Catcher, Cincinnati Reds. Regarded as the best catcher in baseball history. National League Rookie of the Year in his first full season in 1968, he went on to become a leader of the 'Big Red Machine' that dominated the sport in the 1970s. Bench was an outstanding, durable, defensive catcher and won ten consecutive Gold Gloves and two National League MVP titles. He was equally impressive with the bat, hitting 389 home runs. Bench retired in 1983 and was elected to the Hall of Fame in 1989.

Berra, Lawrence Peter ('Yogi')   Born St Louis, Missouri, 12 May 1925. Catcher, New York Yankees, New York Mets. Berra played on 14 pennant-winners and ten world championship teams. The heart of the Yankees for 18 seasons, Berra was three times American League MVP and was selected for the All-Star team every year from 1948 to 1962. He caught Don Larsen's perfect game in the 1956 World Series. After retiring in 1963, he went on to manage the Yankees and the Mets. Elected to the Hall of Fame in 1972.

Bonds, Barry Lamar   Born Riverside, California, 24 July 1964. Outfielder, San Francisco Giants. The all-time single-season home run record holder with

73 in 2001. In 2002 he won the National League batting title with a. 370 average, as well as setting major league records for on-base percentage (.582), walks (198) and intentional walks (68). The same year he was the National League MVP for the fifth time, at the age of 38. Despite putting up record numbers in post-season play for home runs and walks, he missed out on his greatest ambition, when the Giants lost out to the Anaheim Angels in the 2002 World Series. Bonds, eight times a Gold Glove winner, was voted *Sporting News* Player of the Decade for the 1990s.

Carlton, Steven Norman Born Miami, Florida, 22 December 1944. Pitcher, St Louis Cardinals, Philadelphia Phillies, Chicago White Sox, San Francisco Giants, Cleveland Indians, Minnesota Twins. Second on the all-time strike-out list, with 4136. An endurance pitcher, he won in double figures for 18 consecutive seasons, six times winning 20 or more games. Won the National League's Cy Young Award four times over an 11-year period, testament to his durability. His best year was 1972, his first with the Philadelphia Phillies. He won 27 games, struck out 310 batters, posted an ERA of 1.97 and completed 30 games, all figures that led the National League. Carlton seems destined to suffer in the shadow of Nolan Ryan as baseball's top strike-out artist. Retiring in 1988 with a career ERA of 3.22, Carlton was elected to the Hall of Fame in 1994.

Clemens, William Roger Born Dayton, Ohio, 4 August 1962. Pitcher, Boston Red Sox, Toronto Blue Jays, New York Yankees. On 29 April 1986 'The Rocket' became the first pitcher in MLB history to strike out 20 batters. During this record-breaking display Clemens threw 138 pitches and did not walk a batter. Then, ten years later on 18 September 1996, he struck out 20 Detroit Tigers to equal his own record. American League MVP in 1986, he also won the American League Cy Young Award, a feat he repeated in 1987, 1991, 1997, 1998 and 2001.

Clemente (Walker), Roberto Born Carolina, Puerto Rico, 18 August 1934. Outfielder, Pittsburgh Pirates. The first of many great Latin players to make the major leagues, Clemente won four National League batting titles, had a .317 career batting average and played in a Pirates' record 2433 games. Equally brilliant in the field, Clemente won 12 consecutive Gold Gloves. He was the National League MVP in 1966. His most famous exploits were in the 1971 World Series against the Baltimore Orioles, where he hit .414 and two home runs. Just two months later he was killed in a plane crash, flying relief supplies to Nicaraguan earthquake victims. In 1973 he became only the second player (Lou Gehrig being the first) to have the five-year waiting period of eligibility for election to the Hall of Fame waived. He was elected with 92.69 per cent of the total votes cast. He died in San Juan, Puerto Rico, 31 December 1972.

Cobb, Tyrus Raymond (Ty) Born Narrows, Georgia, 18 December 1886. Outfielder, Detroit Tigers, Philadelphia Athletics. Universally acknowledged as the greatest player ever. 'The Georgia Peach' had a lifetime batting average of .367, a figure that may never be beaten. His 297 triples, 4191 hits, 12 American League batting titles (including nine in a row), 23 straight seasons in which he hit over .300, three .400 seasons (topped by a .420 in 1911) and 2245 runs are testament to the man's genius with a bat. These figures are all the more remarkable as most were accumulated in the 'dead-ball era' that heavily favoured the pitcher. An aggressive player in all aspects of the game, Cobb was ruthless on the basepaths, sliding with spikes raised into both bag and player, with little concern for either. He stole 892 bases, including 36 'steals' of home plate, a play rarely contemplated in the modern game. After 22 seasons playing and managing the Tigers he joined the Athletics for the last two years of an incredible career. He went on to hit six for six at-bats (three home runs, a double and two singles), with 16 total bases, setting an American League record that is yet to be surpassed. He was the first inductee into the Hall of Fame in 1936. He died in Atlanta, Georgia, 17 July 1961.

Collins, Edward Trowbridge Born Millerton, New York, 2 May 1887. Second baseman, Philadelphia Athletics, Chicago White Sox. Signed in 1906, 'Eddie' Collins played 25 seasons in the major leagues, a 20th century record for position players. Playing in the same era as Ty Cobb meant Collins never won a batting title, but his 3311 hits stands as eighth of all time. Collins was traded to the Chicago White Sox in 1915, helping them to the World Series in 1917. In 1919 he was part of the infamous 'Black Sox' team that threw the World Series. As one of the 'honest players', he never forgave the eight who sold out, yet described the team as the greatest he played in. Collins managed the White Sox for two years before returning to Philadelphia in 1927. He retired in 1930 with a lifetime batting average of .333. Elected to the Hall of Fame in 1939. He died in Boston, Massachusetts, 25 March 1951.

Dean, Jay Hanna ('Dizzy') Born Lucas, Arkansas, 16 January 1910. Pitcher, St Louis Cardinals, Chicago Cubs, St Louis Browns. A leader of the famous Cardinals, 'Gas House Gang' Dean burst on to the major league scene in 1932. He averaged 24 wins over his first five seasons. In 1934 his record was 30-4, the last National League pitcher to win 30 games. That season he and his brother Paul ('Daffy') led the team to the world championship, and he was named as the National League MVP. A four-time winner of the National League strike-out title, he moved to the Cubs in 1937. Dean never recaptured his previous form. He retired in 1941, returning to play just one game for the Browns in 1947. Elected to the Hall of Fame in 1953. He died in Reno, Nevada, 17 July 1974.

DiMaggio, Joseph Paul Born Martinez, California, 25 November 1914. Outfielder, New York Yankees. Rated by many as the greatest baseball feat of all time, DiMaggio hit safely (had at least one base hit) in 56 consecutive games in 1941. The 'Yankee Clipper' won two American League batting titles and was named MVP in 1941, 1943 and 1947. He played in ten World Series, on the winning side nine times. He retired in 1951 with a lifetime batting average of .325. Joe was married to, and divorced from, actress Marilyn Monroe in 1954. He was elected to the Hall of Fame in 1955. He died in Hollywood, Florida, 8 March 1999.

Feller, Robert William Andrew Born Van Meter, Iowa, 3 November 1918. Pitcher, Cleveland Indians. 'Rapid' Robert Feller gave notice of his blazing fast ball by striking out 15 St Louis Browns batters on his major league debut in 1936. He spent all his 18-year career with the Indians, winning 266 games and racking up 2581 strike-outs, leading the league in strike-outs seven times. He missed four of his prime playing years fighting in World War II. He retired in 1956 with a career ERA of 3.25. Elected to the Hall of Fame in 1962.

B
A
S
E
B
A
L
L

Ford, Edward Charles Born New York City, New York, 21 October 1928. Pitcher, New York Yankees. The 'Money Pitcher' of the great Yankees teams of the 1950s and early 1960s, 'Whitey' Ford's career record of 236 wins and 106 losses gives him the best winning percentage of any 20th-century pitcher. He has the most career wins in the history of the Yankees. The 1961 American League Cy Young Award winner, he still holds many World Series records, including ten wins and 94 strike-outs. He once pitched 33 consecutive scoreless innings in the Fall Classic. He retired in 1967 with a career ERA of 2.74. Elected to the Hall of Fame in 1974.

Foxx, James Emory Born Sudlersville, Maryland, 22 October 1907. First baseman, Philadelphia Athletics, Boston Red Sox, Chicago Cubs, Philadelphia Phillies. A power-hitter, Foxx was an anchor in the Athletics line-up that won pennants from 1929 to 1931. The second player in history to hit 500 home runs, Foxx hit 30 or more homers in a record 12 consecutive seasons and drove in more than a hundred in 13 consecutive years, including a career-best of 175 with Boston in 1938. He won back-to-back American League MVP awards in 1932 and 1933, winning the 'Triple Crown' in the latter year. He retired in 1945 with a .325 lifetime batting average. Elected to the Hall of Fame in 1951. He died in Miami, Florida, 21 July 1967.

Gehrig, Henry Louis Born New York City, New York, 19 June 1903. First baseman, New York Yankees. On 1 June 1925 Yankees first baseman Wally Pipp asked to be taken out of the line-up because of a headache. He was replaced by Lou Gehrig. Some 14 years and 2130 consecutive games later, 'The Iron Horse' was still there. After batting .295 in 1925 he hit .313, the first of 12 consecutive years he hit over .300. He was an integral part of the famous 'murderers' row' Yankee team of 1927, regarded by many as the best ever. Gehrig hit 47 homers that year, but as he seemed destined to do, lived in the shadow of Babe Ruth, who hit 60. Gehrig won the 'Triple Crown' in 1934. His World Series record is spectacular. In 34 games he hit ten home runs, knocked in 35 runs, scored 30 and batted .361. In 1938 Gehrig batted below .300 for the first time since 1925, and it was clear that something was wrong. He started eight games of the 1939 season but then took himself out of the line-up. He was diagnosed with a rare form of a degenerative disease and his career was over. He had a .340 lifetime batting average, 15th on the all-time list. On 4 July 1939, 62,000 fans crowded into Yankee Stadium for 'Lou Gehrig Day'. Although he knew he was dying, he entered into baseball legend when he told the crowd, 'I consider myself the luckiest man alive'. He died of the disease which was named after him. He was elected to the Hall of Fame in 1939 by special election, the five-year rule of eligibility being waived. He died at Riverdale, New York, 2 June 1941.

Gibson, Joshua (Josh) Born Buena Vista, Georgia, 21 December 1911. Catcher, Homestead Greys, Pittsburgh Crawfords (Negro Leagues). Known as 'The Black Babe Ruth', Gibson never played in the major leagues. He died three months before Jackie Robinson made the breakthrough in 1947. Although records were inaccurate in many of the leagues, he has been credited with as many as 84 home runs in a single season and almost 800 in his career. Although it has never been conclusively proven, in

1934 Gibson hit a fair ball out of Yankee Stadium, the only time this feat was achieved. He won nine home run titles and four batting titles. In 1943 he suffered a brain tumour but refused an operation. Playing on despite drinking problems and headaches, he won two more batting titles and four home run crowns. He had an estimated lifetime average over .350. Elected to the Hall of Fame in 1972. He died in Pittsburgh, Pennsylvania, 20 January 1947.

Gibson, Robert Born Omaha, Nebraska, 9 November 1935. Pitcher, St Louis Cardinals. In 17 seasons with the Cardinals, Gibson won 20 games five times. In 1968 he posted an ERA of 1.12, the lowest since 1914 and the fourth best in history. In the World Series that year, in game one, he struck out a series record 17 Detroit Tigers. Having a total of 35 in three games, he was, not surprisingly, the National League MVP and Cy Young Award winner. A versatile sportsman, he also played basketball for the Harlem Globetrotters. He retired in 1975 with a career ERA of 2.91. Elected to the Hall of Fame in 1981.

Grove, Robert Moses ('Lefty') Born Lonaconing, Maryland, 6 March 1900. Pitcher, Philadelphia Athletics, Boston Red Sox. Grove was the backbone of the Athletics' 1929-31 dynasty. He topped the American League in wins four times, winning percentage five times and strike-outs for seven consecutive seasons. Most impressively, he won an astonishing nine ERA titles, easily the greatest total in history. He retired in 1941 with a career ERA of 3.06. Elected to the Hall of Fame in 1947. He died at Norwalk, Ohio, 22 May 1975.

Henderson, Ricky Lee Born Chicago, Illinois, 25 December 1958. Outfielder, Oakland Athletics, New York Yankees, Toronto Blue Jays, San Diego Padres, Anaheim Angels, New York Mets, Seattle Mariners, Boston Red Sox. Widely hailed as the greatest lead-off hitter of all time. He is the leading run scorer in major league history, with 2288. He holds the record for stolen bases with 1403 and he has 12 times led the American League in that category, the last time in 1998 at the age of 39. A veteran of ten All-Star games, he was voted American League MVP in 1990.

Hornsby, Rogers Born Winters, Texas, 27 April 1896. Infielder, St Louis Cardinals, New York Giants, Boston Braves, Chicago Cubs, St Louis Browns. Regarded as the game's most consistent right hand hitter. He captured seven National League batting titles, including six in a row, averaging over .400 three times. His .424 mark in 1924 is the National League record for the 20th century. 'The Rajah' was twice National League MVP, in 1925 and 1929, and won the 'Triple Crown' in 1922 and 1925. In 1926 as player/manager he led the Cardinals to their first World Championship. He retired in 1937 with a career batting average of .357, the second highest ever, and a National League best. Elected to the Hall of Fame in 1942. He died in Chicago, Illinois, 5 January 1963.

Jackson, Joseph Jefferson Born Pickens County, South Carolina, 16 July 1888. Outfielder, Philadelphia Athletics, Cleveland Indians, Chicago White Sox. A power-hitter in the 'dead-ball' era, Jackson could hit, run and throw with the best in baseball. A country boy from South Carolina, he never learned to read or write. He was implicated in the 'Black Sox' scandal of 1919 and despite batting .375 and committing no errors in the series, he was banned for life by commissioner Kenesaw Mountain

Landis. One of the most romantic of baseball heroes, 'Shoeless Joe' has inspired books and films. A campaign is still under way to lift his ban to enable him to take his rightful place in the Hall of Fame. His 13-year career ended in 1921 with a .356 batting average, the third best of all time. He died at Greenville, South Carolina, 5 December 1951.

Jackson, Reginald Martinez Born Wyncote, Pennsylvania, 18 May 1946. Outfielder, Kansas City Athletics, Oakland Athletics, Baltimore Orioles, New York Yankees, California Angels. A hitter of great power, 'Mr October' performed best under the bright lights and cameras of post-season play. In 21 seasons he played for 11 division winners, six pennant winners and five world champions. His World Series average of .357 is almost 100 points better than his regular-season mark. His most remarkable performance came in game six of the 1977 World Series. Trailing 3-2 to the Los Angeles Dodgers in the fourth inning, Jackson put the first pitch over the right-field fence for a two-run shot, to give the Yankees the lead. In his next at-bat he deposited the first pitch even further into the stands. As he came to bat in the eighth the crowd were on their feet. Sure enough, he hit a knuckle ball from Charlie Hough 450 feet into the centre-field bleachers. Three swings, three home runs, another series to the Yankees. He retired in 1987. His 563 career home runs ranked sixth highest at the time. His 2597 strike-outs, however, are an all-time record. Elected to the Hall of Fame in 1993.

Johnson, Byron Bancroft Born Norwalk, Ohio, 5 January 1864. Baseball executive. The founder of the American League, Ban Johnson was baseball's most influential executive for a quarter of a century. As president of the Western League, he changed its name to the American League in 1900 and claimed major league status the following year. The league quickly established itself both on the field and at the gate. Johnson became the most powerful member of the National Commission, baseball's ruling body until 1920. Elected to the Hall of Fame in 1937. He died in St Louis, Missouri, 28 March 1931.

Johnson, Walter Perry Born Humboldt, Kansas, 6 November 1887. Pitcher, Washington Senators. Johnson's fast ball was considered to be in a class by itself. Using a sweeping side-arm delivery, 'The Big Train' struck out 3508 batters over a brilliant 21-year career, and his 110 shut-outs are more than any other pitcher. Despite playing on poor teams for most of his career, he won 417 games, second on the all-time list, and had ten successive seasons of 20 or more victories. Ironically, he won his only World Series game as a relief pitcher in 1924. Coming out of the bull pen in the ninth with the game tied at 3-3 he shut down the New York Giants on just three hits, to win the game and Washington's only world championship. He retired in 1927 with a career ERA of 2.36. Elected to the Hall of Fame in 1936. He died in Washington DC, 10 December 1946.

Keeler, William Henry Born Brooklyn, New York, 3 March 1872. Outfielder, New York Giants, Brooklyn Grooms, Baltimore Orioles, Brooklyn Superbas, New York Highlanders (Yankees). At 1.63m, 'Wee Willie' Keeler was one of the smallest of the game's giants. His motto of 'Hit 'em where they ain't' earned him two batting titles, eight straight years of over 200 hits and a 44-game hitting streak in 1897. His place-hitting prowess resulted in 13 straight seasons of over .300

He retired in 1910 with a career batting average of .345. Elected to the Hall of Fame in 1939. He died in Brooklyn, New York, 1 January 1923.

Koufax, Sanford Born Brooklyn, New York, 30 December 1935. Pitcher, Brooklyn Dodgers, Los Angeles Dodgers. For a period of six years Koufax was as great a pitcher as has ever played the game. For six seasons prior to 1961, he had struggled to find control and harness his fast ball and lethal curve. He led the majors in strike-outs with 269 in 1961 and a year later topped the National League with an ERA of 2.54. In 1963 he finished with a 25-5 record and an ERA of 1.88, struck out 306 batters and pitched 11 shut-outs. Koufax was named MVP, but deserved the award for his World Series performances alone. The Dodgers swept the Yankees 4-0, chiefly because Koufax was impossible to hit. He pitched two complete game victories, allowing three earned runs and struck out 23 batters, walking only three. Koufax topped himself in 1965, winning 26 and losing eight in 41 starts. His ERA was 2.04, the strike-out total a staggering 382. In game five of the 1965 World Series he struck out ten Minnesota Twins, scattering four singles, leading to a 7-0 Dodgers victory. In game seven he pitched his second consecutive shut-out, again striking out ten batters. Arthritis in his throwing arm forced retirement in 1966. He did not post career numbers to rank with the greats, but for six seasons, he was the pitcher of record. In 1972 he became the youngest player to be elected to the Hall of Fame.

Lajoie, Napoleon Born Woonsocket, Rhode Island, 5 September 1874. Infielder, Philadelphia Phillies, Philadelphia Athletics, Cleveland Broncos, Cleveland Naps. Larry Lajoie combined grace in the field with power at the bat. Renowned for hard hitting, he topped .300 in 16 of his 21 big league seasons, ten times batting over .350 for a lifetime average of .339. In 1901 he 'jumped' from the Phillies to the Athletics in the new American League. He dominated the league, winning the 'Triple Crown' and batting .422, still an American League record. He retired in 1916 and was elected to the Hall of Fame in 1937. He died at Daytona Beach, Florida, 7 February 1959.

McGraw, John Born Truxton, New York, 7 April 1873. Manager, Baltimore Orioles (NL), Baltimore Orioles (AL), New York Giants. McGraw was a fiery third baseman with the Orioles in the 1890s but achieved much more recognition as a field manager. In 31 years in charge of the Giants, 'Little Napoleon's' teams won ten pennants, finished second 11 times and won three World Series. He managed 4879 major league games, winning 2840, which ranks second all-time. He retired in 1932, but came back the following year to manage the National League in the first-ever All-Star game. Elected to the Hall of Fame in 1937. He died at New Rochelle, New York, 25 February 1934.

McGwire, Mark David Born Pomona, California, 1 October 1963. First baseman, Oakland Athletics, St Louis Cardinals. In 1998 McGwire and Chicago Cubs slugger Sammy Sosa enthralled baseball fans with a home run bonanza throughout the summer. McGwire started by hitting a grand slam on opening day, and never let up. On 1 September he passed Hack Wilson's National League record of 56, then four days later joined Babe Ruth and Roger Maris in the exclusive 60 homers club. On 8 September McGwire became the all-time home run champion, hitting number 62. He finished this incredible season with 70, pipping Sosa to the crown by four. He hit a home run in every 7.27 at-bats during that incredible summer. He retired at the end of the 2000 season with a career total of 583 home runs and a batting average of .267.

Mack, Cornelius Alexander   Born East Brookfield, Massachusetts, 22 December 1862. Manager, Pittsburgh Pirates, Philadelphia Athletics. After three years in Pittsburgh, 'Connie' Mack assumed control of the Athletics in 1901 and continued for 50 years until his retirement at the age of 88. He won five World Series and built two dynasties, winning four pennants in five years from 1910 to 1914 and three in a row from 1929 to 1931. His 3776 games won is the most by a manager. Elected to the Hall of Fame in 1937. He died in Philadelphia, Pennsylvania, 8 February 1956.

Mantle, Mickey Charles   Born Spavinaw, Oklahoma, 20 October 1931. Outfielder, first baseman, New York Yankees. Mantle was a multi-talented offensive threat. A switch-hitter, he drove in runs from either side of the plate. He got on base by hitting well for average and drawing more than 100 walks in each of ten seasons. He also scored runs with his excellent speed. In spite of a series of devastating injuries, Mantle amassed a long list of impressive accomplishments, finishing his 18-year career with 536 home runs and a .298 batting average. He was voted American League MVP in 1956, 1957 and 1962, the year he appeared in the feature films *Safe at Home* and *That Touch of Mink*. He played in 12 pennant-winning teams and seven world champions in his first 14 years, establishing numerous World Series records including most home runs (18). Retiring in 1968, he was elected to the Hall of Fame in 1974. He died in Dallas, Texas, 13 August 1995.

Mathewson, Christopher   Born Factoryville, Pennsylvania, 12 August 1880. Pitcher, New York Giants, Cincinnati Reds. The dominant pitcher of his era, Mathewson looked like the classic American hero: tall, blond and blue-eyed with a reputation for clean living. He won 373 games over 17 seasons. Using his famous fade-away pitch, 'Matty' won at least 22 games for 12 straight years (four times winning 30 or more). Although playing in four World Series, his only title came in 1905 when he threw three shut-outs in six days to beat the Philadelphia Athletics. His finest season was 1908 when he led the league in wins (37), ERA (1.43), strike-outs (259) and shut-outs (12). He retired in 1916 with a career ERA of 2.62. Elected to the Hall of Fame in 1936. He died at Saranac Lake, New York, 7 October 1925.

Mays, Willie Howard   Born Westfield, Alabama, 6 May 1931. Outfielder, New York Giants, San Francisco Giants, New York Mets. The 'Say Hey Kid' played with enthusiasm and exuberance while excelling in all phases of the game – hitting for average and with power, fielding, throwing and base running. His career statistics include 3283 hits and 660 home runs. He was National League Rookie of the Year in 1951 and MVP in 1964 and 1965. He accumulated 12 Gold Gloves, and played in a record-equalling 24 All-Star games. His spectacular over-the-shoulder catch off Vic Wertz's drive in the 1954 World Series remains one of baseball's most memorable moments. He retired in 1973 with a lifetime batting average of .302. Elected to the Hall of Fame in 1979.

Musial, Stanley Frank   Born Donora, Pennsylvania, 21 November 1920. Outfielder, St Louis Cardinals. After 22 years as a Cardinal, Stan 'The Man' Musial ranked at or near the top of baseball's all-time lists in almost every batting category. He topped the .300 mark 17 times and won seven National League batting titles. He was National League MVP in 1943, 1946 and 1948, and played in 24 All-Star games. He was given his nickname 'The Man' by Dodger fans for the havoc he wrought at Ebbets Field. He retired in 1963 with 475 home runs and a career batting average of .331. Elected to the Hall of Fame in 1969.

Paige, Leroy Robert (Satchel)   Born Mobile, Alabama, 7 July 1906. Pitcher, Birmingham Black Barons, Baltimore Black Sox, Cleveland Cubs, Pittsburgh Crawfords, Kansas City Monarchs, New York Black Yankees, Memphis Red Sox, Philadelphia Stars (Negro Leagues), Cleveland Indians, St Louis Browns, Kansas City A's. A tall, lanky fireballer, Paige was the Negro Leagues' hardest thrower and greatest attraction in the 1930s and 1940s. Sold to the Indians in 1948, on his 42nd birthday, he became the oldest player to make his major league debut. Helping the Indians to the pennant, he became the first black pitcher to play in the World Series. Traded to the St Louis Browns, he retired in 1953. However in 1965 at the age of 59, he pitched three innings for the Kansas City A's, giving up just one hit. Elected to the Hall of Fame in 1971. He died in Kansas City, Missouri, 8 June 1982.

Rickey, Wesley Branch   Born Flat, Ohio, 20 December 1881. General manager, St Louis Cardinals, Brooklyn Dodgers. After a mediocre career as player and manager Rickey spent 50 years in the front office as baseball's greatest visionary executive. In the 1920s and 1930s with the St Louis Cardinals he invented the modern farm system. Moving to the Dodgers, he pioneered the use of baseball statistics. Then, in 1947, he broke the major league colour barrier by signing the first African-American player, Jackie Robinson. Elected to the Hall of Fame in 1967. He died at Columbia, Missouri, 9 December 1965.

Ripken, Calvin Edwin jnr   Born Harve de Grace, Maryland, 24 August 1960. Shortstop, third baseman, Baltimore Orioles. Cal Ripken was one of the greatest-ever shortstops, but will always be remembered for his consecutive game record. His 2632 games spread over 14 seasons will surely never be beaten. At 1.93m he was tall for a shortstop, but combined athleticism with power, hitting more home runs than any other shortstop in history and accumulating the best single-season fielding percentage in that position. American League MVP in 1983 and 1991, he was the Gold Glove winner in 1991 and 1992. He retired in 2001 with a .278 career batting average.

Robinson, Brooks Calbert   Born Little Rock, Arkansas, 18 May 1937. Third baseman, Baltimore Orioles. Acknowledged as the greatest third baseman to play the game, Robinson played 23 seasons in Baltimore, setting major league records for games, put-outs, assists, chances, double plays and fielding percentage. A decent hitter, he had 268 career home runs. He was American League MVP in 1964 and World Series MVP in 1970 when he hit .429 and performed miracles at third base. He retired in 1977. Elected to the Hall of Fame in 1983.

Robinson, Frank   Born Beaumont, Texas, 31 August 1935. Outfielder, Cincinnati Reds, Baltimore Orioles,

Los Angeles Dodgers, California Angels, Cleveland Indians. Frank Robinson is the only man to be voted MVP in both major leagues (with the Reds (NL) in 1961 and the Orioles (AL) in 1966). Rookie of the Year in 1956, he developed into an aggressive outfielder and a hard-charging base runner. A feared hitter, he ranks fifth of all time on the home run list, with 586. In 1975 he created history by becoming the first African-American to manage a major league club, when he skippered the Cleveland Indians. He retired in 1976, with a .294 career batting average. Elected to the Hall of Fame in 1982.

Robinson, Jack Roosevelt Born Cairo, Georgia, 31 January 1919. First baseman, Kansas City Monarchs (Negro Leagues), Brooklyn Dodgers. The most historically significant of baseball players, Jackie Robinson was the first African-American to play in the majors in the 20th century. He was also the first to win the MVP award (1949), play in a World Series and be elected to the Hall of Fame. Breaking the colour barrier by signing for the Dodgers, Robinson soon began to win over the fans with his batting prowess and electrifying speed on the basepaths. An All-Star six times, Robinson's on-field record speaks for itself, but, as the first negro in the leagues, it is for his courage in the face of abuse, threats and intimidation that he will always be remembered. He retired in 1956 with a .311 career batting average. Elected to the Hall of Fame in 1962. He died at Stamford, Connecticut, 24 October 1972.

Rose, Peter Edward Born Cincinnati, Ohio, 14 April 1941. Infielder, outfielder, Cincinnati Reds, Philadelphia Phillies, Montreal Expos; manager, Cincinnati Reds. Pete Rose holds the major league records for hits (4256), singles (3215), at-bats (14,053) and games played (3562). He is the most prolific switch-hitter in history. Rookie of the Year in 1963, 'Charlie Hustle' became a Reds legend in the 'Big Red Machine' of the 1970s. On 11 September 1985, a single took his hits to 4193, passing the immortal Ty Cobb. In 1989, as manager of the Reds, Rose was accused of betting on his own team and as a result he was banned from baseball for life.

Ruth, George Herman ('Babe') Born Baltimore, Maryland, 6 February 1895. Pitcher, outfielder, Boston Red Sox, New York Yankees, Boston Braves. Considered by some as the finest player of all time, Ruth was the prototype of the modern-day superstar. He was the first player to hit 30, 40, 50 and 60 home runs in a season and his slugging style changed for ever the way the game was played. As a pitcher with the Red Sox, he won 89 games in six years, including 29 scoreless innings in the World Series, a record that stood for 42 years. However, his powerful hitting could not be ignored and he moved to right field to allow him to play every day. In 1920 he was sold for $100,000 to the New York Yankees. Ruth responded by shattering his own home run record, with 54, and twice more went on to break the record, with 59 in 1921 and 60 in 1927. As an everyday player Ruth rewrote the record books. The home run leader 12 times, from 1926 to 1931 he averaged better than 50 home runs per year. Over the course of his career he homered once every 11.76 plate appearances. Ruth played in ten World Series, averaging .326 with 15 home runs. In 1933 he hit the first-ever home run in an All-Star game. Traded to the Braves in 1935, he was a shadow of his former self. His 714th and final home run was considered to be among the longest-ever hit in Forbes Field,

Pittsburgh. He retired in 1935 with a career batting average of .342, but his pitching figures of 94-26 and an ERA of 2.28 are also superb. He died of throat cancer at the age of 53, his body lying in state at Yankee Stadium ('The house that Ruth built'). Elected to the Hall of Fame in 1936. He died in New York, 16 August 1948.

Ryan, Lynn Nolan Born Refugio, Texas, 31 January 1947. Pitcher, New York Mets, California Angels, Houston Astros, Texas Rangers. With a blazing fast ball that approached 100mph, he dominated hitters for an unparalleled 27 seasons. Holder of the all-time strike-out record of 5714. During four decades of prominence, he totalled 324 victories and garnered a host of major league records, including seven no-hitters and 383 strike-outs in 1973. He retired in 1993 with a lifetime ERA of 3.19. Elected to the Hall of Fame in 1999.

Schmidt, Michael Jack Born Dayton, Ohio, 27 September 1949. Third baseman, Philadelphia Phillies. An unprecedented combination of power and defence made Schmidt one of the game's all-time great third basemen. He hit 548 home runs, eight times leading the National League in that category. A fine fielder, he won 11 Gold Glove awards and was three times National League MVP. In 1980 he was named World Series MVP with a .381 average and two home runs. He retired in 1989. Elected to the Hall of Fame in 1995.

Seaver, George Thomas Born Fresno, California, 17 November 1944. Pitcher, New York Mets, Cincinnati Reds, Chicago White Sox, Boston Red Sox. Seaver won 311 games in a 20-year career. His 3272 strike-outs set a National League career record. In total, Seaver 'fanned' 3640 batters, including 200 or more a record ten times. He was Rookie of the Year in 1967, and three times a Cy Young Award winner. He retired in 1986 with a career 2.86 ERA. Elected to the Hall of Fame in 1992.

Sosa, Samuel Peralta Born San Pedro de Macoris, Dominican Republic, 12 November 1968. Outfielder, Texas Rangers, Chicago. White Sox, Chicago Cubs. Sammy Sosa became a household name in 1998 by hitting 68 home runs, which is by far the most by any Latin-American baseball player in a single season, and he led the major leagues in RBIs (Runs Batted In) with 158. He was also named as the National League's MVP later that year. In 1999 he became the first player to hit 60 homers in two different major league seasons. In 2001 Sammy became the first player in major league history to have three 60-plus home run seasons.

Speaker, Tristram E. Born Hubbard, Texas, 4 April 1888. Outfielder, Boston Red Sox, Cleveland Indians, Washington Senators, Philadelphia Athletics. Despite spending most of his career in the shadow of Ty Cobb, Speaker's .345 lifetime batting average and his revolutionary defensive play made him one of Cobb's few rivals as the greatest player of the 1910s. His speciality was hitting doubles. He led the American League eight times and his career total of 793 is still a major league record. His shallow play in centre field enabled him to a record 450 assists, easily atop the all-time list. As one of the game's most accomplished managers, he led the Indians to their first world championship in 1920. He retired in 1928, and was elected to the Hall of Fame in 1937. He died at Lake Whitney, Texas, 8 December 1958.

Stengel, Charles Dillon (Casey) Born Kansas City, Missouri, 30 July 1890. Outfielder, Brooklyn

BASEBALL

Dodgers, Pittsburgh Pirates, Philadelphia Phillies, New York Giants, Boston Braves; manager, Brooklyn Dodgers, Boston Braves, New York Yankees, New York Mets. Nicknamed after his home town, Stengel's career spanned 54 years. He played 14 seasons in the majors, retiring with a .284 batting average. But it was as a manager that he achieved his greatest fame. He guided the Yankees to ten pennants and seven world titles, including five in a row, in a 12-year span. Fired by the Yankees in 1960, he took the reins of the newly formed Mets in 1962. He remained in charge until 1965 when a broken hip forced his retirement a week before his 75th birthday. Elected to the Hall of Fame in 1966. He died at Glendale, California, 29 September 1975.

Wagner, John Peter (Honus)   Born Chartiers, Pennsylvania, 24 February 1874. Shortstop, Louisville Colonels, Pittsburgh Pirates. Regarded by many as the game's best-ever in his position, Wagner combined defensive and offensive excellence throughout a 21-year career. He broke into the big leagues in 1897 with the Colonels, hitting .344, the first of 17 consecutive seasons hitting over .300. He was eight times the National League batting champion. Compiling a .329 lifetime average, 'The Flying Dutchman' also stole 722 bases, leading the league in steals on five occasions. He retired in 1917. Elected to the Hall of Fame in 1936. He died at Carnegie, Pennsylvania, 6 December 1955.

Williams, Theodore Samuel   Born San Diego, California, 30 August 1918. Outfielder, Boston Red Sox. One of baseball's greatest hitters, Ted Williams was the last man to have a season batting average of over .400, hitting .406 in 1941. He set several batting records despite missing nearly five full seasons due to military service and two serious injuries. He led the league in batting average six times and was twice named American League MVP (1946 and 1949). He made his debut in 1939, hitting .327 for the season and finally called it a day in 1960, a remarkable career which included 521 home runs and a lifetime average of .344. He marked his last at-bat with a home run at Fenway Park. Elected to the Hall of Fame in 1966. He died at Inverness, Florida, 5 July 2002.

Wilson, Lewis Robert (Hack)   Born Ellwood City, Pennsylvania, 26 April 1900. Outfielder, New York Giants, Chicago Cubs, Brooklyn Dodgers, Philadelphia Phillies. A winner of four home run titles, Wilson is best remembered for his incredible 1930 season – 56 homers (a National League record that stood for 68 years), a .356 batting average and an incredible 191 RBIs, still a major league record. Over 12 major league seasons he hit 244 home runs and compiled a .307 lifetime average. He retired in 1934 and was elected to the Hall of Fame in 1979. He died at Baltimore, Maryland, 23 November 1948.

Yastrzemski, Carl Michael   Born Southampton, New York, 22 August 1939. Outfielder, Boston Red Sox. When 'Yaz' retired in 1982 after 23 seasons in Boston, he was the all-time Red Sox leader in eight major categories. He played more games (3308) than any other American Leaguer. Three times American League batting champion (1963, 1967 and 1968), he also shone in the field, winning seven Gold Gloves in left field. He is the only player in the American League to have 3000 hits and 400 home runs. He was American League MVP in 1967, when he also won the 'Triple Crown', the last player to accomplish that feat. He retired in 1983 with 452 home runs and a career average of .285. Elected to the Hall of Fame in 1989.

Young, Denton True (Cy)   Born Gilmore, Ohio, 29 March 1867. Pitcher, Cleveland Spiders, St Louis Perfectos, St Louis Cardinals, Boston Americans, Pilgrims, Somerset's, Red Sox, Cleveland Naps (Indians), Boston Braves. One baseball record that will almost certainly never be beaten is Cy Young's 511 career wins, almost 100 more than any other pitcher in history. He won 30 games five times and topped 20 wins an amazing 15 times. He had his best season in 1901 when he led the American League in wins, strike-outs and ERA. In 1903 he threw the first-ever pitch in a World Series game, helping Boston to the title with two wins. In 1904 he threw the first perfect game in the American League. Retired in 1911 with a career 2.63 ERA. Elected to the Hall of Fame in 1937. He died at Newcomerstown, Ohio, 4 November 1955.

World Series

Winners			Runners-Up
1903	Boston Red Sox (AL)	5-3	Pittsburgh Pirates (NL)
1904	no series, NL refused to play AL		
1905	New York Giants (NL)	4-1	Philadelphia Athletics (AL)
1906	Chicago White Sox (AL)	4-2	Chicago Cubs (NL)
1907	Chicago Cubs (NL)	4-0	Detroit Tigers (AL)
1908	Chicago Cubs (NL)	4-1	Detroit Tigers (AL)
1909	Pittsburgh Pirates (NL)	4-3	Detroit Tigers (AL)
1910	Philadelphia Athletics (AL)	4-1	Chicago Cubs (NL)
1911	Philadelphia Athletics (AL)	4-2	New York Giants (NL)
1912	Boston Red Sox (AL)	4-3	New York Giants (NL)
1913	Philadelphia Athletics (AL)	4-1	New York Giants (NL)
1914	Boston Braves (NL)	4-0	Philadelphia Athletics (AL)
1915	Boston Red Sox (AL)	4-1	Philadelphia Phillies (NL)
1916	Boston Red Sox (AL)	4-1	Brooklyn Dodgers (NL)
1917	Chicago White Sox (AL)	4-2	New York Giants (NL)
1918	Boston Red Sox (AL)	4-2	Chicago Cubs (NL)
1919	Cincinnati Reds (NL)	5-3	Chicago White Sox (AL)
1920	Cleveland Indians (AL)	5-2	Brooklyn Dodgers (NL)
1921	New York Giants (NL)	5-3	New York Yankees (AL)

1922	New York Giants (NL)	4-0	New York Yankees (AL)
1923	New York Yankees (AL)	4-2	New York Giants (NL)
1924	Washington Senators (AL)	4-3	New York Giants (NL)
1925	Pittsburgh Pirates (NL)	4-3	Washington Senators (AL)
1926	St Louis Cardinals (NL)	4-3	New York Yankees (AL)
1927	New York Yankees (AL)	4-0	Pittsburgh Pirates (NL)
1928	New York Yankees (AL)	4-0	St Louis Cardinals (NL)
1929	Philadelphia Athletics (AL)	4-1	Chicago Cubs (NL)
1930	Philadelphia Athletics (AL)	4-2	St Louis Cardinals (NL)
1931	St Louis Cardinals (NL)	4-3	Philadelphia Athletics (AL)
1932	New York Yankees (AL)	4-0	Chicago Cubs (NL)
1933	New York Giants (NL)	4-1	Washington Senators (AL)
1934	St Louis Cardinals (NL)	4-3	Detroit Tigers (AL)
1935	Detroit Tigers (AL)	4-2	Chicago Cubs (NL)
1936	New York Yankees (AL)	4-2	New York Giants (NL)
1937	New York Yankees (AL)	4-1	New York Giants (NL)
1938	New York Yankees (AL)	4-0	Chicago Cubs (NL)
1939	New York Yankees (AL)	4-0	Cincinnati Reds (NL)
1940	Cincinnati Reds (NL)	4-3	Detroit Tigers (AL)
1941	New York Yankees (AL)	4-1	Brooklyn Dodgers (NL)
1942	St Louis Cardinals (NL)	4-1	New York Yankees (AL)
1943	New York Yankees (AL)	4-1	St Louis Cardinals (NL)
1944	St Louis Cardinals (NL)	4-2	St Louis Browns (AL)
1945	Detroit Tigers (AL)	4-3	Chicago Cubs (NL)
1946	St Louis Cardinals (NL)	4-3	Boston Red Sox (AL)
1947	New York Yankees (AL)	4-3	Brooklyn Dodgers (NL)
1948	Cleveland Indians (AL)	4-2	Boston Braves (NL)
1949	New York Yankees (AL)	4-1	Brooklyn Dodgers (NL)
1950	New York Yankees (AL)	4-0	Philadelphia Phillies (NL)
1951	New York Yankees (AL)	4-2	New York Giants (NL)
1952	New York Yankees (AL)	4-3	Brooklyn Dodgers (NL)
1953	New York Yankees (AL)	4-2	Brooklyn Dodgers (NL)
1954	New York Giants (NL)	4-0	Cleveland Indians (AL)
1955	Brooklyn Dodgers (NL)	4-3	New York Yankees (AL)
1956	New York Yankees (AL)	4-3	Brooklyn Dodgers (NL)
1957	Milwaukee Braves (NL)	4-3	New York Yankees (AL)
1958	New York Yankees (AL)	4-3	Milwaukee Braves (NL)
1959	Los Angeles Dodgers (NL)	4-2	Chicago White Sox (AL)
1960	Pittsburgh Pirates (NL)	4-3	New York Yankees (AL)
1961	New York Yankees (AL)	4-1	Cincinnati Reds (NL)
1962	New York Yankees (AL)	4-3	San Francisco Giants (NL)
1963	Los Angeles Dodgers (NL)	4-0	New York Yankees (AL)
1964	St Louis Cardinals (NL)	4-3	New York Yankees (AL)
1965	Los Angeles Dodgers (NL)	4-3	Minnesota Twins (AL)
1966	Baltimore Orioles (AL)	4-0	Los Angeles Dodgers (NL)
1967	St Louis Cardinals (NL)	4-3	Boston Red Sox (AL)
1968	Detroit Tigers (AL)	4-3	St Louis Cardinals (NL)
1969	New York Mets (NL)	4-1	Baltimore Orioles (AL)
1970	Baltimore Orioles (AL)	4-1	Cincinnati Reds (NL)
1971	Pittsburgh Pirates (NL)	4-3	Baltimore Orioles (AL)
1972	Oakland Athletics (AL)	4-3	Cincinnati Reds (NL)
1973	Oakland Athletics (AL)	4-3	New York Mets (NL)
1974	Oakland Athletics (AL)	4-1	Los Angeles Dodgers (NL)
1975	Cincinnati Reds (NL)	4-3	Boston Red Sox (AL)
1976	Cincinnati Reds (NL)	4-0	New York Yankees (AL)
1977	New York Yankees (AL)	4-2	Los Angeles Dodgers (NL)
1978	New York Yankees (AL)	4-2	Los Angeles Dodgers (NL)
1979	Pittsburgh Pirates (NL)	4-3	Baltimore Orioles (AL)
1980	Philadelphia Phillies (NL)	4-2	Kansas City Royals (AL)
1981	Los Angeles Dodgers (NL)	4-2	New York Yankees (AL)
1982	St Louis Cardinals (NL)	4-3	Milwaukee Brewers (AL)
1983	Baltimore Orioles (AL)	4-1	Philadelphia Phillies (NL)
1984	Detroit Tigers (AL)	4-1	San Diego Padres (NL)
1985	Kansas City Royals (AL)	4-3	St Louis Cardinals (NL)
1986	New York Mets (NL)	4-3	Boston Red Sox (AL)
1987	Minnesota Twins (AL)	4-3	St Louis Cardinals (NL)
1988	Los Angeles Dodgers (NL)	4-1	Oakland Athletics (AL)
1989	Oakland Athletics (AL)	4-0	San Francisco Giants (NL)
1990	Cincinnati Reds (NL)	4-0	Oakland Athletics (AL)
1991	Minnesota Twins (AL)	4-3	Atlanta Braves (NL)
1992	Toronto Blue Jays (AL)	4-2	Atlanta Braves (NL)
1993	Toronto Blue Jays (AL)	4-2	Philadelphia Phillies (NL)

BASEBALL

1994	no series, due to players' strike		
1995	Atlanta Braves (NL)	4-2	Cleveland Indians (AL)
1996	New York Yankees (AL)	4-2	Atlanta Braves (NL)
1997	Florida Marlins (NL)	4-3	Cleveland Indians (AL)
1998	New York Yankees (AL)	4-0	San Diego Padres (NL)
1999	New York Yankees (AL)	4-0	Atlanta Braves (NL)
2000	New York Yankees (AL)	4-1	New York Mets (NL)
2001	Arizona Diamondbacks (NL)	4-3	New York Yankees (AL)
2002	Anaheim Angels (AL)	4-3	San Francisco Giants (NL)
2003	Florida Marlins (NL)	4-2	New York Yankees (AL)

The game of basketball is unusual inasmuch as its roots can be identified with some degree of certainty. In 1891 Dr Luther Gulick, head of Physical Education at the Young Men's Christian Association, gave James Naismith, a physical education instructor at the YMCA Training School in Springfield, Massachusetts, 14 days to create an indoor game that would provide an 'athletic distraction' for a rowdy class during the harsh New England winter. Naismith eventually developed basketball's original 13 rules and, consequently, the game itself.

The game caught on quickly and the first collegiate game was played in 1896 at Iowa City, Iowa, between two teams with five members per side (a rule still existing today). The team consists of a centre (often the tallest player as they must be able to score, take rebounds, draw fouls and defend), point guard (the playmaker responsible for converting defence into attack), power forward (usually marks the opposition centre and picks up rebounds before distributing to the point guard, shooting guard (aka two-guard, responsible for shooting three-pointers), and small forward (fast one-on-one player who can dribble and attack the basket).

Organised basketball began in America in 1898 with the creation of the National Basketball League. In 1946, the Basketball Association of America was formed, and in 1949 the two were merged to create the National Basketball Association (NBA). A third organisation, the National Collegiate Athletic Association (NCAA) governs the sport at college level in the US. The Fédération Internationale de Basketball Amateur (FIBA), formed in 1932, controls international basketball, including the European, World and Olympic championships.

The rules differ slightly among the three organisations: for instance, the international amateur game under FIBA auspices is played over four 10-minute periods, while professional US games of the NBA are played over four 12-minute periods and NCAA games are played over two halves of 20 minutes each, as are all games played by women NBA members.

The court sizes also differ slightly between codes. FIBA games have court dimensions of 28m × 15m, NBA and NCAA games 94ft (28.65m) × 50ft (15.24m). The ball size differs slightly too. FIBA insists on a maximum circumference of 78cm while the NBA specifies 29½ins (74.9cm) to 29¾ins (75.6cm). The pressure of the ball should be between 7½lb and 8½lb (3.4kg to 3.85kg). The basket is 10ft (3.05m) off the ground. Each basket ring should be 18ins (45.8cm) in diameter and painted orange. Every basket scored from within the 6.25m (3-point) line during normal play counts as 2 points. A basket scored from outside the 6.25m line counts as 3 points and a basket scored from the free-throw line after a foul or penalty scores 1 point. The game is controlled by two referees and a crew chief, who has the final say in matters of disputes, and commences with a jump-ball in the centre circle.

The rules of basketball almost guarantee close finishes, perhaps the most memorable being the climax of the 1972 Olympic final in which the Russian team prevailed when the game was thought to be all over. This situation occurs regularly in the NBA and makes basketball one of the most exciting games in the world.

The domestic game in Great Britain has never taken off in a major way. As in ice hockey, there are good teams with excellent facilities but they field few British players and it has become increasingly frustrating to market the game when it is perceived as a substandard version of the NBA. A list of British teams can be found at the end of this section.

Teams in the NBA recruit new players by means of a system called the draft. The best college players are ranked and clubs get draft picks based on the prior season's results, the worst teams getting first pick. Because this system was open to abuse, as teams not vying for championship victory could lose on purpose to ensure the best draft picks for the next season, since 1990 a draft lottery system has been used. The teams involved in the lottery are the 13 teams that fail to make the play-offs. Fourteen balls, numbered from 1 to 14, are placed into a drum. Four balls are drawn. There are 1001 combinations, and each team is assigned the appropriate number of combinations, totalling 1000, based on the order of finish in the standings. The first combination of four balls determines which team gets the no. 1 pick. The balls are then replaced in the drum and the process is repeated for subsequent picks. If the one unassigned combination is drawn, it is ignored. The lottery is used for the first three picks and the remaining ten teams are assigned picks 4 to 13 in reverse order of their final standings.

NBA Championship

	Winners		Runners-Up		Winners		Runners-Up
1947	Philadelphia Warriors	4-1	Chicago Stags	1976	Boston Celtics	4-2	Phoenix Suns
1948	Baltimore Bullets	4-2	Philadelphia Warriors	1977	Portland Trail Blazers	4-2	Philadelphia 76ers
1949	Minneapolis Lakers	4-2	Washington Capitols	1978	Washington Bullets	4-3	Seattle SuperSonics
1950	Minneapolis Lakers	4-2	Syracuse Nationals	1979	Seattle SuperSonics	4-1	Washington Capitols
1951	Rochester Royals	4-3	New York Knicks	1980	LA Lakers	4-2	Philadelphia 76ers
1952	Minneapolis Lakers	4-3	New York Knicks	1981	Boston Celtics	4-2	Houston Rockets
1953	Minneapolis Lakers	4-1	New York Knicks	1982	LA Lakers	4-2	Philadelphia 76ers
1954	Minneapolis Lakers	4-3	Syracuse Nationals	1983	Philadelphia 76ers	4-0	LA Lakers
1955	Syracuse Nationals	4-3	Fort Wayne Pistons	1984	Boston Celtics	4-3	LA Lakers
1956	Philadelphia Warriors	4-3	Fort Wayne Pistons	1985	LA Lakers	4-2	Boston Celtics
1957	Boston Celtics	4-3	St Louis Hawks	1986	Boston Celtics	4-2	Houston Rockets
1958	St Louis Hawks	4-2	Boston Celtics	1987	LA Lakers	4-2	Boston Celtics
1959	Boston Celtics	4-0	Minneapolis Lakers	1988	LA Lakers	4-3	Detroit Pistons
1960	Boston Celtics	4-3	St Louis Hawks	1989	Detroit Pistons	4-0	LA Lakers
1961	Boston Celtics	4-1	St Louis Hawks	1990	Detroit Pistons	4-1	Portland Trail Blazers
1962	Boston Celtics	4-3	LA Lakers	1991	Chicago Bulls	4-1	LA Lakers
1963	Boston Celtics	4-2	LA Lakers	1992	Chicago Bulls	4-1	Portland Trail Blazers
1964	Boston Celtics	4-1	San Francisco Warriors	1993	Chicago Bulls	4-2	Phoenix Suns
1965	Boston Celtics	4-1	LA Lakers	1994	Houston Rockets	4-3	New York Knicks
1966	Boston Celtics	4-3	LA Lakers	1995	Houston Rockets	4-0	Orlando Magic
1967	Philadelphia 76ers	4-2	San Francisco Warriors	1996	Chicago Bulls	4-2	Seattle SuperSonics
1968	Boston Celtics	4-2	LA Lakers	1997	Chicago Bulls	4-2	Utah Jazz
1969	Boston Celtics	4-3	LA Lakers	1998	Chicago Bulls	4-2	Utah Jazz
1970	New York Knicks	4-3	LA Lakers	1999	San Antonio Spurs	4-1	New York Knicks
1971	Milwaukee Bucks	4-0	Baltimore Bullets	2000	LA Lakers	4-2	Indiana Pacers
1972	LA Lakers	4-1	New York Knicks	2001	LA Lakers	4-1	Philadelphia 76ers
1973	New York Knicks	4-1	LA Lakers	2002	LA Lakers	4-0	New Jersey Nets
1974	Boston Celtics	4-3	Milwaukee Bucks	2003	San Antonio Spurs	4-2	New Jersey Nets
1975	Golden State Warriors	4-0	Washington Bullets	2004	Detroit Pistons	4-1	LA Lakers

Olympic Games

Men's Medallists

	Gold	Final	Silver	Bronze		
1936	United States	19-8	Canada	Mexico	26-12	Poland
1948	United States	65-21	France	Brazil	52-47	Mexico
1952	United States	36-25	Soviet Union	Uruguay	68-59	Argentina
1956	United States	89-55	Soviet Union	Uruguay	71-62	France
1960	United States	81-57	Soviet Union	Brazil	78-75	Italy
1964	United States	73-59	Soviet Union	Brazil	76-60	Puerto Rico
1968	United States	65-50	Yugoslavia	Soviet Union	70-53	Brazil
1972	Soviet Union	51-50	United States	Cuba	66-65	Italy
1976	United States	95-74	Yugoslavia	Soviet Union	100-72	Canada
1980	Yugoslavia	86-77	Italy	Soviet Union	117-94	Spain
1984	United States	96-65	Spain	Yugoslavia	88-82	Canada
1988	Soviet Union	76-63	Yugoslavia	United States	78-49	Australia
1992	United States	117-85	Croatia	Lithuania	82-78	Soviet Union
1996	United States	95-69	Yugoslavia	Lithuania	80-74	Australia
2000	United States	85-75	France	Lithuania	89-71	Australia

Women's Medallists

	Gold	Final	Silver	Bronze		
1976	Soviet Union	5-0 (no final)	United States	Bulgaria		
1980	Soviet Union	104-73	Bulgaria	Yugoslavia	68-65	Hungary
1984	United States	85-55	Republic of Korea	Canada	65-63	China
1988	United States	77-70	Yugoslavia	Soviet Union	68-53	Australia
1992	CIS	76-66	China	United States	88-74	Cuba
1996	United States	111-87	Brazil	Australia	66-56	Ukraine
2000	United States	76-54	Australia	Brazil	84-73	South Korea

Men's World Championship

1950	Argentina	1978	Yugoslavia
1954	United States	1982	Soviet Union
1959	Brazil	1986	United States
1963	Brazil	1990	Yugoslavia
1967	Soviet Union	1994	United States
1970	Yugoslavia	1998	Yugoslavia
1974	Soviet Union	2002	Yugoslavia

Biographies of Players and Administrators

Abdul-Jabbar, Kareem   Born Ferdinand Lewis Alcindor, New York, 16 August 1947. Teams: Milwaukee Bucks, Los Angeles Lakers. After winning Rookie of the Year in 1970, Abdul-Jabbar went on to win six NBA Championships, gaining six NBA Most Valuable Player awards and two NBA Final MVP awards, among others. He converted to Islam before the 1971/72 season. After several seasons with the Bucks, he was traded to the Lakers in 1975. Known for the 'sky shot' and his physical fitness regime, he left the game having achieved the highest-ever points total of 38,387, with 17,440 rebounds and 3189 blocks, and having scored double figures in 787 consecutive games. After Magic Johnson joined the Lakers in 1979, they won nine division titles in the final ten years of Abdul-Jabbar's career. Since retiring in 1989, Abdul-Jabbar has worked in the entertainment business, and in 1995 he was elected to the Naismith Memorial Basketball Hall of Fame.

Archibald, Nate   Born New York, 2 September 1948. Teams: Cincinnati Royals, New York Nets, Buffalo Braves, Boston Celtics, Milwaukee Bucks. Nicknamed 'Tiny' after his father 'Big Tiny', Archibald had a 14-year career in the NBA. Selected for the starting line-up of Cincinnati in 1972/73, he led the NBA that year with a 34.0 average and 11.4 assists per game, becoming the only player ever to lead in both categories in the same season. Traded to the New York Nets in 1976, he played in only 34 games due to injury. He then went to the Buffalo Braves, but missed the entire 1977/78 season with a torn Achilles tendon. Appearing for the Boston Celtics until the end of season 1982/83, he finished his career with the Milwaukee Bucks in 1984.

Arizin, Paul   Born Philadelphia, 9 April 1928. Teams: Philadelphia Warriors, Camden Bullets. Paul Arizin 'discovered' the jump shot during practice when he slipped on a waxed floor while trying to carry out a hook shot. Joining the Philadelphia Warriors as the first-round draft choice in 1950, he led the points-scoring league in his second year with an average of 25.4 points per game. Returning after two years' service in Korea, he led the points league for a second time with an average of 25.6 per game. In a ten-year career with the Warriors, during which he suffered from asthma and sinus problems, his average was 22.8 points. After leaving in 1962, Arizin joined the Camden Bullets, a team in the Eastern Basketball League, where his average after three years was 25 points.

Barkley, Charles   Born Leeds, Alabama, 20 February 1963. Teams: Philadelphia 76ers, Phoenix Suns, Houston Rockets. One of four players to have gained over 20,000 points, 10,000 rebounds and 4000 assists, 'Sir' Charles started his career at the 76ers in 1984. He was part of the US 'Dream Team' that won Olympic gold in 1992. A controversial figure throughout his career, he played for eight years at Philadelphia before being traded to the Phoenix Suns. While with the Suns his form returned, and he averaged 25.6 points per game. Injuries were to plague Barkley throughout the rest of his career, limiting his playing time. After joining the Houston Rockets in 1996, he played through back pain for two years, finally retiring after tearing his left quadricep tendon in 1999.

Barry, Rick   Born Elizabeth, New Jersey, 28 March 1944. Teams: San Francisco Warriors, Oakland Oaks, New York Nets, Houston Rockets. After scoring an NCAA Division 1 record of 37.4 points per game, Rick Barry first joined the San Francisco Warriors in the 1965 draft. In his second season, he led the league in scoring with 35.6 points. In 1967 Barry signed a five-year deal with the Oakland Oaks, a team in the newly formed American Basketball League. As he had a year of his contract left at the Warriors, he was forced out of basketball for the year, finally joining Oakland in 1968. When the Oaks became the Washington Capitals, he signed once again with the San Francisco Warriors, but another lawsuit this time kept him at Washington. In 1970, when the team moved to Virginia, he refused to go and was traded to the New York Nets. He returned to the Warriors after his contract with the American Basketball Association (ABA) expired, and was named MVP in the 1975 play-offs when they won the NBA championship. He joined the Houston Rockets as a free agent in 1978, playing there for two years until he retired in 1980.

Bellamy, Walter   Born New Bern, North Carolina, 24 July 1939. Teams: Chicago Packers, New York Knicks, Detroit Pistons, Atlanta Hawks, New Orleans Jazz. After scoring an average 20.6 points per game in three years at the University of Indiana, Bellamy was picked by the Chicago Packers in the first-round draft of 1961. Renamed the Zephyrs in 1962, the team moved to Baltimore, becoming the Bullets in 1963. Bellamy was traded to the New York Knicks in 1965, the Detroit Pistons in 1968, and the Atlanta Hawks in 1970. In 1974 he retired after playing just one game for the New Orleans Jazz.

Bing, David   Born Washington DC, 19 November 1943. Teams: Detroit Pistons, Washington Bullets, Boston Celtics. Bing played for three years at Syracuse College between 1963 and 1966. He joined the Detroit Pistons in 1966, becoming Rookie of the Year. After playing for five years, he held the team scoring and assist records. He missed two months of the 1972 season after suffering a detached retina in a pre-season game, but in 1973 played in all 82 games scoring an average of 22.3 points per game. In 1975 he joined the Washington Bullets for two seasons, finishing his career in 1978 at the Boston Celtics.

BASKETBALL

Bird, Larry   Born French Lick, Indiana, 7 December 1956. Team: Boston Celtics. From playing as a high school sophomore through finishing college, Bird grew from a 1.83m guard to a 2.06m forward. When at Indiana State he averaged 28.6 points per game and although the team lost to Michigan in the NCAA finals, Bird was the college Player of the Year. After Bird signed for the Boston Celtics, they had the greatest turnaround in NBA history, from a record of 29 wins against 53 losses in 1978/79 to 61–21 the following year. Boston won the NBA Championship in 1981, 1984 and 1986; Bird was MVP in the play-offs of 1984 and 1986, and leagues MVP, 1984-86. He began to suffer heel problems in the 1986 season, playing only six games in 1988/89, but continued until the end of the 1991/92 season, making 60 appearances in 1990/91 and 45 in 1991/92.

Chamberlain, Wiltern   Born Philadelphia, Pennsylvania, 21 August 1936. Teams: Philadelphia Warriors, Philadelphia 76ers, Los Angeles Lakers. At 2.11m entering high school, 'Wilt the Stilt' had over two hundred colleges wooing him to join them. The University of Kansas won and in his first game he scored 52 points. He averaged 29.9 points and 18.3 rebounds in three years at Kansas. He joined the Harlem Globetrotters after his junior year, moving to the Philadelphia Warriors in 1959. Now standing 2.18m, he was Rookie of the Year and MVP, setting a league record of 2707 points, while in the 1961 season he scored 4029 points, an average of 50.4 per game. Chamberlain joined the Philadelphia 76ers in 1964, and in 1967 they beat the Boston Celtics to win the NBA Championship. In 1968 he was traded to the Los Angeles Lakers. After a knee injury in 1969, he returned to win the 1972 NBA Championship with the Lakers when they beat the New York Knicks 4-1. Chamberlain was the the first player to score over 30,000 points, averaging 30.1 points per game.

Cousy, Robert   Born New York, 9 August 1928. Teams: Chicago Bears, Boston Celtics, Cincinnati Royals. At Holy Cross in Worcester, MA, Cousy played for an NCAA Championship team as a freshman and was All-American in his senior year. He was to join the NBA's Chicago Bears, but they folded before he played a game. Instead he joined the Boston Celtics after a lottery in which three Bears players' names were pulled out of a hat. Fourth in the league in assists in 1950/51, he was second the following year and led for the next eight seasons. Boston won six championships in seven years from 1956 and he was named MVP in the 1957 season. Cousy was nicknamed 'The Houdini of the Hardwood' because of his playing skills. He retired from playing in 1963, coaching Boston College for six seasons. In 1970 he took over the Cincinnati Royals, who became the Kansas City/Omaha Kings in 1972. He returned to playing in the 1969 season, scoring five points in seven games, but retired after season 1973/74.

Cowens, David W.   Born Newport, Kentucky, 25 October 1948. Teams: Boston Celtics, Milwaukee Bucks. Drafted to the Boston Celtics in 1970, Cowens was named leagues MVP in the 1972/73 season. He helped the Celtics win championships in both 1974 and 1976. Through the 1978/79 season he was player/coach, but quit after achieving a record of only 24 wins against 41 losses. Two years later he joined the Milwaukee Bucks for the 1982/83 season.

Cunningham, J. William   Born Brooklyn, New York, 3 June 1943. Teams: Philadelphia 76ers, Carolina Cougars. At the University of North Carolina, Billy Cunningham was known as 'The Kangaroo Kid' because of his jumping ability. He joined the Philadelphia 76ers as a first-round draft pick in 1964, helping them win the NBA Championship in the 1966/67 season. He joined the American Basketball Association's Carolina Cougars in 1972, becoming the leagues Player of the Year in his first season. After returning to the 76ers in 1974, a knee injury forced him into retirement at the end of season 1975/76. He was the team's coach between 1977 and 1985.

Dantley, Adrian   Born Washington DC, 28 February 1955. Teams: Notre Dame, Buffalo Braves, Indiana Pacers, LA Lakers, Dallas Mavericks, Milwaukee Bucks. Playing for Notre Dame, Dantley scored 2223 points in two years, being named Player of the Year by the US Basketball Writers Association in 1976. He also played in the winning 1976 US Olympic basketball team, averaging 19.3 points per game. Giving up his senior year at Notre Dame to join the Buffalo Braves, he was named Rookie of the Year with an average of 20.3 points per game. Dantley moved from Buffalo to the Indiana Pacers who then traded him to the LA Lakers, and a season and a half later he joined the Utah Jazz. In seasons 1981-84 he had a scoring average over 30 points per game, but after joining the Detroit Pistons in 1986 his average dropped to 20 points per game due to lack of time on court. After being traded again, to the Dallas Mavericks in the 1989/90 season, he joined the Milwaukee Bucks in 1990/91, playing just ten games. He spent his last year playing in Italy.

Debusschere, David A.   Born Detroit, Michigan, 16 January 1940. Teams: Detroit Pistons, New York Knicks. After playing baseball and basketball at the University of Detroit, Debusschere joined both the Chicago White Sox and the Detroit Pistons in 1962. At the age of 24, he left baseball to become the Pistons' player/coach in 1964. He coached until the 1966/67 season, but played on until being traded to the New York Knicks late in 1968. He helped New York win the NBA Championship in 1970 and 1973, being named in the NBA All-Defensive team from 1969-74. He retired from playing in 1974, becoming general manager of the American Basketball Association's New York Nets. A year later he was Commissioner of the ABA, helping the association's merger with the NBA in 1976. In 1982 he became general manager of the New York Knicks.

Drexler, Clyde   Born New Orleans, Louisiana, 22 June 1962. Teams: Portland Trail Blazers, Houston Rockets. At 2m, Drexler averaged 14.4 points per game in his three years as part of the 'Phi Slamma Jamma' team at the University of Houston. Ater his junior year he left, and became a first-round pick by the Portland Trail Blazers in the 1983 draft. He didn't play full time in his first season, but became a starting guard in 1984, coming into his own in the 1987 season when he averaged 27 points per game. Part of the All-NBA third team in 1990 and the second team in both 1988 and 1991, Drexler made the first team in 1992 after averaging 25 points per game. After picking up a back injury, however, he missed most of the 1992/93 season. Traded to the Houston Rockets in the 1994/95 season, he helped them win their second straight championship. He retired in 1998.

English, Alexander   Born Columbia, South Carolina, 5 January 1954. Teams: Milwaukee Bucks, Indiana

Pacers, Denver Nuggets, Dallas Mavericks. While playing as a forward at the University of South Carolina, English scored 1972 points in 111 games. A second-round draft pick for the Milwaukee Bucks in 1976, he then joined the Indiana Pacers, but was traded to the Denver Nuggets during the 1979/80 season. His average rose from 23.8 to a league-leading 28.4 points per game in three years, and in the next six years remained above 25. English joined the Dallas Mavericks in 1990/91 before playing his final season in Italy. In his career he scored 25,613 regular-season points in 1193 games, an average of 21.5 per game.

Erving, Julius Born Roosevelt, New York, 22 February 1950. Teams: Milwaukee Bucks, Virginia Squires, New York Nets, Philadelphia 76ers. Throughout his career, Erving was known as 'Dr J' because of the way he operated on defences. Although only 1.98m, he averaged 27 points per game at the University of Massachusetts, leading him to sign with the American Basketball Association's Virginia Squires. A year later he tried to join the NBA's Atlanta Hawks, but a court ordered him to honour his four-year contract with the Squires. With an average of 31.9 in his second year, Erving was traded to the New York Nets. He became league leading scorer and MVP in both 1974 and 1976, when the Nets won the ABA Championship. By the time he retired, after playing with the Philadelphia 76ers from 1976 until 1987, Erving had become only the third player to score over 30,000 points during his career.

Ewing, Patrick Born Kingston, Jamaica, 5 August 1962. Teams: New York Knicks, Seattle SuperSonics, Orlando Magic. Ewing learned to play basketball when his family moved to America. He had grown to 2.13m by the time he arrived at Georgetown University, Washington DC. While there, he won All-America honours three years in a row, 1983-85, Georgetown winning the NCAA Championship in 1984. Ewing won the Naismith Award, the Eastman Award and the Rupp Trophy in 1985 as college Player of the Year. He helped the US Olympic team win at Seoul in 1984, blocking 18 shots. Drafted in the first round of 1985 by the New York Knicks, Ewing stayed as starter for the next 14 seasons. In 1997, knee problems started to affect his game, and he left New York for the Seattle SuperSonics in 2000. In 2001 he played one year for the Orlando Magic, retiring in 2002.

Frazier, Walter Born Atlanta, Georgia, 29 March 1945. Teams: New York Knicks, Cleveland Cavaliers. After having to sit out his junior year at Southern Illinois due to being academically ineligible, Frazier returned to be MVP at the National Invitation Tournament in 1967. He joined the New York Knicks as first-round draft choice at guard, where in the 1970/71 season he became the team's leading scorer with 21.7 points per game. In ten seasons at the team, the Knicks won NBA Championships in 1970 and 1973. Frazier was traded to the Cleveland Cavaliers in 1977, retiring from the team two seasons later.

Gervin, George Born Detroit, Michigan, 27 April 1952. Teams: Virginia Squires, San Antonio Spurs, Chicago Bulls. After winning a scholarship to Long Beach University, Gervin transferred to Eastern Michigan University after one semester. Having been suspended for brawling, he was expelled and went to play in the Continental Basketball League. After a special draft in the 1972/73 season Gervin was

chosen by the Virginia Squires, being named in the league's All-Rookie team. He left for the San Antonio Spurs in 1974 and after the Spurs joined the NBA in 1976. Gervin led the scoring league four times. He spent one season with the Chicago Bulls after being traded in 1985, finishing his career playing in Italy in 1986/87. Throughout his ABA/NBA career he scored 26,595 points, with an average of 25.1 per game in 1060 season games.

Gilmore, Artis Born Chipley, Florida, 21 September 1949. Teams: Chicago Bulls, Boston Celtics. Gilmore spent two years at Gardner-Webb College before going to Jacksonville University in 1969. While there he scored an average of 24.3 points per game, leading the NCAA Division 1. After joining the American Basketball Association's Kentucky Colonels as their first-round draft choice in 1971, he was named Rookie and Player of the Year. He led the rebounds league for the next four years. When the ABA and NBA merged he joined the Chicago Bulls. He was traded to the San Antonio Spurs in 1982, and back to the Bulls in 1987. Gilmore played for the Boston Celtics in 1987/88 after being released by the Bulls. He played the year after in Italy before retiring. In 17 years he scored 24,041 points in 909 games.

Greer, Harold E. Born Huntington, West Virginia, 26 June 1936. Teams: Syracuse Nationals, Philadelphia 76ers. Greer was the first black player at Marshall University in West Virginia, averaging 23.6 points per game in his senior year. He then joined the Syracuse Nationals, who became the Philadelphia 76ers in 1963. He was part of the team that won the NBA Championship in 1967, averaging 22.1 points per game through the year. Greer retired in 1973 after playing in 1122 games with an average of 19.2 points per game.

Harlem Globetrotters The Globetrotters have their origins in a team of players from Wendell Phillips High School, Chicago, who played in the Negro American Legion League as Giles Post. After they turned professional in 1927 as the Savoy Big Five under manager Dick Hudson, promoter Abe Saperstein bought the team later that year and renamed it the Harlem Globetrotters. Until the late 1930s, the Globetrotters were a serious competitive team but with the acquisition of Inman Jackson they began to work light entertainment and comedy routines into their appearances. They could, however, still play with the best of the professional teams. In 1939, they were runners-up to the New York Rens in the World Professional Basketball Tournament in Chicago, and they won the tournament in 1940.

In 1942, one of the all-time Harlem Globetrotter greats, Reece 'Goose' Tatum, signed for the team. Quickly establishing himself as a basketball genius and an inspired comedian, 'Goose' originated and developed most of the team's classic comedy routines. In 1952, the Globetrotters' silver anniversary was celebrated with a 108-game around-the-world tour, the first in the history of basketball. 'Sweet Georgia Brown' became the team's official theme song later the same year.

The star entertainer with the team is known as The Clown Prince of Basketball, and many players have held that position through the years. (In 1956, there were four units of the Globetrotters on the road, each with their own Clown Prince.) Three men, though, have become internationally famous in this role: 'Goose' Tatum, Meadowlark Lemon and

BASKETBALL

Hubert 'Geese' Ausbie. In 1963, Frederic Douglas 'Curly' Neal (so nicknamed because of his bald head) joined the Globetrotters as a master dribbler and sidekick to Lemon. In 1985 the Globetrotters signed their first female player, Olympic gold medallist Lynette Woodard from Kansas. When, in 1993, Mannie Jackson acquired the Globetrotters, he became the first African-American and former player to own a sports/entertainment organisation.

The team has played over 20,000 games in more than 100 countries around the world. The BBC broadcasts of their games popularised the Globetrotters in the UK and they remain the most entertaining act on the circuit, whether they are considered as sport or showbiz.

Havlicek, John   Born Lansing, Ohio, 8 April 1940. Team: Boston Celtics. 'Hondo' Havlicek was part of an Ohio State team that played in three consecutive NCAA tournament finals, winning one. He was drafted by the NFL's Cleveland Browns and the Boston Celtics, but after being dropped by the Browns joined the Celtics in the 1962/63 season. Playing as either guard or forward, he ran tirelessly up and down the court, scoring consistently from the 20ft range. He played until the 1978 season, averaging 20.8 points per game in 1270 regular games, and was the first player to score over 1000 points per season for 16 years.

Hawkins, Cornelius L.   Born Brooklyn, New York, 17 July 1942. Teams: Harlem Globetrotters, Phoenix Suns, Pittsburgh Rens. After winning two city championships with Brooklyn Boys High School, Connie Hawkins won a scholarship to the University of Iowa. He left the school, however, because of alleged links to game fixers, even though he never faced charges. He joined the Pittsburgh Rens of the American Basketball League in 1961, winning the MVP award as the Rens won the championship. After the ABL ended the year after, he joined the Harlem Globetrotters in 1962 and stayed until 1967. The ABA's Pittsburgh Pipers were his next team; again they won the championship and he was named MVP. After an ongoing lawsuit against the NBA was settled, he joined the Phoenix Suns after the Pipers moved to Minnesota. Playing his rookie year in the NBA at 27, he averaged 24.6 points per game and was named in the All-Star first team. Because of the poor surfaces he played on early in his career, he began to suffer knee problems. However, he played in six more seasons, scoring overall 11,628 points in 616 games.

Hayes, Elvin E.   Born Rayville, Louisiana, 17 November 1945. Teams: San Diego Rockets, Baltimore Rockets, Houston Rockets. After averaging 35 points per game in high school, Hayes went to the University of Houston where he scored 2888 points in his college career. He took part in the college game with the largest-ever attendance, 52,693 spectators, when Houston beat UCLA 71-69 to end their opponents' winning streak of 47 games. Hayes joined the San Diego Rockets, leading the league in scoring with 28.4 points per game in 1969. He stayed with the Rockets when they moved to Houston, but was traded to the Baltimore Bullets in 1972. The Bullets won the NBA championship in 1978, Hayes being named MVP. He later returned to Houston and retired in 1984, having scored a career total of 27,313 points with an average of 21.0 per game.

Heinsohn, Thomas W.   Born Union City, New Jersey, 26 August 1934. Team: Boston Celtics. Playing for Holy Cross in Massachusetts, Heinsohn scored an average of 27.4 points per game and was named in the All-American team during his senior year, 1955/56. Drafted to the Boston Celtics in 1956, he was named Rookie of the Year in 1957. He played well as a rebounder, setting up the Boston offence, and during his tenure the Celtics won eight NBA championships in nine years from 1958-66. Beset by injuries in the 1964/65 season, he retired after playing only 67 games that year. He became head coach of Boston in 1969, where they won NBA championships in 1974 and 1976. At the end of 1977/78 he resigned with a record of 427 wins and 263 losses.

Issel, Daniel P.   Born Batavia, Illinois, 25 October 1948. Teams: Kentucky Colonels, Denver Nuggets. As a starter at the University of Kentucky, Issel scored 2138 points, averaging 25.8 points per game in four years. Joining the ABA's Kentucky Colonels, he was named Rookie of the Year having scored 2480 points in the 1970/71 season and going on to score 2538 the year after. He was traded to the Denver Nuggets just before the 1975 season, where he played until retiring in 1985. In 15 seasons he scored 27,472 points, averaging 18.3 per game. He was twice the Nuggets' coach, first from 1992 until 1995, and then for a second time in 2000. He resigned in December 2001 after being suspended for four games after swearing at a fan.

Johnson, Earvin   Born Lansing, Michigan, 14 August 1959. Team: Los Angeles Lakers. After playing for only two years at Michigan State University, 'Magic' Johnson helped win an NCAA Championship in 1979. He joined the Los Angeles Lakers as a first-round pick in 1979, where he was named in the leagues All-Rookie team in 1980 after they won the NBA Championship. He was the first rookie to win the finals MVP award. With the Lakers, Johnson was part of an NBA Championship-winning team a further four times (1982, 1985, 1987 and 1988), and was named leagues MVP in 1987,1989 and 1990. Although Johnson retired in 1991 after becoming HIV positive, he played in the 1992 'Dream Team' that won the Olympic gold medal. Returning to play again for the Lakers in the 1995/96 season, he appeared in their last 32 games. After the Lakers lost to Houston in the first round of the play-offs, he retired for a second and final time.

Jones, K.C.   Born San Francisco, California, 25 May 1932. Teams: Boston Celtics, Capitol Bullets. Part of the University of San Francisco team that won 55 games in a row and two straight NCAA Championships, Jones played in the gold medal-winning US Olympic team before serving in the army for two years. He was drafted to the Los Angeles Rams, but joined the Boston Celtics. He became starter in 1961, his defensive skills ensuring Boston's success over nine years. In 1968 he retired, becoming head coach at Brandeis University for three years. After that he coached the San Diego Conquistadors in the American Basketball Association, and in 1972 he joined the Capitol Bullets for three years. In 1983 he took over the Celtics, where they won two NBA Championships in his first three seasons. Leaving in 1988, he coached the Seattle SuperSonics from 1990 until 1992.

Jones, Samuel   Born Wilmington, North Carolina, 24 June 1933. Team: Boston Celtics. Jones hadn't yet made a name for himself at North Carolina College when the Boston Celtics made him their first-round draft choice in 1957. After three years as substitute, he became the Celtics' top scorer, with an average over

20 for four seasons in a row. He played for 12 years, helping win ten NBA Championships. In his career he scored a total of 15,411 points, an average of 17.7 per game. The highlight of his career was probably taking an off-balance shot with two seconds to go in the 1969 finals against the Los Angeles Lakers when the Celtics were 88-87 down at home and losing 2-1 in the series. He scored, and Boston went on to win the championship. Jones retired after the finals that year.

Jordan, Michael Born Brooklyn, New York, 17 February 1963. Teams: Chicago Bulls, Washington Wizards. At the University of North Carolina, playing in his freshman year, Jordan made the shot that won the 1982 NCAA Championship over Georgetown. This was just the beginning of one of the most successful careers in basketball history. After joining the Chicago Bulls in 1984, he was named Rookie of the Year in 1985. Having led the league in scoring averages between 1986 and 1993 and won the NBA Championship three years in a row, he retired to play baseball for the Birmingham Barons. After two years he rejoined the Bulls, winning again between 1996 and 1998. He retired once more in 1999, but played for the Washington Wizards from 2001 after selling his shares in the team. Jordan played for the US Olympic team in 1984, 1992 and 1996, winning gold twice, in 1984 and 1992.

Lemon, Meadowlark Born Wilmington, North Carolina, 25 April 1935. Teams: Harlem Globetrotters, Bucketeers, Shooting Stars. As the 'Clown Prince' of the Harlem Globetrotters for 24 seasons, Meadowlark Lemon appeared in more than 7500 consecutive games for the team in red, white and blue, playing in more than 94 countries around the world and in over 1500 North American cities. In April 1952, Lemon sent the Globetrotters a letter asking for a trial. His request was granted and after serving two years in the Army he signed a contract. Lemon played his first season with one of the Globetrotters' developmental teams, the Kansas City Stars, playing his first full season with the Globetrotters in 1954. Part of many special milestones with the Globetrotters during his outstanding 24-year career, in 1971 Lemon became the team's player/coach. In 1978, a nationwide poll named Lemon the fourth most popular personality in America after John Wayne, Alan Alda and Bob Hope. That year he left the Globetrotters to pursue a career in Hollywood, his place as Clown Prince being taken by 'Geese' Ausbie. For a while he had his own basketball/entertainment team; now he is a minister travelling the country to preach.

Lucas, Jerry Born Middletown, Ohio, 30 March 1940. Teams: Cincinnati Royals, San Francisco Warriors, New York Knicks. While at Middletown High School Lucas broke Wilt Chamberlain's scoring record with a total of 2466 points. At Ohio State University, he played in NCAA Championships three times, though winning only once. He helped the team win 78 of 84 games, was named Player of the Year twice and three times made the All-American team. He joined the Cleveland Pipers of the ABA but didn't get a chance to play as the American Basketball League collapsed. The Cincinnati Royals took him on in 1963, where he became Rookie of the Year. In 1969 he was traded to the San Francisco Warriors, and he ended his career at the New York Knicks after leaving the Warriors in 1971. He retired in 1973, but not before playing in the Knicks' first NBA Championship-winning team. In his career he scored 12,894 points in 685 games.

Malone, Karl Born Summerfield, Louisiana, 24 July 1963. Team: Utah Jazz. Nicknamed 'The Mailman' because he always delivers, Malone attended Louisiana Tech University. He was drafted by the Utah Jazz in 1985, where it took him only a short time to establish himself. He was part of the original US 'Dream Team' that won Olympic gold in 1992, and won a second gold medal in 1996. Throughout his career he has scored over 20 points per game in 17 seasons, equalling the record set by Kareem Abdul-Jabbar, and over 2000 points per season 11 times. Malone has played in the NBA Championship finals twice, in 1997 and 1998, losing out to the Chicago Bulls both times.

Malone, Moses Born Petersburg, Virginia, 23 March 1955. Teams: Utah Stars, Spirits of St Louis, Buffalo Braves, Houston Rockets, Philadelphia 76ers, Washington Bullets, Atlanta Hawks, Milwaukee Bucks, San Antonio Spurs. At 2.08m in height at 19, Malone joined the ABA's Utah Stars straight out of high school. After two years in the ABA, he joined the NBA's Buffalo Braves and then the Houston Rockets in 1976. He helped the Rockets into the NBA finals in 1981. Playing for a total of 19 years, Malone's combined ABA and NBA statistics are very impressive, ranking fourth with 29,580 points scored. He was the NBA's MVP in 1979, 1982 and 1983. Part of the Philadelphia 76ers team that won the NBA Championship in 1983, he was named as the finals MVP that year. He ended his career, after a series of injuries, at the San Antonio Spurs in 1995.

Maravich, Pete Born Aliquippa, Pennsylvania, 22 June 1947. Teams: Atlanta Hawks, New Orleans Jazz, Boston Celtics. Maravich attended Louisiana State University. While there, 'Pistol Pete', as he was dubbed, scored 3667 points (44.2 points per game) in three years, scoring 50 points or more in 28 games. He joined the Atlanta Hawks in 1970.

McHale, Kevin Born Hibbing, Minnesota, 19 December 1957. Team: Boston Celtics. After being scouted by various teams while playing for Minnesota University, McHale joined the Boston Celtics as a third-round draft in 1980. Standing 2.11m tall, he became part of one of basketball's greatest frontcourt trios of all time, partnering Robert Parish and Larry Bird. At first he was used as the sixth player, where he helped Boston win the NBA Championship finals in 1981 and took the NBA Sixth Man award two years in a row, in 1984 and 1985. The Celtics won NBA finals again in 1984 and 1986, McHale having become part of the starting line-up in 1985, but injuries to his legs and feet slowed him down. In 1987 the Celtics played in their fourth consecutive Championship series, McHale playing in the final with a broken foot. The Celtics lost, and for the remainder of his career he played less and less, retiring in 1993.

Mikan, George Born Joliet, Illinois, 18 June 1924. Teams: Chicago Gears, Minneapolis Lakers. While playing at DePaul in an era when shorter players were still the norm, 2.08m Mikan caused the NCAA to change the rules regarding goal-tending. No one had previously believed that shots could be blocked above the goal net, but Mikan proved them wrong and goal-tending was afterwards outlawed. Mikan had turned professional in the National Basketball League with the Chicago Gears. When the NBL folded he was distributed to the Minneapolis Lakers. In the next eight years the Lakers won the NBA Championship four times, in 1950, 1952, 1953 and 1954. In 1950 he was instrumental in the introduction of the 24-second clock: when he played for the Lakers against the Fort Wayne Pistons that season, the only way that the Pistons thought they could win the game against a player like Mikan was to keep the ball and make no attempt to score. The outcome was a 19-18 victory for the Pistons, the lowest-scoring game in the NBA's history. He retired in 1954, still in his prime, to help bring up his young family. He returned to the game in the 1955/56 season, but without his earlier success, retiring for good after the Lakers were eliminated from the play-offs.

Monroe, Earl   Born Philadelphia, 21 December 1944. Teams: Baltimore Bullets, New York Knicks. While in college, Monroe was given the nickname 'Earl the Pearl' due to his scoring ability. He joined the Baltimore Bullets in the 1967 NBA draft and after scoring an average 24.3 points per game that season he was named NBA Rookie of the Year. Even though he was only 1.90m tall, the skills he had gained while he was young served him well. A team rivalry had built up between the Bullets and the New York Knicks, and they met six times in play-offs between 1969 and 1974. In 1971, due to a dispute with the Bullets, Monroe was traded to the Knicks. He found it hard adjusting to the system at first, his individual style having to be integrated into the Knicks' gameplan. He entertained the crowds with his extravagant play until the mid-1970s, but soon the Knicks declined and Monroe retired in 1980.

Olajuwon, Hakeem   Born Lagos, Nigeria, 21 January 1963. Teams: Houston Rockets, Toronto Raptors. Hakeem Olajuwon was considered by many the second-best player in the world during the reign of Michael Jordan. The 2.13m, Nigerian-born basketball star is often compared to Jordan. Olajuwon led the University of Houston to three consecutive trips to the final four of the NCAA basketball tournament, although he only began to play basketball when he was fifteen. The Houston Rockets selected him as the first pick in the 1984 NBA draft, ahead of Michael Jordan and Charles Barkley. He quickly made an impact on the league and teamed up in the front court with 2.23m Ralph Sampson to carry the hitherto mediocre Rockets to the play-offs in his rookie season and to the NBA finals in 1986. (They were often referred to as the 'Twin Towers'.) Olajuwon's efforts were largely instrumental in carrying the Rockets to the play-offs in all but one of his seasons with the team, although it was unfortunate that Houston regularly lost in the opening round to more balanced sides. After the Rockets finally found the outside shooting help they needed to complement their star, in 1993 they captured their first Midwest Division title in seven years behind the leadership of Olajuwon, who had the best season of his career to date.

O'Neal, Shaquille   Born Newark, New Jersey, 6 March 1972. Teams: Orlando Magic, Los Angeles Lakers. Noted as one of the most formidable big men in basketball history, Shaquille O'Neal became something of a fixture at All-Star games after just four seasons in the NBA. He had forfeited his senior year in college to enter the 1992 NBA draft, and quickly turned the Orlando Magic into one of the league's premier franchises. Also known for his best-selling rap recordings and a co-starring role in a popular Hollywood movie, he emerged as a multifaceted pop culture icon, promoted by the NBA and his upmarket corporate sponsors as a young superstar. For a short stint the NBA embraced O'Neal as its unofficial ambassador. With his magnetic personality

and signature power slam, Shaq, as he is popularly known, was able to both entertain and dominate in his role as a high-scoring, rebound-snaring basketball icon. O'Neal was one of a dozen NBA stars selected for the United States men's basket-ball team at the 1996 Olympic Games in Atlanta.

Parish, Robert   Born Shreveport, Louisiana, 30 October 1953. Teams: Golden State Warriors, Boston Celtics, Charlotte Hornets, Chicago Bulls. Robert Parish won three NBA Championships in five finals with the Boston Celtics in the 1980s as a centre with remarkable strength, agility and endurance, teaming with Larry Bird and Kevin McHale to form one of the greatest front lines in NBA history. He won yet another championship as a member of the 1996/97 Chicago Bulls, a triumph that capped his successful career. Parish announced his retirement at the age of 43 after playing in 1611 games, more than any other player in NBA history. Ranking 13th in the NBA all-time scoring list with 23,334 points, sixth in rebounds with 14,715, sixth in blocked shots with 2361 and eighth in field goals made with 9614, he is arguably one of the best medium-range shooting big men in the history of basketball.

Pettit, Bob   Born Baton Rouge, Louisiana, 12 December 1932. Team: Milwaukee Hawks. Pettit spent 11 years with the Milwaukee/St Louis Hawks and became the first player in the league to top 20,000 points. He is known to many as the greatest forward of his era. Pettit was an All-Star in each of his 11 seasons, an All-NBA first team selection ten times and a second team pick once. In a NBA scoring race, he never finished below seventh and he left the sport with two MVP awards and an NBA Championship ring. He retired having accumulated 20,880 points (26.4 per game), and he was ranked second of all time with his 12,849 rebounds. His average never amounted to less than 20 points, while his career average for rebounds was 16.2 – in his time third best in league history behind Wilt Chamberlain and Bill Russell. Pettit was elected to the Naismith Memorial Basketball Hall of Fame in 1970, and in 1996 was named in the NBA 50th Anniversary All-Time team.

Pippen, Scottie   Born Hamburg, Arkansas, 25 September 1965. Teams: Chicago Bulls, Portland Trail Blazers. A perennial NBA All-Star and a regular member of the league's All-Defensive team, Pippen is a 6ft 7ins (2m), 210lb (95kg) forward. He was a member of the United States basketball squad, known as the 'Dream Team,' in the 1992 Olympics, but was known as only the Chicago Bulls' second best player until the 1993/94 season. Pippen received little recognition during his college career and when he turned professional his achievements were overshadowed by the dominance of his team-mate Michael Jordan, whose accomplishments seemed either to magnify Pippen's shortcomings or overshadow his victories. Pippen was able to quell doubts about his status as one of the NBA's elite players by leading Chicago to a play-off victory against the challenging New York Knicks. Hurled into the spotlight when, shortly before the beginning of the 1993/94 season, Jordan announced his retirement from basketball, Pippen put up a fantastic performance at the 1994 All-Star game, for which he won the event's MVP trophy.

Reed, Willis   Born Hico, Louisiana, 25 June 1942. Team: New York Knicks. Known for his famous shot in the first few minutes of game seven of the 1970 NBA finals, in the same year Reed was MVP of the

All-Star game, regular season and finals. In his ten years with New York he earned a place in the Knicks' top ten in nearly every category, and he was among the top three in minutes played (23,073), field goals made (4859), rebounds (8414) and total points (12,183). Reed played 19 games in 1973/74 before retiring; he became the first Knicks player to have his uniform number (19) retired in 1976, and the Knicks' dynasty broke up over the next few years. He took over as coach for the 1977/78 season and managed to achieve a 43-39 record out of the squad.

obertson, Oscar Born Charlotte, Tennessee, 24 November 1938. Teams: Cincinnati Royals, Milwaukee Bucks. Passionately devoted to basketball as a youth, Robertson led his high school team to 45 consecutive victories. After an athletically brilliant college career at the University of Cincinnati, Robertson, known as 'The Big O', joined the Cincinnati Royals of the National Basketball Association. Robertson, only 1.93m in height, scored 26,710 points for the Royals (1960-70) and the Milwaukee Bucks (1970-72), while his career total of 9887 assists marks him as a superb playmaker.

obinson, David Born Key West, Florida, 6 August 1965. Team: San Antonio Spurs. Robinson, David Robinson was a college basketball Player of the Year. Robinson, 2.16m tall and nicknamed The Admiral', set NCAA records for blocked shots while playing for the United States Naval Academy. In 1990 he led the San Antonio Spurs to the greatest single-season turnaround in league history, and he was named Rookie of the Year. He went on to become NBA Defensive Player of the Year in 1992. Robinson has also been consistenly among the top ten in the NBA in scoring. A mainstay in the NBA All-Star game, he is one of the few basketball players to have played in two Olympics. He has set high standards, but the Spurs were prevented from taking the final step towards becoming one of the elite teams in the NBA due to a string of serious injuries to key players and numerous coaching changes. Robinson is a devout 'born again' Christian and pursues music as a hobby.

Rodman, Dennis Born Trenton, New Jersey, 13 May 1961. Teams: Detroit Pistons, San Antonio Spurs, Chicago Bulls, Dallas Mavericks, Los Angeles Lakers. A rebounder and defender also known for dyeing his hair various colours, headbutting referees and for getting suspended regularly (in 1997 he was suspended for 11 games for kicking a courtside cameraman), Rodman led the NBA in rebounding seven years in a row (1992-98). A member of five NBA champion teams with Detroit (1989, 1990) and Chicago (1996-98), he was twice defensive Player of the Year (1990 and 1991).

Russell, Bill Born Monroe, Louisiana, 12 February 1934. Teams: St Louis Hawks, Boston Celtics. Until the ascent of Michael Jordan in the 1980s, Bill Russell was acclaimed by many as the greatest player in the history of the NBA. Russell was named the NCAA Tournament Most Outstanding Player in 1955. He averaged 20.7 points and 20.3 rebounds in his three-year varsity career. By his senior season he had matured into a dominant force who could control a game at the defensive end, and he was considered the cornerstone of the Boston Celtics' dynasty of the 1960s. Russell won 11 championships with the Celtics in 13 seasons. Known as the shotblocker who revolutionised NBA defensive play, he was five times NBA MVP and 12 times an All-Star, amassing 21,620 career rebounds (an average of 22.5 per game) and leading the league in rebounding four

times. He had 51 boards in one game, 49 in two others and a dozen consecutive seasons of 1000 or more rebounds.

Schayes, Dolph Born New York, 19 May 1928. Team: Syracuse Nationals. Dolph Schayes was one of professional basketball's early superstars, a crack shooter and top rebounder whose career stretched from the NBA's inaugural year to basketball's emergence as a major sporting attraction. Schayes, who represented a bridge between the old game and the new (he was canning two-handed set shots long after the jumper had come into vogue), was known as the star of the Syracuse Nationals. He was practically the only scoring leader Syracuse ever had – the top scorer 13 times in the club's 17-year existence. Schayes never played for another organisation, logging 15 seasons with Syracuse, following the team as it became the Philadelphia 76ers, and then becoming its coach. Schayes often ranked among the league leaders in free-throw shooting, and he led the Nationals in rebounding 10 years out of 11, averaging double figures in each of those 11 seasons. Schayes retired with 19,249 career points, having played in what was then an NBA record 1059 games. He made the All-NBA first team six times and the second team six times. In 1972 he was elected to the Naismith Memorial Basketball Hall of Fame and in 1996 he was named in the NBA 50th Anniversary All-Time Team. His legacy lasted long after his retirement, his son, Danny, having an extensive NBA career.

Sharman, Bill Born Abilene, Texas, 25 May 1926. Team: Boston Celtics. William Wanton Sharman, arguably the greatest shooter of his era, was one of the first NBA guards to push his field-goal percentage above 0.400 for a season (0.436 in 1952/53). He still ranks among the top free-throw shooters of all time with a spectacular 0.883 lifetime percentage, and he led the league in free-throw shooting for a record seven seasons. Sharman was one of the first guards to shoot better than 40 per cent from the field. In an 11-year NBA career played mostly with the Boston Celtics, Sharman was voted to the All-NBA first or second team seven times, and he played in eight NBA All-Star games. He teamed with Bob Cousy to form one of the most formidable backcourts in league history, helping the Celtics to four championships during his tenure. After retiring as a player in 1961 Sharman distinguished himself as an inspiring and innovative coach, the only one to win championships in three professional leagues – the American Basketball League in 1962, the American Basketball Association in 1971 and the NBA in 1972. He guided the 1971/72 Los Angeles Lakers to the best regular-season record (69-13) in NBA history until the 1995/96 Chicago Bulls finished 72-10. Sharman retired in 1974, and his many contributions to the sport were recognised when he was elected to the Naismith Memorial Basketball Hall of Fame in 1975. In 1996 he was named in the NBA 50th Anniversary All-Time Team.

Stockton, John Born Spokane, Washington, 26 March 1962. Team: Utah Jazz. When John Stockton left the NBA after 19 seasons with the Utah Jazz, he held a mass of assists records, including the career record of 15,806. He led the league in assists twice and, with a career total of 3265, retired as the NBA's all-time leader. He also played all 82 games in 17 of his 19 seasons and his career shooting percentage was 0.515. The Jazz never missed the play-offs during Stockton's career and they reached the Western Conference finals five times in seven years, Stockton himself sinking a last-gasp three-pointer over Houston's Charles Barkley in game six of the 1997 finals to give Utah their first NBA finals berth. Utah went to consecutive NBA finals, losing to the Chicago Bulls in six games in both 1997 and 1998. Stockton finally retired without an NBA title, his final NBA game a play-off loss in Sacramento on 30 April 2003. Stockton finished his career after the 2002/03 season having played in 1504 games, a figure ranked third on the NBA's all-time list after Robert Parish (1611) and Kareem Abdul-Jabbar (1560). His 19,711 points gave him 28th spot on the NBA's all-time scoring list.

Thomas, Isiah   Born Chicago, Illinois, 30 April 1961. Team: Detroit Pistons. Isiah 'Zeke' Thomas, captain of the Detroit Pistons, is widely considered the best point guard of all time. The 1.85m Thomas is the first man under 1.90m to dominate a big man's game since the Boston Celtics' Bob Cousy in the 1950s and the Atlanta Hawks' Lenny Wilkins in the 1960s. He left Indiana University at the age of 20, having already led the Hoosiers to the NCAA championship, to join the professional ranks. During his first few years as a pro, he was noted for both his good works in the public domain and his ability to please a crowd. In 1987, however, Thomas's image suffered when he seemed to agree with a team-mate's assertion that Celtics superstar Larry Bird was overrated because he is white. Putting controversy behind him, Thomas recovered to become the undisputed leader of the Motor City 'Bad Boys', the bruising, defence-oriented Pistons, who in 1989 won their first-ever NBA crown.

Thurmond, Nate   Born Akron, Ohio, 25 July 1941. Teams: San Francisco Warriors, Chicago Bulls, Cleveland Cavaliers. Thurmond was one of the all-time great NBA centres. With a rugged style, he was considered by many to be in the same league as Kareem Abdul-Jabbar and Wilt Chamberlain. The Hall of Famer played 14 professional seasons in the 1960s and 1970s, posting career averages of 15.0 points and 15.0 rebounds per game. Among the all-time NBA leaders in career rebounds and rebounding average, Thurmond was selected to play in seven NBA All-Star games and was chosen for the NBA All-Defensive first or second team five times. The NBA record for most rebounds in a quarter (18) is still his and Thurmond made history as the first player ever to record a quadruple double. Several basketball observers have suggested that the 2.11m Thurmond provided the best mix of offence and defence in basketball history. In 1984 he was elected to the Naismith Memorial Basketball Hall of Fame and in 1996 his 14 years of NBA service earned him a place in the NBA 50th Anniversary All-Time Team. Thurmond settled in San Francisco after leaving basketball, where he opened a restaurant and served as director of community relations for the Golden State Warriors.

Unseld, Wes   Born Louisville, Kentucky, 14 March 1946. Team: Baltimore Bullets. A 2.00m centre, Unseld earned a deserved reputation as a relentless rebounder and laser-beam outlet passer. He did all the unspectacular things that lead to glamorous victories. The league's MVP and Rookie of the Year in 1968/69 and five times an NBA All-Star, he captained the Baltimore and Washington Bullets to four NBA finals appearances in the 1970s and to a championship in 1977/78. He retired in 1980, after which he moved into a front-office position with the Bullets, then coached the team for seven seasons in the late 1980s and early 1990s. Unseld was elected to the Naismith Memorial Basketball Hall of Fame in

1988. In 1996 he was named in the NBA 50th Anniversary All-Time Team.

Walton, Bill   Born La Mesa, California, 5 November 1952. Teams: Portland Trail Blazers, San Diego Clippers, Boston Celtics. In 1973, Bill Walton was hailed as one of greatest college players of his time and by the time he finished his professional career in 1986, most basketball observers considered him to be one of the greatest centres ever. In the championship game of the NCAA tournament against Memphis State, Walton canned 21 of 22 shots, scored 44 points, grabbed 13 rebounds and led UCLA to the NCAA title. That night instantly made him a popular icon. His success continued as he led the Bruins to an 86-4 record and was a vital member of UCLA teams that won 88 straight games. Walton was three times selected for the All-America team, *Sporting News* Player of the Year three years in a row and MVP in the 1972 and 1973 NCAA tournaments. He finished his collegiate career with 1767 points (20.3 per game) and 1370 rebounds (15.7 per game). In 1986 he helped lead the Boston Celtics to the NBA Championship, also winning the NBA Sixth Man award. In 1991, Walton received the prestigious NBA Players Association Oscar Robertson Leadership Award. He remains active in basketball and became a television analyst on NBC professional and collegiate games and on Los Angeles Clippers broadcasts.

West, Jerry   Born Chelyan, West Virginia, 28 May 1938. Team: Minneapolis Lakers. During his 14-year playing career with the Los Angeles Lakers, the name West became synonymous with brilliant basketball – so much so that his silhouette was adopted as the NBA logo. The third player in league history to reach 25,000 points (after Wilt Chamberlain and Oscar Robertson), he was an All-Star every year of his career (1961-74) and led Los Angeles to the NBA finals nine times. He left the game holding records for career post-season scoring and the highest average in a play-off series. West's statistical record only begins to tell his story. When the chips were down, West, with his lightning-quick release, was the man the Lakers turned to for the big basket. Many players have been tagged with the nickname 'Mr Clutch', but none of them lived up to it as well as West did. He was responsible for perhaps the most famous buzzer-beater of all time: a score from 60 feet that tied game three of the 1970 NBA finals against the New York Knicks.

Wilkens, Lenny   Born Brooklyn, New York, 28 October 1937. Teams: St Louis Hawks, Seattle SuperSonics, Cleveland Cavaliers, Portland Trail Blazers. After playing at Providence College, Wilkens joined the St Louis Hawks of the NBA in 1960, beginning a 15-year playing career with four teams. In 1969 he became the Seattle SuperSonics' player/coach. Subsequently he has coached Seattle (1969-72, 1977-85), the Portland Trail Blazers (1974-76), the Cleveland Cavaliers (1986-93), the Atlanta Hawks (1993-2000) and the Toronto Raptors (2000-03). In 1978/79 the SuperSonics won the NBA championship. In 25 seasons, Wilkens methodically established himself as one of the NBA's premier coaches, averaging 45 wins a season and leading his teams to 16 NBA play-off appearances. His 69 play-off victories rank him sixth on the all-time NBA play-off win list – third among active coaches – his overall coaching record earning him his second honour from the Basketball Hall of Fame. On 2 February 1994, Wilkens became only the second coach in NBA history to win 900 games when his Atlanta Hawks defeated the Orlando Magic 118-99. Wilkens was named in the list of the NBA's top ten coaches in league history and was among the group selected as the 50 greatest players in NBA history by an expert panel of media, former players and coaches, current and former general managers and team executives. He was the only NBA member named on both lists.

Worthy, James Born Gastonia, North Carolina, 27 February 1961. Team: Los Angeles Lakers. Arguably one of basketball's greatest fast-break finishers at both college and professional levels, at 2.06m and 102kg he was a powerful forward who could dominate with agility and speed. Worthy was a college star at the University of North Carolina. He went on to lead the Tar Heels to the 1982 NCAA championship in New Orleans and was named MVP of the final four. Named Helms Foundation National Player of the Year, he was selected for the All-America team 11 times throughout his college career by various organisations. Worthy played his entire 12-year professional career with the Los Angeles Lakers, helping them to the 1985, 1987 and 1988 NBA championships and a total of seven NBA finals appearances. He recorded his first triple-double in the biggest game of his career: game seven of the 1988 finals against Detroit, in which he collected 36 points, 16 rebounds and 10 assists. He also holds the all-time record for the highest field goal percentage in a five-game play-off series, 0.721 in the 1985 Western Conference finals against the Denver Nuggets. He was named MVP of the 1988 finals after averaging 22.0 points per game, 7.4 rebounds per game and 4.4 assists per game. He was chosen for seven NBA All-Star games (1986-92) and is one of only seven Lakers to have his number (42) retired. By the time he retired, Worthy owned a Most Outstanding Player award from the 1982 NCAA final four and a MVP award from the 1988 NBA Finals. He was named one of the 50 greatest players in NBA history in 1996.

Yardley, George Born Hollywood, California, 3 November 1928. Teams: Fort Wayne Pistons, Detroit Pistons, Syracuse Nationals, Los Angeles Jets. An offensive-minded player with a knack for scoring, Yardley enjoyed a fruitful seven-year professional career that saw him appear in six All-Star games and average nearly 20 points per game (9063, 19.2 per game). Yardley joined the Pistons in 1953 following a productive three-year career at Stanford (11.5 points per game), after playing one season of AAU ball and serving in the military for two seasons. The 1.96m jump-shooting forward's Fort Wayne teams twice reached the NBA finals, losing in 1955 to Syracuse in seven games. One of Yardley's most significant accomplishments occurred in the 1957/58 season, when he became the first player in NBA history to score 2000 points in one season (2001), breaking the 1932-point record held by George Mikan. That season, Yardley averaged 27.8 points and 10.7 rebounds per game. He shot over 80 per cent from the free-throw line and was an All-NBA first-team selection, though he was relegated to the league's second team in 1956/57.

Zollner, Fred Born Little Falls, Minnesota, 22 January 1901. Teams (owner): Fort Wayne Zollner Pistons, Fort Wayne/Detroit Pistons. The late Fred Zollner played a key role in the early days of the NBA. He was instrumental in the formation of the National Basketball Association following the merger of the Basketball Association of America and the National Basketball League (NBL). His contributions, including financial support, transport and personnel, helped keep the league alive in the early years and were crucial to the NBA's survival. He was the owner of the NBL's Fort Wayne Zollner Pistons and the NBA's Fort Wayne/Detroit Pistons until 1974, which made him the longest-tenured owner of an original NBA team. Zollner was named 'Mr Pro Basketball' at the 1975 Silver Anniversary All-Star game for his status as a founder and long-time supporter of the NBA and in 1996 was the recipient of the Fort Wayne Sports Corporation Lifetime Achievement Award. The NBA Western Conference trophy is named in his honour. Zollner died on 21 June 1982.

BASKETBALL

British Basketball Teams

Bath Romans
Birmingham Aces
Birmingham Bullets
Bournemouth Blitz
Brighton Bears
Brighton Cougars
Bristol Bombers
Brixton Topcats
Bury Wildcats
Cardiff Clippers
Cardiff Phoenix
Chester Jets
Colchester United
Coventry Crusaders
Crystal Palace London
Derby Storm
Derbyshire Arrows
Doncaster Panthers
Dudley Bears
East London Royals
Essex & Herts Leopards

Flintshire Flyers
Hackney White Heat
Haywards Heath Eagles
Hull Stingers
Kingston Wildcats
Leicester Riders
Liverpool ATAC
London Towers
London United
Manchester Giants
Manchester Magic
Mansfield Express
Newcastle Eagles
Northampton Neptunes
NW London Capitals
Oldham Celtics
Oxford Devils
Plymouth Raiders
Portsmouth Pirates
Reading Rockets
Richmond Jaguars

Scottish Rocks
Sheffield Arrows
Sheffield Sharks
Slough Chargers
Solent Stars
Solihull Chiefs
South Bank Univ. London Bulls
Stevenage Rebels
Sunderland Scorpions
Sutton Pumas
Swindon Sonics
Tamar Valley Cannons
Taunton Tigers
Teeside Mohawks
Thames Valley Tigers
Ware Rebels
Westminster Warriors
Worcester Wolves
Worthing Thunder

BATON TWIRLING

The origin of baton twirling is uncertain and the practice probably developed in various guises in different parts of the world. In eastern Europe and Asia, it is thought it started at dance festivals where participants twirled and tossed knives, guns, torches and sticks. The activity was taken up by the armies of some countries where rifles would be twirled during marching. When the army was parading, a rifle twirler would be positioned at the front of the marchers. The rifle was later replaced by a mace, which was originally much larger than the batons of today and unbalanced. The mace bearer or 'drum major' twirled the baton while leading the army or band. The maces were altered for easier twirling, being given smaller ends of light rubber, made from hollow, light metal and balanced to enable greater accuracy. It is thought to be the involvement of females ('drum majorettes') and the development of twirling that necessitated the lightening and balancing of the baton.

In America, it is possible that the idea originated at Millsaps College in Mississippi, founded shortly after the US Civil War by Major Reuben Webster Millsaps. His 'lady athletes' were called the Majorettes, and this may be the origin of the name of the present-day high-stepping majorettes. There is no evidence that actual baton twirling took place; there is, however, some evidence that this is related to the colourful Swiss flag swinging which came to the USA along with the Germans who settled in Pennsylvania.

The first known display of twirling was at the 1893 World's Columbian Exposition in Chicago, which showcased the talents of a gun twirler named Hadji Cheriff. Using a rifle, Hadji performed a routine that resembled a baton twirling routine. It involved two-handed, and even one-handed, twirls and movements that a modern twirler might be able to recognise and name.

On 27 September 1930, in Port Arthur, Texas, a parade showcased the talents of drum majorettes Hazel Dunham and Ethel Thompson, who created a sensation by twirling their batons and performing the drum majorette's strut. This involved picking the feet up at least 12 inches off the ground, and became known as 'high stepping'. It earned majorettes the nickname of 'High Steppers'. Some people referred to the movement as 'lifting their knees', others called it 'prancing' or even 'stomping'. A well-performed strut is graceful and elegant. Many posed photos of majorettes show the girls at the height of a high-stepping strut.

In 1933, Marjorie Domingue became the Red Hussar Marching Band's drum major. Twenty years later, her daughter, Edith, would become the band's drum majorette, and they thus became the first mother and daughter drum majorettes in a world previously dominated by male drum majors. Chicago meanwhile became known as the home of baton twirling when the first baton-twirling contest was held in 1935 as part of the Chicagoland Music Festival.

In 1977, The World Baton Twirling Federation (WBTF) was organised as the number of baton twirlers worldwide continued to increase. The members of the Board gathered in Paris in 1978 to prepare for a worldwide meet, and in 1980 the first World Baton Twirling Championship took place in Seattle, USA. Today, baton twirling is a fully recognised sport which is lobbying for inclusion in the Olympic Games programme.

The following are the results of the 24th WBTF World Baton Twirling Championships, held in Badalona, Spain, 7-10 August 2003. The top performances are as follows:

The World Cup was won by Japan, from USA, France, Canada, Italy and the Netherlands.

The team competition was won by USA, from Japan, France, Canada, Italy and the Netherlands.

BOBSLEIGH

Although the sled has been around for centuries as a mode of transport, the sport of bobsleigh began only in the late 19th century when the Swiss attached a steering mechanism to a toboggan.

In 1897, the world's first bobsleigh club was founded in St Moritz, Switzerland, and the following year the first organised competition was held on the Cresta Run, spurring the growth of the sport in winter resorts throughout Europe. By 1914, bobsleigh races were taking place on a wide variety of natural ice courses. There is a widely held misconception that the Cresta Run, built in 1884, 1320yds (1207m) long, including the notorious bend called the Horse Shoe, and holding the annual Grand National, is the same as the St Moritz Run. In fact, this run is parallel to the Cresta Run, is 1.5 (122m) miles long with a drop of 400 feet (2.41km), and has 14 bends including Sunny Corner.

The first racing sleds were made of wood but were soon replaced by steel sleds that came to be known as bobsleigh, so named because of the way crews bobbed back and forth to increase their speed on the straight. In 1923, the Fédération Internationale de Bobsleigh et de Tobogganing (FIBT) was founded and the following year a four-man race took place at the first-ever Winter Olympics in Chamonix, France. A two-man event was added at the 1932 Olympics in Lake Placid, USA, a format that has remained until the present day.

By the 1950s, however, the sport as we know it today had begun to take shape. As the critical importance of the start was recognised, strong, fast athletes in other sports were drawn to bobsleigh. Also in the 1950s, a one-man version of bobbing, the luge, became popular; the first world championships were held in 1955. Since 1957 the luge has been governed by the Fédération Internationale de Luge. An earlier one-man version, skeleton bob, had been included in the Olympics of 1928 and again in 1948 but it was not until the 1980s that it was revived. The difference between skeleton and luge is the seating position: the luge athlete sits upright while the skeleton athlete lies prone.

In 1952, a critical rule change limiting the total weight of crew and sled ended the era of the super-heavyweight bobsleigh and sealed the future of the sport as an athletic contest of the highest calibre. More athletic crews went hand in hand with advances in sleds and tracks. Today, the world's top teams train year round and compete mostly on artificial ice tracks in sleek high-tech sleds made of fibreglass and steel.

Until the advent of World Cup competition in the mid-1980s, bobsleigh success was deter-mined solely by performance at the Olympics, and the World and European Championships. Since its inception, however, the World Cup series has added an exciting new dimension to the sport whereby versatility on different tracks and season-long consistency are rewarded.

Apart from a British influence in the sport's infancy, a strong US presence from 1928 to 1956, and recent advances by other countries, bobsleigh has been dominated largely by Europe's alpine nations over the years.

By far the most successful bobsleighing nations have been Switzerland and Germany. The Swiss have won more medals in Olympic, World and European Championships than any other nation.

East Germany emerged as the sport's major power in the mid-1970s with its emphasis on sled design and construction. Since reunification, German bobsleighers have remained a formidable group, winning numerous Olympic medals and World Championship titles since 1990.

Italy also has a long and successful track record in the sport, particularly from the mid-1950s to the late 1960s, and Austria has had its shining moments. In World Cup competition the success of the Swiss and Germans has been closely followed by Canadian teams. From the small core of alpine nations who originally embraced bobsleigh, the sport has since expanded around the world to include countries such as Jamaica, Japan, Australia and New Zealand.

In 1985 the following sled standardisation was introduced by the FIBT to place all competitors on an equal footing: maximum length 2.70m, maximum width 0.67m, and maximum weight (including the crew) 390kg. Weight bars may be added to achieve the maximum weight.

Two-man bobsleigh teams include a brakeman and a pilot, while two crewmen/pushers are added for the four-man race. From a standing start, the crew pushes the bobsleigh in unison for up to 50m. This distance is typically covered in less than 6secs and speeds of over 40kph are reached before the crew leap into the bobsleigh.

Although the difference in start times among the top crews is measured in tenths or even hundredths of a second, a fast start is critical. As a rule of thumb, a 0.1sec lead at the start translates into a 0.3sec advantage by the bottom of the course. During a typical 60sec run, speeds of 135kph can be reached and crews are subjected to four or five times the force of gravity.

A seeding system is in place to determine start positions at all major events including the Olympics, World Championships and World Cup events. Since the ice becomes rougher as the competition progresses, it is an advantage to be among the first on the track. The seeding system rewards the top crews (based on previous results) with the best start positions. Similarly, the rest of the field is seeded in additional groups based on previous results. For the remainder of the season, starting groups are based on current World Cup results as follows: Group I − 1 to 10;

Group II − 11 to 20; Group III − 21 to 30 and Group IV − 31 and below.

In the 2004 FIBT Two-Man Bob World Championship at Königssee, Monaco I, with Patrice Servelle and Sebastien Gattuso were placed fourth and thus achieved the best-ever world championship result in any sport for Monaco.

Bobsleigh: Olympic Medallists

Men's Two-Man Bob

	Gold	Silver	Bronze
1932	Hubert Stevens/Curtis Stevens (USA) 8:14.74	Reto Capadrutt/Oscar Geier (SUI) 8:16.28	John Heaton/Robert Minton (USA) 8:29.15
1936	Ivan Brown/Alan Washbond (USA) 5:29.29	Fritz Feierabend/Joseph Beerli (SUI) 5:30.64	Gilbert Colgate/Richard Lawrence (USA) 5:33.96
1948	Felix Endrich/Friedrich Waller (SUI) 5:29.2	Fritz Feierabend/Paul Hans Eberhard (SUI) 5:30.4	Frederick Fortune/Schuyler Carron (USA) 5:35.3
1952	Andreas Ostler/ Lorenz Nieberl (FRG) 5:24.54	Stanley Benham/Patrick Martin (USA) 5:26.89	Fritz Feierabend/Stephan Waser (SUI) 5:27.71
1956	Lamberto Dalla Costa/Giacomo Conti (ITA) 5:30.14	Eugenio Monti/Renzo Alverà (ITA) 5:31.45	Max Angst/Harry Warburton (SUI) 5:37.46
1960	not held		
1964	Tony Nash/Robin Dixon (GBR) 4:21.90	Sergio Zardini/Romano Bonagura (ITA) 4:22.02	Eugenio Monti/Sergio Siorpaes (ITA) 4:22.63
1968	Eugenio Monti/Luciano De Paolis (ITA) 4:41.54	Horst Floth/Pepi Bader (FRG) 4:41.54	Ion Panturu/Nicolae Neagoe (ROM) 4:44.46
1972	Wolfgang Zimmerer/ Peter Utzschneider (FRG) 4:57.07	Horst Floth/Pepi Bader (FRG) 4:58.84	Jean Wicki/Edy Hubacher (SUI) 4:59.33
1976	Meinhard Nehmer/Bernhard Germeshausen (GDR) 3:44.42	Wolfgang Zimmerer/Manfred Schumann (FRG) 3:44.99	Erich Schärer/Josef Benz (SUI) 3:45.70
1980	Erich Schärer/Josef Benz (SUI) 4:09.36	Bernhard Germeshausen Hans-Jürgen Gerhardt (GDR) 4:10.93	Meinhard Nehmer/Bogdan Musiol (GDR) 4:11.08
1984	Wolfgang Hoppe/Dietmar Schauerhammer (GDR) 3:25.56	Bernhard Lehmann/Bogdan Musiol (GDR) 3:26.04	Zintis Ekmanis/Vladimir Alexandrov (URS) 3:26.16
1988	Jânis Kipurs/Vladimir Kozlov (URS) 3:53.48	Wolfgang Hoppe/Bogdan Musiol (GDR) 3:54.19	Bernhard Lehmann/Mario Hoyer (GDR) 3:54.64
1992	Gustav Weder/Donat Acklin (SUI) 4:03.26	Rudolf Lochner/Markus Zimmermann (GER) 4:03.55	Christoph Langen/Günther Eger (GER) 4:03.63
1994	Gustav Weder/Donat Acklin (SUI) 3:30.81	Reto Götschi/Guido Acklin (SUI) 3:30.86	Günther Huber/Stefano Ticci (ITA) 3:31.01
1998	Pierre Lueders/David MacEachern (CAN) 3:37.24 Günther Huber/Antonia Tartaglia (ITA) 3:37.24	Christoph Langen/Markus Zimmermann (GER) 3:37.89	───
2002	Christoph Langen/ Markus Zimmermann (GER) 3:10.11	Christoph Reich/Steve Anderhub (SUI) 3:10.20	Martin Annen/Beat Hefti (SUI) 3:10.62

Men's Four-Man Bob

	Gold	Silver	Bronze
1924	Eduard Scherrer/Alfred Neveu/ Alfred Schläppi/Heinrich Schläppi (SUI) 5:45.54	Ralph Broome/Thomas Arnold/ H. Richardson/Rodney Soher (GBR) 5:48.83	Charles Mulder/René Mortiaux/ Paul van den Broeck/Victor Verschueren/ Henri Willems (BEL) 6:02.29

Men's Five-Man Bob

	Gold	Silver	Bronze
1928	William Fiske/Nion Tocker/Charles Mason/ Clifford Grey/Richard Parke (USA) 3:20.5	Jennison Heaton/David Granger/ Lyman Hine/Thomas Doe/ Jay O'Brien (USA) 3:21.0	Hanns Kilian/Valentin Krempel/ Hans Hess/Sebastian Huber/Hans Nägle (GER) 3:21.9

Men's Four-Man Bob

Gold	Silver	Bronze
1932 William Fiske/Edward Eagan/ Clifford Gray/Jay O'Brien (USA) 7:53.68	Henry Homburger/Percy Bryant/ Paul Stevens/Edmund Horton (USA) 7:55.70	Hanns Kilian/Max Ludwig/ Hans Mehlhorn/Sebastian Huber (GER) 8:00.04
1936 Pierre Musy/Arnold Gartmann/ Charles Bouvier/Joseph Beerli (SUI) 5:19.85	Reto Capadrutt/Hans Aichele/Fritz Feierabend/Hans Bütikofer (SUI) 5:22.73	Frederic McEvoy/James Cardno/Guy Dugdale/Charles Green (GBR) 5:23.41
1948 Francis Tyler/Patrick Martin/ Edward Rimkus/William D'Amico (USA) 5:20.1	Max Houben/Freddy Mansveld/ Louis-Georges Niels/Jacques Mouvet (BEL) 5:21.3	James Bickford/Thomas Hicks/ Donald Dupree/William Dupree (USA) 5:21.5
1952 Andreas Ostler/Friedrich Kühn/ Lorenz Nieberl/Franz Kemser (FRG) 5:07.84	Stanley Benham/Patrick Martin/ Howard Crossett/James Atkinson 5:10.48 (USA)	Fritz Feierabend/Albert Madörin/André Filippini/Stephan Waser (SUI) 5:11.70
1956 Franz Kapus/Gottfried Diener/ Robert Alt/Heinrich Angst (SUI) 5:10.44	Eugenio Monti/Ulrico Giardi/Renzo Alverà/ Renato Morcellini (ITA) 5:12.10	Arthur Tyler/William Dodge/ Charles Butler/James Lamy (USA) 5:12.39
1960 Not held		
1964 Victor Emery/Peter Kirby/ Douglas Anakin/John Emery (CAN) 4:14.46	Erwin Thaler/Adolf Koxeder/Josef Nairz/ Reinhold Durnthaler (AUT) 4:15.48	Eugenio Monti/Sergio Siorpaes/ Benito Rigoni/Gildo Siorpaes (ITA) 4:15.60
1968 Eugenio Monti/Luciano De Paolis/ Roberto Zandonella/Mario Armano (ITA) 2:17.39	Erwin Thaler/Reinhold Durnthaler/ Herbert Gruber/Josef Eder (AUT) 2:17.48	Jean Wicki/Hans Candrian/Willi Hofmann/Walter Graf (SUI) 2:18.04
1972 Jean Wicki/Edy Hubacher/Hans Leutenegger/ Werner Carmichel (SUI) 4:43.07	Nevio De Zordo/Gianni Bonichon/ Adriano Frassinelli/Corrado Dal Fabbro (ITA) 4:43.83	Wolfgang Zimmerer/Peter Utzschneider/ Stefan Gaisreiter/Walter Steinbauer (FRG) 4:43.92
1976 Meinhard Nehmer/Jochen Babock/Bernhard Germeshausen/Bernhard Lehmann (GDR) 3:40.43	Erich Schärer/Ulrich Bächli/Rudolf Marti/Josef Benz (SUI) 3:40.89	Wolfgang Zimmerer/Peter Utzschneider/ Bodo Bittner/Manfred Schumann (FRG) 3:41.37
1980 Meinhard Nehmer/Bogdan Musiol/Bernhard Germeshausen/Hans-Jürgen Gerhardt (GDR) 3:59.92	Erich Schärer/Ulrich Bächli/Rudolf Marti/Josef Benz (SUI) 4:00.87	Horst Schönau/Roland Wetzig/Detlef Richter/Andreas Kirchner (GDR) 4:00.97
1984 Wolfgang Hoppe/Roland Wetzig/Dietmar Schauerhammer/Andreas Kirchner (GDR) 3:20.22	Bernhard Lehmann/Bogdan Musiol/Ingo Voge/Eberhard Weise (GDR) 3:20.78	Silvio Giobellina/Heinz Stettler/Urs Salzmann/Rico Freiermuth (SUI) 3:21.39
1988 Ekkehard Fasser/Kurt Meier/Marcel Fässler/ Werner Stocker (SUI) 3:47.51	Wolfgang Hoppe/Dietmar Schauerhammer/Bogdan Musiol/Ingo Voge (GDR) 3:47.58	Jânis Kipurs/Guntis Osis/Juris Tone/ Vladimir Kozlov (URS) 3:48.26
1992 Ingo Appelt/Harald Winkler/Gerhard Haidacher/ Thomas Schroll (AUT) 3:43.90	Wolfgang Hoppe/Bogdan Musiol/ Axel Kühn/René Hannemann (GER) 3:53.92	Gustav Weder/Donat Acklin/Lorenz Schindelholz/Curdin Morell (SUI) 3:54.13
1994 Harald Czudaj/Karsten Brannasch/Olaf Hampel/ Alexander Szelig (GER) 3:27.78	Gastac Weder/Donat Acklin/Kurt Meier/ Domenico Semeraro (SUI) 3:27.84	Wolfgang Hoppe/Ulf Hielscher/René Hannemann/Carsten Embach (GER) 3:28.01
1998 Christoph Langen/Markus Zimmermann/ Marco Jakobs/Olaf Hampel (GER) 2:39.41	Marcel Rohner/Markus Nüssli/Markus Wasser/Beat Seitz (SUI) 2:40.01	Bruno Mingeon/Emmanuel Hostache/Eric le Chanony/Max Robert (FRA) 2:40.06 Sean Olsson/Dean Ward/Courtney Rumbolt/Paul Attwood (GBR) 2:40.06
2002 André Lange/Lars Behrendt/René Hoppe/ Carsten Embach (GER) 3:07.51	Todd Hays/Randy Jones/Bill Schuffenhauer/Garrett Hines (USA) 3:07.81	Brian Shimer/Mike Kohn/Doug Sharp/ Dan Steele (USA) 3:07.86

Women's Two-Man Bob

Gold	Silver	Bronze
2002 Jill Bakken/Vonetta Flowers (USA) 1:37.76	Sandra Prokoff/Ulrike Holzner (GER) 1:38.06	Susi-Lisa Erdmann/Nicole Herschmann (GER) 1:38.29

Bobsleigh: World Champions

Men's Two-Man Bob

Gold	Silver	Bronze
1931 Hanns Kilian/Sebastian Huber (GER)	Bibo Fischer/Gemmer (GER)	Heinz Volkmer/Anton Kaltenberger (AUT)
1933 Alexandru Papana/Dumitru Hubert (ROM)	Dr Brüme/Heinzel (TCH)	Fritz Grau/Albert Brehme (GER)
1934 Alexandru Frim/Vasile Dumitrescu (ROM)	Hermann von Mumm/Fritz Schwarz (GER)	Alexandru Papana/Dumitru Hubert (ROM)
1935 Reto Capadrutt/Emil Diener (SUI)	Josef Lanzendörfer/Karel Ruzicka (TCH)	Marchese Sforza Brivio/Carlo Soldini (ITA)
1937 Frederick McEvoy/Byran Black (GBR)	Umberto Gilarduzzi/Antonio Gilarduzzi (ITA)	Reto Capadrutt/Hans Aichele (SUI)
1938 Bibo Fischer/Rolf Thielecke (GER)	Frederic McEvoy/Charles Green (GBR)	Fritz Feierabend/Josef Beerli (SUI)
1939 Baron René Lunden/Jean Coops (BEL)	Bibo Fischer/Rolf Thielecke (GER)	Hanns Kilian/Schletter (GER)

B
O
B
S
L
E
I
G
H

Year	Gold	Silver	Bronze
1947	Fritz Feierabend/Stephan Waser (SUI)	Felix Endrich/Fritz Waller (SUI)	Max Houben/Jacques Mouvet (BEL)
1949	Felix Endrich/Fritz Waller (SUI)	Fritz Feierabend/Heinrich Angst (SUI)	Frederick Fortune/John McDonald (USA)
1950	Fritz Feierabend/Stephan Waser (SUI)	Stanley Benham/Patrick Martin (USA)	Frederick Fortune/William d'Amico (USA)
1951	Anderl Ostler/Lorenz Nieberl (FRG)	Stanley Benham/Patrick Martin (USA)	Felix Endrich/Werner Spring (SUI)
1953	Felix Endrich/Fritz Stöckli (SUI)	Anderl Ostler/Franz Kemser (FRG)	Theo Kitt/Lorenz Nieberl (FRG)
1954	Guglielmo Scheibmeier/Andrea Zambelli (ITA)	Italo Petrelli/Luigi Figoli (ITA)	Stanley Benham/James Bickford (USA)
1955	Fritz Feierabend/Harry Warburton (SUI)	Paul Aste/Pepi Isser (AUT)	Franz Kapus/Heinrich Angst (SUI)
1957	Eugenio Monti/Renzo Alvera (ITA)	Arthur Tyler/Charles Thomas Butler (USA)	Marques Alfonso de Portago/Luis Nunoz (ESP)
1958	Eugenio Monti/Renzo Alvera (ITA)	Sergio Zardini/Sergio Siorpaes (ITA)	Paul Aste/Heinz Isser (AUT)
1959	Eugenio Monti/Renzo Alvera (ITA)	Sergio Zardini/Luciano Alberti (ITA)	Arthur Tyler/Thomas Butler (USA)
1960	Eugenio Monti/Renzo Alvera (ITA)	Franz Schelle/Otto Goebl (FRG)	Sergio Zardini/Luciano Alberti (ITA)
1961	Eugenio Monti/Sergio Siorpaes (ITA)	Gary Sheffield/Jerry Tennant (USA)	Sergio Zardini Romano Bonagura (ITA)
1962	Rinaldo Ruatti/Enrico de Lorenzo (ITA)	Sergio Zardini Romano Bonagura (ITA)	Hans Maurer/Adolf Wörmann (FRG)
1963	Eugenio Monti/Sergio Siorpaes (ITA)	Sergio Zardini/Romano Bonagura (ITA)	Anthony Nash/Robin Dixon (GBR)
1965	Anthony Nash/Robin Dixon (GBR)	Rinaldo Ruatti/Enrico de Lorenzo (ITA)	Victor Emery/Mike Young (CAN)
1966	Eugenio Monti/Sergio Siorpaes (ITA)	Gianfranco Gaspari/Leonardo Cavallini (ITA)	Anthony Nash/Robin Dixon (GBR)
1967	Erwin Thaler/Reinhold Durnthaler (AUT)	Nevio de Zordo/Edoardo Tinter de Martin (ITA)	Howard Clifton/James Crall (USA)
1969	Nevio de Zordo/Adriano Frassinelli (ITA)	Ion Panturu/Dumitru Focseneanu (ROM)	Gianfranco Gaspari/Mario Armano (ITA)
1970	Horst Floth/Pepi Bader (FRG)	Wolfgang Zimmerer/Peter Utzschneider (FRG)	Gion Caviezel/Hans Candrian (SUI)
1971	Gianfranco Gaspari/Mario Armano (ITA)	Enzo Vicario/Corrado dal Fabbro (ITA)	Herbert Gruber/Josef Oberhauser (AUT)
1973	Wolfgang Zimmerer/Peter Utzschneider (FRG)	Hans Candrian/Heinz Schenker (SUI)	Ion Panturu/Dumitru Focseneanu (ROM)
1974	Wolfgang Zimmerer/Peter Utzschneider (FRG)	Georg Heibl/Fritz Ohlwärter (FRG)	Fritz Lüdi/Karl Häseli (SUI)
1975	Giorgio Alvera/Franco Perruquet (ITA)	Georg Heibl/Fritz Ohlwärter (FRG)	Fritz Lüdi/Karl Häseli (SUI)
1977	Hans Hiltebrand/Heinz Meier (SUI)	Fritz Lüdi/Hansjörg Trachsel (SUI)	Stefan Gaisreiter/Manfred Schumann (FRG)
1978	Erich Schärer/Josef Benz (SUI)	Meinhard Nehmer/Raimund Bethge (GDR)	Jakob Resch/Walter Barfuss (FRG)
1979	Erich Schärer/Josef Benz (SUI)	Stefan Gaisreiter/Manfred Schumann (FRG)	Toni Mangold/Stefan Späte (FRG)
1981	Bernhard Germeshausen/Hans-Jürgen Gerhardt (GDR)	Horst Schönau/Andreas Kirchner (GDR)	Erich Schärer/Josef Benz (SUI)
1982	Erich Schärer/Max Rüegg (SUI)	Hans Hiltebrand/Ulrich Bächli (SUI)	Horst Schönau/Andreas Kirchner (GDR)
1983	Ralph Pichler/Urs Leuthold (SUI)	Erich Schärer/Max Rüegg (SUI)	Wolfgang Hoppe/Dietmar Schauerhammer (GDR)
1985	Wolfgang Hoppe/Dietmar Schauerhammer (GDR)	Detlef Richter/Steffen Grummt (GDR)	Sintis Ekmanis/Nikolai Schirov (URS)
1986	Wolfgang Hoppe/Dietmar Schauerhammer (GDR)	Ralph Pichler/Celest Poltera (SUI)	Detlef Richter/Steffen Grummt (GDR)
1987	Ralph Pichler/Celest Poltera (SUI)	Hans Hiltebrand/André Kiser (SUI)	Wolfgang Hoppe/Dietmar Schauerhammer (GDR)
1989	Wolfgang Hoppe/Bogdan Musiol (GDR)	Gustav Weder/Bruno Gerber (SUI)	Janis Kipurs/Aldis Intlers (URS)
1990	Gustav Weder/Bruno Gerber (SUI)	Harald Czudaj/Axel Lang (GDR)	Wolfgang Hoppe/Bogdan Musiol (GDR)
1991	Rudi Lochner/Markus Zimmermann (GER)	Gustav Weder/Curdin Morell (SUI)	Wolfgang Hoppe/Rene Hannemann (GER)
1993	Christoph Langen/Peer Jöchel (GER)	Gustav Weder/Donat Acklin (SUI)	Wolfgang Hoppe/Rene Hannemann (GER)
1995	Christoph Langen/Olaf Hampel (GER)	Pierre Lueders/Jack Pyc (CAN)	Eric Alard/Eric le Chanony (FRA)
1996	Christoph Langen/Markus Zimmermann (GER)	Pierre Lueders/Dave MacEachern (CAN)	Reto Götschi/Guido Acklin (SUI)
1997	Reto Götschi/Guido Acklin (SUI)	Günther Huber/Antonio Tartaglia (ITA)	Brian Shimer/Robert Olesen (USA)
1999	Günther Huber/Ubaldo Ranzi (ITA)	Christoph Langen/Markus Zimmermann (GER)	Bruno Mingeon/Emmanuel Hostache (FRA)
2000	Christoph Langen/Markus Zimmermann (GER)	Andre Lange/Rene Hoppe (GER)	Christian Reich/Urs Aeberhard (SUI)
2001	Christoph Langen/Marco Jakobs (GER)	Retö Götschi/Cedric Grand (SUI)	Martin Annen/Beat Hefti (SUI)
2003	André Lange/Kevin Kuske (GER)	Pierre Lueders/Giulio Zardi (CAN)	René Spies/Franz Sagmeister (GER)
2004	Pierre Lueders/Giulio Zardi (CAN)	Christoph Langen/Markus Zimmemann (GER)	André Lange/Kevin Kuske (GER)

Men's Four-Man Bob

	Gold	Silver	Bronze
1930	Franco Zaninetta/Giorgio Biasini/Antonio Dorini/Gino Rossi (ITA)	Jean Moillen/John Schneiter/Andre Moillen/William Pichard (SUI)	Fritz Grau/Picker/Bertram/Albert Brehme (GER)
1931	Werner Zahn/Robert Schmidt/Franz Bock/Emil Hinterfeld (GER)	Rene Fonjallaz/Gustave Fonjallaz/N. Buchheim/Gaston Fonjallaz (SUI)	Dennis Field/P. Coote/R. Wallace/J. Newcobe (GBR)
1934	Hanns Kilian/Fritz Schwarz/Hermann von Valta/Sebastian Huber (GER)	Emil Angelescu/Teodor Popescu/Dumitru Gheorghiu/Ion Gribincea (ROM)	Jean de Suarez d'Aulan/Rheims/Beamish/Jacques Bridou (FRA)
1935	Hanns Kilian/Alexander Gruber/Hermann von Valta/Fritz Schwarz (GER)	Pierre Musy/Noldi Gartmann/Charles Bouvier/Josef Beerli (SUI)	Reto Capadrutt/Fritz Feierabend/A. Lardi/H. Tami (SUI)
1937	Frederic McEvoy/David Looker/Charles Green/Brian Black (GBR)	Gerhard Fischer/Lohfeld/H Fischer/Rolf Thielecke (GER)	Donald Fox/Tippi Gray/Bill Dupree/James Bickford (USA)
1938	Frederic McEvoy/David Looker/Charles Green/Chris Macintosh (GBR)	Hanns Kilian/Dr Werner Windhaus/Bobby Braumüller/Franz Kemser (GER)	Bibo Fischer/Lohfeld/H. Fischer/Rolf Thielecke (GER)
1939	Fritz Feierabend/Heinz Cattani/Alphonse Hörning/Joseph Beerli (SUI)	Frederic McEvoy/Howard/Critchley/Charles Green (GBR)	Hanns Kilian/Werner Windhaus/Hans Schmidt/Franz Kemser (GER)

Year			
1947	Fritz Feierabend/Friedrich Waller/Felix Endrich/Stephan Waser (SUI)	Max Houben/Claude Houben/Albert Lerat/Jacques Mouvet (BEL)	Achille Fould/Henri Evrot/Robert Dumont/William Hirigoyen (FRA)
1949	Stanley Benham/Patrick Martin/William Casey/William d'Amico (USA)	James Bickford/Henry Sterns/Pat Buckley/Donald Dupree (USA)	Fritz Feierabend/Werner Spring/FritzWaller/Heinrich Angst (SUI)
1950	Stanley Benham/Patrick Martin/James Atkinson/William d'Amico (USA)	Fritz Feierabend/Albert Madörin/Romi Spada/Stephan Waser (SUI)	Franz Kapus/Franz Stöckli/Hans Bolli/Heinrich Angst (SUI)
1951	Anderl Ostler/Xaver Leitl/Michel Pössinger/Lorenz Nieberl (FRG)	Stanley Benham/Patrick Martin/James Atkinson/Gary Sheffield (USA)	Franz Kapus/Franz Stöckli/Hans Bolli/Heinrich Angst (SUI)
1953	Lloyd Johnson/Piet Biesiadecki/Hubert Miller/Joseph Smith (USA)	Anderl Ostler/Heinz Wendlinger, Hans Hohenester/Rudi Erben (FRG)	Hans Roesch/Michael Pössinger/Dix Terne/Sylvester Wackerle (FRG) Kjell Holmström/Walter Aronsson/Nils Landgren/Jan Lapidoth (& SWE)
1954	Fritz Feierabend/Harry Warburton/Gottfried Diener/Heinrich Angst (SUI)	Hans Roesch/Michel Pössinger/Dix Terne/Sylvester Wackerle (FRG)	Theo Kitt/Josef Grün/Klaus Koppenberger/Lorenz Nieberl (FRG)
1955	Franz Kapus/Gottfried Diener/Robert Alt/Heinrich Angst (SUI)	Fritz Feierabend/Aby Gartmann/Harry Warburton/Rolf Gerber (SUI)	Franz Schelle/Jakob Nirschl/Hans Henn/Edmund Koller (FRG)
1957	Hans Zoller/Hans Theler/Rolf Küderli/Heinz Leu (SUI)	Eugenio Monti/Ferdinando Piani/Lino Pierdica/Renzo Alvera (ITA)	Arthur Tyler/John Cole/Robert Hagemes/Charles Thomas Butler (USA)
1958	Hans Rösch/Alfred Hammer/Theodor Bauer/Walter Haller (FRG)	Franz Schelle/Eduard Kaltenberger/Josef Sterff/Otto Goebl (FRG)	Sergio Zardini/Massimo Bogana/Renato Mocellini/Alberto Righini (ITA)
1959	Arthur Tyler/Gary Sheffield/Parker Vooris/Charles Thomas Butler (USA)	Segio Zardini/Alberto Righini/Feruccio Della Torre/Romano Bonagura (ITA)	Franz Schelle/Hartl Geiger/Josef Sterff/Otto Goebl (FRG)
1960	Eugenio Monti/Furio Nordio/Sergio Siorpaes/Renzo Alvera (ITA)	Hans Rösch/Alfred Hammer/Theodor Bauer/Albert Kandlbinder (FRG)	Max Angst/Hansjörg Hirschbühl/Gottfried Kottmann/René Kuhl (SUI)
1961	Eugenio Monti/Sergio Siorpaes/Furio Nordio/Benito Rigoni (ITA)	Stanley Benham/Gary Sheffield/Jerry Tennant/Chuck Pandolph (USA)	Gunnar Ahs/Gunnar Carpö/Erik Wennerberg/Börje Bengt Hedblom (SWE)
1962	Franz Schelle/Josef Sterff/Ludwig Siebert/Otto Goebl (FRG)	Sergio Zardini/Ferruccio della Torre/Enrico de Lorenzo/Romano Bonagura (ITA)	Franz Isser/Pepi Isser/Heini Isser/Fritz Isser (AUT)
1963	Sergio Zardini/Ferruccio della Torre/Renato Moce Ilini/Romano Bonagura (ITA)	Angelo Frigerio/Mario Pallua/Luigi de Bettin/Sergio Mocellini (ITA)	Erwin Thaler/Reinhold Durnthaler/Josef Nairz/Adolf Koxeder (AUT)
1965	Victor Emery/Gerald Presley/Michael Young/Peter Kirby (CAN)	Nevio de Zordo/Italo de Lorenzo/Pietro Lesana/Roberto Mocellini (ITA)	Fred Fortune/Richard Knuckles/Joe Wilson/James Lord (USA)
1969	Wolfgang Zimmerer/Peter Utzschneider/Walter Steinbauer/Stefan Gaisreiter (FRG)	Gianfranco Gaspari/Sergio Pompanin/Roberto Zandonella/Mario Armano (ITA)	Les Fenner/Robert William Huscher/Howard Siler/Allen Hachigian (USA)
1970	Nevio de Zordo/Roberto Zandonella/Mario Armano/Luciano de Paolis (ITA)	Wolfgang Zimmerer/Walter Steinbauer/Pepi Bader/Peter Utzschneider (FRG)	Rene Stadler/Hans Candrian/Max Forster/Peter Schärer (SUI)
1971	René Stadler/Max Forster/Erich Schärer/Peter Schärer (SUI)	Oscar d'Andrea/Alessandro Bignozzi/Antonio Brabcaccio/Renzo Caldera (ITA)	Wolfgang Zimmerer/Stefan Gaisreiter/Walter Steinbauer/Peter Utzschneider (FRG)
1973	René Stadler/Werner Camichel/Erich Schärer/Peter Schärer (SUI)	Werner delle Karth/Walter Delle Karth/Hans Eichinger/Fritz Sperling (AUT)	Wolfgang Zimmerer/Stefan Gaisreiter/Walter Steinbauer/Peter Utzschneider (FRG)
1974	Wolfgang Zimmerer/Peter Utzschneider/Manfred Schumann/Albert Wurzer (FRG)	Hans Candrian/Guido Casty/Yves Marchand/Gaudenz Beeli (SUI)	Werner delle Karth/Walter delle Karth/Hans Eichinger/Fritz Sperling (AUT)
1975	Erich Schärer/Peter Schärer/Werner Camichel/Sepp Benz (SUI)	Wolfgang Zimmerer/Peter Utzschneider/Albert Wurzer/Fritz Ohlwärter (FRG)	Manfred Stengl/Gert Krenn/Franz Jakob/Armin Vilas (AUT)
1977	Meinhard Nehmer/Bernhard Germeshausen/Hans-Jürgen Gerhardt/Raimund Bethge (GDR)	Erich Schärer/Ulrich Bächli/Rudolf Marti/Josef Benz (SUI)	Jakob Resch/Herbert Berg/Fritz Ohlwärter/Walter Barfuss (FRG)
1978	Horst Schönau/Horst Bernhard/Harald Seifert/Bogdan Musiol (GDR)	Erich Schärer/Ulrich Bächli/Rudolf Marti/Josef Benz (SUI)	Meinhard Nehmer/Bernhard Germeshausen/Hans-Jürgen Gerhardt/Raimund Bethge (GDR)
1979	Stefan Gaisreiter/Dieter Gebhard/Hans Wagner/Heinz Busche (FRG)	Meinhard Nehmer/Detlef Richter/Bernhard Germeshausen/Hans-Jürgen Gerhardt (GDR)	Erich Schärer/Ulrich Bächli/Hansjörg Trachsel/Josef Benz (SUI)
1981	Bernhard Germeshausen/Hans-Jürgen Gerhardt/Henry Gerlach/Michael Trübner (GDR)	Hans Hiltebrand/Kurt Poletti/Franz Weinberger/Franz Isenegger (SUI)	Erich Schärer/Max Rüegg/Tony Rüegg/Josef Benz (SUI)
1982	Silvio Giobellina/Heinz Stettler/Urs Salzmann/Rico Freiermuth (SUI)	Bernhard Lehmann/Roland Wetzig/Bogdan Musiol/Eberhard Weise (GDR)	Erich Schärer/Franz Isenegger/Tony Rüegg/Max Rüegg (SUI)
1983	Ekkehard Fasser/Hans Maerchy/Kurt Poletti/Rolf Strittmatter (SUI)	Klaus Kopp/Gerhard Öchsle/Günther Neuburger/Hajo Schumacher (FRG)	Detlef Richter/Henry Gerlach/Thomas Forch/Dietmar Jerke (GDR)
1985	Bernhard Lehmann/Matthias Trübner/Ingo Voge/Steffen Grummt (GDR)	Detlef Richter/Dietmar Jerke/Bodo Ferl/Matthias Legler (GDR)	Silvio Giobellina/Heinz Stettler/Urs Salzmann/Rico Freiermuth (SUI)
1986	Erich Schärer/Kurt Meier/Erwin Fassbind/André Kiser (SUI)	Peter Kienast/Franz Siegl/Gerhard Redl/Christian Mark (AUT)	Ralph Pichler/Heinrich Notter/Celest Poltera/Roland Beerli (SUI)
1987	Hans Hiltebrand/Urs Fehlmann/Erwin Fassbind/André Kiser (SUI)	Wolfgang Hoppe/Bogdan Musiol/Roland Wetzig/Dietmar Schauerhammer (GDR)	Ralph Pichler/Heinrich Ott/Edgar Dietsche/Celest Poltera (SUI)
1989	Gustav Weder/Curdin Morell/Bruno Gerber/Lorenz Schindelholz (SUI)	Nico Baracchi/Christian Reich/Donat Acklin/Rene Mangold (SUI)	Wolfgang Hoppe/Bodo Ferl/Bogdan Musiol/Ingo Voge (GDR)
1990	Gustav Weder/Bruno Gerber/Curdin Morell/Lorenz Schindelholz (SUI)	Harald Czudaj/Tino Bonk/Alexander Szelig/Axel Jang (GDR)	Ingo Appelt/Gerhard Redl/Jürgen Mandl/Harald Winkler (AUT)
1991	Wolfgang Hoppe/Bogdan Musiol/Axel Kühn/Christoph Langen (GER)	Gustav Weder/Bruno Gerber/Lorenz Schindelholz/Curdin Morell (SUI)	Harald Czudaj/Tino Bonk/Axel Jang/Alexander Szelig (GER)
1993	Gustav Weder/Donat Acklin/Kurt Meier/Domenico Semeraro (SUI)	Hubert Schösser/Harald Winkler/Gerhard Redl/Gerhard Haidacher (AUT)	Brian Shimer/Bryan Leturgez/Karlos Kirby/Randy Jones (USA)

1995	Wolfgang Hoppe/René Hannemann/Ulf Hielscher/Carsten Embach (GER)	Hubert Schösser/Gerhard Redl/Thomas Schroll/Martin Schützenauer (AUT)	Harald Czudaj/Torsten Voss/Udo Lehmann/ Alexander Szelig (GER)
1996	Christoph Langen/Markus Zimmermann/Sven Rühr/Olaf Hampel (GER)	Marcel Rohner/Markus Wasser/Thomas Schreiber/Roland Tanner (SUI)	Wolfgang Hoppe/Torsten Voss/Sven Peter/ Carsten Embach (GER)
1997	Wolfgang Hoppe/René Hannemann/Carsten Embach/Sven Rühr (GER)	Dirk Wiese/Christoph Bartsch/Torsten Voss/Michael Liekmeier (GER)	Brian Shimer/Chip Minton/Randy Jones/ Robert Olesen (USA)
1999	Bruno Mingeon/Emmanuel Hostache/Eric le Chanony/Max Robert (FRA)	Marcel Rohner/Markus Nüssli/Beat Hefti/ Silvio Schaufelberger (SUI)	Pierre Lueders/Ken Leblanc/Ben Hindle/Matt Hindle (CAN)
2000	André Lange/René Hoppe/Lars Behrendt/ Carsten Embach (GER)	Christoph Langen/Markus Zimmermann/ Tomas Plazter/Sven Rühr (GER)	Christian Reich/Bruno Aeberhard/Urs Aeberhard/Domenic Keller (SUI)
2001	Christoph Langen/Markus Zimmermann/ Sven Peter/Alex Metzger (GER)	André Lange/Lars Behrendt/René Hoppe/Carsten Embach (GER)	Christian Reich/Steve Anderhub/Urs Aeberhard/Domenic Keller (SUI)
2003	André Lange/Kevin Kuske/René Hoppe/ Carsten Embach (GER)	Todd Hays/Bill Schuffenhauer/Randy Jones/Hines Garrett (USA)	Alexandr Zoubkov/Alexei Seliverstov/Sergei Golubev/Dmitri Stepuschkin (RUS)
2004	André Lange/Kevin Kuske/Udo Lehmann/René Hoppe (GER)	Christoph Langen/Christoph Heyder/ Enrico Kühn/Jens Nohka (GER)	Todd Hays/Paule Jovanovic/Bill Schuffenhauer/Steve Mesler (USA)

Women's Two-Man Bob

	Gold	Silver	Bronze
2000	Gabriele Kohlisch/Kathleen Hering (GER)	Jean Racine/Jennifer Davidson (USA)	Francoise Burdet/Katharina Sutter (SUI)
2001	Francoise Burdet/Katharina Sutter (SUI)	Jean Racine/Jennifer Davidson (USA)	Susi Erdmann/Tanja Hess (GER)
2003	Susi Erdmann/Annegret Dietrich (GER)	Sandra Prokoff/Ulrike Holzner (GER)	Cathleen Martini/Yvonne Cernota (GER)
2004	Susi Erdmann/Kristina Bader (IGER)	Sandra Prokoff/Anja Schneiderheinze (GER)	Jean Racine/Vonetta Flowers (USA)

Luge: Olympic Medallists

Men's Singles

	Gold		Silver		Bronze	
1964	Thomas Köhler (GDR)	3:26.77	Klaus Bonsack (GDR)	3:27.04	Hans Plenk (GDR)	3:30.15
1968	Manfred Schmid (AUT)	2:52.48	Thomas Köhler (GDR)	2:52.66	Klaus Bonsack (GDR)	2:53.33
1972	Wolfgang Scheidel (GDR)	3:27.58	Harald Ehrig (GDR)	3:28.39	Wolfram Fiedler (GDR)	3:28.73
1976	Detlef Günther (GDR)	3:27.69	Josef Fendt (FRG)	3:28.20	Hans Rinn (GDR)	3:28.57
1980	Bernhard Glass (GDR)	2:54.80	Paul Hildgartner (ITA)	2:55.37	Anton Winkler (FRG)	2:56.54
1984	Paul Hildgartner (ITA)	3:04.26	Sergey Danilin (URS)	3:04.96	Valeriy Dudin (URS)	3:05.01
1988	Jens Müller (GDR)	3:05.55	Georg Hackl (FRG)	3:05.92	Yuriy Kharchenko (URS)	3:06.27
1992	Georg Hackl (GDR)	3:02.36	Markus Prock (AUT)	3:02.67	Markus Schmid (AUT)	3:02.94
1994	Georg Hackl (GDR)	3:21.57	Markus Prock (AUT)	3:21.58	Armin Zöggeler (ITA)	3:21.83
1998	Georg Hackl (GDR)	3:18.44	Armin Zöggeler (ITA)	3:18.94	Jens Müller (GDR)	3:19.09
2002	Armin Zöggeler (ITA)	2:57.94	Georg Hackl (GDR)	2:58.27	Markus Prock (AUT)	2:58.28

Men's Doubles

	Gold	Silver	Bronze
1964	Josef Feistmantl/Manfred Stengl (AUT) 1:41.62	Reinhold Senn/Helmut Thaler (AUT) 1:41.91	Walter Aussendorfer/ Sigisfredo Mair (ITA) 1:42.87
1968	Klaus Bonsack/Thomas Köhler (GDR) 1:35.85	Manfred Schmid/Ewald Walch (AUT) 1:36.34	Wolfgang Winkler/Fritz Nachmann (FRG) 1:37.29
1972	Horst Hörnlein/Reinhard Bredow (GDR) 1:28.35	——	Klaus Bonsack/Wolfram Fiedler (GDR) 1:29.16
	Paul Hildgartner/Walter Plaikner (ITA) 1:28.35		
1976	Hans Rinn/Norbert Hahn (GDR) 1:25.60	Hans Brandner/Balthasar Schwarm (FRG) 1:25.89	Rudolf Schmid/Franz Schachner (AUT) 1:25.92
1980	Hans Rinn/Norbert Hahn (GDR) 1:19.33	Peter Gschnitzer/Karl Brunner (ITA) 1:19.61	Georg Fluckinger/Karl Schrott (AUT) 1:19.79
1984	Hans Stangassinger/Franz Wembacher (FRG) 1:23.62	Yevgeniy Belousov/ Aleksandr Belyakov (URS) 1:23.66	Jörg Hoffmann/Jochen Pietzsch (GDR) 1:23.89
1988	Jörg Hoffmann/Jochen Pietzsch (GDR) 1:31.94	Stefan Krausse/Jan Behrendt (GDR) 1:32.04	Thomas Schwab/Wolfgang Staudinger (FRG) 1:32.27
1992	Stefan Krausse/Jan Behrendt (GDR) 1:32.05	Yves Mankel/Thomas Rudolph (GDR) 1:32.24	Hansjörg Raffl/Norbert Huber (ITA) 1:32.30
1994	Kurt Brugger/Wilfried Huber (ITA) 1:36.72	Hansjörg Raffl/Norbert Huber (ITA) 1:36.77	Stefan Krausse/Jan Behrendt (GDR)1:36.94
1998	Stefan Krausse/Jan Behrendt (GDR) 1:41.10	Chris Thorpe/Gordy Sheer (USA) 1:41.13	Mark Grimmette/Brian Martin (USA) 1:41.22
2002	Patric-Fritz Leitner/Alexander Resch (GDR) 1:26.08	Mark Grimmette/Brian Martin (USA) 1:26.22	Chris Thorpe/Clay Ives (USA) 1:26.22

Women's Singles

	Gold	Silver	Bronze
1964	Ortrun Enderlein (GDR) 3:24.67	Ilse Geisler (GDR) 3:27.42	Helene Thurner (AUT) 3:29.06
1964	Ortrun Enderlein (GDR) 3:24.67	Ilse Geisler (GDR) 3:27.42	Helene Thurner (AUT) 3:29.06
1968	Erica Lechner (ITA) 2:28.66	Christa Schmuck (FRG) 2:29.37	Angelika Dünhaupt (FRG) 2:29.56
1972	Anna-Maria Müller (GDR) 2:59.18	Ute Rührold (GDR) 2:59.49	Margit Schumann (GDR) 2:59.54
1976	Margit Schumann (GDR) 2:50.62	Ute Rührold (GDR) 2:50.85	Elisabeth Demleitner (FRG) 2:51.06
1980	Vera Zozula (URS) 2:36.54	Melita Sollman (GDR) 2:37.66	Ingrîda Amantova (URS) 2:37.82
1984	Steffi Martin (GDR) 2:46.57	Bettina Schmidt (GDR) 2:46.87	Ute Weiss (GDR) 2:47.25
1988	Steffi Martin Walter (GDR) 3:03.97	Ute Weiss Oberhoffner (GDR) 3:04.10	Cerstin Schmidt (GDR) 3:04.18
1992	Doris Neuner (AUT) 3:06.70	Angelika Neuner (AUT) 3:06.77	Susi Erdmann (GDR) 3:07.11
1994	Gerda Weissensteiner (ITA) 3:15.52	Susi Erdmann (GDR) 3:16.28	Andrea Tagwerker (AUT) 3:16.65
1998	Silke Kraushaar (GDR) 3:23.78	Barbara Niedernhuber (GDR) 3:23.78	Angelika Neuner (AUT) 3:24.25
2002	Sylke Otto (GDR) 2:52.46	Barbara Niedernhuber (GDR) 2:52.78	Silke Kraushaar (GDR) 2:52.86

Luge: World Champions (Artificial Run)

Men's Singles

	Gold	Silver	Bronze
1955	Anton Salvesen (NOR)	Josef Thaler (AUT)	Josef Isser (AUT)
1957	Hans Schaller (FRG)	Bibi Torriani (SUI)	Erich Raffl (AUT)
1958	Jerzy Wojnar (POL)	Ryszard Pedrak (POL)	Reinhold Frosch (AUT)
1959	Herbert Thaler (AUT)	Josef Feistmantl (AUT)	David Moroder (ITA)
1960	Helmut Berndt (FRG)	Reinhold Frosch (AUT)	Hans Plenk (FRG)
1961	Jerzy Wojnar (POL)	Hans Plenk (FRG)	Reinhold Senn (AUT)
1962	Thomas Köhler (GDR)	Jerzy Wojnar (POL)	Jochen Asche (GDR)
1963	Fritz Nachmann (FRG)	Hans Plenk (FRG)	Klaus Bonsack (GDR)
1965	Hans Plenk (FRG)	Mieczyslaw Pawelkiewicz (POL)	Erich Graber (ITA)
1967	Thomas Köhler (GDR)	Klaus Bonsack (GDR)	Josef Feistmantl (AUT)
1969	Josef Feistmantl (AUT)	Manfred Schmid (AUT)	Wolfgang Scheidel (GDR)
1970	Josef Fendt (FRG)	Josef Feistmantl (AUT)	Wolfgang Scheidel (GDR)
1971	Karl Brunner (ITA)	Leonhard Nagenrauft (FRG)	Josef Feistmantl (AUT)
1973	Hans Rinn (GDR)	Wolfram Fiedler (GDR)	Harald Ehrig (GDR)
1974	Josef Fendt (FRG)	Hans Rinn (GDR)	Horst Müller (GDR)
1975	Wolfram Fiedler (GDR)	Manfred Schmid (AUT)	Harald Ehrig (GDR)
1977	Hans Rinn (GDR)	Horst Müller (GDR)	Anton Winkler (FRG)
1978	Paul Hildgartner (ITA)	Anton Winkler (FRG)	Manfred Schmid (AUT)
1979	Detlef Günther (GDR)	Karl Brunner (ITA)	Paul Hildgartner (ITA)
1981	Sergei Danilin (URS)	Michael Walther (GDR)	Ernst Haspinger (ITA)
1983	Miroslav Zajonc (CAN)	Sergei Danilin (URS)	Paul Hildgartner (ITA)
1985	Michael Walther (GDR)	Jörg Hoffmann (GDR)	Jens Müller (GDR)
1987	Markus Prock (AUT)	Jens Müller (GDR)	Sergei Danilin (URS)
1989	Georg Hackl (FRG)	Jens Müller (GDR)	Johannes Schettel (FRG)
1990	Georg Hackl (FRG)	Markus Prock (AUT)	Jens Müller (GDR)
1991	Arnold Huber (ITA)	Georg Hackl (GDR)	Markus Prock (AUT)
1993	Wendell Suckow (USA)	Georg Hackl (GDR)	Wilfried Huber (ITA)
1995	Armin Zöggeler (ITA)	Georg Hackl (GDR)	Markus Prock (AUT)
1996	Markus Prock (AUT)	Georg Hackl (GDR)	Jens Müller (GDR)
1997	Georg Hackl (GDR)	Markus Prock (AUT)	Gerhard Gleirscher (AUT)
1999	Armin Zöggeler (ITA)	Jens Müller (GDR)	Norbert Huber (ITA)
2000	Jens Müller (GDR)	Armin Zöggeler (ITA)	Georg Hackl (GDR)
2001	Armin Zöggeler (ITA)	Georg Hackl (GDR)	Markus Prock (AUT)
2003	Armin Zöggeler (ITA)	Martins Rubenis (LAT)	Rainer Margreiter (AUT)
2004	David Moeller (GER)	Georg Hackl (GER)	Martins Rubenis (LAT)

B
O
B
S
L
E
I
G
H

Men's Doubles

	Gold	Silver	Bronze
1955	Hans Krausner/Josef Thaler (AUT)	Josef Isser/Maria Isser (AUT)	Josef Strillinger/Fritz Nachmann (FRG)
1957	Fritz Nachmann/Josef Strillinger (FRG)	Giorgio Pichler/Giovanni Graber (ITA)	Erich Raffl/Ewald Walch (AUT)
1958	Fritz Nachmann/Josef Strillinger (FRG)	Jerzy Koszla/Janina Suszczewska (POL)	Ryszard Pedrak/Halina Lacheta (POL)
1959	not held		
1960	Reinhold Frosch/Ewald Walch (AUT)	Herbert Thaler/Helmut Thaler (AUT)	Horst Tiedge/Hans Plenk (FRG)
1961	Roman Pichler/Raimondo Prinroth (ITA)	David Maroder/Raimondo Prinot (ITA)	Helmut Thaler/Reinhold Senn (AUT)
1962	Giovanni Graber/Gianpaolo Ambrosi (ITA)	Fritz Nachmann/Max Leo (FRG)	Manfred Novotny/Petr Skrabalek (TCH)
1963	Ryszard Pedrak/Lucjan Kudzia (POL)	Edward Fender/Mieczyslaw Pawelkiewicz (POL)	Anton Venier/Ewald Walch (AUT)

1965	Wolfgang Scheidel/Michael Köhler (GDR)	Klaus Bonsack/Thomas Köhler (GDR)	Horst Hörnlein/Rolf Fuchs (GDR)
1967	Klaus Bonsack/Thomas Köhler (GDR)	Manfred Schmid/Ewald Walch (AUT)	Siegfried Maier/Ernesto Maier (ITA)
1969	Manfred Schmid/Ewald Walch (AUT)	Horst Hörnlein/Reinhard Bredow (GDR)	Klaus Bonsack/Michael Köhler (GDR)
1970	Manfred Schmid/Ewald Walch (AUT)	Klaus Bonsack/Michael Köhler (GDR)	Horst Hörnlein/Reinhard Bredow (GDR)
1971	Paul Hildgartner/Walter Plaikner (ITA)	Manfred Schmid/Ewald Walch (AUT)	Horst Hörnlein/Reinhard Bredow (GDR)
1973	Horst Hörnlein/Reinhard Bredow (GDR)	Hans Rinn/Norbert Hahn (GDR)	Paul Hildgartner/Walter Plaikner (ITA)
1974	Bernd Hahn/Ulrich Hahn (GDR)	Schulze/Neumann (GDR)	Rudolf Schmid/Franz Schachner (AUT)
1975	Hans Rinn/Norbert Hahn (GDR)	Horst Müller/Neumann (GDR)	Rudolf Schmid/Franz Schachner (AUT)
1977	Hans Rinn/Norbert Hahn (GDR)	Karl Brunner/Peter Gschnitzer (ITA)	Hans Brandner/Balthasar Schwarm (FRG)
1978	Dainis Bremse/Aigars Krikis (URS)	Yakuschin/Schitov (URS)	Hans Rinn/Norbert Hahn (GDR)
1979	Hans Brandner/Balthasar Schwarm (FRG)	Hans Rinn/Norbert Hahn (GDR)	Anton Winkler/Anton Wembacher (FRG)
1981	Bernd Hahn/Ulrich Hahn (GDR)	Bernd Oberhoffner/Jörg-Dieter Ludwig (GDR)	Hans Stangassinger/Anton Wembacher (FRG)
1983	Jörg Hoffmann/Jochen Pietzsch (GDR)	Hansjörg Raffl/Norbert Huber (ITA)	Hans Stangassinger/Anton Wembacher (FRG)
1985	Jörg Hoffmann/Jochen Pietzsch (GDR)	Rene Keller/Lutz Kühnlenz (GDR)	Vitali Melnik/Dimitri Alexeyev (URS)
1987	Jörg Hoffmann/Jochen Pietzsch (GDR)	Stefan Ilsanker/Georg Hackl (FRG)	Thomas Schwab/Wolfgang Staudinger (FRG)
1989	Stefan Krausse/Jan Behrendt (GDR)	Hansjörg Raffl/Norbert Huber (ITA)	Jörg Hoffmann/Jochen Pietzsch (GDR)
1990	Hansjörg Raffl/Norbert Huber (ITA)	Kurt Brugger/Wilfried Huber (ITA)	Jörg Hoffmann/Jochen Pietzsch (GDR)
1991	Stefan Krausse/Jan Behrendt (GDR)	Yves Mankel/Thomas Rudolph (GDR)	Hansjörg Raffl/Norbert Huber (ITA)
1993	Stefan Krausse/Jan Behrendt (GDR)	Hansjörg Raffl/Norbert Huber (ITA)	Kurt Brugger/Wilfried Huber (ITA)
1995	Stefan Krausse/Jan Behrendt (GDR)	Chris Thorpe/Gordy Sheer (USA)	Kurt Brugger/Wilfried Huber (ITA)
1996	Tobias Schiegl/Markus Schiegl (AUT)	Chris Thorpe/Gordy Sheer (USA)	Gerhard Plankensteiner/Oswald Hasselrieder (ITA)
1997	Tobias Schiegl/Markus Schiegl (AUT)	Stefan Krausse/Jan Behrendt (GDR)	Steffen Skel/Steffen Wöller (GDR)
1999	Patric Leitner/Alexander Resch (GDR)	Tobias Schiegl/Markus Schiegl (AUT)	Mark Grimmette/Brian Martin (USA)
2000	Patric Leitner/Alexander Resch (GDR)	Steffen Skel/Steffen Wöller (GDR)	Mark Grimmette/Brian Martin (USA)
2001	André Florschütz/Torsten Wustlich (GDR)	Steffen Skel/Steffen Wöller (GDR)	Tobias Schiegl/Markus Schiegl (AUT)
2003	Andreas Linger/Wolfgang Linger (AUT)	Tobias Schiegl/Markus Schiegl (AUT)	Patric Leitner/Alexander Resch (GDR)
2004	Patric Leitner/Alexander Resch (GER)	Andre Florschuetz/Torsten Wustlich (GER)	Mark Grimmette/Brian Martin (USA)

Luge: World Champions (Natural Run)

Men's Doubles

	Gold	Silver	Bronze
1979	Damiano Lugon/Andrea Millet (ITA)	Werner Mücke/Helmut Huter (AUT)	Werner Prantl/Florian Prantl (AUT)
1980	Oswald Pörnbacher/Raimund Pigneter (ITA)	Martin Jud/Harald Steinhauser (ITA)	Werner Mücke/Helmut Huter (AUT)
1982	Andreas Jud/Ernst Oberhammer (ITA)	Alfred Kogler/Franz Huber (AUT)	Werner Prantl/Florian Prantl (AUT)
1984	Andreas Jud/Ernst Oberhammer (ITA)	Martin Jud/Harald Steinhauser (ITA)	Alfred Kogler/Franz Huber (AUT)
1986	Almir Betemps/Corrado Herin (ITA)	Andreas Jud/Ernst Oberhammer (ITA)	Arnold Lunger/Günther Steinhauser (ITA)
1988	not held		
1990	Andreas Jud/Hannes Pichler (ITA)	Almir Betemps/Corrado Herin (ITA)	Walter Mauracher/Georg Eberhardter (AUT)
1992	Almir Betemps/Corrado Herin (ITA)	Roland Wolf/Stefan Kögler (AUT)	Michael Bischofer/Herbert Kögl (AUT)
1994	Manfred Gräber/Günther Steinhauser (AUT)	Jürgen Pezzi/Christian Hafner (ITA)	Roland Niedermaier/Hubert Burger (ITA)
1996	Reinhard Beer/Herbert Kögl (AUT)	Andi Ruetz/Helmut Ruetz (AUT)	Martin Psenner/Arthur Künig (ITA)
1998	Andi Ruetz/Helmut Ruetz (AUT)	Manfred Gräber/Hubert Burger (ITA)	Reinhard Beer/Herbert Kögl (AUT)
2000	Armin Mair/David Mair (ITA)	Reinhard Beer/Herbert Kögl (AUT)	Damian Waniczek/Andrzej Laszczak (POL)
2001	Wolfgang Schopf/Andreas Schopf (AUT)	Armin Mair/David Mair (ITA)	Peter Lechner/Peter Braunegger (AUT)
2003	Wolfgang Schopf/Andreas Schopf (AUT)	Pavel Porschnev/Ivan Lasarev (RUS)	Harald Kleinhofer/Gerhard Mühlbacher (AUT)

Women's Singles

	Gold	Silver	Bronze
1979	Delia Vaudan (ITA)	Ingrid Zarneter (ITA)	Roswitha Fischer (ITA)
1980	Delia Vaudan (ITA)	Christa Fontana (ITA)	Roswitha Fischer (ITA)
1982	Herta Hafner (ITA)	Hilde Fuchs (AUT)	Paula Peintner (ITA)
1984	Delia Vaudan (ITA)	Paula Peintner (ITA)	Irmgard Lanthaler (ITA)
1986	Irmgard Lanthaler (ITA)	Delia Vaudan (ITA)	Helga Pichler (ITA)
1988	not held		
1990	Jeanette Koppensteiner (AUT)	Irene Koch (AUT)	Lyubov Panyutina (URS)
1992	Lyubov Panyutina (EUN)	Elvira Holzknecht (AUT)	Irene Koch (AUT)
1994	Beatrix Mahlknecht (ITA)	Irene Zechner (AUT)	Doris Haselrieder (ITA)
1996	Irene Zechner (AUT)	Elvira Holzknecht (AUT)	Sandra Mariner (AUT)
1998	Lyubov Panjutina (RUS)	Christa Gieti (ITA)	Sonja Steinacher (ITA)
2000	Ekaterina Lavrentyeva (RUS)	Sonja Steinacher (ITA)	Elvira Holzknecht (AUT)
2001	Sonja Steinacher (ITA)	Renate Gietl (ITA)	Sandra Mariner (AUT)
2003	Sonja Steinacher (ITA)	Ekaterina Lavrentyeva (RUS)	Irene Mitterstieler (ITA)

Skeleton Bob: Olympic Medallists

Men

	Gold	Silver	Bronze
1928	Jennison Heaton (USA) 3:01.8	John Heaton (USA) 3:02.8	David, Earl of Northesk (GBR) 3:05.1
1928	Jennison Heaton (USA) 3:01.8	John Heaton (USA) 3:02.8	David, Earl of Northesk (GBR) 3:05.1
1948	Nino Bibbia (ITA) 5:23.2	John Heaton (USA) 5:24.6	John Crammond (GBR) 5:25.1
2002	Jim Shea (USA) 1:41.96	Martin Rettl (AUT) 1:42.01	Gregor Stähli (SUI) 1:42.15

Women

	Gold	Silver	Bronze
2002	Tristan Gale (USA) 1:45.11	Lea Ann Parsley (USA) 1:45.21	Alex Coomber (GBR) 1:45.37

Skeleton Bob: World Championships

Men

	Gold	Silver	Bronze
1982	Gert Elsässer (AUT)	Nico Baracchi (SUI)	Alain Wicki (SUI)
1989	Alain Wicki (SUI)	Christian Auer (AUT)	Franz Plangger (AUT)
1990	Michael Grünberger (AUT)	Andy Schmid (AUT)	Gregor Stähli (SUI)
1991	Christian Auer (AUT)	Andy Schmid (AUT)	Michael Grünberger (AUT)
1992	Bruce Sandford (NZL)	Gregor Stähli (SUI)	Christian Auer (AUT)
1993	Andy Schmid (AUT)	Franz Plangger (AUT)	Gregor Stähli (SUI)
1994	Gregor Stähli (SUI)	Andy Schmid (AUT)	Franz Plangger (AUT)
1995	Jürg Wenger (SUI)	Christian Auer (AUT)	Ryan Davenport (CAN)
1996	Ryan Davenport (CAN)	Franz Plangger (AUT)	Christian Auer (AUT)
1997	Ryan Davenport (CAN)	Jim Shea (USA)	Chris Soule (USA)
1998	Willy Schneider (GDR)	Alain Wicky (SUI)	Felix Poletti (SUI)
1999	Jim Shea(USA)	Andy Böhme (GDR)	Willy Schneider GER
2000	Andy Böhme (GDR)	Gregor Stähli (SUI)	Jim Shea (USA)
			Alexander Müller (AUT)
2001	Martin Rettl (AUT)	Jeff Pain (CAN)	Lincoln DeWitt (USA)
2003	Jeff Pain (CAN)	Chris Soule (USA)	Brady Canfield (USA)

Women

	Gold	Silver	Bronze
2000	Steffi Hanzlik (GDR)	Melissa Hollingsworth (CAN)	Tricia Stumpf (USA)
2001	Maya Pedersen (SUI)	Alex Coomber (GBR)	Tricia Stumpf (USA)
2003	Michelle Kelly (CAN)	Ekaterina Mironova (RUS)	Tristan Gale (USA)

Skeleton Bob: World Cup Winners

Men

1987	Andy Schmid (AUT)	1996	Ryan Davenport (USA)
1988	Andy Schmid (AUT)	1997	Alexander Müller (AUT)
1989	Alain Wicki (SUI)	1998	Willi Schneider (GER)
1990	Christian Auer (AUT)	1999	Andy Böhme (GER)
1991	Christian Auer (AUT)	2000	Andy Böhme (GER)
1992	Christian Auer (AUT)	2001	Lincoln DeWitt (USA)
1993	Franz Plangger (AUT)	2002	Gregor Stähli (SUI)
1994	Christian Auer (AUT)	2003	Chris Soule (USA)
1995	Christian Auer (AUT)		

Women

1997	Steffi Hanzlik (GER)	2001	Alex Coomber (GBR)
1998	Maya Bieri (SUI)	2002	Alex Coomber (GBR)
1999	Steffi Hanzlik (GER)	2003	Michelle Kelly (CAN)
2000	Alexandra Hamilton (GBR)		

BOBSLEIGH

BOCCE

Throwing balls towards a target is the oldest game known to mankind. As early as 5000BC the Egyptians played a form of bocce (also known variously as bocci, or *boccie*, and pronounced 'botchee') with polished rocks. Graphic representations of figures tossing a ball or polished stone have been recorded as early as 5200BC. While bocce today looks quite different from its early predecessors, the unbroken thread of bocce's lineage is the consistent objective of trying to come as close to a fixed target as possible. From this early objective, the basic rules of bocce were born.

From Egypt the game made its way to Greece around 800BC. The Romans learned the game from the Greeks, then introduced it throughout the empire. The Roman influence in bocce is preserved in the game's name; bocce derives from the Vulgate Latin *bottia*, meaning boss.

The early Romans were among the first to play a game resembling what we know as bocce today. In early times they employed coconuts brought back from Africa and later used balls carved out of hard olive wood and covered with iron. Beginning with Emperor Augustus, it became the sport of statesmen and rulers. From the early Greek physician Hippocrates to the great Italian Galileo, participants in bocce have noted that the game's athleticism and spirit of competition rejuvenates the body.

However, as the game enjoyed rapid growth throughout Europe, being the sport of nobility and peasants alike, it began to threaten the health of nations. The popularity of the game was said to interfere with the security of the state because it took too much time away from archery practice and other military exercises.

In 1576, the Republic of Venice publicly condemned the sport, punishing those who played with fines and imprisonment. And perhaps most grave was the game's condemnation by the Catholic Church which deterred the laity and officially prohibited clergymen from playing the game by proclaiming bocce a means of gambling.

Contrary to the rest of Europe, the game thrived in Great Britain, eventually developing into the modern game of bowls.

In modern times, the first bocce clubs were organised in Italy. The first Italian League was formed in 1947 by fifteen teams in and around the town of Rivoli near Turin. The same year also marks the beginning of the yearly Bocce World Championships, although the governing body, the Unione Federazione Italiane Bocce, considered the first world championship to be held in Genoa, Italy, in 1951.

Thanks to many Italian immigrants at the turn of the century, bocce has come to flourish in the United States. During its beginnings in the US there were as many versions of the game as there were towns the immigrants had left. Bringing some order to the game is the Collegium Cosmicum ad Buxeas, the pre-eminent bocce organisation whose headquarters are in Rome.

Italy stages a number of regional competitions, reinforcing the country's strong regional rivalries. International play is largely limited to Italy and France, which occasionally compete at adult and juvenile levels in grandly titled tournaments. There is a cup provided by the Prince of Monaco, whose territory lies between the two main contenders, and the results have long been dominated by Italy. Although it now has the superstructure of a modern sport, bocce is still largely local and recreational in its appeal. Given its peasant origins, it is hardly surprising that it remains male-dominated, although a small number of women play. Despite its growing complexity, its appeal lies in its being a '*sport simpatico e popolare*' in the words of a recent enthusiast – something essentially part of an Italian summer.

Italy and France have produced two main games, codified relatively recently, and with broad similarities. They began and remain predominantly open-air activities, played on long, rectangular pitches originally improvised from rough village spaces during hot, dry summers. These have surfaces of raked sand or gravel on which the tossed balls fall and stick, rather than roll. Both games are still often played informally in the village and café tradition by men of all ages, but they have now acquired national and international competitive networks and, in many cases, dedicated indoor facilities that allow for year-round play in urban areas. The French game is variously called boules or pétanque.

Bocce uses a 'court,' 'alley,' or 'rink' approximately 18.3m long by 2.4m wide. Increasingly, several of these are usually provided side by side, as are dedicated areas found in many public parks. There are foul areas at each end of the court. The small target ball, the *pallino*, is tossed from one end and must land at least 1.25m (5ft) beyond centre. Each player then aims to throw his ball, which is heavier than the *pallino*, as close as possible to the target. This is usually done after a walk-up of several steps within the foul area. The throw is complicated by variations on the way the target is approached, according to regional practices. Competitors comprise two players with two shots each or teams of three to six people using four shots each. If a ball displaces others already in place it is disqualified. The winner of a game is the first to score 9-15 points in pairs, or 9-18 in a team competition.

BOOMERANG

Aerodynamic throwsticks were developed by Stone Age civilisations in various parts of the world thousands of years ago. The Australian aborigines are the best known; however, these special hunting weapons were also developed in other areas including ancient Egypt, the American Southwest, and eastern Europe. While there are many stories of how the returning boomerang came to be (many rooted in myth and misinterpretation), most anthropologists agree that it originated from the throwstick.

The throwstick, called a kylie by the native Australians and a rabbit stick by the Hopi people of pre-European America, was a heavy, non-returning aerodynamic weapon thrown horizontally to kill or stun prey. At some point (perhaps by accident) the stick became more curved and refined (and much lighter) so that, when thrown vertically, it would return to the thrower. These true boomerangs were probably only used for fun and games, not as weapons. Today's modern boomerangs are genuine items of sports equipment and look very different from the L-shaped throwsticks of the past.

A curator at the Smithsonian Museum decided to promote his boomerang exhibition by holding a throwing competition. The Smithsonian tournaments started in the early 1970s, and drew many throwers from around the USA and a few international throwers as well. At first, throwers only had their traditionally shaped boomerangs, made of wood. But a desire for performance pushed the evolution of the boomerang into overdrive. New designs and materials made boomerangs fly higher, faster and farther. Glass, fibreglass, kevlar, phenolic resins and good old plain wood are all used and each has its pros and cons.

Tournaments meanwhile sprang up in other parts of the country. In 1981, the United States fielded a team of ten throwers which travelled to Australia to challenge the Aussies and find out who the best boomerang throwers in the world were. The cross-shaped boomerang became standard due to its ability to be more easily caught, fly more accurately, and hang in the air longer but a variety of other types are used for the very different demands of the world championship events.

The United States initially monopolised the world championships, winning the inaugural event in 1981 (in Australia), and again in 1985 (France), 1987 (USA), May 1988 (Australia), August 1988 (Europe), 1989 (USA), 1991 (Australia), 1992 (Germany) and 1994 (Japan). Only the Australians in 1984 (in the USA) prevented complete domination. Since 1995 the German 'Young Guns' (consisting of Torsten Fredrich, Fridolin Frost, Guenter Möller, Gerrit Lemkau, Oliver Thienhaus, and Harald Steck) have come to the fore and they won in 1996 (in New Zealand), 1998 (USA), and 2000 (Australia), before normal service was resumed and the USA won in 2002. Individual world championships began in 1989 and the first winner was Chet Snouffer of the USA. Subsequent winners are John Koehler (USA, 1991), Fridolin Frost (Germany, 1992), Chet Snouffer (USA, 1994), Rob Croll (Australia, 1996), Fridolin Frost (Germany, 1998) and Manuel Schuetz (Switzerland, 2000 and 2002).

There is also a long-distance world championship which is often held at the same venue as the conventional one.

The events that constitute the team world championships are as follows:

Team Relay: teams run head-to-head against each other. Each thrower, in turn, runs 30m to a bullseye, throws a boomerang which must travel at least 30m, catches it (or tries again!), and races back to tag the next thrower. Teams go through two rounds and the fastest time wins.

Team Endurance Relay: team members sprint to the bullseye, where they have one minute to throw a lightning-fast boomerang and make as many catches as possible. When their minute is up, throwers run a second sprint back to tag the next team-mate. All of the team's catches are added together, and the highest total wins.

Team Supercatch: as in the endurance relay, three team members throw fast catch boomerangs. This time, however, they are not throwing against the clock. Instead, the fourth team member goes to the middle of the field and launches a Maximum Time Aloft (MTA) boomerang. MTAs gain amazing height, and float back to earth very slowly, riding thermals for added time aloft. Once the MTA has been launched, the three fast catchers get to work racking up as many catches as possible while the MTA floats gracefully down, which should take at least 40 seconds. The team stops once the MTA has been caught, and the score for that round is the total number of catches. Four rounds are contested, and the best four-round total wins.

Team Australia Round: tests throwers by assigning points in three categories: catching, distance and accuracy. Two throwers from the same team throw from the bullseye at the same time, trying to achieve distances over 50m, while managing to retain complete accuracy. And, of course, you must catch to receive maximum points. Throwers are scored over five throws; team members' scores are totalled for a team score. Highest total wins.

Team Maximum Time Aloft: utilises the MTA boomerangs from Supercatch. In Team MTA, throwers have three throws to keep a boomerang up as long as possible. Each thrower's best score is added to his team-mates' best scores for a team total. Highest total wins.

Team Accuracy: requires two throwers from the same team to throw at the same time from the bullseye of a ring of concentric circles. Throwers don't try to catch their boomerangs, rather letting them land in the scoring area.

Team Trick Catch/Doubling: tests the throwers in a series of ten trick catches with one boomerang, then ten more trick catches in five throws with a doubling pair. Doublers must be thrown simultaneously, and are tuned to separate in the air, giving the thrower a few seconds between catches to get into position. Trick catches include one-handed catches, one-handed behind-the-back and under-the-leg catches, hackey catches, and even a catch with just the feet! Catches are assigned points based on difficulty, and the thrower's score is his total points for catches completed. Team scores are the total of team members' scores. Highest total wins.

Team Terror: team-mates must sprint, one at a time, to the bullseye. Each team member must complete a different skill. The first thrower must throw for accuracy: the boomerang is thrown and allowed to land untouched, coming to rest in a ring of concentric circles like a dartboard. Points are assigned to each ring, and the thrower must score 30 points before he sprints back to tag the second thrower. The second thrower must complete five trick catches. The third thrower performs five different, more difficult trick catches. The fourth thrower races to the bullseye with a fast catch to complete five throws and catches as fast as possible before returning to stop the clock.

BOULES

The game of boules or pétanque is synonymous with the Italian game of bocce.

The ancient Greeks and Romans played a game resembling pétanque. The Greeks used round stones ('spheristics') while the Romans used wooden balls covered with iron. The Greeks favoured brute strength, throwing their balls as far as possible, while the Romans preferred skill. Thus, the Romans were, in a way, the inventors of the jack or *cochonnet*.

With the barbarian invasions boules disappeared – only to reappear, more popular than ever, in the Middle Ages. During this period, boules players were called 'bouleurs'. The game became so popular that it was forbidden in the 14th century. Later, however, in the early 16th century, boules players found favour in the eyes of Pope Julius II. Seeking to turn the Holy See into an Italian power, he brought together the best bouleurs of his state to form a redoubtable company of rock throwers. They shone in play against the French, the Venetians and the Spaniards.

Boules is derived from the ancient French game *jeu provençal*. The object is to deliver a boule (or boules) from a standing position to land as near the jack (target) as possible. The boule is approximately 8cm in diameter and weighs 620-800g. The standard length of the court, normally with a sand base, is 27.5m.

The men's World Pétanque Championships (for teams of three) have been held annually since 1959. A women's world championship was introduced in 1988 and is held every two years. In 1998 the international governing body, the Confédération Mondiale Sports Boules, had over 70 member countries.

BOWLS

Bowls (from the French *boule*, meaning ball) has close links with the Italian game of bocce and indeed is a derivative of that game. The difference is that the English version of the game necessitates the ball being grounded and rolled as opposed to being flighted through the air.

The first solid evidence of the game dates back to the 13th-century. The Southampton Bowls Club has what is reputed to be the oldest bowling green in the world, founded in 1299, although the Chesterfield Bowling Club claims that its green dates from 1294. The earliest official record of the game describes bowls as 'a game of delicate skill, the object being to get bowls as close as possible to the target'.

In the early 14th century, King Edward III decided to ban the playing of bowls by his bowmen. He feared that their skills were becoming eroded through lack of archery practice as they were too occupied in playing bowls.

The sport's popularity by the 16th century was such that it is mentioned in no less than three of the plays of William Shakespeare – *Richard III*, *Love's Labour's Lost*, and *The Taming of the Shrew*. The last of these even includes a reference to bowls being played by the ladies of that era.

The most renowned player in history, however, must be Sir Francis Drake who, on 15 July 1588, was reputedly playing bowls on Plymouth Hoe and refused to leave for battle against the Spanish Armada until the game was finished.

The sport first came to America in the English version. In accord with how the game was played in Britain, American players threw the ball not on stone dust (as is done today in bocce) but on close-cropped grass; some say this is the origin of the modern lawn. It has been noted that one early American playing field was Bowling Green at the southern tip of Manhattan and that George Washington built a court at Mount Vernon in the 1780s.

The first 'official' rules of the game were written by the Scottish Bowls Association. W.G. Grace, the English cricketer, helped form the English Bowls Association, and was its first president (1903-05). He also helped organise the first international game between Scotland and England.

Today a favoured leisure pursuit of people the world over, bowls has taken its place as one of the most popular sports of all time and the game is now played in over 35 countries – the United Kingdom, Australia, New Zealand, Argentina, Thailand, India, Japan, Spain, Israel, South Africa, the USA and Holland to name but a few.

General Information

bowls: made of	Traditionally a bowl was made of lignum vitae, hence the nickname of 'wood', but nowadays synthetic materials are used. The maximum weight must be 3.5lb (1.6kg) and the maximum diameter 13cm. They are biased on one side.
English Bowling Association governing body	Founded in 1903 with Dr W.G. Grace as its first president. The International Bowling Board (IBB), founded in 1905 (now called the World Bowls Board)
jack: details	White in colour and weighs between 8oz (0.2kg) and 10oz (0.3kg)
Leonard Trophy	Team award, given to the nation with the best overall performances in the men's world championship. Winners: Australia (1966), Scotland (1972), South Africa (1976), England (1980), Scotland (1984), England (1988), Scotland (1992), Scotland (1996), Australia (2000), Scotland (2004).
mat: details	Bowl is delivered from a rubber mat 24 × 14in (61 × 36cm). One foot must be in contact at time of delivery.
rules	Played on a flat lawn or synthetic surface about 40-42yds (37-38m) long and 6-7yds (5.5-6.4m) wide. The jack is rolled to the opposite end of the rink and becomes the target bowl but must travel a minimum of 25yds (22.86m). An end is completed when all four bowls in a singles match are played and all same-coloured woods are scoring. A maximum score of four is therefore possible although rare at top level bowls. Games were played to 21 but recent innovations have included sets played to seven and, less frequently, sets played over a pre-determined number of ends.
top five men 2004/05	1. Alex Marshall (SCO) 2. David Gourlay (SCO) – now playing for Australia 3. Paul Foster (SCO) 4. Andy Thompson (ENG) 5. Robert Weale (WAL)

World Outdoor Championships

Men's singles

966	David Bryant (ENG)
972	Malwyn Evans (WAL)
976	Doug Watson (RSA)
980	David Bryant (ENG)
984	Peter Belliss (NZL)
988	David Bryant (ENG)
992	Tony Allcock (ENG)
996	Tony Allcock (ENG)
000	Jeremy Henry (NIR)
004	Steve Glasson (AUS)

Men's triples

1966	Australia
1972	USA
1976	South Africa
1980	England
1984	Ireland
1988	New Zealand
1992	Israel
1996	Scotland
2000	New Zealand
2004	Scotland

Men's pairs

966	Kelly/Palm (AUS)
972	Delgado/Liddell (HKG)
976	Watson/Moseley (RSA)
980	Sandercock/Reuben (RSA)
984	Adrain (SCO)/Arculli (USA)
1988	Brassey/Belliss (NZL)
1992	Corsie/Marshall (SCO)
1996	Henry/Allen (IRL)
2000	Sneddon/Marshall (SCO)
2004	Bestor/Roney (CAN)

Men's fours

1966	New Zealand
1972	ngland
1976	South Africa
1980	Hong Kong
1984	England
1988	Ireland
1992	Scotland
1996	England
2000	Wales
2004	Ireland

World Indoor Championships

Men's Singles

1979	David Bryant (ENG)
1980	David Bryant (ENG)
1981	David Bryant (ENG)
1982	John Watson (SCO)
1983	Bob Sutherland (SCO)
1984	Jim Baker (IRL)
1985	Terry Sullivan (WAL)
1986	Tony Allcock (ENG)
1987	Tony Allcock (ENG)
1988	Hugh Duff (SCO)
1989	Richard Corsie (SCO)
1990	John Price (WAL)
1991	Richard Corsie (SCO)
1992	Ian Schuback (AUS)
1993	Richard Corsie (SCO)
1994	Andy Thomson (ENG)
1995	Andy Thomson (ENG)
1996	David Gourlay (SCO)
1997	Hugh Duff (SCO)
1998	Paul Foster (SCO)
1999	Alex Marshall (SCO)
2000	Robert Weale (WAL)
2001	Paul Foster (SCO)
2002	Tony Allcock (ENG)
2003	Alex Marshall (SCO)
2004	Alex Marshall (SCO)

Men's Pairs

1986	Bryant/Allcock (ENG)
1987	Bryant/Allcock (ENG)
1988	Schuback/Yates (AUS)
1989	Bryant/Allcock (ENG)
1990	Bryant/Allcock (ENG)
1991	Bryant/Allcock (ENG)
1992	Bryant/Allcock (ENG)
1993	Smith/Thomson (ENG)
1994	Schuback/Curtis (AUS)
1995	Corsie/Marshall (SCO)
1996	Schuback/Kirkow (AUS)
1997	King/Allcock (ENG)
1998	Robertson/Corsie (SCO)
1999	Price/Rees (WAL)
2000	Gourlay/Marshall (SCO)
2001	Gillet/McMahon (ENG)
2002	Duff/Foster (SCO)
2003	Holt/Allcock (ENG)
2004	Henry/McClure (ENG)

B
O
W
L
S

Women's Singles

1988	M. Johnston (IRL)
1989	M. Johnston (IRL)
1990	F. Bougourd (GUE)
1991	M. Price (ENG)
1992	S. Gourlay (SCO)
1993	K. Adams (SCO)
1994	J. Woodley (SCO)
1995	J. Lindores (SCO)
1996	S. Hazell (ENG)

1997	N. Shaw (ENG)
1998	C. McAllister (SCO)
1999	C. McAllister (SCO)
2000	M. Castle (NZL)
2001	E. Brown (SCO)
2002	C. Ashby (ENG)
2003	C. Ashby (ENG)
2004	C. Ashby (ENG)

Commonwealth Games, Manchester 2002

Men's Singles

Gold: Robert Donnelly (RSA)
Silver: Jeremy Henry (NIR)
Bronze: Robert Weale (WAL) and Mike Kernaghan (NZL)

Women's Singles

Gold: Siti Zalina Ahmad (MAL)
Silver: Karen Murphy (AUS)
Bronze: Marlene Castle (NZL) and Lorna Trigwell (RSA)

Men's Pairs

Gold: George Sneddon/Alex Marshall (SCO)
Silver: Dean Morgan/Stephen Farish (ENG)
Bronze: Sean Addinall/Gerry Baker (RSA) and
  Maswadi Aziz/Said Safuan (MAL)

Women's Pairs

Gold: Joanna Edwards/Sharon Sims (NZL)
Silver: Ellen Cawker/Jill Hackland (RSA)
Bronze: Lynne Whitehead/Amy Gowshall (ENG) and
  Joanna Weale/Anwen Butten (WAL)

Men's Fours

Gold: John Ottaway/Simon Skelton/Robert
  Newman/David Holt (ENG)
Silver: Duane Abrahams/Theuns Fraser/Kevin
  Campbell/Neil Burkett (RSA)
Bronze: Ian Slade/Richard Bowen/Jason
  Greenslade/Dai Wilkins (WAL) and Michael Nutt/Noel
  Graham/Neil Booth/Jim Baker (NIR)

Women's Fours

Gold: Ellen Alexander/Shirley Page/Gill Mitchell/Carol
  Duckworth (ENG)
Silver: Shirley Fitzpatrick-Wong/Anita Nivala/Melissa
  Ranger/Andrea Weigand (CAN)
Bronze: Ann Sutherland/Pam John/Nina
  Shipperlee/Gill Miles (WAL) and Wendy
  Jensen/Patsy Jorgensen/Jan Khan, Anne Lomas
  (NZL)

Middleton Inter-County Cup

The English Inter-County Team Championship was originally played as a knockout tournament. It was known as the John Bull Cup until 1922. The round-robin format was introduced in 1959.

1911	Middlesex	1936	Gloucestershire	1962	Middlesex	1984	Somerset
1912	Kent	1937	Surrey	1963	Hampshire	1985	Northumberland
1913	Middlesex	1938	Dorset	1964	Leicestershire	1986	Wiltshire
1914	Surrey	1939	Surrey	1965	Middlesex	1987	Kent
1915-18	not held	1940-44	not held	1966	Norfolk	1988	Northumberland
1919	Bedfordshire	1945	Northumberland	1967	Hampshire	1989	Kent
1920	Surrey	1946	Yorkshire	1968	Hampshire	1990	Yorkshire
1921	Surrey	1947	Yorkshire	1969	Middlesex	1991	Kent
1922	Bedfordshire	1948	Devon	1970	Warwickshire	1992	Norfolk
1923	Surrey	1949	Devon	1971	Hampshire	1993	Kent
1924	Surrey	1950	Devon	1972	Surrey	1994	Cumbria
1925	Middlesex	1951	Northumberland	1973	Yorkshire	1995	Cumbria
1926	Northumberland	1952	Middlesex	1974	Kent	1996	Lincolnshire
1927	Surrey	1953	Yorkshire	1975	Surrey	1997	Norfolk
1928	Surrey	1954	Middlesex	1976	Lincolnshire	1998	Lancashire
1929	Kent	1955	Surrey	1977	Somerset	1999	Cumbria
1930	Northumberland	1956	Sussex	1978	Yorkshire	2000	Durham
1931	Surrey	1957	Surrey	1979	Somerset	2001	Cumbria
1932	Northamptonshire	1958	Surrey	1980	Northamptonshire	2002	Devon
1933	Surrey	1959	Devon	1981	Somerset	2003	Devon
1934	Northamptonshire	1960	Surrey	1982	Berkshire	2004	Devon
1935	Hampshire	1961	Nottinghamshire	1983	Surrey		

BOXING

Although pugilism is an age-old method of settling disputes, the modern prize ring can be traced back to 18th-century England. James Figg, an Oxfordshire-born fighter, is regarded as the first heavyweight champion in the sport's history. He helped popularise boxing by opening a training academy, where he taught the sport to countless pupils. He accepted the challenges of all-comers, retiring as undefeated champion in 1734.

A series of British fighters held the heavyweight crown after Figg. One of the more prominent pugilists was James Broughton, who fought from 1729 to 1750. He was recognised as a heavyweight champion and he too was the proprietor of a successful boxing academy. He is considered the father of boxing because he was the first to establish rules, encouraged the use of gloves and set up the bouts in an area between ropes.

Broughton's rules touched off a chain of reform in boxing that led directly to the Marquis of Queensberry rules. The Queensberry regulations, established in 1867 and the foundation of boxing as we know it today, introduced three-minute rounds and helped facilitate the transition from bare-knuckle fights to gloved contests.

Professional bouts now consist of up to 12 rounds of boxing. Championship fights are always over 12 three-minute rounds with one minute between each round. The ring must be 16 to 20ft (4.9 to 6.1m) square. Gloves must be padded and weigh 6 to 8oz (170 to 227g).

Boxing continued to thrive in England throughout the 19th-century and among the heavyweights who reigned successfully were Jem Belcher, Henry Pearce and Tom Cribb. Cribb (1781-1848) is best remembered for winning a pair of exciting fights against Tom Molineaux, a freed American slave. The bouts were chronicled by the eloquent Pierce Egan, and the rematch is believed to be the first sporting event to garner worldwide attention from the media.

At the close of the century, heavyweight champs Tom Sayer and Jem Mace rose in popularity but English champions were slowly losing their grip on the sport. By 1880, Irish-born Paddy Ryan was recognised as heavyweight champion. He lost the crown to John L. Sullivan, a first-generation American of Irish decent. It was Sullivan's fearless, brawling style and stunning knockout power that was responsible for the rise of boxing's popularity in America.

After a spectacular ten-year reign, Sullivan lost the belt to American James J. Corbett, who in turn lost it to Bob Fitzsimmons. Fitzsimmons was born in England but fought primarily out of Australia and the United States. However, when American James J. Jeffries dethroned him in 1899, it began nearly a century-long drought of British heavyweight champions.

Britain's long periods of disappointment finally ended in 1992 when Lennox Lewis was awarded the WBC heavyweight title after Riddick Bowe refused to honour an agreement to meet Lewis, who had earned the position of mandatory challenger. The success of Lewis has done much to correct American press references to British horizontal heavyweights.

General Information

amateur weight limits	Light fly – 106lb/48kg; fly – 112lb/51kg; bantam – 119lb/54kg; feather – 126lb/57kg; light – 132lb/60kg; light welter – 140lb/63.5kg; welter – 148lb/67kg; light middle – 157lb/71kg; middle – 165lbs/75kg; light heavy – 179lb/81kg; heavy – 201lb/91kg; super heavy over 201lb
British Boxing Board of Control	The BBBC was founded in 1929. It is responsible for licensing professional boxers in Britain. The organisation's rules of governing the licensing of boxers are to minimise risk to the boxers, to ensure boxers are properly fit and to ensure that the two boxers are evenly matched. The BBBC will grant licences if the boxer has had amateur boxing experience and been trained by a licensed trainer (or second), and all must enter into a standard boxer/manager agreement with a licensed manager of the board. The BBBC also has a Medical Council that ensures strict safety procedures and medical criteria that must be met when applying for a licence.
champion at five weights	Sugar Ray Leonard, Thomas Hearns
cigarette celebrations	Ricardo Mayorga of Nicaragua, former world welterweight champion, often celebrates victories by smoking a cigarette in the ring.
Father of Boxing	Jack Broughton
Father of Modern Boxing	'Gentleman Jim' Corbett
first champion	James Figg, who set up his school in 1719, is generally regarded as the first modern champion.
first East European professional	Laszlo Papp

first fight with gloves	Gentleman Jim Corbett defeated John L. Sullivan in 1892
first million-dollar gate	Jack Dempsey v Georges Carpentier in 1921
first main governing bodies	World Boxing Association (WBA), founded 1921; World Boxing Council (WBC), founded 1963; International Boxing Federation (IBF), founded 1983; World Boxing Organisation (WBO), founded 1988
heavyweight champion: longest reign	Joe Louis (1937-49)
last bareknuckle champion	John L. Sullivan
Lonsdale Belt: details	The Lonsdale Belt is the oldest championship belt in boxing, having its origins in 1909 in London. The belt is named after the Earl of Lonsdale, patron of the National Sporting Club and a keen boxing fan who supported the sport for many years. It was originally presented to the champion in each British weight division and the holder could keep the belt if it was won and then defended twice.

The belt was first won by Freddie Welsh in 1909 for winning the British lightweight title. Heavyweight Henry Cooper was the first fighter to win three Lonsdale Belts outright in his 17-year professional career.

The belt is still won today and awarded by the British Boxing Board of Control although to be kept it must be won and defended three times. Belts are crafted from gold and porcelain and are therefore very expensive to produce. Bombadier Billy Wells in 1911 was the first British heavyweight to win a Lonsdale Belt when he beat Ian Hague with a knockout in the sixth round. Wells defended the title 13 times, a record that stood for many years, before losing against Joe Beckett in February 1919. The Lonsdale Belt that he won was the original heavyweight belt and is crafted from 22-carat gold, unlike later belts. The belt is kept at the Royal Artillery Barracks in Woolwich, south-east London.

man who beat the man	In these days of multiple organisations and bodies, a judgement as to who is the champion is at best debatable. One simple way to view the process is by seeing who was the man who beat the previous champion. The list below goes back to John L. Sullivan, the first-ever recognised champion; thereafter the title is given to the man who beat him, and so on.

1885-1892	John L. Sullivan
1892-1897	James J. Corbett
1897-1899	Bob Fitzsimmons
1899-1905	James J. Jeffries (retired as holder; Hart beat Jack Root for vacant title)
1905-1906	Marvin Hart
1906-1908	Tommy Burns
1908-1915	Jack Johnson
1915-1919	Jess Willard
1919-1926	Jack Dempsey
1926-1928	Gene Tunney (retired as holder; Schmeling beat Jack Sharkey for vacant title)
1930-1932	Max Schmeling
1932-1933	Jack Sharkey
1933-1934	Primo Carnera
1934-1935	Max Baer
1935-1937	James J. Braddock
1937-1949	Joe Louis (retired as holder; Ezzard Charles beat Jersey Joe Walcott for title)
1949-1951	Ezzard Charles
1951-1952	Jersey Joe Walcott
1952-1956	Rocky Marciano (retired as holder; Patterson beat Archie Moore for title)
1956-1959	Floyd Patterson
1959-1960	Ingemar Johansson
1960-1962	Floyd Patterson
1962-1964	Charles 'Sonny' Liston
1964-1970	Cassius Clay (stripped of title in 1967; Frazier beat Jimmy Ellis for title)
1970-1973	Joe Frazier
1973-1974	George Foreman
1974-1978	Muhammad Ali
1978	Leon Spinks
1978-1979	Muhammad Ali (retired as holder; Larry Holmes won vacant title from Ken Norton)
1980-1985	Larry Holmes (became undisputed champion after beating Ali)
1985-1988	Michael Spinks
1988-1990	Mike Tyson
1990	James Douglas
1990-1992	Evander Holyfield

1992-1993	Riddick Bowe
1993-1994	Evander Holyfield
1994	Michael Moorer
1994-1997	George Foreman
1997-1998	Shannon Briggs
1998-2001	Lennox Lewis
2001	Hasim Rahman
2001	Lennox Lewis (retired in 2004)

oldest world champion Archie Moore was 49 when he retired as world light-heavyweight champion.

professional weight limits Straw/mini-fly – 105lb/48kg; light fly/junior fly – 108lb/49kg; fly – 112lb/51kg; super fly/junior bantam – 115lb/52kg; bantam – 118lb/54kg; super bantam/junior feather – 122lb/55kg; feather – 126lb/57kg; super feather/junior light – 130lb/59kg; light – 135lb/61kg; super light/junior welter – 140lb/64kg; welter – 147lb/67kg; super welter/junior middle – 154lb/70kg; middle – 160lb/73kg; super middle – 168lb/76kg; light heavy – 175lb/79kg; cruiser/junior heavy – 190lb/86kg; heavy – over 190lb

Queensberry Rules: drafted by John Graham Chambers, a member of the Amateur Athletic Club, drafted the rules in 1865 but they were not published until 1867, under the patronage of John Sholto Douglas, 8th Marquis of Queensbury.

Queensberry Rules: first fight under rules initiated by Jim Corbett beat John L. Sullivan (1892).

Jack Broughton drafted the first rules in 1743 but they were not codified until 1867 by the 8th Marquis of Queensbury.

super-world champions Lennox Lewis, former heavyweight champion of the world, suggested a system of unifying titles to produce undisputed champions. Super champions are those champions who hold the title of two or more of the main four organisations recognised by the WBA, the oldest governing body.

technical knockout A TKO occurs when a boxer fails to answer the bell for the next round and not when the referee stops the fight mid-round. This situation is listed in official records as a knockout.

undefeated heavyweight champion Rocky Marciano (49 fights). Gene Tunney was also undefeated as a heavyweight but lost to Harry Greb as a light heavyweight.

undisputed heavyweight champions John L. Sullivan (1882); James J. Corbett (1892); Bob Fitzsimmons (1897); James J. Jeffries (1899); Marvin Hart (1905); Tommy Burns (1906); Jack Johnson (1908); Jess Willard (1915); Jack Dempsey (1919); Gene Tunney (1926); Max Schmeling (1930); Jack Sharkey (1932); Primo Carnera (1933); Max Baer (1934); James J. Braddock (1935); Joe Louis (1937); Ezzard Charles (1949); Jersey Joe Walcott (1951); Rocky Marciano (1952); Floyd Patterson (1956); Ingemar Johansson (1959); Floyd Patterson (1960); Sonny Liston (1962); Cassius Clay (1964); Joe Frazier (1970); George Foreman (1973); Muhammad Ali (1974); Leon Spinks (1978); Mike Tyson (1988); Riddick Bowe (1992 but not WBO)

youngest world champion Wilfred(o) Benitez was 17 when he won the WBA light-welterweight title.

youngest world heavyweight champion Mike Tyson was 20 years old when he won the WBC crown in 1986.

Muhammad Ali: Professional Record

1960

29 Oct	Tunney Hunsaker	Louisville, KY	W6
27 Dec	Herb Siler	Miami Beach, FL	KO4

1961

17 Jan	Tony Esperti	Miami Beach, FL	KO3
7 Feb	Jim Robinson	Miami Beach, FL	KO1
21 Feb	Donnie Fleeman	Miami Beach, FL	KO7
19 Apr	Lamar Clark	Louisville, KY	KO2
26 Jun	Duke Sabedong	Las Vegas, NV	W10
22 Jul	Alonzo Johnson	Louisville, KY	W10
7 Oct	Alex Miteff	Louisville, KY	KO6
29 Nov	Willi Besmanoff	Louisville, KY	KO7

1962

19 Feb	Sonny Banks	New York, NY	KO4
28 Mar	Don Warner	Miami Beach, FL	KO4
23 Apr	George Logan	Los Angeles, CA	KO6
19 May	Billy Daniels	New York, NY	KO7
20 Jul	Alejandro Lavorante	Los Angeles, CA	KO5
15 Nov	Archie Moore	Los Angeles, CA	KO4

1963

24 Jan	Charlie Powell	Pittsburgh, PA	KO3
13 Mar	Doug Jones	New York, NY	W10
18 Jun	Henry Cooper	London, England	KO5

1964

| 25 Feb | Sonny Liston | Miami Beach, FL | TKO7 |
| | (Won world heavyweight championship) | | |

1965

25 May	Sonny Liston	Lewiston, ME	KO1
	(Retained world heavyweight championship)		
22 Nov	Floyd Patterson	Las Vegas, NV	KO12
	(Retained world heavyweight championship)		

1966

29 Mar	George Chuvalo	Toronto, Canada	W15
	(Retained world heavyweight championship)		
21 May	Henry Cooper	London, England	KO6
	(Retained world heavyweight championship)		
6 Aug	Brian London	London, England	KO3
	(Retained world heavyweight championship)		
10 Sep	Karl Mildenberger	Frankfurt, Germany	KO12
	(Retained world heavyweight championship)		
14 Nov	Cleveland Williams	Houston, TX	KO3
	(Retained world heavyweight championship)		

1967

6 Feb	Ernie Terrell	Houston, TX	W15
	(Retained world heavyweight championship)		
22 Mar	Zora Folley	New York, NY	KO7
	(Retained world heavyweight championship)		

1970

| 26 Oct | Jerry Quarry | Atlanta, GA | KO3 |
| 7 Dec | Oscar Bonavena | New York, NY | KO15 |

1971

8 Mar	Joe Frazier	New York, NY	L15
	(For world championship)		
26 Jul	Jimmy Ellis	Houston, TX	KO12
	(Won vacant NABF heavyweight championship)		
17 Nov	Buster Mathis	Houston, TX	W12
26 Dec	Jurgen Blin	Zurich, Switzerland	KO7

1972

1 Apr	Mac Foster	Tokyo, Japan	W15
1 May	George Chuvalo	Vancouver, Canada	W12
	(Retained NABF heavyweight championship)		
27 Jun	Jerry Quarry	Las Vegas, NV	KO7
	(Retained NABF heavyweight championship)		
19 Jul	Al Lewis	Dublin, Ireland	KO11
20 Sept	Floyd Patterson	New York, NY	KO7
	(Retained NABF heavyweight championship)		
21 Nov	Bob Foster	Stateline, NV	KO8
	(Retained NABF heavyweight championship)		

1973

14 Feb	Joe Bugner	Las Vegas, NV	W12
31 Mar	Ken Norton	San Diego, CA	L12
	(Lost NABF heavyweight championship)		
10 Sep	Ken Norton	Los Angeles, CA	W12
	(Regained NABF heavyweight championship)		
21 Oct	Rudi Lubbers	Jakarta, Indonesia	W12

1974

28 Jan	Joe Frazier	New York, NY	W12
	(Retained NABF heavyweight championship)		
30 Oct	George Foreman	Kinshasa, Zaire	KO8
	(Won world heavyweight championship)		

1975

24 Mar	Chuck Wepner	Cleveland, OH	KO15
	(Retained world heavyweight championship)		
16 May	Ron Lyle	Las Vegas, NV	KO11
	(Retained world heavyweight championship)		
30 Jun	Joe Bugner	Kuala Lumpur, Malaysia	W15
	(Retained world heavyweight championship)		

30 Sep	Joe Frazier (Retained world heavyweight championship)	Manila, Philippines	KO14

1976

20 Feb	Jean Pierre Coopman (Retained world heavyweight championship)	San Juan, PR	KO5
30 Apr	Jimmy Young (Retained world heavyweight championship)	Landover, MD	W15
24 May	Richard Dunn (Retained world heavyweight championship)	Munich, Germany	KO5
25 Jun	Antonio Inoki (above was boxer–wrestler exhibition)	Tokyo, Japan	Exh D15
28 Sep	Ken Norton (Retained world heavyweight championship)	New York, NY	W15

1977

16 May	Alfredo Evangelista (Retained world heavyweight championship)	Landover, MD	W15
29 Sep	Earnie Shavers (Retained world heavyweight championship)	New York, NY	W15

1978

15 Feb	Leon Spinks (Lost world heavyweight championship)	Las Vegas, NV	L15
15 Sep	Leon Spinks (Won world heavyweight championship)	New Orleans, LA	W15

1980

2 Oct	Larry Holmes (For world heavyweight championship)	Las Vegas, NV	KO by 11

1981

11 Dec	Trevor Berbick	Nassau, Bahamas	L10

World Champions

(as at 31 August 2004)

	WBA	WBC	IBF	WBO
Heavyweights	John Ruiz (USA)	Vitali Klitschko (UKR)	Chris Byrd (USA)	Lamon Brewster (USA)
Cruiserweights	Jean Marc Mormeck (FRA)	Wayne Braithwaite (GUY)	Kelvin Davis (USA)	Johnny Nelson (GBR)
Light heavyweights	Fabrice Tiozzo (FRA)	Antonio Tarver (USA)	Glencoffe Johnson (USA)	Zsolt Erdei (HUN)
Super middleweights	Manny Siaca (PUR)	Cristian Sanavia (ITA)	Vacant	Joe Calzaghe (GBR)
Middleweights	Maselino Masoe (NZL)	Bernard Hopkins (USA)	Bernard Hopkins (USA)	Oscar de la Hoya (USA)
Super welterweights	Travis Simms (USA)	Ronald Wright (USA)	Verno Phillips (USA)	Daniel Santos (PUR)
Welterweights	Jose Rivera (USA)	Cory Spinks (USA)	Cory Spinks (USA)	Antonio Margarito (MEX)
Super lightweights	Vivian Harris (USA)	Kostya Tszyu (AUS)	Kostya Tszyu (AUS)	Zab Judah (USA)
Lightweights	Juan Diaz (USA)	José Luis Castillo (MEX)	Julio Diaz (MEX)	Diego Corrales (USA)
Super featherweights	Yodsanan Nanthachai (THA)	Erik Morales (MEX)	Erik Morales (MEX)	Mike Anchondo (USA)
Featherweights	Juan Manuel Marquez (MEX)	Injin Chi (KOR)	Juan Manuel Marquez (MEX)	Scott Harrison (GBR)
Light featherweights	Mahyar Monshipour (FRA)	Oscar Larios (MEX)	Israel Vazquez (MEX)	Joan Guzman (DOM)
Bantamweights	Johnny Bredahl (DEN)	Veeraphol Sahaprom (THA)	Rafael Marquez (MEX)	Ratanachai Vorapin (THA)
Light bantamweights	Alexander Muñoz (VEN)	Masamori Tokuyama (PRK)	Luis Perez (NIC)	Mark Johnson (USA)
Flyweights	Lorenzo Parra (VEN)	Pongsaklek Wonjongkam (THA)	Irene Pacheco (COL)	Omar Narvaez (ARG)
Light flyweights	Beibis Mendoza (COL)	Jorge Arce (MEX)	Jose Victor Burgos (MEX)	Nelson Dieppa (PUR)
Strawweights	Yutaka Niida (JPN)	Eagle Akakura (JPN)	Daniel Reyes (COL)	Ivan Calderon (PUR)

Note: There are several other boxing bodies who put forward fighters as world champions but they are not considered true title-holders inasmuch as none of them are ranked number one in official world lists.

Some of the weight categories are given alternative names by the governing bodies. Super welter is also called junior middle or light middle. Super light is also called junior welter or light welter. Super feather is also called junior light. Light feather is also called super bantam or junior feather. Light bantam is also called junior bantam or super fly. Light fly is also called junior fly.

Biographies

Ali, Laila   Born 30 December 1977. The youngest daughter of Muhammad Ali and Veronica Porsche Anderson. The 1.78m Ali made her ring debut on 8 October 1999 at the Turning Stone Casino Convention Center on the Oneida Indian Nation, in Verona, New York. She beat April Fowler (a waitress) by KO. As at 2003 she is unbeaten in 16 professional fights and has won several noble super-middleweight titles. Ali knocked out her great rival Christy Martin (24 August 2003, Biloxi, Mississippi) to become undisputed queen of the ring. Her nickname is 'She Bee-Stinging Ali'.

Ali, Muhammad   Born Cassius Marcellus Clay, Louisville, Kentucky, 17 January 1942. Started boxing at the age of 12 and turned pro in 1960 after winning Olympic light-heavyweight gold in Rome. After 18 straight victories, Clay fought Henry Cooper. Clay was knocked down at the end of the fourth round and, had his glove not mysteriously split which lengthened the break between rounds, could have lost to Cooper. As it was he stopped Cooper in the next round. He now had a chance at a world title, taking on the ferocious Sonny Liston in 1964. Liston was regarded as such a hot favourite that many bookies refused to take bets on him. But Clay won and ranted afterwards that he 'shook the world'. In the same year Clay changed his name to reflect his new-found belief in Islam. He rejected his 'slave name' and became Muhammad Ali (initially he dubbed himself Muhammud X). The return match against Liston the following year was just as controversial as the first. Liston lost to a seemingly innocuous punch, and was counted out by referee Jersey Joe Walcott. Ali retained the title until it was stripped from him in 1967 because of his refusal to fight in the Vietnam War.

Ali retired officially in 1970 but returned to the ring in 1971 to fight Joe Frazier. Frazier, who had won the vacant title, beat Ali by a close but unanimous decision and inflicted his first-ever defeat. Two years later in a fight with Ken Norton Ali lost again, this time with a broken jaw, although Ali avenged this defeat and then his other loss by beating Frazier on points.

Two of his most memorable fights were still, however, to come. He beat George Foreman in the 'Rumble in the Jungle' in 1974 with an eight-round KO. In the 'Thrilla in Manila' (1975) he overcame Frazier by a stoppage in 14 rounds. In 1978 he lost the title to Leon Spinks but then regained it, beating the same boxer to become the first man to be undisputed heavyweight champion three times. He then retired once more before trying to come back to win the title a fourth time. But age had taken its toll and he lost convincingly to Larry Holmes in 1980. His final fight was against Trevor Berbick the following year. In 61 fights Ali lost only five times.

Ali fought several exhibition matches, the most famous being against a Japanese martial artist, Inoki, which turned into a farcical 15-round holding-on match. Apart from the two ill-advised bouts at the end of his career and a dubious defeat which set up a chance to win the title for the third time, his only losses were against ring greats Frazier and Norton. Self-styled as 'the greatest' and regarded as such by many experts, Ali is a boxing icon. His record breaking, showmanship and pioneering of black rights – not forgetting his inimitable poetry – have made him the most recognisable name ever in sports history.

Antuofermo, Vito   Born Bari, Italy, 1953. Turned pro in 1971, fighting mostly out of New York. In 1976 he won the European light-middleweight title from Eckhard Dagge. In the same year he lost the title to Maurice Hope. In 1979 he won the world middleweight title from Hugo Corro and fought well enough later that same year to defend it successfully against Marvin Hagler. The following year he once again lost to an English boxer, when Alan Minter deprived him of the title over 15 rounds in Las Vegas. Three months later in London, Minter improved on his performance, stopping Antuofermo in nine rounds. Vito fought once more for the title in 1981 when he took on Hagler again, although less than two years since their last meeting the result was very different with a rampant Hagler stopping Antuofermo in four rounds. Antuofermo retired in 1985. Since retiring he has turned to acting and in 1990 he landed a small speaking role in *The Godfather III*.

Arce, Jorge   Born Mexico, 1979. Turned pro in 1996, fighting mostly out of Tijuana, Mexico. In 1998 he beat Juan Domingo Cordoba to win the WBO light-flyweight title, losing this six months later to Michael Carbajal. In 2002 with a victory over Yo-Sam Choi he gained the WBC light-flyweight crown.

Arguello, Alexis   Born Managua, Nicaragua, 1952. Turned professional at the age of 16 and after 38 bouts (Arguello lost his first fight to Cachorro Amaya by a first-round knockout) earned a shot at the WBA featherweight title against Ernesto Marcel in 1974. This he lost on points after 15 rounds. Later that year he returned to take on Ruben Olivares and this time he won. He defended his title four times before giving it up to become a light flyweight. In 1978 he stopped Alberto Escalera, who was making his 11th defence at this weight. He won a third title beating Jim Watt at lightweight in 1981. Having now won at three different weights he attempted to move up to light welterweight and become the first man to win at four weights. He had two great fights with Aaron Pryor (the first of which was suspicious enough for the WBA to grant a rematch) but was not able to make the leap up the scale and eventually retired in 1983. After boxing, Arguello joined the Sandinista rebels in his native land before attempting a few unsuccessful comeback bouts, his last being against Scott Walker in 1995.

Arguello was WBA featherweight champion 1974-76, WBC super-featherweight champion 1978-80, WBC lightweight champion 1981-82 and undisputed lightweight champion 1982-83. He is one of the ring's greatest stars, with 22 world title bouts and 19 wins to his credit.

Armstrong, Henry   Born Henry Jackson jnr, Columbus, Missouri, 1912. Turned pro in 1931 and in his career fought 180 fights, 100 of which he won by KO. He was the first (and still the only) boxer to hold three world titles simultaneously, a feat now unlikely to be equalled given the sparsity of undisputed champions. He was undisputed featherweight champion 1937-38, welterweight champion 1938-40 and lightweight champion 1938-39. Armstrong, known as 'Homicide Hank', first fought in the ring under the name of 'Melody Jackson'. Also known as 'Perpetual Motion,' he dominated feather-, welter- and lightweight opponents with his 'blackout' punch, relentless attack and incredible stamina. For his first title he beat Petey Sarron in 1937; the following year lightweight Lou Ambers and welterweight Barney Ross became his victims. After 150 victories in 14 years, Armstrong retired in 1945. Returning to St Louis in 1972, he became a minister, helped run the Herbert Hoover Boys' Club and trained young boxers. He died aged 75 in 1988.

aer, Max Born Omaha, Nebraska, 11 February 1909. An American of German descent, 'The Livermore Larruper' became undisputed heavyweight champion in 1934 when, giving away 50lb in the process, he easily beat Primo Carnera, knocking him down 11 times. His approach to boxing was lax and in his defence against James J. Braddock in 1935 he was outpointed and lost the title. He also lost in four rounds to a young Joe Louis four months later (his brother Buddy twice fought Louis for the title). After a career in boxing of 72 fights and 52 knockouts he moved into films, appearing in such classics as *The Prize Fighter and the Lady* (also with Primo Carnera). His son, Max Baer jnr, inherited this talent, appearing most famously as Jethro in *The Beverly Hillbillies*. He died 21 November 1959, and was inducted into the International Boxing Hall of Fame in 1995.

arkley, Iran Born New York, 1960. Legend has it that he was taught to box by his sister, Yvonne. He turned pro in 1982. In Las Vegas in 1988 he won the WBC middleweight championship beating Thomas Hearns. He followed up this victory with three straight losses to Roberto Duran, Michael Nunn and Nigel Benn. In 1992 he was back to winning ways gaining the IBF super-middleweight title from Darrin Van Horn. Another win over Thomas Hearns gave him the WBA light-heavyweight title and he had now won titles at three different weights. He lost the IBF super-middleweight title to James 'Lights Out' Toney in 1993. Not renowned as a great technical boxer, 'The Blade' certainly has guts and is unique in being the only boxer to beat Thomas Hearns twice.

Barrera, Marco Antonio Born Mexico City, 1974. Turning pro in 1989 aged only 15, he was unbeaten in his first 34 contests. In 1995 he had a shot at the WBO light-featherweight title. He won, beating Daniel Jimenez in 12 rounds. Nine defences and nine victories later, Barrera was knocked out for the first time in his career, the defeat being inflicted by Junior Jones. Five months later in the rematch Jones won again, this time in 12 rounds.

In 1998 Barrera regained the WBO title only, it seemed, to lose it to Erik Morales in 2000. However, even though Morales won the fight the WBO reinstated Barrera as champion after questioning the decision. In the same year Barrera moved up to super bantamweight and won the WBO title from Jose Luis Valbuena. In 2001, at the Las Vegas MGM Grand, Barrera inflicted the first-ever defeat on Prince Naseem to deprive him of the WBO super-featherweight title. Known as the 'Baby Face Assassin', Barrera is a tough, hard-hitting fighter who has only ever lost four times. But his defeat by Manny Pacquiao in November 2003 prompted his trainer, Rudy Perez, to ask him to hang up his gloves.

Basilio, Carmen Born New York, 1927. Turned pro in 1948. After five years of mixed results he fought Kid Gavilan for the world welterweight title, losing in 15 rounds. Two years later he managed a 12-round KO of Tony DeMarco to attain the title. After beating DeMarco in the rematch he then had three fights with Johnny Saxton. He lost the first on a decision in

1956, but won the next two to regain and retain the title. In 1957 Basilio beat an all-time great when he overcame Sugar Ray Robinson in 15 rounds to become undisputed middleweight champion of the world. A loss to Robinson the following year saw Basilio's career begin to flounder. In 1961, at the age of 34, he lost in 10 rounds to Paul Pender after which he retired. Basilio, undisputed welterweight champion 1955-56 and 1956-57, and undisputed middleweight champion 1957-58, is honoured with a statue in his home town of Canastota, New York.

Belcher, Jim Born Bristol, 1781. Bare-knuckle champion of England from around 1800 when he beat Andrew Gamble, he lost an eye in 1803 which caused him to retire, although he did come back to fight Tom Cribb twice. Retired again, he took over the running of an inn and died in 1811 at the age of 30.

Benitez, Wilfredo Born New York, 1958. Turned pro at the age of 15 and became the youngest-ever world champion when he won the WBA light-welterweight title in 1976, aged 17 years 173 days, beating Antonio 'Kid Pambele' Cervantes. He moved up in weight to beat Carlos Palomino for the WBC welterweight championship on 14 January 1979 and defended the title once before losing it to 'Sugar' Ray Leonard in the last round the same year. He won his third world championship by beating Maurice Hope for the WBC light-middleweight title in 1981, losing the following year to Thomas Hearns. At the time he was only the seventh man in boxing history to win titles in three different weight classes. After losing to Hearns he fought less frequently and suffered six more defeats in 15 fights before hanging up his gloves in 1990. Benitez, who claimed rarely to train for his fights, was an expert in the defensive art of boxing. As undisputed light-welterweight champion 1976-79 and undisputed welterweight champion in 1979 he gained the nicknames of 'The Radar' and 'The Bible of Boxing'. He is now in care suffering from brain damage.

Benn, Nigel Born 22 January 1964. Nigel Benn was one of a group of excellent English middleweight boxers who battled it out during the 1980s and 1990s. He knocked out every one of his first 22 opponents, half of them before the end of the first round. His particular rivals were Chris Eubank, Michael Watson and Herol Graham, Watson being the first and Eubank the second to beat him professionally. WBC super-middleweight champion in 1992, beating Mauro Galvano of Italy, he lost this title four years later to Thulane 'Sugar Boy' Malinga. Benn's nickname was 'The Dark Destroyer'.

Benvenuti, Nino Born Trieste, Italy, 1938. He won the Olympic welterweight championship at Rome in 1960 and turned pro a year later. Three years later he beat Tomaso Truppi to become Italian middleweight champion. His first world title came in 1965 when he beat fellow Italian Sandro Mazzinghi at light middleweight. He held the title only a year, losing it to Ki-Soo Kim, and moved up to middleweight. In 1967 he defeated Emile Griffith over 15 rounds; five months later he lost the rematch. Six months afterwards he regained the same title from Griffith. He finally succumbed to Carlos Monzon in 1970 and after a rematch he retired from the fight game. Benvenuti won 82 of his 90 bouts and was a classical defensive boxer.

Berbick, Trevor Born Port Anthony, Jamaica, 1955. At 21 he represented Jamaica the 1976 Olympics in Montreal. His lack of experience cost him (he had only 11 fights to that date) and he lost to the eventual silver medallist, Mercilius Simon (the winner that year was the great Cuban amateur Teofilo Stevenson). He turned pro in 1976. Five years later he became one of only five men to beat Muhammad Ali, in Ali's last fight. Berbick won in 10 rounds. In 1986 he beat Pinklon Thomas to become WBC heavyweight world champion. He held the title for less than a year, losing it to Mike Tyson in 1986. In 1992 Berbick was imprisoned for rape. On his release he made a comeback with a few minor fights. In 1997 he was deported from the USA. Today Berbick lives in Montreal and trains young fighters.

Berg, Jack Born Judah Bergman, Whitechapel, London, 28 June 1909. 'Kid' Berg left England for America in 1928 and there, two years later, beat Mushy Callahan for the light-welterweight title. Shortly afterwards he inflicted the first-ever loss on 'Kid' Chocolate. Berg, undisputed light-welterweight champion 1930-33, retired in 1945. He had fought 192 bouts in 21 years, losing only eight bouts. He was known as 'The Whitechapel Whirlwind'. He died 22 April 1991.

Bowe, Riddick Born New York, 1967. He had a fine amateur career and lost the super-heavyweight final at the 1988 Seoul Olympics to Lennox Lewis (then of Canada). He turned pro the following year and in November 1992 won a unanimous decision over Evander Holyfield to become WBC, WBA, and IBF heavyweight champion. Just under one year later he lost on a split decision to Holyfield, his first-ever defeat. In 1995 he beat Herbie Hide to win the WBO heavyweight title. The same year he fought the last of his fights against Holyfield and despite an interruption by a paraglider won in eight rounds. Bowe retired in 1997 with a record of 42 fights, 40 wins (32 KOs), one draw and one loss. Nicknamed 'Big Daddy', he was never knocked out in his career.

Braddock, James J. Born James Walter Braddock (the 'J' is erroneous), New York City, 7 June 1906. Started as a welterweight and fought his way up to heavy. His first official fight in a career of over 100 was under the name of Jimmy Ryan in 1923. He was an outstanding amateur middleweight whose fragile hands derailed his career. Since he was tough (he weighed 17lb (7.7kg) at birth) and could take a punch, he continued to fight with severely damaged hands, until, ultimately, he was banned in some jurisdictions. In 1929 he fought and lost to Tommy Loughran for the light-heavyweight championship. Over the next five years he won and lost in seemingly equal measure. In 1934 he fought and defeated Corn Griffin, to put him on track for a shot at the title. On 13 June 1935, in Long Island City, NY, Braddock, as a 10 to 1 underdog, won the heavyweight championship of the world from Max Baer. As a result of his fight with Baer in 1934 Damon Runyon dubbed him 'The Cinderella Man'.

After two years of inactivity Braddock lost his heavyweight title in an eight-round KO to 'The Brown Bomber', Joe Louis. He retired after a final win over Tommy Farr in 1938. He died 29 November 1974.

Briggs, Shannon Born Brooklyn, 1971. He won a silver medal at the Pan American Games in 1991, losing to the superstar of amateur boxing, Felix Savon, in a first-round knockout. He turned pro in 1992 and amassed a large number of wins in his first five years before taking on boxing legend George Foreman. Foreman was making his comeback and lost a contentious fight to Briggs to make 'The Cannon' world heavyweight champion. He lost this title four months later in 1998 to Lennox Lewis.

Briggs has fought sporadically since and against no one of great merit. His last fight was in March 2003 where he scored a first-round KO of Marvin Hill.

Britton, Jack Born William Breslin, New York, 1885. He became welterweight champion in 1915 beating Mike Glover. Almost immediately he relinquished the title to Ted 'Kid' Lewis. Lewis and Britton were almost a double act, sharing the title for the next seven years and fighting each other 20 times. Undisputed welterweight champion 1916-17 and 1919-22. The first mouthpiece was used in his 1915 bout with Lewis. Britton, who fought 299 contests over 22 years, retired to become a boxing instructor and mentor to young athletes in New York City. He died in 1962 aged 76.

Broughton, Jack Born Cirencester, Glos., 1704. He is known as the 'father of boxing'. He was noticed by James Figg and became his protégé, becoming British champion in 1738 with a win over George Taylor. He lost his title in 1750 to Jack Slat. Broughton is most famous as the author of the rules of boxing, published in 1743, that preceded the Queensberry Rules (although the London Prize Ring Rules were drafted in between). He was spurred on to write them by the death of one of his challengers, George Stevenson. Jack was wealthy in his retirement. A Yeoman of the Guard, he is honoured with a stone in Westminster Abbey. He died in 1789.

Brown, Al Born Panama, 1902. Turned pro in 1922. In 1929, Brown challenged Vidal Gregorio for the vacant world bantamweight title and won. He was an exceptionally tall bantamweight, standing 1.8m. Fighting mostly in Europe and Canada he is remembered for his long reach (193cm) and his ability to speak seven languages. Known as 'Panama Al', he died penniless in New York in 1951 aged just 48, after a bout of tuberculosis.

Bruno, Frank Born Hammersmith, London, 16 November 1961. He turned professional in 1982 and was European heavyweight champion by 1985. The popular British heavyweight fought Mike Tyson, Tim Witherspoon (WBA in 1986) and James 'Bonecrusher' Smith for the heavyweight championship before eventually defeating Oliver McCall to win the WBC title in 1995. One year later he lost the crown to a rejuvenated Mike Tyson. His 1989 match against Tyson in Las Vegas was a high point in British boxing although Bruno lost quite easily in five rounds. After a successful career Frank entered the wider world of entertainment and his good-natured banter with boxing commentator Harry Carpenter brought him public acclaim and affection. By the summer of 2003 he was considering a professional comeback but in September of that year he hit the headlines as he was suffering from severe depression. By November, however, he was well enough to give television interviews. Interestingly, Frank was never British heavyweight champion.

Buchanan, Ken Born Edinburgh, 1945. Turning pro in 1965, he won his first 23 fights before beating Maurice Cullen to become British lightweight champion in 1968. He then won his next nine fights before finally losing to Miguel Velasquez in a European lightweight title fight. That same year, 1970, he beat Ismail Laguna to become world lightweight champion. He lost his WBC belt for failing to fight Pedro Carrasco in 1971 and surrendered his other titles to Roberto Duran the following year. Buchanan claimed he was kneed in the groin; referee Johnny LoBianco, however, did not see the infringement and the fight was stopped before the

14th round could begin. He regained the British title in 1973, beating Jim Watt, and added the European title the following year, defeating Antonio Puddu. His last world title fight was against Ishimatsu Suzuki where he lost in 15 rounds. Semi-retired, he returned to fight the occasional bout but after four consecutive losses in 1981 and 1982 retired from the game completely.

Bugner, Joe   Born Hungary, 13 March 1950. He turned pro in 1967 and won the British, European and Commonwealth heavyweight titles from Henry Cooper in 1971 by a controversial decision. Bugner's career was always one of playing second fiddle to Cooper, but he became Commonwealth heavyweight champion again in 1976, beating Richard Dunn. Although not highly regarded in his own country, Bugner found greater acceptance in Australia, eventually emigrating there and becoming a citizen. He remains a boxer who managed to go the distance twice with the great Muhammad Ali and once with Joe Frazier. In 1998, at the age of 48, he made a comeback to boxing and defeated former WBA champ Bonecrusher Smith.

Burns, Tommy   Born Noah Brusso, Ontario, 1881. Burns originally boxed under the name of Brusson and in 1902 he fought Jim Corbett in an exhibition match. His first loss came to the very experienced Mike Schreck. Schreck, a Dutchman, was the first southpaw Burns ever fought. A year later, in 1904, Burns (still fighting as Brusso) beat Ben O'Grady in three rounds in Detroit. O'Grady was seriously injured during this fight, and as a result Brusso adopted the name Burns and left town. He took the heavyweight title in 1906 from Marvin Hart (who had won it when Jim Jeffries retired) in 20 rounds. Over the next two years he managed 11 defences. In 1907 he fought and beat Philadelphia Jack O'Brien. Since both men were under the light-heavyweight limit, he could have claimed this title too but chose not to. In 1908, in Sydney, he lost to Jack Johnson, the first-ever black heavyweight champion of the world. Before his last fight in 1920 he fought only eight bouts in 13 years. Burns, known as 'The Little Giant of Hanover' (he was only 1.70m), died in 1955 aged 73.

Callahan, Mushy   Born Vincent Morris Scheer, New York, 1905. He turned pro in 1923 and fought mostly out of California. In 1926 he fought Pinkey Mitchell for the light-welterweight championship of the world, beating Mitchell in 10 rounds. At his fourth defence in 1930 he lost to Jack 'Kid' Berg after 10 rounds. Callahan fought three more fights, lost the last and retired. Callahan was undisputed light-welterweight champion 1926-30. He died in 1986 aged 80.

Calzaghe, Joe   Born Hammersmith, London, 23 February 1973. Calzaghe is based in Newbridge, Wales, and is known as 'The Pride of Wales'. He turned pro in 1993 after a glittering amateur career which featured three consecutive ABA titles. His first nine contests lasted no longer than the second round, making a grand total of just 11 rounds. In 1997 Calzaghe took on the previously unbeaten Chris Eubank. After 12 rounds Calzaghe was WBO super-middleweight champion of the world. In his second defence he beat Juan Carlos Gimenez, a fighter who had gone the distance with Benn and Eubank. A fast and hard-hitting boxer, not for nothing is Calzaghe nicknamed 'The Terminator'. He is also good at avoiding punches. He was knocked down for the first time in his career in his 36th fight, against Byron Mitchell, but won in the same round. In 2003

he and his manager Frank Warren began making noises about fights with Bernard Hopkins and Roy Jones Jr.

Camacho, Hector   Born Bayamon, Puerto Rico, 24 May 1962. WBC super-featherweight champion 1983-84, WBC lightweight champion 1985-86, and WBO light-welterweight champion in 1989, beating Ray Mancini. He was nicknamed, rather unsurprisingly, 'The Macho Man'.

Canzoneri, Tony   Born Louisiana, 1908. He turned pro in 1925 aged 17. Two years later he fought for the world bantamweight title, first drawing with, then losing to, Bud Taylor. In the same year he beat Johnny Dundee to become American featherweight champion. In 1928 a win over Benny Bass gave him the world title. He lost the title later in the year to Andre Routis in 15 rounds. In 1929 he tried but failed to lift the lightweight world title, losing in 15 rounds to Sammy Mandell before winning the crown in 1930 with a first-round KO of Al Singer. The next year saw him add the light-welterweight title to his list, his third title at different weights. Barney Ross deprived him of the lightweight and light-welterweight titles in 1933. He now concentrated on the lightweight title. Over the next three years he fought Lou Ambers three times, each bout a title match. All three fights went the distance, with Canzoneri winning the first and losing the next two. Canzoneri, undisputed featherweight champion 1928, lightweight champion 1930-33 and 1935-36, and light-welterweight champion 1931-32 and 1933, died in 1959 aged 51.

Carnera, Primo   Born Sequals, nr Venice, Italy, 26 October 1906. Carnera became the first Italian world heavyweight champion when he beat Jack Sharkey to become undisputed champion in 1933. 'The Ambling Alp' lost a year later to Max Baer after only two defences. During the fight Carnera was knocked down 13 times. Carnera stood nearly 6ft 6ins (1.98m) tall and weighed a massive 266lb (120.6kg). He is by far the heaviest world champion boxer ever (indeed it is said that he weighed 22lb (10kg) at birth!). In the late 1930s and early 1940s Carnera took a break from boxing and appeared in numerous films. He made a comeback in 1945 but after two defeats moved into wrestling. Here he fought both Max Baer and Larry Gaines. In 1956 the film *The Harder They Fall* was released, based on the Bud Schulberg novel. Carnera sued over the obvious similarities to his life, but lost. A year later, in Australia at the age of 51, he beat a wrestler called King Kong to claim the heavyweight wrestling crown. Carnera died in his home town on 29 June 1967.

Carpentier, Georges   Born Lens, France, 12 January 1894. Georges 'Orchid Man' Carpentier is perhaps the most famous French boxer ever. He only took up English boxing after first becoming proficient in savate (French kickboxing). He turned pro at the age of 14, and before his 16th birthday he was French lightweight champion. At 18 he was French and European welterweight champion and then became European middleweight champion. In 1912 he fought twice for the world middleweight title, losing to both Frank Klaus and Billy Papke and both times on a foul. The next year, at the age of 19 he became European heavyweight champion with a victory over 'Bombardier' Billy Wells. Unable to compete with the real heavyweight champion of the time, Jack Johnson, Carpentier won the 'white heavyweight championship of the world' by beating Ed 'Gunboat' Smith, again on a foul. During World War I Carpentier served in the air force and won the Croix de Guerre for bravery.

He became undisputed light-heavyweight champion after the war, beating 'Battling' Levinsky, who had held the title for the previous four years. The following year, 1921, he took on Jack Dempsey in the first 'million-dollar gate' fight but lost easily in four rounds. Carpentier lost his light-heavyweight title to Battling Siki in 1922. He fought nine more times, notably against Gene Tunney and Tommy Loughran (both losses) before retiring to open a bar in Paris. Carpentier started as a flyweight and ended as a heavyweight, and during this transformation he fought at every existing weight. Carpentier, undisputed light-heavyweight champion 1920-22, died on 28 October 1975.

Carter, Rubin   Born Clifton, New Jersey, 6 May 1937. In 1961 he fought his first pro fight and in 1964 took on Joey Giardello for the middleweight title. He lost in 15 rounds. His career was cut short prematurely when in 1967 he was jailed for his part in an incident in a bar in which three people were killed. Rubin Carter's story is best known from the recent film *Hurricane* where he is portrayed by Denzel Washington.

Cerdan, Marcel   Born Marcellin Cerdan, Sidi Bel-Abbes, Algeria, 22 July 1916. Cerdan is second only to Georges Carpentier as France's greatest boxing export but is probably remembered as much for a well-publicised affair with Edith Piaf as for his fighting. Cerdan turned pro in 1934 and in a career of 110 fights lost only four times. At the age of 32 he took on Tony Zale for the world middleweight crown. Despite an injury to his hand in the third round Cerdan managed to win. He followed this one-handed victory with a defence against Jake La Motta; this time he pulled a muscle in the third round which led to his retirement in the tenth. Cerdan, undisputed middleweight champion 1948-49, died in a plane crash 27 October 1949 on his way to the return fight.

Charles, Ezzard   Born Lawrenceville, Georgia, 7 July 1921. He turned pro in 1940 after 42 unbeaten amateur fights. Despite his place of birth he is remembered as the 'Cincinnati Flash' or 'Cincinnati Cobra'. He was undisputed heavyweight champion 1949-51. He stands unique as the only man to beat Joe Louis in a world title fight and one of only three men in total. His pro career began at light heavyweight. He won most of his early fights but suffered a loss in 1941 against Ken Overlin over 10 rounds. In 1948 he fought Sam Baroudi and scored a KO in the tenth; Baroudi later died from the injuries sustained. A year later, after Joe Louis's retirement, he fought for the vacant heavyweight title against Jersey Joe Walcott. He won in 15 rounds and then defended the title eight times, including a rematch against Walcott and a defeat of the returning Joe Louis, before eventually losing a third bout with Walcott. He later challenged Walcott (again) and Rocky Marciano twice for the world title, all unsuccessfully. Charles died 28 May 1975 aged 54.

Charnley, Dave   Born Dartford, Kent, 10 October 1935. European, Commonwealth and British lightweight champion 1957-65. He twice made unsuccessful world title challenges against Joe 'Old Bones' Brown, being stopped on a cut eye in Houston, Texas in 1959, and narrowly outpointed over 15 rounds at Earls Court in 1961. Stocky southpaw Dave, undoubtedly one of Britain's all-time great lightweight champions, stopped the veteran American in six rounds in a non-title fight in Manchester on 25 February 1963. He was nicknamed 'The Dartford Destroyer'.

Chocolate, Kid   Born Sergio Eligio Sardinas Montalvo, Cerro, Havana, Cuba, 6 January 1910. After four years as a professional 'The Cuban Bon Bon' lost to Bat Battalino for the featherweight title. He won his junior lightweight title by beating Benny Bass in 1931, but in the same year failed in his bid for the lightweight title, losing to Tony Canzoneri. A skilful, fast-moving boxer but already handicapped by syphilis, 'Kid Chocolate' lost his title in 1933 to Frankie Klick, being knocked out in seven rounds. Although he fought on until 1938 he never again challenged for a world title. Undisputed junior lightweight champion in 1931-33, and featherweight champion in 1932-33, he died in Cuba, 8 August 1988.

Clay, Cassius   See Muhammad Ali.

Cockell, Don   Born Battersea, London, 22 September 1928. A blacksmith by trade, Cockell began boxing in 1946. He beat an ageing Tommy Farr en route to winning the British and Commonwealth crowns and later defeated American contender Roland LaStarza. He challenged heavyweight champ Rocky Marciano on 16 May 1955 at Kezar Stadium in San Francisco. Marciano swarmed over his foe but the British contender managed to withstand the attack until the eighth round. Cockell was dropped in the eighth and twice in the ninth but arose from each knockdown. However, the referee had seen enough and stopped the contest after the third knockdown.

Collins, Steve   Born 1964. 'The Celtic Warrior' became WBO middleweight champion in 1990, beating Chris Pyatt. In the same year he lost a WBA middleweight fight to Mike McCallum. In 1995 he became the first man to beat Chris Eubank professionally, also beating him in the rematch. The following year he defeated Nigel Benn twice to establish himself as the top European middleweight.

Conn, Billy   Born Pittsburgh, Pennsylvania, 1917. Conn started as a professional in 1934, missing out amateur bouts. Two years after turning pro he beat four former champions in the same year (Babe Risko, Vince Dundee, Teddy Yarosz and Young Corbett III). He won the light-heavyweight title from Melio Bettina in the summer of 1939 and defended this three times before moving up to heavyweight. Undisputed light-heavyweight champion 1939-40, his greatest moment duly arrived in 1941 when, having given up the light-heavyweight title, he fought Joe Louis for the heavyweight crown. By all accounts Conn was well ahead in the 13th round when he fell into the trap of trading punches with the heavier and far more powerful Louis. The result was a win for Louis. Conn was scheduled to fight Louis again the following year but his stint in the army intervened. When he returned from active duty in 1946 he took on Louis once more for the title, but lost in eight rounds. His final fight was his third bout with Louis an exhibition match in Chicago. Conn died in 1993.

Conteh, John   Born Liverpool, 27 May 1951. Conteh was WBC light-heavyweight champion 1974-77. He was amateur Commonwealth middleweight champion in 1970 and light-heavyweight ABA champion in 1971 before a disappointing European amateur championship made him decide to turn professional. His shrewd trainer, George Francis, initially campaigned him as a heavyweight and indeed he stopped 15 of his first 18 opponents, but at 182lb he was too light, so after two years he decided to drop down a division to light-heavyweight. His first fight at this weight was for the European light-heavyweight title, which he won from German Rudiger Schmidtge. In his next fight he became British light-heavyweight champion in beating Chris Finnegan. In 1974 Bob Foster was stripped of his title for not defending against Conteh, leaving Conteh to fight, and beat, Argentine Jorge Ahumada for the vacant WBC light-heavyweight crown. As champion, Conteh wanted more control over his destiny and sacked Francis before battling against a chronic hand complaint, the curse of a pro boxer. Conteh was eventually stripped of his light-heavyweight title for failing to fight Miguel Cuello in 1977. He retired from professional boxing in 1980 after 39 pro fights, 34 wins, 1 draw and 4 losses and is now probably one of the best after-dinner speakers on the circuit.

Cooney, Gerry Born Huntingdon, New York, 1956. Turning pro in 1975 Cooney lost his first fight in just three rounds to John Davis. He won the next 25 with a series of KO's, including back-to-back one-rounders against Ron Lyle and Ken Norton, before getting a shot at the title. In 1982 he became one of a long list of victims when he took on Larry Holmes (lasting 13 rounds). A period of inactivity and infrequent fights followed with three fights in three years before he tried again for the heavyweight crown in 1987. Michael Spinks despatched him in five rounds while in 1990 George Foreman did the same in two. Cooney has never fought since, but his record is still impressive. Of his 31 fights he lost only 3 and 24 wins were KOs. Against all but the very best Cooney was a top boxer.

Cooper, Henry Born Bellingham, Kent, 3 May 1934. British heavyweight champion from 1959 (beating Brian London) to 1969. He then relinquished the crown for a short time (Jack Bodell beating Welshman Carl Gizzi for the vacant title) before regaining it in 1970 by defeating Bodell. 'Our 'enery' fought Cassius Clay (Muhammad Ali) on 18 June 1963 at Wembley and knocked him down at the end of the fourth round. Clay's trainer, Angelo Dundee, admitted afterwards that he cut one of Clay's gloves to give him a little more time to recover between rounds. Clay stopped Henry in the next round. In the same year he became European heavyweight champion, beating Brian London. He fought Ali again in 1966 at Highbury and was stopped in the sixth round. Henry's manager was Jim 'The Bishop' Wicks. On 16 March 1971 he lost the British, European and Commonwealth heavyweight titles to Joe Bugner. Cooper, whose punch was known as "enery's 'ammer", retired in 1971, having won 40, lost 14 and drawn one of his 55 bouts. His twin brother, George, was a southpaw who fought under the name of Jim Cooper.

Corbett, James, J. Born San Francisco, California, 1 September 1866. Before boxing Corbett followed the less dangerous profession of bank clerk. He began boxing in 1884 and, although an amateur, fought under the name of Joe Dillon so he could take on professionals while protecting his status. After turning pro in 1889 he fought all the major players of the time, including Joe Choynski and Jake Kilrain. On 7 September 1892 'Gentleman Jim' became the first-ever heavyweight champion under the new Queensberry Rules, knocking out John L. Sullivan in the 21st round in New Orleans. Prior to this most fights he fought were bare-knuckled. He has been called 'The Father of Modern Boxing' because of his innovations in fighting style. He defended the title only once, against Charlie Mitchell, before retiring in 1895. On his retirement he presented his title to Peter Maher. After a short-lived retirement he came

back but officially lost his title on 17 March 1897, when Bob Fitzsimmons knocked him out in the 14th round in Carson City, Nevada. He did challenge again for the world heavyweight title when he fought and lost to James J. Jeffries in 1900 and 1903. He fought only 19 professional bouts, winning 11 (seven by knockout), and losing four (three by knockout). He also had two draws and two no contests. He died 18 February 1933.

Couch, Jane The most famous woman boxer in England and after Laila Ali perhaps the most famous in the world, 'The Fleetwood Assassin' is a rebel with a cause. Couch began boxing after years of drinking, drugs and street fighting. When she was 26 years old, she saw a TV documentary about women's boxing in the United States, and that show inspired her to try her hand at boxing. Couch went on to defeat such top fighters as Leah Mellinger, Andrea De Shong, and Marischa Sjauw of Holland. She made history by being the first woman in British boxing history to fight professionally, in Streatham, London, 25 November 1998. The fight ended in the second round when badly overmatched 18-year-old Simona Lukic from Speyer, Germany was stopped. Couch is currently the welterweight champion of the world.

Criqui, Eugene Born Belleville, France, 1893. He turned pro in 1910, fighting mainly out of Paris. In 1912 he became flyweight champion of France and a year later fought Sid Smith for the world title, losing in 20 rounds. The next year he lost over the same distance to Percy Jones. Criqui fought during World War I and did not box during this period. During the war he was shot in the jaw, which was replaced by a silver plate. In 1921 and 1922 he won the championships of France and Europe and set himself on course for another shot at the world title. In 1923 he knocked out Johnny Kilbane to become undisputed featherweight champion of the world. Just over one month later Johnny Dundee took the title away from him on points. Criqui, now in his thirties, had a few more fights before retiring in 1928. He died in 1977 aged 83.

Cruz, Steve Born Fort Worth, Texas, 1963. He turned pro in 1981. Apart from a blip in 1984 when he suffered a first-round KO to Lenny Valdez, he was unbeaten in his first 28 outings. In 1986 he had his first title fight. Going the distance, he beat Barry McGuigan to win the WBA featherweight championship of the world, but had held this for less than a year when he relinquished it to Antonio Esparragoza. From this moment on his career stuttered and then collapsed. In 1991 and 1992 he fought three times and was knocked out on each occasion. Cruz tried to regain two different versions of the featherweight title against Jorge Paez (IBF) and Paul Hodkinson (WBC) but he would never be champion again. Cruz, WBA featherweight champion 1986-87, last boxed in 1993.

Curry, Don Born Fort Worth, Texas, 7 September 1961. In 1983 he won the first of the disparate divisions of the welterweight titles (WBC) beating Jun-Suk Wang. Three years later, after five defences he managed to unify the titles with a destruction of Milt McCrory. Curry was now described as the best pound-for-pound fighter of his day. Unfortunately the wheels came off his career after this fight and he lost easily to Lloyd Honeyghan (who was a massive outsider) only six months later. In the next two years he moved up to light middleweight and at his second attempt became WBC world champion, beating Gianfranco Rosi. He lost his title at the first defence to

Rene Jacquot. Although he had two more title shots, against Michael Nunn and Terry Norris, he never again reached the levels of performance that he managed to deliver in the mid-1980s. Don Curry is the brother of Bruce, WBC light-welterweight champion 1983-84.

De La Hoya, Oscar   Born Montebello, California, 12 February 1971. In 1992 he won the only US boxing gold medal at the Barcelona Olympics (in the lightweight division). His amateur career was outstanding and he won 223 of 228 bouts with 161 knockouts. Turning pro straight after his Olympic title, he won his first 11 fights in quick order to set up a title fight with Jimmi Bredahl. De La Hoya defeated the previously unbeaten Bredahl and was now WBO junior lightweight champion of the world. Moving up in weight, De La Hoya abandoned the junior lightweight title and won, by beating Jorge Paez, the vacant WBO lightweight title. More wins and defences followed with eventually another move up in weight to light welterweight. A defeat of the great Julio Cesar Chavez in 1996 (in Chavez's 100th fight) gained De La Hoya the WBC welterweight championship and the distinction of being champion at three different weights. A win against Pernell Whitaker in 1997 gave De La Hoya the WBC welterweight championship and a fourth weight category. De La Hoya's victories over Whitaker and Chavez were only the second and third defeats of their respective careers. In 1999, after 32 wins De La Hoya took on Felix Trinidad and lost in 12 rounds. Another defeat followed in 2000 against Shane Mosley (Mosley defeated him again in September 2003). De La Hoya's most recent fight was in June 2004 when he gained a controversial points decision over Felix Sturm of Germany to take the WBO middleweight title.

Delaney, Jack   Born Quebec, 1900. Turned pro in 1919. In 1927 he broke his arm in a street fight when he got drunk one night shortly before his championship fight with Jim Maloney. He kept his injury a secret until he was in the ring, where he fought Maloney with only one hand. Unsurprisingly Maloney won. Close to the end of his career he lost in just one round to future heavyweight champion Jack Sharkey. Delaney never threw a punch and it was speculated that he may have been drunk. After one more fight he retired. Despite these low ebbs in his career, Delaney was undisputed light-heavyweight champion 1926-27. He died in 1948 aged 48.

Dempsey, Jack   Born William Harrison Dempsey, Manassa, Colorado, 14 June 1895. 'The Manassa Mauler' took the name Jack as a tribute to the middleweight Jack 'Nonpareil' Dempsey, who died in the year of his birth. His early career is sketchy. He travelled the country fighting numerous bouts under the name of 'Kid' Blackie. He even took part in wrestling matches. Estimates are that he may have fought up to 100 times during this period. But his career really took off on 4 July 1919 when he beat Jess Willard, the giant heavyweight champion. This, incidentally, was the first-ever fight to be broadcast on radio. Two years later he fought in front of the first million-dollar gate against Georges Carpentier. Known as something of a playboy, Dempsey gave up boxing for a number of years to make films in Hollywood. It was here that he met and married actress Estelle Taylor. In 1926, after five defences of the title, he returned to the ring to fight Gene Tunney. Tunney, a marine, proved an ideal contrast to Dempsey, who had been seen as a war slacker. The

event drew a crowd of over 120,000 to Chicago and they witnessed Tunney outpoint Dempsey.

The return match the following year was one of the most controversial in boxing history. Dempsey lost to Tunney in 'The Battle of the Long Count'. Despite being on the canvas for 14 seconds, Tunney was not counted out, and he got up to stop Dempsey. Though he gave numerous exhibitions, Dempsey never fought again as a pro and his later years were spent as a New York restaurateur (his restaurant was called 'The Meeting Place of the World'). Dempsey, undisputed heavyweight champion 1919-26, had 26 first-round KOs in his career. He died aged 87 in 1983.

Dempsey, Jack   Born John Edward Kelly, Co. Kildare, Ireland, 1862. After emigrating to the USA and trying his hand at wrestling, Jack 'Nonpareil' Dempsey eventually turned to boxing. His first recorded pro fight was in 1883. In 1884 he beat George Fulljames in a bout which gained him the middleweight title of the world. In 1889 he fought and seemingly lost to George LaBlanche, however, LaBlanche had used a 'pivot' punch and so his win was not recognised. Dempsey eventually lost to Englishman Bob Fitzsimmons in 1891. Dempsey, undisputed middleweight champion 1884-91, died aged 32 in 1895.

Dixon, George   Born Halifax, Nova Scotia, 1870. George 'Little Chocolate' Dixon was undisputed bantamweight champion 1890-91, and undisputed featherweight champion 1892-97 and again 1898-1900. His first title, in 1890, came when he beat Nunc Wallace over 18 gruelling rounds. But Dixon, for all of his wins, has created confusion among statisticians and boxing fans for his refusal to accept the loss of his titles when defeated. Dixon was beaten in 1897 by Solly Smith but claimed that the title was not at stake and continued to bill himself as champion. However many title fights he actually enjoyed, Dixon is universally regarded as one of the greatest bantamweights of all time. He was the very first to be undisputed bantamweight champion of the world. Dixon died in 1909 aged only 38.

Douglas, James   Born Columbus, Ohio, 1960. James 'Buster' Douglas turned pro in 1981. Despite a couple of early losses he managed to get a title shot in 1987, fighting Tony Tucker for the IBF heavyweight title but losing in 10 rounds. In 1990, following wins over Trevor Berbick and Oliver McCall, he had another shot at the big time. This time he was to face Mike Tyson. Tyson was unbeaten and in many people's eyes unbeatable. Yet in a shock victory in Tokyo (Tyson was an overwhelming favourite with the bookies), Douglas won the IBF, WBC and WBA titles. His celebrations were short-lived, as later the same year he lost all three titles to Evander Holyfield in a three-round KO. Douglas faded away and although he made a brief comeback in the late 1990s he has never been a threat to the big time again.

Downes, Terry   Born Paddington, London, 9 May 1936. Undisputed middleweight champion 1961-62. Having turned pro in 1957, he won nearly all of his fights by KO. He became British champion in 1958, losing the title but regaining it the following year, both times against Johnny McCormack. His world middleweight crown was won in London in the summer of 1961 when he beat Paul Pender, but Pender exacted his revenge the following year in Boston. Although he managed to take the scalp of an ageing Sugar Ray Robinson in 1962, his last fight was in 1964. In Manchester he lost a light-heavyweight title fight to Willie Pastrano and retired.

Driscoll, Jim Born Cardiff, 1880. One of the greatest Welsh fighters ever, Driscoll was a master of defence and he earned the nickname 'Peerless'. As with other Welsh fighters of the time, Driscoll learned his craft in boxing booths. After losing only one fight, to Harry Mansfield, he fought for the British featherweight title in 1906 against the reigning champion, Joe Bowker. The fight went the full 15 rounds but Bowker was easily beaten. In 1910 Driscoll faced world champion Abe Atell in a no-decision fight. Although contemporary reports give the contest to Driscoll, since there was no knockout the title did not change hands. Driscoll was the first featherweight to win a Lonsdale Belt. His last fight was against Charles Ledoux; although Jim was well ahead after 15 rounds, Ledoux caught him and it was all over at the start of the 16th. Driscoll died in 1925 aged 44.

Dundee, Johnny Born Guiseppe Carrora, Sicily, 1893. In 1910 he turned pro, fighting mostly out of New York. He fought Johnny Kilbane in 1913 for the featherweight championship of the world and drew. Over the next eight years he boxed (mostly no-decision fights) against Benny Leonard (eight times in all), Rocky Kansas and George 'KO' Chaney – all excellent fighters. During this time he never challenged for the title. In 1921 he won the junior lightweight title by beating Chaney on a foul. In 1923 he both lost and regained the lightweight title from Jack Bernstein and beat Eugene Criqui to win the featherweight crown. In 1924 Steve 'Kid' Sullivan took the lightweight honours and Dundee relinquished the featherweight crown. After one more shot at the title in 1927, losing to Tony Canzoneri, Dundee retired. Dundee, undisputed junior lightweight champion 1921-23 and both lightweight and featherweight champion 1923-24, died in 1965 aged 71. The first man ever to be undisputed super-featherweight champion, he is regarded by most experts as one of the greatest featherweights of all time.

Dunn, Richard Born Bradford, 1945. Dunn beat Bunny Johnson in 1975 to become British and Commonwealth heavyweight champion. By knocking out Danny McAlinden in two rounds he became the first person since Henry Cooper to successfully defend the title. Richard became European heavyweight champion in April 1976, beating German Bernd August, but lost to Joe Bugner later the same year. In 1976 he was given a heavyweight title fight with Muhammad Ali in Munich. He lost in five one-sided rounds and was the last man Ali beat inside the distance.

Duran, Roberto Born Guarare, Panama, 1951. He turned pro in 1967, all his early fights taking place in Panama. After 29 wins he took on Ken Buchanan for the world lightweight title, Buchanan lasting 13 rounds before Duran applied the coup de grace. After two more one-round KOs Duran was beaten by Esteban De Jesus. Three defences later he faced Jesus again and defeated him in 11 rounds. At their next meeting in 1978 Duran again beat him, this time in 12 rounds. In 1980 the world was treated to one of the greatest fights ever, when Duran took on Sugar Ray Leonard for the WBC welterweight title. Duran won a fantastic scrap in which Leonard went toe-to-toe with the street-fighting Duran. Five months later Duran was not so fortunate; Leonard had learned from his previous outing and totally outboxed Duran. He purposely exposed Duran's technical deficiencies to the extent that Roberto refused to come out for round nine. In 1982 Duran lost to Wilfredo Benitez trying to win the WBC light-middleweight title.

Continually moving up in weight, he fought Marvin Hagler for the middleweight title but lost in 15 rounds. In 1984 another crack at the light-middleweight title saw him lose against Thomas Hearns. Five years later a resurgent Duran beat Iran Barkley to capture the WBC middleweight crown (his third weight) and a third and final Leonard fight took place. If Duran had won he would have claimed the WBC super-middleweight crown and a title at a fourth weight, but Leonard was a bridge too far. Duran was a great boxer with legendary durability, stubbornness and guts. As undisputed lightweight champion 1972-79, undisputed welterweight champion in 1980, WBA light-middleweight champion 1983-84 and WBC middleweight champion 1989-90, he has a place in history. When he became middleweight champion in 1989 he was the oldest ever to hold such a title at 37 years and 8 months old. Although his record shows 15 losses, when the quality of the opposition is taken into account this is still a fantastic showing. Duran's nicknames included 'Hands of Stone' and 'Stonefist'.

Elorde, Gabriel Born Philippines, 1935. He turned pro in 1951 fighting mostly in Asia until moving to the United States in 1956. Here he won the world featherweight title from Sandy Sadler before moving up to junior lightweight. Back in his native country he beat Harold Gomes in seven rounds to become undisputed junior lightweight champion. In doing so he became the first-ever southpaw to win the title, which he held for the next seven years. During this time he beat Carlos Ortiz twice, before eventually losing the title in 15 rounds to Yoshiaki Numata. A short retirement was followed by an unsuccessful comeback. Elorde retired for good in 1971, and died in Manila in 1985 aged 49.

Erskine, Joe Born Cardiff, Wales, 26 January 1934. Joe won the vacant British heavyweight title on 27 August 1956, beating Johnny Williams on points over 15 rounds. He defended it successfully against Henry Cooper and Joe Bygraves in 1957, both on points, before losing the title on a technical knockout to Brian London the next year. When Cooper won the title in 1959 he defended it against Joe who was stopped in the 12th round. Henry stopped him twice more in 1961 and again in 1962. Joe's trainer was Benny Jacobs. Of his 54 fights he won 45, lost eight and drew one. He retired in 1964 after losing to West Ham's Billy Walker.

Eubank, Chris Born Christopher Livingstone Eubanks, Dulwich, London, 8 August 1966. Now based in Brighton. At an early age he relocated to the United States with his father where he completed his high school education and took up boxing. Here he won the New York Spanish Golden Gloves Tourney in 1984. Turning professional, he fought his first five professional bouts, all four-rounders, in Atlantic City, New Jersey, before returning to Britain. He made his British debut with a first-round stoppage against Darren Parker at Copthorne, West Sussex, on 15 February 1988. Chris became WBO middleweight champion in 1991, beating Nigel Benn. An excellent technical boxer, in the news for his lisp or his fashion sense as often as for his boxing, he was Michael Watson's opponent in the fight which put Watson into a coma. Although he was unbeaten in his first 43 fights, Eubank's career after the fight with Watson was patchy and he recorded his first-ever loss to Steve Collins in 1995.

Farr, Tommy Born Tonypandy, Wales, 1914. Boxing for Farr was the alternative to the mines and he took it. He had an early loss to Eddie Phillips but then beat two former light-heavyweight world champions,

B
O
X
I
N
G

Tommy Loughran and Bob Olin, before becoming British and Empire heavyweight champion by defeating Ben Foord. In what many saw as a mismatch Farr next took on Max Baer. Baer toyed with the Welshman but couldn't put him away and Farr won the verdict. Farr then had a crack at the great Joe Louis on 30 August 1937. It was Louis' first defence and Tommy was never entertained as a real threat. Yet Farr fought a great fight; though Louis got the verdict, Farr went back to Wales a hero. Although Tommy Farr was a wealthy man when he retired in 1940, he was facing bankruptcy when he made a comeback ten years later, at 36 years of age. He regained the Welsh heavyweight title but finally ended his career, three days short of his 39th birthday, when Don Cockell beat him in seven rounds in Nottingham. He died, perhaps fittingly, on St David's Day 1986 aged 71.

Fenech, Jeff   Born Sydney, Australia, 1964. Turned pro in 1984. He won titles in three weight divisions in the span of 20 fights in just three and a half years. He was IBF bantamweight champion in 1985, beating Satoshi Shingaki, WBC light-featherweight champion in 1987, defeating Samart Payakaroon and WBC featherweight champion in 1988, overcoming Victor Callejas. Fighting throughout his career with brittle hands, Fenech retired in 1988. After surgery he made a return and attempted to win at a fourth weight, but it was not to be and he retired for good in 1996. Fenech now trains future greats.

Ferns, James   Born Pittsburgh, Kansas, 1874. 'Rube' Ferns turned pro in 1896. Four years later he beat Eddie Connelly to become undisputed welterweight champion of the world. After losing the title to William 'Matty' Matthews he defeated the same man in 1901 to regain it. Following a series of poor results Ferns retired in 1906. Ferns, credited with being the first man to call his knockout punch a 'haymaker', died in his home town in 1952 aged 78.

Fields, Jackie   Born Jacob Finkelstein, Chicago, Illinois, 9 February 1908. John 'Jackie' Fields was a very gifted amateur. He won the Olympic featherweight gold in 1924 at the age of 16 years and 162 days, the youngest man to win an Olympic title. Turning pro shortly after, he went on to become undisputed welterweight champion 1929-30 and again 1932-33. He died 3 June 1987.

Finnegan, Chris   Born Buckinghamshire, 5 June 1944. Finnegan was a 24-year-old bricklayer when he made his first trip outside Europe to the Mexico Olympics of 1968. He won his first four bouts in Mexico City and in his fifth fight beat Aleksey Kisselyov of the Soviet Union to take the middleweight title. Olympic glory launched Finnegan's professional career although he soon moved up to light heavyweight. He won the British, Commonwealth and European titles but failed to take the world crown despite an heroic effort against the champion and overwhelming favourite, Bob Foster, in an epic 14-round duel at Wembley. Chris lost his British light-heavyweight title to John Conteh in 1973 and retired in 1975. His younger brother, Kevin, was also a British middleweight boxing champion who fought Alan Minter in a series of British title fights but never managed to beat the Crawley man.

Firpo, Louis   Born Louis Angel Firpo, Buenos Aires, Argentina, 1894. In 1919 'The Wild Bull of the Pampas' fought David Mills for the South American heavyweight title and lost narrowly in 15 rounds. A year later against the same opponent he scored a first-round KO. In 1923 he fought Jess Willard and beat him although this was not a title bout. Later the

same year he took on Jack Dempsey but lost easily in two rounds. In his short career he had 38 fights and four losses.

Fitzsimmons, Bob   Born Helston, Cornwall, 26 May 1863. Nicknamed 'Ruby Robert' or 'Speckled Bob', Fitzsimmons is rated among the greatest fighters who ever lived. After moving early in his life to Timaru, New Zealand, he began fighting at a very early age and in New Zealand he often fought numerous bouts in a single day. Some sources, including Fitzsimmons himself, claim he had over 350 fights. From New Zealand he moved to Sydney, Australia and it is here that his pro career started. His first title fight was in 1890 when he fought and lost to Jim Hall for the Australian version of the middleweight crown. Only a year later, now living in the USA, he beat Jack 'Nonpareil' Dempsey for the world middleweight title (and beat him again in 1893 and 1894). Fitzsimmons fought all of the best boxers of the day, including Sullivan, Sharkey, Jeffries and Corbett. On 5 September 1892 he fought 19 rounds of boxing and scored seven KOs. In the ring, Fitzsimmons moved quickly and hit hard from all angles. During an 1894 exhibition fight Con Riordan was knocked out and died at ringside.

During 1895 and 1896 Fitzsimmons tried his hand at the top weight. A fight against Jim Corbett was cancelled and he lost a bout against Sharkey (refereed by Wyatt Earp) on a foul. He had to wait until 1897 to become heavyweight champ, beating Jim Corbett in the process. He lost the title to Jim Jeffries in 1899. In 1903 Fitzsimmons became boxing's first triple world champion although he never held any of the titles simultaneously – that honour goes to Henry Armstrong) when he beat George Gardner to rule the newly created light-heavyweight division. He lost that title to 'Philadelphia' Jack O'Brien two years later.

Having lost all his titles he toured, giving exhibition matches. He fought his last professional fight at the age of 50 and his last-ever fight, an exhibition in New York, was in 1916 against 'Young' Bob Fitzsimmons. He died the following year, on 22 October 1917.

Flowers, Tiger   Born Theodore Flowers, Camille, Georgia, 1895. He turned pro in 1918 and was the first black American since Jack Johnson to hold a world championship. Flowers got his big title shot in 1926. He took on Harry Greb and won the decision over 15 rounds to become middleweight champion of the world. After beating Greb in the rematch he then lost to Mickey Walker, still in 1926. Following an operation in 1927 he died aged only 32. Flowers, undisputed middleweight champion in 1926, was known as 'The Georgia Deacon' (born in Georgia, he was indeed a deacon).

Foreman, George   Born Marshall, Texas, 22 January 1949. He had a distinguished amateur career, capped with the 1968 Olympic heavyweight title. He turned pro in 1969. After 37 wins he took on Joe Frazier and won in two rounds, knocking Joe off his feet at one point. The next year, after disposing of Ken Norton in two, he faced Muhammad Ali in the 'Rumble in the Jungle' fight in Zaire. Ali, a big outsider, stopped him in eight rounds – his first defeat. Six fights later, after a loss to Jimmy Young, Foreman retired. In 1978 he was ordained at the Church of the Lord Jesus Christ in Houston, Texas. In 1987 he returned and strung together 24 wins before meeting Evander Holyfield in 1991. Holyfield won a unanimous points decision over 12 rounds. Two years later against Tommy Morrison the story was exactly the same. A year afterwards, on 5 November

1994, he beat Michael Moorer to win the IBF and WBA titles. He was 45 years old. After three defences he lost the titles again in 1997 to Shannon 'The Cannon' Briggs. A boxing legend, Foreman was only knocked out once, by Ali, and in 2003 said that if Lennox Lewis retired he would come back to the ring.

Foster, Bob Born Alberquerque, New Mexico, 15 December 1938. Foster dominated the light-heavyweight division in the late 1960s and early 1970s. His pro record of 56 wins, 8 defeats and 1 draw (46 KOs), though remarkable, is even better than it looks, as his losses invariably occurred when he took on vastly heavier fighters such as Zora Foley, Ernie Terrell, Joe Frazier and Muhammad Ali. When one discusses the greatest light-heavyweights of all time, Foster is up there with all the greats.

Frazier, Joe Born Beaufort, South Carolina, 12 January 1944. 'Smokiin' Joe was a gifted amateur and at the Tokyo Olympics in 1964 won gold, beating Hans Huber of Germany in the final match. He turned pro in 1965. After 24 unbeaten fights he took on Jimmy Ellis for the vacant heavyweight title, stopping Ellis in four rounds. After a defence against Bob Foster he became, in 1971, the first man to beat Muhammad Ali professionally. Two defences later he met George Foreman in Kingston, Jamaica. Foreman beat him in 12 rounds. Having lost only once in 30 fights he now lost three of his next five, beating Jerry Quarry and Jimmy Ellis but succumbing to Foreman and Ali (twice). The second loss to Ali was on 1 October 1975 at the Araneta Stadium in Manila. In a fight dubbed the 'Thrilla in Manila', Joe retired after 14 pulsating rounds. After a disappointing comeback fight in 1981 against Jumbo Cummings (a draw), Frazier retired once more – this time for good. Since his retirement he has had a strong hand in moulding the talent of his son, Marvis.

Fullmer, Gene Born West Jordan, Utah, 1931. Fullmer turned pro in 1951. After 39 fights, with three losses, in 1957 he got a fight against one of the all time greats, Sugar Ray Robinson. Fullmer won in 15 rounds, but four months later Robinson wreaked his revenge with a five-round stoppage. Fullmer won the American middleweight title and defended it successfully, even against Robinson – twice. His last three fights were all against Dick Tiger. Fullmer lost two and drew one. The final fight was in Tiger's home country of Nigeria, where Fullmer was knocked out in the seventh round, only the second time in his career he suffered a KO. Gene, undisputed middleweight champion in 1957, retired to run a mink farm.

Gans, Joe Born Baltimore, Maryland, 1874. Gans turned pro in 1891 and proceeded to build up a series of wins. After close to 70 fights, and nine years later, he fought Frank Erne for the lightweight title but was forced to retire after 12 rounds. Three years later he fought Erne again, this time stopping him in the first round with a KO. After nine defences he took on Jimmy Britt. Britt was well ahead in the fight when, as a result of a foul, he was disqualified. Gans gave up the title at the end of 1904. He won it back, again on a foul, when he boxed Oscar 'Battling' Nelson in 1906. This time, though, it took 42 rounds before the fight was stopped. Revenge was sweet for Gans when he beat Britt comfortably in six rounds in 1907. It was Nelson who finally dethroned him: in July and September of 1908 Nelson beat him in 17 and then 21 rounds, and Gans fought only once more. Undisputed lightweight champion 1902-04 and 1906-08, he died aged 35 in 1910.

Gavilan, Kid Born Gerardo Gonzalez, Havana, Cuba, 1926. His early fights mostly took place in Cuba and Mexico and apart from a few minor setbacks he won them well. In 1948 he took on Sugar Ray Robinson in a non-title bout, losing in 10 rounds. The following year he fought for the welterweight title and lost in 15. He had to wait until 1951 to win the vacant title, outpointing Johnny Bratton. Over the next three years he put the title on the line seven times before losing it to Johnny Saxton. He put up an extremely good show against Carl 'Bobo' Olson for the middleweight title in the same year but lost over 15 rounds. The next three or four years of his career saw far more losses than wins and he retired in 1958. He died 13 February 2003.

Gomez, Wilfredo Born Puerto Rico, 1956. He turned pro in 1974. After 16 fights, 15 of them KOs, he fought Dong-Kyun Yum for the WBC light-featherweight championship and won with a 12-round knockout. Thereafter he defended his title 17 times. After 33 fights and 32 KOs he lost his first fight to Salvador Sanchez when challenging for the WBC featherweight title, but in 1984 he beat Juan La Porte to become WBC featherweight champion. In one of his three pro defeats Azumah Nelson deprived him of this title the same year. In 1985 he joined the pantheon of three-time champions at different weights with a distance win over Rocky Lockridge for the WBA junior lightweight title, though he lost this the following year to Alfredo Layne. Wilfredo 'Bazooka' Gomez had an incredible record: in 48 bouts he won 44, lost 3 and drew 1. Of his wins, 42 were KOs, as were all his losses; consequently he only ever went the distance three times in his career. Gomez's last fight was in 1989 – unsurprisingly it was a KO in two.

Graham, Herol Born Sheffield, 13 September 1959. Herol 'Bomber' Graham was a middleweight renowned for extremely skilful boxing, equipped with fantastic evasive qualities but with a slightly suspect ability to absorb a punch. One of the plethora of great British middleweights of the 1980s, he was later a mentor to Prince Naseem Hamed. As a light middleweight he became British champion in 1981 and was European middleweight champion 1983-86. His career record boasted 48 wins and six losses.

Graziano, Rocky Born Thomas Rocco Barbella, New York, 7 June 1922. Started boxing professionally in 1942. He was a tremendously destructive boxer, almost all his fights ending in knockouts, whether won or lost. Boxing mostly out of New York and New Jersey, Graziano built his reputation quickly, and after only four years had a chance to win the world middleweight crown. He lost in six rounds to Tony Zale, but less than a year later he inflicted the same loss on Zale and stood triumphant as world champion. His victory was short-lived; less than a year later, he lost again to Zale. His only other title shot was in 1952 against the great Sugar Ray Robinson, when he lost in three. Graziano's life was portrayed in the film *Somebody Up There Likes Me*, where he was played by Paul Newman. After his final fight in 1952 Graziano became an entertainer and is perhaps best remembered for his comedy album *The Maharishi Yoghurt*. He died 22 May 1990.

Greb, Harry Born Pittsburgh, Pennsylvania, 1894. He fought a massive number of fights; although records vary, most sources put the figure at between 300 and 400. Throughout all these Greb lost only

BOXING

eight, a fabulous record, and he is unique in being the only man ever to beat Gene Tunney. Greb gained his nickname, 'The Human Windmill', from his frantic all-action style. After retiring, following his return-bout loss to Tiger Flowers in 1926, he slipped into a coma and died while coming out of anaesthesia following plastic surgery on his nose. It was then that doctors discovered that Greb had fought the majority of his career blind in the right eye and with limited vision in his 'good' eye. He was undisputed middleweight champion 1923-26.

Griffith, Emile Born St Thomas, Virgin Islands, 3 February 1938. He turned pro in 1958 and, despite a few losses, progressed through the rankings to earn a title shot in 1961 against Benny Paret. He beat Paret in 13 rounds to become welterweight champion of the world. Over the next five or six years he won and lost the title several times. Five months after his first win he lost the title but six months later he won it back from Paret in 12. His record stands as follows: he was undisputed welterweight champion in 1961, then 1962-63 and 1963-69. He also held the world middleweight 1966-67, and finally 1967-68. During this seesaw period he had three 15-round fights with Luis Rodriguez and the same number with Nino Benvenuti. He also fought Dick Tiger (two wins, both in 10 rounds), Jose Napoles (a loss in 15) and Carlos Monzon (losses in 14 and 15). After his loss to Monzon in 1973 his win and loss ratio dropped to close on 50 per cent. His final bout was against Alan Minter in 1977 when he lost in 10. A very durable fighter, Griffith was only knocked out twice, by Ruben Carter and Carlos Monzon. In his career, Griffith met ten world champions and boxed 339 title-fight rounds, more than any other fighter in history.

Hagler, Marvin Born Newark, New Jersey, 23 May 1954. He turned pro in 1973. After 48 fights and only two losses he finally had a chance to win a world title when in 1979 he took on Vito Antuofermo for the world middleweight crown. After 15 rounds the fight was declared a draw. The following year Hagler travelled to London to take on Alan Minter, who had subsequently beaten Antuofermo. After he beat Minter at Wembley to become undisputed middleweight champion, the reaction from the crowd was so strong that in the ensuing melee bottles and chairs were thrown into the ring. After 12 defences, including fights against Antuofermo, Tony Sibson, Roberto Duran, Thomas Hearns and John Mugabi, he took on Sugar Ray Leonard. Leonard beat him in 12 rounds. Marvin, a great middleweight champion, changed his name to Marvelous.

Hamed, Naseem Born Sheffield, 12 February 1974. 'Prince' Naseem is of Yemeni descent. His professional career started in 1992 when, managed by Brendan Ingle, he amassed a series of KO wins. After only two years he became European bantamweight champion by beating Vincenzo Belcastro. His first world title came a year later in 1995, when he beat Steve Robinson for the WBO featherweight crown. An explosive fighter, in 1996 he KOed Said Lawal in 35secs. In 1997 he won the IBF version from Tom Johnson and he gained the WBA title in 1998 when he beat Wilfredo Vasquez. That year also saw him abandon his manager as his brother, Riath, took over the reins. The unification of the title occurred in 1999 with a 12-round victory over Cesar Soto. Unbeaten in his first 35 fights (31 of those being KOs), in 2001 he took on the aggressive, hard-hitting Marco Antonio Barrera. Barrera was always ahead and, highlighting

Hamed's defensive shortcomings, won over the distance. Since then the cocky Sheffield boxer has not set foot in the ring.

Harada, Masahiko Born Tokyo, 1943. He turned pro in 1960 fighting almost exclusively out of Tokyo. In 1962 'Fighting' Harada knocked out Pone Kingpetch for the world flyweight title, but three months later he lost the rematch. Harada moved up in weight and won the bantamweight title from Eder Jofre in May 1965. The following year he also got the decision over the great Brazilian. Both fights took place in Tokyo and this may have given Harada a little home advantage. After four defences he lost his bantamweight title to Lionel Rose in 1968. In 1969 Harada took on Johnny Famechon for the WBC featherweight crown but lost on points. Harada, undisputed flyweight champion 1962-63 and undisputed bantamweight champion 1965-68, retired after losing his WBC world featherweight title fight, once more against Johnny Famechon.

Harrison, Audley Born 26 October 1971. After winning the super-heavyweight Olympic gold medal for Great Britain in the 2000 Olympics, he turned professional and sold the rights to cover his first fights to the BBC. Although the initial reaction was favourable, criticism has been levelled at Harrison for his choice of 'inferior' opponents. Harrison's professional career began on 19 May 2001 with a first-round demolition of Florida's Mike Middleton. His fight in 2003 against Matthew Ellis ended in a brawl when former WBO heavyweight champion Herbie Hide was taunted by Harrison from the ring. Known to his supporters as 'The A-Force', his latest fight was on 19 June 2004, when he stopped Poland's Tomasz Bonin in the ninth round, his first defence of the World Boxing Foundation title.

Hart, Marvin Born Fern Creek, Kentucky, 1876. He turned pro in 1899 fighting out of Louisville. In 1905 he beat soon-to-be champion Jack Johnson over 20 rounds and completed the year with a victory over Jack Root to claim the world heavyweight title vacated by Jim Jeffries. Hart, one of the forgotten men of the heavyweight division, lost the title seven months later, in 20 rounds to Tommy Burns. He never scaled the heights again and retired four years and 11 fights later. His last fight was against Carl Morris in 1910. Hart, 'The Fightin' Kentuckian', died aged 55 in 1931.

Hearns, Thomas Born Memphis, Tennessee, 18 October 1958. 'The Hit Man' turned pro in 1977 after a glittering amateur career. Fighting mostly out of Detroit, he set about knocking out all his opponents in double-quick time. His first 17 fights were all KOs and he soon earned his other nickname of the 'Motor City Cobra'. In 1980, 11 more wins saw him challenge and beat Jose 'Pipino' Cuevas for the WBA welterweight title. In 1981, after 32 wins he suffered his first defeat at the hands of Sugar Ray Leonard. Leonard stopped him in 14 rounds, in one of the great clashes in modern boxing. In 1982 a decision over Wilfred Benitez gave him the WBC light-middleweight title. A two-round KO of Roberto Duran in 1984 made him undisputed light-middleweight champion of the world. He was also the first man to knock Duran out.

His move up to middleweight was halted by Marvin Hagler in 1985, Hagler winning in three rounds. In 1987 wins over Dennis Andries (at light heavyweight) and Juan Domingo Roldan (at middleweight) made him the first man to win titles at four weights. In 1988 he lost the WBC middleweight title to Iran Barkley but in 1995 he won at yet another weight. This time the weight was cruiserweight (WBU) and the victim Lenny LaPaglia. Thomas Hearns is one of boxing's all-time great fighters. Strong, fast and an excellent technical boxer, in 64 fights he lost only four, one each to Leonard and Hagler and two to Iran Barkley.

Holmes, Larry   Born Georgia, 3 November 1949. He turned pro in 1973. In 1978, still unbeaten, he fought Earnie Shavers and then Ken Norton, outpointing Norton for the WBC heavyweight title. After seven more defences he became one of only five boxers to beat Muhammad Ali. Holmes continued winning, beating Leon Spinks, Mike Weaver, Gerry Cooney and anyone else who cared to try. In total he won his first 48 contests, losing the 49th – which would have equalled Marciano's record – to Michael Spinks under controversial circumstances. The rematch ended with the same result, although this time Spinks was clearly the better man. After a lay-off of two years Holmes came back to fight Mike Tyson who inflicted the first-ever KO on Holmes in just four rounds. Holmes now retired for three years before making yet another comeback. This time he challenged Evander Holyfield and Oliver McCall but both beat him on unanimous decisions. Holmes was undisputed heavyweight champion from 1980-85. Even with the poor results later in his career, 'The Easton Assassin' won 69 of his 75 fights, 44 of them by knockout.

Holyfield, Evander   Born 19 October 1962. 'The Real Deal' was favourite to win the light-heavyweight gold at the 1984 Olympics, but lost in the semi-finals having knocked out his opponent Kevin Barry after the referee called break. Disqualified, he was forced to settle for bronze. After two years as a pro he had a crack at the WBA world cruiserweight title, beating Dwight Qawi in 15 rounds in 1986. The following year he added the IBF title, beating Ricky Parkey, and the year after the WBC crown to become undisputed cruiserweight champion. He then relinquished these titles and moved up to heavyweight. In 1990, in his 25th fight and still unbeaten, he took on James 'Buster' Douglas and won the IBF, WBC and WBA crowns. Defences followed against Foreman and Holmes until, in November 1992, he lost in 12 rounds in Las Vegas to Riddick Bowe. This was his first defeat in 29 professional fights.

The next year he regained the titles only to lose them to Michael Moorer in 1994. The third and final fight with Bowe saw him knocked out for the only time in his career. In November 1996 Holyfield surprisingly beat Mike Tyson, stopping him in the 11th round to win the WBA heavyweight title. This had originally been scheduled for 1994, but the fight was postponed, first because of an injury to Tyson and then because of Tyson's conviction for rape. The return fight with Tyson is one of the most controversial in boxing history. Tyson, frustrated and behind on points, bit part of Holyfield's ear off in the third round and was disqualified. In 1999 he took part in yet another controversy, this time against Lennox Lewis; with Holyfield out-boxed for most of the 12 rounds, the judges managed to declare a draw. One of the judges was later to say that they were unsighted for part of the match.

In 2000 Holyfield won another controversial decision, beating John Ruiz and thereby regaining the title for a fourth time. His list of titles is impressive: WBA cruiserweight champion 1986-88; WBA, IBF cruiserweight champion 1987-88; WBC, WBA, IBF heavyweight champion 1990-92; WBA, IBF heavyweight champion 1993-94; WBA, IBF heavyweight champion 1996-2000; WBA heavyweight champion 2000-01. Evander Holyfield was the first undisputed cruiserweight champion in history.

Honeyghan, Lloyd   Born Jamaica, 22 April 1960. He turned pro at 20 and after 27 consecutive wins took on Don Curry for the welterweight title of the world. Honeyghan won in seven rounds. In 1987, one year later, he lost the title to Jorge Vaca. In the return match five months later he regained the WBC version. Honeyghan finally lost the title to Marlon Starling when he fought in the heat of Las Vegas. In 1990 he attempted to win the WBA title but was easily beaten by Mark Breland in three rounds. Eleven minor fights later he retired from boxing with only five career losses. Honeyghan was a fast and explosive fighter, winning half of his fights within the distance. He is now a successful trainer and manager.

Hopkins, Bernard   Born Philadelphia, January 1965. Hopkins lost his first pro fight in 1988 to Clinton Mitchell in just six rounds. His next loss was three years later, fighting Roy Jones Jr for the vacant IBF middleweight title. His first title came in 1995 when he beat Segundo Mercado for the IBF middleweight crown, having fought the same man the previous year and recorded a 12-round draw. In a 2001 fight against Keith Holmes he not only kept his IBF crown but won the WBC title too. A win against Felix Trinidad in the same year unified the title. Hopkins was the only man to beat Trinidad in his career. Hopkins gets his nickname, 'The Executioner', from his devastating power and the punishment that he doles out. In 1996 he knocked out Steve Frank in a junior middleweight contest in just 26 seconds. As at the end of December 2003, Hopkins had made 17 successful defences of his middleweight crowns, the last being on 13 December 2003 when he beat William Joppy on a unanimous points decision in Atlantic City, New Jersey. His present record is 43 wins, 2 losses and 1 draw.

Jeffries, Jim   Born Carroll, Ohio, 15 April 1875. Jeffries' fighting style was different from most boxers of the time in that he often fought from a crouching position, springing forward to deliver his punches. He made history in 1900 when he scored the quickest knockout in heavyweight history, beating Jack Finnegan in just 55 seconds. During 1896 in Los Angeles, Jeffries won his first professional fight by knocking out Hank Griffin (although he had fought Hank 'Kid' Lorraine in an unofficial fight a year earlier) in 14 rounds. Jeffries won the heavyweight championship in only his 13th fight when on 9 June 1899, at Coney Island, he knocked out Bob Fitzsimmons in 11 rounds. After winning he beat Jim Corbett, Fitzsimmons (again), Tom Sharkey and John L. Sullivan. He retired unbeaten in 1905. In his prime no one could match Jeffries. He once offered to fight his three top challengers – Fitzsimmons, Corbett and Sharkey – all on the same night. They refused. An astonishing athlete, Jim could run 100 yards in little more than ten seconds and high-jump over six feet. Once retired he took up refereeing, but after five years away from the game he was lured out of retirement in an attempt to beat Jack Johnson. He lost in 15 rounds, his only defeat. Jeffries retired again and toured with Jack Sharkey giving exhibitions. He died 3 March 1953, aged 77.

Jofre, Eder   Born Sao Paulo, Brazil, 1936. A hard-hitting knockout puncher, he turned pro in 1957. In his 40th fight he became world bantamweight champion, beating Eley Sanchez in six rounds. Over the next four years he was undefeated in retaining

B
O
X
I
N
G

the title, until in 1965 he lost a 15-round contest with 'Fighting' Harada in Nagoya, Japan. A year later he lost again over the same distance to the same fighter, this time in Tokyo. At this point Jofre retired. In 1969 he picked up the gloves again and after 14 wins beat Jose Legra to capture the WBC world featherweight title. In 1974 he was stripped of the crown by the WBC for failing to defend against Alfredo Marcano. Still with only two career defeats, he retired permanently in 1974. Jofre, undisputed bantamweight champion 1961-65, and WBC featherweight champion 1973-74, is regarded as one of the greatest fighters in the history of the sport. In Brazil he is an institution; after boxing he went on to become mayor of Sao Paulo.

Johansson, Ingemar Born Gothenburg, Sweden, 22 September 1932. Johansson gained the Olympic heavyweight silver medal in 1952 when he lost to Ed Sanders, but the defeat was a stain on his career; he was disqualified after two rounds for not trying and only received his medal 30 years later. He turned pro in 1952 and knocked out Henry Cooper in 1957 to retain the European heavyweight title that he had won a year earlier from Franco Cavicchi. He beat Floyd Patterson in three rounds to become heavyweight champion of the world in 1959, although he lost the title less than a year later. His 1959 win was ascribed to the use of his magic punch, nicknamed 'Ingo's Bingo' (also 'Hammer of Thor'). Johansson fought Patterson three times, in 1959, 1960 and 1961, but apart from what many saw as his fortuitous first win, Patterson was always on top in their encounters. His last two fights were against Englishmen; in 1962 he beat Dick Richardson to regain the European heavyweight title and the following year his last fight was a win against Brian London.

Although rated by many as a boxer who 'got lucky', Johansson was only ever beaten twice in his professional career, both times by Patterson.

Johnson, Jack Born Galveston, Texas, 31 March 1878. He turned pro just short of his 16th birthday in 1894. In 1903 Johnson won the coloured heavyweight championship of the world, beating Denver Ed Martin with a 20-round decision in Los Angeles. He lost to Marvin Hart in 20 rounds in 1905 but knocked out Bob Fitzsimmons in the 2nd round on 17 July 1907 before becoming the first black heavyweight world champion. He became so, appropriately enough, on Boxing Day 1908 in Sydney, Australia, by beating Tommy Burns. Burns was, according to contemporary reports, suffering from jaundice. Over the next 7 years no one could touch Johnson. As a black man he was not the meek and servile character that the white establishment was used to. He openly cavorted with white women (he married three) and was swaggering and loud. In an attempt to dethrone him Jim Jeffries was coaxed out of retirement. In 1910 he took a bad beating with Johnson toying with the older fighter, eventually finishing it in 15 with a KO. In a demonstration of how much Johnson had in reserve two days after the Jeffries fight he took on and beat 'Fireman' Jim Flynn. On 19 December 1913, his 10-round draw against Jim Johnson was the first ever all-black heavyweight title fight. In the same year he was convicted of contravening the 'White Slave Traffic Act' (Mann Act). To avoid incarceration Johnson fled the US and boxed in Europe and South America. In Havana, Cuba, in 1915 Jess Willard beat Johnson in 26 rounds. Johnson maintained that he threw the fight to be allowed to return to the US. In 1920 he did

return to the US and was promptly imprisoned for one year in Levenworth jail, Kansas. On his release he continued boxing and giving exhibitions. He fought an exhibition match against Joe Ballcort at the age of 67! Johnson, undisputed heavyweight champion from 1908-15, died in a car crash in North Carolina, 10 June 1946, while on his way to watch Joe Louis fight Billy Conn for the title he once held.

Jones, Colin Born Gorseinon, Swansea, 21 March 1959. Jones turned pro in 1977 and was quickly seen as a force to be reckoned with. He was managed by Eddie Thomas, who had previously guided Howard Winstone and Ken Buchanan to world titles. Undefeated in 13 fights (mostly KOs), in 1980 he took on Kirkland Laing for the British welterweight title. The Welshman, a hard-hitting fighter who literally pulled no punches, stopped Laing in the ninth after being outboxed for eight rounds. He moved on to win the Commonwealth title, beating Mark Harris, and then won a rematch with Laing in similar circumstances. Jones then lost controversially to Curtis Ramsey. Nevertheless, after a few more bouts Jones fought Milt 'The Iceman' McCrory for the vacant WBC crown. The result was a draw. The rematch, five months later in Las Vegas, was almost a carbon copy of the first meeting. This time McCrory won on a split decision. In 1985 Jones took on Don Curry, who was at the top of his form and after four rounds had caused a massive gash to open up across the bridge of Jones's nose. The referee stopped the fight and Jones decided it was time to quit. After 30 fights he had won 26, lost 3 and drawn 1.

Jones jnr, Roy Born Pensacola, Florida, 16 January 1969. Jones was robbed of the gold medal at the 1988 Olympics due to an error in scoring, but was still voted outstanding boxer of the games. He won the IBF middleweight crown by beating Bernard Hopkins in 1993. Moving up to super middleweight, he took the IBF title from James Toney in 1994, and then moved up to the light-heavyweight division, winning the WBC (in 1997), WBA (1998) and IBF (1999) titles. He suffered only one pro loss, a disqualification to Montel Griffin which he avenged with a first-round KO five months later. Jones moved up again to the heavyweight division and won the WBA title in 2003 by defeating John Ruiz, although Ruiz was awarded the title later in the year when Jones failed to make a mandatory defence. Often considered to be the best pound-for-pound fighter in the world today, Jones is also an accomplished rapper and actor who has appeared in the *Matrix* series of films. Jones's bubble burst when he was knocked out in the second round by Antonio Tarver (15 May 2004) to lose his WBC light-heavyweight title.

Kane, Peter Born Peter Cain, Heywood, Lancashire, 28 February 1918. His family moved to Golborne, Wigan, and Kane's boxing nickname became 'The Golborne Blacksmith'. He turned pro in 1934. In 1937, after 41 wins, he took on Benny Lynch for the world flyweight title, losing in 13 rounds. The following year he drew with Lynch before taking the title from Jackie Jurich. Kane held the title for five years until deprived of it by Jackie Paterson. Kane, undisputed flyweight champion 1938-43, won 87 of his 97 fights. He died in 1991 aged 73.

Ketchel, Stanley Born Stanislaus Kiecal, Grand Rapids, Michigan, 14 September 1886. Ketchel started fighting as a pro in 1904. Officially he won the world middleweight title in 1908, beating Mike 'Twin' Sullivan with a first-round knockout. His next victory was against Jack 'Twin' Sullivan. Jack was a tougher prospect than Mike and it took Ketchel 20 rounds before he could dispatch him. In September 1908 Ketchel lost the title to Billy Papke but won it back in November. He fought Jack Johnson in 1909 at a time when Johnson was almost unbeatable. Giving away 30lb in weight, Ketchel gave a very good account before losing in 12 rounds. Ketchel was killed on 15 October 1910 by Walter Dipley, a Michigan farmer. The vacant title went to his old rival, Billy Papke. Ketchel, undisputed middleweight champion 1908-10, is rated by some experts as the best middleweight ever.

Kilrain, Jake   Born John Joseph Kilrain, New York, 1859. Jake comes from the golden age of boxing where the old bareknuckle style and the new Queensberry Rules met. He turned pro in 1880 and in 1887 was recognised as heavyweight champion of the world after a fight with Jem Smith. Reports put the number of rounds at 106! On 8 July 1899 Kilrain fought and lost a 75-round bout with John L. Sullivan, the last before the introduction of the Queensberry Rules. This fight was bare knuckle and conducted under London Rules. In 1890 Kilrain lost a six-round decision to Jim Corbett and although he continued to fight he never reached the heights of a title fight again. He died aged 78 in 1937.

Kingpetch, Pone   Born Hui Hui Province, Thailand, 1936. Kingpetch turned pro in 1955. Despite a loss in his first contest he quickly improved and became oriental flyweight champion two years later with a decision over Danny Kid. An attempt to win the bantamweight title the same year failed, Kingpetch losing to Leo Espinosa. In 1960, still having never fought outside Thailand, he beat Pascual Perez to win and then retain the world flyweight title. In 1962 and 1963 he lost to 'Fighting' Harada before winning the rematch and regaining the accompanying title and in 1963 and 1964 repeated the feat, this time against Hiroyuki Ebihara. When he beat Ebihara, he became the first flyweight champion to win the title on three separate occasions. Kingpetch, undisputed flyweight champion 1960-62, 1963 and 1964-65, retired in 1966 with a career record of 28 wins and 6 losses. He died aged 46 in 1982.

Klaus, Frank   Born Pittsburgh, Pennsylvania, 1887. Turning pro in 1904, he got his first title fight in 1912 with a bout against Georges Carpentier. He won on a foul in 19 rounds but the fight was not universally recognised as being for the world title. He was unequivocally recognised when he beat Billy Papke, again on a foul, the following year. A few months later George Chip took his title and Klaus retired from boxing. Klaus, undisputed middleweight champion in 1913, died aged 60 in 1948.

Klitschko, Vitali   Born Belovodsk, Kirghizia, 19 July 1971. Elder brother of Wladimir and, at 2.03m, the bigger of the two. Nicknamed 'Dr Iron Fist', he was a six-time kickboxing champion. Widely tipped as the natural successor to Lennox Lewis (who stopped him in their only fight to date), he has all the attributes to become a dominant champion. He won the WBC belt, vacated by Lewis, on an eighth-round stoppage of South African Corrie Sanders.

Klitschko, Wladimir   Born Ukraine, 25 March 1976. A good amateur, in 1996 he won Olympic super-heavyweight gold. He turned pro immediately afterwards. A 1998 loss to Ross Puritty was the first blip on his career. In 1999 he beat Axel Schulz for the European heavyweight title and the following year fought for the world crown when in Cologne he beat Chris Byrd in 12 rounds to take the WBO title. He lost this title to South African Corrie Sanders in Hanover, Germany, by second-round knockout in 2003 but remains, along with his brother Vitali, one of the leading heavyweights of the day. His nickname is 'Steel Hammer'. A fifth-round stoppage by Lamon Brewster on 10 April 2004 for the vacant WBO belt was unexpected.

La Motta, Jake   Born Giacobe La Motta, New York, 10 July 1921. He turned pro in 1941. In 1942 he had his first fight of six with Sugar Ray Robinson, who won in 10 rounds. The following year they fought twice in February, La Motta winning in 10 before Robinson followed suit. They met twice more in 1945, Robinson winning both (in 10 and 12 rounds). In 1947 La Motta was stopped for the first time in his career by Billy Fox in just four rounds. La Motta later said that the fight had been fixed in order to get him a shot at the world title. A year and a half later La Motta got his chance and took it, beating Marcel Cerdan in 10 rounds. He defended the title twice the following year before, in Chicago on St Valentine's Day 1951, he met Robinson again. Robinson stopped him in the 13th to take his title. After this La Motta, undisputed middleweight champion 1949-51, was never the same fighter.

Lee, Norvel   Born Covington, Kentucky, 1924. Lee was a good amateur and won Olympic light-heavyweight gold in 1952, though he was actually a heavyweight and lost 12 pounds before the competition to make the weight. Despite this he defeated Antonio Pacenza of Argentina. When he returned to the USA he was soon to become aware of the transitory nature of fame. He was arrested in his own home town because he had queued among whites at a bus stop!

Leonard, Benny   Born Benjamin Leiner, New York City, 7 April 1896. In 1911 he started out as a pro and in 1917 fought 'The Welsh Wizard', Freddie Welsh. Leonard knocked Welsh out in the ninth and was crowned world lightweight champion. In 1922 he challenged Jack Britton for the welterweight title but lost on a foul. He retired as champion in 1925. For the next five years he did not box; however, the financial crisis caused by the Wall Street Crash demanded that Leonard return to the ring. On 25 August 1931 one of his comeback fights against Mickey Walker was the first-ever to be televised. His comeback was successful but after 20 or so fights he suffered a loss at the hands of Jimmy McLarnin. After this, Leonard, undisputed lightweight champion for eight years, 1917-25, retired again and became a referee. While officiating on 18 April 1947, he died of a heart attack. Leonard was nicknamed 'The Ghetto Wizard'.

Leonard, Sugar Ray   Born Wilmington, South Carolina, 17 May 1956. After winning light-welterweight gold at the Montreal Olympics in 1976, Sugar Ray turned professional the following year. After 25 wins he took on Wilfredo Benitez and won the WBC welterweight championship in 1979. In 1980 he lost and regained the title in two epic encounters with Roberto Duran, and the WBA light-middleweight crown arrived the following year with a defeat of Ayub Kalule. When he became the first man to beat Thomas Hearns professionally, also in 1981, he gained the WBA welterweight title. With just one defeat on his record, he retired in 1982. Two years later he returned, won one fight and disappeared again for three more years. In 1987 he beat Marvin Hagler to win the WBC middleweight title, his third different weight. In beating Donny Lalonde in 1988 he won the WBC light-heavyweight and super-middleweight titles, his fourth and fifth weights.

In 1989 he drew with Hearns and beat Duran again. Just over a year later he lost to Terry Norris in 12 rounds and retired once more. His final comeback was against Hector 'Macho' Camacho, who stopped him in five rounds; this time Leonard retired hopefully for good. Sugar Ray's record stands up against any fighter in history; he boxed, and beat, some of the all-time greats. His name would top many people's lists as the best pound-for-pound fighter ever. Only Muhammad Ali, Joe Louis, Rocky Marciano and the man from whom he gained his nickname, Sugar Ray Robinson, would contest that title with him.

Lesnevich, Gus Born Cliffside Park, New Jersey, 22 February 1915. In 1934 he turned pro and racked up a series of very quick wins. In 1939, having disposed of Bob Olin he took on Billy Conn for the world light-heavyweight title, getting the decision over 15 rounds. Seven months later the decision went the other way and he was just as quickly dethroned. In 1941 he regained the title from Anton Christoforidis. This time he held it for seven years (although World War II intervened). In 1948 Freddie Mills deprived him of the title over 15 rounds. Three fights later, his last being against Ezzard Charles, he retired. Lesnevich, undisputed light-heavyweight champion 1941-48, died 28 February 1964 aged 49.

Levinsky, Battling Born Barney Lebrovitz, Philadelphia, 10 June 1891. He began fighting as Battling Levinsky in 1913, having previously fought as Barney Williams. In 1914 he lost a light-heavyweight title fight to Jack Dillon in 12 rounds. Two years later he fought Dillon twice more for the title, winning the second bout again in 12. Undisputed light-heavyweight champion 1916-20, he lost in October of that year to Georges Carpentier and never again fought for a world title. His last fight was in 1930 and he died in his home town, 12 February 1949.

Lewis, Lennox Born Lennox Claudius Lewis, London, 2 September 1965. Lewis had a promising amateur career (94 wins and 11 losses) and won super-heavyweight gold at the 1986 Commonwealth Games before fighting in two Olympic Games for Canada. He lost to Tyrell Biggs in LA in 1984 but won super-heavyweight gold at Seoul in 1988, defeating Riddick Bowe in two rounds. He turned pro in 1989 and after a string of impressive victories won the European heavyweight title only a year later, beating Jean-Maurice Chanet. The following year he beat fellow-countryman Gary Mason to retain the European title and win the British. In 1992 he became WBC champion and consequently the first English heavyweight champion since Bob Fitzsimmons in 1899. He defended his title three times (including a fight against Frank Bruno) before being caught by a pearl of a punch from Oliver McCall at Wembley in 1994 and being stopped in the first round. The following year he gained the IBC title by knocking out Tommy Morrison. He now proceeded to fight all the major players – McCall, Golota, Briggs, Holyfield (twice) – and beat them all comfortably. In 2001, overweight and over-confident, he fought Hasim Rahman in South Africa. Rahman beat Lewis for only the second time in his career, in five rounds. In the return fight, later the same year, Lewis KOed Rahman in four.

He has fought Mike Tyson and Vitali Klitschko within the last two years, both being easy victories. Lewis ruled out a rematch with Klitschko and announced his retirement on 6 February 2004. WBC heavyweight champion 1992-94, WBC heavyweight champion 1997-2000, WBA, WBC and IBF heavyweight champion 2000, WBC and IBF heavyweight champion 2000-01, and WBC and IBF heavyweight champion 2001-04, Lewis is regarded by most as one of the great heavyweights of all time.

Lewis, Ted Born Gershon Mendeloff, London, 1894. Lewis had his first pro fight before his 15th birthday. In 1913, after countless fights, he became British featherweight champion, beating Alec Lambert in 17 rounds. The following year he became European champion at the same weight, beating Paul Til on a foul, and the next year world champion. He gained the world championship from Jack Britton and wore the first mouthpiece in this 1915 bout with his great welterweight rival. In total he fought Britton 20 times in his career. Between 1915 and 1919 they shared the title, each defeating the other several times. Having lost the title – to Britton of course – in 1919 he continued to hold welterweight and middleweight titles for Britain and Europe but never again at world level. Undisputed welterweight champion 1915-16 and 1917-19, he had one last world title fight in 1922 when he took on Georges Carpentier. Carpentier beat him in a single round. Lewis died in 1970, four days short of his 76th birthday.

Louis, Joe Born Joseph Louis Barrow, Lafayette, Alabama, 13 May 1914. Louis (pronounced Lewis) is one of the all-time boxing greats. His early professional record is a litany of one- and two-round knockouts. Prior to becoming world champion he beat Primo Carnera, Max Baer, Jack Sharkey and Eddie Simms. Louis became world heavyweight champion in 1937, beating James J. Braddock, and made 25 defences over the 11 years 252 days that he held the title. His phenomenal record is such that he only ever lost one world title fight (to Ezzard Charles) and only three of his 66 professional fights. Max Schmeling became the first person to beat him (in his 28th fight in 1936) when he was knocked out in the 12th round, and Rocky Marciano was the other in 1951. 'The Brown Bomber', as he was known, died 12 April 1981.

Lynch, Benny Born Scotland, 1913. Known as 'The Kid from the Gorbals', he fought all his early bouts in Glasgow. In 1935, after four years as a pro, he became British and world flyweight champion when he beat Jackie Brown. In 1938 he was stripped of the title after failing to make the weight in a fight with Jackie Jurich. His last fight saw the only time that he was knocked out in his career; he retired afterwards and never fought again. Seriously affected by drink, the undisputed flyweight champion of 1935-38 died eight years later in 1946, aged 33.

McCallum, Mike Born Michael McKenzie McCallum, Kingston, Jamaica, 1956. As an impressive amateur, with 240 wins and 10 losses, McCallum won the Commonwealth Games welterweight title in 1978. He turned pro in 1981. Nicknamed 'The Bodysnatcher' for his fierce body punching, he soon set about gaining world titles. He was WBA light-middleweight champion from 1984 (when he beat Sean Mannion) to 1987, WBA middleweight champion from 1989 (beating Herol Graham) to 1991, and WBC light-heavyweight champion from 1994 (beating Jeff Harding) to 1995. McCallum, one of the few boxers to win at three different weights, then retired and is now a boxing trainer in Las Vegas.

McAuliffe, Jack Born Cork, Ireland, 1866. McAuliffe turned pro in 1884, boxing mostly out of New York, and was a protégé of the great Jack 'Nonpareil' Dempsey. In 1886 he beat Billy Frazier to become lightweight champion of America and the following year he went one better, gaining the world title when he overcame Canadian Harry Gilmore. In 1894 he retired from the ring. McAuliffe, undisputed lightweight champion 1886-94, is widely regarded as one of the greatest lightweights of all time. Throughout his career he was undefeated with 33 wins and 9 draws. In a contest against Jem Carney he was close to losing, which would have spoiled his stats, when a gambler with money on McAuliffe intervened and forced the referee to declare a 74-round draw. Known as 'The Napoleon of the Ring', he died aged 71 in 1937.

McCoy, Charles Born Norman Selby, Rush County, Indiana, 13 October 1872. 'Kid' McCoy's fighting style was so variable (often intentionally in order to confuse opponents) that it gave rise to the expression 'the real McCoy': some days an ordinary fighter might show up and on others 'the real McCoy'. He is credited with inventing the corkscrew punch, thrown while rotating the fist. In 1896 McCoy knocked out welterweight champion Tommy Ryan and won by disqualification over former champion 'Mysterious' Billy Smith. In 1897 he won the middleweight crown vacated by Bob Fitzsimmons by KOing Dan Creedon in the 15th round. Six years later he challenged for the light-heavyweight title but lost to Jack Root. After retiring he tried acting but with little success. McCoy was married eight times, and in 1940 he murdered his girlfriend Theresa Mors. He served seven years in prison; in 1940, three years after his release, he committed suicide by means of sleeping pills, 18 April 1940.

McGuigan, Barry Born Clones, Ireland, 28 February 1961. Turned pro in 1981. In 1983 he won the British featherweight title, beating Vernon Penprase in two rounds. The European title followed the same year with a victory over Valerio Nati. After three successful defences of his European crown, McGuigan went one better and fought for the world title. At Loftus Road in June 1985 he beat Eusebio Pedrosa to become WBA featherweight champion. Just over a year later he lost the title to Steve Cruz. Four more fights later and 'The Clones Cyclone' retired. A fast and technical boxer, McGuigan, WBA featherweight champion 1985-86, lost only three times in his career. Only one of these defeats occurred in his prime and of his 32 victories 28 were by KO. His father once represented Ireland in the Eurovision Song Contest.

Mclarnin, Jimmy Born Ireland, 1907. He turned pro in 1924 and went 20 fights unbeaten before losing to Charles Taylor over 10 rounds the following year. 'Baby Face' McLarnin continued to learn his craft and in 1928 fought Sammy Mandell for the world lightweight title, losing in 15 rounds. He fought Mandell twice more, winning both before getting another chance at a world crown. He beat Young Corbett III in the first round to become world welterweight champion in 1933. His next three fights were all against Barney Ross for the same title and saw him lose, win and lose again. After another three fights he retired. McLarnin, undisputed welterweight champion 1933-34 and again 1934-35, lost only 11 times in his career.

McClellan, Gerald Born 1967. 'The G Man' turned pro in 1988. He became WBO middleweight champion in 1991, beating John Mugabi, and was WBC middleweight champion 1993-95. He knocked out Jay Bell in just 20 seconds in a 1993 middleweight bout. In a 1995 fight with Nigel Benn he was severely injured, and as a result he is now wheelchair bound (although his condition is improving) and blind. Two days prior to the fight he said, 'In boxing you are going to war, and in war you must be prepared to die.'

Magri, Charlie Born Tunis, Tunisia, 20 July 1956. Magri turned pro in 1977 and won the British flyweight title in only his third professional bout. After 11 wins and nine KOs he beat Franco Udella to become European flyweight champion in 1979. Now fighting at the top of the tree in flyweight terms, he had a more difficult time of it; his first loss came after 23 fights when he took on Juan Diaz in 1981. A loss to Jose Torres in 1982 was avenged the same year to give him a shot at the world title. On 15 March 1983 he beat Eloncio Mercedes to become WBC world flyweight champion, but lost at his first defence to Frank Cedano later in the year. In 1985 he challenged again and lost, this time to Sot Chitalada. Magri's last fight was against fellow Britain Duke McKenzie, he lost in five rounds and afterwards retired. Magri, WBC flyweight champion in 1983, was an explosive fighter, winning 23 of his 30 victories inside the distance.

Marciano, Rocky Born Brockton, Massachusetts, 1 September 1923. After only a fair amateur record (8 wins from 12) he turned pro in 1948. Coley Wallace can draw some comfort from being the last person to defeat Marciano in a boxing ring when he defeated him as an amateur in March 1948. Of Marciano's first 11 fights not one went past the third round and in 1952 he beat Jersey Joe Walcott to become undisputed champion. His record of 49 unbeaten fights, 43 by knockout, makes Marciano one of the all-time greats. He is remembered for his crouching style and ruthless disposition in the ring. Although his record is formidable, the quality of opposition is not always apparent and he retired only four years after reaching the pinnacle, having fought only six more fights in that time. His nickname was 'The Brockton Blockbuster'. On 31 August 1969, Marciano died tragically in a plane crash near Newton, Iowa, en route to a birthday party.

Marsh, Terry European light-welterweight champion in 1985, and IBF light-welterweight champion in 1987, as an amateur Marsh lost his first nine fights. He is best remembered for the bizarre trial where he was acquitted at the Old Bailey of attempting to kill promoter Frank Warren in 1990. He was also the first British professional to hold a world title and retire undefeated. Marsh is a dedicated member of the Liberal Democrat Party and has maintained aspirations to become an MP.

Maxim, Joey Born Giuseppe Antonio Berardinelli, Cleveland, Ohio, 1922. He turned pro in 1941 and despite a few losses, including two back-to-back against Ezzard Charles and two to Jersey Joe Walcott, progressed through the ranks. In 1949 he became American light-heavyweight champion by beating Gus Levnevich and a year later overcame Freddie Mills to take the world title. In 1951 he fought Ezzard Charles for the heavyweight title but lost in 15 rounds. After two defences of his light-heavyweight crown, including one against Sugar Ray Robinson, he lost to Archie Moore. He had two rematches with Moore but every time he fought him the result was the same, a loss in 15. He had 11 more fights with only three wins (one against Floyd

Patterson) and retired in 1958. Maxim, undisputed light-heavyweight champion 1950-52, was a very good fighter but struggled against top opposition. In total he won 82 fights, lost 29 and drew four times.

Mills, Freddie   Born England, 26 June 1919. A hard-hitting light-heavyweight, he turned pro in 1936. After a mixed set of results he became Commonwealth and British light-heavyweight champion in 1942, beating Len Harvey in two rounds. Two years later he lost both titles to Jack London. His first world title bout was against Gus Lesnevich, but he lost in 10. In 1948 he took on the same man and beat him in 15, but his world crown slipped away when he took on Joey Maxim in 1950. Maxim was too strong for Mills and knocked him out after 10 rounds. Mills, undisputed world light-heavyweight champion 1948-50, never fought again. On 25 July 1965 he was found dead in his car, an apparent suicide.

Minter, Alan   Born Crawley, Sussex, 17 August 1951. Minter won light-middleweight bronze in 1972 at the Munich Olympics. Almost immediately afterwards he turned pro and built up a solid record. Three years later, under the managerial guidance of Doug Bidwell, he defeated Kevin Finnegan for the British middleweight title and also beat him in two rematches the following years (1976 and 1977), all three fights going the distance. His big moment came in 1980 when he became the first British boxer since Ted 'Kid' Lewis to win a world title in America, taking on and outpointing Vito Antuofermo in Las Vegas. He held the title for just six months, losing it the same year to Marvin Hagler at Wembley. His last opponent was Tony Sibson who beat him in three rounds while fighting for the European and British titles. Alan retired after the Sibson fight with a good record of 39 wins and 9 losses, seven of his losses being due to cuts.

Mitchell, Pinkey   Born Myron Mitchell, Milwaukee, 1899. He fought exclusively in the Americas, nearly always in his home town. In 1922 he was awarded the title of light-welterweight champion of the world by popular vote when the readers of *The Boxing Blade* gave him this honour in the newly created division. He lost the title to Mushy Callahan in 1926 and retired four fights later. He died in his home town aged 70 in 1970. His brother, Ritchie Mitchell, was also a boxer.

Monzon, Carlos   Born Argentina, 1942. Monzon first fought as a pro in 1963. In 1970, after almost eighty fights, he fought Nino Benvenuti for the world middleweight title and won with a 12th-round knockout. Over the next seven years he had 19 fights, putting the title up for grabs 14 times, and won them all. He retired as undefeated champion, having dominated his division much as Bob Foster dominated the light-heavyweight division in the 1970s. Monzon, undisputed middleweight champion 1970-77, died in a car crash in 1995 aged 52.

Moore, Archie   Born Archibald Lee Wright, Benoit, Mississippi, 13 December 1913. In 1935, a year after being released from reform school, he had his first organised bout, when he lost in three rounds to Julius Kemp. Fighting mainly in St Louis and San Diego, Moore won most of his fights but had a few losses to add to the tally. In 1936 Moore appeared in 22 bouts, winning all but four of them, 16 by knockout. In 1941 he retired after a long period of stomach problems, having never really made his mark. He returned, however, in 1942 and continued much as before. In the next ten years he fought an amazing number of fights, including 18 in 1951 alone. During this period he also fought and lost to Ezzard Charles three times. He was just over 39 when he beat Joey Maxim to the world light-heavyweight crown. It was reported that he received less than $1,000 for the fight, while Maxim got $100,000. He retained this title until his retirement in 1963, winning two return matches with Maxim.

In an attempt to gain the elusive heavyweight title, he fought and lost to Rocky Marciano and Floyd Patterson and was the only man to fight both Marciano and Muhammad Ali. He fought approximately 200 professional bouts in all, losing only 24. Moore was known variously as 'The 4th of July Kid' and 'The Mongoose' because of his lightning speed and power. In major competition he scored a massive 145 KOs. After leaving boxing Moore tried his hand at films before settling down to training. In 1974 he helped prepare heavyweight boxer George Foreman for his famous 'Rumble in the Jungle' title bout with Ali in Zaire. Moore, undisputed light-heavyweight champion from 1952-62, died 9 December 1998.

Moorer, Michael   Born Brooklyn, New York, 1967. Moorer's pro career started in 1988 when, after 11 wins (all in that year), he became WBO light-heavyweight champion of the world with a five-round victory over Ramzi Hassan. After ten successful defences he relinquished the title in 1991. In 1992 he won the WBO heavyweight title, beating Bert Cooper. The next year saw him give this title up and in 1994 he took on and beat Evander Holyfield for the WBA and IBF titles. He lost seven months later to George Foreman. In 1996 he beat Axel Schulz to gain the vacant IBF heavyweight crown before losing it the next year to Holyfield. Moorer's place in the pantheon of great heavyweights is, however, assured: after a hundred years, he was the first-ever southpaw to become heavyweight champion of the world.

Murphy, Billy   Born Thomas William, Auckland, New Zealand, 1863. 'Torpedo Billy' fought most of his early bouts in New Zealand and then Sydney, Australia. In 1890, after having eventually worked his way to the USA, he beat Ike Weir to win an early accreditation of the world featherweight title. That same year he lost to Young Griffo, a far more talented boxer, in 15 rounds, and the rematch in 1891 led to his disqualification on a foul. His remaining years were unsuccessful. A string of losses saw him retrace his steps, fighting first in Australia and then New Zealand where his last fight took place in 1907; he lost in three rounds. A game, willing and more than skilful fighter, Murphy died in his native Auckland aged 75 in 1939.

Nelson, Azumah   Born Accra, Ghana, 19 September 1958. At the 1976 Montreal Olympics he won featherweight gold under the name of Nelson Azumah. He started as a pro in 1979 and quickly established a reputation as a knockout specialist. In total he had 28 KOs in 46 career fights. In 1984, having won various African and Commonwealth titles, he gained the WBC featherweight title by beating the great Wilfredo Gomez in 11 rounds. In 1988 he added the WBC junior lightweight title, defeating Mario Martinez. His attempt to win at a third weight stalled when in 1990 he took on Pernell Whitaker. Later to win at four weights, Whitaker was too strong for Nelson and he lost in 12, his first defeat in eight years. Over the next six years he fought infrequently, usually for the junior lightweight title and – barring a mishap against James Leija – successfully. After two successive losses Nelson retired in 1998.

Norris, Terry Born Lubbock, Texas, 1967. The brother of WBA world cruiserweight champion, Orlin Norris. Turning pro in 1986, he earned himself a title shot three years later, but lost to Julian Jackson by a second-round KO, the first of his career. In 1990 he beat John 'The Beast' Mugabi to win the WBC light-middleweight championship. 'Terrible' Terry Norris then proved his class with defences against Sugar Ray Leonard and Don Curry. After ten defences he lost the title in 1993 to Simon Brown, regaining it in the 1994 rematch. He then lost it to Luis Santana before winning it back again. He added the IBF title in 1995 with a 12-round win over Paul Vaden, but in 1997 he lost the titles to Keith Mullings in Atlantic City. After two more losses, Norris's last fight was in 1998.

Nunn, Michael Born Davenport, Iowa, 1963. Nunn's pro career started in 1984 and his first 30 fights were all victories, giving him a match against Frank Tate for the IBF middleweight crown in 1988. Nunn knocked Tate out in round nine to take the title. Defences followed against Iran Barkley, Marlon Starling and Don Curry – all wins. Nunn won his first 36 contests but in 1991 he lost the 37th to James 'Lights Out' Toney who knocked him out in round 11. In 1992 he moved up to super middleweight and proceeded to win the WBA title from Victor Cordoba. From 1994 Nunn had three title fights and lost them all, the last for the vacant WBC light-heavyweight crown against Graciano Rocchigiani. Nunn, whose nickname was 'Second To', lost only four fights in his career – all of them for world titles. On 30 January 2004 Nunn was sentenced to 24 years in prison for buying a kilogram of cocaine from an undercover agent in Davenport, Iowa, in August 2002. Nunn won 58 of his 62 fights.

O'Brien, Jack Born James Francis Hagen, Philadelphia, 1878. Turned pro in 1896. During the next eight years 'Philadelphia Jack' fought Marvin Hart, Bob Fitzsimmons, Tommy Burns, Tommy Ryan and a raft of other good fighters. Throughout all these matches (many being no-decision), O'Brien was mostly unscathed with just a handful of losses. In 1905 he fought his first world title bout, defeating Fitzsimmons for the world light-heavyweight title. In 1906 he tried to go one better and win the heavyweight crown and after 20 rounds against Tommy Burns he was awarded a draw. The following year though, Burns beat him, also in 20.

In 1909 he managed to get through 10 rounds against Stanley Ketchel, being saved by the bell in this fight. Showing his versatility, he also fought Jack Johnson the same year; Ketchel was a great middleweight and Johnson an outstanding heavyweight. O'Brien's second fight against Ketchel, however, saw him lose in three. O'Brien, undisputed light-heavyweight champion 1905-12, retired as title holder. He died aged 64 in 1942.

Olson, Bobo Born Carl Olson, Honolulu, Hawaii, 11 July 1928. 'The Hawaiian Swede' turned pro in 1944 at the age of only 16, using fake ID. After eight years fighting mainly out of Hawaii he took on Sugar Ray Robinson for the world middleweight title. He took the champion all the way but lost over 15 rounds. In 1953, having just won the American middleweight crown, he took on Randolph Turpin for the vacant world title. He won in 15 and held it until 1955 when Robinson defeated him in two rounds. After a rematch where he lost in four Olson never again fought for a world title. An excellent fighter, Olson was only ever stopped by a handful of fighters including Robinson (three times), Jose Torres and Archie Moore, whom he challenged for the light-heavyweight championship.

Ortiz, Carlos Born Puerto Rico, 1936. Ortiz started boxing as a pro in 1955. His first defeat came after 28 fights when he took on Johnny Busso, but it was avenged three months later. His next defeat, in the same year, 1958, was against Flash Lane. This defeat was also avenged when in 1959 Ortiz beat Lane for the light-welterweight world title. Ortiz held the title for just over a year before relinquishing it to Duillo Loi in 1960. He fought Loi three times, winning the first and losing the next two; all three fights went the distance. In 1962 Ortiz captured the lightweight crown from Joe Brown. This he defended four times with wins over such stars as Flash Elorde and Kenny Lane, before dropping it to Ismael Laguna. Seven months after losing the title, Ortiz won it back and he now defended it five times before losing, in 1968, to Carlos Cruz over 15 rounds. Ortiz continued to box but never regained the same heights, and after a six-round stoppage by Ken Buchanan in 1972 he retired. Having lost seven fights and being stopped only once, Ortiz was undisputed junior welterweight champion 1959-60, and undisputed lightweight champion 1962-65 and 1965-68.

Owen, Johnny Born Merthyr Tydfil, 1956. Owen's style was one of perpetual motion coupled with skill and great technical expertise. He turned pro in 1976 and after only nine fights beat Paddy Maguire to become British bantamweight champion. No Welsh boxer had held the British bantamweight title for 64 years and a Welsh boxer had never held the Commonwealth bantamweight title, but this duly followed when Owen beat Paul Ferreri in 1978. A victory over Juan Francisco Rodriguez gave Owen the European title too. In his last fight, on 19 September 1980, Owen took on Lupe Pintor for the world title. Pintor won and Owen, just 24 years old, died as a result of the punishment that he had taken. Apart from a dubious decision against Rodriguez this was Owen's only defeat. He had a variety of nicknames – 'The Matchstick Man', 'The Bionic Bantam' and 'The Bionic Skeleton' – all of which give a clear picture of this muscular, paper-thin whirling dervish.

Papke, Billy Born William Herman Papke, Illinois, 1886. Turned pro in 1906. Papke was unbeaten until 1908 when he took on the great Stanley Ketchel, who beat Papke to retain his world middleweight title. The same year Papke was to fight Ketchel twice more and in September he gained the title, though under less than fair circumstances. At the start of the fight, rather than shaking hands or touching gloves Papke hit Ketchel in the throat! Ketchel, game as ever, hung on but was beaten in 12. The rematch, however, was a win for Ketchel in 11. The following year Papke fought Ketchel again, this time losing in 20. He won the world middleweight title twice more, the second time beating Georges Carpentier on a foul. His last world title fight was against Frank Klaus in 1913, when Klaus won on a foul in 15 rounds. Papke, undisputed middleweight champion in 1908, was a fast and hard-hitting fighter who lived up to his nickname of 'The Illinois Thunderbolt'. In 1936, aged 50, he killed his ex-wife and committed suicide.

Papp, László Born Budapest, Hungary, 1926. Papp fought 300 amateur fights and lost only 12, winning gold at three consecutive Olympics with the middleweight crown in 1948 and the light-middleweight title in 1952 and 1956. He turned pro in 1957 and fought solely in Europe. Although he never challenged for the world title he was a great fighter who was never beaten as a pro in 29 fights, with 27 wins and 2 draws. Papp was on the verge of a world middleweight title shot when the Hungarian government revoked his permit to travel abroad, thus ending his pro career. He died 16 October 2003.

Pastrano, Willie   Born New Orleans, 1935. In 1951 he fought his first pro fight. In 1955 he took the scalp of Joey Maxim and in 1962 drew with the great Archie Moore. His first (of three) world title fights came the following year, when he beat Harold Johnson in 15 rounds to become world light-heavyweight champion. After defeating England's Terry Downes by an 11th-round knockout he finally lost the crown to Jose Torres in 1965. Pastrano, undisputed light-heavyweight champion 1963-65, died in 1997 aged 62.

Paterson, Jackie   Born Scotland, 1920. Paterson turned pro in 1938. A year later he won the British flyweight title from Paddy Ryan, and a year after that the Commonwealth title from Kid Tanner. In 1942 he stopped Peter Kane in Glasgow in one round to become world flyweight champion. He held the title for five years until being KOed by Rinty Monaghan in seven rounds in 1948. After four consecutive losses he hung up his gloves in 1951. Paterson, undisputed flyweight champion 1943-48, was murdered in South Africa in 1966, aged just 46.

Patterson, Floyd   Born Waco, North Carolina, 4 January 1935. Patterson is the holder of a number of boxing firsts. In 1952 at the Helsinki Olympic Games he beat Vasile Tita to become middleweight gold medallist. Subsequently he became the first Olympic gold medallist to win the heavyweight world title when in 1956 he beat Archie Moore for the vacant title, becoming at the time the youngest-ever world champion. On defeating Ingemar Johansson in 1960 he became the first boxer to regain the heavyweight crown. Patterson lost eight times in his career, his first to Joey Maxim in 1954 and his last to Muhammad Ali in 1972.

Pedrosa, Eusebio   Born Panama City, 1953. He turned pro in 1973 and three years later lost a bantamweight world title fight with Alfonso Zamora. In 1978 he picked up the WBA featherweight title, beating Cecilio Lastra with a 13-round KO. After 19 defences and ten years later he lost the crown to Barry McGuigan. Semi-retired, Pedrosa fought only five more times, his last fight being in 1992.

Pep, Willie   Born Guiglermo Papaleo, 19 September 1922. Nicknamed 'Will o' the Wisp', Pep won his first 63 fights before losing to Sammy Angott in a non-title bout. He is best remembered for his physical four-fight series against Sandy Saddler. Pep lost his crown to Saddler in 1948, but regained it by decisioning Saddler in a rematch four months later. He managed to keep the title by making defences against Eddie Compo, Charley Riley and Ray Famechon, but a third match with Saddler was inevitable. When they met again, in 1950, Saddler regained the crown with an eighth-round knockout. The two legends would meet once more in 1951 and this time Saddler scored a ninth-round knockout. Undisputed featherweight champion in 1942-48 and1949-50, Willie ended his career having won 230 of his 242 bouts (lost 11 with one drawn).

Quarry, Jerry   Born Los Angeles, 1945. Quarry turned pro in 1965 and suffered his first defeat a year and 21 fights later, losing to Eddie Machen. Quarry fought at a time when there were many excellent heavyweights, and consequently his talents are not universally recognised. In his 66 pro fights he only lost nine, twice each to Joe Frazier and Muhammad Ali. Quarry died in 1999 aged only 53.

Rahman, Hasim   Born Hasim Shariff Rahman, Baltimore, Maryland, 1972. 'The Rock' turned pro in 1994 and became American heavyweight champion three years later. Unbeaten in his first 29 contests, he lost the 30th to David Tua. In 2000 he won the WBU heavyweight title, beating Corrie Sanders in seven rounds. In 2001 he took on Lennox Lewis, a man who had only lost once before and the hot favourite. But an over-confident Lewis weighed in heavy and Rahman stopped him in just five rounds. Since then Rahman has had only four more fights: the first a rematch with Lewis which he lost in four, the next a loss to Evander Holyfield, and then, in March 2003, a draw with the first man to beat him, David Tua. Rahman, WBC and IBF heavyweight champion in 2000, then lost a 12-round unanimous decision against John Ruiz on 13 December 2003, for the interim WBA heavyweight title. He has a record of 35 wins (29 inside the distance), five losses and one draw.

Randall, Frankie   Born Birmingham, Alabama, 25 September 1961. The first man ever to beat Julio Cesar Chavez in a professional bout, thus becoming WBC light-welterweight champion in 1994, Randall was also WBA junior welterweight champion 1994-96 and 1996-97.

Robinson, Steve   Born Cardiff, 1968. Turned pro in 1989. Robinson, nicknamed 'The Cinderella Man' (like James Braddock) had an inauspicious start to his career; in his first 23 fights he won 13 and lost 9. So it was in 1993 that he was given the chance to create his fairytale epithet. The WBO world featherweight champion, Ruben Palacios of Colombia, was scheduled to defend his title against John Davison. However, the champion failed an HIV test during the week of the scheduled fight and was immediately stripped of his title. Into the breach stepped Robinson, who beat Davision for the vacant title and proceeded to prove that the win was no fluke with seven successful defences. In 1995, however, he was stopped by Prince Naseem Hamed and his reign was over. Robinson, former featherweight champion of the world, decided to retire after suffering his sixth loss in a row, making the announcement following his points defeat, over eight rounds, to Steve Conway, in 2002.

Robinson, Sugar Ray   Born Walker Smith, Ailey, Georgia, 3 May 1921. Robinson turned pro in 1940. After 40 wins (including a first victory over Jake La Motta) he lost his first fight. In 10 rounds it was La Motta who inflicted the loss. Just two weeks later Robinson beat Jackie Wilson and a week after that overcame La Motta in the rematch. Two more defeats were inflicted on La Motta in 1945 before, at Christmas 1946, Robinson beat Tommy Bell to become undisputed welterweight champion of the world. He retained this title for the next six years with victories over Bobo Olson, Kid Gavilan and La Motta. In 1951 Robinson, after beating La Motta again for the middleweight title, vacated the welterweight crown. In the same year he lost and regained the title from Randy Turpin. In 1952 he lost only his third fight, to Joey Maxim, when challenging for the light-heavyweight title. At the end of 1952 Robinson retired. He did not fight at all in 1953 but returned to the ring to fight two exhibitions in 1954.

In 1955 he regained the middleweight title from Bobo Olson, while in 1957 and 1958 he lost and regained it against first Gene Fullmer, and then Carmen Basilio. In 1960 Paul Pender deprived him of the crown over 15 rounds and the rematch went the same way. Athough he continued boxing for another five years he never again had a title shot. Robinson, one of the greatest middleweight boxers of all time, retired for good in December 1965. Sugar Ray was a natural fighter and when in shape was awesome. Although the defeats on his record might prevent him being elevated to the top of the all-time great list, he always won when he was well prepared. He died 12 April 1989.

Ruiz, John   Born Chelsea, Massachusetts, 4 January 1972. Ruiz turned pro in 1992. In 1994 he had his first title challenge against Danell Nicholson for the IBO heavyweight title but lost in 12 rounds. His next title outing was six years later; this time the opponent was Evander Holyfield and the version the WBA, but the result was the same – a loss in 12. However, seven months later Ruiz reversed the decision and was heavyweight champion. Early in 2003, after two successful defences, he lost the title to Roy Jones Jr. He became interim WBA champion in December 2003 when Jones failed to make the mandatory defence. A native of Puerto Rico, 'Quiet Man' Ruiz is the first Hispanic heavyweight champion of the world.

Ryan, Paddy   Born Ireland, 1851. Ryan was both a boxer and a wrestler. In 1880 he became heavyweight champion of America when in a marathon match he beat Joe Goss in 87 rounds. In 1882 he lost this title to John L. Sullivan. The remainder of his career comprised mostly exhibition fights. Ryan died in 1900 aged 49.

Ryan, Tommy   Born Joseph Youngs, Redwood, New York, 31 March 1870. Ryan turned pro in 1887. He then produced a series of quick wins, and some slower ones: his 1891 contest against Danny Needham lasted 76 rounds and took five hours to complete. In 1894 he beat 'Mysterious' Billy Smith over 20 rounds to take the welterweight crown. He held the title for the next four years (or two, perhaps) despite the attentions of Smith and Jack 'Nonpareil' Dempsey – with Ryan's fights it is difficult to ascertain exactly when he put his titles on the line. It is generally accepted that in 1896 he lost the title to Kid McCoy and then won it back from Smith. In 1898 he won the middleweight title by beating Jack Bonner. He held the title until 1907, although in 1906 he gave it to Hugo Kelly. The public did not accept this as valid and the next official middleweight champion was the great Stanley Ketchel. Ryan died 3 August 1948, aged 78.

Saldivar, Vicente   Born Mexico, 1943. Turned pro in 1961. A southpaw, he was undisputed featherweight champion from 1964 (beating Sugar Ramos) to 1967 and WBC featherweight champion in 1970. During this period he fought and beat Howard Winstone three times. After their final meeting in 1967 Saldivar announced his retirement. Having made a few comebacks he retired for good after losing to Eder Jofre.

Saxton, Johnny   Born Newark, New Jersey, 1930. Turning pro in 1949, he was unbeaten in his first 40 fights. In 1954 he took on and beat Kid Gavilan for the world welterweight title. He lost this a year later to Tony DeMarco before regaining it in 1956 from Carmen Basilio. Basilio won it back later the same year in nine rounds and in their next bout inflicted a crushing defeat in two. Saxton boxed just four more times before retiring in 1958.

Schmeling, Max   Born Brandenburg, Germany, 28 September 1905. Schmeling turned pro in 1924, the following year he fought Jack Dempsey in an exhibition match and the year after that won the German light-heavyweight title. Two years more and a move up in weight saw him attain the heavyweight crown when he beat Franz Diener. His only fight of 1930 was for the world heavyweight championship. In New York in June he fought Jack Sharkey. His victory is unique as it is the only time that a man has become world heavyweight champion on a disqualification, Sharkey being penalised for a low blow. (The first boxer to win a world title by disqualification was Pedlar Palmer in 25 November 1895 against Billy Plimmer in London.)

Two years later, after one defence against Young Stribling, he lost the title in his return bout with Sharkey. In 1936 he became the first man to beat Joe Louis professionally (though not in a title fight) with a 12th-round knockout. In the rematch two years later Louis knocked Schmeling out in the first round. During the war Schmeling was inactive and after the cessation of hostilities was nowhere near the fighter that he had once been. Five post-war fights later and Schmeling, undisputed heavyweight champion of the world 1930-32, retired. He was nicknamed 'The Black Uhlan of the Rhine'.

Sharkey, Jack   Born 26 October 1902. Sharkey started as a pro in 1924. His early career was varied; a smattering of losses included a seven-round KO by Jack Dempsey. In 1929 he won the American heavyweight title beating Tommy Loughran in three rounds. Two fights later he lost a 1930 contest for the vacant world title to Max Schmeling on a disqualification. In the rematch two years later Sharkey beat Schmeling in 15, but he lost the title at the first defence to a boxer he had previously beaten, Primo Carnera. Seven fights and three years later he retired having lost his last fight, against Joe Louis, in three rounds. Undisputed heavyweight champion 1932-33, Sharkey died 17 August 1994.

Smith, Amos   Born Nova Scotia, 1871. Turning to boxing in 1891, 'Mysterious Billy' Smith had his first title shot a year later and beat Danny Needham to become world welterweight champion. Two years afterwards he met the boxer who was to be his nemesis, Tommy Ryan. Smith had already drawn with Ryan twice when in the third meeting in 1894, Ryan took his title in 20 gruelling rounds. Smith fought Ryan four more times but could never get the better of him. In 1898 he again became undisputed welterweight champion of the world when he beat William 'Matty' Matthews in 25 rounds. In 1899 he fought James 'Rube' Ferns and, even though he had his man on the canvas more than ten times, he lost on a foul in 21 rounds. Smith's career was full of similar incident. In total he lost nine of his career fights on fouls. He lost his title in his last-ever title fight to the man from whom he had won it, William Matthews. Apart from the fouls, Smith's career was also dogged by broken bones and accusations of fixing. He died aged 66 in Portland, Oregon.

Smith, Solly   Born Solomon Garcia Smith, Los Angeles, 1871. Turned pro in 1888. His first loss came in 1893 in seven rounds against George Dixon for the world featherweight title. Four years later he took on Dixon again and beat him in 20, but he held the title for less than a year before losing it to Dave Sullivan. In his next 16 fights he won only one and retired in 1904. Smith, undisputed featherweight champion 1897-98, died in 1933.

Spinks, Leon   Born St Louis, Missouri, 11 July 1953. Brother of Michael, as a boxer he had a great amateur career with a record of 178 wins from 185 fights, 133 of these being by KO. At the Montreal

Olympics in 1976, he won light-heavyweight gold. Turning pro shortly afterwards, in his eighth professional fight he became only the third-ever boxer to defeat Muhammad Ali. Seven months later, he allowed Ali to become the first boxer ever to regain the heavyweight title twice when he lost in 15 rounds, although many thought that Ali had manufactured the situation so that he could set the record. Spinks, undisputed heavyweight champion for seven months in 1978, did fight for the title again when in 1981 he lost in three rounds to Larry Holmes. Spinks continued to make the occasional comeback but fought his last pro fight in 1995 and is now officially retired. He will always be remembered as the man who beat Ali, and he and Michael were the first brothers to become world boxing champions. The family tradition was continued when Leon's son Cory became IBF and WBC world welterweight champion in December 2003.

Spinks, Michael Born St Louis, Missouri, 13 July 1956. Michael won Olympic middleweight gold in 1976 at Montreal. Immediately after the Olympics he turned pro and after 16 wins fought Eddie Mustafa Muhammad for the WBA light-heavyweight title. He won, and with a victory over Dwight Braxton two years later unified the title. In 1985 he managed to prevent Larry Holmes from equalling Rocky Marciano's record of 49 straight wins when he beat him on a controversial points decision. In doing so he became one of the very few boxers to ever hold both light-heavy and heavyweight titles at the same time. Holmes fared no better in their rematch a year later, Spinks getting the decision after 15 rounds. Spinks, although a spoiler of Holmes's record, was himself unbeaten in 31 fights. His first-ever professional defeat was to Mike Tyson in 1988. Tyson took Spinks apart with a first-round KO. Spinks, who had never lost professionally before, decided once was enough and announced his retirement. Spinks was WBA light-heavyweight champion 1981-83, undisputed light-heavyweight champion 1983-85, and heavyweight champion 1985-88.

Starling, Marlon Born Hartford, Connecticut,1959. 'Magic Man' turned pro in 1979 and boxed almost exclusively in his home town. Twenty-five consecutive wins earned him a fight with Don Curry which he duly lost in 12 rounds. Six more wins earned him a shot at the WBA welterweight title, but he again lost to Curry, this time in six. Three years later, in 1987, he finally won a world title, stopping Mark Breland in the 11th round to win the WBA crown. Starling lost his title controversially to a late punch from Tomas Molinares a year later, in 1989. He then won the WBC version from an unprepared Lloyd Honeyghan in the sweltering heat of Las Vegas, holding this title until the following year when in his final fight he lost to Maurice Blocker. Starling did fight for a middleweight title but was never as comfortable in the heavier division and lost in 12 rounds to Michael Nunn. Starling, WBA welterweight champion 1987-88 and WBC champion 1989-90, retired in 1990.

Stracey, John H. Born London, 1950. Stracey's first professional fight was in 1969. He won his first eight by KO and was unbeaten in his first 23 bouts. In 1972 he fought Bobby Arthur for the vacant British welterweight title but lost in seven. The following year he won the title against the same boxer with a four-round stoppage. In 1974 Stracey beat Roger Menetrey to become European champion and in Mexico City on 6 December 1975 he fought Jose Napoles for the world title, winning in just six rounds. After one defence, however, Stracey conceded the title to Carlos Palomino. He fought only twice more, losing to Dave 'Boy' Green and winning his final fight in 1979 against George Warusfel. Stracey, undisputed welterweight champion 1975-76, finished his career with a record of 45 wins, 5 losses and 1 draw with 37 KOs.

Sullivan, John L. Born Boston, Massachusetts, 1858. 'The Boston Strong Boy' had his first pro fight in 1879. Much of his fighting was bare knuckle and he was arrested frequently. In 1882 he became American heavyweight champion by beating Paddy Ryan. As was the norm at the time, Sullivan travelled the country fighting many men in a single day in exhibitions. In 1885 he beat Dominick McCaffrey to win the US title again and in 1889 he defeated Jack Kilrain over a staggering 75 rounds for the same title. In 1892 he lost a 21-round contest to Jim Corbett. A lighter and faster man, Corbett could not match Sullivan the fighter but was equal to him as a boxer. Sullivan continued thereafter to give exhibition matches. His last recorded fight was in 1905 against Jim McCormick, Sullivan winning in two rounds.

Sullivan was a boxing immortal, the link between bare-knuckle and gloved fighting, and the first great American sports idol. He was powerful, quick, could hit with either hand but had exceptional strength in his right, and could take punishment; he is still considered by some to be one of the best heavyweights ever. The undisputed heavyweight champion 1885-92, he died in 1918 aged 59.

Sutherland, Murray Born Edinburgh, 1954. Sutherland turned pro in 1977 and fought out of Canada. In 1981 he challenged Matthew Saad Muhammad for the WBC light-heavyweight title but lost in nine. A year later he lost again, this time in eight rounds to Michael Spinks. In 1984 he won the IBF super-middleweight championship, beating Ernie Singletary, but four months later he lost the title to Chong-Pal Park. Sutherland never again fought a world title bout and retired after eight more bouts, having won 39 of his 63 fights in total.

Terrell, Ernie Born Chicago, Illinois, 4 April 1939. The tall and lanky Terrell earned the heavyweight championship of the world by beating Eddie Machen in 1965 after the WBA stripped Muhammad Ali of the title. Ali defeated Terrell for the 'undisputed title' on 6 February 1967, shouting 'What's my name?', at his opponent throughout the fight – Terrell had insisted on calling Ali by his 'slave name', Cassius Clay. Ernie's sister was one of the Supremes, and he even made a record with her. Terrell became a promoter in Chicago after his retirement from fighting.

Thomas, Eddie Born Merthyr Tydfil, 27 July 1926. Thomas turned pro in 1946. Two years later he secured his first title by taking the Welsh welterweight championship in a 10-round decision over Jack Phillips. Seven months later Thomas faced his toughest opponent to date, Billy Graham. A major contender for world welterweight honours, Graham nevertheless lost a 10-round decision. By beating Pat Patrick and Michele Palermo, Thomas added the Empire and European titles. Three years later, after seven more fights (with mixed success), he hung up his gloves. He now turned to the other side of boxing, becoming a world-renowned cutsman and manager. Under his tutelage both Howard Winstone and Ken Buchanan won world titles. In 48 career fights Thomas won 40, lost 6 and drew 2. He died in 1997 aged 70.

Tiger, Dick Born Amaigbo, Orlu, Nigeria, 14 August 1929. Dick became British Empire middleweight champion in 1958. The WBA middleweight championship followed in 1962 and he became undisputed middleweight champion in 1963, beating Gene Fullmer before losing to him later the same year. He again became undisputed champion in 1965, beating Joey Giardello, but once again lost the title the following year when outpointed by Emile Griffith. He then beat Jose Torres later in 1966 to become the undisputed light-heavyweight champion of the world, a title he held until the great Bob Foster defeated him in 1968. He died 14 December 1971 in Nigeria, soon after announcing his retirement.

Toney, James Nathaniel Born Grand Rapids, Michigan, 24 August 1968. James 'Lights Out' Toney is one of the all-time great fighters. He knocked out Michael Nunn in round 11 to become IBF middleweight champion in 1991 and later that year defeated Mike McCallum on points to become WBA champion. He defeated Iran Barkley in 1993 to win the super-middleweight championship, promptly relinquishing the middleweight crown. Toney's first defeat was at the hands of another boxing legend, Roy Jones Jr, who defeated him on points to take his IBF super-middleweight title on 18 November 1994 in Las Vegas. Three months later, at the same venue, he was beaten on points again by Montell Griffin, a result that was replicated in 1996. His final loss was against Drake Thadzi in 1997. In 2003 he beat Vassiliy Jirov to win the IBF cruiserweight title (later vacated). At the end of 2003 James had a record of 66 wins (42 KOs), four losses and two draws in 72 fights.

Torres, Efren Born Mexico, 1943. Torres turned pro in 1961. In 1968 he had his first world title fight when he took on Chartchai Chionoi for the WBC flyweight crown. Torres lost in 13 rounds to a knockout, but just over a year later he tried again and this time he beat Chionoi in eight. Thirteen months after that he lost the title back to Chionoi in 15. After five more fights, one of them a four-round KO by Ruben Olivares, Torres, undisputed flyweight champion 1969-70, retired.

Trinidad, Felix Born Felix Juan Trinidad Soria, Puerto Rico, 10 January 1973. 'Tito' turned pro in 1990 and in his 20th fight took on Maurice Blocker for the IBF welterweight title, winning in two rounds. He then defended this 15 times over the next six years, including wins over Hector Camacho and Pernell Whitaker before beating Oscar De La Hoya to win the WBC title. In 2000 Trinidad moved up to light middleweight and beat David Reid to win the WBA crown. The following year he won a title at his third weight when he took the WBA middleweight crown from William Joppy. He was finally beaten after 40 fights by Bernard Hopkins when fighting for the middleweight title. Trinidad has been IBF welterweight champion 1993-99, WBC and IBF welterweight champion 1999-2000, WBA and IBF light-middleweight champion 2000-01, and WBA middleweight champion in 2001.

Tunney, Gene Born James Joseph Tunney, New York, 25 May 1897. Undisputed heavyweight champion 1926-28, Gene took up boxing when he received a present of boxing gloves for his 11th birthday. He joined the Marines in 1918 and it was here that he honed his skills, becoming services champion. It was here that he also picked up his nickname of 'The Fighting Marine'. In 1922 he became US light-heavyweight champion, beating Battling Levinsky. He lost this title in his only defeat of his career to Harry Greb, a defeat that was avenged four times. Tunney moved up to heavyweight and became world champion when he outpointed and outboxed Jack Dempsey on 23 September 1926. They fought again on 22 September 1927 in a fight dubbed 'The Battle of the Long Count', but the result was the same – a Tunney victory. He retired after one more defence (against Tom Heeney) to marry well and become a successful businessman. His son later became a US Congressman. Tunney died 7 November 1978.

Turpin, Randolph Born 7 June 1928. He turned pro in 1946 and after moving through the ranks beat Albert Finch for the British middleweight title in 1950. The following year he beat Luc Van Dam for the European middleweight title and 'Sugar' Ray Robinson for the world title. Turpin won in London, but two months later on 12 September 1951 in the return match in New York he lost in 10 rounds. Turpin became British light-heavyweight champion in 1952 when he beat Don Cockell in 11 rounds. He remained a force in Britain and Europe but never again won top honours. Turpin retired in 1964 and took his own life on 16 May 1966.

Tyson, Mike Born Michael Gerard Tyson, Brooklyn, New York, 30 June 1966. He turned pro in 1985. After 27 fights, 25 of them KOs and 15 of those in the first round, he knocked out Trevor Berbick in two rounds to become WBC champion in 1986. The following year he unified the titles by beating James 'Bonecrusher' Smith (WBA) and Tony Tucker (IBF). On 25 February 1989 he stopped Frank Bruno in the fifth round in Las Vegas, although Bruno landed a good punch early in the contest to shake Tyson. After 37 successive wins, and looking unbeatable, he was knocked out by James 'Buster' Douglas in the 10th round in Tokyo in 1990. After four more fights it was no longer his boxing that made headlines. On 9 September 1991, Tyson was indicted on three counts, including one for the rape of Desiree Washington. Tyson was convicted on 10 February 1992 and was imprisoned. He did not fight between 28 June 1991 and 19 August 1995. On his return he beat Frank Bruno in 1996 to regain the WBC heavyweight title. In 1996 he fought Evander Holyfield and lost his second-ever fight. During the rematch in June 1997, Tyson, losing badly, bit off a piece of Holyfield's ear in round three. He was subsequently banned and fined $3m for this incident. In another comeback in 2002 he took on Lennox Lewis and was soundly beaten in eight rounds. Despite the chaos of his personal life, 'Iron' Mike Tyson was 1.76m of pure power and aggression and at his peak was undoubtedly one of the finest heavyweights of all time.

Vaca, Jorge Born Guadalajara, Mexico, 1959. Vaca turned pro in 1978 and quickly demonstrated that his fights were not going to be long drawn out affairs. They were explosive and short; of his first 30 fights only two went the distance. In 1987 he took on Lloyd Honeyghan, who had won the world welterweight title from the seemingly invincible Don Curry in such style that he was widely fancied to make short work of Vaca. Yet Vaca won in 10 rounds, although in a rematch the following year he was demolished by Honeyghan in three. Vaca had held the title for a little over five months. He never again challenged for top honours and by the late 1990s was losing far more fights than he won.

Walcott, Joe Born Barbados, 13 March 1873. Turning pro in 1890 he fought the best lightweights around, including three epic fights with 'Mysterious'

Billy Smith, 15- and 25-round draws and a 20-round loss. He finally got the better of Smith in 1900, beating him twice. In 1901 he beat James 'Rube' Ferns to become welterweight champion of the world, losing the title on a foul three years later to Dixie Kid after 20 rounds. Although he fought twice more for the crown he never again managed to win it. Walcott, undisputed welterweight champion 1901-04, was known as 'The Barbados Demon'. He died in a car crash, 4 October 1935.

Walcott, Jersey Joe Born Arnold Raymond Cream, Merchantville, New Jersey, 31 January 1914. He was undisputed heavyweight champion 1951-52. He turned pro in 1930 and his early fights were all KOs. His first loss came to Henry Taylor in 1933. Thereafter Walcott went up and down the rankings. His first title shots were in 1947 and 1948 against Joe Louis – he lost both. His next two attempts were against Ezzard Charles and here he was more successful, losing the first but winning the second. He defended the title once more against Charles before taking on the great Rocky Marciano, losing in 13 rounds in 1952 and one round in 1953. Humbled by this defeat, Walcott retired immediately afterwards. Jersey Joe became a high-profile boxing referee and presided over the famous Clay–Liston fight of 1964. He died 25 February 1994 in Camden, New Jersey.

Walker, Mickey Born Edward Patrick Walker, Elizabeth, New Jersey, 1901. At 1.70m and with a propensity for KOs he was nicknamed 'The Toy Bulldog'. In 1922 he beat Jack Britton in 15 rounds to become undisputed welterweight champion of the world, a title he held until 1926. In the same year that he lost his welterweight crown he gained the middleweight title, his opponents being Pete Latzo and Tiger Flowers respectively. He held the title for five years until relinquishing it in his attempt to win at a third weight, light heavyweight. At this weight he lost title fights to Tommy Loughran and Maxie Rosenbloom and drew with Jack Sharkey. Although he never achieved success at the higher weight he is still ranked as one of the greatest middleweight boxers of all time. Mickey died in 1981 aged 79.

Watanabe, Jiro Born Okayama, Japan, 1955. Watanabe turned pro in 1979 and won his first ten fights with seven KOs. In 1981 he had his first crack at a world title, fighting Chul-Ho Kim for the WBC super-flyweight crown but lost in 15 rounds. Next year he beat Rafael Pedroza for the same honours, he retaining this title for six defences before unifying it in 1984 when he beat Payao Pooltarat. In 1986 he suffered only his second-ever defeat, losing to Gilberto Roman in 12 rounds. With a career record of 26 wins and 2 losses Watanabe was a top-class bantamweight and the first-ever southpaw to become junior bantamweight world champion.

Watson, Michael A very skilful middleweight who, unlike his fellow boxers Nigel Benn and Chris Eubank, failed to become world champion, he was however Commonwealth middleweight champion in 1989 and the first boxer to beat Benn professionally. After a fight with Eubank in 1991 he was left in a coma and has been attempting to recover ever since. In 2003 he managed to complete the London Marathon and was awarded a Variety Club of Great Britain Award the same year.

Watt, Jim Born 18 July 1948. Watt was WBC lightweight champion 1979-81 and British lightweight champion in 1972, losing his title to fellow Scot Ken Buchanan in 1973. He was again WBC lightweight champion in 1979. A southpaw, he went on from boxing to become a respected commentator and pundit.

Wells, Billy Born William Thomas Wells, London, 1889. In 1910 he turned pro and in 1911 beat William 'Iron' Hague to win the British heavyweight title. The Empire title followed the same year. In 1912 Wells took on Georges Carpentier twice for the European title, but lost both bouts in quick time (four rounds and one round). In 1919, after 14 successful defences, Wells lost his British title to Joe Beckett and he also lost the rematch the following year. 'Bombadier' Billy Wells, better known as the man who banged the gong at the beginning of Rank films, died in 1967 aged 77.

Welsh, Freddie Born Frederick Hall Thomas, Pontypridd, Wales, 1886. Welsh, unlike boxers such as Johnny Owen, was from a well-to-do family and boxed because he loved it. To prevent his family learning that he boxed he chose the name 'Welsh' and turned pro in 1905. Four years and countless fights later, 'The Welsh Wizard' earned a shot for the British lightweight title and won in 20 rounds from Johnny Summers. In 1914 he beat William Ritchie over the same distance to earn the world crown. He kept this for three years until being stopped surprisingly for the only time in his career by Benny Leonard. The story is that Welsh's manager was so confident that he bet the purse on his man to win. A few lacklustre performances later and Welsh hung up his gloves for good. Welsh, undisputed lightweight champion 1914-17, went on to open a health farm and lecture on the sport of boxing. He died aged just 41 in 1927.

Whitaker, Pernell Born Norfolk, Virginia, 2 January 1964. Whitaker had over 200 fights as an amateur before turning pro in 1984. The pinnacle of his amateur career was his defeat of Luis Ortiz in the 1984 Olympics, which won him the gold medal in the lightweight division. His first title fight was against Jose Luis Ramirez in 1988. He lost in 12 rounds, but the following year he won the IBF and WBC titles against Greg Haugen and Ramirez respectively. In 1990 he put both titles on the line against the KO specialist Azumah Nelson and won, adding the WBC version with his defeat of Juan Nazario. Because of his failure to attempt to win the WBO crown he was never undisputed champion (this honour remains with Roberto Duran in 1978). Abandoning his lightweight titles in 1992, he made the move up to light welterweight, where he gained an IBF title by beating Rafael Pinda. In 1993 he won the WBC welterweight title from James McGirt and became one of only a handful of boxers to win at three different weights. Two years later he went one better winning at a fourth weight when he overcame Julio Cesar Vasquez at light middleweight, though he abandoned the title the day after winning it. Whitaker defended his titles regularly until meeting Oscar de la Hoya in 1997. De la Hoya, who had won the 1992 Olympic lightweight title, beat him over 12 rounds to take his WBC welterweight crown. After a fight against Andrei Pestriaev late that year Whitaker was found to have used cocaine and was out of the game for two years. On his return he fought Felix Trinidad for the IBF welterweight title but lost in 12 rounds.

Willard, Jess Born St Clere, Kansas, 29 December 1881. He turned pro in 1911, fighting mostly exhibition matches. Standing almost 6ft 6ins (1.98m), Willard was a very tall boxer (he was known as 'The Pottawatomie Giant') and he weighed between 16 and 18 stone (102-114kg). He was an incredibly hard hitter. In 1913 William 'Bull' Young died from a broken neck sustained during a bout with Willard. He knocked out Jack Johnson in round 26 (45 were scheduled) of a 1915 world heavyweight title fight in Havana, Cuba. Three fights and three years later though, the title was gone, lost in three rounds to Jack Dempsey. Apart from exhibitions Willard had only one more real fight before hanging up his gloves.

After an abortive comeback he finally retired and afterwards tried his hand at acting. He had already appeared in a few films during his career, *The Heart Punch* (1914) and *The Challenge of Chance* (1919) being two notable efforts. In 1933 he appeared in his most well known film, *The Prize Fighter and the Lady* with Max Baer and Myrna Loy. Willard died 15 December 1968.

Winstone, Howard Born Merthyr Tydfil, 1939. He turned professional as a featherweight in 1959 and was unbeaten in his first 34 contests, but in 1962 was stopped in three rounds by the American Leroy Jeffery. Winstone's first attempt to win the world title came in 1965 when he lost on points to Vicente Saldivar. Two more rematches followed, both going the way of the Mexican. After Saldivar retired, Winstone beat Mitsunori Seki in nine rounds to become world featherweight champion but lost the title in quick fashion to Jose Legra in five rounds. Winstone, British featherweight champion in 1968, fought with the top of three fingers on his right hand missing. Nicknamed 'The Welsh Wizard' (he shares the nickname with Freddie Welsh), he died in 2000 aged 61.

Wolfe, Jack Born Jackson Kenneth Wolfe, Cleveland, Ohio, 1895. Turned pro in 1911. After 11 years of boxing, Jack 'Kid' Wolfe became the very first undisputed light-featherweight champion of the world, winning the newly created division when he overcame Joe Lynch over 15 rounds. Carl Duane deprived him of the title in 12 rounds the following year. In 1924, after two consecutive defeats, Wolfe retired. He died aged 79 in 1975.

Zale, Tony Born 29 May 1913. Zale turned pro in 1934 and boxed almost exclusively out of Chicago. After six years he won the American (NBA) middleweight championship from Al Hostak. The following year, 1941, he beat George Abrams to win the world title. In his next fight he lost to Billy Conn, although this contest was not for the title. During the next three years he did not fight due to the war. On his return from active service he strung together ten consecutive KOs including a six-round stoppage of Rocky Graziano. In the summer of 1947 Graziano deprived him of his crown, only to return it a year later. His final fight was in the same year when he took on the great Marcel Cerdan and lost to a 12th-round knockout. He retired soon afterwards but on 8 March 1973, at the age of 59, he fought Graziano again – though only in an exhibition match. He died 20 March 1997.

CANOEING

The canoe is one of the oldest forms of transport, probably second only to the raft. Dugout canoes were being manufactured at least 8000 years ago. But lighter, more manoeuvrable canoes were developed much more recently in North America by covering a frame with animal skins, fabric, or bark. The birchbark canoe used by Native Americans was adopted by French explorers and fur traders during the 17th century. Despite its frail appearance, it is a very strong, durable craft. Its shallow draught will carry through white-water rapids that would demolish most boats, and it can be easily paddled around impassable rapids or across stretches of land from one body of water to another.

The Eskimo kayak, which has a partly enclosed deck with openings for the paddlers' seats, was invented by Europeans much later. While the canoeist uses a single-bladed paddle similar to the oar used in rowing, the kayak paddle has a blade on each end and is gripped in the middle.

Scottish lawyer John MacGregor was chiefly responsible for establishing canoeing as a recreational sport. In 1845, he designed a type of canoe, the Rob Roy, which had a deck and was equipped with a mast and sail as well as paddles. MacGregor went on a series of cruises in Europe and the Holy Land beginning in 1849, and he wrote books and delivered many lectures about his trips. MacGregor and other like-minded enthusiasts founded the Canoe Club in 1866, which became the Royal Canoe Club in 1873. Competitive canoeing began with the club's first regatta in 1867.

The New York Canoe Club was founded in 1871 and was quickly followed by many similar organisations on the east coast of the United States. They organised the American Canoe Association (ACA) in 1880. The Canadian Canoe Association was founded in 1900. During the early part of the 20th century, canoeing became popular in northern and central Europe. Largely through the efforts of Waldemar Van B. Claussen of the ACA, representatives of 19 national clubs met in Copenhagen in 1924 to establish the Internationale Representationschaft des Kanusport (IRK). Also in 1924, canoeing was a demonstration sport at the Paris Olympics. The United States swept the kayak events, while Canada won all four canoeing events.

The IRK's attempt to make canoeing a fully fledged Olympic sport did not succeed, however, until 1936. There were eight events in the 1936 programme: single and pairs canoes at 1000m; single and pairs kayaks at 1000m and 10,000m; and single and pairs folding canoes at 1000m. The IRK headquarters in Munich was destroyed by Allied bombs during World War II; however, the IRK was reorganised as the International Canoe Federation in 1946 and, when the Olympics resumed in 1948, canoeing was again in the programme. The folding canoe events were dropped and the first women's event, the 500m singles kayak, was added.

After the war, white-water canoeing rapidly gained popularity in Central Europe. Originally run through a short stretch of natural rapids, white-water races now take place on artificial rapids. As in Alpine skiing, racers compete in individual time trials. In white-water slalom races, the canoe must pass through a series of gates, including some reverse gates that have to be passed while paddling backwards. Time penalties are awarded for hitting one pole, both poles, or for missing a gate entirely. These penalties are then added to the canoeist's actual time to determine the order of finish. White-water racing (slalom racing over two rounds, best round to count) was in the Olympic programme in 1972. It was dropped after those games, but was restored in 1992.

Olympic races are referred to by a simple code, in which the initial letter is K for kayak or C for Canadian canoe and the number refers to the number of paddlers. For example, C-1 means canoe singles and K-2 means kayak pairs. In flatwater events, men compete in C-1, C-2, K-1 and K-2 races at 500 and 1000m and in K-4 races at 1000m only. Women compete only in K-1, K-2 and K-4, all at the 500m distance. The Olympic white-water slalom events are for the men's C-1, C-2 and K-1 and the women's K-1. There is no standard distance for white-water races, since each course is laid out differently.

In addition to the Olympic events, there are several major long-distance canoe races. Among the best-known are the Sella Descent in northern Spain, a 16.5km race established in 1931; the Liffey Descent, a 28.2km race conducted in Ireland since 1959; and the International White-Water race, established in 1948 and conducted on a 23-mile (37km) downriver course at Salida, Colorado. Flatwater races begin with qualifying heats, and the top two or three finishers in each heat advance to the semi-finals, based on qualifying times. The others go into a repechage round and the top three or four finishers in each heat of that round also move into the semi-finals. Until 1980, the top six finishers in the semi-finals went into the final round to determine the medallists and the next six competed in a petit final for seventh to 12th places. Since 1984, there have been nine finalists in the medal race and the petit final has been eliminated.

The US Canoe Association was founded in 1968 to govern and sanction marathon racing.

Olympic competition is governed by the US Canoe-Kayak Team. The American Canoe Association now operates primarily as an organisation of clubs involved in recreational canoeing, which was always its primary interest. Competition in sailing canoes was popular in the late 19th century. While some sailing races are still conducted by canoe clubs, most such races are now run under the auspices of yachting clubs. One of the first important international yachting trophies, the Seawanhaka International Challenge Cup, was established in 1895 for sailing canoes.

Olympic Medallists

Men's 500m K-1

	Gold	Silver	Bronze
1976	Vasile Dîba (ROM) 1:46.41	Zoltán Sztanity (HUN) 1:46.95	Rüdiger Helm (GDR) 1:48.30
1980	Vladimir Parfenovich (URS) 1:43.43	John Sumegi (AUS) 1:44.12	Vasile Dîba (ROM) 1:44.90
1984	Ian Ferguson (NZL) 1:47.84	Lars-Erik Moberg (SWE) 1:48.18	Bernard Bregeon (FRA) 1:48.41
1988	Zsolt Gyulay (HUN) 1:44.82	Andreas Stähle (GDR) 1:46.38	Paul MacDonald (NZL) 1:46.46
1992	Mikko Kolehmainen (FIN) 1:40.43	Zsolt Gyulay (HUN) 1:40.64	Knut Holmann (NOR) 1:40.71
1996	Antonio Rossi (ITA) 1:37.42	Knut Holmann (NOR) 1:38.34	Piotr Markiewicz (POL) 1:38.61
2000	Knut Holmann (NOR) 1:57.84	Petar Merkov (BUL) 1:58.39	Michael Kolganov (ISR) 1:59.56

Men's 1000m K-1

	Gold	Silver	Bronze
1936	Gregor Hradetzky (AUT) 4:22.9	Helmut Cämmerer (GER) 4:25.6	Jacobus Kraaier (NED) 4:35.1
1948	Gert Fredriksson (SWE) 4:33.2	Johan Frederick Kobberup (DEN) 4:39.9	Henri Eberhardt (FRA) 4:41.4
1952	Gert Fredriksson (SWE) 4:07.9	Thorvald Strömberg (FIN) 4:09.7	Louis Gantois (FRA) 4:20.1
1956	Gert Fredriksson (SWE) 4:12.8	Igor Pissarev (URS) 4:15.3	Lajos Kiss (HUN) 4:16.2
1960	Erik Hansen (DEN) 3:53.00	Imre Szöllösi (HUN) 3:54.02	Gert Fredriksson (SWE) 3:55.89
1964	Rolf Peterson (SWE) 3:57.13	Mihály Hesz (HUN) 3:57.28	Aurel Vernescu (ROM) 4:00.77
1968	Mihály Hesz (HUN) 4:02.63	Aleksandr Shaparenko (URS) 4:03.58	Erik Hansen (DEN) 4:04.39
1972	Aleksandr Shaparenko (URS) 3:48.06	Rolf Peterson (SWE) 3:49.38	Géza Csapó (HUN) 3:49.38
1976	Rüdiger Helm (GDR) 3:48.20	Géza Csapó (HUN) 3:48.84	Vasile Dîba (ROM) 3:49.65
1980	Rüdiger Helm (GDR) 3:48.77	Alain Lebas (FRA) 3:50.20	Ion Bîrladeanu (ROM) 3:50.49
1984	Alan Thompson (NZL) 3:45.73	Milan Janic (YUG) 3:46.88	Gregory Barton (USA) 3:47.38
1988	Gregory Barton (USA) 3:55.27	Grant Davies (AUS) 3:55.28	André Wohllebe (GDR) 3:55.55
1992	Clint Robinson (AUS) 3:37.26	Knut Holmann (NOR) 3:37.50	Gregory Barton (USA) 3:37.93
1996	Knut Holmann (NOR) 3:25.78	Beniamino Bonomi (ITA) 3:27.07	Clint Robinson (AUS) 3:29.71
2000	Knut Holmann (NOR) 3:33.26	Petar Merkov (BUL) 3:34.64	Tim Brabants (GBR) 3:35.05

Men's 500m K-2

	Gold	Silver	Bronze
1976	Joachim Mattern/Bernd Olbricht (GDR) 1:35.87	Sergey Nagorny/Vladimir Romanovsky (URS) 1:36.81	Larion Serghei/Policarp Malihin (ROM) 1:37.43
1980	Vladimir Parfenovich/Sergey Chukhray (URS) 1:32.38	Herminio Menéndez/Guillermo del Riego (ESP) 1:33.65	Rüdiger Helm/Bernd Olbricht (GDR) 1:34.00
1984	Ian Ferguson/Paul MacDonald (NZL) 1:34.21	Per-Inge Bengtsson/Lars-Erik Moberg (SWE) 1:35.26	Hugh Fisher/Alwyn Morris (CAN) 1:35.41
1988	Ian Ferguson/Paul MacDonald (NZL) 1:33.98	Igor Nagayev/Viktor Denisov (URS) 1:34.15	Attila Ábrahám/Ferenc Csipes (HUN) 1:34.32
1992	Kay Bluhm/Torsten Gutsche (GER) 1:28.27	Maciej Freimut/Wojciech Kurpiweski (POL) 1:29.84	Antonio Rossi/Bruno Dreossi (ITA) 1:30.00
1996	Kay Bluhm/Torsten Gutsche (GER) 1:28.70	Beniamino Bonomi/Daniele Scarpa (ITA) 1:28.73	Daniel Collins/Andrew Trim (AUS) 1:29.41
2000	Zoltán Kammerer/Botond Storcz (HUN) 1:47.05	Andrew Trim/Daniel Collins (AUS) 1:47.89	Ronald Rauhe/Tim Wieskötter (GER) 1:48.77

Men's 1000m K-2

	Gold	Silver	Bronze
1936	Adolf Kainz/Alfons Dorfner (AUT) 4:03.8	Ewald Tilker/Fritz Bondroit (GER) 4:08.9	Nicolaas Tates/Willem van der Kroft (NED) 4:12.2
1948	Hans Berglund/Lennart Klingström (SWE) 4:07.3	Ejvind Hansen/Bernhard Jensen (DEN) 4:07.5	Thor Axelsson/Nils Björklof (FIN) 4:08.7
1952	Kurt Wires/Yrjö Hietanen (FIN) 3:51.1	Lars Glassér/Ingemar Hedberg (SWE) 3:51.1	Max Raub/Herbert Wiedermann (AUT) 3:51.4

C
A
N
O
E
I
N
G

1956	Michael Scheuer/Meinrad Miltenberger (GER) 3:49.6	Mikhail Kaaleste/Anatoliy Demitkov (URS) 3:51.4	Max Raub/Herbert Wiedermann (AUT) 3:55.8
1960	Gert Fredriksson/Sven-Olov Sjödelius (SWE) 3:34.73	György Mészáros/András Szente (HUN) 3:34.91	Stefan Kaplaniak/Wladyslaw Zielinski (POL) 3:37.34
1964	Sven-Olov Sjödelius/Nils Gunnar Utterberg (SWE) 3:38.54	Antonius Geurts/Paul Hoekstra (NED) 3:39.30	Heinz Büker/Holger Zander (GER) 3:40.69
1968	Aleksandr Shaparenko/Vladimir Morozov (URS) 3:37.54	Csaba Giczi/István Timár (HUN) 3:38.44	Gerhard Seibold/Günther Pfaff (AUT) 3:40.71
1972	Nikolay Gorbachev/Viktor Kratasyuk (URS) 3:31.23	József Deme/János Rátkai (HUN) 3:32.00	Wladyslaw Szuszkiewicz/ Rafal Piszcz (POL) 3:33.83
1976	Sergey Nagorny/Vladimir Romanovsky (URS) 3:29.01	Joachim Mattern/Bernd Olbricht (GDR) 3:29.33	Zoltán Bakó/István Szabó (HUN) 3:30.56
1980	Vladimir Parfenovich/Sergey Chukhray (URS) 3:26.72	István Szabó/István Joós (HUN) 3:28.49	Luis Ramos Misioné/Herminio Menéndez (ESP) 3:28.66
1984	Hugh Fisher/Alwyn Morris (CAN) 3:24.22	Bernard Bregeon/Patrick Lefoulon (FRA) 3:25.97	Barry Kelly/Grant Kenny (AUS) 3:26.80
1988	Gregory Barton/Norman Bellingham (USA) 3:32.42	Ian Ferguson/Paul MacDonald (NZL) 3:32.71	Peter Foster/Kelvin Graham (AUS) 3:33.76
1992	Kay Bluhm/Torsten Gutsche (GER) 3:16.10	Gunnar Olsson/Karl Sundqvist (SWE) 3:17.70	Grzegorz Kotowicz/Dariusz Bialkowski (POL) 3:18.86
1996	Antonio Rossi/Daniele Scarpa (ITA) 3:09.19	Kay Bluhm/Torsten Gutsche (GER) 3:10.52	Andrian Dushev/Milko Kazanov (BUL) 3:11.21
2000	Antonio Rossi/Beniamino Bonomi (ITA) 3:14.46	Markus Oscarsson/Henrik Nilsson (SWE) 3:16.07	Krisztian Bártfai/Krisztian Veréb (HUN) 3:16.35

Men's 1000m K-4

	Gold	Silver	Bronze
1964	Nikolay Chuzhikov/Anatoliy Grischin/ Vyacheslav Ionov/Vladimir Morozov (URS) 3:14.67	Günther Perleberg/Bernhard Schulze/ Friedhelm Wentzke/Holger Zander (GER) 3:15.39	Simion Cuciuc/Atanase Sciotnic/ Mihal Turcas/Aurel Vernescu (ROM) 3:15.51
1968	Steinar Amundsen/Egil Søby/Tore Berger/Jan Johansen (NOR) 3:14.38	Anton Calenic/Dimitrie Ivanov/ Haralambie Ivanov/Mihai Turcas (ROM) 3:14.81	Csaba Giczi/István Timár/Imre Szöllösi/István Csizmadia (HUN) 3:15.10
1972	Yuriy Filatov/Yuriy Stezenko/Vladimir Morozov/Valeriy Didenko (URS) 3:14.02	Aurel Vernescu/Mihal Zafiu/Roman Vartolomeu/Atanase Sciotnic (ROM) 3:15.07	Egil Søby/Steinar Amundsen/Tore Berger/Jan Johansen (NOR) 3:15.27
1976	Sergey Chuhray/Aleksandr Degtiarev/ Yuriy Filatov/Vladimir Morozov (URS) 3:08.69	José María Estebán/José Ramón López/ Herminio Menéndez/Luis Gregoria Ramos (ESP) 3:08.95	Peter Bischof/Bernd Duvigneau/ Rüdiger Helm/Jürgen Lehnert (GDR) 3:10.76
1980	Rüdiger Helm/Bernd Olbricht/Harald Marg/Bernd Duvigneau (GDR) 3:13.76	Mihal Zafiu/Vasile Dîba/Ion Geant/ Nicusor Esanu (ROM) 3:15.35	Borislav Borissov/Bozhidar Milenkov/Lazar Khristov/Ivan Manev (BUL) 3:15.46
1984	Grant Bramwell/Ian Ferguson/Paul MacDonald/Alan Thompson (NZL) 3:02.28	Per-Inge Bengtsson/Tommy Karls/ Lars-Erik Moberg/Thomas Ohlsson (SWE) 3:02.81	François Barouh/Philippe Boccara/ Pascal Boucherit/Didier Vavasseur (FRA) 3:03.94
1988	Zsolt Gyulay/Ferenc Csipes/Sándor Hódosi/Attila Ábrahám (HUN) 3:00.20	Aleksandr Motusenko/Sergey Kirsanov/ Igor Nagayev/Viktor Denisov (URS) 3:01.40	Kay Bluhm/André Wohllebe/ Andreas Stähle/Hans-Jörg Bliesener (GDR) 3:02.37
1992	Oliver Kegel/Thomas Reineck/Mario von Appen/André Wohllebe (GER) 2:54.18	Attila Ábrahám/Ferenc Csipes/László Fidel/Zsolt Gyulay (HUN) 2:54.82	Ramon Andersson/Kelvin Graham/ Ian Rowling/Steven Wood (AUS) 2:56.97
1996	Detlef Hofmann/Olaf Winter/Thomas Reineck/Mark Zabel (GER) 2:51.53	Attila Adrovicz/Ferenc Csipes/Gábor Horváth/Andras Rajna (HUN) 2:53.18	Sergey Verlin/Oleg Gorobiy/ Anatoliy Tishenko/Georgiy Tsybulnikov (RUS) 2:54.00
2000	Akos Verecki/Gábor Horváth/Zoltán Kammerer/Botond Storcz (HUN) 2:55.18	Jan Schäfer/Mark Zabel/Björn Bach/ Stefan Ulm (GER) 2:55.70	Grzegorz Kotowicz/Adam Seroczynski/Dariusz Bialkowski/ Marek Witkowski (POL) 2:57.19

Men's 500m C-1

	Gold	Silver	Bronze
1976	Aleksandr Rogov (URS) 1:59.23	John Wood (CAN) 1:59.58	Matija Ljubek (YUG)1:59.60
1980	Sergey Postrekhin (URS) 1:53.37	Lyubomir Lyubenov (BUL) 1:53.49	Olaf Heukrodt (GDR) 1:54.38
1984	Larry Cain (CAN) 1:57.01	Henning Jakobsen (DEN) 1:58.45	Costica Olaru (ROM) 1:59.86
1988	Olaf Heukrodt (GDR) 1:56.42	Mikhail Slivinsky (URS) 1:57.26	Martin Marinov (BUL) 1:57.27
1992	Nikolai Bukhalov (BUL) 1:51.15	Mikhail Slivinsky (CIS) 1:51.40	Olaf Heukrodt (GER) 1:53.00
1996	Martin Doktor (CZE) 1:49.93	Slavomir Knazovicky (SVK) 1:50.51	Imre Pulai (HUN) 1:50.76
2000	György Kolonics (HUN) 2:24.81	Maksim Opalev (RUS) 2:25.80	Andreas Dittmer (GER) 2:27.59

Men's 1000m C-1

Gold	Silver	Bronze
1936 Francis Amyot (CAN) 5:32.1	Bohuslav Karlík (TCH) 5:36.9	Erich Koschik (GER) 5:39.0
1948 Josef Holecek (TCH) 5:42.0	Douglas Bennett (CAN) 5:53.3	Robert Boutigny (FRA) 5:55.9
1952 Josef Holecek (TCH) 4:56.3	János Parti (HUN) 5:03.6	Olavi Ojanperä (FIN) 5:08.5
1956 Leon Rotman (ROM) 5:05.3	István Hernek (HUN) 5:06.2	Gennadiy Bukharin (URS) 5:12.7
1960 János Parti (HUN) 4:33.93	Aleksandr Silayev (URS) 4:34.41	Leon Rotman (ROM) 4:35.87
1964 Jürgen Eschert (GER) 4:35.14	Andrei Igorov (ROM) 4:37.89	Yevgeniy Penyayev (URS) 4:38.31
1968 Tibor Tatai (HUN) 4:36.14	Detlef Lewe (FRG) 4:38.31	Vitaliy Galkov (URS) 4:40.42
1972 Ivan Patzaichin (ROM) 4:08.94	Tamás Wichmann (HUN) 4:12.42	Detlef Lewe (FRG) 4:13.63
1976 Matija Ljubek (YUG) 4:09.51	Vasiliy Yurchenko (URS) 4:12.57	Tamás Wichmann (HUN) 4:14.11
1980 Lyubomir Lyubenov (BUL) 4:12.38	Sergey Postrekhin (URS) 4:13.53	Eckhard Leue (GDR) 4:15.02
1984 Ulrich Eicke (FRG) 4:06.32	Larry Cain (CAN) 4:08.67	Henning Jakobsen (DEN) 4:09.51
1988 Ivans Klementjevs (URS) 4:12.78	Jörg Schmidt (GDR) 4:15.83	Nikolai Bukhalov (BUL) 4:18.94
1992 Nikolai Bukhalov (BUL) 4:05.92	Ivans Klementjevs (LAT) 4:06.60	György Zala (HUN) 4:07.35
1996 Martin Doktor (CZE) 3:54.42	Ivans Klementjevs (LAT) 3:54.95	György Zala (HUN) 3:56.37
2000 Andreas Dittmer (GER) 3:54.37	Ledys Frank Balceiro (CUB) 3:56.07	Steve Giles (CAN) 3:56.43

Men's 500m C-2

Gold	Silver	Bronze
1976 Sergey Petrenko/Aleksandr Vinogradov (URS) 1:45.81	Andrzej Gronowicz/Jerzy Opara (POL) 1:47.77	Tamás Buday/Oszkár Frey (HUN) 1:48.35
1980 László Foltán/István Vaskuti (HUN) 1:43.39	Petre Capusta/Ivan Patzaichin (ROM) 1:44.12	Borislav Ananiev/Nikolai Ilkov (BUL) 1:44.63
1984 Matija Ljubek/Mirko Nišovic (YUG) 1:43.67	Ivan Patzaichin/Toma Simionov (ROM) 1:45.68	Enrique Miguez/Narcisco Suárez (ESP) 1:47.71
1988 Viktor Reneisky/Nikolay Zhuravsky (URS) 1:41.77	Marek Dopierala/Marek Lbik (POL) 1:43.61	Philipp Renaud/Joël Bettin (FRA) 1:43.81
1992 Aleksandr Maselkov/Dmitriy Dovgalenok (CIS) 1:41.54	Ulrich Papke/Ingo Spelly (GER) 1:41.68	Martin Marinov/Blagovest Stoyanov (BUL) 1:41.94
1996 Csaba Horvath/György Kolonics (HUN) 1:40.42	Nikolay Zhuravsky/Viktor Reneisky (MDA) 1:40.45	Gheorghe Andriev/Grigore Obreja (ROM) 1:41.33
2000 Ferenc Novák/Imre Pulai (HUN) 1:51.28	Daniel Jedraszko/Pawel Baraszkiewicz (POL) 1:51.53	Mitica Pricop/Florin Popescu (ROM) 1:54.26

Men's 1000m C-2

Gold	Silver	Bronze
1936 Vladimir Syrovátka/Jan Brzák-Felix (TCH) 4:50.1	Rupert Weinstabl/Karl Proisl (AUT) 4:53.8	Frank Saker/Harvey Charters (CAN) 4:56.7
1948 Jan Brzák-Felix/Bohumil Kudma (TCH) 5:07.1	Stephen Lysak/Stephan Macknowski (USA) 5:08.2	Georges Dransart/Georges Gandil (FRA) 5:15.2
1952 Bent Peder Rasch/Finn Haunstoft (DEN) 4:38.3	Jan Brzák-Felix/Bohumil Kudma (TCH) 4:42.9	Egon Drews/Wilfried Soltau (FRG) 4:48.3
1956 Alexe Dumitru/Simion Ismailciuc (ROM) 4:47.4	Pavel Kharine/Gratsian Botev (URS) 4:48.6	Károly Wieland/Ferenc Mohácsi (HUN) 4:54.3
1960 Leonid Geishtor/Sergey Makarenko (URS) 4:17.94	Aldo Dezi/Francesco La Macchia (ITA) 4:20.77	Imre Farkas/András Törö (HUN) 4:20.89
1964 Andrey Khimich/Stepan Oschepkov (URS) 4:04.64	Jean Boudehen/Michel Chapuis (FRA) 4:06.52	Peer Norrbohm Nielsen/John Sørensen (DEN) 4:07.48
1968 Ivan Patzaichin/Serghei Covaliov (ROM) 4:07.18	Tamás Wichmann/Gyula Petrikovics (HUN) 4:08.77	Naum Prokupets/Mikhail Zamotin (URS) 4:11.30
1972 Vladislav Cesiunas/Yuriy Lobanov (URS) 3:52.60	Ivan Patzaichin/Serghei Covaliov (ROM) 3:52.63	Fedia Damianov/Ivan Burchin (BUL) 3:58.10
1976 Sergey Petrenko/Aleksandr Vinogradov (URS) 3:52.76	Gheorghe Danielov/Gheorghe Simionov (ROM) 3:54.28	Tamás Buday/Oszkár Frey (HUN) 3:55.66
1980 Ivan Patzaichin/Toma Simionov (ROM) 3:47.65	Olaf Heukrodt/Uwe Madeja (GDR) 3:49.93	Vasiliy Yurchenko/Yuriy Lobanov (URS) 3:51.28
1984 Ivan Patzaichin/Toma Simionov (ROM) 3:40.60	Matija Ljubek/Mirko Nišovic (YUG) 3:41.56	Didier Hoyer/Eric Renaud (FRA) 3:48.01
1988 Viktor Reneisky/Nikolay Zhuravsky (URS) 3:48.36	Olaf Heukrodt/Ingo Spelly (GDR) 3:51.44	Marek Dopierala/Marek Lbik (POL) 3:54.33
1992 Ulrich Papke/Ingo Spelly (GER) 3:37.42	Arne Nielsson/Christian Frederiksen (DEN) 3:39.26	Didier Hoyer/Olivier Boivin (FRA) 3:39.51
1996 Andreas Dittmer/Gunar Kirchbach (GER) 3:31.87	Antonel Borsan/Marcel Glavan (ROM) 3:32.29	Csaba Horvath/György Kolonics (HUN) 3:32.51
2000 Mitica Pricop/Florin Popescu (ROM) 3:37.35	Ibrahín Rojas/Leobaldo Pereira (CUB) 3:38.75	Stefan Utess/Lars Kober (GER) 3:41.12

CANOEING

Men's K-1 Slalom

Gold	Silver	Bronze
1972 Siegbert Horn (GDR) 268.56	Norbert Sattler (AUT) 270.76	Harald Gimpel (GDR) 277.95
1976-88 not held		
1992 Pierpaolo Ferrazzi (ITA) 106.89	Sylvain Curinier (FRA) 107.06	Jochen Lettmann (GER) 108.52
1996 Oliver Fix (GER) 141.22	Andraz Vehovar (SLO) 141.65	Thomas Becker (GER) 142.79
2000 Thomas Schmidt (GER) 217.25	Paul Ratcliffe (GBR) 223.71	Pierpaolo Ferrazzi (ITA) 225.03

Men's C-1 Slalom

Gold	Silver	Bronze
1972 Reinhard Eiben (GDR) 315.84	Reinhold Kauder (FRG) 327.89	James McEwan (USA) 335.95
1976-88 not held		
1992 Lukáš Pollert (CZE) 113.69	Gareth Marriott (GBR) 116.48	Jacky Avril (FRA) 117.18
1996 Michal Martikan (SVK) 151.03	Lukáš Pollert (CZE) 151.17	Patrice Estanguet (FRA) 152.84
2000 Tony Estanguet (FRA) 231.87	Michal Martikan (SVK) 233.76	Juraj Mincík (SVK) 234.22

Men's C-2 Slalom

Gold	Silver	Bronze
1972 Walter Hofmann/Rolf-Dieter Amend (GDR) 310.68	Hans Otto Schumacher/Wilhelm Baues (FRG) 311.90	Jean-Louis Olry/Jean-Claude Olry (FRA) 315.10
1976-88 not held		
1992 Scott Strausburgh/Joe Jacobi (USA) 122.41	Miroslav Šimek/Jirí Rohan (CZE) 124.25	Franck Adisson/Wilfrid Forgues (FRA) 124.38
1996 Franck Adisson/Wilfrid Forgues (FRA) 158.82	Miroslav Šimek/Jirí Rohan (CZE) 160.16	Andre Ehrenberg/Michael Senft (GER) 163.72
2000 Pavol Hochschorner/Peter Hochschorner (SVK) 237.74	Krzysztof Kolomanski/Michal Staniszewski (POL) 243.81	Marek Jiras/Tomas Mader (CZE) 249.45

Women's 500m K-1

Gold	Silver	Bronze
1948 Karen Hoff (DEN) 2:31.9	Alida van der Anker-Doedens (NED) 2:32.8	Fritzi Schwingl (AUT) 2:32.9
1952 Sylvi Saimo (FIN) 2:18.4	Gertrude Liebhart (AUT) 2:18.8	Nina Savina (URS) 2:21.6
1956 Yelizaveta Dementyeva (URS) 2:18.9	Therese Zenz (GER) 2:19.6	Tove Søby (DEN) 2:22.3
1960 Antonina Seredina (URS) 2:08.08	Therese Zenz(GER) 2:08.22	Daniela Walkowiak (POL) 2:10.46
1964 Lyudmila Khvedosyuk (URS) 2:12.87	Hilde Lauer (ROM) 2:15.35	Marcia Jones (USA) 2:15.68
1968 Lyudmila Pinayeva (URS) 2:11.09	Renate Breuer (GER) 2:12.71	Viorica Dumitru (ROM) 2:13.22
1972 Yuliya Ryabchinskaya (URS) 2:03.17	Mieke Jaapies (NED) 2:04.03	Anna Pfeffer (HUN) 2:05.50
1976 Carola Zirzow (GDR) 2:01.05	Tatyana Korshunova (URS) 2:03.07	Klára Rajnai (HUN) 2:05.01
1980 Birgit Fischer (GDR) 1:57.96	Vania Gesheva (BUL) 1:59.48	Antonina Melnikova (URS) 1:59.66
1984 Agneta Andersson (SWE) 1:58.72	Barbara Schüttpelz (FRG) 1:59.93	Annemiek Derckx (NED) 2:00.11
1988 Vania Gesheva (BUL) 1:55.19	Birgit Schmidt (Fischer) (GDR) 1:55.31	Izabella Dylewska (POL) 1:57.36
1992 Birgit Schmidt (GER) 1:51.60	Rita Kóbán (HUN) 1:51.96	Izabella Dylewska (POL) 1:52.36
1996 Rita Kóbán (HUN) 1:47.65	Caroline Brunet (CAN) 1:47.89	Josefa Idem (ITA) 1:48.731
2000 Josefa Idem-Guerrini (ITA) 2:13.84	Caroline Brunet (CAN) 2:14.64	Katrin Borchert (AUS) 2:15.13

Women's 500m K-2

Gold	Silver	Bronze
1960 Mariya Chubina/Antonina Seredina (URS) 1:54.76	Therese Zenz/Ingrid Hartmann (GER) 1:56.66	Klára Fried-Bánfalvi/Vilma Egresi (HUN) 1:58.22
1964 Roswitha Esser/Annemarie Zimmermann (GER) 1:56.95	Francine Fox/Gloriane Perrier (USA) 1:59.16	Hilde Lauer/Cornelia Sideri (ROM) 2:00.25
1968 Roswitha Esser/Annemarie Zimmermann (FRG) 1:56.44	Anna Pfeffer/Katalin Rozsnyói (HUN) 1:58.60	Lyudmila Pinayeva/Antonina Seredina (URS) 1:58.61
1972 Lyudmila Pinayeva/Ekaterina Kuryshko (URS) 1:53.50	Ilse Kaschube/Petra Grabowski (GDR) 1:54.30	Maria Nichiforov/Viorica Dumitru (ROM) 1:55.01
1976 Nina Gopova/Galina Kreft (URS) 1:51.15	Anna Pfeffer/Klára Rajnai (HUN) 1:51.69	Bärbel Köster/Carola Zirzow (GDR) 1:51.81
1980 Carsta Genäuss/Martina Bischoff (GDR) 1:43.88	Galina Alexeyeva (Kreft)/Nina Trofimova (Gopova) (URS) 1:46.91	Éva Rakusz/Mária Zakariás (HUN) 1:47.95
1984 Agneta Andersson/Anna Olsson (SWE) 1:45.25	Alexandra Barre/Susan Holloway (CAN) 1:47.13	Josefa Idem/Barbara Schüttpelz (FRG) 1:47.32
1988 Birgit Schmidt/Anke Nothnagel (GDR) 1:43.46	Vania Gesheva/Diana Paliiska (BUL) 1:44.06	Annemiek Derckx/Annemarie Cox (NED) 1:46.00

1992 Ramona Portwich/Anke Von Seck (Nothnagel) (GER) 1:40.29	Agneta Andersson/Susanne Gunnarsson (SWE) 1:40.41	Rita Köbán/Éva Dónusz (HUN) 1:40.81
1996 Agneta Andersson/Susanne Gunnarsson (SWE) 1:39.33	Ramona Portwich/Birgit Fischer (Schmidt) (GER) 1:39.59	Katrin Bochert/Anna Wood (AUS) 1:40.64
2000 Birgit Fischer/Katrin Wagner (GER) 1:56.99	Katalin Kovács/Szilvia Szabó (HUN) 1:58.58	Beate Sokolowska/Aneta Pastuszka (POL) 1:58.78

Women's 500m K-4

Gold	Silver	Bronze
1984 Agafia Constantin/Natasia Ionescu/ Tecla Maninescu/Maria Stefan (ROM) 1:38.34	Agneta Andersson/Anna Olsson/ Eva Karlsson/Susanne Wiberg (SWE) 1:38.87	Alexandra Barré/Lucie Guay/ Susan Holloway/Barbara Olmsted (CAN) 1:39.40
1988 Birgit Schmidt/Anke Northnagel/ Ramona Portwich/Heike Singer (GDR) 1:40.78	Erika Géczi/Erika Mészáros/ Éva Rakusz/Rita Köbán (HUN) 1:41.88	Vania Gesheva/Diana Paliiska/ Ogniana Petkova/Borislava Ivanova (BUL) 1:42.63
1992 Éva Dónusz/Kinga Czigány/Rita Köbán/Erika Mészáros (HUN) 1:38.32	Katrin Borchert/Ramona Portwich/Birgit Schmidt/Anke Von Seck (Northnagel) (GER) 1:38.47	Agneta Andersson/Maria Haglund/ Anna Olsson/Susanne Rosenqvist (SWE) 1:39.79
1996 Ramona Portwich/Manuela Mücke/ Birgit Fischer (Schmidt)/Anett Schuck (GER) 1:31.08	Daniela Baumer/Sabine Eichenberger/ Ingrid Haralamow/Gabi Müller (SUI) 1:32.70	Agneta Andersson/Ingela Ericsson/ Anna Olsson/Susanne Rosenqvist (SWE) 1:32.92
2000 Birgit Fischer/Anett Schuck/Manuela Mücke/Katrin Wagner (GER) 1:34.53	Szilvia Szabó/Rita Köbán/Katalin Kovács/ Erzsébet Viski (HUN) 1:34.94	Mariana Limbau/Raluca Andreea Ionita/Elena Radu/Sanda Toma (ROM) 1:37.01

Women's K-1 Slalom

Gold	Silver	Bronze
1972 Angelika Bahmann (GDR) 364.50	Gisela Grothaus (FRG) 398.15	Magdalena Wunderlich (FRG) 400.50
1976-88 not held		
1992 Elisabeth Micheler (GER) 126.41	Danielle Woodward (AUS) 128.27	Dana Chladek (USA) 131.75
1996 Stepanka Hilgertová (CZE) 169.49	Dana Chladek (USA) 169.49	Myriam Fox-Jérusalmi (FRA) 171.00
2000 Stepanka Hilgertová (CZE) 247.04	Brigitte Guibal (FRA) 251.88	Anne-Lise Bardet (FRA) 254.77

Discontinued Events

Men's 10,000m K-1

Gold	Silver	Bronze
1936 Ernst Krebs (GER) 46:01.6	Fritz Landertinger (AUT) 46:14.7	Ernest Riedel (USA) 47:23.9
1948 Gert Fredriksson (SWE) 50:47.7	Kurt Wires (FIN) 51:18.2	Elvind Skabo (NOR) 51:35.4
1952 Thorvald Strömberg (FIN) 47:22.8	Gert Fredriksson (SWE) 47:34.1	Michael Scheuer (FRG) 47:54.4
1956 Gert Fredriksson (SWE) 47:43.4	Ferenc Hatlaczky (HUN) 47:53.3	Michael Scheuer (FRG) 48:00.3

Men's 10,000m K-2

Gold	Silver	Bronze
1936 Paul Wevers/Ludwig Landen (GER) 41:45.0	Viktor Kalisch/Karl Steinhuber (AUT) 42:05.4	Tage Falhborg/Helge Larsson (SWE) 43:06.1
1948 Gunnar Åkerlund/Hans Wetterström (SWE) 46:09.4	Ivar Mathisen/Knut Östbye (NOR) 46:44.8	Thor Axelsson/Nils Björklof (FIN) 46:46.2
1952 Kurt Wires/Yrjö Hietanen (FIN) 44:21.3	Gunnar Åkerlund/Hans Wetterström (SWE) 44:21.7	Ferenc Varga/Jósef Gurovits (HUN) 44:26.6
1956 János Urányi/László Fábián (HUN) 43:37.0	Fritz Briel/Theo Kleine (FRG) 43:40.6	Dennis Green/Walter Brown (AUS) 43:43.2

Men's 10,000m C-1

Gold	Silver	Bronze
1948 František Capek (TCH) 1:02:05	Frank Havens (USA) 1:02:40	Norman Lane (CAN) 1:04:35
1952 Frank Havens (USA) 57:41.1	Gábor Novák (HUN) 57:49.2	Alfréd Jindra (TCH) 57:53.1
1956 Leon Rotman (ROM) 56:41.0	János Parti (HUN) 57:11.0	Gennadiy Bukharin (URS) 57:14.5

CANOEING

Men's 10,000m C-2

1936	Václav Mottl/Zdenek Škrdlant (TCH) 50:35.5	Frank Saker/Harvey Charters (CAN) 51:15.8	Rupert Weinstabl/Karl Proisl (AUT) 51:28.0
1948	Stephen Lysak/Stephan Macknowski (USA) 55:55.4	Václav Havel/Jirí Pecka (TCH) 57:38.5	Georges Dransart/Georges Gandil (FRA) 58:00.8
1952	Georges Turlier/Jean Laudet (FRA) 54:08.3	Kenneth Lane/Donald Hawgood (CAN) 54:09.9	Egon Drews/Wilfried Soltau (FRG) 54:28.1
1956	Pavel Kharine/Gratsian Botev (URS) 54:02.4	Georges Dransart/Marcel Renaud (FRA) 54:48.3	Imre Farkas/József Hunics (HUN) 55:15.6

Men's 10,000m Folding K-1

	Gold	Silver	Bronze
1936	Gregor Hradetzky (AUT) 50:01.2	Henri Eberhardt (FRA) 50:04.2	Xaver Hörmann (GER) 50:06.5

Men's 10,000m Folding K-2

	Gold	Silver	Bronze
1936	Sven Johansson/Eric Bladström (SWE) 45:48.9	Willi Horn/Erich Hanisch (GER) 45:49.2	Cornelis Wijdekop/Pieter Wijdekop (NED) 46:12.4

Men's K-1 4 × 500m Relay

	Gold	Silver	Bronze
1960	Germany 7:39.43	Hungary 7:44.02	Denmark 7:46.09

Coursing

Coursing is the pursuit of game by hounds who hunt by sight and not by scent.

In the 1500s King Henry VIII made it known that he expected all young noblemen to be well versed in the sport of coursing. Not only were they encouraged to keep greyhounds but they were also expected to thoroughly master the art of breeding the best dogs. During the reign of Queen Elizabeth I (1558-1603), competitive coursing was to leave an indelible mark. The Queen, aided by Thomas, Duke of Norfolk, initiated a code of rules, establishing such particulars as the hare's head-start and the ways in which the two hounds' speed, agility and concentration would be judged against one another. By and large these rules are still in force today. Elizabeth favoured both stag and hare coursing and the sport was dubbed 'The Sport of Queens'. Her successor, King James I (1603-25), was a great devotee of hare coursing and had a hunting lodge built close to Newmarket, Suffolk, where he decreed that a hundred hares should be released each year so that the high grade of coursing could continue.

The first known coursing club came into existence in 1776 at Swaffham, Norfolk, through the enterprise of Lord Orford. The famous Waterloo Cup (named after the Waterloo Hotel in Liverpool) was established in 1836, and it has been held annually ever since, except for the war years. It was originally held on the Altcar estate of Earl Sefton and was considered for over a century to be the ultimate test of the coursing greyhound. The National Coursing Club was formed in 1858.

In modern coursing competitions, two greyhounds at a time pursue one hare. The dogs are judged on performance as well as on their success in catching the hare, points being awarded for outracing the other dog and catching up with the hare, for turning it at a right angle, for turning it at less than a right angle (wrenching), for tripping the hare, and for a kill.

Greyhound racing with a mechanical lure is a popular outgrowth of coursing.

CRICKET

Although references to the game have been traced back to Tudor times, it was not until the early 18th century that prestigious matches began to attract spectators – and gamblers. The first great match was between Kent and the Rest of England in 1744, the year in which the first version of the Laws of the game appeared, and in the 1760s the famous Hambledon Club of Hampshire was founded, usually fielding a team of professionals. This club's authority over the game was taken over by the Marylebone Cricket Club (MCC), founded in 1787. Still responsible for the Laws of Cricket, the MCC is based at Lord's, which moved to its present site in St John's Wood Road in 1814. While some of the original regulations remain unchanged (e.g. the pitch still measures 22 yards), later developments included the addition of a third stump in the 1770s and the legalisation of round-arm bowling in 1828, followed by that of over-arm bowling in 1864. Counties had played each other on an unofficial basis for most of the 19th century, but it was not until 1890 that the Championship began on a formalised basis, Durham becoming in 1992 the 18th participant county. The domestic game has been governed since 1997 by the England and Wales Cricket Board.

British expatriates, as well as troops garrisoned overseas, spread the game to the colonies, but before World War I only Australia (where the first-ever Test match was played at Melbourne in 1876-77) and South Africa took part with England in official Tests. These were joined by West Indies (who played their first Test in 1928), New Zealand (1930) and India (1932). After World War II came Pakistan (1952), Sri Lanka (1982) and Zimbabwe (1992), Bangladesh (2000) becoming the tenth full Test-playing country, albeit with scant success to date. Under the aegis of the International Cricket Council (ICC), numerous other countries where the game is less widespread have become associate or affiliate members; some of these take part in the highly successful limited-over World Cup competition, which began in 1975.

Cricket has had its share of crises – the 'bodyline' series in Australia in 1932-33, the 'throwing' controversy of the 1950s and 1960s, the isolation of South Africa between 1969-70 and 1991, the Kerry Packer World Series revolution in 1977, intimidatory bowling and 'sledging'. But it is constantly evolving, notably with the introduction of domestic one-day competitions (starting with the Gillette Cup in 1963) and international games (beginning in 1971 with Australia v England at Melbourne), along with innovations such as coloured clothing and floodlit day–night games, which have mass appeal but which appal the traditionalists. In 2003 the ECB tried out the Twenty20 Cup, an even shorter version of the game with instant thrills for modern short attention spans, and this looks likely to be extended, perhaps even into the international arena. (What it will achieve for players' technique and concentration remains to be seen.) But it is now international cricket, in both Test and one-day forms, which dominates the world cricket calendar, with ever fewer breaks between tournaments.

Cricket Tables 2003 season

Frizzell County Championship – Division One

	P	W	L	D	Bat	Bowl	Deduct	Pts
Sussex	16	10	4	2	62	47	0	257
Lancashire	16	6	2	8	64	43	0	223
Surrey	16	6	3	7	63	44	0	219
Kent	16	6	5	5	47	47	0	198
Warwickshire	16	4	5	7	50	37	2.5	171.5
Middlesex	16	3	3	10	46	41	0	169
Essex	16	3	5	8	34	45	0	156
Nottinghamshire	16	2	8	6	36	45	1	132
Leicestershire	16	1	6	9	36	40	0.5	125.5

Frizzell County Championship – Division Two

	P	W	L	D	Bat	Bowl	Deduct	Pts
Worcestershire	16	10	1	5	42	44	0.25	245.75
Northamptonshire	16	10	2	4	45	44	8	237
Gloucestershire	16	5	2	9	38	46	0	190
Yorkshire	16	4	5	7	54	47	1.5	183.5

	P	W	L	D	NR		NetRR		Pts
Glamorgan	16	5	5	6	45	45	1		183
Durham	16	5	7	4	31	43	0.75		159.25
Somerset	16	4	8	4	41	44	0		157
Hampshire	16	2	6	8	36	44	0		140
Derbyshire	16	2	11	3	30	44	0		114

ECB National Cricket League – Division One

	P	W	L	D	NR	Net RR	Pts
Surrey Lions	16	12	3	0	1	2.99	50
Gloucs Gladiators	16	11	4	0	1	4.48	46
Essex Eagles	16	8	7	1	0	3.8	34
Warwickshire Bears	16	8	8	0	0	-0.57	32
Glamorgan Dragons	16	8	8	0	0	-0.94	32
Kent Spitfires	16	7	8	1	0	3.52	30
Leicester Foxes	16	7	9	0	0	-3.83	28
Yorkshire Phoenix	16	5	11	0	0	-6.96	20
Worcester Royals	16	4	12	0	0	-1.16	16

ECB National Cricket League – Division Two

	P	W	L	D	NR	Net RR	Pts
Lancashire Lightning	18	14	3	0	1	5.81	58
Northants Steelbacks	18	12	5	0	1	11	50
Hampshire Hawks	18	11	7	0	0	4.8	44
Middlesex Crusaders	18	10	7	0	1	-0.27	42
Nottingham Outlaws	18	9	9	0	0	-0.62	36
Derby Scorpions	18	8	8	0	2	-0.36	36
Durham Dynamos	18	7	10	0	1	4.24	30
Sussex Sharks	18	6	12	0	0	-8.17	24
Somerset Sabres	18	5	12	0	1	-4.12	22
Scottish Saltires	18	4	13	0	1	-14	18

CRICKET

County Cricket Club Playing Staffs
details correct at the start of 2004 season

Derbyshire (one-day team known as The Scorpions)

player	date of birth	details
Adnan, Hassan	15.05.1975	right hand bat, right arm off break bowler
Ali, Mohammad	11.08.1973	right hand bat, left arm medium/fast bowler
Bassano, Christopher	11.09.1975	right hand bat, right arm leg break bowler
Botha, Anthony	17.11.1976	left hand bat, slow left arm bowler
Bryant, James	04.02.1976	right hand bat
Chapman, James	19.05.1986	left hand bat, right arm medium bowler
Dean, Kevin	16.10.1975	left hand bat, left arm fast/medium bowler
Dumelow, Nathan	30.04.1981	right hand bat, right arm off break bowler
Gait, Andrew	19.12.1978	right hand bat
Gunter, Neil	12.05.1981	left hand bat, right arm fast/medium bowler
Havell, Paul	04.07.1980	left hand bat, right arm fast/medium bowler
Hewson, Dominic	03.10.1974	right hand bat, right arm medium bowler
Khan, Rawait	05.03.1982	right hand bat, right arm medium bowler
Lungley, Tom	25.07.1979	left hand bat, right arm medium bowler
Moss, Jonathan	04.05.1975	right hand bat, right arm medium bowler
Rogers, Chris	31.08.1977	left hand bat, leg break googly bowler
Selwood, Steve	24.11.1979	left hand bat, left arm slow bowler
Stubbings, Steve	31.03.1978	left hand bat, right arm off break bowler
Sutton, Luke (Capt)	04.10.1976	right hand bat, wicket-keeper
Walker, Nick	07.08.1984	right hand bat, right arm fast/medium bowler
Welch, Graeme	21.03.1972	right hand bat, right arm medium bowler
Wharton, Lian	21.02.1977	left hand bat, left arm slow bowler

Address: Nottingham Road, Derby, DE2 6DA
Telephone: 01332 383211

Durham (one-day team known as The Dynamos)

player	date of birth	details
Akhtar, Shoaib	13.08.1975	right hand bat, right arm fast bowler
Breese, Gareth	09.01.1976	right hand bat, right arm off break bowler
Bridge, Graeme	04.09.1980	right hand bat, left arm slow bowler
Coetzer, Kyle	14.04.1984	right hand bat, right arm medium bowler
Collingwood, Paul	26.05.1976	right hand bat, right arm medium bowler
Davies, Anthony	04.10.1980	right hand bat, right arm medium bowler
Gibbs, Herschelle	23.02.1974	right hand bat, right arm medium and leg break bowler
Hamilton, Gavin	16.09.1974	right hand bat, right arm medium bowler
Harmison, Stephen	23.10.1978	right hand bat, right arm fast bowler
Killeen, Neil	17.10.1975	right hand bat, right arm medium bowler
King, Reon	06.10.1975	right hand bat, right arm fast/medium bowler
Lewis, Jonathan (capt)	21.05.1970	right hand bat, right arm medium bowler
Lowe, James	04.11.1982	right hand bat, wicket-keeper
Muchall, Gordon	02.11.1982	right hand bat, right arm medium bowler
Mustard, Philip	08.10.1982	left hand bat, wicket-keeper
North, Marcus	28.07.1979	left hand bat, right arm off break bowler
Onions, Graham	09.09.1982	right hand bat, right arm fast bowler
Pattison, Ian	05.05.1982	right hand bat, right arm medium bowler
Peng, Nicky	18.09.1982	right hand bat
Plunkett, Liam	06.04.1985	right hand bat, right arm medium bowler
Pratt, Andrew	04.03.1975	left hand bat, wicket-keeper
Pratt, Gary	22.12.1981	left hand bat, right arm off break bowler
Turner, Mark	23.10.1984	right hand bat, right arm fast bowler

Address: Riverside, Chester-le-Street, Co. Durham, DH3 3QR
Telephone: 0191 3871717

Essex (one-day team known as The Eagles)

player	date of birth	details
Bishop, Justin	04.01.1982	left hand bat, left arm medium/fast bowler
Bopara, Ravinder	04.05.1985	right hand bat, right arm medium bowler
Brant, Scott	26.01.1983	right hand bat, left arm medium/fast bowler
Clarke, Andrew	09.11.1975	left hand bat, right arm medium bowler
Cook, Alastair	25.12.1984	left hand bat, right arm off break bowler
Cowan, Ashley	07.05.1975	right hand bat, right arm medium/fast bowler
Doeschate, Ryan ten	30.06.1980	right hand bat, right arm medium/fast bowler
Flower, Andy	28.04.1968	left hand bat, right arm off break bowler, keeper
Foster, James	15.04.1980	right hand bat, wicket-keeper
Gough, Darren	18.09.1970	right hand bat, right arm fast bowler
Grayson, Paul	31.03.1971	right hand bat, left arm slow bowler
Habib, Aftab	07.02.1972	right hand bat, right arm medium/fast bowler
Hussain, Nasser	28.03.1968	right hand bat, right arm leg break bowler
Irani, Ronnie (capt)	26.10.1971	right hand bat, right arm medium bowler
Jefferson, William	25.10.1979	right hand bat, right arm medium bowler
Kaneria, Danish	16.12.1980	right hand bat, right arm leg break bowler
McCoubrey, Adrian	03.04.1980	right hand bat, right arm medium/fast bowler
Middlebrook, James	13.05.1977	right hand bat, right arm off break bowler
Napier, Graham	01.06.1980	right hand bat, right arm medium bowler
Palladino, Tony	29.06.1983	right hand bat, right arm medium/fast bowler
Pettini, Mark	07.08.1983	right hand bat, right arm medium bowler
Phillips, Timothy	13.03.1981	left hand bat, left arm slow bowler
Sharif, Zoheb	22.02.1983	left hand bat, left arm leg break bowler
Stephenson, John	14.03.1965	right hand bat, right arm medium bowler

Address: New Writtle Street, Chelmsford, Essex, CM2 0PG
Telephone: 01245 252420

Glamorgan (one-day team known as The Dragons)

player	date of birth	details
Cherry, Daniel	02.07.1980	left hand bat, right arm medium bowler
Cosker, Dean	01.07.1978	right hand bat, left arm slow bowler
Croft, Robert (capt)	25.05.1970	right hand bat, right arm off break bowler
Dale, Adrian	24.10.1968	right hand bat, right arm medium bowler
Davies, Andrew	11.07.1976	left hand bat, right arm medium bowler
Elliott, Matthew	28.09.1971	left hand bat, left arm medium bowler
Grant, Richard	05.06.1984	right hand bat, right arm medium bowler
Harrison, Adam	30.10.1985	right hand bat, right arm medium bowler

Harrison, David	30.07.1981	right hand bat, right arm medium/fast bowler
Hemp, David	11.08.1970	left hand bat, right arm medium bowler
Hughes, Jonathan	30.06.1981	right hand bat, right arm medium bowler
Jones, Simon	25.12.1978	left hand bat, right arm fast/medium bowler
Kasprowicz, Mike	02.10.1972	right hand bat, right arm medium/fast bowler
Maynard, Matthew	21.03.1966	right hand bat, right arm medium bowler
Powell, Mike	02.03.1977	right hand bat, right arm off break bowler
Shaw, Adrian	17.02.1972	right hand bat, wicket-keeper
Thomas, (Stuart) Darren	25.01.1975	left hand bat, right arm medium bowler
Thomas, Ian	05.09.1979	left hand bat, right arm off break bowler
Wallace, Mark	19.11.1981	left hand bat, wicket-keeper
Watkins, Ryan	09.06.1983	left hand bat, right arm medium bowler
Wharf, Alex	06.04.1975	right hand bat, right arm medium/fast bowler

Address: Sophia Gardens, Cardiff, CF11 9XR
Telephone: 02920 409380

Gloucestershire (one-day team known as The Gladiators)

player	date of birth	details
Adshead, Stephen	29.01.1980	right hand bat, wicket-keeper
Ahmed, Shabbir	21.04.1976	right hand bat, right arm fast/medium bowler
Alleyne, Mark	23.05.1968	right hand bat, right arm medium bowler
Averis, James	28.05.1974	right hand bat, right arm medium bowler
Ball, Martyn	26.04.1970	right hand bat, right arm off break bowler
Bressington, Alastair	28.11.1979	left hand bat, right arm medium bowler
Fisher, Ian	31.03.1976	left hand bat, left arm slow bowler
Gidman, Alexander	22.06.1981	right hand bat, right arm medium bowler
Hancock, Timothy	20.04.1972	right hand bat, right arm medium bowler
Hardinges, Mark	02.05.1978	right hand bat, right arm medium bowler
Lewis, Jonathan	26.08.1975	right hand bat, right arm medium bowler
Malik, Shoaib	01.02.1982	right hand bat, right arm fast/medium bowler
Pearson, James	09.11.1983	left hand bat
Russell, Robert Charles	15.08.1963	left hand bat, wicket-keeper
Sillence, Roger	29.06.1977	right hand bat, right arm medium/fast bowler
Smith, Andrew	10.01.1967	right hand bat, left arm medium/fast bowler
Spearman, Craig	07.04.1972	right hand bat
Taylor, Christopher (capt)	27.09.1976	right hand bat, right arm off break bowler
Weston, William	16.06.1973	left hand bat, left arm medium bowler
Windows, Matthew	04.05.1973	right hand bat, left arm slow bowler

Address: Nevil Road, Bristol, BS7 9EJ
Telephone: 0117 9108000

Hampshire (one-day team known as The Hawks)

player	date of birth	details
Adams, James	23.09.1980	left hand bat, left arm medium bowler
Benham, Chris	24.03.1983	right hand bat, right arm off break bowler
Brown, Michael	09.02.1980	right hand bat, right arm off break bowler
Bruce, James	17.12.1979	right hand bat, right arm medium/fast bowler
Burrows, Thomas	05.05.1985	right hand bat, wicket-keeper
Clarke, Michael	02.04.1981	right hand bat, left arm slow bowler
Crawley, John (capt)	21.09.1971	right hand bat, right arm medium bowler
Hamblin, James	16.08.1978	right hand bat, right arm medium/fast bowler
Kendall, William	18.12.1973	right hand bat, right arm medium bowler
Kenway, Derek	06.12.1978	right hand bat, wicket-keeper
Lamb, Greg	04.03.1980	right hand bat, right arm off break and medium bowler
Latouf, Kevin	07.09.1985	right hand bat, right arm medium bowler
Mascarenhas, Dimitri	30.10.1977	right hand bat, right arm medium/fast bowler
Mullally, Alan	07.12.1969	right hand bat, left arm medium/fast bowler
Pothas, Nic	18.11.1973	right hand bat, wicket-keeper
Prittipaul, Lawrence	19.10.1979	right hand bat, right arm medium bowler
Taylor, Billy	11.01.1977	left hand bat, right arm medium/fast bowler
Tomlinson, James	06.12.1982	left hand bat, left arm medium/fast bowler
Tremlett, Christopher	09.02.1981	right hand bat, right arm medium/fast bowler
Udal, Shaun	18.03.1969	right hand bat, right arm off break bowler
Warne, Shane	13.09.1969	right hand bat, leg break/googly bowler
Watson, Shane	17.06.1981	right hand bat, right arm fast/medium bowler

Address: Rose Bowl, Botley Road, West End, Southampton, SO30 3XH
Telephone: 023 80472002

CRICKET

Kent (one-day team known as The Spitfires)

player	date of birth	details
Carberry, Michael	29.09.1980	left hand bat, right arm off break bowler
Cusden, Simon	21.02.1985	right hand bat, right arm fast bowler
Denly, Joe	16.03.1986	right hand bat, right arm leg break bowler
Dennington, Matthew	16.10.1982	right hand bat, right arm medium/fast bowler
Ferley, Robert	02.04.1982	right hand bat, left arm slow bowler
Fulton, David (capt)	15.11.1971	right hand bat, left arm slow bowler
Jones, Geraint	14.07.1976	right hand bat, wicket-keeper
Joseph, Robbie	20.01.1982	right hand bat, right arm fast bowler
Key, Robert	05.12.1979	right hand bat, right arm off break bowler
Khan, Amjad	14.10.1980	right hand bat, right arm fast bowler
Loudon, Alex	09.06.1980	right hand bat, right arm off break bowler
O'Brien, Niall	08.11.1981	left hand bat, wicket-keeper
Patel, Min	07.07.1970	right hand bat, left arm slow bowler
Saggers, Martin	23.05.1972	right hand bat, right arm fast bowler
Sami, Mohammad	24.02.1981	right hand bat, right arm fast bowler
Sheriyar, Alamgir	15.11.1973	right hand bat, left arm medium/fast bowler
Smith, Ed	19.07.1977	right hand bat, right arm medium bowler
Stiff, David	20.10.1984	right hand bat, right arm fast bowler
Symonds, Andrew	06.09.1975	right hand bat, right arm off break bowler
Tredwell, James	27.02.1982	left hand bat, right arm off break bowler
Trott, Ben	14.03.1975	right hand bat, right arm medium/fast bowler
Walker, Matthew	01.02.1975	left hand bat, right arm medium bowler

Address: St Lawrence Ground, Old Dover Road, Canterbury, CT1 3NZ
Telephone: 01227 456886

Lancashire (one-day team known as The Lightning)

player	date of birth	details
Anderson, James	30.07.1982	left hand bat, right arm fast bowler
Chapple, Glen	23.01.1974	right hand bat, right arm medium bowler
Chilton, Mark	10.02.1976	right hand bat, right arm medium bowler
Cork, Dominic	08.07.1971	right hand bat, right arm medium/fast bowler
Crook, Steven	28.05.1983	right hand bat, right arm medium/fast bowler
Currie, Mark	22.09.1979	right hand bat, right arm off break bowler
Flintoff, Andrew	12.06.1977	right hand bat, right arm medium/fast bowler
Haynes, Jamie	07.05.1974	right hand bat, wicket-keeper
Hegg, Warren (capt)	23.02.1968	right hand bat, wicket-keeper
Hogg, Kyle	07.02.1983	left hand bat, right arm medium/fast bowler
Hooper, Carl	15.12.1966	right hand bat, right arm off break bowler
Horton, Paul	20.09.1982	right hand bat, right arm medium bowler
Keedy, Gary	27.11.1974	left hand bat, left arm slow bowler
Law, Stuart	18.10.1968	right hand bat, right arm slow/medium bowler
Loye, Mal	27.09.1972	right hand bat, right arm off break bowler
Mahmood, Sajid	21.12.1981	right hand bat, right arm medium/fast bowler
Martin, Peter	15.11.1968	right hand bat, right arm medium/fast bowler
Rees, Tim	09.04.1984	right hand bat, right arm off break bowler
Schofield, Chris	10.06.1978	left hand bat, left arm leg break bowler
Sutcliffe, Iain	20.12.1974	left hand bat, left arm off break bowler
Swann, Alec	26.10.1976	right hand bat, right arm off break bowler
Wood, John	22.07.1970	right hand bat, right arm medium/fast bowler
Yates, Gary	20.09.1967	right hand bat, right arm off break bowler

Address: Old Trafford, Manchester, M16 0PX
Telephone: 0161 282 4000

Leicestershire (one-day team known as The Foxes)

player	date of birth	details
Brandy, Damian	14.09.1981	right hand bat, right arm medium bowler
Brignull, David	27.11.1981	right hand bat, right arm medium/fast bowler
Dagnall, Charles	07.10.1976	right hand bat, right arm medium/fast bowler
Dakin, Jon	28.02.1973	left hand bat, right arm medium bowler
DeFreitas, Phillip (capt)	18.02.1966	right hand bat, right arm medium/fast bowler
Ferraby, Nick	31.05.1983	right hand bat, right arm medium bowler
Gibson, Ottis	16.03.1969	right hand bat, right arm fast bowler
Henderson, Claude	14.06.1972	right hand bat, left arm slow bowler
Hodge, Bradley	29.12.1974	right hand bat, right arm off break bowler

Kruger, Garnett	05.01.1977	right hand bat, right arm medium/fast bowler
Liddle, Chris	01.02.1984	right hand bat, left arm slow bowler
Maddy, Darren	23.05.1974	right hand bat, right arm medium bowler
Masters, David	22.04.1978	right hand bat, right arm medium/fast bowler
Maunders, John	04.04.1981	left hand bat, right arm medium bowler
New, Thomas	18.01.1985	left hand bat, wicket-keeper
Nixon, Paul	21.10.1970	left hand bat, wicket-keeper
Robinson, Darren	02.03.1973	right hand bat, right arm medium/fast bowler
Sadler, John	19.11.1981	left hand bat, leg break and googly bowler
Snape, Jeremy	27.04.1973	right hand bat, right arm off break bowler
Stevens, Darren	30.04.1976	right hand bat, right arm medium bowler
Walker, George	05.12.1984	left hand bat, left arm slow bowler

Address: Grace Road, Leicester, LE2 8AD
Telephone: 0116 2832128

Middlesex (one-day team known as The Crusaders)

player	date of birth	details
Betts, Melvyn	26.03.1975	right hand bat, right arm fast/medium bowler
Bloomfield, Timothy	31.05.1973	right hand bat, left arm medium/fast bowler
Compton, Nick	26.06.1983	right hand bat, right arm off break bowler
Cook, Simon	15.01.1977	right hand bat, left arm medium/fast bowler
Dalrymple, James	21.01.1981	right hand bat, right arm off break bowler
Duncan, Ben	21.11.1983	right hand bat, right arm medium bowler
Hayward, Nantie	06.03.1977	right hand bat, right arm fast bowler
Hutchison, Paul	09.06.1977	left hand bat, left arm fast/medium bowler
Hutton, Ben	29.01.1977	left hand bat, right arm medium bowler
Klusener, Lance	04.09.1971	left hand bat, right arm fast/medium bowler
Koenig, Sven	09.12.1973	right hand bat, right arm off break bowler
Joyce, Edmund	22.09.1978	left hand bat, right arm medium bowler
Keegan, Chad	30.07.1979	right hand bat, right arm medium bowler
Morgan, Eoin	10.09.1986	left hand bat, right arm medium bowler
Nash, David	19.01.1978	right hand bat, wicket-keeper
Peploe, Chris	26.04.1981	left hand bat, left arm slow bowler
Rankin, Boyd	05.07.1984	right hand bat, right arm medium/fast bowler
Richards, Mali	02.09.1983	left hand bat, right arm medium bowler
Savill, Thomas	16.05.1983	right hand bat, right arm medium/fast bowler
Scott, Ben	04.08.1981	right hand bat, wicket-keeper
Shah, Owais	22.10.1978	right hand bat, right arm off break bowler
Strauss, Andrew (capt)	03.02.1977	left hand bat, right arm medium bowler
Weekes, Paul	07.08.1969	left hand bat, right arm off break bowler
Whelan, Christopher	08.05.1986	right hand bat, right arm medium/fast bowler

Address: Lord's Cricket Ground, London, NW8 8QN
Telephone: 020 7289 1300

Northamptonshire (one-day team known as The Steelbacks)

player	date of birth	details
Afzaal, Usman	09.06.1977	left hand bat, left arm slow bowler
Anderson, Ricky	22.09.1976	right hand bat, right arm medium/fast bowler
Bailey, Toby	28.08.1976	right hand bat, wicket-keeper
Brophy, Gerard	26.11.1975	right hand bat, wicket-keeper
Brown, Jason	10.10.1974	right hand bat, right arm off break bowler
Cawdron, Michael	10.07.1974	left hand bat, right arm medium/fast bowler
Cook, Jeff	02.02.1972	left hand bat, right arm medium/fast bowler
Greenidge, Carl	20.04.1978	right hand bat, right arm fast bowler
Jones, Philip	09.02.1974	right hand bat, right arm fast bowler
Louw, Johann	12.04.1979	right hand bat, right arm medium/fast bowler
Panesar, Monty	25.04.1982	right hand bat, left arm slow bowler
Phillips, Ben	30.09.1974	right hand bat, right arm medium bowler
Powell, Mark	04.11.1980	right hand bat, right arm medium/off break bowler
Roberts, Timothy	04.03.1978	right hand bat, right arm off break bowler
Sales, David (capt)	03.12.1977	right hand bat, right arm medium bowler
Swann, Graeme	24.03.1979	right hand bat, off break bowler
White, Robert	15.10.1979	right hand bat, right arm leg/off break bowler
Van Jaarsveld, Martin	18.06.1974	right hand bat, right arm medium bowler

Address: Wantage Road, Northampton, NN1 4TJ
Telephone: 01604 514455

CRICKET

Nottinghamshire (one-day team known as The Outlaws)

player	date of birth	details
Alleyne, David	17.04.1976	right hand bat, wicket-keeper
Bicknell, Darren	24.06.1967	left hand bat, left arm slow bowler
Clough, Gareth	25.05.1978	right hand bat, right arm medium bowler
Ealham, Mark	27.08.1969	right hand bat, right arm medium/fast bowler
Franks, Paul	03.02.1979	left hand bat, right arm medium/fast bowler
Gallian, Jason (capt)	25.06.1971	right hand bat, right arm medium bowler
Harris, Andrew	26.06.1973	right hand bat, right arm medium/fast bowler
Hussey, David	15.07.1977	right hand bat, right arm off break bowler
Logan, Richard	28.01.1980	right hand bat, right arm fast bowler
Lucas, David	19.08.1978	left hand bat, left arm medium/fast bowler
MacGill, Stuart	25.02.1971	right hand bat, right arm leg break bowler
McMahon, Paul	12.02.1983	right hand bat, off break bowler
Noon, Wayne	05.02.1971	right hand bat, wicket-keeper
Patel, Samit	30.11.1984	right hand bat, left arm slow bowler
Pietersen, Kevin	27.06.1980	right hand bat, off break bowler
Read, Chris	10.08.1978	right hand bat, wicket-keeper
Shafayat, Bilal	10.07.1984	right hand bat, right arm medium bowler, wicket-keeper
Shreck, Charlie	06.01.1978	right hand bat, right arm medium/fast bowler
Sidebottom, Ryan	15.01.1978	left hand bat, left arm fast/medium bowler
Singh, Anurag	09.09.1975	right hand bat, right arm off break bowler
Smith, Greg	30.10.1971	right hand bat, left arm medium/fast bowler
Warren, Russell	10.09.1971	right hand bat, right arm off break bowler, wicket-keeper

Address: Trent Bridge, Nottingham, NG2 6AG
Telephone: 0115 9823000

Somerset (one-day team known as The Sabres)

player	date of birth	details
Andrew, Gareth	27.12.1983	left hand bat, right arm off break bowler
Blackwell, Ian	10.06.1978	left hand bat, left arm slow bowler
Bowler, Peter	30.07.1963	right hand bat, right arm off break bowler, wicket-keeper
Bryant, James	04.02.1976	right hand bat
Burns, Michael (capt)	06.02.1969	right hand bat, right arm medium bowler, wicket-keeper
Caddick, Andrew	21.11.1968	right hand bat, right arm medium/fast bowler
Cox, Jamie	15.10.1969	right hand bat, right arm off break bowler
Durston, Wesley	06.10.1980	right hand bat, right arm slow bowler
Dutch, Keith	21.03.1973	right hand bat, right arm off break bowler
Edwards, Neil	14.10.1983	left hand bat, right arm medium bowler
Francis, John	13.11.1980	left hand bat, left arm slow bowler
Francis, Simon	15.08.1978	right hand bat, right arm medium/fast bowler
Gazzard, Carl	15.04.1982	right hand bat, wicket-keeper
Hildreth, James	09.09.1984	right hand bat, right arm fast/medium bowler
Hunt, Thomas	19.01.1982	left hand bat, right arm fast/medium bowler
Johnson, Richard	29.12.1974	right hand bat, right arm medium bowler
Laraman, Aaron	10.01.1979	right hand bat, right arm medium/fast bowler
McLean, Nixon	20.07.1973	left hand bat, right arm fast bowler
Munday, Michael	22.10.1984	right hand bat, leg break bowler
Parsons, Keith	02.05.1973	right hand bat, right arm medium bowler
Parsons, Michael	26.11.1984	right hand bat, right arm medium/fast bowler
Ponting, Ricky	19.12.1974	right hand bat
Suppiah, Arul	30.08.1983	right hand bat, left arm slow bowler
Trescothick, Marcus	25.12.1975	left hand bat, right arm medium bowler
Turner, Rob	25.11.1967	right hand bat, wicket-keeper
Webley, Thomas	02.03.1983	left hand bat, right arm medium/fast bowler
Wood, Matthew	30.09.1980	right hand bat, right arm off break bowler

Address: St James St, Taunton, Somerset, TA1 1JT
Telephone: 01823 272946

Surrey (one-day team known as The Lions)

player	date of birth	details
Batty, Jonathan (capt)	18.04.1974	right hand bat, wicket-keeper
Benning, James	04.05.1983	right hand bat, right arm medium bowler
Bicknell, Martin	14.01.1969	right hand bat, right arm medium/fast bowler
Brown, Alistair	02.11.1970	right hand bat, right arm off break, wicket-keeper
Butcher, Mark	23.08.1972	left hand bat, right arm medium bowler

Clarke, Rikki	29.09.1981	right hand bat, right arm medium/fast bowler
Hodd, Andrew	12.01.1984	right hand bat, wicket-keeper
Mahmood, Azhar	28.02.1975	right hand bat, right arm fast/medium bowler
Miller, Daniel	12.06.1983	right hand bat, right arm medium bowler
Murtagh, Tim	02.08.1981	left hand bat, right arm medium/fast bowler
Mushtaq, Saqlain	29.12.1976	right hand bat, right arm off break bowler
Newman, Scott	03.11.1979	left hand bat, right arm medium bowler
Ormond, James	20.08.1977	right hand bat, right arm medium/off break bowler
Ramprakash, Mark	05.09.1969	right hand bat, right arm off break bowler
Saker, Neil	20.09.1984	right hand bat, right arm medium bowler
Salisbury, Ian	21.01.1970	right hand bat, right arm leg break bowler
Sampson, Phil	06.09.1980	right hand bat, right arm medium/fast bowler
Shahid, Nadeem	23.04.1969	right hand bat, right arm leg break bowler
Thorpe, Graham	01.08.1969	left hand bat, right arm medium bowler
Tudor, Alex	23.10.1977	right hand bat, right arm fast bowler

Address: Kennington Oval, London, SE11 5SS
Telephone: 020 7582 6660

Sussex (one-day team known as The Sharks)

player	date of birth	details
Adams, Chris (capt)	06.05.1970	right hand bat, right arm medium bowler
Ahmed, Mushtaq	28.06.1970	right hand bat, right arm leg break bowler
Akram, Mohammad	10.09.1974	right hand bat, right arm fast/medium bowler
Ambrose, Tim	01.12.1982	right hand bat, wicket-keeper
Cottey, Tony	02.06.1966	right hand bat, right arm off break bowler
Davis, Mark	10.10.1971	right hand bat, right arm off break bowler
Goodwin, Murray	11.12.1972	right hand bat, leg break bowler
Hopkinson, Carl	14.09.1981	right hand bat, right arm medium bowler
Innes, Kevin	24.09.1975	right hand bat, right arm medium bowler
Kirtley, James	10.01.1975	right hand bat, right arm medium/fast bowler
Lewry, Jason	02.04.1971	left hand bat, left arm medium bowler
Martin-Jenkins, Robin	28.10.1975	right hand bat, right arm medium bowler
Montgomerie, Richard	03.07.1971	right hand bat, right arm off break bowler
Prior, Matt	26.02.1982	right hand bat, wicket-keeper
Voros, Jason	31.12.1976	left hand bat, left arm fast/medium bowler
Ward, Ian	30.09.1973	left hand bat, right arm slow bowler
Wright, Luke	07.03.1985	right hand bat, right arm medium bowler
Yardy, Michael	27.11.1980	left hand bat, left arm medium bowler

Address: Eaton Road, Hove, BN3 3AN
Telephone: 01273 827100

Warwickshire (one-day team known as The Bears)

player	date of birth	details
Ali, Moeen	18.06.1987	right hand bat
Bell, Ian	11.04.1982	right hand bat, right arm medium bowler
Brown, Dougie	29.10.1969	right hand bat, right arm medium/fast bowler
Carter, Neil	29.01.1975	left hand bat, left arm medium/fast bowler
Clifford, Ian	12.10.1982	right hand bat, wicket-keeper
Frost, Tony	17.11.1975	right hand bat, wicket-keeper
Giles, Ashley	19.03.1973	right hand bat, left arm slow bowler
Hogg, Bradley	06.02.1971	left hand bat, left arm chinaman bowler
Jones, Huw	23.11.1980	right hand bat, leg break bowler
Knight, Nick (capt)	28.11.1969	left hand bat, right arm medium/fast bowler
Mees, Tom	08.06.1981	right hand bat, right arm medium/fast bowler
Ostler, Dominic	15.07.1970	right hand bat, right arm medium bowler, wicket-keeper
Penney, Trevor	12.07.1968	right hand bat, leg break bowler
Piper, Keith	18.12.1969	right hand bat, wicket-keeper
Powell, Michael	05.04.1975	right hand bat, right arm medium bowler
Pretorius, Dewald	06.12.1977	right hand bat, right arm fast bowler
Richardson, Alan	06.05.1975	right hand bat, right arm medium/fast bowler
Spires, Jamie	12.11.1979	right hand bat, left arm slow bowler
Streak, Heath	16.03.1974	right hand bat, right arm fast/medium bowler
Tahir, Naqaash	14.11.1983	right hand bat, right arm medium/fast bowler
Taylor, Stephen	17.12.1985	right hand bat, right arm medium/fast bowler
Trott, Jonathan	22.04.1981	right hand bat, right arm medium/fast bowler
Troughton, Jim	02.03.1979	left hand bat, left arm slow bowler
Wagg, Graham	28.04.1983	right hand bat, left arm medium/fast bowler
Wagh, Mark	20.10.1976	right hand bat, right arm off break bowler

| Warren, Nick | 26.06.1982 | right hand bat, right arm medium/fast bowler |
| Westwood, Ian | 13.07.1982 | left hand bat, right arm off break bowler |

Address: Edgbaston, Birmingham, B5 7QU
Telephone: 0121 4464422

Worcestershire (one-day team known as The Royals)

player	date of birth	details
Ali, Kabir	24.11.1980	right hand bat, right arm fast bowler
Ali, Kadeer	07.03.1983	right hand bat
Batty, Gareth	13.10.1977	right hand bat, right arm off break bowler
Bichel, Andy	27.08.1970	right hand bat, right arm fast/medium bowler
Davies, Steven	17.06.1986	left hand bat, wicket-keeper
Farrow, Jonathan	22.02.1984	right hand bat, right arm fast/medium bowler
Hall, Andrew	31.07.1975	right hand bat, right arm fast/medium bowler
Harrity, Mark	09.03.1974	left hand bat, left arm fast bowler
Hick, Graeme	23.05.1966	right hand bat, right arm off break bowler
Khalid, Shaftab	06.10.1982	off break bowler
Leatherdale, David	26.11.1967	right hand bat, right arm medium bowler
Malik, Nadeem	06.10.1982	right hand bat, right arm fast/medium bowler
Mason, Matt	20.03.1974	right hand bat, right arm fast/medium bowler
Mitchell, Daryl	25.11.1983	right hand bat, right arm medium bowler
Moore, Stephen	04.11.1980	right hand bat
Peters, Stephen	10.12.1978	right hand bat
Pipe, James	16.12.1977	right hand bat, wicket-keeper
Rhodes, Steven	17.06.1964	right hand bat, wicket-keeper
Smith, Ben (capt)	03.04.1972	right hand bat, right arm medium bowler
Solanki, Vikram	01.04.1976	right hand bat, right arm off break bowler
Wigley, David	26.10.1981	right hand bat, right arm medium/fast bowler

Address: New Road, Worcester, WR2 4QQ
Telephone: 01905 748474

Yorkshire (one-day team known as The Phoenix)

player	date of birth	details
Blain, John	04.01.1979	right hand bat, right arm fast/medium bowler
Blakey, Richard	15.01.1967	right hand bat, wicket-keeper
Bresnan, Tim	28.02.1985	right hand bat, right arm medium bowler
Craven, Victor	31.07.1980	left hand bat, right arm medium bowler
Dawson, Richard	04.08.1980	right hand bat, right arm off break bowler
Gale, Andrew	28.11.1983	left hand bat, left arm leg break bowler
Gray, Andy	19.05.1974	right hand bat, right arm off break bowler
Guy, Simon	17.11.1978	right hand bat, wicket-keeper
Harvey, Ian	10.04.1972	right hand bat, right arm medium bowler
Hoggard, Matthew	31.12.1976	right hand bat, right arm fast bowler
Kirby, Steven	04.10.1977	right hand bat, right arm medium/fast bowler
Lawson, Mark	24.10.1985	right hand bat, right arm leg break bowler
Lehmann, Darren	05.02.1970	left hand bat, left arm slow bowler
Lumb, Michael	12.02.1980	left hand bat, right arm medium bowler
McGrath, Anthony (capt)	06.10.1975	right hand bat, right arm medium bowler
Pyrah, Richard	01.11.1982	right hand bat, right arm medium bowler
Sayers, Joe	05.11.1983	left hand bat, right arm off break bowler
Silverwood, Chris	05.03.1975	right hand bat, right arm medium/fast bowler
Taylor, Chris	21.02.1981	right hand bat, right arm fast/medium bowler
Thornicroft, Nick	23.01.1985	left hand bat, right arm fast/medium bowler
Vaughan, Michael	29.10.1974	right hand bat, right arm off break bowler
White, Craig	16.12.1969	right hand bat, right arm medium/fast bowler
Wood, Matthew	06.04.1977	right hand bat, right arm off break bowler

Address: Headingley, Leeds, LS6 3BU
Telephone: 0113 2787394

Trophy Winners from 1946
(for earlier County Championship winners see general information)

	County Championship	ECB National League	Benson & Hedges Cup	Cheltenham & Gloucester Trophy
1946	Yorkshire	–	–	–
1947	Middlesex	–	–	–
1948	Glamorgan	–	–	–
1949	Middlesex/Yorkshire	–	–	–
1950	Lancashire/Surrey	–	–	–
1951	Warwickshire	–	–	–
1952	Surrey	–	–	–
1953	Surrey	–	–	–
1954	Surrey	–	–	–
1955	Surrey	–	–	–
1956	Surrey	–	–	–
1957	Surrey	–	–	–
1958	Surrey	–	–	–
1959	Yorkshire	–	–	–
1960	Yorkshire	–	–	–
1961	Hampshire	–	–	–
1962	Yorkshire	–	–	–
1963	Yorkshire	–	–	Sussex
1964	Worcestershire	–	–	Sussex
1965	Worcestershire	–	–	Yorkshire
1966	Yorkshire	–	–	Warwickshire
1967	Yorkshire	–	–	Kent
1968	Yorkshire	–	–	Warwickshire
1969	Glamorgan	Lancashire	–	Yorkshire
1970	Kent	Lancashire	–	Lancashire
1971	Surrey	Worcestershire	–	Lancashire
1972	Warwickshire	Kent	Leicestershire	Lancashire
1973	Hampshire	Kent	Kent	Gloucestershire
1974	Worcestershire	Leicestershire	Surrey	Kent
1975	Leicestershire	Hampshire	Leicestershire	Lancashire
1976	Middlesex	Kent	Kent	Northamptonshire
1977	Kent/Middlesex	Leicestershire	Gloucestershire	Middlesex
1978	Kent	Hampshire	Kent	Sussex
1979	Essex	Somerset	Essex	Somerset
1980	Middlesex	Warwickshire	Northamptonshire	Middlesex
1981	Nottinghamshire	Essex	Somerset	Derbyshire
1982	Middlesex	Sussex	Somerset	Surrey
1983	Essex	Yorkshire	Middlesex	Somerset
1984	Essex	Essex	Lancashire	Middlesex
1985	Middlesex	Essex	Leicestershire	Essex
1986	Essex	Hampshire	Middlesex	Sussex
1987	Nottinghamshire	Worcestershire	Yorkshire	Nottinghamshire
1988	Worcestershire	Worcestershire	Hampshire	Middlesex
1989	Worcestershire	Lancashire	Nottinghamshire	Warwickshire
1990	Middlesex	Derbyshire	Lancashire	Lancashire
1991	Essex	Nottinghamshire	Worcestershire	Hampshire
1992	Essex	Middlesex	Hampshire	Northamptonshire
1993	Middlesex	Glamorgan	Derbyshire	Warwickshire
1994	Warwickshire	Warwickshire	Warwickshire	Worcestershire
1995	Warwickshire	Kent	Lancashire	Warwickshire
1996	Leicestershire	Surrey	Lancashire	Lancashire
1997	Glamorgan	Warwickshire	Surrey	Essex
1998	Leicestershire	Lancashire	Essex	Lancashire
1999	Surrey	Lancashire	Gloucestershire	Gloucestershire
2000	Surrey	Gloucestershire	Gloucestershire	Gloucestershire
2001	Yorkshire	Kent	Surrey	Somerset
2002	Surrey	Glamorgan	Warwickshire	Yorkshire
2003	Sussex	Surrey	Surrey*	Gloucestershire
2004			Leicestershire	Gloucestershire

*In 2003 the Benson & Hedges Cup was replaced by the Twenty20 Cup.

General Information

Ashes: how the story began	Australia defeated England by seven runs at the Oval in August 1882, and on the following day the *Sporting Times* published an obituary of English cricket. A few months later the Hon. Ivo Bligh (later Earl Darnley) captained the England team which won the second and third Tests of a rubber in Australia and was presented, by some Australian ladies, with a little urn containing the ashes of a burnt stump – and thus the story of the Ashes began. Subsequent Test matches between England and Australia have always been played for the Ashes, which are housed at Lord's.
ball: dimensions	Between 5½oz (159.9g) and 5¾oz (163g) in weight and has a circumference of about 9ins (22.9cm). The ball is made of a core of cork built up with string and encased in polished leather, usually red but also in white leather for night games.
bat throwing controversy	Dermot Reeves (Warks) threw his bat away to avoid giving a bat and pad catch.
Benson & Hedges Cup	A one-day competition of 55 overs per side between the first-class counties, Minor Counties and universities teams, consisting of zonal groups followed by a knockout stage. From 1995 the overs were reduced to 50 per side. In 1999, the Benson & Hedges Super Cup (confined to the counties who had finished in the top eight of the previous season's County Championships) replaced the old format, but the original format was reverted to in 2000. The Twenty20 Cup replaced the competition in 2003.
best Test match bowling figures	Jim Laker 19 for 90, England v Australia at Old Trafford (1956). Tony Lock took the other wicket.
best Test match bowling figures in a single innings	Jim Laker 10 for 53, England v Australia at Old Trafford (1956).
Bodyline series of 1932/33 (Australia v England)	The leading bowler was Harold Larwood (33 wickets) and the England captain was Douglas Jardine, who instructed Larwood to bowl at the leg stump and into the batsman's body.
Bosie	Australian name for the googly (named after its inventor B.J.T. Bosanquet, father of newsreader, Reginald)
bowls for England: played	W.G. Grace
brothers: seven played for Worcestershire	Foster brothers: Basil, Henry, Maurice, Neville, Reginald, Geoffrey, Wilfrid
Cambridge University: youngest debut centurion	Ed Smith (currently playing for Kent) – 101 against Glamorgan in 1996, also scored 50 in each of his first six first-class matches.
captain of England also Olympic boxing gold medallist	J.W.H.T. Douglas
Cheltenham & Gloucester Trophy: details	The C&G Trophy began life in 1963 as the Gillette Cup. Between 1982 and 2000 it was known as the NatWest Trophy before adopting its present sponsors in 2001. It is a 60 over per side one-day competition equivalent to football's FA cup.
chinaman	Googly bowled by a left-hander, i.e. a ball that breaks from off to leg
county captain: longest tenure	W.G. Grace for Gloucestershire (1871-99)
County Championship: details	Officially constituted in 1890, although counties existed prior to that date and claimed a sort of unofficial title. The 1890 Championship was contested by eight counties: Gloucestershire, Kent, Lancashire, Middlesex, Notts, Surrey, Sussex and Yorkshire. The only two counties to join the championship since World War I are Glamorgan in 1921 and Durham in 1992. The County Championship teams were split into two divisions for the 2000 season. The sponsors for the 2003 season were Liverpool Victoria and were branded under their affinity name of Frizzell. Previous sponsors included Schweppes (1977-83), Britannic Assurance (1984-98), PPP Healthcare (1999-2000) and CricInfo (2001-02).

County Championship winners: pre-1946

1890	Surrey	1906	Kent	1926	Lancs
1891	Surrey	1907	Notts	1927	Lancs
1892	Surrey	1908	Yorks	1928	Lancs
1893	Yorks	1909	Notts	1929	Notts
1894	Surrey	1910	Kent	1930	Lancs
1895	Surrey	1911	Warwicks	1931	Yorks
1896	Yorks	1912	Yorks	1932	Yorks
1897	Lancs.	1913	Kent	1933	Yorks
1898	Yorks.	1914	Surrey	1934	Lancs
1899	Surrey	1919	Yorks	1935	Yorks
1900	Yorks	1920	Middlesex	1936	Derby
1901	Yorks	1921	Middlesex	1937	Yorks

1902	Yorks	1922	Yorks	1938	Yorks
1903	Middlesex	1923	Yorks	1939	Yorks
1904	Lancs	1924	Yorks		
1905	Yorks	1925	Yorks		

Denmark: youngest international | Amjad Khan, aged 17 (Amjad currently plays for Kent)

dismissal: methods | Bowled, caught, handled the ball, hit the ball twice, hit wicket, leg before wicket (lbw), obstructing the field, run out, stumped, timed out

Double: first to complete | (1000 runs and 100 wickets in a season) W.G. Grace

Douglas, J.W.H.T.: nickname | Johnny Won't Hit Today

Duckworth/Lewis system | Used to determine the winning score in rain-interrupted one-day matches

ECB (England and Wales Cricket Board): chairman | Lord MacLaurin of Knebworth

England captain: first professional | Len Hutton in 1952

England footballer and cricketer: first | C.B. Fry (England v Ireland in 1901) who also played for Southampton in the 1902 FA Cup final and played for England in 26 Test matches.

FA Cup winner's medal | Denis Compton for Arsenal v Liverpool in 1950

fielding positions | Wicket-keeper, gully, third man, long leg, mid wicket, fine leg, mid-on, mid-off, point, cover point, slip, square leg, long leg, long off, extra cover

fifty: slowest first-class | Trevor Bailey

googly | Off break bowled with a leg break action

highest scorer in first-class cricket | Brian Lara 501no v Durham (1994)

highest scorer in Test cricket | Matthew Hayden 380 v Zimbabwe (2003)

hundred: first recorded | John Minshull, 107 for Duke of Dorset's XI v Wrexham (1769)

last man to take hat-trick in Test match for England | Matthew Hoggard v West Indies at Barbados (2004)

long jump: world record holder | C.B. Fry (23ft 5ins (7.14m)) held for 21 years between 1892 and 1913

Lord's: three locations | St John's Wood, London (1814 to present); North Bank, Regents' Park, London (1811-1814); Dorset Fields, London (1787-1811)

monarch made cricket illegal | Edward IV in 1477 (revoked in 1748)

Olympic champions | Great Britain

one-day internationals: fastest century | Shahid Afridi (Pakistan) scored 100 in 37 balls against Sri Lanka in 1997.

poet: published | John Snow (Sussex and England pace bowler)

rules: general | Played between two teams of 11 players on a large field. Teams take turns at batting (an innings) and bowling. The batting team has two players on the field while the bowling team has all its 11 players on the field, either bowling or fielding. A bowler delivers an overarm delivery to the batsman who stands in front of his wicket. After he bowls six deliveries the umpire calls 'over' and a new bowler delivers a further six balls from the opposite end of the pitch.

The batsman scores runs by hitting the ball into open space in such a way that he has time to run the approximate 58ft (17.68m) between the bowling crease and the popping crease before a fielder can throw the ball to hit the wicket with him out of his ground. If the ball is hit to the boundary, four runs are scored without having to run; if the boundary is reached without the ball hitting the ground then six runs are scored. Runs scored without hitting the bat are known as extras or byes.

Two men must always bat in tandem and must cross each other when they run between wickets. This means a team has 10 wickets before ending their innings as the last man not out is forced to retire. The winner is the team that scores the most runs given either a time or over allotment. The ten methods of dismissal are listed above.

The field of play is usually between 4 and 10 acres (1.6 to 4ha) in area. A wicket consists of three stumps, each 28ins (71.1cm) in height and about 1¼ins (3.1cm) in diameter. The stumps are placed so that the ball cannot penetrate the two gaps without dislodging a bail of wood placed at the top of the stumps. The wicket is therefore 28 x 9ins. The pitch is 22yds (20.12m) long and 10ft (3.05m) wide. A white line 4ft (1.22m) in front of the wicket is called the batsman's popping crease and he must cross this line while running. This line at the other end of the pitch is called the bowling crease. The bat, including the handle, must not be more than 38ins (96.52cm) in length and is usually made of willow. The stumps are often made of ash.

Test matches are played over five days and teams have two innings each. If all four innings fail to be completed then a draw is declared. English county matches are played over four days.

six sixes in over: first | Gary Sobers (for Nottinghamshire v Glamorgan 1968, bowler: Malcolm Nash). Ravi Shastri was the second man to accomplish the feat, during a Ranji Trophy match (1985).

CRICKET

Sunday League	One-day competition originally of 40 overs per side and contested between first-class counties only. CGU National League 1999 and 2000. Norwich Union League 2001 and 2002. ECB National League in 2003. Scotland joined Division Two in 2003. Under current regulations, matches are 45 overs per side.
Sunday League: double century	Ally Brown of Surrey (268 off 160 balls v Glamorgan, 19 June 2002)
swearing incident	Mike Gatting at umpire Shakoor Rana (1987)
TCCB: name change in 1996	England and Wales Cricket Board, formerly Test and County Cricket Board
Test century: fewest balls	Viv Richards (56) against England at St John's,1985/86.
Test century: first	Charles Bannerman (165 retired hurt) for Australia v England, March 1877
Test century: first for England	W.G. Grace (152) for England v Australia at the Oval, 1880
Test cricket: oldest player	Wilfred Rhodes (52 years 165 days on final day, England v West Indies, April 1930)
Test cricket: youngest English player	Brian Close (18 years 149 days on first day, England v New Zealand, 3rd Test, 1949)
Test cricket: youngest player	Hasan Raza (Pakistan) was 14 years 227 days old when he played against Zimbabwe in 1996/97.
Test double century: fewest balls	Nathan Astle (153) for New Zealand v England at Christchurch, March 2002. The first hundred took 114 balls and the second hundred only 39 balls.
Test match: first	Australia v England, Melbourne Cricket Ground, March 1877
Test match: tied	Australia v West Indies (1960) and Australia v India (1986)
Test playing nations	Australia (1877), Bangladesh (2000), England (1877), India (1932), New Zealand (1929/30), Pakistan (1952/53), South Africa (1888/89), Sri Lanka (1982), West Indies (1928), Zimbabwe (1992/93)
Twenty20 Cup	Replaced the Benson & Hedges Cup competition for the 2003 season. It was played over a five-week period commencing 13 June and culminated in a semi-final and final at Trent Bridge on Saturday 19 July 2003. Matches began at 5.30pm and concluded at 8.15pm, with a 15-minute break between innings. The 20-over matches produced thrilling cricket and scores between 150 and 175 were commonplace.
university grounds	Cambridge – Fenners, Oxford – The Parks
West Indies: three Ws	Everton Weekes, Frank Worrell, Clyde Walcott
Wisden: colour	Yellow
Wisden: cover picture 2003	Michael Vaughan
World Cup football winner: played county cricket	Geoff Hurst
World Cup winners	W. Indies beat Australia (1975) W. Indies beat England (1979) India beat W. Indies (1983) Australia beat England (1987) Pakistan beat England (1991) Sri Lanka beat Australia (1996) Australia beat Pakistan (1999) Australia beat India (2003)
World Cup: defeated West Indies	Kenya bowled W. Indies out for 93 in a group match of the 1996 World Cup.

Biographies

Adcock, Neil Born Cape Town, South Africa, 8 March 1931. Hostile right-arm fast bowler for Transvaal (1952/53 to 1959/60), Natal (1960/61 to 1962/63) and South Africa (1953/54 to 1961/62), taking 104 wickets @ 21.10 in his 26 Tests. In the later of his two tours of England (1955 and 1960) he took a then South African Test record 26 wickets @ 22.57 and 108 @ 14.02 in all matches. His best Test analysis was 6-43 v Australia (Durban 1957/58), and he took in all 405 first-class wickets @ 17.25, including 13-65 for Transvaal v Orange Free State at Johannesburg in 1953/54.

Allen, Sir George ('Gubby') Born Sydney, New South Wales, 31 July 1902. Right-arm fast bowler and right-hand batsman for Cambridge University, Middlesex (1921-50) and England, whom he captained in 1936 (v India), 1936/37 (in Australia) and 1947/48 (in West Indies), and later a distinguished administrator. Took all 10 wickets for 40 runs v Lancashire at Lord's in 1929. In the 1932/33 'Bodyline' series he declined Jardine's instruction to bowl fast and short on the leg side. Between 1955 and 1976 he was chairman of Test selectors, president and then treasurer of MCC. In his career he scored 9232 runs @ 28.67 and took 788 wickets @ 22.32. He died 29 November 1989.

Ambrose, Curtly Born Antigua, 21 September 1963. Tall (6ft 7ins) right-arm fast bowler for Leeward Islands, Northamptonshire and, from 1988 to 2000, West Indies. He took 405 Test wickets @ 20.99, including 8-45 v England in Barbados (1989/90), and 6-24 in 1993/94, when England were all out for 46 in

Trinidad. Only Courtney Walsh (519) has taken more wickets for West Indies.

Ames, Leslie Born Eltham, Kent, 3 December 1905. Leading wicket-keeper/batsman for Kent (1926-51) and England (47 Tests from 1929 to 1938/39). The only wicket-keeper to score over a hundred centuries (102), including eight in Tests, he scored 3058 runs in the 1933 season @ 58.80. His 128 dismissals in 1929 remains a record for a season, as do his totals of 64 stumpings in a season (1932) and 418 stumpings in a career total of 1121 dismissals. He scored in all 37,248 runs, including nine double centuries. He later became a Test selector, then manager, secretary and president of Kent. He died 27 February 1990.

Arlott, John Born Basingstoke, Hampshire, 25 February 1914. Famed as 'the voice of cricket' with his almost poetic word-pictures, delivered in a distinctive Hampshire burr – which became more of a growl as the years took their toll. He had spent the years 1934-45 in the local police force, reaching the rank of sergeant. He played no first-class cricket, but did appear for Hampshire Club and Ground in 1937. After the war he joined the BBC, originally as overseas literary producer and then as a cricket commentator. Always aware of the wider world, writing poetry and developing a connoisseur's taste in wines, he fiercely opposed the apartheid South African regime and was instrumental in bringing Basil D'Oliveira to England in 1960 to play at first in league cricket. He retired from commentating during the Centenary Test v Australia at Lord's in 1980, being content to settle in Alderney in 1981 with his wine cellar and his books, and dying there on 14 December 1991.

Asif Iqbal Born Hyderabad, India, 6 June 1943. Fluent right-hand batsman and right-arm medium-pace bowler for Hyderabad, Karachi, PIA, National Bank, Kent and Pakistan from 1959/60 to 1982. He made his Test debut v Australia in 1964/65 batting at number ten, and scored his first Test century (at The Oval 1967) going in at number nine and scoring 146 in 170 minutes. He played for Kent between 1968 and 1982, and was six times captain of Pakistan, for whom he made 3575 runs @ 38.85 in his 58 Tests between 1964/65 and 1979/80, with 11 centuries. His career yielded 23,329 runs @ 37.26 and 291 wickets @ 30.15.

Atherton, Michael Born Manchester, 23 March 1968. Obdurate right-hand batsman for Cambridge University, Lancashire and England between 1987 and 2001, and captain in a record (for England) 54 of his 115 Test matches, in which he played from 1989 until retiring in 2001. He scored 185no for England at Johannesburg in December 1995, and 268no for Lancashire v Glamorgan at Blackpool in 1999 (his highest score). His autobiography, *Opening Up*, was published in 2002. Having scored a career total of 21,929 runs @ 40.83, with 54 centuries, he is now a respected cricketing journalist and television commentator.

Azharuddin, Mohammad Born Hyderabad, India, 8 February 1963. Right-hand batsman for Hyderabad (1981/82), Derbyshire (1991 and 1994) and India (1984/85 to 1999/2000), whom he captained in 47 Tests, winning 14. One of the few Muslims to play for India since partition, he is unique in scoring hundreds in each of his first three Tests (v England 1984/85). He scored 6215 runs @ 45.03 in his 99 Tests, including 22 centuries (his highest being 199 v Sri Lanka at Kanpur in December 1986), as well as

taking 105 catches, and also played in 334 one-day internationals. Banned for life in December 2000 for involvement in a match-fixing scandal, he had by then scored in all 15,855 runs @ 51.98, with 54 centuries.

Bailey, Trevor Born Westcliff-on-Sea, Essex, 3 December 1923. Stubborn right-hand batsman and fast-medium bowler for Cambridge University, Essex (1946-67) and England. The finest post-war English all-rounder until Ian Botham, he is the only player since World War II to score 2000 runs and take 100 wickets in the same season (1959). For England, he scored 2290 runs @ 29.74 and took 132 wickets @ 29.21, including 7-34 v West Indies in Jamaica (1953/54). In a career lasting from 1946 to 1967, he totalled 28,641 runs @ 33.42, scoring 1000 runs in a season 17 times, and took 2082 wickets @ 23.13 (including 10-90 v Lancashire at Clacton in 1949), performing the 'double' eight times. Famous for saving the Ashes Test at Lord's in 1953 by batting 257 minutes for 71, he also took 458 minutes to score 68 at Brisbane in 1958/59. As a footballer, he won an FA Amateur Cup medal with Walthamstow Avenue in 1952.

Barlow, Eddie Born Pretoria, South Africa, 12 August 1940. Pugnacious right-hand opening batsman, right-arm medium-pace bowler and excellent slip fielder for Transvaal, Eastern Province, Western Province and Boland (1959/60 to 1982/83), Derbyshire (1976-78) and South Africa (1961/62 to 1969/70). He scored 2516 runs for his country @ 45.74, with six hundreds, including 201 v Australia (Adelaide 1963/64), and for Rest of the World v England (Leeds 1970) he took four wickets in five balls. His highest score was 217 for Derbyshire (v Surrey, Ilkeston 1976), and his vigorous captaincy revitalised that county.

Barnes, Sydney Born Smethwick, 19 April 1873. Right-arm fast-medium bowler for Warwickshire (1894-96), Lancashire (1899-1903) and England. Regarded by many as the best of all time, he played in 27 Tests between 1901/02 and 1913/14, but only 50 county matches. He took 189 wickets for England @ 16.43, including 9-103 v South Africa at Johannesburg in 1913/14, a tour on which he took a record 49 Test wickets (in only four matches) at 10.93. Preferring league and Minor Counties cricket, he played for Staffordshire until 1935, when he was 62. He died in 1967 at the age of 94.

Barrington, Ken Born Reading, Berkshire, 24 November 1930. Resolute right-hand middle-order batsman for Surrey (1953-68) and England, scoring in all 31,714 runs @ 45.63, with 76 centuries, but significantly his Test match average was 58.67 for his 6806 runs, which included 20 centuries. He averaged 72.75 in the 1962/63 series against Australia, against whom he made his highest career score (256 at Old Trafford in 1964). Later an England selector and tour manager, he died suddenly of a heart attack in March 1981 while assistant manager and coach of the England team in the West Indies.

Bedi, Bishan Born Amritsar, India, 25 September 1946. Skilful left-arm spin bowler for Northern Punjab, Delhi, Northamptonshire and India between 1961/62 and 1980/81, noted for his brightly coloured patkas. He made his first-class debut aged 15, and his Test debut aged 20 v West Indies in Calcutta. He captained India in 22 of his 67 Tests, taking 266 wickets @ 28.71, his career total being 1560 wickets @ 21.69. Bedi twice took 25 wickets in a series against England in India, and 31 wickets in the 1977/78 series in Australia.

Bedser, Alec   Born Reading, Berkshire, 4 July 1918. Outstanding right-arm medium-fast bowler for Surrey (1939-60) and England. He took 11 wickets in each of his first two Tests (v India at Lord's and Old Trafford, 1946) and played his last Test v South Africa in 1955, having taken a then record 236 Test wickets, at an average of 24.89, including his best match performance of 14-99 v Australia at Nottingham in 1953. His first-class wickets totalled 1924 @ 20.41, helping Surrey to seven consecutive Championships (1952-58). He is the only bowler to have dismissed Don Bradman twice for 0 in Test matches. Later a Test selector and England tour manager (in Australia, 1974/75 and 1979/80), he was knighted for his services to cricket in 1997.

Benaud, Richie   Born Penrith, New South Wales, 6 October 1930. An aggressive right-hand batsman and leg-spin bowler for New South Wales (1948/49 to 1963/64) and Australia, he captained his country 28 times during his 63 Tests from 1951/52 to 1963/64. In taking 248 wickets in Tests (then a world record) @ 27.03 and scoring 2201 runs @ 24.45, he became the first player to perform the Test match 'double' of 2000 runs and 200 wickets. On tour in South Africa (1957/58) he took 106 wickets and scored 817 runs; in 1958/59 he first captained Australia, winning the series v England 4-0, and retained the Ashes in England in 1961. He scored three centuries for Australia (his first coming in 78 minutes v W. Indies in Jamaica, 1955) and hit eleven sixes and nine fours in scoring 135 at Scarborough in 1953. His career run total was 11,719 @ 36.50 and he took 945 wickets @ 24.73. He helped set up Kerry Packer's World Series cricket, and is a distinguished cricket journalist and commentator.

Bird, Harold ('Dickie')   Born Barnsley, Yorkshire, 19 April 1933. Right-hand batsman for Yorkshire and Leicestershire 1956-64, scoring 3314 runs @ 20.71, with a highest score of 181no v Glamorgan in 1959 – after which he was left out of Yorkshire's next match. A prominent first-class umpire from 1970 to 1998, he stood in a then record 66 Tests between 1973 and 1998.

Blofeld, Henry   Born Hoverton, Norfolk, 23 September 1939. A right-hand batsman and wicket-keeper for Norfolk in Minor Counties cricket, he also played 17 first-class matches, for Cambridge University in 1958 and 1959 and Free Foresters in 1960, scoring 758 runs @ 24.45 and making one century. Affably addressing fellow commentators and visitors as 'my dear old thing', he is also renowned for his detailed descriptions of passing buses and a variety of bird life, and happily has recovered from heart surgery to continue commentating in his eccentric but informative fashion.

Boon, David   Born Launceston, Tasmania, 29 December 1960. Pugnacious right-hand batsman and brilliant close fielder for Tasmania, Durham (1997-99, captain each season) and Australia. He played in 107 Test matches from 1984/85 to 1995/96, scoring 7422 runs @ 43.65, including 21 centuries (highest score 200 v New Zealand, Perth 1989/90) and 99 catches. On retirement in March 1999 he had scored 23,413 first-class runs @ 44.00, with 68 centuries and 283 catches.

Border, Allan   Born Sydney, New South Wales, 27 July 1955. Determined left-hand batsman, left-arm spin bowler and slip fielder from 1976 to 1996 for New South Wales, Queensland, Gloucestershire (one match), Essex and Australia. He scored a record total of 11,174 runs @ 50.56 in a record 156 Tests, including 27 hundreds, and made 153 consecutive Test appearances from 1979 to 1994 (another record), an unparalleled 93 of these as captain. His highest score is 205 v New Zealand, Adelaide 1987/88. He became the first man to score 150 in both innings of a Test match (150no and 153 v Pakistan, Lahore 1979/80), and scored in his career 27,131 runs @ 51.38, with 70 centuries.

Botham, Ian   Born Heswall, Cheshire, 24 November 1955. Aggressive right-hand batsman and right-arm medium-fast bowler for Somerset, Worcestershire, Durham, Queensland and England from 1974 to 1993. England's outstanding post-war all-rounder, in his 102 Tests he took an English record 383 wickets @ 28.40 (27 times taking five wickets in an innings), scored 5200 runs @ 33.54 including 14 centuries (highest score 208 v India, The Oval 1982) and held 120 catches, an English record he shares with M.C. Cowdrey. In 1979/80 he took 13 for 106 and scored 114 v India in Bombay, the first player to score a century and take ten wickets in the same Test, and later became the first to score 3000 runs and take 300 wickets in Tests. Against Australia in 1981, his famous 149no helped England to an unlikely victory at Headingley, then at Manchester he hit 118 with 13 fours and six sixes. In his career, he totalled 19,399 runs @ 33.97 (with 38 centuries), took 1172 wickets @ 27.22 and held 354 catches. He hit a world record number of sixes in an English season (80 in 1985) and once scored 100 in 52 minutes (v Warwickshire in 1982). He also made 11 Football League appearances for Scunthorpe United (including four as substitute) between 1979/80 and 1984/85.

Bowes, Bill   Born Elland, Yorkshire, 25 July 1908. Right-arm fast-medium bowler for Yorkshire (1929-47) and England. With 68 wickets @ 22.33 in his 15 Tests, including that of Bradman first ball on the 1932/33 tour, he took more career wickets (1,639 @ 16.76) than he scored runs (1,528). He played for England once after the war having been a prisoner of the Germans, later becoming a respected cricket journalist. He died 4 September 1987.

Boycott, Geoffrey   Born Fitzwilliam, Yorkshire, 21 October 1940. Outstanding right-hand opening batsman for Yorkshire (1962-86) and England (1964 to 1981/82). The only player to average over 100 in two English seasons (1971 and 1979), he amassed 48,426 runs (more than any other post-war player) @ 56.83, with 151 centuries (the fifth highest total ever) including 22 in Tests, and was an often controversial captain of Yorkshire from 1971 to 1978. He scored 8114 runs in his 108 Tests @ 47.72 each, his highest being 246no v India (Leeds 1967), when he was dropped from the next Test for slow scoring. He made his hundredth century in the 1977 Test v Australia at Headingley, captaining England four times in 1977/78. Banned from Test cricket for three years after touring South Africa (1981/82), he later became a shrewd if acerbic commentator on the game.

Bradman, Donald   Born Cootamundra, New South Wales, 27 August 1908. Right-hand middle-order batsman for New South Wales (1927/28 to 1933/34), South Australia (1935/36 to 1948/49) and Australia (1928/29 to 1948), and later a distinguished administrator. His achievements defy belief: total runs 28,067 @ 95.14, a century on debut (118 for NSW v S. Australia, Adelaide 1927/28), 117 hundreds in 234 matches, a record 37 double hundreds or more, six double hundreds in an English season (1930), six successive hundreds (1938/39), a feat equalled only by C.B. Fry and M.J. Procter, and a highest score of 452no (NSW v Queensland, Sydney 1929/30), a world record which stood for 29 years. He has the highest batting average for an English season (115.66 in 1938), scoring over 2000 runs in each of his visits there, and over 1000 runs in each of 12 Australian seasons. He scored 1000 runs before the end of May in 1930 and 1938 – the only man to do this twice. In 52 Tests (24 as captain, 1936/37 to 1948) he scored 29 centuries and totalled 6996 runs @ 99.94, an average far exceeding anyone else's, his top score being a then record 334 v England (Leeds 1930), including 309 in a day. He has scored the fastest Test double century in terms of minutes, achieving this in 214 minutes v England at Leeds in 1930. In that series he scored 974 runs – still a record. His series average in 1931/32 v S. Africa was 201.50, and he added 451 for the second wicket with Bill Ponsford v England at The Oval in 1934. Knighted in the 1949 New Year's Honours, he was elected chairman of the Australian Board of Control (1960-63 and 1969-72), and received his country's highest honour, Companion of the Order of Australia, in 1981. He died in Adelaide, 25 February 2001.

Brearley, Mike Born Harrow, Middlesex, 28 April 1942. Right-hand opening batsman and outstanding captain for Cambridge University, Middlesex and England between 1961 and 1983. He captained England in 31 of his 39 Tests, winning three Ashes series (1977, 1978/79, 1981) and scoring 1442 runs @ 22.28 (highest score 91). For MCC v North Zone at Peshawar in 1967 he scored 312no in a day. He captained Middlesex to three outright County Championships (1976, 1980, 1982) and one shared title (1977), scoring 25,185 career runs @ 37.81, with 45 hundreds.

Briggs, Johnny Born Sutton-in-Ashfield, Notts, 3 October 1862. Left-arm spin bowler and right-hand batsman for Lancashire (1879-1900) and England (1884/85 to 1899), for whom he took 118 wickets @ 17.75, including 15 for 28 in a day (8-11 and 7-17) v S. Africa at Cape Town in 1888/89, and 11-74 v Australia at Lord's in 1886. He scored 14,092 career runs @ 18.27 and took 2221 wickets @ 15.95, his best analysis being 10-55 v Worcestershire at Manchester in 1900, his last season. Two years later he died in Cheadle Royal Asylum aged only 39. Only Brian Statham has taken more wickets for Lancashire.

Butcher, Basil Born Port Mourant, British Guiana, 3 September 1933. Consistent right-hand middle-order batsman for British Guiana (1954/55 to 1970/71) and West Indies (1958/59 to 1969). He played in 44 Tests, scoring 3104 runs @ 43.11, with seven hundreds, including 209no at Trent Bridge in 1966 to win the match. In the home series against Australia in 1964/65 he scored 405 runs @ 40.50, and – curiously – had identical figures in Australia in 1968/69. He took 5-34 against England in Port of Spain (1967/68), yet no other Test wickets at all, and had a career record of 11,628 runs @ 49.90, with 31 hundreds.

Caddick, Andrew Born Christchurch, New Zealand, 21 November 1968. Tall right-arm fast-medium bowler for Somerset (debut 1991) and England (debut 1993). His best performances are 9-32 for Somerset v Lancashire (Taunton 1993), and for England 7-46 v S. Africa (Durban 1999/2000). He took 5-14 in West Indies' second innings at Leeds in 2000, including four wickets in one over. He has taken five wickets in an innings more times than any other current English bowler (57 times, equal with Phil DeFreitas by the end of 2002), and in the 2002/03 Ashes series became England's seventh-highest wicket-taker, overtaking Darren Gough.

Chandrasekhar, Bhagwat Born Mysore, India, 17 May 1945. Right-arm medium-pace leg-spin bowler for Mysore and Karnataka (1963/64 to 1979/80) and India (1963/64 to 1979) . Playing in 58 Tests, he took 242 wickets @ 29.74, including 6-38 at The Oval in 1971 in India's first Test victory in England, and 35 wickets @ 18.91 in the 1972/73 series against England. His best analysis was 9-72 for Mysore v Kerala (Bijapur 1969/70) and he took in all 1063 wickets @ 24.04.

Chappell, Greg Born Unley, South Australia, 7 August 1948. Elegant right-hand batsman and fine slip fielder for South Australia (1966/67 to 1972/73), Queensland (1973/74 to 1983/84), Somerset (1968/69) and Australia (1970/71 to 1983/84). He scored 108 on Test debut v England at Perth, 247no and 133 v New Zealand (Wellington 1973/74) and in his first match as captain in 1975/76, succeeding brother Ian, scored 123 and 109 v W. Indies at Brisbane. Returning from Kerry Packer's World Series Cricket, he captained his country again from 1979 to 1981 and scored 182 in his last Test (v Pakistan, Sydney 1983/84), totalling 7110 runs in his 87 Tests @ 53.86, with 24 centuries, and taking a then record 122 catches, including seven in a Test v England (Perth 1974/75). He scored in all 24,535 runs @ 52.20, with 74 hundreds.

Chappell, Ian Born Unley, South Australia, 26 September 1943. Right-hand middle-order batsman for S. Australia (1961/62 to 1979/80), Lancashire (1963, one match) and Australia (1964/65 to 1979/80). An abrasive captain of his country in 30 of his 75 Tests, he regained the Ashes in 1974/75 with shrewd use of the pace of Lillee and Thomson, later helping to set up Packer's World Series cricket. He then returned briefly to Test cricket, where he scored 5345 runs @ 42.42, with 14 hundreds, out of a career total of 19,680 runs @ 48.35, with 59 centuries.

Close, Brian Born Rawdon, Yorkshire, 24 February 1931. Courageous left-hand batsman and right-arm medium pace/off-break bowler for Yorkshire (1949-70), Somerset (1971/77) and England (1949-76), whom he captained in seven of his 22 Tests, scoring 887 runs @ 25.34 (highest score 70 v W. Indies, Lord's 1963) and taking 18 wickets @ 29.55. He achieved the 'double' in his first season, still the youngest player to do so, and also in 1952. He scored 34,994 career runs @ 33.26, with 52 hundreds, and took 1171 wickets @ 26.42 as well as 813 catches – the fifth-highest total in history. He played six Football League games for Bradford City in 1952/53, scoring two goals.

Compton, Denis Born Hendon, 23 May 1918. Brilliant middle-order right-hand batsman and left-arm spin bowler for Middlesex (1936-58) and England (78 Tests, 1937 to 1956/57). He scored 1000 runs in his debut season aged 18, as he did on 16 other occasions (three overseas). In 1947 he

C
R
I
C
K
E
T

made 3816 runs and scored 18 centuries, both records for a season unlikely ever to be beaten. Against South Africa that year he scored 753 runs @ 94.12 in the Tests, and in 1948/49 he scored 300 in 181 minutes v N.E. Transvaal at Benoni, the fastest triple century ever. For England he scored 5807 runs @ 50.06, with 17 centuries, the highest being 278 v Pakistan (Nottingham 1954). In his last Ashes Test he scored 94 and 35no despite the removal of a kneecap following a football injury. He played 54 First Division games for Arsenal, scoring 15 goals from outside left, and won an FA Cup winner's medal v Liverpool in 1950. He died 23 April 1997.

Constantine, Learie   Born Diego Martin, Trinidad, 21 September 1901. Explosive right-hand batsman, right-arm fast bowler and dazzling fielder for Trinidad (1921/22 to 1934/35), Barbados (1938/39) and West Indies (1928-39). He performed the 'double' of 1000 runs and 100 wickets on his country's tour of England in 1928, but spent much of the next decade in the Lancashire League. On tour in England he took 103 wickets @ 17.77, and in his 18 Tests he scored 635 runs @ 19.24 and took 58 wickets @ 30.10 – a modest record for a great cricketer and star attraction. After retiring he was called to the Bar, knighted in 1962, became High Commissioner for Trinidad & Tobago (1962-64) and was created a life peer (Baron Constantine of Maraval and Nelson) in 1969. He died in London, 1 July 1971.

Contractor, Nari   Born Ghodra, India, 7 March 1934. Left-hand opening batsman for Gujarat, Railways and India, captaining his country in 12 of his 31 Tests and scoring 1611 runs @ 31.58 in his Test career from 1955/56 to 1961/62. One of the very few players to score two separate hundreds on debut (152 and 102 for Gujarat v Baroda, Baroda 1952/53), he made 1183 runs @ 31.13 touring England in 1959, and led India to their first series victory over England (2-0, 1961/62). His career – and very nearly his life – ended when a ball from Charlie Griffith, playing for Barbados, fractured his skull in 1961/62.

Cowdrey, Colin   Born Bangalore, India, 24 December 1932. Right-hand batsman and outstanding slip fielder for Kent (1950-76), Oxford University (1952-54) and England (1954/55 to 1974/75). He captained England in 27 of his 114 Tests without ever seeming at ease in the role, scoring 7624 runs @ 44.06, with 22 centuries (highest 182 v Pakistan, The Oval 1962). Added 411 with Peter May for the fourth wicket v W. Indies (Birmingham 1957) – a new record partnership for England. Recalled to Test cricket in an emergency during the torrid tour to Australia in 1974/75 aged 42, he retired soon afterwards, becoming president of MCC in 1986. He was made Lord Cowdrey of Tonbridge in 1997, having seen his son Christopher follow him as England captain. His career yielded 42,719 runs @ 42.89 with 107 centuries, the highest being 307 for MCC v S. Australia (Adelaide 1962/63). He died 4 December 2000.

Cronje, Hansie   Born Bloemfontein, South Africa, 25 September 1969. Right-hand batsman for Orange Free State, Leicestershire (1995) and South Africa. An outstanding captain for his country in 53 of his 68 Tests from 1991/92 to 1999/2000, he scored 3714 runs @ 36.41 (highest 135 v India, Port Elizabeth 1992/93), with six centuries, and a career total of 12,103 runs @ 43.69, including 1362 @ 50.44 in England in 1995. In 2000 he was banned for life after involvement in illegal betting activities, and was killed in a plane crash in South Africa, 1 June 2002.

Crowe, Martin   Born Auckland, New Zealand, 22 September 1962. Splendid right-hand middle-order batsman for Auckland, Central Districts, Somerset, Wellington and New Zealand. Easily New Zealand's heaviest run-scorer in Tests (5444 in 77 Tests between 1981/82 and 1995/96, averaging 45.36, with 17 centuries – also a record for his country), he also took part in a world record partnership for the third wicket of 467 with Andrew Jones (New Zealand v Sri Lanka, Wellington 1990/91), of which his share was 299. In his first season with Somerset (1984), he scored 1870 runs @ 53.42, and in New Zealand in 1986 he scored 1676 runs with eight hundreds, both records for that country.

Davidson, Alan   Born Gosford, New South Wales, 14 June 1929. Left-arm fast-medium bowler, left-hand middle-order batsman and brilliant fielder for New South Wales (1949/50 to 1962/63) and Australia (1953 to 1962/63). With Richie Benaud, he was his country's leading all-rounder from the mid-1950s to the early 1960s, helping his state to 11 championships in his 14 seasons with them. He scored 1328 runs @ 24.59 in his 44 Tests and took 186 wickets @ 20.53; in the 1960/61 series v W. Indies he took 33 wickets @ 18.54, as well as becoming in that series the first player to total 100 runs and take 10 wickets in a Test (the tied game at Brisbane). In all he scored 6804 runs @ 32.86 and took 672 wickets @ 20.90.

de Silva, Aravinda   Born Colombo, Sri Lanka, 17 October 1965. Brilliant right-hand middle-order batsman for Nondescripts, Kent (1995), Auckland and Sri Lanka. His country's leading run-scorer, he totalled 6361 runs @ 42.97 in his 93 Tests between 1984 and 2002, when he retired from Test cricket. He scored 267 v New Zealand (Wellington 1990/91), the highest at the time by a Sri Lankan, as well as 19 other Test centuries. In April 1997 he became the first batsman to score an undefeated century in each innings of a Test (v Pakistan, Colombo). His dazzling 107 v Australia in the 1996 World Cup final won him Man of the Match and helped Sri Lanka to a memorable World Cup trophy.

Dexter, Ted   Born Milan, Italy, 15 May 1935. Lordly right-hand middle-order batsman for Cambridge University (1956-58), Sussex (1957/68) and England, whom he captained between 1961/62 and 1964 in 30 of his 62 Tests. Remembered for a blistering 70 against the West Indies pace attack in 1963, he scored 205 for England v Pakistan (Karachi 1961/62) and eight other hundreds in a Test total of 4502 runs @47.89, an average some way above his career average of 40.75 for 21,150 runs. Also a useful medium-pace bowler, he took 66 Test wickets @ 34.93 out of a career total of 419 @ 29.92. In the 1964 general election, he stood (unsuccessfully) against James Callaghan in Cardiff, and he was appointed chairman of the England Cricket Committee in 1989.

D'Oliveira, Basil   Born Cape Town, South Africa, 4 October 1931. Right-hand middle-order batsman and right-arm medium-pace bowler for Worcestershire (1964-80) and England, qualifying after a period with Middleton in the Central Lancashire League and making five hundreds in his first full Championship season (1965). His England debut came in 1966 and he went on to play 44 Tests until 1972, scoring 2484 runs @ 40.06, with five centuries – the highest 158 v Australia (The Oval 1968). Selected for the 1968/69 tour to South Africa, his entry was refused and the tour was cancelled, bringing the apartheid question to a head and ultimately causing the exclusion of South Africa as a bonafide Test-playing nation. His highest score was 227 (v Yorkshire, Hull 1974) in a career yielding 18,918 runs @ 39.57 and 43 centuries, as well as 548 wickets @ 27.41.

Donald, Allan   Born Bloemfontein, South Africa, 20 October 1966. Right-arm fast bowler for Orange Free State, Warwickshire, Worcestershire and South Africa. The first bowler to take 300 Test wickets for South Africa, he played in 72 Tests from 1991/92 to 2001/02, taking 330 wickets @ 22.25, including 8-71 v Zimbabwe (Harare 1995/96). His analyses include 8-37 for Free State v Transvaal (Johannesburg 1986/87) and 7-37 for Warwickshire v Durham (Birmingham 1992), representing that county from 1987 to 1993, in 1995, 1997 and 1999/2000. He also took 272 wickets in 164 one-day internationals.

Douglas, Johnny   Born Clapton, London, 3 September 1882. Right-hand batsman and right-arm fast-medium bowler for Essex (1901-28), London County and England. The only man to captain England both before and after World War I, he also won a gold medal for boxing as a middleweight at the 1908 Olympic Games. His 23 Tests produced 962 runs @ 29.15, with one century, and 45 wickets @ 33.02. He completed the 'double' five times, scoring in all 24,531 runs @ 27.90 and taking 1893 wickets @ 23.32. He was drowned after a collision at sea in fog, 19 December 1930.

Dravid, Rahul   Born Indore, India, 11 January 1973. Leading right-hand middle-order batsman for Karnataka, Kent (2000) and India (debut 1996). A consistently heavy scorer, he has to date scored almost 7000 Test runs @ over 56, with a highest score of 270 v Pakistan (Rawalpindi 2003/04), the latest of his five double centuries for India. In the four-match series in Australia, also in 2003/04, he scored 619 runs @ 123.80 and was named Man of the Series. He scored 180 v Australia (Calcutta 2000/01), adding 367 with V.V.S. Laxman for the fifth wicket. He also averages over 40 in one-day internationals, often performing as wicket-keeper/batsman.

Dujon, Jeffrey   Born Kingston, Jamaica, 28 May 1956. Wicket-keeper and right-hand middle-order batsman for Jamaica and West Indies. First choice for his country for a decade from 1981/82 to 1991, he played in 81 Tests, scoring 3322 runs @ 31.94 with five centuries, besides claiming 272 victims (267 ct, 5 st) behind the stumps. His first Test century was 110 v India (Antigua 1983/84), putting on 207 with Clive Lloyd for the sixth wicket, and his highest was 139 v Australia (Perth 1984/85). In all matches he scored 9308 runs @ 38.14, with nine hundreds, and dismissed 453 victims (434 ct, 19 st).

Edmonds, Phil   Born Lusaka, Zambia, 8 March 1951. Left-arm spin bowler for Cambridge University, Middlesex (1971-87, 1992), Eastern Province and England, taking five wickets for 17 runs in his first 12 overs of Test cricket (v Australia, Leeds 1975). His 125 Test wickets, taken in 51 Tests from 1975 to 1987, cost 34.18, his best analysis being 7-66 v Pakistan (Karachi 1977/78), and he took 1246 wickets in his career @ 25.66, with a best analysis of 8-53 for Middlesex v Hampshire (Bournemouth 1984). He has since made a successful career in the City.

Edrich, John   Born Blofield, Norfolk, 21 June 1937. Resolute left-hand opening batsman for Surrey (1958-78) and England, playing in 77 Tests from 1963 to 1976 and scoring 5138 runs @ 43.54, with 12 centuries (seven against Australia). His highest Test score of 310no v New Zealand (Leeds 1965) included five sixes and 52 fours. Only the third left-hander to score a hundred centuries, he scored 103 in all in a career total of 39,790 runs @ 45.47, reaching 1000 runs in 19 domestic seasons and twice overseas. He is a cousin of the late W.J. Edrich.

Edrich, W.J. (Bill)   Born Lingwood, Norfolk, 26 March 1916. Determined right-hand batsman and right-arm fast bowler for Middlesex (1937-58) and England (1938 to 1954/55). He scored over 2000 runs in each of his three pre-war seasons for Middlesex, reaching 1000 runs by the end of May in 1938. He scored 219 in the 'timeless' Test at Durban in 1938/39, and played in 39 Tests which produced 2440 runs @ 40.00. In 1947 he scored 3539 runs @ 80.43 (and took 67 wickets @ 22.58), and in 1948 he added 424 with Denis Compton v Somerset at Lord's – still a Middlesex record for the third wicket. His career (interrupted by a war in which he won the DFC as a squadron leader) yielded 36,965 runs @ 42.39 with 479 wickets @ 33.31. He also played 20 Division Two games for Tottenham Hotspur, scoring three goals. He died 24 April 1986.

Emburey, John   Born Peckham, London, 20 August 1952. Right-arm off-break bowler for Middlesex (1973-95), Northamptonshire (1996/97) and England. He played 64 Tests from 1978 to 1995, twice captaining his country and taking 147 wickets @ 38.40, including 7-78 v Australia (Sydney 1986/87). A useful right-hand bat who scored seven centuries in a career total of 12,021 runs @ 23.38, he took in all 1608 wickets @ 26.09, his best season being 1983 – 103 wickets @ only 17.88 each.

Engineer, Farokh   Born Bombay, India, 25 February 1938. Extrovert wicket-keeper and dashing right-hand batsman who often opened for Bombay (1959/60 to 1974/75), Lancashire (1968-76) and India, appearing in 46 Tests, scoring 2611 runs @ 31.08, with two centuries, and claiming 82 victims (66 ct, 16 st). Popular in Lancashire, he played 175 matches for the county, scoring 5942 runs @ 26.64, in addition to making 464 dismissals in a career total of 824 victims. He settled near Manchester as a successful businessman.

Evans, Godfrey   Born Finchley, London, 18 August 1920. Ebullient wicket-keeper and right-hand batsman for Kent (1939-67) and England, for whom he was first choice in the decade following World War II. Often standing up to fast-medium bowlers, he claimed 219 Test victims (173 ct, 46 st) in his 91 Tests, scoring also 2439 runs @ 20.49, with two hundreds. Normally an aggressive bat, he batted for 95 minutes without scoring in the Adelaide Test of 1946/47, a record for over 50 years. His career dismissals totalled 1066 (816 ct, 250 st) and he made in all 14,882 runs @ 21.22, with seven centuries. He died 3 May 1999.

Fleming, Stephen   Born Christchurch, New Zealand, 1 April 1973. Left-hand batsman for Canterbury, Middlesex (2001) and New Zealand, his Test debut being in 1993/94 when he scored 92 v India at Hamilton. The current New Zealand batsman with most runs for his country (4295 by April 2003), his highest Test score is 174no v Sri Lanka (Colombo 1997/98). Long established as New Zealand captain, he holds the record for that country for most catches taken by a non wicket-keeper.

Fletcher, Keith   Born Worcester, 20 May 1944. Right-hand middle-order batsman for Essex (1962-88) and

C
R
I
C
K
E
T

England (59 Tests, seven as captain, from 1968 to 1981/82). A shrewd captain of his county in their heyday from the mid-1970s to the mid-1980s, he led them to four County Championships (1979, 1983, 1984, 1986), one NatWest Trophy (1985) and one Benson & Hedges Cup (1979). He scored in all 37,665 runs @ 37.77, with 63 hundreds, the highest 228no v Sussex (Hastings 1968), while in Test matches he made 3272 runs @ 39.90, with one double century – 216 v New Zealand at Auckland in 1974/75.

Flower, Andy　Born Cape Town, South Africa, 28 April 1968. Outstanding left-hand batsman and wicket-keeper for Mashonaland (debut 1986/87), Essex and Zimbabwe. His country's leading run-scorer since his Test debut in 1992/93, with almost 5000 runs at an average of over 50, he has also claimed over 150 Test dismissals. His highest Test score is 232no v India (Nagpur 2000/01), and he has frequently captained his country. For Essex in 2002 he scored 1048 runs @ 52.40, and disillusioned with the set-up at home he returned as one of Essex's overseas players in 2003.

Fraser, Angus　Born Billinge, Lancashire, 8 August 1965. Dependable right-arm fast-medium bowler for Middlesex (1984-2002) and England. Making his Test debut for England v Australia in 1989 and playing in 46 Tests, he took 177 wickets @ 27.32, including a best performance of 8-53 v W. Indies (Port of Spain 1997/98), the best analysis by an England bowler against that country. On retiring in 2002 and turning to journalism, he had taken 886 wickets in all @ 27.39 each.

Freeman, A.P. ('Tich')　Born Lewisham, 17 May 1888. Diminutive (1.57m) leg-break and googly bowler for Kent (1914-36) and England, playing in a mere 12 Tests between 1924/25 and 1929 despite being a prodigious performer in county cricket, and taking 66 wickets @ 25.86. He is the only bowler to take over 300 wickets in an English season (304 in 1928 @ 18.05), and stands second only to Wilfred Rhodes in the list of all-time wicket-takers (3776 @ 18.42). He captured all ten wickets in an innings three times (1929, 1930, 1931), an unparalleled feat, and took 100 wickets in a season 17 times – bettered only by Rhodes and Derek Shackleton. He died 28 January 1965.

Fry, Charles Burgess　Born West Croydon, Surrey, 25 April 1872. Right-hand batsman for Oxford University, Sussex and England between 1892 and 1921, and distinguished also in public life. He gained a first-class honours degree at Oxford (where he was a triple Blue), played football for England (v Ireland 1901) as well as holding the world long-jump record for 21 years. He was a League of Nations delegate after World War I, founded a boys' training ship and was offered – but declined – the throne of Albania. His 30,886 first-class runs averaged 50.22 and included not only 16 double centuries but also six centuries in succession (1902). In 26 Tests he scored 1223 runs @ 32.18, with two hundreds. His 1939 autobiography was entitled, appropriately, *Life Worth Living*. He died 7 September 1956, aged 84.

Garner, Joel　Born Christ Church, Barbados, 16 December 1952. Right-arm fast bowler for Barbados (1975/76 to 1987/88), Somerset (1977-86), South Australia (1982/83) and West Indies (1976/77 to 1986/87). Taking 25 wickets in his first series (v Pakistan), he captured in all 259 Test wickets at the very low average of 20.97. Using his great height

(2.03m), he was a vital part of his country's attack for ten years, and helped Somerset to a clutch of one-day trophies before being released amid some acrimony. He took in all 881 wickets @ 18.53.

Gatting, Mike　Born Kingsbury, Middlesex, 6 June 1957. Pugnacious right-hand middle-order batsman for Middlesex from 1975 to 1998 (captain 1983-97) and England (1977/78 to 1994/95). He played for his country 79 times and scored 4409 runs @ 35.55 with 10 centuries, the highest being at Madras in 1984/85 (although it had taken him 54 Test innings to reach three figures). The last England captain to date to win an Ashes series (1986/87), he had a much-publicised altercation with umpire Shakoor Rana at Faisalabad the following winter. A prolific scorer in domestic cricket, he totalled 36,549 runs @ 49.52, with 94 centuries, including 258 v Somerset (Bath 1984). A useful medium-pace bowler, he took 158 wickets @ 29.76.

Gavaskar, Sunil　Born Bombay, India, 10 July 1949. Record-breaking right-hand opening batsman for Bombay (1967/68 to 1986/87), Somerset (1980) and India (1970/71 to 1986/87). In his debut series in the West Indies in 1970/71, he made four centuries, and scored in all a world record 34 Test hundreds (the highest being 236no v W. Indies at Madras in 1983/84), as well as being the first man to pass 10,000 Test runs (10,122 in all @ 51.12). He scored over 1000 runs in a calendar year four times (1976, 1978, 1979, 1983) and is the only batsman to score centuries in both innings of a Test on three occasions. In 125 Tests he was captain 47 times and took an Indian record 108 catches. His career produced 25,834 runs @ 51.46, with 81 hundreds.

Gibbs, Lance　Born Georgetown, Guyana, 29 September 1934. Outstanding right-arm off-break bowler for British Guiana, later Guyana (1953-54 to 1974/75), Warwickshire (1967-73), S. Australia (1969/70) and West Indies (1957/58 to 1975/76, 79 matches). He held the then record for Test match wickets (309 @ 29.09), his best analysis being 8-38 v India (Bridgetown 1961/62), including a spell of eight wickets for only six runs. A cousin of Clive Lloyd, he performed the hat-trick v Australia at Adelaide in 1960/61.

Gilchrist, Adam　Born Bellinge, New South Wales, 14 November 1971. Wicket-keeper and explosive left-hand batsman for New South Wales (1992/93 to 1993/94), Western Australia (debut 1994/95) and Australia (debut 1999/2000 v Pakistan at Brisbane). In his highest Test score of 204no v S. Africa (Johannesburg 2001/02) he reached 200 in only 212 balls, with 19 fours and eight sixes. Only the fourth double century by a number seven batsman, in the course of his innings he added 317 with Damien Martyn for the sixth wicket. His 152 v England (Birmingham 2001) took only 143 balls, and he currently averages over 58 in Tests, with his eighth hundred coming in April 2003 v W. Indies at Port of Spain.

Gooch, Graham　Born Leytonstone, Essex, 23 July 1953. Heavy-scoring right-hand opening batsman for Essex (1973-97), Western Province (1982/83 to 1983/84) and England (1975 to 1994/95). His total of 8900 Test runs (@ 42.58) in a then record 118 Tests (34 as captain) is an English record, despite starting with a 'pair' v Australia (Birmingham 1975). His 20 Test centuries include 333 v India (The Oval 1990), the highest score by any England captain; his score of 123 in the second innings makes a record aggregate for a single Test. He was banned from Test cricket for three years after joining a 'rebel' tour to South Africa in 1982. Gooch scored in all 44,841 runs @ 49.11, with 128 hundreds, and in 1990 averaged 101.70 – with Geoffrey Boycott, the only Englishman to average over 100 in an English season.

Gough, Darren Born Barnsley, Yorkshire, 18 September 1970. Right-arm fast bowler for Yorkshire (1989-2003), Essex (2004) and England (debut v New Zealand, Manchester 1994). England's main strike bowler from the mid-1990s, although prolonged knee surgery casts doubt on further Test appearances. In 56 Tests he has taken 228 wickets @ 27.57, including a hat-trick v Australia (Sydney 1998/99), the only Ashes hat-trick by an Englishman in the 20th century. His best Test analysis is 6-42 v S. Africa (Leeds 1998), and he has taken over 700 career wickets with 7-28 v Lancashire (Leeds 1995) his best figures. He has also taken 174 wickets in one-day internationals.

Gower, David Born Tunbridge Wells, Kent, 1 April 1957. Left-hand batsman of elegant insouciance for Leicestershire (1975-89), Hampshire (1990-93) and England, for whom he played 117 times from 1978 to 1992, 32 as captain. His 8231 Test runs – often made in impeccable style – averaged 44.25, with 18 centuries, a total which was a record at the time. He led England to regain the Ashes in 1985, scoring three hundreds in the series, including his highest (215 at Birmingham), but twice lost series 5-0 to a powerful West Indies side (1984, 1985/86). On retiring, having scored 26,339 runs @ 40.08 with 53 centuries, he became a cricket commentator, TV personality and dedicated oenophile.

Grace, William Gilbert 'W.G.' Born Downend, Bristol, 18 July 1848. Right-hand batsman and right-arm medium-pace bowler for Gloucestershire (1870-99), London County (1900-04) and England (1880-99). A Victorian icon who established the game as an English institution, his 'firsts' are legion: aged 23, he scored 2739 runs in a season @ 78.25, both then records, and became the first player to score 10 hundreds in a season (1871), to perform the 'double' (1874), to score 2000 runs and take 100 wickets in the same season (1876), to score a triple century (344 for MCC v Kent, Canterbury 1876), to score the first century for England (152 v Australia, The Oval 1880), to score 1000 runs in May (1895), to score 100 first-class centuries, and to reach 20,000 career runs and 2000 wickets. He scored in all 54,211 runs @ 39.45, with 126 centuries, and took 2809 wickets @ 18.14, his Test figures being 1098 runs @ 32.29 in 22 Tests and 9 wickets @ 26.22. He also represented England at bowls. He died 23 October 1915.

Graveney, Tom Born Riding Mill, Northumberland, 16 June 1927. Attractive right-hand middle-order batsman for Gloucestershire (1948-60), Worcestershire (1961/70), Queensland (1969/70 to 1971/72) and England (1951/69), playing in 79 Tests and scoring 4882 runs @ 44.38 with 11 hundreds. His highest score was 285 v W. Indies (Nottingham 1957). The only player to score over 10,000 runs for two counties, he scored a total of 47,793 runs @ 44.91, with 122 centuries, a total bettered only by Geoffrey Boycott among post-war batsmen.

Greenidge, Gordon Born St Peter, Barbados, 1 May 1951. Attacking right-hand opening batsman for Hampshire (1970/87), Barbados (1972/73 to 1990/91) and West Indies (1974/75 to 1990/91), for whom he played in 108 Tests and scored 7558 runs @ 44.72 with 19 centuries, the highest being 223 v England (Manchester 1984). With D.L. Haynes, he took part in 16 opening partnerships of 100 or more for his country, and in topping 1000 runs in an English season 15 times he amassed in all 37,354 runs @ 45.88, the highest total by any non-English batsman, with 92 hundreds. The best of his five tours to England was in 1976, when his 1952 runs included 592 in the Tests @ 65.77, with three centuries.

Greig, Tony Born Queenstown, South Africa, 6 October 1946. Right-hand batsman and right-arm medium-pace and off-break bowler for Border (1965/66 to 1969/70), Sussex (1966-78), Eastern Province (1970/71 to 1971/72) and England. A charismatic captain in 14 of his 58 consecutive Tests between 1972 and 1977, he scored 3599 runs @ 40.43 for England, also taking 141 wickets @ 32.20. He made eight Test centuries and recorded the best match analysis by an England bowler against West Indies in 1973/74 at Port of Spain (8-86 and 5-70). In 1977 he was revealed to be signing the game's star players for Kerry Packer's World Series cricket, thus effectively ending his Test career. He became a television commentator in Australia, where he settled.

Griffith, Charlie Born St Lucy, Barbados, 14 December 1938. Fearsome right-arm fast bowler for Barbados (1959/60 to 1966/67) and West Indies (1959/60 to 1968/69). On his first-class debut (Barbados v MCC, Bridgetown 1959/60) he dismissed Cowdrey, May and M.J.K. Smith in the space of two overs, and touring England in 1963 he took 119 wickets, including 32 @ only 16.21 in the Test series. Often suspected of throwing his very fast ball, he was – perhaps because of this – less penetrative on later tours and finished his Test career with 94 wickets @ 28.54 in a career yielding 332 wickets @ 21.60.

Grimmett, Clarrie Born Dunedin, New Zealand, 25 December 1891. Right-arm leg-break and googly bowler for Wellington (1911/12 to 1913/14), Victoria (1918/19 to 1923/24), S. Australia (1924/25 to 1940/41) and Australia (1924/25 to 1935/36). The first bowler to take 200 Test wickets, he toured England in 1926, 1930 and 1934, taking over 100 wickets on each occasion. Touring South Africa in 1935/36, in his mid-forties, he took 44 wickets in the five Tests @ only 14.59. He took 216 Test wickets @ 24.21, and 1424 @ 22.28 in all matches. He died 2 May 1980.

Hadlee, Richard Born Christchurch, New Zealand, 3 July 1951. Superb right-arm fast-medium bowler and attacking left-hand lower middle-order batsman for Canterbury (1971/72 to 1988/89), Nottinghamshire (1978-87), Tasmania (1979/80) and New Zealand (1972/73 to 1990). His country's greatest player, he was the first to take 400 Test wickets, finishing with 431 @ 22.29 in his 86 Tests, including 9-52 (15-123 in the match) v Australia (Brisbane 1985/86). He also scored 3124 Test runs @ 27.16 with two centuries, the higher being 151no v Sri Lanka (Colombo 1986/87). In eight English seasons from 1980 to 1987 he topped the national bowling averages five times and came second twice, completing the 'double' in 1984 with 1179 runs @ 51.26 and 117 wickets at only 14.05, and making his highest score of 210no v Middlesex at Lord's. He was knighted during New Zealand's tour of England in 1990, the last of his five tours there.

CRICKET

Hall, Wesley   Born St Michael, Barbados, 12 September 1937. Formidable right-arm fast bowler for Barbados (1955/56 to 1970/71), Trinidad (1966/67 to 1969/70), Queensland (1961/62 to 1962/63) and West Indies (1958/59 to 1968/69). In his 48 Tests he took 192 wickets @ 26.38 and was his country's leading strike bowler throughout the 1960s. He took a career total of 546 wickets @ 26.14, and on retiring became a senator in the Barbados parliament and sports minister for the island.

Hammond, Walter   Born Dover, Kent, 19 June 1903. Majestic right-hand batsman, right-arm medium-pace bowler and superb slip fielder for Gloucestershire (1920-51) and England (1927/28 to 1946/47), whom he led after turning amateur in 1938. He scored 7249 runs @ 58.45 in his 85 Tests, including 336no v New Zealand (Auckland 1932/33), a Test record until beaten by Len Hutton. He scored 36 double hundreds – one fewer than Bradman but far in excess of anyone else – and topped the national averages for eight consecutive seasons from 1933 to 1946. He scored 905 runs @ 113.12 in the Ashes series of 1928/29, and in 1928 held a record 78 catches in an English season, including a record 10 in one match (v Surrey). He made in all 50,551 runs @ 56.10 and took 732 wickets @ 30.58, including a best 9-23 v Worcestershire (Cheltenham 1928), as well as playing several games for Bristol Rovers. He died in South Africa, 1 July 1965.

Hanif Mohammad   Born Junagadh, India, 21 December 1934. Massively patient right-hand opening batsman for Bahawalpur (1953/54), Karachi (1954/55 to 1968/69), PIA (1960/61 to 1975/76) and Pakistan. Playing 55 Tests (11 as captain) between 1952/53 and 1969/70 he scored 3915 runs @ 43.98, including 337 v W. Indies (Bridgetown 1957/58) when he batted for 16hrs 10mins. His innings of 499 for Karachi v Bahawalpur (Karachi 1958/59) was a world record until overtaken by Brian Lara's 501no in 1994. His career runs totalled 17,059 @ 52.32.

Harvey, Neil   Born Fitzroy, Victoria, 8 October 1928. Outstanding left-hand middle-order batsman for Victoria (1946/47 to 1956/57), New South Wales (1958/59 to 1962/63) and Australia (1947/48 to 1962/63). At 19 he became the youngest Australian to score a Test hundred (v India, Melbourne 1947/48) and at Headingley in 1948 he made a brilliant century on a deteriorating pitch to help Australia to a famous victory. He scored 6149 Test runs @ 48.41, with 21 hundreds, including four in each of two series v S. Africa (1949/50 and 1952/53), the latter yielding his Test highest of 205 at Melbourne. He made in all 21,699 runs @ 50.93, with 67 hundreds.

Hawke, Lord   Born Gainsborough, Lincs, 16 August 1860. Right-hand middle-order batsman for Yorkshire (1881-1911), Cambridge University (1882-85) and England. Although playing only five Tests between 1895/96 and 1898/99 and scoring 30 runs @ 7.85, he was an influential captain and then president of Yorkshire, and later president and honorary treasurer of MCC. He introduced winter payments for professionals and insisted in return on proper standards of sobriety. It was he who suggested the idea of a panel of selectors for England's home games. He died in Edinburgh, 10 October 1938.

Hayden, Matthew   Born Kingaroy, Queensland, 29 October 1971. Heavy-scoring left-hand opening batsman for Queensland (debut 1991/92), Hampshire (1997), Northamptonshire (1999/2000)

and Australia. Since his debut for his country at Johannesburg in 1993/94 he had by late 2003 notched 17 centuries, including the highest-ever Test innings of 380, with 11 sixes, v Zimbabwe (Perth 2003/04), thus overtaking Lara's 375 only for Lara to regain the record with his 400no v England in 2003/04. In 2001/02, against New Zealand and South Africa, he and Justin Langer produced a world-record four double-century opening partnerships, and with 1391 runs in 2001 he became the most prolific Test scorer for Australia in one calendar year until overtaken by Ricky Ponting in 2003. He is the only batsman with over 1000 Test runs in each of three consecutive calendar years (2001-03).

Haynes, Desmond   Born St James, Barbados, 15 February 1956. Reliable right-hand opening batsman for Barbados (1976/77 to 1994/95), Middlesex (1989-94) and West Indies, playing in 116 Tests between 1977/78 and 1993/94 and scoring 7487 runs @ 42.29. He opened 89 times with Gordon Greenidge, and they shared 16 opening stands of over 100. The highest of his 18 Test centuries was 184 (Lord's 1980) and his career highest was 255no (v Sussex at Lord's). As well as scoring 25,027 career runs @ 46.17, he is his country's highest scorer in one-day internationals (8648 runs).

Hayward, Tom   Born Cambridge, 29 March 1871. Prolific right-hand opening batsman for Surrey (1893-1914) and England (1895/96 to 1909), and the first professional to score 100 hundreds. He scored 3518 runs in 1906 @ 66.37, a season's record total that stood for 41 years, and reached 1000 runs in 20 consecutive seasons, his highest score being 315no (v Lancashire, The Oval 1898) in a career total of 43,551 @ 41.79. He shared 40 opening partnerships of 100 or more with J.B. Hobbs, and in 35 Tests scored 1999 runs @ 34.46, with three centuries. He died in Cambridge, 19 July 1939.

Headley, George   Born Panama, 30 May 1909. Brilliant right-hand middle-order batsman for Jamaica (1927/28 to 1953/54) and West Indies (1929/30 to 1953/54). His country's greatest pre-war batsman, his Test runs averaged 60.83, with 10 centuries, and this against England or Australia in all but one of his 22 Tests. Scoring 176 in his first Test match (v England, Bridgetown 1929/30), then two hundreds at Georgetown and 223 at Kingston in the same series, he then became in 1939 the first man to hit two hundreds in a Lord's Test and was the first black man to captain his country. His son Ron and grandson Dean both played Test cricket (for West Indies and England respectively). He died in Kingston, Jamaica, 30 November 1983.

Healy, Ian   Born Brisbane, Queensland, 30 April 1964. Wicket-keeper and right-hand middle-order batsman for Queensland (1986/87 to 1998/99) and Australia (1988/89 to 1999). The fourth most-capped Australian (after Allan Border and the Waugh twins), he holds the world record for wicket-keeping dismissals in Tests – 395 victims in 119 matches. His 4356 Test runs @ 27.39 include four centuries, the highest being 161no v W. Indies (Brisbane 1996/97), and he scored in all 8341 first-class runs @ 30.22, retiring in October 1999.

Hendren, E.H. ('Patsy')   Born Elias Henry Hendren, Turnham Green, London, 5 February 1889. Prolific right-hand middle-order batsman for Middlesex (1907-37) and England (1920/21 to 1934/35). The scorer of 170 centuries, second only to Jack Hobbs, his long career produced 57,611 runs – the third highest total ever – @ 50.80. His 3525 Test runs @ 47.63 included seven hundreds, the highest (205no) at Trinidad in 1929/30, a tour on which he scored 1765 runs @ 135.76, with four double centuries. He topped 3000 runs in a season three times, and hit 301no v Worcestershire (Dudley 1933). He died 4 October 1962.

Heyhoe-Flint, Rachel Born 11 June 1939. Cricketer, journalist and broadcaster; a member of the England Women's XI 1960-83, and captain from 1966 to 1977, she became in 1963 the first woman to hit a six in a Test (v Australia, The Oval). She scored 1594 runs in 22 Tests, including three centuries, with a highest score of 179 (v Australia, The Oval 1976) – at the time the highest individual score in women's Test cricket in England. She also captained England to the first Women's World Cup in 1972, and was awarded the MBE for services to women's cricket.

Hick, Graeme Born Salisbury, Rhodesia (now Harare, Zimbabwe), 23 May 1966. Right-hand middle-order batsman for Zimbabwe (1983/84 to 1985/86), Worcestershire (debut 1984), Northern Districts (1987/88 to 1988/89), Queensland (1990/91) and England (debut 1991/92). The only current batsman to have scored over 35,000 runs, presently averaging over 53, in 2002 he scored his 121st century. In 1986 he became the youngest player to score 2000 runs in a season, and in 1988 his 2713 runs @ 77.51 included 1000 runs before the end of May and 405no v Somerset at Taunton. Never consistently an England regular, he scored 3383 runs @ 31.32 in his 65 Tests, with six centuries. He continued to score prolifically in 2004 with two double centuries early in the season.

Hirst, George Born Kirkheaton, Yorkshire, 7 September 1871. Left-arm medium-fast bowler and right-hand batsman for Yorkshire (1891-1929) and England (1897/98 to 1909). The only player to have taken 200 wickets and scored 2000 runs in the same season (1906), he performed the 'double' 14 times (second only to W.G. Grace), and in 1905 made the highest individual score for Yorkshire, 341 v Leicestershire at Leicester. He scored 36,365 runs @ 34.13 and took 2742 wickets @ 18.73, playing 24 times for England, scoring 790 runs @ 22.57 and taking 59 wickets @ 30.00. He died 10 May 1954 aged 82.

Hobbs, Jack Born Cambridge, 16 December 1882. Classical right-hand opening batsman (dubbed 'The Master') for Surrey (1905-34) and England (1907/08 to 1930). Hobbs scored more runs (61,237 @ 50.70) and more centuries (197) than anyone else in history, virtually half his hundreds coming after the age of forty. The first player to pass 5000 runs in Tests, he scored 5410 runs @ 56.94 in 61 appearances for England, with 11 centuries, the highest being 211 v S. Africa (Lord's 1924). He scored 200 or more 16 times, including 316no v Middlesex, Lord's 1926, and in 1925 made 16 centuries, then a record. He was knighted for his services to the game in 1953 and died 21 December 1963.

Holding, Michael Born Kingston, Jamaica, 16 February 1954. Right-arm fast bowler (nicknamed 'Whispering Death' for his silent, deadly run-up) for Jamaica (1972/73 to 1988/89), Lancashire (1981), Tasmania (1982/83), Derbyshire (1983-89), Canterbury (1987/88) and West Indies (1975/76 to 1986/87). His first tour of England in 1976 produced 28 Test wickets @ only 12.71 (including 8-92 and 6-

57 on a placid Oval pitch and 5-17 from 14.5 overs at Manchester), and he claimed 30 wickets @ 22.10 in the series in India in 1983/84. He took 249 wickets @ 23.68 in his 60 Tests and 778 @ 23.43 in all first-class games, and has since become a shrewd and articulate commentator on the game.

Hunte, Conrad Born St Andrew, Barbados, 9 May 1932. Solid right-hand opening batsman for Barbados (1950/51 to 1966/67) and West Indies (1957/58 to 1966/67). In his first Test series (v Pakistan) he scored 142 on debut, then 260 (adding 446 with Sobers) in the third Test, making yet another century in the fourth and totalling 622 runs @ 77.75. Successful also against England and Australia, he made 3245 runs @ 45.06, with eight hundreds, in his 44 Tests, and 8916 runs @ 43.92 in his first-class career. Having devoted much of his life (and income) to the Moral Rearmament cause, he died in Australia, 3 December 1999.

Hussain, Nasser Born Madras, India, 28 March 1968. Right-hand middle-order batsman for Essex (debut 1987) and England (debut 1989/90), succeeding Alec Stewart to the captaincy in 1999. He scored 5764 Test runs, including 14 centuries @ 37.18, including 207 v Australia (Birmingham 1997). He also scored 20,698 first-class runs @ 42.06 with 52 centuries. He retired 27 May 2004, three days after his century gave England victory against New Zealand in the first Test at Lord's.

Hutton, Len Born Pudsey, Yorkshire, 23 June 1916. Superb right-hand opening batsman for Yorkshire (1934-55) and England (1937 to 1954/55). In 79 Tests he scored 6971 runs @ 56.67 with 19 hundreds, which included three double hundreds and one triple. His 364 for England v Australia (The Oval 1938) was a Test record for almost 20 years, and he shared in a then record Test opening stand of 359 with Cyril Washbrook (v S. Africa, Johannesburg 1948/49). Made captain of England in 1952, although a professional, he won back the Ashes in 1953 and retained them in 1954/55. His career total of 40,140 runs @ 55.51, with 129 hundreds, included 3429 in the 1949 season. He was knighted in 1956 and died 6 September 1990.

Illingworth, Raymond Born Pudsey, Yorkshire, 8 June 1932. Right-arm off-break bowler and right-hand middle-order batsman for Yorkshire (1959-68 and 1982-83), Leicestershire (1969-78) and England (1958-73), whom he captained shrewdly from 1969 to 1973 in 31 of his 61 Tests, winning the Ashes in 1970/71 and retaining them in 1972. In Tests he scored 1836 runs @ 23.24 with two centuries, and took 122 wickets @ 31.20, including 6-29 v India in 1967. In 1975 he led Leicestershire to their first County Championship. He did the 'double' six times in a career which produced 24,134 runs @ 28.06 with 22 hundreds, and 2072 wickets @ 20.28, thus becoming one of only nine players to have scored 20,000 runs and taken 2000 wickets. He later became manager of Yorkshire, then chairman of Test selectors, but neither period was an easy one.

Imran Khan Born Lahore, Pakistan, 25 November 1952. Outstanding right-hand batsman and right-arm fast bowler for a number of sides, principally Lahore (1969/70 to 1970/71), Worcestershire (1971-76), Oxford University (1973-75), PIA (1975/76 to 1980/81), Sussex (1977-88) and Pakistan (1971 to 1991/92), whom he captained in 48 of his 88 Tests. The first Pakistan player to take 300 Test wickets (362 in all @ 22.81), he also scored 3807 Test runs

@ 37.69 with six hundreds. In 1987 he led his country to their first series victory in England, taking 21 wickets @ 21.66, and captained them to take the World Cup in 1992. An all-round feat of 111no and 13-99 in a County Championship match v Lancashire in 1976 contributed to career figures of 17,771 runs @ 36.79 and 1287 wickets @ 22.32. On retiring he entered politics and raised funds for charitable causes in his native country.

Inzamam-ul-Haq Born Multan, Pakistan, 3 March 1970. Attacking right-hand middle-order batsman for, inter alia, Multan (debut 1985/86), United Bank (1988/89 to 1990/91) and Pakistan (debut 1992 v England at Birmingham). The second Pakistan batsman to score 6000 Test runs (Javed Miandad being the first), he reached this total during a century before lunch v Zimbabwe (Harare 2002/03), and has also made the tenth-highest Test match score of all time – 329 v New Zealand (Lahore, May 2002).He has scored almost 7000 runs @ over 50 for Pakistan, with 19 centuries – many more than any other current player from that country.

Jackson, F.S. (Stanley) Born Leeds, Yorkshire, 21 November 1870. Right-hand batsman and right-arm fast-medium bowler for Cambridge University (1890-93), Yorkshire (1890-1907) and England, playing in 20 Tests from 1893 to 1905, scoring 1415 runs @ 48.79, with five centuries, and taking 24 wickets @ 33.29. He captained England (though never Yorkshire on a regular basis) on five occasions. His service in the Boer War, as an MP, then as chairman of the Unionist Party and later as governor of Bengal, limited his county appearances, but he still scored in all 15,901 runs @ 33.83, with 31 hundreds, and took 774 wickets @ 20.37. In the 1880s Winston Churchill was his 'fag' at Harrow. He died 9 March 1947.

Jardine, Douglas Born Bombay, India, 23 October 1900. Fine right-hand middle-order batsman for Oxford University (1920-23), Surrey (1921-33) and England (1928 to 1933/34), whom he captained in 15 of his 22 Tests. But he is more often remembered for his controversial captaincy on the 1932/33 tour to Australia, involving fast 'leg-theory' bowling by Larwood and Voce and ultimately straining relations between the two countries. Heading the national batting averages in 1927 and 1928, he scored in all 14,848 runs @ 46.83 with 35 centuries, and for England 1296 runs @ 48.00, including 127 v W. Indies (Manchester 1933). He retired aged only 33 and died 18 June 1958.

Javed Miandad Born Karachi, Pakistan, 12 June 1957. Prolific right-hand middle-order batsman for Karachi, Sind and Habib Bank between 1973/74 and 1990/91, Sussex (1976-79), Glamorgan (1980-85) and Pakistan (1976/77 to 1994/95). His Test total of 8832 runs @ 52.57 (in 124 Tests) is the fifth-highest of all time, and included 23 centuries – six of them double hundreds – with his 280no v India (Hyderabad 1982/83) the highest. He scored 163 on his Test debut v New Zealand (Lahore 1976/77) and captained Pakistan 33 times. In all he scored 28,248 runs @ 53.90, including 2083 @ 69.43 for Glamorgan in 1981, before leaving that county in controversial circumstances. His highest score was 311 for Karachi Whites v National Bank (Karachi 1974/75).

Jayasuriya, Sanath Born Matara, Sri Lanka, 30 June 1969. Aggressive left-hand middle-order batsman for Colombo (1988/89 to 1996/97), Bloomfield (debut 1996/97) and Sri Lanka (debut 1990/91). His 340 v India (Colombo 1997/98) is the fourth-highest Test match innings of all time, adding 576 for the second wicket with R.S. Mahanama – the highest Test partnership for any wicket. The scorer of most runs among current Sri Lankan players since Aravinda de Silva's retirement from Test cricket, he scored 82 from 44 balls versus England in the quarter-final of the 1996 World Cup, which his country won. Only de Silva has scored more runs for Sri Lanka.

Jessop, Gilbert Born Cheltenham, Glos, 19 May 1874. Violent right-hand middle-order batsman and right-arm fast bowler for Gloucestershire (1894-1914), Cambridge University (1896-99) and England (1899-1912). A consistently very fast scorer, he made 1000 runs in a season 14 times and did the 'double' twice. Of his 53 hundreds, one took 40 minutes and another 42, and they were scored at an overall rate of 82 runs an hour. The highest of his five double centuries (v Sussex, Hove 1903) was 286, the 200 being reached in 120 minutes. His 18 Tests produced only one century (104 v Australia, The Oval 1902) when, coming in to bat with England 48 for five and needing 273 to win, he reached 100 in 75 minutes and England won by one wicket. Universally known as 'The Croucher' owing to his stance at the wicket, he died 11 May 1955.

Johnston, Brian Born Little Berkhamstead, Herts, 24 June 1912. Educated at Eton and New College, Oxford, he served in the Grenadier Guards as a tank commander throughout World War II, being involved in the Normandy campaign and crossing the Rhine into Germany. Joining the BBC in 1945, in addition to cricket commentary he made outside broadcasts for TV's *In Town Tonight*, presented *Down Your Way* from 1972 to 1987 and was a commentator on state occasions such as the funeral of George VI in 1952 and the coronation in 1953. BBC cricket correspondent from 1963 to 1972, he was also for a number of years a member of the *Test Match Special* team, loved for his schoolboy sense of humour, his groanworthy puns and his vivid descriptions of chocolate cake sent in by listeners – though not all his fellow commentators approved of such levity. He died 5 January 1994.

Kanhai, Rohan Born Port Mourant, Guyana (then British Guiana), 26 December 1935. Enterprising middle-order batsman for Guyana (1954/55 to 1973/74), Western Australia (1971/72), Trinidad (1964/65), Warwickshire (1968-77), Tasmania (1969/70) and West Indies. Playing in 79 Tests from 1957 (in England) to 1973/74, he scored 6227 runs @ 47.53 with 15 hundreds, including 256 v India (Calcutta 1958/59). Kanhai made over 1000 runs in each of his ten seasons with Warwickshire, his best being 1894 @ 57.39 in 1970, and added 465 for the second wicket with J. Jameson (then a world record for that wicket) v Gloucestershire (Birmingham 1974). He also captained his country 13 times.

Kapil Dev Born Chandigarh, India, 6 January 1959. Right-hand middle-order batsman and right-arm fast-medium bowler for Haryana (1975/76 to 1994/95), Northamptonshire (1981-83), Worcestershire (1984/85) and India (1978/79 to 1993-94). India's greatest all-rounder, with 5248 runs @ 31.05 in 131 Tests including eight centuries, and a then record total of 434 wickets @ 29.64, he also led his country to World Cup victory in 1983, during which he came in with India 17 for five in a group stage match v Zimbabwe at Tunbridge Wells and hit a thunderous

175no. He took 8-106 v Australia (Adelaide 1985/86) and 9-83 v W. Indies (Ahmedabad 1983/84), and once hit Eddie Hemmings for four consecutive sixes in a Test at Lord's (1990), his highest Test score being 163 v Sri Lanka (Kanpur 1986/87). The only player to have scored 5000 runs and taken 400 wickets in Tests, his career yielded 11,356 runs @ 32.91 and 835 wickets @ 27.09.

Knott, Alan Born Belvedere, Kent, 9 April 1946. Brilliant wicket-keeper and middle-order batsman for Kent (1964-85), Tasmania (1969/70) and England, playing in 95 Tests between 1967 and 1981, scoring 4389 runs @ 32.75, with five centuries, and dismissing 269 victims (250 ct, 19 st), an English record. Joining Packer's World Series cricket, and later the controversial SAB tour to South Africa, proved a hindrance to his Test career, but he scored 18,105 career runs @ 29.63, with 17 hundreds (scoring two in a match v Surrey, Maidstone 1972) and claiming 1344 victims behind the stumps.

Kumble, Anil Born Bangalore, India, 17 October 1970. Right-arm leg-break bowler for Karnataka (debut 1989/90), Northamptonshire (1995, taking 105 wickets), Leicestershire (2000) and India (debut 1990). The second Indian bowler to take 300 Test wickets, he is only the second man (after J.C. Laker) to have taken 10 wickets in a Test innings – 10-74 v Pakistan (Delhi 1998/99). His highest Test score is 88 v S. Africa (Calcutta 1996/97), but he has scored centuries for his state.

Laker, Jim Born Bradford, Yorkshire, 9 February 1922. Outstanding right-arm off-break bowler for Surrey (1946-59), Essex (1962-64), Auckland (1951/52) and England. In 46 Tests he took 193 wickets @ 21.24, including an unparalleled 19-90 (10-53 and 9-37) v Australia (Manchester 1956), also taking 10-88 in an innings for Surrey v the Australians at The Oval the same season. He took 1994 career wickets @ 18.41, including a remarkable analysis of eight wickets for two runs in a Test Trial at Bradford in 1950, and helped Surrey to seven consecutive championships in the 1950s. He died 23 April 1986.

Lamb, Allan Born Cape Province, South Africa, 20 June 1954. Aggressive right-hand middle-order batsman for W. Province (1972/73 to 1981/82 and 1992/93), Orange Free State (1987/88), Northamptonshire (1978-95) and England (1982-92), playing in 79 Tests and scoring 4656 runs @ 36.09, with 14 hundreds, including three against West Indies in 1984, his highest score being 142 v New Zealand (Wellington 1991/92). He scored in all 32,502 runs @ 48.94, with 89 hundreds, including 294 for Orange Free State v E. Province (Bloemfontein 1987/88).

Lara, Brian Born Santa Cruz, Trinidad, 2 May 1969. Record-breaking left-hand middle-order batsman of dazzling gifts for Trinidad (debut 1987/88), Warwickshire (1994 and 1998) and West Indies (debut 1987/88). He has made not only the then highest individual score in Test cricket (375 v England, Antigua 1993/94, since beaten by Matthew Hayden) but also the highest score in all first-class cricket (501no for Warwickshire v Durham, Birmingham 1994), the latter including the most fours in one innings (72) and the most runs in one day (390) by anyone. He then regained the Test record with 400no against England (Antigua 2003/04), becoming the only player to exceed 350 in two separate Test innings. He also scored 277 for West Indies v Australia

(Sydney 1992/93), and in his first season with Warwickshire he hit nine centuries in making 2066 runs. In 2003/04 he scored a Test record 28 runs in one over (two sixes, four fours) off Robin Peterson / S. Africa in Johannesburg). With over 9000 runs, and 25 centuries, in Tests, he is now the highest scorer in total for his country, despite media pressure and illness or injuries affecting his form.

Larwood, Harold Born Nuncargate, Notts, 14 November 1904. Right-arm bowler of great pace for Nottinghamshire (1924-38) and England (1926 to 1932/33), who took 78 wickets @ 28.35 in his 21 Tests. He never played for England again after the so-called 'bodyline' tour of Australia in 1932/33, when he was instructed to bowl fast and short on the leg-stump to a leg-side field, provoking Australian outrage at a plan devised by captain Douglas Jardine mainly to curb Bradman's prolific run-scoring. He took in all 1427 wickets @ 17.51 and died 22 July 1995 after settling in Australia.

Lawry, Bill Born Melbourne, Victoria, 11 February 1937. Patiently acquisitive left-hand opening batsman for Victoria (1955/56 to 1971/72) and Australia (1961 to 1970/71), playing in 67 Tests and scoring 5234 runs @ 47.15 with 15 hundreds. His debut tour of England produced 420 Test runs @ 52.50, with two centuries, out of a total of 2019 runs @ 61.18, and against England in 1965/66 he made 592 runs @ 84.57. He captained his country 25 times, but was relieved of the post after losing the Ashes to Illingworth's Englishmen in 1970/71. His highest Test score was 210 (v W. Indies, Bridgetown 1964/65), and his highest in all cricket was 266 for Victoria v NSW (Sydney 1960/61). He scored 50 centuries in a career total of 18,734 runs @ 50.90.

Lillee, Dennis Born Perth, Western Australia, 18 July 1949. Fiery right-arm fast bowler for Western Australia (1969/70 to 1983/84), Tasmania (1987/88), Northamptonshire (1988) and Australia (1970/71 to 1983/84). His country's leading strike bowler for over a decade, he was the first Australian bowler to reach 300 wickets in Test matches, ending with 355 wickets @ 23.92, which included 31 @ 17.87 in the 1972 series in England and 39 @ 22.30 in 1981. Ninety-five of his Test victims were caught by Rodney Marsh – a combination unapproached in Tests. He often defied authority – using an aluminium bat or kicking Javed Miandad were examples of this – but he overcame severe back problems to finish his career with 882 wickets @ 23.46.

Lindwall, Ray Born Sydney, New South Wales, 3 October 1921. Classical right-arm fast bowler for New South Wales (1941/42 to 1953/54), Queensland (1954/55 to 1959/60) and Australia (1945/46 to 1959/60), taking 228 wickets, then an Australian record, in his 61 Tests. In 1948 he took 27 English wickets @ 19.62, including 6-20 at The Oval when England were dismissed for 52. He also scored two Test hundreds, one against England (Melbourne 1946/47), and took in all 794 wickets @ 21.35. He died 23 June 1996.

Lloyd, Clive Born Georgetown, British Guiana (now Guyana), 31 August 1944. Dominating left-hand middle-order batsman for Guyana (1963/64 to 1982/83), Lancashire (1968-86) and West Indies. Playing in 110 Tests from 1966/67 to 1984/85, 74 times as captain, he scored 7515 Test runs @ 46.67, with 19 centuries (including those on his debuts v both England and Australia), his highest being 242no v India (Bombay 1974/75). He made 12,764 runs for

Lancashire @ 44.94, with 30 centuries, in a career total of 31,232 @ 49.26, and led West Indies to World Cup titles in 1975 (scoring a brilliant 102 v Australia in the final) and 1979. For West Indies against Glamorgan (Swansea 1976) he scored 200 in two hours, equalling Gilbert Jessop's record. He settled near Manchester and has been for some years a member of the Lancashire CC committee.

Lock, Tony Born Limpsfield, Surrey, 5 July 1929. Left-arm spin bowler and brilliant close field for Surrey (1946-63), Leicestershire (1965-67), Western Australia (1962/63 to 1970/71) and England (1952 to 1967/68), playing in 49 Tests and taking 174 wickets @ 25.58 (including the one that Jim Laker did not take at Manchester in 1956). The last player to take 200 wickets in a season (212 in 1957), he remodelled his bowling action after accusations of 'throwing', and only Derek Shackleton (Hampshire) has taken more first-class wickets since World War II. With Laker, he helped Surrey to seven consecutive championships (1952-58), and then became a successful captain of Leicestershire and Western Australia. He took 2844 career wickets @ 19.23, including 10-54 v Kent (Blackheath 1956), and his total of 830 catches is bettered only by Frank Woolley and W.G. Grace. He died 29 March 1995.

Lohmann, George Born Kensington, London, 2 June 1865. Right-arm medium-pace bowler for Surrey (1884-96), Western Province (1894/95 to 1896/97) and England, for whom he took 112 wickets in his 18 Tests @ only 10.75, an unequalled feat. In 1895/96 he took 35 wickets in the three-match series in South Africa @ only 5.80, including 8-7 and 7-38 at Port Elizabeth and 9-28 at Johannesburg. In 1886/87 he took 8-25 at Sydney and in 1891/92 8-58, also at Sydney. He took in all 1841 wickets @ 13.73, his best season (1890) yielding 220 wickets @ 13.62. He emigrated to South Africa for his health's sake but died there of tuberculosis on 1 December 1901, aged only 36.

MacLaren, Archie Born Manchester, 1 December 1871. Classical right-hand opening batsman for Lancashire (1890-1914) and England (1894/95), captaining his country in 22 of his 35 Tests and scoring 1931 runs @ 33.87, with five hundreds, including two in one series (1897/98 in Australia) – the first time this had been achieved by an Englishman. His 424 for Lancashire v Somerset (Taunton 1895) was the highest individual innings in England until overtaken by Brian Lara's 501no in 1994, and he scored 22,236 runs in all @ 34.15. He died 17 November 1944.

McCabe, Stan Born Grenfell, New South Wales, 16 July 1910. Consistent right-hand middle-order batsman for New South Wales (1928/29 to 1941/42) and Australia (1930/38), who played two of the great Test match innings of the 1930s – 187no against Larwood and Voce at their most fearsome (Sydney 1932/33) and 232 in under four hours (Nottingham 1938). He scored 2748 Test runs @ 48.21 in a career total of 11,951 @ 49.38. He died falling from a cliff, 25 August 1968.

McGlew, Jackie Born Pietermaritzburg, South Africa, 11 March 1929. Dour right-hand opening batsman for Natal (1947/48 to 1966/67) and South Africa (1951 to 1961/62), for whom he played in 34 Tests (14 as captain), scoring 2440 runs @ 42.06 with seven centuries. He toured England three times (1951, 1955, 1960), and his 255no v New Zealand (Wellington 1952/53) was for 17 years the highest Test innings by a South African; he was also on the field for the whole of that match. His long career produced 12,170 first-class runs @ 45.92. He died 9 June 1998.

McGrath, Glenn Born Dubbo, New South Wales, 9 February 1970. Devastating right-arm fast bowler for New South Wales (debut 1992/93), Worcestershire (2000) and Australia (debut 1993/94), who in 2002/03 became only the second Australian to take 400 wickets in Tests. Touring England in 1997 and 2001, he took 36 Test wickets @ 19.47 (including his best analysis, 8-38 at Lord's) and 32 @ 16.93 respectively. Three Test series v W. Indies yielded 77 wickets – 26 @ 17.42 in 1996/97, 30 @ 16.93 in 1998/99 and 21 @ 17.09 in 2000/01. His Test match wickets have so far been achieved at very low cost – rather less than 20.50.

McDermott, Craig Born Ipswich, Queensland, 14 April 1965. Aggressive right-arm fast bowler for Queensland (1983/84 to 1995/96) and Australia (1984/5 to 1995/96), whose 291 Test wickets @ 28.62 made him then second only in total to Dennis Lillee. In England in 1985 he took 30 wickets in the series aged only 20, including 8-141 at Manchester when he became the youngest Australian to take eight wickets in a Test innings. In India in 1991/92 he took 31 wickets in the series @ only 12.83, and 32 English wickets @ 21.09 in 1994/95, before injury forced him to retire in 1997.

McKenzie, Graham 'Garth' Born Perth, Western Australia, 24 June 1941. Powerfully built right-arm fast bowler for Western Australia (1959/60 to 1973/74), Leicestershire (1969-75) and Australia (1961 to 1970/71), and on each occasion the youngest bowler (at the time) to reach the targets of 100, 150 and 200 wickets in Tests. His 60 Tests produced 246 wickets @ 29.78, including 29 @ 22.55 on the second of his three tours of England (1964), during which he took 7-153 in England's mammoth 611 at Manchester. He helped Leicestershire, for whom he took 465 wickets, to their first County Championship in 1975, and ended his career with 1219 wickets @ 26.96.

Malcolm, Devon Born Kingston, Jamaica, 22 February 1963. Durable right-arm fast bowler for Derbyshire (1984-97), Northamptonshire (1998-2000), Leicestershire (debut 2001) and England (1989-97). He took 128 wickets @ 37.09 in his 40 Tests, including 9-87 v S. Africa (The Oval 1994), and claimed his 1000th first-class wicket at the age of 39. He was still playing for Leicestershire in 2003 at the age of 40.

Marsh, Rodney Born Perth, Western Australia, 11 November 1947. Wicket-keeper and attacking left-hand batsman for Western Australia (1968/69 to 1983/84) and Australia (1970/71 to 1983/84), who claimed 355 victims in his 95 Tests, a record until surpassed by Ian Healy. His 28 dismissals v England in 1982/83 remain a series record for any wicket-keeper, and as a batsman he scored three Test hundreds, with a century on his first-class debut and a top score of 236 for Western Australia against Pakistan (Perth 1972/73). Recently in charge of England's Academy, he has considerable responsibility for the future of English cricket.

Marshall, Malcolm Born Bridgetown, Barbados, 18 April 1958. Splendid right-arm fast bowler for Barbados (1977/78 to 1990/91), Hampshire (1979-93), Natal (1992/93 to 1995/96) and West Indies (1978/79 to 1991), taking a then record 376 wickets @ only 20.94 in his 81 Tests. Two of his four Test series in England (1984 and 1988) yielded 24 wickets @ 18.21 and 35 wickets @ 12.65 respectively, with 20 more @ 22.10 in 1991, his best analysis being 7-22 v England (Manchester 1988). His 134 wickets for Hampshire @ 15.73 in 1982 remain the most by anyone in an English season since the reduction of the number of Championship matches in 1969. He died of cancer, 4 November 1999.

May, Peter Born Reading, Berkshire, 31 December 1929. Outstanding right-hand middle-order batsman for Cambridge University (1950/52), Surrey (1950-63) and England. Playing in 66 Tests from 1951 to 1961, 41 as captain, he scored 138 on his Test debut (v S. Africa, Leeds 1951) and 285no v West Indies at Birmingham in 1957, sharing a Test record fourth-wicket partnership of 411 with Colin Cowdrey and averaging 97.80 in that series. Illness forced his premature retirement from Test cricket at 31, having scored 4537 runs @ 46.77, with 13 hundreds, and after a spell as chairman of Test selectors (1982-88) he died 21 December 1994. He had scored in his career 27,592 runs @ 51.00, with 85 centuries.

Mead, Philip Born Battersea, London, 9 March 1887. Imperturbable left-hand middle-order batsman for Hampshire (1905-36) and England (1911/12 to 1928-29), playing in 17 Tests and scoring 1185 runs @ 49.37, with four hundreds. His career total of 55,061 runs is bettered only by Hobbs, Woolley and Hendren, and he scored more runs for one county (48,892) than anyone else. He died 26 March 1958.

Merchant, Vijay Born Bombay, India, 12 October 1911. Prolific right-hand opening batsman for Hindus (1929/30 to 1945/46), Bombay (1933/34 to 1950/51) and India (1933/34 to 1951/52). In his ten Tests, he scored 859 runs @ 47.72, with three centuries, and on India's tours of England he scored 1745 runs @ 51.32 in 1936 and 2385 @ 74.53 in 1946, with two double centuries. In India's Ranji Trophy matches he made 3639 runs @ 98.75, his highest score being 359no for Bombay v Maharashtra in 1933/34, and his career average of 71.11 (for 13,228 runs) is exceeded only by that of Don Bradman. He died 27 October 1987.

Milburn, Colin Born Burnopfield, Co. Durham, 23 October 1941. Jovially rotund right-hand opening batsman for Northamptonshire (1960-74), Western Australia (1966/67 to 1968/69) and England (1966 to 1968/69), playing in nine Tests and scoring 654 runs @ 46.71 with two centuries. His highest score was a thunderous 243 for W. Australia v Queensland (Brisbane 1968/69) in a career total of 13,262 runs @ 33.07, but his career was cut short by the loss of an eye in a car accident. Though he bravely tried to come back later, he retired in 1974 and died of a heart attack on 28 February 1990, aged only 49.

Miller, Keith Born Melbourne, Victoria, 28 November 1919. Charismatic right-hand middle-order batsman and right-arm fast bowler for Victoria (1937/38 to 1946/47), New South Wales (1947/48 to 1955/56) and Australia (1945/46 to 1956/57). Scoring a century on debut, he also led Australia's pace attack with Lindwall after World War II (taking 7-60 in the first post-war Ashes Test) and scored 2958 runs for his country @ 36.97, in addition to taking 170 wickets @ 22.97. Against West Indies in 1954/55 he scored three centuries and took 20 wickets. He scored in all 14,183 runs @ 48.90 with 41 hundreds (including one in his sole appearance for Nottinghamshire in 1959), as well as taking 497 wickets @ 22.30.

Morris, Arthur Born Bondi, New South Wales, 19 January 1922. Consistent left-hand opening batsman and colleague of Keith Miller for New South Wales (1940/41 to 1954/55) and Australia (1946/47 to 1954/55). The first player to score two separate hundreds on his first-class debut (v Queensland), he also scored two in the Adelaide Test v England in his first series (1946/47). In England in 1948 he made 696 runs @ 87.00 (more than anyone else that series). Scoring in all 3533 runs @ 46.48, with 12 centuries, in his 46 Tests, out of a career total of 12,614 runs @ 53.67 with 47 hundreds, his highest score was 290 v Gloucestershire @ Bristol in 1948.

Muralitharan, Muttiah Born Kandy, Sri Lanka, 17 April 1972. Unfathomable right-arm off-break bowler with a unique action for Tamil Union (debut 1989/90), Lancashire (1999 and 2001), Kent (2003) and Sri Lanka (debut 1992/93), reaching his 400th Test wicket in only 72 Tests – the quickest ever. He took 9-65 and 7-155 v England (The Oval 1998) and 9-51 v Zimbabwe (Kandy 2001/02) – the only bowler besides Jim Laker to take nine or more wickets in a Test innings on two occasions. On his Lancashire debut he took 7-44 and 7-73 v Warwickshire at Southport, finishing with 66 wickets @ 11.77 that season in the six matches in which he bowled. He has taken ten wickets in a Test match 11 times (a record), and five in an innings 41 times. He has also exceeded 300 wickets in one-day internationals, but has suffered some controversy concerning the legality of his bowling action especially for his 'doosra', the ball which spins away to the off. In March 2004 he dismissed G. Kasprowicz of Australia to claim his 500th Test victim, days after Shane Warne had reached 500 in the same series. He became the leading Test match wicket taker on 8 May 2004 when Mluleki Nkala of Zimbabwe became his 520th victim.

Mushtaq Mohammad Born Junagadh, India, 22 November 1943. Right-hand middle-order batsman and right-arm leg-break bowler for Karachi (1956/57 to 1967/68), PIA (1960/61 to 1979-80), Northamptonshire (1964-77) and Pakistan (1958/59 to 1978/79). The youngest-ever Test player at 15 years 124 days (v West Indies, Lahore 1958/59), he had made his first-class debut for Karachi Whites at the age of 13 years 41 days. The first Pakistani player to reach 25,000 first-class runs, he scored in all 31,091 runs @ 42.07, with 72 hundreds and a highest score of 303no (Karachi Blues v Karachi University, Karachi 1967/68), and took 936 wickets @ 24.34. He captained Pakistan in 19 of his 57 Tests, in which he scored 3643 runs @ 39.17 with 10 centuries, and took 79 wickets @ 29.22. His highest Test innings was 201 v New Zealand (Dunedin 1972/73).

Nourse, Dudley Born Durban, South Africa, 12 November 1910. Heavy-scoring right-hand middle-order batsman for Natal (1931/32 to 1952/53) and South Africa (1933-51), playing in 34 Tests (15 as captain) and scoring 2960 runs @ 53.81, with two double hundreds and seven other centuries. His 208 v England (Nottingham 1951) was made with a broken thumb. He scored in all 12,472 runs @ 51.53, with 41 hundreds. He died 14 August 1981.

Nurse, Seymour Born St Michael, Barbados, 10 November 1933. Powerful right-hand middle-order batsman for Barbados (1958/59 to 1971/72) and West Indies (1959/60 to 1968/69). In his 29 Tests he scored 2523 runs @ 47.60, with six centuries, two of which came in England in 1966, when he scored 501 runs @ 62.62 in the five Tests. In the third Test v New Zealand (Christchurch 1968/69) he made 258, his highest-ever score, then promptly announced his retirement from Test cricket. His career had produced 9489 runs @ 43.93, with 26 hundreds.

Oldfield, Bert   Born Sydney, New South Wales, 9 September 1894. Outstanding wicket-keeper and right-hand lower middle-order batsman for New South Wales (1919/20 to 1937/38) and Australia (1920/21 to 1936/37). Often keeping to O'Reilly and Grimmett, his percentage of stumpings (52 of his 130 Test dismissals, or 40 per cent) is unequalled by anyone with over 100 Test victims. In 1932/33 he was knocked unconscious at Adelaide by a short-pitched ball from Larwood, but refused to blame the bowler. He had a career total of 662 victims, of which 262 were stumped. He died 10 August 1976.

O'Reilly, Bill   Born White Cliffs, New South Wales, 20 December 1905. Tall, aggressive right-arm leg-break bowler for New South Wales (1927/28 to 1945/46) and Australia (1931/32 to 1945/46), and one of only two over-forties to represent Australia since World War II. Taking 144 Test wickets @ 22.59 in 27 Tests, he headed the Test match averages in his two tours to England with 28 wickets @ 24.92 in 1934 and 22 @ 27.72 in 1938. He topped the English first-class averages on both occasions, 9-38 v Somerset (Taunton 1934) being his best figures. He also took 27 and 25 wickets respectively during England's two tours of Australia in the 1930s. In his last Test in 1945/46 (v New Zealand at Wellington) he took 5-14 and 3-19, then promptly retired with career figures of 774 wickets @ only 16.60. He died 6 October 1992.

Paynter, Eddie   Born Oswaldtwistle, Lancashire, 5 November 1901. Combative left-hand middle-order batsman for Lancashire (1926-45) and England (1931-39), for whom only Herbert Sutcliffe has a higher Test match batting average. Paynter scored 1540 runs for England @ 59.23, his average against Australia being 84.42 (seven Tests). Two of his four Test hundreds were doubles, and his highest first-class innings was 322 v Sussex (Hove 1937) in his career total of 20,075 runs @ 42.35 with 45 centuries. He died 5 February 1979.

Pollock, Graeme   Born Durban, South Africa, 27 February 1944. Magnificent left-hand middle-order batsman for Eastern Province (1960-61 to 1977-78), Transvaal (1978-79 to 1986-87) and South Africa (1963-64 to 1969-70), whose Test average of 60.97 for his 2256 runs is second only to Bradman. At 16 the youngest century-maker in South Africa's Currie Cup, he became the youngest at 19 to score a Test hundred for his country. Against Australia in 1966-67 he scored 537 runs @ 76.51, and against Australia in 1969/70 he made 517 in four Tests @ 73.85, including 274 at Durban – then the highest innings by a South African in Tests. However, the ban on South Africa then ended his international career after only 23 Tests. In all matches he made 20,940 runs @ 54.67, with 64 hundreds.

Pollock, Shaun   Born Port Elizabeth, South Africa, 16 July 1973. Right-arm fast-medium bowler for Natal (debut 1991-92), Warwickshire (1996 and 2002) and South Africa (debut 1995/96), and nephew of Graeme Pollock. A world-class all-rounder with two Test hundreds (highest 111 v Sri Lanka, Pretoria 2000/01) and over 270 wickets to date (averaging under 21, the lowest average for any bowler with over 200 Test wickets), with a best analysis of 7-87 in 41 overs v Australia (Adelaide 1997/98). He took over as his country's captain after

the ban on Hansie Cronje. His highest score is 150no for Warwickshire v Glamorgan in 1996 at Edgbaston, and his best analysis 7-33 v Border (East London 1995/96).

Ponsford, Bill   Born Melbourne, Victoria, 19 October 1900. Right-hand opening batsman for Victoria (1920/21 to 1933/34) and Australia (1924/25 to 1934), and the only player to score 400 in an innings on two occasions (429 in 1922/23 and 437 in 1927/28, both at Melbourne). Against England in 1924/25 he scored centuries in his first two Tests – then a unique achievement – and in his 29 Tests scored 2122 runs @ 48.22. In 1934 he scored 266 in his last Test match, adding 451 with Bradman for what was a Test second-wicket record until 1997/98. He averaged 65.18 for his 13,189 career runs. He died 6 April 1991.

Ponting, Ricky   Born Launceston, Tasmania, 19 December 1974. Adventurous right-hand middle-order batsman for Tasmania (debut 1992/93, aged 17) and Australia (debut 1995/96). He has scored a century in every fourth Test match in which he has played (20 hundreds by late 2003), and was appointed as his country's one-day captain in 2002, leading them to World Cup victory in 2003, with a Man of the Match innings of 140 (with eight sixes) in the final. In March 2003 he was made vice-captain on Australia's tour of the West Indies, where he scored three Test centuries. His highest first-class score is 257 for Australia v India (Melbourne 2003/04), having scored 242 in the previous Test (at Adelaide), and by the end of 2003 he had scored more runs in one calendar year than any other Australian in history.

Procter, Mike   Born Durban, South Africa, 15 September 1946. Dynamic right-arm fast bowler and vigorous right-hand batsman for Natal (1965/66 to 1988/89), Western Province (1969/70), Rhodesia (1970/71 to 1975/76), Orange Free State (1987/88), Gloucestershire (1965-81) and South Africa (1966/67 to 1969/70). He played in only seven Tests, all against Australia, taking 41 wickets @ only 15.02 and scoring 226 runs @ 25.11, before his country's exclusion from Test cricket. His six successive hundreds for Rhodesia in 1970/71 (a world record shared with Fry and Bradman) included his highest score of 254 v W. Province at Salisbury (now Harare). He took four hat-tricks (and is the only man to have scored a century and taken a hat-trick on two separate occasions), and his best analysis was 9-71 for Rhodesia v Transvaal (Bulawayo 1972/73), in a career total of 1417 wickets @ 19.53, as well as 21,936 runs @ 36.01, with 48 hundreds.

Qadir, Abdul   Born Lahore, Pakistan, 15 September 1955. Skilful and volatile right-arm leg-spin bowler for Punjab, Lahore and Habib Bank (1975/76 to 1995/96) and Pakistan (1977/78 to 1990/91). Often excelling against England, he took 19 wickets @ 23.73 in the 1983/84 series in Pakistan, and in 1987/88 he took 9-56 (13-101 in the match) at Lahore when England were beaten by an innings. He was the first bowler to take 100 wickets in a Pakistan season, and only the second bowler to take 200 Test wickets for his country, for whom he took altogether 236 wickets @ 32.80. He also took 9-49 for Habib Bank v Rawalpindi (Rawalpindi 1982/83).

Ramadhin, Sonny   Born Esperance, Trinidad, 1 May 1929. Enigmatic right-arm off-break and leg-break bowler for Trinidad (1949/50 to 1952/53), Lancashire (1964/65) and West Indies (1950 to 1960/61). Touring England in 1950 with only two first-class matches behind him, he baffled English batsmen with 135 wickets @ 14.88, including 26 @ 23.23 in the four Tests. In West Indies' first-ever Test win in England (Lord's 1950) he took 11-152 in 115 overs (50 maidens), and in England in 1957 he claimed 119 wickets @ 13.98 on the tour, bowling a record 774 deliveries in the Birmingham Test. His Test match tally was 158 wickets @ 28.98 in 43 games, and in all he captured 758 wickets @ 20.24. The Lancashire bowler Kyle Hogg is his grandson.

Randall, Derek   Born Retford, Notts, 24 February 1951. Quirky but entertaining right-hand middle-order batsman for Nottinghamshire (1972-93) and England (1976/77 to 1984), and a brilliant fielder in the covers, his speed and stamina earning him the nickname 'Arkle'. His 2470 runs @ 33.37 in 47 Tests, with seven hundreds, included a dazzling 174 in the Centenary Test (Melbourne 1976/77), and a career total of 28,176 runs @ 38.28, with 52 centuries, featured a knock of 237 for Nottinghamshire v Derbyshire (Nottingham 1988).

Ranjitsinhi, K.S. ('Ranji')   Born Sarodar, India, 10 September 1872. Fluent right-hand middle-order batsman for Cambridge University (1893/94), Sussex (1895-1920) and England (1896-1902). The first batsman to score 3000 runs in a season (3159 @ 63.18 in 1899, and then 3065 @ 87.57 in 1900), he made a hundred on his Test debut, which included the first-ever pre-lunch Test century, and 175 at Sydney in 1897/98, totalling 989 runs @ 44.95 in his 15 Tests. Credited with inventing the leg glance, a stroke he played to perfection, he scored 24,692 runs in his career @ 56.37, his highest innings being 285no for Sussex v Somerset (Taunton 1901). As Jam Sahib of Nawanagar he devoted himself to state affairs and also acted as a delegate to the League of Nations, while playing three more games in 1920, albeit without success, after losing an eye in a shooting accident. He died 2 April 1933.

Rhodes, Wilfred   Born Kirkheaton, Yorkshire, 29 October 1877. Left-arm spin bowler and right-hand batsman of lengthy and distinguished service for Yorkshire (1898-1930) and England (1899 to 1929/30), becoming in the latter series the oldest-ever Test player at the age of 52. The only bowler to take 4000 wickets (4,204 @ 16.72), and performer of the 'double' a record 16 times, he also scored 39,969 runs @ 30.81. With 154 wickets in his first season, he took 100 wickets in a season a record 23 times. For England he took 7-17 v Australia (Birmingham 1902) and 15-124 in the Melbourne Test of 1903/04, taking in all 127 wickets @ 26.96 in his 58 Tests. His total of 2325 Test runs @ 30.19 included a then record opening partnership with Jack Hobbs of 323 (Melbourne 1911/12). He died 8 July 1973 aged 95.

Richards, Barry   Born Durban, South Africa, 21 July 1945. Richly gifted right-hand opening batsman for Natal (1964/65 to 1982/83), Gloucestershire (1965), Hampshire (1968/78), South Australia (1970/71), Transvaal (1970/71) and South Africa (1969/70). Playing in only four Test matches because of the ban on South Africa, he scored 508 runs @ 75.57, with two centuries. His sole season for South Australia produced 1538 runs @ 109.86, including 356 v W. Australia at Perth, and in his first season for Hampshire he scored 2395 runs @ 47.90. He made a century before lunch nine times, and totalled 28,358 runs @ 54.74, while from 1977 to 1979 he starred in World Series cricket. He is

now a respected cricket commentator and summariser.

Richards, Vivian   Born St John's, Antigua, 7 March 1952. Devastating right-hand middle-order batsman for Leeward Islands (1971/72 to 1990/91), Somerset (1974-81), Queensland (1976/77), Glamorgan (1990-93) and West Indies, playing in 121 Tests (50 as captain) and scoring 8540 runs @ 50.23, with 24 centuries, between 1974/75 and 1991. The first – and to date the only – West Indian to score 100 centuries, his aggregate was also a record for his country until exceeded by Brian Lara in November 2003. His 829 runs @ 118.42 in the 1976 Tests in England is also a West Indian record for a series, his century from only 56 balls v England (St John's 1985/86) is the fastest-ever Test hundred in terms of balls received, and his 322 for Somerset v Warwickshire (Taunton 1985) is that county's highest individual innings. He scored in all 36,212 runs @ 49.33 (though this total would have been much higher had he not batted so dashingly), in addition to scoring 6721 runs in one-day internationals, and he was knighted in 1997.

Roberts, Andy   Born Urlings Village, Antigua, 29 January 1951. Impassively menacing right-arm fast bowler for Leeward Islands (1969/70 to 1983/84), Hampshire (1973-78), New South Wales (1976/77), Leicestershire (1981-84) and West Indies (1973/74 to 1983/84). The third West Indian bowler to reach 200 Test wickets, he took 44 wickets in India and Pakistan in 1974/75 (including 12-121 at Madras) and 28 wickets @ 19.17 in the 1976 series in England. His second season for Hampshire produced 119 wickets @ only 13.62 each in 21 matches, and he ended his career with 202 Test wickets @ 25.61 (best analysis: 7-54 v Australia, Perth 1975/76) and 889 in all first-class games @ 21.01.

Russell, R.C. ('Jack')   Born Robert Charles Russell, Stroud, Glos, 15 August 1963. Brilliant wicket-keeper and doughty left-hand lower middle-order batsman for Gloucestershire (debut 1981, aged 17) and England (1988 to 1997/98). He played 54 Test matches, scoring 1897 runs @ 27.10, with two centuries (the higher being 128no v Australia, Manchester 1989). His 165 Test dismissals included a Test record 11 in a match (v S. Africa, Johannesburg 1995/96) as well as an English record 27 victims in that series. In 2002 he created a world record by conceding no byes in a Northamptonshire total of 746-9. Russell retired 22 June 2004, having taken 1319 dismissals for Gloucestershire and scored over 16,000 runs.

Shastri, Ravi   Born Bombay, India, 27 May 1962. Elegant right-hand middle-order batsman and left-arm spin bowler for Bombay (1979/80 to 1993/94), Glamorgan (1987-91) and India (1980/81 to 1992/93). The only batsman besides Garfield Sobers to hit six sixes off one over by Tilak Raj, for Bombay v Baroda, Bombay 1984/85), during the fastest-ever double-century (113 minutes), he scored 3830 runs @ 35.79 in his 80 Tests, including 206 v Australia (Sydney 1991/92), and took 151 wickets @ 40.96. After a career which yielded 13,202 runs @ 44.00 and 509 wickets @ 32.89, he became a respected cricket commentator.

Simpson, Bobby   Born Sydney, New South Wales, 3 February 1936. Reliable right-hand opening batsman, leg-spin bowler and superb slip fielder for New South Wales (1952/53 to 1977/78), Western Australia (1956/57 to 1960/61) and Australia (1957/58 to 1977/78). In 62 Tests (39 as captain) he scored 4869 runs @ 46.10, with 10 hundreds, his first being 311 v England (Manchester 1964), and took 71 wickets @ 42.26, in addition to 110 catches, many of them brilliant. He captained his country against India when in his forties after the defections to Kerry Packer, and later became manager of Leicestershire and then Lancashire. He scored a career total of 21,029 runs @ 56.22 with 60 centuries, including two triples and ten doubles.

Snow, John   Born Peopleton, Worcestershire, 13 October 1941. Hostile right-arm fast bowler for Sussex (1961-77) and England (1965-76), playing in 49 Tests and taking 202 wickets @ 26.66, and part-time poet. He took 27 wickets, including 7-49 in Kingston, in the West Indies in 1967/68, and 31 wickets in the 1970/71 series in Australia when the Ashes were regained. Banned for one Test for knocking Sunil Gavaskar over, he finished his career with 1174 wickets @ 22.72.

Sobers, Garfield   Born Bridgetown, Barbados, 28 July 1936. Perhaps the greatest of all-rounders – a magnificent left-hand middle-order batsman, fast-medium or spin (finger or wrist) left-arm bowler and splendid fielder for Barbados (1952/53 to 1973/74), South Australia (1961/62 to 1963/64), Nottinghamshire (1968-74) and West Indies (1953/54 to 1973/74). He played in 93 Test matches (39 as captain, then a record for his country), scoring 8032 runs @ 57.78 with 26 hundreds, including 365no v Pakistan (Kingston 1957/58), a world record in Tests for 36 years until beaten by Brian Lara. He also captured 235 wickets @ 34.03 and took 109 catches. Against England in 1966 he scored 722 runs @ 103.14 and took 20 wickets, and twice performed the Australian 'double' of 1000 runs and 50 wickets. For Nottinghamshire in 1968 he hit Malcolm Nash of Glamorgan for six sixes in one over at Swansea – the first player to do this and still one of only two to have done so. His career runs totalled 28,315 @ 54.87 with 86 hundreds, and he took in all 1043 wickets @ 27.74, his best analysis being 9-49 for West Indies v Kent (Canterbury 1966). He was knighted by the Queen in Barbados for his services to cricket, an accolade richly deserved and welcomed the world over.

Southerton, James   Born Petworth, Sussex, 16 November 1827. Right-arm slow bowler for Surrey (1854-79), Sussex (1858-72), Hampshire (1861-67) and England (1876/77). He remains, at 49 years 119 days, the oldest Test match debutant, playing in just two Tests and taking seven wickets for 107 runs. After a career which produced 1681 wickets @ 14.44, he became the first Test match cricketer to die, on 16 June 1880.

Spofforth, Fred   Born Balmain, New South Wales, 9 September 1853. Right-arm fast-medium bowler for New South Wales (1874/75 to 1884/85), Victoria (1885/86 to 1887/88), Derbyshire (1889-91) and Australia (1876/77 to 1886/87), and universally called 'The Demon' for his hostile and destructive bowling. He took 94 wickets @ 18.41 in his 18 Tests (all against England), and of his five tours to England, 207 wickets @ 12.82 in 1884 proved the most fruitful. He took in all 853 wickets @ 14.95, his best figures being 9-18 v Oxford University (Oxford 1886). He died 4 June 1926.

Statham, Brian   Born Manchester, 17 June 1930. Fine right-arm fast bowler for Lancashire (1950-68) and England (1950/51 to 1965). Playing in 70 Tests he took 252 wickets @ 24.84, often in tandem with

Trueman or Tyson, including a Test best analysis of 7-39 v S. Africa (Lord's 1955). His best figures for Lancashire, whom he captained from 1965 to 1967, were 8-34 (15-89 in the match) v Warwickshire (Coventry 1957). Taking in all 2260 wickets @ 16.37, he took 15 wickets in a match on two occasions and performed the hat-trick three times. He died 11 June 2000.

Stewart, Alec   Born Merton, Surrey, 8 April 1963. Right-hand middle-order or opening batsman and wicket-keeper for Surrey (debut 1981) and England (debut 1989/90). England's most-capped player after the Ashes series of 2002/03, with 126 appearances, he also in that series joined Gooch and Gower to become the third English player to exceed 8000 runs in Tests. His highest Test score was 190 v Pakistan (Birmingham 1990), and in first-class cricket his highest was 271no v Yorkshire (The Oval 1997) in a career total of over 25,000 runs at an average of almost 40. He also had over 700 victims to his credit – though some of these were not while keeping wicket – including 11 catches in a match v Leicestershire (Leicester 1989).

Streak, Heath   Born Bulawayo, Zimbabwe, 6 March 1974. Right-arm fast-medium bowler for Matabeleland (debut 1992/93), Hampshire (1995) and Zimbabwe (debut 1993/94). Easily the leading wicket-taker in Zimbabwe's short Test history with 180 wickets before his country's tour of England in 2003, he has also scored eight half-centuries in Tests as well as recently captaining the side.

Sutcliffe, Bert   Born Ponsonby, Auckland, New Zealand, 17 November 1923. Prolific and courageous left-hand opening batsman for Auckland (1941/42 to 1948/49), Otago (1946/47 to 1961/62), Northern Districts (1962/63 to 1965/66) and New Zealand (1946/47 to 1965). In 42 Tests his 2727 runs @ 40.10 included five hundreds, his highest being 230no v India (Delhi 1955/56). He scored in all 17,447 runs @ 47.41, with 44 centuries, including scores of 385 and 355 for Otago. On his two tours to England (1949 and 1958) he scored 2627 runs @ 59.70 and 1085 runs @ 31.00 respectively, and he was the mainstay of his country's batting in a period when it was not very strong. He died 20 April 2001.

Sutcliffe, Herbert   Born Harrogate, Yorkshire, 24 November 1894. Outstanding and imperturbable right-hand opening batsman for Yorkshire (1919-45) and England (1924-35). In his 54 Tests he scored 4555 runs, with 16 hundreds @ 60.73 – the highest Test batting average by any Englishman. His achievements are many; he scored 734 runs @ 81.55 in his first Ashes series in 1924/25, scoring two centuries at Melbourne, and 436 @ 87.20 in the 1930 rubber. He made over 1000 runs in each of his 21 full seasons (reaching 2000 14 times), with a highest score of 313 v Essex (Leyton 1932), putting on 555 for the first wicket with Percy Holmes – still a record in England for any wicket. His career total reached 50,138 runs @ 51.95, with 149 hundreds. He died 22 January 1978.

Swanton, E. W. ('Jim')   Born Forest Hill, London, 11 February 1907. Educated at Cranleigh, he worked for the London *Evening Standard* (originally to report on rugby) from 1927 to 1939, and played three matches for Middlesex in 1937 and 1938, scoring 67 runs (highest score 26). An artillery officer in World War II, he was captured at Singapore and spent from 1942 to 1945 in a Japanese prisoner-of-war camp in Thailand. In 1946 he became senior cricket correspondent of the *Daily Telegraph*, a post he held until 1975, although he contributed regularly (and authoritatively) to that newspaper for years thereafter. He was also editorial director of *The Cricketer* magazine from 1967 to 1988, and also organised and managed personally three cricket tours overseas – to the West Indies in 1956 and 1960, and to the Far East in 1964. He died 22 January 2000, always respected for his insistence on the importance of upholding standards in the game

Tate, Maurice   Born Brighton, Sussex, 30 May 1895. Wholehearted right-arm medium-fast bowler and attacking right-hand batsman for Sussex (1912-37) and England (1924-35). He played in 39 Tests, taking 4-12 and 5-83 on debut v S. Africa (Birmingham 1924) and 155 Test match wickets in all @ 26.16. He scored one Test century (v S. Africa, Lord's 1929) among his 1198 Test runs @ 25.48. In England he performed the 'double' eight times, and remains the only player to take 200 wickets and score 1000 runs in a season on three occasions. He scored in all 21,717 runs @ 25.04 (highest score 203 v Northamptonshire, Hove 1921) and took 2784 wickets @ 18.16, including 9-71 v Middlesex (Lord's 1926). He died 18 May 1956.

Taylor, Bob   Born Stoke-on-Trent, Staffs, 17 July 1941. Talented wicket-keeper and lower-order right-hand batsman for Derbyshire (1961-84) and England (1970/71 to 1983/84). His total of 1649 dismissals (1473 ct, 176 st) is a world record for a wicket-keeper. He played 57 Tests, claiming 174 victims, but his Test batting average of 16.28 weighed against him in the selectors' eyes; indeed he scored only one hundred in his 639 first-class matches, averaging 16.92 for his 12,065 career runs. Although officially retired, he came on briefly as substitute wicket-keeper in a Test match v New Zealand (Lord's 1986).

Taylor, Mark   Born Leeton, New South Wales, 27 October 1964. Dependable left-hand opening batsman for New South Wales (1985/86 to 1996/97) and Australia (1988/89 to 1998/99). He captained his country from the series against Pakistan in 1994/95 to the 1998/99 Ashes series, succeeding Allan Border and followed by Steve Waugh. In his 104 Test matches he scored 7525 runs @ 43.49 with 19 centuries, his highest being 334no v Pakistan (Peshawar 1998/99). Having thus equalled Bradman's highest individual innings by an Australian in Tests, he promptly declared! In England in 1989 he scored 839 runs @ 83.90 in the Ashes series, adding 329 – an Ashes record for the first wicket – with Graham Marsh at Nottingham. A fine slip fielder, he took a then record 157 Test catches, and retired after the 1998/99 series with a career total of 17,415 runs @ 41.95.

Tendulkar, Sachin   Born Bombay, India, 24 April 1973. One of the world's outstanding batsmen, a right-hand middle-order batsman for Bombay (debut 1988/89, scoring 100no v Gujarat aged 15 years 232 days), Yorkshire (1992) and India (debut 1989/90, aged 16). He had scored 9265 runs @ 57.19 in 111 Tests by the end of the 2003/04 tour of Australia, with a highest score of 241no at Sydney in that series, as well as 33 Test hundreds – second only to Sunil Gavaskar's 34. He has also scored over 13,000 runs in one-day internationals, and during the 2003 World Cup he became not only the highest run-scorer in its history, but also the highest scorer in any one World Cup (673).

Thomson, Jeff   Born Sydney, New South Wales, 16 August 1950. Right-arm very fast bowler for New South Wales (1972/73 to 1973/74), Queensland (1974/75 to 1985/86), Middlesex (1981) and Australia (1972/73 to 1985). He played in 51 Tests, taking 200 wickets (exactly half against England) @ 28.00, including 33 @ 17.93 v England in 1974/75 and 22 @ 18.68 in the 1982/83 Ashes series, as well as helping Australia to a 5-1 series win in the West Indies with 29 wickets @ 28.65. He took 675 wickets in first-class cricket @ 26.46.

Titmus, Fred   Born Kentish Town, London, 24 November 1932. All-rounder of some longevity – a right-arm off-break bowler and right-hand batsman for Middlesex (1949-82), Surrey (1978, one game) and England (1955 to 1974/75). He did the 'double' eight times, and took 100 wickets in a season 16 times, his best seasons with bat and ball being 1961 (1703 runs @ 37.02) and 1955 (191 wickets @ 16.31) respectively. His Test career (153 wickets @ 32.22 and 1449 runs @ 22.29) was virtually ended by a swimming accident in the Caribbean in 1967/68, when he lost four toes. He played for his county in five different decades, scoring in his career 21,588 runs and taking 2830 wickets @ 22.37.

Trueman, Fred   Born Stainton, Yorkshire, 6 February 1931. Hostile, extrovert right-arm fast bowler for Yorkshire (1949-68), Derbyshire (Sunday League games in 1972) and England (1952-65). The first bowler to take 300 wickets in Test matches, his 67 Tests produced 307 wickets @ 21.57, his best analysis being 8-31 v India (Manchester 1952). He took 100 wickets in a season 12 times, his best season being 1960 with 175 wickets @ 13.98, in addition to performing the hat-trick four times. He took in all 2304 wickets @ 18.29, scored three centuries, and was for many years a summariser on radio's *Test Match Special*.

Trumper, Victor   Born Sydney, New South Wales, 2 November 1877. Graceful right-hand opening batsman for New South Wales (1894/95 to 1913/14) and Australia (1899 to 1911/12), playing in 48 Tests and scoring 3163 runs @ 39.04, his eight hundreds included 214no v S. Africa (Adelaide 1910/11). In 1899 (a wet summer) he made 2570 runs in England @ 48.49 with 11 centuries, including 300no v Sussex at Hove. In the 1903/04 Ashes series he scored 574 runs @ 63.77, and 661 runs @ 94.42 v S. Africa in 1910/11. He died 28 June 1915, aged only 37, having made in all 16,939 runs @ 44.57 with 42 hundreds.

Turner, Glenn   Born Dunedin, New Zealand, 26 May 1947. Right-hand opening batsman for Otago (1964/65 to 1982/83), Northern Districts (1976/77), Worcestershire (1967-82) and New Zealand, scoring 2991 runs in his 41 Tests. Of his seven Test hundreds, his highest was 259 v West Indies (Georgetown 1971/72). The only New Zealander to score over 100 centuries (103), he scored two hundreds in a match four times, and made in all 34,346 runs @ 49.70, his highest score being 311no v Warwickshire (Worcester 1982). In 1977 he scored 141no in Worcestershire's total of 169 v Glamorgan at Swansea – a record 83.4 per cent of his county's total.

Tyson, Frank   Born Farnworth, Lancs, 6 June 1930. Devastatingly fast right-arm bowler for Northamptonshire (1952-60) and England (1954 to 1958/59), taking 76 wickets in his brief Test career @ 18.56, including 28 @ 20.82 in his first Ashes series (1954/55), when his 7-27 at Melbourne routed the Australian batting. Injury hampered his Test career, and on retiring to Australia he had taken 766 wickets in all @ 20.92.

Underwood, Derek Born Bromley, Kent, 8 June 1945. Accurate left-arm slow-medium spin bowler for Kent (1963-87) and England (1966 to 1981/82), his unerring line and length on damp turning wickets earning him the nickname of 'Deadly'. He took 297 wickets @ 25.83 in his Test career (86 matches), which was limited by his departure for World Series cricket (1977) and the SAB tour to South Africa in 1981/82. The youngest player to take 100 wickets in a debut season, he reached 1000 wickets aged only 25, his best figures being 9-28 v Sussex (Hastings 1964) and 9-32 v Surrey (The Oval 1978). He scored a maiden century aged 39, and retired having taken 2465 wickets @ 20.28.

Valentine, Alf Born Kingston, Jamaica, 28 April 1930. Tall, bespectacled left-arm spin bowler for Jamaica (1949/50 to 1964/65) and West Indies (1950 to 1961/62), who played in 36 Tests and took 139 wickets @ 30.32. Virtually unknown, with only two first-class games behind him, he toured England in 1950, claiming 33 wickets @ 20.42 in the four Tests (often bowling in tandem with Ramadhin) as well as 123 wickets @ 17.94 in all matches. He took 8-104 in the first Test at Manchester, his selection confirmed by his 13-67 in the previous match against Lancashire. Touring England again in 1957 and 1963, he never repeated his earlier success, and on retiring had taken altogether 475 wickets @ 26.21. He died 11 May 2004.

Vaughan, Michael Born Manchester, 29 October 1974. Right-hand opening batsman for Yorkshire (debut 1993) and England (debut 1999/2000 v S. Africa). In the calendar year 2002 he scored 1481 Test match runs @ 61.70, with six hundreds (one v Sri Lanka, three v India, two in Australia) – a record total by an English batsman, and the second-highest total in a year behind Vivian Richards. This was followed by another century (183) v Australia in the final Ashes Test of 2002/03. His highest Test score is 197 v India (Nottingham 2002), and he had scored 11 Test hundreds by the start of the 2004 season. Vaughan took over the England captaincy during 2003 and made an immediate impact with a 3-0 whitewash against New Zealand.

Vengsarkar, Dilip Born Bombay, India, 6 April 1956. Skilful right-hand middle-order batsman for Bombay (1975/76 to 1991/92) and India (1975/76 to 1991/92). The only player to score a hundred in each of his first three Lord's Tests (1979, 1982, 1986), he played in 116 Test matches, scoring 6868 runs @ 42.13 – only Gavaskar and Tendulkar have scored more runs for India – with 17 centuries. He scored in all 17,868 runs @ 52.86, with 55 hundreds, the highest being 284 for Bombay v Madhya Pradesh (Bombay 1991/92).

Venkataraghavan, Srinivasaraghavan Born Madras, India, 21 April 1945. Right-arm off-break bowler for Madras (later Tamil Nadu) (1963/64 to 1984/85), Derbyshire (1973/75) and India, playing in 57 Tests from 1964/65 to 1983/84 and taking 156 wickets @ 36.11, including 8-72 v New Zealand at Delhi in his debut series. He captained India in the 1975 World Cup and on the 1979 tour of England. His career total of 1390 wickets @ 24.14 included five or more wickets in an innings 85 times, his best figures being 9-93 for Indians v Hampshire (Bournemouth 1971). He has since umpired in numerous Test matches.

Verity, Hedley Born Leeds, Yorkshire, 18 May 1905. The leading left-arm spin bowler for Yorkshire (1930-39) and England (1931-39) in the decade before World War II, he took 144 wickets @ 24.37 in 40 Tests, including 15-104 in the Lord's Test v Australia in 1934. His best analysis for Yorkshire was a world record 10-10 v Nottinghamshire (Leeds 1931), and he took all ten wickets on one other occasion as well as nine in an innings seven times. He captured, in his ten seasons, 1956 wickets @ 14.90, and two days before war was declared he took 7-9 v Sussex at Hove. He died 31 July 1943 of wounds received in Sicily leading his company of the Green Howards.

Walcott, Clyde Born St Michael, Barbados, 17 January 1926. Powerful right-hand middle-order batsman and wicket-keeper for Barbados (1941/42 to 1955/56), British Guiana (1954/55 to 1963/64) and West Indies (1947/48 to 1959/60), playing in 44 Tests, scoring 3798 runs @ 56.68 with 15 centuries, and making 64 dismissals. Aged only 20, he scored 314no for Barbados v Trinidad at Port of Spain in 1945/46, adding 574 for the fourth wicket with Frank Worrell. Against Australia in 1954/55 he scored 827 runs @ 82.70, with five hundreds in the series. In his career he totalled 11,820 runs @ 56.55, and he was knighted in 1994.

Walsh, Courtney Born Kingston, Jamaica, 30 October 1962. Consistently hostile right-arm fast bowler for Jamaica (1981/82 to 2000/01), Gloucestershire (1984-96 and 1998) and West Indies (1984/85 to 2000/01), and a respected captain of each of these teams. The first bowler to take 500 wickets in Tests, his 519 wickets @ 24.44 include best figures of 7-37 (13-55 in the match) v New Zealand (Wellington 1994/95), and a hat-trick v Australia (Brisbane 1988/89). For Gloucestershire he took 118 wickets @ 18.17 in 1986, including his best analysis of 9-72 v Somerset at Bristol.

Waqar Younis Born Vehari, Pakistan, 16 November 1971. Right-arm fast bowler for Multan (1987/88 to 1990/91 and 1997/98), United Bank (1988/89 to 1996/97), Rawalpindi (1998/99), Redso (debut 1999), Surrey (1990/91 and 1993), Glamorgan (1997/98) and Pakistan (debut 1989/90). With a devastating yorker and command of reverse swing, he retired in 2004 after taking 373 wickets @ 23.56 in his 87 Tests and over 400 in one-day internationals. He took 29 wickets in a three-match series v New Zealand in 1990/91 and 22 wickets in the 1992 series in England, captaining the side in England in 2001. His best analyses are 7-76 in Test matches (v New Zealand, Faisalabad 1990-91) and in all matches 8-17 (Glamorgan v Sussex, Swansea 1997).

Wardle, Johnny Born Ardsley, Yorkshire, 8 January 1923. Talented left-arm finger- and wrist-spinner for Yorkshire (1946-58) and England (1947/48 to 1957), playing in 28 Test matches and taking 102 wickets @ 20.39 – the lowest post-war average for any England bowler with over 100 wickets. He twice took nine wickets in an innings in 1954 (v Lancashire and Sussex), and he claimed in all 1846 wickets @ 18.97 before controversial newspaper articles published under his name ended his career. He died 23 July 1985.

Warne, Shane Born Ferntree Gully, Victoria, 13 September 1969. Peerless right-arm leg-spin bowler for Victoria (debut 1990/91), Hampshire (2000, 2004) and Australia (debut 1991/92). With his first Test delivery in England, he dismissed Mike Gatting with the 'ball of the century' (Manchester 1993), a series in which he took 34 wickets @ 25.79 and revived the art of the leg-spinner. His best Test analysis is 8-71 v England (Brisbane 1994/95) – he took a hat-trick v

England in Melbourne in the same series. His highest Test score is 99 (v New Zealand, Perth 2001/02). Any addition to his Test match wickets haul of 491 @ 25.71 was frustrated by a 12-month ban imposed before the 2003 World Cup; Warne had tested positive for using a prohibited substance after overcoming the effects of surgery on a damaged shoulder. He returned to Test cricket in 2003/04 in Sri Lanka and took 10 wickets in each of his first two Tests, becoming the second bowler after Courtney Walsh to claim 500 Test victims when he dismissed H.P. Tillekeratne in Kandy.

Washbrook, Cyril Born Barrow (near Clitheroe), Lancashire, 6 December 1914. Reliable right-hand opening batsman for Lancashire (1933-59) and England (1937-56). Len Hutton's opening partner for several post-war seasons, he scored 2569 runs @ 42.81 in his 37 Tests. His six Test hundreds included 195 v S. Africa (Johannesburg 1948/49), when he added 359 with Hutton – still an England first-wicket record. His career total was 34,101 runs @ 42.67, with 76 hundreds, the highest being 251no v Surrey (Manchester 1947). He died 27 April 1999.

Wasim Akram Born Lahore, Pakistan, 3 June 1966. Outstanding left-arm fast bowler and left-hand middle-order batsman for PACO (1984/85 to 1985/86), Lahore (1985/86 to 1986/87), PIA (debut 1987/88), Lancashire (1988/98), Hampshire (2003) and Pakistan (debut 1984/85). The only player so far to have taken 400 wickets in both Tests and one-day internationals, he claimed his 500th victim in the latter during the 2003 World Cup. His best Test match analysis is 7-119 v New Zealand (Wellington 1993/94), he took two hat-tricks (in consecutive Tests) v Sri Lanka in 1998-99, and he scored 257no v Zimbabwe (Sheikhupura 1996/97), adding a world Test record for the eighth wicket of 313 with Saqlain Mushtaq. His 374 wickets @ 21.65 for Lancashire included 8-30 v Somerset (Southport 1994) and a hat-trick v Surrey (Southport 1988). He also holds the record for appearances in World Cup matches (38) and wickets taken in that competition (55).

Waugh, Mark Born Sydney, New South Wales, 2 June 1965. Right-hand middle-order batsman for New South Wales (debut 1985/86), Essex (1988-90, 1992, 1995, 2002) and Australia (debut 1990/91). The third Australian batsman to score 8000 runs in Test cricket, he also holds the world record for catches in Tests by a fielder – 181. His highest Test score is 153no v India (Bangalore 1997/98), and his highest first-class innings 229no for New South Wales v W. Australia (Perth 1990/91), adding 464 with twin brother Steve – a record in all cricket for the fifth wicket.

Waugh, Steve Born Sydney, New South Wales, 2 June 1965. Prolific right-hand middle-order batsman and inspirational captain for New South Wales (debut 1985/86), Somerset (1987/88), Kent (2002) and Australia (1985/86 to 2003/04), and twin brother of Mark. In the 2002/03 Ashes series he became only the third player (and second Australian) to score 10,000 runs in Test cricket; he made his 29th Test hundred in that series to equal Bradman's tally, finishing with 32 – only Gavaskar having made more. In April 2003 he set a record by playing in his 157th Test match (v West Indies at Georgetown), finally totalling 168. His top Test score is 200 v West Indies (Kingston 1994/95), and he captained Australia to World Cup victory in 1999. His Test career yielded 10,927 runs @ 51.06, 92 wickets @ 37.44 and 112 catches, with his final Test appearance (at the Sydney Cricket Ground) drawing huge and adoring crowds. He also played in 325 one-day internationals, scoring 7569 runs @ 32.90 with three centuries.

Weekes, Everton Born St Michael, Barbados, 26 February 1925. Pugnacious and free-scoring middle-order batsman for Barbados (1944/45 to 1963/64) and West Indies (1947/48 to 1957/58), appearing in 48 Tests and scoring 4455 runs @ 58.61, with 15 hundreds – five in succession (v England and India). His career total of 12,010 runs @ 55.34 included 304no v Cambridge University at Fenner's in 1950, when his tour of England produced 2310 runs @ 79.65. In 1995 he became the third of the 'Three Ws' to be knighted.

Willis, Bob Born Sunderland, 30 May 1949. Tall (1.98m) right-arm fast bowler for Surrey (1969-71), Warwickshire (1972-84), Northern Transvaal (1972/73) and England (1970/71 to 1984). His total of 325 wickets for England is second only to Ian Botham's, and his 8-43 in the 1981 Ashes Test at Leeds completed England's astounding victory. Captaining his country 18 times, his two Ashes series (1977 and 1981) produced 27 wickets @ 19.77 and 29 @ 22.96 respectively, and he took 899 wickets in all @ 24.99 apiece.

Wisden, John Born Brighton, Sussex, 5 September 1826. Medium-pace round-arm bowler for Sussex, Kent and Middlesex between 1845 and 1863, and producer of the first *John Wisden's Cricketers' Almanack* in 1864. He is also the only bowler to have taken 10 wickets in an innings all bowled (North v South, Lord's 1850). He died 5 April 1884.

Woodfull, Bill Born Malson, Victoria, 22 August 1887. Nicknamed 'The Unbowlable': right-hand opening batsman for Victoria (1921/22 to 1933/34) and Australia (1926-34), playing in 35 Tests (25 as captain) and scoring 2300 runs @ 46.00, with seven centuries, the highest being 161 v S. Africa (Melbourne 1931/32). He also batted courageously in the controversial 'bodyline' series of 1932/33, despite the hostile attentions of Larwood and Voce. Seven of his 49 first-class hundreds were doubles (including 228no v Glamorgan, Swansea 1934), and he shared an opening partnership of 375 with Ponsford for Victoria v New South Wales (Melbourne 1926/27). He died 11 August 1965.

Woolley, Frank Born Tonbridge, Kent, 27 May 1887. Left-hand middle-order batsman, left-arm spin bowler and brilliant slip fielder for Kent (1909-34) and England (1909-34). The complete all-rounder, his total of 58,969 first-class runs @ 40.75 is bettered only by Jack Hobbs, while he took 2068 wickets @ 19.85 and his 1018 catches far outnumber anyone else's. His eight 'doubles' include, uniquely, four seasons yielding 2000 runs and 100 wickets, and in scoring 1000 runs in a season 28 times he is equalled only by W.G. Grace. He played in 64 Tests, scoring 3283 runs @ 36.07 with five hundreds, and taking 83 wickets @ 33.91. He died 18 October 1978 at the age of 91.

Worrell, Frank Born Bridgetown, Barbados, 1 August 1924. Elegant right-hand opening and then middle-order batsman, and left-arm medium-pace bowler, for Barbados (1941/42 to 1946/47), Jamaica (1947/48 to 1963/64) and West Indies. Appearing in 51 Tests (15 as captain) between 1947/48 and 1963, he scored 3860 runs @ 49.48 with nine centuries, the highest being 261 v England (Nottingham 1950). He also took 69 Test wickets @ 38.72. His career runs totalled 15,025 @ 54.24 with 39 hundreds, and

C
R
I
C
K
E
T

he took 349 wickets @ 28.98. The first coloured captain of West Indies for more than one match, he was knighted in 1964 but died of leukaemia on 13 March 1967 aged only 42.

Zaheer Abbas   Born Sialkot, India, 24 July 1947. Attractive and prolific right-hand middle-order batsman for Karachi, PWD, PIA, Sind and Dawood Club between 1965/66 and 1986/87, Gloucestershire (1972-85) and Pakistan (1969/70 to 1985/86). In his second Test match (v England, Birmingham 1971) he scored 274, and his fourth Test double hundred (215 v India, Lahore 1982/83) was his 100th first-class century, making him the first (and so far the only) Pakistan batsman to reach this landmark. He scored two centuries in a match eight times – a world record – and on four of these occasions (all for Gloucestershire) he scored a hundred and a double hundred in the same match (being undefeated in each innings), also a world record. The first Pakistan player to score 5000 Test runs, he scored 5062 @ 44.79, and in his career he totalled 34,843 runs – also a record for a Pakistani batsman – @ 51.54.

CROQUET

games in which a ball was knocked around a course of hoops or obstacles with a mallet were popular in 17th and 18th century France. One of them, *paille maille* ('ball-mallet'), was introduced to London, where it was played in open ground near St James's Palace. The area later became known as Pall Mall, which also gave its name to a nearby street.

During the 1830s, a French doctor developed a new version of the sport as a form of outdoor exercise for his patients. He named it 'croquet', from the French word for a crooked stick, and it was widely played at spas in the South of France. It is likely that English visitors discovered it there and brought it back to their country. Several accounts, however, say that croquet came to England from Ireland in the 1850s, so perhaps the game was first brought from France to Ireland before moving on to England.

The Wimbledon All England Croquet Club, founded in 1868, established the first standardised rules. Croquet was very popular in England until lawn tennis was introduced in 1877. Many of the croquet lawns at Wimbledon were then converted to tennis courts and the club was renamed the Wimbledon All England Lawn Tennis and Croquet Club. The National Croquet Association (NCA), founded in 1879, held its first national tournament in 1882.

While English lawn croquet was played at scattered locations, an American form of croquet had evolved into a very different game from the rather sedate English version. It was played on a court of hard-packed dirt, with hard rubber balls, very narrow wickets, and short mallets. The court was enclosed by a wooden barricade to keep the lively balls on the field of play. In 1899, a new set of rules was standardised for the American version, which was given a new name: roque, formed by clipping the first and last letters from 'croquet'. Like billiards but unlike lawn croquet, roque requires skill in making cannon shots off the boundary board and in the use of side spin to change the path of the shot.

During the early part of the 20th century, roque became the dominant form of the sport in the USA. A new governing body, the American Roque League, was founded in 1916, while the NCA became dormant for many years. Roque reached its peak of popularity during the 1930s, when courts were built at many of the parks and playgrounds constructed by the National Recreation Association and the Works Progress Administration during the Depression. The American Roque League still operates, but its membership is concentrated in the Midwest.

Lawn croquet made something of a comeback during the 1920s, at least among wealthy people

playing on large, flat lawns at estates on Long Island and in Hollywood, the two major hotbeds. Croquet was frequently mentioned in Broadway and movie gossip columns because of the names involved. Among its well-known players were Harpo Marx, George S. Kaufman and Moss Hart of Broadway fame, Hollywood producers Sam Goldwyn, Howard Hawks and Darryl Zanuck, and composer Richard Rodgers – all of whom are now in the Croquet Hall of Fame.

American lawn croquet uses nine hoops (wickets), while British lawn croquet uses only six. Interest in six-hoop croquet was revived during the 1970s. Jack Osborn organised six Eastern clubs into the United States Croquet Association in 1977 and wrote a new rule book for an American version of the sport. In the meantime, the British six-hoop version, often known as 'Association croquet', was evolving into an international sport, played primarily in the British Commonwealth countries: Australia, Great Britain, Ireland, New Zealand, and South Africa.

Yet another governing body, the American Croquet Association (ACA), was founded in 1987 to promote the international form of the sport. Most ACA members also belong to the USCA, and the USCA sanctions many tournaments played under international rules, as well as those played under American rules. In order to promote the sport in general, the USCA promulgates rules for four different versions of croquet: backyard nine-hoop, American six-hoop, international six-hoop, and golf croquet, which uses the nine-hoop layout.

It takes a good deal of experience to reach the top level of croquet play; an unusual combination of physical skills are required, along with strategic and tactical planning. In this respect, croquet resembles billiards more than any other sport. The ability to make shots is only a fraction of the game.

Croquet was on the Olympic programme in 1900, but only French players participated. Roque was included as an Olympic sport at St Louis in 1904, when all the players were from the United States. Some historians have dismissed that as a national championship disguised as an Olympic event, however.

The MacRobertson International Trophy (commonly known as the MacRobertson Shield) is competed for by Great Britain, New Zealand, Australia and the USA. It is held every three or four years. The last competition took place in Palm Beach, Florida in November 2003 and the next will be held in Australia in November 2006.

Association croquet is played with four balls – red, yellow, black and blue – and can be played as singles or doubles. Red and yellow always plays against blue and black (in doubles one partner plays red and the other yellow, in singles competitors play both red and yellow). The object of the game is to get both balls around a course of six hoops twice in a set order, and finish by hitting the centre peg (which has given us the phrase 'pegging out'). The side which first completes this course with both balls wins the game.

A ball scores a hoop point when it passes right through each hoop in its correct order in one or more strokes. Thus the winning side has 26 points to score − 12 hoop points and the peg point with each ball. The point is scored whether the ball is struck directly with the mallet or with another ball. Clips coloured to match the balls are placed on the hoops or peg to indicate the next point for each ball. The clips are placed on the crown of the hoop for the first six hoops and on the side for the second circuit.

A turn usually consists of one stroke only, but extra strokes can be earned in two ways: 1) If the player's ball runs its next hoop, they are entitled to another stroke; 2) If the player's ball hits another ball they place their own ball in contact with the other ball where it comes to rest and then strike their own ball so that the other ball moves. After this the player is entitled to one further stroke. Every turn the player may roquet and then take croquet from each of the other three balls once; however, each time their ball runs its next hoop they may roquet the other balls once more. Thus, by a combination of taking croquet and running hoops, many hoops can be run in a turn and breaks can be built.

A turn ends either when a player has made all the strokes to which they are entitled, or if a ball is sent off the court in a croquet stroke, or if a fault is made as defined in the Laws. A turn does not necessarily end if a ball is sent off the court in any stroke other than the croquet stroke.

After each stroke, any ball which has bee[n] sent off court is placed a yard inside the bound[-]ary nearest to where it went off. Any ball lyin[g] between the boundary and the yard-line (a gre[en] line inside the white boundary line on which ball[s] are replaced after going off court), except th[e] player's own ball, is also replaced on the yard line. At the end of a turn the striker's ball i[s] brought on to the yard-line if it lies within the yard line or had left the court.

When a ball has scored its last hoop point can score the peg point either by the player hittin[g] it on to the peg or by being hit on to the peg b[y] another rover ball. The ball is thus pegged ou[t] and removed from court.

The court is a flat grass area measuring 28yd[s] (25.6m) by 35yds (32m). The peg is 18in (45.7m) tall above ground and 1½ins (3.8cm) i[n] diameter with a smaller dowel extension abou[t] ½in (1.3cm) diameter and 6ins (15cm) lon[g] plugged in the top. The extension may be tem[-] porarily removed if it impedes the striker. The pe[g] is in the centre of the lawn.

Championship hoops are made of ⅝in (1.6cm[)] diameter metal forming a 12ins (30.5cm) hig[h] hoop with a straight top. The gape of the hoop i[s] approximately 3¾ins (10cm) between the jaw[s] (⅛in wider than the balls). Hoops are bare met[al] or painted white, the first hoop having a blue to[p] and the last hoop (rover) having a red to[p] Championship balls are 3⅝ins (9.2cm) in diame[-] ter and weigh 16oz (454g).

Mallets must have parallel and identical end faces made of wood or other material givin[g] similar properties.

The World Croquet Federation (WCF) is th[e] international governing body for croquet. Set up i[n] 1986 it held its first world championships in 1989 although the Open Championship inaugurated i[n] 1897 is still considered by many as the true worl[d] championship.

The Open Championship Winners

Year	Winner	Year	Winner	Year	Winner
1897	C.E. Willis	1921	Leslie O'Callaghan	1947	Humphrey Hicks
1898	Clement Powell	1922	C.E. Pepper	1948	Humphrey Hicks
1899	B.C. Evelagh	1923	H.W.J. Snell	1949	Humphrey Hicks
1900	J.E. Austin	1924	David Joseph	1950	Humphrey Hicks
1901	R.N. Roper	1925	D.D. Steel	1951	Geoffrey Reckitt
1902	Cyril Corbally	1926	Ben Apps	1952	Humphrey Hicks
1903	Cyril Corbally	1927	Duff Mathews	1953	John Solomon
1904	Reginald Beaton	1928	K.H. Coxe	1954	Arthur Ross
1905	Lily Gower	1929	William Du Pre	1955	Patrick Cotter
1906	Cyril Corbally	1930	Ben Apps	1956	John Solomon
1907	Reginald Beaton	1931	Ben Apps	1957	Bobby Wiggins
1908	Cyril Corbally	1932	Humphrey Hicks	1958	Patrick Cotter
1909	G. Ashmore	1933	D.D. Steel	1959	John Solomon
1910	Leslie O'Callaghan	1934	William Du Pre	1960	Hope Rotherham
1911	Edgar Whitaker	1935	D.D. Steel	1961	John Solomon
1912	Leslie O'Callaghan	1936	D.D. Steel	1962	Patrick Cotter
1913	Cyril Corbally	1937	Charles Colman	1963	John Solomon
1914	Duff Mathews	1938	Dudley Hamilton-Miller	1964	John Solomon
1919	Duff Mathews	1939	Humphrey Hicks	1965	John Solomon
1920	Duff Mathews	1946	Dudley Hamilton-Miller	1966	John Solomon

1967	John Solomon	1980	William Prichard	1993	Reg Bamford
1968	John Solomon	1981	David Openshaw	1994	Reg Bamford
1969	Nigel Aspinall	1982	Nigel Aspinall	1995	Reg Bamford
1970	Keith Wylie	1983	Nigel Aspinall	1996	Robert Fulford
1971	Keith Wylie	1984	Nigel Aspinall	1997	Chris Clarke
1972	Bernard Neal	1985	David Openshaw	1998	Robert Fulford
1973	Bernard Neal	1986	Joe Hogan	1999	Reg Bamford
1974	Nigel Aspinall	1987	Mark Avery	2000	Stephen Mulliner
1975	Nigel Aspinall	1988	Stephen Mulliner	2001	Reg Bamford
1976	Nigel Aspinall	1989	Joe Hogan	2002	Reg Bamford
1977	Michael Heap	1990	Stephen Mulliner	2003	Robert Fulford
1978	Nigel Aspinall	1991	Robert Fulford	2004	Robert Fulford
1979	David Openshaw	1992	Robert Fulford		

World Rankings
(as at September 2004)

1 Robert Fulford (ENG)
2 Reg Bamford (RSA)
3 Trevor Bassett (AUS)
4 Peter trimmer (ENG)
5 Jacques Fournier (USA)
6 David Maugham (ENG)
7 Toby Garrison (NZL)
8 Bob Jackson (NZL)
9 Mark Avery (ENG)
10 Jeremy Dyer (ENG)

Olympic Medallists

Singles – One Ball

Gold	Silver	Bronze
1900 Aumoitte (FRA)	Johin (FRA)	Waydelich (FRA)

Singles – Two Ball

Gold	Silver	Bronze
1900 Waydelich (FRA)	Vignerotte (FRA)	Sautareau (FRA)

Doubles

Gold	Silver	Bronze
1900 Aumoitte/Johin (FRA)	—	—

Roque

Gold	Silver	Bronze
1904 Charles Jacobus (USA)	Smith Streeter (USA)	Charles Brown (USA)

WCF World Championships

	Winner	Runner-up	Venue
1989	Joe Hogan	Mark Avery	Hurlingham
1990	Robert Fulford	Mark Saurin	Hurlingham
1991	John Walters	David Openshaw	Hurlingham
1992	Robert Fulford	John Walters	Newport, USA
1994	Robert Fulford	Chris Clarke	Carden Park
1995	Chris Clarke	Robert Fulford	Fontenay le Comte, France
1997	Robert Fulford	Stephen Mulliner	Bunbury, Australia
2001	Reg Bamford	Robert Fulford	Hurlingham
2002	Robert Fulford	Toby Garrison	Wellington, New Zealand

CROQUET

CURLING

In 1565, the Flemish artist Pieter Brueghel (the Elder) painted *Hunters in the Snow* and another work depicting scenes that resemble modern curling. Breughel's paintings support the premise held by some that curling originated in continental Europe, possibly in Holland. As with golf, however, the Scots are the undisputed developers of the modern game. Like golf, curling is both a recreational and an athletic pastime, marked by a strong code of fair play and courtesy. By the 19th century, curling was played by thousands in nearly every Scottish parish. Unfortunately, between the 16th and 20th centuries, Scotland's climate warmed, until today the lochs rarely freeze. The climate change hindered curlers, who played outdoors on natural ice until the 20th century. Nonetheless the Scots had, by the mid-1800s, formalised curling's rules of play and equipment and had established the 'mother club' of curlers worldwide, the Royal Caledonian Curling Club (RCCC). Founded in 1838 as the Grand Caledonian Curling Club, it was given the 'Royal' prefix by Queen Victoria in 1842 after the game was demonstrated to her on the polished floor of the Palace of Scone. The Prince Consort was presented with a pair of curling stones and became patron of the club. The RCCC is today the national governing body of curling in Scotland, with 20,000 active members now playing indoors on refrigerated ice.

The game of curling spread throughout the world through the efforts of thousands of Scottish soldiers and émigrés. In North America, curling's origins probably date to the late 1700s. The first documented record is the founding of the Montreal Curling Club in 1807. In 1832, the Orchard Lake Curling Club, near Detroit, became the first curling club in the United States. Organised at the home of Dr Robert Burns, the Orchard Lake group curled on Lake St Clair. The oldest continuously operating curling club in the United States is the Milwaukee, Wisconsin club, founded in 1845. The largest is the St Paul, Minnesota club, with over 700 members. The United States Curling Association (founded 1958) governs curling in the USA. The USCA is a member of the US Olympic Committee and the World Curling Federation, and has 131 member clubs in 11 regions.

Raymond 'Bud' Somerville, of Superior, Wisconsin, the first inductee into the USCA's Hall of Fame, led his team to its first world championship in 1965, at the age of 28. In 1992, at the age of 55, he skipped his team to a bronze medal in a demonstration competition at the Albertville Olympics. Curling debuted as a medal sport in the 1998 Winter Olympic Games in Japan. Today about 1.5 million people in over 33 countries curl. Curling is often called 'the roaring game' because of the sound made by the stones as they speed towards the tee. There were plenty of roars in Scotland during the 2002 Winter Olympics in Salt Lake City, when Rhona Martin, the Great Britain skip, delivered a perfect final stone to win the first gold medal for Britain since 1984, beating Switzerland 4-3 in the women's curling final. The rest of the Scottish gold medal-winning team were Debbie Knox, Fiona Macdonald, Margaret Morton, and Janice Rankin. Scotland has also produced three world champions: Chuck Hay in the 1960s, David Smith in 1991 and Hammy McMillan in 1999.

The 42lb (19.05kg) granite stones are propelled from a starting block called a hack, or crampit, toward a target at the other end of the ice called the house. The house consists of a series of concentric circles within a 6ft (1.83m) radius from the centre, called the tee, and 38yds (34.74m) from the hack. Two sweepers, equipped with curling brooms or brushes, glide along with the stone and help determine its speed and path by sweeping the ice in front of it to reduce the friction of the moving stone. This manoeuvre is called 'sooping'. The captain, or skip, of the four-person team, determines the strategy of play by calling the shots to be attempted and instructing the sweepers on how to influence the shot's path. The other members of a team, or rink, include the vice-skip, the second and the lead. Each player has two stones per end and plays them alternately with their opponents. A line seven yards from the tee is called the hog-score and any stone not clearing this line is called a hog and removed from the rink. When all 16 stones have been played, each stone lying nearer the centre of the tee than an opposing stone scores a point.

Top curling nations include Australia, Canada, China, France, New Zealand, Scotland, Sweden, Switzerland and the USA.

CYCLING

aron Karl de Draise de Sauerbrun invented the rerunner of the modern bicycle in 1817. The eculiar machine, variously called the Draisienne, aufmaschine, Hobby Horse or Dandy Horse, ad no pedals and on flat ground it was necesary to walk or run astride it.

Earlier machines had been tricycles or four-heeled vehicles, a famous machine being that uilt by Francois Blanchard and M. Masurier in 779. Another Frenchman named de Sivrac is ought to have invented a Célérifère (Celeripede English) in 1790 but this was not commercially eveloped. In 1839 Kirkpatrick Macmillan (1810-3) introduced a system of pedal-driven rear heel although this was never patented or develoed.

In 1845 R.W. Thomson patented a pneumatic re long before J.B. Dunlop's invention, but once gain this went unheralded and largely unnoticed.

1861 Pierre Michaux fitted a crankshaft and edals to the front wheel of a hobby horse and is Michaulines or Vélocifère (velocipede) was ie first machine to resemble the modern bicycle.

The earliest recorded bicycle race was a velociede race over 2km held at the Parc de St-Cloud, aris, on 31 May 1868. It was won by Dr James loore (1847-1935) of Great Britain. This race opularised cycling and Rowley Turner persuaded s uncle at the Coventry Sewing Machine Co to egin making velocipedes later in 1868.

In 1870 the Ariel Ordinary bicycle was patented by James Starley and William Hillman of Coventry, West Midlands. It was the first British all-metal bicycle to be produced in quantity. It sold for £8 and had lever-tension wheels which allowed the spokes to be adjusted. For 15 years the ordinary (penny-farthing) was the most popular cycle of its era but the huge front wheel caused many accidents.

In 1873 John Keen, a world champion cyclist, added brakes for the front wheel and in 1874 James Starley introduced tangential spokes to give a more even distribution of load than the straight spokes used previously. In 1876 the boneshaker became predominant as a practice bike; it had no rubber tyres and was consequently very slow but was therefore perceived as safer for novices, particularly as its wheels were quite small.

Organised races were now commonplace and in 1893 Henri Desgrange set a one-hour record of 21.9 miles (35.24km) at the concrete Buffalo velodrome in Paris. The world sprint championship began in 1895 and the first of the great stage races, the Tour de France, was founded by Desgrange in 1903. Bicycle innovation and development has never ceased and a record of racing achievements of all the various cycle-related personalities and disciplines are included in the following text.

Tour de France

903	Maurice Garin (FRA)	Lucien Pothier (FRA)	Fernand Augereau (FRA)
904	Henri Cornet (FRA)	J.B. Dortignacq (FRA)	Alois Catteau (FRA)
905	Louis Trousselier (FRA)	Hyppolite Aucouturiér (FRA)	J.B. Dortignacq (FRA)
906	René Pottier (FRA)	Georges Passerieu (FRA)	Louis Trousselier (FRA)
907	Lucien Petit-Breton (FRA)	Gustave Garrigou (FRA)	Louis Trousselier (FRA)
908	Lucien Petit-Breton (FRA)	Francois Faber (LUX)	Emile Georget (FRA)
909	Francois Faber (LUX)	Gustave Garrigou (FRA)	Jean Alavoine (FRA)
910	Octave Lapize (FRA)	Francois Faber (LUX)	Gustave Garrigou (FRA)
911	Gustave Garrigou (FRA)	Paul Duboc (FRA)	Emile Georget (FRA)
912	Odile Defraye (BEL)	Eugène Christophe (FRA)	Gustave Garrigou (FRA)
913	Philippe Thijs (BEL)	Gustave Garrigou (FRA)	Marcel Buysse (BEL)
914	Philippe Thijs (BEL)	Henri Pelissier (FRA)	Jean Alavoine (FRA)
915-18	not held		
919	Firmin Lambot (BEL)	Jean Alavoine (FRA)	Eugène Christophe (FRA)
920	Philippe Thijs (BEL)	Hector Heuseghem (BEL)	Firmin Lambot (BEL)
921	Leon Scieur (BEL)	Hector Heuseghem (BEL)	Honore Barthelemy (FRA)
922	Firmin Lambot (BEL)	Jean Alavoine (FRA)	Felix Sellier (FRA)
923	Henri Pelissier (FRA)	Ottavia Bottechia (ITA)	Romain Bellenger (FRA)
924	Ottavio Botecchia (ITA)	Nicolas Frantz (LUX)	Lucien Buysse (BEL)
925	Ottavio Botecchia (ITA)	Lucien Buysse (BEL)	Bartolomeo Aymo (ITA)
926	Lucien Buysse (BEL)	Nicolas Frantz (LUX)	Bartolomeo Aymo (ITA)
927	Nicolas Frantz (LUX)	Maurice Dewaele (BEL)	Julien Vervaecke (BEL)
928	Nicolas Frantz (LUX)	Andre Leducq (FRA)	Maurice Dewaele (BEL)
929	Maurice Dewaele (BEL)	Giuseppe Pancera (ITA)	Jos Demuysere (BEL)
930	Andre Leducq (FRA)	Learco Guerra (ITA)	Antonin Magne (FRA)

1931	Antonin Magne (FRA)	Jos Demuysere (BEL)	Antonio Pesenti (ITA)
1932	Andre Leducq (FRA)	Kurt Stoepel (GER)	Francesco Camusse (ITA)
1933	Georges Speicher (FRA)	Learco Guerra (ITA)	Giuseppe Martano (ITA)
1934	Antonin Magne (FRA)	Giuseppe Martano (ITA)	Roger Lapebie (FRA)
1935	Romain Maes (BEL)	Ambrogio Morelli (ITA)	Felicien Vervaecke (BEL)
1936	Sylvere Maes (BEL)	Antonin Magne (FRA)	Felicien Vervaecke (BEL)
1937	Roger Lapebie (FRA)	Mario Vicini (ITA)	Leo Amberg (SUI)
1938	Gino Bartali (ITA)	Felicien Vervaecke (BEL)	Victor Cosson (FRA)
1939	Sylvere Maes (BEL)	Reno Vietto (FRA)	Lucien Vlaeminck (BEL)
1940-46	not held		
1947	Jean Robic (FRA)	Ed Fachleitner (FRA)	Pierre Brambilla (ITA)
1948	Gino Bartali (ITA)	Briek Schotte (BEL)	Guy Lapébie (FRA)
1949	Fausto Coppi (ITA)	Gino Bartali (ITA)	Jacques Marinelli (FRA)
1950	Ferdi Kübler (SUI)	Stan Ockers (BEL)	Louison Bobet (FRA)
1951	Hugo Koblet (SUI)	Raphael Geminiani (FRA)	Lucien Lazaridès (FRA)
1952	Fausto Coppi (ITA)	Stan Ockers (BEL)	Bernardo Ruiz (ESP)
1953	Louison Bobet (FRA)	Jean Malléjac (FRA)	Giancarlo Astrua (ITA)
1954	Louison Bobet (FRA)	Ferdi Kübler (SUI)	Fritz Schaer (SUI)
1955	Louison Bobet (FRA)	Jean Brankart (BEL)	Charly Gaul (LUX)
1956	Roger Walkowiak (FRA)	Gilbert Bauvin (FRA)	Jan Adriaenssens (BEL)
1957	Jacques Anquetil (FRA)	Marc Janssens (BEL)	Adolf Christian (AUT)
1958	Charly Gaul (LUX)	Vito Favero (ITA)	Raphael Geminiani (FRA)
1959	Federico Bahamontes (ESP)	Henri Anglade (FRA)	Jacques Anquetil (FRA)
1960	Gaston Nencini (ITA)	Graziano Battistini (ITA)	Jan Adriaenssens (BEL)
1961	Jacques Anquetil (FRA)	Guido Carlesi (ITA)	Charly Gaul (LUX)
1962	Jacques Anquetil (FRA)	Jef Planckaert (BEL)	Raymond Poulidor (FRA)
1963	Jacques Anquetil (FRA)	Federico Bahamontes (ESP)	Jose Perez-Frances (ESP)
1964	Jacques Anquetil (FRA)	Raymond Poulidor (FRA)	Federico Bahamontes (ESP)
1965	Felice Gimondi (ITA)	Raymond Poulidor (FRA)	Gianni Motta (ITA)
1966	Lucien Aimar (FRA)	Jan Janssen (NED)	Raymond Poulidor (FRA)
1967	Roger Pingeon (FRA)	Julio Jimenez (ESP)	Franco Balmanion (ITA)
1968	Jan Janssen (NED)	Herman Vanspringel (BEL)	Ferdinand Bracke (BEL)
1969	Eddy Merckx (BEL)	Roger Pingeon (FRA)	Raymond Poulidor (FRA)
1970	Eddy Merckx (BEL)	Joop Zoetemelk (NED)	Gosta Petterson (SWE)
1971	Eddy Merckx (BEL)	Joop Zoetemelk (NED)	Lucien van Impe (BEL)
1972	Eddy Merckx (BEL)	Felice Gimondi (ITA)	Raymond Poulidor (FRA)
1973	Luis Ocana (ESP)	Bernard Thevenet (FRA)	Jose-Manuel Fuente (ESP)
1974	Eddy Merckx (BEL)	Raymond Poulidor (FRA)	Vicente Lopez-Carrill (ESP)
1975	Bernard Thevenet (FRA)	Eddy Merckx (BEL)	Lucien van Impe (BEL)
1976	Lucien van Impe (BEL)	Joop Zoetemelk (NED)	Raymond Poulidor (FRA)
1977	Bernard Thévenet (FRA)	Hennie Kuiper (NED)	Lucien van Impe (BEL)
1978	Bernard Hinault (FRA)	Joop Zoetemelk (NED)	Joaquim Agostinho (POR)
1979	Bernard Hinault (FRA)	Joop Zoetemelk (NED)	Joaquim Agostinho (POR)
1980	Joop Zoetemelk (NED)	Hennie Kuiper (NED)	Raymond Martin (FRA)
1981	Bernard Hinault (FRA)	Lucien van Impe (BEL)	Robert Alban (FRA)
1982	Bernard Hinault (FRA)	Joop Zoetemelk (NED)	Jo Van Der Velde (NED)
1983	Laurent Fignon (FRA)	Angel Arroyo (ESP)	Peter Winnen (NED)
1984	Laurent Fignon (FRA)	Bernard Hinault (FRA)	Greg Lemond (USA)
1985	Bernard Hinault (FRA)	Greg Lemond (USA)	Stephen Roche (IRL)
1986	Greg Lemond (USA)	Bernard Hinault (FRA)	Urs Zimmerman (SUI)
1987	Stephen Roche (IRL)	Pedro Delgado (ESP)	Jean-Francois Bernard (FRA)
1988	Pedro Delgado (ESP)	Steven Rooks (NED)	Fabio Parra (COL)
1989	Greg Lemond (USA)	Laurent Fignon (FRA)	Pedro Delgado (ESP)
1990	Greg Lemond (USA)	Claudio Chiapucci (ITA)	Erik Breukink (NED)
1991	Miguel Indurain (ESP)	Gianni Bugno (ITA)	Claudio Chiapucci (ITA)
1992	Miguel Indurain (ESP)	Claudio Chiapucci (ITA)	Gianni Bugno (ITA)
1993	Miguel Indurain (ESP)	Tony Rominger (SUI)	Zenon Jaskula (POL)
1994	Miguel Indurain (ESP)	Pietr Ugrumov (RUS)	Marco Pantani (ITA)
1995	Miguel Indurain (ESP)	Alex Zülle (SUI)	Bjarne Riis (DEN)
1996	Bjarne Riis (DEN)	Jan Ullrich (GER)	Richard Virenque (FRA)
1997	Jan Ullrich (GER)	Richard Virenque (FRA)	Marco Pantani (ITA)
1998	Marco Pantani (ITA)	Jan Ullrich (GER)	Bobby Julich (USA)
1999	Lance Armstrong (USA)	Alex Zülle (SUI)	Fernando Escartin (ESP)
2000	Lance Armstrong (USA)	Jan Ullrich (GER)	Joseba Beloki (ESP)
2001	Lance Armstrong (USA)	Jan Ullrich (GER)	Joseba Beloki (ESP)
2002	Lance Armstrong (USA)	Joseba Beloki (ESP)	Raimondas Rumsas (LTU)
2003	Lance Armstrong (USA)	Jan Ullrich (GER)	Alexei Vinokourov (KAZ)
2004	Lance Armstrong (USA)	Andréas Klöden (GER)	Ivan Basso (ITA)

Tour of Italy (Giro d'Italia)

Year			
1909	Luigi Ganna (ITA)	Carlo Galetti (ITA)	Giovanni Rossignoli (ITA)
1910	Carlo Galetti (ITA)	Eberardo Pavesi (ITA)	Luigi Ganna (ITA)
1911	Carlo Galetti (ITA)	Giovanni Rossignoli (ITA)	Giovanni Gerbi (ITA)
1912	Team Atala	Team Peugeot	Team Gerbi
1913	Carlo Oriani (ITA)	Eberardo Pavesi (ITA)	Giuseppe Azzini (ITA)
1914	Alfonso Calzolari (ITA)	Pierino Albini (ITA)	Luigi Lucotti (ITA)
1915-18	not held		
1919	Costante Girardengo (ITA)	Gaetano Belloni (ITA)	Marcel Buysse (FRA)
1920	Gaetano Belloni (ITA)	Angelo Gremo (ITA)	Jean Alavoine (FRA)
1921	Giovanni Brunero (ITA)	Gaetano Belloni (ITA)	Bartolomeo Aymo (ITA)
1922	Giovanni Brunero (ITA)	Bartolomeo Aymo (ITA)	Giuseppe Enrici (ITA)
1923	Costante Girardengo (ITA)	Giovanni Brunero (ITA)	Bartolomeo Aymo (ITA)
1924	Giuseppe Enrici (ITA)	Federico Gay (ITA)	Angiolo Gabrielli (ITA)
1925	Alfredo Binda (ITA)	Costante Girardengo (ITA)	Giovanni Brunero (ITA)
1926	Giovanni Brunero (ITA)	Alfredo Binda (ITA)	Arturo Bresciani (ITA)
1927	Alfredo Binda (ITA)	Giovanni Brunero (ITA)	Antonio Negrini (ITA)
1928	Alfredo Binda (ITA)	Giuseppe Pancera (ITA)	Bartolomeo Aymo (ITA)
1929	Alfredo Binda (ITA)	Domenico Piemontesi (ITA)	Leonida Frascarelli (ITA)
1930	Luigi Marchisio (ITA)	Luigi Giacobbe (ITA)	Allegro Grandi (ITA)
1931	Francesco Camusso (ITA)	Luigi Giacobbe (ITA)	Luigi Marchisio (ITA)
1932	Antonio Pesenti (ITA)	Jef Demuysere (BEL)	Remo Bertoni (ITA)
1933	Alfredo Binda (ITA)	Jef Demuysere (BEL)	Domenico Piemontesi (ITA)
1934	Learco Guerra (ITA)	Francesco Camusso (ITA)	Giovanni Cazzulani (ITA)
1935	Vasco Bergamaschi (ITA)	Giuseppe Martano (ITA)	Giuseppe Olmo (ITA)
1936	Gino Bartali (ITA)	Giuseppe Olmo (ITA)	Severino Canavesi (ITA)
1937	Gino Bartali (ITA)	Giovanni Valetti (ITA)	Enrico Mollo (ITA)
1938	Giovanni Valetti (ITA)	Ezio Cecchi (ITA)	Severino Canavesi (ITA)
1939	Giovanni Valetti (ITA)	Gino Bartali (ITA)	Mario Vicini (ITA)
1940	Fausto Coppi (ITA)	Enrico Mollo (ITA)	Giordano Cottur (ITA)
1941-45	not held		
1946	Gino Bartali (ITA)	Fausto Coppi (ITA)	Vito Ortelli (ITA)
1947	Fausto Coppi (ITA)	Gino Bartali (ITA)	Giulio Bresci (ITA)
1948	Fiorenzo Magni (ITA)	Ezio Cecchi (ITA)	Giordano Cottur (ITA)
1949	Fausto Coppi (ITA)	Gino Bartali (ITA)	Giordano Cottur (ITA)
1950	Hugo Koblet (SUI)	Gino Bartali (ITA)	Alfredo Martini (ITA)
1951	Fiorenzo Magni (ITA)	Rik van Steenbergen (BEL)	Ferdy Kübler (SUI)
1952	Fausto Coppi (ITA)	Fiorenzo Magni (ITA)	Ferdy Kübler (SUI)
1953	Fausto Coppi (ITA)	Hugo Koblet (SUI)	Pasquale Fornara (ITA)
1954	Carlo Clerici (SUI)	Hugo Koblet (SUI)	Nino Assirelli (ITA)
1955	Fiorenzo Magni (ITA)	Fausto Coppi (ITA)	Gastone Nencini (ITA)
1956	Charly Gaul (LUX)	Fiorenzo Magni (ITA)	Agostino Coletto (ITA)
1957	Gastone Nencini (ITA)	Louison Bobet (FRA)	Ercole Baldini (ITA)
1958	Ercole Baldini (ITA)	Jean Brankart (BEL)	Charly Gaul (LUX)
1959	Charly Gaul (LUX)	Jacques Anquetil (FRA)	Diego Ronchini (ITA)
1960	Jacques Anquetil (FRA)	Gastone Nencini (ITA)	Charly Gaul (LUX)
1961	Arnaldo Pambianco (ITA)	Jacques Anquetil (FRA)	Antonio Suarez (ESP)
1962	Franco Balmamion (ITA)	Imerio Massignan (ITA)	Nino Defilippis (ITA)
1963	Franco Balmamion (ITA)	Vittorio Adorni (ITA)	Giorgio Zancanaro (ITA)
1964	Jacques Anquetil (FRA)	Italo Zilioli (ITA)	Guido De Rosso (ITA)
1965	Vittorio Adorni (ITA)	Italo Zilioli (ITA)	Felice Gimondi (ITA)
1966	Gianni Motta (ITA)	Italo Zilioli (ITA)	Jacques Anquetil (FRA)
1967	Felice Gimondi (ITA)	Franco Balmamion (ITA)	Jacques Anquetil (FRA)
1968	Eddy Merckx (BEL)	Vittorio Adorni (ITA)	Felice Gimondi (ITA)
1969	Felice Gimondi (ITA)	Claudio Michelotto (ITA)	Italo Zilioli (ITA)
1970	Eddy Merckx (BEL)	Felice Gimondi (ITA)	Martin Vandenbossche (BEL)
1971	Gosta Pettersson (SWE)	Herman van Springel (BEL)	Ugo Colombo (ITA)
1972	Eddy Merckx (BEL)	Jose Manuel Fuente (ESP)	Francisco Galdos (ESP)
1973	Eddy Merckx (BEL)	Felice Gimondi (ITA)	Giovanni Battaglin (ITA)
1974	Eddy Merckx (BEL)	Gianbattista Baronchelli (ITA)	Felice Gimondi (ITA)
1975	Fausto Bertoglio (ITA)	Francisco Galdos (ESP)	Felice Gimondi (ITA)
1976	Felice Gimondi (ITA)	Johan de Muynck (BEL)	Fausto Bertoglio (ITA)
1977	Michel Pollentier (BEL)	Francesco Moser (ITA)	Gianbattista Baronchelli (ITA)
1978	Johan De Muynck (BEL)	Gianbattista Baronchelli (ITA)	Francesco Moser (ITA)
1979	Giuseppe Saronni (ITA)	Francesco Moser (ITA)	Bernt Johansson (SWE)
1980	Bernard Hinault (FRA)	Wladimiro Panizza (ITA)	Giovanni Battaglin (ITA)
1981	Giovanni Battaglin (ITA)	Tommy Prim (SWE)	Giuseppe Saronni (ITA)
1982	Bernard Hinault (FRA)	Tommy Prim (SWE)	Silvano Contini (ITA)
1983	Giuseppe Saronni (ITA)	Roberto Visentini (ITA)	Alberto Fernandez (ESP)

1984	Francesco Moser (ITA)	Laurent Fignon (FRA)	Moreno Argentin (ITA)
1985	Bernard Hinault (FRA)	Francesco Moser (ITA)	Greg Lemond (USA)
1986	Roberto Visentini (ITA)	Giuseppe Saronni (ITA)	Francesco Moser (ITA)
1987	Stephen Roche (IRL)	Robert Millar (SCO)	Erik Breukink (NED)
1988	Andrew Hampsten ((USA)	Erik Breukink (NED)	Urs Zimmermann (SUI)
1989	Laurent Fignon (FRA)	Flavio Giupponi (ITA)	Andrew Hampsten (USA)
1990	Gianni Bugno (ITA)	Charles Mottet (FRA)	Marco Giovannetti (ITA)
1991	Franco Chioccioli (ITA)	Claudio Chiappucci (ITA)	Massimiliano Lelli (ITA)
1992	Miguel Indurain (ESP)	Claudio Chiappucci (ITA)	Franco Chioccioli (ITA)
1993	Miguel Indurain (ESP)	Piotr Ugrumov (LAT)	Claudio Chiappucci (ITA)
1994	Evgeni Berzin (RUS)	Marco Pantani (ITA)	Miguel Indurain (ESP)
1995	Tony Rominger (SUI)	Evgeni Berzin (RUS)	Piotr Ugrumov (RUS)
1996	Pavel Tonkov (RUS)	Enrico Zaina (ITA)	Abraham Olano (ESP)
1997	Ivan Gotti (ITA)	Pavel Tonkov (RUS)	Giuseppe Guerini (ITA)
1998	Marco Pantani (ITA)	Pavel Tonkov (RUS)	Giuseppe Guerini (ITA)
1999	Ivan Gotti (ITA)	Paolo Savoldelli (ITA)	Gilberto Simoni (ITA)
2000	Stefano Garzelli (ITA)	Francesco Casagrande (ITA)	Gilberto Simoni (ITA)
2001	Gilberto Simoni (ITA)	Abraham Olano (ESP)	Unai Osa (ESP)
2002	Paolo Savoldelli (ITA)	Tyler Hamilton (USA)	Pietro Caucchioli (ITA)
2003	Gilberto Simoni (ITA)	Stefano Garzelli (ITA)	Yaroslav Popovych (UKR)
2004	Damiano Cunego (ITA)	Serhiy Honchar (DEN)	Gilberto Simoni (ITA)

Tour of Spain (Vuelta a Espana)

1935	G. Deloor (BEL)	M. Canardo (ESP)	A. Dignef (BEL)
1936	G. Deloor (BEL)	A. Deloor (BEL)	A. Bertola (ESP)
1937-40	not held due to Spanish Civil War		
1941	J. Berrendero (ESP)	F. Trueba (ESP)	J. Jabardo (ESP)
1942	J. Berrendero (ESP)	D. Chafer (ESP)	A. Sancho (ESP)
1945	D. Rodriguez (ESP)	J. Berrendero (ESP)	J. Gimeno (ESP)
1946	D. Langarica (ESP)	J. Berrendero (ESP)	J. Lambrichs (NED)
1947	W. van Dijck (BEL)	M. Costa (ESP)	D. Rodriguez (ESP)
1948	B. Ruiz (ESP)	E. Rodriguez (ESP)	B. Capo (ESP)
1950	E. Rodriguez (ESP)	M. Rodriguez (ESP)	J. Serra (ESP)
1955	J. Dotto (FRA)	J. Quillez (ESP)	R. Geminiani (FRA)
1956	A. Conterno (ITA)	J. Lorono (ESP)	R. Impanis (BEL)
1957	J. Lorono (ESP)	F. Bahamontes (ESP)	B. Ruiz (ESP)
1958	J. Stablinski (FRA)	P. Fornara (ESP)	F. Manzaneque (ESP)
1959	A. Suarez (ESP)	J. Segu (ESP)	R. van Looy (BEL)
1960	F. de Mulder (BEL)	A. Desmet (BEL)	M. Pacheco (ESP)
1961	A. Soler (ESP)	F. Mahe (FRA)	J. Perez-Frances (ESP)
1962	R. Altig (FRG)	J. Perez-Frances (ESP)	S. Elliott (IRL)
1963	J. Anquetil (FRA)	M. Colmenarejo (ESP)	M. Pacheco (ESP)
1964	R. Poulidor (FRA)	L. Ocana (ESP)	J. Perez-Frances (ESP)
1965	R. Wolfshohl (FRG)	R. Poulidor (FRA)	R. van Looy (BEL)
1966	F. Gabica (ESP)	E. Velez (ESP)	C. Echeverria (ESP)
1967	J. Janssen (NED)	J. Ducasse (FRA)	A. Gonzalez (ESP)
1968	F. Gimondi (ITA)	J. Perez-Frances (ESP)	E. Velez (ESP)
1969	R. Pingeon (FRA)	L. Ocana (ESP)	W. Wagtmans (NED)
1970	L. Ocana (ESP)	A. Tamames (ESP)	H. vanspringel (BEL)
1971	F. Bracke (BEL)	W. David (BEL)	L. Ocana (ESP)
1972	J. Fuente (ESP)	M. Lasa (ESP)	A. Tamames (ESP)
1973	E. Merckx (BEL)	L. Ocana (ESP)	B. Thévenet (FRA)
1974	J. Fuente (ESP)	J. Agostinho (POR)	M. Lasa (ESP)
1975	A. Tamames (ESP)	D. Perurena (ESP)	M. Lasa (ESP)
1976	J. Pesarrodona (ESP)	L. Ocana (ESP)	J. Nazabal (ESP)
1977	F. Maertens (BEL)	M. Lasa (ESP)	K. Thaler (FRG)
1978	B. Hinault (FRA)	J. Pesarrodona (ESP)	J. Bernaudeau (FRA)
1979	J. Zoetemelk (NED)	F. Galdos (ESP)	M. Pollentier (BEL)
1980	F. Ruperez (ESP)	P. Torres (ESP)	C. Criquielion (BEL)
1981	G. Battaglin (ITA)	P. Munoz (ESP)	V. Belda (ESP)
1982	M. Lejaretta (ESP)	M. Pollentier (BEL)	S. Nilsson (SWE)
1983	B. Hinault (FRA)	M. Lejarreta (ESP)	A. Fernandez (ESP)
1984	E. Caritoux (FRA)	A. Fernandez (ESP)	R. Dietzen (FRG)
1985	P. Delgado (ESP)	R. Millar (GBR)	F. Rodriguez (COL)
1986	A. Pino (ESP)	R. Millar (GBR)	S. Kelly (IRL)
1987	L. Herrera (COL)	R. Dietzen (FRG)	L. Fignon (FRA)
1988	S. Kelly (IRL)	R. Dietzen (FRG)	A. Fuerte (ESP)
1989	P. Delgado (ESP)	F. Parra (COL)	O. Vargas (COL)
1990	M. Giovannetti (ITA)	P. Delgado (ESP)	A. Fuerte (ESP)
1991	M. Mauri (ESP)	M. Indurain (ESP)	M. Lejaretta (ESP)

92 T. Rominger (SUI)	J. Montoya (ESP)	P Delgado (ESP)
93 T. Rominger (SUI)	A. Zülle (SUI)	L. Cubino (ESP)
94 T. Rominger (SUI)	M. Zarrabeitia (ESP)	P. Delgado (ESP)
95 L. Jalabert (FRA)	A. Olano (ESP)	J. Bruyneel (BEL)
96 A. Zülle (SUI)	L. Dufaux (SUI)	T. Rominger (SUI)
97 A. Zülle (SUI)	F. Escartin (ESP)	L. Dufaux (SUI)
98 A. Olano (ESP)	F. Escartin (ESP)	J.-M. Jiminez (ESP)
99 J. Ullrich (GER)	I. Gonzales de Galdeano (ESP)	H. Heras (ESP)
00 R. Heras (ESP)	A. Casero (ESP)	P. Tonkov (RUS)
01 A. Casero (ESP)	O. Sevilla (ESP)	L. Leipheimer (USA)
02 A. Gonzales (ESP)	R. Heras (ESP)	J. Beloki (ESP)
03 R. Heras (ESP)	I. Nozal (ESP)	A. Valverde (ESP)

World Road Race Champions

Men's

27 Alfredo Binda (ITA)	1957 R. van Steenbergen (BEL)	1981 Freddy Maertens (BEL)
28 Georges Ronsse (BEL)	1958 Ercole Baldini (ITA)	1982 Giuseppe Saronni (ITA)
29 Georges Ronsse (BEL)	1959 André Darrigade (FRA)	1983 Greg Lemond (USA)
30 Alfredo Binda (ITA)	1960 Rik van Looy (BEL)	1984 Claude Criquielion (BEL)
31 Learco Guerra (ITA)	1961 Rik van Looy (BEL)	1985 Joop Zoetemelk (NED)
32 Alfredo Binda (ITA)	1962 Jean Stablinski (FRA)	1986 Moreno Argentin (ITA)
33 Georges Speicher (FRA)	1963 Benoni Beheyt (BEL)	1987 Stephen Roche (IRL)
34 Karel Kaers (BEL)	1964 Jan Janssen (NED)	1988 Maurizio Fondriest (ITA)
35 Jean Aerts (BEL)	1965 Tommy Simpson (GBR)	1989 Greg Lemond (USA)
36 Antonin Magne (FRA)	1966 Rudi Altig (FRG)	1990 Rudy Dhaenens (BEL)
37 Eloi Meulenberg (BEL)	1967 Eddy Merckx (BEL)	1991 Gianni Bugno (ITA)
38 Marcel Kint (BEL)	1968 Vittorio Adorni (ITA)	1992 Gianni Bugno (ITA)
39-45 not held	1969 Harm Ottenbros (NED)	1993 Lance Armstrong (USA)
46 Hans Knecht (SUI)	1970 J.-P. Monsere (BEL)	1994 Luc Leblanc (FRA)
47 Theodore Middelkamp (NED)	1971 Eddy Merckx (BEL)	1995 Abraham Olano (ESP)
48 Briek Schotte (BEL)	1972 Marino Basso (ITA)	1996 Johan Museeuw (BEL)
49 R. van Steenbergen (BEL)	1973 Felice Gimondi (ITA)	1997 Laurent Brochard (FRA)
50 Briek Schotte (BEL)	1974 Eddy Merckx (BEL)	1998 Oscar Camenzind (SUI)
51 Ferdi Kübler (SUI)	1975 Hennie Kuiper (NED)	1999 Oscar Freire Gomez (ESP)
52 Heinz Muller (FRG)	1976 Freddy Maertens (BEL)	2000 Romans Vainsteins (LAT)
53 Fausto Coppi (ITA)	1977 Francesco Moser (ITA)	2001 Oscar Freire Gomez (ESP)
54 Louison Bobet (FRA)	1978 Gerrie Knetemann (NED)	2002 Mario Cipollini (ITA)
55 Stan Ockers (BEL)	1979 Jan Raas (NED)	2003 Igor Astarioa (ESP)
56 R. van Steenbergen (BEL)	1980 Bernard Hinault (FRA)	

Women's

58 E. Jacobs (LUX)	1973 N. Vandenbroeck (NED)	1990 Catherine Marsal (FRA)
59 Yvonne Reynders (BEL)	1974 G. Gambillon (FRA)	1991 L. van Moorsel (NED)
60 Beryl Burton (GBR)	1975 Tr. Fopma (NED)	1993 L. van Moorsel (NED)
61 Yvonne Reynders (BEL)	1976 Cornelia Hage (NED)	1994 Monica Valvik (NOR)
62 M.R. Gaillard (BEL)	1977 J. Bost (FRA)	1995 Jeannie Longo (FRA)
63 Yvonne Reynders (BEL)	1978 Beate Habetz (FRG)	1996 Barbara Heeb (SUI)
64 Em. Sonka (URS)	1979 Petra de Bruin (NED)	1997 Alessandra Cappellotto (ITA)
65 El. Eicholz (GDR)	1980 Beth Heiden (USA)	1998 Diana Ziliute (LTU)
66 Yvonne Reynders (BEL)	1981 Ute Enzenauer (FRG)	1999 Edita Pucinskaite (LTU)
67 Beryl Burton (GBR)	1982 Mandy Jones (GBR)	2000 Zinaida Stahurskaia (BLR)
68 Cornelia Hage (NED)	1983 Marianne Berglund (SUI)	2001 Rasa Polikeviciute (LTU)
69 Audrey McElmury (USA)	1985 Jeannie Longo (FRA)	2002 Susanne Ljungskog (SWE)
70 G. Gambillon (FRA)	1986 Jeannie Longo (FRA)	2003 Susanne Ljungskog (SWE)
71 A. Konkina (URS)	1987 Jeannie Longo (FRA)	
72 G. Gambillon (FRA)	1989 Jeannie Longo (FRA)	

CYCLING

World Sprint Champions

Men's

1895 R. Protin (BEL)	1934 Jef Scherens (BEL)	1973 R. van Lancker (BEL)
1896 Paul Bourillon (FRA)	1935 Jef Scherens (BEL)	1974 P. Pedersen (DEN)
1897 W. Arend (DEN)	1936 Jef Scherens (BEL)	1975 John Nicholson (AUS)
1898 G.A. Banker (USA)	1937 Jef Scherens (BEL)	1976 John Nicholson (AUS)
1899 Major Taylor (USA)	1938 A. van Vliet (NED)	1977 Koichi Nakano (JPN)
1900 E. Jacquelin (FRA)	1939-45 not held	1978 Koichi Nakano (JPN)
1901 Thorvald Ellegaard (DEN)	1946 J Derksen (NED)	1979 Koichi Nakano (JPN)
1902 Thorvald Ellegaard (DEN)	1947 Jef Scherens (BEL)	1980 Koichi Nakano (JPN)
1903 Thorvald Ellegaard (DEN)	1948 A. van Vliet (NED)	1981 Koichi Nakano (JPN)
1904 Yvor Lawson (USA)	1949 Reg Harris (GBR)	1982 Koichi Nakano (JPN)
1905 G. Poulain (FRA)	1950 Reg Harris (GBR)	1983 Koichi Nakano (JPN)
1906 Thorvald Ellegaard (DEN)	1951 Reg Harris (GBR)	1984 Koichi Nakano (JPN)
1907 E. Friol (FRA)	1952 Oscar Plattner (SUI)	1985 Koichi Nakano (JPN)
1908 Thorvald Ellegaard (DEN)	1953 A. van Vliet (NED)	1986 Koichi Nakano (JPN)
1909 V. Dupre (FRA)	1954 Reg Harris (GBR)	1987 Nobuyuki Tawara (JPN)
1910 E. Friol (FRA)	1955 Antonio Maspes (ITA)	1988 Stephen Pate (AUS)
1911 Thorvald Ellegaard (DEN)	1956 Antonio Maspes (ITA)	1989 Claudio Golinelli (ITA)
1912 Frank Kramer (USA)	1957 Jan Derksen (NED)	1990 Michael Hübner (FRG)
1913 W. Rutt (DEN)	1958 M. Rousseau (FRA)	1991 vacated
1920 R. Spears (AUS)	1959 Antonio Maspes (ITA)	1992 Michael Hübner (GER)
1921 Peter Moeskops (NED)	1960 Antonio Maspes (ITA)	1993 Gary Neiwand (AUS)
1922 Peter Moeskops (NED)	1961 Antonio Maspes (ITA)	1994 Marty Nothstein (USA)
1923 Peter Moeskops (NED)	1962 Antonio Maspes (ITA)	1995 Darryn Hill (AUS)
1924 Peter Moeskops (NED)	1963 Sante Gaiardoni (ITA)	1996 Florian Rousseau (FRA)
1925 E. Kaufmann (SUI)	1964 Antonio Maspes (ITA)	1997 Florian Rousseau (FRA)
1926 Peter Moeskops (NED)	1965 Giuseppe Beghetto (ITA)	1998 Florian Rousseau (FRA)
1927 Lucien Michard (FRA)	1966 Giuseppe Beghetto (ITA)	1999 Laurent Gane (FRA)
1928 Lucien Michard (FRA)	1967 Patrick Sercu (BEL)	2000 Jan van Eijden (GER)
1929 Lucien Michard (FRA)	1968 Giuseppe Beghetto (ITA)	2001 Arnaud Tournant (FRA)
1930 Lucien Michard (FRA)	1969 Patrick Sercu (BEL)	2002 Sean Eadie (AUS)
1931 W.F. Hansen (DEN)	1970 Gordon Johnson (AUS)	2003 Laurent Gane (FRA)
1932 Jef Scherens (BEL)	1971 Leijin Loevesijn (NED)	2004 Theo Bos (NED)
1933 Jef Scherens (BEL)	1972 R. van Lancker (BEL)	

Women's

1958 Galina Ermolaeva (URS)	1973 Sheila Young (USA)	1989 Erika Salumaee (URS)
1959 Galina Ermolaeva (URS)	1974 Tamara Piltsikova (URS)	1990 Connie Paraskevin (USA)
1960 Galina Ermolaeva (URS)	1975 Sue Novarra (USA)	1991 Ingrid Haringa (NED)
1961 Galina Ermolaeva (URS)	1976 Sheila Young (USA)	1993 Tanya Dubnicoff (CAN)
1962 Valentina Savina (URS)	1977 Galina Tsareva (URS)	1994 G. Enukhina (RUS)
1963 Galina Ermolaeva (URS)	1978 Galina Tsareva (URS)	1995 Felicia Ballanger (FRA)
1964 Irina Kiritchenko (URS)	1979 Galina Tsareva (URS)	1996 Felicia Ballanger (FRA)
1965 Valentina Savina (URS)	1980 Sue Novarra-Reber (USA)	1997 Felicia Ballanger (FRA)
1966 Irina Kiritchenko (URS)	1981 Sheila Ochowitz-Young (USA)	1998 Felicia Ballanger (FRA)
1967 Valentina Savina (URS)	1982 Connie Paraskevin (USA)	1999 Felicia Ballanger (FRA)
1968 Baguiantz (URS)	1983 Connie Paraskevin (USA)	2000 Natalia Markovnichenko (BLR)
1969 Galina Tsareva (URS)	1984 Connie Paraskevin (USA)	2001 Svetlana Grankovskaia (RUS)
1970 Galina Tsareva (URS)	1985 Isabelle Nicoloso (FRA)	2002 Natallia Tsylinskaya (BLR)
1971 Galina Tsareva (URS)	1986 C. Rothenburger (GDR)	2003 Svetlana Grankovskaia (RUS)
1972 Galina Ermolaeva (URS)	1987 Erika Salumaee (URS)	2004 Svetlana Grankovskaia (RUS)

World Time Trial Champions

Men's	Women's
1994 Chris Boardman (GBR)	1994 Karen Kurreck (USA)
1995 Miguel Indurain (FRA)	1995 Jeannie Longo (FRA)
1996 Alex Zülle (SUI)	1996 Jeannie Longo (FRA)
1997 Laurent Jalabert (FRA)	1997 Jeannie Longo-Ciprelli (FRA)
1998 Abraham Olano (ESP)	1998 Leontien Zijlaard-van Moorsel (NED)
1999 Jan Ullrich (GER)	1999 Leontien Zijlaard-van Moorsel (NED)
2000 Sergei Gontchar (UKR)	2000 Mari Holden (USA)
2001 Jan Ullrich (GER)	2001 Jeannie Longo-Ciprelli (FRA)
2002 Santiago Botero (ESP)	2002 Zoulfia Zabirova (RUS)
2003 Michael Rogers (AUS)	2003 Joane Somarriba Arrola (ESP)

World Track Championships

Men's 4000m Individual Pursuit

1946	Gerrit Peters (NED)	1966	Leandro Faggin (ITA)	1986	Anthony Doyle (GBR)
1947	Fausto Coppi (ITA)	1967	Tiernen Groen (NED)	1987	Hans-Hendrik Oersted (DEN)
1948	Ger Schulte (NED)	1968	Hugh Porter (GBR)	1988	Lech Piasecki (POL)
1949	Fausto Coppi (ITA)	1969	Ferd Bracke (BEL)	1989	Colin Sturgess (GBR)
1950	Antonio Bevilacqua (ITA)	1970	Hugh Porter (GBR)	1990	Vjatceslav Ekimov (RUS)
1951	Antonio Bevilacqua (ITA)	1971	Dirk Baert (BEL)	1991	Francis Moreau (FRA)
1952	Sidney Patterson (AUS)	1972	Hugh Porter (GBR)	1992	Mike McCarthy (USA)
1953	Sidney Patterson (AUS)	1973	Hugh Porter (GBR)	1993	Graeme Obree (GBR)
1954	Guido Messina (ITA)	1974	Roy Schuiten (NED)	1994	Chris Boardman (GBR)
1955	Guido Messina (ITA)	1975	Roy Schuiten (NED)	1995	Graeme Obree (GBR)
1956	Guido Messina (ITA)	1976	Francesco Moser (ITA)	1996	Chris Boardman (GBR)
1957	Roger Riviere (FRA)	1977	Gregor Braun (FRG)	1997	Philippe Ermenault (FRA)
1958	Roger Riviere (FRA)	1978	Gregor Braun (FRG)	1998	Philippe Ermenault (FRA)
1959	Roger Riviere (FRA)	1979	Bert Oosterbosch (NED)	1999	Robert Bartko (GER)
1960	Rudi Altig (FRG)	1980	Anthony Doyle (GBR)	2000	Jens Lehman (GER)
1961	Rudi Altig (FRG)	1981	Alain Bondue (FRA)	2001	Alexandre Symonenko (UKR)
1962	Henk Nijdam (NED)	1982	Alain Bondue (FRA)	2002	Bradley McGee (AUS)
1963	Leandro Faggin (ITA)	1983	Steele Bishop (AUS)	2003	Bradley Wiggins (GBR)
1964	Ferd Bracke (BEL)	1984	Hans-Hendrik Oersted (DEN)	2004	Sergi Escobar Roure (ESP)
1965	Leandro Faggin (ITA)	1985	Hans-Hendrik Oersted (DEN)		

Men's 4000m Team Pursuit

1962	West Germany	Denmark	Soviet Union
	(Ehrenfried Rudolph/Bernd Rohr/Klaus May/Lothar Claesges)		
1963	Soviet Union	West Germany	Denmark
	(Arnold Beljgard/Sergei Teretschenkov/Stanislav Moskvin/Viktor Romanov)		
1964	West Germany	Italy	Soviet Union
	(Lothar Claesges/Karl Link/Karl-Heinz Heinrichs/Ernst Streng)		
1965	Soviet Union	Italy	Czechoslovakia
	(Stanislav Moskvin/Sergey Teretschenkov/Mikhail Kolyuschov/Leonid Vukulov)		
1966	Italy	West Germany	Czechoslovakia
	(Cipriano Chemello/Antonio Castello/Luigi Roncaglia/Gino Pancini)		
1967	Soviet Union	Italy	West Germany
	(Stanislav Moskvin/Mikhail Kolyuschov/Viktor Bykov/Dzintars Latsis)		
1968	Italy	Argentina	Sweden
	(Cipriano Chemello/Lorenzo Bosisio/Giorgio Morbiato/Luigi Roncaglia)		
1969	Soviet Union	Italy	France
	(Stanislav Moskvin/Vladimir Kusnetsov/Viktor Bykov/Sergey Kuskov)		
1970	West Germany	East Germany	Soviet Union
	(Günter Haritz/Peter Vonhof/Hans Lutz/Günter Schumacher)		
1971	Italy	East Germany	West Germany
	(Pietro Algeri/Giacomo Bazzan/Giorgio Morbiato/Luciano Borgognoni)		
1972	not held		
1973	West Germany	Great Britain	Netherlands
	(Günter Schumacher/Peter Vonhof/Hans Lutz/Günter Hatitz)		
	(GB team: Michael Bennett/Richard Evans/Ian Hallam/William Moore)		
1974	West Germany	East Germany	Czechoslovakia
	(Günter Schumacher/Peter Vonhof/Hans Lutz/Dietrich Thurau)		
1975	West Germany	Soviet Union	East Germany
	(Günter Schumacher/Peter Vonhof/Hans Lutz/Dietrich Thurau)		
1976	not held		
1977	East Germany	West Germany	Switzerland
	(Norbert Durpisch/Gerald Mortag/Matthias Wiegand/Volker Winckler)		
1978	East Germany	Soviet Union	Switzerland
	(Uwe Unterwalder/Gerald Mortag/Matthias Wiegand/Volker Winckler)		
1979	East Germany	Soviet Union	Italy
	(Lutz Haueisen/Gerald Mortag/Axel Grosser/Volker Winckler)		
1980	not held		
1981	East Germany	Soviet Union	Czechoslovakia
	(Detlef Macha/Bernd Dittert/Axel Grosser/Volker Winckler)		
1982	Soviet Union	West Germany	East Germany
	(Konstantin Kravzov/Aleksandr Krasnov/Valeriy Novtschan/Sergey Nikitenko)		
1983	West Germany	East Germany	Czechoslovakia
	(Rolf Golz/Detlef Gunther/Gerhard Strittmatter/Michael Marx)		

CYCLING

1984   not held
1985   Italy   Poland   Soviet Union
(Roberto Amadio/Massimo Brunelli/Gianpaolo Grisondi/Silvio Martinello)
1986   Czechoslovakia   East Germany   Soviet Union
(Pavel Soukop/Ales Trcka/Svatopluk Buchta/Teodor Cerny)
1987   Soviet Union   East Germany   Czechoslovakia
(Viatcheslav Ekimov/Aleksandr Krasnov/Viktor Manakov/Sergey Chmelinine)
1988   not held
1989   Germany   Russia   Italy
(Steffen Blochwitz/Carsten Wolf/Thomas Liese/Guido Fulst)
1990   Russia   Germany   Australia
(Valeri Baturo/Evgueni Berzin/Dimitri Neliubin/Alexander Gontchenko)
1991   Germany   Russia   Australia
(Michael Glockner/Stefan Steinweg/Jens Lehmann/Andreas Walzer)
1992   not held
1993   Australia   Germany   Denmark
(Brett Aitken/Tim O'Shannessy/Billy Shearsby/Stuart O'Grady)
1994   Germany   United States   Australia
(Guido Fulst/Andreas Bach/Jens Lehmann/Danilo Hondo)
1995   Australia   Ukraine   United States
(Bradley McGee/Tim O'Shannessy/Rodney McGee/Stuart O'Grady)
1996   Italy   France   Germany
(Andrea Colinelli/Adler Capelli/Cristiano Citton/Mauro Trentin)
1997   Italy   Ukraine   France
(Andrea Colinelli/Adler Capelli/Cristiano Citton/Mario Benetton)
1998   Ukraine   Germany   Italy
(Alexander Simonenko/Sergei Matveiev/Aleksandr Fedenko/Alexander Klimenko)
1999   Germany   France   Russia
(Guido Fulst/Robert Bartko/Daniel Becke/Jens Lehmann)
2000   Germany   Great Britain   France
(Guido Fulst/Sebastian Siedler/Daniel Becke/Jens Lehmann)
(GB team: Paul Manning/Bradley Wiggins/Chris Newton/Jonathan Clay)
2001   Ukraine   Great Britain   Germany
(Alexander Simonenko/Sergey Tscherniovsky/Aleksandr Fedenko/Lubomir Polotajko)
(GB team: Paul Manning/Bradley Wiggins/Chris Newton/Brian Steel)
2002   Australia   Germany   Great Britain
(Peter Dawson/Brett Lancaster/Stephen Woodbridge/Luke Roberts)
(GB team: Paul Manning/Bradley Wiggins/Chris Newton/Brian Steel)
2003   Australia   Great Britain   France
(Peter Dawson/Brett Lancaster/Luke Roberts/G. Brown)
(GB team: Paul Manning/Bradley Wiggins/Rob Hayles/Brian Steel)
2004   Australia   Great Britain   Spain
(Peter Dawson/Ashley Hutchinson/Luke Roberts/Stephen Wooldridge)
(GB team: Paul Manning/Robert Hayles/Chris Newton/Bryan Steel)

Men's 1000m Time Trial

1966 Pierre Trentin (FRA)	1979 Lothar Thoms (GDR)	1994 Florian Rousseau (FRA)
1967 Niels Fredborg (DEN)	1981 Lothar Thoms (GDR)	1995 Shane Kelly (AUS)
1968 Niels Fredborg (DEN)	1982 Fredy Schmidtke (FRG)	1996 Shane Kelly (AUS)
1969 Sartori Gianni (ITA)	1983 Sergei Kopylov (URS)	1997 Shane Kelly (AUS)
1970 Niels Fredborg (DEN)	1985 Jens Glucklich (GDR)	1998 Arnaud Tournant (FRA)
1971 Ed. Rapp (URS)	1986 Malk Malchow (GDR)	1999 Arnaud Tournant (FRA)
1973 J. Kierzkowski (POL)	1987 Martin Vinnicombe (AUS)	2000 Arnaud Tournant (FRA)
1974 Ed. Rapp (URS)	1989 Jens Glucklich (GDR)	2001 Arnaud Tournant (FRA)
1975 K.J. Grunke (GDR)	1990 Aleksander Kiritchenko (URS)	2002 Chris Hoy (GBR)
1977 Lothar Thoms (GDR)	1991 Jose Moreno (ESP)	2003 Stefan Nimke (GER)
1978 Lothar Thoms (GDR)	1993 Florian Rousseau (FRA)	2004 Chris Hoy (GBR)

Men's Keirin

1980 Danny Clark (AUS)	1989 Claudio Golinelli (ITA)	1998 Jens Fiedler (GER)
1981 Danny Clark (AUS)	1990 Michaël Hübner (GDR)	1999 Jens Fiedler (GER)
1982 Gordon Singleton (CAN)	1991 Michaël Hübner (GDR)	2000 Frédéric Magne (FRA)
1983 Urs Freuler (SUI)	1992 Michaël Hübner (GDR)	2001 Ryan Bayley (AUS)
1984 Robert Dill-Bundi (SUI)	1993 Gary Neiwand (AUS)	2002 Jobie Dajka (AUS)
1985 Urs Freuler (SUI)	1994 Marty Nothstein (USA)	2003 Laurent Gane (FRA)
1986 Michel Vaarten (BEL)	1995 Frédéric Magne (FRA)	2004 Jamie Staff (GBR)
1987 Harumi Honda (JPN)	1996 Marty Nothstein (USA)	
1988 Claudio Golinelli (ITA)	1997 Frédéric Magne (FRA)	

Men's Points Race

1980	Stan Tourne (BEL)	1990	Laurent Biondi (FRA)	2000 Rosello Juan Llaneras (ESP)
1981	Urs Freuler (SUI)	1991	Vjatceslav Ekimov (URS)	2001 Bruno Risi (SUI)
1982	Urs Freuler (SUI)	1992	Bruno Risi (SUI)	2002 Chris Newton (GBR)
1983	Urs Freuler (SUI)	1993	Etienne de Wilde (BEL)	2003 Franz Stocher (AUT)
1984	Urs Freuler (SUI)	1994	Bruno Risi (SUI)	2004 Franck Perque (FRA)
1985	Urs Freuler (SUI)	1995	Silvio Martinello (ITA)	
1986	Urs Freuler (SUI)	1996	Juan Llaneras (ESP)	
1987	Urs Freuler (SUI)	1997	Silvio Martinello (ITA)	
1988	Daniel Wyder (SUI)	1998	Rosello Juan Llaneras (ESP)	
1989	Urs Freuler (SUI)	1999	Bruno Risi (SUI)	

Men's Olympic (Team) Sprint

1995	Germany	1999	France	2002 GBR (Chris Hoy, Craig
1996	Australia	2000	France	McLean, Jason Queally)
1997	France	2001	France	2003 Germany
1998	France			2004 France

Women's 3000m Individual Pursuit

1958	L. Kotchetova (URS)	1975	Cornelia Hage (NED)	1993	Rebecca Twigg (USA)
1959	Beryl Burton (GBR)	1976	Cornelia Hage (NED)	1994	Marion Clignet (FRA)
1960	Beryl Burton (GBR)	1977	Vera Kusnetsova (URS)	1995	Rebecca Twigg (USA)
1961	Yvonne Reynders (BEL)	1978	Cornelia Hage (NED)	1996	Marion Clignet (FRA)
1962	Beryl Burton (GBR)	1979	Cornelia Hage (NED)	1997	Judith Arndt (GER)
1963	Beryl Burton (GBR)	1980	Nadia Kibardina (URS)	1998	Lucy Tyler Sharman (AUS)
1964	Yvonne Reynders (BEL)	1981	Nadia Kibardina (URS)	1999	Marion Cligne (FRA)
1965	Yvonne Reynders (BEL)	1982	Rebecca Twigg (USA)	2000	Yvonne McGregor (GBR)
1966	Beryl Burton (GBR)	1983	Connie Carpenter (USA)	2001	Leontien Zijlaard-Van
1967	T. Garkushina (URS)	1984	Rebecca Twigg (USA)		Moorsel (NED)
1968	R. Obodovskaya (URS)	1985	Rebecca Twigg (USA)	2002	Leontien Zijlaard-Van
1969	R. Obodovskaya (URS)	1986	Jeannie Longo (FRA)		Moorsel (NED)
1970	T. Garkushina (URS)	1987	Rebecca Twigg (USA)	2003	Leontien Zijlaard-Van
1971	T. Garkushina (URS)	1988	Jeannie Longo (FRA)		Moorsel (NED)
1972	T. Garkushina (URS)	1989	Jeannie Longo (FRA)	2004	Sarah Ulmer (NZL)
1973	T. Garkushina (URS)	1990	L.van Moorsel (NED)		
1974	T. Garkushina (URS)	1991	Petra Rossner (GER)		

Women's 500m Time Trial

1995	Felicia Ballanger (FRA)	1999	Felicia Ballanger (FRA)	2003	Natallia Tsylinskaya (BLR)
1996	Felicia Ballanger (FRA)	2000	Natalia Markovnichenko (BLR)	2004	Anna Meares (AUS)
1997	Felicia Ballanger (FRA)	2001	Nancy Contreras Reyes (MEX)		
1998	Felicia Ballanger (FRA)	2002	Natallia Tsylinskaya (BLR)		

Women's Points Race

1988	Sally Hodge (GBR)	1994	Ingrid Haringa (NED)	2000	Marion Clignet (FRA)
	(demonstration)	1995	Svetlana Samokhvalova (RUS)	2001	Olga Slusareva (RUS)
1989	Jeannie Longo (FRA)	1996	Svetlana Samokhvalova (RUS)	2002	Olga Slusareva (RUS)
1990	Karen Holliday (NZL)	1997	Natalia Kamirova (RUS)	2003	Olga Slusareva (RUS)
1991	Ingrid Haringa (NED)	1998	Teodora Ruano (ESP)	2004	Olga Slusareva (RUS)
1993	Ingrid Haringa (NED)	1999	Marion Clignet (FRA)		

World Cyclo-Cross Championships

1950	Jean Robic (FRA)	Roger Rondeaux (FRA)		Pierre Jodet (FRA)
1951	Roger Rondeaux (FRA)	André Dufraisse (FRA)		Pierre Jodet (FRA)
1952	Roger Rondeaux (FRA)	André Dufraisse (FRA)		Albert Meier (SUI)
1953	Roger Rondeaux (FRA)	Gilbert Bonvin (FRA)		André Dufraisse (FRA)
1954	André Dufraisse (FRA)	Pierre Jodet (FRA)		Hans Bieri (SUI)
1955	André Dufraisse (FRA)	Hans Bieri (SUI)		Amerigo Severini (ITA)
1956	André Dufraisse (FRA)	Georg Meunier (FRA)		Emanuel Plattner (SUI)
1957	André Dufraisse (FRA)	F. van Kerrebroeck (BEL)		Georg Meunier (FRA)
1958	André Dufraisse (FRA)	Amerigo Severini (ITA)		Rolf Wolfshohl (FRG)
1959	Renato Longo (ITA)	Rolf Wolfshohl (FRG)		Amerigo Severini (ITA)
1960	Rolf Wolfshohl (FRG)	Arnold Hungerbuhler (SUI)		André Aubry (FRA)
1961	Rolf Wolfshohl (FRG)	Renato Longo (ITA)		André Dufraisse (FRA)

CYCLING

1962	Renato Longo (ITA)	Adolphe Gandolfo (FRA)	André Dufraisse (FRA)
1963	Rolf Wolfshohl (FRG)	Renato Longo (ITA)	André Dufraisse (FRA)
1964	Renato Longo (ITA)	Roger de Clercq (BEL)	Jose Mahe (FRA)
1965	Renato Longo (ITA)	Rolf Wolfshohl (FRG)	Jose Mahe (FRA)
1966	Eric de Vlaeminck (BEL)	Hermann Gretener (SUI)	Rolf Wolfshohl (FRG)
1967	Renato Longo (ITA)	Rolf Wolfshohl (FRG)	Hermann Gretener (SUI)
1968	Eric de Vlaeminck (BEL)	Hermann Gretener (SUI)	Michel Pelchat (FRA)
1969	Eric de Vlaeminck (BEL)	Rolf Wolfshohl (FRG)	Renato Longo (ITA)
1970	Eric de Vlaeminck (BEL)	Rolf Wolfshohl (FRG)	Rolf Wolfshohl (FRG)
1971	Eric de Vlaeminck (BEL)	Rolf Wolfshohl (FRG)	René de Clercq (BEL)
1972	Eric de Vlaeminck (BEL)	Rolf Wolfshohl (FRG)	Hermann Gretener (SUI)
1973	Eric de Vlaeminck (BEL)	André Wilhelm (SUI)	Rolf Wolfshohl (FRG)
1974	Albert van Damme (BEL)	Roger de Vlaeminck (BEL)	Peter Frischknecht (SUI)
1975	Roger de Vlaeminck (BEL)	Albert Zweifel (SUI)	Peter Frischknecht (SUI)
1976	Albert Zweifel (SUI)	Peter Frischknecht (SUI)	André Wilhelm (SUI)
1977	Albert Zweifel (SUI)	Peter Frischknecht (SUI)	Eric de Vlaeminck (BEL)
1978	Albert Zweifel (SUI)	Peter Frischknecht (SUI)	Klaus-Peter Thaler (FRG)
1979	Albert Zweifel (SUI)	Gilles Blaser (SUI)	Robert Vermeire (BEL)
1980	Roland Liboton (BEL)	Klaus-Peter Thaler (FRG)	Hennie Stamsnijder (NED)
1981	Hennie Stamsnijder (NED)	Roland Liboton (BEL)	Albert Zweifel (SUI)
1982	Roland Liboton (BEL)	Albert Zweifel (SUI)	Hennie Stamsnijder (NED)
1983	Roland Liboton (BEL)	Albert Zweifel (SUI)	Klaus-Peter Thaler (FRG)
1984	Roland Liboton (BEL)	Hennie Stamsnijder (NED)	Albert Zweifel (SUI)
1985	Klaus-Peter Thaler (FRG)	Adri van der Poel (NED)	Claude Michely (LUX)
1986	Albert Zweifel (SUI)	Pascal Richard (SUI)	Hennie Stamsnijder (NED)
1987	Klaus-Peter Thaler (FRG)	Danny de Bie (BEL)	Charles Lavainne (FRA)
1988	Pascal Richard (SUI)	Adri van der Poel (NED)	Beat Breu (SUI)
1989	Danny di Bie (BEL)	Adri van der Poel (NED)	Charles Lavainne (FRA)
1990	Henk Baars (NED)	Adri van der Poel (NED)	Bruno Lebras (FRA)
1991	Radomir Simunek (CZE)	Adri van der Poel (NED)	Bruno Lebras (FRA)
1992	Mike Kluge (GER)	Karel Camrda (CZE)	Adri van der Poel (NED)
1993	Dominique Arnould (FRA)	Mike Kluge (GER)	Wim de Vos (NED)
1994	Paul Herijgers (BEL)	Richard Groenendaal (NED)	Erwin Vervecken (BEL)
1995	Dieter Runkel (SUI)	Richard Groenendaal (NED)	Beat Wabel (SUI)
1996	Adri van der Poel (NED)	Daniele Pontoni (ITA)	Luca Bramati (ITA)
1997	Daniele Pontoni (ITA)	Thomas Frischknecht (SUI)	Luca Bramati (ITA)
1998	Mario de Clercq (BEL)	Erwin Vervecken (BEL)	Henrik Djernis (DEN)
1999	Mario de Clercq (BEL)	Erwin Vervecken (BEL)	Adri van der Poel (NED)
2000	Richard Groenendaal (NED)	Mario de Clercq (BEL)	Sven Nijs (BEL)
2001	Erwin Vervecken (BEL)	Petr Dlask (CZE)	Mario de Clercq (BEL)
2002	Mario de Clercq (BEL)	Tom Vannoppen (BEL)	Sven Nijs (BEL)
2003	Bart Wellens (BEL)	Mario de Clercq (BEL)	Erwin Vervecken (BEL)
2004	Bart Wellens (BEL)	Mario de Clercq (BEL)	Sven Vanthourenhout (BEL)

British Cyclo-Cross Champions

1954	Alan Jackson	1971	John Atkins	1988	Steve Douce
1955	Alan Jackson	1972	John Atkins	1989	Steve Douce
1956	Alan Jackson	1973	John Atkins	1990	David Baker
1957	Don Stone	1974	John Atkins	1991	Chris Young
1958	Don Stone	1975	Jeff Morris	1992	David Baker
1959	Barry Spence	1976	Keith Mernickle	1993	Steve Douce
1960	D. Briggs	1977	John Atkins	1994	Roger Hammond
1961	John Atkins	1978	Chris Wreghitt	1995	Barrie Clarke
1962	John Atkins	1979	Chris Wreghitt	1996	Nick Craig
1963	Michael Stallard	1980	Chris Wreghitt	1997	Barrie Clarke
1964	Michael Stallard	1981	Chris Wreghitt	1998	Nick Craig
1965	Michael Stallard	1982	Chris Wreghitt	1999	Steve Knight
1966	John Atkins	1983	Steve Douce	2000	Roger Hammond
1967	John Atkins	1984	Chris Young	2001	Roger Hammond
1968	John Atkins	1985	Steve Douce	2002	Roger Hammond
1969	John Atkins	1986	Steve Douce	2003	Roger Hammond
1970	John Atkins	1987	Steve Douce	2004	Roger Hammond

Mountain Bike World Championships

Men's Cross-Country

1990	Ned Overend (USA)	Thomas Frischknecht (SUI)	Tim Gould (GBR)
1991	John Tomac (USA)	Thomas Frischknecht (SUI)	Ned Overend (USA)
1992	Henrik Djernis (DEN)	Thomas Frischknecht (SUI)	David Baker (GBR)
1993	Henrik Djernis (DEN)	Marcel Gerritsen (NED)	Jan Erik Ostergaard (DEN)
1994	Henrik Djernis (DEN)	Tinker Juarez (USA)	Bart Brentjens (NED)
1995	Bart Brentjens (NED)	Miguel Martinez (FRA)	Jan Erik Ostergaard (DEN)
1996	Thomas Frischknecht (SUI)	Rune Hoydahl (NOR)	Hubert Pallhuber (ITA))
1997	Hubert Pallhuber (ITA)	Henrik Djernis (DEN)	Luca Bramati (ITA)
1998	Christophe Dupouey (FRA)	Jèrôme Chiotti (FRA)	Filip Meirhaeghe (BEL)
1999	Michael Rasmussen (DEN)	Miguel Martinez (FRA)	Filip Meirhaeghe (BEL)
2000	Miguel Martinez (FRA)	Roland Green (CAN)	Bart Brentjens (NED)
2001	Roland Green (CAN)	Thomas Frischknecht (SUI)	Christof Sauser (SUI)
2002	Roland Green (CAN)	Filip Meirhaeghe (BEL)	Thomas Frischknecht (SUI)
2003	Filip Meirhaeghe (BEL)	Ryder Hesjedal (CAN)	Roel Paulissen (BEL)

Men's Downhill

1990	Greg Herbold (USA)	Mike Kloser (USA)	Paul Thomasberg (USA)
1991	Albert Iten (SUI)	John Tomac (USA)	Glen Adams (USA)
1992	Dave Cullinan (USA)	Jimmy Deaton (USA)	Christian Taillefer (FRA)
1993	Mike King (USA)	Paolo Caramellino (ITA)	Myles Rockwell (USA)
1994	François Gachet (FRA)	Tommy Johansson (SWE)	Herin Corrado (ITA)
1995	Nicolas Vouilloz (FRA)	François Gachet (FRA)	Mike King (USA)
1996	Nicolas Vouilloz (FRA)	Shaun Palmer (USA)	Bas de Bever (NED)
1997	Nicolas Vouilloz (FRA)	John Tomac (USA)	Cedric Gracia (FRA)
1998	Nicolas Vouilloz (FRA)	Gerwin Peters (NED)	Mickael Pascal (FRA)
1999	Nicolas Vouilloz (FRA)	Mickael Pascal (FRA)	Eric Carter (USA)
2000	Myles Rockwell (USA)	Steve Peat (GBR)	Mickael Pascal (FRA)
2001	Nicolas Vouilloz (FRA)	Steve Peat (GBR)	Greg Minaar (RSA)
2002	Nicolas Vouilloz (FRA)	Steve Peat (GBR)	Chris Kovarik (AUS)
2004	Greg Minaar (RSA)	Mickael Pascal (FRA)	Fabien Barel (FRA)

Women's Cross-Country

1990	Julie Furtado (USA)	Sara Ballantyne (USA)	Ruthie Matthes (USA)
1991	Ruthie Matthes (USA)	Eva Orvosova (SVK)	Silvia Furst (SUI)
1992	Silvia Furst (SUI)	Alison Sydor (CAN)	Ruthie Matthes (USA)
1993	Paula Pezzo (ITA)	Jeannie Longo (FRA)	Ruthie Matthes (USA)
1994	Alison Sydor (CAN)	Susan de Mattei (USA)	Sara Ballantyne (USA)
1995	Alison Sydor (CAN)	Silvia Furst (SUI)	Chantal Daucourt (SUI)
1996	Alison Sydor (CAN)	Ruthie Matthes (USA)	Maria Paola Turcutto (ITA)
1997	Paola Pezzo (ITA)	Nadia de Negri (ITA)	Margarita Fullana (ESP)
1998	Laurence Leboucher (FRA)	Gunn Dahle (NOR)	Alison Sydor (CAN)
1999	Margarita Fullana Riera (ESP)	Alison Sydor (CAN)	Paola Pezzo (ITA)
2000	Margarita Fullana Riera (ESP)	Alison Sydor (CAN)	Paola Pezzo (ITA)
2001	Alison Dunlap (USA)	Alison Sydor (CAN)	Sabine Spitz (GER)
2002	Gunn-Rita Dahle (NOR)	Anna Szafraniec (POL)	Sabine Spitz (GER)
2003	Sabine Spitz (GER)	Alison Sydor (CAN)	Irina Kalentiera (RUS)

Women's Downhill

1990	Cindy Devine (CAN)	Elladee Brown (CAN)	Penny Davidson (USA)
1991	Giovanna Bonazzi (ITA)	Nathalie Fiat (FRA)	Cindy Devine (CAN)
1992	Julie Furtado (USA)	Kim Sonier (USA)	Cindy Devine (CAN)
1993	Giovanna Bonazzi (ITA)	Kim Sonier (USA)	Missy Giove (USA)
1994	Missy Giove (USA)	Sophie Kempf (FRA)	Giovanna Bonazzi (ITA)
1995	Leigh Donovan (USA)	Mercedes Gonzalez (ESP)	Giovanna Bonazzi (ITA)
1996	Anne-Caroline Chausson (FRA)	Leigh Donovan (USA)	Missy Giove (USA)
1997	Anne-Caroline Chausson (FRA)	Marielle Saner (SUI)	Katja Repo (FIN)
1998	Anne-Caroline Chausson (FRA)	Nolvenn le Caer (FRA)	Cheri Elliott (USA)
1999	Anne-Caroline Chausson (FRA)	Katja Repo (FIN)	Sari Jorgensen (SUI)
2000	Anne-Caroline Chausson (FRA)	Katja Repo (FIN)	Marla Streb (USA)
2001	Anne-Caroline Chausson (FRA)	Fionn Griffiths (GBR)	Leigh Donovan (USA)
2002	Anne-Caroline Chausson (FRA)	Fionn Griffiths (GBR)	Missy Giove (USA)
2003	Anne-Caroline Chausson (FRA)	Sabrina Jonnier (FRA)	Nolvenn Le Caer (FRA)

General Information

bloomers: designed for cycling	Named after the American social reformer Amelia Bloomer (1818-94) who advocated a costume called 'rational dress' for women, consisting of a short jacket, full skirt reaching to just below the knee, and trousers down to the ankle. Although designed specifically for cycling, 'bloomers' became the standard women's attire for a variety of sporting pastimes.
BMX racing	The sport of BMX (Bicycle Moto Cross) takes place on purpose-built off-road tracks. Race distance is usually between 300 and 400m. A mechanical start gate is followed by a short downhill then a series of jumps and berms (banked turns). A race consists of one lap and up to eight riders may compete in each heat. BMX racing began in Santa Monica, California, in July 1969 and quickly spread to Europe. Raleigh introduced the BMX in Great Britain in 1983.

BMX: world champions

Men

1982	Greg Hill (USA)	1994	Danny Nelson (USA)
1983	Clint Miller (USA)	1995	Christophe Leveque (FRA)
1984	Phil Hoogendoorn (NED)	1996	Dale Holmes (GBR)
1985	Gary Ellis (USA)	1997	John Purse (USA)
1986	Tommy Brackens (USA)	1998	Thomas Allier (FRA)
1987	Gary Ellis (USA)	1999	Robert de Wilde (NED)
1988	Gary Ellis (USA)	2000	Thomas Allier (FRA)
1989	Charles Townsend (USA)	2001	Dale Holmes (GBR)
1990	Pete Loncarevitch (USA)	2002	Kyle Bennett (USA)
1991	Christophe Leveque (FRA)	2003	Kyle Bennett (USA)
1992	Wilco Groenendaal (NED)	2004	Warwick Stevenson (AUS)
1993	Gary Ellis (USA)		

Women

1993	Corine Dorland (NED)	1999	Audrey Pichol (FRA)
1994	Corine Dorland (NED)	2000	Natarsha Williams (AUS)
1995	Sabine Caballe (FRA)	2001	Gabriela Diaz (ARG)
1996	Natarsha Williams (AUS)	2002	Gabriela Diaz (ARG)
1997	Michelle Cairns (USA)	2003	Elodie Ajinca (FRA)
1998	Rachael Marshall (AUS)	2004	Gabriela Diaz (ARG)

Chopper Mk1: introduced	In 1970 Raleigh introduced the Chopper Mk1, based on their RSW 16 (Raleigh Small Wheels) which had been designed as their rival to the Moulton. It was targeted at 8-14-year-olds and had long vertical handlebars, high saddle, and a knobbly rear tyre.
Classics:	One-day events with top class status within the professional road-race calendar. The following are a list of the most famous classics.
Amstel Gold	Holland's only one-day Classic race was first held in 1966 and takes place around the Limburg province of the Netherlands. Frenchman Jean Stablinski was the first winner of the surprisingly hilly one-day Classic, held on the last Saturday of April.
Flèche Wallonne	Created by the newspaper *Les Sports* in 1936, the first victory going to local Belgian rider Philip Demeersman. Together with the Liège-Bastogne-Liège one-day Classic, known as the Ardennais Classics.
Liège-Bastogne-Liège	Known as La Doyenne as it is the oldest of the one-day Classics. First held in 1892 as an amateur event but by 1894 was established as a professional race, the first winner in 1894 being Belgian Leon Houa. It was not raced again by professionals until 1912 and then 1919-24. Five more years of amateur status followed until it was confirmed as an annual professional race in 1930.
Milan-San Remo	First staged by the newspaper *Gazzetta dello Sport* in 1907, first winner being Frenchman Lucien Petit-Breton. Also known as the Primavera, the one-day Classic is always held on the weekend closest to the first day of spring.
Paris-Roubaix	Launched in 1896 by two Roubaix textile manufacturers, Theo Vienne and Maurice Perez. A total of 188 riders took part in the first race which was won by Josef Fischer. Octave Lapize dominated the race from 1910 but was killed in 1917, while flying a plane in action. The famed cobblestones, narrow roads, farm tracks and mud give the one-day Classic its nickname of 'Hell of the North'.
San Sebastian	First held in 1981 and won by local Spanish rider Marino Lejarreta. The 240km route around the Basque mountains is demanding and follows the Tour de France in August.
cycle racing: became open	Many events were opened for the 1993 season but from 1 January 1996 international cycle sport administered by the UCI became fully open, with no distinction between amateur and professional.
cycle speedway	Cycle speedway traces its origins back to the early post-war years. The bikes are as simple as BMX or track bikes: there are no gears, brakes, brackets or quick-release fittings. Races are short – usually four laps of an outdoor 70-90m

circuit, lasting around 35-40 seconds – and physical contact is allowed. England's Dave Helmsley is the sport's biggest star. Reigning world, European and British champion, he has won the latter title a record five times.

ycleways: pioneered by Eric Claxton, architect of Stevenage New Town, designed Britain's first network of segregated cycleways in 1946 and used his home town as his model. Consequently, Stevenage boasts the proud record of being the only town in Europe with just one set of traffic lights, as his aim was to ensure that a cyclist's progress should not be hampered, thereby encouraging cyclists. In 1995 the British bicycle path charity Sustrans applied for funding from the Millennium Commission for a proposed 6500-mile National Cycle Network. It was awarded £42.5 million and it is hoped that the NCN will be complete by 2005 on the Inverness to Dover, Plymouth to Holyhead and Northern Ireland to Dublin routes.

ycling: governing body The international governing body, the Union Cycliste International (UCI), was formed in 1900.

yclo-cross: introduction The first world championship was won by Jean Robic of France in 1950. He had also won the 1947 Tour de France. Races usually last about an hour and are very demanding, particularly in bad weather. Bikes are carried through the very muddy terrain and over obstacles but most courses have some fast hard ground to show off cycling skills. Three bikes are often used during a race as they become clogged with mud and designated pit areas are seen at the world championships.

isc wheel: first used Disc wheels were first used in 1892 although considered unsafe due to crosswinds. To this day a disc wheel can be a serious problem on windy days and many riders prefer to use them only at indoor meetings or as a back wheel, the front being a conventionally spoked wheel.

our record: progression

11 May 1893	Henri Desgrange	Buffalo, Paris	35.325km
31 Oct 1894	Jules Dubois	Buffalo, Paris	38.220
30 Jul 1897	Oscar van Den Eynde	Vincennes, Paris	39.240
03 Jul 1898	Willie Hamilton	Denver (USA)	40.781
24 Aug 1905	Lucien Petit-Breton	Buffalo, Paris	41.110
20 Jun 1907	Marcel Berthet	Paris	41.520
22 Aug 1912	Oscar Egg	Paris	42.122
07 Aug 1913	Marcel Berthet	Paris	42.741
21 Aug 1913	Oscar Egg	Paris	43.525
20 Sep 1913	Marcel Berthet	Paris	43.775
18 Aug 1914	Oscar Egg	Paris	44.247
25 Aug 1933	Jan van Hout	Roermond	44.588
28 Sep 1933	Maurice Richard	St Trond, Belgium	44.777
31 Oct 1935	Giuseppe Olmo	Vigorelli, Milan	45.090
14 Oct 1936	Maurice Richard	Vigorelli, Milan	45.325
29 Sep 1937	Frans Slaats	Vigorelli, Milan	45.485
03 Nov 1937	Maurice Archambaud	Vigorelli, Milan	45.767
07 Nov 1942	Fausto Coppi	Vigorelli, Milan	45.798
29 Jun 1956	Jacques Anquetil	Vigorelli, Milan	46.159
19 Sep 1956	Ercole Baldini	Vigorelli, Milan	46.394
18 Sep 1957	Roger Rivière	Vigorelli, Milan	46.923
23 Sep 1959	Roger Rivière	Vigorelli, Milan	47.347
30 Oct 1967	Ferdi Bracke	Olympic Velodrome, Rome	48.093
10 Oct 1968	Ole Ritter	Mexico City	48.653
25 Oct 1972	Eddy Merckx	Mexico City	49.431
19 Jan 1984	Francesco Moser	Mexico City	50.808
23 Jan 1984	Francesco Moser	Mexico City	51.151
17 Jul 1993	Graeme Obree	Hamar, Norway	51.596
23 Jul 1993	Chris Boardman	Vélodrome du Lac, Bordeaux	52.270
27 Apr 1994	Graeme Obree	Vélodrome du Lac, Bordeaux	52.713
02 Sep 1994	Miguel Indurain	Vélodrome du Lac, Bordeaux	53.040
22 Oct 1994	Toni Rominger	Vélodrome du Lac, Bordeaux	53.832
05 Nov 1994	Toni Rominger	Vélodrome du Lac, Bordeaux	55.291
07 Sep 1996	Chris Boardman	Manchester, UK	56.375
27 Oct 2000	Chris Boardman	Manchester, UK	49.441

(See 'Athlete's Hour')

our record: Athlete's Hour A major rule change necessitated by the advance in bike technology saw the UCI change its criteria for attempts on the hour record and they reverted to 'Merckx era' standard bikes, creating the so-called 'Athlete's Hour' in the process. Thus Boardman's third record in 2000 is comparable to Merckx's record although the great Belgian's record was set at altitude.

Human Powered Vehicle: pioneer Dr Chester Kyle founded the International Human-Powered Vehicle (HPV) Association in California in 1976. HPVs are also known as recumbents due to the rider pedalling while lying flat on his back.

ersey: colours Blue jersey – the leader of the Intergiro sprint competition at the halfway stage of the Giro d'Italia wears the blue jersey (*maglia azzurra*)

C
Y
C
L
I
N
G

	Green jersey – awarded to the winner of the points prize (most consistent stage placings) in the Tour de France, and worn by the leader in the competition each day. A green jersey (*maglia verde*) is awarded to the King of the Mountains in the Giro d'Italia.
	Maroon jersey – the points leader of the Giro d'Italia wears the maroon jersey (*maglia ciclamina*).
	Pink jersey (*maglia rose*) – worn by the overall leader of the Giro d'Italia
	Polka-dot jersey – the red polka-dot jersey is worn by the leader in the King of the Mountains competition in the Tour de France.
	Rainbow jersey – awarded to the winner of the World Road-Race Championship.
	White jersey – the white jersey (*maglia blanca*) is awarded to the best young rider of the Giro d'Italia and the Tour de France.
	Yellow jersey (*maillot jaune*) – worn by the leading rider in the Tour de France and Vuelta a Espana.
Manchester Velodrome	The UK's first purpose-built indoor cycling stadium. It was built at a cost of £9 million on the site of the Stuart Street power station. It opened in the autumn of 1993 with an individual pursuit race between Chris Boardman and Tony Rominger, in which Boardman was victorious. The 10,000 sq ft building is covered by an aluminium roof supported by a 122m span main arch. The track itself is a 250m circuit of Baltic pine board, designed and constructed by Ron Webb. It is banked at 12.5 degrees on the straight and a maximum 42 degrees on the bends in order to catapult riders down the straight with gravity forces up to 4G. There is seating capacity for 3500 spectators. A bronze statue of Reg Harris, sculpted by James Butler, overlooks the finishing straight.
Moulton: introduced	Alex Moulton introduced the first unisex, mini-wheeled Moulton Stowaway bicycle in 1961.
oldest cycling club	The first recognised cycling club met on 22 June 1870 at the Downs Hotel, Hackney, East London. As the meeting coincided with the death of Charles Dickens it was decided to call the club the Pickwick Club.
plastic bicycle: first	The Swedish-made Itera was the first all-plastic bicycle featuring injection-moulded frame, forks, wheels and handlebars. Despite being rust-proof it was a commercial flop.
pneumatic tyres: first used	In May 1889 the first cycle race using Dunlop pneumatic tyres took place. Solid tyres remained the norm until 1895 after which they became almost obsolete.
rear lights: made compulsory	The use of a red rear light became a requirement by law in 1945 on British roads.
six-day racing events	Two-man team event raced over four main disciplines: Madison, Points, Devil Takes the Hindmost, and the derny-paced race/Keirin. Devil Takes the Hindmost is where the last man across the line at the end of each lap has to drop out. The events rarely last six days any more but the name has remained. On the Continent it was known as *racing à l'Américain*.
Tour de France: alternative names	La Grande Boucle (The Big Loop); Le Tour
first British rider to complete	Brian Robinson and Tony Hoar in 1955
first British rider in yellow	Tommy Simpson, 5 July 1962 (for one day)
first British rider to win stage	Brian Robinson in 1958.
first winner	Maurice Garin (nicknamed The Chimney Sweep)
greatest winning margin	Maurice Garin in the first Tour of 1903 won by 2 hours and 49 minutes.
most stage wins	Eddy Merckx (34)
point scoring system	The yellow jersey – or *maillot jaune* – is worn by the overall race leader, the rider who has covered the overall distance in the least amount of cumulative time. Time bonuses (12secs for winning a road stage, 6secs for winning an intermediate sprint) are deducted, and time penalties (for infringements such as dangerous riding or accepting pushes from spectators on the climbs) are added to riders' stage times before calculating their GC (general classification) times. The green points-leader's jersey is awarded to the best all-around finisher on flat, rolling and mountainous stages, as well as time trials and intermediate 'hot spot' sprints. With the highest points being awarded on flat stage finishes, the points jersey is often thought of as the sprinters' jersey, but a consistent and strategic all-rounder can also be a contender.

Points are scored as follows:

- flat stages: 35 pts, 30, 26, 24, 22, 20 and descending in one-point increments to 25th place
- rolling stages: 25 pts, 22, 20, 18, 16, 15 and descending in one-point increments to 20th place
- mountain stages: 20 pts, 17, 15, 13, 12, 10 and descending in one-point increments to 15th place
- time trials: 15 pts, 12, 10, 8, 6, 5 and descending in one-point increments to 10th place
- intermediate sprints: 6 pts, 4, 2 (three each day in stages 1-10, two each day in stages 11-20)

The polka-dot King of the Mountains jersey is awarded to the rider who most consistently reaches designated summits at the front of the peloton. Points are given not only atop mountainous finishes, but also on smaller climbs.

Climbs in the Tour are classified in five somewhat arbitrary categories:

- category 4 – usually less than 3km in length, an easy pitch that amounts to no more than a sustained rise in the road
- category 3 – slightly harder, up to 5km in length
- category 2 – between 5km and 10km, and steeper than a 4 per cent grade
- category 1 – long and steep. Between 10km and 20km, and steeper than a 5 per cent grade.
- Hors Categorie (HC) or above category – the longest, steepest mountain climbs. Extremely difficult climbs, sometimes 15km to 20km, with grades exceeding 10 per cent.

King of the Mountains points are scored as follows:

- Hors Categorie – to the top 15 riders, in descending order as follows: 40, 35, 30, 26, 22, 18, 16, 14, 12, 10, 8, 6, 4, 2, 1
- category 1 – to the top 12 riders: 30, 26, 22, 18, 14, 12, 10, 8, 6, 4, 2, 1
- category 2 – to the top 10 riders: 20, 15, 12, 10, 8, 6, 4, 3, 2, 1
- category 3 – to the top 5 riders: 10, 7, 5, 3, 1
- category 4 – to the top 3 riders: 5, 3, 1

The white jersey – or *maillot blanc* – is awarded to the best-placed rider aged 25 or under.

Team classification is established by the cumulative time of the top three individuals from each team on each stage.

Signified by a red race number, the most combative award is a somewhat subjective points total given by race judges each day to the riders who demonstrate the most consistent efforts in attacks and breakaways. Each rider's points are cumulative every stage to give an overall classification.

Tour of Britain: first held in 1952

track cycling: disciplines: Sprint A qualifying time trial of 200m of the 250m velodrome decides the pairings for the match sprints. Although two laps are cycled, only the time for the last 200m taken. The riders draw for starting positions in the best-of-three match races. Whoever has the inside lane must lead over the opening lap at walking pace unless an opponent wants to take the front. When the sprint is flat out, the riders have to hold a straight line and the leader has the 'right of way' inside the red sprinter's line that is painted on the track. Tactics are paramount; it is impossible to sprint flat out from the start as the opponent will simply slipstream the leader and pass when exhaustion sets in.

Olympic Sprint This is a three-man event that requires the speed of a sprinter, the strength of a kilometre rider and the ability to power away from the start and maintain a team formation. The race is over three laps of the track. The rider starting from the gate leads for the first lap before pulling off up the banking, the second rider then leads for a lap and, in turn, pulls off up the banking to leave the third rider on his own for the last lap. The event has a time-trial round like the pursuit events; the fastest eight teams go through and the fastest quarter-final winners contest the final. The third and fourth fastest contest the semi-final for the bronze medal.

Keirin This event originated in Japan where it is a sport on which major betting takes place. From six to eight riders follow a small moped-type bike which steadily increases speed before pulling off into the centre of the arena with two and a half laps to go, leaving the riders to sprint for the finish. During the lead-up laps to the finishing sprint the riders can change places in the field as they look for the best position to suit their strengths, however they have to stay behind the back wheel of the pacemaker bike. Keirin literally means 'fight' in Japanese.

Madison This race takes its name from Madison Square Garden in New York. It is a version of the points race except that teams of two riders compete over a distance of 50km. One rider races while the other circles the top of the track taking a rest before his team-mate brings him back into the action with a hand-sling. There are sprints for points every 20 laps but the main objective is to gain a lap on one's opponents. The race requires good team understanding and demands endurance coupled with sprinting ability.

Individual Pursuit 4000m/3000m The pursuit event involves one-on-one competition and the ability to race against the clock. The objective of the pursuit is to catch the rider starting in the opposite straight; if that doesn't happen, then the rider covering the distance in the quickest time is the winner. The first round is a time trial for seeding purposes. The fastest eight riders go through to the second round where the fastest meets the slowest, the second fastest meets the second slowest and so on. The two fastest second-round winners go into the final, the other two second-round winners ride-off for third place. To win in the individual pursuit requires pace judgement, the mental and physical toughness to put three fast rides together over two days and the ability to remain cool under pressure.

Team Pursuit	This event is between teams of four riders, starting on opposite sides of the track, attempting to catch their opponents or completing the ride in the quickest time. As in the individual pursuit event, there is a time-trial round for seeding purposes. The eight fastest teams then race quarter-finals, semi-finals and a final on a knockout basis. The finishing times are taken as the third rider crosses the finishing line; thus a team can lose one rider during the race. The members of a pursuit team must display excellent teamwork skills. Each rider leads for half a lap, or sometimes a whole lap, before riding up the banking to drop back to the end of the line to recover. Slipstreaming can never be underestimated in any cycling event and the ability to 'suck' a wheel is crucial to the success of a team pursuiter.
Points Race	This is a combination of an endurance race – it takes place over 40km (i.e. 160 laps of the track) – and a sprint race, as every 10 laps there is a sprint for additional points. For each sprint, the first four riders across the line at the end of the sprint lap take 5, 3, 2, and 1 point respectively. The last sprint of the race carries double points. Points are in fact a secondary factor; the main objective during the race is to gain a lap on the rest of the field. If more than one rider gains a lap or the whole field finishes on the same lap, then points decide the outcome. This event tends to be a battle between the sprinters, who try to slipstream the other riders, and the strong distance riders, who will try to gain a lap on the rest of the field. With so many riders on the track at the same time, tactics are crucial. Often it is the most tactically aware rider that will gain the day and even the best rider may miss out if forced to do too much work early on. The women's event is raced over 24km.
Triple Crown of cycle racing	The Triple Crown consists of the Giro d'Italia, Tour de France and the World Road-Race title. Only Eddy Merckx (1974) and Stephen Roche (1987) have won the Triple Crown. The three major multi-stage tours are the Tour de France, Giro d'Italia, and Vuelta a Espana but these do not constitute the Triple Crown.
yellow jersey: first wearer	In 1919 Henry Desgranges introduced the idea that the leading rider in the Tour de France should wear a yellow jersey to distinguish him from the rest of the peloton. The first rider to wear the jersey was Eugène Christophe of France, on the Nice–Grenoble stage. Christophe only managed third place in the race that year after an unfortunate accident, the eventual winner being Firmin Lambot of Belgium.

Biographies of Road, Track, BMX and Tricks Riders

Anquetil, Jacques   Born Mont St-Aignan, France, 8 January 1934. Anquetil was known as the man who could not be broken. If he had a weakness it was his lack of sprint at the end of races but he was a great climber and outstanding time triallist. His all-round abilities won him five Tours de France (1957, 1961, 1962, 1963, 1964), an event he concentrated on to the exclusion of other races. In 1956 he broke the world hour record with a distance of 46.159km and in 1967 improved his personal best to 47.493km, although this was not a world record. He retired in 1969 and died of cancer in 1987, aged 53.

Armstrong, Lance   Born Piano, Dallas, Texas, 18 September 1971. Started his sporting career as a promising triathlete before joining the pro peloton when he signed for the American Motorola team. He had an inauspicious start to his pro career, coming last in the 1992 San Sebastian Classic, but then gained second place at the Zurich Meisterschaft before taking his first stage of the Tour de France in 1993. He also won the world road race champion's rainbow jersey in 1993 when he beat Miguel Indurain into second place at Oslo. He avenged his dismal ride in the San Sebastian of 1992 by winning the event in 1995 and propelled himself into 1996 as the number one-ranked cyclist in the world. He started the season by winning the Tour du Pont for the second time and became the first American to win the Belgian Classic Flèche Wallonne race.

In October 1996 Armstrong was forced off his bike in excruciating pain. Tests showed he had advanced testicular cancer which had spread to his lungs and his brain. An operation to remove the malignant testicle and another to remove the growth

from his brain proved successful despite there being less than a 50 per cent chance of recovery. The chemotherapy, coupled with his own enormous will and fitness, proved an irresistible force and Armstrong was back training by March 1997. In May 1998 he won a local race in Austin, Texas, and his rehabilitation was complete. He was offered a contract by the United States Postal Service team and he has remained with them ever since.

He won his first Tour de France in 1999 and proved he was the finest time triallist in the world by winning all three time trials of the Tour; he was also as strong as anyone on the hills. He won the next three Tours de France in emphatic fashion, showing he was clearly the number one rider in the world, and joined Anquetil, Merckx and Indurain as the only men to have won four consecutive Tours.

The 2003 event was by far his greatest challenge. Although he was the overwhelming favourite before the tour began it became obvious that Jan Ullrich of Germany was in superb condition when he won the first time trial proper by 1min 36secs from second-placed Armstrong. Going into the penultimate day's time trial Lance was 1min 7secs ahead of Ullrich and the Tour was poised for a grandstand finale. At the intermediate checkpoints they matched each other second for second in the wet conditions. But Ullrich fell and Armstrong coasted in to take third place, extending his lead and winning his fifth consecutive Tour de France. An historic sixth-consecutive Tour de France victory was gained in emphatic fashion in 2004 with Armstong demonstrating superiority on the climbs and time trials to crush his rivals.

Boardman, Chris Born Clatterbridge, Wirral, 26 August 1968. First came to prominence after winning a Commonwealth Games bronze medal at team pursuit in 1986. This was the platform for a series of national titles and by the time of the Barcelona Olympics in 1992 he was among the favourites for the 4000m pursuit title. Boardman rode quicker in each successive round and in the semi-finals smashed the world record in 4mins 24.496secs. His final ride was even quicker but as he caught his German opponent, Jens Lehman, on the final lap the estimated time of 4mins 22secs could not be ratified.

The following year he broke Graham Obree's newly created hour record at Bordeaux and signed for the Gan team. He immediately had success in time trials for his new team: in 1994 he won the world time trial title and the world 4000m pursuit title. He also won the prologue time trial in his first Tour de France and held the *maillot jaune* (yellow jersey) for three days before retiring from the Tour.

The 1995 season was ruined when he crashed in the prologue time trial he had won the year before in the wet conditions of the Tour de France. In 1996 he was third in the Paris–Nice, took a bronze medal in the Olympic time trial, and then won the 4000m pursuit world championship with a new world record (4mins 11.11secs) beating Andrea Colinelli of Italy. After successfully beating Eddy Merckx's hour record on a conventional bike, Boardman retired from the sport in 2000 after developing osteoporosis (brittle-bone disease).

Bobet, Louison Born St Meen-le-Grand, France, 13 March 1925. Bobet was the first man to win the Tour de France three consecutive times (1953-55), having first worn the *maillot jaune* in 1948. A good all-round cyclist, he won the world road race title in 1954 before retiring in 1959 during the Tour. He died in Biarritz, 13 March 1983.

Burton, Beryl Born Leeds, West Yorkshire, 12 May 1937. Burton was primarily a time triallist but one of the world's best at any discipline. She was all-round British time trial champion 25 times between 1959 and 1983 and also won 14 track pursuit titles and 12 road race titles. In 1967 she covered 446.19km in a 12-hour time trial, 9.25km further than the existing British men's record. In 1968 Burton rode 100 miles in 3hrs 55mins 5secs, a decade after the first British man had broken four hours for the distance. At the World Championships she won five pursuit golds (1959, 1960, 1962, 1963, 1966), as well as three silver and three bronze medals; in 1960 and 1967 she won the road race, also gaining a silver medal.

Burton was the first woman allowed to compete against men at the highest level when she rode in the Grand Prix des Nations. She was awarded the OBE in 1968. Her world outdoor records include 20km (28mins 58.4secs in 1960) and 3000m (4mins 16.6secs and then 4mins 14.9secs) Her daughter Denise (born January 1956) competed with her at the 1972 World Championships.

Carpenter, Connie Born Madison, Wisconsin, 26 February 1957. One of the most versatile athletes in American history, she rowed for the University of California in the national collegiate championships and competed in the 1972 Olympics as a speed skater, finishing seventh in the 1500m. Carpenter turned to cycling after injuring an ankle and won 12 US cycling championships and a world pursuit title in 1983 in a world record time of 3mins 49.53secs. In the 1984 Olympic road race, the first such event for women, she lunged at the line and managed to pip her fellow American Rebecca Twigg to take the gold medal. Carpenter is married to Davis Phinney, a bronze medallist in the team time trial at the same Olympic Games.

Chausson, Anne-Caroline Born Dijon, France, 8 October 1977. The dominant figure in women's BMX racing, having monopolised the downhill mountain-bike championships in recent years. In 1993 she became French, European and world champion BMX racer before addressing her skills to downhill. Apart from winning the world downhill title every year since 1996 she is also the holder of the fastest speed record on a bike of 187.99kph on a downhill course. She also holds world titles in dual slalom and 4-cross.

Cooke, Nicole Born Swansea, South Wales, 13 April 1983. Despite her youth, Cooke has established herself as one of the best cyclists in the world. To date her titles include world junior mountain bike champion, British senior women's cyclo-cross champion, senior British road race champion and the world junior road race title. But the pinnacle came in August 2002 when she won gold for Wales in the road race at the Commonwealth Games in Manchester.

Coppi, Fausto Born Castellania, Italy, 15 September 1919. Undoubtedly the greatest Italian cyclist of all time. Coppi turned professional in 1940 but his early pro career was hampered by World War II. He did though manage to break a string of records in 1942, including the world hour record (45.87km), world 40km record (52mins 19secs) and world 45km record (58mins 51.4secs), also winning the Italian national championship. Coppi was dubbed the *campionissimo* (champion of champions) as he dominated races like no other rider of the day. It is sometimes said that his only weakness was as a sprinter, but he was so strong during races that he was hardly ever called upon to show his ability in a sprint. He won a stage of the 1949 Giro d'Italia (Tour of Italy) by more than 20mins and the 1950 Fleche Wallone by 6mins. Apart from his 1949 and 1952 Tour de France victories he won the Giro d'Italia in 1940, 1947, 1949, 1952 and 1953, and the world pursuit championship in 1947 and 1949. He died from a tropical illness contracted in Upper Volta, 2 January 1960.

Delgado, Pedro Born Segovia, Spain, 15 April 1960. Delgado turned professional in 1982, and after taking second place in 1987, won the Tour de France in 1988. Other major victories included the Vuelta a Espana (Tour of Spain) in 1985 and 1989. A great climber and time triallist, Delgado had several more top-three finishes in the Tour and, as part of the Banesto team, helped Miguel Indurain to several Tour de France victories before retiring at the end of the 1994 season.

de Vlaeminck, Eric Born Eeklo, Belgium, 23 August 1945. Eric won seven world cyclo-cross titles in eight years to establish himself among the great cyclists. He is the elder brother of Roger de Vlaeminck.

de Vlaeminck, Roger Born Eeklo, Belgium, 24 August 1947. One of the great riders but unfortunate to be born in the same era as the greatest of them all, Eddy Merckx. He did manage to inflict several defeats on Merckx, and made the Paris-Roubaix his own with victories in 1972, 1974, 1975 and 1977. He also won the 1968 amateur cyclo-cross world title and the professional title in 1975. He is the younger brother of Eric de Vlaeminck.

Doyle, Tony Born Woking, Surrey, 19 May 1958. Turned professional in 1979 after failing to be

C
Y
C
L
I
N
G

selected to ride in the amateur 4000m pursuit world championship of that year. He had immediate success by winning the 5000m pursuit world championship in 1980, a feat he duplicated in 1986. Two silver medals and a bronze in the intervening years make Doyle one of the greats of the sport and he had further success in six-day competitions, winning 18 events with Danny Clark of Australia and teaming up with Francesco Moser of Italy and Etienne de Wilde of Belgium for further victories. In 1995 he was elected President of the British Cycling Federation.

Egg, Oscar   Born Schlatt, Switzerland, 2 March 1890. One of the great all-round cyclists, who won the 1914 Paris-Tours race and eight six-day races but excelled at sprinting and time trialling. Egg was the Swiss track sprint champion for 12 consecutive years and also held the world one-hour record three times. His greatest distance of 44.247km was set in 1914 and stood until Maurice Richard beat it in 1933. Egg was an early pioneer of a revolutionary gearing system, the Oscgear, a precursor of the derailleur. He later coached Switzerland's only two Tour de France winners, Ferdi Kübler (1950) and Hugo Koblet (1951). He died in Nice, 9 February 1961.

Fignon, Laurent   Born Tournan-en-Brie, France, 16 August 1960. Nicknamed 'The Professor' because of his college background, Fignon won the 1983 Tour de France by over four minutes and triumphed again in 1984, beating Bernard Hinault by 10mins 32secs. Fignon was a great bike-handler and his daredevil descents were breathtaking. In 1989 he led the Tour by 58secs going into the final time trial stage but Greg Lemond overhauled him to win by 8secs, the closest finish in Tour history.

Garkushina, Tamara   Born Lipetsk, Russia, 1 February 1946. Tamara dominated women's pursuit cycling in the late 1960s and early 1970s, first winning the world title in 1967. She did not compete in 1968, finished second to her countrywoman Raisa Obodovskaya in 1969 and then won the title for five consecutive years from 1970-74.

Gaul, Charly   Born Ash, Luxembourg, 18 December 1932. Gaul was the greatest cyclist to be produced by Luxembourg. He excelled on the climbs and was given the nickname 'The Angel of the Mountain' after his performance in the 1955 Tour de France, when he won a mountain stage by 14mins. He became King of the Mountains in the 1955 and 1956 Tours before finally ending the 1958 race in yellow. Other victories included a bronze in the 1954 world professional road race championship and two Giro d'Italia wins in 1956 and 1959.

Harris, Reg   Born Bury, Lancashire, 31 March 1920. Britain's greatest-ever track sprint cyclist. He began racing on the track in 1936 and by 1947 was world amateur champion. Overwhelming favourite for the 1948 Olympic sprint titles, a broken arm early in the season caused him to underperform and he ended with silvers in the individual and tandem sprints. Harris turned pro shortly after this disappointment and in 1949 became the first sprinter to win a world professional championship at the first attempt. He went on to a hat-trick of titles in 1951 and won for the fourth time in 1954. He set world records for the standing start 1000m outdoors, with 1min 9.8secs in 1949 and 1min 8.6secs in 1952, a time which stood for over 21 years. He also set two world records indoors at the 1000m distance with a best time of 1min 8.9secs in 1955. Harris retired in 1957 but 17

years later, in 1974, he returned to racing and won the British sprint championship at the age of 54. He died in Macclesfield, Cheshire, 22 June 1992.

Heiden, Beth   Born Madison, Wisconsin, 27 September 1959. Beth Heiden was another world-class all-round athlete in the mould of Connie Carpenter. She began life as a speed skater, winning world junior titles in 1978 and 1979 and the senior title in 1979. She was favourite for the Olympic title in 1980 but a twisted ankle restricted her to a bronze medal in the 3000m. Later that year Beth became the first American woman to win the world road-race title at cycling, going on to win the NCAA cross-country skiing title. Her brother is Eric Heiden, widely considered the greatest speed skater of all time.

Hinault, Bernard   Born Yffignac, Côtes du Nord, France, 14 November 1954. Hinault was French junior champion in 1972 and turned professional in 1974 with immediate success, winning the French pursuit title in 1975 and 1976. He equalled the record of Jacques Anquetil and Eddy Merckx by winning the Tour de France five times (1978, 1979, 1981, 1982 and 1985) and was unfortunate not to have five consecutive victories when he was forced to retire in 1980 while leading the race. Hinault also won the King of the Mountains title in 1986 and in total gained 28 stage wins. Unlike many recent Tour de France winners who peak purely for that one event, Hinault often raced the other major tours and won the Giro d'Italia in 1980, 1982 and 1985, and the Vuelta a Espana in 1978 and 1983. He also won the world road race title in 1980. Hinault retired on his 32nd birthday in 1986 while still at the top of his profession.

Hoy, Chris   Born Edinburgh, Scotland, 23 March 1976. An all-round athlete at school, excelling as a rugby player and rower. He represented Scotland at rowing and won a British championship silver medal in the junior coxless pairs. Although starting his career on BMX bikes and then progressing to time trials and road races, he found his natural forte was track racing and he left his first club, Dunedin CC, to join the City of Edinburgh Racing Club in 1994. Hoy began to win major championship medals in 1998 and after a silver medal in the team sprint at the 1999 World Championships in Berlin he emulated this feat with silver medals at the 2000 Olympics, the World Championships in Manchester and World Cup in Moscow. In 2002 he set the world alight with some outstanding performances. He won the World Championship team sprint, adding the individual 1000m time trial (a feat he emulated in 2004). He also won the Commonwealth Games gold medal in the individual event and added the World Track Cup in Sydney to end the season as undisputed world number one at this discipline.

Indurain, Miguel   Born Villava, near Pamplona, Spain, 16 July 1974. 'Big Mig' turned professional in 1985 and had an inauspicious start to his Tour de France career, failing to finish in 1985 and 1986 before being placed 97th in 1987 and 47th in 1988. He gained his first stage win during the 1989 Tour, in which he finished 17th, and improved again in 1990 by placing 10th overall. Between 1991 and 1995 Indurain dominated the Tour de France with his fantastic climbing ability and unequalled ability in the time trial stages. In September 1994 Indurain captured Graeme Obree's one-hour record with a distance of 53.04km and the following year he won the world time trial championship in Colombia.

Kelly, Sean Born Carrick-on-Suir, Tipperary, Ireland, 24 May 1956. Kelly turned professional in 1977 and was the world's number one-ranked cyclist between October 1984 and May 1989, due mainly to the numerous one-day Classic wins which earned him the title 'King of the Classics'. His climbing ability was limited and this prevented him from winning the Tour de France, although he was points winner four times (1982, 1983, 1985 and 1989). He also won five stages. His highest overall placing was fourth in 1985 and he wore the yellow jersey for a single day, in 1983. Sean dominated the Paris-Nice stage race, winning it for seven consecutive years (1982-88). He also won the Tour of Lombardy three times. Kelly's last major win was in the 1992 Milan-San Remo. He retired in 1994.

Koblet, Hugo Born Zurich, Switzerland, 21 March 1925. Koblet won the 1951 Tour de France by 22mins, the largest post-war margin of victory after Fausto Coppi's 28mins 17secs success in 1952. On the 177km stage from Brive to Agen on 15 July he made a lone breakaway at 37km. Hard as the peloton tried, they could not catch him and he won the stage by 2mins 35secs. Koblet's nickname was 'The Pedaller of Charm' as his graceful style appeared effortless. Unfortunately he contracted a virus after his win in the Tour and although he managed to win the Tour of Switzerland in 1953 and 1955 he was never the same rider again. He died on 6 November 1964.

Kramer, Frank Born Evansville, Indiana, 20 November 1880. Kramer took up cycling as a therapeutic remedy after contracting tuberculosis as a teenager. He soon established himself as one of the great track sprinters. He won the US amateur sprint title in 1899 and then monopolised the pro title, winning every year between 1901 and 1916 and again in 1918 and 1921. He won the world sprint championship in 1912 when it was held in Newark, New Jersey, and would assuredly have won many more but for the fact that the competitors were generally held in Europe and he disliked travelling. Frank retired on 26 July 1922 at the age of 42, having equalled the world record for ⅙ mile in his final race. He died in East Orange, New Jersey, on 8 October 1958.

Lapize, Octave Born Paris, France, 20 October 1887. Lapize won a bronze medal in the 1908 Olympics in the 100km track race. He went on to win 'The Hell of the North' (Paris-Roubaix) an unprecedented three consecutive times (1909-11) and won the Tour de France in 1910. He died on 14 July 1917 in an aerial dogfight during World War I.

Lemond, Greg Born Lakewood, California, 26 June 1961. Lemond came to prominence in 1979 after winning three gold medals at the world junior championships in the team time trial, individual road-race and individual pursuit. He turned professional in 1981 and joined the Renault team with Bernard Hinault as his team leader. He came second in the world road race championship in 1982, winning the race the following year and again in 1989. He made his Tour de France debut in 1984, finishing third, and in 1985 acted as Hinault's lieutenant in the La Vie Claire team as the great Breton chalked up his fifth victory.

Lemond's time came in 1986 when he beat Hinault by 3mins 10secs in what was expected to be the first of a series of Tour de France victories. Unfortunately, he suffered severe blood loss after a shooting accident and it was thought he would never race again. He confounded the experts by making a successful return to cycling and in the most dramatic Tour de France ever he clawed back 58secs from race leader Laurent Fignon in the final-stage time trial to win the Tour by eight seconds. In 1990 he again won the race, beating Claudio Chiappucci of Italy by a comfortable 2mins 16secs.

He retired in 1994 and will be remembered as the first English-speaking rider to win the Tour de France. He was also the first rider to employ the single-minded approach of peaking for that one event every year, a system that his countryman Lance Armstrong has adopted so successfully.

Longo, Jeannie Born Annecy, France, 31 October 1958. One of the greatest cyclists of all time, Longo won 13 world titles: the pursuit in 1986, 1988 and 1989; road in 1985, 1986, 1987, 1989 and 1995; points in 1989; and the road time trial in 1995, 1996, 1997 and 2001. She was French champion on the road for 11 consecutive years (1979-89), held the pursuit title for 10 consecutive years (1980-89) and again in 1992, and won the points race in 1988, 1989 and 1992. She also won the women's Tour de France in 1987, 1988 and 1989, set numerous world records on the track and gained an Olympic road race gold medal in 1996.

McGregor, Yvonne Born Bradford, West Yorkshire, 9 April 1961. McGregor came to the sport of cycling late in her career after first trying fell running and triathlon. In 1993 she showed her potential by winning the women's 10-mile, 50-mile, and 100-mile UK time trial titles. In 1994 she won a gold medal for England in the 25km points race at the Commonwealth Games in Canada, and in 1995 she set a new one-hour international women's record of 47.4111km. The highlights of her career were undoubtedly her gold medal in the 2000 women's world individual pursuit championship and her bronze medal ride in the women's individual pursuit at the Sydney Olympics.

Maspes, Antonio Born Milan, Italy, 14 January 1932. Maspes first came to prominence when he won a bronze medal in the tandem match sprint at the 1952 Olympic Games with Cesare Pinarello. He subsequently won the world sprint title seven times.

Merckx, Eddy Born Meensel-Kiezegem, Belgium, 17 June 1945. Undoubtedly the greatest cyclist ever, Merckx excelled in every aspect, being the best time triallist and climber as well as being able to hold his own among the great sprint finishers. Nicknamed 'The Cannibal', the 1.93m Merckx became world amateur champion aged 18 and turned professional the following year. He won his first classic aged 21 and totalled 525 victories in 1800 races. In 1969 Merckx became the only man ever to win the yellow jersey, green jersey and polka-dot jersey at the Tour de France. In 1972 he set world records for 10km (11mins 53.2secs), 20km (24mins 6.8secs) and one hour (49.431km) at Mexico City. In 1974 he became the first man to win the Tour de France, the Giro d'Italia and the world professional road race in the same year. In November 1993 his 21-year-old son, Axel (born 8 August 1972), turned professional with the Telekom team.

Millar, David Born in Malta, 4 January 1977, of Scottish parents, and raised in Hong Kong. Millar turned professional in 1997. In 1999 he won the King of the Mountains title during the Tour of Valencia to first show that he had a future as a tour rider rather than just as a time triallist. In the 2000 Tour de France he won the prologue time trial and wore the yellow jersey for three days. He won the prologue time trial in the 2001 Vuelta a Espana as well as a stage victory. In the 2002 Tour de France he won Stage 13 to show he was building up to a significant showing. The 2003 Tour de France started calamitously for him; he saw an assured prologue time trial victory snatched away when his chain came off within sight of the finishing line. Millar soldiered on through the Tour despite a bronchial infection, winning the penultimate day's time trial stage despite falling off his bike. He ended his season by winning the world time trial championship in Canada, October 2003. Millar was subsequently stripped of his title and banned for two years by the British Cycling Federation after admitting taking the blood-boosting drug Erythropoietin (EPO).

Millar, Robert Born Glasgow, Scotland, 13 September 1958. Turned professional in 1980 and is Britain's highest-ever finisher in the Tour de France. A fantastic climber, he took a stage win on his first tour in 1983 and finished 14th overall. In 1984 he also took a stage win but added the King of the Mountains title, the first English-speaking rider to do so, and finished fourth overall. Millar won another stage in the 1989 race and finished 10th that year. His last Tour de France was in 1993 when he finished 24th overall. Only lack of time trial ability prevented him from reaching even greater heights in the main tours but he still managed second place in the 1985 and 1986 Vuelta a Espana and had a similar placing in the 1987 Giro d'Italia. In 1995 he won the UK professional road-race championship on the Isle of Man before retiring.

Mirra, Dave Born Syracuse, New York, 4 April 1974. One of the greatest freestyle BMX racers of all time, Mirra turned professional in 1992. The following year he was hit by a car and required brain surgery. He not only made a remarkable recovery but became a legend of the sport, with numerous tricks records. He was immortalised in 2000 by a video game based on his achievements.

Nakano, Koichi Born Kurume, Fukuoka Prefecture, Japan, 14 November 1955. Nakano dominated the world of track sprinting from the time he won his first world championship at the age of 21. He went on to win the title for 10 consecutive years between 1977 and 1986 and such was his dominance that in his last two victories much of the opposition didn't bother turning up to ride.

Newton, Chris Born Stockton-on-Tees, Cleveland, 29 September 1973. A top British rider on track and road for many years, Newton made the headlines in 2002 by winning the points race at the Commonwealth Games, achieving a scintillating victory in the same event at the World Track Championships.

Obree, Graeme Born Ayr, Scotland, 11 September 1965. Obree hit the headlines on 17 July 1993 when, as an amateur, he took Francesco Moser's ten-year-old world one-hour record of 51.151km, covering a distance of 51.596km on a home-built bike at the Viking Ship Velodrome in Hamar, Norway. His use of the innovative 'Superman position' allowed him to take in more oxygen by not compressing his chest cavity. Six days after Obree's record, Chris Boardman replied with 52.270km in Bordeaux only for Obree to set a new mark of 52.713km on the same track in April 1994. During the 1993 world 4000m pursuit championship at Hamar, Obree set a new world record of 4mins 22.668secs in the semi-final against Boardman and another in the final against Philippe Ermenault of France. A brief period

of riding as a professional with the Le Groupement team followed in 1994 before Obree's riding position was outlawed by the UCI. But he did make a return to pursuiting in 1995, once again capturing the world 4000m pursuit title.

Porter, Hugh Born Wolverhampton, 27 January 1940. Porter won a bronze medal at the 1963 World Championships at the individual pursuit but lost at the quarter-final stage in the 1964 Tokyo Olympics. He improved to win the gold medal at the 1966 Commonwealth Games and this gave him the spur to attain higher peaks. He came second in the 1967 world professional pursuit and improved to win gold in the 1968 event, a feat he repeated in 1970, 1972 and 1973. He was also second in 1969 and third in 1971.) He married swimmer Anita Lonsborough on 1 June 1965.

Queally, Jason Born Great Heywood, Staffordshire, 11 May 1970. A graduate in Biological Science from Lancaster University, Queally represented British Universities at water polo. In 1996 he won a silver medal in the 1000m time trial at the national track championships and in 1998 won a silver medal in the 1000m time trial at the Commonwealth Games in Kuala Lumpur. In 1999 he was placed fifth at the World Championships in the 1000m time trial and, with Chris Hoy and Craig MacLean, won a silver medal in the Olympic team sprint. In 2000 Queally won Britain's first gold medal at the Sydney Olympics in the 1000m time trial in 1min 1.609secs. Following this success he made an attempt on the human powered vehicle record in 2001, attaining a speed of 64.34mph (103.55kph) in his Blue Yonder machine. However, this fell short of Canadian Sam Whittingham's previous mark of 72.3mph (116.36kph), which was later extended to 80.5mph (129.55kph).

Roche, Stephen Born Dublin, Ireland, 20 November 1959. Roche was in the shadow of Sean Kelly throughout his cycling career, his undoubted talent inhibited by a series of knee injuries. After finishing 45th in the 1980 Olympic road race he turned professional in 1981, winning the Paris-Nice and the Tour of Corsica in his first season. He was third in the world professional road race championship in 1983 and attained a similar position in the 1985 Tour de France. In 1987 he had a year only ever matched by the great Eddy Merckx. He won a thrilling Tour de France by 40secs from Pedro Delgado of Spain, having earlier in the season beaten Robert Millar by 3mins 40secs to take the Giro d'Italia. He also won the world road race title that year, but his recurring knee injury prevented him from achieving any further cycling honours.

Simpson, Tommy Born Co. Durham, 30 November 1937. Simpson turned professional in 1960 after a brilliant amateur career where he managed to win bronze at the 1956 Melbourne Olympics at the team pursuit and silver at the 1958 Commonwealth Games at the individual pursuit. In 1962 he became the first British rider to wear the yellow jersey in the Tour de France, although only for a solitary day. In 1965 he won the Tour of Lombardy and the world professional road race title despite recovering from an horrific injury to his arm incurred during a fall in Le Tour. On 13 July 1967, Simpson was climbing Mont Ventoux during a stage in the Tour de France, when he collapsed and fell from his bike. He died soon after and a post-mortem showed his body to contain high levels of stimulants. His death was directly responsible for the anti-drug regulations that are now prevalent across all sports.

ylor, Marshall Walter Born Indianapolis, Indiana, 26 November 1878. Marshall, known as 'Major' Taylor, won the one-mile world professional sprint championship at Queen's Park, Montreal, on 10 August 1899 to become only the second black world champion in any sport, following the lead of boxer George Dixon. He was also the first black person to beat whites in a non-contact sport and was in addition a published poet. He died of heart disease in Chicago on 6 July 1932.

iggins, Bradley Born London, England, 28 April 1980. Wiggins became junior world champion in the individual pursuit in 1998 and soon established himself as one of the leading pursuiters in world cycling. He won a bronze medal in the team pursuit at the Sydney Olympics and another at the same discipline at the 2002 World Track Championships. At the 2003 Championships he was the dominant rider throughout the individual pursuit and despite a slow start in the final came through to beat Luke Roberts of Australia and win gold comfortably.

Zoetemelk, Joop Born The Hague, Netherlands, 3 December 1946. Zoetemelk was the only winner of an Olympic gold medal who also won the Tour de France. He won gold in the 100km team time trial at the 1968 Olympics in Mexico and 12 years later won the Tour after Bernard Hinault was forced out with knee problems. In 1985 he won the rainbow jersey by out-sprinting Greg Lemond to win the world road race championship.

DARTS

The origins of the game of darts in England can never be firmly established, but it dates back to at least the Middle Ages. It seems that bored soldiers took to hurling arrows at the upturned covers of wine casks. As the game became more popular, wine casks were substituted by tree trunks, the rings forming natural segments. The game was initially played outdoors but the extreme winters made an indoor version more attractive; for this the arrows were shortened and the distance thrown reduced. The indoor game became very popular and the noblemen of the day began to play what became known as darts. In 1530 Anne Boleyn presented Henry VIII with a set of ornamented darts. The game maintained a strong military appeal, and the worldwide spread of darts is credited to the British Army who brought the game with them to every corner of the Empire as it grew.

Employees at the brewery firm of Hockey & Sons are credited with establishing the standard throwing distance. It seems that the brewers placed three of their beer crates end to end, drew a line, and threw from that line, a distance of 9ft (2.74m). Eventually Hockey & Sons changed their standard crate size from 3ft (0.91m) to 2ft (0.6m) and so four crates were used. The general international standard today is 7ft 9¼ins (2.37m). The throwing line was called the 'hockey' after the company; later the name was shortened to 'oche' (pronounced 'ockee').

Most dartboards today are made from highly compressed bunches of sisal – the same material used to make heavy ropes.

The establishment of darts as a pub game can be fairly accurately dated. Throughout the Victorian period legislation prohibited 'games of chance' (i.e. gambling) in pubs. In 1908 a pub owner named Anakin in Leeds, Yorkshire, was taken to court for permitting darts to be played in his establishment. He offered to prove that darts was a game of skill. A board was set up in the courtroom, and there Anakin threw three darts into the 20. He challenged any of the magistrates to duplicate his feat. When they could not, the court was forced to accept that darts was indeed a game of skill, not chance, and the laws were eventually changed.

Between the turn of the century and World War II darts grew in popularity as a pub game. Regular leagues were held and competitions took place on a regular basis. The most prestigious of these competitions was that held by the *News of the World* newspaper from 1927. A National Darts Association was formed in 1954, and national championships organised. World championships began in 1978 and today it would be hard to find a pub in Britain without a dartboard.

The outstanding player in the history of the game is the present Professional Darts Council (PDC) champion Phil Taylor, who has dominated the world of darts throughout the 1990s and the start of the new millennium.

World Champions

	Winner		Runner-Up		Winner		Runner-Up
1978	Leighton Rees (WAL)	11-7	John Lowe (ENG)	1996	Steve Beaton (ENG)	6-3	Richie Burnett (WAL)
1979	John Lowe (ENG)	5-0	Leighton Rees (WAL)		Phil Taylor (ENG)	6-4	Dennis Priestley (ENG)
1980	Eric Bristow (ENG)	5-3	Bobby George (ENG)	1997	Les Wallace (SCO)	6-3	Marshall James (WAL)
1981	Eric Bristow (ENG)	5-3	John Lowe (ENG)		Phil Taylor (ENG)	6-3	Dennis Priestley (ENG)
1982	Jocky Wilson (SCO)	5-3	John Lowe (ENG)	1998	Ray Barneveld (NED)	6-5	Richie Burnett (WAL)
1983	Keith Deller (ENG)	6-5	Eric Bristow (ENG)		Phil Taylor (ENG)	6-0	Dennis Priestley (ENG)
1984	Eric Bristow (ENG)	7-1	Dave Whitcombe (ENG)	1999	Ray Barneveld (NED)	6-5	Ronnie Baxter (SCO)
1985	Eric Bristow (ENG)	6-2	John Lowe (ENG)		Phil Taylor (ENG)	6-2	Peter Manley (ENG)
1986	Eric Bristow (ENG)	6-0	Dave Whitcombe (ENG)	2000	Ted Hankey (ENG)	6-0	Ronnie Baxter (SCO)
1987	John Lowe (ENG)	6-4	Eric Bristow (ENG)		Phil Taylor (ENG)	7-3	Dennis Priestley (ENG)
1988	Bob Anderson (ENG)	6-4	John Lowe (ENG)	2001	John Walton (ENG)	6-2	Ted Hankey (ENG)
1989	Jocky Wilson (SCO)	6-4	Eric Bristow (ENG)		Phil Taylor (ENG)	7-0	John Part (CAN)
1990	Phil Taylor (ENG)	6-1	Eric Bristow (ENG)	2002	Tony David (AUS)	6-4	Mervyn King (ENG)
1991	Dennis Priestley (ENG)	6-0	Eric Bristow (ENG)		Phil Taylor (ENG)	7-0	Peter Manley (ENG)
1992	Phil Taylor (ENG)	6-5	Mike Gregory (ENG)	2003	Ray Barneveld (NED)	6-3	Ritchie Davies (WAL)
1993	John Lowe (ENG)	6-3	Alan Warriner (ENG)		John Part (CAN)	7-6	Phil Taylor (ENG)
1994	John Part (CAN)	6-0	Bobby George (ENG)	2004	Andy Fordham (ENG)	6-3	Mervyn King (ENG)
	Dennis Priestley (ENG)	6-1	Phil Taylor (ENG)		Phil Taylor (ENG)	7-6	Kevin Painter (ENG)
1995	Richie Burnett (WAL)	6-3	Ray Barneveld (NED)				
	Phil Taylor (ENG)	6-2	Rod Harrington (ENG)				

NB First named winners are Embassy BDO Champions, second named winners are WDC Champions (now called PDC)

News of the World Champions

1928	Sammy Stone		1964	Tom Barrett
1929	J. Hoare		1965	Tom Barrett
1930	C. Bowley		1966	Wilf Ellis
1931	Tommy Nye		1967	Wally Seaton
1932	Jack Hood		1968	Bill Duddy
1933	Kenny Enever		1969	Barry Twomlow
1934	Fred Metson		1970	Henry Barney
1935	Billy Forecast		1971	Dennis Filkins
1936	Peter Finnigan		1972	Brian Netherton
1937	Stan Outten		1973	Ivor Hodgkinson
1938	Fred Wallis		1974	Peter Chapman
1939	Marmaduke Breckon		1975	Derek White
1948	Harry Leadbetter		1976	Bill Lennard
1949	Jack Boyce		1977	Mick Norris
1950	Dixie Newberry		1978	Stefan Lord (SWE)
1951	Harry Perryman		1979	Bobby George
1952	Tommy Gibbons		1980	Stefan Lord (SWE)
1953	Jimmy Carr		1981	John Lowe
1954	Oliver James		1982	Roy Morgan
1955	Tom Reddington		1983	Eric Bristow
1956	Trevor Peachey		1984	Eric Bristow
1957	Alwyn Mullins		1985	Dave Lee
1958	Tommy Gibbons		1986	Bobby George
1959	Albert Welch		1987	Mike Gregory
1960	Tom Reddington		1988	Mike Gregory
1961	Alec Adamson		1989	Dave Whitcombe
1962	Eddie Brown		1990	Paul Cook
1963	Robbie Rumney		1997	Phil Taylor

NB Prior to 1948 the competition was restricted to players from London and the Home Counties.

General Information

BDO: stands for	British Darts Organisation (founded in 1973 but now vying with the PDC for prestige)
MBE: awarded first	Eric Bristow on 21 February 1989 was the first darts player to be awarded the MBE
News of the World competition	1991-96 suspended sponsorship; ended in 1998
News of the World: best-of-legs	best of three throughout competition
nine-dart 501: first televised	13 October 1984, in the quarter-finals of the MFI World Matchplay Championships the match featured British stars John Lowe and Keith Deller, with Lowe hitting the first televised nine-dart perfect 501 game in the history of the sport. His scores were 180-180-141 and he collected a cheque for £102,000. Ironically, due to complex tax laws, Lowe could not pocket a penny from the jackpot until two years later, as the currency sat in a British bank waiting for final approval.
number sequence: inventor	Brian Gamlin, a carpenter from Bury, Lancashire, came up with the sequence in 1896, at the age of 44. He died in 1903 before patenting the idea. The numbering of a standard dartboard is designed in such a way as to cut down the incidence of 'lucky shots' and reduce the element of chance. The numbers are placed in such a way as to encourage accuracy. The placing of small numbers either side of large numbers, e.g. 3 and 7 either side of 19, 3 and 2 either side of 17, 4 and 1 either side of 18, punishes inaccuracy. Thus, if you shoot for the 20, the penalty for lack of accuracy is to land in either a 1 or a 5. The full clockwise sequence from the top goes: 20, 1, 18, 4, 13, 6, 10, 15, 2, 17, 3, 19, 7, 16, 8, 11, 14, 9, 12, 5.
oche: details	The oche is the throwing line, often raised in top-class games. The name was introduced by The British Darts Organisation in the mid-1970s and is thought to be a corruption of the name Hockey (Hockey & Sons brewery established the throwing distance).
PDC: stands for	Professional Darts Council (established as the World Darts Council in 1992)
venues: Embassy	Heart of Midlands Club, Notts (1978); Jollees Night Club, Stoke (1979-85) Lakeside CC, Frimley Green, Surrey (1986-date)
venue: PDC	Circus Tavern, Purfleet
WDC: stands for	World Darts Council
World Championship: nine-dart leg	Paul Lim (USA) against Jack McKenna (Ireland) in 1990

DUCKPINS

Duckpin bowling was invented in Baltimore, Maryland, in 1900. It was, besides baseball, one of Babe Ruth's favourite games. Duckpin bowling developed from ten-pin bowling, which used to be strictly a winter sport. Most alleys closed down for the summer, but a few remained open so that bowlers could practise with small balls, about 6ins (15cm) in diameter. They usually played odd games called 'back five', using just the 5, 7, 8, 9, and 10 pins, and 'cocked hat', which used only the 1, 7, and 10.

In 1900, summer bowlers at the Diamond Alleys in Baltimore suggested it might be interesting to trim down the standard pins to match the size of the ball. Manager John van Sant liked the idea. He employed a wood turner to do the job and many of his customers enjoyed the new bowling game. At first, the rules of ten-pin bowling were adhered to but gradually the game became sufficiently popular to have its own set of rules.

Van Sant demonstrated the new sport to the owners of the alley, John McGraw and Wilbert Robinson. Though they are much better known as baseball managers, McGraw and Robinson were also avid duck hunters. When they saw the way the small pins flew wildly around the alley, one of them remarked that it looked liked a 'flock of flying ducks'.

Originally a summer sport, duckpin bowling became so popular in the area that winter leagues were organised in Baltimore in 1903 and in Washington, DC in 1904. During the 1920s, duckpin bowling spread along the east coast, from New England to Georgia. While the rules were basically the same everywhere, balls, pins, and lane sizes were not standardised.

The National Duckpin Bowling Congress (NDBC), founded on 8 September 1927, worked with member organisations and manufacturers to bring about standardisation. The NDBC held its first national tournament, patterned after the American Bowling Congress's ten-pin tournament, in the spring of 1928. There were 126 five-person teams, 162 doubles teams and 201 singles entries. Duckpin bowling grew rapidly during the 1930s. By 1938, an estimated 200,000 bowlers were participating in sanctioned league play. Growth continued more slowly after World War II, reaching a peak of 300,000 sanctioned bowlers in 1967. The sport's popularity has declined greatly since then, but it is still strong in a narrow geographical region from Washington and Baltimore to Connecticut and Rhode Island.

The pins are now standardised at 9.4ins (23.3cm) high, and the ball, with no finger holes, is a maximum of 5ins (12cm) in diameter and 3lb 12oz (1.7kg) in weight. As in five-pin bowling, three balls are allowed in each frame of a ten-frame game. A perfect game is 300, the same as in ten-pin bowling.

A variation, rubberband duckpin bowling, developed during the late 1930s. The pins are circled with bands of hard rubber that increase pin action and scores. The ball is the same size as in duckpin bowling but must weigh no more than 3lb 8oz (1.6kg). In 1946, the NDBC created an affiliate, the American Rubberband Duckpin Bowling Congress, to sanction leagues and conduct a national tournament. The rubberband version of the sport never spread very far beyond the Baltimore–Washington area.

EQUESTRIANISM

Horse races employing chariots of varying shapes and sizes were popular among the Egyptians, ancient Greeks and Romans. Chariot races were first held at the ancient Olympiad in 688BC and the welfare of the animals was secondary to the need to triumph. Horses and riders often risked their lives and fatalities of both were commonplace. The sport was a brutal extension of warfare and hunting, in which pursuits the horse was sometimes, of necessity, treated with more respect than it was in races.

That element of the sport stands in bleak contrast to a later development, the dressage. The discipline remains today what it was during the Renaissance. Some see it as the ultimate test of the relationship between rider and horse. The sport of dressage consists of a set of movements performed in an arena 20m × 60m, each movement being marked out of ten. The movements are designed to test the ability of both the rider and the horse.

Jumping events became popular in the 19th century. At that time they consisted mainly of puissance competitions, which were a test of which horse and rider could leap the highest over one fence, similar to the high jump in athletics. Grand Prix show jumping of the kind we know today became popular in France and England in the mid-19th century and in 1900 became part of the modern Olympiad.

The premier British show-jumping competition is the Hickstead Derby. The Hickstead arena, situated between Gatwick Airport and Brighton in Sussex, has been the home of this event since 1961. The two most difficult fences are the Devil's Dykes, where the angle into the obstacle can be crucial to jumping all three fences cleanly, and the famous Derby Bank with its almost vertical drop.

Only 49 clears have been attained as at the conclusion of the 2004 event.

Riders must be at least 18 years of age to compete in three-day and jumping events and at least 16 for dressage. Horses must be at least seven years old and must carry a passport from the International Equestrian Federation. Dressage riders must wear formal dress, although military and police personnel may wear their uniforms.

Three-day eventing features three disciplines: dressage on the first day, cross-country on the second day (a first refusal to jump results in a 40-point penalty, a second refusal one of 80 points and a third refusal elimination) and show jumping on the third day (refusals at fences in show jumping incur three faults, fences down incur four faults but in eventing ten faults are awarded for a refusal and five faults for a fence down). The two most prestigious three-day events in Britain are the Badminton and Burghley horse trials. Vaulting – gymnastics on horseback – became popular in the 1920s in Germany, from whence it spread, as an introduction to equestrianism for children. Competitions comprise two tests, the compulsory and the free, involving a vaulter, a lounger and a horse. In team events (for under-18s) there are eight vaulters. Vaulting – then called Artistic Riding – was included in the 1920 Olympic Games.

The present Royal Family has been fully involved in many aspects of equestrian sport. Princess Anne was a champion three-day eventer, as was her former husband Mark Phillips, and their daughter, Zara, is maintaining the family tradition. Prince Charles has ridden under National Hunt rules and both he and his father are top-flight polo players. Prince Philip was also part of the team that won the 1980 four-in-hand carriage driving World Champion Teamship.

Three-Day Eventing: Olympic Medallists

Individual

	Gold		Silver		Bronze	
1912	Axel Nordlander (SWE)	Lady Artist	Friedrich von Rochow (GER)	Idealist	Jean Cariou (FRA)	Cocotte
1920	Helmer Mörner (SWE)	Germania	Age Lundstrom (SWE)	Ysra	Ettore Caffaratti (ITA)	Caniche
1924	A. v d Noort v Zijp (NED)	Silver Piece	Frode Kirkebjerg (DEN)	Meteor	Sloan Doak (USA)	Pathfinder
1928	C.P. de Mortanges (NED)	Marcroix	Gerard de Kruyff (NED)	Vatten	Bruno Neumann (GER)	Ilja
1932	C.P. de Mortanges (NED)	Marcroix	Earl Thomson (USA)	Jenny Camp	Clarence von Rosen (SWE)	Sunnyside Maid
1936	Ludwig Stubbendorff (GER)	Nurmi	Earl Thomson (USA)	Jenny Camp	Hans Mathiesen-Lunding (DEN)	Jason
1948	Bernard Chevallier (FRA)	Aiglonne	Frank Henry (USA)	Swing Low	Robert Selfelt (SWE)	Claque
1952	H. von Blixen-Finecke II (SWE)	Jubal	Guy Lefrant (FRA)	Verdun	Wilhelm Büsing (GER)	Hutbertus
1956	Petrus Kastenman (SWE)	Iuster	August Lütke-Westhues (GER)	Trux von Kamax	Francis Weldon (GBR)	Kilbarry
1960	Lawrence Morgan (AUS)	Salad Days	Neale Lavis (AUS)	Mirrabooka	Anton Bühler (SUI)	Gay Spark
1964	Mauro Checcoli (ITA)	Surbean	Carlos Moratorio (ARG)	Chalan	Fritz Ligges (GER)	Donkosak
1968	Jean-Jacques Guyon (FRA)	Pitou	Derek Allhusen (GBR)	Lochinvar	Michael Page (USA)	Foster
1972	Richard Meade (GBR)	Laurieston	Alessandro Argenton (ITA)	Woodland	Jan Jönsson (SWE)	Sarajevo
1976	Edmund Coffin (USA)	Bally-Cor	Michael Plumb (USA)	Better and Better	Karl Schultz (FRG)	Madrigal
1980	Frederico Roman (ITA)	Rossinan	Aleksandr Blinov (URS)	Galzun	Yuriy Salnikov (URS)	Pintset

1984	Mark Todd (NZL)	Charisma	Karen Stives (USA)	Ben Arthur	Virginia Holgate (GBR)	Priceless
1988	Mark Todd (NZL)	Charisma	Ian Stark (GBR)	Sir Wattie	Virginia (Holgate) Leng (GBR)	Master Craftsman
1992	Matthew Ryan (AUS)	Kibah Tic Toc	Herbert Blöcker (GER)	Feine Dame	Blyth Tait (NZL)	Messiah
1996	Blyth Tait (NZL)	Ready Teddy	Sally Clark (NZL)	Squirrel Hill	Kerry Millikin (USA)	Out and About
2000	David O'Connor (USA)	Custom Made	Andrew Hoy (AUS)	Swizzle In	Mark Todd (NZL)	Eyespy II

Team

	Gold	Silver	Bronze
1912	Sweden	Germany	United States
1920	Sweden	Italy	Belgium
1924	Netherlands	Sweden	Italy
1928	Netherlands	Norway	Poland
1932	United States	Netherlands	only two completed
1936	Germany	Poland	Great Britain
1948	United States	Sweden	Mexico
1952	Sweden	Germany	United States
1956	Great Britain	Germany	Canada
1960	Australia	Switzerland	France
1964	Italy	United States	West Germany
1968	Great Britain	United States	Australia
1972	Great Britain	United States	Germany
1976	United States	West Germany	Australia
1980	Soviet Union	Italy	Mexico
1984	United States	Great Britain	West Germany
1988	West Germany	Great Britain	New Zealand
1992	Australia	New Zealand	Germany
1996	Australia	United States	New Zealand
2000	Australia	Great Britain	United States

Three-Day Eventing: World Champions

Individual

	Rider	Horse		Rider	Horse
1966	Carlos Moratorio (ARG)	Chalan	1986	Virginia Leng (GBR)	Priceless
1970	Mary Gordon Watson (GBR)	Cornishman V	1990	Blyth Tait (NZL)	Messiah
1974	Bruce Davidson (USA)	Irish Cap	1994	Vaughan Jefferis (NZL)	Bounce
1978	Bruce Davidson (USA)	Night Tango	1998	Blyth Tait (NZL)	Ready Teddy
1982	Lucinda Green (GBR)	Regal Realm	2002	Jean Teulere (FRA)	Espoir de la Mare

Team

1966 Ireland

Virginia Freeman	Jackson Sam Weller
Eddie Boylan	Durlas Eile
Penny Moreton	Loughlin
Tommy Brennan	Kilkenny

1986 Great Britain

Mary Gordon Watson	Cornishman
Richard Meade	The Poacher
Mark Phillips	Chicago
Stuart Stevens	Benson

1974 United States

Bruce Davidson	Irish Cap
J Michael Plumb	Good Mixture
Denny Emerson	Victor Darkin
Donald Sachey	Plain Sailing

1978 Canada

Mark Ishoy	Law and Order
Juliet Bishop	Sumatra
Liz Ashton	Sunrise
Cathy Wedge	Abracadabra

1982 Great Britain

Lucinda Green	Regal Realm
Richard Meade	Kilcashel
Virginia Holgate	Priceless
Rachel Bayliss	Mystic Minstrel

1986 Great Britain

Clarissa Strachan	Delphy Dazzle
Lorna Clarke	Myross
Ian Stark	Oxford Blue
Virginia Leng	Priceless

1990 New Zealand

Andrew Nicholson	Spinning Rhombus
Andrew Scott	Umptee
Blyth Tait	Messiah
Mark Todd	Bahlua

1994 Great Britain

Karen Dixon	Get Smart
Mary Thomson	King William
Charlotte Bathe	The Cool Customer
Kristina Gifford	General Jock

1998 New Zealand

Blyth Tait	Ready Teddy
Mark Todd	Broadcast News
Vaughn Jefferis	Bounce
Sally Clark	Squirrel Hill

2002 United States

John Williams	Carrick
Kimberly Vinoski	Winsome Adanti
David O'Connor	Giltedge
Amy Tryon	Poggio II

Badminton Horse Trial Winners

(Held at Badminton House, Gloucestershire, home of the Dukes of Beaufort)

Rider	Horse	Rider	Horse
1949 John Shedden (GBR)	Golden Willow	1978 Jane (Bullen)	
1950 Tony Collings (GBR)	Remus	Holderness-Roddam (GBR)	Warrior
1951 Hans Schwarzenbach (SUI)	Vae Victis	1979 Lucinda Prior-Palmer (GBR)	Killaire
1952 Mark Darley (IRL)	Emily Little	1980 Mark Todd (NZL)	Southern Comfort III
1953 Lawrence Rook (GBR)	Starlight	1981 Mark Phillips (GBR)	Lincoln
1954 Margaret Hough (GBR)	Bambi	1982 Richard Meade (GBR)	Speculator III
1955*Frank Weldon (GBR)	Kilbarry	1983 Lucinda (Prior-Palmer) Green	
1956 Frank Weldon (GBR)	Kilbarry	(GBR)	Regal Realm
1957 Sheila Willcox (GBR)	High and Mighty	1984 Lucinda Green (GBR)	Beagle Bay
1958 Sheila Willcox (GBR)	High and Mighty	1985 Virginia Holgate (GBR)	Priceless
1959 Sheila (Willcox) Waddington		1986 Ian Stark (GBR)	Sir Wattie
(GBR)	Airs and Graces	1987 not held due to severe weather conditions	
1960 Bill Roycroft AUS	Our Solo	1988 Ian Stark (GBR)	Sir Wattie
1961 Lawrence Morgan AUS	Salad Days	1989 Virginia (Holgate) Leng (GBR)	Master Craftsman
1962 Anneli Drummond-Hay (GBR)	Merely-a-Monarch	1990 Nicola McIrvine (GBR)	Middle Road
1963*Susan Fleet (GBR)	Gladiator	1991 Rodney Powell (GBR)	The Irishman II
1964 James Templer (GBR)	M'Lord Connolly	1992 Mary Thomson (GBR)	King William
1965 Eddie Boylan IRL	Durlas Eile	1993 Virginia Leng (GBR)	Houdini
1966 not held due to severe weather conditions		1994 Mark Todd (NZL)	Horton Point
1967 Celia Ross-Taylor (GBR)	Jonathan	1995 Bruce Davidson (USA)	Eagle Lion
1968 Jane Bullen (GBR)	Our Nobby	1996 Mark Todd (NZL)	Bertie Blunt
1969 Richard Walker (GBR)	Pasha	1997 David O'Connor (USA)	Custom Made
1970 Richard Meade (GBR)	The Poacher	1998 Chris Bartle (GBR)	Word Perfect II
1971 Mark Phillips (GBR)	Great Ovation	1999 Ian Stark (GBR)	JayBee
1972 Mark Phillips (GBR)	Great Ovation	2000 Mary (Thomson) King (GBR)	Star Appeal
1973 Lucinda Prior-Palmer (GBR)	Be Fair	2001 not held due to foot and mouth disease	
1974 Mark Phillips (GBR)	Columbus	2002 Pippa Funnell (GBR)	Supreme Rock
1975 cancelled after dressage due to severe weather		2003 Pippa Funnell (GBR)	Supreme Rock
1976 Lucinda Prior-Palmer (GBR)	Wide Awake	2004 William Fox-Pitt (GBR)	Tamarillo
1977 Lucinda Prior-Palmer (GBR)	George		

*1955 held at Windsor; 1963 reduced to one day due to bad weather

Burghley Horse Trial Winners

(Home of the Marquess of Exeter. The trials replaced those held at Harewood)

Rider	Horse	Rider	Horse
1961 Anneli Drummond-Hay (GBR)	Merely-a-Monarch	1983 Virginia Holgate (GBR)	Priceless
1962 James Templer (GBR)	M'Lord Connolly	1984 Virginia Holgate (GBR)	Night Cap
1963 Harry Freeman-Jackson (IRL)	St Finbarr	1986 Virginia (Holgate) Leng (GBR)	Murphy Himself
1964 Richard Meade (GBR)	Barberry	1987 Mark Todd (NZL)	Wilson Fair
1965 Jeremy Beale (GBR)	Victoria Bridge	1988 Jane Thelwell (GBR)	King's Jester
1967 Lorna Sutherland (GBR)	Popadom	1990 Mark Todd (NZL)	Face the Music
1968 Sheila Willcox (GBR)	Fair and Square	1991 Mark Todd (NZL)	Welton Greylag
1969 Gillian Watson (GBR)	Shaitan	1992 Charlotte Hollingsworth (GBR)	The Cool Customer
1970 Judy Bradwell (GBR)	Don Camillo	1993 Stephen Bradley USA	Sassy Reason
1972 Janet Hodgson (GBR)	Larkspur	1994 William Fox-Pitt (GBR)	Chaka
1973 Mark Phillips (GBR)	Maid Marion	1995 Andrew Nicholson (NZL)	Buckley Province
1975 Aiy Pattinson (GBR)	Carawich	1996 Mary King (GBR)	Star Appeal
1976 Jane Holderness-Roddam		1997 Mark Todd (NZL)	Broadcast News
(GBR)	Warrior	1998 Blyth Tait (NZL)	Chesterfield
1977 Lucinda Prior-Palmer (GBR)	George	1999 Mark Todd (NZL)	Diamond Hall Red
1978 Lorna (Sutherland) Clarke		2000 Andrew Nicholson (NZL)	Mr Smiffy
(GBR)	Greco	2001 Blyth Tait (NZL)	Reddy Teddy
1979 Andrew Hoy (AUS)	Davey	2002 William Fox-Pitt (GBR)	Highland Lad
1980 Richard Walker (GBR)	John of Gaunt	2003 Pippa Funnell* (GBR)	Primmore's Pride
1981 Lucinda Prior-Palmer (GBR)	Beagle Bay	2004 Andrew Hoy (AUS)	Moon Fleet
1982 Richard Walker (GBR)	Ryan's Cross		

*Pippa Funnell won the 'big three' events in three-day eventing in 2003: Badminton, Burghley and Lexington.

E
Q
U
E
S
T
R
I
A
N

Show Jumping: Olympic Medallists

Individual

	Gold		Silver		Bronze	
1900	Aimé Haageman (BEL)	Benton II	Georges van de Poèle (BEL)	Windsor Squire	Louis de Champsavin (FRA)	Terpsichore
1904–08	not held					
1912	Jean Cariou (FRA)	Mignon	Rabod Wilhelm von Kröcher (GER)	Dohna	E. de Blommaert de Soye (BEL)	Clonmore
1920	T. Lequio di Assaba (ITA)	Trebecco	Alessandro Valerio (ITA)	Cento	Carl-Gustaf Lewenhaupt (SWE)	Mon Coeur
1924	Alphonse Gemuseus (SUI)	Lucette	T. Lequio di Assaba (ITA)	Trebecco	Adam Królikiewicz (POL)	Picador
1928	Frantisek Ventura (TCH)	Eliot	P. Bertran de Balanda (FRA)	Papillon	Charley Kuhn (SUI)	Pepita
1932	Takeichi Nishi (JPN)	Uranus	Harry Chamberlin (USA)	Show Girl	Clarence von Rosen (SWE)	Empire
1936	Kurt Hasse (GER)	Tora	Henri Rang (ROM)	Delfis	József Platthy (HUN)	Sello
1948	Humberto Mariles (MEX)	Arete	Rubén Uriza (MEX)	Harvey	Jean d'Orgeix (FRA)	Sucre de Pomme
1952	P. Jonquères d'Oriola (FRA)	Ali Baba	Oscar Cristi (CHI)	Bambi	Fritz Thiedemann (GER)	Meteor
1956	Hans-Günter Winkler (GER)	Haila	Raimondo D'Inzeo (ITA)	Merano	Piero D'Inzeo (ITA)	Uruguay
1960	Raimondo D'Inzeo (ITA)	Posillipo	Piero D'Inzeo (ITA)	The Rock	David Broome (GBR)	Sunsalve
1964	P. Jonquères d'Oriola (FRA)	Lutteur	Hermann Schridde (GER)	Dozent	Peter Robeson (GBR)	Firecrest
1968	William Steinkraus (USA)	Snowbound	Marion Coakes (GBR)	Stroller	David Broome (GBR)	Mister Softee
1972	Graziano Mancinelli (ITA)	Ambassador	Ann Moore (GBR)	Psalm	Neal Shapiro (USA)	Sloopy
1976	Alwin Schockemöhle (FRG)	Warwick Rex	Michel Vaillancourt (CAN)	Branch County	Francois Mathy (BEL)	Gai Luron
1980	Jan Kowalczyk (POL)	Artemor	Nikolay Korolkov (URS)	Espadron	Joaquin Pérez (MEX)	Alymony
1984	Joe Fargis (USA)	Touch of Class	Conrad Homfeld (USA)	Abdullah	Heidi Robbiani (SUI)	Jessica V
1988	Pierre Durand (FRA)	Jappeloup	Greg Best (USA)	Gem Twist	G. Karsten Huck (FRG)	Nepomuk
1992	Ludger Beerbaum (GER)	Classic Touch	Piet Raymakers (NED)	Ratina Z	P. Norman Dello Joio (USA)	Irish
1996	Ulrich Kirchhoff (GER)	Jus de Pommes	Willi Melliger (SUI)	Calvaro	W. Alexandra Ledermann (FRA)	Rochet M
2000	Jeroen Dubbeldam (NED)	Sjiem	Albert Voorn (NED)	Lando	A. Khaled Al-Eid (KSA)	Khashm Al Aan

Team

	Gold	Silver	Bronze
1912	Sweden	France	Germany
1920	Sweden	Belgium	Italy
1924	Sweden	Switzerland	Portugal
1928	Spain	Poland	Sweden
1932	none finished		
1936	Germany	Netherlands	Portugal
1948	Mexico	Spain	Great Britain
1952	Great Britain	Chile	United States
1956	Germany	Italy	Great Britain
1960	Germany	United States	Italy
1964	Germany	France	Italy
1968	Canada	France	West Germany
1972	West Germany	United States	Italy
1976	France	West Germany	Belgium
1980	Soviet Union	Poland	Mexico
1984	United States	Great Britain	West Germany
1988	West Germany	United States	France
1992	Netherlands	Austria	France
1996	Germany	United States	Brazil
2000	Germany	Switzerland	Brazil

Great Britain Team Performances

24 7th

ilip Bowden-Smith
pel Brunker
offrey Brooke

48 Bronze

nry Llewellyn	Foxhunter
nry Nicoll	Kilgeddin
thur Carr	Monty

52 Gold

lfred White	Nizefella
uglas Stewart	Atherfow
nry Llewellyn	Foxhunter

56 Bronze

lfred White	Nizefella
tricia Smythe	Flanagan
ter Robeson	Scorchin

1964 4th

Peter Robeson	Firecrest
David Broome	Jacopo
David Barker	North Flight

1968 8th

David Broome	Mistee Softee
Harvey Smith	Madison Time
Marion Coakes	Stroller

1972 4th

Michael Saywell	Hideaway
Harvey Smith	Summertime
David Broome	Manhattan
Ann Moore	Psalm

1976 7th

Deborah Johnsey	Moxy
Rowland Fernyhough	Bouncer
Peter Robeson	Law Court
Graham Fletcher	Hideaway

1984 Silver

Michael Whitaker	Overton Amanda
John Whitaker	Ryan's Son
Steven Smith	Shining Example
Timothy Grubb	Linky

1988 6th

Nikolas Skelton	Apollo
David Broome	Countryman
Malcolm Pyrah	Anglezarke
Joseph Turi	Vital

1992 7th

John Whitaker	Milton
Michael Whitaker	Monsanta
Timothy Grubb	Denizen
Nick Skelton	Dollar Grit

Show Jumping: World Champions

Individual

	Rider	Horse
53	Francisco Goyoago (ESP)	Quorum
54	Hans-Günter Winkler (FRG)	Halla
55	Hans-Günter Winkler (FRG)	Halla
56	Raimondo d'Inzeo (ITA)	Marano
60	Raimondo d'Inzeo (ITA)	Gowran Girl
66	Pierre Jonquères d'Oriola (FRA)	Pomone B
70	David Broome (GBR)	Beethoven
74	Hartwig Steenken (FRG)	Simona

	Rider	Horse
1978	Gerd Wiltfang (FRG)	Roman
1982	Norbert Koof (FRG)	Fire II
1986	Gail Greenhough (CAN)	Mr T
1990	Eric Navet (FRA)	M. Quito de Baussy
1994	Frankie Sloothaak (GER)	San Patrignano Weihaiwej
1998	Rodrigo Pessoa (BRA)	Gandini Lianos
2002	Dermott Lennon (IRL)	Liscalgot

Team

78 Great Britain

Derek Ricketts	Hydrophane Coldstream
Caroline Bradley	Tigre
Malcolm Pyrah	Law Court
David Broome	Philco

82 France

Michel Robert	Idéal de la Haye
Patrick Caron	Malesan Eole IV
Frédéric Cottier	Flambeau C
Gilles de Balanda	Malesan Galoubet

86 United States

Michael Matz	Chef
Conrad Homfeld	Abdullah
Katie Monahan	Amadia
Katharine Burdsall	The Natural

90 France

Eric Navet	M. Quito de Baussy
Hubert Bourdy	Morgat
Roger-Yves Bost	Norton de Rhuys
Pierre Durand	Jappeloup

1994 Germany

Frankie Sloothaak	San Patrignano Weihaiwej
Soren von Ronne	Taggi
Dirk Hafemeister	PS Priamos
Ludger Beerbaum	Almox Ratina Z

1998 Germany

Lars Niberg	Loro P. Esprit
Markus Beerbaum	Lady Weingard
Franke Sloothaak	San Patrignano Joly
Ludger Beerbaum	PS Priamos

2002 France

Eric Levallois	Diamant de Semilly Ecolit
Reynald Angot	Tialoc M
G. Bertran de Balada	Crocus Graverie
Eric Navet	Dollar du Murier hts de Seine

EQUESTRIAN

Hickstead Show Jumping Derby

(held annually at The All England Jumping Course, Hickstead, Sussex)

	Rider	Horse		Rider	Horse
1961	Seamus Hayes (IRL)	Goodbye III	1982	Paul Schockemöhle (FRG)	Deister
1962	Pat Smythe (GBR)	Flanagan	1983	John Whitaker (GBR)	Ryan's Son
1963	Nelson Pessoa (BRA)	Gran Geste	1984	John Ledingham (GBR)	Gabhran
1964	Seamus Hayes (IRL)	Goodbye III	1985	Paul Schockemöhle (FRG)	Lorenzo
1965	Nelson Pessoa (BRA)	Gran Geste	1986	Paul Schockemöhle (FRG)	Deister
1966	David Broome (GBR)	Mister Softee	1987	Nick Skelton (GBR)	Raffles
1967	Marion Coakes (GBR)	Stroller	1988	Nick Skelton (GBR)	Apollo
1968	Alison Westwood (GBR)	The Maverick VII	1989	Nick Skelton (GBR)	Apollo
1969	Anneli Drummond-Hay		1990	Jozsef Turi (GBR)	Vital
	(GBR)	Xanthos II	1991	Michael Whitaker (GBR)	Mon Santa
1970	Harvey Smith (GBR)	Mattie Brown	1992	Michael Whitaker (GBR)	Mon Santa
1971	Harvey Smith (GBR)	Mattie Brown	1993	Michael Whitaker (GBR)	My Messieur
1972	Hendrik Snoek (FRG)	Shirokko	1994	John Ledingham (GBR)	Kilbala
1973	Alison (Westwood) Dawes		1995	John Ledingham (GBR)	Kilbala
	(GBR)	Mr Banbury	1996	Nelson Pessoa (BRA)	Loro Piana Vivaldi
1974	Harvey Smith (GBR)	Salvador	1997	John Popely (GBR)	Bluebird
1975	Paul Darragh (IRL)	Pele	1998	John Whitaker (GBR)	Gammon
1976	Eddie Macken (IRL)	Boomerang	1999	Rob Hoekstra (GBR)	Lionel II
1977	Eddie Macken (IRL)	Boomerang	2000	John Whitaker (GBR)	Virtual Village Welha
1978	Eddie Macken (IRL)	Boomerang	2001	Peter Charles (IRL)	Corrida
1979	Eddie Macken (IRL)	Boomerang	2002	Peter Charles (IRL)	Corrida
1980	Michael Whitaker (GBR)	Owen Gregory	2003	Peter Charles (IRL)	Corrida
1981	Harvey Smith (GBR)	Sanyo Video	2004	John Whitaker (GBR)	Buddy Bunn

Dressage: World Champions

Individual

1966	Josef Neckermann (FRG)	Mariano
1970	Yelena Petuchkova (URS)	Pepel
1974	Reiner Limke (FRG)	Mehmed
1978	Christine Stuckleberger (SUI)	Granat
1982	Reiner Limke (FRG)	Ahlerich
1986	Anne Grethe Jensen (DEN)	Marzog
1990	Nichole Uphoff (FRG)	Rembrandt
1994	Isabell Werth (GER)	Gigolo
1998	Isabell Werth (GER)	Nissan Gigolo
2002	Nadine Cappelmann (GER)	Farben Froh

Team

1966	West Germany	1982	West Germany	1994	Germany
1970	Soviet Union	1986	West Germany	1998	Germany
1974	West Germany	1990	West Germany	2002	Germany
1978	West Germany				

Vaulting: World Championships

Men

	Gold	Silver	Bronze
1986	Dietmar Otto (GER)	Björn Ahsbahs (GER)	Michael Lehner (GER)
1988	Christoph Lensing (GER)	Michael Lehner (GER)	Dietmar Otto (GER)
1990	Michael Lehner (GER)	Christoph Lensing (GER)	Dietmar Otto (GER)
1992	Christoph Lensing (GER)	Thomas Föcking (GER)	Thomas Fisbaek (GER)
1994	Thomas Fisbaek (GER)	Christoph Lensing (GER)	Thomas Föcking (GER)
1996	Christoph Lensing (GER)	Philipp Lehner (GER)	Devon Maitozo (USA)
1998	Devon Maitozo (USA)	Matthias Lang (FRA)	Henrik Ossenbrink (GER)
2000	Matthias Lang (FRA)	Gero Meyer (GER)	Devon Maitozo (USA)

Women

	Gold	Silver	Bronze
986	Silke Bernhard (GER)	Jeanette Boxall (USA)	Ute Schönian (GER)
988	Silke Bernhard (GER)	Silke Gutermuth (GER)	Christine Otto-Kanstinger (GER)
990	Silke Bernhard (GER)	Silke Michelberger (GER)	Ute Schönian (GER)
992	Barbara Ströbel (GER)	Silke Michelberger (GER)	Tanja Benedetto (GER)
994	Tanja Benedetto (GER)	Kerith Lemon (USA)	Mieke Lorentz (GER)
996	Tanja Benedetto (GER)	Kerith Lemon (USA)	Janine Oswald (GER)
998	Nadia Zülow (GER)	Kerith Lemon (USA)	Janine Oswald (GER)
000	Nadia Zülow (GER)	Nicola Ströh (GER)	Kerith Lemon (USA)
002	Nadia Zülow (GER)	Rikke Laumann (DEN)	Ines Juckstock (GER)

Team

	Gold	Silver	Bronze
986	Germany	Switzerland	Austria
988	Switzerland	West Germany	Poland
990	Switzerland	West Germany	USA
992	Germany	Switzerland	Poland
994	Switzerland	Germany	Sweden
996	Germany	Switzerland	Sweden
998	Germany	Switzerland	USA
000	Germany	Switzerland	Austria

E
Q
U
E
S
T
R
I
A
N

ETON WALL GAME

The first record of the Eton Wall Game was in 1766. The first of the big St Andrew's Day (30 November) matches, however, between the Collegers and the Oppidans (town-dwellers), was played in 1844. By then the rules were more or less agreed, but they were not actually published until five years later.

The rules have been revised from time to time since 1849, but the game has remained essentially the same. The field of play is a narrow strip of land, about 5m wide, running alongside a not-quite-straight brick wall, built in 1717 and about 110m from end to end. As in all forms of football, each side tries to get the ball down to the far end and then score. Players are not allowed to handle the ball, not allowed to let any part of their bodies except feet and hands touch the ground and not allowed to strike or hold their opponents. There are also exceedingly strict 'offside' rules (no passing back and no playing in front). Apart from that, almost anything goes. Non-participating students often sit on the wall to spectate.

Each phase of play starts with a 'bully'. About six of the ten players from each side form up against the wall and against each other, the ball is rolled in and battle is joined. The player in possession of the ball will normally be on all fours, with the ball at his feet or under his knees. Players on his own side will attempt to support him, to establish him in a position where he can pass the ball to them, or to disrupt the opposition.

Likewise, players on the other side will attempt to obstruct his progress, to force him down, to gain possession of the ball themselves. Occasionally the ball becomes 'loose' and a player may be able to kick it out of play: the next bully is then formed opposite where the ball stops or is stopped – quite unlike what happens in soccer or rugby.

At each end of the wall is a special area known as 'calx'. When play reaches this area, the rules alter slightly (passing back becomes legal, for example) and the attacking side can score. The attackers try to raise the ball off the ground and against the wall, and having done so to touch it with the hand. They then shout 'Got it!' and if the umpire is satisfied that all is correct he shouts 'Shy!' and awards them a 'shy', worth one point. The attackers can now attempt to throw a 'goal', which would bring them an extra nine points (the goals are a garden door at one end and a tree at the other). Shies are relatively common, perhaps half a dozen a year, but goals are very uncommon – the last on St Andrew's Day was in 1909.

The Eton Wall Game is exceptionally exhausting and is far more skilful than might appear. The skill consists in the remorseless application of pressure and leverage as one advances inch by painful inch through a seemingly impenetrable mass of opponents.

A keen and successful sportsman, Prince Harry was House Captain of Games in his final year at Eton and took part in the Eton Wall Game.

FENCING

Swords have existed in some form almost as long as humans have walked the earth and swordplay has been practised in many forms in various cultures. Although jousting and tournament combat was a popular sport in the Middle Ages, modern fencing owes more to unarmoured duelling contests that developed from 16th-century rapier combat. Rapiers evolved from cut-and-thrust military swords, but were most popular among civilians who used them for self-defence as well as duelling. Rapiers were edged, but the primary means of attack was the thrust. Rapier fencing spread from Spain and Italy to northwest Europe, in spite of the objections of masters such as George Silver who preferred traditional cutting weapons such as the two-handed English broad sword.

By the 18th century, the rapier had evolved into a simpler, shorter and lighter weapon that was popularised in France as the small sword. Although this often had an edge, it was only to discourage the opponent from grabbing the blade, and the weapon was used exclusively for thrusting. The lightweight design made a more complex and defensive style possible, and the French masters developed a school based on defence with the sword, subtlety of movement, and complex attacks. When buttoned with a leather safety tip that resembled a flower bud, the small sword was known as the *fleuret*, and was identical in use to the modern foil (still known as *le fleuret* in French). Indeed, the French small-sword school forms the basis of most of modern fencing theory.

Meanwhile, another type of sword, the *colichemarde*, had been created for duelling. The blade had a triangular cross-section, with slightly concave sides to reduce weight without reducing strength. The *colichemarde* evolved into the modern épée.

By the mid-19th century, duelling was in decline as a means of settling disputes, not least because victory could lead to a jail term for assault or manslaughter. Emphasis shifted to defeating the opponent without necessarily killing him, and less fatal duelling forms evolved using the duelling sword or *épée de terrain*, an unedged variant of the small sword. Later duels often ended with crippling thrusts to the arm or leg, and resulted in fewer legal difficulties for the participants. This is the basis of fencing as a sport.

The first modern Olympic Games featured foil and sabre fencing for men only. Épée was introduced in 1900. Single stick was featured in the 1904 Games. Épée was electrified in the 1936 Games, foil in 1956, and sabre in 1988. Early Olympic Games featured events for Masters, and until recently fencing was the only Olympic sport that has included professionals. Disruptions in prevailing styles have accompanied the introduction of electric judging, and have most recently transformed sabre fencing. Foil fencing experienced similar upheavals for a decade or two following the introduction of electric judging, which was further complicated by the new, aggressive, athletic style coming out of Eastern Europe at the time.

Women's foil was first contested in the 1924 Olympic Games, but women's épée was only contested for the first time in 1996, although it has been part of the World Championships since 1989. Women's sabre made its first appearance in the 1998 World Championships as a demonstration sport.

The governing body for the sport in Britain is the Amateur Fencing Association, founded in 1902. In the early years there were many disputes as to rules and regulations but these were standardised in 1913 with the foundation of the Fédération Internationale d'Escrime (FIE) in Paris. The stated purpose of the FIE is to codify and regulate the practice of the sport of fencing, particularly for the purpose of international competition.

The first world championships were held in 1921 (although these were called the European Championships until 1936). L. Gaudin of France won the first competition, which was for épée only. The following year the sabre was introduced and A. de Jong of Holland triumphed. The foil was introduced into the World Championships in 1926 and G. Chiavacci of Italy became the first victor. Women's foil began in 1929 and the first world champion was H. Mayer of Germany. World Championships are not held in Olympic years, the Olympic champion being deemed the world champion.

Notable British fencers include Mr H.W.F. Hoskyns who won the World Épée Championship in 1958, and Gillian Sheen who won Olympic gold in 1956.

Olympic Medallists

Men's Foil

Gold	Silver	Bronze
1896 Eugène-Henri Gravelotte (FRA)	Henri Callot (FRA)	Periklis Pierrakos-Mavromichalis (GRE) Athanasios Vouros (GRE)
1900 Emile Coste (FRA)	Henri Masson (FRA)	Marcel Jacques Boulenger (FRA)
1904 Ramón Fonst (CUB)	Albertson van Zo Post (USA)	Charles Tatham (USA)
1906 Georges Dillon-Kavanagh (FRA)	Gustav Casmir (GER)	Pierre d'Hugues (FRA)
1912 Nedo Nadi (ITA)	Pietro Speciale (ITA)	Richard Verderber (AUT)
1920 Nedo Nadi (ITA)	Philippe Cattiau (FRA)	Roger Ducret (FRA)
1924 Roger Ducret (FRA)	Philippe Cattiau (FRA)	Maurice van Damme (BEL)
1928 Lucien Gaudin (FRA)	Erwin Casmir (GER)	Giulio Gardini (ITA)
1932 Gustavo Marzi (ITA)	Joseph Levis (USA)	Giulio Gardini (ITA)
1936 Giulio Gardini (ITA)	Edward Gardère (FRA)	Giorgio Bocchino (ITA)
1948 Jehan Buhan (FRA)	Christian d'Oriola (FRA)	Lajos Maszlay (HUN)
1952 Christian d'Oriola (FRA)	Edoardo Mangiarotti (ITA)	Manlio Di Rosa (ITA)
1956 Christian d'Oriola (FRA)	Giancarlo Bergamini (ITA)	Antonio Spallino (ITA)
1960 Viktor Zhdanovich (URS)	Yuriy Sissikin (URS)	Albert Axelrod (USA)
1964 Egon Franke (POL)	Jean-Claude Magnan (FRA)	Daniel Revenu (FRA)
1968 Ionel Drimba (ROM)	Jenö Kamuti (HUN)	Daniel Revenu (FRA)
1972 Witold Woyda (POL)	Jenö Kamuti (HUN)	Christian Noël (FRA)
1976 Fabio Dal Zotto (ITA)	Aleksandr Romankov (URS)	Bernard Talvard (FRA)
1980 Vladimir Smirnov (URS)	Pascal Jolyot (FRA)	Aleksandr Romankov (URS)
1984 Mauro Numa (ITA)	Matthias Behr (FRG)	Stefano Cerioni (ITA)
1988 Stefano Cerioni (ITA)	Udo Wagner (GDR)	Aleksandr Romankov (URS)
1992 Philippe Omnès (FRA)	Sergey Golubitsky (CIS)	Elvis Gregory (CUB)
1996 Alessandro Puccini (ITA)	Lionel Plumenail (FRA)	Franck Boidin (FRA)
2000 Kim Young-Ho (KOR)	Ralf Bissdorf (GER)	Dmitriy Shevchenko (RUS)

Men's Team Foil

Gold	Silver	Bronze
1904 Cuba	United States	only two teams competed
1920 Italy	France	United States
1924 France	Belgium	Hungary
1928 Italy	France	Argentina
1932 France	Italy	United States
1936 Italy	France	Germany
1948 France	Italy	Belgium
1952 France	Italy	Hungary
1956 Italy	France	Hungary
1960 Soviet Union	Italy	Germany
1964 Soviet Union	Poland	France
1968 France	Soviet Union	Poland
1972 Poland	Soviet Union	France
1976 West Germany	Italy	France
1980 France	Soviet Union	Poland
1984 Italy	West Germany	France
1988 Soviet Union	West Germany	Hungary
1992 Germany	Cuba	Poland
1996 Russia	Poland	Cuba
2000 France	China	Italy

Men's Épée

Gold	Silver	Bronze
1900 Ramón Fonst (CUB)	Louis Perrée (FRA)	Léon Sée (FRA)
1904 Ramón Fonst (CUB)	Charles Tatham (USA)	Albertson van Zo Post (USA)
1906 Georges de la Falaise (FRA)	Georges-Dillon-Kavanagh (FRA)	Hendrik van Blijenburgh (NED)
1908 Gaston Alibert (FRA)	Alexandre Lippmann (FRA)	Eugène Olivier (FRA)
1912 Paul Anspach (BEL)	Ivan Osiier (DEN)	Philippe Le Hardy de Beaulieu (BEL)
1920 Armand Massard (FRA)	Alexandre Lippmann (FRA)	Gustave Buchard (FRA)
1924 Charles Delporte (BEL)	Roger Ducret (FRA)	Nils Hellsten (SWE)
1928 Lucien Gaudin (FRA)	Georges Buchard (FRA)	George Calnan (USA)
1932 Giancarlo Cornaggia-Medici (ITA)	Georges Buchard (FRA)	Carlo Agostini (ITA)

936 Franco Riccardi (ITA)	Saverio Ragno (ITA)	Giancarlo Cornaggia-Medici (ITA)
948 Luigi Cantone (ITA)	Oswald Zappelli (SUI)	Edoardo Mangiarotti (ITA)
952 Edoardo Mangiarotti (ITA)	Dario Mangiarotti (ITA)	Oswald Zappelli (SUI)
956 Carlo Pavesi (ITA)	Giuseppe Delfino (ITA)	Edoardo Mangiarotti (ITA)
960 Giuseppe Delfino (ITA)	Allan Jay (GBR)	Bruno Habarovs (URS)
964 Grigoriy Kriss (URS)	Henry Hoskyns (GBR)	Guram Kostava (URS)
968 Győző Kulcsár (HUN)	Grigoriy Kriss (URS)	Gianluigi Saccaro (ITA)
972 Csaba Fenyvesi (HUN)	Jacques la Degaillerie (FRA)	Győző Kulcsár (HUN)
976 Alexander Pusch (FRG)	Jürgen Hehn (FRG)	Győző Kulcsár (HUN)
980 Johan Harmenberg (SWE)	Ernő Kolczonay (HUN)	Philippe Riboud (FRA)
984 Philippe Boisse (FRA)	Björne Väggö (SWE)	Philippe Riboud (FRA)
988 Arnd Schmidt (FRG)	Philippe Riboud (FRA)	Andrey Shuvalov (URS)
992 Eric Srecki (FRA)	Pavel Kolobkov (CIS)	Jean-Michel Henry (FRA)
996 Aleksandr Beketov (RUS)	Iván Trevejo (CUB)	Geza Imre (HUN)
000 Pavel Kolobkov (RUS)	Hugues Obry (FRA)	Lee Sang-Ki (KOR)

Men's Team Épée

Gold	Silver	Bronze
906 France	Great Britain	Belgium
908 France	Great Britain	Belgium
912 Belgium	Great Britain	Netherlands
920 Italy	Belgium	France
924 France	Belgium	Italy
928 Italy	France	Portugal
932 France	Italy	United States
936 Italy	Sweden	France
948 France	Italy	Sweden
952 Italy	Sweden	Switzerland
956 Italy	Hungary	France
960 Italy	Great Britain	Soviet Union
964 Hungary	Italy	France
968 Hungary	Soviet Union	Poland
972 Hungary	Switzerland	Soviet Union
976 Sweden	West Germany	Switzerland
980 France	Poland	Soviet Union
984 West Germany	France	Italy
988 France	West Germany	Soviet Union
992 Germany	Hungary	CIS
996 Italy	Russia	France
000 Italy	France	Cuba

Men's Sabre

Gold	Silver	Bronze
896 Ioannis Georgiadis (GRE)	Telemachos Karakalos (GRE)	Holger Nielsen (DEN)
900 Georges de la Falaise (FRA)	Léon Thiébaut (FRA)	Siegfried Flesch (AUT)
904 Manuel Díaz (CUB)	William Grebe (USA)	Albertson van Zo Post (USA)
906 Ioannis Georgiadis (GRE)	Gustav Casmir (GER)	Frederico Cesarano (ITA)
908 Jenő Fuchs (HUN)	Béla Zulavsky (HUN)	Vilém Goppold von Lobsdorf (BOH)
912 Jenő Fuchs (HUN)	Béla Békéssy (HUN)	Ervin Mészáros (HUN)
920 Nedo Nadi (ITA)	Aldo Nadi (ITA)	Adrianus de Jong (NED)
924 Sándor Posta (HUN)	Roger Ducret (FRA)	János Garay (HUN)
928 Ödön Tersztyánszky (HUN)	Attila Petschauer (HUN)	Bino Bini (ITA)
932 György Piller (HUN)	Giulio Gaudini (ITA)	Endre Kabos (HUN)
936 Endre Kabos (HUN)	Gustavo Marzi (ITA)	Aladár Gerevich (HUN)
948 Aladár Gerevich (HUN)	Vincenzo Pinton (ITA)	Pál Kovács (HUN)
952 Pál Kovács (HUN)	Aladár Gerevich (HUN)	Tibor Berczelly (HUN)
956 Rudolf Kárpáti (HUN)	Jerzy Pawlowski (POL)	Lev Kuznetsov (URS)
960 Rudolf Kárpáti (HUN)	Zoltán Horváth (HUN)	Wladimiro Calarese (ITA)
964 Tibor Pézsa (HUN)	Claude Arabo (FRA)	Umyar Mavlikhanov (URS)
968 Jerzy Pawlowski (POL)	Mark Rakita (URS)	Tibor Pézsa (HUN)
972 Viktor Sidyak (URS)	Peter Mardyak (URS)	Vladimir Nazlymov (URS)
976 Viktor Krovopuskov (URS)	Vladimir Nazlymov (URS)	Viktor Sidyak (URS)
980 Viktor Krovopuskov (URS)	Mikhail Burtsev (URS)	Imre Gedovari (HUN)
984 Jean-François Lamour (FRA)	Marco Marin (ITA)	Peter Westbrook (USA)
988 Jean-François Lamour (FRA)	Janusz Olech (POL)	Giovanni Scalzo (ITA)
992 Bence Szabó (HUN)	Marco Marin (ITA)	Jean-François Lamour (FRA)
996 Stanislav Pozdnyakov (RUS)	Sergey Sharikov (RUS)	Damien Touya (FRA)
000 Mihai Covaliu (ROM)	Mathieu Gourdain (FRA)	Wiradech Kothny (GER)

F
E
N
C
I
N
G

Men's Team Sabre

Gold	Silver	Bronze
1906 Germany	Greece	Netherlands
1908 Hungary	Italy	Bohemia
1912 Hungary	Austria	Netherlands
1920 Italy	France	Netherlands
1924 Italy	Hungary	Netherlands
1928 Hungary	Italy	Poland
1932 Hungary	Italy	Poland
1936 Hungary	Italy	Germany
1948 Hungary	Italy	United States
1952 Hungary	Italy	France
1956 Hungary	Poland	Soviet Union
1960 Hungary	Poland	Italy
1964 Soviet Union	Italy	Poland
1968 Soviet Union	Italy	Hungary
1972 Italy	Soviet Union	Hungary
1976 Soviet Union	Italy	Romania
1980 Soviet Union	Italy	Hungary
1984 Italy	France	Romania
1988 Hungary	Soviet Union	Italy
1992 CIS	Hungary	France
1996 Russia	Hungary	Italy
2000 Russia	France	Germany

Women's Foil

Gold	Silver	Bronze
1924 Ellen Osiier (DEN)	Gladys Davies (GBR)	Grete Heckscher (DEN)
1928 Helene Mayer (GER)	Muriel Freeman (GBR)	Olga Oelkers (GER)
1932 Ellen Preis (AUT)	Heather 'Judy' Guinness (GBR)	Erna Bogáthy Bogen (HUN)
1936 Ilona Elek (HUN)	Helene Mayer (GER)	Ellen Preis (AUT)
1948 Ilona Elek (HUN)	Karen Lachmann (DEN)	Ellen Müller-Preis (AUT)
1952 Irene Camber (ITA)	Ilona Elek (HUN)	Karen Lachmann (DEN)
1956 Gillian Sheen (GBR)	Olga Orban (ROM)	Renée Garilhe (FRA)
1960 Heidi Schmid (GER)	Valentina Rastvorova (URS)	Maria Vicol (ROM)
1964 Ildikó Ujlaki-Rejtö (HUN)	Helga Mees (GER)	Antonella Ragno (ITA)
1968 Yelena Novikova (URS)	María del Pilar Roldán (MEX)	Ildikó Ujlaki-Rejtö (HUN)
1972 Antonella Ragno-Lonzi (ITA)	Ildikó Bóbis (HUN)	Galina Gorokhova (URS)
1976 Ildikó Schwarczenberger (HUN)	Maria Consolata Collino (ITA)	Yelena Belova (Novikova) (URS)
1980 Pascale Trinquet (FRA)	Magda Maros (HUN)	Barbara Wysoczanska (POL)
1984 Luan Jujie (CHN)	Cornelia Hanisch (FRG)	Donna Vaccaroni (ITA)
1988 Anja Fichtel (FRG)	Sabine Bau (FRG)	Zita-Eva Funkenhauser (FRG)
1992 Giovanna Trillini (ITA)	Wang Huifeng (CHN)	Tatyana Sadovskaya (CIS)
1996 Laura Badea (ROM)	Valentina Vezzali (ITA)	Giovanna Trillini (ITA)
2000 Valentina Vezzali (ITA)	Rita König (GER)	Giovanna Trillini (ITA)

Women's Team Foil

Gold	Silver	Bronze
1960 Soviet Union	Hungary	Italy
1964 Hungary	Soviet Union	Germany
1968 Soviet Union	Hungary	Romania
1972 Soviet Union	Hungary	Romania
1976 Soviet Union	France	Hungary
1980 France	Soviet Union	Hungary
1984 West Germany	Romania	France
1988 West Germany	Italy	Hungary
1992 Italy	Germany	Romania
1996 Italy	Romania	Germany
2000 Italy	Poland	Germany

Women's Épée

Gold	Silver	Bronze
1996 Laura Flessel (FRA)	Valérie Barlois (FRA)	Gyongyi Szalay Horvathne (HUN)
2000 Timea Nagy (HUN)	Gianna Hablützel-Bürki (SUI)	Laura Flessel-Colovic (FRA)

Women's Team Épée

Gold	Silver	Bronze
1996 France	Italy	Russia
2000 Russia	Switzerland	China

Discontinued Events

Masters Foil

Gold	Silver	Bronze
1896 Leon Pyrgos (GRE)	Jean Perronnet (FRA)	only two competitors
1900 Lucien Mérignac (FRA)	Alphonse Kirchhoffer (FRA)	Jean-Baptiste Mimiague (FRA)

Masters Épée

Gold	Silver	Bronze
1900 Albert Ayat (FRA)	Emile Bougnol (FRA)	Henri Laurent (FRA)
1906 Cyril Verbrugge (BEL)	Carlo Gandini (ITA)	Ioannis Raissis (GRE)

Open Épée

Gold	Silver	Bronze
1900 Albert Ayat (FRA)	Ramón Fonst (CUB)	Léon Sée (FRA)

Masters Sabre

Gold	Silver	Bronze
1900 Antonio Conte (ITA)	Italo Santelli (ITA)	Milan Neralic (AUT)
1906 Cyril Verbrugge (BEL)	Ioannis Raissis (GRE)	only two competitors

Sabre – Three Hits

Gold	Silver	Bronze
1906 Gustav Casmir (GER)	George van Rossem (NED)	Péter Tóth (HUN)

Single Sticks

Gold	Silver	Bronze
1904 Albertson van Zo Post (USA)	William Scott O'Connor (USA)	William Grebe (USA)

FENCING

FIVE-PIN BOWLING

When ten-pin bowling was introduced to Toronto in 1905, it became a lunchtime recreation for many people. To speed up the game, they frequently had only five pins set up.

Thomas F. Ryan, owner of the Temperance Street Bowling Club, was inspired in 1909 to create a new sport based on that idea. He had five pins whittled down and he set them up in a V-formation with the point towards the bowler. Each pin was assigned a number of points from one to five. Five-pin bowling caught on quickly. The first league was formed in Toronto in 1910. Two years later, a rubber band circling the throat of the pins was added to increase the amount of action. The first women's league was established in Toronto in 1921 and two years later the sport was introduced to western Canada. Its spread resulted in the founding of the Canadian Bowling Association, based in Toronto, in 1927.

However, bowlers in western Canada adopted their own scoring system in 1930. Whereas Ryan's original system had assigned the values 4, 2, 1, 3 and 5 respectively to the five pins, the western system used the values 1, 4, 5, 3 and 2.

In 1944, the Western Canadian Five-Pin Bowling Association was founded in Regina, Saskatchewan. The two areas of the country continued with their own scoring systems until 1952, when a new national system was established, assigning the values 2, 3, 5, 3 and 2 to the five pins. Most of Ontario, however, stuck to the old scoring system until 1959.

Five-pin bowling throughout Canada was brought under a single governing body, the Canadian Bowling Congress, in 1965. The CBC was replaced by the Canadian 5-Pin Bowlers Association in 1978.

The ball is between 4½ins (11.5cm) and 5ins (12.5cm) in diameter and weighs between 3 (1.4kg) and 4lb (1.8kg). A game consists of frames, in each of which three balls are rolled. The score for knocking down all five pins is 1 and a perfect game is 450.

Although five-pin bowling has been played, times, in Scotland, the British West Indies, the Philippines, Argentina, and small areas of the United States, it now seems to be confined entirely to Canada, where there are more than 500,000 participants.

FIVES

Fives is a British form of handball and belongs to the same family of games as Jai alai. The name is said to have been derived from a slang expression 'a bunch of fives' (meaning a fist) or from an earlier version of the game called *longue paume* in which there were five players on each side, or possibly from the fact that originally the game was played to five points. The sport essentially involves propelling a ball against the walls of a special court using gloved hands and was also known, in the past, as 'hand tennis'. Historically the sport was often played against the walls of church buildings.

There are three common English derivatives of fives and all are played in public schools. The original version, Eton fives, was first played on the steps of Eton Chapel in the early 1700s. Due to the curious geometry of the court it is only practical to play doubles. The court in Eton fives has a step, no back wall and a rather large buttress. From Eton fives, two very different games evolved: Rugby fives and Winchester fives. Although the three games share similar rules, the courts are considerably different. Rugby fives is played in what is essentially a squash court which does have a back wall. In Winchester fives the court has a buttress (resembling the tambour of a real tennis court) on the left-hand wall. Players in all three games wear padded leather gloves, since the ball (which is slightly larger than a golf ball and made of rubber and cork) is quite hard.

In Eton fives, a standard court is divided into two parts, separated by the 'step', which is positioned about one third of the length of the court from the front wall. The front part of the court is known as the front or upper (up) court and is a few inches higher than the rear part, which is known as the back, or lower court. The end of the back court is defined by another small step.

When the game starts, the server alone stands in the upper court. He begins the game by throwing the ball against the front wall so it rebounds to the right-hand wall and then falls to the lower court. The serve is only a method of putting the ball into play and must be made with a single blow of the hand or wrist. The opponent who returns the serve is said to make the 'first cut' and he is not required to do so until he receives a service to his liking. The rally continues with alternate shots being played no later than the first bounce on the floor and which must be returned above the line. Failure to do so results in the award of a point to the opponents.

Each team has one serve per player and both players serve before the team's service is over. Points can only be won on service. A game is won by the first team to score 12 points.

In Rugby fives the person who makes the first return is called the server and he is allowed to throw the ball up for himself or he can require his opponent (called the receiver) to do so. The receiver is 'up' and only a team that is 'up' can score points. The games are usually played to the best of three and to 15 points per game. Both singles and doubles are played in Rugby fives and it is the most popular version.

Winchester fives is a similar game to Rugby fives but the distinct shape of the court adds another dimension to the game.

Fives today is considered a minority sport; there are approximately 4000 active adult players in the United Kingdom, while a similar number play in schools. Over 35 schools are affiliated to the Eton Fives Association (the governing body of the Eton fives variation), and there are numerous Old Boys' and university clubs. The first match on record between schools took place when one Eton pair played at Harrow in 1885 (F. Thomas and C. Barclay of Eton beat E.M. Butler and B.R. Warren of Harrow). Although the image of fives has been dominated by the public schools, courts do exist at state schools, and in recent years many of these have been brought into full use. The advantages of low playing costs (ball and gloves) and economy of space make fives an attractive sport for schools. The game continues to be developed in England and its popularity is growing in the wider community. There are also a number of well-established clubs overseas, such as the Zuoz Fives Club in Switzerland, and the game is also played in northern Nigeria!

There are numerous championships, notably the Eton Fives Kinnaird Cup and the Rugby Fives Singles Open Championship (the Jesters Cup). Other events include schools, university, age-group, Winchester and (recently) women's championships.

Exceptional players in recent times have included the Eton fives pair John Reynolds and Brian Matthews (Old Citizens, Kinnaird Cup) and Rugby Fives champion Wayne Enstone (Manchester YMCA).

FOOTBALL (ASSOCIATION)

I make no apology for this section being the largest in the book. Association football is played all over the world and its popularity and glamour lends itself to a fan-base ranging from school-children to pensioners, heads of state, lords, and an ever-increasing number of women.

Some form of football was probably played many thousands of years ago but it can be traced with certainty to a game called *tsu chu*, played in China from 206BC. The game involved kicking an animal-skin ball between bamboo goalposts and was popular among men and women. The Greeks adapted Tsu Chu into a game called *episkuros* and this was again adapted by the Romans as *harpastum* by the second century BC. Harpastum was more akin to rugby than football but by the end of the first millennium AD a series of kicking games were established throughout Europe. Knappan in Wales, Ba' in the Orkneys, *La Soule* in France and *Calcio* ('kick') in Italy (played in Florence during the Renaissance), were four such games.

Football-type games at this time were community experiences involving up to 100 villagers who would start at a midway point and attempt to advance the ball by any manner or means to an agreed goal area. King Edward II of England issued a proclamation in 1314 banning the game on account of its violence and Richard II again banned the game in 1389 because it interfered with archery practice and consequently jeopardised national security.

By the start of the 19th century football was popular in the public schools of England. In 1843 an attempt to codify rules was made at Cambridge University and adopted by most of the public schools in 1846. A revision of these rules was made in 1863 by representatives of 12 London clubs and at this meeting the Football Association was formed. Association football and rugby football thus became distinct and separate sports. Other football sports are described elsewhere in this book.

The FA Cup began in 1871 and the Football League in 1888. In 1904 the Fédération Internationale de Football Association (FIFA) was formed and it remains the world governing body of the sport.

The following section contains biographies of domestic and world stars past and present as well as statistical information on all major competitions.

World Cup

	Winners		Runners-Up	Venue
1930	Uruguay	4-2	Argentina	Uruguay
1934	Italy	2-1 aet	Czechoslovakia	Italy
1938	Italy	4-2	Hungary	France
1942	not held			
1946	not held			
1950	Uruguay	2-1 deciding match of pool	Brazil	Brazil
1954	West Germany	3-2	Hungary	Switzerland
1958	Brazil	5-2	Sweden	Sweden
1962	Brazil	3-1	Czechoslovakia	Chile
1966	England	4-2 aet	West Germany	England
1970	Brazil	4-1	Italy	Mexico
1974	West Germany	2-1	Holland	West Germany
1978	Argentina	3-1	Holland	Argentina
1982	Italy	3-1	West Germany	Spain
1986	Argentina	3-2	West Germany	Mexico
1990	West Germany	1-0	Argentina	Italy
1994	Brazil	0-0, 3-2 on pens	Italy	USA
1998	France	3-0	Brazil	France
2002	Brazil	2-0	Germany	Japan/South Korea (final played in Japan)

Women's World Cup Winners

1991	USA		1999	USA
1995	Norway		2003	Germany

European Championship

	Winners		Runners-Up	Venue
1960	Soviet Union	2-1	Yugoslavia	Paris
1964	Spain	2-1	Soviet Union	Madrid
1968	Italy	2-0	Yugoslavia	Rome
1972	West Germany	3-0	Soviet Union	Brussels
1976	Czechoslovakia	2-2, 5-3 on pens	West Germany	Belgrade
1980	West Germany	2-1	Belgium	Rome
1984	France	2-0	Spain	Paris
1988	Holland	2-0	Soviet Union	Munich
1992	Denmark	2-0	Germany	Gothenburg
1996	Germany	2-1 aet (golden goal)	Czech Republic	London
2000	France	2-1 aet (golden goal)	Italy	Rotterdam
2004	Greece	1-0	Portugal	Lisbon

Copa America

South American Champions

1910	Argentina	1937	Argentina	1963	Bolivia
1916	Uruguay	1939	Peru	1967	Uruguay
1917	Uruguay	1941	Argentina	1975	Peru
1919	Brazil	1942	Uruguay	1979	Paraguay
1920	Uruguay	1945	Argentina	1983	Uruguay
1921	Argentina	1946	Argentina	1987	Uruguay
1922	Brazil	1947	Argentina	1989	Brazil
1923	Uruguay	1949	Brazil	1991	Argentina
1924	Uruguay	1953	Paraguay	1993	Argentina
1925	Argentina	1955	Argentina	1995	Uruguay
1926	Uruguay	1956	Uruguay	1997	Brazil
1927	Argentina	1957	Argentina	1999	Brazil
1929	Argentina	1959*	Argentina	2001	Colombia
1935	Uruguay		Uruguay	2004	Brazil

*Two tournaments were held in 1959.

African Nations Cup

1957	Egypt	1974	Zaire	1990	Algeria
1959	Egypt	1976	Morocco	1992	Ivory Coast
1962	Ethiopia	1978	Ghana	1994	Nigeria
1963	Ghana	1980	Nigeria	1996	South Africa
1965	Ghana	1982	Ghana	1998	Egypt
1968	Zaire	1984	Cameroon	2000	Cameroon
1970	Sudan	1986	Egypt	2002	Cameroon
1972	Congo	1988	Cameroon	2004	Tunisia

Asian Nations Cup Winners

1956	South Korea	1972	Iran	1988	Saudi Arabia
1960	South Korea	1976	Iran	1992	Japan
1964	Israel	1980	Kuwait	1996	Saudi Arabia
1968	Iran	1984	Saudi Arabia	2000	Japan

Olympic Games

	Winners		Runners-Up		Winners		Runners-Up
1908	Great Britain	2-0	Denmark	1936	Italy	2-1	Austria
1912	Great Britain	4-2	Denmark	1940, 1944 not held			
1916	not held			1948	Sweden	3-1	Yugoslavia
1920	Belgium	2-0	Czechoslovakia	1952	Hungary	2-0	Yugoslavia
1924	Uruguay	3-0	Switzerland	1956	Soviet Union	1-0	Yugoslavia
1928	Uruguay	2-1	Switzerland	1960	Yugoslavia	3-1	Denmark
1932	not held			1964	Hungary	2-1	Czechoslovakia

FOOTBALL

1968	Hungary	4-1	Bulgaria	1988	Soviet Union	2-1	Brazil
1972	Poland	2-1	Hungary	1992	Spain	3-2	Poland
1976	East Germany	3-1	Poland	1996	Nigeria	3-2	Argentina
1980	Czechoslovakia	1-0	East Germany	2000	Cameroon	2-2, 5-3 on pens	Spain
1984	France	2-0	Brazil				

European Champion Clubs' Cup

	Winners		**Runners-Up**	**Venue**
1956	Real Madrid	4-3	Stade de Reims	Paris
1957	Real Madrid	2-0	Fiorentina	Madrid
1958	Real Madrid	3-2 aet	AC Milan	Brussels
1959	Real Madrid	2-0	Stade de Reims	Stuttgart
1960	Real Madrid	7-3	Eintracht Frankfurt	Glasgow
1961	Benfica	3-2	Barcelona	Berne
1962	Benfica	5-3	Real Madrid	Amsterdam
1963	AC Milan	2-1	Benfica	London
1964	Inter Milan	3-1	Real Madrid	Vienna
1965	Inter Milan	1-0	Benfica	Milan
1966	Real Madrid	2-1	Partizan Belgrade	Brussels
1967	Celtic	2-1	Inter Milan	Lisbon
1968	Manchester United	4-1 aet	Benfica	London (Wembley)
1969	AC Milan	4-1	Ajax	Madrid
1970	Feyenoord	2-1 aet	Celtic	Milan
1971	Ajax	2-0	Panathinaikos	London (Wembley)
1972	Ajax	2-0	Inter Milan	Rotterdam
1973	Ajax	1-0	Juventus	Belgrade
1974	Bayern Munich	1-1, 4-0	Atlético Madrid	Brussels
1975	Bayern Munich	2-0	Leeds United	Paris
1976	Bayern Munich	1-0	St Etienne	Glasgow
1977	Liverpool	3-1	Borussia Mönchengladbach	Rome
1978	Liverpool	1-0	FC Bruges	London (Wembley)
1979	Nottingham Forest	1-0	Malmö	Munich
1980	Nottingham Forest	1-0	SV Hamburg	Madrid
1981	Liverpool	1-0	Real Madrid	Paris
1982	Aston Villa	1-0	Bayern Munich	Rotterdam
1983	SV Hamburg	1-0	Juventus	Athens
1984	Liverpool	1-1, 4-2 on pens	AS Roma	Rome
1985	Juventus	1-0	Liverpool	Brussels
1986	Steaua Bucharest	0-0, 2-0 on pens	Barcelona	Seville
1987	FC Porto	2-1	Bayern Munich	Vienna
1988	PSV Eindhoven	0-0, 6-5 on pens	Benfica	Stuttgart
1989	AC Milan	4-0	Steaua Bucharest	Barcelona
1990	AC Milan	1-0	Benfica	Vienna
1991	Red Star Belgrade	0-0, 5-3 on pens	Marseille	Bari
1992	Barcelona	1-0 aet	Sampdoria	London (Wembley)
1993	Marseille*	1-0	AC Milan	Munich
1994	AC Milan	4-0	Barcelona	Athens
1995	Ajax	1-0	AC Milan	Vienna
1996	Juventus	1-1, 4-2 on pens	Ajax	Rome
1997	Borussia Dortmund	3-1	Juventus	Munich
1998	Real Madrid	1-0	Juventus	Amsterdam
1999	Manchester United	2-1	Bayern Munich	Barcelona
2000	Real Madrid	3-0	Valencia	Paris
2001	Bayern Munich	1-1, 5-4 on pens	Valencia	Milan
2002	Real Madrid	2-1	Bayer Leverkusen	Glasgow (Hampden Park)
2003	AC Milan	0-0, 3-2 on pens	Juventus	Manchester (Old Trafford)
2004	FC Porto	3-0	Monaco	Gelsenkirchen

*Marseille were subsequently stripped of the title following a bribery scandal concerning Bernard Tapie, the club president.

NB: The European Cup was established in 1955 and was contested by the respective League champions of the member countries of the Union of European Football Associations (UEFA).
Under current rules, clubs finishing second, third and fourth in the League of those countries with the highest UEFA points coefficients can qualify for the European Champions' Cup.
Since the 1992/93 season the European Cup has changed its format to include qualifying rounds and group stages. A final knockout phase consists of quarter-finals and semi-finals (played over two legs), and a single-match final. The competition since the rule changes is more properly called the UEFA Champions League.

UEFA Cup

Winners			Runners-Up	Venue
1955-58	Barcelona	8-2 agg	London	—
1958-60	Barcelona	4-1 agg	Birmingham City	—
1961	AS Roma	4-2 agg	Birmingham City	—
1962	Valencia	7-3 agg	Barcelona	—
1963	Valencia	4-1 agg	Dynamo Zagreb	—
1964	Real Zaragoza	2-1	Valencia	Barcelona
1965	Ferencvaros	1-0	Juventus	Turin
1966	Barcelona	4-3 agg	Real Zaragoza	—
1967	Dynamo Zagreb	2-0 agg	Leeds United	—
1968	Leeds United	1-0 agg	Ferencvaros	—
1969	Newcastle United	6-2 agg	Ujpest Dozsa	—
1970	Arsenal	4-3 agg	Anderlecht	—
1971	Leeds United	3-3 agg, away goals	Juventus	—
1972	Tottenham Hotspur	3-2 agg	Wolverhampton Wanderers	—
1973	Liverpool	3-2 agg	Borussia Mönchengladbach	—
1974	Feyenoord	4-2 agg	Tottenham Hotspur	—
1975	Borussia Mönchengladbach	5-1 agg	Twente Enschede	—
1976	Liverpool	4-3 agg	FC Bruges	—
1977	Juventus	2-2 agg, away goals	Athletic Bilbao	—
1978	PSV Eindhoven	3-0 agg	Bastia	—
1979	Borussia Mönchengladbach	2-1 agg	Red Star Belgrade	—
1980	Eintracht Frankfurt	3-3 agg, away goals	Borussia Mönchengladbach	—
1981	Ipswich Town	5-4 agg	AZ67 Alkmaar	—
1982	IFK Gothenburg	4-0 agg	SV Hamburg	—
1983	Anderlecht	2-1 agg	Benfica	—
1984	Tottenham Hotspur	2-2 agg, 4-3 on pens	Anderlecht	—
1985	Real Madrid	3-1 agg	Videoton	—
1986	Real Madrid	5-3 agg	Cologne	—
1987	IFK Gothenburg	2-1 agg	Dundee United	—
1988	Bayer Leverkusen	3-3 agg, 3-2 on pens	Espanyol	—
1989	Napoli	5-4 agg	Stuttgart	—
1990	Juventus	3-1 agg	Fiorentina	—
1991	Inter Milan	2-1 agg	AS Roma	—
1992	Ajax	2-2 agg, away goals	Torino	—
1993	Juventus	6-1 agg	Borussia Dortmund	—
1994	Inter Milan	2-0 agg	Casino Salzburg	—
1995	Parma	2-1 agg	Juventus	—
1996	Bayern Munich	5-1 agg	Bordeaux	—
1997	Schalke 04	1-1 agg, 4-1 on pens	Inter Milan	—
1998	Inter Milan	3-0	Lazio	Paris
1999	Parma	3-0	Marseille	Moscow
2000	Galatasaray	0-0, 4-1 on pens	Arsenal	Copenhagen
2001	Liverpool	5-4 (golden goal)	Alavés	Dortmund
2002	Feyenoord	3-2	Borussia Dortmund	Rotterdam
2003	FC Porto	3-2 aet	Celtic	Seville
2004	Valencia	2-0	Marseille	Gothenburg

NB: The competition was originally named the Inter-Cities Fairs Cup and between 1967 and 1971 it was known as the European Fairs Cup. The 1998 UEFA Cup final in Paris was the first, apart from the 1964 and 1965 finals, to be contested as a single match.

European Cup Winners' Cup

Winners			Runners-Up	Venue
1961	Fiorentina	4-1	Rangers	Glasgow/Florence
1962	Atlético Madrid	1-1, 3-0	Fiorentina	Glasgow/Stuttgart
1963	Tottenham Hotspur	5-1	Atlético Madrid	Rotterdam
1964	Sporting Lisbon	3-3, 1-0	MTK Budapest	Brussels/Antwerp
1965	West Ham United	2-0	1860 Munich	London (Wembley)
1966	Borussia Dortmund	2-1 aet	Liverpool	Glasgow
1967	Bayern Munich	1-0 aet	Rangers	Nuremberg
1968	AC Milan	2-0	SV Hamburg	Rotterdam
1969	Slovan Bratislava	3-2	Barcelona	Basle
1970	Manchester City	2-1	Gornik Zabrze	Vienna
1971	Chelsea	1-1, 2-1 aet	Real Madrid	Athens (also replay)
1972	Rangers	3-2	Dynamo Moscow	Barcelona
1973	AC Milan	1-0	Leeds United	Salonika
1974	Magdeburg	2-0	AC Milan	Rotterdam
1975	Dynamo Kiev	3-0	Ferencvaros	Basle
1976	Anderlecht	4-2	West Ham United	Brussels

FOOTBALL

1977	SV Hamburg	2-0	Anderlecht	Amsterdam
1978	Anderlecht	4-0	Austria Vienna	Paris
1979	Barcelona	4-3 aet	Fortuna Düsseldorf	Basle
1980	Valencia	0-0, 5-4 on pens	Arsenal	Brussels
1981	Dynamo Tbilisi	2-1	Carl Zeiss Jena	Düsseldorf
1982	Barcelona	2-1	Standard Liège	Barcelona
1983	Aberdeen	2-1 aet	Real Madrid	Gothenburg
1984	Juventus	2-1	FC Porto	Basle
1985	Everton	3-1	Rapid Vienna	Rotterdam
1986	Dynamo Kiev	3-0	Atlético Madrid	Lyon
1987	Ajax	1-0	Lokomotiv Leipzig	Athens
1988	Mechelen	1-0	Ajax	Strasbourg
1989	Barcelona	2-0	Sampdoria	Berne
1990	Sampdoria	2-0	Anderlecht	Gothenburg
1991	Manchester United	2-1	Barcelona	Rotterdam
1992	Werder Bremen	2-0	AS Monaco	Lisbon
1993	Parma	3-1	Royal Antwerp	London (Wembley)
1994	Arsenal	1-0	Parma	Copenhagen
1995	Real Zaragoza	2-1	Arsenal	Paris
1996	Paris St-Germain	1-0	Rapid Vienna	Brussels
1997	Barcelona	1-0	Paris St-Germain	Rotterdam
1998	Chelsea	1-0	VFB Stuttgart	Stockholm
1999	Lazio	2-1	Real Mallorca	Birmingham (Villa Park)

NB: The European Cup Winners' Cup was established in 1960 and was contested by national cup winners or the runners-up if the winners had qualified for the European Cup. The last competition was held in 1998/99. As from 1999/2000 national cup winners competed in an expanded UEFA Cup.

European Super Cup Winners

1972	Ajax	1983	Aberdeen	1994	AC Milan
1973	Ajax	1984	Juventus	1995	Ajax
1974	not held	1985	not held	1996	Juventus
1975	Dynamo Kiev	1986	Steaua Bucharest	1997	Barcelona
1976	Anderlecht	1987	FC Porto	1998	Chelsea
1977	Liverpool	1988	Mechelen	1999	Lazio
1978	Anderlecht	1989	AC Milan	2000	Galatasaray
1979	Nottingham Forest	1990	AC Milan	2001	Liverpool
1980	Valencia	1991	Manchester United	2002	Real Madrid
1981	not held	1992	Barcelona	2003	AC Milan
1982	Aston Villa	1993	Parma	2004	Valencia

NB: The European Super Cup was originally contested between the winners of the European Champions' Cup and the European Cup Winners' Cup. With the demise of the latter trophy the opponents have been the UEFA Cup winners.

Copa Libertadores

South American Club Cup

1960	Peñarol (Montevideo, URU)	1982	Peñarol
1961	Peñarol	1983	Gremio (Porto Alegre, BRA)
1962	Santos (São Paulo, BRA)	1984	Independiente
1963	Santos	1985	Argentinos Juniors (Buenos Aires, ARG)
1964	Independiente (Buenos Aires, ARG)	1986	River Plate (Buenos Aires, ARG)
1965	Independiente	1987	Peñarol
1966	Peñarol	1988	Nacional
1967	Racing Club (Avellanada, ARG)	1989	Atlético Nacional (Medellin, COL)
1968	Estudiantes (La Plata, ARG)	1990	Olimpia
1969	Estudiantes	1991	Colo Colo (Santiago, CHI)
1970	Estudiantes	1992	São Paulo (BRA)
1971	Nacional (Montevideo, URU)	1993	São Paulo
1972	Independiente (Buenos Aires, ARG)	1994	Velez Sarsfield (Buenos Aires, ARG)
1973	Independiente	1995	Gremio
1974	Independiente	1996	River Plate
1975	Independiente	1997	Cruzeiro
1976	Cruzeiro (Belo Horizonte, BRA)	1998	Vasco da Gama (Rio de Janeiro, BRA)
1977	Boca Juniors (Buenos Aires, ARG)	1999	Palmeiras (São Paulo, BRA)
1978	Boca Juniors	2000	Boca Juniors
1979	Olimpia (Asunción, PAR)	2001	Boca Juniors
1980	Nacional	2002	Olimpia
1981	Flamengo (Rio de Janeiro, BRA)	2003	Boca Juniors

African Champions Cup Winners

1964	Oryx Douala (CMR)	1978	Canon Yaoundé (CMR)	1992	Wydad Casablanca (MAR)
1965	not held	1979	Union Douala (CMR)	1993	Zamalek (EGY)
1966	Stade Abidjan (CIV)	1980	Canon Yaoundé (CMR)	1994	Espérance (TUN)
1967	TP Englebert (COD)	1981	JE Tizi-Ouzou (ALG)	1995	Orlando Pirates (RSA)
1968	TP Englebert (COD)	1982	Al Ahly (EGY)	1996	Zamalek (EGY)
1969	Al Ismaili (EGY)	1983	Asante Kotoko (GHA)	1997	Raja Casablanca (MAR)
1970	Asante Kotoko (GHA)	1984	Zamalek (EGY)	1998	ASEC Abidjan (CIV)
1971	Canon Yaoundé (CMR)	1985	FAR Rabat (MAR)	1999	Raja Casablanca (MAR)
1972	Hafia Conakry (GHA)	1986	Zamalek (EGY)	2000	Hearts of Oak (GHA)
1973	AS Vita Kinshasa (ZAI)	1987	Al Ahly (EGY)	2001	Al Ahly (EGY)
1974	CARA Brazzaville (CGO)	1988	EP Sétif (ALG)	2002	Zamalek (EGY)
1975	Hafia Conakry (GHA)	1989	Raja Casablanca (MAR)	2003	Enyimba Aba (NGR)
1976	MC Algiers (ALG)	1990	JS Kabylie (ALG)		
1977	Hafia Conakry (GHA)	1991	Club Africain (ALG)		

World Club Intercontinental Cup

1960	Real Madrid (ESP)	1975	not held	1990	AC Milan (ITA)
1961	Peñarol (URU)	1976	Bayern Munich (FRG)	1991	Red Star Belgrade (YUG)
1962	Santos (BRA)	1977	Boca Juniors (ARG)	1992	São Paulo (BRA)
1963	Santos (BRA)	1978	not held	1993	São Paulo (BRA)
1964	Inter Milan (ITA)	1979	Olimpia (PAR)	1994	Velez Sarsfield (ARG)
1965	Inter Milan (ITA)	1980	Nacional (URU)	1995	Ajax (NED)
1966	Peñarol (URU)	1981	Flamengo (BRA)	1996	Juventus (ITA)
1967	Racing Club (ARG)	1982	Peñarol (URU)	1997	Borussia Dortmund (GER)
1968	Estudiantes (ARG)	1983	Gremio (BRA)	1998	Real Madrid (ESP)
1969	AC Milan (ITA)	1984	Independiente (ARG)	1999	Manchester United (ENG)
1970	Feyenoord (NED)	1985	Juventus (ITA)	2000	Boca Juniors (ARG)
1971	Nacional (URU)	1986	River Plate (ARG)	2001	Bayern Munich (GER)
1972	Ajax (NED)	1987	FC Porto (POR)	2002	Real Madrid (ESP)
1973	Independiente (ARG)	1988	Nacional (URU)	2003	Boca Juniors (ARG)
1974	Atletico Madrid (ESP)	1989	AC Milan (ITA)		

NB: From 1960 to 1979 the competition was decided over two legs on points, not aggregate scores. From 1980 it was played as a single match in Tokyo. In 2000 the inaugural FIFA Club World Championship took place in Brazil and was won by the Brazilian side Corinthians.

English League Champions

	Division 1	Division 2	Division 3		Division 1	Division 2	Division 3
1889	Preston North End	—	—	1905	Newcastle United	Liverpool	—
1890	Preston North End	—	—	1906	Liverpool	Bristol City	—
1891	Everton	—	—	1907	Newcastle United	Nottingham Forest	—
1892	Sunderland	—	—	1908	Manchester United	Bradford City	—
1893	Sunderland	Small Heath	—	1909	Newcastle United	Bolton Wanderers	—
1894	Aston Villa	Liverpool	—	1910	Aston Villa	Manchester City	—
1895	Sunderland	Bury	—	1911	Manchester United	West Bromwich Albion	—
1896	Aston Villa	Liverpool	—				
1897	Aston Villa	Notts County	—	1912	Blackburn Rovers	Derby County	—
1898	Sheffield United	Burnley	—	1913	Sunderland	Preston North End	—
1899	Aston Villa	Manchester City	—	1914	Blackburn Rovers	Notts County	—
1900	Aston Villa	The Wednesday	—	1915	Everton	Derby County	—
1901	Liverpool	Grimsby Town	—	1916-19	not held	not held	—
1902	Sunderland	West Bromwich Albion	—	1920	West Bromwich Albion	Tottenham Hotspur	—
1903	The Wednesday	Manchester City	—	1921	Burnley	Birmingham City	Crystal Palace
1904	The Wednesday	Preston North End	—				

	Division 1	Division 2	Division 3 North	Division 3 South
1922	Liverpool	Nottingham Forest	Stockport County	Southampton
1923	Liverpool	Notts County	Nelson	Bristol City
1924	Huddersfield Town	Leeds United	Wolverhampton Wanderers	Portsmouth
1925	Huddersfield Town	Leicester City	Darlington	Swansea Town
1926	Huddersfield Town	The Wednesday	Grimsby Town	Reading
1927	Newcastle United	Middlesbrough	Stoke City	Bristol City
1928	Everton	Manchester City	Bradford Park Avenue	Millwall
1929	The Wednesday	Middlesbrough	Bradford City	Charlton Athletic
1930	Sheffield Wednesday	Blackpool	Port Vale	Plymouth Argyle
1931	Arsenal	Everton	Chesterfield	Notts County
1932	Everton	Wolverhampton Wanderers	Lincoln City	Fulham
1933	Arsenal	Stoke City	Hull City	Brentford
1934	Arsenal	Grimsby Town	Barnsley	Norwich City
1935	Arsenal	Brentford	Doncaster Rovers	Charlton Athletic
1936	Sunderland	Manchester United	Chesterfield	Coventry City
1937	Manchester City	Leicester City	Stockport County	Luton Town
1938	Arsenal	Aston Villa	Tranmere Rovers	Millwall
1939	Everton	Blackburn Rovers	Barnsley	Newport County
1940-46	not held	not held	not held	not held
1947	Liverpool	Manchester City	Doncaster Rovers	Cardiff City
1948	Arsenal	Birmingham City	Lincoln City	Queens Park Rangers
1949	Portsmouth	Fulham	Hull City	Swansea Town
1950	Portsmouth	Tottenham Hotspur	Doncaster Rovers	Notts County
1951	Tottenham Hotspur	Preston North End	Rotherham United	Nottingham Forest
1952	Manchester United	Sheffield Wednesday	Lincoln City	Plymouth Argyle
1953	Arsenal	Sheffield United	Oldham Athletic	Bristol Rovers
1954	Wolverhampton Wanderers	Leicester City	Port Vale	Ipswich Town
1955	Chelsea	Birmingham City	Barnsley	Bristol City
1956	Manchester United	Sheffield Wednesday	Grimsby Town	Leyton Orient
1957	Manchester United	Leicester City	Derby County	Ipswich Town
1958	Wolverhampton Wanderers	West Ham United	Scunthorpe United	Brighton & Hove Albion

	Division 1	Division 2	Division 3	Division 4
1959	Wolverhampton Wanderers	Sheffield Wednesday	Plymouth Argyle	Port Vale
1960	Burnley	Aston Villa	Southampton	Walsall
1961	Tottenham Hotspur	Ipswich Town	Bury	Peterborough United
1962	Ipswich Town	Liverpool	Portsmouth	Millwall
1963	Everton	Stoke City	Northampton Town	Brentford
1964	Liverpool	Leeds United	Coventry City	Gillingham
1965	Manchester United	Newcastle United	Carlisle United	Brighton & Hove Albion
1966	Liverpool	Manchester City	Hull City	Doncaster Rovers
1967	Manchester United	Coventry City	Queens Park Rangers	Stockport County
1968	Manchester City	Ipswich Town	Oxford United	Luton Town
1969	Leeds United	Derby County	Watford	Doncaster Rovers
1970	Everton	Huddersfield Town	Orient	Chesterfield
1971	Arsenal	Leicester City	Preston North End	Notts County
1972	Derby County	Norwich City	Aston Villa	Grimsby Town
1973	Liverpool	Burnley	Bolton Wanderers	Southport
1974	Leeds United	Middlesbrough	Oldham Athletic	Peterborough United
1975	Derby County	Manchester United	Blackburn Rovers	Mansfield Town
1976	Liverpool	Sunderland	Hereford United	Lincoln City
1977	Liverpool	Wolverhampton Wanderers	Mansfield Town	Cambridge United
1978	Nottingham Forest	Bolton Wanderers	Wrexham	Watford
1979	Liverpool	Crystal Palace	Shrewsbury Town	Reading
1980	Liverpool	Leicester City	Grimsby Town	Huddersfield Town
1981	Aston Villa	West Ham United	Rotherham United	Southend United
1982	Liverpool	Luton Town	Burnley	Sheffield United
1983	Liverpool	Queens Park Rangers	Portsmouth	Wimbledon
1984	Liverpool	Chelsea	Oxford United	York City
1985	Everton	Oxford United	Bradford City	Chesterfield
1986	Liverpool	Norwich City	Reading	Swindon Town
1987	Everton	Derby County	Bournemouth	Northampton Town
1988	Liverpool	Millwall	Sunderland	Wolverhampton Wanderers
1989	Arsenal	Chelsea	Wolverhampton Wanderers	Rotherham United
1990	Liverpool	Leeds United	Bristol Rovers	Exeter City
1991	Arsenal	Oldham Athletic	Cambridge United	Darlington
1992	Leeds United	Ipswich Town	Brentford	Burnley

	Premier League	Division 1	Division 2	Division 3
1993	Manchester United	Newcastle United	Stoke City	Cardiff City
1994	Manchester United	Crystal Palace	Reading	Shrewsbury Town

1995	Blackburn Rovers	Middlesbrough	Birmingham City	Carlisle United
1996	Manchester United	Sunderland	Swindon Town	Preston North End
1997	Manchester United	Bolton Wanderers	Bury	Wigan Athletic
1998	Arsenal	Nottingham Forest	Watford	Notts County
1999	Manchester United	Sunderland	Fulham	Brentford
2000	Manchester United	Charlton	Preston North End	Swansea City
2001	Manchester United	Fulham	Millwall	Brighton & Hove Albion
2002	Arsenal	Manchester City	Brighton & Hove Albion	Plymouth Argyle
2003	Manchester United	Portsmouth	Wigan Athletic	Rushden & Diamonds
2004	Arsenal	Norwich City	Plymouth Argyle	Doncaster Rovers

Original 12 Football League Clubs

Accrington	Burnley	Preston North End
Aston Villa	Derby County	Stoke City
Blackburn Rovers	Everton	West Bromwich Albion
Bolton Wanderers	Notts County	Wolverhampton Wanderers

English League Clubs

Club	Debut	Nickname(s)	Ground	Previous Name(s)
Arsenal	1893	Gunners	Arsenal Stadium, Highbury	Dial Square, Royal Arsenal, Woolwich Arsenal
Aston Villa	1888	Villans	Villa Park, Birmingham	none
Barnet (NC)	1991	Bees	Underhill	Barnet Alston FC
Barnsley	1898	Tykes, Reds	Oakwell	Barnsley St Peter's Colliers
Birmingham City	1892	Blues	St Andrews	Small Heath Alliance, Small Heath, Birmingham
Blackburn Rovers	1888	Rovers	Ewood Park	none
Blackpool	1896	Seasiders	Bloomfield Road	Blackpool St Johns, Blackpool South Shore
Bolton Wanderers	1888	Trotters	Reebok Stadium	Christ Church FC
Boston United	2002	Pilgrims	York Street Stadium	none
AFC Bournemouth	1923	Cherries	Fitness First Stadium, Dean Court	Boscombe St Johns, Boscombe, Bournemouth and Boscombe Athletic
Bradford City	1903	Bantams	Bradford & Bingley Valley Parade	none
Brentford	1920	Bees	Griffin Park	none
Brighton & Hove Albion	1920	Seagulls	Withdean Stadium	Brighton & Hove Rangers, Brighton & Hove United
Bristol City	1901	Robins	Ashton Gate	Bristol South End
Bristol Rovers	1920	Pirates (originally named Purdown Poachers)	Memorial Ground	Black Arabs, Eastville Rovers, Bristol Eastville Rovers
Burnley	1888	Clarets	Turf Moor	Burnley Rovers
Bury	1894	Shakers	Gigg Lane	none
Cambridge United	1970	U's	Abbey Stadium	Abbey United
Cardiff City	1920	Bluebirds	Ninian Park	Riverside, Riverside Albion
Carlisle United (NC)	1928	Cumbrians, Blues	Brunton Park	amalgamation of Shaddongate United and Carlisle Red Rose
Charlton Athletic	1921	Addicks, Valiants, Robins	The Valley	none
Chelsea	1905	Blues, Pensioners	Stamford Bridge	none
Cheltenham Town	1999	Robins	Whaddon Road	none
Chester City	1931	Blues, City	Deva Stadium	King's School Old Boys and Chester Rovers, Chester
Chesterfield	1899	Spireites, Blues	Recreation Ground, Saltergate	Chesterfield Town
Colchester United	1950	U's	Layer Road	Colchester Town
Coventry City	1919	Sky Blues	Highfield Road	Singers FC
Crewe Alexandra	1892	Railwaymen	Gresty Road	none
Crystal Palace	1920	Eagles	Selhurst Park	none
Darlington	1921	Quakers	Feethams Ground	none
Derby County	1888	Rams	Pride Park	none
Doncaster Rovers	1901	Rovers	Belle Vue	none
Everton	1888	Toffees	Goodison Park	St Domingo FC
Exeter City (NC)	1920	Grecians	St James Park	amalgamation of St Sidwell's United and Exeter United
Fulham	1907	Cottagers	Craven Cottage	Fulham St Andrews
Gillingham	1920	Gills	Priestfield Stadium	Excelsior, New Brompton
Grimsby Town	1892	Mariners	Blundell Park	Grimsby Pelham

F
O
O
T
B
A
L
L

Halifax Town (NC)	1921	Shaymen	Shay Stadium	none
Hartlepool United	1921	Pool	Victoria Ground	Hartlepools United, Hartlepool
Huddersfield Town	1910	Terriers	Alfred McAlpine Stadium, Leeds Road	none
Hull City	1905	Tigers	Kingston Communications Stadium	none
Ipswich Town	1938	Blues, Town, Tractor Boys	Portman Road	Ipswich Association FC
Kidderminster Harriers	2000	Harriers	Aggborough Stadium	none
Leeds United	1920	United, Whites, Peacocks	Elland Road	formed after Leeds City disbanded by FA order
Leicester City	1894	Foxes, Filberts	Walkers Stadium,	Leicester Fosse
Leyton Orient	1905	O's	Leyton Stadium, Brisbane Road	Glyn Cricket and Football Club, Eagle FC, Orient, Clapton Orient
Lincoln City	1892	Red Imps	Sincil Bank	none
Liverpool	1893	Reds, Pool	Anfield	none
Luton Town	1897	Hatters	Kenilworth Road	amalgamation of Luton Town Wanderers and Excelsior
Macclesfield Town	1997	Silkmen	Moss Rose	none
Manchester City	1892	Citizens, Blues	City of Manchester Stadium	Ardwick FC
Manchester United	1892	Red Devils	Old Trafford	Newton Heath
Mansfield Town	1931	Stags	Field Mill	Mansfield Wesleyans
Middlesbrough	1899	Boro	Riverside Stadium	none
Millwall	1920	Lions	New Den, Bermondsey	Millwall Rovers, Millwall Athletic
MK Dons	1977	Dons	National Hockey Stadium, Milton Keynes	Wimbledon Old Centrals, Wimbledon
Newcastle United	1893	Magpies	St James' Park	Stanley, Newcastle East End
Northampton Town	1920	Cobblers	Sixfields Stadium	none
Norwich City	1920	Canaries	Carrow Road	none
Nottingham Forest	1892	Forest, Reds	City Ground	none
Notts County	1888	Magpies	County Ground, Meadow Lane	Notts FC
Oldham Athletic	1907	Latics	Boundary Park	Pine Villa
Oxford United	1962	U's	Kassam Stadium	Headington, Headington United
Peterborough United	1960	Posh	London Road	formed after Peterborough and Fletton disbanded
Plymouth Argyle	1920	Pilgrims	Home Park	Argyle Athletic Club
Portsmouth	1920	Pompey	Fratton Park	none
Port Vale	1892	Valiants	Vale Park	Burslem Port Vale
Preston North End	1888	Lilywhites, North End	Deepdale	none
Queens Park Rangers	1920	Rangers, R's	Rangers Stadium, Loftus Road	St Jude's
Reading	1920	Royals, Biscuitmen	Madejski Stadium	none
Rochdale	1921	Dale	Spotland	none
Rotherham United	1893	Merry Millers	Millmoor	Thornhill United, Rotherham County, Rotherham Town
Rushden & Diamonds	2001	Diamonds	Nene Park	Amalgamation of Rushden Town and Irthlingborough Diamonds
Scarborough (NC)	1987	Boro	McCain Stadium, Seamer Road	Scarborough Cricketers' FC
Scunthorpe United	1950	Iron	Glanford Park	Scunthorpe & Lindsey United
Sheffield United	1892	Blades	Bramall Lane	none
Sheffield Wednesday	1892	Owls	Hillsborough	The Wednesday
Shrewsbury Town	1950	Shrews, Town	Gay Meadow	none
Southampton	1920	Saints	St Mary's Stadium	Southampton St Mary's
Southend United	1920	Shrimpers, Blues	Roots Hall	none
Stockport County	1900	County, Hatters	Edgeley Park	Heaton Norris Rovers
Stoke City	1888	Potters	Britannia Stadium	Stoke
Sunderland	1890	Rokerites, Black Cats	Stadium of Light	Sunderland and District Teachers Association FC
Swansea City	1920	Swans	Vetch Field	Swansea Town
Swindon Town	1920	Robins	County Ground	Spartans and St Mark's Young Men's Friendly Society
Torquay United	1927	Gulls	Plainmoor	Torquay Town
Tottenham Hotspur	1908	Spurs	White Hart Lane	Hotspur FC
Tranmere Rovers	1921	Rovers	Prenton Park, Birkenhead	Belmont AFC
Walsall	1892	Saddlers	Bescot Stadium	Walsall Town Swifts
Watford	1920	Hornets	Vicarage Road	West Herts
West Bromwich Albion	1888	Throstles, Baggies, Albion	The Hawthorns	West Bromwich Strollers

West Ham United	1919	Hammers, Irons	Boleyn Ground, Upton Park	Thames Ironworks FC
Wigan Athletic	1978	Latics	JJB Stadium	none
Wolverhampton Wanderers	1888	Wolves	Molineux	St Luke's
Wrexham	1921	Robins	Racecourse Ground	none
Wycombe Wanderers	1993	Chairboys, Blues	Causeway Stadium	North Town Wanderers
Yeovil Town	2003	Glovers	Huish Park	Yeovil Casuals
York City (NC)	1929	Minstermen	Bootham Crescent	none

(NC) Nationwide Conference

Football Association Cup

Winners		Runners-Up	Winners		Runners-Up
1872 Wanderers	1-0	Royal Engineers	1900 Bury	4-0	Southampton
1873 Wanderers	2-0	Oxford University	1901 Tottenham Hotspur	2-2, 3-1	Sheffield United
1874 Oxford University	2-0	Royal Engineers	(only non-league team		
1875 Royal Engineers	1-1, 2-0	Old Etonians	to win the FA Cup		
1876 Wanderers	1-1, 3-0	Old Etonians	since the League		
1877 Wanderers	2-1 aet	Oxford University	(began in 1888/89 – also		
1878 Wanderers	3-1	Royal Engineers	started the tradition of		
1879 Old Etonians	1-0	Clapham Rovers	decorating the trophy		
1880 Clapham Rovers	1-0	Oxford University	with ribbons in the		
1881 Old Carthusians	3-0	Old Etonians	colours of the		
1882 Old Etonians	1-0	Blackburn Rovers	winning team)		
		(first appearance of a	1902 Sheffield United	1-1, 2-1	Southampton
		northern club in the	1903 Bury	6-0	Derby County
		final)	(record winning margin		
1883 Blackburn Olympic	2-1 aet	Old Etonians	in FA Cup final)		
		(last appearance of	1904 Manchester City	1-0	Bolton Wanderers
		English amateur	1905 Aston Villa	2-0	Newcastle United
		finalists)	1906 Everton	1-0	Newcastle United
1884 Blackburn Rovers	2-1	Queen's Park	1907 The Wednesday	2-1	Everton
1885 Blackburn Rovers	2-0	Queen's Park	1908 Wolverhampton	3-1	Newcastle United
1886 Blackburn Rovers	0-0, 2-0	West Bromwich Albion	Wanderers		
			1909 Manchester United	1-0	Bristol City
1887 Aston Villa	2-0	West Bromwich Albion	1910 Newcastle United	1-1, 2-0	Barnsley
1888 West Bromwich Albion	2-1	Preston North End	(after this final it was		
1889 Preston North End	3-0	Wolverhampton Wanderers	discovered that the		
(first team to win the			trophy had not been		
'double' of League and			copyrighted and had		
FA Cup)			been copied for another		
1890 Blackburn Rovers	6-1	The Wednesday	tournament, therefore		
(William Townley scored			the trophy was		
the first ever FA Cup			presented to Lord		
final hat-trick)			Kinnaird and a new		
			one was commissioned)		
1891 Blackburn Rovers	3-1	Notts County	1911 Bradford City	0-0, 1-0	Newcastle United
1892 West Bromwich Albion	3-0	Aston Villa	(first winners of new		
1893 Wolverhampton Wanderers	1-0	Everton	(present) trophy made		
1894 Notts County	4-1	Bolton Wanderers	by Fattorini & Sons of		
(first 2nd Division team			Bradford)		
to win the FA Cup)			1912 Barnsley	0-0, 1-0 aet	West Bromwich Albion
1895 Aston Villa	1-0	West Bromwich Albion	1913 Aston Villa	1-0	Sunderland
(trophy was stolen on			1914 Burnley	1-0	Liverpool
11 September 1895			1915 Sheffield United	3-0	Chelsea
and was never			1916-19 not held		
recovered)			1920 Aston Villa	1-0 aet	Huddersfield Town
1896 The Wednesday	2-1	Wolverhampton Wanderers	1921 Tottenham Hotspur	1-0	Wolverhampton Wanderers
(new trophy was an					
exact replica of the			1922 Huddersfield Town	1-0	Preston North End
original)			1923 Bolton Wanderers	2-0	West Ham United
1897 Aston Villa	3-2	Everton	(first Wembley final –		
(second team to win			official crowd figure		
the 'double')			126,047; actual figure		
1898 Nottingham Forest	3-1	Derby County	180,000-200,000)		
1899 Sheffield United	4-1	Derby County	1924 Newcastle United	2-0	Aston Villa

FOOTBALL

1925	Sheffield United	1-0	Cardiff City
1926	Bolton Wanderers	1-0	Manchester City (first team to reach the Cup final and be relegated in same season)
1927	Cardiff City (only non-English team to win the Cup)	1-0	Arsenal
1928	Blackburn Rovers	3-1	Huddersfield Town
1929	Bolton Wanderers	2-0	Portsmouth
1930	Arsenal	2-0	Huddersfield Town
1931	West Bromwich Albion	2-1	Birmingham City
1932	Newcastle United	2-1	Arsenal
1933	Everton	3-0	Manchester City
1934	Manchester City	2-1	Portsmouth
1935	Sheffield Wednesday	4-2	West Bromwich Albion
1936	Arsenal	1-0	Sheffield United
1937	Sunderland	3-1	Preston North End
1938	Preston North End	1-0 aet	Huddersfield Town
1939	Portsmouth	4-1	Wolverhampton Wanderers
1940-45 not held			
1946	Derby County (the ball burst during the final; also this was the only season when ties prior to the semi-final stage were played over two legs)	4-1 aet	Charlton Athletic
1947	Charlton Athletic (the ball burst again)	1-0 aet	Burnley
1948	Manchester United (only time winners have played against a team from top flight in every round)	4-2	Blackpool
1949	Wolverhampton Wanderers	3-1	Leicester City
1950	Arsenal	2-0	Liverpool
1951	Newcastle United	2-0	Blackpool
1952	Newcastle United	1-0	Arsenal
1953	Blackpool ('The Matthews Final' – Stan Mortensen hat-trick, winner scored by Bill Perry)	4-3	Bolton Wanderers
1954	West Bromwich Albion	3-2	Preston North End
1955	Newcastle United	3-1	Manchester City
1956	Manchester City	3-1	Birmingham City
1957	Aston Villa	2-1	Manchester United
1958	Bolton Wanderers	2-0	Manchester United
1959	Nottingham Forest	2-1	Luton Town
1960	Wolverhampton Wanderers	3-0	Blackburn Rovers
1961	Tottenham Hotspur (third team to win the 'double', first in 20th century)	2-0	Leicester City
1962	Tottenham Hotspur	3-1	Burnley
1963	Manchester United	3-1	Leicester City
1964	West Ham United	3-2	Preston North End (Preston's Howard Kendall was youngest finalist in 20th century)
1965	Liverpool	2-1 aet	Leeds United
1966	Everton	3-2	Sheffield Wednesday
1967	Tottenham Hotspur (first all-London Wembley final)	2-1	Chelsea
1968	West Bromwich Albion	1-0 aet	Everton
1969	Manchester City	1-0	Leicester City

1970	Chelsea	2-2, 2-1 aet	Leeds United
1971	Arsenal (fourth team to win the 'double')	2-1 aet	Liverpool
1972	Leeds United	1-0	Arsenal
1973	Sunderland (first 2nd Division team to win the Cup since West Brom in 1931)	1-0	Leeds United
1974	Liverpool	3-0	Newcastle United
1975	West Ham United	2-0	Fulham (Bobby Moore played for Fulham against West Ham)
1976	Southampton	1-0	Manchester United
1977	Manchester United	2-1	Liverpool
1978	Ipswich Town (Ipswich only team to have played in every round of Cup including preliminary)	1-0	Arsenal
1979	Arsenal	3-2	Manchester United
1980	West Ham United (most recent 2nd Division winners; West Ham's Paul Allen beat Howard Kendall's 20th century record as youngest finalist)	1-0	Arsenal
1981	Tottenham Hotspur	1-1, 3-2	Manchester City
1982	Tottenham Hotspur	1-1, 1-0	Queens Park Rangers
1983	Manchester United	2-2, 4-0	Brighton & Hove Albion
1984	Everton	2-0	Watford
1985	Manchester United	1-0 aet	Everton
1986	Liverpool	3-1	Everton
1987	Coventry City	3-2 aet	Tottenham Hotspur
1988	Wimbledon	1-0	Liverpool
1989	Liverpool	3-2 aet	Everton
1990	Manchester United	3-3, 1-0	Crystal Palace
1991	Tottenham Hotspur	2-1 aet	Nottingham Forest
1992	Liverpool	2-0	Sunderland
1993	Arsenal (Arsenal also beat Sheffield Wednesday in the League Cup final)	1-1, 2-1 aet	Sheffield Wednesday
1994	Manchester United (sixth team to win the 'double')	4-0	Chelsea
1995	Everton	1-0	Manchester United
1996	Manchester United (first team to win a second 'double'; Eric Cantona – first foreign player to captain the FA Cup winners)	1-0	Liverpool
1997	Chelsea	2-0	Middlesbrough
1998	Arsenal	2-0	Newcastle United
1999	Manchester United (third 'double' and first team to win a treble of League, FA Cup and European Champions' Cup)	2-0	Newcastle United
2000	Chelsea	1-0	Aston Villa
2001	Liverpool	2-1	Arsenal
2002	Arsenal	2-0	Chelsea
2003	Arsenal	1-0	Southampton
2004	Manchester United	3-0	Millwall

Football League Cup (since 2003/04 known as the Carling Cup)

	Winners		Runners-Up		Winners		Runners-Up
1961	Aston Villa	3-2 agg aet	Rotherham United	1982	Liverpool	3-1 aet	Tottenham Hotspur
1962	Norwich City	4-0 agg	Rochdale	1983	Liverpool	2-1 aet	Manchester United
1963	Birmingham City	3-1 agg	Aston Villa	1984	Liverpool	0-0, 1-0 aet	Everton
1964	Leicester City	4-3 agg	Stoke City				
1965	Chelsea	3-2 agg	Leicester City	1985	Norwich City	1-0	Sunderland
1966	'West Brom.' Albion	5-3 agg	West Ham United	1986	Oxford United	3-0	Queens Park Rangers
1967	Queens Park Rangers	3-2	West Brom.' Albion				
1968	Leeds United	1-0	Arsenal	1987	Arsenal	2-1	Liverpool
1969	Swindon Town	3-1 aet	Arsenal	1988	Luton Town	3-2	Arsenal
1970	Manchester City	2-1 aet	'West Brom.' Albion	1989	Nottingham Forest	3-1	Luton Town
1971	Tottenham Hotspur	2-0	Aston Villa	1990	Nottingham Forest	1-0	Oldham Athletic
1972	Stoke City	2-1	Chelsea	1991	Sheffield Wednesday	1-0	Manchester United
1973	Tottenham Hotspur	1-0	Norwich City	1992	Manchester United	1-0	Nottingham Forest
1974	Wolverhampton Wanderers	2-1	Manchester City	1993	Arsenal	2-1	Sheffield Wednesday
				1994	Aston Villa	3-1	Manchester United
1975	Aston Villa	1-0	Norwich City	1995	Liverpool	2-1	Bolton Wanderers
1976	Manchester City	2-1	Newcastle United	1996	Aston Villa	3-0	Leeds United
1977	Aston Villa	0-0, 1-1, 3-2 aet	Everton	1997	Leicester City	1-1,1-0 aet	Middlesbrough
1978	Nottingham Forest	0-0, 1-0 aet	Liverpool	1998	Chelsea	1-0	Middlesbrough
1979	Nottingham Forest	3-2	Southampton	1999	Tottenham Hotspur	1-0	Leicester City
1980	Wolverhampton Wanderers	1-0	Nottingham Forest	2000	Leicester City	2-1	Tranmere Rovers
				2001	Liverpool	1-1, 5-4 on pens	Birmingham City
1981	Liverpool	1-1, 2-1	West Ham United	2002	Blackburn Rovers	2-1	Tottenham Hotspur
				2003	Liverpool	2-0	Manchester United
				2004	Middlesbrough	2-1	Bolton Wanderers

NB: In 1982 the League Cup was renamed the Milk Cup following sponsorship by the Milk Marketing Board. Over the next few seasons it became the Littlewoods, Rumbelows, Coca-Cola and Worthington Cup.

Scottish League Champions

1892	Dumbarton	1925	Rangers	1964	Rangers
1893	Celtic	1926	Celtic	1965	Kilmarnock
1894	Celtic	1927	Rangers	1966	Celtic
1895	Heart of Midlothian	1928	Rangers	1967	Celtic
1896	Celtic	1929	Rangers	1968	Celtic
1897	Heart of Midlothian	1930	Rangers	1969	Celtic
1898	Celtic	1931	Rangers	1970	Celtic
1899	Rangers	1932	Motherwell	1971	Celtic
1900	Rangers	1933	Rangers	1972	Celtic
1901	Rangers	1934	Rangers	1973	Celtic
1902	Rangers	1935	Rangers	1974	Celtic
1903	Hibernian	1936	Celtic	1975	Rangers
1904	Third Lanark	1937	Rangers	1976	Rangers
1905	Celtic	1938	Celtic	1977	Celtic
1906	Celtic	1939	Rangers	1978	Rangers
1907	Celtic	1940-46	not held	1979	Celtic
1908	Celtic	1947	Rangers	1980	Aberdeen
1909	Celtic	1948	Hibernian	1981	Celtic
1910	Celtic	1949	Rangers	1982	Celtic
1911	Rangers	1950	Rangers	1983	Dundee Utd
1912	Rangers	1951	Hibernian	1984	Aberdeen
1913	Rangers	1952	Hibernian	1985	Aberdeen
1914	Celtic	1953	Rangers	1986	Celtic
1915	Celtic	1954	Celtic	1987	Rangers
1916	Celtic	1955	Aberdeen	1988	Celtic
1917	Celtic	1956	Rangers	1989	Rangers
1918	Rangers	1957	Rangers	1990	Rangers
1919	Celtic	1958	Heart of Midlothian	1991	Rangers
1920	Rangers	1959	Rangers	1992	Rangers
1921	Rangers	1960	Heart of Midlothian	1993	Rangers
1922	Celtic	1961	Rangers	1994	Rangers
1923	Rangers	1962	Dundee	1995	Rangers
1924	Rangers	1963	Rangers	1996	Rangers

1997	Rangers	2000	Rangers	2003	Rangers
1998	Celtic	2001	Celtic	2004	Celtic
1999	Rangers	2002	Celtic		

Scottish League Clubs

Club	Ground	Nickname(s)
Aberdeen	Pittodrie Stadium	Dons
Airdrie United	New Broomfield Park	Diamonds, Waysiders
Albion Rovers	Cliffhill Stadium, Coatbridge	Wee Rovers
Alloa Athletic	Recreation Park	Wasps
Arbroath	Gayfield Park	Red Lichties
Ayr United	Somerset Park	Honest Men
Berwick Rangers	Shielfield Park	Borderers
Brechin City	Glebe Park	City
Celtic	Celtic Park (formerly Parkhead), Glasgow	Bhoys
Clyde	Broadwood Stadium, Cumbernauld	Bully Wee
Clydebank	Cappielow Park	Bankies
Cowdenbeath	Central Park	Blue Brazil
Dumbarton	Strathclyde Homes Stadium	Sons
Dundee	Dens Park	Dark Blues/Dee
Dundee United	Tannadice Park	Terrors
Dunfermline Athletic	East End Park	Pars
East Fife	Bayview Park, Methil	Fifers
East Stirlingshire	Firs Park, Falkirk	Shire
Elgin City	Borough Briggs	City, Black and Whites
Falkirk	Brockville Park	Bairns
Forfar Athletic	Station Park	Loons/Sky Blues
Greenock Morton	Cappielow Park	Ton
Gretna	Raydale Park	Black and Whites/Borders
Hamilton Academical	New Douglas Park	Accies
Heart of Midlothian	Tynecastle Park, Edinburgh	Jam Tarts
Hibernian	Easter Road, Edinburgh	Hibees
Inverness Caledonian Thistle	Caledonian Stadium, East Longman	Caley, Jags
Kilmarnock	Rugby Park	Killies
Livingston	West Lothian Courier Stadium	Livi Lions
Montrose	Links Park	Gable Endies
Motherwell	Fir Park	Well
Partick Thistle	Firhill Park, Glasgow	Jags
Peterhead	Balmoor Stadium	Blue Toon
Queen of the South	Palmerston Park, Dumfries	Doonhamers, Queens
Queen's Park	Hampden Park, Glasgow	Spiders
Raith Rovers	Stark's Park, Kirkcaldy	Rovers
Rangers	Ibrox Stadium, Glasgow	Blues, Gers
Ross County	Victoria Park, Dingwall	County
St Johnstone	McDiarmid Park, Perth	Saints
St Mirren	St Mirren Park, Paisley	Buddies
Stenhousemuir	Ochilview Park	Warriors
Stirling Albion	Forthbank Stadium	Binos, The Albion
Stranraer	Stair Park	Blues

NB: Elgin City are now the most northerly club in the Scottish Football League. Airdrie United took over Clydebank (The Bankies) in June 2002 and play in the colours of the former Airdrieonians.

Scottish Cup

	Winners		Runners-Up		Winners		Runners-Up
1874	Queen's Park	2-0	Clydesdale	1882	Queen's Park	2-2, 4-1	Dumbarton
1875	Queen's Park	3-0	Renton	1883	Dumbarton	2-2, 2-1	Vale of Leven
1876	Queen's Park	1-1, 2-0	Third Lanark	1884	Queen's Park	walkover	Vale of Leven
1877	Vale of Leven	0-0, 1-1, 3-2	Rangers		(Queen's Park awarded the cup		
1878	Vale of Leven	1-0	Third Lanark		after Vale of Leven failed to appear)		
1879	Vale of Leven	1-1, walkover	Rangers	1885	Renton	0-0, 3-1	Vale of Leven
(Vale of Leven awarded cup as Rangers				1886	Queen's Park	3-1	Renton
failed to appear for replay after 1-1 draw)				1887	Hibernian	2-1	Dumbarton
1880	Queen's Park	3-0	Thornliebank	1888	Renton	6-1	Cambuslang
1881	Queen's Park	3-1	Dumbarton	1889	Third Lanark	2-1	Celtic
(Dumbarton protested the first result				(Scottish FA ordered a replay because of playing conditions			
in which Queen's Park won 2-1)				after Third Lanark won match 3-0)			

1890	Queen's Park	1-1, 2-1	Vale of Leven
1891	Heart of Midlothian	1-0	Dumbarton
1892	Celtic	5-1	Queen's Park

(In 1892 both teams protested about first game which Celtic won 1-0)

1893	Queen's Park	2-1	Celtic
1894	Rangers	3-1	Celtic
1895	St Bernard's	2-1	Renton
1896	Heart of Midlothian	3-1	Hibernian
1897	Rangers	5-1	Dumbarton
1898	Rangers	2-0	Kilmarnock
1899	Celtic	2-0	Rangers
1900	Celtic	4-3	Queen's Park
1901	Heart of Midlothian	4-3	Celtic
1902	Hibernian	1-0	Celtic
1903	Rangers	1-1, 0-0, 2-0	Heart of Midlothian
1904	Celtic	3-2	Rangers
1905	Third Lanark	0-0, 3-1	Rangers
1906	Heart of Midlothian	1-0	Third Lanark
1907	Celtic	3-0	Heart of Midlothian
1908	Celtic	5-1	St Mirren
1909	cup withheld		

(In 1909 Celtic v Rangers 2-2, 1-1 with riot in extra time – clubs refused to play a third match; Cup was withheld by Scottish FA)

1910	Dundee	2-2, 0-0, 2-1	Clyde
1911	Celtic	0-0, 2-0	Hamilton
1912	Celtic	2-0	Clyde
1913	Falkirk	2-0	Raith Rovers
1914	Celtic	0-0, 4-1	Hibernian
1915-19 not held			
1920	Kilmarnock	3-2	Albion Rovers
1921	Partick Thistle	1-0	Rangers
1922	Morton	1-0	Rangers
1923	Celtic	1-0	Hibernian
1924	Airdrieonians	2-0	Hibernian
1925	Celtic	2-1	Dundee
1926	St Mirren	2-0	Celtic
1927	Celtic	3-1	East Fife
1928	Rangers	4-0	Celtic
1929	Kilmarnock	2-0	Rangers
1930	Rangers	0-0, 2-1	Partick Thistle
1931	Celtic	2-2, 4-2	Motherwell
1932	Rangers	1-1, 3-0	Kilmarnock
1933	Celtic	1-0	Motherwell
1934	Rangers	5-0	St Mirren
1935	Rangers	2-1	Hamilton Academical
1936	Rangers	1-0	Third Lanark
1937	Celtic	2-1	Aberdeen
1938	East Fife	1-1, 4-2 aet	Kilmarnock
1939	Clyde	4-0	Motherwell
1940-46 not held			
1947	Aberdeen	2-1	Hibernian
1948	Rangers	1-1, 1-0 aet	Morton
1949	Rangers	4-1	Clyde

1950	Rangers	3-0	East Fife
1951	Celtic	1-0	Motherwell
1952	Motherwell	4-0	Dundee
1953	Rangers	1-1, 1-0	Aberdeen
1954	Celtic	2-1	Aberdeen
1955	Clyde	1-1, 1-0	Celtic
1956	Heart of Midlothian	3-1	Celtic
1957	Falkirk	1-1, 2-1	Kilmarnock
1958	Clyde	1-0	Hibernian
1959	St Mirren	3-1	Aberdeen
1960	Rangers	2-0	Kilmarnock
1961	Dunfermline Athletic	0-0, 2-0	Celtic
1962	Rangers	2-0	St Mirren
1963	Rangers	1-1, 3-0	Celtic
1964	Rangers	3-1	Dundee
1965	Celtic	3-2	Dunfermline Athletic
1966	Rangers	0-0, 1-0	Celtic
1967	Celtic	2-0	Aberdeen
1968	Dunfermline Athletic	3-1	Heart of Midlothian
1969	Celtic	4-0	Rangers
1970	Aberdeen	3-1	Celtic
1971	Celtic	1-1, 2-1	Rangers
1972	Celtic	6-1	Hibernian
1973	Rangers	3-2	Celtic
1974	Celtic	3-0	Dundee United
1975	Celtic	3-1	Airdrieonians
1976	Rangers	3-1	Heart of Midlothian
1977	Celtic	1-0	Rangers
1978	Rangers	2-1	Aberdeen
1979	Rangers	0-0, 0-0, 3-2 aet	Hibernian
1980	Celtic	1-0	Rangers
1981	Rangers	0-0, 4-1	Dundee United
1982	Aberdeen	4-1 aet	Rangers
1983	Aberdeen	1-0 aet	Rangers
1984	Aberdeen	2-1 aet	Celtic
1985	Celtic	2-1	Dundee United
1986	Aberdeen	3-0	Heart of Midlothian
1987	St Mirren	1-0 aet	Dundee United
1988	Celtic	2-1	Dundee United
1989	Celtic	1-0	Rangers
1990	Aberdeen	0-0, 9-8 on pens	Celtic
1991	Motherwell	4-3 aet	Dundee United
1992	Rangers	2-1	Airdrieonians
1993	Rangers	2-1	Aberdeen
1994	Dundee United	1-0	Rangers
1995	Celtic	1-0	Airdrieonians
1996	Rangers	5-1	Heart of Midlothian
1997	Kilmarnock	1-0	Falkirk
1998	Heart of Midlothian	2-1	Rangers
1999	Rangers	1-0	Celtic
2000	Rangers	4-0	Aberdeen
2001	Celtic	3-0	Hibernian
2002	Rangers	3-2	Celtic
2003	Rangers	1-0	Dundee
2004	Celtic	3-1	Dunfermline Athletic

FOOTBALL

Scottish League Cup

Winners		Runners-Up	Winners		Runners-Up
1947 Rangers	4-0	Aberdeen	1977 Aberdeen	2-1	Celtic
1948 East Fife	0-0, 4-1	Falkirk	1978 Rangers	2-1	Celtic
1949 Rangers	2-0	Raith Rovers	1979 Rangers	2-1	Aberdeen
1950 East Fife	3-0	Dunfermline	1980 Dundee United	0-0, 3-0	Aberdeen
1951 Motherwell	3-0	Hibernian	1981 Dundee United	3-0	Dundee
1952 Dundee	3-2	Rangers	1982 Rangers	2-1	Dundee United
1953 Dundee	2-0	Kilmarnock	1983 Celtic	2-1	Rangers
1954 East Fife	3-2	Partick Thistle	1984 Rangers	3-2	Celtic
1955 Heart of Midlothian	4-2	Motherwell	1985 Rangers	1-0	Dundee United
1956 Aberdeen	2-1	St Mirren	1986 Aberdeen	3-0	Hibernian
1957 Celtic	0-0, 3-0	Partick Thistle	1987 Rangers	2-1	Celtic
1958 Celtic	7-1	Rangers	1988 Rangers	3-3, 5-3 on pens	Aberdeen
1959 Heart of Midlothian	5-1	Partick Thistle			
1960 Heart of Midlothian	2-1	Third Lanark	1989 Rangers	3-2	Aberdeen
1961 Rangers	2-0	Kilmarnock	1990 Aberdeen	2-1	Rangers
1962 Rangers	1-1, 3-1	Heart of Midlothian	1991 Rangers	2-1	Celtic
1963 Heart of Midlothian	1-0	Kilmarnock	1992 Hibernian	2-0	Dunfermline
1964 Rangers	5-0	Morton	1993 Rangers	2-1	Aberdeen
1965 Rangers	2-1	Celtic	1994 Rangers	2-1	Hibernian
1966 Celtic	2-1	Rangers	1995 Raith Rovers	2-2, 6-5 on pens	Celtic
1967 Celtic	1-0	Rangers			
1968 Celtic	5-3	Dundee	1996 Aberdeen	2-0	Dundee
1969 Celtic	6-2	Hibernian	1997 Rangers	4-3	Heart of Midlothian
1970 Celtic	1-0	St Johnstone	1998 Celtic	3-0	Dundee United
1971 Rangers	1-0	Celtic	1999 Rangers	2-1	St Johnstone
1972 Partick Thistle	4-1	Celtic	2000 Celtic	2-0	Aberdeen
1973 Hibernian	2-1	Celtic	2001 Celtic	3-0	Kilmarnock
1974 Dundee	1-0	Celtic	2002 Rangers	4-0	Ayr United
1975 Celtic	6-3	Hibernian	2003 Rangers	2-1	Celtic
1976 Rangers	1-0	Celtic	2004 Livingston	2-0	Hibernian

FIFA World Footballer of the Year

1991	Lothar Matthäus (GER, Inter Milan)
1992	Marco Van Basten (NED, AC Milan)
1993	Roberto Baggio (ITA, Juventus)
1994	Romario (BRA, Barcelona)
1995	George Weah (LBR, AC Milan)
1996	Ronaldo (BRA, Inter Milan)
1997	Ronaldo (BRA, Inter Milan)
1998	Zinedine Zidane (FRA, Juventus)
1999	Rivaldo (BRA, Barcelona)
2000	Zinedine Zidane (FRA, Juventus)
2001	Luis Figo (POR, Real Madrid)
2002	Ronaldo (BRA, Real Madrid)
2003	Zinedine Zidane (FRA, Real Madrid)

European Footballer of the Year

(Le Ballon d'Or – The Golden Ball)

1956	Stanley Matthews (Blackpool)
1957	Alfredo di Stefano (Real Madrid)
1958	Raymond Kopa (Real Madrid)
1959	Alfredo di Stefano (Real Madrid)
1960	Luis Suarez (Barcelona)
1961	Omar Sivori (Juventus)
1962	Josef Masopust (Dukla Prague)
1963	Lev Yashin (Moscow Dynamo)
1964	Denis Law (Manchester Utd)
1965	Eusebio (Benfica)
1966	Bobby Charlton (Manchester Utd)
1967	Florian Albert (Ferencvaros)
1968	George Best (Manchester Utd)
1969	Gianni Rivera (AC Milan)
1970	Gerd Müller (Bayern Munich)
1971	Johan Cruyff (Ajax)
1972	Franz Beckenbauer (Bayern Munich)
1973	Johan Cruyff (Barcelona)
1974	Johan Cruyff (Barcelona)
1975	Oleg Blokhin (Dynamo Kiev)
1976	Franz Beckenbauer (Bayern Munich)
1977	Allan Simonsen (Borussia Mönchengladbach)
1978	Kevin Keegan (SV Hamburg)
1979	Kevin Keegan (SV Hamburg)
1980	Karl-Heinz Rummenigge (Bayern Munich)
1981	Karl-Heinz Rummenigge (Bayern Munich)
1982	Paolo Rossi (Juventus)
1983	Michel Platini (Juventus)
1984	Michel Platini (Juventus)
1985	Michel Platini (Juventus)
1986	Igor Belanov (Dynamo Kiev)
1987	Ruud Gullit (AC Milan)
1988	Marco van Basten (AC Milan)
1989	Marco van Basten (AC Milan)
1990	Lothar Matthäus (Inter Milan)
1991	Jean-Pierre Papin (Marseille)
1992	Marco van Basten (AC Milan)
1993	Roberto Baggio (Juventus)
1994	Hristo Stoichkov (Barcelona)
1995	George Weah (AC Milan)
1996	Matthias Sammer (Borussia Dortmund)
1997	Ronaldo (Inter Milan)

1998	Zinedine Zidane (Juventus)	2001	Michael Owen (Liverpool)
1999	Rivaldo (Barcelona)	2002	Ronaldo (Real Madrid)
2000	Luis Figo (Real Madrid)	2003	Pavel Nedved (Juventus)

PFA Player of the Year

1974	Norman Hunter (Leeds)
1975	Colin Todd (Derby County)
1976	Pat Jennings (Tottenham)
1977	Andy Gray (Aston Villa)
1978	Peter Shilton (Nottm Forest)
1979	Liam Brady (Arsenal)
1980	Terry McDermott (Liverpool)
1981	John Wark (Ipswich)
1982	Kevin Keegan (Southampton)
1983	Kenny Dalglish (Liverpool)
1984	Ian Rush (Liverpool)
1985	Peter Reid (Everton)
1986	Gary Lineker (Everton)
1987	Clive Allen (Tottenham)
1988	John Barnes (Liverpool)
1989	Mark Hughes (Manchester Utd)
1990	David Platt (Aston Villa)
1991	Mark Hughes (Manchester Utd)
1992	Gary Pallister (Manchester Utd)
1993	Paul McGrath (Aston Villa)
1994	Eric Cantona (Manchester Utd)
1995	Alan Shearer (Blackburn)
1996	Les Ferdinand (Newcastle)
1997	Alan Shearer (Newcastle)
1998	Dennis Bergkamp (Arsenal)
1999	David Ginola (Tottenham)
2000	Roy Keane (Manchester Utd)
2001	Teddy Sheringham (Manchester Utd)
2002	Ruud van Nistelrooy (Manchester Utd)
2003	Thierry Henry (Arsenal)
2004	Thierry Henry (Arsenal)

PFA Young Player of the Year

Kevin Beattie (Ipswich)
Mervyn Day (West Ham)
Peter Barnes (Manchester City)
Andy Gray (Aston Villa)
Tony Woodcock (Nottm Forest)
Cyrille Regis (WBA)
Glenn Hoddle (Tottenham)
Gary Shaw (Aston Villa)
Steve Moran (Southampton)
Ian Rush (Liverpool)
Paul Walsh (Luton)
Mark Hughes (Manchester Utd)
Tony Cottee (West Ham)
Tony Adams (Arsenal)
Paul Gascoigne (Newcastle)
Paul Merson (Arsenal)
Matt Le Tissier (Southampton)
Lee Sharpe (Manchester Utd)
Ryan Giggs (Manchester Utd)
Ryan Giggs (Manchester Utd)
Andy Cole (Newcastle)
Robbie Fowler (Liverpool)
Robbie Fowler (Liverpool)
David Beckham (Manchester Utd)
Michael Owen (Liverpool)
Nicolas Anelka (Arsenal)
Harry Kewell (Leeds)
Steven Gerrard (Liverpool)
Craig Bellamy (Newcastle)
Jermaine Jenas (Newcastle)
Scott Parker (Chelsea)

Football Writers' Player of the Year

1948	Stanley Matthews (Blackpool)	1976	Kevin Keegan (Liverpool)
1949	Johnny Carey (Manchester Utd)	1977	Emlyn Hughes (Liverpool)
1950	Joe Mercer (Arsenal)	1978	Kenny Burns (Nottm Forest)
1951	Harry Johnston (Blackpool)	1979	Kenny Dalglish (Liverpool)
1952	Billy Wright (Wolves)	1980	Terry McDermott (Liverpool)
1953	Nat Lofthouse (Bolton)	1981	Frans Thijssen (Ipswich)
1954	Tom Finney (Preston North End)	1982	Steve Perryman (Tottenham)
1955	Don Revie (Manchester City)	1983	Kenny Dalglish (Liverpool)
1956	Bert Trautmann (Manchester City)	1984	Ian Rush (Liverpool)
1957	Tom Finney (Preston North End)	1985	Neville Southall (Everton)
1958	Danny Blanchflower (Tottenham)	1986	Gary Lineker (Everton)
1959	Syd Owen (Luton)	1987	Clive Allen (Tottenham)
1960	Bill Slater (Wolves)	1988	John Barnes (Liverpool)
1961	Danny Blanchflower (Tottenham)	1989	Steve Nicol (Liverpool)
1962	Jimmy Adamson (Burnley)	1990	John Barnes (Liverpool)
1963	Stanley Matthews (Stoke City)	1991	Gordon Strachan (Leeds)
1964	Bobby Moore (West Ham)	1992	Gary Lineker (Tottenham)
1965	Bobby Collins (Leeds)	1993	Chris Waddle (Sheffield Wed)
1966	Bobby Charlton (Manchester Utd)	1994	Alan Shearer (Blackburn)
1967	Jackie Charlton (Leeds)	1995	Jürgen Klinsmann (Tottenham)
1968	George Best (Manchester Utd)	1996	Eric Cantona (Manchester Utd)
1969	Tony Book (Manchester City)	1997	Gianfranco Zola (Chelsea)
	Dave Mackay (Derby County)	1998	Dennis Bergkamp (Arsenal)
1970	Billy Bremner (Leeds)	1999	David Ginola (Tottenham)
1971	Frank McLintock (Arsenal)	2000	Roy Keane (Manchester Utd)
1972	Gordon Banks (Stoke City)	2001	Teddy Sheringham (Manchester Utd)
1973	Pat Jennings (Tottenham)	2002	Robert Pires (Arsenal)
1974	Ian Callaghan (Liverpool)	2003	Thierry Henry (Arsenal)
1975	Alan Mullery (Fulham)	2004	Thierry Henry (Arsenal)

Biographies of Players and Managers

Details correct as at 30 September 2003

Abdullah, Majed Born Jeddah, Saudi Arabia, 11 January 1959. Position: forward. Club: Al-Nassr 1977-98. Honours: Saudi Arabian League Championship 1980, 1981, 1989, 1995; Saudi Arabia Kings Cup 1981, 1986, 1987; Asian Cup 1998. International caps (for Saudi Arabia): 140, 67 goals. Asian Player of the Year 1984, 1985, 1986. Saudi Arabian Player of the Century.

Abedi Pele Born Abedi Pele Ayew, Dome, Ghana, 5 January 1962. Position: forward. Clubs: Real Tamale United 1978-83, 1985-86, Sat Club Qatar 1983-84, Dragons of Benin 1984-85, Chamois Noir 1986-87, Montpellier 1987-88, Lille 1989-90, Olympique Marseille 1990-93, Lyon 1993-94, Torino 1994-96, 1860 Munich 1996-98, Al-Ain 1998-2000. Honours: European Cup 1993 (with Olympique Marseille). International caps (for Ghana): not known. International honours: African Cup of Nations 1982. African Footballer of the Year 1991, 1992, 1993. A goodwill football ambassador for Africa, he also works for FIFA. His younger brother Kwame Ayew plays for Sporting Lisbon and Ghana.

Adams, Tony Born Tony Alexander Adams, Romford, Essex, 10 October 1966. Position: defender. Club: Arsenal 1984-2002. Honours: League Championship/FA Premiership 1989, 1991, 1998, 2002; FA Cup 1993, 1998, 2002; League Cup 1987, 1993; Charity Shield 1998; European Cup Winners' Cup 1994. International caps (for England): 66 (15 as captain), 5 goals. Arsenal's youngest-ever captain. PFA Young Player of the Year 1987. Known to non-Arsenal fans as 'Donkey'. His autobiography *Addicted* recounts his problems with alcohol abuse.

Adamson, Jimmy Born James Adamson, Ashington, Northumberland, 4 April 1929. Position: midfielder. Club (player): Burnley 1946-64. Honours: League Championship 1960. Clubs (manager): Burnley 1970-76, Sparta Rotterdam 1976, Sunderland 1976-78, Leeds United 1978-80. Football Writers' Player of the Year 1962. Adamson made 486 appearances for Burnley. Though never capped by his country, he held the distinction of being England coach in the 1962 World Cup, as well as being picked as a player in the squad. He turned down the chance to replace Walter Winterbottom as England manager.

Ademir, Marques Born Ademir Marques de Meneses, Recife, Brazil, 8 November 1922. Position: forward. Clubs: Recife 1939-42, Vasco da Gama 1942-45, 1948-56, Fluminense 1945-48. Honours: Brazilian League Championship 1945, 1949, 1950, 1952, 1956 (with Vasco da Gama), 1946 (with Fluminense). International caps (for Brazil): 39, 32 goals. Golden Boot winner, World Cup 1950 (9 goals). Having scored 303 goals in 461 games for Vasco da Gama, he went into broadcasting and journalism, on retiring in 1956 through injury. He died 11 May 1996 in Rio de Janeiro.

Ahn Jung Hwan Born Pusan, South Korea, 16 February 1976. Position: midfield. Clubs: Pusan Icons 1994-2000, Perugia 2000-02. First came to prominence in the South Korean student team in the 1994 East Asian games, and was voted Most Valuable Player, K-League in 1999. He scored the Golden Goal winner v Italy in the second round of the 2002 World Cup, for which he was promptly sacked by the owner of Perugia.

Albert, Florian Born Hercegszanto, Hungary, 15 September 1941. Position: forward. Clubs: Ferencvaros 1952-74. Honours: Hungarian League Championship 1963, 1964, 1967, 1968; Inter-cities Fairs Cup 1965 (with Ferencvaros). International caps (for Hungary): 75, 31 goals. Albert is considered the last of the 'Magical Magyars', who illuminated European football in the 1950s. His finest performance was given when Hungary defeated Brazil 3-1 in the 1966 World Cup, this being the Brazilians' first loss since 1954. European Player of the Year 1967. Became a journalist on his retirement in 1974.

Albertini, Demetrio Born Bresana, Brianza, near Milan, Italy, 23 August 1971. Position: midfield. Clubs: AC Milan 1988-2002, Padova 1990-91 (loan), Atlético Madrid 2002-03 (loan), Lazio 2003-present (loan). Honours: Italian League Championship 1992, 1993, 1994, 1996, 1999; UEFA Champions League 1994 (all with AC Milan). International caps (for Italy): 79, 2 goals.

Alberto, Carlos Born Carlos Alberto Torres, Rio de Janeiro, Brazil, 17 July 1944. Position: defender. Clubs (player): Fluminense 1963-65, 1976, Santos 1965-71, 1972-76, Botafogo 1971, Flamengo 1977, New York Cosmos 1977-81, 1982, Newport Beach 1981. Honours: Brazilian Rio League Championship 1964, 1976 (with Fluminense); Brazilian São Paulo League Championship 1965, 1967, 1968, 1969, 1973 (with Santos); Brazilian Cup 1965, 1968 (with Santos); NASL Championship 1977, 1978, 1982 (with New York Cosmos). Clubs (manager): Flamengo 1983-85, 2001-02, Corinthians 1985-86, Clube Nautica Capibaribe 1986-87, Miami Sharks 1987-93, Botafogo 1993-94, 1997-98, 1999-2000, Fluminense 1994-95, Atlético 1998-99, Desportiva Cabonfirense 2001, Violette Athletique Club (Haiti) 2002-present. Honours: Brazilian League Championship 1983 (with Flamengo); Brazilian Rio League Championship 1984 (with Fluminense). International caps (for Brazil): 58, 8 goals. International honours: World Cup 1970 (as captain). International manager (Nigeria): 1995-97; (Oman): 2000-01. He scored the memorable fourth goal in Brazil's 4-1 win over Italy in the 1970 World Cup final. In 2003 he is working to promote a new professional league in Haiti.

Aldair Born Nascimento Santos Aldair, Ilheus, Brazil, 30 November 1965. Position: defender. Clubs: Flamengo 1986-89, Benfica (loan) 1989, Roma 1990-2003, Genoa 2003-present. Honours: Brazilian League Championship 1997 (with Flamengo); Italian League Championship 2001 (with Roma); Italian Cup 2001 (with Roma). International caps (for Brazil): 79. International honours: World Cup 1994. Nicknamed 'Pluto'. Roma retired their no. 6 shirt in June 2003 as a mark of respect for Aldair's 13-year spell at the club. He chose to move to Serie B side Genoa because he did not want to play against Roma.

Aldridge, John Born John William Aldridge, Liverpool, England, 18 September 1958. Position: forward. Clubs (player): South Liverpool 1978-79, Newport County 1979-84 (signed for £3500), Oxford United 1984-87 (signed for £80,000), Liverpool 1987-89 (signed for £750,000), Real Sociedad 1989-91 (signed for £1.1m), Tranmere Rovers 1991-98 (signed or £250,000). Honours: League Championship 1988 (with Liverpool); FA Cup 1989 (with Liverpool); League Cup 1986 (with Oxford United). Clubs (manager): Tranmere Rovers 1996-2001. International caps (for Republic of Ireland): 69, 19 goals. Although he scored 474 goals in all matches in his career, he took Tranmere Rovers to the League Cup final in 2000. Known as 'Aldo'. Aldridge has the unwanted distinction of being the first player to miss an FA Cup final penalty (for Liverpool v Wimbledon 1988).

Allchurch, Ivor Born Ivor John Allchurch, Swansea, Wales, 16 October 1929. Position: forward. Clubs: Swansea Town 1949-58, 1965-67, Newcastle United 1958-61, Cardiff City 1962-64. International caps (for Wales): 68, 23 goals. Considered one of the most skilful players of the 1950s, Allchurch was instrumental in Wales' qualification for the 1958 World Cup. Younger brother Len was also a noted player having the distinction of playing his last season for the newly renamed Swansea City. Awarded the MBE in 1966.

Allen, Clive Born Clive Darren Allen, Stepney, London, 20 May 1961. Position: forward. Clubs: Queens Park Rangers 1978-80, 1981-84 (signed for £400,000), Arsenal 1980 (signed for 1.25m – 63 days), Crystal Palace 1980-81 (signed for £1.25m), Queens Park Rangers 1981-84 (signed for £400,000), Tottenham Hotspur 1984-88 (signed for £700,000), Girondins de Bordeaux 1988-89 (signed for £1m), Manchester City 1989-91 (signed £1.1m), Chelsea 1991-92 (signed for £250,000), West Ham United 1992-94 (signed for £275,000), Millwall 1994-95 (signed for £25,000), Carlisle United 1995. International caps (for England): 5. Football Writers' Player of the Year 1987. PFA Player of the Year 1987. Son of Les Allen. A prolific goalscorer, including 49 in one season for Tottenham Hotspur, and noted for playing for such a wide selection of London clubs. Now works as a TV pundit.

Allen, Les Born Dagenham, Essex, 4 September 1937. Position: forward. Clubs (player): Chelsea 1956-59, Tottenham Hotspur 1959-64, Queens Park Rangers 1965-68. Honours: League Championship 1961 (with Tottenham Hotspur); FA Cup 1961 (with Tottenham Hotspur); League Cup 1967 (with Queens Park Rangers). Clubs (manager): Queens Park Rangers 1969-70, Swindon Town 1972-77, Salonika. Part of a remarkable footballing family. Les's two sons are Clive and Bradley; younger brother Dennis had a long career mainly with Reading and his two sons are Martin and Paul (for some years the youngest player to play in an FA Cup final). On retiring from the game Les worked as a professional model maker.

Altafini, José Born José Joáo Altafini, Piracicaba di São, Brazil, 27 August 1936. Position: forward. Clubs: Palmeiras 1954-58, AC Milan 1958 -65, Napoli 1965-72, Juventus 1972-76, Chiasso. Honours: Italian League Championship 1957, 1959 (with AC Milan), 1972, 1975 (with Juventus); European Cup 1963 (with AC Milan). International caps (for Brazil): 8, 4 goals. International caps (for Italy): 6, 5 goals. International honours: World Cup 1958. One of only six players to appear in the World Cup for two different countries (Brazil 1958, Italy 1962), the others being Luis Monti, Ferenc Puskas, Jose Santamaria, Attilio de Maria and Robert Prosinecki. Nicknamed 'Mazzola' because of his resemblance to the Italian player of the late 1940s.

Amarildo Born Amarildo Tavares da Silva, Rio de Janeiro, Brazil, 29 June 1940. Position: forward.

Clubs: Goytacaz 1958, Flamengo 1959-60, Botafogo 1960-62, AC Milan 1963-67, Fiorentina 1967-71, Roma 1971-72, Vasco da Gama 1972. Honours: Brazilian Rio League Championship 1961, 1962 (with Botafogo); Italian League Championship 1969 (with Fiorentina). International caps (for Brazil): 24, 9 goals. International honours: World Cup 1962.

Amoros, Manuel Born Nimes, France, 1 February 1962. Position: defender. Clubs: Monaco 1977-89, Olympique Marseille 1989-93, 1995-97, Lyon 1993-95. Honours: French League Championship 1982 (with AS Monaco), 1988, 1990, 1991,1992 (with Olympique Marseille); French Cup 1985 (with AS Monaco). International caps (for France): 82, 1 goal.

Anastasi, Pietro Born Catania, Italy, 7 April 1948. Position: forward. Clubs: Massiminiana 1964-66, Varese 1966-68, Juventus 1968-76, Inter Milan, Ascoli. Honours: Italian League Championship 1972, 1973, 1975 (with Juventus). International caps (for Italy): 25, 8 goals. International honours: European Championship 1968. Known as 'Petruzzi', Anastasi first came to attention by scoring a hat-trick against Juventus, who quickly snapped him up. At Juventus he formed a formidable strike partnership with Roberto Bettega. He scored in the final of the 1968 European Championship when Italy beat Yugoslavia 2-1.

Anderson, Viv Born Vivian Alexander Anderson, Nottingham, 29 August 1956. Position: defender. Clubs (player): Nottingham Forest 1972-84, Arsenal 1984-87, Manchester United 1987-90, Sheffield Wednesday 1990-93, Barnsley 1993-94, Middlesbrough 1994-97 (2 appearances when assistant manager). Honours: League Championship 1978; European Cup 1979, 1980 (all with Nottingham Forest). Clubs (manager): Barnsley 1993-94, Middlesbrough 1994-2001 (assistant). International caps (for England): 30, 2 goals. Anderson was the first black player to represent his country, and the second to become a manager in English football after Keith Alexander at Lincoln.

Anderton, Darren Born Darren Robert Anderton, Southampton, 3 March 1972. Position: midfield. Clubs: Portsmouth 1990-92, Tottenham Hotspur 1992-present. Honours: League Cup 1999 (with Tottenham Hotspur). International caps (for England): 30, 7 goals. His susceptibility to injury has led to him being known as 'Sick Note'.

Andrade, Jose Born Jose Leandro Andrade, Salto, Uruguay, 20 November 1898. Position: defender. Clubs: Atlético Misiones, Bella Vista, Nacional, Peñarol, Wanderers. Retired in 1933. Honours: Uruguayan League Championship 1923, 1924, 1926 (with Bella Vista), 1932 (with Peñarol). International caps (for Uruguay): 41, 1 goal. International honours: World Cup 1930; Olympic gold medal 1924, 1928; Copa America 1923, 1924, 1926. Nephew Victor Rodriguez won World Cup winner's medal in 1950. He died October 1957.

Anelka, Nicolas Born Versailles, France, 14 March 1979. Position: forward. Clubs: Paris St-Germain 1994-97, 2000-02, Arsenal 1997-99 (signed for £500,000), Real Madrid 1999-2000 (signed for £22.9m), Liverpool (loan) 2001-02, Manchester City 2002-present (signed for £13m). International honours: FA Premiership 1998 (with Arsenal); FA Cup 1998 (with Arsenal); Charity Shield 1998 (with Arsenal); UEFA Champions League 2000 (with Real Madrid). International caps (for France): 28, 6 goals.

Antognoni, Giancarlo Born Marsciano, Perugia, Italy, 1 April 1954. Position: midfield. Clubs: Astimacobi 1970-72, Fiorentina 1972-87 (signed for

£150,000), Lausanne 1987-89. Honours: Italian Cup 1976 (with Fiorentina). International caps (for Italy): 73, 7 goals. International honours: World Cup 1982. He missed Italy's 1982 World Cup final win because of an injury picked up in the semi-final, and also suffered a double fracture of the skull in a clash with Genoa's goalkeeper. Antognoni was adored by Fiorentina fans who taunted more successful teams with 'You may win the Scudetto but we have Antognoni.'

Archibald, Steve   Born Glasgow, 27 September 1956. Position: forward. Clubs (player): Clyde, Aberdeen 1978-80, Tottenham Hotspur 1980-84 (signed for £800,000), Barcelona 1984 (signed for £1.1m), Hibernian, Espanyol, St Mirren, Reading 1992 (one game), Fulham, Ayr United. Honours: Scottish League Championship 1980 (with Aberdeen); Spanish League Championship 1985 (with Barcelona); FA Cup 1981, 1982 (with Tottenham Hotspur); UEFA Cup 1984 (with Tottenham Hotspur). Clubs (manager): East Fife. International caps (for Scotland): 27, 4 goals. Archibald was involved in a protracted attempt to gain control of Airdrieonians in the early 2000s.

Ardiles, Ossie   Born Osvaldo Cesar Ardiles, Cordoba, Argentina, 3 August 1952. Position: midfield. Clubs (player): National Instituto Cordoba 1969-73, National Belgrano 1974, Huracan 1975-78, Tottenham Hotspur 1978-82,1983-88, Paris St-Germain 1982-83 (loan), Blackburn Rovers 1988, West Bromwich Albion 1988-89, Swindon Town 1989-91. Honours: FA Cup 1981; UEFA Cup 1984 (both with Tottenham Hotspur). Clubs (manager): Swindon Town 1989-91, Newcastle United 1991-92, West Bromwich Albion 1992-93, Tottenham Hotspur 1993-94, Guadalajara 1994, Shimizu S-Pulse 1995-99, Croatia Zagreb 1999, Yokohama Marinos 1999-2001, Al-Ittihad 2002, Racing Club 2002-03, Tokyo Verdy 2003-present. Honours: Tokai Cup 1996, 1998 (with Shimizu S-Pulse). International caps (for Argentina): 42, 8 goals. International honours: World Cup 1978. Known as 'El Piton'. The inspiration for the record 'Ossie's Dream', the Tottenham squad's FA Cup record in 1981, Ardiles was loaned by Tottenham to Paris St-Germain during the Falklands War to avoid any 'unpleasantness'. In a mixed career in management, he won the First Division Two play-off final with Swindon in 1989/90, only for the club's promotion to the First Division to be rescinded by the FA for disciplinary breaches that occurred before he took charge. Had a part in the film *Escape to Victory*.

Armfield, Jimmy   Born James Christopher Armfield, Denton, Manchester, 21 September 1935. Position: defender. Clubs (player): Blackpool, 1954-70. Clubs (manager): Bolton Wanderers 1971-74, Leeds United 1974-78. International caps (for England): 43 (15 as captain). Made 568 League appearances for Blackpool. Considered to be the inventor of the overlapping full-back, he was selected as best full-back of the 1962 World Cup. On leaving management, he became a well-respected football summariser for Radio 5 Live, and has also acted as headhunter for the FA when seeking a replacement manager for England.

Armstrong, George   Born Hebburn, Durham, 9 August 1944. Position: forward. Clubs: Arsenal 1961-77, Leicester City, Stockport County. Honours: English League Championship 1971; FA Cup 1971; Inter-cities Fairs Cup 1970 (all with Arsenal). Coached at Fulham, Aston Villa, Middlesbrough, Queens Park Rangers, Narvik and Kuwait. Reserve team coach at Arsenal 1990-2000. Known as 'Geordie'. A tireless winger who could cross with either foot, he fell foul of Alf Ramsey's 'wingless wonder' system, failing to be capped for his country. He died 1 November 2000.

Armstrong, Gerry   Born Gerard Joseph Armstrong, Belfast, 23 May 1954. Position: forward. Clubs: Bangor (NI), Tottenham Hotspur 1975-80, Watford 1980-83 (signed for £250,000), Real Mallorca 1983-86, West Bromwich Albion, Chesterfield, Brighton & Hove Albion, Millwall. International caps (for Northern Ireland): 63, 12 goals. Famous for his goal against hosts Spain in the 1982 World Cup finals which left Northern Ireland as group winners. Part of an advisory panel developing a soccer strategy for Northern Ireland, he also works as a commentator and analyst of Spanish football on UK television.

Asparuhov, Georgi   Born Bulgaria, 4 May 1943. Position: forward. Clubs: Levski Sofia 1960-61, 1964-71, Botev Plovdiv 1961-63. Honours: Bulgarian League Championship 1965, 1968, 1970 (with Levski Sofia). International caps (for Bulgaria): 50, 19 goals. Bulgarian Player of the Century. Known as 'Gundy'. He died in a car accident, 30 June 1971. Levski Sofia renamed their stadium in his honour and withdrew the no. 9 shirt on 4 May 2003 on the 60th anniversary of his birth.

Astle, Jeff   Born Eastwood, Nottinghamshire, 13 May 1942. Position: forward. Clubs: Notts County 1961-64, West Bromwich Albion 1964-74 (signed for £22,500), Dunstable. Honours: FA Cup 1968; League Cup 1966 (both with West Bromwich Albion). International caps (for England): 5. Known as 'The King'. The first player to score in every round of the FA Cup in one season (1968), Astle was also the first to score in both an FA Cup and a League Cup final. His England career is unfortunately best remembered for a famous miss v Brazil in 1970 when England lost 1-0, although this did not affect the team's qualification for the later stages. He died 19 January 2002.

Aston, John jnr   Born Manchester, 28 June 1947. Position: forward. Clubs: Manchester United 1962-72, Luton Town 1972-77 (signed for £30,000), Mansfield Town 1977-78, Blackburn Rovers 1978-80. Honours: League Championship 1967; European Cup 1968 (both with Manchester United). Played arguably his best game during the 1968 European Cup final.

Aston, John snr   Born Prestwich, Manchester, 3 September 1921. Position: defender. Clubs: Manchester United 1946-54. Honours: FA Cup 1948 (with Manchester United). International caps (for England): 17. Blossomed on being switched from inside-left to full-back by Matt Busby, Aston was forced to retire through injury in 1954 and returned to coach the Manchester United youth team after the Munich air disaster. He acted as chief scout 1970-72.

Athersmith, Charlie   Born William Charles Athersmith, Bloxwich, Staffordshire, 10 May 1872. Position: forward. Clubs: Aston Villa 1891-01, Birmingham City 1901-10. Honours: English League Championship 1894, 1896, 1897, 1899 and 1900. FA Cup 1895, 1897. International caps (for England): 12, 3 goals. He is reported to have played one game against Sheffield United while with Aston Villa, carrying an umbrella as protection from the freezing rain. Known as the fastest man in football, he struck up a formidable partnership with John Devey for Aston Villa. He died 18 September 1910.

Atyeo, John   Born Peter John Walter Atyeo, Dilton, Wiltshire, 7 February 1932. Position: forward. Clubs: Portsmouth 1950, Bristol City 1951-65. International caps (for England): 6, 5 goals. 'Gentleman John', Atyeo scored 315 goals in 597 League games for Bristol City. One of only a few players to be capped for England playing outside the top flight, he put his earlier studying to use when finishing football, becoming a teacher. He died 8 June 1993 in Warminster, Wiltshire.

Auld, Bertie Born Maryhill, Glasgow, 23 February 1938. Position: forward/midfield. Clubs (player): Celtic 1955-61, 1965-71 (signed for £12,000), Dumbarton 1956-57 (loan), Birmingham City 1961-65 (signed for £15,000), Hibernian 1971-73. Honours: Scottish League Championship 1966, 1967, 1968, 1969, 1970, 1971; Scottish Cup 1965, 1967, 1969, 1971; European Cup 1967 (all with Celtic). Clubs (manager): Hibernian 1980-82, Partick Thistle, Hamilton Academical, Dumbarton. International caps (for Scotland): 3.

Baggio, Roberto Born Caldagno, nr Vicenza in Italy. 18 February 1967. Position: forward. Clubs: Vicenza 1982-85, Fiorentina 1985-90, Juventus 1990-95, AC Milan 1995-97, Bologna 1997-2000, Brescia 2000-03. Honours: Italian League Championship 1995; Italian Cup 1995; UEFA Cup 1993 (all with Juventus). International caps (for Italy): 55, 27 goals. European Player of the Year 1993. World Player of the Year 1993. Nicknamed 'The Divine Pony Tail', Baggio needed to use all his skills as a practising Buddhist to overcome the disappointment of missing the decisive penalty against Brazil in the shoot-out for the 1994 World Cup.

Baker, Howard Born Benjamin Howard Baker, Aigburt, Liverpool, 13 February 1892. Position: goalkeeper. Clubs: Northern Nomads, Liverpool, Everton, Chelsea, Marlborough Old Boys, Corinthians, Blackburn Rovers, Preston North End and Oldham Athletic. International caps (for England): 2. Also an accomplished athlete, he held the British high-jump record and was AAA champion. He represented Great Britain at the 1912 and 1920 Olympic Games as a high jumper. He set a British record of 6ft 5ins (1.96m).

Ball, Alan Born Alan James Ball, Farnworth, Lancashire, 12 May 1945. Position: midfield. Clubs (player): Blackpool 1962-66, 1980-81, Everton 1966-71 (signed for £110,000), Arsenal 1971-76 (signed for £220,000), Southampton 1976-79, 1981-82, Bristol Rovers 1982. Honours: League Championship 1970 (with Everton). Clubs (manager): Blackpool 1980-81, Portsmouth 1984-89, 1998-99, Stoke City 1989-91, Exeter City 1991-94, Southampton 1994-95, Manchester City 1995-96. International caps (for England): 72 (6 as captain), 8 goals. International honours: World Cup 1966. Ball will always be remembered for his energy and running in extra time of the 1966 World Cup final, when he created the controversial third goal for England. He had some success as a manager with Portsmouth, but several relegations mar his managerial record. He was the first player to make over 100 First Division appearances for four different teams.

Ballack, Michael Born Chemnitz, West Germany, 26 September 1976. Position: midfield. Clubs: Chemnitzer 1995-97, Kaiserslautern 1997-99, Bayer Leverkusen 1999-2002, Bayern Munich 2002-present. Honours: German League Championship 1998 (with Kaiserslautern), 2003 (with Bayern Munich); German Cup 2003 (with Bayern Munich). International caps (for Germany): 33, 12 goals.

Bambrick, Joe Born Belfast, 3 November 1905. Position: forward. Clubs: Linfield, Chelsea 1934-39, Walsall 1939. International caps (for Northern Ireland): 11, 12 goals. Scored six goals against Wales in 1930 (a Home International record). He died in 1983.

Bambridge, Charles Born Edward Charles Bambridge, Windsor, Berkshire, 30 July 1858. Position: forward. Clubs: Upton Park, Clapham Rovers, Swifts, Corinthians. International caps (for England): 18 (2 as captain), 12 goals. One of five brothers, three of whom (Arthur, Edward and Ernest) were capped for England. He died 8 November 1935 in Wimbledon, London.

Banks, Gordon Born Sheffield, 30 December 1937. Position: goalkeeper. Clubs (player): Rawmarsh, Chesterfield 1955-59, Leicester City 1959-67 (signed for £7,000), Stoke City 1967-72 (signed for £50,000), Fort Lauderdale Strikers. Honours: League Cup 1964 (with Leicester City), 1972 (with Stoke City). Clubs (manager): Telford United. International caps (for England): 73, 57 goals conceded, kept 34 clean sheets. International honours: World Cup 1966. Football Writers' Player of the Year 1972. His early amateur career was disastrous (he was sacked for letting in 15 goals in two games) but by the mid-1960s he was recognised as the best goalkeeper in the world. His most memorable save was against Pelé in the 1970 World Cup but he missed England's defeat by West Germany in León because of illness. England lost only nine of his 73 internationals though within a year of England's 1966 World Cup win Leicester replaced him with Peter Shilton. An eye injury suffered in a car accident in 1972 virtually ended his playing career. Banks later worked as goalkeeping coach at Stoke City. Awarded the OBE in 1970.

Baresi, Franco Born Travagliato, nr Brescia, Italy, 8 May 1960. Position: defender. Clubs: AC Milan 1978-97. Honours: Italian League Championship 1979, 1988, 1992, 1993, 1994, 1996; European Cup/UEFA Champions League 1989, 1990, 1994; European Super Cup 1989, 1990, 1994; World Club Championship 1989, 1990. International caps (for Italy): 81, 1 goal. Baresi made a record 522 appearances for AC Milan. Known as 'Il Capitano', he is considered by many the finest defender ever produced by Italy. He racked up the honours for the *Nerorossi*, despite two seasons spent in Serie B in the early 1980s after relegation for financial irregularities. AC Milan have retired his no. 6 shirt. He appeared in the World Cup final for Italy in 1994, but missed a penalty in the shoot-out. Baresi spent six months at Fulham in 2002 as a technical director, but resigned over difficulties defining the role.

Barkas, Samuel Born Tyne Docks, South Shields, 29 December 1909. Position: defender. Clubs (player): Middle Dock, Bradford City 1927-34, Manchester City 1934-47 (signed for £5000). Honours: League Championship 1937 (with Manchester City). Clubs (manager): Workington Town, Wigan Athletic 1957. International caps (for England): 5 (3 as captain). One of four brothers (Ned, Harry, Jimmy and Sam) who all played League football, he captained Manchester City to the Second Division championship in 1947, later working as a scout for Manchester City and Leeds United.

Barker, Jack Born John William Barker, Mexborough, Yorkshire, 27 February 1907. Position: defender. Club (player): Derby County 1928-39. Clubs (manager): Bradford City 1946-47, Derby County 1953-55. International caps (for England): 11 (1 as captain).

Barmby, Nick Born Nicholas Jonathan Barmby, Hull, 11 February 1974. Position: midfield. Clubs:

Tottenham Hotspur 1991-95, Middlesbrough 1995-96 (signed for £5.25m), Everton 1996-2000 (signed for £5.75m), Liverpool 2000-02 (signed for £6m), Leeds United 2002-present (signed for £2.75m). Honours: English League Cup 2001; Charity Shield 2001; UEFA Cup 2001 (all with Liverpool). International caps (for England): 23, 4 goals.

Barnes, John Born John Charles Bryan Barnes, Kingston, Jamaica, 7 November 1963. Position: midfield. Clubs (player): Sudbury Court 1980-81, Watford 1981-87, Liverpool 1987-97 (signed for £900,000), Newcastle United 1997-99, Charlton Athletic 1999. Honours: League Championship 1988, 1990; FA Cup 1989; English League Cup 1995; Charity Shield 1988, 1989, 1990 (all with Liverpool). Clubs (manager): Celtic 1999-2000. International caps (for England): 79, 11 goals. Football Writers' Player of the Year 1988, 1990. PFA Player of the Year 1988. Awarded the MBE in 1998. Barnes is remembered for a stunning individual goal in the Maracana Stadium when England beat Brazil 2-0. Sacked as manager of Celtic after they lost in the Scottish Cup to Inverness Caledonian Thistle, he returned to punditry for ITV Sport.

Barnes, Peter Born Peter Simon Barnes, Manchester, 10 June 1957. Position: forward. Clubs: Manchester City 1972-79, 1987-88 (signed for £15,000), West Bromwich Albion 1979-81 (signed for £750,000), Leeds United 1981-84 (signed for £930,000), Real Betis 1982 (loan), Melbourne JUST 1984 (loan), Manchester United 1984 (loan), 1985-87, Coventry City 1984-85, Bolton Wanderers 1987 (loan), 1988, Port Vale 1987 (loan), Hull City 1988, Drogheda United 1988, Sporting Farense 1988, Sunderland 1989, Tampa Bay Rowdies 1990, Northwich Victoria 1990, Wrexham 1991, Radcliffe Borough 1991, Mossley 1991, Cliftonville 1992. Honours: League Cup 1976 (with Manchester City). International caps (for England): 22, 4 goals. PFA Young Player of the Year 1976. Son of Ken Barnes, who also played for Manchester City.

Barnes, Walley Born Brecon, Wales, 16 January 1920. Position: defender. Clubs (player): Portsmouth, Southampton, Arsenal 1946-55. Honours: League Championship 1948; FA Cup 1950 (both with Arsenal). Club (manager): Highland Park (South Africa). International caps (for Wales): 22. Became a BBC commentator. He died 4 September 1975 in Hammersmith, London.

Barthez, Fabien Born Fabien Alain Barthez, Lavelanet, France, 28 June 1971. Position: goalkeeper. Clubs: Toulouse 1990-92, Olympique Marseille 1992-95, 2003-present (loan), Monaco 1995-2000, Manchester United 2000-present (signed for £7.8m). Honours: French League Championship 1997 (with Monaco); FA Premiership 2001, 2003 (with Manchester United). International caps (for France): 58. International honours: World Cup 1998; European Championship 2000.

Bartram, Sam Born Simonside, County Durham, 22 January 1914. Position: goalkeeper. Clubs (player): Boldon Villa Colliery, Charlton Athletic 1934-56. Clubs (manager): York City 1956-60, Luton Town 1960-62. Probably the greatest English goalkeeper never to have been capped for his country. A famous story tells of him being found by a policeman still in his goal for Charlton although his team's match with Chelsea had been abandoned because of fog 15 minutes earlier – he thought his team were keeping the opposition pinned in their own half. Bartram made 623 appearances for Charlton Athletic and played in four successive FA Cup finals at Wembley 1944-47 (1944 and 1945 were 'War time finals' and in 1945 he played for Millwall). He died 17 July 1981 in Harpenden.

Bassett, Billy Born William Isaiah Bassett, West Bromwich, 27 January 1869. Position: forward. Club: West Bromwich Albion 1888-1900. Honours: FA Cup 1888, 1892. International caps (for England): 16, 7 goals. Later a director and chairman of West Bromwich Albion. He died 8 April 1937 in West Bromwich.

Bastin, Cliff Born Clifford Sydney Bastin, Exeter, Devon, 14 March 1912. Position: forward. Clubs: Exeter City 1927-29, Arsenal 1929-48. Honours: League Championship 1931, 1933, 1934, 1935, 1938; FA Cup 1930, 1936 (all with Arsenal). International caps (for England): 21, 12 goals. In 1934 he became the youngest FA Cup finalist to date and was nicknamed 'Boy'. He scored 178 goals for Arsenal, a record only broken by Ian Wright in 1998. Bastin became a publican on retirement. He died 3 December 1991 in Exeter.

Batistuta, Gabriel Born Gabriel Omar Batistuta, Avallaneda, Argentina, 1 February 1969. Position: forward. Clubs: Newell's Old Boys 1988-89, River Plate 1989-90, Boca Juniors 1990-91, Fiorentina 1991-2000, Roma 2000-03, Inter Milan 2002-03 (loan). Honours: Italian League Championship 2001 (with Roma). International caps (for Argentina): 78, 56 goals. Sixth in the all-time goalscorers list at World Cup finals with ten. Nicknamed 'Batigol'. A top striker for Fiorentina throughout the 1990s, he eventually won the Scudetto on leaving for Roma.

Batty, David Born Leeds, 2 December 1968. Position: defender. Clubs: Leeds United 1987-93, 1998-present (signed for £4.4m), Blackburn Rovers 1993-96 (signed for £2.75m), Newcastle United 1996-98 (signed for £3.75m). Honours: League Championship 1992; Charity Shield 1992 (both with Leeds United). International caps (for England): 42.

Baxter, Jim Born James Curran Baxter, Hill O' Beath, Fife, Scotland, 29 September 1939. Position: midfield. Clubs: Raith Rovers 1957-59, Rangers 1959-64 (signed for £17,500), Sunderland 1965-67 (signed for £85,000), Nottingham Forest 1967-69, Rangers 1969. Honours: Scottish League Championship 1961, 1963, 1964; Scottish Cup 1962, 1963, 1964; Scottish League Cup 1960, 1961, 1963, 1964 (all with Glasgow Rangers). International caps (for Scotland): 34, 3 goals. Known as 'Slim Jim'. A broken leg in 1964 diminished his skills but he is perhaps best remembered north of the border for performances that bamboozled the Auld Enemy at Wembley in 1963 and 1967. A true 'wayward genius', his heavy drinking led to two liver transplants in 1994. He died 14 April 2001 in Glasgow from cancer.

Beardsley, Peter Born Peter Andrew Beardsley, Longbenton, Newcastle-upon-Tyne, 18 January 1961. Position: forward. Clubs: Carlisle United 1979-81, Vancouver Whitecaps 1981, Manchester United 1982-83, Newcastle United 1983-87, 1993-97 (signed for £1.1m), Liverpool 1987-91 (signed for £1.9m), Everton 1991-93, Bolton Wanderers 1997-98, Manchester City 1998 (loan), Fulham 1998 (loan), Hartlepool United 1998-99, Doncaster Rovers 1999. Honours: League Championship 1988, 1990; FA Cup 1989 (all with Liverpool). International caps: 59 (1 as captain), 9 goals. Remembered for his partnership with Gary Lineker, which enabled England to reach the World Cup semi-final in 1990. Awarded the MBE in 1995. Currently works as youth team coach at Newcastle.

Beattie, James Born James Scott Beattie, Lancaster, 27 February 1978. Position: forward. Clubs: Blackburn Rovers 1995-98, Southampton 1998-present (signed for £1m). International caps (for England): 4.

Beto Born Jose Roberto Gama de Oliveira, Salvador, Brazil, 16 February 1964. Position: forward. Clubs: Vitoria, Flamengo 1983-88, 1996, Vasco da Gama 1988-92, 2002, Deportivo La Coruña 1992-96, Seville 1996, Vitoria 1996-97, 2000-01, Cruzeiro 1997-98, Botafogo 1998-99, Neza Bulls (Mexico) 1999, Kashima Antlers (Japan) 2000, Al-Ittihad (Saudi Arabia) 2002-03. Honours: Brazilian League Championship 1983 (with Flamengo), 1989 (with Vasco da Gama); Spanish Cup 1995 (with Deportivo La Coruña). International caps (for Brazil): 73, 39 goals. International honours: World Cup 1994; Copa America 1989. His partnership with Romario, with whom there were clashes off-field, was a decisive factor in the 1994 World Cup victory. He has spent recent years globe-trotting with short spells at several clubs.

Beckenbauer, Franz Born Munich, West Germany, 11 September 1945. Position: midfield. Clubs (player): Bayern Munich 1962-77, New York Cosmos 1977-80, 1983, SV Hamburg 1980-82. Honours: West German League Championship 1969, 1972, 1973, 1974; West German Cup 1966, 1967, 1969, 1971; European Cup 1974, 1975, 1976 (all with Bayern Munich). International caps (for West Germany): 103, 14 goals. International honours: European Championship 1972; World Cup 1974. International Manager (Germany): 1984-90. International honours: World Cup 1990. First man to captain and coach a World Cup-winning team. Known as 'Der Kaiser'. European Player of the Year 1972, 1976. One of the most influential figures of the 1970s and 80s, he invented the role of attacking sweeper or libero, which brought so much success to the German national team through this period. When taking over the job of national coach on retiring from playing he had no previous coaching experience. He has been a director of Bayern Munich since leaving the national team.

Beckham, David Born David Robert Joseph Beckham, Leytonstone, London, 2 May 1975. Position: midfield. Clubs: Manchester United 1992-2003, Preston North End 1995 (loan), Real Madrid 2003-present (signed for £25m). Honours: FA Premiership 1996, 1997, 1999, 2000, 2001, 2003; FA Cup 1996, 1999; Charity Shield 1996, 1997; UEFA Champions League 1999 (all with Manchester United). International caps (for England): 63 (26 as captain), 13 goals. Beckham scored from 57 yards against Wimbledon on the first day of the 1996/97 season, the longest successful strike in the Premiership. Married to 'Posh Spice', Victoria Adams, and has sons Brooklyn and Romeo. His autobiography *My Side* was published in 2003. Awarded the OBE in 2003. The first British footballer to achieve global superstardom, he has acquired the nickname 'Goldenballs'.

Belanov, Igor Born Odessa, USSR, 25 September 1960. Position: forward. Clubs (player): SKA Odessa 1979-80, Chernomorets Odessa 1981-84, 1995-96, Dynamo Kiev 1985-89, Borussia Mönchengladbach 1989-91, Eintracht Braunschweig 1991-95, Azovetz Mariupol (Ukraine) 1996-97. Honours: USSR Championship 1985, 1986; USSR Cup 1985, 1987; European Cup Winners' Cup 1986 (all with Dynamo Kiev). Club (coach): Azovetz Mariupol 1996-97.

International caps (for USSR): 33, 8 goals. European Player of the Year 1986. Runs a sport dietary business.

Bell, Colin Born Heselden, Co. Durham, 26 February 1946. Position: midfield. Clubs: Bury 1963-66, Manchester City 1966-79 (signed for £45,000). Honours: League Championship 1968; FA Cup 1969; English League Cup 1970; European Cup Winners' Cup 1970 (all with Manchester City). International caps (for England): 48 (1 as captain), 9 goals. The forerunner of contemporary midfield players, where the ability to run the length of the pitch continuously is a prized asset, he was nicknamed 'Nijinsky' (after the horse rather than the ballet dancer) because of his stamina. His career was reduced in impact by an injury sustained in a Manchester derby. On leaving the playing side he worked in the back room at Maine Road until 1998. Bell was voted Manchester City's greatest player in a 2001 poll and has the main stand at the City of Manchester stadium named after him.

Bentley, Roy Born Roy Thomas Frank Bentley, Bristol, 17 May 1924. Position: forward/defender. Clubs: Bristol City, Newcastle United 1946-48 (signed for £8,000), Chelsea 1948-56 (signed for £11,000), Fulham 1956-61, Queens Park Rangers 1961-62. Honours: League Championship 1955 (with Chelsea). International caps (for England): 12, 9 goals. A roving centre-forward, Bentley captained Chelsea to their only League Championship before becoming a centre-half at the end of his career.

Bergkamp, Dennis Born Amsterdam, Holland, 18 May 1969. Position: midfield. Clubs: Ajax 1981-93, Inter Milan 1993-95 (signed for £12m), Arsenal 1995-present (signed for £7.5m). Honours: Dutch League Championship 1990 (with Ajax); FA Premiership 1998, 2002, 2004; FA Cup 2002, 2003; Charity Shield 1998, 2004 (all with Arsenal); UEFA Cup 1992 (with Ajax Amsterdam). International caps (for Holland): 79, 37 goals. Football Writers' Player of the Year 1998. Named after Denis [sic] Law.

Bergomi, Giuseppe Born Milan, Italy, 22 December 1963. Position: defender. Club: Inter Milan 1980-99. Honours: Italian League Championship 1989; Italian Cup 1982; UEFA Cup 1991, 1994, 1998. International caps (for Italy): 89. International honours: World Cup 1982. A one-club servant who was only 18 when part of the victorious Italian side of 1982, he is holder, with 519, of the most League appearances for Internazionale. Until recently also held record for most appearances in European matches, standing at 117.

Best, George Born Belfast, 22 May 1946. Position: midfield. Clubs: Manchester United 1963-74, Dunstable Town 1974, Stockport County 1975, Cork Celtic 1976, Los Angeles Aztecs 1976, 1977, Fulham 1976, Fort Lauderdale Strikers 1978, 1979, Hibernian 1979, San Jose Earthquakes 1980, 1981, AFC Bournemouth 1983, Brisbane Lions 1983. Honours: League Championship 1965, 1967; European Cup 1968 (all with Manchester United). International caps (for Northern Ireland): 37, 9 goals. Nicknamed 'El Beatle' by Portuguese fans. Northern Ireland Player of the Year, Football Writers' Player of the Year and European Player of the Year (the youngest ever) in 1968. He scored six goals in an 8-2 FA Cup win against Northampton Town in 1970. The first superstar of the pop and TV age, Best moved the game away from its flat-cap image of the 1950s and early 60s. That this was achieved at great personal cost is shown by a recent liver transplant in 2002. Currently works in the media.

FOOTBALL

Bettega, Roberto   Born Turin, Italy, 27 December 1950. Position: forward. Clubs: Juventus 1966-83, Varese 1969-70 (loan), Toronto Blizzard 1983-84. Honours: Italian League Championship 1972, 1973, 1975, 1977, 1978, 1981, 1982; Italian Cup 1979, 1983; UEFA Cup 1977 (all with Juventus). International caps (for Italy): 42, 19 goals. After retiring he became a member of the backroom staff at Juventus.

Bierhoff, Oliver   Born Karlsruhe, Germany, 1 May 1968. Position: Centre forward. Clubs: Bayer Uerdingen 1986-88, SV Hamburg 1988-89, Borussia Mönchengladbach 1988-89, SV Saltzburg 1990-93, Ascoli 1993-95, Udinese 1995-98, AC Milan 1998-2001, Monaco 2001-02, Chievo Verona 2002-03. Honours: Italian League Championship 1999 (with AC Milan). International caps (for Germany): 70, 37 goals. International honours: European Championship 1996. Scored the winning Golden Goal for Germany in Euro 96 at Wembley. Bierhoff spent much of his early career at a low level of the game, but eventually won the Scudetto with AC Milan. He called time on his Serie A career by scoring a hat-trick for the 'Flying Donkeys' of Chievo against champions Juventus on the last day of the 2002/03 season.

Binder, Franz   Born St Pölten, Austria, 1 December 1911. Position: forward. Clubs (player): Sturm 19 St Pölten 1921-30, Rapid Vienna 1930-49. Honours: Austrian League Championship 1935, 1938, 1940, 1941, 1946, 1948; Austrian Cup 1946; German League Championship 1941; German Cup 1938 (all with Rapid Vienna). Clubs (manager): Rapid Vienna 1945-51, 1962-66, Nuremburg, Jahn Regensburg, PSV Eindhoven 1960-62, 1860 Munich 1969-70, SC Austria, Vienna 1975-76. Honours: Austrian League Championship 1946, 1948, 1951, 1964 (with Rapid Vienna); Austrian Cup 1946, 1976 (with Rapid Vienna). International caps (for Austria): 19, 16 goals. International caps (for Germany, during Anschluss): 9, 10 goals. Top scorer in Austria six times (1933, 1937, 1938, 1939, 1940, 1941) scored 1151 goals to rank behind Friedenreich and Pelé in the all-time scorers chart. He died 24 April 1989 in Vienna.

Bingham, Billy   Born William Laurie Bingham, Belfast, 5 August 1931. Position: forward. Clubs (player): Glentoran, Sunderland 1950-57, Luton 1958-60 (signed for £15,000), Everton 1960-62 (signed for £20,000), Port Vale 1963-64. Honours: League Championship 1963 (with Everton). Clubs (manager): Southport, Plymouth Argyle 1968-70, Linfield, Everton 1973-77, PAOK Salonika, Mansfield Town 1978-79, Al Nasir. International caps (for Northern Ireland): 56, 10 goals. International manager (Greece): 1971-73; (Northern Ireland): 1968-70, 1980-93. A tricky winger much favoured in the 1950s, as manager he qualified for the World Cup finals of 1982 and 1986. He achieved one of the all-time World Cup upsets when Northern Ireland defeated Spain, the hosts, to progress to the quarter-final group stage in 1982. Awarded the MBE in 1981.

Birtles, Garry   Born Nottingham, 27 July 1956. Position: forward. Clubs (player): Long Eaton, Nottingham Forest 1976-80, 1982-87 (signed for £250,000), Manchester United 1980-82 (signed for £1.25m), Notts County 1987-89, Grimsby Town 1989-92. Honours: League Cup 1979; European Cup 1979, 1980 (all with Nottingham Forest). Club (manager): Gresley Rovers 1995-present (1995-97 assistant). International caps (for England): 3. A prolific scorer for Nottingham Forest, he was unable

to reproduce that form anywhere else. He converted to centre-half in the latter part of his career.

Blanchflower, Danny   Born Robert Dennis Blanchflower, Belfast,10 February 1926. Position: defender. Clubs (player): Glentoran 1945-49, Barnsley 1949-51, Aston Villa 1951-54 (signed for £15,000), Tottenham Hotspur 1954-64. Honours: League Championship 1961; FA Cup 1961, 1962; European Cup Winners' Cup 1963 (all with Tottenham Hotspur). Club (manager): Chelsea 1978-79. International caps (for Northern Ireland): 56, 2 goals. International manager (Northern Ireland): 1976-79. Captain of the Northern Ireland 1958 World Cup squad, which reached the quarter-finals. Football Writers' Player of the Year 1958, 1961. Captain of the first double-winning team of the 20th century. He became a successful journalist with the *Observer* and *Sunday Express* on leaving football and famously refused to appear on 'This is Your Life' He died 9 December 1993 in London.

Blenkinsop, Ernie   Born Ernest Blenkinsop, Cudworth, South Yorkshire, 20 April 1902. Position: defender. Clubs: Cudworth United Methodists, Hull City (signed for £100 plus 80 pints of beer), Sheffield Wednesday 1923-34, Liverpool 1934-37, Cardiff City 1937-38. Honours: League Championship 1929, 1930 (with Sheffield Wednesday). International caps (for England): 26 (4 as captain). He died 24 April 1969 in Sheffield.

Blissett, Luther   Born Luther Loide Blissett, Falmouth, Jamaica, 1 February 1958. Position: forward. Clubs: Watford 1975-83, 1984-89 (signed for £550,000), 1991-93, AC Milan 1983-84, AFC Bournemouth 1988-91 (signed for £60,000), West Bromwich Albion 1992-93 (loan), Bury 1993 (loan), Mansfield Town 1993-94. International caps (for England): 14, 3 goals (hat-trick). His time in Italy was the subject of many odd stories; for instance it was rumoured that Milan actually wanted Watford's John Barnes but bought the wrong player. His name has since been adopted by an Italian anarchist society.

Blokhin, Oleg   Born Kiev, USSR, 5 November 1952. Position: forward. Clubs (player): Dynamo Kiev 1974-86, Vorwarts Styen (Austria) 1988-89, Aris Limassol 1989-90. Honours: USSR League Championship 1974, 1975, 1977, 1980, 1981, 1985, 1986; USSR Cup 1974, 1978, 1982, 1985, 1987; European Cup Winners' Cup 1975, 1986 (all with Dynamo Kiev). Clubs (manager): Olympiakos 1990-93, PAOK Salonika 1993-94, Ionikos 1994-97. Honours: Greek Cup 1992 (with Olympiakos). International caps (for USSR): 101, 35 goals. First Soviet player to play over 100 games for his country. Russian Player of the Year 1973, 1974, 1975. European Player of the Year 1975.

Bloomer, Steve   Born Cradley, Staffordshire, 20 January 1874. Position: forward. Clubs (player): Derby Swift, Derby County 1892-06, 1910-14, Middlesbrough 1906-10. Clubs (manager): Berlin Britannia 1914, Derby County (assistant) 1918-23, Real Irun (Spain) 1923-25, Derby County (junior coach) 1925-38. International caps (for England): 23 (1 as captain), 28 goals. Known as 'The Destroying Angel' and 'The Hammer of the Scots', Bloomer scored five goals against Wales in 1896 and four in 1901. He travelled to Berlin in July 1914 to coach and was interned at the outbreak of World War I, captaining his prison camp team to the 'championship'. 'Steve Bloomer's Watching' is the song to which Derby County run out at all their home matches. Bloomer was an accomplished cricketer who also led the Derby baseball side to the English

Baseball Cup three times in the 1890s. The first superstar of English football, he endorsed many products including 'Bloomer's Lucky Strikers' football boots. Nicknamed 'Paleface' because of his complexion. He died April 1938, Derby.

Boban, Zvonimir Born Imotski, Croatia, 8 October 1968. Position: midfield. Clubs: Dynamo Zagreb 1985-91, AC Milan 1991-2001, Bari 1991-92 (loan), Celta Vigo 2001-02. Honours: Italian League Championship 1993, 1994, 1996, 1999; UEFA Champions League 1994 (all with AC Milan). International caps (for Yugoslavia): 7. International caps (for Croatia): 51, 12 goals. Known as 'Zorro'. During riots after a match against Red Star Belgrade, Boban fought with a Serbian policeman and was dropped from the Yugoslavia national team. He resumed his international career with Croatia when it gained independence.

Bobrov, Vsevolod Born Mershansk, Tambov Oblast, USSR, 1 December 1922. Position: forward. Clubs: Dynamo Leningrad, Moscow Dynamo, Red Army, Spartak Moscow. Probably better known as an ice hockey player, at which sport he won an Olympic gold medal in 1956, together with European Championships in 1954, 1955, 1956 and World Championships in 1954, 1956. He died 1 July 1979 in Moscow.

Bonds, Billy Born William Arthur Bonds, Woolwich, London, 17 September 1946. Position: defender. Clubs (player): Charlton Athletic 1964-67, West Ham United 1967-88 (signed for £50,000). Honours: FA Cup 1975, 1980 (with West Ham United). Clubs (manager): West Ham United 1990-94, Millwall 1997-98. An inspiration to all the teams he captained, Bonds was awarded the MBE in 1988.

Bonetti, Peter Born Putney, London, 27 September 1941. Position: Goalkeeper. Club: Chelsea 1959-78. Honours: FA Cup 1970; European Cup Winners' Cup 1971. International caps (for England): 7, 4 goals conceded. The son of a Swiss restaurateur who settled in London, Bonetti played 600 League games for Chelsea. Nicknamed 'The Cat', he is remembered as the understudy to Gordon Banks who was called into action for the quarter-final of the 1970 World Cup. His handling error allowed West Germany back into the game when trailing 2-0, contributing to England's exit. He later moved with his family to Isle of Mull.

Boniek, Zbigniew Born Zbigniew Kazimezh Boniek, Bydgoszcz, Poland, 3 March 1956. Position: midfield. Clubs: Zawisza Bydgoszcz 1970-75, Widzew Lodz 1975-82, Juventus 1982-85 (signed for £1.1m), Roma 1985-88. Honours: Polish League Championship 1981, 1982 (with Widzew Lodz); Italian League Championship 1984 (with Juventus); Italian Cup 1983 (with Juventus), 1986 (with Roma); European Cup Winners' Cup 1984 (with Juventus); European Cup 1985 (with Juventus). International caps (for Poland): 80, 24 goals. Appeared in three World Cups (1978, 1982 and 1986). Voted Polish Player of the 20th Century. European Player of the Year 1982. Known as 'Zibi' and 'Night Beauty' as he seemed to play better under floodlights. The first star player to appear out of Soviet-controlled Poland, Boniek carried the mantle of the successful World Cup teams of the 1970s, which featured Deyna, Gadocha and Lato.

Boniperti, Giampiero Born Barengo, Novara, Italy, 4 July 1928. Position: forward. Clubs: Momo, Juventus 1947-61. Honours: Italian League Championship 1950, 1952, 1958, 1960, 1961; Italian Cup 1959, 1960 (all with Juventus). International caps (for Italy): 38. Captained Italy in the 1954 World Cup. Boniperti later became president of Juventus.

Bonner, Packie Born Patrick Joseph Bonner, Cloughglass, Burtonport, Co. Donegal, Ireland, 24 May 1960. Position: goalkeeper. Clubs: Keadue Rovers, Celtic 1978-95. Honours: Scottish League Championship 1981, 1982, 1986, 1988; Scottish Cup 1980, 1985, 1988, 1989, 1995; Scottish League Cup 1983 (all with Celtic). International caps (for Republic of Ireland): 80. Jock Stein's last signing for Celtic, he went on to play 642 games for the club, his last being the 1995 Scottish Cup final. His penalty save against Romania in the 1990 World Cup finals helped the Republic of Ireland reach the quarter-finals. He is currently a goalkeeping coach with the Irish national squad and technical director at the FAI.

Book, Tony Born Anthony Keith Book, Bath, 4 September 1935. Position: defender. Clubs (player): Bath City, Plymouth Argyle 1964-66, Manchester City 1966-73 (signed for £17,000). Honours: League Championship 1968; FA Cup 1969; League Cup 1970; European Cup Winners' Cup 1970 (all with Manchester City). Club (manager): Manchester City 1974-79, 1993. Honours: English League Cup 1976. Jointly voted Football Writers' Player of the Year 1969. He began his successful professional career at the age of 29 and worked in the back room at Manchester City until 1996, including a short spell as caretaker manager. He now works as a scout for Sunderland.

Bosman, Jean-Marc Born Belgium, 30 October 1964. Position: midfield. Clubs: RFC Liège. Not noted for his career but rather for his effect on the modern game in Europe; in 1990 Bosman began a dispute with his then club, FC Liège. After a transfer to Dunkerque fell through, Liège refused to let him go but didn't select him. Because he was out of contract he therefore had no club to play for. He sued the club and the Belgian FA for restraint of trade and, after a number of court hearings and appeals, it was ruled that all EU players had the right to a free transfer at the end of their contracts, with the proviso that they were transferring from one EU federation to another. Bosman was supported by both UEFA and FIFA and gained £312,000 compensation for loss of earnings, as his career was over by the time the case was completed. The so-called Bosman Ruling now dominates dealings in the transfer market and has given more power to players in this regard.

Bosman, Johnny Born Bovenquerq, Holland, 1 February 1965. Position: forward. Clubs: Roda '23, RKAVIC, Ajax 1983-88, KV Mechelen 1988-90, PSV Eindhoven 1990-91, Anderlecht 1991-96, Twente Enschede 1996-99, AZ Alkmaar 1999-2002. Honours: Dutch League Championship 1985 (with Ajax), 1991 (with PSV Eindhoven); Belgian League Championship 1989 (with Mechelen), 1993, 1994, 1995 (with Anderlecht); Dutch Cup 1986, 1987 (with Ajax); Belgian Cup 1994 (with Anderlecht); European Cup Winners' Cup 1987 (with Ajax). International caps (for Holland): 30,17 goals. International honours: European Championship 1988. Nicknamed 'The Stork' because of his long neck. In the top ten scorers list for the Dutch national team. Retired from playing in 2002.

Bowles, Stan Born Manchester, 24 December 1948. Position: midfield. Clubs: Manchester City 1967-70, Bury 1970, Crewe Alexandra 1970-71, Carlisle United 1971-72, Queens Park Rangers 1972-79, Nottingham Forest 1979, Leyton Orient 1980-81, Brentford 1981-83. International caps (for England):

5, 1 goal. Known as 'Stan the Man'. Voted Queens Park Rangers' greatest player. Sadly, due to a penchant for betting, Bowles was often cast in the mould of the classic under-achiever.

Bozsik, Jozsef   Born Budapest, Hungary, 28 November 1925. Position: defender. Club (player): Kispest/Honvéd. Honours: Hungarian League Championship 1950, 1952, 1954, 1955. Club (manager): Honvéd. International caps (for Hungary): 101, 11 goals. International honours: Olympic gold medal 1952. Having lived next door to Ferenc Puskas as a teenager, Bozsik captained the 'Magical Magyars' who defeated England at Wembley in 1953. Elected to the Hungarian National Assembly, he chose to stay in Hungary after the 1956 uprising. He had a spell in charge of Honvéd and coached the Hungarian national team for a single match, a 1-0 defeat in Austria in 1974, before retiring because of illness. His son Peter is coach of Zalaegerszegi TE, 2002 Hungarian champions. He died 31 May 1978 in Budapest.

Bradford, Joseph   Born Peggs Green, Leicestershire, 22 January 1901. Position: forward. Clubs: Coleorton, Peggs Green Victoria, Birmingham City 1920-35 (signed for £125), Bristol City 1935-36. International caps (for England): 12, 7 goals. Bradford scored 267 goals in 445 appearances for Birmingham City and played three internationals alongside his cousin Hughie Adcock. He became a publican on retirement. He died 6 September 1980.

Brady, Liam   Born William Brady, Dublin, 13 February 1956. Position: midfield. Clubs (player): Arsenal 1973-80, Juventus 1980-82 (signed for £514,000), Sampdoria 1982-84, Inter Milan 1984-86, Ascoli 1986-87, West Ham United 1987-89. Honours: Italian League Championship 1981, 1982 (with Juventus); FA Cup 1979 (with Arsenal). Clubs (manager): Celtic 1981-83, Brighton & Hove Albion 1993-95. International caps (for Republic of Ireland): 72, 9 goals. Known as 'Chippy'. PFA Player of the Year 1979. His elder brothers Ray and Pat played for Millwall and Queens Park Rangers. Brady is now head of youth development at Arsenal.

Brehme, Andreas   Born Hamburg, West Germany, 9 November 1960. Position: defender. Clubs: Barmbeck-Uhlenhorst, Saarbrucken 1980, Kaiserslautern 1981-86, Bayern Munich 1986-88, Inter Milan 1988-92. Honours: German League Championship 1986 (with Bayern Munich); Italian League Championship 1989 (with Inter Milan); Italian Cup 1989 (with Inter Milan); UEFA Cup 1991 (with Inter Milan). International caps (for West Germany/Germany): 86, 8 goals. International honours: World Cup 1990 (scored winning goal from the penalty spot).

Breitner, Paul   Born Kolbermoor, West Germany, 5 September 1951. Position: defender. Clubs: Freilassung, Bayern Munich 1970-74, 1978-83, Real Madrid 1974-77, Eintracht Brunswick 1977-78. Honours: German League Championship 1972, 1973, 1974, 1980, 1981 (with Bayern Munich); Spanish League Championship 1975, 1976 (with Real Madrid); Spanish Cup 1975 (with Real Madrid); German Cup 1971, 1982 (with Bayern Munich); European Cup 1974 (with Bayern Munich). International caps (for West Germany): 48, 11 goals. International honours: World Cup 1974; European Championship 1972. For a time he was known as 'Der Afro' because of his hairstyle. German Player of the Year 1981. Now a journalist and TV analyst.

Bremner, Billy   Born William John Bremner, Stirling, Scotland, 9 December 1942. Position: midfield. Clubs

(player): Leeds United 1959-76, Hull City 1976-78 (signed for £35,000), Doncaster Rovers 1978-82. Honours: League Championship 1969, 1974 (with Leeds United); FA Cup 1972; Inter-cities Fairs Cup 1968, 1971 (all with Leeds United). Clubs (manager): Doncaster Rovers 1978-85, 1989-92, Leeds United 1985-88. International caps (for Scotland): 54, 3 goals. Football Writers' Player of the Year 1970. Rejected by Arsenal and Chelsea as a youngster as being too small. The title of his autobiography, *You Get Nowt for Coming Second*, sums up the will to win by which he inspired his team-mates. He had a special relationship with 'The Gaffer', Don Revie, who once threatened to resign if Bremner was transferred to raise money. Revie built his team around this 'midfield dynamo'. He died 5 December 1997 in Doncaster and a statue was unveiled outside Elland Road in his honour in August 1999.

Brennan, Shay   Born Seamus Anthony Brennan, Manchester, 6 May 1937. Position: defender. Clubs (player): Manchester United 1955-70, Waterford 1970-73. Honours: League Championship 1965, 1967 (with Manchester United); Irish League Championship 1972, 1973 (with Waterford); European Cup 1968 (with Manchester United). Club (manager): Waterford 1970-73. Honours: Irish League Championship 1972, 1973. International caps (for Republic of Ireland): 19 (5 as captain). Drafted into the Manchester United team after the Munich air disaster, he scored twice in the 1958 FA Cup semi-final, but missed out on the final as more experienced players recovered from their injuries. Bobby Charlton's regular room-mate, he was the first player born outside Ireland to play for the Republic under the parentage rule. On retirement he ran a courier business in Tramore, near Waterford. He died 9 June 2000 in Waterford.

Bridge, Wayne   Born Wayne Michael Bridge, Southampton, 5 August 1980. Position: defender. Clubs: Southampton 1997-2003, Chelsea 2003-present (signed for £7m). International caps (for England): 14.

Broadis, Ivor   Born Ivan Arthur Broadis, Poplar, London, 18 December 1922. Position: forward. Clubs (player): Tottenham Hotspur, Carlisle United 1946-49, Sunderland 1949-51 (signed for £18,000), Manchester City 1951-53 (signed for £25,000), Newcastle United 1953-55 (signed for £20,000), Carlisle United 1955-58 (signed for £3500). Club (manager): Carlisle United 1946-49, 1955-59 (coach), Queen of the South 1959-62 (coach). International caps (for England): 14, 8 goals. The first manager to transfer himself to another club when in 1949, still registered as a player, he moved from Carlisle to Sunderland, raising £18,000 for Carlisle. He was the youngest player-manager at 23. He became a journalist on his retirement in 1962.

Brook, Eric   Born Eric Frederick Brook, Mexborough, South Yorkshire, 27 November 1907. Position: forward. Clubs: Barnsley 1926-28, Manchester City 1928-39. Honours: League Championship 1937; FA Cup 1934 (both with Manchester City). International caps (for England): 18, 10 goals. Scored two goals in the 'Battle of Highbury' against Italy in 1934, a match in which he suffered a broken arm. With 177 goals in all games, he is the highest scorer in Manchester City history. He died 29 March 1965 in Manchester.

Brooking, Trevor   Born Trevor David Brooking, Barking, London, 2 October 1948. Position: midfield. Club (player): West Ham United 1966-84. Honours: FA Cup 1975, 1980. Club (manager): West Ham

United 2003 (caretaker, two spells). International caps (for England): 47, 5 goals. Played 635 games for West Ham. Awarded the MBE in 1981. Chairman of Sport England 1998-2002. Brooking now works in the media as an analyst and commentator. He was knighted in 2004.

uce, Steve Born Corbridge, nr Hexham, Northumberland, 31 December 1960. Position: defender. Clubs (player): Gillingham 1977-84, Norwich City 1984-87, Manchester United 1987-96, Birmingham City 1996-98, Sheffield United 1998-99. Honours: FA Premiership 1993, 1994, 1996 (with Manchester United), FA Cup 1990, 1994, 1996 (with Manchester United), League Cup 1985 (with Norwich City), European Cup Winners' Cup 1991 (with Manchester United). Clubs (manager): Sheffield United 1998-99, Huddersfield Town 1999-2000, Wigan Athletic 2001, Crystal Palace 2001, Birmingham City 2001-present.

uchan, Charles Born Charles Murray Buchan, Plumstead, London, 22 September 1891. Position: forward. Clubs: Clapton Orient 1910, Sunderland 1911-25, Arsenal 1925-28 (signed for £2,000 plus £100 per goal in the first season – he scored 21). Honours: League Championship 1913 (with Sunderland). International caps (for England): 6 (2 as captain), 4 goals. During World War I was awarded the Military Medal while serving with the Grenadier Guards. Played his last game for Arsenal v Everton the day Dixie Dean scored a hat-trick to secure the all-time season scoring record. He became a journalist and broadcaster on his retirement in 1928, and wrote a coaching manual. A founder member of the Football Writers' Association in 1947, he suggested the Footballer of the Year award. Founded *Charles Buchan's Football Monthly* in 1951. He died 25 June 1960 while on holiday in Monte Carlo.

uchan, Martin Born Aberdeen, Scotland, 6 March 1949. Position: defender. Clubs (player): Aberdeen 1965-71, Manchester United 1971-83 (signed for £125,000), Oldham Athletic 1983-84. Honours: Scottish Cup 1970 (with Aberdeen); FA Cup 1977 (with Manchester United). Club (manager): Burnley 1985. International caps (for Scotland): 34. The first player since World War II to captain sides to win both the FA Cup and Scottish Cup.

ull, Steve Born Stephen George Bull, Tipton, Staffordshire, 28 March 1965. Position: forward. Clubs: West Bromwich Albion 1985-86, Wolverhampton Wanderers 1986-99 (signed for £35,000), Hereford United 2001. International caps (for England): 13, 4 goals. Bull scored 50 goals in successive seasons 1987/88, 1988/89 and in total scored 306 goals in 545 games for Wolverhampton Wanderers. He was the last Third Division player to get an England cap when he came on as substitute against Scotland (1988/89) and scored a goal. Awarded the MBE in 2000. He now works in PR at Molineux.

urgess, Ron Born William Arthur Ronald Burgess, Cwm, Ebbw Vale, Wales, 9 April 1917. Position: midfield. Clubs (player): Cwm Villa, Tottenham Hotspur 1937-54, Swansea City 1954-55. Honours: League Championship 1951 (with Tottenham Hotspur). Clubs (manager): Swansea Town 1955-58, Watford 1959-63, Hendon Town. International caps (for Wales): 32.

urns, Kenny Born Glasgow, 23 September 1953. Position: defender. Clubs: Birmingham City 1971-77, Nottingham Forest 1977-81 (signed for £150,000), Leeds United 1981-84 (signed for £400,000), Derby County 1983 (loan), 1984-85, Notts County 1985,

Barnsley 1985-86. Honours: League Championship 1978; European Cup 1979, 1980 (all with Nottingham Forest). International caps (for Scotland): 20, 1 goal. Football Writers' Player of the Year 1978.

Busby, Matt Born Matthew Busby, Orbiston, North Lanarkshire, Scotland, 26 May 1909. Position: midfield. Clubs (player): Deeny Hibernian, Manchester City 1928-36, Liverpool 1936-39 (signed for £8,000). Club (manager): Manchester United 1945-69. Honours: League Championship 1952, 1956, 1957, 1965, 1967; FA Cup 1948, 1963; European Cup 1968. Developed the 'Busby Babes', a richly talented group of young players most of whom were killed in the Munich air disaster of 1958, and during which Busby himself was seriously injured. Became a director and president of Manchester United. Awarded the CBE in 1958 and knighted in 1968. He died 20 January 1994.

Butcher, Terry Born Terrence Ian Butcher, Singapore, 28 December 1958. Position: defender. Clubs (player): Ipswich Town 1976-86, Rangers 1986-90. Honours: Scottish League Championship 1987, 1989, 1990 (with Rangers); Scottish Cup 1987, 1988, 1989 (with Rangers); UEFA Cup 1981 (with Ipswich Town). Clubs (manager): Coventry City 1990-92, Sunderland 1993, Motherwell 2002-present. International caps (for England): 77 (7 as captain), 3 goals. A well-known photograph shows him with his bloodied head bandaged following England's draw in Sweden to qualify for Italia 90.

Butragueno, Emilio Born Emilio Sanches Butragueno, Madrid, 22 July 1963. Position: forward. Clubs: Castilla 1975-83, Real Madrid 1983-95, Atlético Celaya 1995-98. Honours: Spanish League Championship 1986, 1987, 1988, 1989, 1990; UEFA Cup 1985, 1986 (all with Real Madrid). International caps (for Spain): 69, 26 goals. Nicknamed 'The Vulture'. Scored four goals against Denmark in the 1986 World Cup finals.

Butt, Nicky Born Manchester, 21 January 1975. Position: midfield. Clubs: Manchester United 1992-04, Newcastle United 2004-present. Honours: FA Premiership 1996, 1997, 1999, 2000, 2001, 2003; FA Cup 1996; Charity/Community Shield 1996, 1997, 2003; UEFA Champions League 1999. International caps (for England): 29.

Byrne, Johnny Born John Joseph Byrne, West Horsley, Surrey, 13 May 1939. Position: forward. Clubs: Crystal Palace 1956-62, 1967-68, West Ham United 1962-67 (signed for £58,000), Fulham 1968. Honours: FA Cup 1964 (with West Ham United). International caps (for England): 11, 8 goals. Known as 'Budgie'. Capped while playing in the Third Division for Crystal Palace, his transfer in 1962 was then the biggest between two British clubs. He died in South Africa October 1999.

Byrne, Roger Born Gorton, Manchester, 8 February 1929. Position: defender. Club: Manchester United 1951-58. Honours: League Championship 1952, 1956, 1957. International caps (for England): 33. Killed 6 February 1958 in the Munich air disaster.

Callaghan, Ian Born Ian Robert Callaghan, Liverpool, 10 April 1942. Position: midfield. Clubs: Liverpool 1960-78, Swansea City 1978-79, Cork Hibernian, Soudifjord, Crewe Alexandra 1981. Honours: League Championship 1964, 1966, 1973, 1976, 1977; FA Cup 1965, 1974; Charity Shield 1964, 1965, 1966, 1974; UEFA Cup 1973, 1976; European Cup 1977 (all with Liverpool). International caps (for England): 4. International honours: World Cup 1966. Played 856 games for Liverpool (640

League games) and 968 games in total for his clubs. Known as 'Cally'. Football Writers' Player of the Year 1974. Awarded the MBE in 1974.

Campbell, Sol   Born Sulzeer Jeremiah Campbell, Newham, London, 18 September 1974. Position: defender. Clubs: Tottenham Hotspur 1992-2001, Arsenal 2001-present. Honours: FA Premiership 2002, 2004 (with Arsenal); FA Cup 2002 (with Arsenal); League Cup 1999 (with Tottenham Hotspur). International caps (for England): 55 (2 as captain), 1 goal.

Camsell, George   Born George Henry Camsell, Framwellgate Moor, Co. Durham, 27 November 1902. Position: forward. Clubs: Durham City 1924-25, Middlesbrough 1925-39 (signed for £600). International caps (for England): 9, 18 goals. A phenomenal striker, scoring 345 goals in 453 appearances for Middlesbrough, Camsell scored a record 59 League goals in 37 games during season 1926/27 only to see his record broken the following year by Dixie Dean. He might have scored more had he been the team's penalty taker. Unsurprisingly he is Middlesbrough's all-time top scorer. He died in Framwellgate on 7 March 1966.

Caniggia, Claudio   Born Claudio Paul Caniggia, Buenos Aires, Argentina, 9 January 1967. Position: forward. Clubs: River Plate 1985-88, Hellas Verona 1988-89, Atalanta Bergamo 1989-92, Roma 1992-94, Benfica 1994-95, Boca Juniors 1995-2000, Dundee 2000-01, Rangers 2001-03 (signed for £900,000). Honours: Scottish League Championship 2002, 2003; Scottish Cup 2002, 2003 (all with Rangers). International caps (for Argentina): 50, 16 goals. Banned for 13 months in 1993 for testing positive for cocaine.

Cantona, Eric   Born Paris, France, 24 May 1966. Position: forward. Clubs: Auxerre 1983-88, Olympique Marseille 1988-91 (signed for £2.3m), Bordeaux (loan), Montpellier, Nimes 1991-92 (signed for £1m), Leeds United 1992 (signed for £900,000), Manchester United 1992-97 (signed for £1.2m). Honours: French League Championship 1989 (with Olympique Marseille); League Championship/FA Premiership 1992 (with Leeds United), 1993, 1994, 1996, 1997 (with Manchester United); French Cup 1989 (with Olympique Marseille), 1990 (with Montpellier); FA Cup 1994, 1996 (with Manchester United); Charity Shield 1994, 1995, 1997 (with Manchester United). International caps (for France): 45, 19 goals. Won League/Cup doubles in both France and England. PFA Player of the Year 1994, Football Writers' Player of the Year 1996. Repeatedly in trouble because of his temper in France, he was banned for insulting the French national coach, throwing a ball at a referee and calling French FA officials 'idiots'. Having retired briefly in 1991, he was signed by Leeds United after refusing to extend a trial at Sheffield Wednesday. In 1995 a world-wide ban followed his infamous kung-fu style attack on an abusive Crystal Palace fan. He now plays on the beach football circuit and has become a film actor, including the part as the French Ambassador in the 1998 film *Elizabeth*.

Cantwell, Noel   Born Cork, Ireland, 28 February 1932. Position: defender. Clubs (player): Western Rovers, Cork Athletic, West Ham United 1952-60, Manchester United 1960-66 (signed for £29,500). Honours: FA Cup 1963 (with Manchester United). Clubs (manager): Coventry City 1967-72, Peterborough United 1972-77, Boston Tea Men, Peterborough 1986-88. International caps (for Republic of Ireland): 36, 14 goals. Also played cricket

for Ireland. Irish Footballer of the Year 1959. Chairman of the PFA 1966-67. Expected by some to replace Matt Busby at Manchester United, he instead opted to follow Jimmy Hill at Coventry. He became a publican in Peterborough on his retirement from the game.

Carbajal, Antonio   Born Guanajuata, Mexico, 7 June 1929. Position: goalkeeper. Clubs (player): Oviedo 1938-46, Necaxa 1946-48, Espana 1948-50, León 1950-66. Honours: Mexican League Championship 1952, 1956; Mexican Cup 1958 (all with León). Clubs (manager): León, Atlético Morelia. Honours: Mexican League Championship 1970, 1971 (with León). International caps (for Mexico): 47. Carbajal played in five World Cup finals tournaments (1950, 1954, 1958, 1962, 1966), a feat only matched by Lothar Matthäus in 1998. In a total of 11 World Cup matches he was on the winning side only once and only kept a clean sheet in his final game, a 0-0 draw with Uruguay. Known as 'La Tota'. Voted the best goalkeeper of the 20th century in North and Central America.

Carey, Johnny   Born John Joseph Carey, Dublin, 23 February 1919. Position: defender. Clubs (player): Home Farm, St James's Gate 1936, Manchester United 1937-54 (signed for £250). Honours: League Championship 1952; FA Cup 1948 (both with Manchester United). Clubs (manager): Blackburn Rovers 1953-58, Everton 1958-61, Leyton Orient 1961-63, Nottingham Forest 1963-68, Blackburn Rovers 1970-71. International caps (for Northern Ireland): 7; (for Republic of Ireland): 29 (19 as captain), 3 goals. In 1947 captained both Republic of Ireland and Northern Ireland teams. He also captained a Rest of Europe team against Great Britain in 1947. He played in every position for Manchester United except outside left, including goalkeeper against Sunderland in 1953. Football Writers' Player of the Year 1949.

Carragher, Jamie   Born James Lee Duncan Carragher, Bootle, Liverpool, 28 January 1978. Position: defender. Club: Liverpool 1994-present. Honours: FA Cup 2001; League Cup 2001; Charity Shield 2001; UEFA Cup 2001. International caps (for England): 9. Suffered a broken leg in 2003 while playing against Blackburn Rovers.

Carter, Raich   Born Horatio Stratton Carter, Hendon, Sunderland, 21 December 1913. Position: forward. Clubs (player): Sunderland 1931-45, Derby County 1945-48 (signed for £8,000), Hull City 1948-51 (signed for £6,000), Cork Athletic 1953. Honours: League Championship 1936 (with Sunderland); FA Cup 1937 (with Sunderland), 1946 (with Derby County); Irish Cup 1953 (with Cork Athletic); Charity Shield 1936 (with Sunderland). Clubs (manager): Hull City 1948-51, Leeds United 1953-58, Mansfield Town 1960-63, Middlesbrough 1963-66. International caps (for England): 13, 7 goals. Also played cricket for Durham and Derbyshire. Nicknamed 'The Silver Fox' because of his grey hair. The only player to win an FA Cup medal on either side of World War II. He died 9 October 1994 in Willerby, Hull.

Channon, Mick   Born Michael Roger Channon, Orcheston, Wiltshire, 28 November 1948. Position: forward. Clubs: Southampton 1965-77, Manchester City 1977-79, Southampton 1979-82, Caroline Hills (Hong Kong) 1982, Newcastle United 1982, Bristol Rovers 1982, Norwich City 1982-85, Portsmouth 1985-86, Finn Harps. Honours: FA Cup 1976 (with Southampton); League Cup 1985 (with Norwich City). International caps (for England): 46 (2 as captain), 21 goals. Renowned for celebrating his goals with a windmilling arm salute, Channon is since 1990 a very successful racehorse trainer.

Charles, John Born William John Charles, Cwmdu, Swansea, 27 December 1931. Position: forward. Clubs (player): Swansea Town 1947, Leeds United 1947-57, 1962 (signed for £53,000), Juventus 1957-62 (signed for £65,000), Roma 1962-63 (signed for £70,000), Cardiff City 1963-66 (signed for £25,000), Hereford United 1966-71, Merthyr Town. Honours: Italian League Championship 1958, 1959, 1961; Italian Cup 1959, 1960 (all with Juventus). Clubs (manager): Hereford United, Merthyr Town. International caps (for Wales): 38, 15 goals. A great all-round footballer, a world-class centre-forward and centre-half. At Cardiff City he played alongside his brother Mel. Known as 'Il Buon Gigante' (The Gentle Giant), he was revered by fans in both Britain and Italy. The first Briton to make the grade in Italian football, his move to Juventus was negotiated by Kenneth Wolstenholme and he was the only British player to be top scorer in an Italian League season. Awarded the CBE in 2001. He died 21 February 2004.

Charlton, Bobby Born Robert Charlton, Ashington, Northumberland, 11 October 1937. Position: midfield/forward. Clubs (player): Manchester United 1953-73, Preston North End 1974-75. Honours: League Championship 1957, 1965, 1967; FA Cup 1963; European Cup 1968 (all with Manchester United). Clubs (manager): Preston North End 1973-75, Wigan Athletic 1983. International caps (for England): 106 (49 as captain), 49 goals. International honours: World Cup 1966. Football Writers' Player of the Year 1966. European Player of the Year 1966. Renowned for his blistering shot from distance. A survivor of the 1958 Munich air disaster, Charlton was one of the most well-known and admired footballers of his generation. A member of a footballing dynasty, his mother Cissie was the sister of four professional footballers including Jackie Milburn and taught her sons to play football, while Bobby played alongside his elder brother Jack in the World Cup final 1966. Later a director of Manchester United. Awarded the OBE in 1969, the CBE in 1974 and knighted in 1994. In 1959 he won £1000 on the TV show *Double Your Money* answering questions on pop music.

Charlton, Jack Born Ashington, Northumberland, 8 May 1935. Position: defender. Club (player): Leeds United 1952-73. Honours: League Championship 1969; FA Cup 1972; League Cup 1968; Inter-cities Fairs Cup 1968, 1971. Clubs (manager): Middlesbrough 1973-77, 1984, Sheffield Wednesday 1977-83, Newcastle United 1984-85. International caps (for England): 35, 6 goals. International honours: World Cup 1966. International manager (Republic of Ireland): 1986-96. Football Writers' Player of the Year 1967. Awarded honorary Irish citizenship in 1995. Awarded the OBE in 1974. Charlton's other love is angling and he has hosted TV programmes and written books on the subject.

Chastain, Brandi Born Brandi Denise Chastain, San Jose, California, 21 July 1968. Position: midfield. Clubs: Shiroki Serena (Japan) 1993, Sacramento Storm 1997, Bay Area CyberRays 2001-02. International caps (for United States): 106. International honours: Olympic gold medal 1996; Women's World Cup 1991, 1999. A versatile, two-footed player who has played as a defender, midfielder and forward for the national team. Scored the deciding penalty in the shoot-out to win the 1999 Women's World Cup final.

Chedgzoy, Sam Born Ellesmere Port, Cheshire, 1890. Position: forward. Clubs: Burnell's Iron Works, Everton 1910-26. International honours: League Championship 1915 (with Everton). International caps (for England): 8. His main claim to fame is that he spotted a loophole in the corner-kick law which forced it to be changed. In 1924 in a match against Tottenham Hotspur he passed the ball to himself from a corner, dribbled into the area and scored. The goal was disallowed even though it was within the law as it then stood. He died in 1967 in Canada.

Cherry, Trevor Born Trevor John Cherry, Huddersfield, 23 February 1948. Position: defender. Clubs (player): Huddersfield Town 1965-72, Leeds United 1972-82 (signed for £100,000), Bradford City 1982-85 (signed for £10,000). Honours: League Championship 1974. Club (manager): Bradford City 1982-87. International caps (for England): 27 (1 as captain).

Chilavert, Jose Luis Born Jose Luis Felix Chilavert Gonzales, Nu Guazu, Luque, Paraguay, 27 July 1965. Position: goalkeeper. Clubs: Sportivo Luqueno 1983, Guarani 1984, San Lorenzo 1985-88, Real Zaragoza 1988-91, Velez Sarsfield 1991-2000, Strasbourg 2000-03, Peñarol 2003-present. Honours: Paraguayan League Championship 1984 (with Guarani); Argentinian League Championship 1993 (Clausura), 1996 (Apertura), 1998 (Apertura) (with Velez Sarsfield); French Cup 2001 (with Strasbourg); Copa Libertadores 1994 (with Velez Sarsfield). International caps (for Paraguay): 74, 8 goals. A goalkeeper who regularly takes free-kicks and penalties. World Goalkeeper of the Year 1995, 1997. South American Player of the Year 1996. Was in dispute with Strasbourg in 2002 over an unregistered contract.

Chilton, Allenby Born South Hylton, Sunderland, 16 September 1918. Position: defender. Clubs (player): Seaham Colliery 1934-38, Liverpool 1938, Manchester United 1938-55, Grimsby Town 1955-56. Honours: League Championship 1952; FA Cup 1948 (both with Manchester United). Clubs (manager): Grimsby Town 1955-59, Wigan Athletic 1960, Hartlepool United 1962-63. International caps (for England): 2. Considered by Matt Busby to be his best-ever centre half, Chilton played 166 consecutive League games for Manchester United. He trained as a boxer before becoming a footballer. He died 15 June 1996 in Southwick.

Chinaglia, Giorgio Born Carrara, Italy, 24 January 1947. Position: forward. Clubs: Swansea Town 1962-66, Massese 1967, Internapoli 1968-69, Lazio 1969-77 (signed for £140,000), New York Cosmos 1977-83. Honours: Italian League Championship 1974 (with Lazio). International caps (for Italy): 14, 4 goals. Known as 'Little George'. Brought up in Cardiff after his family emigrated from Italy, Chinaglia was the first Serie B player to play for Italy. Named the greatest player in Lazio's history.

Chivers, Martin Born Martin Harcourt Chivers, Southampton, 27 April 1945. Position: forward. Clubs (player): Southampton 1962-68, Tottenham Hotspur 1968-76 (signed for £125,000), Servette 1976-78, Norwich City 1978-79, Brighton & Hove Albion 1979, Dorchester, Vard (Norway) 1980-82, Barnet. Honours: League Cup 1971, 1973; UEFA Cup 1972 (all with Tottenham Hotspur). Clubs (coach): Dorchester Town, Vard 1980-82, Barnet. International caps (for England): 24, 13 goals. Now runs a hotel in Hertfordshire.

Chumpitaz, Hector Born Canete, Peru, 12 April 1944 (some sources 1943). Position: defender.

Clubs: Ocal 1963, Municipal 1964-65, Universitario 1966-75, Sporting Cristal 1977-84. Honours: Peruvian League Championship 1966, 1967, 1969, 1971, 1974 (with Universitario), 1979, 1980, 1983 (with Sporting Cristal). International caps (for Peru): 105. International honours: Copa America 1975. Most-capped player for Peru.

Clarke, Allan   Born Allan John Clarke, Short Heath, nr Wolverhampton, 31 July 1946. Position: forward. Clubs (player): Walsall 1963-66, Fulham 1966-68 (signed for £35,000), Leicester City 1968-69 (signed for £150,000), Leeds United 1969-78 (signed for £165,000), Barnsley 1978-80 (signed for £45,000). Honours: League Championship 1974; FA Cup 1972; UEFA Cup 1971 (all with Leeds United). Clubs (manager): Barnsley 1978-80, Leeds United 1980-82, Scunthorpe 1983-84, Barnsley 1985-89, Lincoln City 1990. International caps (for England): 19, 10 goals. Nicknamed 'Sniffer' because he could sniff out a goalscoring opportunity, Clarke enjoyed a prolific partnership at Leeds United with Mick Jones and scored the winning goal in the 1972 FA Cup final against Arsenal. He now works for a plant hire company.

Clayton, Ronnie   Born Ronald Clayton, Preston, Lancashire, 5 August 1934. Position: midfielder. Clubs (player): Blackburn Rovers 1950-68, Morecambe 1969-70, Great Harwood 1971. Club (manager): Morecambe FC 1969-70. International caps (for England): 35 (5 as captain). Played over 650 games for Blackburn Rovers. His voice provides the commentary for tours of Ewood Park.

Clemence, Ray   Born Raymond Neal Clemence, Skegness, Lincolnshire, 5 August 1948. Position: goalkeeper. Clubs (player): Notts County, Scunthorpe United 1965-67, Liverpool 1967-81 (signed for £18,000), Tottenham Hotspur 1981-88 (signed for £300,000). Honours: League Championship 1973, 1976, 1977, 1979, 1980 (with Liverpool); FA Cup 1974 (with Liverpool) and 1982 (with Tottenham Hotspur); League Cup 1981 (with Liverpool); UEFA Cup 1973, 1976 (with Liverpool), 1984 (with Tottenham Hotspur); Charity Shield 1974, 1976, 1977, 1979, 1980 (with Liverpool); European Cup 1977, 1978, 1981 (with Liverpool). Club (manager): Barnet 1994-96. International caps (for England): 61 (1 as captain). Conceded only 16 goals in Liverpool's 1978/79 League campaign and in total made 1119 appearances for club and country. His son Stephen is currently with Birmingham City, having played for Tottenham Hotspur 1994-2003. Now working as a goalkeeping coach. Awarded the MBE in 1987.

Clough, Brian   Born Brian Howard Clough, Middlesbrough, 21 March 1935. Position: forward. Clubs (player): Middlesbrough 1955-61, Sunderland 1961-64. Clubs (manager): Hartlepool United 1965-67, Derby County 1967-73, Brighton & Hove Albion 1973-74, Leeds United 1974, Nottingham Forest 1975-93. Honours: League Championship 1972 (with Derby County), 1978 (with Nottingham Forest); League Cup 1978, 1989, 1990 (with Nottingham Forest); European Cup 1979, 1980 (with Nottingham Forest). International caps (for England): 2. Clough had the highest goals per game ratio in the Football League – 251 in 274 games – but was forced to retire because of a knee injury. Vice-President of the League Managers' Association. Awarded the OBE in 1991. There is a stand named after him at the City Ground, Nottingham Forest. His forthright, no-nonsense approach was unpopular with officialdom and despite

huge public support he remains the greatest manager never to have managed the England team. Autobiographies *Clough* (1994) and *Cloughie: Walking on Water* (2002). Father of Nigel Clough.

Clough, Nigel   Born Nigel Howard Clough, Sunderland, 19 March 1966. Position: forward/midfield. Clubs (player): Heanor Town 1983-84, Nottingham Forest 1984-93, Liverpool 1993-96 (signed for £2.275m), Manchester City 1996-98 (signed for £1.5m), Nottingham Forest 1996-97 (loan), Sheffield Wednesday 1997 (loan), Burton Albion 1998-present. Honours: League Cup 1989, 1990 (with Nottingham Forest). Club (manager): Burton Albion 1998-present. International caps (for England): 14. Son of Brian Clough.

Coad, Paddy   Born Waterford, Ireland, 1920. Position: forward. Clubs (player): Corinthians, Waterford 1937-38, 1939-42, Glenavon 1938-39, Shamrock Rovers 1942-60. Honours: Irish League Championship 1954, 1957, 1959; Irish Cup 1944, 1945, 1948, 1956 (all with Shamrock Rovers). Clubs (manager): Shamrock Rovers 1949-60, Waterford 1960-66. Honours: Irish League Championship 1954, 1957, 1959 (with Shamrock Rovers), 1966 (with Waterford); Irish Cup 1956 (with Shamrock Rovers). International caps (for Ireland): 11, 3 goals. Believed to be the greatest Irish player never to have played outside Ireland and by some to be the greatest Irish player ever. As a manager he produced a young Shamrock Rovers side known as 'Coad's Colts'.

Coates, Ralph   Born Hetton-le-Hole, Co. Durham, 26 April 1946. Position: midfield/forward. Clubs: Burnley 1963-71, Tottenham Hotspur 1971-78, Orient 1978-80. Honours: League Cup 1973; UEFA Cup 1972 (both with Tottenham Hotspur). International caps (for England): 4.

Cockburn, Henry   Born Ashton-under-Lyne, Manchester, 14 September 1923. Position: defender. Clubs (player): Goslings FC, Manchester United 1946-54, Bury 1954-56, Peterborough United 1956-59, Corby Town 1959-60, Sankeys 1960-61. Honours: FA Cup 1948 (with Manchester United). Clubs (manager/coach): Oldham Athletic 1961-64 (assistant), Huddersfield Town 1964-75 (assistant). International caps (for England): 13. A broken jaw in 1953 led to his replacement at Manchester United by Duncan Edwards.

Cohen, George   Born Kensington, London, 22 October 1939. Position: defender. Club: Fulham 1956-69. International caps (for England): 37. International honours: World Cup 1966. Retired through injury in 1969. According to George Best, 'the best full back I ever played against'. His autobiography *George Cohen* was published in 2000. Awarded the MBE in 2000 along with those other members of the 1966 World Cup squad (Ray Wilson, Alan Ball, Roger Hunt and Nobby Stiles). who had been missed earlier.

Cole, Andy   Born Andrew Alexander Cole, Nottingham, 15 October 1971. Position: forward. Clubs: Arsenal 1989-92, Fulham 1991 (loan), Bristol City 1992-93 (signed for £500,000), Newcastle United 1993-95 (signed for £1.75m), Manchester United 1995-2001 (signed for £6m), Blackburn Rovers 2001-present (signed for £8m). Honours: FA Premiership 1996, 1997, 1999, 2000, 2001 (with Manchester United); FA Cup 1996, 1999 (with Manchester United); League Cup 2002 (with Blackburn Rovers); Charity Shield 1997 (with Manchester United); UEFA Champions League 1999 (with Manchester United). International caps (for

England): 15, 1 goal. Formed a formidable partnership at Manchester United with Dwight Yorke.

le, Ashley   Born Stepney, London, 20 December 1980. Position: defender. Clubs: Arsenal 1998-present, Crystal Palace 2000 (loan). Honours: FA Premiership 2002; FA Cup 2002, 2003 (all with Arsenal). International caps (for England): 21.

le, Joe   Born Joseph John Cole, Islington, London, 8 November 1981. Position: midfield. Clubs: West Ham United 1998-2003, Chelsea 2003-present. International caps (for England): 11, 1 goal.

llins, Bobby   Born Robert Young Collins, Govanhill, Glasgow, 16 February 1931. Position: forward/midfield. Clubs (player): Celtic 1948-58, Everton 1958-62 (signed for £23,500), Leeds United 1962-67 (signed for £25,000), Bury 1967-69, Morton 1969-71, Oldham Athletic 1972-73. Honours: Scottish League Championship 1954; Scottish Cup 1951; Scottish League Cup 1957, 1958 (all with Celtic). Clubs (manager): Oldham Athletic 1972-73 (coach), Huddersfield Town 1974, Hull City 1977-78, Barnsley 1984-85. International caps (for Scotland): 31, 10 goals. Football Writers' Player of the Year 1965 (first Scottish winner). He also played club football in Australia.

llymore, Stan   Born Stanley Victor Collymore, Stone, Staffordshire, 21 January 1971. Position: forward. Clubs: Walsall 1989, Wolverhampton Wanderers 1989, Stafford Rangers 1990-91, Crystal Palace 1991-92 (signed for £100,000), Southend United 1992-93 (signed for £80,000), Nottingham Forest 1993-95 (signed for £2.75m), Liverpool 1995-97 (signed for £8.5m), Aston Villa 1997-2000 (signed for £7m), Fulham 1999-2000 (loan), Leicester City 2000, Bradford City 2000, Real Oviedo 2000. International caps (for England): 3. Nicknamed 'Stan the Man'. An unquestionably talented striker, but at best labelled enigmatic; he flattered to deceive at most of the clubs he played for in the latter part of his career. Retired at the age of 30.

lman, Eddie   Born Salford, Manchester, 1 November 1936. Position: midfielder. Club: Manchester United 1955-58. Honours: League Championship 1956, 1957; Charity Shield 1957. Nicknamed 'Snakehips' because of his mazy runs. One of the 'Busby Babes' killed in the Munich air disaster, 6 February 1958.

luna, Mario   Born Mario Esteves Coluna, Lorenzo Marques, Mozambique, 6 August 1935. Position: forward/midfield. Clubs: Lorenzo Marques 1952-54, Benfica 1954-70, Lyon 1970-71. Honours: Portuguese League Championship 1955, 1957, 1960, 1961, 1963, 1965, 1967, 1968, 1969; Portuguese Cup 1955, 1957, 1959, 1962, 1964, 1969; European Cup 1961, 1962 (all with Benfica). International caps (for Portugal): 58, 8 goals. Captained Benfica to successive European Cup victories and Portugal to third place in the 1966 World Cup. Having held the Mozambique long-jump record for many years, he became Minister of Culture and Sports in Mozambique.

mmon, Alf   Born Alfred Common, Sunderland, 25 May 1880. Position: forward. Clubs: Sunderland, Sheffield United 1901-04 (signed for £325), Sunderland 1904-05 (signed for £520), Middlesbrough 1905-10 (signed for £1000), Woolwich Arsenal 1910-12, Preston North End 1912-15. Subject of the first four-figure transfer when he moved from Sunderland to Middlesbrough in 1905. He became a publican on his retirement and died 3 April 1946 in Darlington.

Connelly, John   Born John Michael Connelly, St Helens, 18 July 1938. Position: forward. Clubs: St Helens Town, Burnley 1956-64, Manchester United 1964-66 (signed for £60,000), Blackburn Rovers 1966-70 (signed for £40,000), Bury 1970-73. Honours: League Championship 1965 (with Manchester United). International caps (for England): 20, 7 goals. A pacy winger, he was nicknamed 'The Flash' after the comic-book character.

Cooper, Davie   Born David Cooper, Hamilton, Scotland, 25 February 1956. Position: forward. Clubs: Hamilton Avondale, Clydebank 1974-77 (signed for £300), Rangers 1977-89 (signed for £100,000), Motherwell 1989-94 (signed for £50,000), Clydebank 1994-95. Honours: Scottish League Championship 1978, 1987, 1989 (with Rangers); Scottish Cup 1978, 1979, 1981 (with Rangers), 1991 (with Motherwell); Scottish League Cup 1978, 1979, 1982, 1984, 1985, 1987, 1988 (with Rangers). International caps (for Scotland): 21, 5 goals. Scorer of what is considered the greatest goal ever scored by Rangers – in the Dryborough Cup final of 1979 when he took a ball on his chest, flicked it four times with his left foot over four Celtic defenders and slotted it home. Called 'The Moody Blue' by the press because he was unwilling to give interviews. He died from a brain haemorrhage while filming a football skills TV programme for children on 22 March 1995, aged 39.

Cooper, Terry   Born Brotherton, 12 July 1944. Clubs (player): Leeds United 1961-75, Middlesbrough 1975-78, Bristol City 1978-79, 1982-85, Bristol Rovers 1979-81, Doncaster Rovers 1981-82, Honours: League Championship 1969, 1974; League Cup 1968 (all with Leeds United). Clubs (manager): Bristol Rovers 1980-81, Bristol City 1982-88, Exeter City 1988-91, 1994-95, Birmingham City 1991-93. International caps (for England): 20. Cooper missed the 1972 FA Cup final with a broken leg which put him out of the game for 20 months. Known as 'TC'. Now works as a scout for Southampton.

Cooper, Tommy   Born Stoke-on-Trent, 9 April 1904. Position: defender. Clubs: Trentham, Port Vale, Derby County 1926-34 (signed for £2500), Liverpool 1934-40 (signed for £7500). International caps (for England): 15 (4 as captain). Known as 'Snowy' because of his grey hair, Cooper formed a strong defensive partnership at Liverpool with Ernie Blenkinsop. He was killed in June 1940 when his military police motorcycle was in a collision with a bus in Suffolk, an incident which led to army despatch riders having to wear crash helmets.

Coppell, Steve   Born Stephen James Coppell, Croxteth, Liverpool, 9 July 1955. Position: forward/midfield. Clubs (player): Liverpool University, Tranmere Rovers 1974-75, Manchester United 1975-83. Honours: FA Cup 1977 (with Manchester United). Clubs (manager): Crystal Palace 1984-93, 1995-96, 1997-98, 1999-2000, Manchester City 1996, Brentford 2001-02, Brighton & Hove Albion 2002-present. International caps (for England): 42, 7 goals. Having played 206 consecutive League games for Manchester United 1977-81, Coppell was forced to retire in 1983 following a knee injury originally picked up playing for England in 1981. He was chief executive of the League Managers' Association 1993-95.

Copping, Wilf   Born Wilfred Copping, Middlecliffe, Barnsley, Yorkshire, 17 August 1909. Position: defender. Clubs (player): Dearne Valley Old Boys, Middlecliffe Rovers, Leeds United 1929-34, 1939-42,

F
O
O
T
B
A
L
L

Arsenal 1934-39 (signed for £8,000). Honours: League Championship 1935, 1938; FA Cup 1936; Charity Shield 1935, 1939 (all with Arsenal). Clubs (coach): Army XI 1945 Antwerp, Southend United 1946-54, Coventry City 1956-59, Bristol City, Southend United. International caps (for England): 20. In 1934 Copping was one of seven Arsenal players in the England team to play Italy in 'The Battle of Highbury'. Known as 'The Iron Man', his motto was 'Get stuck in' and he remarked that 'the first man in a tackle never gets hurt'. Despite his fearsome reputation, enhanced with an equally fearsome appearance (to look even 'harder', he never shaved on match days), he was never booked or dismissed. It is doubtful if his 'famous double-footed tackle' would be treated so leniently now. Copping rejoined Leeds United in 1939 in order to move his family 'back North' at the onset of war. He died June 1980 in Southend.

Corrigan, Joe Born Joseph Thomas Corrigan, Manchester, 18 November 1948. Position: goalkeeper. Clubs: Sale, Manchester City 1966-83, Shrewsbury Town 1968 (loan), Seattle Sounders 1983 (signed for £30,000), Brighton & Hove Albion 1983-86, Stoke City (loan), Norwich City (loan). Honours: League Cup 1970, 1976; European Cup Winners' Cup 1970 (all with Manchester City). International caps (for England): 9. Having worked as goalkeeping coach for Manchester City, since 1994 Corrigan works in the same capacity for Liverpool, having been reserve team coach 1998-2002.

Cowans, Gordon Born Gordon Sidney Cowans, Cornforth, Co. Durham, 27 October 1958. Position: midfield. Clubs: Aston Villa 1975-85, 1988-91, 1993-94, Bari 1985-88, Blackburn Rovers 1991-93, Derby County 1994-95, Wolverhampton Wanderers 1994-96, Sheffield United 1996, Bradford City 1997, Stockport County 1997, Burnley 1998. Honours: League Championship 1981; League Cup 1977; European Cup 1982 (all with Aston Villa). International caps (for England): 10, 2 goals. Missed the 1983/84 season with a serious leg injury.

Crabtree, Jimmy Born James William Crabtree, Burnley, Lancashire, 23 December 1871. Position: defender. Clubs: Burnley, Aston Villa. Honours: League Championship 1894, 1896, 1897, 1899, 1900; FA Cup 1895, 1897 (all with Aston Villa). International caps (for England): 14. His transfer to Aston Villa in 1893 may possibly be the first cash transfer to take place. It was brought on because Burnley could not meet his wage demands.

Crawshaw, Tom Born Thomas Henry Crawshaw, Sheffield, Yorkshire, 27 December 1872. Position: defender. Clubs: Heywood Central, Sheffield Wednesday 1894-1908, Chesterfield. Honours: League Championship 1903, 1904; FA Cup 1896, 1907 (all with Sheffield Wednesday). International caps (for England): 10, 1 goal.

Crerand, Pat Born Patrick Timothy Crerand, Glasgow, 19 February 1939. Position: midfield. Clubs (player): Celtic 1957-62, Manchester United 1962-71 (signed for £55,000). Honours: League Championship 1965, 1967; FA Cup 1963; European Cup 1968 (all with Manchester United). Clubs (manager): Manchester United 1972-76 (assistant), Northampton Town 1976-77. International caps (for Scotland): 16.

Crespo, Hernan Born Florida, Argentina, 5 July 1975. Position: forward. Clubs: River Plate 1993-96, Parma 1997-2000, Lazio 2000-02, Inter Milan 2002-03, Chelsea 2003-present (signed for £16.8m).

Honours: Argentinian League Championship 1994, 1995 (with River Plate); Italian Cup 1999 (with Parma); UEFA Cup 1999 (with Parma). International caps (for Argentina): 36, 19 goals.

Cresswell, Warney Born Warneford Cresswell, South Shields, Tyne & Wear, 5 November 1897. Position: defender. Clubs (player): South Shields 1919-22, Sunderland 1922-27, Everton 1927-36. Honours: League Championship 1928; FA Cup 193 (both with Everton). Clubs (manager): Port Vale 1936-37, Northampton Town 1937-39. International caps (for England): 7. He died 20 October 1973 in South Shields.

Crompton, Bob Born Robert Crompton, Blackburn, Lancashire, 26 September 1879. Position: defende Club (player): Blackburn 1896-1920. Honours: League Championship 1912, 1914. Clubs (manager): Blackburn Rovers 1926-31, 1938-41, Bournemouth & Boscombe Athletic 1935-36. International caps (for England): 41 (22 as captain) He died 15 March 1941.

Crooks, Sam Born Samuel Dickinson Crooks, Durham, 16 January 1908. Position: forward. Clubs (player): Tow Law Town, Durham City, Derby Count 1927-46 (signed for £300). Honours: FA Cup 1946 (with Derby County). Clubs (manager): Retford Tow 1949-50, Shrewsbury Town 1950-54, Gresley Rove 1954-57, 1958-59, Burton Albion 1957-58, Heanor Town 1959-60. International caps (for England): 26 goals. Chairman of the Players' Union 1937-46. Ch scout for Derby County 1946-49, 1960-67. He died February 1981.

Cruyff, Johan Born Amsterdam, 25 April 1947. Position: forward. Clubs (player): Ajax 1964-73, 1981-83, Barcelona 1973-78, Los Angeles Aztecs 1979, Washington Diplomats 1980-81, Levante 1981, Feyenoord 1983-84. Honours: Dutch League Championship 1966, 1967, 1968, 1970, 1972, 197 (with Ajax), 1984 (with Feyenoord); Spanish Leagu Championship 1974 (with Barcelona); Dutch Cup 1967, 1970, 1971, 1972 (with Ajax), 1984 (with Feyenoord); Spanish Cup 1978 (with Barcelona); European Cup 1971, 1972, 1973 (with Ajax). Clubs (manager): Ajax 1985-87, Barcelona 1987-96. Honours: Dutch League Championship 1985 (with Ajax); Spanish League Championship 1991, 1992, 1993 (with Barcelona); Dutch Cup 1986, 1987 (with Ajax); European Cup Winners' Cup 1987 (with Ajax 1989 (with Barcelona); European Cup 1992 (with Barcelona). International caps (for Holland): 48, 33 goals. European Player of the Year 1971, 1973, 1974. Known as 'The Flying Dutchman', he is perhaps most famous for the 'Cruyff turn' which involved dragging the ball behind him with his right foot and then turning 180 degrees and accelerating away from a confused defender. His son Jordi playe for Ajax, Barcelona and Manchester United.

Cubillas, Teofilo Born Puente Piedra, Lima, Peru, 8 March 1949. Position: midfield. Clubs: Alianza Lima 1964-72, 1977-79, 1988, FC Basle 1973, Porto 197 78, Fort Lauderdale Strikers 1979-83, 1989. Honou Peruvian League Championship 1965, 1977, 1978 (with Alianza Lima). International caps (for Peru): 88 38 goals. International honours: Copa America 197 Known as 'El Nene'. South American Player of the Year 1972. The only player to score five goals in two separate World Cup tournaments (1970, 1978). He was appointed Peruvian Minister of Sport in 1999.

Cullis, Stan Born Ellesmere Port, Cheshire, 25 October 1916. Position: defender. Clubs (player): Ellesmere Port Wednesday 1930-34, Wolverhampt

Wanderers 1934-47. Clubs (manager): Wolverhampton Wanderers 1948-64, Birmingham City 1965-70. Honours: League Championship 1954, 1958, 1959; FA Cup 1949, 1960; Charity Shield 1949, 1954, 1959, 1960 (all with Wolverhampton Wanderers). International caps (for England): 12 (1 as captain). Retired in 1970 to work in the photography business. The North Bank stand at Molineux is named in his honour. He died 28 February 2001.

Currie, Tony Born Anthony Williams Currie, Edgware, London, 1 January 1950. Position: midfield. Clubs (player): Watford 1967-68, Sheffield United 1968-76 (signed for £26,500), Leeds United 1976-79 (signed for £250,000), Queens Park Rangers 1979-82 (signed for £400,000), Toronto Nationals 1983, Chesham United, Torquay United 1984-85, Goole Town 1987. Clubs (manager): Goole Town 1987. International caps (for England): 17, 3 goals. Forced to retire by a persistent knee injury. He now works as Football in the Community officer at Sheffield United.

Czibor, Zoltan Born Hungary, 1929. Position: forward. Clubs: Ferencvaros 1945-49, SC Csepel 1949, Honvéd 1950-56, Barcelona 1957-63, Espanyol 1963-65. Honours: Hungarian League Championship 1949 (with Ferencvaros), 1952, 1954, 1955 (with Honvéd); Spanish League Championship 1959, 1960 (with Barcelona); Spanish Cup 1959, 1962 (with Barcelona); Inter-cities Fairs Cup 1960 (with Barcelona). International caps (for Hungary): 43, 17 goals. International honours: Olympic gold medal 1952. Scored in the 1954 World Cup final which Hungary lost 2-3 to West Germany. Moved to Spain following the 1956 Hungarian Uprising. He died 1 September 1997 in Hungary.

Dabizas, Nikos Born Nikolaos Dabizas, Amypeo, Greece, 3 August 1973. Position: defender. Clubs: Pontii Verias, Olympiakos 1994-98, Newcastle United 1998-2004 (signed for £1.3m), Leicester City 2004-present. Honours: Greek League Championship 1997 (with Olympiakos). First Greek player to play in an FA Cup final (1998).

Dalglish, Kenny Born Kenneth Mathieson Dalglish, Dalmarnock, Glasgow, 4 March 1951. Position: forward. Clubs (player): Celtic 1970-77, Liverpool 1977-90 (signed for £440,000). Honours: Scottish League Championship 1972, 1973, 1974, 1977; Scottish Cup 1972, 1974, 1975, 1977; Scottish League Cup 1975 (all with Celtic); League Championship 1979, 1980, 1982, 1983, 1984, 1986, 1988, 1990; FA Cup 1986; League Cup 1981, 1982, 1983, 1984; Charity Shield 1977, 1979, 1980, 1982, 1986; European Cup 1978, 1981, 1984 (all with Liverpool). Clubs (manager): Liverpool 1985-91, Blackburn Rovers 1991-95, Newcastle United 1997-98, Celtic 2000. Honours: English League Championship/FA Premiership 1986, 1988, 1990 (with Liverpool), 1995 (with Blackburn Rovers); FA Cup 1986, 1989 (with Liverpool); Charity Shield 1986 (with Liverpool). International caps (for Scotland): 102, 30 goals. Football Writers' Player of the Year 1979, 1983. PFA Player of the Year 1983. Manager of the Year 1986, 1988, 1990, 1995. One of only three men to lead two different clubs to the League Championship (the others being Herbert Chapman and Brian Clough), Dalglish resigned from Liverpool management in 1991 citing stress resulting from the Hillsborough tragedy. Awarded the MBE in 1985.

Davids, Edgar Born Paramaribo, Surinam, 13 March 1973. Position: midfield. Clubs: Ajax 1991-96, AC Milan 1996-97, Juventus 1997-present. Honours: Dutch League Championship 1994, 1995, 1996 (with Ajax); Dutch Cup 1993 (with Ajax); Italian League Championship 1998, 2002, 2003 (with Juventus); UEFA Cup 1992 (with Ajax); UEFA Champions League 1995 (with Ajax). International caps (for Holland): 54, 6 goals. Known as 'Pitbull' because of his fighting displays, he can sometimes be let down by his temperament. Sometimes called the 'Dutch Roy Keane'. He now plays in special spectacles to combat a problem with glaucoma.

Dean, Dixie Born William Ralph Dean, Birkenhead, Liverpool, 22 January 1907. Position: forward. Clubs: Tranmere 1923-25, Everton 1925-38 (signed for £3,000), Notts County 1938, Sligo Rovers 1938-39. Honours: English League Championship 1928, 1932; FA Cup 1933; Charity Shield 1928, 1932 (all with Everton). International caps (for England): 16, 18 goals. Badly injured in a motorcycle accident in 1926 which seriously jeopardised his career. Dean scored 60 goals in 39 League matches in season 1927/28 to set a record which stands to this day. Needing to score a final-day hat-trick to beat George Camsell's record of 59 goals set only the year before, he netted his third against Arsenal with only five minutes of the season remaining. He totalled 82 goals in all competitions that season. Dean scored 383 goals in 433 appearances for Everton, having scored in each of his first five internationals, and headed 50 per cent of his goals. Though invariably known as 'Dixie', he disliked the name. He died of a heart attack shortly after watching a Liverpool derby on 1 March 1980 at Goodison Park.

Delaney, Jimmy Born James Delaney, Cleland, Lanarkshire, Scotland, 3 September 1914. Position: forward. Clubs (player): Celtic 1933-46, Manchester United 1946-50 (signed for £4000), Aberdeen 1950-51, Falkirk 1951-54, Derry City 1954-55, Cork Athletic 1955-56, Elgin City 1956-57. Honours: Scottish League Championship 1936, 1938 (with Celtic); Scottish Cup 1937 (with Celtic); FA Cup 1948 (with Manchester United); Irish Cup 1954 (with Derry City). Clubs (manager): Cork Athletic 1955-56. International caps (for Scotland): 13, 3 goals. Matt Busby's first purchase as Manchester United manager. Delaney gained cup winner's medals in Scotland, England and Ireland. Nicknamed 'Brittle Bones' after a series of injuries in Scotland. He died 26 September 1989.

del Piero, Alessandro Born Conegliano, Treviso, Italy, 9 November 1974. Position: forward. Clubs: Padova 1991-93, Juventus 1993-present. Honours: Italian League Championship 1995, 1997, 1998, 2002, 2003; Italian Cup 1995; UEFA Champions League 1996 (all with Juventus). International caps (for Italy): 58, 22 goals.

Desailly, Marcel Born Accra, Ghana, 7 September 1968. Position: defender. Clubs: Nantes 1986-92, Olympique Marseille 1992-93, AC Milan 1993-98, Chelsea 1998-present (signed for £4.6m). Honours: Italian League Championship 1994, 1998 (with AC Milan); FA Cup 2000 (with Chelsea); Charity Shield 2000 (with Chelsea); UEFA Champions League 1994 (with AC Milan). International caps (for France): 111, 3 goals. International honours: World Cup 1998; European Championship 2000. Nicknamed 'The Rock'. Most-capped French player.

Deschamps, Didier Born Bayonne, France, 15 October 1968. Position: midfield. Clubs (player): Aviron Bayonnais 1980-83, Nantes 1983-89, Olympique Marseille 1989-90, 1991-94, Bordeaux 1990-91, Juventus 1994-99, Chelsea 1999-2000 (signed for £3m), Valencia 2000-01 (signed for £3.7m). Honours: French League Championship 1990, 1992 (with Olympique Marseille); Italian League Championship 1995, 1997, 1998 (with Juventus); Italian Cup 1995 (with Juventus); UEFA Champions League, 1996 (with Juventus). Clubs (manager): Monaco 2001-present. International caps (for France): 103, 4 goals. International honours: World Cup 1998; European Championship 2000. Second most-capped French player.

Devey, John Born John Henry George Devey, Newtown, Birmingham, 26 December 1866. Position: forward. Clubs: Excelsior 1884-86, Aston Unity 1886-87, Aston Manor 1887-90, Mitchell's St George 1890-91, Aston Villa 1891-1902. Honours: English League Championship 1894, 1896, 1897, 1899, 1900; FA Cup 1895, 1897 (all with Aston Villa). International caps (for England): 2, 1 goal. He formed a sparkling partnership with speedy winger Charlie Athersmith at Aston Villa. It is disputed whether he or Bob Chatt scored the fastest-ever FA Cup final goal (39 seconds in 1895 against West Bromwich Albion). He played first-class cricket for Warwickshire 1894-1907, taking 16 wickets and scoring over 6500 runs, and was also adept at baseball which was being tried in England at the time. A founder member of the Players' Union in 1897, after retiring in 1902 he became a director of Aston Villa and later opened a cinema in Winson Green in partnership with Harry Hampton. He died 11 October 1940 in Moseley, Birmingham.

Deyna, Kazimierz Born Starograd Gdansk, Poland, 23 October 1947. Position: forward. Clubs: Wlokniarz Starograd Gdanski 1960-66, LKS Lodz 1966 (1 game), Legia Warsaw 1966-78, Manchester City 1978-81 (signed for £130,000), San Diego Sockers 1981-87. Honours: Polish League Championship 1969, 1970; Polish Cup 1973 (all with Legia Warsaw). International caps (for Poland): 84, 33 goals. International honours: Olympic gold medal 1972. Nicknamed 'Rogal' (Croissant) because of the swerve in his shot. Polish Player of the Year 1972, 1973, 1976. Had a part in the film *Escape to Victory*. He died in a car accident on 1 September 1989 in San Diego.

Di Canio, Paolo Born Rome, 9 July 1968. Position: forward. Clubs: Terrana 1985-87, Lazio 1987-90, Juventus 1990-93, Napoli 1993-94, AC Milan 1995-96, Celtic 1996-97 (signed for £1m), Sheffield Wednesday 1997-99 (signed for £3m), West Ham United 1999-2003 (signed for £1.75m), Charlton Athletic 2003-present. Honours: Italian League Championship 1995 (with Juventus), 1996 (with AC Milan). Scottish Player of the Year 1997. A volatile and unpredictable player, Di Canio was suspended for 11 matches in October 1998 after pushing referee Paul Alcock while playing for Sheffield Wednesday against Arsenal. In contrast he won the FIFA Fair Play Award in 2001 for stopping play when in a goalscoring position with the opposing goalkeeper injured.

Dickinson, Jimmy Born James William Dickinson, Alton, Hampshire, 24 April 1925. Position: defender. Club (player): Portsmouth 1943-65. Honours: English League Championship 1949, 1950 (with Portsmouth). Club (manager): Portsmouth 1977-79. International caps (for England): 48. Played 764 League games for Portsmouth, never cautioned. On retirement he stayed at Portsmouth in various capacities (PR, scout, secretary) until becoming manager. Awarded the MBE in 1964. He died 8 November 1982 in Alton, Hampshire.

Didi Born Waldyr Pereira, Campos, Brazil, 8 October 1928. Position: midfield. Clubs (player): Rio Branco, Lencoes, Madureiro 1949-50, Fluminense 1950-56, Botafogo 1956-58, 1960-62, Real Madrid 1958-60, Valencia 1959-60 (loan). Honours: Brazilian Championship 1957, 1961, 1962 (with Botafogo). Clubs (manager): Sporting Crystal (Peru), River Plate (Argentina). International caps (for Brazil): 85, 31 goals. International honours: World Cup 1958, 1962. International manager (Peru): 1970. An injury in childhood left him with a limp. Scored the first-ever competitive goal in the Maracana Stadium on 16 June 1950 playing for a representative team from São Paulo against a Carioca team from Rio. A deadly free-kick specialist before this became an essential of the game, he perfected the *folha seca* ('dry leaf') kick which bent around defensive walls. He was loaned to Valencia by Real Madrid after clashes with Alfredo Di Stefano. He died 12 May 2001 in Rio de Janeiro.

Dimmock, Jimmy Born James Henry Dimmock, Tottenham, London, 5 December 1900. Position: forward. Clubs: Tottenham Hotspur 1919-31, Thames, Clapton Orient, Ashford. Honours: FA Cup 1921 (with Tottenham Hotspur). International caps (for England): 3. He died 23 December 1972 in Enfield, London.

Di Stefano, Alfredo Born Barrancas, Argentina, 4 July 1926. Position: forward. Clubs (player): River Plate 1943-49, Huracan 1947 (loan), Millonarios Bogota 1949-53, Barcelona 1953, Real Madrid 1953-64, Espanyol 1964-66. Honours: Colombian League Championship 1951, 1952 (with Millonarios); Spanish League Championship 1954, 1955, 1957, 1958 (with Real Madrid); Spanish Cup 1962 (with Real Madrid); European Cup 1956, 1957, 1958, 1959, 1960 (with Real Madrid). Club (manager): Valencia. Honours: European Cup Winners' Cup 1980. International caps (for Argentina): 8, 6 goals. International honours: Copa America 1947. International caps (for Colombia): 2. International caps (for Spain): 31, 23 goals. European Player of the Year 1957, 1959. Having been transferred to Millonarios in non-FIFA registered Colombia he was at the centre of a tussle for his services between Barcelona and Real Madrid. Barcelona bought him from River Plate and Real Madrid from Millonarios. The Spanish government ordered him to play a year for each but in the event he moved to Real Madrid before his year with Barcelona was up and scored in each of his European Cup final appearances. He is believed by many to be the greatest-ever all-round player. He was a player with both versatility and stamina. Although generally referred to as a forward he was equally adept playing in midfield or defence.

Dixon, Lee Born Lee Michael Dixon, Manchester, 17 March 1964. Position: defender. Clubs: Burnley 1982-84, Chester City 1984-85, Bury 1985-86, Stoke City 1986-88 (signed for £40,000), Arsenal 1988-2002 (signed for £400,000). Honours: English League Championship/FA Premiership 1989, 1991, 1998, 2002; FA Cup 1993, 1998, 2002; Charity Shield 1998, 1999; European Cup Winners' Cup 1994 (all with Arsenal). International caps (for England): 22, 1 goal.

Docherty, Tommy Born Thomas Henderson Docherty, Glasgow, 24 April 1928. Position: defender. Clubs (player): Shettleston Juniors, Celtic 1948-49, Preston North End 1949-58 (signed for £4,000), Arsenal 1958-61 (signed for £28,000), Chelsea 1961. Clubs (manager): Chelsea 1962-67, Rotherham United 1967-68, Queens Park Rangers

1968 (28 days), 1979-80, Aston Villa 1968-70, Porto 1970-71, Manchester United 1972-77, Derby County 1977-79, Sydney Olympic (Australia), Preston North End 1981, South Melbourne (Australia), Wolverhampton Wanderers 1984-85, Altrincham 1987-88. Honours: FA Cup 1977 (with Manchester United); League Cup 1965 (with Chelsea). International caps (for Scotland): 25, 1 goal. International manager (Scotland): 1971-72. Known as 'The Doc'. The 'Gorbals Gob', Docherty once famously said he'd had 'more clubs than Jack Nicklaus.' He was sacked from his post at Manchester United just weeks after their 1977 FA Cup win because of his affair with the club physiotherapist's wife. He still writes a typically opinionated column for Manchester Online and is an after-dinner speaker.

Doherty, Peter Born Peter Dermont Doherty, Magherafelt, Northern Ireland, 5 June 1913. Position: forward. Clubs (player): Coleraine 1930-32, Glentoran 1932-33, Blackpool 1933-36 (signed for £1900), Manchester City 1936-45 (signed for £10,000), Derby County 1946 (signed for £6000), Huddersfield Town 1946-49 (signed for £10,000), Doncaster Rovers 1949-54 (signed for £8000). Honours: League Championship 1937 (with Manchester City); FA Cup 1946 (with Derby County); Northern Irish Cup 1932 (with Glentoran); Charity Shield 1937 (with Manchester City). Clubs (manager): Doncaster Rovers 1949-58, Bristol City 1958-60. International caps (for Northern Ireland): 16, 3 goals. International manager (Northern Ireland): 1957-61. Left three of the clubs he played for because of disputes with the management. Doherty took Northern Ireland to the quarter-finals of the 1958 World Cup. He died 6 April 1990 in Poulton-le-Fylde, Lancashire.

Donaghy, Mal Born Malachy Martin Donaghy, Larne, Co. Antrim, Northern Ireland, 13 September 1957. Position: defender. Clubs: Post Office SC, Cromac Albion, Larne Town 1978, Luton Town 1978-87, 1989-90 (loan), Manchester United 1988-92 (signed for £650,000), Chelsea 1992-94. International caps (for Northern Ireland): 91.

Dorigo, Tony Born Adelaide, Australia, 31 December 1965. Position: defender. Clubs: Aston Villa 1983-87, Chelsea 1987-91 (signed for £475,000), Leeds United 1991-97 (signed for £1.3m), Torino 1997-98, Derby County 1998-2000, Stoke City 2000-01. Honours: League Championship 1992 (with Leeds United). International caps (for England): 15.

Dougan, Derek Born Derek Alexander Dougan, Belfast, 20 January 1938. Position: forward. Clubs (player): Distillery, Portsmouth 1957-59, Blackburn Rovers 1959-61, Aston Villa 1961-63 (signed for £15,000), Peterborough 1963-65, Leicester City 1965-67, Wolverhampton Wanderers 1967-75 (signed for £50,000). Honours: League Cup 1974 (with Wolverhampton Wanderers). Club (manager): Kettering Town. International caps (for Northern Ireland): 43, 8 goals. Chairman of the Professional Footballers' Association 1970-78. Chairman of Wolverhampton Wanderers 1982. He is author of a novel *The Footballer*, a history of professional players titled *On the Spot* and *How Not to Run Football*. Dougan famously put in a transfer request on the eve of the 1960 FA Cup final, which Blackburn lost.

Douglas, Bryan Born Blackburn, Lancashire, 27 May 1934. Position: forward. Clubs: Blackburn Rovers 1952-68, Great Harwood. International caps (for England): 36, 11 goals.

Downie, John Born Lanark, Scotland, 9 July 1925. Position: forward. Clubs: Lanark ATC, Bradford Park Avenue 1942-49, Manchester United 1949-53 (signed for £18,000), Luton Town 1953-54, Hull City 1954-58, Mansfield Town 1958-59, Darlington 1959-60, Hyde United 1960-61, Mossley 1961, Stalybridge Celtic 1961-62. Honours: League Championship 1952 (with Manchester United). On retirement he became a newsagent in Bradford.

Drake, Ted Born Edward Joseph Drake, Southampton, 16 August 1912. Position: forward. Clubs (player): Southampton Gasworks, Winchester City, Southampton 1931-34, Arsenal 1934-45 (signed for £6,000). Honours: League Championship 1935, 1938; FA Cup 1936; Charity Shield 1935, 1938 (all with Arsenal). Clubs (manager): Hendon 1946, Reading 1947-52, Chelsea 1952-61, Barcelona 1970 (assistant). Honours: League Championship 1955 (with Chelsea). International caps (for England): 5, 6 goals. Scorer of the winner in the 'Battle of Highbury' against Italy in 1935, Drake also scored all seven goals (from just eight or nine attempts) against Aston Villa in the same year (the Villa players signed the matchball for him too) and the winning goal in the 1936 FA Cup final. He retired in 1945 with a back injury. He also played first-class cricket for Hampshire 1931-36. He died 30 May 1995.

Dublin, Dion Born Leicester, 22 April 1969. Position: forward/defender. Clubs: Oakham United, Norwich City 1988, Cambridge United 1988-92, Manchester United 1992-94 (signed for £1m), Coventry City 1994-98 (signed for £2m), Aston Villa 1998-present (signed for £5.75m), Millwall 2002 (loan). International caps (for England): 4. Dublin made a remarkable recovery from breaking his neck in a match against Sheffield Wednesday in December 1999, playing with a metal plate in his neck only four months later.

Ducat, Andy Born Brixton, London, 16 February 1886. Position: defender. Clubs (player): Southend Athletic, Woolwich Arsenal 1905-12, Aston Villa 1912-21, Fulham 1921-22, Casuals. Honours: FA Cup 1920 (with Aston Villa). Clubs (manager): Fulham 1924-26. International caps (for England): 6, 1 goal. One of only 12 men to play for England at both football and cricket, he represented Surrey CCC 1906-31 and played one Test Match against Australia in 1921. He was Wisden Cricketer of the Year 1920. Having become a sports journalist, he died 23 July 1942 at Lord's Cricket Ground, St John's Wood, London, after suffering a heart attack while batting for the Home Guard against Surrey and Sussex.

Dunga Born Carlos Caetano Bledorn Verri, in Ijui, Brazil, 31 October 1963. Position: midfield. Clubs: Internacional 1978-84, 1999, Corinthians 1984-85, Santos 1986, Vasco da Gama 1987, Pisa 1987-88, Fiorentina 1988-92, Pescara 1992-93, VfB Stuttgart 1993-94, Jubilo Iwata (Japan) 1994-98. Honours: Brazilian Rio Championship 1983 (with Internacional); Brazilian Paulista Championship 1984 (with Corinthians); Japanese League Championship 1997 (with Jubilo Iwata). International caps (for Brazil): 94. International honours: Copa America 1989, 1997; World Cup 1994. Only three of his games for Brazil were lost. Now acting as technical advisor at Jubilo Iwata.

Dunphy, Eamon Born Dublin, 3 August 1945. Position: midfield. Clubs: Manchester United 1962, York City 1965-66, Millwall 1966-73 (signed for £8000), Charlton Athletic 1973-75 (signed for £20,000), Reading 1975-76. International caps (for Republic of Ireland): 23. Now working as a writer,

F
O
O
T
B
A
L
L

journalist and broadcaster, in 1976 he wrote what some consider to be the best account of a footballer's life in *Only a Game*, which covered his time at Millwall. He later wrote a biography of the group U2 called *Unforgettable Fire*. Also responsible for a biography of Sir Matt Busby, he was the ghostwriter for Roy Keane's autobiography *Keane*.

Durban, Alan Born Port Talbot, Wales, 7 July 1941. Position: forward/midfield. Clubs (player): Cardiff City 1958-63, Derby County 1963-73 (signed for £10,000), Shrewsbury Town 1973-77. Honours: League Championship 1972 (with Derby County). Clubs (manager): Shrewsbury Town 1974-78, Stoke City 1978-81, 1998, Sunderland 1981-84, Cardiff City 1984-86. International caps (for Wales): 27, 2 goals.

Duxbury, Michael Born Accrington, Lancashire, 1 September 1959. Position: defender. Clubs: Manchester United 1976-90, Blackburn Rovers 1990-92, Bradford City 1992-94 (loan then signed), Hong Kong 1994-96. Honours: FA Cup 1983, 1985 (with Manchester United). International caps (for England): 10. Became a PE teacher on retiring from the game.

Dyer, Kieron Born Kieron Courtney Dyer, Ipswich, Suffolk, 29 December 1978. Position: midfield. Clubs: Ipswich Town 1996-99, Newcastle United 1999-present (signed for £6.5m). International caps (for England): 18.

Djazic, Dragan Born Yugoslavia, 30 May 1946. Position: forward. Clubs (player): Red Star Belgrade 1961-75, 1977-78, Bastia 1975-77. Honours: Yugoslav League Championship 1964, 1968, 1969, 1970, 1973; Yugoslav Cup 1964, 1968, 1970, 1971; Yugoslav League Cup 1973 (all with Red Star Belgrade). Club (technical director): Red Star Belgrade 1981-98. Honours: European Cup 1991 (with Red Star Belgrade). International caps (for Yugoslavia): 85, 23 goals. Holds the record number of caps for Yugolsavia. President of Red Star Belgrade since 1998.

Eastham, George jnr Born George Edward Eastham, Blackpool, 23 September 1936. Position: midfield. Clubs (player): Ards 1953-56, Newcastle United 1956-60, Arsenal 1960-66 (signed for £47,500), Stoke City 1966-72 (signed for £35,000), Cape Town Spurs 1971 (loan), Cape Town Hellenic. Honours: League Cup 1972 (with Stoke City). Clubs (manager): Cape Town Hellenic, Stoke City 1977-78. International caps (for England): 19, 2 goals. His transfer to Arsenal was the subject of an historic court case the outcome of which was that Newcastle were guilty of restraint of trade in not allowing Eastham to leave the club. Thus players gained the right to negotiate their own contracts. His father George also played for England (one of only three fathers/sons to do so, the others being the Cloughs and the Lampards). Awarded the OBE in 1975. Eastham now lives in South Africa.

Eastham, George snr Born George Richard Eastham, Blackpool, 13 September 1913. Position: midfield. Clubs (player): Bolton Wanderers 1932-37, Brentford 1937-38 (signed for £4000), Blackpool 1938-45 (signed for £5000), Wigan Athletic 1945-46, Swansea Town 1947-48, Rochdale 1948, Lincoln City 1948-50, Hyde United 1950-53, Ards 1953-55. Clubs (manager): Ards 1953-58, 1964-70, Accrington Stanley 1958-59, Distillery 1959-64, Cape Town Hellenic 1971, Glentoran 1972-74. Honours: Northern Ireland Championship 1958 (with Ards), 1963 (with Distillery); Northern Ireland Cup 1973 (with Glentoran). International caps (for

England): 1. Signed Tom Finney to play one game fo Distillery. Having retired to South Africa, he died in 2000.

Edwards, Duncan Born Dudley, Birmingham, 1 October 1936. Position: midfield. Club: Manchester United 1952-58. Honours: League Championship 1956, 1957. International caps (for England): 18, 5 goals. At the time the youngest player both in the First Division at 16 years and 185 days (4 April 195 v Cardiff City), and for England at 18 years and 183 days (April 1955 v Scotland). He died 21 February 1958 following severe injuries sustained in the Munich air disaster. Bobby Charlton is quoted as describing Edwards as 'the only player who ever made me feel inferior'.

Edwards, Willis Born Newton, Derbyshire, 28 April 1903. Position: defender. Clubs (player): Chesterfiel 1919-25, Leeds United 1925-43 (signed for £1500). Club (manager): Leeds United 1947-48. Internation caps (for England): 16 (5 as captain). He died October 1988, Leeds.

Effenberg, Stefan Born Hamburg, Germany, 2 August 1968. Position: midfield. Clubs: Borussia Mönchengladbach 1986-90, 1994-98, Bayern Munich 1990-92, 1998-2002, Fiorentina 1992-94, VfL Wolfsburg 2002-03, Al-Arahbi (Qatar) 2003-present. Honours: German League Championship 1999, 2000, 2001 (with Bayern Munich); German Cup 1995 (with Borussia Mönchengladbach), 2000 (with Bayern Munich); German League Cup 1999, 2000 (with Bayern Munich); UEFA Champions League 2001 (with Bayern Munich). International caps (for Germany): 35. Known for his strong views on many subjects both inside and outside football which have led to him being suspended and droppe on several occasions, he was sent home from the 1994 World Cup finals for insulting the German fans

Elkjaer, Preben Born Preben Elkjaer-Larsen, Copenhagen, 11 September 1957. Position: forward Clubs: KB Kobenhavn 1976-76, Vanlesse 1977-78, FC Cologne 1976-78, KSK Lorkeren 1978-84, Hella Verona 1984-88, Veille BK 1988-90. Honours: German League Championship (with FC Cologne); German Cup 1977, 1978 (with FC Cologne); Italian League Championship 1985 (with Hellas Verona). International caps (for Denmark): 69, 38 goals. Known as 'Buffalo'. Now owns Danish team B93 Kobenhavn.

England, Mike Born Michael England, Prestatyn, Wales, 2 December 1941. Position: defender. Clubs: Blackburn Rovers 1959-66, Tottenham Hotspur 1966-75 (signed for £95,000), Cardiff City 1975, Seattle Sounders 1975-80. Honours: FA Cup 1967 (for Tottenham Hotspur). International caps (for Wales): 44, 4 goals. International manager (Wales): 1980-88. Awarded the MBE in 1986. Now runs nursing homes in North Wales.

Eusebio Born Eusebio da Silva Ferreira, Lourenço Marques, Mozambique, 25 January 1942. Position: forward. Clubs: Sporting Club of Lourenço Marques 1958-61, Benfica 1961-75, Boston Minutemen 1975 Toronto Metros 1976, Las Vegas Quicksilver 1976. Honours: Portuguese League Championship 1961, 1963, 1964, 1965, 1967, 1968, 1969, 1971, 1972, 1973; Portuguese Cup 1962, 1964, 1969, 1970, 1972; European Cup 1962 (all with Benfica). International caps (for Portugal): 64, 41 goals. Golden Boot winner World Cup 1966. European Player of the Year 1965. European Golden Boot winner 1968, 1973. Known as 'The Black Panther'. On the coaching staff of Benfica since 1977, he is the ambassador for Euro 2004. A film of his life called *His Majesty the King* was released in 1992 and a statue of him stands outside the Estadio da Luz in Lisbon.

Evans, Bobby Born Glasgow, 16 July 1927. Position: defender. Clubs (player): Celtic 1944-60, Chelsea 1960-61 (signed for £12,000), Newport County, Morton, Third Lanark, Raith Rovers. Honours: Scottish League Championship 1954; Scottish Cup 1951, 1954; Scottish League Cup 1957, 1958 (all with Celtic). Clubs (manager): Newport County, Morton, Third Lanark, Raith Rovers. International caps (for Scotland): 48. Known as 'Mr Perpetual Motion'. He is remembered for his captain's role in the 7-1 defeat of Rangers in the Scottish League Cup final of 1957. He died 1 September 2001.

Facchetti, Giacinto Born Treviglio, Italy, 18 July 1942. Position: defender. Club: Inter Milan 1960-78. Honours: Italian League Championship 1963, 1965, 1966, 1971; Italian Cup 1978, European Cup 1964, 1965. International caps (for Italy): 94 (70 as captain), 3 goals. International honours: European Championship 1968.

Falcao Born Paulo Roberto Falcao, Xanxere, Brazil, 16 October 1953. Position: midfield. Clubs: Internacional Porto Alegre 1973-80, Roma 1980-85, São Paulo 1985-86. Honours: Brazilian National Championship 1975, 1976, 1979 (with Internacional Porto Alegre), Italian Championship 1983 (with Roma); Italian Cup 1981, 1984 (with Roma), Brazilian Paulista Championship 1985 (with São Paulo). International caps (for Brazil): 38, 9 goals. International manager (Brazil): 1990-91. Known as 'The Divine One' and 'The Eighth King of Rome'. Now works in the media.

Fenwick, Terry Born Terence William Fenwick, Seaham, Co. Durham, 17 November 1959. Position: defender. Clubs (player): Crystal Palace 1976-80, Queens Park Rangers 1980-87, Tottenham Hotspur 1987-90, Leicester City 1990-91, Swindon Town 1993-95. Clubs (manager): Portsmouth 1995-98, Crystal Palace (assistant), CL Financial San Juan Jabloteh (Trinidad & Tobago) 2001-02, Northampton Town 2003 (49 days). Honours: Trinidad & Tobago League Championship 2002 (with CL Financial San Juan Jabloteh). International caps (for England): 20.

Ferdinand, Les Born Acton, London, 18 December 1966. Position: forward. Clubs: Queens Park Rangers 1987-95, Hayes 1987-88 (loan), 1988-89 (loan), Brentford 1988 (loan), Newcastle United 1995-97 (signed for £6m), Tottenham Hotspur 1997-2003 (signed for £6m), West Ham United 2003, Leicester City 2003-04, Bolton Wanderers 2004-present. Honours: Turkish Cup 1989 (with Besiktas); League Cup 1999 (with Tottenham Hotspur). International caps (for England): 17, 5 goals. PFA Player of the Year 1996.

Ferdinand, Rio Born Rio Gavin Ferdinand, Peckham, London, 7 November 1978. Position: defender. Clubs: West Ham United 1995-2000, AFC Bournemouth 1996-97 (loan), Leeds United 2000-02 (signed for £18m), Manchester United 2002-present (signed for £30m). Honours: FA Premiership 2003 (with Manchester United). International caps (for England): 33, 1 goal. Twice signed for a then world record fee for a defender. Suspended in 2004 for failing to take a drugs test.

Ferguson, Alex Born Alexander Chapman Ferguson, Govan, Glasgow, 31 December 1941. Position: forward. Clubs (player): Queen's Park 1957-60, St Johnstone 1960-64, Dunfermline 1964-67, Rangers 1967-69 (signed for £65,000), Falkirk 1969-73 (signed for £20,000), Ayr United 1973-74, East Stirlingshire 1974. Clubs (manager): East Stirlingshire 1974, St Mirren 1974-77, Aberdeen 1977-86, Manchester United 1986-present. Honours: Scottish League Championship 1980, 1984, 1985 (with Aberdeen); Scottish Cup 1982, 1983, 1984, 1986 (with Aberdeen); Scottish League Cup 1986 (with Aberdeen); League Championship/FA Premiership 1993, 1994, 1996, 1997, 1999, 2000, 2001, 2003 (with Manchester United); FA Cup 1990, 1994, 1996, 1999 (with Manchester United); League Cup 1992 (with Manchester United); European Cup Winners' Cup 1983 (with Aberdeen), 1991 (with Manchester United); UEFA Champions League 1999 (with Manchester United). International manager (Scotland): 1986 (caretaker). Awarded the OBE in 1985, the CBE in 1995 and knighted in 1999. Autobiography *Managing my Life*. Co-owner of record-breaking racehorse Rock of Gibraltar.

Ferguson, Barry Born Glasgow, 2 February 1978. Position: forward. Clubs: Rangers 1994-2003, Blackburn Rovers 2003-present (signed for £7.5m). Honours: Scottish League Championship 1999, 2000, 2003; Scottish Cup 1999, 2000, 2002, 2003; Scottish League Cup 1998, 2001, 2003 (all with Rangers). International caps (for Scotland): 18, 2 goals.

Ferrari, Giovanni Born Alessandria, Italy, 6 December 1907. Position: forward. Clubs: Alessandria 1923-25, 1926-30, Internaples 1925-26, Juventus 1930-35, 1941-42, Ambrosiana (Inter Milan) 1935-40, Bologna 1940-41. Honours: Italian League Championship 1931, 1932, 1933, 1934, 1935 (with Juventus), 1938, 1940 (with Ambrosiana), 1941 (with Bologna); Italian Cup 1942 (with Juventus). International caps (for Italy): 44, 14 goals. International honours: World Cup 1934, 1938. International manager (Italy): 1962. Holds the record number of Italian Championship medals (along with Guiseppe Furino). He died 1982.

Figo, Luis Born Lisbon, Portugal, 4 November 1972. Position: midfield/forward. Clubs: Sporting Lisbon 1989-95, Barcelona 1995-2000 (signed for £4.2m), Real Madrid 2000-present (signed for £37m). Honours: Portuguese Cup 1995 (with Sporting Lisbon); Spanish League Championship 1998, 1999 (with Barcelona), 2001, 2003 (with Real Madrid); Spanish Cup 1997, 1998 (with Barcelona); European Cup Winners' Cup 1997 (with Barcelona); UEFA Champions League 2002 (with Real Madrid). International caps (for Portugal): 96, 28 goals. European Player of the Year 2000. World Player of the Year 2001. Married to Swedish fashion model Helen Swedin.

Figueroa, Elias Born Elias Figueroa Brander, Valparaiso, Chile, 25 October 1946. Position: defender. Clubs (player): Peñarol 1967-72, Internacional Porto Alegre 1972-77, Palestino (Santiago), 1977-81, Fort Lauderdale Strikers 1981-82, Colo Colo (Santiago) 1982-83. Honours: Uruguayan League Championship 1967, 1968 (with Peñarol), Brazilian National Championship 1975, 1976 (with Internacional Porto Alegre); Chilean League Championship 1978 (with Palestino). Club (manager): Internacional Porto Alegre 1996. International caps (for Chile): 47, 2 goals. Chilean Player of the Year 1965. Uruguayan Player of the Year 1967, 1968, 1969. South American Player of the Year 1974, 1975, 1976. Brazilian Player of the

Year 1976. Voted Chilean Player of the Century. Known as 'Don Elias'.

Fillol, Ubaldo Born Ubaldo Matildo Fillol, San Miguel del Monte, Argentina, 21 July 1950. Position: goalkeeper. Clubs: Quilmes 1969-71, Racing Club 1972-73, 1987-89, River Plate 1973-83, Argentinos Juniors 1983, Flamengo 1983-85, Atlético Madrid 1985-86, Velez Sarsfield 1989-90. Honours: Argentinian Metropolitan League Championship 1975, 1977, 1979, 1980; Argentinian National League Championship 1975, 1979, 1981 (all with River Plate). International caps (for Argentina): 58. International honours: World Cup 1978. Argentinian Player of the Year 1977. Known as 'El Pato' ('The Duck').

Finney, Tom Born Preston, Lancashire, 5 April 1922. Position: forward. Clubs: Preston North End 1941-60, Distillery 1963 (one game). International caps (for England): 76, 30 goals. Football Writers' Player of the Year 1954, 1957 (first to get the award twice). Finney worked as a plumber throughout his career. Injury forced him to switch from winger to centre-forward in 1956. Never having been booked, he retired in 1960 but played one last game for George Eastham snr's Distillery team in a home European Cup match against Benfica which ended 3-3. Awarded the OBE in 1961, the CBE in 1992 and knighted in 1998.

Fleming, Harold Born Harold John Fleming, Downton, nr Salisbury, Wiltshire, 30 April 1887. Position: forward. Clubs: St Marks, Swindon Town 1907-24. International caps (for England): 11. Possibly the last man to be capped by England playing non-League football, he would have had more caps but for World War I. A devoutly religious man, he refused to play at Easter or Christmas. A main street in Swindon is named in his honour. He died 23 August 1955.

Flowers, Ron Born Edlington, nr Doncaster, South Yorkshire, 28 July 1934. Position: defender. Clubs (player): Doncaster Rovers, Wolverhampton Wanderers 1952-66, Northampton Town 1967-68, Telford United. Honours: League Championship 1954, 1958, 1959; FA Cup 1960 (all with Wolverhampton Wanderers). Clubs (manager): Northampton Town 1967-68, Wellington Town/Telford United 1969-71. International caps (for England): 49 (3 as captain), 10 goals.

Flowers, Tim Born Timothy David Flowers, Kenilworth, 3 February 1967. Position: goalkeeper. Clubs: Wolverhampton Wanderers 1984-86, Southampton 1986-93 (signed for £70,000), Swindon Town 1987 (loan – two spells), Blackburn Rovers 1993-99 (signed for £2.4m), Leicester City 1999-2003 (signed for £1.1m), Stockport County 2001 (loan), Coventry City 2002 (loan), Manchester City 2002 (loan). Honours: FA Premiership 1995 (with Blackburn Rovers); League Cup 2000 (with Leicester City). International caps (for England): 11.

Flynn, Brian Born Port Talbot, Wales, 12 October 1955. Position: midfield. Clubs (player): Burnley 1972-77, Leeds United 1977-82 (signed for £175,000), Burnley 1982-84 (loan, then signed for £60,000), Cardiff City 1984-85 (signed for £15,000), Doncaster Rovers 1985-86, 1987-88, Bury 1986-87, Limerick 1988, Wrexham 1988-93. Clubs (manager): Wrexham 1989-2001, Swansea City 2002-present. Honours: FAW Premier Cup 1998, 2000 (with Wrexham). International caps (for Wales): 66.

Fontaine, Just Born Marrakesh, Morocco, 1933. Position: forward. Clubs (player): Marocaine Casablanca 1950-53, Nice 1953-56, Reims 1956-62. Honours: French League Championship 1956 (with Nice), 1958, 1960, 1962 (with Reims); French Cup 1954 (with Nice), 1958 (with Reims). Clubs (manager): Paris St-Germain 1973-76. International caps (for France): 21, 30 goals. Golden Boot winner, World Cup 1958 (13 goals). International manager (France): 1967 (two games); (Morocco). Retired from playing in 1962 after breaking his leg in two places and again only five games after his recovery from the earlier injury, having scored 200 goals in 213 games. At one time he was president of the French Footballers' Union.

Ford, Trevor Born Swansea, 1 October 1923. Position: forward. Clubs: Swansea Town 1945-47, Aston Villa 1947-50 (signed for £9500), Sunderland 1950-54 (signed for £29,500), Cardiff City 1954-57 (signed for £29,500), PSV Eindhoven 1957-60, Newport County 1960, Romford. International caps (for Wales): 38, 23 goals. Having been suspended from playing in England following suggestions of illegal payments to players made in his autobiography, he spent three years in Holland with PSV Eindhoven. Retiring from the game in 1961, he went into the car trade. He died 29 May 2003 in Swansea.

Forrest, James Born James Henry Forrest, Blackburn, Lancashire, 1862. Clubs: Blackburn Rovers, Darwen 1895-96. Honours: FA Cup 1884, 1885, 1886, 1890, 1891 (all with Blackburn Rovers). International caps (for England): 11 (1 as captain). The first professional footballer to play for England, and one of only three players to win five FA Cup winners' medals (along with Lord Kinnaird and Charles Wollaston). Retiring in 1896, he became a publican and was later a director of Blackburn Rovers. He died 1925.

Foulke, Billy Born William Henry Foulk(e), Old Park, Dawley, Shropshire, 12 April 1874. Position: goalkeeper. Clubs: Sheffield United 1894-1904, Chelsea 1904-07, Bradford City 1907. Honours: League Championship 1898; FA Cup 1899, 1902 (all with Sheffield United). International caps (for England): 1. Known as 'Tiny', 'Two Ton' and 'Fatty', he is allegedly both the heaviest (at 22st (140kg)) and tallest (at 6ft 6ins (1.98m)) man to have played for England. He may also be the heaviest man to have played first-class cricket, representing Derbyshire in 1900, taking two wickets and scoring one 50. A character of massive proportions, he was known for arguing with fans, opponents (he supposedly held strikers up by their ankles and bounced them in the mud), referees and equipment (breaking crossbars by swinging on them when bored). One of his enormous jerseys can be seen at the Sheffield United 'Hall of Fame'. Returning to Sheffield on his retirement to run a pub near Bramall Lane, he died of pneumonia in the city on 1 May 1916. Reportedly the illness was contracted while he earned a living challenging members of the public to score penalties against him on Blackpool beach.

Foulkes, Bill Born William Anthony Foulkes, St Helens, Lancashire, 5 January 1932. Position: defender. Club (player): Manchester United 1952-70. Honours: League Championship 1956, 1957, 1965, 1967; FA Cup 1963; European Cup 1968. Clubs (manager): Manchester United 1970-75 (coach), Chicago Sting 1975-77 (coach), Tulsa Roughnecks 1978 (coach), Witney Town 1979-80, San Jose Earthquakes 1980 (coach), Stenjker (Norway), Lillestrom (Norway), Viking Stavanger (Norway), Mazda Hiroshima. International caps (for England): 1. He played 61 consecutive FA Cup matches for

Manchester United 1954-67, and played in a League match only two weeks after the Munich air disaster.

owler, Robbie Born Robert Bernard Fowler, Toxteth, Liverpool, 9 April 1975. Position: forward. Clubs: Liverpool 1992-2001, Leeds United 2001-03 (signed for £11m), Manchester City 2003-present (signed for £6m). Honours: League Cup 1995 (with Liverpool). International caps (for England): 26, 7 goals. PFA Young Player of the Year 1995 and 1996.

rancescoli, Enzo Born Enzo Francescoli Uriarte, Montevideo, Uruguay, 12 November 1961. Position: forward. Clubs: Wanderers 1980-82, River Plate 1983-86, 1994-97, Racing Club de Paris 1986-89, Olympique Marseille 1989-90, Cagliari 1990-93, Torino 1993-94. Honours: French League Championship 1989 (with Olympique Marseille); Argentinian League Championship 1994 (Apertura), 1995 (Apertura), 1997 (Apertura and Clausura) (with River Plate); French Cup (with Olympique Marseille); Copa Libertadores 1996 (with River Plate). International caps (for Uruguay): 72, 15 goals. International honours: Copa America 1983, 1987, 1995. Known as 'El Principe' (The Prince). Argentinian Player of the Year 1985, 1995. South American Player of the Year 1985.

rancis, Gerry Born Gerald Charles James Francis, Hammersmith, London, 6 December 1951. Position: midfield. Clubs (player): Queens Park Rangers 1969-79, 1981-82 (signed for £15,000), Crystal Palace 1979-81 (signed for £465,000), Coventry City 1982-83 (signed for £165,000), Exeter City 1983-84, Cardiff City 1984, Swansea 1984, Portsmouth 1985, Bristol Rovers 1987-88. Clubs (manager): Exeter City 1983-84, Wimbledon (assistant coach) 1986, Bristol Rovers 1987-91, Queens Park Rangers 1991-94, Tottenham Hotspur 1994-97, Bristol Rovers 2001. International caps (for England): 12 (8 as captain), 3 goals.

rancis, Trevor Born Trevor John Francis, Plymouth, Devon, 19 April 1954. Position: forward. Clubs (player): Birmingham City 1971-78, Detroit Express 1978, 1979, Nottingham Forest 1979-81 (signed for £1m), Manchester City 1981-82 (signed for £1m), Sampdoria 1982-86 (signed for £700,000), Atalanta 1986-87, Rangers 1987-88 (signed for £75,000), Queens Park Rangers 1988-90, Sheffield Wednesday 1990-94 . Honours: League Cup 1980 (with Nottingham Forest), Italian Cup 1985 (with Sampdoria); Scottish League Cup 1988 (with Rangers); European Cup 1979, 1980 (with Nottingham Forest). Clubs (manager): Queens Park Rangers 1988-90, Sheffield Wednesday 1991-95, Birmingham City 1996-2001, Crystal Palace 2001-03. International caps (for England): 52, 12 goals. Britain's first £1m footballer.

ranklin, Neil Born Cornelius Franklin, Stoke-on-Trent, 24 January 1922. Position: defender. Clubs (player): Stoke City 1945-60, Santa Fe Bogota 1960, Hull City, Crewe Alexandra, Stockport County. Club (manager): Colchester United 1963-68. International caps (for England): 27. He flew to Bogota in 1960 with a promise of high wages only to find that Colombia was not to his liking, after which he was banned by the FA until January 1961. He died 9 February 1996.

riedenreich, Artur Born São Paulo, Brazil, 1892. Position: forward. Clubs: Germania 1911, Mackenzie 1912, Ypiranga 1913-18, Paulistano 1918-29, São Paulo 1930-35, Flamengo 1935. Honours: Brazilian Paulista Championship 1918, 1919, 1921, 1926, 1927, 1929 (with Paulistano), 1931 (with São Paulo).

International caps (for Brazil): 22, 10 goals. Honours: Copa America 1919 (Brazil's first national honour). Known as 'The Tiger', he reportedly scored 1239 goals in competitive competition, the most by any player. He died 1969.

Froggatt, Jack Born Sheffield, 17 November 1922. Position: forward/defender. Clubs (player): Portsmouth 1946-53, Leicester City 1954-57, Kettering Town 1960-61. Honours: League Championship 1949, 1950 (with Portsmouth). Club (manager): Kettering Town 1960-61. International caps (for England): 13, 2 goals. Known as 'Jolly Jack'. His second cousin Redfern Froggatt also played for England (4 caps, 2 goals). Together with Stan Milburn, he is credited with the only joint own goal, while playing for Leicester City against Chelsea in 1955. Retired from the game to become a hotelier. He died February 1993.

Futre, Paulo Born Paulo Jorge dos Santos Futre, Montijo, Portugal, 28 February 1966. Position: forward. Clubs: Sporting Lisbon 1983-84, Porto 1984-87, Atlético Madrid 1987-93, 1997-98, Benfica 1993, Olympique Marseille 1993-94, Reggiana 1994-95, AC Milan 1995-96, West Ham United 1996, Yokohama Flugels 1998-99. Honours: Portuguese League Championship 1985, 1986 (with Porto); Portuguese Cup 1984, 1986 (with Porto); Spanish Cup 1991, 1992 (with Atlético Madrid); Italian League Championship 1996 (with AC Milan); European Cup 1987 (with Porto). International caps (for Portugal): 41, 6 goals. Portuguese Footballer of the Year 1986, 1987. Sporting director of Atlético Madrid 2000-03.

Gallacher, Hughie Born Hugh Kilpatrick Gallacher, Bellshill, North Lanarkshire, Scotland, 2 February 1903. Position: forward. Clubs: Airdrieonians 1921-25, Newcastle United 1925-30 (signed for £6500), Chelsea 1930-34 (signed for £10,000), Derby County 1934-36 (signed for £2750), Notts County 1936-38, Grimsby Town 1938, Gateshead 1938-39. Honours: League Championship 1927 (with Newcastle United); Scottish Cup 1924 (with Airdrieonians). International caps (for Scotland): 20, 22 goals. One of the 1928 'Wembley Wizards', he scored five times for Scotland against Northern Ireland in 1929. Scored 387 goals in 543 League games, including 133 in 160 games for Newcastle United. Derby County paid off his debts as part of the transfer deal with Chelsea. He suffered from alcohol problems, and committed suicide 11 June 1957 in Low Fell, Tyne & Wear, by throwing himself under a train.

Garrincha Born Manoel Francisco dos Santos, Pau Grande, Brazil, 28 October 1933. Position: forward. Clubs: Pau Grande 1948-52, Botafogo 1953-64, Corinthians São Paulo 1965-68, Atlético Junior Barranquilla 1968, Flamengo 1969, Bangu, Red Star Paris 1971-72, Olaria 1972. Honours: Brazilian League Championship 1957, 1961, 1962 (with Botafogo). International caps (for Brazil): 54, 34 goals. International honours: World Cup 1958, 1962. Known as 'Little Bird'. Born with deformed legs, his left leg was distorted even after surgery. A car crash in 1965 severely affected his form. He died 20 January 1983 in Rio de Janeiro as the result of alcohol poisoning.

Gascoigne, Paul Born Paul John Gascoigne, Gateshead, Tyne & Wear, 27 May 1967. Position: midfield. Clubs: Newcastle United 1985-88, Tottenham Hotspur 1988-92 (signed for £2m), Lazio 1992-95 (signed for £5.5m), Rangers 1995-98 (signed for £4.3m), Middlesbrough 1998-2000 (signed for £3.45m), Everton 2000-02, Burnley 2002,

Gansu Tianma (China) 2002-03. Honours: FA Cup 1991 (with Tottenham Hotspur); Scottish League Championship 1996, 1997 (with Rangers); Scottish Cup 1996 (with Rangers); Scottish League Cup 1997 (with Rangers). International caps (for England): 57, 10 goals. Known as 'Gazza'. A brilliant midfielder who was let down by a temperament which endeared and infuriated in equal measure.

Gemmill, Archie   Born Paisley, Scotland, 24 March 1947. Clubs (player): St Mirren 1963-67, Preston North End 1967-70 (signed for £13,000), Derby County 1970-77 (signed for £66,000), Nottingham Forest 1977-79, Birmingham City 1979-81, Jacksonville 1981, Wigan Athletic 1982, Derby County 1982-84. Club (manager): Rotherham United 1994-96. International caps (for Scotland): 43, 8 goals. The first official substitute in Scottish football (13 August 1966, St Mirren v Clyde), he became a legend in Scotland following his brilliant solo goal against Holland in the 1978 World Cup finals. The goal was recreated in a dance choreographed by Andy Howitt of 200 schoolchildren at Hampden Park in 2001. Gemmill now works as a scout for Derby County and the Scottish Football Association. His son Scot Gemmill also plays professionally (Nottingham Forest, Everton).

Gento, Francisco   Born Francisco Gento Lopez, Guarnizo, Santander, Spain, 21 October 1933. Position: forward. Clubs (player): Rayo Cantabria, Real Santander 1951-53, Real Madrid 1953-71. Honours: Spanish League Championship 1954, 1955, 1957, 1958, 1961, 1962, 1963, 1964, 1965, 1967, 1968, 1969; Spanish Cup 1962, 1970; European Cup 1956, 1957, 1958, 1959, 1960, 1966 (all with Real Madrid). Clubs (manager): Castille, Castellon, Palencia, Granada. International caps (for Spain): 43, 5 goals. Gento, who played in eight European Cup finals, reportedly once ran 100m in 10.9secs with the ball at his feet!

Germano   Born Germano de Figueiredo, Lisbon, Portugal, 18 January 1933. Position: defender. Clubs: Atlético Club de Portugal, Benfica. Honours: Portuguese League Championship 1961, 1963, 1964, 1965; Portuguese Cup 1962, 1964; European Cup 1961, 1962 (all with Benfica). International caps (for Portugal): 23.

George, Charlie   Born Frederick Charles George, Islington, London, 10 October 1950. Position: forward. Clubs: Arsenal 1968-75, Derby County 1975-78 (signed for £90,000), Southampton 1978-80, Nottingham Forest 1980-82, Bulova (Hong Kong), Dundee United, AFC Bournemouth 1982, Derby County 1982. Honours: League Championship 1971; FA Cup 1971; Inter-cities Fairs Cup 1970 (all with Arsenal). International caps (for England): 1. He scored the winning goal in the 1971 FA Cup final. Became a publican before working at Highbury in the museum and as matchday host.

Gerrard, Steven   Born Whiston, Liverpool, 30 May 1980. Position: midfield. Club: Liverpool 1998-present. Honours: FA Cup 2001; League Cup 2001, 2003; UEFA Cup 2001. International caps (for England): 20, 3 goals.

Gerson   Born Gerson de Oliveira Nunes, Niteroi, Brazil, 11 January 1941. Position: midfield. Clubs: Flamengo 1955-63, Botafogo 1963-69, São Paulo 1969-72, Fluminense 1972-74. Honours: Brazilian League Championship 1967, 1968 (with Botafogo). International caps (for Brazil): 98, 28 goals. International honours: World Cup 1970. Forced to retire in 1974 because of an ankle injury.

Giggs, Ryan   Born Ryan Joseph Wilson, Cardiff, 29 November 1973. Position: midfield. Club: Manchester United 1990-present. Honours: FA Premiership 1993, 1994, 1996, 1997, 1999, 2000, 2001, 2003; FA Cup 1994, 1996, 1999, 2004; League Cup 1992; Charity/Community Shield 1996, 1997, 2003; UEFA Champions League 1999. International caps (for Wales): 40, 8 goals. PFA Young Player of the Year 1992, 1993. In 1991 became youngest-ever Welsh international, having captained England Schoolboys. He changed his surname from Wilson to Giggs (his mother's maiden name) when his parents separated. His father, Danny Wilson, played rugby for Wales. Giggs published his autobiography in 1994, aged 21.

Giles, Johnny   Born Michael John Giles, Cabra, Dublin, 6 January 1940. Position: midfield. Clubs (player): Home Farm, Manchester United 1957-63, Leeds United 1963-74 (signed for £33,000), West Bromwich Albion 1975-77, Shamrock Rovers 1977-78, Philadelphia Fury 1978-80, Vancouver Whitecaps 1980. Honours: League Championship 1969, 1974 (with Leeds United); FA Cup 1963 (with Manchester United), 1972 (with Leeds United); League Cup 1968 (with Leeds United); Inter-cities Fairs Cup 1968, 1971 (with Leeds United). Clubs (manager): West Bromwich Albion 1975-77, 1984-85, Shamrock Rovers 1977-78, Vancouver Whitecaps. Honours: Irish Cup 1978 (with Shamrock Rovers). International caps (for Republic of Ireland): 59. International manager (Republic of Ireland): 1973-80. Now works as a journalist.

Gillespie, Billy   Born Ballintrae, Co. Derry, Ireland, 6 August 1892. Position: midfield. Clubs (player): Leeds City, Sheffield United. Honours: FA Cup 1925 (with Sheffield United). Club (manager): Derry City. International caps (for Ireland): 25. He played with a silver plate in his leg following an injury in 1914, which had kept him out of Sheffield United's 1915 FA Cup-winning team. In 1925 he captained United to another FA cup win. Derry City now play in red and white stripes in honour of Gillespie and Sheffield United. He died 2 July 1981 in Bexley, London.

Gilmar   Born Gilmar Neves dos Santos, São Paulo, Brazil, 22 August 1930. Position: goalkeeper. Clubs: Jabaquara 1950-51, Corinthians 1951-61, Santos 1961-70. Honours: Brazilian São Paulo League Championship 1951, 1952, 1954 (with Corinthians), 1962, 1964, 1965, 1967, 1968, 1969 (with Santos); Rio-São Paulo Tournament 1953, 1954 (with Corinthians), 1963, 1964, 1966 (with Santos); South American Cup 1962, 1963 (with Santos); World Club Championship 1962, 1963 (with Santos). International caps (for Brazil): 96. International honours: World Cup 1958, 1962.

Ginola, David   Born Gassin, France, 25 January 1967. Position: forward. Clubs: Nice 1983-84, Toulon 1984-88, Racing Club Paris 1988-90, Brest Armorique 1990-91, Paris St-Germain 1991-95, Newcastle United 1995-97 (signed for £2.5m), Tottenham Hotspur 1997-2000 (signed for £2m), Aston Villa 2000-02 (signed for £3m), Everton 2002. Honours: French Cup 1993, 1995 (with Paris St-Germain); French League Cup 1995 (with Paris St-Germain); League Cup 1999 (with Tottenham Hotspur). International caps (for France): 17, 3 goals. French Player of the Year 1994. PFA Player of the Year 1999. Football Writers' Player of the Year 1999. International spokesperson for the Red Cross Anti-Landmine Campaign.

Giresse, Alain   Born Langoiran, France, 2 August 1952. Position: midfield. Clubs (player): Bordeaux

1970-86, Olympique Marseille 1988-90. Honours: French League Championship 1984, 1985; French Cup 1986 (all with Bordeaux). Clubs (manager): Toulouse 1993-97 (sporting director 1993-95), Paris St-Germain 1998, Toulouse 1998-2000, FAR Rabat 2001-03. International caps (for France): 47, 6 goals. International honours: European Championship 1984. International manager (Georgia): 2004-present. French Player of the Year 1982, 1983, 1987. His son Thibault plays for Toulouse.

Givens, Don Born Daniel Joseph Givens, Limerick, Ireland, 9 August 1949. Position: forward. Clubs (player): Dublin Rangers, Manchester United 1965-70, Luton Town 1970-72, Queens Park Rangers 1972-78, Birmingham City 1978-81, AFC Bournemouth 1980 (loan), Sheffield United 1981, Xamax Neuchatel (Switzerland) 1981-87. Clubs (manager/coach): Xamax Neuchatel 1993-97, Arsenal 1997-2000 (youth team coach). International caps (for Republic of Ireland): 56, 19 goals. International manager (Republic of Ireland): 2000-present (U-21), 2002-03 (caretaker, one game).

Goater, Shaun Born Leonardo Shaun Goater, Hamilton, Bermuda, 25 February 1970. Position: forward. Clubs: Manchester United 1989, Rotherham United 1989-96, Notts County 1993 (loan), Bristol City 1996-98 (signed for £175,000), Manchester City 1998-2003 (signed for £400,000), Reading 2003-present (signed for £500,000). International caps (for Bermuda): 32, 26 goals. A prolific scorer for Manchester City, he inspired the cry 'Feed the goat and he will score' (sung to 'Cwm Rhondda'). Has the freedom of Hamilton, and 21 June each year is designated 'Leonardo Shaun Goater Day' in Bermuda. He has organised the 'Shaun Goater Grassroots Football Festival'. Awarded an MBE in 2003.

Goodall, Archie Born Ireland, 1865. Position: defender. Clubs: Preston North End, Aston Villa, Derby County 1889-1903. Born in Ireland but raised in Kilmarnock, Scotland, by his stepfather. He stood outside the ground trying to sell tickets before the 1898 FA Cup final. He once refused to play extra time because his contract ended after 90 minutes. After finishing his playing career he toured Europe and America with a strongman act. He was the younger brother of John Goodall, with whom he played at Preston North End and Derby County.

Goodall, John Born Westminster, London, 19 June 1863. Position: forward. Clubs (player): Kilmarnock Burns, Kilmarnock Athletic, Great Lever, Preston North End 1885-89, Derby County 1889-99, New Brighton Tower 1900-01, Glossop 1901-03. Honours: League Championship 1889 (with Preston North End); FA Cup 1889 (with Preston North End). Clubs (manager): Watford 1903-10. International caps (for England): 14 (2 as captain), 12 goals. Born in England, like his brother he was brought up in Kilmarnock, Scotland, by his stepfather. Known as 'Johnny All-Good', he played in the 'Invincible' Preston North End double-winning side. He also played cricket as wicket-keeper for Derbyshire 1895-96. He died 20 May 1942 in Watford, Hertfordshire.

Goram, Andy Born Andrew Lewis Goram, Bury, Lancashire, 13 April 1964. Position: goalkeeper. Clubs: West Bromwich Albion 1980-81, Oldham Athletic 1981-87, 2002, Hibernian 1987-91, Rangers 1991-98 (signed for £1m), Notts County 1998, Sheffield United 1998, Motherwell 1999-2001, Manchester United 2001 (loan), Coventry City 2001-02, Queen of the South 2002-03. Honours: Scottish League Championship 1992, 1993, 1994, 1995,

1996, 1997; Scottish Cup 1992, 1993, 1996; Scottish League Cup 1993, 1994, 1997 (all with Rangers). International caps (for Scotland): 43. Having kept 107 clean sheets in 258 games for Rangers, he was voted the club's greatest-ever goalkeeper in 1999. He also represented Scotland at cricket. His father Lew played 111 League games for Bury.

Gough, Richard Born Charles Richard Gough, Stockholm, Sweden, 5 April 1962. Position: defender. Clubs: Dundee United 1980-86, Tottenham Hotspur 1986-87, Rangers 1987-96, 1997-98, Kansas City Wizz 1996-97, San Jose Clash 1998-99, 2001-present (player/coach), Nottingham Forest 1999 (loan), Everton 1999-2001. Honours: Scottish League Championship 1983 (with Dundee United), 1989, 1990, 1991, 1992, 1993, 1994, 1995, 1996, 1997 (with Rangers); Scottish Cup 1992, 1993, 1996 (with Rangers); Scottish League Cup 1987, 1988, 1989, 1991, 1993, 1994 (with Rangers). International caps (for Scotland): 61, 6 goals. Scottish Player of the Year 1989. Nicknamed 'The Old Man of Hoy' and 'Captain Blood'. His father, Charles, played for Charlton Athletic.

Graham, George Born Bargeddie, North Lanarkshire, 30 November 1944. Position: midfield/forward. Clubs (player): Aston Villa 1959-64, Chelsea 1964-66, Arsenal 1966-72, Manchester United 1972-74, Portsmouth 1974-76, Crystal Palace 1976-80, California Surf 1978 (loan). Honours: League Championship 1971; FA Cup 1971; Inter-cities Fairs Cup 1970 (all with Arsenal). Clubs (manager): Queens Park Rangers 1980-82 (coach), Millwall 1982-86, Arsenal 1986-95, Leeds United 1996-98, Tottenham Hotspur 1998-2001. Honours: League Championship 1989, 1991; FA Cup 1993; League Cup 1993; European Cup Winners' Cup 1994 (all with Arsenal). International caps (for Scotland): 12, 3 goals. Nicknamed 'Stroller'. Graham was banned from the game for one year in 1995 following financial misconduct.

Gray, Andy Born Andrew Mullen Gray, Glasgow, 30 November 1955. Position: forward. Clubs: Clydebank Strollers 1970-73, Dundee United 1973-75, Aston Villa 1975-77 (signed for £110,000), 1985-87 (signed for £150,000), Wolverhampton Wanderers 1979-83 (signed for £1.47m), Everton 1983-85 (signed for £250,000), Notts County 1987 (loan), West Bromwich Albion, Rangers 1988-89, Cheltenham Town 1989. Honours: League Championship 1985 (with Everton); FA Cup 1984 (with Everton); League Cup 1977 (with Aston Villa), 1980 (with Wolverhampton Wanderers); Scottish Premiership 1989 (with Rangers); Scottish League Cup 1989 (with Rangers); European Cup Winners' Cup 1985 (with Everton). International caps (for Scotland): 20, 7 goals. PFA Player of the Year 1977. Now works as a TV commentator and analyst.

Gray, Eddie Born Holyrood, 17 January 1948. Position: forward. Club (player): Leeds United 1965-84. Honours: League Championship 1969, 1974; FA Cup 1972; League Cup 1968; Inter-cities Fairs Cup 1968, 1971. Clubs (manager): Leeds United 1982-85, Rochdale 1986-88, Hull City 1988-89, Leeds United 1995-2003 (youth team/reserve team coach/assistant manager 1998-2003). International caps (for Scotland): 12, 3 goals. He also worked for BBC Radio Leeds as sports editor. Autobiography *Marching on Together*.

Greaves, Jimmy Born James Peter Greaves, Poplar, London, 20 February 1940. Position: forward. Clubs: Chelsea 1957-60, AC Milan 1961 (signed for

£80,000 stayed four months), Tottenham Hotspur 1961-70 (signed for £99,999), West Ham United 1970-71 (signed for £54,000 and exchange with Martin Peters), Barnet, Chelmsford City, Brentwood Town and Woodford Town. Honours: FA Cup 1962, 1967; European Cup Winners' Cup 1963 (all with Tottenham Hotspur). International caps (for England): 57, 44 goals. Greaves scored on his debut for each of his clubs, for England and for England Under-23, The first player to score 100 goals in League football before the age of 21, he holds the Tottenham Hotspur season scoring record 37 (1962). He missed out on the latter stages of the 1966 World Cup finals after being injured against France and was replaced by in-form Geoff Hurst. He later presented *Saint and Greavsie* with Ian St John. He admitted alcohol problems later in life and his autobiography, *Greavsie*, was published in 2003.

Greenhoff, Jimmy   Born Barnsley, South Yorkshire, 19 June 1946. Position: forward. Clubs (player): Leeds United 1961-68, Birmingham City 1968-69, Stoke City 1969-76, Manchester United 1976-80 (signed for £120,000), Crewe Alexandra 1980-81, Toronto Blizzard 1981, Port Vale 1981-83, Rochdale 1983-84. Honours: FA Cup 1977 (with Manchester United). Clubs (manager): Toronto Blizzard 1981 (coach), Rochdale 1983-84. Younger brother Brian played alongside him in the 1977 FA Cup final.

Gregg, Harry   Born Henry Gregg, Magherafelt, Co. Derry, Northern Ireland, 25 October 1932. Position: goalkeeper. Clubs (player): Linfield Rangers, Linfield Swifts, Coleraine, Doncaster Rovers 1952-57, Manchester United 1957-66 (signed for £23,500), Stoke City 1966 (two games). Clubs (manager/coach): Shrewsbury Town 1968-72, Swansea City 1972-75, 1982 (coach), Crewe Alexandra 1975-78, Kitan Sports Club (Kuwait) 1978, Manchester United 1978-81 (coaching staff), Swindon Town 1984-85 (assistant manager), Carlisle United 1986-87. International caps (for Northern Ireland): 32. After surviving the Munich air disaster he refused to fly to an international in Madrid and never played for Northern Ireland again. Awarded the MBE in 1995.

Greig, John   Born Edinburgh, 11 September 1942. Position: defender/midfield. Club (player): Rangers 1960-78. Honours: Scottish League Championship 1963, 1964, 1975, 1976, 1978; Scottish Cup 1963, 1964, 1966, 1973, 1976, 1978; Scottish League Cup 1964, 1965, 1976, 1978; European Cup Winners' Cup 1972. Club (manager): Rangers 1978-83. Honours: Scottish Cup 1979, 1981; Scottish League Cup 1979, 1982. International caps (for Scotland): 44, 3 goals. Awarded the MBE in 1977. He holds the record for most League appearances for Rangers (496) and made the second-highest number of appearances in all competitions (857). Won the Scottish 'treble' three times (1964, 1976, 1978). Voted the greatest-ever Rangers player in 1999, he now works in public relations for the club.

Gren, Gunnar   Born Gothenburg, Sweden, 31 October 1920. Position: forward. Clubs: IFK Gothenburg, AC Milan 1949-53, Fiorentina 1953-55, Genoa 1955-56, GAIS Gothenburg 1956-59. Honours: Italian League Championship 1951 (with AC Milan). International caps (for Sweden): 57, 32 goals. International honours: Olympic gold medal 1948. Formed the 'Gre-No-Li' attacking combination at AC Milan with fellow Swedes Gunnar Nordahl and Niels Lindholm. Known as 'The Professor'. He died 1 November 1991.

Grimsdell, Arthur   Born Watford, Hertfordshire, 23 March 1894. Position: defender. Clubs: St Albans City 1910-11, Watford 1911-15, Tottenham Hotspur 1915-29, Clapton Orient 1929-30. Honours: FA Cup 1921 (with Tottenham Hotspur). International caps (for England): 6 (3 as captain). His brother Ernest was an England amateur international. Grimsdell became a director of Watford, and also played as wicket-keeper for Hertfordshire CCC. He died 12 March 1963 in Watford.

Grobbelaar, Bruce   Born Durban, South Africa, 6 October 1957. Position: goalkeeper. Clubs (player): Vancouver Whitecaps 1979-81, Crewe Alexandra 1979 (loan), Liverpool 1981-94 (signed for £250,000), Stoke City 1993 (loan), Southampton 1994-96, Plymouth Argyle 1996-97, Oxford United 1997, Sheffield Wednesday 1997, Oldham Athletic 1997-98, Chesham United 1998, Bury 1998, Lincoln City 1998, Northwich Victoria 1998. Honours: League Championship 1982, 1983, 1984, 1986, 1988, 1990; FA Cup 1986, 1989, 1992; League Cup 1982, 1983, 1984; Charity Shield 1982, 1986, 1988, 1989, 1990; European Cup 1984 (all with Liverpool). Club (manager): Seven Stars (South Africa) 1999. International caps (for Zimbabwe): 9. International manager (Zimbabwe): 1997 (acting manager). Known for his madcap antics on the field – including going 'all weak at the knees' facing a penalty in the 1984 European Cup final shoot-out – he unfortunately became embroiled in a long investigation into match-fixing alongside Wimbledon's Hans Segers and John Fashanu.

Gronkjaer, Jesper   Born Nuuk, Denmark, 12 August 1977. Position: forward. Clubs: Aalborg 1995-98, Ajax 1998-2000, Chelsea 2000-present (signed for £7.8m). International caps (for Denmark): 35, 2 goals.

Gudjohnsen, Eidur   Born Reykjavik, Iceland, 15 September 1978. Position: forward. Clubs: Valur Reykjavik 1994-95, PSV Eindhoven 1995-97, KR Reykjavik 1997-98, Bolton Wanderers 1998-2000, Chelsea 2000-present. International caps (for Iceland): 19, 4 goals.

Gullit, Ruud   Born Amsterdam, Holland, 1 September 1962. Position: midfield. Clubs (player): Haarlem 1978-82, Feyenoord 1982-85, PSV Eindhoven 1935-87 (signed for £400,000), AC Milan 1987-93 (signed for £5.5m), 1994, Sampdoria 1993-94, 1994-95, Chelsea 1995-97. Honours: Dutch League Championship 1986, 1987 (with PSV Eindhoven); Dutch Cup 1984 (with Feyenoord); Italian League Championship 1988, 1992, 1993 (with AC Milan); Italian Cup 1994 (with Sampdoria); European Cup 1989, 1990 (with AC Milan); World Club Championship 1990 (with AC Milan). Clubs (manager): Chelsea 1996-98, Newcastle United 1998-99. Honours: FA Cup 1997 (with Chelsea). International caps (for Holland): 66, 16 goals. International Honours: European Championship 1988. Dutch Player of the Year 1986, 1987. European Player of the Year 1987. World Player of the Year 1987, 1989. Gullit was the first non-British manager (and the youngest) to win the FA Cup.

Hagi, Gheorghe   Born Sacele, Romania, 5 February 1965. Position: midfield. Clubs: Farul Constanta 1979-80, 1982-83, Luceafarul Bucharest 1980-82, Sportul Bucharest 1983-86, Steaua Bucharest 1986-89, Real Madrid 1990-92, Brescia 1992-94, Barcelona 1994-96, Galatasaray 1996-2001. Honours: Romanian League Championship 1987, 1988, 1989 (with Steaua Bucharest); Romanian Cup 1987, 1988, 1989 (with Steaua Bucharest); Turkish

League Championship 1997, 1998, 1999, 2000 (with Galatasaray); Turkish Cup 1999, 2000 (with Galatasaray); Anglo-Italian Cup 1994 (with Brescia). International caps (for Romania): 125, 35 goals. Known as 'The Maradona of the Carpathians'. Romanian Player of the Year 1985, 1987, 1993, 1994, 1997, 1999, 2000. Voted Romanian Player of the Century.

Hall, Willie   Born George William Hall, Newark, Nottinghamshire, 12 March 1912. Position: forward. Clubs (player): Notts County, Tottenham Hotspur 1932-39. Clubs (manager): Clapton Orient, Chingford. International caps (for England): 10, 9 goals. Having retired through injury in 1944, he had both legs amputated due to acute thrombosis. Scored three goals in three and a half minutes in the match between England and Ireland in 1938, going on to score five in the game. He died 22 May 1967 in Newark.

Halse, Harold   Born Harold James Halse, Stratford, London, 1 January 1886. Position: forward. Clubs: Newportians, Wanstead, Barking Town, Clapton Orient 1905-06, Southend United 1906-07, Manchester United 1907-12, Aston Villa 1912-13, Chelsea 1913-21, Charlton Athletic 1921-23. Honours: League Championship 1908, 1911 (with Manchester United); FA Cup 1909 (with Manchester United), 1913 (with Aston Villa); Charity Shield 1911 (with Manchester United). International caps (for England): 1, 2 goals. Scored six goals in the 1911 Charity Shield match. Halse acted as scout for Manchester United 1923-25. He died 25 March 1949 in Colchester.

Hamilton, Bryan   Born Belfast, 31 December 1946. Position: midfield. Clubs (player): Linfield, Ipswich Town 1971-75, Everton 1975-77, Millwall 1977-78, Swindon Town 1978-80, Tranmere Rovers 1980-83. Clubs (manager): Tranmere Rovers 1980-85, Wigan Athletic 1985-86, 1989, Leicester City 1986-87, Ipswich Town 1990 (coach), 2001-02 (coach), Norwich City 2000 (technical director/manager), Pittsburgh Riverhounds 2002-present (assistant coach). International caps (for Northern Ireland): 50. International manager (Northern Ireland): 1994-98. Hamilton served on the committee to find a replacement for Mick McCarthy as manager of the Republic of Ireland in 2002.

Hamm, Mia   Born Mariel Margaret Hamm, Selma, Alabama, 17 March 1972. Position: forward. Clubs: University of North Carolina 1989-93, Washington Freedom 2001-present. Honours: NCAA Championship 1989, 1990, 1992, 1993 (with University of North Carolina). International caps (for USA): 221, 140 goals. International honours: Olympic gold medal 1996; World Cup 1991, 1999. Youngest player to play for the USA, aged 15. Nicknamed 'Jordan' after Michael Jordan. US Soccer Female Athlete of the Year 1994, 1995, 1996, 1997, 1998. In 1999 Nike named the largest building on its corporate campus in Beaverton, Oregon, after her. She formed the Mia Hamm Foundation to benefit bone marrow research and is author of *Go for the Goal: A Champion's Guide to Winning in Soccer and Life*. FIFA Women's World Player of the Year 2001, 2002. World's leading scorer (male or female) in international competition.

Hampson, Jimmy   Born Little Hulton, Manchester, 1906. Position: forward. Clubs: Nelson, Blackpool 1927-38 (signed for £2,000). International caps (for England): 3, 5 goals. Record scorer in a season for Blackpool (45 in 1929/30 season). He died 10

January 1938 in a fishing accident in Morecambe Bay, when the boat he was on was in collision with a Fleetwood trawler. His body was never recovered.

Hampton, Harry   Born Harry Joseph Hampton, Wellington, Shropshire, 21 April 1885. Position: forward. Clubs (player): Wellington Town 1903, 1924-25, Aston Villa 1904-20, Birmingham City 1920-22, Newport County 1922-24. Honours: League Championship 1910; FA Cup 1905, 1913 (all with Aston Villa). Club (manager): Preston North End 1925-26. International caps (for England): 4, 2 goals. He died March 1963 in Wrexham.

Hamrin, Kurt   Born Stockholm, Sweden, 14 November 1934. Position: forward. Clubs: AIK Stockholm 1952-56, Juventus 1956-57, Padova 1957-58 (loan), Fiorentina 1958-67, AC Milan 1967-69, Napoli 1969-71. Honours: Italian League Championship 1968 (with AC Milan); Italian Cup 1961, 1966 (with Fiorentina); European Cup Winners' Cup 1961 (with Fiorentina), 1968 (with AC Milan); European Cup 1969 (with AC Milan). International caps (for Sweden): 32, 16 goals. Known in Italy as 'L'Uccellino' (little bird). Even though a winger, he scored 150 goals for Fiorentina, bettered only by Gabriel Batistuta in 2000. His record of 190 goals in Serie A was equalled by Roberto Baggio in February 2003 and he now lies sixth in the list of all-time scorers. Lives in Florence.

Hanappi, Gerhard   Born Vienna, Austria, 9 July 1929. Position: defender/midfield/forward. Clubs: Wacker Vienna 1946-50, SK Rapid Vienna 1950-65. Honours: Austrian League Championship 1947 (with Wacker Vienna); 1951, 1952, 1954, 1956, 1957, 1960, 1964 (with Rapid Vienna); Austrian Cup 1961 (with Rapid Vienna). International caps (for Austria): 93,12 goals. Capped in every position except goalkeeper and left-wing. Austrian Footballer of the Year eight times. Hanappi became an architect and designed the West-Stadion in Vienna. He died 23 August 1980 in Vienna, after which the West-Stadion was renamed the 'Gerhard Hanappi Stadium'.

Hancocks, Johnny   Born Jonathon Hancocks, Oakengates, Shropshire, 30 April 1919. Position: midfield/forward. Clubs (player): Oakengates Town, Walsall 1938-46, Wolverhampton Wanderers 1946-56 (signed for £4000), Wellington Town 1957-59, Cambridge United 1960, Oswestry Town 1960, GKN Sankey's 1960-61. Honours: League Championship 1954; FA Cup 1949 (both with Wolverhampton Wanderers). Clubs (manager): Wellington Town 1957-59. International caps (for England): 3, 2 goals. Known as 'The Mighty Atom' because he stood only 5ft 4ins (1.63m) and wore a size 2 boot but could produce thunderous shots. As well as a prodigious goalscorer he was an exceptional crosser of the ball. Fellow Wolves player Jessie Pye once joked that he had missed a goal because the ball had arrived with the laces facing him but that after complaining to Hancocks it had never happened again. Hancocks retired from playing in 1961 and worked in an iron foundry until retiring in 1979. He died 19 February 1994 in Oakengates.

Hansen, Alan   Born Alan David Hansen, New Sauchie, Clackmannan, Scotland, 13 June 1955. Position: defender. Clubs: Partick Thistle 1973-77, Liverpool 1977-90 (signed for £100,000). Honours: League Championship 1979, 1980, 1982, 1983, 1984, 1986, 1988, 1990; FA Cup 1986, 1989; League Cup 1981, 1983, 1984; Charity Shield 1979, 1980, 1982, 1986, 1989. European Cup 1978, 1981, 1984 (all with Liverpool). International caps (for

Scotland): 26. Represented Scotland at Under-18 level in golf, squash and volleyball. Now works as a sports presenter and pundit in TV. His elder brother John was also a Scottish international.

Hapgood, Eddie Born Edris Albert Hapgood, Bristol, 24 September 1908. Position: defender. Clubs (player): Kettering Town, Arsenal 1927-44. Honours: League Championship 1931, 1933, 1934, 1935, 1938; FA Cup 1930, 1936 (all with Arsenal). Clubs (manager): Blackburn Rovers 1944-47, Watford 1948-50, Bath City. International caps (for England): 30 (21 as captain). Also worked as a tennis coach. He died 20 April 1973 in Leamington Spa, Warwickshire.

Hardwick, George Born George Francis Moutret Hardwick, Saltburn, Cleveland, 2 February 1920. Position: defender. Clubs (player): South Bank, Middlesbrough 1937-50 (signed for £15,000), Oldham Athletic 1950-55 (signed for £15,000). Clubs (manager): Oldham Athletic 1950-55, PSV Eindhoven, Sunderland 1964-65. International caps (for England): 13 (13 as captain). International manager (Holland): 1957. Known as 'Gentleman George'.

Hardy, Sam Born Newbold, Chesterfield, 26 August 1883. Position: goalkeeper. Clubs: Newbold White Star 1901-03, Chesterfield 1903-05, Liverpool 1905-12 (signed for £500), Aston Villa 1912-21 (signed for £650), Nottingham Forest 1921-25. Honours: League Championship 1906 (with Liverpool); FA Cup 1913, 1920 (with Aston Villa). International caps (for England): 21. Nicknamed 'Safe and Steady Sam'. Retiring in 1925, he became a hotelier in Chesterfield. He died 24 October 1966 in Chesterfield.

Hargreaves, Owen Born Owen Lee Hargreaves, Calgary, Canada, 20 January 1981. Position: midfield. Club: Bayern Munich 1997-present. Honours: German League Championship 2001, 2003; German Cup 2003; European Cup 2001. International caps (for England): 15. Chose to play for England (his father is English) even though he has a Welsh mother, was born and raised in Canada and has a residential qualification to play for Germany.

Harris, Ron Born Hackney, London, 13 November 1944. Position: defender. Clubs (player): Chelsea 1961-79, Brentford 1980-83. Honours: FA Cup 1970; League Cup 1965; European Cup Winners' Cup 1971 (all with Chelsea). Club (manager): Aldershot 1984-85. International manager (Jersey): 2002-03. Known as 'Chopper' because of his hard-tackling style. He captained England's youth team to a World Cup win in 1962.

Hartford, Asa Born Richard Asa Hartford, Clydebank, Scotland, 24 October 1950. Position: midfield. Clubs (player): West Bromwich Albion 1967-74, Manchester City 1974-79 (signed for £250,000), 1981-84 (signed for £350,000), Nottingham Forest 1979 (signed for £500,000 – three games), Everton 1979-81 (signed for £400,000), Fort Lauderdale Strikers 1984-85, Norwich City 1984-85, Bolton Wanderers 1985-86, Stockport County 1987-89. Honours: League Cup 1976 (with Manchester City), 1985 (with Norwich City). Clubs (manager): Stockport County 1987-89, Shrewsbury Town 1990-91, Boston United 1991, Blackburn Rovers 1991-93 (reserve team coach), Stoke City 1993-95 (assistant manager), Manchester City 1995-present (assistant manager/coach – caretaker 1996). International caps (for Scotland): 50, 4 goals. A transfer from West

Bromwich Albion to Leeds United in 1971 was cancelled when it was discovered he had a hole in the heart.

Hateley, Mark Born Mark W. Hateley, Wallasey, Liverpool, 7 November 1961. Position: forward. Clubs (player): Coventry City 1978-83, Portsmouth 1983-84 (signed for £180,000), AC Milan 1984-87 (signed for £915,000), Monaco 1987-90 (signed for £2m), Rangers 1990-96 (signed for £500,000), 1997 (signed for £300,000), Queens Park Rangers 1995-97 (signed for £1.5m), Leeds United 1996 (loan), Hull City 1997-98, Ross County 1999. Honours: French League Championship 1988 (with Monaco); Scottish League Championship 1990, 1991, 1992, 1993, 1994, 1997; Scottish Cup 1993; Scottish League Cup 1991, 1993, 1994 (all with Rangers). International caps (for England): 32, 9 goals. Scored 115 goals in 222 games for Glasgow Rangers. First Englishman to be voted Scottish Football Writers' Player of the Year (1994). Son of Tony Hateley.

Hateley, Tony Born Anthony Hateley, Derby, 13 April 1941. Position: forward. Clubs: Notts County 1958-63, 1970-72, Aston Villa 1963-66, Chelsea 1966-67 (signed for £100,000), Liverpool 1967-68 (signed for £96,000), Coventry City 1968-69 (signed for £80,000), Birmingham City 1969-70, Oldham Athletic 1972-73, Bromsgrove Rovers 1974, Prescot Town 1976-77. Father of Mark Hateley.

Hatton, Bob Born Hull, 10 April 1947. Position: forward. Clubs: Wolverhampton Wanderers 1964-67, Bolton Wanderers 1967-68, Northampton Town 1968-69, Carlisle United 1969-71 (signed for £8000), Birmingham City 1971-76 (signed for £82,500), Blackpool 1976-78 (signed for £60,000), Luton Town 1978-80, Sheffield United 1980-82, Cardiff City 1982. Scored 217 goals in 602 League games.

Haynes, Johnny Born John Norman Haynes, Kentish Town, London, 17 October 1934. Position: forward. Clubs: Fulham 1952-69, Durban City 1970. International caps (for England): 56 (22 as captain), 18 goals. The first £100-a-week player in Britain, he represented England at all five international levels (schoolboy, youth, Under-23, 'B' and senior). Haynes missed the 1962 season as the result of a serious car crash. He now lives in South Africa.

Hector, Kevin Born Leeds, 2 November 1944. Position: forward. Clubs: Bradford Park Avenue 1962-66, Derby County 1966-77 (signed for £40,000), 1980-81, Vancouver Whitecaps, Boston United, Burton Albion, Belper Town 1984-85. Honours: League Championship 1972, 1975 (with Derby County). International caps (for England): 2. Derby's second-highest goalscorer (201 in 589 games) behind Steve Bloomer. Known as 'King Kev' to Derby fans. Reportedly he is now a postman in Derby.

Henry, Thierry Born Paris, 17 August 1977. Position: forward. Clubs: Monaco 1995-99, Juventus 1999, Arsenal 1999-present (signed for £10.5m). Honours: French League Championship 1997 (with Monaco); FA Premiership 2002, 2004 (with Arsenal); FA Cup 2002, 2003 (with Arsenal). International caps (for France): 49, 20 goals. International honours: World Cup 1998; European Championship 2000. Football Writers' Player of the Year 2003. PFA Player of the Year 2003.

Herd, David Born David George Herd, Hamilton, Scotland, 15 April 1934. Position: forward. Clubs (player): Stockport County 1950-54, Arsenal 1954-61 (signed for £8000), Manchester United 1961-68 (signed for £35,000), Stoke City 1968-70, Waterford 1970-71. Honours: League Championship 1965,

1967; FA Cup 1963 (all with Manchester United). Club (manager): Lincoln City 1971-72. International caps (for Scotland): 5, 3 goals. Having played alongside his father Alec at Stockport County, Herd scored twice in the 1963 FA Cup final. He missed the1968 European Cup final through injury but was awarded a medal (along with Denis Law). He also played cricket for Cheadle Hulme.

Heskey, Emile Born Emile William Ivanhoe Heskey, Leicester, 11 January 1978. Position: forward. Clubs: Leicester City 1994-2000, Liverpool 2000-present (signed for £11m). Honours: FA Cup 2001 (with Liverpool); League Cup 1997, 2000 (with Leicester City), 2001 (with Liverpool); Community Shield 2001 (with Liverpool); UEFA Cup 2001 (with Liverpool). International caps (for England): 35, 5 goals.

Hibbitt, Kenny Born Bradford, Yorkshire, 3 January 1951. Position: midfield. Clubs (player): Bradford Park Avenue 1968, Wolverhampton Wanderers 1968-84 (signed for £5000), Coventry City 1984-86, Bristol Rovers 1986-88. Honours: League Cup 1974, 1980 (with Wolverhampton Wanderers). Clubs (manager): Bristol Rovers 1988-90 (assistant), Walsall 1990-94, Cardiff City 1996, 1998, Hednesford Town 2001-present.

Hibbs, Harry Born Henry Edward Hibbs, Wilnecote, Staffordshire, 27 May 1906. Position: goalkeeper. Club (player): Birmingham City 1924-40. Club (manager): Walsall 1944-51. International caps (for England): 25. Kept 10 clean sheets. Made up for being only 5ft 9ins (1.75m) by supreme agility and positioning skills. He died 23 April 1984 in Hatfield, Hertfordshire.

Hidegkuti, Nandor Born Budapest, Hungary, 3 March 1922. Position: forward. Clubs (player): Gazm Vek 1940-43, Elektromos 1943-45, Herminamezei 1945-47, MTK Budapest 1947-58. Honours: Hungarian League Championship 1951, 1953, 1958 (with MTK Budapest). Clubs (manager): BTK Budapest 1959-60, Fiorentina 1960-62, Mantova 1962-63, Györi ETO 1963-65, Tatabanya 1966, MTK Budapest 1967-68, Spartacus 1968-71, Stal Rzeszow 1972, Egri Dozsa 1973, Al Ahly (Egypt) 1973-80, Al Ahly (Dubai) 1983-85, Ittihad (Egypt) 1997. Honours: Hungarian League Championship 1963 (with Györi ETO); Hungarian Cup 1952 (with MTK Budapest); Egyptian League Championship 1975, 1976, 1977, 1979, 1980 (with Al Ahly); Egyptian Cup 1978 (with Al Ahly); European Cup Winners' Cup 1961 (with Fiorentina). International caps (for Hungary): 69, 39 goals. International honours: Olympic gold medal 1952. Hidegkuti scored 222 goals in 302 matches for MTK Budapest. A member of the 'Magical Magyars' of the early 1950s, he scored a hat-trick in Hungary's historic 6-3 win over England at Wembley in 1953. He died 14 February 2002 in Budapest and the MTK Budapest stadium has been renamed in his honour.

Hilditch, Lal Born Clarence George Hilditch, Hartford, Cheshire, 2 June 1894. Position: defender. Clubs (player): Hartford FC, Northwich FC, Witton Albion, Altrincham, Manchester United 1916-32. Club (manager): Manchester United 1926-27. The only player/manager in Manchester United's history. He died 31 October 1977 in Hartford.

Hill, Gordon Born Gordon Alex Hill, Sunbury, 1 April 1954. Position: forward. Clubs (player): Millwall 1973-75, Chicago Sting 1975 (loan), Manchester United 1975-78 (signed for £80,000), Derby County 1978-79, Queens Park Rangers 1979-81, Montreal Manic 1981-82, Chicago Sting 1982, New York Arrows,

Kansas City Comets 1984, Tacoma Stars 1985, Twente Enschede 1985-86, Northwich Victoria 1986-87, Stafford Rangers 1987-88, Radcliffe Borough 1990. Clubs (manager/coach): Northwich Victoria 1986 (caretaker), 1988, Chester City 2001 (director of football/manager), Stenhousemuir 2002 (director of football). International caps (for England): 6 Known as 'Merlin'.

Hoddle, Glenn Born Hayes, London, 27 October 1957. Position: midfield. Clubs (player): Tottenham Hotspur 1975-88, Monaco 1988-91, Swindon Town 1991-93. Honours: FA Cup 1981, 1982 (with Tottenham Hotspur). Clubs (manager): Swindon Town 1991-93, Chelsea 1993-96, Southampton 2000-01, Tottenham Hotspur 2001-03. International caps (for England): 53, 8 goals. International manager (England): 1996-99. PFA Young Footballer of the Year 1980. Reached number 12 in the UK pop charts in 1987 with the song 'Diamond Lights' alongside his team-mate Chris Waddle. Hoddle lost his England managership following comments in a newspaper interview, having written a controversial account of the 1998 World Cup in *My World Cup Story*.

Hollins, John Born Guildford, Surrey, 16 July 1946. Position: midfield. Clubs (player): Chelsea 1963-75, 1983-85, Queens Park Rangers 1975-79, Arsenal 1979-83. Honours: FA Cup 1970; European Cup Winners' Cup 1971 (both with Chelsea). Clubs (manager): Chelsea 1985-88, Queens Park Rangers 1997, Swansea City 1998-2001, Rochdale 2001-02, Stockport County 2003, Stockport Tiger Star (China) 2004-present. International caps (for England): 1. Elder brother Dave also played professional football as a goalkeeper for, among others, Brighton & Hove Albion and Newcastle United. Having been born in Bangor, Dave opted to be a Welsh international, being capped 11 times.

Hopkinson, Eddie Born Royton, Lancashire, 29 October 1935. Position: goalkeeper. Clubs (player): Oldham Athletic 1951-52, Bolton Wanderers 1952-69. Honours: FA Cup 1958 (with Bolton Wanderers). Club (manager): Stockport County 1974 (assistant). International caps (for England): 14. Only 5ft 9ins (1.75m) tall, known as 'Hoppie'. Having made a club record 519 appearances for Bolton Wanderers, he was goalkeeping coach at the club for a short time before retiring from the game.

Houghton, Ray Born Raymond James Houghton, Glasgow, 9 January 1962. Position: midfield. Clubs: West Ham United 1979-82, Fulham 1982-85, Oxford United 1985-87 (signed for £147,000), Liverpool 1987-92 (signed for £800,000), Aston Villa 1992-95 (signed for £825,000), Crystal Palace 1995-97 (signed for £300,000), Reading 1997-99, Stevenage 1999-2000. Honours: League Championship 1988, 1990 (with Liverpool); FA Cup 1989, 1992 (with Liverpool); League Cup 1986 (with Oxford United), 1994 (with Aston Villa). International caps (for Republic of Ireland): 73, 6 goals. Now works in the media.

Hughes, Emlyn Born Emlyn Walter Hughes, Barrow-in-Furness, Cumbria, 28 August 1947. Position: midfield. Clubs (player): Blackpool 1964-67, Liverpool 1967-79 (signed for £65,000), Wolverhampton Wanderers 1979-81, Rotherham United 1981-83, Hull City 1983, Mansfield Town 1983, Swansea City 1983. Honours: League Championship 1973, 1976, 1977, 1979 (with Liverpool); FA Cup 1974 (with Liverpool); League Cup 1980 (with Wolverhampton Wanderers); UEFA Cup 1973, 1976 (with Liverpool); European Cup 1977, 1978 (with Liverpool). Club (manager):

Rotherham United 1981-83. International caps (for England): 62 (23 as captain), 1 goal. Football Writers' Player of the Year 1977. Awarded the OBE in 1980. Nicknamed 'Crazy Horse', he was a popular team captain on the BBC's *A Question of Sport*.

Hughes, Mark   Born Leslie Mark Hughes, Wrexham, Wales, 1 November 1963. Position: forward. Clubs: Manchester United 1978-86, 1988-95 (signed for £1.8m), Barcelona 1986-88 (signed for £2.3m), Bayern Munich 1987-88 (loan), Chelsea 1995-98 (signed for £1.5m), Southampton 1998-2000 (signed for £650,000), Everton 2000, Blackburn Rovers 2000-02. Honours: FA Premiership 1993, 1994 (with Manchester United); FA Cup 1985, 1990, 1994 (with Manchester United), 1997 (with Chelsea); League Cup 1992 (with Manchester United), 1998 (with Chelsea), 2002 (with Blackburn Rovers); Charity Shield 1993, 1994 (with Manchester United); European Cup Winners' Cup 1991 (with Manchester United), 1998 (with Chelsea). International caps (for Wales): 72, 16 goals. International manager (Wales): 1999-present. PFA Player of the Year 1989, 1991. Known as 'Sparky'. The first player to score in four different club matches at Wembley in one season (1994 Charity Shield, League Cup final, FA Cup semi-final and final), he is the only player to win four FA Cup winner's medals.

Hulme, Joe   Born Joseph Harold Anthony Hulme, Stafford, 26 August 1904. Position: forward. Clubs (player): York City, Hull City, Blackburn Rovers 1924-26, Arsenal 1926-38, Huddersfield Town. Honours: League Championship 1931; FA Cup 1930, 1936 (all with Arsenal). Club (manager): Tottenham Hotspur 1945-49. International caps (for England): 9. Having played in five FA Cup finals – 1927, 1930, 1932, 1936 (for Arsenal), 1938 (for Huddersfield Town), he subsequently worked as a sports journalist. He also played first-class cricket for Middlesex CCC 1929-39, scoring over 8000 runs and taking 89 wickets. He died 27 September 1991 in Winchmore Hill, London.

Hunt, Roger   Born Golborne, Manchester, 20 July 1938. Position: forward. Clubs: Stockton Heath, Liverpool 1959-69, Bolton Wanderers 1969-72. Honours: League Championship 1964, 1966; FA Cup 1965 (all with Liverpool). International caps (for England): 34, 18 goals. International honours: World Cup 1966. Scored 245 League goals for Liverpool, a club record. Retired in 1972 and joined the family haulage business.

Hunter, Archie   Born Ayr, 23 September 1859. Position: forward. Clubs: Third Lanark, Ayr Thistle, Aston Villa 1878-91. Honours: FA Cup 1887 (with Aston Villa). International caps (for Scotland): 73, 42 goals. Having suffered a heart attack while playing for Aston Villa against Everton at Anfield on 4 January 1890, he never really recovered and died in 1894. His gravestone reads 'Erected by his football comrades and the club as a lasting tribute to his ability on the field and his sterling worth as a man'.

Hunter, Norman   Born Eighton Banks, Middlesbrough, 29 October 1943. Position: defender. Clubs (player): Leeds United 1961-76, Bristol City 1976-79, Barnsley 1979-83. Honours: League Championship 1969, 1974; FA Cup 1972; League Cup 1968; Inter-cities Fairs Cup 1968, 1971 (all with Leeds United). Clubs (manager): Barnsley 1980-84, Rotherham United 1985-87. International caps (for England): 28. PFA Player of the Year 1974. Given the nickname 'Bites Yer Legs' Hunter because of his uncompromising tackling style.

Hurley, Charlie   Born Cork, Ireland, 4 October 1936. Position; defender. Clubs (player): Millwall 1953-57, Sunderland 1957-69 (signed for £18,000), Bolton Wanderers 1969-70. Club (manager): Reading 1972-77. International caps (for Republic of Ireland): 40, 2 goals. Known as 'Big Charlie' even as a youngster, Hurley was reckoned by many to be the best centre back in Britain in the early 1960s. Voted Sunderland's Player of the Century. The club's training ground is named after him.

Hurst, Geoff   Born Geoffrey Charles Hurst, Ashton-under-Lyne, Lancashire, 8 December 1941. Position: forward. Clubs (player): West Ham United 1959-72, Stoke City 1972-75, West Bromwich Albion 1975, Cork Celtic, Telford United. Honours: FA Cup 1964; European Cup Winners' Cup 1965 (both with West Ham United). Clubs (manager): Cork Celtic, Telford United, Chelsea. International caps (for England): 49, 24 goals. International honours: World Cup 1966. Played first-class cricket for Essex CCC in 1962 (one match). He is the only player to score a hat-trick in a World Cup final.

Hutchinson, Ian   Born Derby, 4 August 1948. Position: forward. Clubs: Burton Albion 1966, Cambridge United 1966-68 (signed for £2000), Chelsea 1968-76 (signed for £5000). Honours: FA Cup 1970; European Cup Winners' Cup 1971 (both with Chelsea). Famous for his long throws, one of which set up the winning goal in the 1970 FA Cup final. Out of action for two seasons through a series of injuries, including a broken arm and a broken leg, he was forced to retire in 1976. He died 19 September 2002 after a long illness.

Hutchison, Tommy   Born Cardenden, Scotland, 22 September 1947. Position: forward. Clubs (player): Alloa Athletic, Blackpool 1968-72, Coventry City 1972-80, Manchester City 1980-82, Bulova (Hong Kong) 1982-83, Burnley, Swansea City. Club (manager): Swansea City 1985-86. International caps (for Scotland): 17, 1 goal. Known as 'Hutch'. He notably scored for both sides in the 1981 FA Cup final against Tottenham Hotspur. Retired from playing in 1991 and is now working as Football in the Community Officer for Bristol City.

Ince, Paul   Born Paul Emerson Carlyle Ince, Ilford, Essex, 21 October 1967. Position: midfield. Clubs: West Ham United 1985-89, Manchester United 1989-95 (signed for £2m), Inter Milan 1995-97 (signed for £7m), Liverpool 1997-99 (signed for £4.2m), Middlesbrough 1999-2002 (signed for £1m), Wolverhampton Wanderers 2002-present (free transfer). Honours: FA Premiership 1993, 1994; FA Cup 1990, 1994; League Cup 1992; Charity Shield 1993, 1994; European Cup Winners' Cup 1991; European Super Cup 1991 (all with Manchester United). International caps (for England): 54 (7 as captain), 2 goals. Retired from international football after Euro 2000. Nicknamed 'The Guv'nor', Ince was the first black player to captain England.

Inzaghi, Filippo   Born Piacenza, Italy, 9 August 1973. Position: forward. Clubs: Piacenza 1991-92, 1994-95, Leffe 1992-93, Hellas Verona 1993-94, Parma 1995-96, Atalanta 1996-97, Juventus 1997-2001, AC Milan 2001-present. Honours: Italian League Championship 1998 (with Juventus); Italian Super Cup 1997 (with Juventus); UEFA Champions League 2003 (with AC Milan). International caps (for Italy): 44, 15 goals. Known as 'Super Pippo'. His brother Simone is also an Italian international.

Irwin, Denis   Born Denis Joseph Irwin, Cork, Ireland, 31 October 1965. Position: defender. Clubs: Leeds

United 1983-86; Oldham Athletic 1986-90, Manchester United 1990-2002 (signed for £625,000), Wolverhampton Wanderers 2002-04. Honours: FA Premiership 1993, 1994, 1996, 1997, 1999, 2000, 2001; FA Cup 1994, 1996, 1999; League Cup 1992; FA Charity Shield 1993, 1996, 1997; European Cup Winners' Cup 1991; European Super Cup 1991; UEFA Champions League 1999; Intercontinental Cup 1999 (all with Manchester United). International caps (for Ireland): 56, 4 goals. Retired from international football in 2001 and club football in 2004.

Izzet, Muzzy Born Mustafa Kemal Izzet, Mile End, London, 31 October 1974. Position: midfield. Clubs: Chelsea 1993-96, Leicester City 1996-present (signed for £650,000). Honours: League Cup 1997, 2000 (with Leicester City). International caps (for Turkey): 8.

Jack, David Born David Bone Nightingale Jack, Bolton, Lancashire, 3 April 1899. Position: forward. Clubs (player): Plymouth Argyle, Bolton Wanderers, Arsenal 1929-34 (signed for £10,890, the first five-figure transfer fee). Honours: League Championship 1931, 1933, 1934 (with Arsenal); FA Cup 1923, 1926 (with Bolton), 1930 (with Arsenal). International caps (for England): 9 (4 as captain), 3 goals. Clubs (manager): Southend 1939-40, Middlesbrough 1944-52, Shelbourne 1953-55. Scored the first FA Cup final goal at Wembley in 1923 and also scored in the 1926 final. Retired from playing in 1934 and managed Sunderland greyhound stadium during the war. He died 10 September 1958 in London.

Jackson, Alec Born Alexander Skinner Jackson, Renton, Dumbartonshire, 12 May 1905. Position: forward. Clubs: Aberdeen 1923-25, Huddersfield Town 1925-30, Chelsea 1930-32, Ashton Nationals 1932, Margate, Nice. Honours: League Championship 1926 (with Huddersfield Town). International caps (for Scotland): 17, 8 goals. Having emigrated to the USA he returned to Scotland in 1923. One of the 1925 Scottish 'Wembley Wizards', a dispute with the management at Chelsea led to his retirement from top-flight football. He retired to manage a pub and was killed in a car crash in Cairo, Egypt, on 15 November 1946 while on active service.

Jairzinho Born Jair Ventura Filho, Caxias, Rio de Janeiro, Brazil, 25 December 1944. Position: forward. Clubs: Botafogo 1959-71, Olympique Marseille (France) 1971-73, Cruzeiro 1973-76, Portuguesa de Acarigua (Venezuela) 1976-78, Fast (USA), Wilstermann (Bolivia). Honours: South American Cup 1976 (with Cruzeiro). International caps (for Brazil): 80, 33 goals. International honours: World Cup 1970. Played in three World Cup tournaments (1966, 1970, 1974), scoring in every Brazil match at the 1970 finals. Known as 'The Hurricane'. He retired from playing in 1981 and became a scout and agent, famously spotting the teenage Ronaldo and helping launch his career.

James, Alex Born Alexander Wilson James, Mossend, Lanarkshire, 14 September 1901. Position: forward/midfield. Clubs: Brandon Amateurs, Orbison Celtic, Ashfield, Raith Rovers 1922-25, Preston North End 1925-29 (signed for £3000), Arsenal 1929-37 (signed for £8750). Honours: League Championship 1931, 1933, 1934, 1935; FA Cup 1930, 1936; Charity Shield 1931, 1934 (all with Arsenal). International caps (for Scotland): 8. Nicknamed 'Wee Alex', he always wore extra-long shorts that made him look even shorter. Retiring in 1937, having scored 106 goals (26 for Arsenal), he coached in Poland and for Arsenal. He died on 1 June 1953 in London.

James, David Born David Benjamin James, Welwyn Garden City, Hertfordshire, 1 August 1970. Position: goalkeeper. Clubs: Watford 1988-92, Liverpool 1992-99 (signed for £1m), Aston Villa 1999-2001 (signed for £1.7m), West Ham 2001-04 (signed for £3.5m), Manchester City 2004-present. Honours: League Cup 1995 (with Liverpool). International caps (for England): 18. Known as 'Calamity James' during his last days at Liverpool.

Jeffers, Francis Born Liverpool, 25 January 1981. Position: forward. Clubs: Everton 1997-2001, Arsenal 2001-present (signed for £8m). Honours: FA Premiership 2002; FA Cup 2002 (both with Arsenal). International caps (for England): 1.

Jennings, Pat Born Patrick Anthony Jennings, Newry, Co. Down, Northern Ireland, 12 June 1945. Position: Goalkeeper. Clubs: Newry Town 1961-63, Watford 1963-64, Tottenham Hotspur 1964-77 (signed for £27,000), Arsenal 1977-84. Honours: FA Cup 1967 (with Tottenham Hotspur), 1979 (with Arsenal); League Cup 1971 (with Tottenham Hotspur); UEFA Cup 1972 (with Tottenham Hotspur). International caps (for Northern Ireland): 119. Football Writers' Player of the Year 1973. PFA Player of the Year 1976. First British player to record over 1000 first-class appearances, he is also Northern Ireland's most-capped player. Scored a goal from his own penalty area in the 1967 Charity Shield (against Manchester United's Alex Stepney). Now goalkeeping consultant for Tottenham, his son (also called Pat) is also a goalkeeper. Awarded both the MBE (1976) and OBE (1986).

Johanneson, Albert Born Johannesburg, South Africa, 13 March 1940. Position: forward. Clubs: Germiston (South Africa), Leeds United 1961-70, York City 1970-72. The first black player to appear in an FA Cup final (1965). Known as 'Hurry, Hurry' and 'The Black Flash'. Johanneson went into a sad decline after retiring in 1972 and had a continual fight against alcoholism until his death in September 1995.

John, Bob Born Robert Frederick John, Barry, Wales, 3 February 1899. Position: defender. Club: Arsenal 1922-37. Honours: League Championship 1931, 1933, 1934; FA Cup 1930. International caps (for Wales): 15. Retired in 1937. Coach for West Ham, Torquay, Crystal Palace and Cardiff City.

Johnston, Harry Born Henry Johnston, Droylsden, Manchester, 26 September 1919. Position: defender. Club (player): Blackpool 1935-55. Honours: FA Cup 1953. Clubs (manager): Reading 1955-63, Blackpool (caretaker manager). International caps (for England): 10. Football Writers' Player of the Year 1951. He died 12 October 1973.

Johnstone, Jimmy Born James Connolly Johnstone, Viewpark, Lanarkshire, Scotland, 30 September 1944. Clubs: Celtic 1961-75, San Jose Earthquakes 1975, Sheffield United 1975-77, Dundee Shelbourne 1977, Elgin City. Honours: Scottish League Championship 1966, 1967, 1968, 1969, 1970, 1971, 1972, 1973, 1974; Scottish Cup 1965, 1967, 1969, 1971, 1972; Scottish League Cup 1967, 1968; European Cup 1967 (all with Celtic). International caps (for Scotland): 23, 4 goals. Known as 'Wee Jinky' Johnstone, he was known for his fiery temperament. He was diagnosed with motor neurone disease in 2001. Voted the greatest-ever Celtic player in a fans' poll in 2002.

Jones, Bryn Born Brynmor Jones, Pentard, Wales, 14 February 1912. Position: forward. Clubs: Wolverhampton Wanderers 1933-38, Arsenal 1938-49 (signed for £14,000 – a then record), Norwich

City 1949-50. International caps (for Wales): 17. His transfer fee led to 'questions in the House of Commons' about the 'outrageous' level fees had reached. The attendant publicity is believed to have affected his game. Retired in 1950 to run a newsagent's. Uncle of Cliff Jones. He died on 18 October 1985 in Wood Green, London.

Jones, Cliff Born Clifford William Jones, Swansea, 7 February 1935. Position: forward. Clubs: Swansea Town 1952-58, Tottenham Hotspur 1958-68 (signed for £35,000), Fulham 1968-70. Retired briefly before playing for King's Lynn, Wealdstone, Bedford Town, Cambridge City and Wingate. Honours: League Championship 1961; FA Cup 1961, 1962, 1967; European Cup Winners' Cup 1963 (all with Tottenham). International caps (for Wales): 59. In the 1967 FA Cup final he became the first substitute to gain a winner's medal. Played in World Cup finals 1958. After retirement he became a sports teacher. His father Ivor was also a Welsh international and Bryn Jones was his uncle.

Jones, Cobi Born Detroit, Michigan, USA, 16 June 1970. Position: midfield. Clubs: Coventry City 1994-95, Vasco da Gama 1996, Los Angeles Galaxy 1996-present. Honours: MLS Cup 1996, 2002 (with Los Angeles Galaxy). International caps (for USA): 160, 14 goals. Youngest player in the world to reach 100 caps, at the age of 27 in 1998.

Jones, Mick Born Michael David Jones, Worksop, Nottinghamshire, 24 April 1945. Position: forward. Clubs: Sheffield United 1962-67, Leeds United 1967-75 (signed for £100,000). Honours: League Championship 1969; FA Cup 1972; League Cup 1968; Inter-cities Fairs Cup 1968, 1971; Charity Shield 1969 (all with Leeds United). International caps (for England): 3. Retired through injury in 1975.

Jones, T.G. Born Thomas George Jones, Connahs Quay, Wales, 12 October 1917. Position: defender. Clubs (player): Flint, Wrexham, Everton (signed for £3000), Bangor City. Honours: League Championship 1939 (with Everton). Clubs (manager): Bangor City 1958-67, Rhyl. Honours: Welsh Cup 1962 (with Bangor City). International caps (for Wales): 17. Known as 'TG' and 'The Prince of Centre Halves'. He founded Connahs Quay Juniors in 1946, and coached Bangor City to a home win against AC Napoli in a 1962 European Cup Winners' Cup tie before losing in a play-off.

Jones, Vinnie Born Vincent Peter Jones, Watford, Hertfordshire, 5 January 1965. Position: defender. Clubs: Wealdstone 1985-86, Wimbledon 1986-89 (signed for £10,000), 1992-98 (signed for £700,000), IFK Holmsund 1986 (loan), Leeds United 1989-90 (signed for £650,000), Sheffield United 1990-91 (signed for £700,000), Chelsea 1991-92 (signed for £575,000), Queens Park Rangers 1998-99 (signed for £750,000). Honours: FA Cup 1988 (with Wimbledon). International caps (for Wales): 9. Noted for his fiery demeanour and reputation as a 'hard man', he was once famously booked after only 4 seconds in a match against Chelsea. Given a suspended six-month ban in 1993 for fronting the video *Soccer's Hard Men*. Retiring in 1999, he successfully turned to acting.

Jordan, Joe Born Carluke, Scotland, 15 December 1951. Position: striker. Clubs (player): Blantyre Victoria, Morton 1968-70, Leeds 1970-78 (signed for £15,000), Manchester United 1978-81 (signed for £350,000), AC Milan 1981-82 (signed for £325,000), Hellas Verona 1982-84, Southampton 1984-87 (signed for £150,000), Bristol City 1987-90. Clubs (manager): Bristol City

1988-90, 1994-97, Heart of Midlothian 1990-93, Celtic (assistant) 1993, Stoke 1993-94, Huddersfield Town (assistant) 2000-02. International caps (for Scotland): 52, 11 goals. International manager (Northern Ireland): 1998-99 (assistant). He is the only British player to score in three World Cups (1974, 1978 and 1982). His son Andy has played for Bristol City and Cardiff.

Juninho Born Osvaldo Giroldo Júnior Juninho Paulista, São Paulo, Brazil, 22 February 1973. Position: midfielder. Clubs: São Paulo 1993-95, Middlesbrough 1995-97 (signed for £4.75m), 1999-2000 (loan), 2002-present (signed for £6m), Atlético Madrid 1997-2002 (signed for £12m), Vasco da Gama 2000-01 (loan), Flamengo 2001-02 (loan). Honours: Brazilian League Championship 2001 (with Vasco da Gama). International caps (for Brazil): 49, 5 goals. International honours: World Cup 2002.

Kahn, Oliver Born Karlsruhe, West Germany, 15 June 1969. Position: goalkeeper. Clubs: Karlsruhe SC 1975-84, Bayern Munich 1994-present. Honours: German League Championship 1997, 1999, 2000, 2001, 2003; German League Cup 1997, 1998, 1999, 2000; UEFA Champions League 2001; UEFA Cup 1996; World Club Championship 2001 (all with Bayern Munich). International caps (for Germany): 60. International honours: European Championship 1996. World Goalkeeper of the Year 1999, 2001. Won Golden Ball award at World Cup 2002.

Kanu, Nwankwo Born Oweri, Nigeria, 1 August 1976. Position: forward. Clubs: Federation Works 1991-92, Iwuanyanwo Nationale 1992-93, Ajax 1994-96, Inter Milan 1996-99, Arsenal 1999-present (signed for £4.5m). Honours: FA Premiership 2002; FA Cup 2002; Charity Shield 1999 (all with Arsenal); Nigerian League Championship 1992 (with Iwuanyanwo Nationale); Dutch League Championship 1994, 1995, 1996; Dutch Cup 1994, 1995; UEFA Champions League 1995 (all with Ajax); UEFA Cup 1998 (with Inter Milan). International caps (for Nigeria): 38, 6 goals. International honours: Olympic gold medal 1996. Voted African Player of the Year 1996. Suffered from a heart defect while at Inter Milan which was corrected by an operation in the USA. Awarded Order of the Niger for services to Nigerian football in 2002. Patron and founder of the Kanu Nwankwo Heart Foundation.

Keane, Robbie Born Robert David Keane, Dublin, 8 July 1980. Position: forward. Clubs: Wolverhampton Wanderers 1997-99, Coventry City 1999 (signed for £6m), Inter Milan 1999-2000 (signed for £13m), Leeds United 2000-02 (loan, then signed for £12m), Tottenham Hotspur 2002-present (signed for £7m). International caps (for Republic of Ireland): 40, 14 goals.

Keane, Roy Born Roy Maurice Keane, Cork, Ireland, 10 August 1971. Position: midfield. Clubs: Cobh Ramblers 1989-90, Nottingham Forest 1990-93 (signed for £10,000), Manchester United 1993-present (signed for £3.75m). Honours: FA Premiership 1994, 1996, 1997, 1999, 2000, 2001; FA Cup 1994, 1996, 1999; Charity/Community Shield 1993, 1996, 1997, 2003 (all with Manchester United); Full Members Cup 1992 (with Nottingham Forest); Intercontinental Cup 1999 (with Manchester United). International caps (for Republic of Ireland): 58, 9 goals. PFA and Football Writers' Player of the Year 2000. Missed UEFA Champions League final 1999 through suspension. Retired from international football on medical grounds in 2003. One of only four players to win the 'double' three times, he appeared in five FA Cup finals during the 1990s (one with

Nottingham Forest and four with Manchester United). A well-publicised disagreement with the then Irish manager Mick McCarthy led to him walking out during the 2002 World Cup in Korea/Japan. Autobiography *Keane* published in 2002.

Keegan, Kevin Born Joseph Kevin Keegan, Armthorpe, Yorkshire, 14 February 1951. Position: forward. Clubs (player): Scunthorpe United 1968-71, Liverpool 1971-77 (signed for £35,000), SV Hamburg 1977-80 (signed for £500,000), Southampton 1980-82 (signed for £420,000), Newcastle United 1982-84 (signed for £100,000). Honours: League Championship 1973, 1976, 1977 (with Liverpool); FA Cup 1974 (with Liverpool); German League Championship 1979 (with SV Hamburg); German Cup 1979 (with SV Hamburg); European Cup 1977 (with Liverpool); UEFA Cup 1973, 1976 (with Liverpool). Clubs (manager): Newcastle United 1992-97, Fulham 1998-99, Manchester City 2001-present. International caps (for England): 63 (31 as captain), 21 goals. Played only 27 minutes of football in the World Cup finals in 1972. International manager (England): 1999-2000. Nicknamed 'The Mighty Mouse'. Football Writers' Player of the Year 1976. European Player of the Year 1978, 1979. PFA Player of the Year 1982. Awarded the OBE in 1982. With the shortest tenure and worst record of any 'permanent' England manager, Keegan resigned, 7 October 2000, following England's 1-0 defeat by Germany in the last game to be played at the old Wembley stadium.

Keller, Kasey Born Lacey, Washington, USA, 29 November 1969. Position: goalkeeper. Clubs: University of Portland 1991-92, Millwall 1992-96, Leicester City 1996-99 (signed for £900,000), Rayo Vallecano 1999-2001, Tottenham Hotspur 2001-present. Honours: League Cup 1997 (with Leicester City). International caps (for USA): 60.

Kempes, Mario Born Cordoba, Argentina, 15 July 1954. Position: forward. Clubs (player): Instituto de Cordoba 1971-73, Rosario Central 1974-76, Valencia 1976-81, 1982-84, River Plate 1981-82, Hercules de Alicante 1984-86, First Vienna (Austria) 1986-87, St Pölten 1987-90, Kremser 1990-92, Fernandez Vial (Chile) 1995, Pelita Hyatt (Indonesia) 1996. Honours: Spanish Cup 1978, 1979 (with Valencia); European Cup Winners' Cup 1979, 1980 (with Valencia); Argentine Championship 1981 (with River Plate). Clubs (coach/manager): Pelita Hyatt 1996, SK Lushnja (Albania) 1996, Mineros de Guayana (Venezuela) 1997-98, The Strongest (Bolivia) 1999, Independiente Petrolero (Bolivia) 2000-01. International caps (for Argentina): 43, 20 goals. International honours: World Cup 1978. Golden Boot winner and Player of the Tournament, World Cup 1978. Scored two goals in the 1978 final. Known as 'El Matador'.

Kendall, Howard Born Ryton, Tyne & Wear, 22 May 1946. Position: midfield. Clubs (player): Preston North End 1962-67, Everton 1967-74, Birmingham City 1974-77, Stoke City 1977-79, Blackburn Rovers 1979-81. Honours: League Championship 1970 (with Everton). Clubs (manager): Blackburn Rovers 1979-81, Everton 1981-87, 1990-93, 1997-98, Athletic Bilbao 1987-89, Manchester City 1989-90, Xanthi (Greece), Notts County 1995, Sheffield United 1995-97. Honours: League Championship 1985, 1987; FA Cup 1984; European Cup Winners' Cup 1985 (all with Everton). Played for Preston in the 1964 FA Cup final aged 17 years and 345 days, at the time the youngest player to appear in an FA Cup final.

Keown, Martin Born Martin Raymond Keown, Oxford, 24 July 1966. Position: defender. Clubs: Arsenal 1984-86, 1993-present (signed for £2m), Brighton & Hove Albion 1985 (loan), Aston Villa 1986-89 (signed for £200,000), Everton 1989-93 (signed for £750,000). Honours: FA Premiership 1998, 2002; FA Cup 1998, 2002; Charity Shield 1998, 1999 (all with Arsenal). International caps (for England): 43 (1 as captain), 2 goals.

Kewell, Harry Born Harold Kewell, Smithfield, Australia, 22 September 1978. Position: midfield. Clubs: Australian Institute of Sport 1994-95, Leeds United 1995-2003, Liverpool 2003-present. International caps (for Australia): 13, 3 goals.

Kidd, Brian Born Collyhurst, Manchester, 29 May 1949. Position: forward. Clubs (player): Manchester United 1964-74, Arsenal 1974-76 (signed for £110,000), Manchester City 1976-79 (signed for £100,000), Everton 1979-80 (signed for £150,000), Bolton Wanderers 1980-82 (signed for £150,000), Atlanta Chiefs 1981, Fort Lauderdale Strikers 1982-83, Minnesota Strikers 1984. Honours: Charity Shield 1967; European Cup 1968 (both with Manchester United). Clubs (manager): Barrow 1984-85, Swindon (assistant) 1985-86, Preston North End 1986, Manchester United (youth coach) 1988-91, (assistant manager) 1991-98, Blackburn Rovers 1998-99, Leeds United (youth/head coach) 2000-present. International caps (for England): 2, 1 goal. England assistant coach 2003-present. Scored in the European Cup final on his 19th birthday.

Kinkladze, Georgi Born Georgiou Kinkladze, Tbilisi, Georgia, 6 July 1973. Position: midfield. Clubs: Mrettebi Tbilisi 1989-92, Dynamo Tbilisi 1992-95, Saarbrucken 1993-94 (loan), Manchester City 1995-98 (signed for £2m), Ajax 1998-2000 (signed for £5m), Derby County 1999-present (loan then signed for £3m). Honours: Georgian League Championship 1993, 1994, 1995; Georgian Cup 1993, 1994, 1995 (all with Dynamo Tbilisi). International caps (for Georgia): 46, 8 goals. Georgian Player of the Year 1993.

Kinnaird, Arthur Born Arthur Fitzgerald Kinnaird, Kensington, London, 16 February 1847. Clubs: Wanderers, Old Etonians. Honours: FA Cup 1873, 1877, 1878 (with Wanderers), 1879, 1882 (with Old Etonians). International caps (for Scotland): 1. He played in the first unofficial England-Scotland match. An all-round sportsman – Cambridge Blue at football, fives, real tennis and swimming. Kinnaird played in nine FA Cup finals and was the scorer of the first own goal in a final (1877). Appointed president of the Football Association in 1890, he remained in that position until his death and was presented with the second version of the FA Cup in 1911 in recognition of his 21 years as president. He was also president of the YWCA which had been co-founded by his mother. He died 30 January 1923.

Kirkland, Chris Born Leicester, 2 May 1981. Position: goalkeeper. Clubs: Coventry City 1997-2001, Liverpool 2001-present (signed for £6m).

Klinsmann, Jürgen Born Goppingen, Germany, 30 July 1964. Position: forward. Clubs: Stuttgart Kickers 1978-84, VfB Stuttgart 1984-89, Inter Milan 1989-92, Monaco 1992-94, Tottenham 1994-95 (signed for £2m), 1997-98 (loan), Bayern Munich 1995-97, Sampdoria 1997-98. Honours: German League Championship 1984 (with VfB Stuttgart), 1997 (with Bayern Munich); UEFA Cup 1991 (with Inter Milan), 1996 (with Bayern Munich). International caps (for Germany): 108, 47 goals. International honours:

World Cup 1990; European Championship 1996. German Player of the Year 1988, 1994. English Football Writers' Player of the Year 1995. Retired from the game in 1998 after the World Cup.

Kluivert, Patrick   Born Patrick Stephan Kluivert, Amsterdam, Holland, 1 July 1976. Position: forward. Clubs: Schellingwoude 1993-94, Ajax 1994-97, AC Milan 1997-98, Barcelona 1998-present. Honours: Dutch League Championship 1995, 1996 (with Ajax); Spanish League Championship 1999 (with Barcelona); UEFA Champions League 1995 (with Ajax); World Club Cup 1995 (with Ajax). Scored the winning goal for Ajax in the Champions League final against AC Milan. International caps (for Holland): 72, 39 goals.

Knowles, Cyril   Born Cyril Barry Knowles, Fitzwilliam, Yorkshire, 13 July 1944. Position: defender. Clubs (player): Middlesbrough 1962-63, Tottenham Hotspur 1964-75. Honours: FA Cup 1967 (with Tottenham Hotspur). Clubs (coach/manager): Hertford Town, Doncaster Rovers (coach) 1977-81, Middlesbrough (coach/assistant) 1981-83, Darlington 1983-87, Torquay United 1987-89, Hartlepool United 1989-91. International caps (for England): 4. Inspiration for the catchphrase 'Nice one, Cyril' which spawned a top 20 hit for the Cockerel Chorus before the 1973 League Cup final). Made 403 appearances for Tottenham Hotspur. His brother Peter, who played for Wolverhampton Wanderers, retired from the game on religious grounds. Cyril died 31 August 1991 in Middlesbrough, aged 47 .

Kocsis, Sandor   Born Budapest, Hungary, 23 September 1929. Position: forward. Clubs: Ferencvaros 1946-49, EDOSZ Budapest 1949-50, Honvéd 1950-56, Young Boys Zurich 1957, Barcelona 1958-66. Honours: Hungarian League Championship 1949 (with Ferencvaros), 1950-55 (with Honvéd); Spanish League Championship 1959 and 1960 (with Barcelona); Spanish Cup 1959 and 1963 (with Barcelona); UEFA Cup 1960 (with Barcelona). International caps (for Hungary): 68, 75 goals. International honours: Olympic gold medal 1952. Golden Boot winner, World Cup 1954. Kocsis defected to Spain in 1956 during the Hungarian uprising. Known as 'The Man with the Golden Head'. Retired in 1966. He died 21 July 1979 in Barcelona.

Koeman, Ronald   Born Zaandam, Holland, 21 March 1963. Position: defender. Clubs (player): Groningen 1980-83, Ajax 1983-86, PSV Eindhoven 1986-89, Barcelona 1989-95, Feyenoord 1995-97. Honours: Dutch League Championship 1985 (with Ajax), 1987, 1988, 1989 (with PSV Eindhoven); Dutch Cup 1986 (with Ajax), 1988, 1989 (with PSV Eidhoven); Spanish League Championship 1991, 1992, 1993, 1994 (with Barcelona); Spanish Cup 1990 (with Barcelona); European Cup 1988 (with PSV Eindhoven), 1992 (with Barcelona). Clubs (manager): Vitesse Arnhem 2000-01, Ajax 2001-present. International caps (for Holland): 78, 14 goals. International honours: European Championship 1988. First player to win the European Cup with two different teams.

Kopa, Raymond   Born Raymond Kopaszewski, Noueux-les-Mines, Pas de Calais, France, 13 October 1931. Position: forward. Clubs: US Noueux-les-Mines 1946-49, SCO Angers 1949-51, Stade de Reims 1951-56, 1959-67, Real Madrid 1956-59. Honours: French League Championship 1953, 1955, 1960, 1962 (with Stade de Reims); Spanish League Championship 1957, 1958 (with Real Madrid);

European Cup 1957, 1958, 1959 (with Real Madrid). International caps (for France): 45, 18 goals. European Player of the Year 1958. First footballer to be awarded the Legion of Honour (1970). Nicknamed 'The Little Napoleon' and 'The French Stanley Matthews'. His parents were Polish.

Krankl, Hans   Born Johann Krankl, Vienna, Austria, 14 February 1953. Position: forward. Clubs (player): Rapid Vienna 1971-78, 1980-86, Barcelona 1978-79, First Vienna 1979-80, Rapid Vienna 1980-86, Sportclub Vienna 1986-88, Kremser 1988, Austria Salzburg 1988-89. Honours: Austrian League 1982, 1983 (with Rapid Vienna); Austrian Cup 1972, 1976, 1983, 1984, 1985 (with Rapid Vienna); European Cup Winners' Cup 1979 (with Barcelona). Clubs (manager): Sportclub Vienna, Rapid Vienna 1989-92, VfB Mödling 1992-94, 1995-96, Tirol 1994-95, Gerasdorf 1997, Austria Salzburg, Fortuna Cologne 2000, VfB Admira Wacker Mödling 2000-02. International caps (for Austria): 69, 39 goals. International manager (Austria): 2002-present. Scored six goals for Austria in a game against Malta in 1977. Austrian Footballer of the Year 1973, 1974, 1977, 1982, 1983.

Krol, Rudi   Born Rudolf Jozef Krol, Amsterdam, Holland, 24 March 1949. Position: defender. Clubs (player): Ajax 1968-80, Vancouver Whitecaps 1980, Napoli 1980-84, Cannes 1984-86. Retired from playing in 1987. Honours: Dutch League Championship 1968, 1970, 1972, 1973, 1977, 1979, 1980, 1981; Dutch Cup 1970, 1971, 1972, 1979; European Cup 1971, 1972, 1973 (all with Ajax). Clubs (manager): Mechelen 1989, Servette Geneva, Zamalek Cairo, Al Wahad (UAE), SK Beveren, Ajax (assistant). International caps (for Holland): 83, 4 goals. International manager (Egypt): 1995-96.

Kubala, Ladislav   Born Budapest, Hungary, 10 June 1927. Position: forward. Clubs (player): Ferencvaros 1945-46, SK Bratislava 1947, Vasas 1948-49, Barcelona 1950-63, Espanyol 1964-65. Honours: Spanish League Championship 1952, 1953, 1959, 1960; Spanish Cup 1951, 1952, 1953, 1957, 1959, Inter-cities Fairs Cup 1958, 1960 (all with Barcelona). Clubs (coach/manager): Barcelona 1963-64, 1980-82, Espanyol 1964-65, FC Zurich 1966-67, Toronto Falcons 1967-68, FC Cordoba 1968-69, al-Hilal 1982-86, Murcia 1986-87, Malaga 1987-89. International caps (for Hungary): 6; (for Czechoslovakia): 11, 4 goals; (for Spain): 19, 11 goals. International honours: Olympic gold medal 1952 (with Hungary). International manager (Spain): 1969-80; (Spain Olympic Team): 1991-92; (Paraguay): 1995. The only man apart from Alfredo Di Stefano to play for three nations, Kubala was voted the greatest player in Barcelona's history in a poll conducted during the club's centenary year. He died 17 May 2002.

Labruna, Angel   Born Buenos Aires, Argentina, 26 September 1918. Position: forward. Clubs (player): River Plate 1939-59, Rangers (Chile) 1960, Rampla Juniors (Uruguay) 1960, Platense 1961. Honours: Argentinian League Championship 1941, 1942, 1945, 1947, 1952, 1953, 1955, 1956, 1957; South American Championship 1946, 1955 (all with River Plate). Clubs (manager): Platense, River Plate. Honours: Argentinian League Championship 1971 (with Platense), 1975, 1977, 1979, 1980 (with River Plate). International caps (for Argentina): 36, 17 goals. Played in the 1958 World Cup at the age of 40. Known as 'El Feo', 'The Ugly One' (because of his teeth), 'Angelito', or 'The Eternal One' (because of his longevity). During his time the River Plate team were known as 'The Machine'. He died 19 September 1983 in Buenos Aires.

alas, Alexi Born Detroit, Michigan, 1 June 1970. Position: defender. Clubs: Padova 1994-95, New England Revolution 1996-97, MetroStars 1998, Kansas City Wizards 1999, Los Angeles Galaxy 2001-present. International caps (for United States): 96, 9 goals. Having come to prominence during the 1994 World Cup with his red hair and billy-goat beard, he was the first United States player to play in Italy's Serie A.

ampard, Frank jnr Born Frank James Lampard, Romford, 21 June 1978. Position: midfield. Clubs: West Ham United 1992-2001, Swansea City 1995 (loan), Chelsea 2001-present (signed for £11m). International caps (for England): 12, 1 goal.

ampard, Frank snr Born Frank Richard George Lampard, West Ham, London, 20 September 1948. Clubs (player): West Ham United 1967-85, Southend United 1985-86. Honours: FA Cup 1975, 1980 (with West Ham United). Club (coach): West Ham (assistant) 1994-2001. International caps (for England): 2 (eight years between these caps 1972, 1980).

arsson, Henrik Born Helsingborg, Sweden, 20 September 1971. Position: forward. Clubs: Hogaborg BK 1988-92, Helsingborg 1992-93, Feyenoord 1993-97 (signed for £295,000), Celtic 1997-2004 (signed for £650,000), Barcelona 2004-present. Honours: Dutch Cup 1994, 1995 (with Feyenoord); Scottish League Championship 1998, 2000, 2001; Scottish Cup 2001; Scottish League Cup 2000, 2001(all with Celtic). International caps (for Sweden): 72, 24 goals. Suffered a serious leg injury in 1999 in a UEFA Cup game against Olympique Lyonnais. Winner of the Adidas Golden Boot for the top scorer in Europe 2001. Scottish Player of the Year 1999, 2001. His father is from Cape Verde, his mother is Swedish.

atchford, Bob Born Robert Dennis Latchford, Birmingham, 18 January 1951. Position: forward. Clubs: Birmingham City 1968-73, Everton 1973-80 (signed for £350,000), Swansea City 1981-84 (signed for £125,000), NAC Breda 1984, Coventry City 1985, Lincoln City 1985-86, Newport County 1986 (loan), Merthyr Tydfil 1986. Honours: Welsh Cup 1986 (with Merthyr Tydfil). International caps (for England): 12, 5 goals. Won a £10,000 prize from the *Daily Express* in 1978 by scoring 30 goals in Division 1. Now lives in Germany.

ato, Grzegorz Born Grzegorz Boleslaw Lato, Malbork, Poland, 8 April 1950. Position: forward. Clubs (player): Stal Mielec, Lokeren 1980-83, Atlante (Mexico) 1983-85, Toronto 1985. Retired from playing 1988. Honours: Polish League Championship 1973, 1976 (with Stal Mielec). Clubs (trainer/coach): Stal Mielec, Olympia Poznan, Amika Wronki, Widzew Lodz. International caps (for Poland): 95, 42 goals. Golden Boot winner World Cup 1974. Known as 'Bolek'. Now a member of the Polish Senate.

audrup, Michael Born Copenhagen, Denmark, 15 June 1964. Position: forward. Clubs (player): Brondby 1971-79, 1981-83, BK Copenhagen 1979-81, Lazio 1983-85, Juventus 1985-89, Barcelona 1989-94, Real Madrid 1994-96, Vissel Kobe (Japan) 1996-97, Ajax 1997-98. Honours: Italian League Championship 1986 (with Juventus); Spanish League Championship 1991, 1992, 1993, 1994 (with Barcelona), 1995 (with Real Madrid); Dutch League Championship 1998 (with Ajax); Dutch Cup 1998

(with Ajax); European Cup 1992 (with Barcelona). Club (manager): Brondby. International caps (for Denmark): 104, 37 goals. International manager (Denmark): 2000-present (assistant). Danish Player of the Year 1982, 1985. Refused to play for Denmark in the European Championships in 1992 after falling out with the manager. His younger brother Brian (born 22 February 1969 in Angreb, Austria) was also a Danish international (82 caps, 21 goals) and was a member of the 1992 European Championship-winning side.

Law, Denis Born Aberdeen, 24 February 1940. Position: forward. Clubs: Huddersfield Town 1955-60, Manchester City 1960-61 (signed for £55,000), 1973-74, Torino 1961-62 (signed for £110,000), Manchester United 1962-73 (signed for £115,000). Honours: League Championship 1965, 1967; FA Cup 1963; European Cup 1968 (all with Manchester United). International caps (for Scotland): 55, 30 goals. European Player of the Year 1964. Law missed the 1968 European Cup final through injury but was still awarded a medal. He scored the only goal for a Rest of the World side which played England to celebrate the 100th anniversary of the FA in June 1963. He retired in 1974 having scored the goal that relegated Manchester United from Division 1, and in total scored 300 goals in 585 games, including all six in an FA Cup tie between Manchester City and Luton which was abandoned with City leading 6-2. They lost the rearranged game. Currently works in the media.

Lawrenson, Mark Born Preston, 2 June 1957. Position: defender/midfield. Clubs (player): Preston North End 1974-77, Brighton & Hove Albion 1977-81, Liverpool 1981-88 (signed for £900,000). Honours: League Championship 1982, 1983, 1984, 1986, 1988; FA Cup 1986; League Cup 1982, 1983, 1984; European Cup 1984 (all with Liverpool). Clubs (manager): Oxford United 1988, Peterborough United 1989-90. International caps (for Republic of Ireland): 38. Having retired from playing in 1988 through injury, he is now an analyst and pundit on TV and radio.

Lawton, Tommy Born Bolton, Lancashire, 6 October 1919. Position: forward. Clubs (player): Burnley 1936-37, Everton 1937-45 (signed for £6,500), Chelsea 1945-47, Notts County 1947-52 (signed for £20,000), Brentford 1952-53, Arsenal 1953-55, Kettering Town 1955-57. Honours: League Championship 1939 (with Everton). Clubs (manager): Brentford 1952-53, Kettering Town 1955-57, Notts County 1957-58. International caps (for England): 23, 22 goals. The youngest player to score a hat-trick in the Football League at 17 years and 4 days, he worked after retirement as a columnist for the *Nottingham Evening Post*. He died of pneumonia 6 November 1996 in Nottingham.

Lee, Francis Born Francis Henry Lee, Westhoughton, Lancashire, 29 April 1944. Position: forward. Clubs: Bolton Wanderers 1960-67, Manchester City 1967-73, Cape Town City 1971 (summer loan), Derby County 1974-75. Honours: League Championship 1968 (with Manchester City), 1975 (with Derby County); FA Cup 1969; League Cup 1970; European Cup Winners' Cup 1970 (all with Manchester City). International caps (for England): 27, 10 goals. A successful businessman in the paper industry, he was also for a time a racehorse trainer. Acquired the nickname 'Lee Won Pen' for his ability to 'win' penalties, scoring 13 during the 1971-72 season.

Leighton, Jim Born Johnstone, Renfrewshire, 24 July 1958. Position: goalkeeper. Clubs: Dalry Thistle, Aberdeen 1977-88, Deveronvale 1977-78 (loan), Manchester United 1988-92 (signed for £750,000), Arsenal 1991 (loan), Reading 1991-92 (loan), Dundee 1992-93, Sheffield United 1993, Hibernian 1993-97, Aberdeen 1997-99. Honours: Scottish League Championship 1980, 1984, 1985; Scottish Cup 1982, 1983, 1984, 1986; Scottish League Cup 1986; European Cup Winners' Cup 1983 (all with Aberdeen). International caps (for Scotland): 91, 47 clean sheets. Retired from playing in 1997 to take up a coaching post with Aberdeen and is also Scottish Under-21 goalkeeping coach. He played in the 1990 FA Cup final for Manchester United but was dropped for the replay. Biography: *In the Firing Line*. Awarded the MBE in 1998.

Lennox, Bobby Born Saltcoats, Ayrshire, Scotland, 30 August 1943. Position: forward. Clubs: Celtic 1961-78, 1979-80, Houston Hurricanes 1978. Honours: Scottish League Championship 1966, 1967, 1968, 1970, 1971, 1972, 1973, 1974, 1977, 1979; Scottish Cup 1965, 1967, 1969, 1971, 1975; Scottish League Cup 1966, 1967, 1968, 1969, European Cup 1967 (all with Celtic). International caps (for Scotland): 10, 3 goals. Known as 'Buzz Bomb' or 'Lemon' (he made defenders look like suckers!). Awarded the MBE in 1981.

Le Saux, Graeme Born Graeme Pierre Le Saux, Jersey, 17 October 1968. Position: defender. Clubs: St Paul's Jersey, Chelsea 1987-93, Blackburn Rovers 1993-97 (signed for £750,000), Chelsea 1997-2003 (signed for £5m), Southampton 2003-present. Honours: FA Premiership 1995 (with Blackburn Rovers); League Cup 1998 (with Chelsea); Charity Shield 2000 (with Chelsea). International caps (for England): 36, 1 goal.

Le Tissier, Matt Born Matthew Paul Le Tissier, Guernsey, 14 October 1968. Position: forward. Club: Southampton 1986-2002. International caps (for England): 8. Scored the last goal at The Dell before Southampton's move to a new stadium at St Mary's. Known as 'Le God'. Retired in 2002.

Leonidas Born Leonidas da Silva, São Christovao, Brazil, 6 September 1913. Position: forward. Clubs (player): São Christovao, Nacional 1933, Vasco da Gama 1934, Botafogo 1935, Flamengo 1936-42, São Paulo 1942-50. Honours: Uruguayan League Championship 1933 (with Nacional); Brazilian Carioca League Championship 1934 (with Vasco da Gama), 1935 (with Botafogo), 1939 (with Flamengo); Brazilian Paulista League Championship 1943, 1945, 1946, 1948, 1949 (with São Paulo). Club (manager): São Paulo 1953. International caps (for Brazil): 22, 23 goals. Leading scorer in World Cup 1938. Known as 'The Black Diamond' and 'The Rubber Man', he is believed to have 'invented' the bicycle kick. He died 24 January 2004.

Liddell, Billy Born William Beveridge Liddell, Townhill, nr Dunfermline, Fife, 10 January 1922. Position: forward. Club: Liverpool 1939-61 (but did not make League debut until 1946). Honours: League Championship 1947. International caps (for Scotland): 30, 6 goals. Along with Stanley Matthews, he was the only player to play for Great Britain select teams in both 1947 and 1955. He scored 229 goals in 537 games for Liverpool, while working part-time in the accounts office of the club throughout his playing career. He later became a youth worker, lay preacher and Justice of the Peace before becoming an assistant bursar at Liverpool University.

Liedholm, Nils Born Waldemarsvik, Sweden, 8 October 1922. Position: midfield/forward. Clubs (player): IFK Norrkoping 1947-49, AC Milan 1949-61. Honours: Swedish League Championship 1947, 1948 (with IFK Norrkoping); Italian League Championship 1951, 1955, 1957, 1959 (with AC Milan). Clubs (manager): Verona, Varese, Fiorentina 1971-73, Roma 1974-77, 1980-84, 1987-89, AC Milan 1977-79, 1984-87. Honours: Italian League Championship 1979 (with AC Milan), 1983 (with Roma); Italian Cup 1980, 1981, 1984 (with Roma). International caps (for Sweden): 23, 11 goals. International honours: Olympic gold medal 1948. Captain of Sweden in 1958 World Cup finals, he was a member of the 'Gre-No-Li' line-up of strikers for both Sweden and AC Milan. Known as 'Liddas' at Milan and later 'The Baron' after marrying into Italian nobility. He was among the first footballers to begin a serious training regime to improve fitness.

Lineker, Gary Born Gary Winston Lineker, Leicester, 30 November 1960. Position: forward. Clubs: Leicester City 1978-85, Everton 1985-86 (signed for £800,000), Barcelona 1986-89 (signed for £2.3m), Tottenham Hotspur 1989-92, Nagoya Grampus 8 (Japan) 1992-94. Honours: Spanish Cup 1988, European Cup Winners' Cup 1989 (both with Barcelona); FA Cup 1991 (with Tottenham Hotspur). International caps (for England): 80 (18 as captain), 48 goals. Golden Boot winner, World Cup 1986. Football Writers' Player of the Year 1986, 1992. PFA Player of the Year 1986. Top British scorer in World Cups. After retirement in 1994 he now works in TV. Awarded the OBE in 1992.

Litmanen, Jari Born Lahti, Finland, 20 February 1971. Position: midfield. Clubs: Reipas Lahti 1987-91, HJK Helsinki 1991-92, MyPa-47 1992-93, Ajax 1993-99, 2003-present, Barcelona 1999-2001, Liverpool 2001-03. Honours: Dutch League Championship 1994, 1995, 1996, 1998; Dutch Cup 1993, 1998, 1999; UEFA Champions League 1995 (all with Ajax); FA Cup 2001 (with Liverpool); League Cup 2001 (with Liverpool). International caps (for Finland): 78, 22 goals. Dutch Player of the Year 1993.

Lloyd, Larry Born Lawrence Lloyd, Bristol, 6 October 1948. Position: defender. Clubs (player): Bristol Rovers 1967-69, Liverpool 1969-74 (signed for £50,000), Coventry City 1974-76 (signed for £225,000), Nottingham Forest 1976-81 (signed for £60,000), Wigan Athletic 1981-83. Honours: League Championship 1973 (with Liverpool), 1978 (with Nottingham Forest); UEFA Cup 1973 (with Liverpool); European Cup 1979, 1980 (with Nottingham Forest). Clubs (manager): Wigan Athletic 1981-83, Notts County 1983-84. International caps (for England): 4.

Lofthouse, Nat Born Nathaniel Lofthouse, Bolton, Lancashire, 27 August 1925. Position: forward. Club (player): Bolton Wanderers 1939-60 (League debut 1946). Honours: FA Cup 1958. Club (manager): Bolton Wanderers 1968-70, 1971, 1985. International caps (for England): 33, 30 goals. Scored in every round of the 1953 FA Cup. Football Writers' Player of the Year 1953. Known as 'The Lion of Vienna' after his display against Austria in 1952 which culminated in his being knocked unconscious by the opposition goalkeeper while in the process of scoring the winning goal. Appointed President of Bolton 1986. Awarded the OBE in 1994. In his early years he played while still working full-time as a coal miner.

Lorimer, Peter Born Dundee, Scotland, 14 December 1946. Position: forward. Clubs: Leeds United 1962-78, 1984-85, York City 1979-80 (signed for £25,000), Toronto Blizzard 1979-80, Vancouver Whitecaps 1981-83, Whitby, Hapoel Haifa. Honours: League Championship 1969, 1974; FA Cup 1972; League Cup 1968; Inter-cities Fairs Cup 1968, 1971 (all with Leeds United). International caps (for Scotland): 21, 4 goals. Known as 'Hot Shot' for his shots which could reach 90mph.

Ljungberg, Freddie Born Fredrik Ljungberg, Vittsjo, Sweden, 16 April 1977. Position: midfield. Clubs: BK Halmstad 1994-98, Arsenal 1998-present (signed for £3m). Honours: FA Premiership 2002; FA Cup 2002; Charity Shield 1999 (all with Arsenal). International caps (for Sweden): 35, 2 goals.

Mabbutt, Gary Born Gary Vincent Mabbutt, Bristol, 23 August 1961. Position: midfield. Clubs: Bristol Rovers 1977-82, Tottenham Hotspur 1982-98 (signed for £105,000). Honours: FA Cup 1991; Charity Shield 1991; UEFA Cup 1984 (all with Tottenham Hotspur). International caps (for England):16, 1 goal. Retired from playing through injury in 1998. His father Ray played for Bristol Rovers and Newport County and his brother Kevin for Bristol City and Crystal Palace. Awarded the MBE in 1994.

McAllister, Gary Born Motherwell, Scotland, 25 December 1964. Position: midfield. Clubs (player): Motherwell 1981-85, Leicester City 1985-90 (signed for £125,000), Leeds United 1990-96 (signed for £1m), Coventry City 1996-2000 (signed for £3m), 2002-present, Liverpool 2000-02. Honours: League Championship 1992 (with Leeds United); FA Cup 2001 (with Liverpool); League Cup 2001 (with Liverpool); UEFA Cup 2001 (with Liverpool). Club (manager): Coventry City 2002-04. International caps (for Scotland): 57, 5 goals.

Macari, Lou Born Luigi Macari, Aberdeen, Scotland, 4 June 1949. Position: forward. Clubs (player): Kilwinning Amateurs, Celtic 1970-73, Manchester United 1973-84, Swindon Town 1984-85. Honours: Scottish League Championship 1970, 1971, 1972, 1973; Scottish Cup 1971, 1972 (all with Celtic); FA Cup 1977 (with Manchester United). Clubs (manager): Swindon Town 1984-89, West Ham United 1989-90, Birmingham City 1991, Stoke City 1991-93, 1994-97, Celtic 1993-94, Huddersfield Town 2000-02. International caps (for Scotland): 24, 5 goals.

McAteer, Jason Born Jason Wynn McAteer, Birkenhead, Cheshire, 18 June 1971. Position: defender. Clubs: Marine 1991-92, Bolton Wanderers 1992-95, Liverpool 1995-99 (signed for £4.5m), Blackburn Rovers 1999-2001 (signed for £4m), Sunderland 2001-present (signed for £1m). International caps (for Republic of Ireland): 51, 3 goals.

McAuley, James Born 1860. Position: goalkeeper. Club: Dumbarton. Originally a centre forward he scored for Dumbarton in the Scottish Cup final 1881. International caps (for Scotland): 8. Known as 'The Prince of Goalkeepers'. He died 1943.

McCall, Stuart Born Andrew Stuart Murray McCall, Leeds, 10 June 1964. Position: midfield. Clubs: Bradford City 1982-88, 1998-2002 (free transfer), Everton 1988-91 (signed for £850,000), Rangers 1991-98 (signed for £1.2m), Sheffield United 2002-present. Honours: Scottish League Championship 1992, 1993, 1994, 1995, 1996; Scottish Cup 1992, 1993, 1996; Scottish League Cup 1992, 1993 (all with Glasgow Rangers). International caps (for Scotland): 40, 1 goal.

McCalliog, Jim Born Glasgow, 23 September 1946. Position: midfield. Clubs (player): Leeds United 1963, Chelsea 1963-65, Sheffield Wednesday 1965-68, Wolverhampton Wanderers 1969-74 (signed for £70,000), Manchester United 1974-75 (signed for £60,000), Southampton 1975-77, Chicago Sting 1977, Lynn Oslo 1977-78, Lincoln City 1978-79. Honours: FA Cup 1976 (with Southampton). Clubs (manager): Lynn Oslo 1977-78, Lincoln City 1978-79, Runcorn 1979, Halifax Town 1990-91, Leyton Orient 1992 (scout). International caps (for Scotland): 5, 1 goal. Runs a pub in Wetherby, Yorkshire.

McCann, Gavin Born Gavin Peter McCann, Blackpool, 1 October 1978. Position: midfield. Clubs: Everton 1995-98, Sunderland 1998-present (signed for £500,000). International caps (for England): 1.

McCarthy, Mick Born Barnsley, Yorkshire, 7 February 1959. Clubs (player): Barnsley 1973-83, Manchester City 1983-87, Celtic 1987-89, Olympique Lyonnais 1989-90, Millwall 1990-92. Honours: Scottish League Championship 1988; Scottish Cup 1988, 1989 (all with Celtic). Clubs (manager): Millwall 1992-96, Sunderland 2003-present. International caps (for Republic of Ireland): 57, 2 goals. International manager (Republic of Ireland): 1996-2002.

McClair, Brian Born Airdrie, Scotland, 8 December 1963. Position: forward. Clubs (player): Aston Villa 1980-81, Motherwell 1981-83, 1998, Celtic 1983-87 (signed for £75,000), Manchester United 1987-98 (signed for £850,000). Honours: Scottish League Championship 1986; Scottish Cup 1985 (both with Celtic); FA Premiership 1993, 1994, 1996, 1997; FA Cup 1990, 1994, 1996; League Cup 1992; European Cup Winners' Cup 1991 (all with Manchester United). Clubs (manager): Blackburn Rovers (assistant) 1998-2001, Manchester United 2001-present (reserve team). International caps (for Scotland): 30, 2 goals. Scottish Player of the Year 1987. Known as 'Choccy' (as in eclair).

McCoist, Ally Born Alistair Murdoch McCoist, Bellshill, North Lanarkshire, Scotland, 24 September 1962. Position: forward. Clubs: St Johnstone 1978-81, Sunderland 1981-83 (signed for £400,000), Rangers 1983-98 (signed for £185,000), Kilmarnock (free transfer). Retired in 2001. Honours: Scottish League Championship 1987, 1989, 1990, 1991, 1992, 1993, 1994, 1995, 1996, 1997; Scottish Cup 1992, 1993, 1996; Scottish League Cup 1984, 1985, 1987, 1988, 1989, 1991, 1993, 1994, 1997 (all with Rangers). International caps (for Scotland): 61, 19 goals. Known as 'Super Ally'. First player to score 200 goals in the Scottish Premiership. Winner of Adidas Golden Boot for top scorer in Europe 1992, 1993. Scottish Player of the Year 1992. Awarded the MBE in 1996. He now works in TV, and won the Television Radio Industry Club's Sports Presenter of the Year award in 2001. Appeared in the film *A Shot at Glory* with Robert Duvall.

McCracken, Billy Born Belfast, 29 January 1883. Position: defender. Clubs (player): Distillery, Newcastle United. Honours: Irish Cup 1903 (with Distillery); English League Championship 1907, 1909; FA Cup 1910 (all with Newcastle United). Clubs (manager): Hull City, Gateshead 1932-33, Millwall 1933-36, Aldershot 1937-49. Later became a scout for Watford and Newcastle. International caps (for Ireland): 15. An early exponent of the offside law whose actions precipitated a change to the original law in 1925. He died 20 January 1979 in Hull.

FOOTBALL

McCreery, David Born Belfast, Northern Ireland, 16 September 1957. Position: midfield. Clubs (player): Manchester United 1974-79, Queens Park Rangers 1979-81, Tulsa Roughnecks (USA) 1981-82, Newcastle 1982-89, Heart of Midlothian 1989-92, Hartlepool United 1991-92, Carlisle United 1992-95. Honours: FA Cup 1977 (with Manchester United). Clubs (manager): Hartlepool 1991-92, Coleraine 1992, Carlisle United 1992-93, Hartlepool Town 1994-95. International caps (for Northern Ireland): 67. Nicknamed 'Roadrunner'.

McDermott, Terry Born Kirkby, Liverpool, 8 December 1951. Position: midfield. Clubs (player): Bury 1969-73, Newcastle United 1973-74 (signed for £22,000), 1982-85 (signed for £100,000), Liverpool 1974-82 (signed for £170,000), Cork City, Apoel FC. Honours: League Championship 1977, 1979, 1980, 1982; League Cup 1981, 1982; European Cup 1977, 1978, 1981 (all with Liverpool). Club (manager): Newcastle United 1997 (four days). International caps (for England): 25, 3 goals. Football Writers' Player of the Year 1980. PFA Player of the Year 1980. Joined Kevin Keegan as assistant coach at Newcastle United.

Macdonald, Malcolm Born Malcolm Ian Macdonald, Fulham, London, 7 January 1950. Position: forward. Clubs (player): Tonbridge 1967, Fulham 1968-69, Luton Town 1969-71 (signed for £17,500), Newcastle United 1971-76 (signed for £180,000), Arsenal 1976-79, Djurgarden (Sweden) 1979. Clubs (manager): Fulham 1980-84, Huddersfield Town 1987-88. International caps (for England): 14, 6 goals. He scored 121 goals in 242 appearances for Newcastle and 57 goals in 108 games for Arsenal, also scoring all five England goals in a 5-0 win over Cyprus in 1975. Known as 'Supermac'. Having recovered from a decline in health due to alcohol abuse brought on by his retirement through a knee injury, he is currently working in the media. His autobiography, *Supermac*, was published in 2003.

McGovern, John Born Montrose, Scotland, 28 October 1949. Position: midfield. Clubs (player): Hartlepool United 1965-68, Derby County 1968-74 (signed for £7,500), Leeds United 1974-75 (signed for £75,000), Nottingham Forest 1975-82 (signed for £35,000), Bolton Wanderers 1982-84. Honours: League Championship 1972 (with Derby County), 1978 (with Nottingham Forest); League Cup 1978, 1979 (with Nottingham Forest); European Cup 1979, 1980 (with Nottingham Forest). Club (manager): Bolton Wanderers 1984-85. Managed by Brian Clough at Hartlepool United, Derby County, Leeds United and Nottingham Forest.

McGrain, Danny Born Daniel Fergus McGrain, Glasgow, 1 May 1950. Position: defender. Clubs: Queen's Park Victoria, Celtic 1967-87, Hamilton Academical. Honours: Scottish League Championship 1973, 1974, 1977, 1979, 1981, 1982, 1986; Scottish Cup 1974, 1975, 1977, 1980, 1985; Scottish League Cup 1974, 1982 (all with Celtic). International caps (for Scotland): 62 (10 as captain). Played in World Cup finals 1974, 1982. Voted Scottish Player of the Year 1977. Awarded the MBE in 1983. McGrain suffered from diabetes and arthritis while playing, and fractured his skull in a game against Falkirk in 1972.

McGrath, Paul Born Greenford, London, 4 December 1959. Position: defender. Clubs (player): St Patricks Athletic, Manchester United 1982-89 (signed for £30,000), Aston Villa 1989-96 (signed for £450,000), Derby County 1996-97 (signed for £200,000), Sheffield United 1997-98 (free transfer). Honours: FA Cup 1985 (with Manchester United); League Cup 1994 (with Aston Villa). Retired from playing through injury 1998. International caps (for Republic of Ireland): 75, 7 goals. PFA Player of the Year 1993.

McGrory, Jimmy Born James Edward McGrory, Glasgow, Scotland, 26 April 1904. Position: forward. Clubs (player): Celtic 1922-37, Clydebank 1923 (loan). Honours: Scottish League Championship 1926, 1936; Scottish Cup 1925, 1931, 1933, 1937 (all with Celtic). Clubs (manager): Kilmarnock 1937-39, Celtic 1945-65. International caps (for Scotland): 7, 6 goals. Retired in 1937. A prolific goal scorer, McGrory scored 397 goals for Glasgow Celtic in 378 league games. Scored eight goals in a game against Dunfermline in 1928 and a three-minute hat-trick against Motherwell in 1936. He died 20 October 1982 in Glasgow.

McIlroy, Jimmy Born Lambeg, Co. Antrim, Northern Ireland, 25 October 1931. Position: forward. Clubs (player): Glentoran 1947-50, Burnley 1950-62, Stoke City 1962-65, Oldham Athletic 1965-67. Honours: League Championship 1960 (with Burnley). Club (manager): Oldham Athletic 1966-68. International caps (for Northern Ireland): 55, 10 goals. Played in World Cup finals 1958. After retiring from the game he became a sports journalist. A stand named in his honour was opened at Turf Moor in 1999.

McIlroy, Sammy Born Belfast, 2 August 1954. Position: midfield. Clubs (player): Manchester United 1971-82, Stoke City 1982-85, Manchester City 1985-87, Orgryte IS 1986 (loan), Bury 1987-88, VfB Mödling 1988, Preston North End 1988-90. Honours: FA Cup 1977 (with Manchester United). Clubs (manager): Preston North End 1988-90, Northwich Victoria 1991-92, Ashton United 1992-93, Macclesfield Town 1993-2000, Stockport County 2003-present. International caps (for Northern Ireland): 88, 5 goals. International manager (Northern Ireland): 2000-03. Matt Busby's last signing for Manchester United. Led Macclesfield Town from the Conference into the League in 1997.

Mackay, Dave Born David Craig Mackay, Musselburgh, Midlothian, Scotland, 14 November 1934. Position: defender. Clubs (player): Heart of Midlothian 1952-59, Tottenham Hotspur 1959-68, Derby County 1968-71, Swindon Town 1971-72. Honours: Scottish League Championship 1958; Scottish Cup 1956; Scottish League Cup 1955, 1959 (all with Heart of Midlothian); League Championship 1961; FA Cup 1961; 1962, 1967 (all with Tottenham Hotspur). Clubs (manager): Swindon Town 1971-72, Nottingham Forest 1972-73, Derby County 1973-76, Walsall 1977-78, Doncaster Rovers 1987-89, Birmingham City 1989-91, Zamalek (Egypt) 1991-93. Coached in Kuwait and Dubai 1979 to 1987. Honours: League Championship 1975 (with Derby County); Egyptian League Championship 1992, 1993 (with Zamalek). International caps (for Scotland): 22, 4 goals. Scottish Player of the Year 1958. Football Writers' Player of the Year 1969 (joint). Broke a leg twice in 1963.

McLeish, Alex Born Alexander McLeish, Glasgow, 21 January 1959. Position: defender. Club (player): Aberdeen 1976-93. Honours: Scottish League Championship 1980, 1984, 1985; Scottish Cup 1982, 1983, 1984, 1986, 1990; Scottish League Cup 1986, 1990; European Cup Winners' Cup 1983. Clubs (manager): Motherwell 1994-98, Hibernian 1998-2001, Rangers 2001-present. Honours: Scottish

League Championship 2003; Scottish Cup 2003; Scottish League Cup 2003 (all with Rangers). International caps (for Scotland): 77. Scottish Player of the Year 1990.

cLintock, Frank Born Francis McLintock, Glasgow, 28 December 1939. Position: defender. Clubs (player): Leicester City 1959-64, Arsenal 1964-73 (signed for £80,000), Queens Park Rangers 1973-77 (signed for £20,000). Honours: League Championship 1971; FA Cup 1971; Inter-cities Fairs Cup 1970 (all with Arsenal). Clubs (coach/manager): Leicester City 1977, Queens Park Rangers 1982-84, Brentford 1984-87, Millwall (assistant) 1988-90. International caps (for Scotland): 9. Football Writers' Player of the Year 1971. Awarded the MBE in 1972.

cMahon, Steve Born Liverpool, 20 August 1961. Clubs (player): Everton 1979-83, Aston Villa 1983-85 (signed for £175,000), Liverpool 1985-91 (signed for £375,000), Manchester City 1991-94 (signed for £900,000), Swindon Town 1994-98 (free transfer). Honours: League Championship 1986, 1988, 1990; FA Cup 1986, 1989 (all with Liverpool). Clubs (manager): Swindon Town 1994-98, Blackpool 2000-04. International caps (for England): 17.

cManaman, Steve Born Bootle, Liverpool, 11 February 1972. Position: midfield. Clubs: Liverpool 1990-99, Real Madrid 1999-2003 (free transfer), Manchester City 2003-present. Honours: FA Cup 1992 (with Liverpool); League Cup 1995 (with Liverpool); Spanish League Championship 2001, 2003 (with Real Madrid); UEFA Champions League 2000, 2002 (with Real Madrid). International caps (for England): 37, 3 goals.

cMullan, Jimmy Born Denny, Stirling, Scotland, 26 March 1895. Position: defender. Clubs (player): Partick Thistle 1913-21, 1923-26, Maidstone United 1921-23, Manchester City 1926-33 (signed for £4700). Clubs (manager): Oldham Athletic 1933-34, Aston Villa 1934-36, Notts County 1936-37, Sheffield Wednesday 1937-42. International caps (for Scotland): 16. Captained the Scottish side dubbed the 'Wembley Wizards' after their 5-1 win over England in 1928. Left the game in 1942 to work in the Sheffield steel works. He died on 28 November 1964 in Sheffield.

cNeill, Billy Born Bellshill, North Lanarkshire, Scotland, 2 March 1940. Position: defender. Clubs (player): Blantyre Victoria, Celtic 1957-75 (signed for £250). Honours: Scottish League Championship 1966, 1967, 1968, 1969, 1970, 1971, 1972, 1973, 1974; Scottish Cup 1965, 1967, 1969, 1971, 1972, 1974, 1975; Scottish League Cup 1966, 1967, 1968, 1969, 1970, 1975; European Cup 1967 (all with Celtic). Clubs (manager): Clyde 1977, Aberdeen 1977-78, Celtic 1978-83, Manchester City 1983-86, Aston Villa 1986-87. Honours: Scottish League Championship 1979, 1981, 1982, 1988; Scottish Cup 1980, 1988, 1989; Scottish League Cup 1983 (all with Celtic). International caps (for Scotland): 29, 3 goals. Known as 'Caesar'. Scottish Player of the Year 1965. Awarded the MBE in 1974.

cQueen, Gordon Born Kilbirnie, Scotland, 26 June 1952. Position: defender. Clubs (player): Largs Thistle, St Mirren 1970-72, Leeds United 1972-78 (signed for £30,000), Manchester United 1978-85 (signed for £495,000). Honours: League Championship 1974 (with Leeds United); FA Cup 1983 (with Manchester United). Clubs (manager): Seiko Hong Kong 1985-87, Airdrieonians 1987-89, St Mirren (coach) 1989-94, Middlesbrough (coach) 1994-2001. International caps (for Scotland): 30, 5

goals. His father Tom played in goal for Queen of the South and Accrington Stanley.

McStay, Paul Born Paul Michael Lyons McStay, Hamilton, South Lanarkshire, Scotland, 22 October 1964. Position: midfield. Club: Celtic 1981-97. Retired from playing through injury in 1997. Honours: Scottish League Championship 1986, 1988; Scottish Cup 1985, 1988, 1989, 1995; Scottish League Cup 1983 (all with Celtic). International caps (for Scotland): 76, 9 goals. Scottish Player of the Year 1988. Two great-great-uncles and his brothers Willie and Raymond also played for Celtic.

McWilliam, Peter Born Inveravon, Aberdeenshire, Scotland, 21 September 1878. Position: midfield. Club (player): Newcastle United 1902-11. Honours: League Championship 1905, 1907, 1909; FA Cup 1910. Retired from playing through injury 1911. Clubs (manager): Tottenham Hotspur 1912-27, 1937-42, Middlesbrough 1927-34, Arsenal (advisor) 1934-37. Honours: FA Cup 1921 (with Tottenham Hotspur). International caps (for Scotland): 8.

Madeley, Paul Born Paul Edward Madeley, Beeston, Yorkshire, 20 September 1944. Position: defender. Club: Leeds United 1962-80. Honours: League Championship 1969, 1974; FA Cup 1972; League Cup 1968. International caps (for England): 24. During his career at Leeds he played in every outfield position. After retiring in 1980 he opened a sports shop.

Maier, Sepp Born Josef-Dieter Maier, Metten, Germany, 28 February 1944. Position: goalkeeper. Club: Bayern Munich 1958-79. Honours: German League Championship 1969, 1972, 1973, 1974; German Cup 1966, 1967, 1969, 1971; European Cup 1974, 1975, 1976; European Cup Winners' Cup 1967; World Club Championship 1976. International caps (for West Germany): 95. International honours: World Cup 1974; European Championship 1972. Retired in 1979 following a car accident. Goalkeeping coach at Bayern Munich 1994-present, he is also goalkeeping coach for the German national team.

Maldini, Paolo Born Milan, Italy, 26 June 1968. Position: defender. Club: AC Milan 1984-present. Honours: Italian League Championship 1988, 1992, 1993, 1994, 1996, 1999; European Cup/UEFA Champions League 1989, 1990, 1994, 2003. International caps (for Italy): 126, 7 goals. World Player of the Year 1994. Italy's most-capped player, he played in World Cup finals 1990, 1994, 1998 (as captain), 2002. Son of ex-AC Milan and ex-Italian national team manager Cesare Maldini, he made his debut for AC Milan at 16.

Male, George Born West Ham, London, 8 May 1910. Position: defender. Clubs: Clapton FC, Arsenal 1930-48. Honours: League Championship 1933, 1934, 1935, 1938; FA Cup 1936; Charity Shield 1934, 1935, 1939 (all with Arsenal). International caps (for England): 19 (6 as captain). On the coaching staff and also a scout for Arsenal until 1975; in all he spent 45 years at Highbury in some connection. As scout he spotted the early talent of Charlie George. He died 19 February 1998.

Mannion, Wilf Born Wilfred James Mannion, South Bank, Middlesbrough, 16 May 1918. Position: forward. Clubs: Middlesbrough 1937-54, Hull City 1955, various non-league clubs. International caps (for England): 26, 11 goals. Part of England's attacking spearhead in post-World War II internationals alongside Raich Carter and Tommy Lawton, a dispute with Middlesbrough harmed his career and cost him his England place. He died 14 April 2000.

Maradona, Diego　Born Diego Armando Maradona, Lanus, Buenos Aires, Argentina, 30 October 1960. Position: midfield. Clubs (player): Argentinos Juniors 1976-81, Boca Juniors 1981-82, 1995-97, Barcelona 1982-84 (signed for £4.8m), Napoli 1984-91 (signed for £6.9m), Seville 1992-93 (signed for £4.48m), Newell's Old Boys 1993-94. Honours: Argentine League Championship 1981 (with Boca Juniors), Italian League Championship 1987, 1990; Italian Cup 1987; UEFA Cup 1989 (all with Napoli). Clubs (coach): Mandiyu de Corrientes 1994, Racing Club de Avellaneda 1995. International caps (for Argentina): 91, 34 goals, including the so-called 'hand of God' goal against England during the 1986 World Cup when he fisted the ball into the net. International honours: World Cup 1986. Golden Ball for Player of the Tournament, World Cup 1986. Played in World Cup finals 1982, 1986, 1990, 1994. Expelled from World Cup 1994 after failing a drugs test. Argentine Football Writers' Footballer of the Year 1979, 1980, 1981. Argentine Sports Writers' Footballer of the Year 1979, 1980, 1981, 1986. The Argentine Sports Personality of the Year 1979, 1980, 1986. South American Footballer of the Year 1979, 1986, 1989, 1990, 1992. Argentine Sports Writers' Sportsman of the Century 1999. Argentine Football Federation has retired the no. 10 shirt from the squad. Known as 'El Grande'. Ill health has plagued him and he suffered a mild heart attack in April 2004.

Marindin, Arthur　Born Arthur Francis Marindin, Weymouth, Dorset, 1839. Position: defender/goalkeeper. Clubs: Royal Engineers, Old Etonians. Known as 'The Major'. Founder of both Royal Engineers and Old Etonians, he withdrew from playing in the 1875 FA Cup final so as not to offend either of the teams contesting the match despite having played in both the Engineers' previous losing finals. He refereed nine FA Cup finals; in the 1884 final the Scots of Queen's Park were bemused when he ruled two of their perfectly legal goals offside while allowing a Blackburn Rovers goal when it was clearly offside. Marindin, who was apparently using the English offside law (which at the time was different from the Scottish one), claimed that if the Scots players had protested he would have disallowed the Blackburn goal. Blackburn won 2-1. A major in the Royal Engineers and president of the Football Association 1874-90. Marindin withdrew from the game at the onset of professionalism. He also helped establish the International Board of the home unions in rugby in 1889 and was later knighted.

Marsh, Rodney　Born Rodney William Marsh, Hatfield, Hertfordshire, 11 October 1944. Position: forward. Clubs (player): Fulham 1962-65, Queens Park Rangers 1965-72 (signed for £15,000), Manchester City 1972-75 (signed for £200,000), Tampa Bay Rowdies 1976-79 (signed for £45,000), Fulham 1976 (loan). Honours: League Cup 1967 (with Queens Park Rangers); US Championship 1976, 1977, 1978, 1979 (with Tampa Bay Rowdies). Clubs (manager): Tampa Bay Rowdies 1984. International caps (for England): 9, 1 goal. Now working in the media, his autobiography *Priceless* was published in 2001.

Martyn, Nigel　Born Antony Nigel Martyn, St Austell, Cornwall, 11 August 1966. Position: goalkeeper. Clubs: St Blazey, Bristol Rovers 1987-89, Crystal Palace 1989-96 (signed for £1m), Leeds United 1996-2003 (signed for £2.25m), Everton 2003-present. Honours: Full Members Cup 1991 (with Crystal Palace). International caps (for England): 23.

Masopust, Josef　Born Most, Bohemia, 9 February 1931. Position: midfield. Clubs (player): Union Teplice 1948-51, Dukla Prague 1951-68, Crossing Molenbeek 1968-71. Honours: Czech League Championship 1956, 1958, 1961, 1962, 1963, 1964, 1966; Prague Czech Cup 1961, 1965, 1966 (all with Dukla Prague). Club (manager): Dukla Prague (assistant). International caps (for Czechoslovakia): 63, 10 goals. International manager (Czechoslovakia): 1984-87. European Player of the Year 1962.

Matthäus, Lothar　Born Erlangen, West Germany, 21 March 1961. Position: midfield. Clubs: FC Herzogenaurach, Borussia Mönchengladbach 1979-84, Bayern Munich 1984-88, 1992-2000, Inter Milan 1988-92 (signed for £2.4m), New Jersey Metrostars 2000-present. Honours: German League Championship 1985, 1986, 1987, 1994, 1997, 1999, 2000 (with Bayern Munich); German League Cup 1986, 1998, 2000 (with Bayern Munich); Italian League Championship 1989 (with Inter Milan); UEFA Cup 1991 (with Inter Milan), 1996 (with Bayern Munich). International caps (for Germany): 150, 22 goals. International honours: World Cup 1990; European Championship 1980. German Player of the Year 1990, 1999. European Player of the Year 1990. World Player of the Year 1991. Appeared in five World Cup finals (1982, 1986, 1990, 1994, 1998).

Matthews, Sir Stanley　Born Hanley, Stoke-on-Trent, 1 February 1915. Position: forward. Clubs (player): Stoke City 1932-47, 1961-65, Blackpool 1947-61. Honours: FA Cup 1953 (with Blackpool). Clubs (manager): Port Vale 1965-68, Hibernian (Malta) 1969. Also coached in South Africa. International caps (for England): 54, 11 goals. First Football Writers' Player of the Year 1948, also 1963. First European Player of the Year 1956. First footballer awarded a CBE (1957). First footballer to be knighted (1965). Aged 50 years and 5 days when he played his final League game for Stoke v Fulham in 1965. Known as 'The Wizard of Dribble', 'The King of Soccer' and 'The Maestro'. He died 23 February 2000.

May, David　Born Oldham, Lancashire, 24 June 1970. Position: defender. Clubs: Blackburn Rovers 1988-94, Manchester United 1994-2003 (signed for £1.25m), Huddersfield Town 1999 (loan). Honours: FA Premiership 1996, 1997, 1999; FA Cup 1996, 1999; Charity Shield 1994, 1996; UEFA Champions League 1999 (all with Manchester United).

Mazzola, Sandro　Born Alessandro Mazzola, Turin, Italy, 8 November 1942. Position: forward/midfield. Club: Inter Milan 1960-77. Honours: Italian League Championship 1963, 1965, 1966, 1971; European Cup 1964, 1965. International caps (for Italy): 70, 22 goals. International honours: European Championship 1968. Played in World Cup finals 1966, 1970, 1974. Son of Valentino Mazzola.

Mazzola, Valentino　Born Cassano d'Adda, Milan, Italy, 26 January 1919. Position: midfield/forward. Clubs: Alfa Romeo Milan, Venezia 1939-42, Torino 1942-49. Honours: Italian League Championship 1943, 1946, 1947, 1948, 1949 (with Torino); Italian Cup 1941 (with Venezia), 1943 (with Torino). International caps (for Italy): 12 (5 as captain), 4 goals. Mazzola was killed along with 18 other members of the Torino team in the Superga air crash, 4 May 1949. With Torino just four matches from winning their fourth consecutive Scudetto the season was played out between Torino's youth team and the youth teams of their opponents.

Meazza, Giuseppe Born Milan, Italy, 23 August 1910. Position: forward. Clubs (player): Inter Milan 1927-39, 1946-47, AC Milan 1940-42, Juventus 1942-43, Atalanta 1945-46. Honours: Italian Championship 1930, 1938; Italian Cup 1939 (all with Inter Milan). Club (manager): Inter Milan 1946-47. International caps (for Italy): 53, 33 goals. International honours: World Cup 1934, 1938 (as captain). International manager (Italy): 1952-53. Known as 'Peppino', he was deplored by the Fascist government for his popularity with the masses. On one occasion the entire Italian team excepting Meazza were honoured by the government in an attempt to humiliate him. The San Siro Stadium, the home of Inter Milan, was officially renamed the Giuseppe Meazza Stadium in his memory. He died 21 August 1979.

Meisl, Hugo Born Vienna, Austria, 16 November 1881. Clubs: Cricketers, Austria FK. Known as 'The Father of Austrian Football', Meisl brought English coach Jimmy Hogan to Vienna to run the national side – the 'Wunderteam'. He died 17 February 1937 in Vienna.

Mendieta, Gaizka Born Gaizka Mendieta Zabala, Bilbao, Spain, 27 March 1974. Position: midfield. Clubs: Castellon 1990-92, Valencia 1992-2001, Lazio 2001-present (signed for £28.9m), Barcelona 2002 (loan), Middlesbrough 2003-present (loan). Honours: Spanish Cup 1999 (with Valencia). International caps (for Spain): 39, 8 goals.

Mercer, Joe Born Ellesmere Port, Cheshire, 9 August 1914. Position: midfield. Clubs (player): Everton 1932-46, Arsenal 1946-54. Honours: League Championship 1939 (with Everton), 1948, 1953 (with Arsenal); FA Cup 1950 (with Arsenal). Playing career ended by injury in April 1954. Clubs (manager): Sheffield United 1955-58, Aston Villa 1958-64, Manchester City 1965-72, Coventry City 1972-75. Honours: League Championship 1968 (with Manchester City); FA Cup 1969 (with Manchester City); League Cup 1960 (with Aston Villa), 1970 (with Manchester City), European Cup Winners' Cup 1970 (with Manchester City). International manager (England): 1974 (caretaker). Football Writers' Player of the Year 1950. Awarded the OBE in 1976. He died on his 76th birthday, 9 August 1990, at Hoylake, Merseyside.

Meredith, Billy Born William Henry Meredith, Chirk, nr Wrexham, Wales, 30 July 1874. Position: forward. Clubs (player): Black Park 1890-92, Northwich Victoria 1892-94, Manchester City 1894-1906, 1921-24, Manchester United 1906-21, Stalybridge Celtic 1915-19 (wartime). Honours: League Championship 1908, 1911 (with Manchester United); FA Cup 1904 (with Manchester City), 1909 (with Manchester United); Welsh Cup 1892 (with Black Park). Clubs (manager): Manchester City 1921-24, Manchester United (coach) 1931. International caps (for Wales): 48, 11 goals. Played his last international at the age of 48. Meredith was at the centre of a scandal in 1905 when, while playing for Manchester City, he was accused of attempting to bribe an Aston Villa opponent. He was suspended for a year as a result and sold to Manchester United. He was a founder member of the Players' Union in Manchester in 1907. Always played with a toothpick in his mouth. Known as 'The Prince of Wingers', 'The Welsh Wizard' and 'Old Skinny'. He died 19 April 1958 in Manchester.

Merson, Paul Born Paul Charles Merson, Northolt, Middlesex, 20 March 1968. Position: midfield. Clubs: Arsenal 1985-97, Brentford 1987 (loan), Middlesbrough 1997-98 (signed for £4.5m), Aston Villa 1998-2002 (signed for £6.75m), Portsmouth 2002-03 (free transfer), Walsall 2003-present (free transfer). Honours: League Championship 1989, 1991; FA Cup 1993; League Cup 1993; European Cup Winners' Cup 1994 (all with Arsenal). International caps (for England): 21, 3 goals.

Milburn, Jackie Born John Edward Thompson Milburn, Ashington, Northumberland, 11 May 1924. Position: forward. Clubs (player): Newcastle United 1946-57, Linfield 1957-60. Honours: FA Cup 1951, 1952, 1955 (with Newcastle United); Northern Irish League Championship 1959 (with Linfield); Northern Ireland Cup 1960 (with Linfield). Clubs (manager): Linfield, Ipswich Town 1963-65. International caps (for England): 13, 10 goals. Known as 'Wor Jackie'. Four of his cousins (George, Jack, Jim and Stanley) played League football; a fifth, Cissie, was the mother of Bobby and Jack Charlton. Milburn once ran 200yds in 19.7secs. As a result of fibrositis he rarely headed the ball although in the 1955 FA Cup final he scored after 45 seconds with a header (then the quickest Wembley Cup final goal). Scored in every round of the FA Cup in 1951. Ulster Player of the Year 1958, he played in the European Cup for Linfield. After retirement he worked as a journalist for the *News of the World*. Milburn was granted the Freedom of the City of Newcastle (2 January 1980), where a statue of him stands. He died 8 October 1988 in Ashington and his ashes are scattered on the Gallowgate end of St James' Park.

Milla, Roger Born Albert Roger Milla, Yaoundé, Cameroon, 20 May 1952. Position: forward. Clubs: Eclair de Douala 1965-70, Leopard Douala 1970-73, Tonnerre Yaoundé 1974-77, Valenciennes (France) 1977-79, Monaco 1979-80, Bastia 1980-84, St-Etienne 1984-86, Montpellier 1986-89, St Pierre (Reunion Islands) 1990-94. Honours: Cameroon League Championship 1972 (with Leopard Douala); Cameroon Cup 1974 (with Tonnerre Yaoundé); African Cup Winners' Cup 1976 (with Tonnerre Yaoundé); French Cup 1980 (with Monaco), 1981 (with Bastia); Reunion Islands Championship 1990 (with St Pierre). International caps (for Cameroon): 81. International honours: African Cup of Nations 1984, 1988. Winner of African Golden Ball 1976. African Footballer of the Year 1976, 1990. Having retired from French League football in 1989, he came back to play in the World Cup finals of 1990, 1994, and became the oldest scorer in the World Cup finals 1994 (aged 42). He is now an ambassador for African football.

Miller, Kenny Born Edinburgh, 23 December 1979. Position: forward. Clubs: Hutchison Vale BC, Hibernian 1996-2000, Stenhousemuir 1998 (loan), Rangers 2000-01 (signed for £2m), Wolverhampton Wanderers 2001-present (loan, then signed for £3m). International caps (for Scotland): 2, 1 goal.

Miller, Willie Born Glasgow, 1955. Position: defender. Club (player): Aberdeen 1971-90. Honours: Scottish League Championship 1980, 1984, 1985; Scottish Cup 1982, 1983, 1984, 1986, 1990; Scottish League Cup 1986, 1990; European Cup Winners' Cup 1983. Club (manager): Aberdeen 1992-95. International caps (for Scotland): 65, 1 goal. Scottish Player of the Year 1984. Voted the greatest-ever Aberdeen player in 2003.

Mills, Danny Born Daniel John Mills, Norwich, 18 May 1977. Position: defender. Clubs: Norwich City 1994-98, Charlton Athletic 1998-99 (signed for

£350,000), Leeds United 1999-present (signed for £4.37m), Middlesbrough 2003-present (loan). International caps (for England): 18.

Mills, Mick Born Michael Denis Mills, Godalming, Surrey, 4 January 1949. Position: defender. Clubs (player): Ipswich Town 1966-82, Southampton 1982-85, Stoke City 1985-87. Honours: FA Cup 1978; UEFA Cup 1981 (both with Ipswich). Clubs (manager): Stoke City 1985-89, Colchester United 1990, Coventry City (assistant) 1991, Birmingham City 2001. International caps (for England): 42 (8 as captain). Awarded the MBE in 1984.

Milne, Gordon Born Preston, Lancashire, 29 March 1937. Position: midfield. Clubs (player): Morecambe, Preston North End 1956-60, Liverpool 1960-67 (signed for £16,000), Blackpool 1967-69. Honours: League Championship 1964, 1966; Charity Shield 1964, 1965 (all with Liverpool). Clubs (manager): Blackpool 1969-70, Wigan Athletic 1970-72, Coventry City 1974-81, Leicester City 1982-86, Besiktas, Nagoya Grampus 8. International caps (for England): 14. Currently working at Newcastle United.

Moncur, Bobby Born Perth, Scotland, 19 January 1945. Position: defender. Clubs (player): Newcastle United 1963-74, Sunderland 1974-76 (signed for £30,000), Carlisle United 1976-77. Honours: Inter-cities Fairs Cup 1969 (with Newcastle United). Clubs (manager): Carlisle United 1976-77, Heart of Midlothian 1980-81, Plymouth Argyle 1981-83, Whitley Bay, Hartlepool United 1988-89. International caps (for Scotland): 16. Scored a hat-trick to help Newcastle win the Fairs Cup final in 1969. Having retired from the game in 1989, he now runs a yacht business and has taken part in the Fastnet Race.

Monti, Luis Born Luisito Felipe Monti, Buenos Aires, Argentina, 15 May 1901. Position: defender. Clubs: Huracan, Boca Juniors 1922, Nacional San Lorenzo de Almagro 1922-30, Juventus 1931-39. Honours: Argentinian Championship 1921 (with Huracan), 1923, 1924, 1927 (with San Lorenzo); Italian League Championship 1932, 1933, 1934, 1935 (with Juventus); Italian Cup 1938 (with Juventus). International caps (for Argentina): 16, 5 goals International caps (for Italy): 18. International honours: 1 goal, World Cup 1934 (with Italy). Played in the 1930 World Cup for Argentina and in the 1934 World Cup for Italy. Nicknamed 'Doble Ancho' (double wide) for his ability to cover so much of the pitch. He died on 9 September 1983.

Moore, Bobby Born Robert Frederick Chelsea Moore, Barking, Essex, 12 April 1941. Position: defender. Clubs (player): West Ham United 1958-74, Fulham 1974-77, San Antonio Thunder 1976, Seattle Sounders 1978. Honours: FA Cup 1964; European Cup Winners' Cup 1965 (both with West Ham United). Clubs (manager): Herning (Denmark) 1978, Oxford City 1979-80, Southend 1984-86. International caps (for England): 108 (90 as captain), 2 goals. International honours: World Cup 1966. Played in World Cup finals 1962, 1966, 1970. Football Writers' Player of the Year 1964. BBC Sports Personality of the Year 1966. Awarded the OBE in 1967. His 90 appearances as captain of his country are a world record (shared with Billy Wright). Worked for the *Sunday Sport* as a journalist and on promotions. Had a part in the film *Escape to Victory*. He died 24 February 1993 in Putney, London.

Morena, Fernando Born Montevideo, Uruguay, 2 February 1952. Position: forward. Clubs: River Plate, Peñarol, Rayo Vallecano, Flamengo. Honours: Copa Libertadores 1982 (with Peñarol). International caps (for Uruguay): 49, 20 goals. International honours: Copa America 1983.

Morientes, Fernando Born Carceres, Spain, 5 April 1976. Position: forward. Clubs: Albacete 1993-95, Real Zaragoza 1995-97, Real Madrid 1997-present. Honours: Spanish League Championship 2001, 2003; Spanish Cup 2003; UEFA Champions League 1998, 2000, 2002 (all with Real Madrid). International caps (for Spain): 27, 17 goals.

Mortensen, Stan Born Stanley Harding Mortensen, South Shields, Tyne & Wear, 26 May 1921. Position: forward. Clubs (player): Blackpool 1937-55, Hull City 1955-56, Southport 1956-57, Southampton, Bath City, Lancaster City. Honours: FA Cup 1953 (with Blackpool). Retired from playing 1962. Club (manager): Blackpool 1962-64. International caps (for England): 25, 23 goals. Seriously injured when his bomber crashed during World War II. Known as 'The Blackpool Bombshell' and 'The Electric Eel'. He scored four goals in his full England debut against Portugal 25 May 1947. He died May 1991 in Blackpool.

Morton, Alan Born Alan Lauder Morton, Partick, Glasgow, 24 April 1893. Position: forward. Clubs: Queen's Park 1913-20, Rangers 1920-33. Honours: Scottish League Championship 1921, 1923, 1924, 1925, 1927, 1928, 1929, 1930, 1931; Scottish Cup 1928, 1930 (all with Rangers). International caps (for Scotland): 31. One of the 'Wembley Wizards', he later became a director of Rangers. Nicknamed 'The Wee Blue Devil'. He died 15 December 1971 in Glasgow.

Müller, Gerd Born Gerhardt Muller, Zinsen, Germany, 3 November 1945. Position: forward. Clubs: TSV Nordlingen, Bayern Munich 1964-79, Fort Lauderdale Strikers 1979-81. Honours: German League Championship 1969, 1972, 1973, 1974; European Cup 1974, 1975, 1976; European Cup Winners' Cup 1967; World Club Championship 1976 (all with Bayern Munich). Scored 365 goals in 427 League games. International caps (for West Germany): 62, 68 goals. International honours: World Cup 1974; European Championship 1972. Golden Boot winner, World Cup 1970. German Player of the Year 1967, 1969. European Player of the Year 1970. European Golden Boot winner 1970, 1972. Known as 'Der Bomber'. He is currently youth team coach at Bayern Munich.

Mullery, Alan Born Alan Patrick Mullery, Notting Hill, London, 23 November 1941. Position: midfield. Clubs (player): Fulham 1958-64, Tottenham Hotspur 1964-72 (signed for £72,000), Fulham 1972-76. Honours: FA Cup 1967; League Cup 1971; UEFA Cup 1972 (all with Tottenham Hotspur). Clubs (manager): Brighton & Hove Albion 1976-81, 1986-87, Charlton Athletic 1981-82, Crystal Palace 1982-84, Queens Park Rangers 1984, Barnet. International caps (for England): 35 (1 as captain), 1 goal. First England player to be sent off – against Yugoslavia in 1968. Football Writers' Player of the Year 1975. Awarded the MBE 1976. Retired from the game in 1987.

Murdoch, Bobby Born Robert White Murdoch, Bothwell, Scotland, 17 August 1944. Position: midfield. Clubs (player): Celtic 1959-73, Middlesbrough 1973-76. Honours: Scottish League Championship 1966, 1967, 1968, 1969, 1970, 1971, 1972, 1973; Scottish Cup 1965, 1967, 1969, 1971, 1972; Scottish League Cup 1966, 1967, 1968, 1969, 1970; European Cup 1967 (all with Celtic). Club (manager): Middlesbrough 1976-81 (juniors), 1981-82. International caps (for Scotland): 12, 6 goals. Scottish Player of the Year 1969. He died 15 May 2001 in Glasgow.

Murphy, Danny Born Daniel Benjamin Murphy, Chester, 18 March 1977. Position: midfield. Clubs: Crewe Alexandra 1994-97, 1999 (loan), Liverpool 1997-present (signed for £1.5m). Honours: FA Cup 2001; League Cup 2001, 2003; Charity Shield 2001; UEFA Cup 2001 (all with Liverpool). International caps (for England): 8, 1 goal.

Nadal, Miguel Angel Born Manacor, Spain, 28 July 1966. Position: defender. Clubs: Real Mallorca 1986-91, 1999-present, Barcelona 1990-99. Honours: Spanish League Championship 1991, 1992, 1993, 1994, 1998; European Cup Winners' Cup 1997; European Cup 1992 (all with Barcelona). International caps (for Spain): 59, 3 goals.

Nakata, Hidetoshi Born Kofu City, Yamanashi Prefecture, Japan, 22 January 1977. Position: midfield. Clubs: Bellmare Hiratsuka (now Shonan Bellmare) 1995-98, Perugia 1998-2000, Roma 2000-01, Parma 2001-present. Honours: Asian Cup Winners' Cup 1996 (with Bellmare Hiratsuka). Italian League Championship 2001 (with Roma); Italian Cup 2002 (with Parma). International caps (for Japan): 54, 10 goals. Asian Player of the Year 1997, 1998.

Nasazzi, Jose Born Montevideo, Uruguay, 24 May 1901. Position: defender. Clubs: Lito FC, Bella Vista. International caps (for Uruguay): not known. International honours: Olympic gold medal 1924, 1928; World Cup 1930; Copa America 1923, 1924, 1926, 1935. Retired in 1937. Known as 'El Mariscal' (The Marshal). He died 1968.

Neal, Phil Born Philip George Neal, Irchester, Northants, 20 February 1951. Clubs (player): Northampton Town 1967-74, Liverpool 1974-85 (signed for £65,000), Bolton Wanderers 1985-89. Honours: League Championship 1976, 1977, 1979, 1980, 1982, 1983, 1984; League Cup 1981, 1982, 1983, 1984; European Cup 1977, 1978, 1981, 1984; UEFA Cup 1976 (all with Liverpool). Clubs (manager): Bolton Wanderers 1985-92, Coventry City 1993-95, Cardiff City 1996, Manchester City 1996. International caps (for England): 50 (1 as captain), 5 goals.

Nedved, Pavel Born Cheb, Czechoslovakia, 30 August 1972. Position: midfield. Clubs: Dukla Prague 1991-92, Sparta Prague 1992-97, Lazio 1997-2001, Juventus 2001-present (signed for £25m). Honours: Czechoslovakian Championship 1993 (with Sparta Prague); Czech Championship 1994, 1995 (with Sparta Prague); Czech Cup 1996 (with Sparta Prague); Italian Championship 2000 (with Lazio), 2002 (with Juventus); Italian Cup 1998, 2000 (with Lazio); Italian Super Cup 1998, 2000 (with Lazio), 2002 (with Juventus); European Cup Winners' Cup 1999 (with Lazio). International caps (for Czech Republic): 70, 16 goals. Czech Player of the Year 1998, 2000, 2001. European Footballer of the Year 2003.

Needham, Ernest Born Newbold Moor, Chesterfield, Derbyshire, 21 January 1873. Position: midfield/defender. Club: Sheffield United 1891-1910. Honours: League Championship 1898; FA Cup 1899, 1902 (all with Sheffield United). International caps (for England): 16 (1 as captain), 3 goals. Known as 'Nudger Needham', he captained Sheffield United to their Championship and FA Cup victories. He was also called 'The Prince of Half-backs'. First Sheffield United player to captain England. Author of a book, *Association Football*, in which he recalled a game during which Charlie Athersmith of Aston Villa carried an umbrella because of the freezing conditions, several Villa players turned out in overcoats and

Needham himself stopped playing with 30 minutes left to play in fear of catching pneumonia. Also played first-class cricket for Derbyshire 1901-12, scoring over 6500 runs at an average of 20.15. He died 8 March 1936 in Chesterfield.

Neeskens, Johan Born Heemstede, Holland, 15 September 1951. Position: midfield. Clubs (player): RCH Heemdale 1968-70, Ajax 1970-74, Barcelona 1974-79, New York Cosmos 1979-84, FC Groningen 1984-85, Fort Lauderdale Sun 1986, Lowenbrau 1986-87, FC Baar (Switzerland) 1987-90, FC Zug (Switzerland) 1990-91. Honours: Dutch League Championship 1972, 1973; Dutch Cup 1971, 1972; European Cup 1971, 1972, 1973 (all with Ajax); Spanish Cup 1978 (with Barcelona); European Cup Winners' Cup 1979 (with Barcelona). Clubs (manager): FC Baar 1987-90, FC Zug 1990-93, FC Stafa 1993-95, FC Singen 1995-96, Nujmegen NEC 2000-present. International caps (for Holland): 49, 17 goals. International manager (Holland): 1997-2000 (co-manager and youth team coach). Scored the first penalty in a World Cup final (1974).

Nesta, Alessandro Born Rome, 19 March 1976. Position: defender. Clubs: Lazio 1993-2002, AC Milan 2002-present. Honours: Italian Championship 2000; Italian Cup 1998, 2000; European Cup Winners' Cup 1999 (all with Lazio); UEFA Champions League 2003 (with AC Milan). International caps (for Italy): 50.

Netto, Igor Born Moscow, USSR, 9 January 1930. Position: midfield. Club: Spartak Moscow 1948-66. Honours: USSR League Championship 1952, 1953, 1956, 1958, 1962; USSR Cup Winners' Cup 1950, 1958, 1963, 1965. International caps (for USSR): 58, 4 goals. International honours: Olympic gold medal 1956; European Championship 1960. Having retired in 1966 he became an ice-hockey trainer. International manager (Iran): 1970. Voted in at number 71 in a 2004 UEFA poll of best-ever European players, just ahead of Paul Gascoigne. He died 30 March 1999 in Moscow.

Netzer, Gunter Born Mönchengladbach, Germany, 14 September 1944. Position: midfield. Clubs (player): Borussia Mönchengladbach 1961-73, Real Madrid 1973-76, Grasshoppers Zurich 1976-78. Honours: German League Championship 1970, 1971 (with Borussia Mönchengladbach); German Cup 1973 (with Borussia Mönchengladbach); Spanish League Championship 1975, 1976 (with Real Madrid); Spanish Cup 1974, 1975 (with Real Madrid). Clubs (manager): SV Hamburg 1978-86. Honours: German League Championship 1979, 1982, 1983. International caps (for West Germany): 38, 6 goals. International honours: World Cup 1974; European Championship 1972. Netzer today is one of the powerful figures in German football. He is the country's most influential TV soccer commentator and writes a column for a top trade magazine, *Sport Bild*. In 2002 the KirchMedia Group was taken over by a company headed by Netzer, who was already a manager at KirchSport.

Neville, Gary Born Gary Alexander Neville, Bury, Lancashire, 18 February 1975. Position: defender. Club: Manchester United 1992-present. Honours: FA Premiership 1996, 1997, 1999, 2000, 2001, 2003; FA Cup 1996, 1999, 2004; Charity/Community Shield 1996, 2003; UEFA Champions League 1999. International caps (for England): 56. Brother of Phil Neville.

Neville, Phil Born Philip John Neville, Bury, Lancashire, 21 January 1977. Position: defender.

F
O
O
T
B
A
L
L

Club: Manchester United 1994-present. Honours: FA Premiership 1996, 1997, 1999, 2000, 2001, 2003; FA Cup 1996, 1999; Charity/Community Shield 1996, 1997, 2003; UEFA Champions League 1999. International caps (for England): 41. Brother of Gary Neville.

Nicholas, Charlie Born Cowcaddens, Scotland, 30 December 1961. Position: forward. Clubs (player): Celtic 1980-83, Arsenal 1984-88, Aberdeen 1988-90 (signed for £400,000), Clyde 1995-96. Honours: Scottish League Championship 1982, 1983 (with Celtic); League Cup 1987 (with Arsenal). International caps (for Scotland): 20, 5 goals. Scottish Player of the Year 1983. Nicknamed 'Champagne Charlie'. Now a pundit on TV.

Nicholl, Jimmy Born James Michael Nicholl, Hamilton, Canada, 28 February 1956. Clubs (player): Manchester United 1974-82, Sunderland 1981-82 (loan), Toronto Blizzard (Canada) 1982, Sunderland 1982, Rangers 1983-84 (loan), 1986-89, West Bromwich Albion 1984-86, Dunfermline Athletic 1989-90, Raith Rovers 1990-96. Honours: FA Cup 1977 (with Manchester United); Scottish League Championship 1987 (with Rangers); Scottish League Cup 1987, 1988 (with Rangers). Clubs (manager): Rangers (reserve team) 1986-89, Raith Rovers 1990-96, 1997-99, Millwall 1996-97, Dunfermline Athletic (assistant) 1999-present. Honours: Scottish League Cup 1995 (with Raith Rovers). International caps (for Northern Ireland): 73, 2 goals. Scottish Manager of the Year 1995.

Nicholson, Bill Born William Edward Nicholson, Scarborough, Yorkshire, 26 January 1919. Position: defender. Club (player): Tottenham Hotspur 1938-54. Honours: League Championship 1951. Club (manager): Tottenham Hotspur 1955-58 (assistant), 1958-74. Honours: League Championship 1961; FA Cup 1961, 1962, 1967; League Cup 1971, 1973; European Cup Winners' Cup 1963; UEFA Cup 1972. International caps (for England): 1, 1 goal. Awarded the OBE in 1975. Scout for West Ham 1975-76. Appointed club president of Tottenham Hotspur 1991. The road leading to the main gates at White Hart Lane is named Bill Nicholson Way.

Nicol, Steve Born Irvine, Scotland, 11 December 1961. Position: defence/midfield. Clubs (player): Ayr United, Liverpool 1981-94 (signed for £300,000), Notts County 1995, Sheffield Wednesday, Doncaster Rovers. Honours: League Championship 1984, 1986, 1988, 1990; FA Cup 1986, 1989, 1992; Charity Shield 1989 (all with Liverpool). Clubs (coach): Notts County 1995, New England Revolution 2002-03, Boston Bulldogs 2003-present. International caps (for Scotland): 27. Football Writers' Player of the Year 1989. Major League Soccer (MLS) Coach of the Year 2002.

Nordahl, Gunnar Born Hornefors, Sweden, 19 October 1921. Position: forward. Clubs (player): Hornefors, Degefors 1940-44, IFK Norrkoping 1944-49, AC Milan 1949-56, Roma 1956-59. Honours: Swedish League Championship 1945, 1946, 1947, 1948 (with IFK Norrkoping); Swedish Cup 1945 (with IFK Norrkoping); Italian League Championship 1951, 1955 (with AC Milan). Club (manager): Karlstad. International caps (for Sweden): 33, 43 goals. International honours: Olympic gold medal 1948. A member of the 'Gre-No-Li' forward line for both Sweden and AC Milan, he scored 473 goals in 518 games. One of five brothers who all played in the top flight in Sweden, he worked as a fireman while playing there. Retired from playing in 1959 and took up coaching in Sweden. He died 1995.

Oakley, William Born Shrewsbury, Shropshire, 27 April 1873. Position: defender. Clubs: Oxford University, Corinthians. International caps (for England): 16 (1 as captain). Also an athlete he was AAA long-jump champion in 1895, jumping 6.56m (equivalent).

Ocwirk, Ernst Born Vienna, Austria, 7 March 1926. Position: midfield. Clubs (player): Austria FAC, FK Austria Vienna 1947-56, 1961-63, Sampdoria 1956-61. Honours: Austrian Championship 1949, 1950, 1953, 1962, 1963 (all with Austria Vienna). Clubs (manager): Sampdoria 1962-65, Austria Vienna 1965-70, IF Cologne 1970-71, Admira-Energie 1972-76. Honours: Austrian Championship 1969, 1970 (with Austria Vienna). International caps (for Austria): 62. Nicknamed 'Clockwork' and 'Ossi'. He died 23 January 1980 in Kleinpochlarn, Lower Austria.

O'Flanagan, Kevin Born Kevin Patrick O'Flanagan, Dublin, 10 June 1919. Clubs: Bohemians 1935-39, Arsenal 1945-49, Brentford 1950. International caps (for Republic of Ireland): 1. While playing for Arsenal he also played rugby union for London Irish and played for Arsenal as an amateur while practising as a doctor. An all-round sportsman, he also won one cap at rugby union and was Irish 100yds and long-jump champion. Medical Officer for the Irish Olympic teams 1960, 1964, 1968, and a member of the International Olympic Committee.

O'Hare, John Born Renton, Scotland, 24 September 1946. Position: forward. Clubs (player): Sunderland 1963-67, Derby County 1967-74 (signed for £20,000), Leeds United 1974-75, Nottingham Forest 1975-80, Dallas Tornado 1997. Honours: League Championship 1972 (with Derby County), 1978 (with Nottingham Forest); League Cup 1978 (with Nottingham Forest); European Cup 1979, 1980 (with Nottingham Forest). International caps (for Scotland): 13. Nicknamed 'Solly'.

O'Leary, David Born David Anthony O'Leary, Stoke Newington, London, 2 May 1958. Position: defender. Clubs (player): Shelbourne, Arsenal 1973-93, Leeds United 1993-94. Honours: League Championship 1989, 1991; FA Cup 1979, 1993 (all with Arsenal). Retired from playing 1995. Clubs (manager): Leeds United 1996-98 (assistant), 1998-2002, Aston Villa 2003-present. International caps (for Republic of Ireland): 67. Wrote a controversial account of his time as Leeds United manager, *Leeds United on Trial*.

O'Neill, Martin Born Martin Hugh Michael O'Neill, Kilrea, Co. Derry, Northern Ireland, 1 March 1952. Position: midfield. Clubs (player): Derry City, Nottingham Forest 1971-81, Norwich City 1981, 1982-83 (signed for £150,000), Manchester City 1981, Notts County 1983-84, Chesterfield 1984, Fulham 1984-85. Honours: League Championship 1978; League Cup 1978, 1979; European Cup 1979, 1980 (all with Nottingham Forest). Clubs (manager): Grantham Town 1987-89, Shepshed Charterhouse 1989-90, Wycombe Wanderers 1990-95, Norwich City 1995, Leicester City 1995-2000, Celtic 2000-present. Honours: League Cup 2000 (with Leicester City); Scottish League Championship 2001, 2002; Scottish Cup 2001; Scottish League Cup 2001 (all with Celtic). International caps (for Northern Ireland) 64, 8 goals.

Osgood, Peter Born Peter Leslie Osgood, Windsor, Berkshire, 20 February 1947. Position: forward. Clubs: Chelsea 1965-76, 1978-79, Southampton 1973-77, Norwich City 1976 (loan), Philadelphia Fury 1978. Honours: FA Cup 1970 (with Chelsea), 1976 (with Southampton); European Cup Winners'

Cup 1971 (with Chelsea). International caps (for England): 4. Scored in every round of the 1970 FA Cup. Now an after-dinner speaker.

O'Shea, John　Born John Francis O'Shea, Waterford, Ireland, 30 April 1981. Clubs: Waterford United, Manchester United 1998-present, AFC Bournemouth 2000 (loan), Royal Antwerp 2001 (loan). Honours: FA Premiership 2003; Community Shield 2003 (both with Manchester United). International caps (for Republic of Ireland): 7.

Overath, Wolfgang　Born Seigberg, Germany, 29 September 1943. Position: midfield. Clubs: SV Seigburg 04, FC Cologne 1963-77. Honours: German Championship 1964; German Cup 1968, 1977 (all with FC Cologne); International caps (for West Germany): 81. International honours: World Cup 1974. Retired in 1977 after the German Cup final.

Overmars, Marc　Born Emst, Holland, 29 March 1973. Position: midfield. Clubs: SV Epe 1979-87, Go Ahead Eagles 1987-91, Willem II 1991-92, Ajax 1992-97, Arsenal 1997-2000, Barcelona 2000-present. Honours: Dutch League Championship 1994, 1995, 1996 (with Ajax); Dutch Cup 1993 (with Ajax); English Premiership 1998 (with Arsenal); FA Cup 1998 (with Arsenal); UEFA Champions League 1995 (with Ajax); World Club Cup 1995 (with Ajax). International caps (for Holland): 74, 16 goals. Known variously as 'The Flying Dutchman', 'Overdrive' and 'Quickfoot'.

Owen, Michael　Born Michael James Owen, Chester, 14 December 1979. Club: Liverpool 1996-2004, Real Madrid 2004-present. Honours: FA Cup 2001; League Cup 2001, 2003; Charity Shield 2001; UEFA Cup 2001. International caps (for England): 53 (6 as captain), 24 goals. Football Writers' Player of the Year 2001. European Player of the Year 2001.

Owen, Syd　Born Sydney William Owen, Small Heath, Birmingham, 29 February 1922. Position: defender. Clubs (player): Birmingham City, Luton Town 1947-59. Club (manager): Luton Town 1959-60. International caps (for England): 3. Football Writers' Player of the Year 1959. Captained Luton Town to their 1959 FA Cup final appearance. Assistant to Don Revie at Leeds United, he was also youth team coach at Manchester United. He died January 1999.

Pahars, Marian　Born Marians Pahars, Riga, Latvia, 5 August 1976. Position: forward. Clubs: Pardaugava Riga 1994, Skonto Riga 1994-99, Southampton 1999-present (signed for £800,000). International caps (for Latvia): 53, 14 goals. Latvian Player of the Year 1999, 2000, 2001.

Paine, Terry　Born Terence Lionel Paine, Winchester, Hampshire, 23 March 1939. Position: forward. Clubs (player): Winchester City, Southampton 1957-74, Hereford United 1974-77. Clubs (manager): Cheltenham Town 1979. International caps (for England): 19, 7 goals. A member of the 1966 World Cup squad, he made a record 713 appearances for Southampton. There is a Terry Paine Suite at St Mary's Stadium. Paine now lives in South Africa and works as a presenter for South African television on the biggest football show in Africa, alongside ex-Manchester United goalkeeper Gary Bailey.

Paisley, Bob　Born Hetton-le-Hole, Tyne & Wear, 23 January 1919. Position: midfield. Clubs (player): Bishop Auckland, Liverpool 1945-54. Honours: FA Amateur Cup 1939 (with Bishop Auckland); League Championship 1947 (with Liverpool). Club (manager): Liverpool 1954-74 (coach & physio),

1974-83 (manager). Honours: League Championship 1976, 1977, 1979, 1980, 1982, 1983; League Cup 1981, 1982, 1983; Charity Shield 1974, 1976, 1977, 1980, 1982; UEFA Cup 1976; European Cup 1977, 1978, 1981. Voted Manager of the Year six times (1976, 1977, 1979, 1980, 1982, 1983). Became a director of Liverpool 1985. Awarded the OBE in 1977. He died 12 February 1996 in Liverpool, and the Paisley Gateway was opened on 8 April 1999.

Pallister, Gary　Born Ramsgate, Kent, 30 August 1965. Position: defender. Clubs: Billingham Town, Middlesbrough 1984-89, 1998-2001, Darlington 1985 (loan), Manchester United 1989-98 (signed for £2.3m). Honours: FA Premiership 1993, 1994, 1996, 1997; FA Cup 1990, 1994, 1996; League Cup 1992 (all with Manchester United). International caps (for England): 22. PFA Player of the Year 1992.

Palmer, Carlton　Born Carlton Lloyd Palmer, Rowley Regis, West Midlands, 5 December 1965. Position: midfield. Clubs (player): West Bromwich Albion 1984-89, Sheffield Wednesday 1989-94 (signed for £750,000), 2001 (loan), Leeds United 1994-97 (signed for £2.6m), Southampton 1997-99 (signed for £1m), Nottingham Forest 1999 (signed for £1.1m), Coventry City 1999-2001 (free transfer), Watford 2000 (loan), Stockport County 2001-04. Clubs (manager): Stockport County 2001-04. International caps (for England): 18.

Papin, Jean-Pierre　Born Boulogne-sur-Mer, France, 5 November 1963. Position: forward. Clubs: Jeumont 1970-78, Trith St-Leger 1978-81, INF Vichy 1981-84, Valenciennes 1984-85, FC Bruges 1985-86, Olympique Marseille 1986-92, AC Milan 1992-94, Bayern Munich 1994-96, Bordeaux 1996-98, EA Guincamp 1998, St-Pierre de la Réunion. Honours: French League Championship 1989, 1990, 1991, 1992 (with Olympique Marseille); French Cup 1989 (with Olympique Marseille); Belgian Cup 1986 (with FC Bruges); Italian League Championship 1993 (with AC Milan); UEFA Cup 1996 (with Bayern Munich). International caps (for France): 54, 30 goals. European Player of the Year 1991.

Parlour, Ray　Born Romford, Essex, 7 March 1973. Position: midfield. Club: Arsenal 1991-present. Honours: FA Premiership 1998, 2002; FA Cup 1993, 1998, 2002; League Cup 1993; Charity Shield 1998, 1999; European Cup Winners' Cup 1994. International caps (for England): 10.

Passarella, Daniel　Born Chacabuco, Buenos Aires, Argentina, 25 May 1953. Position: defender/midfield. Clubs (player): Argentino de Chacabuco 1966-73, Sarmiento de Junin 1973-74, River Plate 1974-82, 1988-89, Fiorentina 1982-86, Inter Milan 1986-88. Honours: Argentinian League Championship (Metropolitan) 1975, 1977, 1979, 1980 (with River Plate); Argentinian League Championship (National) 1975, 1979, 1981 (with River Plate). Clubs (manager): River Plate 1989-94, Parma 2001. Honours: Argentinian League Championship 1990 (with River Plate); Argentinian League Championship (Apertura) 1992 (with River Plate). International caps (for Argentina): 70, 22 goals. International honours: World Cup 1978, 1986 (squad member but did not play). International manager (Argentina): 1994-98; (Uruguay): 1999-2001. Known as 'El Gran Capitan' as he captained Argentina to their 1978 World Cup win. Lost his job as manager of Parma when his first five games ended in defeat.

Pearce, Stuart　Born Hammersmith, London, 24 April 1962. Position: defender. Clubs: Wealdstone,

Coventry City 1983-85 (signed for £25,000), Nottingham Forest 1985-97 (signed for £200,000), Newcastle United 1997-99 (free transfer), West Ham United 1999-2001 (free transfer), Manchester City 2002 (free transfer). Honours: League Cup 1989, 1990; Full Members Cup 1989, 1992 (all with Nottingham Forest). International caps (for England): 78 (9 as captain), 4 goals. Retired in July 2002.

Pearson, Stuart Born Hull, Yorkshire, 21 June 1949. Position: forward. Clubs (player): Hull City 1966-74, Manchester United 1974-79 (signed for £200,000), West Ham United 1979-81 (signed for £220,000). Honours: FA Cup 1977 (with Manchester United), 1980 (with West Ham United). Clubs (manager): Stockport County (coach) 1985-86, Northwich Victoria 1986, West Bromwich Albion (assistant) 1988-92, Bradford City (assistant) 1992-94. International caps (for England): 15, 5 goals. Known as 'Pancho'. Works as an agent and for the Manchester United television channel, MUTV.

Pelé Born Edson Arantes do Nascimento, Tres Coracoes, Minas Gerais, Brazil, 23 October 1940. Position: forward. Clubs: Santos 1956-74, New York Cosmos 1975-77. Honours: São Paulo League Championship 1956, 1958, 1960, 1961, 1962, 1964, 1965, 1967, 1968, 1969, 1973; Brazilian Cup 1961, 1962, 1963, 1964, 1965, 1968; World Club Championship 1962, 1963 (all with Santos). International caps (for Brazil): 91, 77 goals. International honours: World Cup 1958, 1962, 1970. South American Player of the Year 1973. Retired in 1974 but returned to play for New York Cosmos in 1975. He scored 1281 goals in 1363 matches, including Brazil's 100th goal in the World Cup in the 1970 final against Italy. Became a sporting ambassador for Brazil and later Sports Minister. Had parts in the films *Escape to Victory* and *Mike Bassett, England Manager*. Known as 'The Black Pearl' and believed by many to be the best footballer ever to have played the game, Pelé was declared the best player of the previous 70 years by FIFA in 2000 – an award shared with Diego Maradona.

Pennington, Jesse Born West Bromwich, 23 August 1883. Position: defender. Clubs: Aston Villa, West Bromwich Albion 1903-22. Honours: League Championship 1920 (with West Bromwich Albion, captain). International caps (for England): 25 (2 as captain). Captained WBA to their 1920 Championship success. He died 5 September 1970 in Kidderminster.

Perry, Bill Born Johannesburg, South Africa, 10 September 1930. Position: forward. Clubs: Blackpool 1949-62, Stockport County, Hereford United. Honours: FA Cup 1953 (with Blackpool). International caps (for England): 3, 2 goals. Scored the winning goal in the FA Cup final 1953 (The Matthews Final), and was the first South African to win an FA Cup winner's medal. Qualified to play for England as his father was English. Known as 'Champagne Perry'. He still lives in Blackpool after retiring from his printing business.

Perryman, Steve Born Stephen John Perryman, Ealing, London, 21 December 1951. Position: defender. Clubs (player): Tottenham Hotspur 1967-86, Oxford United 1986, Brentford 1986-90. Honours: FA Cup 1981, 1982; League Cup 1971, 1973; UEFA Cup 1984; Inter-cities Fairs Cup 1972 (all with Tottenham Hotspur). Clubs (manager): Brentford 1986-90, Watford 1990-93, Tottenham Hotspur (assistant, one match as manager November 1994) 1993-95, Shimizu S-Pulse

(assistant/manager) 1995-2000, Kashiwa Reysol 2000-02. Honours: Asian Cup Winners' Cup 2000 (with Shimizu S-Pulse). International caps (for England): 1. Football Writers' Player of the Year 1982. Awarded the MBE in 1986.

Peschisolido, Paul Born Paolo Pasquale Peschisolido, Scarborough, Canada, 25 May 1971. Position: forward. Clubs: Toronto Blizzards, Birmingham City 1992-94 (signed for £25,000), 1996 (signed for £400,000), Stoke City 1994-96 (signed for £400,000), West Bromwich Albion 1996-97 (signed for £600,000), Fulham 1997-2001 (signed for £1.1m), Queens Park Rangers 2000 (loan), Sheffield United 2001 (loan), 2001-present (signed for £150,000), Norwich City 2001 (loan). International caps (for Canada): 45, 9 goals. Married to Karren Brady, managing director of Birmingham City.

Peters, Martin Born Martin Stanford Peters, Plaistow, London, 8 November 1943. Position: midfield. Clubs (player): West Ham United 1962-70, Tottenham Hotspur 1970-75 (signed for £200,000), Norwich City 1975-80 (signed for £50,000), Sheffield United 1980-81, Gorleston 1981-82. Honours: League Cup 1971, 1973 (with Tottenham Hotspur); European Cup Winners' Cup 1965 (with West Ham United); UEFA Cup 1972 (with Tottenham Hotspur). Club (manager): Sheffield United 1980-81. International caps (for England): 67 (4 as captain), 20 goals. Honours: World Cup 1966. Scored England's second goal in the World Cup final. The first £200,000 player, he was famously said to be 'ten years ahead of his time' by Sir Alf Ramsey. Having retired from the game in 1982, he now works in the insurance business. Awarded the MBE in 1978.

Petit, Emmanuel Born Dieppe, France, 22 September 1970. Position: midfield. Clubs: Monaco 1985-97, Arsenal 1997-2000 (signed for £3.5m), Barcelona 2000-01 (signed for £5m), Chelsea 2001-present (signed for £7.5m). Honours: French League Championship 1997 (with Monaco); French Cup 1991 (with Monaco); FA Premiership 1998; FA Cup 1998; Charity Shield 1998, 1999 (all with Arsenal). International caps (for France): 63, 6 goals. International honours: World Cup 1998; European Championship 2000.

Phillips, Kevin Born Kevin Mark Phillips, Hitchin, Hertfordshire, 25 July 1973. Position: forward. Clubs: Baldock, Watford 1994-97 (signed for £10,000), Sunderland 1997-2003 (signed for £325,000), Southampton 2003-present. International caps (for England): 8

Pires, Robert Born Reims, France, 29 October 1973 (some sources say 29 January). Position: midfield. Clubs: Reims 1991-92, Metz 1992-98, Olympique Marseille 1998-2000, Arsenal 2000-present (signed for £6m). Honours: FA Premiership 2002 (with Arsenal); FA Cup 2003 (with Arsenal); French League Cup 1996 (with Metz). International caps (for France): 57, 11 goals. International honours: World Cup 1998; European Championship 2000. Football Writers' Player of the Year 2002.

Planicka, Frantisek Born Prague, Bohemia, 2 July 1904. Position: goalkeeper. Club: Slavia Prague 1923-39. International caps (for Czechoslovakia): 73. Having captained his national team in the World Cup 1934, he broke his arm towards the end of his last international, a World Cup quarter-final against Brazil in 1938, but stayed on the pitch until the end of the match. Played more than 1000 matches for Slavia Prague. He was awarded the UNESCO International Fair Play Award in 1985 for never having been booked or sent off during his playing career. He died 20 July 1996 in Prague.

Platini, Michel   Born Joeuf, France, 21 June 1955. Position: midfield. Clubs: Joeuf 1966-76, Nancy-Lorraine 1976-79, AS St-Etienne 1979-82, Juventus 1982-87. Honours: French League Championship 1981 (with St-Etienne); French Cup 1978 (with Nancy-Lorraine), 1979, 1982 (with St-Etienne); Italian League Championship 1983, 1984, 1985, 1986; Italian Cup 1983; European Cup 1985; European Cup Winners' Cup 1984, European Super Cup 1984; Intercontinental Cup 1985 (all with Juventus). International caps (for France): 72 (49 as captain), 41 goals. International honours: European Championship 1984. International manager (France): 1988-92. Formed the '*carré magique*' (magic square) with Giresse, Tigana and Fernandez in the French midfield. European Player of the Year 1983, 1984, 1985. Known as 'Platoche'. Co-president of the Organising Committee for the 1998 World Cup. Vice-president of the French Football Federation.

Platt, David   Born David Andrew Platt, Chadderton, Lancashire, 10 June 1966. Position: midfield. Clubs (player): Manchester United 1984-85, Crewe Alexandra 1985-88 (free transfer), Aston Villa 1988-91 (signed for £200,000), Bari 1991-92 (signed for £5.5m), Juventus 1992-93 (signed for £6.5m), Sampdoria 1993-95 (signed for £5.2m), Arsenal 1995-98 (signed for £4.75m). Clubs (manager): Sampdoria 1998-99 (seven weeks), Nottingham Forest 1999-2001. International caps (for England): 62 (19 as captain), 27 goals. International manager (England Under-21): 2001-04. PFA Player of the Year 1990. His combined transfer fees, totalling over £22 million, represented a record at the time.

Popescu, Gheorghe   Born Calafat, Romania, 10 September 1967. Position: defender. Clubs: Universidat Craiova 1984-88, 1988-90, Steaua Bucharest 1988, PSV Eindhoven 1990-95, Tottenham Hotspur 1995, Barcelona 1995-97, Galatasaray 1997-2002, Lecce 2002-present. Honours: Romanian League Championship 1988 (with Steaua Bucharest); Dutch League Championship 1991, 1992 (with PSV Eindhoven); Turkish League Championship 1998, 1999 (with Galatasaray); Spanish Cup 1997 (with Barcelona), Turkish Cup 1999 (with Galatasaray); European Cup Winners' Cup 1997 (with Barcelona). International caps (for Romania): 115, 16 goals. Romanian Player of the Year 1989, 1990, 1991, 1992, 1995, 1996. Brother-in-law of Gheorghe Hagi.

Powell, Chris   Born Christopher George Robin Powell, Lambeth, London, 8 September 1969. Position: defender. Clubs: Crystal Palace 1987-90, Aldershot 1990 (loan), Southend United 1990-96 (free transfer), Derby County 1996-98 (signed for £800,000), Charlton Athletic 1998-present (signed for £800,000). International caps (for England): 5.

Poyet, Gus   Born Gustavo Augusto Poyet, Dominguez, Montevideo, Uruguay, 15 November 1967. Position: midfield. Clubs: River Plate 1986-88, Grenoble 1988-90, Bella Vista 1990, Real Zaragoza 1990-97, Chelsea 1997-2001, Tottenham Hotspur 2001-present. Honours: FA Cup 2000 (with Chelsea); Charity Shield 2000 (with Chelsea); European Cup Winners' Cup 1995 (with Real Zaragoza), 1998 (with Chelsea). International caps (for Uruguay): 26, 3 goals.

Prosinecki, Robert   Born Schwenningen, Germany, 12 November 1969. Position: midfield. Clubs: Red Star Belgrade 1987-91, Real Madrid 1991-94, Real Oviedo 1994-96, Barcelona 1995-96, Seville 1996-97, Dynamo Zagreb 1997-2000, Dragovoljac 2000, Standard Liege 2000-01, Portsmouth 2001-02 (free transfer), Olympija Ljubljana 2002-present. Honours: Yugoslav Championship 1988, 1990, 1991; Yugoslav Cup 1990; European Cup 1991 (all with Red Star Belgrade). International caps (for Yugoslavia): 15, 4 goals; (for Croatia): 49, 11 goals.

Puskas, Ferenc   Born Ferenc Purczeld, Budapest, Hungary, 2 April 1927. Position: forward. Clubs (player): Kispest-Honvéd 1943-56, Real Madrid 1958-66. Honours: Hungarian League Championship 1948 (with Kispest), 1950, 1952, 1954, 1955 (with Honvéd); Spanish League Championship 1961, 1962, 1963, 1964, 1965; Spanish Cup 1961; European Cup 1960, 1962; World Club Championship 1960 (all with Real Madrid). Clubs (manager/coach): San Francisco Gales, Vancouver Royals 1968, Panathinaikos 1971, Colo Colo (Chile), AEK Athens, South Melbourne Hellas 1989-92. International caps (for Hungary): 84, 83 goals. International honours: Olympic gold medal 1952. International caps (for Spain): 4. International manager (Hungary): 1983 (caretaker). Defected to Spain in 1956 following the Hungarian uprising. Known as 'The Galloping Major'. He scored 35 goals in 39 European Cup matches.

Quinn, Micky   Born Liverpool, 2 May 1962. Position: forward. Clubs: Wigan Athletic 1980-82, Stockport County 1982-84, Oldham Athletic 1984-86, Portsmouth 1986-89, Newcastle United 1989-92 (signed for £600,000), Coventry City 1992-95, Thessaloniki 1995. Retired from playing in 1995 and worked as an assistant to Mick Channon as a race trainer. Obtaining his own training licence in 1997. Suspended for negligence in 2000, he was reinstated in 2003. Known as 'Sumo' because of his weighty appearance, his autobiography *Who Ate All the Pies* was published in 2003.

Quinn, Niall   Born Dublin, 6 October 1966. Position: forward. Clubs: Arsenal 1983-90, Manchester City 1990-96 (signed for £800,000), Sunderland 1996-2002 (signed for £1.3m). Honours: League Cup 1987 (with Arsenal). International caps (for Republic of Ireland): 91, 21 goals. Donated the entire proceeds of his 2002 testimonial match to charity.

Quixall, Albert   Born Sheffield, 9 August 1933. Position: forward. Clubs: Sheffield Wednesday 1948-58, Manchester United 1958-64 (signed for £45,000, then a British record fee), Oldham Athletic 1964-66, Stockport County 1966-67, Altrincham 1967, Radcliffe Borough. Honours: FA Cup 1963 (with Manchester United). International caps (for England): 5. Matt Busby's first signing after the Munich air disaster.

Race, Roy   Born Melchester, c.1936. Position: forward. Clubs (player): Melchester Rovers 1954-83, 1984-93, Walford Rovers 1983-84. Honours: League Championship 1958, 1960, 1963, 1968, 1972, 1977, 1980, 1988, 1992; FA Cup 1959, 1961, 1966, 1970, 1972, 1974, 1984, 1990; League Cup 1974, 1986, 1987; European Cup Winners' Cup 1971, 1975, 1985; UEFA Cup 1978; European Cup 1964, 1967, 1969, 1973; World Club Cup 1965, 1970 (all with Melchester Rovers). Clubs (manager): Melchester Rovers 1974-83, 1984-93, 1996-present, Walford Rovers 1983-84, AC Monza 1994-95. Honours: FA Cup 1984, 1990, 1999. International caps (for England): too numerous to count. International Manager (England): 1978 (caretaker). After being shot in 1982 he missed the

F
O
O
T
B
A
L
L

1986 World Cup finals after being kidnapped in Basran. His left foot was amputated following a helicopter crash in 1993. Many consider him to be a one-dimensional player but his record speaks for itself. Son Roy Race jnr also plays for Melchester Rovers.

Radford, John   Born Hemsworth, Yorkshire, 22 February 1947. Position: forward. Clubs (player): Arsenal 1964-76, West Ham United 1976-78, Blackburn Rovers 1978, Bishops Stortford. Honours: League Championship 1971; FA Cup 1971 (both with Arsenal). Club (manager): Bishops Stortford 1987-98 (three spells). International caps (for England): 2.

Rahn, Helmut   Born Alten-Hessen, Germany, 16 August 1929. Position: forward. Clubs: BV Altenessen, Olde 09, Sportfreunde Katernberg, Rot-Weiss Essen, FC Cologne, Twente Enschede, MSV Duisburg. Honours: West German League Championship 1955 (with Rot-Weiss Essen); West German Cup 1953 (with Rot-Weiss Essen). International caps (for West Germany): 40, 21 goals. International honours: World Cup 1954. Scored twice including the winning goal in the World Cup final 1954. Known as 'The Boss'. Retired in 1965 to become a second-hand car salesman. He died 13 August 2003 in Essen.

Ramsey, Alf   Born Alfred Ernest Ramsey, Dagenham, Essex, 22 January 1920. Position: defender. Clubs (player): Southampton 1946-49, Tottenham Hotspur 1949-55. Honours: League Championship 1951 (with Tottenham Hotspur). Clubs (manager): Ipswich Town 1955-63, Birmingham City 1977. Honours: League Championship 1962 (with Ipswich Town). International caps (for England): 32 (3 as captain), 3 goals. International Manager (England): 1963-74. Honours: World Cup 1966. Knighted in 1967. He died 28 April 1999 in Ipswich.

Ramsey, George   Born George Burrell Ramsey, Glasgow, 4 March 1855. Position: forward. Club: Aston Villa 1876-80. Forced to retire through injury, he was club secretary of Aston Villa 1884-1926, and was instrumental in the development of the club, being responsible for the purchase of Villa Park. He died 1935.

Raul   Born Raul Gonzalez Blanco, Madrid, Spain, 27 June 1977. Position: forward. Clubs: San Cristobal de los Angeles 1988-89, Atlético Madrid 1990-92, Real Madrid 1992-present. Honours: Spanish League Championship 1995, 1997, 2001, 2003; UEFA Champions League 1998, 2000, 2002 (all with Real Madrid). International caps (for Spain): 65, 34 goals.

Ravanelli, Fabrizio   Born Perugia, Italy, 11 December 1968. Position: forward. Clubs: Perugia 1986-89, Avellino 1989-90, Casertana 1989 (loan), Reggiana 1990-92, Juventus 1992-96, Middlesbrough 1996-97 (signed for £7m), Olympique Marseille 1997-2000 (signed for £5.3m), Lazio 2000-01, Derby County 2001-03, Dundee 2003-present. Honours: Italian League Championship 1995 (with Juventus), 2000 (with Lazio); Italian Cup 1995; UEFA Cup 1993; UEFA Champions League 1996 (all with Juventus). International caps (for Italy): 22, 8 goals. Known as 'The White Feather', a term relating to his hair colour rather than his bravery.

Ravelli, Thomas   Born Vastervik, Sweden, 13 August 1959. Position: goalkeeper. Clubs: Osters Vaxjo 1976-89, IFK Gothenburg 1989-97, Tampa Bay Mutiny 1997-99. Honours: Swedish League Championship 1980, 1981 (with Osters Vaxjo), 1990, 1991, 1993, 1994, 1995, 1996 (with IFK Gothenburg); Swedish Cup 1992 (with IFK Gothenburg). International caps (for Sweden): 143.

Most-capped player for Sweden and second in the all-country male list behind Lothar Matthäus. A joker both on and off the field, he is known as the 'Clown Prince' of Swedish football. His twin brother Andreas played alongside him at Osters Vaxjo.

Redknapp, Harry   Born Poplar, London, 2 March 1947. Position: midfield. Clubs (player): West Ham United 1964-72, AFC Bournemouth 1972-76, Brentford 1976. Also one League appearance for AFC Bournemouth in 1982-83 (in emergency). Clubs (manager): AFC Bournemouth 1983-92, West Ham United 1994-2001, Portsmouth 2002-present. Father of Jamie Redknapp.

Redknapp, Jamie   Born Jamie Frank Redknapp, Barton-on-Sea, Hampshire, 25 June 1973. Position: midfield. Clubs: AFC Bournemouth 1990-91, Liverpool 1991-2002 (signed for £350,000), Tottenham Hotspur 2002-present. Honours: League Cup 1995 (with Liverpool). International caps (for England): 18, 2 goals. Son of the successful manager Harry Redknapp.

Reid, Peter   Born Huyton, Liverpool, 20 June 1956. Position: midfield. Clubs (player): Bolton Wanderers 1974-82, Everton 1982-89 (signed for £60,000), Queens Park Rangers 1989, Manchester City 1989-93, Southampton 1993-94, Notts County 1994, Bury 1994-95. Honours: League Championship 1985; FA Cup 1984; European Cup Winners' Cup 1985 (all with Everton). Clubs (manager): Manchester City 1990-93, Sunderland 1995-2002, Leeds United 2003. International caps (for England): 13. PFA Player of the Year 1985. Subject of a fly-on-the-wall TV documentary during a particularly tense season in the Premiership when managing Sunderland.

Reilly, Laurie   Born Lawrence Reilly, Edinburgh, 28 October 1928. Position: forward. Club: Hibernian 1945-58. Honours: Scottish League Championship 1951, 1952. International caps (for Scotland): 38, 22 goals. Known as 'Last-Minute Reilly' because of his habit of scoring close to the end of games. Forced to retire through injury in 1958 and became a licensee.

Revie, Don   Born Donald George Revie, Middlesbrough, 10 July 1927. Position: forward. Clubs (player): Leicester City 1944-49, Hull City 1949-51, Manchester City 1951-56, Sunderland 1956-58, Leeds United 1958-62. Honours: FA Cup 1956 (with Manchester City). Club (manager): Leeds United 1961-74. Honours: League Championship 1969, 1974; FA Cup 1972; League Cup 1968; UEFA Cup 1968, 1971. International caps (for England): 6, 4 goals. International manager (England): 1974-77; (United Arab Emirates): 1977-80. Football Writers' Player of the Year 1955. Awarded the OBE in 1970. He died 26 May 1989 in Edinburgh.

Rideout, Paul   Born Paul David Rideout, Bournemouth, 14 August 1964. Position: forward/midfield. Clubs (player): Swindon Town 1981-83, 1991 (loan), Aston Villa 1983-85 (signed for £200,000), Bari 1985-88 (signed for £400,000), Southampton 1988-91 (signed for £430,000), Notts County 1991-92 (signed for £250,000), Rangers 1992 (signed for £500,000), Everton 1992-97 (signed for £500,000), Huang Dao Vanguards (China) 1997-98 (signed for £250,000), Kansas City Wizards 1998-99, Shengzhen Pingan Shanghai 1999-2000, Tranmere Rovers 2000-02 (free transfer). Honours: FA Cup 1995; Charity Shield 1995 (both with Everton). Clubs (coach): KCFC Alliance 90/91 Boys (Kansas) 2003. Best Overseas Player in Chinese League 1998. Scored the winning goal in the 1995 FA Cup final against Manchester United.

Riise, Jon Arne Born Molde, Norway, 24 September 1980. Position: midfield. Clubs: Aalesund, Monaco 1998-2001, Liverpool 2001-present (signed for £3.77m). Honours: French League Championship 2000 (with Monaco); Charity Shield 2001 (with Liverpool). International caps (for Norway): 25, 3 goals.

Rijkaard, Frank Born Franklin Edmundo Rijkaard, Amsterdam, Holland, 30 September 1962. Position: midfield. Clubs (player): Ajax 1980-87, 1993-95, Real Zaragoza 1988, AC Milan 1988-93 (signed for £2.5m). Honours: Dutch League Championship 1982, 1983, 1985, 1994, 1995 (with Ajax); Italian League Championship 1992, 1993 (with AC Milan); Dutch Cup 1983, 1986, 1987 (with Ajax); European Cup Winners' Cup 1987 (with Ajax); European Cup 1989, 1990 (with AC Milan), 1995 (with Ajax). Clubs (manager): Sparta Rotterdam 2001-02, Barcelona 2003-present. International caps (for Holland): 73, 10 goals. International honours: European Championship 1988. International manager (Holland): 1998-2000.

Riva, Luigi Born Leggiuno, Italy, 7 November 1944. Position: forward. Clubs: Legnano 1962-63, Cagliari 1963-76. Honours: Italian Championship 1970 (with Cagliari). International caps (for Italy): 42, 35 goals. International honours: European Championship 1968. Retired through injury in 1977. He is Italy's leading goalscorer.

Rivaldo Born Victor Borba Ferreira Rivaldo, Recife, Brazil, 19 April 1972. Position: forward. Clubs: Paulista 1989-90, Santa Cruz 1991, Mogi-Mirim, Corinthians 1993, Palmeiras 1994-96, Deportivo La Coruña 1995-97, Barcelona 1997-2002 (signed for £16m), AC Milan 2002-present. Honours: Brazilian Paulista League Championship 1994, 1996 (with Palmeiras); Spanish League Championship 1998 (with Barcelona); Spanish Cup 1998 (with Barcelona); Italian Cup 2003 (with AC Milan); UEFA Champions League 2003 (with AC Milan). International caps (for Brazil): 71, 33 goals. International honours: World Cup 2002. European Player of the Year 1999. World Player of the Year 1999.

Rivelino, Roberto Born São Paulo, Brazil, 19 January 1946. Position: midfield/forward. Clubs: Corinthians 1964-75, Fluminense 1975-78, Al-Ahly (Saudi Arabia) 1979-81. Honours: Brazilian Rio League Championship 1975, 1976 (with Fluminense). International caps (for Brazil): 94, 26 goals. International honours: World Cup 1970. Much admired for his long-range shooting and bending of free-kicks.

Rivera, Gianni Born Valle S. Bartolomeo, Alessandria, Italy, 18 August 1943. Position: forward. Clubs: Alessandria 1958-60, AC Milan 1960-79 (signed for £65,000). Honours: Italian Championship 1962, 1968, 1979; Italian Cup 1967, 1972, 1973, 1977; European Cup Winners' Cup 1968, 1973; European Cup 1963, 1969 (all with AC Milan). International caps (for Italy): 60, 14 goals. International honours: European Championship 1968. Known as 'The Golden Boy'. European Player of the Year 1969. After retirement he became an Italian MP.

Roberto Carlos Born Roberto Carlos da Silva, Garca, Brazil, 10 April 1973. Position: defender. Clubs: Uniao São Joao de Arras 1990-91, Palmeiras 1992-94, Inter Milan 1995-96, Real Madrid 1996-present. Honours: Brazilian Paulista League Championship 1993, 1994 (with Palmeiras); Spanish League Championship 1997, 2001, 2003 (with Real Madrid); UEFA Champions League 1998, 2000, 2002 (with Real Madrid). International caps (for Brazil): 97, 7 goals. International honours: World Cup 1996, 2002; Copa America 1997. An attacking defender known for his thunderous free-kicks.

Roberts, Charlie Born Charles Roberts, Darlington, Co. Durham, 6 April 1883. Position: defender. Clubs (player): Rise Carr Rangers, Darlington St Augustine's, Bishop Auckland, Grimsby Town 1903-04, Manchester United 1904-13 (signed for £600), Oldham Athletic 1913-15. Honours: League Championship 1908, 1911; FA Cup 1909 (all with Manchester United). Club (manager): Oldham Athletic 1921-22. International caps (for England): 3. The first Manchester United player to be capped for England, and one of the founders of the Players' Union. On leaving football he opened a wholesale tobacconist's. He died 7 August 1939.

Roberts, Herbie Born Herbert Roberts, Oswestry, Shropshire, 19 February 1905. Position: defender. Club: Arsenal 1926-38. Honours: League Championship 1931, 1933, 1934, 1935; FA Cup 1936. International caps (for England): 1. Known as 'Policeman' Roberts because of his wholly defensive centre-half play. He died while on active service, 19 June 1944.

Robinson, John Born John William Robinson, Derby, 22 April 1870. Position: goalkeeper. Clubs: Derby County 1891-97, New Brighton Tower 1897-98, Southampton. International caps (for England): 11, 11 goals conceded. Known as Jack Robinson. Caused a furore by joining New Brighton Tower, a non-affiliated club, for the extra money they could pay.

Robinson, Paul Born Beverley, Yorkshire, 15 October 1979. Position: goalkeeper. Clubs: Leeds United 1997-2004, Tottenham Hotspur 2004-present. International caps (for England): 3.

Robson, Bobby Born Robert William Robson, Langley Park, Co. Durham, 18 February 1933. Position: forward/defender. Clubs (player): Fulham 1950-56, 1962-67, West Bromwich Albion 1956-62, Vancouver Royals 1967. Clubs (manager): Vancouver Royals 1967, Fulham 1968, Ipswich Town 1969-82, PSV Eindhoven 1990-93, 1998, Sporting Lisbon 1993-94, Porto 1994-97, Barcelona 1997, Newcastle United 1999-2004. Honours: Dutch League Championship 1991, 1992 (with PSV Eindhoven); Portuguese League Championship 1995, 1996 (with Porto); FA Cup 1978 (with Ipswich Town); Portuguese Cup 1994 (with Porto); Spanish Cup 1997 (with Barcelona); UEFA Cup 1981 (with Ipswich Town); European Cup Winners' Cup 1997 (with Barcelona). International caps (for England): 20, 4 goals. International manager (England): 1982-90. Vice-president of the League Managers' Association. Awarded the CBE in 1990 and knighted in 2002. Awarded the PFA Merit Award 2003. A statue in his honour stands outside Portman Road.

Robson, Bryan Born Chester-le-Street, Co. Durham, 11 January 1957. Position: midfield. Clubs (player): West Bromwich Albion 1974-81, Manchester United 1981-94 (signed for £1.5m), Middlesbrough 1994-98. Honours: FA Premiership 1993, 1994; FA Cup 1983, 1985, 1990, 1994; European Cup Winners' Cup 1991 (all with Manchester United). Club (manager): Middlesbrough 1998-2001. International caps (for England): 90 (65 as captain), 26 goals. Awarded the OBE in 1990.

F
O
O
T
B
A
L
L

Rocastle, David Born David Carlyle Rocastle, Lewisham, London, 2 May 1967. Position: midfield. Clubs: Arsenal 1985-92, Leeds United 1992-93 (signed for £2m), Manchester City 1993-94, Chelsea 1994-98, Norwich City 1997 (loan), Hull City 1997, Sabah (Malaysia) 1998-2000. Honours: League Championship 1989, 1991; League Cup 1987 (all with Arsenal). International caps (for England): 14. Known as 'Rocky'. Retired through injury in 2000. His attitude is summed up by a story told by Alan Hansen. Rocastle had been badly brought down by Hansen's mistimed tackle. He stood up, dusted himself down, smiled and said 'Getting old, Alan?'. He died 31 March 2001 of cancer at the age of 33.

Rocha, Pedro Born Pedro Virgillio Rocha Franchetti, Salto, Uruguay, 3 December 1942. Position: midfield. Clubs: Peñarol 1959-70, São Paulo 1970-77, Cortiba 1978, Palmeiras 1979, Bangu 1979, Monterrey 1980, Al-Nassr 1980. Honours: Uruguayan League Championship 1960, 1961, 1962, 1964, 1965, 1967, 1968 (with Peñarol); Brazilian Paulista League Championship 1971, 1975 (with São Paulo); Brazilian National League Championship (National) 1977 (with São Paulo). International caps (for Uruguay): 75, 16 goals. International honours: Copa America 1967.

Rogers, Don Born Donald Rogers, Paulton, Somerset, 25 October 1945. Position: forward. Clubs: Swindon Town 1962-72, 1976, Crystal Palace 1972-74 (signed for £147,000), Queens Park Rangers 1974-76 (signed for £200,000). Honours: League Cup 1969 (with Swindon Town). Best known for scoring two goals in Swindon's 3-1 victory over Arsenal in the 1969 League Cup final. Probably failed to gain international honours because he did not fit into Alf Ramsey's 'wingless wonder' scheme. Now runs a sports shop in Swindon and is manager of Hungerford Town.

Romario Born Romario Da Souza Faria, Rio de Janeiro, Brazil, 26 January 1966. Position: forward. Clubs: Olario 1979, Vasco da Gama 1980-88, PSV Eindhoven 1988-93, Barcelona 1993-94, Flamengo 1995-96, 1997, 1998-99, Valencia 1996, 1997. Honours: Rio League Championship 1987, 1988 (with Vasco da Gama), 1996, 1999 (with Flamengo); Dutch League Championship 1988, 1989, 1991, 1992 (with PSV Eindhoven); Dutch Cup 1988, 1989, 1990 (with PSV Eindhoven); Spanish League Championship 1993, 1994 (with Barcelona); Rio State Championship 1987, 1988 (with Vasco da Gama), 1996, 1999 (with Flamengo). International caps (for Brazil): 69, 54 goals. International honours: World Cup 1994; Copa America 1989, 1997; Confederations Cup 1997. World Player of the Year 1994.

Ronaldinho Born Ronaldo de Assis Moreira, Porto Alegre, Brazil, 21 March 1980. Position: midfield. Clubs: Gremio 1997-2001, Paris St-Germain 2001-03, Barcelona 2003-present (signed for £21.25m). International caps (for Brazil): 39, 15 goals. International honours: World Cup 2002; Copa America 1999.

Ronaldo Born Ronaldo Luiz Nazario de Lima, Bento Ribeiro, Brazil, 22 September 1976. Position: forward. Clubs: São Cristovao, Cruzeiro Belo Horizonte 1993-94, PSV Eindhoven 1994-96 (signed for £4m), Barcelona 1996-97, Inter Milan 1997-2002 (signed for £18m), Real Madrid 2002-present (signed for £20m). Honours: Brazilian Cup 1993 (with Cruzeiro); Dutch Cup 1996 (with PSV Eindhoven); Spanish League Championship 2003 (with Real Madrid); Spanish Cup 1997 (with Barcelona); European Cup Winners' Cup 1997 (with Barcelona); UEFA Cup 1998 (with Inter Milan); UEFA Champions League 2002 (with Real Madrid). International caps (for Brazil): 71, 48 goals. International honours: World Cup 1994, 2002; Copa America 1997. Golden Boot winner, World Cup 2002. European Player of the Year 1997, 2002. World Player of the Year 1996, 1997, 2002. Named after the doctor who delivered him. Nicknamed 'El Fenomeno'.

Ronaldo, Cristiano Born Madeira, 5 February 1985. Position: forward. Clubs: Sporting Lisbon 2001-03, Manchester United 2003-present (signed for £12.24m). Honours: Portuguese League Championship 2002; Portuguese Cup 2002 (both with Sporting Lisbon); FA Cup 2004 (with Manchester United).

Rooney, Wayne Born Liverpool, 24 October 1985. Position: forward. Club: Everton 2002-2004, Manchester United 2004-present. International caps (for England): 7, 2 goals. Became youngest goalscorer for England at the tender age of 17 years and 317 days when scoring against Macedonia in a World Cup qualifier in 2003.

Rossi, Paolo Born Prato, Italy, 23 September 1956. Position: forward. Clubs: Juventus 1977-85, Como 1975 (loan), Lanerossi Vicenza 1977-79 (loan), Perugia 1979 (loan), AC Milan 1985-86, Hellas Verona 1986-87. Honours: Italian League Championship 1982, 1984; Italian Cup 1983; European Cup Winners' Cup 1984; European Cup 1985 (all with Juventus). International caps (for Italy): 48, 20 goals. International honours: World Cup 1982. Golden Boot winner, World Cup 1982. European Player of the Year 1982. Known as 'Pablito'. Suspended in 1979 after allegations of match-fixing a game between Perugia and Avellino, and three-year sentence was later reduced to two years, which crucially allowed him to play for Italy in the 1982 World Cup.

Rowley, Arthur Born George Arthur Rowley, Wolverhampton, 21 April 1926. Position: forward. Clubs (player): Wolverhampton Wanderers, West Bromwich Albion 1946-48, Fulham 1948-50, Leicester City 1950-58, Shrewsbury Town 1958-65. Clubs (manager): Shrewsbury Town 1958-65, Sheffield United 1968-69, Southend United 1970-76. Scored 434 goals in 619 League games, scoring 20 or more goals in every season 1950-63. Brother of Jack Rowley.

Rowley, Jack Born John Frederick Rowley, Wolverhampton, 7 October 1920. Position: forward. Clubs (player): Wolverhampton Wanderers 1935-37, Cradley Heath 1936 (loan), Bournemouth & Boscombe Athletic 1937, Manchester United 1937-55, Plymouth Argyle 1955-57. Honours: League Championship 1952; FA Cup 1948 (both with Manchester United). Clubs (manager): Plymouth Argyle 1955-60, Oldham Athletic 1960-63, 1968-69, Wrexham 1966-67, Ajax. International caps (for England): 6, 6 goals. Known as 'Gunner' because of his powerful shot. He died 27 June 1998.

Ruddock, Neil Born Wandsworth, London, 9 May 1968. Position: defender. Clubs: Millwall 1986, 1988-89 (signed for £300,000), Tottenham Hotspur 1986-88 (signed for £50,000), 1992-93 (signed for £75,000), Southampton 1989-92 (signed for £250,000), Liverpool 1993-98 (signed for £2.5m), Queens Park Rangers 1998 (loan), West Ham United 1998-2000 (signed for £100,000), Crystal Palace 2000-01, Swindon Town 2001-03. Honours: League Cup 1995 (with Liverpool). International caps (for England): 1. Known as 'Razor'.

Rummenigge, Karl-Heinz Born Lippstadt, Westphalia, West Germany, 25 September 1955. Position: forward. Clubs: Borussia Lippstadt, Bayern Munich 1973-83, Inter Milan 1983-87 (signed for £2.5m), Servette Geneva 1987-89. Honours: European Cup 1976 (with Bayern Munich). International caps (for West Germany): 95, 45 goals. International honours: European Championship 1980. European Player of the Year 1980, 1981. Became a TV commentator.

Rush, Ian Born Ian James Rush, St Asaph, Denbighshire, Wales, 20 October 1961. Position: forward. Clubs: Chester City 1979-80, Liverpool 1980-86 (signed for £300,000), 1986-87 (loan), 1988-96 (signed for £2.8m), Juventus 1986-88 (signed for £3.2m), Leeds United 1996-97, Newcastle United 1997-98, Sheffield United 1998 (loan), Wrexham 1998-99. Honours: League Championship 1982, 1983, 1984, 1986, 1990; FA Cup 1986, 1989, 1992; League Cup 1981, 1982, 1983, 1984, 1995; European Cup 1984 (all with Liverpool). International caps (for Wales): 73, 28 goals. Football Writers' Player of the Year 1984. PFA Player of the Year 1984. European Golden Boot winner, 1984. One of six brothers, the other five of whom all played for Flint Town. Awarded the MBE in 1996 and now runs his own finishing school for strikers.

Rutherford, Jock Born John Rutherford, Percy Main, Northumberland, 12 October 1884. Position: forward. Clubs (player): Newcastle United 1902-13, Arsenal 1913-23, 1923-26, Stoke City 1923. Honours: League Championship 1905, 1907, 1908; FA Cup 1910 (all with Newcastle United). Club (manager): Stoke City 1923. International caps (for England): 11, 3 goals. Known as 'The Newcastle Flyer'. The oldest-ever Arsenal player at 41 years 236 days v Manchester City, March 1926. On retirement he became a shop owner. His son John James Rutherford played for Arsenal 1925-26. He died 21 April 1963 in Neasden.

Sadler, David Born Yalding, Kent, 5 February 1946. Position: defender. Clubs: Maidstone United, Manchester United 1963-74, Miami Toros 1973 (loan), Preston North End 1973-77. Honours: League Championship 1967; European Cup 1968 (both with Manchester United). International caps (for England): 4.

Sagar, Ted Born Edward Sagar, Moorends, Doncaster, 7 February 1910. Position: goalkeeper. Clubs: Thorne Colliery, Everton 1929-53. Honours: League Championship 1932, 1939; FA Cup 1933; Charity Shield 1932 (all with Everton). International caps (for England): 4, 7 goals conceded. His record of 463 League games (over 24 years and 1 month) for Everton was beaten only in 1994 by Neville Southall. He played in goal for Northern Ireland when they were short of a goalkeeper for a wartime international. Became a publican upon retirement. He died October 1986.

St John, Ian Born Motherwell, Scotland, 7 June 1938. Position: forward. Clubs (player): Motherwell, Liverpool 1961-71 (signed for £37,500), Coventry City 1971-72, Tranmere Rovers 1972. Honours: League Championship 1964, 1966; FA Cup 1965; Charity Shield 1965, 1966 (all with Liverpool). Club (manager): Motherwell 1972-75. International caps (for Scotland): 21, 9 goals. Scored the 1965 FA Cup winner. Won a BBC competition to find a new commentator for the 1970 World Cup. Works in the media and presented *Saint and Greavsie* with Jimmy Greaves.

Salako, John Born John Akin Salako, Nigeria, 11 February 1969. Position: forward. Clubs: Crystal Palace 1986-95, Swansea City 1989 (loan), Coventry City 1995-98 (signed for £1.5m), Bolton Wanderers 1998 (loan), Fulham 1998-99, Charlton Athletic 1999-2001 (loan, then signed for £150,000), Reading 2001-present (loan, then signed for £50,000). Honours: Full Members Cup 1991 (with Crystal Palace). International caps (for England): 5.

Salas, Marcelo Born Jose Marcelo Salas Melinao, Temuco, Chile, 24 December 1974. Position: forward. Clubs: Universidad de Chile 1993-96, River Plate 1996-98, Lazio 1998-2001, Juventus 2001-present. Honours: Chilean League Championship 1994, 1995 (with Universidad de Chile); Argentinian League Championship 1997 (Apertura and Clausura), 1998 (Apertura) (with River Plate); Italian League Championship 2000 (with Lazio), 2002, 2003 (with Juventus); Italian Cup 2000 (with Lazio); European Cup Winners' Cup 1999 (with Lazio). International caps (for Chile): 58, 34 goals. Known as 'The Matador'. In 1996 his contract was sold to an Argentinian businessman who then sold him to River Plate.

Sammer, Matthias Born Dresden, East Germany, 5 September 1967. Position: midfield. Clubs (player): Dresden, VfB Stuttgart 1991-92, Inter Milan 1992-93, Borussia Dortmund 1993-98. Honours: German League Championship 1992 (with VfB Stuttgart), 1995, 1996 (with Borussia Dortmund); European Cup 1997 (with Borussia Dortmund). Clubs (manager): Borussia Dortmund 2000-present. International caps (for Germany): 51, 8 goals. International honours: European Championship 1996. Along with Andreas Thom the first East Germans to play in a unified German team. Captained Borussia Dortmund to their 1997 European Cup victory. Youngest coach in the history of the Bundesliga. European Player of the Year 1996.

Sanchez, Hugo Born Hugo Sanchez Marquez, Mexico City, 11 June (some sources 11 July) 1958. Position: forward. Clubs (player): Pumas de la Unam 1975-79, 1980-81, San Diego Soccers 1979-80, Atlético Madrid 1981-85, Real Madrid 1985-92, Rayo Vallecano 1993-94, Linz 1995-96, Dallas Burns 1996, Atletica Celaya 1996-97. Honours: Mexican League Championship 1977, 1981 (with Pumas de la Unam); Spanish League Championship 1986, 1987, 1988, 1989, 1990 (with Real Madrid); Spanish Cup 1985 (with Atlético Madrid), 1989 (with Real Madrid); UEFA Cup 1986 (with Real Madrid). Club (manager): Pumas de la Unam 2000-present. International caps (for Mexico): 75, 46 goals. Celebrated his goals with extravagant somersaults.

Sansom, Kenny Born Kenneth Graham Sansom, Camberwell, London, 26 September 1958. Position: defender. Clubs: Crystal Palace 1975-80, Arsenal 1980-88, Newcastle United 1988-89 (signed for £300,000), Queens Park Rangers 1989-92, Coventry City 1992-93, Everton 1993, Brentford, Watford 1994 (player/coach). Honours: League Cup 1987 (with Arsenal). International caps (for England): 86, 1 goal.

Santos, Djalma Born São Paulo, Brazil, 27 February 1929. Position: defender. Clubs: Portuguesa de Desportos 1948-58, Palmeiras 1958-68, Atlético Paranaense 1968-72. Honours: Brazilian League Championship 1959, 1963, 1966 (with Palmeiras). International caps (for Brazil): 98, 3 goals. International honours: World Cup 1958, 1962. Played in the 1966 World Cup at the age of 38.

FOOTBALL

Sarosi, Gyorgy Born Gyorgy Stefancsis, Budapest, Hungary, 16 September 1912. Position: forward. Clubs (player): Mugyetemi Atletikai 1927-29, Ferencvaros 1929-48, Juventus 1951-53. Clubs (manager): Bologna, Roma, Juventus. International caps (for Hungary): 62, 42 goals. He died 20 June 1993 in Genoa, Italy.

Saunders, Dean Born Dean Nicholas Saunders, Swansea, 21 June 1964. Position: forward. Clubs: Swansea City 1982-85, Cardiff City 1985 (loan), Brighton & Hove Albion 1985-87, Oxford United 1987-88 (signed for £60,000), Derby County 1988-91 (signed for £1m), Liverpool 1991-92 (signed for £2.9m), Aston Villa 1992-95 (signed for £2.3m), Galatasaray 1995-96 (signed for £2.35m), Nottingham Forest 1996-97 (signed for £1.5m), Sheffield United 1997-98, Benfica 1998-99 (signed for £500,000), Bradford City 1999-2001. Honours: FA Cup 1992 (with Liverpool); League Cup 1994 (with Aston Villa). International caps (for Wales): 75, 22 goals. Father Roy also played for Liverpool and Swansea City.

Saunders, Ron Born Birkenhead, Merseyside, 6 November 1932. Position: forward. Clubs (player): Everton 1951-54, Tonbridge 1954-57, Gillingham 1957-58, Portsmouth 1958-64, Watford 1964-65, Charlton Athletic 1965-66. Clubs (manager): Yeovil Town, Oxford United 1969, Norwich City 1969-73, Manchester City 1973-74, Aston Villa 1974-82, Birmingham City 1982-86, West Bromwich Albion 1986-87. Honours: League Championship 1981; League Cup 1975, 1977 (all with Aston Villa).

Savage, Robbie Born Robert William Savage, Wrexham, Wales, 18 October 1974. Position: midfield. Clubs: Manchester United 1993-94, Crewe Alexandra 1994-97, Leicester City 1997-2002 (signed for £400,000), Birmingham City 2002-present (signed for £1.25m). Honours: League Cup 2000 (with Leicester City). International caps (for Wales): 29, 2 goals.

Schiaffino, Juan Alberto Born Montevideo, Uruguay, 28 July 1925. Position: forward. Clubs: Peñarol 1943-54, AC Milan 1954-60 (signed for £72,000 – then a world record), Roma 1960-62. Honours: Uruguayan League Championship 1944, 1945, 1949, 1951, 1953, 1954 (with Peñarol); Italian League Championship 1955, 1957, 1959 (with AC Milan); UEFA Cup 1961 (with Roma). International caps (for Uruguay): 45; (for Italy): 4. International honours: World Cup 1950 (with Uruguay). Scored three goals against Bolivia in the World Cup finals 1950.

Schmeichel, Peter Born Peter Boleslaw Schmeichel, Gladsaxe, Denmark, 18 November 1963. Position: goalkeeper. Clubs: Hvidovre 1984-87, Brondby 1987-91, Manchester United 1991-99 (signed for £550,000), Sporting Lisbon 1999-2001, Aston Villa 2001-02, Manchester City 2002-03. Honours: Danish League Championship 1987, 1989 (with Brondby); Portuguese League Championship 2000 (with Sporting Lisbon); FA Premiership 1993, 1994, 1996, 1997, 1999; FA Cup 1994, 1996, 1999; League Cup 1992; Charity Shield 1993, 1994, 1996, 1997; UEFA Champions League 1999 (all with Manchester United). International caps (for Denmark): 129, 1 goal. International honours: European Championships 1992. Danish Player of the Year 1990, 1993. European Goalkeeper of the Year 1995. Captained Manchester United in the Champions League final 1999.

Schnellinger, Karl-Heinz Born Duren, Germany, 31 March 1939. Position: defender. Clubs: FC Dueren 99, FC Cologne 1958-63, Mantua 1963-64, Roma 1964-65, AC Milan 1965-74, TeBe Berlin 1974-75. Honours: German League Championship 1962 (with FC Cologne); Italian League Championship 1968; Italian Cup 1967, 1972, 1973; European Cup Winners' Cup 1968, 1973; European Cup 1969; World Club Championship 1969 (all with AC Milan). International caps (for West Germany): 48. Nicknamed 'Volkswagen' when playing for AC Milan. German Player of the Year 1962.

Scholes, Paul Born Salford, 16 November 1974. Position: midfield. Club: Manchester United 1993-present. Honours: FA Premiership 1996, 1997, 1999, 2000, 2001, 2003; FA Cup 1996, 1999, 2004; Charity/Community Shield 1996, 1997, 2003; UEFA Champions League 1999. International caps (for England): 57, 13 goals.

Scifo, Enzo Born Vincenzo Scifo, La Louvière, Belgium, 19 February 1966. Position: midfield/forward. Clubs (player): La Louvière, Anderlecht 1982-87, 1997-2000, Inter Milan 1987-88, Bordeaux 1988-89, Auxerre 1989-91, Torino 1991-93, Monaco 1993-97, Charleroi 2000. Honours: Belgian League Championship 1985, 1986, 1987 (with Anderlecht); Italian Cup 1993 (with Torino). Clubs (coach): Charleroi 2000-02. International caps (for Belgium): 84, 18 goals. Belgian Player of the Year 1984. Retired in 2000 having been diagnosed with chronic arthritis of the hip.

Scirea, Gaetano Born Cernusco sul Naviglio, Italy, 25 May 1953. Position: defender. Clubs: Atalanta 1972-74, Juventus 1974-88. Honours: Italian League Championship 1975, 1977, 1978, 1981, 1982, 1984, 1986; Italian Cup 1979, 1983; European Cup Winners' Cup 1984; UEFA Cup 1977; European Cup 1985 (all with Juventus). International caps (for Italy): 78 (10 as captain), 2 goals. International honours: World Cup 1982. Killed in a road accident in Poland 3 September 1989 while travelling to observe Juventus' next European opponents.

Scott, Elisha Born Belfast, Northern Ireland, 24 August 1894. Position: goalkeeper. Clubs (player): Liverpool 1913-34, Belfast Celtic 1934-36. Honours: League Championship 1921, 1922 (with Liverpool). Club (manager): Belfast Celtic 1934-49. International caps (for Northern Ireland): 31. Rated by many of his contemporaries as the greatest goalkeeper of the era he gained his 31 caps only against the other 'home countries' as neither Ireland nor Northern Ireland then played abroad. His brother William, also a goalkeeper, was also an Irish international. He died 16 May 1959 in Belfast.

Scott, Laurie Born Laurence Scott, Sheffield, 23 April 1917. Position: defender. Clubs: Bradford City, Arsenal 1945-51, Crystal Palace 1951-52. Honours: League Championship 1948; FA Cup 1950 (both with Arsenal). Clubs (manager): Crystal Palace 1951-54, Hitchin Town. International caps (for England): 17. He died 23 July 1999.

Seaman, David Born David Andrew Seaman, Rotherham, Yorkshire, 19 September 1963. Position: goalkeeper. Clubs: Leeds United 1981-82, Peterborough United 1982-84 (signed for £4000), Birmingham City 1984-86 (signed for £100,000), Queens Park Rangers 1986-90 (signed for £225,000), Arsenal 1990-2003 (signed for £1.3m), Manchester City 2003-04. Honours: FA Premiership 1998, 2002; FA Cup 1993, 1998, 2002; League Cup 1993; European Cup Winners' Cup 1994; Charity Shield 1998 (all with Arsenal). International caps (for England): 75 (1 as captain).

Seed, Jimmy Born James Marshall Seed, Blackhill, Co. Durham, 25 March 1895. Position: forward. Clubs (player): Mid-Rhondda, Tottenham Hotspur 1919-27, Sheffield Wednesday 1927-31. Honours: League Championship 1929, 1930 (with Sheffield Wednesday); FA Cup 1921 (with Tottenham Hotspur). Clubs (manager): Clapton Orient 1931-33, Charlton Athletic 1933-56, Bristol City (consultant), Millwall 1958-59. Honours: FA Cup 1947 (with Charlton Athletic). International caps (for England): 5, 1 goal. He died 16 July 1966 in Bromley, Kent, and a stand is named after him at The Valley.

Seeler, Uwe Born Hamburg, Germany, 5 November 1936. Position: forward. Club: SV Hamburg 1953-71. Honours: West German League Championship 1960; West German Cup 1963. International caps (for West Germany): 72, 43 goals. After retiring in 1971, he became a businessman in the clothing industry. Seeler is the only man besides Pelé to score in four World Cups 1958-70.

Setters, Maurice Born Honiton, Devon, 16 December 1936. Position: defender. Clubs (player): Exeter City 1954-55, West Bromwich Albion 1955-60, Manchester United 1960-64, Stoke City 1964-67, Coventry City 1967-70, Charlton Athletic 1970. Honours: FA Cup 1963 (with Manchester United). Clubs (manager): Doncaster Rovers 1971-74, Sheffield Wednesday 1983. Acted as assistant manager to Jack Charlton for the Republic of Ireland national team.

Shackleton, Len Born Leonard Francis Shackleton, Bradford, West Yorkshire, 3 May 1922. Position: forward. Clubs (player): Kippax United, Arsenal (ground staff), London Paper Mills 1939 (loan), Bradford Park Avenue 1945-46, Newcastle United 1946-48 (signed for £13,000), Sunderland 1948-58 (signed for £20,050). International caps (for England): 5, 1 goal. Scored six goals on his debut for Newcastle United. Known as 'The Clown Prince of Soccer', also the title of his autobiography which famously included a chapter entitled 'The Average Director's Knowledge of Football', consisting of a single blank page. Worked as a journalist. He died 28 November 2000 in Grange-over-Sands.

Shankly, Bill Born William Shankly, Glenbuck, South Lanarkshire, 2 September 1913. Position: midfield. Clubs (player): Cronberry Eglinton 1931-32, Carlisle United 1932-33, Preston North End 1933-49. Honours: FA Cup 1938 (with Preston North End). Clubs (manager): Carlisle United 1949-51, Grimsby Town 1951-53, Workington 1953-55, Huddersfield Town 1955-59, Liverpool 1959-74. Honours: League Championship 1964, 1966, 1973; FA Cup 1965, 1974; English Charity Shield 1964, 1965, 1966; UEFA Cup 1973 (all with Liverpool). International caps (for Scotland): 5. Awarded the OBE in 1974. A statue of him stands outside the Kop End at Anfield. He died 28 September 1981 in Liverpool.

Sharpe, Lee Born Lee Stuart Sharpe, Halesowen, 27 May 1971. Position: forward. Clubs: Torquay United 1988, Manchester United 1988-96 (signed for £185,000), Leeds United 1996-99 (signed for £4.5m), Sampdoria 1998-99 (loan), Bradford City 1999-2002 (loan then signed for £200,000), Portsmouth 2001 (loan), Exeter City 2002. Honours: FA Premier League 1993, 1994, 1996; League Cup 1992; Charity Shield 1994; European Cup Winners' Cup 1991 (all with Manchester United). International caps (for England): 8.

Shearer, Alan Born Newcastle-upon-Tyne, 13 August 1970. Position: forward. Clubs: Southampton 1988-92, Blackburn Rovers 1992-96 (signed for £3.6m), Newcastle United 1996-present (signed for £15m). Honours: FA Premiership 1995 (with Blackburn Rovers). International caps (for England): 63 (34 as captain), 30 goals. First player to score 100 goals in the Premiership, then 200 goals in the Premiership and then the first player to score 100 goals in the Premiership with two different clubs. Football Writers' Player of the Year 1994. PFA Player of the Year 1995. Voted Premiership Player of the Decade (1992-2002). Awarded the OBE in 2001.

Sheringham, Teddy Born Edward Paul Sheringham, Highams Park, London, 2 April 1966. Position: forward. Clubs: Millwall 1984-91, Djurgaarden 1985 (loan), Aldershot 1985 (loan), Nottingham Forest 1991-92 (signed for £2m), Tottenham Hotspur 1992-97 (signed for £2.1m), Manchester United 1997-2001 (signed for £3.5m), Tottenham Hotspur 2001-03 (free transfer), Portsmouth 2003-present. Honours: FA Premiership 1999, 2000, 2001; FA Cup 1999; Charity Shield 1997; UEFA Champions League 1999 (all with Manchester United). International caps (for England): 51, 11 goals. PFA Player of the Year 2001.

Shevchenko, Andriy Born Dvirkivshchyna, Ukraine, 29 September 1976. Position: forward. Clubs: Dynamo K2 1993-94, Dynamo Kiev 1994-99, AC Milan 1999-present. Honours: Ukrainian League Championship 1995, 1996, 1997, 1998, 1999; Ukrainian Cup 1996, 1998, 1999 (all with Dynamo Kiev); Italian Cup 2003; UEFA Champions League 2003 (both with AC Milan). International caps (for Ukraine): 50, 22 goals. Won a pair of Ian Rush's boots as a 14-year-old at a tournament in Wales and later played against Rush in the Champions League.

Shilton, Peter Born Peter Leslie Shilton, Leicester, 18 September 1949. Position: goalkeeper. Clubs (player): Leicester City 1966-74, Stoke City 1974-77 (signed for £300,000), Nottingham Forest 1977-82 (signed for £270,000), Southampton 1982-87 (signed for £325,000), Derby County 1987-92 (signed for £90,000), Plymouth Argyle 1992-95, Wimbledon 1995, Bolton Wanderers 1995 (one game), Coventry City 1995-96, West Ham United 1996, Leyton Orient 1996-97. Honours: League Championship 1978; League Cup 1979; European Cup 1979, 1980 (all with Nottingham Forest). Club (manager): Plymouth Argyle 1992-94. International caps (for England): 125 (15 as captain). PFA Player of the Year 1978. Awarded the MBE in 1986 and the OBE in 1990. His 125 caps are a record for England.

Simonian, Nikita Born Armavir, USSR, 12 October 1926. Position: forward. Clubs (player): Georgia, Krilia Sovietov 1946-49, Spartak Moscow 1949-58. Honours: USSR League Championship 1952, 1953, 1956, 1958; USSR Cup 1950, 1958 (all with Spartak Moscow). Club (manager): Spartak Moscow. International caps (for USSR): 23, 12 goals. International honours: Olympic gold medal 1956.

Simonsen, Allan Born Allan Rodenkam Simonsen, Vejle, Denmark, 15 December 1952. Position: midfield. Clubs (player): Vejle BK 1968-72, 1983-89, Borussia Mönchengladbach 1972-79, Barcelona 1979-82, Charlton Athletic 1982-83. Honours: Danish League Championship 1971, 1972, 1984 (with Vejle BK); Danish Cup 1972 (with Vejle BK); German League Championship 1975, 1976, 1977 (with Borussia Mönchengladbach); Spanish Cup 1981 (with Barcelona); UEFA Cup 1975, 1979 (with Borussia Mönchengladbach); European Cup Winners' Cup 1982 (with Barcelona). Clubs (coach/manager): Vejle BK 1990-91. International caps (for Denmark): 56, 20 goals. International

manager (Faroe Islands): 1994-2001;
(Luxembourg): 2001-present. European Player of
the Year 1977.

Sinclair, Trevor Born Dulwich, London, 2 March
1973. Position: midfield. Clubs: Blackpool 1990-93,
Queens Park Rangers 1993-98 (signed for
£600,000), West Ham United 1998-2003 (signed for
£2.3m), Manchester City 2003-present (signed for
£2.5m). International caps (for England): 12.

Sindelar, Matthias Born Kozlornext-Iglau, Moravia, 10
February 1903. Position: forward. Club: Austria Vienna
1924-38. Honours: Austrian League Championship
1926; Austrian Cup 1925, 1926, 1933, 1935, 1936;
Mitropa Cup 1933, 1936. International caps (for
Austria): 44, 27 goals. Known as 'Der Papierene' (The
Paper Man) because of his slender build and his ability
to skip through defences as if they weren't there. A
goal against England in 1932 would purportedly have
put Maradona's second in 1986 in the shade. Part of
the 'Austrian Wonderteam' of the early 1930s, in April
1938 Sindelar captained an 'old Austria' team to a 2-0
win against an 'Austro-German' team after the
Anschluss. Much disliked by the new Nazi regime as
he was Jewish, he was nevertheless invited to play for
'Greater Germany'. He failed to appear for training,
citing injury and age. Austrian Sportsman of the
Century. He died 29 January 1939 of carbon monoxide
poisoning, possibly in an accident although his death
may equally have been the result of foul play. He is
honoured every year on the anniversary of his death
by Austrian players and officials, who gather at his
graveside to pay their respects.

Sinton, Andy Born Cramlington, Northumberland,
19 March 1966. Position: midfield. Clubs: Cambridge
United 1983-85, Brentford 1985-89 (signed for
£25,000), Queens Park Rangers 1989-93 (signed for
£350,000), Sheffield Wednesday 1993-96 (signed for
£2.75m), Tottenham Hotspur 1996-99 (signed for
£1.5m), Wolverhampton Wanderers 1999-2002,
Burton Albion 2002-present. Honours: League Cup
1999 (with Tottenham Hotspur). International caps
(for England): 12.

Sivori, Omar Born Enrique Omar Sivori, San
Nicolas, Argentina, 2 October 1935. Position:
forward. Clubs: River Plate 1952-57, Juventus 1957-
65, Napoli 1965-69. Honours: Argentinian League
Championship 1955, 1956 (with River Plate); Italian
League Championship 1958, 1960, 1961 (with
Juventus); Italian Cup 1959, 1960, 1965 (with
Juventus). International caps (for Argentina): 19, 9
goals. International honours: Copa America 1955,
1957. International caps (for Italy): 9, 8 goals.
European Player of the Year 1961. Sivori formed a
productive partnership at Juventus with John
Charles.

Slater, Bill Born William John Slater, Clitheroe,
Lancashire, 29 April 1927. Position: defender. Clubs:
Blackpool 1944-51, Brentford 1951, Wolverhampton
Wanderers 1952-63, Brentford 1963. Honours:
League Championship 1954, 1958, 1959; FA Cup
1960 (all with Wolverhampton Wanderers).
International caps (for England): 12. Played in the
1951 FA Cup final for Blackpool as an amateur.
Football Writers' Player of the Year 1960. Became
deputy director of Crystal Palace Sports Centre and
later Director of Physical Education at Liverpool and
Birmingham Universities. Awarded the OBE in 1982
and the CBE in 1998.

Smith, Alan Born Alan Martin Smith, Bromsgrove,
21 November 1962. Position: forward. Clubs:
Alvechurch, Leicester City 1982-87, Arsenal 1987-95

(signed for £800,000). Honours: League
Championship 1989, 1991; FA Cup 1993; Charity
Shield 1991; European Cup Winners' Cup 1994 (all
with Arsenal). He scored the winning goal in the Cup
Winners' Cup final. International caps (for England):
13, 2 goals. Retired through injury in 1995. He
infamously replaced Gary Lineker in Sweden in a
crucial European Championship game in the 1992
finals when Graham Taylor brought a premature end
to the latter's international career.

Smith, Bobby Born Robert Alfred Smith, Langdale,
North Yorkshire, 22 February 1933. Position: forward.
Clubs: Chelsea 1950-55, Tottenham Hotspur 1955-
64, Brighton & Hove Albion 1964. Honours: League
Championship 1961; FA Cup 1961, 1962 (all with
Tottenham Hotspur). International caps (for
England): 15, 13 goals. Smith had an excellent goal-
scoring ratio: 217 League goals in 376 appearances
for Tottenham Hotspur.

Smith, G.O. Born Gilbert Oswald Smith, Croydon,
Surrey, 25 November 1872. Position: forward. Clubs:
Oxford University, Old Carthusians, Corinthians.
International caps (for England): 20 (15 as captain),
11 goals. Smith scored a record five goals against
Ireland in 1899, having also played cricket for Oxford
University and Surrey 1893-96. He died 6 December
1943 in Yaldhurst, Lymington, Hampshire.

Smith, Tommy Born Liverpool, 5 April 1945. Position:
defender/midfield. Clubs: Liverpool 1962-78,
Swansea City 1978-79. Honours: League
Championship 1966, 1973, 1976, 1977; FA Cup
1965, 1974; Charity Shield 1965, 1966, 1974; UEFA
Cup 1973, 1976; European Cup 1977 (all with
Liverpool). International caps (for England): 1. Scored
a goal in the 1977 European Cup final, his 600th
appearance for Liverpool. Awarded the MBE in 1977.

Socrates Born Socrates Brasileiro Sampaio de
Sousa Vieira de Oliveira, Belem, Brazil, 19 February
1954. Position: forward. Clubs: Botafogo 1974-76,
Corinthians 1977-84, Fiorentina 1984-85, Flamengo
1985-87, Santos 1988-90. Honours: São Paulo
League Championship 1979, 1982, 1983 (with
Corinthians); Rio League Championship 1986 (with
Flamengo). International caps (for Brazil): 63, 25
goals. Known as 'The Doctor' or 'Doctor Socrates'
because he held a medical degree. South American
Player of the Year 1983.

Solskjaer, Ole Born Ole Gunnar Solskjaer,
Kristiansund, Norway, 26 February 1973. Position:
forward. Clubs: Clausenengen FK, Molde 1995-96,
Manchester United 1996-present (signed for £1.5m).
Honours: FA Premiership 1997, 1999, 2000, 2001,
2003; FA Cup 1999; Charity Shield 1997, 2003; UEFA
Champions League 1999 (all with Manchester
United). International caps (for Norway): 55, 20 goals.

Souness, Graeme Born Graeme James Souness,
Edinburgh, 6 May 1953. Position: midfield. Clubs
(player): Tottenham Hotspur 1970-72, Middlesbrough
1972-78 (signed for £30,000), Liverpool 1978-84
(signed for £352,000), Sampdoria 1984-86 (signed for
£650,000), Rangers 1986-91. Honours: League
Championship 1979, 1980, 1982, 1983, 1984; League
Cup 1981, 1982, 1983, 1984 (all with Liverpool);
Scottish League Championship 1987, 1989, 1990
(with Rangers). Clubs (manager): Rangers 1986-91,
Liverpool 1991-94, Galatasaray 1994-96,
Southampton 1996-97, Torino 1997, Benfica 1997-99,
Blackburn Rovers 2000-04, Newcastle United 2004-
present. Honours: Scottish League Championship
1987, 1989, 1990 (with Rangers); FA Cup 1992
(with Liverpool); League Cup 2002 (with Blackburn

Rovers); Turkish Cup 1996 (with Galatasaray). International caps (for Scotland): 54, 4 goals.

Southall, Neville   Born Llandudno, Wales, 16 September 1958. Position: goalkeeper. Clubs (player): Winsford United 1979-80, Bury 1980-81, Everton 1981-98 (signed for £150,000), Port Vale 1983 (loan), Southend United 1997-98 (loan), Stoke City 1998 (loan, then free transfer), Torquay United 1998-2000, Huddersfield Town 1999 (loan), Bradford City 2000, York City 2001, Rhyl 2001, Shrewsbury Town 2001, 2002, Dover Athletic 2001, Dagenham & Redbridge 2002. Honours: League Championship 1985, 1987; FA Cup 1984, 1995; Charity Shield 1984, 1985, 1987, 1995; European Cup Winners' Cup 1985 (all with Everton). Clubs (manager): Dover Athletic 2001-present. International caps (for Wales): 93. Football Writers' Player of the Year 1985. Wales' most-capped player, Southall also made a record 750 appearances for Everton. Known as 'Big Nev'.

Southgate, Gareth   Born Watford, Hertfordshire, 3 September 1970. Position: defender. Clubs: Crystal Palace 1989-95, Aston Villa 1995-2001 (signed for £2.5m), Middlesbrough 2001-present (signed for £6.5m). Honours: League Cup 1996 (with Aston Villa). International caps (for England): 49, 1 goal.

Spence, Joe   Born Joseph Walter Spence, Throckley, Northumberland, England, 15 December 1898. Position: forward. Clubs: Newburn FC, Scotswood, Manchester United 1919-33, Bradford City 1933-35, Chesterfield 1935-38. International caps (for England): 2, 1 goal. Known as 'Mr Soccer' in Manchester. 'Give it to Joe' was a catchprase of the Manchester United crowd during his time there. He died 31 December 1966.

Springett, Ron   Born Ronald Derrick G. Springett, Fulham, London, 22 July 1935. Position: goalkeeper. Clubs: Victoria United, Queens Park Rangers 1953-58, 1967-68, Sheffield Wednesday 1958-67. International caps (for England): 33, 48 goals conceded.

Sproston, Bert   Born Sandbach, Cheshire, 22 June 1915. Position: defender. Clubs: Leeds United 1933-38, Tottenham Hotspur 1938 (signed for £9500), Manchester City 1938-50 (signed for £10,000). International caps (for England): 11. Sproston signed for Manchester City the day before they were due to play his former team, Tottenham Hotspur. He travelled to Manchester with the Spurs team and was listed in the programme as a Spurs player – but played for Manchester City.

Stam, Jaap   Born Kampen, Holland, 17 July 1972. Position: defender. Clubs: Dos Kampen, PEC Zwolle 1992-93, Cambuur Leeuwarden 1993-95, Willem II 1995-96, PSV Eindhoven 1996-98, Manchester United 1998-2001 (signed for £10.75m), Lazio 2001-present (signed for £16.5m). Honours: Dutch League Championship 1997 (with PSV Eindhoven); FA Premiership 1999, 2000, 2001; FA Cup 1999; UEFA Champions League 1999 (all with Manchester United). International caps (for Holland): 52, 3 goals. Stam left Manchester United after publication of his autobiography, *Head to Head*. He was banned for five months in 2002 for using the steroid nandrolone.

Stapleton, Frank   Born Francis Anthony Stapleton, Dublin, 10 July 1956. Position: forward. Clubs (player): St Martins, Bolton Athletic, Arsenal 1973-81, Manchester United 1981-87 (signed for £800,000), Ajax 1987-88, Derby County 1988 (loan), Le Havre 1988-89, Blackburn Rovers 1989-91, Aldershot 1991, Huddersfield Town 1991, Bradford City 1991-94, New England Revolution 1996-97.

Honours: FA Cup 1979 (with Arsenal), 1983, 1985 (with Manchester United). Clubs (manager): Bradford City 1991-94, New England Revolution 1996. International caps (for Republic of Ireland): 71, 20 goals. The first player to score for two different clubs in Wembley FA Cup finals – in 1979 for Arsenal and in 1983 for Manchester United.

Staunton, Steve   Born Drogheda, Ireland, 19 January 1969. Position: defender. Clubs: Dundalk 1985-86, Liverpool 1986-91 (signed for £2000), 1998-2000, Bradford City 1987-88 (loan), Aston Villa 1991-98 (signed for £1.1m), 2000-03, Crystal Palace 2000, Coventry City 2003-present. Honours: League Championship 1990 (with Liverpool); FA Cup 1989 (with Liverpool); League Cup 1994, 1996 (with Aston Villa). International caps (for Republic of Ireland): 102, 8 goals.

Steel, Billy   Born William Steel, Dunipace, Stirling, 1 May 1923. Position: forward. Clubs: Bo'ness Cadora, Leicester City, St Mirren, Morton 1941-47, Derby County 1947-50 (signed for £15,500, a then record fee for British clubs), Dundee 1950-54 (signed for £23,000). Honours: Scottish League Cup 1952, 1953 (with Dundee). International caps (for Scotland): 30, 12 goals. Not a favourite with his fellow Derby County players, not least because he commuted from Scotland for each of his games. He was the first Scottish international to be sent off while representing his country. Steel emigrated to USA in 1954 where he worked in advertising. He died 13 May 1982 in San Francisco.

Stein, Jock   Born John Stein, Hamilton, South Lanarkshire, Scotland, 6 October 1922. Clubs (player): Albion Rovers, Llanelli, Celtic 1951-55. Honours: Scottish League Championship 1954; Scottish FA Cup 1954 (both with Celtic). Clubs (manager): Dunfermline Athletic, Hibernian, Celtic 1965-78, Leeds United 1978. Honours: Scottish League Championship 1966, 1967, 1968, 1969, 1970, 1971, 1972, 1973, 1974, 1977; Scottish FA Cup 1965, 1967, 1969, 1971, 1972, 1974, 1975, 1977; Scottish League Cup 1966, 1967, 1968, 1969, 1970, 1975; European Cup 1967 (all with Celtic). International manager (Scotland): 1978-85. Awarded the CBE in 1970. He died 10 September 1985 at Ninian Park, Cardiff, only hours after Scotland qualified for the 1986 World Cup finals by drawing 1-1 with Wales.

Stephenson, Clem   Born New Delaval, Co. Durham, Northumberland, 6 February 1890. Position: forward. Clubs (player): Aston Villa 1910-21, Huddersfield 1921-30. Honours: League Championship 1924, 1925, 1926 (with Huddersfield Town). Clubs (manager): Huddersfield Town 1929-42. International caps (for England): 1. Captained Huddersfield Town to their hat-trick of League Championship wins.

Stepney, Alex   Born Mitcham, Surrey, 18 September 1942. Position: goalkeeper. Clubs: Tooting & Mitcham 1958-63, Millwall 1963-66, Chelsea 1966 (signed for £50,000, played only one League game), Manchester United 1966-78 (signed for £55,000), Dallas Tornado 1979, 1980, Altrincham 1979-80 (player/coach). Honours: League Championship 1967; FA Cup 1977; European Cup 1968 (all with Manchester United). International caps (for England): 1, one goal conceded. Chosen 20 times to play for England but was on the subs' bench on 19 occasions. Mainly remembered for his save from Eusebio near the end of the 1968 European Cup final with the score at 1-1. He also scored twice from the penalty spot for Manchester United in 1975. He is now working as a goalkeeping coach.

Steven, Trevor　Born Trevor McGregor Steven, Berwick-upon-Tweed, Northumberland, 21 September 1963. Position: midfield. Clubs: Burnley 1981-83, Everton 1983-89, Rangers 1989-91 (signed for £1.5m), 1992-97, Olympique Marseille 1991-92 (signed for £5.6m). Honours: League Championship 1985, 1987 (with Everton); Scottish League Championship 1990, 1991, 1993, 1994, 1995, 1996 (with Rangers); French League Championship 1992 (with Olympique Marseille); FA Cup 1984 (with Everton); Scottish League Cup 1989, 1991, 1994 (with Rangers); European Cup Winners' Cup 1985 (with Everton). International caps (for England): 36, 4 goals. Won League Championships in three different countries (England, Scotland and France).

Stevens, Gary　Born Michael Gary Stevens, Barrow-in-Furness, Cumbria, 27 March 1963. Position: defender. Clubs: Everton 1981-88, Rangers 1988-94 (signed for £1m), Tranmere Rovers 1994-98. Honours: League Championship 1985, 1987 (with Everton); FA Cup 1984 (with Everton); Scottish League Championship 1989, 1990, 1991, 1992, 1993, 1994; Scottish Cup 1992; Scottish League Cup 1989, 1991, 1994 (all with Rangers); European Cup Winners' Cup 1985 (with Everton). International caps (for England): 46. Retired through injury 1998.

Stiles, Nobby　Born Norbert Peter Stiles, Collyhurst, Manchester, 18 May 1942. Position: defender. Clubs (player): Manchester United 1957-71, Middlesbrough 1971-73, Preston North End 1973-74. Honours: League Championship 1965, 1967; European Cup 1968 (all with Manchester United). Clubs (manager/coach): Preston North End 1977-81, Vancouver Whitecaps 1981-84, West Bromwich Albion 1984-86. International caps (for England): 28, 1 goal. International honours: World Cup 1966. Remembered for his jig around Wembley in 1966 with the Jules Rimet Trophy in close attendance. Youth team coach at Manchester United 1989-93. Awarded the MBE in 2000.

Stock, Alec　Born Peasedown St John, nr Radstock, Somerset, 30 March 1917. Position: forward. Clubs (player): Tottenham Hotspur, Charlton Athletic 1936-38, Queens Park Rangers 1938-39, Yeovil Town 1945-49. Clubs (manager): Yeovil Town 1945-49, Leyton Orient 1949-56, Arsenal 1956, 1956-57, 1958-59, Roma 1957, Queens Park Rangers 1959-68, 1978, Luton Town 1968-72, Fulham 1972-76, AFC Bournemouth 1979-80. Honours: League Cup 1967 (with Queens Park Rangers). Stock is known mainly for the giant-killing exploits of the teams he managed, especially Yeovil's defeat of First Division Sunderland in the 1949 FA Cup – the first time a non-league team had beaten one from the top flight. Autobiography *A Little Thing Called Pride*. He died 16 April 2001 aged 84. He also bought both Malcolm Macdonald and Rodney Marsh at the beginning of their careers.

Stoichkov, Hristo　Born Plovdiv, Bulgaria, 8 February 1966. Position: forward. Clubs: CSKA Sofia 1984-86, 1989-90, 1997-98, CFKA Sredets 1986-89, Barcelona 1990-95, 1996-98, Parma 1995-96, Al-Ansar 1998 (loan), Reysol 1999, Chicago Fire 2000-03, DC United 2003-present. Honours: Bulgarian League Championship 1987, 1989 (with CFKA Sredets), 1990 (with CSKA Sofia); Bulgarian Cup 1985 (with CSKA Sofia), 1987, 1988, 1989 (with CFKA Sredets); Spanish League Championship 1991, 1992, 1993, 1994; Spanish Cup 1997; European Cup Winners' Cup 1997; European Cup 1992 (all with Barcelona). International caps (for Bulgaria): 83, 37 goals. Golden Boot winner (shared), World Cup 1994. Bulgarian Player of the Year 1989, 1990, 1991, 1992, 1994. European Player of the Year 1994. Stoichkov was suspended for a season for his part in a riot during the 1985 Bulgarian Cup final which also led to CSKA Sofia being disbanded and becoming CFKA Sredets for three seasons.

Storey, Peter　Born Peter Edwin Storey, Farnham, Surrey, 7 September 1945. Position: defender. Clubs: Arsenal 1962-77, Fulham 1977. Honours: League Championship 1971; FA Cup 1971; Inter-cities Fairs Cup 1970 (all with Arsenal). International caps (for England): 19. After his retirement in 1977 Storey embarked on a life of crime which included being found guilty of running a brothel, being involved with counterfeiting gold coins and car theft.

Strachan, Gordon　Born Gordon David Strachan, Edinburgh, 9 February 1957. Position: midfield. Clubs (player): Dundee 1975-77, Aberdeen 1977-83 (signed for £50,000), Manchester United 1984-89 (signed for £500,000), Leeds United 1989-95 (signed for £300,000), Coventry City 1995-97. Honours: Scottish League Championship 1980, 1984 (with Aberdeen); Scottish Cup 1982, 1983, 1984 (with Aberdeen); League Championship 1992 (with Leeds United); FA Cup 1985 (with Manchester United); European Cup Winners' Cup 1983 (with Aberdeen). Clubs (manager): Coventry City 1996-2001, Southampton 2001-04. International caps (for Scotland): 50, 5 goals. Football Writers' Player of the Year 1991. Awarded the OBE in 1993.

Strange, Alfred　Born Alfred Henry Strange, Marehey, Derbyshire, 2 April 1900. Position: defender. Club: Sheffield Wednesday 1927-35. International caps (for England): 20 (2 as captain). He died in 1978.

Suarez, Claudio　Born Texcoco, Mexico, 17 December 1968. Position: defender. Clubs: Pumas de la Unam 1988-95, Chivas del Guadalajara 1996-2000, Tigres 2000-present. Honours: Mexican League Championship 1991 (with Pumas de la Unam), 1997 (summer) (with Chivas del Guadalajara). International caps (for Mexico): 170, 8 goals. Known as 'El Emperador', he is the most-capped male player in the world.

Suarez, Luis　Born Luis Suarez Miramonte, La Coruña, Spain, 2 May 1935. Position: forward. Clubs (player): Barcelona 1953-61, Inter Milan 1961-70, Sampdoria 1970-73. Honours: Italian League Championship 1963, 1965, 1966; European Cup 1964, 1965; World Club Championship 1964, 1965 (all with Inter Milan). Clubs (manager): Genoa, Cagliari, Como. International caps (for Spain): 32, 14 goals. International honours: European Championship 1964. International manager (Spain): 1988-91. European Player of the Year 1960.

Suker, Davor　Born Osijek, Croatia, 1 January 1968. Position: forward. Clubs: Osijek 1984-89, Dinamo Zagreb 1989-91, Seville 1991-96, Real Madrid 1996-99, Arsenal 1999-2000 (signed for £500,000), West Ham United 2000-01, 1860 Munich 2001-present. Honours: Spanish League Championship 1997; UEFA Champions League 1998 (both with Real Madrid). International caps (for Yugoslavia): 2, 1 goal; (for Croatia): 69, 45 goals. Golden Boot winner, World Cup 1998.

Sukur, Hakan　Born Adapazari, Turkey, 1 September 1971. Position: forward. Clubs: Sakaryaspor, Bursaspor 1990-92, Galatasaray 1992-95, 1995-2000, 2003-present, Torino 1995 (five games), Inter Milan 2000-02, Parma 2002, Blackburn Rovers

2002-03. Honours: Turkish League Championship 1993, 1994, 1997, 1998, 1999, 2000; Turkish Cup 1993, 1996, 1999, 2000 (all with Galatasaray). International caps (for Turkey): 87, 40 goals. He scored the fastest goal ever in the World Cup 2002 third place play-off against South Korea at 10.8secs.

Swan, Peter Born South Elmsall, Yorkshire, 8 October 1936. Position: defender. Clubs: Sheffield Wednesday 1953-73, Bury 1973. International caps (for England): 19. In 1965 Sheffield Wednesday players Swan, David 'Bronco' Layne and Tony Kay bet £50 that they would lose to opponents Ipswich Town. The bet was revealed by the *Sunday People* and the case went to court. All three were found guilty of 'conspiracy to defraud' (though oddly Kay had been named as man of the match by the *Sunday People* in that game). They were banned for life from English football and served four-month jail terms. The life ban was later commuted and in August 1973 Swan took the field for Sheffield Wednesday again. He went on to be player/coach for Matlock Town and, with Layne and his son Carl in the team, took the 1975 FA Challenge Trophy.

Swift, Frank Born Frank Victor Swift, Blackpool, Lancashire, 24 December 1913. Position: goalkeeper. Club: Manchester City 1932-49. Honours: League Championship 1937; FA Cup 1934 (both with Manchester City). International caps (for England): 19 (2 as captain), conceded 18 goals. First goalkeeper to captain England. Collapsed from nervous exhaustion after the 1934 FA Cup final. Swift pioneered throwing the ball to his team-mates rather than punting it upfield, and campaigned for better wages and conditions. After retirement from the game he became a sports reporter for the *Sunday Empire News*. He died in the Munich air disaster, 1958.

Tardelli, Marco Born Capanne di Careggine, Italy, 24 September 1954. Position: midfield. Clubs (player): Pisa 1972-74, Como 1974-75, Juventus 1975-85, Inter Milan 1985-87, San Gallo 1987-88. Honours: Italian League Championship 1977, 1978, 1981, 1982, 1984; Italian Cup 1979, 1983; UEFA Cup 1977; European Cup Winners' Cup 1984; European Cup 1985 (all with Juventus). Clubs (coach): Cesena, Como. International caps (for Italy): 81, 6 goals. International honours: World Cup 1982. Known as 'Schizzo' (The Spurt) for his forceful runs into the penalty area. Tardelli scored in Italy's 3-1 win over West Germany in the 1982 World Cup final, and was coach of the Italian team which won the Under-21 European Championship in 2000.

Taylor, Tommy Born Barnsley, South Yorkshire, 29 January 1932. Position: forward. Clubs: Smithies United 1948, Barnsley 1949-53, Manchester United 1953-58 (signed for £29,999). Honours: League Championship 1956, 1957 (with Manchester United). International caps (for England): 19, 16 goals. Unwilling to label Taylor as the first £30,000 footballer, Matt Busby gave £1 to a dinner lady and paid £29,999 for him. Known as 'The Smiling Executioner', Taylor was described by Alfredo Di Stefano as 'Magnifico'. He died 6 February 1958 in the Munich air disaster.

Thompson, Peter Born Carlisle, Cumbria, 27 November 1942. Position: forward. Clubs: Preston North End 1959-63, Liverpool 1963-74 (signed for £40,000), Bolton Wanderers 1974-77. Honours: League Championship 1964, 1966; FA Cup 1965; Charity Shield 1964, 1966 (all with Liverpool). International caps (for England): 16. Retired in 1977 to become an hotelier in the Lake District.

Thompson, Phil Born Philip Bernard Thompson, Liverpool, 21 January 1954. Position: defender. Clubs (player): Liverpool 1971-84, Sheffield United 1984-86. Honours: League Championship 1973, 1976, 1977, 1979, 1980, 1982, 1983; FA Cup 1974; League Cup 1981, 1982; Charity Shield 1974, 1976, 1977, 1979, 1980, 1982; UEFA Cup 1973, 1976; European Cup 1978, 1981 (all with Liverpool). Clubs (manager): Liverpool 1986-92 (reserve team coach), 1998-2004 (assistant), 2001-02 (caretaker). International caps (for England): 42 (6 as captain), 1 goal.

Thuram, Lilian Born Pointe-à-Pierre, Guadeloupe, 1 January 1972. Position: defender. Clubs: Monaco 1990-96, Parma 1996-2001, Juventus 2001-present. Honours: Italian League Championship 2002, 2003 (with Juventus); French Cup 1991 (with Monaco); Italian Cup 1999 (with Parma); UEFA Cup 1999 (with Parma). International caps (for France): 92, 2 goals. International honours: World Cup 1998; European Championship 2000.

Todd, Colin Born Chester-le-Street, Co. Durham, 12 December 1948. Position: defender. Clubs (player): Sunderland 1966-71, Derby County 1971-78, Everton 1978-79, Birmingham City 1979-82, Nottingham Forest 1982-84, Oxford United 1984, Vancouver Whitecaps 1984, Luton Town 1984. Honours: League Championship 1972, 1975 (with Derby County). Clubs (manager): Middlesbrough 1987-91 (assistant 1987-90), Bradford City 1991-92 (coach), Bolton Wanderers 1992-99 (assistant 1992-95), Swindon Town 2000, Derby County 2001-02. International caps (for England): 27. PFA Player of the Year 1975.

Toshack, John Born Cardiff, 22 March 1949. Position: forward. Clubs (player): Cardiff City 1966-70, Liverpool 1970-79, Swansea City 1979-84. Honours: League Championship 1973, 1976, 1977 (with Liverpool); FA Cup 1974 (with Liverpool); Welsh Cup 1968, 1969, 1970 (with Cardiff City); UEFA Cup 1973, 1976 (with Liverpool). Clubs (manager): Swansea City 1979-84, Sporting Lisbon 1984-85, Real Sociedad 1985-89, 1991-94, Real Madrid 1989-90, 1999, Deportivo La Coruña 1995-97, Besiktas 1997-99. Honours: Spanish League Championship 1990 (with Real Madrid); Welsh Cup 1981, 1982, 1983 (with Swansea City); Spanish Cup 1987 (with Real Sociedad). International caps (for Wales): 40, 13 goals. International manager (Wales): 1994 (one game).

Tostao Born Eduardo Gonçalves de Andrade, Belo Horizonte, Minas Gerais, Brazil, 25 January 1947. Position: forward. Clubs: Cruzeiro, Vasco da Gama. Honours: Brazilian League Championship (Mineiro) 1965, 1966, 1967, 1968, 1969; Brazilian Cup 1966 (all with Cruzeiro). International caps (for Brazil): 53, 31 goals. International honours: World Cup 1970. South American Player of the Year 1971. His playing career was ended by an eye injury in 1974. Known as 'Mineirinho D'Ouro' (Little Miner of Gold), he now works as a sports journalist.

Trautmann, Bert Born Bernhard Carl Trautmann, Bremen, Germany, 22 October 1923. Position: goalkeeper. Clubs (player): St Helens Town, Manchester City 1949-64, Wellington Town. Honours: FA Cup 1956 (with Manchester City). Club (manager): Stockport County 1965-66. Football Writers' Player of the Year 1956. His is an extraordinary tale. During World War II he was a paratrooper in the Wehrmacht. In 1945 he was court-martialled for sabotage; captured by the Russians,

F
O
O
T
B
A
L
L

he escaped and was recaptured by the Free French. Escaping twice more he was captured again by the Americans and finally by the British. He had also been in the Hitler Youth and won the Iron Cross, first class. He was imprisoned in England and decided to settle. Despite serious criticism from many sides when he was signed by Manchester City he overcame the prejudice to become an incredibly popular figure, renowned for playing out the final 15 minutes of the 1956 FA Cup final having unknowingly suffered a broken neck following a challenge. He later became German FA overseas coach and retired in Germany in the 1980s.

Urrutikoetxea, Javier Gonzalez Born San Sebastian, Spain, 17 February 1952. Position: goalkeeper. Clubs: Real Sociedad 1973-76, Espanyol 1976-81, Barcelona 1981-88. Honours: Spanish Championship 1985; Spanish Cup 1983, 1988; European Cup Winners' Cup 1982 (all with Barcelona). International caps (for Spain): 5. Known as 'Urruti'. He was killed in a car accident, 24 May 2001.

Valderrama, Carlos Born Carlos Alberto Valderrama Palacio, Santa Marta, Colombia, 2 September 1961. Position: midfield. Clubs: Union Magdalena 1981-84, Millonarios 1984-85, Deportivo Cali 1985-88, SCP Montpellier 1988-90 (signed for $1.5m), Real Valladolid 1990-92, Deportivo Independiente Medellin 1992-93, Atlético Juniors 1993-96, Tampa Bay Mutiny 1996-98, 1999-2001, Miami Fusion 1998-99, Colorado Rapids 2001-present. Honours: French Cup 1990 (with Montpellier). International caps (for Colombia): 111, 10 goals. South American Footballer of the Year 1987, 1994. Named Colombian Player of the Century in 2000. Easily recognisable by his shock of blond hair, he is known as 'El Pibe' (The Kid). The 10m tall bronze statue of Valderrama, unveiled in his home town of Santa Marta in November 2002, is believed to be the biggest statue ever dedicated to a sports personality.

Van Basten, Marco Born Utrecht, Holland, 31 October 1964. Position: forward. Clubs: Ajax 1981-87, AC Milan 1987-95. Honours: Dutch League Championship 1982, 1983, 1985 (with Ajax); Dutch Cup 1983, 1986, 1987 (with Ajax); Italian League Championship 1988, 1992, 1993, 1994 (with AC Milan); European Cup Winners' Cup 1987 (with Ajax); European Cup/UEFA Champions League 1989, 1990, 1994 (with AC Milan). International caps (for Holland): 58, 24 goals. International honours: European Championship 1988. European Golden Boot winner, 1986. European Player of the Year 1988, 1989, 1992. FIFA World Player of the Year 1992. Retired in 1995 because of an ankle injury. Known as 'Marco Goalo'. His volleyed goal in the European Championship final in 1988 against USSR was voted best ever goal in the competition.

Van Bronckhorst, Giovanni Born Rotterdam, Holland, 5 February 1975. Position: midfield. Clubs: Feyenoord 1993-98, RKC 1993-94, 1998 (loan), Rangers 1998-2001 (signed for £5m), Arsenal 2001-present (signed for £8.5m). Honours: Dutch Cup 1995 (with Feyenoord); Scottish League Championship 1999, 2000; Scottish Cup 1999, 2000; Scottish League Cup 1999 (all with Rangers); FA Premiership 2002 (with Arsenal); FA Cup 2002 (with Arsenal). International caps (with Holland): 29, 3 goals. Known as 'Gio Force' in Holland.

Van Himst, Paul Born Leeuw-St-Pierre, Belgium, 2 October 1943. Position: forward. Clubs (player): Anderlecht 1960-75, RWD Molenbeek 1975-76,

Alost 1976-77. Honours: Belgian League Championship 1962, 1964, 1965, 1966, 1967, 1968, 1972, 1974; Belgian Cup 1965, 1972, 1973, 1975 (all with Anderlecht). Clubs (coach/director): Anderlecht 1982-85 (trainer), RWD Molenbeek 1987-89 (technical director). Honours: Belgian League Championship 1985; UEFA Cup 1983 (both with Anderlecht). International caps (for Belgium): 81, 30 goals. International manager (Belgium): 1991-96. Belgian Player of the Year 1960, 1962, 1965. Having declined to play for the national side 1967-68, van Himst retired from international football in 1970 but returned in 1972. Belgian Footballer of the Century. Had a part in the film *Escape to Victory*.

Van Hooijdonk, Pierre Born Steenbergen, Holland, 29 November 1969. Position: forward. Clubs: SC Welberg, Steenbergen, NAC Breda, RBC Roosendaal 1989-91, NAC Breda 1991-94, Celtic 1995-97 (signed for £1.2m), Nottingham Forest 1997-99 (signed for £4.5m), Vitesse Arnhem 1999-2000 (signed for £3.5m), Benfica 2000-01, Feyenoord 2001-present. Honours: Scottish Cup 1995 (with Celtic). International caps (for Holland): 30, 10 goals.

van Nistelrooy, Ruud Born Rutgerus van Nistelrooy, Oss, Holland, 1 July 1976. Position: forward. Clubs: Nooit Gedacht, Magriet, Den Bosch 1993-97, SC Herenveen 1997-98, PSV Eindhoven 1998-2000, Manchester United 2000-present. Honours: FA Premiership 2003; FA Cup 2004; FA Community Shield 2003 (all with Manchester United). International caps (for Holland): 25, 11 goals. Dutch Footballer of the Year 1999.

Varadi, Imre Born Paddington, London, 8 July 1959. Position: forward. Clubs (player): Sheffield United 1978-79, Everton 1979-81 (signed for £80,000), Newcastle United 1981-83 (signed for £100,000), Sheffield Wednesday 1983-85 (signed for £150,000), West Bromwich Albion 1985-86 (signed for £285,000), Manchester City 1986-88 (signed for £50,000), Leeds United 1990-92 (signed for £50,000), Luton Town 1992 (loan), Rotherham United 1992-95, Oxford United 1993 (loan), Mansfield Town 1995, Boston United 1995, Scunthorpe United 1995, Matlock Town 1995-96. Clubs (manager): Matlock Town 1995-96

Varela, Obdulio Born Obdulio Jacinto Varela, Uruguay, 1917. Position: defender. Clubs (player): Wanderers 1938-42, Peñarol 1942-54. Clubs (manager): Peñarol 1954-56. International caps (for Uruguay): 52. International honours: World Cup 1950 (as captain). He was never on the losing side in a World Cup match.

Vassell, Darius Born Sutton Coldfield, West Midlands, 13 June 1980. Position: forward. Club: Aston Villa 1998-present. International caps (for England): 8, 3 goals.

Vava Born Edvaldo Izidio Neto, Recife, Pernambuco, Brazil, 12 November 1934. Position: forward. Clubs (player): Recife 1949-52, Vasco da Gama 1952-58, Atlético Madrid 1958-60, Palmeiras 1960-63, America (Mexico) 1964-67, San Diego Toros 1967-69, Portuguesa 1969. Honours: Rio League Championship 1956, 1958 (with Vasco da Gama); Spanish Cup 1960, 1961 (with Atlético Madrid); São Paulo League Championship 1963 (with Palmeiras). International caps (for Brazil): 20, 15 goals. Honours: World Cup 1958, 1962. Vava scored in both the 1958 and 1962 World Cup finals (a feat equalled only by Pelé and Paul Breitner). International manager (Qatar). Had the nicknames 'Chest of Steel' and 'Lion of Brazil'. He died 19 January 2002 in the São Victor clinic in Rio.

Venables, Terry   Born Terence Frederick Venables, Dagenham, London, 6 January 1943. Position: midfield. Clubs (player): Chelsea 1958-66, Tottenham Hotspur 1966-69 (signed for £80,000), Queens Park Rangers 1969-74 (signed for £70,000), Crystal Palace 1974-76 (signed for £70,000). Honours: FA Cup 1967 (with Tottenham Hotspur); League Cup 1965 (with Chelsea). Clubs (manager): Crystal Palace 1976-80, Queens Park Rangers 1980-84, Barcelona 1984-87, Tottenham Hostpur 1987-93, Portsmouth 1996 (director of football), Crystal Palace 1998-99 (coach), Middlesbrough 2000-01, Leeds United 2002-03. Honours: Spanish League Championship 1985 (with Barcelona); FA Cup 1991 (with Tottenham Hotspur). International caps (for England): 2. Represented England at five levels – schoolboy, youth, amateur, Under-23 and senior. International manager (for England): 1994-96; (for Australia): 1996-97. Nicknamed 'El Tel' after his spell at Barcelona. Co-author of the *Hazell* detective novels, Venables also co-authored a novel *They Used To Play on Grass* which foresaw a sporting future in which artificial surfaces had taken over, and designed a football game called *The Manager*. Introduced an artificial pitch at Queens Park Rangers while manager there.

Veron, Juan   Born Juan Sebastian Veron, La Plata, Argentina, 9 March 1975. Position: midfield. Clubs: Estudiantes de la Plata 1993-95, Boca Juniors 1995-96, Sampdoria 1996-98 (signed for £3m), Parma 1998-99 (signed for £13m), Lazio 1999-2001 (signed for £18m), Manchester United 2001-03 (signed for £28.1m), Chelsea 2003-present. Honours: Italian Cup 1999 (with Parma); Italian League Championship 2000 (with Lazio); FA Premiership 2003 (with Manchester United); UEFA Cup 1999 (with Parma). International caps (for Argentina): 51, 8 goals. Son of 1960s Argentine international Juan Ramon Veron who was nicknamed 'The Witch'; Juan Sebastian therefore became 'The Little Witch'; He has a tattoo of Che Guevara on his right arm.

Vialli, Gianluca   Born Cremona, Italy, 9 July 1964. Position: forward. Clubs (player): Cremonese 1980-84, Sampdoria 1984-92, Juventus 1992-96 (signed for £12m), Chelsea 1996-2000. Honours: Italian League Championship 1991 (with Sampdoria), 1995 (with Juventus); FA Cup 1997 (with Chelsea); European Cup Winners' Cup 1990 (with Sampdoria); UEFA Cup 1993 (with Juventus); UEFA Champions League 1996 (with Juventus). Clubs (manager): Chelsea 1998-2000, Watford 2001-02. Honours: FA Cup 2000; European Cup Winners' Cup 1998 (both with Chelsea). International caps (for Italy): 59, 16 goals.

Viduka, Mark   Born Melbourne, Australia, 9 October 1975. Position: forward. Clubs: Melbourne Knights 1993-95, Croatia Zagreb 1995-98, Celtic 1998-2000 (signed for £3.5m), Leeds United 2000-04 (signed for £6.5m), Middlesbrough 2004-present. Honours: Scottish League Cup 2000 (with Celtic). International caps (for Australia): 21, 2 goals. Australian NSL Player of the Year 1994, 1995. Scottish Player of the Year 2000. Oceania Player of the Year 2001. Nicknamed 'The V-Bomber' in Australia.

Vieira, Patrick   Born Dakar, Senegal, 23 June 1976. Position: midfield. Clubs: Cannes 1993-95, AC Milan 1995-96, Arsenal 1996-present (signed for £3.5m). Honours: Italian Championship 1996 (with AC Milan); FA Premiership 1998, 2002; FA Cup 1998, 2002,

2003; Charity/Community Shield 1998, 1999, 2002 (all with Arsenal). International caps (for France): 62, 4 goals. International honours: World Cup 1998; European Championship 2000; Confederations Cup 2001.

Vieri, Christian   Born Bologna, Italy, 12 July 1973. Position: forward. Clubs: Prato 1989-90, Torino 1990-93, Pisa 1993, Ravenna 1993-94, Venezia 1994-95, Atalanta 1995-96, Juventus 1996-97, Atlético Madrid 1997-98, Lazio 1998-99, Inter Milan 1999-present (signed for £32m). Honours: European Cup Winners' Cup 1999 (with Lazio). International caps (for Italy): 30, 13 goals.

Viollet, Denis   Born Dennis Sydney Viollet, Manchester, 20 September 1933. Position: forward. Clubs (player): Manchester United 1952-62, Stoke City 1962-67, Baltimore Bays 1967-68, Witton Albion 1969, Linfield 1969-70. Honours: League Championship 1956, 1957 (with Manchester United). Clubs (coach): Linfield 1969-70, Preston North End 1970-71, Crewe Alexandra 1971, Washington Diplomats 1974-77, Jackson University 1981-86, University of North Florida 1986-95, Richmond Kickers 1995-96. International caps (for England): 2, 1 goal. A survivor of the Munich air disaster 1958. Viollet was awarded the Freedom of the City of Jackson, and the Dennis Viollet Memorial Cup is played at the University of North Florida. He died in Jacksonville, 6 March 1999.

Vogts, Bertie   Born Hans-Hubert Vogts, Buttgen, Lower Rhine, Germany, 30 December 1946. Position: defender. Clubs (player): VfR Buttgen, Borussia Mönchengladbach 1966-79. Honours: German League Championship 1970, 1971, 1975, 1976, 1977; German Cup 1973; UEFA Cup 1975, 1979 (all with Borussia Mönchengladbach). Club (coach/manager): Bayer Leverkusen 2000-01. International caps (for West Germany): 96 (20 as captain). International honours: World Cup 1974. International manager (Germany): 1990-98. Honours: European Championships 1996. International manager (Kuwait): 2001-02; (Scotland): 2002-present. Known as 'Der Terrier'.

Völler, Rudi   Born Rudolf Völler, Hanau, Germany, 13 April 1960. Position: forward. Clubs (player): Kickers Offenbach 1977-80, 1860 Munich 1980-82, Werder Bremen 1982-87, Roma 1987-92, Olympique Marseille 1992-94, Bayer Leverkusen 1994-96. Honours: French League Championship 1993 (with Olympique Marseille); Italian Cup 1991 (with Roma). Club (manager): Bayer Leverkusen 1996-2000 (general manager). International caps: 90, 47 goals. International honours: World Cup 1990. International manager (Germany): 2000-present. Known as 'Tante Kathe' (Aunt Kath) in the German press.

Waddle, Chris   Born Christopher Roland Waddle, Hepworth, Tyne & Wear, 14 December 1960. Position: forward. Clubs (player): Tow Law Town 1979-80, Newcastle United 1980-85, Tottenham Hotspur 1985-89, Olympique Marseille 1989-92 (signed for £4.25m), Sheffield Wednesday 1992-96 (signed for £1m), Falkirk 1996 (free transfer), Bradford City 1996-97 (monthly contract), Sunderland 1997 (signed for £75,000), Burnley 1997-98, Torquay United 1999, Worksop Town 2000-01, Glapwell 2002-03. Honours: French League Championship 1990, 1991, 1992 (with Olympique Marseille). Club (manager): Burnley 1997-98. International caps (for England): 62, 6 goals. Football Writers' Player of the Year 1993. Nicknamed 'Le Dribbleur Fou' (The Mad

Dribbler) by the French. Reached number 12 in the UK pop charts in 1987 with the song 'Diamond Lights', along with his team-mate Glenn Hoddle.

Walker, Billy Born William Henry Walker, Wednesbury, West Midlands, 29 October 1897. Position: forward. Clubs (player): Aston Villa 1914-33. Honours: FA Cup 1924. Clubs (manager): Sheffield Wednesday 1933-37, Chelmsford City 1937-39, Nottingham Forest 1939-60. Honours: FA Cup 1935 (with Sheffield United), 1959 (with Nottingham Forest). International caps (for England): 18 (3 as captain), 9 goals. He retired from the game due to ill health in 1960, and died 28 November 1964 in Sheffield.

Walker, Des Born Hackney, London, 26 November 1965. Position: defender. Clubs: Nottingham Forest 1983-92, 2002-present, Sampdoria 1992-93, Sheffield Wednesday 1993-2002 (signed for £2.7m). International caps (for England): 59.

Walker, Ian Born Ian Michael Walker, Watford, Hertfordshire, 31 October 1971. Position: goalkeeper. Clubs: Tottenham Hotspur 1989-2001, Oxford United 1990 (loan), Leicester City 2001-present. Honours: League Cup 1999 (with Tottenham Hotspur). International caps (for England): 3, 1 goal conceded.

Wallace, Rod Born Rodney Seymour Wallace, Greenwich, London, 2 October 1969. Position: forward. Clubs: Southampton 1988-91, Leeds United 1991-98 (signed for £1.6m), Rangers 1998-2001 (free transfer), Bolton Wanderers 2001-02 (free transfer), Gillingham 2002-present. Honours: Charity Shield 1992 (with Leeds United); Scottish League Championship 1999, 2000; Scottish Cup 1999, 2000; Scottish League Cup 1998 (all with Rangers). On 22 October 1988, Rod and brothers Ray and Danny played in the same Southampton team.

Walter, Fritz Born Kaiserslautern, Germany, 31 October 1920. Position: midfield. Club: Kaiserslautern 1937-60. Honours: German League Championship 1951, 1953. International caps (for West Germany): 61 (30 as captain), 33 goals. International honours: World Cup 1954 (as captain). A POW in Russia during World War II, Walter was known as 'The Hero of Berne' for his part in West Germany's 1954 World Cup triumph. Kaiserslautern renamed their stadium the Fritz-Walter-Stadion in 1985 to mark his 65th birthday. Franz Beckenbauer described him as 'the most important German football player of the last century'. He died 18 June 2002 in Kaiserslautern aged 81.

Wanchope, Paulo Born Paulo Cesar Wanchope, Heridia, Costa Rica, 31 July 1976. Position: forward. Clubs: CS Heridiano 1995-97, Derby County 1997-99 (signed for £600,000), West Ham United 1999-2000 (signed for £3.5m), Manchester City 2000-present (signed for £3.65m). International caps (for Costa Rica): 51, 35 goals.

Wark, John Born Glasgow, 4 August 1957. Position: forward/midfield. Clubs: Ipswich Town 1974-84, 1988-96 (signed for £100,000), Liverpool 1984-88 (signed for £450,000), Middlesbrough 1990-91. Honours: League Championship 1986 (with Liverpool); FA Cup 1978 (with Ipswich Town); UEFA Cup 1981 (with Ipswich Town). International caps (for Scotland): 29, 7 goals. PFA Player of the Year 1981. Appeared in the film *Escape to Victory*.

Watson, Dave Born David Vernon Watson, Stapleford, Notts, 5 October 1946. Position: defender. Clubs: Notts County 1966-67 and 1984-85, Rotherham United 1967-70, Sunderland 1970-74,

Manchester City 1975-78, Werder Bremen 1979-80, Southampton 1980-81, Stoke City 1981-82, Vancouver Whitecaps 1983, Derby County 1983-84, Kettering Town. Honours: FA Cup 1973 (with Sunderland). International caps (for England): 65 (3 as captain), 4 goals.

Watson, Dave Born Liverpool, 20 January 1961. Position: defender. Clubs (player): Liverpool 1979-80, Norwich City 1980-86 (signed for £50,000), Everton 1986-2000 (signed for £1.23m). Honours: League Championship 1987 (with Everton); FA Cup 1995 (with Everton); League Cup 1985 (with Norwich City); Charity Shield 1987, 1995 (with Everton). Clubs (manager): Everton 1997-98, Tranmere Rovers 2001-02. International caps (for England): 12.

Watson, Willie Born Bolton-on-Dearne, South Yorkshire, 7 March 1920. Position: midfielder. Clubs: Huddersfield Town, Sunderland 1946-53, Halifax Town 1954-55. International caps (for England): 4. Watson also played cricket for Yorkshire and Leicestershire, representing England 23 times between 1951 and 1959. He shared a stand of 163 with Trevor Bailey to save the 1953 Lord's Test against Australia, and was a Test selector 1962-64.

Weah, George Born Monrovia, Liberia, 1 October 1966. Position: forward. Clubs: Young Survivors 1981-84, Bongrange 1984, Barolle 1985-86, Invincible Eleven 1986-87, Tonnerre Klarra 1987-88, Monaco 1988-92, Paris St Germain 1992-95, AC Milan 1995-2000 (signed for £5m), Chelsea 2000, Manchester City 2000 (free transfer), Olympique Marseille 2000-01 (free transfer), Al Jazira 2001-02. Honours: Liberian Championship 1987 (with Invincible Eleven); Cameroon Championship 1988 (with Tonnerre Klarra); French Championship 1994; French Cup 1991, 1993; French League Cup 1995 (all with Paris St-Germain); Italian Championship 1995, 1999 (with AC Milan); FA Cup 2000 (with Chelsea); European Cup Winners' Cup 1992 (with Monaco). International caps (for Liberia): 96, 33 goals. International manager (Liberia): 2002. African Player of the Year 1989, 1994, 1995, 1996. European Player of the Year 1995. World Player of the Year 1995. Now a UNICEF ambassador.

Webb, David Born East Ham, London, 9 April 1946. Position: defender. Clubs (player): Leyton Orient 1964-65, Southampton 1965-67, Chelsea 1967-73, Queens Park Rangers 1974-77, Leicester City 1977-78, Derby County 1978-80, AFC Bournemouth 1980-82. Honours: FA Cup 1970; European Cup Winners' Cup 1971 (both with Chelsea). Clubs (manager): AFC Bournemouth 1980-82, Torquay 1984-85, Southend United 1986-87, 1988-92, 2000-01, Chelsea 1993, Brentford 1993-97. Webb scored the winning goal for Chelsea in the 1970 FA Cup final. His son Daniel has played for Southend United and Brighton & Hove Albion.

Wedlock, Billy Born William John Wedlock, Bristol, 1879. Position: defender. Club: Bristol City. International caps (for England): 26, 2 goals. Retired 1921. Nicknamed 'Fatty' (although this was an exaggeration) he remains the most-capped Bristol City player.

Westcott, Dennis Born Wallasey, Cheshire, 2 July 1917. Position: forward. Clubs: New Brighton 1932-37, Wolverhampton Wanderers 1937-47, Blackburn Rovers 1948-50, Manchester City 1950-52, Chesterfield 1952, Stafford Rangers. A prolific goalscorer who averaged two goals every three games throughout his career. Westcott scored 43 goals in 43 League and Cup matches for

Wolverhampton Wanderers in season 1938-39. He died of leukaemia in 1960, aged 43.

Westerveld, Sander Born Enschede, Holland, 23 October 1974. Position: goalkeeper. Clubs: De Tubanters 1980-88, Twente Enschede 1988-96, Vitesse Arnhem 1996-99, Liverpool 1999-2001 (signed for £4m), Real Sociedad 2001-present (signed for £3.49m). Honours: FA Cup 2001; League Cup 2001; English Charity Shield 2001; UEFA Cup 2001 (all with Liverpool). International caps (for Holland): 6.

Wharton, Arthur Born Accra, Gold Coast (now Ghana), 1865. Position: goalkeeper. Clubs: Darlington 1887, Preston North End 1887-88, Rotherham Town 1889-94, Sheffield United 1894-97, Ashton North End 1897-98, Stalybridge Rovers 1898-1900, Stockport County 1901-02. The first black professional footballer in Britain, his mother was a member of the Fante tribe (the Gold Coast royal family) and his father was a missionary. An excellent athlete, before turning professional as a footballer he won the AAA 100yds in 10.1secs in 1886, a record that stood for 30 years (he also won in 10.1secs in 1887). Wharton also played professional league cricket in Rotherham. Retired from playing in 1902, becoming a publican in Rotherham and then a coal miner at Yorkshire Main Colliery in Edlington, nr Doncaster. He died a relative pauper on 12 December 1930 at Springwell House Sanatorium and was buried in Edlington cemetery. He is the subject of a recent exhibition entitled 'In a League of His Own' and his portrait was included in an exhibition of British sporting heroes at the National Portrait Gallery. A 1997 campaign raised enough money to provide a headstone for his previously unmarked grave.

Whelan, Noel Born Noel David Whelan, Leeds, 30 December 1974. Position: forward. Clubs: Leeds United 1993-95, Coventry City 1995-2000 (signed for £2m), Middlesbrough 2000-03 (signed for £2.2m), Crystal Palace 2003 (loan), Millwall 2003-present.

White, John Born Musselburgh, Midlothian, Scotland, 28 April 1937. Position: forward. Clubs: Alloa Athletic 1956-58, Falkirk 1958-59, Tottenham Hotspur 1959-64 (signed for £20,000). Honours: League Championship 1961; FA Cup 1961 (both with Tottenham Hotspur). International caps (for Scotland): 22, 3 goals. Known as 'The Ghost'. White was killed when struck by lightning sheltering under a tree while playing golf at Crews Hill Golf Course on 21 July 1964. The John White Memorial Trophy is awarded to the winners of the annual Musselburgh five-a-side tournament.

Whiteside, Norman Born Belfast, 7 May 1965. Position: forward/midfield. Clubs (player): Manchester United 1982-89, Everton 1989-91 (signed for £750,000). Honours: FA Cup 1983, 1985 (with Manchester United). Clubs (manager): Northwich Victoria (assistant) 1991-92. International caps (for Northern Ireland): 38, 9 goals. The youngest player to appear in the World Cup finals, he was also the youngest to score in an FA Cup final. Known in the press as 'The Shankhill Skinhead' and 'Nasty Norman'. Forced into retirement by injury, he went to university and became a specialist in sports injuries to the feet.

Wilcox, Jason Born Jason Malcolm Wilcox, Farnworth, Lancashire, 15 July 1971. Position: midfield. Clubs: Blackburn Rovers 1989-99, Leeds United 1999-present (signed for £3m). International caps (for England): 3.

Wilkins, Ray Born Raymond Colin Wilkins, Hillingdon, London, 14 September 1956. Position: midfield. Clubs (player): Chelsea 1971-79, Manchester United 1979-84, AC Milan 1984-87, Paris St-Germain 1987, Rangers 1987-89, Queens Park Rangers 1989-94, 1994-96, Crystal Palace 1994, Wycombe Wanderers 1996, Hibernian 1996, Millwall 1997, Leyton Orient 1997. Honours: FA Cup 1983 (with Manchester United); Scottish League Championship 1988, 1989 (with Rangers); Scottish League Cup 1989 (with Rangers); Clubs (manager): Queens Park Rangers 1994-96, Fulham 1997-98, Chelsea (coach) 1998, Watford (coach) 2001-02. International caps (for England): 84 (10 as captain), 3 goals. Nicknamed 'The Crab' and 'Butch'. Awarded the MBE in 1993.

Wilson, Andrew Born Andrew Nesbit Wilson, Irvine, Scotland, 11 January 1880. Position: forward. Clubs: Clyde, Sheffield Wednesday 1900-20. Honours: League Championship 1903, 1904; FA Cup 1907 (all with Sheffield Wednesday). International caps (for Scotland): 6. Wilson captained Wednesday to the FA Cup triumph in 1907 and made 501 appearances, a record for the club. He died 13 March 1945.

Wilson, George Born Blackpool, Lancashire, 14 January 1892. Position: defender. Clubs: Sheffield Wednesday 1920-25. International caps (for England): 12 (7 as captain). He died 25 November 1961.

Wilson, Ray Born Ramon Wilson, Shirebrook, Derbyshire, 17 December 1934. Position: defender. Clubs (player): Huddersfield Town 1952-64, Everton 1964-69 (signed for £35,000), Oldham Athletic 1969-70, Bradford City 1970-71. Honours: FA Cup 1966 (with Everton). Clubs (manager): Bradford City 1970-71. International caps (for England): 63. International honours: World Cup 1966. Retired from the game in 1971 to join the family undertaking business. Awarded the MBE in 2000.

Wiltord, Sylvain Born Neuilly-sur-Marne, France, 10 May 1974. Position: forward. Clubs: Stade Rennais 1991-97, Deportivo La Coruña 1997-98, Bordeaux 1998-2000, Arsenal 2000-present (signed for £13m). Honours: French League Championship 1999 (with Bordeaux); FA Premiership 2002; FA Cup 2002, 2003; Community Shield 2002 (all with Arsenal). International caps (for France): 55, 17 goals. International honours: European Championship 2000; Confederations Cup 2001, 2003.

Winterbottom, Walter Born Oldham, Lancashire, 31 January 1913. Position: defender. Clubs (player): Royton Amateurs, Manchester City (amateur), Mossley, Manchester United 1936-38. Club (manager): Mossley FC. International manager (England): 1946-62. Forced to retire from playing in 1939 through a spinal disease, he later launched the England Under-23 team. Statistically England's most successful coach with only 28 losses from 139 games, he was also director-general of the Sports Council 1965-78. Awarded the OBE in 1962, CBE in 1972 and knighted in 1978. He died 16 February 2002 in Guildford.

Winterburn, Nigel Born Nuneaton, Warwickshire, 11 December 1963. Position: defender. Clubs: Birmingham City 1981-83, Oxford United 1983, Wimbledon 1983-87 (free transfer), Arsenal 1987-2000 (signed for £407,000), West Ham United 2000-03. Honours: League Championship 1989, 1991; FA Premiership 1998; FA Cup 1993, 1998; League Cup 1993; Charity Shield 1998, 1999; European Cup Winners' Cup 1994 (all with Arsenal). International caps (for England): 2. Retired from playing July 2003.

FOOTBALL

Wise, Dennis Born Dennis Frank Wise, Kensington, London, 15 December 1966. Position: midfield. Clubs: Southampton, Wimbledon 1985-90, Chelsea 1990-2001 (signed for £1.6m), Leicester City 2001-02 (signed for £1.6m), Millwall 2002-present (free transfer). Honours: FA Cup 1988 (with Wimbledon), 1997, 2000 (with Chelsea); League Cup 1998 (with Chelsea); Charity Shield 2000 (with Chelsea); European Cup Winners' Cup 1998 (with Chelsea). International caps (for England): 21, 1 goal. His career has been blighted by off-field indiscretions, including being dismissed from Leicester City after an incident involving team-mate Callum Davidson in 2002. He has now appeared in FA Cup finals for three different clubs: Wimbledon, Chelsea and Millwall.

Withe, Peter Born Liverpool, 30 August 1951. Position: forward. Clubs (player): Southport 1971, Barrow 1971, Arcadia Shepherds (South Africa), Wolverhampton Wanderers 1973-75, Birmingham City 1975-76, 1987-88, Portland Timbers 1975, Nottingham Forest 1976-78, Newcastle United 1978-80, Aston Villa 1980-85 (signed for £500,000), Sheffield United 1985-87, Huddersfield Town 1988-89. Honours: League Championship 1981; European Cup 1982; European Super Cup 1982 (all with Aston Villa). Clubs (manager): Wimbledon 1991-92. International caps (for England): 11, 1 goal. International manager (for Thailand): 1998-present.

Wollaston, Charles Born Charles Henry Reynolds Wollaston, Felpham, Sussex, 31 July 1849. Position: forward. Club: Wanderers. Honours: FA Cup 1872, 1873, 1876, 1877, 1878. International caps (for England): 4 (1 as captain), 1 goal. All his four England caps were against Scotland. He later became a referee and stood in the England-Scotland match of April 1879 which England won 5-4, having been 4-1 down at half-time. He scored in the FA Cup finals of 1873, 1876 and captained Wanderers in 1876. Wollaston trained as a solicitor and was also a keen alpine climber. He died 1926.

Woodburn, Willie Born Edinburgh, 1919. Position: defender. Club: Rangers 1938-54. Honours: Scottish League Championship 1947, 1949, 1950, 1953; Scottish Cup 1948, 1949, 1950, 1953; Scottish League Cup 1947, 1949. International caps (for Scotland): 24. Often in trouble because of his temper, he was banned for 21 days and then 6 weeks in 1953 for serious foul play. In 1954 he was again in trouble, this time for punching an opponent (all in matches against Stirling Albion). At the subsequent tribunal, which lasted four minutes, he was given a life ban by the Scottish Football Association. He failed to contest the decision and it was not lifted until 1957, by which time he was too old to play on. He worked briefly as a *News of the World* reporter in the 1980s. Nicknamed 'Big Ben' – not because of his size but because of his exuberant celebration after a victory over Benfica. He died 1 December 2001.

Woodcock, Tony Born Anthony Stewart Woodcock, Nottingham, 6 December 1955. Position: forward. Clubs (player): Nottingham Forest 1974-79, Lincoln City 1975 (loan), Doncaster Rovers 1976 (loan), FC Cologne 1979-82 (signed for £650,000), 1986-88, Arsenal 1982-86, Honours: League Championship 1978; League Cup 1978, 1979; European Cup 1979 (all with Nottingham Forest). Clubs (manager): SCB Bruck, VfB Leipzig 1994-95, Eintracht Frankfurt 2001-02. International caps (for England): 42, 16 goals.

Woodgate, Jonathan Born Jonathan Simon Woodgate, Middlesbrough, 22 January 1980. Position: defender. Clubs: Leeds United 1997-2003, Newcastle United 2003-present (undisclosed fee). International caps (for England): 1. Career blighted by well-publicised off-the-field matters but presently resurrecting his England career at Newcastle.

Woods, Chris Born Christopher Charles Eric Woods, Swineshead, nr Boston, Lincolnshire, 14 November 1959. Position: goalkeeper. Clubs: Nottingham Forest 1976-79, Queens Park Rangers 1979-81, Norwich City 1981-86 (signed for £225,000), Rangers 1986-91 (signed for £600,000), Sheffield Wednesday 1991-96, Reading 1995-96 (loan), Colorado Rapids 1996-97, Southampton 1996-97 (loan), Sunderland 1996-97, Burnley 1997-98. Honours: League Cup 1978 (with Nottingham Forest), 1983 (with Norwich City); Scottish League Championship 1987, 1989, 1990; Scottish League Cup 1987, 1988, 1989, 1991 (all with Rangers). International caps (for England): 43. Now goalkeeping coach with Everton. Holds British record for conceding no goals 26 November 1986 to 31 January 1987 – a clean sheet for 1196 minutes.

Woodward, Vivian Born Vivian John Woodward, Kennington, London, 3 June 1879. Position: forward. Clubs: Tottenham Hotspur 1902-09, Chelsea 1909-16. International caps (for England): 23 (14 as captain), 29 goals. International honours: Olympic gold medal 1908, 1912. Woodward scored 44 goals in 30 amateur internationals, while his 29 goals in full internationals for England set a record which stood until 1958. Granted leave to play in the 1915 FA Cup final, he declined so as not to deprive a regular team member of his place. Retired from the game after being wounded in action during World War I, and became a farmer. He died 31 January 1954 in Ealing, London.

Worthington, Frank Born Frank Stuart Worthington, Halifax, Yorkshire, 23 November 1948. Position: forward. Clubs: Huddersfield Town 1966-72, Leicester City 1972-77 (signed for £80,000), Bolton Wanderers 1977-79 (signed for £87,000), Philadelphia Fury 1979, Birmingham City 1979-82 (signed for £150,000), Tampa Bay Rowdies 1981 (loan), Leeds United 1982 (player exchange), Sunderland 1982-83 (signed for £50,000), Southampton 1983-84 (signed for £30,000), Brighton & Hove Albion 1984-85, Tranmere Rovers 1985-87, Preston North End 1987, Stockport County 1987-88. Also played in South Africa after 1988. International caps (for England): 8, 2 goals. Now works as an after-dinner speaker.

Wright, Billy Born William Ambrose Wright, Ironbridge, Shropshire, 6 February 1924. Position: defender. Club: Wolverhampton Wanderers 1941-59. Honours: League Championship 1954, 1958, 1959; FA Cup 1949. International caps (for England): 105 (90 as captain), 3 goals. His record of 90 appearances as his country's captain was equalled only by Bobby Moore. Played in World Cup finals in 1950, 1954, 1958. Football Writers' Player of the Year 1952. Retired 7 August 1959. He died 3 September 1994 in Barnet, London.

Wright, Ian Born Ian Edward Wright, Woolwich, London, 3 November 1963. Position: forward. Clubs: Greenwich Borough 1984-85, Crystal Palace 1985-91, Arsenal 1991-98 (signed for £2.5m), West Ham United 1998-99 (signed for £500,000), Nottingham Forest 1999 (loan), Celtic 1999-2000 (free transfer), Burnley 2000 (free transfer). Honours: FA Cup 1993;

League Cup 1993 (both with Arsenal). International caps (for England): 31, nine goals. Broke Cliff Bastin's Arsenal record of 178 goals in 1999. Now pursuing a career in the media.

Wright, Mark Born Dorchester-on-Thames, Oxfordshire, 1 August 1963. Position: defender. Clubs (player): Oxford United 1981-82, Southampton 1982-87 (signed for £80,000), Derby County 1987-91 (signed for £760,000), Liverpool 1991-98 (signed for £2.2m). Honours: FA Cup 1992 (with Liverpool). Clubs (manager): Southport 1999-2001, Oxford United 2001, Chester City 2002-present. International caps (for England): 45 (1 as captain), 1 goal.

Wright, Richard Born Richard Ian Wright, Ipswich, Suffolk, 5 November 1977. Position: forward. Clubs: Ipswich Town 1995-2001, Arsenal 2001-02, Everton 2002-present. Honours: FA Premiership 2002; FA Cup 2002 (both with Arsenal). International caps (for England): 2.

Xavier, Abel Born Abel Luis da Silva Costa Xavier, Mozambique, 30 November 1972. Position: defender. Clubs: Estrela Amadora 1990-93, Benfica 1993-95, Bari 1995-96, Real Oviedo 1996-98, PSV Eindhoven 1998-99, Everton 1999-2002 (signed for £1.5m), Liverpool 2002-present (signed for £800,000), Galatasaray 2003 (loan). International caps (for Portugal): 20, 2 goals. Recognisable by his eccentric hairstyle he has several nicknames, such as 'Santa Claus', 'Neptune' and 'Zeus'. Xavier was banned from all European matches for nine months following his protests after giving away a penalty during the Euro 2000 semi-final against France.

Yashin, Lev Born Lev Ivanovich, Moscow, 22 October 1929. Position: goalkeeper. Club (player) Moscow Dynamo 1951-71. Honours: USSR League Championship 1954, 1955, 1957, 1959, 1963; USSR Cup 1953, 1954. Club (manager): Moscow Dynamo from 1971. International caps (for USSR): 78. International honours: Olympic gold medal 1956; European Championship 1960. European Player of the Year 1963 (the only goalkeeper so honoured). Awarded the Order of Lenin in 1968. Variously known as 'The Black Panther', 'The Black Spider' and 'The Black Octopus' (he usually played in a black strip). Yashin always took two caps on to the playing field, one to wear and one for luck. He died of cancer on 21 March 1990 in Moscow.

Yeats, Ron Born Aberdeen, Scotland, 15 November 1937. Position: defender. Clubs (player): Dundee United, Liverpool 1961-71 (signed for £22,000), Tranmere Rovers 1971-73. Honours: League Championship 1964, 1966; FA Cup 1965; Charity Shield 1964, 1965, 1966 (all with Liverpool). Clubs (manager): Tranmere Rovers 1971-75, Stalybridge Celtic, Barrow 1976-77. International caps (for Scotland): 2. Chief scout for Liverpool 1986-present. Known as 'Rowdy' after Clint Eastwood's character Rowdy Yates from the TV series *Rawhide*.

Yeboah, Tony Born Anthony Yeboah, Kumasi, Ghana, 6 June 1966. Position: forward. Clubs: Kumasi Corner Stones, Okwawu United, Saarbrucken 1988-90, Eintracht Frankfurt 1990-95, Leeds United 1995-97 (signed for £3.4m), SV Hamburg 1997-2002 (signed for £1m), Al-Itthiad (Qatar) 2002-present. International caps (for Ghana): 36. Top scorer in Ghana 1986, 1987.

Yorath, Terry Born Cardiff, Wales, 27 March 1950. Position: midfield. Clubs (player): Leeds United 1967-76, Coventry City 1976-79 (signed for £125,000), Tottenham Hotspur 1979-82 (signed for £300,000), Vancouver Whitecaps 1981, Bradford City 1982-86.

Honours: League Championship 1974 (with Leeds United). Clubs (manager): Bradford City 1982-86, Swansea City 1986-89, 1990-91, Bradford City 1989-90, Cardiff City 1994-95, Huddersfield Town 1997-99, Sheffield Wednesday 2001-02. International caps (for Wales): 59. International manager (Wales): 1988-93; (Lebanon): 1995-97. His daughter Gabby presents football programmes on TV.

Yorke, Dwight Born Canaan, Tobago, 3 November 1971. Position: forward. Clubs: Signal Hill 1988-89, Aston Villa 1989-98 (signed for £120,000), Manchester United 1998-2002 (signed for £12.6m), Blackburn Rovers 2002-present (signed for £2m). Honours: FA Premiership 1999, 2000, 2001 (with Manchester United); FA Cup 1999 (with Manchester United); League Cup 1994, 1996 (with Aston Villa); UEFA Champions League 1999 (with Manchester United). International caps (for Trinidad and Tobago): 55, 19 goals. Tommy Docherty is quoted as saying, 'If that lad makes a first division player, my name is Mao-Tse Tung.' In 1999 he finished top scorer with 29 goals and joint top-scorer in the Champions League, while helping United to their historic 'treble'.

Young, Alex Born Loanhead, Scotland, 3 February 1937. Position: forward. Clubs (player): Heart of Midlothian, Everton 1960-68 (signed for £40,000), Glentoran 1968, Stockport County 1968. Honours: League Championship 1963; FA Cup 1966; Charity Shield 1963 (all with Everton). Club (manager): Glentoran 1968. International caps (for Scotland): 8. Known as 'The Golden Vision' (the title of Ken Loach's 1968 television film about Everton and its fans).

Young, George Born George Lewis Young, Grangemouth, Falkirk, Scotland, 27 October 1922. Position: defender. Club (player): Rangers 1941-57. Honours: Scottish League Championship 1947, 1949, 1950, 1953, 1956, 1957; Scottish Cup 1948, 1949, 1950, 1953; Scottish League Cup 1947, 1949. Club (manager): Third Lanark 1959-62. International caps (for Scotland): 53 (48 as captain). Nicknamed 'Corky'. He died 1997.

Zagallo, Mario Born Mario Jorge Lobo Zagallo, Maceio, Brazil, 10 March 1928. Position: forward. Clubs (player): Flamengo 1947-59, Botafogo 1959-64. Honours: Brazilian League Championship 1962 (with Botafogo). Clubs (manager): Botafogo 1964-70, Fluminense 1970-71, Flamengo 1971-74, 1984, 2000-01, El Elal 1979, Portuguesa 1999. Honours: Brazilian League Championship 1971 (with Fluminense), Rio Cup 1971 (with Fluminense), Saudi Arabian Championship 1979 (with El Elal). International caps (for Brazil): 35. International honours: World Cup 1958, 1962. International manager (Brazil): 1970-74, 1993-95, 1995-98 (technical director), 2002 (caretaker), 2003-present (technical director); (Kuwait): 1975-78; (Saudi Arabia) 1980-84; (United Arab Emirates): 1989-90. Honours: World Cup 1970 (with Brazil); Gulf Cup 1976 (with Kuwait). Zagallo was the first winner of World Cup as both player and manager. Nicknamed 'The Little Ant' and 'Wolf'.

Zambrotta, Gianluca Born Como, Italy, 19 February 1977. Position: midfield. Clubs: Como 1995-98, Bari 1998-99, Juventus 1999-present. Honours: Italian Championship 2002, 2003 (with Juventus). International caps (for Italy): 27.

Zamora, Ricardo Born Ricardo Zamora Martinez, Barcelona, Spain, 21 January 1901. Position: goal-keeper. Clubs (player): Espanyol 1915-19, 1922-31,

Barcelona 1919-22, Real Madrid 1931-36, Nice 1936-38. Honours: Spanish League Championship 1920, 1922 (with Barcelona), 1929 (with Espanyol); Spanish Cup 1929 (with Espanyol), 1934, 1936 (with Real Madrid). Clubs (manager): Atlético Madrid 1939-45, Celta Vigo 1946-49, Malaga 1949-52, Espanyol 1957-78 (technical director/public relations director). Honours: Spanish League Championship 1940, 1941 (with Atlético Madrid). International caps (for Spain): 46, 40 goals conceded. International manager (Spain): 1952. Known as 'The Man in Black' and 'El Divino', Zamora conceded seven goals against England in 1931, but was the first goalkeeper to save a penalty in a World Cup (1934 against Brazil). The Zamora Award is given annually to the best Spanish goalkeeper. He died 18 September 1978 in Barcelona.

Zenden, Boudwijn   Born Maastricht, Holland, 15 August 1976. Position: forward. Clubs: Leonidas 1983-88, MVV 1988-90, PSV Eindhoven 1994-99, Barcelona 1999-2001, Chelsea 2001-present (signed for £7.5m). Honours: Dutch League Championship 1997; Dutch Cup 1996 (both with PSV Eindhoven). International caps (for Holland): 45, 6 goals.

Zenga, Walter   Born Milan, Italy, 28 April 1960. Position: goalkeeper. Clubs (player): Inter Milan 1977, 1982-94, Salernitana 1978-79, Savona 1979-80, Sambenedettese 1980-82, Sampdoria 1994-96, Padova 1996, New England Revolution 1997-99. Honours: Italian League Championship 1989; UEFA Cup 1991, 1994 (all with Inter Milan). Clubs (manager): New England Revolution 1998-99, Brera Milan 2000-02, National Bucharest 2002-03. International caps (for Italy): 58, 38 clean sheets. Nicknamed 'Spiderman'. He has performed as an actor in commercials, soap operas and TV mini-series.

Zico   Born Artur Antunes Coimbra, Rio de Janeiro, Brazil, 3 March 1953. Position: midfield/forward. Clubs (player): Flamengo 1971-82, 1985-90, Udinese 1982-85, Antlers of Kashima (Japan) 1991-94. Honours: South American Championship 1981; World Club Championship (both with Flamengo), J-League Championship 1993 (with Antlers of Kashima). Club (manager): Antlers of Kashima 1994-2002 (general manager). Honours: J-League Championship 1996, 1998, 2000, 2001 (with Antlers of Kashima). International caps (for Brazil): 71, 48 goals. International manager (Brazil): 1998 (assistant); (Japan): 2002-present. Retired in 1990 but returned to play in Japan in 1991. Voted South American Footballer of the Year 1977, 1981, 1982. Known as 'The White Pelé'.

Zito   Born Jose Eli de Miranda, Roseira, Brazil, 8 August 1932. Position: midfield. Clubs: Taubate, Santos 1952-68. Honours: São Paulo Championship 1955, 1956, 1958, 1960, 1961, 1962, 1964, 1965, 1967, 1968; Brazilian Cup 1961, 1962, 1963, 1964, 1965 (all with Santos). International caps (for Brazil): 46, 3 goals. International honours: World Cup 1958, 1962.

Zidane, Zinedine   Born Marseilles, France, 23 June 1972. Position: midfield. Clubs: US St Henri, Sport Olympique, Cannes 1986-93, Bordeaux 1993-96, Juventus 1996-2001, Real Madrid 2001-present (signed for £45.62m). Honours: Italian League Championship 1997, 1998 (with Juventus); Spanish League Championship 2003 (with Real Madrid); UEFA Champions League 2002 (with Real Madrid); European Super Cup 1996 (with Juventus), 2002 (with Real Madrid); Intercontinental Cup 1996 (with Juventus), 2002 (with Real Madrid). International caps (for France): 82, 22 goals. International honours: World Cup 1998; European Championship 2000. European Player of the Year 1998. World Player of the Year 1998, 2000, 2003. Made his French First Division debut aged 17. Scored twice in the World Cup final in 1998. Known as 'Zizou'.

Zmuda, Wladyslaw   Born Lublin, Poland, 6 June 1954. Position: defender. Clubs: Motor Lublin 1970-73, Gwardia Warsaw 1973-75, Slask Wroclaw 1975-79, Widzew Lodz 1979-82, Hellas Verona 1982-84, Cremonese 1984-87, New York Cosmos 1984. Honours: Polish League Championship 1981, 1982 (with Widzew Lodz); Polish Cup 1976 (with Slask Wroclaw). International caps (for Poland): 92.

Zoff, Dino   Born Mariano del Friuli, Gorizia, Italy, 22 February 1942. Position: goalkeeper. Clubs (player): Udinese 1961-63, Mantova 1963-67, Napoli 1967-72, Juventus 1972-83. Honours: Italian League Championship 1973, 1975, 1977, 1978, 1979; Italian Cup 1979, 1983; UEFA Cup 1977 (all with Juventus). Clubs (manager): Juventus 1988-90, Lazio 1990-94, 1997, 2001. International caps (for Italy): 112 (59 as captain). International honours: World Cup 1982 (as captain); European Championship 1968. International manager (Italy): 1998-2000. Played in 12 consecutive internationals (1972-74) without conceding a goal (1143 minutes). The oldest player (aged 40) to win the World Cup, he made 570 appearances in Serie A.

Zola, Gianfranco   Born Oliena, Sardinia, 5 July 196 Position: forward. Clubs: Nuorese 1986-87, Torres 1987-89, Napoli 1989-93, Parma 1993-96, Chelsea 1996-2003 (signed for £4.5m), Cagliari 2003-present. Honours: Italian League Championship 1990 (with Napoli); English FA Cup 1997, 2000; League Cup 1998; Charity Shield 2000 (all with Chelsea); UEFA Cup 1995 (with Parma); European Cup Winners' Cup 1998; European Super Cup 199 (both with Chelsea). International caps (for Italy): 3 7 goals. Football Writers' Player of the Year 1997.

Zubizarreta, Andoni   Born Vitoria, Spain, 23 Octob 1961. Position: goalkeeper. Clubs: UD Aretxabaleta 1977-79, CD Alavés Aficionades Vitoria 1979-81, Athletic Bilbao 1981-86, Barcelona 1986-94, Valencia 1994-98. Honours: Spanish League Championship 1983, 1984 (with Athletic Bilbao), 1991, 1992, 1993, 1994 (with Barcelona); Spanish Cup 1984 (with Athletic Bilbao), 1988, 1990 (with Barcelona); European Cup Winners' Cup 1989 (with Barcelona); European Cup 1992 (with Barcelona). International caps (for Spain): 126.

Football: General Information

AFC

Asian Football Confederation, founded in 1954. Its headquarters are in Kuala Lumpur, Malaysia. The AFC is responsible for the Asian Cup, Asian Games, Asian Super League and Asian Women's Championship

Argentinian championship

Argentina has a two-stage championship; an autumn-spring season wi the Torneo Apertura (opening tournament) from July to December, and the Torneo Clausura (closing tournament) from February to May/June.

each tournament every club plays each of the other clubs once. The Apertura and Clausura winners are officially regarded as co-national champions.

Arsenal: unbeaten in League	2003/04 season (played 38, won 26, drew 12)
Arsenal tube station: former name	Gillespie Road (one of the innovative Herbert Chapman's ideas)
artificial turf: first team to use	Queens Park Rangers (1981). Luton Town followed soon after.
ball: dimensions	The circumference must be 27-28ins (69-71cm) and the weight between 410-450g. The internal pressure of the ball must be between 0.6 and 1.1 atmospheres.
Battle of Highbury	In a friendly international between England and Italy on 14 November 1934, the Italians were reduced to ten men within minutes of the start after Luis Monti broke his foot in a tackle with Ted Drake. Convinced that the injury had been inflicted deliberately, the Italians spent the rest of the match retaliating. As a result, among many injuries England captain Eddie Hapgood suffered a broken nose and Eric Brook a broken arm. England, 3-0 up after 12 minutes, finally won 3-2.
black player: first in British football	Arthur Wharton
black player: first to manage English League side	Eddie Stein (when he succeeded Barry Fry as Barnet boss in April 1993)
black player: first to play for England	Viv Anderson while playing for Nottingham Forest (v Czechoslovakia, 1978).
CAF	Confédération Africaine de Football, founded in 1957. Its headquarters are in Cairo, Egypt.
caps: first awarded for England internationals	1886
cards: meaning	A yellow card is shown as a caution to a player and a red card is shown when a referee sends a player off. If a player has already received a yellow card the second caution is an automatic sending-off.
celebrity footballers	Des O'Connor was on the club books of Northampton Town, Rod Stewart played for Brentford, Julio Iglesias for Real Madrid.
city that has never had a Premiership (Division 1) team	Hull
CONMEBOL	Confederación Sudamericana de Fútbol, founded in 1916, its headquarters are in Asunción, Paraguay. It is responsible for the Copa America, Copa Libertadores and Copa Pan-Americana.
corner kick	A corner kick is awarded to the attacking team when the ball crosses the goal line of the opposition either side of the goalposts when the last player to touch the ball was a defender. A corner kick is also awarded if the ball enters the goal from a throw-in or an indirect free kick. When the corner kick is taken, the ball is placed within a small arc around the corner flag on the side of the pitch where the ball crossed the goal line. Defenders must be 10yds away and the taker cannot touch the ball again until another player has touched the ball.
cricket and football League: played first-class	Ian Botham, Raich Carter, Ted Drake, John Devey, Billy Foulke, John Goodall, Andy Goram, Geoff Hurst, Ernest Needham, G.O. Smith, Willie Watson
cricket: represented England	Willie Watson and Arthur Milton played both cricket and football for England post World War II.
cricket: represented Ireland	Noel Cantwell played both cricket and football for Ireland.
cricket: represented Scotland	Andy Goram played both cricket and football for Scotland.
crossbar introduced	1875
Derby: derivation of term	Village football matches were often played on Shrove Tuesday. The game between the parishes of St Peter and All Saints in Derby was notorious for its fierce competitiveness and gave rise to the term for all such keenly fought local contests.
duration of play	The game is divided into two halves of 45 minutes each. Extra time may be played in Cup matches.
England: captained every time he played	George Hardwick played 13 times for England and was captain on each occasion.
fathers and sons played for	George Eastham snr and jnr, Brian and Nigel Clough, Frank Lampard snr and jnr
first goalkeeper to captain	Frank Swift (v Italy, 1947)
first home loss to foreign side	In 1953 Hungary defeated England 6-3 at Wembley.
first loss to foreign side	In 1929 Spain beat England 4-3 in Madrid.
heaviest man to play for	Billy Foulke (22st (140kg))
international: first to be sent off	Alan Mullery was the first player to be sent off for England (v Yugoslavia in 1968).
tallest man to play for	Billy Foulke (6ft 6ins (1.98m))
team from one club	In 1894 Corinthians supplied all eleven players for England (v Wales at Wrexham)
European Footballer of the Year: first	Stanley Matthews (1956)
FA Charity Shield: contestants	FA Cup winners v League winners
FA Cup: 15 original teams	Barnes, Civil Service, Clapham Rovers, Crystal Palace (not the present

FOOTBALL

club), Donnington School (Spalding), Great Marlow, Hampstead Heathens, Harrow Chequers, Hitchin, Maidenhead, Queens Park, Reigate Priory, Royal Engineers (Chatham), Upton Park, Wanderers

final: broke neck	Bert Trautmann of Manchester City (1956)
final: fastest goal scored	It is uncertain whether Bob Chatt or John Devey scored the 39sec goal for Aston Villa against WBA in 1895. (Roberto di Matteo's 42sec goal for Chelsea in 1997 is only Wembley's fastest.)
final: first goal at Wembley	David Jack scored the first-ever goal at a Wembley Cup final while playing for Bolton Wanderers in 1923.
final: first monarch to attend	King George V (1914)
final: first own goal	Arthur Kinnaird playing for Wanderers in the 1877 final
first player sent off	Kevin Moran of Manchester United (1985)
final: first replay (Wembley)	In 1970 (draw at Wembley, replayed at Old Trafford)
final: horse cleared pitch	PC George Scorey on a white horse called Billy cleared the overcrowded pitch at Wembley's first Cup final (1923).
final: youngest player in	Curtis Weston (Millwall substitute who came on to replace Dennis Wise in the 2000 final. He was 17 years 119 days). Previous youngest was Paul Allen for West Ham in the 1980 final.
final: youngest to score in	Norman Whiteside (18 years and 19 days) for Manchester United v Brighton & Hove Albion (1983)
first floodlit tie	Kidderminster Harriers v Brierley Hill (preliminary round, 1955)
first scorer	M.P. Betts (Harrow Chequers) scored the first goal in an FA Cup tie.
four winner's medals	Mark Hughes (Manchester United 1985, 1990, 1994; Chelsea 1997) is the only player to achieve this distinction.
manager: youngest	Ruud Gullit (who was also the first non-British manager to win the FA Cup) with Chelsea (1997)
non-League winner	Tottenham Hotspur (1901)
played every year	Great Marlow (now Marlow) and Maidenhead have played in every FA Cup since 1872.
stolen	In 1895 (from a Birmingham shop)
winner's medals either side of World War II	Raich Carter (1937 Sunderland, 1946 Derby) is the only man to have winning medals.
FIFA	Fédération Internationale de Football Association, founded in 1904. Its headquarters are in Zurich, Switzerland. Its current president is Joseph Sepp Blatter of Switzerland. FIFA is responsible for the World Cup, Women's World Cup, World Club Championship, Confederations Cup, World Youth Championship and Under-17 World Championship.
floodlit game: first	1887
floodlit international: first	England v Spain at Wembley (1955)
Football Association: address	25 Soho Square, London W1D 4FA; tel: 020 7745 4545
Football Association: established	Freemason's Tavern, Lincoln's Inn Fields (1863)
free kick	Awarded for fouls or violations of rules. All players of the offending side must be 9.5m (10yds) from the ball. Free kicks may be either direct, from which a goal may be scored, for serious fouls such as kicking or tripping an opponent, or handling the ball; or indirect, from which goals cannot be scored until after the ball has touched another player. Indirect free kicks are awarded for lesser violations such as obstruction (interfering with an opponent while not playing the ball).
goal: dimensions	Height: 2.44m (8ft), width: 7.32m (8yds). The goal area runs from a point 5.5m (6 yds) either side of the goalposts and the same distance upfield giving an area of 100.75m^2 (120 sq yds).
goal: how scored	When the whole of the ball has crossed the goal line between the goalposts and under the crossbar, provided no infringement has taken place, a goal has been scored.
goal kick	A goal kick is awarded to the defending team when the ball crosses its own goal line, wide of the posts, and the last person to touch the ball was an attacker. A goal kick is taken from within the goal area and must leave the penalty area or be retaken. All opposition players must be outside the penalty area when the kick is taken and the taker cannot touch the ball again until another player has touched it. A goal cannot be scored from a goal kick.
goal nets used: first time	1891 (North v South match)
goal-scoring record for a season	In the 1927/28 season Dixie Dean scored 60 goals in 39 League matches for Everton.
hat-trick: youngest in English League	Tommy Lawton (17 years and 4 days) for Burnley v Spurs, 1936
high-jump champion	Howard Baker was an international footballer for England but also represented his country at the 1912 and 1920 Olympics in the high jump.
home internationals: first played	In 1883 (Scotland v Ireland was the first match)
home internationals: last played	In 1984 (Ireland won on goal difference after all four teams finished on three points)
£100 a week player: first	Johnny Haynes
international at five levels: first	Johnny Haynes was capped at schoolboy, youth, Under-23, 'B' and senior level while Terry Venables was also capped at five levels: schoolboy,

youth, amateur, Under-23 and senior.

international: first official	England v Scotland (1872)
international in four sports	Alan Hansen (Liverpool) was a Scottish international golf, squash, volleyball and football player.
international in three sports	Kevin O'Flanagan was an Irish international footballer, rugby union player and athlete.
internationals: scored in first five	Dixie Dean
Ireland: captained both teams	Johnny Carey captained both Northern Ireland and the Republic of Ireland in 1947.
Ireland (Northern): FA founded	The Irish Football Association was founded in 1880. Its first League champion in 1881 was Linfield who are the most successful club in both League and Cup competitions.
Ireland (Republic of): FA founded	The Football Association of Ireland was founded in 1921. Its first champion in 1922 was St James' Gate. The most successful club in both League and Cup competitions has been Shamrock Rovers.
Irish club: first founded	Cliftonville (1879)
League and Cup double: first	In 1989 Preston North End won the FA Cup without conceding a goal and the League without losing a game.
League Championship in three countries	Trevor Steven won championship medals in England, France and Scotland.
lightning: killed by	John White (Tottenham Hotspur), while sheltering under a tree at Crews Hill golf course (21 July 1964).
linesmen: now called	Assistant referees (linesmen were first introduced in 1891)
long-jump champion	England International William Oakley was AAA long-jump champion in 1895.
managed two Division 1/ Premiership-winning teams	Herbert Chapman (Huddersfield Town, Arsenal), Brian Clough (Derby County, Nottingham), Kenny Dalglish (Liverpool, Blackburn Rovers)
Milan teams: full names	AC Milan – Associazione Calcio Milan
	Inter Milan – Internazionale
nicknames: famous	

Donkey	Tony Adams
Sick Note	Darren Anderton
Divine Pony Tail	Roberto Baggio
Boy	Cliff Bastin
Slim Jim	Jim Baxter
Der Kaiser	Franz Beckenbauer
Goldenballs	David Beckham
Nijinsky	Colin Bell
Zorro	Zvonimir Boban
Cat	Peter Bonetti
Zibi, Night Beauty	Zbigniew Boniek
Chippy	Liam Brady
Der Afro	Paul Breitner
Budgie	Johnny Byrne
La Tota	Antonio Carbajal
Sniffer	Allan Clarke
Stan the Man	Stan Collymore and before him Stan Bowles
Iron Man	Wilf Copping
Flying Dutchman	Johan Cruyff
Rock	Marcel Desailly
Black Panther	Eusebio
Divine One, Eighth King of Rome	Falcao
Preston Plumber	Tom Finney
El Principe	Enzo Francescoli
Tiger	Artur Friedenreich
Little Bird	Garrincha
Old Man of Hoy, Captain Blood	Richard Gough
Stroller	George Graham
Professor	Gunnar Gren
Maradona of the Carpathians	Gheorghe Hagi
Merlin	Gordon Hill
Crazy Horse	Emlyn Hughes
Sparky	Mark Hughes
Bites Yer Legs	Norman Hunter
Hurricane	Jairzinho
Wee Jinky	Jimmy Johnstone
Mighty Mouse	Kevin Keegan
El Matador	Mario Kempes
The Man with the Golden Head	Sandor Kocsis
Lee Won Pen	Francis Lee
Buzz Bomb, Lemon	Bobby Lennox
Le God	Matt Le Tissier
Lion of Vienna	Nat Lofthouse

Hot Shot	Peter Lorimer
Choccy	Brian McClair
Roadrunner	David McCreery
Supermac	Malcolm Macdonald
Caesar	Billy McNeill
El Grande	Diego Maradona
Major	Arthur Marindin
King of Soccer, Maestro, Wizard of Dribble	Sir Stanley Matthews
Father of Austrian Football	Hugo Meisl
Prince of Wingers, Welsh Wizard, Old Skinny	Billy Meredith
Blackpool Bombshell, Electric Eel	Stanley Mortensen
Der Bomber	Gerd Muller
Clockwork, Ossi	Ernst Ocwirk
Solly	John O'Hare
Overdrive, Quickfoot, Flying Dutchman	Marc Overmars
Pancho	Stuart Pearson
Black Pearl	Pelé
Galloping Major	Ferenc Puskas
Sumo	Micky Quinn
Boss	Helmut Rahn
White Feather	Fabrizio Ravanelli
Golden Boy	Gianni Rivera
El Fenomeno	Ronaldo
Razor	Neil Ruddock
Newcastle Flyer	Jock Rutherford
Matador	Marcelo Salas
Volkswagen	Karl-Heinz Schnellinger
Paper Man	Matthias Sindelar
Doctor	Socrates
Little Miner of Gold	Tostao
Kid	Carlos Valderrama
Marco Goalo	Marco van Basten
Chest of Steel, Lion of Brazil	Vava
El Tel	Terry Venables
Little Witch	Juan Veron
V-Bomber	Mark Viduka
Der Terrier	Bertie Vogts
Aunt Kath	Rudy Voller
Mad Dribbler	Chris Waddle
Hero of Berne	Fritz Walter
Ghost	John White
Butch, Crab	Ray Wilkins
Big Ben	Willie Woodburn
Santa Claus, Neptune, Zeus	Abel Xavier
Black Spider, Black Panther, Black Octopus	Lev Yashin
Rowdy	Ron Yeats
Golden Vision	Alex Young
Corky	George Young
Little Ant, Wolf	Mario Zagallo
Man in Black, El Divino	Ricardo Zamora
Spiderman	Walter Zenga
White Pelé	Zico

numbering of players	Introduced by Herbert Chapman, manager of Arsenal (1928) (not the norm until Football League voted in favour for 1938/39 season)
OFC	Oceania Football Confederation, founded in 1966. Its headquarters are in Auckland, New Zealand.
offside rule	Offside is an illegal position taken up by a player relative to the ball, the field of play and opposition players at the moment when the ball is played by an attacking team-mate. A player is deemed offside when a) they are in the opposition's half of the field b) they are closer to the opponent's goal line than there are fewer than two defenders, including the goalkeeper, who are closer to the goal line than the attacking player. A player is penalised for being offside if they are deemed to be interfering with play or with an opponent and they can gain some advantage from being in that position.
oldest club: founded	Sheffield (1857)
oldest English League club: founded	Notts County (1862)
oldest Scottish club: founded	Queen's Park (1867)
Olympic Games: 1920 controversy	In 1920 the silver medal was awarded to Spain after Czechoslovakia were disqualified for walking off the pitch after 39 minutes of the final complaining about refereeing decisions. The referee was a Mr Lewis of Great Britain. Spain actually won a mini-tournament to earn their medal.
out of play	The ball is designated out of play when the whole ball, whether in the air or on the ground, has crossed either touchline or goal line.
penalty area: dimensions	A rectangular area in front of the goal 40.2m (44 yds) wide and extending

	16.5m (18yds) into the field.	
penalty kick introduced	1891 (at request of the Irish FA). A penalty kick is a direct free kick awarded when the violation is inside the offending team's own penalty area. The kick is taken from the penalty spot. If the ball rebounds off the post another player (standing 9.15m (10yds) away from the penalty spot at the time of taking) may then score but the taker can only score after another player, of either side, has touched the ball.	
penalty spot: distance from goal	11m (12yds)	
pitch: dimensions	The width of the pitch must be between 45m and 90m (50-100yds). For international matches it must be between 64m and 75m (70-82yds). The length of the pitch must be between 90m and 120m (100-130yds) and for international matches between 100m and 110m (109-120yds). The centre circle must have a radius of 9.15m (10yds).	
players in a team: maximum and minimum	A team consists of 11 players but may begin a game with only seven players.	
points: first club to score over 100 in League	York City (101), season 1983/84	
points: League record	Sunderland (105), season 1998/99	

Premiership club managers

		from
Arsenal	Arsene Wenger	September 1996
Aston Villa	David O'Leary	May 2003
Birmingham City	Steve Bruce	December 2001
Blackburn Rovers	to be decided	
Bolton Wanderers	Sam Allardyce	October 1999
Charlton Athletic	Alan Curbishley	July 1991
Chelsea	Jose Mourinho	June 2004
Crystal Palace	Iain Dowie	December 2003
Everton	David Moyes	March 2002
Fulham	Chris Coleman	April 2003
Liverpool	Rafael Benitez	June 2004
Manchester City	Kevin Keegan	May 2001
Manchester United	Sir Alex Ferguson	November 1986
Middlesbrough	Steve McClaren	June 2001
Newcastle United	Graeme Souness	September 2004
Norwich City	Nigel Worthington	December 2000
Portsmouth	Harry Redknapp	March 2002
Southampton	Steve Wigley	replaced Paul Sturrock in August 2004
Tottenham Hotspur	Jacques Santini	June 2004
West Bromwich Albion	Gary Megson	March 2000

Rangers: won every League match	Season 1898/99. (Won all 18 games to attain maximum 36 points.)
referee: famous bald-headed	Pierluigi Collina of Italy, who is generally recognised as the world's leading referee at present (2004). He retired from the international scene after the 2004 European Championship.
religious support: Glasgow	Traditionally Catholics follow Celtic and Protestants follow Rangers.
rules: codified	At Cambridge University (1846)
Scotland FA: founded	Scottish Football Association was founded in 1873.
Scottish international: first to be sent off	Billy Steel
Scudetto (literally, 'shield')	Name given to the Italian League Premier Division (Serie A)
shinguards introduced	1874

stadiums: famous world football

Amsterdam Arena, Amsterdam (Ajax)	Olympic Stadium, Munich (Bayern Munich)
Azteca Stadium, Mexico	Parc des Princes, Paris (Paris St-Germain)
Bernabeu, Madrid (Real Madrid)	
Giuseppe Meazza, San Siro (AC and Inter Milan)	Stade de France, St Denis
	Stadio Delle Alpi, Turin (Juventus)
Lansdowne Road, Dublin	Stadium of Light, Lisbon (Benfica)
Maracana, Rio de Janeiro	Windsor Park, Belfast (Linfield)
Nou Camp, Barcelona	

start of play	A coin is tossed and the winning team chooses ends for the first half while the losing team takes the kick-off. The second half is kicked off by the winner of the toss and the ends are reversed. The kick-off must be taken from the centre spot and the ball must move into the opposition's half of the field. All players must be in their own halves at commencement of play and the opposition must be at least 10yds from the ball. The ball must be touched by another player before the player who kicks off can touch the ball again.
substitute in Scottish football: first	Archie Gemmill (13 August 1966, St Mirren v Clyde)
substitutes	A squad of up to seven substitutes are allowed, any three of which may be used during a game. Substitutes may only enter the game at the halfway line during a stoppage after another player has left the field.
Sunday football: first League game	20 January 1974 (Millwall v Fulham)
Superga air crash	On 4 May 1949, a Fiat G212 airliner left Lisbon with the Torino squad on

board after a friendly against Benfica in honour of the Portuguese club's former player Francisco Ferreira. The plane, carrying 31 passengers, including 18 Torino squad members plus officials, crashed into an embankment below the Superga mountainside basilica. There were no survivors.

televised football: first	The match between Arsenal and Everton on 29 August 1936 was shown by the BBC the same evening.
televised football: first live	On 30 April 1938 the Wembley FA Cup final between Huddersfield Town and Preston North End was shown by the BBC.
ten-goal Payne	On 13 April 1936 (Easter Monday) Joe Payne scored ten goals during Luton's 12-0 defeat of Bristol Rovers in a Division 3 South League match. He was thereafter always referred to as 'Ten-Goal Payne'.
three points for League wins awarded: first	Season 1981/82 in England, 1994/95 in Scotland
throw-in	Awarded to a team when the ball has crossed the touchline and an opposition player was the last to touch it. The throw-in is taken from the point where the ball crossed the touchline. The taker must have both feet on the ground, use two hands, throw the ball from behind and over the head and be facing the field of play. A goal cannot be scored directly from a throw-in.
tragedies: Bolton	9 March 1946 (FA Cup tie, Bolton Wanderers v Stoke City), 33 died when a wall and barrier collapsed before the match.
Bradford	11 May 1985 (League Division 3, Bradford City v Lincoln City), 56 died after fire broke out in the main stand during the match.
Heysel (Brussels)	29 May 1985 (European Cup final, Liverpool v Juventus), 41 died when a wall collapsed after Liverpool fans attacked those of Juventus.
Hillsborough (Sheffield)	15 April 1989 (FA Cup semi-final, Nottingham Forest v Liverpool), 96 died when fans were unable to escape the seriously overcrowded Leppings Lane end before the game.
Ibrox (Glasgow)	5 April 1902 (Scotland v England), 25 died when a stand collapsed. 2 January 1971 (Celtic v Rangers), 66 died when crash barriers gave way after Rangers equalised in the final minute.
train: threw himself under	Hughie Gallacher (11 June 1957, in Low Fell, Tyne & Wear)
transfer: first £1000	Alf Common from Sunderland to Middlesbrough (1905)
first £10,000	David Jack from Bolton to Arsenal (1928)
first £50,000	Denis Law from Huddersfield to Manchester City (1960) (actual transfer price £55,000)
first £100,000	Denis Law from Torino to Manchester Utd (1962)
first £100,000 (between English clubs)	Alan Ball from Blackpool to Everton (1966) (actual transfer price £110,000)
first £200,000	Martin Peters from West Ham to Spurs (1970)
first £500,000	Gordon McQueen from Leeds to Manchester Utd (1978)
first £1 million	Trevor Francis from Birmingham to Nottingham Forest (1979)
first £2 million	Paul Gascoigne from Newcastle to Spurs (1988)
first £5 million	Chris Sutton from Norwich City to Blackburn Rovers (1994)
first £10 million and £15 million	Alan Shearer from Blackburn to Newcastle Utd (1996)
first £30 million*	Rio Ferdinand from Leeds to Manchester Utd (2002)
two-handed throw introduced	1895
UEFA	Union of European Football Associations, founded in 1954. Its headquarters are in Nyon, Switzerland. UEFA is responsible for the European Championships, Champions League, UEFA Cup, Intertoto Cup, European Super Cup and European Women's Championship.
Wales FA: founded	The Football Association of Wales was founded in 1876
war: started by football match	El Salvador v Honduras (1969)
white ball legalised	1950
World Club Championship: inaugural	The FIFA World Club Championship was inaugurated in 2000 and in a disappointing competition Corinthians beat their countrymen from Brazil, Vasco da Gama, 4-3 on penalties after a 0-0 draw
World Cup: England first played	In 1950 (England were beaten in the qualifying competition in Brazil)
World Cup final: first penalty scorer	Johan Neeskens scored the first penalty in a World Cup final in 1974.
World Cup final: oldest scorer	Roger Milla of Cameroon was 42 years, 39 days when he scored in 1994
World Cup finals: played in five	Antonio Carbajal (Mexico), 1950, 1954, 1958, 1962, 1966; Lothar Matthäus (West Germany/Germany), 1982, 1986, 1990, 1994, 1998
World Cup finals: scored most goals in a match	O. Salenko (five goals for Russia against Cameroon in 1994)
World Cup finals: youngest to play in	Norman Whiteside (17 years, 42 days) for Northern Ireland, 1982
World Cup match: first played	13 July 1930, France v Mexico
World Cup: top scorer in single tournament	Just Fontaine (France), 13 in 1958

*This deal included several unquantifiable dependents and the package is often quoted as being worth £29.1 million. Similarly, the Wayne Rooney transfer from Everton to Manchester United in August 2004 is estimated at £29.85 million but could exceed £30 million depending on future events.

GAELIC FOOTBALL

Gaelic football is Ireland's most popular sport. The Statute of Galway (1527) banning football in Ireland is our first record of the game in that country, though references to hurling are even older. The effect of this legislation banning all games 'except alone football with the grate ball', was to elevate football above hurling in popularity. The first known football match was between Meath and Louth in 1712 at Slane.

The Gaelic Athletic Association was founded in 1884 by Michael Cusack to promote Irish sport and culture. The first patron of the association was Archbishop T.W. Croke of Cashel. The association standardised the game's rules in 1887 and remains the governing body.

The sport is a mixture of soccer and rugby. Traditionally teams are comprised of three full-forwards, three half-forwards, two midfielders, three halfbacks, three full-backs and a goal-keeper. It is played on grass pitches 130m-145m in length and 80m-90m in width. The scoring posts are 6.5m apart and 7m high. At a height of 2.5m from the ground there is a crossbar. The ball is similar to a soccer ball, while the goals are like those in rugby.

Single points are scored for getting the ball over the crossbar, and goals scored under the crossbar are worth three points. Scores are recorded in the form Team A 2-10, Team B 1-15. This means Team A has scored 2 three-point goals and 10 one-pointers, totalling 16 points. Team B has 1 three-point goal and 15 one-pointers, totalling 18 points. Each half lasts for 30 or 35 minutes.

Variations of the game may involve between 7 and 13 players per side. International Rules combines aspects of both Australian and Gaelic football and an annual competition between Australia and Ireland (although it is a common misconception that Australian Rules derives from Gaelic football). The Ladies' Gaelic Football Association was founded in 1974.

The All-Ireland Championships bring together the provincial champions of Connacht, Leinster, Munster, and Ulster. Recently the runners-up from Leinster and Munster have also been included in the championship play-offs. Winners since 1928 have been presented with the Sam MacGuire Trophy. A new trophy for the 1988 final replaced the original trophy.

Croke Park, Dublin has been the venue for the championships since 1914.

All-Ireland Senior Football Championship Finals

Year	Winners		Runners-Up		Year	Winners		Runners-Up	
1887	Limerick	1-4	Louth	0-3	1917	Wexford	0-9	Clare	0-5
1888	not held				1918	Wexford	0-5	Tipperary	0-4
1889	Tipperary	3-6	Laois	0-0	1919	Kildare	2-5	Galway	0-1
1890	Cork	2-4	Wexford	0-1	1920	Tipperary	1-6	Dublin	1-2
1891	Dublin	2-1	Cork	1-9	1921	Dublin	1-9	Mayo	0-2
1892	Dublin	1-4	Kerry	0-3	1922	Dublin	0-6	Galway	0-4
1893	Wexford	1-1	Cork	0-2	1923	Dublin	1-5	Kerry	0-1
1894	Dublin	0-6	Cork	1-1	1924	Kerry	0-4	Dublin	0-3
1895	Tipperary	0-4	Meath	0-3	1925	Galway declared champions			
1896	Limerick	1-5	Dublin	0-7	1926	Kerry*	1-4	Kildare	0-4
1897	Dublin	2-6	Cork	0-2	1927	Kildare	1-7	Kerry	0-3
1898	Dublin	2-8	Waterford	0-4	1928	Kildare	2-6	Cavan	2-5
1899	Dublin	1-10	Cork	0-6	1929	Kerry	1-8	Kildare	1-5
1900	Tipperary	3-7	Galway	0-1	1930	Kerry	3-11	Monaghan	0-2
1901	Dublin	1-2	Cork	0-4	1931	Kerry	1-11	Kildare	0-8
1902	Dublin	0-6	Tipperary	0-5	1932	Kerry	2-7	Mayo	2-4
1903	Kerry	0-8	Kildare	0-2	1933	Cavan	2-5	Galway	1-4
1904	Kerry	0-5	Dublin	0-2	1934	Galway	3-5	Dublin	1-9
1905	Kildare	1-7	Kerry	0-5	1935	Cavan	3-6	Kildare	2-5
1906	Dublin	0-5	Cork	0-4	1936	Mayo	4-11	Laois	0-5
1907	Dublin	0-6	Cork	0-2	1937	Kerry*	4-4	Cavan	1-7
1908	Dublin	0-10	Kerry	0-3	1938	Galway*	2-4	Kerry	0-7
1909	Kerry	1-9	Louth	0-6	1939	Kerry	2-5	Meath	2-3
1910	Louth	w/o	Kerry		1940	Kerry	0-7	Galway	1-3
1911	Cork	6-6	Antrim	1-2	1941	Kerry	1-8	Galway	0-7
1912	Louth	1-7	Antrim	1-2	1942	Dublin	1-10	Galway	1-8
1913	Kerry	2-2	Wexford	0-3	1943	Roscommon*	2-7	Cavan	2-2
1914	Kerry*	2-3	Wexford	0-6	1944	Roscommon*	1-9	Kerry	2-4
1915	Wexford	2-4	Kerry	2-1	1945	Cork	2-5	Cavan	0-7
1916	Wexford	2-4	Mayo	1-2	1946	Kerry*	2-8	Roscommon	0-10

1947	Cavan	2-11	Kerry	2-7		1976	Dublin	3-8	Kerry	0-10
1948	Cavan	4-5	Mayo	4-4		1977	Dublin	5-12	Armagh	3-6
1949	Meath	1-10	Cavan	1-6		1978	Kerry	5-11	Dublin	0-9
1950	Mayo	2-5	Louth	1-6		1979	Kerry	3-13	Dublin	1-8
1951	Mayo	2-8	Meath	0-9		1980	Kerry	1-9	Roscommon	1-6
1952	Cavan*	0-9	Meath	0-5		1981	Kerry	1-12	Offaly	0-8
1953	Kerry	0-13	Antrim	1-6		1982	Offaly	1-14	Kerry	0-17
1954	Meath	1-13	Kerry	1-7		1983	Dublin	1-10	Galway	1-8
1955	Kerry	0-12	Dublin	1-6		1984	Kerry	0-14	Dublin	1-6
1956	Galway	2-13	Cork	3-7		1985	Kerry	2-12	Dublin	2-8
1957	Louth	1-9	Cork	1-7		1986	Kerry	2-15	Tyrone	1-10
1958	Dublin	2-12	Down	1-9		1987	Meath	1-14	Cork	0-11
1959	Kerry	3-7	Galway	1-4		1988	Meath	0-13	Cork	0-12
1960	Down	2-10	Kerry	0-8		1989	Cork	0-17	Mayo	1-11
1961	Down	3-6	Offaly	2-8		1990	Cork	0-11	Meath	0-9
1962	Kerry	1-12	Roscommon	1-6		1991	Down	1-16	Meath	1-14
1963	Dublin	1-9	Galway	0-10		1992	Donegal	0-18	Dublin	0-14
1964	Galway	0-15	Kerry	0-10		1993	Derry	1-14	Cork	2-8
1965	Galway	0-12	Kerry	0-9		1994	Down	1-12	Dublin	0-13
1966	Galway	1-10	Meath	0-7		1995	Dublin	1-10	Tyrone	0-12
1967	Meath	1-9	Cork	0-9		1996	Meath	2-9	Mayo	1-11
1968	Down	2-12	Kerry	1-13		1997	Kerry	0-13	Mayo	1-7
1969	Kerry	0-10	Offaly	0-7		1998	Galway	1-14	Kildare	1-10
1970	Kerry	2-19	Meath	0-18		1999	Meath	1-11	Cork	1-8
1971	Offaly	1-14	Galway	2-8		2000	Kerry*	0-17	Galway	1-10
1972	Offaly*	1-19	Kerry	0-13		2001	Galway	0-17	Meath	0-8
1973	Cork	3-17	Galway	2-13		2002	Armagh	1-12	Kerry	0-14
1974	Dublin	0-14	Galway	1-6		2003	Tyrone	0-12	Armagh	0-9
1975	Kerry	2-12	Dublin	0-11						

*won following replay

All-Ireland Ladies' Football Champions

1974	Tipperary		1984	Kerry		1994	Waterford
1975	Tipperary		1985	Kerry		1995	Waterford
1976	Kerry		1986	Kerry		1996	Monaghan
1977	Cavan		1987	Kerry		1997	Monaghan
1978	Roscommon		1988	Kerry		1998	Waterford
1979	Offaly		1989	Kerry		1999	Mayo
1980	Tipperary		1990	Kerry		2000	Mayo
1981	Offaly		1991	Waterford		2001	Laois
1982	Kerry		1992	Waterford		2002	Mayo
1983	Kerry		1993	Kerry		2003	Mayo

GOALBALL

Goalball is a highly competitive sport played by two teams of three, indoors on a gym floor, primarily by blind and visually impaired athletes. Games are keenly fought and exciting to watch and scoring goals is very difficult.

Two teams play in either half of a 18m × 9m court. Players are blindfolded to make the game fair. The object is to throw a 1.25kg goalball past the opposing team. The goalball is similar in size and shape to a basketball but significantly heavier and it has jingle bells attached to enable the sightless players to listen for it.

When players hear the ball coming towards their end of the court, they dive, usually head first, towards it hoping to block it with their body and stop it. If all three players miss the ball and it goes past the back line, a goal is scored. The team scoring the most goals wins the game.

Goalball was invented in 1946 by Austrian Hanz Lorenzen and German Sepp Reindle, in an effort to help in the rehabilitation of blinded war veterans. The game was introduced to the world in 1976 at the Paralympics in Toronto, Canada, and has been played at every Paralympics since.

The success of the initial competition was overwhelming and in 1978 a world championship was held in Austria; this has been subsequently held every four years. Since that time the popularity of goalball has risen to such an extent that it is played competitively in all International Blind Sports Association (IBSA) regions.

GOLF

It is impossible to date the origin of the game of golf with any accuracy although it is known to have existed in Scotland as early as the 15th century. There is some evidence that a Dutch game called *kolven* was played even earlier than this. Kolven, or *kolf* (from the name given to the club) and the Flemish game of *chole* were early precursors of modern golf. In these games the ball was directed towards a pre-arranged target, such as a well, or church door, from a starting point a huge distance away; reaching this target would require many strokes. The earliest written reference to the sport was made in 1457 when the Parliament of King James II of Scotland decreed that both 'fute-ball and golfe be utterly cryed downe'. This decree was made because the games interfered with the practice of archery, which was necessary for the defence of the realm.

James I (VI of Scotland) is believed to have introduced the game to Blackheath in London c. 1608. The oldest club is the Company of Gentlemen Golfers, now called the Honourable Company of Edinburgh Golfers, which was formed in 1744. Around the same time golf began to be played in Charleston, North Carolina, and in Virginia. In 1754 the Society of St Andrews, now the Royal & Ancient Golf Club of St Andrews (R&A), became the second golf club to be established and in 1766 the Royal Blackheath Club became the first organised golf club in England.

The 19th century saw a proliferation of clubs established all over the world. The first Irish club was founded at Royal Belfast in 1881 and the first Welsh club at Tenby in 1888. The same year the St Andrews club was formed in Yonkers, New York, to become the first American golf club. The Royal Liverpool Club organised Great Britain's first Amateur Championship in 1885 and in 1919 the Royal & Ancient Golf Club accepted the management of the championships as well as the Open.

Golf balls were originally made of wood but compressed feather balls were introduced at the turn of the 17th century. In 1848 the gutta-percha ball revolutionised the game. Gutta-percha, the evaporated milky juice or latex of various South American and South Pacific islands trees, becomes hard when boiled and allowed to cool. Apart from the advantage that the substance keeps its shape, gutta-percha balls were far cheaper to produce than those made of feathers. Coburn Haskell and Bertam G. Work patented the rubber ball, consisting of a rubber thread wound under tension around a solid rubber core in the early 20th century and this further popularised the game as vast distances could be attained with such balls.

Iron clubs began to replace many of the traditional wooden ones by the 1920s. Technological advances in equipment have meant that club golfers can hit huge distances with great accuracy and course designers have had to display ever-greater ingenuity to prevent professionals from reducing their courses to glorified pitch-and-putts.

The following biographies, results and general information provide a historic record of the development of a game that has confounded and frustrated millions but delighted many more in their search for that perfect swing.

Major Championship Winners

	Open Championship	Venue	US Open	US PGA	US Masters
1860	W. Park (SCO)	Prestwick	——	——	——
1861	T. Morris snr (SCO)	Prestwick	——	——	——
1862	T. Morris snr (SCO)	Prestwick	——	——	——
1863	W. Park (SCO)	Prestwick	——	——	——
1864	T. Morris snr (SCO)	Prestwick	——	——	——
1865	A. Strath (SCO)	Prestwick	——	——	——
1866	W. Park (SCO)	Prestwick	——	——	——
1867	T. Morris snr (SCO)	Prestwick	——	——	——
1868	T. Morris jnr (SCO)	Prestwick	——	——	——
1869	T. Morris jnr (SCO)	Prestwick	——	——	——
1870	T. Morris jnr (SCO)	Prestwick	——	——	——
1871	not held		——	——	——
1872	T. Morris jnr (SCO)	Prestwick	——	——	——
1873	T. Kidd (SCO)	St Andrews	——	——	——
1874	M. Park (SCO)	Musselburgh	——	——	——
1875	W. Park (SCO)	Prestwick	——	——	——
1876	R. Martin (SCO)	St Andrews	——	——	——
1877	J. Anderson (SCO)	Musselburgh	——	——	——
1878	J. Anderson (SCO)	Prestwick	——	——	——
1879	J. Anderson (SCO)	St Andrews	——	——	——
1880	R. Ferguson (SCO)	Musselburgh	——	——	——
1881	R. Ferguson (SCO)	Prestwick	——	——	——
1882	R. Ferguson (SCO)	St Andrews	——	——	——
1883	W. Fernie (SCO)	Musselburgh	——	——	——
1884	J. Simpson (SCO)	Prestwick	——	——	——
1885	R. Martin (SCO)	St Andrews	——	——	——
1886	D. Brown (SCO)	Musselburgh	——	——	——
1887	W. Park jnr (SCO)	Prestwick	——	——	——
1888	J. Burns (SCO)	St Andrews	——	——	——
1889	W. Park jnr (SCO)	Musselburgh	——	——	——
1890	J. Ball (ENG)	Prestwick	——	——	——
1891	H. Kirkcaldy (SCO)	St Andrews	——	——	——
1892	H. Hilton (ENG)	Muirfield	——	——	——
1893	W. Auchterlonie (SCO)	Prestwick	——	——	——
1894	J. Taylor (SCO)	Sandwich	——	——	——
1895	J. Taylor (SCO)	St Andrews	H. Rawlins (USA)	——	——
1896	H. Vardon (SCO)	Muirfield	J. Foulis (USA)	——	——
1897	H. Hilton (SCO)	Hoylake	J. Lloyd (USA)	——	——
1898	H. Vardon (SCO)	Prestwick	F. Herd (USA)	——	——
1899	H. Vardon (SCO)	Sandwich	W. Smith (USA)	——	——
1900	J. Ball (SCO)	St Andrews	H. Vardon (SCO)	——	——
1901	H. Kirkcaldy (SCO)	Muirfield	W. Anderson (USA)	——	——
1902	A. Herd (SCO)	Hoylake	L. Auchterlonie (USA)	——	——
1903	H. Vardon (SCO)	Prestwick	W. Anderson (USA)	——	——
1904	J. White (SCO)	Sandwich	W. Anderson (USA)	——	——
1905	J. Braid (SCO)	St Andrews	W. Anderson (USA)	——	——
1906	J. Braid (SCO)	Muirfield	A. Smith (USA)	——	——
1907	A. Massy (FRA)	Hoylake	A. Ross (USA)	——	——
1908	J. Braid (SCO)	Prestwick	F. McLeod (USA)	——	——
1909	J. Taylor (SCO)	Deal	G. Sargent (USA)	——	——
1910	J. Braid (SCO)	St Andrews	A. Smith (USA)	——	——
1911	H. Vardon (SCO)	Sandwich	J. McDermott (USA)	——	——
1912	E. Ray (ENG)	Muirfield	J. McDermott (USA)	——	——
1913	J. Taylor (SCO)	Hoylake	F. Ouimet (USA)	——	——
1914	H. Vardon (SCO)	Prestwick	W. Hagen (USA)	——	——
1915	not held		J. Travers (USA)	——	——
1916	not held		C. Evans jnr (SCO)	J. Barnes (USA)	——
1917	not held		not held	not held	——
1918	not held		not held	not held	——
1919	not held		W. Hagen (USA)	J. Barnes (USA)	——
1920	G. Duncan (ENG)	Deal	E. Ray (ENG)	J. Hutchison (USA)	——
1921	J. Hutchison (USA)	St Andrews	J. Barnes (USA)	W. Hagen (USA)	——
1922	W. Hagen (USA)	Sandwich	G. Sarazen (USA)	G. Sarazen (USA)	——
1923	A.G. Havers (ENG)	Troon	R. Jones (USA)	G. Sarazen (USA)	——
1924	W. Hagen (USA)	Hoylake	C. Walker (USA)	W. Hagen (USA)	——
1925	J. Barnes (USA)	Prestwick	W. McFarlane (USA)	W. Hagen (USA)	——
1926	R. Jones (USA)	Royal Lytham	R. Jones (USA)	W. Hagen (USA)	——
1927	R. Jones (USA)	St Andrews	T. Armour (USA)	W. Hagen (USA)	——

	Open Championship	Venue	US Open	US PGA	US Masters
1928	W. Hagen (USA)	Sandwich	J. Farrell (USA)	L. Diegel (USA)	——
1929	W. Hagen (USA)	Muirfield	R. Jones (USA)	L. Diegel (USA)	——
1930	B. Jones (USA)	Hoylake	R. Jones (USA)	T. Armour (USA)	——
1931	T. Armour (USA)	Carnoustie	B. Burke (USA)	T. Creavy (USA)	——
1932	G. Sarazen (USA)	Prince's	G. Sarazen (USA)	O. Dutra (USA)	——
1933	D. Shute (USA)	St Andrews	J. Goodman (USA)	G. Sarazen (USA)	——
1934	H. Cotton (ENG)	Sandwich	O. Dutra (USA)	P. Runyan (USA)	H. Smith (USA)
1935	A. Perry (ENG)	Muirfield	S. Parks jnr (SCO)	J. Revolta (USA)	G. Sarazen (USA)
1936	A. Padgham (ENG)	Hoylake	T. Manero (USA)	D. Shute (USA)	H. Smith (USA)
1937	H. Cotton (ENG)	Carnoustie	R. Guldahl (USA)	D. Shute (USA)	B. Nelson (USA)
1938	R. Whitcombe (ENG)	Sandwich	R. Guldahl (USA)	P. Runyan (USA)	H. Picard (USA)
1939	R. Burton (ENG)	St Andrews	B. Nelson (USA)	H. Picard (USA)	R. Guldahl (USA)
1940	not held		L. Little (USA)	B. Nelson (USA)	J. Demaret (USA)
1941	not held		C. Wood (USA)	V. Ghezzi (USA)	C. Wood (USA)
1942	not held		not held	S. Snead (USA)	B. Nelson (USA)
1943	not held		not held	not held	not held
1944	not held		not held	B. Hamilton (USA)	not held
1945	not held		not held	B. Nelson (USA)	not held
1946	S. Snead (USA)	St Andrews	L. Mangrum (USA)	B. Hogan (USA)	H. Keiser (USA)
1947	F. Daly (IRL)	Hoylake	L. Worsham (USA)	J. Ferrier (USA)	J. Demaret (USA)
1948	H. Cotton (ENG)	Muirfield	B. Hogan (USA)	B. Hogan (USA)	C. Harmon (USA)
1949	B. Locke (SAF)	Sandwich	C. Middlecoff (USA)	S. Snead (USA)	S. Snead (USA)
1950	B. Locke (SAF)	Troon	B. Hogan (USA)	C. Harper (USA)	J. Demaret (USA)
1951	M. Faulkner (ENG)	Portrush	B. Hogan (USA)	S. Snead (USA)	B. Hogan (USA)
1952	B. Locke (SAF)	Royal Lytham	J. Boros (USA)	J. Turnesa (USA)	S. Snead (USA)
1953	B. Hogan (USA)	Carnoustie	B. Hogan (USA)	W. Burkemo (USA)	B. Hogan (USA)
1954	P. Thomson (AUS)	Royal Birkdale	E. Furgol (USA)	C. Harbert (USA)	S. Snead (USA)
1955	P. Thomson (AUS)	St Andrews	J. Fleck (USA)	D. Ford (USA)	C. Middlecoff (USA)
1956	P. Thomson (AUS)	Hoylake	C. Middlecoff (USA)	J. Burke (USA)	J. Burke jnr (USA)
1957	B. Locke (SAF)	St Andrews	D. Mayer (USA)	L. Hebert (USA)	D. Ford (USA)
1958	P. Thomson (AUS)	Royal Lytham	T. Bolt (USA)	D. Finsterwald (USA)	A. Palmer (USA)
1959	G. Player (SAF)	Muirfield	W. Casper (USA)	B. Rosburg (USA)	A. Wall jnr (USA)
1960	K. Nagle (AUS)	St Andrews	A. Palmer (USA)	J. Hebert (USA)	A. Palmer (USA)
1961	A. Palmer (USA)	Royal Birkdale	G. Littler (USA)	J. Barber (USA)	G. Player (RSA)
1962	A. Palmer (USA)	Troon	J. Nicklaus (USA)	G. Player (RSA)	A. Palmer (USA)
1963	R. Charles (NZL)	Royal Lytham	J. Boros (USA)	J. Nicklaus (USA)	J. Nicklaus (USA)
1964	T. Lema (USA)	St Andrews	K. Venturi (USA)	B. Nichols (USA)	A. Palmer (USA)
1965	P. Thomson (AUS)	Royal Birkdale	G. Player (RSA)	D. Marr (USA)	J. Nicklaus (USA)
1966	J. Nicklaus (USA)	Muirfield	W. Casper (USA)	A. Geiberger (USA)	J. Nicklaus (USA)
1967	R. de Vicenzo (ARG)	Hoylake	J. Nicklaus (USA)	D. January (USA)	G. Brewer (USA)
1968	G. Player (RSA)	Carnoustie	L. Trevino (USA)	J. Boros (USA)	R. Goalby (USA)
1969	A. Jacklin (ENG)	Royal Lytham	O. Moody (USA)	R. Floyd (USA)	G. Archer (USA)
1970	J. Nicklaus (USA)	St Andrews	A. Jacklin (ENG)	D. Stockton (USA)	W. Casper (USA)
1971	L. Trevino (USA)	Royal Birkdale	L. Trevino (USA)	J. Nicklaus (USA)	C. Coody (USA)
1972	L. Trevino (USA)	Muirfield	J. Nicklaus (USA)	G. Player (RSA)	J. Nicklaus (USA)
1973	T. Weiskopf (USA)	Troon	J. Miller (USA)	J. Nicklaus (USA)	T. Aaron (USA)
1974	G. Player (RSA)	Royal Lytham	H. Irwin (USA)	L. Trevino (USA)	G. Player (RSA)
1975	T. Watson (USA)	Carnoustie	L. Graham (USA)	J. Nicklaus (USA)	J. Nicklaus (USA)
1976	J. Miller (USA)	Royal Birkdale	J. Pate (USA)	D. Stockton (USA)	R. Floyd (USA)
1977	T. Watson (USA)	Turnberry	H. Green (USA)	L. Wadkins (USA)	T. Watson (USA)
1978	J. Nicklaus (USA)	St Andrews	A. North (USA)	J. Mahaffey (USA)	G. Player (RSA)
1979	S. Ballesteros (ESP)	Royal Lytham	H. Irwin (USA)	D. Graham (AUS)	F. Zoeller (USA)
1980	T. Watson (USA)	Muirfield	J. Nicklaus (USA)	J. Nicklaus (USA)	S. Ballesteros (ESP)
1981	W. Rogers (USA)	Sandwich	D. Graham (AUS)	L. Nelson (USA)	T. Watson (USA)
1982	T. Watson (USA)	Troon	T. Watson (USA)	R. Floyd (USA)	C. Stadler (USA)
1983	T. Watson (USA)	Royal Birkdale	L. Nelson (USA)	H. Sutton (USA)	S. Ballesteros (ESP)
1984	S. Ballesteros (ESP)	St Andrews	F. Zoeller (USA)	L. Trevino (USA)	B. Crenshaw (USA)
1985	A. Lyle (SCO)	Sandwich	A. North (USA)	H. Green (USA)	B. Langer (FRG)
1986	G. Norman (AUS)	Turnberry	R. Floyd (USA)	B. Tway (USA)	J. Nicklaus (USA)
1987	N. Faldo (ENG)	Muirfield	S. Simpson (USA)	L. Nelson (USA)	L. Mize (USA)
1988	S. Ballesteros (ESP)	Royal Lytham	C. Strange (USA)	J. Sluman (USA)	A. Lyle (SCO)
1989	M. Calcavecchia (USA)	Troon	C. Strange (USA)	P. Stewart (USA)	N. Faldo (ENG)
1990	N. Faldo (ENG)	St Andrews	H. Irwin (USA)	W. Grady (AUS)	N. Faldo (ENG)
1991	I. Baker-Finch (AUS)	Royal Birkdale	P. Stewart (USA)	J. Daly (USA)	I. Woosnam (WAL)
1992	N. Faldo (ENG)	Muirfield	T. Kite (USA)	N. Price (ZIM)	F. Couples (USA)
1993	G. Norman (AUS)	Sandwich	L. Janzen (USA)	P. Azinger (USA)	B. Langer (GER)
1994	N. Price (ZIM)	Turnberry	E. Els (RSA)	N. Price (ZIM)	J. M. Olazabal (ESP)
1995	J. Daly (USA)	St Andrews	C. Pavin (USA)	S. Elkington (USA)	B. Crenshaw (USA)
1996	T. Lehman (USA)	Royal Lytham	S. Jones (USA)	M. Brooks (USA)	N. Faldo (ENG)
1997	J. Leonard (USA)	Troon	E. Els (RSA)	D. Love III (USA)	T. Woods (USA)
1998	M. O'Meara (USA)	Royal Birkdale	L. Janzen (USA)	V. Singh (FIJ)	M. O'Meara (USA)
1999	P. Lawrie (SCO)	Carnoustie	P. Stewart (USA)	T. Woods (USA)	J.M. Olazabal (ESP)
2000	T. Woods (USA)	St Andrews	T. Woods (USA)	T. Woods (USA)	V. Singh (FIJ)
2001	D. Duval (USA)	Royal Lytham	R. Goosen (RSA)	D. Toms (USA)	T. Woods (USA)

	Open Championship	Venue	US Open	US PGA	US Masters
2002	E. Els (RSA)	Muirfield	T. Woods (USA)	R. Beem (USA)	T. Woods (USA)
2003	B. Curtis (USA)	Sandwich	J. Furyk (USA)	S. Micheel (USA)	M. Weir (USA)
2004	T. Hamilton (USA)	Troon	R. Goosen (RSA)	V. Singh (FIJ)	P. Mickelson (USA)

World Matchplay Championship (Wentworth)

	Winner	Runner-Up
1964	Arnold Palmer (USA)	Neil Coles (ENG)
1965	Gary Player (RSA)	Peter Thomson (AUS)
1966	Gary Player (RSA)	Jack Nicklaus (USA)
1967	Arnold Palmer (USA)	Peter Thomson (AUS)
1968	Gary Player (RSA)	Bob Charles (NZL)
1969	Bob Charles (NZL)	Gene Littler (USA)
1970	Jack Nicklaus (USA)	Lee Trevino (USA)
1971	Gary Player (RSA)	Jack Nicklaus (USA)
1972	Tom Weiskopf (USA)	Lee Trevino (USA)
1973	Gary Player (RSA)	Graham Marsh (AUS)
1974	Hale Irwin (USA)	Gary Player (RSA)
1975	Hale Irwin (USA)	Al Geiberger (USA)
1976	David Graham (AUS)	Hale Irwin (USA)
1977	Graham Marsh (AUS)	Ray Floyd (USA)
1978	Isao Aoki (JPN)	Simon Owen (NZL)
1979	Bill Rogers (USA)	Isao Aoki (JPN)
1980	Greg Norman (AUS)	Sandy Lyle (SCO)
1981	Severiano Ballesteros (ESP)	Ben Crenshaw (USA)
1982	Severiano Ballesteros (ESP)	Sandy Lyle (SCO)
1983	Greg Norman (AUS)	Nick Faldo (ENG)
1984	Severiano Ballesteros (ESP)	Bernhard Langer (FRG)
1985	Severiano Ballesteros (ESP)	Bernhard Langer (FRG)
1986	Greg Norman (USA)	Sandy Lyle (SCO)
1987	Ian Woosnam (WAL)	Sandy Lyle (SCO)
1988	Sandy Lyle (SCO)	Nick Faldo (ENG)
1989	Nick Faldo (ENG)	Ian Woosnam (WAL)
1990	Ian Woosnam (WAL)	Mark McNulty (NZL)
1991	Severiano Ballesteros (ESP)	Nick Price (ZIM)
1992	Nick Faldo (ENG)	Jeff Sluman (USA)
1993	Corey Pavin (USA)	Nick Faldo (ENG)
1994	Ernie Els (RSA)	Colin Montgomerie (SCO)
1995	Ernie Els (RSA)	Steve Elkington (AUS)
1996	Ernie Els (RSA)	Vijay Singh (FIJ)
1997	Vijay Singh (FIJ)	Ernie Els (RSA)
1998	Mark O'Meara (USA)	Tiger Woods (USA)
1999	Colin Montgomerie (SCO)	Mark O'Meara (USA)
2000	Lee Westwood (ENG)	Colin Montgomerie (SCO)
2001	Ian Woosnam (WAL)	Padraig Harrington (IRL)
2002	Ernie Els (RSA)	Sergio Garcia (ESP)
2003	Ernie Els (RSA)	Thomas Bjorn (DEN)

G
O
L
F

Ryder Cup

	Winner	Venue
1927	USA	Worcester, Massachusetts
1929	Great Britain	Moortown, North Yorkshire
1931	USA	Scioto, Ohio
1933	Great Britain	Southport & Ainsdale, Lancashire
1935	USA	Ridgewood, New Jersey
1937	USA	Southport & Ainsdale, Lancashire
1947	USA	Portland, Oregon
1949	USA	Ganton, Yorkshire
1951	USA	Pinehurst, North Carolina
1953	USA	Wentworth, Surrey
1955	USA	Thunderbird CC, California
1957	Great Britain	Lindrick, Yorkshire
1959	USA	Eldorado CC, California
1961	USA	Royal Lytham, Lancashire
1963	USA	Atlanta, Georgia
1965	USA	Royal Birkdale, Lancashire
1967	USA	Houston, Texas
1969	Tie	Royal Birkdale, Lancashire
1971	USA	St Louis, Missouri

1973	USA	Muirfield, Scotland
1975	USA	Laurel Valley, Pennsylvania
1977	USA	Royal Lytham, Lancashire
1979	USA	Greenbrier, Virginia
1981	USA	Walton Heath, Surrey
1983	USA	Palm Beach, Florida
1985	Europe	The Belfry, Warwickshire
1987	Europe	Muirfield Village, Ohio
1989	Tie	The Belfry, Warwickshire
1991	USA	Kiawah Island, South Carolina
1993	USA	The Belfry, Warwickshire
1995	Europe	Oak Hill CC, New York
1997	Europe	Valderrama, Spain
1999	USA	Boston, Massachusetts
2002	Europe	The Belfry, Warwickshire
2004		Oakland Hills, Michigan

NB: Since 1979 the Ryder Cup has been contested by USA and Europe. The 2001 event was cancelled due to the terrorist attack of 11 September

Golf: General Information

Augusta National: designers	Bobby Jones and Scottish architect Alister Mackenzie in 1933
Bonallack family	In 1968, Michael Bonallack won the English amateur championship in the same year that his sister, Sally, won the English women's championship. Michael's wife, Angela, was twice English women's champion and her sister, Shirley Ward, won the English girls championship in 1964.
British Open: correct title	The Open Championship (as it was the first championship open to the world)
bunker: biggest in the world	Hell's Half Acre on the 585yds par five at the Pine Valley course, Clementon, New Jersey, USA
clubs: maximum number allowed	14
Curtis Cup	Biennial tournament instituted in 1932 and played between amateur women's teams from the United States and Great Britain & Ireland. Teams consist of six players, two substitutes and a captain. The first British victory was at Muirfield in 1952 and the first on US soil was in 1986.
forms of play	The two forms of golf are match play and stroke play, often called medal play. In match play the golfers play together and against one another, the winner being the player who wins the most holes. In medal play each competitor is playing against every other golfer in the tournament, and the winner is the player with the lowest aggregate score. In professional tournaments medal competitions are played over 72 holes.
golf balls: dimensions	maximum weight 1.62oz (45.93g), minimum diameter of 1.68ins (4.27cm)
number of pimples	332
golf club makers: famous	The Dickson family of Leith in the late 18th century were the first great family of clubmakers. Other famous names of the 19th century were the McEwans of Leith, Forgans of St Andrews, Patricks of Leven, Morrises of St Andrews, Parks of Musselburgh and Dunns of North Berwick. Simon Cossar and Hugh Philp were well-known individuals in the club-making trade.

golf club names

1 wood – driver	1 iron – driving iron
2 wood – brassie	2 iron – midiron
3 wood – spoon	3 iron – mid-mashie
4 wood – baffy	4 iron – mashie iron
5 wood – equivalent to 3 or 4 iron	5 iron – mashie
	6 iron – spade mashie
	7 iron – mashie-niblick
	8 iron – pitching niblick
	9 iron – niblick
	10 iron – wedge
	putter

golf clubs: first in Australia	The Royal Adelaide Golf Club (founded in 1870)
first in New Zealand	Christchurch Golf Club (founded in 1873)
first in South Africa	Maritzburg Golf Club, Natal (founded in 1884)
oldest outside Great Britaiin	The Royal Calcutta Golf Club (founded in 1829)
golf glove pioneer	Henry Cotton began to use a left-hand glove to help his grip in 1930.
golf hole: dimensions	4¼ins (108mm) diameter and at least 4ins (102mm) deep
golfing all-rounders	Bob Falkenburg, Brazilian amateur golf champion in 1959, 1960 and 1961, was also Wimbledon tennis champion in 1948.
	Charlotte Dod, British ladies' golf champion in 1904, won the Wimbledon singles title five times and also a silver medal at archery in the 1908 Olympics.
	Robert Gardner, twice US amateur golf champion, also held the world record for the pole vault at 13ft (3.96m).
	Ellsworth Vines, who won majors at tennis, later turned professional at golf and became one of the top 15 American players.

Ted Dexter won the President's Putter at Rye in 1983 and 1985 after a very successful cricket career in which he captained the England team.

Althea Gibson became a regular on the LPGA tour after her very successful tennis career.

Babe Zaharias won the British and American Amateur championships and the American Women's Open three times but found time to win two gold medals at the 1932 Olympic Games in Los Angeles, in the javelin and the high hurdles; in both she broke the world record. She also won silver in the high jump.

handicap	Golf has a marvellous method of enabling players of differing standards to compete against one another by use of a handicap system. The better the player the lower their handicap. Professionals play off zero handicap (scratch) and would need to give an 18-handicap player a stroke a hole.
hole lengths: rule of thumb	Generally par three holes are up to 249yds (228m) long, par fours between 250yds (229m) and 474yds (433m) and par fives in excess of 474yds (433m). With modern technology these parameters are under close inspection and many courses now adapt these yardages for professional competitions. Par threes and in particular par fours are now playing easier in some circumstances and there is nothing in the rules of the game to prevent designers deeming a 499yds (456m) hole a par four.
longest hole in the world	The 7th hole (par 7) of the Sano Course, Satsuki Golf Club, Japan, measures 909yds (831m).
Open Championship: founded	In October 1860 by the Prestwick Club, Ayrshire. There was no championship in 1871 because 'Young' Tom Morris had won the previous three and thus made the belt his own. In 1872, a new trophy, a silver claret jug, was presented to the winner and the organisation became a joint effort of the Prestwick club, the Royal & Ancient Golf Club (R&A) and the Honourable Company of Edinburgh Golfers. Until 1892, the championship was played over 36 holes in one day but from then on it became a 72-hole competition. The R&A took over sole organisation in 1920.
Carnoustie: first Open	The first Open to be contested at Carnoustie was in 1931.
hole-in-one: first	In 1868 'Young' Tom Morris scored the first hole-in-one in championship golf at Prestwick's 8th hole.
Hoylake: first Open	In 1897 Hoylake hosted its first Open, won by Harold Hilton, a local member.
largest winning margin	In 1862 'Old' Tom Morris won by 13 strokes.
live television coverage	In 1955 the BBC televised the Open live for the first time and the first prize reached £1000.
newsreel of Open	In 1914 the first newsreel was made of the Open.
1957 controversy	The 1957 championship was transferred from Muirfield to St Andrews owing to a petrol shortage during the Suez crisis. Bobby Locke marked his ball a putter's head length from the spot on the 72nd green, but replaced it on the marker's spot in error. He holed the putt for a three-shot win. In theory he could have been disqualified but the more likely punishment was a two-stroke penalty. Common sense prevailed and no action was taken against him. This championship was the first where the leaders went out last in the final two rounds.
non-Scottish winner: first	John Ball in 1890 broke the Scottish monopoly by becoming the first Englishman to win the Open. Ball was also the first amateur to win the Open but perhaps his most remarkable achievement was his placing of fifth in the 1878 Open at the age of 14!
oldest winner	'Old' Tom Morris (46)
overseas winner: first	Arnaud Massy of France in 1907. The first time the Claret Jug was taken to America was in 1921 when US-based Scotsman Jock Hutchison won the championship at St Andrews.
Portrush: Open held in	The 1951 Open was held in Portrush, Northern Ireland, the only time it has been contested outside Great Britain.
Prestwick: last Open	The last Open to be staged at Prestwick was in 1925.
qualifying cut introduced	In 1898 Harry Vardon won the Open, the first time it was won with four rounds under 80. This championship was also the first one where a qualifying cut was made after two rounds.
Royal Lytham: first Open	The first Open to be contested at Royal Lytham & St Annes was in 1926.
rubber ball: first used	The rubber-cored ball was first used by a winner of the Open championship in 1902 (Sandy Herd).
St Andrews: first Open	From 1860-72 the Open was played at Prestwick but in 1873 St Andrews hosted its first Open.
Sandwich: first Open	In 1894 Sandwich hosted the Open, the first time the championship was held in England.
sub-300 aggregate: first	Jack White won the 1904 Open with an aggregate of 296, the first four-round score under 300. John Henry Taylor scored the first round under 70 during these championships.
Sunday finish: first	The first Open in which the last round was played on Sunday was in 1980.
Turnberry: first Open	The first Open to be contested at Turnberry was in 1977.
United States winner: first	Walter Hagen in 1922
youngest winner	'Young' Tom Morris (17)
youngest winner in 20th century	Severiano Ballesteros (22)
qualified pilots: famous golfers	Bill Campbell (1964 US Amateur champion), Jerilyn Britz (1979 US Women's Open champion), and Arnold Palmer are all qualified pilots and Bobby Locke flew as a bomber pilot with the South African Air Force during World War II.

G
O
L
F

retired aged 28	Bobby Jones
Ryder Cup: brothers-in-law in team	Jerry Pate and Bruce Lietzke were members of the 1981 US Ryder Cup team. Lietzke married Pate's sister.
father and sons played	Percy and Peter Alliss, Antonio and Ignacio Garrido
inauguration year	The Ryder Cup began in 1927 and was contested between the professional players of the United States and those of Great Britain & Ireland. In 1979 the the format was changed, the British team being replaced by a European select.
Samuel Ryder: profession	Seed-merchant from Manchester, England
Solheim Cup	A biennial tournament instituted in 1990 and played between professional women's teams from the United States and Europe. It takes its name from Karsten Solheim, owner of golf club manufacturer Ping. Teams consist of 12 players and a non-playing captain.
Stableford system	Originated by Dr Frank Stableford (1870-1959) and first used on 16 May 1932 at Wallasey Golf Club, Cheshire. The scoring was 1 point for a bogey, 2 points for a par, 3 points for a birdie, 4 points for an eagle and 5 points for an albatross.
stymie: year outlawed	In 1951 the practice of purposely hitting one's ball in the line of an opponent's shot, thus preventing them having a direct putt into the hole, was abolished.
tee pegs: originating year	1938
Triumvirate of Golf	Name given to the three British professionals that dominated golf at the turn of the 20th century: James Braid, John Henry Taylor and Harry Vardon.
US Amateur: famous champion	Nathaniel Crosby, son of Bing Crosby, won the 1981 US Amateur championship.
US Masters: founder	Bobby Jones
first hole-in-one	Ross Somerville, a Canadian amateur, scored the first hole-in-one at the Masters in 1934.
first overseas winner	Gary Player in 1961
oldest winner	Jack Nicklaus (46)
youngest winner	Tiger Woods (21)
US Open: first held	On 4 October 1895, at Newport, Rhode Island, the first winner being Englishman Horace Rawlins.
first amateur to win	Francis Ouimet in 1913
first American to win	Johnny McDermott in 1911
first bespectacled winner	Willie Macfarlane of Scotland in 1925
first round under 70	Dave Hunter made 68 in the opening round of the 1909 championship.
first to break 80 in four rounds	Laurie Auchterlonie in 1902. The new Haskell rubber-cored ball helped his cause.
last amateur to win	Johnny Goodman in 1933
longest championship	The 1931 championship was won by Billy Burke who required a 72-hole play-off (36 holes twice) before seeing off the challenge of George von Elm.
oldest winner	Hale Irwin (45)
youngest winner	John McDermott (19)
US PGA: first held	In 1916 and was a matchplay event until 1958 when it became a 72-hole strokeplay event. The first winner was Englishman Jim Barnes residing in the United States.
first American-born winner	Walter Hagen in 1921
oldest winner	Julius Boros (48)
youngest winner	Gene Sarazen (20)
US Women's Open: first UK winner	Laura Davies in 1987
waggled at address of ball	Sandy Herd was the first golfer to introduce the waggle of the club while addressing the ball.
Walker Cup	Inaugurated in 1921 and played between amateur teams from the United States and the British Isles. It was proposed by George Walker, president of the USGA, as the International Challenge Trophy but took its present name in 1922. It became a biennial event in 1924. Teams consist of eight players, two substitutes and a captain. The first British victory was at St Andrews in 1938 and the first time the British did not lose on US soil was in 1965 when they tied 12-12.
World Matchplay Championship	Inaugurated in 1964 and sponsored first by Piccadilly, then by Colgate, Suntory, Cisco, and from 2003, HSBC. All matches are played over 36 holes at Wentworth, Surrey. The Andersen Consulting World Matchplay Championship was first staged in 1996 and won by Britain's Barry Lane. Other winners have included Colin Montgomerie (1998), Darren Clarke (2000), Steve Stricker (2001), Kevin Sutherland (2002) and Tiger Woods (2003). The field consists of the world's top 64 golfers.
yips: coined by	Scottish professional Tommy Armour in the 1920s. The term describes an inability to release the putter through the ball.

Golf: Biographies of Post-War Major Tournament Winners and Other Notable Golfers

Aaron, Tommy Born Gainesville, Georgia, USA, 22 February 1937. In the 1968 US Masters, Aaron filled in the card of playing partner Roberto de Vicenzo incorrectly, writing four instead of three at the 17th on the last day. This let in Bob Goalby who won the tournament by one shot.

Archer, George Born San Francisco, California, USA, 1 October 1939. Won 12 titles on the US tour. He was a fantastic putter which helped him tremendously to win his only major, the 1969 US Masters when his 281 total left him seven under par.

Armour, Tommy Born Edinburgh, Scotland, 24 September 1895. Armour became a professional golfer in 1924 and soon established a reputation as a respected teacher, Bobby Jones being a notable pupil. He won the US Open in 1927, in a play-off against Henry Cooper, and the US PGA in 1930. His Open victory in 1931 meant he had won all three of the professional majors existing at the time. He died 11 September 1968.

Azinger, Paul Born Hoylake, Massachusetts, USA, 6 January 1960. Azinger developed cancer at the age of 33 just as he was likely to become a huge star. He lost the 1987 British Open to Nick Faldo by one shot after dropping strokes at the last two holes. He won his only major when he triumphed in the 1993 US PGA tournament at Inverness Club, Toledo, Ohio, by defeating Greg Norman at the second extra hole of a sudden death play-off.

Baker-Finch, Ian Born Nambour, Australia, 24 October 1960. In 1991 at Royal Birkdale, Baker-Finch became the first-ever player with a double-barrelled surname to prevail in a major when he won the Open Championship, defeating fellow-countryman Mike Harwood by one shot. Since then his fall from grace has been dramatic, most particularly because of an inability to use his driver with any great confidence.

Ballesteros, Seve Born Padrena, Spain, 9 April 1957. Ballesteros can rightly claim to have been one of the greatest players the world has ever seen. He announced himself to the world in 1976 when as a precocious 19-year-old he led the Open at Royal Birkdale after three rounds, only to finish joint runner-up (with Jack Nicklaus) to Johnny Miller. Later in the year he had his first European tour win in the Dutch Open. From 1979-88 he won five majors (three Opens and two Masters). His first Open Championship was won at Royal Lytham in 1979, when he became the first continental European to win the championship since Arnaud Massy in 1907. He was the first player to win 50 tournaments on the official European tour and he was the non-playing captain of the 1997 European Ryder Cup team that successfully defended the trophy at Valderrama, Spain.

Barber, Jerry Born Woodson, Illinois, USA, 25 April 1916. He won his only major in 1961 when he captured the US PGA title at Olympic Fields, Illinois, defeating Don January by one shot in an 18-hole play-off. At the age of 45 he became the oldest man to win the PGA title. Later that year he was the playing captain of the US team that won the Ryder Cup 14½-9½ at Royal Lytham.

Beem, Rich Born Phoenix, Arizona, USA, 24 August 1970. Beem's first US tour win was the 1999 Kemper Open but he did not fulfil his real talent in a major until 2002 when he won the US PGA title by one shot from Tiger Woods. He quit golf temporarily in 1995 and sold mobile phones and car stereo systems until he gained renewed interest from watching his friend, J.P. Hayes win the 1998 Buick Classic.

Bolt, Tommy Born Haworth, Oklahoma, USA, 31 March 1918. A fine player who had a fiery temperament on the golf course, hence his nickname 'Thunder' Bolt. Once playing partner Porky Oliver threw Bolt's putter into a lake to stop him hurling it further. He won his sole major at Southern Hills, Tulsa, Oklahoma in 1958, when he took the US Open by one shot from a very young and then unknown Gary Player.

Boros, Julius Nicholas Born Fairfield, Connecticut, USA, 3 March 1920. Nicknamed 'The Moose' and of Hungarian extraction, Boros had a great record considering he did not turn professional until 30, after giving up an accountancy career. He won 18 tournaments on the US tour including three majors, the last being the 1968 US PGA when he became, aged 48, the oldest-ever golfer to win a major. He was a great wedge and bunker player.

Brewer, Gay Born Middleburn, Ohio, 19 March 1932. At Augusta National in 1967 Brewer won his only major when he took the US Masters by a stroke from Bobby Nicholls after a fine last-round 67. He won 11 US tour victories and in Britain won the Alcan Championship in both 1967 and 1968.

Brooks, Mark Born Fort Worth, Texas, USA, 25 March 1961. Brooks won his only major in 1996 when he defeated Kenny Perry in a play-off to win the US PGA title at Valhalla Golf Club, Louisville, Kentucky. Three weeks earlier he had a creditable joint fifth place in the Open Championship at Royal Lytham.

Burke, Jack Born Fort Worth, Texas, USA, 29 January 1923. Burke's best spell of golf was in 1952 when he won four events in just over three weeks. In 1956 he won two majors, the US Masters after pulling back eight shots in the last round from Ken Venturi and the US PGA title when he defeated Ted Kroll 3 & 2 in the final. He was captain of the US Ryder Cup team in 1957 and 1973.

Burkemo, Walter Born Detroit, Michigan, USA, 9 October 1918. A Ryder Cup player in 1953, he won the US PGA title that year when he defeated unknown Felice Torza 2 & 1 in the final. He lost in the final of the same major the following year, going down 4 & 3 to Chick Harbert. During World War II he was an infantry sergeant – hence his nickname 'Sarge'.

Calcavecchia, Mark Born Laurel, Nebraska, USA, 12 June 1960. Calcavecchia won his only major in 1989 when he captured the Open Championship at Royal Troon after a four-hole play-off against Wayne Grady and Greg Norman. In 1988 he had been runner-up in the US Masters.

Casper, Billy Born San Diego, California, USA, 24 June 1931. Nicknamed 'Buffalo Bill' because of a diet which included buffalo steaks, Casper had an amazing 51 career wins on the US tour from 1956-75. The winner of two US Opens and a US Masters title, he was one of the all-time great putters, using a wristy action which is deemed out of date nowadays. Indeed in the 1959 US Open, which he won, he needed only 112 putts.

GOLF

Charles, Bob Born Carterton, New Zealand, 14 March 1936. The first left-hander to win a major, Charles is a former bank clerk come good. A fantastic putter in his prime, he captured the Open Championship at Royal Lytham in 1963 after defeating the American Phil Rodgers by eight shots in a 36-hole play-off. In 1972 he won both the John Player Classic and the Dunlop Masters in successive weeks in Britain. He had five wins on the regular US tour 1963-74.

Clarke, Darren Born Dungannon, Northern Ireland, 14 August 1968. Clarke became the first European to win one of the World Golf Championships events, capturing the Accenture Match Play Championship in February 2000 by beating David Duval in the semi-final and Tiger Woods in the final at La Costa Resort and Spa. He led the 2000 Volvo Order of Merit race going into the final week of the season but was only in a tie for 17th place in the WGC-American Express Championship, which was not enough to stop Lee Westwood claiming the title of Europe's number one. Clarke won in South Africa for the first time at the start of 2001, capturing the Dimension Data Pro-Am. His first European tour title of the year was gained on home soil in the Smurfit European Open at the K Club in July, making him the first Irishman to win in Ireland since John O'Leary 19 years earlier. He was part of a winning European Ryder Cup team for the second time when he helped beat the United States 15½-12½ at The Belfry in September, 2002. He won the NEC International at the Firestone Country Club, Akron, Ohio, in August 2003.

Coody, Billy Charles Born Stamford, Texas, USA, 13 July 1937. Charles (as he was known) joined the US tour in 1963 after a fine amateur career. He won only three times on the regular US tour, one of his successes being the 1971 US Masters when he finished two shots in front of runners-up Johnny Miller and Jack Nicklaus. He had two wins in Europe, both in 1973, at King's Norton near Birmingham and in the John Player Classic at Turnberry. On the second day he had a remarkable round of 74 when most scores were in the 80s due to gales.

Cotton, Thomas Henry Born Holmes Chapel, Cheshire, England, 26 January 1907. Arguably the greatest player produced in Great Britain, Cotton won the Open Championship on three occasions, twice before the war and once in 1948. His win at Royal St George's, Sandwich in 1934 included a remarkable round of 65 which broke the record for the championship until Mark Hayes shot a 63 at Turnberry in 1977. The Dunlop 65 ball was named after his great round. He captained Great Britain's Ryder Cup teams in 1947 and 1953 and at the age of 49 came sixth in the Open in 1956. He won his last tournament, the 1954 Penfold, at the age of 47. He died 22 December 1987 and was knighted posthumously.

Couples, Fred Born Seattle, Washington, USA, 3 October 1959. A very long hitter, hence his nickname 'Boom Boom', Couples should have won more than his single major. He took the 1992 US Masters by two shots from 49-year-old Ray Floyd. In 1995 he and Davis Love III became the first pairing to win the World Cup on four successive occasions.

Crenshaw, Ben Born Austin, Texas, USA, 11 January 1952. Crenshaw has a reputation as one of the greatest-ever putters in the game and his two major victories in the US Masters of 1984 and 1995 bear testament to that. In 1984 he collected the first-ever $100,000-plus winner's cheque. He won the 1995 title just a few days after the death of his friend and mentor Harvey Penick, to whom he dedicated the victory. He is nicknamed 'Gentle Ben'.

Curtis, Ben Born Ostranda, Ohio, USA, 26 May 1977. Curtis was born only 50 yards from the practice putting green at Millcreek golf course, which his grandfather built and where his father remains as superintendent. A virtual unknown, he won the 2003 Open Championship at Royal St George's when he held off the challenge of some of the game's great players – including world number one Tiger Woods, Thomas Bjorn, Davis Love III and Vijay Singh – to gain victory by one shot in only his 16th career professional tournament.

Daly, Fred Born Portrush, Northern Ireland, 11 October 1911. When Fred Daly won the Open Championship at Royal Liverpool (Hoylake) in 1947 he became the only Ulsterman to take the title. He also finished second in 1948, third in 1950, fourth in 1951 and third in 1952. He was an ever-present in the Ryder Cup 1947-53. An excellent match player, he three times took the Professional Matchplay Championship, in 1947, 1948 and 1952.

Daly, John Born Carmichael, California, USA, 28 April 1966. Nicknamed 'The Wild Thing' partly due to his ability to hit the ball huge distances and partly due to his often excessive lifestyle, he is one of the very few players to win two majors before the age of 30. At the 1991 US PGA Championship he was ninth reserve, but a combination of late withdrawals due to unavailability and injury put Daly into the competition. Despite not having played a practice round, he won by three shots from fellow-countryman Bruce Lietzke. He won the Open Championship at St Andrews in 1995 in a four-hole play-off with Costantino Rocca of Italy. John emerged on the scene as a breath of fresh air, often reducing par five holes to a drive and a wedge, but a combination of personal problems and injury sadly prevented him from dominating the world of golf as once seemed likely.

Davies, Laura Born Coventry, England, 10 May 1963. Britain's greatest-ever female golfer, Davies is the only professional, male or female, to have won on five different tours in the same year. In 1987 she won the US Women's Open and during the 1990s she was consistently high on, if not on top of, the money list. Indeed she is the first woman golfer to have topped $1m in prize money in a single year. In recognition of her contribution to golf, she was awarded an MBE in 1988. Laura has also been an effective team player and has been a member of several Curtis and Solheim Cup squads.

Demaret, James Born Houston, Texas, USA, 24 May 1910. In 1950 Jimmy Demaret became the first man to win the US Masters on three occasions, having previously prevailed in 1940 and 1947. He was one of nine children of a carpenter, three of whom became pro golfers. His best season was 1947 when he captured six titles and won the Vardon Trophy for the lowest stroke average. For a spell he was a band singer in nightclubs. He died in Houston, Texas, 28 December 1983.

Duval, David Born Jacksonville, Florida, USA, 9 November 1971. Duval was brought up around golf; his father Bob still competes on the US Senior Tour. His only major win to date is the 2001 Open Championship at Royal Lytham when he finished three shots in front of Sweden's Niclas Fasth.

Elkington, Steve Born Inverell, New South Wales, Australia, 8 December 1962. Elkington's greatest triumph was his only major victory when he took the 1995 US PGA title, coming from six shots behind on the final day to defeat Colin Montgomerie. Elkington holed a 25-foot putt on the first extra hole of a sudden death play-off to deny the Scot, both men having finished on a record low score of 267. Elkington also won the Players Championship in the USA in 1991 and 1997.

Els, Ernie   Born Johannesburg, South Africa, 17 October 1969. Els lives up to his nickname 'The Big Easy' due to his relaxed manner and demeanour on the course. His first two majors were both US Open titles, in 1994 and 1997. In 1994 he defeated Colin Montgomerie and Loren Roberts in a play-off and in 1997 he again relegated Montgomerie to the runner-up spot. His first win in the Open Championship was in 2002 at Muirfield. Els first came to the attention of his home country in 1992 when, aged only 23, he equalled Gary Player's record of winning the South African Open, South African PGA and South African Masters all in the same year. In the 1993 Open at Royal St George's he became the first player in the history of the event to record four rounds in the 60s.

Faldo, Nick   Born Welwyn Garden City, Hertfordshire, England, 18 July 1957. Faldo has played more Ryder Cup matches than any other player, won six majors and has reigned supreme on both sides of the Atlantic to make him one of the greatest golfers of all time. His first Open win was at Muirfield in 1987 when 18 straight pars in the final round gave him the title. He won the Open at St Andrews in 1990 by five shots and again captured the championship at Muirfield in 1992 by one shot from American John Cook. In 1990 he became the first man since Jack Nicklaus in 1972 to successfully defend his US Masters title. He won his third Masters in remarkable fashion in 1996 when he forced Greg Norman to surrender a six-shot overnight lead on the final day. In his first Ryder Cup singles match aged only 20 he defeated Tom Watson.

Faulkner, Max   Born Bexhill, Sussex, England, 29 July 1916. Max Faulkner is the only player to date to have won the Open Championship outside England and Scotland, doing so at Royal Portrush in Northern Ireland in 1951. After two rounds of the championship, eccentric Max was signing autographs 'Open Champion 1951'. He played on five occasions in the Ryder Cup but never won a singles match. At the age of 52 he won the Portuguese Open. His son-in-law is ex-Ryder Cup golfer Brian Barnes.

Ferrier, James   Born Sydney, Australia, 24 February 1915. Ferrier became in 1947 the first winner of the US PGA title born outside the United States when he defeated Chick Harbert in the final. Thirteen years later he finished second to Jay Herbert when the event had become a strokeplay competition.

Finsterwald, Dow   Born Athens, Georgia, USA, 6 September 1929. In 1958 Finsterwald was the winner of the first US PGA title to be contested as a strokeplay tournament, his 276 aggregate putting him two shots in front of Billy Casper. A good match player, he made four Ryder Cup appearances as a player and was non-playing captain of the 1977 American team.

Fleck, Jack   Born Bettendorf, Iowa, USA, 8 November 1921. Virtually unknown and unheralded, Fleck caused one of golf's greatest upsets when he won the 1955 US Open after a play-off with Ben Hogan. Five years later he finished third to Arnold Palmer.

Floyd, Ray   Born Fort Bragg, North Carolina, USA, 4 September 1942. The Open Championship title eluded Floyd but he still won at each of the other three majors. Allied to the fact that he won on 22 occasions on the US tour, played eight Ryder Cup matches and had a successful Seniors career, Floyd is definitely among the cream of the world's golfers; indeed he competed in the 1993 Ryder Cup at the age of 51. A noted front runner and streak putter, he won the 1976 US Masters having led from start to finish. He relegated Gary Player to runner-up in the 1969 US PGA Championship and won his only US Open title in 1986 at Shinnecock Hills, Southampton, New York.

Ford, Doug   Born West Haven, Connecticut, USA, 6 August 1922. Ford was an American Ryder Cup regular between 1955 and 1961 during which period he won two majors. He defeated Gary Middlecoff 4 & 3 in the final to take the 1955 US PGA title and in 1957, in the first-ever US Masters to employ a cut after 36 holes, he prevailed by three shots from Sam Snead.

Furgol, Ed   Born New York Mills, New York, USA, 22 March 1917. Despite the handicap of a withered left arm after a childhood accident, Fergol won the 1954 US Open at Baltusrol, New Jersey, by one shot from Gene Littler. He was a top-60 money winner in the USA in every year but one between 1945 and 1957.

Furyk, Jim   Born West Chester, Pennsylvania, USA, 12 May 1970. Furyk's swing has been described as like an octopus playing golf in a telephone box but there is no doubting its pedigree. Always a fine player on the US Tour, he was becoming known as one of the best players never to have won a major when all came good at the 2003 US Open at Olympia Fields, Illinois. His two-over-par score of 72 in the final round was enough to give him a three-shot win over Stephen Leaney. His caddie was Mike 'Fluff' Cowan who carried the bag of Tiger Woods for much of his early career.

Garcia, Sergio   Born Borriol, Spain, 9 January 1980. Garcia turned professional on 21 April 1999 and won the Murphys Irish Open in his sixth start as a professional. His second-place finish to Tiger Woods in the 1999 US PGA Championship highlighted his potential. He collected three and a half points out of five in a brilliant Ryder Cup debut at Brookline before returning to Europe to win the Linde German Masters and help Spain capture the Alfred Dunhill Cup. He claimed his third European tour title when he came from four strokes behind with four holes to play to edge ahead of defending champion Retief Goosen and win the Trophée Lancôme in September 2001. Garcia made his big breakthrough in America in 2001, winning his first tournament on the US PGA tour, the Mastercard Colonial, and followed that with a second victory by capturing the Buick Classic a month later. In January 2002 won the first event on the US PGA Tour, the Mercedes Championships, and added the Canarias Open de España title in Gran Canaria in April, finishing the year as the only player to finish in the top ten in all four major championships.

Geiberger, Al   Born Red Bluff, California, USA, 1 September 1937. The first player to card a round of 59 in an American PGA official tour event (the 1977 Danny Thomas Memphis event). His biggest win was in the 1966 US PGA championship at Firestone, Akron, Ohio, when he was the only player to achieve par.

Goalby, Bob   Born Belleville, Illinois, USA, 14 March 1929. Of his 11 victories in 20 years on the tour,

G
O
L
F

Goalby's success in the 1968 US Masters was the most memorable, with Argentinian Roberto de Vicenzo signing for a wrong score to miss a play-off.

Goosen, Retief Born Pietersburg, South Africa, 3 February 1969. Made his professional tournament debut in 1990 and had six wins in his first five years. His real breakthrough came when he won the 1995 South African Open. His first major was the 2001 US Open played at Southern Hills when he defeated Mark Brooks in a play-off. In that year he also became the first non-European to win the Volvo Order of Merit (in Europe) since Greg Norman in 1982 and the first South African to win the Harry Vardon Trophy since Dale Hayes in 1975. He retained his Volvo Order of Merit title in 2002. He won his second US Open title at Shinnecock Hills, New York, in 2004.

Grady, Wayne Born Brisbane, Australia, 26 July 1957. Won his first tournament in the USA when he took the Westchester Classic title in 1989 and captured his first major in 1990 when he won the US PGA title in fine style by three shots from Fred Couples. He became the third Australian to hold the title after Jim Ferrier and David Graham. In 1989 he (along with Greg Norman) lost a four-hole play-off for the Open at Troon to the eventual winner, Mark Calcavecchia. He now commentates for the BBC at the Open Championship.

Graham, David Born Windsor, Victoria, Australia, 23 May 1946. Despite winning the Japanese Open in 1971 and his first American tour title in 1972, Graham had to wait until 1979 to win his first major when he took the US PGA title at Oakland Hills, Birmingham, Michigan, defeating Ben Crenshaw at the third extra hole of a sudden death play-off. Two years later he captured the US Open at Merion in Pennsylvania. He was the first Australian to win the title and the first overseas winner since Tony Jacklin in 1970.

Graham, Lou Born Nashville, Tennessee, USA, 7 January 1938. A top US professional in the 1970s, he made three Ryder Cup appearances in 1973, 1975 and 1977 and had six US tour wins. The pinnacle of his career, however, was victory in the 1975 US Open when he defeated John Mahaffey in a play-off.

Green, Hubert Born Birmingham, Alabama, USA, 28 December 1946. In 1976 Green won three successive tournaments on the US tour which gave him confidence to win the US Open the following year, despite death threats from an anonymous telephone caller. He had a distinct putting style in which he stood over the ball with legs splayed wide apart, a method used to great effect when he won the US PGA title in 1985 by two shots from Lee Trevino.

Hagen, Walter Born Rochester, New York, 21 December 1892. Hagen was one of the early 'greats' of the game. In an age when professional golfers were deemed second-class citizens by golf clubs, Hagen shone like a beacon. He led an opulent lifestyle, pioneered colourful clothing on the course and insisted on being paid appearance money for plying his trade. Professionals were not allowed in the clubhouse in his day and so Walter would often change into his plus-fours in his Rolls-Royce, to the amusement of spectators. He won two US Opens (1914 and 1919), four Opens (1922, 1924, 1928 and 1929), five PGA Championships (1921, 1924-1927) and five Western Opens. He retired with 40 PGA wins and was six times US Ryder Cup captain. He died 5 October 1969.

Hamilton, Todd Born Galesburg, Illinois, USA, 18 October 1985. Turned pro in 1987 and played on the Canadian in 1988 and 1989 before joining the Asian Tour and becoming the top money earner in 1992. Hamilton won 11 Asian titles and finally won his PGA Tour card in 2003 at his eighth attempt. In 2004 he won the Honda Classic and became Open Champion at Royal Troon.

Harbert, Melvin R. Born Dayton, Ohio, USA, 20 February 1915. Going by the nickname 'Chick', Harbert turned professional in 1940 and was known as a long hitter of the ball. He won the 1954 US PGA title by defeating Walter Burkemo 4 & 3 in the final, having been runner-up two years earlier. He captained the 1955 US Ryder Cup team.

Harmon, Claude Born Savannah, Georgia, USA, 1916. Harmon won the 1948 US Masters despite not being a tour regular. In 1959 he finished third in the US Open behind the eventual winner, Billy Casper. Harmon's son Butch is now a respected golf coach who worked for a long time with Tiger Woods.

Harper, Chandler Born Portsmouth, Virginia, USA, 1914. Harper won his only major in 1950 when he captured the US PGA title at Scioto, Columbus, Ohio, chiefly due to the fact that Ben Hogan did not play and Sam Snead was defeated in the second round. His single Ryder Cup appearance was in 1955 when in his only match, paired with Jerry Barber, he lost to Johnny Fallon and John Jacobs.

Harrington, Padraig Born Dublin, Republic of Ireland, 31 August 1971. Harrington completed an accountancy degree before turning professional and has become a permanent fixture in the top ten of the official world golf rankings since arriving there in November 2001, shortly after winning the Volvo Masters Andalucia. He won his first tournament in 1996, the Peugeot Open de España, but had to wait until the 2000 season for his second victory. He has won twice in 2000, once each in 2001 and 2002, and twice in the 2003 season (the BMW Asian Open and the Deutsche Bank-SAP Open TPC of Europe). He teamed up with Paul McGinley at Kiawah Island in 1997 to win the World Cup for Ireland for the first time in 39 years, and in 2002 played the last two rounds of the Target World Challenge in California with tournament host Tiger Woods before beating the world number one by two shots. He made his Ryder Cup debut in 1999 and was part of the successful team in the 34th Ryder Cup at the Belfry. It was the second time he had been part of a team that defeated the Americans, having first tasted success in his amateur days in the Walker Cup of 1995 at Royal Porthcawl.

Hebert, Jay Born St Martinville, Louisiana, USA, 1923. Both Hebert and his brother Lionel won the US PGA title, Jay's victory coming in 1960 when he beat the 1947 winner, Jim Ferrier, into second place. As a player he represented his country in the 1959 and 1961 Ryder Cups and was non-playing captain in 1971, when his team ran out 18½-13½ winners.

Hebert, Lionel Born Lafayette, Louisiana, USA, 1928. Five years younger than his brother Jay, Lionel won the US PGA title in 1957, the last time it was a match-play event, defeating Dow Finsterwald in the final. As a Ryder Cup player in 1957 he lost his singles match to Ken Bousefield at Lindrick in Yorkshire.

Hogan, Ben Born Dublin, Texas, USA, 13 August 1912. Undoubtedly one of the great names of golf, as emphasised by his career record of 63 US tour wins and nine major titles. He won all four majors at least once in a period from 1946-53. He was the dominant force in the golf world in this period and it was altogether more remarkable because in 1949 he was severely injured when his car collided with a Greyhound bus. He survived despite doubts that he would ever walk again. The story of his crash and recovery were told in the 1951 film *Follow the Sun* with Glenn Ford playing Hogan. In 1953 he won the Open, US Open and US Masters but was denied the chance of a grand slam because the dates of the Open and the US PGA championship coincided. At his only appearances in Britain he won the Open at Carnoustie in 1953 and the individual title in the 1956 Canada (World) Cup at Wentworth. Sometimes nicknamed 'The Wee Ice Man', in the USA he was known as 'The Hawk'. In 1967 at the age of 54 he scored a 66 in the US Masters. He died at Fort Worth, Texas, 25 July 1997.

Irwin, Hale   Born Joplin, Missouri, USA, 3 June 1945. Irwin's three major victories were all achieved at the US Open, the first being at Winged Foot in 1974 when steady play gave him a two-shot victory over Forrest Fezler. On a tough course Irwin's winning score was a remarkable seven over par. His second win in 1979 was again on a difficult course, his level-par aggregate giving him another two-shot victory. His third victory, in a play-off against Mike Donald in 1990, made him at the age of 45 the oldest-ever winner of the event. He won the World Matchplay Championship at Wentworth in 1974 and 1975. Since turning 50 he has been a prolific winner on the US Seniors tour.

Jacklin, Tony   Born Scunthorpe, England, 7 July 1944. Jacklin's exploits in the 1960s and 1970s showed British golfers that they could take on and beat the Americans in their own backyard. Although a tournament player in Europe, he won his first US tournament, the Jacksonville Open, in 1968. He was one of the favourites for the 1969 Open at Royal Lytham and duly obliged his fans with a two-shot victory over Bob Charles. The Claret Jug was back in English hands for the first time since 1951. He took the US Open in 1970 at Haseltine, Minnesota, with a seven-shot victory, becoming the first Englishman since Ted Ray to capture the title. Although a regular winner in the 1970s, he never dominated world golf again. After competing in seven successive Ryder Cups as a player from 1967 he took over as non-playing captain in 1983, when his team lost by a single point. In 1985 they won the match amid historic scenes at The Belfry, retained the trophy (15-13) at Muirfield Village in 1987 and kept it once more at The Belfry in 1989 with a 14-14 draw. He recorded a famous hole-in-one at Royal St George's, Sandwich, in the 1967 Dunlop Masters.

January, Don   Born Plainview, Texas, USA, 20 November 1929. The monster golf course at Columbine, Denver, Colorado (7436yds (6799m)) hosted its one and only major in 1967, when Don January won an 18-hole play-off against Don Massingale. January made two Ryder Cup appearances and in 1980 was the first man to win a US Seniors tour event, when he took the inaugural Atlantic City Senior title.

Janzen, Lee   Born Austin, Minnesota, USA, 28 August 1964. Janzen's two major titles were both US Open wins: in 1993 at Baltusrol, New Jersey, and in 1998 at the Olympic Club in San Francisco. On both occasions Payne Stewart was runner-up.

Jones, Robert Tyre   Born Atlanta, Georgia, USA, 17 March 1902. At the turn of the 20th century, the majors were considered to be the British and US Opens and Amateur Championships. Bobby Jones played his first major tournament, the US Amateur, when he was 14 and finished in the top ten. However, it was not until 1923 that he won his first major, the US Open. By the time he retired from competitive golf in 1930, Jones had won the Open three times, the British Amateur once, the US Open four times and the US Amateur four times. In 1930 he was the first golfer to win all the majors in a single year (the US PGA still not being a major at this time). In all he won 13 national championships in eight years; in addition he played in every Walker Cup from its inauguration in 1922 until his retirement. Jones devoted only three months of every year to golf. The remaining time was spent acquiring first-class honours degrees in law, English literature and mechanical engineering – all from different universities. When he retired he set up his own law practice in Atlanta. He never turned professional but rivals the likes of Jack Nicklaus and Tiger Woods as the greatest of players. He died 18 December 1971.

Jones, Steve   Born Artesia, New Mexico, USA, 27 December 1958. With three wins on the US tour in 1989, Jones's future in golf looked assured, but an accident with a motorcycle in 1991 put him out of the game for three years. Worse still, the accident meant he could no longer grip the club in the normal way, so it was a complete surprise that, having pre-qualified, he won the 1996 US Open at Oakland Hills with a 278 aggregate.

Keiser, Herman   Born Springfield, Missouri, USA, 1914. When Keiser won the 1946 US Masters he inflicted upon the great Ben Hogan the longest reign of any golfer as runner-up in a major. Hogan had been runner-up in the Masters in 1942 and again finished in second place when the championship was next played in 1946 after the war. Keiser played in the 1947 Ryder Cup, in which he was the only American to lose his singles match – to Sam King.

Kite, Tom   Born Austin, Texas, USA, 9 December 1949. After years of being described as the best player never to win a major, Kite finally laid the bogey by winning the US Open in 1992 at Pebble Beach, 20 years after joining the US tour. In addition to his US wins, Kite also won the European Open in 1980 and has racked up numerous other honours, including Rookie of the Year in 1973 and PGA Player of the Year in 1989. Perhaps his greatest honour, however, was captaining the US Ryder Cup team at Valderrama in 1997 following his seven Ryder Cup campaigns as a player.

Langer, Bernhard   Born Anhausen, West Germany, 27 August 1957. Without doubt the greatest-ever golfer to come from Germany, he is also one of Europe's top players of all time. His two major victories recorded in the US Masters of 1985 and 1993 were unusual in that he twice recorded bogey fives on the last hole. In the 1991 Ryder Cup at Kiawah Island, Langer missed a putt from 5½ft against Hale Irwin, resulting in the USA winning the trophy. Langer was the first player to be number one in the official world rankings when they were introduced by Sony in April 1986.

Lawrie, Paul   Born Aberdeen, Scotland, 1 January 1969. The 1999 Open Championship at Carnoustie takes some beating for pure sporting drama. Qualifier Paul Lawrie won the championship, beating Justin Leonard and Jean van de Velde in the four-hole play-off after Van de Velde made a triple bogey at the 72nd hole around the Barry Burn when leading by three shots. Lawrie has since won the inaugural Dunhill Links championship and the 2002 Welsh Open at Celtic Manor. He had a magnificent Ryder Cup at Brookline, Boston in 1999, when he claimed 3½ points.

Lehman, Tom   Born Austin, Missouri, USA, 7 March 1959. In 1996 Lehman became the first American to win the Open at Royal Lytham since Bobby Jones in 1926. Rounds of 67, 67, 64 and 73 gave him a 271 aggregate and a comfortable two-shot victory over Ernie Els and Mark McCumber.

Lema, Tony   Born Oakland, California, USA, 25 February 1934. After three rounds of the 1962 Orange County California Open, Lema led by three shots and promised the press champagne if he won. He did and he became 'Champagne' Tony Lema to them thereafter. In 1964 he decided to enter the Open at St Andrews but had no time to get to know the course. That did not matter because he romped to a five-shot victory over Jack Nicklaus with a closing round of 70, to win his only major. He famously lost a match to Gary Player in the World Matchplay Championship at Wentworth having been seven up with 17 holes to play. He died in a plane crash along with his wife on 24 July 1966 on his way to play a pro-am tournament after the US PGA championship.

Leonard, Justin   Born Dallas, Texas, USA, 15 June 1972. Won his only major in 1997, taking the Open Championship at Royal Troon in convincing style by recording a last-round 65. His three-shot victory gave him a winner's cheque of £250,000. His 45-foot putt on the 17th green against Jose Maria Olazabal caused the infamous and controversial scenes at the 1999 Ryder Cup at Brookline, Boston, when the American team prematurely congratulated Leonard for securing the point required to win the trophy although Olazabal had a putt to keep the match alive.

Littler, Gene   Born San Diego, California, USA, 21 July 1930. Littler's 29 US tour victories, seven Ryder Cup appearances, many Senior tour wins and 1961 US Open victory make him a great player by any standards. His first tour win was the 1954 San Diego Open which he won as an amateur. He was nicknamed 'Gene the Machine', and Gene Sarazen once said of him as a youngster, 'Here's a kid with a perfect swing like Sam Snead's . . . only better'.

Locke, Bobby   Born Germiston, Transvaal, South Africa, 20 November 1917. Born Arthur D'Arcy Locke, he took the name Bobby from his great hero Bobby Jones. He was a dominant figure in world golf in the 1940s and 1950s as his Open Championship record of four wins between 1949 and 1957 bears witness. In 1949 he defeated Harry Bradshaw after a play-off to land the title, in 1950 he won by two shots from Roberto di Vicenzo, in 1952 he beat Peter Thomson by one shot and in 1957 he again relegated Thomson to runner-up with a comfortable three-shot victory. Nicknamed 'Old Muffin Face' by the Americans, he had 11 wins on the US tour. He also won the South African Open championship nine times (1935, 1937-40, 1946, 1950, 1951). He died in Johannesburg on 9 March 1987.

Lopez, Nancy   Born Torrance, California, USA, 6 January 1957. Lopez dominated the women's game in the late 1970s and 1980s. She turned professional in 1977 and in 1978, her first full season, won eight tournaments including the US LPGA and was nominated Rookie of the Year. She won the US LPGA again in 1985 and 1989, recorded 49 wins on the PGA tour and represented the USA in the World Cup and Curtis Cup. Throughout her career, she has collected more than $4.5m in prize money and has earned as much again from her endorsements and other commercial interests including her post as playing editor of *Golf* magazine.

Love III, Davis   Born Charlotte, North Carolina, USA, 13 April 1964. To date Davis Love III has won only one major, the 1997 US PGA title at Winged Foot when he destroyed the field with a closing round of 66 to give him a five-shot victory. The same year also saw him make his third Ryder Cup appearance on the trot, losing all of his four matches. In 1995 he and Fred Couples became the first pairing to win the World Cup on four successive occasions.

Lyle, Sandy   Born Shrewsbury, England, 9 February 1958. Up there with the best-ever British golfers, Sandy Lyle's best years were the mid and late 1980s. During this period he had two major wins, the first being at Royal St George's, Sandwich, in the 1985 Open and the second the US Masters in 1988. His Masters victory is famous for the seven-iron he hit from a fairway trap some 150 yards from the 72nd green. He duly made his ten-foot birdie putt to prevail over Mark Calcavecchia by one shot. In 1992 he won the Volvo Masters at Valderrama, Spain.

Mahaffey, John   Born Kerville, Texas, USA, in 1948. A short but accurate hitter, Mahaffey seemed destined not to win a major. Having lost a play-off to Lou Graham in the 1975 US open, in 1976 he led the eventual winner, Jerry Pate, by two shots going into the last round only to fail at the final hurdle. However, he made amends in 1978, taking the US PGA title in a sudden death play-off with Pate and Tom Watson.

Mangrum, Lloyd   Born Trenton, Texas, USA, 1 August 1914. Lloyd Eugene Mangrum made four successive appearances in the Ryder Cup from 1947, captaining the team in 1953. He won the US Open in 1946 after a play-off with Byron Nelson and Vic Ghezzi, and was defeated by Hogan in a play-off for the title in 1950. He died in Apple Valley, California, 17 November 1973.

Marr, Dave   Born Houston, Texas, USA, 27 December 1933. Laurel Valley golf club in Pennsylvania was the setting for Marr's 1965 US PGA victory, when a four-under-par total of 280 gave him a two-shot victory over Billy Casper and Jack Nicklaus. In retirement Marr became a respected television commentator who worked for the BBC at the Open on many occasions.

Mayer, Dick   Born Stamford, Connecticut, USA, 29 August 1924. Mayer won the 1957 US Open after a play-off with Cary Middlecoff. Aware of Middlecoff's slow play, Mayer took out a camping stool, on which he sat as Middlecoff laboriously set himself up for shots.

Micheel, Shaun   Born Orlando, Florida, USA, 5 January 1969. Micheel turned professional in 1992 but with little success. After trying the Japanese tour he returned to the US tour, winning the 1998 Singapore Open and the 1999 Nike Greensboro Open. Despite these victories he ended the 2002 season ranked 105th on the US money list. However, 2003 was a better year and even before the US PGA Championship he had won $640,172. He came to the 72nd hole at Oakhill with a one-stroke lead over Chad Campbell and played his approach shot to within four inches of the pin for a simple birdie and a winning score of four under par, two shots clear of Campbell.

Mickelson, Phil   Born San Diego, California, USA, 16 June 1970. Turned pro in 1992 and within a year gained US PGA Tour wins in the Buick Open and The International. With 20 US PGA victories and a number two world ranking Mickelson had been dubbed 'the greatest player never to win a Major' by the start of the 2004 season. Victory in the Masters has thankfully made that epithet a distant memory.

Middlecoff, Cary   Born Halls, Tennessee, USA, 6 January 1921. Nicknamed 'Doc' because he was a qualified dentist, Middlecoff had 40 wins on the US tour including three majors. His most remarkable victory was the 1955 US Masters, when he obliterated the field with a seven-shot victory over runner-up Ben Hogan. He made three Ryder Cup appearances.

Miller, Johnny   Born San Francisco, California, USA, 29 April 1947. Miller's best years were the mid-1970s. In 1973 he won the US Open with an astonishing final round of 63. The following year he won eight events on the US tour, headed the money list and was PGA Player of the Year. In 1976 he won the Open Championship at Royal Birkdale and saw 19-year-old Spaniard by the name of Severiano Ballesteros come to the fore in a major championship.

Mize, Larry   Born Augusta, Georgia, USA, 23 September 1958. Mize's 1987 US Masters victory is famous for the 140ft chip which gave him victory over Greg Norman on the second hole of a sudden death play-off, Severiano Ballesteros having departed on the first hole. Mize is also an accomplished pianist.

Montgomerie, Colin   Born Glasgow, Scotland, 23 June 1963. One of the best players never to have won a major. Raised in Yorkshire where his father, James, was a company director. Montgomerie attended Houston Baptist University. His father retired as Royal Troon secretary in 1997. Colin lost out in a play-off for the 1994 US Open Championship and was runner-up again, this time to Ernie Els, in 1997. He was also defeated in sudden death by Steve Elkington for the US PGA title in 1995. Awarded the MBE in 1998, he won six times in 1999 to claim his seventh successive Volvo Order of Merit crown. Having won the Ericsson Masters at the start of 2001 to capture his first title Down Under, he claimed his first in Asia the following year. One week after sharing the 2002 Volvo Masters Andalucia with Bernhard Langer in the season-ending event at Valderrama – his 27th European title – he won the TCL Classic in China.

Moody, Orville   Born Chickasha, Oklahoma, USA, 9 December 1933. A part-Cherokee Indian, Moody was a staff sergeant in the army with 14 years experience behind him when he won the 1969 US Open. Scores of 71, 70, 68 and 72 gave him a 281 aggregate and a one-shot victory over Denne Beaman, Al Geiberger and Bob Rosburg.

Morris, 'Old' Tom   Born St Andrews, Fife, Scotland, 16 June 1821. 'Old' Tom is remembered as a true pioneer of golf. He was an accomplished champion, course designer and club-maker. In 1851, Morris moved to Prestwick as greenkeeper; the same year, his son, the great 'Young' Tom Morris, was born. He helped to set up the Open and finished second to Willie Park in the inaugural event of 1860. Morris competed in every Open until 1896 and was four times winner. He returned to St Andrews in 1865 as greenkeeper and later as professional. Morris was associated with St Andrews until his death on 24

May 1908, a few months after he sustained injuries falling down the stairs at the clubhouse. A measure of his popularity is that his funeral was attended by hundreds of admirers. In recognition of his service, the R&A has hung his portrait on permanent display in its clubhouse.

Morris, 'Young' Tom   Born St Andrews, Fife, Scotland, 20 April 1851. 'Young' Tom was a professional from the age of 13 in an era where amateurs were far more appreciated. In 1868, Morris won the first of four consecutive Opens aged just 17, and he remains the youngest winner in the history of the event. After winning his third Open 1870 and therefore taking the championship belt outright, the authorities suspended the event. The Open was not played in 1871 while they figured out a way of overcoming such unexpected domination of the championship. They decided to rotate it between three courses and to award the famous claret jug on a yearly basis as prize. Morris nevertheless won the Open yet again in 1872! The story of 'Young' Tom is ultimately a tragic one. His wife of one year was taken ill during childbirth and a telegram was dispatched to call Morris to her bedside. It was given to him as he came off the course at North Berwick. While he was in transit home, another telegram arrived with the grim news that she had died. Morris never recovered from the shock; he died a few months later on Christmas Day 1875.

Nagle, Kelvin   Born Sydney, Australia, 21 December 1920. Kel Nagle was 40 years old when he won his first major in 1960, taking the centenary championship at St Andrews. Five years later he lost a play-off to Gary Player for the US Open. In contrast, at the 1968 Alcan tournament in Britain in atrocious conditions, he carded a second-round score of 105!

Nelson, Byron   Born Fort Worth, Texas, USA, 4 February 1912. Only Snead, Hogan, Palmer and Nicklaus have won more US tour titles than Byron Nelson. In 1945 he won 19 tournaments including a streak of 11 consecutive wins. His five major wins included the 1945 US PGA title, when he beat Claude Harmon 5 & 4 in the semi-final and Sam Byrd 4 & 3 in the final. In 1965, aged 53, he had rounds of 70, 74, 72 and 74, good enough for 15th place in the US Masters. For many years he played the ceremonial opening nine holes of the US Masters.

Nelson, Larry   Born Fort Payne, Alabama, USA, 10 September 1947. Although Nelson won only ten tournaments on the regular US tour, three of these were majors. A veteran of the Vietnam War, he captured the US PGA title in 1981 at the Atlanta Athletic Club situated only a few minutes from his front door. He won the same title again in 1987 by defeating Lanny Wadkins in a sudden death play-off. He won the 1983 US Open at Oakmont, shooting 132 for the last 36 holes.

Nichols, Bobby   Born Louisville, Kentucky, USA, 14 April 1936. Nichols was a long hitter who suffered two significant injuries in his career. In 1952 a car crash left him with a broken pelvis and for a time he was paralysed from the waist down. In 1975 he was one of three golfers – the others were Lee Trevino and Jerry Heard – who were struck by lightning during the 1975 Western Open. He won the 1964 US PGA Championship in Columbus, Ohio, with a 271 aggregate.

Nicklaus, Jack   Born Columbus, Ohio, USA, 21 January 1940. Nicklaus is simply the most

GOLF

successful player of all time in major championship golf. He won three Open Championships, four US Opens, five US PGA titles and a phenomenal six US Masters Championships. Remarkably he also finished in the top three in majors on another 28 occasions. His total of 70 US tour wins is topped only by Sam Snead. Nicknamed 'The Golden Bear', he was famed for his fantastic driving ability from the tee, great long irons and a sure and steady putting action. Nicklaus won his first major when he defeated Arnold Palmer in a play-off over 18 holes for the 1962 US Open. He was the first player since Bobby Jones to hold the US Amateur and US Open titles at the same time. He won his sixth US Masters title at the age of 46. A Ryder Cup player on many occasions, he was captain of his country when they lost their first-ever match at home in the Ryder Cup in 1987, at his own Muirfield Village club.

Norman, Greg   Born Queensland, Australia, 10 February 1955. 'The Great White Shark' can count himself unfortunate to have won only two majors, despite a phenomenal career. He lost the 1986 US PGA Championship after Bob Tway sensationally holed a bunker shot on the 72nd hole (Norman had led every major that year at the start of the final round), lost the 1987 US Masters to an audacious chip by Larry Mize on a play-off hole, and in 1996 lost an 11-stroke swing in the final round of the US Masters to let in Nick Faldo to win. In addition to his defeat to Mize, he also lost play-offs in each of the other three majors. The undoubted world number one golfer for several years, Norman had a remarkable record of career wins in Europe, the USA and around the rest of the world. When winning the 1986 Open at Turnberry he had a 63 on the second day and at Royal St George's, Sandwich, in 1993, he set the lowest aggregate score in majors history, when his 64 in the last round gave him a two-shot victory over Nick Faldo.

North, Andy   Born Thorpe, USA, 9 March 1950. To win only three US tour titles indicates merely an average career, but when two of these victories were in the US Open, that career appears more substantial. That is Andy North's legacy. He won in 1978 at Cherry Hills, Denver, with a one-over-par aggregate of 285. His second win was in 1985 at Oakland Hills, Michigan, when his one-under-par aggregate left him champion, one shot in front of Dave Barr, Tze-Chung Chen and Denis Watson.

Olazabal, Jose Maria   Born Fuenterrabia, Spain, 5 February 1966. Two victories on the European tour in his first year and a second place in the Order of Merit in 1986 marked out Olazabal as a force to be reckoned with. He has certainly fulfilled that potential despite a serious foot injury that threatened to ruin his career and well-publicised problems using a driver from the tee. To date his two major successes have been in the US Masters. In 1994 a 69 in the final round gave him a two-shot victory over Tom Lehman. He played the last 54 holes in 11 under par. In 1999 his 280 aggregate, eight under par, was enough to prevail over Davis Love III by two shots.

O'Meara, Mark   Born Goldsboro, North Carolina, USA, 13 January 1957. A regular US tour player since 1981, O'Meara did not win a major until aged 41 when first he captured the US Masters title and then the Open championship at Royal Birkdale. In the Open O'Meara defeated US exile Brian Watts in a four-hole play-off.

Palmer, Arnold   Born Latrobe, Pennsylvania, USA, 10 September 1929. Many players have nicknames but only Arnold Daniel Palmer's followers had a special name, 'Arnie's Army'. His first professional win was the 1955 Canadian Open but soon majors were coming thick and fast. Between 1958 and 1964 he won seven majors, with only the US PGA title eluding him. His first major was the US Masters in 1958 when, by taking the $11,250 first prize, he became the first golfer to win a five-figure purse at the championship. In Britain he will be remembered for revitalising a waning Open championship by committing himself to the tournament in the early 1960s. In 1960 he was runner-up to Kel Nagle, and in 1961 and 1962 he was champion at Royal Birkdale and Troon respectively. Hordes of Americans subsequently made the journey across the Atlantic. His last major victory was in the 1964 US Masters, in which he led all the way to gain a six-shot victory. Arnie managed a top 30 finish in the Open in 1982 (he led for a while) and beat Neil Coles in the first-ever World Matchplay Championship at Wentworth in 1964.

Pate, Jerry   Born Macon, Georgia, USA, 16 September 1953. Winning the US Open at the age of 22 in 1976 (the youngest since Bobby Jones in 1923) promised to mark the beginning of a fantastic career for Jerry Pate. Sadly it did not work out and his victory at Atlanta Club in his home state of Georgia was to be his only major success. The crowd over the four days in 1976 numbered more than 100,000 for the first time.

Pavin, Corey   Born Oxnard, California, USA, 16 November 1959. Pavin has had a successful career despite being one of the shortest hitters on the US tour. His 1995 US Open victory is famed for a great four wood on the 72nd, from 220 yards, which ended 5ft from the hole, enabling him to pip Greg Norman to the title. He had a chance to win the 1993 Open at Royal St George's but his last-round 70 left him five shots behind Norman, this time the winner, in a tie for fourth place. He defeated Nick Faldo (1 up) to take the 1993 World Matchplay Championship.

Player, Gary   Born Johannesburg, South Africa, 1 November 1935. Along with Nicklaus and Palmer, Gary Player made up the famous 'Big Three' of golf in the 1960s. A terrific competitor with a magnificent short game, he is one of golf's greats. He first made the world aware of his prowess when in 1956 he finished fourth in the Open aged only 20. Two years later he finished runner-up at the US Open. In 1959 he won the first Open championship at Muirfield. His prize money was a paltry £1000. From then until 1978 he won a career total of nine majors. In 1965, he became the first overseas winner of the US Open since Ted Ray when he defeated Kel Nagle in an 18-hole play-off. By becoming champion he joined Gene Sarazen and Ben Hogan as only one of three players (at the time) to have won all four majors. His final major victory was in 1978 when a last round of 64 in the US Masters, including seven birdies in the last ten holes, set up his third Masters victory. He won five World Matchplay titles at Wentworth between 1965 and 1973. He is rated as one of the best bunker players the world has seen.

Price, Nick   Born Durban, South Africa, 28 January 1957. Runner-up in the Open Championship in 1982 and 1988, Nick Price had his first major win in 1992 when he captured the US PGA title; his 278 aggregate gave him a three-shot win over John Cook, Nick Faldo, Jim Gallagher jnr and Gene Sauers. He won the same title in 1994, which was also the year of his Open Championship victory at

Turnberry on the Ayrshire coast, when Jesper Parnevik bogeyed the last to lose by one shot. Price had a remarkable six victories on the US tour in 1994, the first time anyone had won so many since Tom Watson in 1980.

Rogers, Bill   Born Waco, Texas, USA, 10 September 1951. As an amateur Bill Rogers was a member of the 1973 US Walker Cup team and in 1979, as a virtual unknown, he defeated Isao Aoki in the final of the World Matchplay. However, 1981 was to be the pinnacle of his career. He was named Player of the Year, made his only Ryder Cup appearance and won the Open Championship at Royal St George's, Sandwich, by four shots from Bernhard Langer.

Rosburg, Bob   Born San Francisco, California, USA, 21 October 1926. Not a great striker of the ball and with one of the ugliest swings in the game, Rosburg was a great putter who gave the ball a wristy wrap. At the 1959 Pensacola Open he took only 19 putts in one round. His 1959 US PGA victory was his sole major, but he featured prominently in both the 1969 and 1971 US Opens and in 1972 won the Bob Hope Desert Classic.

Sarazen, Gene   Born Eugene Saraceni, New York, USA, 27 February 1902. Gene turned professional in 1920 and won seven major titles including the Open and US Open in the same year (1932). At this time he was the highest-paid sportsman in the world. Sarazen was a member of the American Ryder Cup team on six occasions. He regretted that he never captained the team, the authorities preferring Walter Hagen instead. As the twilight fell on his career in later years, he became a radio commentator. However, he continued to play golf all his life and recorded very good scores into his seventies. He died 13 May 1999, having teed off for the last time at that year's Masters aged 97.

Simpson, Scott   Born San Diego, California, USA, 17 September 1955. A former Walker Cup player, Simpson won the 1980 Western Open in his second year as a pro. In 1987 he took the US Open when birdies at 14, 15 and 16 on the final stretch gave him a one-shot victory over Tom Watson. He almost won a second US Open in 1991 but lost an 18-hole play-off to Payne Stewart.

Singh, Vijay   Born Lautoka, Fiji, 22 February 1963. One of golf's most determined and hardest-working players, Singh's first prominent victory was in the 1997 World Matchplay Championship when he defeated Ernie Els by one stroke. He won the US PGA title in 1998 with a one-over-par total of 271 and in 2000 clinched his first US Masters title. In 2003 he finished joint runner-up, with Thomas Bjorn, to Ben Curtis in the Open Championship at Royal St George's, Sandwich. Singh's third Major came in the 2004 US PGA after a three-hole playoff with Chris DiMarco and Justin Leonard.

Sluman, Jeff   Born Rochester, New York, USA, 11 September 1957. With a final-round 65, Sluman made up six shots on Paul Azinger to clinch the 1988 US PGA Championship at Oak Tree, Edmund, Oklahoma.

Snead, Sam   Born Hot Springs, Virginia, USA, 27 May 1912. Sam Snead's record of 81 victories on the US tour will take some beating. He won his first tournament in 1937 and in 1965 at the age of 52 took the Greensboro Open. In between he had seven major successes. He never won the US Open, although he lost a play-off to Lew Worsham in 1947. He won the first Open after World War II at St Andrews with a 290 aggregate, receiving the grand

sum of £150. His third US Masters victory in 1954 was achieved after an 18-hole play-off with his old adversary Ben Hogan. He made seven Ryder Cup appearances and in 1974, aged 62, finished third behind Nicklaus and Trevino at the US PGA Championship. He died 23 May 2002.

Sorenstam, Annika   Born Stockholm, Sweden, 9 October 1970. Annika made her debut as a full-time member of the LPGA Tour in February 1994. In 1995 she became US Open champion, finished second in the Open and in September, at the GHP Heartland Classic, blew away the field for a ten-stroke win. A week later at the World Championship of Women's Golf, she beat Laura Davies with a birdie in a play-off on the first extra hole. She topped the money lists for the US, European and Australian tours, a triple never before accomplished. In 1996 she won the US Open again by eight shots. Majors eluded her for a few years but in 2001 she posted a 59 during the second round of the Standard Register Ping in Arizona and followed up with the season's first major, the LPGA Nabisco Championship.

In 2002 she defended her title at the Kraft Nabisco Championship, capturing the fourth major of her career. Annika's 2002 performance of 13 wins in 25 events spurred her on to try her hand in a men's tournament. In the annual Fort Worth event, in May 2003, she made 71 and 74 to narrowly miss the cut but, playing off the men's tees, she showed just how good she was. In June 2003 she won the McDonald's LPGA Championship in her return to the women's circuit. Less than two months later she took the Women's British Open to finish off her career grand slam.

Stadler, Craig   Born San Diego, California, USA, 2 June 1953. Nicknamed 'The Walrus' and weighing over 108kg, Stadler has had an amazing career. His first US tour win was in 1976 but in 1982 he took the US Masters title, defeating Dan Pohl in a sudden death play-off. He continued to win his share of American tournaments and in 2003 joined the Seniors circuit, perceiving some rich pickings. In the space of a couple of weeks he was to win on both the regular and Seniors US tours.

Stockton, Dave   Born San Bernardino, California, USA, 2 November 1941. When he won the 1970 US PGA championship Stockton denied Arnold Palmer the chance to win each of the four majors (it was Palmer's third runner-up spot in the event). On a tough course the winner was the only player to finish under par. He proved his win was no fluke by repeating his victory in the tournament in 1976 at Congressional, Bethesda, Minnesota. A Ryder Cup player, he was also non-playing captain in 1991's 'The War on the Shore' at Kiawah Island.

Stewart, Payne   Born Springfield, Missouri, USA, 30 January 1957. With his distinct plus-fours and garish outfits, Payne Stewart was never going to go unnoticed on a golf course. At one time he was sponsored to wear colours of American football teams. Even without those colourful outfits his golf was good enough for people to stand and take note as his three major victories testify. He was runner-up to both Sandy Lyle (1985) and Nick Faldo (1990) at the Open Championship. In 1989 he was the victor at the US PGA by one shot and 1991 saw him clinch the US Open when he beat Scott Simpson in a play-off. He won his second US Open at Pinehurst, North Carolina, as a 42-year-old in 1999. Two months later (25 October 1999) he was to die in a tragic, bizarre flying accident.

Strange, Curtis Born Norfolk, Virginia, USA, 30 January 1955. When he won his second US Open in 1989 Curtis Strange became the first golfer since Ben Hogan to retain the title. He first won the title in an 18-hole play-off against Nick Faldo at Brookline, Massachusetts, his play-off score of 71 beating Faldo by four shots. His one-shot victory over Chip Beck, Mark McCumber and Ian Woosnam in 1989 saw a series of freak shots at the 167yds (152m) 6th hole where, within a few hours during round two, Doug Weaver, Mark Wiebe, Jerry Pate and Nick Price all scored holes-in-one. Strange was captain of the 2002 US Ryder Cup team. He has an identical twin brother, Allen, who was at one time a US tour regular.

Sutton, Hal Born Shreveport, California, USA, 28 April 1958. Sutton has been nicknamed 'Halimony', because of the number of times he has been married. After two Walker Cup appearances he turned pro in 1981 and two years later captured the US PGA title, his only major win. His six-figure dollar victory cheque was the first in golf history in a major. He also won the Tournament Players Championship in 1983, repeating that success 17 years later, after he had played a significant part in America's 2000 Ryder Cup win. He will captain the 2004 Ryder Cup team.

Thomson, Peter Born Melbourne, Australia, 23 August 1929. Thomson's forte was the Open championship and from 1952 to 1958 he was never out of the top two, with a hat-trick of wins from 1954. His fifth and last victory in the Open in 1965 at Royal Birkdale (returning to the scene of his first Open victory in 1954), silenced critics who said his wins in the 1950s were devalued because of the poor American attendance. Furthermore, on reaching 53 he decided to try his luck on the US Seniors circuit and in 1985 he won nine times and topped their money list.

Toms, David Born Monroe, Louisiana, USA, 4 January 1967. In 2001 David Toms had his best season on the US Tour when his three tour victories were second only to Tiger Woods' five. He also had nine top-ten finishes and captured the US PGA title, after a tremendous battle with Phil Mickelson in the last round, to finish third place on the money list. In round three Toms scored a hole-in-one on the par three 15th hole.

Trevino, Lee Born Dallas, Texas, USA, 1 December 1939. With six major championship victories, 'Supermex' sits among the golfing greats. Born into an impoverished family, he was brought up by his mother Juanita and his grandfather, neither of whom could read or write. He has an unorthodox 'out-to-in' swing and a hooker's grip but is possessed of great touch and feel around the greens. He won his first major in 1968 when he took the US Open and in so doing became the first man in history to win any major with all four rounds under par and below 70. In 1971, in the space of a few months he won the US Open, Open Championship and Canadian Open. A year later he retained his Open Championship at Muirfield, famously chipping in on the 71st hole after missing the green with his fourth shot, to deny Jack Nicklaus and Tony Jacklin. In 1984 he won his last major at the age of 44 and took $125,000 prize money for victory in the US PGA championship. All of his four rounds were in the 60s. Trevino played in every Ryder Cup from 1969 to 1981 except 1977. He was non-playing captain in 1985 when Europe won 16½-11½ at The Belfry.

Turnesa, James Born Elmsford, New York, USA, 1912. Jim Turnesa was one of seven golfing brothers, two of whom, Joe and Mike, finished runners-up in majors. Jim finally won a major for the family by capturing the 1952 US PGA title when he beat Chick Harbert in the final at Big Spring, Louisville, Kentucky.

Tway, Bob Born Edmond, Oklahoma, USA, 4 May 1959. Tway won the 1986 US PGA title by two shots from Greg Norman after the latter had squandered a four shot lead after 54 holes. Tway's chip-in from a bunker on the 72nd hole at the Inverness Club, Toledo, Ohio, gave him a six-under-par aggregate 276. In the 1994 Memorial, Tway scored two holes-in-one in the same tournament.

Vardon, Harry Born Grouville, Jersey, 9 May 1870. Vardon's rise to the top was progressive rather than instant. In 1896, he beat J.H. Taylor and later that year won his first Open. Not only was he the first Englishman to win the event, he would go on to record an unbeaten six victories. He also beat Taylor to win the US Open in 1900. He did not invent the overlapping grip which bears his name but certainly popularised it. J. Laidley used it before Vardon to win the Amateur Championship. Vardon's strength was in the power and accuracy of his swing. However a bout of tuberculosis in 1903 permanently affected his health. His illness manifested itself on the course when the club head would shake in an erratic manner whilst putting. Despite this, he did go on to win the Open for the sixth time in 1914 and indeed was second in the 1920 US Open to Ted Ray. On both the European and US PGA Tours, the Vardon Trophy is awarded annually to the professional with the lowest stroke average. He died 20 March 1937.

Venturi, Ken Born San Francisco, California, USA, 15 May 1931. A last-round 80 robbed Ken Venturi of victory in the 1956 US Masters while still an amateur, losing out to Jack Burke jnr by one shot. He was to finish runner-up in the 1960 US Masters thanks to Palmer's birdie-birdie finish, but made amends by taking the 1964 US Open when his 278 aggregate score gave him a two-shot victory over Tommy Jacobs.

Vicenzo, Roberto de Born Buenos Aires, Argentina, 14 April 1923. De Vicenzo was a magnificent striker of a golf ball who won over 200 tournaments worldwide, including 100 significant titles. Had his putting been better he would surely have added to his lone major victory, the 1967 Open at Hoylake (Royal Liverpool); at 44 years of age, he was the oldest 20th-century winner of the championship. He would have won the 1968 Masters but on the last day inadvertently signed a score card that his playing partner Tommy Aaron had filled in incorrectly. The score of four written down by Aaron instead of the three De Vincenzo had made at the 17th gave Goalby the title by one shot.

Wadkins, Lanny Born Richmond, Virginia, USA, 5 December 1949. Ability-wise Lanny Wadkins should have won more than his lone major trophy, the 1977 US PGA title. A winner of over 20 titles on the US tour, he finally laid his majors ghost when he defeated Gene Littler in a sudden-death play-off. He was non-playing captain of the 1995 US Ryder Cup team.

Wall, Art jnr Born Homesdale, Pennsylvania, USA, 23 November 1923. By scoring a superb 66 in round four of the 1959 US Masters, Art Wall edged out Cary Middlecoff to win his only major. At the age of 51 he won the Greater Milwaukee Open, nine years after his previous tour victory. He also claims the world record for holes-in-one, an astonishing 42.

Watson, Tom Born Kansas City, Missouri, USA, 4 September 1949. Watson was the world's number one golfer in the late 1970s and early 1980s, as his eight major victories in that period indicate. His favourite major was the Open Championship which he won five times, but he was not to win in England until his last victory at Royal Birkdale in 1983, having won his previous four in Scotland. An unforgettable battle with Jack Nicklaus at Turnberry in 1977 was won by Watson when they finished respectively 11 and 10 shots in front of third-placed Hubert Green. After a contest dubbed 'The Duel in the Sun', Green was later to say, 'I won the 1977 at Turnberry – the other two (Watson and Nicklaus) were playing a different game to the rest of the field.' In 1993 he was non-playing captain of the American team that triumphed 15-13 in the Ryder Cup at the Belfry. The only major Watson failed to win was the US PGA championship. His final major victory on American soil was the 1981 US Masters, his eight-under-par total giving him a two-shot victory over Johnny Miller and Jack Nicklaus. He is still playing well in majors and has earned big money on the Seniors circuit.

Weir, Bob Born Sarnia, Ontario, Canada, 12 May 1970. Weir's 2003 victory in the US Masters made him, after Bob Charles, only the second left-hander to win a major title. In doing so he recorded just the fourth bogey-free final round by a winner in the 67-year history of the Masters, and the first since Doug Ford in 1957. When he defeated Len Mattiace on the first play-off hole, he also became the first Canadian to win a major.

Weiskopf, Tom Born Massillon, Ohio, USA, 9 November 1942. At 1.93m, Tom Weiskopf was nicknamed 'The Towering Inferno' because of his habit of losing his temper on the golf course. However, there is no doubting the fact that he had one of the greatest swings the game has known. His talent was such that he should have won more than his solitary major, the Open at Royal Troon in 1973.

Westwood, Lee Born Worksop, Notts, England, 24 April 1973. Westwood rounded off 2000 by securing his first Volvo Order of Merit crown, so ending Colin Montgomerie's seven-year tenure at the top. In the process he edged his close friend and stablemate, Darren Clarke, into second place after a dramatic race which went down to the wire. In January of that year Westwood won the Dimension Data Pro-Am tournament (partnering his father) in South Africa to give him a victory in every continent, before going on to emulate the feats of Seve Ballesteros, Nick Faldo and Montgomerie by winning six times in Europe. He had broken through in America in 1998 by taking the Freeport McDermott Classic. Lee married Laura Coltart, sister of fellow Ryder Cup player Andrew, in January 1999. His pairing with Sergio Garcia in the 34th Ryder Cup in 2002 claimed three points out of four. Lee scored his first hole-in-one in professional play during the Damova British Masters on 6 June 2003.

Woods, Tiger Born Eldrick Woods, Cypress, California, USA, 30 December 1975. Born to an Afro-American father and a Thai mother, Woods started playing golf at the age of five. At the age of 15 he won his first US Junior Amateur title and went on to win three in a row. He then stepped up to the full US Amateur Championship and again won three in a row. Woods has a delicate touch around the greens, is a dedicated professional and a tremendously long driver. He dominated the amateur game and has dominated the professional game to date. He was the first player to win four consecutive majors – the 2000 Open, 2000 US Open, 2000 US PGA and 2001 US Masters. Along with Lee Trevino he is one of only two players in history to win the Open, US Open and Canadian Open in the same season, and is only the fifth player in history to win all four majors, joining Gene Sarazen, Ben Hogan, Gary Player and Jack Nicklaus. The youngest player to win a career grand slam (24 years 7 months), surpassing Nicklaus (26 years 6 months), when winning the Open in 2000 he joined Greg Norman (1993) and Nick Price (1994) as the only Open champions to shoot all four rounds in the 60s. When he won the 1997 US Masters he tore apart the record books by becoming the youngest champion and recording the lowest aggregate total – only 270.

Woosnam, Ian Born Oswestry, Shropshire, England, 2 March 1958. Ian Woosnam is without doubt the best Welsh player to take up golf and can rightly claim to be one of Europe's best ever. A regular tour winner, some of his successes include the European Open (1988), the Scottish Open (1987 and 1990) and the Irish Open (1988 and 1989). However, his big year was 1991 when he won the US Masters, clinching victory on the 72nd hole with a five-foot par putt to beat Jose-Maria Olazabal by one shot. In 1987 he became the first British player to win the World Matchplay Championship and he again won the championship in 1990 and 2001. In 2001 he had a great chance to win the Open Championship, but, by mistake, was found to be carrying 15 clubs in his bag at the start of his fourth round.

Worsham, Lewis Elmer Born Alta Vista, Virginia, USA, 1917. Sam Snead never won the US Open but had a great chance in 1947 after tying with Lew Worsham after 72 holes. Worsham, however, won the 18-hole play-off in controversial circumstances. He asked for a measure after Snead had addressed his 2½ft putt. The measure still meant that Snead was first to putt. He missed, and Worsham made his putt to win. He later became a renowned teacher.

Zaharias, Babe Didrikson see entry in Athletics section

Zoeller, Fuzzy Born Frank Urban Zoeller, New Albany, Indiana, USA, 11 November 1951. A great talent with a fine record, Zoeller could have achieved even greater success with a more single-minded approach to the game. As it is he won two majors, the first being the 1979 US Masters when he defeated Tom Watson and Ed Sneed at the third hole of a sudden death play-off. In the 1984 US Open at Winged Foot, Mamaroneck, New York, he defeated Greg Norman by eight shots in an 18-hole play-off.

GOLF

GREYHOUND RACING

Greyhounds can be traced back to ancient Egypt and are the only breed of dog to be mentioned in the Bible (Proverbs 30:31). They have been much revered throughout history; it is documented that the Greek conqueror, Alexander the Great (356-323BC) of Macedon, owned a greyhound bitch named Peritas. In Britain, for hundreds of years, it was a crime for a peasant to own such an animal – a greyhound was solely the property of the aristocracy.

The first greyhound race run after an artificial hare took place at the Welsh Harp, Hendon, in 1876. In fact this was a more humane form of coursing, the races being held over a straight track of 400yds. Racing on a circular track was patented in America in 1890 although Owen Smith did not demonstrate the sport until 1919 at Emeryville, California, having perfected the operation of the mechanical hare. The first organised meeting took place in Oklahoma in 1923 and the first established track opened at St Petersburg, Florida, in 1925.

Greyhound racing in its present form started at Belle Vue, Manchester, in 1926, and is governed by the National Greyhound Racing Club (NGRC, founded 1928). Races were originally run on grass but following the American lead the tracks are now made from a special sand-based substance manufactured in Leighton Buzzard. Circuits vary in distance but are generally in the region of 400m. The Derby is now run over a distance of 480m.

The British Greyhound Racing Board (BGRB) is an independent body responsible for the promotion of greyhound racing in the UK. All rule changes, licence and registration issues must be discussed with the board.

Greyhound racing was a massive spectator sport in the first half of the 20th century and crowds of 30,000 were commonplace at the White City. The legalisation of betting shops in 1961 created a decline in attendances, although there has been an upward trend in recent years and crowds are gradually returning to a sport which offers betting opportunities via an ever-increasing number of races.

Famous Greyhounds

Ballyregan Bob Sired by Ballyheigue Moon. Raced between August 1984 and December 1986. In a career that began with four successive defeats, Bob's overall record of 42 wins from 48 races looks all the better. He did not win a classic but surely would have won the Leger if injury had not forced him out of that competition. In total he scored at 11 different tracks, breaking 16 track records and winning a world record 32 consecutive races.

Trainer George Curtis described Ballyregan Bob as 'the perfect racing machine'. After four unlucky defeats, on 25 October 1984 Bob came from off the pace to finally win his first race in Britain. Rattling off another seven straight wins to finish the year, he had arrived in spectacular style and his seasonal debut the following year was eagerly awaited. On 15 April 1985 a battering at the traps saw his chance gone in a race at Wembley, yet that was the last time Ballyregan Bob was to see the rear of another greyhound at the finish line. Having been beaten in that race, however, he then began to establish his impressive record. His crowning glory came at Hove on 9 December 1986 when he raced for the last time and for the new world record.

Entry Badge Sired by Jamie. A handsome brindle weighing 69lb (31.3kg) when he won the first-ever Greyhound Derby, Entry Badge was the sire of Mutton Cutlet and the first important sire of racing greyhounds. He was one of three dogs and a bitch born to Beaded Nora in January 1926, the year track racing began in Britain. One of the fastest-ever from the traps, in addition he possessed intelligence on a par with that of Mick The Miller, moving to the rails whenever there was the slightest opportunity in order to steer clear of first-bend crowding. Entered

for the first Derby, at White City on 15 October 1927, he won the final by six and a half lengths, one of the biggest margins ever at that time, having set off at the shortest odds to that date of 1-4. He had started from trap 5 and not until Daw's Dancer won in 1953 was a dog again successful from this trap. Entry Badge raced for the best part of two years and was beaten only once. In all he won 11 out of 12 races, all in top class, and was odds-on favourite in every race he ran. He generally won by three lengths or more and in very fast times, and thus can truly be classed as one of the all-time greats of the sport.

Mick The Miller Sired by Glorious Event. Raced between April 1928 and October 1931. Undoubtedly the best-known greyhound of all time, Mick The Miller's 15 victories from 20 races in his native Ireland were supplemented by a further 46 wins and 10 second places in England and Wales. He won the Derby twice, plus a St Leger, a Cesarewitch and a Welsh Derby. Mick broke five track records and won 19 races in a row. He became a film star and, until recently, stood embalmed at the Natural History Museum before being moved to the museum at Tring, Hertfordshire, where he still takes pride of place. Bred by Father Martin Brophy, a parish priest in Ireland, and named after Mick Miller, the odd-job man at the vicarage, he was one of a litter of 12 and lived the usual life of a young greyhound until he was struck down by distemper, a highly contagious viral disease which primarily affects dogs. There were no vaccines in the 1920s and his career was in jeopardy for some time; it was not until April 1928 that the then two-year-old made his racing debut. He won with ease and went on to compete in a total of 20 races in Ireland. Trainer Mick Horan and Father

Brophy brought Mick The Miller to England in May 1929. His first trial at White City was a sensation and he was duly sold for 800 guineas to a London bookmaker, the sale making the evening papers. He drew a huge audience for his first race, the first round of the 1929 Derby, and not only did he win, he smashed through the previously unachievable 30-second barrier for the 525yds distance at White City. Flying through the second round and semi-finals with impressive success, he was naturally hot favourite for the final. In fact, he was beaten into second by Palatinus but a no-race was declared. He found his best form again in the re-run just half an hour later and this time beat Palatinus by three lengths in 29.96secs. The dog took up residence at the kennels of Sidney Orton, who was based at Wimbledon.

In 1930 Mick The Miller enjoyed another vintage year, winning countless races and taking the Derby again, going through the event, as he had the previous year, with an unblemished record. A hectic schedule followed with unbeaten runs through the Cesarewitch at West Ham and the Welsh Derby at Cardiff in July. So much racing eventually took its toll and he was eliminated in the first round of the Laurels at Wimbledon. Mick The Miller was not seen in action again until the spring of 1931 when he went unbeaten through the Spring Cup at Wembley. He was then lightly raced in preparation for his third Derby attempt. His passage to the final was not impressive but on the big night, he ran the race of his life to land his third successive Derby. But the title was cruelly taken away from him once more with another no-race decision. The re-run was held less than an hour after the first race and he was soundly beaten into fourth by Seldom Led, who had finished last in the original final. It was the twilight of Mick The Miller's career on the track but he still had a treat to serve up. Well over five years old, he was entered for the 1931 St Leger at Wembley and duly went through the event unbeaten.

Patricia's Hope For any greyhound to win a Derby is exceptional; to win three in the same year is almost unprecedented. Patricia's Hope, though, was that exception, a greyhound blessed with remarkable all-round pace and craft. Trained by Adam Jackson, he embarked on his British career at the end of 1971 where he won at the first time of asking at Clapton. He duly reached the 1972 English Derby final but was considered something of a no-hoper after a couple of defeats in the event and was sent off at 7-1 to clinch the sport's greatest prize. Super Rory, who had set a new world speed record in the semi-finals, was the warm favourite but nothing else had a chance as Patricia's Hope blasted clear from the traps and into what was to prove an unassailable lead. His next target was the Welsh Derby at Cardiff, which he went through unbeaten, and then on to Shawfield for the Scottish Derby where he was again to face Super Rory, once more favourite in the final. This time Patricia's Hope did not make the break and was crowded early. However, he was nothing if not a battler and he gradually clawed his way back into the race to beat Priory Hi and his rival Super Rory in a thrilling finish that saw barely a length and a half covering them.

Winning three classics was a fantastic achievement but the gruelling schedule had taken its toll and the decision to retire him to stud was made in November 1972 but connections still had tremendous faith in their star and were keen to emulate Mick The Miller by twice winning the English Derby. Now trained by Jim O'Connor, in the 1973 race, one of the most exciting spectacles ever seen on a greyhound track. Patricia's Hope was away like a shot but favourite Say Little was ominously close, as were Black Banjo and a bitch named Softly. In a pulsating finish, Patricia's Hope refused to yield and scraped home. His double Derby success ensures Patricia's Hope his place in the greyhound Hall of Fame.

Pigalle Wonder Sired by Champion Prince out of the famous dam Prairie Peg. Pigalle Wonder was whelped in March 1956. A brindle dog, he was bred and reared in Co. Kilkenny, Ireland, by Tom Murphy, who originally named him Prairie Champion. He ran his first race at Kilkenny in a heat for the famous McCalmont Cup on 10 October 1957, winning by ten lengths in 29.80secs; he went on to win the final, showing just how good he was at only 18 months of age. A law unto himself, handsome, with great track craft and electric speed from the traps, he never knew when he was beaten. All tracks came alike to him and he set new records wherever he ran.

Having been placed with trainer Jim Syder jnr at Wembley, Pigalle Wonder's first big event was the 1958 Derby. He won his second round heat and semi-final (in which he set the track record) and went on to take the final by three lengths. His next contest was the Pall Mall at Haringey, which he also won comfortably. Showing himself outstanding over middle distances, Pigalle Wonder was to end a wonderful year by dead-heating for the Cesarewitch. That year he set new records on every track he raced. His last race was at Shelbourne Park on 13 August 1960 in the final of the Irish Derby. Having reached the final by coming second to Perry's Apple in his semi-final, he was again beaten by the same greyhound after running into trouble at the first bend. His longer-term career, though, was only just beginning; he spent nearly ten years at stud, during which time his influence on modern greyhound racing was to prove considerable.

Quare Times Quare Times, weighing in at 67lb (30.4kg), was in the 1940s one of the fastest greyhounds ever to race at any track and the first to break 29secs over 525yds in a race (though Bahs Choice had done so previously in a trial at White City). By Ballydancer, an Irish 550yds national record holder, out of the dam Quite Welcome, and whelped in 1944, he first came to prominence when finishing second to Shaggy Lad in the 1945 Irish Puppy Derby. Owned, bred and trained by Mr and Mrs Quinn of Killenaule, Co. Tipperary, Ireland, Quare Times was the fastest since Mr Quinn's star of earlier days, Brilliant Bob, but his early races set the pattern for his whole career. He had amazing speed but his track craft left a lot to be desired and led to an inconsistency that prevented true greatness. In the final of the 1946 Easter Cup at Shelbourne Park he was second to the bitch Astra, having previously beaten her in the second round by six lengths. Coming to England in May 1946 after his Easter Cup disappointment, Quare Times was placed with Sidney Orton at Wimbledon and entered for the Derby. It was in heat four of the second round that he clocked a new world record time of 28.95secs. At White City, in an England v Ireland match against Bahs Choice on Bank Holiday Monday, run over 550yds, Quare Times was the winner by three and a half lengths in the world's fastest time for the distance of 30.38secs. Quare Times was undoubtedly the fastest dog of his generation but, rather like the recently retired Top Savings, he will always be regarded as an under-achiever through lack of major competition wins.

Scurlogue Champ Sired by Sand Man. Raced between July 1984 and August 1986. With 51 wins from 63 races, this phenomenal marathon runner would tail himself off for a circuit and then cut through the field like a hot knife through butter. It wasn't so much that the black dog increased his speed at the finish, more that he maintained a pace while others tired. At one stage he won 16 consecutive races, while classic victory came in the Cesarewitch at Belle Vue. Scurlogue Champ started life on a farm in Co. Wexford. Bred by Francis Kent from Levittstown, he was one of a litter of six dogs and two bitches. Trainer Ken Peckham flew to Dublin at the beginning of May 1984 where he saw Scurlogue Champ win his sales trial. Peckham thrashed out a deal with his Irish trainer and the Champ was on his way back to England for the start of one of greyhound racing's most remarkable careers. The newcomer was soon busy trialling at Peterborough and Walthamstow before making his debut at White City. Scurlogue Champ duly won. Remarkably, he started favourite in 60 of his 63 races and, in the process, set 20 new track records at the 23 tracks where he raced, over distances ranging from 663m at Hall Green to 888m at Catford.

Some Picture Sired by Slaneyside Hare. The ultimate that can be achieved by any greyhound in modern-day racing is the 'triple crown' of the Scottish, English and Irish Derbies. Some Picture was within a whisker of becoming one of the most celebrated greyhounds ever, had he not struggled with illness in the Irish race. Trained by Charlie Lister, he first came to prominence at the end of 1996 when winning the Eclipse at Nottingham in superb style. That success was enough to gain him an invitation to the Select Stakes and he hacked up. The following year Some Picture confirmed himself as one of the outstanding greyhounds of the 1990s. The Regal Scottish Derby seemed a natural for this gloriously gifted animal. He breezed through the competition with hardly a blemish and was equally impressive in winning the English Derby. Installed as one of the favourites for the Irish Derby.

Trev's Perfection Sired by Trev's Despatch. A handsome brindle, he was whelped in April 1944 out of a Beef Cutlet bitch. Named Friar Tuck, he was bred and reared in Cumberland by Mr H.G. Nunn, who renamed him Highland Perfection and from whom he was purchased, when ready to race, by Nora Roth. During 1946 he won a batch of open races but later that year, he went down with distemper and pneumonia. After a patient convalescence, he made it back to the track and reached the final of the Wandsworth Spring Stakes. Purchased by Fred Trevillion, a haulage contractor from Dartford, and after another name change, Trev's Perfection's first big race was on 22 March 1947 at White City when he beat Parish Model by one and a half lengths. He was next at Walthamstow for the Circuit, which he won in 28.80secs. Then, early in June 1947, he contested the Gold Collar at Catford. After winning his heat, he was beaten by Monday's News in his semi, the winner setting a new track record, but Trev's Perfection gained revenge in the final. At White City for the Derby, he produced devastating form. He won his heat very impressively by five lengths from Mad Midnight in 29.50secs and his semi by three lengths from Slaney Record in 29.30secs, to qualify for a final in which he was the only English-bred greyhound. This, too, he won by two lengths to show at last his true ability; it was the first time 29secs had been broken in the Derby final. It was also the first time the Derby had been won from trap 2. The following week Trev's Perfection travelled to Glasgow for the Scottish Derby and duly won. He then created history by winning the Welsh Derby the following week to establish a remarkable Triple Crown.

On 1 April 1948 Trevillion and his head kennel-man Arthur Hancock left with Trev's Perfection for the USA. But the dog was a comparative failure and in five races did not win one. Trev's Perfection must nevertheless be regarded as one of the most remarkable dogs of all time.

Westpark Mustard Sired by Newdown Heather. It was in 1974 that Westpark Mustard set the then record winning sequence of 20 consecutive victories to beat Mick The Miller's long-standing record and therefore carve herself a special niche in the history books. Trained by Tommy Johnston at Wembley, her remarkable sequence was achieved in the space of ten months, a period including four months off the course in the middle of that season. All Westpark Mustard's wins were recorded in open races. Her run began in a four-bend event at Wemble and she had amassed an impressive 15 victories by the time she broke down at the beginning of May. Connections were in no rush to bring her back from season but, when she did return, she duly completed the record.

Grand National Winners

	Venue	Distance	Winner	Breeding	Trainer and Training Base	Winning Time	Starting Price
1927	White City	500yds	Bonzo	Bon Marche-Bertha	J. Buck, Belle Vue	31.42	13-8F
1928	White City	525yds	Cormorant	Stormont-Ballyveney Maid	S. Probert, Wembley	31.16	4-1
1929	White City	525yds	Levator	Spalding Bishop-Lisgreen	M. Burls, Wembley	31.09	2-1
1930	White City	525yds	Stylish Cutlet	Mutton Cutlet-Style Kid	J.T. Hutchinson, Wimbledon	30.94	11-4
1931	White City	525yds	Rule The Roost	Jamie-Road Head Rally	J. Harmon, White City	31.17	5-2
1932	White City	525yds	Long Hop	Macoma-Bright Emblem	I. McCorkindale, Harringay	31.44	3-1
1933	White City	525yds	Scapegoat	Macoma-Bright Emblem	A. Jonas, White City	31.20	6-1
1934	White City	525yds	Lemonition	Golden Splendour-Green Gown	D. Costello, Wimbledon	30.84	11-4
1935	White City	525yds	Quarter Cross	Open Steak-For Ever	S. Probert, Wembley	30.76	7-2
1936	White City	525yds	Kilganny Bridge	Red Cloud-Killemalla	P.J. Higgins, Clapton	30.70	3-1
1937	White City	525yds	Flying Wedge	Beginner-Brannock Queen	S. Biss, West Ham	30.61	EvsF
1938	White City	525yds	Juvenile Classic	Beef Cutlet-Lady Eleanor	J. Harmon, Wimbledon	30.35	2-1
1939	White City	525yds	Valiant Bob	Valiant Cutlet-Winged Maiden	P. Fortune, Wimbledon	30.50	8-1
1940	White City	525yds	Juvenile Classic	Beef Cutlet-Lady Eleanor	J. Harmon, Wimbledon	30.23	EvsF
1941-45 not held							

Year	Venue	Distance	Winner	Breeding	Trainer and Training Base	Winning Time	Starting Price
1946	White City	525yds	Barry From Limerick	Cherry Grove Cross-Connor May	E. Davidson, unattached	30.61	2-1
1947	White City	525yds	Baytown Pigeon	Manhattan Midnight-Little Nettle	P. McEllistrim, Wimbledon	30.67	25-1
1948	White City	525yds	Jove's Reason	Mooncoin Fiddler-Anxious Mate	K. Appleton, West Ham	30.37	2-1
1949	White City	525yds	Blossom Of Annagura	Speedy Dancer-Orchard Blossom	J. Sherry, Ramsgate	30.20	8-1
1950	White City	525yds	Blossom Of Annagura	Speedy Dancer-Orchard Blossom	J. Sherry, Ramsgate	29.97	5-2
1951	White City	525yds	XPDNC	Bella's Prince-Here Comes Eliza	L. Parry, White City	29.80	11-4JF
1952	White City	525yds	Whistling Laddie	Lone Seal-Whistling Rum	S. Martin, Wimbledon	30.13	20-1
1953	White City	525yds	Denver Berwick	Humming Bee-Baytown Fir	D. Geggus, Walthamstow	30.26	10-11F
1954	White City	525yds	Prince Lawrence	Dangerous Prince-Knight's Romance	J. Pickering, White City	30.29	10-1
1955	White City	525yds	Barrowside	Ballymac Ball-Nifty Bella	H. Harvey, Wembley	29.43	1-3F
1956	White City	525yds	Blue Sand	Sandown Champion-Fast And Beautiful	K. Appleton, West Ham	29.70	15-8F
1957	White City	525yds	Tanyard Tulip	Despot O'Leer-Knockeevan Tulip	H. Harvey, Wembley	29.85	2-1
1958	White City	525yds	Fodda Champion	Champion Prince-Wimble Lady	J. Jowett, Clapton	30.20	7-4F
1959	White City	525yds	Prince Poppit	Champion Prince-Greenane Darkie	D. Hannafin, Wimbledon	30.10	3-1
1960	White City	525yds	Bruff Chariot	Cheerful Chariot-Really Bold	J. Jowett, Clapton	29.50	EvsF
1961	White City	525yds	Ballinatona Special	Superman-Orange Queen	S. Martin, Wimbledon	29.50	6-4F
1962	White City	525yds	Corsican Reward	Solar Prince-Rose Confection	G. Hodson, unattached	30.15	9-4F
1963	White City	525yds	Indoor Sport	Champion Prince-Yoblstrap	B. O'Connor, Walthamstow	29.98	4-5F
1964	White City	525yds	Two Aces	Crazy Parachute-Penicola	J. Rimmer, Wembley	30.42	10-11F
1965	White City	525yds	I'm Crazy	Crazy Parachute-Misfortunate	R. Singleton, White City	29.60	11-4
1966	White City	525yds	Halfpenny King	Crazy Parachute-The Baw Wee	J. Shevlin, New Cross	30.28	7-2
1967	White City	525yds	The Grange Santa	The Grand Prince-Grange Delienne	N. Gleeson, Wimbledon	29.72	9-4F
1968	White City	525yds	Ballintore Tiger	Prairie Flash-Not Landing	N. Chambers, New Cross	29.50	1-3F
1969	White City	525yds	Tony's Friend	Prairie Flash-Maggie from Cork	R. Singleton, White City	30.16	EvsF
1970	White City	525yds	Sherry's Prince	Mad Era-Nevasca	J. Shevlin, West Ham	30.02	4-6F
1971	White City	525yds	Sherry's Prince	Mad Era-Nevasca	C. West, West Ham	29.22	1-3F
1972	White City	525yds	Sherry's Prince	Mad Era-Nevasca	C. West, White City	29.80	5-4F
1973	White City	525yds	Killone Flash	Forward Flash-Dancing Barrier	R. Singleton, White City	29.35	5-2
1974	White City	525yds	Shanney's Darkie	Monalee Champion-Shanney's Jet	C. West, White City	29.43	10-1
1975	White City	500yds	Pier Hero	Tender Hero-Helena's Girl	F. Melville, Harringay	30.65	EvsF
1976	White City	500yds	Weston Pete	Monalee Champion-New Kashmir	C. West, White City	30.60	4-5F
1977	White City	500yds	Salerno	Clerihan Venture-Fish Pond	J. Coleman, Wembley	30.43	5-4F
1978	White City	500yds	Topothetide	Westpark Mint-Lady In Love	T. Forster, Harringay	30.23	8-11F
1979	White City	500yds	Topothetide	Westpark Mint-Lady In Love	T. Lanceman, Southend	31.60	6-4F
1980	White City	500yds	Gilt Edge Flyer	Monalee Expert-Proud Secretary	E. Pateman, unattached	30.22	4-5F
1981	White City	500yds	Bobcol	Westpark Mint-Black Katty	N. McEllistrim, Wimbledon	30.64	1-2F
1982	White City	500yds	Face The Mutt	Mutt's Silver-Mill Road Cast	N. McEllistrim, Wimbledon	30.71	11-10F
1983	White City	500yds	Sir Winston	Myrtown-King's Comet	G. Curtis, Hove	31.09	5-1
1984	White City	500yds	Kilcoe Foxy	Hume Highway-Aghadown Liz	G. Curtis, Hove	30.32	4-5F
1985	Hall Green	474m	Seaman's Star	Hume Highway-Sleepy Nell	A.E. Boyce, Catford	30.08	14-1
1986	Hall Green	474m	Castlelyons Cash	Belvedere Bran-Kick On Susie	D. Luckhurst, unattached	29.51	5-4F
1987	Hall Green	474m	Cavan Town	Sail On Il-Leafy Glade	M. Cumner, Maidstone	30.01	4-1
1988	Hall Green	474m	Breeks Rocket	Noble Brigg-Sandville Lady	D. Luckhurst, Crayford	30.09	5-1
1989	Hall Green	474m	Lemon Chip	Sinbad-Lemon Lisa	P. Rees, Wimbledon	29.84	EvsF
1990	Hall Green	474m	Gizmo Pasha	Whisper Wishes-If And When	L. Mullins, Romford	29.62	4-6F
1991	Hall Green	474m	Ballycarney Dell	Track Man-Ballycarney Blue	A. Gifkins, Yarmouth	29.81	14-1
			dead heat Ideal Man	Clayderman-Ideal Honeygar	J McGee, Peterborough	29.81	3-1JF
1992	Hall Green	474m	Kildare Slippy	Track Man-Kildare Elm	P. Hancox, Hall Green	28.52	EvsF
1993	Hall Green	474m	Arfur Daley	Pond Mirage-Blue Mint II	F. Meadows, unattached	28.89	5-4F
1994	Hall Green	474m	Randy Savage	Randy-Sooty Foot	K. Connor, Canterbury	29.50	8-1
1995	Hall Green	474m	Elegant Brandy	Murlen's Slippy-Elegant Dream	E. Gaskin, Walthamstow	29.24	10-1
1996	Hall Green	474m	Dynamic Display	Aulton Slippy-Liquid Asset	B. O'Sullivan, Crayford	29.23	7-2
1997	Hall Green	474m	Tarn Bay Flash	Airmount Grand-Highmoor Mist	P. McCombe, Belle Vue	29.07	4-1
1998	Hall Green	474m	El Tenor	Ratify-Ballygar Rose	L. Mullins, Walthamstow	29.20	11-10F
1999	Wimbledon	460m	Hello Buttons	Trade Official-Pal Sal	L. Mullins, Walthamstow	28.13	9-4JF
			dead heat Potto's Storm	Droopy's Fintan-Certain Way	D. Mullins, Romford	28.13	9-4JF
2000	Wimbledon	460m	Tuttle's Minister	Alpine Minister-Tuttle's Snowie	T. Foster, Wimbledon	28.36	3-1
2001	Wimbledon	460m	Kish Jaguar	Deenside Spark-Bansha Lough	N. McEllistrim, Wimbledon	28.80	10-1
2002	Wimbledon	460m	Ballyvorda Class	No Road Back-Group Class	T. Foster, Wimbledon	28.24	7-4F
2003	Wimbledon	460m	Selby Ben	Vintage Prince-Farloe Crib	T. Foster, Wimbledon	28.45	12-1
2004	Wimbledon	480m	Droopys Scholes	Top Honcho-Droopys Kristin	I. Reilly, unattached	28.62	7-2

GREYHOUND RACING

Television Trophy Winners

	Venue	Distance	Winner	Breeding	Trainer and Training Base	Winning Time	Starting Price
1958	Wimbledon	500yds	Town Prince	Small Town-Orphan Princess	L. Reynolds, Wembley	28.14	20-1
1959	West Ham	700yds	Don't Divulge	The Grand Champion-Ennell Gale	L. Reynolds, Wembley	38.72	5-1
1960	Harringay	880yds	Crazy Paving	Magourna Reject-Minorca's Judy	C.C. Payne, unattached	51.22	100-7
1961	Belle Vue	880yds	Chantilly Lace	Coolkill Nigger-Fire Beat	J. Clubb, unattached	52.38	3-1
1962	Wembley	880yds	Avis	Polonius-Twenty Smackers	J. Rimmer, Wembley	51.30	8-13F

1963	Wimbledon	880yds	Curraheen Bride	Hi There-Tallow Bride	W. Kelly, Clapton	52.32	4-1
1964	Powderhall	880yds	Hillstride	Knock Hill Chieftain-Miss Lorraine	T.J. Perry, unattached	51.37	6-4F
1965	Wimbledon	880yds	Lucky Hi There	Hi There-Olive's Bonny	J. Jowett, Clapton	51.35	13-8F
1966	Walthamstow	880yds	Bedford	Steady The Man-Over Beyond	R.G. Thomson, Romford	52.46	20-1
1967	Hove	880yds	Spectre	Crazy Parachute-Supreme Witch	J. Hookway, Sheffield	50.09	EvsF
1968	Romford	880yds	Shady Begonia	Pigalle Wonder-Castle Swan	N. Oliver, Brough Park	50.53	2-1F
1969	White City	880yds	Cash For Dan	Movealong Donal-Cash For Carrick	B. Parsons, Nottingham	49.44	5-4F
1970	Belle Vue	880yds	Hi Diddle	Spectre-Scintilla's Spark	P. Heasman, unattached	51.95	10-1
1971-72 not held							
1973	Wimbledon	880yds	Leading Pride	Spectre-Conigar Goddess	G. Curtis, Hove	51.16	2-1F
1974	White City	880yds	Stage Box	The Grand Silver-Crubs Up	N. Savva, Bletchley	51.75	16-1
1975	Monmore	815m	Lizzies Girl	Newdown Heather-Knock Rose Lady	E.F. Williams, unattached	52.16	7-4JF
1976	Belle Vue	815m	Aughadonagh Jock	Blackrath Motion-Levalley Flash	B. Jay, Perry Barr	52.77	12-1
1977	Walthamstow	820m	Montreen	Moordyke Spot-Avondale	H. Bamford, Belle Vue	52.40	13-2
1978	Walthamstow	820m	Westown Adam	Westmead County-Adamstown Belle	N. Savva, Bletchley	52.27	11-4
1979	Hall Green	815m	Weston Blaze	Westmead County-Weston Star	R.A. Young, Bletchley	53.16	5-1
1980	Wembley	850m	Tread Fast	Glin Bridge-Edenvale Lady	G. Sharp, Walthamstow	53.20	12-1
1981	Perry Barr	830m	Decoy Boom	Westmead County-Ka Boom	J. Cobbold, Ipswich	54.27	7-4F
1982	Belle Vue	815m	Alfa My Son	Alfa Boy-Tough Jackie	L. Steed, Cambridge	52.41	9-2
1983	Walthamstow	820m	Sandy Lane	Maplehurst Star-Pla Irish Imp	G. Curtis, Hove	52.43	7-4
1984	Wimbledon	820m	Weston Prelude	Gaily Noble-Weston Princess	A. Hitch, Oxford	52.14	4-1
1985	Monmore	815m	Scurlogue Champ	Sand Man-Old Rip	K. Peckham, Ipswich	51.64	1-5F
1986	Brough Park	825m	Scurlogue Champ	Sand Man-Old Rip	K. Peckham, Ipswich	52.65	2-5F
1987	Oxford	845m	Glenowen Queen	Yellow Ese-Rikasso Monica	D. Hawkes, Walthamstow	53.37	7-1
1988	Hall Green	815m	Minnies Siren	Easy And Slow-Fenian's Minnie	T. Duggan, Hackney	52.50	16-1
1989	Catford	850m	Proud To Run	Mathews World-Run With Pride	H. White, Canterbury	55.25	4-5F
1990	Walthamstow	820m	Shropshire Lass	Ballyregan Bob-Chocolate Satin	Hubble, unattached	52.48	11-4
1991	Monmore	815m	Jenny's Wish	Kyle Jack-Easy Mary	E. Jordan, Hove	52.44	12-1
1992	Belle Vue	855m	Fortunate Man	Ben G Cruiser-Linda's Dance	Fell, unattached	55.70	6-4F
1993	Wimbledon	820m	Heavenly Lady	Manorville Sand-Black Sancisco	L. Mullins, Walthamstow	51.40	6-1
1994	Sunderland	827m	Jubilee Rebecca	Pond Mirage-Lively Bid	G. Rooks, Brough Park	53.13	2-1
1995	Oxford	845m	Last Action	Chet-Sunshine Penny	J. Wileman, Monmore	53.68	10-11F
1996	Walthamstow	820m	Suncrest Sail	Low Sail-Sarah's Surprise	C. Lister, Nottingham	51.75	7-2
1997	Hall Green	815m	Thornfield Pride	Fearless Mustang-Thornfield Sophi	R. Morris, unattached	52.17	12-1
1997	Wimbledon	820m	Moanrue Slippy	Murlen's Slippy-Athea's Delight	K. Rockman, Harlow	51.35	5-1
1998	Wimbledon	868m	Note Book	Ratify-Book Shelf	G. Adams, Peterborough	54.75	5-1
1999	Wimbledon	868m	Hollinwood Poppy	Dempsey Duke-Hollinwood Major	M. Clarke, Stainforth	54.89	10-1
2000	Wimbledon	868m	Sexy Delight	Some Picture-Spring Rose	C. Lister, unattached	54.51	9-4F
2001	Wimbledon	868m	Killeacle Phoebe	Smooth Rumble-Blonde Returns	B. Clemenson, Hove	54.27	EvsF
2002	Wimbledon	868m	Serious Dog	Top Honcho-Fly Venue	P. Young, Romford	55.14	4-1
2003	Wimbledon	872m	Ericas Equity	Smooth Rumble-Mosney Flyer	P. Young, Romford	54.62	6-4
2004	Wimbledon	872m	Double Take	Carlton Bale-Metric Flower	A.P. Heyes	55.22	11-10F

English Greyhound Derby Winners

	Venue	Distance	Winner	Breeding	Trainer and Training Base	Winning Time	Starting Price
1927	White City	500yds	Entry Badge	Jamie-Beaded Nora	J. Harmon, White City	29.01	1-4F
1928	White City	525yds	Boher Ash	Over The Water-Honey Bee II	T. Johnson, Powderhall	30.48	5-1
1929	White City	525yds	Mick The Miller	Glorious Event-Na Boc Lei	P. Horan, Dublin	29.96	4-7F
1930	White City	525yds	Mick The Miller	Glorious Event-Na Boc Lei	S. Orton, Wimbledon	30.24	4-9F
1931	White City	525yds	Seldom Led	Society Boy-Pity	W.H. Green, West Ham	30.04	7-2
1932	White City	525yds	Wild Woolley	Hautley-Wild Witch	J. Rimmer, White City (Man)	29.72	5-2
1933	White City	525yds	Future Cutlet	Mutton Cutlet-Wary Guide	S. Probert, Wembley	29.80	6-1
1934	White City	525yds	Davesland	Kick Him Down-Hasty Go	H. Harvey, Harringay	29.81	3-1
1935	White City	525yds	Greta Ranee	Doumergue-Parrein	A. Jonas, White City	30.18	4-1
1936	White City	525yds	Fine Jubilee	Silver Seal-Harissi	M. Yate, unattached	29.48	10-11F
1937	White City	525yds	Wattle Bark	Secret Chance-Helena Kane	J.P. Syder, Wembley	29.26	5-2
1938	White City	525yds	Lone Keel	Lone Man-Lucky Plum	S.W. Wright, unattached	29.62	9-4
1939	White City	525yds	Highland Rum	Rum Ration-Liagh Lady	P. Fortune, Wimbledon	29.35	2-1F
1940	Harringay	525yds	G R Archduke	Ataxy-Gay Revels	C.W. Ashley, Harringay	29.66	100-7
1941-44 not held							
1945	White City	525yds	Ballyhennessy Seal	Lone Seal-Canadian Glory	S. Martin, Wimbledon	29.56	EvsF
1946	White City	525yds	Monday's News	Orlucks Best-Monday Next	F.G. Farey, unattached	29.24	5-1
1947	White City	525yds	Trev's Perfection	Trev's Despatch-Friar Tuck	F. Trevillion, unattached	28.95	4-1
1948	White City	525yds	Priceless Border	Clonahard Border-Priceless Sandills	L. Reynolds, Wembley	28.78	1-2F
1949	White City	525yds	Narrogar Ann	Dutton Swordfish-Winnie Of Berrow	L. Reynolds, Wembley	28.95	5-1
1950	White City	525yds	Ballymac Ball	Lone Seal-Raging Tornado	S. Martin, Wimbledon	28.72	7-2
1951	White City	525yds	Ballylanigan Tanist	Mad Tanist-Fly Dancer	L. Reynolds, Wembley	28.62	11-4
1952	White City	525yds	Endless Gossip	Priceless Border-Narrogar Ann	L. Reynolds, Wembley	28.50	EvsF
1953	White City	525yds	Daw's Dancer	The Daw-Castleview Dancer	P.J. McEvoy, unattached	29.20	10-1

1954	White City	525yds	Paul's Fun	Sandown Champion-All Fun	L. Reynolds, Wembley	28.84	8-15F
1955	White City	525yds	Rushton Mac	Rushton News-Rushton Panda	F. Johnston, unattached	28.97	5-1
1956	White City	525yds	Dunmore King	Shaggy Lad-Dunmore Dancer	P.J. McEvoy, Clapton	29.22	7-2
1957	White City	525yds	Ford Spartan	Polonius-Harrow Glamour	D. Hannafin, Wimbledon	28.84	EvsF
1958	White City	525yds	Pigalle Wonder	Champion Prince-Prairie Peg	J.P. Syder, Wembley	28.65	4-5F
1959	White City	525yds	Mile Bush Pride	The Grand Champion-Witching Dancer	J. Harvey, Wembley	28.76	EvsF
1960	White City	525yds	Duleek Dandy	Flash Jack-Flower Of Duleek	W.H. Dash, unattached	29.15	25-1
1961	White City	525yds	Palm's Printer	The Grand Champion-Palm Shadow	P.J. McEvoy, Clapton	28.84	2-1
1962	White City	525yds	The Grand Canal	Champion Prince-The Grand Duchess	P.J. Dunphy, Ireland	29.09	2-1F
1963	White City	525yds	Lucky Boy Boy	Superman-Grange Maiden	J. Bassett, Clapton	29.00	EvsF
1964	White City	525yds	Hack Up Chieftain	Knock Hill Chieftain-Bunclody Queen	P. Stagg, Belle Vue	28.92	20-1
1965	White City	525yds	Chittering Clapton	Noted Crusader-Chittering Hope	A. Jackson, Clapton	28.82	5-2
1966	White City	525yds	Faithful Hope	Solar Prince-Millie Hawthorn	P. Keane, Clapton	28.52	8-1
1967	White City	525yds	Tric Trac	Crazy Parachute-Supreme Witch	R. Hookway, Owlerton	29.00	9-2
1968	White City	525yds	Camira Flash	Prairie Flash-Duet Fire	R. Singleton, White City	28.89	100-8
1969	White City	525yds	Sand Star	Bauhus-Direct Lead	H. Orr, Ireland	28.76	6-1
1970	White City	525yds	John Silver	Faithful Hope-Trojan Silver	B. Tompkins, unattached	29.01	11-4
1971	White City	525yds	Dolores Rocket	Newdown Heather-Come On Dolores	H. White, unattached	28.74	11-4
1972	White City	525yds	Patricia's Hope	Silver Hope-Patsicia	A. Jackson, Clapton	28.55	7-1
1973	White City	525yds	Patricia's Hope	Silver Hope-Patsicia	J. O'Connor, Ireland	28.66	7-2
1974	White City	525yds	Jimsun	Monalee Champion-Lady Expert	G. De Mulder, Hall Green	28.76	5-2
1975	White City	500m	Tartan Khan	Spectre-Chilled Sweet	G. Lynds, Bletchley	29.57	25-1
1976	White City	500m	Mutts Silver	The Grand Silver-Simple Pride	P. Rees, Wimbledon	29.38	6-1
1977	White City	500m	Balliniska Band	Lively Band-Certral	E. Moore, Belle Vue	29.16	EvsF
1978	White City	500m	Lacca Champion	Itsachampion-Highland Finch	P. Mullins, unattached	29.42	6-4F
1979	White City	500m	Sarah's Bunny	Jimsun-Sugarloaf Bunny	G. De Mulder, Hall Green	29.53	3-1
1980	White City	500m	Indian Joe	Brave Bran-Minnatonka	J. Hayes, Ireland	29.68	13-8JF
1981	White City	500m	Parkdown Jet	Cairnville Jet-Gabriel Ruby	G. McKenna, Ireland	29.57	4-5F
1982	White City	500m	Laurie's Panther	Shamrock Sailor-Lady Lucey	T. Duggan, Romford	29.60	6-4F
1983	White City	500m	I'm Slippy	Laurdella Fun-Glenroe Bess	B. Tompkins, Coventry	29.40	6-1
1984	White City	500m	Whisper Wishes	Sand Man-Micklem Drive	C. Coyle, Maidstone	29.43	7-4F
1985	Wimbledon	480m	Pagan Swallow	Black Earl-Acres of Apples	P.C. Rees, Wimbledon	29.04	9-1
1986	Wimbledon	480m	Tico	The Stranger-Derry Linda	A. Hitch, Slough	28.69	6-4JF
1987	Wimbledon	480m	Signal Spark	Echo Spark-Balbec Duchess	G. Baggs, Walthamstow	28.83	14-1
1988	Wimbledon	480m	Hit The Lid	Soda Fountain-Cailin Dubh	J. McGee, Canterbury	28.53	3-1
1989	Wimbledon	480m	Lartigue Note	One To Note-Lartigue Spark	G. McKenna, Ireland	28.79	EvsF
1990	Wimbledon	480m	Slippy Blue	I'm Slippy-Valoris	K. Linzell, Walthamstow	28.70	8-1
1991	Wimbledon	480m	Ballinderry Ash	Kyle Jack-Ballinderry Sand	P. Byrne, Wimbledon	28.78	5-1
1992	Wimbledon	480m	Farloe Melody	Lodge Prince -Chini Chin Chin	M. O'Donnell, Ireland	28.88	6-4F
1993	Wimbledon	480m	Ringa Hustle	Midnight Hustle-Ring U Back	T. Meek, Oxford	28.62	5-2
1994	Wimbledon	480m	Moral Standards	Flag Star-No Way Jose	T. Meek, Hall Green	28.59	9-4F
1995	Wimbledon	480m	Moaning Lad	Kyle Jack-Lady Bellamy	T. Mentzis, unattached	28.66	5-2
1996	Wimbledon	480m	Shanless Slippy	Murlen's Slippy-Lisnakill Flyer	D. Ruth, Ireland	28.66	4-9F
1997	Wimbledon	480m	Some Picture	Slaneyside Hare-Spring Season	C. Lister, Nottingham	28.23	8-13F
1998	Wimbledon	480m	Tom's The Best	Frightful Flash-Lady's Guest	N. Savva, Milton Keynes	28.75	4-5F
1999	Wimbledon	480m	Chart King	Trade Official-Clarinka Sand	R. Hewitt, Ireland	28.76	8-11F
2000	Wimbledon	480m	Rapid Ranger	Come On Ranger-Rapid Vienna	C. Lister, unattached	28.71	7-4F
2001	Wimbledon	480m	Rapid Ranger	Come On Ranger-Rapid Vienna	C. Lister, unattached	28.71	7-4
2002	Wimbledon	480m	Allen Gift	In Question-Raceline Claire	C. Gardiner, Hove	29.04	16-1
2003	Wimbledon	480m	Droopys Hewitt*	Top Honcho-Droopy's Cheryl	A. Ioannou, unattached	28.82	16-1
2004	Wimbledon	480m	Droopys Scholes	Top Honcho-Droopys Kristin	I. Reilly, unattached	28.62	7-2

*Droopy's Hewitt was subsequently disqualified and Farloe Verdict awarded the 2003 Derby.

British Greyhound Tracks

Track	Location	Telephone	Race Days	Circuit
Belle Vue	Manchester	0870 8407557	Tues, Thurs, Fri, Sat	395m
Brighton & Hove	Hove	01273 204601	Tues, Wed, Thurs, Sat, Sun	455m
Brough Park	Newcastle	0191 2105300	Tues, Thurs, Sat	415m
Crayford	Kent	01322 557836	Mon, Thurs, Sat	334m
Hall Green	Birmingham	0870 8407400	Tues, Fri, Sat	412m
Harlow	Essex	01279 426804	Wed, Fri, Sat	354m
Henlow	Bedford	01462 815593	Mon, Fri	410m
Hull	Yorkshire	01482 374131	Fri, Sat	415m
Kinsley	Pontefract	01977 610946	Tues, Fri, Sat	380m
Mildenhall	Suffolk	01638 711777	Tues, Fri	325m
Milton Keynes	Bucks.	01908 670150	Tues, Thurs, Sat, Sun	375m

GREYHOUND RACING

Monmore Green	Wolverhampton	01902 452648	Mon, Thurs, Fri, Sat	419m
Nottingham	Notts.	0115 9103333	Mon, Tues, Thurs, Sat	437m
Oxford	Oxon.	01865 778222	Tues, Thurs, Fri, Sat	395m
Perry Barr	Birmingham	0121 3562324	daily	434m
Peterborough	Cambs.	01733 296930	Tues, Wed, Fri, Sat	370m
Poole	Dorset	01202 677449	Tues, Thurs, Sat	450m
Portsmouth	Hampshire	02392 698000	Tues, Fri, Sat	354m
Reading	Berkshire	01189 750746	Tues, Thurs, Sat	385m
Romford	Essex	01708 762345	Mon, Wed, Fri, Sat	350m
Rye House	Hertford	01992 469000	Fri, Sun	410m
Shawfield	Glasgow	0141 6474121	Tues, Thurs, Fri, Sat	432m
Sheffield	Yorkshire	0114 2343074	Mon, Tues, Thurs, Fri, Sat	425m
Sittingbourne	Kent	01795 475547	Fri, Sat, Sun	443m
Stainforth	Yorkshire	01302 351639	Tues, Fri to Sat	430m
Sunderland	Tyne & Wear	0191 5367250	Mon, Tues, Wed, Fri, Sat	378m
Swindon	Wiltshire	01793 721253	Mon, Wed, Fri, Sat	452m
Walthamstow	London	020 84983300	Mon, Tues, Thurs, Fri, Sat	405m
Wimbledon	London	020 89468000	Tues, Fri, Sat	408m
Yarmouth	Great Yarmouth	01493 720343	Mon, Wed, Sat	382m

General Information

British Greyhound Racing Board	The BGRB is the representative body for greyhound racing in the UK. Directors of the board include greyhound owners, breeders, trainers, track owners and the senior steward of the NGRC. The board primarily exists to promote the best interests of greyhound racing.
Derby: first run	The Greyhound Derby was first run at the White City, London, on 1 October 1927. Entry Badge, trained by J. Harmon and owned by Mr E. Baxter, was the first winner.
Derby: royal owners	Camira Flash, the 1968 Derby winner, was owned by HRH Prince Philip, the Duke of Edinburgh. Druid's Johno, the 1990 Derby favourite and runner-up, was owned by HRH Prince Edward, Earl of Wessex.
Forest Laws	In 1016 King Cnut passed the 'Forest Laws' forbidding commoners to keep greyhounds. The penalty for abuse of this law was public execution. This English law lasted until the 14th century.
famous greyhound owners	Anne Boleyn owned a jet-black greyhound named Satan. Vinnie Jones has owned several racing greyhounds, the most famous of which is Smoking Bullet, a star marathon champion.
hare: types	Swaffham, Swaffham McGee, Fannon Swaffham, Bramich, Sumner
jacket colours	Races in the UK usually consist of six runners boxed in traps. Each greyhound wears a coloured jacket with a number printed on it: trap 1 – red, trap 2 – blue, trap 3 – white, trap 4 – black, trap 5 – orange, trap 6 – black and white stripes. Experiments with eight-dog races have taken place, notably at Monmore Green, but the inevitable crowding at the first bend has ensured that the exercise has never been taken off with the public or animal lovers. For the record, trap 7 – green, trap 8 – yellow and black.
mechanical hare	In 1912 an American named Owen Patrick Smith invented a mechanical hare which ran in a circular path.
National Greyhound Racing Club	The NGRC was established in 1928 and is the governing body of the sport of greyhound racing. Address: Twyman House, 16 Bonny Street, London NW1 9QD. Tel: (020) 7267 9256.
Television Trophy	First run in 1958 and for almost 40 years broadcast live on BBC television, the Television Trophy was rescued by Sky Sports and the *Evening Standard* when the BBC pulled the plug in 1997. In fact, two Television Trophies were staged that year, Thornfield Pride winning the BBC version in March and Moanrue Slippy claiming the Sky race in October. Town Prince, trained by Les Reynolds, made his mark as the race's first winner, the only time the race was run over four bends (500yds (457m)), BBC executives taking an early view that a long-distance event would make for better television. The race was initially run at a different track every year but since the Sky takeover it has been held at Wimbledon.
tracks owned by bookmakers	Ladbrokes – Crayford, Monmore Green Corals – Hove, Romford William Hill – Brough Park, Sunderland
virtual greyhound track	Millersfield became the first computerised virtual reality track in 2003, followed by Brushwood, a virtual jumps track.

GYMNASTICS

Gymnastics, as an activity sport, was developed by the Greeks in the eighth century BC and formed a prominent part of the ancient Olympic Games. The name of the sport comes from *gymnos*, the Greek word for naked; in ancient Greece, male athletes trained and competed in the nude. The *gymnasium* ('place for exercising naked'), originally an area for physical training, came to be a school for training both the mind and the body.

After the Olympics deteriorated into gladiatorial spectacles, it was not until the 18th century that the beauty, strength and grace of gymnasts were once again enjoyed by the masses. Johann Friedrich GutsMuths (1759-1839), who taught at the Schnepfenthal Educational Institute near Gotha, Germany, developed a complete programme of exercises designed to improve balance and suppleness as well as muscular strength. His book, *Gymnastics for the Young*, published in 1793 and soon translated into Danish, English, French and Dutch, became a manual for a generation of physical education teachers in several countries.

In 1881 the Bureau of the European Gymnastics Federation was formed. Later renamed the International Gymnastics Federation (FIG), this organisation pioneered international competition. The Amateur Athletic Union (AAU), formed in the United States in 1883, took control of gymnastics along with most other amateur sports in United States.

The first large-scale gymnastics competition was held at the 1896 Olympics in Athens, Greece. The men's competition included horizontal bar, parallel bars, pommel horse, rings, rope climb and vault. The next international event following the Olympics was held in 1903 in Antwerp, Belgium. This event is now considered the first World Championship. The first men's team competition was held at the 1904 Olympics at St Louis under the name 'turnverein' (tumbling association).

The first women's gymnastic team debuted during the 1928 Olympics, the competition being dominated by Dutch gymnasts. The first full women's programme began at the 1936 Olympics in Berlin, Germany.

In 1962, rhythmic gymnastics was recognised as a sport by the FIG. In 1963 in Budapest, Hungary, the first Rhythmic World Championship took place. It included 28 athletes from 10 countries. During the 1984 Olympics in Los Angeles, the rhythmic individual all-around competition was held for the first time and rhythmic gymnastics became a medal sport at the centennial Olympics in Atlanta in 1996. Men's gymnastic competition today consists of rings, high bar, vault (lengthways), pommel horse, parallel bars and floor exercises. Women's events are the asymmetric (uneven) bars, beam, vault (sideways) and floor exercises.

Gymnastics gained a massively higher profile in the 1970s when a young Russian girl called Olga Korbut (born Grodno, Belarus, 16 May 1955) captivated the hearts of all nations at the Munich Olympics. The diminutive Soviet gymnast invented two new moves (the Korbut Salto, an aerial backflip on the beam, and the Korbut Flip, a backflip-to-catch on the asymmetric bars) but it was her delightful floor routine with its final flick of her wrist that totally enamoured both the judges and an international audience.

By 1976 a new superstar had elevated gymnastics to the highest of profiles. Nadia Comaneci (born Onesti, Moldavia, 12 November 1961) was coached by Bela Karolyi, a controversial man obsessed with the weight of his gymnasts but even more so with the achievement of perfection. Karolyi expected his athletes to ignore pain and injury in striving for this erstwhile impossible perfection. In Comaneci he had the perfect pupil, 1.5m and 39kg, and able to follow his work ethic to the letter. On that historic day in Montreal 16,000 spectators could be heard to gasp as Nadia flew between the two poles of the asymmetric bars, then whooped with delight as the seemingly impossible biomechanical routine was completed perfectly and the maximum score of 10 was given for the first time in the history of the modern Olympic Games.

Olympic Medallists

Men's Horizontal Bar

	Gold	Silver	Bronze
1896	Hermann Weingärtner (GER)	Alfred Flatow (GER)	only two competitors
1900	not held		
1904	Anton Heida (USA)	—	
	Edward Hennig (USA)		George Eyser (USA)
1906-20	not held		
1924	Leon Stukelj (YUG)	Jean Gutweniger (SUI)	André Higelin (FRA)

1928	Georges Miez (SUI)	Romeo Neri (ITA)	Eugen Mack (SUI)
1932	Dallas Bixler (USA)	Heikki Savolainen (FIN)	Einari Teräsvirta (FIN)
1936	Aleksanteri Saarvala (FIN)	Konrad Frey (GER)	Alfred Schwarzmann (GER)
1948	Josef Stalder (SUI)	Walter Lehmann (SUI)	Veikko Huhtanen (FIN)
1952	Jack Günthard (SUI)	Josef Stalder (SUI)	——
		Alfred Schwarzmann (FRG)	
1956	Takashi Ono (JPN)	Yuriy Titov (URS)	Masao Takemoto (JPN)
1960	Takashi Ono (JPN)	Masao Takemoto (JPN)	Boris Shakhlin (URS)
1964	Boris Shakhlin (URS)	Yuriy Titov (URS)	Miroslav Cerar (YUG)
1968	Akinori Nakayama (JPN)	——	Eizo Kenmotsu (JPN)
	Mikhail Voronin (URS)		
1972	Mitsuo Tsukahara (JPN)	Sawao Kato (JPN)	Shigeru Kasamatsu (JPN)
1976	Mitsuo Tsukahara (JPN)	Eizo Kenmotsu (JPN)	Henry Boërio (FRA)
			Eberhard Gienger (FRG)
1980	Stoyan Deltchev (BUL)	Aleksandr Dityatin (URS)	Nikolay Andrianov (URS)
1984	Shinji Morisue (JPN)	Tong Fei (CHN)	Koji Gushiken (JPN)
1988	Vladimir Artemov (URS)	——	Holger Behrendt (GDR)
	Valeriy Lyukin (URS)		Marius Gherman (ROM)
1992	Trent Dimas (USA)	Grigoriy Misyutin (CIS)	——
		Andreas Wecker (GER)	
1996	Andreas Wecker (GER)	Krasimir Dunev (BUL)	Fan Bin (CHN)
			Aleksey Nemov (RUS)
2000	Aleksey Nemov (RUS)	Benjamin Varonian (FRA)	Lee Joo-Hyung (KOR)

Men's Parallel Bars

	Gold	**Silver**	**Bronze**
1896	Alfred Flatow (GER)	Louis Zutter (SUI)	Conrad Böcker (GER)
			Hermann Weingärtner (GER)
1900	not held		
1904	George Eyser (USA)	Anton Heida (USA)	John Duha (USA)
1908-20	not held		
1924	August Güttinger (SUI)	Robert Prasak (TCH)	Giorgio Zampori (ITA)
1928	Ladislav Vácha (TCH)	Josip Primozic (YUG)	Hermann Hänggi (SUI)
1932	Romeo Neri (ITA)	István Pelle (HUN)	Heikki Savolainen (FIN)
1936	Konrad Frey (GER)	Michael Reusch (SUI)	Alfred Schwarzmann (GER)
1948	Michael Reusch (SUI)	Veikko Huhtanen (FIN)	Christian Kipfer (SUI)
			Josef Stalder (SUI)
1952	Hans Eugster (SUI)	Viktor Chukarin (URS)	Josef Stalder (SUI)
1956	Viktor Chukarin (URS)	Masami Kubota (JPN)	Takashi Ono (JPN)
			Masao Takemoto (JPN)
1960	Boris Shakhlin (URS)	Giovanni Carminucci (ITA)	Takashi Ono (JPN)
1964	Yukio Endo (JPN)	Shuji Tsurumi (JPN)	Franco Menichelli (ITA)
1968	Akinori Nakayama (JPN)	Mikhail Voronin (URS)	Viktor Klimenko (URS)
1972	Sawao Kato (JPN)	Shigeru Kasamatsu (JPN)	Eizo Kenmotsu (JPN)
1976	Sawao Kato (JPN)	Nikolay Andrianov (URS)	Mitsuo Tsukahara (JPN)
1980	Aleksandr Tkachyov (URS)	Aleksandr Dityatin (URS)	Roland Brückner (GDR)
1984	Bart Conner (USA)	Nobuyoki Kajitani (JPN)	Mitch Gaylord (USA)
1988	Vladimir Artemov (URS)	Valeriy Lyukin (URS)	Sven Tippelt (GDR)
1992	Vitaliy Scherbo (CIS)	Li Jing (CHN)	Guo Linyao (CHN)
			Igor Korobchinsky (CIS)
1996	Rustam Sharipov (UKR)	Jair Lynch (USA)	Vitaliy Scherbo (BLR)
2000	Li Xiaopeng (CHN)	Lee Joo-Hyung (KOR)	Aleksey Nemov (RUS)

Men's Vault

	Gold	**Silver**	**Bronze**
1896	Karl Schuhmann (GER)	Louis Zutter (SUI)	Hermann Weingärtner (GER)
1900	not held		
1904	George Eyser (USA)	——	William Merz (USA)
	Anton Heida (USA)		
1924	Frank Kriz (USA)	Jan Koutny (TCH)	Bohumil Morkovsky (TCH)
1928	Eugen Mack (SUI)	Emanuel Löffler (TCH)	Stane Durganc (YUG)
1932	Savino Guglielmetti (ITA)	Alfred Jochim (USA)	Edward Carmichael (USA)
1936	Alfred Schwarzmann (GER)	Eugen Mack (SUI)	Matthias Volz (GER)
1948	Paavo Aaltonen (FIN)	Olavi Rove (FIN)	János Mogyorósi-Klencs (HUN)
			Ferenc Pataki (HUN)
			Leo Sotorník (TCH)
1952	Viktor Chukarin (URS)	Masao Takemoto (JPN)	Takashi Ono (JPN)
			Tadao Uesako (JPN)

1956	Helmut Bantz (GER)	——	Yuriy Titov (URS)
	Valentin Mouratov (URS)		
1960	Takashi Ono (JPN)	——	Vladimir Portnoy (URS)
	Boris Shakhlin (URS)		
1964	Haruhiro Yamashita (JPN)	Viktor Lisitsky (URS)	Hannu Rantakari (FIN)
1968	Mikhail Voronin (URS)	Yukio Endo (JPN)	Sergey Diomidov (URS)
1972	Klaus Köste (GDR)	Viktor Klimenko (URS)	Nikolay Andrianov (URS)
1976	Nikolay Andrianov (URS)	Mitsuo Tsukahara (JPN)	Hiroshi Kajiyama (JPN)
1980	Nikolay Andrianov (URS)	Aleksandr Dityatin (URS)	Roland Brückner (GDR)
1984	Lou Yun (CHN)	Mitch Gaylord (USA)	——
		Koji Gushiken (JPN)	
		Li Ning (CHN)	
		Shinji Morisue (JPN)	
1988	Lou Yun (CHN	Sylvio Kroll (GDR)	Park Jong-Hoon (KOR)
1992	Vitaliy Scherbo (EUN)	Grigoriy Misyutin (CIS)	Yoo Ok-Ryul (KOR)
1996	Aleksey Nemov (RUS)	Yeo Hong-Chul (KOR)	Vitaliy Scherbo (BLR)
2000	Gervasio Deferr (ESP)	Aleksey Bondarenko (RUS)	Leszek Blanik (POL)

Men's Pommel Horse

	Gold	**Silver**	**Bronze**
1896	Louis Zutter (SUI)	Hermann Weingärtner (GER)	only two competitors
1900	not held		
1904	Anton Heida (USA)	George Eyser (USA)	William Merz (USA)
1906-20	not held		
1924	Josef Wilhelm (SUI)	Jean Gutweniger (SUI)	Antoine Rebetez (SUI)
1928	Hermann Hänggi (SUI)	Georges Miez (SUI)	Heikki Savolainen (FIN)
1932	István Pelle (HUN)	Omero Bonoli (ITA)	Frank Haubold (USA)
1936	Konrad Frey (GER)	Eugen Mack (SUI)	Albert Bachmann (SUI)
1948	Paavo Aaltonen (FIN)	——	——
	Veikko Huhtanen (FIN)		
	Heikki Savolainen (FIN)		
1952	Viktor Chukarin (URS)	Yevgeniy Korolkov (URS)	——
		Grant Shaginyan (URS)	
1956	Boris Shakhlin (URS)	Takashi Ono (JPN)	Viktor Chukarin (URS)
1960	Eugen Ekman (FIN)	——	Shuji Tsurumi (JPN)
	Boris Shakhlin (URS)		
1964	Miroslav Cerar (YUG)	Shuji Tsurumi (JPN)	Yuriy Tsapenko (URS)
1968	Miroslav Cerar (YUG)	Olli Eino Laiho (FIN)	Mikhail Voronin (URS)
1972	Viktor Klimenko (URS)	Sawao Kato (JPN)	Eizo Kenmotsu (JPN)
1976	Zoltán Magyar (HUN)	Eizo Kenmotsu (JPN)	Nikolay Andrianov (URS)
			Michael Nikolay (GDR)
1980	Zoltán Magyar (HUN)	Aleksandr Dityatin (URS)	Michael Nikolay (GDR)
1984	Li Ning (CHN)	——	Timothy Daggett (USA)
	Peter Vidmar (USA)		
1988	Dmitriy Bilozercher (URS)	——	——
	Zsolt Borkai (HUN)		
	Lyubomir Geraskov (BUL)		
1992	Pae Gil-Su (PRK)	——	Andreas Wecker (GER)
	Vitaliy Scherbo (CIS)		
1996	Donghua Li (SUI)	Marius Urzica (ROM)	Aleksey Nemov (RUS)
2000	Marius Urzica (ROM)	Eric Poujade (FRA)	Aleksey Nemov (RUS)

Men's Rings

	Gold	**Silver**	**Bronze**
1896	Ioannis Mitropoulos (GRE)	Hermann Weingärtner (GER)	Petros Persakis (GRE)
1900	not held		
1904	Hermann Glass (USA)	William Merz (USA)	Emil Voigt (USA)
1906-20	not held		
1924	Francesco Martino (ITA)	Robert Prasak (TCH)	Ladislav Vácha (TCH)
1928	Leon Stukelj (YUG)	Ladislav Vácha ((TCH)	Emanuel Löffler (TCH)
1932	George Gulack (USA)	William Denton (USA)	Giovanni Lattuada (ITA)
1936	Alois Hudec (TCH)	Leon Stukelj (YUG)	Matthias Volz (GER)
1948	Karl Frei (SUI)	Michael Reusch (SUI)	Zdenek Ruzicka (TCH)
1952	Grant Shaginyan (URS)	Viktor Chukarin (URS)	Hans Eugster (SUI)
			Dmitriy Leonkin (URS)
1956	Albert Azaryan (URS)	Valentin Mouratov (URS)	Masami Kubota (JPN)
			Masao Takemoto (JPN)

1960	Albert Azaryan (URS)	Boris Shakhlin (URS)	Velik Kapsazov (BUL)
			Takashi Ono (JPN)
1964	Takuji Haytta (JPN)	Franco Menichelli (ITA)	Boris Shakhlin (URS)
1968	Akinori Nakayama (JPN)	Mikhail Voronin (URS)	Sawao Kato (JPN)
1972	Akinori Nakayama (JPN)	Mikhail Voronin (URS)	Mitsuo Tsukahara (JPN)
1976	Nikolay Andrianov (URS)	Aleksandr Dityatin (URS)	Danut Grecu (ROM)
1980	Aleksandr Dityatin (URS)	Aleksandr Tkachyov (URS)	Jirí Tabák (TCH)
1984	Koji Gushiken (JPN)	——	Mitch Gaylord (USA)
	Li Ning (CHN)		
1988	Holger Behrendt (GDR)	——	Sven Tippelt (GDR)
	Dmitriy Bilozerchev (URS)		
1992	Vitaliy Scherbo (CIS)	Li Jing (CHN)	Li Xiaoshuang (CHN)
			Andreas Wecker (GER)
1996	Jury Chechi (ITA)	Dan Burinca (ROM)	——
		Szilveszter Csollány (HUN)	
2000	Szilveszter Csollány (HUN)	Dimosthenis Tampakos (GRE)	Jordan Jovtchev (BUL)

Men's Floor Exercise

	Gold	Silver	Bronze
1932	István Pelle (HUN)	Georges Miez (SUI)	Mario Lertora (ITA)
1936	Georges Miez (SUI)	Josef Walter (SUI)	Konrad Frey (GER)
			Eugen Mack (SUI)
1948	Ferenc Pataki (HUN)	János Mogyorósi-Klencs (HUN)	Zdenek Ruzicka (TCH)
1952	William Thoresson (SWE)	Jerzy Jokiel (POL)	——
		Tadao Uesako (JPN)	
1956	Valentin Muratov (URS)	Nobuyuki Aihara (JPN)	——
		Viktor Chukarin (URS)	
		William Thoresson (SWE)	
1960	Nobuyuki Aihara (JPN)	Yuriy Titov (URS)	
1964	Franco Menichelli (ITA)	Yukio Endo (JPN)	Franco Menichelli (ITA)
		Viktor Lisitsky (URS)	
1968	Sawao Kato (JPN)	Akinori Nakayama (JPN)	Takeshi Kato (JPN)
1972	Nikolay Andrianov (URS)	Akinori Nakayama (JPN)	Shigeru Kasamatsu (JPN)
1976	Nikolay Andrianov (URS)	Vladimir Marchenko (URS)	Peter Kormann (USA)
1980	Roland Brückner (GDR)	Nikolay Andrianov (URS)	Aleksandr Dityatin (URS)
1984	Li Ning (CHN)	Lou Yun (CHN)	Koji Sotomura (JPN)
			Philippe Vatuone (FRA)
1988	Sergey Kharkov (URS)	Vladimir Artemov (URS)	Yukio Iketani (JPN)
			Lou Yun (CHN)
1992	Li Xiaoshuang (CHN)	Yukio Iketani (JPN)	——
		Grigoriy Misyutin (CIS)	
1996	Ioannis Melissanidis (GRE)	Li Xiaoshuang (CHN)	Aleksey Nemov (RUS)
2000	Igors Vihrovs (LAT)	Aleksey Nemov (RUS)	Jordan Jovtchev (BUL)

Men's Team

	Gold	Silver	Bronze
1906	Norway	Denmark	Italy
1908	Sweden	Norway	Finland
1912	Italy	Hungary	Great Britain
1920	Italy	Belgium	France
1924	Italy	France	Switzerland
1928	Switzerland	Czechoslovakia	Yugoslavia
1932	Italy	United States	Finland
1936	Germany	Switzerland	Finland
1948	Finland	Switzerland	Hungary
1952	Soviet Union	Switzerland	Finland
1956	Soviet Union	Japan	Finland
1960	Japan	Soviet Union	Italy
1964	Japan	Soviet Union	Germany
1968	Japan	Soviet Union	German Democratic Republic
1972	Japan	Soviet Union	German Democratic Republic
1976	Japan	Soviet Union	German Democratic Republic
1980	Soviet Union	German Democratic Republic	Hungary
1984	United States	China	Japan
1988	Soviet Union	German Democratic Republic	Japan
1992	CIS	China	Japan
1996	Russia	China	Ukraine
2000	China	Ukraine	Russia

Women's All-Around

	Gold	Silver	Bronze
1952	Mariya Gorokhovskaya (URS)	Nina Bocharova (URS)	Margit Korondi (HUN)
1956	Larisa Latynina (URS)	Ágnes Keleti (HUN)	Sofia Muratova (URS)
1960	Larisa Latynina (URS)	Sofia Mouratova (URS)	Polina Astakhova (URS)
1964	Vera Cáslavská (TCH)	Larisa Latynina (URS)	Polina Astakhova (URS)
1968	Vera Cáslavská (TCH)	Zinaida Voronina (URS)	Natalya Kuchinskaya (URS)
1972	Lyudmila Turischeva (URS)	Karin Janz (GDR)	Tamara Lazakovich (URS)
1976	Nadia Comaneci (ROM)	Nelli Kim (URS)	Lyudmila Turischeva (URS)
1980	Yelena Davydova (URS)	Nadia Comaneci (ROM)	——
		Maxi Gnauck (GDR)	
1984	Mary Lou Retton (USA)	Ekaterina Szabo (ROM)	Simona Pauca (ROM)
1988	Yelena Shushunova (URS)	Daniela Silivas (ROM)	Svetlana Boginskaya (URS)
1992	Tatyana Gutsu (CIS)	Shannon Miller (USA)	Lavinia Milosovici (ROM)
1996	Liliya Podkopayeva (UKR)	Gina Gogean (ROM)	Simona Amanar (ROM)
			Lavinia Milosovici (ROM)
2000	Simona Amanar (ROM)	Maria Olaru (ROM)	Liu Xuan (CHN)

Women's (Asymmetric) Uneven Bars

	Gold	Silver	Bronze
1952	Margit Korondi (HUN)	Mariya Gorokhovskaya (URS)	Ágnes Keleti (HUN)
1956	Ágnes Keleti (HUN)	Larisa Latynina (URS)	Sofia Muratova (URS)
1960	Polina Astakhova (URS)	Larisa Latynina (URS)	Tamara Lyukhina (URS)
1964	Polina Astakhova (URS)	Katalin Makray (HUN)	Larisa Latynina (URS)
1968	Vera Cáslavská (TCH)	Karin Janz (GDR)	Zinaida Voronina (URS
1972	Karin Janz (GDR)	Olga Korbut (URS)	——
		Erika Zuchold (GDR)	
1976	Nadia Comaneci (ROM)	Teodora Ungureanu (ROM)	Márta Egervári (HUN)
1980	Maxi Gnauck (GDR)	Emilia Eberle (ROM)	Mariya Filatova (URS)
			Steffi Kräker (GDR)
			Melita Rühn (ROM)
1984	Ma Yanhong (CHN)	——	Mary Lou Retton (USA)
	Julianne McNamara (USA)		
1988	Daniela Silivas (ROM)	Dagmar Kersten (GDR)	Yelena Shushunova (URS)
1992	Lu Li (CHN)	Tatyana Gutsu (CIS)	Shannon Miller (USA)
1996	Svetlana Khorkina (RUS)	Bi Wenjiing (CHN)	——
		Amy Chow (USA)	
2000	Svetlana Khorkina (RUS)	Ling Jie (CHN)	Yang Yun (CHN)

G
Y
M
N
A
S
T
I
C
S

Women's Balance Beam

	Gold	Silver	Bronze
1952	Nina Bocharova (URS)	Mariya Gorokhovskaya (URS)	Margit Korondi (HUN)
1956	Ágnes Keleti (HUN)	Eva Bosáková (TCH)	——
		Tamara Manina (URS)	
1960	Eva Bosáková (TCH)	Larisa Latynina (URS)	Sofia Mouratova (URS)
1964	Vera Cáslavská (TCH)	Tamara Manina (URS)	Larisa Latynina (URS)
1968	Natalya Kuchinskaya (URS)	Vera Cáslavská (TCH)	Larisa Petrik (URS)
1972	Olga Korbut (URS)	Tamara Lazakovich (URS)	Karin Janz (GDR)
1976	Nadia Comaneci (ROM)	Olga Korbut (URS)	Teodora Ungureanu (ROM)
1980	Nadia Comaneci (ROM)	Yelena Davydova (URS)	Natalya Shaposhnikova (URS)
1984	Simona Pauca (ROM)	——	Kathy Johnson (GBR)
	Ekaterina Szabo (ROM)		
1988	Daniela Silivas (ROM)	Yelena Shushunova (URS)	Phoebe Mills (USA)
			Gabriela Potorac (ROM)
1992	Tatyana Lysenko (CIS)	Lu Li (CHN)	——
		Shannon Miller (USA)	
1996	Shannon Miller (USA)	Liliya Podkopayeva (UKR)	Gina Gogean (ROM)
2000	Liu Xuan (CHN)	Yekaterina Lobazniouk (RUS)	Yelena Prodounova (RUS)

Women's Vault

	Gold	Silver	Bronze
1952	Yekaterina Kalinchuk (URS)	Mariya Gorokhovskaya (URS)	Galina Minaicheva (URS)
1956	Larisa Latynina (URS)	Tamara Manina (URS)	Ann-Sofi Colling-Pettersson (SWE)
			Olga Tass (HUN)
1960	Margarita Nikolayeva (URS)	Sofia Muratova (URS)	Larisa Latynina (URS)
1964	Vera Cáslavská (TCH)	Larisa Latynina (URS)	——
		Birgit Radochia (GER)	

1968	Vera Cáslavská (TCH)	Erika Zuchold (GDR)	Zinaida Voronina (URS)
1972	Karin Janz (GDR)	Erika Zuchold (GDR)	Lyudmila Turischeva (URS)
1976	Nelli Kim (URS)	Carola Dombeck (GDR)	—
		Lyudmila Turischeva (URS)	
1980	Natalya Shaposhnikova (URS)	Steffi Kräker (GDR)	Melita Rühn (ROM)
1984	Ekaterina Szabo (ROM)	Mary Lou Retton (USA)	Lavinia Agache (ROM)
1988	Svetlana Boginskaya (URS)	Gabriela Potorac (ROM)	Daniela Silivas (ROM)
1992	Lavinia Milosovici (ROM)		Tatyana Lysenko (CIS)
	Henrietta Ónodi (HUN)		
1996	Simona Amanar (ROM)	Mo Hiulan (ROM)	Gina Gogean (ROM)
2000	Yelena Zamoldtchikova (RUS)	Andreea Raducan (ROM)	Yekaterina Lobazniouk (RUS)

Women's Floor Exercise

	Gold	**Silver**	**Bronze**
1952	Ágnes Keleti (HUN)	Mariya Gorokhovskaya (URS)	Margit Korondi (HUN)
1956	Ágnes Keleti (HUN)	—	Elena Leustean (ROM)
	Larisa Latynina (URS)		
1960	Larisa Latynina (URS)	Polina Astakhova (URS)	Tamara Lyukhina (URS)
1964	Larisa Latynina (URS)	Polina Astakhova (URS)	Anikó Jánosi-Ducza (HUN)
1968	Vera Cáslavská (TCH)		Natalya Kuchinskaya (URS)
	Larisa Petrik (URS)		
1972	Olga Korbut (URS)	Lyudmila Turischeva (URS)	Tamara Lazakovich (URS)
1976	Nelli Kim (URS)	Lyudmila Turischeva (URS)	Nadia Comaneci (ROM)
1980	Nadia Comaneci (ROM)	—	Maxi Gnauck (GDR)
	Nelli Kim (URS)		Natalya Shaposhnikova (URS)
1984	Ekaterina Szabo (ROM)	Julianne McNamara (USA)	Mary Lou Retton (USA)
1988	Daniela Silivas (ROM)	Svetlana Boginskaya (URS)	Diana Dudeva (BUL)
1992	Lavinia Milosovici (ROM)	Henrietta Ónodi (HUN)	Christina Bontas (ROM)
			Tatyana Gutsu (CIS)
			Shannon Miller (USA)
1996	Liliya Podkopayeva (UKR)	Simona Amanar (ROM)	Dominique Dawes (USA)
2000	Yelena Zamoldtchikova (RUS)	Svetlana Khorkina (RUS)	Simona Amanar (ROM)

Women's Team

	Gold	**Silver**	**Bronze**
1928	Netherlands	Italy	Great Britain
1932	not held		
1936	Germany	Czechoslovakia	Hungary
1948	Czechoslovakia	Hungary	United States
1952	Soviet Union	Hungary	Czechoslovakia
1956	Soviet Union	Hungary	Romania
1960	Soviet Union	Czechoslovakia	Romania
1964	Soviet Union	Czechoslovakia	Japan
1968	Soviet Union	Czechoslovakia	German Democratic Republic
1972	Soviet Union	German Democratic Republic	Hungary
1976	Soviet Union	Romania	German Democratic Republic
1980	Soviet Union	Romania	German Democratic Republic
1984	Romania	United States	China
1988	Soviet Union	Romania	German Democratic Republic
1992	CIS	Romania	United States
1996	United States	Russia	Romania
2000	Romania	Russia	China

Discontinued Events

Men's Team – Free Exercises & Apparatus

	Gold	**Silver**	**Bronze**
1912	Norway	Finland	Denmark
1920	Denmark	Norway	only two teams competed

Men's Team – Swedish System

	Gold	**Silver**	**Bronze**
1912	Sweden	Denmark	Norway
1920	Sweden	Denmark	Belgium

Men's Team – Horizontal Bar

Gold	Silver	Bronze
1896 Germany	only one team competed	

Men's Team Parallel Bars

Gold	Silver	Bronze
1896 Germany	Panhellenic Club (Athens) (GRE)	National G.C. (Athens) (GRE)

Men's Vault – Side Horse

Gold	Silver	Bronze
1924 Albert Séguin (FRA)	François Gangloff (FRA) Jean Gounot (FRA)	—

Men's Rope Climbing

Gold	Silver	Bronze
1896 Nikolaos Andriakopoulos (GRE)	Thomas Xenakis (GRE)	Fritz Hofmann (GER)
1900 not held		
1904 George Eyser (USA)	Charles Krause (USA)	Emil Voigt (USA)
1906 Georgios Aliprantis (GRE)	Béla Erödy (HUN)	Konstantinos Kozanitas (GRE)
1908-20 not held		
1924 Bedrich Supcík (TCH)	Albert Séguin (FRA)	August Güttinger (SUI) Ladislav Vácha (TCH)
1928 not held		
1932 Raymond Bass (USA)	William Galbraith (USA)	Thomas Connelly (USA)

Men's Club Swinging

Gold	Silver	Bronze
1904 Edward Hennig (USA)	Emil Voigt (USA)	Ralph Wilson (USA)
1908-28 not held		
1932 George Roth (USA)	Philip Erenberg (USA)	William Kuhlmeier (USA)

Men's Tumbling

Gold	Silver	Bronze
1932 Rowland Rolfe (USA)	Edward Gross (USA)	William Hermann (USA)

Men's All-Around Turnverein

Gold	Silver	Bronze
1904 Julius Lenhart (AUT)	Wilhelm Weber (GER)	Adolf Spinnler (SUI)

Men's Team Turnverein

Gold	Silver	Bronze
1904 Philadelphia Turngemeinde (USA)	New York Turnverein (USA)	Central Turnverein (Chicago) (USA)

Men's Athletic Triathlon

Gold	Silver	Bronze
1904 Max Emmerich (USA)	John Grieb (USA)	William Merz (USA)

Men's Gymnastic Triathlon

Gold	Silver	Bronze
1904 Adolf Spinnler (SUI)	Julius Lenhart (AUT)	Wilhelm Weber (GER)

Women's Team – Portable Apparatus

	Gold	**Silver**	**Bronze**
1952	Sweden	Soviet Union	Hungary
1956	Hungary	Sweden	Poland
			Soviet Union

World Champions

Men's All-Around

1903	Joseph Martinez (FRA)
1905	Marcel Lalu (FRA)
1907	Josef Cada (TCH)
1909	Marco Torrès (FRA)
1911	Ferdinand Steiner (TCH)
1913	Marco Torrès (FRA)
1922	Peter Sumi (YUG)
	Frantisek Pechacek (TCH) (tie)
1926	Peter Sumi (YUG)
1930	Josip Primozic (YUG)
1934	Eugen Mack (SUI)
1938	Jan Gajdos (TCH)
1950	Walter Lehmann (SUI)
1954	Viktor Chukarin (URS)
	Valentin Mouratov (URS) (tie)
1958	Boris Schachlin (URS)
1962	Yuriy Titov (URS)
1966	Michail Woronin (URS)
1970	Eizo Kenmotsu (JPN)

1974	Shigeru Kasamatsu (JPN)
1978	Nikolai Andrianov (URS)
1979	Alexandr Dityatin (URS)
1981	Juriy Korolev (URS)
1983	Dimitri Bilosertchev (URS)
1985	Yury Korolev (URS)
1987	Dimitri Bilosertschev (URS)
1989	Igor Korobtschinski (URS)
1991	Grigoriy Misyutin (URS)
1992	not held
1993	Vitaliy Scherbo (BLR)
1994	Ivan Ivankov (BLR)
1995	Li Xiaoshuang (CHN)
1996	not held
1997	Ivan Ivankov (BLR)
1999	Nikolai Krukov (RUS)
2001	Feng Jing (CHN)
2002	not held
2003	Paul Hamm (USA)

Men's Horizontal Bar

1903	Joseph Martinez (FRA)
	Pierre Payssé (FRA) (tie)
1905	Marcel Lalu (FRA)
1907	Georges Charmoille (FRA)
	Frantisek Erben (TCH) (tie)
1909	Joseph Martinez-France
	Josef Cada (TCH)
	Frantisek Erben (FRA) (tie)
1911	Josef Cada (TCH)
1913	Josef Cada (TCH)
1922	Miroslav Klinger (TCH)
1926	Leon Stukelj (YUG)
1930	István Pelle (HUN)
1934	Ernst Winter (GER)
1938	Michael Reusch (SUI)
1950	Paavo Aaltonen (FIN)
1954	Valentin Mouratov (URS)
1958	Boris Schachlin (URS)
1962	Takashi Ono (JPN)
1966	Akinori Nakayama (JPN)
1970	Eizo Kenmotsu (JPN)

1974	Eberhard Gienger (FRG)
1978	Shigeru Kasamatsu (JPN)
1979	Kurt Thomas (USA)
1981	Aleksandr Tkatschev (URS)
1983	Dimitri Bilosertschev (URS)
1985	Tong Fei (CHN)
1987	Dimitri Bilosertschev (URS)
1989	Li Chunyang (CHN)
1991	Li Chunyang (CHN)
	Ralf Büchner (GER) (tie)
1992	Grigoriy Misyutin (CIS)
1993	Sergey Charkov (RUS)
1994	Vitaliy Scherbo (BLR)
1995	Andreas Wecker (GER)
1996	Jesus Carballo (ESP)
1997	Jani Tanskanen (FIN)
1999	Jesus Carballo (ESP)
2001	Vlasios Maras (GRE)
2002	Vlasios Maras (GRE)
2003	Takehiro Kashima (JPN)

Men's Parallel Bars

1903	Joseph Martinez (FRA)
	Francois Hentges (LUX) (tie)
1905	Joseph Martinez (FRA)
1907	Jos Lux (FRA)
1909	Joseph Martinez (FRA)
1911	Giorgio Zampori (ITA)
1913	Giorgio Zampori (ITA)
	Guido Boni (ITA) (tie)
1922	Leon Stukelj (YUG)
	Stane Derganc (YUG)

	N. Jindrich (TCH)
	Miroslav Klinger (TCH)
	Vlado Simoncic (YUG) (tie)
1926	Ladislav Vácha (TCH)
1930	Josip Primozic (YUG)
1934	Eugen Mack (SUI)
1938	Michael Reusch (SUI)
1950	Hans Eugster (SUI)
1954	Viktor Chukarin (URS)
1958	Boris Schachlin (URS)

1962	Miroslav Cerar (YUG)
1966	Sergey Diomidov (URS)
1970	Akinori Nakayama (JPN)
1974	Eizo Kenmotsu (JPN)
1978	Eizo Kenmotsu (JPN)
1979	Bart Conner (USA)
1981	Alexandr Dityatin (URS)
	Koji Gushiken (JPN) (tie)
1983	Vladimir Artemov (URS)
	Lou Yun (CHN) (tie)
1985	Silvio Kroll (GDR)
	Valentin Mogilny (URS) (tie)
1987	Vladimir Artemov (URS)
1989	Li Jing (CHN)

	Vladimir Artemov (URS) (tie)
1991	Li Jing (CHN)
1992	Li Jing (CHN)
	Alexey Voropayev (BLR) (tie)
1993	Vitaliy Scherbo (BLR)
1994	Huang Liping (CHN)
1995	Vitaliy Scherbo (BLR)
1996	Rustam Charipov (UKR)
1997	Zhang Jinjing (CHN)
1999	Joo-Hyung Lee (PRK)
2001	Sean Townsend (USA)
2002	Li Xiaopeng (CHN)
2003	Li Xiaopeng (CHN)

Men's Vault

1903	G. de Jaeghere (FRA)
	Jos Lux (LUX)
	N. Thysen (NED) (tie)
1905	G. de Jaeghere (FRA)
1907	Frantisek Erben (TCH)
1909	not held
1911	not held
1913	Karel Stary (TCH)
	Ben Sadoun (FRA)
	Osvaldo Palazzi (ITA)
	Stane Vidmar (YUG) (tie)
1922	not held
1926	not held
1930	not held
1934	Eugen Mack (SUI)
1938	Eugen Mack (SUI)
1950	Ernst Gebendinger (SUI)
1954	Leo Sotornik (TCH)
1958	Yuriy Titov (URS)
1962	Premysel Krbec (TCH)
1966	Haruhiro Matsuda (JPN)

1970	Mitsuo Tsukahara (JPN)
1974	Shigeru Kasamatsu (JPN)
1978	Junichi Shimizu (JPN)
1979	Alexandr Dityatin (URS)
1981	Ralf-Peter Hemmann (GDR)
1983	Artur Akopjan (URS)
1985	Yury Korolev (URS)
1987	Silvio Kroll (GDR)
	Lou Yun (CHN) (tie)
1989	Jörg Behrendt (GDR)
1991	You Ok-Yul (KOR)
1992	You Ok-Yul (KOR)
1993	Vitaliy Scherbo (BLR)
1994	Vitaliy Scherbo (BLR)
1995	Aleksey Nemov (RUS)
1996	Aleksey Nemov (RUS)
1997	Sergey Fedorschenko (KAZ)
1999	Li Xiaopeng (CHN)
2001	Marian Dragulescu (ROM)
2002	Li Xiaopeng (CHN)
2003	Li Xiaopeng (CHN)

Men's Pommel Horse

1911	Osvaldo Palazzi (ITA)
1913	Giorgio Zampori (ITA)
	N. Aubrey (FRA)
	Osvaldo Palazzi (ITA) (tie)
1922	Miroslav Klinger (TCH)
	N. Jindrich (TCH)
	Leon Stukelj (YUG) (tie)
1926	Jan Karafiat (TCH)
1930	Josip Primozic (YUG)
1934	Eugen Mack (SUI)
1938	Michael Reusch (SUI)
	Vratislav Petracek (TCH) (tie)
1950	Josef Stalder (SUI)
1954	Grant Shaginyan (URS)
1958	Boris Schakhlin (URS)
1962	Miroslav Cerar (YUG)
1966	Miroslav Cerar (YUG)
1970	Miroslav Cerar (YUG)
1974	Zoltán Magyar (HUN)
1978	Zoltán Magyar (HUN)

1979	Zoltán Magyar (HUN)
1981	Michael Nikolay (GDR)
	Li Xiaoping (CHN) (tie)
1983	Dmitri Bilozechev (URS)
1985	Valentin Mogilny (URS)
1987	Dmitri Bilozechev (URS)
	Zsolt Borkai (HUN) (tie)
1989	Valentin Mogilny (URS)
1991	Valeriy Belenki (URS)
1992	Gil Su-Pae (PRK)
1993	Gil Su-Pae (PRK)
1994	Marius Urzica (ROM)
1995	Li Donghua (SUI)
1996	Gil Su-Pae (PRK)
1997	Valeriy Belenki (GER)
1999	Aleksey Nemov (RUS)
2001	Marius Urzica (ROM)
2002	Marius Urzica (ROM)
2003	Teng Haibin (CHN)

Men's Rings

1903	Joseph Martinez (FRA)
	Jos Lux (LUX) (tie)
1905	not held
1907	not held
1909	Guido Romano (ITA)
	Marco Torres (FRA) (tie)

1911	Ferdinand Steiner (TCH)
	Dominique Follacci (FRA)
	Pietro Bianchi (ITA) (tie)
1913	Laurent Grech (FRA)
	Marco Torres (FRA)
	Giorgio Zampori (ITA)
	Guido Boni (ITA) (tie)

G
Y
M
N
A
S
T
I
C
S

1922	Laurent Karasek (TCH)	1981	Alexandr Dityatin (URS)
	Josef Maly (TCH)	1983	Dimitri Bilosertschev (URS)
	Leon Stukelj (YUG)		Koji Gushiken (JPN) (tie)
	Peter Sumi (YUG) (tie)	1985	Li Ning (CHN)
1926	Leon Stukelj (YUG)		Yury Korolev (URS) (tie)
1930	Emanuel Löffler (TCH)	1987	Yury Korolev (URS)
1934	Alois Hudec (TCH)	1989	Andreas Aguilar (FRG)
1938	Alois Hudec (TCH)	1991	Grigory Misyutin (URS)
1950	Walter Lehmann (SUI)	1992	Vitaly Scherbo (BLR)
1954	Albert Azaryan (URS)	1993	Juri Chechi (ITA)
1958	Albert Azaryan (URS)	1994	Juri Chechi (ITA)
1962	Yuriy Titov (URS)	1995	Juri Chechi (ITA)
1966	Mikhail Voronin (URS)	1996	Juri Chechi (ITA)
1970	Akinori Nakayama (JPN)	1997	Juri Chechi (ITA)
1974	Nikolay Andrianov (URS)	1999	Zhen Dong (CHN)
	Dan Grecu (ROM) (tie)	2001	Jordan Jovtchev (BUL)
1978	Nikolay Andrianov (URS)	2002	Szilveszter Csollany (HUN)
1979	Alexandr Dityatin (URS)	2003	Jordan Jovtchev (BUL)

Men's Floor Exercise

1913	Giorgio Zampori (ITA)	1981	Yuriy Korolev (URS)
	V. Rabic (TCH) (tie)		Li Yuejiu (CHN) (tie)
1922	not held	1983	Tong Fei (CHN)
1926	not held	1985	Tong Fei (CHN)
1930	Josip Primozic (YUG)	1987	Lou Yun (CHN)
1934	Georges Miez (SUI)	1989	Igor Korobchinsky (URS)
1938	Jan Gajdos (TCH)	1991	Igor Korobchinsky (URS)
1950	Josef Stalder (SUI)	1992	Igor Korobchinsky (CIS)
1954	Valentin Mouratov (URS)	1993	Grigori Misjutin (UKR)
	Masao Takemoto (JPN) (tie)	1994	Vitaliy Scherbo (BLR)
1958	Masao Takemoto (JPN)	1995	Vitaliy Scherbo (BLR)
1962	Nobuyuki Aihara (JPN)	1996	Vitaliy Scherbo (BLR)
	Yukio Endo (JPN) (tie)	1997	Alexey Nemov (RUS)
1966	Akinori Nakayama (JPN)	1999	Alexey Nemov (RUS)
1970	Akinori Nakayama (JPN)	2001	Marian Dragulescu (ROM)
1974	Shigeru Kasamatsu (JPN)		Jordan Jovtchev (BUL) (tie)
1978	Kurt Thomas (USA)	2002	Marian Dragulescu (ROM)
1979	Kurt Thomas (USA)	2003	Paul Hamm (USA)
	Roland Brückner (GDR) (tie)		

Men's Team

1903	France	1958	Soviet Union	1992	not held
1905	France	1962	Japan	1993	not held
1907	Czechoslovakia	1966	Japan	1994	China
1909	France	1970	Japan	1995	China
1911	Czechoslovakia	1974	Japan	1996	not held
1913	Czechoslovakia	1978	Japan	1997	China
1922	Czechoslovakia	1979	Soviet Union	1999	China
1926	Czechoslovakia	1981	Soviet Union	2000	not held
1930	Czechoslovakia	1983	China	2001	Belarus
1934	Switzerland	1985	Soviet Union	2002	not held
1938	Czechoslovakia	1987	Soviet Union	2003	China
1950	Switzerland	1989	Soviet Union		
1954	Soviet Union	1991	Soviet Union		

Women's All-Around

1934	Vlasta Dekanova (TCH)
1938	Vlasta Dekanova (TCH)
1950	Helena Rakoczy (POL)
1954	Galina Roudiko (URS)
1958	Larissa Latynina (URS)
1962	Larissa Latynina (URS)
1966	Vera Caslavska (TCH)
1970	Lyudmila Turischeva (URS)
1974	Lyudmila Turischeva (URS)
1978	Yelena Mukhina (URS)
1979	Nelli Kim (URS)
1981	Olga Bitcherova (URS)
1983	Natalya Yuschenko (URS)
1985	Oksana Omeljantschik (URS)
	Yelena Shushunova (URS) (tie)

1987	Aurelia Dobre (ROM)
1989	Svetlana Boginskaya (URS)
1991	Kim Zmeskal (USA)
1992	not held
1993	Shannon Miller (USA)
1994	Shannon Miller (USA)
1995	Lilya Podkopayeva (UKR)
1996	not held
1997	Svetlana Khorkina (RUS)
1999	Maria Olaru (ROM)
2001	Svetlana Khorkina (RUS)
2002	not held
2003	Svetlana Khorkina (RUS)

Women's Horizontal Bar

1938	Matylda Palfyova (TCH)
	Marta Majowska (TCH) (tie)

Women's Uneven Bars

1950	Helena Rakoczy (POL)
1954	Agnes Keleti (HUN)
1958	Larissa Latynina (URS)
1962	Irina Pervuschina (URS)
1966	Natalya Kuchinskaya (URS)
1970	Karin Janz (GDR)
1974	Annelore Zinke (GDR)
1978	Marcia Frederick (USA)
1979	Ma Yanhong (CHN)
	Maxi Gnauck (GDR) (tie)
1981	Maxi Gnauck (GDR)
1983	Maxi Gnauck (GDR)
1985	Gabriela Fähnrich (GDR)
1987	Daniela Silivas (ROM)
	Dörthe Tümmler (GDR) (tie)

1989	Fan Di (CHN)
	Daniela Silivas (ROM) (tie)
1991	Kim Gwang-Suk (PRK)
1992	Lavinia Milosovici (ROM)
1993	Shannon Miller (USA)
1994	Luo Li (CHN)
1995	Svetlana Khorkina (RUS)
1996	Svetlana Khorkina (RUS)
	Yelena Piskun (BLR) (tie)
1997	Svetlana Khorkina (RUS)
1999	Jie Ling (CHN)
2001	Svetlana Khorkina (RUS)
2002	Courtney Kupets (USA)
2003	Hollie Vise (USA)

Women's Balance Beam

1938	Vlasta Dekanova (TCH)
1950	Helena Rakoczy (POL)
1954	Keiko Tanaka (JPN)
1958	Larissa Latynina (URS)
1962	Eva Bosakova (TCH)
1966	Natalya Kuchinskaya (URS)
1970	Erika Zuchold (GDR)
1974	Lyudmila Turischeva (URS)
1978	Nadia Comaneci (ROM)
1979	Vera Cerna (TCH)
1981	Maxi Gnauck (GDR)
1983	Olga Mostepanova (URS)
1985	Daniela Silivas (ROM)

1987	Aurelia Dobre (ROM)
1989	Daniela Silivas (ROM)
1991	Svetlana Boginskaya (URS)
1992	Kim Zmeskal (USA)
1993	Lavinia Milosovici (ROM)
1994	Shannon Miller (USA)
1995	Mo Huilan (CHN)
1996	Dina Kochetkova (RUS)
1997	Gina Gogean (ROM)
1999	Svetlana Khorkina (RUS)
2001	Andreea Raducan (ROM)
2002	Ashley Postell (USA)
2003	Fan Ye (CHN)

GYMNASTICS

Women's Vault

1938	Vlasta Dekanova (TCH)		1989	Olessia Dudnik (URS)
1950	Helena Rakoczy (POL)		1991	Lavinia Milosovici (ROM)
1954	Tamara Manina (URS)		1992	Henrietta Onodi (HUN)
	Anna Petersson (SWE) (tie)			Lavinia Milosovici (ROM) (tie)
1958	Larissa Latynina (URS)		1993	Yelena Piskun (BLR)
1962	Vera Caslavska (TCH)		1994	Gina Gogean (ROM)
1966	Vera Caslavska (TCH)		1995	Simona Amanar (ROM)
1970	Erika Zuchold (GDR)			Lilya Podkopayeva (UKR) (tie)
1974	Olga Korbut (URS)		1996	Gina Gogean (ROM)
1978	Nelli Kim (URS)		1997	Simona Amanar (ROM)
1979	Dumitrata Turner (ROM)		1999	Yelena Zamoldtchikova (RUS)
1981	Maxi Gnauck (GDR)		2001	Svetlana Khorkina (RUS)
1983	Boriana Stojanova (BUL)		2002	Yelena Zamoldtchikova (RUS)
1985	Yelena Shushunova (URS)		2003	Oksana Chusovitina (UZB)
1987	Yelena Shushunova (URS)			

Women's Floor Exercise

1938	Matylda Palfyova (TCH)		1989	Daniela Silivas (ROM)
1950	Helena Rakoczy (POL)			Svetlana Boginskaya (URS) (tie)
1954	Tamara Manina (URS)		1991	Cristina Bontas (ROM)
1958	Eva Bosakova (TCH)			Oksana Shusovitina (URS) (tie)
1962	Larissa Latynina (URS)		1992	Kim Zmeskal (USA)
1966	Natalya Kuchinskaya (URS)		1993	Shannon Miller (USA)
1970	Lyudmila Turischeva (URS)		1994	Dina Koschetkova (RUS)
1974	Lyudmila Turischeva (URS)		1995	Gina Gogean (ROM)
1978	Nelli Kim (URS)		1996	Gina Gogean (ROM)
	Yelena Mukhina (URS) (tie)			Kui Yuanyuan (CHN) (tie)
1979	Emilia Eberle (ROM)		1997	Gina Gogean (ROM)
1981	Natalya Iyenko (URS)		1999	Andreea Raducan (ROM)
1983	Ecaterina Szabo (ROM)		2001	Andreea Raducan (ROM)
1985	Oksana Omelianchik (URS)		2002	Elena Gomez (ESP)
1987	Yelena Shushunova (URS)		2003	Daiane dos Santos (BRA)
	Daniela Silivas (ROM) (tie)			

Women's Team

1934	Czechoslovakia		1974	Soviet Union		1991	Soviet Union
1938	Czechoslovakia		1978	Soviet Union		1994	Romania
1950	Sweden		1979	Romania		1995	Romania
1954	Soviet Union		1981	Soviet Union		1997	Romania
1958	Soviet Union		1983	Soviet Union		1999	Romania
1962	Soviet Union		1985	Soviet Union		2001	Romania
1966	Czechoslovakia		1987	Romania		2003	United States
1970	Soviet Union		1989	Soviet Union			

HANDBALL

Handball is the generic name for any game played in a walled court or against a single wall, with a small rubber ball that is struck with hand or fist against the wall, the object being to cause the ball to rebound in such a way that the opposition cannot return it.

Handball can be traced back to ancient times. A simple, naturally evolving game, it was the precursor of many ball games including fives, tennis, squash, rackets, pelota and jai alai.

Many accounts of handball are given by 18th century writers who indicate that one-wall handball was being played in Ireland from at least 1700. Contemporary accounts of the 1798 Irish rebellion describe John Murphy, leader of the rebels in the south-east, as a famous handballer and many of the courts were venues for meetings of his followers.

Irish migrants moving to England introduced the game to the English and while some one-wall play took place, indoor tennis courts became popular sites for three-wall handball. In these, play off the side wall became a feature – the courts were too long for back-wall play. In London, John Cavanagh, a resident Irishman, was recognised as a peerless handballer. His obituary, written by William Hazlitt in 1819, indicated the high regard in which he was held. 'It is not likely that anyone will now see the game of handball played in its perfection for many years to come – for Cavanagh is dead and has not left his like behind him.'

Organised games were not a feature of this era, but there was what may be seen as the earliest professional tour. As early as 1850, players such as Martin Butler of Kilkenny and William Baggs of Tipperary, with seemingly no fixed occupation, would travel all over Ireland to play for money against the local champions. Handball and other Gaelic sports were fostered by Catholic teaching orders such as the Christian Brothers. Many of these men later brought the game to South Africa, America and Australia.

A number of the handball champions of this era excelled in other sports, especially those requiring strength and endurance – essential attributes for matches which sometimes involved 21 games. The top player of the 1880s, David Browning of Limerick, was also a champion rower, weight thrower and boxer. He was finally defeated by American born John Lawlor in 1885, who immediately claimed to be champion of Ireland and was soon challenged by Phil Casey of New York for the world title and a purse of $1000. In Cork Lawlor won six games to Casey's three, but the return at Casey's own court in Brooklyn saw Casey win the required eight games to claim the title eleven games to six.

This meeting between the US and Irish champions seemed to be the beginning of an ongoing exchange between the two countries. Interest was high but the difficulty of travel, differences in courts, rules and balls, and interference by backers and promoters made it difficult to organise such challenges on a regular basis. Casey Fitzgerald of Ireland, Michael Eagan and James Kelly of New York were in turn recognised as world champions, but often the title matches were unsatisfactory. Eagan's victory over Oliver Drew from Cork was marred by arguments over gate receipts and a walkout by Drew. Kelly, in his match against J.J. Bowles of Limerick, had a clause in his contract compelling the latter to serve all balls to his dominant left hand. Such controversies and bad feeling soon led to the abandonment of the series and almost 20 years were to elapse before the resumption of Irish/American challenges.

The Gaelic Athletic Association attempted to bring order to the game by codifying rules and organising tournaments. Similarly, the Amateur Athletic Union (AAU), which controlled many amateur sports in America, arranged in 1897 the first official tournament between Eagan and James Dunne of Brooklyn. Eagan won this match easily and for the next nine years travelled widely in America playing all challengers for his title.

When James Kelly of New York defeated Bowles for the world title in 1909 it was to be the last occasion for the champions of both countries to play each other until the modern World Championships were inaugurated in 1964. During this period of separation the game in America began to move away from its Irish roots and when the Americans returned to Ireland in the 1970s they brought a much changed game back with them.

The Gaelic Athletic Association, founded fifty years earlier to promote Gaelic games, began to take a more active interest in handball and helped to set up the Irish Amateur Handball Association in 1924. One of their first tasks was to arrange trials and organise competitions for that year's Tailteann Games (a festival of Irish sport and culture). A team of Americans arrived and to the amazement of the Irish their players, McDonagh, O'Donnell and Meeney, made a clean sweep of the invitational events both in hardball and softball (a game played with a larger ball similar to a tennis ball).

The amateur status of the new association brought it into direct opposition with the semi-professional Irish Handball Union (IHU), but the majority of players quickly transferred to the new body. The IHU continued to hold national and even world championships up until 1936. The new association attracted the support of state bodies, particularly the army and police. Handballers became national figures and top players such as Soye, O'Neill and Perry were featured on sport cards and in advertising. The Tailteann Games continued but American players no longer attended.

Handball is today played mainly in the United States, Canada and Ireland and to a lesser extent in Argentina, Australia, France, Mexico, New Zealand and South Africa.

Standard four-wall courts are 40ft (12.2m) long, 20ft (6.1m) wide and 20ft (6.1m) high, with a back wall 14ft (4.27m) high. A short line, parallel to the front wall, divides the court in half. The service line is parallel to and 5ft (1.52m) in front of the short line. Between these two lines on each side of the court is a service box, formed by a line parallel to and 18ins (46cm) from each side wall. The serving area is the space between the outer edges of the short and service lines. A vertical line marked on each side wall, 5ft (1.52m) behind the short line, indicates the front edge of the back court receiving zone.

In one-wall handball, the front wall is 20ft (6.1m) wide and 16ft (4.87m) high, with a playing area 34ft (10.36m) long and 20ft (6.1m) wide. The sidelines extend 3ft (0.9m) further from the wall than the long line. The short line runs parallel to and 16ft (4.87m) from the wall. Service lines 6ins (15cm) long run parallel to and midway between the long and short lines and extend inward from the sidelines. The imaginary joining of these lines forms the service line. The serving zone of 20ft (6.1m) by 9ft (2.75m) includes the long and side lines.

Traditionally, the Irish used a hard ball with a cork or wood centre covered by a wool base. This ball was 1⅛ ins (4.7cm) in diameter and weighed between 1½oz (43g) and 1¾oz (50g). Today the ball is of the same size but made of black rubber and weighs 65g.

To commence a game the server stands within the service area, drops the ball to the ground, and strikes it against the front wall on the firs bounce with one hand. In the four-wall game, th rebounding ball must land on the floor behind th short line, either before or after striking one of th side walls. If it fails to do so it is deemed a sho ball, and a fault. Two faults constitute an 'out after which service is passed to the opposition. I the one-wall game, if the ball lands beyond th long line, it is deemed a 'long ball', also a fault. it goes outside the sidelines it is a 'handout'. Th receiving side may return the ball on the volley c on the first bounce; the return may hit the sid walls but must hit the front wall. The server score points until becoming handout. The gaining of 2 points ends the game.

Team handball originated in Europe in the 1900 and is a completely different sport from tha described above. The International Handba Federation (IHF) is the governing body and has i excess of 140 member countries. Team handba first appeared in the Olympics in 1936 as an ou door field sport with 11 players per side. It wa not included again until the Munich Games c 1972 when it became an indoor sport of 7 pe side. Women's handball was introduced into th Olympic programme in 1976. Team handba combines elements of both soccer and basket ball. It is played on a court 20m × 40m by team of seven players per side. The basketball aspec of the game is in the method of play whereby th ball may be dribbled or held for up to three sec onds before passing. A player may also run wit the ball for up to three steps before and after th commencement of a dribble. Goals are scored, a in water polo, by hand into an area 2m high an 3m wide. The net is 1m deep at the base of th goal. A handball is made of leather and weigh 15-17oz (425-481g) with a circumference of 23 24ins (58.4-61cm) (Men), or 12-14oz (340-396g with a circumference of 21-22ins (53.3-55.9cm (Women and Juniors). The game is played ove two halves of 30 minutes each.

Team Handball: Olympic Medallists

Men's

	Gold	Silver	Bronze
1972	Yugoslavia	Czechoslovakia	Romania
1976	Soviet Union	Romania	Poland
1980	German Democratic Republic	Soviet Union	Romania
1984	Yugoslavia	West Germany	Romania
1988	West Germany	West Germany	Yugoslavia
1992	CIS	Sweden	France
1996	Croatia	Sweden	Spain
2000	Russia	Sweden	Spain

Women's

	Gold	Silver	Bronze
1976	Soviet Union	German Democratic Republic	Hungary
1980	Soviet Union	Yugoslavia	German Democratic Republic
1984	Yugoslavia	South Korea	China
1988	South Korea	Norway	Soviet Union
1992	South Korea	Norway	CIS
1996	Denmark	South Korea	Hungary
2000	Denmark	Hungary	Norway

HOCKEY

The origins of hockey can be traced to ancient Egypt and Greece. A drawing on a tomb dating from about 2000BC, buried deep in Egypt's Nile Valley in the village of Beni Hasan, shows two men standing over a ball holding sticks with curved ends. In Athens, on a wall built by Themistocles around 500BC, another drawing depicts six athletes poised to play a game with sticks curved at the lower end.

After many centuries of informal play in England, London's Blackheath Hockey Club was organised in 1861. The first to hold proper meetings with minutes, it can therefore be considered the first hockey club, although it was the Wimbledon club in London that first standardised the rules in 1883. Modern hockey (known as field hockey where there is a need to distinguish it from ice hockey) was truly born with the formation of the Hockey Association in England on 18 January 1886. It was during this period that hockey spread to other countries, particularly those in Europe and the British Empire. The Fédération Internationale de Hockey (International Hockey Federation, FIH), the current governing body of the global game, was founded in 1924.

Constance M.K. Applebee of England introduced hockey to American women in 1901 and she remained in the US as a physical educator, teaching the sport at several schools and at a summer camp that she established in 1922. (Applebee was also active in establishing lacrosse as a women's sport in the US.) The international governing body, the International Federation of Women's Hockey Association (IFWHA), was formed in 1927 but women's hockey, despite being played in schools and colleges, did not become internationally popular until the first Women's World Cup in 1974. In Olympic competition, while men's hockey first appeared in 1908, a women's Olympic event has only been held since 1980.

The Olympic Games is undoubtedly the most prestigious tournament in hockey and men's hockey has been an event at every Games since 1928. Historically, Indian and Pakistani teams dominated the men's game for many years. Before the introduction of women's hockey at the Olympics, the best international women's team was the Netherlands. From the early 1990s, however, the Australian women's team has been by far the best on the international scene, although Argentina are currently in the ascendancy as a hockey nation.

The World Cup was instituted in 1971 for men and 1974 for women and the Champions Trophy in 1978 for men and 1987 for women. Many countries also have extensive club competitions for both junior and senior players. Club hockey, despite the huge number of participants, does not attract large numbers of spectators and very few players can afford to play professionally.

Hockey was traditionally played on ordinary grass, but 'synthetic grass', a smooth, carpet-like material, is used for most modern games. The goals are 2.13m (7ft) high and 3.66m (4yds) wide, and are surrounded by a semicircle 14.63m (16yds) from the goal known as the 'shooting circle'. A line is marked 22.9m across the field 20.9m (25yds) from each end and there is also a centre line. The game is played between two teams of eleven players (five forwards, three half-backs, two full-backs and a goalkeeper) on a 91.4m × 55m (100yds × 60yds) rectangular field.

A 'stick', traditionally made of wood and about 90cm (36in) to 96cm (38ins) long, is carried by each player. Today hockey sticks are made with fibreglass, kevlar and carbon fibre composites, with a rounded handle of approximately 2.5cm (1in) diameter at the top, flattening out on one side and with a hook at the bottom. The stick is used to dribble, push, or hit a hard plastic ball. Hockey balls, usually dimpled, are approximately 7cm (2.5ins) in diameter.

A face-off (often called a bully-off) in the centre of the field starts the game; two opposing players alternately tap the ground and then each other's sticks three times before striking the ball with the aim of getting possession. Teams direct their play towards advancing the ball down the field with their sticks. A point is scored by putting the ball between the goalposts.

Players are permitted to push, dribble, or hit the ball only with the flat side of the stick, which is always on the 'natural' side for a right-handed person – there are no 'left-handed' hockey sticks. It is against the rules to let the ball strike any part of an outfield player's body. Fouls result in penalty strokes and free hits.

Within their defensive circle goalkeepers are permitted to play the ball with any part of their body. Extensive protective equipment is worn by goalkeepers, including chest guards, helmets, body armour, heavily padded gloves, and leg and foot guards designed both to protect the goalkeeper and to allow them to propel the ball away without the use of the stick. The rules for men and women are fundamentally the same, although men play two halves of 35 minutes' duration while women play two halves of 30 minutes.

Biographies

Abbas, Sohail Born Karachi, Pakistan, 9 June 1977. Abbas is already the holder of three world records in his seven-year international career. He is the scorer of the highest number of goals (60) in a calendar year, as well as the maker of the fastest century and double-century of goals in international hockey. He reached his double-century of goals in his 165th match on 17 August 2003 at Amstelveen's Wagener stadium when he struck twice in a thrilling 6-5 win over Argentina during the 25th Champions Trophy. Despite such achievements, Abbas is yet to win gold in a major event. He represented Pakistan in the 2000 Olympics and the 1998 and 2002 World Cup, but Pakistan failed to win a medal. He was silver and bronze medallist in the Champions Trophy of 1998 and 2003 respectively and he also appeared in the tournament in 1999 and 2001. With more than 200 international caps to his name Sohail is recognised as the world's finest penalty corner expert.

Allen, Richard James Born India, 4 June 1902. An outstanding goalkeeper for India and Port Commissioners (Calcutta), Allen did not concede a single goal at the Amsterdam Olympics (1928), and only five at Los Angeles (1932) and Berlin (1936).

Anders, Beth Born Norristown, USA, 13 November 1951. Recognised for her past contributions to the US national team, Anders is a two-time Olympian, scoring star of the 1984 Olympic Games, and also team captain – but her most noteworthy contributions to the sport result from the sidelines as head coach of Old Dominion University hockey team. Anders has twice been named National Coach of the Year by the National Field Hockey Coaches Association and five times Colonial Athletic Association (CAA) Coach of the Year. Anders was inducted into the United States Field Hockey Association Hall of Fame in 1989 and into the Pennsylvania Sports Hall of Fame in 1998. She is also the author of *Field Hockey – Steps to Success*, published in 1998.

Annan, Alyson Born New South Wales, Australia, 21 June 1973. Considered by many as the 'sharpest shooter in international women's hockey' and the 'best female hockey player in the world', Alyson Annan first made history at the 1998 Commonwealth Games when she became Australia's highest-ever goal scorer with 110 goals. With 218 caps, Annan has the highest number of international goals, 162. Her credits include four Champions Trophy gold medals, two World Cup gold medals, two Olympic gold medals and a Commonwealth Games gold medal. In addition to her contributions to the Australian team effort, Annan has earned numerous individual honours over the years. She was the top goal scorer at the 1999 Champions Trophy, as well as at the 1998 World Cup where she was selected as Player of the Tournament. She was also the first-ever recipient of the International Hockey Federation's Player of the Year Award in 1998 and again won the award in 2000. First selected in the Australian team in June 1991 to play in a Test series against South Korea in Hobart and Melbourne, Alyson has been a key contributor to the many championships won by the Australian women's hockey team in recent years.

Aymar, Luciana Paula Born Rosario, Argentina, 10 August 1977. Aymar plays as an attacking midfielder for Jockey Club Rosario and Argentina. She won gold at the 2001 Champions Trophy and the 2002 World Cup and was named as FIH Player of the Year in 2001.

Benninga, Carina Born Amsterdam, Holland, 18 August 1962. A gold medallist for the Dutch hockey team at the 1984 Olympic Games in Los Angeles. Benninga earned additional Olympic honours with a bronze at the 1988 Olympics in Seoul. In her third Olympic appearance, she was named as flag bearer for the Netherlands at the 1992 opening ceremony in Barcelona, thus becoming the first woman to present Holland's colours at an Olympic Games. She served as captain of the 1990 Netherlands World Cup team and earned two World Championships with the Netherlands in 1983 and 1990. After her playing days, Benninga became an assistant coach and consultant for the US national team, 1993-95. In 1994, she was a member of the US coaching staff and helped lead the Americans to the bronze medal in the World Cup in Dublin. She served as interim head coach of the US women's national field hockey team from November 1998 to January 1999. Benninga was knighted by the Queen of Holland in 1994.

Chand, Dhyan Born Allahabad, India, 29 August 1905. Dhyan Chand, nicknamed 'The Wizard', was a hockey genius and an icon of Indian sport. His international career, which began with the Army tour of New Zealand in April/June 1926, spanned 22 years. During an era in which the Olympics was the only international tournament, Chand won gold medals at Amsterdam (1928), Los Angeles (1932) and as captain in Berlin in 1936. As a centre-forward, he scored 36 goals in 12 Olympic matches. India scored 338 goals in 1932, before and after the Los Angeles Olympics, of which Chand's share was 133. In 1935, on the New Zealand/Australia tour, he scored 201 goals in 48 matches.

After Indian independence, Chand made a tour of East Africa at the age of 42, scoring 61 goals in 22 matches. He was honoured with the Padma Bhushan in 1956 and took charge as chief coach of NIS (National Institute of Sports), Patiala, between 1961 and 1969. Chand, undoubtedly one of India's most legendary strikers, died 3 December 1979. A year after his demise the government of India issued a commemorative stamp in his honour. India's National Sports Day is observed on his birthday.

Charlesworth, Richard Born Subiaco, Perth, Western Australia, 6 December 1952. A doctor by profession and thrice elected to the Australian Federal Parliament, Charlesworth began his illustrious Olympic career as a powerful forward in 1972. On moving into the sports arena he played cricket for Western Australia, once as captain. As a hockey player his achievements are considerable. He was part of Australia's bronze medal-winning 1978 and 1982 World Cup teams, capping those two bronzes with a gold in 1986 in London. He played in three Olympics, gaining a silver in 1976. When Australia won the title in the London World Cup, he was 36 years old and in his 16th year in international hockey. He went on to become a successful national hockey coach; under him Australia's women had a golden run in the 1990s, winning numerous titles including the Olympics, the World Cup and the Champions Trophy. He is widely considered the greatest of Australian hockey players.

HOCKEY

Claudius, Leslie   Born Bilaspur, India, 25 March 1927. Hockey's first quadruple Olympian, Claudius was a member of the Indian hockey teams that won gold at London (1948), Helsinki (1952) and Melbourne (1956), and silver at Rome (1960). Though he did not play in the 1948 final, he was the team's captain in Rome.

Francis, Ranganandhan   Born Madras, India, 15 March 1920. Goalkeeper of the Indian hockey team that won Olympic gold in 1948, 1952 and 1956, although he did not play in the finals in 1948 or 1956. He is considered by some as India's best-ever goalkeeper.

Gentle, Singh Randhir   Born India, 1923. An outstanding full-back for Independent SC (Delhi) and India, Gentle was also a remarkable scorer of penalties. During the Melbourne Olympics he deputised as captain in the absence of Balbir Singh and scored six goals, including the decisive goal in the final against Pakistan. On retiring he proved an outstanding coach and prepared national teams in India, Malaya and Spain, also becoming an international umpire. He played for the Indian team that won Olympic gold in 1948, 1952 and 1956.

Green, Michael   Born 1972. A midfielder with strong defence, and foresight and perception in passing. Green started playing at the age of 14. He then joined the Braunschweig club in his home town, moving to Hamburg in 1992. He now plays for HTHC Hamburg, who have been German and European club champions several times. Highlights of his career include performances at the Atlanta and Sydney Olympics, gold at the 2002 men's World Cup and three gold, three silver and three bronze Champions Trophy medals. In addition, he qualified as a doctor of medicine in 1999 and started practising after the Sydney Olympics. The FIH made Green its Player of the Year for 2002.

Hawkes, Rechelle   Born Albany, Australia, 30 May 1967. The winner of three Olympic gold medals (1988, 1996 and 2000), the first of which was instrumental in launching a sustained period of success for Australian women's hockey. Hawkes was inducted as a Hall of Fame member and singled out for praise when the 1988 Hockeyroos were recognised among six outstanding teams from the past. A midfield player with great stick skill and pace to match, Hawkes was a master reader of the game.

Kerly, Sean   Born England, 29 January 1960. Kerly learnt his hockey at Chatham House School and polished it to a sparkle at the Southgate Club. Having earned his first senior international cap in 1981 after a successful junior international career, he was drafted into the Great Britain Olympic team for the 1984 Los Angeles Olympics. His goals helped the side to a bronze medal and this rekindled the passion for the game back home and sowed the seed of revival of British hockey. The 1986 World Cup, played on home ground, turned the spotlight on Kerly and he once again proved his hunger for goals. In the first match he netted twice against New Zealand, while two more goals came later as England reached a World Cup final for the first time. After scoring a hat-trick against the mighty Pakistan in the 1987 Champions Trophy and eight goals

against Espeoo Club of Finland in the European Cup for Club Champions in 1986-87, Kerly was something of a superstar even before the glory of Seoul in 1988. In the Olympic semi-final against Australia, Great Britain showed their fighting qualities. With Great Britain leading 2-0, thanks to two Kerly strikes, Australia pulled the game level, but the British team fought back to win as Kerly completed his hat-trick late in the match. The final was a match for fans to savour – Great Britain v West Germany – and for once the glory did not go to the Germans as Imran Sherwani (2) and Kerly put the Brits 3-0 up on the way to a 3-1 victory. Kerly was hailed as a true sporting superstar following the Seoul Olympics but unfortunately the Great Britain team did not have the strength in depth of other top nations and the revival was short-lived.

Kunz, Florian   Born Germany, 22 February 1972. Kunz has been striking terror into the hearts of the opposition since he began playing hockey at five years old. Nicknamed 'Floh', scored 143 goals in 39 international matches between his first international cap in March 1994 and the 2002 World Cup. His 2001 performances contributed to his team's gold medals at both the European Nations Cup indoors in Lucerne and the 23rd Men's Champions Trophy in Rotterdam. The FIH voted him Player of the Year in 2001.

Rognoni, Cecilia   Born 1977. Banned from international competition for a year in 1999 for throwing a ball at English umpire Gill Clarke during the Pan-Am Games, Argentinian defender Rognoni was voted FIH Player of the Year in 2002. Playing for Ciudad de Buenos Aires Hockey Club, Rognoni is a commanding defender with a fearsome hit which she employs at both ends of the field, having scored over 50 goals for Argentina. She has won silver medals at the Sydney Olympics and 2002 Women's Champions Trophy, and gold at the Women's Champions Trophy in 2001.

Schubert, Grant   Born Loxton, Australia, 1 August 1980. Schubert joined the Junior World Cup as a strong-running forward, the event being his first major competition in the hockey arena. Before the 2003 Champions Trophy, he had scored seven goals in six internationals, and he became the fifth scorer of a hat-trick for Australia in the 25-year history of the tournament when he netted three times in a 4-1 win against India in their encounter on 19 August 2003 at Wagener Stadium, Amstelveen. He also struck twice against Pakistan and Germany and at one point was leading the scorers' chart with seven goals. Schubert is set to be a giant of the game and was the FIH Young Player of the Year in 2003.

Veen, Stephan   Born Groningen, Amsterdam, 27 July 1970. Captain of the Dutch national team since 1996, Veen is known to many as the best male player in the world. He has a long list of championships to his credit, winning Olympic gold in 1996, several World Cup trophies and Champions Trophy gold medals, European championship golds and an Intercontinental Cup. He received the FIH Player of the Year award in 1998 and 2000. He retired in 2001 having scored 166 goals in 275 international matches.

Olympic Medallists

Men's

	Gold	Silver	Bronze	Venue
1908	Great Britain (England)	Ireland	Great Britain (Wales)	London
1920	Great Britain	Denmark	Belgium	Antwerp
1928	India	Netherlands	Germany	Amsterdam
1932	India	Japan	United States	Los Angeles
1936	India	Germany	Netherlands	Berlin
1948	India	Great Britain	Netherlands	London
1952	India	Netherlands	Great Britain	Helsinki
1956	India	Pakistan	Federal Republic of Germany	Melbourne
1960	Pakistan	India	Spain	Rome
1964	India	Pakistan	Australia	Tokyo
1968	Pakistan	Australia	India	Mexico City
1972	Federal Republic of Germany	Pakistan	India	Munich
1976	New Zealand	Australia	Pakistan	Montreal
1980	India	Spain	Soviet Union	Moscow
1984	Pakistan	Federal Republic of Germany	Great Britain	Los Angeles
1988	Great Britain	Federal Republic of Germany	Netherlands	Seoul
1992	Germany	Australia	Pakistan	Barcelona
1996	Netherlands	Spain	Australia	Atlanta
2000	Australia	Argentina	Netherlands	Sydney

Women's

	Gold	Silver	Bronze	Venue
1980	Zimbabwe	Czechoslovakia	Soviet Union	Moscow
1984	Netherlands	Federal Republic of Germany	United States	Los Angeles
1988	Australia	South Korea	Netherlands	Seoul
1992	Spain	Germany	Great Britain	Barcelona
1996	Australia	South Korea	Netherlands	Atlanta
2000	Netherlands	Argentina	Australia	Sydney

World Cup Medallists

Men's

	Gold	Silver	Bronze	Venue
1971	Pakistan	Spain	India	Barcelona
1973	Netherlands	India	West Germany	Amsterdam
1975	India	Pakistan	West Germany	Kuala Lumpur
1978	Pakistan	Netherlands	Australia	Buenos Aires
1982	Pakistan	West Germany	Australia	Bombay
1986	Australia	Great Britain	West Germany	London
1990	Netherlands	Pakistan	Australia	Lahore
1994	Pakistan	Netherlands	Australia	Sydney
1998	Netherlands	Spain	Germany	Utrecht
2002	Germany	Australia	Netherlands	Kuala Lumpur

Women's

	Gold	Silver	Bronze	Venue
1974	Netherlands	Argentina	West Germany	Mandelieu
1976	West Germany	Argentina	Netherlands	Berlin
1978	Netherlands	West Germany	Argentina/Belgium	Madrid
1981	West Germany	Netherlands	Soviet Union	Buenos Aires
1983	Netherlands	Canada	Australia	Kuala Lumpur
1986	Netherlands	West Germany	Canada	Amsterdam
1990	Netherlands	Australia	South Korea	Sydney
1994	Australia	Argentina	United States	Dublin
1998	Australia	Netherlands	Germany	Utrecht
2002	Argentina	Netherlands	China	Perth

HOCKEY

Champions Trophy

Men's Results

	Gold	Silver	Bronze	Venue
1978	Pakistan	Australia	Great Britain	Lahore
1980	Pakistan	West Germany	Australia	Karachi
1981	Netherlands	Australia	West Germany	Karachi
1982	Netherlands	Australia	India	Amsterdam
1983	Australia	Pakistan	West Germany	Karachi
1984	Australia	Pakistan	Great Britain	Karachi
1985	Australia	Great Britain	West Germany	Perth
1986	West Germany	Australia	Pakistan	Karachi
1987	West Germany	Netherlands	Australia	Amsterdam
1988	West Germany	Pakistan	Australia	Lahore
1989	Australia	Netherlands	West Germany	Berlin
1990	Australia	Netherlands	West Germany	Melbourne
1991	Germany	Pakistan	Netherlands	Berlin
1992	Germany	Australia	Pakistan	Karachi
1993	Australia	Germany	Netherlands	Kuala Lumpur
1994	Pakistan	Germany	Netherlands	Lahore
1995	Germany	Australia	Pakistan	Berlin
1996	Netherlands	Pakistan	Germany	Madras
1997	Germany	Australia	Spain	Adelaide
1998	Netherlands	Pakistan	Australia	Lahore
1999	Australia	South Korea	Netherlands	Brisbane
2000	Netherlands	Germany	South Korea	Amstelveen
2001	Germany	Australia	Netherlands	Rotterdam
2002	Netherlands	Germany	Pakistan	Cologne
2003	Netherlands	Australia	Pakistan	Amsterdam

Women's Results

	Gold	Silver	Bronze	Venue
1987	Netherlands	Australia	South Korea	Amsterdam
1989	South Korea	Australia	West Germany	Frankfurt
1991	Australia	Germany	Netherlands	Berlin
1993	Australia	Netherlands	Germany	Amstelveen
1995	Australia	South Korea	United States	Mar del Plata (Argentina)
1997	Australia	Germany	Netherlands	Berlin
1999	Australia	Netherlands	Germany	Brisbane
2000	Netherlands	Germany	Australia	Amstelveen
2001	Argentina	Netherlands	Australia	Amstelveen
2002	China	Argentina	Netherlands	Macau (China)
2003	Australia	China	Netherlands	Sydney

Horse Racing

It is recorded that the earliest horse race in England took place about AD210 at Netherby in Yorkshire under the auspices of the Roman emperor Septimus Severus. In King Henry II's reign races were held on the site where Smithfield meat market now stands and the sport became fashionable during the reign of his son, King Richard I. In 1377, the Prince of Wales (later King Richard II) raced against the Earl of Arundel, but the 'Sport of Kings' remained largely a pursuit followed for the amusement of the nobility.

Chester is the oldest racecourse in Britain, being established in 1540 during the reign of King Henry VIII, and later that century racing took place at Croydon and on Salisbury Plain with Elizabeth I a frequent visitor. The royal connection was maintained with races at Garterley and Enfield being attended by James I, who also had studs at Tutbury, Hampton Court, Eltham and Cole Park. At this time the sport began to boom and meetings were held at Newmarket, York, Doncaster, Liverpool and Lincoln.

When Charles I came to the throne (in 1625) the sport began to develop a structure. Where previously only silver and golden bells were given as prizes, now prize money and cups were being offered, while wagers were struck and rules implemented. Races were often graded between four and six miles long and weights varied between 10st and 17st.

Council of State under the Commonwealth prohibited racing in 1654 but it was restored when Charles II came to the throne. The Merry Monarch proclaimed Newmarket as the headquarters of racing and in June 1711 Queen Anne founded Royal Ascot. Epsom racecourse was opened in 1730. The Jockey Club was formed in 1750 and by the time that the St Leger was first run in 1776 the sport had become mainstream with racing colours becoming compulsory in 1762. The first official judge was appointed in 1772.

Biographies of Racehorses, Jockeys, Trainers and Owners

Abdullah, Khalid Born 1924. Saudi Arabian prince who owned the 1980 2000 Guineas winner Known Fact, the first Arab-owned English classic winner. Prince Khalid has subsequently owned winners of all five British classics and his most famous horses include Rousillon, Warning, Rainbow Quest, Quest For Fame, Commander-In-Chief, Sanglamore, Wince, Reams of Verse, Toulon, Zafonic, Xaar and Dancing Brave.

Abernant Grey colt foaled 1946 by Owen Tudor out of Rustum Mahal. Trained by Sir Noel Murless. High-class sprinter 1948-50. Champion 2-year-old, European Champion 3-year-old and 4-year-old and twice European Horse of the Year. Winner of the Champagne Stakes, Middle Park Stakes, Somerset Stakes, King's Stand Stakes, July Cup (twice), King George Stakes (twice), Bedford Stakes, Chesham Stakes, Nunthorpe Sweepstake (twice) and National Breeders' Stakes, he lost the 1949 2000 Guineas by a short head. Won 14 from 17 starts. Died in 1970 aged 24. The Abernant Stakes, named in his memory, is run over six furlongs at Newmarket's Craven Meeting in April. He was described by Sir Noel Murless as 'the fastest horse I ever saw'.

Affirmed Chestnut colt foaled 1975 by Exclusive Native out of Won't Tell You. Trained by Laz Barrera. Won the US Triple Crown in 1978, beating Alydar into second in all three races. Champion 2-year-old and champion 3-year-old. Champion Handicap Horse 1979. Horse of the Year 1978, 1979. Won 22 from 29 starts. Died January 2001.

Aga Khan Born 1936. His Highness Prince Karim, the Aga Khan, is the grandson of the Aga Khan, whose horses won the Derby five times, and son of Prince Aly Khan, the owner of Petite Etoile. As Aga Khan he is Imam (spiritual leader) of the Ismaili sect of Shia Muslims. Classic winners owned by him include Doyoun, Shergar, Shahrastani, Kahyasi and Sinndar. He was leading owner in 1981 and 2000, and his breeding interests are divided between the Gillstown Stud in Co. Kildare and the Haras de Bonneval in France.

Alleged Bay colt foaled 1974 by Hoist the Flag out of Princess Pout. Owned by Robert Sangster. Trained by Vincent O'Brien. Champion 3-year-old in Europe, 1977. Champion Older Horse in Europe, 1978. Won the Prix de l'Arc de Triomphe in 1977 and 1978. Won 9 from 10 starts.

Aly Khan Born 1911. Son of the 'old' Aga Khan who owned Derby winners Blenheim, Bahram, Mahmoud, My Love and Tulyar. Aly Khan's best colt was Taboun and his best filly Petite Etoile. He was married first to the Hon. Mrs Loel Guinness, mother of his son Karim, the present Aga Khan, and then to the film actress Rita Hayworth. He died in a car crash near Paris, May 1960.

Archer, Fred Born Frederick James Archer, Cheltenham, Gloucestershire, 11 January 1857. Nicknamed 'The Tin Man'. Archer rode 2748 winners from 8084 rides between 1869 and 1886. His first winner was in a steeplechase at Bangor at just 12 years of age and weighing just 4st 11lb (30.4kg). He rode 21 classic winners, including five Epsom Derby winners – Silvio (1877), Bend Or (1880), Iroquois (1881), Melton (1885) and Ormonde (1886). Champion Flat jockey for 13 consecutive years, he topped the 200 mark eight times. Archer was very tall for a jockey, 5ft 10ins (1.78m), and naturally weighed 11st (69.9kg). Only a draconian diet and a purgative, known as Archer's mixture, got him down to his racing weight of 8st (50.8kg). He shot himself on 8 November 1886 at Falmouth House, Newmarket, using a silver pistol given to him after a win at Aintree. He was 29 years old and suffering from depression following the death of his wife and a fever brought on by weight wasting before the Cambridgeshire. His ghost is said still to ride Newmarket racecourse.

Arkle   Bay gelding foaled 1957 by Archive out of Bright Cherry. Bred by Mary Baker. Owned by Anne, Duchess of Westminster. Trained by Tom Dreaper. Named after a mountain facing the Duchess's house by Loch Stack in Sutherland. He had the highest *Timeform* rating, at 212, ever awarded to a steeplechaser. Won the Cheltenham Gold Cup three times (1964, 1965, 1966), the Irish Grand National (1964), the King George VI Chase (1965), the Hennessy Gold Cup (1964, 1965) and the Whitbread Gold Cup (1965). Won 27 from 35 starts, including several epic duels with Mill House, and never fell on the racecourse. After cracking a pedal bone he retired in 1966. Put down 31 May 1970, his skeleton is preserved in the Irish Horse Museum at the Irish National Stud.

Asmussen, Cash   Born Brian Keith Asmussen, Agar, South Dakota, USA, 1962. His nickname of 'Cash' was bestowed upon him by his father but he formally adopted it in 1977. To date the only foreigner to become champion jockey in France, he was leading rider there five times (1985, 1986, 1988, 1989, 1990). His best rides included Suave Dancer, In the Wings, Soviet Star, April Run, Mairzy Doates, Kingmambo, Hernando, Dream Well, Spinning World and Montjeu. He retired in 2001.

Assault   Bay colt foaled 1943 by Bold Venture out of Igual. Owned and bred by King Ranch. Trained by Max Hirsch. Won the US Triple Crown in 1946. Having injured a foot as a foal, he was known as 'The Clubfooted Comet'. Won 18 from 42 starts. Sterile at stud, Assault was still racing as a seven-year-old. Died in 1971.

Bahram   Bay colt foaled 1932 by Blandford out of Friar's Daughter. Owned and bred by HH Aga Khan III. Trained by Frank Butters. Won the English Triple Crown in 1935. Unbeaten from 9 starts. Died 1956.

Bailey, Jerry   Born Dallas, Texas, USA, 29 August 1957. Bailey has ridden more than 5000 winners, including success in four Dubai World Cups on Cigar (1996), Singspiel (1997), Captain Steve (2001) and Street Cry (2002). He has won the Kentucky Derby twice, the Preakness Stakes twice and the Belmont Stakes once, and partnered Dubai Millennium to win the Prince of Wales' Stakes at Royal Ascot in June 2000.

Balding, Ian   Born 7 November 1938. The younger brother of trainer Toby and father of BBC racing presenter Clare and fellow trainer Andrew. He was leading trainer in 1971, largely due to the exploits of his greatest horse Mill Reef, his only classic winner. Paul Mellon was his principal patron for several years and he has also sent out many winners for Her Majesty the Queen from his Kingsclere stables near Newbury in Berkshire. The great sprinter Lochsong was also trained by Balding. Ian retired in 2002 and his son Andrew trained the 2003 Oaks winner Casual Look.

Balding, Toby   Born Gerald Barnard Balding, September 1936. Balding first took out a licence in 1957. His Flat successes include winning the Stewards' Cup and Ayr Gold Cup in 1986 with Green Ruby but he is better known as a National Hunt trainer, having won the Grand National twice with Highland Wedding (1969) and Little Polveir (1989), the Champion Hurdle with Beech Road (1989) and Morley Street (1991), and the Cheltenham Gold Cup with Cool Ground (1992).

Ballymoss   Chestnut colt foaled 1954 by Mossborough out of Indian Call. Owned by John McShain. Trained by Vincent O'Brien. Finished second to Crepello in the Derby (1957) but went on to win the Irish Derby and the St Leger at Doncaster, the first Irish-trained horse to do so. As a four-year-old he won the Coronation Cup, Eclipse Stakes, King George VI & Queen Elizabeth Diamond Stakes and Prix de l'Arc de Triomphe, once again being the first Irish-trained horse to win the French race. Sired Royal Palace. Died 1979.

Barry, Ron   Born Co. Limerick, Ireland, 28 February 1943. First winner: Final Approach in a novice hurdle (Ayr, 19 October 1964). Barry became champion National Hunt jockey in 1973 and again in 1974 and won the Cheltenham Gold Cup in 1973 and Whitbread Gold Cup in 1974 on The Dikler, the latter race on the disqualification of John Oaksey's mount, Proud Tarquin. Another notable victory was on the New Zealand-bred Grand Canyon in the Colonial Cup in South Carolina in 1976. Retired in 1983.

Beasley, Bobby   Grandson of Harry Beasley, who won the Grand National on Come Away in 1891, and one of only four jockeys since World War II to have won the Grand National, Cheltenham Gold Cup and Champion Hurdle. Alcohol addiction brought about his premature retirement but he made a successful comeback and won a second Cheltenham Gold Cup in 1974 before finally retiring for good.

Beaverbrook, Lady   Popular owner who took up racing after the death of her husband Max, proprietor of the *Daily Express*, in 1964. Her best-known horse was Bustino, who won the 1974 St Leger and 1975 Coronation Cup before running second to Grundy in the so-called 'race of the century', the 1975 King George VI & Queen Elizabeth Stakes. Other classic winners include Minster Son and Mystiko as well as Boldboy, Relkino, Niniski, and Terimon. Lady Beaverbrook died in 1994, aged 85.

Bend Or   Owned and bred by the first Duke of Westminster and trained by Robert Peck. Name is a heraldic term for a diagonal band in gold. Bend Or won the 1880 Derby by a head from Robert the Devil when ridden by Fred Archer with one arm (following a savaging by a horse a month earlier). As a stallion his best son was 1886 Triple Crown winner Ormonde, while his daughters included Ornament, Dam of Sceptre. Arkle traces to Bend Or on both sides of his pedigree, and interestingly, Arkle's owner Anne, Duchess of Westminster was the fourth wife of the second Duke of Westminster, grandson of Bend Or's owner.

Biddlecombe, Terry   Born 1941. After a successful amateur career he turned pro in 1960. His first winner under rules: Burnella, in a novice hurdle (Wincanton, March 1958). Attached to the Fred Rimell yard for most of his career, he won many top races on horses such as Charlie Potheen, Coral Diver, Red Thorn, Game Spirit and Gay Trip, although the Grand National eluded him as he was injured for Gay Trip's win. He retired in 1974 after riding 905 winners and is now part of a successful training partnership with his wife Henrietta Knight.

Bolger, Jim   Born Co. Wexford, Ireland, 25 December 1941. Bolger trained only one English classic winner, Jet Ski Lady, but was a prolific winner in his native country with horses such as Give Thanks, Park Appeal, Park Express, Polonia, Condessa, Flame of Tara, and the greatest of all, St Jovite, runner-up to Dr Devious in the 1992 Derby before reversing the form by 12 lengths in the Irish Derby. He was champion trainer in Ireland by prize money in 1991 and 1992, and by number of winners trained in 1990, 1992, 1994 and 1996.

outin, François Born 1937. Took out his first licence in 1964. He enjoyed early English classic success with La Lagune in the 1968 Oaks, while Nonoalco brought him further success in the 1974 2000 Guineas. His Nureyev was disqualified after winning the 1980 2000 Guineas but further English classic wins were attained by Zino (2000 Guineas, 1982) and Miesque (1000 Guineas, 1987). Arazi was a brilliant winner of the Juvenile at Churchill Downs in 1991 while French classic wins included the 1976 French Derby with Caracolero. His greatest horse though was Sagaro, who with Lester Piggott aboard won the Ascot Gold Cup three times in successive years, 1975-77. He died in 1995, aged 58.

reasley, Scobie Born Arthur Breasley, Wagga Wagga, New South Wales, Australia, 1914. Known as 'Scobie' after Australian trainer James Scobie. At 14 he began racing in Melbourne, and won his first major race, the 1930 AJC Metropolitan, on Cragford, at the age of 16. Breasley went to England after World War II. In 1951 he won his first classic – the 2000 Guineas at Newmarket – on Ki Ming. Won the 1954 1000 Guineas on Festoon and the 1957 Prix de l'Arc de Triomphe on Oroso. He also won the Epsom Derby twice, on Santa Claus (1964) and Charlottown (1966). He won the jockeys' championship four times (1957, 1961, 1962, 1963). From 1955 until his retirement in 1969, Breasley averaged more than 100 winners each year in Britain as well as being highly successful in Australia. His career total of 3251 winners included 2161 in England.

rigadier Gerard Bay colt foaled 1968 by Queen's Hussar out of La Paiva. Bred and owned by Mr and Mrs J. Hislop. Trained by Dick Hern. Brigadier Gerard became a superstar by beating the two 'wonderhorses' Mill Reef (by three lengths, inflicting his only defeat) and My Swallow in the 1971 2000 Guineas. Champion Miler in England, 1971. Champion Older Horse, Miler and Horse of the Year in England, 1972. Six times Group One winner in England. His wins included the Middle Park Stakes, St James's Palace Stakes, Sussex Stakes, Goodwood Mile, Queen Elizabeth II Stakes, Champion Stakes, Lockinge Stakes, Prince of Wales Stakes, Eclipse Stakes and King George VI Stakes. Won 17 from 18 starts. Died 1989. A race named after him is run at Sandown Park.

rown Jack Brown gelding foaled 1924 by Jackdaw out of Querquidella. Bred by George Webb. Trained by Aubrey Hastings (until 1929), then Ivor Anthony. One of the best-loved horses of the 1920s and 1930s, he won the Champion Hurdle in 1928 before being switched to Flat racing. Partnered by Steve Donoghue, Brown Jack won the long distance (2m 6f) Queen Alexandra Stakes at Ascot six times in succession (1929-34). Died in 1948.

uckle, Frank Born Francis Buckle, Newmarket, Suffolk, 1766. Known as 'The Pocket Hercules', Buckle rode a total of 27 classic winners including the Derby five times on John Bull (1792), Daedalus (1794), Tyrant (1802), Phantom (1811) and Emilius (1823). He also won the Oaks nine times, St Leger twice, 1000 Guineas six times and 2000 Guineas five times and continued race riding until he was 65.

udgett, Arthur Born 1916. Only the second person in racing history to own, breed and train two Derby winners, after William L'Anson in the mid-19th century. Blakeney was his first Derby winner and this horse helped him to become leading trainer in 1969. His second success came with Morston, also a son of Windmill Girl, whom Budgett had trained to be runner-up in the 1964 Oaks. Other notable Budgett horses include Commissar, Blast, Derring-Do, Huntercombe, Petty Officer, Dominion and Daring Boy.

Byerley Turk Foaled in the late 1670s and one of the three founding stallions of the thoroughbred breed (see Darley Arabian and Godolphin Arabian), he is said to have been ridden by Captain Byerley at the Battle of the Boyne before being brought to England in 1689 and sent to stud in Co. Durham. Became the sire of Jigg and, through him, the great-great-grandsire of Herod, the greatest stallion of the latter 1800s. Other distinguished descendants include The Tetrarch, Blakeney and Dr Devious.

Carson, Willie Born William Fisher Hunter Carson, Stirling, Scotland, 16 November 1942. The first Scotsman to be champion jockey. His first ride was on Marija at Redcar (fifth). First winner: Pinker's Pond (Catterick, 19 July 1962). His first classic success came on High Top (2000 Guineas, 1972). He won four Epsom Derbys, on Troy (1979), Henbit (1980), Nashwan (1989) and Erhaab (1994), and was champion jockey five times (1972, 1973, 1978, 1980, 1983). In total he rode 3828 winners, including 17 UK classics, before retiring in 1997, making him the fourth highest winning rider after Richards, Eddery and Piggott.

Cauthen, Steve Born Covington, New York, USA, 1 May 1960. Nicknamed 'Stevie Wonder' and 'The Million Dollar Man'. First ride: King of Swat (Churchill Downs, Kentucky, 1976). First winner: Red Piper (River Downs, Kentucky, 1976, aged 16). In 1978 he was the youngest winner of the US Triple Crown on Affirmed. Having hit a disastrous patch of form in 1979, riding 110 consecutive losers, Cauthen's career was resurrected when he crossed the Atlantic. Champion jockey three times (1984, 1985, 1987), he won the 2000 Guineas on Tap On Wood (1979), the fillies' Triple Crown on Oh So Sharp (1985), and the Epsom Derby twice, on Slip Anchor (1985) and Reference Point (1987). The only jockey to win the Kentucky, Epsom, Irish, French, and Italian Derby, he is also the only jockey to win both US and British champion jockey titles.

Cazalet, Peter Born 1907. Cazalet took up training at Fairlawne, near Tonbridge in Kent, in 1939. He was leading trainer in 1950, 1960 and 1965 although he never won any of the 'Big Three' National Hunt races, suffering desperate luck in the Grand National in particular. Davy Jones, ridden by Anthony Mildmay, ran out between the last two fences when leading the 1936 race and the same jockey had a severe bout of cramp when looking an assured winner in 1948 aboard Cromwell, but worst of all was when the Queen Mother's Devon Loch lost his legs 50 yards from certain victory in 1956. Other notable horses Cazalet trained included Statecraft, Rose Park, Lochroe, Dunkirk, Monaveen, Manicou, Double Star, Silver Dome, Makaldar, Laffy, Antiar and The Rip. He died in 1973, having trained over 1100 winners including 250 for the Queen Mother.

Cecil, Henry Born Henry Richard Amherst Cecil, 11 January 1943 (ten minutes before his identical twin brother David). He became Captain Cecil Boyd-Rochfort's assistant trainer in 1964 and took over the stables at Freemason Lodge in 1968 when his stepfather retired. His first winner was Celestial

Cloud at Ripon on 17 May 1969 and his first classic success came with Bolkonski in the 1975 2000 Guineas. The following year he won the race again with Wollow to help him to his first championship. On the retirement of Sir Noel Murless, whose daughter Julie he had married in 1966 (they divorced in 1990 and Cecil was remarried to Natalie Payne in 1992), he moved into Murless's stables at Warren Place in Newmarket. He won his first Derby, with Slip Anchor, in 1985, and followed up with Reference Point in 1987, Commander-In-Chief in 1993 and Oath in 1999. Fillies include Oh So Sharp, Bosra Sham, Indian Skimmer, One In A Million, Fairy Footsteps, Diminuendo, Ramruma, Wince, Sleepytime, Snow Bride, Lady Carla, Reams Of Verse and Love Divine. His most famous stayers were Le Moss, who won the Ascot Gold Cup, Goodwood Cup and Doncaster Cup in both 1979 and 1980, and Ardross, who won the Ascot Gold Cup in 1981 and 1982. Other notable horses included Old Vic, French and Irish Derby winner in 1989, and Kris, who won 14 of his 16 races between 1978 and 1980. Cecil was leading trainer ten times (1976, 1978, 1979, 1982, 1984, 1985, 1987, 1988, 1990, 1993).

Champion, Bob   Born 4 June 1948. The rider of 421 winners as a bread-and-butter National Hunt jockey, he is notable for his 1981 Grand National success on Aldaniti following his fight against testicular cancer. His book *Champion's Story*, written with Jonathan Powell, was made into the film *Champions*, starring John Hurt.

Channon, Mick   Born Orcheston, Wiltshire, 28 November 1948. One of very few sportsmen to reach the top in two completely different fields, after retiring from a footballing career which saw him win 46 England caps and score 21 goals between 1973 and 1978, he became assistant to John Baker and Ken Cunningham-Brown before taking out his own licence in 1990. Based in West Ilsley, his Group One horses include Piccolo, Tobougg, Seazun, Bint Allayl, Josr Algarhoud and the ill-fated Queen's Logic.

Cigar   Bay colt foaled 1990 by Palace Music out of Solar Slew. Bred in the USA with owner Allen Paulson. Trained for most of his career by Bill Mott. Winner of 16 consecutive stakes, including the Breeders' Cup classic and the Dubai World Cup, to equal the US record set by Citation in 1948, and world record-holder for most money won in one season ($4.9 million in 1996). Horse of the Year and Champion Older Horse in the US in 1995 and 1996.

Citation   Brown colt foaled 1945 by Bull Lea out of Hydroplane II. Owned and bred by Calumet Farm. Trained by Ben Jones. Won the US Triple Crown in 1948. First horse to win $1 million in prize money. Won 32 from 45 starts, including 27 from his first 28 starts, and joint record holder with Cigar for the most consecutive races (16) won in the US. Died 1970.

Cochrane, Ray   Born Ulster, 18 June 1957. First winner: Romany Way (Windsor, August 1974). He won the Epsom Derby on Kahyasi (1988). With 1600 career wins, he retired 6 November 2000. Now agent for Frankie Dettori, he rescued Dettori after the plane crash at Newmarket on 1 June 2000 which killed pilot Patrick Mackey.

Common   Brown colt foaled 1888 by Isonomy out of Thistle. Bred by the 1st Baron Alington. Owned by Sir Frederick Johnstone. Trained by John Porter. Won the English Triple Crown in 1891. Won 4 from 5 starts. Died 1912.

Cottage Rake   Brown gelding foaled 1939 by Cottage out of Hartingo. Owned by F.L. Vickerman. Trained Vincent O'Brien. Won three successive Cheltenha Gold Cups (1948, 1949, 1950) ridden by Aubrey Brabazon. Also won the Irish Cesarewitch (1947) and King George VI Chase (1949).

Count Fleet   Brown colt foaled 1940 by Reigh Cou out of Quickly. Bred by Stoner Creek stud. Owned Mrs J.D. Hertz, wife of the founder of the Hertz re car company. Trained by Don Cameron. Won the Triple Crown in 1943. Won 16 from 21 starts. Died 1973.

Crisp   Owned and bred by Sir Chester Manifold, o of the most prominent figures in Australian racing Trained by Fred Winter. An outstanding winner of Two Mile Champion Chase in 1971 and fifth in the Cheltenham Gold Cup of 1972, but the race he w always be remembered for is the 1973 Grand National where he led the great Red Rum until the shadow of the post, giving away 23lb (10.4kg). Aft Richard Pitman's memorable front-running performance, Crisp did gain some small consolati when defeating Red Rum by an easy eight length a level-weight match the following November.

Crump, Neville   Born 27 December 1910. Middleham-based trainer of three Grand National winners, Sheila's Cottage (1948), Teal (1952) and Merryman II (1960), as well as the Scottish Natior five times with Wot No Sun (1949), Merryman II (1959), Arcturus (1968), Salkeld (1980) and Cant (1983). Crump also trained the enigmatic Dorman beat Mill House (albeit in receipt of 3st (19kg)) in 1964 Whitbread Gold Cup. Crump retired in 1989 and died in January 1997, at the age of 86.

Cumani, Luca   Born Milan, Italy, April 1949. After successful amateur riding career culminating in a win on the Ian Balding-trained Meissen in the 197 Moet & Chandon Silver Magnum at Epsom, he began his training career as assistant to Henry C before taking out his own licence in 1976. Two English Derby wins, with Kahyasi (1988) and High Rise (1998), were the highlights of his career and also gave Lester Piggott his record-beating 28th classic victory on Comanche Run in 1984. Fellow Italian Frankie Dettori joined Cumani as an apprentice in 1987 and gave him two Group One winners in Mark of Distinction and Shamsir.

Cummings, Bart   Born 1927. The Australian traine won the Melbourne Cup 11 times, Light Fingers being his first success in 1965 and Rogan Josh hi last in 1999.

Dancing Brave   Bay colt foaled 1983 by Lyphard c of Navajo Princess. Won both the 2000 Guineas a the Prix de l'Arc de Triomphe in 1986. Finished second to Shahrastani in the 1986 Epsom Derby amid criticism that Greville Starkey had given him too much to do. Also won the Eclipse Stakes and King George VI & Queen Elizabeth Stakes. Won 8 from 10 starts. Retired to stud in 1986.

Darley Arabian   Foaled in 1700. Like Byerley Turk never raced, but from the age of four until he died aged 30 he was a prolific stallion at Aldby Park. S of Flying Childers, the first great racehorse, and great-great-grandsire of Eclipse.

Darley, Kevin   Born Kevin Paul Darley, Tettenhall, Staffordshire, 1960. Apprenticed to Reg Hollinshe First winner: Dust Up (Haydock, 5 August 1977). Champion apprentice in 1978, his biggest win can in the 1995 Prix du Jockey Club (French Derby) o Celtic Swing. In 2000 he became the first English-born champion jockey since 1982 and he was runner-up in 2001. In 2004 he won both the Englis and Irish 1000 Guineas on Attraction (trained by Mark Johnston), the first horse to complete this double.

Darling, Fred Born 1884. One of the most successful trainers of the 20th century, he began his career training jumpers for Lady de Bathe (Lily Langtry) before turning to the Flat and ultimately securing 19 classic winners including seven Derby wins with Captain Cuttle (1922), Manna (1925), Coronach (1926), Cameronian (1931), Bois Roussel (1938), Pont L'Eveque (1940) and Owen Tudor (1941) He also trained fillies' Triple Crown winner Sun Chariot (1942). He died 1953.

Dawn Run Bay mare foaled 1978 by Deep Run out of Twilight Slave. Owned by Charmaine Hill. Trained by Paddy Mullins. The only horse to have won both the Champion Hurdle (1984) and the Cheltenham Gold Cup (1986), she also won the French and Irish Champion Hurdles in 1984. Won 21 of 35 starts. Killed in a fall at Auteuil in 1986.

Day, Pat Born Brush, Colorado, USA, 13 October 1953. Day rode his first winner in 1973. Camden Park's win at Churchill Downs, Kentucky, on 31 May 2001 gave him his 8000th winner, a feat only before achieved by Willie Shoemaker and Laffit Pincay. Day rode five Preakness Stakes winners (1985, 1990, 1994-96), three Belmont Stakes winners (1989, 1994, 2000) and a Kentucky Derby winner on Lil E Tee (1992).

Desert Orchid Grey gelding foaled 1979 by Grey Mirage out of Flower Child. Owned by Richard Burridge. Trained by David Elsworth. Ridden by Colin Brown, then Simon Sherwood (to April 1989) who won on nine out of his ten rides on the horse, and finally Richard Dunwoody. Won the Cheltenham Gold Cup (1989), King George VI Chase four times (1986, 1988, 1989, 1990) and the Irish Grand National (1990). Won the Whitbread Gold Cup (1988) and 34 from 70 starts.

Dettori, Frankie Born Lanfranco Dettori, Milan, Italy, 15 November 1970. First winner: Rif (Turin, Italy, 16 November 1986). First British winner: Lizzy Hare (Goodwood, 9 June 1987). Dettori has been champion jockey twice (1994, 1995). Though he has never won the Derby, he has seven classics to his name: Oaks (1994 on Balanchine, 1995 on Moonshell); St Leger (1995 on Classic Cliche, 1996 on Shantou); 2000 Guineas (1996 on Mark of Esteem, 1999 on Island Sands); 1000 Guineas (1998 on Cape Verdi). Dettori's greatest claim to fame is the day (28 September 1996) he rode all seven winners on the card at Ascot, clocking up a 25,095-1 accumulator in the process, the seven being Wall Street (Cumberland Lodge Stakes), Diffident (Diadem Stakes), Decorated Hero (Tote Festival Handicap), Mark of Esteem (Queen Elizabeth II Stakes), Fatefully (Rosemary Rated Stakes), Lochangel (Blue Seal Conditions Stakes) and Fujiyama Crest (Gordon Carter Handicap). Other notable victories have included Prix de l'Arc de Triomphe wins on Lammtarra, Sakhee and Marienbad, a Breeders' Cup Turf victory aboard Daylami and a Dubai World Cup win aboard Dubai Millennium. He was awarded the MBE in 2000.

Diamond Jubilee Bay colt foaled 1897 by St Simon out of Perdita. Bred and owned by HRH The Prince of Wales. Trained by Richard Marsh. Won the English Triple Crown (2000 Guineas, Derby, St Leger) in 1900. Won 6 from 15 starts. Sold to Argentina in 1906. Leading sire in Argentina 1914-16. Died 1923.

Dickinson's Tony Dickinson (1915-91) and his wife

Monica (formerly Miss Birtwistle) began a successful training partnership in the 1960s and 1970s which was taken over by their son Michael in 1980. Silver Buck was inherited from his father and maintained his form to complete a King George double (1979 and 1980) before going on to win the Cheltenham Gold Cup in 1982. Michael's reputation grew and culminated in his record first five placings in the 1983 Gold Cup. A brief spell as private trainer to Robert Sangster ended when Dickinson moved to America and the Harewood yard was taken over by his mother. Michael sent out Da Hoss to win the Breeders' Cup Mile in 1996 and 1998.

Donoghue, Steve Born 1884 in Warrington. Known as 'Our Steve'. Donoghue struggled at the beginning of his career and had to ply his trade first in France, and then Ireland, before returning to England. Donoghue was champion jockey ten years in succession between 1914 and 1923. Won 14 classics, including six Derbys: Pommern (1915), Gay Crusader (1917), Humorist (1921), Captain Cuttle (1922), Papyrus (1923) and Manna (1925). Donoghue was also associated with two great horses: The Tetrarch, who only ran as a two-year-old and, in 1913 it is believed, was the fastest horse who has ever raced in England; and Brown Jack, who Donoghue rode to six consecutive victories in the Queen Alexandra Stakes at Royal Ascot (1929-34). During his career he never committed a single riding offence. His autobiography was titled *Donoghue Up!* He died 1945.

Doumen, François Born 1940. The top French trainer, he made it fashionable for foreign raiders to make successful plunders of the top British National Hunt races, beginning when Nupsala won the 1987 King George VI Stakes at Kempton. The Fellow won the Cheltenham Gold Cup in 1994 and other notable British successes included Algan's 1994 King George success and First Gold's impressive win in the 2000 race.

Dreaper, Tom Born 1898. Arguably the greatest Irish trainer of the 20th century, Dreaper bought Greenogue farm in Kilsallaghan, Dublin, and turned it into a training establishment. Prince Regent won the 1946 Cheltenham Gold Cup for him and Fort Leney the 1968 race but his greatest triumphs were with Flyingbolt, winner of the 1966 Irish Grand National, and the great Arkle. When Dreaper died in 1975 his son, Jim, took over the yard and himself had great success, winning the Gold Cup with Ten Up (1975) and three Irish Nationals with Brown Lad (1975, 1976, 1978).

Dubai Millennium Bay colt foaled 1996 by Seeking the Gold out of Colorado Dancer. Owned and bred by Sheikh Mohammed Al Maktoum, and originally named Yazzer. Trained by David Loder as a two-year-old; transferred to Godolphin and trained by Saeed Bin Suroor. After winning a maiden race impressively under Loder at Yarmouth in 1998, he won his two preparation races for the 1999 Derby with Bin Suroor, but it is thought he simply did not act on the vagaries and undulations of the Epsom Downs course, and he finished ninth. He remained unbeaten after this defeat and the manner of his victory in the 2000 Dubai World Cup from a world-class field suggested that this was one of the all-time great horses. Having won 9 of his 10 starts a training accident prevented a match with the other great horse of the day, Montjeu, and Dubai Millennium, who had suffered a broken hind leg, was saved for breeding purposes. Soon after taking up duties at

HORSE RACING

the Dalham Hall Stud, however, he was struck down with grass sickness and died 29 April 2001.

Duffield, George   Born Wakefield, Yorkshire, 30 November 1946. Holds a Guinness world record for the most consecutive wins on a horse (11, and 13 in total) when riding Spindrifter in 1980. A long association with Sir Mark Prescott has ensured a steady flow of big winners although his first classic win on User Friendly in the 1992 Oaks was trained by Clive Brittain.

Dunlop, John   Born John Leeper Dunlop, 1939. Began as assistant to Gordon Smyth before taking out his training licence in 1966. Based at Castle Stables, Arundel, West Sussex, Dunlop has trained two Derby winners to date, Shirley Heights (1978) and Erhaab (1994), and his Salsabil won the 1000 Guineas, Oaks and Irish Derby in 1990. Other notable horses he has trained include Quick as Lightning, Shadayid, Circus Plume, Moon Madness, Silver Patriarch, Millenary and Habibti. Sheikh Hamdan Al Maktoum is his chief patron and he was leading trainer in 1995. Recovering from a life-threatening illness in 2001, his son Ed Dunlop trains at Newmarket.

Dunwoody, Richard   Born Thomas Richard Dunwoody, Belfast, 18 January 1964. Known as 'The Prince'. First winner: Game Trust (Cheltenham, 4 May 1983). Dunwoody held the record for the greatest number of career wins for a National Hunt jockey in Britain (1699 from 9399 rides) until Tony McCoy beat it in 2002. Dunwoody broke the previous record (1679) with a win on Yorkshire Edition at Wincanton, 5 April 1999. Champion jockey for three seasons (1993, 1994, 1995), he is one of only four post-war jockeys (the others are Fred Winter, Willie Robinson and Bobby Beasley) to have captured the triple crown of Cheltenham Gold Cup (Charter Party, 1986), Champion Hurdle (Kribensis, 1990) and Grand National (West Tip, 1986; Minnehoma, 1994). Awarded the MBE in 1993. Dunwoody retired in December 1999. His autobiography was titled *Obsessed*.

Easterby's   Born 1929, Miles Henry (M.H.) Easterby, better known as Peter, took out his first training licence in 1950. Very successful on the Flat, while his jumping successes include the Cheltenham Gold Cup with Alverton (1979) and Little Owl (1981), and the Champion Hurdle with Night Nurse (1976, 1977) and Sea Pigeon (1980, 1981). On his retirement in 1995 his Malton yard was taken over by his son, Tim. Peter's younger brother Michael William (M.W.) Easterby trains at Sheriff Hutton, near York, and took out his licence in 1961. His only classic success came with Mrs McArdy in the 1977 1000 Guineas but he will be best remembered for training the great sprinter Lochnager, who won the King's Stand Stakes, July Cup and William Hill Sprint (Nunthorpe) in 1976.

Eclipse   Chestnut colt foaled 1764 by Marske out of Spiletta. Bred by HRH William, the Duke of Cumberland (the third son of King George II). Owned by William Wildman and Dennis O'Kelly. Foaled during the great solar eclipse of 1764, Eclipse was unbeaten and never headed in 18 starts including seven walkovers. Retired in 1771, he sired 344 winners, including the Derby winners Young Eclipse, Saltram, and Sergeant, as well as important runners and sires such as Pot-8-Os and King Fergus whose lines survive to this day. It is estimated that among all living thoroughbreds, at least 95 per cent can trace their direct tail-male line back to Eclipse. Died

1789. His skeleton is now on display in the Jockey Club Museum in Newmarket.

Eddery, Pat   Born Patrick James John Eddery, Newbridge, Co. Galway, Ireland, 18 March 1952. First winner: Alvaro (Epsom, 29 April 1969). Won 14 classics including three Derby wins, Grundy (1975), Golden Fleece (1982) and Quest for Fame (1990). In 1974 he became the youngest champion jockey for 50 years, and he was champion jockey 11 times (1974-77, 1986, 1988-91, 1993, 1996). He missed out twice on a century of winners in the UK, in 1982 when he was champion jockey in Ireland and in 2002 when he managed 99 wins. During the 1980s Eddery won the Prix de l'Arc de Triomphe four times, on Detroit (1980), Rainbow Quest (1985), Dancing Brave (1986) and Trempolino (1987). He retired in November 2003 with a total of 4632 winners, only Gordon Richards having ridden more among British jockeys.

Elliott, Charlie   Born Edward Charles Elliott, 1904. Champion jockey in 1923, sharing the title with Steve Donoghue, but notable for winning the title in 1924 while still an apprentice. He spent much of his career riding in France but still won 14 English classics: the Derby three times (1927, 1938, 1949); the Oaks twice (1931, 1943); the 2000 Guineas five times (1923, 1928, 1940, 1941, 1949); and the 1000 Guineas four times (1924, 1931, 1932, 1944). Retiring from riding in 1953, he trained in France and England for the next ten years. He died 1979.

Fabre, André   Born December 1945. First took out a licence in 1977. Won four English classics, with Toulon (St Leger, 1991), Zafonic (2000 Guineas, 1993), Intrepidity (Oaks, 1993) and Pennekamp (2000 Guineas, 1995) as well as five Prix de l'Arc de Triomphe wins with Trempolino (1987), Subotica (1992), Carnegie (1994), Peintre Célèbre (1997) and Sagamix (1998). He has monopolised the French trainers' championship since 1988.

Fallon, Kieren   Born Kieren Francis Fallon, Crusheen, Co. Clare, Ireland, 22 February 1965. Apprenticed to Kevin Prendergast in 1983. First winner: Piccadilly Lord (Navan, 18 June 1984). Moved to be apprenticed to Jimmy Fitzgerald and his first winner in England was Evichstar (Thirsk, 16 April 1988). Champion jockey in 1997, 1998, 1999, 2001, 2002 and 2003. Stable jockey to Henry Cecil, 1997-99, he was first jockey to Sir Michael Stoute in 2000 and 2001. He won the Derby on Oath (1999), Kris Kin (2002) and North Light (2003) the 1000 Guineas on Sleepytime (1997), Wince (1999) and Russian Rhythm (2003), the 2000 Guineas on King's Best (2000) and Golan (2001), and the Oaks on Reams Of Verse (1997), Ramruma (1999) and Ouija Board (2004).

Fitzgerald, Mick   Born Cork, Ireland, 10 May 1970. Grand National on Rough Quest (1996), and the Cheltenham Gold Cup on See More Business (1999). His autobiography is titled *A Jump Jockey's Life*. He rode his 1000th winner in November 2003.

Flyingbolt   Chestnut colt foaled in 1959 by Airborne out of East Lock. Owned by T. Wilkinson. Trained by Tom Dreaper. Rated only 2lb (0.9kg) inferior to his stablemate Arkle at his peak, in 1966 he won the Two Mile Champion Chase as well as the Massey Ferguson Gold Cup and the Thyestes Chase at Gowran Park.

Flying Fox   Bay colt foaled 1896 by Orme out of Vampire. Owned and bred by the 1st Duke of Westminster. Trained by John Porter. In 1899 Flying Fox became John Porter's third English Triple Crown winner. Won 9 from 11 starts. Died 1911.

Forster, Tim Born 1934. One of the most popular trainers of his generation, Captain Tim Forster will be remembered for his successful partnership with champion National Hunt jockey Graham Thorner. He took out his licence in 1962 and specialised in the big chase events, winning the Grand National three times with Well To Do (1972), Ben Nevis (1980) and Last Suspect (1985). He retired in 1998 having trained 1346 winners and was succeeded by Henry Daly. He died 21 April 1999, aged 65.

Francis, Dick Born Richard Stanley Francis, Pembrokeshire, Wales, 31 October 1920. Rode his first winner on Wrenbury Tiger at Bangor-on-Dee (3 May 1947) and his last on Crudwell at Leicester (7 January 1957). Champion National Hunt jockey in 1954, he never won a major race; the inexplicable collapse of his mount in the 1956 Grand National, the Queen Mother's Devon Loch, when clear and 50yds from the post, is part of racing folklore. Published his autobiography *The Sport of Queens* in 1957 and his first novel *Dead Cert* in 1962, establishing a career as a best-selling thriller writer.

Francome, John Born Swindon, Wiltshire, 13 December 1952. Originally worked as a panel beater. Won gold medal at the European Showjumping Championships 1969. Won his very first National Hunt race in 1970 on Multigrey and remained as first jockey to Fred Winter throughout his career. He retired in 1985 having ridden 1138 winners from 5072 mounts. Won the Cheltenham Gold Cup on Midnight Court (1978) and the Champion Hurdle on Sea Pigeon (1981). Champion jockey 1976, 1979, 1981, 1982 (he stopped riding that year when level with the injured Peter Scudamore and they shared the title), 1983, 1984, 1985. His autobiography *Born Lucky* was published in 1985 and he has written numerous novels. Awarded the MBE in 1986.

Further Flight Grey gelding foaled 1986 by Pharly out of Flying Nelly. Owned by Simon Wingfield Digby. Trained by Barry Hills. Son of the 1974 Cambridgeshire winner, Further Flight won the Group Three Jockey Club Cup at Newmarket every year between 1991 and 1995, the only horse to win the same pattern race five years in a row. The splendid grey animal became whiter with the passing of the years and also won the Ebor (1990), Goodwood Cup (1991, 1992) and Doncaster Cup (1992). Put down in July 2001, aged 15.

Gainsborough Bay colt foaled 1915 by Bayardo out of Rosedrop. Owned and bred by Lady James Douglas. Trained by Alec Taylor. Won the English Triple Crown in 1918. Won 5 from 8 starts. Sire of Hyperion, he was the leading sire in 1932 and 1933. Died 1945.

Gallant Fox Bay colt foaled 1927 by Sir Galahad III out of Marguerite. Bred at Claiborne Farm. Owned by William Woodward. Trained by James Fitzsimmons. Champion 3-year-old. Won the US Triple Crown in 1930. Won 11 from 17 starts. Only Triple Crown winner to sire another – Omaha. Died 1954.

Galtee More Bay colt foaled 1894 by Kendal out of Morganette. Owned and bred by John Gubbins. Trained by Sam Darling. Won the English Triple Crown in 1897. Won 11 from 13 starts. Sold to the Russian government in 1897, he was sold on to Germany in 1904. Died 1917.

Gay Crusader Bay colt foaled 1914 by Bayardo out of Gay Laura. Owned and bred by Alfred Cox. Trained by Alec Taylor. Won the English Triple Crown in 1917. Jockey Steve Donoghue said he was the best horse he ever rode. Won 8 from 10 starts. Died 1932.

Gifford, Josh Born Great Stukeley, nr Huntingdon, 1941. Apprenticed to Cliff Beechener and then Fred Armstrong as a Flat jockey, Gifford joined Ryan Price as a National Hunt jockey in the late 1950s, riding his first winner at Wincanton on Kingmaker (17 December 1959). Taking over from Fred Winter as Price's stable jockey, he had immediate success, winning the jockeys' title four times. He never won the big three National Hunt races and indeed never had a ride in the Cheltenham Gold Cup, but was placed second on Honey End in the 1967 Grand National and second on Major Rose in the 1970 Champion Hurdle. Taking over from Ryan Price at Findon in 1970, he trained the 1981 National winner Aldaniti (Edward Woodward played Gifford in the film *Champions*). Famous for having great success during the autumn months, he is still producing winners with his limited stock. Gifford's brother, Macer, was also a top-class jockey whose life was ended prematurely.

Gladiateur Bay colt foaled 1862 by Monarque out of Miss Gladiator. Owned and bred by Comte Frederic De Lagrange. Trained by Tom Jennings. Won the English Triple Crown in 1865, the Ascot Gold Cup in 1866 and four Grands Prix at Longchamps. Won 16 from 19 starts despite being almost continuously lame. Died 1875.

Godolphin Training operation begun by Sheikh Mohammed Al Maktoum in Dubai in 1994. After the recruitment of Saeed Bin Suroor as trainer in 1995 the stable began to plunder the world's Group One races with winners including Balanchine (Oaks and Irish Derby, 1994), Lammtarra (Derby, 1995, in the colours of the Sheikh's son, Saeed Maktoum Al Maktoum, King George and Prix de l'Arc de Triomphe, 1995), Moonshell (Oaks, 1995), Classic Cliché (St Leger, 1996) and numerous others. Frankie Dettori is Godolphin's principal jockey in Europe. Two stars which should perhaps be given special mention are Daylami, winner of the Eclipse in 1998 as well as the King George, Irish Champion Stakes and Breeders' Cup Turf in 1999, and Dubai Millennium, the Sheikh's pride and joy and winner of all his races bar the 1999 English Derby.

Godolphin Arabian Foaled in 1724. Said to have been found pulling a water cart in Paris, he was the direct ancestor of Man O' War and Santa Claus.

Golden Miller Bay gelding foaled 1927 by Goldcourt out of Miller's Pride. Owned by Dorothy Paget. Trained by Basil Briscoe. The only horse to win both the Grand National and the Cheltenham Gold Cup in the same year (1934), he set a National course record that stood until broken by Red Rum. Ran four other times in the National, but did not finish the course. Won Cheltenham Gold Cup a record five times (1932-36), the last time trained by Owen Anthony after an acrimonious split between his owner and previous trainer. Won 29 from 55 starts. Died 1957.

Gosden, John Born 30 March 1951. Following spells as assistant to Noel Murless and then Vincent O'Brien he took out his own licence in California in 1980 and produced Royal Heroine to win the Mile at the Inaugural Breeders' Cup at Hollywood Park in 1984. Returning to Britain in 1988 he set up at Newmarket. His first classic winner was Shantou (St Leger, 1996) and further successes include Benny the Dip (Derby, 1997) and Lahan (1000 Guineas, 2000). He moved to Manton, near Marlborough, Wiltshire in 1999.

Greaves, Alex Born Alex Ann Greaves, 14 May 1968. First winner: Andrews First (Southwell, 1 December 1989). The first female jockey to ride out her claim by reaching 100 winners, she was also the first woman to ride in the Derby, on Portuguese Lil (1996) and the first, and currently the only, female jockey to win a Group race (Group One Nunthorpe Stakes on Ya Malak). She also won the Lincoln Handicap on Amenable (1991).

Guest, Raymond American owner of Sir Ivor, winner of the 2000 Guineas, Derby, Champion Stakes and Washington DC International in 1968. His other successes included Larkspur (Derby, 1962), and L'Escargot (Gold Cup, 1970, 1971; Grand National, 1975). He also won the 1965 Preakness with Tom Rolfe. Former US Ambassador to Ireland. He died December 1991, aged 84

Guest, Richard Born Andover, Hampshire, 10 July 1965. First winner: Coral Leisure (Cheltenham, October 1986). Won the Grand National on Red Marauder (2001) and the Champion Hurdle on Beech Road (1989). Guest announced his retirement from race riding after being found guilty of breaching the non-triers' rule (Rule 151) at Perth in April 1998 – his third such offence that season – but had a change of heart.

Hammond, John Born Bromley, Kent, 1960. Educated at Rugby and Trinity College, Dublin. Hammond began his career working for Susan Piggott's bloodstock agency before becoming assistant trainer to Patrick Haslam at Newmarket. He took out his own licence in 1987 in Chantilly, France, following brief spells working for Jim Dreaper in Ireland and then André Fabre. The success of Suave Dancer in the 1991 French Derby and Prix de l'Arc de Triomphe assured his place in turf history but his best horse was Montjeu, winner of the 1999 French Derby, Arc and Irish Derby as well as the 2000 King George.

Harwood, Guy Born 10 June 1939. Harwood took out his training licence in 1966 having been an assistant to Bryan Marshall. His notable performers include To-Agori-Mou, Recitation, Kalaglow, Lear Fan, Rousillon and Warning, but his greatest horse was undoubtedly Dancing Brave. He retired in 1998 and handed over his yard in Pulborough, Sussex, to his daughter Amanda Perrett.

Head's Born 1924, Alec Head began training in Chantilly in 1947, producing three English classic wins on Lavandin (Derby, 1956), Rose Royale II (1000 Guineas, 1957) and Taboun (2000 Guineas, 1959), and four Prix de l'Arc de Triomphe wins on Nuccio (1952), Saint Crespin II (1959), Ivanjica (1976) and Gold River (1981). His son Freddie, born in 1947, was one of the greatest French jockeys, winning the French Derby four times: on Goodly (trained by his grandfather, Willie) in 1969, Roi Lear (trained by his father) in 1973, Val de l'Orne (trained by his father) in 1975 and Youth in 1976. He also won the Prix de l'Arc de Triomphe four times: on Bon Mot (trained by Willie Head) in 1966, San San in 1972, Ivanjica in 1976 and Three Troikas (trained by his sister, Criquette) in 1979. He also won three English classics. Criquette (christened Christiane) Head-Maarek was born in 1948 and took out her first licence in 1977. She has won the 1000 Guineas with Ma Biche (1983), Ravinella (1988) and Hatoof (1992) and became the first and so far the only woman to train an Arc winner in 1979.

Henderson, Nicky Born 1950. Began as assistant trainer to Fred Winter between 1974 and 1978, combining this with a successful amateur jockey career that culminated in winning the Fox Hunters' Chase at Aintree on Happy Warrior in 1977. He took out his first licence in 1978 and trains at Seven Barrows near Lambourn, Berkshire. The best of his numerous high-class animals have been See You Then (Champion Hurdle, 1985, 1986, 1987) and Remittance Man (Queen Mother Champion Chase, 1992).

Hern, Major Dick Born William Richard Hern, 20 January 1921. From 1952-57 Hern was assistant to trainer Michael Pope before being taken on by Major Lionel Holliday as private trainer. Hethersett was his first classic win (St Leger, 1962, in the Holliday colours). He moved to West Ilsley in Berkshire (owned by the Queen) at the end of 1962 and proceeded to form great partnerships with Joe Mercer and then Willie Carson. Brigadier Gerard was undoubtedly his greatest horse but he also trained three English Derby winners (Troy, Henbit and Nashwan) as well as Bustino (St Leger, 1974), Sun Princess (Oaks and St Leger, 1983), Highclere (1000 Guineas, 1974) and numerous others. The 'Major' was injured in a hunting accident in 1984 which left him partially paralysed and, suffering from a heart complaint in 1988, he temporarily handed his licence to his assistant Neil Graham, who won the 1988 St Leger with Minster Son while deputising for Hern. When the 'Major's' lease at West Ilsley ran out he moved operations to Kingwood, near Lambourn, and thanks to the patronage of Sheikh Hamdan Al Maktoum, continued his classic success with Harayir (1000 Guineas, 1995). He was champion trainer in 1962, 1972, 1980, 1983. He retired in 1997 and died 22 May 2002.

Hide, Edward Born Shropshire, 1937. First winner: Ritornello (Chepstow, September 1951). He rode six classic winners and was 'Cock of the North' (leading northern jockey) 16 times. Altogether he rode 2591 winners, the last being Hi-Tech Leader at Nottingham on 13 August 1985.

Hills, Barry Born Barrington William Hills, 1937. Apprenticed to George Colling before working for Fred Rimell and then as head lad to John Oxley at Newmarket, he took out his first training licence in 1969 at Lambourn and soon struck success, winning the 1973 Prix de l'Arc de Triomphe with Rheingold. He has won three classics to date: the 1000 Guineas in 1978 with Enstone Spark, the 1979 2000 Guineas with Tap On Wood and the 1994 St Leger with Moonax. Barry has three sons; John trains at Upper Lambourn and twins Michael and Richard are top-class jockeys in their own right.

Hills, Michael Born Newmarket, 22 January 1963. Ten minutes older than twin brother Richard. First winner: Sky Thief (Nottingham, 13 August 1979). Had classic success when he won the 1996 Epsom Derby on Shaamit.

Hills, Richard Born Richard John Hills, Newmarket, 22 January 1963. Apprenticed with Tom Jones. First winner: Border Dawn (Doncaster, 26 October 1979). Hills has four classic wins: the 1000 Guineas (1995 Harayir, 2000 Lahan), the St Leger (1999 Mutafaweq) and the 2000 Guineas (2004 Haafhd). He also won the 1999 Dubai World Cup on Almutawakel, and took over as number one jockey to Sheikh Hamdan Al Maktoum on the retirement of Willie Carson.

Howard de Walden, Lord Born 27 November 1912. Owner of the 1985 Derby winner Slip Anchor and the brilliant miler Kris, his most famous horse was arguably Lanzarote, the winner of the 1974

Champion Hurdle who was fatally injured during the 1977 Cheltenham Gold Cup. Lord Howard de Walden died in 1999, aged 86.

Hunt, Nelson Bunker　Texas oil magnate who used on the purchase of bloodstock the considerable wealth accrued by his monopoly of silver mining. He began by buying a share in Vaguely Noble, later owning such equine luminaries as Dahlia (King George VI & Queen Elizabeth Stakes, 1973, 1974) and Empery (Derby, 1976).

Hyperion　Chestnut colt foaled 1930 by Gainsborough out of Selene. Owned and bred by the 17th Earl of Derby. Trained by George Lambton. Champion 3-year-old. Winner of the Derby and St Leger (1933), New Ham Stakes, Chester Vase, Dewhurst Stakes, Prince of Wales 2-year-old Stakes and Prince of Wales Stakes. Leading British sire in 1940, 1941, 1942, 1945, 1946, 1954. Sired seven classic winners including Owen Tudor and Aureole. Died 1960 but is immortalised by the magnificent John Skeaping statue outside the Jockey Club Rooms in Newmarket High Street.

Isinglass　Bay colt foaled 1888 by Isonomy out of Dead Lock. Owned and bred by Harry McCalmont. Trained by James Jewitt. Won the English Triple Crown in 1893. Also won the Eclipse Stakes and Ascot Gold Cup. Won 11 from 12 starts. Died 1911.

Istabraq　Bay gelding foaled 1992 by Sadler's Wells out of Betty's Secret. Owned by J.P. McManus. Trained by Aidan O'Brien. Ridden by Charlie Swan. Istabraq won the Champion Hurdle three times (1998, 1999, 2000) and was deprived of a record fourth successive win by the outbreak of foot and mouth disease. First National Hunt horse to have won over £1 million. Won 23 from 29 starts. Retired in 2002 after being pulled up in attempting to win his fourth Champion Hurdle.

Jarnet, Thierry　Born 24 March 1967. French champion jockey four times (1992-95). He won the Oaks on Pennekamp (1995), and the Prix de l'Arc de Triomphe on Subotica (1992) and Carnegie (1994).

Joel, Jim　Born 1894. Winner of five classics with Picture Play, Royal Palace, Light Cavalry and Fairy Footsteps. Joel became leading owner on the Flat in 1967 when Royal Palace won the 2000 Guineas and Derby. Other notable Flat horses he owned included Connaught, Welsh Pageant and Predominate. Twice leading owner over jumps (1980, 1987), he became the first owner since Raymond Guest to win both the Grand National and the Derby when Maori Venture won the 1987 National. Other jumping stars under his auspices included The Laird, Summerville and his top-flight hurdler Beacon Light. He died March 1992, aged 97.

Kelleway's　Born 1940, Paul Kelleway rode his first winner on Golovine on the Flat at Haydock Park (October 1955). He later won the Cheltenham Gold Cup on What A Myth (1969) and the Queen Mother Champion Chase on Crisp (1971) but his greatest triumphs were on the Champion Hurdler of 1971 and 1972, Bula. Bula beat the great Persian War in his first Champion Hurdle and went on to become, alongside Captain Christy, the top chaser of his day. Kelleway turned to training in 1977 and had great success on very limited resources. He died of cancer in April 1999, aged 58. His daughter Gay Kelleway was a top amateur jockey, becoming the first woman to ride a winner at Royal Ascot (Sprowston Boy, Queen Alexandra Stakes, 1987), before turning to training and proving that with the right material she can compete with the best.

Kinane, Michael　Born Michael Joseph Kinane, Cashel, Co.Tipperary, Ireland, 22 June 1959. Son of Tommy Kinane, who won the 1978 Champion Hurdle on Monksfield. First winner: Muscari (Leopardstown, 19 March 1975). Apprenticed with Liam Browne. Champion Irish apprentice (1978) and Irish champion jockey 11 times to date, he has eight English classic wins: the Derby on Commander-In-Chief (1993) and Galileo (2001); the Oaks on Shahtoush (1998) and Imagine (2001); the 2000 Guineas on Tirol (1990), Entrepreneur (1997) and King of Kings (1998); and the St Leger on Milan (2001); as well as numerous Irish classics. He has also won the Prix de l'Arc de Triomphe twice, on Carroll House (1989) and Montjeu (1999); the Melbourne Cup on Vintage Crop in 1993; the Japan Cup on Pilsudski in 1997; and the Belmont Stakes on Go and Go in 1990, the first European-based rider to ride the winner of a US Triple Crown race.

Kincsem　Chestnut filly foaled 1874 in Hungary by Cambuscan out of Waternymph. Unbeaten in 54 races all over Europe, including the 1878 Goodwood Cup in England. Died 1887.

Knight, Henrietta　Born 15 December 1946. Took out her first training licence in 1989. Her stables at West Lockinge, near Wantage, Oxfordshire, have housed some top-class individuals including Champion Chaser Edredon Bleu. Married to former champion National Hunt jockey Terry Biddlecombe, she is famous for watching her horses with eyes closed from behind trees, grandstands, anything to spare her the agonies that she believes may befall her beloved animals. Her greatest horst is undoubtedly triple Gold Cup winner Best Mate.

Lammtarra　Chestnut colt foaled 1992 by Nijinsky out of Snow Bride. First English Derby winner to have a Derby winner as a sire (Nijinsky won in 1970) and an Oaks winner as a dam (Snow Bride was awarded the 1989 race on the disqualification of Aliysa after a post-race dope test). Owned by Saeed Maktoum Al Maktoum. Trained as a two-year-old by Alex Scott (one run in the Washington Singer Stakes at Newbury). Following the murder of Scott in September 1994 his training was taken over by Saeed bin Suroor at Godolphin. Won the 1995 Derby on his seasonal debut (the first to do so since Grand Parade in 1919) in a time of 2mins 32.31secs, beating the record of Mahmoud in 1936. Walter Swinburn lost the ride for the King George VI & Queen Elizabeth Stakes, Frankie Dettori winning impressively before also landing the Prix de l'Arc de Triomphe. Retired to stud unbeaten in his four races and was eventually exported to Japan.

Lewis, Geoff　Born nr Brecon, 21 December 1935. Apprenticed to Ron Smyth at Epsom. First winner: Eastern Imp (Epsom, 23 April 1953). Lewis quickly became one of the leading jockeys in Britain. His first classic winner was aboard Right Tack in the 1969 2000 Guineas but he will always be remembered for his association with the brilliant Mill Reef whom he rode in all his 14 races, winning 12 of them. Lewis won five English classics in all and on retiring in 1979 became a very successful Epsom-based trainer, saddling a winner at his first attempt (Concert Hall at Doncaster, 20 March 1980). He retired in 1999.

Llewellyn, Carl　Born Pembrokeshire, Wales, 29 July 1965. First winner: Starjestic (Wolverhampton, 14 March 1986). Won the Grand National on Party Politics (1992) and Earth Summit (1998).

Lord Lyon　Bay colt foaled 1863 by Stockwell out of

H
O
R
S
E

R
A
C
I
N
G

Paradigm. Bred by Mark Pearson. Owned by Richard Sutton. Trained by James Dover. Won the English Triple Crown in 1866. Won 15 from 19 starts. Died 1887.

McCoy, Tony Born Anthony Peter McCoy, Ballymena, Co. Antrim, Northern Ireland, 4 May 1974. First winner in England: Chickabiddy (Exeter, 7 September 1994). Beginning as conditional jockey for Toby Balding, McCoy has broken countless records since he started riding in England in 1994. Champion National Hunt jockey 1995-2004. Having become the fastest jockey to reach the 1000-winners mark, he then beat Sir Gordon Richards' record for winners in a season for all types of racing in 2002 with a new high of 289. Won the Champion Hurdle on Make a Stand (1997); the Cheltenham Gold Cup on Mister Mulligan (1997); the Scottish Grand National on Belmont King (1997); and the Queen Mother Champion Chase on Edredon Bleu (2000). McCoy appears set to rewrite the record books over the coming seasons; he broke Richard Dunwoody's record of 1699 wins during the 2003 season and rode his 2000th winner on 17 January 2004. McCoy resigned his position as stable jockey to Martin Pipe in 2004 to join Jonjo O'Neill.

Maguire, Adrian Born Kilmessan, Co. Meath, Ireland, 29 April 1971. Maguire started his career pony racing at the age of nine. He rode over 200 winners and was champion pony race rider. First winner under National Hunt rules: Gladtogetit (Sligo, 23 April 1990). He won the Fulke Walwyn Kim Muir Chase on Omerta at Cheltenham on his first ride in Britain (1991), and the Irish Grand National aboard the same horse, as well as the Cheltenham Gold Cup on Cool Ground (1992).

Maktoum's The four Maktoum brothers, Sheikh Maktoum, Sheikh Hamdan, Sheikh Mohammed and Sheikh Ahmed, have monopolised the buying and breeding of the world's top thoroughbreds in the last twenty years or so. Their father was Sheikh Rashid Bin Saeed Al Maktoum, the ruler of Dubai, who was succeeded by his eldest son Sheikh Maktoum Al Maktoum on his death in 1991. He was the first to have a classic success when Touching Wood won the 1982 St Leger. Sheikh Hamdan, the Dubai Minister of Finance, has owned horses of the calibre of Unfuwain and Nashwan, and was leading owner in 1990, 1994 and 1995. Sheikh Mohammed owned Dubai Millennium, Daylami, Swain, Oh So Sharp, Pebbles, Unite, Diminuendo, Indian Skimmer, Carnegie and Old Vic, as well as Champion Hurdlers Kribensis and Royal Gait. He has been leading owner on the Flat nine times (1985-89, 1991-93, 1997). Sheikh Ahmed has owned Wassl, Mtoto and Ameerat.

Mandarin Bay gelding foaled 1951 by Deux Pour Cent out of Manada. Owned by Mme K. Hennessy. Won the inaugural Hennessy Gold Cup at Cheltenham in 1957 and landed a second Hennessy at Newbury in 1961. Won the Cheltenham Gold Cup in 1962, aged 11, and is remembered for an heroic effort three months later when he won the Grand Steeple-Chase de Paris at Auteuil after his bit snapped; jockey Fred Winter, with no steering, also had to contend with the horse going slightly lame in a foreleg. Died 1976, aged 25.

Man O' War Chestnut colt foaled 1917 by Fair Play out of Mahubah. Bred by Nursery Stud (USA). Owned by Sam Riddle. Known as 'Big Red'. Champion 2-year-old and 3-year-old. Won both the Preakness Stakes and Belmont Stakes but did not run in the Kentucky Derby as his owner thought the course was too far west. Won 20 from 21 starts. Rather appropriately, the horse that beat him as a two-year-old was named Upset. Sired US Triple Crown winner War Admiral. Leading sire in 1926. Died 1947.

Mellor, Stan Born 10 April 1937. The first National Hunt jockey to ride over 1000 winners (Final total 1035 on retiring), his 1000th winner being Ouzo (Nottingham, 18 December 1971). He won many important races, although none of the big three (Grand National, Cheltenham Gold Cup, Champion Hurdle). His greatest moment was probably riding the brilliant grey Stalbridge Colonist to victory over the mighty Arkle in the 1966 Hennessy Gold Cup. He became a successful trainer and retired in 2001.

Mercer's Born 1934, Joe Mercer won his first race under National Hunt rules in September 1950 while apprenticed to Major Fred Sneyd. Champion apprentice in 1952, he won the Oaks in 1953 on Ambiguity while apprenticed to R.J. Colling. His many top-class rides included Le Moss, Bustino, Time Charter, Kris and Cut Above, but his greatest mount was undoubtedly Brigadier Gerard, arguably the greatest eight to ten furlong horse of all time. Mercer became champion jockey in 1979 and retired in 1985, having ridden 2810 winners in Britain. He is now racing manager to Sheikh Maktoum Al Maktoum. Emmanuel (Manny) Mercer, born in 1930, was Joe's elder brother and equally brilliant in the saddle. He won the 1953 1000 Guineas on Happy Laughter and the 1954 2000 Guineas on Darius, as well as the inaugural running of the Washington DC International in 1952 on Wilwyn. He was tragically killed in September 1959 when thrown from Priddy Fair on the way to the start of a race at Ascot.

Mildmay, Anthony Born 1909. As a jockey, Lord Mildmay of Flete had two of the all-time great hard-luck stories of the Grand National. In the 1936 race he was leading Reynoldstown over the second-last on the 100-1 outsider Davy Jones when the buckle on the reins came loose and the horse ran out at the last fence. In 1948 he suffered a severe cramp in his neck aboard Cromwell and came a gallant third despite not being able to lift his head from the horse's neck. In spite of these setbacks he managed to win the amateur championship every year from 1946-50. He was instrumental in introducing Queen Elizabeth, the Queen Mother, to the sport by persuading her to buy a horse.

Mill House Bay colt foaled 1957 in Co. Kildare by King Hal out of Nas Na Riogh. Owned by Bill Gollings. Won the 1963 Gold Cup as a six-year-old and was touted at the time as being the greatest of them all; however, another Irish superstar, Arkle, was beginning to flourish at the same time. The first time they met, in the 1963 Hennessy at Newbury, Mill House gained the expected victory but Arkle then came into his own and the aggregate tally ended 4-1 in Arkle's favour. Many experts believe that the constant defeats by Arkle took their toll on the precocious Mill House, but he lost the 1964 Whitbread by only a neck, conceding 42lb (19kg) to Dormant, and won the 1967 race to show what a talent he was in his own right. Died October 1975.

Mill Reef Bay colt foaled 1968 by Never Bend out of Milan Mill. Bred and owned by Paul Mellon (USA). Trained by Ian Balding. Won on his debut, beating the highly regarded Fireside Chat, and his only reverse was a short-head defeat by My Swallow in the Prix Robert Papin at Maisons-Laffitte. The much-awaited return of the two superstars in the 1971 2000 Guineas lived up to expectations, but they raced only for second place as the great Brigadier Gerard came of age on that day. Mill Reef won the Derby and the Prix de l'Arc de Triomphe in 1971, along with the Eclipse Stakes and King George VI & Queen Elizabeth Stakes. Won 12 from 14 starts. Sired two Derby winners: Shirley Heights (1978) and Reference Point (1987). Died 1986.

oore, George   Born Mackay, Queensland, Australia, 5 July 1923. Moore dominated the Sydney racing scene, winning ten Jockeys' Premierships between 1957 and 1969. He won the Epsom Derby on Royal Palace (1967) and the Prix de l'Arc de Triomphe on Saint Crespin II (1959). He retired in 1971, becoming a trainer in Hong Kong.

urless, Noel   One of the greatest trainers of all time. Murless took out his first licence in 1935 and in 1947 took over the Beckhampton stables of Fred Darling before relocating to Warren Place, Newmarket, in 1952. He won 19 classics with horses such as Crepello (Derby and 2000 Guineas, 1957), St Paddy (Derby and St Leger, 1960), Royal Palace (Derby and 2000 Guineas, 1967), Petite Etoile (1000 Guineas, 1959), Altesse Royale (1000 Guineas and Oaks, 1971), Mysterious (1000 Guineas and Oaks, 1973), Carozza (Oaks, 1957) and Lupe (Oaks, 1970). He was leading trainer nine times (1948, 1957, 1959, 1960, 1961, 1967, 1968, 1970, 1973). Murless retired in 1976 and handed over his yard to Henry Cecil, the then husband of his daughter, Julie. He died 1987, aged 77.

urtagh, Johnny   Born John Patrick Murtagh, Co. Meath, Ireland, 14 May 1970. First winner: Chicago Style (Limerick, 6 July 1987). He has three British classic wins to date: the Derby (2000 on Sinndar, 2002 on High Chaparral) and the 2000 Guineas (2002 on Rock Of Gibraltar). He also won the Prix de l'Arc de Triomphe in 2000 on Sinndar. Champion Irish apprentice in 1989, he was champion jockey in Ireland in 1995, 1996 and 1998, and has also been champion in Dubai. He was first jockey to John Oxx to whom he was apprenticed but left in 2004 to take up a short tenure as David Loder's stable jockey.

ashwan   Chestnut colt foaled by Blushing Groom out of Height of Fashion. Owned and bred by Sheikh Hamdan Al Maktoum. The only horse ever to have won the 2000 Guineas, Derby, Eclipse and King George in the same season (1989).

ative Dancer   Grey colt foaled 1950 by Polynesian out of Geisha. Bred by Dan Scott. Owned by A.G. Vanderbilt. Trained by Bill Winfrey. Known as 'The Gray Ghost'. Won the Belmont Stakes and Preakness Stakes in 1952, and was beaten by a head in the Kentucky Derby. Horse of the Year in 1952 and 1954. Won 21 from 22 starts. Travelled everywhere with a cat called 'Black Cat'. An outstanding sire, he died 1967. His ghost is said to haunt Churchill Downs.

icholson, David   Born 19 March 1939. The son of 'Frenchie' Nicholson, the famed teacher of young jockeys such as Pat Eddery and Walter Swinburn, 'The Duke', as he has always been known, first rode in a Flat race at Newmarket at the age of 12. His first mount, and winner, under National Hunt rules, was Fairval at Chepstow on 11 April 1955; he also rode his first and only Flat winner that year on Desertcar at Wolverhampton. He had many big-race wins but the highlight of his riding career was undoubtedly winning the 1967 Whitbread on the great Mill House. Nicholson retired in 1974, having ridden 583 winners

over jumps, to become one of the top National Hunt trainers in the country. Top-class chasers he has trained include Charter Party (Gold Cup, 1988), Viking Flagship (Queen Mother Champion Chase, 1994, 1995) and Barton Bank (King George VI Chase, 1993), as well as the brilliant hurdlers Broadsword, Very Promising, Relkeel and Mysilv. He retired in 1999.

Nijinsky   Bay colt foaled 1967 by Northern Dancer out of Flaming Page. Bred by Edward Taylor in Canada. Owned by Charles Engelhard. Trained by Vincent O'Brien. Won the English Triple Crown in 1970. Also won the Irish Derby and was second in the Prix de l'Arc de Triomphe and Champion Stakes when many good experts believed he had gone over the top for the season. Won 11 from 13 starts. Sire of three Derby winners: Golden Fleece (1982), Shahrastani (1986) and Lammtarra (1995). Died 1992.

Northern Dancer   Bay colt foaled 1961 by Nearctic out of Natalma. Owned and bred by E.P. Taylor in Canada. Trained by Horatio Luro. Northern Dancer won 14 of his 18 races including the 1964 Preakness Stakes and Kentucky Derby, but his limited stamina made the Belmont an impossible task. Sired numerous classic winners including Nijinsky, El Gran Senor, The Minstrel and Secreto; his son Sadler's Wells assumed his mantle of most influential sire in the world. Retired from stud duties in 1987 and died November 1990, aged 29.

Oaksey, Lord   Born John Lawrence, 1929. Educated at Eton, Oxford and Yale. Winner of the amateur riders' championship over jumps in 1958 and 1971, Lawrence was associated with many good-class horses, notably Taxidermist (who won the Whitbread and Hennessy Gold Cups in 1958) and Carrickbeg (who led until caught on the run-in by Ayala in the 1963 Grand National). On retiring from the saddle he became racing correspondent for the *Daily Telegraph* and wrote a weekly column for *Horse and Hound* under the name of Audax. His father, Geoffrey, was presiding judge at the Nuremberg war trials and was rewarded with an hereditary peerage for his efforts, a title inherited by his son on his death. 'My Noble Lord', as Oaksey was dubbed by racing pundit John McCririck, remains a popular figure in the racing world, and he and his wife have raised the profile of the Injured Jockeys Fund as well as its bank balance.

O'Brien, Aidan   Born Aidan Patrick O'Brien, Co. Wexford, Ireland, 1969. Began as an amateur jockey, winning the Irish amateur title in 1994, but always showed an aptitude for training racehorses while assistant to Jim Bolger and his own wife Anne-Marie Crowley, who was champion National Hunt trainer in Ireland in 1993. His rise through the training ranks has been nothing short of astounding, winning five National Hunt championships before concentrating on the Flat. He moved to Ballydoyle, near Cashel, Co. Tipperary, in 1995 to take over the yard of Vincent O'Brien. Notable horses he has trained include King of Kings (2000 Guineas, 1998), Shahtoush (Oaks, 1998), Imagine (Oaks, 2001), Galileo (Derby, 2001), Giant's Causeway (five Group One races in 2000), Rock of Gibraltar (2000 Guineas, 2000), High Chaparral (English and Irish Derby, 2002) and Hawk Wing (Eclipse Stakes, 2002). His dominance in his home country can be measured by the fact that he trained the first three home in the 2001 Irish 2000 Guineas. Despite all these achievements, O'Brien will always be

HORSE RACING

remembered as the trainer of the triple Champion Hurdler, Istabraq.

O'Brien, Vincent Born Michael Vincent O'Brien, Co. Cork, Ireland, 1917. The world's greatest trainer for three decades, he began training at Churchtown, Co. Cork, his first winner being Oversway at Limerick Junction (now renamed Tipperary) on 20 May 1943. He concentrated on jumpers at the start of his career, winning three successive Gold Cups (1948-50) with Cottage Rake and three successive Champion Hurdles (1949-51) with Hatton's Grace, and became the only man to train three successive National winners, with Early Mist (1953), Royal Tan (1954) and Quare Times (1955). He won a fourth Gold Cup with Knock Hard in 1953 but in the meantime moved to Ballydoyle and began training Flat horses. Ballymoss was his first English classic winner when he took the 1957 St Leger but O'Brien won a further 15 English classics with horses such as Sir Ivor, Nijinsky, Lomond, El Gran Senor, Glad Rags, Larkspur, Roberto, The Minstrel, Golden Fleece, Long Look, Valoris and Boucher. He also trained Sadler's Wells, Caerleon and Royal Academy. His last winner was Mysterious Ways at the Curragh on 17 September 1994 and he retired later that year. The leading trainer in Britain on the Flat in 1966 and 1977 and over jumps in 1953 and 1954, a record second to none.

Omaha Chestnut colt foaled 1932 by Gallant Fox out of Flambino. Owned and bred by Belair Stud. Trained by James Fitzsimmons. Won the US Triple Crown (Kentucky Derby, Preakness Stakes and Belmont Stakes) in 1935. Ran in England in 1936, winning two races and finishing second in the Ascot Gold Cup. Won 9 from 22 starts. Died 1959.

O'Neill, Jonjo Born John Joseph O'Neill, Castletownroche, Co. Cork, Ireland, 13 April 1952. First winner: Lana at the Curragh on 9 September 1970. O'Neill's 149 winners in 1977/78 was the then record for a National Hunt season. O'Neill won the Gold Cup on Alverton (1984) and the Champion Hurdle on Sea Pigeon (1980). He also won the Champion Hurdle (1984) and Gold Cup (1986) on Dawn Run, the first horse ever to win both races. Champion jockey in 1978 and 1980.

Ormonde Bay colt foaled 1883 by Bend Or out of Lily Agnes. Owned and bred by the 1st Duke of Westminster. Trained by John Porter. Won the English Triple Crown in 1886, ridden in the Derby and St Leger by Fred Archer. Won the Champion Stakes when priced at 100-1 Unbeaten from 16 starts. Died 1904.

O'Sullevan, Sir Peter Born Kenmare, Co. Kerry, Ireland, 3 March 1918. Known for six decades as the voice of racing, O'Sullevan made his first BBC broadcast in 1946 and commentated on the first live televised Grand National in 1960. He also wrote for the *Daily Express* between 1950 and 1986. O'Sullevan owned a few good-class racehorses over the years, notably Be Friendly and Attivo. He retired after calling home Suny Bay in the Hennessy Gold Cup in November 1997. He was knighted in his retirement year.

Paget, Dorothy Eccentric owner of some top-class jumpers such as Roman Hackle (Cheltenham Gold Cup, 1940), Insurance (Champion Hurdle, 1932, 1933), Solford (Champion Hurdle, 1940), Distel (Champion Hurdle,1946) and particularly Golden Miller, who won the Cheltenham Gold Cup for five successive years between 1932 and 1936. Lack of convention was Ms Paget's byword: she was known

to dine at 7am and sleep during the day only to rise for breakfast at 8.30pm when she would ring her bookie and place bets for the afternoon racing that had just taken place. Her love of food made her swe to over 20st (127kg) and her dislike of the male species was legendary. She died 1960, aged 54.

Pebbles Chestnut filly foaled 1981 by Sharpen Up out of La Dolce. Bred by Marcos Lemos. Owned by Sheikh Mohammed. Trained by Clive Brittain. Won the 1000 Guineas and the Coronation Cup. First filly to win the Eclipse Stakes. Beat the Derby winner (Slip Anchor) and the St Leger winner (Comanche Run) to win the Champion Stakes (1985). Won the Breeders' Cup Turf in 1985. Won 8 from 15 starts.

Persian War Foaled by Persian Gulf out of Warning, a Chanteur II mare. Bred by Jakie Astor. Trained on the Flat by Major Dick Hern, Persian War showed a lot of promise but his true potential was realised when he was sold to trainer Tom Masson and then David Naylor-Leyland, and ultimately on to Henry Alper who ran him in the claret and blue colours of his beloved West Ham United. Colin Davies began train Persian War with immediate success and in 1968 he became the first hurdler to be voted Horse of the Year, following a spectacular season in which he carried 11st 13lb (76kg) to win the Schweppes Gold Trophy at Newbury (a weight-carrying record that still stands) – the first of his three Champion Hurdle successes. Jimmy Uttley, a hurdle specialist, was the great horse's regular jockey. Persian War was retired in 1974 while in considerable decline an died in 1984, aged 21.

Persimmon Bay colt foaled 1893 by St Simon out o Perdita. Bred and owned by HRH The Prince of Wales. Trained by Richard Marsh. Won the Epsom Derby and St Leger in 1896, and the Ascot Gold Cu and Eclipse Stakes in 1897. Won 7 from 9 starts. Sired five classic winners. Champion sire four times (1902, 1906, 1908, 1912). Died 1908.

Peslier, Olivier Born Cossé-le-Vivien, France, 12 January 1971. First winner: Cavallo d'Oro (Rouen, March 1989). French champion jockey 1996, 1997, 1999 and 2000. He won consecutive Prix de l'Arc de Triomphes on Helissio (1996), Peintre Célèbre (1997) and Sagamix (1998). Won the Derby on High Rise (1998).

Phar Lap Chestnut gelding foaled 1926 by Night Raid out of Entreaty. Bred by A.F. Roberts in New Zealand. Owned by David Davis and Harry Telford. Trained by Harry Telford. Known variously as 'Big Red' (also a nickname for Secretariat), 'The Red Terror', 'The Wonder Horse' and 'The Big Fellow'. Won all the major Australian races including the Melbourne Cup in 1930. Winner of the richest horse race in the world at that time, the Agua Caliente Handicap, in Mexico in 1932. Won 37 from 51 starts. Died mysteriously in 1932 just weeks after the Mexican win, though claims of poisoning were unproven.

Piggott, Lester Born Lester Keith Piggott, Wantage, Berkshire, 5 November 1935. Known as 'Old Stoneface' and 'The Long Fellow'. Apprenticed to his father Keith Piggott. First winner: The Chase (Northampton, 18 August 1948 at the age of 12). In 1954 he won his first Derby on Never Say Die. Champion jockey 1960, 1964-71, 1981, 1982. His record 30 classic wins included nine Derbys, spread over thirty years, on: Never Say Die (1954), Crepelle (1957), St Paddy (1960), Sir Ivor (1968), Nijinsky (1970), Roberto (1972), Empery (1976), The Minstr (1977) and Teenoso (1983). In total he recorded

4493 winners in the UK. Having announced his retirement as a jockey in 1985, in 1987 he was found guilty of a £3.25 million tax fraud and imprisoned. After his release in 1988 he worked for a time as a trainer before staging a comeback as a jockey in 1990. He finally retired in 1995.

Pincay, Laffit Born Panama, 29 December 1946. Rode his first winner, Panama in 1964. First winner in the USA: Teacher's Art (Arlington Park, Chicago, July 1966). He registered his 8834th win on Irish Nip at Hollywood Park on 10 December 1999 to become the jockey with the most winners in US history, beating Willie Shoemaker's record. To date he has won over 9300 races.

Pipe, Martin Born Wellington, Somerset, 29 May 1945. Britain's 12-time champion National Hunt trainer began his working life as assistant to his bookmaker father, David. From humble training origins as a permit holder, Pipe has built a phenomenally successful operation at Nicholashayne in Somerset. His first winner was Hit Parade in a selling hurdle at Taunton on 9 May 1975 and he has now trained over 3000 more. Like his former stable jockey Tony McCoy, it is difficult to quantify his achievements as he breaks records on a regular basis. He has won the Grand National in 1994 with Minnehoma and the Champion Hurdle with Granville Again (1993) and Make A Stand (1997). Other notable horses he has trained include Sabin Du Loir, Rolling Ball, Pridwell, Challenger Du Luc, Unsinkable Boxer, Blowing Wind, Cyfor Malta, Omerta, Bonanza Boy and Baron Blakeney. Pipe narrowly beat Paul Nicholls to retain his champion trainer title in 2004.

Pitman, Jenny Born Leicestershire, 11 June 1946. Jenny left school at 15 for a job as a stable girl. She met and married Richard Pitman at the age of 19 and the couple moved to Wiltshire where they purchased a plot of land on which to build stables. In 1975 she gained her first training licence and had her first winner that same year. The pressure took its toll on her marriage and Jenny and Richard divorced in 1977. She moved to Lambourn, Berkshire, and became the first woman to train a Grand National winner when Corbiere won the 1983 race. She also won in 1995 with Royal Athlete as well as winning the 1993 'race that never was' with Esha Ness, when two false starts had voided the race. Other notable successes include two Cheltenham Gold Cups on Burrough Hill Lad in 1984 and Garrison Savannah in 1991. In 1997 she was diagnosed with thyroid cancer and, although in remission, she announced her retirement before the 1999 Cheltenham Festival. Jenny married her second husband, David Stait, in 1997. Her son from her first marriage, Mark, has proven to be a shrewd trainer in his own right.

Potoooooooo (Pot-8-Os) Chestnut colt foaled 1773 by Eclipse out of Sportsmistress. Bred by the 4th Earl of Abingdon. Owned by the 1st Earl of Grosvenor. Supposedly named after the mispelling of 'potato' by a stable lad, the horse ran under both spellings. Running between 1777 and 1783, mainly in four-mile races, he won 30 races including 28 at Newmarket, a record number of wins at one course. Sired three Epsom Derby winners (Waxy in 1793, Champion in 1800 and Tyrant in 1802). In all sired 165 winners and established the Eclipse line. Died 1800.

Prendergast, Paddy Born Co. Carlow, Ireland, 1909. Began training in 1940. Known variously as 'PJ' or 'Darkie'. He won 17 Irish classics, while his four English classic successes were Martial (2000

Guineas, 1960), Noblesse (Oaks, 1963), Ragusa (St Leger, 1963) and Pourparler (1000 Guineas, 1964). The leading trainer in Britain three times (1963, 1964, 1965). He died 22 June 1980 and his sons Kevin and Paddy jnr have kept the training tradition of the family alive.

Prescott, Sir Mark Born March 1948. After working as an assistant to Jack Waugh, he took out his first licence in 1971. Prescott has a reputation for shrewdness second to none and is known for his attention to detail in preparing horses for major races. Alborada won the Champion Stakes for him in 1998 and 1999, and he has had a host of high-class horses, mostly ridden by his stable jockey, George Duffield. His Spindrifter won 13 races in 1980, including 11 in a row.

Price, Ryan Born 16 August 1912. Price became private trainer to Lord Nunburnholme in Yorkshire in 1937. After distinguished war service as a commando he resumed training at Wisborough Green and Lavant, West Sussex, before moving to Findon, West Sussex, in 1951. He won the Champion Hurdle three times (Clair Soleil in 1955, Fare Time in 1959, Eborneezer in 1961), the Grand National with Kilmore (1962), and the Cheltenham Gold Cup with What A Myth (1969). Price won the Schweppes Gold Trophy four times, the last win coming from Hill House which caused some controversy over the horse's improvement on his previous run. The leading National Hunt trainer five times (1955, 1959, 1962, 1966, 1967), he also won two classics on the Flat with Ginevra (Oaks, 1972) and Bruni (St Leger, 1975). He retired in 1982 and died 1986.

Queen Elizabeth II Inherited her love of racing from her father, King George VI, who owned Sun Chariot, the fillies' Triple Crown winner of 1942. The Queen registered her first racing colours in 1949 (scarlet, purple hooped sleeves, black cap) and took over the royal colours on her accession to the throne in 1952. Her first classic winner was Carozza in the 1957 Oaks and further classic wins came from Pall Mall (2000 Guineas, 1958), Highclere (1000 Guineas, 1974), and Dunfermline (Oaks and St Leger, 1977), but she has owned no Derby winner as yet.

Queen Elizabeth, the Queen Mother The Queen Mother without doubt popularised the sport of horse racing more than anyone in turf history. Her notable horses include Manicou, The Rip, Silver Dome, Makaldar, Laffy, Double Star, Gay Record, Antiar, Oedipe, Escalus, Inch Arran, Colonius, Isle of Man, Game Spirit, Sunyboy, Tammuz, Special Cargo, The Argonaut and Devon Loch.

Quinn, Richard Born Thomas Richard Quinn, Stirling, Scotland, 2 December 1961. Apprenticed to Paul Cole. First winner: Bolivar Baby (Kempton, 21 October 1981). Champion European apprentice in 1983 and champion British apprentice in 1984, Quinn has two classic wins, the St Leger on Snurge (1990) and the Oaks on Love Divine (2000).

Red Rum Bay gelding foaled 1965 by Quorum out of Mared. Bred by Martyn McEnery. Owned by Noel Le Mare. Trained by Ginger McCain. Won the Grand National three times (1973, 1974, 1977), the only horse ever to do so, and was second in both his other starts in 1975 and 1976. Won the Scottish Grand National in 1974. Won 27 from 110 starts. Died 1995 and was buried by the winning post at Aintree.

Reid, John Born John Andrew Reid, Co. Down, Northern Ireland, 6 August 1955. First winner: Eyry

HORSE RACING

(Goodwood, 16 May 1973). He has four classic wins: the Derby on Dr Devious (1992), the 1000 Guineas on On The House (1982) and Las Meninas (1994), and the St Leger on Nedawi (1998).

Ribot Brown colt foaled 1952 at the English National Stud in West Grinstead, Sussex, by Tenerani out of Romanella. Bred by Frederico Tesio. Owned by Dormello-Orgiata Stud. Trained by Ugo Penco. Won the Prix de l'Arc de Triomphe twice (1955, 1956), and won the King George VI & Queen Elizabeth Diamond Stakes in 1956. Unbeaten from 16 starts. Champion English sire 1963, 1967, 1968. Died 1972.

Richards, Sir Gordon Born Oakengates, Shropshire, 5 May 1904. Having begun as a stable apprentice in 1919, from the mid-1920s until his retirement in 1954 Richards was champion jockey 26 times. In 1943 he became the all-time record British winner, surpassing Fred Archer's 2749 wins; in all he won 4870 races from 21,843 rides. On 3-5 October 1947 Richards had a world record 12 winners in succession: having won the final race at Nottingham on 3 October, the next day he won all six at Chepstow; on the following day, 5 October, he rode the first five winners at Chepstow again, narrowly losing the last. In 1953 he became the first jockey ever to be knighted following his first Derby win on Pinza at his 28th attempt. Richards was a trainer from 1955 to 1970, after which he became a racing manager. He died 10 November 1986.

Rimell, Fred Born 1913. Apprenticed to his father Tom, who trained the 1932 Grand National winner, Forbra. Champion National Hunt jockey four times (1939, 1940, 1945, 1946), his riding career was ended when he broke his neck twice in 1947. As a trainer he won four Grand Nationals, with E.S.B. (1956), Nicolaus Silver (1961), Gay Trip (1970) and Rag Trade (1976); two Cheltenham Gold Cups (Woodland Venture in 1967 and Royal Frolic in 1976); two Champion Hurdles with Comedy of Errors (1973, 1975); and had numerous other big-race successes. He was leading trainer five times (1951, 1961, 1969, 1970, 1976). He died suddenly in 1981 and his stable at Kinnersley, Worcestershire, was taken over by his wife Mercy who trained the 1983 Champion Hurdler Gaye Brief before retiring in 1989.

Roberts, Michael Born Michael Leonard Roberts, Cape Town, South Africa, 17 May 1954. Known as 'Mouse'. First winner: Smyrn (Pietermaritzburg, 30 August 1969). He had two classic wins, the 2000 Guineas on Mystiko (1991) and the Oaks on Intrepidity (1993). Champion jockey 11 times in South Africa, he was champion Flat jockey in Britain in 1992.

Robinson, Jem Born James Robinson, Newmarket. Robinson won the Epsom Derby six times on Azor (1817), Cedric (1824), Middleton (1825), Mameluke (1827), Cadland (1828) and Bay Middleton (1836). He also won the St Leger twice, the Oaks twice and the 2000 Guineas a record nine times in his career.

Rock Sand Brown colt foaled 1900 by Sainfoin out of Roquebrune. Owned and bred by Sir James Miller. Trained by George Blackwell. Won the English Triple Crown in 1903. Won 16 from 20 starts. Sold to the USA in 1906, where he sired the dam of Man O'War, he was again sold onto France in 1912. Died 1914.

Sadler's Wells Bay colt foaled 1981 by Northern Dancer out of Fairy Bridge. Top-class racehorse who won the 1984 Irish 2000 Guineas, Eclipse and Champion Stakes, but for all this his real ability has been shown as a stallion at stud. Champion sire in 1990 and every year since 1992, his progeny have included Galileo, Imagine, Old Vic, Salsabil, King Of Kings, Opera House, Dream Well, Intrepidity, In The Wings, Barathea, Carnegie, Entrepreneur, King's Theatre, Moonshell, Montjeu and Istabraq.

Saint-Martin, Yves Born France, 8 September 1941. Fell off on his first ride in public in 1958 but rode his first winner later that year on Royalic at Le Tremblay. Champion jockey 15 times in France and he also won 29 French classics and all five English classics. He retired in 1987.

Sangster, Robert Born 23 May 1936. Sangster began owning horses at a very young age, his first winner, Chalk Stream, winning a Haydock Park handicap in 1960 when he was 24 years old. He founded the famous Coolmore Stud in Co. Tipperary with John Magnier in the early 1970s and in 1975 formed a conglomerate of racehorse owners, including Stavros, Niarchos and Danny Schwartz, dedicated to representing the best American blood, with Vincent O'Brien the trainer. In 1984 he bought the training establishment at Manton, Wiltshire, which has had some top trainers as residents including Michael Dickinson, Barry Hills, Peter Chapple-Hyam and presently John Gosden. The leading owner on the Flat five times (1977, 1978, 1982-84). Notable horses he has owned include The Minstrel, Alleged, Detroit, Golden Fleece, Lomond, Caerleon, El Gran Senor, Sadler's Wells, Rodrigo De Triano, Las Meninas and Turtle Island. He died 7 April 2004.

Sceptre Bay filly foaled 1899 by Persimmon out of Ornament. Bred by the 1st Duke of Westminster. Owned and trained by Robert Siever. The only horse to win four English classics, in 1902 she won the 2000 Guineas, then two days later the 1000 Guineas. She ran fourth when favourite for the Epsom Derby but the next day won the Oaks. Finally she won the St Leger. Won 13 from 25 starts.

Scudamore, Peter Born Hereford, 13 June 1958. Known as 'Scu'. His career totals of 1678 winners from 7521 mounts plus 221 winners in a season (1988/89) both stood as records at the time of his retirement. He was champion jockey a record eight times alongside John Francome, the last seven in succession (1986-92).

Sea Bird II Chestnut colt foaled 1962 by Dan Cupid out of Sicalade. Bred and owned by Jean Ternynck. Trained by Etienne Pollet. Won the Epsom Derby and Prix de l'Arc de Triomphe in 1965. Won 7 from 8 starts. Sired Allez France. Died 1973.

Sea Pigeon Bay gelding foaled 1970 by Sea Bird II out of Around the Roses. Bred by Jock Whitney (USA). Owned by Pat Muldoon. Trained by Peter Easterby. Began as a Flat runner (finishing seventh in the Derby in 1973) but eventually transferred to National Hunt. On the Flat he won the Chester Cup and Ebor Handicap. Won the Champion Hurdle twice (1980, 1981) and both Welsh and Scottish Champion Hurdles. Won 37 from 85 starts. Died 2000.

Seattle Slew Brown colt foaled 1974 by Bold Reasoning out of My Charmer. Bred by Ben Castleman (USA). Owned by Karen and Mickey Taylor. Trained by Billy Turner. Won the US Triple Crown in 1977. Champion 2-year-old and 3-year-old. Horse of the Year, 1977. Champion Handicap Horse, 1978. Won 14 from 17 starts. Died 2002.

Secretariat Chestnut colt foaled 1970 by Bold Ruler out of Somethingroyal. Bred by Meadow Stud (USA). Known as 'Big Red' or 'Super Red'. Won the US Triple Crown in 1972, all in track record times.

Champion 2-year-old and 3-year-old. Horse of the Year in 1972 and 1973. Won 16 from 21 starts. Died 1989.

Shergar Bay colt foaled 1978 by Great Nephew out of Sharmeen. Owned and bred by HH Aga Khan IV. Trained by Michael Stoute. Won the 2000 Guineas and Epsom Derby in 1981, recording the biggest winning margin (ten lengths) in the latter. Also won the Irish Derby and King George VI & Queen Elizabeth Stakes. Kidnapped by the IRA in 1983, his ultimate fate remains unknown.

Shoemaker, Willie Born Billy Lee Shoemaker, Fabens, Texas, 19 August 1931. Nicknamed 'The Shoe'. First winner: Shafter V (Golden Gate Fields, California, 20 April 1949). Shoemaker won on nearly 22 per cent of his mounts. After suffering serious injuries in 1968 and 1969, he came back for many more successful years of riding before retiring in 1990. His last winner was Beau Genius (Gulfstream Park, Florida, 20 January 1990). His 8833 winners from 40,350 starts included four Kentucky Derbys, five Belmont Stakes and two Preakness Stakes. In 1991 a car accident left him paralysed. He died 12 October 2003.

Sir Barton Chestnut colt foaled 1916 by Star Shoot out of Lady Sterling. Bred by Maddon and Gooch. Owned by J.K.L. Ross. Trained by H.G. Bedwell. First winner of the US Triple Crown in 1919. Won 13 from 31 starts. Lost in a match race to Man O'War in 1920. Died 1937.

Sir Ivor Bay colt foaled 1965 by Sir Gaylord out of Attica. Owned by Raymond Guest. Trained by Vincent O'Brien. Sir Ivor is worthy of note, if only because Lester Piggott often mentioned that he could be the best horse he ever rode. Won a high-class 2000 Guineas in 1968 from the likes of Petingo and Jimmy Reppin and was an odds-on winner of that year's Derby, collaring the brilliant Connaught with a terrific late run. Placed in all the top races that year and ended by winning the Champion Stakes and the Washington DC International, to prove he was one of the toughest horses ever to race. He was retired at the end of his three-year-old season and died in 1995, aged 30.

Smirke, Charlie Born Charles James William Smirke, Lambeth, 1906. Apprenticed to Epsom trainer Stanley Wootton. Rode his first winner in April 1922 and his last in November 1959. In between he rode 11 classic winners, including My Babu, Palestine, Rose Royale II, Windsor Lad, Mahmoud, Tulyar, Hard Ridden and Bahram, and deputised for Lester Piggott when winning the 1954 St Leger on Never Say Die. His career suffered a terrible setback when he was banned for five years after his mount Welcome Gift refused to start at Gatwick in August 1928. He died 1993.

Smith, Doug Born 1917. Apprenticed to Fred Sneyd, he rode his first winner in 1932 and had classic triumphs aboard Our Babu (2000 Guineas, 1955), Pall Mall (2000 Guineas, 1958), Hypericum (1000 Guineas, 1946) and Petite Etoile (1000 Guineas, 1959). He specialised in long-distance races and monopolised the cup races in the 1950s. Champion jockey five times (1954, 1955, 1956, 1958, 1959), he retired in 1967 having ridden 3112 winners in Britain. After turning to training he had further classic success with Sleeping Partner (Oaks, 1969). Having retired in 1979 he was found dead in his Newmarket swimming pool in 1989, aged 71. His elder brother, Eph Smith (1915-72), was also a successful jockey, winning three classics with Blue Peter (2000

Guineas and Derby, 1939) and Premonition (St Leger, 1953).

Spectacular Bid Grey colt foaled 1976 by Bold Bidder out of Spectacular. Bred by Mrs W. Gilmour and Mrs W.M. Jason. Owned by Hawksworth Farm. Trained by Grover 'Buddy' Delp. Known as 'The Bid'. Won the Kentucky Derby and Preakness Stakes but could only finish third in the Belmont Stakes in 1979, ending a 12-race winning streak. Won 26 from 30 starts.

Spencer, Jamie Born Co. Tipperary, Ireland, 8 June 1980. First winner: Huncheon Chance (Downpatrick, 11 May 1996). Won the 1998 Irish 1000 Guineas on Tarascon at the age of 17, and the Irish 2000 Guineas on Gossamer (2002). His latest classic success was aboard Brian Boru in the 2003 St Leger.

Stoute, Sir Michael Born Barbados, 1945. He moved to Britain aged 19 to join the Yorkshire stable of Pat Rohan and spent brief spells with Doug Smith and Tom Jones at Newmarket before claiming his own training licence there in 1972. He has 13 English classic successes to date with Fair Salinia (Oaks, 1978), Shergar (Derby, 1981), Entrepreneur (2000 Guineas, 1997), Shadeed (2000 Guineas, 1985), King's Best (2000 Guineas, 2000), Doyoun (2000 Guineas, 1988), Musical Bliss (1000 Guineas, 1989), Unite (Oaks, 1987), Golan (1000 Guineas 2001), Shahrastani (Derby, 1986), Russian Rhythm (2000 Guineas, 2003), Kris Kin (Derby, 2003) and Northern Light (Derby, 2004). Leading trainer on the Flat in Britain six times (1981, 1986, 1989, 1994, 1997, 2000). His brief sorties into the jumping world have been successful, notably with Kribensis when winning the 1990 Champion Hurdle.

Suroor, Saeed Bin Born 10 October 1967. Following a brief spell as a policeman, Bin Suroor took out his first training licence in Dubai in 1994 and replaced Hilal Ibrahim as principal trainer for Godolphin the following year. Classic successes include Mark of Esteem (2000 Guineas, 1996), Island Sands (2000 Guineas, 1999), Cape Verdi (1000 Guineas, 1998), Kazzia (1000 Guineas and Oaks, 2002), Lammtarra (Derby, 1995), Moonshell (Oaks, 1995), Classic Cliché (St Leger, 1995), Nedawi (St Leger, 1998) and Mutafaweq (St Leger, 1999). His numerous Group One winners include Halling, Kayf Tara, Daylami and Dubai Millennium. The leading trainer in Britain in 1996, 1998 and 1999.

Swinburn, Walter Born Oxford, 7 August 1961. Son of Wally Swinburn, champion jockey of Ireland. Known as 'The Choirboy'. First winner: Paddy's Luck (Kempton, 12 July 1978). He won the Epsom Derby on Shergar (1981), Shahrastani (1986) and Lammtarra (1995); the Prix de l'Arc de Triomphe on All Along (1983); the Oaks on Unite (1987); the 2000 Guineas on Doyoun (1988); and the 1000 Guineas on Musical Bliss (1989), Hatoof (1992) and Sayyedati (1993). He had a serious accident in 1996 while riding a two-year-old in Hong Kong but made a full recovery. His last winner was Sir Francis at Brighton on 13 April 2000 and he retired having ridden 1391 winners in Britain.

Taaffe, Pat Born Rathcoole, Co. Dublin, 1930. First winner: Ballincora (Phoenix Park, Easter Saturday 1946). He became first jockey to trainer Tom Dreaper in 1949 and together they won many of the top National Hunt races, including three Gold Cups with Arkle. Taaffe rode a fourth Cheltenham Gold Cup winner on Fort Leney in 1968 and two Grand Nationals on Quare Times in 1955 and Gay Trip in

*H
O
R
S
E
R
A
C
I
N
G*

1970. Champion jockey in Ireland in 1952 and 1953. He retired in 1970 and as a trainer produced Captain Christy to win the 1974 Cheltenham Gold Cup. He died 7 July 1992.

Take, Yutaka Born Kyoto, Japan, 15 March 1969. First winner: Dyna Bishop (Hanshin, 7 March 1987). Japanese champion 11 times, he moved to the USA to ride in 2000 and to France in 2001.

Tetrarch, The Grey colt foaled by Roi Herode out of Vahren. Bred in Ireland. Trained by Atty Persse. Nicknamed 'The Spotted Wonder' and the most precocious horse of all time. As a two-year-old in 1913 he dominated all his races in a manner never seen before or since. Ridden by Steve Donoghue, he won all his races, including the Coventry Stakes at Royal Ascot by ten lengths. Injury prevented a three-year-old career. Died 1935, aged 24.

Tree, Jeremy Born 1925. Began as assistant to Dick Warden at Newmarket before training in his own right at Beckhampton in 1952. His four classic wins were with Only For Life (2000 Guineas, 1963), Known Fact (2000 Guineas, 1980), Juliette Marny (Oaks, 1975) and Scintillate (Oaks, 1979). He also won the 1985 Prix de l'Arc de Triomphe with Rainbow Quest, after the disqualification of Sagace. Tree also trained the great sprinter Sharpo to win three successive Nunthorpe Stakes (1980-82). He died in 1993, aged 67.

Tudor Minstrel Bay colt foaled 1944 by Owen Tudor out of Sansonnet. Owned and bred by J.A. Dewar. Trained by Fred Darling. The brilliant colt won the 1947 2000 Guineas by no less than eight lengths which made him the shortest-priced Derby favourite of all time at 4-7. Unfortunately he did not stay 12 furlongs and was beaten into fourth place by Pearl Diver. Peerless as a miler, only the great Brigadier Gerard could be considered his superior.

Voltigeur Brown colt foaled 1847 by Voltaire out of Martha Lynn. Bred at Hartlepool by Robert Stephenson. Owned by the Earl of Zetland. Trained by Robert Hill and won his solitary two-year-old race in 1849. His next race was the Derby which he duly won and then dead-heated with Russborough in the St Leger before winning the run-off. Two days later he beat The Flying Dutchman, who had won the previous year's Derby and St Leger, in the Doncaster Cup. The Flying Dutchman reversed the result in a famous match race at York in May 1851. He died after being kicked by a mare in 1874.

War Admiral Brown colt foaled 1934 by Man O'War out of Brushup. Owned and bred by Sam Riddle. Trained by George Conway. Won the US Triple Crown in 1937. Won 21 from 26 starts. Died 1959.

West Australian Bay colt foaled 1850 by Melbourne out of Mowerina. Owned and bred by John Bowes. Trained by John Scott. First horse to win the English Triple Crown in 1853. Won the Ascot Gold Cup in 1854. Known as 'The West'. Won 9 from 10 starts. Died 1870.

Whirlaway Chestnut colt foaled 1938 by Blanheim II out of Dustwhirl. Owned and bred by Calumet Farm. Trained by Ben Jones. Won the US Triple Crown in 1941. Won 32 from 60 starts. Whirlaway's trainer developed new-style blinkers for the horse, who was known for erratic running. Sent to stud in France. Died 1953.

Williamson, Norman Born Co. Cork, Ireland, 16 January 1969. Apprenticed to Dermot Weld. First winner: Jack 'N' Jill (Clonmel, March 1987). He won the Champion Hurdle on Alderbrook (1995), the Cheltenham Gold Cup on Master Oats (1995) and the Welsh Grand National on Master Oats (1994).

Winter, Fred Born Andover, Hampshire, 20 September 1926. The son of a trainer also called Fred. First winner: Tam O'Shanter (Salisbury, 15 May 1940, aged 13). His first National Hunt winner was Carton at Kempton on 27 December 1947, while his last was Vultrix at Wolverhampton on 25 March 1964. Winter is the only man in National Hunt racing to have both ridden and trained winners of the Grand National, Cheltenham Gold Cup and Champion Hurdle. Champion jockey four times (1953, 1956, 1957, 1958), he rode 929 winners from 4298 mounts. As a trainer his yard was at Uplands, Upper Lambourn, and housed such luminaries as Bula, Crisp, Pendil, Lanzarote and the ill-fated Killiney (killed at Ascot in 1973). He trained successive National winners with Jay Trump (1965) and Anglo (1966). He was leading trainer eight times (1971-75, 1977, 1978, 1985). He retired in 1985 following a stroke and was succeeded by Charlie Brooks. He died 6 April 2004.

Wragg, Harry Born 1902. One of the few individuals who made it to the top both as a jockey and a trainer, he rode his first winner in 1919 and by the time of his retirement from the saddle in 1946 had ridden 1762 winners in Britain, including 13 classic victories. He only won the champion jockey title once (1941), largely due to the genius of Gordon Richards. His nickname, given him because of his great judgement of when to make a challenge, was 'The Head Waiter'. He began training at Newmarket in 1947 and won six classics with Darius (2000 Guineas, 1954), Psidium (Derby ,1961), Abermaid (1000 Guineas, 1962), Full Dress II (1000 Guineas, 1969), Intermezzo (St Leger, 1969) and On the House (1000 Guineas, 1982). He died in 1985 and his son Geoff (born 1930) has continued the tradition, having the distinction of becoming the first man to train a classic winner in the same year as he first took out a licence when Teenoso won the 1983 Derby.

Xaar Bay colt sired by Zafonic out of Monroe. Owned by Khalid Abdullah. Trained by André Fabre. An equally precocious two-year-old as his sire, his seven-length win in the Dewhurst made him an odds-on chance for the 1998 2000 Guineas. Like his father, however, his career ended in disappointment with defeats in the Guineas and two other races before being retired, having never recaptured the brilliance of his first season.

Zafonic Bay colt foaled 1990 by Gone West out of Zaizafon. Owned by Khalid Abdullah. Trained in France by André Fabre. Unbeaten as a two-year-old in 1992, he suffered his first defeat at the hands of Kingmambo in his prep-race for the Guineas but won the 1993 2000 Guineas pulling the proverbial cart. Broke a blood vessel in his next outing and was retired having run only seven times.

English Classic Flat Race Winners

	St Leger		Oaks		Derby	
	Horse	**Jockey**	**Horse**	**Jockey**	**Horse**	**Jockey**
1776	Allabaculia	J. Singleton	——	——	——	——
1777	Bourbon	J. Cade	——	——	——	——
1778	Hollandaise	G. Hearon	——	——	——	——
1779	Tommy	G. Lowrey snr	Bridget	R. Goodisson	——	——
1780	Ruler	J. Mangle	Teetotum	R. Goodisson	Diomed	S. Arnull
1781	Serina	R. Forster	Faith	R. Goodisson	Young Eclipse	C. Hindley
1782	Imperatrix	G. Searle	Ceres	S. Chifney snr	Assassin	S. Arnull
1783	Phoenomenon	A. Hall	Maid Of Oakes	S. Chifney snr	Saltram	C. Hindley
1784	Omphale	J. Kirton	Stella	C. Hindley	Sergeant	J. Arnull
1785	Cowslip	G. Searle	Trifle	J. Bird	Aimwell	C. Hindley
1786	Paragon	J. Mangle	Yellow Filly	J. Edwards	Noble	J. White
1787	Spadille	J. Mangle	Annette	D. Fitzpatrick	Sir Peter Teazle	S. Arnull
1788	Young Flora	J. Mangle	Nightshade	D. Fitzpatrick	Sir Thomas	W. South
1789	Pewett	J. Singleton	Tag	S. Chifney snr	Skyscraper	S. Chifney snr
1790	Ambidexter	G. Searle	Hippolyta	S. Chifney snr	Rhadamanthus	J. Arnull
1791	Young Traveller	J. Jackson	Portia	J. Singleton	Eager	M. Stephenson
1792	Tartar	J. Mangle	Volante	C. Hindley	John Bull	F. Buckle
1793	Ninety-three	W. Peirse	Caelia	J. Singleton	Waxy	W. Clift
1794	Beningborough	J. Jackson	Hermione	S. Arnull	Daedalus	F. Buckle
1795	Hambletonian	R.D. Boyes	Platina	D. Fitzpatrick	Spreadeagle	A. Wheatley
1796	Ambrosio	J. Jackson	Parisot	J. Arnull	Didelot	J. Arnull
1797	Lounger	J. Shepherd	Nike	F. Buckle	Fidget Colt	J. Singleton
1798	Symmetry	J. Jackson	Bellissima	F. Buckle	Sir Harry	S. Arnull
1799	Cockfighter	T. Fields	Bellina	F. Buckle	Archduke	J. Arnull
1800	Champion	F. Buckle	Ephemera	D. Fitzpatrick	Champion	W. Clift
1801	Quiz	J. Shepherd	Eleanor	J. Saunders	Eleanor	J. Saunders
1802	Orville	J. Singleton jnr	Scotia	F. Buckle	Tyrant	F. Buckle
1803	Remembrancer	B. Smith	Theophania	F. Buckle	Ditto	W. Clift
1804	Sancho	F. Buckle	Pelisse	W. Clift	Hannibal	W. Arnull
1805	Staveley	J. Jackson	Meteora	F. Buckle	Cardinal Beaufort	D. Fitzpatrick
1806	Fyldener	T. Carr	Bronze	W. Edwards	Paris	J. Shepherd
1807	Paulina	W. Clift	Briseis	S. Chifney jnr	Election	J. Arnull
1808	Petronius	B. Smith	Morel	W. Clift	Pan	F. Collinson
1809	Ashton	B. Smith	Maid Of Orleans	J. Moss	Pope	T. Goodison
1810	Octavian	W. Clift	Oriana	W. Peirse	Whalebone	W. Clift
1811	Soothsayer	B. Smith	Sorcery	S. Chifney jnr	Phantom	F. Buckle
1812	Ottrington	R. Johnson	Manuella	W. Peirse	Octavius	W. Arnull
1313	Altisidora	J. Jackson	Music	T. Goodison	Smolensko	T. Goodison
1814	William	J. Shepherd	Medora	S. Barnard	Blucher	W. Arnull
1815	Filho Da Puta	J. Jackson	Minuet	T. Goodison	Whisker	T. Goodison
1816	The Duchess	B. Smith	Landscape	S. Chifney jnr	Prince Leopold	W. Wheatley
1817	Ebor	R. Johnson	Neva	F. Buckle	Azor	J. Robinson
1818	Reveller	R. Johnson	Corinne	F. Buckle	Sam	S. Chifney jnr
1819	Antonio	J. Nicholson	Shoveler	S. Chifney jnr	Tiresias	W. Clift
1820	St Patrick	J. Johnson	Caroline	H. Edwards	Sailor	S. Chifney jnr
1821	Jack Spigot	W. Scott	Augusta	J. Robinson	Gustavus	S. Day
1822	Theodore	J. Jackson	Pastille	H. Edwards	Moses	T. Goodison
1823	Barefoot	T. Goodison	Zinc	F. Buckle	Emilius	F. Buckle
1824	Jerry	B. Smith	Cobweb	J. Robinson	Cedric	J. Robinson
1825	Memnon	W. Scott	Wings	S. Chifney jnr	Middleton	J. Robinson
1826	Tarrare	G. Nelson	Lilias	T. Lye	Lapdog	G. Dockeray
1827	Matilda	J. Robinson	Gulnare	F. Boyce	Mameluke	J. Robinson
1828	The Colonel	W. Scott	Turquoise	J.B. Day	Cadland	J. Robinson
1829	Rowton	W. Scott	Green Mantle	G. Dockeray	Frederick	J. Forth
1830	Birmingham	P. Conolly	Variation	G. Edwards	Priam	S. Day
1831	Chorister	J.B. Day	Oxygen	J.B. Day	Spaniel	W. Wheatley
1832	Margrave	J. Robinson	Galata	P. Conolly	St Giles	W. Scott
1833	Rockingham	S. Darling	Vespa	J. Chapple	Dangerous	J. Chapple
1834	Touchstone	G. Calloway	Pussy	J.B. Day	Plenipotentiary	P. Conolly
1835	Queen Of Trumps	T. Lye	Queen Of Trumps	T. Lye	Mundig	W. Scott
1836	Elis	J.B. Day	Cyprian	W. Scott	Bay Middleton	J. Robinson
1837	Mango	S. Day jnr	Miss Letty	J. Holmes	Phosphorus	G. Edwards
1838	Don John	W. Scott	Industry	W. Scott	Amato	J. Chapple
1839	Charles The Twelfth	W. Scott	Deception	J.B. Day	Bloomsbury	S. Templeman
1840	Launcelot	W. Scott	Crucifix	J.B. Day	Little Wonder	W. Macdonald
1841	Satirist	W. Scott	Ghuznee	W. Scott	Coronation	P. Conolly
1842	Blue Bonnet	T. Lye	Our Nell	T. Lye	Attila	W. Scott

Year	St Leger Horse	Jockey	Oaks Horse	Jockey	Derby Horse	Jockey
1843	Nutwith	J. Marson	Poison	F. Butler	Cotherstone	W. Scott
1844	Faugh Ballagh	H. Bell	The Princess	F. Butler	Orlando	E. Flatman
1845	The Baron	F. Butler	Refraction	H. Bell	The Merry Monarch	F. Bell
1846	Sir Tatton Sykes	W. Scott	Mendicant	S. Day	Pyrrhus The First	S. Day
1847	van Tromp	J. Marson	Miami	S. Templeman	Cossack	S. Templeman
1848	Surplice	E. Flatman	Cymba	S. Templeman	Surplice	S. Templeman
1849	The Flying Dutchman	C. Marlow	Lady Evelyn	F. Butler	The Flying Dutchman	C. Marlow
1850	Voltigeur	J. Marson	Rhedycina	F. Butler	Voltigeur	J. Marson
1851	Newminster	S. Templeman	Iris	F. Butler	Teddington	J. Marson
1852	Stockwell	J. Norman	Songstress	F. Butler	Daniel O'Rourke	F. Butler
1853	West Australian	F. Butler	Catherine Hayes	C. Marlow	West Australian	F. Butler
1854	Knight Of St George	R. Basham	Mincemeat	J. Charlton	Andover	A. Day
1855	Saucebox	J. Wells	Marchioness	S. Templeman	Wild Dayrell	R. Sherwood
1856	Warlock	E. Flatman	Mincepie	A. Day	Ellington	T. Aldcroft
1857	Imperieuse	E. Flatman	Blink Bonny	J. Charlton	Blink Bonny	J. Charlton
1858	Sunbeam	L. Snowden	Governess*	T. Ashmall	Beadsman	J. Wells
1859	Gamester	T. Aldcroft	Summerside	G. Fordham	Musjid	J. Wells
1860	St Albans	L. Snowden	Butterfly	J. Snowden	Thormanby	H. Custance
1861	Caller Ou	T. Chaloner	Brown Duchess	L. Snowden	Kettledrum	R. Bullock
1862	The Marquis	T. Chaloner	Feu De Joie	T. Chaloner	Caractacus	J. Parsons
1863	Lord Clifden	J. Osborne	Queen Bertha	T. Aldcroft	Macaroni	T. Chaloner
1864	Blair Athol	J. Snowden	Fille De L'Air	A. Edwards	Blair Athol	J. Snowden
1865	Gladiateur	H. Grimshaw	Regalia	J. Norman	Gladiateur	H. Grimshaw
1866	Lord Lyon	H. Custance	Tormentor	J. Mann	Lord Lyon	H. Custance
1867	Achievement	T. Chaloner	Hippia	J. Daley	Hermit	J. Daley
1868	Formosa	T. Chaloner	Formosa	G. Fordham	Blue Gown	J. Wells
1869	Pero Gomez	J. Wells	Brigantine	T. Cannon	Pretender	J. Osborne
1870	Hawthornden	J. Grimshaw	Gamos	G. Fordham	Kingcraft	T. French
1871	Hannah	C. Maidment	Hannah	C. Maidment	Favonius	T. French
1872	Wenlock	C. Maidment	Reine	G. Fordham	Cremorne	C. Maidment
1873	Marie Stuart	T. Osborne	Marie Stuart	T. Cannon	Doncaster	F. Webb
1874	Apology	J. Osborne	Apology	J. Osborne	George Frederick	H. Custance
1875	Craig Millar	T. Chaloner	Spinaway	F. Archer	Galopin	J. Morris
1876	Petrarch	J. Goater	Enguerrandee**	Hudson	Kisber	C. Maidment
			Camelia	T. Glover		
1877	Silvio	F. Archer	Placida	H. Jeffrey	Silvio	F. Archer
1878	Jannette	F. Archer	Jannette	F. Archer	Sefton	H. Constable
1879	Rayon D'Or	J. Goater	Wheel Of Fortune	F. Archer	Sir Bevys	G. Fordham
1880	Robert The Devil	T. Cannon	Jenny Howlet	J. Snowden	Bend Or	F. Archer
1881	Iroquois	F. Archer	Thebais	G. Fordham	Iroquois	F. Archer
1882	Dutch Oven	F. Archer	Geheimniss	T. Cannon	Shotover	T. Cannon
1883	Ossian	J. Watts	Bonny Jean	J. Watts	St Blaise	C. Wood
1884	The Lambkin	F. Archer	Busybody	T. Cannon	St Gatien/Harvester	C. Wood/S. Loates
1885	Melton	F. Archer	Lonely	F. Archer	Melton	F. Archer
1886	Ormonde	F. Archer	Miss Jummy	J. Watts	Ormonde	F. Archer
1887	Kilwarlin	W. Robinson	Reve D'Or	C. Wood	Merry Hampton	J. Watts
1888	Seabreeze	W. Robinson	Seabreeze	W. Robinson	Ayrshire	F. Barrett
1889	Donovan	F. Barrett	L'Abbesse De Jouarre	J. Woodburn	Donovan	T. Loates
1890	Memoir	J. Watts	Memoir	J. Watts	Sainfoin	J. Watts
1891	Common	G. Barrett	Mimi	F. Rickaby	Common	G. Barrett
1892	La Fleche	J. Watts	La Fleche	G. Barrett	Sir Hugo	F. Allsopp
1893	Isinglass	T. Loates	Mrs Butterwick	J. Watts	Isinglass	T. Loates
1894	Throstle	H. Cannon	Amiable	W. Bradford	Ladas	J. Watts
1895	Sir Visto	S. Loates	La Sagesse	S. Loates	Sir Visto	S. Loates
1896	Persimmon	J. Watts	Canterbury Pilgrim	F. Rickaby	Persimmon	J. Watts
1897	Galtee More	C. Wood	Limasol	W. Bradford	Galtee More	C. Wood
1898	Wildfowler	C. Wood	Airs And Graces	W. Bradford	Jeddah	H. Madden
1899	Flying Fox	H. Cannon	Musa	H. Madden	Flying Fox	H. Cannon
1900	Diamond Jubilee	H. Jones	La Roche	M. Cannon	Diamond Jubilee	H. Jones
1901	Doricles	K. Cannon	Cap And Bells II	M. Henry	Volodyovski	L. Reiff
1902	Sceptre	F.W. Hardy	Sceptre	H. Randall	Ard Patrick	J. Martin
1903	Rock Sand	D. Maher	Our Lassie	H. Cannon	Rock Sand	D. Maher
1904	Pretty Polly	W. Lane	Pretty Polly	W. Lane	St Amant	K. Cannon
1905	Challacombe	O. Madden	Cherry Lass	H. Jones	Cicero	D. Maher
1906	Troutbeck	G. Stern	Keystone II	D. Maher	Spearmint	D. Maher
1907	Wool Winder	W. Halsey	Glass Doll	H. Randall	Orby	J. Reiff
1908	Your Majesty	W. Griggs	Signorinetta	W. Bullock	Signorinetta	W. Bullock
1909	Bayardo	D. Maher	Perola	F. Wootton	Minoru	H. Jones
1910	Swynford	F. Wootton	Rosedrop	C. Trigg	Lemberg	B. Dillon
1911	Prince Palatine	F. O'Neill	Cherimoya	F. Winter	Sunstar	G. Stern
1912	Tracery	G. Bellhouse	Mirska	J. Childs	Tagalie	J. Reiff

St Leger

	Horse	Jockey
1913	Night Hawk	E. Wheatley
1914	Black Jester	W. Griggs
1915	Pommern	S. Donoghue
1916	Hurry On	C. Childs
1917	Gay Crusader	S. Donoghue
1918	Gainsborough	J. Childs
1919	Keysoe	B. Carslake
1920	Caligula	A. Smith
1921	Polemarch	J. Childs
1922	Royal Lancer	R. Jones
1923	Tranquil	T. Weston
1924	Salmon-Trout	B. Carslake
1925	Solario	J. Childs
1926	Coronach	J. Childs
1927	Book Law	H. Jellis
1928	Fairway	T. Weston
1929	Trigo	M. Beary
1930	Singapore	G. Richards
1931	Sandwich	H. Wragg
1932	Firdaussi	F. Fox
1933	Hyperion	T. Weston
1934	Windsor Lad	C. Smirke
1935	Bahram	C. Smirke
1936	Boswell	P. Beasley
1937	Chulmleigh	G. Richards
1938	Scottish Union	B. Carslake
1939	not held	
1940	Turkhan	G. Richards
1941	Sun Castle	G. Bridgland
1942	Sun Chariot	G. Richards
1943	Herringbone	H. Wragg
1944	Tehran	G. Richards
1945	Chamossaire	T. Lowrey
1946	Airborne	T. Lowrey
1947	Sayajirao	E. Britt
1948	Black Tarquin	E. Britt
1949	Ridge Wood	M. Beary
1950	Scratch II	W.R. Johnstone
1951	Talma II	W.R. Johnstone
1952	Tulyar	C. Smirke
1953	Premonition	E. Smith
1954	Never Say Die	C. Smirke
1955	Meld	W.H. Carr
1956	Cambremer	F. Palmer
1957	Ballymoss	T.P. Burns
1958	Alcide	W.H. Carr
1959	Cantelo	E. Hide
1960	St Paddy	L. Piggott
1961	Aurelius	L. Piggott
1962	Hethersett	W.H. Carr
1963	Ragusa	G. Bougoure
1964	Indiana	J. Lindley
1965	Provoke	J. Mercer
1966	Sodium	F. Durr
1967	Ribocco	L. Piggott
1968	Ribero	L. Piggott
1969	Intermezzo	R. Hutchinson
1970	Nijinsky	L. Piggott
1971	Athens Wood	L. Piggott
1972	Boucher	L. Piggott
1973	Peleid	F. Durr
1974	Bustino	J. Mercer
1975	Bruni	A. Murray
1976	Crow	Y. Saint-Martin
1977	Dunfermline	W. Carson
1978	Julio Mariner	E. Hide
1979	Son Of Love	A. Lequeux
1980	Light Cavalry	J. Mercer
1981	Cut Above	J. Mercer
1982	Touching Wood	P. Cook
1983	Sun Princess	W. Carson

Oaks

Horse	Jockey
Jest	F. Rickaby jnr
Princess Dorrie	W. Huxley
Snow Marten	W. Griggs
Fifinella	J. Childs
Sunny Jane	H. Madden
My Dear	S. Donoghue
Bayuda	J. Childs
Charlebelle	A. Whalley
Love In Idleness	J. Childs
Pogrom	E. Gardner
Brownhylda	V. Smyth
Straitlace	F. O'Neill
Saucy Sue	F. Bullock
Short Story	R.A. Jones
Beam	T. Weston
Toboggan	T. Weston
Pennycomequick	H. Jelliss
Rose Of England	G. Richards
Brulette	E.C. Elliott
Udaipur	M. Beary
Chatelaine	S. Wragg
Light Brocade	B. Carslake
Quashed	H. Jelliss
Lovely Rosa	T. Weston
Exhibitionist	S. Donoghue
Rockfel	H. Wragg
Galatea II	R.A. Jones
Godiva	D. Marks
Commotion	H. Wragg
Sun Chariot	G. Richards
Why Hurry	E.C. Elliott
Hycilla	G. Bridgland
Sun Stream	H. Wragg
Steady Aim	H. Wragg
Imprudence	W.R. Johnstone
Masaka	W. Nevett
Musidora	E. Britt
Asmena	W.R. Johnstone
Neasham Belle	S. Clayton
Frieze	E. Britt
Ambiguity	J. Mercer
Sun Cap	W.R. Johnstone
Meld	W.H. Carr
Sicarelle	F. Palmer
Carrozza	L. Piggott
Bella Paola	M. Garcia
Petite Etoile	L. Piggott
Never Too Late II	R. Poincelet
Sweet Solera	W. Rickaby
Monade	Y. Saint-Martin
Noblesse	G. Bougoure
Homeward Bound	G. Starkey
Long Look	J. Purtell
Valoris	L. Piggott
Pia	E. Hide
La Lagune	G. Thiboeuf
Sleeping Partner	J. Gorton
Lupe	A. Barclay
Altesse Royale	G. Lewis
Ginevra	A. Murray
Mysterious	G. Lewis
Polygamy	P. Eddery
Juliette Marny	L. Piggott
Pawneese	Y. Saint-Martin
Dunfermline	W. Carson
Fair Salinia	G. Starkey
Scintillate	P. Eddery
Bireme	W. Carson
Blue Wind	L. Piggott
Time Charter	W. Newnes
Sun Princess	W. Carson

Derby

Horse	Jockey
Aboyeur	E. Piper
Dubar II	M. MacGee
Pommern	S. Donoghue
Fifinella	J. Childs
Gay Crusader	S. Donoghue
Gainsborough	J. Childs
Grand Parade	F. Templeman
Spion Kop	F. O'Neill
Humorist	S. Donoghue
Captain Cuttle	S. Donoghue
Papyrus	S. Donoghue
Sansovino	T. Weston
Manna	S. Donoghue
Coronach	J. Childs
Call Boy	E.C. Elliott
Felstead	H. Wragg
Trigo	J. Marshall
Blenheim	H. Wragg
Cameronian	F. Fox
April The Fifth	F. Lane
Hyperion	T. Weston
Windsor Lad	C. Smirke
Bahram	F. Fox
Mahmoud	C. Smirke
Mid-day Sun	M. Beary
Bois Roussel	E.C. Elliott
Blue Peter	E. Smith
Pont L'Eveque	S. Wragg
Owen Tudor	W. Nevett
Watling Street	H. Wragg
Straight Deal	T. Carey
Ocean Swell	W. Nevett
Dante	W. Nevett
Airborne	T. Lowrey
Pearl Diver	G. Bridgland
My Love	W.R. Johnstone
Nimbus	E.C. Elliott
Galcador	W.R. Johnstone
Arctic Prince	C. Spares
Tulyar	C. Smirke
Pinza	G. Richards
Never Say Die	L. Piggott
Phil Drake	F. Palmer
Lavandin	W.R. Johnstone
Crepello	L. Piggott
Hard Ridden	C. Smirke
Parthia	W.H. Carr
St Paddy	L. Piggott
Psidium	R. Poincelet
Larkspur	N. Sellwood
Relko	Y. Saint-Martin
Santa Claus	A. Breasley
Sea Bird II	T.P. Glennon
Charlottown	A. Breasley
Royal Palace	G. Moore
Sir Ivor	L. Piggott
Blakeney	E. Johnson
Nijinsky	L. Piggott
Mill Reef	G. Lewis
Roberto	L. Piggott
Morston	E. Hide
Snow Knight	B. Taylor
Grundy	P. Eddery
Empery	L. Piggott
The Minstrel	L. Piggott
Shirley Heights	G. Starkey
Troy	W. Carson
Henbit	W. Carson
Shergar	W. Swinburn
Golden Fleece	P. Eddery
Teenoso	L. Piggott

HORSE RACING

St Leger

	Horse	Jockey
1984	Comanche Run	L. Piggott
1985	Oh So Sharp	S. Cauthen
1986	Moon Madness	P. Eddery
1987	Reference Point	S. Cauthen
1988	Minster Son	W. Carson
1989	Michelozzo	S. Cauthen
1990	Snurge	T. Quinn
1991	Toulon	P. Eddery
1992	User Friendly	G. Duffield
1993	Bob's Return	P. Robinson
1994	Moonax	P. Eddery
1995	Classic Cliché	L. Dettori
1996	Shantou	L. Dettori
1997	Silver Patriarch	P. Eddery
1998	Nedawi	J. Reid
1999	Mutafaweq	R. Hills
2000	Millenary	T. Quinn
2001	Milan	M.J. Kinane
2002	Bollin Eric	K. Darley
2003	Brian Boru	J. Spencer
2004		

Oaks

	Horse	Jockey
1984	Circus Plume	L. Piggott
1985	Oh So Sharp	S. Cauthen
1986	Midway Lady	R. Cochrane
1987	Unite	W. Swinburn
1988	Diminuendo	S. Cauthen
1989	Snow Bride	S. Cauthen
1990	Salsabil	W. Carson
1991	Jet Ski Lady	C. Roche
1992	User Friendly	G. Duffield
1993	Intrepidity	M. Roberts
1994	Balanchine	L. Dettori
1995	Moonshell	L. Dettori
1996	Lady Carla	P. Eddery
1997	Reams Of Verse	K. Fallon
1998	Shahtoush	M.J. Kinane
1999	Ramruma	K. Fallon
2000	Love Divine	T. Quinn
2001	Imagine	M.J. Kinane
2002	Kazzia	L. Dettori
2003	Casual Look	M. Dwyer
2004	Ouija Board	K. Fallon

Derby

	Horse	Jockey
1984	Secreto	C. Roche
1985	Slip Anchor	S. Cauthen
1986	Shahrastani	W. Swinburn
1987	Reference Point	S. Cauthen
1988	Kahyasi	R. Cochrane
1989	Nashwan	W. Carson
1990	Quest Of Fame	P. Eddery
1991	Generous	A. Munro
1992	Dr Devious	J. Reid
1993	Commander-In-Chief	M.J. Kinane
1994	Erhaab	W. Carson
1995	Lammtarra	W. Swinburn
1996	Shaamit	M. Hills
1997	Benny The Dip	W. Ryan
1998	High Rise	O. Peslier
1999	Oath	K. Fallon
2000	Sinndar	J. Murtagh
2001	Galileo	M.J. Kinane
2002	High Chaparral	J. Murtagh
2003	Kris Kin	K. Fallon
2004	North Light	K. Fallon

*The 1858 Oaks was a dead heat for first place, Governess beat Gildermere (ridden by T. Alcroft) in the decider.
**the 1876 Oaks was a dead heat for first place, Enguerrande subsequently walked over but the stakes were divided.

2000 Guineas

	Horse	Jockey
1809	Wizard	W. Clift
1810	Hephestion	F. Buckle
1811	Trophonius	S. Barnard
1812	Cwrw	S. Chifney jnr
1813	Smolensko	H. Miller
1814	Olive	W. Arnull
1815	Tigris	W. Arnull
1816	Nectar	W. Arnull
1817	Manfred	W. Wheatley
1818	Interpreter	W. Clift
1819	Antar	E. Edwards
1820	Pindarrie	F. Buckle
1821	Reginald	F. Buckle
1822	Pastille	F. Buckle
1823	Nicolo	W. Wheatley
1824	Schahriar	W. Wheatley
1825	Enamel	J. Robinson
1826	Dervise	J.B. Day
1827	Turcoman	F. Buckle
1828	Cadland	J. Robinson
1829	Patron	F. Boyce
1830	Augustus	P. Conolly
1831	Riddlesworth	J. Robinson
1832	Archibald	A. Pavis
1833	Clearwell	J. Robinson
1834	Glencoe	J. Robinson
1835	Ibrahim	J. Robinson
1836	Bay Middleton	J. Robinson
1837	Achmet	E. Edwards
1838	Grey Momus	J.B. Day
1839	The Corsair	W. Wakefield
1840	Crucifix	J.B. Day
1841	Ralph	J.B. Day
1842	Meteor	W. Scott
1843	Cotherstone	W. Scott
1844	The Ugly Buck	J. Day jnr
1845	Idas	E. Flatman
1846	Sir Tatton Sykes	W. Scott
1847	Conyngham	J. Robinson
1848	Flatcatcher	J. Robinson
1849	Nunnykirk	F. Butler
1850	Pitsford	A. Day
1851	Hernandez	E. Flatman
1852	Stockwell	J. Norman

1000 Guineas

	Horse	Jockey
1809	———	———
1810	———	———
1811	———	———
1812	———	———
1813	———	———
1814	Charlotte	W. Clift
1815	brown filly by Selim	W. Clift
1816	Rhoda	S. Barnard
1817	Neva	W. Arnull
1818	Corinne	F. Buckle
1819	Catgut	unknown
1820	Rowena	F. Buckle
1821	Zeal	F. Buckle
1822	Whizgig	F. Buckle
1823	Zinc	F. Buckle
1824	Cobweb	J. Robinson
1825	Tontine	walkover
1826	Problem	J.B. Day
1827	Arab	F. Buckle
1828	Zoe	J. Robinson
1829	Young Mouse	W. Arnull
1830	Charlotte West	J. Robinson
1831	Galantine	P. Conolly
1832	Galata	W. Arnull
1833	Tarantella	E. Wright
1834	May Day	J.B. Day
1835	Preserve	E. Flatman
1836	Destiny	J.B. Day
1837	Chapeau D'Espagne	J.B. Day
1838	Barcarolle	E. Edwards
1839	Cara	G. Edwards
1840	Crucifix	J.B. Day
1841	Potentia	J. Robinson
1842	Firebrand	S. Rogers
1843	Extempore	S. Chifney jnr
1844	Sorella	J. Robinson
1845	Pic-Nic	W. Abdale
1846	Mendicant	S. Day
1847	Clementina	E. Flatman
1848	Canezou	F. Butler
1849	Flea	A. Day
1850	Lady Orford	F. Butler
1851	Aphrodite	J. Marson
1852	Kate	A. Day

2000 Guineas

	Horse	Jockey
1853	West Australian	F. Butler
1854	The Hermit	A. Day
1855	Lord Of The Isles	T. Aldcroft
1856	Fazzoletto	E. Flatman
1857	Vedette	J. Osborne
1858	Fitz-Roland	J. Wells
1859	The Promised Land	A. Day
1860	The Wizard	t. Ashmall
1861	Diophantus	A. Edwards
1862	The Marquis	T. Ashmall
1863	Macaroni	T. Chaloner
1864	General Peel	T. Aldcroft
1865	Gladiateur	H. Grimshaw
1866	Lord Lyon	R. Thomas
1867	Vauban	G. Fordham
1868	Moslem*	T. Chaloner
1869	Pretender	J. Osborne
1870	Macgregor	J. Daley
1871	Bothwell	J. Osborne
1872	Prince Charlie	J. Osborne
1873	Gang Forward	T. Chaloner
1874	Atlantic	F. Archer
1875	Camballo	J. Osborne
1876	Petrarch	H. Luke
1877	Chamant	J. Goater
1878	Pilgrimage	T. Cannon
1879	Charibert	F. Archer
1880	Petronel	G. Fordham
1881	Peregrine	F. Webb
1882	Shotover	T. Cannon
1883	Galliard	F. Archer
1884	Scot Free	W. Platt
1885	Paradox	F. Archer
1886	Ormonde	G. Barrett
1887	Enterprise	T. Cannon
1888	Ayrshire	J. Osborne
1889	Enthusiast	T. Cannon
1890	Surefoot	J. Liddiard
1891	Common	G. Barrett
1892	Bona Vista	W. Robinson
1893	Isinglass	T. Loates
1894	Ladas	J. Watts
1895	Kirkconnel	J. Watts
1896	St Frusquin	T. Loates
1897	Galtee More	C. Wood
1898	Disraeli	S. Loates
1899	Flying Fox	H. Cannon
1900	Diamond Jubilee	H. Jones
1901	Handicapper	W. Halsey
1902	Sceptre	H. Randall
1903	Rock Sand	J.H. Martin
1904	St Amant	K. Cannon
1905	Vedas	H. Jones
1906	Gorgos	H. Jones
1907	Slieve Gallion	W. Higgs
1908	Norman III	H. Madden
1909	Minoru	H. Jones
1910	Neil Gow	D. Maher
1911	Sunstar	G. Stern
1912	Sweeper II	D. Maher
1913	Louvois	J. Reiff
1914	Kennymore	G. Stern
1915	Pommern	S. Donoghue
1916	Clarissimus	J. Clark
1917	Gay Crusader	S. Donoghue
1918	Gainsborough	J. Childs
1919	The Panther	R. Cooper
1920	Tetratema	B. Carslake
1921	Craig An Eran	J. Brennan
1922	St Louis	G. Archibald
1923	Ellangowan	E.C. Elliott

1000 Guineas

Horse	Jockey
Mentmore Lass	J. Charlton
Virago	J. Wells
Habena	S. Rogers
Manganese	J. Osborne
Imperieuse	E. Flatman
Governess	T Ashmall
Mayonnaise	G. Fordham
Sagitta	T. Aldcroft
Nemesis	G. Fordham
Hurricane	T. Ashmall
Lady Augusta	A. Edwards
Tomato	J. Wells
Siberia	G. Fordham
Repulse	T. Cannon
Achievement	H. Custance
Formosa	G. Fordham
Scottish Queen	G. Fordham
Hester	J. Grimshaw
Hannah	C. Maidment
Reine	H. Parry
Cecilia	J. Morris
Apology	J. Osborne
Spinaway	F. Archer
Camelia	T. Glover
Belphoebe	H. Jeffery
Pilgrimage	T. Cannon
Wheel Of Fortune	F. Archer
Elizabeth	C. Wood
Thebais	G. Fordham
St Marguerite	C. Wood
Hauteur	G. Fordham
Busybody	T. Cannon
Farewell	G. Barrett
Miss Jummy	J. Watts
Reve D'Or	C. Wood
Briar Root	W. Warne
Minthe	J. Woodburn
Semolina	J. Watts
Mimi	F. Rickaby
La Fleche	G. Barrett
Siffleuse	T. Loates
Amiable	W. Bradford
Galeottia	F. Pratt
Thais	J. Watts
Chelandry	J. Watts
Nun Nicer	S. Loates
Sibola	J.F. Sloan
Winifreda	S. Loates
Aida	D. Maher
Sceptre	H. Randall
Quintessence	H. Randall
Pretty Polly	W. Lane
Cherry Lass	G. McCall
Flair	B. Dillon
Witch Elm	B. Lynham
Rhodora	L. Lyne
Electra	B. Dillon
Winkipop	B. Lynham
Atmah	F. Fox
Tagalie	L.H. Hewitt
Jest	F. Rickaby jnr
Princess Dorrie	W. Huxley
Vaucluse	F. Rickaby jnr
Canyon	F. Rickaby jnr
Diadem	F. Rickaby jnr
Ferry	B. Carslake
Roseway	A. Whalley
Cinna	W. Griggs
Bettina	G. Bellhouse
Silver Urn	B. Carslake
Tranquil	E. Gardner

HORSE RACING

2000 Guineas

	Horse	Jockey
1924	Diophon	G. Hulme
1925	Manna	S. Donoghue
1926	Colorado	T. Weston
1927	Adam's Apple	J. Leach
1928	Flamingo	E.C. Elliott
1929	Mr Jinks	H. Beasley
1930	Diolite	F. Fox
1931	Cameronian	J. Childs
1932	Orwell	R. Jones
1933	Rodosto	R. Brethes
1934	Colombo	W. Johnstone
1935	Bahram	F. Fox
1936	Pay Up	R. Dick
1937	Le Ksar	C. Semblat
1938	Pasch	G. Richards
1939	Blue Peter	E. Smith
1940	Djebel	E.C. Elliott
1941	Lambert Simnel	E.C. Elliott
1942	Big Game	G. Richards
1943	Kingsway	S. Wragg
1944	Garden Path	H. Wragg
1945	Court Martial	C. Richards
1946	Happy Knight	T. Weston
1947	Tudor Minstrel	G. Richards
1948	My Babu	C. Smirke
1949	Nimbus	E.C. Elliott
1950	Palestine	C. Smirke
1951	Ki Ming	A. Breasley
1952	Thunderhead II	R. Poincelet
1953	Nearula	E. Britt
1954	Darius	E. Mercer
1955	Our Babu	D. Smith
1956	Gilles De Retz	F. Barlow
1957	Crepello	L. Piggott
1958	Pall Mall	D. Smith
1959	Taboun	G. Moore
1960	Martial	R. Hutchinson
1961	Rockavon	N. Stirk
1962	Privy Councillor	W. Rickaby
1963	Only For Life	J. Lindley
1964	Baldric II	W. Pyers
1965	Niksar	D. Keith
1966	Kashmir II	J. Lindley
1967	Royal Palace	G. Moore
1968	Sir Ivor	L. Piggott
1969	Right Tack	G. Lewis
1970	Nijinsky	L. Piggott
1971	Brigadier Gerard	J. Mercer
1972	High Top	W. Carson
1973	Mon Fils	F. Durr
1974	Nonoalco	Y. Saint-Martin
1975	Bolkonski	G. Dettori
1976	Wollow	G. Dettori
1977	Nebbiolo	G. Curran
1978	Roland Gardens	F. Durr
1979	Tap On Wood	S. Cauthen
1980	Known Fact	W. Carson
1981	To-Agori-Mou	G. Starkey
1982	Zino	F. Head
1983	Lomond	P. Eddery
1984	El Gran Senor	P. Eddery
1985	Shadeed	L. Piggott
1986	Dancing Brave	G. Starkey
1987	Don't Forget Me	W. Carson
1988	Doyoun	W. Swinburn
1989	Nashwan	W. Carson
1990	Tirol	M.J. Kinane
1991	Mystiko	M. Roberts
1992	Rodrigo De Triano	L. Piggott
1993	Zafonic	P. Eddery
1994	Mister Baileys	J. Weaver

1000 Guineas

	Horse	Jockey
1924	Plack	E.C. Elliott
1925	Saucy Sue	F. Bullock
1926	Pillion	R. Perryman
1927	Cresta Run	A. Balding
1928	Scuttle	J. Childs
1929	Taj Mah	W. Sibbritt
1930	Fair Isle	T. Weston
1931	Four Course	E.C. Elliott
1932	Kandy	E.C. Elliott
1933	Brown Betty	J. Childs
1934	Campanula	H. Wragg
1935	Mesa	W.R. Johnstone
1936	Tideway	R. Perryman
1937	Exhibitionist	S. Donoghue
1938	Rockfel	S. Wragg
1939	Galatea II	R.A. Jones
1940	Godiva	D. Marks
1941	Dancing Time	R. Perryman
1942	Sun Chariot	G. Richards
1943	Herringbone	H. Wragg
1944	Picture Play	E.C. Elliott
1945	Sun Stream	H. Wragg
1946	Hypericum	D. Smith
1947	Imprudence	W.R. Johnstone
1948	Queenpot	G. Richards
1949	Musidora	E. Britt
1950	Camaree	W.R. Johnstone
1951	Belle Of All	G. Richards
1952	Zabara	K. Gethin
1953	Happy Laughter	E. Mercer
1954	Festoon	A. Breasley
1955	Meld	W.H. Carr
1956	Honeylight	E. Britt
1957	Rose Royale II	C. Smirke
1958	Bella Paola	S. Boullenger
1959	Petite Etoile	D. Smith
1960	Never Too Late	R. Poincelet
1961	Sweet Solera	W. Rickaby
1962	Abermaid	W. Williamson
1963	Hula Dancer	R. Poincelet
1964	Pourparler	G. Bougoure
1965	Night Off	W. Williamson
1966	Glad Rags	P. Cook
1967	Fleet	G. Moore
1968	Caergwrle	A. Barclay
1969	Full Dress II	R. Hutchinson
1970	Humble Duty	L. Piggott
1971	Altesse Royale	Y. Saint-Martin
1972	Waterloo	E. Hide
1973	Mysterious	G. Lewis
1974	Highclere	J. Mercer
1975	Nocturnal Spree	J. Roe
1976	Flying Water	Y. Saint-Martin
1977	Mrs McArdy	E. Hide
1978	Enstone Spark	E. Johnson
1979	One In A Million	J. Mercer
1980	Quick As Lightning	B. Rouse
1981	Fairy Footsteps	L. Piggott
1982	On The House	J. Reid
1983	Ma Biche	F. Head
1984	Pebbles	P. Robinson
1985	Oh So Sharp	S. Cauthen
1986	Midway Lady	R. Cochrane
1987	Miesque	F. Head
1988	Ravinella	G. Moore
1989	Musical Bliss	W. Swinburn
1990	Salsabil	W. Carson
1991	Shadayid	W. Carson
1992	Hatoof	W. Swinburn
1993	Sayyedati	W. Swinburn
1994	Las Meninas	J. Reid

2000 Guineas

	Horse	Jockey
1995	Pennekamp	T. Jarnet
1996	Mark Of Esteem	L. Dettori
1997	Entrepreneur	M.J. Kinane
1998	King Of Kings	M.J. Kinane
1999	Island Sands	L. Dettori
2000	King's Best	K. Fallon
2001	Golan	K. Fallon
2002	Rock Of Gibraltar	J. Murtagh
2003	Refuse To Bend	P. Smullen
2004	Haafhd	R. Hills

1000 Guineas

	Horse	Jockey
	Harayir	R. Hills
	Bosra Sham	P. Eddery
	Sleepytime	K. Fallon
	Cape Verdi	L. Dettori
	Wince	K. Fallon
	Lahan	R. Hills
	Ameerat	P. Robinson
	Kazzia	L. Dettori
	Russian Rhythm	K. Fallon
	Attraction	K. Darley

*The 1868 running of the 2000 Guineas was in fact a dead heat between Moslem and Formosa, but there was no run-off and Moslem walked over to claim victory.

Prix de l'Arc de Triomphe Winners

	Horse	Jockey		Horse	Jockey
1920	Comrade	Frank Bullock	1962	Soltikoff	Marcel Depalmas
1921	Ksar	George Stern	1963	Exbury	Jean Deforge
1922	Ksar	Frank Bullock	1964	Prince Royal II	Roger Poincelet
1923	Parth	Frank O'Neill	1965	Sea Bird II	Pat Glennon
1924	Massine	Fred Sharpe	1966	Bon Mot	Freddie Head
1925	Priori	Marcel Allemand	1967	Topyo	Bill Pyers
1926	Biribi	Domingo Torterolo	1968	Vaguely Noble	Bill Williamson
1927	Mon Talisman	Charles Semblat	1969	Levmoss	Bill Williamson
1928	Kantar	Arthur Esling	1970	Sassafras	Yves Saint-Martin
1929	Ortello	Paolo Caprioli	1971	Mill Reef	Geoff Lewis
1930	Motrico	Marcel Fruhinsholtz	1972	San San	Freddie Head
1931	Pearl Cap	Charles Semblat	1973	Rheingold	Lester Piggott
1932	Motrico	Charles Semblat	1974	Allez France	Yves Saint-Martin
1933	Crapom	Paolo Caprioli	1975	Star Appeal	Greville Starkey
1934	Brantôme	Charles Bouillon	1976	Ivanjica	Freddie Head
1935	Samos	Wally Sibbritt	1977	Alleged	Lester Piggott
1936	Corrida	Charlie Elliott	1978	Alleged	Lester Piggott
1937	Corrida	Charlie Elliott	1979	Three Troikas	Freddie Head
1938	Eclair au Chocolat	Charles Bouillon	1980	Detroit	Pat Eddery
1939	not held		1981	Gold River	Gary Moore
1940	not held		1982	Akiyda	Yves Saint-Martin
1941	La Pacha	Paul Francolon	1983	All Along	Walter Swinburn
1942	Djebel	Jacko Doyasbère	1984	Sagace	Yves Saint-Martin
1943	Verso II	Guy Duforez	1985	Rainbow Quest	Pat Eddery
1944	Ardan	Jacko Doyasbère	1986	Dancing Brave	Pat Eddery
1945	Nikellora	Rae Johnstone	1987	Trempolino	Pat Eddery
1946	Caracalla	Charlie Elliott	1988	Tony Bin	John Reid
1947	Le Paillon	Fernand Rochetti	1989	Carroll House	Michael Kinane
1948	Migoli	Charlie Smirke	1990	Saumarez	Gerald Mosse
1949	Coronation	Roger Poincelet	1991	Suave Dancer	Cash Asmussen
1950	Tantième	Jacko Doyasbère	1992	Subotica	Thierry Jarnet
1951	Tantième	Jacko Doyasbère	1993	Urban Sea	Eric Saint-Martin
1952	Nuccio	Roger Poincelet	1994	Carnegie	Thierry Jarnet
1953	La Sorellina	Maurice Larraun	1995	Lammtarra	Frankie Dettori
1954	Sica Boy	Rae Johnstone	1996	Helissio	Olivier Peslier
1955	Ribot	Enrico Camici	1997	Peintre Célèbre	Olivier Peslier
1956	Ribot	Enrico Camici	1998	Sagamix	Olivier Peslier
1957	Oroso	Serge Boullenger	1999	Montjeu	Michael Kinane
1958	Ballymoss	Scobie Breasley	2000	Sinndar	Johnny Murtagh
1959	Saint Crespin II	George Moore	2001	Sakhee	Frankie Dettori
1960	Puissant Chef	Max Garcia	2002	Marienbard	Frankie Dettori
1961	Molvedo	Enrico Camici	2003	Dalakhani	Christophe Soumillon

Grand National

	Horse	Jockey		Horse	Jockey
1837	The Duke	Mr H. Potts	1847	Matthew	D. Wynne
1838	Sir William	A. McDonough	1848	Chandler	Capt Josey Little
1839	Lottery	Jem Mason	1849	Peter Simple	T. Cunningham
1840	Jerry	Mr B. Bretherton	1850	Abd-El-Kader	C. Green
1841	Charity	Mr H. Powell	1851	Abd-El-Kader	T. Abbot
1842	Gay Lad	T. Olliver	1852	Miss Mowbray	Mr A. Goodman
1843	Vanguard	T. Olliver	1853	Peter Simple	T. Olliver
1844	Discount	Mr H. Crickmere	1854	Bourton	J. Tasker
1845	Cure-All	Mr W.G. Loft	1855	Wanderer	J. Hanlon
1846	Pioneer	W. Taylor	1856	Freetrader	G. Stevens

HORSE RACING

	Horse	Jockey		Horse	Jockey
1857	Emigrant	C. Boyce	1931	Grakle	R. Lyall
1858	Little Charley	W. Archer	1932	Forbra	J. Hamey
1859	Half Caste	C. Green	1933	Kellsboro Jack	D. Williams
1860	Anatis	Mr T. Pickernell	1934	Golden Miller	G. Wilson
1861	Jealousy	J. Kendall	1935	Reynoldstown	Mr F.C. Furlong
1862	Huntsman	H. Lamplugh	1936	Reynoldstown	Mr F.T. Walwyn
1863	Emblem	G. Stevens	1937	Royal Mail	E. Williams
1864	Emblematic	G. Stevens	1938	Battleship	Bruce Hobbs
1865	Alcibiade	Capt H. Coventry	1939	Workman	T. Hyde
1866	Salamander	Mr A. Goodman	1940	Bogskar	M. Jones
1867	Cortolvin	J. Page	1941-45 not held		
1868	The Lamb	Mr G. Ede-Edwards	1946	Lovely Cottage	Capt R. Petre
1869	The Colonel	G. Stevens	1947	Caughoo	E. Dempsey
1870	The Colonel	G. Stevens	1948	Sheila's Cottage	A.P. Thompson
1871	The Lamb	Mr T. Pickernell	1949	Russian Hero	L. McMorrow
1872	Casse Tete	J. Page	1950	Freebooter	J. Power
1873	Disturbance	Mr J.M. Richardson	1951	Nickel Coin	J.A. Bullock
1874	Reugny	Mr J.M. Richardson	1952	Teal	A.P. Thompson
1875	Pathfinder	Mr T. Pickernell	1953	Early Mist	B. Marshall
1876	Regal	J. Cannon	1954	Royal Tan	B. Marshall
1877	Austerlitz	Mr F.G. Hobson	1955	Quare Times	P. Taaffe
1878	Shifnal	J. Jones	1956	E.S.B.	D.V. Dick
1879	The Liberator	Mr G. Moore	1957	Sundew	F. Winter
1880	Empress	Mr T. Beasley	1958	Mr What	A.R. Freeman
1881	Woodbrook	Mr T. Beasley	1959	Oxo	M. Scudamore
1882	Seaman	Lord Manners	1960	Merryman II	G. Scott
1883	Zoedone	Count K. Kinsky	1961	Nicolaus Silver	R. Beasley
1884	Voluptuary	Mr E.P. Wilson	1962	Kilmore	F. Winter
1885	Roquefort	Mr E.P. Wilson	1963	Ayala	P. Buckley
1886	Old Joe	T. Skelton	1964	Team Spirit	W. Robinson
1887	Gamecock	W. Daniels	1965	Jay Trump	Mr C. Smith
1888	Playfair	C. Mawson	1966	Anglo	T. Norman
1889	Frigate	Mr T. Beasley	1967	Foinavon	J. Buckingham
1890	Ilex	A. Nightingall	1968	Red Alligator	B. Fletcher
1891	Come Away	Mr H. Beasley	1969	Highland Wedding	E. Harty
1892	Father O'Flynn	Capt R. Owen	1970	Gay Trip	P. Taaffe
1893	Cloister	W. Dollery	1971	Specify	J. Cook
1894	Why Not	A. Nightingall	1972	Well To Do	G. Thorner
1895	Wild Man From Borneo	Mr J. Widger	1973	Red Rum	B. Fletcher
1896	The Soarer	D. Campbell	1974	Red Rum	B. Fletcher
1897	Manifesto	T. Kavanagh	1975	L'Escargot	T. Carberry
1898	Drogheda	J. Gourley	1976	Rag Trade	J. Burke
1899	Manifesto	G. Williamson	1977	Red Rum	T. Stack
1900	Ambush II	A. Anthony	1978	Lucius	R. Davies
1901	Grudon	A. Nightingall	1979	Rubstic	M. Barnes
1902	Shannon Lass	D. Read	1980	Ben Nevis	Mr C. Fenwick
1903	Drumcree	P. Woodland	1981	Aldaniti	R. Champion
1904	Moifaa	A. Birch	1982	Grittar	Mr R. Saunders
1905	Kirkland	F. Mason	1983	Corbiere	B. De Haan
1906	Ascetic's Silver	Hon. A. Hastings	1984	Hallo Dandy	N. Doughty
1907	Eremon	A. Newey	1985	Last Suspect	H. Davies
1908	Rubio	H.B. Bletsoe	1986	West Tip	R. Dunwoody
1909	Lutteur III	G. Parfrement	1987	Maori Venture	S. Knight
1910	Jenkinstown	R. Chadwick	1988	Rhyme 'N' Reason	B. Powell
1911	Glenside	J.R. Anthony	1989	Little Polveir	J. Frost
1912	Jerry M	E. Piggott	1990	Mr Frisk	Mr M. Armytage
1913	Covertcoat	P. Woodland	1991	Seagram	N. Hawke
1914	Sunloch	W.J. Smith	1992	Party Politics	C. Llewellyn
1915	Ally Sloper	J.R. Anthony	1993	race void*	
1916	Vermouth	J. Reardon	1994	Minnehoma	R. Dunwoody
1917	Ballymacad	E. Driscoll	1995	Royal Athlete	J. Titley
1918	Poethlyn	E. Piggott	1996	Rough Quest	M. Fitzgerald
1919	Poethlyn	E. Piggott	1997	Lord Gyllene	A. Dobbin
1920	Troytown	J.R. Anthony	1998	Earth Summit	C. Llewellyn
1921	Shaun Spadah	F.B. Rees	1999	Bobbyjo	P. Carberry
1922	Music Hall	F.B. Rees	2000	Papillon	R. Walsh
1923	Sgt Murphy	Capt G.H. Bennett	2001	Red Marauder	R. Guest
1924	Master Robert	R. Trudgill	2002	Bindaree	J. Culloty
1925	Double Chance	Major J. Wilson	2003	Monty's Pass	B. Geraghty
1926	Jack Horner	W. Watkinson	2004	Amberleigh House	G. Lee
1927	Sprig	T.E. Leader			
1928	Tipperary Tim	Mr W.P. Dutton			
1929	Gregalach	R. Everett			
1930	Shaun Goilin	T. Cullinan			

*The 150th Aintree Grand National on 3 April 1993 was declared void after two false starts.

Cheltenham Gold Cup Winners

	Horse	Jockey		Horse	Jockey
1924	Red Splash	Dick Rees	1965	Arkle	Pat Taaffe
1925	Ballinode	Ted Leader	1966	Arkle	Pat Taaffe
1926	Koko	Tim Hamey	1967	Woodland Venture	Terry Biddlecombe
1927	Thrown In	Hugh Grosvenor	1968	Fort Leney	Pat Taaffe
1928	Patron Saint	Dick Rees	1969	What A Myth	Paul Kelleway
1929	Easter Hero	Dick Rees	1970	L'Escargot	Tommy Carberry
1930	Easter Hero	Tommy Cullinan	1971	L'Escargot	Tommy Carberry
1931	not held		1972	Glencaraig Lady	Frank Berry
1932	Golden Miller	Ted Leader	1973	The Dikler	Ron Barry
1933	Golden Miller	Billy Stott	1974	Captain Christy	Bobby Beasley
1934	Golden Miller	Gerry Wilson	1975	Ten Up	Tommy Carberry
1935	Golden Miller	Gerry Wilson	1976	Royal Frolic	John Burke
1936	Golden Miller	Evan Williams	1977	Davy Lad	Dessie Hughes
1937	not held		1978	Midnight Court	John Francome
1938	Morse Code	Danny Morgan	1979	Alverton	Jonjo O'Neill
1939	Brendan's Cottage	George Owen	1980	Master Smudge	Richard Hoare
1940	Roman Hackle	Evan Williams	1981	Little Owl	Mr Jim Wilson
1941	Poet Prince	Roger Burford	1982	Silver Buck	Robert Earnshaw
1942	Médoc II	Frenchie Nicholson	1983	Bregawn	Graham Bradley
1943	not held		1984	Burrough Hill Lad	Phil Tuck
1944	not held		1985	Forgive 'N' Forget	Martin Dwyer
1945	Red Rower	Davy Jones	1986	Dawn Run	Jonjo O'Neill
1946	Prince Regent	Tim Hyde	1987	The Thinker	Ridley Lamb
1947	Fortina	Dick Black	1988	Charter Party	Richard Dunwoody
1948	Cottage Rake	Aubrey Brabazon	1989	Desert Orchid	Simon Sherwood
1949	Cottage Rake	Aubrey Brabazon	1990	Norton's Coin	Graham McCourt
1950	Cottage Rake	Aubrey Brabazon	1991	Garrison Savannah	Mark Pitman
1951	Silver Fame	Martin Molony	1992	Cool Ground	Adrian Maguire
1952	Mont Tremblant	Dave Dick	1993	Jodami	Martin Dwyer
1953	Knock Hard	Tim Molony	1994	The Fellow	Adam Kondrat
1954	Four Ten	Tommy Cusack	1995	Master Oats	Norman Williamson
1955	Gay Donald	Tony Grantham	1996	Imperial Call	Conor O'Dwyer
1956	Limber Hill	Jimmy Power	1997	Mister Mulligan	Tony McCoy
1957	Linwell	Michael Scudamore	1998	Cool Dawn	Andrew Thornton
1958	Kerstin	Stan Hayhurst	1999	See More Business	Mick Fitzgerald
1959	Roddy Owen	Bobby Beasley	2000	Looks Like Trouble	Richard Johnson
1960	Pas Seul	Bill Rees	2001	not held	(foot and mouth
1961	Saffron Tartan	Fred Winter			epidemic)
1962	Mandarin	Fred Winter	2002	Best Mate	Jim Culloty
1963	Mill House	Willie Robinson	2003	Best Mate	Jim Culloty
1964	Arkle	Pat Taaffe	2004	Best Mate	Jim Culloty

Champion Hurdle Winners

	Horse	Jockey		Horse	Jockey
1927	Blaris	George Duller	1947	National Spirit	Danny Morgan
1928	Brown Jack	Bilbie Rees	1948	National Spirit	Ron Smyth
1929	Royal Falcon	Dick Rees	1949	Hatton's Grace	Aubrey Brabazon
1930	Brown Tony	Tommy Cullinan	1950	Hatton's Grace	Aubrey Brabazon
1931	not held		1951	Hatton's Grace	Tim Molony
1932	Insurance	Ted Leader	1952	Sir Ken	Tim Molony
1933	Insurance	Billy Stott	1953	Sir Ken	Tim Molony
1934	Chenango	Danny Morgan	1954	Sir Ken	Tim Molony
1935	Lion Courage	Gerry Wilson	1955	Clair Soleil	Fred Winter
1936	Victor Norman	Frenchie Nicholson	1956	Doorknocker	Harry Sprague
1937	Free Fare	Georges Pellerin	1957	Merry Deal	Grenville Underwood
1938	Our Hope	Perry Harding	1958	Bandalore	George Stack
1939	African Sister	Keith Piggott	1959	Fare Time	Fred Winter
1940	Solford	Sean Magee	1960	Another Flash	Bobby Beasley
1941	Seneca	Ron Smyth	1961	Eborneezer	Fred Winter
1942	Forestation	Ron Smyth	1962	Anzio	Willie Robinson
1943	not held		1963	Winning Fair	Mr Alan Lillingston
1944	not held		1964	Magic Court	Pat McCarron
1945	Brains Trust	Fred Rimell	1965	Kirriemuir	Willie Robinson
1946	Distel	Bobby O'Ryan	1966	Salmon Spray	Johnny Haine

HORSE RACING

Horse	Jockey		Horse	Jockey
1967 Saucy Kit	Roy Edwards	1986	See You Then	Steve Smith-Eccles
1968 Persian War	Jimmy Uttley	1987	See You Then	Steve Smith-Eccles
1969 Persian War	Jimmy Uttley	1988	Celtic Shot	Peter Scudamore
1970 Persian War	Jimmy Uttley	1989	Beech Road	Richard Guest
1971 Bula	Paul Kelleway	1990	Kribensis	Richard Dunwoody
1972 Bula	Paul Kelleway	1991	Morley Street	Jimmy Frost
1973 Comedy Of Errors	Ken White	1992	Royal Gait	Graham McCourt
1974 Lanzarote	Richard Pitman	1993	Granville Again	Peter Scudamore
1975 Comedy Of Errors	Ken White	1994	Flakey Dove	Mark Dwyer
1976 Night Nurse	Paddy Broderick	1995	Alderbrook	Norman Williamson
1977 Night Nurse	Paddy Broderick	1996	Collier Bay	Graham Bradley
1978 Monksfield	Tommy Kinane	1997	Make A Stand	Tony McCoy
1979 Monksfield	Dessie Hughes	1998	Istabraq	Charlie Swan
1980 Sea Pigeon	Jonjo O'Neill	1999	Istabraq	Charlie Swan
1981 Sea Pigeon	John Francome	2000	Istabraq	Charlie Swan
1982 For Auction	Mr Colin Magnier	2001	not held	(foot and mouth epidemic)
1983 Gaye Brief	Richard Linley	2002	Hors La Loi	Dean Gallagher
1984 Dawn Run	Jonjo O'Neill	2003	Rooster Booster	Richard Johnson
1985 See You Then	Steve Smith-Eccles	2004	Hardy Eustace	Conor O'Dwyer

Champion Jockeys: Flat

(no. of winners in parentheses)

1840 E. Flatman (50)	1886 F. Archer (170)	1932 G. Richards (190)
1841 E. Flatman (68)	1887 C. Wood (151)	1933 G. Richards (259)
1842 E. Flatman (42)	1888 F. Barrett (108)	1934 G. Richards (212)
1843 E. Flatman (60)	1889 T. Loates (167)	1935 G. Richards (210)
1844 E. Flatman (64)	1890 T. Loates (147)	1936 G. Richards (177)
1845 E. Flatman (81)	1891 H. Cannon (137)	1937 G. Richards (214)
1846 E. Flatman (81)	1892 H. Cannon (182)	1938 G. Richards (206)
1847 E. Flatman (89)	1893 T. Loates (222)	1939 G. Richards (155)
1848 E. Flatman (104)	1894 H. Cannon (167)	1940 G. Richards (68)
1849 E. Flatman (94)	1895 H. Cannon (184)	1941 H. Wragg (71)
1850 E. Flatman (88)	1896 H. Cannon (164)	1942 G. Richards (67)
1851 E. Flatman (78)	1897 H. Cannon (145)	1943 G. Richards (65)
1852 E. Flatman (92)	1898 H. Madden (161)	1944 G. Richards (88)
1853 J. Wells (86)	1899 S. Loates (160)	1945 G. Richards (104)
1854 J. Wells (82)	1900 L. Reiff (143)	1946 G. Richards (212)
1855 G. Fordham (70)	1901 H. Madden (130)	1947 G. Richards (269)
1856 G. Fordham (108)	1902 W. Lane (170)	1948 G. Richards (224)
1857 G. Fordham (84)	1903 H. Madden (154)	1949 G. Richards (261)
1858 G. Fordham (91)	1904 H. Madden (161)	1950 G. Richards (201)
1859 G. Fordham (118)	1905 E. Wheatley (124)	1951 G. Richards (227)
1860 G. Fordham (146)	1906 W. Higgs (149)	1952 G. Richards (231)
1861 G. Fordham (106)	1907 W. Higgs (146)	1953 G. Richards (191)
1862 G. Fordham (166)	1908 D. Maher (139)	1954 D. Smith (129)
1863 G. Fordham (103)	1909 F. Wootton (165)	1955 D. Smith (168)
1864 J. Grimshaw (164)	1910 F. Wootton (137)	1956 D. Smith (155)
1865 G. Fordham (142)	1911 F. Wootton (187)	1957 A. Breasley (173)
1866 S. Kenyon (123)	1912 F. Wootton (118)	1958 D. Smith (165)
1867 G. Fordham (143)	1913 D. Maher (115)	1959 D. Smith (157)
1868 G. Fordham (110)	1914 S. Donoghue (129)	1960 L. Piggott (170)
1869 G. Fordham (95)	1915 S. Donoghue (62)	1961 A. Breasley (171)
1870 W. Gray/C. Maidment (76)	1916 S. Donoghue (43)	1962 A. Breasley (179)
1871 G. Fordham/C. Maidment (86)	1917 S. Donoghue (42)	1963 A. Breasley (176)
1872 T. Cannon (87)	1918 S. Donoghue (66)	1964 L. Piggott (140)
1873 H. Constable (110)	1919 S. Donoghue (129)	1965 L. Piggott (166)
1874 F. Archer (147)	1920 S. Donoghue (143)	1966 L. Piggott (191)
1875 F. Archer (172)	1921 S. Donoghue (141)	1967 L. Piggott (117)
1876 F. Archer (207)	1922 S. Donoghue (102)	1968 L. Piggott (139)
1877 F. Archer (218)	1923 S. Donoghue/E.C. Elliott (89)	1969 L. Piggott (163)
1878 F. Archer (229)	1924 E.C. Elliott (106)	1970 L. Piggott (162)
1879 F. Archer (197)	1925 G. Richards (118)	1971 L. Piggott (162)
1880 F. Archer (120)	1926 T. Weston (95)	1972 W. Carson (132)
1881 F. Archer (220)	1927 G. Richards (164)	1973 W. Carson (163)
1882 F. Archer (210)	1928 G. Richards (148)	1974 P. Eddery (148)
1883 F. Archer (232)	1929 G. Richards (135)	1975 P. Eddery (164)
1884 F. Archer (241)	1930 F. Fox (129)	1976 P. Eddery (162)
1885 F. Archer (246)	1931 G. Richards (145)	1977 P. Eddery (176)

1978	W. Carson (182)	1987	S. Cauthen (197)	1996	P. Eddery (186)
1979	J. Mercer (164)	1988	P. Eddery (183)	1997	K. Fallon (202)
1980	W. Carson (165)	1989	P. Eddery (171)	1998	K. Fallon (204)
1981	L. Piggott (179)	1990	P. Eddery (209)	1999	K. Fallon (202)
1982	L. Piggott (188)	1991	P. Eddery (165)	2000	K. Darley (155)
1983	W. Carson (159)	1992	M. Roberts (206)	2001	K. Fallon (166)
1984	S. Cauthen (130)	1993	P. Eddery (169)	2002	K. Fallon (151)
1985	S. Cauthen (195)	1994	L. Dettori (233)	2003	K. Fallon (221)
1986	P. Eddery (177)	1995	L. Dettori (216)		

Champion Jockeys: National Hunt

(no. of winners in parentheses)

1900	Mr. H.S. Sidney (53)	1935	G. Wilson (73)	1970	R. Davies (91)
1901	F. Mason (58)	1936	G. Wilson (57)	1971	G. Thorner (74)
1902	F. Mason (67)	1937	G. Wilson (45)	1972	R. Davies (89)
1903	P. Woodland (54)	1938	G. Wilson (59)	1973	R. Barry (125)
1904	F. Mason (59)	1939	F. Rimell (61)	1974	R. Barry (94)
1905	F. Mason (73)	1940	F. Rimell (24)	1975	T. Stack (82)
1906	F. Mason (58)	1941	G. Wilson (22)	1976	J. Francome (96)
1907	F. Mason (59)	1942	R. Smyth (12)	1977	T. Stack (97)
1908	P. Cowley (65)	1943	not held	1978	J.J. O'Neill (149)
1909	R. Gordon (45)	1944	not held	1979	J. Francome (95)
1910	E. Piggott (67)	1945	H. Nicholson/F. Rimell (15)	1980	J.J. O'Neill (115)
1911	W. Payne (76)	1946	F. Rimell (54)	1981	J. Francome (105)
1912	I. Anthony (78)	1947	J. Dowdeswell (58)	1982	J. Francome/P. Scudamore (120)
1913	E. Piggott (60)	1948	B. Marshall (66)	1983	J. Francome (106)
1914	Mr. J.R. Anthony (60)	1949	T. Molony (60)	1984	J. Francome (131)
1915	E. Piggott (44)	1950	T. Molony (95)	1985	J. Francome (101)
1916	C. Hawkins (17)	1951	T. Molony (83)	1986	P. Scudamore (91)
1917	W. Smith (15)	1952	T. Molony (99)	1987	P. Scudamore (123)
1918	G. Duller (17)	1953	F. Winter (121)	1988	P. Scudamore (132)
1919	Mr. H. Brown (48)	1954	R. Francis (76)	1989	P. Scudamore (221)
1920	F.B. Rees (64)	1955	T. Molony (67)	1990	P. Scudamore (170)
1921	F.B. Rees (65)	1956	F. Winter (74)	1991	P. Scudamore (141)
1922	J. Anthony (78)	1957	F. Winter (80)	1992	P. Scudamore (175)
1923	F.B. Rees (64)	1958	F. Winter (82)	1993	R. Dunwoody (173)
1924	F.B. Rees (108)	1959	T. Brookshaw (83)	1994	R. Dunwoody (198)
1925	E. Foster (76)	1960	S. Mellor (68)	1995	R. Dunwoody (160)
1926	T. Leader (61)	1961	S. Mellor (118)	1996	A.P. McCoy (175)
1927	F.B. Rees (59)	1962	S. Mellor (80)	1997	A.P. McCoy (190)
1928	W. Stott (88)	1963	J. Gifford (70)	1998	A.P. McCoy (253)
1929	W. Stott (76)	1964	J. Gifford (94)	1999	A.P. McCoy (186)
1930	W. Stott (77)	1965	T. Biddlecombe (114)	2000	A.P. McCoy (245)
1931	W. Stott (81)	1966	T. Biddlecombe (102)	2001	A.P. McCoy (191)
1932	W. Stott (77)	1967	J. Gifford (122)	2002	A.P. McCoy (289)
1933	G. Wilson (61)	1968	J. Gifford (82)	2003	A.P. McCoy (256)
1934	G. Wilson (56)	1969	T. Biddlecombe/R. Davies (77)		

United Kingdom and Ireland Racecourse Details

Flat = Flat racing only

NH = National Hunt racing only

mixed = Flat and National Hunt racing in season

Aintree (NH)

Ormskirk Road, Aintree, Liverpool L9 5AS
Tel: 0151 523 2600
Fax: 0151 522 2920
Email: aintree@rht.net
Web: www.aintree.co.uk

Two left-handed courses. The Grand National course of 2¼ miles (3.6km) round is the longest of any British track, and completely flat; the Foxhunters' Chase and the John Hughes Trophy are run over 2¾ miles (4.4km) of the Grand National fences.
Famous fences include Becher's Brook, the Chair, Valentine's Brook and the Canal Turn.
The Mildmay Course of 1½ miles (2.4km) has traditional fences and is much sharper.

Ascot (mixed)	Ascot, Berkshire SL5 7JN
	Tel: 01344 622211
	Fax: 01344 628299
	Email: enquiries@ascot.co.uk
	Web: www.ascot.co.uk
	Founded in 1711 by Queen Anne and was solely a Flat race track until April 1965 when it held its first jump meeting. The circuit is a right-handed triangle of 1¾ miles (2.8km) round. Swinley Bottom is a famous part of the track.
Ayr (mixed)	Whitletts Road, Ayr KA8 0JE
	Tel: 01292 264179
	Fax: 01292 610140
	Email: info@ayr-racecourse.co.uk
	Web: www.ayr-racecourse.co.uk
	Left-handed oval of 1½ miles (2.4km) which has held flat and jump meetings since 1907.
Bangor-On-Dee (NH)	Bangor-On-Dee, near Wrexham, Clwyd LL13 0DA
	Tel: 01978 780323
	Fax: 01978 780985
	Email: racing@bangordee.sagehost.co.uk
	Web: www.bangorraces.co.uk
	Famed for being the only British racetrack without a grandstand. Track 1½ miles (2.4km) round.
Bath (Flat)	Lansdown, Bath, Somerset BA1 9BU
	Tel: 01225 424609
	Fax: 01225 444415
	Web: www.bath-racecourse.co.uk
	Left-handed circuit of 1½ miles (2.4km) round with a sharp bend two furlongs out. Highest Flat course in England at 780ft (237m) above sea level.
Beverley (Flat)	The Grandstand, York Road, Beverley, East Yorkshire HU17 8QZ
	Tel: 01482 867488
	Fax: 01482 863892
	Email: info@beverleyracecourse.co.uk
	Web: www.beverley-racecourse.co.uk
	Right-handed oval course of 1 mile 3 furlongs (2.2km).
Brighton (Flat)	Freshfield Road, Racehill, Brighton, East Sussex BN2 9XZ
	Tel: 01273 603580
	Fax: 01273 673267
	Email: info@brighton-racecourse.co.uk
	Web: www.brighton-racecourse.co.uk
	Left-handed crescent-shaped course of just under 1½ miles (2.4km), one of only four in England (along with Epsom, Newmarket and York) that is not a complete circuit.
Carlisle (mixed)	Durdar Road, Carlisle, Cumbria CA2 4TS
	Tel: 01228 554700
	Fax: 01228 554747
	Email: info@carlisle-races.co.uk
	Web: www.carlisle-races.co.uk
	Right-handed pear-shaped course of just over 1½ miles (2.4km) for mixed racing.
Cartmel (NH)	Cartmel, Cumbria LA11 6QF
	Tel: 01539 536340
	Left-handed circuit of just over 1 mile (1.6km), the shortest track in National Hunt racing, and the longest run-in at ½ mile (0.8km) of any course.
Catterick (mixed)	Catterick Bridge, Richmond, North Yorkshire DL10 7PE
	Tel: 01748 811478
	Fax: 01748 811082
	Email: info@catterickbridge.co.uk
	Web: www.catterickbridge.co.uk
	Flat course of 9 furlongs (1.8km) and a jump track of 1¼ miles (2km).
Cheltenham (NH)	Prestbury Park, Cheltenham, Gloucestershire GL50 4SH
	Tel: 01242 513014
	Fax: 01242 224227
	Email: cheltenham@rht.net
	Web: www.cheltenham.co.uk
	Left-handed oval of 1½ miles (2.4km) round. Although there are three courses proper, Old, New and Park, there is also a cross-country course that has been used since 1995.
Chepstow (mixed)	Chepstow, Gwent NP6 5YH
	Tel: 01291 622260
	Fax: 01291 625550
	Email: info@chepstow-racecourse.co.uk
	Web: www.chepstow-racecourse.co.uk
	Opened in 1926, left-handed undulating circuit of just under 2 miles (3.2km).

Chester (Flat)	Chester, Cheshire CH1 2LY Tel: 01244 304600 Fax: 01244 304649 Email: sales@chester-races.com Web: www.chester-races.co.uk Left-handed circuit of 1 mile (1.6km) round, the shortest Flat course in England. Chester is also the oldest track in Britain.
Clonmel (mixed)	Powerstown Park Racecourse, Clonmel Co. Tipperary, Ireland Tel: 052 72481 Fax: 052 26446 Email: info@clonmelraces.ie Web: www.powerstownpark.com Right-handed course of 1¼ miles (2km) round, situated at the foot of the Comeragh Mountains in the valley of the River Suir.
Cork (mixed)	Cork Racecourse, Mallow, Co. Cork, Ireland Tel: 022 50207 Fax: 022 50213 Email: info@corkracecourse.ie Web: www.corkracecourse.ie Founded in 1924 and known as Mallow until renamed in 1997. Right-handed track of 1½ miles (2.4km) round.
Curragh (Flat)	The Curragh, Co. Kildare, Ireland Tel: 045 441205 Fax: 045 441442 Email: info@curragh.ie Web: www.curragh.ie The headquarterss of Flat racing in Ireland. Horseshoe-shaped circuit of 2 miles (3.2km). Rather aptly its name is a corruption of the Gaelic word *culreach*, meaning racecourse.
Doncaster (mixed)	The Grandstand, Leger Way, Doncaster, South Yorkshire DN2 6BB Tel: 01302 320066 Fax: 01302 323271 Email: administration@doncasterracing.co.uk Web: www.doncaster-racecourse.com Left-handed pear-shaped circuit of just under 2 miles (3.2km) round. The Town Moor course has a small rise and fall at Rose Hill about ten furlongs out.
Down Royal (mixed)	Maze, Co. Antrim, Northern Ireland BT27 5BW Tel: 028 9262 1256 Fax: 028 9262 1433 Email: info@downroyal.com Web: www.downroyal.com Right-handed circuit of 1 mile 7 furlongs (3km). One of only two courses in Northern Ireland.
Downpatrick (mixed)	Ballyduggan Road, Downpatrick, Co. Down, Northern Ireland BT30 7SP Tel: 01396 612054 Fax: 01396 842227 Right-handed circuit of 1 mile 5 furlongs (2.6km). One of only two courses in Northern Ireland.
Dundalk (mixed)	Dowdallshill, Dundalk, Co. Louth, Ireland Tel: 042 937 1271 Fax: 042 937 1271 Left-handed circuit of 1¼ miles (2km) at the foot of the Cooley Mountains.
Epsom Downs (Flat)	Epsom Downs, Surrey KT18 5LQ Tel: 01372 726311 Fax: 01372 748253 Email: epsom@rht.net Web: www.epsomderby.co.uk Left-handed undulating course of 1½ miles (2.4km). Five-furlong course is slightly down hill. Indigenous clocked 53.6secs in 1960, a world record that still stands.
Exeter (NH)	Kennford, nr Exeter, Devon EX6 7XS Tel: 01392 832599 Fax: 01392 833454 Email: exeter.races@eclipse.co.uk Web: www.exeter-racecourse.co.uk Right-handed course of just under 2 miles (3.2km). Formerly Devon and Exeter until 1992.
Fairyhouse (mixed)	Fairyhouse Club Ltd, Ratoath, Co. Meath, Ireland Tel: 01 825 6167 Fax: 01 825 6051 Email: info@fairyhouseracecourse.ie Web: fairyhouseracecourse.ie Right-handed course of 1¾ miles (2.8km) round. Home of the Irish Grand National.

HORSE RACING

Fakenham (NH)   Fakenham, Norfolk NR21 7NY
                       Tel: 01328 862388
                       Fax: 01328 855908
                       Email: info@falkenhamracecourse.co.uk
                       Left-handed rectangular circuit of 1 mile (1.6km). Known as the West Norfolk Hunt until
                       1963.
Folkestone (Flat)   Westhanger, Hythe, Kent CT21 4HY
                       Tel: 0870 220 0023
                       Fax: 01342 836815
                       Web: www.folkestone-racecourse.co.uk
                       Right-handed circuit of 1 mile 3 furlongs (2.2km) round. Founded in 1898 and the only track
                       in Kent.
Fontwell Park (NH)   Fontwell, nr Arundel, West Sussex BN18 0SX
                       Tel: 01243 543335
                       Fax: 01243 543904
                       Email: enquiries@fontwellpark.co.uk
                       Web: www.fontwellpark.co.uk
                       Figure-of-eight course of about 1 mile (1.6km). Founded in 1924.
Galway (mixed)   Ballybrit, Co. Galway, Ireland
                       Tel: 091 753870
                       Fax: 091 752592
                       Email: information@galwayraces.com
                       Web: www.galwayraces.com
                       Right-handed course of 1¼ miles (2km), famed for its six-day festival meeting in late
                       July/early August.
Goodwood (Flat)   Goodwood, Chichester, West Sussex PO18 0PS
                       Tel: 01243 755022
                       Fax: 01243 755025
                       Email: racing@goodwood.co.uk
                       Web: www.goodwood.co.uk
                       Undulating pan-handle track with a fast downhill five furlongs. Glorious Goodwood takes
                       place in July.
Gowran Park (mixed)   Gowran, Co. Kilkenny, Ireland
                       Tel: 056 26225
                       Fax: 056 26173
                       Right-handed undulating course of 1½ miles (2.4km) famous for receiving the first-ever
                       racecourse commentary in Ireland in 1952.
Great Leighs   Near Chelmsford, Essex
(Flat)   Left-handed polytrack of 1 mile (1.6km). The first new British racecourse in 75 years,
                       scheduled to open in 2004.
Hamilton Park (Flat)   Bothwell Road, Hamilton, Lanarkshire ML3 0DW
                       Tel: 01698 283806
                       Fax: 01698 286621
                       Email: morag@hamilton-park.co.uk
                       Web: www.hamilton-park.co.uk
                       Right-handed course of 1 mile 5 furlongs (2.6km), famous for holding the first-ever evening
                       meeting in Great Britain on 18 July 1947 and also the first-ever Saturday morning meeting
                       on 8 May 1971.
Haydock Park (mixed)   Newton-le-Willows, Merseyside WA12 0HQ
                       Tel: 01942 725963
                       Fax: 01942 270879
                       Email: haydockpark@rht.net
                       Web: www.haydock-park.com
                       Left-handed oval of 1 mile 5 furlongs (2.6km) round.
Hereford (NH)   Roman Road, Holmer, Hereford HR4 9QU
                       Tel: 01432 273560
                       Fax: 01432 352807
                       Email: info@hereford-racecourse.co.uk
                       Web: www.hereford-racecourse.co.uk
                       Right-handed rectangular circuit of 1½ miles (2.4km).
Hexham (NH)   High Yarridge, Hexham, Northumberland NE46 2JP
                       Tel: 01434 606881
                       Fax: 01434 605814
                       Email: hexrace@aol.com
                       Web: www.hexham-racecourse.co.uk
                       Left-handed circuit of 1½ miles (2.4km) round. Stiff uphill climb between the last two fences.

Huntingdon (NH)	Brampton, Huntingdon, Cambridgeshire PE18 8NN Tel: 01480 453373 Fax: 01480 455275 Email: huntingdon@rht.net Web: www.huntingdon-racecourse.co.uk Right-handed circuit of 1½ miles (2.4km) round.
Kelso (NH)	Kelso, Roxburghshire TD5 7SX Tel: 01668 280800 Fax: 01668 281113 Email: trish@kelso-races.co.uk Web: www.kelso-races.co.uk Left-handed circuit hurdle of 1¼ miles (2km) round, the steeplechase course is 1 furlong further.
Kempton Park (mixed)	Staines Road East, Sunbury-on-Thames, Middlesex TW16 5AQ Tel: 01932 782292 Fax: 01932 782044 Email: kempton@rht.net Web: www.kempton.co.uk Right-handed triangular course of 1 mile 5 furlongs (2.6km). The Jubilee Course of 1¼ miles (2km) forms a long spur that joins the round course at around 3½ furlongs out.
Kilbeggan (NH)	Loughnagore, Kilbeggan, Co. Westmeath, Ireland Tel: 0506 32176 Fax: 0506 32125 Email: kilbegganracecourse@eircom.net Right-handed course of 9 furlongs (1.8km) round. The only course in Ireland that stages just National Hunt races.
Killarney (mixed)	Killarney, Co. Kerry, Ireland Tel: 064 31125 Fax: 064 31860 Left-handed circuit of 9½ furlongs (1.9km). One of the most scenic courses in the world.
Laytown (Flat)	Laytown, Co. Meath, Ireland Tel: 041 984 2111 Fax: 041 983 7566 Straight 1¼ mile (2km) track on the beach. The annual spring meeting is very popular.
Leicester (mixed)	Oadby, Leicester LE2 4AL Tel: 0116 271 6515 Fax: 0116 271 1746 Email: info@leicester-racecourse.co.uk Web: www.leicester-racecourse.co.uk Right-handed oval course of 1¾ miles (2.8km).
Leopardstown (mixed)	Foxrock, Dublin 18, Ireland Tel: 01 289 3607 Fax: 01 289 2634 Email: info@leopardstown.com Web: www.leopardstown.com Left-handed circuit of 1¾ miles (2.8km) round.
Limerick (mixed)	Greenmount Park, Patrickswell, Co. Limerick, Ireland Tel: 061 320000 Fax: 061 355766 Email: info@limerick-racecourse.com Web: www.limerick-racecourse.com Right-handed course of 1¼ miles (2km).
Lingfield Park (mixed)	Lingfield, Surrey RH7 6PQ Tel: 01342 834800 Fax: 01342 832833 Email: info@lingfieldpark.co.uk Web: www.lingfield-racecourse.co.uk Turf course is a left-handed triangular track of 1½ miles (2.4km). The all-weather course is just under 1¼ miles (2km).
Listowel (mixed)	Listowel, Co. Kerry, Ireland Tel/Fax: 068 21144 Left-handed circuit of 1 mile (1.6km) round.
Ludlow (NH)	Bromfield, Ludlow, Shropshire SY8 2BT Tel: 01584 856221 Fax: 01584 856217 Email: mail@ludlow-racecourse.co.uk Web: www.ludlow-racecourse.co.uk Right-handed course of 1½ miles (2.4km) round.

HORSE RACING

Market Rasen (NH)	Legsby Road, Market Rasen, Lincolnshire LN8 3EA
	Tel: 01673 843434
	Fax: 01673 844532
	Email: marketrasen@rht.net
	Web: www.marketrasenraces.co.uk
	Right-handed course of 1¼ miles (2km) round.
Musselburgh (mixed)	Linkfield Road, Musselburgh, East Lothian EH21 7RG
	Tel: 0131 665 2859
	Fax: 0131 653 2083
	Email: info@musselburgh-racecourse.co.uk
	Web: www.musselburgh-racecourse.co.uk
	Right-handed oval of 1¼ miles (2km). Known as Edinburgh until 1 January 1996.
Naas (mixed)	Woodlands Park, Tipper Road, Naas, Co. Kildare, Ireland
	Tel: 045 897391
	Fax: 045 879486
	Email: goracing@naasracecourse.com
	Web: www.naasracecourse.com
	Left-handed circuit of 1½ miles (2.4km) round.
Navan (mixed)	Proudstown, Navan, Co. Meath, Ireland
	Tel: 046 21350
	Fax: 046 27964
	Left-handed circuit of 1½ miles (2.4km) round.
Newbury (mixed)	Newbury, Berkshire RG14 7NZ
	Tel: 01635 40015
	Fax: 01635 528354
	Email: info@newbury-racecourse.co.uk
	Web: www.newbury-racecourse.co.uk
	Founded in 1905, left-handed course of 1 mile 7 furlongs (3km) round. Home of both the John Porter Stakes on the Flat and the Hennessy Cognac Gold Cup over jumps.
Newcastle (mixed)	High Gosforth Park, Newcastle upon Tyne NE3 5HP
	Tel: 0191 236 2020
	Fax: 0191 236 7761
	Email: info@gknowles@newcastle-racecourse.co.uk
	Web: www.newcastle-racecourse.co.uk
	Left-handed triangular circuit of 1¾ miles (2.8km).
Newmarket (Flat)	Westfield House, The Links, Newmarket, Suffolk CB8 0TG
	Tel: 01638 663482/01638 662762 (Rowley Mile office)/01638 662752 (July Course office)
	Fax: 01638 663044
	Email: newmarket@rht.net
	Web: www.newmarketracecourses.co.uk
	Rowley Mile Course is 2¼ miles (3.6km) long with a right-hand bend after 1 mile (1.6km). The July course has a shorter run-in from the right-hand bend.
Newton Abbot (NH)	Kingsteignton Road, Newton Abbot, Devon TQ12 3AF
	Tel: 01626 353235
	Fax: 01626 336972
	Email: management@newtonabbotracing.com
	Web: www.newtonabbotracing.com
	Left-handed track of 1¼ miles (2km). Traditionally the opening fixture of the new jumping season.
Nottingham (Flat)	Colwick Park, Nottingham NG2 4BE
	Tel: 0115 958 0620
	Fax: 0115 958 4515
	Email: nottingham@rht.net
	Web: www.nottinghamracecourse.co.uk
	Left-handed oval of 1½ miles (2.4km) round. National Hunt racing was discontinued in 1996.
Perth (NH)	Scone Palace Park, Perth, Perthshire PH2 6BB
	Tel: 01738 551597
	Fax: 01738 553021
	Email: sam@perth-races.co.uk
	Web: www.perth-races.co.uk
	Opened in 1908 and the most northerly racecourse in Britain. Right-handed circuit of 1½ miles (2.4km) round.
Plumpton (NH)	Plumpton Green, East Sussex BN7 3AL
	Tel: 01273 890383
	Fax: 01273 891557
	Email: racing@plumptonracecourse.co.uk
	Web: www.plumptonracecourse.co.uk
	Left-handed track of 9 furlongs (1.8km).

Pontefract (Flat)   Park Lane, Pontefract, West Yorkshire WF8 1LE
Tel: 01977 781307
Fax: 01977 781333
Email: info@pontefract-races.co.uk
Web: www.pontefract-races.co.uk
Left-handed circuit of about 2 miles (3.2km).

Punchestown (mixed)   Naas, Co. Kildare, Ireland
Tel: 045 897704
Fax: 045 897319
Email: info@punchestown.com
Web: www.punchestown.com
Right-handed circuit of 2 miles (3.2km).

Redcar (Flat)   Redcar, Cleveland TS10 2BY
Tel: 01642 484068
Fax: 01642 488272
Email: info@redcarracing.co.uk
Web: www.redcarracing.co.uk
Left-handed track of 1 mile 5 furlongs (2.6km).

Ripon (Flat)   Boroughbridge Road, Ripon, North Yorkshire HG4 1UG
Tel: 01765 602156
Fax: 01765 690018
Email: cwpy@hutchbuch.demon.co.uk
Web: www.ripon-races.co.uk
Right-handed circuit of 5 furlongs (2.6km).

Roscommon (mixed)   Racecourse Road, Co. Roscommon, Ireland
Tel: 0903 63494/0903 26231 (racedays)
Fax: 0903 63608
Right-handed circuit of 1¼ miles (2km).

Salisbury (Flat)   Netherhampton, Salisbury, Wiltshire SP2 8PN
Tel: 01722 326461
Fax: 01722 412710
Email: biburyclub@salisburyracecourse.fs.net
Web: www.salisburyracecourse.co.uk
Right-handed course with loop for longer races.

Sandown Park (mixed)   Esher, Surrey KT10 9AJ
Tel: 01372 463072
Fax: 01372 465205
Email: sandown@rht.net
Web: www.sandown.co.uk
Right-handed oval of 1 mile 5 furlongs (2.6km).

Sedgefield (NH)   Sedgefield, Stockton-on-Tees, Cleveland TS21 2HW
Tel: 01740 621925
Fax: 01740 620663
Email: info@sedgefield-racecourse.co.uk
Web: www.sedgefield-racecourse.co.uk
Left-handed track of 1¼ miles (2km) round.

Sligo (mixed)   Cleveragh, Connaught, Ireland
Tel: 071 62484
Fax: 071 83342
Right-handed oval circuit of 1 mile (1.6km).

Southwell (mixed)   Rolleston, Newark, Nottinghamshire NG25 0TS
Tel: 01636 814481
Fax: 01636 812271
Email: info@southwell-racecourse.co.uk
Web: www.southwell-racecourse.co.uk
All-weather left-handed track of 1¼ miles (2km) with jumping course inside.

Stratford-on-Avon (NH)   Luddington Road, Stratford-on-Avon, Warwickshire CV37 9SE
Tel: 01789 267949
Fax: 01789 415850
Email: info@stratfordracecourse.net
Web: www.stratfordracecourse.net
Left-handed triangular course of 1¼ miles (2km).

HORSE RACING

Taunton (NH)	Orchard Portman, Taunton Somerset TA3 7BL
	Tel: 01823 337172
	Fax: 01823 325881
	Email: info@tauntonracecourse.co.uk
	Web: www.tauntonracecourse.co.uk
	Right-handed sausage-shaped course of 1¼ miles (2km).
Thirsk (Flat)	Station Road, Thirsk, North Yorkshire YO7 1QL
	Tel: 01845 522276
	Fax: 01845 525353
	Email: info@thirskraces.fsnet.co.uk
	Web: www.thirskracecourse.net
	Left-handed oval of about 1¼ miles (2km).
Thurles (mixed)	Thurles, Co. Tipperary, Ireland
	Tel: 0504 22253
	Fax: 0504 24565
	Right-handed oval circuit of 1¼ miles (2km).
Tipperary (mixed)	Limerick Junction, Co. Tipperary, Ireland
	Tel: 062 51357
	Fax: 062 51303
	Email: info@tipperaryraces.ie
	Web: www.tipperaryraces.ie
	Left-handed course of 1¼ miles (2km) round. Formerly called Limerick Junction until 1986.
Towcester (NH)	London Road, Towcester, Northants NN12 7HS
	Tel: 01327 353414
	Fax: 01327 358534
	Email: info@towcester.racecourse.co.uk.
	Web: www.towcester-racecourse.co.uk
	Right-handed track of 1¾ miles (2.8km) round.
Tralee (mixed)	Ballybeggan Park, Tralee, Co. Kerry, Ireland
	Tel: 066 36148
	Fax: 066 28007
	Left-handed circuit of 1¼ miles (2km).
Tramore (mixed)	Waterford and Tramore Racecourse, Tramore, Co, Waterford, Ireland
	Tel: 051 381425
	Fax: 051 390928
	Email: racing@tramore.ie
	Web: www.tramore-racecourse.com
	Right-handed circuit of 1 mile (1.6km). Founded in 1911.
Uttoxeter (NH)	Wood Lane, Uttoxeter, Staffordshire ST14 8BD
	Tel: 01889 562561
	Fax: 01889 562786
	Email: info@uttoxeter-racecourse.co.uk
	Web: www.uttoxeter-racecourse.co.uk
	Left-handed circuit of about 1¼ miles (2km) with a right-hand kink in the back straight.
Warwick (mixed)	Hampton Street, Warwick CV34 6HN
	Tel: 01926 491553
	Fax: 01926 403223
	Email: warwick@rht.net
	Web: www.warwickracecourse.co.uk
	Left-handed circuit of 1¾ miles (2.8km).
Wetherby (NH)	York Road, Wetherby, West Yorkshire LS22 5EJ
	Tel: 01937 582035
	Fax: 01937 580565
	Email: info@wetherbyracing.co.uk
	Web: www.wetherbyracing.co.uk
	Left-handed oval circuit of 1½ miles (2.4km).
Wexford (mixed)	Wexford, Co. Wexford, Ireland
	Tel: 051 42307 (racedays)/051 421681 (general)
	Fax: 051 421830
	Email: info@wexfordraces.ie
	Web: www.wexfordraces.ie
	Right-handed track of 9 furlongs (1.8km).
Wincanton (NH)	Wincanton, Somerset BA9 8BJ
	Tel: 01963 32344
	Fax: 01963 34668
	Email: wincanton@rht.net
	Web: www.wincantonracecourse.co.uk
	Right-handed track of 1 mile 3 furlongs (2.2km) round.

Windsor (Flat)	Windsor, Berkshire SL4 5JJ Tel: 01753 865234 Fax: 01753 830156 Email: office@windsor-racecourse.co.uk Web: www.windsor-racecourse.co.uk Figure-of-eight of about 1½ miles (2.4km).
Wolverhampton (mixed)	Dunstall Park, Goresbrook Road, Wolverhampton, West Midlands WV6 0PE Tel: 01902 421421 Fax: 01902 716626 Email: enquiries@dunstallpark.com Web: www.wolverhampton-racecourse.co.uk Left-handed all-weather circuit of just under 1 mile (1.6km) round, with turf track for jump racing on the outside of the all-weather course.
Worcester (NH)	Pitchcroft, Worcester WR1 3EJ Tel: 01905 25364 Fax: 01905 617563 Email: info@worcester-racecourse.co.uk Web: www.worcester-racecourse.co.uk Left-handed circuit of 1 mile 5 furlongs (2.8km).
Yarmouth (Flat)	Jellicoe Road, North Denes, Great Yarmouth, Norfolk NR30 4AU Tel: 01493 842527 Fax: 01493 843254 Web: www.greatyarmouthracecourse.co.uk Left-handed oval of 1¾ miles (2.8km) round.
York (Flat)	York YO2 1EX Tel: 01904 620911 Fax: 01904 611071 Email: enquiries@yorkracecourse.co.uk Web: www.yorkracecourse.co.uk Left-handed track of about 2 miles (3.2km). Known as 'The Knavesmire'

HORSE RACING

General Information

Alexandra Park	The only racecourse in London until its closure in 1970. Alexandra Park was nicknamed 'The Frying Pan' because of its circular track with a spur into the home straight.
all-weather courses (UK)	Lingfield Park, Southwell, Wolverhampton. The first race on an all-weather surface was won by Niklas Angel at Lingfield Park on 30 October 1989. Southwell held the second fixture the next day and Wolverhampton followed suit on 27 December 1993, this fixture including two races under floodlights, the first illuminated races in Britain. National Hunt races on all-weather courses were suspended indefinitely in February 1994 due to a spate of equine deaths. Lingfield is a polytrack, while Southwell and Wolverhampton are fibresand.
apprentice jockeys	Apprentices may ride at the age of 16 but cannot remain so after the age of 24. Allowances of 7lb (3.1kg) may be claimed until they have ridden 10 winners, 5lb (2.3kg) up to 50 winners, and 3lb (1.4km) up to 75 winners. The last English classic to be won by an apprentice was the 1982 Oaks when Billy Newnes partnered Time Charter.
Arlington Million	Inaugurated in 1981 and run over 1 mile 2 furlongs (2km) in the autumn on the Chicago racetrack, the first running being won by John Henry.
Australian Jockey Club: founded	In 1842
autumn double	Cesarewitch and Cambridgeshire
Belmont Stakes	Run over 1 mile 4 furlongs (2.4km) at Belmont Park in Elmont, NY, the largest track in the United States. The oldest of the three Triple Crown races, first run in 1867 at Jerome Park but moved to Morris Park in 1889 and then Belmont Park in 1890. It takes place three weeks after the Preakness Stakes and five weeks after the Kentucky Derby.
betting: accumulator bets, names	A Yankee is the term for backing four horses in six doubles, four trebles and an accumulator, a total of 11 bets. A Super Yankee is five horses in 10 doubles, 10 trebles, 5 fourfold accumulators and a 5-horse accumulator, a total of 26 bets. This bet is also called a Canadian. A Heinz is six horses in 15 doubles, 20 trebles, 15 fourfolds, 6 fivefolds and a 6-horse accumulator, a total of 57 bets. A Super Heinz is seven horses in 21 doubles, 35 trebles, 35 fourfolds, 21 fivefolds, 7 sixfolds and a 7-horse accumulator, a total of 120 bets. A Goliath is eight horses in 28 doubles, 56 trebles, 70 fourfolds, 56 fivefolds, 28 sixfolds, 8 sevenfolds and an 8-horse accumulator, a total of 247 bets.

betting slang				
	1-1	evens	9-2	on the shoulders
	11-10	tips/bits	5-1	hand
	5-4	wrist	11-2	hand and a half
	11-8	up the arm	6-1	exes
	6-4	ear 'ole	13-2	exes and a half
	13-8	bits on the ear 'ole	7-1	neves
	7-4	shoulder	8-1	T.H.
	15-8	double taps	9-1	enin
	2-1	bottle	10-1	cockle
	9-4	top of the head	11-1	elef
	5-2	face/bottle and a half	12-1	net and bice
	11-4	elef a vier	14-1	net and rouf
	3-1	carpet	16-1	net and ex
	100-30	burlington bertie	20-1	score/double net
	7-2	carpet and a half	25-1	pony
	4-1	rouf	33-1	double carpet

bookmaker: first	The first reported bookmaker was a man named Ogden, who set up a market at Newmarket in 1795. The Betting Houses Act resulted in the closing down of betting offices, until they were legalised on 1 May 1961.
Breeders' Cup: details	Founded in 1984 and administered by breeders with the aim of stimulating thoroughbred racing in North America. The series offers in excess of $20 million annually for the autumn races, the top purse being allocated to the Breeders' Cup classic. The inaugural event was run at Hollywood Park and the series includes a 6 furlongs (1.2km) race, a juvenile fillies' event over 1 mile 110 yards (1.7km), a distaff race over 1 mile 1 furlong (1.8km), a juvenile colts race over 1 mile 110 yards (1.7km), the Breeders' Cup Mile, the Breeders' Cup Turf over 1 mile 4 furlongs (2.4km) and the Classic run over 1 mile 2 furlongs (2km).
British Horseracing Board: address	42 Portman Square, London W1H 6EN Tel: 020 7396 0011 Fax: 020 7935 0131 Email: info@bhb.co.uk Web: www.thebhb.co.uk
Caulfield Cup	Run over 1 mile 4 furlongs (2.4km) at Caulfield, Melbourne, in October. First raced in 1879. The first-ever winner trained outside Australia was Taufan's Melody in 1998, trained at Arundel by Lady Herries and ridden by Ray Cochrane.
Champion Hurdle	Run over 2 miles 110 yards (3.3km) at Cheltenham during the Spring Festival. Sponsored by Waterford Crystal 1978-92, and Smurfit from 1993. Four-year-olds carry 11st 6lb (72.6kg), older horses 12st (76.2kg) but there is a 5lb (2.3kg) mares' allowance.
champion jockey: 13 times in a row	Elnathan Flatman (1840-52), Fred Archer (1874-86)
champion jockey: shot himself	Fred Archer (aged 29)
Cheltenham Gold Cup	Steeplechase run over 3 miles 2 furlongs 110 yards (5.3km), all horses carry 12st (76.2kg) over 22 fences. Sponsored by the Horserace Totalisator Board since 1980.
Cheltenham Gold Cup: trained first five home	Michael Dickinson (1983): Bregawn (1), Captain John (2), Wayward Lad (3), Silver Buck (4), Ashley House (5)
classics: jockey won most	Lester Piggott (30)
colours: Prince Khalid Abdullah	Green, pink sash and cap, white sleeves
Lady Beaverbrook	Beaver-brown, maple-leaf green crossbelts and cap
Lord Howard de Walden	Apricot
Godolphin	Royal blue
Paul Mellon	Black with gold cross front and back, black cap with gold stripe
Queen Elizabeth II	Purple, gold braid, scarlet sleeves, black velvet cap, gold fringe
Queen Elizabeth, the Queen Mother	Blue, buff stripes, blue sleeves, black cap, gold tassel
Sheikh Ahmed Al Maktoum	Yellow, black epaulets
Sheikh Hamdan Al Maktoum	Royal blue, white epaulets, striped cap
Sheikh Maktoum Al Maktoum	Royal blue, white chevron, light blue cap
Sheikh Mohammed Al Maktoum	Maroon, white sleeves, maroon cap, white star
conditional jockeys	National Hunt jockey equivalent of flat race apprentice jockeys
consecutive wins in Britain	Johnny Gilbert (1959) and Phil Tuck (1986) both recorded 10 wins over fences but Gordon Richards holds the world's longest sequence, having 12 consecutive flat wins in 1933.
Coolmore Stud	Situated near Fethard, Co. Tipperary, Ireland, this is the principal stud farm in Europe.
crash helmets: made compulsory	In 1924
Derby: fewest runners	Daedalus in 1794 beat only three rivals.
first filly to win	Sir Charles Bunbury's Eleanor in 1801, who went on to win the Oaks the next day at 4-7.

first Irish-trained winner	Orby (1907), owned by Boss Croker and trained by Fred McCabe in Sandyford
first royal winner	Sir Thomas, owned by HRH The Prince of Wales, in 1788
first winner to be sired by previous winner	Sir Harry in 1798 was sired by Sir Peter Teazle, the winner in 1787.
inaugurated by	Sir Charles Bunbury
longest winning distance	Shergar (ten lengths)
where run during WWII	Newmarket (1940-45)
winner that never was	Although the record books show Orlando as the winner of the 1844 race, the race was actually won by Running Rein. Subsequently, however, this horse was found to be a four-year-old named Maccabeus.
distance, a	A winning margin in excess of 30 lengths (220m)
distance, the	An unidentified spot 240yds (220m) from the finish of a race. It has come into parlance mainly for commentators to identify the approach of the final furlong, 220yds (201m) from the finish.
Dubai World Cup	Inaugurated in 1996, this immediately became the world's richest race with a total prize fund of $4 million and $2.4 million to the winner. It is run on a dirt track over 1 mile 2 furlongs (2km).
English classics: 1000 Guineas	Usually the first classic of the season, run over 1 mile (1.6km) at Newmarket. For fillies only, carrying 9st (57kg). Sponsored by General Accident (1984-92), Madagans (1993-95), Pertemps (1996-97), and Sagitta (from 1998).
2000 Guineas	Traditionally the second classic of the season, for colts carring 9st (57kg) and fillies both carrying 8st 9lb (55kg). Also run at Newmarket. It has the same sponsors as the 1000 Guineas. Seven fillies have won the 2000 Guineas.
Oaks	Run over 1 mile 4 furlongs (2.4km) at Epsom, for fillies only, carrying 9st. (57kg) The Oaks was run at Newmarket during both World War I and II. Sponsored by Gold Seal (1984-92), Energizer (1993-94), Vodafone (from 1995).
Derby	Run over 1 mile 4 furlongs (2.4 km) at Epsom, for colts carrying 9st (57kg) and fillies carrying 8st 9lb (55kg). Run at Newmarket during World War I and II. Sponsored by Ever Ready (1984-94), Vodafone (from 1995). Six fillies have won the Derby.
St Leger	Run over 1 mile 6 furlongs 132yds (2.92km) at Doncaster, for colts carrying 9st (57kg) and fillies carrying 8st 11lb (55.8kg). Run at Newmarket during during World War I and II except 1940 (Thirsk), 1941 (Manchester) and 1945 (York). In 1989 it was moved to Ayr (the first time an English classic had been held in Scotland) due to damage to the Doncaster track. Sponsored by Holsten Pils (1984-88), Coalite (1991-93), Teleconnection (1994), Pertemps (1995-97) and Rothmans Royals (from 1998).
evening meeting: first in Britain	Hamilton Park, 18 July 1947
Fasig-Tipton	US sale company based near Lexington, Kentucky, whose yearling sales are second only to Keeneland in importance in America.
fillies: year all five classics won by	1882
flat jockey: champion most times	Gordon Richards (26)
flat race: longest in the UK	Queen Alexandra Stakes at Ascot, run over 2¾ miles (4.4km)
French classics	Poule d'Essai des Pouliches (1000 Guineas), run over 1600m at Longchamp. Poule d'Essai des Poulains (2000 Guineas), run over 1600m at Longchamp. Prix de Diane Hermès (Oaks), run over 2100m at Chantilly. Prix du Jockey Club (Derby), run over 1 mile 4 furlongs (2.4km) at Chantilly. Prix Royal Oak (St Leger), run over 3100m at Longchamp. Prix de l'Arc de Triomphe, run over 2400m at Longchamp on the first Sunday in October, the most prestigious race in Europe. The Lucien Barrière leisure group now sponsors the Arc.
Gary Bardwell: nickname	The Angry Ant
Goffs: details	Founded in 1866 and based at Kill, Co. Kildare, Goffs is the leading bloodstock sales company in Ireland. Its Orby Sale in October is the most important Irish sale.
Grand National: first woman jockey	Charlotte Brew on Barony Fort (1977)
first woman jockey to complete	Geraldine Rees on Cheers (1982)
future monarch owned winner	Ambush II (King Edward VII in 1900)
number of fences	30
officially named	In 1847
race that never was	In 1993 the race was cancelled after two false starts. The flagman was Ken Evans and the starter was Captain Keith Brown. Many of the horses completed the course and the first past the post was Esha Ness ridden by John White and trained by Jenny Pitman.
royal horse that collapsed	Devon Loch, ridden by Dick Francis
where run during World War I	Gatwick (1916-18) as the Race Course Association Chase (1916) and the War National Chase (1917-18)
youngest winning rider	Bruce Hobbs on Battleship, aged 17 (1938)
Group One races in England: names and venues	Coronation Cup, run over 1 mile 4 furlongs (2.4km) at the Derby meeting St James' Palace Stakes, three-year-olds, run over 1 mile (1.6km) at Royal Ascot in June Coronation Stakes, three-year-old fillies, run over 1 mile at Royal Ascot in June Ascot Gold Cup, run over 2 miles 4 furlongs (4km) at Royal Ascot in June

Eclipse Stakes, run over 1 mile 2 furlongs (2km) at Sandown Park in July
July Cup, run over 6 furlongs (1.2km) at Newmarket
King George VI & Queen Elizabeth Diamond Stakes, run over 1 mile 4 furlongs at Ascot in July
Sussex Stakes, run over 1 mile at Glorious Goodwood
Juddmonte International Stakes, run over 1 mile 2 furlongs at York
Yorkshire Oaks, run over 1 mile 4 furlongs at York
Nunthorpe Stakes, run over 5 furlongs (1km) at York
Queen Elizabeth II Stakes, run over 1 mile at Royal Ascot
Cheveley Park Stakes, two-year-old fillies, 6 furlongs at Newmarket
Middle Park Stakes, two-year-olds, run over 6 furlongs at Newmarket
Champion Stakes, run over 1 mile 2 furlongs at Newmarket
Dewhurst Stakes, two-year-olds, run over 7 furlongs (1.4km) at Newmarket
Racing Post Trophy, two-year-olds, run over 1 mile at Doncaster

Guineas: run on the same day	In 1921 both the 1000 and 2000 Guineas were run on the same day.
handicap race: first	The Oatlands handicap run at Ascot in 1791
harness racing: gaits	Trotting (striding with horse's left front and right rear leg synchronised)
	Pacing (moving both legs on one side of the body at the same time)
harness racing: vehicle pulled	Sulky
height of horses: measured in	A horse's height is measured, at the shoulder, in hands (1 hand = 4 ins (10cm)).
Hennessy Cognac Gold Cup:	Began in 1957. Now run over 3 miles 2 furlongs 82yds (5.27km) at Newbury, although initially run at Cheltenham from 1957-59. Winners include Mandarin (1957), Mill House (1963), Arkle (1964-65), Stalbridge Colonist (1966) and One Man (1994).
Horse Racing Levy Board	Created on 1 September 1961 along with the Horserace Totalisator Board.
hurdle race: first recorded	In 1821 a race over five hurdles took place at Durdham Down, near Bristol, over a 1 mile (1.6km) course.
Injured Jockeys Fund	Founded in 1964 as a result of injuries sustained by Paddy Farrell and Tim Brookshaw, two well-known National Hunt jockeys. John Lawrence, now Lord Oaksey, is a prime fundraiser for the IJF. Address: 1 Lynx Court, Victoria Way, Newmarket, Suffolk CB8 7SH Tel: 01638 662246 Fax: 01638 668988 Email: kh@ijf.org.uk Web: www. ijf. org.uk
Irish classics: where run	All Irish classics are run at the Curragh.
Irish Derby: first run	In 1866 over an extended 1¾ miles (2.8km) and won by Selim
Irish Grand National	Run over 3 miles 5 furlongs (5.8km) at Fairyhouse, for five-year-olds and over
Irish Grand National: woman jockey won	Ann Ferris (1984) on Bentom Boy
Japan Cup: details	Run each November in Tokyo over 1 mile 4 furlongs (2.4km). It was the world's richest race until the Dubai World Cup began in 1996.
Jockey Club: address	42 Portman Square, London W1H 6EN Tel: 020 7486 4921 Fax: 020 7935 8703 Email info@thejockeyclub.co.uk Web: www.thejockeyclub.co.uk
Jockey Club formed	In 1750. Women were allowed membership in 1977.
jockey: first knighted	Gordon Richards
Keeneland: details	Racetrack in Lexington, Kentucky, founded in 1936 and best known for its yearling sales, especially the September sale.
Kentucky Derby: details	Nicknamed 'The Run for the Roses', the Kentucky Derby is run over 1 mile 2 furlongs (2km) at Churchill Downs, Louisville, Kentucky. It takes place on the first Saturday in May and is the longest continuously held sporting contest in the US, first run in 1875.
King George VI Chase: details	Traditional Boxing Day fixture over 3 miles (4.8km) at Kempton Park, first run in 1947. Winners include Mandarin (1957), Mill House (1963), Arkle (1965), Titus Oates (1969), Wayward Lad (1982, 1983, 1985), Desert Orchid (1986, 1988, 1989, 1990), One Man (1995, 1996). The 1995 win by One Man actually took place at Sandown Park in January 1996
Lester Piggott: first winner	The Chase (1948) at Haydock Park. Piggott was 12 years old
Lester Piggott: nickname	The Long Fellow, Old Stoneface
Lincoln handicap: woman jockey won	Alex Greaves on Amenable in 1991
Mackeson Gold Cup: details	Began in 1960 and run over 2 miles 4 furlongs (4km) at Cheltenham in the autumn. Its name was changed in 1996 to the Murphys Gold Cup.
mare: age filly becomes	Five
Melbourne Cup: details	Held on the first Tuesday in November at Flemington Park, and inaugurated in 1861. Traditionally run over 2 miles, since 1972 it has been raced over the slightly shorter metric distance of 3200m. The race is now sponsored by Fosters.
most prolific winning horse	Catherina won 79 of her 176 races before retiring in 1841.
most runners in a British race	The record Flat race field was 58 in the 1948 Lincoln Handicap. The record National Hunt field was 66 in the 1929 Grand National.

Newmarket Town Plate: details	Founded by Charles II in about 1665 and won by him in 1671 and 1674, the only reigning monarch to ride a winner in the plate.
New Zealand: first race run	The first official meeting was in 1842 on the Epsom racetrack in Auckland.
oldest racecourse in Britain	The Roodee at Chester held its first meeting on 9 February 1540.
overnight declarations: introduced in Britain	1961
pacing: US Triple Crown	William H. Cane Futurity (commenced 1955); Messenger Stake (1957); Little Brown Jug (1946)
pari-mutuel	French totaliser system devised in 1865 by Frenchman Pierre Oller
photo-finish: first used in Britain	On 22 April 1947 at Epsom
Preakness Stakes	Known as 'The Middle Jewel of the Triple Crown', the Preakness Stakes is run over 1 mile 1 furlong 110yds (1.9km) at Pimlico Racecourse, Baltimore, Maryland. It takes place two weeks after the Kentucky Derby. The tropy is the Woodlawn Vase, valued at $1 million and the most valuable trophy in American sport.
Prince Charles: first racecourse appearance	In the Madhatters' Private Sweepstakes over 2 miles at Plumpton on 4 March 1980, Prince Charles rode the favourite Long Wharf into second place behind Classified, ridden by Derek Thompson. His first ride over fences was on the unplaced Sea Swell four days later. After a fall from Good Prospect at the 1981 Cheltenham Festival, he was advised to give up the sport.
Princess Royal: first victory	Gulfland in the Mommessin Stakes at Redcar on 5 August 1986 when Princess Anne. Her first win as the Princess Royal was Ten No Trumps in the 1 mile Dresden Diamond Stakes at Ascot on 25 July 1987. She also won the Queen Mother's Cup at York in 1988 on Insular.
racehorse birthdays	1 January (northern hemisphere) and 1 August (southern hemisphere). This convention began at Newmarket in 1834 and was universally adopted in 1858.
racehorses: maximum number of letters in name	18
Scottish Grand National:	Run over 4 miles 1 furlong (6.6km) at Ayr
spring double	Lincoln Handicap and Grand National
stallion: age colt becomes	Five
starting stalls: first used in Britain	Newmarket, Chesterfield Stakes on 8 July 1965
steeplechase: first recorded in England	In 1792 a race took place in Leicestershire between Barkby Holt and Billesdon Coplow and back, a total distance of eight miles being recorded.
suffragette: killed during Derby	Emily Davison threw herself under the King's horse Anmer in 1913. The race had further drama, winner Craganour being disqualified.
thoroughbred: ancestry	Darley Arabian, Byerley Turk, Godolphin Arabian (aka Barb)
Timeform Ratings	Founded by the late Phil Bull in 1948, Timeform Ratings are an expression in pounds for use as a guide to compare the merits of racehorses. Flat horses are given separate ratings to jumpers. Sea Bird was given the highest-ever Flat rating (145) and Arkle the highest National Hunt (212)
tipster: famous	Prince Ras Monolulu (1881-1965). Real name Peter McKay. Born in Abyssinia, he was famous for parading around racecourses in his trademark ostrich-feather headdress screaming 'I Gotta Horse'.
trainer: first woman in Britain to become	Mrs Florence Nagle was awarded her licence on 28 July 1966.
trainer within M25	Andrew Reid at Mill Hill, London, is the only trainer with a stable within the M25.
trotting: US Triple Crown	Hambleton (commenced 1926), Yonkers Futurity (1958), Kentucky Futurity (1893)
Triple Crown: English	2000 Guineas, Derby, St Leger
Triple Crown: US	Kentucky Derby (first of the season), Preakness Stakes, Belmont Stakes (last of the season). Belmont's inaugural race was in 1867 at Jerome Park, pre-dating the Preakness by six years and the Derby by eight.
US Triple Crown: only woman to win a race	Julie Krone became the first and only woman to date to win a leg of the Triple Crown when she won the Belmont Stakes on Colonial Affair in 1993.
virtual racing: name of tracks	Portman Park (Flat), Steepledowns (Jump). (Computerised races piped into betting shops for betting purposes.)
walk over	Term used to denote races in which only one runner is declared. Traditionally the runner is not required to run the whole distance of the race but merely to walk across the winning line.
weighed-in signal	The signal given for bookmakers to settle bets as the result is official. The equivalent in Ireland is 'winner all right'.
Welsh Grand National: run	Chepstow
Whitbread Gold Cup: details	Inaugurated in 1957, run at Sandown over 3 miles 5 furlongs 18yds (3.6km). Winners include Arkle (1965), Mill House (1967), Desert Orchid (1988).
women jockeys: firsts in Britain	Meriel Tufnell won the first women's race on Scorched Earth at Kempton in May 1972. In 1974 Linda Goodwill was the first to beat male jockeys. In 1976 women were allowed to compete in National Hunt races.
yearling races: abolished	1860

HORSE RACING

HURLING

Hurling, also called hurley, has been played in Ireland for thousands of years and is believed to have been part of the ancient Tailteann Games. Tracing back to approximately 1800BC, these are the oldest recorded organised sporting event in the world. The most famous early reference to hurling is from a 12th-century document which recounts the legend of Cu Chulainn, one of the greatest Irish mythological heroes. The story is told in *Táin Bo Cuailnge* (The Cattle Raid of Cooley) when, as a young boy, known as Setanta, the hero defeated a vicious hound by hitting his ball through its mouth with his hurley. For this feat he won the name Cu Chulainn (the Hound of Chulainn).

In 1882 Michael Cusack founded the Dublin Hurling Club (which later became the Metropolitan Hurling Club), and on 1 November 1884 the Gaelic Athletic Association (GAA) was founded in Thurles, Co. Tipperary. Charles Stuart Parnell was its early patron. The late 19th century also saw the emergence of shinty, a Scottish version of hurling, and bandy, a Welsh version. The first All-Ireland Senior Hurling final was played in 1887.

The winners of the All-Ireland Senior Hurling Championship are presented with the Liam McCarthy Cup. The trophy was first presented for the 1921 final between Dublin and Limerick, though this was not actually played until 4 March 1923. Dublin were then defending champions and holders of the previous trophy, the Great Southern Cup, but on that day it was Limerick who emerged as the champions and first winners of the new trophy.

Hurling is a game similar to hockey, in that it is played with a small ball and a curved wooden stick. Each team consists of 15 players, lining up as follows: one goalkeeper, three full-backs, three half-backs, two midfielders, three half-forwards and three full-forwards. The stick, or 'hurley' (called the *camán* in Irish), is made of young pliable ash, approximately 0.9m (3ft) long and 13cm (5ins) wide at its blade, which is curved outwards at the end to provide the striking surface. The ball, or *sliothar*, is similar in size to a hockey ball but has raised ridges. It is fashioned from cork, wound with wool and covered with leather, and is 23-25cm (9-10ins) in circumference. Hurling is played on a pitch approximately 137m (150yds) long and 82m (90yds) wide. The goalposts are the same shape as on a rugby pitch, 6.4m (21ft) high and 6.4m (21ft) apart, with the crossbar 2.4m (8ft) above the ground.

The ball may be struck on the ground or in the air. Unlike hockey, the ball can be picked up with the hurley and carried in the hand for not more than four steps. After those steps the ball may be bounced on the hurley and back to the hand, but it is forbidden to catch the ball more than twice. To get around this, one of the skills is running with the ball balanced on the hurley. A single point is scored by putting the ball over the crossbar with the hurley; a goal, worth three points, is scored by putting the ball under the crossbar and into the net. Physical contact is allowed, shoulder to shoulder.

The women's equivalent of hurling is called camogie and is played according to the same basic rules. A smaller pitch and smaller sticks are used, however, and a camogie team has only 12 players.

ICE HOCKEY

The origins of ice hockey can be traced back to the second century AD although the first organised game was played by Englishmen on the frozen expanse of Kingston Harbour, Ontario, in 1860. These pioneers of the game were predominantly Crimean War veterans serving in a regiment of the Royal Canadian Rifles. Montreal became the centre for the early development of the game.

Although the game has maintained a very strong Canadian link there has been a revival of interest in Great Britain in recent years. Grosvenor House became the first British National League champions in 1934 and the leading teams in Britain after World War II included Brighton Tigers,

Harringay Racers, Nottingham Panthers, Paisley Pirates, Streatham and Wembley Lions. In recent years the league has been dominated by teams such as Cardiff Devils, Dundee Stars, Durham Wasps, Fife Flyers, Guildford Flames, Murrayfield Racers, Sheffield Steelers and Slough Jets. A British Championship was played in 1930 and again in 1960 before becoming an annual event in 1966. A British Superleague was established in 1997 (it became the British Elite Ice Hockey League in 2003).

The following is a list of results, biographies and general information about a sport often described as the fastest team game on earth.

Biographies of Players, Coaches and Owners

Apps, Charles Joseph Sylvanus (Syl)   Born Paris, Ontario, 18 January 1915. Centre, Toronto Maple Leafs 1936-48. Winner of the Calder Trophy in 1937 and the Lady Byng Trophy in 1942. Won the pole vault at the 1934 Empire Games, and placed sixth in the 1936 Olympics in Berlin. Apps served in the Ontario Legislature and the Ontario cabinet as Minister of Correctional Services. He died 24 December 1998.

Belfour, Ed   Born Carman, Manitoba, 21 April 1965. Goalkeeper, Chicago Blackhawks 1988-97, San Jose Sharks 1996-97, Dallas Stars 1997-2002, Toronto Maple Leafs 2002-03. He won the Stanley Cup in 1999. Balfour was also a winner of the Olympic gold for Canada in 2002. Won Calder Trophy in 1991 and the Vezina Trophy in 1991 and 1993.

Béliveau, Jean   Born Trois Rivières, Quebec, 31 August 1931. Centre, Montreal Canadiens 1950/51 and 1951-71, winning ten Stanley Cups. He won the Hart Memorial Trophy (1956 and 1964), the Art Ross Trophy (1956), and the first Conn Smythe Trophy to be awarded in 1965.

Bossy, Mike   Born Montreal, Quebec, 22 January 1957. Forward, New York Islanders 1977-87, winning four Stanley Cups (1980-83). Won the Conn Smythe Trophy in 1982. His no. 22 jersey was retired by New York Islanders.

Bourque, Ray   Born Montreal, Quebec, 28 December 1960. Defenceman, Boston Bruins 1980-2000, Colorado Avalanche 1999-2001. Bourque won the Stanley Cup in 2001 and the Calder Memorial Trophy in 1980. He represented Canada at the 1998 Olympics in Nagano.

Brodeur, Martin   Born Montreal, Quebec, 6 May 1972. Goalkeeper, New Jersey Devils 1991-2004. Played in their three Stanley Cup wins (1995, 2000 and 2003). He won the Calder Memorial Trophy in 1994 and played for Canada in the 1998 and 2002 Olympics winning gold in 2002.

Carbonneau, Guy   Born Sept-Iles, Quebec, 18 March 1960. Centre, Montreal Canadiens 1982-94 (winning Stanley Cups in 1986 and 1993); St Louis

Blues 1994-95, Dallas Stars 1995-2000 (winning the Stanley Cup in 1999). He won the Selke Trophy in 1988, 1989 and 1992.

Chelios, Chris   Born Chicago, Illinois, 25 January 1962. Defenceman, Montreal Canadiens 1983-90, Chicago Blackhawks 1990-99, Detroit Red Wings 1998-2003. Won the Stanley Cup in 1986 and 2002, and represented USA at the Olympics in 1984 and 1998 before winning silver in 2002.

Clarke, Bobby   Born Flin Flon, Manitoba 13 August 1949. Centre, Philadelphia Flyers 1969-84. Clarke won the Stanley Cup in 1974 and 1975, the Hart Memorial Trophy in 1973, 1975 and 1976, the Lester B. Pearson Award in 1973 and the Selke Trophy in 1983.

Coffey, Paul   Born Weston, Ontario, 1 June 1961. Defenceman, Edmonton Oilers 1980-87, Pittsburgh Penguins 1987-92, LA Kings 1991-93, Detroit Red Wings 1992-96, Hartford Whalers 1996-97, Philadelphia Flyers 1996-98, Chicago Blackhawks 1998-99, Carolina Hurricanes 1999-2000, Boston Bruins 2000-01. Coffey won the Stanley Cup with Edmonton Oilers three times (1984, 1985, 1987) and Pittsburgh Penguins in 1991.

Dionne, Marcel   Born Drummondville, Quebec, 3 August 1951. Forward, Detroit Red Wings 1971-75, LA Kings 1975-87, New York Rangers 1987-89. Won the Lady Byng Memorial Trophy in 1975 and 1977, the Lester B. Pearson Award in 1979 and 1980, and the Art Ross Trophy in 1980.

Dryden, Ken   Born Hamilton, Ontario, 8 August 1947. Goalkeeper, Montreal Canadiens 1970-79. Dryden won six Stanley Cups and the Conn Smythe Trophy in 1971. He also won the Calder Memorial Trophy in 1972 and the Vezina Trophy five times (1973, 1976, 1977, 1978, 1979).

Durnan, Bill   Born Toronto, Ontario, 22 January 1916. Goalkeeper, Montreal Royals 1940-43, Montreal Canadiens 1943-50. Durnan won the Stanley Cup in 1944 and 1946, and was the first goalkeeper to win the Vezina Trophy six times (1944-7, 1949, 1950). He died 31 October 1972.

Esposito, Phil   Born Sault Ste. Marie, Ontario, 20 February 1942. Centre, Chicago Blackhawks 1963-67, Boston Bruins 1967-76, New York Rangers 1976-81. Won the Stanley Cup in 1970 and 1972, the Hart Memorial Trophy in 1969 and 1974, the Ross Trophy in 1969, 1971, 1972, 1973 and 1974, and the Lester B. Pearson Award in 1971 and 1975. His no. 7 jersey was retired by Boston Bruins. Brother of Tony Esposito.

Espisito, Tony   Born Sault Ste. Marie, Ontario, 23 April 1942. Goalkeeper, Montreal Canadiens 1968-69, Chicago Blackhawks 1969-84. Won the Calder Memorial Trophy in 1970, and the Vezina Trophy in 1970, 1972 and 1974. Brother of Phil Esposito.

Fedorov, Sergei   Born Pskov, Russia, 13 December 1969. Centre, CSKA Moscow 1986-90, Detroit Red Wings 1990-2003 (winning three Stanley Cups), Anaheim Mighty Ducks 2003. Won Olympic silver with Russia in 1998, and bronze in 2002. He also won the Hart Memorial Trophy in 1994, the Lester B. Pearson Award in 1994, and the Selke Trophy in 1994 and 1996. Was married to tennis player Anna Kournikova.

Gainey, Bob   Born Peterborough, Ontario, 13 December 1953. Forward, Montreal Canadiens 1973-89, winning five Stanley Cups and the Conn Smythe Trophy in 1979. Gainey won the Selke Trophy in 1978, 1979, 1980 and 1981.

Gartner, Mike   Born Ottawa, Ontario, 29 October 1959. Right-wing, Washington Capitals 1979-89, Minnesota North Stars 1989-90, New York Rangers 1990-94, Toronto Maple Leafs 1994-96, Phoenix Coyotes 1996-98.

Geoffrion, Bernie   Born Montreal, Quebec, 16 February 1931. Right-wing, Montreal Canadiens (1950-4), winning six Stanley Cups, New York Rangers (1966-68). Geoffrion won the Calder Memorial Trophy in 1952, the Art Ross Trophy in 1955 and 1961, and the Hart Memorial Trophy in 1961. He also coached Quebec Aces, Atlanta Flames and Montreal Canadiens. Nicknamed 'Boom Boom'.

Gretzky, Wayne   Born Brantford, Ontario, 26 January 1961. Centre, Edmonton Oilers 1978-88, LA Kings 1988-96, St Louis Blues 1996, New York Rangers 1996-99. Considered by most experts to have been the best ice hockey player of all time. Gretzky won the Stanley Cup four times (1984, 1985, 1987 and 1988) and the Conn Smythe Trophy in 1985 and 1988. He also won the Art Ross Trophy a record ten times (1981-87, 1990, 1991, 1994), the Hart Memorial Trophy a record nine times (1980-87, 1989), the Lester B. Pearson award 1982-85 and 1987, and the Lady Byng Memorial Trophy 1982-85 and 1987. He played for Canada in the 1998 Olympics when they disappointingly finished outside the medals. General manager of the Olympic gold-winning team in 2002. Became joint owner of Phoenix Coyotes in 2001. His number, 99, was retired by Edmonton Oilers, LA Kings and the NHL. Known as 'The Great One'.

Hainsworth, George   Born Toronto, Ontario, 26 June 1895. Goalkeeper, Montreal Canadiens 1926-33 and 1936-37, Toronto Maple Leafs 1933-36. Won the Stanley Cup in 1930 and 1931, and the first three Vezina Trophies, 1927-29.

Harvey, Doug   Born Montreal, Quebec, 19 December 1924. Defenceman, Montreal Canadiens 1947-61, winning six Stanley Cups. Also played for New York Rangers 1961-64, Detroit Red Wings 1966-67, St Louis Blues 1967-69. He won the James Norris Memorial Trophy seven times (1955-58,1960-62). He died in 1989.

Hasek, Dominik   Born Pardubice, Czechoslovakia, 29 January 1965. Goalkeeper, Chicago Blackhawks 1990-92, Buffalo Sabres 1992-2001, Detroit Red Wings 2001-02. Hasek won the Stanley Cup in 2002. He also won a gold medal at the 1998 Olympics with the Czech Republic. He won the Hart Memorial Trophy in 1997 and 1998 (the first goalkeeper to win in consecutive seasons), the Lester B. Pearson Award in 1997 and 1998, and the Vezina Trophy a record-equalling six times (1994, 1995, 1997, 1998, 1999 and 2001).

Howe, Gordie   Born Floral, Saskatchewan, 31 March 1928. Centre, Detroit Red Wings 1946-71, Houston Aeros 1973-77, New England Whalers 1977-79, Hartford Whalers 1979-80. Holds NHL record for most seasons (26) and most games played (1767). Howe finished in the top five in NHL scoring for 20 straight seasons. He won the Art Ross Trophy a then record six times (1951, 1952, 1953, 1954, 1957, 1963), the Hart Memorial Trophy a then record six times (1952, 1953, 1957, 1958, 1960, 1963), and the James Norris Memorial Trophy in 1967. Nicknamed 'Mr Hockey'.

Hull, Bobby   Born Point Anne, Ontario, 3 January 1939. Left-wing, Chicago Blackhawks 1957-72, Winnipeg Jets 1972-80, Hartford Whalers 1980. Won the Stanley Cup in 1961, the Art Ross Trophy in 1960, 1962 and 1966, the Hart Memorial Trophy in 1965 and 1966, and the Lady Byng Memorial Trophy in 1965.

Hull, Brett   Born Belleville, Ontario, 9 August 1964. Right-wing, Calgary Flames 1986-88, St Louis Blues 1987-98, Dallas Stars 1998-2001, Detroit Red Wings 2001-2003. Scored the winning goal in the 1999 Stanley Cup finals. Represented USA in the Olympics in 1998 and 2002, winning silver in 2002. Hull won the Lady Byng Memorial Trophy in 1990, the Hart Memorial Trophy in 1991 and the Lester B. Pearson Award in 1991. Son of Bobby Hull.

Jagr, Jaromir   Born Kladno, Czech Republic, 15 February 1972. Right-wing, Pittsburgh Penguins 1990-2001, Washington Capitals 2001-03. Represented Czechoslovakia from 1990-93 and the Czech Republic from 1993-2003. Won Olympic gold in 1998. Jagr also won the Stanley Cup in 1991 and 1992, the Art Ross Trophy in 1995, 1998, 1999, 2000 and 2001, the Lester B. Pearson Award in 1999 and 2000, and the Hart Memorial Trophy in 1999.

Johnson, Ivan (Ching)   Born Winnipeg, Manitoba, 7 December 1898. Defenceman, New York Rangers 1926-37, New York Americans 1937-38. Johnson won the Stanley Cup in 1928 and 1933. He died 16 June 1979.

Kariya, Paul   Born Vancouver, British Columbia, 16 October 1974. Left-wing, Anaheim Mighty Ducks 1994-2003. Born of Japanese parents, he is the most revered NHL player in Japan. Kariya was selected to play for Canada in the 1998 Olympics (held in his ancestral homeland) but suffered an injury just two weeks before the tournament and did not play again for seven months. Won gold for Canada at the 2002 Olympics. Also winner of the Lady Byng Memorial Award in 1996 and 1997.

Kurri, Jari   Born Helsinki, Finland, 18 May 1960. Right-wing, Edmonton Oilers 1980-90, LA Kings 1991-95, New York Rangers 1995-96, Anaheim Mighty Ducks 1996-97, Colorado Avalanche 1997-98. Kurri is the top European scorer of all time in the NHL, with 601 goals, 797 assists and 1398 points in 1251 games. He is also the first European to lead the NHL in most goals scored (1986). He won the

Lady Byng Memorial Trophy in 1985. Kurri represented Finland internationally.

Lafleur, Guy Born Thurso, Quebec, 20 September 1951. Right-wing, Montreal Canadiens 1971-85 (winning five Stanley Cups and the Conn Smythe Trophy in 1977), New York Rangers 1988-89, Quebec Nordiques 1989-91. He won the Art Ross Trophy in 1976, 1977 and 1978, the Lester B. Pearson Award in 1976, 1977 and 1978, and the Hart Memorial Trophy in 1977 and 1978. His no. 10 jersey was retired by the Canadiens.

Langway, Rod Born Taipei, Taiwan, 3 May 1957. Defenceman, Montreal Canadiens 1978-82 (winning the Stanley Cup in 1979), Washington Capitals 1982-93. Washington Capitals retired his no. 5 jersey.

Lemieux, Mario Born Montreal, Quebec, 5 October 1965. Centre, Laval Voisins (Quebec Major Junior Hockey League) 1981-84. Pittsburgh Penguins 1984-97, 2000-03. Number one draft pick in 1984. Won the Stanley Cup and the Conn Smythe Trophy in 1991 and 1992. Out of the game from 1997 to 2000, due to injury, he returned in 2000. Lemieux became the owner of Pittsburgh Penguins in 1999. He won the Calder Memorial Trophy in 1985, the Lester B. Pearson Trophy in 1986, 1988, 1993 and 1996, the Art Ross Trophy in 1988, 1989, 1992, 1993, 1996 and 1997, and the Hart Memorial Trophy in 1988, 1993 and 1996. Played for Canada at the 2002 Olympics. Jersey 66 for Pittsburgh Penguins.

Lindros, Eric Born London, Ontario, 28 February 1973. Centre, Philadelphia Flyers 1992-2000, New York Rangers 2001-03. Represented Canada at the Olympics in 1992 (winning silver), 1998 and 2002 (winning gold). Won the Hart Memorial Trophy in 1995 and the Lester B. Pearson Award in 1995.

Messier, Mark Born Edmonton, Alberta, 18 January 1961. Centre, Edmonton Oilers 1979-91, New York Rangers 1991-97, 2000-03, Vancouver Canucks 1997-2000. Messier won six Stanley Cups, five with the Oilers and one with Rangers. He also won the Conn Smythe Award in 1984, the Lester B. Pearson Trophy in 1990 and 1992, and the Hart Memorial Trophy in 1990 and 1992.

Mikita, Stan Born Sokoice, Slovakia, 20 May 1940. Right-wing, Chicago Blackhawks 1958-80. Won the Stanley Cup in 1961, the Hart Memorial Trophy in 1967 and 1968, the Art Ross Trophy in 1964, 1965, 1967 and 1968 and the Lady Byng Memorial Trophy in 1967 and 1968. Appeared as himself in the 1992 movie *Wayne's World*.

Morenz, Howie Born Mitchell, Ontario, 21 June 1902. Centre, Montreal Canadiens 1923-34, 1936-37 Chicago Blackhawks 1934-36, New York Rangers 1936. Morenze won the Stanley Cup in 1924, 1930 and 1931, and the Hart Memorial Trophy in 1928, 1931 and 1932. One of the outstanding players of the 1920s and 1930s, a fast skater and a goal scorer – the NHL's top marksman in 1927-28 and 1930-31. He broke his leg in a game on 28 January 1937 and died in hospital on 8 March 1937. His no. 7 jersey was retired by Montreal Canadiens.

Orr, Bobby Born Parry Sound, Ontario, 20 March 1948. Defenceman, Bonson Bruins 1966-76, Chicago Blackhawks 1976-79. He won the Conn Smythe Trophy in 1970 and 1972, the first player to win the award twice.

Parent, Bernie Born Montreal, Quebec, 3 April 1945. Goalkeeper, Boston Bruins 1966-67, Philadelphia Flyers 1967-71, 1973-79, Toronto Maple Leafs 1970-72. Won the Stanley Cup in 1974 and 1975. He also

won the Conn Smythe Trophy in 1974 and 1975, the first player to win the award in consecutive years, and the Vezina Trophy in 1974 and 1975.

Plante, Jacques Born Shawinigan Falls, Quebec, 17 January 1929. Goalkeeper, Montreal Canadiens 1952-63 (winning six Stanley Cups), Montreal Royals, Buffalo Bisons 1953-54, New York Rangers 1963-65, Baltimore Clippers 1964-65, St Louis Blues 1968-70, Toronto Maple Leafs 1970-73, Edmonton Oilers 1974-75. In a career that spanned 29 years from 1947-75, he won a record seven Vezina Trophies (1956-60, 1962, 1969) and the Hart Memorial Trophy in 1962. Credited with being the first goalie to wear a face mask. He died 27 February 1986.

Potvin, Denis Born Hull, Ottawa, Quebec, 29 October 1953. Defenceman, New York Islanders 1973-88. Potvin was the first pick in the 1973 NHL amateur draft. Won four Stanley Cups (1980-83), and the Calder Memorial Trophy in 1974.

Richard, Maurice (Rocket) Born Montreal, Quebec, 4 August 1921. Defenceman, Montreal Canadiens 1942-60 (winning eight Stanley Cups). Richard was the first NHL player to score 50 goals in a season (1944/45). He inspired the 'Richard Riots' on 17 March 1955 after being suspended by an 'Anglo-Canadian' official. Won the Hart Memorial Trophy in 1947. He died 27 May 2000.

Robinson, Larry Born Winchester, Ontario, 2 June 1951. Defenceman, Montreal Canadiens 1972-89 (winning six Stanley Cups and the Conn Smythe Trophy in 1978), LA Kings 1989-92. Coached New Jersey Devils 1992-95 and 1999-2000 and LA Kings 1995-98 in the NHL.

Roy, Patrick Born Quebec City, Quebec, 5 October 1965. Goalkeeper, Montreal Canadiens 1984-96, Colorado Avalanche 1995-2003. He won four Stanley Cups (1986, 1993, 1996, 2001), as well as the Conn Smythe Trophy in 1986, 1993 (with Montreal) and 2001 (with Colorado). Roy is the only player to have won the award three times and for two different teams. He represented Canada at the 1998 Olympics, and won the Vezina Trophy in 1989, 1990 and 1992.

Sawchuk, Terry Born Winnipeg, Manitoba, 28 December 1927. Goalkeeper, Detroit Red Wings 1949-55, 1957-64, 1968-69, Boston Bruins 1955-57, Toronto Maple Leafs 1964-67, LA Kings 1968-69, New York Rangers 1969-70. Sawchuk won four Stanley Cups (1952, 1954, 1955, 1967), the Calder Memorial Trophy in 1951 and the Vezina Trophy four times (1952, 1953, 1955, 1965). His no. 1 jersey was retired by Detroit Red Wings. He died 31 May 1970.

Shore, Eddie Born Fort Qu'Appelle, Saskatchewan, 25 November 1902. Defenceman, Boston Bruins 1926-39. Shore won the Stanley Cup in 1929 and 1939 and the Hart Memorial Trophy in 1933, 1935, 1936 and 1938. He died 16 March 1986.

Stevens, Scott Born Kitchener, Ontario, 1 April 1964. Defenceman, Washington Capitals 1982-90, St Louis Blues 1990-91, New Jersey Devils 1991-2003. Stevens played in the Devils' Stanley Cup victories in 1995, 2000 and 2003, and won the Conn Smythe Trophy in 2000. He represented Canada at the 1998 Olympics.

Trottier, Brian Born Val Marie, Saskatchewan, 17 July 1956. Centre, New York Islanders 1975-90, Pittsburgh Penguins 1990-92, 1993-94. Won six Stanley Cups (1980, 1981, 1982, 1983, 1991 and 1992), the Conn Smythe Trophy in 1980, the Calder Memorial Trophy in 1976, the Art Ross Trophy in

ICE HOCKEY

1979 and the Hart Memorial Trophy in 1979.

Tretiak, Vladislav   Born Dimitrov, nr Moscow, 25 April 1952. Goalkeeper. He participated in four Olympics for the USSR (winning gold in 1972, 1976 and 1984, and silver in 1980). Tretiak was the first non-NHL player to be inducted into the Hockey Hall of Fame, in 1989.

Yzerman, Steve   Born Cranbrook, Ontario, 9 May 1965. Centre, Detroit Red Wings 1983-2004. Yzerman won the Stanley Cup three times (1997, 1998 and 2002) and the Conn Smythe Trophy in 1998. He also won the Lester B. Pearson Award in 1989 and the Selke Trophy in 2000. He represented Canada at the 1998 and 2002 Olympics (winning gold in 2002).

General Information

British Championship: trophy played for	1930 – Patton Cup 1966-81 – Icy Smith Cup 1982-93 – Heineken Championship 1999 onwards – Sekonda Playoff Championship
equipment: puck	Circular Solid vulcanized rubber Diameter: 3ins (7.6cm) Thickness: 1in (2.5cm) Weight: approx. 5½ oz (156g)
stick	Handle length: maximum 53ins (135cm) Blades: maximum 14½ins (37cm) Goalkeepers are allowed larger sticks
European Championships	Began in 1910 and were last held in 1991. They were often run as part of the World Championships or Olympics, as follows: 1928 – Combined with World Championships and Olympics 1930-31 – Combined with World Championships 1933-81 – Combined with World Championships or Olympics 1982-91 – Combined with World Championships
history timeline: 1879	First rules formulated by W.F. Robertson and R.F. Smith, students at McGill University in Montreal. Teams would use a square puck, with nine players on each side.
1880	First recognised team formed – McGill University Hockey Club.
1886	8 December – Amateur Hockey Association of Canada (AHAC) formed in Montreal. Charter members: Montreal A.A.A. McGill University Montreal Victorias Ottawa Hockey Club Montreal Crystals
1893	Hockey first played in USA, at Yale University and Johns Hopkins University.
1893	Stanley Cup donated as a permanent senior trophy by Frederick Arthur, Lord Stanley of Preston, the Governor-General of Canada. Originally cost CAN$48.67. The Stanley Cup is the oldest trophy competed for by professional athletes in North America.
1896	United States Amateur Hockey League founded.
1905	British Ice Hockey Federation founded.
1908	International Ice Hockey Federation (IIHF) formed. Founder members: Belgium Bohemia France Great Britain Switzerland
1910	National Hockey Association (NHA) founded in eastern Canada.
1911	Pacific Coast Hockey Association (PCHA) founded, the league lasting until 1924.
1914	British Ice Hockey Association (BIHA) formed. Replaced by Ice Hockey UK in 1999.
1917	National Hockey League (NHL) replaced the NHA. Founder members were: Montreal Canadiens Montreal Wanderers (withdrew in 1918 after their stadium burnt down) Ottawa Senators Quebec Bulldogs (did not play in the first season) Toronto Arenas
1961	26 August – Hockey Hall of Fame officially opened in Toronto. There are over 300 members in three categories – Players, Builders and Referees/Linesmen.
1977	The movie *Slap Shot* released. Acknowledged as one of the best US sports movies ever, it follows the hockey team, the Charlestown Chiefs, their head coach Reggie Dunlop (Paul Newman) and the players 'the Hanson brothers'.
NHL divisions	1967/68 to 1973/74 – East and West 1974/75 to 1992/93 – Prince of Wales Conference (comprising: Norris Division,

I
C
E

H
O
C
K
E
Y

	Adams Division) and Clarence Campbell Conference (comprising: Patrick Division, Smythe Division)	
	1993/94-present – Eastern Conference (comprising: Northeast Division, Atlantic Division, Southeast Division (from 1998/99)) and Western Conference (comprising: Central Division, Pacific Division, Northwest Division (from 1998/99))	
NHL history	A National Hockey League existed from 1908 until it was disbanded at the end of the 1916/17 season. The National Hockey League of North America (NHL) in its present form was formed in Montreal in November 1917. Inaugural five teams:	
	Montreal Canadiens	
	Montreal Wanderers	
	Ottawa Senators	
	Quebec Bulldogs	
	Toronto Arenas	
	There were numerous changes in teams playing in the NHL, until the roster stabilised in 1942/43. Members from the 1942/43 season:	
	Boston Bruins	
	Chicago Blackhawks	
	Detroit Red Wings	
	Montreal Canadiens	
	New York Rangers	
	Toronto Maple Leafs	
	First expansion – 1967/68 season, formed East (existing teams) and West (new teams) Divisions. West Division members:	
	Los Angeles Kings	
	Minnesota North Stars	
	California Seals (renamed Oakland Seals in 1967, California Golden Seals in 1970)	
	Philadelphia Flyers	
	Pittsburgh Penguins	
	St Louis Blues	
	New NHL teams after 1967/68 and date joined:	
	Buffalo Sabres	1970
	Vancouver Canucks	1970
	Atlanta Flames	1972
	New York Islanders	1972
	Kansas City Scouts	1974
	Washington Capitals	1974
	Cleveland Barons	1976
	Colorado Rockies	1976
	Edmonton Oilers	1979
	Hartford Whalers	1979
	Quebec Nordiques	1979 (became Colorado Avalanche in 1995/96)
	Winnipeg Jets	1979
	New Jersey Devils	1982
	San Jose Sharks	1991
	Ottawa Senators	1992
	Tampa Bay Lightning	1992
	Florida Panthers	1993
	Dallas Stars	1993
	Anaheim Mighty Ducks	1993
	Phoenix Coyotes	1996
	Carolina Hurricanes	1997
	Nashville Predators	1998
	Atlanta Thrashers	1999
	Columbus Blue Jackets	2000
	Minnesota Wild	2000
Olympic Games: first gold medal missed by Canada	Won by the Winnipeg Falcons, representing Canada (1920)	
	Canada withdrew from international amateur competition in 1969 due to their objection to playing the 'professional' amateurs from the eastern bloc. As a result they missed the Olympics in 1972 and 1976.	

most gold medals			
	Vitaliy Davidov	(URS)	1964, 1968, 1972
	Anatoliy Firssov	(URS)	1964, 1968, 1972
	Viktor Kuzkin	(URS)	1964, 1968, 1972
	Alexsandr Ragulin	(URS)	1964, 1968, 1972
	Vladislav Tretiak	(URS)	1972, 1976, 1984
	Andrey Khomutov	(URS/CIS)	1984, 1988, 1992

nine university students	1960 – nine USA squad members were from the University of Minnesota.
oldest medallist	Carl Erhardt (GBR) in 1936, aged 39 years, 1 day
tennis champion won medal	The 1954 Wimbledon champion, Jaroslav Drobny, won a silver medal for Czechoslovakia in 1948.
two gold medals, first	1968 – nine members of the USSR squad became the first to win two Olympic gold medals.

USA v USSR	USA beat the Soviet Union in the 1980 Olympic final group match. It is often erroneously thought that this was the final. In fact they had to beat Finland in the final group game to win the gold medal.
youngest gold medallist	John Kilpatrick (GBR) in 1936, aged 18 years, 224 days
youngest medallist	Richard Torriani (SUI) in 1928, aged 16 years, 141 days
Richard Riots	Following NHL President Clarence Campbell's suspension of Maurice Richard for allegedly striking a linesman, fans threw tomatoes and tear gas at Campbell at the next game at the Forum and there were riots on nearby Sainte-Catherine Street.
rules:	Length of game – three periods of 20 minutes each (time when the puck is in play) Red light – light behind goal which is lit up when the referee awards a goal Zones of play – Defence, Neutral (centre), Attacking
Goal area	IIHF – 6ft (1.8m) radius semicircle NHL – 4ft (1.2m) rectangle
Goals	4ft (1.2m) high 6ft (1.8m) wide 2ft+ (0.6m) deep Blue lines – divide rink into three zones Red centre line Centre spot – blue, surrounded by 15ft (4.6m) diameter face-off circle Face-off circles – two in each half
penalties	Players must leave the rink for two minutes (for body-checking, charging, elbowing, high stick, tripping, deliberately shooting out of the rink). Five-minute and ten-minute penalties or total expulsion are incurred for more serious offences.
players	Six players each side are permitted on the ice at any time: goalkeeper, two defencemen, three forwards
playing area	200ft (61m) long 85ft (26m) wide Barrier boards – 3ft 4ins (1m) to 4ft (1.2m) high Red goal lines – 11ft (3.4m) to 15ft (4.6m) from end of rink
start of play	Play begins with a 'face-off'
trophies and awards	Allan Cup – Donated in 1908 by Sir Montague Allan to the Victoria Hockey Club in Montreal (Victorias). The most prestigious senior amateur hockey award, it is made to the Canadian senior amateur champions. Until 1963, the winner of the Allan Cup often represented Canada in the World Championships. Art Ross Trophy – Given to the top points scorer at the end of the regular NHL season. Calder Memorial Trophy – For the best player in debut season, awarded by the Professional Hockey Writers' Association. Named after Frank Calder, president of the NHL between 1917 and 1943. Conn Smythe Trophy – Presented to the MVP (Most Valuable Player) in Stanley Cup play-off matches, as selected by the Professional Hockey Writers' Association. The trophy is named after the former coach, general manager, president and owner of the Toronto Maple Leafs. Hart Memorial Trophy – Awarded annually 'to the player adjudged to be the most valuable to his team'. Named after Cecil Hart, the manager/coach of the Montreal Canadiens from 1926 to 1939. Jack Adams Award – Awarded annually 'to the NHL coach adjudged to have contributed the most to his team's success'. The winner is selected by the National Hockey Broadcasters' Association. Named after Jack Adams, former player, and general manager of the Detroit Red Wings in the late 1940s and early 1950s. James Norris Memorial Trophy – For the best defenceman throughout the season. Decided by the Professional Hockey Writers' Association. Lady Byng Memorial Trophy – Awarded annually 'to the player adjudged to have shown the best sportsmanship and gentlemanly conduct combined with a high standard of playing ability. Lester B. Pearson Award – To the most outstanding player of the year, as chosen by the NHL Players' Association. Named after the former Canadian prime minister. Lester Patrick Trophy – For outstanding service to ice hockey in the United States. Presidents' Trophy – The overall winner of the NHL regular season has been awarded the Presidents' Trophy since 1986. Selke Trophy – Awarded annually 'to the forward who best excels in the defensive aspects of the game'. The winner is selected by the Professional Hockey Writers Association. Stanley Cup Vezina Trophy – Awarded annually 'to the goalkeeper adjudged to be the best at his position'. The general managers of the NHL teams vote for this award.
World Championships	Originally held every four years from 1920, and annually from 1930 onwards. From 1920 to 1968, in Olympic years, the Olympic competition doubled as the World Championships. No competition was held in the Olympic years of 1980, 1984 and 1988. Canada appeared in the first 13 finals up to World War II.

Stanley Cup

		Winner		Runner-Up
1893		Montreal A.A.A.	-	A.A.A. declared champions
1894		Montreal A.A.A.		Ottawa Capitals
1895		Montreal Victorias		Victorias declared champions
1896	(Dec)	Montreal Victorias	1-0	Winnipeg Victorias
	(Feb)	Winnipeg Victorias	1-0	Montreal Victorias
1897		Montreal Victorias	1-0	Ottawa Capitals
1898		Montreal Victorias	-	Victorias declared champions
1899	(Feb)	Montreal Victorias	2-0	Winnipeg Victorias
	(Mar)	Montreal Shamrocks	1-0	Queen's University
1900		Montreal Shamrocks	2-0	Halifax Crescents
1901		Winnipeg Victorias	2-0	Montreal Shamrocks
1902	(Jan)	Winnipeg Victorias	2-0	Toronto Wellingtons
	(Mar)	Montreal A.A.A.	2-1	Winnipeg Victorias
1903	(Feb)	Montreal A.A.A.	3-1	Winnipeg Victorias
	(Mar)	Ottawa Silver Seven	2-0	Rat Portage Thistles
1904		Ottawa Silver Seven	2-0	Brandon Wheat Kings
1905		Ottawa Silver Seven	2-1	Rat Portage Thistles
1906	(Feb)	Ottawa Silver Seven	2-0	Smith Falls
	(Mar)	Montreal Wanderers	2-0	Ottawa Silver Seven
1907	(Jan)	Kenora Thistles	2-0	Montreal Wanderers
	(Mar)	Montreal Wanderers	2-0	Kenora Thistles
1908		Montreal Wanderers	2-0	Ottawa Victorias
1909		Ottawa Senators	2-0	Edmonton Eskimos
1910		Montreal Wanderers	1-0	Berlin Union Jacks
1911		Ottawa Senators	1-0	Port Arthur Bearcats
1912		Quebec Bulldogs	2-0	Moncton Victorias
1913		Quebec Bulldogs	2-0	Sydney Miners
1914		Toronto Blueshirts	3-0	Victoria Cougars
1915		Vancouver Millionaires	3-0	Ottawa Senators
1916		Montreal Canadiens	3-2	Portland Rosebuds
1917		Seattle Metropolitans	3-1	Montreal Canadiens
1918		Toronto Arenas	3-2	Vancouver Millionaires
1919		No decision – Montreal Canadiens/Seattle Metropolitans, abandoned at 2-2, influenza epidemic		
1920		Ottawa Senators	3-2	Seattle Metropolitans
1921		Ottawa Senators	3-2	Vancouver Millionaires
1922		Toronto St Patrick's	3-2	Vancouver Millionaires
1923		Ottawa Senators	2-0	Edmonton Eskimos
1924		Montreal Canadiens	3-1	Calgary Tigers
1925		Victoria Cougars	3-1	Montreal Canadiens
1926		Montreal Maroons	3-1	Victoria Cougars
1927		Ottawa Senators	2-0	Boston Bruins
1928		New York Rangers	3-2	Montreal Maroons
1929		Boston Bruins	2-0	New York Rangers
1930		Montreal Canadiens	2-0	Boston Bruins
1931		Montreal Canadiens	3-2	Chicago Blackhawks
1932		Toronto Maple Leafs	3-0	New York Rangers
1933		New York Rangers	3-1	Toronto Maple Leafs
1934		Chicago Blackhawks	3-1	Detroit Red Wings
1935		Montreal Maroons	3-0	Toronto Maple Leafs
1936		Detroit Red Wings	3-1	Toronto Maple Leafs
1937		Detroit Red Wings	3-2	New York Rangers
1938		Chicago Blackhawks	3-1	Toronto Maple Leafs
1939*		Boston Bruins	4-1	Toronto Maple Leafs
1940		New York Rangers	4-2	Toronto Maple Leafs
1941		Boston Bruins	4-0	Detroit Red Wings
1942		Toronto Maple Leafs	4-3	Detroit Red Wings
1943		Detroit Red Wings	4-0	Boston Bruins
1944		Montreal Canadiens	4-0	Chicago Blackhawks
1945		Toronto Maple Leafs	4-3	Detroit Red Wings
1946		Montreal Canadiens	4-1	Boston Bruins
1947		Toronto Maple Leafs	4-2	Montreal Canadiens
1948		Toronto Maple Leafs	4-0	Detroit Red Wings
1949		Toronto Maple Leafs	4-0	Detroit Red Wings
1950		Detroit Red Wings	4-3	New York Rangers
1951		Toronto Maple Leafs	4-1	Montreal Canadiens
1952		Detroit Red Wings	4-0	Montreal Canadiens

	Winner		Runner-Up
1953	Montreal Canadiens	4-1	Boston Bruins
1954	Detroit Red Wings	4-3	Montreal Canadiens
1955	Detroit Red Wings	4-3	Montreal Canadiens
1956	Montreal Canadiens	4-1	Detroit Red Wings
1957	Montreal Canadiens	4-1	Boston Bruins
1958	Montreal Canadiens	4-2	Boston Bruin
1959	Montreal Canadiens	4-1	Toronto Maple Leafs
1960	Montreal Canadiens	4-0	Toronto Maple Leafs
1961	Chicago Blackhawks	4-2	Detroit Red Wings
1962	Toronto Maple Leafs	4-2	Chicago Blackhawks
1963	Toronto Maple Leafs	4-1	Detroit Red Wings
1964	Toronto Maple Leafs	4-3	Detroit Red Wings
1965	Montreal Canadiens	4-3	Chicago Blackhawks
1966	Montreal Canadiens	4-2	Detroit Red Wings
1967	Toronto Maple Leafs	4-2	Montreal Canadiens
1968	Montreal Canadiens	4-0	St Louis Blues
1969	Montreal Canadiens	4-0	St Louis Blues
1970	Boston Bruins	4-0	St Louis Blues
1971	Montreal Canadiens	4-3	Chicago Blackhawks
1972	Boston Bruins	4-2	New York Rangers
1973	Montreal Canadiens	4-2	Chicago Blackhawks
1974**	Philadelphia Flyers	4-2	Boston Bruins
1975	Philadelphia Flyers	4-2	Buffalo Sabres
1976	Montreal Canadiens	4-0	Philadelphia Flyers
1977	Montreal Canadiens	4-0	Boston Bruins
1978	Montreal Canadiens	4-2	Boston Bruins
1979	Montreal Canadiens	4-1	New York Rangers
1980	New York Islanders	4-2	Philadelphia Flyers
1981	New York Islanders	4-1	Minnesota North Stars
1982	New York Islanders	4-0	Vancouver Canucks
1983	New York Islanders	4-0	Edmonton Oilers
1984	Edmonton Oilers	4-1	New York Islanders
1985	Edmonton Oilers	4-1	Philadelphia Flyers
1986	Montreal Canadiens	4-1	Calgary Flames
1987	Edmonton Oilers	4-3	Philadelphia Flyers
1988	Edmonton Oilers	4-0	Boston Bruins
1989	Calgary Flames	4-2	Montreal Canadiens
1990	Edmonton Oilers	4-1	Boston Bruins
1991	Pittsburgh Penguins	4-2	Minnesota North Stars
1992	Pittsburgh Penguins	4-0	Chicago Blackhawks
1993	Montreal Canadiens	4-1	Los Angeles Kings
1994	New York Rangers	4-3	Vancouver Canucks
1995	New Jersey Devils	4-0	Detroit Red Wings
1996	Colorado Avalanche	4-0	Florida Panthers
1997	Detroit Red Wings	4-0	Philadelphia Flyers
1998	Detroit Red Wings	4-0	Washington Capitals
1999	Dallas Stars	4-2	Buffalo Sabres
2000	New Jersey Devils	4-2	Dallas Stars
2001	Colorado Avalanche	4-3	New Jersey Devils
2002	Detroit Red Wings	4-1	Carolina Hurricanes
2003	New Jersey Devils	4-3	Anaheim Mighty Ducks
2004	Tampa Bay Lightning	4-3	Calgary Flames

NB Prior to the formation of the NHL in 1917, there were a number of occasions when the Stanley Cup was awarded more than once in one year. All recognised winners have been listed.

*The final was the best of seven games from 1938/39 season.

**Philadelphia Flyers first expansion team to win the Stanley Cup.

Presidents' Trophy

	Winners			Winners
1986	Edmonton Oilers		1996	Detroit Red Wings
1987	Edmonton Oilers		1997	Colorado Avalanche
1988	Calgary Flames		1998	Dallas Stars
1989	Calgary Flames		1999	Dallas Stars
1990	Boston Bruins		2000	St Louis Blues
1991	Chicago Blackhawks		2001	Colorado Avalanche
1992	New York Rangers		2002	Detroit Red Wings
1993	Pittsburgh Penguins		2003	Ottawa Senators
1994	New York Rangers		2004	Detroit Red Wings
1995	Detroit Red Wings			

Conn Smythe Trophy

	Player	Team		Player	Team
1965	Jean Beliveau	Montreal Canadiens	1985	Wayne Gretzky	Edmonton Oilers
1966	Roger Crozier	Detroit Red Wings	1986	Patrick Roy	Montreal Canadiens
1967	Dave Keon	Toronto Maple Leafs	1987	Ron Hextall	Philadelphia Flyers
1968	Glenn Hall	St Louis Blues	1988	Wayne Gretzky	Edmonton Oilers
1969	Serge Savard	Montreal Canadiens	1989	Al MacInnis	Calgary Flames
1970	Bobby Orr	Boston Bruins	1990	Bill Ranford	Edmonton Oilers
1971	Ken Dryden	Montreal Canadiens	1991	Mario Lemieux	Pittsburgh Penguins
1972	Bobby Orr	Boston Bruins	1992	Mario Lemieux	Pittsburgh Penguins
1973	Yvan Cournoyer	Montreal Canadiens	1993	Patrick Roy	Montreal Canadiens
1974	Bernie Parent	Philadelphia Flyers	1994	Brian Leetch	New York Rangers
1975	Bernie Parent	Philadelphia Flyers	1995	Claude Lemieux	New Jersey Devils
1976	Reggie Leach	Philadelphia Flyers	1996	Joe Sakic	Colorado Avalanche
1977	Guy Lafleur	Montreal Canadiens	1997	Mike Vernon	Detroit Red Wings
1978	Larry Robinson	Montreal Canadiens	1998	Steve Yzerman	Detroit Red Wings
1979	Bob Gainey	Montreal Canadiens	1999	Joe Nieuwendyk	Dallas Stars
1980	Bryan Trottier	New York Islanders	2000	Scott Stevens	New Jersey Devils
1981	Butch Goring	New York Islanders	2001	Patrick Roy	Colorado Avalanche
1982	Mike Bossy	New York Islanders	2002	Nicklas Lidström	Detroit Red Wings
1983	Bill Smith	New York Islanders	2003	Jean-Sébastien Giguère	Anaheim Mighty Ducks
1984	Mark Messier	Edmonton Oilers	2004	Brad Richards	Tampa Bay Lightning

ICE HOCKEY

Jack Adams Award

	Player	Team		Player	Team
1974	Fred Shero	Philadelphia Flyers	1990	Bob Murdoch	Winnipeg Jets
1975	Bob Pulford	Los Angeles Kings	1991	Brian Sutter	St Louis Blues
1976	Don Cherry	Boston Bruins	1992	Pat Quinn	Vancouver Canucks
1977	Scotty Bowman	Montreal Canadiens	1993	Pat Burns	Toronto Maple Leafs
1978	Bobby Kromm	Detroit Red Wings	1994	Jacques Lemaire	New Jersey Devils
1979	Al Arbour	New York Islanders	1995	Marc Crawford	Quebec Nordiques
1980	Pat Quinn	Philadelphia Flyers	1996	Scotty Bowman	Detroit Red Wings
1981	Red Berenson	St Louis Blues	1997	Ted Nolan	Buffalo Sabres
1982	Tom Watt	Winnipeg Jets	1998	Pat Burns	Boston Bruins
1983	Orval Tessier	Chicago Blackhawks	1999	Jacques Martin	Ottawa Senators
1984	Bryan Murray	Washington Capitals	2000	Joel Quenneville	St Louis Blues
1985	Mike Keenan	Philadelphia Flyers	2001	Bill Barber	Philadelphia Flyers
1986	Glen Sather	Edmonton Oilers	2002	Bob Francis	Phoenix Coyotes
1987	Jacques Demers	Detroit Red Wings	2003	Jacques Lemaire	Minnesota Wild
1988	Jacques Demers	Detroit Red Wings	2004	John Tortorella	Tampa Bay Lightning
1989	Pat Burns	Montreal Canadiens			

Olympic Medallists

Men's

	Gold	Silver	Bronze
1920*	Canada	USA	Czechoslovakia
1924	Canada	USA	Great Britain
1928	Canada	Sweden	Switzerland
1932	Canada	USA	Germany
1936	Great Britain	Canada	USA
1948	Canada	Czechoslovakia	Switzerland
1952	Canada	USA	Sweden
1956	USSR	USA	Canada
1960	USA	Canada	USSR
1964	USSR	Sweden	Czechoslovakia
1968	USSR	Czechoslovakia	Canada
1972	USSR	USA	Czechoslovakia
1976	USSR	Czechoslovakia	West Germany
1980	USA	USSR	Sweden
1984	USSR	Czechoslovakia	Sweden
1988	USSR	Finland	Sweden
1992	CIS	Canada	Czech Republic
1994	Sweden	Canada	Finland
1998	Czech Republic	Russia	Finland
2002	Canada	USA	Russia

*The 1920 ice hockey competition was held at the summer Games.

Women's

	Gold	Silver	Bronze
1998	USA	Canada	Finland
2002	Canada	USA	Sweden

World Championships

Men's

	Gold	Silver	Bronze
1920	Canada	USA	Czechoslovakia
1924	Canada	USA	Great Britain
1928	Canada	Sweden	Switzerland
1930	Canada	Germany	Switzerland
1931	Canada	USA	Austria
1932	Canada	USA	Germany
1933	USA	Canada	Czechoslovakia
1934	Canada	USA	Germany
1935	Canada	Switzerland	Great Britain
1936	Great Britain	Canada	USA
1937	Canada	Great Britain	Switzerland
1938	Canada	Great Britain	Czechoslovakia
1939	Canada	USA	Switzerland
1940-46	not held		
1947	Czechoslovakia	Sweden	Austria
1948	Canada	Czechoslovakia	Switzerland
1949	Czechoslovakia	Canada	USA
1950	Canada	USA	Switzerland
1951	Canada	Sweden	Switzerland
1952	Canada	USA	Sweden
1953	Sweden	West Germany	Switzerland
1954	USSR	Canada	Sweden
1955	Canada	USSR	Czechoslovakia
1956	USSR	USA	Canada
1957	Sweden	USSR	Czechoslovakia
1958	Canada	USSR	Sweden
1959	Canada	USSR	Czechoslovakia
1960	USA	Canada	USSR
1961	Canada	Czechoslovakia	USSR

1962	Sweden	Canada	USA
1963	USSR	Sweden	Czechoslovakia
1964	USSR	Sweden	Czechoslovakia
1965	USSR	Czechoslovakia	Sweden
1966	USSR	Czechoslovakia	Canada
1967	USSR	Sweden	Canada
1968	USSR	Czechoslovakia	Canada
1969	USSR	Sweden	Czechoslovakia
1970	USSR	Sweden	Czechoslovakia
1971	USSR	Czechoslovakia	Sweden
1972	Czechoslovakia	USSR	Sweden
1973	USSR	Sweden	Czechoslovakia
1974	USSR	Czechoslovakia	Sweden
1975	USSR	Czechoslovakia	Sweden
1976	Czechoslovakia	USSR	Sweden
1977	Czechoslovakia	Sweden	USSR
1978	USSR	Czechoslovakia	Canada
1979	USSR	Czechoslovakia	Sweden
1980	not held		
1981	USSR	Sweden	Czechoslovakia
1982	USSR	Czechoslovakia	Canada
1983	USSR	Czechoslovakia	Canada
1984	not held		
1985	Czechoslovakia	Canada	USSR
1986	USSR	Sweden	Canada
1987	Sweden	USSR	Czechoslovakia
1988	not held		
1989	USSR	Canada	Czechoslovakia
1990	USSR	Sweden	Czechoslovakia
1991	Sweden	Canada	Czechoslovakia
1992	Sweden	Finland	Czech Republic
1993	Russia	Sweden	Czech Republic
1994	Canada	Finland	Sweden
1995	Finland	Sweden	Canada
1996	Czech Republic	Canada	USA
1997	Canada	Sweden	Czech Republic
1998	Sweden	Finland	Czech Republic
1999	Czech Republic	Finland	Sweden
2000	Czech Republic	Slovakia	Finland
2001	Czech Republic	Finland	Sweden
2002	Slovakia	Russia	Sweden
2003	Canada	Sweden	Slovakia
2004	Canada	Sweden	USA

Women's

	Gold	Silver	Bronze
1990	Canada	USA	Finland
1992	Canada	USA	Finland
1994	Canada	USA	Finland
1997	Canada	USA	Finland
1999	Canada	USA	Finland
2000	Canada	USA	Finland
2001	Canada	USA	Russia
2003	cancelled due to SARS virus in China		
2004	Canada	USA	Finland

European Championships

Men's

	Gold	Silver	Bronze
1910	Great Britain	Germany	Belgium
1911	Bohemia	Germany	Belgium
1912	Bohemia	Germany	Austria
1913	Belgium	Bohemia	Germany
1914	Bohemia	Germany	Belgium
1915-20	not held		
1921	Sweden	Czechoslovakia	only two teams entered
1922	Czechoslovakia	Sweden	Switzerland
1923	Sweden	France	Czechoslovakia

ICE HOCKEY

1924	France	Sweden	Switzerland
1925	Czechoslovakia	Austria	Switzerland
1926	Switzerland	Czechoslovakia	Austria
1927	Austria	Belgium	Germany
1928	Sweden	Switzerland	Great Britain
1929	Czechoslovakia	Poland	Austria
1930	Germany	Switzerland	Austria
1931	Austria	Poland	Czechoslovakia
1932	Sweden	Austria	Switzerland
1933	Czechoslovakia	Austria	Germany
1934	Germany	Switzerland	Czechoslovakia
1935	Switzerland	Great Britain	Czechoslovakia
1936	Great Britain	Czechoslovakia	Germany
1937	Great Britain	Switzerland	Germany
1938	Great Britain	Czechoslovakia	Germany
1939	Switzerland	Czechoslovakia	Germany
1940-46	not held		
1947	Czechoslovakia	Sweden	Austria
1948	Czechoslovakia	Switzerland	Sweden
1949	Czechoslovakia	Sweden	Switzerland
1950	Switzerland	Great Britain	Sweden
1951	Sweden	Switzerland	Norway
1952	Sweden	Czechoslovakia	Switzerland
1953	Sweden	Germany	Switzerland
1954	USSR	Sweden	Czechoslovakia
1955	USSR	Czechoslovakia	Sweden
1956	USSR	Sweden	Czechoslovakia
1957	Sweden	USSR	Czechoslovakia
1958	USSR	Sweden	Czechoslovakia
1959	USSR	Czechoslovakia	Sweden
1960	USSR	Czechoslovakia	Sweden
1961	Czechoslovakia	USSR	Sweden
1962	Sweden	Finland	Norway
1963	USSR	Sweden	Czechoslovakia
1964	USSR	Sweden	Czechoslovakia
1965	USSR	Czechoslovakia	Sweden
1966	USSR	Czechoslovakia	Sweden
1967	USSR	Sweden	Czechoslovakia
1968	USSR	Czechoslovakia	Sweden
1969	USSR	Sweden	Czechoslovakia
1970	USSR	Sweden	Czechoslovakia
1971	Czechoslovakia	USSR	Sweden
1972	Czechoslovakia	USSR	Sweden
1973	USSR	Sweden	Czechoslovakia
1974	USSR	Czechoslovakia	Sweden
1975	USSR	Czechoslovakia	Sweden
1976	Czechoslovakia	USSR	Sweden
1977	Czechoslovakia	Sweden	USSR
1978	USSR	Czechoslovakia	Sweden
1979	USSR	Czechoslovakia	Sweden
1980	not held		
1981	USSR	Sweden	Czechoslovakia
1982	USSR	Czechoslovakia	Sweden
1983	USSR	Czechoslovakia	Sweden
1984	not held		
1985	USSR	Czechoslovakia	Finland
1986	USSR	Sweden	Finland
1987	USSR	Sweden	Czechoslovakia
1988	not held		
1989	USSR	Czechoslovakia	Sweden
1990	Sweden	USSR	Czechoslovakia
1991	USSR	Sweden	Finland

Women's

Year	Gold	Silver	Bronze
1989	Finland	Sweden	West Germany
1991	Finland	Sweden	Denmark
1993	Finland	Sweden	Norway
1995	Finland	Sweden	Switzerland
1996	Sweden	Russia	Finland

This competition has been replaced by the Pool B Qualification section of the Women's World Championships.

British Superleague Champions

1997	Cardiff Devils		2001	Sheffield Steelers
1998	Ayr Scottish Eagles		2002	Belfast Giants
1999	Manchester Storm		2003	Sheffield Steelers
2000	Bracknell Bees			

British Championship

	Winners		**Runners-Up**	**Venue**
1930	London Lions	2-1	Glasgow Mohawks	
1960	Brighton Tigers	6-5*	Nottingham Panthers	
1966	Murrayfield Racers	11-8	Durham Hornets	
1967	Glasgow Dynamos	12-10	Murrayfield Racers	
1968	Paisley Mohawks	12-11	Durham Wasps	
1969	Murrayfield Racers	9-5	Glasgow Dynamos	
1970	Murrayfield Racers	14-9	Glasgow Dynamos	
1971	Murrayfield Racers	21-8	Durham Wasps	
1972	Murrayfield Racers	18-5	Fife Flyers	
1973	Whitley Warriors	21-9	Murrayfield Racers	
1974	Whitley Warriors	18-5	Streatham	
1975	Murrayfield Racers	12-9	Streatham Redskins	
1976	Ayr Bruins	14-8*	Streatham Redskins	
1977	Fife Flyers	27-11*	Southampton Vikings	
1978	Fife Flyers	23-5*	Southampton Vikings	
1979	Murrayfield Racers	10-2	Streatham Redskins	Billingham
1980	Murrayfield Racers	21-2	Solihull Barons	Crowtree
1981	Murrayfield Racers	8-4	Streatham Redskins	Billingham
1982	Dundee Rockets	3-2	Streatham Redskins	Streatham
1983	Dundee Rockets	6-2	Durham Wasps	Streatham
1984	Dundee Rockets	5-4	Murrayfield Racers	Wembley
1985	Fife Flyers	9-4	Murrayfield Racers	Wembley
1986	Murrayfield Racers	4-2	Dundee Rockets	Wembley
1987	Durham Wasps	9-5	Murrayfield Racers	Wembley
1988	Durham Wasps	8-5	Fife Flyers	Wembley
1989	Nottingham Panthers	6-3	Ayr Bruins	Wembley
1990	Cardiff Devils	6-6**	Murrayfield Racers	Wembley
1991	Durham Wasps	7-4	Peterborough Pirates	Wembley
1992	Durham Wasps	7-6	Nottingham Panthers	Wembley
1993	Cardiff Devils	7-4	Humberside Seahawks	Wembley
1994	Cardiff Devils	12-1	Sheffield Steelers	Wembley
1995	Sheffield Steelers	7-2	Edinburgh Racers	Wembley
1996	Sheffield Steelers	3-3**	Nottingham Panthers	Wembley
1997	Sheffield Steelers	3-1	Nottingham Panthers	Nynex Arena
1998	Ayr Scottish Eagles	3-2***	Cardiff Devils	Nynex Arena
1999	Cardiff Devils	2-1	Nottingham Panthers	MEN Arena
2000	London Knights	7-3	Newcastle Riverkings	MEN Arena
2001	Sheffield Steelers	2-1	London Knights	National Ice Centre
2002	Sheffield Steelers	3-3**	Manchester Storm	National Ice Centre
2003	Belfast Giants	5-3	London Knights	National Ice Arena

*aggregate scores (1960 – 3-2, 3-3; 1976 – 5-5, 9-3; 1977 – 9-5, 18-6; 1978 – 13-0, 10-5)
**decided by penalty shoot-out
***won in overtime

ICE
HOCKEY

ICE SKATING (FIGURE SKATING AND SPEED SKATING)

Ice skating has taken place as a pastime for thousands of years but was naturally developed in the cold belts of Scandinavia as a more competitive sport over the course of a few hundred years, beginning in the 18th century.

Until the 16th century skates were made from wood, which was waxed to give a greater gliding facility. In 1572 the first iron-bladed skates were introduced and speed skating competitions began to be held. The world's first skating club was formed in Edinburgh in 1642 and in 1850, E.W. Bushnell from Philadelphia invented the first all-iron skate. John Gamgee built the first refrigerated ice rink (the Glaciarum) in the King's Road, Chelsea, in 1876. In 1879 the National Skating Association of Great Britain was founded and in 1892 the International Skating Union (ISU), formed of 15 European nations, followed. It expanded to include Canada in 1894. The first World Championships in speed skating were held in 1893 in Amsterdam. The World Figure Skating Championships were first held in St Petersburg in 1896, the inaugural year of the modern Olympic Games, although it was not until 1908 in London that figure skating was included at the Olympics.

Olympic figure skaters compete in singles, pairs or, since 1976, in ice dancing. Pairs and singles are normally required to complete two elements: a short programme of certain prescribed moves, and free skating, where skaters perform their own combinations to music.

The greatest figure skater of all time is arguably Sonja Henie. Henie was born 8 April 1912, in Kristiana (now Oslo), Norway. She was coached by Oscar Holte who realised early on that she possessed a prodigious talent. Sonja was a great all-round athlete, winning her national championships at tennis as well as being a skilled horse rider and gymnast. In 1924, the 12-year-old Henie won the Norwegian figure skating championships and later that year competed in the inaugural Winter Olympics in Chamonix, France, coming last. In 1926 Sonja was runner-up in the World Championships but from that moment on dominated figure skating in a manner that has rarely been seen in any sport. Introducing balletic movements learnt from her favourite ballerina, Anna Pavlova, a dynamic interpretation of music and eye-catching costumes, Sonja was a class apart from her rivals. She won three successive Olympic titles (1928, 1932 and 1936) and ten successive World Championship titles (1927-36).

Cecilia Colledge of Great Britain had a tremendous tussle with Henie towards the end of the Norwegian's career but always fell short of Henie's brilliance. Sonja turned to films on her retirement and *One in a Million* (1936), her first film, made her as big a film star as she was a sports star. She died of leukaemia, 12 October 1969.

Speed skating has been a part of every Winter Olympics since their inception in 1924. Races are held on a 400m oval course and known as long track; competitors race in pairs against the clock over distances between 500m and 10,000m. Although the European nations have an excellent record at the Games, perhaps the most memorable contribution came at Lake Placid in 1980 when one man, an American, dominated. Eric Heiden (born Madison, Wisconsin, 14 June 1958), first competed at the 1976 Olympics in Innsbruck, coming seventh in the 1500m and 19th in the 5000m, but the following year began to rule the sport in an extraordinary manner. Heiden won every world title available at the time; the measure of this performance can be compared to asking a 100m track athlete to compete in the mile . . . and win! By the 1980 Olympics Heiden appeared invincible and indeed he was. He won all five gold medals and in the process smashed the world record for 10,000m (14mins 28.13secs) in his final race. His sister Beth Heiden won the bronze in the 3000m.

Long track was joined as an Olympic event by short track speed skating in 1992. Long track skaters had for some time used smaller indoor rinks in order to train all year round – short track developed from this and was formally added to the Winter Olympic programme at Albertville, France. The short-track circuit is 111.12m long and races are head-to-head – up to four racers compete against each other. The shortest race is the 500m sprint, the longest the 5000m relay for men.

The 1992 Olympic short track competition was unfortunately a little too late for the British 1991 world champion Wilf O'Reilly, who was in decline by the time of its acceptance (he had, however, won two gold medals at the 1988 games when the sport debuted as a demonstration event). Nicky Gooch of Great Britain won a bronze in the 500m sprint in 1994 in Lillehammer and was unfortunate on more than one occasion when he fell at crucial stages of his best middle-distance events.

Speed Skating (Long Track): Olympic Medallists

Men's 500m

	Gold	Silver	Bronze
1924	Charles Jewtraw (USA)	Oskar Olsen (NOR)	Roald Larsen (NOR)
			Clas Thunberg (FIN)
1928	Bernt Evensen (NOR)	——	John O'Neil Farrell (USA)
	Clas Thunberg (FIN)		Jaako Friman (FIN)
			Roald Larsen (NOR)
1932	John Shea (USA)	Bernt Evensen (NOR)	Aleksandr Hurd (CAN)
1936	Ivar Ballangrud (NOR)	Georg Krog (NOR)	Leo Freisinger (USA)
1948	Finn Helgesen (NOR)	Kenneth Bartholomew (USA)	——
		Thomas Byberg (NOR)	
		Robert Fitzgerald (USA)	
1952	Kenneth Henry (USA)	Donald McDermott (USA)	Gordon Audley (CAN)
			Arne Johansen (NOR)
1956	Yevgeny Grishin (URS)	Rafael Gratch (URS)	Alv Gjestvang (NOR)
1960	Yevgeny Grishin (URS)	William Disney (USA)	Rafael Gratch (URS)
1964	Richard 'Terry' McDermott (USA)	Alv Gjestvang (NOR)	——
		Yevgeny Grishin (URS)	
		Vladimir Orlov (URS)	
1968	Erhard Keller (FRG)	Richard 'Terry' McDermott (USA)	——
		Magne Thomassen (NOR)	
1972	Erhard Keller (FRG)	Hasse Börjes (SWE)	Valeriy Muratov (URS)
1976	Yevgeny Kulikov (URS)	Valeriy Muratov (URS)	Daniel Immerfall (USA)
1980	Eric Heiden (USA)	Yevgeny Kulikov (URS)	Lieuwe de Boer (NED)
1984	Sergey Fokichev (URS)	Yoshihiro Kitazawa (JPN)	Gaétan Boucher (CAN)
1988	Uwe-Jens Mey (GDR)	Jan Ykema (NED)	Akira Kuroiwa (JPN)
1992	Uwe-Jens Mey (GDR)	Toshiyuki Kuroiwa (JPN)	Junichi Inoue (JPN)
1994	Aleksandr Golubev (RUS)	Sergey Klevchenya (RUS)	Manabu Horii (JPN)
1998	Hiroyasu Shimizu (JPN)	Jeremy Wotherspoon (CAN)	Kevin Overland (CAN)
2002	Casey FitzRandolph (USA)	Hiroyasu Shimizu (JPN)	Kip Carpenter (USA)

Men's 1000m

	Gold	Silver	Bronze
1976	Peter Mueller (USA)	Jørn Didriksen (NOR)	Valeriy Muratov (URS)
1980	Eric Heiden (USA)	Gaétan Boucher (CAN)	Vladimir Lobanov (URS)
			Frode Rønning (NOR)
1984	Gaétan Boucher (CAN)	Sergey Khlebnikov (URS)	Kai Arne Engelstad (NOR)
1988	Nikolay Gulyaev (URS)	Uwe-Jens Mey (GDR)	Igor Zhelezovsky (URS)
1992	Olaf Zinke (GER)	Kim Yoon-Man (KOR)	Yukinori Miyabe (JPN)
1994	Dan Jansen (USA)	Igor Zhelezovsky (BLR)	Sergey Klevchenya (RUS)
1998	Ids Postma (NED)	Jan Bos (NED)	Hiroyasu Shimizu (JPN)
2002	Gerard van Velde (NED)	Jan Bos (NED)	Joey Cheek (USA)

Men's 1500m

	Gold	Silver	Bronze
1924	Clas Thunberg (FIN)	Roald Larsen (NOR)	Sigurd Moen (NOR)
1928	Clas Thunberg (FIN)	Bernt Evensen (NOR)	Ivar Ballangrud (NOR)
1932	John Shea (USA)	Aleksandr Hurd (CAN)	William Logan (CAN)
1936	Charles Mathisen (NOR)	Ivar Ballangrud (NOR)	Birger Wasenius (FIN)
1948	Sverre Farstad (NOR)	Åke Seyffarth (SWE)	Odd Lundberg (NOR)
1952	Hjalmar Andersen (NOR)	Willem van der Voort (NED)	Roald Aas (NOR)
1956	Yevgeny Grishin (URS)	——	Toivo Salonen (FIN)
	Yuriy Mikhailov (URS)		
1960	Roald Aas (NOR)	——	Boris Stenin (URS)
	Yevgeny Grishin (URS)		
1964	Ants Antson (URS)	Kees Verkerk (NED)	Willy Haugen (NOR)
1968	Kees Verkerk (NED)	Ivar Eriksen (NOR)	——
		Ard Schenk (NED)	
1972	Ard Schenk (NED)	Roar Grønvold (NOR)	Göran Claesson (SWE)
1976	Jan Egil Storholt (NOR)	Yuriy Kondakov (URS)	Hans van Helden (NED)
1980	Eric Heiden (USA)	Kay Arne Stenshjemmet (NOR)	Terje Andersen (NOR)
1984	Gaétan Boucher (CAN)	Sergey Khlebnikov (URS)	Oleg Bozhyev (URS)

ICE SKATING

1988	André Hoffmann (GDR)	Eric Flaim (USA)	Michael Hadschieff (AUT)
1992	Johan Olav Koss (NOR)	Ådne Søndrål (NOR)	Leo Visser (NED)
1994	Johan Olav Koss (NOR)	Rintje Ritsma (NED)	Falko Zandstra (NED)
1998	Ådne Søndrål (NOR)	Ids Postma (NED)	Rintje Ritsma (NED)
2002	Derek Parra (USA)	Jochem Uytdehaage (NED)	Ådne Søndrål (NOR)

Men's 5000m

	Gold	Silver	Bronze
1924	Clas Thunberg (FIN)	Julius Skutnabb (FIN)	Roald Larsen (NOR)
1928	Ivar Ballangrud (NOR)	Julius Skutnabb (FIN)	Bernt Evensen (NOR)
1932	Irving Jaffee (USA)	Edward Murphy (USA)	William Logan (CAN)
1936	Ivar Ballangrud (NOR)	Birger Wasenius (FIN)	Antero Ojala (FIN)
1948	Reidar Liaklev (NOR)	Odd Lundberg (NOR)	Göthe Hedlund (SWE)
1952	Hjalmar Andersen (NOR)	Kees Broekman (NED)	Sverre Haugli (NOR)
1956	Boris Shilkov (URS)	Sigvard Ericsson (SWE)	Oleg Goncharenko (URS)
1960	Viktor Kosichkin (URS)	Knut Johannesen (NOR)	Jan Pesman (NED)
1964	Knut Johannesen (NOR)	Per Ivar Moe (NOR)	Fred Anton Maier (NOR)
1968	Fred Anton Maier (NOR)	Kees Verkerk (NED)	Petrus Nottet (NED)
1972	Ard Schenk (NED)	Roar Grønvold (NOR)	Sten Stensen (NOR)
1976	Sten Stensen (NOR)	Piet Kleine (NED)	Hans van Helden (NED)
1980	Eric Heiden (USA)	Kay Arne Stenshjemmet (NOR)	Tom Erik Oxholm (NOR)
1984	Tomas Gustafson (SWE)	Igor Malkov (URS)	René Schöfisch (GDR)
1988	Tomas Gustafson (SWE)	Leo Visser (NED)	Gerard Kemkers (NED)
1992	Geir Karlstad (NOR)	Falko Zandstra (NED)	Leo Visser (NED)
1994	Johan Olav Koss (NOR)	Kjell Storelid (NOR)	Rintje Ritsma (NED)
1998	Gianni Romme (NED)	Rintje Ritsma (NED)	Bart Veldkamp (BEL)
2002	Jochem Uytdehaage (NED)	Derek Parra (USA)	Jens Boden (GER)

Men's 10,000m

	Gold	Silver	Bronze
1924	Julius Skutnabb (FIN)	Clas Thunberg (FIN)	Roald Larsen (NOR)
1928	Irving Jaffee (USA)	Bernt Evensen (NOR)	Otto Polacsek (AUT)
1932	Irving Jaffee (USA)	Ivar Ballangrud (NOR)	Frank Stack (CAN)
1936	Ivar Ballangrud (NOR)	Birger Wasenius (FIN)	Max Stiepl (AUT)
1948	Åke Seyffarth (SWE)	Lauri Parkkinen (FIN)	Pentti Lammio (FIN)
1952	Hjalmar Andersen (NOR)	Kees Broekman (NED)	Carl-Erik Asplund (SWE)
1956	Sigvard Ericsson (SWE)	Knut Johannesen (NOR)	Oleg Goncharenko (URS)
1960	Knut Johannesen (NOR)	Viktor Kosichkin (URS)	Kjell Bäckman (SWE)
1964	Jonny Nilsson (SWE)	Fred Anton Maier (NOR)	Knut Johannesen (NOR)
1968	Johnny Höglin (SWE)	Fred Anton Maier (NOR)	Örjan Sandler (SWE)
1972	Ard Schenk (NED)	Kees Verkerk (NED)	Sten Stensen (NOR)
1976	Piet Kleine (NED)	Sten Stensen (NOR)	Hans van Helden (NED)
1980	Eric Heiden (USA)	Piet Kleine (NED)	Tom Erik Oxholm (NOR)
1984	Igor Malkov (URS)	Tomas Gustafson (SWE)	René Schöfisch (GDR)
1988	Tomas Gustafson (SWE)	Michael Hadschieff (AUT)	Leo Visser (NED)
1992	Bart Veldkamp (NED)	Johan Olav Koss (NOR)	Geir Karlstad (NOR)
1994	Johan Olav Koss (NOR)	Kjell Storelid (NOR)	Bart Veldkamp (NED)
1998	Gianni Romme (NED)	Bob de Jong (NED)	Rintje Ritsma (NED)
2002	Jochem Uytdehaage (NED)	Gianni Romme (NED)	Lasse Sætre (NOR)

Men's Combined (discontinued)

	Gold	Silver	Bronze
1924	Clas Thunberg (FIN)	Roald Larsen (NOR)	Julius Skutnabb (FIN)

Women's 500m

	Gold	Silver	Bronze
1960	Helga Haase (GDR)	Natalya Donchenko (URS)	Jeanne Ashworth (USA)
1964	Lidya Skoblikova (URS)	Irina Yegorova (URS)	Tatyana Sidorova (URS)
1968	Lyudmila Titova (URS)	Jennifer Fish (USA)	——
		Dianne Holum (USA)	
		Mary Meyers (USA)	
1972	Anne Henning (USA)	Vera Krasnova (URS)	Lyudmila Titova (URS)
1976	Sheila Young (USA)	Cathy Priestner (CAN)	Tatyana Averina (URS)
1980	Karin Enke (GDR)	Leah Mueller (USA)	Natalya Petruseva (URS)

1984	Christa Rothenburger (GDR)	Karin Enke (GDR)	Natalya Chive (URS)
1988	Bonnie Blair (USA)	Christa Rothenburger (GDR)	Karin (Enke) Kania (GDR)
1992	Bonnie Blair (USA)	Ye Qiaobo (CHN)	Christa (Rothenburger) Luding (GER)
1994	Bonnie Blair (USA)	Susan Auch (CAN)	Franziska Schenk (GER)
1998	Catriona LeMay Doan (CAN)	Susan Auch (CAN)	Tomomi Okazaki (JPN)
2002	Catriona LeMay Doan (CAN)	Monique Garbrecht-Enfeldt (GER)	Sabine Völker (GER)

Women's 1000m

	Gold	**Silver**	**Bronze**
1960	Klara Guseva (URS)	Helga Haase (GDR)	Tamara Rylova (URS)
1964	Lidya Skoblikova (URS)	Irina Yegorova (URS)	Kaija Mustonen (FIN)
1968	Carry Geijssen (NED)	Lyudmila Titova (URS)	Dianne Holum (USA)
1972	Monika Pflug (FRG)	Atje Keulen-Deelstra (NED)	Anne Henning (USA)
1976	Tatyana Averina (URS)	Leah Poulos (USA)	Sheila Young (USA)
1980	Natalya Petruseva (URS)	Leah (Poulos) Mueller (USA)	Silvia Albrecht (GDR)
1984	Karin Enke (GDR)	Andrea Schöne (GDR)	Natalya Petruseva (URS)
1988	Christa Rothenburger (GDR)	Karin (Enke) Kania (GDR)	Bonnie Blair (USA)
1992	Bonnie Blair (USA)	Ye Qiaobo (CHN)	Monique Garbrecht (GER)
1994	Bonnie Blair (USA)	Anke Baier (GER)	Ye Qiaobo (CHN)
1998	Marianne Timmer (NED)	Chris Witty (USA)	Catriona LeMay Doan (CAN)
2002	Chris Witty (USA)	Sabine Völker (GER)	Jennifer Rodriguez (USA)

Women's 1500m

	Gold	**Silver**	**Bronze**
1960	Lidya Skoblikova (URS)	Elwira Seroczynska (POL)	Helena Pilejczyk (POL)
1964	Lidya Skoblikova (URS)	Kaija Mustonen (FIN)	Berta Kolokoltseva (URS)
1968	Kaija Mustonen (FIN)	Carry Geijssen (NED)	Christina 'Stien' Kaiser (NED)
1972	Dianne Holum (USA)	Christina 'Stien' Baas-Kaiser (NED)	Atje Keulen-Deelstra (NED)
1976	Galina Stepanskaya (URS)	Sheila Young (USA)	Tatyana Averina (URS)
1980	Annie Borckink (NED)	Ria Visser (NED)	Sabine Becker (GDR)
1984	Karin Enke (GDR)	Andrea Schöne (GDR)	Natalya Petruseva (URS)
1988	Yvonne van Gennip (NED)	Karin (Enke) Kania (GDR)	Andrea Ehrig (Schöne) (GDR)
1992	Jacqueline Börner (GER)	Gunda Niemann-Kleemann (GER)	Seiko Hashimoto (JPN)
1994	Emese Hunyady (AUT)	Svetlana Fedotkina (RUS)	Gunda Niemann-Kleemann (GER)
1998	Marianne Timmer (NED)	Gunda Niemann-Stirnemann (GER)	Chris Witty (USA)
2002	Anni Friesinger (GER)	Sabine Völker (GER)	Jennifer Rodriguez (USA)

Women's 3000m

	Gold	**Silver**	**Bronze**
1960	Lidya Skoblikova (URS)	Valentina Stenina (URS)	Eevi Huttunen (FIN)
1964	Lidya Skoblikova (URS)	Han Pil-Hwa (PRK) Valentina Stenina (URS)	——
1968	Johanna 'Ans' Schut (NED)	Kaija Mustonen (FIN)	Christina 'Stien' Kaiser (NED)
1972	Christina 'Stien' Baas-Kaiser (NED)	Dianne Holum (USA)	Atje Keulen-Deelstra (NED)
1976	Tatyana Averina (URS)	Andrea Mitscherlich (GDR)	Lisbeth Korsmo (NOR)
1980	Bjørg Eva Jensen (NOR)	Sabine Becker (GDR)	Beth Heiden (USA)
1984	Andrea Schöne (Mitscherlich) (GDR)	Karin Enke (GDR)	Gabi Schönbrunn (GDR)
1988	Yvonne van Gennip (NED)	Andrea (Schöne) Ehrig (GDR)	Gabi (Schönbrunn) Zange (GDR)
1992	Gunda Niemann-Kleemann (GER)	Heike Warnicke (GER)	Emese Hunyady (AUT)
1994	Svetlana Bazhanova (RUS)	Emese Hunyady (AUT)	Claudia Pechstein (GER)
1998	Gunda Niemann-Stirnemann (GER)	Claudia Pechstein (GER)	Anni Friesinger (GER)
2002	Claudia Pechstein (GER)	Renate Groenewold (NED)	Cindy Klassen (CAN)

Women's 5000m

	Gold	**Silver**	**Bronze**
1988	Yvonne van Gennip (NED)	Andrea Ehrig (GDR)	Gabi Zange (GDR)
1992	Gunda Niemann-Kleemann (GER)	Heike Warnicke (GER)	Claudia Pechstein (GER)
1994	Claudia Pechstein (GER)	Gunda Niemann-Kleemann (GER)	Hiromi Yamamoto (JPN)
1998	Claudia Pechstein (GER)	Gunda Niemann-Stirnemann (GER)	Lyudmila Prokasheva (KAZ)
2002	Claudia Pechstein (GER)	Gretha Smit (NED)	Clara Hughes (CAN)

ICE SKATING

Speed Skating (Short Track): Olympic Medallists

Men's 500m

	Gold	Silver	Bronze
1994	Chae Ji-Hoon (KOR)	Mirko Vuillermin (ITA)	Nicky Gooch (GBR)
1998	Takafumi Nishitani (JPN)	An Yulong (CHN)	Hitoshi Uematsu (JPN)
2002	Marc Gagnon (CAN)	Jonathan Guilmette (CAN)	Rusty Smith (USA)

Men's 1000m

	Gold	Silver	Bronze
1992	Kim Ki-Hoon (KOR)	Frédéric Blackburn (CAN)	Lee Joon-Ho (KOR)
1994	Kim Ki-Hoon (KOR)	Chae Ji-Hoon (KOR)	Marc Gagnon (CAN)
1998	Kim Dong-Sung (KOR)	Li Jiajun (CHN)	Éric Bédard (CAN)
2002	Steven Bradbury (AUS)	Apolo Anton Ohno (USA)	Mathieu Turcotte (CAN)

Men's 1500m

	Gold	Silver	Bronze
2002	Apolo Anton Ohno (USA)	Li Jiajun (CHN)	Marc Gagnon (CAN)

Men's 5000m Relay

	Gold	Silver	Bronze
1992	South Korea	Canada	Japan
1994	Italy	United States	Australia
1998	Canada	South Korea	China
2002	Canada	Italy	China

Women's 500m

	Gold	Silver	Bronze
1992	Cathy Turner (USA)	Li Yan (CHN)	Hwang Ok-Sil (PRK)
1994	Cathy Turner (USA)	Zhang Yanmei (CHN)	Amy Peterson (USA)
1998	Annie Perreault (CAN)	Yang Yang (S) (CHN)*	Chun Lee-Kyung (KOR)
2002	Yang Yang (A) (CHN)	Evgenia Radanova (BUL)	Wang Chunlu (CHN)

Women's 1000m

	Gold	Silver	Bronze
1994	Chun Lee-Kyung (KOR)	Nathalie Lambert (CAN)	Kim So-Hee (KOR)
1998	Chun Lee-Kyung (KOR)	Yang Yang (S) (CHN)	Won Hye-Kyung (KOR)
2002	Yang Yang (A) (CHN)	Ko Gi-Hyun (KOR)	Yang Yang (S) (CHN)

Women's 1500m

	Gold	Silver	Bronze
2002	Ko Gi-Hyun (KOR)	Choi Eun-Kyung (KOR)	Evgenia Radanova (BUL)

Women's 3000m Relay

	Gold	Silver	Bronze
1992	Canada	United States	CIS
1994	South Korea	Canada	United States
1998	South Korea	China	Canada
2002	South Korea	China	Canada

*The two Yang Yangs in the Chinese team were suffixed '(A)' and '(S)' to distinguish them.

Figure Skating: Olympic Medallists

Men's Singles

	Gold	Silver	Bronze
1908	Ulrich Salchow (SWE)	Richard Johannson (SWE)	Per Thorén (SWE)
1920	Gillis Grafström (SWE)	Andreas Krogh (NOR)	Martin Stixrud (NOR)
1924	Gillis Grafström (SWE)	Willy Böckl (AUT)	Georges Gautschi (SUI)
1928	Gillis Grafström (SWE)	Willy Böckl (AUT)	Robert von Zeebroeck (BEL)
1932	Karl Schäfer (AUT)	Gillis Grafström (SWE)	Montgomery Wilson (CAN)
1936	Karl Schäfer (AUT)	Ernst Baier (GER)	Felix Kaspar (AUT)
1948	Dick Button (USA)	Hans Gerschwiler (SUI)	Edi Rada (AUT)
1952	Dick Button (USA)	Helmut Seibt (AUT)	James Grogan (USA)
1956	Hayes Alan Jenkins (USA)	Ronnie Robertson (USA)	David Jenkins (USA)
1960	David Jenkins (USA)	Karol Divin (TCH)	Don Jackson (CAN)
1964	Manfred Schnelldorfer (GDR)	Alain Calmat (FRA)	Scott Allen (USA)
1968	Wolfgang Schwarz (AUT)	Tim Wood (USA)	Patrick Pera (FRA)
1972	Ondrej Nepela (TCH)	Sergey Chetveroukhin (URS)	Patrick Pera (FRA)
1976	John Curry (GBR)	Vladimir Kovalev (URS)	Toller Cranston (CAN)
1980	Robin Cousins (GBR)	Jan Hoffman (GDR)	Charles Tickner (USA)
1984	Scott Hamilton (USA)	Brian Orser (CAN)	Josef Sbovcík (TCH)
1988	Brian Boltano (USA)	Brian Orser (CAN)	Viktor Petrenko (URS)
1992	Viktor Petrenko (CIS)	Paul Wylie (USA)	Petr Barna (TCH)
1994	Aleksey Umanov (RUS)	Elvis Stojko (CAN)	Philippe Candeloro (FRA)
1998	Ilya Kulik (RUS)	Elvis Stojko (CAN)	Philippe Candeloro (FRA)
2002	Aleksey Yagudin (RUS)	Yevgeny Plushenko (RUS)	Timothy Goebel (USA)

Men's Special Figures (discontinued)

	Gold	Silver	Bronze
1908	Nikolay Panin (Kolomenkin) (URS)	Arthur Cumming (GBR)	Geoffrey Hall-Say (GBR)

Women's Singles

	Gold	Silver	Bronze
1908	Florence 'Madge' Syers (GBR)	Eisa Rendschmidt (GER)	Dorothy Greenhough-Smith (GBR)
1912	not held		
1920	Magda Julin-Mauroy (SWE)	Svea Norén (SWE)	Theresa Weld (USA)
1924	Herma Szabó (AUT)	Beatrix Loughran (USA)	Ethel Muckelt (GBR)
1928	Sonja Henie (NOR)	Fritzi Burger (AUT)	Beatrix Loughran (USA)
1932	Sonja Henie (NOR)	Fritzi Burger (AUT)	Maribel Vinson (USA)
1936	Sonja Henie (NOR)	Cecilia Colledge (GBR)	Vivi-Anne Hultén (SWE)
1948	Barbara Ann Scott (CAN)	Eva Pawlik (AUT)	Jeannette Altwegg (GBR)
1952	Jeannette Altwegg (GBR)	Tenley Albright (USA)	Jacqueline du Bief (FRA)
1956	Tenley Albright (USA)	Carol Heiss (USA)	Ingrid Wendl (AUT)
1960	Carol Heiss (USA)	Sjoukje Dijkstra (NED)	Barbara Roles (USA)
1964	Sjoukje Dijkstra (NED)	Regine Heitzer (AUT)	Petra Burka (CAN)
1968	Peggy Fleming (USA)	Gabriele Seyfert (GDR)	Hana Masková (TCH)
1972	Beatrix Schuba (AUT)	Karen Magnussen (CAN)	Janet Lynn (USA)
1976	Dorothy Hamill (USA)	Dianne de Leeuw (NED)	Christine Errath (GDR)
1980	Anett Pötzsch (GDR)	Linda Fratianne (USA)	Dagmar Lurz (FRG)
1984	Katarina Witt (GDR)	Rosalynn Sumners (USA)	Kira Ivanova (URS)
1988	Katarina Witt (GDR)	Elizabeth Manley (CAN)	Debra Thomas (USA)
1992	Kristi Yamaguchi (USA)	Midori Ito (JPN)	Nancy Kerrigan (USA)
1994	Oksana 'Pasha' Baiul (UKR)	Nancy Kerrigan (USA)	Chen Lu (CHN)
1998	Tara Lipinski (USA)	Michelle Kwan (USA)	Chen Lu (CHN)
2002	Sarah Hughes (USA)	Irina Slutskaya (RUS)	Michelle Kwan (USA)

Pairs

	Gold	Silver	Bronze
1908	Anna Hübler/Heinrich Burger (GDR)	Phyllis Johnson/James Johnson (GBR)	Florence 'Madge' Syers/Edgar Syers (GBR)
1912	not held		
1920	Ludovika Jakobsson-Eilers/ Walter Jakobsson (FIN)	Alexia Bryn-Schøyen/ Yngvar Bryn (NOR)	Phyllis Johnson/Basil Williams (GBR)

ICE SKATING

1924	Helene Engelmann/ Alfred Berger (AUT)	Ludovika Jakobsson-Eilers/ Walter Jakobsson (FIN)	Andrée Joly/Pierre Brunet (FRA)
1928	Andrée Joly/Pierre Brunet (FRA)	Lilly Scholz/Otto Kaiser (AUT)	Melitta Brunner/Ludwig Wrede (AUT)
1932	Andrée (Joly) Brunet/ Pierre Brunet (FRA)	Beatrix Loughran/ Sherwin Badger (USA)	Emília Ratter/László Szollás (HUN)
1936	Maxi Herber/Ernst Baier (GDR)	Ilse Pausin/Erik Pausin (AUT)	Emília Rotter/László Szollás (HUN)
1948	Micheline Lannoy/ Pierre Baugniet (BEL)	Andrea Kékessy/Ede Király (HUN)	Suzanne Morrow/ Wallace Diestelmeyer (CAN)
1952	Ria Falk/Paul Falk (GDR)	Karol Kennedy/Michael Kennedy (USA)	Marianna Nagy/László Nagy (HUN)
1956	Elisabeth Schwartz/ Kurt Oppelt (AUT)	Frances Dafoe/ Norris Bowden (CAN)	Marianna Nagy/László Nagy (HUN)
1960	Barbara Wagner/Bob Paul (CAN)	Marika Kilius/ Hans-Jürgen Bäumler (GDR)	Nancy Ludington/Ronald Ludington (CAN)
1964	Lyudmila Belousova/ Oleg Protopopov (URS)	Marika Kilius/ Hans-Jürgen Bäumler (GDR)	Debbi Wilkes/Guy Revell (CAN)
1968	Lyudmila Belousova/ Oleg Protopopov (URS)	Tatyana Zhuk/Aleksandr Gorelik (URS)	Margot Glockshuber/ Wolfgang Danne (FRG)
1972	Irina Rodnina/ Aleksey Ulanov (URS)	Lyudmila Smirnov/ Andrey Suraikin (URS)	Manuela Gross/Uwe Kagelmann (GDR)
1976	Irina Rodnina/ Aleksandr Zaitsev (URS)	Romy Kermer/Rolf Österreich (GDR)	Manuela Gross/Uwe Kagelmann (GDR)
1980	Irina Rodnina/ Aleksandr Zaitsev (URS)	Marina Cherkosova/ Sergey Shakrai (URS)	Manuela Mager/ Uwe Bewersdorff (GDR)
1984	Yelena Valova/Oleg Vasilyev (URS)	Caitlin 'Kitty' Carruthers/ Peter Carruthers (USA)	Larisa Selezneva/Oleg Makarov (URS)
1988	Yekaterina Gordeyeva/ Sergey Grinkov (URS)	Yelena Valova/Oleg Vasilyev (URS)	Jill Watson/Peter Oppegard (USA)
1992	Natalya Mishkutenok/ Artur Dmitriev (CIS)	Yelena Bechke/Denis Petrov (CIS)	Isabelle Brasseur/Lloyd Eisler (CAN)
1994	Yekaterina Gordeyeva/ Sergey Grinkov (RUS)	Natalya Mishkutenok/ Artur Dmitriev (RUS)	Isabelle Brasseur/Lloyd Eisler (CAN)
1998	Oksana Kazakova/ Artur Dmitriyev (RUS)	Yelena Berezhnaya/ Anton Sikharulidze (RUS)	Mandy Wötzel/Ingo Steuer (GER)
2002	Yelena Berezhnaya/ Anton Sikharulidze (URS) Jamie Salé/David Pelletier (CAN)*	——	Shen Xue/Zhao Hongbo (CHN)

*Salé and Pelletier were originally placed second, but were later awarded a gold medal because of judging irregularities.

Ice Dance

	Gold	Silver	Bronze
1976	Lyudmila Pakhomova/ Aleksandr Gorshkov (URS)	Irina Moiseyeva/Andrey Minenkov (URS)	Colleen O'Connor/James Millns (USA)
1980	Natalya Linichuk/ Gennadiy Karponosov (URS)	Krisztina Regöczy/András Sallay (HUN)	Irina Moiseyeva/ Andrey Minenkov (URS)
1984	Jayne Torvill/ Christopher Dean (GBR)	Natalya Bestemianova/Andrey Bukin (URS)	Marina Klimova/ Sergey Ponomarenko (URS)
1988	Natalya Bestemianova/ Andrey Bukin (URS)	Marina Klimova/ Sergey Ponomarenko (URS)	Tracy Wilson/Rob McCall (CAN)
1992	Marina Klimova/ Sergey Ponomarenko (CIS)	Isabelle Duchesnay-Dean/ Paul Duchesnay (FRA)	Maia Usova/Aleksandr Zhulin (CIS)
1994	Oksana Grischuk/ Yevgeny Platov (RUS)	Maia Usova/Aleksandr Zhulin (RUS)	Jayne Torvill/Christopher Dean (GBR)
1998	Oksana Grischuk/ Yevgeny Platov (RUS)	Anzhelika Krylova/Oleg Ovsyannikov (RUS)	Marina Anissina/ Gwendal Peizerat (FRA)
2002	Marina Anissina/ Gwendal Peizerat (FRA)	Irena Lobicheva/Iliya Averbukh (RUS)	Barbara Fusar Poli/ Maurizio Margaglio (ITA)

Figure Skating: World Champions

Men's Singles

1896	Gilbert Fuchs (GER)	1935	Karl Schäfer (AUT)	1974	Jan Hoffman (GDR)
1897	Gustav Hügel (AUT)	1936	Karl Schäfer (AUT)	1975	Sergey Volkov (URS)
1898	Henning Grenander (SWE)	1937	Felix Kaspar (AUT)	1976	John Curry (GBR)
1899	Gustav Hügel (AUT)	1938	Felix Kaspar (AUT)	1977	Vladimir Kovalev (URS)
1900	Gustav Hügel (AUT)	1939	Graham Sharp (GBR)	1978	Charles Tickner (USA)
1901	Ulrich Salchow (SWE)	1940-46	not held	1979	Vladimir Kovalev (URS)
1902	Ulrich Salchow (SWE)	1947	Hans Gerschwiler (SUI)	1980	Jan Hoffman (GDR)
1903	Ulrich Salchow (SWE)	1948	Dick Button (USA)	1981	Scott Hamilton (USA)
1904	Ulrich Salchow (SWE)	1949	Dick Button (USA)	1982	Scott Hamilton (USA)
1905	Ulrich Salchow (SWE)	1950	Dick Button (USA)	1983	Scott Hamilton (USA)
1906	Gilbert Fuchs (GER)	1951	Dick Button (USA)	1984	Scott Hamilton (USA)
1907	Ulrich Salchow (SWE)	1952	Dick Button (USA)	1985	Aleksandr Fadeev (URS)
1908	Ulrich Salchow (SWE)	1953	Hayes Alan Jenkins (USA)	1986	Brian Boitano (USA)
1909	Ulrich Salchow (SWE)	1954	Hayes Alan Jenkins (USA)	1987	Brian Orser (CAN)
1910	Ulrich Salchow (SWE)	1955	Hayes Alan Jenkins (USA)	1988	Brian Boitano (USA)
1911	Ulrich Salchow (SWE)	1956	Hayes Alan Jenkins (USA)	1989	Kurt Browning (CAN)
1912	Fritz Kachler (AUT)	1957	David Jenkins (USA)	1990	Kurt Browning (CAN)
1913	Fritz Kachler (AUT)	1958	David Jenkins (USA)	1991	Kurt Browning (CAN)
1914	Gösta Sandahl (SWE)	1959	David Jenkins (USA)	1992	Viktor Petrenko (CIS)
1915-21	not held	1960	Alain Giletti (FRA)	1993	Kurt Browning (CAN)
1922	Gillis Grafström (SWE)	1961	not held	1994	Elvis Stojko (CAN)
1923	Fritz Kachler (AUT)	1962	Donald Jackson (CAN)	1995	Elvis Stojko (CAN)
1924	Gillis Grafström (SWE)	1963	Don McPherson (CAN)	1996	Todd Eldredge (USA)
1925	Willy Böckl (AUT)	1964	Manfred Schnelldorfer (GDR)	1997	Elvis Stojko (CAN)
1926	Willy Böckl (AUT)	1965	Alain Calmat (FRA)	1998	Aleksey Yagudin (URS)
1927	Willy Böckl (AUT)	1966	Emmerich Danzer (AUT)	1999	Aleksey Yagudin (URS)
1928	Willy Böckl (AUT)	1967	Emmerich Danzer (AUT)	2000	Aleksey Yagudin (URS)
1929	Gillis Grafström (SWE)	1968	Emmerich Danzer (AUT)	2001	Yvgeny Plushenko (URS)
1930	Karl Schäfer (AUT)	1969	Tim Wood (USA)	2002	Aleksey Yagudin (URS)
1931	Karl Schäfer (AUT)	1970	Tim Wood (USA)	2003	Yevgeny Plushenko (URS)
1932	Karl Schäfer (AUT)	1971	Ondrej Nepela (TCH)	2004	Yevgeny Plushenko (URS)
1933	Karl Schäfer (AUT)	1972	Ondrej Nepela (TCH)		
1934	Karl Schäfer (AUT)	1973	Ondrej Nepela (TCH)		

Women's Singles

1906	Florence 'Madge' Syers (GBR)	1939	Megan Taylor (GBR)	1975	Dianne de Leeuw (NED)
1907	Florence 'Madge' Syers (GBR)	1940-46	not held	1976	Dorothy Hamill (USA)
1908	Lily Kronberger (HUN)	1947	Barbara Ann Scott (CAN)	1977	Linda Fratianne (USA)
1909	Lily Kronberger (HUN)	1948	Barbara Ann Scott (CAN)	1978	Anett Pötzsch (GDR)
1910	Lily Kronberger (HUN)	1949	Alena Vrzánová (TCH)	1979	Linda Fratianne (USA)
1911	Lily Kronberger (HUN)	1950	Alena Vrzánová (TCH)	1980	Anett Pötzsch (GDR)
1912	Opika von Méray Horváth (HUN)	1951	Jeannette Altwegg (GBR)	1981	Denise Biellmann (SUI)
1913	Opika von Méray Horváth (HUN)	1952	Jacqueline du Bief (FRA)	1982	Elaine Zayak (USA)
1914	Opika von Méray Horváth (HUN)	1953	Tenley Albright (USA)	1983	Rosalynn Sumners (USA)
1915-21	not held	1954	Gundi Busch (FRA)	1984	Katarina Witt (GDR)
1922	Herma Szabó (AUT)	1955	Tenley Albright (USA)	1985	Katarina Witt (GDR)
1923	Herma Szabó (AUT)	1956	Carol Heiss (USA)	1986	Debra Thomas (USA)
1924	Herma Szabó (AUT)	1957	Carol Heiss (USA)	1987	Katarina Witt (GDR)
1925	Herma Szabó (AUT)	1958	Carol Heiss (USA)	1988	Katarina Witt (GDR)
1926	Herma Szabó (AUT)	1959	Carol Heiss (USA)	1989	Midori Ito (JPN)
1927	Sonja Henie (NOR)	1960	Carol Heiss (USA)	1990	Jill Trenary (USA)
1928	Sonja Henie (NOR)	1961	not held	1991	Kristi Yamaguchi (USA)
1929	Sonja Henie (NOR)	1962	Sjoukje Dijkstra (NED)	1992	Kristi Yamaguchi (USA)
1930	Sonja Henie (NOR)	1963	Sjoukje Dijkstra (NED)	1993	Oksana Baiul (UKR)
1931	Sonja Henie (NOR)	1964	Sjoukje Dijkstra (NED)	1994	Yuka Sato (JPN)
1932	Sonja Henie (NOR)	1965	Petra Burka (CAN)	1995	Lu Chen (CHN)
1933	Sonja Henie (NOR)	1966	Peggy Fleming (USA)	1996	Michelle Kwan (USA)
1934	Sonja Henie (NOR)	1967	Peggy Fleming (USA)	1997	Tara Lipinski (USA)
1935	Sonja Henie (NOR)	1968	Peggy Fleming (USA)	1998	Michelle Kwan (USA)
1936	Sonja Henie (NOR)	1969	Gabriele Seyfert (GDR)	1999	Maria Butyrskaya (RUS)
1937	Cecilia Colledge (GBR)	1970	Gabriele Seyfert (GDR)	2000	Michelle Kwan (USA)
1938	Megan Taylor (GBR)	1971	Beatrix Schuba (AUT)	2001	Michelle Kwan (USA)
		1972	Beatrix Schuba (AUT)	2002	Irina Slutskaya (RUS)
		1973	Karen Magnussen (CAN)	2003	Michelle Kwan (USA)
		1974	Christine Errath (GDR)	2004	Shizuka Arakawa (JPN)

ICE SKATING

Pairs

1908	Anna Hübler/Heinrich Burger (GER)	1963	Marika Kilius/Hans-Jürgen Bäumler (GDR)
1909	Phyllis Johnson/James H. Johnson (GBR)	1964	Marika Kilius/Hans-Jürgen Bäumler (GDR)
1910	Anna Hübler/Heinrich Burger (GER)	1965	Lyudmila Belousova/Oleg Protopopov (URS)
1911	Ludovika Eilers/Walter Jakobsson (GER)	1966	Lyudmila Belousova/Oleg Protopopov (URS)
1912	Phyllis Johnson/James Johnson (GBR)	1967	Lyudmila Belousova/Oleg Protopopov (URS)
1913	Helene Engelmann/Karl Mejstrik (AUT)	1968	Lyudmila Belousova/Oleg Protopopov (URS)
1914	Ludovika Jakobsson/Walter Jakobsson (FIN)	1969	Irina Rodnina/Alexey Ulanov (URS)
1922	Helene Engelmann/Alfred Berger (AUT)	1970	Irina Rodnina/Alexey Ulanov (URS)
1923	Ludovika Jakobsson/Walter Jakobsson (FIN)	1971	Irina Rodnina/Alexey Ulanov (URS)
1924	Helene Engelmann/Alfred Berger (AUT)	1972	Irina Rodnina/Alexey Ulanov (URS)
1925	Herma Szabó/Ludwig Wrede (HUN)	1973	Irina Rodnina/Aleksandr Zaitsev (URS)
1926	Andrée Joly/Pierre Brunet (FRA)	1974	Irina Rodnina/Aleksandr Zaitsev (URS)
1927	Herma Szabó/Ludwig Wrede (HUN)	1975	Irina Rodnina/Aleksandr Zaitsev (URS)
1928	Andrée Joly/Pierre Brunet (FRA)	1976	Irina Rodnina/Aleksandr Zaitsev (URS)
1929	Lilly Scholz/Otto Kaiser (AUT)	1977	Irina Rodnina/Aleksandr Zaitsev (URS)
1930	Andrée Brunet/Pierre Brunet (FRA)	1978	Irina Rodnina/Aleksandr Zaitsev (URS)
1931	Emília Rotter/László Szollás (HUN)	1979	Tai Babilonia/Randy Gardner (USA)
1932	Andrée Brunet/Pierre Brunet (FRA)	1980	Marina Tcherkasova/Sergey Schakhrai (URS)
1933	Emília Rotter/László Szollás (HUN)	1981	Irina Vorobieva/Igor Lisovski (URS)
1934	Emília Rotter/László Szollás (HUN)	1982	Sabine Baess/Tassilo Thierbach (GDR)
1935	Emília Rotter/László Szollás (HUN)	1983	Yelena Valova/Oleg Vasilyev (URS)
1936	Maxi Herber/Ernst Baier (GER)	1984	Barbara Underhill/Paul Martini (CAN)
1937	Maxi Herber/Ernst Baier (GER)	1985	Yelena Valova/Oleg Vassiliev (URS)
1938	Maxi Herber/Ernst Baier (GER)	1986	Yekaterina Gordeyeva/Sergey Grinkov (URS)
1939	Maxi Herber/Ernst Baier (GER)	1987	Yekaterina Gordeyeva/Sergey Grinkov (URS)
1940-46 not held		1988	Yelena Valova/Oleg Vassiliev (URS)
1947	Micheline Lannoy/Pierre Baugniet (BEL)	1989	Yekaterina Gordeyeva/Sergey Grinkov (URS)
1948	Micheline Lannoy/Pierre Baugniet (BEL)	1990	Yekaterina Gordeyeva/Sergey Grinkov (URS)
1949	Andrea Kékessy/Ede Király (HUN)	1991	Natalya Mishkutenok/Artur Dmitriev (URS)
1950	Karol Kennedy/Michael Kennedy (USA)	1992	Natalya Mishkutenok/Artur Dmitriev (UKR)
1951	Ria Baran/Paul Falk (GDR)	1993	Isabelle Brasseur/Lloyd Eisler (CAN)
1952	Ria Falk/Paul Falk (GDR)	1994	Evgenia Shishkova/Vadim Naumov (RUS)
1953	Jennifer Nicks/John Nicks (GBR)	1995	Radka Kovariková/Rene Novotny (TCH)
1954	Frances Dafoe/Norris Bowden (CAN)	1996	Marina Eltsova/Sergey Bushkov (RUS)
1955	Frances Dafoe/Norris Bowden (CAN)	1997	Mandy Wötzel/Ingo Steuer (GER)
1956	Elisabeth Schwarz/Kurt Oppelt (AUT)	1998	Yelena Berezhnaya/Anton Sikharulidze (RUS)
1957	Barbara Wagner/Bob Paul (CAN)	1999	Yelena Berezhnaya/Anton Sikharulidze (RUS)
1958	Barbara Wagner/Bob Paul (CAN)	2000	Maria Petrova/Alexey Tichonov (RUS)
1959	Barbara Wagner/Bob Paul (CAN)	2001	Jamie Salé/David Pelletier (CAN)
1960	Barbara Wagner/Bob Paul (CAN)	2002	Shen Xue/Zhao Hongbo (CHN)
1961	not held	2003	Shen Xue/Zhao Hongbo (CHN)
1962	Maria Jelinek/Otto Jelinek (CAN)	2004	Tatiana Totmianina/Maxim Marinin (RUS)

Ice Dance

1952	Jean Westwood/Lawrence Demmy (GBR)	1976	Lyudmila Pakhomova/Aleksandr Gorshkov (URS)
1953	Jean Westwood/Lawrence Demmy (GBR)	1977	Irina Moiseyeva/Andrey Minenkov (URS)
1954	Jean Westwood/Lawrence Demmy (GBR)	1978	Natalya Linichuk/Gennadiy Karponosov (URS)
1955	Jean Westwood/Lawrence Demmy (GBR)	1979	Natalya Linichuk/Gennadiy Karponosov (URS)
1956	Pamela Wright/Paul Thomas (GBR)	1980	Krisztina Regőczy/András Sallay (HUN)
1957	June Markham/Courtney Jones (GBR)	1981	Jayne Torvill/Christopher Dean (GBR)
1958	June Markham/Courtney Jones (GBR)	1982	Jayne Torvill/Christopher Dean (GBR)
1959	Doreen Denny/Courtney Jones (GBR)	1983	Jayne Torvill/Christopher Dean (GBR)
1960	Doreen Denny/Courtney Jones (GBR)	1984	Jayne Torvill/Christopher Dean (GBR)
1961	not held	1985	Natalya Bestemianova/Andrey Bukin (URS)
1962	Evá Romanová/Pavel Roman (TCH)	1986	Natalya Bestemianova/Andrey Bukin (URS)
1963	Evá Romanová/Pavel Roman (TCH)	1987	Natalya Bestemianova/Andrey Bukin (URS)
1964	Evá Romanová/Pavel Roman (TCH)	1988	Natalya Bestemianova/Andrey Bukin (URS)
1965	Evá Romanová/Pavel Roman (TCH)	1989	Marina Klimova/Sergey Ponomarenko (URS)
1966	Diane Towler/Bernard Ford (GBR)	1990	Marina Klimova/Sergey Ponomarenko (URS)
1967	Diane Towler/Bernard Ford (GBR)	1991	Isabelle Duchesnay/Paul Duchesnay (FRA)
1968	Diane Towler/Bernard Ford (GBR)	1992	Marina Klimova/Sergey Ponomarenko (UKR)
1969	Diane Towler/Bernard Ford (GBR)	1993	Maia Usova/Aleksandr Zhulin (RUS)
1970	Lyudmila Pakhomova/Aleksandr Gorshkov (URS)	1994	Oksana 'Pasha' Grishuk/Yevgeny Platov (RUS)
1971	Lyudmila Pakhomova/Aleksandr Gorshkov (URS)	1995	Oksana 'Pasha' Grishuk/Yevgeny Platov (RUS)
1972	Lyudmila Pakhomova/Aleksandr Gorshkov (URS)	1996	Oksana 'Pasha' Grishuk/Yevgeny Platov (RUS)
1973	Lyudmila Pakhomova/Aleksandr Gorshkov (URS)	1997	Oksana 'Pasha' Grishuk/Yevgeny Platov (RUS)
1974	Lyudmila Pakhomova/Aleksandr Gorshkov (URS)	1998	Anzhelika Krylova/Oleg Ovsyannikov (RUS)
1975	Irina Moiseyeva/Andrey Minenkov (URS)	1999	Anzhelika Krylova/Oleg Ovsyannikov (RUS)

2000	Marina Anissina/Gwendal Peizeirat (FRA)
2001	Barbara Fusar Poli/Maurizio Margaglio (ITA)
2002	Irina Lobacheva/Ilya Averbukh (RUS)

| 2003 | Shae-Lynn Bourne/Victor Kraatz (CAN) |
| 2004 | Tatiana Navka/Roman Kostomarov (RUS) |

Synchronised

2000	Sweden
2001	Sweden
2002	Finland

| 2003 | Sweden |
| 2004 | Finland |

ICE SKATING

JAI ALAI

Jai alai evolved from the game of handball. It is often referred to as the fastest of all ball games – professional players have clocked shots at speeds in excess of 180mph (290kph). Jai alai originated in the Basque region of northern Spain at least 300 years ago. It is played in a three-walled arena, called the fronton, with two players or with several teams of players. Called *pelota vasca* (Basque ball) in Spain, the western hemisphere name jai alai (Basque for 'merry festival') was given to the game when it was imported to Cuba around 1900. The players use a wicker basket (*cesta*) attached to their right arm to launch a small ball, called the *pelota* (Spanish for 'ball'), against the front wall of the court (*cancha*) so that when the ball returns, the opponent will be unable to play it. At that point the successful player or team gains a point.

Each cesta is custom made using Pyrenees mountain reeds woven over a light, ribbed frame of Spanish chestnut; a leather glove (guante) sewn to the outside holds the player's hand securely. The cesta is approximately 2½ft (76cm) long and enables the player to hurl the pelota at much higher speeds than would be possible by unaided arm. The pelota itself is harder and heavier than a golf ball. It is made of hand-wound virgin rubber covered with a layer of linen or nylon thread which is then overlaid with two layers of hardened goat skin. The sheer weight and hardness of the pelota has made the wearing of helmets essential – there have been in excess of 30 fatalities in the game.

The cancha is usually 176ft (59m) long, 50ft (15m) wide and 40ft (12m) high (there are no standard dimensions). The front wall is called the *frontis* and is made of granite blocks. The back wall is called the *rebote*, and the side wall is called the *lateral*. Both the rebote and the lateral are made of a pressurised cement called *gunite*. The fourth side of the court has a clear screen, through which spectators can watch the game. The floor and side wall of the court are divided into 15 numbered areas by lines evenly spaced between the frontis and the rebote. The serving zone – the area the ball must first rebound into after it has been served against the frontis – is the space between lines 4 (marked 'Overserve') and 7 (marked 'Underserve'). Players serve from behind the line. Each game's three judges stand opposite lines 4, 7 and 11. The officials carry rackets to protect themselves from the pelota. The game can be played as singles, doubles, or triples, with the players on each team spaced out alternately down the length of the court. There are, however, no limitations on a player's movement about the court.

A match is played to a pre-designated number of points ranging from 7 to 35. After a player has served, the pelota must be caught in the cesta and thrown in a continuous motion. It may be returned before it bounces or when it has bounced once after hitting the frontis. The ball must be returned directly to the frontis and be played on the three walls or the floor. Play continues until one team loses a point. Points are gained when the opponent (a) returns the ball after it has bounced more than once, (b) misses the ball, (c) does not return the ball on to the frontis, or (d) fails to catch the ball and throw it again in a continuous motion. In a rotating game, with more than two teams, the team that loses the point returns to the end of the players' bench, and the next team in line replaces them on the court. The game proceeds in this manner, with the winner staying on the court, until one team achieves the required number of points to win. Play-offs determine the winner in the case of a tie.

JUDO

Judo is derived from ju-jitsu (in Japanese *jūjutsu*, meaning 'gentle art'), a martial art developed by the samurai class of warriors in 17th-century Japan. It was created by Professor Jigoro Kano, who was born in Japan on 28 October 1860 and who died 4 May 1938 after a lifetime of promoting judo. Mastering several styles of ju-jitsu including *Kito-Ryu* and *Tenjin-shinyo Ryu* in his youth, Kano began to develop his own system based on modern sports principles. In 1882 he founded the Kodokan Judo Institute in Tokyo where he began teaching and which still is the international authority for judo. Various aspects of Kodokan judo were introduced over time, such as the Kangeiko (winter training) in 1894, the Shochugeiko (summer training) in 1896, and the spring and autumn Red and White contests which began in 1884. In 2004, the Red and White tournament promotes itself as the longest-running competitive sporting event in the world.

The word 'judo' means 'gentle way' and its basis lies in the theory of turning an opponent's force to one's own advantage. There are two principal ways of practising judo, i.e. *Kata* and *Randori*. *Kata*, which literally means 'form', is practised using a formal system of prearranged structured exercise, while *randori*, meaning 'free exercise', is practised freely. Judo consists primarily of throws (*nage-waza*) and grappling (*katame-waza*), which includes pins (*osaekomi-waza*), chokes (*shime-waza*) and joint locks (*kansetsu-waza*). Additional techniques, including striking (*atemi-waza*), various joint locks, self-defence and weapons training, can also be used in kata and randori.

Achievement in judo is recognised by a series of ranks. The student ranks (*kyu*) are usually differentiated by coloured belts (*obi*). Different colours may be used around the world and in some countries there are more than six *kyu* ranks. The ten black belt, or expert, ranks are called *dan*. The traditional *kyu* ranks are as follows: *ikkyu* (1st grade), *nikyu* (2nd), *sankyu* (3rd), *yonkyu* (4th), *gokyu* (5th), *rokyu* (6th). The expert ranks are: *shodan* (1st degree), *nidan* (2nd), *sandan* (3rd), *yodan* (4th), *godan* (5th), *rokudan* (6th), *shichidan* (7th), *hachidan* (8th), *kudan* (9th) and *judan* (10th). The traditional colours of the belts are white (beginner), yellow, orange, green, blue, brown then black. Sixth dans to 8th dans are entitled to use red-and-white belts and 9th and 10th dans (the highest possible grade), red belts.

While the Kodokan remains the sport's technical authority, since 1951 judo's organising body has been the International Judo Federation (IJF). It oversaw the first World Judo Championships in Tokyo in 1956 and men's judo's entry into the Olympics in 1964. Women's judo, a demonstration sport in 1988, was added to the Olympic programme in 1992. In Olympic judo competition, there are two pools, each with its own single-elimination tournament. The two pool winners compete for the gold medal, with the loser winning the silver medal. In each pool, the competitors who lost to the pool winner enter a repêchage round for another single-elimination tournament. The winners of the repêchage pools are both awarded bronze medals. Weight categories have changed through the years: the limits shown in the following records are those used at the 2000 Olympic Games in Sydney.

Olympic Medallists

Men's Extra Lightweight (60kg)

	Gold	Silver	Bronze
1980	Thierry Rey (FRA)	Rafael Rodríguez (CUB)	Tibor Kincses (HUN)
			Aramby Yernizh (URS)
1984	Shinji Hosokawa (JPN)	Kim Jae-Yup (KOR)	Neil Eckersley (GBR)
			Edward Liddle (USA)
1988	Kim Jae-Yup (KOR)	Kevin Asano (USA)	Shinji Hosokawa (JPN)
			Amiran Tokiuashvili (URS)
1992	Nazim Guseynov (CIS)	Yoon Hyun (KOR)	Tadanori Koshino (JPN)
			Richard Trautmann (GER)
1996	Tadahiro Nomura (JPN)	Girolamo Giovinazzo (ITA)	Dorjpalan Narmandakh (MGL)
			Richard Trautmann (GER)
2000	Tadahiro Nomura (JPN)	Jung Bu-Kyung (KOR)	Manolo Poulot (CUB)
			Aidyn Smagulov (KGZ)

Men's Half Lightweight (66kg)

	Gold	Silver	Bronze
1980	Nikolay Solodukhin (URS)	Tsendying Damdin (MGL)	Ilian Nedkov (BUL)
			Janusz Pawlowski (POL)
1984	Yoshiyuki Matsuoka (JPN)	Hwang Jung-Oh (KOR)	Marc Alexandre (FRA)
			Josef Reiter (AUT)
1988	Lee Kyung-Keun (KOR)	Janusz Pawlowski (POL)	Bruno Carabetta (FRA)
			Yosuke Yamamoto (JPN)
1992	Rogério Sampaio Cardoso (BRA)	József Csák (HUN)	Israel Hernández (CUB)
			Udo Quellmalz (GER)
1996	Udo Quellmalz (GER)	Yukimasa Nakamura (JPN)	Carlos Henrique Guimãres (BRA)
			Israel Hernández (CUB)
2000	Hüseyin Özkan (TUR)	Larbi Benboudaoud (FRA)	Girolamo Giovinazzo (ITA)
			Georgiy Vazagashvili (GEO)

Men's Lightweight (73kg)

	Gold	Silver	Bronze
1964	Takehide Nakatani (JPN)	Eric Hänni (SUI)	Arons Bogolubovs (URS)
			Oleg Stepanov (URS)
1972	Takao Kawaguchi (JPN)	(disqualified)*	Kim Yong-Ik (PRK)
			Jean-Jacques Mounier (FRA)
1976	Héctor Rodríguez (CUB)	Chang Eun-Kyung (KOR)	Felice Mariani (ITA)
			József Tuncsik (HUN)
1980	Ezio Gamba (ITA)	Neil Adams (GBR)	Ravdan Davaadalai (MGL)
			Karl-Heinz Lehmann (GDR)
1984	Ahn Byeong-Keun (KOR)	Ezio Gamba (ITA)	Kerrith Brown (GBR)
			Luis Onmura (BRA)
1988	Marc Alexandre (FRA)	Sven Loll (GDR)	Michael Swain (USA)
			Georgiy Tenadze (URS)
1992	Toshihiko Koga (JPN)	Bertalan Hajtós (HUN)	Chung Se-Hoon (KOR)
			Shay Oren Smadga (ISR)
1996	Kenzo Nakamura (JPN)	Kwak Dae-Sung (KOR)	Christophe Gagliano (FRA)
			James Pedro (USA)
2000	Giuseppe Maddaloni (ITA)	Tiago Camilo (BRA)	Anatoliy Larukov (BLR)
			Vsevolods Zelonijs (LAT)

*Bakhaavaa Buidaa (MGL) was disqualified for failing a drugs test.

Men's Welterweight (70kg) (discontinued)

	Gold	Silver	Bronze
1972	Toyokazu Nomura (JPN)	Antoni Zajkowski (POL)	Diermar Hötger (GDR)
			Anatoliy Novikov (URS)
1976	Vladimir Nevzorov (URS)	Koji Kuramoto (JPN)	Marian Talaj (POL)
			Patrick Vial (FRA)

Men's Half Middleweight (81kg)

	Gold	Silver	Bronze
1980	Shota Khabareli (URS)	Juan Ferrer (CUB)	Harald Heinke (GDR)
			Bernard Tchoullyan (FRA)
1984	Frank Wieneke (FRG)	Neil Adams (GBR)	Mircea Fratiça (ROM)
			Michel Nowak (FRA)
1988	Waldemar Legien (POL)	Frank Wieneke (FRG)	Torsten Bréchôt (GDR)
			Bashir Varayev (URS)
1992	Hidehiko Yoshida (JPN)	Jason Morris (USA)	Bertrand Damaisin (FRA)
			Kim Byung-Joo (KOR)
1996	Djamel Bouras (FRA)	Toshihiko Koga (JPN)	Cho In-Chul (KOR)
			Soso Liparteliani (GEO)
2000	Makoto Takimoto (JPN)	Cho In-Chul (KOR)	Aleksey Budolin (EST)
			Nuño Delgado (POR)

Men's Middleweight (90kg)

	Gold	Silver	Bronze
'64	Isao Okano (JPN)	Wolfgang Hofmann (GDR)	James Bregman (USA)
			Kim Eui-Tae (KOR)
'72	Shinobu Sekine (JPN)	Oh Seung-Lip (KOR)	Jean-Paul Coché (FRA)
			Brian Jacks (GBR)
'76	Isamu Sonoda (JPN)	Valeriy Dvoinikov (URS)	Slavko Obadov (YUG)
			Park Young-Chul (KOR)
'80	Jürg Röthlisberger (SUI)	Isaac Azcuy (CUB)	Aleksandrs Jackevics (URS)
			Detlef Ultsch (GDR)
'84	Peter Seisenbacher (AUT)	Robert Berland (USA)	Walter Carmona (BRA)
			Seiki Nose (JPN)
'88	Peter Seisenbacher (AUT)	Vladimir Shestakov (URS)	Akinobu Osako (JPN)
			Ben Spijkers (NED)
'92	Waldemar Legien (POL)	Pascal Tayot (FRA)	Nicolas Gill (CAN)
			Hirotaka Okada (JPN)
'96	Jeon Ki-Young (KOR)	Armen Bagdasarov (UZB)	Mark Huizinga (NED)
			Marko Spittka (GER)
'00	Mark Huizinga (NED)	Carlos Honorato (BRA)	Frédéric Demontfaucon (FRA)
			Ruslan Mashurenko (UKR)

Men's Half Heavyweight (100kg)

(titled Light Heavyweight in 1972 and 1976)

	Gold	Silver	Bronze
'72	Shota Chochoshvili (URS)	David Starbrook (GBR)	Paul Barth (FRG)
			Chiaki Ishii (BRA)
'76	Kazuhiro Ninomiya (JPN)	Ramaz Kharshiladze (URS)	Jürg Röthlisberger (SUI)
			David Starbrook (GBR)
'80	Robert van de Walle (BEL)	Tengiz Khubuluri (URS)	Dietmar Lorenz (GDR)
			Henk Numan (NED)
'84	Ha Hyoung-Zoo (KOR)	Douglas Vieira (BRA)	Bjarni Fridriksson (ISL)
			Günther Neureuther (FRG)
'88	Aurélio Miguel (BRA)	Marc Melling (FRG)	Dennis Stewart (GBR)
			Robert van de Walle (BEL)
'92	Antal Kovács (HUN)	Ray Stevens (GBR)	Theo Meijer (NED)
			Dmitriy Sergeyev (CIS)
'96	Pawel Nastula (POL)	Kim Min-Soo (KOR)	Aurélio Miguel (BRA)
			Stéphane Traineau (FRA)
'00	Kosei Inoue (JPN)	Nicolas Gill (CAN)	Yuriy Stepkine (RUS)
			Stéphane Traineau (FRA)

Men's Heavyweight (over 100kg)

	Gold	Silver	Bronze
'64	Isao Inokuma (JPN)	Douglas Rogers (CAN)	Pamaoz Chikviladze (URS)
			Anzor Kiknadze (URS)
'72	Willem Ruska (NED)	Klaus Glahn (FRG)	Motoki Nishimura (JPN)
			Givi Onashvili (URS)
'76	Sergey Novikov (URS)	Günther Neureuther (FRG)	Allen Coage (USA)
			Sumio Endo (JPN)
'80	Angelo Parisi (FRA)	Dimitar Zapryanov (BUL)	Radomir Kovacevic (YUG)
			Vladimír Kocman (TCH)
'84	Hitoshi Saito (JPN)	Angelo Parisi (FRA)	Mark Berger (CAN)
			Cho Yong-Chul (KOR)
'88	Hitoshi Saito (JPN)	Henry Stöhr (GDR)	Cho Yong-Chul (KOR)
			Grigoriy Verichev (URS)
'92	David Khakhaleishvili (CIS)	Naoya Ogawa (JPN)	Imre Csosz (HUN)
			David Douillet (FRA)
'96	David Douillet (FRA)	Ernesto Pérez (ESP)	Frank Möller (GER)
			Harry van Barneveld (BEL)
'00	David Douillet (FRA)	Shinichi Shinohara (JPN)	Indrek Pertelson (EST)
			Tamerlan Tmenov (RUS)

JUDO

Men's Open (no weight restriction)

	Gold	Silver	Bronze
1964	Anton Geesink (NED)	Akio Kaminaga (JPN)	Theodore Boronovskis (AUS)
			Klaus Glahn (FRG)
1972	Willem Ruska (NED)	Vitaliy Kusnetzov (URS)	Jean-Claude Brondani (FRA)
			Angelo Parisi (GBR)
1976	Haruki Uemura (JPN)	Keith Remfry (GBR)	Jeaki Cho (KOR)
			Shota Chochoshvili (URS)
1980	Dietmar Lorenz (GDR)	Angelo Parisi (FRA)	Arthur Mapp (GBR)
			András Ozsvár (HUN)
1984	Yasuhiro Yamashita (JPN)	Mohamed Ali Rashwan (EGY)	Mihai Cloc (ROM)
			Arthur Schnabel (FRG)

Women's Extra Lightweight (48kg)

	Gold	Silver	Bronze
1992	Cécile Nowak (FRA)	Ryoko Tamura (JPN)	Amarilys Savón (CUB)
			Hülya Senyurt (TUR)
1996	Kye Sun-Hi (PRK)	Ryoko Tamura (JPN)	Amarilys Savón (CUB)
			Yolanda Soler (ESP)
2000	Ryoko Tamura (JPN)	Lyubov Brouletova (RUS)	Anna-Maria Gradante (GER)
			Ann Simons (BEL)

Women's Half Lightweight (52kg)

	Gold	Silver	Bronze
1992	Almudena Múñoz (ESP)	Noriko Mizoguchi (JPN)	Li Zhongyun (CHN)
			Sharon Rendle (GBR)
1996	Marie-Claire Restoux (FRA)	Hyun Sook-Hee (KOR)	Noriko Sugawara (JPN)
			Legna Verdecia (CUB)
2000	Legna Verdecia (CUB)	Noriko Narazaki (JPN)	Kye Sun-Hui (PRK)
			Liu Yuxiang (CHN)

Women's Lightweight (57kg)

	Gold	Silver	Bronze
1992	Miriam Blasco (ESP)	Nicola Fairbrother (GBR)	Driulys González (CUB)
			Chiyori Tateno (JPN)
1996	Driulys González (CUB)	Jung Sun-Yong (KOR)	Isabel Fernández (ESP)
			Marisabel Lomba (BEL)
2000	Isabel Fernández (ESP)	Driulys González (CUB)	Kie Kusakabe (JPN)
			Maria Pekli (AUS)

Women's Half Middleweight (63kg)

	Gold	Silver	Bronze
1992	Catherine Fleury (FRA)	Yael Arad (ISR)	Yelena Petrova (CIS)
			Zhang Di (CHN)
1996	Yuko Emoto (JPN)	Gella Vandecaveye (BEL)	Jenny Gal (NED)
			Jung Sung-Sook (KOR)
2000	Séverine Vandenhende (FRA)	Li Shufang (CHN)	Jung Sung-Sook (KOR)
			Gella Vandecaveye (BEL)

Women's Middleweight (70kg)

	Gold	Silver	Bronze
1992	Odalys Revé (CUB)	Emanuela Pierantozzi (ITA)	Kate Howey (GBR)
			Heidi Rakels (BEL)
1996	Cho Min-Sun (KOR)	Aneta Szczepanska (POL)	Wang Xianbo (CHN)
			Claudia Zwiers (NED)
2000	Sibelis Veranis (CUB)	Kate Howey (GBR)	Cho Min-Sun (KOR)
			Ylenia Scapin (ITA)

Women's Half Heavyweight (78kg)

	Gold	Silver	Bronze
1992	Kim Mi-Jung (KOR)	Yoko Tanabe (JPN)	Irene de Kok (NED)
1996	Ulla Werbrouck (BEL)	Yoko Tanabe (JPN)	Laetitia Meignan (FRA) Diadenys Luna (CUB)
2000	Tang Lin (CHN)	Céline Lebrun (FRA)	Ylenia Scapin (ITA) Emanuela Pierantozzi (ITA) Simona Marcela Richter (ROM)

Women's Heavyweight (over 78kg)

	Gold	Silver	Bronze
1992	Zhuang Xiaoyan (CHN)	Estela Rodríguez (CUB)	Natalina Lupino (FRA)
1996	Sun Fuming (CHN)	Estela Rodríguez (CUB)	Yoko Sakaue (JPN) Christine Cicot (FRA)
2000	Yuan Hua (CHN)	Daima Mayelis Beltrán (CUB)	Johanna Hagn (GER) Kim Seon-Young (KOR) Mayumi Yamashita (JPN)

World Championships

Men's Extra Lightweight (60kg)

	Gold	Silver	Bronze
1979	Thierry Rey (FRA)	Koa Woo-Jong (KOR)	Yasuhiko Moriwaki (JPN)
1981	Yasuhiko Moriwaki (JPN)	Pavel Petrikov (TCH)	Felice Mariani (ITA) Felice Mariani (ITA)
1983	Khazret Tletseri (URS)	Tamás Bujko (HUN)	Philip Takahashi (CAN) Klaus-Peter Stollberg (GDR)
1985	Shinji Hosokawa (JPN)	Peter Jupke (FRG)	Kenichi Haraguchi (JPN) Khazret Tletseri (URS)
1987	Jae-Yup Kim (KOR)	Shinji Hosokawa (JPN)	Tamas Bujko (HUN) Patrick Roux (FRA)
1989	Amiran Tokiuaschvili (URS)	Tadanori Koshino (JPN)	Kevin Asano (USA) Yoon Hyun (KOR)
1991	Tadanori Koshino (JPN)	Yoon Hyun (KOR)	Dashgombyn Battulga (MGL) Philippe Pradayrol (FRA)
1993	Ryuji Sonoda (JPN)	Nazim Guseynov (AZE)	Nazim Guseynov (URS) Richard Trautmann (GER)
1995	Nikolay Oyegine (RUS)	Georgiy Vazagashvili (GEO)	Georgiy Vazagashvili (GEO) Ryuji Sonoda (JPN)
1997	Tadahiro Nomura (JPN)	George Revasishvili (GEO)	Natik Bagirov (BLR) Cédric Taymans (BEL)
1999	Manolo Poulot (CUB)	Kazuhiko Tokuno (JPN)	Fúlvio Miyata (BRA) Natik Bagirov (BLR)
2001	Anis Lounifi (TUN)	Cédric Taymans (BEL)	Nestor Khergiani (GEO) John Buchanan (GBR)
2003	Min Ho Choi (KOR)	Craig Fallon (GBR)	Kazuhiko Tokuno (JPN) Tadahiro Nomura (JPN) Anis Lounifi (TUN)

Men's Half Lightweight (66kg)

	Gold	Silver	Bronze
1979	Nikolay Solodukhin (URS)	Yves Delvingt (FRA)	Janusz Pawlowski (POL)
1981	Katsushiko Kashiwazaki (JPN)	Constantin Niculae (ROM)	Sahara (JPN) Petr Ponomaryov (URS)
1983	Nikolay Solodukhin (URS)	Yoshiyuki Matsuoka (JPN)	Jung-Oh Hwang (KOR) Janusz Pawlowski (POL)
1985	Yuriy Sokolov (URS)	Lee Kyung-Keun (KOR)	Sandro Rosati (ITA) Stephen Gawthorpe (GBR)
1987	Yosuke Yamamoto (JPN)	Yuriy Sokolov (URS)	Yoshiyuki Matsuoka (JPN) Tamás Bujko (HUN)
1989	Dragomir Becanovic (YUG)	Udo Quellmalz (GDR)	Janusz Pawlowski (POL) Sergey Kosmynin (URS)
1991	Udo Quellmalz (GER)	Masahiko Okuma (JPN)	Bruno Carabetta (ITA) Sergey Kosmynin (URS) Jimmy Pedro (USA)

JUDO

1993	Yukimasa Nakamura (JPN)	Eric Born (SUI)	Udo Quellmalz (GER)
			Sergey Kosmynin (RUS)
1995	Udo Quellmalz (GER)	Yukimasa Nakamura (JPN)	Bektas Demirel (TUR)
			Kim Dae-Ik (KOR)
1997	Kim Hyuk (KOR)	Larbi Benboudaoud (FRA)	Georgiy Vasagashvili (GEO)
			Viktor Bivol (MDA)
1999	Larbi Benboudaoud (FRA)	Hüseyin Özkan (TUR)	Patrick van Kalken (NED)
			Jordanis Arencibia (CUB)
2001	Arash Miresmaili (IRI)	Musa Nastuyev (UKR)	Jordanis Arencibia (CUB)
			Kim Hyung-Ju (KOR)
2003	Arash Miresmaili (IRI)	Larbi Benboudaoud (FRA)	Jordanis Arencibia (CUB)
			Magomed Dzhafarov (RUS)

Men's Lightweight (73kg)

	Gold	**Silver**	**Bronze**
1965	Hirofumi Matsuda (JPN)	Hiroshi Minatoya (JPN)	Park Kid-Soon (KOR)
			Oleg Stepanov (URS)
1967	Takafumi Shigeoka (JPN)	Hirofumi Matsuda (JPN)	Sergey Suslin (URS)
			Chung-Sik Kim (KOR)
1969	Yoshio Sonoda (JPN)	Toyokazu Nomura (JPN)	Sergey Suslin (URS)
			Sang-Chul Kim (KOR)
1971	Takao Kawaguchi (JPN)	Toyokazu Nomura (JPN)	Sergey Suslin (URS)
			Choi Jong Sam (KOR)
1973	Yoshiharu Minami (JPN)	Takao Kawaguchi (JPN)	Héctor Rodríguez (CUB)
			Schengeli Pitschelauri (URS)
1975	Yoshiharu Minami (JPN)	Katsuhiko Kashiwazaki (JPN)	Torsten Reissmann (GDR)
			Felice Mariani (ITA)
1979	Hiro Katsuki (JPN)	Ezio Gamba (ITA)	Neil Adams (GBR)
			Tomaz Namgalauri (URS)
1981	Chong-Hak Park (KOR)	Serge Dyot (FRA)	Karl-Heinz Lehmann (GDR)
			Vojo Vujevic (YUG)
1983	Hidetoshi Nakanishi (JPN)	Ezio Gamba (ITA)	Tarnat Namgalauri (URS)
			Steffen Stranz (FRG)
1985	Byeong Keun Ahn (KOR)	Mikel Swain (USA)	Steffen Stranz (FRG)
			Wieslaw Blach (POL)
1987	Mikel Swain (USA)	Marc Alexandre (FRA)	Kerrith Brown (GBR)
			Steffen Stranz (FRG)
1989	Toshihiko Koga (JPN)	Mike Swain (USA)	Li Chang-Su (KOR)
			Georgiy Tenadze (URS)
1991	Toshihiko Koga (JPN)	Joaquín Ruíz (ESP)	Chung Se-Hoon (KOR)
			Vladimir Dgebuadse (URS)
1993	Chung Se-Hoon (KOR)	Bertalan Hajtós (HUN)	Daisuke Hideshima (JPN)
			Rogério Cardoso (BRA)
1995	Daisuke Hideshima (JPN)	Kwak Dee-Sung (KOR)	Jimmy Pedro (USA)
			Diego Brambilla (ITA)
1997	Kenzo Nakamura (JPN)	Christophe Gagliano (FRA)	Guilherme Bentes (POR)
			Vsevolod Zelenschi (LAT)
1999	Jimmy Pedro (USA)	Vitaliy Makarov (RUS)	Sebastian Pereira (BRA)
			George Reyazishvili (GEO)
2001	Vitaliy Makarov (RUS)	Yusuke Kanamaru (JPN)	Askhat Shakharov (KAZ)
			Krzysztof Wilkomirski (POL)
2003	Lee Won-Hee (KOR)	Daniel Fernandes (FRA)	João Neto (POR)
			Vitaliy Makarov (RUS)

Men's Welterweight (70kg) (discontinued)

	Gold	**Silver**	**Bronze**
1967	Hiroshi Minatoya (JPN)	Kid-Soon Park (KOR)	Takehide Nakatani (JPN)
			Park Chung-Sam (KOR)
1969	Hiroshi Minatoya (JPN)	Yashimitsu Kono (JPN)	David Rudman (URS)
			Kim Chil-Bok (KOR)
1971	Hisashi Tsuzawa (JPN)	Hiroshi Minatoya (JPN)	Dietmar Hötger (GDR)
			Antoniy Zajkovski (POL)
1973	Toyokazu Nomura (JPN)	Dietmar Hötger (GDR)	Kazuro Yoshimura (JPN)
			Anatoli Novikov (URS)
1975	Vladimir Nevzorov (URS)	Valeriy Dvoinikov (URS)	Katsunari Akimoto (JPN)
			Koji Kuramoto (JPN)

Men's Half Middleweight (81kg)

	Gold	Silver	Bronze
1979	Shozo Fujii (JPN)	Bernard Toullouyan (FRA)	Harald Heinke (GDR)
			Park Young-Chul (KOR)
1981	Neil Adams (GBR)	Jiro Kase (JPN)	Georgi Petrov (BUL)
			Kevin Doherty (CAN)
1983	Nobutoshi Hikage (JPN)	Neil Adams (GBR)	Shota Khabareli (URS)
			Mircea Fratiça (ROM)
1985	Nobutoshi Hikage (JPN)	Torsten Bréchôt (GDR)	Neil Adams (GBR)
			Vladimir Shestakov (URS)
1987	Hirotaka Okada (JPN)	Bashir Varayev (URS)	Lee Koai-Hwa (KOR)
			Waldemar Legien (POL)
1989	Byung-Ju Kim (KOR)	Tatsuto Moshida (JPN)	Bashir Varayev (URS)
			Waldemar Legien (POL)
1991	Daniel Lascau (GER)	Johan Laats (BEL)	Bashir Varayev (URS)
			Hidehiko Yoshida (JPN)
1993	Chung Ki-Young (KOR)	Hidehiko Yoshida (JPN)	Jason Morris (USA)
			Darcel Yandzi (FRA)
1995	Toshihiko Koga (JPN)	Shay Oren Smadga (ISR)	Patrick Reiter (AUT)
			Djamel Bouras (FRA)
1997	Cho In-Chul (KOR)	Djamel Bouras (FRA)	Chol Ok Kwak (PRK)
			Patrick Reiter (AUT)
1999	Graeme Randall (GBR)	Farkhod Turayev (UZB)	Chol Ok Kwak (PRK)
			Cho In-Chul (KOR)
2001	Cho In-Chul (KOR)	Aleksey Budolin (EST)	Sergey Aschwanden (SUI)
			Elkhan Rajabli (AZE)
2003	Florian Wanner (GER)	Sergey Aschwanden (SUI)	Robert Krawczyk (POL)
			Aleksey Budolin (EST)

Men's Middleweight (90kg)

	Gold	Silver	Bronze
1965	Isao Okano (JPN)	Kinishi Yamanaka (JPN)	Kim Eui-Tae (KOR)
			Jim Bregman (USA)
1967	Eiji Maruki (JPN)	Martin Poglajen (NED)	Brian Jacks (GBR)
			Takehide Nakatani (JPN)
1969	Isamu Sonoda (JPN)	Katsuya Hirao (JPN)	Martin Poglajen (NED)
			Oh Seung-Lip (KOR)
1971	Shozo Fujii (JPN)	Masashiga Shigematsu (JPN)	David Starbrook (GBR)
			Guy Auffray (FRA)
1973	Shozo Fujii (JPN)	Isamu Sonoda (JPN)	Bernd Look (GDR)
			Antoni Reiter (POL)
1975	Shozo Fujii (JPN)	Yoshimi Hara (JPN)	Jean-Paul Coche (FRA)
			Adam Adamczyk (POL)
1979	Detlef Ultsch (GDR)	Michel Sanchis (FRA)	Masao Takahashi (JPN)
			Walter Carmona (BRA)
1981	Bernard Thoullouyan (FRA)	Seiki Nose (JPN)	Detlef Ultsch (GDR)
			Minda Bodayeli (URS)
1983	Detlef Ultsch (GDR)	Fabien Canu (FRA)	Bobby Berland (USA)
			Seiki Nose (JPN)
1985	Peter Seisenbacher (AUT)	Georgi Petrow (BUL)	Vitaliy Pesnyak (URS)
			Fabien Canu (FRA)
1987	Fabien Canu (FRA)	Park Jong-Chul (PRK)	Densign White (GBR)
			Masao Murata (JPN)
1989	Fabien Canu (FRA)	Ben Spijkers (NED)	Axel Lobenstein (GDR)
			Stefan Freudenberg (FRG)
1991	Hirotaka Okada (JPN)	Joey Wanag (USA)	Giorgio Vismara (ITA)
			Waldemar Legien (POL)
1993	Yoshio Nakamura (JPN)	Nicolas Gill (CAN)	Adrian Croitoru (ROM)
			Leon Villar (ESP)
1995	Jeon Ki-Young (KOR)	Hidehiko Yoshida (JPN)	Oleg Maltsev (RUS)
			Nicolas Gill (CAN)
1997	Jeon Ki-Young (KOR)	Marko Spittka (GER)	Brian Olson (USA)
			Michele Monti (ITA)
1999	Hidehiko Yoshida (JPN)	Viktor Florescu (MDA)	Sung-Yeon Yoo (KOR)
			Adrian Croitoru (ROM)
2001	Frédéric Demontfaucon (FRA)	Zurab Zviadauri (GEO)	Rassoul Salimow (AZE)
			Dong-Sik Yoon (KOR)
2003	Hwang Hee-Tae (KOR)	Zurab Zviadauri (GEO)	Sergey Kukharenko (BLR)
			Carlos Honorato (BRA)

JUDO

Men's Half Heavyweight (100kg)

(titled Light Heavyweight 1967-75)

	Gold	Silver	Bronze
1967	Nobuyuki Sato (JPN)	Osamu Sato (JPN)	Peter Herrmann (FRG)
			Ernst Eugster (NED)
1969	Fumio Sasahara (JPN)	Peter Herrmann (FRG)	Kawabata (JPN)
			Tomoyuki Vladimir Pokatayev (URS)
1971	Fumio Sasahara (JPN)	Nobuyuki Sato (JPN)	Chiaki Ishili (BRA)
			Helmut Howiller (GDR)
1973	Nobuyuki Sato (JPN)	Takafumi Ueguchi (JPN)	David Starbrook (GBR)
			Dietmar Lorenz (GDR)
1975	Jean-Luc Rougé (FRA)	Michinori Ishibashi (JPN)	Viktor Betanov (URS)
			Ramaz Harshiladze (URS)
1979	Tengiz Khouboulouri (URS)	Robert van de Walle (BEL)	Henk Numan (NED)
			Günther Neureuther (FRG)
1981	Tengiz Khouboulouri (URS)	Robert van de Walle (BEL)	Ha Hyung-Joo (KOR)
			Roger Vachon (FRA)
1983	Andreas Preschel (GDR)	Valeriy Divissenkov (URS)	Günther Neureuther (FRG)
			Robert van de Walle (BEL)
1985	Hitoshi Sugai (JPN)	Ha Hyung-Joo (KOR)	Günther Neureuther (FRG)
			Robert van de Walle (BEL)
1987	Hitoshi Sugai (JPN)	Theo Meijer (NED)	Aurelio Miguel Fernandes (BRA)
			Ha Hyung-Joo (KOR)
1989	Koba Kurtanidze (URS)	Baljinnyam Odvogiin (MGL)	Robert van de Walle (BEL)
			Marc Meiling (FRG)
1991	Stéphane Traineau (FRA)	Pawel Nastula (POL)	Marc Meiling (GER)
			Jirí Sosna (TCH)
1993	Antal Kovács (HUN)	Aurélio Miguel Fernandes (BRA)	Marc Meiling (GER)
			Stéphane Traineau (JPN)
1995	Pawel Nastula (POL)	Dimitriy Sergeyev (RUS)	Shigeru Okaizumi (JPN)
			Stephane Traineau (FRA)
1997	Pawel Nastula (POL)	Aurelio Miguel Fernandes (BRA)	Ghislain Lemaire (FRA)
			Yoshio Nakamura (JPN)
1999	Kosei Inoue (JPN)	Jang Sung-Ho (KOR)	Aleksandr Mikhailin (RUS)
			Nicolas Gill (CAN)
2001	Kosei Inoue (JPN)	Antal Kovács (HUN)	Jang Sung-Ho (KOR)
			Askhat Zhitkeyev (KAZ)
2003	Kosei Inoue (JPN)	Ghislain Lemaire (FRA)	Mário Sabino jnr (BRA)
			Igor Makarau (BLR)

Men's Heavyweight (over 100kg)

	Gold	Silver	Bronze
1965	Anton Geesink (NED)	Matsuo Matsunaga (JPN)	Alfred Douglas Rogers (CAN)
			Seiji Sakaguchi (JPN)
1967	Willem Ruska (NED)	Nobuyuki Majima (JPN)	Anzor Kiknadse (URS)
			Takeshi Matsusaka (JPN)
1969	Shuji Suma (JPN)	Klaus Glahn (FRG)	Givi Onashvili (URS)
			Mitsuo Matsunaga (JPN)
1971	Willem Ruska (NED)	Klaus Glahn (FRG)	Hisakazu Iwata (JPN)
			Keith Remfry (GBR)
1973	Chonusuke Tagaki (JPN)	Ramaz Nizharadze (URS)	Keith Remfry (GBR)
			Sergey Novikov (URS)
1975	Sumio Endo (JPN)	Sergey Novikov (URS)	Park Gil-Jong (PRK)
			Chonusuke Tagaki (JPN)
1979	Yasuhiro Yamashita (JPN)	Jean-Luc Rouge (FRA)	Imre Varga (HUN)
			Cho Jae-Ki (KOR)
1981	Yasuhiro Yamashita (JPN)	Grigoriy Verichev (URS)	Vladimir Kocman (TCH)
			Juha Salonen (FIN)
1983	Yasuhiro Yamashita (JPN)	Wil Wilhelm (NED)	Henry Stöhr (GDR)
			Mihai Cioc (ROM)
1985	Cho Yong-Chul (KOR)	Hitoshi Saito (JPN)	Grigoriy Verichev (URS)
			Dimitar Zaprianov (BUL)
1987	Grigoriy Verichev (URS)	Mohamed Ali Rashwan (EGY)	Jochen Plate (FRG)
			Guoqing Xu (CHN)
1989	Naoya Ogawa (JPN)	Frank Moreno (CUB)	Grigoriy Verichev (URS)
			Rafael Kubacki (POL)
1991	Sergey Kossorotov (URS)	Frank Moreno (CUB)	Naoya Ogawa (JPN)
			Kim Kun-Soo (KOR)

1993	David Douillet (FRA)	David Khakhaleishvili (GEO)	Frank Möller (GER)
			Sergey Kosorotov (RUS)
1995	David Douillet (FRA)	Frank Möller (GER)	Naoya Ogawa (JPN)
			David Khakhaleishvili (GEO)
1997	David Douillet (FRA)	Shinichi Shinohara (JPN)	Pan Song (CHN)
			Tamerlan Tmenov (RUS)
1999	Shinichi Shinohara (JPN)	Indrek Pertelson (EST)	Pan Song (CHN)
			Selim Tataroglu (TUR)
2001	Aleksandr Mikhailin (RUS)	Selim Tataroglu (TUR)	Mahmoud Miranfashandi (IRI)
			Shinichi Shinohara (JPN)
2003	Yasuyuki Muneta (JPN)	Dennis van der Geest (NED)	Tamerlan Tmenov (RUS)
			Yevgeniy Sotnikov (UKR)

Men's Open (no weight restriction)

	Gold	Silver	Bronze
1956	Shokichi Natsui (JPN)	Yoshihiko Yoshimatsu (JPN)	Anton Geesink (NED)
			Henri Courtine (FRA)
1958	Koji Sone (JPN)	Akio Kaminaga (JPN)	Kimiyoshi Yamashiki (JPN)
			Bernard Pariset (FRA)
1961	Anton Geesink (NED)	Koji Sone (JPN)	Takeshi Koga (JPN)
			Kim Tong-Pae (PRK)
1965	Isao Inokuma (JPN)	Anzor Kibrosachvili (URS)	Anzor Kiknadze (URS)
			Peter Snijders (NED)
1967	Matsuo Matsunaga (JPN)	Klaus Glahn (FRG)	Masatoshi Shinomaki (JPN)
			Peter Herrmann (FRG)
1969	Masatoshi Shinomaki (JPN)	Willem Ruska (NED)	Ernst Eugster (NED)
			Sato (JPN)
1971	Masatoshi Shinomaki (JPN)	Vitaliy Kusnetsov (URS)	Shinobu Sekine (JPN)
			Klaus Glahn (FRG)
1973	Kazuhiro Ninomiya (JPN)	Haruki Uemura (JPN)	Wolfgang Zuckschwerdt (GDR)
			Klaus Glahn (FRG)
1975	Haruki Uemura (JPN)	Kazuhiro Ninomiya (JPN)	Shota Chochoshvili (URS)
			Dietmar Lorenz (GDR)
1979	Sumio Endo (JPN)	Vitaliy Kusnetsov (URS)	Radomir Kovacevic (YUG)
			Jean-Luc Rougé (FRA)
1981	Yasuhiro Yamashita (JPN)	Wojciech Reszko (POL)	Robert van de Walle (BEL)
			Andras Ozsvar (HUN)
1983	Hitoshi Saito (JPN)	Vladimír Kocman (TCH)	Andras Ozsvar (HUN)
			Robert van de Walle (BEL)
1985	Yoshimi Masaki (JPN)	Mohamed Ali Rashwan (EGY)	Wil Wilhelm (NED)
			Khabil Biktachev (URS)
1987	Naoya Ogawa (JPN)	Elvis Gordon (GBR)	Jorge Castro (CUB)
			Henry Stöhr (GDR)
1989	Naoya Ogawa (JPN)	Akaky Kibordiladze (URS)	Kim Kun-Soo (KOR)
			Alexander van der Groeben (FRG)
1991	Naoya Ogawa (JPN)	David Khakaleishvili (URS)	Imre Csosz (HUN)
			Georges Mathonnet (FRA)
1993	Rafael Kubacki (POL)	Henry Stöhr (GER)	David Khakhaleishvili (GEO)
			Naoya Ogawa (JPN)
1995	David Douillet (FRA)	Sergey Kosorotov (RUS)	Shinichi Shinohara (JPN)
			Selim Tataroglu (TUR)
1997	Rafael Kubacki (POL)	Yoshida Makishi (JPN)	Harry van Barneveld (BEL)
			Dennis van der Geest (NED)
1999	Shinichi Shinohara (JPN)	Selim Tataroglu (TUR)	Dennis van der Geest (NED)
			Harry van Barneveld (BEL)
2001	Aleksandr Mikhailin (RUS)	Ariel Zeevi (ISR)	Frank Möller (GER)
			Dennis van der Geest (NED)
2003	Keiji Suzuki (JPN)	Indrek Petelson (EST)	Abdullo Tangriev (UZB)
			Movlud Miraliyev (AZE)

Women's Extra Lightweight (48 kg)

	Gold	Silver	Bronze
1980	Jane Bridge (GBR)	Anna de Novellis (ITA)	Marie-France Colignon (FRA)
			Mary Lewis (USA)
1982	Karen Briggs (GBR)	Marie-France Colignon (FRA)	H. Nakahara (JPN)
			Jola Bink (NED)
1984	Karen Briggs (GBR)	Marie-France Colignon (FRA)	Julie Reardon (AUS)
			Darlene Anaya (USA)

JUDO

1986	Karen Briggs (GBR)	Fumiko Esaki (JPN)	Zhangyun Li (CHN)
			Fabienne Boffin (FRA)
1987	Li Zhongyun (CHN)	Fumiko Esaki (JPN)	Chou Yu-Ping (TPE)
			Jessica Gal (NED)
1989	Karen Briggs (GBR)	Fumiko Esaki (JPN)	Jessica Gal (NED)
			Cécile Nowak (FRA)
1991	Cécile Nowak (FRA)	Karen Briggs (GBR)	Ryoko Tamura (JPN)
			Legna Verdecia (CUB)
1993	Ryoko Tamura (JPN)	Li Aiyue (CHN)	Giovanna Tortora (ITA)
			Joyce Heron (GBR)
1995	Ryoko Tamura (JPN)	Li Aiyue (CHN)	Amarilys Savón (CUB)
			Malgorzata Roszkowska (POL)
1997	Ryoko Tamura (JPN)	Amarilys Savón (CUB)	Monika Kurath (SUI)
			Dong-Suk Pae (PRK)
1999	Ryoko Tamura (JPN)	Amarilys Savón (CUB)	Sarah Nichilo-Rosso (FRA)
			Anna-Maria Gradante (GER)
2001	Ryoko Tamura (JPN)	Ri Kyong-Ok (KOR)	Danieska Carrión (CUB)
			Giuseppina Macri (ITA)
2003	Ryoko Tamura (JPN)	Frédérique Jossinet (FRA)	Danieska Carrión (CUB)
			Nese Sensoy (TUR)

Women's Half Lightweight (52kg)

	Gold	Silver	Bronze
1980	Edith Hrovat (AUT)	Kaori Yamaguchi (JPN)	Bridgette McCarthy (GBR)
			Pascale Doger (FRA)
1982	Loretta Doyle (GBR)	Kaori Yamaguchi (JPN)	Pascale Doger (FRA)
			Christina Boyd (AUS)
1984	Kaori Yamaguchi (JPN)	Edith Hrovat (AUT)	Christina Boyd (AUS)
			Joanna Majdan (POL)
1986	Dominique Brun (FRA)	Kaori Yamaguchi (JPN)	Sharon Rendle (GBR)
			Ok Kyung-Sook (KOR)
1987	Sharon Rendle (GBR)	Kaori Yamaguchi (JPN)	Alessandra Giungi (ITA)
			Dominique Brun (FRA)
1989	Sharon Rendle (GBR)	Alessandra Giungi (ITA)	Maritza Pérez (CUB)
			Cho Min-Jun (KOR)
1991	Alessandra Giungi (ITA)	Sharon Rendle (GBR)	Maritza Pérez (CUB)
			Mitsumi Ueda (JPN)
1993	Legna Verdecia (CUB)	Almudena Munoz (ESP)	Cécile Nowak (FRA)
			Wakaba Suzuki (JPN)
1995	Marie-Claire Restoux (FRA)	Carolina Mariani (ARG)	Legna Verdecia (CUB)
			Sharon Rendle (GBR)
1997	Marie-Claire Restoux (FRA)	Kye Sun-Hui (PRK)	Hyun Sook-Hee (KOR)
			Nicole Flagothier (BEL)
1999	Noriko Narasaki (JPN)	Legna Verdecia (CUB)	Kye Sun-Hui (PRK)
			Marie-Claire Restoux (FRA)
2001	Kye Sun-Hui (KOR)	Raffaella Imbriani (GER)	Liu Yuxiang (CHN)
			Legina Verdecia Rodriguez (CUB)
2003	Amarilys Savón (CUB)	Annabelle Euranie (FRA)	Raffaella Imbriani (GER)
			Yuki Yokosawa (JPN)

Women's Lightweight (57kg)

	Gold	Silver	Bronze
1980	Gerda Winklbauer (AUT)	L. Panza (FRA)	Loretta Doyle (GBR)
			Jeannine Meulemans (BEL)
1982	Béatrice Rodriguez (FRA)	Suzanne Williams (AUS)	Diane Bell (GBR)
			Eve Aronoff (USA)
1984	Ann-Maria Burns (USA)	Suzanne Williams (AUS)	Gerda Winklbauer (AUT)
			Catherine Arnaud (FRA)
1986	Ann Hughes (GBR)	Maria Gontowicz (POL)	Béatrice Rodriguez (FRA)
			Chita Gross (NED)
1987	Catherine Arnaud (FRA)	Suzanne Williams (AUS)	Ann Hughes (GBR)
			Regina Philips (FRG)
1989	Catherine Arnaud (FRA)	Ann Hughes (GBR)	Miriam Blasco (ESP)
			Jung Sun-Yong (KOR)
1991	Miriam Blasco (ESP)	Nicole Flagothier (FRA)	Nicola Fairbrother (GBR)
			Li Zhongyun (CHN)
1993	Nicola Fairbrother (GBR)	Chiyori Tateno (JPN)	Driulys González (CUB)
			Jessica Gal (NED)

1995	Driulys Gonzales-Morales (CUB)	Jung Sun-Yong (KOR)	Danielle Zangrando (BRA)
1997	Isabel Fernandez (ESP)	Driulys González (CUB)	Filipa Cavalleri (POR)
			Chiyori Tateno (JPN)
1999	Driulys Gonzales-Morales (CUB)	Isabel Fernández (ESP)	Magali Baton (FRA)
			Jessica Gal (NED)
2001	Yurisleidis Lupetey (CUB)	Deborah Gravenstijn (NED)	Michaela Vernerová (CZE)
			Isabel Fernández (ESP)
2003	Kye Sun-Hui (PRK)	Yvonne Boenisch (GER)	Kie Kusakabe (JPN)
			Yurisleidis Lupetey (CUB)
			Deborah Gravenstijn (NED)

Women's Half Middleweight (63kg)

	Gold	**Silver**	**Bronze**
1980	Anita Staps (NED)	Laura Di Toma (ITA)	Inge Berg (FRG)
			Martine Rottier (FRA)
1982	Martine Rottier (FRA)	Inger Lise Solheim (NOR)	Jeannine Peeters (BEL)
			Gabriele Ritschel (FRG)
1984	Natasha Hernandez (VEN)	Chantal Han (NED)	Martine Rottier (FRA)
			Kaori Hachinoche (JPN)
1986	Diane Bell (GBR)	Céline Geraud (FRA)	Donna Guy (NZL)
			Ryoko Fujimoto (JPN)
1987	Diane Bell (GBR)	Lynn Roethke (USA)	Noriko Mochida (JPN)
			Boguslawa Olechnowicz (POL)
1989	Catherine Fleury (FRA)	Yelena Petrova (URS)	Gabriele Ritschel (FRG)
			Takako Kobayashi (JPN)
1991	Frauke Eickoff (GER)	Diane Bell (GBR)	Catherine Fleury (FRA)
			Yael Arad (ISR)
1993	Gella Vandecavaye (BEL)	Yael Arad (ISR)	Zulue Beltram (CUB)
			Diane Bell (GBR)
1995	Jung Sung-Sook (KOR)	Jenny Gal (NED)	Gella Vandecavaye (BEL)
			Catherine Fleury (FRA)
1997	Séverine Vandenhende (FRA)	Gella Vandecavaye (BEL)	Sara Álvarez (ESP)
			Jung Sung-Sook (KOR)
1999	Keiko Maeda (JPN)	Gella Vandecavaye (BEL)	Sara Álvarez (ESP)
			Karen Roberts (GBR)
2001	Gella Vandecavaye (BEL)	Sara Álvarez (ESP)	Anaisis Hernandez (CUB)
			Ayumi Tanimoto (JPN)
2003	Daniela Krukower (ARG)	Driulys Gonzalez (CUB)	Anna Von Harnier (CUB)
			Ylenia Scapin (ITA)

Women's Middleweight (70kg)

	Gold	**Silver**	**Bronze**
1980	Edith Simon (AUT)	Dawn Netherwood (GBR)	Catherine Pierre (FRA)
			Christine Pernick (USA)
1982	Brigitte Deydier (FRA)	Karin Krüger (FRG)	Heidi Andersen (NOR)
			Anita Staps (NED)
1984	Brigitte Deydier (FRA)	Irene de Kok (NED)	Dawn Netherwood (GBR)
			Shinobu Kandori (JPN)
1986	Brigitte Deydier (FRA)	Elisabeth Karlsson (SWE)	Alexandra Schreiber (FRG)
			Anita Staps (NED)
1987	Alexandra Schreiber (FRG)	Brigitte Deydier (FRA)	Roswitha Hartl (AUT)
			Hikari Sasaki (JPN)
1989	Emanuela Pierantozzi (ITA)	Hikari Sasaki (JPN)	Claire Lecat (FRA)
			Odalys Revé (CUB)
1991	Emanuela Pierantozzi (ITA)	Odalys Revé (CUB)	Ryoko Fujimoto (JPN)
			Kate Howey (GBR)
1993	Cho Min-Sun (KOR)	Liloko Ogasawa (USA)	Odalys Revé (CUB)
			Zhang Di (CHN)
1995	Cho Min-Sun (KOR)	Odalys Revé (CUB)	Aneta Szczepanska (POL)
			Liliko Ogasawara (USA)
1997	Kate Howey (GBR)	Anja von Rekowski (GER)	Emanuela Pierantozzi (ITA)
			Cho Min-Sun (KOR)
1999	Sibelis Veranes (CUB)	Ulla Werbrouck (BEL)	Kate Howey (GBR)
			Ylenia Scapin (ITA)
2001	Masae Ueno (JPN)	Kate Howey (GBR)	Regla Leyen (CUB)
			Ulla Werbrouck (BEL)
2003	Masae Ueno (JPN)	Regla Leyen (CUB)	Edith Bosch (NED)
			Annet Börhm (GER)

JUDO

Women's Half Heavyweight (78kg)

	Gold	Silver	Bronze
1980	Jocelyne Triadou (FRA)	Barbara Classen (FRG)	Avril Malley (GBR)
			Jolanda van Meggelen (NED)
1982	Barbara Classen (FRG)	Ingrid Berghmans (BEL)	Jocelyne Triadou (FRA)
			Karin Posch (AUT)
1984	Ingrid Berghmans (BEL)	Barbara Classen (FRG)	Anita Staps (NED)
			Véronique Vigneron (FRA)
1986	Irene de Kok (NED)	Liu Aixiang (CHN)	Barbara Classen (FRG)
			Ingrid Berghmans (BEL)
1987	Irene de Kok (NED)	Ingrid Berghmans (BEL)	Yoko Tanabe (JPN)
			Barbara Classen (FRG)
1989	Ingrid Berghmans (BEL)	Yoko Tanabe (JPN)	Aline Batailler (FRA)
			Wu Wiefeng (CHN)
1991	Kim Mi-Jung (KOR)	Yoko Tanabe (JPN)	Marion van Dorssen (NED)
			Laetitia Meignan (FRA)
1993	Leng Chunhui (CHN)	Kate Howey (GBR)	Victoria Kasunina (RUS)
			Kim Mi-Jung (KOR)
1995	Diadenys Luna (CUB)	Ulla Werbrouck (BEL)	Yoko Tanabe (JPN)
			Tatyana Belyayeva (UKR)
1997	Noriko Anno (JPN)	Diadenys Luna (CUB)	Ednaci da Silva (BRA)
			Ulla Werbrouck (BEL)
1999	Noriko Anno (JPN)	Yin Yufeng (CHN)	Celine Lebrun (FRA)
			Diadenys Luna (CUB)
2001	Noriko Anno (JPN)	Yurisel Laborde (CUB)	Céline Lebrun (FRA)
			Lee So-Yeon (KOR)
2003	Noriko Anno (JPN)	Yurisel Laborde (CUB)	Ednanci Silva (BRA)
			Esther San Miguel (ESP)

Women's Heavyweight (over 78kg)

	Gold	Silver	Bronze
1980	Margherita De Cal (ITA)	Paulette Fouillet (FRA)	Ingrid Berghmans (BEL)
			Christiane Kieburg (FRG)
1982	Natalina Lupino (FRA)	Margaret Castro (USA)	Marjolein van Unen (NED)
			Maria Teresa Motta (ITA)
1984	Maria Teresa Motta (ITA)	Gao Fengliang (CHN)	Margaret Castro (USA)
			Marjolein van Unen (NED)
1986	Gao Fengliang (CHN)	Marjolein van Unen (NED)	Nilmari Santini (PUR)
			Isabelle Paque (FRA)
1987	Gao Fengliang (CHN)	Regins Sigmund (FRG)	Angelique Seriese (NED)
			Margaret Castro-Gomez (USA)
1989	Gao Fengliang (CHN)	Regins Sigmund (FRG)	Natalina Lupino (FRA)
			Beata Maksymow (POL)
1991	Moon Ji-Yoon (KOR)	Zhang Ying (CHN)	Monique van der Lee (NED)
			Beata Maksymow (POL)
1993	Johanna Hagn (GER)	Moriko Anno (JPN)	Monique van der Lee (NED)
			Svetlana Goundarenko (RUS)
1995	Angelique Seriese (NED)	Zhang Ying (CHN)	Shon Hyun-Me (KOR)
			Daina Beltrán (CUB)
1997	Christine Cicot (FRA)	Miho Ninomiya (JPN)	Beata Maksymow (POL)
			Sun Fuming (CHN)
1999	Beata Maksymow (POL)	Yuan Hua (CHN)	Miho Ninomiya (JPN)
			Karina Bryant GBR)
2001	Yuan Hua (CHN)	Midori Shintani (JPN)	Daina Beltran (CUB)
			Sandra Köppen (GER)
2003	Sun Fuming (CHN)	Maki Tsukada (JPN)	Tea Donguzashvili (RUS)
			Karina Bryant (GBR)

Women's Open (no weight restriction)

	Gold	Silver	Bronze
1980	Ingrid Berghmans (BEL)	Paulette Fouillet (FRA)	Barbara Classen (FRG)
			Barbara Fest (USA)
1982	Ingrid Berghmans (BEL)	Hiromi Tateishi (JPN)	Jocelyne Triadou (FRA)
			Regina Sigmund (FRG)
1984	Ingrid Berghmans (BEL)	Marjolein van Unen (NED)	Natalina Lupino (FRA)
			Gao Fengliang (CHN)

1986	Ingrid Berghmans (BEL)	Li Jinlin (CHN)	Laetitia Meignan (FRA)
1987	Gao Fengliang (CHN)	Ingrid Berghmans (BEL)	Karin Kutz (FRG)
1989	Estella Rodriguez (CUB)	Sharon Lee (GBR)	Isabelle Paque (FRA)
1991	Zhuang Xiaoyan (CHN)	Estela Rodríguez (CUB)	Karin Kutz (FRG)
1993	Beata Maksymow (POL)	Angelique Seriese (NED)	Yoko Tanabe (JPN)
1995	Monique van der Lee (NED)	Sun Fuming (CHN)	Zhang Di (CHN)
1997	Daina Beltrán (CUB)	Raquel Barrientos (ESP)	Claudia Weber (GER)
1999	Daina Beltrán (CUB)	Miho Ninomiya (JPN)	Natalina Lupino (FRA)
2001	Céline Lebrun (FRA)	Karina Bryant (GBR)	Zhang Ying (CHN)
2003	Tong Wen (CHN)	Karina Bryant (GBR)	Moon Ji-Yoon (KOR)

Laetitia Meignan (FRA)
Karin Kutz (FRG)
Isabelle Paque (FRA)
Karin Kutz (FRG)
Yoko Tanabe (JPN)
Zhang Di (CHN)
Claudia Weber (GER)
Natalina Lupino (FRA)
Zhang Ying (CHN)
Moon Ji-Yoon (KOR)
Lee Hyun-Kyung (KOR)
Estela Rodriguez (CUB)
Yuan Hua (CHN)
Miho Ninomiya (JPN)
Tsvetlana Bojilova (BUL)
Choi Sook-le (KOR)
Catarina Rodrígues (POR)
Tong Wen (CHN)
Mara Kovacevic (SCG)
Daima Beltrán (CUB)

KABADDI

Kabaddi is primarily an Indian game, though it is played with minor variations all over Asia and is especially popular in Nepal, Bangladesh, Sri Lanka, Japan and Pakistan. The origins of kabaddi are obscure, however it is thought that it was originally used to develop self defence, responses to attack and reflexes of counter-attack by individuals, in groups or teams. It is a simple and inexpensive game that requires neither a massive playing area nor any expensive equipment. It is precisely for this reason that the game is so popular in rural India.

Kabaddi is known by various names: *chedugudu* or *hu-tu-tu* in southern parts of India, *hadudu* (men's version) and *chu-kit-kit* (women's version) in eastern India, and simply kabaddi in northern India.

The kabaddi playing area is 12.5m × 10m and is divided by a line into two halves. The side that wins the toss sends a 'raider' into the opponents' court continuously chanting 'kabaddi'. The raider's aim is to touch any or all players on the opposing side and return to his court without taking a breath, while still chanting 'kabaddi'. All players touched by the raider are out. The aim of the opposing team is to hold the raider and stop him from returning to his own court before he takes a breath. If the raider cannot return to his court in one breath he is declared out and leaves the court. Each team in turn sends a player into their opponents' court. If a player crosses the boundary line during the course of play, or if any part of his body touches the ground outside the boundary, he is out, except during a struggle. Matches are staged on the basis of age groups and weight. Seven officials supervise a match – one referee, two umpires, two linesmen, a time keeper and a scorer.

There are three main forms of kabaddi: Surjeevani, Amar and Gaminee. In the Surjeevani form, one player is revived each time a player of the opposing team is out. i.e. each time one team loses a player, one of their opponents returns to the court. In the Amar form, when a player is out he does not leave the court but stays inside, and one point is awarded to the team that touched him. There is a fixed time limit. In Gaminee kabaddi no players are revived and the game ends when all the players of one team are out; unlike both other forms there is no time limit.

The Kabaddi Federation of India (KFI) was founded in 1950. It compiled a standard set of rules and regulates the Surjeevani form of kabaddi. The Amateur Kabaddi Federation of India (AKFI), founded in 1973, has given new shape to the rules, and it also holds the rights of modification to the rules. The Asian Kabaddi Federation was founded under the chairmanship of Mr. Sharad Pawar (Maharashtra). The England Kabaddi Federation was founded in 1969, while Channel 4 television brought kabaddi to a wider British audience in the early 1990s.

The first world kabaddi championship was held in Hamilton, Ontario, Canada, with approximately 14,000 people packing Copps Coliseum to watch stars from India, Pakistan, Canada, England and the United States compete. India has maintained its dominance in kabaddi, winning the gold medal in all four Asian Games since the event made its debut in 1990. In the 2002 Games in Busan, the Indian team took gold by defeating Pakistan 37-7. The championship game is played between two teams of 12, although only seven players are allowed on the court at any one time. The game has two periods of 20 minutes each.

KARATE

According to legend, the evolution of karate began over a thousand years ago, possibly as early as the fifth century AD when Bodhidharma arrived at the Shaolin temple in China from India to teach Zen Buddhism. At the same time he introduced a systematised set of exercises designed to strengthen the mind and body. With these supposedly originated the Shaolin style of temple boxing, and Bodhidharma's teachings later became the basis for the majority of Chinese martial arts. In truth, however, the origins of karate appear to be somewhat obscure and little is known about the early development of karate until it appeared in Okinawa.

A small island of the group that comprises modern-day Japan, Okinawa, is the main island in the chain of Ryuku Islands stretching from Japan to Chinese Taipei. Being at the crossroads of major trading routes, it developed as a trade centre for south-east Asia, trading with Japan, China, Indo-China, Thailand, Malaysia, Borneo and the Philippines.

In its earliest stages, the martial art known as 'karate' was an indigenous form of closed-fist fighting which was developed in Okinawa and called *te*, or 'hand'. Weapons bans, imposed on the Okinawans at various points in their history, encouraged the refinement of so-called 'empty hand' techniques which, for this reason, were developed in secret until modern times. Further refinement came with the influence of other martial arts brought by nobles and trade merchants to the island.

Te continued to develop over the years, primarily in three Okinawan cities: Shuri, Naha and Tomari. Each of these places was the centre for a different sector of society: kings and nobles, merchants and business people, and farmers and fishermen respectively. For this reason, different forms of self-defence developed within each city, subsequently becoming known as *Shuri-te*, *Naha-te* and *Tomari-te*. Collectively they were called *Okinawa-te* or *Tode*, 'Chinese hand'. Gradually, karate was divided into two main groups: *Shorin-ryu*, which developed around Shuri and Tomari, and *Shorei-ryu*, which came from the Naha area. The close proximity of the three towns, however, meant that the differences between their arts were essentially ones of emphasis, not of kind. It is possible that the two styles were developed based on different physical requirements, Shorin-ryu being quick and linear with natural breathing while Shorei-ryu emphasised steady, rooted movements, breathing being synchronised with each movement.

The Chinese character used to write *Tode* could also be pronounced 'kara' thus the name was replaced with *kara te-jutsu* or 'Chinese hand art' by the Okinawan masters. This was later changed to *karate-do* by the first great karate master, Gichin Funakoshi (1868-1957), who adopted an alternative meaning for the Chinese character for *kara*. From this point on the term *karate* came to mean 'empty hand'. The *do* in *karate-do* means 'way' or 'path', and is indicative of the discipline and philosophy of karate with its moral and spiritual connotations.

The first public demonstration of karate in Japan was in 1917 by Gichin Funakoshi, at the Butoku-den in Kyoto. This and subsequent demonstrations greatly impressed many Japanese, including Crown Prince Hirohito, who was very enthusiastic about the Okinawan art. In 1922, Dr Jigoro Kano, founder of the Japanese art of judo, invited Funakoshi to demonstrate at the Kodokan Dojo, the training hall for judo in Tokyo, and to remain in Japan to teach karate. Kano's sponsorship was instrumental in establishing a base for karate in Japan. As an Okinawan 'peasant art', karate would have been scorned by the Japanese without the backing of so formidable a martial arts master.

Today there are four main styles of karate-do in Japan: *Goju-ryu*, *Shito-ryu*, *Shotokan* and *Wado-ryu* (ryu literally means 'style').

Goju-ryu developed out of Naha-te, its popularity being due primarily to the success of Kanryo Higaonna (1853-1915). Higaonna opened a dojo in Naha using eight forms brought from China. His best student, Chojun Miyagi (1888-1953), later founded Goju-ryu, 'hard soft way' in 1930. In Goju-ryu much emphasis is placed on combining soft circular blocking techniques with quick, strong counter-attacks delivered in rapid succession.

Shito-ryu was founded by Kenwa Mabuni (1889-1952) in 1928 and was influenced directly by both Naha-te and Shuri-te. The name 'Shito' is constructively derived from the combination of the Japanese characters of Mabuni's teachers' names – Ankoh Itosu and Kanryo Higaonna. Shito-ryu schools use a large number (about fifty) of prearranged sets of movements, *kata*, characterised by an emphasis on power in the execution of techniques.

Shotokan was founded by Gichin Funakoshi in Tokyo in 1938. Funakoshi is considered to be the founder of modern karate. Born in Okinawa, he began to study karate with Yasutsune Azato, one of Okinawa's greatest experts in the art. In 1921 Funakoshi first introduced karate to Tokyo. In 1936, at nearly 70 years of age, he opened his own training hall. The dojo was called Shotokan after the pen name used by Funakoshi to sign poems written in his youth. Shotokan karate is characterised by powerful linear techniques and deep, strong stances.

Wado-ryu, 'way of harmony', founded in 1939, is a system of karate developed from ju-jitsu and karate by Hienori Otsuka as taught by Funakoshi. This style of karate combines basic movements of ju-jitsu with techniques of evasion, placing a strong emphasis on softness and the 'way of harmony' or spiritual discipline.

KENDO

Kendo is the traditional Japanese style of fencing with wooden swords. It is a composite word composed of two *kanji* or pictograms: *Ken*, meaning sword, and *Do*, meaning 'the way of'. Together the term is literally 'the way of the sword'. It is a martial arts practice spawned by the traditional schools of swordsmanship (*ryu*) of ancient Japan, and was performed mainly by the *bushi*, or samurai class, of the era.

As practice with real blades is inherently dangerous, the schools developed a dummy sword called a *shinai*, and a set of protective equipment called *bogu* which protects the face and head (*men*), wrists (*kote*), chest (*do*), and groin (*tare*). Before the Showa period (1926-89), it was customarily referred to as *kenjutsu* (fencing) or *gekken*.

Kendo went into decline after World War II as General Douglas McArthur outlawed its practice. It was thought that it had agitated the rise of nationalism and militarism in Japan during the war. However, in 1953, the year of the US–Japan Peace Treaty, kendo was reprieved and thereafter flourished to the extent that it was included as a mandatory subject in all high-school curriculums.

Kendo training is based on a variety of movements of attack and defence known as *waza*. Most fundamental are stance, footwork, cuts, thrusts, feints and parries. Although kendo is physically demanding, it also acts as a great source for self-discipline in order to strengthen both mind and body. It is this aspect of kendo that attracts many of its most devoted *kendoka* (kendo players). A kendo bout between skilled opponents is an intense experience. For a moment in time concentration is absolute, conscious thought is suppressed and action is instinctive. Such training develops in the serious student powers of resolution and endurance under pressure that frequently affect his or her life in a positive way.

The rules of kendo are fairly simple: strike one of a handful of targets with your shinai before your opponent strikes yours. The strike must be delivered with proper form and power, such that the proper part of the shinai makes contact with the target area just as the right foot strikes the floor, and must be accompanied by a shout of the name of the point aimed for.

The equipment is as follows (in the order it is donned): *keikogi* (shirt), *hakama* (skirt), *tare* (waist protector), *do* (chest protector), *hachimaki*, or more recently *mentoweru* (headscarf), *men* (one-piece helmet with wire face-shield and neck/shoulder protectors) and *kote* (padded gloves).

Kendo begins with three basic stances which are dependent on the skill of the fighters involved. *Chudan no kamae* is the most common and conservative stance; in this stance the shinai is held with the hands at waist level and its tip pointed at the opponent's throat. *Jodan no kamae* is an aggressive stance in which the shinai is raised above the head ready to attack; it is often used by a more skilled (or simply more aggressive) fighter against a lesser opponent. *Gedan no kamae* is a defensive stance where the shinai is held with the point towards the floor. It takes great skill and timing to go from the gedan into a successful attack.

Points are scored by striking any one of eight areas on an opponent: the men (three places to score), kote (two places), do (two places), and tsuki (neck area protected by men, one place). Tsuki is the only area where a thrusting motion is allowed, indeed required.

The match area is a square or rectangle of 9-11m, and the centre of the court must be marked with an 'X' made of two pieces of white tape each 30cm in length. The shinai must be made from four split pieces of bamboo or permissible synthetic material and be a maximum of 120cm in length with a maximum weight of 500g.

A typical match commences as follows: contestants step on to the court, place themselves approximately nine steps apart and exchange *rei* (bow), then move three steps forward to take the *sonkyo* (knee bend squat), at the same time drawing the shinai with the tips about one inch apart and getting into the *kamae* (ready position). At the *hajime* (start) command from the chief referee they stand up and begin fighting. Kendo bouts are judged over a set period of time or by the first person to score two points; hence if one fighter is 1-0 in the lead when the allocated time elapses then they are deemed the winner. The standard duration of a match is five minutes but with time-outs this can be extended considerably.

Today kendo has ten ranks and three teaching degrees, the higher ranks being regulated by the All-Japan Kendo Federation (formed in 1928). The International Kendo Federation oversees all international kendo tournaments and orchestrates the World Kendo Championships which take place once every three years and have been dominated by Japanese fighters.

KICKBOXING

Thousands of years ago in East Asia, Muay Thai kickboxing (see separate section) was commonly practised as a self-defence discipline. However, modern kickboxing has its origins largely in the desire among many Western martial arts practitioners for a full-contact sport without the rigid rules and boundaries of karate. There is no doubt that the popularity of kung fu films, and in particular those featuring Bruce Lee, gave momentum to the rise of kickboxing, providing it with exposure around the world. Film stars such as Jean-Claude van Damme and Dolph Lundgren are former kickboxing protagonists.

The initial international championship for full-contact kickboxing was held in Los Angeles in 1974. This development was regarded favourably by many leading karate masters at the time, some of whom encouraged and eagerly participated in the newly recognised sport. Joe Lewis, Bill Wallace, Jeff Smith and Isuena Duenas were its first champions.

In the early days of the sport the most formally constituted and widely recognised international sanctioning group was the Professional Kickboxing Association (PKA), founded in the United States. Its founders were the first to organise televised reports of championships being held around the globe, and the group also formed the first fighter's rating systems. Among the stars of this new syndicate were Jean-Yves Theriault, Jerry Trimble and Brad Hefton.

In 1975 Georges Bruckner created the first European amateur organisation, named the World All Style Karate Organisation (WAKO). It was soon seen as a strong rival to the PKA and in recent years, since the Italian Ennio Falsoni took control from WAKO's German founder, has become the most widely recognised amateur federation in the sport.

In 1976, Howard Hanson, a Shorin-ryu karate black belt and student of karate grandmaster Mike Stone, created his own group, the World Kickboxing Association (WKA). At first the WKA had many successes and achievements, even developing its own regulations on low kicks in the sport, and producing champions like Fred Royers, Ronnie Green and Rob Kaman.

As a result of legal problems faced by the PKA, a new international governing body, the International Sports Kickboxing Association (ISKA), was founded in 1986 by five promoters and PKA executives.

Today there are four divisions within the sport of kickboxing: Full Contact (FC), Freestyle Rules (FR), Oriental Rules (OR), and Muay Thai (MT). Great Britain has a super-welterweight world champion in the Full Contact division in the person of Jim Caldecourt, a Brighton-based fighter.

KORFBALL

The origins of korfball, a game similar to basketball and netball, can be traced back to a Dutch schoolteacher, Nico Broekhuysen, who devised the game in Amsterdam in 1902, having been inspired by a game he had played during a summer course in Nääs, Sweden. He named his new version after the Dutch word for a basket, *korf*. It was designed to be played by both sexes on equal terms.

The Dutch Korfball Association was founded in 1903 and korfball was demonstrated at the Olympic Games of 1920 (Antwerp) and 1928 (Amsterdam). However, it was only after the formation of the International Korfball Federation in 1933 (comprising the Dutch and Belgian associations), an organisation committed to the expansion of the sport, that further development came to be seriously considered.

In the first half of the 20th century, the sport's underlying philosophy of gender equality perhaps appeared to be too progressive. In the 21st century, however, there is greater parity between the sexes and, as one of the few mixed team sports, korfball both satisfies and confirms this trend. Hence, korfball is gradually establishing itself and gaining popularity around the globe by holding true to its twin principles of coeducation and co-operation. The sport's expansion has taken it into the Americas, Eastern Europe and South-east Asia.

The sport's growth in Central and Eastern Europe is particularly spectacular and the overall level of skills is improving dramatically. In international competition countries like Poland, Hungary and the Czech Republic have become serious competitors.

World championships have been held since 1978 and korfball featured in the World Games (a multi-sport competition including about 45 disciplines) from 1985 onwards. In 1991 Chinese Taipei became the first non-European country to win world championship medals and four years later the World Cup competition was for the first time held outside Europe, in India.

The first British korfball club was founded in Croydon in 1946 but in Great Britain it remains a minority sport. Testament to that is the appearance of the word 'korfball' on the television show *Call My Bluff* in 1997.

The game is played on a 40m × 20m pitch indoors, and one of up to 60m × 30m outdoors. It is contested between two teams of eight, with two pairs of men and women in each of the two zones of attack and defence. A goal is scored by throwing the ball through the opponents' basket which is atop a 3.5m post. After every two goals, attackers and defenders change position. The pairing of women versus women and men versus men makes korfball the only truly integrated sport, giving no advantage to male physical strength. The game itself is simple; its few set rules are similar to those of netball and basketball.

World Championships

	Gold	Silver	Bronze	Venue
1978	Netherlands	Belgium	West Germany	Rotterdam
1984	Netherlands	Belgium	West Germany	Antwerp
1987	Netherlands	Belgium	Great Britain	Rotterdam
1991	Belgium	Netherlands	Chinese Taipei	Antwerp
1995	Netherlands	Belgium	Portugal	New Delhi
1999	Netherlands	Belgium	Great Britain	Adelaide
2003	Netherlands	Belgium	Czech Republic	Rotterdam

LACROSSE

Lacrosse is the oldest sport in North America, its origin dating back to the 1400s when it was played by the Six Nations of the Iroquois in what became upper New York State and lower Ontario. It did not become generally known about, however, until 1636 when a Jesuit missionary named Jean de Brebeuf saw the Huron Indians play it near Thunder Bay, Ontario. In a report to his ecclesiastical superiors he likened the stick with which the Indians competed to the crosier carried at religious ceremonies by a bishop. Thus, the name *la crosse* evolved, and this later became simply lacrosse.

Another Jesuit, Pierre de Charlevoix, described the game as played by the Algonquins in 1721. Indian lacrosse was known as 'baggataway' and was a mass participation game, with teams often made up of one hundred to one thousand braves on each side. The goals were usually 500m to 800m apart. On occasion, the goals could be separated by several miles. Usually a large rock or tree was considered the goal and a score was recorded by hitting the rock or tree with a ball. Some tribes used goalposts 2-3m apart, and the ball had to pass between them for a score, much like today's game. These games lasted as long as two or three days, starting at sunrise and ending at sunset.

Lacrosse was played not only for recreation but also as a means of training warriors (the Cherokee referred to it as 'the little brother of war'). The roughness of the game served to accustom players to conditions of close combat, and its length to develop endurance for war and hunting parties.

Modern lacrosse is a field game played by two opposing teams, with a ball and a special netted stick, or crosse, with which the ball is caught, carried and thrown. It was not until the early 1800s that the French pioneers started playing lacrosse seriously. Europeans in Canada started playing the game about 1840, and the first lacrosse organisation, the Olympic Club, was founded in Montreal in 1842. Canadian dentist W. George Beers standardised the game in 1867 with the adoption of set field dimensions, limits to the number of players per team, and other basic rules. He became known as the 'Father of Lacrosse'.

New York University fielded America's first college team in 1877, and Philips Andover Academy, Massachusetts, Philips Exeter Academy, New Hampshire, and the Lawrenceville School, New Jersey, were the nation's first high school teams in 1882.

The English Lacrosse Union was founded in 1892 and in the sport's formative years England, Canada and the United States played each other in international competitions. The game has now become popular all over the world and playing nations include Scotland, Wales, Ireland, Argentina, Australia, the Czech Republic, Finland, Germany, Hong Kong, Japan, Holland, South Korea, Sweden, Tonga, New Zealand, the Iroquois Nation and South Africa.

The National Lacrosse League (NLL) was organised in 1997 as a group of independently owned teams who began play the following year. After much negotiation, the Major Indoor Lacrosse League (MILL) merged with the NLL.

The Englishwoman Constance M.K. Applebee, who introduced hockey to American women in 1901, and remained in the United States as a physical educator, was active in establishing lacrosse as a women's sport in the US. The U.S. Women's Lacrosse Association (USWLA) was founded at her summer camp in 1931. The USWLA governed the sport on collegiate and club levels until 1981, when the NCAA (National Collegiate Athletic Association) inaugurated its national championship tournament for women.

Lacrosse was an Olympic sport in 1904 at St Louis and in 1908 at London. Only three countries, Canada, England and the United States, were represented and Canada won both gold medals.

The International Lacrosse Federation has conducted a men's world championship tournament since 1967. The women's world championship, inaugurated in 1969, was replaced in 1982 by the World Cup tournament for women.

The USA have been victorious in eight of the nine men's world championships: Toronto 1967, Melbourne 1974, Baltimore 1982, Toronto 1986, Perth 1990, Manchester 1994, Baltimore 1998 and Perth 2002. The only other winner has been Canada, in 1978, when the competition was held in Stockport. The 2006 championship will be held in London, Ontario.

The inaugural indoor championships took place in 2003 in a variety of venues in Ontario, Canada, in the towns of Oshawa, Mississauga, Kitchener and Hamilton. Six nations took part in this first event of its kind, with the hosts being hot favourites. Hoping to transfer their international reputation from the outdoor game were USA, Iroquois Nation and Australia. Always capable of causing upsets, the Czech Republic and Scotland completed the group. After a series of round-robin matches Canada were duly declared winners.

Men's lacrosse is played on a field 60yds (55m) wide and 110yds (100m) long, including 15yds (14m) of clear space behind each goal so that the area between opposing goals is 80yds (73m). Each goal consists of two poles 6ft (1.83m) tall, with a 6ft (1.83m) crossbar at the top.

A pyramid-shaped netting, open at the front, is attached to the poles and crossbar and is fastened to the ground at its apex, 7ft (2.1 m) beyond the goal line. The object of the game is to score more goals than one's opponents. A player may run with the ball, pass it in any direction and catch it, but, with the exception of the goalkeeper, may not touch it by hand. Defensive players are allowed to prod the player in possession with their stick or slap at the ball-carrier's stick to dislodge the ball from the net attached to the stick.

The rules for women's lacrosse stipulate no boundaries, but a field of 120yds × 70yds (110m × 64m) is preferable. The women's game allows no bodily contact whatsoever.

The lacrosse ball is made of hard rubber, generally 8ins (20cm) in circumference and 5oz (141g) to 5¼oz (148g) in weight.

Players carry a stick, or crosse, 40-42ins (102-107cm) long for men, and 35½-43¼ins (90-110cm) long for women. Defenders may use a crosse 52-72ins (132-183cm) long. The stick is hooked on top, with strings woven of rawhide, gut, clock string or linen cord strung diagonally across the hooked portion to form a network.

Players in field lacrosse today use a stick that has an aluminum, graphite, or wood handle; only the goalkeeper's crosse may exceed a width of 10ins (25cm).

Men's teams have ten players; women's teams are composed of 12 players.

In field lacrosse the 60-minute playing time is divided into four periods, or quarters, with each team being allowed two time-outs per half.

The women's game consists of two 25-minute halves with a 10-minute rest period between.

Another form of the game is called box lacrosse. It consists of six players per side on a hard, enclosed surface 90ft (27m) by 180-200ft (54-61m). This form of lacrosse has a professional league in the United States, the Major Indoor Lacrosse League. The Mann Cup, originally donated by Sir Donald Mann in 1910 as a challenge trophy for the Canadian amateur champion team, was transferred to box lacrosse in the 1930s.

LAWN TENNIS

Racket sports go back many centuries. The origin of lawn tennis can perhaps be traced to a 12th- and 13th-century French game called *jeu de paume* (game of the palm), although many popular racket sports have contributed to the development of what we now call tennis. In some places the game is still referred to as lawn tennis, since it was first played on the lawns of Victorian England.

Modern tennis is derived mainly from the old game of court tennis or real (i.e. royal) tennis, and partly from rackets and badminton. Major Walter Clopton Wingfield, of Nantclwyd in north Wales, patented a game he called 'Sphairistike' (in Greek, 'ball playing') in 1874. The popularity of tennis grew rapidly. The US Lawn Tennis Association was formed in 1881 and held its first championship the same year, while national championships were established in France (1891) and Australia (1905).

In England the Marylebone Cricket Club, which at the time was also the ruling body for real tennis, adapted Wingfield's first rules almost immediately. The new rules were in turn adapted by the All England Croquet and Lawn Tennis Club which in 1877 had decided to hold a championship event, a men's tournament. The first women's championship followed in 1884.

The Lawn Tennis Association (LTA) became the ruling body for British tennis in 1888, while the International Lawn Tennis Federation was formed in 1913. This organisation, later renamed the International Tennis Federation (ITF), has governed international tennis since the outbreak of World War I.

The International Lawn Tennis Challenge Trophy, introduced in 1900, was originally contested between the United States and Great Britain. It soon became known as the Davis Cup after a benefactor of the game, Dwight Davis, donated a trophy to the tennis community. Davis was a doubles specialist, and the bowl he donated has remained the dominant men's team trophy in the game. Over 100 countries now participate in the competition.

The Ladies' International Lawn Tennis Championship, more usually known as the Wightman Cup, was instigated in 1923 by Hazel Hotchkiss Wightman and was played between Great Britain and the United States. It was last held in 1990.

The true women's international team competition today is the Federation Cup, inaugurated in 1963. Nell Hopman, wife of Australian Davis Cup captain Harry Hopman, took up Hazel Hotchkiss Wightman's original idea of an international team event. In 1962 the ITF was finally persuaded that a women's team championship was feasible. Since 1994 the event has been known as the Fed Cup.

Biographies

Agassi, Andre   Born Las Vegas, USA, 29 April 1970. Known for having the best return of serve in professional tennis, Agassi achieved a no. 1 ranking on the ATP (Association of Tennis Professionals) tour in 1999 and by 2000 had won over $19 million in prize money. Agassi has won eight Grand Slam singles titles (Wimbledon 1992; US Open 1994, 1999; Australian Open 1995, 2000, 2001, 2003; French Open 1999). He has represented the USA in the Davis Cup in 21 ties, compiling a lifetime record of 30 wins and 5 losses. Agassi is currently married to Steffi Graf.

Austin, Tracy   Born Rolling Hills, California, USA, 12 December 1962. The youngest-ever winner of the US Open women's championship in 1979 at the age of 16 years, 9 months. In 1981 she won a second US Open but her career was curtailed by injury. She was the youngest player ever inducted into the Tennis Hall of Fame. Currently she works as a television commentator.

Ashe, Arthur   Born Richmond, Virginia, USA, 10 July 1943. The first African-American selected for the United States Davis Cup team (1963). In 1965, Ashe won the individual National Collegiate Athletic Association (NCAA) championship and was a chief contributor to UCLA's victory in the team NCAA championship the same year. Winner of the inaugural US Open in 1968, he was later one of the key players behind the formation of the Association of Tennis Professionals (ATP). He defeated Jimmy Connors in the 1975 Wimbledon final, earning for himself the no.1 ranking in the world and becoming the only black player ever to win the Wimbledon men's singles. Ashe died after complications with AIDS, 6 February 1993.

Becker, Boris   Born Leimen, Heidelberg, West Germany, 22 November 1967. Won his first Wimbledon championship when unseeded in 1985, the first German and the youngest-ever man to become Wimbledon champion. In all Becker won six Grand Slam titles (Wimbledon 1985, 1986, 1989; US Open 1989; Australian Open 1991, 1996), only the French Open eluding him. He is currently an active senior ATP player.

Borg, Björn   Born Södertälje, Sweden, 6 June 1956. Borg, dubbed 'The Ice Man' for his calm demeanour on court, won 11 Grand Slam singles titles and a total of 62 singles tournaments during his career. He won five consecutive Wimbledon championships (1976-80) and six French Open titles (1974, 1975, 1978-81). Perhaps his most remarkable match was the 1980 Wimbledon final in which he defeated John McEnroe 1-6, 7-5, 6-3, 6-7 (16-18), 8-6. Borg was the no. 1-ranked player six times between 1977 and

1981, totalling 109 weeks. He retired at the age of 26 in 1983 but still occasionally plays on the senior tour.

Budge, Donald   Born Oakland, California, USA, 13 June 1915. Ranked according to *Tennis* magazine as one of the 20 greatest players of the 20th century, Budge left university in 1933 to play tennis with the US Davis Cup auxiliary team. In 1937 he enjoyed a series of victories during the Wimbledon championships, winning the singles title, the men's doubles title with Gene Mako, and the mixed doubles crown with Alice Marble. He went on to win the US National singles and the mixed doubles with Sarah Palfrey Fabyan. In 1938 he became the first man to complete the Grand Slam of all four major titles. He is particularly remembered for his match against Gottfried Von Cramm in the 1937 Davis Cup inter-zone finals where, after trailing 1-4 in the final set, he came back to win 8-6. He became the first tennis player to be given the James E. Sullivan Award as America's top amateur athlete. In 2000 he was injured in an automobile accident from which he never fully recovered. He died shortly afterwards in a nursing home in Scranton, Pennsylvania, 26 January 2000.

Capriati, Jennifer   Born Long Island, USA, 29 March 1976. Turning professional on 5 March 1990 at the age of 13, Capriati reached the final of the French Open that same year and in 1991 became the youngest-ever women's semi-finalist at the Wimbledon championships. She went on to win the singles gold medal at the 1992 Olympics, defeating Steffi Graf. After some disappointing losses in 1993 and legal and personal problems in the following years she put her career on hold, returning to the tour in 1996. Capriati won the singles title in Luxembourg in 2000 and in 2001 began an earnest comeback, winning both the Australian Open and the French Open. She successfully defended her Australian Open title the following year but lost her first match defending the title in 2003. Capriati was ranked no. 1 in the world for brief periods in 2001 and 2002.

Chang, Michael   Born Hoboken, New Jersey, USA, 22 February 1972. Chang won his first national title, the USTA Junior Hardcourt Singles, aged 12. His only Grand Slam success came in the 1989 French Open at the age of 17, while his highest singles world ranking was no. 2 (9 September 1996). In 2000 his world ranking dropped to no. 31. In 2003 Chang announced his retirement from the game.

Clijsters, Kim   Born Bilzen, Belgium, 8 June 1983. One of the best current players yet to win a major title, Clijsters' recent Grand Slam achievements include reaching the French Open final in 2001, losing to Jennifer Capriati, and the French Open and US Open finals in 2003 which she lost to fellow Belgian Justine Henin-Hardenne. On 10 August 2003 she achieved the no. 1 world ranking on the Women's Tennis Association (WTA) list, but lost it to Henin-Hardenne soon afterwards.

Connolly, Maureen   Born Maureen Catherine Connolly, San Diego, California, USA, 17 September 1934. 'Little Mo' was a natural at tennis from a very young age. At the age of 14 she won 56 consecutive matches and the following year she became the youngest-ever player to win the United States under-18 championship. She entered her first US national championship in 1951 at Forest Hills, New York, and in the finals defeated Shirley Fry, becoming at the age of 16 years, 11 months the youngest-ever to win America's most prestigious tennis tournament. She

was named 'Woman Athlete of the Year' by the Associated Press three years in a row, 1951-53, her achievements having made her enormously popular with the media. In 1952 Connolly defended her US title and won the Wimbledon championship. In 1953 she became the first woman, and only the second person ever, to win the world's four Grand Slam titles in the same year. In all she won nine Grand Slam singles titles (Wimbledon 1952, 1953, 1954; US Open 1951, 1952, 1953; Australian Open 1953; French Open 1953, 1954). Connolly married Norman Brinker, a member of the 1952 United States Olympic equestrian team. She was diagnosed with cancer in 1966 and after a long battle with the disease died in Dallas, Texas, 21 June 1969.

Connors, Jimmy   Born Illinois, USA, 2 September 1952. Known for his brash conduct on and off court, for five straight years (1974-78) Jimmy Connors was ranked no. 1 in the world. The first high-profile tennis player to use a metal racket, along with Bjorn Börg he made the two-handed backhand shot an accepted part of the game. He won the Wimbledon men's singles title twice (1974 and 1982). During the 1991 US Open Connors celebrated his 39th birthday, having only made the event as a wild-card entry, but managed to reach the semi-finals, before losing to eventual champion Stefan Edberg. Connors also had a celebrated doubles partnership with fellow rebel Ilie Nastase; the pair won the Wimbledon title in 1973. Undoubtedly one of the finest players of all time, Connors ranks alongside Andre Agassi as one of the best-ever returners of serve.

Cooper, Charlotte   Born Charlotte Reinagle Cooper, Ealing, Middlesex, England, 22 September 1871. Nicknamed 'Chattie', Cooper won the first of her five Wimbledon singles titles in 1895. In the 1900 Olympics in Paris, where women were allowed to participate for the first time, she won the tennis singles, thus becoming the first woman to win an Olympic gold medal. She followed this up with a second gold, winning the mixed doubles with partner Reginald Doherty. In 1908 she won her fifth Wimbledon singles title at the age of 37, an age record that still stands. In 1912, at the age of 41, she yet again reached the Wimbledon singles final. Her husband, Alfred Sterry, became President of the Lawn Tennis Association (LTA) and their daughter, Gwen, played in Britain's Wightman Cup tennis team. Cooper continued to play in championship events and remained active in competitive tennis well into her fifties. She died in 1967 at the age of 96.

Court, Margaret   Born Margaret Jean Smith, Albury, New South Wales, Australia, 16 July 1942. One of the dominant women's tennis players of the 1960s, Margaret Smith began playing tennis at the age of eight and was 17 when she won the first of seven straight Australian Open singles titles in 1960. She went to Wimbledon in 1962 as strong favourite for the singles title, but in a famous battle lost to American Billie-Jean Moffit. The following year, however, she became the first Australian woman to win the Wimbledon championship and also the first, with partner Ken Fletcher, to win the Grand Slam in mixed doubles. In total, Court won 62 Grand Slam events (singles and doubles), a record that still stands. She was ranked no.1 in the world seven times (1962-65, 1969, 1970, 1973). Her victories included 24 Grand Slam singles titles (Wimbledon 1963, 1965, 1970; US Open 1962, 1965, 1969, 1970, 1973; Australian Open 1960-66, 1969, 1970, 1971, 1973; French Open 1962, 1964, 1969, 1970, 1973). In 1991 she was ordained as a Christian minister and founded the Victory Life Church. Court now lives in Perth, Western Australia, and runs a Christian ministry.

Davenport, Lindsay Born Palos Verdes, California, USA, 8 June 1976. Winner of three Grand Slam singles titles (Wimbledon 1999; US Open 1998; Australian Open 2000), Davenport also won the Olympic gold medal in 1996. She was the no. 1-ranked women's singles player in the world several times between 1998 and 2001. Davenport married investment banker and former professional footballer Jon Leach, brother of tennis player Rick Leach, in 2003.

Federer, Roger Born Basel, Switzerland, 8 August 1981. Federer joined the ATP professional tour at the age of 17 and has made a rapid rise through the ranks. In 2001 he reached the quarter-final stages at Wimbledon and the French Open. By 2003 he seemed the complete player: having begun the year by winning four Davis Cup matches out of four, he then won the BMW Open, Dubai Open, Open 13, and the Gerry Webber International, before on 6 July 2003 defeating Mark Philippoussis in the Wimbledon final, 7-6 (7-5), 6-2, 7-6 (7-3), with irresistible tennis. He became the world no. 1-ranked player (1 February 2004) after winning the Australian Open and then he successfully defended his Wimbledon crown, beating Andy Roddick in four sets.

Gibson, Althea Born Silver, South Carolina, USA, 25 August 1927. The first African-American woman to play at the United States championships and at Wimbledon, with her victory at the French championships of 1956 Gibson became the first black woman ever to win a major singles title. In 1957 and 1958 she won back-to-back titles at the US championships at Forest Hills, New York, and at Wimbledon. She also won three consecutive Wimbledon doubles titles (1956-58). Gibson retired from tennis after the 1958 season, having become an acclaimed public figure. In 1964 she became the first African-American woman to play in the Ladies Professional Golf Association (LPGA). After retirement she worked in various government advisory positions for physical fitness. She died in East Orange, New Jersey, 28 September 2003.

Goolagong, Evonne Born Evonne Fay Goolagong, Griffith, New South Wales, Australia, 31 July 1951. A member of the Wiradjuri people, Goolagong in 1971 was the first indigenous Australian to win a Wimbledon title. She is considered to be one of the greatest Australian tennis players, having won Wimbledon twice (1971 and 1980), the Australian Open four times (1974-77), the French Open once (1971), and being runner-up for four years in a row at the US Open (1973-76). She represented Australia seven times in the Federation Cup, winning in 1971, 1973 and 1974. She married British businessman Roger Cawley in 1975.

Graf, Steffi Born Stefanie Maria Graf, Mannheim, West Germany, 14 June 1969. Graf turned professional in 1982. Famous for her forehand (she was affectionately known as 'Fraulein Forehand') and her excellent fitness, she won 22 Grand Slam titles during her great career (Wimbledon 1988, 1989, 1991, 1992, 1993, 1995, 1996; US Open 1988, 1989, 1993, 1995, 1996; Australian Open 1988, 1989, 1990, 1994; French Open 1987, 1988, 1993, 1995, 1996, 1999). In 1988 she became only the third woman to win the Grand Slam when she defeated Chris Evert in the Australian Open final, Natalia Zvereva in the French Open final, Martina

Navratilova at Wimbledon and Gabriela Sabatini at the US Open. She completed the 'golden slam' by defeating Sabatini again to win the gold medal at the 1988 Olympics in Seoul.

Altogether she won 107 WTA tournaments and was the tour's no. 1-ranked player for 377 weeks, longer than any other player. She retired in August 1999, following the TIG Tennis Classic in San Diego. Graf married the American tennis player Andre Agassi in 2001 and moved to Las Vegas.

Henin-Hardenne, Justine Born Liège, Belgium, 1 June 1982. Henin-Hardenne turned professional in 1999 and established herself as a major competitor in 2001, regularly reaching late rounds of international competitions. She won her first Grand Slam tournament, the French Open, on 7 June 2003, defeating her Flemish compatriot Kim Clijsters, and her second, the US Open, on 7 September of the same year, once again defeating Clijsters. In October 2003 she replaced Clijsters to take the no. 1 ranking on the WTA list and in January 2004 again beat Clijsters to take the Australian Open title.

Henman, Tim Born Oxford, England, 6 September 1974. Henman (known as 'Tiger Tim' in some circles) was a member of the David Lloyd Slater Squad, where he trained alongside a number of other young British tennis hopefuls. While at school he was diagnosed with osteochondritis, a bone disease, but continued to pursue tennis and in 1992 won the national junior titles in singles and doubles. Joining the professional tour in 1993, by 1996 he became England's highest-ranked player and won the Most Improved Player trophy at the ATP awards. He was later elected to the ATP Tour Player Council and went on to win his first championship in January 1997. In 1998 he was ranked as one of the top ten ATP players. In the same year he reached Wimbledon's semi-finals for the first time, having been a quarter-finalist in 1996 and 1997. He has come close to reaching the final at Wimbledon on a number of subsequent occasions, bowing out in semi-finals in 1999, 2001 and 2002 and in the quarter-finals again in 2003 and 2004.

Hewitt, Lleyton Born Adelaide, South Australia, 24 February 1981. Became the youngest winner of an ATP tournament when he won the 1998 Adelaide Open as an almost unknown youngster. In 2001 he won the US Open and in 2002 the Wimbledon men's singles title. He topped the world rankings in 2001 and 2003 and was a member of Australia's 2003 Davis Cup-winning team, but he has not reached a Grand Slam final since his Wimbledon win.

Hingis, Martina Born Košice, Czechoslovakia, 30 September 1980. Hingis, sometimes referred to as 'The Swiss Miss', started entering tournaments at the age of five. In 1996 she partnered Helena Sukova in the women's doubles at Wimbledon and made history by becoming the youngest person ever to win a Wimbledon title. She won both the Wimbledon singles title and the US Open in 1997, and the Australian Open in 1997, 1998 and 1999. In 1998 she won all four Grand Slam doubles events. At one time ranked no. 1 in the world, Hingis last played in October 2002. She was forced to retire in February 2003 due to chronic ankle injuries.

Ivaniševic, Goran Born Split, Yugoslavia (now Croatia), 13 September 1971. Left-hander with a thunderous serve. A losing finalist in the Wimbledon men's singles three times (1992, 1994 and 1998) before his popular victory at the 2001 championships. A wild-card entry for the tournament

L
A
W
N

T
E
N
N
I
S

that year, he overcame Tim Henman in the semi-final in a rain-delayed five sets before defeating Patrick Rafter in another epic five-set match to take the title.

Jaušovec, Mima   Born Maribor, Yugoslavia, 20 July 1956. Best known as the 1977 French Open women's singles champion. In the following year, she once again reached the final but was defeated by Virginia Ruzici. Her playing career spanned 15 years, from 1973 to 1988.

King, Billie-Jean   Born Billie-Jean Moffitt, Long Beach, California, USA, 22 November 1943. One of the greatest female tennis players and female athletes in history, during the course of her career King won the triple crown for singles, doubles and mixed doubles both in the US Open (1967) and at Wimbledon (1973). One of only eight players to hold a singles title in each of the Grand Slam tennis events, King is also the only woman to win US singles titles on all four surfaces on which it has been played (grass, clay, indoor and hard). She won a total of 12 Grand Slam singles titles (Wimbledon 1966, 1967, 1968, 1972, 1973, 1975; US Open 1967, 1971, 1972, 1974; Australian Open 1968; French Open 1972). In all she won 20 Wimbledon titles and was the world no. 1-ranked player 1966-68, 1971 and 1974.

She is credited for speaking out against sexual inequality in sport and raising the prize money offered in the women's game. In the so-called 'Battle of the Sexes' on 20 September 1973, she defeated Bobby Riggs (winner of the Wimbledon men's singles title in 1939 and the US title in 1939 and 1941) 6-4, 6-4, 6-3, before 30,492 spectators in the Houston Astrodome and television viewers in over 37 countries.

Kournikova, Anna   Born Moscow, Soviet Union, 7 June 1981. As well known for her beauty and fashion sense as for her tennis skills, Kournikova won her first Grand Slam title in 1999 at the Australian Open in the women's doubles with partner Martina Hingis, where they were dubbed 'The Spice Girls'. Her other major title was also with Hingis at the Australian Open in 2002. While consistently ranked in the top 20 in the WTA tour rankings, she has never won a professional singles tournament. Her serve is notably weak for a top-level tennis player. She was named one of *People* magazine's 50 most beautiful people in 1998. Persistent back injuries curtailed her 2003 season.

Laver, Rod   Born Rockhampton, Queensland, Australia, 9 August 1938. Also known as 'The Rockhampton Rocket', Laver is considered by many to be the greatest tennis player of all time. A left-hander, he began playing tennis as a young boy. Having turned professional in 1963, he did not play at the US championship, Wimbledon or any of the other major tournaments for five years before tennis became open to professional players in 1968. He nevertheless became the first tennis player to surpass the $1 million mark in lifetime prize money, and still won 11 Grand Slam singles titles (Wimbledon 1961, 1962, 1968, 1969; US Open 1962, 1969; Australian Open 1960, 1962, 1968; French Open 1962, 1969), including the singles Grand Slam in 1962 and 1969. He was clearly the world's no. 1 player throughout the 1960s. Laver suffered a stroke in 1998 but made a speedy comeback, tennis being instrumental in his recovery. In 2003 he was honoured, along with fellow Australian tennis superstar Margaret Court, on a postage stamp as recipients of the Australia Post Australian Legends Award.

Lendl, Ivan   Born Ostrava, Czechoslovakia, 7 March 1960. Lendl is best remembered for his perennial attempts to win the Wimbledon title – he was twice runner-up and five times losing semi-finalist – and also for his eight straight finals in the US Open from 1982 to 1989. It is thought that one reason for his US success was the hardcourt surface used at Flushing Meadows, although he managed to convert only three of these finals into victories. Lendl was an outstanding tennis player, as his eight major titles (US Open 1985, 1986, 1987; Australian Open 1989, 1990; French Open 1984, 1986, 1987) hold testimony, but his austere approach and severe expression never endeared him to the crowds.

McEnroe, John   Born Wiesbaden, Germany, 16 February 1959. Famous for his epic matches against rivals Björn Borg, Jimmy Connors and Ivan Lendl and also for his highly strung on-court demeanour, left-hander McEnroe's career ended with 77 singles titles and another 77 in men's doubles (57 of them with long-time doubles partner Peter Fleming). His seven major titles included four US Opens (1979, 1980, 1981, 1984) and three Wimbledon championships (1981, 1983, 1984). As well as being the no. 1 singles player between 1981 and 1984 he was undoubtedly the world's top doubles player, and in fact won more major doubles titles than singles. After retiring as a player, McEnroe coached the US Davis Cup team, of which he was formerly a perennial member. Now a successful tennis commentator and television presenter, he still plays tennis to a high level and is the no. 1 player on the seniors tour.

Muster, Thomas   Born Leibnitz, Austria, 2 October 1967. Muster, known as 'The King of Clay', turned professional in 1985. A left-hander, he captured seven ATP tour titles. He won the French Open in 1995 and on 12 February 1996 became (at 28 years, 4 months) the second-oldest player to rank no. 1 for the first time. Muster holds a 42-16 career Davis Cup record (33-7 in singles). Having earned $2,887,979 in prize money, he is now retired and owns a farm in Australia where he lives with his wife and son.

Nastase, Ilie   Born Bucharest, Romania, 19 July 1946. Nastase was one of the top players of the 1970s, being twice ranked no. 1 in 1972 and 1973. Among his 57 singles titles are the US Open in 1972 and the French Open in 1973. In doubles he won at the French Open in 1970, Wimbledon in 1973 and the US Open in 1975. At Wimbledon in 1972 he was the runner-up in the men's singles, losing a classic final against Stan Smith in five sets. Nastase acquired the nickname 'Nasty' after several incidents where his temper got the better of him. He entered politics in the 1990s, making an unsuccessful bid for election as mayor of Bucharest in 1996.

Navratilova, Martina   Born Prague, Czechoslovakia, 18 October 1956. Became a US citizen in 1981, although playing under the auspices of the USA from the end of 1978. Powerful left-hander Navratilova turned professional in 1973, reaching the quarter-finals of her first Grand Slam event. She went on to dominate women's tennis in the first half of the 1980s, winning 18 major singles titles from 1978-90 (Wimbledon 1978, 1979, 1982-87, 1990; US Open 1983, 1984, 1986, 1987; Australian Open 1981, 1983, 1985; French Open 1982, 1984). In 1991 Navratilova lost in three major finals, every time to Monica Seles, and her last major victory was in 1993, when she beat Seles to win the French Open. In 1994 she announced her intention to retire from singles competition but that year she still reached two Open finals (Rome and Wimbledon), losing both to Conchita Martinez.

She later returned to the professional tennis circuit as a doubles player and in January 2003 won the Australian Open mixed doubles title with Leander Paes, thus becoming only the third player (after Doris Hart and Margaret Court) to win every possible title (singles, women's doubles, mixed doubles) in the four Grand Slam tournaments. At the same time, at 46 years, 3 months, she became the oldest player, male or female, to win a Grand Slam title. Later in 2003 Navratilova equalled the record of Billie-Jean King in winning her 20th Wimbledon title, partnering Leander Paes in the mixed doubles.

Paes, Leander Born Goa, India, 17 June 1973. Son of Jennifer Paes, a renowned basketball player and captain of the Indian team in the 1980 Asian Basketball Championships, and Vece Paes, a hockey midfielder who represented the Indian team that won bronze in the 1972 Olympics. Paes turned professional in 1991 after winning the 1990 Wimbledon junior title and rose to no. 1 in the junior world rankings. Specialising primarily in doubles, he was ranked no. 1 along with Mahesh Bhupathi. In 1999 he reached the finals of all four Grand Slam doubles events, winning at Wimbledon and the French Open. In 2003 he won the Wimbledon and Australian Open mixed doubles titles with Martina Navratilova. He resumed his career in 2004 after recovering from surgery on a brain cyst.

Perry, Fred Born Stockport, Cheshire, England, 18 May 1909. Three times Wimbledon champion who only took up tennis at the age of 18. Perry became the first player to hold all four Grand Slam singles titles at the same time, though not in the same year. The last English-born male player to win the Wimbledon title, in 1933 Perry also helped lead his team to victory over France in the Davis Cup final, Britain's first success in 21 years. Perry won eight Grand Slam titles in total (Wimbledon 1934, 1935, 1936; US Open 1933, 1934, 1936; Australian Open 1934; French Open 1935) and was also a world champion at table tennis, the sport at which he initially excelled. On retiring he became involved in the design of tennis clothing, giving his name to the famous brand. He died 2 February 1995.

Philippoussis, Mark Born Melbourne, Victoria, Australia, 7 November 1976. Philippoussis turned professional in 1994. A powerful serve and sturdy groundstrokes, which earned him the nickname 'Scud', are the hallmark of his game. His highest singles ranking to date is no. 8 (19 April 1999), after he lost in the US Open final to fellow countryman Patrick Rafter. A regular member of the Australian Davis Cup squad, in 1999 Philippoussis, along with doubles partner Jelena Dokic, won Australia's first-ever Hopman Cup title by beating Sweden 2-1 in the final. In 2003 he broke a two-year singles title drought by winning the Shanghai Open. He also made the 2003 Wimbledon final, losing to Roger Federer 7-6, 6-2, 7-6.

Roddick, Andy Born Omaha, Nebraska, USA, 30 August 1982. In the 2003 US Open Roddick won his first Grand Slam title when he beat Juan Carlos Ferrero in straight sets. He had shown battling qualities in the semi-finals, rallying from two sets down to beat David Nalbandian. Roddick ended 2003 as the world no. 1 but lost it to Roger Federer on 1 February 2004 following Federer's success in the Australian Open. Federer went on to defeat Roddick in the Wimbledon singles final of 2004.

Rusedski, Greg Born Montreal, Quebec, Canada, 6 September 1973. Eligible to play for Great Britain through his English mother (born in Dewsbury, Yorkshire) so it was not unnatural for him to decide to play his senior tennis for Great Britain as opposed to his native Canada. In 1997 Rusedski had his most successful year, winning the Nottingham Open and the indoor tournament at Basel and also reaching the quarter-final of Wimbledon and the final of the US Open. He became the British no. 1 and reached no. 4 in the world rankings, he was named BBC Sports Personality of the Year, LTA Player of the Year and ITV Champion of Sport. Rusedski then suffered recurring ankle injuries and was forced to restructure his game. His hard work appeared to be paying off when, against the odds, he beat top seed Gustavo Kuerten in the 2001 Australian Open and won the San Jose Open in California, defeating Andre Agassi in the final. Other injuries spoilt the 2003 season and he is again seeking to rebuild his tennis career after failing a drug test for excessive nandrolone levels, although he was eventually cleared of any wrongdoing.

Safin, Marat Born Marat Mikhailovich Safin, Moscow, Russia, 27 January 1980. Winner of the US Open title in 2000, in recent years Safin has struggled with various injuries which have prevented him becoming a dominant force. He has twice been runner-up in the Australian Open (2002 and 2004), however, and another Grand Slam victory is a distinct possibility.

Sampras, Pete Born Washington DC, USA, 12 August 1971. Nicknamed 'Pistol Pete', after his powerful serve, Sampras is widely considered one of the best players in tennis history. He holds the record for the most wins in Grand Slam events with 14 (Wimbledon 1993, 1994, 1995, 1997-2000; US Open 1990, 1993, 1995, 1996, 2002; Australian Open 1994, 1997), and was the no. 1-ranked player for six consecutive years, 1993-98. His professional career began in 1988 and his first victory in a Grand Slam tournament came at the US Open in 1990, when he defeated Andre Agassi, his long-term rival, in straight sets. In the 2002 US Open final he again defeated Agassi, 6-3, 6-4, 5-7, 6-4, in yet another memorable battle. He officially retired on 25 August 2003.

Seles, Monica Born Novi Sad, Yugoslavia, 2 December 1973. Became a US citizen in 1994. Seles achieved great success while still a teenager, being ranked the women's no. 1 at the age of 17 in 1991. Having won the European junior championship at the age of 10 she moved to the United States in 1986 to attend a tennis academy in Florida. She turned professional in 1989 and went on to reach the semi-finals of her first tournament, winning the second. In 1990 she won her first Grand Slam title, the French Open, which she also won in 1991 and 1992. In 1991 Seles also won the Australian and US Opens, repeating the feat of winning three Grand Slam titles in 1992. After Seles won the Australian Open in early 1993, her appearances were limited by a series of injuries. She returned to tournament play in April 1993 but was stabbed on the court by a spectator during a tournament in Germany. Subsequent to this incident Seles cancelled her participation in tournaments in 1993 and 1994. She came back to win her ninth major title, the 1996 Australian Open, although she was not the same player she had been before the attack.

Srichaphan, Paradorn Born Khon Kaen, Thailand, 14 June 1979. Srichaphan turned professional in 1998 and stayed in the lower parts of the ATP top

100 for some years. In 2002 he reached the top 30 after defeating Andre Agassi at Wimbledon, and the following year became the first Asian player to attain a place in the top ten.

Wilander, Mats   Born Växjö, Sweden, 22 August 1964. Winner of seven Grand Slam titles (US Open 1988; Australian Open 1983, 1984, 1988; French Open 1982, 1985, 1988), Wilander was ranked no. 1 in the world between September 1988 and January 1989. In the 1982 Davis Cup quarter-finals, he lost to John McEnroe in a 6hrs 22mins, five-set marathon, 7-9, 2-6, 17-15, 6-3, 6-8. It remains the longest Davis Cup match in history. He officially retired in 1996, but now competes occasionally on the senior tour. He coached Marat Safin during the 2001 season.

Williams, Serena   Born Saginaw, Michigan, USA, 26 September 1981. In 1995, aged 14, Serena played her first professional match in Quebec City, losing to Annie Miller. Her ranking climbed from 304 to 102 after she beat two top ten players in a 1997 tournament in Chicago. In 1999 Serena won five singles titles including her first Grand Slam, the US Open, going on to win three doubles titles with her sister including the French Open and the US Open. She won Wimbledon and Olympic doubles titles with Venus in 2000. In 2002 Serena defeated her sister 7-5, 6-3, to win the French Open, her second Grand

Slam singles title. She subsequently reached no. 1 in the WTA world rankings. Serena won the Wimbledon championship in 2002, retaining the title in 2003. Her second US Open title was won in 2002 and she cemented her domination of the women's game by taking the Australian Open in 2003. She was injured for the remainder of 2003 and lost her no. 1 ranking to Justine Henin-Hardenne. She reached the final of Wimbledon in 2004 but lost 6-1, 6-4 to the 17-year-old Russian Maria Sharapova.

Williams, Venus   Born Lansing, Michigan, USA, 17 June 1980. Venus won the Wimbledon and US Open championships and a gold medal at the Sydney Olympics in 2000, winning the same two Grand Slam titles in 2001 to establish herself as the world's no. 1 player. When Venus and her sister won the 1999 French Open doubles title, they became the first pair of sisters to win a doubles title in the 20th century. In 2003 Venus played in the Wimbledon singles final despite suffering stomach cramps, losing to her sister, 6-4, 4-6, 2-6. On 14 September 2003 the Williams sisters suffered the loss of their older sister, Yetunde Price, in a shooting incident in the Compton area of Los Angeles. Venus has struggled with injuries in 2004 and was beaten in the second round at Wimbledon by Croat Karolina Sprem.

Wimbledon Champions

	Men's Singles	Women's Singles	Men's Doubles	Women's Doubles
1877	S.W. Gore (GBR)	——	——	
1878	P.F. Hadow (GBR)	——	——	
1879	J.T. Hartley (GBR)	——	——	
1880	J.T. Hartley (GBR)	——	——	
1881	W. Renshaw (GBR)	——	——	
1882	W. Renshaw (GBR)	——	——	
1883	W. Renshaw (GBR)	——	——	
1884	W. Renshaw (GBR)	M. Watson (GBR)	W. Renshaw/E. Renshaw (GBR)	——
1885	W. Renshaw (GBR)	M. Watson (GBR)	W. Renshaw/E. Renshaw (GBR)	——
1886	W. Renshaw (GBR)	B. Bingley (GBR)	W. Renshaw/E. Renshaw (GBR)	——
1887	H.F. Lawford (GBR)	C. Dod (GBR)	H.W. Wilberforce/P.B. Lyon (GBR)	——
1888	E. Renshaw (GBR)	C. Dod (GBR)	W. Renshaw/E. Renshaw (GBR)	——
1889	W. Renshaw (GBR)	B. (Bingley) Hillyard (GBR)	W. Renshaw/E. Renshaw (GBR)	——
1890	W.J. Hamilton (GBR)	L. Rice (GBR)	J. Pim/F.O. Stoker (GBR)	——
1891	W. Baddeley (GBR)	C. Dod (GBR)	W. Baddeley/H. Baddeley (GBR)	——
1892	W. Baddeley (GBR)	C. Dod (GBR)	E.W. Lewis/H.S. Barlow (GBR)	——
1893	J. Pim (GBR)	C. Dod (GBR)	J. Pim/F.O. Stoker (GBR)	——
1894	J. Pim (GBR)	B. Hillyard (GBR)	W. Baddeley/H. Baddeley (GBR)	——
1895	W. Baddeley (GBR)	C.R. Cooper (GBR)	W. Baddeley/H. Baddeley (GBR)	——
1896	H.S. Mahony (GBR)	C.R. Cooper (GBR)	W. Baddeley/H. Baddeley (GBR)	——
1897	R.F. Doherty (GBR)	B. Hillyard (GBR)	R.F. Doherty/L.H. Doherty (GBR)	——
1898	R.F. Doherty (GBR)	C.R. Cooper (GBR)	R. F. Doherty/L.H. Doherty (GBR)	——
1899	R.F. Doherty (GBR)	B. Hillyard (GBR)	R.F. Doherty/L.H. Doherty (GBR)	——
1900	R.F. Doherty (GBR)	B. Hillyard (GBR)	R.F. Doherty/L.H. Doherty (GBR)	——
1901	A.W. Gore (GBR)	C.R. (Cooper) Sterry (GBR)	R.F. Doherty/L.H. Doherty (GBR)	——
1902	L.H. Doherty (GBR)	M.E. Robb (GBR)	S.H. Smith/F.L. Riseley (GBR)	——
1903	L.H. Doherty (GBR)	D.K. Douglass (GBR)	R.F. Doherty/L.H. Doherty (GBR)	——
1904	L.H. Doherty (GBR)	D.K. Douglass (GBR)	R. F. Doherty/L.H. Doherty (GBR)	——
1905	L.H. Doherty (GBR)	M. Sutton (USA)	R. F. Doherty/L.H. Doherty (GBR)	——
1906	L.H. Doherty (GBR)	D.K. Douglass (GBR)	S. H. Smith/F.L. Riseley (GBR)	——
1907	N.E. Brookes (AUS)	M. Sutton (USA)	N.E. Brookes (AUS)/A.F. Wilding (GBR)	——
1908	A.W. Gore (GBR)	C. R. Sterry (GBR)	A.F. Wilding/M.J.G. Ritchie (GBR)	——
1909	A.W. Gore (GBR)	D.P. Boothby (GBR)	A. W. Gore/H. Roper Barrett (GBR)	——
1910	A.F. Wilding (NZL)	D.K. Douglass Chambers (GBR)	A.F. Wilding (NZL)/M.J.G. Ritchie (GBR)	——
1911	A.F. Wilding (NZL)	D.K. Douglass Chambers (GBR)	A.H. Gobert/M. Decugis (GBR)	——
1912	A.F. Wilding (NZL)	E.W. Larcombe (GBR)	H. Roper Barrett/C.P. Dixon (GBR)	——
1913	A.F. Wilding (NZL)	D.K. Douglass Chambers (GBR)	H. Roper Barrett/C.P. Dixon (GBR)	R.J. McNair/D.P. Boothby (GBR)
1914	N.E. Brookes (AUS)	D.K. Douglass Chambers (GBR)	N.E. Brookes (AUS)/A.F. Wilding (NZL)	E. Ryan (USA)/A.M. Morton (GBR)

	Men's Singles	Women's Singles	Men's Doubles	Women's Doubles
1915-18	not held	not held	not held	not held
1919	G.L. Patterson (AUS)	S. Lenglen (FRA)	R.V. Thomas (GBR)/P. O'Hara Wood (AUS)	S. Lenglen (FRA)/E. Ryan (USA)
1920	W.T. Tilden (USA)	S. Lenglen (FRA)	R.N. Williams (GBR)/C.S. Garland (USA)	S. Lenglen (FRA)/E. Ryan (USA)
1921	W.T. Tilden (USA)	S. Lenglen (FRA)	R. Lycett/M. Woosnam (GBR)	S. Lenglen(FRA)/E. Ryan (USA)
1922	G.L. Patterson (AUS)	S. Lenglen (FRA)	J.O. Anderson (AUS)/R. Lycett (GBR)	S. Lenglen (FRA)/E. Ryan (USA)
1923	W.M. Johnston (USA)	S. Lenglen (FRA)	L.A. Godfree/R. Lycett (GBR)	S. Lenglen (FRA)/E. Ryan (USA)
1924	J. Borotra (FRA)	K. McKane (GBR)	F.T. Hunter/V. Richards (USA)	H.V. Hotchkiss Wightman/H.N. Wills (USA)
1925	R. Lacoste (FRA)	S. Lenglen (FRA)	J. Borotra/R. Lacoste (FRA)	S. Lenglen (FRA)/E. Ryan (USA)
1926	J. Borotra (FRA)	K. (McKane) Godfree (GBR)	J. Brugnon/H. Cochet (FRA)	M.K. Browne/E. Ryan (USA)
1927	H. Cochet (FRA)	H.N. Wills (USA)	F.T. Hunter/W.T. Tilden (USA)	H.N. Wills/E. Ryan (USA)
1928	R. Lacoste (FRA)	H.N. Wills (USA)	J. Brugnon/H. Cochet (FRA)	P. Saunders/M. Watson (GBR)
1929	H. Cochet (FRA)	H.N. Wills (USA)	W.L. Allison/J. Van Ryn (USA)	P. (Saunders) Michell/M. Watson (GBR)
1930	W.T. Tilden (USA)	H.N. Wills Moody (USA)	W.L. Allison/J. Van Ryn (USA)	H.N. Wills Moody/E. Ryan (USA)
1931	S.B. Wood (USA)	C. Aussem (GER)	G.M. Lott/J. Van Ryn (USA)	P. Mudford/D. Shepherd Barron (GBR)
1932	H.E. Vines (USA)	H.N. Wills Moody (USA)	J. Borotra/J. Brugnon (FRA)	D. Metaxa (FRA)/J. Sigart (BEL)
1933	J. H. Crawford (AUS)	H.N. Wills Moody (USA)	J. Borotra/J. Brugnon (FRA)	E. Ryan (USA)/R. Mathieu (FRA)
1934	F.J. Perry (GBR)	D.E. Round (GBR)	G.M. Lott/L.R. Stoefen (USA)	E. Ryan (USA)/R. Mathieu (FRA)
1935	F.J. Perry (GBR)	H.N. Wills Moody (USA)	J.H. Crawford/A.K. Quist (AUS)	F. James/K.E. Stammers (GBR)
1936	F.J. Perry (GBR)	H.H. Jacobs (USA)	G.P. Hughes/C.R.D. Tuckey (GBR)	F. James/K.E. Stammers (GBR)
1937	J.D. Budge (USA)	D. Round (GBR)	J.D. Budge/G. Mako (USA)	R. Mathieu (FRA)/B. Yorke (GBR)
1938	J.D. Budge (USA)	H.N. Wills Moody (USA)	J.D. Budge/G. Mako (USA)	S. Palfrey Fabyan/A. Marble (USA)
1939	R.L. Riggs (USA)	A. Marble (USA)	E.T. Cooke/R.L. Riggs (USA)	S. Palfrey Fabyan/A. Marble (USA)
1940-45	not held	not held	not held	not held
1946	Y. Petra (FRA)	P. Betz (USA)	T. Brown/J.A. Kramer (USA)	A.L. Brough/M.E. Osborne (USA)
1947	J.A. Kramer (USA)	M.E. Osborne (USA)	B. Falkenburg/J.A. Kramer (USA)	P. Todd/D.J. Hart (USA)
1948	B. Falkenburg (USA)	A.L. Brough (USA)	J.E. Bromwich/F.A. Sedgman (AUS)	A.L. Brough/M.E. (Osborne) Du Pont (USA)
1949	T. Schroeder (USA)	A.L. Brough (USA)	P. Gonzales/F. Parker (USA)	A.L. Brough/M.E. Du Pont (USA)
1950	B. Patty (USA)	A.L. Brough (USA)	J.E. Bromwich/A.K. Quist (AUS)	A.L. Brough/M.E. Du Pont (USA)
1951	D. Savitt (USA)	D.J. Hart (USA)	K.B. McGregor/F.A. Sedgman (AUS)	D.J. Hart/S.J. Fry (USA)
1952	F.A. Sedgman (AUS)	M. Connolly (USA)	K.B. McGregor/F.A. Sedgman (AUS)	D.J. Hart/S.J. Fry (USA)
1953	E.V. Seixas (USA)	M. Connolly (USA)	L.A. Hoad/K.R. Rosewall (AUS)	D.J. Hart/S.J. Fry (USA)
1954	J. Drobny (EGY)	M. Connolly (USA)	R.N. Hartwig/M.G. Rose (AUS)	A.L. Brough/M.E. Du Pont (USA)
1955	T. Trabert (USA)	A.L. Brough (USA)	R.N. Hartwig/L.A. Hoad (AUS)	A. Mortimer/A. Shilcock (GBR)
1956	L.A. Hoad (AUS)	S.J. Fry (USA)	L.A. Hoad/K. R. Rosewall (AUS)	A. Buxton/A. Gibson (USA)
1957	L.A. Hoad (AUS)	A. Gibson (USA)	B. Patty/G. Mulloy (USA)	A. Gibson/D.R. Hard (USA)
1958	A.J. Cooper (AUS)	A. Gibson (USA)	S. Davidson/U. Schmidt (SWE)	M.E. Bueno (BRA)/A. Gibson (USA)
1959	A. Olmedo (PER)	M.E. Bueno (BRA)	R.S. Emerson/N.A. Fraser (AUS)	J.M. Arth/D.R. Hard (USA)
1960	N.A. Fraser (AUS)	M.E. Bueno (BRA)	R. H. Osuna (MEX)/D. Ralston (USA)	M.E. Bueno (BRA)/D.R. Hard (USA)
1961	R.G. Laver (AUS)	A. Mortimer (GBR)	R.S. Emerson/N.A. Fraser (AUS)	K. Hantze/B.-J. Moffitt (USA)
1962	R.G. Laver (AUS)	K. Susman (USA)	R.A. Hewitt (RSA)/F.S. Stolle (AUS)	B-J. Moffitt/K. (Hantze) Susman (USA)
1963	C. McKinley (USA)	M. Smith (AUS)	R.H. Osuna/A. Palafox (MEX)	M.E. Bueno (BRA)/D.R. Hard (USA)
1964	R.S. Emerson (AUS)	M.E. Bueno (BRA)	R.A. Hewitt (RSA)/F.S. Stolle (AUS)	M. Smith (AUS)/L. Turner (USA)
1965	R.S. Emerson (AUS)	M. Smith (AUS)	J.D. Newcombe/A.D. Roche (AUS)	M.E. Bueno (BRA)/B-J. Moffitt (USA)
1966	M. Santana (ESP)	B.-J. King (USA)	K. Fletcher/J.D. Newcombe (AUS)	M.E. Bueno (BRA)/N. Richey (USA)
1967	J.D. Newcombe (AUS)	B.-J. King (USA)	R.A. Hewitt/F. McMillan (RSA)	R. Casals/B.-J. King (USA)
1968	R.G. Laver (AUS)	B.-J. King (USA)	J.D. Newcombe/A.D. Roche (AUS)	R. Casals/B.-J. King (USA)
1969	R.G. Laver (AUS)	A.S. Jones (GBR)	J.D. Newcombe/A.D. Roche (AUS)	M. (Smith) Court/J. Tegart (AUS)
1970	J.D. Newcombe (AUS)	M. (Smith) Court (AUS)	J.D. Newcombe/A.D. Roche (AUS)	R. Casals/B.-J. King (USA)
1971	J.D. Newcombe (AUS)	E. Goolagong (AUS)	R.S. Emerson/R.G. Laver (AUS)	R. Casals/B.-J. King (USA)
1972	S.R. Smith (USA)	B.-J. King (USA)	R.A. Hewitt/F. McMillan (RSA)	B.-J. King (USA)/B. Stove (NED)
1973	J. Kodes (TCH)	B.-J. King (USA)	J.S. Connors (USA)/I. Nastase (ROM)	R. Casals/B-J. King (USA)
1974	J.S. Connors (USA)	C.M. Evert (USA)	J.D. Newcombe/A.D. Roche (AUS)	E. Goolagong (AUS)/P. Michel (USA)
1975	A.R. Ashe (USA)	B.-J. King (USA)	V. Gerulaitis/S. Mayer (USA)	A. Kiyomura (JPN)/K.Sawamatsu (USA)
1976	B. Borg (SWE)	C.M. Evert (USA)	B. Gottfried (USA)/R. Ramirez (MEX)	C.M. Evert (USA)/M. Navratilova (TCH)
1977	B. Borg (SWE)	S.V. Wade (GBR)	R. Case/G. Masters (AUS)	H. Gourlay Cawley (AUS)/J. Russell (USA)
1978	B. Borg (SWE)	M. Navratilova (TCH)	R.A. Hewitt/F. McMillan (RSA)	K. Reid/W.H. Turnbull (AUS)
1979	B. Borg (SWE)	M. Navratilova (USA)	J.P. McEnroe/P. Fleming (USA)	B.-J. King/M. Navratilova (USA)
1980	B. Borg (SWE)	E. (Goolagong) Cawley (AUS)	P. McNamara/P. McNamee (AUS)	K. Jordan/A. Smith (USA)

	Men's Singles	Women's Singles	Men's Doubles	Women's Doubles
1981	J.P. McEnroe (USA)	C.M. Evert Lloyd (USA)	J.P. McEnroe/P. Fleming (USA)	M. Navratilova/P. Shriver (USA)
1982	J.S. Connors (USA)	M. Navratilova (USA)	P. McNamara/P. McNamee (AUS)	M. Navratilova/P. Shriver (USA)
1983	J.P. McEnroe (USA)	M. Navratilova (USA)	J.P. McEnroe/P. Fleming (USA)	M. Navratilova/P. Shriver (USA)
1984	J.P. McEnroe (USA)	M. Navratilova (USA)	J.P. McEnroe/P. Fleming (USA)	M. Navratilova/P. Shriver (USA)
1985	B. Becker (FRG)	M. Navratilova (USA)	H. Gunthard (SUI)/B. Taroczy (HUN)	K. Jordan (USA)/E. Smylie (AUS)
1986	B. Becker (FRG)	M. Navratilova (USA)	J. Nystrom/M. Wilander (SWE)	M. Navratilova/P. Shriver (USA)
1987	P. Cash (AUS)	M. Navratilova (USA)	R. Seguso/K. Flach (USA)	C. Kohde-Kilsche (FRG)/H. Sukova (TCH)
1988	S. Edberg (SWE)	S. Graf (FRG)	R. Seguso/K. Flach (USA)	S. Graf (FRG)/G. Sabatini (ARG)
1989	B. Becker (FRG)	S. Graf (FRG)	J.B. Fitzgerald (AUS)/A. Jarryd (SWE)	J. Novotna/H. Sukova (TCH)
1990	S. Edberg (SWE)	M. Navratilova (USA)	R. Leach/J. Pugh (USA)	J. Novotna/H. Sukova (TCH)
1991	M. Stich (GER)	S. Graf (GER)	J.B. Fitzgerald (AUS)/A. Jarryd (SWE)	L. Savchenko/N. Zvereva (URS)
1992	A. Agassi (USA)	S. Graf (GER)	J.P. McEnroe (USA)/M. Stich (GER)	G. Fernandez (USA)/N. Zvereva (CIS)
1993	P. Sampras (USA)	S. Graf (GER)	T. Woodbridge/M. Woodforde (AUS)	G. Fernandez (USA)/N. Zvereva (BLR)
1994	P. Sampras (USA)	C. Martinez (ESP)	T. Woodbridge/M. Woodforde (AUS)	G. Fernandez (USA)/N. Zvereva (BLR)
1995	P. Sampras (USA)	S. Graf (GER)	T. Woodbridge/M. Woodforde (AUS)	J. Novotna (CZE)/A. Sanchez Vicario (ESP)
1996	R. Krajicek (NED)	S. Graf (GER)	T. Woodbridge/M. Woodforde (AUS)	M. Hingis (SUI)/H. Sukova (CZE)
1997	P. Sampras (USA)	M. Hingis (SUI)	T. Woodbridge/M. Woodforde (AUS)	G. Fernandez (USA)/N. Zvereva (BLR)
1998	P. Sampras (USA)	J. Novotna (CZE)	J. Eltingh/P. Haarhuis (NED)	M. Hingis (SUI)/J. Novotna (CZE)
1999	P. Sampras (USA)	L. Davenport (USA)	M. Bhupathi/L. Paes (IND)	L. Davenport/C. Morariu (USA)
2000	P. Sampras (USA)	V. Williams (USA)	T. Woodbridge/M. Woodforde (AUS)	V. Williams/S. Williams (USA)
2001	G. Ivanisevic (CRO)	V. Williams (USA)	D. Johnson/J. Palmer (USA)	L. Raymond (USA)/R. Stubbs (AUS)
2002	L. Hewitt (AUS)	S. Williams (USA)	T. Woodbridge (AUS)/J. Bjorkman (SWE)	V. Williams/S. Williams (USA)
2003	R. Federer (SUI)	S. Williams (USA)	T. Woodbridge (AUS)/J. Bjorkman (SWE)	K. Clijsters (BEL)/A. Sugiyama (JPN)
2004	R. Federer (SUI)	M. Sharapova (RUS)	T. Woodbridge (AUS)/J. Bjorkman (SWE)	C. Black (ZIM)/R. Stubbs (AUS)

US Open

	Men's Singles	Women's Singles	Men's Doubles	Women's Doubles
1881	R.D. Sears (USA)	——	C.M. Clark/F.W. Taylor (USA)	——
1882	R.D. Sears (USA)	——	R.D. Sears/J. Dwight (USA)	——
1883	R.D. Sears (USA)	——	R.D. Sears/J. Dwight (USA)	——
1884	R.D. Sears (USA)	——	R.D. Sears/J. Dwight (USA)	——
1885	R.D. Sears (USA)	——	R.D. Sears/J. Dwight (USA)	——
1886	R.D. Sears (USA)	——	R.D. Sears/J. Dwight (USA)	——
1887	R.D. Sears (USA)	E. Hansell (USA)	R.D. Sears/J. Dwight (USA)	——
1888	H.W. Slocum (USA)	B.L. Townsend (USA)	O.S. Campbell/V.G. Hall (USA)	——
1889	H.W. Slocum (USA)	B.L. Townsend (USA)	H.W. Slocum/H.A. Taylor (USA)	M. Ballard/B.L. Townsend (USA)
1890	O.S. Campbell (USA)	E.C. Roosevelt (USA)	V.G. Hall/C. Hobart (USA)	E.C. Roosevelt/G.W. Roosevelt (USA)
1891	O.S. Campbell (USA)	M.E. Cahill (USA)	O.S. Campbell/R.P Huntington (USA)	M.E. Cahill/W.F. Morgan (USA)
1892	O.S. Campbell (USA)	M.E. Cahill (USA)	O.S. Campbell/R.P. Huntington (USA)	M.E. Cahill/A.M. McKinley (USA)
1893	R.D. Wrenn (USA)	A.M. Terry (USA)	C. Hobart/F.H. Hovey (USA)	A.M. Terry/H. Butler (USA)
1894	R.D. Wrenn (USA)	H.R. Hellwig (USA)	C. Hobart/F.H. Hovey (USA)	H.R. Helwig/J.P. Atkinson (USA)
1895	F.H. Hovey (USA)	J.P. Atkinson (USA)	M. G. Chace/R.D. Wrenn (USA)	H.R. Helwig/J.P. Atkinson (USA)
1896	R.D. Wrenn (USA)	E.H. Moore (USA)	C.B. Neel/S R. Neel (USA)	E.H. Moore/J.P. Atkinson (USA)
1897	R.D. Wrenn (USA)	J.P. Atkinson (USA)	L.E. Ware/G.P. Sheldon (USA)	J.P. Atkinson/K. Atkinson (USA)
1898	M.D. Whitman (USA)	J.P. Atkinson (USA)	L.E. Ware/G.P. Sheldon (USA)	J.P. Atkinson/K. Atkinson (USA)
1899	M.D. Whitman (USA)	M. Jones (USA)	H. Ward/D.F. Davis (USA)	J.W. Craven/M. McAteer (USA)
1900	M.D. Whitman (USA)	M. McAteer (USA)	H. Ward/D.F. Davis (USA)	E. Parker/H. Champlin (USA)
1901	W.A. Larned (USA)	E.H. Moore (USA)	H. Ward/D.F. Davis (USA)	J.P. Atkinson/M. McAteer (USA)
1902	W.A. Larned (USA)	M. Jones (USA)	R.F. Doherty/H.L. Doherty (GBR)	J.P. Atkinson/M. Jones (USA)
1903	H.L. Doherty (GBR)	E.H. Moore (USA)	R.F. Doherty/H.L. Doherty (GBR)	E.H. Moore/C.B. Neely (USA)
1904	H. Ward (USA)	M.G. Sutton (USA)	H. Ward/B.C. Wright (USA)	M.G. Sutton/M. Hall (USA)
1905	B.C. Wright (USA)	E.H. Moore (USA)	H. Ward/B.C. Wright (USA)	H. Homans/C.B. Neely (USA)
1906	W.J. Clothier (USA)	H.Homans (USA)	H. Ward/B.C. Wright (USA)	L.S. Coe/D.S. Platt (USA)
1907	W.A. Larned (USA)	E. Sears (USA)	F.B. Alexander/H.H. Hackett (USA)	M. Wimer/C.B. Neely (USA)
1908	W.A. Larned (USA)	M. Barger-Wallach (USA)	F.B. Alexander/H.H. Hackett (USA)	E. Sears/M. Curtis (USA)
1909	W.A. Larned (USA)	H.V. Hotchkiss (USA)	F.B. Alexander/H.H. Hackett (USA)	H.V. Hotchkiss/E. Rotch (USA)
1910	W.A. Larned (USA)	H.V. Hotchkiss (USA)	F.B. Alexander/H.H. Hackett (USA)	H.V. Hotchkiss/E. Rotch (USA)
1911	W.A. Larned (USA)	H.V. Hotchkiss (USA)	R.D. Little/G.F. Touchard (USA)	H.V. Hotchkiss/E. Sears (USA)
1912	M.E. McLoughlin (USA)	M.K. Browne (USA)	M.E. McLoughlin/T.C. Bundy (USA)	D. Greene/M.K. Browne (USA)
1913	M.E. McLoughlin (USA)	M.K. Browne (USA)	M.E. McLoughlin/T.C. Bundy (USA)	M.K. Browne/L. Williams (USA)

	Men's Singles	Women's Singles	Men's Doubles	Women's Doubles
1914	R.N. Williams (USA)	M.K. Browne (USA)	M.E. McLoughlin/T.C. Bundy (USA)	M.K. Browne/L. Williams (USA)
1915	W.M. Johnston (USA)	M. Bjurstedt (NOR)	W.M. Johnston/C.J. Griffin (USA)	H.V. Hotchkiss Wightman/ E. Sears (USA)
1916	R.N. Williams (USA)	M. Bjurstedt (NOR)	W. M. Johnston/C.J. Griffin (USA)	M. Bjurstedt (NOR)/E. Sears (USA)
1917	R.L. Murray (USA)	M. Bjurstedt (NOR)	F.B. Alexander/H.A. Throckmorton (USA)	M. Bjurstedt (NOR)/E. Sears (USA)
1918	R.L. Murray (USA)	M. Bjurstedt (NOR)	W.T. Tilden/V. Richards (USA)	M. Zinderstein/E.E. Goss (USA)
1919	W.M.Johnston (USA)	H.V. (Hotchkiss) Wightman (USA)	N.E. Brookes/G.L. Patterson (AUS)	M. Zinderstein/E.E. Goss (USA)
1920	W.T. Tilden (USA)	M. (Bjurstedt) Mallory (USA)	W.M. Johnston/C.J. Griffin (USA)	M. Zinderstein/E.E. Goss (USA)
1921	W.T. Tilden (USA)	M. Mallory (USA)	W.T. Tilden/V. Richards (USA)	M.K. Browne/L. Williams (USA)
1922	W.T. Tilden (USA)	M. Mallory (USA)	W.T. Tilden/V. Richards (USA)	M. (Zinderstein) Jessup/H.N. Wills (USA)
1923	W.T. Tilden (USA)	H.N. Wills (USA)	W.T. Tilden/B.I.C. Norton (USA)	K. McKane/P.H. Covell (USA)
1924	W.T. Tilden (USA)	H.N. Wills (USA)	H.O. Kinsey/R.G. Kinsey (USA)	H. Wightman/H.N. Wills (USA)
1925	W.T. Tilden (USA)	H.N. Wills (USA)	R.N. Williams/V. Richards (USA)	M.K. Browne/H.N. Wills (USA)
1926	R. Lacoste (FRA)	M. Mallory (USA)	R.N. Williams/V. Richards (USA)	E. Ryan/E.E. Goss (USA)
1927	R. Lacoste (FRA)	H.N. Wills (USA)	W.T. Tilden/F.T. Hunter (USA)	K. (McKane) Godfree (GBR)/E.H. Harvey (USA)
1928	H. Cochet (FRA)	H.N. Wills (USA)	G.M. Lott/J.F. Hennessey (USA)	H. Wightman/H.N. Wills (USA)
1929	W.T. Tilden (USA)	H.N. Wills (USA)	G.M. Lott/J.H. Doeg (USA)	M. Watson/P. (Saunders) Michell (GBR)
1930	J.H. Doeg (USA)	B. Nuthall (GBR)	G. Lott/J.H. Doeg (USA)	B. Nuthall (GBR)/S. Palfrey (USA)
1931	H.E. Vines (USA)	H.N. Wills Moody (USA)	W.L. Allison/J. Van Ryn (USA)	B. Nuthall (GBR)/E.B. Whittingstall (USA)
1932	H.E. Vines (USA)	H.H. Jacobs (USA)	H.E. Vines/K. Gledhill (USA)	H.H. Jacobs/S. Palfrey (USA)
1933	F.J. Perry (GBR)	H.H. Jacobs (USA)	G.M. Lott/L.R. Stoefen (USA)	B. Nuthall (GBR)/F. James (GBR)
1934	F.J. Perry (GBR)	H.H. Jacobs (USA)	G.M. Lott/L.R. Stoefen (USA)	H.H. Jacobs/S. Palfrey (USA)
1935	W.L. Allison (USA)	H.H. Jacobs (USA)	W.L. Allison/J. Van Ryn (USA)	H.H. Jacobs/S. Palfrey Fabyan (USA)
1936	F.J. Perry (GBR)	A. Marble (USA)	J.D. Budge/G. Mako (USA)	M. Van Ryn/C.A. Babcock (USA)
1937	J.D. Budge (USA)	A. Lizana (CHI)	G. Von Cramm/H. Henkel (GER)	S. Palfrey Fabyan/A. Marble (USA)
1938	J.D. Budge (USA)	A. Marble (USA)	J.D. Budge/G. Mako (USA)	S. Palfrey Fabyan/A. Marble (USA)
1939	R.L. Riggs (USA)	A. Marble (USA)	A.K. Quist/J.E. Bromwich (AUS)	S. Palfrey Fabyan/A. Marble (USA)
1940	W.D. McNeill (USA)	A. Marble (USA)	J.A. Kramer/F.R. Schroeder (USA)	S. Palfrey Fabyan/A. Marble (USA)
1941	R.L. Riggs (USA)	S. Palfrey Cooke (USA)	J.A. Kramer/F.R. Schroeder (USA)	S. Palfrey Cooke/M.E. Osborne (USA)
1942	F.R. Schroeder (USA)	P. M. Betz (USA)	G. Mulloy/W.F. Talbert (USA)	A.L. Brough/M.E. Osborne (USA)
1943	J.R. Hunt (USA)	P. M. Betz (USA)	J.A. Kramer/F.A. Parker (USA)	A.L. Brough/M.E. Osborne (USA)
1944	F.A. Parker (USA)	P. M. Betz (USA)	W.D. McNeill/R. Falkenburg (USA)	A.L. Brough/M.E. Osborne (USA)
1945	F.A. Parker (USA)	S. Palfrey Cooke (USA)	G. Mulloy/W.F. Talbert (USA)	A.L. Brough/M.E. Osborne (USA)
1946	J.A. Kramer (USA)	P. M. Betz (USA)	G. Mulloy/W.F. Talbert (USA)	A.L. Brough/M.E. Osborne (USA)
1947	J.A. Kramer (USA)	A.L. Brough (USA)	J.A. Kramer/F.R. Schroeder (USA)	A.L. Brough/M.E. Osborne (USA)
1948	R.A. Gonzales (USA)	M.E. (Osborne) Du Pont (USA)	G. Mulloy/W.F. Talbert (USA)	A.L. Brough/M.E. (Osborne) Du Pont (USA)
1949	R.A. Gonzales (USA)	M.E. Du Pont (USA)	J.E. Bromwich/O.W. Sidwell (AUS)	A.L. Brough/M.E. Du Pont (USA)
1950	A. Larsen (USA)	M.E. Du Pont (USA)	J.E. Bromwich/F.A. Sedgman (AUS)	A.L. Brough/M.E. Du Pont (USA)
1951	F.A. Sedgman (AUS)	M. Connolly (USA)	K.B. McGregor/F.A. Sedgman (AUS)	D.J. Hart/S.J. Fry (USA)
1952	F.A. Sedgman (AUS)	M. Connolly (USA)	M.G. Rose (AUS)/E.V. Seixas (USA)	D.J. Hart/S.J. Fry (USA)
1953	M.A. Trabert (USA)	M. Connolly (USA)	R.N. Hartwig/M.G. Rose (AUS)	D.J. Hart/S.J. Fry (USA)
1954	E.V. Seixas (USA)	D.J. Hart (USA)	E.V. Seixas/M.A. Trabert (USA)	D.J. Hart/S.J. Fry (USA)
1955	M.A. Trabert (USA)	D.J. Hart (USA)	K. Kamo/A. Miyagi (JPN)	A.L. Brough/M.E. Du Pont (USA)
1956	K.R. Rosewall (AUS)	S.J. Fry (USA)	L.A. Hoad/K.R. Rosewall (AUS)	A.L. Brough/M.E. Du Pont (USA)
1957	M.J. Anderson (AUS)	A. Gibson (USA)	A.J. Cooper/N.A. Fraser (AUS)	A.L. Brough/M.E. Du Pont (USA)
1958	A.J. Cooper (AUS)	A. Gibson (USA)	A. Olmedo/H. Richardson (USA)	A.L. Brough/M.E. Du Pont (USA)
1959	N.A. Fraser (AUS)	M.E. Bueno (BRA)	N.A. Fraser/R.S. Emerson (AUS)	J.M. Arth/D.M. Hard (USA)
1960	N.A. Fraser (AUS)	D.R. Hard (USA)	N.A. Fraser/R.S. Emerson (AUS)	M.E. Bueno (BRA)/D.R. Hard (USA)
1961	R.S. Emerson (AUS)	D.R. Hard (USA)	C. McKinley/R.D. Ralston (USA)	D.R. Hard/L. Turner (USA)
1962	R.G. Laver (AUS)	M. Smith (AUS)	R.H. Osuna/A. Palafox (MEX)	M.E. Bueno (BRA)/D.R. Hard (USA)
1963	R.H. Osuna (MEX)	M.E. Bueno (BRA)	C. McKinley/R.D. Ralston (USA)	R. Ebbern/M. Smith (AUS)
1964	R.S. Emerson (AUS)	M.E. Bueno (BRA)	C. McKinley/R.D. Ralston (USA)	B.-J. Moffitt/K. (Hantze) Susman (USA)
1965	M. Santana (ESP)	M. Smith (AUS)	R.S. Emerson/F.S. Stolle (AUS)	C.A. Graebner/N. Richey (USA)
1966	F.S. Stolle (AUS)	M.E. Bueno (BRA)	R.S. Emerson/F.S. Stolle (AUS)	M.E. Bueno (BRA)/N. Richey (USA)
1967	J.D. Newcombe (AUS)	B.-J. King (USA)	J.D. Newcombe/A.D. Roche (AUS)	R. Casals/B.-J. King (USA)
1968*	A.R. Ashe (USA) (O/N)	S.V. Wade (GBR) (O) M. (Smith) Court (AUS) (N)	R.C. Lutz/S.R. Smith (USA) (O/N)	M.E. Bueno (BRA)/M. (Smith) Court (AUS) (O/N)
1969*	R.G. Laver (AUS) (O) S.R. Smith (USA) (N)	M. Court (AUS) (O/N)	K.R. Rosewall/F.S. Stolle (AUS) (O) D. Crealy/A. Stone (AUS) (N)	F. Durr (FRA)/D. Hard (USA) (O) M. Court (AUS)/S.V. Wade (GBR) (N)
1970	K.R. Rosewall (AUS)	M. Court (AUS)	P. Barthes (FRA)/N. Pilic (YUG)	M. Court (AUS)/J. Dalton (AUS)
1971	S.R. Smith (USA)	B.-J. King (USA)	J.D. Newcombe (AUS)/R. Taylor (GBR)	R. Casals (USA)/J. Dalton (AUS)
1972	I. Nastase (ROM)	B.-J. King (USA)	C.E. Drysdale (RSA)/R. Taylor (GBR)	F. Durr (FRA)/B. Stove (NED)
1973	J.D. Newcombe (AUS)	M. Court (AUS)	O.K. Davidson/J.D. Newcombe (AUS)	M. Court(AUS)/S. V. Wade (GBR)

1974	J.S. Connors (USA)	B.-J. King (USA)	R.C. Lutz/S.R. Smith (USA)	R. Casals/B.-J. King (USA)
1975	M. Orantes (ESP)	C.M. Evert (USA)	J.S. Connors (USA)/I. Nastase (ROM)	M. Court(AUS)/S.V. Wade (GBR)
1976	J.S. Connors (USA)	C.M. Evert (USA)	T.S. Okker (NED)/M.C. Riessen (USA)	L. Boshoff/I. Kloss (RSA)
1977	G. Vilas (ARG)	C.M. Evert (USA)	R.A.J. Hewitt/F.D. McMillan (RSA)	M. Navratilova (TCH)/B. Stove (NED)
1978	J.S. Connors (USA)	C.M. Evert (USA)	R.C. Lutz/S.R. Smith (USA)	B.-J. King (USA)/M. Navratilova (TCH)
1979	J.P. McEnroe (USA)	T.A. Austin (USA)	J.P. McEnroe/P. Fleming (USA)	W.H. Turnbull (AUS)/B. Stove (NED)
1980	J.P. McEnroe (USA)	C.M. Evert Lloyd (USA)	R.C. Lutz/S.R. Smith (USA)	B.-J. King/M. Navratilova (USA)
1981	J.P. McEnroe (USA)	T.A. Austin (USA)	J.P. McEnroe/P. Fleming (USA)	K. Jordan/A. Smith (USA)
1982	J.S. Connors (USA)	C.M. Evert Lloyd (USA)	K. Curren (RSA)/S. Denton (USA)	R. Casals (USA)/W. M. Turnbull (AUS)
1983	J.S. Connors (USA)	M. Navratilova (USA)	J.P. McEnroe/P. Fleming (USA)	M. Navratilova/P. Shriver (USA)
1984	J.P. McEnroe (USA)	M. Navratilova (USA)	J.B. Fitzgerald (AUS)/T. Smid (TCH)	M. Navratilova/P. Shriver (USA)
1985	I. Lendl (TCH)	H. Mandlikova (TCH)	K. Flach (AUS)/R. Seguso (ECU)	C. Kohde-Kilsche(FRG)/H. Sukova (TCH)
1986	I. Lendl (TCH)	M. Navratilova (USA)	A. Gomez(ECU)/S. Zivojinovic (YUG)	M. Navratilova/P. Shriver (USA)
1987	I. Lendl (TCH)	M. Navratilova (USA)	S. Edberg/A. Jarryd (SWE)	M. Navratilova/P. Shriver (USA)
1988	M. Wilander (SWE)	S. Graf (FRG)	S. Casal/E. Sanchez (ESP)	G. Fernandez/R. White (USA)
1989	B. Becker (FRG)	S. Graf (FRG)	J.P. McEnroe(USA)/M. Woodforde (AUS)	H. Mandlikova (TCH)/ M. Navratilova (USA)
1990	P. Sampras (USA)	G. Sabatini (ARG)	P. Aldrich/D. Visser (RSA)	G. Fernandez/M. Navratilova (USA)
1991	S. Edberg (SWE)	M. Seles (YUG)	J. B. Fitzgerald (AUS)/A. Jarryd (SWE)	P. Shriver (USA)/N. Zvereva (URS)
1992	S. Edberg (SWE)	M. Seles (YUG)	J. Grabb/R. Reneberg (USA)	G. Fernandez/N. Zvereva (URS)
1993	P. Sampras (USA)	S. Graf (GER)	K. Flach/R. Leach (USA)	A. Sanchez Vicario (ESP)/ H. Sukova (CZE)
1994	A. Agassi (USA)	A. Sanchez Vicario (ESP)	J.Eltingh/P. Haarhuis (NED)	J. Novotna (CZE)/ A. Sanchez Vicario (ESP)
1995	P. Sampras (USA)	S. Graf (GER)	T. Woodbridge/M. Woodforde (AUS)	G. Fernandez (USA)/ N. Zvereva (BLR)
1996	P. Sampras (USA)	S. Graf (GER)	T. Woodbridge)/M. Woodforde (AUS)	G. Fernandez (USA)/ N. Zvereva (BLR)
1997	P. Rafter (AUS)	M. Hingis (SUI)	Y. Kafelnikov (RUS)/D. Vacek (USA)	J. Novotna (CZE)/ L. Davenport (USA)
1998	P. Rafter (AUS)	L. Davenport (USA)	S. Stolle (AUS)/C. Suk (USA)	M. Hingis (SUI)/J. Novotna (CZE)
1999	A. Agassi (USA)	S. Williams (USA)	S. Lareau (CAN)/A. O'Brien (USA)	V. Williams/S. Williams (USA)
2000	M. Safin (RUS)	V. Williams (USA)	L. Hewitt (AUS)/M. Mirnyl (BLR)	A. Sugiyama (JPN)/J. Halard-Decugis (FRA)
2001	L. Hewitt (AUS)	V. Williams (USA)	W. Black (ZIM)/K. Ullyett (USA)	L. Raymond (USA)/ R. Stubbs (AUS)
2002	P. Sampras (USA)	S. Williams (USA)	M.Bhupathi (IND)/M. Myrnyl (USA)	V. Ruano Pascual (ESP)/ P. Suarez (USA)
2003	A. Roddick (USA)	J. Henin-Hardenne (BEL)	T. Woodbridge (AUS)/ J. Bjorkman (SWE)	V. Ruano Pascual (ESP)/ P. Suarez (USA)

*In 1968 and 1969 two US championships were held: national (which was closed to professionals) and open. (O) denotes winners of the open championship, (N) winners of the national.
The US championship became fully open to professionals in 1970.

Australian Open

	Men's Singles	Women's Singles		Men's Singles	Women's Singles
1891	———	———	1907	H.M. Rice (AUS)	———
1892	———	———	1908	F.B. Alexander (USA)	———
1893	———	———	1909	A.F. Wilding (NZL)	———
1894	———	———	1910	R.W. Heath (AUS)	———
1895	———	———	1911	N.E. Brookes (AUS)	———
1896	———	———	1912	J.C. Parke (GBR)	———
1897	———	———	1913	E.F. Parker (AUS)	———
1898	———	———	1914	A.O'Hara Wood (AUS)	———
1899	———	———	1915	F.G. Lowe (GBR)	———
1900	———	———	1916-18 not held		
1901	———	———	1919	A.R.F. Kingscote (GBR)	———
1902	———	———	1920	P.O'Hara Wood (AUS)	———
1903	———	———	1921	R.H. Gemmell (AUS)	———
1904	———	———	1922	J.O. Anderson (AUS)	M. Molesworth (AUS)
1905	R.W. Heath (AUS)	———	1923	P.O'Hara Wood (AUS)	M. Molesworth (AUS)
1906	A.F. Wilding (NZL)	———	1924	J.O. Anderson (AUS)	S. Lance (AUS)

1925	J.O. Anderson (AUS)	D.S. Akhurst (AUS)	
1926	J.B. Hawkes (AUS)	D.S. Akhurst (AUS)	
1927	G.L. Patterson (AUS)	E.F. Boyd (AUS)	
1928	J. Borotra (FRA)	D.S. Akhurst (AUS)	
1929	J.C. Gregory (GBR)	D.S. Akhurst (AUS)	
1930	E.F. Moon (AUS)	D.S. Akhurst (AUS)	
1931	J.H. Crawford (AUS)	C. Buttsworth (AUS)	
1932	J.H. Crawford (AUS)	C. Buttsworth (AUS)	
1933	J.H. Crawford (AUS)	J. Hartigan (AUS)	
1934	F.J. Perry (GBR)	J. Hartigan (AUS)	
1935	J.H. Crawford (AUS)	D.E. Round (GBR)	
1936	A.K. Quist (AUS)	J. Hartigan (AUS)	
1937	V.B. McGrath (AUS)	N.M. Wynne (AUS)	
1938	J.D. Budge (USA)	D.M. Bundy (USA)	
1939	J.E. Bromwich (AUS)	E. Westacott (AUS)	
1940	A.K. Quist (AUS)	N.M. Wynne Bolton (AUS)	
1941-45	not held	not held	
1946	J.E. Bromwich (AUS)	N.M. Bolton (AUS)	
1947	D. Pails (AUS)	N.M. Bolton (AUS)	
1948	A.K. Quist (AUS)	N.M. Bolton (AUS)	
1949	F.A. Sedgman (AUS)	D.J. Hart (USA)	
1950	F.A. Sedgman (AUS)	A.L.Brough (USA)	
1951	R. Savitt (USA)	N.M. Bolton (AUS)	
1952	K.B. McGregor (AUS)	T. Long (AUS)	
1953	K.R. Rosewall (AUS)	M. Connolly (USA)	
1954	M.G. Rose (AUS)	T. Long (AUS)	
1955	K.R. Rosewall (AUS)	B. Penrose (AUS)	
1956	L.A. Hoad (AUS)	M. Carter (AUS)	
1957	A.J. Cooper (AUS)	S.J. Fry (USA)	
1958	A.J. Cooper (AUS)	A. Mortimer (GBR)	
1959	A. Olmedo (PER)	M. (Carter) Reitano (AUS)	
1960	R.G. Laver (AUS)	M. Smith (AUS)	
1961	R.S. Emerson (AUS)	M. Smith (AUS)	
1962	R.G. Laver (AUS)	M. Smith (AUS)	
1963	R.S. Emerson (AUS)	M. Smith (AUS)	
1964	R.S. Emerson (AUS)	M. Smith (AUS)	
1965	R.S. Emerson (AUS)	M. Smith (AUS)	
1966	R.S. Emerson (AUS)	M. Smith (AUS)	
1967	R.S. Emerson (AUS)	N. Richey (USA)	
1968	W.W. Bowrey (AUS)	B.-J. King (USA)	
1969	R.G. Laver (AUS)	M. (Smith) Court (AUS)	
1970	A.R. Ashe (USA)	M. Court (AUS)	
1971	K.R. Rosewall (AUS)	M. Court (AUS)	
1972	K.R. Rosewall (AUS)	S.V. Wade (GBR)	
1973	J.D. Newcombe (AUS)	M. Court (AUS)	
1974	J.S. Connors (USA)	E. Goolagong (AUS)	
1975	J.D. Newcombe (AUS)	E. Goolagong (AUS)	
1976	M. Edmondson (AUS)	E. (Goolagong) Cawley (AUS)	
1977*	R. Tanner (USA)	K. Reid (AUS)	
	V. Gerulaitis (USA)	E. (Goolagong) Cawley (AUS)	
1978	G. Vilas (ARG)	C. O'Neill (AUS)	
1979	G. Vilas (ARG)	B. Jordan (USA)	
1980	B. Teacher (USA)	H. Mandlikova (TCH)	
1981	J. Kriek (RSA)	M. Navratilova (USA)	
1982	J. Kriek (RSA)	C.M. Evert Lloyd (USA)	
1983	M. Wilander (SWE)	M. Navratilova (USA)	
1984	M. Wilander (SWE)	C.M. Evert Lloyd (USA)	
1985	S. Edberg (SWE)	M. Navratilova (USA)	
1986	not held	not held	
1987	S. Edberg (SWE)	H. Mandlikova (TCH)	
1988	M. Wilander (SWE)	S. Graf (FRG)	
1989	I. Lendl (TCH)	S. Graf (FRG)	
1990	I. Lendl (TCH)	S. Graf (FRG)	
1991	B. Becker (GER)	M. Seles (YUG)	
1992	J. Courier (USA)	M. Seles (YUG)	
1993	J. Courier (USA)	M. Seles (YUG)	
1994	P. Sampras (USA)	S. Graf (GER)	
1995	A. Agassi (USA)	M. Pierce (FRA)	
1996	B. Becker (GER)	M. Seles (USA)	
1997	P. Sampras (USA)	M. Hingis (SUI)	
1998	P. Korda (CZE)	M. Hingis (SUI)	
1999	Y. Kafelnikov (RUS)	M. Hingis (SUI)	
2000	A. Agassi (USA)	L. Davenport (USA)	
2001	A. Agassi (USA)	J. Capriati (USA)	
2002	T. Johansson (SWE)	J. Capriati (USA)	
2003	A. Agassi (USA)	S. Williams (USA)	
2004	R. Federer (SUI)	J. Henin-Hardenne (BEL)	

LAWN TENNIS

*In 1977 the Australian Open was moved to December, having until then taken place in January, so there were two tournaments that year. In 1987 it was moved back to January; thus there was no tournament in 1986.

French Open

	Men's Singles	Women's Singles		Men's Singles	Women's Singles
1891	H. Briggs (GBR)	——	1915	not held	not held
1892	J. Schopfer (FRA)	——	1916-18	not held	not held
1893	L. Riboulet (FRA)	——	1919	not held	not held
1894	A. Vacherot (FRA)	——	1920	A.H. Gobert (FRA)	S. Lenglen (FRA)
1895	A. Vacherot (FRA)	——	1921	J. Samazeuilh (FRA)	S. Lenglen (FRA)
1896	A. Vacherot (FRA)	——	1922	H. Cochet (FRA)	S. Lenglen (FRA)
1897	P. Ayme (FRA)	C. Masson (FRA)	1923	P. Blanchy (FRA)	S. Lenglen (FRA)
1898	P. Ayme (FRA)	C. Masson (FRA)	1924	J. Borotra (FRA)	D. Vlasto (FRA)
1899	P. Ayme (FRA)	C. Masson (FRA)	1925	R. Lacoste (FRA)	S. Lenglen (FRA)
1900	P. Ayme (FRA)	Y. Prevost (FRA)	1926	H. Cochet (FRA)	S. Lenglen (FRA)
1901	A. Vacherot (FRA)	P. Girod (FRA)	1927	R. Lacoste (FRA)	K. Bouman (NED)
1902	A. Vacherot (FRA)	C. Masson (FRA)	1928	H. Cochet (FRA)	H.N. Wills (USA)
1903	M. Decugis (FRA)	C. Masson (FRA)	1929	R. Lacoste (FRA)	H.N. Wills (USA)
1904	M. Decugis (FRA)	K. Gillou (FRA)	1930	H. Cochet (FRA)	H.N. Wills Moody (USA)
1905	M. Germot (FRA)	K. Gillou (FRA)	1931	J. Borotra (FRA)	C. Aussem (GER)
1906	M. Germot (FRA)	K. (Gillou) Fenwick (FRA)	1932	H. Cochet (FRA)	H.N. Wills Moody (USA)
1907	M. Decugis (FRA)	M. de Kermel (FRA)	1933	J. Crawford (AUS)	M.C. Scriven (GBR)
1908	M. Decugis (FRA)	K. Fenwick (FRA)	1934	G. Von Cramm (GER)	M.C. Scriven (GBR)
1909	M. Decugis (FRA)	J. Mattley (FRA)	1935	F.J. Perry (GBR)	H. Sperling (DEN)
1910	M. Germot (FRA)	J. Mattley (FRA)	1936	G. Von Cramm (GER)	H. Sperling (DEN)
1911	A.H. Gobert (FRA)	J. Mattley (FRA)	1937	H. Henkel (GER)	H. Sperling (DEN)
1912	M. Decugis (FRA)	J. Mattley (FRA)	1938	J.D. Budge (USA)	S. Mathieu (FRA)
1913	M. Decugis (FRA)	M. Broquedis (FRA)	1939	W.D. McNeill (USA)	S. Mathieu (FRA)
1914	M. Decugis (FRA)	M. Broquedis (FRA)	1940	not held	not held

1941-45 not held	not held	1974	B. Borg (SWE)	C.M. Evert (USA)
1946 M. Bernard (FRA)	M.E. Osborne (USA)	1975	B. Borg (SWE)	C.M. Evert (USA)
1947 J. Asboth (HUN)	P. Todd (USA)	1976	A. Panatta (ITA)	S. Barker (GBR)
1948 F.A. Parker (USA)	N. Landry (BEL)	1977	G. Vilas (ARG)	M. Jaušovec (YUG)
1949 F.A. Parker (USA)	M.E. (Osborne) Du Pont	1978	B. Borg (SWE)	V. Ruzici (ROM)
	(USA)	1979	B. Borg (SWE)	C.M. Evert Lloyd (USA)
1950 J.E. Patty (USA)	D.J. Hart (USA)	1980	B. Borg (SWE)	C.M. Evert Lloyd (USA)
1951 J. Drobny (EGY)	S.J. Fry (USA)	1981	B. Borg (SWE)	H. Mandlikova (TCH)
1952 J. Drobny (EGY)	D.J. Hart (USA)	1982	M. Wilander (SWE)	M. Navratilova (USA)
1953 K.R. Rosewall (AUS)	M. Connolly (USA)	1983	Y. Noah (FRA)	C.M. Evert Lloyd (USA)
1954 M.A. Trabert (USA)	M. Connolly (USA)	1984	I. Lendl (TCH)	M. Navratilova (USA)
1955 M.A. Trabert (USA)	A. Mortimer (GBR)	1985	M. Wilander (SWE)	C.M.Evert Lloyd (USA)
1956 L. A. Hoad (AUS)	A. Gibson (USA)	1986	I. Lendl (TCH)	C.M. Evert Lloyd (USA)
1957 S. Davidson (SWE)	S.J. Bloomer (GBR)	1987	I. Lendl (TCH)	S. Graf (FRG)
1958 M.G. Rose (AUS)	S. Kormoczy (HUN)	1988	M. Wilander (SWE)	S. Graf (GER)
1959 N. Pietrangeli (ITA)	C.C. Truman (GBR)	1989	M. Chang (USA)	A. Sanchez Vicario (ESP)
1960 N. Pietrangeli (ITA)	D.R. Hard (USA)	1990	A. Gomez (ECU)	M. Seles (YUG)
1961 M. Santana (ESP)	A.S. Haydon (GBR)	1991	J. Courier (USA)	M. Seles (YUG)
1962 R.G. Laver (AUS)	M. Smith (AUS)	1992	J. Courier (USA)	M. Seles (YUG)
1963 R.S. Emerson (AUS)	L.R. Turner (AUS)	1993	S. Bruguera (ESP)	S. Graf (GER)
1964 M. Santana (ESP)	M. Smith (AUS)	1994	S. Bruguera (ESP)	A. Sanchez Vicario (ESP)
1965 F. S. Stolle (AUS)	L.R. Turner (AUS)	1995	T. Muster (AUT)	S. Graf (GER)
1966 A.D. Roche (AUS)	A.S. (Haydon) Jones	1996	Y. Kafelnikov (RUS)	S. Graf (GER)
	(GBR)	1997	G. Kuerten (BRA)	I. Majoli (CRO)
1967 R.S. Emerson (AUS)	F. Durr (FRA)	1998	C. Moya (ESP)	A. Sanchez Vicario (ESP)
1968 K.R. Rosewall (AUS)	N. Richey (USA)	1999	A. Agassi (USA)	S. Graf (GER)
1969 R.G. Laver (AUS)	M. (Smith) Court (AUS)	2000	G. Kuerten (BRA)	M. Pierce (FRA)
1970 J. Kodes (TCH)	M. Court (AUS)	2001	G. Kuerten (BRA)	J. Capriati (USA)
1971 J. Kodes (TCH)	E. Goolagong (AUS)	2002	A. Costa (ESP)	S. Williams (USA)
1972 A. Gimeno (ESP)	B.-J. King (USA)	2003	J.C. Ferrero (ESP)	J Henin-Hardenne (BEL)
1973 I. Nastase (ROM)	M. Court (AUS)	2004	G. Gaudio (ARG)	A. Myskina (RUS)

General Information

Australian Open: venue	Melbourne Park (formerly known as Flinders Park)
ball dimensions	Balls must be between 2½ins (6.35cm) and 2⅝ins (6.67cm) and weigh between 1.975oz (56g) and 2.095oz (59.4g).
court dimensions	For singles play the dimensions are 78ft × 27ft (23.77m × 8.23m) and for doubles 78ft by 36ft (23.77m × 10.97m). The service line is 21ft (6.4m) from the net and the base line a further 18ft (5.5m).
Davis Cup: inaugurated	1900
most wins	USA (31)
official title	The International Men's Team Championship of the World
played for Italy	Martin Mulligan (Australia)
Egyptian citizenship adopted	Jaroslav Drobny (born in Czechoslovakia) became an Egyptian citizen in 1949.
Federation Cup	Women's equivalent of the Davis Cup. Inaugurated in 1963, the United States defeated Australia 2-1 in the first final.
'Four Musketeers'	Jean Borotra, Jacques 'Toto' Brugnon, Henri Cochet, René Lacoste
French championships: made open	Before 1925 the French championships were only open to members of French clubs.
French Open: venue	The French Open has been played at Roland Garros Stadium, Paris, since 1928.
Grand Slam: definition	Winning all four major titles (Australian Open, French Open, Wimbledon, US Open) consecutively, irrespective of calendar year (the feat formerly had to be achieved in a calendar year)
winners	Donald Budge (1938), Maureen Connolly (1953), Margaret Court (1970), Steffi Graf (1988), Rod Laver (1962, 1969), Martina Navratilova (1983, 1984)
junior winner	Earl Buchholz won all four junior titles in 1958, as did Stefan Edberg in 1983.
Hopman Cup	An international event for mixed teams first held between 28 December 1988 and 1 January 1989. Czechoslovakia defeated Australia in the first championship.
net: height in middle	3ft (0.91m), supported by posts each side of 3½ft (1.07m) high and 3ft (0.91m) outside the court
nicknames:	The Bounding Basque – Jean Borotra; Poker Face – Helen Wills-Moody; The Ghost – Harold Mahony; The Two Helens – Helen Wills-Moody and Helen Jacobs (the two were great rivals and were born on the same street in Berkeley, California)
Olympic champions: 2000	Venus Williams (USA) and Yevgeny Kafelnikov (Russia)

Olympic Games: ice hockey player	Jaroslav Drobny (1948)
tennis challenge: battle of the sexes	Bobby Riggs had beaten Margaret Court in 1973 but was then beaten by Billie-Jean King (and famously presented with a pig).
'Three Musketeers'	Jean Borotra, Henri Cochet, René Lacoste
US Open: venue	The US Open has been played at Flushing Meadows, New York, since 1978. The finals showcourt is named after Arthur Ashe.
Wimbledon:	
boycott year	1973 (due to suspension of Nikki Pilic of Yugoslavia)
champion at first and the only attempt	Bobby Riggs (USA) won all three titles on his only appearance in the championships (1939).
first American woman competitor	Marion Jones (lost in the 2nd round)
first black champion	Althea Gibson (1957)
first black men's champion	Arthur Ashe (1975)
first professional champion	Rod Laver (1968)
last amateur champion	John Newcombe (1967)
longest match	5hrs 12mins: Pancho Gonzales beat Charlie Pasarell 22-24, 1-6, 16-14, 6-3, 11-9, in 1969. (This match hastened the need for the tie-break system)
lost in first round of defence: first	Manuel Santana lost to Charlie Pasarell in 1967.
mixed doubles: brother and sister	John and Tracy Austin won the 1981 championship. Wayne and Cara Black won the 2004 championship.
mixed doubles: man and wife	Mr and Mrs L.A. Godfree won the 1926 championship.
oldest men's champion	Arthur Gore (41 in 1910)
original sport played at venue	croquet
represented Brazil in Davis Cup	Robert Falkenburg (USA)
unseeded champion	Boris Becker (West Germany) in 1985
unseeded player in two finals	Kurt Nielsen (Denmark) beaten in 1953 and 1955
youngest champion	Lottie Dod (Great Britain) aged 15 years, 285 days (1887)
youngest men's champion	Boris Becker (West Germany) aged 17 years, 227 days (1985)

MARBLES

Marbles is one of the earliest games ever played and its origins can be traced back to ancient times. Earthen monuments of the Mound Builders, a race of people who lived on the American continent before the American Indians arrived, contained marbles along with other ancient artefacts. The earliest marbles were made of flint or clay and although crude in form were often uniquely decorated by their makers. It is thought these first spheres were used in games, though it is possible they were either used for decorative purposes or held religious significance.

In the Roman Empire marbles seem to have reached a peak of popularity about the time of the Emperor Augustus, in the century before the beginning of the Christian era. There are references to the use of marbles in various games and sports in Roman literature of this period. The Romans probably popularised the game throughout their empire. In this way, the game appeared in England around the latter part of the first century AD, after the final conquest of Britain by the Romans. About this period, the writings of Britain reveal that both adults and their children used marbles made from stone in their games. As marbles became more popular in Britain, they were made from real marble as well as from other more common stones and from dried or baked clay. The British Museum contains marbles used by both Egyptian and Roman children.

A 15th-century manuscript mentions 'the little yellow balls with which school boys played, and which were very cheap'. Some sources claim that glass marbles had their origin in Venice with the old glassmakers.

Marbles was played throughout Europe in pre-Elizabethan times. In 1503 the town council of Nürnberg limited the playing of marbles games to a meadow outside the town's limits; and in the English village of St Gall, the town council statutes authorised the sacristan of St Laurence to use a cat-o'-nine-tails on boys 'who played at marbles under the fish stand and refused to be warned off'. In France the game of Troule-en-Madame, in which small marbles were rolled into holes at one end of a board, was popular, and it moved across the English Channel to be corrupted into the children's marbles game called Troll-My-Dame.

Shakespeare mentions the game of 'Cherry Pit', in which polished stones were tossed into holes in the ground, and in Henry V he talks of times when 'the boys went to span-counter for French Crowns'. Pieter Breughel the Elder's 1560 painting Kinderspiele (Children's Games), which depicts about eighty of these, is regarded by historians as a prime source for information about children's games. It shows children playing mar-

bles. Francis Beaumont and John Fletcher in Monsieur Thomas (c.1607), Thomas Dekker and John Webster in Northward Ho (c.1605) and John Donne in his fourth Satire (c.1597) all mention marbles games.

Daniel Defoe, author of Robinson Crusoe, wrote in 1720, of a marbles player, that:

> Marbles, (which he used to call children playing at bowls) yielded him a mighty diversion, and he was so dextrous an artist at shooting that little alabaster globe from between the end of his forefinger and knuckle of his thumb that he seldom missed hitting plumb.

Marbles games usually fall into three categories: chase games, in which two or more players alternately shoot at each other along a makeshift meandering course; enclosure games, in which marbles are shot at other marbles contained within a marked-off area; and hole games, in which marbles are shot or bowled into a series of holes. In the United States the varieties of marbles are virtually infinite and the game is called, variously, 'Ringer', 'Immies', or 'Mibs'. In England, Scotland and Ireland it is also 'Taw', 'Boss', 'Span'. In Brazil children play it as Gude; in parts of Africa it is Jorrah and in Italy, Pallina di vetro. In West Virginia it is played with agate or glass balls, in parts of Australia with balls of polished wood, and on the streets of New York City even with steel ball-bearings. In Iran, Turkey and Syria marbles is played with balls of baked clay or with the knucklebones of sheep. Chinese children play at 'kicking the marbles' and youngsters in Tasmania play at Pyramids.

Good Friday in England was once celebrated as 'Marbles Day', a ploy by the English clergy who considered a countrywide marbles day preferable to 'more boisterous and mischievous enjoyments'. Pubs, inns and taverns had built-in marbles 'bowling alleys' for their patrons' pleasure. This tradition is maintained in the Crawley suburb of Tinsley Green in West Sussex where, every Good Friday, the World Marbles Championship is held in the car park of the Greyhound public house. Local teams such as the Toucan Terribles and the Black Dog Boozers have often won the title although many of the players only 'knuckle-down' once a year. To start, 49 marbles are placed in the centre of a ring and the winning team is the first to knock 25 out of the ring. Overseas teams have rarely attended this event but when they do it is sometimes with 'professional' squads that demolish the home contingent. In recent years the Americans and the Germans have made the trip and duly taken the trophy.

MODERN PENTATHLON

The modern pentathlon was devised in 1912 at the Stockholm Olympic Games by Baron Pierre de Coubertin, founder of the modern Olympics. His goal was to create a sport that could be used as a symbol of the Olympic Ideal. The phrase 'Citius Altius Fortius' (Faster – Higher – Stronger) was acquiring strength and sports were increasing in variety. Pierre de Coubertin soon realised that 'his' games needed to assimilate a new range of values in addition to physical ability, such as skill and the athlete's psychological capacity, in order to create a sport that would reward the complete athlete.

The modern pentathlon came into being as a fusion of five sports: shooting, swimming, fencing, running and horse riding. It has participants worldwide but is most popular in Europe.

Even today, in 2004, after nearly 100 years the modern pentathlon remains faithful to its roots. Since the Atlanta Games in 1996 it has been contested in a single day, in what is called the 'one-day event', which mercilessly eliminates less-prepared contestants. The shooting event starts at 7.30am with a compressed air pistol at a distance of 10m from the target. The pentathlete is required to make 20 shots (with approximately one minute for each shot). This is followed by fencing, which starts at 10.00am. By 1.00pm the athletes commence the swimming event in an Olympic distance pool (50m) or short pool (25m) for a distance of 200m. At 2.00pm the horse riding event, a cross-country steeplechase, begins. By 6.00pm the athletes start the running event over a 3000m cross-country course. For each event the athlete's score in points is attributed proportionally to his or her performance using a system similar to athletic decathlon and heptathlon tables. After the five events the pentathlete who has collected most points is declared the winner.

Britain's Stephanie Cook won the women's title in its inauguration into the Olympics in 2000, overhauling leader Emily de Riel of the US in the final event with a storming run that took her through the field to victory.

Olympic Medallists

Men's Individual

	Gold	Silver	Bronze
1912	Gösta Lilliehöök (SWE)	Gösta Åsbrink (SWE)	Georg de Laval (SWE)
1920	Gustaf Dyrssen (SWE)	Erik de Laval (SWE)	Gösta Runö (SWE)
1924	Bo Lindman (SWE)	Gustaf Dyrssen (SWE)	Berth Uggla (SWE)
1928	Sven Thofelt (SWE)	Bo Lindman (SWE)	Helmuth Kahl (GER)
1932	Johan Oxenstierna (SWE)	Bo Lindman (SWE)	Richard Mayo (USA)
1936	Gotthardt Handrick (GER)	Charles Leonard (USA)	Silvano Abba (ITA)
1948	William Grut (SWE)	George Moore (USA)	Gösta Gärdin (SWE)
1952	Lars Hall (SWE)	Gábor Benedek (HUN)	István Szondy (HUN)
1956	Lars Hall (SWE)	Olavi Mannonen (FIN)	Väinö Korhonen (FIN)
1960	Ferenc Németh (HUN)	Imre Nagy (HUN)	Robert Beck (USA)
1964	Ferenc Török (HUN)	Igor Novikov (URS)	Albert Mokeyev (URS)
1968	Björn Ferm (SWE)	András Balczó (HUN)	Pavel Lednev (URS)
1972	András Balczó (HUN)	Boris Onischenko (URS)	Pavel Lednev (URS)
1976	Janusz Pyciak-Peciak (POL)	Pavel Lednev (URS)	Jan Bártu (TCH)
1980	Anatoliy Starostin (URS)	Tamás Szombathelyi (HUN)	Pavel Lednev (URS)
1984	Daniele Masala (ITA)	Svante Rasmuson (SWE)	Carlo Massullo (ITA)
1988	János Martinek (HUN)	Carlo Massullo (ITA)	Vakhtang Yagorashvili (URS)
1992	Arkadiusz Skrzypaszek (POL)	Attila Mizsér (HUN)	Eduard Zenovka (CIS)
1996	Aleksandr Parygin (KAZ)	Eduard Zenovka (RUS)	János Martinek (HUN)
2000	Dmitriy Svatkovsky (RUS)	Gábor Balogh (HUN)	Pavel Dovgal (BLR)

Women's Individual

	Gold	Silver	Bronze
2000	Stephanie Cook (GBR)	Emily de Riel (USA)	Kate Allenby (GBR)

Men's Team

	Gold	Silver	Bronze
1952	Hungary	Sweden	Finland
1956	Soviet Union	United States	Finland
1960	Hungary	Soviet Union	United States
1964	Soviet Union	United States	Hungary
1968	Hungary	Soviet Union	France
1972	Soviet Union	Hungary	Finland
1976	Great Britain	Czechoslovakia	Hungary
1980	Soviet Union	Hungary	Sweden
1984	Italy	United States	France
1988	Hungary	Italy	Great Britain
1992	Poland	CIS	Italy

World Champions

Men's

	Individual	Team		Individual	Team
1949	Tage Bjurfeldt (SWE)	Sweden	1978	Pavel Lednev (URS)	Poland
1950	Lars Hall (SWE)	Sweden	1979	Robert Niemann (USA)	United States
1951	Lars Hall (SWE)	Sweden	1981	Janusz Pyciak-Peciak (POL)	Poland
1953	Gábor Benedek (HUN)	Sweden	1982	Daniele Masala (ITA)	Soviet Union
1954	Björn Thofelt (SWE)	Hungary	1983	Anatoliy Starostin (URS)	Soviet Union
1955	Konstantin Salnikov (URS)	Hungary	1985	Attila Miszér (HUN)	Soviet Union
1957	Igor Novikov (URS)	Soviet Union	1986	Carlo Massullo (ITA)	Italy
1958	Igor Novikov (URS)	Soviet Union	1987	Joel Bouzou (FRA)	Hungary
1959	Igor Novikov (URS)	Soviet Union	1989	László Fabian (HUN)	Hungary
1961	Igor Novikov (URS)	Soviet Union	1990	Gianluca Tiberti (ITA)	Soviet Union
1962	Edward Sdobnikov (URS)	Soviet Union	1991	Arkadiusz Skrzypaszek (POL)	Soviet Union
1963	András Balczó (HUN)	Hungary	1993	Richard Phelps (GBR)	not held
1965	András Balczó (HUN)	Hungary	1994	Dmitriy Svatkovsky (RUS)	France
1966	András Balczó (HUN)	Hungary	1995	Dmitriy Svatkovsky (RUS)	Hungary
1967	András Balczó (HUN)	Hungary	1997	Sébastien Deleigne (FRA)	Hungary
1969	András Balczó (HUN)	Soviet Union	1998	Sébastien Deleigne (FRA)	Mexico
1970	Peter Kelemen (HUN)	Hungary	1999	Gábor Balogh (HUN)	Hungary
1971	Boris Onischenko (URS)	Hungary	2000	Andrejus Zadneprovskis (LTU)	United States
1973	Pavel Lednev (URS)	Soviet Union	2001	Gábor Balogh (HUN)	Hungary
1974	Pavel Lednev (URS)	Soviet Union	2002	Michal Sedlecky (CZE)	Hungary
1975	Pavel Lednev (URS)	Hungary	2003	Eric Walther (GER)	Hungary
1977	Janusz Pyciak-Peciak (POL)	Poland			

NB: Men's World Championships were not held in Olympic years until the year 2000.

Women's

	Individual	Team		Individual	Team
1981	Anne Ahlgren (SWE)	Great Britain	1993	Eva Fjellerup (DEN)	not held
1982	Wendy Norman (GBR)	Great Britain	1994	Eva Fjellerup (DEN)	Italy
1983	Lynn Chernobrywy (CAN)	Great Britain	1995	Kerstin Danielsson (SWE)	Poland
1984	Sveta Jakovleva (URS)	Soviet Union	1996	Janna Dolgascheva-Schubenok (BLR)	Russia
1985	Barbara Kotevska (POL)	Poland			
1986	Irina Kisseleva (URS)	France	1997	Jelisaveta Suvorova (RUS)	Italy
1987	Irina Kisseleva (URS)	Soviet Union	1998	Anna Sulima (POL)	Poland
1988	Dorota Idzi (POL)	Poland	1999	Zsuzsanna Vörös (HUN)	Russia
1989	Lori Norwood (USA)	Poland	2000	Pernille Svarre (DEN)	Poland
1990	Eva Fjellerup (DEN)	Poland	2001	Stephanie Cook (GBR)	Great Britain
1991	Eva Fjellerup (DEN)	Poland	2002	Bea Simoka (HUN)	Hungary
1992	Iwona Kowalewska (POL)	Poland	2003	Szuzsa Vörös (HUN)	Great Britain

Motorcycles are descended from the first bicycles to have front and rear wheels of the same size and a pedal crank mechanism to drive the rear wheel. Gottlieb Daimler (who later teamed up with Karl Benz to form the Daimler-Benz Corporation) is credited with building the first motorcycle in 1885. Using one wheel at the front and one at the back, with a smaller spring-loaded outrigger wheel on each side, it was constructed mostly of wood. The wheels were iron-banded and wooden-spoked.

According to Eric W. Walford's *Early Days in the British Motorcycle Industry* (1931), a 1000-mile trial run in the spring of 1900 was motorcycling's first organised competitive event. In 1903 the Auto-Cycle Club (which became the Auto-Cycle Union (ACU) in 1907) was founded to control the sport. In 1904 the FICM (Fédération Internationale des Clubs Motorcyclistes) was established in Paris as motorcycling's first international federation (it was renamed the FIM (Fédération Internationale de Motocyclisme) in 1949). In 1907 the ACU organised the first of the now-famous Isle of Man Tourist Trophy (TT) races. Now sadly defunct as a world Grand Prix venue, due to the high incidence of injuries on the road circuit, the Isle of Man still holds annual Manx Grand Prix and TT Formula One races. The Grand Prix began life as the Amateur Road Race Championships in 1923, before being renamed in 1930.

In 1928 speedway was imported to Britain from Australia and it remains one of the most popular motorcycling sports. More than 300 tracks were constructed. Speedway is normally raced on an oval shale circuit, using bikes that have fixed gears and no brakes. Ice speedway developed from the sport. Raced on an ice rink, the bikes have spikes inserted into the tyres to grip the ice.

After World War II, scrambling (now called motocross or supercross, which is a stadium dirt-track version), enduro and trial riding also became popular and Grand Prix races and world championships began to be held in these formats. All are sanctioned by the FIM which, in 2004, has over 85 affiliated national federations, including the AMA (American Motorcyclist Association). There are more than 90 classifications of motorcycle competition.

The following is an A-Z of biographies of champions, tracks and machines in the sports of enduro, ice speedway, motocross, road racing, speedway, supercross, trial riding and cross-country rallying. A results section is also included for the main road racing and speedway events, and for an at-a-glance guide to motorcycling's 2003 champions.

Road Racing World Championships

500cc

	Winner	Manufacturer	Second	Third
1949	Leslie Graham (GBR)	AJS	Nello Pagani (ITA)	Arciso Artesiani (ITA)
1950	Umberto Masetti (ITA)	Gilera/Norton	Geoff Duke (GBR)	Leslie Graham (GBR)
1951	Geoff Duke (GBR)	Norton	Alfredo Milani (ITA)	Umberto Masetti (ITA)
1952	Umberto Masetti (ITA)	Norton	Leslie Graham (GBR)	Reginald Armstrong (IRL)
1953	Geoff Duke (GBR)	Gilera	Reginald Armstrong (IRL)	Alfredo Milani (ITA)
1954	Geoff Duke (GBR)	Gilera	Ray Amm (RHO)	Ken Kavanagh (AUS)
1955	Geoff Duke (GBR)	Gilera	Reginald Armstrong (IRL)	Umberto Masetti (ITA)
1956	John Surtees (GBR)	MV Agusta	Walter Zeller (FRG)	John Hartle (GBR)
1957	Libero Liberati (ITA)	Gilera	Bob McIntyre (GBR)	John Surtees (GBR)
1958	John Surtees (GBR)	MV Agusta	John Hartle (GBR)	Dickie Dale (GBR)
1959	John Surtees (GBR)	MV Agusta	Remo Venturi (ITA)	Bob Brown (AUS)
1960	John Surtees (GBR)	MV Agusta	Remo Venturi (ITA)	John Hartle (GBR)
1961	Gary Hocking (RHO)	MV Agusta	Mike Hailwood (GBR)	Frank Perris (GBR)
1962	Mike Hailwood (GBR)	MV Agusta	Alan Shepherd (GBR)	Phil Read (GBR)
1963	Mike Hailwood (GBR)	MV Agusta	Alan Shepherd (GBR)	John Hartle (GBR)
1964	Mike Hailwood (GBR)	MV Agusta	Jack Ahearn (AUS)	Phil Read (GBR)
1965	Mike Hailwood (GBR)	MV Agusta	Giacomo Agostini (ITA)	Paddy Driver (RSA)
1966	Giacomo Agostini (ITA)	MV Agusta/Honda	Mike Hailwood (GBR)	Jack Findlay (AUS)
1967	Giacomo Agostini (ITA)	MV Agusta	Mike Hailwood (GBR)	John Hartle (GBR)
1968	Giacomo Agostini (ITA)	MV Agusta	Jack Findlay (AUS)	Gyula Marszovsky (SUI)
1969	Giacomo Agostini (ITA)	MV Agusta	Gyula Marszovsky (SUI)	Godfrey Nash (GBR)
1970	Giacomo Agostini (ITA)	MV Agusta	Ginger Molloy (NZL)	Angelo Bergamonti (ITA)
1971	Giacomo Agostini (ITA)	MV Agusta	Keith Turner (GBR)	Rob Bron (NED)
1972	Giacomo Agostini (ITA)	MV Agusta	Alberto Pagani (ITA)	Bruno Kneubühler (SUI)
1973	Phil Read (GBR)	MV Agusta	Kim Newcombe (NZL)	Giacomo Agostini (ITA)

	Winner	Manufacturer	Second	Third
1974	Phil Read (GBR)	MV Agusta/Yamaha	Gianfranco Bonera (ITA)	Teuvo Länsivuori (FIN)
1975	Giacomo Agostini (ITA)	Yamaha	Phil Read (GBR)	Hideo Kanaya (JPN)
1976	Barry Sheene (GBR)	Suzuki	Teuvo Länsivuori (FIN)	Pat Hennen (USA)
1977	Barry Sheene (GBR)	Suzuki	Steve Baker (USA)	Pat Hennen (USA)
1978	Kenny Roberts (USA)	Yamaha/Suzuki	Barry Sheene (GBR)	Johnny Cecotto (VEN)
1979	Kenny Roberts (USA)	Yamaha/Suzuki	Virginio Ferrari (ITA)	Barry Sheene (GBR)
1980	Kenny Roberts (USA)	Yamaha/Suzuki	Randy Mamola (USA)	Marco Lucchinelli (ITA)
1981	Marco Lucchinelli (ITA)	Suzuki	Randy Mamola (USA)	Kenny Roberts (USA)
1982	Franco Uncini (ITA)	Suzuki	Graeme Crosby (NZL)	Freddie Spencer (USA)
1983	Freddie Spencer (USA)	Honda	Kenny Roberts (USA)	Randy Mamola (USA)
1984	Eddie Lawson (USA)	Yamaha/Honda	Randy Mamola (USA)	Raymond Roche (FRA)
1985	Freddie Spencer (USA)	Honda	Eddie Lawson (USA)	Christian Sarron (FRA)
1986	Eddie Lawson (USA)	Yamaha	Wayne Gardner (AUS)	Randy Mamola (USA)
1987	Wayne Gardner (AUS)	Honda/Yamaha	Randy Mamola (USA)	Eddie Lawson (USA)
1988	Eddie Lawson (USA)	Yamaha	Wayne Gardner (AUS)	Wayne Rainey (USA)
1989	Eddie Lawson (USA)	Honda	Wayne Rainey (USA)	Christian Sarron (FRA)
1990	Wayne Rainey (USA)	Yamaha	Kevin Schwantz (USA)	Michael Doohan (AUS)
1991	Wayne Rainey (USA)	Yamaha	Michael Doohan (USA)	Kevin Schwantz (USA)
1992	Wayne Rainey (USA)	Yamaha/Honda	Michael Doohan (USA)	John Kocinski (USA)
1993	Kevin Schwantz (USA)	Suzuki/Yamaha	Wayne Rainey (USA)	Derryl Beattle (AUS)
1994	Michael Doohan (AUS)	Honda	Luca Cadalora (ITA)	John Kocinski (USA)
1995	Michael Doohan (AUS)	Honda	Derryl Beattle (AUS)	Luca Cadalora (ITA)
1996	Michael Doohan (AUS)	Honda	Alex Criville (ESP)	Luca Cadalora (ITA)
1997	Michael Doohan (AUS)	Honda	Tadayuki Okada (JPN)	Nobuatu Aoki (JPN)
1998	Michael Doohan (AUS)	Honda	Max Biaggi (ITA)	Alex Crivillé (ESP)
1999	Alex Crivillé (ESP)	Honda	Kenny Roberts jnr (USA)	Tadayuki Okada (JPN)
2000	Kenny Roberts jnr (USA)	Suzuki/Yamaha	Valentino Rossi (ITA)	Max Biaggi (ITA)
2001	Valentino Rossi (ITA)	Honda	Max Biaggi (ITA)	Loris Capirossi (ITA)

MotoGP

	Winner	Manufacturer	Second	Third
2002	Valentino Rossi (ITA)	Honda	Max Biaggi (ITA)	Tohru Ukawa (JPN)
2003	Valentino Rossi (ITA)	Honda	Sete Gibernau (ESP)	Max Biaggi (ITA)

350cc

	Winner	Manufacturer	Second	Third
1949	Freddie Frith (GBR)	Velocette	Reginald Armstrong (IRL)	Bob Foster (GBR)
1950	Bob Foster (GBR)	Velocette	Geoff Duke (GBR)	Leslie Graham (GBR)
1951	Geoff Duke (GBR)	Norton	Bill Doran (GBR)	Johnny Lockett (GBR)
1952	Geoff Duke (GBR)	Guzzi/Norton	Reginald Armstrong (IRL)	Ray Amm (RHO)
1953	Fergus Anderson (GBR)	Guzzi/Moto Guzzi	Enrico Lorenzetti (ITA)	Ray Amm (RHO)
1954	Fergus Anderson (GBR)	Guzzi	Ray Amm (RHO)	Rod Coleman (NZL)
1955	Bill Lomas (GBR)	Moto Guzzi	Dickie Dale (GBR)	August Hobl (GER)
1956	Bill Lomas (GBR)	Moto Guzzi	August Hobl (FRG)	Dickie Dale (GBR)
1957	Keith Campbell (AUS)	Gilera	Libero Liberati (ITA)	Bob McIntyre (GBR)
1958	John Surtees (GBR)	MV Agusta	John Hartle (GBR)	Geoff Duke (GBR)
1959	John Surtees (GBR)	MV Agusta	John Hartle (GBR)	Bob Brown (AUS)
1960	John Surtees (GBR)	MV Agusta	Gary Hocking (RHO)	John Hartle (GBR)
1961	Gary Hocking (RHO)	MV Agusta	Frantisek Stastny (TCH)	Gustav Havel (TCH)
1962	Jim Redman (RHO)	Honda	Tommy Robb (IRL)	Mike Hailwood (GBR)
1963	Jim Redman (RHO)	Honda	Mike Hailwood (GBR)	Luigi Taveri (SUI)
1964	Jim Redman (RHO)	Honda	Bruce Beale (RHO)	Mike Duff (CAN)
1965	Jim Redman (RHO)	Honda	Giacomo Agostini (ITA)	Mike Hailwood (GBR)
1966	Mike Hailwood (GBR)	Honda	Giacomo Agostini (ITA)	Renzo Pasolini (ITA)
1967	Mike Hailwood (GBR)	Honda	Giacomo Agostini (ITA)	Ralph Bryans (IRL)
1968	Giacomo Agostini (ITA)	MV Agusta	Renzo Pasolini (ITA)	Kel Carruthers (AUS)
1969	Giacomo Agostini (ITA)	MV Agusta	Silvio Grasseti (ITA)	Giuseppe Vicenzi (ITA)
1970	Giacomo Agostini (ITA)	MV Agusta	Kel Carruthers (AUS)	Renzo Pasolini (ITA)
1971	Giacomo Agostini (ITA)	MV Agusta	Jarno Saarinen (FIN)	Curt-Ivan Carlsson (SWE)
1972	Giacomo Agostini (ITA)	MV Agusta	Jarno Saarinen (FIN)	Renzo Pasolini (ITA)
1973	Giacomo Agostini (ITA)	MV Agusta/Yamaha	Teuvo Länsivuori (FIN)	Phil Read (GBR)
1974	Giacomo Agostini (ITA)	Yamaha	Dieter Braun (FRG)	Patrick Pons (FRA)
1975	Johnny Cecotto (VEN)	Yamaha	Giacomo Agostini (ITA)	Pentti Korhonen (FIN)
1976	Walter Villa (ITA)	Harley/Yamaha	Johnny Cecotto (VEN)	Chas Mortimer (GBR)
1977	Takazumi Katayama (JPN)	Yamaha	Tom Herron (IRL)	Jon Ekerold (RSA)
1978	Kork Ballington (RSA)	Kawasaki	Katazumi Katayama (JPN)	Gregg Hansford (AUS)
1979	Kork Ballington (RSA)	Kawasaki	Patrick Fernandez (FRA)	Gregg Hansford (AUS)
1980	Jon Ekerold (RSA)	Kawasaki/Bimota-Yamaha	Anton Mang (FRG)	Jean-Francois Balde (FRA)

| 1981 | Anton Mang (FRG) | Yamaha/Kawasaki | Jon Ekerold (RSA) | Jean-Francois Balde (FRA) |
| 1982 | Anton Mang (FRG) | Kawasaki | Didier de Radigues (BEL) | Jean-Francois Balde (FRA) |

250cc

	Winner	Manufacturer	Second	Third
1949	Bruno Ruffo (ITA)	Moto Guzzi	Dario Ambrosini (ITA)	Ron Mead (GBR)
1950	Dario Ambrosini (ITA)	Benelli	Maurice Cann (GBR)	Bruno Ruffo (ITA)
				Fergus Anderson (GBR)
1951	Bruno Ruffo (ITA)	Moto Guzzi	Tommy Wood (GBR)	Dario Ambrosini (ITA)
1952	Enrico Lorenzetti (ITA)	NSU/Moto Guzzi	Fergus Anderson (GBR)	Leslie Graham (GBR)
1953	Werner Haas (FRG)	NSU	Reginald Armstrong (IRL)	Fergus Anderson (GBR)
1954	Werner Haas (FRG)	NSU	Rupert Hollaus (AUT)	Hermann Müller (FRG)
1955	Herman Müller (FRG)	NSU/MV Agusta	Bill Lomas (GBR)	Cecil Sandford (GBR)
1956	Carlo Ubbiali (ITA)	MV Agusta	Luigi Taveri (SUI)	Enrico Lorenzetti (ITA)
1957	Cecil Sandford (GBR)	Mondial	Tarquinio Provini (ITA)	Sammy Miller (IRL)
1958	Tarquinio Provini (ITA)	MV Agusta	Horst Fügner (GDR)	Carlo Ubbiali (ITA)
1959	Carlo Ubbiali (ITA)	MV Agusta	Gary Hocking (RHO)	——
			Tarquinio Provini (ITA)	
1960	Carlo Ubbiali (ITA)	MV Agusta	Gary Hocking (RHO)	Luigi Taveri (SUI)
1961	Mike Hailwood (GBR)	Honda	Tom Phillis (AUS)	Jim Redman (RHO)
1962	Jim Redman (RHO)	Honda	Bob McIntyre (GBR)	Arthur Wheeler (GBR)
1963	Jim Redman (RHO)	Honda	Tarquinio Provini (ITA)	Fumio Ito (JPN)
1964	Phil Read (GBR)	Yamaha	Jim Redman (RHO)	Alan Shepherd (GBR)
1965	Phil Read (GBR)	Yamaha	Mike Duff (CAN)	Jim Redman (RHO)
1966	Mike Hailwood (GBR)	Honda	Phil Read (GBR)	Jim Redman (RHO)
1967	Mike Hailwood (GBR)	Honda	Phil Read (GBR)	Billy Ivy (GBR)
1968	Phil Read (GBR)	Yamaha	Billy Ivy (GBR)	Heinz Rosner (GDR)
1969	Kel Carruthers (AUS)	Benelli	Kent Andersson (SWE)	Santiago Herrero (ESP)
1970	Rodney Gould (GBR)	Yamaha	Kel Carruthers (AUS)	Kent Andersson (SWE)
1971	Phil Read (GBR)	Yamaha	Rodney Gould (GBR)	Jarno Saarinen (SWE)
1972	Jarno Saarinen (FIN)	Yamaha	Renzo Pasolini (ITA)	Rodney Gould (GBR)
1973	Dieter Braun (FRG)	Yamaha	Teuvo Länsivuori (FIN)	John Dodds (AUS)
1974	Walter Villa (ITA)	Harley-Davidson/Yamaha	Dieter Braun (FRG)	Patrick Pons (FRA)
1975	Walter Villa (ITA)	Harley-Davidson	Michel Rougerie (FRA)	Dieter Braun (FRG)
1976	Walter Villa (ITA)	Harley-Davidson	Katazumi Katayama (JPN)	Gianfranco Bonera (ITA)
1977	Mario Lega (ITA)	Morbidelli/Yamaha	Franco Uncini (ITA)	Walter Villa (ITA)
1978	Kork Ballington (RSA)	Kawasaki	Gregg Hansford (AUS)	Patrick Fernandez (FRA)
1979	Kork Ballington (RSA)	Kawasaki	Gregg Hansford (AUS)	Graziano Rossi (ITA)
1980	Anton Mang (FRG)	Kawasaki	Kork Ballington (RSA)	Jean-François Balde (FRA)
1981	Anton Mang (FRG)	Kawasaki	Jean-François Balde (FRA)	Roland Freymond (SUI)
1982	Jean-Louis Tournadre (FRA)	Yamaha	Anton Mang (FRG)	Roland Freymond (SUI)
1983	Carlos Lavado (VEN)	Yamaha	Christian Sarron (FRA)	Didier de Radiguès (BEL)
1984	Christian Sarron (FRA)	Yamaha	Manfred Herweh (FRG)	Carlos Lavado (VEN)
1985	Freddie Spencer (USA)	Honda	Anton Mang (FRG)	Carlos Lavado (VEN)
1986	Carlos Lavado (VEN)	Yamaha/Honda	Alfonso Pons (ESP)	Christian Sarron (FRA)
1987	Anton Mang (FRG)	Honda	Reinhold Roth (FRG)	Alfonso Pons (ESP)
1988	Alfonso Pons (ESP)	Honda	Juan Garriga (ESP)	Jacques Cornu (FRA)
1989	Alfonso Pons (ESP)	Honda	Reinhold Roth (FRG)	Jacques Cornu (FRA)
1990	John Kocinski (USA)	Yamaha	Carlos Cadus (ESP)	Luca Cadalora (ITA)
1991	Luca Cadalora (ITA)	Honda	Helmut Bradl (GER)	Carlos Cadus (ESP)
1992	Luca Cadalora (ITA)	Honda	Loris Reggiani (ITA)	Pierfrancesco Chili (ITA)
1993	Tetsuya Harada (JPN)	Yamaha/Honda	Loris Capirossi (ITA)	Loris Reggiani (ITA)
1994	Max Biaggi (ITA)	Aprilia/Honda	Tadayuki Okada (JPN)	Loris Capirossi (ITA)
1995	Max Biaggi (ITA)	Aprilia	Tetsuya Harada (JPN)	Ralf Waldmann (GER)
1996	Max Biaggi (ITA)	Aprilia/Honda	Ralf Waldmann (GER)	Olivier Jacque (FRA)
1997	Max Biaggi (ITA)	Honda	Ralf Waldmann (GER)	Tetsuya Harada (JPN)
1998	Loris Capirossi (ITA)	Aprilia	Valentino Rossi (ITA)	Tetsuya Harada (JPN)
1999	Valentino Rossi (ITA)	Aprilia	Tohru Ukawa (JPN)	Loris Capirossi (ITA)
2000	Olivier Jacque (FRA)	Yamaha	Shinya Nakano (JPN)	Daijiro Kato (JPN)
2001	Daijiro Kato (JPN)	Honda	Tetsuya Harada (JPN)	Marco Melandri (ITA)
2002	Marco Melandri (ITA)	Aprilia	Fonsi Nieto (ESP)	Roberto Rolfo (ITA)
2003	Manuel Poggiali (ITA)	Aprilia	Roberto Rolfo (ITA)	Toni Elras (ESP)

125cc

	Winner	Manufacturer	Second	Third
1949	Nello Pagani (ITA)	Mondial	Renato Magi (ITA)	Umberto Masetti (ITA)
1950	Bruno Ruffo (ITA)	Mondial	Carlo Ubbiali (ITA)	——
			Gianni Leoni (ITA)	

	Winner	Manufacturer	Second	Third
1951	Carlo Ubbiali (ITA)	Mondial	Gianni Leoni (ITA)	Cromie McCandless (IRL)
1952	Cecil Sandford (GBR)	MV Agusta	Carlo Ubbiali (ITA)	Emilio Mendogni (ITA)
1953	Werner Haas (GER)	NSU/MV Agusta	Cecil Sandford (GBR)	Carlo Ubbiali (ITA)
1954	Rupert Hollaus (AUT)	NSU	Carlo Ubbiali (ITA)	Hermann Müller (FRG)
1955	Carlo Ubbiali (ITA)	MV Agusta	Luigi Taveri (SUI)	Remo Venturi (ITA)
1956	Carlo Ubbiali (ITA)	MV Agusta	Romolo Ferri (ITA)	Luigi Taveri (SUI)
1957	Tarquinio Provini (ITA)	Mondial	Luigi Taveri (SUI)	Carlo Ubbiali (ITA)
1958	Carlo Ubbiali (ITA)	MV Agusta	Alberto Gandossi (ITA)	Luigi Taveri (SUI)
1959	Carlo Ubbiali (ITA)	MV Agusta	Tarquinio Provini (ITA)	Mike Hailwood (GBR)
1960	Carlo Ubbiali (ITA)	MV Agusta	Gary Hocking (RHO)	Ernst Degner (GDR)
1961	Tom Phillis (AUS)	Honda	Ernst Degner (GDR)	Jim Redman (RHO)
1962	Luigi Taveri (SUI)	Honda	Jim Redman (RHO)	Tommy Robb (IRL)
1963	Hugh Anderson (NZL)	Suzuki	Luigi Taveri (SUI)	Jim Redman (RHO)
1964	Luigi Taveri (SUI)	Honda	Jim Redman (RHO)	Hugh Anderson (NZL)
1965	Hugh Anderson (NZL)	Suzuki	Frank Perris (GBR)	Derek Woodman (GBR)
1966	Luigi Taveri (SUI)	Honda	Billy Ivy (GBR)	Ralph Bryans (IRL)
1967	Billy Ivy (GBR)	Yamaha	Phil Read (GBR)	Stuart Graham (GBR)
1968	Phil Read (GBR)	Yamaha	Billy Ivy (GBR)	Ginger Molloy (NZL)
1969	Dave Simmonds (GBR)	Kawasaki	Dieter Braun (FRG)	Cees van Dongen (NED)
1970	Dieter Braun (FRG)	Suzuki	Ángel Nieto (ESP)	Börje Jansson (SWE)
1971	Ángel Nieto (ESP)	Derbi	Barry Sheene (GBR)	Börje Jansson (SWE)
1972	Ángel Nieto (ESP)	Derbi	Chas Mortimer (GBR)	Kent Andersson (SWE)
1973	Kent Andersson (SWE)	Yamaha	Chas Mortimer (GBR)	Jos Schurgers (NED)
1974	Kent Andersson (SWE)	Yamaha	Bruno Kneubühler (SUI)	Ángel Nieto (ESP)
1975	Paolo Pileri (ITA)	Morbidelli	Pierpaolo Bianchi (ITA)	Kent Andersson (SWE)
1976	Pierpaolo Bianchi (ITA)	Morbidelli	Ángel Nieto (ESP)	Paolo Pileri (ITA)
1977	Pierpaolo Bianchi (ITA)	Morbidelli	Eugenio Lazzarini (ITA)	Ángel Nieto (ESP)
1978	Eugênio Lazzarini (ITA)	MBA/Minarelli	Ángel Nieto (ESP)	Pierpaolo Bianchi (ITA)
1979	Ángel Nieto (ESP)	Minarelli	Maurizio Massimiani (ITA)	Hans Müller (SUI)
1980	Pierpaolo Bianchi (ITA)	MBA/Minarelli	Guy Bertin (FRA)	Ángel Nieto (ESP)
1981	Ángel Nieto (ESP)	Minarelli	Loris Reggiani (ITA)	Pierpaolo Bianchi (ITA)
1982	Ángel Nieto (ESP)	Garelli	Eugenio Lazzarini (ITA)	Ivan Palazzese (ITA)
1983	Ángel Nieto (ESP)	Garelli/MBA	Bruno Kneubühler (SUI)	Eugenio Lazzarini (ITA)
1984	Ángel Nieto (ESP)	Garelli	Eugenio Lazzarini (ITA)	Fausto Gresini (ITA)
1985	Fausto Gresini (ITA)	Garelli/MBA	Pierpaolo Bianchi (ITA)	August Auinger (AUT)
1986	Luca Cadalora (ITA)	Garelli	Fausto Gresini (ITA)	Domenico Brigaglia (ITA)
1987	Fausto Gresini (ITA)	Garelli	Bruno Casanova (ITA)	Paolo Casoli (ITA)
1988	Jorge Martínez (ESP)	Derbi	Ezio Gianola (ITA)	Hans Spaan (NED)
1989	Alex Crivillé (ESP)	JJ Cobas/Honda	Hans Spaan (NED)	Ezio Gianola (ITA)
1990	Loris Capirossi (ITA)	Honda	Hans Spaan (NED)	Stefan Prein (FRG)
1991	Loris Capirossi (ITA)	Honda	Fausto Gresini (ITA)	Ralf Waldmann (GER)
1992	Alessandro Gramigni (ITA)	Aprilia/Honda	Fausto Gresini (ITA)	Ralf Waldmann (GER)
1993	Dirk Raudes (GER)	Honda	Kazuto Sakata (JPN)	Takashi Tsujimura (JPN)
1994	Kazuto Sakata (JPN)	Aprilia/Honda	Noburo Ueda (JPN)	Takashi Tsujimura (JPN)
1995	Haruchika Aoki (JPN)	Honda	Kazuto Sakata (JPN)	Emilio Alzamora (ESP)
1996	Haruchika Aoki (JPN)	Honda/Aprilia	Masaki Tokudome (JPN)	Tomomi Manako (JPN)
1997	Valentino Rossi (ITA)	Aprilia	Noburo Ueda (JPN)	Tomomi Manako (JPN)
1998	Kazuto Sakata (JPN)	Aprilia/Honda	Tomomi Manako (JPN)	Marco Melandri (ITA)
1999	Emilio Alzamora (ESP)	Honda	Marco Melandri (ITA)	Massao Azuma (JPN)
2000	Roberto Locatelli (ITA)	Aprilia/Honda	Youichi Ui (JPN)	Emilio Alzamora (ESP)
2001	Manuel Poggiali (RSM)	Gilera/Honda	Youichi Ui (JPN)	Toni Elías (ESP)
2002	Arnaud Vincent (FRA)	Aprilia	Manuel Poggiali (ITA)	Daniel Pedrosa (ESP)
2003	Daniel Pedrosa (ESP)		Alex de Ángelis (SMR)	Héctor Barberá (ESP)
				Stefano Perugini (ITA)

80cc

	Winner	Manufacturer	Second	Third
1984	Stefan Dörflinger (SUI)	Zündapp	Hubert Abold (FRG)	Pierpaolo Bianchi (ITA)
1985	Stefan Dörflinger (SUI)	Krauser	Jorge Martínez (ESP)	Gerd Kafka (AUT)
1986	Jorge Martínez (ESP)	Derbi	Manuel Herreros (ESP)	Stefan Dörflinger (SUI)
1987	Jorge Martínez (ESP)	Derbi	Manuel Herreros (ESP)	Gerhard Waibel (FRG)
1988	Jorge Martínez (ESP)	Derbi	Alex Crivillé (ESP)	Stefan Dörflinger (SUI)
1989	Manuel Herreros (ESP)	Derbi/Krauser	Stefan Dörflinger (SUI)	Peter Öttl (FRG)

50cc

	Winner	Manufacturer	Second	Third
1962	Ernst Degner (GER)	Suzuki	Hans-Georg Anscheidt (FRG)	Luigi Taveri (SUI)
1963	Hugh Anderson (NZL)	Suzuki	Hans-Georg Anscheidt (FRG)	Ernst Degner (GER)

1964	Hugh Anderson (NZL)	Suzuki	Ralph Bryans (IRL)	Hans-Georg Anscheidt (FRG)
1965	Ralph Bryans (IRL)	Honda	Luigi Taveri (SUI)	Hugh Anderson (NZL)
1966	Hans-Georg Anscheidt (FRG)	Suzuki/Honda	Ralph Bryans (IRL)	Luigi Taveri (SUI)
1967	Hans-Georg Anscheidt (FRG)	Suzuki	Yoshimi Katayama (JPN)	Stuart Graham (GBR)
1968	Hans-Georg Anscheidt (FRG)	Suzuki	Paul Lodewijk (NED)	Barry Smith (GBR)
1969	Ángel Nieto (ESP)	Derbi	Aalt Toersen (NED)	Rudolf Kunz (FRG)
1970	Ángel Nieto (ESP)	Derbi	Aalt Toersen (NED)	Jos Schurgers (NED)
1971	Jan de Vries (NED)	Kreidler	Ángel Nieto (ESP)	Theo Timmer (NED)
1972	Ángel Nieto (ESP)	Derbi/Kreidler	Jan de Vries (NED)	Theo Timmer (NED)
1973	Jan de Vries (NED)	Kreidler	Bruno Kneubühler (SUI)	Julien van Zeebroeck (BEL)
1974	Henk van Kessel (NED)	Kreidler	Herbert Rittberger (FRG)	Julien van Zeebroeck (BEL)
1975	Ángel Nieto (ESP)	Kreidler	Eugenio Lazzarini (ITA)	Ulrich Graf (SUI)
1976	Ángel Nieto (ESP)	Bultaco	Herbert Rittberger (FRG)	Ricardo Tormo (ESP)
1977	Ángel Nieto (ESP)	Bultaco	Eugenio Lazzarini (ITA)	Patrick Plisson (FRA)
1978	Ricardo Tormo (ESP)	Bultaco	Eugenio Lazzarini (ITA)	Patrick Plisson (FRA)
1979	Eugenio Lazzarini (ITA)	Kreidler	Rolf Blatter (SUI)	Hans-Jürgen Hummel (AUT)
1980	Eugenio Lazzarini (ITA)	Kreidler	Stefan Dörflinger (SUI)	Stefan Dörflinger (SUI)
1981	Ricardo Tormo (ESP)	Bultaco	Theo Timmer (NED)	Claudio Lusuardi (ITA)
1982	Stefan Dörflinger (SUI)	MBA/Kreidler	Eugenio Lazzarini (ITA)	Claudio Lusuardi (ITA)
1983	Stefan Dörflinger (SUI)	Garelli	Eugenio Lazzarini (ITA)	

World Superbikes

	Winner	Manufacturer		Winner	Manufacturer
1988	Fred Merkel (USA)	Honda	1996	Troy Corser (AUS)	Ducati
1989	Fred Merkel (USA)	Honda	1997	John Kocinski (USA)	Honda
1990	Raymond Roche (FRA)	Honda	1998	Carl Fogarty (ENG)	Ducati
1991	Doug Polen (USA)	Ducati	1999	Carl Fogarty (ENG)	Ducati
1992	Doug Polen (USA)	Ducati	2000	Colin Edwards (USA)	Ducati
1993	Scott Russell (USA)	Ducati	2001	Troy Bayliss (AUS)	Ducati
1994	Carl Fogarty (ENG)	Ducati	2002	Colin Edwards (USA)	Ducati
1995	Carl Fogarty (ENG)	Ducati	2003	Neil Hodgson (ENG)	Ducati

Formula 750

	Winner	Manufacturer	Second	Third
1973	Barry Sheene (GBR)	Suzuki	Johnny Dodds (AUS)	Jack Findlay (AUS)
1974	Johnny Dodds (AUS)	Yamaha	Patrick Pons (FRA)	Jack Findlay (AUS)

Formula 750 (European)

	Winner	Manufacturer	Second	Third
1975	Jack Findlay (AUS)	Yamaha	Barry Sheene (GBR)	Patrick Pons (FRA)
1976	Victor Palomo (ESP)	Yamaha	Gary Nixon (USA)	John Newbold (GBR)

Formula 750 (World)

	Winner	Manufacturer	Second	Third
1977	Steve Baker (USA)	Yamaha	Christian Sarron (FRA)	Giacomo Agostini (ITA)
1978	Johnny Cecotto (VEN)	Yamaha	Kenny Roberts (USA)	Christian Sarron (FRA)
1979	Patrick Pons (FRA)	Yamaha	Michel Frutschi (SUI)	Johnny Cecotto (VEN)

TT Formula One

	Winner	Manufacturer		Winner	Manufacturer
1977	Phil Read (GBR)	Honda	1984	Joey Dunlop (GBR)	Honda
1978	Mike Hailwood (GBR)	Ducati	1985	Joey Dunlop (GBR)	Honda
1979	Ron Haslam (GBR)	Honda	1986	Joey Dunlop (GBR)	Honda
1980	Graeme Crosby (NZL)	Suzuki	1987	Virginio Ferrari (ITA)	Yamaha
1981	Graeme Crosby (NZL)	Suzuki	1988	Carl Fogarty (GBR)	Honda
1982	Joey Dunlop (GBR)	Honda	1989	Carl Fogarty (GBR)	Honda
1983	Joey Dunlop (GBR)	Honda	1990	Carl Fogarty (GBR)	Honda

MOTORCYCLING

TT Formula Two

	Winner	Manufacturer		Winner	Manufacturer
1977	Alan Jackson (GBR)	Honda	1982	Tony Rutter (GBR)	Ducati
1978	Alan Jackson (GBR)	Honda	1983	Tony Rutter (GBR)	Ducati
1979	Alan Jackson (GBR)	Honda	1984	Tony Rutter (GBR)	Ducati
1980	Charles Williams (GBR)	Yamaha	1985	Brian Reid (GBR)	Yamaha
1981	Tony Rutter (GBR)	Ducati	1986	Brian Reid (GBR)	Yamaha

TT Formula Three

	Winner	Manufacturer		Winner	Manufacturer
1977	Joh Kidson (GBR)	Honda	1980	Ron Haslam (GBR)	Honda
1978	William A. Smith (GBR)	Honda	1981	Barry Smith (AUS)	Yamaha
1979	Barry Smith (AUS)	Yamaha			

Sidecar World Road Racing Champions

	Winners	Manufacturer
1949	Eric Oliver/Denis Jenkinson (GBR)	Norton
1950	Eric Oliver (GBR)/Lorenzo Dobelli (ITA)	Norton
1951	Eric Oliver (GBR)/Lorenzo Dobelli (ITA)	Norton
1952	Cyril Smith/Bob Clements (GBR)	Norton
1953	Eric Oliver/Stanley Dibben (GBR)	Norton
1954	Wilhelm Noll/Fritz Cron (FRG)	BMW
1955	Willy Faust/Karl Remmert (FRG)	BMW
1956	Wilhelm Noll/Fritz Cron (FRG)	BMW
1957	Fritz Hillebrand/Manfred Grunwald (FRG)	BMW
1958	Walter Schneider/Hans Strauss (FRG)	BMW
1959	Walter Schneider/Hans Strauss (FRG)	BMW
1960	Helmut Fath/Alfred Wohlgemut (FRG)	BMW
1961	Max Deubel/Emil Hörner (FRG)	BMW
1962	Max Deubel/Emil Hörner (FRG)	BMW
1963	Max Deubel/Emil Hörner (FRG)	BMW
1964	Max Deubel/Emil Hörner (FRG)	BMW
1965	Fritz Scheidegger (SUI)/John Robinson (GBR)	BMW
1966	Fritz Scheidegger (SUI)/John Robinson (GBR)	BMW
1967	Klaus Enders/Rolf Engelhardt (FRG)	BMW
1968	Helmut Fath/Wolfgang Kalauch (FRG)	BMW
1969	Klaus Enders/Rolf Engelhardt (FRG)	BMW
1970	Klaus Enders/Wolfgang Kalauch (FRG)	BMW
1971	Horst Owesle (FRG)//Peter Rutterfort (GBR)	Münch-Urs
1972	Klaus Enders/Rolf Engelhardt (FRG)	BMW
1973	Klaus Enders/Rolf Engelhardt (FRG)	BMW
1974	Klaus Enders/Rolf Engelhardt (FRG)	Busch-BMW
1975	Rolf Steinhausen/Joseph Huber (FRG)	Busch-König
1976	Rolf Steinhausen/Joseph Huber (FRG)	Busch-König
1977	George O'Dell/Cliff Holland/Kenny Arthur (GBR)	Yamaha
1978	Rolf Biland (SUI)/Kenny Williams (GBR)	BEO-Yamaha
1979*	Rolf Biland/Kurt Waltisperg (B2A) (SUI)	LCR-Yamaha
	Bruno Holzer/Carl Meierhaus (B2B) (SUI)	LCR-Yamaha
1980	Jock Taylor GBR)/Benga Johansson (SWE)	Yamaha
1981	Rolf Biland/Kurt Waltisperg (SUI)	LCR-Yamaha
1982	Werner Schwärzel/Joseph Huber (GER)	Seymaz-Yamaha
1983	Rolf Biland/Kurt Waltisperg (SUI)	LCR-Yamaha
1984	Egbert Streuer/Bernie Schneiders (NED)	LCR-Yamaha
1985	Egbert Streuer/Bernie Schneiders (NED)	LCR-Yamaha
1986	Egbert Streuer/Bernie Schneiders (NED)	LCR-Yamaha
1987	Steve Webster/Tony Hewitt (GBR)	LCR-Krauser
1988	Steve Webster/Tony Hewitt/Gavin Simmons (GBR)	LCR-Krauser
1989	Steve Webster/Tony Hewitt (GBR)	LCR-Krauser
1990	Alain Michel (FRA)/Simon Birchall (GBR)	LCR-Krauser
1991	Steve Webster/Gavin Simmons (GBR)	LCR-Krauser
1992	Rolf Biland/Kurt Waltisperg (SWE)	LCR-Krauser
1993	Rolf Biland/Kurt Waltisperg (SWE)	LCR-Krauser
1994	Rolf Biland/Kurt Waltisperg (SWE)	LCR-Krauser
1995	Darren Dixon/Andy Hetherington (GBR)	Windle-ADM
1996	Darren Dixon/Andy Hetherington (GBR)	Windle-ADM
1997	Steve Webster/David James (GBR)	LCR-ADM

*In 1979 B2A was the 'Classix' and B2B the 'Modern' sidecar category

Superside

Winners		Manufacturer
1998	Steve Webster/David James (GBR)	LCR-Honda
1999	Steve Webster/David James (GBR)	LCR-Suzuki
2000	Steve Webster/Paul Woodhead (GBR)	LCR-Suzuki
2001	Klaus Klaffenbock/Christian Parzer (AUT)	LCR-Suzuki
2002	Steve Abbott/Jamie Biggs (GBR)	Yamaha
2003	Steve Webster/Paul Woodhead (GBR)	LCR-Suzuki

Speedway World Championships

Individual

	Winner	Venue
1936	Lionel van Praag (AUS)	Wembley
1937	Jack Milne (USA)	Wembley
1938	Bluey Wilkinson (AUS)	Wembley
1939-48 not held		
1949	Tommy Price (GBR)	Wembley
1950	Freddie Williams (GBR)	Wembley
1951	Jack Young (AUS)	Wembley
1952	Jack Young (AUS)	Wembley
1953	Freddie Williams (GBR)	Wembley
1954	Ronnie Moore (NZL)	Wembley
1955	Peter Craven (GBR)	Wembley
1956	Ove Fundin (SWE)	Wembley
1957	Barry Briggs (NZL)	Wembley
1958	Barry Briggs (NZL)	Wembley
1959	Ronnie Moore (NZL)	Wembley
1960	Ove Fundin (SWE)	Wembley
1961	Ove Fundin (SWE)	Malmö
1962	Peter Craven (GBR)	Wembley
1963	Ove Fundin (SWE)	Wembley
1964	Barry Briggs (NZL)	Göteborg
1965	Bjørn Knutsson (SWE)	Wembley
1966	Barry Briggs (NZL)	Göteborg
1967	Ove Fundin (SWE)	Wembley
1968	Ivan Mauger (NZL)	Göteborg
1969	Ivan Mauger (NZL)	Wembley
1970	Ivan Mauger (NZL)	Wroclaw
1971	Ole Olsen (DEN)	Göteborg
1972	Ivan Mauger (NZL)	Wembley
1973	Jerzy Szczakiel (POL)	Chorzow
1974	Anders Michanek (SWE)	Göteborg
1975	Ole Olsen (DEN)	Wembley
1976	Peter Collins (GBR)	Chorzow
1977	Ivan Mauger (NZL)	Göteborg
1978	Ole Olsen (DEN)	Wembley
1979	Ivan Mauger (NZL)	Chorzow
1980	Michael Lee (GBR)	Göteborg
1981	Bruce Penhall (USA)	Wembley
1982	Bruce Penhall (USA)	Los Angeles
1983	Egon Müller (FRG)	Norden
1984	Erik Gundersen (DEN)	Göteborg
1985	Erik Gundersen (DEN)	Bradford
1986	Hans Nielsen (DEN)	Chorzow
1987	Hans Nielsen (DEN)	Amsterdam
1988	Erik Gundersen (DEN)	Vojens
1989	Hans Nielsen (DEN)	Munich
1990	Per Jonsson (SWE)	Bradford
1991	Jan O. Pedersen (DEN)	Göteborg
1992	Gary Havelock (GBR)	Wroclaw
1993	Sam Ermolenko (USA)	Pocking
1994	Tony Rickardsson (SWE)	Vojens
1995*	Hans Nielsen (DEN)	
1996	Billy Hamill (USA)	
1997	Greg Hancock (USA)	
1998	Tony Rickardsson (SWE)	
1999	Tony Rickardsson (SWE)	

MOTORCYCLING

2000 Mark Loram (GBR)
2001 Tony Rickardsson (SWE)
2002 Tony Rickardsson (SWE)
2003 Nicki Pedersen (DEN)

*Since 1995 the title has been decided by a series of GP races.

Long Track

(replaced the European Sand Track Championship)

	Winner	Venue
1971	Ivan Mauger (NZL)	Oslo
1972	Ivan Mauger (NZL)	Mühldorf
1973	Ole Olsen (DEN)	Oslo
1974	Egon Müller (FRG)	Scheessel
1975	Egon Müller (FRG)	Radgona
1976	Ivan Mauger (NZL)	Mariánské Lázně
1977	Anders Michanek (SWE)	Aalborg
1978	Egon Müller (FRG)	Möhldorf
1979	Alois Wiesboeck (FRG)	Mariánské Lázně
1980	Karl Maier (FRG)	Scheessel
1981	Michael Lee (GBR)	Radgona
1982	Karl Maier (FRG)	Korsko
1983	Shawn Moran (USA)	Mariánské Lázně
1984	Erik Gundersen (DEN)	Herxheim
1985	Simon Wigg (GBR)	Korsko
1986	Erik Gundersen (DEN)	Pfarrkirchen
1987	Karl Maier (FRG)	Möhldorf
1988	Karl Maier (FRG)	Scheessel
1989	Simon Wigg (GBR)	Mariánské Lázně
1990	Simon Wigg (GBR)	Herxheim
1991	Gerd Riss (GER)	Mariánské Lázně
1992	Marcel Gerhard (SUI)	Pfarrkirchen
1993	Simon Wigg (GBR)	Möhldorf
1994	Simon Wigg (GBR)	Mariánské Lázně
1995	Kelvin Tatum (GBR)	Scheessel
1996	Gerd Riss (GER)	Herxheim
1997*	Tommy Dunker (GER)	
1998	Kelvin Tatum (GBR)	
1999	Gerd Riss (GER)	
2000	Kelvin Tatum (GBR)	
2001	Gerd Riss (GER)	
2002	Robert Barth (GER)	
2003	Robert Barth (GER)	

*In 1997, this competition was amalgamated with the European Grass Track Championship. The title is now decided by a final series.

2003 Motorcycling Champions

2003 MotoGP Championship

Valentino Rossi (ITA), Honda

2003 250cc GP Championship

Manuel Poggiali (ITA), Aprilia

2003 125cc GP Championship

Daniel Pedrosa (ESP), Honda

2003 US AMA Superbike Championship

Mat Mladin (AUS), Suzuki

2003 British Superbike Championship

Shane Byrne (GBR), Ducati

2003 World Superbike Championship

1 Neil Hodgson (GBR), Ducati 999R, 489pts
2 Ruben Xaus (ESP), Ducati 999R, 386pts
3 James Toseland (GBR), Ducati 998R, 271pts

2003 World Supersport Championship

Chris Vermeulen (AUS), Honda

2003 World Trials Championship

Dougie Lampkin (GBR) (outdoor)
Adam Raga (ESP) (indoor)

2003 World Speedway Championship

Nicki Pedersen, (DEN)

2003 World Motocross Championship

Stefan Everts (BEL), Yamaha (MXGP)
Joël Smets (BEL), KTM (650)

2003 AMA Motocross Championship

Ricky Carmichael (USA), Honda (250cc)
Grant Langston (RSA) KTM (125cc)

2003 World Supercross Championship

Chad Reed (AUS), Yamaha

2003 AMA Supercross Championship

Ricky Carmichael (USA), Honda (250cc)
James Stewart (USA), Kawasaki (125cc West Region)
Branden Jesseman (USA), Suzuki (125cc East Region)

2003 Australian Formula Xtreme Championship

Kevin Curtain (AUS), Yamaha

2003 Australian Superbike Championship

Craig Coxhell (AUS), Suzuki

Motorcycling: Biographies, Tracks and Machines

(Details correct as at 31 December 2003)

Abbreviations: enduro (EN), cross-country rallying (CC), trial riding (TR), ice speedway (ISP), motocross (MX), road racing (RR), speedway (SP), supercross (SX), trial riding (TR)

Abbot, Steve   (RR) Born Derbyshire, England. First GP: sidecar Belgian, 1982. First GP win: 2000. Sidecar world champion: with Jamie Biggs (Yamaha). Abbot won the World Championship 20 years after his first race in the competition. He won six GPs, with another 33 podium finishes (to end 2003).

Abe, Norick   (RR) Born Tokyo, Japan, 7 September 1975. First GP: 500cc Japanese, 1994. First GP win: 500cc Japanese, 1996. The first Japanese winner of the Japanese GP. He has won three GPs and been on the podium a further 14 times.

Aberg, Bengt   (MX) Born Sweden. World champion: 500cc, 1969 and 1970. Winner of Motocross des Nations (Sweden) in 1970, 1971 and 1974.

Adams, Leigh   (SP) Born Mildura, Australia, 28 April 1971. World under-21 champion 1992. World team champion: 1999, 2001 and 2002 (Australia). Australian champion: 1992-94, 1997, 2000, 2002 and 2003. Australian long track champion: 1992 and 2000. Teams represented: Swindon (1990-92, 1997-99), Essex (1993-95), Hackney (1996), King's Lynn (2000), Oxford (2001-02), Poole (1989), Leszno (Poland) (1996-2004), Indianerna Sweden (1998-99), Masarna (Sweden) (2000-04), Lublin (Poland) (1991-94), Vetlanda (Sweden) (1995-96).

Aerts, Albert   (RR) Born Baasrode, Belgium, 2 July 1972. Endurance world champion: 2001. Known as 'Beire'. He died 30 May 2004 in a racing accident at Chimay, Belgium.

Agostini, Giacomo   (RR) Born Brescia, Italy, 16 June 1942. Agostini took part in hill-climbs in 1961 at the age of 19. He won the 1964 250cc Italian title on a Morini, and joined MV Agusta in 1965. First GP: 250cc West German, 1964. First GP win: 500cc Finnish, 1965. World champion: 350cc 1968-73 (MV Agusta) and 1974 (Yamaha); 500cc 1966-72 (MV Agusta) and 1975 (Yamaha). In 1972 Agostini's friend Gilberto Parlotti was killed racing the Isle of Man TT and from then on Agostini refused to race there. He won the Daytona 200 in 1974 and joined Yamaha for whom he took the 1975 500cc World Championship. He won seven successive 500cc and 350cc World Championships. Agostini rode briefly for Suzuki before retiring in 1977. In all he won a record 15 world titles, 122 GPs and 10 Isle of Man TTs. Recipient of the FIM Gold Medal in 1993.

Ahvala, Tommi   (TR) Born Helsinki, Finland, 13 November 1971. Finnish champion: 1989-96. US champion: 1999. World outdoor champion: 1992. World indoor champion: 1993.

AJS   Founded in the early 1900s by the Stevens brothers – Harry, George, Jack and Joe. The brothers produced motorcycles using engines manufactured by their father's company. The name AJS was chosen as these were the initials of the eldest brother, Albert John (Jack) Stevens, the only brother to have a middle name. After building engines for other manufacturers, Jack Stevens and his brothers finally produced a complete machine with the AJS logo in 1911. They won the Junior IOM TT in 1914. By 1931 the company also manufactured radio sets, cars and commercial vehicles but during the Depression the company was sold to Matchless and production moved from Wolverhampton to Plumstead in south-east London. After World War II AJS machines became little more than a Matchless with a different badge. However, Leslie Graham took the inaugural 500cc World Championship in 1949, with AJS taking the manufacturers' title. AJS production finally ceased in 1967.

Albertyn, Greg   (MX) Born Johannesburg, South Africa, 13 October 1972. South African champion: 125cc, 1988 and 1989. US champion: 250cc, 1999. World champion: 125cc, 1992; 250cc, 1993 and 1994. Known as 'Albee'. Albertyn retired in 2000.

Allen, Oliver   (SP) Born Norwich, England, 27 May 1982. Teams represented: Peterborough (1998), Swindon (1999-2002), Wolverhampton (2003). World under-21 finalist in 2002 and member of the Young England Team. His father, Dave Allen, raced between 1976 and 1986.

Alzamora, Emilio   (RR) Born Lleida, Spain, 22 May 1973. First GP: 125cc Malaysian, 1994. First GP win: 125cc Argentinian, 1995. World champion: 125cc, 1999 (Honda). Alzamora moved to 250cc in 2001 with Team Fortuna Honda Gresini. He won four GPs.

Ambrosini, Dario   (RR) Born Cesena, Italy, 7 March 1918. First GP: 250cc, Swiss, 1949. First GP win: 250cc GP des Nations, 1949. World champion: 250cc, 1950 (Benelli). Ambrosini won five GPs. He also won the Lightweight TT in 1950. He was killed during practice for the French GP at Albi in July 1951.

Anderson, Fergus   (RR) Born Great Britain 9 February 1909. Lived most of his life abroad, mainly in Italy. He worked as a journalist in Hamburg before World War II. First GP: 250cc Swiss, 1949. Joined Moto Guzzi in 1950. First GP win: 250cc Swiss, 1951. World champion: 350cc, 1953 and 1954 (Moto Guzzi). Won 250cc Lightweight ICM TT in 1952 and 1953. Anderson won 12 GPs and was placed 12 times, retiring in 1955 to head the Moto Guzzi competition department. He returned to racing with BMW but was killed on 6 May 1956 racing at Floreffe in Belgium.

Anderson, Hugh   (RR) Born Auckland, New Zealand, 18 January 1936. He won four World Championships and was a renowned rider of small-capacity machines. Anderson began his European racing career in the early 1960s riding AJS and Norton machines. First GP: 350cc Ulster, 1961. Joined Suzuki in 1961. First GP wins: 1962 Argentinian 50cc and 125cc. World champion: 50cc, 1963 and 1964; 125cc, 1963 and 1965 (with seven wins from the seven counting results), all for Suzuki. Anderson had an impressive record in TTs, winning the 1963 Lightweight (125cc) TT and the 1964 Lightweight (50cc) TT. Overall he won 25 GPs and was on the podium a further 23 times.

Andersson, Hakan   (MX) Born Sweden. World champion: 250cc, 1973. Winner of Motocross des Nations (Sweden), 1974.

Andersson, Kent   (RR) Born Sweden, 1 August 1942. First GP: 250cc Finnish, 1966. First GP win: 250cc West German, 1969. World champion: 125cc, 1973 and 1974 (Yamaha). Andersson won 18 GPs and had a further 35 podium finishes.

Andrews, Bob   (SP) Born Edmonton, London, England, 27 October 1935. Emigrated to New Zealand. World pairs champion: 1969 (with Ivan Mauger). Teams represented: Wimbledon (1956-64), Wolverhampton (1965), Cradley Heath (1968-69, 1971-72), Hackney (1970).

Anscheidt, Hans-Georg   (RR) Born Konigsberg, Germany, 23 December 1935. First GP: 50cc ICM TT, 1962. First GP win: 50cc Belgian, 1962. World champion: 50cc 1966-68 (Suzuki). Anscheidt won 14 GPs and was on the podium another 20 times.

Aoki, Haruchika   (RR) Born Gunma, Japan, 28 March 1976. First GP: 125cc Australian, 1993. First GP win: 125cc Australian, 1995. World champion: 125cc, 1995 and 1996 (Honda). Aoki won nine GPs, and retired at the end of the 2003 season.

Aprilia   (RR) The company was founded in Noale, near Venice, Italy. Originally a bicycle firm, it began producing motorcycles in 1973. Aprilia began GP racing in 1985. First GP win: 250cc Italian (Loris Reggiani). World champion (riders): (125cc) Gramigni 1992, Sakata 1994 and 1998, Rossi 1997 and 1999, Locatelli 2000, Vincent 2002; (250cc) Biaggi 1994-96, Capirossi 1998, Rossi 1999, Melandri 2002. World champion (manufacturer): (125cc) 1996, 1997 and 2002; (250cc) 1995, 1998, 1999 and 2002.

Arbekov, Viktor   (MX) Born Soviet Union. World champion: 250cc, 1965.

Aro, Samuli   (EN) Born Järvenpää, Finland, 10 April 1975. Two days enduro world champion: two-stroke 250cc, 2002. Enduro world team champion: 2003 (Finland).

Ashby, Martin   (SP) Born Marlborough, England, 5 February 1944. World team champion: 1968 (Great Britain) and 1975 (England). Known as 'Crash'. Teams represented: Swindon (1961-67, 1971-79), Exeter (1968-70), Reading (1980). His younger brother, David John Ashby, also raced between 1972 and 1979.

Assen   (RR) Circuit in Assen, Holland. First used for World Championship in 1949 and the only venue to have hosted a GP in every year since. Circuit (Circuit van Drenthe) was opened in 1955. Modified in 2002. It held its first World Superbike round in 1992. Length: 6027m. Width: 10m. Left turns: 7. Right turns: 9. Named corners include: Madijk, De Strubben, Stekkenvaal. Assen is the longest GP circuit currently in use (2004).

Autódromo Nelson Piquet   (RR) Circuit at Jacarepaguá near Rio de Janeiro, Brazil. Opened in 1978. Modified in 1995. Length: 4933m. Width: 18m. Left turns: 8. Right turns: 4.

Baeten, René   (MX) Born Belgium, 1927. World champion: 500cc, 1958. Baeten was killed during competition in 1960.

Baker, Steve   (RR) Born Bellingham, Washington, United States, 5 September 1952. First GP: 500cc Venezuelan, 1977. Scored seven GP podium finishes. World champion: 750cc, 1977 (Yamaha). Runner-up in the 500cc World Championship in 1977. He won the Daytona 200 in 1976. Injuries sustained in an accident in Canada at the end of 1978 forced his retirement.

Balashov, Alexandre   (ISP) Born Soviet Union, 28 May 1967. World champion: 1994, 1996 and 1998. World team champion: 1992-94 and 1996-99 (Russia).

Ballington, Kork   (RR) Born Hugh Neville Ballington, Salisbury, Rhodesia, 10 April 1951. Ballington rode as a South African. First GP: 250cc West German, 1976. First GP win: 350cc Spanish, 1976. World champion: 250cc, 1978 and 1979; 350cc, 1978 and 1979 (Kawasaki). He won 31 GPs, with a further 15 podium finishes. Ballington retired in 1983.

Barros, Alex   (RR) Born São Paulo, Brazil, 18 October 1970. First GP: 80cc, Spanish, 1986. First GP win: 500cc, FIM, 1993. Barros has won six GPs and gained another 19 podium finishes.

Barth, Robert   (SP) Born Dickenreishausen, West Germany, 10 August 1968. World long track champion: 2002 and 2003.

Bartolini, Andrea   (MX) Born Imola, Italy, 4 November 1968. Italian champion: 125cc, 1990. World champion: 500cc, 1999.

Bayle, Jean-Michel   (MX) Born Manosque, France, 1 April 1969. US champion: 250cc (supercross), 1991. US champion: 250cc and 500cc, 1991. World champion: 125cc, 1988; 250cc, 1989. After motocross Bayle took up road racing. He won the Le Mans 24hrs in 2002.

Bayliss, Troy   (RR) Born Taree, Australia, 30 March 1969. World champion: Superbike 2001 (Ducati). Bayliss won 22 World Superbike races and finished on the podium another 24 times from 76 starts. He was British Superbike champion in 1999 (Ducati), and replaced the injured Carl Fogarty in the Ducati World Superbike team in April 2000. Bayliss moved to MotoGP in 2003 and gained three podium finishes. Known as 'The Wonder from Down Under'.

Benelli   (RR) Founded by the six Benelli brothers in Pesaro, Italy. The company produced its first bike in 1921. World champion (rider): (250cc) Ambrosini 1950, Carruthers 1969. Ambrosini's death in 1951 put a halt to the firm's participation in racing, but it did return in the 1960s. World champion (manufacturer): (250cc), 1950 and 1969. The Benelli family sold the firm shortly afterwards and the marque made no more significant contributions to racing.

Bergvall, Peter   (EN) Born Örebro, Sweden, 16 September 1975. Two days enduro world champion: four-stroke 250cc, 2002 and 2003.

Betts, Terry   (SP) Born Harlow, England, 1943. World pairs champion: 1972 (with Ray Wilson). Teams represented: Norwich (1960-63), Wolverhampton, King's Lynn.

Biaggi, Max   (RR) Born Massimiliano Biaggi, Rome, Italy, 26 June 1971. First GP: 250cc European, 1991.

First GP win: 250cc South African, 1992. World champion: 250cc, 1994-96 (Aprilia) and 1997 (Honda). Runner-up in the 500cc World Championship in 2001 (Honda), and the MotoGP World Championship in 2002 (Honda). Biaggi won 41 GPs, plus a further 57 podium places.

Bianchi, Pierpaolo (RR) Born Rimini, Italy, 11 March 1952. First GP: 125cc National, 1973. First GP win: 125cc Austrian, 1976. World champion: 125cc, 1976, 1977 (Morbidelli) and 1980 (MBA). Won 27 GPs plus a further 34 podium finishes.

Bickers, Dave (MX) Born Gipping, Suffolk, England, 17 January 1938. First GP win: 250cc Swiss, 1960. British champion: 250cc, 1960 and 1962-65; 500cc, 1966. European champion: 250cc, 1960 and 1961. Winner Motocross des Nations (Britain) in 1966 and 1967. Bickers retired in 1976 and set up 'Bickers Action', a successful film stunt co-ordinating company.

Biland, Rolf (RR) Born Birmenstorf, Switzerland, 1 April 1951. Sidecar world champion: 1978 (with Kenny Williams), 1979, 1981, 1983 and 1992-94 (all with Kurt Waltisperg). The wins in 1978, 1979, 1981 and 1983 were for Yamaha, with the rest for LCR. Biland won 81 GPs, making him the third most successful GP rider after Giacomo Agostini and Ángel Nieto.

Bimota (RR) Formed in Rimini, Italy, 1973 by Valerio Bianchi, Guiseppe Morri and Massimo Tamburini. Bimota is best known for building the frames used on the Yamaha ridden by Johnny Cecotto to win the 1975 350cc world title, and the Harley-Davidson of Walter Villa who won the 1976 350cc world title and the 250cc world titles between 1974 and 1976. Jon Ekerold won the 1980 350cc World Championship on a Bimota-Yamaha.

BMW (RR) Post-World War I restrictions on the manufacturing of aircraft forced aircraft engine manufacturer BMW (Bayerische Motoren Werke) to diversify. The first BMW motorcycle, the R32, was produced in 1923. In the 1930s supercharged competition machines established new speed records. In 1939 Schorsch Meier, riding a BMW, became the first foreign rider to win the Manx TT. Although they failed to achieve major success in the solo classes, they dominated World Championship sidecar racing for 20 years between 1954 and 1974, winning 19 of the 21 championships with drivers such as Max Deubel and Klaus Enders.

Bolley, Frederic (MX) Born Marseille, France, 17 February 1974. World champion: 250cc, 1999 and 2000. Retired from motocross in 2002 to turn to road racing. Known as 'Bobol'.

Bondarenko, Anatoly (ISP) Born Soviet Union. World champion: 1979 and 1980. World team champion: 1979 and 1980 (Russia).

Boocock, Eric (SP) Born 1943. Chairman of the Speedway Riders Association. Teams represented: Middlesbrough, Halifax. Boocock retired from riding in 1975. Managed Hull Vikings. Brother of Nigel.

Boocock, Nigel (SP) Born Wakefield, England, 17 September 1937. Qualified for eight WC finals. World team champion: 1968 (Great Britain). Teams represented: Bradford, Birmingham, Ipswich, Coventry, Exeter, Canterbury. Boocock rode in 151 Test matches. He retired in 1979. Nickname: 'Little Boy Blue' because of the colour of his leathers. Brother of Eric.

Brands Hatch (RR) Circuit in Kent, England. Length: 4221m. Left turns: 3. Right turns: 6. Named corners: Druids Hill, Surtees, Hawthorn, Dingle Dell, Stirlings.

Named straights: Brabham, Clearways, Minter. Brands Hatch held its first World Superbike round in 1993.

Braun, Dieter (RR) Born Ulm, Germany, 2 February 1943. First GP: 125cc West German, 1968. First GP win: 125cc Yugoslav, 1969. World champion: 125cc, 1970 (Suzuki); 250cc, 1973 (Yamaha). Braun won 14 GPs and was on the podium another 35 times.

Briggs, Barry (SP) Born Christchurch, New Zealand, 30 December 1934. Briggs came to England in 1952. He was known as an unpredictable rider in his early days as his impetuosity caused several crashes and almost led to him being banned. World champion: 1957, 1958, 1964 and 1966. He made 17 consecutive appearances in the World Championship finals (1954-70), never finishing lower than seventh. He only lost one heat during his four winning years. World team champion: 1968, 1971 (Great Britain) and 1979 (New Zealand). A total of seven world titles. British League riders champion: 1965-70. Teams represented: Wimbledon (1952-59, 1974-75), New Cross (1960), Southampton (1961-63), Swindon (1964-72), Hull. After retiring in 1976 Briggs formed World Superstars Inc. with Ivan Mauger which helped to popularise the sport in the United States. Retired in 1976. He was the first speedway rider to be awarded the MBE (1973).

Brno (RR) Circuit in the Czech Republic. Automotodrom Brno was built in the 1980s and opened in 1987. It was modified in 1996. The previous circuit, named after President T.G. Masaryk, was used from the 1930s onwards. It was first used for the World Championships in 1965. Length: 5403m. Width: 15m. Left turns: 6. Right turns: 8.

Broadbanks, Mike (SP) Born Hoddesdon, England, 25 September 1934. Teams represented: Rye House (1954-56), Wembley (1956), Swindon (1957-71), Stoke (1972-73), Hackney (1974), Crayford, Newport. Broadbanks retired in 1977. He was known as 'Red Devil' because of his red leathers.

Bryans, Ralph (RR) Born Belfast, Northern Ireland, 7 March 1942. First GP: 50cc Ulster, 1963. Joined the Honda team in 1964. First GP win: 50cc Dutch, 1964. World champion: 50cc, 1965 (Honda). Won the 50cc TT in 1966. Bryans won ten GPs and was on the podium a further 30 times. Ulster's only world champion.

BSA In June 1861 the Birmingham Small Arms Company was formed and in 1863 a factory was built at Small Heath. By 1880, the market for guns had declined and the company started to make bicycles and tricycles. Its first motorcycle was produced in 1903. By World War II the company consisted of 67 factories and during the war produced 126,000 M20 motorcycles. The purchase of Triumph in 1951 made the BSA Group the largest producer of motorcycles in the world. Due to intense competition from Germany and Japan, by the 1970s the company was struggling and Norton's Wolverhampton factory, together with BSA's Small Heath plant, was closed. However, a BSA company did survive to produce lightweight bikes, mainly for the Third World, including the popular BSA Bushman. In 1991 BSA Group was formed and purchased Norton Spares, becoming BSA Regal Group in 1994. Based in Southampton, the company specialises in hand-built and limited edition models.

Bultaco (RR) Founded in Barcelona in 1958 by Francisco Bulto after he left Montesa (a motorcycle company he had earlier founded, in 1944, with Pedro Permanyer), Bultaco originally produced 124cc, single-cylinder two-stroke road and racing motorcycles. In 1976 Bultaco returned to Grand Prix racing with 50cc and 125cc bikes based on Piovaticci designs. World champion (riders): (50cc) Nieto 1976 and 1977, Tormo 1978 and 1981. World champion (manufacturer): 1976-78 and 1981. Bultaco shut down permanently in 1983.

Burgat, Gilles (TR) Born France. World outdoor champion: 1961 and 1981.

Byrne, Shane (RR) Born Lambeth, London, England, 10 December 1976. British Superbike (BSB) champion, 2003. First BSB GP: Snetterton, 1999. First BSB GP win: Donington, 2002. Known as 'Shakey'. Made his debut in MotoGP in 2004, riding for Aprilia.

Cabestany, Albert (TR) Born Tarragona, Spain, 26 June 1980. World indoor champion: 2002. Winner of Trial des Nations (Spain) 2000 and 2001.

Cadalora, Luca (RR) Born Modena, Italy, 17 May 1963. First GP: 125cc San Marino, 1984. First GP win: 125cc West German, 1986. World champion: 125cc, 1986 (Garelli); 250cc 1991 and 1992 (Honda). Cadalora won 32 GPs. He was on the podium another 35 times.

Cagiva (RR) Founded by the Castiglioni brothers in 1950 at Varese, Italy. The company began as a small machine shop, but entered the motorcycle business in 1978 when it bought the Aermacchi factory from AMF-Harley-Davidson, Italy. It now owns Ducati, Moto Morini, Husqvarna, MV Agusta and others. Raced in the 500cc class in the early 1990s but withdrew from GP racing in 1995.

Campbell, Keith (RR) Born Australia, 2 October 1938. First GP: 250cc Ulster, 1950. First GP win: 350cc Dutch, 1957. World champion: 350cc, 1957 (Moto Guzzi). Campbell won three GPs and had five other podium positions. He was killed racing at Cadours, France, on 13 July 1958.

Capirossi, Loris (RR) Born Bologna, Italy, 4 April 1973. First GP: 125cc Japanese, 1990. First GP win: 125cc British, 1991. World champion: 125cc, 1990 and 1991 (Honda) – youngest winner of the 125cc world title; 250cc, 1998 (Aprilia). Has won 23 GPs with a further 58 podium positions. Capirossi joined Honda in 1999 and moved on to Ducati in 2003.

Carlqvist, Hakan (MX) Born Sweden, 15 January 1954, World champion: 250cc, 1979; 500cc, 1983. Known as 'Carla'.

Carlsson, Bjorne (EN) Born Sweden, 22 January 1975. Enduro world champion: 400cc, 1998.

Carruthers, Kel (RR) Born Australia, 3 January 1931. First GP: 350cc Ulster, 1966. First GP win: 250cc IOM TT, 1969. World champion: 250cc, 1969 (Benelli). Carruthers won seven GPs and was on the podium another 15 times.

Carter, Kenny (SP) Born Halifax, England, 1961. World pairs champion: 1983 (with Peter Collins). British League riders champion: 1981 and 1982. Teams represented: Newcastle, Halifax. He committed suicide in May 1986.

Cecotto, Johnny (RR) Born Caracas, Venezuela, 25 January 1956. First GP: 250cc French, 1975. First GP win: 250cc French, 1975 (win on debut). World champion: 350cc, 1975 (Yamaha); 750cc, 1978 (Yamaha). Won 14 GPs and featured on the podium another 12 times. Cecotto won the Daytona 200 in 1976. He retired from two-wheel racing in 1981. Returned to drive in Formula One in 1983 and 1984 at Toleman with Ayrton Senna as his team-mate. However, a heavy crash in the British GP at Brands

Hatch ended Cecotto's F1 career. He raced touring cars from 1985 to 2002.

Checa, Carlos (RR) Born Sant Fruitos, Spain, 15 October 1972. First GP: 125cc European, 1993. First GP win: 500cc Catalonian, 1996. Checa has won two GPs and been on the podium a further 21 times. Known as 'Chubby' Checa.

Chili, Pierfrancesco (RR) Born Bologna, Italy, 20 June 1964. First GP: 500cc National, 1986. First GP win: 500cc National, 1989. European champion: 125cc, 1985. Chili won five GPs and had six other podium finishes. His first World Superbike win came at Monza in 1995. He won 16 World Superbike races and gained another 36 podium finishes from 217 starts.

Chiodi, Alessio (MX) Born Salo, Italy, 17 March 1973. European champion: 125cc, 1991. World champion: 125cc, 1997-99. Winner of Motocross des Nations (Italy) 1999. Known as 'Chicco'.

Circuit de Catalunya (RR) Circuit near Barcelona, Spain. Opened in 1995. Modified in 1995. Length: 4727m. Width: 12m. Left turns: 5. Right turns: 8.

Collier, Charlie (RR) Born Plumstead, Kent, 1886. Co-developer of the Matchless motorcycle. Set four world speed records on his Matchless in 1910 and 1911. Collier was the first winner of the IOM TT in 1907. He died 28 August 1954 in Plumstead, London.

Collins, Les (SP) Born Manchester, England, 24 May 1958. British League riders champion: 1980. Teams represented: Crewe, Belle Vue, Stoke, Leicester, Sheffield, Edinburgh, Cradley Heath, Glasgow. One of five racing brothers: Peter, Les, Neil, Phil and Steve. Known as 'The Beard'. Collins raced alongside his son, Aidan, for Glasgow in the late 1990s.

Collins, Peter (SP) Born Urmston, Manchester, England, 24 March 1954. World champion: 1976 (at Katowice, Poland). World pairs champion: 1977 (with Malcolm Simmons), 1980 (with David Jessup), 1983 (with Kenny Carter) and 1984 (with Chris Morton). World team champion: 1973-75, 1977 and 1980 (for England/Great Britain). British League riders champion: 1974 and 1975. Teams represented: Rochdale, Belle Vue. One of five racing brothers. Awarded the MBE in 2001.

Colomer, Marc (TR) Born Sant Esteve den Bas, Spain, 17 August 1974. Spanish champion: 1995 and 1997-2000. World outdoor champion: 1996. World indoor champion: 1994-96. Winner of Trial des Nations (Spain) in 1991-96, 1998, 2000 and 2001.

Comunitat Valenciana Ricardo Tormo (RR) Circuit at Cheste, Spain, named after local racer Ricardo Tormo. Opened in 1999. Held its first World Superbike round in 2000. Length: 4005m. Width: 12m. Left turns: 9. Right turns: 5.

Correy, Ronnie (SP) Born California, United States. World pairs champion: 1992 (with Greg Hancock and Sam Ermolenko). Teams represented: Wolverhampton, Peterborough (1997, 1999-2000), Long Eaton, Belle Vue, King's Lynn. Known as 'Rocket Ronnie'. Correy retired in 2001.

Corser, Troy (RR) Born Wollongong, Australia, 27 November 1971. Australian Superbike champion: 1993 (Honda). AMA Superbike champion: 1994 (Ducati). World Superbike champion: 1996 (Ducati). Corser won 23 World Superbike races and gained another 65 podium places from 181 starts. He rode in seven 500cc GP races in 1997. Joined the Foggy Petronas Superbike team in 2002.

Cotton (RR) This motorcycle firm was founded in Gloucester in 1918 by Francis Willoughby Cotton. The early machines became popular following success in the IOM TTs in the 1920s. The famous 'coTTon' badge was inspired by Stanley Woods's IOM TT win in 1923. The original firm went bankrupt in 1940. A new company was formed at the old factory in the 1950s and some road racing success followed in Britain in the early 1960s. The company finally ceased to exist in 1980.

Craven, Peter (SP) Born Liverpool, England, 21 June 1934. World champion: 1955 and 1962. Teams represented: Liverpool, Belle Vue. Craven was killed in a crash at Meadowbank, Edinburgh, in 1963. He is the only Englishman to win two world titles.

Crivillé, Alex (RR) Born Seva, Spain, 4 March 1970. First GP: 80cc Belgian, 1987 (for Derbi). First GP win: 125cc Australian, 1989. World champion: 125cc, 1989 (Kobas); 500cc, 1999 (Honda). Crivillé joined Honda in 1994, and moved to Yamaha in 2002 but was unable to race due to illness. He announced his retirement in May 2002. He won 20 GPs and achieved another 44 podium places.

Crump, Jason (SP) Born Bristol, England, 16 August 1975. World under-21 champion: 1995. World team champion: 1999, 2001 and 2002 (Australia). Australian champion: 1995. Elite League riders champion: 1999 and 2001. Teams represented: Peterborough, Oxford, Belle Vue, Zielona Góra, (Poland), Pila (Poland), Vargarna (Sweden). Son of four times Australian champion, Phil Crump.

de Coster, Roger (MX) Born Brussels, Belgium, 28 August 1944. Belgian champion: 500cc, 1966. Trans-AMA champion: 1974-77. World champion: 500cc, 1971-73, 1975 and 1976. Winner of Motocross des Nations (Belgium) in 1969, 1972, 1973, 1976, 1977 and 1979. Team manager (USA), Motocross des Nations 1981-90. A total of 37 GP wins. Retired from riding in 1980. He has worked as team manager for Honda and Suzuki. Named Motocrosser of the Century by *Cycle News*. Known simply as 'The Man'.

de Vries, Jan (RR) Born Netherlands, 5 January 1944. First GP: 50cc, Dutch, 1968. First GP win: 50cc Nations, 1970. World champion: 50cc, 1971 and 1973 (Kreidler). He won 14 GPs and made another 13 podium appearances.

Degner, Ernst (RR) Born Gleiwitz, Germany, 22 September 1931. First GP: 125cc West German, 1957. First GP win: 125cc Nations, 1959. World champion: 50cc, 1962 (inaugural season – Suzuki). An East German by birth, Degner defected to West Germany in 1961 and from there went to Japan, carrying with him a wealth of information about the preparation and design of two-stroke race engines developed by MZ (Motortadwerk Zschopau). This is considered to be a turning point in the development of Japanese lightweight racing bikes. Degner won 15 GPs and made a further 23 podium finishes. He died 10 September 1983.

Derbi (RR) Founded in 1922 in Barcelona, Spain. The name Derbi derives from DERivados de BIcicletus. The company was originally a producer of pedal cycles but eventually began to produce small-capacity road racing bikes. First GP win: Australian, 1966 (Barry Smith). World champion (riders): (125cc) Nieto 1971 and 1972, Martínez 1988; (80cc), Martínez 1986-88, Herreros 1989; (50cc) Nieto 1969, 1970 and 1972. World champion (manufacturer): (125cc) 1971, 1972 and 1988; (80cc) 1986-88; (50cc) 1969 and 1970. Derbi withdrew from road racing in 1972 to concentrate on road bikes and

motocross but returned in the late 1980s to record more world titles.

Despres, Cyril (CC) Born Fontainebleau, France, 24 January 1974. World cross-country rally champion: 2003. Winner in Dubai Rally in 2001 and 2002.

Deubel, Max (RR) Born Germany, 5 February 1935. First GP: sidecar German, 1959. First GP win: sidecar German, 1961. Sidecar world champion: 1961-64 (with Emil Hörner for BMW). Deubel won 12 GPs and finished on the podium a further 16 times. He retired in 1966. In 2004 he is an official of the governing body of the sport, the FIM.

Dixon, Darren (RR) Born England, 1960. Sidecar world champion 1995 and 1996 (with Andy Hetherington for Windle). Dixon won seven GPs and finished on the podium another 11 times.

Dobb, James (MX) Born Ripley, England, 2 January 1972. British champion: 125cc, 1989, 1998 and 1999; 250cc, 1990. World champion: 125cc, 2001.

Donington Park (RR) Near Castle Donington, England. Built in 1931, closed during World War II and not reopened until 1977. Modified in 1985. Length: 4023m. Width: 10m. Left turns: 4. Right turns: 7. Named corners: McLeans, Coppice, Redgate, Crainer Curves, Melbourne Hairpin.

Doohan, Michael (RR) Born Brisbane, Australia, 4 June 1965. First GP: 500cc Japanese, 1989 (Honda). First GP win: 500cc Hungarian, 1990. World champion: 500cc, 1994-98 (Honda) and runner-up in 1991 and 1992. A major accident at Assen in 1992 nearly ended his career and another, in 1999, led to his retirement. Doohan was voted Australian Sports Personality of the Year, 1998. Became Honda racing manager after retiring in 1999. He had 54 GP wins plus 41 podium finishes from 137 starts. He also won three World Superbike races from four starts.

Dörflinger, Stefan (RR) Born Nagold, Germany (although he raced as a Swiss). First GP: 50cc Yugoslavian, 1973. First GP win: 50cc Belgian, 1980. World champion: 50cc, 1982 and 1983 (Kreidler); 125cc, 1984 (Zundapp) and 1985 (Krauser). Dörflinger won 18 GPs and finished on the podium a further 40 times.

Drabik, Slawomir (SP) Born Poland. World pairs champion: 1996 (with Tomasz Gollob and Piotr Protasiewicz). Teams represented: Poole, Terow (Germany), Vastervik (Sweden), Wroclaw (Poland).

Drogalin, Kyril (ISP) Born Moscow, Soviet Union, 21 February 1963. World champion: 1997, 2000 and 2001. World team champion: 1997-2000 (Russia).

Dryml, Lukas (SP) Born Pardubice, Czechoslovakia, 16 April 1981. World Junior champion: 2002. Teams represented: Oxford, Poole, Mariestad (Sweden), Vetlanda (Sweden), Leszno (Poland).

Ducati (RR) Founded by the Ducati brothers, Adriano and Marcello, at Bologna in 1926 to make electrical components. After World War II the company turned to motorcycle manufacture. Ducati established a name in the racing world following first- and second-place finishes (Paul Smart and Bruno Spaggiari respectively) in the Imola 200 in April 1972. Mike Hailwood won the 1978 IOM F1 TT on a Ducati. World champion (rider): (Superbike) Raymond 1990, Polen 1991 and 1992, Fogarty 1994, 1995, 1998 and 1999, Corser 1996, Bayliss 2001. World champion (manufacturer): (Superbike) 1991-96 and 1998-2002. Facing financial difficulties in 1985, the state-owned firm was taken over by Cagiva and went on to score continued success in Superbike racing throughout the 1990s.

Duggan, Vic (SP) Born West Maitland, Australia, 10 August 1910. Australian champion: 1945, 1947 and 1948. British champion: 1948. Qualified for the cancelled World Championships of 1939. Injury cost Duggan the chance to compete in the first post-war World Championships in 1949 and he withdrew from the sport in 1950 following the death of his brother Ray in a crash at Sydney. Team represented: Harringay (for whom, in 1947, he won 297 out of 348 races in the British League).

Duke, Geoff (RR) Born St. Helens, England, 29 March 1923. Duke learnt to ride a motorcycle during World War II as a despatch rider, and after leaving the forces he rode in trials on a BSA before taking up road racing. Made his road racing debut on a 350cc Norton at the 1948 IOM GP. Came to prominence after winning the 1949 Senior Clubmans TT and the Senior IOM GP. In 1950 he finished second in the Junior TT and broke the lap and race records on winning the Senior, his first World Championship victory. First GP: 500cc IOM TT, 1950. First GP win: 500cc IOM TT, 1950. World champion: 350cc, 1951 and 1952 (Norton); 500cc, 1951 (Norton) and 1953-55 (Gilera). The first man to win the world 350cc and 500cc in the same year (1951). After dabbling with motor racing he signed for Gilera. He was banned for six months for supporting a riders' strike. He retired in 1960. Duke was six times a TT winner and six times world champion. He won 33 GPs overall. He was also the first rider to wear one-piece leathers, designed by a St Helens tailor. Awarded the OBE in 1953 in recognition of his services to motorcycling.

Dunlop, Joey (RR) Born William Joseph Dunlop, Ballymoney, Co. Antrim, Northern Ireland, 25 February 1952. Dunlop began racing at the age of 18. He won the Jubilee IOM TT in 1977 on a Yamaha and the Classic TT in 1980. He broke Mike Hailwood's record of 14 IOM TT wins in 1992. Eventually took his tally to 26 TT wins, winning the TT Formula One world title from 1982 to 1986. He was awarded the MBE in 1986 and the OBE in 1995. Dunlop was killed while taking part in a 125cc race outside Tallinn, Estonia, on 2 July 2000.

Edmondson, Paul (EN) Born Otley, England, 17 July 1969. Enduro world champion: 125cc, 1990, 1993 and 1994; 250cc, 1996.

Edwards, Colin (RR) Born Houston, Texas, United States, 27 February 1974. World Superbike champion 2000 and 2002 (Honda), and runner-up in 1999 and 2001. Edwards won 31 World Superbike races and finished on the podium a further 44 times from 175 races. Moved to race MotoGP for Aprilia in 2003. He also won the Suzuka eight-hour race in 1996 (with Noriyuki Haga).

80cc, GP class (RR) World championship class 1984-89. Champion manufacturer: Derbi (3), Krauser (2), Zundapp (1). Champion rider: Jorge Martínez (3), Stefan Dörflinger (2), Manuel Herreros (1). Nationalities (total wins): Spanish (4), Swiss (2).

Ekerold, Jon (RR) Born South Africa, 8 October 1948. First GP: 350cc Austrian, 1975. First GP win: 250cc French, 1977. World champion: 350cc, 1980 (Yamaha). He won seven GPs plus a further 12 podium finishes. Ekerold retired in 1983 and lives in Germany. His autobiography is entitled *The Privateer.*

Enders, Klaus (RR) Born Giessen, Germany, 2 May 1937. Sidecar world champion 1967 and 1969 (with Rolf Engelhardt), 1970 (with Wolfgang Kalauch) and 1972-74 (again with Engelhardt), all for BMW.

Enders won IOM TTs in 1969, 1970 and 1973. He won 27 GPs, 23 times partnered by Rolf Engelhardt and four times by Wolfgang Kalauch. He also raced BMW cars during a short 'retirement' from sidecars in 1971.

Eriksson, Anders (EN) Born Falkoping, Sweden, 14 May 1973. Enduro world champion: 350cc, 1995; up to 400cc, 1996. Two days enduro world champion: four-stroke 500cc, 1998, 1999, 2001, 2002 and 2003.

Ermolenko, Sam (SP) Born Guy Allen Ermolenko, Maywood, California, United States, 23 November 1960. World champion: 1993. World team champion: 1992 (United States). British League riders champion: 1991, 1994 and 1996. Teams represented: Poole (1983, 1984), Sheffield (1996), Belle Vue (1997, 2002), Hull (1999), Wolverhampton (1986-95, 1998, 2000, 2001, 2003). Severe leg injuries from a crash in Germany in July 1989 forced Ermolenko to miss riding for a year and he suffered further injuries later in his career. Known as 'Sudden Sam'.

Estoril (RR) Circuit near Lisbon in Portugal. Opened in 1972 and modified in 1999. First used for MotoGP in 2000. Length: 4182m. Width 14m. Left turns: 4. Right turns: 9.

Everts, Harry (MX) Born Noeroeteren, Belgium, 6 February 1952. World champion: 125cc, 1979-81; 250cc, 1975. Winner of Motocross des Nations (Belgium) in 1976 and 1979. Father of Stefan Everts.

Everts, Stefan (MX) Born Noeroeteren, Belgium, 25 November 1972. Belgian champion: 125cc, 1988, 1990, 1991 and 1993. World champion: 125cc, 1991; 250cc, 1995-97; 500cc, 2001 and 2002. World champion, MXGP: 2003. Winner of Motocross des Nations (Belgium) in 1995 and 1997. Nicknamed 'Stefun'. Everts broke Joël Robert's record number of GP wins in 2002 and by the end of 2003 had 69 GP wins to his credit. The first rider to win GPs in three different classes on the same day (2003). 'Officially' the greatest-ever world motocross rider, having won seven titles. Son of Harry Everts.

Fadeev, Vladimir (ISP) Born Soviet Union, 26 April 1958. World champion: 1993 and 1999. World team champion: 1993, 1994, 1996, 1999 and 2000 (Russia).

Farioli, Fabio (EN) Born Italy, 20 January 1970. Enduro world champion: 500cc, 1993.

Farndon, Tom (SP) Born Coventry, England, 1909. Considered the best rider of the early 1930s. Teams represented: Coventry, Crystal Palace. Farndon was killed in a crash at New Cross on 30 August 1935.

Fath, Helmut (RR) Born Germany, 24 May 1929. Sidecar world champion 1960 (with Alfred Wohlgemut for BMW) and 1968 (with Wolfgang Kalauch for URS). Involved in a serious accident at Nürburgring in 1961 in which Wohlgemut was killed. Fath only returned to racing in 1967 with a machine designed and built by himself (the URS). He won 11 GPs with another six podium finishes.

Faust, Willy (RR) Born Germany, 10 January 1924. Sidecar world champion 1955 (with Karl Remmert for BMW). Faust retired in 1956 after his passenger Remmert was killed in an accident. He won three GPs and gained another three podium finishes. He died 27 November 1992.

50cc, GP class (RR) World championship class 1962-83. Champion manufacturer: Kreidler (7), Suzuki (5), Bultaco (4), Derbi (2), Honda (2), Garelli (1). Not awarded in 1982. Champion rider: Ángel

Nieto (6), Hans-Georg Anscheidt (3), Hugh Anderson (2), Jan de Vries (2), Stefan Dörflinger (2), Eugenio Lazzarini (2), Ricardo Tormo (2), Ralph Bryans (1), Ernst Degner (1), Hank van Kessel (1). Nationalities (total wins): Spanish (8), German (4), Dutch (3), Italian (2), New Zealand (2), Northern Irish (1), Swiss (2).

FIM Governing body of the sport: Fédération Internationale de Motocyclisme. Founded in 1904 in Paris as the Fédération Internationale des Clubs Motocyclistes, FICM. Founding members: France, England, Germany, Austria, Belgium and Denmark.

500cc, GP class (RR) World Championship class 1949-2001 (replaced in 2002 by MotoGP). Champion manufacturer: MV Agusta (16), Honda (13), Yamaha (9), Suzuki (7), Gilera (3), Norton (3), AJS (1). Not awarded in 1954. Champion rider: Giacomo Agostini (8), Michael Doohan (5), Geoff Duke (4), Mike Hailwood (4), Eddie Lawson (4), John Surtees (4), Wayne Rainey (3), Kenny Roberts snr (3), Umberto Masetti (2), Phil Read (2), Barry Sheene (2), Freddie Spencer (2), Alex Criville (1), Wayne Gardner (1), Leslie Graham (1), Gary Hocking (1), Libero Liberati (1), Marco Lucchinelli (1), Kevin Schwantz (1), Kenny Roberts jnr (1), Valentino Rossi (1), Franco Uncini (1). Nationalities (total wins): British (17), Italian (14), United States (14), Australian (6), Rhodesian (1), Spanish (1).

Fogarty, Carl (RR) Born Blackburn, England, 1 July 1965. World champion: TT Formula One 1988-90 (Honda); endurance 1992 (Yamaha); Superbike, 1994, 1995, 1998 and 1999 (Ducati). Fogarty won a record 59 World Superbike races and gained another 50 podium places from 219 races. He suffered a serious arm injury on 23 April 2000 in a World Superbike race at Phillip Island, Australia, which eventually forced him to retire in September of that year. Formed the Foggy Petronas Superbike team to compete in 2003.

Foret, Fabien (RR) Born Aix-en-Provence, France, 29 January 1973. World supersport champion: 2002. Foret won seven Supersport GPs with a further three podium finishes.

Foster, Bob (RR) Born England, 16 March 1911. First GP: 350cc Dutch, 1949. First GP win: 350cc, Belgian, 1950. World champion: 350cc, 1950 (Velocette). He won five GPs and was on the podium three more times. Foster retired in 1951. He died March 1982.

Friedrichs, Paul (MX) Born Germany, 21 March 1940. World champion: 500cc, 1966-68. He won 27 GPs.

Frith, Freddie (RR) Born Grimsby, England, 30 May 1909. First GP: 350cc Swiss, 1949. First GP win: 350cc IOM TT, 1949. World champion: 350cc, 1949 (Velocette). He won five GPs. In 1949 Frith became the first motorcyclist to be awarded the OBE. He died 25 May 1988.

Fundin, Ove (SP) Born Tranås, Sweden, 23 May 1933. World champion: 1956, 1960, 1961, 1963 and 1967. Never worse than third in the World Championship between 1956 and 1965. Fundin appeared in 15 world finals. World team champion: 1960, 1962-64, 1967 and 1970 (Sweden). World pairs champion: 1968 (with Torbjorn Harryson). He won a total of 12 world titles. Swedish champion: 1956, 1957, 1960, 1962, 1964, 1966, 1967, 1969 and 1970. Teams represented: Norwich, Long Eaton, Belle Vue. Known as 'The Fox'. The World Cup trophy is named in his honour.

Gardner, Wayne (RR) Born Woolongong, Australia,

11 October 1959. First GP: 500cc Dutch, 1983. First GP win: 500cc Spanish, 1986. World champion: 500cc, 1987 (Honda). Gardner also won the Suzuka eight-hour on four occasions (1985, 1986, 1991 and 1992). He won 18 GPs with a further 34 podium finishes. He retired from two-wheel racing in 1993 and turned to touring cars. Announced his retirement from motorsport in February 2003.

Garelli (RR) Began production in 1913. World champion (riders): (50cc) Dörflinger 1982 and 1983; (125cc) Nieto 1982 and 1984, Gresini 1985 and 1987, Cadalora 1987. World champion (manufacturer): (50cc) 1983; (125cc) 1982, 1984, 1986, 1987.

Geboers, Eric (MX) Born Belgium, 5 August 1962. World champion: 125cc, 1982 and 1983; 250cc, 1987; 500cc, 1988 and 1990. The first and, along with Stefan Everts, the only rider to win titles at 125cc, 250cc and 500cc. Known as 'Mister 875' (125+250+500). Moved to race GT and touring cars in 2001.

Gerhard, Marcel (SP) Born Switzerland, 25 August 1955. World long track champion: 1992. He retired in 1999.

Gibernau, Sete (RR) Born Barcelona, Spain, 15 December 1972. First GP: 250cc Spanish, 1992. First GP win: 500cc Valencian, 2001. He has won five GPs and been on the podium a further 11 times. The grandson of Francisco 'Paco' Bulto, the founder of the Bultaco factory.

Gilera (RR) Founded in 1909 by 22-year-old Giuseppe Gilera in Acore, Milan. Purchased the Rondine equipe in 1935 and in 1937 Piero Taruffi broke the world speed record on a Gilera. World champion (riders): (500cc) Masetti 1950, 1952, Duke 1953-55, Liberati 1957; (125cc) Poggiali 2001. World champion (manufacturer): (125cc) 1953, 1955 and 1957; (350cc) 1957; (500cc) 2001. In 1957 Bob McIntyre riding a Gilera became the first man to lap the IOM Mountain Course at over 100mph. Gilera withdrew from road racing in 1957 and was purchased by Piaggio in 1969. The company made an abortive return to GP in 1992 and the original factory was forced to close. It re-entered GP in 2001, in conjunction with Derbi, and took the 125cc world manufacturers' and riders' titles, the first such success for 44 years.

Gollob, Tomasz (SP) Born Bydgoszcz, Poland, 11 April 1971. World pairs champion: 1996 (with Slawomir Drabik and Piotr Protsiewicz). World team champion: 1996 (Poland). Teams represented: Bydgoszcz (Poland), Vastervik (Sweden).

Gould, Rodney (RR) Born England, 10 March 1943. First GP: 500cc East German, 1967. First GP win: 250cc French, 1970. World champion: 250cc, 1970 (Yamaha). He won ten GPs with a further 24 podium finishes.

Graham, Leslie (RR) Born Wallasey, England, 14 September 1911. First GP: 500cc Swiss, 1949. First GP win: 500cc Swiss, 1949. World champion: 500cc, 1949 (AJS). Graham moved to Italy and joined MV Agusta in 1950. He served in the RAF during World War II (a bomber pilot in 166 Squadron) and won the DFC (Distinguished Flying Cross) on 8 December 1944. He won eight GPs. He was killed during the IOM Senior TT in 1953.

Gramigni, Alessandro (RR) Born Florence, Italy, 29 December 1968. First GP: 125cc Spanish, 1990. First GP win: 125cc Czech, 1991. World champion: 125cc, 1992 (Aprilia). He won three GPs and scored nine other podium finishes.

Gresini, Fausto (RR) Born Italy, 23 January 1961. First GP: 125cc Nations, 1983. First GP win: 125cc Swedish, 1984. World champion: 125cc, 1985 and 1987 (Garelli). He won 21 GPs with a further 26 podium finishes.

Gundersen, Erik (SP) Born Esbjerg, Denmark, 8 October 1959. Danish champion: 1983-86 and 1989. World champion: 1984, 1985 and 1988. World pairs champion: 1985 (with Tommy Knudsen) and 1986-89 (with Hans Nielsen). World team champion: 1981 and 1983-88 (Denmark). World long track champion: 1984 and 1986. In 1985 he became the first man to hold all the World Championships simultaneously. A total of 17 world titles. British League riders champion: 1983 and 1985. Team represented: Cradley Heath (1979-89). Gundersen retired from riding in 1989 following injuries sustained in a crash during the World Team Cup final. Manager of Danish Test team.

Gustafsson, Henrik (SP) Born Sweden, 14 August 1970. World pairs champion: 1993 (with Tony Rickardsson and Per Jonsson) and 1994 (with Tony Rickardsson). Teams represented: Bydgoszcz (Poland), Indianerna (Sweden).

Haas, Werner (RR) Born Germany, 30 May 1927. First GP: 125cc West German, 1952. First GP win: 125cc West German, 1952 (win on debut). World champion: 125cc, 1953; 250cc, 1953 and 1954 (NSU). Haas won 11 GPs and finished on the podium another seven times. He was killed in a light plane crash, 13 December 1955.

Haga, Noriyuki (RR) Born Nagoya, Japan, 2 March 1975. Won Suzuka eight-hour race, 1996 (with Colin Edwards). Runner-up in World Superbike championship, 2000 (Aprilia). Haga won 11 World Superbike races and finished on the podium a further 20 times from 110 starts. He raced MotoGP in 2001, returning to Superbikes in 2002 and then going back to MotoGP in 2003.

Hailwood, Mike (RR) Born Stanley Michael Bailey Hailwood, Great Milton, England, 2 April 1940. The son of a motorcycle dealer. In 1958 Hailwood came third in his first IOM TT 250cc race. Between 1958 and 1960 he won 11 out of a possible 12 ACU Star championships. In 1961 he won the IOM TT 125cc, 250cc and 500cc races on a Honda, the first rider to do this. He joined MV Agusta in 1962. First GP: 250cc IOM TT, 1958. First GP win: 125cc Ulster, 1959. World champion: 250cc, 1961 (Honda), 1966 and 1967 (MV Agusta); 350cc, 1966 and 1967 (MV Agusta); 500cc, 1962-65 (MV Agusta). He won 76 GPs and was on the podium another 36 times. In 1965 Hailwood raced cars and motorcycles. He retired from motorcycling in 1967, but raced Formula One 1971-74. He was awarded the OBE in 1967 for his services to motorcycling and also received the George Medal for Bravery after rescuing Clay Regazzoni from his blazing Ferrari at Kyalami, South Africa, in 1973. A bad crash at Nürburgring forced Hailwood to retire in 1974. He did, though, return to race in the Isle of Man, where he won the 1000cc Formula One TT on a Ducati. Retired finally in 1979. He was killed on 23 March 1981, along with his daughter Michelle, in a car accident near his home. He won 13 TTs and 76 GPs. Known as 'Mike the Bike'.

Hallman, Torsten (MX) Born Uppsala, Sweden, 12 August 1940. World champion: 500cc, 1962, 1963, 1966 and 1967. Hallman moved to the United States in the late 1960s and helped introduce motocross to the American public. He started a company producing the 'Thor' brand of motocross clothing. Wrote a book, *Mr Moto-cross*.

Hamill, Billy (SP) Born Arcadia, United States, 23 May 1970. World champion: 1996. World pairs champion: 1998 (with Greg Hancock). World team champion: 1990, 1992, 1993 and 1998 (United States). Teams represented: Cradley Heath, Stoke, Belle Vue, Coventry (1998 onwards), Zielona Góra (Poland), Smederna (Sweden). Known as 'Billy The Bullet'.

Hampel, Jarek (SP) Born Łódź, Poland, 17 April 1982. Under-21 world champion 2003. Teams represented: Ipswich, Pila (Poland).

Hancock, Greg (SP) Born Whittier, California, United States, 3 June 1970. World champion: 1997. World pairs champion: 1992 (with Sam Ermolenko and Ronnie Correy) and 1998 (with Billy Hamill). World team champion: 1990, 1992 and 1993 (United States). British League riders champion: 1997. US national champion: 1998 and 2000. Teams represented: Cradley Heath (1989-91), Coventry, Oxford, Wroclaw (Poland), Rospiggarna (Sweden). Variously known as 'The Grin', 'The Californian Flash', or 'Herbie'.

Harada, Tetsuya (RR) Born Chiba, Japan, 14 June 1970. First GP: 250cc Japanese, 1990. First GP win: 250cc Australian, 1993. World champion: 250cc, 1993 (Yamaha). He won his 500cc, GP debut in 1999 for Aprilia. Runner-up, 250cc World Championship, 2001. Harada rode MotoGP for Honda in 2002 before announcing his retirement. He won 17 GPs with a further 38 podium finishes.

Harley-Davidson (RR) Founded in 1901 by William Harley and Arthur Davidson. Its output grew from eight machines in 1904 to 50 in 1906. The company started its own racing division in 1914. It dominated US dirt track racing of the time. In 1923 a Harley-Davidson motorcycle set the world speed record when British rider Freddie Dixon achieved a speed of 106.8mph (171.9kph). Harley-Davidson won the first nine US AMA championships (1954-62) and dominated the Daytona 200 prior to the arrival of the Japanese machines. He won 24 GPs in total. World champion (rider): (350cc) Villa 1976; (250cc) Villa 1974-76. World champion (manufacturer): (250cc) 1975.

Harryson, Törbjorn (SP) Born Sweden. Nordic champion: 1969. World pairs champion: 1968 (with Ove Fundin). Team represented: Newport (1966-69). A broken leg in the 1969 World Cup final at Wembley eventually led to his retirement. Harryson went on to be a coach.

Haslam, Ron (RR) Born Langley Mill, England, 22 June 1956. First GP: 500cc South African, 1983. Podium finishes: nine. World champion: F1 TT, 1979 and 1981; F3 TT, 1980. Runner-up in British championship on a Norton in 1991. Haslam formed Team GB for new British riders in 1993. Set up the Ron Haslam Race School, and in 2004 is still racing (as is his son, Leon). Known as 'Rocket' Ron.

Havelock, Gary (SP) Born Eaglescliffe, Co. Durham, England, 4 November 1966. British champion: 1991. World champion: 1992. British League riders champion: 1995. Teams represented: Middlesbrough, Bradford, Poole, Masarna (Sweden). Once called 'The Vivienne Westwood of Speedway' because of his flamboyant fashion sense.

Herreros, Manuel (RR) Born Spain, 20 April 1963. First GP: 125cc Spanish, 1984. First GP win: 80cc West German, 1986. World champion: 80cc, 1989. Herreros won two GPs and had 20 podium finishes.

Hillebrand, Fritz (RR) Born Germany, 22 November 1917. First GP: sidecar Italian, 1953. First GP win:

sidecar IOM TT, 1956. Sidecar world champion 1957 (with Manfred Grunwald for BMW). Hillebrand won five GPs and gained another four podium places. He was killed in testing at Bilbao, Spain, on 24 August 1957. Posthumous world champion.

Hirvasoja, Jarmo (ISP) Born Finland. World champion: 1990.

Hislop, Steve (RR) Born Hawick, Scotland, 11 January 1962. Twice winner of three IOM TTs in the same year (equalling Mike Hailwood and Joey Dunlop). British champion: 250cc, 1990. British Superbike (BSB) champion: 1995 and 2002 (for Ducati). Hislop moved to Yamaha for the 2003 BSB season. Known as 'Hizzy', he was killed in a helicopter crash near Hawick on 29 July 2003.

Hocking, Gary (RR) Born Rhodesia, 30 September 1937. First GP: 500cc Dutch. First GP win: 250cc Swedish, 1959. World champion: 350cc and 500cc, 1961 (MV Agusta). Hocking won 19 GPs. He was killed while testing an F1 Lotus at Durban, South Africa on 21 December 1962.

Hodgson, Neil (RR) Born Burnley, England, 20 November 1973. British Superbike champion: 2000. First GP: 250cc British, 1992. First World Superbike (WSB): Misano, 1996. First WSB win: Donington Park, 2000. World Superbike champion: 2003. Hodgson won 16 WSB races and had another 25 podium finishes from 147 starts. He moved to MotoGP in 2004 to race for the D'Antin Ducati team.

Hollaus, Rupert (RR) Born Traisen, Austria, 4 September 1931. First GP: 125cc Spanish, 1953. First GP win: 125cc IOM TT, 1954. World champion: 125cc, 1954 (NSU). He won five GPs. He was killed in practice at Monza, 11 September 1954. Posthumous world champion.

Holta, Rune Born Randaberg, Norway, 29 August 1973. Norwegian champion: 1994, 1996, 1997 and 2000. Scandinavian champion: 1999 and 2000. Teams represented: Vetlanda (Sweden), Czestochowa (Poland).

Holzer, Bruno (RR) Born Switzerland, 9 February 1947. Sidecar world champion (B2B) 1979 (with Carl Meierhaus for LCR-Yamaha). He won the championship without winning a GP but finished second in every race. Holzer won one GP and was on the podium another eight times in his career.

Honda (RR) Founded in 1948 by Soichiro Honda with 34 employees. By 1968 this had risen to 16,000 employees. Honda's road race championship debut was on 3 June 1959 in the 125cc IOM TT. The first win came in the 1961 125cc Spanish at Montjuich, ridden by Tom Phillis. This was also the first GP victory for a Japanese machine. The first 250cc GP win came in the 1962 West German, at Hockenheim. This was the first GP victory for a Japanese rider (Kunimitsu Takahashi). Honda's first world manufacturers' and riders' titles came in 1961 (125cc for Tom Phillis and 250cc for Mike Hailwood). In 1966 Honda became the first manufacturer to win the manufacturers' title in all five classes (50cc, 125cc 250cc, 350cc and 500cc), with Luigi Taveri (125cc) and Mike Hailwood (250cc and 500cc) winning riders' titles. A break followed before Honda returned to road racing in 1979. The first victory of this new era came for Freddie Spencer in the 500cc Belgian GP in July 1982 on a two-stroke NS500. Honda was the first manufacturer to win 500 GPs.

World champion (riders): (125cc): Phillis 1961, Taveri 1962, 1964 and 1966, Capirossi 1990 and 1991, Raudies 1993, Aoki 1995 and 1996, Sakata 1998, Alzamora 1999; (250cc) Hailwood 1961, 1966

and 1967, Redmond 1962 and 1963, Spencer 1985, Mang 1987, Pons 1988 and 1989, Cadalora 1991 and 1992, Biaggi 1997; (350cc) Redmond 1962-65, Hailwood 1966 and 1967; (500cc/MotoGP) Bryans 1965, Spencer 1983 and 1985, Gardner 1987, Lawson 1989, Doohan 1994-98, Crivillé 1999, Rossi 2001 and 2002; (Superbike) Merkel 1988 and 1989, Kocinski 1997, Edwards 2000 and 2002. World champion (manufacturer): (125cc) 1961, 1962, 1964, 1966, 1989-95 and 1998-2000; (250cc) 1961-63, 1966, 1967, 1985-89, 1991-94, 1996, 1997 and 2001; (350cc) 1962-67; (500cc) 1966, 1983-85, 1989, 1992, 1994, 2001, 2002 and 2003; (Superbike) 1988, 1989, 1997, 2000 and 2002.

Hudson, Neil (MX) Born Bristol, England. World champion: 250cc, 1981.

Imola (RR) Circuit near Faenza, Italy. Known as Autodromo Enzo e Dino Ferrari. First GP held: Nations, 1969. Held seven Nations GPs (1969, 1972, 1974, 1975, 1977, 1979 and 1988), two San Marino GPs (1981 and 1983) and three City of Imola GPs (1996, 1997 and 1998). Length: 4933m.

Indian (RR) Founded in 1901 in Springfield, Massachusetts, by George Hendee and Oscar Hedstrom. The factory was known as the 'Wigwam' and the logo was a native American headdress. Indian machines dominated early American racing and in 1911 filled the first three places in the IOM TT. In 1914 Erwin 'Cannonball' Baker rode from San Diego to New York in 11 days, 12hrs and 10mins. Jack de Rosier broke the speed record at Brooklands. The firm hit financial difficulties after World War II and ceased production in 1953. New Indian machines were being produced in 1999.

Isle of Man (IOM) (RR) Motor racing on the IOM started in 1904 after the Manx authorities passed legislation to enable the closing of public roads for motor racing. The first TTs, held on short course in 1907, were won by Rem Fowler (twin-cylinder) and Charlie Collier (single-cylinder). The mountain circuit, still in use in 2004, was introduced in 1911. It is 37.73 miles (60.7km) long. Course: Braddan, Union Mills, Glen Vine, Crosby, Ballacraine, Glen Helen, Kirk Michael, Ballaugh, Sulby, Ramsey, Ramsey Hairpin, the Waterworks, Gooseneck, Guthries Memorial, East Mountain Gate, Black Hut, Verandah, Bungalow, Brandywell (427m above sea level), Windy Corner, 33rd Milestone, Keppel Gate, Creg-ny-Baa, Brandish, Hillbery, Signpost Corner, Bedstead Corner, the Nook, Governors Residence, Governors Bridge, Glencrutchery Road. First fatality 1913. First World Championship GPs held in 1949. Clypse Course on the outskirts of Douglas was introduced in 1954 for 125cc, 250cc (1955-59) and sidecar. It was discontinued as a World GP circuit in 1976 after being adjudged too dangerous by many top riders.

Ivanov, Juri (ISP) Born Soviet Union. World champion: 1986, 1987 and 1992. World team champion: 1986-92 (Russia).

Ivanov, Sergei (ISP) Born Soviet Union. World champion: 1991. World team champion: 1987 and 1991 (Russia).

Ivy, Bill (RR) Born Maidstone, England, 27 August 1942. First GP: 125cc Dutch, 1965. First GP win: 125cc Spanish, 1966. World champion: 125cc, 1967 (Yamaha). He won 21 GPs with a further 21 podium finishes. Ivy was the first man to lap the IOM TT course at over 100mph (161kph) on a 125cc machine. After falling out with team-mate Phil Read he announced his retirement in 1968 but later returned with Jawa, the Czechoslovakian team. Ivy drove Formula Two for Brabham during his 'retirement' from motorcycling in 1968. He was killed during practice for the East German GP at the Sachsenring on 12 July 1969.

Jacque, Olivier (RR) Born Villerupt, France, 29 August 1973. First GP: 250cc, Australian, 1995. First GP win: 250cc Brazilian, 1996. World champion: 250cc, 2000 (Yamaha). Jacque won seven GPs with another 27 podium finishes. Known as 'OJ'.

Janniro, Billy (SP) Born Vallejo, United States, 3 July 1980. Teams represented: Coventry (2001 onwards), Valsarma (Sweden), Zielona-Gora (Poland).

Jansson, Tommy (SP) Born Sweden. World pairs champion: 1973 and 1975 (with Anders Michanek). Team represented: Wimbledon (1972-76). Jansson was killed in a crash in Sweden on 20 May 1976.

Jerez (RR) Circuit at Jerez, Spain. Opened in 1986. Modifications made in 2002. Length: 4423m. Width: 11m. Left turns: 5. Right turns: 8. Named corners: Ángel Nieto, Michelin, Dry Sack.

Jobé, Georges (MX) Born Retinne, Belgium, 6 January 1961. Winner of Motocross des Nations (Belgium), 1980. World champion: 250cc, 1980 and 1983; 500cc, 1987, 1991 and 1992.

Jonsson, Andreas (SP) Born Hallstavik, Sweden, 3 September 1980. World under-21 champion: 2000. Teams represented: Coventry (1998 onwards), Czestochowa (Poland), Rospiggarna (Sweden).

Jonsson, Per (SP) Born Stockholm, Sweden, 21 March 1966. World champion: 1990. World pairs champion: 1993 (with Tony Rickardsson and Henrik Gustafsson). British League riders champion: 1993. Teams represented: Reading (1984-90, 1992-94), Torun (Poland) (1991-94), Rospiggarna (Sweden) (1994). Jonsson was forced to retire through injury in 1994.

Kadyrov, Gabdrakhman (ISP) Born Ufa, Bashkortostan, 1941. European champion: 1963. World champion: 1966, 1968, 1969 and 1971-73. Recipient of the FIM Bronze Medal in 1990.

Karger, Brian (SP) Born Horsans, Denmark, 9 February 1967. World pairs champion: 1995 (with Tommy Knudsen and Hans Nielsen). Teams represented: Swindon (1986-91 and 1995-98), Essex (1992-94), Belle Vue (2000 and 2002).

Karlson, Ulf (TR) Born Sweden. Swedish champion: 1976-83. World outdoor champion: 1980 (Montesa).

Karlsson, Mikael (SP) Born Gullspang, Sweden, 21 August 1973. World team champion: 1994 and 2000 (Sweden). World Under-21 champion: 1994. Teams represented: Wolverhampton (1993 onwards), Rybnik, Warsaw (Poland), Luxo Stars and Valsarma (Sweden). The younger brother of Peter Karlsson, he now rides as Mikael Max (taking his mother's maiden name).

Karlsson, Peter (SP) Born Gullspang, Sweden, 17 December 1969. World team champion: 2000 (Sweden). Teams represented: Wolverhampton (1990, 1992-97, 1999, 2002 onwards), Peterborough (2000), King's Lynn (2001), Belle Vue (2001). Known as 'The Milky Bar Kid'. Elder brother of Mikael Karlsson. Peter, Mikael and their youngest brother, Magnus (born 28 December 1981), all ride for Wolverhampton in 2004.

Kasakov, Sergei (ISP) Born Soviet Union. World champion: 1982 and 1983. World team champion: 1982, 1984, 1988 and 1990 (Russia).

Katayama, Takazumi (RR) Born Korea, 16 April 1951. Raced for Japan. First GP: 250cc Belgian,

1974. First GP win: 250cc Swedish, 1976. World champion: 350cc, 1977 (Yamaha). Katayama won 11 GPs and had a further 24 podium places. The first Japanese world champion.

Kato, Daijiro (RR) Born Saitama, Japan, 4 July 1976. First GP: 250cc Japanese, 1996. First GP win: 250cc Japanese, 1997. World champion: 250cc, 2001 (Honda). Kato won 17 GPs with a further ten podium finishes. He won the Suzuka eight-hour race in 2000. He rode MotoGP in 2002, and was nominated Rookie of the Year. He died from injuries received in a crash during the Japanese, at Suzuka on 20 April 2003. Inducted into the MotoGP Hall of Fame in October 2003.

Kawasaki (RR) Part of Kawasaki Heavy Industries. Kawasaki's first motorcycle was built in 1960. Debut GP: 125cc Japanese, 1965. World champion (riders): (125cc) Simmonds 1969; (250cc) Ballington 1978 and 1979, Mang 1980 and 1981; (350cc) Ballington 1978 and 1979, Mang 1981 and 1982. World champion (manufacturer): (125cc) 1969 and 1978-81; (350cc) 1978, 1979, 1981 and 1982. The company gained its first IOM TT win in 1969.

Kessel, Henk van (RR) Born Netherlands, 25 June 1946. First GP: 50cc Swedish, 1972. First GP win: 50cc French, 1974. World champion: 50cc, 1974 (Kreidler). Kessell won seven GPs with a further 18 podium finishes.

Khomitsevich, Vitali (ISP) Born Soviet Union. World champion: 2003. World team champion: 2003 (Russia).

Kilby, Bob (SP) Born Swindon, England, 23 September 1944. Teams represented: Exeter (1971-73), Oxford (1973-74), Swindon (1964-70, 1975-83). Kilby retired in 1983.

King, Shayne (MX) Born New Plymouth, New Zealand, 9 September 1970. New Zealand champion: 250cc, 1990, 1992-94 and 1997; 500cc, 1993, 1994 and 1997. World champion: 500cc, 1996.

Kinigadner, Heinz (MX/EN) Born Uderns, Austria, 28 January 1960. Motocross world champion : 250cc, 1984 and 1985. Kinigadner also raced in the Paris–Dakar rally.

Klaffenbock, Klaus (RR) Born Austria, 24 July 1968. First GP: sidecar Italian, 1990. First GP win: sidecar Czech, 1997. Sidecar world champion 2001 (with Christian Parzer for LCR-Yamaha). Klaffenbock won 16 GPs, with another 42 podium finishes.

Klingberg, Niklas (SP) Born Varing, Sweden, 6 February 1973. World team champion: 2000 (Sweden). Teams represented: King's Lynn, Leszno (Poland), Masarna (Sweden).

Knutsson, Björn (SP) Born Sweden. World champion: 1965. Known as 'The Crown Prince'.

Kobas/Cobas (RR) Designed by Spaniard Antonio Cobas using Rotax engines. World champion (rider): (125cc) Crivillé 1989.

Kocinski, John (RR) Born North Little Rock, Arkansas, United States, 20 March 1968. AMA champion: 250cc, 1987, 1988 and 1989. First GP: 250cc Japanese, 1988. First GP win: 250cc Japanese, 1989. World champion: 250cc, 1990 (Yamaha); Superbike, 1997 (Honda). Kocinski won 13 GPs and gained 18 more podium positions. He won 14 World Superbike races and finished on the podium another 15 times in 48 starts.

Krauser (RR) Founded by motorcycle luggage designer Mike Krauser in Germany. Performance racers based on BMW powerplants. World champion (rider): 80cc, Dörflinger 1985, Herreros 1989;

(sidecar) Webster 1988 and 1989, Michel 1990. World champion (manufacturer): (80cc) 1985 and 1989; (sidecar) 1988-90.

Kreidler (RR) Started making bikes in 1951 in Germany and ceased production in 1983. Garelli rebadged some of their small-engined bikes as Kreidler until around 1988. World champion (riders): (50cc) de Vries 1971 and 1973, Nieto 1975, van Kessel 1974, Lazzarini 1979. World champion (manufacturer): (50cc) 1971-75, 1979 and 1980.

Kujawa, David (SP) Born Zielona Góra, Poland, 13 April 1981. World under-21 champion: 2001. Team represented: Zielona Góra (Poland).

Lackey, Brad (MX) Born Berkeley, California, United States, 8 July 1953. US AMA champion: 500cc, 1972. World champion: 500cc, 1982. First American to win the 500cc world motocross title. He retired in 1982 after winning the world title.

Laguna Seca Raceway (RR) Circuit at Laguna Seca, California, United States. First World Superbike round held 1995. Length: 3610m. Left turns: 6. Right turns: 4, plus one ess. Named corner: The Corkscrew (ess).

Lampkin, Dougie (TR) Born Silsden, England, 23 March 1976. British champion: 1994, 1996-2000 and 2002. Spanish champion: 2001. European champion: 1993. World outdoor champion: 1997-2003. World indoor champion: 1997-2001. Winner of Trial des Nations (Great Britain), 1997, 1999 and 2002. Son of Martin Lampkin and nephew of top scrambler Arthur Lampkin. Awarded the MBE in 2002.

Lampkin, Martin (TR) Born Silsden, England, 28 December 1950. World champion: 1975. Father of Dougie Lampkin.

Langston, Grant (MX) Born Durban, South Africa, 17 June 1982. South African champion: 80cc, 1995 and 1996. Dutch champion: 125cc, 1999 and 2000. World champion: 125cc, 2000. Began riding in supercross in United States in 2002.

Laporte, Danny (MX) Born United States. US champion: 500cc, 1979. World champion: 250cc, 1982. Winner of Motocross des Nations (USA), 1981.

Lavado, Carlos (RR) Born Caracas, Venezuela, 25 May 1956. First GP: 250cc Venezuelan, 1978. First GP win: 250cc Venezuelan, 1979. World champion: 250cc, 1983 and 1986 (Yamaha). Lavado won 19 GPs, with another 23 podium places.

Lavieille, Christian (RR) Born Villefranche, France, 16 December 1965. Endurance world champion: 1998. Winner of the Bol d'Or in 1996, 1999 and 2001. Driver in FIA (Fédération Internationale de l'Automobile) GT championship, 2001 onwards

Lawson, Aub (SP) Born Warialda, Australia, 1916. Lawson began racing in Australia in 1937 before moving to England to join Wembley. Qualified for the cancelled World Championship in 1939. Took part in nine post-war WC finals without success. Australian champion: 1949, 1950 and 1953-55. Teams represented: Wembley, West Ham, Norwich. He died 21 January 1977 in Northam, Western Australia.

Lawson, Eddie (RR) Born Upland, California, United States, 11 March 1958. AMA Superbike champion: 1981 and 1982 (Kawasaki). AMA champion: 250cc, 1980 and 1981 (Kawasaki). First GP: 500cc South African, 1983. First GP win: 500cc South African, 1984. World champion: 500cc, 1984, 1986, and 1988 (Yamaha) and 1989 (Honda). Lawson won the Suzuka eight-hours race in 1990. Switched to Cagiva in 1991. He retired from racing in 1992 but returned

to win the Daytona 200 in 1993, having previously won it in 1986. Raced Indycars during the mid-1990s, largely with uncompetitive equipment. Known as 'Steady Eddie'. Record of 31 GP wins and 47 other podium finishes.

Lazzarini, Eugenio (RR) Born Urbino, Italy, 26 March 1945. First GP: 250cc French, 1969. First GP win: 125cc Dutch, 1973. World champion: 50cc, 1979 (Kreidler) and 1980 (Ipreme); 125cc, 1978 (MBA). Lazzarini won 27 GPs, with another 56 GP podium finishes.

LCR (RR) Stands for Louis Christen Racing, a Swiss firm specialising in building sidecar chassis. First design produced in 1976. LCR has collaborated with a number of manufacturers, and produced monocoque frames for Zundapp and Krauser.

Le Mans (RR) Circuit 5km from Le Mans, France. Circuit Bugatti. Opened in 1966. Modified in 2002. Built inside existing 24-hour track. Use of the track was suspended from 1996 until 1999 after a serious accident involving Alberto Puig. Length 4305m. Named corners: Du Musée, Dunlop Curve, Virage du Garage Vert, Virage des 'S' Bleus, Virage de Raccordement, Virage du Chemin aux Boeufs.

Lee, Michael (SP) Born Cambridge, England, 11 December 1958. World champion: 1980. World long track champion: 1981. World team champion: 1977 and 1980 (Great Britain). Teams represented: Kings Lynn, Poole.

Lega, Mario (RR) Born Rome, Italy, 20 February 1949. First GP: 250cc Yugoslavian, 1973. First GP win: 250cc Yugoslavian, 1977. World champion: 250cc, 1977 (Morbidelli). Lega won one GP and gained another eight podium finishes.

Lejeune, Eddy (TR) Born Verviers, Belgium, 1961. World outdoor champion: 1982-84.

Liberati, Libero (RR) Born Terni, Italy, 20 September 1926. First GP: 500cc Nations, 1953. First GP win: 500cc Nations, 1956. World champion: 500cc, 1957 (Gilera). Liberati won six GPs and finished on the podium a further eight times. He was killed in an accident at Terni on 5 March 1962. A football stadium was named in his memory in Terni, Umbria, Italy.

Lioubitch, Vladimir (ISP) Born Soviet Union. World champion: 1981. World team champion: 1980, 1982 and 1984 (Russia).

Locatelli, Roberto (RR) Born Bergamo, Italy, 5 July 1974. First GP: 125cc Italian, 1994. First GP win: 125cc French, 1999. World champion: 125cc, 2000 (Aprilia). Locatelli won seven GPs, with another nine podium places.

Lomas, Bill (RR) Born Alfreton, England, 1928. First GP: 350cc Dutch, 1950. First GP win: 250cc IOM TT, 1955. World champion: 350cc, 1955 and 1956 (Moto Guzzi). He won nine GPs with a further seven GP podium finishes.

Loram, Mark (SP) Born Malta, 12 January 1971. British champion: 1999. World champion: 2000. Teams represented: Eastbourne, Bydgoszcz (Poland), Team Svelux (Sweden).

Lorenzetti, Enrico (RR) Born Rome, Italy, 4 January 1911. First GP: 500cc Belgian. First GP win: 250cc National, 1951. World champion: 250cc, 1952 (Moto Guzzi). Lorenzetti won seven GPs and gained another 14 podium finishes. He died August 1989.

Louis, Chris (SP) Born Ipswich, England, 9 September 1969. World under-21 champion: 1990. British champion: 1998. Teams represented: Ipswich, Pila (Poland), Ornarna (Sweden). Son of John Louis.

Louis, John (SP) Born Ipswich, England. Originally a successful scrambler, Louis was persuaded to try his hand at speedway by his local club at Ipswich in 1969. He qualified for his first WC final in 1972 and finished fourth. World pairs champion: 1976 (with Malcolm Simmons). British League riders champion: 1979. Father of Chris Louis.

Lucchinelli, Marco (RR) Born Ceparana, Italy, 26 June 1954. First GP: 350cc Nations, 1975. First GP win: 500cc West German, 1980. World champion: 500cc, 1981 (Suzuki). He won six GPs and was on the podium another 13 times. He also won two World Superbike races and gained another two podium finishes from 18 starts.

Lundin, Sten (MX) Born Stockholm, Sweden, 1931. Swedish champion: 1955. World champion: 500cc, 1959 and 1961. Winner of Motocross des Nations (Sweden), 1955. Known as 'Storken'. In the 1970s Lundin developed the HL-500 motocross motorcycle with Torsten Hallman.

Lyda, Katrin (CC) Born Hof, Germany, 9 November 1962. Women's World Cross-Country Cup winner, 2003. Lyda became a journalist for motorsport publications and has also participated in cross-country rallies since 1994.

Lyons, Jason (SP) Born Mildura, Victoria, Australia, 15 June 1970. World team champion: 1999, 2001 and 2002 (Australia). Teams represented: Glasgow, Belle Vue (UK), Novrköping (Sweden), Pila (Poland).

Maier, Karl (SP) Born Munich, West Germany, 24 August 1974. World long track champion: 1980, 1982, 1987 and 1988.

Malherbe, Andre (MX/EN) Born Huy, Belgium, 29 March 1956. World champion: 500cc, 1980, 1981 and 1984. Winner of Motocross des Nations (Belgium), 1977, 1979 and 1980. Malherbe was paralysed after a crash in the 1988 Paris–Dakar Rally.

Mang, Anton (RR) Born Inning, Germany, 29 September 1949. First GP: 350cc Austrian, 1975. First GP win: 125cc West German, 1976. World champion: 250cc, 1980 and 1981 (Kawasaki) and 1987 (Honda); 350cc, 1981 and 1982 (Kawasaki). Mang won 42 GPs, with a further 42 podium finishes.

Martens, Jacky (MX) Born Belgium, 3 July 1963. World champion: 500cc, 1993. Head of the Husaberg factory team, 2002-03. Head of the KTM team, 2004.

Martínez, Jorge (RR) Born Valencia, Spain, 29 August 1962. First GP: 50cc Spanish, 1982. First GP win: 80cc Dutch, 1984. World champion: 80cc, 1986-88 (Derbi). He won 37 GPs, with 24 other podium finishes, and retired in 1997. Nicknamed 'Aspar' (The Cobbler), after his father's occupation.

Maschio, Mickael (MX) Born Digne, France, 19 May 1973. French Supercross champion: 125cc, 1994; 250cc, 1997. French MX champion: 125cc, 2002. World champion: 125cc, 2002.

Masetti, Umberto (RR) Born Parma, Italy, 4 May 1926. First GP: 125cc Swiss, 1949. First GP win: 500cc Belgian, 1950. World champion: 500cc, 1950 and 1952 (Gilera). Masetti won six GPs, with a further 15 podium finishes.

Matchless (RR) The firm was founded in 1899 in Plumstead, London, by H.H. Collier and his sons Charlie and Harry. Charlie won the inaugural IOM TT in 1907 and Harry won in 1909. Charlie won again in 1910. Matchless bought AJS from the Stevens brothers in 1931 to become Associated Motor Cycles (AMC), a firm which would eventually absorb Norton. AMC collapsed in 1967.

Mauger, Ivan (SP) Born Christchurch, New Zealand, 4 October 1939. Mauger came to Britain in 1957, returning to New Zealand in 1959 but coming back to England to ride for Newcastle in 1963. World champion: 1968-70, 1972, 1977 and 1979. World pairs champion: 1969 (with Bob Andrews) and 1970 (with Ronnie Moore). World team champion: 1968, 1971, 1972 (Great Britain) and 1979 (New Zealand). World long track champion: 1971, 1972 and 1976. A total of 15 world titles. British League riders champion: 1971 and 1973. Teams represented: Wimbledon, Newcastle, Belle Vue, Exeter. Recipient of the FIM Gold Medal in 1983. Awarded the MBE in 1976.

Max, Mikael (SP) see Karlsson, Mikael.

MBA (RR) Founded in Pesaro, Italy (also the home of Benelli and Morbidelli). World champion (riders): (125cc) Lazzarini 1978, Bianchi 1980. World champion (manufacturer): (125cc) 1983 and 1985.

McIntyre, Bob (RR) Born Glasgow, Scotland, 7 November 1928. First GP: 350cc Ulster, 1953. First GP win: 500cc IOM TT, 1957. McIntyre won five GPs, with another 20 podium finishes. In 1957 he was the first rider to lap the IOM TT circuit at over 100mph (161kph) (on a 500cc Gilera). He set the one-hour speed record on a 350cc Gilera at Monza in 1957. McIntyre was killed while riding an experimental five-speed Norton at Oulton Park in August 1962.

Melandri, Marco (RR) Born Ravenna, Italy, 8 August 1982. First GP: 125cc Czech, 1997. First GP win: 125cc Dutch, 1998. World champion: 250cc, 2002 (Aprilia). Melandri has won 17 GPs, with another 25 podium finishes. The youngest winner of a GP, aged 15 years and 324 days when he won the 125cc Dutch in 1998.

Merkel, Fred (RR) Born Stockton, United States, 28 September 1962. AMA Superbike champion: 1984-86 (Honda). World Superbike champion: 1988 and 1989 (Honda). Merkel won eight World Superbike races and finished on the podium another 16 times from 114 starts. He went on to ride for Kawasaki and Suzuki, and retired in 1995.

Merriman, Stefan (TR/EN) Born Tauranga, New Zealand, 24 March 1973. Australian enduro champion: 1994. Two days enduro world champion: two-stroke 250cc, 2000 and 2003; four-stroke 400cc, 2001. Merriman began in trial riding and was world junior trial champion, 1989.

Mertens, Stephane (RR) Born Belgium, 14 May 1959. Endurance world champion: 1995 and 2002. Runner-up in World Superbikes in 1989 before moving to endurance racing. Mertens has seven wins in World endurance and 11 wins in World Superbikes.

Michalik, Roman (EN) Born Czechoslovakia, 2 May 1974. Enduro world champion: 125cc, 1998.

Michanek, Anders (SP) Born Stockholm, Sweden, 30 May 1943. World champion: 1974. He contested 11 WC finals (1967-78). World pairs champion: 1973 and 1975 (with Tommy Jansson), 1974 (with Soren Sjosten). World team champion: 1970 (Sweden). World long track champion: 1977. A total of six world titles. As a teenager Michanek spent three years as a competitive ski jumper. Teams represented: Long Eaton (1967), Leicester (1968), Newcastle (1970), Reading (1972-76), Cradley Heath (1977), Ipswich (1979).

Michaud, Thierry (TR) Born France, 11 September 1963. World outdoor champion: 1985, 1986 and 1988. Trainer of the French Trial des Nations team.

Michel, Alain (RR) Born France, 23 December 1953. First GP: sidecar French, 1976. First GP win: sidecar

French, 1977. Sidecar world champion 1990 (with Simon Birchall for Krauser). Michel won 18 GPs and finished on the podium another 50 times between 1976 and 1991.

Mikkola, Heikki (MX) Born Mikkeli, Finland, 6 July 1945. World champion: 250cc, 1976; 500cc, 1974, 1977 and 1978.

Miller, Sammy (TR) Born Ireland, 11 November 1935. One of the most successful trial riders, with over 1300 victories, including 11 British championships. He rode for Ariel in the 1950s and in the 1960s he developed winning machines for Bultaco, including the Sherpa, and Honda. Started the Sammy Miller Museum, New Milton, Hampshire, England, which houses a collection of fully restored motorcycles, including factory racers and exotic prototypes.

Milne, Jack (SP) Born Pasadena, California, United States. World champion: 1937. The Jack Milne Cup is held at Costa Mesa, California, in his honour and was won by his grand-nephew Gary Hicks in 1999 and 2001. Costa Mesa was opened by Milne in 1970. The first American to win a motorsports world championship of any kind. His brother Cordy finished third in the 1937 World Championship. Team represented: New Cross.

Minarelli (RR) Motori Minarelli based in Bologna, Italy. World champion (rider): (125cc) Nieto 1979 and 1981. World champion (manufacturer): (125cc) 1979, 1980 and 1981. The company holds the land speed record for a 50cc-engined motorcycle.

Minter, Derek (RR) Born Littlebourne, Kent, England, 27 April 1932. British champion: 500cc, 1961-64. Known as 'The Mint' and 'The King of Brands' (a straight is named in his honour at Brands Hatch). He retired in 1987.

Misano (RR) Circuit at Misano, Italy. First World Superbike round in 1991. Length: 4060m. Named corners: Variante Arena, Curva del Rio, Tramonto, Curva del Carro.

Moiseev, Guennady (MX) Born St Petersburg, Russia, 3 February 1948. World champion: 250cc, 1974, 1977 and 1978. Winner of Motocross des Nations (Soviet Union), 1978.

Mondial (RR) The Italian firm FB Mondial was founded in Bologna in 1929 by the four Boselli brothers. World champion (rider): (125cc) Pagani 1949, Ruffo 1950, Provini 1957; (250cc) Sandford 1957. World champion (manufacturer): (125cc) 1949-51 and 1957; (250cc) 1957. Mondial withdrew from racing in 1957.

Monza (RR) Circuit at Monza, Italy. First World Superbike round in 1990. Length: 5793m. Left turns: 5. Right turns: 8.

Moore, Bobby (MX) Born United States. World champion: 125cc, 1994. In 2004 managed Chad Reed. Co-founder of the Road 2 Recovery Foundation.

Moore, Ronnie (SP) Born Hobart, Tasmania, Australia, 8 March 1933. At the age of 11 Moore rode pillion in his father's touring 'Wall of Death' act. He settled with his family in New Zealand, but came to Britain in 1950 to ride for Wimbledon. He reached that year's WC final at the age of 17. World champion: 1954 and 1959. He contested 14 WC finals. Moore retired in 1963 after breaking his leg, but returned to riding in 1969. World pairs champion: 1970 (with Ivan Mauger). He finally retired from league riding in 1972 and from international riding in 1975 after suffering a fractured skull in a crash during a world champions' series in Australia. He

rode with a strapped-up broken leg to win his 1954 world title and with a broken foot when he won in 1959. Team represented: Wimbledon.

Moran, Shawn (SP) World team champion: 1982 (United States). World long track champion: 1983. British League riders champion: 1989.

Morbidelli (RR) Financed by Giancarlo Morbidelli from his woodwork machinery firm in Pesaro, Italy. World champion (riders): (125cc) Pileri 1975, Bianchi 1976, 1977; (250cc) Lega 1977. World champion (manufacturer): (125cc) 1975-77.

Motegi (RR) Circuit in Motegi, Kanto district, Japan. It was built by Honda as a test facility. It opened in 1997 and was modified in 1999. Length: 4801m. Width: 15m. Left turns: 6. Right turns: 8.

Moto Guzzi (RR) Formed by three Italian air corps friends, Carlo Guzzi, Giorgio Parodi and Giovanni Ravelli. On Ravelli's death the company adopted the air corps' eagle symbol. Company headquarters were in Como, Italy, with a wind tunnel facility at Mandello del Lario. The first bike was designed in 1920. Debuting in GP in the early 1920s, Moto Guzzi quickly became one of the outstanding racing teams between the wars. It won the first 250cc World Championship in 1949 with Bruno Ruffo taking the riding honours. World champion (riders): (125cc) Ruffo 1949 and 1951, Lorenzetti 1952; (350cc) Fergus Anderson 1953 and 1954, Lomas 1955 and 1956, Campbell 1957. World champion (manufacturer): (350cc) 1953, 1955 and 1956. Lack of success in the 500cc class led to a withdrawal from racing in 1957. A revival in the 1960s was short-lived.

MotoGP class (RR) Replaced 500cc class in 2002. Inaugural champions: Valentino Rossi (Honda) and Honda, who both repeated the feat in 2003.

Mugello (RR) Circuit in Mugello, Tuscany, Italy. It opened in 1974. Modified in 1999. Length: 5245m. Width: 14m. Left turns: 6. Right turns: 9. Owned by Ferrari since 1988.

Müller, Egon (SP) Born Kiel, West Germany, 26 November 1948. World champion: 1983. World long track champion: 1974, 1975 and 1978. Considered an expert at long track rather than conventional speedway. In 1977 Müller set world records at 1000m in sandtrack, grass and speedway racing. Teams represented: Coatbridge (1973), Hull (1976), Brokstedt (Germany).

Müller, Herman (RR) Born Germany, 21 November 1909. First GP: 125cc Spanish, 1952. First GP win: 250cc West German, 1955. World champion: 250cc, 1955 (NSU). The oldest world champion (aged 46). Müller won one GP and was placed on the podium six times. He died 30 December 1975.

MV Agusta (RR) One of the all-time greatest racing marques. Began in 1923 as an aircraft company. After World War II Count Domenico Agusta founded the Meccanica Verghera Agusta motorcycle factory at Gallarate, near Milan. The first racing bike was produced in 1948. World champion (riders): (125cc) Standford 1952, Ubbiali 1955, 1956 and 1958-60; (250cc) Ubbiali 1956, 1959 and 1960, Provini 1958; (350cc) Surtees 1958-60, Hocking 1961, Agostini 1968-72; (500cc) Surtees 1956, 1958-60, Hocking 1961, Hailwood 1962-65, Agostini (1966-72), Read 1973 and 1974. World champion (manufacturer): (125cc) 1952, 1953, 1955, 1956 and 1958-60; (250cc) 1955, 1956 and 1958-60; (350cc) 1958-61 and 1968-72; (500cc) 1956, 1958-65 and 1967-73. Ironically, Agostini took the 1975 title on a Yamaha to end Agusta's run of victories. The team won 38 riders' world titles, 39 manufacturers' championships and over 3000 international races. Bikes were known as 'Gallarate fire engines'. Production ended in 1977 and the name was bought by Cagiva.

Naveau, Laurent (RR) Born Belgium, 29 December 1966. Endurance world champion: 2001. Known as 'Boldy'.

Nielsen, Hans (SP) Born Brovst, Denmark, 26 December 1959. World champion: 1986, 1987, 1989 and 1995. World pairs champion: 1979 (with Ole Olsen), 1986-89 (with Erik Gundersen), 1990 and 1991 (with Jan Pedersen), 1995 (with Tommy Knudsen and Brian Karger) and 1997 (with Tommy Knudsen). World team champion: 1978, 1981, 1983-88 and 1991 (Denmark). A total of 22 world titles. British League riders champion: 1986, 1987 and 1990. Team represented: Oxford. Known as 'The Main Dane'.

Nieto, Ángel (RR) Born Zamora, Spain, 25 January 1947. Began riding at the age of 13. He gained a reputation for being 'wild' by contesting with riders on faster machines, falling five times in one race. Nieto first joined Bultaco and then Derbi. First GP: 50cc Spanish, 1964. First GP win: 50cc East German, 1969. World champion: 50cc, 1969, 1970 and 1972 (Derbi), 1975 (Kreidler), 1976 and 1977 (Bultaco); 125cc, 1971 and 1972 (Derbi), 1979, 1981 (Minarelli), and 1982-84 (Garelli). He retired in 1986. He was six times 50cc world champion and seven times 125cc world champion, a total of 13 titles, with 90 GP wins, second only to Giacomo Agostini. He was known as 'The King of the Lightweights' and 'El Niño'. Recipient of the FIM Gold Medal in 1983.

Nilsson, Bill (MX) Born Hallstavik, Sweden, 1932. World champion: 500cc, 1957 and 1960. Winner of Motocross des Nations (Sweden) in 1955, 1958 and 1961. Known as 'Buffalo Bill'.

Nischenko, Nikolai (ISP) Born Soviet Union. World champion: 1989. World team champion: 1989-91 (Russia).

Noll, Wilhelm (RR) Born Germany, 15 March 1926. First GP: sidecar German, 1952. First GP win: sidecar German, 1954. Sidecar world champion 1954 and 1956 (with Fritz Cron for BMW). Noll won eight GPs and finished on the podium another seven times.

Norton (RR) The Norton factory was established in 1902 by James Landsdowne Norton at Bracebridge Street, Birmingham. Rem Fowler rode a privately entered Norton to win the very first IOM TT in 1907. Norton's Brooklands Special (BS) was the world's first production racing bike and was sold with a certificate confirming it had exceeded 75mph (121kph). The first factory success in the TT came in 1924. The development of an overhead camshaft engine made Norton a dominant marque during the 1930s, taking both the senior and junior TTs in every year bar two between 1931 and 1938. A 'featherbed' frame helped the bikes remain competitive in the immediate post-war years. World champion (riders): (350cc) Duke 1951 and 1952; (500cc) Duke 1951; (sidecar) Oliver 1949-51 and 1953, Cyril Smith 1952. World champion (manufacturer): (350cc) 1951 and 1952; (500cc) 1950-52; (sidecar) 1949-53. Norton withdrew from road racing in 1955. The company had been taken over by Associated Motor Cycles (AMC) in 1953, who also owned AJS and Matchless. Production was moved to south London. The marque was restructured as Norton Villiers in 1966 but was liquidated in the late 1970s.

Nowland, Warwick (RR) Born Sydney, Australia, 3 October 1972. Endurance world champion: 2000. Known as 'Wokka'.

Noyce, Graham (MX) Born Winchester, England, 1958. British champion: 500cc, 1976 and 1977. World champion: 500cc, 1979.

NSU (RR) Originally a knitting machine manufacturer. The first motorcycle was produced in 1901. In 1929 Norton's Walter Moore joined the firm and produced the 500SS. NSU was taken over by Audi and ceased motorcycle production in 1969. World champion (riders): (250cc) Haas 1953 and 1954, Müller (1955). World champion (manufacturer): (250cc) 1953.

O'Dell, George (RR) Born Hemel Hempstead, Hertfordshire, England, 13 November 1945. First GP: sidecar IOM TT, 1972. Sidecar world champion 1977 (without winning a race) (with Arthur Kenny and Cliff Holland for Yamaha). O'Dell committed suicide in March 1981.

Oliver, Eric (RR) Born Sussex, England. 1911. First GP: sidecar Swiss, 1949. First GP win: sidecar Swiss, 1949. Sidecar world champion 1949 (with Denis Jenkinson), 1950 and 1951 (with Lorenzo Dobelli) and 1953 (with Stanley Dibben), all for Norton. Introduced the first kneeler sidecar in 1954. Oliver retired in 1955 after recording 17 GP wins and two podium places. He died in 1981.

Olsen, Ole (SP) Born Haderslev, Denmark, 16 November 1946. World champion: 1971 (first Danish winner), 1975 and 1978. World pairs champion: 1979 (with Hans Nielsen). World team champion: 1978, 1981 and 1983 (Denmark). World long track champion: 1973. A total of eight world titles. He became manager of the Danish team. British League riders champion: 1972 and 1976-78. Teams represented: Newcastle (1967-69), Wolverhampton (1970-75), Coventry. Known as 'The Great Dane'. Recipient of the FIM Gold Medal in 1990.

125cc, GP Class (RR) World Championship class 1949 onwards. Champion manufacturer: Honda (14), MV Agusta (7), Garelli (4), Mondial (4), Yamaha (4), Aprilia (4), Derbi (3), Minarelli (3), Morbidelli (3), Suzuki (3), MBA (3), Gilera (1), Kawasaki (1). Not awarded in 1954 and 1978. Champion rider: Ángel Nieto (7), Carlo Ubbiali (6), Pierpaolo Bianchi (3), Luigi Taveri (3), Hugh Anderson (2), Kent Andersson (2), Haruchika Aoki (2), Loris Capirossi (2), Fausto Gresini (2), Kazuto Sakarta (2), Emilio Alzamora (1), Dieter Braun (1), Luca Cadalora (1), Alex Crivillé (1), Alessandro Gramigni (1), Werner Haas (1), Rupert Hollaus (1), Billy Ivy (1), Eugenio Lazzarini (1), Roberto Locatelli (1), Jorge Martínez (1), Nello Pagani (1), Daniel Pedrosa (1), Tom Phillis (1), Paolo Pileri (1), Manuel Poggiali (1), Tarquinio Provini (1), Dirk Raudies (1), Phil Read (1), Valentino Rossi (1), Bruno Ruffo (1), Cecil Sandford (1), Dave Simmonds (1), Arnaud Vincent (1). Nationalities (total wins): Italian (21), Spanish (11), British (4), Japanese (4), German (3), Swiss (3), New Zealand (2), Swedish (2), Austrian (1), Australian (1), French (1), San Marino (1).

Owesle, Horst (RR) Born Germany. First GP: sidecar IOM TT, 1970. First GP win: sidecar Finnish, 1971. Sidecar world champion 1971 (with Peter Rutterford for BMW). Owesle won three GPs and finished on the podium another three times.

Pagani, Nello (RR) Born Milan, Italy, 11 October 1911. First GP: 125cc Swiss, 1949. First GP win: 125cc Swiss, 1949 (win on debut). World champion: 125cc, 1949 (Mondial). Pagani won four GPs and was placed another seven times.

Parker, Jack (SP) Born Aston Manor, Warwickshire, England, 9 October 1908. Runner-up to Tommy Price in the 1949 WC final. Worked in the design team for BSA. Brother of Norman Parker. Teams represented: Coventry, Southampton, Clapton, Harringay, Belle Vue. He died 31 December 1989 in Rugby, Warwickshire.

Parker, Norman (SP) Born Solihull, England, 14 January 1910. Managed Swindon to win the British League title in 1967. Teams represented: Coventry (1929-30), Southampton (1931), Clapton (1932-34), Harringay (1934-39), Wimbledon (1946-53). He died 27 April 2001. Brother of Jack Parker.

Parker, Trampas (MX) Born United States. Italian champion: 125cc, 1991; 250cc, 1989 and 1991; 500cc, 1991. World champion: 125cc, 1989; 250cc, 1991. Known as 'Chad'.

Pastrana, Travis (SX) Born Annapolis, United States, 8 October 1983. Freestyle MX rider and SX rider. MX freestyle world champion: 1988, aged 14. Gold medallist in Summer-X games, 1999-2001.

Pedersen, Jan O. (SP) Born Middlefart, Denmark, 9 November 1962. World champion: 1991. World pairs champion: 1990 and 1991 (with Hans Nielsen). A total of seven world titles. British League riders champion: 1988. Teams represented: Cradley Heath (1983, 1985-92), Sheffield (1984). He retired through injury. He managed Oxford, Cradley Heath and Stoke in the 1990s.

Pedersen, Nicki (SP) Born Odense, Denmark, 2 April 1977. World champion: 2003. Teams represented: Wolverhampton, Eastbourne, Oxford, Rybnik (Poland).

Pedrosa, Daniel (RR) Born Sabadell, Spain, 29 September 1985. First GP: 125cc Japanese, 2001. First GP win: 125cc Dutch, 2002. World champion: 125cc, 2003. Eight GP wins from 46 starts plus a further nine podium finishes. The second youngest rider to win the 125cc world title (after Loris Capirossi).

Penhall, Bruce (SP) Born Balboa, United States, 17 August 1960. World champion: 1981 and 1982. World pairs champion: 1981 (with Bobby Schwartz). World team champion: 1982 (United States). A total of four world titles. Team represented: Cradley Heath (1978-82). Penhall retired in 1982 after his second world title win. He became a successful powerboat racer (with Dennis Sigalos). Penhall also turned his hand to acting, appearing in at least ten films and the TV series *CHiPs*, in which he played the character Bruce Penway Nelson.

Peterhansel, Stephane (EN) Born Vesoul, France, 6 August 1965. French enduro champion: 250cc, 1984, 1989, 1991 and 1993-97; 500cc, 1985-87. Two days enduro world champion: over 175cc, 1997; four-stroke 250cc, 2001. Winner of the Tunisian Rally in 1990 and 1994; the Paris–Dakar Rally 1991-93, 1995-97 and 2000; and the Paris–Beijing Rally in 1992.

Phakisa Freeway (RR) Circuit at Welkom, South Africa. It opened in 1999. Length: 4242m. Width 12m. Left turns: 5. Right turns: 9. The complex includes a football stadium. 1350m above sea level.

Phillip Island (RR) Circuit in Victoria, Australia. It opened in 1956. Modified in 1988. Length: 4448m. Width: 13m. Left turns: 7. Right turns: 5. Held its first World Superbike round in 1990.

Phillis, Tom (RR) Born Australia, 9 April 1934. First GP: 350cc Ulster, 1959. First GP win: 125cc Spanish, 1961. World champion: 125cc, 1961 (Honda). Phillis won six GPs and had a further 14 podium finishes. He was killed riding in the IOM TT on 6 June 1962.

Pichon, Mickael (MX) Born Le Mans, France, 13 February 1976. First GP: 125cc, 1992. World champion: 250cc, 2001 and 2002.

Pileri, Paolo (RR) Born Italy, 31 July 1944. First GP: 125cc, Austrian, 1973. First GP win: 125cc Spanish, 1975. World champion: 125cc, 1975 (Morbidelli). Pileri won eight GPs and gained another 12 podium places.

Platacis, Heinz (RR) Born Australia, 10 August 1960. Endurance world champion: 2001. Known as 'Heinzi'.

Poggiali, Manuel (RR) Born San Marino, 14 February 1983. First GP: 125cc City of Imola, 1998. First GP win: 125cc French, 2001. World champion: 125cc, 2001 (Gilera); 250cc, 2003. He has won 11 GPs with a further 21 podiums.

Pohjamo, Petri (EN) Born Vandaa, Finland, 1 August 1973. Spanish enduro champion: 125cc, 2001 and 2002. Enduro world champion: 125cc, 2003.

Polen, Doug (RR) Born Detroit, Michigan, United States, 2 September 1960. Polen retired after an accident in the early 1980s but returned in 1986. Japan Superbike champion, 1989 (Suzuki). AMA Superbike champion: 1993 (Ducati). World Superbike champion: 1991 and 1992 (Ducati). He won 27 World Superbike races and finished on the podium another 13 times from 79 starts. World endurance champion: 1997 and 1998. He retired in 1998.

Pons, Alfonso (RR) Born Barcelona, Spain, 9 November 1959. First GP: 250cc Belgian, 1981. First GP win: 250cc Spanish, 1984. World champion: 250cc, 1988 and 1989 (Honda). Pons won 15 GPs and gained another 26 podium finishes.

Pons, Patrick (RR) Born Paris, France, 24 December 1952. World champion: 750cc, 1979 (Yamaha). Competed in 250cc and 350cc, gaining 11 podium finishes. Pons won the Daytona 200 in 1980. He died 12 August 1980 after an accident at the British GP at Silverstone.

Price, Tommy (SP) Born Cambridge, England, 11 June 1911. World champion: 1949 (first Englishman). Team represented: Wembley. Price emigrated to Australia.

Protasiewicz, Piotr (SP) Born Zielona Góra, Poland, 25 January 1975. World pairs champion: 1996 (with Tomasz Gollob and Slawomir Drabik). Team represented: Bydgoszcz (Poland).

Provini, Tarquinio (RR) Born Italy, 19 May 1933. First GP: 125cc Nations, 1954. First GP win: 125cc Spanish, 1954. World champion: 125cc, 1957 (Mondial); 250cc, 1958 (MV Agusta). He won 20 GPs and made 19 further podium finishes.

Puzar, Alessandro (MX) Born Ceva, Italy, 19 November 1968. World champion: 250cc, 1990; 125cc, 1995. Winner of Motocross des Nations (Italy), 2002.

Raga, Adam (TR) Born Ulldecona, Spain, 5 April 1982. European champion: 2000. World junior champion: 2001. World indoor champion: 2003. Winner of Trial des Nations (Spain) 2001.

Rahier, Gaston (MX/EN) Born Belgium, 1945. World champion: 125cc, 1975-77. Winner of Motocross des Nations (Belgium), 1976. Winner of Paris–Dakar Rally in 1984 and 1985; Rally of the Pharaohs in 1984, 1985 and 1988.

Rainey, Wayne (RR) Born Los Angeles, United States, 23 October 1960. AMA Superbike champion: 1983 (Kawasaki) and 1987 (Honda). First GP: 250cc

Nations, 1984. First GP win: 500cc British, 1988. World champion: 500cc 1990-92 (Team Kenny Roberts Yamaha). Rainey won 24 GPs and gained another 41 podium places. He won the Daytona 200 in 1987, but was forced to retire in 1993 after a crash at Misano, Italy. Headed his own team from 1994 to 1998. Recipient of the FIM Gold Medal in 1993.

Ramon, Steve (MX) Born Brugge, Belgium, 29 December 1979. Belgian champion: 125cc, 2001. World champion: 125cc, 2003.

Raudies, Dirk (RR) Born Biberach, West Germany, 17 June 1964. First GP: 125cc West German, 1989. First GP win: 125cc Brazilian, 1992. World champion: 125cc, 1993 (Honda). He won 14 GPs and made another nine podium finishes. Raudies retired in 1997 to run his own team.

Read, Phil (RR) Born Luton, England, 1 January 1939. His first race was on a 350cc BSA at Mallory Park. He won the Senior IOM GP in 1960 and the Junior TT in 1961. Read joined Yamaha in 1964. He won 250cc world titles in 1964, 1965, 1968 and 1971 for Yamaha and also the 125cc title in 1968. In the 1965 IOM TT he became the first man to lap the mountain course at over 100mph (161kph) on a 250cc machine. He joined MV Agusta and ended team-mate Giacomo Agostini's run of successive 500cc world titles by winning in both 1973 and 1974. He moved to Suzuki in 1975 before retiring in 1976, but came out of retirement in 1977 to win Senior and Formula One IOM TTs. Finally retired in 1982. Read recorded 52 GP wins.

Redman, Jim (RR) Born Hampstead, England, 8 November 1931. He emigrated to Rhodesia (now Zimbabwe) in 1949. He ran a garage in Bulawayo. Redman had a brief spell racing in England in 1958 before returning to Rhodesia. He rode Nortons and Ducatis before signing for Honda in 1960. First GP: 500cc Dutch, 1959. First GP win: 250cc Belgian, 1961. World champion: 250cc, 1962 and 1963; 350cc, 1962-65 (all Honda). He won both the Junior and Lightweight IOM TTs between 1963 and 1965. Following an accident in the Belgian GP, he retired to South Africa in 1966. Redman registered 45 GP wins, and was awarded the MBE in 1964.

Reed, Chad (SX) Born Newcastle, Australia, 15 March 1982. World supercross GP champion: 2003. Nicknamed 'Skippy'.

Reynolds, John (RR) Born Nottingham, England, 27 June 1965. British Superbike champion: 1991, 1992 and 2001. Won one World Superbike race (Brands Hatch, 2000) and had one other podium finish.

Richardson, Lee (SP) Born Hastings, England, 25 April 1979. World under-21 champion: 1999. Teams represented: Reading, Poole, Coventry (2000 onwards), Lublin (Poland), Rospiggarna (Sweden).

Rickardsson, Tony (SP) Born Grylas, Sweden, 17 August 1970. World champion: 1994, 1998, 1999, 2001 and 2002. World pairs champion: 1993 (with Henrik Gustafsson and Per Jonsson). World team champion: 1994 and 2000 (Sweden). Swedish champion: 1997-99. Teams represented: Ipswich, Kings Lynn, Poole, Torun (Poland), Masarna (Sweden).

Rinaldi, Mario (EN) Born Rovato, Italy, 17 March 1966. Enduro world champion: 350cc, 1992; four-stroke 400cc, 1994, 1997 and 2000.

Rinaldi, Michele (MX) Born Parma, Italy, March 1959. Italian champion: 250cc, 1985 and 1986; 500cc, 1985. World champion: 125cc, 1984. Runs Yamaha factory motocross team.

Riss, Gerd (SP) Born Leutkirch, Germany, 17 March 1965. World long track champion: 1991, 1996, 1999 and 2001.

Robert, Joël (MX) Born Grandieu, Belgium, 23 October 1943. World champion: 250cc, 1964 and 1968-72. Winner of Motocross des Nations (Belgium), 1969. Robert held the record number of GP wins (50) until 2002 when it was beaten by Stefan Everts. Team manager (Belgium), Motocross des Nations 2003.

Roberts, Kenny (RR) Born Modesto, California, United States, 31 December 1951. Roberts began racing at the age of 14. He moved to the European circuit in 1974 but became a serious competitor in 1978, riding for Yamaha. First GP: 250cc Dutch, 1974. First GP win: 250cc Venezuelan, 1978. World champion: 500cc, 1978-80 (first US winner). Won the Daytona 200 three times (1978, 1983 and 1984). He registered 24 GP wins and 20 more podium finishes, and retired from riding in 1983 to head Team Roberts Yamaha. In 1996 Roberts created his own GP bike, the Modenas KR3.

Roberts, Kenny, jnr (RR) Born Mountain View, United States, 25 July 1973. First GP 250cc United States, 1993. First GP: win: 500cc Malaysian, 1999. World champion: 500cc 2000 (Suzuki). He has won eight GPs and gained another 11 podium places. Son of Kenny Roberts.

Roche, Raymond (RR) Born Ollioules, France, 21 February 1957. First GP: 250cc French, 1978. World Superbike champion 1990 (Ducati). Roche won 23 World Superbike races and finished on the podium another 34 times in 95 starts.

Rossi, Valentino (RR) Born Urbino, Italy, 16 February 1979. First GP: 125cc Malaysian, 1996. First GP win: 125cc Czech, 1996. World champion: 125cc, 1997 (Aprilia); 250cc, 1999 (Aprilia); 500cc, 2001 (Honda); MotoGP, 2002 and 2003 (Honda). Rossi has won 59 GPs and gained another 31 podium finishes. He is the youngest rider to win all three world titles at 125cc, 250cc and 500cc. The second youngest winner of the 125cc title in 1997, and the youngest winner of the 250cc world title in 1999. He joined Honda in 1999 and won the 500cc world title in 2001. Repeated the feat in 2002 by winning the inaugural MotoGP championship. Son of Graziano Rossi, a former Italian champion.

Rubin, Matteo (EN) Born Italy, 2 October 1973. Enduro world champion: four-stroke 250cc, 2000.

Ruffo, Bruno (RR) Born Verona, Italy, 9 December 1920. First GP: 250cc Swiss, 1949. First GP win: 250cc Swiss, 1949 (win on debut). World champion: 125cc, 1950 (Mondial); 250cc, 1949 and 1951 (Moto Guzzi). Ruffo won four GPs, with another six podium places.

Russell, Scott (RR) Born College Park, Georgia, United States, 28 October 1964. AMA Superbike champion: 1992. World Superbike champion: 1993 (Kawasaki). Runner-up in World Superbike championship, 1994. Russell won 14 World Superbike races and finished on the podium a further 23 times from 39 starts. He won the Daytona 200 in 1992, 1994, 1995, 1997 and 1998. First GP: 500cc Italian, 1995. Rode 500cc GP, 1996 (Suzuki).

Rymer, Terry (RR) Born England, 28 February 1967. World Superbike endurance champion: 1992 and 1999. Winner of the Bol d'Or in 1995, 1997 and 1998. Retired from bike racing in 2000.

Saarinen, Jarno (RR) Born Turku, Finland, 11 December 1945. First GP: 250cc West German, 1970. First GP win: 250cc Spanish, 1971. World champion: 250cc, 1972 (Yamaha). Saarinen won 15

GPs, with 17 further podium finishes. He won the Daytona 200 in 1973. He was killed during the 250cc Nations at Monza on 29 May 1973. Known as 'The Flying Finn'.

Sachsenring (RR) Circuit near Chemnitz, Germany. It opened in 1996. Modified in 2001. Length: 3074m. Replaced an existing public-road-based circuit.

Sakata, Kazuto (RR) Born Tokyo, Japan, 15 August 1966. First GP: 125cc Japanese, 1991. First GP win: 125cc Spanish, 1993. World champion: 125cc, 1994 and 1998 (Aprilia). Sakata won 11 GPs and gained another 30 podium places.

Sala, Giovanni (EN) Born Bergamo, Italy, 23 November 1963. Italian enduro champion: 250cc, 1994-2002; 500cc, 1993. Overall Italian enduro champion: 1994-99. Enduro world champion: two-stroke 250cc, 1994, 1995 and 1998; four-stroke 400cc, 1999; 500cc, 1993. Overall enduro world champion: 1998.

Salminen, Juha (EN) Born Vantaa, Finland, 27 September 1976. Two days enduro world champion: 125cc, 1999 and 2000; 250cc, 2001; four-stroke 400cc, 2002; four-stroke 500cc, 2003. Overall enduro world team champion: 2000-03. Enduro world team champion: 2003 (Finland).

Samorodov, Boris (ISP) Born Ufa, Bashkortostan. World champion: 1967.

Sandford, Cecil (RR) Born Gloucestershire, England, 21 February 1928. First GP: 350cc Ulster, 1950. First GP win: 125cc IOM TT, 1952. World champion: 125cc, 1952 (MV Agusta); 250cc, 1957 (Mondial). Sandford won five GPs and gained another 16 podium finishes. The first British rider to win the World Championship at 125cc and 250cc. He retired in 1957.

Sanz, Laia (TR) Born Cordoba de Llobregat, Spain, 11 December 1985. Women's European champion: 2002 and 2003. Women's world champion: 2000-03.

Sarron, Christian (RR) Born France, 27 March 1955. First GP: 350cc West German, 1976. First GP win: 250cc West German, 1977. World champion: 250cc, 1984 (Yamaha). Sarron won seven GPs and had a further 30 podium finishes.

Scheidegger, Fritz (RR) Born Switzerland, 30 December 1930. Sidecar world champion 1965 and 1966 (with John Robinson for BMW). He won 16 GPs. Scheidegger was killed 26 March 1967 at Mallory Park.

Schmit, Donnie (MX) Born United States, 17 January 1967. World champion: 125cc, 1990; 250cc, 1992. He died 19 January 1996 from a brain haemorrhage.

Schneider, Walter (RR) Born Germany, 15 January 1927. Sidecar world champion 1958 and 1959 (with Hans Strauss for BMW). He won seven GPs.

Schreiber, Bernie (TR) Born Southern California, United States, 1959. US champion: 1978, 1982, 1983 and 1987. World outdoor champion: 1979. He wrote *Observed Trials*, the 'trials bible'.

Schwantz, Kevin (RR) Born Houston, Texas, United States, 19 June 1964. He won the Daytona 200 in 1988 despite breaking his left arm in practice. First GP: 500cc Dutch, 1986. First GP win: 500cc Japanese, 1988. World champion: 500cc, 1993 (Suzuki). Schwantz won 24 GPs and gained another 24 podium places. He had a series of closely fought races with Wayne Rainey. He retired unexpectedly early in the 1995 season. Afterwards Schwantz drove in NASCAR and touring car races. Recipient of the FIM Silver Medal in 1995.

Schwartz, Bobby (SP) Born Santa Barbara, California, United States, 10 August 1956. World pairs champion: 1981 (with Bruce Penhall) and 1982 (with Dennis Sigalos). World team champion: 1982 (United States). Known as 'Boogaloo' and 'Captain America'.

Schwärzel, Werner (RR) Born Germany, 6 September 1948. First GP: sidecar French, 1973. First GP win: sidecar German, 1974. Sidecar world champion 1982 (with Joseph Huber for Seymaz) without winning a race. He won ten GPs and finished on the podium another 42 times.

Scovolo, Fausto (EN) Born Provezze, Italy, 2 November 1967. Enduro world champion: 125cc, 1996.

Screen, Joe (SP) Born Warrington, England, 27 November 1972. World under-21 champion: 1993. British League riders champion: 1992. British champion: 1996 and 2004. Teams represented: Bradford, Belle Vue, Hull, Eastbourne, Bydgoszcz (Poland), Luxo (Sweden). Known as 'The Screen Machine'.

Seel, Eddy (MX) Born Verviers, Belgium, 23 April 1970. World champion: supermoto 2003.

Sepang (RR) Circuit at Sepang, Malaysia, 50km south of Kuala Lumpur. It opened in 1998. Modified in 1999. Length: 5548m. Width: 25m. Left turns: 5. Right turns: 10. Longest lap in MotoGP.

Serenius, Per-Olov (ISP) Born Avesta, Sweden, 9 March 1948. Raced motorcycle sidecar and speedway before taking up ice racing in 1977. World champion: 1995 and 2002. World team champion: 1985, 1995 and 2002 (Sweden).

Sergis, Kristers (MX) Born Cēsis, Latvia, 18 January 1974. Latvian sidecar champion: 1991, 1994 and 1995. Sidecar world champion: 1997, 1998, 2000-02 (all with Artis Rasmasis as passenger).

750cc, GP class (RR) World championship class 1977-79. Champion manufacturer: Yamaha (3). Champion rider: Steve Baker (1), Johnny Cecotto (1), Patrick Pons (1). Nationalities (total wins): French (1), United States (1), Venezuelan (1).

Sheene, Barry (RR) Born Holborn, London, England, 11 September 1950. Introduced to motorsport at the age of five, with his father Frank building him his first ever motorbike. Sheene took up professional racing on a 125cc Bultaco in 1968. He won the British 750cc title in 1969-70 and the European 750cc title in 1973. First GP: 125cc Spanish, 1970. First GP win: 125cc Belgian, 1971. World champion: 500cc, 1976 and 1977 (Suzuki). Between 1975 and 1982 he won more international 500cc and 750cc Grand Prix titles than any other rider. He is renowned for spectacular crashes, including a near-fatal 175mph (282kph) crash at Daytona in 1973. He is the only man to have won GPs at both 50cc and 500cc. Sheene won 23 GPs and gained a further 29 podium places. He left Suzuki to run his own team of Yamaha machines in 1980. He broke both legs in a crash at Silverstone in 1982. Sheene retired in 1984 and took up media work and truck racing before emigrating to Queensland, Australia. Awarded the MBE in 1978. He died from cancer 10 March 2003.

Sidecar class (RR) World championship class 1949 onwards. Not given World Championship status 1997-2000 but run as 'world cup'. Champion manufacturer: BMW (19), Yamaha (including LCR-Yamaha) (11), Norton (5), LCR-Krauser (3), LCR (3), Suzuki (3), Busch (2). Not awarded in 1954, 1976 and 1993-98. Champion rider: Steve Webster (8),

Rolf Biland (7), Klaus Enders (6), Max Deubel (4), Eric Oliver (4), Egbert Streuer (3), Darren Dixon (2), Helmut Fath (2), Wilhelm Noll (2), Fritz Scheidegger (2), Bernie Schneiders (2), Rolf Steinhausen (2), Steve Abbott (1), Willy Faust (1), Fritz Hillebrand (1), Klaus Klaffenböeck (1), Alain Michel (1), George O'Dell (1), Horst Owesle (1), Werner Schwärzel (1), Cyril Smith (1), Jock Taylor (1). Nationalities (total wins): German (22), British (18), Swiss (9), Dutch (3), Austrian (1), French (1).

Silvan, Petteri   (EN) Born Jämsä, Finland, 21 October 1972. Two days' enduro world champion: 125cc, 1995, 2001 and 2002; 250cc, 1999. Overall enduro world champion: 1999. Enduro world team champion: 2003 (Finland).

Silverstone   (RR) Circuit in Northamptonshire, England. First used for World Championships in 1977. First World Superbike race in 2002. Length 5094m. Left turns: 7. Right turns: 8. Named corners: Copse, Maggotts, Becketts, Chapel, Stowe, Club, Abbey, Woodcote. Named straight: Hanger Straight.

Simmonds, Dave   (RR) Born Britain, 25 October 1939. First GP: 50cc Dutch, 1966. First GP win: 125cc West German, 1969. World champion: 125cc, 1969 (Kawasaki). He won 11 GPs and finished on the podium another 11 times. Simmonds died 23 October 1972.

Simmons, Malcolm   (SP) Born 1947. World pairs champion: 1976 (with John Louis), 1977 (with Peter Collins) and 1978 (with Gordon Kennett). A total of seven world titles.

Slight, Aaron   (RR) Born Masterton, New Zealand, 19 January 1966. Australian Superbike champion: 1991. Runner-up in the World Superbike championship in 1996 and 1998 and third 1993-95 and 1997. Slight won 13 World Superbike races and gained another 74 podium finishes from 229 races. He won the Suzuka eight-hour in 1993, 1994 and 1995.

Smets, Joël   (MX) Born Mol, Belgium, 6 April 1969. First GP: 500cc Dutch, 1989. Belgian champion: 500cc, 1995 and 1996. World champion: 500cc, 1995, 1997, 1998 and 2000; 650cc, 2003. Winner of Motocross des Nations (Belgium) 1995, 1997 and 1998. Known as 'The Flemish Lion'. Named after Joël Robert. The most successful 500cc rider in the history of motocross.

Smith, Cyril   (RR) Born Britain, 2 January 1919. First GP: sidecar Belgian, 1951. First GP win: sidecar German, 1952. Sidecar world champion 1952 (with Bob Clements for Norton). Smith won two GPs and gained another 16 podium finishes. He died 24 December 1962.

Smith, Jeff   (MX) Born Colne, Lancashire, England, 14 October 1934. British champion: 500cc, 1955, 1956, 1960-65 and 1967. Motocross des Nations (Britain) 1956, 1957, 1959, 1960, 1963, 1965 and 1967. World champion: 500cc, 1964 and 1965. Smith rode a BSA virtually throughout his career. He was awarded the MBE in 1970, the first non-road race motorcyclist to receive the honour. He emigrated to Canada in 1972.

Spencer, Freddie   (RR) Born Shreveport, Louisiana, United States, 20 December 1961. The youngest winner of an AMA race in 1979 at the age of 18 (on a Kawasaki). He joined Honda in 1980. First GP: 500cc Argentinian, 1982. First GP win: 500cc Belgian, 1982. World champion: 250cc, 1985 (Honda); 500cc, 1983 and 1985 (Honda). Won 27 GPs and gained another 12 podium places. He won the Daytona 200 in 1985. Spencer retired from GP

racing in 1988 but made a couple of comebacks before officially retiring in 1996. He became a commentator and founded a performance riding school. Known as 'Fast Freddie'.

Spinka, Milan   (ISP) Born Czechoslovakia, 5 May 1951. World champion: 1974. Became a speedway referee and event organiser.

Sportsland SUGO   (RR) Circuit at Sugo, Japan. Held its first World Superbike round in 1988. Length: 3737m. Width: 10m-12.5m. Left turns: 6. Right turns: 9.

Steinhausen, Rolf   (RR) Born Germany, 27 June 1943. First GP: sidecar French, 1972. First GP win: sidecar Belgian, 1974. Sidecar world champion: 1975 and 1976 (with Joseph Huber for Busch-König). Steinhausen won ten GPs and gained another 12 podium finishes.

Stenlund, Erik   (ISP) Born Uppsala, Sweden, 1962. World champion: 1984 and 1988. World team champion: 1985 (Sweden). Team represented: Rospiggarna (Sweden)

Stonehewer, Carl   (SP) Born Manchester, England, 16 May 1972. Premier League riders champion: 2000 and 2001. Teams represented: Workington, Zielona Gora (Poland), Pila (Poland), Smederna (Sweden).

Streuer, Egbert   (RR) Born Netherlands, 1 February 1954. First GP: sidecar Czech, 1978. First GP win: sidecar British, 1982. Sidecar world champion 1984-86 (with Bernt Schneiders for Yamaha). Streuer won 22 GPs and finished on the podium another 33 times. He retired in 1993.

Strijbos, Dave   (MX) Born Netherlands, 8 November 1967. World champion: 125cc, 1986.

Suchov, Vladimir   (ISP) Born Soviet Union. World champion: 1985. World team champion: 1981, 1982, 1984, 1986 and 1987 (Russia).

Sullivan, Ryan   (SP) Born Melbourne, Australia, 20 January 1975. World team champion: 1999, 2001 and 2002 (Australia). Elite League riders champion: 2000. Teams represented: Poole, Peterborough, Torun (Poland), Czestochowa (Poland), Rospiggarna (Sweden), Kaparna (Sweden). He was forced to quit racing between 1992 and 1997 because of serious injury.

Superbike class (RR)   World Championship class 1988 onwards. Champion manufacturer: Ducati (10), Honda (5), Kawasaki (1). Champion rider: Carl Fogarty (4), Colin Edwards (2), Fred Merkel (2), Doug Polen (2), Troy Bayliss (1), Troy Corser (1), Neil Hodgson (1), John Kocinski (1), Raymond Roche (1), Scott Russell (1). Nationalities (total wins): United States (8), British (5), Australian (2), French (1).

Surtees, John   (RR) Born Tatsfield, Surrey, England, 11 February 1934. His father was a motorcycle dealer. Surtees started racing at the age of 17, first on a Vincent and then on Nortons, and regularly won short circuit races. First GP: 500cc Ulster, 1952. First GP win: 250cc Ulster, 1955. He joined MV Agusta in 1956. World champion: 350cc, 1958-60; 500cc, 1956 and 1958-60. In 1958 and 1959 he won all 25 GPs he entered. He also won both the 1959 Junior and Senior IOM TT races and became only the second rider to do 'the double' two years running. The first rider to win the Senior TT in three successive years (1958-60). He won 38 GPs and finished on the podium another seven times. After retiring from motorcycle racing in 1960 Surtees began in Formula One. He became F1 world champion in 1964 – the only man to win world titles on both two and four wheels. He retired from racing in 1971 and ran his own team until 1978. Voted BBC Sports Personality of the Year in 1959.

Suzuka (RR) Circuit at Suzuka, Japan. It opened in 1961. Modified in 2002. Length: 5859m. Width: 15m. Left turns: 10. Right turns: 11. Named turns: Spoon Curve, Casio Triangle. The course has a unique crossover feature, the Degner Crossing.

Suzuki (RR) The Suzuki factory at Hamamatsu near Nagoya, Japan, began life as a clothing factory in 1909. During the depression following World War II the factory diversified, producing its first motorcycles in 1952. After the arrival of East German Ernst Degner in 1962, Suzuki found success in the 50cc class. In the 1970s the company produced its four-square 500cc machine. World champion (riders): (50cc) Degner 1952, Hugh Anderson 1963 and 1964, Anscheidt 1966, 1967 and 1968 (privately entered); (125cc) Hugh Anderson 1963 and 1965, Braun 1970; 500cc, Sheene 1976 and 1977, Lucchinelli 1981, Uncini 1982. World champion (manufacturer): (50cc) 1962, 1963, 1964, 1967, 1968; (125cc) 1963, 1965 and 1970; (500cc) 1976-82.

Svab, Antonin (ISP) Born Czechoslovakia. World champion: 1970.

Szczakiel, Jerzy (SP) Born Grudziadz, Poland, 28 January 1949. World champion: 1973. World pairs champion: 1971 (with Andrzej Wyglenda).

Tarabanko, Sergei (ISP) Born Soviet Union. World champion: 1975-78. World team champion: 1979-81 (Russia).

Tarres, Jordi (TR) Born Manresa, Spain, 10 September 1966. Spanish champion: 1986-94. World outdoor champion: 1987, 1989-91 and 1993-95. Winner Trial des Nations (Spain) in 1989, 1991-96. He retired in 1997.

Tatum, Kelvin (SP) Born Epsom, Surrey, England, 8 February 1964. World long track champion: 1995, 1998 and 2000. World Championship qualifier seven times. Teams represented: Wimbledon, Essex (1994 and 2002 onwards). Tatum became a TV commentator. He was awarded the MBE in 2002.

Taveri, Luigi (RR) Born Horen, Switzerland, 19 September 1929. First GP: 250cc Swiss, 1954. First GP win: 125cc Spanish, 1955. World champion: 125cc, 1962, 1964 and 1966 (Honda). Taveri won 30 GPs and finished on the podium another 59 times. He also raced as a sidecar passenger.

Taylor, Jock (RR) Born Pencaitland, Scotland, 9 March 1954. First GP win: sidecar Swedish, 1979. Sidecar world champion: 1980 (with Benga Johansson for Windle-Yamaha). Taylor won six GPs. He was killed on 15 August 1982 while racing in the Finnish GP at Imatra.

Thorpe, Dave (MX) Born England, 29 October 1962. British champion: 1976 and 1977. World champion: 500cc, 1985, 1986 and 1989.

350cc, GP class (RR) World Championship class 1949-82. Champion manufacturer: MV Agusta (9), Honda (6), Yamaha (6), Kawasaki (4), Moto Guzzi (3), Norton (2), Velocette (2), Gilera (1). Not awarded in 1954. Champion rider: Giacomo Agostini (7), Jim Redman (4), John Surtees (3), Fergus Anderson (2), Kork Ballington (2), Geoff Duke (2), Mike Hailwood (2), Bill Lomas (2), Anton Mang (2), Keith Campbell (1), Johnny Cecotto (1), Jon Ekerold (1), Bob Foster (1), Freddie Frith (1), Gary Hocking (1), Takazumi Katayama (1), Walter Villa (1). Nationalities (total wins): British (13), Italian (8), Rhodesian (5), South African (3), German (2), Australian (1), Japanese (1), Venezuelan (1).

Tiainen, Kari (EN) Born Riihimaki, Finland, 26 August 1966. Finnish enduro champion: 250cc, 1989 and 1990. Spanish enduro champion: four-stroke 500cc, 2000 and 2001. Enduro world champion: 250cc, 1990 and 1991; four-stroke 500cc, 1992, 1994, 1995, 1997 and 2000. Enduro world team champion: 1996, 1998, 1999 and 2003 (Finland).

Tibblin, Rolf (MX) Born Stockholm, Sweden, 7 May 1937. World champion: 500cc, 1962 and 1963. Winner of Motocross des Nations (Sweden) in 1961 and 1962.

Tormo, Ricardo (RR) Born Valencia, Spain, 7 September 1952. First GP: 50cc Spanish, 1973. First GP win: 50cc Swedish, 1977. World champion: 50cc, 1978 and 1981 (Bultaco). Tormo won 19 GPs and gained another 17 podium places. Serious injuries to both legs incurred in an accident while testing a new Derbi in 1984 forced him to retire. He died of leukaemia on 28 December 1998. Circuit Comunitat Valenciana is named in his honour.

Tortelli, Sebastien (MX) Born Agen, France, 19 August 1978. French champion: 125cc (supercross), 1995; 125cc, 1996. World champion: 125cc, 1996; 250cc, 1998. Known as 'Dyno'.

Toseland, James (RR) Born Sheffield, England, 5 October 1980. Toseland has won one World Superbike race and made another four podium finishes from 74 starts.

Tournadre, Jean-Louis (RR) Born Clermont, France, 17 November 1958. First GP: 250cc Czech, 1980. First GP win: 250cc French, 1982. World champion: 250cc, 1982 (Yamaha). Tournadre won one GP and finished on the podium another eight times.

Tragter, Pedro (MX) Born Netherlands. World champion: 125cc, 1993.

Triumph (RR) Founded by Siegfried Bettmann and Mauritz Schulte, both originally from Nürnberg, in 1888 in Coventry to make pedal cycles. Produced its first motorcycle in 1902. In 1936 the company was sold to Jack Sangster, the owner of Ariel Motorcycles. In 1951 it was in turn sold to BSA. The Triumph Bonneville was produced in 1959. The Triumph factory at Meriden closed in 1973 despite a workers' sit-in. The company went into liquidation in 1983. It was resurrected under John Bloor in 1990 with a new factory at Hinckley, Leicestershire.

250cc, GP class (RR) World Championship class 1949 onwards. Champion manufacturer: Honda (17), Yamaha (14), MV Agusta (5), Aprilia (5), Kawasaki (4), Moto Guzzi (3), Benelli (2), Harley-Davidson (1), Mondial (1), NSU (1). Not awarded in 1954 and 1976. Champion rider: Max Biaggi (4), Phil Read (4), Mike Hailwood (3), Anton Mang (3), Carlo Ubbiali (3), Walter Villa (3), Kork Ballington (2), Luca Cadalora (2), Werner Haas (2), Carlos Lavado (2), Alfonso Pons (2), Jim Redman (2), Bruno Ruffo (2), Dario Ambrosini (1), Dieter Braun (1), Loris Capirossi (1), Kel Carruthers (1), Rodney Gould (1), Tetsuya Harada (1), Olivier Jacque (1), Daijiro Kato (1), John Kocinski (1), Mario Lega (1), Enrico Lorenzetti (1), Marco Melandri (1), Herman Müller (1), Manuel Poggiali (1), Tarquinio Provini (1), Valentino Rossi (1), Jarno Saarinen (1), Cecil Sandford (1), Christian Sarron (1), Freddie Spencer (1), Jean-Louis Tournadre (1). Nationalities (total wins): Italian (21), British (9), German (7), French (3), Japanese (2), Rhodesian (2), South African (2), Spanish (2), United States (2), Venezuelan (2), Australian (1), Finnish (1), San Marino (1).

Ubbiali, Carlo (RR) Born Bergamo, Italy, 22

September 1929. First GP: 125cc Swiss, 1949. First GP win: 125cc Ulster, 1950. World champion: 125cc, 1951 (Mondial) and 1955-60 (MV Agusta); 250cc, 1956, 1959 and 1960 (MV Agusta). Ubbiali won 39 GPs and finished on the podium another 29 times.

Ukawa, Tohru   (RR) Born Chiba Prefecture, Japan, 18 May 1973. First GP: 250cc Japanese, 1994. First GP win: 250cc French, 1999. Won five GPs and gained another 34 podium places. He also won the Suzuka eight-hour race in 1997, 1998 and 2000 (Honda). Runner-up 250cc World Championship, 1999. Ukawa announced his retirement on 3 November 2003.

Uncini, Franco   (RR) Born Recanati, Italy, 9 March 1955. First GP: 250cc Dutch, 1976. First GP win: 250cc Nations, 1977. World champion: 500cc, 1982 (Suzuki). Uncini won seven GPs and took 14 more podium places.

URS   (RR) Founded by sidecar world champion Helmut Fath in 1964. World champion (sidecar) (rider): 1968 Fath. Closed in 1971.

van den Berk, John   (MX) Born Netherlands. World champion: 125cc, 1987; 250cc, 1988. Team manager (Netherlands), Motocross des Nations, 2003. Became head coach of the Royal Dutch Motorcyclist Federation.

van den Bosch, Thierry   (SX) Born Agen, France, 8 July 1974. European supermoto champion: 2000 and 2002. World supermoto champion: 2002.

van Kessel, Hank   (RR) Born Netherlands, 25 June 1946. First GP: 50cc Swedish, 1972. First GP win: 50cc French, 1974. World champion: 50cc, 1974 (Kreidler). He won seven GPs and finished on the podium a further 18 times.

van Praag, Lionel   (SP) Born Sydney, Australia, 17 December 1908. World champion: 1936 (inaugural champion), after race-off with Eric Langton. He came to Britain in 1931. Team represented: Wembley. Served in the RAF during World War II and was awarded the George Medal in 1941. He retired in 1954 and returned to Australia to run the International Speedway Club in Sydney. He died 19 May 1987 in Sydney.

Vehkonen, Pekka   (MX) Born Helsinki, Finland, 27 May 1964. World champion: 125cc, 1985.

Velocette   (RR) The firm of Veloce Ltd was founded in Hall Green, Birmingham, in 1904 by German immigrant Johannes Gütgemann, who subsequently anglicised his name to John Goodman. His sons Percy and Eugene and his grandsons Bertie and Peter were all involved in both testing and racing the firm's machines. The first motorcycle was produced in 1905. The 'Velocette', a smaller version of a 1911 VMC, was first produced in 1913. This name was eventually applied to all the machines produced by the company. Velocettes had a great deal of success at the IOM TTs of the late 1920s, 1930s and 1940s. The KTT model became the private racers' 'mount of choice' in the 350cc class. World champion (riders): (350cc) Frith 1949, Foster 1950. World champion (manufacturer): (350cc) 1949 and 1950. Along with many other British manufacturers the firm ran into problems in the late 1960s and the factory was closed on 5 February 1971.

Vermeulen, Chris   (RR) Born Brisbane, Australia, 19 June 1982. World champion Supersport: 2003. He has won four Supersport GPs and gained six further podium places.

Vesterinen, Yrjo   (TR) Born Kokkola, Finland, 7 December 1952. World outdoor champion: 1976-78.

Villa, Walter   (RR) Born Italy, 13 August 1943. First GP: 125cc West German, 1967. First GP win: 250cc Nations, 1974. World champion: 250cc, 1975-76 (Harley-Davidson); 350cc, 1976 (Harley-Davidson). Villa died in June 2002.

Vimond, Jacky   (MX) Born France, 18 July 1961. World champion: 250cc, 1986.

Vincent, Arnaud   (RR) Born Nancy, France, 30 November 1974. First GP: 125cc French, 1996. First GP win: 125cc Catalonian, 1999. World champion: 125cc, 2002 (Aprilia). Vincent has won seven GPs and finished on the podium a further 12 times.

Walker, Chris   (RR) Born Nottingham, England, 25 March 1972. Runner-up in British Superbike championship, 1997-2000.

Watanabe, Akira   (MX) Born Japan. World champion: 125cc, 1978.

Webster, Steve   (RR) Born York, England, 7 January 1960. First GP: sidecar British, 1983. First GP win: sidecar Belgian, 1986. Sidecar world champion 1987-89 (with Tony Hewitt for Yamaha), 1991 (with Gavin Simmons for LCR-Krauser), 1997-99 (with David James for Suzuki), 2000 and 2003 (with Paul Woodhead for Suzuki). Webster has won 51 GPs and finished on the podium a further 68 times. He was awarded an MBE in 1990.

Wigg, Simon   (SP) Born Aylesbury, England, 15 October 1960. World long track champion: 1985, 1989, 1990, 1993 and 1994. Teams represented: Weymouth, Birmingham, Cradley Heath, Oxford, Hackney, Bradford, Coventry, Exeter, King's Lynn. Wigg retired in 1998. He died from a brain tumour, aged 40, on 23 November 2000.

Wilkinson, Bluey   (SP) Born Millthorpe, Australia, 27 August 1911. Wilkinson came to Britain in 1927. World champion: 1938. Team represented: West Ham (1929-39). He retired in 1938. He was killed in a road accident on 27 July 1940 at Roes Bay, Australia.

Williams, Freddie   (SP) Born Port Talbot, Wales, 12 March 1926. World champion: 1950 and 1953 (first British rider to win two WC finals). Williams won the 1950 title without having passed his motorcycle driving test. His brother Ian (born Port Talbot, 4 August 1931) rode for Swindon.

Wiltshire, Todd   (SP) Born Sydney, Australia, 26 September 1968. Australian champion: 2001. Intercontinental champion: 1999. World team champion: 2000-02 (Australia). Teams represented: Wimbledon (1988-89), Reading (1990-91), Oxford (2000-01), Bydgoszcz (Poland), Vastervik (Sweden), Landshut (Germany). Known as 'The Freak'.

Woods, Stanley   (RR) Born Dublin, November 1903. Held the record of most TT wins (10) until passed by Mike Hailwood and Joey Dunlop. He rode for Cotton, Norton, Moto Guzzi and Velocette. Known as 'King of the TT'. He died 1993 in Downpatrick, Co. Down, Northern Ireland.

World Individual Speedway Championship   (SP) 1936-38, 1949 onwards. Since 1995, World Speedway GP. Winners : Ivan Mauger (6), Ove Fundin (5), Tony Rickardsson (5), Barry Briggs (4), Hans Nielsen (4), Erik Gundersen (3), Ole Olsen (3), Peter Craven (2), Ronnie Moore (2), Bruce Penhall (2), Freddie Williams (2), Jack Young (2), Peter Collins (1), Sam Ermolenko (1), Billy Hamill (1), Greg Hancock (1), Gary Havelock (1), Per Jonsson (1), Björn Knutsson (1), Michael Lee (1), Mark Loram (1), Anders Michanek (1), Jack Milne (1), Egon Muller (1), Jan O. Pedersen (1), Nicki Pedersen (1), Tommy Price (1), Jerzy Szczakiel (1), Lionel van Praag (1), Bluey Wilkinson (1).

Nationalities (total wins): Swedish (13), New Zealand (12), Danish (11), British (9), United States (6), Australian (4), German (1), Polish (1).

World Long Track Championship (SP) 1971 onwards. Winners: Simon Wigg (5), Karl Maier (4), Gerd Riss (4), Ivan Mauger (3), Egon Müller (3), Kelvin Tatum (3), Erik Gundersen (2), Robert Barth (1), Tommy Dunker (1), Marcel Gerhard (1), Michael Lee (1), Anders Michanek (1), Ole Olsen (1), Shawn Moran (1), Alois Wiesböck (1). Nationalities (total wins): German (14), British (9), Danish (3), New Zealand (3), Swedish (1), Swiss (1), United States (1).

World Pairs Championship (SP) 1968-93 (1968 and 1969 are considered unofficial). Amalgamated with World Team Championship in 1994. National wins: Denmark (8), Great Britain (7), Sweden (5), United States (3), New Zealand (2), Poland (1).

World Team Championship (SP) 1960 onwards. From 2001 classified as the Speedway World Cup. National wins: Denmark (11), Great Britain (9), Sweden (8), Poland (5), United States (5), Australia (4), New Zealand (1).

Wyglenda, Andrzej (SP) Born Poland, 4 May 1941. World pairs champion: 1971 (with Jerzy Szczakiel).

Xaus, Ruben (RR) Born Barcelona, Spain, 18 February 1978. World Superbike debut: Nürburgring 1988. First World Superbike win: Oschersleben, 2001. Xaus has won nine World Superbike races and made another 22 podium finishes from 77 starts. Raced in MotoGP in 2004.

Yamaha (RR) Founded by Torakusu Yamaha in 1888 as a producer of musical instruments. Yamaha began producing motorcycles in 1955 with the first racing machine built in 1961. World champion (riders): (125cc) Ivy 1967, Read 1968, Kent Anderson 1973 and 1974; (250cc) Read 1964, 1965, 1968 and 1971, Gould 1970, Saarinen 1972, Braun 1973, Tournadre 1982, Lavado 1983 and 1986, Sarron 1984, Kocinski 1990, Harada 1993, Jacque 2000; (350cc) Agostini 1974, Katayama 1977; (500cc) Agostini 1975, Roberts 1978-80, Lawson 1984, 1986 and 1988, Rainey 1990, 1991 and 1993; (sidecar) O'Dell 1977, Biland 1978, 1979, 1981 and 1983, Taylor 1980, Schwärzel 1982, Streuer 1984-86, Webster 1987, Abbott 2002. World champion (manufacturer): (125cc) 1967, 1968, 1973, 1974; (250cc) 1964, 1965, 1968, 1970-74, 1977, 1982-84, 1990, 2000; (350cc) 1973-77; (500cc) 1974, 1975, 1986-88, 1990, 1991, 1993 and 2000; 750cc, 1977-79; (sidecar) 1977-87.

Young, Jack (SP) Born Adelaide, Australia, 16 April 1924. World champion: 1951 (while riding for a second division team) and 1952 (the first rider to win twice). Teams represented: Edinburgh (1951), West Ham (1952). He died November 1987 in Adelaide.

Zundapp (RR) Founded in 1917 in Germany, initially to make gun parts. Stefan Dörflinger won the 80cc world title for Zundapp in 1984. A year later the company went into liquidation.

M
O
T
O
R
C
Y
C
L
I
N
G

MOTOR RACING

The petrol car was invented in 1888 by Karl Benz and it did not take long before cars were raced competitively. The first Grand Prix was held in France, near Le Mans, in 1906. The winner was Hungarian François Szisz in a Renault at an average speed of 117.93kph (73.3mph). The Indianapolis 500 began in 1911, as did the Monte Carlo Rally.

In 1923 the Le Mans 24-Hour race began and car racing became a universally accepted sport.

In 1950 both the Formula One World Championship and the NASCAR Championships began and today motor racing is among the most popular and well-rewarded sports in the world.

The following history of the sport, through biographies of famous drivers and records of race results, concentrates on the most popular arm of motor racing, Formula One, but other four-wheeled motor sports are also included.

Biographies

Alboreto, Michele   Born Milan, Italy, 23 December 1956. Made his debut for Tyrrell in the 1981 San Marino Grand Prix. Alboreto drove for Tyrrell from 1981 to 1983, gaining his maiden victory at the US Grand Prix in 1982. After two wins for the team he moved to Ferrari for whom he drove between 1984 and 1988, winning a further three races. In 1989 he returned to Tyrrell, but after five races that season moved to Lola for a further five. The following year saw him with Arrows, 1991 and 1992 with Footwork, 1993 back with Lola and 1994 with Minardi. After the Australian Grand Prix that year, his 194th, he retired. He scored a total of 186.5 points, with five wins, two pole positions and five fastest laps. In 1997 he won the Le Mans 24-Hour race. He died 25 April 2001 while testing for Le Mans in an Audi R8 on the Lausitzring circuit, Germany.

Alesi, Jean   Born Montfavet, France, 11 June 1964. After success at Formula 3000 Alesi made his debut for Tyrrell in the 1989 French Grand Prix, finishing fourth. He drove for Tyrrell (1989-90), Ferrari (1991-95), Benetton (1996-97), Sauber (1998-99) and Prost (2000-01), finishing his racing career with Jordan in 2001, although 2002 saw him as a test driver with McLaren. He competed in 201 Grands Prix, with a solitary win (Canada, 1995), two pole positions, four fastest laps and a career total of 241 points.

Amon, Chris   Born Bulls, New Zealand, 20 July 1943. Made his Formula One debut for Lola in the 1963 Belgian Grand Prix. After five Grands Prix for Lola he moved to Lotus for the Mexican Grand Prix that year. He drove for Lotus until 1965 and for Cooper in the 1966 French Grand Prix; the same year he won Le Mans. He then drove for Ferrari (1967-69), March (1970), Matra (1971-72), Tecno (1973) and Tyrrell (1973 Canadian Grand Prix only). Having entered his own Amon car at the 1974 Spanish Grand Prix but failed to finish, he drove for BRM in Canada and the United States in 1974, and for Ensign in Austria and Italy in 1975 and for eight races in 1976. He withdrew from the 1976 German Grand Prix after Niki Lauda's near-fatal crash and never raced again. Probably the best driver never to win a Grand Prix, he had three second places, five pole positions and three fastest laps in his 96 Grands Prix, in which he scored 83 points.

Anderson, Bob   Born Hendon, England, 19 May 1931. Former motorcycle racer, who won the Rome Grand Prix in 1963, the year he made his Formula One debut at Silverstone for Lola. He drove as a private entrant in a Brabham from 1964 to 1967, winning the Von Trips Memorial Trophy for most successful private entrant in 1964. That year he achieved his best result, third in the Austrian Grand Prix. In total he raced in 25 Grands Prix, scoring 8 points, before dying in a testing crash at Silverstone on 14 August 1967.

Andretti, Mario   Born Montona, Italy (now Croatia), 28 February 1940. Having emigrated to America in 1955 and become a US citizen, Andretti first entered Formula One for Lotus at the 1968 US Grand Prix. He drove occasionally until 1974, for Lotus (1968-69), March (1970), Ferrari (1971-72) and Parnelli (1974). Continuing for Parnelli in 1975, he then joined Lotus in 1976, staying with them until 1980 and winning the World Championship in 1978. In 1981 he moved to Alfa Romeo for his last full season, and the following year he drove one race for Williams and two for Ferrari, ending his career, after 128 races, at the 1982 United States Grand Prix. He won 12 races, had 17 poles and 10 fastest laps, and accumulated 180 points in that time. Outside Formula One he also won the Indianapolis 500 in 1969, the Indycar Championship four times (1965, 1966, 1969 and 1984), the Daytona 500 (1967) and the Sebring 12 Hours (1967, 1970 and 1972).

Andretti, Michael   Born Bethlehem, Pennsylvania, USA, 5 October 1962. Son of Mario, Michael achieved success in Indycar racing, winning the championship in 1991. McLaren were impressed enough to sign him for the 1993 season, but he found Formula One a struggle and left after only 13 races, ironically achieving his best result of third in his last race in Italy. He scored only 7 points overall.

Ascari, Alberto   Born Milan, Italy, 13 July 1918. The son of Antonio, a driver for Alfa Romeo in the 1920s, he won five Grands Prix in the 1940s before racing for Ferrari from 1950 to 1953. Winner of the World Championship in 1952 and 1953, he had nine straight Grand Prix wins straddling those seasons. In 1954 he drove for Maserati, Ferrari and Lancia, as well as winning the Mille Miglia, and 1955 saw him continue the partnership with Lancia. At the 1955 Monaco Grand Prix he drove into the harbour but survived, only to be killed in a testing accident at Monza four days later on 26 May 1955. In total he drove 32 Grands Prix, winning 13, gaining 14 poles and 13 fastest laps and scoring 140.14 points.

Attwood, Dickie   Born Wolverhampton, England, 4 April 1940. Made his debut for Lotus in the 1965 Monaco Grand Prix, but at the end of that season was dropped. Attwood drove one race for Cooper in 1967, before driving for BRM in 1968. His final Formula One drive came at Monaco in 1969, when he temporarily replaced Jochen Rindt at Lotus. In all he drove 17 races, scoring 11 points. In 1970 he won the Le Mans 24-Hour race.

Baghetti, Giancarlo   Born Milan, Italy, 25 December 1934. Made a spectacular debut for Ferrari, winning the 1961 French Grand Prix, but would never win another race. After drives for Ferrari in 1961 and 1962, he drove for ATS in 1963 and BRM in 1964 but then only made guest appearances at the Italian Grand Prix, for Brabham (1965), Ferrari (1966) and Lotus (1967). He drove 21 races in total, garnering one fastest lap to go with his solitary win, and scored 14 points. He died 27 November 1995.

Barrichello, Rubens   Born São Paulo, Brazil, 23 May 1972. Joined Jordan for the 1993 season and spent four seasons with them, gaining the team's first pole position. Having moved to the new Stewart team in 1997, he then joined Ferrari in 2000 as number two to Michael Schumacher.

Bell, Derek   Born Pinner, Middlesex, England, 31 October 1941. Made his debut for Ferrari at the 1968 Italian Grand Prix, and also drove for the team in America that year, failing to finish on both occasions. He subsequently had sporadic drives for McLaren at the 1969 British Grand Prix, Brabham at the 1970 Belgian, Surtees at the 1970 American, where he got his best finish of sixth, and the 1971 British Grand Prix. He drove for Tecno for two races in 1972 and finally for Surtees at the 1974 German Grand Prix, his ninth and last. However, he was rather more successful in sports car racing, winning Le Mans five times and the World Championship twice.

Bellof, Stefan   Born Giessen, Germany, 20 November 1957. Raced for Tyrrell in the 1984 and 1985 seasons in 20 races. Although he finished third at Monaco in 1984 this result was later stripped from him when the team was disqualified for the year, as were the five points he had gained. His best official finish was fourth at the 1985 United States Grand Prix and he had managed four points up to the Dutch Grand Prix that year. A week later, on 1 September 1985, he was competing at Spa in a sports car race, having been sports car world champion in 1984, and was killed in an accident there.

Berger, Gerhard   Born Austria, 27 August 1959. Made his debut for ATS at the 1984 Austrian Grand Prix, driving in four races for them that year. Berger moved to Arrows for the 1985 season and then to Benetton in 1986, achieving his first win in Mexico that year, before joining Ferrari in 1987. He joined McLaren in 1990 for a further three years before returning to Ferrari in 1993 for another three-year spell. He rejoined Benetton in 1996. He raced in 210 Grands Prix, with 10 victories, 12 pole positions, 21 fastest laps and a total of 384 points, coming third in the Drivers' Championship on three occasions. After retiring he worked for BMW as director of motor sport.

Bira, Prince   Born Prince Birabongse Bhanuban, Bangkok, Thailand, 15 July 1914. A Siamese prince and a successful private owner, he made his Formula One debut at the 1950 British Grand Prix for Maserati, for whom he drove in four races that year.

He drove for OSCA at the 1951 Spanish Grand Prix, two races each for Simca and Gordini in 1952, three for Connaught and one for Maserati in 1953, and six for Maserati in 1954. In his 19-race career he scored 8 points with a best finish of fourth achieved twice (Switzerland in 1950, France in 1954). He died 23 December 1985.

Blundell, Mark   Born Barnet, Hertfordshire, England, 8 April 1966. Having driven for Brabham in 1991 Blundell was dropped for 1992, however his win in the Le Mans 24-Hour race earned him a place with Ligier for 1993. In 1994 he joined Tyrrell and he drove all but two races of the 1995 season for McLaren as a replacement for Nigel Mansell. Dropped in favour of David Coulthard for 1996, he eventually raced Indycars as he was unable to find a further Formula One drive. In a total of 61 races he scored 32 points, with a best finish of third on three occasions, and tenth place in the Drivers' Championship twice.

Boutsen, Thierry   Born Brussels, Belgium, 13 July 1957. Made his debut for Arrows at the 1983 Belgian Grand Prix, replacing Chico Serra. Boutsen stayed with the team until 1986, switching to Benetton in 1987. After two years there he moved to Williams in 1989, departing to Ligier in 1991 for another two seasons. In all he drove 162 Grands Prix, winning three times while with Williams, with one pole position, one fastest lap and a total of 132 points. His best position in the Drivers' Championship was fourth in 1988.

Brabham, Jack   Born Sydney, Australia, 2 April 1926. Made his debut at the 1955 British Grand Prix in a Cooper, driving for Maserati in 1956 before returning to Cooper for a number of races in 1957. He stayed with Cooper until 1961, becoming the first man to win the Drivers' Championship in a rear-engined car in 1959 and retaining the title in 1960. Brabham moved to Lotus in 1962, but in mid-season launched his own team in Germany. He drove for his own team until 1970, in 1966 becoming the first person to win a race, and later a Drivers' Championship, in a car of his own design. In all he drove in 126 Grands Prix, with 14 victories, 13 pole positions and 12 fastest laps, gaining 261 points and three championships. He later sold his team. His sons David, Geoffrey and Gary all raced.

Brise, Tony   Born Dartford, Kent, England, 28 March 1952. Made his debut with Williams at the 1975 Spanish Grand Prix as a temporary replacement for Jacques Laffite, before signing for Hill with whom he saw out the season, driving in ten races in total that year. A best finish of sixth in Sweden garnered him his solitary championship point. His career was cut short when he died in the plane crash that ended Graham Hill's life on 29 November 1975.

Brooks, Tony   Born Dunkinfield, Cheshire, England, 25 February 1932. Having won at Syracuse with a Connaught in 1955, the first Grand Prix win in a British car since 1932, he made his Formula One debut at the 1956 British Grand Prix for BRM. Brooks drove for Vanwall in 1957 and 1958 before switching to Ferrari for the 1959 season. He was at Cooper in 1960 and BRM in 1961, the final race of that season being his 38th and last. In that time he had won six races, with four pole positions and three fastest laps, gaining 75 points with a best Drivers' Championship placing of second in 1959.

Brundle, Martin   Born King's Lynn, Norfolk, England, 1 June 1959. Made his debut for Tyrrell in the 1984 Brazilian Grand Prix, finishing fifth but subsequently saw his results for that year, including a second place in the US Grand Prix, annulled when Tyrrell were disqualified from the championship. After missing the latter half of 1984 he continued with Tyrrell for the whole of 1985 and 1986, before moving to Zakspeed for the 1987 season. In 1988 he was without a Formula One drive, guesting for Williams in Belgium and winning the Sports Car World Championship, before he returned with Brabham in 1989 and 1991. He moved to Benetton in 1992, Ligier in 1993 and McLaren in 1994, returning to Ligier in 1995 – as a replacement during the season for Aguri Suzuki – and driving for Jordan in 1996. In total he drove in 158 Grands Prix, with a best place of second in Italy in 1992 and Monaco in 1994, scoring 97 points with a best Drivers' Championship placing of sixth in 1992. He also won Le Mans in 1990, and after retiring became a respected commentator for British television's coverage of the sport.

Burns, Richard   Born Reading, Berkshire, England, 17 January 1971. Made his debut in the World Rally Championship of 1990 at the RAC Rally. As at the end of 2003 he has competed in 77 world rallies, with ten wins. He became world rally champion in 2002. His co-driver is Robert Reid.

Button, Jenson   Born Frome, Somerset, England, 19 January 1980. After a race-off with Bruno Junquiera, Button was signed by Williams for the 2000 season, and had a good year, being voted young driver of the year by his peers. Even so, the signing of Juan Pablo Montoya meant that he lost his place for 2001 and was loaned for two seasons to Benetton (who were renamed Renault in 2002). Being surplus to requirements at both Williams and Renault, at the end of 2002 he moved to British American Racing (BAR) for 2003, and is team leader in 2004. He had his first podium finish in the Malaysian GP, placing third, and bettered that result at Imola with a second place after starting on pole.

Castellotti, Eugenio   Born Milan, Italy, 10 October 1930. Made his debut for Lancia at the 1955 Argentinian Grand Prix, but after the team folded in mid-season he continued for Ferrari, and drove for the team until he was killed in a testing crash in Modena on 14 March 1957. In Castellotti's 14 races his best place was second twice, in Monaco (1955) and France (1956), and he had one pole while accruing 19.5 points. His 12 points in 1955 gave him third place in the Drivers' Championship that year. He also won the Mille Miglia in 1956.

Chimeri, Ettore   Born Cuba, 4 June 1921. A Venezuelan national, Chimeri drove for Maserati in the 1960 Argentinian Grand Prix, retiring with exhaustion after 23 laps, and died 20 days later on 27 February 1960.

Chiron, Louis   Born Monaco, 3 August 1899. First drove in Grands Prix in 1923. He competed for Maserati in the inaugural Formula One World Championship in 1950, and in the first two races of 1951, before finishing the season with Talbot. In 1953 he drove in France and Italy for OSCA, and in 1955 for Lancia in Monaco, finishing sixth in his 15th and last Formula One Grand Prix. In that race he became the oldest driver to start a Grand Prix. His best finish was third in Monaco in 1950, which gave him his only points score of four. Chiron also won the Monte Carlo Rally in 1954 and helped organise the race, along with the Monaco Grand Prix, after his retirement. He died 22 June 1979.

Clark, Jim   Born Kilmany, Scotland, 4 March 1936.

One of the greats of Formula One, he made his debut for Lotus in the 1960 Dutch Grand Prix, and would drive for the team throughout his 72-race career. In that time he had 25 victories (including six straight wins in 1965, during which he also won the Indianapolis 500), 33 poles and 28 fastest laps, accruing 274 points and winning the Drivers' Championship in 1963 and 1965. After winning the South African Grand Prix in 1968, he was killed in a Formula Two race at Hockenheim on 7 April that year.

Collins, Peter   Born Kidderminster, Worcestershire, England, 6 November 1931. He drove for HWM in 1952 and 1953, then in the British and Italian Grands Prix of 1954 for Vanwall and 1955 for Maserati, before getting a full season's drive in 1956 and 1957 with Lancia-Ferrari. Continuing with Ferrari in 1958, he had a fatal accident at the Nürburgring on 3 August 1958, cutting short a career of 32 races, in which he had three victories (including his last completed race, the 1958 British Grand Prix) and scored 47 points, coming third in the Drivers' Championship in 1956.

Coulthard, David   Born Twynholm, Scotland, 27 March 1971. Made his debut for Williams at the 1994 Spanish Grand Prix, taking the seat left vacant after Ayrton Senna's fatal crash until Nigel Mansell's return later in the season. Kept on at Williams in 1995, he moved to McLaren for the 1996 season, and has been with the team ever since. Coulthard has won many Grands Prix and pole positions but has so far been thwarted for the championship by the brilliance of Michael Schumacher.

Courage, Piers   Born Colchester, Essex, England, 27 May 1942. A member of the brewing family, he made his debut driving a Formula Two Lotus at the 1966 German Grand Prix. He drove for Lotus in 1967's season-opening South African Grand Prix and for BRM in Monaco, but had to wait a further year for another opportunity in the BRM, driving for most of the 1968 season for the team. Switching to Brabham in 1969, he then moved to De Tomaso for 1970 but four races in at Zandvoort perished on 21 June in a fatal accident in his 28th Grand Prix. In that time he had achieved a best finish of second twice (Monaco and United States in 1969) and scored 20 points, 16 of these in 1969 when he was eighth in the Drivers' Championship.

Dalmas, Yannick   Born Toulon, France, 28 July 1961. Made his debut for Lola in the 1987 Mexican Grand Prix, staying with the team for 1988 but only driving for them at San Marino in 1989. Moving to AGS in 1990 brought little further success and he moved to sports cars, becoming sports car world champion in 1992 and winning Le Mans in 1992, 1994 and 1995. Dalmas briefly returned to Formula One with Larrousse in 1994 for two races. The Portuguese Grand Prix that year was his 24th and last, in which time his best finish had been fifth in Australia in 1987, but as he was not entered for the whole season he was ineligible to score points, and so ended up pointless.

de Angelis, Elio   Born Rome, Italy, 26 March 1958. Made his debut with Shadow in the 1979 season, moving to Lotus in 1980 and staying with the team for six seasons. Switching to Brabham in 1986, he drove in the first four races that season before being killed in testing at the Paul Ricard circuit on 15 May, the Monaco Grand Prix four days earlier proving to be his 108th and last. In that time he won twice (Austria in 1982 and San Marino in 1985), with three poles and a total of 122 points, and a best placing in the Drivers' Championship of third in 1984.

de Beaufort, Carel Godin Born Netherlands, 10 April 1934. Having made his debut in a Formula Two car for Porsche in the 1957 German Grand Prix, de Beaufort drove for the team twice in 1958 and once in 1959, as well as a further race for Maserati that year and one for Cooper in 1960. In 1961, 1962 and 1963 he found a more regular drive with Porsche, but his last Grand Prix was for the team in the Netherlands in 1964, as he crashed in practice for the German Grand Prix and died of his injuries the day after the race on 3 August 1964. Notable for driving without shoes, he drove in 28 Grands Prix with a best position of sixth on four occasions, gaining him 4 points in total.

de Cesaris, Andrea Born Rome, Italy, 31 May 1959. Made his debut for Alfa Romeo in the 1980 Canadian Grand Prix, also driving for the team in the next, and season-ending, race in America. He moved to McLaren in 1981, but returned to Alfa Romeo for 1982 and 1983. Driving for Ligier in 1984 and 1985, he failed to complete the 1985 season, being dropped after the Dutch Grand Prix. He then drove for Minardi (1986), Brabham (1987), Rial (1988), Dallara (1989, 1990), the newly formed Jordan (1991), and Tyrrell (1992, 1993), while in 1994 he drove two races for Jordan and then moved to Sauber. Dropped for the final two races of the season, the European Grand Prix that year proved to be his last. Despite one pole position and one fastest lap his best finish was second twice (Germany and South Africa in 1983); his 208 Grands Prix are a record number for a driver without a win. He scored a total of 59 points, with a best Drivers' Championship placing of eighth in 1983.

de Fillipis, Maria Teresa Born Italy, 11 November 1926. The first woman to compete in Formula One, her first Grand Prix start was for the Maserati team in the Belgian Grand Prix of 1958 where she was placed tenth. She later drove in the Portuguese and Italian Grands Prix, but failed to finish.

de Tomaso, Alessandro Born Buenos Aires, Argentina, 10 July 1928. De Tomaso drove for Ferrari in the 1957 Argentinian Grand Prix, coming ninth, and for Cooper in the 1959 US Grand Prix, failing to finish. Settling in Italy, he constructed racing cars and supercars for the road.

Diniz, Pedro Born Sao Paulo, Brazil, 22 May 1970. After seasons in Formula Ford (1989), South American Formula Three (1990/91) and European Formula 3000 (1992-94), he made his Formula One debut with Forti for the 1995 season, moving to Ligier in 1996 and Arrows in 1997. After two seasons with the team he spent a further two with Sauber before being dropped at the end of 2000 after 99 Grands Prix. His best finish was fifth twice (Luxembourg in 1997 and Belgium in 1998) and he accumulated a total of 10 points in his career.

Fabi, Teo Born Milan, Italy, 3 September 1955. Fabi drove for Toleman in the 1982 season, making his debut at San Marino after failing to qualify in the three earlier races, but had to sit out 1983, returning with Brabham in 1984. He returned to Toleman in 1985 before joining the newly formed Benetton team in 1986, driving with them for two seasons. The Australian Grand Prix of 1987 proved to be his 64th and last, in which time he had three pole positions and two fastest laps, but only managed a best finish of third twice (US in 1984 and Austria in 1987), scoring a total of 23 points with a best Drivers'

Championship placing of 9th in 1987. He became sports car world champion in 1991.

Fagioli, Luigi Born Osimo, Italy, 9 June 1898. Fagioli drove for Alfa Romeo in 1950, finishing second in four races, third in another and only failing to finish at Monaco when he was caught up in the aftermath of Giuseppe Farina's crash on the first lap. Sharing an Alfa Romeo with Fangio, he won the 1951 French Grand Prix, becoming the oldest driver to win a Formula One race in the process. This proved to be his seventh and last Grand Prix, in which time he had netted 32 points and come third in the 1950 Drivers' Championship. He died after a crash in practice at Monaco, 20 June 1952.

Fangio, Juan Manuel Born Balcarce, Argentina, 24 June 1911. One of the greats of Formula One, he drove for Alfa Romeo in the 1950 and 1951 seasons, missed 1952 through injury but returned with Maserati in 1953. He started with Maserati in 1954 but switched to Mercedes because they had the better car, staying with the team until 1955 when they withdrew from Formula One. He moved to Lancia-Ferrari in 1956 but returned to Maserati in 1957, driving a Maserati for Scuderia Sud Americana in Argentina in 1958 and a privately entered Maserati in the 1958 French Grand Prix. This was his 51st and last Grand Prix as he retired after the race. Helped by picking the team with the strongest car during his career, he notched up a remarkable 24 victories in his races, with 29 poles and 23 fastest laps, accumulating 277.14 points and winning the Drivers' Championship in 1951 and 1954-7. He died 17 July 1995 in Balcarce, Argentina.

Farina, Giuseppe Born Turin, Italy, 30 October 1906. 'Nino' drove for Alfa Romeo in 1950, winning the first Drivers' Championship, and continued with the team in 1951 before switching to Ferrari in 1952. After two full seasons he drove only the first two races of 1954 and the first three of 1955 for the team. The Belgian Grand Prix that year was his 33rd and the last of his career, in which he had five wins, five poles and five fastest laps, accumulating a total of 127.33 points. He died 30 June 1966 in a road accident in Aiguebelle, France.

Fisichella, Giancarlo Born Rome, Italy, 14 January 1973. After three years in Italian Formula Three from 1992, winning the championship in 1994, Fisichella joined Minardi as a test driver in 1995 and drove in eight races for the team in the following season, before becoming Ferrari's test driver. He also won the 1996 Bologna F1 Supersprint with Benetton, and his success led to him joining Jordan for the 1997 season. He switched to Benetton in 1998, staying four seasons before rejoining Jordan in 2002, swapping seats with Jarno Trulli who went in the opposite direction. His maiden win came in 2003 in Brazil. He has also had one pole and one fastest lap in his 123-race career to date, scoring a total of 94 points with a best placing in the Drivers' Championship of sixth in 2000. He drives for Sauber in 2004.

Fittipaldi, Christian Born São Paulo, Brazil, 18 January 1971. The son of Wilson and nephew of Emerson, he was European Formula 3000 champion in 1991, leading to a drive for Minardi in 1992 and 1993 before he switched to Footwork in 1994. In his 40 races his best finish was fourth on three occasions and he scored a total of 12 points. Subsequently he switched to Indycar racing.

Fittipaldi, Emerson Born São Paulo, Brazil, 12 December 1946. Made his debut for Lotus in the 1970

British Grand Prix, staying with the team until 1973, when he moved to McLaren. After two seasons at McLaren (1974, 1975) he moved to his brother Wilson's team, where he spent five seasons as a lesser force in Formula One before retiring at the end of 1980 after 144 Grands Prix. In that time he had won 14 races, with six poles and six fastest laps, winning the Drivers' Championship in 1972 (becoming the youngest driver to do so) and 1974, and accumulating 284 points. Subsequently he drove in Indycar racing, winning the Indianapolis 500 and the championship in 1989 and the Indianapolis 500 in 1993.

Fittipaldi, Wilson   Born São Paulo, Brazil, 25 December 1943. Made his debut for Brabham at the 1972 Spanish Grand Prix, continuing with the team until the end of 1973. Having no drive in 1974 he founded his own team, Fittipaldi, for the 1975 season and drove his own car that season, before retiring from driving to manage the team, which stayed in Formula One until 1982. In his 35 Grands Prix as a driver his best finish was fifth in Germany in 1973, the year in which he scored his sole 3 points in Formula One.

Frentzen, Heinz-Harald   Born Mönchengladbach, West Germany, 18 May 1967. After competing in Japanese Formula 3000 in 1992 and acting as a test driver for Tyrrell in 1993 he joined Sauber for the 1994 season, staying there three years before replacing Damon Hill at Williams in 1997. After two years at Williams he was dropped and moved to Jordan in 1999, finding the success that had eluded him at Williams and would elude him afterwards. Jordan dropped him after 11 races in 2001, his third season with the team, and he finished the season with Prost, replacing Jean Alesi who had taken his place at Jordan. With the Prost team quitting at the end of 2001 he moved to Arrows, but they had financial problems and after 11 races of the 2002 season were unable to take further part. After guesting for Sauber in America he rejoined Arrows for 2003, but failed to keep his seat for 2004 and may have driven his last race. In his 156 Grands Prix he had three wins, two pole positions and six fastest laps, accruing 174 points in total with a best placing in the Drivers' Championship of third in 1999.

Frere, Paul   Born Le Havre, France 30 January 1917. Belgian national, a journalist and technical writer, who raced as an adjunct to that career. After winning the 1952 Grand Prix des Frontières he made his Formula One debut at the 1952 Belgian Grand Prix in a HW car. He drove a further race for them and one for Simca-Gordini that year, making two appearances for HW in 1953, three for Gordini in 1954 and two for Ferrari in 1955. He drove for Lancia-Ferrari at the 1956 Belgian Grand Prix, in which he achieved his best placing of second. In his 11 Grands Prix he scored a total of 11 points. He later won Le Mans in 1960 in a Ferrari.

Gachot, Bertrand   Born Luxembourg, 23 December 1962. French national, who, after winning the British Formula Ford 2000 in 1986 and finishing runner-up in British Formula Three in 1987, joined the new Onyx team in 1989. It was not until seven races into the season in France that he qualified for a race, and later that year he was dropped from the team and moved to Rial for the last two races, failing to qualify in either. Moving to Coloni in 1990, he failed to qualify for a single race, but managed to move to Jordan in 1991. However, while he won Le Mans in a Mazda that year he was also sentenced to six

months in prison for assaulting a taxi driver in Britain the previous winter and lost his seat with the team, giving Michael Schumacher his break. Returning in Australia with Lola, he failed to qualify. He moved to Larrousse in 1992, but with little success and 1993 saw him without a drive. His return came in 1994 as part-owner of Pacific, with whom he spent two unsuccessful seasons. The 1995 Australian Grand Prix proved to be his 47th and last. His best place was fifth in Canada in 1991, and he scored a total of 4 points.

Galicia, Davina   Born Great Britain, 13 August 1946. Former British ski champion who became a Formula One Grand Prix driver. The only British woman to race in Formula One, in 1976 Galicia raced for the Surtees team, and in 1978 for the Hesketh team. Unfortunately she never led a race or scored any championship points.

Ganley, Howden   Born Hamilton, New Zealand, 24 December 1941. After competing in Formula Three he raced for BRM in 1971 and 1972, moving to Williams in 1973 and March in 1974. However he left the team after two races of that season, and after failing to qualify in Germany for the Maki team and crashing badly in practice he retired after 35 Grands Prix. In that time his best place was fourth twice (United States in 1971, Germany in 1972) and he scored 10 points. He then established the Tiga team with Tim Schenken and later served as secretary of the British Racing Drivers' Club.

Gethin, Peter   Born Ewell, Surrey, England, 21 February 1940. Son of jockey Ken Gethin, he made his debut for McLaren in the 1970 Dutch Grand Prix, staying with the team in 1971 but switching to BRM for the last four races of the season. He stayed with BRM for 1972 but only guested for them in Canada in 1973. His 30th and last Grand Prix was a guest appearance for the Embassy Lola team in the 1974 British Grand Prix, when he retired on the first lap through discomfort. He won a single Grand Prix, in Italy in 1971, when he set records for the fastest average speed (only beaten in 2003) and closest finish, winning by 0.01secs. He scored a total of 11 points, and later went into driver management and ran a driving school at Goodwood.

Hailwood, Mike   Born Birmingham, England, 2 April 1940. The former 500cc motorcycle world champion made less of an impact in Formula One racing. The best he managed was leading a Grand Prix for five laps and finishing runner-up in one. He died in a road accident on 23 March 1981.

Häkkinen, Mika   Born Helsinki, Finland, 28 September 1968. World champion in 1998 and 1999 (both with McLaren-Mercedes), he made his Formula One debut in the 1991 US Grand Prix driving a Lotus-Judd. His career statistics are 20 Grand Prix wins and 26 pole positions.

Hawthorn, Mike   Born John Michael Hawthorn, Mexborough, Yorkshire, England, 10 April 1929. Made his Formula One debut in the 1952 Belgian Grand Prix and was world champion in 1958. Hawthorn had three Grand Prix victories and four pole positions from 47 starts. He died in a road accident, 22 January 1959.

Herbert, Johnny   Born Brentwood, Essex, England, 25 June 1964. Made his Formula One debut in the 1989 Brazilian GP driving a Tyrrell, after becoming British Formula Three champion in 1987. Herbert had 161 Grand Prix starts and three wins, achieving no poles but leading races four times. He also won the Le Mans 24-Hour race in 1991.

Hill, Damon Born Hampstead, London, England, 17 September 1960. Son of Graham Hill, he made his Formula One debut in the British Grand Prix in 1992, driving for Williams. He was world champion in 1996 driving for Williams-Renault. Hill's last Grand Prix was the Italian GP at Monza in 1999. He drove in 99 Grands Prix, with 22 victories, 20 pole positions and 19 fastest laps.

Hill, Graham Born Norman Graham Hill, Hampstead, London, England, 15 February 1929. Made his Formula One debut in the 1958 Monaco Grand Prix. His first win was the Dutch Grand Prix in 1962. World champion in 1962 (with BRM) and 1968 (with Lotus). Hill had a career total of 14 Grand Prix wins. He died in a plane crash along with Tony Brise, 29 November 1975.

Hill, Phil Born Miami, Florida, USA, 20 April 1927. Made his Formula One debut in the 1958 French Grand Prix. World champion in 1961. Hill is the only American-born driver to win the Formula One World Championship.

Hulme, Denny Born Nelson, New Zealand, 18 June 1936. Made his Formula One debut in the 1965 Monaco Grand Prix. World Champion in 1967, he was also CanAm Series champion in 1968 and 1970. He died of a heart attack, 4 October 1992.

Hunt, James Born Belmont, Surrey, England, 29 August 1947. Made his Formula One debut in the 1973 Monaco Grand Prix for March. World champion in 1976 driving a McLaren, Hunt's career statistics include 10 Grand Prix victories from 93 starts, with 14 pole positions. He died of a heart attack, 15 June 1993.

Ickx, Jacky Born Brussels, Belgium, 1 January 1945. Made his Formula One debut in the German Grand Prix of 1996 driving a Matra. He drove in 116 Grands Prix, gaining eight victories and 13 pole positions. Ickx was runner-up in the 1969 championship, driving for Brabham, and again in 1970, driving for Ferrari. Formula Two champion in 1967, he also won six Le Mans 24-Hour races (1969, 1975-77, 1981, 1982).

Irvine, Eddie Born Bangor, Northern Ireland, 10 November 1965. Made his Formula One debut in Japan in 1993 driving for Jordan. Irvine won four Grands Prix from 147 starts, finishing second in the 1999 championship (for Ferrari). Retired after the 2002 season.

Jones, Alan Born Melbourne, Australia, 2 October 1946. Made his Formula One debut for Hesketh in the 1975 Spanish Grand Prix. World champion in 1980 driving a Williams, Jones raced in a total of 116 Grands Prix, attaining 12 victories and six pole positions.

Lauda, Niki Born Vienna, Austria, 22 February 1949. His Formula One debut was in the 1971 Austrian Grand Prix, driving a March. British Formula Two champion in 1972, he was Formula One world champion in 1975 and 1977 (for Ferrari) and 1984 (for McLaren). In his 170 Grands Prix he managed 25 victories and had 24 pole positions. Lauda had an horrific crash at the Nürburgring, Germany, in 1976 and after hitting an earth-bank, his car burst into flames and was hit by two other cars, one head-on. He was badly burned but made a miraculous recovery. He retired for the 1980 and 1981 seasons but came back to win a third title before starting his own team.

Lombardi, Lella Born Rome, Italy, 26 March 1943. Made her first Grand Prix start in the South African Grand Prix in 1975, driving a Williams. Lombardi's best performance was sixth place in the 1975 Spanish Grand Prix where she scored 0.5 championship points, her only points tally. She drove in 12 Grands Prix. She died of cancer, 3 March 1992.

McLaren, Bruce Born Auckland, New Zealand, 30 August 1937. Made his Formula One debut in the 1958 German Grand Prix for Cooper. McLaren won four Grands Prix and was runner-up in the 1960 Formula One Drivers' Championship and third in 1969. In 1966 he began to use the car he had himself developed and which is now established as one of the greatest in the sport. He died as a result of a testing crash at Goodwood, 2 June 1970.

McRae, Colin Born Lanark, Scotland, 5 August 1968. Made his world rally debut in the Swedish rally of 1987 driving a Vauxhall Nova and won the World Rally Championship in 1995 driving a Subaru Impreza. Undoubtedly one of the most talented drivers of modern times, McRae attained a record 25 world rally victories (equal with Carlos Sainz), although he is currently without a drive for 2004. Derek Ringer is his usual co-driver.

Mäkinen, Tommi Born Puuppola, Finland, 26 June 1964. Having made his world rally debut in the 1000 Lakes rally of 1987, driving a Lancia Delta, Mäkinen won the World Rally Championship in four consecutive years (1996-99), driving a Mitsubishi Lancer with co-driver Risto Mannisenmaki. Now retired.

Mansell, Nigel Born Upton-on-Severn, Worcestershire, England, 8 August 1953. Made his Formula One debut in the 1980 Austrian Grand Prix for Lotus. World champion in 1992 driving a Williams, he was CART champion and Rookie of the Year in 1993. Mansell's 187 Formula One starts gleaned 31 victories and 32 pole positions.

Mass, Jochen Born Munich, Germany, 30 September 1940. Made his Formula One debut in the Great British Grand Prix. German racing/sports car champion in 1985.

Montoya, Juan Pablo Born Bogota, Colombia, 20 September 1975. One of the few top drivers who does not live in Monaco, choosing to live in Miami, Florida, and the UK for parts of the year. Montoya joined Williams-BMW in 2001, debuting in the Australian Grand Prix. He took the seat of Britain's Jenson Button but immediately proved that it was the correct decision. He is several times a Grand Prix winner and is always among the favourites for every race he competes in.

Moss, Stirling Born Stirling Caulfield Moss, London, England, 17 September 1929. Made his Formula One debut in the 1951 Swiss Grand Prix and was British Formula Two champion in 1959. Of his 66 Grand Prix starts he can boast 16 victories and 16 pole positions. Runner-up in the World Drivers' Championship four consecutive years (1955-58) and third in 1959 and 1960, Moss is often referred to as being the greatest driver never to have won the world title. His near-fatal crash at Goodwood in 1962 caused severe head injuries and although he eventually made a full recovery, he decided to retire.

Oliver, Jackie Born Romford, Essex, England, 14 August 1942. Made his Formula One debut in the German Grand Prix in 1967. He won the Le Mans 24-Hour race in 1969 and was CanAm series champion in 1974.

Palmer, Jonathan Born London, England, 7 October 1956. Made his Formula One debut in the 1983 European Grand Prix for Williams. British Formula Three champion in 1981 and Formula Two champion in 1983, Palmer never made a successful transition to Formula One, scoring a mere 14 points in his 84 Grands Prix. A qualified doctor, he became an articulate and informed broadcaster on the sport.

Piquet, Nelson   Born Rio de Janeiro, Brazil, 17 August 1952. Made his Formula One debut in the German Grand Prix of 1978 and was world champion in 1981, 1983 and 1987. Piquet's 204 Grand Prix starts included 23 victories and 24 pole positions.

Prost, Alain   Born Lorette, France, 25 February 1955. French Formula Three champion in 1978 and 1979 and European Formula Three champion in 1979. Prost made his Formula One debut in Argentina, 1980, driving a McLaren. World champion in 1985, 1986, 1989 (all with McLaren) and 1993 (with Williams). 198 Grand Prix starts included 51 victories and 33 pole positions. Nicknamed 'The Professor' for his calm, methodical driving style, he always managed to be in the right place at the right time, and is a true great of the sport.

Purley, David   Born Bognor Regis, Sussex, England, 26 January 1945. Made his Formula One debut in the 1973 Monaco Grand Prix and was Shellsport Group 8 champion 1976. He died in a plane crash, 2 July 1985.

Ratzenberger, Roland   Born Salzburg, Austria, 4 July 1962. Made his debut in the Pacific Grand Prix of 1994, his only start. He died in a crash while qualifying for the San Marino Grand Prix at Imola, Italy, 30 April 1994.

Regazzoni, Clay   Born Gianclaudio Regazzoni, Lugano, Switzerland, 5 September 1939. Made his Formula One debut in the 1970 Dutch Grand Prix driving for Ferrari, becoming Formula Two champion the same year. Regazzoni had 132 Grand Prix starts, five wins and five pole positions.

Reutemann, Carlos   Born Sante Fé, Argentina, 12 April 1942. Made his Formula One debut at his home Grand Prix in 1972, driving for Brabham. His career totals of 146 starts, 12 victories and six pole positions make him one of the best drivers never to win a championship.

Revson, Peter   Born New York, USA, 27 February 1939. Revson made his debut at the Belgian Grand Prix of 1964. He had 30 Grand Prix starts, two wins, and one pole position. Always an underrated driver, mainly because he came from a wealthy family who owned the Revlon cosmetic empire, he died while testing for the South African Grand Prix, 22 March 1974.

Rindt, Jochen   Born Mainz, Germany, 18 April 1942. Austrian national, made his Formula One debut in the Austrian Grand Prix of 1964 and was British Formula Two champion in 1967. Rindt made 60 Grand Prix starts, with six wins and ten pole positions. He died during practice for the Italian Grand Prix, 5 September 1970, but had a winning lead in the World Drivers' Championship, the first and only posthumous champion to date.

Rosberg, Keke   Born Keijo Rosberg, Stockholm, Sweden, 6 December 1948. Finnish national. Made his first Formula One start in the South African Grand Prix of 1978. With 114 Grand Prix starts and five wins, his best year was in 1982 for Williams when he won the Swiss Grand Prix and finished high up in almost all the other races to win the World Drivers' Championship.

Scheckter, Jody   Born East London, South Africa, 29 January 1950. His Formula One debut was in the United States Grand Prix, 1972. Scheckter had ten Grand Prix wins and won the World Championship in 1979, driving for Ferrari. He later became a

world *Superstars* champion, his success advertising the level of fitness required to become a top driver.

Schumacher, Michael   Born Hurth-Hermulheim, Cologne, West Germany, 3 January 1969. Made his first Grand Prix start in Belgium, 1991 (for Jordan), after becoming German Formula Three champion in 1990. Schumacher joined Benetton later in 1991 and in 1992 gained his first Grand Prix win. World champion in 1994, 1995 (both with Benetton), 2000, 2001, 2002 and 2003 (all with Ferrari), his career statistics are unparalleled. In 195 Grand Prix starts he has had 70 wins from 55 pole positions, proving he can win from the front or behind. As at July 2004 he has won all ten GPs he has completed, only Jarno Trulli's win in the Monaco GP preventing a 100 per cent record. In this race Schumacher crashed out behind the safety car. Michael duly clinched the 2004 world drivers' championship by placing second to Kimi Raikkonen at the Belgian Grand Prix at Spa 29 August.

Schumacher, Ralf   Born Hurth-Hermulheim, Cologne, West Germany, 30 June 1975. His career began in 1978 with his participation in go-karts, at the age of three. Schumacher came to prominence in 1996 by winning the Japanese Formula Nippon Championship and subsequently made his Formula One debut in Australia in 1997, driving for Jordan. He joined Williams in 1999 and has risen through the ranks to become one of the best drivers in the world.

Senna, Ayrton   Born Ayrton da Silva, São Paulo, Brazil, 21 March 1960. After winning the British Formula Three Championship in 1983 he made his debut in Formula One in 1984 for Toleman, before driving for Lotus between 1985 and 1987. His fortunes rose when he joined McLaren in 1988 and he immediately won the World Drivers' Championship, a feat he repeated in 1990 and 1991. In total he started in 161 Grands Prix, and had 41 wins and 65 pole positions. He died 1 May 1994 at Imola, Italy, during the San Marino Grand Prix weekend.

Stewart, Jackie   Born John Young Stewart, Dumbarton, Scotland, 11 June 1939. Made his Formula One debut in the South African Grand Prix in 1965. British Formula One champion in 1969, he was World champion in 1969 (with Matra MS80), 1971 and 1973 (with Tyrrell-Ford). Stewart had 99 Grand Prix starts, 27 wins and 17 pole positions. He retired in 1975.

Surtees, John   Born Tatsfield, Surrey, England, 11 February 1934. Surtees is the only man to become world champion on both two wheels and four. His first Grand Prix start was in Monaco in 1960, driving for Lotus, and he went on to become world champion in 1964 with Ferrari. Before all this he was 500cc motorcycle world champion (1956, 1958-60) and 350cc motorcycle world champion (1958-60) a total of seven world titles on two wheels. Undoubtedly he is one of the all-time great all-rounders of sport.

Trulli, Jarno   Born Pescara, Italy, 13 January 1974. Made his Formula One debut in the Australian Grand Prix in 1997 (driving for Minardi) after becoming German Formula Three champion in 1996. Trulli moved to Prost in 1998, Jordan in 2000 and Renault in 2002. He achieved his first Grand Prix win in 2004, winning in Monaco from pole position.

Verstappen, Jos   Born Montfort, Netherlands, 4 March 1972. Made his debut in the 1994 Brazilian Grand Prix driving a Benetton-Ford, before moving to Stewart in 1998 and Arrows in 2000. He drove for Minardi in 2003.

Villeneuve, Gilles Born Berthierville, Quebec, Canada, 18 January 1950. His first Grand Prix start was in Canada in 1977 and he had six Grand Prix wins and two pole positions. In 1979 he was runner-up to Jody Scheckter in the Formula One World Drivers' Championship. He died 8 May 1982 while qualifying for the Belgian Grand Prix at Zolder.

Villeneuve, Jacques Born St-Jean-sur-Richelieu, Quebec, Canada, 9 April 1971. The son of Gilles Villeneuve, he made his Formula One debut in the Australian Grand Prix of 1996 driving for the Williams team. Jacques went on to become world champion in 1997 still driving for Williams. IndyCar CART Rookie of the Year in 1994, in 1995 he was both CART champion and winner of the Indianapolis 500. Unfortunately he has not had the car in which to compete successfully since his win in 1997.

Warwick, Derek Born Alresford, Hampshire, England, 27 August 1954. His debut in Formula One was in the United States Grand Prix in 1981, a year in which he failed to score any championship points. He went on to become the winner of the Le Mans 24-Hour and the FIA World Sports Car/Sports-Prototype Championship in 1992.

Watson, John Born Belfast, Northern Ireland, 4 May 1946. His first Grand Prix start was in Great Britain in 1973 driving a Brabham-Ford. Watson's first

Grand Prix win came in 1976 for Penske. He had five Grand Prix wins in his career plus two pole positions. His best season was 1982 when he had two victories and finished runner-up in the championship, driving for McLaren. He retired in 1985.

Williams, Frank Born South Shields, Tyne & Wear, England, 16 April 1942. Chief executive of the Williams team, founded in 1977. The team's first Grand Prix win was in Argentina in 1978 and the following year Clay Regazzoni secured its first win in Britain. A serious car crash just before the start of the 1986 season, just outside the Paul Ricard circuit in France, left Williams confined to a wheelchair, but his skill and determination, at first in tandem with his driver and great friend, Piers Courage, and then in 1975 when teaming up with designer Patrick Head, make Williams one of the most powerful characters in Formula One.

Wilson, Justin Born Sheffield, England, 31 July 1978. Made his Formula One debut in the Australian Grand Prix in 2003. British Formula Vauxhall Junior Challenge champion in 1995 and runner-up in the British Formula Vauxhall Championship in 1996, he was Formula Palmer Audi champion in 1998 and winner of the International Formula 3000 Championship in 2001. Wilson is yet to make an impression in Formula One.

Formula One Championship

	Winner	Car	Runner-up	Constructor's Championship
1950	Guiseppe Farina (ITA)	Alfa Romeo	Juan Manuel Fangio (ARG)	—
1951	Juan Manuel Fangio (ARG)	Alfa Romeo	Alberto Ascari (ITA)	—
1952	Alberto Ascari (ITA)	Ferrari	Guiseppe Farina (ITA)	—
1953	Alberto Ascari (ITA)	Ferrari	Juan Manuel Fangio (ARG)	—
1954	Juan Manuel Fangio (ARG)	Maserati/Mercedes	Jose Gonzalez (ARG)	—
1955	Juan Manuel Fangio (ARG)	Mercedes-Benz	Stirling Moss (GBR)	—
1956	Juan Manuel Fangio (ARG)	Lancia-Ferrari	Stirling Moss (GBR)	—
1957	Juan Manuel Fangio (ARG)	Maserati	Stirling Moss (GBR)	—
1958	Mike Hawthorn (GBR)	Ferrari	Stirling Moss (GBR)	Vanwall
1959	Jack Brabham (AUS)	Cooper-Climax	Tony Brooks (GBR)	Cooper-Climax
1960	Jack Brabham (AUS)	Cooper-Climax	Bruce McLaren (NZL)	Cooper-Climax
1961	Phil Hill (USA)	Ferrari	Wolfgang Von Trips (FRG)	Ferrari
1962	Graham Hill (GBR)	BRM	Jim Clark (GBR)	BRM
1963	Jim Clark (GBR)	Lotus-Climax	Graham Hill (GBR)	Lotus-Climax
1964	John Surtees (GBR)	Ferrari	Graham Hill (GBR)	Ferrari
1965	Jim Clark (GBR)	Lotus-Climax	Graham Hill (GBR)	Lotus-Climax
1966	Jack Brabham (AUS)	Brabham-Repco	John Surtees (GBR)	Brabham-Repco
1967	Denny Hulme (NZL)	Brabham-Repco	Jack Brabham (AUS)	Brabham-Repco
1968	Graham Hill (GBR)	Lotus-Ford	Jackie Stewart (GBR)	Lotus-Ford
1969	Jackie Stewart (GBR)	Matra-Ford	Jacky Ickx (BEL)	Matra-Ford
1970	Jochen Rindt (AUT)	Lotus-Ford	Jacky Ickx (BEL)	Lotus-Ford
1971	Jackie Stewart (GBR)	Tyrrell-Ford	Ronnie Peterson (SWE)	Tyrrell-Ford
1972	Emerson Fittipaldi (BRA)	Lotus-Ford	Jackie Stewart (GBR)	Lotus-Ford
1973	Jackie Stewart (GBR)	Tyrrell-Ford	Emerson Fittipaldi (BRA)	Lotus-Ford
1974	Emerson Fittipaldi (BRA)	McLaren-Ford	Clay Regazzoni (SUI)	McLaren-Ford
1975	Niki Lauda (AUT)	Ferrari	Emerson Fittipaldi (RSA)	Ferrari
1976	James Hunt (GBR)	McLaren-Ford	Niki Lauda (AUT)	Ferrari
1977	Niki Lauda (AUT)	Ferrari	Jody Scheckter (RSA)	Ferrari
1978	Mario Andretti (USA)	Lotus-Ford	Ronnie Peterson (SWE)	Lotus-Ford
1979	Jody Scheckter (RSA)	Ferrari	Gilles Villeneuve (CAN)	Ferrari
1980	Alan Jones (AUS)	Williams-Ford	Nelson Piquet (BRA)	Williams-Ford
1981	Nelson Piquet (BRA)	Brabham-Ford	Carlos Reutemann (ARG)	Williams-Ford
1982	Keke Rosberg (FIN)	Williams-Ford	John Watson (GBR) Didier Pironi (FRA)	Ferrari
1983	Nelson Piquet (BRA)	Brabham-BMW	Alain Prost (FRA)	Ferrari
1984	Niki Lauda (AUT)	McLaren-Porsche	Alain Prost (FRA)	McLaren-Porsche
1985	Alain Prost (FRA)	McLaren-TAG	Michele Alboreto (ITA)	McLaren-TAG
1986	Alain Prost (FRA)	McLaren-TAG	Nigel Mansell (GBR)	Williams-Honda

1987	Nelson Piquet (BRA)	Williams-Honda	Nigel Mansell (GBR)	Williams-Honda
1988	Ayrton Senna (BRA)	McLaren-Honda	Alain Prost (FRA)	McLaren-Honda
1989	Alain Prost (FRA)	McLaren-Honda	Ayrton Senna (BRA)	McLaren-Honda
1990	Ayrton Senna (BRA)	McLaren-Honda	Alain Prost (FRA)	McLaren-Honda
1991	Ayrton Senna (BRA)	McLaren-Honda	Nigel Mansell (GBR)	McLaren-Honda
1992	Nigel Mansell (GBR)	Williams-Renault	Riccardo Patrese (ITA)	Williams-Renault
1993	Alain Prost (FRA)	Williams-Renault	Ayrton Senna (BRA)	Williams-Renault
1994	Michael Schumacher (GER)	Benetton-Ford	Damon Hill (GBR)	Williams-Renault
1995	Michael Schumacher (GER)	Benetton-Renault	Damon Hill (GBR)	Benetton-Renault
1996	Damon Hill (GBR)	Williams-Renault	Jacques Villeneuve (CAN)	Williams-Renault
1997	Jacques Villeneuve (CAN)	Williams-Renault	Michael Schumacher (GER)	Williams-Renault
1998	Mika Häkkinen (FIN)	McLaren-Mercedes	Michael Schumacher (GER)	McLaren-Mercedes
1999	Mika Häkkinen (FIN)	McLaren-Mercedes	Eddie Irvine (GBR)	Ferrari
2000	Michael Schumacher (GER)	Ferrari	Mika Häkkinen (FIN)	Ferrari
2001	Michael Schumacher (GER)	Ferrari	David Coulthard (GBR)	Ferrari
2002	Michael Schumacher (GER)	Ferrari	Rubens Barrichello (BRA)	Ferrari
2003	Michael Schumacher (GER)	Ferrari	Kimi Raikkonen (FIN)	Ferrari
2004	Michael Schumacher (GER)	Ferrari	Not yet known	Ferrari

2003 Car Racing Champions

2003 Formula One Championship
Michael Schumacher (GER), Ferrari

2003 American Le Mans Series
Frank Biela (GER)/Marco Werner (GER)

2003 World Rally Championship
Petter Solberg (NOR), Subaru; co-driver Phil Mills (WAL)

2003 British Touring Car Championship (BTCC)
Yvan Muller (FRA), Vauxhall

2003 Champcar (CART) Championship
Paul Tracy (CAN)

2003 German Touring Car Championship (DTM)
Bernd Schneider (GER), Mercedes

2003 Indycar (IRL) Championship
Scott Dixon (NZL), Toyota

2003 European Touring Car Championship (ETCC)
Gabriele Tarquini (ITA), Alfa Romeo

2003 NASCAR Winston Cup
Matt Kenseth (USA), Ford

2003 Porsche Supercup Championship
Wolf Henzler (GER)

2003 International Formula 3000 Championship
Björn Wirdheim (SWE)

2003 Australian Rally Championship
Cody Crocker (AUS), Subaru

2003 British Formula Three Championship
Alan Van Der Merwe (RSA)

2003 Australian Touring Car (V8 Supercar)
Marcos Ambrose (AUS), Ford

2003 Formula Nippon Championship
Satoshi Motoyama (JPN)

General Information

drag racing	Approximately five seconds of sheer speed over a distance of a quarter of a mile (402m). Santa Pod is the British venue for this popular sport but unfortunately lack of sponsorship and political issues have prevented any formal world championships of late.
Formula One: first woman driver	Maria Teresa de Filippis (1958)
flags	black – disqualification of a driver
	black and white chequered – end of race
	blue – car about to overtake
	red – premature end of race
	yellow – danger, no overtaking
	yellow and red diagonal stripes – oil on track
fuel used	Before 1961 nitro-methane was used, but since then ordinary commercial fuel has been compulsory (Indianapolis still uses nitro-methane).
most consecutive wins	Alberto Ascari (9)
oldest champion	Juan Manuel Fangio (46)
points system	From the 2003 season points are awarded for the top eight finishers, thus: 10, 8, 6, 5, 4, 3, 2, 1.
posthumous champion	Jochen Rindt (1970)
teams for 2004 season	Ferrari: Michael Schumacher and Rubens Barrichello
	McLaren: Kimi Raikkonen and David Coulthard
	Williams: Ralf Schumacher and Juan Pablo Montoya
	BAR: Takuma Sato and Jenson Button
	Sauber: Giancarlo Fisichella and Felipe Massa

Jaguar: Mark Webber and Christian Klien
Renault: Jarno Trulli and Fernando Alonso
Minardi: Gianmaria Bruni and Zsolt Baumgartner
Toyota: Olivier Panis and Cristiano da Matta
Jordan: Nick Heidfeld and Giorgio Pantano.

technical regulations
The engine of the car may be a maximum of 3 litres and must be normally aspirated. The engine must be ten cylinders. The tyres used must be declared at the start of an event and uniquely marked. There are four types of tyres a team may use, depending on weather conditions: Grooved tyres, used on dry tracks. (Each tyre, whether front or rear, has four grooves which run around the tyre.) Intermediate tyres, used on damp tracks. (Intermediate tyres are basically slicks with grooves cut across the tyre.) Wet-Weather tyres, which have full tread to enable water to be dispersed in much the same way as a road car. Monsoon tyres, which are similar to wets but are more heavily treaded to allow more water to be dispersed. A car may have a maximum of seven forward gears (a minimum of four) and must have a reverse gear. With the exception of rollover structures, no part of the car may be higher than 95cm from the reference plane. The overall width of the car may not exceed 180cm.

Grand Prix circuits: Formula One
Argentinian – Buenos Aires
Australian – Adelaide, Melbourne
Austrian – A1 Ring, Spielberg
Bahrain – Bahrain International Circuit
Belgian – Spa-Francorchamps, Zolder
Brazilian – São Paulo, Interlagos (Rio de Janeiro)
British – Silverstone
Canadian – Gilles Villeneuve Circuit, Montreal
Chinese – Shanghai International Circuit
Dutch – Zandvoort
French – Magny Cours, Dijon
German – Hockenheim
Hungarian – Hungaroring, Budapest
Italian – Monza
Japanese – Suzuka
European – Nürburgring (Bonn, Germany)
Malaysian – Sepang
Mexican – Mexico City
Monaco – Monte Carlo
Portuguese – Estoril
San Marino – Imola
Spanish – Catalunya, Montjuich (Barcelona)
United States – Detroit, Long Beach, Indianapolis
The Nürburgring is no longer used for the German Grand Prix but has been the venue of the European Grand Prix in recent years. Similarly, Aida in Japan is no longer used for its own Grand Prix but has been the venue for the Pacific Grand Prix.

Indianapolis 500: first winner
Ray Harroun in Marmon Wasp (1911). Throughout the 1950s the race was part of the World Drivers' Championship.

laps
200 (although the race is 500 miles (800km) in length, hence the name). The circuit is nicknamed 'The Brickyard'.

Formula One winners
Jim Clark (1965), Graham Hill (1966), Mario Andretti (1969), Emerson Fittipaldi (1989, 1993), Jacques Villeneuve (1995)

land speed record: holder
Andy Green in Thrust SSC (714mph)

first over 100 mph
Louis Rigolly in 1904

Le Mans 24-Hour race
Raced over a circuit of 13.84km (8.48 miles). First held in 1923, since 1953 the race has been part of the Sports Car World Championship. The most successful driver has been Jacky Ickx (BEL) with six wins (1969, 1975, 1976, 1977, 1981, 1982).

Monaco Grand Prix: five times winner
Graham Hill

NASCAR
National Association for Stock Car Auto Racing. The first races in America began in 1948. The main event, the Winston Cup, was officially founded in 1950. Top drivers have included Richard Petty and Dale Earnhardt, both winning seven championships. Petty gained 27 wins in 1967 to dominate the season. Engine details: V8, 350-358 cu in, 770bhp. Maximum speeds are well in excess of 200mph. The cars have a steel chassis and roll cage, with a four-speed manual gearbox. The maximum weight must be 3400lb (1542kg). A restrictor plate limits power to 450bhp, 190mph (306kph) at superspeedways but more at faster tracks.

Paris to Dakar rally
First raced in 1979. The route of over 10,000km from Paris to Dakar crosses the Sahara desert, though the actual route sometimes varies due to the political situation in Africa. The starting order each day is motorcycles first, cars second, trucks last. Each day consists of a special stage averaging 480km. Besides factory-sponsored cars, motorcycles and trucks, many competitors are amateur racers.

Rally world champions			
	1977*	Sandro Munari (ITA)	Lancia
	1978*	Markku Alén (FIN)	Fiat-Lancia Stratos
	1979	Björn Waldegaard (SWE)	Ford Escort-Mercedes
	1980	Walter Röhrl (DEN)	Fiat
	1981	Ari Vatanen (FIN)	Ford
	1982	Walter Röhrl (DEN)	Opel
	1983	Hannu Mikkola (FIN)	Audi
	1984	Stig Blomqvist (SWE)	Audi
	1985	Timo Salonen (FIN)	Peugeot
	1986	Juha Kankkunen (FIN)	Peugeot
	1987	Juha Kankkunen (FIN)	Lancia
	1988	Massimo Biasion (ITA)	Lancia
	1989	Massimo Biasion (ITA)	Lancia
	1990	Carlos Sainz (ESP)	Toyota
	1991	Juha Kankkunen (FIN)	Lancia
	1992	Carlos Sainz (ESP)	Toyota
	1993	Juha Kankkunen (FIN)	Toyota
	1994	Didier Auriol (FRA)	Lancia
	1995	Colin McRae (SCO)	Subaru
	1996	Tommi Mäkinen (FIN)	Mitsubishi
	1997	Tommi Mäkinen (FIN)	Mitsubishi
	1998	Tommi Mäkinen (FIN)	Mitsubishi
	1999	Tommi Mäkinen (FIN)	Mitsubishi
	2000	Marcus Grönholm (FIN)	Peugeot
	2001	Richard Burns (ENG)	Subaru
	2002	Marcus Grönholm (FIN)	Peugeot
	2003	Petter Solberg (NOR)	Subaru

*For FIA cup.

UK motor racing circuit: first   Brooklands, Surrey, opened in 1907

MUAY THAI

Muay Thai kickboxing is currently one of the fastest growing full contact sports in the world. In Thailand, Muay Thai, which translates as 'Thai boxing' is known to have flourished since the Sukhothai period (AD1257-1377). It is as popular as football is in the United Kingdom. Thousands of camps around Thailand provide teaching and training in the sport to eager students.

Most of what is known about the early history of Thai boxers comes from Burmese accounts of warfare between Myanmar (formerly known as Burma) and Thailand during the 15th and 16th centuries. A reference (from AD1411) mentions a ferocious style of unarmed combat that decided the fate of the Thai kings, while a later description tells how Nai Khanom Tom, Thailand's first famous boxer and a prisoner of war in Myanmar, gained his freedom by defeating a dozen Burmese warriors before a Burmese court.

King Naresuan the Great (AD1555-1605) was a great Thai boxer himself, and he made Muay Thai a required part of military training for all Thai soldiers. Later another Thai king, Phra Chao Seua (the Tiger King), further promoted Thai boxing as a national sport by encouraging prize fights and the development of training camps in the early 18th century. King Seua himself is said to have been an incognito participant in many of the matches during the early part of his reign.

Contestants' fists were wrapped in thick horsehide for maximum impact with minimum knuckle damage. They also used cotton soaked in glue and ground glass and hemp bindings. Tree bark and seashells were used to protect the groin area during fights. There are accounts of massive wagers and bouts to the death during this time. Because of the high mortality rate among fight-ers, the government banned Muay Thai in the 1920s but it was revived in the 1930s with a stricter set of rules based on a Western-style boxing code. Bouts were standardised as five three-minute rounds with a two-minute break between rounds. Gloves were worn and the boxers fought in shorts, either red or blue in colour. Shoes were not worn but feet were taped.

Despite these concessions Muay Thai remains an extreme form of fighting. All parts of the body may be struck and only the head is considered illegal for striking purposes. Knee and elbow strikes can be decisive although kicks to the calf and knees to the thighs often wear down an opponent before the *coup de grâce*.

Thai boxing is becoming increasingly popular outside Thailand. It has enthusiasts and practi-tioners in the Americas, Australia, the Netherlands, Finland, Russia and Japan, as well as in many other countries around the world. Training camps have been set up in many coun-tries, creating large numbers of professional and amateur Muay Thai boxers, coached by Thai as well as non-Thai instructors. The International Amateur Muay Thai Federation (IAMTF) organ-ised the first World Amateur Muay Thai Championships in 1995, while the International Federation of Muay Thai Amateurs (IFMA) organ-ised the 2000 World Cup. Amateur Muay Thai fighters wear protective helmets and padded vests. Professional Muay Thai is run by the World Muaythai Council (WMC).

There are 16 weight divisions in Thai boxing, ranging from mini-flyweight to heavyweight. As in western-style boxing, matches take place on a $7.3m^2$ canvas-covered floor with rope retainers supported by four padded posts.

NETBALL

Netball was first played in England in 1895 at Madame Ostenburg's College. In the first half of the 20th century, netball's popularity grew continuously, with the game reaching many Commonwealth countries. There were no standard rules at that time and both nine-a-side and five-a-side versions of the game were played.

The origins of netball can be traced to 1891. In Springfield, Massachusetts, a 30-year-old Canadian immigrant to the United States, James Naismith, was asked to invent an indoor game for students at the School for Christian Workers (later known as the YMCA), where he worked as a physical education instructor.

The first games that he tried ended with injuries to players, so he devised a game in which a ball had to be lobbed into a high peach basket (he reasoned that if the ball had to be dropped into the 'goal', it couldn't be thrown at breakneck speed).

It was thus that basketball was born. The original game featured nine players – three forwards, three centres and three guards – simply because at the time Naismith had 18 youths to keep amused.

Women's indoor basketball began very soon after when female teachers at the gym were captivated by the game. It wasn't until 1895, however, that the current game of netball was shaped. When Clara Baer, a sports teacher in New Orleans, wrote to Naismith asking for a copy of the rules, she received a package that contained a drawing of the court, with lines pencilled across it to show the areas various players could best patrol. Baer misinterpreted the lines and assumed players could not leave those areas. In 1899 her mistake was integrated into the rules of women's basketball, as the system of zones.

Three-bounce dribbling had quickly been established in the men's game (which did not have no-go zones), but it was seldom used in the women's version when it reached Britain and the Commonwealth. There was no pressure to use that form of ball movement more frequently and as a result dribbling eventually ceased to exist.

During an Australian tour of England in 1957, discussions took place to consider standardising the rules of the sport and this led to representatives from England, Australia, New Zealand, South Africa and the West Indies meeting in Ceylon, (now Sri Lanka) in 1960, to establish the International Federation of Women's Basketball and Netball. This was later renamed the International Federation of Netball Associations (IFNA). Formal rules were established at this inaugural meeting and it was decided to hold world championship tournaments every four years, beginning in Eastbourne, England, in 1963.

The World Championships have since been held in Australia (1967, 1991 and 1999), England (1995), Jamaica (1971 and 2003), New Zealand (1975), Scotland (1987), Singapore (1983) and Trinidad and Tobago (1979). Throughout this period, Australia dominated, winning the event in 1963, 1971, 1975, 1983, 1991, 1995 and 1999. New Zealand won in 1967, 1987 and 2003. The 1979 championship was a three-way tie between Australia, New Zealand, and Trinidad and Tobago. The nations that took part in the 2003 World Championship were: Antigua, Australia, Barbados, Bermuda, Canada, Cayman Islands, Cook Islands, England, Fiji, Grenada, Hong Kong, Jamaica, New Zealand, Niue, Northern Ireland, Samoa, Scotland, South Africa, Sri Lanka, St Lucia, St Vincent and the Grenadines, Trinidad and Tobago, United States and Wales.

As part of the Australian bicentenary celebrations in 1988, a youth tournament took place in Canberra, for players aged under 21. Its success led to this event being held once every four years. Fiji hosted the Second World Youth Netball Championship, Canada the third and the fourth took place in Wales. Australia won in 1988, 1996 and 2000, and New Zealand in 1992. In 1995 netball became a recognised Olympic sport.

In 1998, for the first time, netball was included in the Commonwealth Games programme in Kuala Lumpur. In a ten-team competition Australia took the gold medal, New Zealand the silver and England the bronze. Australia retained the title in the 2002 Manchester Commonwealth Games. In preparation for the 2006 Commonwealth Games in Melbourne, Australia, the IFNA negotiated for a greater number of teams (12) to participate. Netball is now recognised as a core Commonwealth Games sport.

General Information

famous England player of the past

Sheila Lerwill (née Alexander) of Surrey and England (also held the world high jump record)

famous goal shooters

Australia: Catherine Cox, Jacqui Delaney, Alex Hodge, Sharelle McMahon, Cynna Neele, Eloise Southby

England: Alex Astle, Lyn Carpenter, Abby Teare, Tracey Neville (the goal attack and sometimes wing attack for Bury and England is the sister of footballers Gary and Phil Neville), Jo Steed

New Zealand: Belinda Colling, Tania Dalton, Irene van Dyk

positions on the court

Goal shooter (GS), goal attack (GA), wing attack (WA), centre (C), wing defence (WD), goal defence (GD), goal keeper (GK)

rules

Netball is played on a hard-surface court 100ft (30.5m) long by 50ft (15.2m) wide, by two teams of seven players, using a ball made of leather, rubber or similar material, that weighs 14-16oz (400-450g) and measures 27-28ins (69-71cm) in circumference.

The court is divided into three equal parts (a defensive third, a centre third and an attacking third), and has a centre spot 3ins (7.6cm) in diameter from which the game must commence. A semi-circle with a radius of 16ft (4.9m) is marked around each goalpost; these are called the shooting circles. The goalposts have a ring 15ins (38cm) in diameter placed 10ft (3m) off the ground and 6ins (15.2cm) from the supporting post. The top of the post, unlike that in basketball, is on the same level as the ring. The shooters and attacks may only play in the shooting areas. The six centre court players may only play in the centre court and must not enter the shooting areas. Penalties are awarded if these boundaries are crossed.

Once holding the ball, a player cannot take a step. This means that once the player has landed, with the ball in hand, they must keep at least one foot planted on the ground. The player cannot jump, step or drag their foot. A player who is defending must be at least 3ft (0.9m) away from the player who holds the ball. Netball is considered a non-contact sport, which means that a player cannot make physical contact with another player if it hinders that person's ability to play the ball. A player is considered to be offside if any part of their body touches the ground in an area where they are not permitted to play. Once a player has caught the ball they have three seconds either to pass it, or to shoot for a goal. If a player holds the ball for longer than three seconds they are penalised. A penalty awarded to an attacker within the attacker's goal circle can be taken as either a pass or a shot for goal. The opponent who infringed must stand out of the way (where the umpire has indicated).

The game is played over four quarters of 15 minutes each, but at school level may be over two halves of 20 minutes per half.

senior rankings (as at end 2003)

1. Australia
2. New Zealand
3. England
4. Jamaica
5. South Africa
6. Fiji
7. Cook Islands
8. Trinidad and Tobago
9. Samoa
10. Barbados

N
E
T
B
A
L
L

ORIENTEERING

Orienteering began in Scandinavia in the 19th century. It was primarily a military exercise and was part of military training in Sweden and Norway. In 1919 the modern version of orienteering was born as a competitive sport in Sweden when Ernst Killander, then president of the Stockholm Amateur Athletic Association, conceived a cross-country race in which runners could choose their own route using a map and a compass. He is rightly considered the father of orienteering.

In the early 1930s, orienteering received a technical boost with the invention of a new compass which was precise and fast to use when direction-finding. The Kjellström brothers, Björn and Alvan, and their friend, Gunnar Tillander, were responsible for this new device. They were among the best Swedish orienteers of the thirties and shared several individual orienteering championships among themselves. In 1946 orienteering was introduced to the United States by Björn Kjellström.

A terrain suitable for orienteering should traditionally be heavily wooded, preferably uninhabited, and diverse enough to suit different levels of competition. The area must also be accessible to competitors and its use should be coordinated with appropriate terrain and range control offices.

Competitions begin with each orienteer being given a 1:50,000 topographic map on which the various control points are circled. The ideal map for an orienteering course is a multi-coloured, large-scale topographic map that portrays the shape and elevation of the terrain using contour lines.

The International Orienteering Federation (IOF), the sport's governing body, was founded in 1961 and has approximately 60 affiliated nations. The first World Championships were held in Fiskars, Finland, in 1966. They are held every two years, and races take place over several distances in individual and relay competitions. Scandinavian countries have traditionally dominated, although other nations, including Switzerland, have also had success. The 1999 World Championships were held in Inverness, Scotland, and Yvette Baker of Great Britain won the short distance event. In 2003 at Rapperswil-Jona, Switzerland, Jamie Stevenson won the sprint event gold medal for Great Britain.

World Championships

Men's Classic Distance

	Gold	Silver	Bronze
1966	Åge Hadler (NOR)	Aimo Tepsell (FIN)	Anders Morelius (SWE)
1968	Karl Johanssson (SWE)	Sture Björk (SWE)	Åge Hadler (NOR)
1970	Stig Berge (NOR)	Karl John (SUI)	Dieter Hulliger (SUI)
1972	Åge Hadler (NOR)	Stig Berge (NOR)	Bernt Frilen (SWE)
1974	Bernt Frilen (SWE)	Jan Fjärested (NOR)	Eystein Weltzien (NOR)
1976	Egil Johansen (NOR)	Rolf Pettersson (SWE)	Svein Jacobsen (NOR)
1978	Egil Johansen (NOR)	Risto Nuuros (FIN)	Simo Nurminen (FIN)
1979	Öyvin Thon (NOR)	Egil Johansen (NOR)	Tore Sagvolden (NOR)
1981	Öyvin Thon (NOR)	Tore Sagvolden (NOR)	Morten Berglia (NOR)
1983	Morten Berglia (NOR)	Öyvin Thon (NOR)	Sigurd Dähli (NOR)
1985	Kari Sallinen (FIN)	Tore Sagvolden (NOR)	Egil Iversen (NOR)
1987	Kent Olsson (SWE)	Tore Sagvolden (NOR)	Urs Fluhmann (SUI)
1989	Petter Thoresen (NOR)	Kent Olsson (SWE)	Håvard Tveite (NOR)
1991	Jörgen Mårtensson (SWE)	Kent Olsson (SWE)	Sixten Sild (URS)
1993	Allan Mogensen (DEN)	Jörgen Mårtensson (SWE)	Petter Thoresen (NOR)
1995	Jörgen Mårtensson (SWE)	Janne Salmi (FIN)	Carsten Jörgensen (DEN)
1997	Petter Thoresen (NOR)	Jörgen Mårtensson (SWE)	Kjetil Bjørlo (NOR)
1999	Björnar Valstad (NOR)	Carl-Henrik Björseth (NOR)	Alain Berger (SUI)
2001	Jörgen Rostrup (NOR)	Jani Lakanen (FIN)	Carl-Henrik Björseth (NOR)
2003	Thomas Bührer (SUI)	Yuri Omeltchenko (UKR)	Emil Wingstedt (SWE)

Men's Short Distance

	Gold	Silver	Bronze
1991	Petr Kovak (CZE)	Kent Olsson (SWE)	Martin Johansson (SWE)
1993	Petter Thoresen (NOR)	Timo Karppinen (FIN)	Martin Johansson (SWE)
1995	Yuri Omeltchenko (UKR)	Jörgen Mårtensson (SWE)	Björnar Valstad (NOR)
1997	Janne Salmi (FIN)	Timo Karppinen (FIN)	Björnar Valstad (NOR)
1999	Jörgen Rostrup (NOR)	Juha Peltola (FIN)	Janne Salmi (FIN)
2001	Pasi Ikonen (FIN)	Tore Sandvik (NOR)	Jörgen Rostrup (NOR)

Men's Sprint

	Gold	Silver	Bronze
2001	Jimmy Birklin (SWE)	Pasi Ikonen (FIN)	Jörgen Olsson (SWE)
2003	Jamie Stevenson (GBR)	Rudolf Ropek (CZE)	Thierry Georgiou (FRA)

Women's Classic Distance

	Gold	Silver	Bronze
1966	Ulla Lindkvist (SWE)	Käthy Perch-Nielsen (SUI)	Raila Hovi (FIN)
1968	Ulla Lindkvist (SWE)	Ingrid Hadler (NOR)	Kerstin Granstedt (SWE)
1970	Ingrid Hadler (NOR)	Ulla Lindkvist (SWE)	Kristin Danielsen (NOR)
1972	Sarolta Monspart (HUN)	Pirjo Seppä (FIN)	Birgitta Larsson (SWE)
1974	Mona Nørgaard (DEN)	Kristin Cullman (SWE)	Outi Borgenström (FIN)
1976	Liisa Veijalainen (FIN)	Kristin Cullman (SWE)	Anne Lundmark (SWE)
1978	Anne Berit Eid (NOR)	Liisa Veijalainen (FIN)	Wenche Jacobsen (NOR)
1979	Outi Borgenstrom (FIN)	Liisa Veijalainen (FIN)	Monica Andersson (SWE)
1981	Annichen Kringstad (SWE)	Brit Volden (NOR)	Karin Rabe (SWE)
1983	Annichen Kringstad (SWE)	Marita Skogum (SWE)	Annariita Kottonen (FIN)
1985	Annichen Kringstad (SWE)	Brit Volden (NOR)	Christina Blomqvist (SWE)
1987	Arja Hannus (SWE)	Karin Rabe (SWE)	Jana Galikova (TCH)
1989	Marita Skogum (SWE)	Jana Galikova (TCH)	Alida Abola (URS)
1991	Katalin Olah (HUN)	Christina Blomqvist (SWE)	Jana Galikova (CZE)
1993	Marita Skogum (SWE)	Annika Viilo (FIN)	Yvette Hague (GBR)
1995	Katalin Olah (HUN)	Yvette Hague (GBR) Eija Koskivaara (FIN)	——
1997	Hanne Staff (NOR)	Katarina Borg (SWE)	Hanne Sandstad (NOR)
1999	Kirsi Bostrom (FIN)	Hanne Staff (NOR)	Johanna Asklöf (FIN)
2001	Simone Luder (SUI)	Marika Mikkola (FIN)	Reeta Kolkkala (FIN)
2003	Simone Luder (SUI)	Karolina Höjsgaard (SWE)	Brigitte Wolf (SUI)

Women's Short Distance

1991	Jana Cieslarova (CZE)	Ada Kucharova (CZE)	Marita Skogum (SWE)
1993	Anna Bogren (SWE)	Marita Skogum (SWE)	Eija Koskivaara (FIN)
1995	Marie-Luce Romanens (SUI)	Yvette Hague (GBR)	Marlena Jansson (SWE)
1997	Lucie Böhm (AUT)		Anna Bogren (SWE) Hanne Staff (NOR)
1999	Yvette Baker (GBR)	Hanne Sandstad (NOR)	Frauke Schmitt Gran (GER)
2001	Hanne Staff (NOR)	Lucie Böhm (AUT) Jenny Johansson (SWE)	Gunilla Svörd (SWE)

Women's Sprint

	Gold	Silver	Bronze
2001	Vroni König-Salmi (SUI)	Johanna Asklöf (FIN)	Simone Luder (SUI)
2003	Simone Luder (SUI)	Marie-Luce Romanens (SUI)	Jenny Johansson (SWE)

ORIENTEERING

PADDLE TENNIS

Paddle tennis was invented in 1898 by Frank Peer Beale, a child from Albion, Michigan, USA. When Beale became the Episcopal minister of a Manhattan church in 1915 he persuaded city officials to build a series of paddle tennis courts to provide children with an introduction to the game of tennis. The first proper tournament was held in 1922. In 1923 the United States Paddle Tennis Association was formed and it remains the governing body for the sport. A New Yorker, Murray Geller, developed the game in the 1940s to make it an adult game as well as a children's recreation. The adult version was played on a larger court and instead of two serves only one was allowed. Adults also had to serve underhand while children served overhand.

Instead of rackets, rectangular wooden bats with short handles are used. The sponge-rubber ball is not as lively as the ball used in lawn tennis. The court measures 50ft (15.24m) by 20ft (6.1m). The service line is 3ft (0.9m) within the base line. The net is 31ins (78.7cm) high. The ball must be a pressurised tennis ball which has its internal pressure reduced by being punctured so that when dropped from a height of 6ft (1.83m) to the playing court surface, the bounce will be not less than 31ins (78.7cm) and not more than 33ins (83.8cm). Puncturing with a hypodermic needle or safety pin is a simple method of achieving the required bounce.

The paddle must be made of solid materials, and must not be more than 9½ins (24cm) × 18ins (45.7cm). It may be perforated or textured, but must contain no strings. The children's court measures 39ft (11.9m) by 18ft (5.5m).

The game is played primarily on the east and west coasts of the USA. Great Wimbledon tennis champions such as Althea Gibson and Bobby Riggs were paddle tennis champions and it used to be a popular winter game for touring tennis players. Now tennis is played all year round, paddle tennis has become a dedicated sport.

The outstanding player of the last decade is undoubtedly Scott Freedman, who has won the triple crown of the sport.

PADDLEBALL

Paddleball is a generic name for various forms of a game derived from handball and racquetball. One-wall paddleball was started in upstate New York by handball players who found their hands were too brittle and painful to play, due to the extremely cold winters. A wooden paddle with no holes and a taped handle was introduced and the game of one-wall paddleball was born. The game was played on one-wall handball courts in New York City alongside handball players.

The sport of paddleball gained popularity in the mid-1900s. The top players in history have included Harold Salomon, John Bruchi, Chris Leacakes, Howie Hammer, Eddie Acevedo, Wellington Cabrera, Freddy Diaz, Godfrey Brown, Donny Ciaffone, Glen Winokur, Gregg Sgarlata, Nelson Deida, Sammy Cesareo, Jesus Barretto, Frank Savino, Mike Petry, Robert Sostre, and the twins John and Arty Randon. Sostre, with his huge serves over 130mph (209kph), lays claim to be the greatest player of all time.

Originally a black Seamco ball was used but in the late 1970s the Spalding green ball emerged; this ball has a bounce which no other company has been able to match and it is now the official ball of paddleball.

One-wall paddleball is a game contested by two individuals or two teams in which a ball is hit by a paddle against a wall in such a manner that it creates an exchange or volley between the two teams. Each point or volley begins with the ball being served against the wall. The volleying continues back and forth until one team fails to return the ball in accordance with the rules. Each team must hit the ball in consecutive order. Any member of the team can hit for the team. Play is usually to 11, 15 or 21 points, with a margin of two points required to win. A score of 9-0 for a 21-point game might be considered a shutout – an automatic win.

The court consists of a wall, floor, non-court area and boundary lines. The wall is 16ft (4.88m) in height from the bottom to the top edge of the boundary line. The floor is 20ft (6.1m) in width from the outside edge of the right boundary line to the outside edge of the left boundary line. The short line runs parallel with the wall and extends from the right boundary line to the left boundary line. It is 16ft (4.88m) from the back outside edge to the wall. The long line also runs parallel with the wall and extends from the right boundary line to the left boundary line. It is 34ft (10.36m) from the back outside edge to the wall. Service markers are lines 6ins (15cm) in length, located midway between the short line and the long line. The court is usually coloured a light shade of grey, blue, beige or white and all lines are black.

Four-wall paddleball was created at the University of Michigan in 1930 by Earl Riskey, a PE instructor, to enable paddleball to be played indoors. It is primarily an American-based game played on racquetball courts during the winter months.

Many racquetball players are switching to four-wall paddleball, which they find a faster, more demanding game. The game is played by teams of two, three, or four players to 21 points. A match is normally the best of three games.

The ball used is made of rubber, pressureless, slightly smaller than a tennis ball (and similar to a racquetball ball), with a small pinhole. Black in colour, the ball should have a bounce of no more than 3ft 6ins (1.07m) when dropped from 6ft (1.83m).

PIGEON RACING

The earliest record of the domestication of pigeons dates from the fifth Egyptian dynasty, around 3000BC. The great empires of Carthage, Egypt and Rome made full use of the birds in many ways, including the production of squabs (young pigeons) as a culinary delicacy, as well as high-grade fertiliser for their fields from pigeon droppings.

The main use of pigeons, though, was in a great network of advanced communication. They kept emperors in touch with the most remote areas of their lands during a time when horse and riders or caravans would have taken weeks to deliver the same information. Julius Caesar made use of them during his conquest of Gaul. The Sultan of Baghdad established a pigeon-post system in AD1150 and Genghis Khan relied on pigeons to control his empire. When Napoleon was defeated at Waterloo, Count Rothschild knew of his defeat long before anyone else in England, having received this critical information via carrier pigeon. This advance knowledge allowed him to make critical financial decisions that made an enormous fortune possible. Later in the 19th century Julius Reuter founded as a line of pigeon posts the news service that globally still carries his name.

The modern racing pigeon has been developed over the past 150 years to fly farther, faster and more often. The racing pigeon is the product of the mixing together of several different breeds of pigeons including Horseman, Dragoon, Smerle and the carrier pigeon. The modern homing pigeon is in fact, from an ornithological point of view, a dove. In Dutch it is more correctly referred to as a *postduiven* (messenger dove).

The most successful modern racing pigeons were developed in Belgium, where in 1818 the first long-distance race of more than 100 miles (160km) took place. The homing pigeon of Belgium is the result of the crossing of the Cumulet of Antwerp with the Smerle of Liège. The Cumulet, of Flemish origin with white eyes, had a habit of flying so high that it was out of sight for several hours; the Smerle, with a short beak and several recurved feathers on its neck, did not fly as high or as long as the Cumulet, but it was much faster. Finally, in Belgium, the Bec-Anglais (Dragoons) were also crossed, the three varieties forming the basis for the appearance of the better-built, stronger, faster modern homing pigeon with a more precisely cultivated homing instinct.

Racing pigeons are trained, by repetitive practice, to return to their home loft when released at varying distances. They are banded before being loosed in order to establish the time in flight. Much research has been carried out on the means whereby a pigeon orients itself as it soars high into the sky, the latest theory being that it uses permanent countryside fixtures as a sighting guide. Motorways are thought to be a popular device used by homers.

POLO

The name 'polo' is derived from the Tibetan word *pulu* (ball game). It is the oldest team sport still in existence and was first played by nomadic warriors over 2000 years ago. Used for training cavalry, the game was played from Constantinople to Japan in the Middle Ages. The Mongol conqueror Tamerlane (1336-1405) ordered his men to play with the decapitated heads of their foes, His polo grounds can still be seen in Samarkand.

The first recorded polo tournament was in 600BC when the Turkomans beat the Persians in a public match. The poet Firdausi (AD935-1020) described this match in his *Shahnahmah* (Book of Kings). The Persians and the Mogul conquerors of India spread the game of polo across the eastern world. King Darius (c. 525BC) sent Alexander the Great a polo stick (called a *Chaugān*) and ball, to which Alexander prophetically replied that the ball was the earth and he was going to be the polo stick.

Emperor John VI Cantacuzenus, ruler of Byzantium 1341-54, was one of the earliest recorded casualties of the sport. Akbar the Great, ruler of India in the 16th century, played polo and his stables at Agra still exist. In the ancient city of Ispahan, in modern Iran, a polo field was built in front of Ali Ghapu Palace by Shah Abbas the Great (ruled 1585-1628). Today, still used as a public park, it is the same size as a modern polo field with its original stone goalposts in place.

Captain Robert Stewart and Major General Joe Sherer were the men responsible for introducing the West to the game. They saw it while they were stationed in Manipur in northern India, and in 1859 called the inaugural meeting of the first polo club, the Silehar, known as the first white man's polo club. When Sherer retired as a major general he was known as the father of English polo.

The British Army and British tea planters in India quickly took up the game and in 1862 the Calcutta Polo Club, the oldest active club in the world today, was founded. The oldest clubs outside India are today the Malta Club (founded 1868), the All Ireland Club in Dublin (1872), the Monmouthshire Club in England (1872), and the Meadowbrook Polo Club in the United States (1877).

In England, the first match was organised by Captain Edward 'Chicken' Hartopp, 10th Hussars, on Hounslow Heath in 1869, although a detachment of the regiment had played a scratch game near Limerick a year earlier. By the 1870s, the game was well established in England. In the same decade an Irishman, Captain John Watson, a cavalryman in the 13th Hussars, created the first set of written rules for polo on behalf of the Monmouthshire Club. In 1874 the Hurlingham Rules were created. These included the offside rule and limited the number of players to five on a team (this was eventually reduced to four).

In 1876, James Gordon Bennett, a noted American publisher, introduced polo to New York City and organised the first game in the United States at Dickel's Riding Academy on 39th Street and Fifth Avenue. On 13 May 1876, the Jerome Park racetrack in Westchester County was the site of the first outdoor polo match in the United States.

In 1878 the first Oxford vs. Cambridge match took place and ended in an Oxford victory.

From the early 1880s the Meadowbrook Polo Club played polo regularly on the infield of the racetrack at the Mineola Fair Grounds of Long Island. The club's first polo field was built in 1884, setting the stage for Long Island's role as 'Polo Capital of the World' during the 1920s and 1930s.

In 1886 the Westchester Cup matches commenced between Great Britain and the USA. Britain dominated in the early years but in 1909 the USA managed their first victory when Mr H.P. Whitney brought over his team known as the 'big four' (L. Waterbury, J. Waterbury, H.P. Whitney and D. Milburn).

In 1891 handicaps and player ratings were added to polo in the United States so that teams could be more evenly matched in games. Ratings were determined by a single handicapper named H.L. Herbert, who rated the best players at 10 goals and the lowest at 0 goals. In 1910 the American handicap system was universally accepted, albeit adjusted so that minus ratings could be given. (The offside law was also dispensed with in 1910 in order to make the game faster and more exciting.) The highest handicap of a 10-goal rating is currently held by only two Americans: Mike Azzaro and Owen Rinehart. A number of professional Argentinian players (including Mariano Aguerre, Pite Merlos, Memo Gracida, Lolo Castagnola, Marcos Heguy and Adolfo Cambiaaso) also currently hold 10-goal ratings. The highest-rated English professional is Henry Brett, at 8 goals.

In 1904 another important tournament began, the United States Open. The first Open was won by the Wanderers, who scored 4½ to the Freebooters' 3. The tournament resumed in 1910 and continued every year with the exception of 1911, 1915, 1917, 1918 and 1942-45. The US Open would become polo's most prestigious tournament.

Polo is played on an outdoor grass field 300yds (274.3m) long by 160yds (146.3m) wide. Goalposts at each end of the field are 8yds (7.3m) apart. A goal is scored by hitting the ball between the posts with the polo stick while on horseback. Play commences with all four players in one team facing the four opposition players in the centre of the field and one of the two referees bowling the ball between the sides. The four players are numbered, no. 1 often being the weakest player, no. 2 the scrambler, no. 3 the caller of tactics, and consequently often the best player, and no. 4 the defensive player.

The ball is traditionally made from bamboo or willow root, 3¼ins (8.3cm) in diameter and weighing 4oz (113.4g). The mallet has a rubber-wrapped grip with a webbed thong for wrapping around the hand, and a bamboo shaft and head 9½ins (24.2cm) in length. The whole stick weighs about 7oz (198.1g) and varies from 48ins (122cm) to 53ins (135cm) in length. The ball is struck with the side of the mallet and not the end.

The game in England is played over four periods (chukkas) of 7½ minutes each and in Argentina over eight chukkas. Polo is unique inasmuch as it discriminates against left-handed players, who are disallowed for obvious logistical and safety reasons. Since 1915 there has been an indoor game hugely popular in the United States with basically the same rules although the playing area is 100yds (91.44m) by 50yds (45.72m) and teams consist of three players instead of four.

From 1909 to 1950 the United States was dominant in the world of polo but since then the top nation has been Argentina. From 1900 to 1936 polo was an Olympic sport.

There remains a great royal tradition in polo and both Prince Philip, the Duke of Edinburgh, and Prince Charles, the Prince of Wales, were notable players.

The competitions for the British Open Gold Cup and the Silver Jubilee Cup are both played at Cowdray Park, Midhurst, Sussex, the home of British polo. Azzurra beat Dubai 17-9 to win the 2004 Veuve Clicquot Gold Cup, the British Open.

POWERBOAT RACING

A year after its founding in 1903, the American Power Boat Association (APBA) established a race on the Hudson river for a trophy called the Gold Challenge Cup. The first race, in June 1904, consisted of three 32-mile heats run on consecutive days. A 59-foot boat, *Standard*, was the winner with an average speed of 23.160mph (37.264kph). Lightweight hulls were excluded from the race, which left out some of the fastest powerboats of the day. The APBA decided to stage a second race in September, allowing lightweight hulls. One of the lightweights, *Vingt-Et-Un II*, won with an average speed of 24.900mph (40.064kph), setting a record of 25.367mph (40.816kph) in the second heat. Originally the race was hosted by the defending champion's boat club, but during the 1920s the APBA began to hold races at a neutral site, often Detroit, and the trophy became known simply as the Gold Cup.

Regulations for the types of boat that could be entered have changed several times. Between 1922 and 1928, only displacement hulls were allowed and engines were limited to 625cu. ins (10,241cc) in piston displacement. The intention was to lower the cost and allow more entries, but that didn't happen and hydroplanes were readmitted to the race in 1929, although engine displacement was still limited. Competition was suspended during World War II. When the race resumed in 1946, the APBA lifted its restriction on engine displacement, mainly because none of the smaller engines had been produced during the war. The unlimited hydroplanes quickly became very popular with spectators and the Gold Cup has been a race for the unlimiteds ever since.

Powerboat racing was revolutionised in 1981 when Formula One racing was recognised by the International Powerboating Union in Monte Carlo. Up to that time the main categories were the OZ unlimited capacity (usually from 3600-4500cc) and the ON outboard-engined, whose capacity was 2000cc. This class was later named Formula Grand Prix. From 1981 to 1989, Formula One and Grand Prix races were held in parallel. There were three world powerboat champions, Italian Renato Molinari in Formula One, the American Bill Seebold (who now produces racing cats) in ON and Englishman Tony Williams in Formula Two, which was later named Grand Prix. The difference was more bureaucratic than technical: the American and European international powerboating authorities and racing courses officials could not agree terms. The present scoring system for Formula One is 20 points for first place, 15 points for second, 12 points for third, 9 points for fourth, 7 points for fifth, 5 points for sixth and then down to 1 point for tenth place. Great Britain has had its share of world champions in Formula One. This form of racing is now referred to as circuit racing.

The most prestigious form of powerboat racing is organised by the UIM (Union Internationale Motonautique). The UIM Class 1 World Offshore Championships have been won several times by co-pilots Bjorn Gjelsten of Norway and Steve Curtis of Great Britain. Throttleman Curtis had a fantastic 2003, winning the world championship aboard *Spirit of Norway* and the Segrave Trophy (awarded to a British subject for outstanding achievements by land, sea or air). Curtis was also honoured by the Royal Yacht Association and named Yachtsman of the Year.

The oldest powerboat race still in existence is Britain's Harmsworth Trophy. It was the most prestigious event in the world for many years after its inaugural event in 1903. Formula One racing caused its decline and it lay dormant between 1995 and 2002 when it was then relaunched. Dale Van Wyk aboard *Miss Seattle* won the 2004 event.

Formula One World Champions

1981	Renato Molinari (ITA)
1982	Roger Jenkins (GBR)
1983	Renato Molinari (ITA)
1984	Renato Molinari (ITA)
1985	Bob Spalding (GBR)
1986	Gene Thibodaux (USA)
1987-89	not held
1990	John Hill (GBR)
1991	Jonathan Jones (GBR)
1992	Fabrizio Bocca (ITA)
1993	Guido Cappellini (ITA)
1994	Guido Cappellini (ITA)
1995	Guido Cappellini (ITA)
1996	Guido Cappellini (ITA)
1997	Scott Gillman (USA)
1998	Jonathan Jones (GBR)
1999	Guido Cappellini (MON)
2000	Scott Gillman (USA)
2001	Guido Cappellini (ITA)
2002	Guido Cappellini (ITA)
2003	Guido Cappellini (ITA)
2004	Scott Gillman (USA)

Gold Cup

	Boat	Drivers		Boat	Drivers
1904	*Standard* (June)	Carl Riotte	1956	*Miss Thriftway*	Bill Muncey
1904	*Vingt-Et-Un II* (Sept.)	W. Sharpe Kilmer	1957	*Miss Thriftway*	Bill Muncey
1905	*Chip I*	J.M. Wainwright	1958	*Hawaii Kai III*	Jack Regas
1906	*Chip II*	J.M. Wainwright	1959	*Maverick*	Bill Stead
1907	*Chip II*	J.M. Wainwright	1960	not held	
1908	*Dixie II*	E.J. Schroeder	1961	*Miss Century 21*	Bill Muncey
1909	*Dixie II*	E.J. Schroeder	1962	*Miss Century 21*	Bill Muncey
1910	*Dixie III*	F.K. Burnham	1963	*Miss Bardahl*	Ron Musson
1911	*MIT II*	J.H. Hayden	1964	*Miss Bardahl*	Ron Musson
1912	*P.D.Q. II*	A.G. Miles	1965	*Miss Bardahl*	Ron Musson
1913	*Ankle Deep*	C.S. Mankowski	1966	*Tahoe Miss*	Mira Slovak
1914	*Baby Speed Demon II*	Jim Blackton/Bob Edgren	1967	*Miss Bardahl*	Bill Shumacher
1915	*Miss Detroit*	Johnny Milot/Jack Beebe	1968	*Miss Bardahl*	Bill Shumacher
1916	*Miss Minneapolis*	Bernard Smith	1969	*Miss Budweiser*	Bill Sterett
1917	*Miss Detroit II*	Gar Wood	1970	*Miss Budweiser*	Dean Chenoweth
1918	*Miss Detroit II*	Gar Wood	1971	*Miss Madison*	Jim McCormick
1919	*Miss Detroit III*	Gar Wood	1972	*Atlas Van Lines*	Bill Muncey
1920	*Miss America I*	Gar Wood	1973	*Miss Budweiser*	Dean Chenoweth
1921	*Miss America I*	Gar Wood	1974	*Pay 'n' Pak*	George Henley
1922	*Packard Chriscraft*	J.G. Vincent	1975	*Pay 'n' Pak*	George Henley
1923	*Packard Chriscraft*	Caleb Bragg	1976	*Miss U.S.*	Tom D'Eath
1924	*Baby Bootlegger*	Caleb Bragg	1977	*Atlas Van Lines*	Bill Muncey
1925	*Baby Bootlegger*	Caleb Bragg	1978	*Atlas Van Lines*	Bill Muncey
1926	*Greenwich Folly*	George Townsend	1979	*Atlas Van Lines*	Bill Muncey
1927	*Greenwich Folly*	George Townsend	1980	*Miss Budweiser*	Dean Chenoweth
1928	not held		1981	*Miss Budweiser*	Dean Chenoweth
1929	*Imp*	Richard Hoyt	1982	*Atlas Van Lines*	Chip Hanauer
1930	*Hotsy Totsy*	Vic Kliesrath	1983	*Atlas Van Lines*	Chip Hanauer
1931	*Hotsy Totsy*	Vic Kliesrath	1984	*Atlas Van Lines*	Chip Hanauer
1932	*Delphine IV*	Bill Horn	1985	*Miller American*	Chip Hanauer
1933	*El Lagarto*	George Reis	1986	*Miller American*	Chip Hanauer
1934	*El Lagarto*	George Reis	1987	*Miller American*	Chip Hanauer
1935	*El Lagarto*	George Reis	1988	*Miss Circus Circus*	Chip Hanauer/Jim Prevost
1936	*Impshi*	Kaye Don	1989	*Miss Budweiser*	Tom D'Eath
1937	*Notre Dame*	Clell Perry	1990	*Miss Budweiser*	Tom D'Eath
1938	*Alagi*	Theo Rossi	1991	*Winston Eagle*	Mark Tate
1939	*My Sin*	Z.G. Simmons jnr	1992	*Miss Budweiser*	Chip Hanauer
1940	*Hotsy Totsy III*	Sidney Allen	1993	*Miss Budweiser*	Chip Hanauer
1941	*My Sin*	Z.G. Simmons jnr	1994	*Smokin' Joe's*	Mark Tate
1942-45	not held		1995	*Miss Budweiser*	Chip Hanauer
1946	*Tempo VI*	Guy Lombardo	1996	*Pico/American Dream*	Dave Villwock
1947	*Miss Peps V*	Danny Foster	1997	*Miss Budweiser*	Dave Villwock
1948	*Miss Great Lakes*	Danny Foster	1998	*Miss Budweiser*	Dave Villwock
1949	*My Sweetie*	Bill Cantrell	1999	*Miss Pico*	Chip Hanauer
1950	*Slo-Mo-Shun IV*	Ted Jones	2000	*Miss Budweiser*	Dave Villwock
1951	*Slo-Mo-Shun V*	Lou Fageol	2001	*Miss Tubby's Subs*	Michael Hanson
1952	*Slo-Mo-Shun IV*	Stan Dollar	2002	*Miss Budweiser*	Dave Villwock
1953	*Slo-Mo-Shun IV*	Joe Taggart/Lou Fageol	2003	*Miss Fox Hills*	Ed Cooper/Mitch Evans
1954	*Slo-Mo-Shun V*	Lou Fageol	2004	*Miss DYC*	Nate Brown
1955	*Gale V*	Lee Schoenith			

RACKETS

In its earliest form during the 18th century, rackets was played in the open on the walls of the yards of the two main debtors' prisons: the King's Bench and the Fleet. Gentlemen, imprisoned until they could find the wherewithal to repay their creditors, amused themselves with many different activities around the prison yard. These included skittles and fives, which was played both with the hand and a bat (as at Westminster School), while some brought tennis rackets with them and improvised against any convenient wall, sometimes with no side walls and always without a back wall.

There is mention of rackets at the Fleet in a poem of 1749 and in John Howard's report on the state of prisons in England and Wales published in 1780. It is not until the early 1800s that rackets becomes part of life outside the prisons. In Pierce Egan's *Book of Sports and Mirror of Life*, published in 1832, there is a long description of rackets mentioning several open rackets courts other than the King's Bench and the Fleet. One of these was at the Belvedere Tavern, Pentonville, where most of the open court championships were played. Among others in London (all public houses) were the Eagle Tavern on the City Road, The White Bear, Kennington, White Conduit House, Islington, and the Rosemary Branch, Peckham.

There are also records of courts at Bristol, Bath, Birmingham and Belfast. Egan states that if a gentleman sought a game at a tavern he would have to mix with those not of the highest rank in society. Implicit in this observation is that the debtors' prison may have had a higher class of player (in both meanings of the word), indeed of spectator as well, as visitors often came to watch matches in the prisons (mention is made of a Major Campbell who was the best player in the King's Bench, having been incarcerated there for 14 years).

Dickens mentions rackets in *The Pickwick Papers*, Mr Pickwick being unlucky enough to be put into the Fleet. From Dickens's description of the court it appears to have had a front wall and one side wall similar to a jai alai *fronton*. In 1814 there were four courts at the King's Bench and six racket masters to look after them. Early courts outside the prisons had a front wall only, about 40ft (12.2m) wide and 45ft (13.7m) high.

Outside prisons and taverns, Harrow was the first school at which rackets was played, probably from the early 1820s when the schoolyard was enlarged. When the first lawn tennis championships were played at Wimbledon later in the century, Old Harrovian rackets player Spencer Gore would win the singles.

In the middle of the 19th century, rackets played in covered courts began to predominate. The Marylebone Cricket Club (MCC) built a court in 1844 next to the old tennis court and Old Princes Club opened in 1853 with several courts as well as two tennis courts. The main competition court at Princes set the standard dimensions for most closed courts built from then up to the present day, being 60ft (18.3m) long by 30ft (9.14m) wide. Before this on the open courts, doubles was played on a court of 80ft × 40ft (24.4m × 12.2m) with two playing at the front and two at the back.

At around this time, the growing popularity of the indoor game caused rackets at the open courts attached to public houses to decline and rackets became more and more a game for the wealthy. Although Lord West built a court at Buckhurst Park in Sussex in the 1850s and the Earl of Eglinton and Winton built one at Eglinton Castle, his home in Scotland, rackets did not take off as a private country house game to the same extent as tennis did later in the century.

Both Oxford and Cambridge universities had courts by 1855, the date of the first Varsity match. There were courts built at Torquay in 1859 and the first covered court at Harrow School, built in 1865, is still in use today. Devonshire Park at Eastbourne included a rackets court built in 1870 as part of its general recreational facilities. Between 1870 and 1890, courts were built at the new Princes Club, Manchester, Liverpool and in 1888 the courts at Queens were opened. Rugby School has the distinction of having nurtured no less than three world champions of whom David Milford was the first, holding the title from 1937 to 1947. In 1933 and 1934 Rugby won the public schools championship, repeating this feat in 1938 and 1939. In 1933 R.A. Gray, son of the professional Harry Gray, was the first string playing with R.F. Lumb. Rugby's next world champion, although never a winner of the public schools championship, was arguably the best player that the school produced. Geoffrey Atkins held the world championship for 17 years, from 1954-70, and retired undefeated. Rugby next won at Queens in 1952 and then in 1965. The first string in 1965 was W.M.C. Surtees playing with A.M.A. Hankey. Surtees went on to hold the world championship in 1972-73 and then from 1975-81. James Male of Great Britain has been at the top of the world rankings for large parts of the last two decades.

Real Tennis

Also called royal tennis and court tennis, the sport has been played since the Middle Ages when it is said to have been cursed by the sovereign. In February 1437, James I of Scotland supposedly tried to hide down the royal drains while attempting to evade conspirators led by Walter, Earl of Atholl, but the drains were blocked by real tennis balls. He was subsequently found and assassinated. Real tennis was popularised by Henry VIII in the early 16th century when he frequently enjoyed a game at Hampton Court. Most of the Tudor and Stuart monarchs enjoyed playing real tennis. Charles I built a new court at Hampton Court in 1625 and this is still used for championship matches today.

The 16th and 17th centuries were a golden age for real tennis: it was played by the nobility throughout France as well as England. There were reputedly as many as 1800 courts in Paris during the game's heyday, although many of these were probably quite rough structures. It is even recorded that a court was built on a 2000-ton French ship in the 16th century. The court at Versailles was built in 1686 at a cost of 45,403 francs. By the 1700s the game had begun to decline. On 21 July 1788, in Vizille castle's 'real tennis' room, the assembly of the three orders of the Dauphiné held the meeting that gave birth to the revolutionary process in France, and on 20 June 1789 the *Serment du Jeu de paume* (oath of the real tennis court), the pledge which marks the birth of the French Revolution, was signed in the real tennis court at Versailles. By 1800, partly due to the revolution, the game in France was practically non-existent.

The court itself is complex and few are still in use around the world. There are no standard dimensions, but the following are recommended by the Tennis & Rackets Association (founded 1907). The overall length should be 110ft (33.5m) and the overall width 39ft (11.9m). The penthouse width should be 7ft 6ins (2.29m), its lower edge height 7ft (2.13m) and its upper edge height 10ft 6ins (3.2m). The height of the playline is 18ft (5.5m) and the height of the building at the eaves 30ft (9.14m). The net is 5ft (1.52m) high at the sides and 3ft (0.91m) at the middle. As in lawn tennis, scoring proceeds as love, 15, 30, 40 and game, probably derived from a sexagesimal monetary system that was convenient for betting purposes. A set is won by the first player to reach six games.

Although there are numerous constituents (rules and features of the court), the complexity of the game is often exaggerated. However, the system of *chases* is an essential difference from other modern games. A key element of real tennis, which it shares with squash (but not lawn tennis), is playing the ball to good 'length' – that is, so that the ball's second bounce occurs near the end (penthouse) or back wall of the court. Chases primarily occur when the ball bounces a second time. A good chase is made on an opponent's side if it is near the end wall, while a poorer chase is near the net – the lines on the floor acting as a means to mark and remember the chases made (e.g. chase one yard or chase six yards). The areas where chases can be made are different on the two sides of the court, and chases also occur when the ball enters the side galleries (except for the 'winning' gallery). When two chases are made, or if there is one chase and game point is reached, then players change ends and the chases are played off. Since service is made from one end of the court, the playing off of chases is the only mechanism by which change of service occurs – giving chases great tactical importance.

Originally the game was played with the bare hand, later with a glove, then someone had the idea of attaching cord or tendons to the fingers. It was a short step to attaching these cords to a frame and adding a handle to form a racket. Today, Grays of Cambridge is the only real tennis racket-maker, the pear-shaped face being very distinctive. The ball, although similar in appearance to a lawn tennis ball, is made with a core of cork, covered in cloth, tightly bound in string and covered in felt. The balls are all hand-stitched and last for about two weeks. This method has been used throughout history, although other substances such as hair or wool were used for the centre, and the balls are a good deal lighter at 1oz (28g), as opposed to nearly 3oz (85g), before the advent of the racket.

The world real tennis championships are played on a challenge basis. Pieter Etchebaster held the world title from 1938 to 1954, when he retired at the age of 61, although the longest reign was by Frenchman Edmond Barre (1829-62). Robert Fahey of Australia is the present world champion having dominated the game since 1994. The women's game has been dominated by Penny Lumley of Great Britain since 1989 when she first won the world title as Penny Fellows.

ROLLER SKATING

Often regarded as a relatively new sport, roller skating has actually existed for several hundred years.

Inspired by ice skating, and the desire to move equally quickly across land during summer, a Dutchman, Hans Brinkner, was the first to produce a type of roller skate at the beginning of the 18th century, by buckling wooden spools under his boots. However, the first real inventor is generally considered to have been Joseph Merlin (b. 1735), a Belgian manufacturer of musical instruments, who produced the first design with metal wheels shortly after 1760. In 1813, Jean Garcin constructed a skate consisting of a simple wooden board to which rollers were fastened and which was strapped to the foot as a unit. Other innovative designs were soon patented, but the skates still remained difficult to master, both in balance and direction. In 1863, Garcin's design was picked up by industrial engineers and demonstrated at the World's Fair in Paris. Suitably inspired, James Leonard Plympton of New York designed roller skates, which were sold under the trade name 'Rocking Skate'. Plympton opened the first successful roller rink at Newport, Rhode Island, in 1866.

The National Skating Association of Great Britain (founded in 1879), previously concentrating on ice skating, assumed control of roller skating in 1893. At around this time improved roller skates led to various competitions and the different disciplines of speed skating, artistic skating and roller hockey began to evolve. The first British figure championship was won by W. Stanton in 1910 at Maida Vale and the competition was open to men and women until 1939 when the sexes had dedicated championships. European championships were inaugurated in 1937 and World Championships in 1947 in Washington. Donald Mounce of the USA and Ursula Wehrli of Switzerland were the first champions of the world.

We owe today's superior roller skates and the ensuing techniques to the German/American space scientist Wernher von Braun and his colleagues. While developing their space programme in the 1960s, they discovered a synthetic material whose extraordinary properties made it ideally suited for sealing rockets – it was rock-hard but absorbed shocks and impacts without shattering or crumbling. Its name was polyurethane and this is now the substance used to fill the wheels on almost all new roller skates.

Modern champions include Luca Lallai and Luca D'Alisera of Italy who have won several men's singles titles at the Artistic World Championships but also pioneered triple loop combinations, D'Alisera being the first athlete to perform a triple axel in competition. Other star performers include Scott Cohen and Jason Cohen of the United States, Tanja Romano of Italy, Heather Mulkey of the United States, and the famed Italian pair of Patrick Venerucci and Beatrice Palazzi Rossi who have won numerous world titles together and almost as many perfect 10.0 scores.

ROWING

Today rowing is mainly a form of recreation and sport. However, for centuries it was the most dependable form of water transport. There is historical evidence of rowing as a mode of travel from about 2500BC. Early warships (galleys) were powered by oarsmen. Biremes, triremes and quadriremes had two, three and four banks of rowers respectively. Races between galleys were held in ancient Egypt and Rome. As recently as 7 October 1571 oared galleys featured in major sea battles when, in the Gulf of Lepanto (now the Gulf of Corinth), a Christian alliance defeated the fleet of the Ottoman empire.

It is generally thought that rowing was used as a means of transport on the River Thames from as early as the 13th century. Impromptu races amongst the watermen possibly began in the 16th century. By the early 18th century there were an estimated 40,000 liveried watermen at work on the Thames. Doggett's Coat and Badge, one of the world's oldest continuing rowing races, held annually between London Bridge and Chelsea, began in 1715. The contest was instituted in that year by Thomas Doggett, an English comic actor, to commemorate the accession of George I in 1714.

Rowing as a school and university amateur sport began in England in the early 19th century. There were organised races at Oxford and Cambridge in the 1820s. On 12 March 1829, Cambridge challenged Oxford and a tradition was born, the annual University Boat Race. The first Henley Regatta was held in 1839 and, under the patronage of Prince Albert, it became the Henley Royal Regatta in 1851. Henley-style events have since been held in the USA, Canada and Australia. The highlights at Henley are the Grand Challenge Cup (established 1839) for eights and the Diamond Challenge Sculls (established 1844) for individual rowers.

Local and national rowing organisations were also formed, the Amateur Rowing Association (ARA) being established in 1882. Today the ARA is the governing body for the sport of rowing in Great Britain, and is responsible for representing British interests to the Fédération Internationale des Sociétés d'Aviron (FISA), the world's governing body which was established in 1892. (*Aviron* being French for oar or rowing).

Rowing has been an Olympic sport for men since 1900 and for women since 1976. It had been scheduled for 1896 but bad weather forced its cancellation. The first World Championships were held at Lucerne in 1962, events for women and lightweight men being introduced in 1974.

The sport consists of two main categories, rowing and sculling. In rowing (also known as sweep rowing) the lightweight craft or 'shell' is propelled by means of a single oar grasped in both hands, whereas in sculling two oars are used, one held in each hand. Early shells and sculls were made of wood and had fixed seats. Nowadays lightweight materials are used; the sliding seat was introduced in the USA in 1857 and in Britain in 1871. Modern Olympic, World and European Championship races are held over a 2000m course. In rowing there are races for two, four or eight rowers and in sculling for one, two or four scullers.

Biographies of Rowers and Coaches

Abbagnale brothers Giuseppe born Pompeii, Italy, 24 July 1959; Carmine born Pompeii, 5 January 1962; Agostino born Pompeii 25 August 1966. Giuseppe and Carmine Abbagnale, together with cox Giuseppe di Capua, formed a formidable partnership; winning the world title seven times between 1981 and 1991, and Olympic gold twice (1984, 1988). Undefeated since 1986, they were expected to win gold again at Barcelona in 1992 but were beaten into second place by the British brothers Jonny and Greg Searle. The Abbagnales' long, powerful strokes usually put them in command of their races well before the finish but they tended to be a one-pace crew and, under attack from the younger Searle brothers, they were unable to raise their rate of striking and were beaten by half a length. Younger brother Agostino eclipsed his elder brothers' Olympic record by winning gold at three different Olympics (1988, 1996, 2000), in the quadruple sculls in Seoul, the double sculls in Atlanta, with Davide Tizzano, and the quadruple sculls again in Sydney.

Adam, Karl Born 1911. West German coach. The most influential coach of the second half of the 20th century, Adam, like Hiram Conibear, had no real experience of rowing when he accepted a coaching post with the Ratzeburg Rowing Club near Lübeck; he had been a former world student boxing champion and high school teacher. In the 1950s he successfully introduced new training methods based on *Fahrtspiel* ('speed play', originally used for training runners), and on interval training (short sprints alternated with long runs). In addition his oarsmen used heavy weights in the gymnasium. His use of 'cybernetics', in which learning is done through instinctive processes, was similar to the ideas of the great Australian coach, Steve Fairbairn. In 1958 Adam's Ratzeburg eight, which won the West German national championships, contained five 18-year-olds. Adam also pioneered advances in equipment, including the use of longer oars with shovel-shaped blades. He produced many outstanding crews such as the eight which won the 1959 European Championship and the 1960 Olympic gold, ending the American domination of the event which had begun in 1920. He retired in

1968 after his eight had won another Olympic title using a shell 75lb (34kg) lighter than any of the others used in the race. He died in 1975.

Baillieu, Chris Born Marylebone, London, 12 December 1949. While at Jesus College, Cambridge, he became the only Light Blue to win four Boat Races in the 20th century (1970-73). Turning his attention to sculling, in partnership with Michael Hart he won four double sculls World Championship medals – bronze in 1974 and 1975, silver in 1978 and gold in 1977 – and the pair won the silver medal at the 1976 Olympics behind the Norwegian brothers Frank and Alf Hansen. At the 1980 Olympics with a new partner, Tim Clark, Baillieu just missed out on the medals, finishing in fourth place. As a single sculler he enjoyed much success at Henley, winning the Diamond Sculls on three occasions (1981, 1982, 1984), but his best placing in the World Championships was fourth in 1981. He was awarded the MBE and later became a steward of Henley Royal Regatta.

Beresford, Jack Born Jack Beresford Wiszniewski, Chiswick, London, 1 January 1899. Educated at Bedford School, he saw active service in the latter years of World War I. His father, Julius, won an Olympic silver medal in the eights in 1912. Beresford had an outstanding record as an amateur sculler and as an oarsman with Thames, Leander and Kingston Rowing Clubs: champion sculler of Great Britain from 1920 to 1926, he won the Diamond Sculls at Henley Royal Regatta four times during the same period. He won the silver medal at the Olympic Games in Antwerp in 1920, losing the sculling final by one second to the American Jack Kelly. He was renowned for his tactical acumen, and his ability to do just enough to beat his opponents. He won the Philadelphia Gold Cup for the world amateur title in 1924 and 1925 and after 1920 won four more medals in the next four Olympic Games: the single sculling title in 1924 in Paris, silver in the British eight at Amsterdam in 1928, gold in the British four at Los Angeles in 1932, and, at the age of 37, the double sculls gold, with L.F. ('Dick') Southwood, at Berlin in 1936, ahead of the German crew. He continued to enjoy domestic success at Henley and devoted considerable efforts to coaching and sports administration. For his services to rowing, he was awarded the gold medal of the International Rowing Federation (FISA) in 1947, and the Olympic diploma of merit in 1949 after helping to organise the Games in London and Henley-on-Thames in 1948. Beresford managed the British rowing team at the 1952 Olympics. He was appointed CBE in 1960. He died at his home, Highlands House, Shiplake, 3 December 1977.

Conibear, Hiram Born Mineral, Illinois, USA, 5 September 1871. US rowing coach. Along with Australian Steve Fairbairn and German Karl Adam, Conibear was one of the most influential rowing coaches. A former professional cyclist and athletics and baseball coach, he was hired by the University of Washington as rowing coach. Although he had no previous knowledge of rowing, during his time there (1907-17) he developed a distinctive style that stressed physical training and was based on powerful leg drive, upright finish and fast recovery. He produced rowers noted for their strength and stamina and the Conibear stroke dominated American rowing so successfully that the eights in every Olympic Games from 1920 to 1956 were won by US collegiate crews. Unfortunately Conibear died

before these triumphs after a fall from a fruit tree in Seattle, 9 September 1917.

Cracknell, James Born Sutton, Surrey, 5 May 1972. Cracknell began rowing at Kingston Grammar School. In 1990 he won gold in the coxless fours at the World Junior Championships and was selected at senior level the following year for the World Championships. In 1995 he switched to sculling and in the double sculls finished seventh at the 1995 World Championships. Returning to sweep rowing, he won gold at the 1997 World Championships in the coxless fours, retaining the world title in 1998 and 1999. However, his greatest triumph came with Foster, Pinsent and Redgrave in the coxless fours at the Sydney Olympics in 2000. He was awarded the MBE in the New Year's Honours List in 2001. In the 2001 season he switched to the coxless pairs with Matthew Pinsent, a partnership which completed a unique double at the World Championships. They won both this event and the coxed pairs (with cox Neil Chugani) held less than two hours earlier, eclipsing the performance of Redgrave and Holmes who won gold and silver in the 1987 World Championships. They retained their coxless pairs title in 2002 in a world best time, also winning the Silver Goblets coxless pairs at Henley for three successive years (2001-03). However, the seemingly unassailable partnership could finish only fourth in the 2003 World Championships in Milan. Cracknell, a qualified geography teacher, has contributed a rowing column to the *Daily Telegraph.*

Fairbairn, Steve Born Melbourne, Australia, 25 August 1862. Australian rower and coach. Unlike the other outstanding coaches, Hiram Conibear and Karl Adam, Fairbairn had a background in rowing, having come from Sydney to Cambridge University (Jesus College) for whom he rowed four times in the 1880s. As a coach at Cambridge, he enjoyed great success with an innovative approach, settling in England in 1905. In contrast to the orthodox school, which emphasised body swing as the main source of power, Fairbairn's stroke concentrated on leg drive, arm pull and smooth blade work, and was short on the water; his technique demanded a high degree of physical fitness. The success of his Cambridge and Thames Rowing Club crews influenced international rowing and led to a number of equipment modifications and developments. Slides were lengthened, swivel rowlocks replaced fixed pins, and crews sat in straight lines rather than in staggered positions. In 1926 Fairbairn organised the first Head of the River Race on the Thames, which quickly became a fixture in the sport. His *Rowing Notes* (1926) is considered a seminal rowing book. In 1931 his autobiography *Fairbairn of Jesus* was published. He died in London, 16 May 1938.

Foster, Tim Born Hillingdon, Middlesex, 19 January 1970. Foster began rowing at Bedford Modern School and went on to become the first Briton to win gold medals at successive World Junior Championships, in 1987 in the coxless fours and in 1988 in the coxless pairs with Matthew Pinsent. From 1989 to 1992 he had considerable success in eights. In the 1989 World Championships he won a bronze medal, repeating the achievement in 1991 as stroke. Foster had to make several comebacks from career-threatening injuries, the first of these requiring a major back operation in 1993. He recovered to win World Championship bronze and silver (1994,1995) in the coxless fours with Rupert Obholzer and the Searle brothers, the foursome also winning bronze in the Atlanta Olympics (1996). In

1997 Foster was in the Oxford crew that lost to Cambridge in the University Boat Race. In the same year he was chosen with Pinsent, Redgrave and Cracknell to form a new British coxless four. They won both the 1997 World Cup regatta series and the World Championships. Having missed much of the 1998 season through injury, he rejoined the crew in time for a successful defence of their world title, before undergoing back surgery for a second time later that year. He recovered sufficiently to win silver in the British eight at the 1999 World Championships while Ed Coode took his place in the winning coxless four. Foster won his place back in the coxless fours which won the memorable race at the Sydney Olympics in 2000, giving him a record of two Olympic and seven World Championship medals. In 2001, after a succession of injuries, he decided to retire and concentrate on coaching.

Grobler, Jürgen Born Magdeburg, Germany, 31 July 1946. He moved to Britain from the former East Germany in 1991 to be the head coach at Leander Club. He was appointed chief coach for men by the Amateur Rowing Association after the 1992 Olympic Games, a position he still holds. From 1991 he was the coach to Matthew Pinsent and Steven Redgrave who in the coxless pair won four World Championship gold medals and two Olympic golds from 1991 to 1996. Since 1996 he has been coach of the men's coxless four and has taken them to gold medals in the 1997, 1998 and 1999 World Championships and finally to Olympic glory in Sydney 2000. To mark his achievements over the years Jürgen was awarded the International Rowing Federation (FISA) 2000 'Coach of the Year' award and in the same year he was nominated as Coach of the Year in BBC Television's *Sports Review of the Year*. He was awarded the Freedom of Henley, where he lives, on his return from the Atlanta Olympics.

Grubor, Luka Born Zagreb, Croatia, 27 December 1973. His father played basketball for Yugoslavia in the 1960s. Grubor began rowing as a 14-year-old. Within three years he was selected to represent Yugoslavia at the World Junior Championships. While attending Imperial College, London, he gained selection for the Croatian team in 1993. In 1996 he began studies at Oxford University and in 1997 rowed in the University Boat Race. He became a British citizen and now belongs to the Tower Boat Club. He was a member of the British eight who won silver at the 1999 World Championships, gold at the Sydney Olympics (the first British win in the event for 88 years) and in 2001 the overall World Cup for a second successive year.

Holmes, Andrew Born 15 October 1959. Holmes's considerable achievements have been overshadowed by the exploits of Redgrave, Pinsent and others. He was a gold medallist at the 1984 Olympics in the coxed fours with Martin Cross, Richard Budgett, Redgrave and cox Adrian Ellison. Though Holmes and Redgrave were double gold winners (coxless pairs and coxed fours) in the 1986 Commonwealth Games in Edinburgh, Redgrave again stole the headlines by winning a third gold medal, this time in the single sculls. Redgrave and Holmes were the world champions in the coxless pairs in 1987. Holmes was a gold medallist again at Seoul in 1988, this time with Redgrave in the coxless pairs. Less than 23 hours later they were back on the water in the coxed fours with cox Patrick Sweeney and finished in bronze medal position. After Seoul, Holmes dropped out of rowing, disillusioned with the

'hype' and fame surrounding Redgrave after the 1998 Olympics.

Ivanov, Vyacheslav Born Moscow, Soviet Union, 30 July 1938. Soviet army officer who was the first man to win the prestigious Olympic single sculls event on three occasions (1956, 1960, 1964). His first victory, on Lake Wendouree, Melbourne, was achieved at the age of 18. After beating Australian sculler Stuart MacKenzie into second place, Ivanov was so excited he dropped his medal in the lake. It was never recovered and eventually the IOC issued him with a replacement. In the Rome and Tokyo Olympics he beat East German Achim Hill on both occasions. On the latter occasion he briefly lost consciousness 50m from the finishing line. He recovered to find himself still ahead and went on to win by nearly four seconds. Ivanov won 11 consecutive USSR single sculls titles (1956-66), was four times European champion and won the inaugural World Championships at Lucerne in 1962. In his races, he was usually last after 500m, but his judgement was excellent and he would make his way through the field to win.

Karppinen, Pertti Born Vehmaa, Finland, 17 February 1953. Standing 6ft 9ins (2.05m), the Finnish fireman equalled the feat of Ivanov by winning the Olympic single sculls three times (1976, 1980, 1984). He was also world champion in 1979 and 1985 and had three second places (1977, 1981, 1986) and one third place (1987). With his brother Reina (born 27 January 1958) he was second in the double sculls at the World Championships. During his career he was often in competition with Peter-Michael Kolbe of Germany, who won the World Championships five times compared to Karppinen's two. The Finn, however, seemed to save his best for the Olympics, beating Kolbe twice. The combination of Karppinen's immense power and easy strokes made him a strong finisher; like Ivanov, he often stayed at the back of the field before putting on a sustained sprint in the last 500m of a race.

Kelly, John, snr Born Philadelphia, USA, 4 October 1889. Known as Jack and the father of Grace Kelly, the film actress, who became Princess Grace of Monaco. He won 126 consecutive races in single sculls in 1919 and 1920, a record that included a gold medal at the 1920 Olympic Games in Antwerp, beating Briton Jack Beresford. Kelly also won the double sculls event (with his cousin Paul Costello) at the 1920 Games. These two races were only 30 minutes apart. He repeated his double sculls success with Costello at the 1924 Games in Paris. The Philadelphia Challenge Cup was inaugurated in his honour for being the first American to win the single sculls race in Olympic competition. Kelly never rowed at Henley, a fact attributed by some to the claim that he was not an amateur, and by others to the fact that his trade as a bricklayer was socially unacceptable. His son, Jack Kelly jnr, redressed the Henley situation. Coached by his father, he won the Diamond Sculls in 1947 and 1949, and went on to win Olympic bronze in 1956. John Kelly snr died in his home city of Philadelphia, 20 June 1960.

Lange, Thomas Born Eisleben, East Germany, 27 February 1964. A sculler renowned for his technical brilliance, Lange was a product of the East German sporting machine. He might have emulated the feat of Ivanov by winning three gold medals for single sculls and deprived Karppinen of doing so, but for the East German boycott of the 1984 Olympics. He won the event for the German Democratic Republic in 1988 and in 1992 for the re-unified Germany.

Between 1980 and 1992, apart from the years he did not compete (1984 and 1990 when completing medical studies), Lange won a gold medal each year at junior or senior level in World Championships and the Olympics. In total at the World Championships, he won the single sculls three times and the double sculls twice with fellow countryman Uwe Hepper. In 1993 he won the Diamond Sculls at Henley, defeating the Czech, Vaclav Chalupa. In the 1996 Olympics he had to be content with the bronze medal.

Lipa, Elisabeta   Born Elisabeta Olenivic, Siret, Romania, 26 October 1964. Lipa has won seven Olympic medals, more than any other rower (four gold, two silver and one bronze). She won gold and silver respectively in the double sculls in 1984 and 1988, also winning bronze in the quadruple sculls. In 1992 this Romanian civil servant won her second gold in the single sculls. In the next two Olympics, 1996 and 2000, she was a member of the Romanian eight that won gold on both occasions. From 1981 to 2003 she won a total of 14 medals at the FISA World Championships, two gold, nine silver and three bronze – the highlight being when she won the single sculls gold in 1989.

Mackenzie, Stuart   Born Sydney, Australia, 1937. Educated at King's School, Sydney. A chicken sexer by trade, he came to prominence in 1956 by winning the Australian single sculls championship. At the Olympics that year he took the silver medal behind Ivanov. In 1957 he won the Australian, New Zealand, Belgian and European championships as well as the Diamond Sculls. In 1958 he successfully defended his European title and also won the Commonwealth Games gold. From 1956 he consistently beat Ivanov and was the favourite to win the Olympic title in 1960. However, he fell ill in Rome and had to scratch from the competition. His greatest triumphs were at Henley where he won the Diamond Sculls six years in succession (1957-62), thus breaking an 80-year-old Henley record. In 1959 he became the first man in history to win both the single and double sculls at Henley. Mackenzie regularly upset the Henley establishment with some outrageous mocking behaviour, once wearing a bowler hat in a race and, on another occasion, stopping in mid-race to adjust his cap before pulling away again to win easily. Two of his Henley wins were controversial as he steered in front of his opponents giving them his wash. The international rules, which would have resulted in his disqualification, did not apply at Henley. He continued to race in Europe until his retirement in 1965.

Nickalls, Guy   Born Horton Kirby, Kent, 12 November 1866. Regarded in his youth as being of delicate constitution, Nickalls nevertheless became an oarsman of tremendous power and endurance. He rowed for two years for Eton, winning the Ladies' Plate in 1885, and five years for Oxford (1887-91), being a member of the winning crew in the last two years. His Henley successes are unlikely to be surpassed. Over this course he rowed 81 races, of which he won 67 and lost 13, one being a dead heat. This extraordinary achievement includes the following victories: Diamond Sculls (7), Goblets or pair-oared races (6), Stewards' or four-oared races (7), Grand Challenge Cups (4), Olympic eights (1), and Ladies' Plate (1). The Nickalls family (Guy, his brother Vivian and his son Guy Oliver) had 43 Henley wins between them. The most notable of Guy senior's achievements was his rowing at no. 4 in the victorious Leander eight at the age of 42 in the 1908 Olympics. He died in Leeds on 7 July 1935 from injuries received in a motoring accident the previous day.

Nitsch, Jo   Born Aldershot, Hampshire, 18 March 1969. A member of the Leander Club, Nitsch started rowing at the Bedford Rowing Club in 1991. One of the top lightweight women rowers in Britain in both sweep and sculling events, Nitsch has a total of four World Championship medals. She won consecutive silver medals in the women's lightweight coxless fours in the 1995 and 1996 World Championships, and in 1998 and 2001 won gold (with Juliet Machan and Sarah Birch respectively) in the women's lightweight coxless pairs. Remarkably she had spent the previous two years sculling and was at the World Championships as a member of the British lightweight women's four. The day before the pairs final, the stroke was forced to withdraw through injury and Nitsch was asked to substitute for her. She produced an outstanding performance as the scratch pairing rowed away from the field to win gold.

Pinsent, Matthew   Born Holt, Norfolk, 10 October 1970. Educated at Eton and St Catherine's College, Oxford, Pinsent took up rowing at Eton. Steve Redgrave's legendary record has, to some extent, overshadowed Pinsent's amazing achievements at the highest level. Over a 12-year period (1991-2002), he won a gold medal every year in either the World Championships or the Olympics and won two in 2001. Prior to that he won gold with Tim Foster in 1988 in the coxless pairs at the World Junior Championships. Since 1989 he has been a member of the Leander Club. In that year, at senior level, he won a World Championship bronze in the coxed fours. Replacing the injured Simon Berrisford, he teamed up with Redgrave in 1990. As a coxless pair they won the World Championship bronze in 1990 and went on to win gold in the World Championships of 1991, 1993, 1994 (in world-record time) and 1995. At the Barcelona Olympics in 1992 they won their final by the biggest margin of the regatta. From 1992 to 1996 they were unbeaten anywhere and in fact were Britain's only gold medal winners at the 1996 Olympics in Atlanta. On the domestic front Pinsent rowed in three University Boat Races for Oxford, where he was president 1992-93. The first two (1990 and 1991) were wins but 1993 ended in defeat. To date he has a total of 15 wins at Henley including seven Silver Goblets for coxless pairs. After Redgrave changed his mind about retiring in 1996, it was decided they would switch to coxless fours. In 1997 they were unbeaten in the World Cup series and also claimed the World Championship gold. The latter was retained in 1998 and in 1999 they had another unbeaten run in the World Cup and World Championships. At the 2000 Olympics Pinsent was chosen as Britain's flag-bearer in the opening ceremony. In Sydney in the race which will be remembered for Redgrave's fifth Olympic gold, Pinsent was himself winning his third. Since Sydney he has returned to coxless pairs, this time teaming up with James Cracknell. In 2001 they achieved a unique British double at the World Championships by winning gold in both the coxless and coxed pairs. In retaining the 2002 world coxless pairs crown they set a new world-record time of 6mins 14.27secs, beating the 1994 mark set when Pinsent was partnering Redgrave. In the same year Pinsent was elected as an athlete's representative on the International Olympic Committee. His remarkable 'gold run' finally came to an end in 2003 when he and Cracknell could finish only fourth in the World Championships in Milan. To maximise Britain's chances of rowing gold in Athens 2004 Jürgen Grobler decided Pinsent and Cracknell should compete in the coxless four.

Redgrave, Steve Born Amersham, Buckinghamshire, 23 March 1962. Britain's greatest-ever Olympian took up rowing at Marlow School and became a member of the Marlow Rowing Club. He set out originally to be a sculler and won a silver medal at the World Junior Championships in 1980 in the double sculls. At senior level he competed in the 1981 and 1982 World Championships in the quadruple sculls. His record at Henley of 19 titles (64 race wins out of 67) is the best of the modern era. He won the Wingfield sculls (the amateur championship of the Thames and Great Britain) five years in succession (1985-89) and the Diamond Sculls twice (1983, 1985). He also won the single sculls as part of a unique treble at the Commonwealth Games of 1986 – the other two gold medals being with Andrew Holmes in the coxless and coxed pairs (cox Patrick Sweeney). At Henley, he also has a record seven victories in the Silver Goblets and Nickalls Cup for coxless pairs (twice with Holmes, once with Berrisford and four times with Pinsent). Redgrave has medals in all senior Henley events except the Grand Challenge Cup for eights. He also as a record 11 wins with Leander (whom he joined in 1987) in the Head of the River Race. At World Championships he won nine gold medals, a British record until Pinsent won his tenth in 2002. He won in the coxed pairs in 1986 and coxless pair in 1987 with Holmes – they also won silver in the coxed pairs. However, it is his partnership with Pinsent that will be long remembered. After Holmes retired and new partner Simon Berrisford (with whom he won world silver in 1989) became injured, Redgrave and Pinsent teamed up. They won their first World Championship medal, a bronze in 1990. In the same year Redgrave won the Indoor World Rowing Championship. Back on water with Pinsent, he won the World Championship gold in 1991 and they completed a treble of victories in 1993 and 1995, the pair remaining unbeaten anywhere in the world between 1992 and 1996. As part of the British coxless four crew, he won gold at the World Championships three years in succession, 1997-99. The World Cup was also won in 1997 and 1999. The only sportsman in an endurance event to win gold at five different Olympics, Redgrave's achievements were marked at the Sydney Olympics by a presentation from IOC President Samaranch. At Los Angeles in 1984 he won gold in the coxed fours (with Holmes, Richard Budgett, Adrian Ellison and Martin Cross) and in 1988 gold in the coxless pairs with Holmes and bronze in the coxed pairs with Holmes and cox Patrick Sweeney. Chosen as Britain's flag-bearer in Barcelona in 1992 and Atlanta in 1996 (the first Briton to be given this honour twice), he won gold on both occasions with Pinsent. At Atlanta he stated his

intention to quit when he famously said, 'If anyone sees me anywhere near a boat, they have permission to shoot me'. Fortunately he had a change of heart and at Sydney in the coxless fours his fifth gold medal was won. Redgrave's achievements have been recognised by the award of the MBE (1986), CBE (1997) and a knighthood in 2001. Not surprisingly, he was voted BBC Sports Personality of the Year in 2000. He was elected honorary president of the Amateur Rowing Association in 2001. He has published two books: *Redgrave's Complete Book of Rowing* (1992) and his autobiography *A Golden Age* (2000). In 1989, Redgrave also took up bobsledding and was a member of the team which won the British four-man championship.

Searle brothers Jonathan (Jonny) born Walton-on-Thames, Surrey, 8 May 1969. Greg(ory) born Ashford, Kent, 20 March 1972. The brothers attended Hampton School and became members of the Molesey Boat Club. Jonny won a silver medal (1986) and a gold (1987) in the coxless fours at the World Junior Championships. As a senior, he twice won bronze medals in eights at the World Championships (1989, 1981). He was President of the Oxford University Boat Club and rowed in the winning Oxford boat on three occasions (1988-90). Greg was twice a world junior gold medallist in coxless fours (1989, 1990). He was only the second Briton to achieve the feat, the first being Tim Foster. Greg was the first British rower to gain selection in the same year (1990) at both the junior and senior World Championships. He was in the same eight as Jonny which won the world bronze in 1991. The greatest performances by the Searle brothers were achieved when they rowed together. In an epic race against the Italian Abbagnale brothers, they won the coxed pairs at the 1992 Olympics. Together with cox Garry Herbert (born 3 October 1969), they were awarded the MBE after their Barcelona triumph. Again beating the Abbagnales, they won gold at the 1993 World Championships in the same event. In the 1994 World Championships, the brothers won bronze in the coxless fours with Rupert Obholzer and Tim Foster, the quartet picking up bronze and silver respectively at the 1994 and 1995 World Championships and bronze at the 1996 Olympics. Jonny semi-retired but came back to win a silver medal at the 1999 World Championships in the coxed fours. After Atlanta, Greg switched his attention to single sculling. He won the bronze medal at the 1997 World Championships and in the same year won the Diamond Sculls at Henley. In preparation for the 2000 Olympics, he decide to return to sweep rowing and teamed up with Ed Coode (born Falmouth, 19 June 1975) in the coxless pairs. The partnership promised much but finished in fourth place at Sydney.

General Information

abbreviations

The following list of abbreviations is used by FISA to denote the current range of events held at World Championships:

M1x – men's single sculls	W1x – women's single sculls
M2x – men's double sculls	W2x – women's double sculls
M4x – men's quadruple sculls	W4x – women's quadruple sculls
M2– – men's coxless pairs	W2– – women's coxless pairs
M2+ – men's coxed pairs	W4– – women's coxless fours
M4– – men's coxless fours	W4+ – women's coxed fours
M4+ – men's coxed fours	W8+ – women's eights
M8+ – men's eights	

LM1x – lightweight men's single sculls	LW1x – lightweight women's single sculls
LM2x – lightweight men's double sculls	LW2x – lightweight women's double sculls
LM4x – lightweight men's quadruple sculls	LW4x – lightweight women's quadruple sculls
LM2– – lightweight men's coxless pairs	LW2– – lightweight women's coxless pairs
LM4– – lightweight men's coxless fours	
LM8+ – lightweight men's eights	

adaptive rowing

Rowing or sculling in boats adapted for people with physical limitations or disabilities. At the 2002 FISA World Championships in Seville two events – a coxed four and a double scull – were open to mixed crews made up of 50 per cent men and 50 per cent women. Both events were raced over 1000m. The races attracted 38 disabled athletes from Europe, Australia and the USA. This event was a first step in the process of including rowing in the Paralympic Games in Beijing in 2008. Three adaptive boat classes raced during the 2003 FISA World Championships in Milan.

Amateur Rowing Association

The Amateur Rowing Association is the governing body of rowing in Britain. Address: 6 Lower Mall, Hammersmith, London W6 9DJ. Website: www.ara-rowing.org

Formed in 1882, it prescribed that an amateur must be an officer in the fighting or civil service, educated at a university or public school, or a member of the liberal professions. In 1890 the National Amateur Rowing Association (NARA) was formed with similar rules to the ARA but did not bar competitors from other social classes. The NARA was much more active in promoting rowing than the ARA, and the two associations existed alongside each other for 65 years, finally merging in 1956.

Boat Race

The first University Boat Race was the result of a challenge issued to Oxford by Cambridge in 1829. Two friends, Charles Merival (Cambridge) and Charles Wordsworth (Oxford), a nephew of the poet William Wordsworth, were involved. It was rowed on the Thames from Hambledon Lock to Henley Bridge. Oxford were the first winners. The second race was staged in 1836 and was rowed on a 5¾ mile (9.25km) stretch of the Thames between Westminster and Putney. The same course was used in the races from 1839 to 1842. In 1846, 1856 and 1863 the course was from Mortlake to Putney and on all other occasions the race has been rowed from Putney to Mortlake over a distance of 4 miles 374yds (6.779km). The race became an annual event in 1854. The race is held in March or early April. The captain of the previous year's losing team issues a formal challenge. The first women's race was in 1927 and the first lightweight races were in 1975. The current score stands at 78 to Cambridge, 71 to Oxford, with one dead heat. In 1849 two races were held, Cambridge winning in March and Oxford in December.

brothers in opposing crews

Two sets of brothers rowed in opposing boats in the 2003 race for the first time. David Livingston and Matt Smith were in the winning Oxford crew, while James Livingston and Ben Smith rowed for Cambridge. The last time brothers were in opposing boats was 1900 when Raymond Etherington-Smith was president of the Cambridge crew while his younger brother Thomas was a freshman at Oxford.

coach, most successful

Dan Topolski (Oxford), who had ten successive wins between 1976 and 1985.

cox, most successful

C.R.W. Tottenham (Oxford) steered five winning crews in the 1860s.

dead heat

The 2003 race, won by Oxford by just a foot, is believed to have been an even closer finish than the controversial 'dead heat' of 1877. The story goes that the judge at the finish, 'Honest John' Phelps, was asleep under a bush as the crews raced past. When awakened and asked the result he said: 'Dead heat to Oxford by four feet.'

famous competitors

Some famous people have competed in the race including: the former Australian Prime Minister, Lord Bruce of Melbourne (Cambridge 1907); the photographer, Lord Snowdon (who as Anthony Armstrong-Jones coxed Cambridge 1950); the comedian, Hugh Laurie (Cambridge 1980); the recent Olympic gold medallists, Matthew Pinsent (Oxford 1992-93) and Jonny Searle (Oxford 1988-89); and Sydney Olympic gold medallists, Tim Foster (Oxford 1997), Luka Grubor (Oxford 1997), Kieran West (Cambridge 1999 and 2001) and Andrew Lindsay (Oxford 1997-99).

records

Lightest oarsman – Alfred Higgins (Oxford), 9st 6½lb (60.1kg) (1882)
Heaviest oarsman – Chris Heathcote (Cambridge), 17st 5lb (110.2kg) (1990)
Heaviest crew – Cambridge, average weight 94.8kg (1998)
Most successful oarsman – Boris Rankov (Oxford), six wins (1978-83)

Youngest oarsman – Matthew Brittin (Cambridge), 18 years, 208 days (1987)
Oldest oarsman – Donald MacDonald (Oxford), 31 years, 3 months (1987)
Tallest oarsman – Josh West (Cambridge), 6ft 9ins (2.06m) (1999-2001)
Fastest time – Cambridge, 16mins 19secs (1998)
Greatest margin of victory – Cambridge, 20 lengths (1900)
Longest winning streak – Cambridge, 13 wins (1924-36)

reserve crews
Men's – Goldie (Cambridge) v Isis (Oxford)
Women's – Blondie (Cambridge) v Osiris (Oxford)

sinkings
There have been six sinkings but the race result has only been determined by a sinking on three occasions: Cambridge twice (1859 and 1978) and Oxford once (1925). On 31 March 1912, both boats sank and the race was held again on 1 April. On 24 March 1951, Oxford sank and the race was rescheduled for 26 March, when Cambridge won. The most recent sinking occurred in 1984, when Cambridge sank after ramming a barge before they were even under starter's orders.

sponsors
Prior to 1976 there was no official race sponsor.
1976-86 Ladbrokes
1987-98 Beefeater Gin
1999-date Aberdeen Asset Management

television and radio
The event has a huge worldwide television audience, estimated in 2003 at 400 million. The first radio broadcast was in 1927 and the first television coverage in 1938. John Snagge (1904-96), the long-serving BBC broadcaster, covered the Boat Race for many years on radio and is often remembered for the following observation during the 1949 race: 'I can't tell who's leading. It's either Oxford or Cambridge.'

women coxes
Oxford made history in 1981 with the selection of the first female cox, Sue Brown. She coxed crews to victory in 1981 and 1982. The first time both boats were coxed by women was in 1989, with Alison Norrish (Oxford) and Leigh Weiss (Cambridge).

Commonwealth Games
Rowing has featured in the Commonwealth Games on seven occasions (1930, 1938, 1950, 1954, 1958, 1962, 1986). Women's and lightweight events were included for the only time in 1986. All the events have been won by competitors from either Australia (16 wins), Canada (7), England (14) or New Zealand (9). The most notable performance was that of Steve Redgrave who won three gold medals in 1986 (M1x, M2–, M4–). Mervyn Wood, the Australian sculler who was Olympic champion in 1948, also won three Commonwealth gold medals (1950 M1x and M2x, 1954 M2x).

coxswain
Usually shortened to 'cox'. Coxes form part of the crew in sweep rowing in eights and also in coxed pairs and fours. The minimum weights for coxswains in championship rowing are: 55kg for Senior Open, Veteran Open, J18, J16 and mixed crews; 50kg for Senior Women, Veteran Women, WJ18 and WJ16 crews; 45kg for all J15 and younger crews. To make up this weight a lighter coxswain has to carry dead weight.

Doggett's Coat and Badge
The right to wear Doggett's Coat and Badge is the prize in a rowing race held annually since 1715 between London Bridge and Cadogan Pier, Chelsea, in London, a distance of 4 miles 5 furlongs (7.4km). The event is a sculling race between skiffs, which were originally used to ferry passengers across the river, and is contested by newly qualified Thames watermen. It was initiated by Thomas Doggett, a comic actor, to commemorate the accession of George I and the House of Hanover in 1714. Doggett himself organised the race until his death in 1721. He provided for a cash prize and an orange-coloured livery with a silver badge, showing the white horse of Hanover representing Liberty, to be awarded to the winner. Since his death the Worshipful Company of Fishmongers has funded the race. The colour of the uniform has changed from orange to red and the cash prize is no longer awarded, but in all other respects Doggett's decree continues to be fulfilled. The name of the first winner is not known; the winner of the 2003 race was Liam Cairns (from Greenwich Rowing Club), who finished in 29mins 15secs.

equipment
There are no restrictions on length or weight of craft. However, in practice, shells range in length from 16m to 18.9m (52ft to 62ft) and single sculls are usually 8.2m (27ft). Oars are usually 3.6m to 3.9m (12ft to 13ft) in length and sculls are normally 2.9m (9.5ft) long.

European Championships
FISA held the first European Championships at Lake Orta in Italy, September 1893. The championships ran continuously until 1973 with the exception of the war years, 1914-19 and 1939-46. They have now been superseded by the World Championships. Britain entered the men's events in 1950 and British women competed from 1954, the year that women's events were held for the first time. In total, British women won three medals (two silver, one bronze) and British men won ten medals (two gold, four silver, four bronze). The gold medallists were the men's eight in 1951 (David Jennens, James Crowden, William Windham, J.R. Dingle, John Jones, Nicholas Clack, David Macklin, Harry Almond and John Hinde) and the men's coxless pair in 1957 (Christopher Davidge and David Leadley).

FISA
Rowing's international governing body is the Fédération Internationale des Sociétés d'Aviron.
Address: Avenue de Cour 135, Case Postale 18, 1000 Lausanne 3, Switzerland
Website: www.worldrowing.com
It was founded in 1892 in Turin by representatives from France, Switzerland, Belgium, Adriatica (now a part of Italy) and Italy. The oldest international sports federation in

the Olympic movement, it now has over 100 member nations. FISA held its first official European Championships in 1893 and the first World Championships in 1962.

Head of the River Race

Founded in 1926 by Steve Fairbairn, the Head of the River Race is for eights every March over the reverse University Boat Race course, i.e. Mortlake to Putney. Since 1979 the race has been restricted to 420 crews.

Henley Royal Regatta

Established in 1839, the event gained its 'royal' prefix when, in 1851, Prince Albert became its patron. Henley Royal Regatta is an annual four-day series of rowing races held in the first week in July on the River Thames at Henley-on-Thames, Oxfordshire. The traditional length of the course is 1 mile 550yds (2112m), which was the longest distance of open water that could be obtained in 1839 on the Henley Reach. Owing its existence to the fact that the first Oxford and Cambridge Boat Race took place there in 1829, it soon developed into a fashionable sporting and social event. The full list of current Henley events is as follows, in chronological order of their inauguration:

Grand Challenge Cup: dates from 1839, in which year the stewards resolved that a silver cup, value 100 guineas, to be called the 'Henley Grand Challenge Cup', be rowed for annually by amateur crews in eight-oared boats. The oldest of the Henley events, it has over the years attracted many of the world's finest eights. Most wins: Leander Club (27). Fastest time: Hansa Dortmund R.C. 5mins 58secs (1989).

Stewards' Challenge Cup: second only to the Grand Challenge Cup in seniority, having been instituted in 1841. For fours and subject to the same rules of entry. In early days the boats were coxed. In 1873 the event became a coxless race.

Diamond Challenge Sculls: introduced in 1844 'for amateurs, open to all England', it remains one of the world's top single sculls events. Most wins: Stuart Mackenzie (1957-62), Guy Nickalls (1888-91, 1893-94). Record time: Václav Chalupa (CZE), 7mins 23secs (1989).

Ladies' Challenge Plate: in 1845 a new challenge prize was offered for eight-oared crews which, in the following year, was named the Ladies' Challenge Plate. Up to the 1966 Regatta, entries for this event were restricted to certain academic institutions within the United Kingdom, together with Trinity College, Dublin. The rules were then widened to permit entries from academic institutions throughout the world. Since 1985 the event has been open to crews from any club and is now the second most senior event for men's eights at the Regatta.

Silver Goblets & Nickalls Cup: has its origin in a pairs event instituted in 1845. In 1850 silver goblets were given as presentation prizes. In 1895 Tom Nickalls donated a challenge trophy to commemorate the achievements of his sons, Guy and Vivien, who between them won eleven goblets in the 1890s, a feat only bettered a century later when Steve Redgrave won the event for a record seventh time in 1995.

Visitors' Challenge Cup: originally called the 'District Fours' and awarded for a local four-oared coxed race. The event was renamed in 1847 and the qualification rules of that time remained in force until 1970. From 1971 to 2000 the event was open to boat clubs of any academic institution throughout the world. In 2000 the Visitors' Challenge Cup was opened to clubs as well as to students.

Wyfold Challenge Cup: for coxless fours, presented to the Regatta in 1847. Originally this prize was awarded to the winning challenger for the Grand Challenge Cup. In 1855 the race was changed to a four-oared race. In December 1995 new qualification rules were brought in to ensure that the 'Wyfold' is an event for 'genuine' club crews.

Thames Challenge Cup: instituted for eights in 1868, the race attracted entries from home and overseas crews of 'club', rather than 'Grand', standard. Since 1995 the 'Thames' has become an event for 'genuine' club crews.

Double Sculls Challenge Cup: dates from Henley's centenary regatta in 1939. In the first final between Beresford and Southwood of Thames Rowing Club and the Italians, Scherli and Broschi, then champions of Europe, the result was a dead heat.

The Princess Elizabeth Challenge Cup: for eights, instituted in 1946 for public schools in the United Kingdom and was opened to entries from overseas in 1964.

Prince Philip Challenge Cup: for coxed fours, instituted in 1963. The trophy was presented to the Regatta by Prince Philip, the Duke of Edinburgh.

Britannia Challenge Cup: presented in 1969 by Nottingham Britannia Rowing Club to mark its centenary, this replaced the Henley Prize, introduced in the previous year, as an event for coxless fours not up to the standard of competitors for the Prince Philip Challenge Cup.

Queen Mother Challenge Cup: for quadruple sculls, introduced in 1981 to mark the occasion of the Queen Mother's 80th birthday the year before.

Temple Challenge Cup instituted in 1990 for the eights of single colleges, of smaller university boat clubs and of schools.

Fawley Challenge Cup: for quadruple sculls, offered for the first time at the 1992 Regatta. It is for under-19s and is open to crews from boat clubs as well as those from schools.

Princess Royal Challenge Cup: in 1993 an event for women's single sculls was introduced. The cup itself was presented for the first time in 1997.

Remenham Challenge Cup: in the 1998 and 1999 Regattas an invitation race for women's eights was held which became an open women's eights event. Known originally as the Henley Prize, its current name was adopted in 2002.

Princess Grace Challenge Cup: at the 2001 Regatta an event for women's quadruple sculls was introduced. In 2003 this event was named in memory of Princess Grace of Monaco.

Men's quadruple sculls: introduced in 2001.

Henley-style regattas are held in the USA, Canada and Australia. The American Rowing Association ends its season each year with the 'American Henley', a regatta at the regulation Henley distance, alternately at Philadelphia and Boston. The Royal Canadian Henley was held at various sites from 1880 and since 1903 has been held annually at St Catharines, Ontario. An Australian Henley at Melbourne was first held in 1904.

indoor rowing

The sport of indoor rowing was created in 1981 when the US rowing equipment manufacturer Concept 2 developed its first rowing machine and the first world championship took place in 1982. The sport is exclusively performed on Concept 2 indoor rowers. There is an annual world championship in Boston, USA, every February and national championships throughout Europe and worldwide each winter. The 'blue riband' championship race distance is 2000m and there are recognised age-group world records for this and other distances, even for 90-year-olds!

British Records (2000m)	World Records (2000m)
Men:	
Matthew Pinsent (Leander) 5:42.6 (1999)	Rob Waddell (NZL) 5:38.3 (1999)
Lightweight Men:	
Tim Male (Tideway Scullers) 6:07.2 (1997)	Eskild Ebbesen (DEN) 6:03.2 (2002)
Women:	
Catherine Bishop (Marlow RC) 6:32.6 (2001)	Georgina Evers-Swindells (NZL) 6:28.6 (2002)
Lightweight Women:	
Jo Hammond (Rob Roy BC) 6:59.9 (2003)	Lisa Schlenker (USA) 6:56.7 (2002)

lightweight rowing

Lightweight events were introduced into the World Championships for men and women in 1974 and 1985 respectively. They also featured in the Olympic rowing programme for the first time in 1996. Lightweight men must weigh no more than 72.5kg and the average of the whole crew must not exceed 70kg (single sculler maximum, 72.5kg). Lightweight women must weigh no more than 59kg and the average of the whole crew must not exceed 57kg (single sculler maximum, 59kg). With the introduction of lightweight classes the career of Briton Peter Haining (born St Andrews, 3 April 1962) prospered when he transferred from sweep rowing to sculling. The high point of his career was successive golds in the lightweight single sculls at the 1993, 1994 and 1995 World Championships. The introduction of lightweight rowing also benefited Britain's leading oarswoman of the early 1980s, Beryl Mitchell (later Crockford, born London, 26 June 1950). Having won the silver medal in the single sculls at the World Championships in 1981, as a lightweight in 1985 she won the lightweight double sculls gold with Lin Clark. In 1982 she had won the first sculling event for women at Henley.

National Water Sports Centre

Purpose-built venue located in 270 acres of parkland at Holme Pierrepoint on the River Trent, three miles from Nottingham. Its facilities include a 2000m × 135m regatta lake (opened in 1973), used for racing and as a training ground. Along with the other main water-based governing bodies, the Amateur Rowing Association has a base at the centre. The FISA World Championships of 1975 and 1986 were held at Nottingham.

Olympic Games and World Championships: length of course

In 1900 the Olympic course was 1750m long, in 1904 3218m (2 miles), in 1908 2414m (1.5 miles) and in 1948, 1883m. In the intercalated Games of 1906 the courses varied. In all other years, including 2000, all races have been over 2000m. Women's races at the Olympics are also rowed on a 2000m course, but prior to 1988 courses were 1000m. Each lane is 13.5m wide. The water must be at least 3.5m deep.

Olympic Games: British medallists

	1900 single sculls – bronze	St George Ashe
	1908 single sculls – gold	Henry Blackstaffe
	1908 single sculls – silver	Alexander McCulloch
	1908 coxless pairs – gold	Reginald Fenning/Gordon Thomson
	1908 coxless pairs – silver	George Fairbairn/Philip Verdon
	1908 coxless fours – gold	C. Robert Cudmore/James Gillan/Duncan MacKinnon/Robert Somers-Smith (Magdalen College, Oxford)
	1908 coxless fours – silver	Philip Filleul/Harold Barker/Reginald Fenning/Gordon Thomson (Leander Club)

1908 eights – gold	Albert Gladstone/Frederick Kelly/Banner Johnstone/Guy Nickalls/Charles Burnell/ Ronald Sanderson/Raymond Etherington-Smith/Henry Bucknall/Gilchrist Maclagan (Leander Club)
1912 single sculls – gold	William Kinnear
1912 coxed fours – silver	Julius Beresford/Karl Vernon/Charles Rought/Bruce Logan/Geoffrey Carr (Thames R.C.)
1912 eights – gold	Edgar Burgess/Sidney Swann/Leslie Wormwald/Ewart Horsfall/J. Angus Gillan/Arthur Garton/Alister Kirby/Philip Fleming/Henry Wells (Leander Club)
1912 eights – silver	William Fison/William Parker/Thomas Gillespie/Beaufort Burdekin/Frederick Pitman/Arthur Wiggins/Charles Littlejohn/Robert Walker/John Walker (New College, Oxford)
1920 single sculls – silver	Jack Beresford
1920 eights – silver	Ewart Horsfall/Guy Oliver Nickalls/Richard Lucas/Walter James/John Campbell/Sebastian Earl/Ralph Shove/Sidney Swann/Robin Johnstone
1924 single sculls – gold	Jack Beresford
1924 coxless fours – gold	Charles Eley/James Macnabb/Robert Morrison/Terence Sanders
1928 single sculls – bronze	Theodore Collet
1928 coxless pairs – silver	Terence O'Brien/Robert Archibald Nisbet
1928 coxless fours – gold	John Lander/Michael Warriner/Richard Beesly/Edward Bevan
1928 eights – silver	James Hamilton/Guy Oliver Nickalls/Donald Gollan/John 'Felix' Badcock/Harold Lane/Gordon Killick/Jack Beresford/Harold West/Arthur Sulley
1932 coxless pairs – gold	Hugh 'Jumbo' Edwards/Lewis Clive
1932 coxless fours – gold	John 'Felix' Badcock/Hugh 'Jumbo' Edwards/Jack Beresford/Rowland George
1936 double sculls – gold	Jack Beresford/Leslie Southwood
1936 coxless fours – silver	Thomas Bristow/Alan Barrett/Peter Jackson/John Duncan Sturrock
1948 double sculls – gold	Richard Burnell/Bertie Bushnell
1948 coxless pairs – gold	John Wilson/William 'Ran' Laurie
1948 eights – silver	Christopher Barton/Michael Lepage/Guy Richardson/Ernest Paul Bircher/Paul Massey/David Meyrick/Charles Brian Lloyd/Alfred Mellows/Jack Dearlove
1964 coxless fours – silver	John Michael Russell/Hugh Arthur Wardell-Yerburgh/William Barry/John James
1976 double sculls – silver	Chris Baillieu/Michael Hart
1976 eights – silver	Richard Lester/John Yallop/Timothy Crooks/Hugh Matheson/David Maxwell/R. James Clark/Frederick Smallbone/Leonard Robertson/Patrick Sweeney
1980 coxless pairs – bronze	Charles Wiggin/Malcolm Carmichael
1980 coxless fours – bronze	John Beattie/Ian McNuff/David Townsend/Martin Cross
1980 eights – silver	Duncan McDougall/Allan Whitwell/J. Henry Clay/Christopher Mahoney/Andrew Justice/John Pritchard/Malcolm McGowan/Richard Stanhope/Colin Moynihan
1984 coxed fours – gold	Martin Cross/Richard Budgett/Andrew Holmes/Steve Redgrave/Adrian Ellison
1988 coxless pairs – gold	Steve Redgrave/Andrew Holmes
1988 coxed pairs – bronze	Steve Redgrave/Andrew Holmes/Patrick Sweeney
1992 coxed pairs – gold	Jonathan Searle/Gregory Searle/Garry Herbert
1996 coxless pairs – gold	Steve Redgrave/Matthew Pinsent
1996 coxless fours – bronze	Rupert Obholzer/Jonathan Searle/Gregory Searle/Tim Foster
2000 coxless fours – gold	Steve Redgrave/Matthew Pinsent/James Cracknell/Tim Foster
2000 eights – gold	Andrew Lindsay/Ben Hunt-Davis/Simon Dennis/Louis Attrill/Luka Grubor/Kieran West/Fred Scarlett/Steve Trapmore/Rowley Douglas
2000 quadruple sculls (women) – silver	Guin Batten/Katherine Grainger/Gillian Lindsay/ Miriam Batten

R
O
W
I
N
G

The above medal was the first ever won by British oarswomen at the Olympics.
At the 1908 Olympic rowing events, held at Henley, British crews won four gold medals, an achievement since unsurpassed.
British father and son Charles and Richard Burnell each won Olympic gold – Charles in the eights in 1908 and Richard in the double sculls in 1948.

Hugh 'Jumbo' Edwards won two golds in one day in 1932 in the coxless pairs and the coxless fours. During World War II while in the RAF he rowed his dinghy four miles from his ditched plane to safety.

William 'Ran' Laurie, who won gold in the 1948 coxless pairs, was the father of the comic actor Hugh Laurie who rowed in the University Boat Race for Cambridge in 1980.

Guy Nickalls was the oldest oarsman to win a gold medal, in the eights in 1908 at the age of 42 years and 170 days.

Steve Redgrave has the most Olympic gold medals in rowing, a total of five (plus one bronze).

Philadelphia Challenge Cup
The Philadelphia Challenge Cup was first awarded to John B. (Jack) Kelly by the Schuylkill Navy of Philadelphia in recognition of his feat of becoming the first American to win the Olympic single sculls gold medal (1920). It was to be awarded to the winner of the Olympic single sculls final. Between Olympiads, a suitable opponent could challenge the holder to a special match race. In 1924 Jack Beresford acquired the Cup by defeating the holder Paul Costello at the 1924 Olympics in Paris. Beresford made a successful defence in 1925. Henry 'Bobby' Pearce (AUS) won it at the 1928 and 1932 Olympics and was never beaten for it. The great Soviet sculler Vyacheslav Ivanov won it as Olympic champion in 1956. The Cup disappeared in mysterious circumstances around 1960, reappearing in 1996 in an antique store with the name of Don Spero (USA) engraved on it. Spero recalled beating Ivanov at the 1966 World Championships at Bled but had no recollection of a formal challenge being issued for the trophy. The legal battle to recover the Cup in time for the Atlanta Olympics in 1996 failed and the winner of the single sculls, Xeno Müller (SUI), was presented with a photograph of the Cup.

regatta
A term applied to a rowing as well as a sailing meeting. Originally the name given to races held between gondoliers in Venice, the word comes from a Venetian dialect word meaning 'strife' or 'contention'. According to the Amateur Rowing Association, the oldest regatta in the rowing calendar is Chester, which dates back to the 18th century (possibly as early as 1733). The first known regatta on the Thames was at Ranelagh Gardens, Putney, in 1775. The most famous of all regattas is Henley.

repêchage
Repêchage (French, lit. 'fishing out again') in rowing and other sports is a supplementary heat, giving competitors eliminated in the first heat a second chance to progress to the final. In rowing those who finish second in their heats are allowed a row-off for a place in the final. When the system was introduced in the 1924 Olympics, Jack Beresford qualified for the single sculls final through the repêchage. Having finished second in his opening round behind William Gilmore of the USA, Beresford avenged his earlier defeat to take the gold medal with Gilmore second.

River & Rowing Museum
Address: Mill Meadows, Henley-on-Thames, Oxfordshire RG9 1BF
Website: www.rrm.co.uk
The museum has three main galleries devoted to the River Thames, the sport of rowing and the town of Henley. The rowing gallery covers the history of rowing in its progression from a working tool to a recreation and sport. Its Hall of Fame features coaches as well as rowers.

rowing clubs
In Great Britain over 500 rowing clubs are affiliated to the Amateur Rowing Association. Founded in 1818, Leander Club is the world's oldest and best-known rowing club. In the 19th century the club was based in London but by the end of the century had moved its headquarters to its current site by Henley Bridge. Leander was established with membership offered only by invitation. The first open rowing club was founded in Chester on 9 July 1838 as Chester Victoria Rowing Club; it later became the Royal Chester Rowing Club. The first open club on the Thames was Henley Rowing Club, founded in 1839.

Torpids
At Oxford University, college second crews made a brief appearance in Eights Week in 1836 and 1837, but in 1838 were given their own event, 'Torpids'. Originally this took place on a fairly casual basis, either on the intervening nights between the eights races, or after Eights Week had finished. However, when the event was moved to Lent (Hilary) Term in 1852, and also fixed as a six-day event, its status increased in recognition of its importance in providing feeder crews for the eights. Various rules were subsequently required to ban or restrict members of college (first) eights rowing in the following year's Torpids. Both Torpids and eights are held on the same course on the Thames at Oxford (Isis).

Wingfield sculls
The Wingfield sculls were inaugurated by Henry C. Wingfield in 1830 to be raced annually on his birthday (10 August) on the half-tide between Westminster and Putney. The course was changed in 1849 to Putney to Kew and then, in 1861, to its present course, Putney to Mortlake. A race has been held every year except during the world wars; the title 'Amateur Championship of the Thames' was added in the 1840s and the 'British Amateur Sculling Championship' in 1952. The 2002 winner was Greg Searle. Steve Redgrave won the race five times in succession (1985-89).

World Championships
The first FISA World Rowing Championships took place in 1962 and were held in Lucerne, Switzerland. Until 1974, the event took place every four years. It then became an annual event except for Olympic Games years until 1996. The events in 1996 (Strathclyde) and 2000 (Zagreb) were restricted to non-Olympic boat classes. Women's events were first introduced in 1974, lightweight events for men also began

in 1974 and those for lightweight women were added in 1985.
For key to event abbreviations, see earlier in this section.

British winners

Men's
1977 M2x Chris Baillieu/Michael Hart
1986 M2+ Steve Redgrave/Andrew Holmes/Patrick Sweeney
1987 M2– Steve Redgrave/Andrew Holmes
1991 M2– Steve Redgrave/Matthew Pinsent
1993 M2+ Greg Searle/Jonny Searle/Garry Herbert
1993 M2– Steve Redgrave/Matthew Pinsent
1994 M2– Steve Redgrave/Matthew Pinsent
1995 M2– Steve Redgrave/Matthew Pinsent
1997 M4– Steve Redgrave/Matthew Pinsent/Tim Foster/James Cracknell
1998 M4– Steve Redgrave/Matthew Pinsent/Tim Foster/James Cracknell
1999 M4– Steve Redgrave/Matthew Pinsent/Ed Coode/James Cracknell
2000 M4+ Tom Stallard/Steve Trapmore/Luka Grubor/Simon Fieldhouse/Kieran West
2001 M4– Stephen Williams/Toby Garbett/Ed Coode/Richard Dunne
2001 M2– Matthew Pinsent/James Cracknell
2001 M2+ Matthew Pinsent/James Cracknell/Neil Chugani
2002 M4+ Tom Stallard/Steve Trapmore/Luka Grubor/Christian Cormack/Kieran West
2002 M2– Matthew Pinsent/James Cracknell
Lightweight Men's
1979 LM4– Ian Wilson/Stuart Wilson/Colin Barratt/Nicholas Howe
1986 LM2x Carl Smith/Alan Whitwell
1991 LM4– Thomas Kay/Toby Hessian/Christopher Bates/Carl Smith
1992 LM4– Thomas Kay/Toby Hessian/Christopher Bates/Carl Smith
1993 LM1x Peter Haining
1994 LM1x Peter Haining
1994 LM8+ Toby Hessian/Stephen Ellis/Simon Cox/John Deakin/Christopher Bates/Carl Smith/Tom Kay/James McNiven/David Lemon
1995 LM1x Peter Haining
Women's
1997 W4– Lisa Eyre/Alexandra Beever/Elisabeth Henshilwood/Susan Walker
1998 W2x Miriam Batten/Gillian Lindsay
2003 W2– Cath Bishop/Katharine Grainger
Lightweight Women's
1985 LW2x Beryl Mitchell/Linn Clark
1993 LW4– Jane Hall/Annamarie Dryden/Alison Brownless/Tonia Williams
1998 LW2– Juliet Machan/Jo Nitsch
2000 LW2– Malindi Myers/Miriam Taylor
2001 LW2– Jo Nitsch/Sarah Birch
2002 LW2– Naomi Ashcroft/Leonie Barron

venues

1962 Lucerne, Switzerland	1990 Lake Barrington, Australia
1966 Bled, Yugoslavia (now Slovenia)	1991 Vienna, Austria
1970 St Catharine's, Canada	1992 Montreal, Canada (lightweight events only)
1974 Lucerne, Switzerland	1993 Roudnice, Czech Republic
1975 Nottingham, England	1994 Indianapolis, USA
1977 Amsterdam, Netherlands	1995 Tampere, Finland
1978 Karapiro, New Zealand	1996 Strathclyde, Scotland (non-Olympic events only)
1979 Bled, Yugoslavia (now Slovenia)	1997 Aiguebelette, France
1981 Munich, West Germany	1998 Cologne, Germany
1982 Lucerne, Switzerland	1999 St Catharine's, Canada
1983 Duisburg, West Germany	2000 Zagreb, Croatia, (non-Olympic events only)
1985 Hazewinkel, Belgium	2001 Lucerne, Switzerland
1986 Nottingham, England	2002 Seville, Spain
1987 Copenhagen, Denmark	2003 Milan, Italy
1989 Bled, Yugoslavia (now Slovenia)	2004 Banyoles, Spain (non-Olympic events only)

World Cup

In 1997 FISA introduced a World Cup based on three regattas. Germany were the overall winners. The World Cup venues have been as follows:

1997 Munich, Paris, Lucerne	2001 Princeton (USA), Vienna, Munich
1998 Munich, Hazewinkel, Lucerne	2002 Hazewinkel, Lucerne, Munich
1999 Hazewinkel, Vienna, Lucerne	2003 Milan, Munich, Lucerne

World Sculls Cup

Held from 1990 to 1995 for both men's and women's single sculls over a series of races.

ROWING

Olympic Medallists

Men's Single Sculls

	Gold	Silver	Bronze
1896	not held		
1900	Hermann Barrelet (FRA)	André Gaudin (FRA)	St George Ashe (GBR)
1904	Frank Greer (USA)	James Juvenal (USA)	Constance Titus (USA)
1906	Gaston Delaplane (FRA)	Joseph Larran (FRA)	only two competitors
1908	Henry Blackstaffe (GBR)	Alexander McCulloch (GBR)	Bernhard von Gaza (GER)
			Károly Levitzky (HUN)
1912	William Kinnear (GBR)	Polydore Veirman (BEL)	Everard Butler (CAN)
			Mihkel Kuusik (EST)
1920	John Kelly (USA)	Jack Beresford (GBR)	Clarence Hadfield D'Arcy (NZL)
1924	Jack Beresford (GBR)	William Garrett Gilmore (USA)	Josef Schneider (SUI)
1928	Henry Pearce (AUS)	Kenneth Myers (USA)	Theodore Collet (GBR)
1932	Henry Pearce (AUS)	William Miller (USA)	Guillermo Douglas (URU)
1936	Gustav Schäfer (GER)	Josef Hasenöhrl (AUT)	Daniel Barrow (USA)
1948	Mervyn Wood (AUS)	Eduardo Risso (URU)	Romolo Catasta (ITA)
1952	Yuriy Tyukalov (URS)	Mervyn Wood (AUS)	Teodor Kocerka (POL)
1956	Vyacheslav Ivanov (URS)	Stuart Mackenzie (AUS)	John Kelly jnr (USA)
1960	Vyacheslav Ivanov (URS)	Achim Hill (GER)	Teodor Kocerka (POL)
1964	Vyacheslav Ivanov (URS)	Achim Hill (GER)	Gottfried Kottmann (SUI)
1968	Henri Jan Wienese (NED)	Jochen Meissner (FRG)	Alberto Demiddi (ARG)
1972	Yuriy Malishev (URS)	Alberto Demiddi (ARG)	Wolfgang Güldenpfennig (GDR)
1976	Pertti Karppinen (FIN)	Peter-Michael Kolbe (FRG)	Joachim Dreifke (GDR)
1980	Pertti Karppinen (FIN)	Vasiliy Yakusha (URS)	Peter Kersten (GDR)
1984	Pertti Karppinen (FIN)	Peter-Michael Kolbe (FRG)	Robert Mills (CAN)
1988	Thomas Lange (GDR)	Peter-Michael Kolbe (FRG)	Eric Verdonk (NZL)
1992	Thomas Lange (GER)	Václav Chalupa (CZE)	Kajetan Broniewski (POL)
1996	Xeno Müller (SUI)	Derek Porter (CAN)	Thomas Lange (GER)
2000	Rob Waddell (NZL)	Xeno Müller (SUI)	Marcel Hacker (GER)

Men's Double Sculls

	Gold	Silver	Bronze
1896	not held		
1900	not held		
1904	John Mulcahy/William Varley (USA)	James McLoughlin/John Hoben (USA)	Joseph Ravanack/John Wells (USA)
1906-12	not held		
1920	John Kelly/Paul Costello (USA)	Erminio Dones/Pietro Annoni (ITA)	Alfred Plé/Gaston Giran (FRA)
1924	Paul Costello/John Kelly (USA)	Marc Detton/Jean-Pierre Stock (FRA)	Rudolf Bosshard/Heinrich Thoma (SUI)
1928	Paul Costello/Charles McIlvaine (USA)	Joseph Wright/Jack Guest (CAN)	Leo Losert/Viktor Flessl (AUT)
1932	Kenneth Myers/William Garrett Gilmore (USA)	Herbert Buhtz/Gerhard Boetzelen (GER)	Charles Pratt/Noël de Mille (CAN)
1936	Jack Beresford/Leslie Southwood (GBR)	Willy Kaidel/Joachim Pirsch (GER)	Roger Verey/Jerzy Ustupski (POL)
1948	Richard Burnell/Bertie Bushnell (GBR)	Ebbe Parsner/Aage Larsen (DEN)	William Jones/Juan Rodríguez (URU)
1952	Tranquilo Cappozzo/Eduardo Guerrero (ARG)	Georgiy Zhilin/Igor Yemchuk (URS)	Miguel Seijas/Juan Rodríguez (URU)
1956	Aleksandr Berkutov/Yuriy Tyukalov (URS)	Bernard Paul Costello jnr/James Gardiner (USA)	Murray Riley/Mervyn Wood (AUS)
1960	Václav Kozák/Pavel Schmidt (TCH)	Aleksandr Berkutov/Yuriy Tyukalov (URS)	Ernst Hürlimann/Rolf Larcher (SUI)
1964	Oleg Tyurin/Boris Dubrovskiy (URS)	Seymour Cromwell/James Storm (USA)	Vladimír Andrš/Pavel Hofmann (TCH)
1968	Anatoliy Sass/Aleksandr Timoshinin (URS)	Leendert Frans van Dis/Henricus Droog (NED)	William Maher/John Nunn (USA)
1972	Aleksandr Timoshinin/Gennadiy Korshikov (URS)	Frank Hansen/Svein Thøgersen (NOR)	Joachim Böhmer/Hans-Ulrich Schmied (GDR)
1976	Frank Hansen/Alf Hansen (NOR)	Chris Baillieu/Michael Hart (GBR)	Hans-Ulrich Schmied/Jürgen Bertow (GDR)
1980	Joachim Dreifke/Klaus Kröppelien (GDR)	Zoran Pancic/Milorad Stanulov (YUG)	Zdenek Pecka/Václav Vochoska (TCH)
1984	Bradley Lewis/Paul Enquist (USA)	Pierre-Marie Deloof/Dirk Crois (BEL)	Zoran Pancic/Milorad Stanulov (YUG)
1988	Ronald Florijn/Nicolaas Rienks (NED)	Beat Schwerzmann/Ueli Bodenmann (SUI)	Aleksandr Marchenko/Vasiliy Yakusha (URS)
1992	Stephen Hawkins/Peter Antonie (AUS)	Arnold Jonke/Christoph Zerbst (AUT)	Henk-Jan Zwolle/Nicolaas Rienks (NED)
1996	Davide Tizzano/Agostino Abbagnale (ITA)	Kjetil Undset/Steffen Skår Størseth (NOR)	Frédéric Kowal/Samuël Barathay (FRA)
2000	Luka Spik/Iztok Cop (SLO)	Olaf Tufte/Fredrik Bekken (NOR)	Giovanni Calabrese/Nicola Sartori (ITA)

Men's Quadruple Sculls

	Gold	Silver	Bronze
1976	German Democratic Republic	Soviet Union	Czechoslovakia
1980	German Democratic Republic	Soviet Union	Bulgaria
1984	Federal Republic of Germany	Australia	Canada
1988	Italy	Norway	German Democratic Republic
1992	Germany	Norway	Italy
1996	Germany	United States	Australia
2000	Italy	Netherlands	Germany

Men's Coxless Pairs

	Gold	Silver	Bronze
1904	Robert Farnam/ Joseph Ryan (USA)	John Mulcahy/ William Varley (USA)	John Joachim/ Joseph Buerger (USA)
1906	not held		
1908	Reginald Fenning/Gordon Thomson (GBR)	George Fairbairn/Philip Verdon (GBR)	Frederick Toms/ Norwey Jackes (CAN) Martin Stahnke/ Willy Düskow (GER)
1912-20	not held		
1924	Antonie Beijnen/Wilhelm Rösingh (NED)	Maurice Bouton/Georges Piot (FRA)	only two pairs competed
1928	Bruno Müller/Kurt Moeschter (GER)	Terence O'Brien/Robert Archibald Nisbet (GBR)	Paul McDowell/John Schmitt (USA)
1932	Hugh 'Jumbo' Edwards/Lewis Clive (GBR)	Cyril Stiles/Frederick Thompson (NZL)	Henryk Budzynski/Janusz Mikolajczak (POL)
1936	Willi Eichhorn/Hugo Strauss (GER)	Richard Olsen/Harry Larsen (DEN)	Horacio Podestá/Julio Curatella (ARG)
1948	John Wilson/William 'Ran' Laurie (GBR)	Hans Kalt/Josef Kalt (SUI)	Felice Fanetti/Bruno Boni (ITA)
1952	Charles Logg/Thomas Price (USA)	Michel Knuysen/Robert Baetens (BEL)	Kurt Schmid/Hans Kalt (SUI)
1956	James Fifer/Duvall Hecht (USA)	Igor Buldakov/Viktor Ivanov (URS)	Alfred Sageder/Josef Kloimstein (AUT)
1960	Valentin Boreyko/Oleg Golovanov (URS)	Alfred Sageder/Josef Kloimstein (AUT)	Veli Lehtelä/Toimi Pitkänen (FIN)
1964	George Hungerford/Roger Jackson (CAN)	Steven Blaisse/Ernst Veenemans (NED)	Michael Schwan/Wolfgang Hottennrott (GER)
1968	Jörg Lucke/Hans-Jürgen Bothe (GDR)	Lawrence Hough/Philip 'Tony' Johnson (USA)	Peter Christiansen/Ib Ivan Larsen (DEN)
1972	Siegfried Brietzke/Wolfgang Mager (GDR)	Heinrich Fischer/Alfred Bachmann (SUI)	Roelof Luynenburg/Rudolf Stokvis (NED)
1976	Jörg Landvoigt/Bernd Landvoigt (GDR)	Calvin Coffey/Michael Staines (USA)	Peter Van Roye/Thomas Strauss (FRG)
1980	Bernd Landvoigt/Jörg Landvoigt (GDR)	Yuriy Pimenov/Nikolay Pimenov (URS)	Charles Wiggin/Malcolm Carmichael (GBR)
1984	Petru Iosub/Valer Toma (ROM)	Fernando Climent/Luis María Lasúrtegui (ESP)	Hans Magnus Grepperud/Sverre Løken (NOR)
1988	Andrew Holmes/Steve Redgrave (GBR)	Dragos Neagu/Danut Dobre (ROM)	Bojan Prešeren/Sadik Mujkic (YUG)
1992	Steve Redgrave/Matthew Pinsent (GBR)	Peter Höltzenbein/Colin von Ettingshausen (GER)	Iztok Cop/Denis Zvegelj (SLO)
1996	Steve Redgrave/Matthew Pinsent (GBR)	David Weightman/Robert Scott (AUS)	Michel Andrieux/Jean-Christophe Rolland (FRA)
2000	Michel Andrieux/Jean-Christophe Rolland (FRA)	Ted Murphy/Sebastian Bea (USA)	Matthew Long/James Tomkins (AUS)

Men's Coxed Pairs

	Gold	Silver	Bronze
1896	not held		
1900	Minerva Amsterdam (NED)	Soc. Nautique de la Marne (FRA)	R.C. de Castillon (FRA)
1904	not held		
1906A	Bucintoro (Venice) (ITA)	Barion (Bari) (ITA)	Soc. Nautique de la Basse Seine (FRA)
1906B	Bucintoro (Venice) (ITA)	R.C. Nautique de Gand (BEL)	Soc. Nautique de Bayonne (FRA)
1908-12	not held		
1920	Ercole Olgeni/Giovanni Scatturin/ Guido De Filip (ITA)	Gabriel Poix/Maurice Bouton/ Ernest Barberolle (FRA)	Édouard Candeveau/Alfred Felber/ Paul Piaget (SUI)
1924	Edouard Candeveau/Alfred Felber/ Emile Lachapelle (SUI)	Ercole Olgeni/Giovanni Scatturin/ Gino Sopracordevole (ITA)	Leon Butler/Harold Wilson/ Edward Jennings (USA)
1928	Hans Schöchlin/Karl Schöchlin/ Hans Bourquin (SUI)	Armand Marcelle/Édouard Marcelle/ Henri Préaux (FRA)	Léon Flament/François De Coninck/ Georges Anthony (BEL)
1932	Joseph Schauers/Charles Kieffer/ Edward Jennings (USA)	Jerzy Braun/Janusz Slazak/ Jerzy Skolimowski (POL)	Anselme Brusa/André Giriat/ Pierre Brunet (FRA)
1936	Gerhard Gustmann/Herbert Adamski/ Dieter Arend (GER)	Almiro Bergamo/Guido Santin/ Luciano Negrini (ITA)	Georges Tapie/Marceau Fourcade/ Noël Vandernotte (FRA)

ROWING

1948	Finn Pedersen/Tage Henriksen/ Carl-Ebbe Andersen (DEN)	Giovanni Steffe/Aldo Tarlao/ Alberto Radi (ITA)	Antal Szendey/Béla Zsitnik/ Róbert Zimonyi (HUN)
1952	Raymond Salles/Gaston Mercier/ Bernard Malivoire (FRA)	Heinz-Joachim Manchen/Helmut Heinhold/Helmut Noll (GER)	Svend Pedersen/Poul Svendsen/ Jørgen Frandsen (DEN)
1956	Arthur Ayrault/Conn Findlay/ Kurt Seiffert (USA)	Karl-Heinrich von Groddeck/Horst Arndt/Rainer Borkowsky (GER)	Igor Yemchuk/Georgiy Zhilin/ Vladimir Petrov (URS)
1960	Bernhard Knubel/Heinz Renneberg/ Klaus Zerta (GER)	Antanas Bagdanavicius/Zigmas Jukna/Igor Rudakov (URS)	Richard Draeger/Conn Findlay/ Kent Mitchell (USA)
1964	Edward Ferry/Conn Findlay/ Kent Mitchell (USA)	Jacques Morel/Georges Morel/ Jean-Claude Darouy (FRA)	Jan Bos/Herman Rouwé/ Frederick Hartsuiker (NED)
1968	Primo Baran/Renzo Sambo/ Bruno Cipolla (ITA)	Herman Suselbeek/Hadriaan van Nes/ Roderick Rijnders (NED)	Jørn Krab/Harry Jørgensen/ Preben Krab (DEN)
1972	Wolfgang Gunkel/Jörg Lucke/ Klaus-Dieter Neubert (GDR)	Oldrich Svojanovský/Pavel Svojanovský/ Vladimír Petrícek (TCH)	Stefan Tudor/Petre Ceapura/ Ladislau Lovrenschi (ROM)
1976	Harold Jährling/Friedrich-Wilhelm Ulrich/Georg Spohr (GDR)	Dmitriy Bekhterev/Yuriy Shurkalov/ Yuriy Lorentson (URS)	Oldrich Svojanovský/Pavel Svojanovský/ Ludvík Vébr (TCH)
1980	Harold Jährling/Friedrich-Wilhelm Ulrich/Georg Spohr (GDR)	Viktor Pereverzev/Gennadiy Kryuchkin/ Aleksandr Lukyanov (URS)	Dusko Mrduljas/Zlatko Celent/ Josip Reic (YUG)
1984	Carmine Abbagnale/Giuseppe Abbagnale/Giuseppe di Capua (ITA)	Dimitrie Popescu/Vasile Tomoiaga/ Dumitru Raducanu (ROM)	Kevin Still/Robert Espeseth/ Doug Herland (USA)
1988	Carmine Abbagnale/Giuseppe Abbagnale/Giuseppe di Capua (ITA)	Mario Streit/Detlef Kirchhoff/ René Rensch (GDR)	Andrew Holmes/Steve Redgrave/ Patrick Sweeney (GBR)
1992	Jonathan Searle/Greg Searle/ Garry Herbert (GBR)	Carmine Abbagnale/Giuseppe Abbagnale/ Giuseppe di Capua (ITA)	Dimitrie Popescu/Nicolaie Taga/ Dumitru Raducanu (ROM)

NB: Two races were held in 1906, over 1000m (A) and 1 mile (B). The event was discontinued after 1992.

Men's Coxless Fours

	Gold	Silver	Bronze
1904	Century B.C. (St Louis) (USA)	Mound City R.C. (St Louis) (USA)	Western R.C. (St Louis) (USA)
1906	not held		
1908	Magdalen College (Oxford) (GBR)	Leander Club (GBR)	Argonaut R.C. (Toronto) (CAN)/ Amstel Amsterdam (NED)
1912-20	not held		
1924	Great Britain	Canada	Switzerland
1928	Great Britain	United States	Italy
1932	Great Britain	Germany	Italy
1936	Germany	Great Britain	Switzerland
1948	Italy	Denmark	United States
1952	Yugoslavia	France	Finland
1956	Canada	United States	France
1960	United States	Italy	Soviet Union
1964	Denmark	Great Britain	United States
1968	German Democratic Republic	Hungary	Italy
1972	German Democratic Republic	New Zealand	Federal Republic of Germany
1976	German Democratic Republic	Norway	Soviet Union
1980	German Democratic Republic	Soviet Union	Great Britain
1984	New Zealand	United States	Denmark
1988	German Democratic Republic	United States	Federal Republic of Germany
1992	Australia	United States	Slovenia
1996	Australia	France	Great Britain
2000	Great Britain	Italy	Australia

Men's Coxed Fours

	Gold	Silver	Bronze
1896	not held		
1900	Cercle de l'Aviron de Roubaix (FRA) Germania RC (Hamburg) (GER)	Club Nautique de Lyon (FRA) Minerva Amsterdam (NED)	R.C. Favorite Harmonia (Hamburg) (GER) Ludwigshafener Ruderverein (GER)
1904	not held		
1906	Bucintoro (Venice) (ITA)	Soc. Nautique de la Basse Seine (FRA)	Soc. Nautique de Bayonne (FRA)
1908	not held		
1912	Ludwigshafener Ruderverein (GER)	Thames R.C. (GBR)	Polyteknisk Roklub (DEN)
1920	Switzerland	United States	Norway
1924	Switzerland	France	United States
1928	Italy	Switzerland	Poland
1932	Germany	Italy	Poland
1936	Germany	Switzerland	France
1948	United States	Switzerland	Denmark
1952	Czechoslovakia	Switzerland	United States

1956	Italy	Sweden	Finland
1960	Germany	France	Italy
1964	Germany	Italy	Netherlands
1968	New Zealand	German Democratic Republic	Switzerland
1972	Federal Republic of Germany	German Democratic Republic	Czechoslovakia
1976	Soviet Union	German Democratic Republic	Federal Republic of Germany
1980	German Democratic Republic	Soviet Union	Poland
1984	Great Britain	United States	New Zealand
1988	German Democratic Republic	Romania	New Zealand
1992	Romania	Germany	Poland

NB: Two finals were held in 1900 due to confusion over qualification. The event was discontinued after 1992.

Men's Eights

	Gold	Silver	Bronze
1896	not held		
1900	Vesper B.C. (Philadelphia) (USA)	R.C. Nautique de Gand (BEL)	Minerva Amsterdam (NED)
1904	Vesper B.C. (Philadelphia) (USA)	Argonaut R.C. (Toronto) (CAN)	only two teams competed
1906	not held		
1908	Leander Club (GBR)	R.C. Nautique de Gand (BEL)	Argonaut R.C. (Toronto) (CAN)/ Cambridge University B.C. (GBR)
1912	Leander Club (GBR)	New College (Oxford) (GBR)	Berliner Rudergesellschaft (GER)
1920	United States	Great Britain	Norway
1924	United States	Canada	Italy
1928	United States	Great Britain	Canada
1932	United States	Italy	Canada
1936	United States	Italy	Germany
1948	United States	Great Britain	Norway
1952	United States	Soviet Union	Australia
1956	United States	Canada	Australia
1960	Germany	Canada	Czechoslovakia
1964	United States	Germany	Czechoslovakia
1968	Federal Republic of Germany	Australia	Soviet Union
1972	New Zealand	United States	German Democratic Republic
1976	German Democratic Republic	Great Britain	New Zealand
1980	German Democratic Republic	Great Britain	Soviet Union
1984	Canada	United States	Australia
1988	Federal Republic of Germany	Soviet Union	United States
1992	Canada	Romania	Germany
1996	Netherlands	Germany	Russia
2000	Great Britain	Australia	Croatia

Men's Lightweight Double Sculls

	Gold	Silver	Bronze
1996	Markus Gier/ Michael Gier (SUI)	Maarten van der Linden/ Pepijn Aardewijn (NED)	Anthony Edwards/ Bruce Hick (AUS)
2000	Tomasz Kucharski/ Robert Sycz (POL)	Elia Luini/ Leonardo Pettinari (ITA)	Pascal Touron/ Thibaud Chapelle (FRA)

Men's Lightweight Coxless Fours

	Gold	Silver	Bronze
1996	Denmark	Canada	United States
2000	France	Australia	Denmark

Discontinued Events

Men's Coxed Fours Inriggers

	Gold	Silver	Bronze
1912	Denmark	Sweden	Norway

Men's Naval Rowing Boats (6 Man) – 2000m

	Gold	Silver	Bronze
1906	Varese (ITA)	Spetsai (GRE)	Hydra (GRE)

ROWING

Naval Rowing Boats (17 Man) – 3000m

	Gold	Silver	Bronze
1906	Poros (GRE)	Hydra (GRE)	Varese (ITA)

Women's Single Sculls

	Gold	Silver	Bronze
1976	Christine Scheiblich (GDR)	Joan Lind (USA)	Yelena Antonova (URS)
1980	Sanda Toma (ROM)	Antonina Makhina (URS)	Martina Schröter (GDR)
1984	Valeria Racila (ROM)	Charlotte Geer (USA)	Ann Haesebrouck (BEL)
1988	Jutta Behrendt (GDR)	Anne Marden (USA)	Magdalena Georgieva (BUL)
1992	Elisabeta Lipa (ROM)	Annelies Bredael (BEL)	Silken Laumann (CAN)
1996	Yekaterina Khodotovich (BLR)	Silken Laumann (CAN)	Trine Hansen (DEN)
2000	Yekaterina Karsten (Khodotovich) (BLR)	Rumyana Neykova (BUL)	Katrin Rutschow-Stomporowski (GER)

Women's Double Sculls

	Gold	Silver	Bronze
1976	Svetla Otsetova/ Zdravka Yordanova (BUL)	Sabine Jahn/ Petra Boesler (GDR)	Leonora Kaminskaité/ Genovaité Ramoškiené (URS)
1980	Yelena Khloptseva/ Larissa Popova (URS)	Cornelia Linse/ Heidi Westphal (GDR)	Olga Homeghi/ Valeria Racila-Rosca (ROM)
1984	Mariora Popescu/ Elisabeta Oleniuc (ROM)	Greet Hellemans/ Nicolette Hellemans (NED)	Daniele Laumann/ Silken Laumann (CAN)
1988	Birgit Peter/ Martina Schröter (GDR)	Elisabeta Lipa (Oleniuc)/ Veronica Cogeanu (ROM)	Violeta Ninova/ Stefka Madina (BUL)
1992	Kerstin Köppen/ Kathrin Boron (GER)	Veronica Cochela (Cogeanu)/ Elisabeta Lipa (ROM)	Gu Xiaoli/ Lu Huali (CHN)
1996	Marnie McBean/ Kathleen Heddle (CAN)	Cao Mianying/ Zhang Xiuyun (CHN)	Irene Eijs/ Eeke van Nes (NED)
2000	Jana Thieme/ Kathrin Boron (GER)	Pieta van Dishoeck/ Eeke van Nes (NED)	Biruté Sakickiené/ Kristina Poplavskaja (LTU)

Women's Quadruple Sculls

	Gold	Silver	Bronze
1976	German Democratic Republic	Soviet Union	Romania
1980	German Democratic Republic	Soviet Union	Bulgaria
1984	Romania	United States	Denmark
1988	German Democratic Republic	Soviet Union	Romania
1992	Germany	Romania	Soviet Union
1996	Germany	Ukraine	Canada
2000	Germany	Great Britain	Russia

NB: 1976-84 with cox, 1988-date without cox

Women's Coxless Pairs

	Gold	Silver	Bronze
1976	Siika Kelbecheva/ Stoyanka Gruicheva (BUL)	Angelika Noack/ Sabine Dähne (GDR)	Edith Eckbauer/ Thea Einöder (FRG)
1980	Ute Steindorf/ Cornelia Klier (GDR)	Malgorzata Dluzewska/ Czeslawa Kocianska (POL)	Siika Barbulova (Kelbecheva)/ Stoyanka Kurbatova (Gruicheva) (BUL)
1984	Rodica Arba/ Elena Horvat (ROM)	Elizabeth Craig/ Tricia Smith (CAN)	Ellen Becker/ Iris Völkner (FRG)
1988	Rodica Arba/ Olga Homeghi (ROM)	Radka Stoyanova/ Lalka Berberova (BUL)	Nicola Payne/ Lynley Hannen (NZL)
1992	Marnie McBean/ Kathleen Heddle (CAN)	Stefanie Werremeier/ Ingeburg Schwerzmann (GER)	Anna Seaton/ Stephanie Pierson (USA)
1996	Megan Still/ Kate Slatter (AUS)	Missy Schwen/ Karen Kraft (USA)	Christine Gossé/ Hélène Cortin (FRA)
2000	Georgeta Damian/ Doina Ignat (ROM)	Rachael Taylor/ Kate Slatter (AUS)	Missy Ryan (Schwen)/ Karen Kraft (USA)

Women's Eights

Gold	Silver	Bronze
1976	German Democratic Republic	Soviet Union	United States
1980	German Democratic Republic	Soviet Union	Romania
1984	United States	Romania	Netherlands
1988	German Democratic Republic	Romania	China
1992	Canada	Romania	Germany
1996	Romania	Canada	Belarus
2000	Romania	Netherlands	Canada

Women's Lightweight Double Sculls

	Gold	Silver	Bronze
1996	Constanta Burcica/ Camelia Macoviciuc (ROM)	Teresa Bell/ Lindsay Burns (USA)	Rebecca Joyce/ Virginia Lee (AUS)
2000	Constanta Burcica/ Angela Alupei (ROM)	Valerie Viehoff/ Claudia Blasberg (GER)	Christine Collins/ Sarah Garner (USA)

Discontinued Events

Women's Coxless Fours

	Gold	Silver	Bronze
1992	Canada	United States	Germany

Women's Coxed Fours

	Gold	Silver	Bronze
1976	German Democratic Republic	Bulgaria	Soviet Union
1980	German Democratic Republic	Bulgaria	Soviet Union
1984	Romania	Canada	Australia
1988	German Democratic Republic	China	Romania

World Champions

Men's Single Sculls

1962	Vyachesav Ivanov (URS)	1989	Thomas Lange (GDR)
1966	Don Spero (USA)	1990	Yuriy Yanson (URS)
1970	Alberto Demiddi (ARG)	1991	Thomas Lange (GDR)
1974	Wolfgang Honig (GDR)	1993	Derek Porter (CAN)
1975	Peter-Michael Kolbe (FRG)	1994	André Willms (GER)
1977	Joachim Dreifke (FRG)	1995	Iztok Cop (SLO)
1978	Peter-Michael Kolbe (FRG)	1996	not held
1979	Pertti Karppinen (FIN)	1997	Jamie Koven (USA)
1981	Peter-Michael Kolbe (FRG)	1998	Rob Waddell (NZL)
1982	Rudiger Reiche (GDR)	1999	Rob Waddell (NZL)
1983	Peter-Michael Kolbe (FRG)	2000	not held
1985	Pertti Karppinen (FIN)	2001	Olaf Tufte (DEN)
1986	Peter-Michael Kolbe (FRG)	2002	Marcel Hacker (GER)
1987	Thomas Lange (GDR)	2003	Olaf Tufte (DEN)

ROWING

Men's Double Sculls

1962	René Duhamel/Bernard Monnereau (FRA)	1989	Lars Bjonness/Rol Bent Thorsen (NOR)
1966	Melchior Burgin/Martin Studach (SUI)	1990	Christophe Zerbst/Arnold Jonke (AUT)
1970	Jorgen Engelbrecht/Niels Secher (DEN)	1991	Henk-Jan Zwolle/Nicolaas Rienks (NED)
1974	Christof Kreuziger/Hans-Ulrich Schmied (GDR)	1993	Yves Lamarque/Samuel Barathay (FRA)
1975	Alf Hansen/Frank Hansen (NOR)	1994	Ralf Thorsen/Lars Bjonness (NOR)
1977	Chris Baillieu/Michael Hart (GBR)	1995	Lars Christensen/Martin Halabo-Hansen (DEN)
1978	Alf Hansen/Frank Hansen (NOR)	1996	not held
1979	Alf Hansen/Frank Hansen (NOR)	1997	Stephan Volkert/Andreas Hajek (GER)
1981	Klaus Kröppelien/Joachim Dreifke (GDR)	1998	Stephan Volkert/Andreas Hajek (GER)
1982	Alf Hansen/Rolf Thorsen (NOR)	1999	Iztok Cop/Luka Spik (SLO)
1983	Thomas Lange/Uwe Heppner (GDR)	2000	not held
1985	Thomas Lange/Uwe Heppner (GDR)	2001	Tibor Peto/Akos Haller (HUN)
1986	Alberto Belgori/Igor Pescialli (ITA)	2002	Tibor Peto/Akos Haller (HUN)
1987	Vasil Radeyev/Danatyl Yordanov (BUL)	2003	Sebastien Vielledant/Adrien Hardy (FRA)

Men's Quadruple Sculls

1962	not held	1983	West Germany	1996	not held
1966	not held	1985	Canada	1997	Italy
1970	not held	1986	Soviet Union	1998	Italy
1974	East Germany	1987	Soviet Union	1999	Germany
1975	East Germany	1989	Romania	2000	not held
1977	East Germany	1990	Soviet Union	2001	Germany
1978	East Germany	1991	Soviet Union	2002	Germany
1979	East Germany	1993	Germany	2003	Germany
1981	East Germany	1994	Italy		
1982	East Germany	1995	Italy		

Men's Coxless Pairs

1962	Dieter Bender/Gunther Zumkeller (FRG)	1989	Thomas Jung/Uwe Kellner (GDR)
1966	Peter Gorny/Werner Klatt (GDR)	1990	Thomas Jung/Uwe Kellner (GDR)
1970	Peter Gorny/Werner Klatt (GDR)	1991	Steve Redgrave/Matthew Pinsent (GBR)
1974	Bernd Landvoigt/Jörg Landvoigt (GDR)	1993	Steve Redgrave/Matthew Pinsent (GBR)
1975	Bernd Landvoigt/Jörg Landvoigt (GDR)	1994	Steve Redgrave/Matthew Pinsent (GBR)
1977	Vitaliy Yeliseyev/Aleksandr Kulagin (URS)	1995	Steve Redgrave/Matthew Pinsent (GBR)
1978	Bernd Landvoigt/Jörg Landvoigt (GDR)	1996	not held
1979	Bernd Landvoigt/Jörg Landvoigt (GDR)	1997	Michel Andrieux/Jean-Christophe Rolland (FRA)
1981	Yuriy Pimenov/Nikolay Pimenov (URS)	1998	Robert Sens/Detlef Kirchhoff (GER)
1982	Hans Magnus Grepperud/Sverre Løken (NOR)	1999	Drew Ginn/James Tomkins (AUS)
1983	Carl Ertel/Ulf Sauerbrey (GDR)	2000	not held
1985	Yuriy Pimenov/Nikolay Pimenov (URS)	2001	Matthew Pinsent/James Cracknell (GBR)
1986	Yuriy Pimenov/Nikolay Pimenov (URS)	2002	Matthew Pinsent/James Cracknell (GBR)
1987	Andrew Holmes/Steven Redgrave (GBR)	2003	Drew Ginn/James Tomkins (AUS)

Men's Coxed Pairs

1962	West Germany	1983	East Germany	1996	France
1966	Netherlands	1985	Italy	1997	United States
1970	Romania	1986	Great Britain	1998	Australia
1974	Soviet Union	1987	Italy	1999	United States
1975	East Germany	1989	Italy	2000	United States
1977	Bulgaria	1990	Italy	2001	Great Britain
1978	East Germany	1991	Italy	2002	Germany
1979	East Germany	1993	Great Britain	2003	United States
1981	Italy	1994	Croatia		
1982	Italy	1995	Italy		

Men's Coxless Fours

1962	West Germany	1983	West Germany	1996	not held
1966	East Germany	1985	West Germany	1997	Great Britain
1970	East Germany	1986	United States	1998	Great Britain
1974	East Germany	1987	East Germany	1999	Great Britain
1975	East Germany	1989	East Germany	2000	not held
1977	East Germany	1990	Australia	2001	Great Britain
1978	Soviet Union	1991	Australia	2002	Germany
1979	East Germany	1993	France	2003	Canada
1981	Soviet Union	1994	Italy		
1982	Switzerland	1995	Italy		

Men's Coxed Fours

1962	West Germany	1983	New Zealand	1996	Romania
1966	East Germany	1985	Soviet Union	1997	France
1970	West Germany	1986	East Germany	1998	Australia
1974	East Germany	1987	East Germany	1999	United States
1975	Soviet Union	1989	Romania	2000	Great Britain
1977	East Germany	1990	East Germany	2001	France
1978	East Germany	1991	Germany	2002	United States
1979	East Germany	1993	Romania	2003	United States
1981	East Germany	1994	Romania		
1982	East Germany	1995	United States		

Men's Eights

1962	West Germany	1983	New Zealand	1996	not held
1966	West Germany	1985	Soviet Union	1997	United States
1970	East Germany	1986	Australia	1998	United States
1974	United States	1987	Soviet Union	1999	United States
1975	East Germany	1989	West Germany	2000	not held
1977	East Germany	1990	West Germany	2001	Romania
1978	East Germany	1991	Germany	2002	Canada
1979	East Germany	1993	Germany	2003	Canada
1981	Soviet Union	1994	United States		
1982	New Zealand	1995	Germany		

Lightweight Men's Single Sculls

1974	William Belden (USA)	1989	Frans Goebel (NED)
1975	Reto Wyss (SUI)	1990	Frans Goebel (NED)
1976	Raimund Haberl (AUT)	1991	Niall O'Toole (IRL)
1977	Reto Wyss (SUI)	1992	Jens Mohr Ernst (DEN)
1978	José Antonio Montosa (ESP)	1993	Peter Haining (GBR)
1979	William Belden (USA)	1994	Peter Haining (GBR)
1980	Christian Georg Wahrlich (FRG)	1995	Peter Haining (GBR)
1981	Scott Roop (USA)	1996	Karsten Nielsen (DEN)
1982	Raimund Haberl (AUT)	1997	Karsten Nielsen (DEN)
1983	Bjarne Eltang (DEN)	1998	Stefano Basalini (ITA)
1984	Bjarne Eltang (DEN)	1999	Karsten Nielsen (DEN)
1985	Ruggero Verroca (ITA)	2000	Michal Vabrousek (CZE)
1986	Peter Antoine (AUS)	2001	Sam Lynch (IRL)
1987	Willem Van Belleghem (BEL)	2002	Sam Lynch (IRL)
1988	Alwin Otten (FRG)	2003	Stefano Basalini (ITA)

ROWING

Lightweight Men's Double Sculls

1974-77 not held
1978 Pal Bornick/Arne Gilje (NOR)
1979 Pal Bornick/Arne Gilje (NOR)
1980 Francesco Esposito/Ruggero Verroca (ITA)
1981 Francesco Esposito/Ruggero Verroca (ITA)
1982 Francesco Esposito/Ruggero Verroca (ITA)
1983 Francesco Esposito/Ruggero Verroca (ITA)
1984 Francesco Esposito/Ruggero Verroca (ITA)
1985 Luc Crispon/Thierry Renault (FRA)
1986 Carl Smith/Allan Whitwell (GBR)
1987 Enrico Gandola/Giovanni Calabrese (ITA)
1988 Enrico Gandola/Francesco Esposito (ITA)
1989 Christoph Schmolzer/Walter Rantasa (AUT)
1990 Steve Peterson/Robert Dreher (USA)

1991 Kai Von Warburg/Michael Buchheit (GER)
1992 Gary Lynagh/Bruce Hick (AUS)
1993 Gary Lynagh/Bruce Hick (AUS)
1994 Francesco Esposito/Michelangelo Crispi (ITA)
1995 Michael Gier/Markus Gier (SUI)
1996 not held
1997 Tomasz Kucharski/Robert Sycz (POL)
1998 Tomasz Kucharski/Robert Sycz (POL)
1999 Michelangelo Crispi/Leonardo Pettinari (ITA)
2000 not held
2001 Elia Luini/Leonardo Pettinari (ITA)
2002 Elia Luini/Leonardo Pettinari (ITA)
2003 Elia Luini/Leonardo Pettinari (ITA)

Lightweight Men's Quadruple Sculls

1974-88 not held
1989 West Germany
1990 Italy
1991 Australia
1992 Italy
1993 Austria

1994 Austria
1995 Austria
1996 Italy
1997 Italy
1998 Italy

1999 Italy
2000 Japan
2001 Italy
2002 Italy
2003 Italy

Lightweight Men's Coxless Pairs

1974-92 not held
1993 Fernando Climent/Fernando Molina (ESP)
1994 Leonardo Pettinari/Carlo Gaddi (ITA)
1995 Carlo Grande/Pasquale Marigliano (ITA)
1996 Thomas Ebert/Bo Svendsen (DEN)
1997 Mathias Binder/Benedikt Schmidt (SUI)

1998 Vincent Montabel/Jean-Christophe Bette (FRA)
1999 Paolo Pittino/Stefano Basalini (ITA)
2000 Ed Winchester/Ben Storey (CAN)
2001 Gearold Towey/Tony O'Connor (IRL)
2002 C.R.Yantani Garces/M.A.Cerda Silva (CHI)
2003 Bo Helleberg/Mads Anderssen (DEN)

Lightweight Men's Coxless Fours

1974 Australia
1975 France
1976 France
1977 France
1978 Switzerland
1979 Great Britain
1980 Australia
1981 Australia
1982 Italy
1983 Spain

1984 Spain
1985 West Germany
1986 Italy
1987 West Germany
1988 Italy
1989 West Germany
1990 West Germany
1991 Great Britain
1992 Great Britain
1993 United States

1994 Denmark
1995 Italy
1996 not held
1997 Denmark
1998 Denmark
1999 Denmark
2000 not held
2001 Austria
2002 Denmark
2003 Denmark

Lightweight Men's Eights

1974 United States
1975 West Germany
1976 West Germany
1977 Great Britain
1978 Great Britain
1979 Spain
1980 Great Britain
1981 Denmark
1982 Italy
1983 Spain

1984 Denmark
1985 Italy
1986 Italy
1987 Italy
1988 Italy
1989 Italy
1990 Italy
1991 Italy
1992 Denmark
1993 Canada

1994 Great Britain
1995 Denmark
1996 Germany
1997 Australia
1998 Germany
1999 United States
2000 United States
2001 France
2002 Italy
2003 Germany

Women's Single Sculls

1974	Christine Scheiblich (GDR)	1991	Silken Laumann (CAN)
1975	Christine Scheiblich (GDR)	1993	Jana Thieme (GER)
1977	Christine Scheiblich (GDR)	1994	Trine Hansen (DEN)
1978	Christine Scheiblich (GDR)	1995	Maria Brandin (SWE)
1979	Sanda Toma (ROM)	1996	not held
1981	Sanda Toma (ROM)	1997	Yekaterina Khodotovich (BLR)
1982	Irina Fetissova (URS)	1998	Irina Fedotova (RUS)
1983	Jutta Hampe (GDR)	1999	Ekaterina Karsten (BLR)
1985	Cornelia Linse (GDR)	2000	not held
1986	Jutta Hampe (GDR)	2001	Katrin Rutschow-Stomporowski (GER)
1987	Magdalena Georgieva (BUL)	2002	Rumyana Neykova (BUL)
1989	Elisabeta Lipa (ROM)	2003	Rumyana Neykova (BUL)
1990	Birgit Peter (GDR)		

Women's Double Sculls

1974	Yelena Antonova/Galina Yermoleyeva (URS)	1993	Philippa Baker/Brenda Lawson (NZL)
1975	Yelena Antonova/Galina Yermoleyeva (URS)	1994	Philippa Baker/Brenda Lawson (NZL)
1977	Anke Borchmann/Roswietha Zobelt (GDR)	1995	Marnie McBean/Kathleen Heddle (CAN)
1978	Svetla Otsetova/Zdravka Yordanova (BUL)	1996	not held
1979	Cornelia Linse/Heidi Westphal (GDR)	1997	Meike Evers/Kathrin Boron (GER)
1981	Margarita Kokarevitha/Antonina Makhina (URS)	1998	Miriam Batten/Gillian Lindsay (GBR)
1982	Yelena Braticko/Antonina Makhina (URS)	1999	Kathrin Boron/Jana Thieme (GER)
1983	Jutta Scheck/Martina Schröter (GDR)	2000	not held
1985	Sylvia Schurabe/Martina Schröter (GDR)	2001	Kathrin Boron/Kerstin Kowalski (GER)
1986	Sylvia Schurabe/Beate Schramm (GDR)	2002	Georgina Evers-Swindell/
1987	Steska Madina/Violeta Ninova (BUL)		Caroline Evers-Swindell (NZL)
1989	Jana Sorgers/Beate Schramm (GDR)	2003	Georgina Evers-Swindell/
1990	Kathrin Boron/Beate Schramm (GDR)		Caroline Evers-Swindell (NZL)
1991	Kathrin Boron/Beate Schramm (GER)		

Women's Quadruple Sculls

1974	East Germany	1986	East Germany	1997	Germany
1975	East Germany	1987	East Germany	1998	Germany
1977	East Germany	1989	East Germany	1999	Germany
1978	Bulgaria	1990	East Germany	2000	not held
1979	East Germany	1991	Germany	2001	Germany
1981	Soviet Union	1993	China	2002	Germany
1982	Soviet Union	1994	Germany	2003	Australia
1983	Soviet Union	1995	Germany		
1985	East Germany	1996	not held		

Women's Coxless Pairs

1974	Marilena Ghita/Cornelia Neascu (ROM)	1991	Marnie McBean/Kathleen Heddle (CAN)
1975	Sabine Dähne/Angelika Noack (GDR)	1993	Hélène Cortin/Christine Gossé (FRA)
1977	Sabine Dähne/Angelika Noack (GDR)	1994	Hélène Cortin/Christine Gossé (FRA)
1978	Cornelia Bugel/Ute Steindorf (GDR)	1995	Megan Still/Kate Slatter (AUS)
1979	Cornelia Bugel/Ute Steindorf (GDR)	1996	not held
1981	Sigrid Anders/Iris Rudolph (GDR)	1997	Emma Robinson/Alison Korn (CAN)
1982	Silvia Fröhlich/Marita Sandig (GDR)	1998	Emma Robinson/Theresa Luke (CAN)
1983	Silvia Fröhlich/Marita Sandig (GDR)	1999	Emma Robinson/Alison Korn (CAN)
1985	Rodica Arba/Elena Florea (ROM)	2000	not held
1986	Rodica Arba/Olga Homeghi (ROM)	2001	Georgeta Damian/Viorica Susanu (ROM)
1987	Rodica Arba/Olga Homeghi (ROM)	2002	Georgeta Andrunache/Viorica Susanu (ROM)
1989	Kathrin Haaker/Judith Zeidler (GDR)	2003	Cath Bishop/Katharine Grainger (GBR)
1990	Stefanie Werremeier/Ingeburg Althoff (FRG)		

Women's Coxless Fours

1974-85	not held	1993	China	1999	Belarus
1986	United States	1994	Netherlands	2000	Belarus
1987	not held	1995	United States	2001	Australia
1989	East Germany	1996	United States	2002	Australia
1990	Romania	1997	Great Britain	2003	United States
1991	Canada	1998	Ukraine		

ROWING

Women's Eights

1974	East Germany	1986	Soviet Union	1997	Romania
1975	East Germany	1987	Romania	1998	Romania
1977	East Germany	1989	Romania	1999	Romania
1978	Soviet Union	1990	Romania	2000	not held
1979	Soviet Union	1991	Canada	2001	Australia
1981	Soviet Union	1993	Romania	2002	United States
1982	Soviet Union	1994	Germany	2003	Germany
1983	Soviet Union	1995	United States		
1985	Soviet Union	1996	not held		

Lightweight Women's Single Sculls

1974-84	not held	1994	Constanta Pipota (ROM)
1985	Adair Ferguson (AUS)	1995	Rebecca Joyce (AUS)
1986	Maria Sava (ROM)	1996	Constanta Burcica (ROM)
1987	Magdalena Georgieva (BUL)	1997	Sarah Garner (USA)
1988	Kris Karlson (USA)	1998	Pia Vogel (SUI)
1989	Kris Karlson (USA)	1999	Pia Vogel (SUI)
1990	Mette Bloch Jensen (DEN)	2000	Laila Finska-Bezerra (FIN)
1991	Philippa Baker (NZL)	2001	Sinead Jennings (IRL)
1992	Mette Bloch Jensen (DEN)	2002	Vikoriya Dimitrova (BUL)
1993	Michelle Darvill (CAN)	2003	Fiona Milne (CAN)

Lightweight Women's Double Sculls

1974-84	not held	1994	Colleen Miller/Wendy Wiebe (CAN)
1985	Lin Clark/Beryl Crockford (GBR)	1995	Colleen Miller/Wendy Wiebe (CAN)
1986	Chris Ernst/Cary Beth Sands (USA)	1996	not held
1987	Stefka Madina/Violeta Ninova (BUL)	1997	Michelle Darville/Angelika Brand (GER)
1988	Lauren Vermuist/Ellen Meliese (NED)	1998	Christine Collins/Sarah Garner (USA)
1989	Cary Beth Sands/Kris Karlson (USA)	1999	Constanta Burcica/Camelia Macoviciuc (ROM)
1990	Ulla Jensen/Regitze Siggaard (DEN)	2000	not held
1991	Christiane Weber/Claudia Waldi (GER)	2001	Janet Radunzel/Claudia Blasberg (GER)
1992	Christiane Weber/Claudia Waldi (GER)	2002	Sally Causby/Amber Halliday (AUS)
1993	Colleen Miller/Wendy Wiebe (CAN)	2003	Marie-Louise Draeger/Claudia Blasberg (GER)

Lightweight Women's Quadruple Sculls

1974-96	not held	1999	United States	2002	Australia
1997	Germany	2000	Germany	2003	China
1998	Germany	2001	Australia		

Lightweight Women's Coxless Pairs

1985-86	not held	1999	Linda Muri/Rachel Anderson (USA)
1987	Rodica Arba/Olga Homeghi (ROM)	2000	Malindi Myers/Miriam Taylor (GBR)
1989-95	not held	2001	Jo Nitsch/Sarah Birch (GBR)
1996	Christine Smith/Ellen Munzner (USA)	2002	Naomi Ashcroft/Leonie Barron (GBR)
1997	Eliza Blair/Justine Joyce (AUS)	2003	Liliana Niga/Elena Scurto (ROM)
1998	Juliet Machan/Jo Nitsch (GBR)		

Discontinued Events

Women's Coxed Fours

1974	East Germany	1979	Soviet Union	1985	East Germany
1975	East Germany	1981	Soviet Union	1986	Romania
1977	East Germany	1982	Soviet Union	1987	Romania
1978	East Germany	1983	East Germany		

Lightweight Women's Coxed Fours

1985   West Germany
1986   United States
1987   Romania

Lightweight Women's Coxless Fours

1985-95 not held
1996   China

Henley Royal Regatta

Grand Challenge Cup

1839	Trinity College, Cambridge
1840	Leander Club
1841	Cambridge Subscription Rooms, London
1842	Cambridge Subscription Rooms, London
1843	Oxford University Boat Club
1844	Etonian Boat Club, Oxford
1845	Cambridge University Boat Club
1846	Thames Club, London
1847	Oxford University Boat Club
1848	Oxford University Boat Club
1849	Wadham College, Oxford
1850	Oxford University
1851	Oxford University Boat Club
1852	Oxford University Boat Club
1853	Oxford University Boat Club
1854	First Trinity, Cambridge
1855	Cambridge University Boat Club
1856	Royal Chester Rowing Club
1857	London Rowing Club
1858	Cambridge University Boat Club
1859	London Rowing Club
1860	First Trinity, Cambridge
1861	First Trinity, Cambridge
1862	London Rowing Club
1863	University College, Oxford
1864	Kingston Rowing Club
1865	Kingston Rowing Club
1866	Oxford Etonian Club
1867	Oxford Etonian Club
1868	London Rowing Club
1869	Oxford Etonian Club
1870	Oxford Etonian Club
1871	Oxford Etonian Club
1872	London Rowing Club
1873	London Rowing Club
1874	London Rowing Club
1875	Leander Club
1876	Thames Rowing Club
1877	London Rowing Club
1878	Thames Rowing Club
1879	Jesus College, Cambridge
1880	Leander Club
1881	London Rowing Club
1882	Exeter College, Oxford
1883	London Rowing Club
1884	London Rowing Club
1885	Jesus College, Oxford
1886	Trinity Hall, Cambridge
1887	Trinity Hall, Cambridge
1888	Thames Rowing Club
1889	Thames Rowing Club
1890	London Rowing Club
1891	Leander Club

Diamond Sculls

1839	——
1840	——
1841	——
1842	——
1843	——
1844	T.B. Bumsted, Scullers Club, London
1845	S. Wallace, Leander Club
1846	E.G. Moon, Magdalen College, Oxford
1847	W. Maule, Trinity College, Cambridge
1848	W.L. Bagshawe, Trinity College, Cambridge
1849	T.R. Bone, Thames Club, London
1850	T.R. Bone, Thames Club, London
1851	E.G. Peacock, Thames Club, London
1852	E. MacNaghten, Trinity College, Cambridge
1853	S. Rippingall, Peterhouse, Cambridge
1854	H.H. Playford, Wandle Club
1855	A.A. Casamajor, Wandle Club
1856	A.A. Casamajor, Argonaut Club
1857	A.A. Casamajor, London Rowing Club
1858	A.A. Casamajor, London Rowing Club
1859	E.D. Brickford, Richmond
1860	H.H. Playford, London Rowing Club
1861	A.A. Casamajor, London Rowing Club
1862	E.D. Brickord, Brasenose College, Oxford
1863	C.B. Lawes, Third Trinity, Cambridge
1864	W.B. Woodgate, Brasenose College, Oxford
1865	E.B. Michell, Magdalen College, Oxford
1866	E.B. Michell, Magdalen College, Oxford
1867	W.C. Crofts, Brasenose College, Oxford
1868	W. Stout, London Rowing Club
1869	W.C. Crofts, Brasenose College, Oxford
1870	John B. Close, First Trinity, Cambridge
1871	W. Fawcus, Tynemouth Rowing Club
1872	C.C. Knollys, Oxford
1873	A.C. Dicker, Lady Margaret B.C., Cambridge
1874	A.C. Dicker, Cambridge
1875	A.C. Dicker, Cambridge
1876	F.L. Playford, London Rowing Club
1877	T.C. Edwards-Moss, Brasenose College, Oxford
1878	T.C. Edwards-Moss, Brasenose College, Oxford
1879	F.L. Playford, London Rowing Club
1880	J. Lowndes, Derby
1881	J. Lowndes, Derby
1882	J. Lowndes, Derby
1883	J. Lowndes, Twickenham Rowing Club
1884	W.S. Unwin, Magdalen College, Oxford
1885	W.S. Unwin, Magdalen College, Oxford
1886	F.I. Pitman, Third Trinity, Cambridge
1887	J.C. Gardner, Emmanuel College, Cambridge
1888	G. Nickalls, Magdalen College, Oxford
1889	G. Nickalls, Magdalen College, Oxford
1890	G. Nickalls, Magdalen College, Oxford
1891	G. Nickalls, Magdalen College, Oxford

ROWING

1892	Leander Club	J.J.K. Ooms, Neptune Rowing Club (NED)
1893	Leander Club	G. Nickalls, Magdalen College, Oxford
1894	Leander Club	G. Nickalls, Formosa Boat Club
1895	Trinity Hall, Cambridge	R. Guinness, Leander Club
1896	Leander Club	Hon. R. Guinness, Leander Club
1897	New College, Oxford	E.H. TenEyck, Wachusett Boat Club (USA)
1898	Leander Club	B.H. Howell, Trinity Hall, Cambridge
1899	Leander Club	B.H. Howell, Thames Rowing Club
1900	Leander Club	E.G. Hemmerde, University College, Oxford
1901	Leander Club	C.V. Fox, Guards Brigade Rowing Club
1902	Third Trinity, Cambridge	F.S. Kelly, Balliol College, Oxford
1903	Leander Club	F.S. Kelly, Leander Club
1904	Leander Club	L.F. Scholes, Toronto Rowing Club (CAN)
1905	Leander Club	F.S. Kelly, Leander Club
1906	Club Nautique de Gand (BEL)	H.T. Blackstaffe, Vesta Rowing Club
1907	Sport Nautique de Gand (BEL)	Capt. W.H. Darrell, Household Brigade Boat Club
1908	Christ Church, Oxford	A. McCulloch, Leander Club
1909	Royal Nautique de Gand (BEL)	A.A. Stuart, Kingston Rowing Club
1910	Magdalen College, Oxford	W.D. Kinnear, Kensington Rowing Club
1911	Magdalen College, Oxford	W.D. Kinnear, Kensington Rowing Club
1912	Sydney Rowing Club (AUS)	E.W. Powell, Vikings Club
1913	Leander Club	C. McVilly, Derwent Rowing Club, Tasmania (AUS)
1914	Harvard Athletics Association Boat Club (USA)	G. Sinigaglia, Lario Club, Como (ITA)
1920	Magdalen College, Oxford	J. Beresford jnr, Thames Rowing Club
1921	Magdalen College, Oxford	F.E. Eyken, Delft University Boat Club (NED)
1922	Leander Club	W.M. Hoover, Deluth Boat Club (USA)
1923	Thames Rowing Club	M.K. Morris, London Rowing Club
1924	Leander Club	J. Beresford jnr, Thames Rowing Club
1925	Leander Club	J. Beresford jnr, Thames Rowing Club
1926	Leander Club	J. Beresford jnr, Thames Rowing Club
1927	Thames Rowing Club	R.T. Lee, Worcester College, Oxford
1928	Thames Rowing Club	J. Wright, Argonaut Rowing Club (CAN)
1929	Leander Club	L.H.F. Gunther (NED)
1930	London Rowing Club	J.S. Guest, Don Rowing Club (CAN)
1931	London Rowing Club	R. Pearce, Leander B.C. of Hamilton (CAN)
1932	Leander Club	H. Buhtz, Berliner R.C. (GER)
1933	London Rowing Club	T.G. Askwith, Peterhouse, Cambridge
1934	Leander Club	H. Buhtz, Berliner R.C. (GER)
1935	Pembroke College, Cambridge	E. Rufli, Zurich Rowing Club (SUI)
1936	Zurich Rowing Club (SUI)	E. Rufli, Zurich Rowing Club (SUI)
1937	Rudergesellschaft 'Wiking' (GER)	J. Hasenohrl (AUS)
1938	London Rowing Club	J.W. Burk, Pennsylvania Athletic Club (USA)
1939	Harvard University (USA)	J.W. Burk, Pennsylvania Athletic Club (USA)
1946	Leander Club	J. Sepheriades, SN Basse Seine (FRA)
1947	Jesus College, Oxford	J.B. Kelly, University of Pennsylvania (USA)
1948	Thames Rowing Club	M.T. Wood, NSW Police (AUS)
1949	Leander Club	J.B. Kelly, University of Pennsylvania (USA)
1950	Harvard University (USA)	A.D. Rowe, Leander Club
1951	Lady Margaret Boat Club, Cambridge	T.A. Fox, Pembroke College, Oxford
1952	Leander Club	M.T. Wood, Sydney Rowing Club (AUS)
1953	Leander Club	T.A. Fox, London Rowing Club
1954	Krylia Sovetov (URS)	P. Vlasic, Mornar Club (YUG)
1955	University of Pennsylvania (USA)	T. Kocerka, AZS Bydgoszcz (POL)
1956	Centre Sportif des Forces Armés (FRA)	T. Kocerka, AZS Bydgoszcz (POL)
1957	Cornell University (USA)	S.A. MacKenzie, Sydney Rowing Club (AUS)
1958	Trud Club (USA)	S.A. MacKenzie, Sydney Rowing Club (AUS)
1959	Harvard University (USA)	S.A. MacKenzie, Sydney Rowing Club (AUS)
1960	Molesey Boat Club	S.A. MacKenzie, Leander Club
1961	Central Sport Club of the USSR Navy, Moscow (URS)	S.A. MacKenzie, Mossman Rowing Club (AUS)
1962	Central Sport Club of the USSR Navy, Moscow (URS)	S.A. MacKenzie, Leander Club
1963	University of London	G. Knottmann, Belvoir Ruder Club (SUI)
1964	Club Zjalghiris Viljnjus, (URS)	S. Cromwell, Non Pareil Rowing Club (USA)
1965	Ratzeburger Ruderclub (GER)	D.M. Spero, New York Athletic Club (USA)
1966	TSC Berlin (GER)	A. Hill, BSC Motor Baumschulenweg (GER)
1967	SS Wissenschaft DHfK, Leipzig (GDR)	M. Studach, Grasshopper Club, Zurich (SUI)
1968	University of London	H.A. Wardell-Yerburgh, Eton Vikings Club
1969	SC Einheit, Dresden (GDR)	H-J. Bohmer, SC Dynamo, Berlin (GER)
1970	ASK Vorwarts, Rostock (GDR)	J. Meissner, Mannheimer Rv Amicitia (FRG)
1971	The Tideway Scullers' School	A Demiddi, Club de Regattas, Rosario (ARG)
1972	WMF Moscow (URS)	A. Timoschinin, WMF Moscow (URS)
1973	Trud Kolomna (URS)	S. Drea, Neptune Rowing Club (IRL)
1974	Trud Kolomna (URS)	S. Drea, Neptune Rowing Club (IRL)

1975	Leander Club/Thames Tradesmen's Rowing Club	S. Drea, Neptune Rowing Club (IRL)
1976	Thames Tradesmen's Rowing Club	E.O. Hale, Sydney Rowing Club (AUS)
1977	University of Washington (USA)	T.J. Crooks, Leander Club
1978	Trakia Club (BUL)	T.J. Crooks, Leander Club
1979	Thames Tradesmen/London Rowing Club	H.P. Matheson, Nottingham Boat Club
1980	Charles River Rowing Association (USA)	R.D. Ibarra (ARG)
1981	Oxford University/Thames Tradesmen's R.C.	C.L. Baillieu, Leander Club
1982	Leander Club/London Rowing Club	C.L. Baillieu, Leander Club
1983	London Rowing Club/University of London	S.G. Redgrave, Marlow Rowing Club
1984	Leander Club/London Rowing Club	C.L. Baillieu, Leander Club
1985	Harvard University (USA)	S.G. Redgrave, Marlow Rowing Club
1986	Nautilus Rowing Club	B. Eltang, Danske Studenters Roklub (DEN)
1987	Soviet Army (URS)	P.-M. Kolbe, R.C. Hamburg (FRG)
1988	Leander Club/University of London	G.H. McGlashan, Melbourne University B.C. (AUS)
1989	Hansa Dortmund (FRG)	V. Chalupa, Duka Praha (TCH)
1990	Hansa Dortmund (FRG)	E.F.M. Verdonk, Koru Rowing Club (NZL)
1991	Leander Club/Star Club	W. van Belleghem, Koninklijke Rv, Ghent (BEL)
1992	University of London	R.G.F. Henderson, Leander Club
1993	Hansa Dortmund (GER)	T. Lange, Ruderverein Bollberg-Halle (GER)
1994	Charles River Rowing Association/San Diego (USA)	X.R. Müller, Grasshopper Club, Zurich (SUI)
1995	San Diego Training Center (USA)	J. Jaanson, Parnu R.C. (EST)
1996	Imperial College London/Queen's Tower B.C.	M.L.O. Vervoorn, Delftsche SP P-R (NED)
1997	Australian/NSW Institutes of Sport (AUS)	G.M.P. Searle, Molesey Boat Club
1998	Hansa Dortmund/Berliner R.C. (GER)	J.W. Koven, Brown Alumni (USA)
1999	Hansa Dortmund/Berliner R.C. (GER)	M. Hacker, R.C. Magdeburg (GER)
2000	Australian Institute of Sport	A.H. Abdullah, Princeton Training Center (USA)
2001	HAVK Mladost/VK Croatia, Croatia	D.S. Free, Surfers Paradise Rowing Club (AUS)
2002	Victoria City R.C./University of Victoria (CAN)	P.J.C. Wells, University of London
2003	Victoria City Rowing Club (CAN)	A.W. Campbell, The Tideway Scullers' School
2004	Hollandia Roeiclub (NED)	M. Hacker (GER)

Head of the River Race

1926	London R.C.	1963	University of London B.C.
1927	London R.C./Thames R.C.	1964-72	Tideway Scullers' School
1928-35	London R.C.	1975-76	ARA National Squad
1936	Thames R.C.	1977	Leander Club
1937	not held	1978	London R.C.
1938	Cambridge Univ B.C. (Goldie)	1979-80	ARA National Squad
1939	London R.C.	1981	Thames Tradesmen's R.C.
1940-45	not held	1982	ARA National Squad
1946	Imperial College B.C.	1983	Thames Tradesmen's R.C.
1947	Jesus College, Cambridge B.C.	1984-90	GBR national squad*
1948	Thames R.C.	1991	Leander Club
1949-50	London R.C.	1992	Molesey B.C.
1951-52	Jesus College, Cambridge B.C.	1993-94	RV Munster von 1882 (GER)
1953	Thames R.C.	1995	Netherlands Rowing Federation
1954	Royal Air Force	1996-98	Leander Club
1955-56	Thames R.C.	1999-2001	Queens Tower
1957	Oxford University B.C. (Isis)	2002-03	Leander Club
1958-62	Barn Cottage B.C.	2004	cancelled due to bad weather

*Record time 1989 – 16mins 37secs.

University Boat Race

Cambridge wins

1836	1884	1953
1839-41	1886-89	1955-58
1845-46	1899-1900	1961-62
1849	1902-04	1964
1856	1906-08	1968-73
1858	1914	1975
1860	1920-22	1986
1870-74	1924-36	1993-99
1876	1939	2001
1879	1947-51	2004

NB: 1877 race was a dead-heat.

Oxford wins

1829	1880-83	1954
1842	1885	1959-60
1849	1890-98	1963
1852	1901	1965-67
1854	1905	1974
1857	1909-13	1976-85
1859	1923	1987-92
1861-69	1937-38	2000
1875	1946	2002-03
1878	1952	

ROWING

World Sculls Cup Champions

	Men's	Women's
1990	Václav Chalupa (TCH)	Birgit Peter (GDR)
1991	Václav Chalupa (TCH)	Silken Laumann (CAN)
1992	Thomas Lange (GER)	Beate Schramm (GER)
1993	Václav Chalupa (CZE)	Annelies Bredael (BEL)
1994	Xeno Müller (SUI)	Marnie McBean (CAN)
1995	Juri Jaanson (EST)	Trine Hansen (DEN)

RUGBY LEAGUE

Rugby league is unusual among sports in that its formation can be dated exactly, and the reasons for its existence are clearly defined. Throughout the 1880s and 1890s, rugby was booming in the industrial heartlands of Yorkshire and Lancashire. Crowds flocked to the game – the Yorkshire Cup final attracted as many as 40,000 spectators. In contrast to the gentlemen amateurs playing the game in the south, the teams were made up mainly of working men. In those days, the working week included Saturday mornings, and players were often left with a dilemma when travelling to an away match as this would mean missing a morning's work, and hence a morning's pay. Certain teams began to offer 'broken time' payments to compensate the men for the shortfall in their weekly income.

The Rugby Football Union (RFU) refused to sanction broken time payments, so on 29 August 1895, when 21 clubs were represented at the George Hotel, Huddersfield, it was decided that those clubs would break away from the RFU and form what was originally called the Northern Union (NU). Rules for payments were strictly enforced – certain lines of work were not permitted, and payments could be made only if a man was genuinely missing a morning's work and was not sick.

The costs of payment to players meant that clubs needed to maximise their income by attracting crowds to the games. Rugby union was considered by some a game for the player, rather than the spectator, so the NU tried to improve the entertainment value in order to keep the crowd numbers high. In the early days there were experiments with 15-man teams and a round ball, but eventually a decision was made to remove two forwards from each team, thus creating more space on the field and more opportunity for open, running play. Even a century later, changes were still being made to the rules to make the game ever more entertaining.

Try as it might, rugby league has always struggled to break away from its heartland. In the main, it is confined to what is now the M62 corridor and Cumbria in England, and to New South Wales and Queensland in Australia. There have always been accusations that those involved in rugby union and the southern-based press have tried to do the game down, but rugby league continues to thrive in its heartlands, and to attract good television audiences, drawn by the skills and fitness on offer. A major advantage is that the ball is always visible.

In 1929 the crucial decision was made to play the Challenge Cup final at Wembley. The annual pilgrimage became a highlight for many rugby league fans. In 1996 the game at its top echelon went fully professional.

World Cup

	Winners		Runners-Up	Venue
1954	Great Britain	16-12	France	Paris
1957	Australia	——	——	——
1960	Great Britain	——	——	——
1968	Australia	20-2	France	Sydney
1970	Australia	12-7	Great Britain	Headingley
1972	Great Britain*	10-10	Australia	Lyon
1975	Australia	——	——	——
1977	Australia	13-12	Great Britain	Sydney
1988	Australia	25-12	New Zealand	Auckland
1992	Australia	10-6	Great Britain	Wembley
1995	Australia	16-8	England	Wembley
2000	Australia	40-12	New Zealand	Old Trafford

*Great Britain won won by having better results in preceding league matches.

Challenge Cup

	Winners		Runners-Up	Venue	Attendance
1897	Batley	10-3	St Helens	Leeds	13,492
1898	Batley	7-0	Bradford	Leeds	27,941
1899	Oldham	19-9	Hunslet	Manchester	15,763
1900	Swinton	16-8	Salford	Manchester	17,864
1901	Batley	6-0	Warrington	Leeds	29,563
1902	Broughton	25-0	Salford	Rochdale	15,006

Year	Winner	Score	Runner-up	Venue	Attendance
1903	Halifax	7-0	Salford	Leeds	32,507
1904	Halifax	8-3	Warrington	Salford	17,041
1905	Warrington	6-0	Hull KR	Leeds	19,638
1906	Bradford	5-0	Salford	Leeds	15,834
1907	Warrington	17-3	Oldham	Broughton	18,500
1908	Hunslet	14-0	Hull	Huddersfield	18,000
1909	Wakefield	17-0	Hull	Leeds	23,587
1910	Leeds	7-7	Hull	Huddersfield	19,413
	Leeds	26-12 (replay)	Hull	Huddersfield	11,608
1911	Broughton	4-0	Wigan	Salford	8,000
1912	Dewsbury	8-5	Oldham	Leeds	15,271
1913	Huddersfield	9-5	Warrington	Leeds	22,754
1914	Hull	6-0	Wakefield	Halifax	19,000
1915	Huddersfield	37-3	St Helens	Oldham	8,000
1916-19	not held				
1920	Huddersfield	21-10	Wigan	Leeds	14,000
1921	Leigh	13-0	Halifax	Broughton	25,000
1922	Rochdale	10-9	Hull	Leeds	32,596
1923	Leeds	28-3	Hull	Wakefield	29,335
1924	Wigan	21-4	Oldham	Rochdale	41,831
1925	Oldham	16-3	Hull KR	Leeds	28,335
1926	Swinton	9-3	Oldham	Rochdale	27,000
1927	Oldham	26-7	Swinton	Wigan	33,448
1928	Swinton	5-3	Warrington	Wigan	33,909
1929	Wigan	13-2	Dewsbury	Wembley	41,500
1930	Widnes	10-3	St Helens	Wembley	36,544
1931	Halifax	22-8	York	Wembley	40,368
1932	Leeds	11-8	Swinton	Wigan	29,000
1933	Huddersfield	21-17	Warrington	Wembley	41,874
1934	Hunslet	11-5	Widnes	Wembley	41,280
1935	Castleford	11-8	Huddersfield	Wembley	39,000
1936	Leeds	18-2	Warrington	Wembley	51,250
1937	Widnes	18-5	Keighley	Wembley	47,699
1938	Salford	7-4	Barrow	Wembley	51,243
1939	Halifax	20-3	Salford	Wembley	55,453
1940	not held				
1941	Leeds	19-2	Halifax	Bradford	28,500
1942	Leeds	15-10	Halifax	Bradford	15,250
1943	Dewsbury	16-9	Leeds	Dewsbury	10,470
	Dewsbury	0-6	Leeds	Leeds	16,000
	(Dewsbury won 16-15 on aggregate)				
1944	Bradford	0-3	Wigan	Wigan	22,000
	Bradford	8-0	Wigan	Bradford	30,000
	(Bradford won 8-3 on aggregate)				
1945	Huddersfield	7-4	Bradford	Huddersfield	9,041
	Huddersfield	6-5	Bradford	Bradford	17,500
	(Huddersfield won 13-9 on aggregate)				
1946	Wakefield	13-12	Wigan	Wembley	54,730
1947	Bradford	8-4	Leeds	Wembley	77,605
1948	Wigan	8-3	Bradford	Wembley	91,465
1949	Bradford	12-0	Halifax	Wembley	95,050
1950	Warrington	19-0	Widnes	Wembley	94,249
1951	Wigan	10-0	Barrow	Wembley	94,262
1952	Workington	18-10	Featherstone	Wembley	72,093
1953	Huddersfield	15-10	St Helens	Wembley	89,588
1954	Warrington	4-4	Halifax	Wembley	81,841
	Warrington	8-4 (replay)	Halifax	Bradford	102,569
1955	Barrow	21-12	Workington	Wembley	66,513
1956	St Helens	13-2	Halifax	Wembley	79,341
1957	Leeds	9-7	Barrow	Wembley	76,318
1958	Wigan	13-9	Workington	Wembley	66,109
1959	Wigan	30-13	Hull	Wembley	79,811
1960	Wakefield	38-5	Hull	Wembley	79,773
1961	St Helens	12-6	Wigan	Wembley	94,672
1962	Wakefield	12-6	Huddersfield	Wembley	81,263
1963	Wakefield	25-10	Wigan	Wembley	84,492
1964	Widnes	13-5	Hull KR	Wembley	84,488
1965	Wigan	20-16	Hunslet	Wembley	89,016
1966	St Helens	21-2	Wigan	Wembley	98,536
1967	Featherstone	17-12	Barrow	Wembley	76,290
1968	Leeds	11-10	Wakefield	Wembley	87,100
1969	Castleford	11-6	Salford	Wembley	97,939

Year	Winner	Score	Loser	Venue	Attendance
1970	Castleford	7-2	Wigan	Wembley	95,255
1971	Leigh	24-7	Leeds	Wembley	85,514
1972	St Helens	16-13	Leeds	Wembley	89,495
1973	Featherstone	33-14	Bradford	Wembley	72,395
1974	Warrington	24-9	Featherstone	Wembley	77,400
1975	Widnes	14-7	Warrington	Wembley	85,098
1976	St Helens	20-5	Widnes	Wembley	89,982
1977	Leeds	16-7	Widnes	Wembley	80,871
1978	Leeds	14-12	St Helens	Wembley	96,000
1979	Widnes	12-3	Wakefield	Wembley	94,218
1980	Hull KR	10-5	Hull	Wembley	95,000
1981	Widnes	18-9	Hull KR	Wembley	92,496
1982	Hull	14-14	Widnes	Wembley	92,147
	Hull	18-9 (replay)	Widnes	Leeds	41,171
1983	Featherstone	14-12	Hull	Wembley	84,969
1984	Widnes	19-6	Wigan	Wembley	80,116
1985	Wigan	28-25	Hull	Wembley	97,801
1986	Castleford	15-15	Hull KR	Wembley	82,134
1987	Halifax	19-18	St Helens	Wembley	91,267
1988	Wigan	32-12	Halifax	Wembley	94,273
1989	Wigan	27-0	St Helens	Wembley	78,000
1990	Wigan	36-14	Warrington	Wembley	77,729
1991	Wigan	13-8	St Helens	Wembley	75,532
1992	Wigan	28-12	Castleford	Wembley	77,286
1993	Wigan	20-14	Widnes	Wembley	77,684
1994	Wigan	26-16	Leeds	Wembley	78,348
1995	Wigan	30-10	Leeds	Wembley	78,550
1996	St Helens	40-32	Bradford	Wembley	75,994
1997	St Helens	32-22	Bradford	Wembley	78,022
1998	Sheffield	17-6	Wigan	Wembley	60,699
1999	Leeds	52-16	London	Wembley	73,242
2000	Bradford	22-18	Leeds	Edinburgh	75,356
2001	St Helens	13-6	Bradford	Twickenham	68,250
2002	Wigan	21-12	St Helens	Edinburgh	62,140
2003	Bradford	22-20	Leeds	Cardiff	71,212
2004	St Helens	32-16	Wigan	Cardiff	73,734

RUGBY LEAGUE

Lance Todd Trophy Winners

Year	Player	Club		Year	Player	Club
1946	Billy Stott	Wakefield		1975	Ray Dutton	Widnes
1947	Willie Davies	Bradford		1976	Geoff Pimblett	St Helens
1948	Frank Whitcombe	Bradford		1977	Steve Pitchford	Leeds
1949	Ernest Ward	Bradford		1978	George Nicholls	St Helens
1950	Gerry Helme	Warrington		1979	David Topliss	Wakefield
1951	Cec Mountford	Wigan		1980	Brian Lockwood	Hull
1952	Billy Ivison	Workington		1981	Mick Burke	Widnes
1953	Peter Ramsden	Huddersfield		1982	Eddie Cunningham	Widnes
1954	Gerry Helme	Warrington		1983	David Hobbs	Featherstone
1955	Jack Grundy	Barrow		1984	Joe Lydon	Widnes
1956	Alan Prescott	St Helens		1985	Brett Kenny	Wigan
1957	Jeff Stevenson	Leeds		1986	Bob Beardmore	Castleford
1958	Rees Thomas	Wigan		1987	Graham Eadie	Halifax
1959	Brian McTigue	Wigan		1988	Andy Gregory	Wigan
1960	Tommy Harris	Hull		1989	Ellery Hanley	Wigan
1961	Dick Huddart	St Helens		1990	Andy Gregory	Wigan
1962	Neil Fox	Wakefield		1991	Denis Betts	Wigan
1963	Harold Poynton	Wakefield		1992	Martin Offiah	Wigan
1964	Frank Collier	Widnes		1993	Dean Bell	Wigan
1965	Ray Ashby	Wigan		1994	Martin Offiah	Wigan
	Brian Gabbitas	Hunslet		1995	Jason Robinson	Wigan
1966	Len Killeen	St Helens		1996	Robbie Paul	Bradford
1967	Carl Dooler	Featherstone		1997	Tommy Martyn	St Helens
1968	Don Fox	Wakefield		1998	Mark Aston	Sheffield
1969	Malcolm Reilly	Castleford		1999	Leroy Rivett	Leeds
1970	Bill Kirkbride	Castleford		2000	Henry Paul	Bradford
1971	Alex Murphy	Leigh		2001	Sean Long	St Helens
1972	Kel Coslett	St Helens		2002	Kris Radlinski	Wigan
1973	Steve Nash	Featherstone		2003	Gary Connolly	Leeds
1974	Derek Whitehead	Warrington		2004	Sean Long	St Helens

Harry Sunderland Trophy Winners

1965	Terry Fogerty	Halifax v St Helens	1985	Harry Pinner	St Helens v Hull KR
1966	Albert Halsall	St Helens v Halifax	1986	Les Boyd	Warrington v Halifax
1967	Ray Owen	Wakefield v St Helens	1987	Joe Lydon	Wigan v Warrington
1968	Gary Cooper	Wakefield v Hull KR	1988	David Hulme	Widnes v St Helens
1969	Bev Risman	Leeds v Castleford	1989	Alan Tait	Widnes v Hull
1970	Frank Myler	St Helens v Leeds	1990	Alan Tait	Widnes v Bradford
1971	Bill Ashurst	Wigan v St Helens	1991	Greg Mackey	Hull v Widnes
1972	Terry Clawson	Leeds v St Helens	1992	Andy Platt	Wigan v St Helens
1973	Mick Stephenson	Dewsbury v Leeds	1993	Chris Joynt	St Helens v Wigan
1974	Barry Philbin	Warrington v St Helens	1994	Sam Panapa	Wigan v Castleford
1975	Mel Mason	Leeds v St Helens	1995	Kris Radlinski	Wigan v Leeds
1976	George Nicholls	St Helens v Salford	1996	Andy Farrell	Wigan v St Helens
1977	Geoff Pimblett	St Helens v Warrington	1997	Andy Farrell	Wigan v St Helens
1978	Bob Haigh	Bradford v Widnes	1998	Jason Robinson	Wigan v Leeds
1979	Kevin Dick	Leeds v Bradford	1999	Henry Paul	Bradford v St Helens
1980	Mal Aspey	Widnes v Bradford	2000	Chris Joynt	St Helens v Wigan
1981	Len Casey	Hull KR v Hull	2001	Michael Withers	Bradford v Wigan
1982	Mick Burke	Widnes v Hull	2002	Paul Deacon	Bradford v St Helens
1983	Tony Myler	Widnes v Hull	2003	Stuart Reardon	Bradford v Wigan
1984	John Dorahy	Hull KR v Castleford	2004	Michael Withers	Bradford v Wigan

Man of Steel

1977	David Ward (Leeds)	1991	Gary Schofield (Leeds)
1978	George Nicholls (St Helens)	1992	Dean Bell (Wigan)
1979	Doug Laughton (Widnes)	1993	Andy Platt (Wigan)
1980	George Fairbairn (Wigan)	1994	Jonathan Davies (Warrington)
1981	Ken Kelly (Warrington)	1995	Denis Betts (Wigan)
1982	Mick Morgan (Carlisle)	1996	Andy Farrell (Wigan)
1983	Allan Agar (Featherstone)	1997	James Lowes (Bradford)
1984	Joe Lydon (Widnes)	1998	Iestyn Harris (Leeds)
1985	Ellery Hanley (Bradford)	1999	Adrian Vowles (Castleford)
1986	Gavin Miller (Hull KR)	2000	Sean Long (St Helens)
1987	Ellery Hanley (Wigan)	2001	Paul Sculthorpe (St Helens)
1988	Martin Offiah (Widnes)	2002	Paul Sculthorpe (St Helens)
1989	Ellery Hanley (Wigan)	2003	Jamie Peacock (Bradford)
1990	Shaun Edwards (Wigan)		

World Club Challenge

	Winners		Runners-Up	Venue
1976	Eastern Suburbs	25-2	St Helens	Sydney
1987	Wigan	8-2	Manly-Warringah	Central Park
1989	Widnes	30-18	Canberra	Old Trafford
1991	Wigan	21-4	Penrith	Anfield
1992	Brisbane	22-8	Wigan	Central Park
1994	Wigan	20-14	Brisbane	ANZ Stadium
1997	Brisbane	36-12	Hunter	Ericsson Stadium
2000	Melbourne	44-6	St Helens	JJB Stadium
2001	St Helens	20-18	Brisbane	Reebok Stadium
2002	Bradford	41-26	Newcastle Knights	McAlpine Stadium
2003	Sydney City	38-0	St Helens	Reebok Stadium
2004	Bradford	22-4	Penrith	McAlpine Stadium

Clubs: Details

Team	Nicknames	Ground	Colours
Barrow Raiders	Shipbuilders	Craven Park	blue and white
Batley Bulldogs	Gallant Youth	Mount Pleasant	cerise and fawn
Bradford Bulls	Northern	Odsal	white, red, gold and black
Castleford Tigers	Glassblowers	The Jungle (Wheldon Road)	white, amber and black
Chorley Lynx		Victory Park	black and white
Dewsbury Rams		Ram Stadium	red, gold and black (New Crown Flatt)
Doncaster Dragons		Belle Vue	blue and yellow
Featherstone Rovers	Colliers	Lionheart Stadium	navy blue and white (Post Office Road)
Gateshead Thunder		Gateshead International Stadium	purple and yellow
Halifax	Blue Sox, Thrum Hallers	The Shay	blue and white
Huddersfield Giants	Barracudas, Fartowners	McAlpine Stadium	maroon and gold
Hull	Sharks, Airlie Birds	Kingston Communications Stadium	black and white
Hull Kingston Rovers	Robins	New Craven Park	white and red
Hunslet Hawks	Parksiders	South Leeds Stadium	myrtle, flame and white
Keighley Cougars		Cougar Park	red, green and white (Lawkholme Lane)
Leeds Rhinos	Loiners	Headingley	blue and amber
Leigh Centurions		Hilton Park	red and white
London Broncos	Crusaders	Griffin Park	red, blue and white
London Skolars		New River Stadium	black, green and red
Oldham Roughyeds	Bears	Boundary Park	red, white and blue
Rochdale Hornets		Spotland	red, blue and white
St Helens Saints		Knowsley Road	white and red
Salford City Reds	Red Devils	The Willows	red and white
Sheffield Eagles		Don Valley	black
Swinton Lions		Moor Lane	blue and white
Wakefield Trinity Wildcats	Dreadnoughts	Belle Vue	white, red, gold and black
Warrington Wolves	Wire	Wilderspool	primrose and blue
Whitehaven Warriors	Haven	Recreation Grounds	white, yellow, blue and chocolate
Widnes Vikings	Chemics	Halton Stadium	black and white
Wigan Warriors	Riversiders	JJB Stadium	cherry and white
Workington Town		Derwent Park	blue and white
York City Knights	Wasps, Vikings	Ryedale Stadium	light and dark blue

RUGBY LEAGUE

General Information

George Hotel

Built 1851, the George Hotel in Huddersfield is the birthplace of rugby league. There, on 29 August 1895, 21 clubs met to agree to break away from the Rugby Football Union and form the Northern Union, thus allowing them to compensate players who had to miss work in order to be able to play rugby.

Grand Final: history

The Grand Final concept was introduced to the English game for the 1998 Super League season, having been successfully used in Australian rugby league for a number of years. The Grand Final play-offs replaced the previous premiership system, and saw only the top six teams at the end of the weekly rounds involved (as opposed to the previous eight clubs), with the winning team being given a prestigious ring instead of a medal. Old Trafford was retained as the venue for the Grand Final, with a series of matches (over three weeks) deciding the two teams to compete in the final. The system involved in the play-offs means that the top two teams in the final Super League placings will not necessarily win through to the Grand Final, although whoever is on top is exempt from the first week of the series and home advantage is always decided by final Super League placings. The first two Grand Finals, however, did involve the teams who finished at the top of the table, and the first four years saw only five teams involved in the play-offs. In 1998, Wigan Warriors and Leeds Rhinos contested the inaugural Grand Final, and it was Wigan who emerged victorious in a tight game, Jason Robinson's try and three Andy Farrell goals giving them a 10-4 win.

Harry Sunderland Trophy

Awarded to the man of the match in the Super League Grand Final, as voted for by members of the Rugby League Writers' Association. Queensland-born Harry Sunderland was an Australian tour manager, broadcaster and journalist, and this award recognises his work in rugby league (he was also influential in the introduction of the Lance Todd Trophy). The trophy has been awarded since 1965, from the then Championship Final, and the Premiership Final since its inception in 1975. In 1998 the trophy was awarded to Jason Robinson, in the inaugural Grand Final of the Super League season. In 2002, a Bradford Bulls player became the second winner in four years to be awarded the Harry Sunderland Trophy despite losing to St Helens (Paul Deacon in 2002 and Henry Paul in 1999).

Lance Todd Trophy: details	Awarded to the man of the match at the Challenge Cup final
Man of Steel award	Awarded to an outstanding rugby league player as voted for by broadcasters and journalists
nicknames	Australia – Kangaroos, Great Britain – Lions, New Zealand – Kiwis
positions and numbers	1 full-back; 2 winger/three-quarter; 3 centre/three-quarter; 4 centre/three-quarter; 5 winger/three-quarter; 6 five-eighth/stand off; 7 half-back/scrum half; 8 front row/prop forward; 9 hooker; 10 front row/prop forward; 11 second row; 12 second row; 13 lock/loose forward.
rules	Two teams take part in a game of rugby league with 13 players on each team at kick-off. Each team also has four substitutes available to bring on at any appropriate moment in the game. Each team's 'thirteen' is made up of seven backs and six forwards. The backs are generally regarded as the attacking players and usually have more pace than the bigger, more powerful forwards who are normally the 'yard' makers. The object of the game is for one team to score more points than the other within the 80 minutes game time. A team can score points through scoring a try or kicking a goal. Each team is given six tackles or chances to score. If after six tackles the team has not achieved this then the ball is given to the opposing team and the cycle begins again. If a team has not scored by the fifth/last tackle then the 'acting half-back' will generally pass the ball to the team's kicker who will punt it downfield in order to gain territorial advantage. The only disadvantage to this tactic is that if the ball goes out of play on the 'full' (before bouncing), the opposition gain possession of the ball from where the kick was originally made.
Super League: history	Super League came to fruition in 1996, a year after Rupert Murdoch's News Corporation invested £87 million in the European game (to be spread over five years). Murdoch's vision of running a European Super League in tandem with the Australian competition has seen the game expanded to new boundaries at the top level, with teams from Paris and Gateshead joining London, as clubs from outside of the heartland, in the top flight. After a move to play games in summer rather than winter, March 1996 saw Super League kick off and Paris played host to Sheffield Eagles in the first-ever game, benefiting from an increased and improved service from Sky television, with a giant screen at live televised games enabling the use of a video referee to adjudicate on tries. Clubs adopted nicknames and pre-match entertainment also helped to market and popularise the sport. The inaugural Super League champions were Shaun McRae's St Helens, who had adapted to the new competition to such an extent that they achieved the Challenge Cup double in 1996.
Wembley Stadium	Opened in 1923 and the venue of every peacetime Challenge Cup final from 1929 to 1999, with the exception of 1932. Up to 90,000 people regularly made the pilgrimage south.
World Club Challenge	As a result of the success of the European Super League a World Club Championship was begun in 1997. Brisbane Broncos emerged as the inaugural winners of the competition, defeating the Hunter Mariners in the final, with no European sides making the final four. Wigan put up the best show, losing to the Mariners at Central Park.
World Cup: details	The rugby league World Cup was first contested in 1954 between Great Britain, France, Australia and New Zealand. It was played as a one-leg league competition, with a play-off final because Great Britain and France were the joint league leaders. Great Britain beat France 16-12 in the play-off in Paris. Australia headed the table in the second World Cup in 1957 and in the third competition in 1960 Great Britain came out on top. The cup was revived under a new format in 1968 when the final was played by the top two nations. In this fourth World Cup competition Australia beat France 20-2 at the Sydney Cricket Ground. In 1970 Australia defeated Great Britain 12-7 at Headingley and in 1972 Great Britain gained revenge, drawing 10-10 with the Kangaroos in Lyon but winning the tournament by having better results in the league matches. In 1975 the league format again decided the winner and the Australians were victorious, beginning their long dominance of the competition. The 1977 World Cup was won in a tight 13-12 struggle against Great Britain in Sydney but the ninth competition took place between 1985 and 1988 under a four-season home-and-away system and culminated in a very comfortable 25-12 victory for the Kangaroos over the Kiwis, in Auckland. The four-year system was retained for the tenth World Cup and in a titanic final battle held in front of a record crowd of 73,641 at Wembley in October 1992 Australia beat Great Britain 10-6. The 1995 World Cup returned to a tournament format and amid the centenary celebrations and Super League dramas, the Cup kicked off with home side England beating the Kangaroos in the first game. However, normal service was resumed in the final and the Aussies defeated England 16-8 at Wembley. The 12th World Cup in 2000 was staged in Great Britain and France, and Great Britain divided itself again into four home nations, while teams from Lebanon, Russia, Fiji, South Africa, New Zealand Maori, and Cook Islands were also included for the first time. Australia once again proved strongest in the final and beat the Kiwis 40-12 at Old Trafford. The next World Cup is due to be held in 2005.

Biographies of Players, Coaches, Managers and Commentators

Ah Kuoi, Fred   Stand off, Auckland, Hull, New Zealand. One of several Kiwis who played for Hull in the 1980s, Fred was New Zealand Player of the Year in 1979 and 1980. He could play at stand off or anywhere in the three-quarter line and played 29 Tests for New Zealand between 1975 and 1985.

Anderson, Chris   Wing, Canterbury, Widnes, Hull KR, Halifax, Australia. Anderson has had an extremely successful career, both as a player (1970-84), and as coach for Canterbury, Melbourne, Halifax, Cronulla and Australia.

Ashcroft, Ernie   Centre, Wigan, Huddersfield, Warrington, Great Britain. Ashcroft played 691 games for Wigan, Huddersfield and Warrington between 1942 and 1962, playing 11 Tests.

Ashcroft, Kevin   Hooker, Leigh, Warrington, Great Britain. He was subsequently coach of Salford and Leigh.

Ashton, Eric   Born St Helens, England. Centre, Wigan, Great Britain. Ashton played all his club rugby for Wigan. A fine centre, who captained Wigan and the Lions, he later returned to St Helens as coach and chairman. He played 26 internationals. In 1966 he was the first rugby league player ever to be honoured with the MBE.

Atkinson, John   Wing, Leeds, Great Britain. A police officer, Atkinson played left wing for Leeds from 1966 to 1983 and scored 401 tries. The leading finisher of his era, he also played 26 internationals.

Baskerville, Albert   Born 1883. Coach, New Zealand. His influence on the game of rugby league in the southern hemisphere cannot be overstated. He virtually single-handedly raised the first team from New Zealand to tour Australia and the UK, which they did in 1907/08. Although primarily the manager, he also played in one Test against Australia in 1908 but succumbed to pneumonia and died 20 May 1908.

Bath, Harry   Born 1924. Second row/prop, Brisbane, Balmain, Barrow, Warrington, St George. Said by some to be the best player never to play for Australia, Bath played between 1946 and 1959. A goal-kicking second row or prop, he was the first foreign captain of a Challenge Cup-winning side, having the honour when Warrington won the replayed final of 1954. Bath later coached Balmain and was coach of Australia in the 1968 and 1970 World Cups.

Batten, Billy   Born Fitzwilliam, West Yorkshire, England. Centre, Hunslet, Hull, Wakefield, Castleford. Father of Eric and one of the first inductees into the Hall of Fame in 1988. His career lasted from 1907, at the age of 17, to 1927. A centre who was sold by Hunslet to Hull for a then record transfer of £600. He was famous for his 'leap' over potential tacklers rather than the more traditional dummy around them.

Batten, Eric   Wing, Wakefield Trinity, Hunslet, Bradford Northern, Featherstone Rovers, Great Britain. Son of Billy, Eric's 21-season career from 1933 to 1954 gained him only four Test caps but his 443 tries, for Wakefield, Hunslet, Bradford and Featherstone, put him fifth on the all-time list.

Beetson, Artie   Born Roma, Australia, 1945. Second row, Balmain, Parramatta, Easts (Sydney), Hull KR, Queensland, Australia. He played 28 times for Australia between 1966 and 1977, and is thought by many to be the best ball-playing forward produced by that country. In 1980 he captained Queensland in the first-ever State of Origin game – which would become an annual interstate rugby league contest – and later coached the state. Inducted into the Australian Hall of Fame in 2002.

Bell, Dean   Born 29 April 1962. Centre, Wigan, Easts (Sydney), Auckland, Leeds, New Zealand. He played with the great Wigan side of the 1980s and 1990s. He later coached Leeds before taking on an administrative role at Wigan.

Bevan, Brian   Born Sydney, Australia, 1924. Wing, Warrington, Blackpool. Scorer of 796 tries in 688 matches for Warrington and Blackpool between 1946 and 1964, over 200 more than anybody else. In home games at Wilderspool, his strike rate was more than 1.5 tries a game. Australian-born, he stayed on in the UK after World War II. Bevan is remembered still in Warrington by the Brian Bevan Stand at Wilderspool and there is a statue in his honour near the ground. A very small and wiry figure, who looked the antithesis of a successful athlete, elusiveness and speed were his hallmarks. Inducted into the Hall of Fame in 1988.

Bevan, John   Born Tylorstown, Wales, 28 October 1950. Wing, Warrington, Wales, Great Britain. He played in the famous Barbarians against All Blacks game in 1972 before going north the following year to ply his trade as a strong, powerful try-scoring winger for Warrington, where he stayed for 13 years, scoring over 200 tries.

Boston, Billy   Born Tiger Bay, Cardiff, Wales, 1934. Wing, Wigan, Blackpool, Wales, Great Britain. Associated mainly with Wigan, where he played from 1953 to 1968 before finishing his career at Blackpool. He scored 478 tries in 487 games for Wigan, and 34 tries in 31 internationals, as part of a career total of 571 tries in 465 matches, second on the all-time try-scoring list. In those days a huge man to be playing on the wing, his speed and power were enough to take him over for many scores. A legend in Wigan, his grandson Wes Davies has also represented the club. Boston became the first black rugby player to play in Australia when he was chosen for the 1954 Lions tour. A freeman of the borough, he was awarded the MBE in 1996. Inducted into the Hall of Fame in 1988.

Botica, Frano   Born Mangakino, New Zealand, 3 August 1963. Wing, Wigan, Auckland, New Zealand. Botica was a New Zealand All Black who signed for Wigan, before returning to rugby union. He also represented Croatia in the rugby union World Cup. Usually playing on the wing, although he could play in any position behind the scrum, he was a phenomenally successful goal kicker, so much so that it was a surprise when he missed a goal from anywhere on the pitch. He holds the record of 21 goals and 46pts in all Challenge Cup finals.

Boyd, Les   Born Nyngan, Australia. Prop forward, Wests (Sydney), Manly, Warrington, Australia. A fearsome Australian prop forward who made 17 appearances for the Kangaroos. He played for Wests and Manly before signing for Warrington, winning the 1986 Harry Sunderland Trophy.

Brough, Jim   Born Silloth, England, 5 November 1903. Full-back, Leeds. Known as 'Gentleman Jim', the Cumbrian full-back played 442 games for Leeds between 1925 and 1944, after having previously played rugby union for England.

Brown, Dave   Born Sydney, Australia, 1913. Centre, Easts (Sydney), Warrington, Australia. Dave Brown has often been described as 'the Bradman of rugby league', due to his propensity for breaking scoring records. His three remaining records are 285pts on the 1933/34 Kangaroo Tour from 19 tries and 114 goals; his 38 tries scored in the 1935 season for Eastern Suburbs; and his 45pts scored in a club game in 1935. It is unlikely that those records will ever be broken. Until the introduction of the Clive Churchill Medal in 1986 for the best Grand Final player, the award was known as the 'Dave Brown Medal'. He died in 1974. Inducted into the Australian Hall of Fame in 2002.

Burge, Frank   Born 1894. Loose forward, Glebe, St George, Australia. He played 13 Tests for Australia as a strong-tackling and speedy loose forward. Burge scored 33 tries in 23 games on the 1921/22 tour of Britain. He died in 1958.

Carlson, Brian   Born 1933. Carlson played in and around Newcastle and Sydney from 1951 to 1963, and in 23 internationals. A natural in any back position, his abilities as a kicker also meant he finished with over 1000 career points. He died in 1987.

Churchill, Clive   Born 21 January 1927. Full-back, Newcastle (Australia), Souths (Sydney), New South Wales, Australia. A member of the Australian Hall of Fame, he played 37 Tests for Australia as an attacking full-back. Churchill also played for Souths, captaining them to five Premierships. At various times, he captained and coached the national team. Inducted into the Australian Hall of Fame in 2002.

Clarkson, Geoff   Born 1943. He played first-team rugby from 1966 to 1983, and is believed to be the player who was transferred most times – 12 in total. He died in 2001.

Clay, Eric   Famous referee who stood no nonsense from anyone. Known as the 'Sergeant Major'.

Clues, Arthur   Second row/loose forward, Wests (Sydney), Leeds, Hunslet, Australia. This Australian international played in the second row and at loose forward for Leeds from 1947 to 1955, before joining Hunslet. He also played cricket for Leeds and is believed to be the only man to have scored a century and scored a try at Headingley. Clues died in 1998.

Clyde, Bradley   Born Sydney, Australia. Second row, Canberra, Canterbury, Leeds, Australia. One of the greatest forwards in the Australian game. He played 178 games for Canberra and 35 for Canterbury. The only player ever to have been awarded the Clive Churchill Medal on two occasions as the man of the match in the Australian Grand Final.

Connolly, Gary   Born St Helens, England, 22 June 1971. Full-back/centre, St Helens, Wigan, Leeds, England, Great Britain. He started his career as St Helens' full-back, playing in the 1989 Challenge Cup final. Connolly left for Wigan in 1993 and became the finest defensive centre of his generation. In 2003 he moved to Leeds and resumed the full-back role, winning the 2003 Lance Todd Trophy.

Cooper, Lionel   In only nine seasons, Cooper scored 420 tries for Huddersfield to become their leading try scorer ever, topping the season's charts three times, in the era of Brian Bevan. In the same period he scored another 21 tries in representative matches. In

1951 Cooper scored ten tries against Keighley – the record against a professional side.

Coote, Ron   Born 25 October 1944. Loose forward, Souths (Sydney), Easts (Sydney), Australia. He played for Souths and Easts from 1963 to 1977. An automatic choice as loose forward for the Australian side of the time.

Coslett, Kel   Born Bynea, Wales, 14 January 1942. Full-back/prop forward, St Helens, Wales. Holder of goals, points and appearances records for St Helens. Coslett was one of the many Welshmen who travelled north to play for St Helens. Lance Todd Trophy winner in 1972. Coslett coached Rochdale and later moved into administrative roles with St Helens and Wales.

Cronin, Mick   Centre, Parramatta, New South Wales, Australia. This Australian centre of the 1970s and 1980s was famed for the accuracy of his goal-kicking. Cronin scored a record 1971pts for Parramatta.

Crooks, Lee   Born 18 September 1963. Prop forward, Hull, Leeds, Castleford, Great Britain. A goal-kicking prop forward, his touchline penalty in the dying minutes of the 1985 Elland Road Test against New Zealand was selected as the best kick of the 1980s.

Cunningham, Keiron   Born 28 October 1976. Hooker, St Helens, Wales, Great Britain. The youngest of a rugby-playing family (brother Eddie won the 1982 Lance Todd Trophy). A strong-running and powerful hooker capable of scoring tries from halfway but at his best using his power close to the line. Cunningham turned down a huge amount of money from Welsh rugby union club Swansea to stay in rugby league.

Daley, Laurie   Born 20 October 1969. Stand off, Canberra and Australia. This great player spent his entire senior career at Canberra. He also played 25 Tests for Australia and was Australian Player of the Year in 1996.

Davies, Jonathan   Born Trimsaran, Wales, 24 October 1962. Stand off, Widnes, Warrington, Canterbury Bulldogs, Wales, Great Britain. A brilliant signing from Welsh rugby union (he joined from Llanelli in 1989, having played for Neath and for the national side). Davies later became the first player to return to union (for Cardiff) after captaining Wales to the 1995 World Cup semi-final, and was subsequently capped again by the WRU. He played for Warrington after his shock signing by Widnes. Primarily a stand off, he could play in any position behind the pack, including full-back, where he scored a famous try in the 12-man Great Britain team's 8-4 victory over Australia in 1994.

Dixon, Colin   Born Cardiff, Wales, 1944. Centre/second row, Halifax, Salford, Hull KR, Wales, Great Britain. He signed for Halifax in 1961. During his 20-year career with Halifax, Salford and Hull KR, he played 738 first-team games. Dixon won 14 Great Britain and 15 Wales caps, playing mostly in the back row. He was quick and strong and an important member of any team he played for. He died in 1999.

Drummond, Des   Born 17 June 1958. Wing, Leigh, Warrington. The quickest winger of his era, Drummond played mainly for Leigh (1976-86) and Warrington. He also gave the game a high profile, appearing on BBC's *Superstars* in 1983, where he was unbeaten in the 100m.

Edwards, Shaun   Born Wigan, England, 17 October 1967. Full-back/half-back, Wigan, London Broncos, Bradford Bulls, England, Great Britain. Signed by Alex Murphy for Wigan at midnight on his 17th birthday, he was an extremely fine player at home at either full-back or at half-back. He became a coach at Wasps rugby union club. Edwards holds the record for the most Cup final appearances (11) and wins (9), his first coming in 1985.

Ellaby, Alf   Born St Helens, England, 24 November 1902. Wing, St Helens, Wigan, England, Great Britain. A legendary winger, Ellaby scored 446 tries in the 14 seasons leading up to the outbreak of World War II.

Elwell, Keith   Hooker, Widnes, England, Great Britain. Known as 'Chiefy', he holds the record for most consecutive appearances, 239 (242 if appearances as a substitute are included), between 1977 and 1982, and for total appearances (588). An excellent distributor and drop goal king. Elwell received 32 winners' and runners'-up medals in major competitions, which is believed to be a world record.

Ettingshausen, Andrew   Born 29 June 1969. Wing/centre, Cronulla, New South Wales, Leeds, Australia. Known as 'ET', he played a record 328 games for Cronulla as winger or centre, scoring 165 tries. He also had a brief spell with Leeds.

Fairbairn, George   Full-back, Wigan, Hull KR, England, Great Britain. Scots-born goal-kicking full-back who gave sterling service to Wigan, Hull KR (as player and coach) and the Lions. As Scotland did not have a team in the 1975 World Cup, he played for England in that competition. He later became involved with rugby league in Scotland.

Fallowfield, Bill   Fallowfield was secretary of the rugby league from 1945 to 1973. He also commentated on the game for ITV. During his time as secretary, his innovations included televising matches, the World Cup and the limited tackle rule.

Farrell, Andy   Born Wigan, England, 20 May 1975. Loose forward, Wigan, England, Great Britain. An extremely hard-working loose forward cum second row and prolific goal kicker. Captain of home town team Wigan and Great Britain at 21; in fact no man has been captain of Great Britain more often than his 21 appearances. The first player to score 1000 Super League points.

Ferguson, Joe   Front row, Oldham, England. A Cumbrian forward who played 682 games for Oldham between 1899 and 1923. He played for England in 15-man, 13-man and 12-man teams (the latter being a short-lived experiment).

Fielding, Keith   Born Birmingham, England, 8 July 1949. Wing, Salford. He holds the season record of tries for Salford – 46 in 1973/74, when he topped the league charts. Former England rugby union winger who was the first man to score four tries in a World Cup match. Fielding's all-round fitness was ably demonstrated in the BBC's *Superstars* series and his success highlighted the speed, strength and stamina required of a rugby league player.

Fish, Jack   Born 1879. Wing, Warrington. Fish played in four Challenge Cup finals for Warrington and coached them to another. He played over 300 games for Warrington between 1898 and 1911, scoring over 200 tries from the wing and kicking over 200 goals. He regularly won sprint races.

Fittler, Brad   Born Sydney, Australia, 5 February 1972. Stand off/lock, Penrith, Sydney City, New South Wales, Australia. He made his international debut at the age of 18. Throughout the 1990s Fittler was one of the best players in the world, equally at home at centre, stand off and loose forward. He played for Penrith and Sydney City, captaining the latter to a Grand Final success in 2002.

Fletcher, Geoff   Nicknamed 'Piggy' because he owned a pig farm near St Helens' ground, Fletcher is best known for his unstinting efforts to keep the club, variously known as Huyton, Runcorn, Highfield and Prescot Panthers, going for many years in the face of consistently poor playing performances, small crowds and no income. An unsung hero, he embodies the spirit of rugby league by putting far more into the game than he ever took out.

Foster, Trevor   Born Newport, Wales, 1916. Second row/loose forward, Bradford Northern, Wales, Great Britain. Universally known as 'Mr Bradford Northern', Foster served the club in virtually every capacity, even in his late eighties as president and timekeeper. He signed for Bradford in 1938 from Newport rugby union club. He played 428 games as a second row and loose forward, scoring 128 tries, and played three games for Great Britain. Awarded the MBE for his services to the game in 2001, he led the Bradford team out at the 2003 Cup final in Cardiff.

Fox, Don   Born Sharlston, England. Scrum half/loose forward, Featherstone Rovers, Wakefield Trinity, Great Britain. Brother of Neil and Peter. A former coach of the international side, Fox played initially as a scrum half, before moving into the pack. He still holds the Featherstone career record of 162 tries. He won the Lance Todd Trophy for Wakefield in 1968, but is most remembered for missing a last-minute conversion in front of the posts which would have given Wakefield the cup.

Fox, Neil   Born Sharlston, England, 1939. Centre, Wakefield, Bradford, Hull KR, York, Bramley, Huddersfield, Great Britain. Fox, who played mostly for Wakefield at centre before moving into the pack, is the top points scorer of all time with 6220pts made up of 358 tries and 2575 goals (second only to Jim Sullivan) in 828 games. His career lasted from 1956 to 1979 and included Championship and Cup final wins, and the Lance Todd Trophy in 1962. He holds the record of scoring the most points in a Challenge Cup final – 20 against Hull in 1960. Inducted into the International Rugby Hall of Fame as a founder member in 1989.

French, Ray   Born St Helens, England, 23 December 1939. Second row, St Helens, Widnes, Great Britain. An English teacher, French played for St Helens and England (in rugby union) before turning pro with league club St Helens in 1961. He subsequently gained international honours in the second row in rugby league, and ended his career at Widnes. French started his commentary career with BBC Radio Merseyside before replacing Eddie Waring in 1981 as 'the voice of rugby league'.

Fulton, Bobby   Born Warrington, England, 1948. Stand off/centre, Manly, Easts (Sydney), New South Wales, Australia. His parents emigrated while he was still a baby. He played for Manly and Easts, and 20 Tests for Australia, at stand off and centre. Fulton subsequently became a very successful coach of Manly and Australia. Inducted into the International Rugby Hall of Fame in 2002.

Furner, David   Born Queanbeyan, Australia, 6 February 1971. Second row, Canberra, New South Wales, Wigan, Leeds, Australia. A goal-kicking second row, Furner scored over 1200pts for Canberra.

Ganley, Bernard   Full-back, Oldham, Great Britain. Ganley represented Oldham from 1950 to 1961, and is holder of all goal-scoring records for that club. In total he scored 1398 goals and 2844pts.

Gasnier, Reg   Born 12 May 1939. Centre, St George, Australia. Gasnier played 36 Tests for Australia, but his career lasted only nine seasons (between 1957 and 1968), before a repeat injury to his leg caused his premature retirement. At 22, this magnificent St George centre was Australia's youngest-ever captain. Inducted into the International Rugby Hall of Fame in 2002.

Gibson, Kerry　In all other respects a rather run-of-the-mill Australian import, Gibson, who played briefly for Springfield Borough and Runcorn in the late 1980s, was remarkable because he played professional rugby while having only one arm.

Goldthorpe, Albert　Born 3 November 1871. Full-back/centre, Hunslet. His career (1888-1910) spanned the break away from rugby union, and his greatest success was in 1907/08 when he captained the Hunslet side to all four cups – Yorkshire League and Cup, Challenge Cup and League Championship. Goldthorpe often played in a team with his three brothers. He was the first man to kick 100 goals in a season, and was seven times top of the goalscoring charts. He died in 1943.

Goulding, Bobby　Born 4 February 1972. Scrum half/hooker, Wigan, Widnes, Leeds, St Helens, Salford, Leigh, England, Great Britain. A brilliant scrum half cum hooker, and excellent goal-kicker, Goulding's career was hampered by disciplinary problems on and off the park. He captained St Helens to successive Cup final wins in 1996 and 1997.

Grayshon, Jeff　Second row/prop forward, Dewsbury, Bradford, Leeds, Featherstone Rovers, Batley, England, Great Britain. Grayshon played 776 first-team games and captained Great Britain. At 36 he is the oldest man to have represented Great Britain in a Test match. His son Paul also played at a professional level.

Gregory, Andy　Born 2 June 1961. Scrum half, Widnes, Warrington, Wigan, Salford, Great Britain. The finest British scrum half of the 1980s, his ability lay in creating openings for other people with his darting runs along the line.

Grothe, Eric　Wing, Parramatta, Leeds. He was Parramatta Rookie of the Year in 1978. His son Eric jnr played for Parramatta and Sydney City, before returning to Parramatta for the start of the 2004 season.

Gunney, Geoff　Born 1934. Second row/loose forward, Hunslet, Great Britain. He is often called 'Mr Hunslet'. He played for the south Leeds side on 606 occasions between 1951 and 1973 and later coached the club. When the old Hunslet club folded, he was instrumental in the founding of New Hunslet. Gunney played 11 Tests as a second row or loose forward, and was only the second rugby league player to be awarded the MBE. He later coached Wakefield.

Haigh, Bob　Loose forward, Wakefield Trinity, Leeds, Bradford, Great Britain. The first forward to top the try-scorers chart, scoring 40 tries in 1970/71. He played five Tests.

Hanley, Ellery　Born Bradford, England, 27 March 1962. Stand off/loose forward, Bradford Northern, Wigan, Leeds, Great Britain. One of the greatest players ever to pull on a shirt, he started life as a back (he could play in any position), but found his most effective role at loose forward. A native of Bradford, he left his home town club to join the all-conquering Wigan team of the late 1980s and 1990s, where he became the star player and inspirational captain. Hanley subsequently moved to Leeds in the first £250,000 transfer deal, and also captained

Great Britain. Later he coached Great Britain to a win over the Australians in 1994, before guiding St Helens to victory in the 1999 Grand Final.

Harris, Eric　Born Toowoomba, Australia. Wing, Leeds. Nicknamed the 'Toowoomba Ghost', Harris played on the wing in the 1930s for Leeds, scoring 391 tries at a rate of more than one a game, including 63 in the 1935/36 season.

Harris, Iestyn　Born Oldham, England, 25 June 1976. Stand off/full-back, Warrington, Leeds, Wales, Great Britain. Born of Welsh parents, Harris played with great distinction for Warrington and Leeds before joining Cardiff rugby union club to fulfil a long-standing ambition to play international union for Wales. He usually played at stand off or full-back, often in the same match. His eight goals and 20pts in the 1999 Challenge Cup final both equalled records.

Harrison, Jack　Born 1891. Wing, Hull. The only rugby league player to be awarded the Victoria Cross. He scored 52 tries for Hull in 1914/15, still a club record. He enlisted in the East Yorkshire Regiment in 1914, becoming a second lieutenant and being awarded the Military Medal. At the Battle of Oppy Wood on 3 May 1917, he single-handedly attacked a German machine-gun post, but was killed in the process. He has no known grave. He received a posthumous VC for his actions.

Helme, Gerry　Scrum half, Warrington, England, Great Britain. The first man to win the Lance Todd Trophy twice (1950 and 1954). A diminutive scrum half, his try was a decisive moment in the 1954 Challenge Cup replay at Odsal. He also won 12 Great Britain caps. He died December 1981.

Hey, Vic　Born 1912. Stand off, Wests (Sydney), Leeds, Dewsbury, Hunslet, Australia. One of the best stand offs produced by Australia, he played only six internationals as he spent most of his career in England. He later coached Australia to their first Ashes win for 30 years in 1950. He died in 1995.

Hodgson, Martin　Second row, Swinton and Great Britain. Best remembered for his all-time record goal kick of 77¾yds (71m), Hodgson was an excellent second row forward for Swinton in the years before World War II, playing in 16 Test matches, often terrorising the Australians. Typical of many rugby league players of the time, he was a native of Cumberland.

Holmes, John　Born 1951. No man has played more games for Leeds than John Holmes – a total of 625 between 1968 and 1989. A fine distributor of the ball and a good goal kicker, Holmes is co-holder of the Lions record for most goals in a game (ten against New Zealand in 1972), and scored more than 1500pts for Leeds.

Horder, Harold　Born 1894. Wing, Norths (Sydney), Souths (Sydney), Queensland, New South Wales, Australia. The greatest Australian winger of the inter-war years. Speedy and elusive with a great sidestep, Horder played 13 times for Australia. He scored over 1700pts in his career, and was one of the few men to play for both Queensland and New South Wales. He died in 1978.

Horne, Willie　Born Barrow, England, 1924. Stand off, Barrow, Great Britain. A legendary Barrow player between 1943 and 1958. A one-club man who played eight Tests, including two as captain, he holds Barrow's goal- and points-scoring records. A stand at the ground and a road in his home town are named after him.

Huddart, Dick   Born 22 June 1936. Second row, Whitehaven, St Helens, St George, Great Britain. He won a full collection of medals with Saints and an Australian Grand Final, as well as 16 Test caps playing as a strong-running, rangy second row.

Hynes, Sid   Centre, Leeds, Great Britain. Captain of the strong Leeds team of the 1960s and early 1970s and subsequent coach of the club. Hynes, a fine centre, made headlines for all the wrong reasons when he became the first player to be sent off in a Challenge Cup final, against Leigh in 1971. He played 13 Tests for Great Britain.

Idle, Graham   Born 10 March 1950. Idle played 740 games for nine clubs, fifth on the all-time appearances list, before finally retiring at the age of 43. He started his career in the back row before moving up to prop.

Iro, Kevin   Born 25 May 1968. Centre, Mount Albert, Wigan, Manly, Leeds, St Helens, Mariners, New Zealand. Generally known as 'Beast', this Kiwi is the only man to score two tries in a Cup final on three occasions, doing so for Wigan in 1988, 1989 and 1990. His brother Tony played for Wigan and New Zealand.

Irvine, Ken   Born 1940. Wing, Norths (Sydney), Manly, Australia. One of the quickest wingers ever to play for Australia, Irvine was a sprinter, good enough to be co-holder of the world record at 100yds for professionals, who decided to concentrate on rugby. He played 31 Tests, scoring 33 tries, and in 236 Premiership games for Norths and Manly scored 216 tries. He once converted his own try from the touchline to complete a Test victory against Great Britain. He died in 1990.

Jackson, Phil   Born Canada, 1932. Centre, Barrow, Great Britain. He played 27 Tests for Great Britain in the 1950s, and also played 226 games in the centre for Barrow between 1950 and 1959. Jackson was born in Canada but moved to Barrow at the age of three.

Johns, Andrew   Born Cessnock, Australia, 19 May 1974. Half-back/hooker, Newcastle (Australia), Australia. Three times a winner of the Dally M Medal, and twice voted the best player in the world. Half back or hooker, Johns has won trophy after trophy – 23pts on his debut for Newcastle was the sign of things to come. Player of the Series in the 1995 World Cup and man of the match in the final, he has scored over 1500 career points.

Jones, Lewis   Born Gorseinon, Wales, 11 April 1931. Stand off, Leeds, Great Britain. Known as 'The Golden Boy', Jones was a Welsh rugby union club international who came north to play for Leeds in 1952. He made an immediate impact as a stand off. He played 15 Tests, kicking 66 goals and scoring 147pts. Jones still holds the record of 496pts in a season, when he scored 36 tries and 194 goals in 1956/57. He scored 3445pts in 13 seasons for Leeds.

Joynt, Chris   Born Wigan, England, 7 December 1971. Second row, Oldham, St Helens, Great Britain. Twice winner of the Harry Sunderland Trophy, and captain of Saints from 1998 to 2003.

Karalius, Vince   Born Widnes, England, 15 October 1932. Loose forward, St Helens, Widnes, Great Britain. The Australians called him 'The Wild Bull of the Pampas'. Loose forward with St Helens and Widnes from 1952 to 1966, he also played in 12 Tests for Great Britain. Inducted into the International Rugby Hall of Fame in 2000.

Kellett, Cyril   Full-back, Hull KR, Featherstone Rovers. With 1768 goals for Hull KR and Featherstone between 1956 and 1974, as a goal-kicking full-back, Kellett lies third on the all-time list. He co-holds the record of eight goals in a single Wembley final (with Iestyn Harris).

Kenny, Brett   Stand off, Parramatta, Wigan, Australia. Elected Parramatta Rookie of the Year in 1980, his early promise was fulfilled. He was a brilliant stand off with Parramatta and Wigan – Kenny holds appearances (265) and tries (110) records for Parramatta. Lance Todd Trophy winner in 1985.

Killeen, Len   Wing, St Helens, Balmain. The only man ever to top the goal- and try-scorers charts in the same season, scoring 32 tries and 120 goals in 1965/66. Killeen scored over 1000pts in five seasons with Saints, including 13 in the 1966 Challenge Cup final, when he won the Lance Todd Trophy. He later signed for Balmain.

Lam, Adrian   Born Rabaul, Papua New Guinea, 25 August 1970. Scrum half, Easts (Sydney), Sydney City, Queensland, Wigan, Papua New Guinea. The star Papua New Guinea player of all time. He played for Easts and Sydney City before moving to Wigan in 2001. Lam is a mercurial scrum half, capable of making and scoring tries, and is a fine exponent of the drop goal.

Langer, Allan   Born Ipswich, Australia, 30 July 1966. Scrum half, Norths (Sydney), Brisbane, Queensland, Warrington, Australia. 'Alfie' was a fantastic scrum half who played in a record 34 State of Origin games. A key member of the Brisbane Broncos side which, in 1992, was the first non-New South Wales side to win the Grand Final.

Langlands, Graeme   Born 2 September 1941. Full-back/centre, St George, Australia. Langlands played for St George from 1963 to 1976, and in 34 Tests for Australia. He had a big, deceptive sidestep and was a courageous full-back with flair and dash, a record-breaking goal kicker, and captain and coach of his country. Though his position was traditionally at full-back, Langlands played most of his Test career in the centres, scoring 17 tries and 69 goals. Inducted into the International Rugby Hall of Fame in 2002.

Laughton, Doug   Born Widnes, England. Laughton played for St Helens, Wigan, Widnes, Canterbury and Great Britain, but is probably more famous as a coach, especially at Widnes and Leeds. He played 15 Tests, five as captain.

Lewis, Wally   Born Brisbane, Queensland, Australia, 1 December 1959. Five-eighth, Valleys (Brisbane), Wynnum Manly, Wakefield Trinity, Brisbane Broncos, Gold Coast Seagulls, Australia. Variously known as 'The King', 'The Emperor of Lang Park' or 'The High Priest of the Spectacular', Lewis is undoubtedly a true great of the game. He represented Australian Schoolboys at rugby union in 1977 before switching codes in 1978. Lewis represented Australia in 33 Tests (23 as captain) between 1981 and 1991. He also captained Queensland in 30 State of Origin matches between 1980 and 1991. His brilliant career has included the Best Player in the World Award and a statue of him proudly adorns Lang Park.

Leytham, Jim   Wing, Wigan, Great Britain. The first man to score four tries in an international. Three times top try scorer, Leytham scored 314 tries in a career lasting from 1901 to 1912.

Lindsay, Maurice   Born 1941. A bookmaker who has had long spells as vice-chairman and chairman of Wigan, interrupted by a spell as chief executive of the Rugby Football League (RFL), and as chief executive of Super League Europe. During his spell as chief executive of the RFL, Lindsay oversaw the introduction of the Super League.

Lomas, Jim   Born Cumberland, 1879. Centre, Bramley, Salford, Oldham, Great Britain. One of the earliest stars of the game, he was the first man to be transferred for £100 (from Bramley to Salford in 1902), and for £300 (to Oldham ten years later). Lomas topped the points-scorers lists on five occasions and scored 310 tries between 1902 and 1923. He was captain of the first-ever Lions tour in 1910.

Lydon, Joe   Born Wigan, England, 26 November 1963. Full-back/centre, Widnes, Wigan, Easts (Sydney), Great Britain. Lydon scored two tries for Widnes in the 1984 Challenge Cup final before joining home town club Wigan for the first-ever £100,000 transfer fee. Playing mainly full-back or centre, he also became the first full-back to score a try for Great Britain against Australia, doing so in 1986, after 78 years of internationals.

McTigue, Brian   Prop forward, Wigan, Great Britain. McTigue played 25 Test matches between 1958 and 1963.

Meninga, Mal   Born Bundaberg, Australia, 8 July 1960. Centre, Souths (Brisbane), St Helens, Canberra, Australia. Meninga first hit the big time as a member of the 1982 Australian tour to Great Britain. Also a goal kicker, he had a phenomenally successful season with St Helens, and later played for Canberra. Inducted into the International Rugby Hall of Fame in 2002.

Messenger, Herbert 'Dally'   Born 12 April 1883. Centre, Easts (Sydney), Australia, New Zealand. The Dally M Medal in Australia is named after him. He played centre for Easts in Sydney, and for both Australia (seven caps) and New Zealand (three caps) in internationals. A gifted ball-player, while touring Great Britain in 1907/08, both Spurs and Manchester United offered him terms to play football. His goals and points-scoring achievements remained records for many years. Inducted into the International Rugby Hall of Fame in 2002.

Mills, Jim   Prop forward, Widnes, Norths (Sydney), Great Britain. Always known as 'Big Jim', Mills came north to Widnes in 1972, and was to be associated with the club in virtually every capacity. He scored 39 tries in 188 League games, an extremely fine return for a prop forward. Among his medal collection are three Cup final medals.

Millward, Roger   Born Castleford, England, 1947. Stand off, Castleford, Hull KR, England, Great Britain. 'Roger the Dodger' played for Castleford and Hull KR from 1963 to 1981, and later coached Hull KR for 14 years. Elected to the Hall of Fame immediately on becoming eligible in 1990. Of small stature, his runs from half-back were extremely elusive. He was also a fine goal kicker.

Mitchell, Tom   Mitchell will always be associated with Workington Town. Instantly recognisable from his hat, dark glasses and flowing white beard, he also managed the 1958 Ashes tour and was a leading light in the evolution of the British Amateur Rugby League Association (BARLA), without which the amateur game might have withered away.

Monie, John   Coach, Wigan, London, Parramatta, Auckland. He had two extremely successful spells as coach of Wigan, doing the double in four consecutive seasons. Monie is the only man to have coached clubs to all the cups available in a single season in both Britain and Australia.

Murphy, Alex   Born St Helens, England, 1939. Scrum half, St Helens, Leigh, Warrington, Great Britain. Indubitably one of the greatest players of all time. A scrum half who could play successfully at stand off or centre, he made his debut at the age of 17 in 1956 and his international debut at 18. Murphy won Cup finals for St Helens in 1961 and 1966, when he captained the Saints to four trophies, before moving to win the 1971 Cup final with Leigh and the 1974 Cup final with Warrington, both as player/coach. He later coached Wigan, St Helens and Huddersfield, as well as the national team. Inducted into the International Rugby Hall of Fame in 1998.

Newlove, Paul   Born Pontefract, England, 10 August 1971. Centre, Featherstone Rovers, Bradford Northern, St Helens, Great Britain. Son of John and brother of Richard, who both played for Featherstone. Paul was undoubtedly the best British attacking centre of the 1990s. He moved from Bradford to St Helens in a record deal (£500,000), and was the youngest player ever to play for Britain (aged 18 years, 72 days).

Norton, Steve   Forward, Castleford, Hull, Manly, Great Britain. A ball-playing forward, 'Knocker' was a regular pick for the international team.

Offiah, Martin   Born London, England, 29 December 1966. Wing, Widnes, Wigan, London, Salford, England, Great Britain. 'Chariots' signed for Widnes from Rosslyn Park rugby union club. He later moved to Wigan for the then record transfer fee of £440,000. The best winger of his era, he is the only English-born player to have scored over 500 tries, and lies third on the all-time try-scorers list. While pace was his prime asset, he also had sidestep and a good awareness of the lines to run.

Oliver, Joe   Full-back/centre, Huddersfield, Batley, Hull, Hull KR, Great Britain. One of the many Cumbrian-born players who played a prominent role in inter-war rugby. Oliver only played four Tests, but holds the goals- (687) and points-scoring (1842) career records for Hull from full-back or centre. He played for Huddersfield and Batley before joining Hull, and later rejoined Hull after a spell with Hull KR. He scored over 2250pts and holds the record for most appearances for Cumberland, with 35.

Parkin, Jonty   Born Sharlston, England. Scrum half, Wakefield, Hull KR, England, Great Britain. Made his debut at 16 in 1913, his career lasting until 1932. The only man to captain two Lions tours to Australia (1924 and 1928). Parkin won a total of 17 caps. Inducted into the International Rugby Hall of Fame in 1998.

Paul, Henry   Born Tokoroa, New Zealand, 10 February 1974. Stand off, Wakefield Trinity, Wigan, Bradford Bulls, New Zealand. A Kiwi who has also appeared for England at rugby union, especially in the Sevens team. A devastating runner from half-back for Wigan before joining younger brother Robbie at Bradford. At one stage he held the record of 35 consecutive successful goal attempts.

Paul, Robbie   Born Tokoroa, New Zealand, 3 February 1976. Full-back/stand off, Bradford Bulls, New Zealand. Younger brother of Henry. Winner of the Lance Todd Trophy in 1996 when scoring the first hat-trick in a Wembley Cup final, despite being on the losing side. Paul has given years of service to Bradford and New Zealand. He is versatile enough to play anywhere behind the scrum, but plays mainly at full-back or stand off.

Pearce, Wayne   Born Balmain, Australia, 1960. Loose forward, Balmain, New South Wales, Australia.

Pearce played 18 Tests while representing Balmain and New South Wales. One of his colleagues described him as 'the toughest bloke I ever saw'. He was much rewarded during his career as a loose forward despite its being cut short by injury. He subsequently coached New South Wales.

Pinner, Harry   Loose forward, St Helens, Great Britain. A brilliant ball distributor who played mainly for St Helens at loose forward in the 1970s and 1980s. He also captained Great Britain in the 1986 Test series against New Zealand.

Platt, Andy   Born St Helens, England, 9 October 1963. Centre/prop forward, Wigan, England, Great Britain. Platt started life as a centre before moving into the pack. He spent the best years of his career as prop for Wigan and was an automatic choice for the international side.

Prescott, Alan   Born Widnes, England, 17 June 1927. Prop forward, Halifax, St Helens, Great Britain. Capped 28 times, captaining the side on 17 occasions (including the 1958 Ashes tour), Prescott is most remembered for playing the majority of a match with a broken arm, tackling one-handed. He captained St Helens to their first Challenge Cup win in 1956, also winning the Lance Todd Trophy.

Price, Ray   Born St Leonards, Australia, 4 March 1953. Lock, Parramatta, Australia. Price played rugby union for Australia before embarking on a ten-year career with Parramatta. He was a magnificent back row who toured with the 1978 Australians and the 1982 'Invincibles', playing 25 Tests. Twice player of the year in Australia, he played over 250 games for Parramatta. In 2004 he is still playing veterans rugby.

Prigg, Wally   Born 1908. Loose forward, Newcastle (Australia), Australia. He played for Newcastle from 1927 to 1939. Prigg was the first Australian to go on three Ashes tours – he was captain on the third – and played in 17 Tests. A great ball player who formed an effective link between forwards and backs. He died in 1980. Inducted into the International Rugby Hall of Fame in 2002.

Puig-Aubert   Born Aubert Puig. Full-back, France. The most famous French player of all time. So many people in the area he grew up in had the surname Puig, that he changed the name round. A full-back and a great kicker for goal and out of hand, he captained France in the inaugural World Cup of 1954.

Quinn, Steve   Centre, York, Featherstone Rovers. Goal-kicking centre between 1970 and 1988, his two late tries helped Featherstone to win the 1983 Challenge Cup against favourites Hull. He kicked 1578 goals in his career.

Ramsden, Peter   Born 1934. Stand off, Huddersfield. At 19, Ramsden became the youngest winner of the Lance Todd Trophy when his two tries helped Huddersfield win the 1953 Challenge Cup final.

Raper, John   Born 12 April 1939. Lock/loose forward, Newton, St George, Australia. Raper played 33 Tests for Australia – a record for a forward. Playing at loose forward, he captained Australia in the 1968 World Cup. He spent most of his career with St George, playing while they won eight successive Australian Premierships (1959-66). His son Stuart coached Castleford and Wigan. Inducted into the International Rugby Hall of Fame in 2002.

Reilly, Mal   Loose forward, Castleford, Manly, Great Britain. He won the 1969 Lance Todd Trophy while playing in his usual position of loose forward. Subsequently coached Castleford, Leeds, Huddersfield, Halifax, Newcastle Knights and the Lions. He only played nine internationals, all in 1970, as he spent a large part of his career in Australia.

Risman, Gus   Born Cardiff, Wales, 1911. Centre, Salford, Workington Town, Batley, Wales, Great Britain. His career spanned 25 years from 1929 to 1954. He captained Salford to the 1938 Challenge Cup win, and then captained and coached Workington to the same trophy in 1952, at the age of 41. Risman kicked 1677 goals and scored 4050pts in 873 games to put him third on the all-time scorers list. Inducted into the International Rugby Hall of Fame in 1998.

Rivett, Leroy   Born Leicester, England, 17 December 1976. Wing, Leeds, Huddersfield, Warrington. Rivett won the Lance Todd Trophy after becoming the only man to score four tries in a Wembley Cup final (against London in 1999). However, the rest of his career has failed to match its early promise.

Robinson, Jason   Born Leeds, England, 30 July 1974. Wing, Wigan, Sale, Great Britain. Robinson was initially a scrum half before his exceptional pace and elusiveness found him a place on Wigan's wing. His try won the first Grand Final in 1997. He later went on to play rugby union for Sale, England and the British Lions.

Rosenfeld, Albert   Born Sydney, Australia. Wing, Huddersfield, Wakefield Trinity, Bradford Northern. Rosenfeld is most associated with Huddersfield, who stayed in Yorkshire after touring in 1908 to marry a local girl. Rosenfeld scored 386 tries in 378 matches. His most successful season was 1913/14 when he scored a remarkable 80 tries, including seven in one match, five in two more, four in two and another ten hat-tricks. He also scored 78 tries two seasons earlier and topped the try-scorers list for each of the five years before World War I. Inducted into the International Rugby Hall of Fame in 1998.

Schofield, Garry   Born Hunslet, England, 1 July 1965. Centre/stand off, Hull, Leeds, England, Great Britain. Schofield played for Hull as a youngster before signing for Leeds. His total of 46 caps puts him joint top of the list of most international appearances (with Mick Sullivan). His greatest achievement in a British shirt was scoring four tries against New Zealand in the Wigan Test in 1985.

Sculthorpe, Paul   Born Oldham, England. Loose forward/stand off, Warrington, St Helens, England, Great Britain. The only man to be named Man of Steel in successive years (2001 and 2002).

Southward, Ike   Wing, Workington Town, Oldham, Great Britain. Southward was the first man to command a £10,000 transfer fee when moving from Workington to Oldham in 1959. He was transferred back three years later for another record fee of £11,002 10s.

Stephenson, Mick   Hooker, Dewsbury, Penrith, Great Britain. He became known as a commentator with trenchant views, and it is often forgotten that 'Stevo' was an excellent hooker, captaining Dewsbury to the 1973 Championship and winning the Harry Sunderland Trophy, before moving to play in Australia for Penrith. He won five international caps.

Stephenson, Nigel   Stand off, Dewsbury. The first man to ensure that a match finished 1-0, when he scored the only point of a game against York. A star in Dewsbury's Championship-winning team of 1973, his son Francis later played for Wigan and London.

Sterling, Peter   Born Toowoomba, Australia, 1960. Scrum half, Parramatta, New South Wales, Hull, Australia. Toured with Australia in 1982. Sterling was considered the best scrum half in the world at the time, and won four Grand Finals with Parramatta. He also had a spell with Hull. A dislocated shoulder ended his career in 1992.

Sullivan, Anthony Born 23 November 1968. Wing, Hull KR, St Helens, Wales. Son of Clive. Sullivan was signed by St Helens from Hull KR. Inheriting his father's pace, he scored over 200 tries for Saints from the left wing, before playing a few games for Cardiff rugby union club.

Sullivan, Clive Born Cardiff, Wales, 1943. Wing, Hull, Hull KR, Oldham, Doncaster, Wales, Great Britain. An extremely quick Welsh winger who was also the first black captain of a British national team in any sport. He played 17 internationals. He was the only man to score more than 100 tries for both Hull (250) and Hull KR (118). Sullivan scored 406 tries in total, finishing his career at Oldham and Doncaster, before dying tragically young. The main road into Hull from the M62 is named Clive Sullivan Way in his honour.

Sullivan, Jim Born Cardiff, Wales, 1903. Full-back, Wigan, Wales, Great Britain. Signed for Wigan in 1921 at 17 for £750, Sullivan holds the records for most appearances (928) and goals (2867) in a career and lies second only to Neil Fox in the number of career points. He once kicked 22 goals in a Challenge Cup game, and kicked at least 100 goals in each season between 1921/22 and the outbreak of World War II. He later became a successful coach with Wigan and St Helens. Sullivan topped the goal-scorers list 17 times and the points-scorers list 14 times. He also played 25 internationals and captained the Lions on an Ashes tour. Inducted into the International Rugby Hall of Fame in 1998.

Sullivan, Mick Born 12 January 1934. Wing, Huddersfield, Wigan, St Helens, York, England, Great Britain. Co-holder of the Great Britain record of 46 international appearances, including 36 in succession, scoring a record 41 tries.

Tait, Alan Born Kelso, Scotland, 2 July 1964. Full-back, Widnes, Leeds, Great Britain. A Scotland rugby union full-back who followed his father into rugby league. Tait won consecutive Harry Sunderland Trophies before returning to Scotland to resume his rugby union club career.

Tallis, Gordon Born Townsville, Australia, 27 July 1973. Second row, Brisbane, Queensland, Australia. A fearsomely aggressive second row forward.

Todd, Lance Born 1883. Todd toured with the 1907/08 New Zealand squad before signing for Wigan at the end of their tour. However, he had a bigger impact after his retirement. He was appointed secretary of Salford, and moulded the team into one of the greatest ever seen. He also worked as a radio commentator. He was killed in a wartime car crash in 1942. When rugby restarted after World War II, it was decided that the man of the match award in the Challenge Cup final should be named after him.

Traill, Ken Born 1926. Loose forward, Hunslet, Bradford Northern, Halifax, Great Britain. Unusually among rugby league players, Traill was Northumberland-born, although his father had played for Hunslet. Traill joined Bradford from Hunslet. One of the best loose forwards of his generation, he later played for Halifax, but reached even greater heights as coach of the great Wakefield side of the 1960s. He played in nine internationals. While in charge of Wakefield he appeared in the film *This Sporting Life*, location shots for which were filmed at the club's Belle Vue ground. He died in 2002.

Turner, Rocky Born Derek Turner. Loose forward, Hull KR, Oldham, Wakefield, Great Britain. A strong loose forward and natural leader, Turner, always known as 'Rocky', played for Hull KR, Oldham and Wakefield, captaining the latter to three Challenge Cup wins in 1960, 1962 and 1963.

Valentine, Dave Born Hawick, Scotland, 12 September 1926. Loose forward, Huddersfield, Great Britain. A former Scotland rugby union international who turned pro with Huddersfield and captained the Lions to victory in the inaugural World Cup in 1954, immediately after a gruelling Ashes tour. He played 15 Tests in total. The only Scot to lift a World Cup in a major sport.

van Vollenhoven, Tom Born Orange Free State, South Africa, 29 April 1935. Wing, St Helens. Flying South African winger who gave 12 years of sterling service to St Helens. 'The Voll' scored 392 tries in 409 games for Saints. After seven matches for the Springboks, he was chased by several English clubs before signing for Saints in 1957. His two most famous tries came in the 1959 Championship final and the 1961 Challenge Cup final. Inducted into the International Rugby Hall of Fame in 2000.

Wagstaff, Harold Born Holmfirth, England, 1891. Centre, Huddersfield, Great Britain. Known as 'The Prince of Centres', was a founder member of the Hall of Fame in 1988. Turning pro at 15 with Huddersfield, he made his international debut at 18, captained Huddersfield at 20, when they were known as 'The Team of all the Talents', and the Lions at 23. Wagstaff was captain in the famous 'Rorke's Drift' Test in 1914 when the Lions had only ten fit men. He scored over 200 career tries.

Ward, Ernest Centre, Bradford Northern, Great Britain. Captain of Great Britain on nine occasions. He was centre and goal kicker when Bradford became the first team in any sport to appear in three consecutive Wembley finals, from 1947-49. Ward, a Welshman, won the Lance Todd Trophy on the last of these occasions for his general play as well as his four goals, in a time when games were much more low-scoring.

Ward, Kevin Prop forward, Castleford, Manly, St Helens, Great Britain. This magnificent craggy prop played 17 times for the Lions. He is held in high esteem by supporters at all his former clubs. Ward was forced to retire after an appalling leg injury in the 1993 Wigan v St Helens title decider.

Waring, Eddie Mostly remembered as the BBC commentator for many years, Waring had previously been a print journalist and Dewsbury manager. While not always popular with the rugby league public, some of whom felt he didn't take the game seriously enough, he popularised the game outside its heartlands and loved it dearly. Much impersonated, he also found a niche in light entertainment, being a commentator for many years on *Jeux sans Frontières*. The BBC award for 'try of the season' is named in his memory.

Watkins, David Born Bloina, Wales, 5 March 1942. Centre, Salford, Swinton, Cardiff, Wales, Great Britain. Previously a brilliant fly half with Newport, Watkins turned professional with Salford in 1967. He holds the record of 221 goals in a season, in 1972/73, scoring 493pts, and another record of scoring in 92 consecutive games between August 1972 and April 1974. He later played for Swinton and was the driving force behind the short-lived Cardiff Blue Dragons team. He is still, in 2004, closely associated with both codes.

Watson, Cliff Born London, England. Prop forward, St Helens, Cronulla, Great Britain. Watson signed for St Helens in 1960 in response to an advert that had been placed in the press. He played 30 Tests between 1963 and 1971 before emigrating to Australia to play for Cronulla.

West, George Born 1882. Wing, Hull KR. Holder of the records for tries and points in a match – 11 tries and 53pts for Hull KR against Brooklands in 1905.

Woods, John Born 14 September 1956. Stand off, Leigh, Bradford, Warrington, Rochdale. Mainly associated with Leigh, where he is the club's all-time leading points scorer, Woods also had a successful career with Bradford, Warrington and Rochdale. He scored 3985pts including 1591 goals.

RUGBY UNION

According to tradition, rugby union was invented in November 1823 by a 17-year-old schoolboy named William Webb Ellis at Rugby School, Warwickshire, England. He is believed to have cheated technically during a game of the crude mob football then played at the school, when, 'with a fine disregard for the rules of football as played in his time, [he] first took the ball in his arms and ran with it'. In fact, there were other handling games long before Webb Ellis's alleged infringement: for example, camp, played in East Anglia in the 15th century; hurling (without sticks), played in Ireland and Cornwall (this was a form of handball); Shrovetide football; and the traditional Scottish game of Jethart Ba' (Ball). More exact historians trace the origin of rugby to about 1838-39 and identify the frustrated runner as one Jem Mackie.

Whatever the truth, the game was played at Cambridge University in 1839, and in 1843 Guy's Hospital Rugby Football Club was founded (the oldest rugby union club in existence). In the next 30 years many other clubs were founded in England, Scotland, Ireland and Wales. In 1871 the Rugby Football Union (RFU) was created and a code of rules drawn up. In the same year the first international match was played (England against Scotland, 20-a-side). In 1872 the first Oxford against Cambridge match took place (Oxford won). This became an annual fixture (except during World War I) which, from 1922, was held at Twickenham, London. The two universities had a considerable influence on the game and many of their students have become international players. The Scottish Rugby Union (SRU) was formed in 1873, the Irish Rugby Football Union (IRFU) in 1879 and the Welsh Rugby Union (WRU) in 1880. In 1877 the number of players in international matches was reduced from 20 to 15 a side. The International Championships, now known as the Six Nations Championship, began in 1883 although France did not compete until the 1909/10 season and also missed the tournaments between the 1931/32 and 1938/39 seasons when the Home Unions suspended relations with them.

The International Rugby Board (IRB) was founded in 1886 and is the governing body of international rugby union. Its headquarters are in Dublin and it is responsible for the organisation of the Rugby World Cup.

A rugby union pitch should be a maximum of 100m long and 69m wide. The goal should be 5.6m wide and the goal posts approximately 5m high with a crossbar at 3m. The in-goal is the area behind the goalposts running the width of the pitch. A try is scored by first grounding the ball in the opponents' in-goal. A try is also awarded if one would probably have been scored but for foul play by the opposing team. A goal is scored by kicking the ball over the opponents' crossbar and between the goalposts from the field of play by any place kick or drop kick, except a kick-off, drop-out or free kick, without touching the ground or any player of the kicker's team. A goal may also be scored if the ball has crossed the bar notwithstanding a prior offence by the opposing team. A goal is awarded if the ball has crossed the bar, even though it may have been blown backwards afterwards, and whether it has touched the crossbar or either upright. A goal may be awarded if the ball is illegally touched by any player of the opposing team and if the referee considers that a goal would otherwise probably have been scored. The scoring values are as follows: a try – 5pts; a goal scored after a try – 2pts; a goal from a penalty kick – 3pts; a drop(ped) goal otherwise obtained but not from a free kick or after a scrum taken in lieu of a free kick – 3pts.

World Cup

	Winners	Winning Captain/Coach	Score	Runners-Up	Venue
1987	New Zealand	David Kirk/Brian Lochore	29-9	France	New Zealand/Australia
1991	Australia	Nick Farr-Jones/Bob Dwyer	12-6	England	England
1995	South Africa	François Pienaar/Kitch Christie	15-12	New Zealand	South Africa
1999	Australia	John Eales/Rod Macqueen	35-12	France	Wales
2003	England	Martin Johnson/Clive Woodward	20-17 aet	Australia	Australia

2003 World Cup

The 2003 World Cup kicked off on 14 October when Australia played Argentina and ended on 22 November when the hosts faced England in the final. In total, 48 games between 20 different countries were played. Games were played in ten different Australian cities.

Format:

The number of participating countries in 2003 was increased from 65 to 90. After qualification, 20 teams faced each other in four pools:
Pool A: Australia, Argentina, Ireland, Romania, Namibia
Pool B: France, Scotland, Fiji, Japan, United States
Pool C: South Africa, England, Samoa, Uruguay, Georgia
Pool D: New Zealand, Wales, Canada, Italy, Tonga
The top two teams in each of the four pools progressed to the quarter-final. Losing quarter-final and semi-final teams were eliminated, with the semi-final winning teams progressing to the final at Stadium Australia on 22 November in Sydney.

Pool A

	Pl	W	D	L	F	A	PD	BP	Pts
Australia	4	4	0	0	273	32	+239	2	18
Ireland	4	3	0	1	141	45	+85	3	15
Argentina	4	2	0	2	140	57	+83	3	11
Romania	4	1	0	3	65	192	-127	1	5
Namibia	4	0	0	4	28	310	-281	0	0

Australia	24-8	Argentina	Stadium Australia
Ireland	45-17	Romania	Central Coast Stadium
Argentina	67-14	Namibia	Central Coast Stadium
Australia	90-8	Romania	Suncorp Metway Stadium
Ireland	64-7	Namibia	Aussie Stadium
Argentina	50-3	Romania	Aussie Stadium
Australia	142-0	Namibia	Adelaide Oval
Ireland	16-15	Argentina	Adelaide Oval
Romania	37-7	Namibia	York Park
Australia	17-16	Ireland	Telstra Dome

Pool B

	Pl	W	D	L	F	A	PD	BP	Pts
France	4	4	0	0	204	70	+134	4	20
Scotland	4	3	0	1	102	97	+5	2	14
Fiji	4	2	0	2	98	114	-16	2	10
United States	4	1	0	3	86	125	-39	2	6
Japan	4	0	0	4	79	163	-71	0	0

France	61-18	Fiji	Suncorp Metway Stadium
Scotland	32-11	Japan	Dairy Farmers Stadium
Fiji	19-18	United States	Suncorp Metway Stadium
France	51-29	Japan	Dairy Farmers Stadium
Scotland	39-15	United States	Suncorp Metway Stadium
Fiji	41-13	Japan	Dairy Farmers Stadium
France	51-9	Scotland	Stadium Australia
United States	39-26	Japan	Central Coast Stadium
France	41-14	United States	WIN Stadium
Scotland	22-20	Fiji	Aussie Stadium

Pool C

	Pl	W	D	L	F	A	PD	BP	Pts
England	4	4	0	0	255	47	+208	3	19
South Africa	4	3	0	1	184	60	+124	3	15
Samoa	4	2	0	2	138	117	+21	2	10
Uruguay	4	1	0	3	56	255	-199	0	4
Georgia	4	0	0	4	46	200	-154	0	0

South Africa	72-6	Uruguay	Subiaco Oval
England	84-6	Georgia	Subiaco Oval
Samoa	60-13	Uruguay	Subiaco Oval
England	25-6	South Africa	Subiaco Oval
Samoa	46-9	Georgia	Subiaco Oval
South Africa	46-19	Georgia	Aussie Stadium
England	35-22	Samoa	Telstra Dome
Uruguay	24-12	Georgia	Aussie Stadium
South Africa	60-10	Samoa	Suncorp Metway Stadium
England	111-13	Uruguay	Suncorp Metway Stadium

Pool D

	Pl	W	D	L	F	A	PD	BP	Pts
New Zealand	4	4	0	0	282	57	+225	4	20
Wales	4	3	0	1	132	98	+34	2	14
Italy	4	2	0	2	77	123	-46	0	8
Canada	4	1	0	3	54	135	-81	1	5
Tonga	4	0	0	4	46	178	-132	1	1

New Zealand	70-7	Italy	Telstra Dome
Wales	41-10	Canada	Telstra Dome
Italy	36-12	Tonga	Canberra Stadium
New Zealand	68-6	Canada	Telstra Dome
Wales	27-20	Tonga	Canberra Stadium
Italy	19-14	Canada	Canberra Stadium
New Zealand	91-7	Tonga	Suncorp Metway Stadium
Wales	27-15	Italy	Canberra Stadium
Canada	24-7	Tonga	WIN Stadium
New Zealand	53-37	Wales	Stadium Australia

Quarter-finals

New Zealand	29-9	South Africa	Telstra Dome
Australia	33-16	Scotland	Suncorp Metway Stadium
France	43-21	Ireland	Telstra Dome
England	28-17	Wales	Suncorp Metway Stadium

Semi-finals

Australia	22-10	New Zealand	Stadium Australia
England	24-7	France	Stadium Australia

Third place play-off

New Zealand	40-13	France	Stadium Australia

Final

England	20-17 aet	Australia	Stadium Australia

Stadiums

Adelaide Oval
built 1871, Adelaide, 33,597 capacity
Aussie Stadium
built 1988, Sydney, 42,000 capacity
Canberra Stadium
built 1977, Canberra, 25,000 capacity
Central Coast Stadium
built 2000, Gosford, 20,000 capacity
Dairy Farmers Stadium
built 1996, Townsville, 31,500 capacity
Stadium Australia
built 1999, Sydney, 80,000 capacity

Subiaco Oval
built 1908, Perth, 43,000 capacity
Suncorp Metway Stadium
built 2003, Brisbane, 52,500 capacity
Telstra Dome
built 2000, Melbourne, 52,000 capacity
WIN Stadium
built 1992, Wollongong, 20,000 capacity
York Park
built 2001, Launceston, 20,000 capacity

Six Nations Championship Winners

1883	England	1949	Ireland
1884	England	1950	Wales
1885	not completed	1951	Ireland
1886	England/Scotland	1952	Wales
1887	Scotland	1953	England
1888	not completed	1954	England
1889	not completed	1955	Wales/France
1890	England/Scotland	1956	Wales
1891	Scotland	1957	England
1892	England	1958	England
1893	Wales	1959	France
1894	Ireland	1960	France/England
1895	Scotland	1961	France
1896	Ireland	1962	France
1897	not completed	1963	England
1898	not completed	1964	Scotland/Wales
1899	Ireland	1965	Wales
1900	Wales	1966	Wales
1901	Scotland	1967	France
1902	Wales	1968	France
1903	Scotland	1969	Wales
1904	Scotland	1970	Wales/France
1905	Wales	1971	Wales
1906	Ireland/Wales	1972	not completed
1907	Scotland	1973	England/France/Ireland/Scotland/Wales
1908	Wales	1974	Ireland
1909	Wales	1975	Wales
1910	England	1976	Wales
1911	Wales	1977	France
1912	England/Ireland	1978	Wales
1913	England	1979	Wales
1914	England	1980	England
1915-19	not held	1981	France
1920	England/Scotland/Wales	1982	Ireland
1921	England	1983	France/Ireland
1922	Wales	1984	Scotland
1923	England	1985	Ireland
1924	England	1986	France/Scotland
1925	Scotland	1987	France
1926	Scotland/Ireland	1988	Wales/France
1927	Scotland/Ireland	1989	France
1928	England	1990	Scotland
1929	Scotland	1991	England
1930	England	1992	England
1931	Wales	1993	France
1932	England/Wales/Ireland	1994	Wales
1933	Scotland	1995	England
1934	England	1996	England
1935	Ireland	1997	France
1936	Wales	1998	France
1937	England	1999	Scotland
1938	Scotland	2000*	England
1939	England/Wales/Ireland	2001	England
1940-46	not held	2002	France
1947	Wales/England	2003	England
1948	Ireland	2004	France

*In 2000 Italy joined the competition, previously known as the Five Nations Championship.

R
U
G
B
Y

U
N
I
O
N

Teams	Coach (in 2004)	Venue	Grand Slams
England	Clive Woodward	Twickenham	1913, 1914, 1921, 1923, 1924, 1928, 1957, 1980, 1991, 1992, 1995, 2003
France	Bernard Laporte	Stade de France	1968, 1977, 1981, 1987, 1997, 1998, 2002, 2004
Ireland	Eddie O'Sullivan	Lansdowne Road	1948
Italy	John Kirwan	Stadio Flaminio	
Scotland	Matt Williams	Murrayfield	1925, 1984, 1990
Wales	Mike Ruddock	Millennium Stadium	1908, 1909, 1911, 1950, 1952, 1971, 1976, 1978

Tri-Nations

	Winners	Runners-Up	Third place
1996	New Zealand	South Africa	Australia
1997	New Zealand	South Africa	Australia
1998	South Africa	Australia	New Zealand
1999	New Zealand	Australia	South Africa
2000	Australia	New Zealand	South Africa
2001	Australia	New Zealand	South Africa
2002	New Zealand	Australia	South Africa
2003	New Zealand	Australia	South Africa
2004	South Africa	Australia	New Zealand

World Cup Sevens

1993	England
1997	Fiji
2001	New Zealand

IRB Sevens

2000	New Zealand
2001	New Zealand
2002	New Zealand
2003	New Zealand
2004	New Zealand

Heineken/European Cup

	Winners		Runners-Up	Venue	Attendance
1996	Toulouse	21-18 aet	Cardiff	Cardiff Arms Park	21,800
1997	Brive	28-9	Leicester	Cardiff Arms Park	41,664
1998	Bath	19-18	Brive	Stade Lescure	36,500
1999	Ulster	21-6	Colomiers	Lansdowne Road	49,000
2000	Northampton	9-8	Munster	Twickenham	68,441
2001	Leicester	34-30	Stade Français	Parc des Princes	44,000
2002	Leicester	15-9	Munster	Millennium Stadium	74,000
2003	Toulouse	22-17	Perpignan	Lansdowne Road	28,600
2004	Wasps	27-20	Toulouse	Twickenham	73,057

Parker Pen Cup

1997	Bourgoin
1998	Colomiers
1999	Montferrand
2000	Castres
2001	Harlequins
2002	Sale
2003	Wasps
2004	Harlequins

NB: It was introduced as the European Shield in 1997 but changed its name in 2002.

Super 12 Finals

	Winners		Runners-Up	Venue
1996	Auckland Blues	45-21	Natal Coastal Sharks	Auckland
1997	Auckland Blues	23-7	ACT Brumbies	Auckland
1998	Canterbury Crusaders	20-13	Auckland Blues	Auckland
1999	Canterbury Crusaders	24-19	Otago Highlanders	Dunedin
2000	Canterbury Crusaders	20-19	ACT Brumbies	Canberra
2001	ACT Brumbies	36-6	Natal Coastal Sharks	Canberra
2002	Canterbury Crusaders	31-12	ACT Brumbies	Christchurch
2003	Auckland Blues	21-17	Canterbury Crusaders	Auckland
2004	ACT Brumbies	47-38	Canterbury Crusaders	Canberra

Premiership Winners

1988	Leicester		1997	Wasps
1989	Bath		1998	Newcastle
1990	Wasps		1999	Leicester
1991	Bath		2000	Leicester
1992	Bath		2001	Leicester
1993	Bath		2002	Leicester
1994	Bath		2003	Wasps
1995	Leicester		2004	Bath
1996	Bath			

NB 1988-97 – Courage League Division One
1998-2000 – Allied Dunbar Premiership
2001-date – Zurich Premiership

RFU Knockout Cup

1972	Gloucester	17-6	Moseley		1989	Bath	10-6	Leicester
1973	Coventry	27-15	Bristol		1990	Bath	48-6	Gloucester
1974	Coventry	26-6	London Scottish		1991	Harlequins	25-13 aet	Northampton
1975	Bedford	28-12	Rosslyn Park		1992	Bath	15-12 aet	Harlequins
1976	Gosforth	23-14	Rosslyn Park		1993	Leicester	23-16	Harlequins
1977	Gosforth	27-11	Waterloo		1994	Bath	21-9	Leicester
1978	Gloucester	6-3	Leicester		1995	Bath	36-16	Wasps
1979	Leicester	15-12	Moseley		1996	Bath	16-15	Leicester
1980	Leicester	21-9	London Irish		1997	Leicester	9-3	Sale
1981	Leicester	22-15	Gosforth		1998	Saracens	48-18	Wasps
1982	Gloucester	12-12 aet	Moseley		1999	Wasps	29-19	Newcastle
1983	Bristol	28-22	Leicester		2000	Wasps	31-23	Northampton
1984	Bath	10-9	Bristol		2001	Newcastle	30-27	Harlequins
1985	Bath	24-15	London Welsh		2002	London Irish	38-7	Northampton
1986	Bath	25-17	Wasps		2003	Gloucester	40-22	Northampton
1987	Bath	19-12	Wasps		2004	Newcastle	37-33	Sale
1988	Harlequins	28-22	Bristol					

NB: 1972-88 – John Player Cup
1989-97 – Pilkington Cup
1998-2000 – Tetley's Bitter Cup
2000-date – Powergen Cup

RUGBY UNION

County Championship Winners

1889	Yorkshire		1913	Gloucestershire
1890	Yorkshire		1914	Midlands
1891	Lancashire		1915-19	not held
1892	Yorkshire		1920	Gloucestershire
1893	Yorkshire		1921	Gloucestershire
1894	Yorkshire		1922	Gloucestershire
1895	Yorkshire		1923	Somerset
1896	Yorkshire		1924	Cumberland
1897	Kent		1925	Leicestershire
1898	Northumberland		1926	Yorkshire
1899	Devon		1927	Kent
1900	Durham		1928	Yorkshire
1901	Devon		1929	Middlesex
1902	Durham		1930	Gloucestershire
1903	Durham		1931	Gloucestershire
1904	Kent		1932	Gloucestershire
1905	Durham		1933	Hampshire
1906	Devon		1934	East Midlands
1907	Durham/Devon		1935	Lancashire
1908	Cornwall		1936	Hampshire
1909	Durham		1937	Gloucestershire
1910	Gloucestershire		1938	Lancashire
1911	Devon		1939	Warwickshire
1912	Devon		1940-46	not held

1947	Lancashire	1976	Gloucestershire
1948	Lancashire	1977	Lancashire
1949	Lancashire	1978	North Midlands
1950	Cheshire	1979	Middlesex
1951	East Midlands	1980	Lancashire
1952	Middlesex	1981	Northumberland
1953	Yorkshire	1982	Lancashire
1954	Middlesex	1983	Gloucestershire
1955	Lancashire	1984	Gloucestershire
1956	Middlesex	1985	Middlesex
1957	Devon	1986	Warwickshire
1958	Warwickshire	1987	Yorkshire
1959	Warwickshire	1988	Lancashire
1960	Warwickshire	1989	Durham
1961	Cheshire	1990	Lancashire
1962	Warwickshire	1991	Cornwall
1963	Warwickshire	1992	Lancashire
1964	Warwickshire	1993	Lancashire
1965	Warwickshire	1994	Yorkshire
1966	Middlesex	1995	Warwickshire
1967	Durham/Surrey	1996	Gloucestershire
1968	Middlesex	1997	Cumbria
1969	Lancashire	1998	Cheshire
1970	Staffordshire	1999	Cornwall
1971	Surrey	2000	Yorkshire
1972	Gloucestershire	2001	Yorkshire
1973	Lancashire	2002	Gloucestershire
1974	Gloucestershire	2003	Lancashire
1975	Gloucestershire	2004	Devon

Biographies of Players, Clubs and Coaches

Allen, Fred   Born Oamaru, South Island, New Zealand, 9 February 1920. Loose forward, Canterbury, Marlborough, Waikato, Auckland, New Zealand (1946-49), 6 caps. An outstanding back row and coach. 'Fred the Needle' toured Britain in the New Zealand army team, 'The Kiwis', 1945/46, and captained the All Blacks in 1946 against Australia. He captained two All Black tours, to Australia in 1947 and South Africa in 1949. Allen was dropped for the two final Tests against the Springboks – at his own suggestion. After retiring he became selector/coach of Auckland (1957-63) in one of its most successful periods, defending the Ranfurly Shield 25 times between 1960 and 1963. An All Black selector (1964/65), he was coach from 1966 to 1968 when the team won all 14 Tests played. With Charlie Saxton, Allen took the All Blacks through an unbeaten British tour in 1967.

Andrew, Rob   Born Richmond, North Yorkshire, England, 18 February 1963. Fly half, Cambridge University, Nottingham, Wasps, Newcastle, England (1985-97), 71 caps (2 as captain). Test points: 396, tries: 2, penalties: 86, conversions: 33, drop goals: 21. British Lions (1989-93), 5 caps. Test debut against Romania in 1985, scoring 16pts from six kicks. His strengths were pinpoint touch kicking and exceptional defence, and he became a goal-kicking machine. Scored a last-minute penalty in his second Test, a 9-9 draw with France. He played in only two World Cup matches in 1987. He was expected to take the captaincy, but head coach Geoff Cooke appointed Will Carling instead, and in 1988 England won 28-19 against Australia at Twickenham. A late replacement for the Lions' 1989 Australian tour, Andrew scored three goals to help win the second Test 19-12. In the third Test, an error by David Campese, after Andrew's drop goal attempt, led to

Ieuan Evans' match- and series-winning try. Andrew won the Courage League Division One championship with Wasps in 1990, and England Grand Slams in 1991, 1992 and 1995. He played in all of the 1991 World Cup matches, scoring a late drop goal to win the semi-final against Scotland, 9-6.

Andrew won three British Lions caps in 1993 in New Zealand. At the 1995 World Cup in South Africa, he scored 24pts against Argentina and 17pts against Italy, and a last-minute drop goal to win the quarter-final 25-22 against Australia. In 1997 he joined Newcastle, and won the Premiership in 1998. On retirement he held several Test records – most capped stand off; English record points and penalty goals; world record international drop goals; and a world record 30pts in a match (60-19 against Canada, 1994, at Twickenham). He was awarded the MBE in 1995. He coached Jonny Wilkinson, who broke his England points-scoring record in 2003.

Andrews, Mark   Born Elliot, South Africa, 22 February 1972. Lock, Natal, Aurillac (France), Newcastle, South Africa (1994-2002), 77 caps. Test points: 60, tries 12. Test debut against England in 1994. The most-capped Springbok forward. Captained Natal Sharks to the semi-final of the 2001 Super 12 and the final of the 2001 Currie Cup. He played no. 8 during the 1995 World Cup semi-final and final. A gifted athlete and devastating forward standing 2m tall and 116kg in weight, he also represented South Africa in water polo. Andrews was an excellent source of possession in the line-out and allied this with mobility and ball skills in general play. He was one of South Africa's strongest performers in the 1999 World Cup.

Barbarians   William Percy Carpmael was the inspiration behind the Barbarians, a unique club that has no natural home, where membership is by invitation only and the playing philosophy is based on adventure and attack. 'Tottie', as Carpmael was nicknamed, loved the culture behind the rugby tour and came up with the idea of regular short tours involving players of the highest skill levels. In 1890 he took the Southern Nomads – mainly made up of players from Blackheath – on a tour to the north of England. In Leuchters Restaurant, Bradford, the concept of the Barbarians was agreed on. Over the years the concept took hold and the nearest thing to a club home became a hotel called the Esplanade in Penarth. This was where the Barbarians always stayed on their Easter tours of Wales. The first international match came on 31 January 1948, when the 'Baa-Baas' beat the Wallabies 9-6. Since that first international match many of the world's greatest players have played for the Barbarians.

Batty, Grant   Born Greytown, New Zealand, 31 August 1951. Wing, Tauranga, Marist-St Pat's, Wellington, Bay of Plenty, New Zealand (1972-77), 15 caps. Test points: 16, tries 4. As a schoolboy Batty scored nine tries against Masterton. Test debut on the 1972/73 tour of the British Isles and France, where he played in Test victories over Wales, Scotland and England. He played in New Zealand's 16-10 defeat to England in 1973. In the 1974 All Black tour of Australia, Batty played in 11 wins and one draw. Later in that season he won the Ranfurly Shield (from South Canterbury) with Wellington. On the 1976 tour to South Africa he played all four Tests, but the first Test against the 1977 Lions was to be his last. A serious knee injury finished his career at the age of 25. Batty won the game for the All Blacks with a 50m run and try, after intercepting a Trevor Evans pass, when a Lions score had seemed certain. He later moved to Australia as rugby manager of the Brisbane Easts club and other Queensland sides.

Beaumont, Bill   Born William Blackledge Beaumont, Preston, Lancashire, England, 9 March 1952. Lock, Fylde, England (1975-82), 34 caps (21 as captain). British Lions (1977-80), 7 caps. After touring South Africa with Lancashire in 1974, he played the touring Tongans for the England under-23 team. He made his Test debut for England against Ireland. His second Test, in Australia, was memorable – he left the field injured after the first line-out, but Mike Burton was sent off, so Beaumont returned to play prop. He then played 33 consecutive matches, until his final cap against Scotland in 1982. He won three British Lions caps against New Zealand in 1977. Appointed captain in 1978, he led England to its first Grand Slam for 23 years in 1980. Beaumont also captained the 1980 Lions tour to South Africa, the first Englishman for 23 years, winning four caps. Although the series was lost, he showed good ball skills and excellent line-out play. He became a much-loved television personality, and was awarded the OBE in 1982. In 2003 he became the second Englishman inducted into the International Rugby Hall of Fame, after 1920s hero Wavell Wakefield.

Bennett, Phil   Born Felinfoel, South Wales, 24 October 1948. Fly half, Llanelli, Wales (1969-78), 29 caps. Test points: 166, tries: 4, penalties: 36, conversions: 18, drop goals: 2. British Lions (1974-77), 8 caps. Test debut, aged 20, against France (Paris) in 1969 in an 8-8 draw, the first Welsh replacement to be capped. A superb runner with a unique hunched style, twinkling feet and a devastating sidestep, he was also a superb kicker. The pressure of Barry John restricted his chances, but he won caps at full-back and centre. He started the famous Barbarians try against the All Blacks in 1973, fielding a punt and sidestepping the marauding chasers. On the Lions tour of South Africa in 1974, he was the star player, scoring 103pts, including a 50-yard try in the 28-9 second Test victory in Pretoria. In 1977, he became the second Welshman to skipper a Lions tour, after captaining Wales that season. The tour was disappointing, but, not for the first time, he scored over 100pts. In 1976 he had scored a record-equalling 38pts in the Five Nations Championship. With Wales he won two Grand Slams (1976 and 1978), three Five Nations Championships (1970, 1973 and 1975) and one Triple Crown (1977). Bennett retired from Test rugby in 1978, holding the world record for international points (210). He was awarded the OBE in 1978.

Bettarello, Stefano   Born 1958. Fly half, Rovigo, Italy (1979-88), 55 caps (1 as captain). Test points: 483, tries: 7, penalties: 104, conversions: 46, drop goals: 17. The son of Romano and nephew of Ottorino, both Italian internationals. Bettarello was the first player to score more than 400pts in full internationals. He was coached at Rovigo by Carwyn James. As well as having good kicking skills, he was an attacking fly half who was quick and had a sidestep that was legendary in Italian rugby.

Blanco, Serge   Born Caracas, Venezuela, 31 August 1958. Full-back, Biarritz, France (1980-91), 93 caps. Test points: 233, tries: 38, penalties: 21, conversions: 6, drop goals: 2. Test debut against South Africa (Pretoria) in 1980, losing 37-15. Somewhat inconsistent, a superb running full-back and goal kicker, he scored a record 36pts in the 1983 Five Nations, beating Didier Camberabero's 1967 mark. Although injured, Blanco scored the match-winning try against Australia in the 1987 World Cup semi-final, and made the final. He captained France on the 1990 Australia tour, scoring a stupendous 90m try in the second Test at Brisbane. Skipper and assistant coach for All Blacks home series in 1990. He retired as the world record cap-winner after a 19-10 defeat by England in the 1991 World Cup quarter-final in Paris, and became Biarritz club president. Inducted into the International Rugby Hall of Fame in 1997.

Botha, Naas   Born Breyten, South Africa, 27 February 1958. Fly half, Northern Transvaal, South Africa (1980-92), 28 caps. Test points: 312, tries: 2, penalties: 50, conversions: 50, drop goals: 18. Test debut, aged 22, against South America (Johannesburg), winning 24-9. Played four Tests against the Lions in 1980, winning three, thanks to his goal kicking. He toured New Zealand in 1981, his accurate goal kicking bringing 20pts in the second Test, a record in a Test against the All Blacks. Almost unbelievably Botha missed a simple conversion in the deciding third Test in Auckland at 22-22, and the All Blacks clinched the series. He was tried out as a kicker for Dallas Cowboys, but returned to South African rugby. He twice scored three drop goals in a Test, against South America in 1980 and the second Test in a 12-10 win against Ireland in 1981. He kicked all 24pts in the 1987 Currie Cup final against Transvaal – four penalties and four drop goals. His last Test appearance was against England at Twickenham in 1992, losing 33-16.

Brooke, Zinzan   Born Waiuku, New Zealand, 14 February 1965. No. 8, Auckland, New Zealand (1987-97) 58 caps. Test points: 89, tries: 17, drop goals: 3. The leading forward in world rugby and possibly the best player in any position in the mid-1990s. Test debut, aged 22, against Argentina (Wellington) in the 1987 World Cup, winning 46-15. He displaced captain Wayne Shelford at number eight and played the 1990 French tour with a broken ankle. Brooke established himself in the 1991 World Cup, and, in the 1992 Test against South Africa, was named the 'Colossus of Ellis Park', scoring from a quick tap when the Springboks expected a shot at goal. In 1993 he toured Britain, playing flanker, and scored four tries against South of Scotland. The 1994 New Zealand Player of the Year starred at home against the Springboks and his performance almost retrieved a hopeless cause in the Bledisloe Cup. Although injured, in the 1995 World Cup semi-final he dropped a goal from 40m. He was impressive in the All Blacks' first series win in South Africa in 1996, which included another crucial drop goal. He scored two tries against Australia in his 50th Test in 1997. The All Blacks toured Britain unbeaten in 1997, and drew the last Test, against England, 26-26. *Rugby World* magazine voted Brooke the second best number eight of all time to the great Mervyn Davies.

Brown, Gordon   Born Troon, Scotland, 1 November 1947. Lock, West of Scotland, Scotland (1969-76), 30 caps. British Lions (1971-77), 8 caps. Test debut against South Africa (Murrayfield) in 1969, winning 6-3. A fine two-handed line-out catcher, who played in two of the 1971 Lions Tests in New Zealand. He enjoyed the 1974 Lions tour of South Africa, scoring eight tries and helping in a series win. Sent off in 1977, Brown was suspended for the international season, but went on the Lions' New Zealand tour. There he teamed up in the second row with Bill Beaumont. His final Scotland Test had been in 1976 against Ireland in Dublin, winning 15-6. The son of Jock, a Scottish international goalkeeper, and brother of Peter (27 Scotland caps, 1964-73), whose unorthodox round-the-corner kicking style was surprisingly successful. He died 19 March 2001. Inducted into the International Rugby Hall of Fame in 2001.

Brownlie, Maurice   Born Wanganui, New Zealand, 6 August 1895. Loose forward, Hawke's Bay and New Zealand (1924-28), 8 caps (4 as captain). Test points: 6, tries: 2. One of three brothers to wear All Black. Laurie, the youngest, represented New Zealand against New South Wales in 1921, but was never capped. Maurice toured Britain and France in 1924 and 1925, and captained the 1928 tour of South Africa which was tied 2-2. Cyril, the eldest and biggest of the brothers, stood 6ft 3ins (1.9m), weighed 15st (96kg) and won three caps. He joined Maurice's two tours, playing flanker with him in the All Blacks' three-man second row. Following a fracas early in an England game in 1925, the referee, Albert Freethy, ordered Cyril from the pitch. He was the first and only man sent off in a Test, until Colin Meads was sent off against Scotland in 1967.

Calder, Finlay   Born Haddington, Scotland, 20 August 1957. Flanker, Scotland (1986-91), 34 caps (4 as captain). Test points: 8, tries: 2, Test debut against France at Murrayfield in January 1986. Scotland won 18-17. His final appearance came in the World Cup on 30 October 1991 against New Zealand at Cardiff, losing 13-6.

Campese, David   Born Queanbeyan, Australia, 21 October 1962. Wing/full-back, Randwick, New South Wales and Australia (1982-96), 101 caps. Test points: 315, tries: 64, penalties: 7, conversions: 8, drop goals: 2. Test debut against New Zealand in Christchurch in August 1982, losing 23-16. Campese was an unknown 19-year-old working in a sawmill when his career began in 1982, and by the time he retired, fourteen years later, the proud possessor of 101 caps and a world record 64 tries, he was the most recognisable and bemedalled player in the game. Campese was one of the finest all-round footballers that Australia has produced, known mostly for his phenomenal try-scoring ratio and his trademark move the 'goose step' – a technique that fooled opponents into thinking he was slowing down when in fact he was speeding up.

His spectacular gaffe in the third Test against the British Lions in 1989 was a temporary blip in his relentless try-scoring ability. With the series tied at one apiece and the Wallabies clinging on to a slender lead in the Sydney decider, Campese threw a suicidal goal line pass to Greg Martin which the full-back had no chance of catching. Lions winger Ieuan Evans capitalised on the error and downed the ball in what became known as 'Campo's Corner'. That match was eventually lost 19-18 and with it Australia's chance of recording a first victory over the Lions. Campese did not allow the setback to upset him unduly, and his brilliance was the linchpin of Australia's dominance of the game in the 1990s. He made his final appearance on 1 December 1996 against Wales in Cardiff, winning 28-19. Inducted into the International Rugby Hall of Fame in 2001.

Carling, Will   Born Bradford-on-Avon, Wiltshire, England, 12 December 1965. Centre, Sedbergh School, Harlequins, England (1988-97), 72 caps (59 as captain – a world record, including three Grand Slams). Test points: 54, tries: 12. Test debut, aged 22, against France (Paris) in 1988, losing 10-9. Controversially sacked as captain for describing the RFU committee as '57 old farts'. Carling's final appearance was on 15 March 1997 when England beat Wales 34-13.

Catchpole, Ken   Born Paddington, Australia, 21 June 1939. Scrum half, New South Wales, Australia (1961-68), 27 caps (13 as captain). Test points: 9, tries: 3. Brilliant half-back who linked well with fly half partner, Phil Hawthorne. Captained Australia on his debut against Fiji, aged 21, and was vice-captain thereafter. Played his part in three great wins: in 1964 at Wellington against New Zealand, and in 1966 against Wales at Cardiff, and England at Twickenham. In the first Test against New Zealand in 1968 he was hit hard by the Kiwi forwards and his knee was seriously injured when Colin Meads tried to pull him out of a ruck. He retired shortly after and later commentated for ABC. Inducted into the International Rugby Hall of Fame in 2001.

Clarke, Don   Born Pihama, New Zealand, 10 November 1933. Full-back, Kereone, Morrinsville, Waikato, North Island, New Zealand (1956-64), 31 caps. Test points: 207, tries: 2, penalties: 38, conversions: 32, drop goals: 5. A solid, reliable defender, 'The Boot's' kicking would punish virtually any opposition transgression in its own half. One of five brothers who played for Waikato (his older brother Ian was also an All Black). Clarke scored 8pts on his Test debut in August 1956 against South Africa in Christchurch. He played against Australia home and away in 1957 and 1958, and scored a then world record six penalty goals to beat the Lions in Dunedin, 18-17. In the second Test at Wellington, he scored the winning try. On the South Africa tour in 1960, he came in for rough treatment, but was a key player in the second Test win, and his last minute conversion drew the third. He retired after playing in all five Tests on the 1963/64 tour to the British Isles and France. His world record of total Test points stood for over 20 years until passed by Andy Irvine. It remained the New Zealand record until passed by Grant Fox in 1988. Clarke died in Johannesburg, 29 December 2002. Inducted into the International Rugby Hall of Fame in 2001.

Clohessy, Peter Born Limerick, Ireland, 22 March 1966. Prop, Munster, Ireland (1993-2002), 54 caps. Test points: 20, tries: 4. Test debut against France, February 1993 in Dublin, in a 21-6 defeat, aged 26.

Cobner, Terry Born Blaenavon, Wales, 10 January 1946. Flanker, Pontypool, Wales (1974-78), 19 caps (as captain). Test debut against Scotland (Cardiff) in January 1974, winning 6-0. After Mervyn Davies had to retire in 1976, Cobner took on the role of leader. A shuddering tackler who was an intelligent leader on the field, he could control the match from the back of the line-out or scrum. He skippered the Wales win over Argentina in 1976. After an injury he did not captain the side again until 1978, when he led the tour of Australia. His greatest moment was on the 1977 Lions tour of New Zealand. After losing the first Test, 'Cobs' ensured the Lions forwards dominated and won the Christchurch Test. He missed the third Test through injury and the series was lost. He retired after Wales' 18-8 defeat by Australia on the tour of 1978. In the 1980s he became a Wales selector.

Colclough, Maurice Born Oxford, England, 2 September 1953. Lock, Wasps, Angoulême, Swansea, England (1978-86), 25 caps. Test points: 4, tries: 1. British Lions (1980-83), 8 caps. Test debut against Scotland at Murrayfield in March 1978, winning 15-0, aged 24. With Bill Beaumont, Colclough formed a solid second row in the 1980 Grand Slam side and on tour to South Africa in 1980. The pair performed well, although the Lions narrowly lost three of the four Tests. Colclough played in all four Tests of the 1983 Lions tour of New Zealand. Later that year he scored his only Test try when England beat New Zealand 15-9 at Twickenham, the first home win over New Zealand in 47 years. He retired after the 29-10 defeat against France in Paris in 1986, the last of the 1980 Grand Slam team to do so.

Cotton, Fran Born Francis Cotton, Wigan, Lancashire, England, 3 January 1947. Prop, Loughborough College, Sale, Coventry, England (1971-81), 31 caps (3 as captain). Test points: 4, tries: 1. British Lions (1974-77), 7 caps. Test debut against Scotland in the 1971 centenary Test. He played in all four matches in the 1973 Five Nations and in the England team that beat New Zealand 16-10 in Auckland, its only tour win, and Australia 20-3 at Twickenham. The first-choice Lions tight-head prop in South Africa in 1974, Cotton also played three of the four Tests in New Zealand in 1977 as a loose-head prop, and returned to South Africa on the 1980 Lions tour. He captained the North Division which beat New Zealand 21-9 at Otley, in 1979, the first English provincial team ever to do so. He was a member of the 1980 Grand Slam team. Cotton suffered an on-field heart attack in South Africa in

1980. In his last Test (in 1981) he sustained a hamstring injury against Wales in Cardiff. Cotton retired as England's most-capped prop and with former team-mate Steve Smith he set up the Cotton Traders clothing company. He managed the victorious 1997 Lions tour to South Africa. His father played rugby league for Great Britain.

Craven, Danie Born Lindley, South Africa, 11 October 1910. Scrum half, Western Province, South Africa (1931-38), 16 caps (4 as captain). Test points: 6, tries: 2. Craven was educated at Stellenbosch University, where he was influenced by August Markotter (called 'Oubaas' – old master), and later lectured at the institution. A leading scrum half of the 1930s, he developed the dive pass, an invention of Dauncey Devine. He played Tests in four positions – scrum half, centre, fly half and loose forward. In a touring match against Queensland, he also played full-back. A shrewd tactician, he retired at the age of 28 in 1938. He became a national selector, a coach in the 1950s, the manager of the Springboks and president of the white SA Rugby Football Board in 1956 (until 1990). Craven worked for racial integration of the sport. 'Craven Week', a schools teams competition, started in 1964, and became multiracial from 1980. He was executive president of the South African Rugby Football Union until he died in January 1993, aged 82. Inducted into the International Rugby Hall of Fame in 1997.

Culhane, Simon Born Invercargill, New Zealand, 10 March 1968. Fly half, New Zealand (1995-96), 6 caps. Test points: 114, tries: 1, penalties: 15, conversions: 32. Made one of the most remarkable Test debuts ever, aged 27, against Japan in the 1995 World Cup. His personal total of 45pts included 20 conversions (and one miss) as well as a try. Incredibly, he was dropped for the next match, to be replaced by regular fly half Andrew Mehrtens. His brief career ended in Johannesburg, a 32-22 defeat by South Africa in August 1996.

Cullen, Christian Born Paraparaumu, New Zealand, 12 February 1976. Full-back, Wellington, Hurricanes, New Zealand (1996-), 58 caps. Test points: 236, tries: 46, conversions: 3. Test debut against Samoa (Napier) winning 51-10 in 1996. New Zealand's highest Test try-scorer, a devastating attacker with pace allied to strength. He threatened Gareth Edwards' record of 53 consecutive Tests from debut, until he was stopped by a knee operation after 51 appearances. With 46 tries, Cullen is, in 2004, the third-highest try scorer in internationals, three behind Rory Underwood (49), and 18 behind David Campese (64). He has scored twice as many tries as any other player against South Africa (ten plus one for the Barbarians). His 51 consecutive Test matches put him fifth behind Sean Fitzpatrick (63), Joe Roff (62), Willie John McBride and Gareth Edwards (53). In the Tri-Nations he had scored 16 tries to the end of 2003 – more than twice as many as any other player.

Dallaglio, Lawrence Born Lawrence Bruno Nero Dallaglio, Shepherds Bush, London, England, 10 August 1972. Flanker/no. 8, Wasps, England (1995-), 65 caps (14 as captain) (to end 2003). Test points: 65, tries: 13. British Lions (1997), 3 caps. Test debut as a replacement against South Africa (Twickenham) in November 1995, losing 24-14. He is also qualified to play for Italy. Educated at Ampleforth College and Kingston University. A powerful and forthright back row, 'Lol' came to prominence as a member of the

1993 World Cup-winning England Sevens side. As a British Lion in 1997 he played in all three Tests against South Africa. He formed a powerful back row with Neil Back and Richard Hill in 41 internationals. Dallaglio played in all of England's matches during the 1999 World Cup. He captained England 14 times, before resigning after newspaper stories of drugs use in 1999. He played a hugely influential part in England's two wins over New Zealand in Wellington, and Australia in Melbourne in June 2003. At the 2003 World Cup he was the only player of any nation to play in every minute of all his team's games. The final was his 26th consecutive England victory.

Dalton, Andy   Born Dunedin, New Zealand, 16 November 1951. Hooker, Bombay, New Zealand (1977-85), 35 caps (17 as captain). Test points: 12, tries: 3. The son of an All Black. Test debut, aged 26, against France (Paris), winning 15-3. The first All Black hooker to throw at the line-out. Dalton formed the world's best front row with Gary Knight and John Ashworth, for 20 Tests between 1978 and 1985, and they became known as 'The Geriatrics', the title of their 1986 joint autobiography. Unavailable for the 1980 Australia tour, Dalton was appointed captain against the touring South Africans in 1981 when Graham Mourie would not play. The series was ferocious, and was disrupted by anti-apartheid demonstrations. In the deciding Test at Auckland, after a flour bomb was dropped from an aeroplane and flattened an All Black player, the referee called the skippers and offered to abandon the match. Neither spoke and New Zealand won 25-22. Dalton captained the All Blacks to 15 wins in 17 Tests between 1981 and 1985. The 1983 British Lions were soundly beaten 4-0. Further successes followed against Australia, England and Argentina. He joined the 1986 rebel Cavaliers to tour South Africa, where he broke his jaw, and so missed the series against Australia. He was appointed skipper for the 1987 World Cup at home, but injury kept him out. Sean Fitzpatrick replaced him at hooker and David Kirk became captain. His last Test was in 1985 against Australia in Auckland, a 10-9 win.

Davies, Gerald   Born Llansaint, Wales, 7 February 1945. Wing, Cambridge University, Cardiff, London Welsh and Wales (1966-78), 46 caps (2 as captain). Test points: 72, tries: 20. British Lions (1968-71), 5 caps. A truly great attacking player with great pace and sidestep. Test debut, a 14-11 loss against Australia at Cardiff in 1966. He played centre for his first 12 Tests. He toured South Africa with the Lions in 1968, but played only one Test through injury. In 1971 at Murrayfield he scored the crucial try against Scotland in a 19-18 win. On the 1969 tour of Australia and New Zealand, Wales coach Clive Rowlands switched Davies to the wing. He was a great success on the victorious 1972 Lions tour of New Zealand, playing in all four Tests. He scored two tries in the second Test at Christchurch and the first try in the 13-3 win at Wellington in the third. He also scored four tries in a memorable display against Hawke's Bay. Davies was unavailable for the 1974 and 1977 Lions tours. After Wales's 1978 Grand Slam, his final Wales caps were as captain against Australia, scoring a try in both Tests. He held the Welsh record of 20 tries, tied with Gareth Edwards, until it was broken by Ieuan Evans. He won three Grand Slams, five Championships and five Triple Crowns. Inducted into the International Rugby Hall of Fame in 1999.

Davies, Jonathan   Born Trimsaran, Wales, 24 October 1962. Fly half, Neath, Llanelli, Cardiff, Wales (1985-88), 32 caps (4 as captain). Test points: 81, tries: 5, penalties: 6, conversions: 2, drop goals: 13. British Lions (1996-97), 5 caps. An elusive runner and superb kicker. He scored two tries on his Test debut against England at Cardiff in 1985. Welsh record 13 drop goals. Davies played all six games in the 1987 World Cup, captaining against Canada, and was masterful as Wales clinched third place against Australia. He ran England ragged and dropped two goals against Scotland at Cardiff as Wales took the Triple Crown in 1988. Wales endured a miserable 1988 New Zealand tour, although captain Davies stood out. He scored a fantastic 90m try in the second Test. He was voted *Rugby World* Player of the Year in 1987 and 1988. In 1989, Davies moved from Llanelli to Widnes rugby league club for a world record fee of £225,000. He was Rugby League Player of the Year in 1991 and 1993, and a 'Man of Steel' winner, earning 13 Wales caps in rugby league and 13 Great Britain caps. He also played for Warrington and Canterbury Bull Dogs before returning to union with Cardiff. He was awarded the MBE in 1995. Davies is the only player to captain Wales at both rugby union and league.

Davies, Mervyn   Born Swansea, Wales, 9 December 1946. No. 8, London Welsh, Swansea, Wales (1969-76), 38 caps (9 as captain). Test points: 7, tries: 2. British Lions (1971-74), 8 caps. Test debut against Scotland (Murrayfield), winning 17-3. 'Merv the Swerve', in a distinctive white headband, played 38 consecutive Tests. He controlled the forwards from the back of the scrum and the line-out, had superb ball handling and was usually first to the breakdown. In 1971, he played 13 games on the Lions tour of New Zealand and formed part of a back row which was too mobile for the All Blacks. The Lions won the Test series 3-1. In 1974, he was on the Lions tour of South Africa, and kept out Andy Ripley. His surging breaks were a feature of the series victory. He first captained Wales in 1975. Playing for Swansea against Pontypool in the Welsh Cup semi-final he collapsed with a brain haemorrhage and never played again. Davies retired as the world's most-capped no. 8 and wrote for a newspaper. Inducted into the International Rugby Hall of Fame in 2001.

Dawes, John   Born Abercarn, Wales, 29 June 1940. Centre, London Welsh, Wales (1964-71), 22 caps (6 as captain). British Lions (1971), 4 caps. Scored a try on his Test debut in 1964, aged 23, against Ireland (Dublin) in a 15-6 win. A steady rather than a quick player whose well-timed passes gave his winger the best chance of scoring. Dawes toured South Africa with Wales and won the 1965 Triple Crown. Dropped in 1966, he was recalled as captain, and toured New Zealand as vice-captain of Wales in 1969. He skippered both Wales' 1971 Grand Slam and the Lions' successful 1971 New Zealand tour, the first Welsh Lions captain (and the All Blacks' first home series defeat since 1937). He then retired from Tests, and in 1977 coached the Lions on their return to New Zealand. He coached Wales (1974-79), winning two Grand Slams, four Championships and four successive Triple Crowns. WRU National Coaching Director, 1980-90. He was awarded the OBE in 1972.

Dawson, Matt   Born Birkenhead, England, 31 October 1972. Scrum half, Northampton, England (1995-), 57 caps (9 as captain) (to end 2003). Test points: 91, tries: 14, penalties: 3, conversions: 6.

British Lions (1997-2001), 3 caps. Test debut against Western Samoa (Twickenham) in December 1995, winning 27-9. England's most-capped scrum half, despite competing with Kyran Bracken for the Test spot. In 2000 and 2001 he stood in as England captain for the injured Martin Johnson, losing the Six Nations Grand Slam in both seasons. He first came to notice in the Lions' first Test in South Africa in 1997. Ten minutes from time, with the Lions losing, Dawson broke on the blind side, and as the tacklers closed, he successfully dummied an overhead pass to score the match-winning try. Dawson also won praise on the 1998 'tour from hell', of the southern hemisphere, when England lost every Test heavily. Formed the half-back partnership with Jonny Wilkinson that won the 2003 Grand Slam and World Cup.

Deans, Colin   Born Hawick, Scotland, 3 May 1955. Hooker, Scotland (1978-87), 52 caps (13 as captain). Test points: 8, tries: 2. Test debut, aged 22, against France in February 1978, and missed only two of 54 internationals between 1978 and 1987. He retired in 1987 as the world's most-capped hooker and joint Scotland record cap-holder with Jim Renwick. Deans toured New Zealand with the British Lions in 1983, captained by hooker Ciaran Fitzgerald, and consequently never played a Test. The All Blacks won all four matches. Small but mobile, his pinpoint line-out throws and linkage with David Leslie at the tail were key ingredients in the 1984 Scotland Grand Slam team. His last Test was the 30-3 defeat by New Zealand in the 1987 World Cup at Christchurch. He was awarded the MBE in 1988.

Dodge, Paul   Born Leicester, England, 26 February 1958. Centre, Leicester, England (1978-85), 32 caps (8 as captain). Test points: 15, tries: 1, penalties: 3, conversions: 1. British Lions 1980, 2 caps. Test debut, aged 19, against Wales in 1978, one of England's youngest caps. Left out of the 1980 Grand Slam team, he came in for the final Tests against Wales and Scotland. Called up as a replacement for the 1980 Lions in South Africa, he played in the third-Test defeat in Port Elizabeth and in the fourth-Test in Pretoria which the Lions won 17-13, in a 3-1 series defeat. In 1982, when England beat Australia 15-11 at Twickenham, he kicked three penalties and converted Nick Jeavons' try. In 1983 he played in England's first win over New Zealand for ten years, although England were last in the Five Nations. A broken leg caused him to miss the 1984 season. In 1985 he became England's 100th captain and he led a tour to New Zealand, where, after a close first Test, England lost the second by a record 42-15. He retired from Tests aged 27, with a record number of caps for an English centre. He represented Leicester (1975-91) in 436 matches, was a John Player Cup winner (1979-81), and with Leicester the first Courage League Championship winner in 1988.

Dooley, Wade   Born Warrington, Lancashire, England, 2 October 1957. Lock, Preston, England (1985-93), 55 caps. Test points: 12, tries: 3. British Lions (1989), 2 caps. Test debut, aged 27, against Romania. A player who turned to union after playing league, the 'Blackpool Tower' was a policeman whose size made him a handful at line-outs and scrums. On his Test debut he was the then tallest England player at 2.03m. A member of the 1991 and 1992 Grand Slam teams, on his 50th appearance, in 1992 (aged 34), Dooley scored the final try in

England's 24-0 win over Wales at Twickenham to secure the second Slam. On tour in Australia in 1991 he broke his hand against Queensland. He played in the 1991 World Cup final at Twickenham, losing to Australia. Dooley was selected for the 1993 New Zealand Lions tour, but came home for his father's funeral and was not asked to return. On retirement Martin Johnson took his England place.

Duckham, David   Born Coventry, England, 28 June 1946. Wing, Coventry, England (1969-76), 36 caps. Test points: 36, tries: 10. British Lions (1971), 3 caps. Test debut, aged 22, against Ireland (Dublin) in 1969. Big for a winger, at 6ft 1in (1.85m) and 14st (90kg), he scored on his England debut. Known for his outside swerves and inside cuts, Duckham specialised in tries from broken play. His peak was the 1971 Lions tour of New Zealand, with 11 tries, including a record six tries against West-Coast Buller Combined (later equalled by J.J. Williams). He starred in the 1973 Barbarians v All Blacks match and captained Coventry to the 1973 RFU Cup. The title of his autobiography, *Dai for England*, was a nod to those from Wales who said he played like a Welshman.

du Plessis, Morné   Born Krugersdorp, South Africa, 21 October 1949. No. 8, Western Province, South Africa (1971-80), 22 caps (15 as captain). Test points: 12, tries: 3. Attended Stellenbosch University, where the legendary Danie Craven suggested he switch from tight forward. Test debut came on the disrupted Australian tour of 1971, but he was dropped after the 28-9 second Test disaster against the Lions in 1974. He captained the successful 3-1 series against the touring All Blacks in 1976. He also led the Springboks against the 1980 Lions, another 3-1 series win, and against a World XV in 1977. His father, Felix, and he were the first father and son to captain the Springboks. His playing style was often criticised by his countrymen, but he retired at the age of 31 after five successful years as skipper. Inducted into the International Rugby Hall of Fame in 1999.

du Preez, Frik   Born Frederik du Preez, Rustenberg, South Africa, 28 November 1935. Lock/wing, Northern Transvaal, South Africa (1961-71), 38 caps. Test points: 11, tries: 1, penalties: 2, conversions: 1. Test debut, aged 25, at Twickenham against England in 1961, winning 5-0. Versatile enough to play at lock and flank in Tests, he made up for a lack of size with an all-round game. He was fast enough to catch Test wingers in full flight, and was also a prodigious, if inconsistent, goal kicker. He drop kicked a 77m penalty in Pretoria. Du Preez enjoyed several epic tussles against the All Blacks' Colin Meads and Ireland's Willie John McBride. He played his final Test at Sydney in an 18-6 win over Australia. Inducted into the International Rugby Hall of Fame in 1997.

Eales, John   Born Brisbane, Australia, 27 June 1970. Lock, Queensland, Australia (1991-2001), 86 caps (a record 55 as captain). Test points: 173, tries: 2, penalties: 34, conversions: 31. Nicknamed 'Nobody' because 'Nobody's Perfect'. Test debut against Wales (Brisbane) in 1991, where he dominated the line-out in a 63-6 win. Eales had a superb all-round game – height, strength, mobility, technical skills in the line-out and scrum, and ball-handling and kicking. In the 1991 World Cup, with second row partner Rod McCall, the team won 28 of 30 line-outs against Wales. He took on Michael Lynagh's goal-kicking duties against Romania in the 1995 World Cup. Eales was appointed skipper in 1996, but had the worst possible start – a record 43-6 defeat by New Zealand in Dunedin. He kicked a last-minute penalty to beat New Zealand 24-23 in Wellington to win the 2000 Tri-Nations title. After Australia's first series win against the British Lions in 2001, he ended with a second successive Tri-Nations. His last game was in Sydney, a 29-26 win against New Zealand before a capacity 91,000 crowd.

Edwards, Gareth Born Pontardawe, Wales, 12 July 1947. Scrum half, Cardiff, Wales (1967-78), 53 caps (13 as captain). Test points: 88, tries: 20, drop goals: 2. British Lions (1968-74), 10 caps. Test debut, aged 19, against France (Paris) in 1967, losing 20-14. Edwards played the next 52 consecutive games – then a world record. He won his first game as captain 5-0, aged 20 in February 1968, against Scotland in Cardiff (becoming the youngest-ever Welsh captain). He emulated the All Black Chris Laidlaw, and perfected the spin pass. He was a superb kicker and try scorer. Partnered 'The King', Barry John, at half-back for 23 Tests, in a period of Welsh domination. He won three Grand Slams, five successive Triple Crowns and five Championships (plus two shared). In 1971 Edwards toured New Zealand with the Lions and was a major factor in a series win. He also scored what some consider the game's greatest-ever try for the Barbarians against the All Blacks in 1973. Phil Bennett caught a kick deep in his own 22, sidestepped twice and passed. The ball was passed again and again, until Edwards took it on the left wing at halfway, and dived over in the corner. Edwards toured South Africa in 1974 with the Lions who were undefeated. His final Test was a 16-7 win against France at Cardiff in 1978. Inducted into the International Rugby Hall of Fame in 1997.

Ella, Mark Born Sydney, Australia, 5 June 1959. Fly half, Randwick, New South Wales, Australia (1980-84), 25 caps (10 as captain). Test points: 78, tries: 6, penalties: 8, conversions: 3, drop goals: 8. Test debut, aged 21, against New Zealand (Sydney) winning 13-9. A naturally gifted all-round player, he could run, pass and kick. With twin Glen and brother Gary, Ella toured the UK with the Australian Schoolboys in 1977/78, scoring against every home nation. All three toured Britain in 1981/82 and New Zealand in 1982 (when Mark was Australia's captain), although they never played in a Test together. In the 1980 Bledisloe Cup series, Ella's round-the-body pass in the third Test led to Peter Grigg's try. After a defeat by the All Blacks in 1984, he toured the UK again, and scored a try in every Test match, as Australia made a clean sweep of the Tests. Aged 25, he shocked the game by retiring, his last Test being the 37-12 win over Scotland at Murrayfield in 1984. He became a sports broadcaster and journalist, ignoring lucrative offers to join the league game, and later coached in Italy and Sydney. Inducted into the International Rugby Hall of Fame in 1997.

Ellis, William Webb Born Salford, England, 24 November 1806. Webb Ellis is credited with originating the game of rugby football, after catching the ball and running towards the opposition in 1823, while training at his school, Rugby, in Warwickshire. The convention had previously been to take a mark and punt the ball. There is no contemporaneous evidence that Ellis was the first to do so. He was considered as a cricketer rather than a footballer until 1876, when Matthew Bloxam, a former pupil, wrote an account in *Meteor*, the Rugby School magazine. Another past pupil had told him about the

incident, although neither had witnessed it. In 1890 the school put up a commemorative tablet. Webb Ellis was at Rugby School from 1816 to 1825, where headmaster Thomas Arnold encouraged football as part of his creed of muscular Christianity. From 1825 he attended Brasenose College, Oxford, earning a cricket Blue in 1827. Webb Ellis eventually became an Anglican chaplain at St George's, Albermarle, London, and a minister at St Clement Dane, London. Late in his life he travelled to Menton, France to convalesce, but died there on 24 January 1872. His grave was discovered in 1969 and a replica of the school tablet added in 1972, the centenary of his death.

Evans, Ieuan Born Swansea, Wales, 21 March 1964. Wing, Llanelli, Bath, Wales (1987-98), 72 caps (28 as captain). Tries: 33. British Lions (1989-97), 7 caps. Test debut, aged 22, against France (Paris) in February 1987, losing 16-9. He set Welsh records for points and caps. His last cap came when he moved to play for Bath, at Stradey Park in a 23-20 win over Italy in 1998. *Rugby World and Post* Player of the Year 1992/93. Evans played all three Tests in the 1989 Lions series win (2-1) in Australia, scoring the series-clinching try in the final Test (won 19-18), and all three Tests in New Zealand with the 1993 Lions. He became a national hero when running in the winning try against England in December 1993. He played in the first three World Cups, and was one of few to play on three Lions tours. In 1993 he was the top try scorer with a total of four tries scored against New Zealand. On the Lions tour of South Africa he scored three tries. However, his trip to South Africa was to end prematurely thanks to a groin injury. After retirement he ran his own public relations marketing company, and later entered broadcasting. He was awarded the MBE in 1996.

Farr-Jones, Nick Born Carringbah, New South Wales, Australia, 18 April 1962. Scrum half, Australia (1984-93), 63 caps (36 as captain). Test points: 37, tries: 9. Test debut against England, in November 1984 at Twickenham, part of the famous 'Grand Slam' UK tour, playing alongside Mark Ella, he scored his first Test try against Scotland in the final Test. Formed the 'Holy Trinity' with Michael Lynagh and David Campese (and contributed to most of Campese's 64 Test tries). After a poor 1987 World Cup, he replaced Andrew Slack as captain, aged 25. Although his first Tests as skipper in 1988 were wins against England in Brisbane and Sydney, defeats followed in the Bledisloe Cup, a shambolic tour of the UK, and a 2-1 series loss in 1989 to the Lions. After losing the first two Tests in the 1990 Bledisloe Cup, Farr-Jones and his team stood up to the All Blacks at the Haka, and won the third, 21-9. He skippered the 1991 World Cup winners, although he was forced to leave the field in the dying minutes of the Ireland match, missing Michael Lyngah's winning try. After the 1992 victory in the Bledisloe Cup, came a Test win in Cape Town. He retired, but returned for the 1993 South Africa series, winning 2-1. Inducted into the International Rugby Hall of Fame in 1997.

Fatialofa, Papaliitele Peter Born Apia, Samoa, 26 April 1959. Prop, Ponsonby, Auckland, Samoa (1988-96), 32 caps (13 as captain). Test points: 4, tries: 1. 'Fats' led Samoa in its first World Cup in 1991, incredibly winning its first match against Wales in Cardiff, and reaching the quarter-final. His last Test came against New Zealand in June 1996. He coached King Country and with Bryan Williams helped Samoa's progress as a world rugby nation.

Fenwick, Steve   Born Caerphilly, Wales, 23 July 1951. Centre, Bridgend, Wales (1975-81), 30 caps (3 as captain). Test points: 152, tries: 4, penalties: 35, conversions: 11, drop goals: 3. British Lions (1977), 4 caps. Test debut, aged 23, against France in Paris in January 1975, winning 25-10. Fenwick scored a try within five minutes, and finished with 9pts. Robust and direct rather than fast, he was never an elegant runner or goal kicker, but broke Arthur Gould's 1897 record for Wales caps at centre. He played in all four Tests on the 1977 Lions tour of New Zealand. He scored 38pts in the 1978-79 Five Nations, equalling the highest for any country, and went on to form a formidable centre partnership for Wales with Ray Gravell, captaining Wales in the 1980 centenary game against New Zealand. After a 15-6 loss to Scotland at Murrayfield in 1981, he joined the Blue Dragons rugby league team, and won Welsh caps, setting many points records.

Fitzpatrick, Sean   Born Auckland, New Zealand, 4 January 1963. Hooker, Auckland, New Zealand (1986-97), 92 caps (a record 51 as captain). Test points: 55, tries: 12. The son of 1950s All Black centre Brian Fitzpatrick. Test debut, aged 23, against France (Christchurch) in 1986. The team was called the 'Baby Blacks', after many senior players had been suspended after the rebel Cavaliers tour to South Africa. Fitzpatrick only played in the 1987 World Cup pool matches when captain Andy Dalton was injured, but went on to keep him out, as New Zealand triumphed at home. He earned a record 63 consecutive Test caps in eight years, a run only ended when he was rested for the 1995 World Cup pool game against Japan. In 1991 the World Cup holders were beaten by a David Campese-inspired Australia in the semi-final. Fitzpatrick and his fellow forwards were hardly to blame, providing more than sufficient possession to win. Acclaimed as the world's greatest forward in the 1990s, he became All Black captain in 1992, and led them, as expected, to the 1995 World Cup final.

The squad succumbed to food poisoning before the match and lost in extra time, but Fitzpatrick led them on to the first two Tri-Nations titles in 1996 and 1997. In 1996 he captained the first All Blacks team to win a Test series in South Africa, after five failures. His last Test was at Wembley in November 1997 as a replacement against Wales, having played in a world record number of Tests for a forward. Knee problems led to his retirement in 1998. New Zealand's sponsors presented Fitzpatrick with a limited edition crate of beer called 'Seanlager' in his honour. Inducted into the International Rugby Hall of Fame in 1997.

Fox, Grant   Born New Plymouth, New Zealand, 6 June 1962. Fly half, Auckland, New Zealand (1985-93), 46 caps. Test points: 645, tries: 1, penalties: 128, conversions: 118, drop goals: 7. Dropped a goal in a 33-20 win against Argentina in Buenos Aires, on his Test debut in October 1985. Fox scored 100pts in only six Tests, and after 12 games he passed Donald Clarke's New Zealand points record of 207 (which Clarke had taken 32 Tests to reach). In the 1987 World Cup Fox was the highest points scorer with 126pts in six matches, 17pts coming in the 29-9 final victory over France. He scored a tournament record 30 conversions. Against Wales in 1988 he kicked 10 conversions in a 54-9 victory. He scored his only Test try against Scotland in 1990. After playing in the 1991 Bledisloe Cup, he scored 44pts in the World Cup. He was dropped after the first Test against a World XV in 1992 and was a replacement in the second. He came back for the Bledisloe Cup, which was lost 2-1. However, in the 1993 victory against the Lions he scored 32pts, half New Zealand's total, including a last-minute kick to win the first Test 20-18. His last two Tests were against Australia and Samoa.

Gallagher, John   Born Lewisham, London, England, 29 January 1964. Full-back, Wellington, New Zealand (1987-89), 18 caps. Test points: 52, tries: 13. Although qualified for England, Gallagher made his All Blacks debut, aged 23, in the 70-6 World Cup win in Auckland against Italy. Then he scored a record-equalling four tries against Fiji in the group stages, as did team-mate Craig Green. He missed only one of the next 18 Tests, and never lost. In the three years after winning the World Cup, came series victories over Australia, Wales and Argentina, and romps in Wales and Ireland. His final Test was a 23-6 win against Ireland in Dublin. Following a rare defeat in the Hong Kong Sevens final in 1990 by Fiji, he signed for Leeds rugby league club, with modest success. He titled his autobiography *The World's Greatest Rugby Player?*

Gallaher, Dave   Born Ramelton, Ireland, 30 October 1873. Hooker/wing, Auckland, New Zealand (1903-06), 6 caps. Having fought in the Boer War, Gallaher did not make his Test debut until aged 28. Originally a hooker, he switched to 'rover' or wing forward, a position New Zealand created by using only seven forwards in the scrum. He toured Australia in 1903, where New Zealand were unbeaten in 20 matches. Gallaher captained the 1905 New Zealand tour – 'The Originals' – losing only one match of 35 (to Wales, 3-0). He was greatly criticised for his spoiling play at scrums, and was heavily penalised. He introduced modern methods of preparation, asking his players to contemplate the match ahead, using liniment and even chewing gum. Set moves were given code names, and some new plays devised, such as miss passes, decoy runners and extra men in the backs. He retired after the tour, and was the Auckland selector from 1906 to 1916 and for New Zealand from 1907 to 1914. He died on active service in World War I at Passchendaele in 1917. In 1922 the Auckland senior club championship was named the Gallaher Shield in his honour.

Gibbs, Scott   Born Ian Scott Gibbs, Bridgend, Wales, 23 January 1971. Centre, Neath, St Helens (RL), Wales (1991-2001), 53 caps (1 as captain). Test points: 50, tries: 10. British Lions (1993-97), 5 caps. Test debut, aged 19, against England at Cardiff in January 1991, losing 25-6. Gibbs was described by Jeremy Guscott as 'the world's fastest prop'. Short, barrel-chested and strong, at 5ft 8ins (1.73m) and 216lb (98kg), he feared nobody. On his first Lions tour to New Zealand in 1993, played in the last two Tests. He left union for rugby league at St Helens in 1994, his career highlight being a win over Bradford Bulls in the 1996 Wembley Challenge Cup final. He returned to international rugby union in 1996 against Italy in Rome. Gibbs was Man of the Series on the victorious 1997 tour to South Africa – in one unforgettable incident he crashed into the huge prop Os du Randt, dropped him and rampaged on. His finest moment for Wales came at Wembley in 1999, when his 83rd-minute try against England helped overturn a 31-25 lead. In 2001, his last Test was a 33-23 win in Rome against Italy.

Gibson, Mike   Born Michael Cameron Gibson, Belfast, Northern Ireland, 3 December 1942. Centre,

Dublin University, Wanderers, Cambridge University, NIFC, Ireland (1964-79), 69 caps (5 as captain). Test points: 112, tries: 9, penalties: 16, conversions: 7, drop goals: 6. British Lions (1966-71), 12 caps. A direct runner, quick over the first 10 or 20 yards, with a fine sidestep, he was an all-rounder and good tactical kicker. Test debut, aged 21, in an 18-5 win against England at Twickenham in February 1964. Gibson was the world's most-capped player, first winning 25 at fly half, then 40 at centre, and 4 on the wing. Shares with Tony O'Reilly the longest Irish international career, 16 seasons. He made five Lions tours, including series wins in New Zealand in 1971 and South Africa in 1974. He won the fourth-most Lions caps ever. He joined Ireland's tours of Australia in 1967 and 1979, and New Zealand in 1976. His last two Tests were wins in Australia, ending with the 9-3 second Test in Sydney. An all-time great, Gibson was a sportsman and ambassador, one of few players to score over 100 Test points for Ireland. He was awarded the MBE. Inducted into the International Rugby Hall of Fame in 1997.

Going, Sid   Born Kawakawa, New Zealand, 9 August 1943. Scrum half, North Auckland, New Zealand (1967-77), 29 caps. Test points: 44, tries: 10, penalties: 2, conversions: 1. Test debut against Australia in August 1967. The balding 'Super Sid' had a low centre of gravity. He would run the ball with pace from the scrum or line-out, using blind-side breaks and multiple dummies to set up his forwards. An astute tactical kicker, Going was Maori Player of the Year from 1967 to 1972. When playing with his brothers Ken and Brian, their planned intricate moves were named Maramaku Special, after their home town. His style contrasted with that of Chris Laidlaw, a superb passer across the line and his rival for the scrum half jersey until Laidlaw retired in 1970. Going became New Zealand's most-capped scrum half. Some of his greatest battles were with the Wales and British Lions scrum half, Gareth Edwards. In 1971 the Lions won the series in New Zealand with a back row specifically chosen to counter Going's attacking style. He was the goal kicker in South Africa on the 1976 tour, and when the Lions next toured, in 1977, he scored in the first Test. New Zealand's defeat in the Second Test was his last international match.

Gould, Arthur   Born Newport, Wales, 10 October 1864. Centre/full-back, Newport, Southampton, London Welsh, Richmond, Hampshire, Middlesex, South Wales, Wales, 27 caps (18 as captain). Test tries: 4. Perhaps rugby's first superstar, a fast, elusive back, he specialised in drop goals, and set records for total first class appearances, tries and drop goals. In 1893, with Wales trailing England 11-0 at Cardiff, 'Monkey' Gould scored two tries as he skippered Wales to their first Triple Crown. In 1896 his testimonial raised over £500. Following just a year after the Northern Union breakaway, the home unions and IRB were up in arms, and Wales played no internationals for 14 months. Gould was presented with a detached house in Newport and was retired, ending the Welsh exile. He became a referee and Wales selector. Of his brothers, Bert and Bob played for Wales, and Harry, Gus and Wyatt played for Newport.

Gould, Roger   Born Brisbane, Australia, 4 April 1957. Full-back, Australia (1980-87), 25 caps. Test points: 86, tries: 4, penalties: 12, conversions: 14, drop goals: 2. Test debut against New Zealand in 1980, winning 13-9. His towering clearance kicks helped Australia to the win and a 2-1 series victory. Tall,

strong and mentally resilient, the rock on which Australia's 1980s team was built, he was one of the last 'toe end' goal kickers, which led to occasional lapses. Injury and illness prevented him touring New Zealand in 1978, aged 21, and France in 1981, and limited him to four caps after 1984. Selected for the Wallabies' visit to Britain in 1981, Gould played in the first three Tests, but was dropped for the 15-11 defeat by England. Before the 1984 season, he moved to Argentina, only being persuaded out of exile by coach Alan Jones. Australia again lost the Bledisloe Cup, however, with Gould's kicking off form in the deciding third Test. The winter tour of the British Isles was a greater success – the Australians set new standards in modern attacking rugby – and Gould played superbly in all four Tests. In his final game he came on as a replacement for Andrew Leeds in the defeat of England in the 1987 World Cup.

Gravell, Ray   Born Cydweli, Wales, 12 September 1951. Centre, Llanelli, Wales (1975-82), 23 caps. Test points: 4, tries: 1. Test debut against France (Paris) in 1975 – a match in which Wales scored five tries to France's one. A barnstorming crash-ball centre, passionately Welsh, his philosophy was 'if you can't go round them, go through them'. In his debut the bearded Llanelli stalwart made an instant impression after one shuddering tackle that allowed Graham Price, the Welsh prop, to hack and run 70 yards to score a try. During the next five years, Wales made two Grand Slams, four Championships and four Triple Crowns. Gravell missed the 1977 British Lions tour of New Zealand because of a shoulder injury. He played in all four Tests on the 1980 Lions tour to South Africa, although a substitute in the first Test. He started the second and scored a try. He would also star in the 17-13 victory in Pretoria against the Springboks. He became a popular broadcaster, and acted in a Louis Malle film and with Oscar-winning actor Jeremy Irons.

Gregan, George   Born Lusaka, Zambia, 19 April 1973. Scrum half, Randwick, ACT Brumbies, Transvaal, Australia (1994-), 99 caps (31 as captain) (as at 31 July 2004). Test points: 81, tries: 15, drop goals: 2. Gregan has lived in Sydney since he was one year old. He made an immediate international impact when famously tackling All Black Jeff Wilson to save the game for Australia during the 1994 Bledisloe Cup Test. Since his Test debut in 1994 v Italy, Gregan has become the most-capped scrum half in the history of Test rugby with all of his internationals played in the no. 9 jersey. He passed South African great Joost Van Der Westhuizen's 89 Tests in 2003.

Guscott, Jeremy   Born Bath, England, 7 July 1965. Centre, Bath, England (1989-99), 65 caps. Test points: 143, tries: 30, drop goals: 2. British Lions (1989-95), 8 caps. Test debut against Romania in May 1989. 'The Prince of Centres', cool and poised, Guscott could tackle, score tries, drop goals and make opportunities for others. His acceleration was allied to a superb football brain. He bagged a hat-trick of tries on his England debut in Romania. Two months later he joined the British Lions tour of Australia. After losing the first Test, he and Scott Hastings replaced the centres, and the Lions won the second Test 19-12, with Guscott scoring his only Lions try. The third Test was also won, 19-17. Against Fiji at Twickenham in 1989 he played alongside Will Carling, the first of a record 45-cap pairing, scored a try and assisted in all five of Rory Underwood's tries.

In 1990 he scored tries against Ireland, France and Scotland in the Five Nations and a fine solo try against Australia in Sydney, in England's record 40-15 loss in 1991. At the World Cup that year he scored two tries against Italy.

Guscott featured in a second consecutive Grand Slam in 1992, scoring a try against Ireland at Twickenham, and his first drop goal, against Scotland at Murrayfield. He starred for the British Lions in New Zealand in 1993, partnering Welshman Scott Gibbs. He failed to score in the 1995 South Africa World Cup, but in England's 1996 Five Nations Championship win he scored against Wales after charging a kick. On his third consecutive Lions tour, to South Africa in 1997, his last-minute drop goal in the second Test secured both an 18-15 win and a Lions series win. He broke his arm in the third Test. Guscott helped Bath win their first European Cup in 1998 and scored four tries in England's 110-0 win against Holland, one against Australia at Twickenham, and another a week later as England beat South Africa (who had won 17 consecutive games). After the 1999 World Cup games against Italy, New Zealand and Fiji, he retired, as England's then second highest try scorer. He was awarded the MBE in 2000.

Haden, Andy Born Wanganui, New Zealand, 26 September 1950. Lock, Auckland, New Zealand (1977-86), 41 caps. Test points: 8, tries: 2. An inspirational figure, standing at 2m, then the tallest All Black ever. Excellent in the line-out and scrum, and mobile in the loose, in 1977 he played in all four Lions matches for the All-Blacks, and scored his first Test try in the third. He toured France later that year. At Cardiff Arms Park in November 1978, with Wales leading 12-10 and time almost up, New Zealand had a line-out deep in opposition territory. The locks, Haden and Frank Oliver, both fell as if they had been pushed. The referee awarded a penalty, which Brian McKechnie scored to win the game. Relations were soured between the two countries for years to come. After losing a Bledisloe Cup decider 12-6 to Australia in Sydney in 1979, he handed his shirt to the Australian coach. The 1980 Bledisloe Cup was lost 2-1 in Australia, but the trophy was regained by New Zealand in 1982.

Haden's second British Lions series in 1983 was won 4-0 (in the fourth Test he scored his second and last Test try). He missed the 1987 World Cup group games through a hamstring injury, and although captain, he could not displace Sean Fitzpatrick at hooker. Published a book, *Boots 'n' All!*, and became the All Blacks' first professional marketing agent in the late 1980s and occasional national team line-out coach.

Hare, Dusty Born William Hare, Newark, Nottinghamshire, England, 29 November 1952. Full-back, Nottingham, Leicester, England (1974-84), 25 caps. Test points: 240, tries: 2, penalties: 67, conversions: 14, drop goals: 1. Test debut against Wales in March 1974. World record 7337pts in first-class matches (1971-89), (1800 for Nottingham, 4427 for Leicester, 240 for England, 88 for the Lions and 782 in other matches). Reliable and consistent as a player and goal kicker, Hare's debut in a surprise 16-12 win over Wales in March 1974 was his only cap for four years. In 1980 he kicked all England's points in a 9-8 victory over Wales, the winner from wide in the dying stages, as the Grand Slam was completed. Facing Wales in 1981, however, he was both hero and villain, scoring all 19 of England's points (a try and five penalties), but

missing an injury-time kick in a 21-19 defeat. Against France in 1982 Hare set a then Five Nations record for points in a match (19 in a 27-15 win). In 1984 he set a Five Nations record for a season's total, with 44pts. On retirement, he was England's leading points scorer and most-capped full-back. Toured with British Lions to New Zealand, but played in no Tests. Hare played for Leicester until 1989, winning three John Player Cup finals. He also played county cricket for Nottinghamshire. He was awarded the MBE in 1989.

Hastings, Gavin Born Edinburgh, Scotland, 3 January 1962. Full-back, Cambridge University, Watsonians, Scotland (1986-95), 61 caps (20 as captain). Test points: 733 (Scottish record), tries: 17, penalties: 140, conversions: 86. British Lions (1989-93), 6 caps. Test debut against France at Murrayfield, conceding a first-minute try after he kicked straight into touch, but scored all Scotland's points in an 18-17 win. Championship record 52pts in 1986, and he later scored 21pts against both Romania and England. In the 1987 World Cup he scored 27pts against Romania and 19 against Zimbabwe. He played all three Lions Tests in Australia in 1989, scoring 28pts. Hastings helped Scotland win the Grand Slam in 1990, unexpectedly beating England 13-7 at Murrayfield, but England gained revenge in the 1991 World Cup semi-final, winning 9-6 (Hastings missed a penalty under the posts at 6-6). In the third place play-off against New Zealand, he made one of the tackles of the tournament.

Hastings succeeded David Sole as captain of Scotland in 1992 and was named British Lions captain for New Zealand, a series narrowly lost 2-1. However, he set Lions individual records, including 35pts (series), 12 penalty goals, 6 penalty goals in a match, 66pts (career), and his 18pts in a match equalled that of Ireland's Tony Ward in 1980. In 1994 Scotland lost 15-14 to England at Murrayfield after he missed two penalties but Hastings fared better in 1995. Scotland won in Paris for the first time since 1969, Hastings scoring the decisive try at the death, and he totalled 56pts for the Championship, breaking his own record. At the World Cup that year he harvested 44pts from the Ivory Coast and 31 against Tonga, before losing to New Zealand in the quarter-final. He retired Scotland's most-capped player, until brother Scott overtook him in 1996. He was awarded the OBE in 1994. Inducted into the International Rugby Hall of Fame in 2003.

Hastings, Scott Born Edinburgh, Scotland, 4 December 1964. Centre, Watsonians, Scotland (1986-97), 5 caps. Test points: 43, tries: 10. Test debut, aged 21, against France (Murrayfield) (also elder brother Gavin's debut), winning 18-17. Last Test was against England at Twickenham in 1997, losing 41-13. He remained Scotland's most-capped player until passed by Gregor Townsend in 2002.

Hewson, Allan Born Lower Hutt, New Zealand, 6 June 1954. Full-back, Wellington, New Zealand (1981-84), 19 caps. Test points: 201, tries: 4, penalties: 43, conversions: 22, drop goals: 4. Test debut, aged 27, against Scotland (Dunedin) in June 1981, winning 11-4. Slightly built, but quick, and a phenomenal points machine. Against the 1981 Springboks, in the last seconds of the third Test, with the series at 1-1 and the game at 22-22, Naas Botha missed a conversion and New Zealand were awarded a penalty. Hewson's kick clinched the series. The following year against Australia, he scored 26pts out of 33, then a world record. The

Australian full-back Roger Gould ran in a great try in the first minute, but Hewson scored five minutes later in the opposite corner, and converted. His final Test came in July 1984 against Australia in Sydney, a 16-9 loss. His total of 201pts was only six behind Donald Clarke's then All Black record.

Hickie, Denis   Born Dublin, Ireland, 13 February 1976. Wing, St Mary's College, Leinster, Ireland (1997-), 44 caps (to end 2003). Test points: 115, tries: 23. Test debut against Wales (Cardiff), in February 1997, winning 26-25. He relies on pure pace rather than eluding the defence. Hickie lost his place on the 1998 South Africa tour, and was not recalled until 2000. He scored three tries in three matches at the 2003 World Cup, before being injured against Australia.

Hill, Richard   Born Dormansland, Surrey, England, 23 May 1973. Flanker, Saracens, England (1997-), 63 caps (to end 2003). Test points: 55, tries: 11. British Lions (1997-2001), 4 caps. Represented England at every level. Test debut, aged 23, against Scotland at Twickenham in February 1997, winning 41-13. He formed a formidable back row with Lawrence Dallaglio and Neil Back in 41 internationals. Nicknamed 'The Silent Assassin', he is a mobile breakdown forward, who is strong in the maul, a thunderous tackler and a good line-out jumper. Hill missed the vital third Lions Test in Australia in 2001 after a collision with Australian centre Nathan Grey in the second Test. The Lions without Hill lost 23-29. He also missed several of England's opening 2003 World Cup matches after injuring himself against Georgia in the first pool game, and England missed him. He returned for the semi-final win over France. He could not stop Serge Betsen's dash from a 22m line-out for France's try, but compensated with impressive games in the semi-final and final.

Hiller, Bob   Born Woking, Surrey, England, 14 October 1942. Full-back, Harlequins, England (1968-72), caps: 19 (7 as captain). Test points: 138, tries: 3, penalties: 32, conversions: 12, drop goals: 2. Test debut, aged 25, against Wales at Twickenham, January 1968, an 11-11 draw. He played in England's remaining matches in that Championship, scoring 22pts. One of the last toe-end kickers, he scored in every international he played and his career 138pts was a then English record. He was England's most-capped full-back until Dusty Hare. Hiller went on both the 1968 and 1971 Lions tours, and although he did not play a Test, scored over 100pts in both tours. In 1969 he played in all four Championship matches, scoring 36pts, only two less than Roger Hosen's 1967 England record. He notched 5pts as England defeated South Africa for the first time, 11-8 at Twickenham. Against Ireland in 1970, he scored two spectacular drop goals, close to touch, and just beyond halfway, as England triumphed 9-3. After the 1971 Lions tour, he earned one last cap in February 1972 against Ireland at Twickenham, losing 16-12.

Horan, Tim   Born Darlinghurst, New South Wales, Australia, 18 May 1970. Centre/fly half, Queensland, Australia (1989-2000). 80 caps (1 as captain). Test points: 140, tries: 30. Test debut, aged 19, against New Zealand (Auckland) in August 1989, losing 24-12. In 1994 his international career almost came to an end when he suffered a severe knee injury in a Super 10s game for Queensland. It was predicted that he would never play top-flight rugby again, but after months of gruelling rehabilitation he made an amazing comeback. A double World Cup-winner with Australia, his final appearance was on 17 June 2000 against Argentina (Brisbane), winning 53-6. Inducted into the International Rugby Hall of Fame in 2003.

Irvine, Andrew   Born Edinburgh, Scotland, 16 September 1951. Full-back, Edinburgh, Scotland (1972-82), 51 caps (15 as captain). Test points: 273, tries: 10, penalties: 61, conversions: 25. British Lions (1974-77), 6 caps. Test debut against New Zealand (Murrayfield) in December 1972, losing 14-9. Irvine won two British Lions caps in 1974 (South Africa) and four in 1977 (New Zealand). In March 1982 he led Scotland to their first win in Cardiff for 20 years (34-18) which was Wales's first Championship defeat in Cardiff for 27 games. In July 1982 he led Scotland to their first-ever win in Australia (in Brisbane), winning 12-7), and made his last appearance for Scotland later in the series, losing 33-9 to Australia in Sydney. Inducted into the International Rugby Hall of Fame in 1990.

Jenkins, Neil   Born Church Village, Wales, 8 July 1971. Fly half/centre/full-back, Pontypridd, Cardiff, Wales, 87 caps. Test points: 1049, tries: 11, penalties: 235, conversions: 130, drop goals: 10. Jenkins made his Welsh international debut aged 19 against England (19 January 1991). His final international appearance was on 1 November 2002 against Romania. In between, and largely due to his extremely accurate kicking, he became world rugby's all-time highest points scorer.

John, Barry   Born Cefneithin, Wales, 6 January 1945. Fly-half, Llanelli, Cardiff, Wales (1966-72), 25 caps. Test points: 90, tries: 5, penalties: 13, conversions: 6, drop goals: 8. British Lions (1968-71), 5 caps. Test debut, aged 21 and still a student, against Australia in 1966, replacing the Lions captain David Watkins. Inspired by Carwyn James, another notable Cefneithin rugby man. An air of reserve belied John's keen football brain, great kicking ability and legendary hip swerve. His half-back partnership with Gareth Edwards, playing 23 international matches together, was among the game's greatest. He toured South Africa in 1968 with the Lions, but broke his collarbone in the first Test. He dominated the 1971 Lions series win in New Zealand, his tactical kicking winning the first Test, and scored 30 of the Lions' 48pts in four matches. His 188 tour points were over 100 more than the previous record. In 1971/72 Wales were unbeaten in the Five Nations; 'King' John scored 35pts in three games and amassed a final total of 90pts, both records. He scored a crucial try in Paris to win the Grand Slam (9-5). He retired aged 27. Compared by some to Bjorn Borg or George Best, as a genius whose light burned all too briefly. Inducted into the International Rugby Hall of Fame in 1997.

Johnson, Martin   Born Solihull, West Midlands, England, 9 March 1970. Lock, Leicester, England (1993-2003), 84 caps (39 as captain). Test points: 10, tries: 2. British Lions (1993-2001), 8 caps. Test debut against France (Twickenham) in January 1993, winning 16-15. Johnson captained the England team in a victorious World Cup campaign in 2003. He was runner-up to Jonny Wilkinson as 2003 BBC Television Sports Personality of the Year, and was awarded the CBE.

Jones, Michael   Born Auckland, New Zealand, 8 April 1965. Flanker, Auckland, Blues, New Zealand (1987-98), 55 caps. Test points: 56, tries: 13. Test debut against Italy in May 1987. Michael Jones was one of those once-in-a-lifetime rugby legends who changed the way the game was played. As the All Blacks dominated the inaugural World Cup in 1987, it was Jones more than anyone who caught the rugby world's attention. He was the complete player. He had more pace than many wingers, the ball skills of an inside back and yet could anticipate the breakdown, make tackles and maul more effectively than any other flanker on display. He marked his debut by scoring the first try by an individual in the World Cup. His impact was such that he became an automatic selection for New Zealand despite his unavailability for Sunday Test matches due to his religious convictions. In 1988 Jones continued his sublime form against Wales and Australia but in 1989, after dominating France and Argentina, he encountered his greatest challenge when he endured a knee injury so horrific it was feared amputation might be necessary.

Quite remarkably he was to regain the fitness needed to grace the New Zealand no. 7 shirt again when he toured France in 1990. In the 1991 World Cup he again scored the tournament's first try. His absence was a crucial factor in the Sunday semi-final loss to Australia. Injuries again removed him from the UK tour in 1993 and Tests against South Africa in 1994. In the final Test of that series, Jones re-emerged as a replacement. He continued this excellence against Australia but in 1995 he was, for the first time, to miss an All Black rugby World Cup squad due to the number of Sunday games. Despite Josh Kronfeld's emergence, Jones was quickly reinstated into the squad for the following Bledisloe Cup series and then for the tour to France. It was there that he began the switch to blind-side flanker that would pay huge dividends for New Zealand. Jones's transition from flyer to huge-hitting defender was remarkable.

Alongside Kronfeld and Zinzan Brooke, he formed a trio that provided the perfect link and helped to ensure New Zealand's first-ever series victory in South Africa in 1996. Sadly Jones's final years in 1997 and 1998 were blighted by injury, including another major knee operation. He was voted New Zealand's third-greatest player ever, behind Colin Meads and Sean Fitzpatrick, in a millennium poll and *Rugby World* magazine also named him the greatest open-side flanker of all time. Inducted into the International Rugby Hall of Fame in 2003.

Kennedy, Ken Born Rochester, Kent, England, 10 May 1941. Hooker, Queens University Belfast, London Irish, Ireland (1965-75), 45 caps, British Lions (1966 and 1974), 4 caps. Test debut, aged 23, against France (Dublin), a 3-3 draw. A doctor who was enthusiastic and a ceaseless talker on the field, he would tend the injured of either team. He enjoyed two Lions tours – in 1966 to New Zealand, and to South Africa in 1974 (when the Lions were unbeaten). He missed the 1968 Lions tour of South Africa through injury, enabling John Pullin to establish himself, and he was not selected for the 1971 New Zealand tour. In the match in Dublin against New Zealand in 1974, he passed Australian Peter Johnson's world record 42 caps by a hooker. John Pullin equalled his record in 1976, and it was finally beaten by Colin Deans during the 1987 World Cup.

Kiernan, Michael Born Cork, Ireland, 17 January 1961. Centre/wing, Dolphin, Lansdowne, Ireland (1982-91), 43 caps. Test points: 308, tries: 6, penalties: 62, conversions: 40, drop goals: 6. British

Lions (1983), 5 caps. His uncle, Tom Kiernan, took him on Ireland's tour to South Africa in 1981, and he earned his first cap in January 1982 against Wales in Dublin, aged 21. In 1983 he played centre in three Lions Tests in New Zealand. After 11 Tests he took over kicking duties from Ollie Campbell and set several records. He was switched to the wing by Ireland in 1988. Although lacking outright speed, his strength and timing made him dependable. His last game was a 21-13 defeat against France in Dublin.

Kiernan, Tom Born Cork, Ireland, 7 January 1939. Full-back, University College, Cork, Cork Constitution, Ireland (1960-73), 54 caps (24 as captain). Test points: 158, tries: 2, penalties: 31, conversions: 26, drop goals: 2. British Lions (1962-68), 5 caps. Test debut against England in February 1960. A dependable full-back who started as a centre and first played full-back for Ireland in 1960 before doing so at club level. Ireland won only one game in his first two seasons, but he scored 38 of his team's 59pts, and was selected to go to South Africa with the Lions in 1962. He returned to South Africa in 1968 as captain. Despite Kiernan scoring 17pts in the first Test, and 35 in the series overall, both of which set records, the Lions did not win a Test. His final Test for Ireland was against Scotland at Murrayfield where he scored a try at the corner. He coached Munster to victory over New Zealand in 1978 and became Ireland's coach in 1980. Ireland visited South Africa, and won the Five Nations outright in 1982 and jointly with France in 1983.

Kirk, David Born Wellington, New Zealand, 5 October 1960. Scrum half, New Zealand (1985-87), 17 caps (11 as captain). Test points: 24, tries: 6. Test debut against England in June 1985. Educated and articulate, a Rhodes scholar and a doctor. Kirk was a New Zealand colt, and he joined the All Blacks' British tour in 1983 before his Test debut in 1985. The next year he declined to join the rebel Cavalier team touring South Africa. With many misgivings, he skippered New Zealand in four Tests, a series loss to Australia and a bruising encounter at home to France. He surprised many, possibly none more than himself, by retaining the captaincy when the rebels returned. When hooker and captain Andy Dalton withdrew from the 1987 World Cup because of a training injury. In the final, Kirk scored a try and set up another for winger John Kirwan, as New Zealand triumphed against France 29-9. He played his final Test against Australia later the same year, a 30-16 win. He represented Oxford University in the varsity match in 1987 and 1988. In retirement Kirk entered television and journalism and also wrote a book, *Black and Blue*.

Kirkpatrick, Ian Born Gisborne, New Zealand, 24 May 1946. Flanker, Canterbury, New Zealand (1967-77), 39 caps (9 as captain). Test points: 57, tries: 16 (then record). Test debut, aged 21, against France, a 19-15 win in which he scored a try. A back row stalwart of his era. An All Black tourist to Britain and France in 1967, in 1968, as a replacement, Kirkpatrick scored three tries in the first Test against Australia. After losing the first Test to the British Lions in 1971, he scored a memorable individual try from 60m. He starred in the 1972 whitewash of Australia, and captained New Zealand in 1973, touring the UK and losing only one Test (in Dublin). After sensationally losing 16-10 to England in Auckland, Kirkpatrick was sacked as skipper and replaced by Andy Leslie. His form returned on the

Australia tour and in 1976 he played in all four Tests in South Africa. The following year the Lions returned, and were beaten 3-1. Following 37 consecutive All Black appearances, Kirkpatrick retired. Inducted into the International Rugby Hall of Fame in 2003.

Kirwan, John   Born Auckland, New Zealand, 16 December 1964. Wing, Marist, Auckland Warriors (RL), New Zealand (1984-94), 63 caps. Test points: 143, tries: 35. Test debut against France in June 1984. An oustanding attacking player, quick and big for a winger. He broke New Zealand's try-scoring record, 19 by Stu Wilson. He was then third in the all-time list, behind Campese (then on 37) and Blanco (then on 33). In 1986 he and David Kirk refused to join the rebel Cavalier team to South Africa. The 1986 Bledisloe Cup began his great rivalry with David Campese. Australia won it for the first time in New Zealand 2-1. However, in the 1988 Bledisloe Cup, Kirwan was outstanding, giving Campese such a torrid time that it badly damaged the Australian's confidence. That was followed by two thrashings of Wales, 52-3 and 54-9. In 1989 damaged knee ligaments ended Kirwan's tour of Wales and Ireland. He was surprisingly not selected for the 1993 tour to Britain. His Test career finished at Auckland with an 18-18 draw against South Africa. He played club rugby in Italy and after a stint as assistant coach of Super 12 side Auckland Blues in 2001, he became Italy's national team coach in 2002. Inducted into the International Rugby Hall of Fame in 2003.

Knight, Gary   Born Wellington, New Zealand, 26 August 1951. Prop, Manawatu, New Zealand (1977-86), 36 caps. Test points: 4, tries: 1. Knight endured a baptism of fire on his Test debut in 1977 against French forward and amateur boxer Gerard Cholley who poked him in both eyes, tearing an eyelid. He formed a formidable front row with Andy Dalton and John Ashworth, earning 'The Geriatrics' soubriquet. He twice toured Britain, in 1978 and 1980. In 1981 South Africa toured New Zealand, sparking a heated campaign that culminated in a Cessna flying over the stadium at the final Test in Auckland, dropping flour bombs. One felled 'Axle', who had earlier scored his only Test try. A farmer and amateur wrestler, he enjoyed series wins against the Lions, England and Australia.

Kronfeld, Josh   Born Hastings, New Zealand, 20 June 1971. Flanker, Otago, New Zealand (1995-2000), 54 caps. Test points: 70, tries: 14. Test debut against Canada in April 1995. Described himself as a German-Samoan, his great uncles, Frank and Dave Solomon, were All Blacks. At the 1995 World Cup, Kronfeld flourished in the absence for Sunday matches of devout Christian Michael Jones, scoring three tries, including one in the semi-final against England. Although South Africa won the final, New Zealand won the inaugural Tri-Nations in 1996, the formidable back row of Jones, Kronfeld and Christian Cullen ensuring an ample supply of ball. Mobile and undaunted, Kronfeld was an attack-minded player and was rewarded with many important tries.

Laidlaw, Chris   Born Dunedin, New Zealand, 16 November 1943. Scrum half, Otago, New Zealand (1964-70), 20 caps (1 as captain). Test points: 12, tries: 3, drop goals: 1. Test debut against France in February 1964. A brilliant half-back with astute tactical sense, and a strong and long passer who gave his stand offs space. His two main rivalries

were with Sid Going, for New Zealand's scrum half position, and Dawie de Villiers, South Africa's scrum half and captain. Laidlaw replaced injured Brian Lochore as the All Blacks' captain in 1968. As a Rhodes scholar he led Oxford University to victory over the touring 1969/70 Springboks. His autobiography, *Mud In Your Eye*, was critical of rugby's administration, especially contact with South Africa. He ardently opposed apartheid. Laidlaw became the first New Zealand High Commissioner to Zimbabwe.

Leonard, Jason   Born Barking, Essex, England, 14 August 1968. Prop, Harlequins, England (1990-2004), 114 caps. Test points: 125, tries: 30. Test debut in the 25-12 victory against Argentina in Buenos Aires, 28 July 1990. Became a double Grand Slam-winner in 1991 and 1992 before gaining his first British Lion's cap in 1993 against New Zealand. Leonard became England's most-capped prop with his 38th cap against Scotland at Twickenham as England claimed another Five Nations Grand Slam, 18 March 1995. He became the youngest England player to win 50 caps, against Italy at Twickenham, 23 November 1996. Leonard equalled Philippe Sella's world record of 111 caps v Wales in the quarter-finals of the 2003 Rugby World Cup and beat it in the semi-final match against France. His final mternational match at Twickenham was for the Barbarians v England in May 2004 where he scored the first try in a 32-12 victory before exiting in the 67th minute. He was awarded the MBE in 2002.

Loane, Lars   Born Ipswich, Queensland, Australia, 11 July 1954. No. 8, Ballymore, Queensland, Australia (1973-82), 28 caps (6 as captain). tries: 2. Test debut against Tonga (Sydney) winning 30-12, three weeks before his 19th birthday. Loane was the second-youngest Australia international (Brian Ford, the Queensland winger, played against New Zealand in 1957 aged 18 years 3 months), and the youngest Wallaby forward. After a shock defeat in the second Test against Tonga, 16-11, he missed the tour of England, Wales. A powerful and rumbustious runner and a shuddering tackler, he was the archetypal hard man beloved by the fans. Loane played a large part in Queensland's inter-state success and was a fixture in the Wallaby side from 1974, captaining against New Zealand and on the Argentina tour in 1979. He spent a year in Natal in 1980 and became a firm favourite, before returning to Australia and the tour to Britain. He regained the captaincy for the England match and for Scotland's visit in 1982, but retired soon after this and returned to medicine.

Lochore, Sir Brian   Born Masterton, New Zealand, 3 September 1940. No. 8/lock, Wairarapa-Bush, New Zealand (1964-71), 25 caps (18 as captain). Test points: 6, tries: 2. A quiet farmer, he distinguished himself for Wairarapa-Bush against the Lions in 1959 and made his All Black debut at no. 8 against England and Scotland on the 1963/64 tour. He established himself against South Africa in 1965 and was appointed captain in 1966, suffering just three losses in 18 Tests. He led the unbeaten tourists to Britain and France in 1967. His two losing series coincided with his injuries – against Australia in 1968 he suffered a broken thumb in the first Test, and against South Africa in 1970 he missed the first five games through a hand injury – and he retired afterwards. He captained the President's XV against England to celebrate the centenary of the Rugby Union in 1971 and was dramatically called from retirement to play lock in the third Test against the Lions. Lochore became an All Black selector and national coach (1985-87), winning the first World Cup. He retired from rugby after winning the Bledisloe Cup 30-16. Honoured with the OBE, Sir Brian was knighted in 1999. Inducted into the International Rugby Hall of Fame in 1999.

Loe, Richard   Born Chevot, New Zealand, 6 April 1960. Prop, Waikato, New Zealand (1987-95), 49 caps. Test points: 25, tries: 6. Test debut against Italy in May 1987. He played in the 1987, 1991 and 1995 World Cups, an immense physical presence, who derived his strength from working on the land and notably applied it in the maul. Loe first joined the New Zealand squad in France in 1986, finally making his bow in 1987 against Italy and Argentina in the World Cup. In 1988 he became established, playing five Tests against Australia, Wales, and formed a daunting front row with Steve McDowell and Sean Fitzpatrick (in fact they were unbeaten until losing the third Test against Australia in 1990). Loe missed only the United States match in the 1991 World Cup, before losing the semi-final against Australia. The 1992 Bledisloe Cup was narrowly lost 2-1, but Loe broke Paul Carozza's nose with a late hit after the winger scored in the corner. Later that season he was suspended for six months for eye gouging and missed the 1993 Lions matches. In 1994 he played six Tests against Australia and South Africa and came on in the 1995 World Cup final against South Africa. He played his final game in November of that year in a 37-12 win in Paris.

Lomu, Jonah   Born Pukehoe, Auckland, New Zealand, 12 May 1975. Wing, Wellington, New Zealand (1994-2002), 63 caps. Test points: 185, tries: 37. Test debut against France at Christchurch in June 1994. His 15 World Cup tries, and a haul of eight at the 1999 tournament, when he scored in five consecutive games, are World Cup records. At the 1995 World Cup he became the first All Black since 1905 to score four tries in a Test match against England. The youngest-ever All Black Test match player and the youngest player in the world to score ten Test match tries, he became in 1995 the first player in the world to score 12 Test match tries in a calendar year. Lomu dominated rugby both on and off the field after the game turned professional, becoming the game's first truly global star. After the highs of 1995, the following year saw his career hampered by injury and, more seriously, illness. At the end of that year he was diagnosed as having a rare and serious kidney disorder, nephrotic syndrome. After a long fight, Lomu returned to rugby and was back in the All Black side for the tour of the UK at the end of 1997. Despite the All Blacks crashing out at the semi-final stage of the World Cup in 1999, Lomu was still one of the stars of the tournament.

Lynagh, Michael   Born Brisbane, Australia, 25 October 1963. Fly half, Australia (1984-95), 72 caps (15 as captain). Test points: 911, tries: 117, penalties: 177, conversions: 140, drop goals: 9. Test debut against Fiji (Suva) in June 1984, winning 16-3. Lynagh was one-third of the so-called 'Holy Trinity' of Australia's back division in the 1980s and 1990s, a formidable line-up that also included David Campese and Nick Farr-Jones. During his 11-year career, 'Noddy' was also the heaviest scorer in world rugby,

amassing a mighty 911pts in 72 Tests at a rate of almost 13pts per game. He played his last game against England in the 1995 World Cup, losing 25-22. Inducted into the International Rugby Hall of Fame in 1995.

MacLagan, Bill   Born 1858. Educated at the Edinburgh Academy (1869-75). He represented Scotland in 26 international matches between 1878 and 1890, playing as captain in eight of them. A stockbroker, he moved to London in 1880 and played a prominent part in the development of the London Scottish club (founded in 1878), both as player and office bearer. Bill MacLagan could be regarded as one of the main contributors to the development of Scottish rugby. At the start of his career, rugby union was in the process of turning from a 20-a-side game into a 15-a-side game. In the 20-a-side version, teams played with two full-backs instead of one. In 1878, with Ireland the opposition, MacLagan became only the second single full-back for Scotland. It was his first cap for his country. He would go on to score three tries and four conversions.

During an unbroken run as full-back for five internationals he again made rugby history when, against Ireland in 1881, he was joined by two team-mates to form the first-ever three-man three-quarter line in a rugby international. In 1891, even though he had retired from playing for Scotland, MacLagan took the opportunity to captain a British Isles team touring South Africa. The team enjoyed a remarkable record and won all 19 of their matches, scoring 224pts while conceding only 1pt. MacLagan played in all but one of these matches.

McBride, Willie John   Born Toomebridge, Co. Antrim, Northern Ireland, 6 June 1940. Lock, Ballymena, Ulster, Ireland (1962-77), 63 caps (12 as captain). Test points: 4, tries: 1. Test debut against England (Twickenham) in February 1962, losing 16-0. His final appearance came in March 1975 against Wales (Cardiff), losing 32-4. Inducted into the International Rugby Hall of Fame in 1997.

Marshall, Reverend Frank   A stocky, bearded man who smoked cigars while refereeing and handed them to the players afterwards. Marshall was appointed headmaster at Almondbury Grammar School near Huddersfield in 1878, treasurer of the Yorkshire Rugby Union in 1888, president in 1890 and its RFU representative, and he actively opposed players' payments and organised committee inquiries into any alleged breaches. As match attendances rose during a period of major industrial unrest, the pressure to pay players increased. After Marshall retired from the RFU, a proposal by the Yorkshire Union to allow 'broken time' payments – to be given to players to compensate for loss of earnings – was defeated at the RFU in 1893. Encouraged to continue his campaign, in 1894 the Huddersfield, Leeds, Salford and Wigan clubs were suspended. On 29 August 1895, a meeting held at the George Hotel, Huddersfield, formed the Northern Union (NU) of 21 clubs. By 1898 they had become nearly 100. Within ten years the number of RFU member clubs halved. English rugby union was greatly weakened and Wales took advantage. Marshall wrote *Football – The Rugby Game*, a history to 1892.

McLaren, Bill   Born Hawick, Scotland, 1923. From the relatively humble beginnings of a ten-minute slot during South of Scotland's match against the touring South Africans in Hawick, McLaren rose to exert an influence on the game as profound as that of any one of the great players whose exploits he so inimitably described.

It was always his ambition to play for Scotland and he was quickly immersed in the rugby culture of the Borders. A talented flanker, he soon made the Hawick first XV before World War II. He qualified as a physical education teacher in 1947 and played in a Scotland trial. On the verge of that elusive cap, he was struck down with tuberculosis. Despite the doctors' prediction of four years in hospital he was out within 19 months thanks to a new wonder drug.

While waiting for a teaching post, McLaren joined the *Hawick Express* in 1950, and during a nine-year spell there he fell into broadcasting and was invited by the BBC to attend a commentary audition. He was soon given his first full game – Glasgow against Edinburgh in 1952 – and began to perfect the research techniques and meticulous preparation that have been his hallmark and also at times his salvation.

His first international was at Lansdowne Road in 1953 when Ireland met France. In 1959 he transferred to television, the year he also landed his first teaching post. He taught for 40 years, combining his duties at Hawick High School and four local primary schools with commentating. McLaren's sense of duty to his pupils and his employers meant he never covered a British Isles tour. He retired 6 April 2002 after commentating on Scotland's 27-22 defeat of Wales. Inducted into the International Rugby Hall of Fame in 2001.

Meads, Colin Born Cambridge, New Zealand, 3 June 1936. Lock/forward, King Country, New Zealand (1957-71), 55 caps (4 as captain). Test points: 21, tries: 7. Test debut, aged 20, against Australia in May 1957. A 6ft 4ins (1.93m) raw, tough sheep farmer, from Te Kuite, somewhat dour, 'Pinetree' epitomised the All Blacks. He was once famously photographed carrying a sheep under each arm. An all-time great, outstanding line-out jumper and superb in open play, he often formed the New Zealand second row with his brother Stan. In his second Test he played on the wing, scoring a try. After a successful series against Australia in 1958, he missed the first 1959 Lions Test, but was recalled and scored a try in an 11-8 win. The series was won 3-1. In 1960 he toured South Africa, losing 2-1. South Africa visited in 1965 and were defeated 3-1. Meads played when the All Blacks soundly beat the 1966 British Lions 4-0, and scored in the second Test. On the UK tour in 1967, he was sent off against Scotland, only the second Test dismissal in history (the first was Cyril Brownlie of New Zealand, against England in 1925). Worse was to come for Meads; in 1968 in Sydney, with New Zealand leading 19-3, Ken Catchpole was trapped in a ruck over the ball. Meads hauled his leg sideways, and ended the Australian scrum half's career. On the 1970 South African tour Meads had his arm broken, missing the first two Tests after 31 consecutive internationals, and New Zealand lost their first series since 1960. He was captain against the 1971 British Lions, and was notably gracious in defeat. He became New Zealand's national selector and coach, but after coaching the 1986 New Zealand Cavaliers on the rebel tour of South Africa, he was sacked. Meads was later appointed New Zealand team manager. Inducted into the International Rugby Hall of Fame in 1997, he was named New Zealand Player of the Century in 1999.

Moore, Brian Born Birmingham, England, 11 January 1962. Hooker, Harlequins, England (1987-95), 64 caps. Test points: 4, tries: 1. Test debut against Scotland (Twickenham) in April 1987, winning 21-12. A passionate player who gave everything to the England cause. Moore was a member of the the the victorious 1989 Lions and the 1991 Grand Slam team. He was also a member of the 1991 World Cup final side. England's defeat by France in the 1995 World Cup third place play-off was his final appearance.

Morgan, Cliff Born Trebanog, Wales, 7 April 1930. Fly half, Cardiff, Wales (1951-58), 29 caps (4 as captain). Test points: 9, tries: 3. Test debut against Ireland in March 1951. A great player for Wales and the British Lions, Morgan is even better known as a rugby pundit and commentator, television personality and team captain on *A Question of Sport*, opposite Henry Cooper. Inducted into the International Rugby Hall of Fame in 1997.

Neary, Tony Born Manchester, England, 25 November 1948. Flanker, Broughton Park, England (1971-80), 43 caps (7 as captain). Test points: 19, tries: 5. British Lions (1977), 1 cap. Test debut against Wales (Cardiff) in January 1971, losing 22-6. The Broughton flanker was the one constant presence in the frequently changing England sides throughout most of the 1970s. He won one British Lions cap against New Zealand in 1977, and was a member of the 1980 Grand Slam-winning team. He played his last Test against Scotland in March 1980 in a 30-18 win for England.

Nepia, George Born Wairoa, New Zealand, 25 April 1905. Full-back, Hawkes Bay, East Coast, New Zealand (1924-30), 9 caps. Test points: 5, penalties: 1, conversions: 1. Test debut against Ireland in November 1924. A fearless tackler, superb runner and great kicker. A 19-year-old full-back on the 1924 'Invincibles' tour of Australia, Britain, Ireland, France and Canada, he played all 38 games, and the team was unbeaten. Nepia earned great praise for his rock-like defence. A bogus telegram caused his omission from the 1927 Maori tour of Britain, and his final series was in 1930 against the touring Lions. As a Maori, he was, shamefully, never selected to play against South Africa, and he described a Maori match against South Africa as 'more than just rugby. It was racial conflict'. Nepia was a dairy farmer, and played rugby league in England for Streatham and Mitcham for two seasons from 1935, and also for New Zealand. In 1950, when Olympians played Poverty Bay, the opposing full-backs and captains were George Nepia, the father and son. He later became a referee. Nepia finally visited South Africa in 1976 as guest of its Rugby Union. He died 27 August 1986. Inducted into the International Rugby Hall of Fame in 1997.

Obolensky, Prince Alexander Born St Petersburg, Russia, 17 February 1916. Wing, White Russia, Oxford University, Rosslyn Park, Barbarians, England (1936), 4 caps. Test points: 6, tries: 2. A speedy winger, he scored a memorable try in 1936 against New Zealand. England won 13-0, and newsreels showed his two tries, the second a now legendary solo run, cutting diagonally from the right wing to the left corner; it became Obolensky's match. He scored a world record 17 tries in a tour match against Brazil. He was killed on 29 March 1940 when his RAF Hurricane crashed in East Anglia, the first of 111 internationals to die in World War II.

O'Reilly, Tony Born Dublin, Ireland, 7 May 1936. Wing, Old Belvedere, Ireland (1955-70), 29 caps. Test points: 12, tries: 4. British Lions (1955-59), 10 caps. Test debut against France in January 1955. A dashing and stylish wing, red-haired and a crowd favourite. O'Reilly went on Lions tours to South Africa in 1955, aged 19, and Australia/New Zealand in 1959, where he became a local favourite. He was recalled to the Irish team in 1970 after an absence of eight years. After retiring from rugby he became one of Ireland's richest men: a highly successful businessman, he was chairman of Irish Dairy Produce Marketing Board and chief executive of Heinz Food Corporation. He later became the executive chairman of Independent News and Media in Ireland. Inducted into the International Rugby Hall of Fame in 1997.

Orr, Phil Born Dublin, Ireland, 14 December 1950. Prop, Old Wesley, Leinster, Ireland (1976-87), 58 caps (then world record for a prop). British Lions (1977), 1 cap. Test debut against France in February 1976. He played 49 consecutive international matches between 1976 and 1984, and went on four Ireland tours (another record) and two Lions tours (winning one cap against the All Blacks in 1977). He retired after Ireland's defeat by Australia in the 1987 World Cup quarter-final.

Osler, Bennie Born Rondenbosch, South Africa, 23 November 1901. Fly half, Western Province, South Africa (1924-33), 17 caps (5 as captain). Test points: 46, tries: 2, penalties: 4, conversions: 6, drop goals: 4. Test debut against Britain in August 1924. 'Mr King of Rugby' was a fly half who revolutionised the kicking game, when drop goals were worth 4pts – one more than a try. In 1928 he scored 14pts against the touring All Blacks – a world record until Okey Geffin in 1949 – in a record-breaking 17-0 defeat of New Zealand. He captained the 1931 tour of Britain, where his tactical kicking was heavily criticised, although it was very effective. The Springboks lost only one of 26 games – when Osler did not play. He lost the captaincy to Flip Nel for Australia's 1933 tour. However, Nel's injury after a victorious first Test enabled Osler to regain the job. In the second Test South Africa ran every ball, and lost. Osler lost the captaincy for the last time. He died in 1961.

Owen, Dicky Born Richard Owen, Llandore, Wales, 17 November 1876. Scrum half, Swansea, Wales (1901-12), 35 caps (3 as captain). Test points: 6, tries: 2. Test debut against Ireland in March 1901. 'The Little Wonder' won 35 caps, a record until beaten by Ken Jones in 1955, and six Championships including four Triple Crowns. Although tiny, just 5ft 2ins (1.57m) tall and about 9½st (60kg), he was a tough player and an innovator, the first scrum half to combine with his loose forwards in attack. He invented the reverse pass, most famously used against New Zealand in 1905 to produce Teddy Morgan's try in a 3-0 win. Probably the greatest scrum half of his time and a notable tactician, he was fearless at tackling or falling on to the ball. He was carried off shoulder-high after a superb performance as player and captain in his last game for Wales – aged 35 – against Scotland at Swansea in 1912.

Poidevin, Simon Born Goulburn, New South Wales, Australia, 31 October 1958. Flanker, Australia (1980-91), 59 caps (4 as captain). Test points: 24, tries: 6. Test debut against Fiji (Suva) in May 1980, winning 22-9. His final appearance came in the 1991 World Cup final against England (Twickenham), winning 12-6.

Porta, Hugo Born Buenos Aires, Argentina, 11 September 1951. Fly half, Banco Nacion, Argentina (1971-90), 57 caps (34 as captain). Test points: 529, tries: 10, penalties: 88, conversions: 78, drop goals: 25. Test debut against Chile (Montevideo) in October 1971, winning 20-3. Final appearance came in November 1990 against Scotland (Murrayfield), losing 49-3. Inducted into the International Rugby Hall of Fame in 1997.

Price, Graham Born Moascar, Egypt, 24 November 1951. Prop, Wales (1975-83), 41 caps. Test points: 8, tries: 2. Test debut against France (Paris) in January 1975, winning 25-10. His final appearance came on 16 July 1983 against France (Paris), losing 16-9.

Quinnell, Derek Born Llanelli, Wales, 22 May 1949. No. 8, Llanelli, Wales (1972-80), 23 caps. Test points: 4, tries: 1. Test debut against France in March 1972. Quinnell and his sons Scott and Craig have provided the only instance of a father and two sons playing for Wales. A third son, Gavin Quinnell, made his senior debut for the club in 2002. The three brothers are nephews of Barry John. Derek Quinnell joined Llanelli youth in 1964. He played for the Scarlets for 18 years, in 366 premier games, scoring 44 tries and captaining the club. He also played for and captained the Barbarians, and went on three British Lions tours. He is the only British player ever to have played in four winning teams against New Zealand – twice for the Lions (1971 and 1977) and for Llanelli and the Barbarians in 1972 and 1973.

Richards, Dean Born Nuneaton, England, 11 July 1963. No. 8, Leicester, England, 48 caps. Test points: 24, tries: 6. Following his international debut against Ireland in 1986, when he scored a brace of tries, he went on to become the most-capped no. 8 in world rugby and also made six Lions appearances. Richards was on the first official Lions tour of Australia in 1989, when the tourists won 11 of the 12 games they played. After retiring as a player, Richards continued in a coaching capacity and as director of rugby at Leicester Tigers he masterminded four successive English Premiership titles, and coached his side to their first-ever Heineken European Cup win in Paris, in May 2001, by beating Stade Français in the final in Paris. The following year Richards was at the helm as the Midlands club made history by successfully defending their European title, beating Munster in Cardiff.

Ripley, Andrew Born Liverpool, England, 1 December 1947. No. 8, Rosslyn Park, England (1972-76), 24 caps. Test points: 8, tries: 2. Test debut against Wales (Twickenham) losing 12-3 January 1972. Ripley was a larger-than-life character who in the 1970s brought skill and excitement to England sides that were otherwise dull and unimaginative. The Rosslyn Park no. 8 played 24 Tests for England between 1972 and 1976 before being dumped unceremoniously by the selection committee during the whitewash of that year. Upon his introduction to the England set-up, Ripley formed an excellent understanding with flanker Tony Neary and their intricate combinations were the highlight of many an England performance. Like the Broughton Park player, Ripley was an excellent ball handler and even scored the winning try against Wales in 1974, England's sole triumph over the red dragon during the 1970s. He also touched down in England's 20-3 win over Australia in 1973, the third leg of a clean sweep of victories for England over the southern hemisphere nations in the space of 16 months. Unlike the understated and clean-cut Neary, Ripley was a consummate extrovert at a time when English rugby players had a distinctly low profile. Ripley toured with the Lions in 1974, but was kept out of the Test side by Davies. At the end of his England career he was the mastermind behind the Barbarians' historic victory in the 1981 Hong Kong Sevens and led Rosslyn Park to two cup finals. A fitness fanatic and superb athlete, he made frequent appearances on the BBC *Superstars* programme and was victorious in the 1980 competition. Later on he channelled his energies into rowing and in 1997 came close to earning a Blue for Cambridge University at the age of 49.

Rives, Jean-Pierre   Born Toulouse, France, 31 December 1952. Flanker, France (1975-84), 59 caps (34 as captain). Test points: 20, tries: 5. Test debut against England (Twickenham) in February 1975, winning 27-20. His final appearance was on 17 March 1984 against Scotland (Murrayfield) in a 21-12 loss. Inducted into the International Rugby Hall of Fame in 1997.

Salmon, Jamie   Born Hong Kong, 16 October 1959. Centre, Wellington, Harlequins, New Zealand (1981), 3 caps, England (1985-87), 12 caps. Test points (New Zealand): 4, tries: 1. Test points (England): 4, tries: 1. Test debut for New Zealand against Romania in October 1981 and for England against New Zealand (Christchurch) in June 1985, losing 18-13. Salmon had the distinction of being a dual international, appearing for both New Zealand and England between 1981 and 1987. He first appeared for the All Blacks on their 1981 European tour in a victory in Bucharest, and also played in both Tests of their 2-0 series victory against France. When Salmon next took the field in an international four years later it was against the All Blacks, now wearing the white shirt of England.

Sella, Philippe   Born Tonneins, France, 4 February 1962. Centre/wing, 111 caps (4 as captain). Test points: 125, tries: 30. Sella made his international debut on 31 October 1982 v Romania (in Bucharest) and lost 13-9. His final Test appearance was on 22 June 1995 v England (in Pretoria), winning 19-9 to claim third place in the World Cup. He was the first player to gain 100 caps and his final tally of 111 caps (gained between 1982 and 1995) remained a record until Jason Leonard beat it during the World Cup campaign of 2003. Of those 111 matches Sella won 72, drew 5 and lost 34. After his international career was over he went on to join a stable of world-class talent at big-spending English club Saracens, earning instant cult status for his wholehearted approach and helping to steer the team to victory over Wasps in the showpiece Tetley Bitter Cup Final at Twickenham in 1997 – his last competitive match. Perhaps former French coach Jacques Fouroux said it best when he described Sella as having, 'the strength of a bull but the touch of a piano player'.

Slattery, Fergus   Born Dún Laoghaire, Ireland, 12 March 1949. Flanker, Ireland (1970-84), 61 caps (17 as captain). Test points: 12, tries: 3. Test debut against South Africa (Dublin) in January 1970, an 8-8 draw. Ireland and British Lions legend, Slattery played with an intensity and level of professionalism that would not have looked out of place in the

modern era, keeping up a remarkable level of performance for 14 years. His 61 caps made him the most-capped flanker of all time on his retirement.

Sole, David   Born Aylesbury, Buckinghamshire, England, 8 May 1962. Prop, Edinburgh, Scotland (1986-92), 44 caps (25 as captain). Test points: 12, tries: 3. Test debut against France (Murrayfield) In January 1986, winning 18-17. Edinburgh prop David Sole has entered Scottish rugby folklore as one of his country's best captains and the man who wrested the Grand Slam from England in 1990, leading the now famous slow march on to the pitch, for the deciding match with the Auld Enemy. Aside from his habitual headband, the trademarks of Sole's game were his superb handling ability and tenacity in the loose.

Teague, Mike   Born Gloucester, England, 8 October 1960. Flanker, Gloucester, England (1985-93), 27 caps. Test points: 12, tries: 3. British Lions (1989-93), 3 caps. Test debut against France (Twickenham) in February 1985 in a 9-9 draw. Of Teague's three British Lions caps, two came in 1989 against Australia and one in 1993 against New Zealand. Against Australia he played in both of the Lions' 1989 Test victories, and was Player of the Series. On 19 January 1991 he scored the only try of England's 25-6 win against Wales in Cardiff (the first win in Cardiff for 28 years). He was also a member of that year's Grand Slam team, and was a World Cup finalist.

Thomas, Delme   Born Bancyfelin, Carmarthenshire, Wales, 12 September 1942. Prop, Wales (1966-74), 25 caps (1 as captain). Test debut against Australia (Cardiff) in December 1966, losing 14-11. In 1966 (aged 23) during the British Lions tour to New Zealand, he was selected before having been capped by Wales, and was promoted to the Test team ahead of captain Mike Campbell-Lamerton for the first two Tests. He moved from lock to prop for the third Test so that the skipper could play. He was a member of the 1971 Grand Slam team.

Underwood, Rory   Born Middlesbrough, England, 19 June 1963. Wing, Leicester, England (1984-96), 85 caps. Test points: 210, tries: 49. Test debut against Ireland (Twickenham) in February 1984, winning 12-9. An RAF flight-lieutenant, Rory Underwood played his rugby with all the speed and skill associated with his day job. He burst on to the international scene in 1984 and would remain as England's premier winger for the next 12 seasons. Such longevity enabled him to gain the honour of becoming the first man to play 50 times for England, a milestone reached in the epic 1991 World Cup semi-final against Scotland. Blessed with searing pace and capable of scoring spectacular tries, he was equally at home on either the right or left wing. A darling of the Leicester crowds, Underwood scored his first international try in only his second game – an opportunist try in which he displayed the exhilarating turn of pace which would become his hallmark. In November 1992 in a 33-16 win against South Africa at Twickenham, he and Tony Underwood became the first brothers to play together for England for 55 years. Rory played his last game against Ireland in March 1996 in a 28-15 victory. On his retirement he was the all-time most-capped Englishman and most-capped wing, the second-highest try scorer in international rugby (49 tries), and he had the most Five Nations appearances (50) and tries (18). He was awarded the MBE in 1992.

Ward, Tony Born Dublin, Ireland, 8 October 1954. Fly half, Ireland (1978-87), 19 caps. Test points: 113, penalties: 29, conversions: 7, drop goals: 4. Test debut against Scotland (Dublin) in January 1978, winning 12-9. In 1978 he kicked two drop goals and a conversion as Munster became the first Irish side to beat the All-Blacks in Ireland (12-0). His final appearance came in June 1987 when Ireland beat Tonga 32-9 in the World Cup.

Webb, Jonathan Born London, England, 24 August 1963. Full-back, Bristol and England (1987-93), 33 caps. Test points: 296, tries: 4, penalties: 66, conversions: 41. Test debut against Australia (Sydney) in the 1987 World Cup, losing 19-6. England were perhaps lucky in that their resurgence in the late 1980s coincided with the presence of two excellent kicking full-backs – Simon Hodgkinson and Jonathan Webb. The two were both medical men, but had different qualities on the field. Hodgkinson was the slightly more reliable with the boot while Webb was more threatening with ball in hand.

Wilkinson, Jonny Born Frimley, Surrey, England, 25 May 1979. Fly half/centre, Newcastle and England (1998-), 52 caps (1 as captain) (to end 2003). Test points: 817, tries: 5, penalties: 161, conversions: 123, drop goals: 21. Test debut against Ireland (Twickenham) in April 1998, winning 35-17. The Newcastle Falcons fly half is the only player in Test rugby to average over 15pts a game. The highlight of his career to the end 2003 was his drop goal in the dying seconds of extra time in the final of the 2003 World Cup that gave England a 20-17 victory over Australia. Predictably, he was crowned BBC Television Sports Personality of the Year the following month. Wilkinson's success rate of kicking between the posts is phenomenal and unequalled in rugby (90 per cent success in 2003). Subsequent to the World Cup final, Jonny was diagnosed as having played the match with a broken bone in his neck.

Williams, Bryan Born Auckland, New Zealand, 3 October 1950. Wing, Auckland, New Zealand (1970-78), 38 caps. Test points: 71, tries: 10, penalties: 9, conversions: 2, drop goals: 1. Test debut against South Africa in July 1970. The first Polynesian All Black, he retired as New Zealand's most-capped wing. He created a sensation touring South Africa as a 19-year-old law student in 1970, and scored a try on his debut, a 17-6 defeat. He went on to score 14 tries and 6 goals in 13 tour matches. Of the next 31 Tests he missed only the third Test against the 1971 Lions, because of injury. He toured Europe in 1972/73, Australia in 1974 and South Africa in 1976. In 1977 the Lions were beaten 3-1. Williams played the first Test in France later that year, before suffering a serious hip injury. In 1978 the touring All Blacks beat the four home nations, and he won his final cap against Scotland, retiring from internationals at the age of 28. He coached Auckland and later Western Samoa in the 1991 World Cup.

Williams, Chester Born Paarl, South Africa, 8 August 1970. Wing, Western Province, Golden Lions, South Africa (1993-2000), 27 caps. Test points: 70, tries: 14. Test debut against Argentina (Buenos Aires) in November 1993, winning 52-23. 'The Black Pearl' was a wing of searing pace and finishing ability that brought him 13 tries in his first 16 Tests, while his superb tackling made him a key player for Western Province in the Currie Cup and South Africa's World Cup campaign of 1995. He became

the first non-white player to don a Springbok shirt since Errol Tobias in the early 1980s. A year later he played in the 1-1 draw with England, but injury meant that he was dropped from the 1995 World Cup squad, only to be dramatically recalled at the last-minute.

This incident fuelled speculation that Chester was merely a token black player in South Africa's effort to present a united front to the world. However, his four tries against the ultra-physical Western Samoans in the quarter-finals proved beyond doubt that he was no passenger. Injuries prevented him from reaching his full potential and after retiring he went on to become a coach, leading the South African Sevens squad to bronze at the 2002 Commonwealth Games and a runners-up place in the World Sevens Championship. Then, prior to the Springboks' tour of the UK and Europe in autumn 2002, Williams released a controversial autobiography which provided his own perspective on his status within South African rugby, particularly at the time of the 1995 World Cup.

Williams, J.J. Born Nantyffyllon, Wales, 1 April 1948. Wing, Wales (1973-79), 30 caps. Test points: 48, tries: 12. Test debut against France (Paris) in March 1973, losing 12-3. His final appearance came on 17 March 1979 against England (Cardiff) in a 27-3 win.

Williams, J.P.R. Born John Peter Rhys Williams, Bridgend, Wales, 2 March 1949, Full-back, Bridgend, London Welsh, Wales (1969-81), 55 caps (5 as captain). Test points: 36, tries: 6, penalties: 3, conversions: 2. Test debut against Scotland (Murrayfield) in March 1969, winning 17-3. Educated at Bridgend County School, Millfield School and St Mary's Hospital. In 1966 he won the Wimbledon Junior Championships and in 1968 qualified for the British Tennis Open. Williams switched to rugby and played for Bridgend and London Welsh. He was a very competitive and committed player who made his last Test appearance at Cardiff Arms Park, 7 February 1981, equalling the then world record of 54 appearances for a full-back (his total of 55 games included one as flanker). Williams was awarded the MBE in 1977 for his services to rugby. Inducted into the International Rugby Hall of Fame in 1997.

Wilson, Jeff Born Invercargill, New Zealand, 24 October 1973. Wing, New Zealand (1993-2001), 60 caps. Test points: 234, tries: 44, penalties: 3, conversions: 1, drop goals: 1. Test debut against Scotland (Murrayfield) in November 1993, winning 51-15. Jeff 'Goldie' Wilson is one of the most gifted all-round sportsmen that New Zealand has produced, and it is likely that he would have excelled in whatever discipline he chose to specialise. Wilson had already represented New Zealand in one-day cricket internationals before he made his debut for the All Blacks in 1993, and it was a sport to which he would later return.

Windsor, Bobby Born Newport, Wales, 31 January 1946. Hooker, Wales (1973-79), 28 caps. Test points: 4, tries: 1. Test debut against Australia (Cardiff) in November 1973, winning 24-0. Bobby 'the Duke' Windsor was part of the legendary Pontypool front row, immortalised in a song by Max Boyce. He began his career as a full-back and outside half but would move into the front row, winning 28 caps for his country.

Winterbottom, Peter Born Horsforth, Yorkshire, England, 31 May 1960. Flanker, Harlequins, England (1982-93), 58 caps. Test points: 13, tries: 3. British Lions (1983 and 1993), 4 caps. Test debut against

Australia (Twickenham) in January 1982, winning 15-11. Peter Winterbottom was the second player, after Rory Underwood, to reach 50 caps for his country. He was a member of the 1991 and 1992 Grand Slam teams, and won British Lions caps in 1983 (1) and on the 1993 tour to New Zealand (3).

Woodward, Sir Clive   Born Ely, Cambridgeshire, England, 6 January 1956. Centre, Leicester, England (1980-84), 21 caps. Test points: 16, tries: 4. British Lions (1980-83), 2 caps. Test debut

against Ireland (Twickenham) in January 1980, winning 24-9. Woodward was a member of the 1980 Grand Slam team, playing in all four games, having made his debut as a replacement in the first game against Ireland. He won his two British Lions caps in 1980 against South Africa. He became England coach in 1997, winning the Six Nations Grand Slam in 2003. Later that year his England team won the World Cup in Australia. He was knighted for his achievements.

SAILING

King Charles II is often considered to have been the father of British sailing. In 1662 there was a record of the first race between the King and the Duke of York, Charles winning over a course from Greenwich to Gravesend and back for the sum of £100. The first sailing club to be formed in the British Isles, and indeed the world, was the Royal Cork Club in 1720. In 1815, the Yacht Club was formed at the Thatched House Tavern, St James's Street, London, and this club became the Royal Yacht Squadron.

In 1851 a silver cup worth 100 guineas was presented by the Royal Yacht Squadron for an eastward race around the Isle of Wight between the schooner *America* and 15 British yachts. The Hundred Guineas Cup, as it was originally called, soon became the America's Cup. In 1945 the first Sydney to Hobart race was launched with Captain J.H. Illingworth skippering *Rani*. In 1957 the first Admiral's Cup was raced for and won by Great Britain.

The sport was alternatively known as yachting (derived from the Dutch *yaghten*, meaning to hunt) until 2000, when its name was officially changed for competitions. When sailing first became an Olympic sport in 1900, the boats really were yachts, i.e. large boats with as many as ten crew members. Over the years, the large yachts were gradually replaced by smaller, one-design sailboats that put the premium on the skill of the sailors rather than the inherent speed of the vessel.

Results were determined by a series of seven races from 1936 to 1988. In 1992, the Soling class had six round-robin races leading up to match races based on the round-robin standings, and sailboarding had a series of ten races. All classes except Soling went to an 11-race series in 1996. The Soling competition consisted of ten round-robin races that year. In 2000, there were 16 races for the new 49er class.

At the 2000 Olympics Britain was very successful, winning gold medals in the Europe Dinghy class with Shirley Robertson, the Laser class with Ben Ainslie and the Finn class with Ian Percy.

Two different points systems have been used. In the simplest system, each boat is given points equivalent to its placing in a race; that is, one point for first place, two points for second, and so forth. Between 1968 and 1992, negative points were awarded, based on the following scale: first place, 0; second, 3; third, 5.7; fourth, 8; fifth, 10; sixth, 11.7; seventh, 13. One point was added for each subsequent place below seventh.

The sport was traditionally one of few to have no sex discrimination, but in 1988, separate men's and women's competitions were added in some events, while others remain open to either sex.

Olympic Medallists

Men's Boardsailing

	Gold	Silver	Bronze
1984	Stephan van den Berg (NED)	Randall Scott Steele (USA)	Bruce Kendall (NZL)
1988	Bruce Kendall (NZL)	Jan Boersma (AHO)	Michael Gebhardt (USA)
1992	Franck David (FRA)	Michael Gebhardt (USA)	Lars Kleppich (AUS)
1996	Nikolaos Kaklamanakis (GRE)	Carlos Espinola (ARG)	Gal Fridman (ISR)
2000	Christoph Sieber (AUT)	Carlos Espinola (ARG)	Aaron McIntosh (NZL)

Men's Finn
(mixed prior to 1988)

	Gold	Silver	Bronze
1952	Paul Elvstrøm (DEN)	Charles Currey (GBR)	Richard Sarby (SWE)
1956	Paul Elvstrøm (DEN)	André Nelis (BEL)	John Marvin (USA)
1960	Paul Elvstrøm (DEN)	Aleksandr Tšutšelov (URS)	André Nelis (BEL)
1964	Wilhelm Kuhweide (GER)	Peter Barrett (USA)	Henning Wind (DEN)
1968	Valentin Mankin (URS)	Hubert Raudaschl (AUT)	Fabio Albarelli (ITA)
1972	Serge Maury (FRA)	Ilias Chatzipavlis (GRE)	Viktor Potapov (URS)
1976	Jochen Schümann (GDR)	Andrey Balashov (URS)	John E. Bertrand (AUS)
1980	Esko Rechardt (FIN)	Wolfgang Mayrhofer (AUT)	Andrey Balashov (URS)
1984	Russell Coutts (NZL)	John E. Bertrand (USA)	Terry Neilson (CAN)
1988	José Luis Doreste (ESP)	Peter Holmberg (ISV)	John Cutler (NZL)
1992	José María van der Ploeg (ESP)	Brian Ledbetter (USA)	Craig Monk (NZL)
1996	Mateusz Kusznierewicz (POL)	Sébastien Godefroid (BEL)	Roy Heiner (NED)
2000	Iain Percy (GBR)	Luca Devoti (ITA)	Fredrik Lööf (SWE)

Men's 470
(mixed prior to 1988)

	Gold	Silver	Bronze
1976	Frank Hübner/ Harro Bode (FRG)	Antonio Gorostegui/ Pedro Millet (ESP)	Ian Brown/Ian Ruff (AUS)
1980	Marcos Rizzo/ Eduardo Penido (BRA)	Jörn Borowski/ Egbert Swensson (GDR)	Jouko Lindgren/Georg Tallberg (FIN)
1984	Luis Doreste/Roberto Molina (ESP)	Stephan Benjamin/ Christopher Steinfeld (USA)	Thierry Peponnet/Luc Pillot (FRA)
1988	Thierry Peponnet/Luc Pillot (FRA)	Tõnu Tõniste/ Toomas Tõniste (URS)	John Shadden/Charlie McKee (USA)
1992	Jordi Calafat/Francisco Sánchez (ESP)	Morgan Reeser/ Kevin Burnham (USA)	Tõnu Tõniste/Toomas Tõniste (EST)
1996	Yevgeniy Braslavets/ Igor Matviyenko (UKR)	John Merricks/Ian Walker (GBR)	Vitor Rocha/Nuño Barreto (POR)
2000	Tom King/Mark Turnbull (AUS)	Paul Foerster/ Robert Merrick (USA)	Javier Conte/Juan de la Fuente (ARG)

Women's Boardsailing
(Lechner Division II 1992, Mistral 1996/2000)

	Gold	Silver	Bronze
1992	Barbara Kendall (NZL)	Zhang Xiaodong (CHN)	Dorien de Vries (NED)
1996	Lee Lai-Shan (HKG)	Barbara Kendall (NZL)	Alessandra Sensini (ITA)
2000	Alessandra Sensini (ITA)	Amelie Lux (GER)	Barbara Kendall (NZL)

Women's Europe

	Gold	Silver	Bronze
1992	Linda Andersen (NOR)	Natalia Vía Dufresne (ESP)	Julia Trotman (USA)
1996	Kristine Roug (DEN)	Margriet Matthijsse (NED)	Courtney Becker-Dey (USA)
2000	Shirley Robertson (GBR)	Margriet Matthijsse (NED)	Serena Amato (ARG)

Women's 470

	Gold	Silver	Bronze
1988	Allison Jolly/Lynne Jewell (USA)	Marit Söderström/ Brigitta Bengtsson (SWE)	Larisa Moskalenko/ Irina Chunikhovskaya (URS)
1992	Theresa Zabell/Patricia Guerra (ESP)	Leslie Egnot/Jan Shearer (NZL)	Jennifer 'JJ' Isler/Pamela Healy (USA)
1996	Theresa Zabell/ Begoña Vía Dufresne (ESP)	Yumiko Shige/Alicia Kinoshita (JPN)	Ruslana Taran/ Yelena Pakholchik (UKR)
2000	Jenny Armstrong/Belinda Stowell (AUS)	Jennifer 'JJ' Isler/ Sarah Glaser (USA)	Ruslana Taran/ Yelena Pakholchik (UKR)

Laser

	Gold	Silver	Bronze
1996	Robert Scheidt (BRA)	Ben Ainslie (GBR)	Peer Moberg (NOR)
2000	Ben Ainslie (GBR)	Robert Scheidt (BRA)	Michael Blackburn (AUS)

Star

	Gold	Silver	Bronze
1932	Gilbert Gray/Andrew Libano (USA)	Colin Ratsey/Peter Jaffe (GBR)	Gunnar Asther/ Daniel Sundén-Cullberg (SWE)
1936	Peter Bischoff/Hans-Joachim Weise (GER)	Arvid Laurin/Uno Wallentin (SWE)	Willem de Vries-Lentsch/ Adriaan Maas (NED)
1948	Hilary Smart/Paul Smart (GBR)	Carlos De Cárdenas snr/ Carlos De Cárdenas jnr (CUB)	Adriaan Maas/ Edward Stutterheim (NED)
1952	Agostino Straulino/Nicolo Rode (ITA)	John Reid/John Price (USA)	Joaquim De Mascarenhas/ Francisco Rebelo (POR)
1956	Herbert Williams/Lawrence Low (USA)	Agostino Straulino/ Nicolo Rode (ITA)	Durward Knowles/ Sloan Farrington (BAH)
1960	Timir Pinegin/Fyodor Shutkov (URS)	José Quina/Mário Quina (POR)	William Parks/Robert Halperin (USA)
1964	Durward Knowles/Cecil Cooke (BAH)	Richard Stearns/ Lynn Williams (USA)	Pelle Pettersson/ Holger Sundström (SWE)

1968	Lowell North/Peter Barrett (USA)	Peder Lunde/ Per Olav Wiken (NOR)	Franco Cavallo/Camillo Gargano (ITA)
1972	David Forbes/John Anderson (AUS)	Pelle Pettersson/ Stellan Westerdahl (SWE)	Wilhelm Kuhweide/ Karsten Meyer (FRG)
1976	not held		
1980	Valentin Mankin/ Aleksandr Muzicenko (URS)	Hubert Raudaschl/Karl Ferstl (AUT)	Giorgio Gorla/Alfio Peraboni (ITA)
1984	William Buchan snr/ Stephen Erickson (USA)	Joachim Griese/ Michael Marcour (FRG)	Giorgio Gorla/ Alfio Peraboni (ITA)
1988	Michael McIntyre/Bryn Vaile (GBR)	Mark Reynolds/Hal Haenel (USA)	Torben Grael/Nelson Falcão (BRA)
1992	Mark Reynolds/Hal Haenel (USA)	Rod Davies/Donald Cowie (NZL)	Ross MacDonald/Eric Jespersen (CAN)
1996	Marcelo Ferreira/Torben Grael (BRA)	Bobbie Lohse/Hans Wallen (SWE)	Colin Beashel/David Giles (AUS)
2000	Mark Reynolds/Magnus Liljedahl (USA)	Ian Walker/Mark Covell (GBR)	Marcelo Ferreira/Torben Grael (BRA)

Tornado

	Gold	Silver	Bronze
1976	Reg White/John Osborn (GBR)	David McFaull/ Michael Rothwell (USA)	Jörg Spengler/Jörg Schmall (FRG)
1980	Alexandre Welter/ Lars Sigurd Björkström (BRA)	Peter Due/Per Kjergard (DEN)	Göran Marström/ Jörgen Ragnarsson (SWE)
1984	Rex Sellers/Christopher Timms (NZL)	Randy Smyth/Jay Glaser (USA)	Chris Cairns/John Anderson (AUS)
1988	Jean-Yves Le Déroff/ Nicolas Hénard (FRA)	Rex Sellers/ Christopher Timms (NZL)	Lars Grael/ Clinlo Freitas (BRA)
1992	Yves Loday/Nicolas Hénard (FRA)	Randy Smyth/Keith Notary (USA)	Mitch Booth/John Forbes (AUS)
1996	José Luis Ballester/ Fernando León Boissier (ESP)	Mitch Booth/ Andrew Landenberger (AUS)	Lars Grael/ Henrique Kiko Pellicano (BRA)
2000	Roman Hagara/ Hans Peter Steinacher (AUT)	John Forbes/ Darren Bundock (AUS)	Roland Gäbler/René Schwall (GER)

49er

	Gold	Silver	Bronze
2000	Jyrki Järvi/Thomas Johanson (FIN)	Ian Barker/Simon Hiscocks (GBR)	Jonathan McKee/Charlie McKee (USA)

Soling

	Gold	Silver	Bronze
1972	Harry Melges/William Bentsen/ William Allen (USA)	Stig Wennerström/ Lennart Roslund/Bo Knape/ Stefan Krook (SWE)	David Miller/John Ekels/ Paul Cote (CAN)
1976	Poul Jensen/Valdemar Bandolowski/ Erik Hansen (DEN)	John Kolius/Walter Glasgow/ Richard Hoepfner (USA)	Dieter Below/Michael Zachries/ Olaf Engelhard (GDR)
1980	Poul Jensen/Valdemar Bandolowski/ Erik Hansen (DEN)	Boris Budnikov/Aleksandr Budnikov/ Nikolay Pohyakov (URS)	Anastasios Boudouris/ Anastasios Gavrilis/ Aristidis Rapanakis (GRE)
1984	Robert Haines/Edward Trevelyan/ Roderick Davis (USA)	Torben Grael/Daniel Adler/ Ronaldo Senfft (BRA)	Hans Marius Fogh/John Kerr/ Steve Calder (CAN)
1988	Jochen Schümann/Thomas Flach/ Bernd Jäkel (GDR)	John Kostecki/William Baylis/ Robert Billingham (USA)	Jesper Bank/Jan Dupont Mathiasen/ Steen Secher (DEN)
1992	Jesper Bank/Steen Secher/ Jesper Seier (DEN)	Kevin Mahaney/James Brady/ Doug Kern (USA)	Lawrie Smith/Robert Cruikshank/ Simon Stewart (GBR)
1996	Jochen Schümann/Thomas Flach/ Bernd Jäkel (GER)	Georgiy Shayduko/ Dmitriy Shabanov/ Igor Skalin (RUS)	Jeff Madrigali/Jim Barton/ Kent Massey (USA)
2000	Jesper Bank/Henrik Blakskjær/ Thomas Jacobsen (DEN)	Jochen Schümann/Gunnar Bahr/ Ingo Borkowski (GER)	Herman Horn Johannessen/ Paul Davis/Espen Stokkeland (NOR)

Discontinued Events
Firefly 1948

	Gold	Silver	Bronze
1924	Léon Huybrechts (BEL)	Henrik Robert (NOR)	Hans Dittmar (FIN)
1928	Sven Thorell (SWE)	Henrik Robert (NOR)	Bertil Broman (FIN)
1932	Jacques Lebrun (FRA)	Adriaan Maas (NED)	Santiago Amat Cansino (ESP)
1936	Daniel Kagchelland (NED)	Werner Krogmann (GER)	Peter Scott (GBR)
1948	Paul Elvstrøm (DEN)	Ralph Evans (USA)	Jacobus de Jong (NED)

Two-Handed Centreboard Dinghy – 12 Feet

	Gold	Silver	Bronze
1920	Johannes Hin/Franciscus Hin (NED)	Arnoud Van Der Biesen/ Petrus Beukers (NED)	——

Two-Handed Centreboard Dinghy – 18 Feet

	Gold
1920	Francis Richards/Tom Hedberg (GBR)

12 Square Metre

	Gold	Silver	Bronze
1956	Peter Mander/John Cropp (NZL)	Roland Tasker/John Scott (AUS)	Jasper Blackall/Terence Smith (GBR)

Flying Dutchman

	Gold	Silver	Bronze
1960	Peder Lunde/Bjørn Bergvall (NOR)	Hans Fogh/Ole Erik Petersen (DEN)	Rolf Mulka/Ingo Von Bredow/ Achim Kadelbach (GER)
1964	Helmer Pedersen/Earle Wells (NZL)	Franklyn Musto/ Arthur Morgan (GBR)	Harry Melges/ William Bentsen (USA)
1968	Rodney Pattison/ Iain Macdonald-Smith (GBR)	Ullrich Libor/ Peter Naumann (FRG)	Reinaldo Conrad/ Burkhard Cordes (BRA)
1972	Rodney Pattison/ Christopher Davies (GBR)	Yves Pajot/Marc Pajot (FRA)	Ullrich Libor/Peter Naumann (FRG)
1976	Jörg Diesch/Eckart Diesch (FRG)	Rodney Pattison/Julian Brooke Haughton (GBR)	Reinaldo Conrad/ Peter Eicker (BRA)
1980	Alesandro Abascal/ Miguel Noguer (ESP)	David Wilkins/ James Wilkinson (IRL)	Szabolcs Detre/ Zsolt Detre (HUN)
1984	Jonathan McKee/ William Buchan jnr (USA)	Terry McLaughlin/ Evert Bastet (CAN)	Jonathan Richards/ Peter Allam (GBR)
1988	Jørgen Bojsen Møller/ Christian Grønborg (DEN)	Ole Petter Pollen/ Erik Bjorkum (NOR)	Frank McLaughlin/ John Millen (CAN)
1992	Luis Doreste/Domingo Manrique (ESP)	Paul Foerster/ Stephen Bourdow (USA)	Jørgen Bojsen Møller/ Jens Bojsen Møller (DEN)

Swallow

	Gold	Silver	Bronze
1948	Stewart Morris/David Bond (GBR)	Duarte de Almeida/ Fernando Pinto Coelho (POR)	Lockwood Pine/Owen Torry (USA)

Tempest

	Gold	Silver	Bronze
1972	Valentin Mankin/Vitaliy Dyrdyra (URS)	Alan Warren/David Hunt (GBR)	Glen Foster/Peter Dean (USA)
1976	John Albrechtson/Ingvar Hansson (SWE)	Valentin Mankin/Vladislav Akimenko (URS)	Dennis Conner/Conn Findlay (USA)

Dragon

Gold	Silver	Bronze
1948	Thor Thorvaldsen/Sigve Lie/ Håkon Barfod (NOR)	Folke Bohlin/Hugo Jonsson/ Gösta Brodin (SWE)	William Berntsen/Ole Berntsen/ Klaus Baess (DEN)
1952	Thor Thorvaldsen/Sigve Lie/ Håkon Barfod (NOR)	Per Gedda/Sidney Boldt-Christmas/ Erland Almkvist (SWE)	Theodor Thomsen/Erich Natusch/ Georg Nowka (GER)
1956	Folke Bohlin/Bengt Palmquist/ Leif Wikström (SWE)	Ole Berntsen/Cyril Andresen/ Christian von Bülow (DEN)	Graham Mann/Ronald Backus/ Jonathan Janson (GBR)
1960	Crown Prince Constantin/ Odysseus Eskitzoglou/ Georgios Zaimis (GRE)	Jorge Salas Chávez/ Héctor Calegaris/ Jorge del Río (ARG)	Antonio Cosentino/ Antonio Ciciliano/ Giulio De Stefano (ITA)
1964	Ole Berntsen/Christian von Bülow/ Ole Poulsen (DEN)	Peter Ahrendt/Ulrich Mense/ Wilfried Lorenz (GER)	Lowell North/Charles Rogers/ Richard Deaver (USA)
1968	Shelby Friedrichs/Barton Jahncke/ Gerald Schreck (USA)	Aage Birch/Paul Høj Jensen/ Niels Markussen (DEN)	Paul Borowski/Karl-Heinz Thun/ Konrad Weichert (GDR)
1972	John Cuneo/Thomas Anderson/ John Shaw (AUS)	Paul Borowski/Karl-Heinz Thun/ Konrad Weichert (GDR)	Donald Cohan/Charles Horter/ John Marshall (USA)

5.5 Metre

	Gold
1952	United States
1956	Sweden
1960	United States
1964	Australia
1968	Sweden

6 Metre (1906 Rating)

	Gold
1908	Great Britain
1912	France
1920	Belgium

6 Metre (1919 Rating)

	Gold
1920	Norway
1924	Norway
1928	Norway
1932	Sweden
1936	Great Britain
1948	United States
1952	United States

6.5 Metre

	Gold
1920	Netherlands

7 Metre

	Gold
1908	Great Britain
1912	not held
1920	Great Britain

8 Metre (1906 Rating)

	Gold
1908	Great Britain
1912	Norway
1920	Norway

8 Metre (1919 Rating)

	Gold
1920	Norway
1924	Norway
1928	France
1932	United States
1936	Italy

10 Metre (1906 Rating)

	Gold
1912	Sweden
1920	Norway

10 Metre (1919 Rating)

	Gold
1920	Norway

12 Metre (1906 Rating)

	Gold
1908	Great Britain
1912	Norway
1920	Norway

12 Metre (1919 Rating)

	Gold
1920	Norway

30 Square Metre

	Gold
1920	Sweden

40 Square Metre

	Gold
1920	Sweden

SAILING

0.5 Ton

	Gold
1900A	*Baby* (FRA)
1900B	*Fantlet* (FRA)

0.5-1 Ton

	Gold
1900A	*Scotia* (GBR)
1900B	*Carabinier* (FRA)

1-2 Tons

	Gold
1900A	*Lerina* (SUI)
1900B	*Aschenbrodel* (GER)

2-3 Tons

	Gold
1900A	*Olle* (FRA)/(GBR)
1900B	*Olle* (FRA)/(GBR)

3-10 Tons

	Gold
1900A	*Femur* (FRA)
1900B	*Bona Fide* (GBR)

10-20 Tons

	Gold
1900	*Estérel* (FRA)

20+ Tons

	Gold
1900	*Cicely* (GBR)

Open

	Gold
1900	*Scotia* (GBR)

Olympic Yachting/Sailing Venues

1900	Meulan, Le Havre, France
1908	Ryde, Firth of Clyde, Great Britain
1912	Nynashamn, Sweden
1920	Ostend, Belgium, and Amsterdam, Netherlands
1924	Le Havre, France
1928	Zuidersee, Netherlands
1932	Los Angeles, United States
1936	Kiel, Germany
1948	Torquay, Great Britain
1952	Harmaja, Finland
1956	Port Philip, Australia
1960	Naples, Italy
1964	Fujisawa, Enoshima, Japan
1968	Acapulco, Mexico
1972	Kiel, Federal Republic of Germany
1976	Kingston, Ontario, Canada
1980	Tallinn, Soviet Union
1984	Long Beach, United States
1988	Pusan, South Korea
1992	Barcelona, Spain
1996	Savannah, United States
2000	Sydney, Australia
2004	Athens, Greece

America's Cup

	Winner	Score	Winning Skipper	Loser
1851	*America*	—	Richard Brown	*Aurora* (GBR)
1870	*Magic*	1-0	Andrew Comstock	*Cambria* (GBR)
1871	*Columbia*	2-1	Nelson Comstock	*Livonia* (GBR)
	Sappho	2-0	Sam Greenwood	
1876	*Madeline*	2-0	Josephus Williams	*Countess of Dufferin* (CAN)
1881	*Mischief*	2-0	Nathanael Clock	*Atalanta* (CAN)
1885	*Puritan*	2-0	Aubrey Crocker	*Genesta* (GBR)
1886	*Mayflower*	2-0	Martin Stone	*Galatea* (GBR)
1887	*Volunteer*	2-0	Henry Haff	*Thistle* (GBR)
1893	*Vigilant*	3-0	William Hansen	*Valkyrie II* (GBR)
1895	*Defender*	3-0	Henry Haff	*Valkyrie III* (GBR)
1899	*Columbia*	3-0	Charles Barr	*Shamrock* (GBR)
1901	*Columbia*	3-0	Charles Barr	*Shamrock II* (GBR)
1903	*Reliance*	3-0	Charles Barr	*Shamrock III* (GBR)
1920	*Resolute*	3-2	Charles F. Adams	*Shamrock IV* (GBR)
1930	*Enterprise*	4-0	Harold Vanderbilt	*Shamrock V* (GBR)
1934	*Rainbow*	4-2	Harold Vanderbilt	*Endeavour* (GBR)
1937	*Ranger*	4-0	Harold Vanderbilt	*Endeavour II* (GBR)
1958	*Columbia*	4-0	Briggs Cunningham	*Sceptre* (GBR)
1962	*Weatherly*	4-1	Bus Mosbacher	*Gretel* (AUS)
1964	*Constellation*	4-0	Bob Bavier/Eric Ridder	*Sovereign* (AUS)
1967	*Intrepid*	4-0	Bus Mosbacher	*Dame Pattie* (AUS)

1970	*Intrepid*	4-1	Bill Ficker	*Gretel II* (AUS)
1974	*Courageous*	4-0	Ted Hood	*Southern Cross* (AUS)
1977	*Courageous*	4-0	Ted Turner	*Australia* (AUS)
1980	*Freedom*	4-1	Dennis Conner	*Australia* (AUS)
1983	*Australia II*	4-3	John Bertrand	*Liberty* (USA)
1987	*Stars & Stripes*	4-0	Dennis Conner	*Kookaburra III* (AUS)
1988	*Stars & Stripes*	2-0	Dennis Conner	*New Zealand* (NZL)
1992	*America*	4-1	Bill Koch/Buddy Melges	*Il Moro di Venezia* (ITA)
1995	*Black Magic* (NZL)	5-0	Russell Coutts	*Young America* (USA)
2000	*Black Magic* (NZL)	5-0	Russell Coutts/Dean Barker	*Luna Rossa* (ITA)
2003	*Alinghi* (SUI)	5-0	Russell Coutts	*Black Magic* (NZL)

SHOOTING

There is evidence that shooting clubs were first formed in the 13th century and that competition using firearms with rifled barrels has existed from the 16th century. In 1860 the National Rifle Association (NRA) was founded. In the same year, its first competition was held on Wimbledon Common, the first shot being fired by Queen Victoria. The NRA moved to Bisley Camp, Surrey, in 1890 and HRH The Princess of Wales fired the first shot at what still remains the home of shooting in the UK. The premier award at Bisley is the Queen's Prize which was inaugurated at Wimbledon in 1860 and is still much coveted. Arthur Fulton MBE was the first competitor to win the Queen's Prize on three occasions (1912, 1926 and 1931).

In 1876 the first World Long Range Championships for the Palma Trophy were held in Creedmore, USA, and in 1896 the sport was included in the first modern Olympics. The following year, rifle shooting held its first world championship at Lyon in France. In 1907 the Union des Fédérations et Associations Nationales de Tir (International Shooting Union, UIT) was founded with its base in Zurich, Switzerland. The organisation was renamed the International Shooting Sport Federation (ISSF) in 1998. Women's shooting events were included for the first time at the World Shooting Championships of 1958 and in 1966 shooting events were included for the first time in the Commonwealth Games at Kingston, Jamaica.

In 1968 clay target (skeet) shooting was included for the first time in the Olympics at Mexico City, when Bob Braithwaite won the Olympic gold in the trap event. In 1976 Margaret Thompson Murdock of the USA became the first woman to win an Olympic medal in open competition against both men and women, in the small-bore three positions in Montreal, Canada, when she won silver behind fellow countryman Lanny Bassham. In the 1986 Commonwealth Games in Edinburgh, husband and wife Malcolm and Sarah Cooper won the three positions rifle pairs event.

Olympic Medallists

Men's Trap
(a – single shot; b – double shot)

	Gold	Silver	Bronze
1900	Roger de Barbarin (FRA)	René Guyot (FRA)	Justinien de Clary (FRA)
1904	not held		
1906a	Gerald Merlin (GBR)	Ioannis Peridis (GRE)	Sidney Merlin (GBR)
1906b	Sidney Merlin (GBR)	Anastasios Metaxas (GRE)	Gerald Merlin (GBR)
1908	Walter Ewing (CAN)	George Beattie (CAN)	Alexander Maunder (GBR)
			Anastasios Metaxas (GRE)
1912	James Graham (USA)	Alfred Göldel (GER)	Harry Blau (RUS)
1920	Mark Arie (USA)	Frank Troeh (USA)	Frank Wright (USA)
1924	Gyula Halasy (HUN)	Konrad Huber (FIN)	Frank Hughes (USA)
1928-48	not held		
1952	George Généreux (CAN)	Knut Holmqvist (SWE)	Hans Liljedahl (SWE)
1956	Galliano Rossini (ITA)	Adam Smelczynski (POL)	Alessandro Ciceri (ITA)
1960	Ion Dumitrescu (ROM)	Galliano Rossini (ITA)	Sergey Kalinin (URS)
1964	Ennio Mattarelli (ITA)	Pâvels Senicevs (URS)	William Morris (USA)
1968	John 'Bob' Braithwaite (GBR)	Thomas Garrigus (USA)	Kurt Czekalla (GDR)
1972	Angelo Scalzone (ITA)	Michel Carrega (FRA)	Silvano Basagni (ITA)
1976	Donald Haldeman (USA)	Armando da Silva Marques (POR)	Ubaldesco Baldi (ITA)
1980	Luciano Giovannetti (ITA)	Rustam Yambulatov (URS)	Jörg Damme (GDR)
1984	Luciano Giovannetti (ITA)	Francisco Boza (PER)	Dan Carlisle (USA)
1988	Dmitriy Monakov (URS)	Miroslav Bednařík (TCH)	Franz Peeters (BEL)
1992	Petr Hrdlicka (CZE)	Kazumi Watanabe (JPN)	Marco Venturini (ITA)
1996	Michael Diamond (AUS)	Joshua Lakatos (USA)	Lance Bade (USA)
2000	Michael Diamond (AUS)	Ian Peel (GBR)	Giovanni Pellielo (ITA)

Men's Double Trap

	Gold	Silver	Bronze
1996	Russell Mark (AUS)	Albano Pera (ITA)	Zhang Bing (CHN)
2000	Richard Faulds (GBR)	Russell Mark (AUS)	Fehaid Al-Deehani (KUW)

Men's Skeet

	Gold	Silver	Bronze
1968	Yevgeniy Petrov (URS)	Romano Garagnani (ITA)	Konrad Wirnhier (FRG)
1972	Konrad Wirnhier (FRG)	Yevgeniy Petrov (URS)	Michael Buchheim (GDR)
1976	Josef Panacek (TCH)	Eric Swinkels (NED)	Wieslaw Gawlikowski (POL)
1980	Hans Kjeld Rasmussen (DEN)	Lars-Göran Carlsson (SWE)	Roberto Castrillo (CUB)
1984	Matt Dryke (USA)	Ole Riber Rasmussen (DEN)	Luca Scribani Rossi (ITA)
1988	Axel Wegner (GDR)	Alfonso de Iruarrizaga (CHI)	Jorge Guardiola (ESP)
1992	Zhang Shan (CHN)	Juan Giha Yarur (PER)	Bruno Rossetti (ITA)
1996	Ennio Falco (ITA)	Miroslaw Rzepkowski (POL)	Andrea Benelli (ITA)
2000	Mikola Milchev (UKR)	Petr Málek (CZE)	James Graves (USA)

Men's Free Pistol (Mixed 1968-80)
(1896, 30m; 1906, 1912- 50m; 1908, 50yds)

	Gold	Silver	Bronze
1896	Sumner Paine (USA)	Holger Nielsen (DEN)	Ioannis Frangoudis (GRE)
1900-04	not held		
1906	Georgios Orphanidis (GRE)	Jean Fouconnier (FRA)	Aristidis Rangavis (GRE)
1908	Paul van Asbroeck (BEL)	Réginald Storms (BEL)	James Gorman (USA)
1912	Alfred Lane (USA)	Peter Dolfen (USA)	Charles Stewart (GBR)
1920	Karl Frederick (USA)	Afranio da Costa (BRA)	Alfred Lane (USA)
1924-32	not held		
1936	Torsten Ullman (SWE)	Erich Krempel (GER)	Charles des Jammonières (FRA)
1948	Edwin Vásquez (PER)	Rudolf Schnyder (SUI)	Torsten Ullman (SWE)
1952	Huelet Benner (USA)	Ángel León (ESP)	Ambrus Balogh (HUN)
1956	Pentti Linnosvuo (FIN)	Makhmud Umarov (URS)	Offutt Pinion (USA)
1960	Aleksey Gushchin (URS)	Makhmud Umarov (URS)	Yoshihisa Yoshikawa (JPN)
1964	Väinö Markkanen (FIN)	Franklin Green (USA)	Yoshihisa Yoshikawa (JPN)
1968	Grigoriy Kosykh (URS)	Heinz Mertel (FRG)	Harald Vollmar (GDR)
1972	Ragnar Skanåker (SWE)	Dan Iuga (ROM)	Rudolf Dollinger (AUT)
1976	Uwe Potteck (GDR)	Harald Vollmar (GDR)	Rudolf Dollinger (AUT)
1980	Aleksandr Melentyev (URS)	Harald Vollmar (GDR)	Lyubcho Diakov (BUL)
1984	Xu Haifeng (CHN)	Ragnar Skanåker (SWE)	Wang Yifu (CHN)
1988	Sorin Babii (ROM)	Ragnar Skanåker (SWE)	Igor Basinskiy (URS)
1992	Konstantin Lukashik (CIS)	Wang Yifu (CHN)	Ragnar Skanåker (SWE)
1996	Boris Kokorev (RUS)	Igor Basinskiy (BLR)	Roberto Di Donna (ITA)
2000	Tanyu Kiriakov (BUL)	Igor Basinskiy (BLR)	Martin Tenk (CZE)

Men's Rapid-Fire Pistol (Mixed 1968-80)
(1920, 30m; 1924- , 25m)

	Gold	Silver	Bronze
1920	Guilherme Paraense (BRA)	Raymond Bracken (USA)	Fritz Zulauf (SUI)
1924	Henry Bailey (USA)	Wilhelm Carlberg (SWE)	Lennart Hannelius (FIN)
1928	not held		
1932	Renzo Morigi (ITA)	Heinz Hax (GER)	Domenico Matteucci (ITA)
1936	Cornelius van Oyen (GER)	Heinz Hax (GER)	Torsten Ullman (SWE)
1948	Károly Takács (HUN)	Carlos Enrique Díaz Sáenz Valiente (ARG)	Sven Lundqvist (SWE)
1952	Károly Takács (HUN)	Szilárd Kun (HUN)	Gheorghe Lichiardopol (ROM)
1956	Stefan Petrescu (ROM)	Yevgeniy Cherkasov (URS)	Gheorghe Lichiardopol (ROM)
1960	William McMillan (USA)	Pentti Linnosvuo (FIN)	Aleksandr Zabelin (URS)
1964	Pentti Linnosvuo (FIN)	Ion Tripsa (ROM)	Lubomír Nácovský (TCH)
1968	Józef Zapedzki (POL)	Marcel Rosca (ROM)	Renart Suleimanov (URS)
1972	Józef Zapedzki (POL)	Ladislav Falta (TCH)	Viktor Torshin (URS)
1976	Norbert Klaar (GDR)	Jürgen Wiefel (GDR)	Roberto Ferraris (ITA)
1980	Corneliu Ion (ROM)	Jürgen Wiefel (GDR)	Gerhard Petritsch (AUT)
1984	Takeo Kamachi (JPN)	Corneliu Ion (ROM)	Rauno Bies (FIN)
1988	Afanasijs Kuzmins (URS)	Ralf Schumann (GDR)	Zoltán Kovács (HUN)
1992	Ralf Schumann (GER)	Afanasijs Kuzmins (LAT)	Vladimir Vokhmyanin (CIS)
1996	Ralf Schumann (GER)	Emil Milev (BUL)	Vladimir Vokhmyanin (KAZ)
2000	Sergey Alifirenko (RUS)	Michel Ansemet (SUI)	Iulian Raicea (ROM)

SHOOTING

Men's Air Pistol
(10m)

	Gold	Silver	Bronze
1988	Taniu Kiriakov (BUL)	Erich Buljung (USA)	Xu Haifeng (CHN)
1992	Wang Yifu (CHN)	Sergey Pyzhyanov (CIS)	Sorin Babii (ROM)
1996	Roberto Di Donna (ITA)	Wang Yifu (CHN)	Taniu Kiriakov (BUL)
2000	Franck Dumoulin (FRA)	Wang Yifu (CHN)	Igor Basinskiy (BLR)

Men's Small-Bore Rifle, Prone (Mixed 1968-80)
(50m)

	Gold	Silver	Bronze
1924	Pierre Coquelin de Lisle (FRA)	Marcus Dinwiddie (USA)	Josias Hartmann (SUI)
1928	not held		
1932	Bertil Rönnmark (SWE)	Gustavo Huet (MEX)	Zoltán Hradetzky-Soós (HUN)
1936	Willy Røgeberg (NOR)	Ralph Berzsenyi (HUN)	Wladyslaw Karas (POL)
1948	Arthur Cook (USA)	Walter Tomsen (USA)	Jonas Jonsson (SWE)
1952	Iosif Sârbu (ROM)	Boris Andreyev (URS)	Arthur Jackson (USA)
1956	Gérald Ouellette (CAN)	Vasiliy Borisov (URS)	Gilmour Boa (CAN)
1960	Peter Kohnke (GER)	James Hill (USA)	Enrico Forcella (VEN)
1964	László Hammerl (HUN)	Lones Wigger (USA)	Tommy Pool (USA)
1968	Jan Kurka (TCH)	László Hammerl (HUN)	Ian Ballinger (NZL)
1972	Li Ho-Jun (PRK)	Victor Auer (USA)	Nicolae Rotaru (ROM)
1976	Karlheinz Smieszek (FRG)	Ulrich Lind (FRG)	Gennadiy Lushchikov (URS)
1980	Károly Varga (HUN)	Hellfried Heilfort (GDR)	Petar Zaprianov (BUL)
1984	Ed Etzel (USA)	Michel Bury (FRA)	Mike Sullivan (GBR)
1988	Miroslav Varga (CZE)	Cha Young-Chul (KOR)	Attila Záhonyi (HUN)
1992	Lee Eun-Chul (KOR)	Harald Stenvaag (NOR)	Stevan Pletikosic (IOP)
1996	Christian Klees (GER)	Sergey Belyayev (KAZ)	Jozef Gönci (SVK)
2000	Jonas Edman (SWE)	Torben Grimmel (DEN)	Sergey Martynov (BLR)

Men's Small-Bore Rifle, Three Positions (Mixed 1968-80)
(50m)

	Gold	Silver	Bronze
1952	Erling Kongshaug (NOR)	Vilho Ylönen (FIN)	Boris Andreyev (URS)
1956	Anatoliy Bogdanov (URS)	Otakar Horinek (TCH)	Nils Johan Sundberg (SWE)
1960	Viktor Shamburkin (URS)	Marat Niyazov (URS)	Klaus Zähringer (GER)
1964	Lones Wigger (USA)	Velichko Velichkov (BUL)	László Hammerl (HUN)
1968	Bernd Klingner (FRG)	John Writer (USA)	Viktor Parkhimovich (URS)
1972	John Writer (USA)	Lanny Bassham (USA)	Werner Lippoldt (GDR)
1976	Lanny Bassham (USA)	Margaret Murdock (USA)	Werner Siebold (FRG)
1980	Viktor Vlasov (URS)	Bernd Hartstein (GDR)	Sven Johansson (SWE)
1984	Malcolm Cooper (GBR)	Daniel Nipkow (SUI)	Alister Allan (GBR)
1988	Malcolm Cooper (GBR)	Alister Allan (GBR)	Kirill Ivanov (URS)
1992	Hrachya Petikyan (CIS)	Robert Foth (USA)	Ryohei Koba (JPN)
1996	Jean-Pierre Amat (FRA)	Sergey Belyayev (KAZ)	Wolfram Waibel (AUT)
2000	Rajmond Debevec (SLO)	Juha Hirvi (FIN)	Harald Stenvaag (NOR)

Men's Air Rifle
(10m)

	Gold	Silver	Bronze
1984	Philippe Hébérle (FRA)	Andreas Kronthaler (AUT)	Barry Dagger (GBR)
1988	Goran Maksimovic (YUG)	Nicolas Berthelot (FRA)	Johann Riederer (FRG)
1992	Yuriy Fedkin (CIS)	Franck Badiou (FRA)	Johann Riederer (GER)
1996	Artem Khadzhibekov (RUS)	Wolfram Waibel (AUT)	Jean-Pierre Amat (FRA)
2000	Cai Yalin (CHN)	Artem Khadzhibekov (RUS)	Yevgeniy Aleinikov (RUS)

Men's Running Target (Mixed 1968-80)
(1900, running boar; 1908, small-bore rifle 25yds; 1972-88, 50m; 1992- , air rifle 10m)

	Gold	Silver	Bronze
1900	Louis Debray (FRA)	Pierre Nivet (FRA)	Comte de Lambert (FRA)
1904-06	not held		
1908	John Fleming (GBR)	Michael Matthews (GBR)	William Marsden (GBR)
1912-68	not held		
1972	Lakov Zheleznyak (URS)	Helmut Bellingrodt (COL)	John Kynoch (GBR)
1976	Aleksandr Gazov (URS)	Aleksandr Kedyarov (URS)	Jerzy Greszkiewicz (POL)
1980	Igor Sokolov (URS)	Thomas Pfeffer (GDR)	Aleksandr Gazov (URS)
1984	Li Yuwei (CHN)	Helmut Bellingrodt (COL)	Huang Shiping (CHN)

1988	Tor Heiestad (NOR)	Huang Shiping (CHN)	Gennadiy Avramenko (URS)
1992	Michael Jakosits (GER)	Anatoliy Asrabayev (CIS)	Luboš Racanskš (CZE)
1996	Yang Ling (CHN)	Xiao Jun (CHN)	Miroslav Januš (CZE)
2000	Yang Ling (CHN)	Oleg Moldovan (MDA)	Niu Zhiyaun (CHN)

Women's Trap

	Gold	Silver	Bronze
2000	Daina Gudzineviciuté (LTU)	Delphine Racinet (FRA)	Gao En (CHN)

Women's Double Trap

	Gold	Silver	Bronze
1996	Kim Rhode (USA)	Susanne Kiermayer (GER)	Deserie Huddleston (AUS)
2000	Pia Hansen (SWE)	Deborah Gelisio (ITA)	Kim Rhode (USA)

Women's Skeet

	Gold	Silver	Bronze
2000	Zemfira Meftakhetdinova (AZE)	Svetlana Demina (RUS)	Diána Igaly (HUN)

Women's Sport Pistol

	Gold	Silver	Bronze
1984	Linda Thom (CAN)	Ruby Fox (USA)	Patricia Dench (AUS)
1988	Nino Salukvadze (URS)	Tomoko Hasegawa (JPN)	Jasna Šekaric (YUG)
1992	Marina Logvinenko (CIS)	Li Duihong (CHN)	Dorzhsuren Munkhbayar (MGL)
1996	Li Duihong (CHN)	Diana Yorgova (BUL)	Marina Logvinenko (RUS)
2000	Maria Grozveda (BUL)	Tao Luna (CHN)	Lalita Yauhleuskaya (BLR)

Women's Air Pistol
(10m)

	Gold	Silver	Bronze
1988	Jasna Šekaric (YUG)	Nino Salukvadze (URS)	Marina Dobrancheva (URS)
1992	Marina (Dobrancheva) Logvinenko (CIS)	Jasna Šekaric (IOP)	Maria Grozdeva (BUL)
1996	Olga Klochneva (RUS)	Marina Logvinenko (RUS)	Maria Grozdeva (BUL)
2000	Tao Luna (CHN)	Jasna Šekaric (YUG)	Annemarie Forder (AUS)

Women's Small-Bore Rifle, Three Positions
(50m)

	Gold	Silver	Bronze
1984	Wu Xiaoxuan (CHN)	Ulrike Holmler (FRG)	Wanda Jewell (USA)
1988	Sylvia Sperber (FRG)	Vessela Letcheva (BUL)	Valentina Cherkasova (URS)
1992	Launi Meili (USA)	Nonka Matova (BUL)	Malgorzata Ksiazkiewicz (POL)
1996	Aleksandra Ivošev (YUG)	Irina Gerasimenok (RUS)	Renata Mauer (POL)
2000	Renata Mauer (POL)	Tatyana Goldobina (RUS)	Mariya Feklistova (RUS)

Women's Air Rifle
(10m)

	Gold	Silver	Bronze
1984	Pat Spurgin (USA)	Edith Gufler (ITA)	Wu Xiaoxuan (CHN)
1988	Irina Shilova (URS)	Sylvia Sperber (FRG)	Anna Malukhina (URS)
1992	Yeo Kab-Soon (KOR)	Vessela Letcheva (BUL)	Aranka Binder (IOP)
1996	Renata Mauer (POL)	Petra Horneber (GER)	Aleksandra Ivošev (YUG)
2000	Nancy Johnson (USA)	Kang Cho-Hyun (KOR)	Gao Jing (CHN)

Discontinued Events

Men's Team Free Pistol

	Gold	Silver	Bronze
1908	United States	Belgium	Great Britain
1912	United States	Sweden	Great Britain
1920	United States	Sweden	Brazil

SHOOTING

Men's Duelling Pistol
(1906a, 20m; 1906b, 25m; 1912, 30m)

	Gold	Silver	Bronze
1906a	Konstantinos Skarlatos (GRE)	Johann Hübner von Holst (SWE)	Wilhelm Carlberg (SWE)
1906a	Léon Moreaux (FRA)	Cesare Liverziani (ITA)	Maurice Lecoq (FRA)
1908	not held		
1912	Alfred Lane (USA)	Paul Palén (SWE)	Johan Hübner von Holst (SWE)

Men's Team Duelling Pistol

	Gold	Silver	Bronze
1912	Sweden	Russia	Great Britain

Men's Free Revolver
(1896, 25m; 1900, 50m; 1906, 25m)

	Gold	Silver	Bronze
1896	Ioannis Frangoudis (GRE)	Georgios Orphanidis (GRE)	Holger Nielsen (DEN)
1900	Conrad Röderer (SUI)	Achille Paroche (FRA)	Konrad Stäheli (SUI)
1904	not held		
1906	Maurice Lecoq (FRA)	Léon Moreaux (FRA)	Aristidis Rangavis (GRE)

Men's Team Free Revolver

	Gold	Silver	Bronze
1900	Switzerland	France	Netherlands

Men's Military Revolver
(1896-1900, 25m; 1906, 20m)

	Gold	Silver	Bronze
1896	John Paine (USA)	Sumner Paine (USA)	Nikolaos Dorakis (GRE)
1900	Maurice Larrouy (FRA)	Léon Moreaux (FRA)	Eugène Balme (FRA)
1904	not held		
1906	Louis Richardet (SUI)	Alexandros Theofilakis (GRE)	Georgios Skotadis (GRE)

Men's Military Revolver (1873-74 Model Gras)
(20m)

	Gold	Silver	Bronze
1906	Jean Fouconnier (FRA)	Raoul de Boigne (FRA)	Hermann Martin (FRA)

Men's Team Rapid-Fire Pistol

	Gold	Silver	Bronze
1920	United States	Greece	Switzerland

Men's Small-Bore Rifle
(1908, 50+100yds; 1912, 50m)

	Gold	Silver	Bronze
1908	Arthur Carnell (GBR)	Harry Humby (GBR)	George Barnes (GBR)
1912	Frederick Hird (USA)	William Milne (GBR)	Harold Burt (GBR)

Men's Team Small-Bore Rifle

	Gold	Silver	Bronze
1908	Great Britain	Sweden	France
1912	Great Britain	Sweden	United States

Men's Small-Bore Rifle, Standing
(50m)

	Gold	Silver	Bronze
1920	Lawrence Nuesslein (USA)	Arthur Rothrock (USA)	Dennis Fenton (USA)

Men's Team Small-Bore Rifle, Standing

	Gold	Silver	Bronze
1920	United States	Sweden	Norway

Men's Free Rifle
(1896-1906, 300m; 1924, 600m)

	Gold	Silver	Bronze
1896	Georgios Orphanidis (GRE)	Ioannis Frangoudis (GRE)	Viggo Jensen (DEN)
1900-04	not held		
1906	Marcel Meyer de Stadelhofen (SUI)	Konrad Stäheli (SUI)	Léon Moreaux (FRA)
1908-20	not held		
1924	Morris Fisher (USA)	Carl Osburn (USA)	Niels Larsen (DEN)

Men's Team Free Rifle
(400+600+800m)

	Gold	Silver	Bronze
1924	United States	France	Haiti

Men's Free Rifle, Standing
(300m)

	Gold	Silver	Bronze
1900	Lars Jørgen Madsen (DEN)	Ole Østmo (NOR)	Charles Paumier du Verger (BEL)
1904	not held		
1906	Gudbrand Skatteboe (NOR)	Julius Braathe (NOR)	Albert Helgerud (NOR)

Men's Free Rifle, Kneeling
(300m)

	Gold	Silver	Bronze
1900	Konrad Stäheli (SUI)	Emil Kellenberger (SUI)	—
1904	not held	Anders Peter Nielsen (DEN)	
1906	Konrad Stäheli (SUI)	Louis Richardet (SUI)	Marcel Meyer de Stadelhofen (SUI)

Men's Free Rifle, Prone
(300m)

	Gold	Silver	Bronze
1900	Achille Paroche (FRA)	Anders Peter Nielsen (DEN)	Ole Østmo (NOR)
1904	not held		
1906	Gudbrand Skatteboe (NOR)	Louis Richardet (SUI)	Konrad Stäheli (SUI)

Men's Free Rifle, Three Positions
(300m)

	Gold	Silver	Bronze
1900	Emil Kellenberger (SUI)	Anders Peter Nielsen (DEN)	Paul van Asbroeck (BEL) Ole Østmo (NOR)
1904	not held		
1906	Gudbrand Skatteboe (NOR)	Konrad Stäheli (SUI)	Jean Reich (SUI)
1908	Albert Helgerud (NOR)	Harry Simon (USA)	Ole Sæther (NOR)
1912	Paul Colas (FRA)	Lars Jørgen Madsen (DEN)	Niels Larsen (DEN)
1920	Morris Fisher (USA)	Niels Larsen (DEN)	Østen Østensen (NOR)
1924-36	not held		
1948	Emil Grünig (SUI)	Pauli Janhonen (FIN)	Willy Røgeberg (NOR)
1952	Anatoliy Bogdanov (URS)	Robert Bürchler (SUI)	Lev Vainshtein (URS)
1956	Vasiliy Borisov (URS)	Allan Erdman (URS)	Vilho Ylönen (FIN)
1960	Hubert Hammerer (AUT)	Hans Spillman (SUI)	Vasiliy Borisov (URS)
1964	Gary Anderson (USA)	Shota Kveliashvili (URS)	Martin Gunnarsson (USA)
1968	Gary Anderson (USA)	Vladimir Kornev (URS)	Kurt Müller (SUI)
1972	Lones Wigger (USA)	Boris Melnik (URS)	Lajos Papp (HUN)

SHOOTING

Men's Team Free Rifle, Three Positions

	Gold	Silver	Bronze
1900	Switzerland	Norway	France
1904	not held		
1906	Switzerland	Norway	France
1908	Norway	Sweden	France
1912	Sweden	Norway	Denmark
1920	United States	Norway	Switzerland

Men's Military Rifle
(1896, 200m; 1908, 1000yds; 1912a, 300m; 1912b, 600m)

	Gold	Silver	Bronze
1896	Pantelis Karasevdas (GRE)	Paulos Pavlidis (GRE)	Nikolaos Trikoupes (GRE)
1908	Joshua 'Jerry' Milner (GBR)	Kellogg Casey (USA)	Maurice Blood (USA)
1912a	Alexander Prokopp (HUN)	Carl Osburn (USA)	Embret Skogen (NOR)
1912b	Paul Colas (FRA)	Carl Osburn (USA)	John Jackson (USA)

Men's Team Military Rifle

	Gold	Silver	Bronze
1908	United States	Great Britain	Canada
1912	United States	Great Britain	Sweden

Men's Military Rifle, Standing or Kneeling
(300m)

	Gold	Silver	Bronze
1906	Louis Richardet (SUI)	Jean Reich (SUI)	Raoul de Boigne (FRA)

Men's Military Rifle, 1873-74 Model Gras, Standing or Kneeling

	Gold	Silver	Bronze
1906	Léon Moreaux (FRA)	Louis Richardet (SUI)	Jean Reich (SUI)

Men's Military Rifle, Standing
(300m)

	Gold	Silver	Bronze
1920	Carl Osburn (USA)	Lars Jørgen Madsen (DEN)	Lawrence Nuesslein (USA)

Team Military Rifle, Standing

	Gold	Silver	Bronze
1920	Denmark	United States	Sweden

Men's Military Rifle, Prone
(1920a, 300m; 1920b, 600m)

	Gold	Silver	Bronze
1920a	Otto Olsen (NOR)	Léon Johnson (FRA)	Fritz Kuchen (SUI)
1920b	Carl Hugo Johansson (SWE)	Mauritz Eriksson (SWE)	Lloyd Spooner (USA)

Team Military Rifle, Prone
(1920a, 300m; 1920b, 600m; 1920c, 300+600m)

	Gold	Silver	Bronze
1920a	United States	France	Finland
1920b	United States	South Africa	Sweden
1920c	United States	Norway	Switzerland

Men's Disappearing Target
(small-bore rifle – 1908, 25yds; 1912, 25m)

	Gold	Silver	Bronze
1908	William Styles (GBR)	Harold Hawkins (GBR)	Edward Amoore (GBR)
1912	Wilhelm Carlberg (SWE)	Johan Hübner von Holst (SWE)	Gustaf Ericsson (SWE)

Team Disappearing Target

	Gold	Silver	Bronze
1912	Sweden	Great Britain	United States

Men's Running Deer, Single Shot
(1908, 100yds; 1912-24, 100m)

	Gold	Silver	Bronze
1908	Oscar Swahn (SWE)	Thomas 'Ted' Ranken (GBR)	Alexander Rogers (GBR)
1912	Alfred Swahn (SWE)	Åke Lundeberg (SWE)	Nestori Toivonen (FIN)
1920	Otto Olsen (NOR)	Alfred Swahn (SWE)	Harald Natvig (NOR)
1924	John Boles (USA)	Cyril Mackworth-Praed (GBR)	Otto Olsen (NOR)

Men's Team Running Deer, Single Shot

	Gold	Silver	Bronze
1908	Sweden	Great Britain	only two teams competed
1912	Sweden	United States	Finland
1920	Norway	Finland	United States
1924	Norway	Sweden	United States

Men's Running Deer, Double Shot
(1908, 100yds; 1912-24, 100m)

	Gold	Silver	Bronze
1908	Walter Winans (USA)	Thomas 'Ted' Ranken (GBR)	Oscar Swahn (SWE)
1912	Åke Lundeberg (SWE)	Edvard Benedicks (SWE)	Oscar Swahn (SWE)
1920	Ole Andreas Lilloe-Olsen (NOR)	Fredrik Landelius (SWE)	Einar Liberg (NOR)
1924	Ole Andreas Lilloe-Olsen (NOR)	Cyril Mackworth-Praed (GBR)	Alfred Swahn (SWE)

Men's Team Running Deer, Double Shot

	Gold	Silver	Bronze
1920	Norway	Sweden	Finland
1924	Great Britain	Norway	Sweden

Men's Running Deer, Single and Double Shot
(100m)

	Gold	Silver	Bronze
1952	John Larsen (NOR)	Per Olof Sköldberg (SWE)	Tauno Mäki (FIN)
1956	Vitaliy Romanenko (URS)	Per Olof Sköldberg (SWE)	Vladimir Sevryugin (URS)

Men's Team Trap

	Gold	Silver	Bronze
1908	Great Britain	Canada	Great Britain
1912	United States	Great Britain	Germany
1920	United States	Belgium	Sweden
1924	United States	Canada	Finland

Men's Live Pigeon

	Gold	Silver	Bronze
1900	Léon de Lunden (BEL)	Maurice Faure (FRA)	Donald Mackintosh (AUS)
			Crittenden Robinson (USA)

SHOOTING

SKIING

Skiing competitions have been taking place for hundreds of years. The biathlon, which combines cross-country skiing and rifle shooting, originated in Norway as a training exercise for soldiers. The first known competition took place in 1767 between companies of guards who patrolled the border with Sweden. Late in the 19th century, local rifle and ski clubs in Norway and other Scandinavian countries practised the sport to keep their members prepared for combat. An early form of the biathlon, called 'military ski patrol', was a demonstration sport at the first Winter Olympics in 1924 and a medal sport in 1928, 1936 and 1948. The first world championship was held in 1957 and biathlon was added to the Winter Olympic programme in 1960, when Klas Lestander of Sweden won the men's 20km event.

Modern skiing can be said to originate from the invention of ski bindings in 1889 by a Norwegian, Sondre Nordheim, often described as 'the father of skiing'.

Nordic skiing, which is essentially cross-country skiing, was included in the Winter Olympics at Chamonix in 1924, as were ski jumping events. Alpine skiing, which comprises downhill events such as the slalom, became an Olympic sport in 1948.

Freestyle skiing gained popularity in the 1980s and was added to the Olympic programme in 1992. A combination of the disciplines of alpine skiing and acrobatics, its two main events are moguls, which entails the performance at speed of various manoeuvres on a downhill slope covered with 'moguls' or large bumps, and aerials, a form of ski jumping with emphasis on gymnastic ability.

Who is the greatest skier of all time? There are numerous contenders. Perhaps the sheer speed and skill required in Alpine skiing should be the deciding factor. For all their brilliance and domination in slalom events, neither Ingemar Stenmark (Sweden) nor Alberto Tomba (Italy) were more than competent downhill skiiers. Conversely, great downhillers such as Austrian Franz Klammer, Maria Walliser (Switzerland) and Annemarie Moser-Pröll (Austria) were average slalom skiers. Both Pirmin Zurbriggen (Switzerland) and Marc Girardelli (Luxembourg) were great all-rounders although Zurbriggen favoured downhill skiing and Girardelli slalom. Hermann Maier (Austria) must also be a contender, especially since his successful comeback in the 2003/04 season after a near-fatal motorcycle accident in 2001. Two names that would be top of many people's lists are Christel Cranz of Germany, who dominated all aspects of women's skiing before World War II, and the great Frenchman, Jean-Claude Killy, who managed an unprecedented clean sweep of all the gold medals available at the 1968 Winter Olympics.

Olympic Medallists

Alpine Skiing

Men's Downhill

	Gold	Silver	Bronze
1948	Henri Oreiller (FRA) 2:55.0	Franz Gabl (AUT) 2:59.1	Karl Molitor (SUI) Rolf Olinger (SUI) 3:00.3
1952	Zeno Colò (ITA) 2:30.8	Othmar Schneider (AUT) 2:32.0	Christian Pravda (AUT) 2:32.4
1956	Toni Sailer (AUT) 2:52.2	Raymond Fellay (SUI) 2:55.7	Andreas Molterer (AUT) 2:56.2
1960	Jean Vuarnet (FRA) 2:06.0	Hans-Peter Laing (GER) 2:06.5	Guy Périllat (FRA) 2:06.9
1964	Egon Zimmermann (AUT) 2:18.16	Léo Lacroix (FRA) 2:18.90	Wolfgang Bartels (GER) 2:19.48
1968	Jean-Claude Killy (FRA) 1:59.85	Guy Périllat (FRA) 1:59.93	John-Daniel Dätwyler (SUI) 2:00.32
1972	Bernhard Russi (SUI) 1:51.43	Roland Collombin (SUI) 1:52.07	Heinrich Messner (AUT) 1:52.40
1976	Franz Klammer (AUT) 1:45.73	Bernhard Russi (SUI) 1:46.06	Herbert Plank (ITA) 1:46.59
1980	Leonhard Stock (AUT) 1:45.50	Peter Wirnsberger (AUT) 1:46.12	Steve Podborski (CAN) 1:46.62
1984	Bill Johnson (USA) 1:45.59	Peter Müller (SUI) 1:45.86	Anton Steiner (AUT) 1:45.95
1988	Pirmin Zurbriggen (SUI) 1:59.63	Peter Müller (SUI) 2:00.14	Franck Piccard (FRA) 2:01.24
1992	Patrick Ortlieb (AUT) 1:50.37	Franck Piccard (FRA) 1:50.42	Günther Mader (AUT) 1:50.47
1994	Tommy Moe (USA) 1:45.75	Kjetil André Aamodt (NOR) 1:45.79	Ed Podivinsky (CAN) 1:45.87
1998	Jean-Luc Cretier (FRA) 1:50:11	Lasse Kjus (NOR) 1:50.51	Hannes Trinkl (AUT) 1:50.63
2002	Fritz Ströbl (AUT) 1:39:13	Lasse Kjus (NOR) 1:39.35	Stephan Eberharter (AUT) 1:39.41

Men's Slalom

Gold	Silver	Bronze
1948	Edi Reinalter (SUI) 2:10.3	James Couttet (FRA) 2:10.8	Henri Oreiller (FRA) 2:12.8
1952	Othmar Schneider (AUT) 2:00.0	Stein Eriksen (NOR) 2:01.2	Guttorm Berge (NOR) 2:01.7
1956	Toni Sailer (AUT) 3:14.7	Chiharu Igaya (JPN) 3:18.7	Stig Sollander (SWE) 3:20.2
1960	Ernst Hinterseer (AUT) 2:08.9	Matthias Leitner (AUT) 2:10.3	Charles Bozon (FRA) 2:10.4
1964	Josef 'Pepi' Stiegler (AUT) 2:11.13	William Kidd (USA) 2:11.27	James Heuga (USA) 2:11.52
1968	Jean-Claude Killy (FRA) 1:39.73	Herbert Huber (AUT) 1:39.82	Alfred Matt (USA) 1:40.09
1972	Francisco Fernández Ochoa (ESP) 1:49.27	Gustav Thöni (ITA) 1:50.28	Roland Thöni (ITA) 1:50.30
1976	Piero Gros (ITA) 2:03.29	Gustav Thöni (ITA) 2:03.73	Willy Frommelt (LIE) 2:04.28
1980	Ingemar Stenmark (SWE) 1:44.26	Phil Mahre (USA) 1:44.76	Jacques Lüthy (SUI) 1:45.06
1984	Phil Mahre (USA) 1:39.41	Steve Mahre (USA) 1:39.62	Didier Bouvet (FRA) 1:40.20
1988	Alberto Tomba (ITA) 1:39.47	Frank Wörndl (FRG) 1:39.53	Paul Frommelt (LIE) 1:39.84
1992	Finn Christian Jagge (NOR) 1:44.39	Alberto Tomba (ITA) 1:44.67	Michael Tritscher (AUT) 1:44.85
1994	Thomas Stangassinger (AUT) 2:02.02	Alberto Tomba (ITA) 2:02,17	Jure Košir (SLO) 2:02.53
1998	Hans Fetter Buraas (NOR) 1:49.31	Ole Kristian Furuseth (NOR) 1:50.64	Thomas Sykora (AUT) 1:50.68
2002	Jean-Pierre Vidal (FRA) 1:41.06	Sébastien Amiez (FRA) 1:41.82	Benjamin Raich (AUT) 1:42.41

Men's Giant Slalom

Gold	Silver	Bronze
1952	Stein Eriksen (NOR) 2:25.0	Christian Pravda (AUT) 2:26.9	Toni Spiss (AUT) 2:28.8
1956	Toni Sailer (AUT) 3:00.1	Andreas Molterer (AUT) 3:06.3	Walter Schuster (AUT) 3:07.2
1960	Roger Staub (SUI) 1:48.3	Josef Stiegler (AUT) 1:48.7	Ernst Hinterseer (AUT) 1:49.1
1964	François Bonlieu (FRA) 1:46.71	Karl Schranz (AUT) 1:47.09	Josef Stiegler (AUT) 1:48.05
1968	Jean-Claude Killy (FRA) 3:29.28	Willy Favre (SUI) 3:31.50	Heinrich Messner (AUT) 3:31.83
1972	Gustav Thöni (ITA) 3:09.62	Edmund Bruggmann (SUI) 3:10.75	Werner Mattle (SUI) 3:10.99
1976	Heini Hemmi (SUI) 3:36.97	Ernst Good (SUI) 3:27.17	Ingemar Stenmark (SWE) 3:27.41
1980	Ingemar Stenmark (SWE) 2:40.74	Andreas Wenzel (LIE) 2:41.49	Hans Enn (AUT) 2:42.51
1984	Max Julen (SUI) 2:41.18	Jure Franko (YUG) 2:41.41	Andreas Wenzel (LIE) 2:41.75
1988	Alberto Tomba (ITA) 2:06.37	Hubert Strolz (AUT) 2:07.41	Pirmin Zurbriggen (SUI) 2:08.39
1992	AlbertoTomba (ITA) 2:06.98	Marc Girardelli (LUX) 2:07.30	Kjetil André Aamodt (NOR) 2:07.82
1994	Markus Wasmeier (GER) 2:52.46	Urs Kälin (SUI) 2:52.48	Christian Mayer (AUT) 2:52.58
1998	Hermann Maier (AUT) 2:38.51	Stephan Eberharter (AUT) 2:39.36	Michael von Grüningen (SUI) 2:49.82
2002	Stephan Eberharter (AUT) 2:23.28	Bode Miller (USA) 2:24.16	Lasse Kjus (NOR) 2:24.32

Men's Super Giant Slalom

Gold	Silver	Bronze
1988	Franck Piccard (FRA) 1:39.66	Helmut Mayer (AUT) 1:40.96	Lars-Börge Eriksson (SWE)
1992	Kjetil André Aamodt (NOR) 1:13.04	Marc Girardelli (LUX) 1:13.77	Jan Einar Thorsen (NOR)
1994	Markus Wasmeier (GER) 1:32.53	Tommy Moe (USA) 1:32.61	Kjetil André Aamodt (NOR)
1998	Hermann Maier (AUT) 1:34.82	Didier Cuche (SUI)	——
		Hans Knauss (AUT) 1:35.43	
2002	Kjetil André Aamodt (NOR) 1:21.58	Stephan Eberharter (AUT) 1:21.68	Andreas Schifferer (AUT)

Men's Combined

Gold	Silver	Bronze
1936	Franz Pfnür (GER) 99.25	Gustav Lantschner (GER) 96.26	Emile Allais (FRA) 94.69
1948	Henri Oreiller (FRA) 3.27	Karl Molitor (SUI) 6.44	James Couttet (FRA) 6.95
1952-84	not held		
1988	Hubert Strolz (AUT) 36.55	Bernhard Gstrein (AUT) 43.45	Paul Accola (SUI) 48.24
1992	Josef Polig (ITA) 14.58	Gianfranco Martin (ITA) 14.90	Steve Locher (SUI) 18.16
1994	Lasse Kjus (NOR) 3:17.53	Kjetil André Aamodt (NOR) 3:18.55	Harald Christian Strand Nilsen (NOR) 3:19.14
1998	Mario Reiter (AUT) 3:08.06	Lasse Kjus (NOR) 3:08.65	Christian Mayer (AUT) 3:10.11
2002	Kjetil André Aamodt (NOR) 3:17.56	Bode Miller (USA) 3:17.84	Benjamin Raich (AUT) 3:18.26

Women's Downhill

Gold	Silver	Bronze
1948	Hedy Schlunegger (SUI) 2:28.3	Trude Beiser (AUT) 2:29.1	Resi Hammer (AUT) 2:30.2
1952	Trude Jochum-Beiser (AUT) 1:47.1	Annemarie Buchner (GER) 1:48.0	Giuliana Minuzzo (ITA) 1:49.0
1956	Madeleine Berthod (SUI) 1:40.7	Frieda Dänzer (SUI) 1:45.4	Lucile Wheeler (CAN) 1:45.9
1960	Heidi Biebl (GER) 1:37.6	Penny Pitou (USA) 1:38.6	Traudl Hecher (AUT) 1:38.9
1964	Christl Haas (AUT) 1:55.39	Edith Zimmermann (AUT) 1:56.42	Traudl Hecher (AUT) 1:56.66

SKIING

1968	Olga Pall (AUT) 1:40.87	Isabelle Mir (FRA) 1:41.33	Christl Haas (AUT) 1:41.41
1972	Marie-Thèrèse Nadig (SUI) 1:36.68	Annemarie Pröll (AUT) 1:37.00	Susan Corrock (USA) 1:37.68
1976	Rosi Mittermaier (FRG) 1:46.16	Brigitte Totschnigg (AUT) 1:46.68	Cynthia Nelson (USA) 1:47.50
1980	Annemarie Moser-Pröll (AUT) 1:37.52	Hanni Wenzel (LIE) 1:38.22	Marie-Thérèse Nadig (SUI) 1:38.36
1984	Michela Figini (SUI) 1:13.36	Maria Walliser (SUI) 1:13.41	Olga Charvátová (TCH) 1:13.53
1988	Marina Kiehl (FRG) 1:25.86	Brigitte Oertli (SUI) 1:26.61	Karen Percy (CAN) 1:26.62
1992	Kerrin Lee-Gartner (CAN) 1:52.55	Hilary Lindh (USA) 1:52.61	Veronica Wallinger (AUT) 1:52.64
1994	Katja Seizinger (GER) 1:35.93	Picabo Street (USA) 1:36.59	Isolde Kostner (ITA) 1:36.85
1998	Katja Seizinger (GER) 1:28.89	Pernilla Wiberg (SWE) 1:29.18	Florence Masnada (FRA) 1:29.37
2002	Carole Montillet (FRA) 1:39.56	Isolde Kostner (ITA) 1:40.01	Renate Götschl (AUT) 1:40.39

Women's Slalom

	Gold	Silver	Bronze
1948	Gretchen Fraser (USA) 1:57.2	Antoinette Meyer (SUI) 1:57.7	Erika Mahringer (AUT) 1:58.0
1952	Andrea Mead Lawrence (USA) 2:10.6	Ossi Reichert (GER) 2:11.4	Annemarie Buchner (GER) 2:13.3
1956	Renée Colliard (SUI) 1:52.3	Regina Schöpf (AUT) 1:55.4	Yevgeniya Sidorova (URS) 1:56.7
1960	Anne Heggtveit (CAN) 1:49.6	Betsy Snite (USA) 1:52.9	Barbara Henneberger (GER) 1:56.6
1964	Christine Goitschel (FRA) 1:29.86	Marielle Goitschel (FRA) 1:30.77	Jean Saubert (USA) 1:31.36
1968	Marielle Goitschel (FRA) 1:25.86	Nancy Greene (CAN) 1:26.15	Annie Famose (FRA) 1:27.89
1972	Barbara Cochran (USA) 1:31.24	Danièlle Debernard (FRA) 1:31.26	Florence Steurer (FRA) 1:32.69
1976	Rosi Mittermaier (FRG) 1:30.54	Claudia Giordani (ITA) 1:30.87	Hanni Wenzel (LIE) 1:32.20
1980	Hanni Wenzel (LIE) 1:25.09	Christa Kinshofer (FRG) 1:26.50	Erika Hess (SUI) 1:27.89
1984	Paoletta Magoni (ITA) 1:36.47	Perrine Pelen (FRA) 1:37.38	Ursula Konzett (LIE) 1:37.50
1988	Vreni Schneider (SUI) 1:36.69	Mateja Svet (YUG) 1:38.37	Christa Kinshofer-Güthlein (FRG) 1:38.40
1992	Petra Kronberger (AUT) 1:32.68	Annelise Coberger (NZL) 1:33.10	Blanca Fernández Ochoa (ESP) 1:33.35
1994	Vreni Schneider (SUI) 1:56.01	Elfriede Eder (AUT) 1:56.35	Katja Koren (SLO) 1:56.61
1998	Hilde Gerg (GER) 1:32.40	Deborah Compagnoni (ITA) 1:32.46	Zali Steggall (AUS) 1:32.67
2002	Janica Kostelic (CRO) 1:46.10	Laure Péquegnot (FRA) 1:46:17	Anja Pärson (SWE) 1:47.09

Women's Giant Slalom

	Gold	Silver	Bronze
1952	Andrea Mead Lawrence (USA) 2:06.8	Dagmar Rom (AUT) 2:09.0	Annemarie Buchner (GER) 2:10.0
1956	Ossi Reichert (GER) 1:56.5	Josefine Frandl (AUT) 1:57.8	Dorothea Hochleitner (AUT) 1:58.2
1960	Yvonne Rugg (SUI) 1:39.9	Penny Pitou (USA) 1:40.0	Giuliana Chenal-Minuzzo (ITA) 1:40.2
1964	Marielle Goitschel (FRA) 1:52.24	Christine Goitschel (FRA) Jean Saubert (USA) 1:53.11	—
1968	Nancy Greene (CAN) 1:51.71	Annie Famose (FRA) 1:54.61	Fernande Bochatay (SUI) 1:54.74
1972	Marie-Thérèse Nadig (SUI) 1:29.90	Annemarie Pröll (AUT) 1:30.75	Wiltrud Drexel (AUT) 1:32.35
1976	Kathy Kreiner (CAN) 1:29.13	Rosi Mittermaier (FRG) 1:29.25	Danièlle Debernard (FRA) 1:29.95
1980	Hanni Wenzel (LIE) 2:41.66	Irene Epple (FRG) 2:42.12	Perrine Pelen (FRA) 2:42.41
1984	Debbie Armstrong (USA) 2:20.98	Christin Cooper (USA) 2:21.38	Perrine Pelen (FRA) 2:21.40
1988	Vreni Schneider (SUI) 2:06.49	Christa Kinshofer-Güthlein (FRG) 2:07.42	Maria Walliser (SUI) 2:07.72
1992	Pernilla Wiberg (SWE) 2:12.74	Diann Roffe (USA) Anita Wachter (AUT) 2:13.71	—
1994	Deborah Compagnoni (ITA) 2:30.97	Martina Erti (GER) 2:32.19	Vreni Schneider (SUI) 2:32.97
1998	Deborah Compagnoni (ITA) 2:50.59	Alexandra Meissnitzer (AUT) 2:52.39	Katja Seizinger (GER) 2:52.61
2002	Janica Kostelic (CRO) 2:30.01	Anja Pärson (SWE) 2:31.33	Sonja Nef (SUI) 2:31.67

Women's Super Giant Slalom

	Gold	Silver	Bronze
1988	Sigrid Wolf (AUT) 1:19.03	Michela Figini (SUI) 1:20.03	Karen Percy (CAN) 1:20.29
1992	Deborah Compagnoni (ITA) 1:21.22	Carole Merle (FRA) 1:22.63	Katja Seizinger (GER) 1:23.19
1994	Diann Roffe (USA) 1:22.55	Svetlana Gladisheva (RUS) 1:22.44	Isolde Kostner (ITA) 1:22.45
1998	Picabo Street (USA) 1:18.02	Michaela Dorfmeister (AUT) 1:18.03	Alexandra Meissnitzer (AUT) 1:18.09
2002	Daniela Ceccarelli (ITA) 1:13.59	Janica Kostelic (CRO) 1:13.64	Karen Putzer (ITA) 1:13.86

Women's Combined

	Gold	Silver	Bronze
1936	Christl Cranz (GER) 97.06	Käthe Grasegger (GER) 95.26	Laila Schou Nilsen (NOR) 93.48
1948	Trude Beiser (AUT) 6.58	Gretchen Fraser (USA) 6.95	Erika Mahringer (AUT) 7.04
1952-84	not held		

1988	Anita Wachter (AUT) 29.25	Brigitte Oertli (SUI) 29.48	Maria Walliser (SUI) 51.28
1992	Petra Kronberger (AUT) 2.55	Anita Wachter (AUT) 19.39	Florence Masnada (FRA) 21.38
1994	Pernilla Wiberg (SWE) 3:05.16	Vreni Schneider (SUI) 3:05.29	Alenka Dovzan (SLO) 3:06.64
1998	Katja Seizinger (GER) 2:40.74	Martina Ertl (GER) 2:40.92	Hilde Gerg (GER) 2:41.50
2002	Janica Kostelic (CRO) 2:43.28	Renate Götschl (AUT) 2:44.77	Martina Ertl (GER) 2:45.16

Nordic Skiing

Men's 1.5km Freestyle Sprint

	Gold	Silver	Bronze
2002	Tor Arne Hetland (NOR) 2:56.9	Peter Schlickenrieder (GER) 2:57.0	Christian Zorzi (ITA) 2:57.2

Men's 10km

	Gold	Silver	Bronze
1992	Vegard Ulvang (NOR) 23:36.0	Marco Albarello (ITA) 27:55.2	Christer Majbäck (SWE) 27:56.4
1994	Bjørn Dæhlie (NOR) 24:20.1	Vladimir Smirnov (KAZ) 24:38.3	Marco Albarello (ITA) 24:42.3
1998	Bjørn Dæhlie (NOR) 27:24.5	Markus Gandler (AUT) 27:32.5	Mika Myllylä (FIN) 27:40.1

Men's 15km
(1988, classical)

	Gold	Silver	Bronze
1956	Hallgeir Brenden (NOR) 49:39	Sixten Jernberg (SWE) 50:14	Pavel Kolchin (URS) 50:17
1960	Haakon Brusveen (NOR) 51:55.5	Sixten Jernberg (SWE) 51:58.6	Veikko Hakulinen (FIN) 52:03.0
1964	Eero Mäntyranta (FIN) 50:54.1	Harald Grønningen (NOR) 51:34.8	Sixten Jernberg (SWE) 51:42.2
1968	Harald Grønningen (NOR) 47:54.2	Eero Mäntyranta (FIN) 47:56.1	Gunnar Larsson (SWE) 48:33.7
1972	Sven-Ake Lundbäck (SWE) 45:28.2	Fedor Simashev (URS) 46:00.8	Ivar Formo (NOR) 46:02.7
1976	Nikolay Bazhukov (URS) 43:58.5	Yevgeniy Belyaev (URS) 44:01.1	Arto Koivisto (FIN) 44:19.2
1980	Thomas Wassberg (SWE) 41:57.6	Juha Mieto (FIN) 41:57.6	Ove Aunli (NOR) 42:28.6
1984	Gunde Svan (SWE) 41:25.6	Aki Karvonen (FIN) 41:34.9	Harri Kirvesniemi (FIN) 41:45.6
1988	Mikhail Devyatyarov (URS) 41:18.9	Pål Gunnar Mikkelsplass (NOR) 41:33.4	Vladimir Smirnov (URS) 41:48.5
1992-98	not held		
2002	Andrus Veerpalu (EST) 37:07.4	Frode Estil (NOR) 37:43.4	Jaak Mae (EST) 37:50.8

Men's 18km

	Gold	Silver	Bronze
1924	Thorleif Haug (NOR) 1:14:31	Johan Grøttumsbråten (NOR) 1:51:15	Tapani Niku (FIN) 1:16:26
1928	Johan Grøttumsbråten (NOR) 1:37:01	Ole Hegge (NOR) 1:39:01	Reidar Ødegaard (NOR) 1:40:11
1932	Sven Utterström (SWE) 1:23:07	Axel Wikström (SWE) 1:25:07	Veli Saarinen (FIN) 1:25:24
1936	Erik-August Larsson (SWE) 1:14:38	Oddbjørn Hagen (NOR) 1:15:33	Pekka Niemi (FIN) 1:16:59
1948	Martin Lundström (SWE) 1:13:50	Nils Östensson (SWE) 1:14:22	Gunnar Eriksson (SWE) 1:16:06
1952	Hallgeir Brenden (NOR) 1:01:34	Tapio Mäkelä (FIN) 1:02:09	Paavo Lonkila (FIN) 1:02:20

Men's 30km
(1988-92, 1998, classical; 1994, freestyle; 1998, 2002, freestyle mass start)

	Gold	Silver	Bronze
1956	Veikko Hakulinen (FIN) 1:44:06	Sixten Jernberg (SWE) 1:44:30	Pavel Kolchin (URS) 1:45:45
1960	Sixten Jernberg (SWE) 1:51:03.9	Rolf Rämgård (SWE) 1:51:16.9	Nikolay Anikin (URS) 1:52:28.2
1964	Eero Mäntyranta (FIN) 1:30:50.7	Harald Grønningen (NOR) 1:32:02.3	Igor Voronchikin (URS) 1:32:15.8
1968	Franco Nones (ITA) 1:35:39.2	Odd Martinsen (NOR) 1:36:28.9	Eero Mäntyranta (FIN) 1:36:55.3
1972	Vyacheslav Vedenine (URS) 1:36:31.1	Pål Tyldum (NOR) 1:37:25.3	Johs Harviken (NOR) 1:37:32.4
1976	Sergey Savelyev (URS) 1:30:29.4	Bill Koch (USA) 1:30:57.8	Ivan Garanin (URS) 1:31:09.3
1980	Nikolay Zimyatov (URS) 1:27:02.8	Vasiliy Rochev (URS) 1:27:34.2	Ivan Lebanov (BUL) 1:28:03.9
1984	Nikolay Zimyatov (URS) 1:28:56.3	Aleksandr Zavyalov (URS) 1:29:23.3	Gunde Svan (SWE) 1:29:35.7
1988	Aleksey Prokurorov (URS) 1:24:26.3	Vladimir Smirnov (URS) 1:24:35.1	Vegard Ulvang (NOR) 1:25:11.6
1992	Vegard Ulvang (NOR) 1:22:27.8	Bjørn Dæhlie (NOR) 1:23:14.0	Terje Langli (NOR) 1:23:42.5
1994	Thomas Alsgaard (NOR) 1:12:26.4	Bjørn Dæhlie (NOR) 1:13:13.6	Mika Myllylä (FIN) 1:14:14.5
1998	Mika Myllylä (FIN) 1:33:55.8	Erling Jevne (NOR) 1:35:27.1	Silvio Fauner (ITA) 1:36:08.5
2002	Christian Hoffmann (AUT) 1:11:31.0	Mikhail Botwinow (AUT) 1:11:32.3	Kristen Skjeldal (NOR) 1:11:42.7

S
K
I
I
N
G

Men's 50km
(1988-92, 1998, freestyle; 1994, classical; 2002, classical)

	Gold	Silver	Bronze
1924	Thorleif Haug (NOR) 3:44:32	Thoralf Strømstad (NOR) 3:46:23	Johan Grøttumsbråten (NOR) 3:47:46
1928	Per Erik Hedlund (SWE) 4:52:03	Gustaf Jonsson (SWE) 5:05:30	Volger Andersson (SWE) 5:05:46
1932	Veli Saarinen (FIN) 4:28:00	Väinö Likkanen (FIN) 4:28:20	Arne Rustadstuen (NOR) 4:31:53
1936	Elis Wiklund (SWE) 3:30:11	Axel Wikström (SWE) 3:33:20	Nils-Joel Englund (SWE) 3:34:10
1948	Nils Karlsson (SWE) 3:47:48	Harold Eriksson (SWE) 3:52:20	Benjamin Vanninen (FIN) 3:57:28
1952	Veikko Hakulinen (FIN) 3:33:33	Eero Kolehmainen (FIN) 3:38:11	Magnar Estenstad (NOR) 3:38:28
1956	Sixten Jernberg (SWE) 2:50:27	Veikko Hakulinen (FIN) 2:51:45	Fedor Terentyev (URS) 2:53:32
1960	Kalevi Hämäläinen (FIN) 2:59:06.3	Veikko Hakulinen (FIN) 2:59:26.7	Rolf Rämgård (SWE) 3:02:46.7
1964	Sixten Jernberg (SWE) 2:43:52.6	Assar Rönnlund (SWE) 2:44:58.2	Arto Tiainen (FIN) 2:45:30.4
1968	Ole Ellefsæther (NOR) 2:28:45.8	Vyacheslav Vedenine (URS) 2:29:02.5	Josef Haas (SUI) 2:29:14.8
1972	Pål Tyldum (NOR) 2:43:14.7	Magne Myrmo (NOR) 2:43:29.4	Vyacheslav Vedenine (URS) 2:44:00.2
1976	Ivar Formo (NOR) 2:37:30.0	Gert-Dietmar Klause (GDR) 2:38:13.2	Benny Södergren (SWE) 2:39:39.2
1980	Nikolay Zimyatov (URS) 2:27:24.6	Juha Mieto (FIN) 2:30:20.5	Aleksandr Zavyalov (URS) 2:30:51.5
1984	Thomas Wassberg (SWE) 2:15:55.8	Gunde Svan (SWE) 2:16:00.7	Aki Karvonen (FIN) 2:17:04.7
1988	Gunde Svan (SWE) 2:04:30.9	Maurilio De Zolt (ITA) 2:05:36.4	Andreas Grünenfelder (SUI) 2:06:01.9
1992	Bjørn Dæhlie (NOR) 2:03:41.5	Maurilio De Zolt (ITA) 2:04:39.1	Giorgio Vanzetta (ITA) 2:06:42.1
1994	Vladimir Smirnov (KAZ) 2:07:20.3	Mika Myllylä (FIN) 2:08:41.9	Sture Sivertsen (NOR) 2:08:49.0
1998	Bjørn Dæhlie (NOR) 2:05:08.2	Niklas Jonsson (SWE) 2:05:16.3	Christian Hoffmann (AUT) 2:06:01.8
2002	Mikhail Ivanov (RUS) 2:06:20.8	Andrus Veerpalu (EST) 2:06:44.5	Odd-Bjørn Hjelmeset (NOR) 2:08:41.5

Men's Combined Pursuit
(1992-98, 10km classical/15km freestyle; 2002, 10km classical/10km freestyle)

	Gold	Silver	Bronze
1992	Bjørn Dæhlie (NOR) 1:05:37.9	Vegard Ulvang (NOR) 1:06:31.3	Giorgio Vanzetta (ITA) 1:06:32.2
1994	Bjørn Dæhlie (NOR) 1:00:08.8	Vladimir Smirnov KAZ 1:00:38.0	Silvio Fauner (ITA) 1:01:48.6
1998	Thomas Alsgaard (NOR) 1:07:01.7	Bjørn Dæhlie (NOR) 1:07:02.8	Vladimir Smirnov (KAZ) 1:07:31.5
2002	Thomas Alsgaard (NOR) Frode Estil (NOR) 49:48.9	—	Per Olfsson (SWE)

Men's 4 × 10km Relay

	Gold	Silver	Bronze
1936	Finland 2:41:33	Norway 2:41:39	Sweden 2:43:03
1948	Sweden 2:32:08	Finland 2:41:06	Norway 2:44:33
1952	Finland 2:20:16	Norway 2:23:13	Sweden 2:24:13
1956	Soviet Union 2:15:30	Finland 2:16:31	Sweden 2:17:42
1960	Finland 2:18:45.6	Norway 2:18:46.4	Soviet Union 2:21:21.6
1964	Sweden 2:18:34.6	Finland 2:18:42.4	Soviet Union 2:18:46.9
1968	Norway 2:08:33.5	Sweden 2:10:13.2	Finland 2:10:56.7
1972	Soviet Union 2:04:47.9	Norway 2:04:57.1	Switzerland 2:07:00.6
1976	Finland 2:07:59.7	Norway 2:09:58.4	Soviet Union 2:10:51.5
1980	Soviet Union 1:57:03.5	Norway 1:58:45.8	Finland 2:00:00.2
1984	Sweden 1:55:06.3	Soviet Union 1:55:16.5	Finland 1:56:31.4
1988	Sweden 1:43:58.6	Soviet Union 1:44:11.3	Czechoslovakia 1:45:22.7
1992	Norway 1:39:26.0	Italy 1:40:52.7	Finland 1:41:22.9
1994	Italy 1:41:15.0	Norway 1:41:15.4	Finland 1:42:15.6
1998	Norway 1:40:55.7	Italy 1:40:55.9	Finland 1:42:15.5
2002	Norway 1:32:45.5	Italy 1:32:45.8	Germany 1:33:34.5

Men's Nordic Combined Sprint
(K120 jump/7.5km cross-country)

	Gold	Silver	Bronze
2002	Samppa Lajunen (FIN)	Ronny Ackermann (GER) +9.0	Felix Gottwald (AUT) +40.2

Men's Nordic Combined

(1924-52, jump/18km cross-country; 1956, jump/15km cross-country; 1960, K80 jump/15km cross-country; 1964-88, K70 jump/15km cross-country; 1992- , K90 jump/15km cross-country)

	Gold	Silver	Bronze
1924	Thorleif Haug (NOR) 18.906	Thoralf Strømstad (NOR) 18.219	Johan Grøttumsbråten (NOR) 17.854
1928	Johan Gröttumsbråten (NOR) 17.833	Hans Vinjarengen (NOR) 15.303	Jon Snersrud (NOR) 15.021
1932	Johan Gröttumsbråten (NOR) 446.00	Ole Stenen (NOR) 436.05	Hans Vinjarengen (NOR) 434.60
1936	Oddbjørn Hagen (NOR) 430.30	Olav Hoffsbakken (NOR) 419.80	Sverre Brodahl (NOR) 408.10
1948	Heikki Hasu (FIN) 448.80	Martti Huhtala (FIN) 433.65	Sven Israelsson (SWE) 433.40
1952	Simon Slåttvik (NOR) 451.621	Heikki Hasu (FIN) 447.500	Sverre Stenersen (NOR) 436.335
1956	Sverre Stenersen (NOR) 455.000	Bengt Eriksson (SWE) 437.400	Franciszek Gasienica-Gron (POL) 436.800
1960	Georg Thoma (GER) 457.952	Tormod Knutsen (NOR) 453.000	Nikolay Gusakov (URS) 452.000
1964	Tormod Knutsen (NOR) 469.280	Nikolay Kiselyov (URS) 453.040	Georg Thoma (GER) 452.880
1968	Franz Keller (FRG) 449.040	Alois Kälin (SUI) 447.990	Andreas Kunz (GDR) 444.100
1972	Ulrich Wehling (GDR) 413.340	Rauno Miettinen (FIN) 405.505	Karl-Heinz Luck (GDR) 398.800
1976	Ulrich Wehling (GDR) 423.390	Urban Hettich (FRG) 418.900	Konrad Winkler (GDR) 417.470
1980	Ulrich Wehling (GDR) 432.200	Jouko Karjalainen (FIN) 429.500	Konrad Winkler (GDR) 425.320
1984	Tom Sandberg (NOR) 422.295	Jouko Karjalainen (FIN) 416.900	Jukka Ylipulli (FIN) 410.825
1988	Hippolyt Kempf (SUI)	Klaus Sulzenbacher (AUT) +19.0	Allar Levandi (URS) +1:04.3
1992	Fabrice Guy (FRA)	Sylvain Guillaume (FRA) +48.4	Klaus Sulzenbacher (AUT) +1:06.3
1994	Fred Børre Lundberg (NOR)	Takanori Kono (JPN) +1:17.5	Bjarte Engen Vik (NOR) +1:18.3
1998	Bjarte Engen Vik (NOR)	Samppa Lajunen (FIN) +27.5	Valeriy Stolyarov (RUS) +28.2
2002	Samppa Lajunen (FIN)	Jaakko Tallus (FIN) +24.7	Felix Gottwald (AUT) +54.8

Men's Team Nordic Combined

(K90 Jump/4 × 5km relay)

	Gold	Silver	Bronze
1988	West Germany	Switzerland +3.4	Austria +30.9
1992	Japan	Norway +1:26.4	Austria +1:40.1
1994	Japan	Norway +4:49.1	Switzerland +7:48.1
1998	Norway	Finland +1:18.9	France +1:41.9
2002	Finland	Germany +7.5	Austria +11.0

Women's 1.5km Freestyle Sprint

	Gold	Silver	Bronze
2002	Yuliya Chepalova (RUS) 3:10.6	Evi Sachenbacher (GER) 3:12.2	Anita Moen (NOR) 3:12.7

Women's 5km

(1988, classical)

	Gold	Silver	Bronze
1964	Klavdia Boyarskikh (URS) 17:50.5	Mirja Lehtonen (FIN) 17:52.9	Alevtina Kolchina (URS) 18:08.4
1968	Toini Gustafsson (SWE) 16:45.2	Galina Kulakova (URS) 16:48.4	Alevtina Kolchina (URS) 16:51.6
1972	Galina Kulakova (URS) 17:00.5	Marjatta Kajosmaa (FIN) 17:05.5	Helena Šikolová (TCH) 17:07.3
1976	Helena Takalo (FIN) 15:48.7	Raisa Smetanina (URS) 15:49.7	Nina Baldycheva (URS) 16:12.8
1980	Raisa Smetanina (URS) 15:06.9	Hilkka Riihivuori (FIN) 15:12.0	Kvetoslava Jeriová (TCH) 15:23.4
1984	Marja-Liisa Hämäläinen (FIN) 17:04.0	Berit Aunli (NOR) 17:14.1	Kvetoslava Jeriová (TCH) 17:18.3
1988	Marjo Matikainen (FIN) 15:04.0	Tamara Tikhonova (URS) 15:05.3	Vida Venciené (URS) 15:11.1
1992	Marjut Lukkarinen (FIN) 14:13.8	Lyubov Yegorova (CIS)14:14.7	Yelena Välbe (CIS) 14:22.7
1994	Lyubov Yegorova (RUS) 14:08.8	Manuela Di Centa (ITA) 14:28.3	Marja-Liisa Kirvesniemi (FIN) 14:36.0
1998	Larisa Lazutina (RUS) 17:37.9	Katerina Neumannová (CZE) 17:42.7	Bente Martinsen (NOR) 17:49.4

Women's 10km

(1988, classical)

	Gold	Silver	Bronze
1952	Lydia Wideman (FIN) 41:40	Merja Hietamies (FIN) 42:39	Siiri Rantanen (FIN) 42:50
1956	Lyubov Kozyreva (URS) 38:11	Radya Yeroshina (URS) 38:16	Sonja Edström (SWE) 38:23
1960	Maria Gusakova (URS) 39:46.6	Lyubov Baranova Kozyreva (URS) 40:04.2	Radya Yeroshina (URS) 40:06.0
1964	Klavdiya Boyarskikh (URS) 40:24.3	Yevdoyka Mekshilo (URS) 40:26.6	Maria Gusakova (URS) 40:46.6
1968	Toini Gustafsson (SWE) 36:46.5	Berit Mørdre (NOR) 37:54.6	Inger Aufles (NOR) 37:59.9
1972	Galina Kulakova (URS) 34:17.8	Alevtina Olunina (URS) 34:54.1	Marjatta Kajosmaa (FIN) 34:56.4
1976	Raisa Smetanina (URS) 30:13.4	Helena Takalo (FIN) 30:14.3	Galina Kulakova (URS) 30:38.6
1980	Barbara Petzold (GDR) 30:31.5	Hilkka Riihivuori (FIN) 30:35.0	Helena Takalo (FIN) 30:45.2
1984	Marja-Liisa Hämäläinen (FIN) 31:44.2	Raisa Smetanina (URS) 32:02.9	Brit Pettersen (NOR) 32:12.7

S
K
I
N
G

1988	Vida Venciené (URS) 30:08.3	Raisa Smetanina (URS) 30:17.0	Marjo Matikainen (FIN) 30:20.5
1992-98	not held		
2002	Bente Skari (NOR) 28:05.6	Olga Danilova (RUS) 28:08.1	Yuliya Chepalova (RUS) 28:09.9

Women's 15km
(1992, 1998, classical; 1994, freestyle; 2002, freestyle mass start)

	Gold	Silver	Bronze
1992	Lyubov Yegorova (CIS) 42:20.8	Marjut Lukkarinen (FIN) 43:29.9	Yelena Välbe (CIS) 43:42.3
1994	Manuela Di Centa (ITA) 39:44.6	Lyubov Yegorova (RUS) 41:03.0	Nina Gavrilyuk (RUS) 41:10.4
1998	Olga Danilova (RUS) 46:55.4	Larisa Lazutina (RUS) 47:01.0	Anita Moen Guidon (NOR) 47:52.6
2002	Stefania Belmondo (ITA) 39:54.4	Larisa Lazutina (RUS) 39:56.2	Katerina Neumannová (CZE) 40:01.3

Women's 20km
(1988, freestyle)

	Gold	Silver	Bronze
1984	Marja-Liisa Hämäläinen (FIN) 1:01:45.0	Raisa Smetanina (URS) 1:02:26.7	Anne Jahren (NOR) 1:03:13.6
1988	Tamara Tikhonova (URS) 55:53.6	Anfisa Reztsova (URS) 56:12.8	Raisa Smetanina (URS) 57:22.1

Women's 30km
(1992, 1998, freestyle; 1994, classical; 2002, classical)

	Gold	Silver	Bronze
1992	Stefania Belmondo (ITA) 1:22:30.1	Lyubov Yegorova (CIS) 1:22:52.0	Yelena Välbe (CIS) 1:24:13.9
1994	Manuela Di Centa (ITA) 1:25:41.6 1:26:13.6	Marit Wold (NOR) 1:25:57.8	Marja-Liisa Kirvesniemi (FIN)
1998	Yuliya Chepalova (RUS) 1:22:01.5	Stefania Belmondo (ITA) 1:22:11.7	Larisa Lazutina (RUS) 1:23:15.7
2002	Gabriella Paruzzi (ITA) 1:30:57.1	Stefania Belmondo (ITA) 1:31:01.6	Bente Skari (NOR) 1:31:36.3

Women's Combined Pursuit
(1992-98, 5km classical/10km freestyle; 2002, 5km classical/5km freestyle)

	Gold	Silver	Bronze
1992	Lyubov Yegorova (CIS) 40:07.7	Stefania Belmondo (ITA) 40:31.8	Yelena Välbe (CIS) 40:51.7
1994	Lyubov Yegorova (RUS) 41:38.1	Manuela Di Centa (ITA) 41:46.4	Stefania Belmondo (ITA) 42:21.1
1998	Larisa Lazutina (RUS) 46:06.9	Olga Danilova (RUS) 46:13.4	Katerina Neumannová (CZE) 46:14.2
2002	Olga Danilova (RUS) 24:52.1	Larisa Lazutina (RUS) 24:59.0	Beckie Scott (CAN) 25:09.9

Women's 3 × 5km Relay

	Gold	Silver	Bronze
1956	Finland 1:09:01	Soviet Union 1:09:28	Sweden 1:09:48
1960	Sweden 1:04:21.4	Soviet Union 1:05:02.6	Finland 1:06:27.5
1964	Soviet Union 59:20.2	Sweden 1:01:27.0	Finland 1:02:45.1
1968	Norway 57:30.0	Sweden 57:51.0	Soviet Union 58:13.6
1972	Soviet Union 48:46.15	Finland 49:19.37	Norway 49:51.49

Women's 4 × 5km Relay

	Gold	Silver	Bronze
1976	Soviet Union 1:07:49.7	Finland 1:08:36.6	East Germany 1:09:57.9
1980	East Germany 1:02:11.1	Soviet Union 1:03:18.3	Norway 1:04:13.5
1984	Norway 1:06:49.7	Czechoslovakia 1:07:34.7	Finland 1:07:36.7
1988	Soviet Union 59:51.1	Norway 1:01:33.0	Finland 1:01:53.8
1992	CIS 59:34.8	Norway 59:56.4	Italy 1:00:25.9
1994	Russia 57:12.5	Norway 57:42.6	Italy 58:42.6
1998	Russia 55:13.5	Norway 55:38.0	Italy 56:53.3
2002	Germany 49:30.6	Norway 49:31.9	Switzerland 50:03.6

Ski Jumping

Men's Normal Hill
(1964-88, K70; 1992- , K90)

	Gold	Silver	Bronze
1924	Jacob Tullin Thams (NOR)	Narve Bonna (NOR)	Anders Haugen (USA)
1928	Alf Andersen (NOR)	Sigmund Ruud (NOR)	Rudolf Burkert (TCH)
1932	Birger Ruud (NOR)	Hans Beck (NOR)	Kaare Wahlberg (NOR)
1936	Birger Ruud (NOR)	Sven Eriksson (SWE)	Reidar Andersen (NOR)
1948	Petter Hugstedt (NOR)	Birger Ruud (NOR)	Thorleif Schelderup (NOR)
1952	Arnfinn Bergmann (NOR)	Torbjørn Falkanger (NOR)	Karl Holmström (SWE)
1956	Antti Hyvärinen (FIN)	Aulis Kallakorpi (FIN)	Harry Glass (GER)
1960	Helmut Recknagel (GER)	Niilo Halonen (FIN)	Otto Leodolter (AUT)
1964	Veikko Kankkonen (FIN)	Thoralf Engan (NOR)	Torgeir Brandtzæg (NOR)
1968	Jirí Raška (TCH)	Reinhold Bachler (AUT)	Baldur Preiml (AUT)
1972	Yukio Kasaya (JPN)	Akitsugu Konno (JPN)	Seiji Aochi (JPN)
1976	Hans-Georg Aschenbach (GDR)	Jochen Danneberg (GDR)	Karl Schnabl (AUT)
1980	Anton Innauer (AUT)	Manfred Deckert (GDR)	——
		Hirokazu Yagi (JPN)	
1984	Jens Weissflog (GDR)	Matti Nykänen (FIN)	Jari Puikkonen (FIN)
1988	Matti Nykänen (FIN)	Pavel Ploc (TCH)	Jirí Malec (TCH)
1992	Ernst Vettori (AUT)	Martin Höllwarth (AUT)	Toni Nieminen (FIN)
1994	Espen Bredesen (NOR)	Lasse Ottesen (NOR)	Dieter Thoma (GER)
1998	Jani Soininen (FIN)	Kazuyoshi Funaki (JPN)	Andreas Widhölzl (AUT)
2002	Simon Ammann (SUI)	Sven Hannawald (GER)	Adam Malysz (POL)

Men's Large Hill
(1960-64, K80; 1968-88, K90; 1992- , K120)

	Gold	Silver	Bronze
1960	Helmut Recknagel (GER)	Niilo Haloner (FIN)	Otto Leodolter (AUT)
1964	Thoralf Engan (NOR)	Veikko Kankkonen (FIN)	Torgeir Brandtzæg (NOR)
1968	Vladimir Belousov (URS)	Jirí Raška (TCH)	Lars Grini (NOR)
1972	Wojciech Fortuna (POL)	Walter Steiner (SUI)	Rainer Schmidt (GDR)
1976	Karl Schnabl (AUT)	Anton Innauer (AUT)	Henry Glass (GDR)
1980	Jouko Törmänen (FIN)	Hubert Neuper (AUT)	Jari Puikkonen (FIN)
1984	Matti Nykänen (FIN)	Jens Weissflog (GDR)	Pavel Ploc (TCH)
1988	Matti Nykänen (FIN)	Erik Johnsen (NOR)	Matjaz Debelak (YUG)
1992	Toni Nieminen (FIN)	Martin Höllwarth (AUT)	Heinz Kuttin (AUT)
1994	Jens Weissflog (GER)	Espen Bredesen (NOR)	Andreas Goldberger (AUT)
1998	Kazuyoshi Funaki (JPN)	Jani Soininen (FIN)	Masahiko Harada (JPN)
2002	Simon Ammann (SUI)	Adam Malysz (POL)	Matti Hautamäki (FIN)

Men's Team
(1988, K90; 1992- , K120)

	Gold	Silver	Bronze
1988	Finland 634.4	Yugoslavia 625.5	Norway 596.1
1992	Finland 644.4	Austria 642.9	Czech Republic 620.1
1994	Germany 970.1	Japan 956.9	Austria 918.9
1998	Japan 933.0	Germany 897.4	Australi 881.5
2002	Germany 974.1	Finland 974.0	Slovenia 946.3

Freestyle Skiing

Men's Aerials

	Gold	Silver	Bronze
1994	Andreas Schönbächler (SUI) 234.67	Philippe LaRoche (CAN) 228.63	Lloyd Langlois (CAN) 222.44
1998	Eric Bergoust (USA) 255.64	Sébastien Foucras (FRA) 248.79	Dmitriy Dashchinsky (BLR) 240.79
2002	Aleš Valenta (CZE) 257.02	Joe Pack (USA) 251.64	Aleksey Grichin (BLR) 251.19

Men's Moguls

	Gold	Silver	Bronze
1992	Edgar Grospiron (FRA) 25.81	Olivier Allamand (FRA) 24.87	Nelson Carmichael (USA) 24.82
1994	Jean-Luc Brassard (CAN) 27.24	Sergey Shupletsov (RUS) 26.90	Edgar Grospiron (FRA) 26.64

S
K
I
I
N
G

| 1998 | Jonny Moseley (USA) 26.93 | Janne Lähtela (FIN) 26.00 | Sami Mustonen (FIN) 25.76 |
| 2002 | Janne Lähtela (FIN) 27.97 | Travis Mayer (USA) 27.59 | Richard Gay (FRA) 26.91 |

Women's Aerials

	Gold	Silver	Bronze
1994	Lina Cheryazova (UZB) 166.84	Marie Lindgren (SWE) 165.88	Hilde Synnøve Lid (NOR) 164.13
1998	Nikki Stone (USA) 193.00	Xu Nannan (CHN) 186.97	Colette Brand (SUI) 171.83
2002	Alisa Camplin (AUS) 193.47	Veronica Brenner (CAN) 190.02	Deidra Dionne (CAN) 189.26

Women's Moguls

	Gold	Silver	Bronze
1992	Donna Weinbrecht (USA) 23.69	Yelizaveta Kozhevnikova (CIS) 23.50	Stine Lise Hattestad (NOR) 23.04
1994	Stine Lise Hattestad (NOR) 25.97	Elizabeth McIntyre (USA) 25.89	Yelizaveta Kozhevnikova (RUS) 25.81
1998	Tae Satoya (JPN) 25.06	Tatjana Mittermayer (GER) 24.62	Kari Traa (NOR) 24.09
2002	Kari Traa (NOR) 25.94	Shannon Bahrke (USA) 25.06	Tae Satoya (JPN) 24.85

World Championships

Alpine Skiing

Men's Downhill

	Gold	Silver	Bronze
1931	Walter Prager (SUI)	Otto Furrer (SUI)	Willi Steuri (SUI)
1932	Gustav Lantschner (GER)	David Zogg (SUI)	Otto Furrer (SUI)
1933	Walter Prager (SUI)	David Zogg (SUI)	Hans Hauser (AUT)
1934	David Zogg (SUI)	Franz Pfnür (GER)	Ido Cattaneao (ITA)
			Heinz von Allmen (SUI)
1935	Franz Zingerle (AUT)	Emile Allais (FRA)	Willi Steuri (SUI)
1936	Rudolf Rominger (SUI)	Gianfranco Sertorelli (ITA)	Heinz von Allmen (SUI)
1937	Emile Allais (FRA)	Maurice Lafforque (FRA)	——
		Gianfranco Sertorelli (ITA)	
1938	James Couttet (FRA)	Emile Allais (FRA)	Gustav Lantschner (GER)
1939	Gustav Lantschner (GER)	Josef Jennewein (GER)	Karl Molitor (SUI)
1941	Josef Jennewein (GER)	Alberto Marcellin (ITA)	Rudi Cranz (GER)
1942–49	not held		
1950	Zeno Colo (ITA)	James Couttet (FRA)	Egon Schöpf (AUT)
1954	Christian Pravda (AUT)	Martin Strolz (AUT)	Ernst Obereigner (AUT)
1958	Anton Sailer (AUT)	Roger Staub (SUI)	Jean Vuarnet (FRA)
1962	Karl Schranz (AUT)	Emile Viollat (FRA)	Egon Zimmermann (AUT)
1966	Jean-Claude Killy (FRA)	Léo Lacroix (FRA)	Franz Vogler (FRG)
1970	Bernhard Russi (SUI)	Karl Cordin (AUT)	Malcolm Milne (AUS)
1974	David Zwilling (AUT)	Franz Klammer (AUT)	Willy Frommelt (LIE)
1978	Josef Walcher (AUT)	Michael Veith (FRG)	Werner Grissmann (AUT)
1982	Harti Weirather (AUT)	Conradin Cathomen (SUI)	Erwin Resch (AUT)
1985	Pirmin Zurbriggen (SUI)	Peter Müller (SUI)	Douglas Lewis (USA)
1987	Peter Müller (SUI)	Pirmin Zurbriggen (SUI)	Karl Alpiger (SUI)
1989	Hansjörg Tauscher (FRG)	Peter Müller (SUI)	Karl Alpiger (SUI)
1991	Franz Heinzer (SUI)	Peter Runggaldier (ITA)	Daniel Mahrer (SUI)
1993	Urs Lehmann (SUI)	Atle Skårdal (NOR)	A.J. Kitt (USA)
1996	Patrick Ortlieb (AUT)	Kristian Ghedina (ITA)	Luc Alphand (FRA)
1997	Bruno Kernen (SUI)	Lasse Kjus (NOR)	Kristian Ghedina (ITA)
1999	Hermann Maier (AUT)	Lasse Kjus (NOR)	Kjetil André Aamodt (NOR)
2001	Hannes Trinkl (AUT)	Hermann Maier (AUT)	Florian Eckert (GER)
2003	Michael Walchhofer (AUT)	Kjetil André Aamodt (NOR)	Bruno Kernen (SUI)

Men's Slalom

	Gold	Silver	Bronze
1931	David Zogg (SUI)	Anton Seelos (AUT)	Friedl Däuber (GER)
1932	Friedl Däuber (GER)	Otto Furrer (SUI)	Hans Hauser (AUT)
1933	Anton Seelos (AUT)	Gustav Lantschner (AUT)	Willi Steuri (SUI)
1934	Franz Pfnür (GER)	David Zogg (SUI)	Willi Steuri (SUI)
1935	Anton Seelos (AUT)	David Zogg (SUI)	Friedl Pfeiffer (AUT)
			Francois Vignole (FRA)

1936	Rudolf Matt (AUT)	Eberhard Kneissl (AUT)	Rudolf Rominger (SUI)
1937	Emile Allais (FRA)	Willi Walch (AUT)	Roman Wörndle (GER)
1938	Rudolf Rominger (SUI)	Emile Allais (FRA)	Gustav Lantschner (GER)
1939	Rudolf Rominger (SUI)	Josef Jennewein (GER)	Willi Walch (AUT)
1941	Vittorio Chierroni (ITA)	——	Alberto Marcellin (ITA)
	Albert Pfeiffer (GER)		
1942-49	not held		
1950	Georges Schneider (SUI)	Zeno Colo (ITA)	Stein Eriksen (NOR)
1954	Stein Eriksen (NOR)	Beni Obermüller (AUT)	Toni Spiss (AUT)
1958	Josi Rieder (AUT)	Anton Sailer (AUT)	Chiharu Igaya (JPN)
1962	Charles Bozon (FRA)	Guy Périllat (FRA)	Gerhard Nenning (AUT)
1966	Carlo Senoner (ITA)	Guy Périllat (FRA)	Louis Jauffret (FRA)
1970	Jean-Noël Augert (FRA)	Patrick Russel (FRA)	Billy Kidd (USA)
1974	Gustavo Thöni (ITA)	David Zwilling (AUT)	Francisco Fernandez-Ochoa (ESP)
1978	Ingemar Stenmark (SWE)	Piero Gros (ITA)	Paul Frommelt (LIE)
1982	Ingemar Stenmark (SWE)	Bojan Krizaj (YUG)	Bengt Fjällberg (SWE)
1985	Jonas Nilsson (SWE)	Marc Girardelli (LUX)	Robert Zoller (AUT)
1987	Frank Wörndl (FRG)	Günther Mader (AUT)	Armin Bittner (FRG)
1989	Rudolf Nierlich (AUT)	Armin Bittner (FRG)	Marc Girardelli (LUX)
1991	Marc Girardelli (LUX)	Thomas Stangassinger (AUT)	Ole Kristian Furuseth (NOR)
1993	Kjetil André Aamodt (NOR)	Marc Girardelli (LUX)	Thomas Stangassinger (AUT)
1996	Alberto Tomba (ITA)	Mario Reiter (AUT)	Michael von Grünigen (SUI)
1997	Tom Stiansen (NOR)	Sébastien Amiez (FRA)	Alberto Tomba (ITA)
1999	Kalle Palander (FIN)	Lasse Kjus (NOR)	Christian Mayer (AUT)
2001	Mario Matt (AUT)	Benjamin Raich (AUT)	Mitja Kunc (SLO)
2003	Ivica Kostelic (CRO)	Silvan Zurbriggen (SUI)	Giorgio Rocca (ITA)

Men's Giant Slalom

	Gold	**Silver**	**Bronze**
1950	Zeno Colo (ITA)	Fernand Grosjean (SUI)	James Couttet (FRA)
1954	Stein Eriksen (NOR)	Francois Bonlieu (FRA)	Andreas Molterer (AUT)
1958	Anton Sailer (AUT)	Josi Rieder (AUT)	François Bonlieu (FRA)
			Roger Staub (SUI)
1962	Egon Zimmermann (AUT)	Karl Schranz (AUT)	Martin Burger (AUT)
1966	Guy Périllat (FRA)	Georges Mauduit (FRA)	Karl Schranz (AUT)
1970	Karl Schranz (AUT)	Werner Bleiner (AUT)	Dumeng Giovanoli (SUI)
1974	Gustavo Thöni (ITA)	Hans Hinterseer (AUT)	Piero Gros (ITA)
1978	Ingemar Stenmark (SWE)	Andreas Wenzel (LIE)	Willy Frommelt (LIE)
1982	Steve Mahre (USA)	Ingemar Stenmark (SWE)	Boris Strel (YUG)
1985	Markus Wasmeier (FRG)	Pirmin Zurbriggen (SUI)	Marc Girardelli (LUX)
1987	Pirmin Zurbriggen (SUI)	Marc Girardelli (LUX)	Alberto Tomba (ITA)
1989	Rudolf Nierlich (AUT)	Helmut Mayer (AUT)	Pirmin Zurbriggen (SUI)
1991	Rudolf Nierlich (AUT)	Urs Kälin (SUI)	Johan Wallner (SWE)
1993	Kjetil André Aamodt (NOR)	Rainer Salzgeber (AUT)	Johan Wallner (SWE)
1996	Alberto Tomba (ITA)	Urs Kälin (SUI)	Michael von Grünigen (SUI)
1997	Michael von Grünigen (SUI)	Lasse Kjus (NOR)	Andreas Schifferer (AUT)
1999	Lasse Kjus (NOR)	Marco Büchel (LIE)	Steve Locher (SUI)
2001	Michael von Grünigen (SUI)	Kjetil André Aamodt (NOR)	Frédéric Covili (FRA)
2003	Bode Miller (USA)	Hans Knauss (AUT)	Erik Schlopy (USA)

Men's Super Giant Slalom

	Gold	**Silver**	**Bronze**
1987	Pirmin Zurbriggen (SUI)	Marc Girardelli (LUX)	Markus Wasmeier (FRG)
1989	Martin Hangl (SUI)	Pirmin Zurbriggen (SUI)	Tomas Cizman (YUG)
1991	Stephan Eberharter (AUT)	Kjetil André Aamodt (NOR)	Franck Piccard (FRA)
1996	Atle Skårdal (NOR)	Patrik Järbyn (SWE)	Kjetil André Aamodt (NOR)
1997	Atle Skårdal (NOR)	Lasse Kjus (NOR)	Günther Mader (AUT)
1999	Hermann Maier (AUT)	——	Hans Knaus (AUT)
	Lasse Kjus (NOR)		
2001	Daron Rahlves (USA)	Stephan Eberharter (AUT)	Hermann Maier (AUT)
2003	Stephan Eberharter (AUT)	Bode Miller (USA)	——
		Hermann Maier (AUT)	

Men's Combined

	Gold	Silver	Bronze
1932	Otto Furrer (SUI)	Hans Hauser (AUT)	Gustav Lantschner (GER)
1933	Anton Seelos (AUT)	Fritz Steuri (SUI)	Otto Furrer (SUI)
1934	David Zogg (SUI)	Franz Pfnür (GER)	Heinz von Allmen (SUI)
1935	Anton Seelos (AUT)	Emile Allais (FRA)	Birger Ruud (NOR)
1936	Rudolf Rominger (SUI)	Heinz von Allmen (SUI)	Eberhard Kneissl (AUT)
1937	Emile Allais (FRA)	Maurice Lafforgue (FRA)	Willi Steuri (SUI)
1938	Emile Allais (FRA)	Rudolf Rominger (SUI)	Gustav Lantschner (GER)
1939	Josef Jennewein (GER)	Willi Walch (GER)	Rudolf Rominger (SUI)
1941	Josef Jennewein (GER)	Alberto Marcellin (ITA)	Vittori Chierroni (ITA)
1942-53	not held		
1954	Stein Eriksen (NOR)	Christian Pravda (AUT)	Stig Sollander (SWE)
1956	Anton Sailer (AUT)	Charles Bozon (FRA)	Stig Sollander (SWE)
1958	Anton Sailer (AUT)	Josi Rieder (AUT)	Roger Staub (SUI)
1960	Guy Périllat (FRA)	Charles Bozon (FRA)	Hans-Peter Lanig (FRG)
1962	Karl Schranz (AUT)	Gerhard Nenning (AUT)	Ludwig Leitner (FRG)
1964	Ludwig Leitner (FRG)	Gerhard Nenning (AUT)	Billy Kidd (USA)
1966	Jean-Claude Killy (FRA)	Leo Lacroix (FRA)	Ludwig Leitner (FRG)
1968	Jean-Claude Killy (FRA)	Dumeng Giovanoli (SUI)	Heinrich Messner (AUT)
1970	Billy Kidd (USA)	Patrick Russel (FRA)	Andrzej Bachleda (POL)
1972	Gustav Thöni (ITA)	Walter Tresch (SUI)	Jim Hunter (CAN)
1974	Franz Klammer (AUT)	Andrzej Bachleda (POL)	Wolfgang Junginger (FRG)
1976	Gustav Thöni (ITA)	Willy Frommelt (LIE)	Greg Jones (USA)
1978	Andreas Wenzel (LIE)	Josef Ferstl (FRG)	Peter Patterson (USA)
1980	Phil Mahre (USA)	Andreas Wenzel (LIE)	Leonhard Stock (AUT)
1982	Michel Vion (FRA)	Peter Lüscher (SUI)	Anton Steiner (AUT)
1985	Pirmin Zurbriggen (SUI)	Ernst Riedelsberger (AUT)	Thomas Bürgler (SUI)
1987	Marc Girardelli (LUX)	Pirmin Zurbriggen (SUI)	Günther Mader (AUT)
1989	Marc Girardelli (LUX)	Paul Accola (SUI)	Günther Mader (AUT)
1991	Stephan Eberharter (AUT)	Kristian Ghedina (ITA)	Günther Mader (AUT)
1993	Lasse Kjus (NOR)	Kjetil André Aamodt (NOR)	Marc Girardelli (LUX)
1996	Marc Girardelli (LUX)	Lasse Kjus (NOR)	Günther Mader (AUT)
1997	Kjetil André Aamodt (NOR)	Bruno Kernen (SUI)	Mario Reiter (AUT)
1999	Kjetil André Aamodt (NOR)	Lasse Kjus (NOR)	Paul Accola (SUI)
2001	Kjetil André Aamodt (NOR)	Mario Matt (AUT)	Paul Accola (SUI)
2003	Bode Miller (USA)	Lasse Kjus (NOR)	Kjetil André Aamodt (NOR)

Women's Downhill

	Gold	Silver	Bronze
1931	Esme MacKinnon (GBR)	Nell Carroll (GBR)	Irma Schmiedegg (AUT)
1932	Paola Wiesinger (ITA)	Inge Wersin-Lantschner (AUT)	Hady Lantschner (AUT)
1933	Inge Wersin-Lantschner (AUT)	Nini Arx-Zogg (SUI)	Gerda Paumgarten (AUT)
1934	Anny Rüegg (SUI)	Christel Cranz (GER)	Lisa Resch (GER)
1935	Christel Cranz (GER)	Hady Pfeiffer (GER)	Anny Rüegg (SUI)
1936	Evelyn Pinching (GBR)	Elvira Osirning (SUI)	Nini Arx-Zogg (SUI)
1937	Christel Cranz (GER)	Nini Zogg (SUI)	Käthe Grasegger (GER)
1938	Lisa Resch (GER)	Christel Cranz (GER)	Käthe Grasegger (GER)
1939	Christel Cranz (GER)	Lisa Resch (GER)	Helga Gödl (GER)
1941	Christel Cranz (GER)	Käthe Grasegger (GER)	Anneliese Proxauf (SUI)
1942-49	not held		
1950	Trude Beiser (AUT)	Erika Mahringer (AUT)	Therese Miller (FRA)
1954	Ida Schöpfer (AUT)	Trude Klecker (AUT)	Lucienne Schmidt (FRA)
1958	Lucille Wheeler (CAN)	Frieda Dänzer (SUI)	Carla Marchelli (ITA)
1962	Christel Haas (AUT)	Pia Riva (ITA)	Barbara Ferries (USA)
1966	Erika Schinegger (AUT)	Marielle Goitschel (FRA)	Annie Famose (FRA)
1970	Annerösli Zryd (SUI)	Isabelle Mir (FRA)	Annemarie Moser-Pröll (AUT)
1974	Annemarie Moser-Pröll (AUT)	Betsy Clifford (CAN)	Wiltrud Drexel (AUT)
1978	Annemarie Moser-Pröll (AUT)	Irene Epple (FRG)	Doris de Agostini (SUI)
1982	Gerry Sörensen (USA)	Cindy Nelson (USA)	Laurie Graham (CAN)
1985	Michela Figini (SUI)	Ariane Ehrat (SUI)	Katrin Gutensohn (AUT)
1987	Maria Walliser (SUI)	Michela Figini (SUI)	Regina Mösenlechner (FRG)
1989	Maria Walliser (SUI)	Karen Percy (CAN)	Karin Dedler (FRG)
1991	Petra Kronberger (AUT)	Nathalie Bouvier (FRA)	Svetlana Gladyscheva (RUS)
1993	Kate Pace (CAN)	Astrid Lødemel (NOR)	Anja Haas (AUT)
1996	Picabo Street (USA)	Katja Seizinger (GER)	Hilary Lindh (USA)
1997	Hilary Lindh (USA)	Heidi Zurbriggen (SUI)	Pernilla Wiberg (SWE)
1999	Renate Götschl (AUT)	Michaela Dorfmeister (AUT)	Stefanie Schuster (AUT)
2001	Michaela Dorfmeister (AUT)	Renate Götschl (AUT)	Selina Heregger (AUT)
2003	Melanie Turgeon (CAN)	Corinne Rey-Bellet (SUI)	Alexandra Meissnitzer (AUT)

Women's Slalom

	Gold	Silver	Bronze
1931	Esme MacKinnon (GBR)	Inge Wersin-Lantschner (AUT)	Jeanette Kessler (GBR)
1932	Rösli Streiff (SUI)	Audrey Sale-Barker (GBR)	Doreen Elliott (GBR)
1933	Inge Wersin-Lantschner (AUT)	Helen Boughton-Leigh (GBR)	Helen Zingg (SUI)
1934	Christel Cranz (GER)	Lisa Resch (GER)	Rösli Rominger (SUI)
1935	Anny Rüegg (SUI)	Christel Cranz (GER)	Käthe Grasegger (GER)
1936	Gerda Paumgarten (AUT)	Evelyn Pinching (GBR)	Grete Weichert (AUT)
1937	Christel Cranz (GER)	Käthe Grasegger (GER)	Lisa Resch (GER)
1938	Christel Cranz (GER)	Nini Arx-Zogg (SUI)	Erna Steuri (SUI)
1939	Christel Cranz (GER)	Margrit Schaad (SUI)	May Nilsson (SWE)
1941	Celina Seghi (ITA)	Christel Cranz (GER)	Anneliese Proxauf (SUI)
1942-49	not held		
1950	Dagmar Rom (AUT)	Erika Mahringer (AUT)	Celina Seghi (ITA)
1954	Trude Klecker (AUT)	Ida Schöpfer (AUT)	Sarah Thomasson (SWE)
1958	Inger Bjørnbakken (NOR)	Josefine Frandl (AUT)	Annemarie Waser (SUI)
1962	Marianne Jahn (AUT)	Marielle Goitschel (FRA)	Erika Netzer (AUT)
1966	Annie Famose (FRA)	Marielle Goitschel (FRA)	Peggy McCoy (USA)
1970	Ingrid Lafforgue (FRA)	Barbara Cochran (USA)	Michèle Jacot (FRA)
1974	Hanni Wenzel (LIE)	Michèle Jacot (FRA)	Lise-Marie Morerod (SUI)
1978	Lea Sölkner (AUT)	Pamela Behr (FRG)	Monika Kaserer (AUT)
1982	Erika Hess (SUI)	Christin Cooper (USA)	Daniela Zini (ITA)
1985	Perrine Pelen (FRA)	Christelle Guignard (FRA)	Paoletta Magoni (ITA)
1987	Erika Hess (SUI)	Roswitha Steiner (AUT)	Mateja Svet (YUG)
1989	Mateja Svet (YUG)	Vreni Schneider (SUI)	Tamara McKinney (USA)
1991	Vreni Schneider (SUI)	Natasja Bokal (YUG)	Ingrid Salvenmoser (AUT)
1993	Karin Buder (AUT)	Julie Parisien (USA)	Elfriede Eder (AUT)
1996	Pernilla Wiberg (SWE)	Patricia Chauvet (FRA)	Urska Hrovat (SLO)
1997	Deborah Compagnoni (ITA)	Lara Magoni (ITA)	Karin Roten (SUI)
1999	Zali Steggall (AUT)	Pernilla Wiberg (SWE)	Trine Bakke (NOR)
2001	Anja Paerson (SWE)	Christel Saioni (FRA)	Hedda Berntsen (NOR)
2003	Janica Kostelic (CRO)	Marlies Schild (AUT)	Nicole Hosp (AUT)

Women's Giant Slalom

	Gold	Silver	Bronze
1950	Dagmar Rom (AUT)	Trude Beiser (AUT)	Lucienne Schmidt (FRA)
1954	Lucienne Schmidt (FRA)	Madeleine Berthod (SUI)	Jannette Burr (USA)
1958	Lucille Wheeler (CAN)	Sally Deaver (USA)	Frieda Dänzer (SUI)
1962	Marianne Jahn (AUT)	Erika Netzer (AUT)	Joan Hannah (USA)
1966	Marielle Goitschel (FRA)	Heide Zimmermann (AUT)	Florence Steurer (FRA)
1970	Betsy Clifford (CAN)	Ingrid Lafforgue (FRA)	Françoise Macchi (FRA)
1974	Fabienne Serrat (FRA)	Traudl Treichl (FRA)	Jacqueline Rouvier (FRA)
1978	Maria Epple (FRG)	Lise-Marie Morerod (SUI)	Annemarie Moser-Pröll (AUT)
1982	Erika Hess (SUI)	Christin Cooper (USA)	Ursula Konzett (LIE)
1985	Diann Roffe (USA)	Elisabeth Kirchler (AUT)	Ewa Twardokens (USA)
1987	Vreni Schneider (SUI)	Mateja Svet (YUG)	Maria Walliser (SUI)
1989	Vreni Schneider (SUI)	Carole Merle (FRA)	Christelle Guignard (FRA)
1991	Pernilla Wiberg (SWE)	Ulrike Maier (AUT)	Traudl Hächer (GER)
1993	Carole Merle (FRA)	Anita Wachter (AUT)	Martina Ertl (GER)
1996	Deborah Compagnoni (ITA)	Karin Roten (SUI)	Martina Ertl (GER)
1997	Deborah Compagnoni (ITA)	Karin Roten (SUI)	Leila Piccard (FRA)
1999	Alexandra Meissnitzer (AUT)	Andrine Flemmen (NOR)	Anita Wachter (AUT)
2001	Sonja Nef (SUI)	Karen Putzer (ITA)	Anja Paerson (SWE)
2003	Anja Paerson (SWE)	Denise Karbon (ITA)	Allison Forsyth (CAN)

Women's Super Giant Slalom

	Gold	Silver	Bronze
1987	Maria Walliser (SUI)	Michela Figini (SUI)	Mateja Svet (YUG)
1989	Ulrike Maier (AUT)	Sigrid Wolf (AUT)	Michaela Gerg (FRG)
1991	Ulrike Maier (AUT)	Carole Merle (FRA)	Anita Wachter (AUT)
1993	Katja Seizinger (GER)	Sylvia Eder (AUT)	Astrid Lødemel (NOR)
1996	Isolde Kostner (ITA)	Heidi Zurbriggen (SUI)	Picabo Street (USA)
1997	Isolde Kostner (ITA)	Katja Seizinger (GER)	Hilde Gerg (GER)
1999	Alexandra Meissnitzer (AUT)	Renate Götschl (AUT)	Michaela Dorfmeister (AUT)
2001	Regine Cavagnoud (FRA)	Isolde Kostner (ITA)	Hilde Gerg (GER)
2003	Michaela Dorfmeister (AUT)	Kirsten Clark (USA)	Jonna Mendes (USA)

SKIING

Women's Combined

	Gold	Silver	Bronze
1932	Rösli Streiff (SUI)	Inge Wersin-Lantschner (AUT)	Hady Lantschner (AUT)
1933	Inge Wersin-Lantschner (AUT)	Gerda Paumgarten (AUT)	Jeanette Kessler (GBR)
1934	Christel Cranz (GER)	Lisa Resch (GER)	Anny Rüegg (SUI)
1935	Christel Cranz (GER)	Anny Rüegg (SUI)	Käthe Grasegger (GER)
1936	Evelyn Pinching (GBR)	Elvira Osirning (SUI)	Gerda Paumgarten (SUI)
1937	Christel Cranz (GER)	Nini Arx-Zogg (SUI)	Käthe Grasegger (GER)
1938	Christel Cranz (GER)	Lisa Resch (GER)	Käthe Grasegger (GER)
1939	Christel Cranz (GER)	Margrit Schaad (SUI)	Lisa Resch (GER)
1941	Christel Cranz (GER)	Celina Seghi (ITA)	Anneliese Proxauf (SUI)
1942-53	not held		
1954	Ida Schöpfer (AUT)	Madeleine Berthod (SUI)	Lucienne Schmidt (FRA)
1956	Madeleine Berthod (SUI)	Frieda Dänzer (SUI)	Giuliana Chenal-Minuzzo (ITA)
1958	Frieda Dänzer (SUI)	Lucille Wheeler (CAN)	Josefine Frandl (AUT)
1960	Anne Heggtveit (CAN)	Sonja Sperl (FRG)	Barbi Henneberger (FRG)
1962	Marielle Goitschel (FRA)	Marianne Jahn (AUT)	Erika Netzer (AUT)
1964	Marielle Goitschel (FRA)	Christel Haas (AUT)	Edith Zimmermann (AUT)
1966	Marielle Goitschel (FRA)	Annie Famose (FRA)	Heide Zimmermann (AUT)
1968	Nancy Greene (CAN)	Marielle Goitschel (FRA)	Annie Famose (FRA)
1970	Michèle Jacot (FRA)	Florence Steurer (FRA)	Marilyn Cochran (USA)
1972	Annemarie Moser-Pröll (AUT)	Florence Steurer (FRA)	Toril Førland (NOR)
1974	Fabienne Serrat (FRA)	Hanni Wenzel (LIE)	Monika Kaserer (AUT)
1976	Rosi Mittermaier (FRG)	Danielle Debernard (FRA)	Hanni Wenzel (LIE)
1978	Annemarie Moser-Pröll (AUT)	Hanni Wenzel (LIE)	Fabienne Serrat (FRA)
1980	Hanni Wenzel (LIE)	Cindy Nelson (USA)	Ingrid Eberle (AUT)
1982	Erika Hess (SUI)	Perrine Pelen (FRA)	Christin Cooper (USA)
1985	Erika Hess (SUI)	Sylvia Eder (AUT)	Tamara McKinney (USA)
1987	Erika Hess (SUI)	Sylvia Eder (AUT)	Tamara McKinney (USA)
1989	Tamara McKinney (USA)	Vreni Schneider (SUI)	Brigitte Örtli (SUI)
1991	Chantal Bournissen (SUI)	Ingrid Stöckl (AUT)	Vreni Schneider (SUI)
1993	Miriam Vogt (GER)	Picabo Street (USA)	Anita Wachter (AUT)
1996	Pernilla Wiberg (SWE)	Anita Wachter (AUT)	Marianne Kjørstad (NOR)
1997	Renate Götschl (AUT)	Katja Seizinger (GER)	Hilde Gerg (GER)
1999	Pernilla Wiberg (SWE)	Renate Götschl (AUT)	Florence Masnada (FRA)
2001	Martina Ertl (GER)	Christine Sponring (AUT)	Karen Putzer (ITA)
2003	Janica Kostelic (CRO)	Nicole Hosp (AUT)	Marlies Öster (SUI)

Ski Jumping

Men's Normal Hill

	Gold	Silver	Bronze
1925	Wilen Dick (TCH)	Henry Ljungmann (NOR)	Frantisek Wende (TCH)
1926	Jacob Tullin Thams (NOR)	Otto Aasen (NOR)	Georg Østerholt (NOR)
1927	Tore Edman (SWE)	Wilen Dick (TCH)	Bertil Carlsson (SWE)
1929	Sigmund Ruud (NOR)	Kristian Johansson (NOR)	Hans Kleppen (NOR)
1930	Gunnar Andersen (NOR)	Reidar Andersen (NOR)	Sigmund Ruud (NOR)
1931	Birger Ruud (NOR)	Fritz Kaufmann (SUI)	Sven Selånger (Eriksson) (SWE)
1933	Marcel Reymond (SUI)	Rudolf Purkert (TCH)	Sven Selånger (Eriksson) (SWE)
1934	Kristian Johansson (NOR)	Arne Hovde (NOR)	Sven Selånger (Eriksson) (SWE)
1935	Birger Ruud (NOR)	Reidar Andersen (NOR)	Alf Andersen (NOR)
1937	Birger Ruud (NOR)	Reidar Andersen (NOR)	Sigurd Solid (NOR)
1938	Asbjørn Ruud (NOR)	Stanislaw Marusarz (POL)	Hilmar Myhra (NOR)
1939	Josef Bradl (GER)	Birger Ruud (NOR)	Arnholdt Kongsgaard (NOR)
1941	Paavo Vierto (FIN)	Leo Laakso (FIN)	Sven Selånger (Eriksson) (SWE)
1950	Hans Bjørnstad (NOR)	Thure Lindgren (SWE)	Arnfinn Bergmann (NOR)
1954	Matti Pietikäinen (FIN)	Veikko Heinonen (FIN)	Bror Östman (SWE)
1958	Juhani Kärkinen (FIN)	Ensio Hyytiä (FIN)	Helmut Recknagel (GDR)
1962	Toralf Engan (NOR)	Antoni Laciak (POL)	Helmut Recknagel (GDR)
1966	Bjørn Wirkola (NOR)	Dieter Neuendorf (GDR)	Paavo Lukkariniemi (FIN)
1970	Gari Napalkov (URS)	Yukio Kasaya (JPN)	Lars Grini (NOR)
1974	Hans-Georg Aschenbach (GDR)	Dietrich Kampf (GDR)	Aleksey Borovitin (URS)
1978	Matthias Buse (GDR)	Henry Glass (GDR)	Aleksey Borovitin (URS)
1982	Armin Kogler (AUT)	Jari Puikkonen (FIN)	Ole Bremseth (NOR)
1985	Jens Weissflog (GDR)	Andreas Felder (AUT)	Per Bergerud (NOR)
1987	Jirí Parma (TCH)	Matti Nykänen (FIN)	Vegard Opaas (NOR)
1989	Jens Weissflog (GDR)	Ari-Pekka Nikkola (FIN)	Heinz Kuttin (AUT)
1991	Heinz Kuttin (AUT)	Kent Johansen (NOR)	Ari-Pekka Nikkola (FIN)
1993	Masahiko Harada (JPN)	Andreas Goldberger (AUT)	Jaroslav Sakala (CZE)

	Gold	Silver	Bronze
1995	Takanobu Okabe (JPN)	Hiroya Saito (JPN)	Mika Laitinen (FIN)
1997	Janne Ahonen (FIN)	Masahiko Harada (JPN)	Andreas Goldberger (AUT)
1999	Kazuyoshi Funaki (JPN)	Hideharu Miyahira (JPN)	Masahiko Harada (JPN)
2001	Adam Malysz (POL)	Martin Schmitt (GER)	Martin Höllwarth (AUT)

Men's Large Hill

	Gold	Silver	Bronze
1962	Helmut Recknagel (GDR)	Nikolay Kamensky (URS)	Niilo Halonen (FIN)
1966	Bjørn Wirkola (NOR)	Takashi Futisawa (JPN)	Kjell Sjöberg (SWE)
1970	Gari Napalkov (URS)	Jirí Raška (TCH)	Stanislaw Daniel-Gasienica (POL)
1974	Hans-Georg Aschenbach (GDR)	Heinz Wossipiwo (GDR)	Rudolf Höhnl (TCH)
1978	Tapio Räisänen (FIN)	Alois Lipburger (AUT)	Falko Weisspflog (GDR)
1982	Matti Nykänen (FIN)	Olav Hansson (NOR)	Armin Kogler (AUT)
1985	Per Bergerud (NOR)	Jari Puikkonen (FIN)	Matti Nykänen (FIN)
1987	Andreas Felder (AUT)	Vegard Opaas (NOR)	Ernst Vettori (AUT)
1989	Jari Puikkonen (FIN)	Jens Weissflog (GDR)	Matti Nykänen (FIN)
1991	Franci Petek (YUG)	Rune Olijnyk (NOR)	Jens Weissflog (GER)
1993	Espen Bredesen (NOR)	Jaroslav Sakala (CZE)	Andreas Goldberger (AUT)
1995	Tommy Ingebretsen (NOR)	Andreas Goldberger (AUT)	Jens Weissflog (GER)
1997	Masahiko Harada (JPN)	Dieter Thoma (GER)	Sylvain Freiholz (SUI)
1999	Martin Schmitt (GER)	Sven Hannawald (GER)	Hideharu Miyahira (JPN)
2001	Martin Schmitt (GER)	Adam Malysz (POL)	Janne Ahonen (FIN)
2003	Adam Malysz (POL)	Tommy Ingebrigtsen (NOR)	Noriaki Kasai (JPN)

Men's K120 Hill (often called ski-flying)

	Gold	Silver	Bronze
1972	Walter Steiner (SUI)	Heinz Wossipiwo (GDR)	Jiri Raska (TCH)
1973	Hans-Georg Aschenbach (GDR)	Walter Steiner (SUI)	Karel Kodejska (TCH)
1974	Walter Steiner (SUI)	Esko Rautionaha (FIN)	Dag Fossum (NOR)
1975	Karel Kodejska (TCH)	Rainer Schmidt (GDR)	Karl Schnabl (AUT)
1976	Toni Innauer (AUT)	Heinz Wossipiwo (GDR)	Hans Wallner (AUT)
1977	Walter Steiner (SUI)	Toni Innauer (AUT)	Henry Glass (GDR)
1979	Armin Kogler (AUT)	Axel Zitzman (GDR)	Piotr Fijas (POL)
1981	Jari Puikkonen (FIN)	Armin Kogler (AUT)	Tom Levorstad (NOR)
1983	Klaus Ostwald (GDR)	Pavel Ploc (TCH)	Matti Nykänen (FIN)
1985	Matti Nykänen (FIN)	Jens Weissflog (GDR)	Pavel Ploc (TCH)
1986	Andreas Felder (AUT)	Franz Neuländtner (AUT)	Matti Nykänen (FIN)
1988	Ole Gunnar Fidjestøl (NOR)	Primuz Ulaga (YUG)	Matti Nykänen (FIN)
1990	Dieter Thoma (GER)	Matti Nykänen (FIN)	Jens Weissflog (GER)
1992	Noriaki Kasai (JPN)	Andreas Goldberger (AUT)	Roberto Cecon (ITA)
1994	Jaroslav Sakala (CZE)	Espen Bredesen (NOR)	Roberto Cecon (ITA)
1996	Andreas Goldberger (AUT)	Janne Ahonen (FIN)	Urban Franc (SLO)
1998	Kazuyoshi Funaki (JPN)	Sven Hannawald (GER)	Dieter Thoma (GER)
2000	Sven Hannawald (GER)	Andreas Widhölzl (AUT)	Janne Ahonen (FIN)
2002	Sven Hannawald (GER)	Martin Schmitt (GER)	Matti Hautamäki (FIN)
2003	Adam Malysz (POL)	Matti Hautamäki (FIN)	Noriaki Kasai (JPN)

Men's Team Large Hill

	Gold	Silver	Bronze
1982	Norway	Austria	Finland
1984	Finland	East Germany	Czechoslovakia
1985	Finland	Austria	East Germany
1987	Finland	Norway	Austria
1989	Finland	Norway	Czechoslovakia
1991	Austria	Finland	Germany
1993	Norway	Czechoslovakia	Austria
1995	Finland	Japan	Germany
1997	Finland	Japan	Germany
1999	Germany	Japan	Austria
2001	Germany	Finland	Austria
2003	Finland	Japan	Norway

S
K
I
N
G

Four Hills Champions

1953	Sepp Bradl (AUT)		1979	Pentti Kokkonen (FIN)
1954	Olav Bjomstad (NOR)		1980	Hubert Neuper (AUT)
1955	Torbjom Ruste (NOR)		1981	Hubert Neuper (AUT)
1956	Nikolai Kamensik (URS)		1982	Manfred Dockert (GDR)
1957	Pentti Uotina (FIN)		1983	Matti Nykaenen (FIN)
1958	Helmut Recknagl (GDR)		1984	Jens Weissflog (GDR)
1959	Helmut Recknagl (GDR)		1985	Jens Weissflog (GDR)
1960	Max Bolkert (FRG)		1986	Ernst Vettori (AUT)
1961	Helmut Recknagl (GDR)		1987	Ernst Vettori (AUT)
1962	Eino Kirjonen (FIN)		1988	Matti Nykaenen (FIN)
1963	Toralf Engen (NOR)		1989	Risto Laakonen (FIN)
1964	Veikko Kankkonen (FIN)		1990	Dieter Thoma (GER)
1965	Torgar Brandtzag (NOR)		1991	Jens Weissflog (GER)
1966	Veikko Kankkonen (FIN)		1992	Toni Nieminen (FIN)
1967	Bjorn Wirkola (NOR)		1993	Andreas Goldberger (AUT)
1968	Bjorn Wirkola (NOR)		1994	Espen Bredersen (NOR)
1969	Bjorn Wirkola (NOR)		1995	Andreas Goldberger (AUT)
1970	Horst Queck (GDR)		1996	Jens Weissflog (GER)
1971	Jiri Raska (TCH)		1997	Primoz Peterka (SLO)
1972	Ingolf Mork (NOR)		1998	Kazuyoshi Funaki (JPN)
1973	Rainer Schmidt (GDR)		1999	Janne Ahonen (FIN)
1974	Hans-Georg Aschenbach (GDR)		2000	Andreas Wiodholzl (AUT)
1975	Willi Purstl (AUT)		2001	Adam Malysz (POL)
1976	Jochen Danneburg (GDR)		2002	Sven Hannewald (GER)
1977	Jochen Danneburg (GDR)		2003	Janne Ahonen (FIN)
1978	Kari Yiantilla (FIN)		2004	Sigurd Pettersen (NOR)

Freestyle Skiing

Men's Aerials

	Gold	Silver	Bronze
1986	Lloyd Langlois (CAN)	Yves Laroche (CAN)	Jean-Marc Bacquin (FRA)
1988	Jean-Marc Rozon (CAN)	Didier Meda (FRA)	Lloyd Langlois (CAN)
1989	Lloyd Langlois (CAN)	Didier Meda (FRA)	Philippe Laroche (CAN)
1991	Philippe Laroche (CAN)	John Ross (CAN)	Dave Valenti (USA)
1993	Philippe Laroche (CAN)	Richard Cobbing (GBR)	Jean-Marc Bacquin (FRA)
1995	Trace Worthington (USA)	Christian Rijavec (AUT)	Sebastien Foucras (FRA)
1997	Nicholas Fontaine (CAN)	Eric Bergoust (USA)	Andy Capicik (CAN)
1999	Eric Bergoust (USA)	Christian Rijavec (AUT)	Joe Pack (USA)
2001	Aleksey Grishin (BLR)	Dimitriy Dashinski (BLR)	Joe Pack (USA)
2003	Dimitriy Archipov (RUS)	Aleksey Grishin (BLR)	Steve Omischl (CAN)

Men's Moguls

	Gold	Silver	Bronze
1986	Eric Berthon (FRA)	Petsch Moser (SUI)	Martti Kellokumpu (FIN)
1988	Hakan Hansson (SWE)	Elde Hans Engelsen (NOR)	Edgar Grospiron (FRA)
1989	Edgar Grospiron (FRA)	Jörg Biner (SUI)	Eric Berthon (FRA)
1991	Edgar Grospiron (FRA)	Bernard Brandt (SUI)	Chuck Martin (USA)
1993	Jean-Luc Brassard (CAN)	Fabien Bertrand (FRA)	Olivier Cotte (FRA)
1995	Edgar Grospiron (FRA)	Jean-Luc Brassard (CAN)	Sergey Schupletsov (RUS)
1997	Jean-Luc Brassard (CAN)	Stephane Rochon (CAN)	Jesper Rönnbäck (SWE)
1999	Janne Lahtela (FIN)	Lauri Lassila (FIN)	Sami Mustonen (FIN)
2001	Mikko Ronkainen (FIN)	Pierre-Alexandre Rousseau (CAN)	Stephane Rochon (CAN)
2003	Mikko Ronkainen (FIN)	Jeremy Bloom (USA)	Toby Dawson (USA)

Dual Moguls

	Gold	Silver	Bronze
1999	Johann Grégoire (FRA)	Janne Lahtela (FIN)	Lauri Lassila (FIN)
2001	Stéphane Yonnet (FRA)	Patrick Sundberg (SWE)	Johann Gregoire (FRA)
2003	Jeremy Bloom (USA)	Yugo Tsukita (JPN)	Toby Dawson (USA)

Men's Acro (Ballet)

	Gold	Silver	Bronze
1986	Richard Schabl (FRG)	Lane Spina (USA)	——
1988	Hermann Reitberger (FRG)	Lane Spina (USA)	Rune Kristiansen (NOR)
1989	Hermann Reitberger (FRG)	Lane Spina (USA)	Dave Walker (CAN)
1991	Lane Spina (USA)	Roberto Franco (ITA)	Dave Walker (CAN)
1993	Fabrice Becker (FRA)	Rune Kristiansen (NOR)	Lane Spina (USA)
1995	Rune Kristiansen (NOR)	Fabrice Becker (FRA)	Heini Baumgartner (SUI)
1997	Fabrice Becker (FRA)	Ian Edmondson (USA)	Heini Baumgartner (SUI)
1999	Ian Edmondson (USA)	Mike McDonald (CAN)	Heini Baumgartner (SUI)

Men's Combined

	Gold	Silver	Bronze
1986	Alain Laroche (CAN)	John Witt (USA)	Eric Labureux (FRA)
1989	Chris Simboli (CAN)	Scott Ogren (USA)	Marti Rafel (ESP)
1991	Sergey Shupletsov (URS)	Jeff Viola (CAN)	Youri Gilg (FRA)
1993	Sergey Shupletsov (RUS)	Trace Worthington (USA)	Hugo Bonatti (AUT)
1995	Trace Worthington (USA)	Darcy Downs (CAN)	Jonny Moseley (USA)
1997	Darcy Downs (CAN)	Toben Sutherland (CAN)	Oleg Kuleshov (BLR)

Women's Aerials

	Gold	Silver	Bronze
1986	Maria Quintana (USA)	Carin Hernskog (SWE)	Meredith Gardner (CAN)
1988	Melanie Palenik (USA)	Sonja Reichart (FRG)	Carin Hernskog (SWE)
1989	Catherine Lombard (FRA)	Sonja Reichart (FRG)	Melanie Palenik (USA)
1991	Vasilisa Semenchuk (URS)	Elfi Simchen (GER)	Lieselotte Johansson (SWE)
1993	Lina Cheryassova (UZB)	Marie Lindgren (SWE)	Kristean Porter (USA)
1995	Nikki Stone (USA)	Marie Lindgren (SWE)	Kirstie Marshall (AUS)
1997	Kirstie Marshall (AUS)	Michele Rohrbach (SUI)	Veronica Brenner (CAN)
1999	Jacqui Cooper (AUS)	Hilde Synnöve Lid (NOR)	Nikki Stone (USA)
2001	Veronika Bauer (CAN)	Michèle Rohrbach (SUI)	Deidra Dionne (CAN)
2003	Alisa Camplin (AUS)	Veronika Bauer (CAN)	Deidra Dionne (CAN)

Women's Moguls

	Gold	Silver	Bronze
1986	Mary Jo Tiampo (USA)	Hayley Wolff (USA)	Silvia Marciandi (ITA)
1988	Tatjana Mittermayer (FRG)	Raphaelle Monod (FRA)	Conny Kissling (SUI)
1989	Raphaelle Monod (FRA)	Donna Weinbrecht (USA)	Tatjana Mittermayer (FRG)
1991	Donna Weinbrecht (USA)	Tatjana Mittermayer (GER)	Birgit Stein (GER)
1993	Stine Lise Hattestad (NOR)	Petra Moroder (ITA)	Bronwen Thomas (CAN)
1995	Candice Gilg (FRA)	Raphaelle Monod (FRA)	Tatjana Mittermayer (GER)
1997	Candice Gilg (FRA)	Donna Weinbrecht (USA)	Tatjana Mittermayer (GER)
1999	Ann Battelle (USA)	Kari Traa (NOR)	Corinne Bodmer (SUI)
2001	Kari Traa (NOR)	Maria Despas (AUS)	Aiko Uemura (JPN)
2003	Kari Traa (NOR)	Michelle Roark (USA)	Stephanie St Pierre (CAN)

Women's Dual Moguls

	Gold	Silver	Bronze
1999	Sandra Schmidt (GER)	Kari Traa (NOR)	Ann Battelle (USA)
2001	Kari Traa (NOR)	Corinne Bodmer (SUI)	Tami Bradley (CAN)
2003	Kari Traa (NOR)	Marina Cherkasova (RUS)	Shannon Bahrke (USA)

Women's Acro (Ballet)

	Gold	Silver	Bronze
1986	Jan Bucher (USA)	Christine Rossi (FRA)	Lucy Barma (CAN)
1988	Christine Rossi (FRA)	Jan Bucher (USA)	Conny Kissling (SUI)
1989	Jan Bucher (USA)	Conny Kissling (SUI)	Lucy Barma (CAN)
1991	Ellen Breen (USA)	Jan Bucher (USA)	Cathy Fechoz (FRA)
1993	Ellen Breen (USA)	Sharon Petzold (USA)	Cathy Fechoz (FRA)
1995	Elena Batalova (RUS)	Ellen Breen (USA)	Annika Johansson (SWE)
1997	Oksana Kutschenko (RUS)	Asa Magnusson (SWE)	Annika Johansson (SWE)
1999	Natalya Rasumovskaya (RUS)	Oksana Kutschenko (RUS)	Annika Johansson (SWE)

Women's Combined

	Gold	Silver	Bronze
1986	Conny Kissling (SUI)	Anna Fraser (CAN)	Silvia Marciandi (ITA)
1989	Melanie Palenik (USA)	Conny Kissling (SUI)	Meredith Gardner (CAN)
1991	Maja Schmid (SUI)	Conny Kissling (SUI)	Kristean Porter (USA)
1993	Katherina Kubenk (CAN)	Natalya Orechova RUS	Kristean Porter (USA)
1995	Kristean Porter (USA)	Maja Schmid (SUI)	Katherina Kubenk (CAN)

Grass Skiing
Men's Slalom

	Gold	Silver	Bronze
1979	Vincent Riewe (FRG)	——	——
1981	Richi Christen (SUI)	——	——
1983	Erwin Gansner (SUI)	——	——
1985	Richi Christen (SUI)	——	——
1987	Klaus Spinka (AUT)	Uwe Kalliwoda (FRG)	Richi Christen (SUI)
1989	Klaus Spinka (AUT)	Rainer Grossmann (FRG)	Marcus Peschek (AUT)
1991	Rainer Grossmann (GER)	Klaus Spinka (AUT)	Marcus Peschek (AUT)
1993	Klaus Spinka (AUT)	Richard Höllbacher (AUT)	Oscar Bazzi (ITA)
1995	Richard Höllbacher (AUT)	Juri Donini (ITA)	Michal Macat (CZE)
			Roland Mathys (SUI)
1997	Christian Balek (AUT)	Stefano Sartori (ITA)	Richard Höllbacher (AUT)
1999	Christian Balek (AUT)	Jan Nemec (CZE)	Stefano Sartori (ITA)
2001	Jan Nemec (CZE)	Stefano Sartori (ITA)	Richard Höllbacher (AUT)

Men's Giant Slalom

	Gold	Silver	Bronze
1979	Vincent Riewe (FRG)	——	——
1981	Erwin Gansner (SUI)	——	——
1983	Marcus Dejori (ITA)	——	——
1985	Rainer Grossmann (FRG)	——	——
1987	Erwin Gansner (SUI)	Claudio Faccioli (ITA)	Marcus Peschek (AUT)
1989	Marcus Peschek (AUT)	Werner Fagerer (AUT)	Claudio Faccioli (ITA)
1991	Rainer Grossmann (GER)	Kurt Schweinberger (AUT)	Werner Fagerer (AUT)
1993	Rainer Grossmann (GER)	Erwin Gansner (SUI)	Marcus Peschek (AUT)
1995	Roland Mathys (SUI)	Michal Macat (CZE)	Christian Balek (AUT)
1997	Christian Balek (AUT)	Stefano Sartori (ITA)	Fausto Cerentin (ITA)
1999	Fausto Cerentin (ITA)	Christian Balek (AUT)	Jan Nemec (CZE)
2001	Stefano Sartori (ITA)	Jan Nemec (CZE)	Christian Ring (GER)

Men's Super Giant Slalom

	Gold	Silver	Bronze
1987	Erwin Gansner (SUI)	Klaus Spinka (AUT)	Richi Christen (SUI)
1989	Oscar Bazzi (ITA)	Klaus Spinka (AUT)	Werner Fagerer (AUT)
1991	Rainer Grossmann (GER)	Werner Fagerer (AUT)	Ivan Magni (ITA)
1993	Rainer Grossmann (GER)	Marcus Peschek (AUT)	Juri Donini (ITA)
1995	Götz Scheffler (GER)	Marcus Peschek (AUT)	Hans Eckler (AUT)
1997	Michal Macat (CZE)	Christian Balek (AUT)	Fausto Cerentin (ITA)
1999	Stefano Sartori (ITA)	Christian Balek (AUT)	Christian Ring (GER)
2001	Stefano Sartori (ITA)	Michal Macat (CZE)	Christian Ring (GER)

Men's Combined

	Gold	Silver	Bronze
1979	Vincent Riewe (FRG)	——	——
1981	Erwin Gansner (SUI)	——	——
1983	Erwin Gansner (SUI)	——	——
1985	Richi Christen (SUI)	——	——
1987	Erwin Gansner (SUI)	Klaus Spinka (AUT)	Richi Christen (SUI)
1989	Marcus Peschek (AUT)	Rainer Grossmann (FRG)	Erwin Christen (SUI)
1991	Rainer Grossmann (GER)	Marcus Peschek (AUT)	Oscar Bazzi (ITA)
1993	Klaus Spinka (AUT)	Götz Scheffler (GER)	Thomas Schretzmayer (AUT)
1995	Richard Höllbacher (AUT)	Roland Mathys (SUI)	Michal Macat (CZE)

1997	Christian Balek (AUT)	Fausto Cerentin (ITA)	Richard Höllbacher (AUT)
1999	Christian Balek (AUT)	Stefano Sartori (ITA)	Jan Nemec (CZE)
2001	Jan Nemec (CZE)	Stefano Sartori (ITA)	Richard Höllbacher (AUT)

Women's Slalom

	Gold	Silver	Bronze
1979	Ingrid Hirschhofer (AUT)	—	—
1981	Carole Petitjean (FRA)	—	—
1983	Bettina Dongue (FRG)	—	—
1985	Ingrid Hirschhofer (AUT)	—	—
1987	Ingrid Hirschhofer (AUT)	Gabi Pimper (AUT)	Martina Bauknecht (FRG)
1989	Martina Bauknecht (FRG)	Carole Petitjean (FRA)	Steffi Schmidt (FRG)
1991	Katja Krey (GER)	Christina Mauri (ITA)	Ulrike Kölle (GER)
1993	Ingrid Hirschhofer (AUT)	Claudia Däpp (SUI)	Michaela Kaiser (AUT)
1995	Ingrid Hirschhofer (AUT)	Patrizia Mauri (ITA)	Sabine Hengelage (GER)
1997	Paola Bazzi (ITA)	Christina Mauri (ITA)	Ingrid Hirschhofer (AUT)
1999	Paola Bazzi (ITA)	Bettina Schweighofer (AUT)	Ingrid Hirschhofer (AUT)
2001	Ingrid Hirschhofer (AUT)	Sylva Lipcikova (CZE)	Anna-Lena Büdenbender (GER)

Women's Giant Slalom

	Gold	Silver	Bronze
1979	Brigitte Single (FRG)	—	—
1981	Ingrid Hirschhofer (AUT)	—	—
1983	Ingrid Hirschhofer (AUT)	—	—
1985	Claudia Otratowitz (AUT)	—	—
1987	Cinzia Valt (ITA)	Ingrid Hirschhofer (AUT)	Katja Krey (FRG)
1989	Katja Krey (FRG)	Ingrid Hirschhofer (AUT)	Martina Bauknecht (FRG)
1991	Cristina Mauri (ITA)	Katja Krey (GER)	Sandra Pohl (GER)
1993	Ingrid Hirschhofer (AUT)	Erika Bircher (SUI)	Cristina Mauri (ITA)
1995	Cristina Mauri (ITA)	Erika Bircher (SUI)	Ingrid Hirschhofer (AUT)
1997	Paola Bazzi (ITA)	Erika Bircher (SUI)	Ingrid Hirschhofer (AUT)
1999	Paola Bazzi (ITA)	Ingrid Hirschhofer (AUT)	Cristina Mauri (ITA)
2001	Sylva Lipcikova (CZE)	Paola Bazzi (ITA)	Ingrid Hirschhofer (AUT)

Women's Super Giant Slalom

	Gold	Silver	Bronze
1987	Cinzia Valt (ITA)	Agnes Koch (HUN)	Sigrid Schweinberger (AUT)
1989	Ingrid Hirschhofer (AUT)	Katja Krey (FRG)	Christina Grimalda (ITA)
1991	Katja Krey (GER)	Michaela Kaiser (AUT)	Christina Mauri (ITA)
1993	Ingrid Hirschhofer (AUT)	Bettina Schweighofer (AUT)	Michaela Kaiser (AUT)
1995	Paola Bazzi (ITA)	Christina Mauri (ITA)	Ingrid Hirschhofer (AUT)
1997	Paola Bazzi (ITA)	Erika Bircher (SUI)	Silvia Lipcikova (CZE)
1999	Paola Bazzi (ITA)	Ingrid Hirschhofer (AUT)	Silvia Lipcikova (CZE)
2001	Nicole Portmann (SUI)	Paola Bazzi (ITA)	—
		Ingrid Hirschhofer (AUT)	
		Silvia Lipcikova (CZE)	

Women's Combined

	Gold	Silver	Bronze
1979	Ingrid Hirschhofer (AUT)	—	—
1981	Carole Petitjean (FRA)	—	—
1983	Ingrid Hirschhofer (AUT)	—	—
1985	Ingrid Hirschhofer (AUT)	—	—
1987	Ingrid Hirschhofer (AUT)	Martina Bauknecht (FRG)	Katja Krey (FRG)
1989	Martina Bauknecht (FRG)	Sigrid Schweinberger (AUT)	Katja Krey (FRG)
1991	Katja Krey (GER)	Christina Mauri (ITA)	Tanja Storz (GER)
1993	Ingrid Hirschhofer (AUT)	Michaela Kaiser (AUT)	Claudia Däpp (SUI)
1995	Ingrid Hirschhofer (AUT)	Sabine Hengelage (GER)	Alessandra Sartori (ITA)
1997	Paola Bazzi (ITA)	Christina Mauri (ITA)	Ingrid Hirschhofer (AUT)
1999	Paola Bazzi (ITA)	Ingrid Hirschhofer (AUT)	Christina Mauri (ITA)
2001	Ingrid Hirschhofer (AUT)	Sylva Lipcikova (CZE)	Anna-Lena Büdenbender (GER)

S
K
I
N
G

SNOOKER AND BILLIARDS

The precise origins of the games of snooker and billiards are uncertain.

References to billiards were made in the 14th century but this was an outdoor game similar to croquet. Louis XI of France (1423-83) is often credited with first playing the game indoors on a table, while Mary Queen of Scots (1542-87) was known to have owned a billiard table. Billiards was a popular pastime with army officers; and it was one of them, Neville Bowes Chamberlain, later General Sir Neville Chamberlain (no relation to the British Prime Minister), who is thought to have invented the game of snooker. Chamberlain named his derivative of billiards 'pyramids' and this game was played with a white ball and 15 reds, the six colours being added over time. While playing pyramids with a fellow officer at Jubbulpore, India, in 1875, Chamberlain referred to him as a 'snooker' after he failed to pot a simple ball, and the name stuck. The term was in fact a mildly derogatory name given to new recruits at the Royal Military Academy in Woolwich.

Billiards remained the more popular sport, having held World Championships since 1870, but Joe Davis was instrumental in the formation of a structure to the snooker scene and the World Professional Championship was first held in 1927. In 1952 a dispute caused the professional players to organise their own tournaments and between 1952 and 1957 the World Championship was renamed the Professional Match-Play Championship.

No Championships were held between 1958 and 1963 due to lack of interest; when they were resumed in 1964 they were run on a challenge match basis until 1969. The BBC *Pot Black* series had now begun and, after this proved very popular, edited highlights of the battles between Ray Reardon and John Spencer began to be shown on television. When the Championships were transferred to the Crucible Theatre, Sheffield, in 1977, they were covered more extensively.

Already more popular than billiards by about the mid-1940s, by the mid-1980s snooker had become more popular than any sport barring perhaps football. The game continues to thrive and develop and although originally a very British pastime it has now become an international sport shortlisted for Olympic inclusion.

Biographies of Players, Referees and Administrators

Baynton, Maureen   Born Maureen Barrett, Peckham, London, 1937. Schoolgirl snooker champion in 1947, she was equally proficient at billiards, winning eight national titles at snooker and seven at billiards.

Charlton, Eddie   Born Merewether, New South Wales, Australia, 31 October 1929. Nicknamed 'Steady Eddie' for his consistent, if unexciting, style of play, Charlton dominated Australian snooker from the time he turned professional in 1963 and won the Australian Professional Championship for 19 out of the next 20 years, his only defeat being at the hands of Warren Simpson in 1968. He never won a major ranking title but was runner-up in both the snooker and billiards World Championship and was ranked no. 3 snooker player for five consecutive years between 1976/77 and 1980/81. Charlton won the BBC's *Pot Black* series in 1972, 1973 and 1980 and also achieved the highest all-time *Pot Black* break of 110 during the 1973 series. In 1975 he was beaten 31-30 by Ray Reardon in the final of the World Snooker Championship. A good all-round sportsman, he carried the Australian flag for part of its journey during the 1956 Olympics in Melbourne.

Davis, Fred   Born Whittingham Moor, nr Chesterfield, Derbyshire, 13 August 1913. Right-hander often in the shadow of his more illustrious brother but flourished after Joe's retirement from tournament play. Fred only met his brother once in the World Championship but this 1940 matching was a classic that Joe won 37-36. Fred won the world professional title three times becoming only the second player after his brother to win both the snooker and billiards world titles when he won the latter in 1980. Fred won the Professional Match-Play Championship five consecutive times from 1952-56. Another epic encounter ensued in the 1965 World Championship when John Pulman beat him 37-36. He was also the only player to beat Joe on level terms, a feat he accomplished on four occasions. Fred suffered two heart attacks, the first in 1970 and the second in 1974, but despite ill-health he was ranked no. 4 in the first world ranking list in 1976. At the age of 65 he made the World Championship semi-finals in 1978. He was awarded the OBE in 1977 and by the time he put away his famous swivel-lensed glasses, due to arthritis, in 1992, he was the oldest active professional sportsman in the world. He died 16 April 1998.

Davis, Joe   Born Whitwell, Derbyshire, 15 April 1901. Right-hand master cue-man who is often considered the greatest-ever all-round player, being equally proficient at billiards and snooker. Joe became Chesterfield and District amateur billiards champion aged 13 and turned professional aged 18. In 1926 he was instrumental in persuading the Billiards Association and Control Club to stage a world snooker championship. He became the first-ever world snooker champion in 1927 when he defeated Tom Dennis in the final at Camkin's Hall in Birmingham, receiving prize money of £6 10s (£6.50). From 1927 until his retirement in 1946 Joe remained unbeaten through 34 World Championship matches, his closest match being against his brother

Fred who held him to 37-36 in the 1940 final. During this period Joe also won the World Billiards Championship four times. He made his first century break against Fred Pugh at Manchester in 1928 and his 500th against Jackie Rea in 1953, and achieved the first-ever maximum snooker break on 22 January 1955 at Leicester Square Hall against Willie Smith. On his retirement in 1964 his tally of century breaks was 687, plus 83 billiard breaks of 1000 or more. In 1935 he compiled the first century in the World Championships. He was awarded the OBE in 1963. He died 10 July 1978.

Davis, Steve   Born Brentwood, Essex, 22 August 1957. Turned professional in 1978 and totally dominated the game throughout the 1980s, winning the world title six times and holding the no. 1 world ranking between the 1983/84 and 1989/90 seasons. Davis also won six UK titles, three Masters, eight Irish Masters, four world doubles titles with Tony Meo, four Matchroom League titles, and numerous other ranking tournaments, as well as being crowned *Pot Black* champion in 1982 and 1983. His name became synonymous with Barry Hearn who spotted his great potential and developed his cutting edge by inviting a host of top professionals to play him at his Romford club. Davis made the first televised 147 maximum break in January 1982 while playing John Spencer in the Lada Classic and, after a brief spell out of the top 16, has recently returned to the top echelon of the game. He is also a world-class nine-ball pool player who has consistently beaten the cream of the world's players and played a leading part in the European Mosconi Cup victory over the Americans in December 2002. More recently 'The Nugget' (as he is affectionately known) has become a witty and informative member of the BBC snooker commentary team.

Doherty, Ken   Born Dublin, Ireland, 17 September 1969. Right-hand player who turned professional in 1990. Doherty won the World Amateur Championship in 1989, and in 1997 became the first player to win both the amateur and professional world titles when he was successful at the Crucible, Sheffield.

Donaldson, Walter   Born Coatbridge, Scotland, 1907. Donaldson won the national under-16 billiards title in 1922 and the following year turned professional. He was unfortunate to be around during the era of Joe Davis but when Davis retired in 1946 he vied for the no. 1 spot with Joe's brother Fred. A slow, methodical player, his game was good enough to win the 1947 and 1950 World Championships and gain the runner-up spot six times. His highest break of 142 against John Pulman in 1946 was a record at the time. He died in Buckinghamshire,1973.

Drago, Tony   Born Valletta, Malta, 22 September 1965. Right-hand cueist whose highly strung temperament has often led to him losing matches that he should probably have won. One of the most naturally talented players on the circuit, Drago is also the quickest, having completed a century break in 3mins 31secs (1996). He turned professional in 1985 and his only major tournament final was in the 1997 International Open where he was beaten heavily by Stephen Hendry. His highest tournament break is 144 and his highest world ranking was 10th in 1998/99.

Ebdon, Peter   Born London, 27 August 1970. A brilliant junior player, Ebdon joined the professional ranks in 1991 and made an immediate impact by attaining a world ranking of 47 in his first season. Flamboyant and pony-tailed in those days, he was often criticised for his intensity which would sometimes be accompanied by a great shout of elation when winning an important frame. His first ranking victory came in the 1993 Grand Prix. Ebdon's powers of concentration are second to none and his choice of brave and telling pots brought him the world title in 2002. Several ranking victories make him one of the current crop of elite players always challenging for top honours and his outside interests of racehorse breeding and crooning do not appear to have affected his form. His highest ranking to date is no. 3 in the 1996/97 season.

Edmonds, Ray   Born Grimsby, Humberside, 28 May 1936. A top amateur snooker and billiards player, Edmonds won world amateur titles in 1972 and 1974, before turning professional in 1978 at the age of 42. His knowledge of the game is supreme and he has become a regular member of television commentary teams.

Fisher, Allison   Born Cheshunt, London, 24 February 1968. Possibly the greatest female player of all time. Fisher turned professional in 1991 after winning the UK Championship every year from 1985 to 1990. She also won the World Championship in 1985, 1986, 1988, 1989, 1991, 1993 and 1994. Her dominance was such that she began to lose her motivation to play snooker. Taking up the fresh challenge of American pool, she quickly became the leading light and has so far won several WPBA nine-ball world championships.

Fisher, Kelly   Born Carlisle, Cumbria, 26 August 1978. Currently the dominant female snooker player, having won the World Championship in 1998, 1999, 2000, 2002 and 2003. She has a tournament high break of 143 although she has scored a 147 maximum in practice.

Francisco, Silvino   Born Cape Town, South Africa, 4 May 1946. The son of a Portuguese fisherman whose restaurant in Cape Town housed two snooker tables, both Silvino and his elder brother Mannie became top amateur snooker and billiards players in South Africa. Francisco turned professional in 1978 but also held down a job as an oil executive to boost his earnings. His spoiling, unorthodox style of play gained him many victories though he was never a fluent break-builder. His one ranking success was in the 1985 Dulux British Open against Kirk Stevens of Canada, the first major final without a UK representative. This match was shrouded in controversy, Stevens being strong favourite but losing 12-9 amid accusations of drug-taking and illegal betting. Francisco was fined £6000 for accusing Stevens of playing under the influence of forbidden substances, but later that year Stevens admitted his addiction to cocaine. Known to be a heavy gambler, Francisco was declared bankrupt in December 1996, and in 1997 he was jailed for smuggling cannabis. His nephew, Peter Francisco (born 14 February 1962), was also a top professional snooker player who was banned in the mid-1990s after being accused of giving 'a performance not consistent with his standing as a professional player'.

Fu, Marco   Born Happy Valley, Hong Kong, 8 January 1978. Fu beat England's Stuart Bingham to win the 1997 IBSF World Amateur Championship in Bulawayo, Zimbabwe, and turned professional soon afterwards. He made an immediate impact, reaching the 11th qualifying round of the World Championship and gaining a ranking of 377. In his first full season on the main tour Fu reached the final of the first ranking event, the 1998 Grand Prix. After a couple of fallow years where his only notable achievement was making a 147 maximum against Ken Doherty in the 2000 Regal Scottish Masters, the 2002/03 season saw him to the fore with a good run in the World Championship and victory in the Hasseroder Premier Snooker League.

Ganley, Len   Born Lurgan, nr Belfast, Northern Ireland. An accomplished player with a highest break of 136, with his large frame and thick Irish brogue, Ganley later became the most famous snooker referee in the world. He moved to Burton-on-Trent in 1971 and obtained his Grade 'A' refereeing certificate in 1979. His other claim to fame, which subsequently gave him the nickname of 'Ball-crusher', was his appearance in a Carling Black Label lager television advert where he is seen crushing a snooker ball into dust.

Griffiths, Terry   Born Llanelli, Wales, 16 October 1947. A late developer, Griffiths won his first title in 1975 with success in the Welsh Amateur Championship. He went on to win the English Amateur Championships in 1977 and 1978 and then turned professional. His first event was a 9-8 loss to Rex Williams, after leading 8-2 and thus losing the last seven frames, his second the 1979 World Professional Championships at the Crucible where victories over Perrie Mans, Alex Higgins, Eddie Charlton and Dennis Taylor gave him the title. He soon became a contender for every major title and considering the dominance of Steve Davis throughout this period, his string of titles is impressive. He reached a highest ranking of no. 3 in the 1981/82 season. Griffiths is now a leading coach and helped Mark Williams to success in the 2003 World Championship.

Hann, Quinten   Born Wagga Wagga, New South Wales, Australia, 4 June 1977. Brilliant yet enigmatic all-round cueist who turned professional in 1995. Despite winning no major titles Hann has improved his world ranking every year and is now firmly established as an elite player, reaching no. 14 in the 2002/03 season. He became world eight-ball pool champion in 1999 and this might explain his occasional propensity to smash the pack of reds to all corners of the table. Moody and unpredictable on and off the table, his first ranking title may ultimately depend on him reconciling his temperamental shortcomings. He fought, and beat, fellow snooker professional Mark King in a much-publicised charity boxing match in 2004.

Hearn, Barry   Born Dagenham, Essex, 19 June 1948. Hearn has done more to popularise snooker in the UK and around the world than any other person. An accountant by profession, the youngest fellow of the Institute of Chartered Accountants, he began his involvement with snooker in 1974 when his company purchased the 17 Lucania snooker halls. Although Hearn had other promising players on his managerial books, notably Geoff Foulds and Vic Harris, his partnership with Steve Davis was to dominate the world of snooker throughout the 1980s. Once Davis had won several championships Hearn expanded his camp with other major stars, notably Dennis Taylor, Terry Griffiths and Jimmy White. In recent years Hearn has branched out to promote sports as diverse as angling, darts, poker, pool and boxing, and he is chairman of Leyton Orient Football Club.

Hendry, Stephen   Born Auchterarder, Perthshire, Scotland, 13 January 1969. Right-hand player who turned professional in 1985 and has subsequently rewritten the record books. The youngest-ever world snooker champion in 1990, he is often considered the greatest exponent of the game in history. Hendry dominated snooker in the 1990s and, apart from his seven World Championships to date, he holds the record for most century breaks (587), most major titles (34 as at the end of the 2002/03 season), most 147s in professional tournaments (7) and most seasons at no. 1 in the rankings (eight consecutive years from 1990-98). He was awarded the MBE in 1994.

Higgins, Alex   Born Belfast, Northern Ireland, 18 March 1949. Higgins honed his skills at the Jampot Club in Belfast. Originally destined to be a jockey, his increase in weight and undoubted snooker talent led him to move to Manchester in 1971 to become a professional snooker player. He took the snooker world by storm immediately, defeating John Spencer to become the 1972 world champion. A promoter's dream in many respects, his flamboyant game and speed around the table gave rise to his nickname of 'Hurricane'. Unfortunately he often upset other players by his braggadocio statements. Higgins's genius was often revealed in the face of adversity; with his developing drinking problems and bad-boy image he was perceived as a loveable rogue by the public and supported like no other player before or since. Having defeated Ray Reardon in the 1982 world final, he came from 7-0 down to beat Steve Davis 16-15 in the 1983 Coral UK Championship. Not always gracious in defeat, his frustration at losing matches that he felt he should have won often led to off-table incidents; a series of fines, bans and docked ranking points sealed his fate in the top echelons of snooker. Higgins has recently fought back from throat cancer. He has found it hard to adjust to life away from the game but he will always have a place in the hearts of the snooker public. Apart from his ranking victories, Higgins won the Irish professional title in 1972, 1978, 1979, 1983 and 1989, the world doubles title in 1984 with Jimmy White and was a member of the winning Irish World Cup teams in 1985, 1986 and 1987.

Higgins, John   Born Wishaw, Lanarkshire, Scotland, 18 May 1975. Right-hand player who turned professional in 1992. 'The Wizard of Wishaw', as he is affectionately known, captured the World Professional Championship in 1998. Higgins is always among the favourites for every tournament and apart from his numerous ranking victories he attained the world no. 1 slot in 1998, retaining it the following year.

Hillyard, Stacey   Born Christchurch, Dorset, 1970. Hillyard won the World Amateur Championship in 1984 but will always be remembered for becoming the first woman to make a century break in competitive play. This feat was accomplished on 15 January 1985, playing against 45-year-old Bill Scorer in the Walter C. Clark League, Premier Division, in Bournemouth, aged 14!

Hunter, Paul   Born Leeds, West Yorkshire, 14 October 1978. Hunter turned professional in 1995 and achieved his first ranking success in 1998 by winning the Regal Welsh Open. An elite top eight player always in contention for the major prizes, in 2004 he won the Masters title for the third time, beating Ronnie O'Sullivan 10-9.

Johnson, Joe Born Bradford, West Yorkshire, 29 July 1952. Johnson turned professional in 1979 after being runner-up to Cliff Wilson in the 1978 World Amateur Championship, but had an inauspicious start to his professional career: it was not until the Mercantile Credit Classic of 1985 that he won his first televised match. The following season he arrived at the Crucible never having won a match there and was made a 150-1 outsider. Johnson was a revelation and on countless occasions made frame-winning breaks, often from behind. Following wins over Dave Martin, Mike Hallett, Terry Griffiths and Tony Knowles, he faced Steve Davis, still smarting from his dramatic loss against Dennis Taylor in 1985. Johnson was in irresistible form and ran out a deserved 18-12 winner. The following season was something of a disaster for Johnson but when he arrived at the Crucible to defend his title he struck a rich vein of form to reach the final again against Davis. This time, however, it proved to be an insurmountable hurdle. Despite winning the Scottish Masters the following season, his ranking of no. 5 was to be the highest he attained and by 1990 he had dropped out of the top 16. Heart and sight problems plagued Johnson around this time and it is to his credit that he has been able to overcome these setbacks and still play a respectable game.

Karnehm, Jack Born Crowthorne, Berkshire, 18 June 1917. A good snooker player, Karnehm excelled at billiards and in the latter sport reached the final of the World Championship in both 1971 and 1973. He also won the English and World Amateur Billiards Championship in 1969 and the UK Championship in 1980. He was, however, better known as a national coach for the Billiards and Snooker Foundation and as a great commentator on the game of snooker. His informative and good-humoured observations are sadly missed. He died 28 July 2002.

Knowles, Tony Born Bolton, Greater Manchester, 13 June 1955. Knowles turned professional in 1979 after an in-and-out amateur career, making the headlines in 1982 when he beat defending champion Steve Davis 10-1 in the first round of the World Championship at the Crucible. He eventually lost to Eddie Charlton 13-11 in the quarter-finals but he had done enough to establish himself as an elite player. Knowles became the pin-up boy of world snooker and was frequently pictured in the tabloids; this did not affect his snooker, however, and with three world semi-finals and two other ranking event victories he rose to no. 2 in the rankings by the mid-1980s. Poor form in the 1990s has made his television appearances infrequent, the demands of qualifying matches taking their toll, but he remains a solid performer.

Lee, Stephen Born Trowbridge, Wiltshire, 12 October 1974. Turned professional in 1992 after an illustrious amateur career. His cue action is second to none although his class has taken time to show through. His first ranking victory came in the 1998 Grand Prix event and he is now established as one of the elite players.

Lindrum, Horace Born Horace Morell, Australia, 1912. The nephew of the great billiards player Walter Lindrum, it was at snooker that Horace was to excel. Although his only world title was in the 1952 challenge match against Clark McConachy he had many great encounters with Joe Davis, but never managed to beat Davis except when given a black start. He retired from tournament play in 1957 and concentrated on exhibitions, but came out of retirement in 1963 and won the Australian Open in that year. In 1970 he became the first man to make 1000 centuries in public. He died in 1974.

Lindrum, Walter Born Kalgoorlie, Australia, 1908. Walter compiled the world record billiards break in 1932 when, playing against Joe Davis at Thurston's, Leicester Square, he made 4137 in 2hrs 55mins over three sessions. A fast-scoring player, he once made a century break in 29 seconds. He competed in two World Championships, in 1933 and 1934, beating Joe Davis on both occasions. Having retired from tournament play in 1950 to concentrate on exhibitions, he was awarded the OBE in 1958 for his considerable charity work. He died 30 July 1960.

Lowe, Ted Born Edwin Charles Ernest Lowe, Lambourn, Berkshire, 1 November 1920. Lowe began broadcasting on snooker in 1954 after a ten-year stint as general manager of the famous Leicester Square Hall. Lowe devised the format for the BBC *Pot Black* series and recruited the players for the competition. The BBC began extensive coverage of the World Championship following Lowe's urgings. Until then he had been the lone voice of snooker but with the two-week coverage he required help, which came in the form of Clive Everton and Jack Karnehm. Known as 'Whispering' Ted Lowe because of his dulcet tones, he was awarded the MBE in 2004.

McManus, Alan Born Glasgow, Scotland, 29 January 1971. McManus turned professional at the start of the 1991 season and attained a world ranking of no. 41 by the end of the year, the highest of all that year's debutants. The following season he reached the top 16 and he won his first ranking tournament in 1994 with victory in the Dubai Classic. His safety game and knowledge of angles have ensured his status as a top player even when his form has been patchy. A resurgence in form in the 2002/03 season has once again made him a player to be feared by all.

Mans, Perrie Born Pierre Mans, Johannesburg, South Africa, 14 October 1940. Mans was the son of a top South African snooker professional. A left-hand player, he was not a prolific break-builder but was thought to be the best single-ball potter in the game. His greatest success before the 1978 World Championship was to have won the BBC *Pot Black* title but in the first round at the Crucible that year he beat the holder John Spencer and went all the way to the final. His other major successes include 19 South African professional titles and victory in the 1979 Masters.

Miles, Graham Born Birmingham, West Midlands, 11 May 1941. Miles turned professional in 1969 but did not set the world alight in his first few seasons although always a difficult match-player to overcome. When Fred Davis was forced to pull out of the 1974 series of *Pot Black* Miles came in as a last-minute replacement and won the series, the result giving him a great confidence boost. He reached the final of that year's World Championship and after successfully defending his *Pot Black* title in 1975 he was firmly established as a top player. His peculiar sighting action, placing his chin to the right of the cue rather than in the centre, was his trademark and his wit and charm made him increasingly popular, although he eventually struggled to live up to public expectations distorted by his *Pot Black* success. His highest world ranking was no. 5 in the very first ranking list in 1976, but despite maintaining his form for much of the 1970s, wins became rarer in the 1980s and he retired from the main tour in 1991.

Mountjoy, Doug   Born Tir-y-Berth, Glamorgan, South Wales, 8 June 1942. Turned professional in 1976 immediately after winning the World Amateur Championship and made an impact in his first tournament by winning the Masters. Mountjoy won numerous tournaments, including *Pot Black* in 1978 and 1985, but his form tapered off in the mid-1980s and he returned to his coaching guru Frank Callan to help him. This was a resounding success at the start of 1988/89 and after two tournament victories he ended the following season ranked no. 5, his highest-ever placing. Unfortunately he began to suffer ill-health and his eyesight deteriorated. His last battle was against cancer, and his fighting spirit has been seen to the full in his long battle to regain health.

O'Sullivan, Ronnie   Born Essex, 5 December 1975. Right-hand player who is reckoned good enough with his left hand to maintain a position in the world's top 16. O'Sullivan turned professional in 1992, aged 16, and made an immediate impact by remaining unbeaten for the first few weeks of his professional career. His first major title was the 1993 UK Championship, aged 17, and his speed around the table soon earned him the nickname 'The Rocket'. Despite winning the World Championship in 2001, he will always be remembered for his first-round match against Mick Price in the 1997 tournament when he compiled the fastest-ever maximum 147 break in 5mins 20secs. He captured his second World Championship in 2004.

Parrott, John   Born Liverpool, 11 May 1964. Turned professional in 1983 after winning the *Junior Pot Black* title for the second successive year. Parrott quickly established himself as a top player and remained in the world top 16 from the 1987/88 season until 2000/01. Tournament success did not come quickly, perhaps because of the genius of Steve Davis, Alex Higgins and Cliff Thorburn; Parrott achieved his first ranking victory in the 1989 European Open, the pinnacle of his career coming in 1991 when he played inspired snooker to beat a rampant Jimmy White in the World Championship. He remained a major threat in every tournament of the 1990s but the presence of Stephen Hendry prevented the glut of victories that might otherwise have materialised. Parrott's hard-hitting, positive play made him exciting on the table and his humour off it has made him a natural for a media job. He now splits his time between playing snooker and appearing on television as quiz-show panellist, snooker commentator and horse racing pundit.

Pulman, John   Born Devon, England, 13 August 1926. Turned professional in 1946 after winning the English Amateur Championship and was one of only a handful of professionals on the circuit during the sport's decline in the 1950s. He won the *News of the World* title in 1954 and 1957 and in that year he effectively became world champion when he won the Professional Match-Play Championship. In 1964 the World Championship was reintroduced and Pulman beat Fred Davis for the title. The Championship was held on a challenge basis during his tenure and between 1964 and 1968 he defended it successfully six times, against Fred Davis (twice), Rex Williams (twice), Freddie van Rensburg and Eddie Charlton. Pulman became part of the ITV snooker commentary team and a well-respected coach. He died 25 December 1998.

Rea, Jackie   Born Dungannon, Northern Ireland, 6 April 1921. Having turned professional in 1947 after winning the Irish Amateur Championship, Rae won the Northern Ireland Championship every year between 1948 and 1971 apart from 1951, and only the genius of Alex Higgins prevented him from lengthening that record. He was nevertheless denied the ultimate prize, his peak in the late 1950s and early 1960s coinciding with an era when no World Championships were held. Still a tournament contender throughout the 1960s and early 1970s, he became better known on the exhibition circuit where his series of trick shots and clever banter made him a popular act. He rarely played tournaments in the mid-1970s and early 1980s but made a brief return to tournament play in the mid-1980s.

Reardon, Ray   Born Tredegar, South Wales, 8 October 1932. Right-hand player who at the age of 14 went to work down the mines where he was once buried alive for three hours. He subsequently left the pit and joined the police force in Stoke-on-Trent. He won the *News of the World* amateur title in 1949 at the age of 17 and the Welsh amateur title for six successive years from 1950 to 1955 before moving to Stoke. In 1964 he won the English amateur title and in 1967 he turned professional. In his first World Championship in 1969 he lost in the first round by the odd frame in 49 to Fred Davis, but he won the *Pot Black* series that year and in 1970 claimed the first of his six world titles with a 39-34 victory over John Pulman. John Spencer beat him in the semi-finals of the next Championship and he only reached the quarter-finals in 1972, but then won four successive titles and a sixth in 1978. A regular at the Pontins Festival, he won the professional title there on four occasions and the Welsh professional title three times. His only ranking title outside the World Championship came in the Professional Players' Tournament in 1982 and his final two wins were the Yamaha International Masters and his third Welsh professional title in 1983. Reardon was the first world no. 1 when the rankings were introduced in 1976, a position he held for five years. After a year gap, he regained the top slot in 1982/83, the first player to have done so. Reardon reached the World Championship semi-final in 1985 but, like his great rival John Spencer, began to have vision problems and eventually retired in 1992. He was affectionately known as 'Dracula'.

Selby, Vera   Born Newcastle, 1931. Selby won five national women's snooker titles and eight national billiards titles during the 1970s but the pinnacle of her career was winning the 1976 World Snooker Championship, a feat she repeated in 1981. The most remarkable feature of her career is that she did not take up either sport until she was 37 years of age.

Spencer, John   Born Radcliffe, Lancashire, 18 June 1935. Right-hand player who, with his great friend and rival, Ray Reardon, dominated the game for ten years from 1969, when he won the first of the newly reorganised World Championships. Affectionately known as 'Sniffer', he was one of the first players to perfect the 'deep screw' shot and in 1977 became the first player to win the World Championship using a two-piece cue. Spencer began playing snooker aged 15 and was compiling centuries within a year. National Service forced him to give the game up in 1953 and he did not take it up again seriously until 1963. The following year he entered the English Amateur Championship, reaching the final only to lose to Ray Reardon. He made the final again the next year and in 1966 beat Marcus Owen to win the title. Runner-up in that year's World Amateur

Championships in Karachi, where he lost to Marcus's older brother, Gary, he then turned professional along with Gary Owen and Ray Reardon, the three becoming the first new professionals since 1951. In his first World Championship, in 1969, he gained his revenge over Gary Owen, beating him 37-24 to become champion. Reardon beat him in the semi-final in April 1970 but when the next Championships were played in Australia in November 1970, Spencer took his second world title, beating local man Warren Simpson in the final. He reached the final again in 1972, losing to Alex Higgins, but he won the Norwich Union Open in 1973 and 1974, adding the inaugural Masters in 1975. He also took the first World Championship to be held at the Crucible in 1977, beating Cliff Thorburn 25-21 and the first-ever Irish Masters in 1978. Three *Pot Black* titles also came his way. He started to experience double vision and won only one more title, the Holsten Lager International in 1979. In the quarter-finals he made the first-ever 147 maximum in tournament play but the television cameras were not running, and the break was never recognised for record purposes due to oversize pockets. As Spencer's eye problems became worse, he slipped down the rankings, but in 1987 reached the quarter-finals of the Dulux British Open, eventually losing to Jimmy White. Spencer began to commentate and announced his retirement in 1992. He was chairman of the WPBSA between 1990 and 1996.

Stevens, Kirk Born Toronto, Canada, 17 August 1958. Turned professional in 1978 following defeat by Cliff Wilson in the semi-finals of the World Amateur Championship. Stevens won the Canadian professional championship in 1979, 1981 and 1983 and was a semi-finalist in the World Championships in 1980 and 1984. His highest world ranking was no. 4 in the 1984/85 season. During the 1984 Masters semi-final against Jimmy White he managed a 147 maximum. Following his unexpected loss to South African Silvino Francisco in the final of the 1985 Dulux Open he admitted to having a cocaine habit. Stevens' ranking began to fall and although he has beaten his addiction problems he has never regained the standard of consistency demanded of a top player.

Stevens, Matthew Born Carmarthen, Wales, 11 September 1977. Turned professional in 1994, aged 16. His first tournament victory came in the Regal Scottish Masters in 1999 and he finished that season ranked no. 6 in the world, his highest ranking to date. Stevens won his first ranking title, the UK Championship, in November 2003, defeating Stephen Hendry 10-8 in the final.

Taylor, Dennis Born Coalisland, Co. Tyrone, Northern Ireland, 19 January 1949. A top amateur at both snooker and billiards, after moving to his Blackburn base Taylor decided to turn professional in 1972. He never won a tournament of note during the 1970s but his consistency had moved him up to no. 2 in the world rankings by the end of the decade. In 1980 he beat his great rival Alex Higgins in the final of the Irish professional championship and won this title again in 1981, 1982, 1985, 1986 and 1987. In his third Irish final against Higgins, Taylor's fighting spirit came to the fore after Higgins had made unfortunate personal remarks against him. Though lacking the touch of genius that Higgins brought to the game, Taylor's determination and will to succeed took him to victory that day. In the 1983 Benson & Hedges Irish Masters his new trademark glasses

were unveiled. Designed by Jack Karnehm, the spectacles were twice the size of ordinary lenses and sat higher on the nose so sighting was not impaired by the rim. Taylor's first ranking victory followed in the 1984 Rothmans Grand Prix against his good friend Cliff Thorburn. However, he will always be remembered for his epic battle against Steve Davis in the final of the 1985 World Championship. Having been 8-0 down at one stage, Taylor pulled back to 17-17 before potting the final black of the final frame to win the title in the early hours of the morning. The match gained what is still a record television audience (18.5 million) for any programme broadcast after midnight. Taylor remained in the top 16 until the 1993/94 season, his 18th successive year, and eventually retired in 2000 to become a popular commentator on the game.

Thorburn, Cliff Born Victoria, British Columbia, Canada, 16 January 1948. Turned professional in 1973 following victories in the North American Championships in 1971 and 1972. Thorburn, nicknamed 'The Grinder' for his slow methodical approach, soon became a leading contender for every major title. In 1977 he was beaten in the first-ever final of the World Championships at the Crucible, Sheffield, but defeated Alex Higgins in the 1980 final to become the first overseas player to win the title. He won the Canadian Open in 1974, 1978 and 1979 and the Canadian professional title in 1980, 1984, 1985, 1986 and 1987. Other successes included the Masters in 1983, 1985 and 1986 and the Scottish Masters in 1985 and 1986. Thorburn also won the BBC *Pot Black* series in 1981 and was world no. 1 in the 1981/82 season. He gained immortality by shooting the first-ever maximum 147 break during the 1983 World Championship.

Thorne, Willie Born Leicester, 4 March 1954. 'The Great WT' as he is affectionately known, was one of the most prolific break-builders in the history of the game, having made over 100 maximums. However, only one of these, in the 1987 UK Championships, was made in tournament play, and Thorne never consistently emulated the form shown in his Leicester club when under the gaze of television cameras. He turned professional in 1975 but had to wait until the 1985 Mercantile Credit Classic for his first ranking tournament victory. He should have won the UK Open the following season but missed a simple blue against Steve Davis in the final when five frames ahead and never recovered. Thorne's highest world ranking was no. 7 in 1983/84 and 1986/87. One of the most popular characters in the game, he is now a respected commentator.

Virgo, John Born Rochdale, Greater Manchester, 3 March 1946. Turned professional in 1976 after an excellent amateur career. Used to television exposure through his involvement in a teaching snooker programme, his highest ranking was no. 10 at the end of the 1978/79 season after he reached the semi-finals of the World Championship. He won his only major tournament the following season when he beat Terry Griffiths 14-13 in the final of the UK Championship. Despite his dour outward appearance, Virgo had a great sense of humour and the ability to observe and mimic his fellow professionals. In the 1982 World Championships he demonstrated his act while the television cameras were rolling, and a star was born. Virgo remained in the world's top 16 throughout the 1980s but after succeeding Rex Williams as chairman of the WPBSA for two years victories became scarcer. He beat Steve Davis in the 1987 Dulux Open, the first time

Davis had been defeated before the televised stages of any tournament, but eventually retired from the tour at the end of the 1993/94 season. The following year the BBC asked him to co-host its new game-show *Big Break* with Jim Davidson, through which Virgo's impressive range of trick shots reached a large general audence. He is now a regular member of the BBC commentary team.

Wattana, James   Born Wattana Pu-Orb-Orm, Bangkok, Thailand, 17 January 1970. Wattana turned professional in 1988 after winning that year's World Amateur Championship. He won his first ranking tournament when he defeated John Parrott 9-5 in the final of the Strachan Open in 1992 and finished that season ranked no. 7. His highest ranking so far has been no. 3 in 1994/95. Unfortunately, the burden of a nation's expectations and problems with his eyesight resulted in a loss of form in the new millennium and Wattana is no longer a top 16 player.

Werbeniuk, Bill   Born Winnipeg, Manitoba, Canada, 14 January 1947. Along with Cliff Thorburn and Kirk Stevens, one of the triumvirate of great Canadian players. Werbeniuk began playing in Vancouver, aged nine, and turned professional in 1973, winning the North American and Canadian Championships in his first season. He was a quarter-finalist in the 1978, 1979, 1981 and 1983 World Championships and his highest world-ranking was no. 8 in the 1984/85 season. Based in England at the height of his career and travelling to tournaments in a converted bus, Werbeniuk was known for his average intake of 20 pints of lager per session of a match. This 'medication', deemed necessary by the Inland Revenue, was required because of a nerve-related illness causing severe shaking of his hands. He won the World Team Cup in 1982 with Cliff Thorburn and Kirk Stevens and substituted the alcohol with a drug called Inderal, but unfortunately this was banned by the WPBSA and he was suspended. He died 20 January 2003.

White, Jimmy   Born James Warren White, London, 2 May 1962. Nicknamed 'The Whirlwind', White is a left-hander touched with genius. He won the English amateur title before his 17th birthday and this qualified him for the 1980 World Amateur Championships in Tasmania. He won this title aged 18 and after winning the Indian national championships on his way home turned professional. Although he won numerous non-ranking events, including the world doubles title with his great friend Alex Higgins, his first ranking event success did not come until the 1986 Mercantile Credit Classic. He also won the BBC *Pot Black* series that year. Many titles were to follow but White will always be remembered as the best player never to have won a World Professional Championship. He has been runner-up six times, including five consecutive years from 1990 to 1994, and only inspired snooker by his opponents has prevented him from winning a title he richly deserved. White's highest ranking of no. 2 was reached in 1987. Like his rival Steve Davis he has achieved some fine

results in nine-ball pool and poker. Both White and Davis made the final of the 2003 Poker Million series on Sky television and White was victorious. White has wrested the mantle of 'people's champion' from Alex Higgins and remains the most popular player on the circuit.

Williams, Mark   Born Cwm, South Wales, 21 March 1975. Turned professional in 1992. His first ranking tournament victory came in 1995 when he beat John Parrott 9-3 in the Regal Welsh Open and in 2000 he became the first left-handed player to win the world title. Williams became world no. 1 in the 2000/01 season and following his second Crucible win in 2003 was the no. 1-ranked player in the world going into the 2003/04 season. A consistent potter with the ability to appear relaxed in the most tense of circumstances, he is one of the most formidable of current players.

Williams, Rex   Born Stourbridge, West Midlands, 20 July 1933. One of the game's great all-rounders, equally proficient at snooker or billiards, Williams won the national under-16 titles in both disciplines and in 1951 won the English amateur snooker title before turning professional. As a billiards player he won the UK title in 1979 and 1983 and the world professional billiards title in 1968, 1971, 1973, 1974, 1976, 1982 and 1983. His highest snooker ranking was no. 7 in the 1981/82 season and he was the oldest ranking finalist when beaten by Jimmy White in the 1986 Rothmans Grand Prix at the age of 53. Instrumental in the formation of the Professional Billiards Players Association (which became the WPBSA in May 1968), Williams was its chairman between 1968 and 1987 and again from 1997 to 1999.

Wilson, Cliff   Born Tredegar, South Wales, 10 May 1934. Right-hand player who was born in the same Welsh town as Ray Reardon and who shared in many battles with him as an amateur. Reardon would usually gain the upper hand in the Welsh Amateur Championships but Wilson returned the compliment in the English amateur competition. Wilson won the Welsh amateur title in 1956 but then retired, disillusioned with the game when its popularity was at an all-time low. Fifteen years later a workmate asked him to turn out for the local league team and this revived his interest in the game. By now his eyesight had deteriorated considerably – he resorted to wearing a patch for some time as he was short-sighted in one eye and long-sighted in the other – yet he was soon back at the top of the sport and in 1977 again won the Welsh amateur title. The following year he won the World Amateur Championship and after winning the Welsh title again in 1979 he decided to turn professional at the age of 45. Blessed with outrageous talent, his laid-back demeanour, wise-cracking manner and quick, fluent potting made him one of the most popular players on the circuit. Consistent results brought him a ranking in the top 16 by the 1988/89 season but his health then began to suffer again, although he won the world seniors title in 1991 and in 1992 beat Ronnie O'Sullivan in the UK Championships. He died in June 1994.

Snooker: Ranking Tournaments

World Professional Championship

	Winner		Runner-Up
1927	Joe Davis (ENG)	20-11	Tom Dennis (ENG)
1928	Joe Davis (ENG)	16-13	Fred Lawrence (ENG)
1929	Joe Davis (ENG)	19-14	Tom Dennis (ENG)
1930	Joe Davis (ENG)	25-12	Tom Dennis (ENG)
1931	Joe Davis (ENG)	25-21	Tom Dennis (ENG)
1932	Joe Davis (ENG)	30-19	Clark McConachy (NZL)
1933	Joe Davis (ENG)	25-18	Willie Smith (ENG)
1934	Joe Davis (ENG)	25-23	Tom Newman (ENG)
1935	Joe Davis (ENG)	25-20	Willie Smith (ENG)
1936	Joe Davis (ENG)	34-27	Horace Lindrum (AUS)
1937	Joe Davis (ENG)	32-29	Horace Lindrum (AUS)
1938	Joe Davis (ENG)	37-24	Sidney Smith (ENG)
1939	Joe Davis (ENG)	43-30	Sidney Smith (ENG)
1940	Joe Davis (ENG)	37-36	Fred Davis (ENG)
1941-45	not held		
1946	Joe Davis (ENG)	78-67	Horace Lindrum (AUS)
1947	Walter Donaldson (SCO)	82-63	Fred Davis (ENG)
1948	Fred Davis (ENG)	84-61	Walter Donaldson (SCO)
1949	Fred Davis (ENG)	80-65	Walter Donaldson (SCO)
1950	Walter Donaldson (SCO)	51-46	Fred Davis (ENG)
1951	Fred Davis (ENG)	58-39	Walter Donaldson (SCO)
1952	Horace Lindrum (AUS)	94-49	Clark McConachy (NZL)
1952	Fred Davis (ENG)	38-35	Walter Donaldson (SCO)
1953	Fred Davis (ENG)	37-34	Walter Donaldson (SCO)
1954	Fred Davis (ENG)	39-21	Walter Donaldson (SCO)
1955	Fred Davis (ENG)	37-34	John Pulman (ENG)
1956	Fred Davis (ENG)	38-35	John Pulman (ENG)
1957	John Pulman (ENG)	39-34	Jackie Rea (NIR)
1958-63	not held		
1964	John Pulman (ENG)	19-16	Fred Davis (ENG)
1964	John Pulman (ENG)	40-33	Rex Williams (ENG)
1965	John Pulman (ENG)	25-22	Rex Williams (ENG)
1965	John Pulman (ENG)	37-36	Fred Davis (ENG)
1965	John Pulman (ENG)	39-12	Freddie van Rensburg (RSA)
1966	John Pulman (ENG)	5-2 (match series)	Fred Davis (ENG)
1967	not held		
1968	John Pulman (ENG)	39-34	Eddie Charlton (AUS)
1969	John Spencer (ENG)	37-24	Gary Owen (ENG)
1970	Ray Reardon (WAL)	37-33	John Pulman (ENG)
1971	John Spencer (ENG)	37-29	Warren Simpson (AUS)
1972	Alex Higgins (NIR)	37-32	John Spencer (ENG)
1973	Ray Reardon (WAL)	38-32	Eddie Charlton (AUS)
1974	Ray Reardon (WAL)	22-12	Graham Miles (ENG)
1975	Ray Reardon (WAL)	31-30	Eddie Charlton (AUS)
1976	Ray Reardon (WAL)	27-16	Alex Higgins (NIR)
1977	John Spencer (ENG)	25-21	Cliff Thorburn (CAN)
1978	Ray Reardon (WAL)	25-18	Perrie Mans (RSA)
1979	Terry Griffiths (WAL)	24-16	Dennis Taylor (NIR)
1980	Cliff Thorburn (CAN)	18-16	Alex Higgins (NIR)
1981	Steve Davis (ENG)	18-12	Doug Mountjoy (WAL)
1982	Alex Higgins (NIR)	18-15	Ray Reardon (WAL)
1983	Steve Davis (ENG)	18-6	Cliff Thorburn (CAN)
1984	Steve Davis (ENG)	18-16	Jimmy White (ENG)
1985	Dennis Taylor (NIR)	18-17	Steve Davis (ENG)
1986	Joe Johnson (ENG)	18-12	Steve Davis (ENG)
1987	Steve Davis (ENG)	18-14	Joe Johnson (ENG)
1988	Steve Davis (ENG)	18-11	Terry Griffiths (WAL)
1989	Steve Davis (ENG)	18-3	John Parrott (ENG)
1990	Stephen Hendry (SCO)	18-12	Jimmy White (ENG)
1991	John Parrott (ENG)	18-11	Jimmy White (ENG)
1992	Stephen Hendry (SCO)	18-14	Jimmy White (ENG)
1993	Stephen Hendry (SCO)	18-5	Jimmy White (ENG)
1994	Stephen Hendry (SCO)	18-17	Jimmy White (ENG)
1995	Stephen Hendry (SCO)	18-9	Nigel Bond (ENG)

1996	Stephen Hendry (SCO)	18-12	Peter Ebdon (ENG)
1997	Ken Doherty (IRL)	18-12	Stephen Hendry (SCO)
1998	John Higgins (SCO)	18-12	Ken Doherty (IRL)
1999	Stephen Hendry (SCO)	18-11	Mark Williams (WAL)
2000	Mark Williams (WAL)	18-16	Matthew Stevens (WAL)
2001	Ronnie O'Sullivan (ENG)	18-14	John Higgins (SCO)
2002	Peter Ebdon (ENG)	18-17	Stephen Hendry (SCO)
2003	Mark Williams (WAL)	18-16	Ken Doherty (IRL)
2004	Ronnie O'Sullivan (ENG)	18-8	Graeme Dott (SCO)

NB: From 1952 to 1957 the competition was named the Professional Match-Play Championship. Between 1964 and 1968 it was organised on a challenge basis. The knockout format was introduced in 1969.

United Kingdom Championship

	Winner		**Runner-Up**
1977	Patsy Fagan (IRL)	12-9	Doug Mountjoy (WAL)
1978	Doug Mountjoy (WAL)	15-9	David Taylor (ENG)
1979	John Virgo (ENG)	14-13	Terry Griffiths (WAL)
1980	Steve Davis (ENG)	16-6	Alex Higgins (NIR)
1981	Steve Davis (ENG)	16-3	Terry Griffiths (WAL)
1982	Terry Griffiths (WAL)	16-15	Alex Higgins (NIR)
1983	Alex Higgins (NIR)	16-15	Steve Davis (ENG)
1984*	Steve Davis (ENG)	16-8	Alex Higgins (NIR)
1985	Steve Davis (ENG)	16-14	Willie Thorne (ENG)
1986	Steve Davis (ENG)	16-7	Neal Foulds (ENG)
1987	Steve Davis (ENG)	16-14	Jimmy White (ENG)
1988	Doug Mountjoy (WAL)	16-12	Stephen Hendry (SCO)
1989	Stephen Hendry (SCO)	16-12	Steve Davis (ENG)
1990	Stephen Hendry (SCO)	16-15	Steve Davis (ENG)
1991	John Parrott (ENG)	16-13	Jimmy White (ENG)
1992	Jimmy White (ENG)	16-9	John Parrott (ENG)
1993	Ronnie O'Sullivan (ENG)	10-6	Stephen Hendry (SCO)
1994	Stephen Hendry (SCO)	10-5	Ken Doherty (IRL)
1995	Stephen Hendry (SCO)	10-3	Peter Ebdon (ENG)
1996	Stephen Hendry (SCO)	10-9	John Higgins (SCO)
1997	Ronnie O'Sullivan (ENG)	10-6	Stephen Hendry (SCO)
1998	John Higgins (SCO)	10-6	Matthew Stevens (WAL)
1999	Mark Williams (WAL)	10-8	Matthew Stevens (WAL)
2000	John Higgins (SCO)	10-4	Mark Williams (WAL)
2001	Ronnie O'Sullivan (ENG)	10-1	Ken Doherty (IRL)
2002	Mark Williams (WAL)	10-9	Ken Doherty (IRL)
2003	Matthew Stevens (WAL)	10-8	Stephen Hendry (SCO)

* The championship became open to overseas players in 1984.

Grand Prix

	Winner		**Runner-Up**
1982*	Ray Reardon (WAL)	10-5	Jimmy White (ENG)
1983*	Tony Knowles (ENG)	9-8	Joe Johnson (ENG)
1984	Dennis Taylor (NIR)	10-2	Cliff Thorburn (CAN)
1985	Steve Davis (ENG)	10-9	Dennis Taylor (NIR)
1986	Jimmy White (ENG)	10-6	Rex Williams (WAL)
1987	Stephen Hendry (SCO)	10-7	Dennis Taylor (NIR)
1988	Steve Davis (ENG)	10-6	Alex Higgins (NIR)
1989	Steve Davis (ENG)	10-0	Dean Reynolds (ENG)
1990	Stephen Hendry (SCO)	10-5	Nigel Bond (ENG)
1991	Stephen Hendry (SCO)	10-6	Steve Davis (ENG)
1992	Jimmy White (ENG)	10-9	Ken Doherty (IRL)
1993	Peter Ebdon (ENG)	9-6	Ken Doherty (IRL)
1994	John Higgins (SCO)	9-6	Dave Harold (ENG)
1995	Stephen Hendry (SCO)	9-5	John Higgins (SCO)
1996	Mark Williams (WAL)	9-5	Euan Henderson (SCO)
1997	Dominic Dale (WAL)	9-6	John Higgins (SCO)
1998	Stephen Lee (ENG)	9-2	Marco Fu (HKG)
1999	John Higgins (SCO)	9-8	Mark Williams (WAL)
2000	Mark Williams (WAL)	9-5	Ronnie O'Sullivan (ENG)

Tournament discontinued after 2000/01 season
*Called the Professional Players' Tournament.

British Open

	Winner		Runner-Up
1985	Silvino Francisco (RSA)	12-9	Kirk Stevens (CAN)
1986	Steve Davis (ENG)	12-7	Willie Thorne (ENG)
1987	Jimmy White (ENG)	13-9	Neal Foulds (ENG)
1988	Stephen Hendry (SCO)	13-2	Mike Hallett (ENG)
1989	Tony Meo (ENG)	13-6	Dean Reynolds (ENG)
1990	Bob Chaperon (CAN)	10-8	Alex Higgins (NIR)
1991	Stephen Hendry (SCO)	10-9	Gary Wilkinson (ENG)
1992	Jimmy White (ENG)	10-7	James Wattana (THA)
1993	Steve Davis (ENG)	10-2	James Wattana (THA)
1994	Ronnie O'Sullivan (ENG)	9-4	James Wattana (THA)
1995	John Higgins (SCO)	9-6	Ronnie O'Sullivan (ENG)
1996	Nigel Bond (ENG)	9-8	John Higgins (SCO)
1997	Mark Williams (WAL)	9-2	Stephen Hendry (SCO)
1998	John Higgins (SCO)	9-8	Stephen Hendry (SCO)
1999	Fergal O'Brien (IRL)	9-7	Anthony Hamilton (ENG)
1999*	Stephen Hendry (SCO)	9-5	Peter Ebdon (ENG)
2000	Peter Ebdon (ENG)	9-6	Jimmy White (ENG)
2001	John Higgins (SCO)	9-6	Graeme Dott (SCO)
2002	Paul Hunter (ENG)	9-4	Ian McCulloch (ENG)
2003	Stephen Hendry (SCO)	9-6	Ronnie O'Sullivan (ENG)

*Changed from spring tournament to autumn in 1999/2000.

Welsh Open

	Winner		Runner-Up
1992	Stephen Hendry (SCO)	9-3	Darren Morgan (WAL)
1993	Ken Doherty (IRL)	9-7	Alan McManus (SCO)
1994	Steve Davis (ENG)	9-6	Alan McManus (SCO)
1995	Steve Davis (ENG)	9-3	John Higgins (SCO)
1996	Mark Williams (WAL)	9-3	John Parrott (ENG)
1997	Stephen Hendry (SCO)	9-2	Mark King (ENG)
1998	Paul Hunter (ENG)	9-5	John Higgins (SCO)
1999	Mark Williams (WAL)	9-8	Stephen Hendry (SCO)
2000	John Higgins (SCO)	9-8	Stephen Lee (ENG)
2001	Ken Doherty (IRL)	9-2	Paul Hunter (ENG)
2002	Paul Hunter (ENG)	9-7	Ken Doherty (IRL)
2003	Stephen Hendry (SCO)	9-5	Mark Williams (WAL)

Scottish Open

	Winner		Runner-Up
1981*	Steve Davis (ENG)	9-0	Dennis Taylor (NIR)
1982	Tony Knowles (ENG)	9-6	David Taylor (ENG)
1983	Steve Davis (ENG)	9-4	Cliff Thorburn (CAN)
1984	Steve Davis (ENG)	9-2	Tony Knowles (ENG)
1985	Cliff Thorburn (CAN)	12-10	Jimmy White (ENG)
1986	Neal Foulds (ENG)	12-9	Cliff Thorburn (CAN)
1987	Steve Davis (ENG)	12-5	Cliff Thorburn (CAN)
1988	Steve Davis (ENG)	12-6	Jimmy White (ENG)
1989	Steve Davis (ENG)	9-4	Stephen Hendry (SCO)
1993	Stephen Hendry (SCO)	10-6	Steve Davis (ENG)
1994	John Parrott (ENG)	9-5	James Wattana (THA)
1995	John Higgins (SCO)	9-5	Steve Davis (ENG)
1996	John Higgins (SCO)	9-3	Rod Lawler (ENG)
1997	Stephen Hendry (SCO)	9-1	Tony Drago (MLT)
1998	Ronnie O'Sullivan (ENG)	9-5	John Higgins (SCO)
1999	Stephen Hendry (SCO)	9-1	Graeme Dott (SCO)
2000	Ronnie O'Sullivan (ENG)	9-1	Mark Williams (WAL)
2001	Peter Ebdon (ENG)	9-7	Ken Doherty (IRL)
2002	Stephen Lee (ENG)	9-2	David Gray (ENG)
2003	David Gray (ENG)	9-7	Mark Selby (ENG)
2004	Jimmy White (ENG)	9-7	Paul Hunter (ENG)

Before 1998 the Scottish Open was called the International Open. From 2004 the event became the *Daily Record* Players' Championship.
*Non-ranking.

European Open

	Winner		Runner-Up
1988	John Parrott (ENG)	9-8	Terry Griffiths (WAL)
1989	John Parrott (ENG)	10-6	Stephen Hendry (SCO)
1990	Tony Jones (ENG)	9-7	Mark Johnston-Allen (ENG)
1991	Jimmy White (ENG)	9-3	Mark Johnston-Allen (ENG)
1992	Steve Davis (ENG)	10-4	Stephen Hendry (SCO)
1993	Stephen Hendry (SCO)	9-5	Ronnie O'Sullivan (ENG)
1994	Stephen Hendry (SCO)	9-3	John Parrott (ENG)
1996	John Parrott (ENG)	9-7	Peter Ebdon (ENG)
1997	John Higgins (SCO)	9-5	John Parrott (ENG)
2001	Stephen Hendry (SCO)	9-2	Joe Perry (ENG)
2003	Ronnie O'Sullivan (ENG)	9-6	Stephen Hendry (SCO)
2004	Stephen Maguire (ENG)	9-3	Jimmy White (ENG)

Irish Masters

	Winner		Runner-Up
1978	John Spencer (ENG)	5-3	Doug Mountjoy (WAL)
1979	Doug Mountjoy (WAL)	6-5	Ray Reardon (WAL)
1980	Terry Griffiths (WAL)	9-8	Doug Mountjoy (WAL)
1981	Terry Griffiths (WAL)	9-7	Ray Reardon (WAL)
1982	Terry Griffiths (WAL)	9-5	Steve Davis (ENG)
1983	Steve Davis (ENG)	9-2	Ray Reardon (WAL)
1984	Steve Davis (ENG)	9-1	Terry Griffiths (WAL)
1985	Jimmy White (ENG)	9-5	Alex Higgins (NIR)
1986	Jimmy White (ENG)	9-5	Willie Thorne (ENG)
1987	Steve Davis (ENG)	9-1	Willie Thorne (ENG)
1988	Steve Davis (ENG)	9-4	Neal Foulds (ENG)
1989	Alex Higgins (NIR)	9-8	Stephen Hendry (SCO)
1990	Steve Davis (ENG)	9-4	Dennis Taylor (NIR)
1991	Steve Davis (ENG)	9-5	John Parrott (ENG)
1992	Stephen Hendry (SCO)	9-6	Ken Doherty (IRL)
1993	Steve Davis (ENG)	9-4	Alan McManus (SCO)
1994	Steve Davis (ENG)	9-8	Alan McManus (SCO)
1995	Peter Ebdon (ENG)	9-8	Stephen Hendry (SCO)
1996	Darren Morgan (WAL)	9-8	Steve Davis (ENG)
1997	Stephen Hendry (SCO)	9-8	Darren Morgan (WAL)
1998*	Ken Doherty (IRL)		
1999	Stephen Hendry (SCO)	9-8	Stephen Lee (ENG)
2000	John Higgins (SCO)	9-4	Stephen Hendry (SCO)
2001	Ronnie O'Sullivan (ENG)	9-8	Stephen Hendry (SCO)
2002	John Higgins (SCO)	10-3	Peter Ebdon (ENG)
2003	Ronnie O'Sullivan (ENG)	10-9	John Higgins (SCO)

*Ronnie O'Sullivan beat Ken Doherty 9-3 in the 1998 final, but was later stripped of the title after failing a drug test.

LG Cup

	Winner		Runner-Up
2001	Stephen Lee (ENG)	9-4	Peter Ebdon (ENG)
2002	Chris Small (SCO)	9-5	Alan McManus (SCO)
2003	Mark Williams (WAL)	9-5	John Higgins (SCO)

China Open

	Winner		Runner-Up
1999 (Mar)	John Higgins (SCO)	9-3	Billy Snaddon (SCO)
1999 (Dec)	Ronnie O'Sullivan (ENG)	9-2	Stephen Lee (ENG)
2000	Ronnie O'Sullivan (ENG)	9-3	Mark Williams (WAL)
2002	Mark Williams (WAL)	9-8	Anthony Hamilton (ENG)

Thailand Masters

	Winner		Runner-Up
1995	James Wattana (THA)	9-6	Ronnie O'Sullivan (ENG)
1996	Alan McManus (SCO)	9-8	Ken Doherty (IRL)
1997	Peter Ebdon (ENG)	9-7	Nigel Bond (ENG)
1998	Stephen Hendry (SCO)	9-6	John Parrott (ENG)
1999	Mark Williams (WAL)	9-7	Alan McManus (SCO)
2000	Mark Williams (WAL)	9-5	Stephen Hendry (SCO)
2001	Ken Doherty (IRL)	9-3	Stephen Hendry (SCO)
2002	Mark Williams (WAL)	9-4	Stephen Lee (ENG)

Snooker: Non-Ranking Tournaments

Benson & Hedges Masters

	Winner		Runner-Up
1975	John Spencer (ENG)	9-8	Ray Reardon (WAL)
1976	Ray Reardon (WAL)	7-3	Graham Miles (ENG)
1977	Doug Mountjoy (WAL)	7-6	Ray Reardon (WAL)
1978	Alex Higgins (NIR)	7-5	Cliff Thorburn (CAN)
1979	Perrie Mans (RSA)	8-4	Alex Higgins (NIR)
1980	Terry Griffiths (WAL)	9-5	Alex Higgins (NIR)
1981	Alex Higgins (NIR)	9-6	Terry Griffiths (WAL)
1982	Steve Davis (ENG)	9-5	Terry Griffiths (WAL)
1983	Cliff Thorburn (CAN)	9-7	Ray Reardon (WAL)
1984	Jimmy White (ENG)	9-5	Terry Griffiths (WAL)
1985	Cliff Thorburn (CAN)	9-6	Doug Mountjoy (WAL)
1986	Cliff Thorburn (CAN)	9-5	Jimmy White (ENG)
1987	Dennis Taylor (NIR)	9-8	Alex Higgins (NIR)
1988	Steve Davis (ENG)	9-0	Mike Hallett (ENG)
1989	Stephen Hendry (SCO)	9-6	John Parrott (ENG)
1990	Stephen Hendry (SCO)	9-4	John Parrott (ENG)
1991	Stephen Hendry (SCO)	9-8	Mike Hallett (ENG)
1992	Stephen Hendry (SCO)	9-4	John Parrott (ENG)
1993	Stephen Hendry (SCO)	9-5	James Wattana (THA)
1994	Alan McManus (SCO)	9-8	Stephen Hendry (SCO)
1995	Ronnie O'Sullivan (ENG)	9-3	John Higgins (SCO)
1996	Stephen Hendry (SCO)	10-5	Ronnie O'Sullivan (ENG)
1997	Steve Davis (ENG)	10-8	Ronnie O'Sullivan (ENG)
1998	Mark Williams (WAL)	10-9	Stephen Hendry (SCO)
1999	John Higgins (SCO)	10-8	Ken Doherty (IRL)
2000	Matthew Stevens (WAL)	10-8	Ken Doherty (IRL)
2001	Paul Hunter (ENG)	10-9	Fergal O'Brien (IRL)
2002	Paul Hunter (ENG)	10-9	Mark Williams (WAL)
2003	Mark Williams (WAL)	10-4	Stephen Hendry (SCO)

Scottish Masters

	Winner		Runner-Up
1981	Jimmy White (ENG)	9-4	Cliff Thorburn (CAN)
1982	Steve Davis (ENG)	9-4	Alex Higgins (NIR)
1983	Steve Davis (ENG)	9-6	Tony Knowles (ENG)
1984	Steve Davis (ENG)	9-4	Jimmy White (ENG)
1985	Cliff Thorburn (CAN)	9-7	Willie Thorne (ENG)
1986	Cliff Thorburn (CAN)	9-8	Alex Higgins (NIR)
1987	Joe Johnson (ENG)	9-7	Terry Griffiths (WAL)
1989	Stephen Hendry (SCO)	10-1	Terry Griffiths (WAL)
1990	Stephen Hendry (SCO)	10-6	Terry Griffiths (WAL)
1991	Mike Hallett (ENG)	9-6	Steve Davis (ENG)
1992	Neal Foulds (ENG)	10-8	Gary Wilkinson (ENG)
1993	Ken Doherty (IRL)	10-9	Alan McManus (SCO)
1994	Ken Doherty (IRL)	9-7	Stephen Hendry (SCO)
1995	Stephen Hendry (SCO)	9-5	Peter Ebdon (ENG)
1996	Peter Ebdon (ENG)	9-6	Alan McManus (SCO)
1997	Nigel Bond (ENG)	9-8	Alan McManus (SCO)
1998	Ronnie O'Sullivan (ENG)	9-7	John Higgins (SCO)
1999	Matthew Stevens (WAL)	9-7	John Higgins (SCO)
2000	Ronnie O'Sullivan (ENG)	9-6	Stephen Hendry (SCO)

SNOOKER AND BILLIARDS

2001	John Higgins (SCO)	9-6	Ronnie O'Sullivan (ENG)
2002	Ronnie O'Sullivan (ENG)	9-4	John Higgins (SCO)

German Open

	Winner		**Runner-Up**
1995	John Higgins (SCO)	9-3	Ken Doherty (IRL)
1996	Ronnie O'Sullivan (ENG)	9-7	Alain Robidoux (CAN)
1997*	John Higgins (SCO)	9-4	John Parrott (ENG)

* Ranking event.

Ladies' World Championship

1976	Vera Selby (ENG)	4-0	Muriel Hazeldine (ENG)
1980	Lesley McIlraith (AUS)	4-2	Agnes Davies (WAL)
1981	Vera Selby (ENG)	3-0	Mandy Fisher (ENG)
1984	Stacey Hillyard (ENG)	4-1	Natalie Stelmach (CAN)
1985	Allison Fisher (ENG)	5-1	Stacey Hillyard (ENG)
1986	Allison Fisher (ENG)	5-0	Sue LeMaich (CAN)
1987	Ann-Marie Farren (ENG)	5-0	Stacey Hillyard (ENG)
1988	Allison Fisher (ENG)	6-1	Ann-Marie Farren (ENG)
1989	Allison Fisher (ENG)	6-5	Ann-Marie Farren (ENG)
1990	Karen Corr (NIR)	7-4	Stacey Hillyard (ENG)
1991	Allison Fisher (ENG)	8-2	Karen Corr (NIR)
1993	Allison Fisher (ENG)	9-3	Stacey Hillyard (ENG)
1994	Allison Fisher (ENG)	7-3	Stacey Hillyard (ENG)
1995	Karen Corr (NIR)	6-3	Kim Shaw (ENG)
1996	Karen Corr (NIR)	6-3	Kelly Fisher (ENG)
1998	Kelly Fisher (ENG)	4-0	Karen Corr (NIR)
1999	Kelly Fisher (ENG)	4-2	Karen Corr (NIR)
2000	Kelly Fisher (ENG)	4-1	Lisa Ingall (ENG)
2001	Lisa Quick (ENG)	4-2	Lynette Horsburgh (SCO)
2002	Kelly Fisher (ENG)	4-1	Lisa Quick (ENG)
2003	Kelly Fisher (ENG)	4-1	Lisa Quick (ENG)
2003	Kelly Fisher (ENG)	4-1	Lisa Quick (ENG)

NB: In 2003 two championships were held, the Embassy in Sheffield under the auspices of the World Ladies Billiards & Snooker Association (WLBSA) and the IBSF event in China.

Men's Top 32 World Rankings for 2004/05 Season

1	Ronnie O'Sullivan (ENG)	17	Ian McCulloch (ENG)
2	Mark Williams (WAL)	18	Quinten Hann (AUS)
3	Stephen Hendry (SCO)	19	Ali Carter (ENG)
4	Paul Hunter (ENG)	20	Joe Perry (ENG)
5	John Higgins (SCO)	21	Barry Pinches (ENG)
6	Matthew Stevens (WAL)	22	Tony Drago (MLT)
7	Ken Doherty (IRL)	23	Mark King (ENG)
8	Peter Ebdon (ENG)	24	Stephen Maguire (ENG)
9	Stephen Lee (ENG)	25	Anthony Hamilton (ENG)
10	Alan McManus (SCO)	26	Gerard Greene (ENG)
11	Jimmy White (ENG)	27	Drew Henry (SCO)
12	Chris Small (SCO)	28	Robert Milkins (ENG)
13	Steve Davis (ENG)	29	Michael Holt (ENG)
14	David Gray (ENG)	30	Joe Swail (NIR)
15	Graeme Dott (SCO)	31	John Parrott (ENG)
16	Marco Fu (HKG)	32	Dominic Dale (WAL)

Billiards and Pool

World Professional Billiards Championship

	(English unless stated)		
1870	William Cook	bt	John Roberts snr
1870	John Roberts jnr	bt	William Cook
1870	John Roberts jnr	bt	A. Bowles
1870	Joseph Bennett	bt	John Roberts jnr
1871	John Roberts jnr	bt	Joseph Bennett

1871	William Cook	bt	Joseph Bennett
1872	William Cook	bt	John Roberts jnr
1875	John Roberts jnr	bt	William Cook
1877	John Roberts jnr	bt	William Cook
1880	Joseph Bennett	bt	William Cook
1881	Joseph Bennett	bt	Tom Taylor
1885	John Roberts jnr	bt	William Cook
1885	John Roberts jnr	bt	Joseph Bennett
1889	Charles Dawson	bt	J. North
1900	Charles Dawson	bt	H.W. Stevenson
1901	H.W. Stevenson	bt	Charles Dawson
1901	Charles Dawson	bt	H.W. Stevenson
1901	H.W. Stevenson	(declared champion)	
1903	Charles Dawson	bt	H.W. Stevenson
1908	Melbourne Inman	(declared champion)	
1909	Melbourne Inman	bt	A. Williams
1909	H.W. Stevenson	(declared champion)	
1910	H.W. Stevenson	bt	Melbourne Inman
1910	H.W. Stevenson	bt	Melbourne Inman
1911	H.W. Stevenson	bt	Melbourne Inman
1912	Melbourne Inman	bt	Tom Reece
1913	Melbourne Inman	bt	Tom Reece
1914	Melbourne Inman	bt	Tom Reece
1919	Melbourne Inman	bt	H.W. Stevenson
1920	Willie Smith	bt	Claude Falkiner
1921	Tom Newman	bt	Tom Reece
1922	Tom Newman	bt	Claude Falkiner
1923	Willie Smith	bt	Tom Newman
1924	Tom Newman	bt	Tom Reece
1925	Tom Newman	bt	Tom Reece
1926	Tom Newman	bt	Joe Davis
1927	Tom Newman	bt	Joe Davis
1928	Joe Davis	bt	Tom Newman
1929	Joe Davis	bt	Tom Newman
1930	Joe Davis	bt	Tom Newman
1931	not held		
1932	Joe Davis	bt	Clark McConachy (NZL)
1933	Walter Lindrum (AUS)	bt	Joe Davis
1934	Walter Lindrum (AUS)	bt	Joe Davis
1935-50	not held		
1951	Clark McConachy (NZL)	bt	John Barrie
1952-67	not held		
1968	Rex Williams	bt	Clark McConachy (NZL)
1971	Leslie Driffield	bt	Jack Karnehm
1971	Rex Williams	bt	Bernard Bennett
1973	Leslie Driffield	bt	Albert Johnson
1974	Rex Williams	bt	Eddie Charlton (AUS)
1976	Rex Williams	bt	Eddie Charlton (AUS)
1980	Fred Davis	bt	Rex Williams
1981	Fred Davis	bt	Mark Wildman
1982	Rex Williams	bt	Mark Wildman
1983	Rex Williams	bt	Fred Davis
1984	Mark Wildman	bt	Eddie Charlton (AUS)
1985	Ray Edmonds	bt	Norman Dagley
1986	Robbie Foldvari (AUS)	bt	Norman Dagley
1987	Norman Dagley	bt	Robbie Foldvari (AUS)
1988	Norman Dagley	bt	Eddie Charlton (AUS)
1989	Mike Russell	bt	Peter Gilchrist
1990	not held		
1991	Mike Russell	bt	Robbie Foldvari (AUS)
1992	Geet Sethi (IND)	bt	Mike Russell
1993	Geet Sethi (IND)	bt	Mike Russell
1994	Peter Gilchrist	bt	Mike Russell
1995	Geet Sethi (IND)	bt	Devendra Joshi (IND)
1996	Mike Russell	bt	Geet Sethi (IND)
1997	not held		
1998	Geet Sethi (IND)	bt	Mike Russell
1999	Mike Russell	bt	Peter Gilchrist
2000	not held		
2001	Peter Gilchrist	bt	Mike Russell
2002	Mike Russell	bt	Peter Gilchrist
2003	Mike Russell	bt	Peter Gilchrist

World Ladies' Billiards Championship

(English unless stated)

1998	Karen Corr (NIR)	bt	Emma Bonney
1999	Karen Corr (NIR)	bt	Kelly Fisher
2000	Emma Bonney	bt	Caroline Walch
2001	Kelly Fisher	bt	Emma Bonney
2002	Emma Bonney	bt	Kelly Fisher
2003	Kelly Fisher	bt	Emma Bonney

World 9-Ball Pool Champions

1990	Earl Strickland (USA)		1999*	Nick Varner (USA)
1991	Earl Strickland (USA)			Efren Reyes (PHI)
1992	Johnny Archer (USA)		2000	Fong-Pang Chao (TPE)
1993	Fong-Pang Chao (TPE)		2001	Mika Immonen (FIN)
1994	Takeshi Okumuru (JPN)		2002	Earl Strickland (USA)
1995	Oliver Ortmann (GER)		2003	Thorsten Hohmann (GER)
1996	Ralf Souquet (GER)		2004	Alex Pagulayan (CAN)
1997	Johnny Archer (USA)			
1998	Kunihiko Takahashi (JPN)			*Two championships played.

World 8-Ball Pool Champions

1993	Kevin Wright (ENG)		1999	Quinten Hann (AUS)
1994	Rob McKenna (SCO)		2000	Jason Twist (ENG)
1995	Daz Ward (ENG)		2001	Chris Melling (ENG)
1996	Greg Farren (IRL)		2002	Jason Twist (ENG)
1997	Rob McKenna (SCO)		2003	Chris Melling (ENG)
1998	Carl Morris (ENG)		2004	Mick Hill (ENG)

Ladies' World 9-Ball Pool Champions

1990	Robin Bell (USA)		1997	Allison Fisher (ENG)
1991	Robin Bell (USA)		1998	Allison Fisher (ENG)
1992	Franziska Stark (GER)		1999	Liu Hsin-Mei (TPE)
1993	Loree Jon Jones (USA)		2000	Julie Kelly (IRL)
1994	Ewa Mataya-Laurance (SWE)		2001	Allison Fisher (ENG)
1995	Gerda Hofstatter (AUT)		2002	Liu Hsin-Mei (TPE)
1996	Allison Fisher (ENG)			

Ladies' World 8-Ball Pool Champions

1993	Linda Moffat (ENG)		1999	Lisa Quick (ENG)
1994	Linda Moffat (ENG)		2000	Sue Thompson (SCO)
1994	Linda Leadbitter (ENG)		2001	Lisa Quick (ENG)
1996	Sue Thompson (SCO)		2002	Sue Thompson (SCO)
1997	Sue Thompson (SCO)		2003	Sue Thompson (SCO)
1998	Linda Leadbitter (ENG)		2004	Sue Thompson (SCO)

World Carom Champions
(also known as 3-cushion billiards)

1974	Nobuaki Kobayashi (JPN)		1991	Torbjorn Blomdahl (SWE)
1975	Raymond Ceulemans (BEL)		1992	Torbjorn Blomdahl (SWE)
1976	Raymond Ceulemans (BEL)		1993	Sang Chun Lee (USA)/Rini van Bracht (NED)
1977	Raymond Ceulemans (BEL)		1994	Torbjorn Blomdahl (SWE)
1978	Raymond Ceulemans (BEL)		1995	Torbjorn Blomdahl (SWE)/Jozef Philipoon (BEL)
1979	Raymond Ceulemans (BEL)		1996	Torbjorn Blomdahl (SWE)/Christian Rudolph (GER)
1980	Raymond Ceulemans (BEL)			
1981	Ludo Dielis (BEL)		1997	Dick Jaspers (NED)/Torbjorn Blomdahl (SWE)
1982	Rini van Bracht (NED)		1998	Torbjorn Blomdahl (SWE)/Daniel Sánchez (ESP)
1983	Raymond Ceulemans (BEL)		1999	Dick Jaspers (NED)/Frédéric Caudron (BEL)
1984	Nobuaki Kobayashi (JPN)		2000	Dick Jaspers (NED)
1985	Raymond Ceulemans (BEL)		2001	Torbjorn Blomdahl (SWE)/Raymond Ceulemans (BEL)
1986	Avelino Rico (ESP)			
1987	Torbjorn Blomdahl (SWE)		2002	Marco Zanetti (ITA)
1988	Torbjorn Blomdahl (SWE)		2003	Semih Sayginer (TUR)
1989	Ludo Dielis (BEL)			
1990	Raymond Ceulemans (BEL)			NB: In years with two champions it is because there were two versions held.

World Bar Billiards Championships

1981	Harry Siddal	bt	Derek Payne
1982	Graham Bisson	bt	Clarrie Queree
1983	Tim Ringsdore	bt	Micky Daw
1984	Peter Noel	bt	Don Cadec
1985	Bernie McCluskey	bt	Paul Webb
1986	Dave Harris	bt	Peter Noel
1987	Wayne Poingdestre	bt	Kevin Tunstall
1988	Alan Le Blond	bt	Micky Daw
1989	Trevor Gallienne	bt	Bob Taylor
1990	Steve Ahier	bt	Terry Race
1991	Steve Ahier	bt	Simon Tinto
1992	Dennis Helleur	bt	Harry Barbet
1993	Kevin Tunstall	bt	Graham Bisson
1994	Kevin Tunstall	bt	Tony Walsh
1995	Tony Walsh	bt	Mark Brewster
1996	Terry Oakley	bt	Don Cadec
1997	Jim Millward	bt	Steve Ahier
1998	Keith Sheard	bt	Nick Barnett
1999	Peter Noel	bt	Terry Race
2000	Bernie McCluskey	bt	Bob King
2001	Jim Millward	bt	Kevin Tunstall
2002	Terry Race	bt	Nigel Ryall
2003	Jim Millward	bt	Terry Race

General Information

balls: dimensions	The balls shall be of an approved composition and shall each have a diameter of 52.5mm with a tolerance of +/– 0.05mm. They should be of equal weight within a tolerance of 3g per set.
bar billiards	Bar billiards most likely developed from the game of bagatelle. It was popularised by English businessman David Gill in the 1930s. The British Isles Open Bar Billiards Championship became the World Championships in 2000. The tournament is played in Jersey.
cue: dimensions	A cue must be not less than 3ft (914mm) in length and must show no substantial departure from the traditional shape and form.
Mosconi Cup	Annual 9-ball pool competition between the USA and Europe. Inaugurated in 1994, USA have won every year bar 1995 and 2002.
pool: history	Pool originated in the USA as the American form of pocket billiards. Eight-ball pool was invented at the turn of the 20th century. The object is to pot either the seven red balls or seven yellow balls followed by the final black to win the frame. Nine-ball pool developed from 8-ball and in the 1920s was very much a gambling game. In 9-ball the balls are potted in sequence commencing with the 1-ball.
Pot Black: referee	Sydney Lee (English amateur billiards champion 1931-34, world champion 1933)
rules of snooker	Snooker is played by two or more players, either independently or in teams. Each player uses the same white cue ball and there are 21 balls which require potting into six pockets, i.e. 15 reds worth 1 point each; yellow – 2 points; green – 3 points; brown – 4 points; blue – 5 points; pink – 6 points; black – 7 points. A red must be potted before each colour and once potted remains in the pocket. The colours are replaced on their positions at the start of the game until all the reds are cleared and then they are potted in ascending order from yellow to black. A maximum break is therefore 147, being 15 reds and blacks and all the colours. At the start of the game the coloured balls are positioned on their spots: on the baulk line green, brown and yellow (a useful mnemonic being God Bless You), blue in the centre of the table, pink in the centre of the bottom half of the table and black on the remaining spot beneath the pink. The 15 reds are racked in a triangle and placed with the top red as close to the pink spot as possible without touching it. The cue ball is placed in the 'D' and is usually struck from between the brown and yellow to hit the reds to break them up. If a ball is not potted then the next player takes their turn and plays the cue ball from where it rests unless it is potted unintentionally, in which case it is played from the 'D'. Foul shots carry a minimum penalty of four points but fouls on blue ball and above carry a penalty of the ball value. Points awarded for fouls are added to the opponent's score. A successful snooker is where a player forces their opponent to make a foul shot by leaving them with no direct shot from cue ball to object ball. A free ball is awarded following an unsuccessful

SNOOKER AND BILLIARDS

attempt to escape from a snooker where the opponent is left unable to see both sides of the object ball. In a free-ball situation a colour can be nominated and potted as a red and then a colour potted. This means that in theory the highest possible clearance is 155. Theoretically the lowest possible clearance is 44, i.e. the 15 reds potted in one shot, followed by a yellow and then all the colours.

Push shots are not allowed in snooker. A push shot is where two balls are almost touching and the cue, cue ball and object ball make contact at the same time. When the cue ball comes to rest against a potential object ball the player must play away without disturbing the touching ball.

The winner of a frame of snooker is the player accruing the most points after the final black is potted. The first foul on the final black ends the game unless the scores are then equal, in which case play continues until a further score is made. If one player is over seven points in front, the pink is the final ball that must be potted.

table: dimensions	The playing area within the cushion-faces on the inner perimeter measures 11ft 8½ins × 5ft 10ins (3.57m × 1.78m) with a tolerance on both dimensions of +/– ½in (+/– 13mm). The height of the table from the floor to the top of the cushion rail should be from 2ft 9½ins (85.1cm) to 2ft 10½ins (87.6cm). A straight line drawn 29ins (73.7cm) from the bottom cushion and parallel to it is called the baulk line, and that line and the intervening space is termed the baulk. The 'D' is a semi-circle described in baulk with its centre at the middle of the baulk line and with a radius of 11½ins (29.2cm).

Four spots are marked on the centre longitudinal line of the table: the spot (known as the black spot), 12¾ins (32.4cm) from a point perpendicularly below the face of the top cushion; the centre spot (known as the blue spot), located midway between the faces of the top and bottom cushions; the pyramid spot (known as the pink spot), located midway between the centre spot and the face of the top cushion; and the middle of the baulk line (known as the brown spot). The two other spots used are located at the corners of the 'D'. Viewed from the baulk end, the one on the right is known as the yellow spot and the one on the left as the green spot.

television: first player to be shown on United Kingdom Championship: sponsors	Sydney Lee in a demonstration from Alexandra Palace The 1977 sponsor was Super Crystalate From 1978-85 the sponsor was Coral From 1986-88 the sponsor was Tennents From 1989-90 the sponsor was Stormseal From 1992-95 the sponsor was Royal Liver Insurance From 1997-2000 the sponsor was Liverpool Victoria From 2001-02 the sponsor was PowerHouse In 2003 the sponsor was Travis Perkins
World Championships: first woman referee	Michaela Tabb (2003)
World Confederation of Billiard Sports (WCBS)	Founded in January 1992, incorporating the primary cue sports of snooker, pool and carom. The WPBSA was a founding member of the WCBS. The remit of the WCBS is to fulfil International Olympic Committee conditions.
World Professional Billiards and Snooker Association (WPBSA)	The WPBSA is the governing body of professional snooker and billiards throughout the world. Its current president is golfer Ian Woosnam.
World Professional Snooker Championship: sponsor	Since 1976 Embassy has sponsored the World Championship.
World Snooker Association: address	Ground Floor, Albert House, 111-117 Victoria St, Bristol BS1 6AX Tel: 0117 3178200. Fax: 0117 3178300. Website: www.worldsnooker.com
youngest world snooker champion	Stephen Hendry, 21 years, 106 days (1990)

SQUASH

The precise origins of the game of 'squash' are elusive, although squash rackets, as it was known until recently, is clearly a member of the extensive family of racket games. The first known reference to a rebounding-ball game was made by an English schoolmaster in 1581. More recently, in 1865, a game which had evolved from the English game of rackets (see separate section) was played in an enclosed court at Harrow School. This led to the building of similar courts at Rugby School and at various private houses and clubs.

At that time there was no standard size for courts, this finally being formalised only after World War I. The process was started by the Tennis and Rackets Association in 1911 but it was not until 1922 that championships were played. The rackets used at the turn of the 20th century were not unlike those used today (although not nearly as efficient), but the balls differed greatly.

Balls were constructed of thin rubber and were quite soft. They also had a number of holes in them which caused the ball to collapse when hit hard. It is from this 'squashy' ball, along with the rackets connection that the name of 'squash rackets' probably originated. Squash quickly spread and is now played worldwide in over 120 countries.

In 1929 the Squash Rackets Association was formed in Britain. The first squash courts in Australia were built in 1913 at the Melbourne Club in Collins Street, and in 1934 an official squash association was formed, named the Squash Rackets Association of Australia (SRAA). It was nevertheless mainly concerned with local competition. In 1938, the SRAA took on a national role when 18 clubs from Victoria, New South Wales and South Australia joined.

The game is played indoors on an enclosed rectangular four-walled court. The singles court is 6.40m wide by 9.75m. The doubles court is almost 50 per cent longer than the singles court and 20 per cent wider. Most squash courts are single courts. Because the squash court is three-dimensional, the ball can be bounced off the four walls which surround the floor of the court. The entry door when closed forms part of the back wall. The floor consists of parallel hardwood planks.

In the singles game, two players take turns to hit the ball on to the front wall, in an area defined by an 'out' line at the top of the court and the top of the 'tin', an area which extends across and near the bottom of the front wall. A rally begins when the server, standing in one of the service boxes, hits the ball directly to the front wall (above the service or 'cut' line and below the 'out' line) to rebound into the opposite quarter of the court bounded by the side and back wall and two lines (the short line and the half court line). The player receiving may choose to hit the ball before it bounces but must hit it before it bounces twice. The rally continues so long as the ball goes on to the front wall before going down or out, down being into the 'tin' or into the floor, and out being on or above the 'out' line which surrounds the court at the top of each of the four walls. After the serve, the ball may hit any wall before hitting the front wall so long as it does not go down or out.

The doubles game is similar except that instead of players taking turns to hit the ball, either member of each team must hit the ball in turn.

Squash has two scoring systems: the nine-point system and the rally system, which are both used at international as well as local level. In the traditional nine-point scoring system, players must gain the serve before being able to score a point. If receivers win a rally they win the serve, but if servers win the rally they score a point. The first player to nine points wins the game unless the score is eight-all. In that case, the player who scored eight points first can choose whether to play to nine or ten points. A match consists of the best of five games. The nine-point system is generally employed in international competition in singles matches.

In the rally scoring system a point is scored after each rally. Instead of going to nine points, each game goes to 15 except when it is 14-all. In this case, the first player to reach 14 chooses whether to go to 15 or 17 points. Again, a match consists of the best of five games. The rally system is employed in international competition in doubles matches.

Jonah Barrington of Great Britain and Geoff Hunt of Australia were the greatest players during the 1970s, the balance of power afterwards resting with Pakistan and in particular, Jahingar Khan and then Jansher Khan. The women's game was dominated throughout this period by Australian Heather McKay who was undefeated between 1962 and 1980.

The Professional Squash Association (PSA) is the governing body of the men's game and the 2003 world champion is Amr Shabana of Egypt. The current world no. 1 player according to the PSA Rankings of September 2004 is Scottish-born Peter Nicol of England. Lee Beachill of England is no. 2 in the rankings and Shabana places fifth. The Women's International Squash Players Association (WISPA) governs the women's game. Carol Owens of New Zealand won the 2003 world championship and then announced her retirement. The current world no. 1 player according to the WISPA Rankings of September 2004 is Rachael Grinham of Australia. England's Cassie Jackman is ranked second.

SUMO

The national sport of Japan is almost as old as the race itself although the earliest written mention of sumo is found in the *Record of Ancient Matters* (*Kojiki*), a book dating from the beginning of the Nara period (710AD), and the oldest example of Japanese writing. The *Kojiki* relates a legend about how possession of the Japanese islands was determined by a sumo match 2500 years ago. The sport was under imperial patronage throughout the Nara and Heian periods (710-1185) and this heritage explains the ritualistic prevalence in sumo. Each match is an historical recreation and precise formalities are observed before, during and after a session. The *rikishi* (wrestlers sometimes referred to as *sumotori*) are paraded in ranking order before each day's competition and the yokozuna (grand champion) performs the *dohyo-iri* ceremony. After first clapping his hands together to attract the attention of the gods, he extends his arms to the sides and turns palms upward to show he is concealing no weapons. Then at the climax he lifts first one leg to the side high in the air, then the other, bringing each down with a resounding stamp on the ground symbolically driving evil from the *dohyo*. After the final bout a highly skilled person (*makushita*) will perform the 'bow dance', where an ornamental bow is twirled in a graceful and very entertaining manner.

Modern professional sumo began in the early 17th century and the first yokozuna was Akashi Shiganosuke in 1632. Since then there have been another 66 Yokozunas, the 67th being Hawaiian-born Koyo Musashimaru (born 2 May 1971). Two outstanding yokozunas of the past are Taiho and Chiyonofuji. Taiho was born in Hokkaido, 29 May 1940, as Koki Naya. He won 32 tournaments (*bashos*) and won almost 80 per cent of his over 1000 fights. Chiyonofuji was born in Hokkaido, 1 June 1955, as Mitsugu Akimoto. He won 31 *bashos* and of his over 1500 fights he won 70 per cent, an amazing statistic considering, at 17 stone (108kg), he was one of the smallest wrestlers on the circuit.

The sumo area is called the *dohyo* and takes its name from the straw rice bags that mark out its different parts. The greater portion of each bale is firmly buried in the earth. The *dohyo* is 18ft (5.5m) square and 2ft (0.6m) high and is constructed of a special kind of clay. The hard surface is covered with a thin layer of sand. The bout commences with the *rikishi* being led into the *dohyo* by the referee (*gyoji*). This man is specially trained not only to have a discerning eye but also a particularly high-pitched voice used to announce the fighters. It is traditional for each *rikishi* to choose a poetic sumo name for himself. Some adopt a name derived from the name of their sumo master or their place of birth. Most frequently chosen are names ending in '*yama*' (mountain), '*gawa*' (river) or '*umi*' (sea). When it is time for the combatants to begin, the *gyoji* gives the signal with his fan. The *rikishi* will customarily 'size-up' his opponent by staring him out during several trial runs before the actual commencement of hostilities. At this time salt is thrown into the *dohyo* by the fighters. This preparatory ritual must be performed within four minutes and then finally the *rikishi* will squat down with their weight on their clenched fists. When all four fists touch the ground battle commences. This part of the ritual is called the '*shikiri*'. The *dohyo* has an inner circle a little over 15ft (4.6m) in diameter. Over the *dohyo* suspended from the ceiling by cables is a roof resembling a Shinto shrine with four giant tassels. *Rikishi* wear only a silken loin cloth (*mawashi*) and a match is often won by the *rikishi* who establishes an early grip on his opponent's *mawashi*. A match is won by forcing the opponent out of the inner circle or throwing him in the *dohyo*. To lose the match it is not necessary to fall in the circle or to be pushed completely out. The *rikishi* who touches the ground with any part of his body, his knee or even the tip of his finger or his top-knot, loses the match. He need only put one toe or his heel over the straw bales marking the circle. Striking with fists, hair pulling, eye gouging, choking and kicking in the stomach or chest are prohibited. The most common method of winning a bout is by grabbing the opponent by the *mawashi* and forcing him out of the ring (*yorikiri*). A useful move at the *shikiri* is to sidestep the opponent when he springs forward and push him out of the ring (*hataki-komi*). When it is not clear who has won the match the *gyoji* will refer to the five judges, who then make a decision to award the bout to the *rikishi* or to have a rematch. Occasionally the judges will overrule a referee's decision.

There are six main *bashos* held each year, three in Tokyo, one in Osaka, Nagoya and Kyushu. A tournament lasts for fifteen days, each *rikishi* fighting once every day with a different opponent. The winner of the tournament is the *rikishi* with the best record of wins over losses, and this person is awarded the Emperor's Cup. As well as the Emperor's Cup awards are given for fighting spirit (*kanto sho*), outstanding performance (*shukun sho*) and technical accomplishment (*gino sho*). An award is also given if a yokozuna is beaten by a maegashira over and above the *shukun sho* prize, this is called '*kinboshi*'.

There are about 800 professional *rikishi* at present and they are subject to a ranking (*banzuke*) system and this is reviewed after every *basho*. The top five ranks are referred to as the *maku-uchi* and are, in order, yokozuna, ozeki, sekiwake, komusubi, and maegashira. The top ranks form about five percent of all *rikishi* and only these get to fight on all 15 days of a *basho*, the junior ranks of juryo and below are accommodated where possible. Although the rankings are adjusted after every *basho*, yokozunas can never be demoted and if they begin to perform consistently badly they are expected to retire and go through the very emotional ceremony of having their topknot cut off in the centre of the *dohyo*. This appears harsh but if one considers the work involved in becoming a yokozuna (the minimum requirement is to win two successive *bashos* at ozeki level) and the prestige, honour and uniqueness (on average only one *rikishi* is made yokozuna every five years!) then you realise that the chosen few are very special indeed.

SURFING

The idea of riding waves with a wooden board originated in Western Polynesia over three thousand years ago. Fishermen favoured this method of transportation as an efficient method of returning to shore with their catch, and at some point they realised that 'catching waves' could be fun and began to ride for pleasure. Records of surfing first appear in 1777 when explorer Captain James Cook described how a Tahitian caught waves with his outrigger canoe. In 1821 surfing was banned by European missionaries who deemed it immoral, and it was not until 1920 that the Hawaiian Duke Paoa Kahanamoku (1890-1968) ('Duke' being his – and his father's – first name), the Olympic freestyle swimming champion of 1912 and 1920, formed the first surfing club in Waikiki (where Kahanamoku was born). The world amateur surfing championships began in 1964 and the world professional championships in 1970 when the competition was decided over a single event. In 1976 the International Professional Surfing Tour was formed and the competition evolved into the Association of Surfing Professionals World Championship Tour (WCT) circuit.

The two outstanding surfers of recent years are Kelly Slater and Layne Beachley. Slater (born 11 March 1972), from Cocoa Beach, Florida, was six-times world professional champion (1992, 1994-98). He developed existing moves and invented new moves such as the 'rodeo clown'. Florida was the home of 'freeboarding' (riding a board behind a boat, also known as wakeboarding) and this tow-in style of surfing lent itself to innovation. (Slater also took part in a series of the television programme *Baywatch*.) Layne 'the Beast' Beachley (born 24 May 1972), from Sydney, Australia, has dominated women's surfing, winning the last six world championships (1998-2003).

Since the days of the long, narrow wooden 'Malibu' boards (measuring between 6ft (1.83m) and 7½ft (2.28m), great strides have been made to ensure that materials such as fibre-glass and designs of board (thickness and angle of rail, fin placement and shape) enable surfers to ride enormous 'barrels' (a 'barrel' is a wave that is hollow when it breaks. It is also called a 'tube'). Scores for surfing events are out of a possible 10 marks per barrel run: maximum scores are rare.

SWIMMING

Swimming as a competitive sport began in the late 19th century. Matthew Webb's swimming of the English Channel in 1875 brought the sport to prominence and it was included in the first modern Olympic programme in 1896. The Amateur Swimming Association (ASA) was founded in 1886 and the Fédération International de Natation Amateur (International Amateur Swimming Federation, FINA) was formed at the Manchester Hotel, London, on 19 July 1908 by George Hearn. Today FINA governs international competition in swimming, diving and water polo.

The sport has produced its fair share of characters over the years. Duke Kahanamoku (1890-1968) was an early high-profile swimmer. A member of the Hawaiian Royal family who won three gold and two silver medals in the 1912, 1920 and 1924 Olympic Games, he also played water polo and was a pioneer in the sport of surfing. Duke also introduced the crawl stroke to America and later became the sheriff of Honolulu.

Johnny Weissmuller (1904-84) was the next superstar swimmer. Born in Freidorf, Hungary (now Romania), he won three golds at the 1924 Olympics and two more at the 1928 Games, collecting numerous world records. He never lost a race and was the first person to swim 100m in under a minute. However, he is perhaps best remembered for his portrayal of the lead role in several *Tarzan* movies.

Clarence Lindon Crabbe (1908-83), better known as 'Buster', followed in Weissmuller's footsteps as both a swimmer and a film star. The only non-Japanese male swimmer to win a gold medal at the 1932 Los Angeles Olympics, winning the 400m freestyle, he went on to star as the title character in the early *Flash Gordon* serials, also starring in some *Tarzan* movies.

Australian Dawn Fraser (born 1937) was another character of the sport. Known for her rebellious behaviour, Fraser won eight Olympic and eight Commonwealth Games medals. In October 1962 she became the first woman to swim 100m in less than a minute, a record that remained unbroken for eight years after her retirement. She was named Australian of the Year in 1964. In 1965 she retired from swimming after being banned for breaches of discipline by the Australian Swimming Union. Fraser later became a swimming coach and in 1988 a Member of the Legislative Assembly (MLA) for the New South Wales seat of Balmain. In 1998 she was appointed an Officer of the Order of Australia (AO).

British swimming heroes include Scot David Wilkie and Duncan Goodhew, but the sport has generally been dominated by the United States and Australia. However, the present British squad, under the exacting coaching methods of Australian Bill Sweetenham, is the strongest ever and is fancied to win several medals at forthcoming championships.

Olympic Medallists

Men's 50m Freestyle
(50yds in 1904)

	Gold		Silver		Bronze	
1904	Zoltán Halmaj (HUN)	28.2	Scott Leary (USA)	28.6	Charles Daniels (USA)	——
1906-84	not held					
1988	Matt Biondi (USA)	22.14	Thomas Jager (USA)	22.36	Gennadiy Prigoda (URS)	22.71
1992	Aleksandr Popov (CIS)	21.91	Matt Biondi (USA)	22.09	Thomas Jager (USA)	22.30
1996	Aleksandr Popov (RUS)	22.13	Gary Hall jnr (USA)	22.26	Fernando Scherer (BRA)	22.29
2000	Anthony Ervin (USA)	21.98			Pieter van den Hoogenband (NED)	22.03
	Gary Hall jnr (USA)					

Men's 100m Freestyle
(100yds in 1904)

	Gold		Silver		Bronze	
1896	Arnold Guttmann (HUN)	1:22.2	Otto Herschmann (AUT)	1:22.8	——	
1900	not held					
1904	Zoltán Halmaj (HUN)	1:02.8	Charles Daniels (USA)	——	Scott Leary (USA)	——
1906	Charles Daniels (USA)	1:13.6	Zoltán Halmaj (HUN)	——	Cecil Healy (AUS)	——
1908	Charles Daniels (USA)	1:05.4	Zoltán Halmaj (HUN)	1:06.2	Harald Julin (SWE)	1:08.0
1912	Duke Paoa Kahanamoku (USA)	1:03.4	Cecil Healy (AUS)	1:04.6	Kenneth Huszagh (USA)	1:05.6
1920	Duke Paoa Kahanamoku (USA)	1:01.4	Pua Kela Kealoha (USA)	1:02.6	William Harris (USA)	1:03.0
1924	Johnny Weissmuller (USA)	59.0	Duke Paoa Kahanamoku (USA)	1:01.4	Samuel Kahanamoku (USA)	1:01.8

1928	Johnny Weissmuller (USA)	58.6	István Bárány (HUN)	59.8	Katsuo Takaishi (JPN)	1:00.0
1932	Yasuji Miyazaki (JPN)	58.2	Tatsugo Kawaishi (JPN)	58.6	Albert Schwartz (USA)	58.8
1936	Ferenc Csík (HUN)	57.6	Masanori Yusa (JPN)	57.9	Shigeo Arai (JPN)	58.0
1948	Walter Ris (USA)	57.3	Alan Ford (USA)	57.8	Géza Kádas (HUN)	58.1
1952	Clarke Scholes (USA)	57.4	Hiroshi Suzuki (JPN)	57.4	Göran Larsson (SWE)	58.2
1956	Jon Henricks (AUS)	55.4	John Devitt (AUS)	55.8	Gary Chapman (AUS)	56.7
1960	John Devitt (AUS)	55.2	Lance Larson (USA)	55.2	Manuel Dos Santos (BRA)	55.4
1964	Don Schollander (USA)	53.4	Robert McGregor (GBR)	53.5	Hans-Joachim Klein (GER)	54.0
1968	Mike Wenden (AUS)	52.2	Kenneth Walsh (USA)	52.8	Mark Spitz (USA)	53.0
1972	Mark Spitz (USA)	51.22	Jerry Heidenreich (USA)	51.65	Vladimir Bure (URS)	51.77
1976	Jim Montgomery (USA)	49.99	Jack Babashoff (USA)	50.81	Peter Nocke (FRG)	51.31
1980	Jörg Woithe (GDR)	50.40	Per Holmertz (SWE)	50.91	Per Johansson (SWE)	51.29
1984	Rowdy Gaines (USA)	49.80	Mark Stockwell (AUS)	50.24	Per Johansson (SWE)	50.31
1988	Matt Biondi (USA)	48.63	Chris Jacobs (USA)	49.08	Stephan Caron (FRA)	49.62
1992	Aleksandr Popov (CIS)	49.02	Gustavo Borges (BRA)	49.43	Stephan Caron (FRA)	49.50
1996	Aleksandr Popov (RUS)	48.74	Gary Hall jnr (USA)	48.81	Gustavo Borges (BRA)	49.02
2000	Pieter van den Hoogenband (NED)	48.30	Aleksandr Popov (RUS)	48.69	Gary Hall jnr (USA)	48.73

Men's 200m Freestyle
(220yds in 1900, 1904)

	Gold		Silver		Bronze	
1900	Freddie Lane (AUS)	2:25.2	Zoltán Halmaj (HUN)	2:31.4	Karl Ruberl (AUT)	2:32.0
1904	Charles Daniels (USA)	2:44.2	Francis Galley (USA)	2:46.0	Emil Rausch (GER)	2:56.0
1906-64	not held					
1968	Mike Wenden (AUS)	1:55.2	Don Schollander (USA)	1:56.8	John Nelson (USA)	1:58.1
1972	Mark Spitz (USA)	1:52.78	Steven Genter (USA)	1:53.73	Werner Lampe (FRG)	1:53.99
1976	Bruce Furniss (USA)	1:50.29	John Naber (USA)	1:50.50	Jim Montgomery (USA)	1:50.58
1980	Sergey Kopliakov (URS)	1:49.81	Andrey Krylov (URS)	1:50.76	Graeme Brewer (AUS)	1:51.60
1984	Michael Gross (FRG)	1:47.44	Michael Heath (USA)	1:49.10	Thomas Fahrner (FRG)	1:49.68
1988	Duncan Armstrong (AUS)	1:47.25	Anders Holmertz (SWE)	1:47.89	Matt Biondi (USA)	1:47.99
1992	Yevgeniy Sadovyi (CIS)	1:46.70	Anders Holmertz (SWE)	1:46.89	Antti Kasvio (FIN)	1:47.64
1996	Danyon Loader (NZL)	1:47.63	Gustavo Borges (BRA)	1:48.08	Dan Kowalski (AUS)	1:48.26
2000	Pieter van den Hoogenband (NED)	1:45.35	Ian Thorpe (AUS)	1:45.83	Massimiliano Rosolino (ITA)	1:46.65

Men's 400m Freestyle

	Gold		Silver		Bronze	
1904	Charles Daniels (USA)	6:16.2	Francis Galley (USA)	6:22.0	Otto Wahle (AUT)	6:39.0
1906	Otto Scheff (AUT)	6:24.0	Henry Taylor (GBR)	6:26.0	John Arthur Jarvis (GBR)	
1908	Henry Taylor (GBR)	5:36.8	Francis Beaurepaire (AUS)	5:44.2	Otto Scheff (AUT)	5:46.0
1912	George Hodgson (CAN)	5:24.4	John Hatfield (GBR)	5:25.8	Harold Hardwick (AUS)	5:31.2
1920	Norman Ross (USA)	5:26.8	Ludy Langer (USA)	5:29.0	George Vernot (CAN)	5:29.6
1924	Johnny Weissmuller (USA)	5:04.2	Arne Borg (SWE)	5:05.6	Andrew 'Boy' Charlton (AUS)	5:06.6
1928	Alberto Zorrilla (ARG)	5:01.6	Andrew 'Boy' Charlton (AUS)	5:03.6	Arne Borg (SWE)	5:04.6
1932	Clarence 'Buster' Crabbe (USA)	4:48.4	Jean Taris (FRA)	4:48.5	Tsutomo Oyokota (JPN)	4:52.3
1936	Jack Medica (USA)	4:44.5	Shumpei Uto (JPN)	4:45.6	Shozo Makino (JPN)	4:48.1
1948	William Smith (USA)	4:41.0	James McLane (USA)	4:43.4	John Marshall (AUS)	4:47.4
1952	Jean Boiteux (FRA)	4:30.7	Ford Konno (USA)	4:31.3	Per-Olof Östrand (SWE)	4:35.2
1956	Murray Rose (AUS)	4:27.3	Tsuyoshi Yamanaka (JPN)	4:30.4	George Breen (USA)	4:32.5
1960	Murray Rose (AUS)	4:18.3	Tsuyoshi Yamanaka (JPN)	4:21.4	John Konrads (AUS)	4:21.8
1964	Don Schollander (USA)	4:12.2	Frank Wiegand (GER)	4:14.9	Allan Wood (AUS)	4:15.1
1968	Mike Burton (USA)	4:09.0	Ralph Hutton (CAN)	4:11.7	Alain Mosconi (FRA)	4:13.3
1972	Brad Cooper (AUS)	4:00.27	Steven Genter (USA)	4:01.94	Tom McBreen (USA)	4:02.64
1976	Brian Goodell (USA)	3:51.93	Tim Shaw (USA)	3:52.54	Vladimir Raskatov (URS)	3:55.76
1980	Vladimir Salnikov (URS)	3:51.31	Andrey Krylov (URS)	3:53.24	Ivar Stukolkin (URS)	3:53.95
1984	George DiCarlo (USA)	3:51.23	John Mykkanen (USA)	3:51.49	Justin Lemberg (AUS)	3:51.79
1988	Uwe Dassler (GDR)	3:46.95	Duncan Armstrong (AUS)	3:47.15	Artur Wojdat (POL)	3:47.34
1992	Yevgeniy Sadovyi (CIS)	3:45.00	Kieren Perkins (AUS)	3:45.16	Anders Holmertz (SWE)	3:46.77
1996	Danyon Loader (NZL)	3:47.97	Paul Palmer (GBR)	3:49.00	Dan Kowalski (AUS)	3:49.39
2000	Ian Thorpe (AUS)	3:40.59	Massimiliano Rosolino (ITA)	3:43.40	Klete Keller (USA)	3:47.00

Men's 1500m Freestyle
(1 mile in 1904)

	Gold		Silver		Bronze	
1904*	Emil Rausch (GER)	27:18.2	Géza Kiss (HUN)	28:28.2	Francis Galley (USA)	28:54.0
1906	Henry Taylor (GBR)	28:28.0	John Arthur Jarvis (GBR)	30:07.6	Otto Scheff (AUT)	30:53.4
1908	Henry Taylor (GBR)	22:48.4	Thomas Battersby (GBR)	22:51.2	Francis Beaurepaire (AUS)	22:56.2
1912	George Hodgson (CAN)	22:00.0	John Hatfield (GBR)	22:39.0	Harold Hardwick (AUS)	23:15.4
1920	Norman Ross (USA)	22:23.2	George Vernot (CAN)	22:36.4	Francis Beaurepaire (AUS)	23:04.0
1924	Andrew 'Boy' Charlton (AUS)	20:06.6	Arne Borg (SWE)	20:41.4	Francis Beaurepaire (AUS)	21:48.4
1928	Arne Borg (SWE)	19:51.8	Andrew 'Boy' Charlton (AUS)	20:02.6	Clarence 'Buster' Crabbe (USA)	20:28.8
1932	Kusio Kitamura (JPN)	19:12.4	Shozo Makino (JPN)	19:14.1	James Cristy (USA)	19:39.5
1936	Noboru Terada (JPN)	19:13.7	Jack Medica (USA)	19:34.0	Shumpei Uto (JPN)	19:34.5
1948	Jimmy McLane (USA)	19:18.5	John Marshall (AUS)	19:31.3	György Mitró (HUN)	19:43.2
1952	Ford Konno (USA)	18:30.3	Shiro Hashizume (JPN)	18:41.4	Tetsuo Okamoto (JPN)	18:51.3
1956	Murray Rose (AUS)	17:58.9	Tsuyoshi Yamanaka (JPN)	18:00.3	George Breen (USA)	18:08.2
1960	John Konrads (AUS)	17:19.6	Murray Rose (AUS)	17:21.7	George Breen (USA)	17:30.6
1964	Robert Windle (AUS)	17:01.7	John Nelson (USA)	17:03.0	Allan Wood (AUS)	17:07.7
1968	Mike Burton (USA)	16:38.9	John Kinsella (USA)	16:57.3	Gregory Brough (AUS)	17:04.7
1972	Mike Burton (USA)	15:52.58	Graham Windeatt (AUS)	15:58.48	Douglas Northway (USA)	16:09.25
1976	Brian Goodell (USA)	15:02.40	Bobby Hackett (USA)	15:03.91	Steve Holland (AUS)	15:04.66
1980	Vladimir Salnikov (URS)	14:58.27	Aleksandr Chayev (URS)	15:14.30	Max Metzker (AUS)	15:14.49
1984	Mike O'Brien (USA)	15:05.20	George DiCarlo (USA)	15:10.59	Stefan Pfeiffer (FRG)	15:12.11
1988	Vladimir Salnikov (URS)	15:00.40	Stefan Pfeiffer (FRG)	15:02.69	Uwe Dassler (GDR)	15:06.15
1992	Kieren Perkins (AUS)	14:43.48	Glen Housman (AUS)	14:55.29	Jörg Hoffmann (GER)	15:02.29
1996	Kieren Perkins (AUS)	14:56.04	Dan Kowalski (AUS)	15:02.43	Graeme Smith (GBR)	15:02.48
2000	Grant Hackett (AUS)	14:48.33	Kieren Perkins (AUS)	14:53.59	Chris Thompson (USA)	14:56.81

Men's 100m Backstroke
(100yds in 1904)

	Gold		Silver		Bronze	
1904	Walter Brack (GER)	1:16.8	Georg Hoffmann (GER)	——	Georg Zacharias (GER)	——
1906	not held					
1908	Arno Bieberstein (GER)	1:24.6	Ludvig Dam (GER)	1:26.6	Herbert Haresnape (GBR)	1:27.0
1912	Harry Hebner (USA)	1:21.2	Otto Fahr (GER)	1:22.4	Paul Kellner (GER)	1:24.0
1920	Warren Paoa Kealoha (USA)	1:15.2	Ray Kegeris (USA)	1:16.8	Gérard Blitz (BEL)	1:19.0
1924	Warren Paoa Kealoha (USA)	1:13.2	Paul Wyatt (USA)	1:15.4	Károly Bartha (HUN)	1:17.8
1928	George Kojac (USA)	1:08.2	Walter Laufer (USA)	1:10.0	Paul Wyatt (USA)	1:12.0
1932	Masaji Kiyokawa (JPN)	1:08.6	Toshio Irie (JPN)	1:09.8	Kentaro Kawazu (JPN)	1:10.0
1936	Adolf Kiefer (USA)	1:05.9	Albert Vandeweghe (USA)	1:07.7	Masaji Kiyokawa (JPN)	1:08.4
1948	Allen Stack (USA)	1:06.4	Robert Cowell (USA)	1:06.5	Georges Vallerey (FRA)	1:07.8
1952	Yoshinobu Oyakawa (USA)	1:05.4	Gilbert Bozon (FRA)	1:06.2	Jack Taylor (USA)	1:06.4
1956	David Theile (AUS)	1:02.2	John Monckton (AUS)	1:03.2	Frank McKinney (USA)	1:04.5
1960	David Theile (AUS)	1:01.9	Frank McKinney (USA)	1:02.1	Robert Bennett (USA)	1:02.3
1964	not held					
1968	Roland Matthes (GDR)	58.7	Charles Hickcox (USA)	1:00.2	Ronald Mills (USA)	1:00.5
1972	Roland Matthes (GDR)	56.58	Michael Stamm (USA)	57.70	John Murphy (USA)	58.35
1976	John Naber (USA)	55.49	Peter Rocca (USA)	56.34	Roland Matthes (GDR)	57.22
1980	Bengt Baron (SWE)	56.33	Viktor Kuznetsov (URS)	56.99	Vladimir Dolgov (URS)	57.63
1984	Rick Carey (USA)	55.79	David Wilson (USA)	56.35	Mike West (CAN)	56.49
1988	Daichi Suzuki (JPN)	55.05	David Berkoff (USA)	55.18	Igor Polyansky (URS)	55.20
1992	Mark Tewksbury (CAN)	53.98	Jeff Rouse (USA)	54.04	David Berkoff (USA)	54.78
1996	Jeff Rouse (USA)	54.10	Rodolfo Falcón (CUB)	54.98	Neisser Bent (CUB)	55.02
2000	Lenny Krayzelburg (USA)	53.72	Matthew Welsh (AUS)	54.07	Stev Theloke (GER)	54.82

Men's 200m Backstroke

	Gold		Silver		Bronze	
1900	Ernst Hoppenberg (GER)	2:47.0	Karl Ruberl (AUT)	2:56.0	Johannes Drost (NED)	3:01.0
1904-60	not held					
1964	Jed Graef (USA)	2:10.3	Gary Dilley (USA)	2:10.5	Robert Bennett (USA)	2:13.1
1968	Roland Matthes (GDR)	2:09.6	Mitchell Ivey (USA)	2:10.6	Jack Horsley (USA)	2:10.9
1972	Roland Matthes (GDR)	2:02.82	Michael Stamm (USA)	2:04.09	Mitchell Ivey (USA)	2:04.33
1976	John Naber (USA)	1:59.19	Peter Rocca (USA)	2:00.55	Dan Harrigan (USA)	2:01.35
1980	Sándor Wladár (HUN)	2:01.93	Zoltán Verrasztó (HUN)	2:02.40	Mark Kerry (AUS)	2:03.14
1984	Rick Carey (USA)	2:00.23	Frédéric Delcourt (FRA)	2:01.75	Cameron Henning (CAN)	2:02.37
1988	Igor Polyansky (URS)	1:59.37	Frank Baltrusch (GDR)	1:59.60	Paul Kingsman (NZL)	2:00.48
1992	Martín López-Zubero (ESP)	1:58.47	Vladimir Selkov (CIS)	1:58.87	Stefano Battistelli (ITA)	1:59.40
1996	Brad Bridgewater (USA)	1:58.54	William 'Tripp' Schwenk (USA)	1:59.99	Emanuele Merisi (ITA)	1:59.18
2000	Lenny Krayzelburg (USA)	1:56.76	Aaron Peirsol (USA)	1:57.35	Matthew Welsh (AUS)	1:57.59

SWIMMING

Men's 100m Breaststroke

	Gold		Silver		Bronze	
1968	Donald McKenzie (USA)	1:07.7	Vladimir Kosinsky (URS)	1:08.0	Nikolay Pankin (URS)	1:08.0
1972	Nobutaka Taguchi (JPN)	1:04.94	Thomas Bruce (USA)	1:05.43	John Hencken (USA)	1:05.61
1976	John Hencken (USA)	1:03.11	David Wilkie (GBR)	1:03.43	Arvydas Juozaitis (URS)	1:04.23
1980	Duncan Goodhew (GBR)	1:03.44	Arsens Miskarovs (URS)	1:03.82	Peter Evans (AUS)	1:03.96
1984	Steve Lundquist (USA)	1:01.65	Victor Davis (CAN)	1:01.99	Peter Evans (AUS)	1:02.97
1988	Adrian Moorhouse (GBR)	1:02.04	Károly Güttler (HUN)	1:02.05	Dmitriy Volkov (URS)	1:02.20
1992	Nelson Diebel (USA)	1:01.50	Norbert Rózsa (HUN)	1:01.68	Phil Rogers (AUS)	1:01.76
1996	Frédérik Deburghgraeve (BEL)	1:00.65	Jeremy Linn (USA)	1:00.77	Mark Warnecke (GER)	1:01.33
2000	Domenico Fioravanti (ITA)	1:00.46	Ed Moses (USA)	1:00.73	Roman Sloudnov (RUS)	1:00.91

Men's 200m Breaststroke

	Gold		Silver		Bronze	
1908	Frederick Holman (GBR)	3:09.2	William Robinson (GBR)	3:12.8	Pontus Hanson (SWE)	3:14.6
1912	Walther Bathe (GER)	3:01.8	Wilhelm Lützow (GER)	3:05.0	Kurt Mahlisch (GER)	3:08.0
1920	Håkan Malmroth (SWE)	3:04.4	Thor Henning (SWE)	3:09.2	Arvo Aaltonen (FIN)	3:12.2
1924	Robert Skelton (USA)	2:56.6	Joseph De Combe (BEL)	2:59.2	William Kirschbaum (USA)	3:01.0
1928	Yoshiyuki Tsuruta (JPN)	2:48.8	Erich Rademacher (GER)	2:50.6	Teofilo Yldefonzo (PHI)	2:56.4
1932	Yoshiyuki Tsuruta (JPN)	2:45.4	Reizo Koike (JPN)	2:46.6	Teofilo Yldefonzo (PHI)	2:47.1
1936	Tetsuo Hamuro (JPN)	2:41.5	Erwin Sietas (GER)	2:42.9	Reizo Koike (JPN)	2:44.2
1948	Joseph Verdeur (USA)	2:39.3	Keith Carter (USA)	2:40.2	Robert Sohl (USA)	2:43.9
1952	John Davies (AUS)	2:34.4	Bowen Stassforth (USA)	2:34.7	Herbert Klein (GER)	2:35.9
1956	Masaru Furukawa (JPN)	2:34.7	Masahiro Yoshimura (JPN)	2:36.7	Kharis Yunichev (URS)	2:36.8
1960	Bill Mulliken (USA)	2:37.4	Yoshihiko Osaki (JPN)	2:38.0	Wieger Mensonides (NED)	2:39.7
1964	Ian O'Brien (AUS)	2:27.8	Georgiy Prokopenko (URS)	2:28.2	Chester Jastremski (USA)	2:29.6
1968	Felipe 'Pepe' Múñoz (MEX)	2:28.7	Vladimir Kosinsky (URS)	2:29.2	Brian Job (USA)	2:29.9
1972	John Hencken (USA)	2:21.55	David Wilkie (GBR)	2:23.67	Nobutaka Taguchi (JPN)	2:23.88
1976	David Wilkie (GBR)	2:15.11	John Hencken (USA)	2:17.26	Richard Colella (USA)	2:19.20
1980	Robertas Zulpa (URS)	2:15.85	Albán Vermes (HUN)	2:16.93	Arsens Miskarovs (URS)	2:17.28
1984	Victor Davis (CAN)	2:13.34	Glenn Beringen (CAN)	2:15.79	Etienne Dagon (SUI)	2:17.41
1988	József Szabó (HUN)	2:13.52	Nick Gillingham (GBR)	2:14.12	Sergio López (ESP)	2:15.21
1992	Mike Barrowman (USA)	2:10.16	Norbert Rózsa (HUN)	2:11.23	Nick Gillingham (GBR)	2:11.29
1996	Norbert Rózsa (HUN)	2:12.57	Károly Güttler (HUN)	2:13.03	Andrey Korneyev (RUS)	2:13.17
2000	Domenico Fioravanti (ITA)	2:10.87	Terence Parkin (RSA)	2:12.50	Davide Rummolo (ITA)	2:12.73

Men's 100m Butterfly

	Gold		Silver		Bronze	
1968	Doug Russell (USA)	55.9	Mark Spitz (USA)	56.4	Ross Wales (USA)	57.2
1972	Mark Spitz (USA)	54.27	Bruce Robertson (CAN)	55.56	Jerry Heidenreich (USA)	55.74
1976	Matt Vogel (USA)	54.35	Joe Bottom (USA)	54.50	Gary Hall (USA)	54.65
1980	Pär Arvidsson (SWE)	54.92	Roger Pyttel (GDR)	54.94	David López-Zubero (ESP)	55.13
1984	Michael Gross (FRG)	53.08	Pablo Morales (USA)	53.23	Glenn Buchanan (AUS)	53.85
1988	Anthony Nesty (SUR)	53.00	Matt Biondi (USA)	53.01	Andy Jameson (GBR)	53.30
1992	Pablo Morales (USA)	53.32	Rafal Szukala (POL)	53.35	Anthony Nesty (SUR)	53.41
1996	Denis Pankratov (RUS)	52.27	Scott Miller (AUS)	52.53	Vladislav Kulikov (RUS)	53.13
2000	Lars Frölander (SWE)	52.00	Michael Klim (AUS)	52.18	Geoff Huegill (AUS)	52.22

Men's 200m Butterfly

	Gold		Silver		Bronze	
1956	William Yorzyk (USA)	2:19.3	Takashi Ishimoto (JPN)	2:23.8	György Tumpek (HUN)	2:23.9
1960	Michael Troy (USA)	2:12.8	Neville Hayes (AUS)	2:14.6	David Gillanders (USA)	2:15.3
1964	Kevin Berry (AUS)	2:06.6	Carl Robie (USA)	2:07.5	Fred Schmidt (USA)	2:09.3
1968	Carl Robie (USA)	2:08.7	Martin Woodroffe (GBR)	2:09.0	John Ferris (USA)	2:09.3
1972	Mark Spitz (USA)	2:00.70	Gary Hall (USA)	2:02.86	Robin Backhaus (USA)	2:03.33
1976	Mike Bruner (USA)	1:59.23	Steven Gregg (USA)	1:59.54	Bill Forrester (USA)	1:59.56
1980	Sergey Fesenko (URS)	1:59.76	Phil Hubble (GBR)	2:01.20	Roger Pyttel (GDR)	2:01.49
1984	Jon Sieben (AUS)	1:57.04	Michael Gross (FRG)	1:57.40	Rafael Vidal (VEN)	1:57.51
1988	Michael Gross (FRG)	1:56.94	Benny Nielsen (DEN)	1:58.24	Anthony Mosse (NZL)	1:58.28
1992	Melvin Stewart (USA)	1:56.26	Danyon Loader (NZL)	1:57.93	Franck Esposito (FRA)	1:58.51
1996	Denis Pankratov (RUS)	1:56.51	Tom Malchow (USA)	1:57.44	Scott Goodman (AUS)	1:57.48
2000	Tom Malchow (USA)	1:55.35	Denis Sylantyev (UKR)	1:55.76	Justin Norris (AUS)	1:56.17

Men's 200m Individual Medley

Gold		Silver		Bronze	
1968	Charles Hickcox (USA)	2:12.0	Gregory Buckingham (USA)	2:13.0	John Ferris (USA)	2:13.3
1972	Gunnar Larsson (SWE)	2:07.17	Alexander 'Tim' McKee (USA)	2:08.37	Steven Furniss (USA)	2:08.45
1976-80 not held						
1984	Alex Baumann (CAN)	2:01.42	Pablo Morales (USA)	2:03.05	Neil Cochran (GBR)	2:04.38
1988	Tamás Darnyi (HUN)	2:00.17	Patrick Kühl (GDR)	2:01.61	Vadim Yaroshchuk (URS)	2:02.40
1992	Tamás Darnyi (HUN)	2:00.76	Gregory Burgess (USA)	2:00.97	Attila Czene (HUN)	2:01.00
1996	Attila Czene (HUN)	1:59.91	Jani Sievinen (FIN)	2:00.13	Curtis Myden (CAN)	2:01.13
2000	Massimiliano Rosolino (ITA)	1:58.98	Tom Dolan (USA)	1:59.77	Tom Wilkins (USA)	2:00.87

Men's 400m Individual Medley

Gold		Silver		Bronze	
1964	Richard Roth (USA)	4:45.4	Roy Saari (USA)	4:47.1	Gerhard Hetz (GER)	4:51.0
1968	Charles Hickcox (USA)	4:48.4	Gary Hall (USA)	4:48.7	Michael Holthaus (FRG)	4:51.4
1972	Gunnar Larsson (SWE)	4:31.98	Alexander 'Tim' McKee (USA)	4:31.98	András Hargitay (HUN)	4:32.70
1976	Rod Strachan (USA)	4:23.68	Alexander 'Tim' McKee (USA)	4:24.62	Andrey Smirnov (URS)	4:26.90
1980	Aleksandr Sidorenko (URS)	4:22.89	Sergey Fesenko (URS)	4:23.43	Zoltán Verrasztó (HUN)	4:24.24
1984	Alex Baumann (CAN)	4:17.41	Ricardo Prado (BRA)	4:18.45	Robert Woodhouse (AUS)	4:20.50
1988	Tamás Darnyi (HUN)	4:14.75	David Wharton (USA)	4:17.36	Stefano Battistelli (ITA)	4:18.01
1992	Tamás Darnyi (HUN)	4:14.23	Eric Namesnik (USA)	4:15.57	Luca Sacchi (ITA)	4:16.34
1996	Tom Dolan (USA)	4:14.90	Eric Namesnik (USA)	4:15.25	Curtis Myden (CAN)	4:16.28
2000	Tom Dolan (USA)	4:11.76	Erik Vendt (USA)	4:14.23	Curtis Myden (CAN)	4:15.33

Men's 4 × 100m Freestyle Relay

Gold		Silver		Bronze	
1964	United States	3:32.2	Germany	3:37.2	Australia	3:39.1
1968	United States	3:31.7	Soviet Union	3:34.2	Australia	3:34.7
1972	United States	3:26.42	Soviet Union	3:29.72	German Democratic Republic	3:32.42
1976-80 not held						
1984	United States	3:19.03	Australia	3:19.68	Sweden	3:22.69
1988	United States	3:16.53	Soviet Union	3:18.33	German Democratic Republic	3:19.82
1992	United States	3:16.74	CIS	3:17.56	Germany	3:17.90
1996	United States	3:15.41	Russia	3:17.06	Germany	3:17.20
2000	Australia	3:13.67	United States	3:13.86	Brazil	3:17.40

Men's 4 × 200m Freestyle Relay

Gold		Silver		Bronze	
1908	Great Britain	10:55.6	Hungary	10:59.0	United States	11:02.8
1912	Australia/New Zealand	10:11.6	United States	10:20.0	Great Britain	10:28.2
1920	United States	10:04.4	Australia	10:25.4	Great Britain	10:37.2
1924	United States	9:53.4	Australia	10:02.2	Sweden	10:06.8
1928	United States	9:36.2	Japan	9:41.4	Canada	9:47.8
1932	Japan	8:58.4	United States	9:10.5	Hungary	9:31.4
1936	Japan	8:51.5	United States	9:03.0	Hungary	9:12.3
1948	United States	8:46.0	Hungary	8:48.4	France	9:08.0
1952	United States	8:31.1	Japan	8:33.5	France	8:45.9
1956	Australia	8:23.6	United States	8:31.5	Soviet Union	8:34.7
1960	United States	8:10.2	Japan	8:13.2	Australia	8:13.8
1964	United States	7:52.1	Germany	7:59.3	Japan	8:03.8
1968	United States	7:52.33	Australia	7:53.77	Soviet Union	8:01.66
1972	United States	7:35.69	Federal Republic of Germany	7:41.69	Soviet Union	7:45.76
1976	United States	7:23.22	Soviet Union	7:27.97	Great Britain	7:32.11
1980	Soviet Union	7:23.50	German Democratic Republic	7:28.60	Brazil	7:29.30
1984	United States	7:15.69	Federal Republic of Germany	7:15.73	Great Britain	7:24.78
1988	United States	7:12.51	German Democratic Republic	7:13.68	Federal Republic of Germany	7:14.35
1992	CIS	7:11.95	Sweden	7:15.51	United States	7:16.23
1996	United States	7:14.84	Sweden	7:17.56	Germany	7:17.71
2000	Australia	7:07.05	United States	7:12.64	Netherlands	7:12.70

S
W
I
M
M
I
N
G

Men's 4 × 100m Medley Relay

	Gold		Silver		Bronze	
1960	United States	4:05.4	Australia	4:12.0	Japan	4:12.2
1964	United States	3:58.4	Germany	4:01.6	Australia	4:02.3
1968	United States	3:54.9	German Democratic Republic	3:57.5	Soviet Union	4:00.7
1972	United States	3:48.16	German Democratic Republic	3:52.12	Canada	3:52.26
1976	United States	3:42.22	Canada	3:45.94	Federal Republic of Germany	3:47.29
1980	Australia	3:45.70	Soviet Union	3:45.92	Great Britain	3:47.71
1984	United States	3:39.30	Canada	3:43.23	Australia	3:43.25
1988	United States	3:36.93	Canada	3:39.28	Soviet Union	3:39.96
1992	United States	3:36.93	CIS	3:38.56	Canada	3:39.56
1996	United States	3:34.84	Russia	3:37.55	Australia	3:39.56
2000	United States	3:33.73	Australia	3:35.27	Germany	3:35.88

Women's 50m Freestyle

	Gold		Silver		Bronze	
1988	Kristin Otto (GDR)	25.49	Yang Wenyi (CHN)	25.64	Katrin Meissner (GDR)	25.71
					Jill Sterkel (USA)	
1992	Yang Wenyi (CHN)	24.79	Zhuang Yong (CHN)	25.06	Angelino Martino (USA)	25.23
1996	Amy Van Dyken (USA)	24.87	Le Jingyi (CHN)	24.90	Sandra Völker (GER)	25.14
2000	Inge de Bruijn (NED)	24.32	Therese Alshammar (SWE)	24.51	Dara Torres (USA)	24.63

Women's 100m Freestyle

	Gold		Silver		Bronze	
1912	Sarah 'Fanny' Durack (AUS)	1:22.2	Wilhelmina Wylie (AUS)	1:25.4	Jennie Fletcher (GBR)	1:27.0
1920	Ethelda Bleibtrey (USA)	1:13.6	Irene Guest (USA)	1:17.0	Frances Schroth (USA)	1:17.2
1924	Ethel Lackie (USA)	1:12.4	Mariechen Wehselau (USA)	1:12.8	Gertrude Ederle (USA)	1:14.2
1928	Albina Osipowich (USA)	1:11.0	Eleanor Garatti (USA)	1:11.4	Joyce Cooper (GBR)	1:13.6
1932	Helene Madison (USA)	1:06.8	Willemijntje den Ouden (NED)	1:07.8	Eleanor Saville (Garatti) (USA)	1:09.3
1936	Hendrika 'Rie' Mastenbroek (NED)	1:05.9	Jeannette Campbell (ARG)	1:06.4	Gisela Arendt (GER)	1:06.6
1948	Greta Andersen (DEN)	1:06.3	Ann Curtis (USA)	1:06.5	Marie-Louise Vaessen (NED)	1:07.6
1952	Katalin Szöke (HUN)	1:06.8	Johanna Termeulen (NED)	1:07.0	Judit Temes (HUN)	1:07.1
1956	Dawn Fraser (AUS)	1:02.0	Lorraine Crapp (AUS)	1:02.3	Faith Leech (AUS)	1:05.1
1960	Dawn Fraser (AUS)	1:01.2	Christine Von Saltza (USA)	1:02.8	Natalie Steward (GBR)	1:03.1
1964	Dawn Fraser (AUS)	59.5	Sharon Stouder (USA)	59.9	Kathleen Ellis (USA)	1:00.8
1968	Jan Henne (USA)	1:00.0	Susan Pedersen (USA)	1:00.3	Linda Gustavson (USA)	1:00.3
1972	Sandra Neilson (USA)	58.59	Shirley Babashoff (USA)	59.02	Shane Gould (AUS)	59.06
1976	Kornelia Ender (GDR)	55.65	Petra Priemer (GDR)	56.49	Enith Brigitha (NED)	56.65
1980	Barbara Krause (GDR)	54.79	Caren Metschuck (GDR)	55.16	Ines Diers (GDR)	55.65
1984	Nancy Hogshead (USA)	55.92			Annemarie Verstappen (NED)	56.08
	Carrie Steinseifer (USA)					
1988	Kristin Otto (GDR)	54.93	Zhuang Yong (CHN)	55.47	Catherine Plewinski (FRA)	55.49
1992	Zhuang Yong (CHN)	54.64	Jenny Thompson (USA)	54.84	Franziska van Almsick (GER)	54.94
1996	Le Jingyi (CHN)	54.50	Sandra Völker (GER)	54.88	Angelino Martino (USA)	54.93
2000	Inge de Bruijn (NED)	53.83	Therese Alshammar (SWE)	54.33	Dara Torres (USA)	54.43
					Jenny Thompson (USA)	

Women's 200m Freestyle

	Gold		Silver		Bronze	
1968	Debbie Meyer (USA)	2:10.5	Jan Henne (USA)	2:11.0	Jane Barkman (USA)	2:11.2
1972	Shane Gould (AUS)	2:03.56	Shirley Babashoff (USA)	2:04.33	Keena Rothhammer (USA)	2:04.92
1976	Kornelia Ender (GDR)	1:59.26	Shirley Babashoff (USA)	2:01.22	Enith Brigitha (NED)	2:01.40
1980	Barbara Krause (GDR)	1:58.33	Ines Diers (GDR)	1:59.64	Carmela Schmidt (GDR)	2:01.44
1984	Mary Wayte (USA)	1:59.23	Cynthia Woodhead (USA)	1:59.50	Annemarie Verstappen (NED)	1:59.69
1988	Heike Friedrich (GDR)	1:57.65	Silvia Poll (CRC)	1:58.67	Manuela Stellmach (GDR)	1:59.01
1992	Nicole Haislett (USA)	1:57.90	Franziska van Almsick (GER)	1:58.00	Kerstin Kielgass (GER)	1:59.67
1996	Claudia Poll (CRC)	1:58.16	Franziska van Almsick (GER)	1:58.57	Dagmar Hase (GER)	1:59.56
2000	Susie O'Neill (AUS)	1:58.24	Martina Moravcová (SVK)	1:58.32	Claudia Poll (CRC)	1:58.81

Women's 400m Freestyle

	Gold		Silver		Bronze	
1924	Martha Norelius (USA)	6:02.2	Helen Wainwright (USA)	6:03.8	Gertrude Ederle (USA)	6:04.8
1928	Martha Norelius (USA)	5:42.8	Maria Braun (NED)	5:57.8	Josephine McKim (USA)	6:00.2

1932	Helene Madison (USA)	5:28.5	Lenore Kight (USA)	5:28.6	Jennie Maakal (SAF)	5:47.3
1936	Hendrika 'Rie' Mastenbroek (NED)	5:26.4	Ragnhild Hveger (DEN)	5:27.5	Lenore Wingard (Kight) (USA)	5:29.0
1948	Ann Curtis (USA)	5:17.8	Karen Margrete Harup (DEN)	5:21.2	Catherine Gibson (GBR)	5:22.5
1952	Valéria Gyenge (HUN)	5:12.1	Éva Novák (HUN)	5:13.7	Evelyn Kawamoto (USA)	5:14.6
1956	Lorraine Crapp (AUS)	4:54.6	Dawn Fraser (AUS)	5:02.5	Sylvia Ruuska (USA)	5:07.1
1960	Christine Von Saltza (USA)	4:50.6	Jane Cederqvist (SWE)	4:53.9	Catherina Lagerberg (NED)	4:56.9
1964	Virginia Duenkel (USA)	4:43.3	Marilyn Ramenofsky (USA)	4:44.6	Terri Stickles (USA)	4:47.2
1968	Debbie Meyer (USA)	4:31.8	Linda Gustavson (USA)	4:35.5	Karen Moras (AUS)	4:37.0
1972	Shane Gould (AUS)	4:19.04	Novella Calligaris (ITA)	4:22.44	Gudrun Wegner (GDR)	4:23.11
1976	Petra Thümer (GDR)	4:09.89	Shirley Babashoff (USA)	4:10.46	Shannon Smith (CAN)	4:14.60
1980	Ines Diers (GDR)	4:08.76	Petra Schneider (GDR)	4:09.16	Carmela Schmidt (GDR)	4:10.86
1984	Tiffany Cohen (USA)	4:07.10	Sarah Hardcastle (GBR)	4:10.27	June Croft (GBR)	4:11.49
1988	Janet Evans (USA)	4:03.85	Heike Friedrich (GDR)	4:05.94	Anke Möhring (GDR)	4:06.62
1992	Dagmar Hase (GER)	4:07.18	Janet Evans (USA)	4:07.37	Hayley Lewis (AUS)	4:11.22
1996	Michelle Smith (IRL)	4:07.25	Dagmar Hase (GER)	4:08.30	Kirsten Vlieghuis (NED)	4:08.70
2000	Brooke Bennett (USA)	4:05.80	Diana Munz (USA)	4:07.17	Claudia Poll (CRC)	4:07.83

Women's 800m Freestyle

	Gold		Silver		Bronze	
1968	Debbie Meyer (USA)	9:24.0	Pamela Kruse (USA)	9:35.7	María Teresa Ramírez (MEX)	9:38.5
1972	Keena Rothhammer (USA)	8:53.68	Shane Gould (AUS)	8:56.39	Novella Calligaris (ITA)	8:57.46
1976	Petra Thümer (GDR)	8:37.14	Shirley Babashoff (USA)	8:37.59	Wendy Weinberg (USA)	8:42.60
1980	Michelle Ford (AUS)	8:28.90	Ines Diers (GDR)	8:32.55	Heike Dähne (GDR)	8:33.48
1984	Tiffany Cohen (USA)	8:24.95	Michele Richardson (USA)	8:30.73	Sarah Hardcastle (GBR)	8:32.60
1988	Janet Evans (USA)	8:20.20	Astrid Strauss (GDR)	8:22.09	Julie McDonald (AUS)	8:22.93
1992	Janet Evans (USA)	8:25.52	Hayley Lewis (AUS)	8:30.34	Jana Henke (GER)	8:31.09
1996	Brooke Bennett (USA)	8:27.89	Dagmar Hase (GER)	8:29.91	Kirsten Vlieghuis (NED)	8:30.84
2000	Brooke Bennett (USA)	8:19.67	Yana Klochkova (UKR)	8:22.66	Kaitlin Sandeno (USA)	8:24.29

Women's 100m Backstroke

	Gold		Silver		Bronze	
1924	Sybil Bauer (USA)	1:23.2	Phyllis Harding (GBR)	1:27.4	Aileen Riggin (USA)	1:28.2
1928	Maria Braun (NED)	1:22.0	Ellen King (GBR)	1:22.2	Joyce Cooper (GBR)	1:22.8
1932	Eleanor Holm (USA)	1:19.4	Philomena Mealing (AUS)	1:21.3	Elizabeth Valerie Davies (GBR)	1:22.5
1936	Dina 'Nida' Senff (NED)	1:18.9	Hendrika 'Rie' Mastenbroek (NED)	1:19.2	Alice Bridges (USA)	1:19.4
1948	Karen Margrete Harup (DEN)	1:14.4	Suzanne Zimmerman (USA)	1:16.0	Judy-Joy Davies (AUS)	1:16.7
1952	Joan Harrison (SAF)	1:14.3	Geertje Wielema (NED)	1:14.5	Jean Stewart (NZL)	1:15.8
1956	Judy Grinham (GBR)	1:12.9	Carin Cone (USA)	1:12.9	Margaret Edwards (GBR)	1:13.1
1960	Lynn Burke (USA)	1:09.3	Natalie Steward (GBR)	1:10.8	Satoko Tanaka (JPN)	1:11.4
1964	Cathy Ferguson (USA)	1:07.7	Christine Caron (FRA)	1:07.9	Virginia Duenkel (USA)	1:08.0
1968	Kaye Hall (USA)	1:06.2	Elaine Tanner (CAN)	1:06.7	Jane Swagerty (USA)	1:08.1
1972	Melissa Belote (USA)	1:05.78	Andrea Gyarmati (HUN)	1:06.26	Susan Atwood (USA)	1:06.34
1976	Ulrike Richter (GDR)	1:01.83	Birgit Treiber (GDR)	1:03.41	Nancy Garapick (CAN)	1:03.71
1980	Rica Reinisch (GDR)	1:00.86	Ina Kleber (GDR)	1:02.07	Petra Riedel (GDR)	1:02.64
1984	Theresa Andrews (USA)	1:02.55	Betsy Mitchell (USA)	1:02.63	Jolanda De Rover (NED)	1:02.91
1988	Kristin Otto (GDR)	1:00.89	Krisztina Egerszegi (HUN)	1:01.56	Cornelia Sirch (GDR)	1:01.57
1992	Krisztina Egerszegi (HUN)	1:00.68	Tünde Szabó (HUN)	1:01.14	Lea Loveless (USA)	1:01.43
1996	Beth Botsford (USA)	1:01.19	Whitney Hedgepeth (USA)	1:01.47	Marianne Kriel (RSA)	1:02.12
2000	Diana Iuliana Mocanu (ROM)	1:00.21	Mai Nakamura (JPN)	1:00.55	Nina Zhivanevskaya (ESP)	1:00.89

Women's 200m Backstroke

	Gold		Silver		Bronze	
1968	Lillian Watson (USA)	2:24.8	Elaine Tanner (CAN)	2:27.4	Kaye Hall (USA)	2:28.9
1972	Melissa Belote (USA)	2:19.19	Susan Atwood (USA)	2:20.38	Donna Gurr (CAN)	2:23.22
1976	Ulrike Richter (GDR)	2:13.43	Birgit Treiber (GDR)	2:14.97	Nancy Garapick (CAN)	2:15.6
1980	Rica Reinisch (GDR)	2:11.77	Cornelia Polit (GDR)	2:13.75	Birgit Treiber (GDR)	2:14.14
1984	Jolanda De Rover (NED)	2:12.38	Amy White (USA)	2:13.04	Aneta Patrascoiu (ROM)	2:13.29
1988	Krisztina Egerszegi (HUN)	2:09.29	Kathrin Zimmerman (GDR)	2:10.61	Cornelia Sirch (GDR)	2:11.45
1992	Krisztina Egerszegi (HUN)	2:07.06	Dagmar Hase (GER)	2:09.46	Nicole Stevenson (AUS)	2:10.20
1996	Krisztina Egerszegi (HUN)	2:07.83	Whitney Hedgepeth (USA)	2:12.98	Cathleen Rund (GER)	2:12.06
2000	Diana Iuliana Mocanu (ROM)	2:08.16	Roxana Maracineanu (FRA)	2:10.25	Miki Nakao (JPN)	2:11.05

SWIMMING

Women's 100m Breaststroke

	Gold		Silver		Bronze	
1968	Djurdjica Bjedov (YUG)	1:15.8	Galina Prozumenshikova (URS)	1:15.9	Sharon Wichman (USA)	1:16.1
1972	Catherine Carr (USA)	1:13.58	Galina Stepanova (Prozumenshikova) (URS)	1:14.99	Beverley Whitfield (AUS)	1:15.73
1976	Hannelore Anke (GDR)	1:11.16	Lyubov Rusanova (URS)	1:13.04	Marina Koshevaya (URS)	1:13.30
1980	Ute Geweniger (GDR)	1:10.22	Elvira Vasilkova (URS)	1:10.41	Susanne Nielsson (DEN)	1:11.16
1984	Petra van Staveren (NED)	1:09.88	Anne Ottenbrite (CAN)	1:10.69	Cathérine Poirot (FRA)	1:10.70
1988	Tanya Dangalakova (BUL)	1:07.95	Antoaneta Frenkeva (BUL)	1:08.74	Silke Hörner (GDR)	1:08.83
1992	Yelena Rudkovskaya (CIS)	1:08.00	Anita Nall (USA)	1:08.17	Samantha Riley (AUS)	1:09.25
1996	Penny Heyns (RSA)	1:07.73	Amanda Beard (USA)	1:08.09	Samantha Riley (AUS)	1:09.18
2000	Megan Quann (USA)	1:07.05	Leisel Jones (AUS)	1:07.49	Penny Heyns (RSA)	1:07.55

Women's 200m Breaststroke

	Gold		Silver		Bronze	
1924	Lucy Morton (GBR)	3:33.2	Agnes Geraghty (USA)	3:34.0	Gladys Carson (GBR)	3:35.4
1928	Hildegard Schrader (GER)	3:12.6	Mietje 'Marie' Baron (NED)	3:15.2	Lotte Mühe (GER)	3:17.6
1932	Clare Dennis (AUS)	3:06.3	Hideko Maehata (JPN)	3:06.4	Else Jacobsen (DEN)	3:07.1
1936	Hideko Maehata (JPN)	3:03.6	Martha Geneger (GER)	3:04.2	Inge Sørensen (DEN)	3:07.8
1948	Petronella van Vliet (NED)	2:57.2	Beatrice Lyons (AUS)	2:57.7	Éva Novák (HUN)	3:00.2
1952	Éva Székely (HUN)	2:51.7	Éva Novák (HUN)	2:54.4	Elenor Gordon (GBR)	2:57.6
1956	Ursula Happe (GER)	2:53.1	Éva Székely (HUN)	2:54.8	Eva-Maria Ten Elsen (GER)	2:55.1
1960	Anita Lonsbrough (GBR)	2:49.5	Wiltrud Urselmann (GER)	2:50.0	Barbara Göbel (GER)	2:53.6
1964	Galina Prozumenshikova (URS)	2:46.4	Claudia Kolb (USA)	2:47.6	Svetlana Babanina (URS)	2:48.6
1968	Sharon Wichman (USA)	2:44.4	Djurdjica Bjedov (YUG)	2:46.4	Galina Prozumenshikova (URS)	2:47.0
1972	Beverley Whitfield (AUS)	2:41.71	Dana Schoenfield (USA)	2:42.05	Galina Stepanova (Prozumenshikova) (URS)	2:42.36
1976	Marina Koshevaya (URS)	2:33.35	Marina Yurchenya (URS)	2:36.08	Lyubov Rusanova (URS)	2:36.22
1980	Lina Kaciušyté (URS)	2:29.54	Svetlana Varganova (URS)	2:29.61	Yuliya Bogdanova (URS)	2:32.39
1984	Anne Ottenbrite (CAN)	2:30.38	Susan Rapp (USA)	2:31.15	Ingrid Lempereur (BEL)	2:31.40
1988	Silke Hörner (GDR)	2:26.71	Huang Xiaomin (CHN)	2:27.49	Antoaneta Frenkeva (BUL)	2:28.34
1992	Kyoko Iwasaki (JPN)	2:26.65	Lin Li (CHN)	2:26.85	Anita Nall (USA)	2:26.88
1996	Penny Heyns (RSA)	2:25.41	Amanda Beard (USA)	2:25.75	Ágnes Kovács (HUN)	2:26.57
2000	Ágnes Kovács (HUN)	2:24.35	Kristy Kowal (USA)	2:24.56	Amanda Beard (USA)	2:25.35

Women's 100m Butterfly

	Gold		Silver		Bronze	
1956	Shelly Mann (USA)	1:11.0	Nancy Ramey (USA)	1:11.9	Mary Sears (USA)	1:14.4
1960	Carolyn Schuler (USA)	1:09.5	Marianne Heemskerk (NED)	1:10.4	Janice Andrew (AUS)	1:12.2
1964	Sharon Stouder (USA)	1:04.7	Ada Kok (NED)	1:05.6	Kathleen Ellis (USA)	1:06.0
1968	Lynette McClements (AUS)	1:05.5	Ellie Daniel (USA)	1:05.8	Susan Shields (USA)	1:06.2
1972	Mayumi Aoki (JPN)	1:03.34	Roswitha Beier (GDR)	1:03.61	Andréa Gyarmati (HUN)	1:03.73
1976	Kornelia Ender (GDR)	1:00.13	Andrea Pollack (GDR)	1:01.98	Wendy Boglioli (USA)	1:01.17
1980	Caren Metschuck (GDR)	1:00.42	Andrea Pollack (GDR)	1:00.90	Christiane Knacke (GDR)	1:01.44
1984	Mary T. Meagher (USA)	59.26	Jenna Johnson (USA)	1:00.19	Karin Seick (FRG)	1:01.36
1988	Kristin Otto (GDR)	59.00	Birte Weigang (GDR)	59.45	Qian Hong (CHN)	59.52
1992	Qian Hong (CHN)	58.62	Christine Ahmann-Leighton (USA)	58.74	Catherine Plewinski (FRA)	59.01
1996	Amy van Dyken (USA)	59.13	Liu Limin (CHN)	59.14	Angelino Martino (USA)	59.23
2000	Inge de Bruijn (NED)	56.61	Martina Moravcová (SVK)	57.97	Dara Torres (USA)	58.20

Women's 200m Butterfly

	Gold		Silver		Bronze	
1968	Ada Kok (NED)	2:24.7	Helga Lindner (GDR)	2:24.8	Ellie Daniel (USA)	2:25.9
1972	Karen Moe (USA)	2:15.57	Lynn Colella (USA)	2:16.34	Ellie Daniel (USA)	2:16.74
1976	Andrea Pollack (GDR)	2:11.41	Ulrike Tauber (GDR)	2:12.50	Rosemarie Gabriel (GDR)	2:12.86
1980	Ines Geissler (GDR)	2:10.44	Sybille Schönrock (GDR)	2:10.55	Michelle Ford (AUS)	2:11.66
1984	Mary T. Meagher (USA)	2:06.90	Karen Phillips (AUS)	2:10.56	Ina Beyermann (FRG)	2:11.91
1988	Kathleen Nord (GDR)	2:09.51	Birte Weigang (GDR)	2:09.91	Mary T. Meagher (USA)	2:10.80
1992	Summer Sanders (USA)	2:08.67	Wang Xiaohong (CHN)	2:09.02	Susie O'Neill (AUS)	2:09.03
1996	Susie O'Neill (AUS)	2:07.76	Petria Thomas (AUS)	2:09.82	Michelle Smith (IRL)	2:09.91
2000	Misty Hyman (USA)	2:05.88	Susie O'Neill (AUS)	2:06.58	Petria Thomas (AUS)	2:07.12

Women's 200m Individual Medley

	Gold		Silver		Bronze	
1968	Claudia Kolb (USA)	2:24.7	Susan Pedersen (USA)	2:28.8	Jan Henne (USA)	2:31.4
1972	Shane Gould (AUS)	2:23.07	Kornelia Ender (GDR)	2:23.59	Lynn Vidali (USA)	2:24.6
1976-80	not held					
1984	Tracy Caulkins (USA)	2:12.64	Nancy Hogshead (USA)	2:15.17	Michele Pearson (AUS)	2:15.92
1988	Daniela Hunger (GDR)	2:12.59	Yelena Dendeberova (URS)	2:13.31	Noemi Lung (ROM)	2:14.85
1992	Lin Li (CHN)	2:11.65	Summer Sanders (USA)	2:11.91	Daniela Hunger (GER)	2:13.92
1996	Michelle Smith (IRL)	2:13.93	Marianne Limpert (CAN)	2:14.35	Lin Li (CHN)	2:14.74
2000	Yana Klochkova (UKR)	2:10.68	Beatrice Caslaru (ROM)	2:12.57	Cristina Teuscher (USA)	2:13.32

Women's 400m Individual Medley

	Gold		Silver		Bronze	
1964	Donna De Varona (USA)	5:18.7	Sharon Finneran (USA)	5:24.1	Martha Randall (USA)	5:24.2
1968	Claudia Kolb (USA)	5:08.5	Lynn Vidali (USA)	5:22.2	Sabine Steinbach (GDR)	5:25.3
1972	Gail Neall (AUS)	5:03.97	Leslie Cliff (CAN)	5:03.57	Novella Calligaris (ITA)	5:03.99
1976	Ulrike Tauber (GDR)	4:42.77	Cheryl Gibson (CAN)	4:48.10	Becky Smith (CAN)	4:50.48
1980	Petra Schneider (GDR)	4:36.29	Sharron Davies (GBR)	4:46.83	Agnieszka Czopek (POL)	4:48.17
1984	Tracy Caulkins (USA)	4:39.24	Suzanne Landells (AUS)	4:48.30	Petra Zindler (FRG)	4:48.57
1988	Janet Evans (USA)	4:37.76	Noemi Lung (ROM)	4:39.46	Daniela Hunger (GDR)	4:39.76
1992	Krisztina Egerszegi (HUN)	4:36.54	Lin Li (CHN)	4:36.73	Summer Sanders (USA)	4:37.58
1996	Michelle Smith (IRL)	4:39.18	Allison Wagner (USA)	4:42.03	Krisztina Egerszegi (HUN)	4:42.53
2000	Yana Klochkova (UKR)	4:33.59	Yasuko Tajima (JPN)	4:36.96	Beatrice Caslaru (ROM)	4:37.18

Women's 4 × 100m Freestyle Relay

	Gold		Silver		Bronze	
1912	Great Britain	5:52.8	Germany	6:04.6	Austria	6:17.0
1920	United States	5:11.6	Great Britain	5:40.8	Sweden	5:43.6
1924	United States	4:58.8	Great Britain	5:17.0	Sweden	5:35.6
1928	United States	4:47.6	Great Britain	5:02.8	South Africa	5:13.4
1932	United States	4:38.0	Netherlands	4:47.5	Great Britain	4:52.4
1936	Netherlands	4:36.0	Germany	4:36.8	United States	4:40.2
1948	United States	4:29.2	Denmark	4:29.6	Netherlands	4:31.6
1952	Hungary	4:24.4	Netherlands	4:29.0	United States	4:30.1
1956	Australia	4:17.1	United States	4:19.2	South Africa	4:25.7
1960	United States	4:08.9	Australia	4:11.3	Germany	4:19.7
1964	United States	4:03.8	Australia	4:06.9	Netherlands	4:12.0
1968	United States	4:02.5	German Democratic Republic	4:05.7	Canada	4:07.2
1972	United States	3:55.19	German Democratic Republic	3:55.55	Federal Republic of Germany	3:57.93
1976	United States	3:44.82	German Democratic Republic	3:45.50	Canada	3:48.81
1980	German Democratic Republic	3:42.71	Sweden	3:48.93	Netherlands	3:49.51
1984	United States	3:43.43	Netherlands	3:44.40	Federal Republic of Germany	3:45.56
1988	German Democratic Republic	3:40.63	Netherlands	3:43.39	United States	3:44.26
1992	United States	3:39.46	China	3:40.12	Germany	3:41.60
1996	United States	3:39.29	China	3:40.48	Germany	3:41.48
2000	United States	3:36.61	Netherlands	3:39.83	Sweden	3:40.30

4 × 200m Freestyle Relay

	Gold		Silver		Bronze	
1996	United States	7:59.87	Germany	8:01.55	Australia	8:05.47
2000	United States	7:57.80	Australia	7:58.52	Germany	7:58.64

Women's 4 × 100m Medley Relay

	Gold		Silver		Bronze	
1960	United States	4:41.1	Australia	4:45.9	Germany	4:47.6
1964	United States	4:33.9	Netherlands	4:37.0	Soviet Union	4:39.2
1968	United States	4:28.3	Australia	4:30.0	Federal Republic of Germany	4:36.4
1972	United States	4:20.75	German Democratic Republic	4:24.91	Federal Republic of Germany	4:26.46
1976	German Democratic Republic	4:07.95	United States	4:14.55	Canada	4:15.22
1980	German Democratic Republic	4:06.67	Great Britain	4:12.24	Soviet Union	4:13.61
1984	United States	4:08.34	Federal Republic of Germany	4:12.97	Canada	4:12.98
1988	German Democratic Republic	4:03.74	United States	4:07.90	Canada	4:10.49
1992	United States	4:02.54	Germany	4:05.19	CIS	4:06.44

SWIMMING

| 1996 | United States | 4:02.88 | Australia | 4:05.08 | China | 4:07.34 |
| 2000 | United States | 3:58.30 | Australia | 4:01.59 | Japan | 4:04.16 |

Discontinued Events

Men's 100m Freestyle – Sailors

	Gold		Silver		Bronze	
1896	Ioannis Maloknis (GRE)	2:20.4	Spyridon Chazapis (GRE)	——	Dimitrios Drivas (GRE)	——

Men's 500m Freestyle

	Gold		Silver		Bronze	
1896	Paul Neumann (AUT)	8:12.6	Antonios Pepanos (GRE)	9:57.6	Eustathios Korafas (GRE)	——

Men's 880yds Freestyle

	Gold		Silver		Bronze	
1904	Emil Rausch (GER)	13:11.4	Francis Galley (USA)	13:23.4	Géza Kiss (HUN)	——

Men's 1000m Freestyle

	Gold		Silver		Bronze	
1900	John Arthur Jarvis (GBR)	13:40.2	Otto Wahle (AUT)	14:53.6	Zoltán Halmaj (HUN)	15:16.4

Men's 1200m Freestyle

	Gold		Silver		Bronze	
1896	Arnold Guttmann (HUN)	18:22.1	Ioannis Andreou (GRE)	21:03.4	Eustathios Korafas (GRE)	——

Men's 4000m Freestyle

	Gold		Silver		Bronze	
1900	John Arthur Jarvis (GBR)	58:24.0	Zoltán Halmaj (HUN)	1:08:55.4	Louis Martin (FRA)	1:13:08.4

Men's 400m Breaststroke
(440yds in 1904)

	Gold		Silver		Bronze	
1904*	Georg Zacharias (GER)	7:23.6	Walter Brack (GER)	——	Jamison Handy (USA)	——
1906-08	not held					
1912	Walther Bathe (GER)	6:29.6	Thor Henning (SWE)	6:35.6	Percy Courtman (GBR)	6:36.4
1920	Håkan Malmroth (SWE)	6:31.8	Thor Henning (SWE)	6:45.2	Arvo Aaltonen (FIN)	6:48.0

Men's 60m Underwater

	Gold		Silver		Bronze	
1900	Charles de Vendeville (FRA)	188.4pts	André Six (FRA)	185.4pts	Peter Lykkeberg (DEN)	147pts

Men's 200m Obstacle

	Gold		Silver		Bronze	
1900	Freddie Lane (AUS)	2:38.4	Otto Wahle (AUT)	2:40.0	Peter Kemp (GBR)	2:47.4

Men's 4 × 50yds Freestyle Relay

	Gold		Silver		Bronze	
1904	New York A.C. 'A' (USA)	2:04.6	Chicago A.C. (USA)	——	Missouri A.C. (USA)	——

Men's 4 × 250m Freestyle Relay

	Gold		Silver		Bronze	
1906	Hungary	16:52.4	Germany	17:16.2	Great Britain	——

Men's 200m Team

	Gold		Silver		Bronze	
1900	Germany	33pts	Pupilles de Neptune de Lille (FRA) 53pts		Tritons Lillois (FRA)	59pts

Men's Plunge for Distance

	Gold		Silver		Bronze	
1904	William Dickey (USA)	19.05m	Edgar Adams (USA)	17.53m	Leo 'Budd' Goodwin (USA)	17.37m

Women's 300m Freestyle

	Gold		Silver		Bronze	
1920	Ethelda Bleibtrey (USA)	4:34.0	Margaret Woodbridge (USA)	4:42.8	Frances Schroth (USA)	4:52.0

World Champions

Men's 50m Freestyle

		Time				Time
1973-82	not held			1998	Bill Pilczuk (USA)	22.29
1986	Tom Jager (USA)	22.49		2001	Anthony Ervin (USA)	22.09
1991	Tom Jager (USA)	22.16		2003	Aleksandr Popov (RUS)	21.92
1994	Aleksandr Popov (RUS)	22.17				

Men's 100m Freestyle

		Time				Time
1973	Jim Montgomery (USA)	51.70		1991	Matt Biondi (USA)	49.18
1975	Tim Shaw (USA)	51.25		1994	Aleksandr Popov (RUS)	49.12
1978	David McCagg (USA)	50.24		1998	Aleksandr Popov (RUS)	48.93
1982	Jörg Woithe (GDR)	50.18		2001	Anthony Ervin (USA)	48.33
1986	Matt Biondi (USA)	48.94		2003	Aleksandr Popov (RUS)	48.42

Men's 200m Freestyle

		Time				Time
1973	Jim Montgomery (USA)	1:53.02		1991	Giorgio Lamberti (ITA)	1:47.27
1975	Tim Shaw (USA)	1:51.04		1994	Antti Kasvio (FIN)	1:47.32
1978	Billy Forrester (USA)	1:51.02		1998	Michael Klim (AUS)	1:47.41
1982	Michael Gross (FRG)	1:49.84		2001	Ian Thorpe (AUS)	1:44.06
1986	Michael Gross (FRG	1:47.92		2003	Ian Thorpe (AUS)	1:45.14

Men's 400m Freestyle

		Time				Time
1973	Rick DeMont (USA)	3:58.18		1991	Jörg Hoffman (GER)	3:48.04
1975	Tim Shaw (USA)	3:54.88		1994	Kieren Perkins (AUS)	3:43.80
1978	Vladimir Salnikov (URS)	3:51.94		1998	Ian Thorpe (AUS)	3:46.29
1982	Vladimir Salnikov (URS)	3:51.30		2001	Ian Thorpe (AUS)	3:40.17
1986	Rainer Henkel (FRG)	3:50.05		2003	Ian Thorpe (AUS)	3:42.58

SWIMMING

Men's 800m Freestyle

		Time
1973-98	not held	
2001	Ian Thorpe (AUS)	7:39.16
2003	Grant Hackett (AUS)	7:43.82

Men's 1500m Freestyle

		Time			Time
1973	Stephen Holland (AUS)	15:31.85	1991	Jörg Hoffman (GER)	14:50.36
1975	Tim Shaw (USA)	15:28.92	1994	Kieren Perkins (AUS)	14:50.52
1978	Vladimir Salnikov (URS)	15:03.99	1998	Grant Hackett (AUS)	14:51.70
1982	Vladimir Salnikov (URS)	15:01.77	2001	Grant Hackett (AUS)	14:34.56
1986	Rainer Henkel (FRG)	15:05.31	2003	Grant Hackett (AUS)	14:43.14

Men's 50m Backstroke

		Time
1973-98	not held	
2001	Randall Bal (USA)	25.34
2003	Thomas Rupprath (GER)	24.80

Men's 100m Backstroke

		Time			Time
1973	Roland Matthes (GDR)	57.47	1991	Jeff Rouse (USA)	55.23
1975	Roland Matthes (GDR)	58.15	1994	Martín López-Zubero (ESP)	55.17
1978	Bob Jackson (USA)	56.36	1998	Lenny Krayzelburg (USA)	55.00
1982	Dirk Richter (GDR)	55.95	2001	Matt Welsh (AUS)	54.31
1986	Igor Polyansky (URS)	55.58	2003	Aaron Peirsol (USA)	53.61

Men's 200m Backstroke

		Time			Time
1973	Roland Matthes (GDR)	2:01.87	1991	Martín López-Zubero (ESP)	1:59.52
1975	Zoltán Verrasztó (HUN)	2:05.05	1994	Vladimir Selkov (RUS)	1:57.42
1978	Jesse Vassallo (USA)	2:02.16	1998	Lenny Krayzelburg (USA)	1:58.84
1982	Rick Carey (USA)	2:00.82	2001	Aaron Peirsol (USA)	1:57.13
1986	Igor Polyansky (URS)	1:58.78	2003	Aaron Peirsol (USA)	1:55.92

Men's 50m Breaststroke

		Time
1973-98	not held	
2001	Oleg Lisogor (UKR)	27.52
2003	James Gibson (GBR)	27.56

Men's 100m Breaststroke

		Time			Time
1973	John Hencken (USA)	1:04.02	1991	Norbert Rózsa (HUN)	1:01.45
1975	David Wilkie (GBR)	1:04.26	1994	Norbert Rózsa (HUN)	1:01.24
1978	Walter Kusch (FRG)	1:03.56	1998	Frédérik Deburghgraeve (BEL)	1:01.34
1982	Steve Lundquist (USA)	1:02.75	2001	Roman Sloudnov (RUS)	1:00.16
1986	Victor Davis (CAN)	1:02.71	2003	Kosuke Kitajima (JPN)	59.78

Men's 200m Breaststroke

		Time			Time
1973	David Wilkie (GBR)	2:19.28	1991	Mike Barrowman (USA)	2:11.23
1975	David Wilkie (GBR)	2:18.23	1994	Norbert Rózsa (HUN)	2:12.81
1978	Nick Nevid (USA)	2:18.37	1998	Kurt Grote (USA)	2:13.40
1982	Victor Davis (CAN)	2:14.77	2001	Brendan Hansen (USA)	2:10.69
1986	József Szabó (HUN)	2:14.27	2003	Kosuke Kitajima (JPN)	2:09.42

Men's 50m Butterfly

		Time
2001	Geoff Huegill (AUS)	23.50
2003	Matt Welsh (AUS)	23.43

Men's 100m Butterfly

		Time			Time
1973	Bruce Robertson (CAN)	55.69	1991	Anthony Nesty (SUR)	53.29
1975	Greg Jagenburg (USA)	55.63	1994	Rafal Szukala (POL)	53.51
1978	Joe Bottom (USA)	54.30	1998	Michael Klim (AUS)	52.25
1982	Matt Gribble (USA)	53.88	2001	Lars Frölander (SWE)	52.10
1986	Pablo Morales (USA)	53.54	2003	Ian Crocker (USA)	50.98

Men's 200m Butterfly

		Time			Time
1973	Robin Backhaus (USA)	2:03.32	1991	Melvin Stewart (USA)	1:55.69
1975	Bill Forrester (USA)	2:01.95	1994	Denis Pankratov (RUS)	1:56.54
1978	Mike Bruner (USA)	1:59.38	1998	Denis Sylantyev (UKR)	1:56.61
1982	Michael Gross (FRG)	1:58.85	2001	Michael Phelps (USA)	1:54.58
1986	Michael Gross (FRG)	1:56.53	2003	Michael Phelps (USA)	1:54.35

Men's 200m Individual Medley

		Time			Time
1973	Gunnar Larsson (SWE)	2:08.36	1991	Tamás Darnyi (HUN)	1:59.36
1975	András Hargitay (HUN)	2:07.72	1994	Jani Sievinen (FIN)	1:58.16
1978	Graham Smith (CAN)	2:03.65	1998	Marcel Wouda (NED)	2:01.18
1982	Aleksandr Sidorenko (URS)	2:03.30	2001	Massimiliano Rosolino (ITA)	1:59.71
1986	Tamas Darnyi (HUN)	2:01.57	2003	Michael Phelps (USA)	1:56.04

Men's 400m Individual Medley

		Time			Time
1973	András Hargitay (HUN)	4:31.11	1991	Tamás Darnyi (HUN)	4:12.36
1975	András Hargitay (HUN)	4:32.57	1994	Tom Dolan (USA)	4:12.30
1978	Jesse Vassallo (USA)	4:20.05	1998	Tom Dolan (USA)	4:14.95
1982	Ricardo Prado (BRA)	4:19.78	2001	Alessio Boggiatto (ITA)	4:13.15
1986	Tamas Darnyi (HUN)	4:18.98	2003	Michael Phelps (USA)	4:09.09

Men's 4 × 100m Freestyle Relay

		Time			Time
1973	United States	3:27.18	1991	United States	3:17.15
1975	United States	3:24.85	1994	United States	3:16.90
1978	United States	3:19.74	1998	United States	3:16.69
1982	United States	3:19.26	2001	Australia	3:14.10
1986	United States	3:19.89	2003	Russia	3:14.06

Men's 4 × 200m Freestyle Relay

		Time			Time
1973	United States	7:33.22	1991	Germany	7:13.50
1975	Federal Republic of Germany	7:39.44	1994	Sweden	7:17.74
1978	United States	7:20.82	1998	Australia	7:12.48
1982	United States	7:21.09	2001	Australia	7:04.66
1986	German Democratic Republic	7:15.91	2003	Australia	7:08.58

Men's 4 × 100m Medley Relay

		Time			Time
1973	United States	3:49.49	1991	United States	3:39.66
1975	United States	3:49.00	1994	United States	3:37.74
1978	United States	3:44.63	1998	Australia	3:38.98
1982	United States	3:40.84	2001	Australia	3:35.35
1986	United States	3:41.25	2003	United States	3:31.54

SWIMMING

Women's 50m Freestyle

	Time			Time
1973-82 not held			1998 Amy van Dyken (USA)	25.15
1986 Tamara Costache (ROM)	25.28		2001 Inge de Bruijn (NED)	24.47
1991 Zhuang Yong (CHN)	25.47		2003 Inge de Bruijn (NED)	24.47
1994 Le Jingyi (CHN)	24.51			

Women's100m Freestyle

	Time			Time
1973 Kornelia Ender (GDR)	57.54		1991 Nicole Haislett (USA)	55.17
1975 Kornelia Ender (GDR)	56.50		1994 Le Jingyi (CHN)	54.01
1978 Barbara Krause (GDR)	55.68		1998 Jenny Thompson (USA)	54.95
1982 Birgit Meineke (GDR)	55.79		2001 Inge de Bruijn (NED)	54.18
1986 Kristin Otto (GDR)	55.05		2003 Hanna-Maria Seppala (FIN)	54.37

Women's 200m Freestyle

	Time			Time
1973 Keena Rothhammer (USA)	2:05.99		1991 Hayley Lewis (AUS)	2:00.48
1975 Shirley Babashoff (USA)	2:02.50		1994 Franziska van Almsick (GER)	1:56.78
1978 Cynthia Woodhead (USA)	1:58.53		1998 Claudia Poll (CRC)	1:58.90
1982 Annemarie Verstappen (NED)	1:59.53		2001 Giaan Rooney (AUS)	1:58.57
1986 Heike Friedrich (GDR)	1:58.26		2003 Alena Popchanka (BEL)	1:58.32

Women's 400m Freestyle

	Time			Time
1973 Heather Greenwood (USA)	4:20.28		1991 Janet Evans (USA)	4:08.63
1975 Shirley Babashoff (USA)	4:16.87		1994 Yang Aihua (CHN)	4:09.64
1978 Tracey Wickham (AUS)	4:06.28		1998 Chen Yan (CHN)	4:06.72
1982 Carmela Schmidt (GDR)	4:08.98		2001 Yana Klochkova (UKR)	4:07.30
1986 Heike Friedrich (GDR)	4:07.45		2003 Hannah Stockbauer (GER)	4:06.75

Women's 800m Freestyle

	Time			Time
1973 Novella Calligaris (ITA)	8:52.97		1991 Janet Evans (USA)	8:24.05
1975 Jenny Turrall (AUS)	8:44.75		1994 Janet Evans (USA)	8:29.85
1978 Tracey Wickham (AUS)	8:25.94		1998 Brooke Bennett (USA)	8:28.71
1982 Kim Linehan (USA)	8:27.48		2001 Hannah Stockbauer (GER)	8:24.66
1986 Astrid Strauss (GDR)	8:28.24		2003 Hannah Stockbauer (GER)	8:23.66

Women's 1500m Freestyle

	Time
1973-98 not held	
2001 Hannah Stockbauer (GER)	16:01.02
2003 Hannah Stockbauer (GER)	16.00.18

Women's 50m Backstroke

	Time
1973-98 not held	
2001 Haley Cope (USA)	28.51
2003 Nina Zhivanevskaya (ESP)	28.48

Women's 100m Backstroke

	Time			Time
1973 Ulrike Richter (GDR)	1:05.42		1991 Krisztina Egerszegi (HUN)	1:01.88
1975 Ulrike Richter (GDR)	1:03.30		1994 He Cihong (CHN)	1:00.57
1978 Linda Jezek (USA)	1:02.55		1998 Lea Maurer (USA)	1:01.16
1982 Kristin Otto (GDR)	1:01.30		2001 Natalie Coughlin (USA)	1:00.37
1986 Betsy Mitchell (USA)	1:01.74		2003 Antje Buschschulte (GER)	1:00.50

Women's 200m Backstroke

		Time				Time
1973	Melissa Belote (USA)	2:20.52		1991	Krisztina Egerszegi (HUN)	2:09.15
1975	Birgit Treiber (GDR)	2:15.46		1994	He Cihong (CHN)	2:07.40
1978	Linda Jezek (USA)	2:11.93		1998	Roxanna Maracineanu (FRA)	2:11.26
1982	Cornelia Sirch (GDR)	2:09.91		2001	Diana Mocanu (ROM)	2:09.94
1986	Cornelia Sirch (GDR)	2:11.37		2003	Katy Sexton (GBR)	2:08.74

Women's 50m Breaststroke

		Time
1973-98 not held		
2001	Luo Xuejuan (CHN)	30.84
2003	Luo Xuejuan (CHN)	30.67

Women's 100m Breaststroke

		Time				Time
1973	Renate Vogel (GDR)	1:13.74		1991	Linley Frame (AUS)	1:08.81
1975	Hannalore Anke (GDR)	1:12.72		1994	Samantha Riley (AUS)	1:07.69
1978	Julia Bogdanova (URS)	1:10.31		1998	Kristy Kowal (USA)	1:08.42
1982	Ute Geweniger (GDR)	1:09.14		2001	Luo Xuejuan (CHN)	1:07.18
1986	Sylvia Gerasch (GDR)	1:08.11		2003	Luo Xuejuan (CHN)	1:06.80

Women's 200m Breaststroke

		Time				Time
1973	Renate Vogel (GDR)	2:40.01		1991	Yelena Volkova (URS)	2:29.53
1975	Hannalore Anke (GDR)	2:37.25		1994	Samantha Riley (AUS)	2:26.87
1978	Lina Kaciušyté (URS)	2:31.42		1998	Ágnes Kovács (HUN)	2:25.45
1982	Svetlana Varganova (URS)	2:28.82		2001	Ágnes Kovács (HUN)	2:24.90
1986	Silke Hörner (GDR)	2:27.40		2003	Amanda Beard (USA)	2:23.99

Women's 50m Butterfly

		Time
1973-98 not held		
2001	Inge de Bruijn (NED)	25.90
2003	Inge de Bruijn (NED)	25.84

Women's 100m Butterfly

		Time				Time
1973	Kornelia Ender (GDR)	1:02.53		1991	Qian Hong (CHN)	59.68
1975	Kornelia Ender (GDR)	1:01.24		1994	Liu Limin (CHN)	58.98
1978	Joan Pennington (USA)	1:00.20		1998	Jenny Thompson (USA)	58.46
1982	Mary T. Meagher (USA)	59.41		2001	Petria Thomas (AUS)	58.27
1986	Kornelia Gressler (GDR)	59.51		2003	Jenny Thompson (USA)	57.99

Women's 200m Butterfly

		Time				Time
1973	Rosemarie Kother (GDR)	2:13.76		1991	Summer Sanders (USA)	2:09.24
1975	Rosemarie Kother (GDR)	2:15.92		1994	Liu Limin (CHN)	2:07.24
1978	Tracy Caulkins (USA)	2:09.87		1998	Susie O'Neill (AUS)	2:07.25
1982	Ines Geissler (GDR)	2:08.66		2001	Petria Thomas (AUS)	2:06.73
1986	Mary T. Meagher (USA)	2:08.41		2003	Otylia Jedrzejczak (POL)	2:07.56

S
W
I
M
M
I
N
G

Women's 200m Individual Medley

		Time				Time
1973	Andre Hübner (GDR)	2:20.51	1991	Lin Li (CHN)		2:13.40
1975	Kathy Heddy (USA)	2:19.80	1994	Lu Bin (CHN)		2:12.34
1978	Tracy Caulkins (USA)	2:14.07	1998	Wu Yanyan (CHN)		2:10.88
1982	Petra Schneider (GDR)	2:11.79	2001	Martha Bowen (USA)		2:11.93
1986	Kristin Otto (GDR)	2:15.56	2003	Yana Klochkova (UKR)		2:10.75

Women's 400m Individual Medley

		Time				Time
1973	Gudrun Wegner (GDR)	4:57.51	1991	Lin Li (CHN)		4:41.45
1975	Ulrike Tauber (GDR)	4:52.76	1994	Dai Guohong (CHN)		4:39.14
1978	Tracy Caulkins (USA)	4:40.83	1998	Chen Yan (CHN)		4:36.66
1982	Petra Schneider (GDR)	4:36.10	2001	Yana Klochkova (UKR)		4:36.98
1986	Kathleen Nord (GDR)	4:43.75	2003	Yana Klochkova (UKR)		4:36.74

Women's 4 × 100m Freestyle Relay

		Time			Time
1973	East Germany	3:52.45	1991	United States	3:43.26
1975	East Germany	3:49.37	1994	China	3:37.91
1978	United States	3:43.43	1998	United States	3:42.11
1982	East Germany	3:43.97	2001	Germany	3:39.58
1986	East Germany	3:40.57	2003	United States	3:38.09

Women's 4 × 200m Freestyle Relay

		Time			Time
1973-82	not held		1998	Germany	8:01.46
1986	East Germany	7:59.33	2001	Great Britain	7:58.69
1991	Germany	8:02.56	2003	United States	7:55.70
1994	China	7:57.96			

Women's 4 × 100m Medley Relay

		Time			Time
1973	East Germany	4:16.84	1991	United States	4:06.51
1975	East Germany	4:14.74	1994	China	4:01.67
1978	United States	4:08.21	1998	United States	4:01.93
1982	East Germany	4:05.88	2001	Australia	4:01.50
1986	East Germany	4:04.82	2003	China	3:59.89

Diving Olympic Gold Medallists

Men's Springboard

1908	Albert Zürner (GER)
1912	Paul Günther (GER)
1920	Louis Kuehn (USA)
1924	Albert White (USA)
1928	Pete Desjardins (USA)
1932	Michael Galitzen (USA)
1936	Richard Degener (USA)
1948	Bruce Harlan (USA)
1952	David Browning (USA)
1956	Bob Clotworthy (USA)
1960	Gary Tobian (USA)
1964	Ken Sitzberger (USA)
1968	Bernie Wrightson (USA)
1972	Vladimir Vasin (URS)
1976	Phil Boggs (USA)
1980	Aleksandr Portnov (URS)
1984	Greg Louganis (USA)
1988	Greg Louganis (USA)
1992	Mark Lenzi (USA)
1996	Xiong Ni (CHN)
2000	Xiong Ni (CHN)

Men's Platform

1904	George Sheldon (USA)
1906	Gottlob Walz (GER)
1908	Hjalmar Johansson (SWE)
1912	Erik Adlerz (SWE)
1920	Clarence Pinkston (USA)
1924	Albert White (USA)
1928	Pete Desjardins (USA)
1932	Harold Smith (USA)
1936	Marshall Wayne (USA)
1948	Sammy Lee (USA)
1952	Sammy Lee (USA)
1956	Joaquin Capilla (MEX)
1960	Bob Webster (USA)
1964	Bob Webster (USA)
1968	Klaus Dibiasi (ITA)
1972	Klaus Dibiasi (ITA)
1976	Klaus Dibiasi (ITA)
1980	Falk Hoffmann (GDR)
1984	Greg Louganis (USA)
1988	Greg Louganis (USA)
1992	Sun Shuwei (CHN)
1996	Dmitri Sautin (RUS)
2000	Tian Liang (CHN)

Women's Springboard

1920	Aileen Riggin (USA)
1924	Elizabeth Becker (USA)
1928	Helen Meany (USA)
1932	Georgia Coleman (USA)
1936	Marjorie Gestring (USA)
1948	Vicki Draves (USA)
1952	Pat McCormick (USA)
1956	Pat McCormick (USA)
1960	Ingrid Krämer (GER)
1964	Ingrid Engel-Krämer (GER)
1968	Sue Gossick (USA)
1972	Micki King (USA)
1976	Jennifer Chandler (USA)
1980	Irina Kalinina (URS)
1984	Sylvie Bernier (CAN)
1988	Gao Min (CHN)
1992	Gao Min (CHN)
1996	Fu Mingxia (CHN)
2000	Fu Mingxia (CHN)

Women's Platform

1912	Greta Johansson (SWE)
1920	Stefani Fryland-Clausen (DEN)
1924	Caroline Smith (USA)
1928	Elizabeth Becker Pinkston (USA)
1932	Dorothy Poynton (USA)
1936	Dorothy Poynton Hill (USA)
1948	Vicki Draves (USA)
1952	Pat McCormick (USA)
1956	Pat McCormick (USA)
1960	Ingrid Krämer (GER)
1964	Lesley Bush (USA)
1968	Milena Duchková (TCH)
1972	Ulrika Knape (SWE)
1976	Elena Vaytsekhovskaya (URS)
1980	Martina Jäschke (GDR)
1984	Zhou Jihong (CHN)
1988	Xu Yanmei (CHN)
1992	Fu Mingxia (CHN)
1996	Fu Mingxia (CHN)
2000	Laura Wilkinson (USA)

SWIMMING

TABLE TENNIS

The game was developed from tennis at the end of the 19th century to enable tennis players to keep active during bad weather. In early forms of table tennis players used cigar lids as bats, a row of books as a net and a wine cork for a ball.

Pioneers of the game include Charles Barter and James Gibb, and names such as 'Gossima', 'Whiff Whaff', 'Flim Flam' and the most widely used of all, 'Ping Pong', were early, or alternative, names for the game. In 1901 the short-lived Ping Pong Association was founded and later that year the Table Tennis Association was formed (it became defunct at the outset of World War I but reformed in 1922). In 1926 the Fédération Internationale de Tennis de Table (ITTF) was formed in Berlin.

The World Championships started in 1927, in London, and many of the early winners came from Hungary. By the end of the 20th century the Chinese had come to dominate the sport, winning the majority of titles available.

As the game has developed, rule changes have been introduced to make the sport more attractive, particularly to television viewers; the scoring system has changed, reducing the number of points required to win a game to 11 (down from the traditional 21). This is thought to create more crisis points and therefore more excitement. The ball has increased in size from 38mm in diameter to 40mm, with the intention of slowing its flight and therefore increasing the length of rallies. Several changes have also been made to the rules covering the service action, to make it easier for the receiver to return serve.

An Olympic sport since 1988, table tennis is hugely popular internationally, with 186 countries currently competing in the ITTF structure. British world champions include Fred Perry (1929), Johnny Leach (1949 and 1951), and twins Diane and Rosalind Rowe (doubles, 1951 and 1954). The Rowe twins were prodigious talents; Rosalind was the youngest-ever England no. 1 player when she achieved that feat in 1951, aged 17. The twins were identical but were easily picked out on the table tennis table as Diana was left-handed and Rosalind right-handed.

Katie Parker became the youngest player ever to represent England at a World Championship (Manchester 1997, when she was only 12 years old). Three days short of her 18th birthday, she became the youngest player for over 50 years to be ranked England women's top player. Her mother was the 1976 European champion, Jill (Hammersley) Parker, and her father Don, a former international himself, managed the England team. Jill was a great defensive player and her style was a great advertisement for the 'expedite rule', which comes into play in long games and means points must be won within a certain number of strikes or the receiver is awarded the point.

Other high-profile British players include Chester Barnes, the British no. 1 player in the early 1960s (who carved out a new career as assistant to race-horse trainer Martin Pipe), and Ann Haydon Jones who, in 1956, and just short of her 18th birthday, became England no. 1. She also played in five World Table Tennis Championship matches, including three in the 1957 World Championships (losing all of them), before achieving greater fame in tennis as the 1969 Wimbledon champion.

Biographies

Barna, Victor Born Budapest, Hungary, 24 August 1911. Barna dominated the game in the early 1930s. His famous backhand flick shot helped him to contest six consecutive world finals from 1930 to 1935, winning five of them (his only loss being to fellow countryman Miklos Szabados, with whom Barna won seven men's doubles titles). He died 28 February 1972.

Bergmann, Richard Born Vienna, Austria, 1919. Bergmann became famous for his impenetrable hard-bat defence, uncanny ball control and a superb mental tenacity. He was the first true tactician of the game, who studied the strengths and weaknesses of his opponents. He could also attack on both wings and break up the rhythm of players. He won the world title in 1937 and then left Austria, due to the German invasion, and settled in Britain. He won further world titles in 1939, 1948 and 1950, representing England. Bergmann was probably the greatest hard-bat player of all time.

Cooke, Alan Born Chesterfield, Derbyshire, England, 23 March 1966. Right-handed all-round attacking player, five times English national champion (1988, 1989, 1996, 2003 and 2004). Cooke became Commonweath champion in Cardiff in 1989, and was three times English Top Twelve champion. As a regular member of the English national team he won two European team medals and three European bronze medals.

Douglas, Desmond Born Kingston, Jamaica, 20 July 1955. A legendary player in the domestic game having won the English national title a record 11 times, including nine in a row between 1979 and 1987. A left-handed attacking player who thrived on containing his opponents while waiting to create angles to launch his own attack. Internationally, Douglas won the English Open twice plus the European Top Twelve in 1987 in Basle.

Hilton, John Born Hyde, Cheshire, England, 25 June 1947. Surprise winner of the European

Championships while ranked no. 4 in England in 1980, beating Josef Dvoracek of Czechoslovakia in the final. Hilton perfected the art of using a bat with black rubber on both sides, imparting spin to the ball with one side but not the other. By twiddling the racket around in his hand during each rally, he was able to confuse his opponents as to whether or not there was any spin on the ball.

Leach, Johnny Born Hackney, London, England, 20 November 1922. World champion twice, in 1949 and 1951, and member of the victorious English men's team in the Swaythling Cup in 1953. A right-handed all-round player who tended to defend more than attack. He became the only English player ever to win the US Open.

Perry, Fred Born Stockport, Greater Manchester, England, 18 May 1909. The greatest-ever British tennis player began his sporting life as a table tennis player of some repute, winning the world title in 1929. He died 2 February 1995.

Prean, Carl Born Newport, Isle of Wight, England, 20 August 1967. This right-handed attacking player who employed long-pimpled rubber on the backhand became European junior champion in 1985 beating Tomar of Romania in the final. Three times national champion (1991, 1993 and 1995), Prean spent the majority of his professional career abroad, playing 16 years in Germany and two years in France.

Syed, Matthew Born Bromley, Kent, England, 2 November 1970. Right-handed defensive player renowned for his spectacular ability to retrieve attacking drives. Four times English national champion (1997, 1998, 2000 and 2001). He also won three Commonwealth titles and the Czechoslovakian Open in 1991. Syed stood for Parliament in 2001 for the Labour Party in Wokingham, losing to John Redwood.

Waldner, Jan-Ove Born Stockholm, Sweden, 3 October 1965. Waldner was a precocious player who won his first national title, in his age-group, aged nine. He became a professional player at the age of 15 and remained at the top of the game for 20 years, winning two world titles and becoming Olympic champion in 1992, as well as winning the Europe Top Twelve title seven times and the European Championships in 1996. Still playing top-class table tennis in 2004, Jan-Ove Waldner lays claim to being the greatest player of all time.

Olympic Medallists

Men's Singles

1988	Yoo Nam Kyu (KOR)
1992	Jan-Ove Waldner (SWE)
1996	Liu Guoliang (CHN)
2000	Kong Linghui (CHN)

Men's Doubles

1988	Chen Longcan/Wei Qingguang (CHN)
1992	Wang Tao/Lu Lin (CHN)
1996	Kong Linghui/Liu Guoliang (CHN)
2000	Wang Liqin/Yan Sen (CHN)

Women's Singles

1988	Chen Jing (CHN)
1992	Deng Yaping (CHN)
1996	Deng Yaping (CHN)
2000	Wang Nan (CHN)

Women's Doubles

1988	Hyan Jung Hwa/Yang Young Ja (CHN)
1992	Deng Yaping/Qiao Hong (CHN)
1996	Deng Yaping/Qiao Hong (CHN)
2000	Wang Nan/Li Ju (CHN)

World Championships

	Men's Singles	Women's Singles	Men's Doubles
1926	Roland Jacobi (HUN)	Maria Mednyánszky (HUN)	Roland Jacobi/Daniel Pecsi (HUN)
1928	Zoltán Mechlovits (HUN)	Maria Mednyánszky (HUN)	Alfred Liebster/Robert Thum (AUT)
1929	Fred Perry (ENG)	Maria Mednyánszky (HUN)	Victor Barna/Miklos Szabados (HUN)
1930	Victor Barna (HUN)	Maria Mednyánszky (HUN)	Victor Barna/Miklos Szabados (HUN)
1931	Miklos Szabados (HUN)	Maria Mednyánszky (HUN)	Victor Barna/Miklos Szabados (HUN)
1932	Victor Barna (HUN)	Anna Sipos (HUN)	Victor Barna/Miklos Szabados (HUN)
1933	Victor Barna (HUN)	Anna Sipos (HUN)	Victor Barna/S. Glanncz (HUN)
1934	Victor Barna (HUN)	Marie Kettnerová (TCH)	Victor Barna/Miklos Szabados (HUN)
1935	Victor Barna (HUN)	Marie Kettnerová (TCH)	Victor Barna/Miklos Szabados (HUN)
1936	Stanislav Kolar (TCH)	Ruth Aarons (USA)	R.G. Blattner/Jimmy McClure (USA)
1937	Richard Bergmann (AUT)		R.G. Blattner/Jimmy McClure (USA)
1938	Bohumil Vana (TCH)	Gertrude Pritzi (AUT)	Jimmy McClure/Sol Schiff (USA)
1939	Richard Bergmann (ENG)	Vlasta Depetrisova (TCH)	Victor Barna (HUN)/Richard Bergman (ENG)
1947	Bohumil Vana (TCH)	Gizella Farkas (HUN)	Adolf Slar/Bohumil Vana (TCH)
1948	Richard Bergmann (ENG)	Gizella Farkas (HUN)	Ladislav Stipek/Bohuma Vana (TCH)
1949	Johnny Leach (ENG)	Gizella Farkas (HUN)	Ivan Andreadis/Frantisek Tokar (TCH)
1950	Richard Bergmann (ENG)	Angelica Rozeanu (ROM)	Ferenc Sido/Ferenc Soos (HUN)
1951	Johnny Leach (ENG)	Angelica Rozeanu (ROM)	Ivan Andreadis/Bohumil Vana (TCH)
1952	Hiroji Satoh (JPN)	Angelica Rozeanu (ROM)	Norizaku Fujii/Tadaki Hayashi (JPN)
1953	Ferenc Sido (HUN)	Angelica Rozeanu (ROM)	Jozsef Koczian (YUG)/Ferenc Sido (HUN)

1954	Ichiro Ogimura (JPN)	Angelica Rozeanu (ROM)	Zarko Dolinar/Vilim Harangozo (YUG)
1955	Toshio Tanaka (JPN)	Angelica Rozeanu (ROM)	Ivan Andreadis/Ladislav Stipek (TCH)
1956	Ichiro Ogimura (JPN)	Tommi Okawa (JPN)	Ichiro Ogimura/Yoshio Tomita (JPN)
1957	Toshio Tanaka (JPN)	Fuji Eguchi (JPN)	Ivan Andreadis/Ladislav Stipek (TCH)
1959	Rong Guotang (CHN)	Kimiyo Matsuzaki (JPN)	Ichiro Ogimura/Teruo Murakami (JPN)
1961	Zhuang Zedong (CHN)	Giu Zhonghui (CHN)	Nobuya Hoshino/Koji Kimura (JPN)
1963	Zhuang Zedong (CHN)	Kimiyo Matsuzaki (JPN)	Zhang Xielin/Wang Zhiliang (CHN)
1965	Zhuang Zedong (CHN)	Naoko Fakuzu (JPN)	Zhang Xielin/Xu Yinsheng (CHN)
1967	Nobuhiku Hasegawa (JPN)	Sachiko Morisawa (JPN)	Hans Alser/Kjell Johansson (SWE)
1969	Shigeo Itoh (JPN)	Toshiko Kowada (JPN)	Hans Alser/Kjell Johansson (SWE)
1971	Stellan Bengsston (SWE)	Lin Huiqing (CHN)	István Jonyer/Tibor Klampar (HUN)
1973	Xi Enting (CHN)	Hu Yu-Lan (CHN)	Stellan Bengsston/Kjell Johansson (SWE)
1975	István Jonyer (HUN)	Pak Yung Sun (PRK)	Gabor Gergely/István Jonyer (HUN)
1977	Mitsuru Kohno (JPN)	Pak Yung Sun (PRK)	Li Zhenshi/Liang Geliang (CHN)
1979	Seiji Ono (JPN)	Ge Xinai (CHN)	Dragutin Surbek/Anton Stipancic (YUG)
1981	Guo Yuehua (CHN)	Tong Ling (CHN)	Li Zhenshi/Cai Zhenhua (CHN)
1983	Guo Yuehua (CHN)	Cao Yanhua (CHN)	Dragutin Surbek/Zoran Kalinic (YUG)
1985	Jiang Jialiang (CHN)	Cao Yanhua (CHN)	Mikael Appelgren/Ulf Carlsson (SWE)
1987	Jiang Jialiang (CHN)	He Zhili (CHN)	Chen Longcan/Wei Qingguang (CHN)
1989	Jan-Ove Waldner (SWE)	Qiao Hong (CHN)	Jörg Rosskopf/Steffen Fetzner (FRG)
1991	Jörgen Persson (SWE)	Deng Yaping (CHN)	Peter Karlsson/Thomas von Scheele (SWE)
1993	Jean-Philippe Gatien (FRA)	Hyun Jung Hwa (KOR)	Wang Tao/Lu Lin (CHN)
1995	Kong Linghui (CHN)	Deng Yaping (CHN)	Wang Tao/Lu Lin (CHN)
1997	Jan-Ove Waldner (SWE)	Deng Yaping (CHN)	Kong Linghui/Liu Guoliang (CHN)
1999	Liu Guoliang (CHN)	Wang Nan (CHN)	Kong Linghui/Liu Guoliang (CHN)
2001	Wang Liqin (CHN)	Wang Nan (CHN)	Wang Liqin/Yan Sen (CHN)
2003	Werner Schalger (AUT)	Wang Nan (CHN)	Wang Liqin/Yan Sen (CHN)

Women's Doubles

1926	not held	1959	Taeko Namba/Kozuko Yamaizuma (JPN)
1928	Fanchette Flamm (AUT)/Maria Mednyánszky (HUN)	1961	Maria Alexandru/Georgita Pitica (ROM)
1929	Erika Metzger/E.Ruster (GER)	1963	Kimiyo Matsuzaki/Masako Seki (JPN)
1930	Maria Mednyánszky/Anna Sipos (HUN)	1965	Zheng Minzhi/Lin Huiquing (CHN)
1931	Maria Mednyánszky/Anna Sipos (HUN)	1967	Shaeko Hirota/Sachito Morisawa (JPN)
1932	Maria Mednyánszky/Anna Sipos (HUN)	1969	Svetlana Grinberg/Zoya Rudnova (URS)
1933	Maria Mednyánszky/Anna Sipos (HUN)	1971	Zheng Minzhi/Lin Huiquing (CHN)
1934	Maria Mednyánszky/Anna Sipos (HUN)	1973	Maria Alexandru (ROM)/Miho Hamada (JPN)
1935	Maria Mednyánszky/Anna Sipos (HUN)	1975	Maria Alexandru (ROM)/Shoko Takahashi (JPN)
1936	Marie Ketnerová/Anna Smidova (TCH)	1977	Yang Ying (CHN)/Pak Yong Ok (PRK)
1937	Vlasta Depetrisova/Vera Votrubcova (TCH)	1979	Zhang Li/Zhang Deying (CHN)
1938	Vlasta Depetrisova/Vera Votrubcova (TCH)	1981	Zhang Deying/Cao Yanhua (CHN)
1939	Hilde Bussman (HUN)/Gertrude Pritzi (GER)	1983	Shen Jianping/Dai Lili (CHN)
1947	Gizella Farkas (HUN)/Gertrude Pritzi (AUT)	1985	Dai Lili/Geng Lijuan (CHN)
1948	Margaret Franks/Vera Thomas (ENG)	1987	Hyan Jung Hwa/Yang Young Ja (KOR)
1949	Helen Elliott (SCO)/Gizella Farkas (HUN)	1989	Deng Yaping/Qiao Hong (CHN)
1950	Dora Beregi (ENG)/Helen Elliott (SCO)	1991	Chen Zhi/Gao Jun (CHN)
1951	Diane Rowe/Rosalind Rowe (ENG)	1993	Liu Wei/Qiao Yunping (CHN)
1952	Shizuku Narahara/Tomi Nishimura (JPN)	1995	Deng Yaping/Qiao Hong (CHN)
1953	Gizella Farkas (HUN)/Angelica Rozeanu (ROM)	1997	Deng Yaping/Yang Ying (CHN)
1954	Diane Rowe/Rosalind Rowe (ENG)	1999	Wang Nan/Li Ju (CHN)
1955	Angelica Rozeanu/Ella Zeller (ROM)	2001	Wang Nan/Li Ju (CHN)
1956	Angelica Rozeanu/Ella Zeller (ROM)	2003	Wang Nan/Zhang Yining (CHN)
1957	Livia Mosoczy/Agnes Simon (HUN)		

Mixed Doubles

1926	Zoltan Mechlovits/Maria Mednyánszky (HUN)	1947	Ferenc Soos/Gizella Farkas (HUN)
1928	Zoltan Mechlovits/Maria Mednyánszky (HUN)	1948	Richard Miles/Thelma Thall (USA)
1929	István Kelen/Anna Sipos (HUN)	1949	Ferenc Sido/Gizella Farkas (HUN)
1930	Miklas Svabados/Maria Mednyánszky (HUN)	1950	Ferenc Sido/Gizella Farkas (HUN)
1931	Miklas Svabados/Maria Mednyánszky (HUN)	1951	Bohumil Vana (TCH)/Angelica Rozeanu (ROM)
1932	Viktor Barna/Anna Sipos (HUN)	1952	Ferenc Sido (HUN)/Angelica Rozeanu (ROM)
1933	István Kelen/Maria Mednyánszky (HUN)	1953	Ferenc Sido (HUN)/Angelica Rozeanu (ROM)
1934	Miklas Svabados/Maria Mednyánszky (HUN)	1954	Ivan Andreadis (TCH)/Gizella Farkas (HUN)
1935	Viktor Barna/Anna Sipos (HUN)	1955	Kalman Szepesi/Eva Koczian (HUN)
1936	Miloslav Hamr/Gertrude Kleinova (TCH)	1956	Ervin Klein/Leah Neuberger (USA)
1937	Bohumil Vana/Vera Votrubcová (TCH)	1957	Ichuro Ogimura/Fujie Eguchi (JPN)
1938	László Bellak (HUN)/Wendy Woodhead (ENG)	1959	Ichuro Ogimura/Fujie Eguchi (JPN)
1939	Bohumil Vana/Vera Votrubcová (TCH)	1961	Ichuro Ogimura/Kimiyo Matsuzaki (JPN)

1963	Koji Kimura/Kazuk Ito (JPN)	1985	Cai Zhenhua/Cao Yanhua (CHN)
1965	Koji Kimura/Kazuko Ito (JPN)	1987	Hui Jun/Geng Lijuan (CHN)
1967	Nobuhiko Hasegawa/Noriko Yamanka (JPN)	1989	Yoo Nam Kyu/Hyan Jung Hwa (KOR)
1969	Nobuhiko Hasegawa/Yasuko Kohno (JPN)	1991	Wang Tao/Liu Wei (CHN)
1971	Zhang Xielin/Lin Huiqing (CHN)	1993	Wang Tao/Liu Wei (CHN)
1973	Liang Geliang/Li Li (CHN)	1995	Wang Tao/Liu Wei (CHN)
1975	Stanislav Gomozkov/Tatyana Ferdman (URS)	1997	Liu Guoliang/Wu Na (CHN)
1977	Jacques Secretin/Claude Bergeret (FRA)	1999	Ma Lin/Zhang Yining (CHN)
1979	Liang Geliang/Ge Xinai (CHN)	2001	Qin Zhijan/Yang Ying (CHN)
1981	Xie Saike/Huang Junqun (CHN)	2003	Ma Lin/Wang Nan (CHN)
1983	Guo Yuehua/Ni Xialian (CHN)		

Men's Team (Swaythling Cup)

1926	Hungary	1950	Czechoslovakia	1975	China
1928	Hungary	1951	Czechoslovakia	1977	China
1929	Hungary	1952	Hungary	1979	Hungary
1930	Hungary	1953	England	1981	China
1931	Hungary	1954	Japan	1983	China
1932	Czechoslovakia	1955	Japan	1985	China
1933	Hungary	1956	Japan	1987	China
1934	Hungary	1957	Japan	1989	Sweden
1935	Hungary	1959	Japan	1991	Sweden
1936	Austria	1961	China	1993	Sweden
1937	United States	1963	China	1995	China
1938	Hungary	1965	China	1997	China
1939	Czechoslovakia	1967	Japan	2000	Sweden
1947	Czechoslovakia	1969	Japan	2001	China
1948	Czechoslovakia	1971	China	2004	China
1949	Hungary	1973	Sweden		

Women's Team (Corbillon Cup)

1926-33	not held	1954	Japan	1979	China
1934	Germany	1955	Romania	1981	China
1935	Czechoslovakia	1956	Romania	1983	China
1936	Czechoslovakia	1957	Japan	1985	China
1937	United States	1959	Japan	1987	China
1938	Czechoslovakia	1961	Japan	1989	China
1939	Germany	1963	Japan	1991	Korea
1947	England	1965	China	1993	China
1948	England	1967	Japan	1995	China
1949	United States	1969	Japan	1997	China
1950	Romania	1971	China	2000	China
1951	Romania	1973	Korea	2001	China
1952	Japan	1975	China	2004	China
1953	Romania	1977	China		

European Championships

	Men's Singles	Women's Singles	Men's Doubles
1958	Zoltán Berczik (HUN)	Eva Koczian (HUN)	Ladislav Stipiek/Ludvik Vyhnanovsky (TCH)
1960	Zoltán Berczik (HUN)	Eva Koczian (HUN)	Zoltán Berczik/Ferenc Sido (HUN)
1962	Hans Alser (SWE)	Agnes Simon (GER)	Vojiszlav Markovic/Janez Teran (YUG)
1964	Kjell Johansson (SWE)	Eva Földy (HUN)	Jaroslav Stanek/Vldimir Miko (TCH)
1966	Kjell Johansson (SWE)	Marta Alexandru (ROM)	Hans Alser/Kjell Johansson (SWE)
1968	Dragutin Surbek (YUG)	Ilona Vostova (TCH)	Anton Stipancic/Edvard Vecko (YUG)
1970	Hans Alser (SWE)	Zoya Rudnova (URS)	Anton Stipancic/Dragutin Surbek (YUG)
1972	Stellan Bengtsson (SWE)	Zoya Rudnova (URS)	István Joyner/Peter Rozsas (HUN)
1974	Milan Orlowski (TCH)	Judi Magos (HUN)	István Joyner/Tibor Klampar (HUN)
1976	Jacques Secretin (FRA)	Jill Hammersley (ENG)	Stellan Bengtsson/Kjell Johansson (SWE)
1978	Gabor Gergely (HUN)	Judi Magos (HUN)	Milan Orlowski (TCH)/Gabor Gergely (HUN)
1980	John Hilton (ENG)	Valentina Popova (URS)	Jacques Secretin/Patrick Birocheau (FRA)
1982	Mikael Appelgren (SWE)	Bettine Vriesekoop (NED)	Dragutin Surbek/Zoran Kalinic (YUG)
1984	Ulf Bengtsson (SWE)	Valentina Popova (URS)	Dragutin Surbek/Zoran Kalinic (YUG)

1986	Jörgen Persson (SWE)	Csilla Batorfi (HUN)	Jan-Ove Waldner/Erik Lindh (SWE)
1988	Mikael Appelgren (SWE)	Fliura Bulatova (URS)	Jan-Ove Waldner/Mikael Appelgren (SWE)
1990	Mikael Appelgren (SWE)	Daniela Guergelcheva (BUL)	Ilija Lupulescu/Zoran Primorac (YUG)
1992	Jörg Rosskopf (GER)	Bettine Vriesekoop (NED)	Jörgen Persson/Erik Lindh (SWE)
1994	Jean-Michel Saive (BEL)	Marie Svensson (SWE)	Kalinikos Kreanga (GRE)/Zoran Kalinic (YUG)
1996	Jan-Ove Waldner (SWE)	Nicole Struse (GER)	Jan-Ove Waldner/Jörgen Persson (SWE)
1998	Vladimir Samsonov (BLR)	Ni Xia Lian (LUX)	Vladimir Samsonov (BLR)/Jörg Rosskopf (GER)
2000	Peter Karlsson (SWE)	Qianhong Gotsch (GER)	Patrick Chila/Jean-Philippe Gatien (FRA)
2002	Timo Boll (GER)	Ni Xia Lian (LUX)	Timo Boll/Zoltán Fejer-Konnerth (GER)
2003	Vladimir Samsonov (BLR)	Otilia Badescu (ROM)	Weixing Chen (AUT)/Yevgeniy Shetinin (BLR)

Women's Doubles

1958	Angelica Rozeanu/Ulla Zeller (ROM)	1982	Fliura Bulatova/Inna Kovalenko (URS)
1960	Angelica Rozeanu/Maria Alexandru (ROM)	1984	Valentina Popova/Narine Antonyan (URS)
1962	Mary Shannon/Diane Rowe (ENG)	1986	Fliura Bulatova/Yelena Kovtun (URS)
1964	Mary Shannon/Diane Rowe (ENG)	1988	Csilla Batorfi/Edit Urban (HUN)
1966	Eva Koczian/Erzsebet Jurik (HUN)	1990	Csilla Batorfi/Gabriella Wirth (HUN)
1968	Marta Luzova/Jitka Karlikova (TCH)	1992	Jasna Fazlic/Gordana Perkucin (YUG)
1970	Zoya Rudnova/Svetlana Grinberg (URS)	1994	Csilla Batorfi/Krisztina Toth (HUN)
1972	Judit Magos/Henritte Lotaller (HUN)	1996	Nicole Struse/Elke Schall (GER)
1974	Judit Magos/Henritte Lotaller (HUN)	1998	Nicole Struse/Elke Schall (GER)
1976	Jill Hammersley/Linda Howard (ENG)	2000	Csilla Batorfi/Krisztina Toth (HUN)
1978	Maria Alexandru/Liana Mihut (ROM)	2002	Tamara Boros (CRO)/Mihaela Steff (ROM)
1980	Valentina Popova/Liana Antonian (URS)	2003	Tamara Boros (CRO)//Mihaela Steff (ROM)

Mixed Doubles

1958	Zoltán Berzik/Gizella Lantos (HUN)	1984	Jacques Secretin (FRA)/Valentina Popova (URS)
1960	Gheorghe Corbizan/Maria Alexandru (ROM)	1986	Jindrich Pansky/Marie Hrachova (TCH)
1962	Hans Alser (SWE)/Inge Harst (FRG)	1988	Ilija Lupulescu/Jasna Fazlic (YUG)
1964	Peter Rozsas/Sarolta Lukacs (HUN)	1990	Jean-Pierre Gatien/Xiaoming Wang (FRA)
1966	Vladimir Miko/Marta Luzova (TCH)	1992	Kalinikos Kreanga(GRE)/Otilia Badescu (ROM)
1968	Stanislav Gomozkov/Zoya Rudnova (URS)	1994	Zoran Primorac (CRO)/Csilla Batorfi (HUN)
1970	Stanislav Gomozkov/Zoya Rudnova (URS)	1996	Vladimir Samsonov (BLR)/Krisztina Toth (HUN)
1972	Stanislav Gomozkov/Zoya Rudnova (URS)	1998	Ilija Lupulescu (YUG)/Otilia Badescu (ROM)
1974	Stanislav Gomozkov/Zoya Rudnova (URS)	2000	Alexander Karakasevic (YUG)/
1976	Anton Stipancic/Erzsebet Palatinus (YUG)		Ruta Garkauskaite-Budiene (LTU)
1978	Wilfried Lieck/Wiebke Hendriksen (FRG)	2002	Lucjan Blaszczyk (POL)/Ni Xia Lian (LUX)
1980	Milan Orlovski/Iona Uhlikova (TCH)	2003	Werner Schlager (AUT)/Krisztina Toth (HUN)
1982	Andrzej Grubba (POL)/Bettine Vriesekoop (NED)		

Men's Team

1958	Hungary	1982	Hungary
1960	Hungary	1984	France
1962	Yugoslavia	1986	Sweden
1964	Sweden	1988	Sweden
1966	Sweden	1990	Sweden
1968	Sweden	1992	Sweden
1970	Sweden	1994	France
1972	Sweden	1996	Sweden
1974	Sweden	1998	Sweden
1976	Yugoslavia	2000	Sweden
1978	Hungary	2002	Sweden
1980	Sweden	2003	Belarus

Women's Team

1958	England		1982	Hungary
1960	Hungary		1984	Soviet Union
1962	West Germany		1986	Hungary
1964	England		1988	Soviet Union
1966	Hungary		1990	Hungary
1968	West Germany		1992	Romania
1970	Soviet Union		1994	Russia
1972	Hungary		1996	Germany
1974	Soviet Union		1998	Germany
1976	Soviet Union		2000	Hungary
1978	Hungary		2002	Romania
1980	Soviet Union		2003	Italy

English National Championships

Men's Singles

1960	Bryan Merrett		1983	Desmond Douglas
1961	Ian Harrison		1984	Desmond Douglas
1962	Bobby Stevens		1985	Desmond Douglas
1963	Chester Barnes		1986	Desmond Douglas
1964	Chester Barnes		1987	Desmond Douglas
1965	Chester Barnes		1988	Alan Cooke
1966	Denis Neale		1989	Alan Cooke
1967	Ian Harrison		1990	Desmond Douglas
1968	Denis Neale		1991	Carl Prean
1969	Denis Neale		1992	Chen Xinhua
1970	Denis Neale		1993	Carl Prean
1971	Chester Barnes		1994	Chen Xinhua
1972	Trevor Taylor		1995	Carl Prean
1973	Trevor Taylor		1996	Alan Cooke
1974	Chester Barnes		1997	Matthew Syed
1975	Denis Neale		1998	Matthew Syed
1976	Desmond Douglas		1999	Alex Perry
1977	Denis Neale		2000	Matthew Syed
1978	Paul Day		2001	Matthew Syed
1979	Desmond Douglas		2002	Andrew Baggaley
1980	Desmond Douglas		2003	Alan Cooke
1981	Desmond Douglas		2004	Alan Cooke
1982	Desmond Douglas			

Men's Doubles

1960	Johnny Leach/Mike Thornhill		1983	Desmond Douglas/Paul Day
1961	Ian Harrison/Bryan Merrett		1984	Desmond Douglas/Paul Day
1962	Bobby Raybould/Bobby Stevens		1985	Desmond Douglas/Paul Day
1963	Bobby Raybould/Bobby Stevens		1986	Desmond Douglas/Carl Prean
1964	David Creamer/Johnny Leach		1987	Skylet Andrew/Nicky Mason
1965	Chester Barnes/Ian Harrison		1988	Skylet Andrew/Nicky Mason
1966	Chester Barnes/Ian Harrison		1989	Skylet Andrew/Nicky Mason
1967	Chester Barnes/Ian Harrison		1990	Alan Cooke/Desmond Douglas
1968	Chester Barnes/Ian Harrison		1991	Skylet Andrew/Nicky Mason
1969	Alan Hydes/Denis Neale		1992	Alan Cooke/Desmond Douglas
1970	Alan Hydes/Denis Neale		1993	Skylet Andrew/Nicky Mason
1971	Chester Barnes/Trevor Taylor		1994	Skylet Andrew/Nicky Mason
1972	Alan Hydes/Denis Neale		1995	Alan Cooke/Desmond Douglas
1973	Denis Neale/Trevor Taylor		1996	Aian Cooke/Desmond Douglas
1974	Alan Hydes/Denis Neale		1997	Alan Cooke/Desmond Douglas
1975	Andy Barden/Paul Day		1998	Alan Cooke/Desmond Douglas
1976	Desmond Douglas/Denis Neale		1999	Alex Perry/Gareth Herbert
1977	Desmond Douglas/Denis Neale		2000	Alex Perry/Gareth Herbert
1978	Andy Barden/Paul Day		2001	Alan Cooke/Bradley Billington
1979	Desmond Douglas/J. Walker		2002	Gareth Herbert/Andrew Baggaley
1980	Paul Day/Nick Jarvis		2003	Alex Perry/Terry Young
1981	Desmond Douglas/Paul Day		2004	Alan Cooke/Bradley Billington
1982	Desmond Douglas/Paul Day			

TABLE TENNIS

Women's Singles

1960	Diane Rowe	1983	Karen Witt
1961	Diane Rowe	1984	Alison Gordon
1962	Diane Rowe	1985	Lisa Bellinger
1963	Mary Shannon	1986	Joy Grundy
1964	Diane Rowe	1987	Fiona Elliot
1965	Mary Shannon	1988	Andrea Holt
1966	Mary (Shannon) Wright	1989	Lisa Lomas
1967	Mary Wright	1990	Fiona Elliot
1968	Mary Wright	1991	Andrea Holt
1969	J. Williams	1992	Alison Gordon
1970	Mary Wright	1993	Andrea Holt
1971	Karenza Matthews	1994	Lisa Lomas
1972	Karenza Matthews	1995	Andrea Holt
1973	Jill Hammersley	1996	Alison Broe
1974	Jill Hammersley	1997	Nicola Deaton
1975	Jill Hammersley	1998	Lisa Lomas
1976	Jill Hammersley	1999	Nicola Deaton
1977	Carole Knight	2000	Nicola Deaton
1978	Jill Hammersley	2001	Nicola Deaton
1979	Jill Hammersley	2002	Nicola Deaton
1980	Carole Knight	2003	Andrea Holt
1981	Jill Hammersley	2004	Andrea Holt
1982	Carole Knight		

Women's Doubles

1960	Diane Rowe/J. Rook	1983	Jill Hammersley/Karen Witt
1961	Elsie Carrington/J. McCree	1984	Alison Gordon/Mandy Sainsbury
1962	A. Mills/Diane Rowe	1985	Lisa Bellinger/Jackie Bellinger
1963	Diane Rowe/Mary Shannon	1986	Joy Grundy/J. Parker
1964	Diane Rowe/Mary Shannon	1987	Lisa Lomas/Jackie Bellinger
1965	Diane Rowe/Mary Shannon	1988	Fiona Elliot/Lisa Lomas
1966	K. Smith/Mary (Shannon) Wright	1989	Fiona Elliot/Lisa Lomas
1967	K. Smith/Mary Wright	1990	Fiona Elliot/Lisa Lomas
1968	J. Billington/Elsie Carrington	1991	Fiona Elliot/Lisa Lomas
1969	J. Heaps/Pauline Piddock	1992	Fiona Elliot/Lisa Lomas
1970	Karenza Matthews/Mary Wright	1993	K. Goodall/Andrea Holt
1971	Karenza Matthews/Jill Shirley	1994	Lisa Lomas/Fiona (Elliot) Mommessin
1972	Karenza Matthews/Jill (Shirley) Hammersley	1995	K. Goodall/Andrea Holt
1973	Linda Howard/Karenza Matthews	1996	Alison Broe/Nicola Deaton
1974	Linda Howard/Karenza Matthews	1997	Andrea Holt/Kubrat Owolabi
1975	Carole Knight/Karenza Matthews	1998	Lisa Lomas/Andrea Holt
1976	Jill Hammersley/Linda Howard	1999	Nicola Deaton/Helen Lower
1977	Jill Hammersley/Linda Howard	2000	Nicola Deaton/Helen Lower
1978	Jill Hammersley/Linda Howard	2001	Nicola Deaton/Helen Lower
1979	Jill Hammersley/Linda Howard	2002	Nicola Deaton/Helen Lower
1980	Carole Knight/A. Stevenson	2003	Nicola Deaton/Kubrat Owolabi
1981	Jill Hammersley/Linda Jarvis	2004	Helen Lower/Georgina Walker
1982	Carole Knight/A. Stevenson		

Mixed Doubles

1960	Johnny Leach/Diane Rowe	1975	N. Jarvis/Jill Hammersley
1961	M. Maclaren/N. Piper	1976	Desmond Douglas/Linda Howard
1962	Johnny Leach/Diane Rowe	1977	P. Day/M. Ludi
1963	B. Wright/Mary Shannon	1978	N. Eckersley/K. Witt
1964	I. Harrison/Diane Rowe	1979	Desmond Douglas/Linda Howard
1965	G.C. Barnes/Diane Rowe	1980	J. Hilton/Jill Hammersley
1966	B. Wright/M. Wright	1981	Desmond Douglas/L. Jarvis
1967	S Gibbs/M. Wright	1982	Desmond Douglas/L. Jarvis
1968	D. Neale/K. Smith	1983	N. Eckersley/J. Grundy
1969	D. Neale/K. Mathews	1984	S. Andrew/C. Moore
1970	D. Neale/M. Wright	1985	G. Sandley/A. Gordon
1971	G.C. Barnes/K. Mathews	1986	S. Andrew/F. Elliot
1972	D. Neale/K. Mathews	1987	S. Andrew/F. Elliot
1973	A. Hydes/Linda Howard	1988	S. Andrew/F. Elliot
1974	D. Neale/K. Mathews	1989	J. Holland/J. Billington

1990	S. Andrew/F. Elliot
1991	Chen Xinhua/Nicola Deaton
1992	S. Andrew/F. Elliot
1993	S. Andrew/F. Mommessin
1994	S. Andrew/F. Mommessin
1995	D. Holland/L. Radford
1996	Alan Cooke/Nicola Deaton
1997	Alex Perry/Andrea Holt

1998	Alan Cooke/Nicola Deaton
1999	Alex Perry/Nicola Deaton
2000	Alex Perry/H. Lower
2001	Alan Cooke/Nicola Deaton
2002	Alex Perry/H. Lower
2003	Alex Perry/H. Lower
2004	Alex Perry/H. Lower

TENPIN BOWLING

The sport of tenpin bowling has a long and fascinating history. Archaeological evidence points to bowling's existence around 7000 years ago, with the discovery in an Egyptian child's grave of bowling balls, pins and other implements for playing a game decidedly similar to modern tenpin. The date of this child's burial has been placed at 5200BC. Another discovery was of the ancient Polynesian game of 'ula maika', which also used pins and balls of stone. The stones were rolled at targets some 60ft (about 18m) away, a distance which is still one of the basic requirements in tenpin bowling. Bowling was practised by crown heads of state and clerics, including Henry VIII and Martin Luther. It has survived and grown into the world's second most played sport, with over 100 million participants annually.

Records in Sydney's Mitchell Library show that the game of tenpin bowling began in Australia in 1885 at the Washington Bowling Saloon in Ballarat, Victoria. The game spread throughout Australia with bowling centres appearing in many major population areas. With the advent of automatic pinsetting machinery the popularity of the game exploded. The first fully automatic centre opened in Hurstville, Sydney, in 1960.

On 9 September 1895 the American Bowling Congress (ABC) was founded in New York City, establishing rules and equipment standards, and began promoting bowling as a wholesome form of recreation and competition. The first ABC tournament was held in 1901. In 1916, the Women's International Bowling Congress (WIBC) was established. It has sponsored annual tournaments since 1917 and as well as regulating the sport, provides recognition of achievements in women's bowling. The popularity of bowling increased even more in the 1950s with the help of television and in 1958 the Professional Bowlers' Association (PBA) was founded. The PBA developed a star system and a tournament tour, and was followed in 1959 by the organisation of the Professional Women Bowlers' Association (it became known as the Ladies' Pro Bowlers Tour). In 1961 the British Tenpin Bowling Association (BTBA) was formed to act as the sport's governing body in Great Britain.

Modern tenpin bowling is an indoor sport in which a ball between 6lb (2.7kg) and 16lb (7.3kg) in weight is rolled down a lane approximately 42ins (107cm) wide by 60ft (18.2m) long from the foul line to the head pin, in an effort to knock down ten pins (nine until 1842) set in a triangular array at the other end of the lane. There are ten frames in a game, and each frame consists of two balls bowled unless a strike is recorded. Scoring is based on the number of pins knocked down, the highest possible score being 300.

Tenpin bowling was an exhibition sport at the 1988 Seoul Olympic Games. In 1992 and 1996, modern bowling facilities were installed in the athletes' villages at Barcelona and Atlanta, where champion bowlers conducted exhibitions, competed, and offered instructional sessions for the benefit of Olympic athletes.

In September 1998, the sport made its historic inaugural appearance at the Commonwealth Games, held in Malaysia. Eighteen Commonwealth countries in a state-of-the-art centre, Pyramid Bowl, in Kuala Lumpur, took part in the competition. Medals were awarded in five events: men's and women's singles, men's and women's doubles, and mixed doubles. Australia's team performed spectacularly, achieving the highest tenpin bowling medal tally in the Games with three gold, one silver and one bronze.

TRAMPOLINING

The word trampoline literally means 'stilts' (Italian: *trampolino*) and is suggestive of the heights that can be achieved on the 7ft × 14ft (2.13m × 4.27m) canvas beds as well as the great circus acrobat tradition. Although rebound tumbling has been in existence for centuries it was not until 1936 that an American gymnast and diver, George Nissen, developed a sprung canvas bed and began to give demonstrations of tumbling routines.

The first competitions were held in colleges and schools in the United States, the first US championships being held in 1954. Trampolining was included in the Pan-American Games for the first time in 1955. Its European pioneers were Kurt Baechler of Switzerland and Ted Blake of England. The first-ever televised British championships were held in 1958 and the inaugural World Championships were held in London in 1964. The following year saw the first meeting of prominent trampolinists in Frankfurt, Germany, to discuss the formation of an International Trampoline Federation. This was ratified later that year in Twickenham, England, and the Federation was formally recognised as the international governing body for the sport. Subsequently, the International Trampoline Federation has been merged with FIG – Fédération Internationale de Gymnastique, the international governing body of gymnastics. By 1969 the first European Championship was held in Paris and Paul Luxon of London was the winner at the age of 18.

A trampoline competition consists of one optional and one compulsory routine. Each routine is limited to ten moves (formerly eight contacts with the trampoline bed) although the warm-up bounces are not counted as moves but merely necessary to attain the required height. Competitors are scored on difficulty tariff, execution and form. The winners of the two routines often perform a further optional routine to decide the winner. In 2000, trampolining featured for the first time in the Olympic Games in Sydney and is the only sport to have its number of competitors increased for the Athens Games of 2004.

Olympic Medallists

Men's Individual

	Gold	Score	Silver	Score	Bronze	Score
2000	Aleksandr Moskalenko (RUS)	41.7	Ji Wallace (AUS)	39.3	Mathieu Turgeon (CAN)	39.1

Women's Individual

	Gold	Score	Silver	Score	Bronze	Score
2000	Irina Karavaeva (RUS)	38.9	Oksana Tsyhuleva (UKR)	37.7	Karen Cockburn (CAN)	37.4

World Champions

	Men's	Women's	Venue
1964	Danny Millman (USA)	Judy Willis Cline (USA)	London, Great Britain
1965	Gary Erwin (USA)	Judy Willis Cline (USA)	London, Great Britain
1966	Wayne Miller (USA)	Judy Willis Cline (USA)	Lafayette, Los Angeles, United States
1967	David Jacobs (USA)	Judy Willis Cline (USA)	London, Great Britain
1968	David Jacobs (USA)	Judy Willis Cline (USA)	Amersfoort, Netherlands
1970	Wayne Miller (USA)	Renee Ramson (USA)	Bern, Switzerland
1972	Paul Luxon (GBR)	Alexandra Nicholson (USA)	Stuttgart, West Germany
1974	Richard Tison (FRA)	Alexandra Nicholson (USA)	Johannesburg, South Africa
1976	Eugeni Janes (URS)	Svetlana Levina (URS)	Tulsa, Oklahoma, United States
	Richard Tison (FRA)		
1978	Eugeni Janes (URS)	Tatiana Anisimova (URS)	Newcastle, Australia
1980	Stewart Matthews (GBR)	Ruth Keller (SUI)	Brig, Switzerland
1982	Carl Furrer (GBR)	Ruth Keller (SUI)	Bozeman, Missouri, United States
1984	Lionel Pioline (FRA)	Susan Shotton (GBR)	Osaka, Japan
1986	Lionel Pioline (FRA)	Tatiana Lushina (URS)	Paris, France
1988	Vadim Krasnochapka (URS)	Rusudan Khoperia (URS)	Birmingham, Alabama, United States
1990	Alexander Moskalenko (RUS)	Elena Merkulova (RUS)	Essen, Germany
1992	Alexander Moskalenko (RUS)	Elena Merkulova (RUS)	Auckland, New Zealand
1994	Alexander Moskalenko (RUS)	Irina Karavaeva (RUS)	Porto, Portugal

Men's	Women's	Venue
1996	Dimitri Poliarush (BLR)	Tatiana Kovaleva (RUS)	Vancouver, Canada
1998	German Knytshev (RUS)	Irina Karavaeva (RUS)	Sydney, Australia
1999	Alexander Moskalenko (RUS)	Irina Karavaeva (RUS)	Sun City, South Africa
2001	Alexander Moskalenko (RUS)	Anna Dogonadze-Lilkendey (GER)	Odense, Denmark
2003	Henrik Stehik (GER)	Karen Cockburn (CAN)	Hannover, Germany

VOLLEYBALL

The game of volleyball (originally called 'Mintonette' as it was patterned after badminton) originated in the United States and is thought to have come about when William G. Morgan, an instructor at the Young Men's Christian Association (YMCA) in Holyoke, Massachusetts, decided to create a game which would require less physical contact than basketball. This was perhaps owing to the fact that the majority of his clients were middle-aged businessmen. Morgan's new game blended elements of basketball, baseball, badminton, tennis and handball.

In his original rules, the court was 25ft (7.6m) by 50ft (15.2m) and the net was 6ft 6ins (1.98m) high. In a bow to baseball, a match was made up of nine innings, with three serves for each team per inning. There was no limit to the number of players in a team. Later on, during one of the earliest demonstration games, it was observed that the ball was being 'volleyed back and forth over the net'. 'Volleyball' was thus deemed the most appropriate name for the sport.

The first game of volleyball was played at Springfield College on 7 July 1896 and, after the founding in 1947 of the sport's international governing body, the Fédération Internationale de Volleyball (FIVB), the first World Championships were held in Prague in 1949. By 1951 volleyball was played by over 50 million people each year in over 60 countries. The Pan-American Games went on to include volleyball in 1955. In 1957 the game achieved Olympic status when the International Olympic Committee (IOC) designated volleyball as an Olympic team sport, to be included in the 1964 Tokyo Olympic Games.

The 1960s saw new techniques added to the game including the soft spike (dink), forearm pass (bump), blocking across the net, and defensive diving and rolling. The Japanese volleyball used in the 1964 Olympics consisted of a rubber carcass with leather panelling. A similarly constructed ball is used in most modern competitions. Beach volleyball became an Olympic sport in the Atlanta Olympics of 1996.

Olympic Medallists

Men's

	Gold	Silver	Bronze
1964	Soviet Union	Czechoslovakia	Japan
1968	Soviet Union	Japan	Czechoslovakia
1972	Japan	German Democratic Republic	Soviet Union
1976	Poland	Soviet Union	Cuba
1980	Soviet Union	Bulgaria	Romania
1984	United States	Brazil	Italy
1988	United States	Soviet Union	Argentina
1992	Brazil	Netherlands	United States
1996	Netherlands	Italy	Yugoslavia
2000	Yugoslavia	Russia	Italy

Men's Beach Volleyball

	Gold	Silver	Bronze
1996	Charles 'Karch' Kiraly/ Kent Steffes (USA)	Michael Dodd/ Michael Whitmarsh (USA)	John Child/Mark Heese (CAN)
2000	Dan Blanton/ Eric Fonoimoana (USA)	José Marco de Melo/ Ricardo Santos (BRA)	Jörg Ahmann/ Axel Hager (GER)

Women's

	Gold	Silver	Bronze
1964	Japan	Soviet Union	Poland
1968	Soviet Union	Japan	Poland
1972	Soviet Union	Japan	North Korea
1976	Japan	Soviet Union	South Korea
1980	Soviet Union	German Democratic Republic	Bulgaria
1984	China	United States	Japan
1988	Soviet Union	Peru	China
1992	Cuba	CIS	United States
1996	Cuba	China	Brazil
2000	Cuba	Russia	Brazil

Women's Beach Volleyball

	Gold	Silver	Bronze
1996	Sandra Pires/ Jackie Silva (BRA)	Monica Rodrigues/ Adriana Samuel Ramos (BRA)	Natalie Cook/ Kerri-Ann Pottharst (AUS)
2000	Natalie Cook/ Kerri-Ann Pottharst (AUS)	Adriana Behar/ Shelda Bede (BRA)	Adriana Samuel Ramos/ Sandra Pires (BRA)

WATER POLO

There is little documentation about the origins of water polo. In the 1860s, and possibly before that, primitive games of 'water football' were played in rivers and lakes in Great Britain. However, it was not until 1870 that the London Swimming Association drew up official rules to govern the game. Originally it was thought that water polo would provide a new attraction for swimming galas. The term 'polo' comes from the vulcanised India rubber ball which was used in early games. In Hindi, the word 'pulu', mispronounced by the English, was the word for 'ball'. There is no historical connection between water polo and the game played on horses.

The first recorded description of 'aquatic football' concerned a match played in the open water, outside London on 13 July 1876. By 1879, keen observers of the game realised that if it were developed under proper conditions, it could prove of immense value as a pastime among swimmers.

Early games were generally exhibitions of brute strength and aquatic wrestling. Passing and dribbling were scarcely practised and only infrequently attempted. Games were fought on individual lines: players considered it their sole duty, without regard to position, to score goals. A goal was scored by placing the ball, with two hands, on the top end of the pool. A favourite trick of these early games was to place the small India rubber ball (which ranged from 5ins (12.7cm) to 9ins

(22.8cm) in diameter) inside the drawers, dive under the water and then 'appear' again as near the goal as possible. This mode of scoring had its disadvantages however, as the goalkeeper was permitted to stand on the pool deck and protect the goal. Should the forward come up too near the goal, he could be jumped on by the goalkeeper.

In the mid 1880s, the game was revolutionised by the introduction of the 'Trudgeon Stroke'. This new swimming technique enabled water polo to become a faster moving, more wide-open game. Rules, previously influenced by rugby, now allowed a style of play akin to soccer. Goals became cages of 10ft (3m) by 3ft (0.9m) and a goal could be scored by throwing the ball. Players could only be tackled when holding the ball, which could no longer be taken under water. A leather soccer ball replaced the small rubber ball.

Water polo is played by teams of seven active players and four substitutes. Each team wears either blue or white caps (except the goalkeeper who wears a red cap with a blue or white no. 1 on it). The other team members are numbered from 2 to 11. The minimum depth of the pool must be 1m. FINA (Fédération International de Natation Amateur) is the governing body responsible for water polo's administration.

Water polo was first included at the Olympics in 1900. In 2000 at Sydney, women's water polo became a new Olympic event.

Olympic Games

	Gold	Silver	Bronze
Men's			
1900	GreatBritain	Belgium	France
1904	United States	United States	United States
1908	Great Britain	Belgium	Sweden
1912	Great Britain	Sweden	Belgium
1914-18	not held		
1920	Great Britain	Belgium	Sweden
1924	France	Belgium	United States
1928	Germany	Hungary	France
1932	Hungary	Germany	United States
1936	Hungary	Germany	Belgium
1940-44	not held		
1948	Italy	Hungary	Netherlands
1952	Hungary	Yugoslavia	Italy
1956	Hungary	Yugoslavia	Soviet Union
1960	Italy	Soviet Union	Hungary
1964	Hungary	Yugoslavia	Soviet Union
1968	Yugoslavia	Soviet Union	Hungary
1972	Soviet Union	Hungary	United States
1976	Hungary	Italy	Netherlands
1980	Soviet Union	Yugoslavia	Hungary
1984	Yugoslavia	United States	West Germany
1988	Yugoslavia	United States	Soviet Union
1992	Italy	Spain	CIS
1996	Spain	Croatia	Italy
2000	Hungary	Russia	Yugoslavia
Women's			
2000	Australia	United States	Russia

WEIGHTLIFTING

The genealogy of lifting can be traced back to the beginning of recorded history where evidence of humankind's fascination with physical prowess can be found among numerous ancient writings. A 5000-year-old Chinese text tells of prospective soldiers having to pass lifting tests. Ancient Greek sculptures also depict lifting feats. The weights were generally stones, but these later gave way to dumb-bells. The word 'dumb-bells' comes from the practice of removing clappers from bells, rendering them soundless during lifting.

Lawrence Levy from England was the sport's first world champion in 1891, when the competition was held at the Café Monica, Piccadilly, London. The International Weightlifting Federation (IWF), the sport's governing body, was founded in 1905.

Weightlifting was included in the first modern Olympics, held in 1896. The sport did not appear in the 1900 Games, but returned in 1904, and has been a regular event since 1920. Three lifts were standard in 1932: the press (eliminated in 1972), the snatch, and the clean and jerk. In 1932, there were five weight classes; today there are eight weight classes for men and seven for women.

Women's weightlifting has been conducted at the World Championships since 1987 and was included for the first time in the 2000 Olympics in Sydney, Australia. Tara Nott, a US lifter in the 48kg class, was the first woman to earn an Olympic gold medal in weightlifting and the first US lifter for 40 years to win a gold medal in the sport.

In 1951, John Davis from the United States was the first weightlifter to lift over 180kg. He was world champion six times and won gold medals at the 1948 and 1952 Olympics. In 1954 Norbert Chemanski, also from the United States, broke the world record by lifting 190kg. At the Rome Olympics in 1960, Yuri Vlassov from the Soviet Union became the first man to lift more than 200kg, while Vasiliy Alekseyev, another Russian, increased the world record by 25kg during the 1970s. A giant of a man, 1.86m tall and weighing 162kg, he won Olympic gold at super heavyweight in 1972 and 1976 and was the strongest man in the world throughout that decade, also winning the world title eight times.

Aleksandr Kurlovich continued the Russian tradition in the over-110kg category when he won Olympic gold in Seoul (1988) and Barcelona (1992). His compatriot, Andrey Chemerkin, left his mark in the heavyweight category when he won the gold medal in Atlanta (1996), also winning six world titles.

Among the greatest weightlifters outside the heavyweight divisions are the Japanese brothers Yusiyuki and Yoshinobu Miyake, who prevailed in the under-60kg category throughout the 1960s; Mohamet Nasiri from Iran, under-56kg gold medallist in 1968 and world champion four times; Americans Charles Vintsi, who won Olympic gold in the same category in 1956 and 1960, and Stanley Stanchick who won the gold medal in 1948 and was five times world champion; Yurik Vardanian of the Soviet Union, who won the gold medal in 1980 and was seven times world champion, breaking 40 world records during his career; and Cuban Daniel Núñez, who won the gold medal in Moscow (1980) in the under-56kg category as well as world titles in 1977, 1978, 1980 and 1981. Louis Martin of Great Britain won world titles in the under-90k mid-heavyweight class in 1959, 1962, 1963 and 1965 although he never won Olympic gold.

But the best pound-for-pound weightlifter of all time, as proclaimed by the IWF, is Naim Süleymanoglu of Turkey. Süleymanoglu was born in 1967 in Bulgaria of ethnic Turkish parents. Standing 1.47m tall, the so-called 'pocket Hercules' quickly attracted attention for his weightlifting ability. He set his first adult world record when he was only 15 years old. During the period between 1982, when he first participated in an international weightlifting competition in the under-56kg division, and 1996, the year of the Atlanta Olympics, where he won his last gold medal, he was considered to be unbeatable. Süleymanoglu won three successive gold medals, in 1988, 1992 and 1996, and seven world championships, despite a two-year ban from international competition after his defection to Turkey in 1986. One of the greatest athletes at the 1984, 1985 and 1986 World Championships, he also collected 21 gold medals, three silver and one bronze at various European Championships.

Although it does not require the same degree of technical competence, powerlifting is a true test of pure strength. The sport is divided into three elements: bench press, squat, and dead lift. World championships are held in each division but the existence of so many different governing bodies in 2004 means that it is hard to discern who the real world beaters are.

Olympic Champions

Men's Bantamweight
(1948-92, under-56kg; 1996, under-59kg; 2000, under-56kg)

1948	Joseph Di Pietro (USA)	1976	Norair Nurikian (BUL)
1952	Ivan Udodov (URS)	1980	Daniel Núñez (CUB)
1956	Charles Vinci (USA)	1984	Wu Shude (CHN)
1960	Charles Vinci (USA)	1988	Oksen Mirzoyan (URS)
1964	Aleksey Vakhonin (URS)	1992	Chun Byung-Kwan (KOR)
1968	Mohammad Nasiri (IRN)	1996	Tang Ningsheng (CHN)
1972	Imre Földei (HUN)	2000	Halil Mutlu (TUR)

Men's Featherweight
(1920-62, under-60kg; 1996, under-64kg; 2000, under-62kg)

1920	François de Haes (BEL)	1968	Yoshinobu Miyake (JPN)
1924	Pierino Gabetti (ITA)	1972	Norair Nurikian (BUL)
1928	Franz Andrysek (AUT)	1976	Nikolay Kolesnikov (URS)
1932	Raymond Suvigny (FRA)	1980	Viktor Mazin (URS)
1936	Anthony Terlazzo (USA)	1984	Chen Weiqiang (CHN)
1948	Mahmoud Fayad (EGY)	1988	Naim Süleymanoglu (TUR)
1952	Rafael Chimiskyan (URS)	1992	Naim Süleymanoglu (TUR)
1956	Isaac Berger (USA)	1996	Naim Süleymanoglu (TUR)
1960	Yevgeniy Minayev (URS)	2000	Nikolay Peshalov (CRO)
1964	Yoshinobu Miyake (JPN)		

Men's Lightweight
(1920-92, under-67.5kg; 1996, under-70kg; 2000, under-69kg)

1920	Alfred Neuland (EST)	1964	Waldemar Baszanowski (POL)
1924	Edmund Décottignies (FRA)	1968	Waldemar Baszanowski (POL)
1928	Kurt Helbig (GER)	1972	Mukharbiy Kirzhinov (URS)
	Hans Haas (AUT)	1976	Pyotr Korol (URS)
1932	René Duverger (FRA)		Zbigniew Kaczmarek (POL)
1936	Anwar Mohammad Mesbah (EGY)	1980	Yanko Rusev (BUL)
	Robert Fein (AUT)	1984	Yao Jingyuan (CHN)
1948	Ibrahim Shams (EGY)	1988	Joachim Kunz (GDR)
1952	Tommy Kono (USA)	1992	Israil Militosyan (CIS)
1956	Igor Rybak (URS)	1996	Zhang Xugang (CHN)
1960	Viktor Bushuyev (URS)	2000	Galabin Boevski (BUL)

Men's Middleweight
(1920-92, under-75kg; 1996, under-76kg; 2000, under-77kg)

1920	Henri Gance (FRA)	1968	Viktor Kurentsov (URS)
1924	Carlo Galimberti (ITA)	1972	Yordan Bikov (BUL)
1928	Roger François (FRA)	1976	Yordan Mitkov (BUL)
1932	Rudolf Ismayr (GER)	1980	Assen Zlatev (BUL)
1936	Khadr El Touni (EGY)	1984	Karl-Heinz Radschinsky (FRG)
1948	Frank Spellman (USA)	1988	Borislav Gidikov (BUL)
1952	Peter George (USA)	1992	Fyodor Kassapu (CIS)
1956	Fyodor Bogdanovskiy (URS)	1996	Pablo Lara (CUB)
1960	Aleksandr Kurynov (URS)	2000	Zhan Xugang (CHN)
1964	Hans Zdrazila (TCH)		

WEIGHTLIFTING

Men's Light Heavyweight
(1920-92, under-82.5kg; 1996, under-83kg; 2000, under-85kg)

1920	Ernest Cadine (FRA)	1968	Boris Selitskiy (URS)
1924	Charles Rigoulot (FRA)	1972	Leif Jenssen (NOR)
1928	El Sayed Nosseir (EGY)	1976	Valeriy Shary (URS)
1932	Louis Hostin (FRA)	1980	Yurik Vardanyan (URS)
1936	Louis Hostin (FRA)	1984	Petre Becheru (ROM)
1948	Stanley Stanczyk (USA)	1988	Israil Arsamakov (URS)
1952	Trofim Lomakin (URS)	1992	Pyrros Dimas (GRE)
1956	Tommy Kono (USA)	1996	Pyrros Dimas (GRE)
1960	Ireneusz Palinski (POL)	2000	Pyrros Dimas (GRE)
1964	Rudolf Plukfelder (URS)		

Men's Middle Heavyweight
(1952-92, under-90kg; 1996, under-91kg; 2000, under-94kg)

1952	Norbert Schemansky (USA)	1980	Péter Baczakó (HUN)
1956	Arkadiy Vorobyov (URS)	1984	Nicu Vlad (ROM)
1960	Arkadiy Vorobyov (URS)	1988	Anatoliy Khrapaty (URS)
1964	Vladimir Golovanov (URS)	1992	Kakhi Kakhiachvili (CIS)
1968	Kaarlo Kangasniemi (FIN)	1996	Aleksey Petrov (RUS)
1972	Andon Nikolov (BUL)	2000	Akakios Kakhiashvilis (GRE)
1976	David Rigert (URS)		

Men's Heavyweight
(1920-48, over-82.5kg; 1952-68, over-90kg; 1972-92, under 110kg; 1996, under-108kg; 2000, under-105kg)

1920	Filipo Bottino (ITA)	1968	Leonid Zhabotinskiy (URS)
1924	Guiseppe Tonani (ITA)	1972	Jaan Talts (URS)
1928	Josef Strassberger (GER)	1976	Yuriy Zaitsev (URS)
1932	Jaroslav Skobla (TCH)	1980	Leonid Taranenko (URS)
1936	Josef Manger (AUT)	1984	Norberto Oberburger (ITA)
1948	John Davis (USA)	1988	Yuriy Zkaharevich (URS)
1952	John Davis (USA)	1992	Ronny Weller (GER)
1956	Paul Anderson (USA)	1996	Timur Taimazov (UKR)
1960	Yuriy Vlasov (URS)	2000	Hossein Tavakoli (IRI)
1964	Leonid Zhabotinskiy (URS)		

Men's Super Heavyweight
(1972-92, over-110kg; 1996, over-108kg; 2000, under-105kg)

1972	Vasiliy Alekseyev (URS)	1988	Aleksandr Kurlovich (URS)
1976	Vasiliy Alekseyev (URS)	1992	Aleksandr Kurlovich (CIS)
1980	Sultan Rakhmanov (URS)	1996	Audrey Chemerkin (RUS)
1984	Dean Lukin (AUS)	2000	Hossein Rezazadeh (IRI)

Discontinued Events

Men's Flyweight
(1972-92, under-52kg; 1996, under-54kg)

1972	Zygmunt Smalcerz (POL)	1988	Sevdalin Marinov (BUL)
1976	Aleksandr Voronin (URS)	1992	Ivan Ivanov (BUL)
1980	Kanybek Osmanaliev (URS)	1996	Halil Mutlu (TUR)
1984	Zeng Guoqiang (CHN)		

Men's Sub Heavyweight
(1980-92, under-100kg; 1996, under-99kg)

1980	Ota Zaremba (TCH)	1992	Viktor Tregubov (CIS)
1984	Rolf Milser (FRG)	1996	Akakios Kakhiashuilis (GRE)
1988	Pavel Kuznetsov (URS)		

Men's One-Hand Lift

1896	Launceston Elliot (GBR)
1900-04	not held
1906	Josef Steinbach (AUT)

Men's Two-Hand Lift

1896	Viggo Jensen (DEN)
1900	not held
1904	Periklis Kakousis (GRE)
1906	Dimitrios Tofalos (GRE)

Men's All-Round Dumb-bell

1904	Oscar Osthoff (USA)

Women's Flyweight
(under-48kg)

2000	Tara Nott (USA)

Women's Featherweight
(under-53kg)

2000	Yang Xia (CHN)

Women's Lightweight
(under-58kg)

2000	Soraya Jiménez (MEX)

Women's Middleweight
(under-63kg)

2000	Chen Xiaomin (CHN)

Women's Light Heavyweight
(under-69kg)

2000	Lin Weining (CHN)

Women's Heavyweight
(under-75kg)

2000	María Isabel Urrutia (COL)

Women's Super Heavyweight
(over-75kg)

2000	Ding Meiyuan (CHN)

WEIGHTLIFTING

WORLD'S STRONGEST MAN

The World's Strongest Man competition has been covered by BBC Television almost since its beginning. It is based on all aspects of strength and not just the lifting of weights, although most of the very best competitors have also been champion weightlifters. Geoff Capes of Great Britain, previously a shot-putter, ushered in a new breed of athlete who was not only very large but also very fit and very quick. The competitions have featured many great personalities over the years, from the bullish Bill Kazmaier to the extrovert John Pall Sigmarsson (sadly no longer with us) with his 'Viking' chant and, of course, the other great Icelander, Magnus Ver Magnusson. The 2003 champion, Mariusz Pudzianowski, showed outstanding aerobic abilities and strength that belied his relatively small frame.

Winners

1977	Bruce Wilhelm (USA)	1991	Magnus Ver Magnusson (ISL)
1978	Bruce Wilhelm (USA)	1992	Ted van Der Parre (NED)
1979	Don Reinhoudt (USA)	1993	Gary Taylor (GBR)
1980	Bill Kazmaier (USA)	1994	Magnus Ver Magnusson (ISL)
1981	Bill Kazmaier (USA)	1995	Magnus Ver Magnusson (ISL)
1982	Bill Kazmaier (USA)	1996	Magnus Ver Magnusson (ISL)
1983	Geoff Capes (GBR)	1997	Jouko Ahola (FIN)
1984	Jon Pall Sigmarsson (ISL)	1998	Magnus Samuelsson (SWE)
1985	Geoff Capes (GBR)	1999	Jouko Ahola (FIN)
1986	Jon Pall Sigmarsson (ISL)	2000	Janne Virtanen (FIN)
1987*	Jon Pall Sigmarsson (ISL)	2001	Sven Karlssen (NOR)
1988	Jon Pall Sigmarsson (ISL)	2002	Mariusz Pudzianowski (POL)
1989	Jamie Reeves (GBR)	2003	Mariusz Pudzianowski (POL)
1990	Jon Pall Sigmarsson (ISL)		

* Competition known as Pure Strength

WORLD SUPERSTARS

The World Superstars competition ran for six years on the BBC and made stars of athletes such as Canadian footballer Brian Budd, who treated the competition with the same professional approach as his own sport. Brian Hooper won the last of the international competitions, while the British *Superstars* series ran between 1973 and 1985 and was won by fine athletes such as Lynn Davies, Andy Ripley, John Conteh, David Hemery, Keith Fielding and the most famous of all, judo champion Brian Jacks, who set remarkable dip-bar records. The series also presented memorable spectacles such as the painful demise of Kevin Keegan on a bike. Austin Healey won a 2001 one-off special and the BBC revived the series in 2003, when athlete Duane Ladejo triumphed. The champions are listed below together with their original sport.

Winners

1977	Bob Seagren (USA) – pole vault		1983	Renaldo Nehemiah – hurdles
1978	Brian Budd (CAN) – football		1984	Tom Petranoff – javelin
1979	Brian Budd (CAN) – football		1985	Mark Gastineau – American football
1980	Brian Budd (CAN) – football		1986	Renaldo Nehemiah – hurdles
1981	Jody Sheckter (RSA) – motor racing		1987	Herschel Walker – American football
1982	Brian Hooper (GBR) – pole vault		1988	Herschel Walker – American football
			1989	Willie Gault – American football

The competition still takes place in the USA and US winners are as follows:

1973	Bob Seagren – pole vault		1990	Willie Gault – American football
1974	Kyle Rote jnr – football		1991	Kelly Gruber – baseball
1975	O.J. Simpson – American football		1992	Mike Powell – long jump
1976	Kyle Rote jnr – football		1993	Dave Johnson – decathlon
1977	Kyle Rote jnr – football		1994	Dave Johnson – decathlon
1978	Wayne Grimditch – water skiing		1998	Jason Sehorn – American football
1979	Greg Pruitt – American football		1999	Jason Sehorn – American football
1980	Charles White – American football		2000	Jason Sehorn – American football
1981	Renaldo Nehemiah – hurdles		2001	Hermann Maier – alpine skiing
1982	Renaldo Nehemiah – hurdles		2002	Bode Miller – alpine skiing
			2003	Jeremy Bloom – freestyle skiing

WRESTLING

Modern Olympic wrestling competition has two disciplines, freestyle and Graeco-Roman. Freestyle wrestling was on the first Olympic programme in 1896, with just two weight classes. It was dropped in 1900, but restored in 1904, and has been on the programme ever since.

Although the heavyweight competition at the 1896 Olympics was billed as Graeco-Roman wrestling, it was actually freestyle, since leg holds were allowed. True Graeco-Roman wrestling, in which holds below the waist are prohibited, was introduced to the Olympic Games in 1906.

From 1938 until 1980, medals were based on round-robin competition. The wrestler with the fewest penalty points in the final round won the gold medal. If two or more wrestlers had the same number of penalty points in the final round, standings were based on the number of penalty points in previous rounds. Wrestling weight limits have changed a number of times through the years. The limits shown in the Olympic results are those used at the Sydney Games in 2000.

Although not in Olympic competition, the modern sport of arm wrestling is a genuinely international sport. Based on a Native American game, it was usually called 'Indian wrestling' when practised by frontiersmen during the 19th century and by children in the 20th century.

Opponents are seated at a table, facing one another. They lock hands (usually the right hand, but there is also left-handed competition), with their elbows firmly planted on the flat surface, and each attempts to force the other's arm down to the table. In the United States the sport received a major boost from *Peanuts* cartoonist Charles Schulz in 1968. Schulz drew a series of comic strips in which the character of Snoopy was headed to Petaluma to try to win the arm wrestling championship. Largely because of that publicity, the championship was televised on ABC Television's *Wide World of Sports* in 1969 and became an annual event on the programme for 16 years. In Britain, Fred Trueman's sports programme *Indoor League* featured arm wrestling at the same time and this helped to make it a true international sport. The American Armwrestling Association, now the American Armsports Association (AAA), was organised by Bob O'Leary during the 1960s. In 2004 it has 56 member associations across the US. O'Leary was also largely responsible for the founding of the World Armsport Federation (WAF), with the United States, Canada, Brazil and India as the first four members. There are now more than 70 member countries. The WAF held its first World Championships in 1992 in Switzerland.

Graeco-Roman Wrestling: Olympic Champions

Light Flyweight
(under 48kg)

1972	Gheorghe Berceanu (ROM)		1988	Vincenzo Maenza (ITA)
1976	Aleksey Shumakov (URS)		1992	Oleg Kucherenko (CIS)
1980	Zaksylik Ushkempirov (URS)		1996	Sim Kwon-Ho (KOR)
1984	Vincenzo Maenza (ITA)			

Flyweight
(under 55kg)

1948	Pietro Lombardi (ITA)		1976	Vitaliy Konstantinov (URS)
1952	Boris Gurevich (URS)		1980	Vakhtang Blagidze (URS)
1956	Nikolay Solovyov (URS)		1984	Atsuji Miyahara (JPN)
1960	Dumitru Pirvulescu (ROM)		1988	Jon Rønningen (NOR)
1964	Tsutomu Hanahara (JPN)		1992	Jon Rønningen (NOR)
1968	Petar Kirov (BUL)		1996	Armen Nazaryan (ARM)
1972	Petar Kirov (BUL)		2000	Sim Kwon-Ho (KOR)

Bantamweight
(55-60kg)

1924	Eduard Pütsep (EST)		1968	János Varga (HUN)
1928	Kurt Leucht (GER)		1972	Rustem Kazakov (URS)
1932	Jakob Brendel (GER)		1976	Pertti Ukkola (FIN)
1936	Márton Lörincz (HUN)		1980	Shamil Serikov (URS)
1948	Kurt Pettersén (SWE)		1984	Pasquale Passarelli (FRG)
1952	Imre Hódos (HUN)		1988	András Sike (HUN)
1956	Konstantin Vyrupayev (URS)		1992	An Han-Bong (KOR)
1960	Oleg Karavayev (URS)		1996	Yuriy Melnichenko (KAZ)
1964	Masamitsu Ichiguchi (JPN)		2000	Armen Nazaryan (ARM)

Featherweight
(under 63kg)

1912	Kaarlo Koskelo (FIN)		1964	Imre Polyák (HUN)
1920	Oskar Friman (FIN)		1968	Roman Rurua (URS)
1924	Kaarlo 'Kalle' Anttila (FIN)		1972	Georgi Markov (BUL)
1928	Voldemar Väli (EST)		1976	Kazimierz Lipien (POL)
1932	Giovanni Gozzi (ITA)		1980	Stylianos Mygiakis (GRE)
1936	Yasar Erkan (TUR)		1984	Kim Weon-Kee (KOR)
1948	Mehmet Oktav (TUR)		1988	Kamandar Madzhidov (URS)
1952	Yakov Punkin (URS)		1992	Akif Pirim (TUR)
1956	Rauno Mäkinen (FIN)		1996	Wlodzimierz Zawadzki (POL)
1960	Müzahir Sille (TUR)		2000	Varteras Samourgachev (RUS)

Lightweight
(60-66kg)

1906	Rudolf Watzl (AUT)		1960	Avtandil Koridze (URS)
1908	Enrico Porro (ITA)		1964	Kazim Ayvaz (TUR)
1912	Eemeli Väre (FIN)		1968	Munji Mumemura (JPN)
1920	Eemeli Väre (FIN)		1972	Shamil Khisamutdinov (URS)
1924	Oskar Friman (FIN)		1976	Suren Nalbandyan (URS)
1928	Lajos Keresztes (HUN)		1980	Stefan Rusu (ROM)
1932	Erik Malmberg (SWE)		1984	Vlado Lisjak (YUG)
1936	Lauri Koskela (FIN)		1988	Levon Dzhulfalakyan (URS)
1948	Gustav Freij (SWE)		1992	Attila Repka (HUN)
1952	Shazam Safin (URS)		1996	Ryszard Wolny (POL)
1956	Kyösti Lehtonen (FIN)		2000	Filiberto Azcuy (CUB)

Welterweight
(66-74kg)

1928	Väinö Kokkinen (FIN)		1972	Vitezslav Mácha (TCH)
1932	Ivar Johansson (SWE)		1976	Anatoliy Bykov (URS)
1936	Rudolf Svedberg (SWE)		1980	Ferenc Kocsis (HUN)
1948	Gösta Andersson (SWE)		1984	Jouko Salomäky (FIN)
1952	Miklós Szilvási (HUN)		1988	Kim Young-Nam (KOR)
1956	Mithat Bayrak (TUR)		1992	Mnatsakan Iskandaryan (CIS)
1960	Mithat Bayrak (TUR)		1996	Filiberto Azcuy (CUB)
1964	Anatoliy Kolesov (URS)		2000	Mourat Kardanov (RUS)
1968	Rudolf Vesper (GDR)			

Middleweight
(74-84kg)

1906	Verner Weckman (FIN)		1960	Dimitar Dobrev (BUL)
1908	Frithiof Mårtensson (SWE)		1964	Branislav Simic (YUG)
1912	Claes Johanson (SWE)		1968	Lothar Metz (GDR)
1920	Carl Westergren (SWE)		1972	Csaba Hegedüs (HUN)
1924	Edvard Westerlund (FIN)		1976	Momir Petkovic (YUG)
1928	Ibrahim Mustapha (EGY)		1980	Gennadiy Korban (URS)
1932	Väinö Kokkinen (FIN)		1984	Ion Draica (ROM)
1936	Ivar Johansson (SWE)		1988	Mikhail Mamiashvili (URS)
1948	Axel Grönberg (SWE)		1992	Péter Farkas (HUN)
1952	Axel Grönberg (SWE)		1996	Hamza Yerlikaya (TUR)
1956	Givy Kartoziya (URS)		2000	Hamza Yerlikaya (TUR)

WRESTLING

Light Heavyweight
(84-96kg)

1908	Verner Weckman (FIN)	1960	Tevfik Kis (TUR)
1912	Alders Ahlgren (SWE)	1964	Boyan Radev (BUL)
	Ivar Böhling (FIN)	1968	Boyan Radev (BUL)
1920	Claes Johanson (SWE)	1972	Valeriy Rezantsev (URS)
1924	Carl Westergren (SWE)	1976	Valeriy Rezantsev (URS)
1928	not held	1980	Norbert Növényi (HUN)
1932	Rudolf Svensson (SWE)	1984	Steven Fraser (USA)
1936	Axel Cadier (SWE)	1988	Atanas Komchev (BUL)
1948	Karl-Erik Nilsson (SWE)	1992	Maik Bullmann (GER)
1952	Kaelpo Gröndahl (FIN)	1996	Vyacheslav Oloynik (UKR)
1956	Valentin Nikolayev (URS)	2000	Mikael Ljungberg (SWE)

Heavyweight
(under 100kg)

1896	Carl Schuhmann (GER)	1956	Anatoliy Parfenov (URS)
1900-04	not held	1960	Ivan Bogdan (URS)
1906	Søren Marius Jensen (DEN)	1964	István Kozma (HUN)
1908	Richárd Weisz (HUN)	1968	István Kozma (HUN)
1912	Yrjö Saarela (FIN)	1972	Nicolae Martinescu (ROM)
1920	Adolf Lindfors (FIN)	1976	Nikolay Balboshin (URS)
1924	Henri Deglane (FRA)	1980	Georgi Raikov (BUL)
1928	Rudolf Svensson (SWE)	1984	Vasile Andrei (ROM)
1932	Carl Westergren (SWE)	1988	Andrzej Wronski (POL)
1936	Kristjan Palusalu (EST)	1992	Héctor Milián (CUB)
1948	Ahmet Kireçci (TUR)	1996	Andrzej Wronski (POL)
1952	Johannes Kotkas (URS)	2000	Mikael Ljingberg (SWE)

Super Heavyweight
(96-120kg)

1972	Anatoliy Roshin (URS)	1988	Aleksandr Karelin (URS)
1976	Aleksandr Kolchinsky (URS)	1992	Aleksandr Karelin (CIS)
1980	Aleksandr Kolchinsky (URS)	1996	Aleksandr Karelin (RUS)
1984	Jeff Blatnick (USA)	2000	Rulon Gardner (USA)

All-Around

1906	Søren Marius Jensen (DEN)

Freestyle Wrestling: Olympic Champions

Light Flyweight
(under 48kg)

1896	Robert Curry (USA)	1984	Bobby Weaver (USA)
1900-68	not held	1988	Takashi Kobayashi (JPN)
1972	Roman Dmitryev (URS)	1992	Kim Il (PRK)
1976	Hasan Isayev (BUL)	1996	Kim Il (PRK)
1980	Claudio Pollio (ITA)		

Flyweight
(under 55kg)

1904	Robert Curry (USA)	1972	Kiyomi Kato (JPN)
1908-36	not held	1976	Yuji Takada (JPN)
1948	Lennart Viitala (FIN)	1980	Anatoliy Beloglazov (URS)
1952	Hasan Gemici (TUR)	1984	Šaban Trstena (YUG)
1956	Mirian Tsalkalamanidze (URS)	1988	Mitsuru Sato (JPN)
1960	Ahmet Bilek (TUR)	1992	Li Hak-Son (PRK)
1964	Yoshikatsu Yoshida (JPN)	1996	Valentin Yordanov (BUL)
1968	Shigeo Nakata (JPN)	2000	Namik Abdullayev (AZE)

Bantamweight
(55-60kg)

1904	George Mehnert (USA)		1964	Yojiro Uetake (JPN)
1906	not held		1968	Yojiro Uetake (JPN)
1908	George Mehnert (USA)		1972	Hideaki Yanagida (JPN)
1912-20	not held		1976	Vladimir Yumin (URS)
1924	Kustaa Pihlajamäki (FIN)		1980	Sergey Beloglazov (URS)
1928	Kaarlo Mäkinen (FIN)		1984	Hideaki Tomiyama (JPN)
1932	Robert Pearce (USA)		1988	Sergey Beloglazov (URS)
1936	Ödön Zombori (HUN)		1992	Alejandro Puerto (CUB)
1948	Nasuh Akar (TUR)		1996	Kendall Cross (USA)
1952	Shohachi Ishii (JPN)		2000	Alireza Dabir (IRI)
1956	Mustafa Dagistanli (TUR)			
1960	Terry McCann (USA)			

Featherweight
(under 63kg)

1904	Isador Niflot (USA)		1960	Mustafa Dagistanli (TUR)
1906	not held		1964	Osamu Watanabe (JPN)
1908	George Dole (USA)		1968	Masaaki Kaneko (JPN)
1912	not held		1972	Zagalav Abdulbekov (URS)
1920	Charles Ackerly (USA)		1976	Yang Jung-Mo (KOR)
1924	Robin Reed (USA)		1980	Magomedgasan Abushev (URS)
1928	Allie Morrison (USA)		1984	Randy Lewis (USA)
1932	Hermanni Pihlajamäki (FIN)		1988	John Smith (USA)
1936	Kustaa Pihlajamäki (FIN)		1992	John Smith (USA)
1948	Gazanfer Bilge (TUR)		1996	Tom Brands (USA)
1952	Bayram Sit (TUR)		2000	Daniel Igali (CAN)
1956	Shozo Sasahara (JPN)			

Lightweight
(60-66kg)

1904	Benjamin Bradshaw (USA)		1960	Shelby Wilson (USA)
1906	not held		1964	Enyu Vulchev (Dimov) (BUL)
1908	George de Relwyskow (GBR)		1968	Abdollah Movahed (IRN)
1912-20	not held		1972	Danny Gable (USA)
1920	Kaarlo 'Kalle' Anttila (FIN)		1976	Pavel Pinigin (URS)
1924	Russell Vis (USA)		1980	Saipulla Absaidov (URS)
1928	Osvald Käpp (EST)		1984	You In-Tak (KOR)
1932	Charles Pacôme (FRA)		1988	Arsen Fadzayev (URS)
1936	Károly Kárpáti (HUN)		1992	Arsen Fadzayev (CIS)
1948	Celal Atik (TUR)		1996	Vadim Bogiyev (RUS)
1952	Olle Anderberg (SWE)		2000	Mourad Oumakhnov (RUS)
1956	Imam-Ali Habibi (IRN)			

Welterweight

(66-74kg)

1904	Otto Roehm (USA)		1964	Ismail Ogan (TUR)
1906-20	not held		1968	Mahmut Atalay (TUR)
1924	Hermann Gehri (SUI)		1972	Wayne Wells (USA)
1928	Arvo Haavisto (FIN)		1976	Jiichiro Date (JPN)
1932	Jack van Bebber (USA)		1980	Valentin Angelov (BUL)
1936	Frank Lewis (USA)		1984	Dave Schultz (USA)
1948	Yasar Dogu (TUR)		1988	Kenny Monday (USA)
1952	Bill Smith (USA)		1992	Park Jang-Soon (KOR)
1956	Mitsuo Ikeda (JPN)		1996	Buvaysa Saytyev (RUS)
1960	Doug Blubaugh (USA)		2000	Brandon Slay (USA)

Middleweight
(74-84kg)

1908	Stanley Bacon (GBR)	1964	Prodan Gardzhev (BUL)
1912	not held	1968	Boris Gurevich (URS)
1920	Eino Leino (FIN)	1972	Levan Tediashvili (URS)
1924	Fritz Hagman (SUI)	1976	John Peterson (USA)
1928	Ernst Kyburz (SUI)	1980	Ismail Abilov (BUL)
1932	Ivar Johansson (SWE)	1984	Mark Schultz (USA)
1936	Emile Poilvé (FRA)	1988	Han Myung-Woo (KOR)
1948	Geln Brand (USA)	1992	Kevin Jackson (USA)
1952	David Tsimakuridze (URS)	1996	Khadzhimurad Mongomedor (RUS)
1956	Nikola Stancher (BUL)	2000	Adam Saitiev (RUS)
1960	Hasan Güngör (TUR)		

Light Heavyweight
(84-96kg)

1920	Anders Larsson (SWE)	1968	Ahmet Ayik (TUR)
1924	John Spellman (USA)	1972	Ben Peterson (USA)
1928	Thure Sjöstedt (SWE)	1976	Levan Tediashvili (URS)
1932	Peter Mehringer (USA)	1980	Sanasar Oganisyan (URS)
1936	Knut Fridell (SWE)	1984	Lou Banach (USA)
1948	Henry Wittenberg (USA)	1988	Makharbek Khadartsev (URS)
1952	Wiking Palm (SWE)	1992	Makharbek Khadartsev (CIS)
1956	Gholamreza Takhti (IRN)	1996	Rasoul Khadem (IRI)
1960	Ismet Atli (TUR)	2000	Saghid Mourtasaliyev (RUS)
1964	Aleksandr Medved (URS)		

Heavyweight
(under 100kg)

1904	Bernhuff Hansen (USA)	1956	Hamit Kaplan (TUR)
1906	not held	1960	Wilfried Dietrich (GER)
1908	George 'Con' O'Kelly (GBR)	1964	Aleksandr Ivanitsky (URS)
1912	not held	1968	Aleksandr Medved (URS)
1920	Robert Roth (SUI)	1972	Ivan Yargin (URS)
1924	Harry Steel (USA)	1976	Ivan Yargin (URS)
1928	Johan Richthoff (SWE)	1980	Ilya Mate (URS)
1932	Johan Richthoff (SWE)	1984	Lou Banach (USA)
1936	Kristjan Palusalu (EST)	1988	Vasile Puscasu (ROM)
1948	Gyula Bóbis (HUN)	1992	Leri Khabelov (CIS)
1952	Arsen Mekokishvili (URS)	1996	Kurt Angle (USA)

Super Heavyweight
(96-120kg)

1972	Aleksandr Medved (URS)	1988	David Gobezhishvili (URS)
1976	Soslan Andiyev (URS)	1992	Bruce Baumgartner (USA)
1980	Soslan Andiyev (URS)	1996	Mahmut Demir (TUR)
1984	Bruce Baumgartner (USA)	2000	David Moussoulbes (RUS)

Arm Wrestling: World Champions

Men's Right-handed

50kg
(2003, 52kg)

1992	Emile Gachet (SUI)		1999	Vyocheslav Dzoblayev (RUS)
1994	Roine Eklund (SWE)		2000	Dmitriy Bezkorovaini (UKR)
1995	Michel Clauet (CAN)		2001	Vadim Tagoyev (RUS)
1996	Temuri Lipartashvili (GEO)		2002	Dmitriy Bezkorovaini (UKR)
1997	Dmitriy Bezkorovaini (UKR)		2003	Fabio Manfrinato (BRA)
1998	Temuri Lipartashvili (GEO)			

55kg

1992	Vyacheslav Chivanin (RUS)		1998	Gurami Gigolashvili (GEO)
1993	Alan Berget (USA)		1999	Vladimir Bolotayev (RUS)
1994	Terzi Engin (TUR)		2000	Aleksander Sokolov (RUS)
1995	Totraz Tamayev (RUS)		2001	Gokhan Galisirisgi (TUR)
1996	Lorenzo Martinez (ESP)		2002	Michael Moore (USA)
1997	Gucha Gobosov (RUS)		2003	Hiroshi Kotera (JPN)
	Ivan Portela Giner (ESP)			

60kg
(2003, 57kg)

1992	Leslie Whims (USA)		1998	Engin Terzi (TUR)
1993	Joaquin Garrido-Laso (ESP)		1999	Valeriy Gusov (RUS)
1994	Georgi Khachidze (GEO)		2000	Totraz Tamayev (RUS)
1995	Joaquin Garrido-Laso (ESP)		2001	Vladimir Bolotayev (RUS)
1996	Georgi Khachidze (GEO)		2002	Topi Saaranlvoma (FIN)
1997	Taimuraz Tsakhilov (RUS)		2003	Akhmed Aliev (KAZ)

65kg
(2003, 63kg)

1992	Brian Shea (USA)		1998	Taimuraz Tsakhilov (RUS)
1993	Haydar Gildil (TUR)		1999	Taimuraz Tsakhilov (RUS)
1994	Tomas Chucherashvili (GEO)		2000	Engin Terzi (TUR)
1995	Igor Grushnikov (RUS)		2001	Ozgur Kizgin (TUR)
1996	Aslan Bitarov (RUS)		2002	Carlos Rodrigues (BRA)
1997	Igor Grushnikov (RUS)		2003	Vladimir Bolotayev (RUS)

70kg

1992	Telly Janing (USA)		1999	Aslan Bitarov (RUS)
1993	Chad Silvers (USA)		2000	Ivan Levitskiy (KAZ)
1994	Vepkhavia Samkharadze (GEO)		2001	Engin Terzi (TUR)
1995	Shamil Karazhayev (RUS)		2002	Ruslan Babayev (UKR)
1996	Vepkhavia Samkharadze (GEO)		2003	Hadzimurat Zoloev (RUS)
1998	Alex Mundgishvili (RUS)			

75kg
(2003, 78kg)

1992	Serge Usereau (CAN)		1998	Gildil Haydar (TUR)
1993	Andrew Rhodes (USA)		1999	Abdula Eldarov (RUS)
1994	Andreas Rundström (SWE)		2000	Andrew Rhodes (USA)
1995	Mayerbek Zolovyev (BLR)		2001	Taimuraz Tsakhilov (RUS)
1996	Mindia Petviashvili (GEO)		2002	Shamil Karazhayev (RUS)
1997	Vepkhavia Samkharadze (GEO)			

WRESTLING

80kg
(2003, 78kg)

1992	Andrew Rhodes (USA)		1998	Kurt Niyazi (TUR)
1993	Phil Stoppert (CAN)		1999	Yoshinobu Kanai (JPN)
1994	Djimgher Merabishvili (GEO)		2000	Kurt Niyazi (TUR)
1995	Kazbek Solovyev (RUS)		2001	Gennadiy Fardzinov (RUS)
1996	Kazbek Solovyev (RUS)		2002	Artjom Klimenko (RUS)
1997	Aslanbek Khugayev (RUS)		2003	Shamil Karazhayev (RUS)

85kg
(2003, 86kg)

1992	Nir Harel (ISR)		1999	Aslanbek Khugayev (RUS)
1993	Tony Senger (CAN)		2000	Thor Moiseyev (UKR)
1994	Jan Germanus (SVK)		2001	Neil Pickup (ENG)
1995	Anatoliy Sodtayev (RUS)		2002	Gennadiy Fardzinov (RUS)
1996	Anatoliy Sodtayev (RUS)		2003	Gennadiy Fardzinov (RUS)
1998	Aslanbek Khugayev (RUS)			

90kg
(2003, 95kg)

1992	Sharon Remez (ISR)		1998	Jan Germanus (SVK)
1993	Andrey Yurikov (RUS)		1999	Jan Germanus (SVK)
1994	Koba Todadze (GEO)		2000	Jan Germanus (SVK)
1995	Bill Brzenk (USA)		2001	Jan Germanus (SVK)
1996	Bill Brzenk (USA)		2002	Tara Iakin (UKR)
1997	Anatoliy Sodtayev (RUS)			

100kg
(2003, 95kg)

1992	Aleksandr Kusnezov (RUS)		1998	Ruslan Kokoyev (RUS)
1993	Jose Carlis Vidal (BRA)		1999	Jan Germanus (SVK)
1994	Aleksandr Kusnezov (RUS)		2000	Russul Chochayer (RUS)
1995	Ruslan Saryev (RUS)		2001	Russul Chochayer (RUS)
1996	David Chelidze (GEO)		2002	Jan Germanus (SVK)
1997	Erekle Gurchiani (GEO)		2003	Arsen Zoloyev (RUS)

110kg
(2003, 105kg)

1992	Emanuele Bruni (ITA)		1998	Erekle Gurchiani (GEO)
1993	Eli Sappiashvili (ISR)		1999	Ruslan Kokoyev (RUS)
1994	David Chelidze (GEO)		2000	Jerry Codorette (USA)
1995	Kurt Kvikstaad (NOR)		2001	Sergey Kodzasov (RUS)
1996	Jerry Cadorette (USA)		2002	Peter Gatzdarica (SVK)
1997	David Chelidze (GEO)		2003	Slavik Kochmazov (RUS)

Over-110kg
(2003, over-105kg)

1992	Zaur Ghodedze (GEO)		1998	Vakhtang Yavakhadze (GEO)
1993	Gary Goodridge (CAN)		1999	Alan Karayev (RUS)
1994	Zaur Ghodedze (GEO)		2000	Frantisek Zivny (CZE)
1995	Glauco Prior (BRA)		2001	Alan Karayev (RUS)
1996	Alan Karayev (RUS)		2002	Sergey Kodzasov (RUS)
1997	Alan Karayev (RUS)		2003	Alan Karayev (RUS)

Men's Left-handed

50kg
(2003, 52kg)

1993	David Bauer (USA)		1999	Fabio Manfrinato (BRA)
1994	Vladimir Lasarov (RUS)		2000	Dmitriy Bezkorovaini (UKR)
1995	Vladimir Lasarov (RUS)		2001	Vadim Togoyev (RUS)
1996	Dmitriy Bezkorovaini (UKR)		2002	Dmitriy Bezkorovaini (UKR)
1998	Bezko Rbvayniyi (UKR)		2003	Fabio Manfrinato (FRA)

55kg

1993   (blank)

2002   David Bauer (USA)

60kg
(2003, 57kg)

1993	Leslie Whims (USA)		1999	Totraz Tamayev (RUS)
1994	Georgi Kchachidze (GEO)		2000	Totraz Tamayev (RUS)
1995	Joaquin Garrido-Laso (ESP)		2001	Gocha Gobozov (RUS)
1996	Michael Clarke (USA)		2002	Ivan Portello (ESP)
1998	Totraz Tamayev (RUS)		2003	Chociev Ibragim (RUS)

65kg

2002   Pavel Sasonov (RUS)

70kg

1993	Michael Barrett (CAN)		1999	Bondo Khouboulov (RUS)
1994	Mairam Solovyev (RUS)		2000	Taimuraz Tsakhilov (RUS)
1995	Anatoliy Mayransayev (RUS)		2001	Engin Terzi (TUR)
1997	Shamil Karazhayev (RUS)		2002	Rustam Babayev (UKR)
1998	Bondo Khouboulov (RUS)		2003	Maxim Cherski (RUS)

75kg

2002   Cvetan Gaschewski (BUL)

80kg
(2003, 78kg)

1993	Bill Ballinger (USA)		1999	Soslan Kudziev (AZE)
1994	Kazbek Solovyev (RUS)		2000	Abdula Eldarov (RUS)
1995	Kazbek Solovyev (RUS)		2001	Aleksey Semerenko (UKR)
1996	Marat Asainov (KAZ)		2002	Alex Matskevich (BLR)
1998	Kazbek Solovyev (RUS)		2003	Shamil Karazhayev (RUS)

85kg

2002   Maksim Maksimov (RUS)

90kg
(2003, 86kg)

1993	Steve Morneau (CAN)		1999	Eduard Kramtsov (RUS)
1994	Koba Totadze (GEO)		2000	Aleksandr Ter (RUS)
1995	Marcio Barbosa (BRA)		2001	Jan Germanus (SVK)
1997	Marcia Barbosa (BRA)		2002	Slavic Rachmazov (RUS)
1998	Ivakin Taras (UKR)		2003	Vacheslav Muriev (RUS)

WRESTLING

100kg
(2003, 95kg)

1993	Jose Carlis Vidal (BRA)		1999	Zaurbek Bitayev (RUS)
1994	Mike Gould (CAN)		2000	Aleksandr Fugarov (KAZ)
1995	Ruslan Saryev (RUS)		2001	Rassul Chochayev (RUS)
1996	Vladimir Nikolski (BLR)		2002	Jan Germanus (SVK)
1998	Rassoul Chochayev (UKR)		2003	Tameryan Dzukayev (RUS)

110kg
(2003, 105kg)

1993	Garvin Lewis (CAN)		1999	Ruslan Kokoyev (RUS)
1994	Artur Khadonov (RUS)		2000	Don Victor (USA)
1995	Artur Khadonov (RUS)		2001	Ruslan Kokoyev (RUS)
1997	Mitch Cady (USA)		2002	Aleksey Semerenko (RUS)
1998	Erekle Gurchiani (GEO)		2003	Oleg Chegodayev (KAZ)

Over-110kg
(2003, over-105kg)

1993	Gary Goodridge (CAN)		2000	Frantizek Zivny (CZE)
1994	Cleve Dean (USA)		2001	Alan Karayev (RUS)
1995	Mayerbek Gioyev (RUS)		2002	Sergey Kodzasov (RUS)
1999	Mikel Gould (CAN)		2003	Sergey Kodzasov (RUS)

Women's Right-handed

45kg

1994	Stine Karlsen (NOR)		1999	Yelena Shubina (RUS)
1996	Tatyana Onufrieva (RUS)		2000	J. Merkulova (RUS)
1997	Nadezda Ryazanova (RUS)		2001	Maria Menendes (BRA)
1998	Maria Menendes (BRA)		2002	Martins Galquiria (BRA)

50kg
(2003, 49kg)

1992	Selene Belise (USA)		1998	Inga Kodzasova (RUS)
1993	Chrissy Baliko (USA)		1999	Caren Cooley (USA)
1994	Yelena Shubina (RUS)		2000	Marina Pavlova (RUS)
1995	Chrissi Baliko (USA)		2001	Nuran Pehlivan (TUR)
1996	Pia Forsstrom (FIN)		2002	Marina Pavlova (RUS)
1997	Chrissy Baliko (USA)		2003	Dzerasa Boloyeva (RUS)

55kg
(2003, 54kg)

1992	Shirley Isaac (CAN)		1998	Valina Bagayeva (RUS)
1993	Katherine Monbiot (GBR)		1999	Tatyana Istomina (RUS)
1994	Margie Cziria (USA)		2000	Lina Khamidulina (RUS)
1995	Margie Cziria (USA)		2001	Sandra Bumsaite (LTU)
1996	Tamara Kelly (CAN)		2002	Veronika Bonkova (RUS)
1997	Svetlana Yakimova (RUS)		2003	Luiza Gabueva (RUS)

60kg

1992	Dola Akanmu (GBR)		1998	Sandra Bumsaite (LTU)
1993	Barb Schlegel (CAN)		1999	Heidi Andersson (SWE)
1994	Oksana Odarenko (RUS)		2000	Heidi Andersson (SWE)
1995	Oksana Odarenko (RUS)		2001	Svetlana Yakmova (RUS)
1996	Barb Zalepa (CAN)		2002	Heidi Andersson (SWE)
1997	Alena Kondratova (BLR)		2003	Svetlana Yakmova (RUS)

65kg

2000	Elaine Pickup (GBR)		2002	Susan Owen (GBR)
2001	Irina Celadkay (RUS)		2003	Gabriela Vasconcelos (BRA)

70kg
(2003, 75kg)

1992	Anna Pettersson (SWE)		1998	Regina Enaldyeva (RUS)
1993	Cornelia Wüthrich (SUI)		1999	Ludmila Shestakova (RUS)
1994	Grace Ann Swift (USA)		2000	Regina Enaldyeva (RUS)
1995	Sharon Brandes (CAN)		2001	Christine Gfeller (SUI)
1996	Liama Janutiene (LTU)		2002	Barb Zalepa (CAN)
1997	Parela Tarja (FIN)		2003	Ekaterina Yaskevich (RUS)

80kg
(2003, 83kg)

1992	Maristella Avanzini (ITA)		1998	Albina Gusalova (RUS)
1993	Irina Turchinskaya (RUS)		1999	Margarita Smirnova (BLR)
1994	Vika Gabakova (RUS)		2000	Margarita Smirnova (BLR)
1995	Sylvie Dufresne (CAN)		2001	Albina Gusalova (RUS)
1996	Albina Gusalova (RUS)		2002	Dalia Medsiausyte (LTU)
1997	Albina Gusalova (RUS)		2003	Nicole Cisco (USA)

Over-80kg
(2003, over-83kg)

1992	Liane Dufresne (CAN)		1998	Lilia Khamidulina (RUS)
1993	Heitje van Arendenk (NED)		1999	Vika Gabakova (RUS)
1994	Liane Dufresne (CAN)		2000	Vika Gabakova (RUS)
1995	Vika Gabakova (RUS)		2001	Nurcihan Gonul (TUR)
1996	Vika Gabakova (RUS)		2002	Vika Gabakova (RUS)
1997	Vika Gabakova (RUS)		2003	Jocilene Bassanelli (FRA)

Women's Left-handed

50kg
(2003, 49kg)

1993	Chrissy Baliko (USA)		1999	Nadezhda Rezanova (RUS)
1994	E. Shubina (RUS)		2000	Marina Pavlova (RUS)
1995	Chrissy Baliko (USA)		2001	Yana Onishchenko (UKR)
1997	Erizhe Khamidulina (RUS)		2002	Marina Pavlova (RUS)
1998	Inga Kodzasova (RUS)		2003	Dzerasa Boloyeva (RUS)

55kg

2002	Fia Reisek (SWE)

60kg
(2003, 57kg)

1993	Dola Akanmu (GBR)		1999	Kathy Defeche (BEL)
1994	Margie Cziria (USA)		2000	Kathy Defeche (BEL)
1995	Alena Kondratova (BLR)		2001	Sandra Bumsaite (LTU)
1996	Alena Kondratova (BLR)		2002	Petra Spatz (GER)
1998	Sandra Bumsaite (LTU)		2003	Ekaterina Larina (RUS)

65kg

2002	Olga Fedotova (RUS)

70kg
(2003, 67kg)

1993	Cecilie Knutsen (NOR)	1999	Ludmila Shestakova (BLR)
1994	Tanila Pirkko (FIN)	2000	Regina Enaldyeva (RUS)
1995	Sharon Brandes (CAN)	2001	Gabriela Noskova (CZE)
1996	Ludmila Shestakova (BLR)	2002	Anastasia Lvova (RUS)
1997	Ludmila Shestakova (BLR)	2003	Gabriela Vasconcelos (BRA)

80kg
(2003, 75kg)

1993	Irina Turchinskaya (RUS)	2001	Egle Vaitkute (LTU)
1999	Natalia Chrustaleva (RUS)	2002	Dalia Medsiausyte (LTU)
2000	Margarita Smirnova (BLR)	2003	Ekaterina Yaskevich (RUS)

Over-80kg
(2003, over-83kg)

1992	Liane Dufresne (CAN)	1999	Vika Gabakova (RUS)
1993	Rose Jowsey (CAN)	2000	Vika Gabakova (RUS)
1994	Liane Dufresne (CAN)	2001	Oksana Arschayeva (RUS)
1995	Vika Gabakova (RUS)	2002	Vika Gabakova (RUS)
1997	Vika Gabakova (RUS)	2003	Karina Bozyeva (RUS)
1998	Lili Khamidulina (RUS)		

Miscellaneous

Sporting Terms

Sporting Trophies

Sporting Quotations

Sporting Record 2003

Obituaries of Sporting Persons 2003

Sporting Record 2004

Obituaries of Sporting Persons 2004

Olympic Games: British Gold Medallists

BBC Sports Personalities of the Year

Sporting Terms

acey-deucey	Horse racing	Riding style in the US whereby the left stirrup leather is longer than the right to maintain balance on left-hand tracks
acting half-back	Rugby league	Play from the attacking team in which a player (generally the *hooker*) picks up the ball immediately following a play-the-ball situation and passes it to a team-mate or makes an attacking run
adolph	Trampolining	Front somersault with a half twist
advantage	Rugby	When play is allowed by the referee to proceed to the benefit of a team which would have been awarded a penalty if play had stopped. Advantage allows a team to catch their opponents either *offside* or off guard, thus allowing them to gain more ground than if they had taken a *penalty*. It also allows a team to gain momentum in attack
air shot	Golf	Complete missing of the ball which constitutes a stroke (unless a *mulligan* is awarded)
albatross	Golf	Score of three under par on a single hole
amar	Kabaddi	A form of Kabaddi where if the player has been touched out he need not leave the court. The team that 'touched' him is awarded 1 point
antis	Kabaddi	The opposing player or players to the *raider*
appel	Fencing	Beating or stamping of the foot during a contest
apron	Golf	Grass cut short between the *fairway* and the approach to the green
arab spring	Gymnastics	Cartwheel with a quarter turn
arabesque	Figure skating	A sustained *edge*, usually curved, with the free foot extended to form a line or an upward curve with the body
assist	Basketball	Final pass given to the shooter of a basket
assist	Ice hockey	Individual point-scoring credit to the player who makes the final pass to the goalscorer
axel	Ice skating	One-and-a-half turn *jump* from the forward outside edge of one skate to the backward outside edge of the other (named after Norwegian skater Axel Paulser)
Ba(u)lk	Baseball	Illegal action whereby a pitcher feints a throw to base or a pitch
back alley	Badminton	The area at the back of the court
back bowl	Bowls	Wood deliberately played beyond the *jack* to ensure good position if the jack is later sprung or moved on in any way
backcourt	Basketball	Consists of the entire midcourt line and the rest of the court to include the opponent's basket and inbounds part of the backboard
backline	Rugby	Players who are not involved in the scrum. Wingers, centres, full-backs, five-eighths/standoffs and halfbacks/scrum halfs are included in the backline
backward pumping	Figure skating	Movement in which the skater glides on the outside edge of the inside foot, while pushing with the outside foot
bai-hou	Karate	White crane stance with one knee raised high
balestra	Fencing	Attack after an *appel*
bank shot	Bocce	A standard bocce court provides the facility to bank a shot off the sideboards. The use of this shot is advantageous when other balls are blocking a direct shot to the *pallino*
banzuki	Sumo wrestling	Title given to the list of rankings
barani	Trampolining	Three and a half front twisting somersault
barrier	Figure skating	The low wooden or plastic wall which marks the edge of the ice surface that surrounds the rink
basho	Sumo wrestling	The name of a sumo tournament
battery	Baseball	Originally a term for the *pitcher*; now incorporates both the pitcher and catcher
baulk	Billiards	Line from which a game begins
baulk line	Kabaddi	Line that runs down the centre of the court dividing the playing area into two
beamer	Cricket	Ball bowled higher than a full toss, often endangering the batsman
beanball	Baseball	Pitch aimed at the ear area of the batter, causing him to duck under the ball
bed	Trampolining	The sprung area from which jumps are performed
behind	Australian Rules	Awarded when the ball passes between the goal posts and the behind posts (scores 1 point)
behind line	Australian Rules	The white lines marked on the field of play between the goal posts and the behind posts
besom	Curling	Type of broom used to sweep the ice to gain more distance
bias	Bowls	Lateral force of the wood caused by its weighting, which creates an arc when played
bib	Netball	Tie-up over top on which player's position is labelled
bintsuke	Sumo wrestling	Hair oil used by all wrestlers to hold their hair in place while competing
birdie	Golf	Score of one under par on a single hole

blade	Figure skating	The metal runner on the boot with which the skater glides over the ice
blind side	Rugby	The side of the playing area between the *scrum* and touch line
blitz	American football	Defensive tactic in which players, other than linemen, are assigned specifically to make attacks on the *quarterback*
block	Basketball	Illegal personal contact that impedes the progress of an opponent who does not have the ball
block	Volleyball	Basic return at the net employed to counter an opponent's *spike*
blood-bin	Rugby league	When a player has an injury from which blood is openly flowing, the referee may instruct him to leave the pitch for treatment. The player is substituted temporarily but must return within ten minutes, otherwise the temporary substitution becomes a permanent one
board-check	Ice hockey	To deliberately push a player on to the barrier boards
body-check	Ice hockey	To throw oneself in front of an opponent to block his progress
bogey	Golf	Score of one over par on a single hole
bomb	American football	Long pass often used either at the start of play or as an offensive tactic if a team is behind towards the end of a game
bonk	Cycling	Tiredness caused by lack of food
bonspiel	Curling	An important tournament, usually consisting of several events
boom	Sailing	Long spar or pole hinged at one end, securing the bottom of a boat's sail
boot	Figure skating	The leather part of the skate that laces up and reaches up to the ankle
bosey/bosie	Cricket	Australian name for a *googly* (named after B.J.T. Bosanquet (1877-1936), an English cricketer)
Boston crab	Wrestling	Manoeuvre whereby one fighter sits on the back of the other with legs tucked under his or her arms
bouncer	Cricket	Ball bowled short and fast in order to cause batsman to take evasive action
bowling crease	Cricket	Line extended from the stumps sideways and 4ft (1.22m) behind the *popping crease*; the ball must be delivered between these two lines
brakeman	Bobsleigh	Person who operates the brakes in the sleigh
Brill Bend	High jump	Equivalent to the *Fosbury Flop*; named after Debbie Brill (CAN)
brush	Curling	Implement with which the ice is swept, thereby causing the stone to travel further
bunt	Baseball	To let the ball hit the bat without swinging at it in order to force a fielder away from the base and give the batter an opportunity to make first base or a third-base runner to reach home base during a *squeeze play*
burgee	Sailing	Ornamental flag used for identification of a team or club
butsukari-geiko	Sumo wrestling	The pushing technique used during the competition. Most common one used
button	Rowing	Moveable collar fitted to the shaft of the oar so that it does not slip through the rowlock
button	Skiing	One-person drag lift that uses a supporting disc instead of a bar
buttonhook	American football	Type of pass which requires the receiver to run straight downfield and then double back a few steps to receive it
bye	Cricket	*Extra* gained by batting side when the batsmen complete a run or the ball crosses the boundary after no contact with bat has taken place
bye	Figure skating	Allows a skater to compete in a higher level of competition without qualifying at a lower level. Term now has general usage in sport.
calx	Eton wall game	Area behind the goal line
caman	Shinty	Stick used for striking the ball
camel spin	Figure skating	One-foot spin performed with the body in one continuous line with the free leg extended behind so that both are parallel to the ice
cannon	Billiards	Shot causing the object ball to hit the opponent's ball and the red ball (scores 3 points)
capriole	Dressage	Movement in which the horse jumps straight upward with its forelegs drawn in, kicking back with its hind legs horizontal
carriage	Figure skating	Term used to describe the poise and the posture of a skater
carrot	Croquet	The part of a hoop that is beneath the ground
catch	Real tennis	Obsolete former name for the game
catch a crab	Rowing	To get an oar trapped underwater or to miss the water with a stroke
catenaccio	Association football	Defensive system employing a *sweeper*, first used in Italy (Italian 'bolt, lock')
centring	Figure skating	Technique of maintaining a spin over one point on the ice without travelling from that spot
change-foot spin	Figure skating	A spin where a change of foot is needed
charge-down	Rugby	Block by an opposition player of a kick using either the hands, arm or body, thus eliminating any significant territorial advantage from the kick
check	Figure skating	To stop the rotation of a spin or *jump* by extending the arms and free leg
checking	Ice hockey	Legal use of physical contact to gain control of the *puck*
chicane	Motor racing	A sharp double bend
chinaman	Cricket	Left-arm bowler's *googly* to a right-handed batsman

chistera	Pelota/Jai alai	Curved glove with a chestnut or ash frame (also called the cesta)
chon-mage	Sumo wrestling	The top-knot sumo wrestlers wear in their hair to keep it out of the way
chopper	Table tennis	Player who uses a chopping action to hit the ball
Christiania	Skiing	Turn in which the skis are kept in parallel, used for stopping short (also called a Christie)
Christmas tree	Drag racing	Starting system
Christmas tree	Football	4-3-2-1 formation
chui	Judo	Warning that incurs a penalty of 5 points
chukka	Polo	Each of the 7½-minute periods into which a game is divided. Also spelt 'chucker' or 'chukker'
claw grip	Bowls	The usual method of holding the wood. The thumb is high up on the side of the bowl so that it rests comfortably on the palm and fingers
clean	Figure skating	A programme with no errors; an unmarked skating surface
closed position	Figure skating	Otherwise known as the waltz. Partners face each other, one skating backwards and the other forwards
cody	Trampolining	One and a quarter back somersault to the feet, i.e. the move starts with a front face-down landing
compulsory dance	Figure skating	First of three parts in an *ice dancing* competition. Two compulsory dances must be selected out of a possible 21, with every competitor performing the same routine to the same music
compulsory figures	Figure skating	Include steps, edges and turns performed on specific points of the ice
continuation stroke	Croquet	Extra stroke allowed after taking croquet
conversion	Canadian football	Method of adding to the score after touchdown has been scored
conversion	Rugby	Method of adding to the score after a *try* has been scored by kicking the ball between the goal posts (scores 2 points)
corpse	Trampolining	Where back, seat and legs all hit the *bed* at the same time. Also known as a flatback, this position is almost impossible to get up to feet from
count	Bowls	The number of scoring shots that count to a player during an *end*
courbet/curvet	Dressage	A jump forward at the *levade*
cover	Cricket	Fielding position midway between the wicket and the boundary in which a good fielder may save a single
cover point	Cricket	Fielding position on the off side and nearer the batsman than the non-striker
cradle grip	Bowls	Grip used with the thumb lowered, thus enabling a slingshot delivery; useful when driving but less accurate for finesse play and drawing
cradling	Lacrosse	Method of keeping the ball attached to the netted stick by spinning the stick in the hand so that centrifugal force has an adhesive effect
crampon	Curling	Device formerly used to enable a steady delivery
crampon	Rock-climbing	Frame with 10 or 12 metal spikes, strapped to boots to give a firmer footing
cross buttock	Wrestling	Throw in which a wrestler throws an opponent head first over his or her hip
crosse	Lacrosse	Hooked and netted stick used for carrying the ball
crossovers	Figure skating	Movement from the outside edge of one skate to the inside edge of the other
crucifix	Gymnastics (rings)	Basic position with the arms held outstretched to the sides
crysal	Archery	A transverse crack in the belly of a wooden bow, caused by constant compression of the fibres
curveball	Baseball	Ball which deviates from a straight path because of the spin imparted by the *pitcher*. The ball is wedged between the thumb and forefinger, with the wrist cocked to the left. On release, the ball is snapped down and towards the pitcher's body, and the resulting pitch drops and curves to the left
cut line	Squash	Line above which a served ball must strike the wall
dan	Martial arts	Each of the numbered grades of the advanced level of proficiency in many martial arts
dead ball	Rugby	Any ball which goes out of play
death spiral	Figure skating	High-speed manoeuvre by a pair in which the woman is swung around by the man with her head almost on the ice
deshi	Sumo wrestling	An apprentice wrestler
diamond	Baseball	The area formed by the four bases within the infield
differential penalty	Rugby	*Penalty* in which the receiving team cannot opt to kick at goal
dig	Volleyball	Defensive motion of forcing the ball up from below net height with two hands to counter a *spike*
ditch	Bowls	The channel around the rink
dogleg	Golf	Hole that bends sharply to one side, so ensuring that a positional shot is required
dohyo	Sumo wrestling	The sumo ring. It is a hard clay platform which measures 18ft (5.49m) square with a height of 2ft (0.6m)
domestiques	Cycling	Team members of tour teams whose responsibility is to ensure a high position for their team leader

double eagle	Golf	Score of three under par on a particular hole (US term)
double foul	Basketball	Situation in which two opponents commit *personal* or *technical fouls* against each other at approximately the same time
double jump	Figure skating	*Jump* with two complete mid-air rotations
double play	Baseball	Defensive manoeuvre involving first and second basemen and shortstop, designed to put out two opponents in a single action
down	American football	Each of a fixed number of attempts to advance the ball 10yds
draft	American football	The pre-season signing by professional teams of players who have just completed their college careers
draw	American football	A run play where the *quarterback* takes a pass before handing off to the running back, who moves into the gap left by the defensive linemen
draw	Bowls	Basic shot whereby a wood is played as close to the *jack* as possible
drive	Bowls	Shot played at high speed which decreases the bias of the bowl; used in order to remove one or more scoring bowls or to spring the *jack*
drop-kick	Rugby	Kick made by dropping the ball and kicking it as it rebounds from the ground
drop-kick	Wrestling	Two-footed aerial kick to an opponent's chest or head
drop-line	Angling	Weighted line used when fishing near the bottom of a waterway
drop-out	Rugby	*Drop-kick* made from within the defending team's 22m line in order to restart play after the ball has become dead
dropped goal	Rugby	Goal scored with a *drop-kick* that propels the ball over the crossbar
dummy, sell a	Rugby	To successfully feign a pass
dunk	Basketball	To shoot a basket by jumping so that the hands are above the ring and the ball is dropped down through the *hoop*
eagle	American football	Defensive formation
eagle	Golf	Score of two under par on a single hole
edge	Figure skating	The sharp side of the blade that comes into contact with the ice
egg position	Skiing	Tucked position that ensures a fast glide
eight-second rule	Basketball	A team must not be in continuous possession of a ball in its *backcourt* for more than eight consecutive seconds
en garde	Fencing	Call to a fencer to adopt a defensive stance in readiness for an attack or bout
encroachment	American football	An offence for which the offending team is penalised 5yds
end	Bowls/Curling	Division of a match consisting of the delivery of all players' woods or stones. The next *end* is played from the other end of the rink
English	Pool	The use of *side* on the cue ball
Eskimo roll	Canoeing	A 360-degree roll starting and finishing above water but 180 degrees of which is under water
expedite	Table tennis	To bring a match to a conclusion after a series of long rallies or deuces by setting a limit to the number of strokes per point
extras	Cricket	Generic name for all types of *byes* and penalty runs scored other than by the batsman hitting the ball
face-off	Ice hockey	Method of starting or restarting play, when the referee drops the *puck* on to the ice between two opposing players
face-off	Lacrosse	Method of starting or restarting play
fairway	Golf	Part of a golf course between *tee* and green in which the grass is cut short to reward accuracy
false start	American football	Penalty given should any lineman move before the *snap*, after assuming a three-point stance. The offending team is penalised 5yds
false start	Athletics	Movement of an athlete before the gun is fired to start an event. Under current regulations a single false start by any athlete means that the entire field is cautioned and a further infringement means the automatic disqualification of the second offending athlete
fastball	Baseball	High-speed pitch held on the ends of the fingers and thumb. The ball leaves the fingers with a backward spin and will tend to rise slightly, although the sheer power of delivery will ensure a flatter trajectory than other types of pitch
field goal	American football	A field goal may be taken at any time and can either be a *place-kick* or *drop-kick*. To score, the ball must go between the two posts and over the crossbar (scores 3 points)
field goal	Basketball	A successful *field goal attempt* from the area on or inside the three-point field goal line counts 2 points. A successful *field goal attempt* from the area outside the three-point field goal line counts 3 points
field goal attempt	Basketball	Player's attempt to shoot the ball into the basket for a field goal.
fifty-metre arc	Australian Rules	Line drawn in the shape of an arc at each end of the field of play to show that the distance to the centre of the goal line is 50m
fifty-metre penalty	Australian Rules	The act of advancing by 50m towards the centre of the goal line, the position on the field of play where a player has been awarded a free-kick or a mark
fine leg	Cricket	Fielding position between wicket-keeper and square leg but deeper
fistmele	Archery	The breadth of a fist and extended thumb, used by an archer to check bracing height, i.e. the distance between bow and strings

flag	American football	A yellow flag is thrown on to the field by any official who sees what they interpret as a penalty
flanker	American football	The wide receiver on the tight end's side of the field. Flankers generally line up about a yard behind the line of *scrimmage*
flea-flicker	American football	Trick play where the *quarterback* tosses the ball to a back who fakes a run, then tosses the ball back to the quarterback for a surprise pass
flèche	Archery	Obsolete name for an arrow
flèche	Fencing	A running attack
flic-flac	Gymnastics	A simple back flip
flip jump	Figure skating	Toe *jump* in which the skater leaps back from a back outside edge while turning in mid-air to land on the back outside edge of the other foot
flying mare	Wrestling	Throw in which one wrestler throws the other over his or her back using the other's arm as a lever
flying spin	Figure skating	A spin that starts with a *jump*
flying wedge	American football	Tactic used at the start of a half whereby the kicker, instead of kicking off, nudges the ball with his toe and then picks it up and runs with it as his team-mates form a V-shaped wedge over which he leaps to gain yardage
40/20 rule	Rugby league	Introduced to reward excellence in kicking for touch. If a player kicks the ball and is within 40m of his own line, or if the ball bounces into touch within the 20m area of his opponents' half, then the side whose player kicked the ball will have head and feed at the resulting *scrum*. This virtually guarantees the team possession in an attacking position
forward pass	Rugby	A pass travelling in the direction of the opposition's *dead-ball* line, thus going to a player standing in front of the one with the ball
Fosbury Flop	High jump	Technique named after Dick Fosbury, whereby head and shoulders are thrown over the bar first and legs pulled back to ensure an economical clearance
free dance	Figure skating	The third and final phase of an *ice dancing* competition, making up half of the final score. Lasts 4mins and competitors are allowed their own music and routines
free skate	Figure skating	Otherwise known as the long programme. The second and last phase of singles and pairs competitions, worth two-thirds of the final score. For men and pairs the phase lasts 4½mins and for women's singles the phase lasts 4mins
free throw	Basketball	Free shot at basket due to an infringement by the opposition (scores 1 point)
frontcourt	Basketball	Consists of that part of the court between its endline and the nearer edge of the midcourt line, including the basket and inbounds part of the backboard
fukuro shinai	Kendo	Wooden sword often covered in cloth or leather
full nelson	Wrestling	Two-handed hold whereby the arms are placed under the arms of the opponent and interlocked behind his or her neck, immobilising the upper body
fullback	American football	The most important member of the backfield, whose main role is to block running plays and to protect the *quarterback* on pass plays
gaff	Sailing	Spar situated on the after side of a mast and supporting the head of a fore-and-aft sail
garryowen	Rugby	Alternative name for an *up and under*
genoa	Sailing	Large *jib* with a low foot
goalposts	American football	Bright yellow Y-shaped posts placed at the end of the endzone. Each upright is 30ft (9.14m) in height, and the horizontal crossbar is 10ft (3m) above the ground
gojo-ryu	Karate	Hard/soft technique
gokuhi	Martial arts	Techniques and 'secrets' of masters relayed to gifted students
googly	Cricket	Off-break ball bowled with an apparent leg-break action
goongi	Kabaddi	Form of kabaddi not played on a court, in which two players wrestle each other
goosewinged	Yachting	Square-rigged boats having the topsail spread for scudding under when the wind is strong, the bunt of the sail being hauled up to the yard
gridiron	American football	The field of play
ground the ball	Rugby	To place a ball on the ground with either one or both hands; to exert downwards pressure on a ball on the ground with either one's hand(s) or arm(s), covering the ball with the part of the body above the waist and below the neck
gully	Cricket	Fielding position a little wider than the *slips*
gybe	Sailing	Of a fore-and-aft sail or its boom, to swing from one side of a vessel to the other
gyoji	Sumo wrestling	The referee
hack	Curling	Notch made in the ice used to steady the foot when delivering a *stone*
hackamore	Horse racing	Bitless bridle with a hard oval noseband which allows pressure to be exerted on the nose by means of the reins attached just in front of a heavy counterbalancing knot

hail mary	American football	A long pass to the endzone where multiple wide receivers converge to increase the possibility of catching the pass. This play is often reserved for the end of a game
half nelson	Wrestling	Hold whereby the arm of the opponent is bent behind his or her back and pushed upwards
halfback	American football	Situated behind the *quarterback*, in the backfield. The halfback is usually the quickest member of the backfield and the featured running back
half-turn	Figure skating	Spin that starts with a *jump*
halyard	Sailing	Rope or tackle for raising or lowering a sail
hammer grip	Table tennis	Rarely used method of holding the bat whereby no fingers touch the face
hand-in	Squash	The server
hand-out	Squash	When a player loses a point on his service he becomes hand-out
handover	Rugby league	Surrender of the ball to the opposition; this usually takes place after the sixth tackle
hashmarks	American football	Marks 1yd (0.9m) and 70ft 9ins (21.56m) from each sideline, used to mark the spot where the next play will start
hataki-komi	Sumo wrestling	Slap-down technique
haute école	Dressage	Advanced training methods (French, lit. 'high school')
head	Bowls	The grouping of the woods around the *jack*
hecht	Gymnastics	Dismount of the asymmetric bars head and body first between bars
held ball	Basketball	Called when two opponents have one or two hands so firmly upon the ball that neither can gain possession
helicopter	Figure skating	Pairs lift in which the woman skates forwards and the man skates backwards. Once in the air, she is held parallel to the ice with her back arched and her legs held in a 'V' shape so that as the man turns, she looks like the blades of a helicopter
herringboning	Skiing	Method of climbing a slope by walking with the skis pointing outwards
high-sticking	Ice hockey	Illegal carrying of the stick above shoulder level
hikiwake	Kendo	A draw in a competitive match
hitting shot	Bocce	A smash shot, also referred to as a *spock* or *raffa* shot
hog line	Curling	Line behind which the *stone* must be delivered
hog's back	Equestrianism	Sharp-ridged natural mound, forming part of a jumping course
hollow	Figure skating	The *blade* of the skate with its concave groove between the two edges
honk	Cycling	To cycle out of the saddle
hooker	Rugby	Player in the front row of the *scrum* supported between the two *props* who attempts to hook ball back with his feet to be used by his team
hooking	Ice hockey	Illegal use of the blade of a stick to hook an opponent from behind
hoop	Basketball	The metal ring of the 'basket'
hoop	Croquet	Arch through which the ball must be driven
house	Curling	The round target area of concentric circles on the rink
hurley	Hurling	Curved stick with a broad blade, used to strike the ball
I-formation	American football	Offensive formation in which two backs line up directly behind the *quarterback*
ice dancing	Figure skating	Figure-skating phase in which the couple dance without turns and lifts
illegal assist	Basketball	A player may not assist himself to score by using the basket ring or backboard to lift, hold or raise himself, nor may he assist a team-mate to gain height in attempting to score
in touch	Rugby	Out of play
inside edge	Figure skating	The edge of the *blade* that corresponds to the inside of that particular foot
interchange area	Australian Rules	The area marked on the boundary line through which players enter and leave the field of play
interchange players	Australian Rules	The player(s) of a team who are not on the field of play but who are listed on the team sheet and available to replace a player on the field
ippon	Judo	Japanese, 'full point'; a match-winning throw or hold (scores 10 points in competition)
Irish whip	Wrestling	One-handed throw whereby the arm is whipped back and forth forcing a somersault in the air by the opponent
jack	Bowls	White ball which is the target for the woods
jamming	Baseball	Pitch aimed into the body of the batter, cramping his swing and thereby robbing him of power as the ball misses the sweet spot of his bat and often makes contact high up near the handle
jib	Sailing	Triangular staysail stretching from the outer end of the jib-boom to the fore-topmast
judogi	Judo	Judo suit
judoka	Judo	A judo practitioner, known as a player
jump	Figure skating	Entails the skater taking off from the ice and rotating in mid-air before landing
jump ball	Basketball	Method of putting the ball into play whereby the referee tosses it up between two opponents who try to tap it to a team-mate

MISCELLANEOUS

kachi-koshi	Sumo wrestling	A score of 8/7 or more. In this case the wrestler has more wins than losses
kanto-sho	Sumo wrestling	The fighting spirit prize
katame-waza	Judo	Basic hold
keikoku	Judo	Warning incurring a penalty of 7 points
ketaguri	Sumo wrestling	A leg sweep technique
kiggle-caggle	Curling	The rocking movement of the *stone* when it has not been thrown squarely on the ice
kimarite	Sumo wrestling	A general term for sumo technique
kinsa	Judo	Small advantage (scores 3 points)
kip	Gymnastics	Movement whereby the body is straightened from a piked position by pushing the hips forward and the legs back
kitty litter	Motorcycling	Slang term for gravel traps used to slow down bikes if they crash off the track
knock-back	Rugby	Loss of control of the ball by a player where the ball bounces backwards behind the player, thus allowing the game to continue
knock-on	Rugby	Loss of control of the ball by a player where the ball bounces in front of the player or moves forward. As a result a *scrum* or *handover* will be called
knuckleball	Baseball	Flat throw with no spin. The speed and method of delivery with the seam of the ball upwards, creating an uneven flow of air over its surface, makes it impossible for the batter to predict as it often deflects randomly through its flight
koka	Judo	Hold maintained between 10 and 20 seconds
komusubi	Sumo wrestling	A junior champion who is in the second class
kote-nage	Sumo wrestling	The forearm throw technique
kubi-nage	Sumo wrestling	The neck throw technique
kyokai	Sumo wrestling	Japan's official sumo wrestling association
kyu	Martial arts	Student
lateral twist jump	Figure skating	Used in *pairs* skating where the woman is tossed and spun in the air while parallel to the ice
laundry	Drag racing	Parachute employed to slow cars down
layback spin	Figure skating	One-foot spin where the body is bent backwards so that the trunk is parallel to the ice
lazy back	Trampolining	Three quarter back somersault (270°) starting from feet to land on front
leg side	Cricket	The side of the wicket on which the receiving batsman stands and towards which his back is turned; also called the *on side*
leg bye	Cricket	Run scored after the ball has touched any part of the batsman's body except the hand
levade	Dressage	Movement in which the horse raises and draws in its forelegs, standing balanced on its bent hind legs
lift	Figure skating	Manoeuvre in *pairs* skating where the man lifts the woman into the air above his head
line-out	Rugby	Method of throwing the ball back into play between two lines of opposing forwards after it has gone out of play over the touch line
lobe	Figure skating	Part of a circular figure
lock	Rugby	One of two forwards in the second row of the *scrum*
lona	Kabaddi	A bonus of 2 points awarded if the entire opposing team is out
long hop	Cricket	Ball bowled flat and short so as almost to bounce twice before reaching the batsman
loop	Figure skating	A jump with a mid-air rotation through 360 degrees
loose arm	Rugby	An offence by the *hooker* in which one of the player's arms is not packed into the *scrum* correctly
loose ball	Rugby	When the ball is in play and not held by any player
loose ball foul	Basketball	Illegal contact, after the ball is live, when team control does not exist
loose head	Rugby	Refers to the front-row forwards closest to the referee (hence the area from which the ball is fed into the *scrum*)
luff	Sailing	The edge of a fore-and-aft sail next to the mast or stay; it is also a term for obstructing the opposition attempting to pass on the windward side by sailing closer to the wind
lutz	Ice skating	*Jump* in which the skater takes off from the outside back edge of one skate and lands, after full rotation, on the outside back edge of the other
lutz jump	Figure skating	Toe *jump* in which the skater makes a clockwise turn from a backside edge
maegashira	Sumo wrestling	The senior wrestlers in the top division
maiden	Cricket	An over in which no runs have been scored
makunouchi	Sumo wrestling	The top division. There are 36 contenders in this class
mallet	Croquet	Striking implement used to manoeuvre the ball through the *hoops*
mark	Rugby	Point at which a *penalty*/free kick is awarded, or where a *scrum* is formed
mashie	Golf	Obsolete colloquial name for a no. 5 iron

mashie niblick	Golf	Obsolete colloquial name for a no. 7 iron
mat	Bowls	Black rubber pad from which the wood is played
mata	Judo	Break of a hold
maul	Rugby	Distinguished from a *ruck* by the ball being held off the ground
men	Kendo	Armour that covers the head and face
mid-off	Cricket	Fielding position on the off side, halfway to the boundary: in the case of a right-handed batsman, to the left of the bowler during his run-up
mid-on	Cricket	Fielding position on the leg side, halfway to the boundary: in the case of a right-handed batsman, to the right of the bowler during his run-up
mid-wicket	Cricket	Fielding position opposite a point halfway between the two sets of stumps
mirror skating	Figure skating	The precise mirroring of each other's movements by a pair of skaters
mohawk	Figure skating	Turn made by moving from the skating foot to the free foot
monkey climb	Wrestling	Move by which one wrestler climbs up and wraps himself around the other to immobilise him
mulligan	Golf	Free stroke awarded after a poor shot, usually an *air shot*
nage-waza	Judo	Collective name for the basic throwing techniques
niblick	Golf	Obsolete colloquial name for a sand wedge or sometimes a wedge
night watchman	Cricket	Lower-order batsman who comes in high up the order to protect a key player if a wicket is lost near close of play
no side	Rugby	Official name for the end of a game (no longer commonly used)
nock	Archery	Notch at the end of an arrow through which the bowstring is run
nocking point	Archery	Point of a bowstring to which the notch of an arrow is applied
non-flying spin	Figure skating	Spin that starts without a *jump*
Notre Dame shift	American football	Offensive manoeuvre whereby the backs move just before the *snap* of the ball from their *T-formation*
nutmeg	Association football	To play the ball between the legs of a player and run around him to collect it
O'Brien shift	Shot-put	Common technique of gliding across the circle, named after shot-putter Parry O'Brien
obstruction	Rugby	Offence of impeding an opponent who does not have the ball
offensive foul	Basketball	Illegal contact committed by an offensive player after the ball is live
offside	Ice hockey	Occurs either when an attacking player precedes the *puck* into the attacking zone, or when the puck travels untouched over more than one line. The position of a player is taken from his skate, not his stick
offside	Rugby	A player is offside and cannot participate in the current plays, despite being on the field, were they either in front of the referee when a tackle is made or in front of a kicker on their team
Oklahoma	American football	Defensive formation
on side	Cricket	Alternative name for the *leg side*
open position	Figure skating	Otherwise known as the foxtrot. The couple skate slightly away from each other
open side	Rugby	The opposite side to the *blind side*, i.e. the side furthest away from the touch line at a *scrum*
ordinal	Figure skating	A skater's ranking position within a group of other skaters
original dance	Figure skating	The second of three phases in an ice skating competition. It lasts for 2mins and competitors must perform an original choreographed programme to pre-set music
OT	American football	Overtime: additional 15-minute period played in event of score being tied. The first team to score in this period wins the game.
out of bounds	Australian Rules	Occurs when the ball passes completely over the boundary line or touches a behind post but before doing so, touches the ground or is touched by a player
out of bounds on full	Australian Rules	Occurs when the football, having been kicked, crosses the boundary line, or touches or passes over the behind post, without touching the ground within the field of play or being touched by a player
outside position	Figure skating	Also known as the tango. Two partners facing each other stand hip to hip with the man to the woman's right
oxer	Equestrianism	Brush fence with a guard rail on one side
ozeki	Sumo	The second rank after yokozuna (lit. 'great barrier')
pack	Rugby	The collection of forwards in a team which pack down into the *scrum*
painter	Yachting	Short rope or chain by which the shank of an anchor is held fast
pairs	Figure skating	Competition in which a man and a woman skate together as a couple
pallino	Bocce	The target ball in a game of bocce, also called the boccino
par	Golf	Benchmark score an expert would be expected to make on a hole (coined in the USA c.1900; used to compute handicaps)
parallel spin	Figure skating	An alternative name for the *sit spin*
parallelogram	Gaelic football	The playing area
parry	Fencing	To ward off an attack, especially with a counter
passage	Dressage	Cadenced high-stepping trot
pebble	Curling	Alternative name for a *stone*
penalty	Rugby	Advantage such as a chance to kick at goal, kick for touch, or (in rugby

		league) start a new set of six tackles from a tap, given to the opposing team when a player commits an offence
penalty shot	Ice hockey	A clear shot at goal, awarded if an attacking player is pulled down or tripped when in a scoring position. A goal cannot be scored from a rebound after a penalty shot
penholder grip	Table tennis	Method of holding the bat like a pencil, popularised by the Chinese; quick footwork is essential as backhands are impossible to play. Also known as the Eastern grip
penthouse	Real tennis	Sloping roof of the corridor or gallery running around three sides of the court
personal foul	Basketball	Illegal physical contact whereby a player holds, pushes, or impedes the progress of an opponent. The offending team is charged with a team foul if the illegal contact was caused by the defender. Up to three *free throws* may be awarded against the offending team
piaffe	Dressage	A trot in pace
pick	Basketball	Action of a player who, without causing contact, delays or prevents an opponent from reaching his desired position
pick-up	Sprinting	Second phase of a race after a start from blocks in which the head is raised and relaxation starts
pile-driver	Wrestling	Manoeuvre in which the opponent is upended and his head driven into the canvas
pinch-hitter	Baseball/Cricket	Technically limited player capable of hitting out forcefully; in cricket often used to open the innings
pirouette	Figure skating	A spin in *ice dancing*. Skaters must not make more than three rotations
piste	Fencing	The total area in which a fencing bout takes place
piste	Skiing	Course on which a skiing competition takes place
pitcher	Baseball	Specialist thrower of the ball towards the opposing batter
pivot	Basketball	Movement in which a player with the ball steps once or more in any direction with the same foot while the other foot is kept at its point of contact with the floor
pivot	Figure skating	A turn around the toe pick of one skate while the other traces a circle on the ice
place-kick	Rugby	A kick from either a *tee* or sand mound
planche	Gymnastics	Support position from where the body is horizontal and facing downwards. It is supported from straight arms above the apparatus
plastron	Fencing	Padded, leather-covered breastplate
play the ball	Rugby league	The act of bringing the ball into play after a tackle has been completed by the team with the ball
point	Cricket	Off side fielding position wide of *gully*
pop	Figure skating	To cut short the number of pre-planned rotations of a *jump* by landing early
popping crease	Cricket	Line 4ft (1.22m) in front of and parallel to the wicket within which the batsman must remain unless the ball is dead or a run is being taken
power play	Ice hockey	Sustained attack by one team, usually when the opposition is one or more men short
press	Basketball	Defensive technique of harassing players into hurried play
prop	Rugby	One of the two forwards in the front row of the *scrum* who support the *hooker*
puck	Ice hockey	Flat rubber disc used in place of a ball
puissance	Show jumping	Event that entails the jumping of a single high fence in a rapid movement
pull through	Figure skating	Manoeuvre whereby the man pulls his partner through his position to the opposing side in a rapid movement
punt	American football	Kick used by the offensive team to relinquish possession of the ball if it has not gained the yardage required for a first *down*. The kick is performed by the punter, who is a speciality player
punt	Rugby	A ball dropped from the hand(s) of a player and kicked before it hits the ground
put out	Baseball	To cause a batter or base runner to be out
quad	Figure skating	Jump that has four revolutions
quarterback	American football	Player stationed behind the centre who directs a team's attacking play
rack	Pool	Implement used for setting the red balls at the start of a frame (also the name used for an individual frame)
raffa	Bocce	Also known as a *hitting shot* or *spock*, a raffa is thrown after taking a few running steps before releasing the ball prior to crossing the hitting foul line
raider	Kabaddi	Name given to the player who enters the court to try and touch the opposing players and tag them out
randolph (randi)	Trampolining	Two and a half twisting front somersault
repêchage	Rowing	A second chance for the best of the losing rowers in eliminating heats to progress to a final
return crease	Cricket	The lines on either side of the wicket at right angles to the *bowling crease*

reverse lasso	Figure skating	*Pairs* lift in which the woman begins the lift while facing backward
reversed killian	Figure skating	Dance manoeuvre in which the woman stands on the left side of the man
reversed tango	Figure skating	Configuration in which the man stands to the woman's left. Also called the reverse outside position
riposte	Fencing	Lunge or quick thrust after a *parry*
rocker	Figure skating	The curve from heel to toe on the *blade*. Also known as the rock of the blade
rocker	Ice skating	Skate with a curved blade
roquet	Croquet	To strike another player's ball with one's own
rover	American football	Defensive linebacker assigned to move about in anticipation of opponents' plays
rover	Archery	Target chosen at random and at an undetermined range (also a mark for long-distance shooting)
rover	Australian Rules	Player forming part of the *ruck*
rover	Croquet	Ball that has passed through all the *hoops* but not pegged out (also a player whose ball has done this)
ruck	Rugby	Occurs when progress of the ball is checked and two or more players struggle to gain possession. Distinguished from a *maul* by the ball being on the ground and legally playable only with the feet
rudolph (rudy)	Trampolining	Front somersault with one and a half twists
run a hoop	Croquet	A ball runs a *hoop* when it passes right through each hoop in its correct order in one or more strokes. A point is scored whether the ball is struck directly with the *mallet* or with another ball
rush	Ice hockey	Sudden attack on goal, often from a defensive position
Russian split	Figure skating	*Jump* that begins in the sitting position with the legs spread wide and the knees straight, with the toes pointed and the hands holding the ankles
salchow	Ice skating	Full-turn *jump* from the inside back edge of one skate to the outside back edge of the other
schuss	Skiing	The starting gate or housing
scissors	High jump	Training technique of clearing the bar with legs only and without rotating the hips
scissors	Rugby	Change of direction of an attack by a player running diagonally opposite to the line of attacking play when receiving the ball
screen	Basketball	see *pick*
screwball	Baseball	Thrown like a *curveball* except that the wrist action and spin are reversed, moving away from the pitcher's body. The ball breaks downwards and to the right
scrimmage	American football	Phase of play, beginning with the *snap* and ending when the ball becomes dead, in which offence and defence face each other
scrum(mage)	Rugby	Formation by six (rugby league) or eight (rugby union) forwards of each side into a pushing mass in three ranks for purpose of gaining possession of the ball with the feet
serpentine	Dressage	Series of half-circles performed alternately to the right and left
shadow skating	Figure skating	A *pairs* partnership who dance in unison without actual physical contact
shido	Judo	Judge's warning with no point deduction
shime-waza	Judo	Strangulation technique
shinai	Kendo	Sword made up of four bamboo sticks bound together
shobu-ari	Kendo	The end of a match
shopping, go	Billiards	To pot one's opponent's ball
short leg	Cricket	Fielding position close to the batsman and on the *leg side*
shotgun	American football	Offensive formation
shroud	Sailing	The set of ropes supporting the mainsail
shukokai	Karate	A karate school
shuriken	Karate	One of various designs of throwing weapon, often eight-sided and sharp
shut-out	Ice hockey	The goalkeeper not conceding a goal in a match or period
side	Billiards	Spin imparted to the cue ball by striking it off centre in order to make an angle in positional play
silly mid-off	Cricket	Close fielding position short of *mid-off*
silly mid-on	Cricket	Close fielding position short of *mid-on*
sin-bin	Ice hockey	Common term referring to the penalty box in which suspension is served during a match
sin-bin	Rugby league	Punishment incurred when a player commits an offence deemed to be more serious than an ordinary foul; the referee shows the offending player a yellow card and the player must leave the field for a period of 10 minutes
sit spin	Figure skating	Spin performed on one foot. The skater sinks down to a sitting position with free leg extending forward
sleeper	Wrestling	Application of pressure on the nerves in the neck which can cause loss of consciousness

slider	Baseball	Pitch thrown like an American football pass, with the wrist cocked at a 90-degree angle and curved slightly down and to the left. It is thrown harder than a *curveball*, and consequently breaks less and closer to the batter
sliothar	Hurling	Ball (Gaelic)
slip	Cricket	Fielding position next to the wicket-keeper
snap	American football	To put the ball into play on the ground by a quick backward movement
soigneur	Cycling	General assistant to a team, responsible for its physical and mental preparation
solo lift	Figure skating	Manoeuvre in which the woman holds one position when in the air
soop	Curling	To assist the progress of a curling *stone* by sweeping the ice in front of it
southpaw	Boxing	Boxer who leads with the right hand
spare	Ten pin bowling	Second shot used to knock down any pins standing after a player's first bowl has been delivered
spider	Billiards	Implement used when bridging directly over a ball
spider	Darts	The wire frame around the board
spike	Volleyball	One-handed attacking shot from above and across the net. Spike serves are common at high levels of the game
spin	Cycling	US term for twiddle, now commonly used in the UK
spinnaker	Sailing	Large triangular sail carried forward of or opposite the mainsail
spinner	Angling	Real or artificial bait or lure fixed so as to revolve when pulled through the water
spiral	Figure skating	A glide on one leg in either direction, the skater extending the free leg behind them
split	Tenpin bowling	Attempt to knock down pins which are wide apart
split	Weightlifting	Action of thrusting forward with one foot and backward with the other to aid leverage during a lift
split T	American football	Offensive formation
split twist lift	Figure skating	Manoeuvre in *pairs* dancing in which the woman's legs are split during her spin into the air
spock	Bocce	A *hitting shot* whereby the bocce ball is hurled with an underhand movement in a ferocious manner in order to disrupt an undesirable ball formation
spoon	Angling	Artificial bait in the shape of the bowl of a spoon, used in spinning or *trolling*
spoon	Golf	Any club with a slightly concave wooden head but often specifically a 3 wood
spreadeagle	Figure skating	Two-footed glide with the skater's heels turned inwards together and the toes pointing out
spring the jack	Bowls	To play a wood so that it hits another bowl that is touching the *jack* and thus moves the jack away
squeeze play	Baseball	Tactical play used by the offensive team to get the man on third base safely home. The preferred method is for the batter to *bunt* the ball about 25ft (7.6m) down the third-base line and gamble that the runner beats the throw of the third-baseman. This play is risky as the runner must set off as the pitch is made; if the batter misses the bunt then the runner can be left stranded mid-base
star lift	Figure skating	*Pairs* lift in which the man holds his partner hand-to-hand with one arm and hand-to-hip with the other. The woman holds a scissor position while parallel to the ice
steal bases	Baseball	To reach a base without the striker hitting the ball
stick-handling	Ice hockey	Retention of possession of the *puck* while in motion, by flicking it alternately with each side of the blade
stone	Curling	The heavy 'top' with a handle which is aimed at the *house*
straddle	High jump	Similar to the *western roll* but the straddle jumper keeps their legs wide apart and body straight
strike	Baseball	Complete miss of the ball
strike	Tenpin bowling	To knock down all the pins with one ball by the bowler
stroking	Figure skating	Gliding strides over the ice, alternate feet propelling the skater
suicide squad	American football	Specialist players who deliberately block attacks
sulky	Harness racing	Vehicle used in harness racing
sweeper	Association football	A player who plays just behind the central defenders and is used as a spare man. A good sweeper can read the game well, is a good passer of the ball, and sees opportunities to create attacking play as well as providing an extra defensive option
sweeper	Curling	Team member who sweeps the ice to gain distance for the *stone*
sweet spot	Baseball/Golf	The point on the bat or club where, if timed correctly, maximum power will be attained when striking the ball
sweet spot	Figure skating	The place on the *blade* of the skate where a skater balances when spinning
switch-hitting	Boxing	Changing from orthodox to *southpaw* during a bout
swizzle	Figure skating	A two-footed movement that takes the skater backwards

tack	Equestrianism	A horse's riding harness, consisting of saddle, bridle and bit
tack	Sailing	Zigzag movement of a boat
tagged out	Baseball	Self explanatory term for a situation where a runner fails to touch base before being tagged
take croquet	Croquet	Following a *roquet* a player may place their own ball in contact with another ball where it comes to rest and then strike their own ball so that the other ball moves
tame-shiwari	Karate	The practice of board-breaking techniques
tariff	Diving/Trampolining	The difficulty rating of a dive or routine. The higher the tariff, the harder the dive or routine but consequently the greater the potential for high scores
taw	Marbles	The line from which a player shoots; also another name for the game itself and formerly a name for a large marble
technical foul	Basketball	Penalty for unsportsmanlike conduct or violations by team members on the floor or seated on the bench. It may also be awarded for illegal contact which occurs with an opponent before the ball becomes live
tee	Curling	The centre point of the *house*
tee	Golf	Small peg on which to rest the ball when driving; also the name for the area where the initial drive is made
T-formation	American football	Offensive formation
third man	Cricket	Fielding position close to the boundary behind the *slip* area
three-second rule	Basketball	An offensive player must not stand for more than three seconds in the *free throw* lane when the ball is in his team's control
tice	Cricket	Obsolete term for a *yorker*
tice	Croquet	Stroke tempting an opponent to aim at one's ball
tiger country	Golf	Deep rough, usually on high ground
timeouts	Basketball	Agreed break in play during a game. The regulations governing timeouts allow many variations, depending on conditions such as whether the game is televised
tin	Squash	Lower line on the back wall above which all shots must be played
tkachyov	Gymnastics	One-handed 360-degree swing on horizontal (high) bar
tolley	Marbles	Portmanteau word from '*taw*' and '*alley*'
touchdown	American football	Equivalent of a *try* in rugby, except that the ball need not touch the ground when carried or received inside the opponents' endzone (scores 6 points)
touchdown	Rugby league	Grounding of the ball by a defending player in his own in-goal/try region; results in a line *drop-out*
touché	Fencing	Acknowledgment that a scoring hit has been made in a bout
toucher	Bowls	Wood that has touched the *jack* in its travels. Such a wood is marked with chalk until the end is completed and will remain live even if it ends up in the *ditch*, as long as it stays within the width of the rink
trace	Figure skating	The marking out of the outline of a figure on the ice with the *blade* of the skate
tram lines	Tennis	The outer lines at each side of the court; these become part of the court in doubles matches
trapeze	Sailing	Sliding support used for outboard balancing on a yacht
travel	Basketball	To run with the ball without bouncing it
triangle	Angling	Set of three hooks fastened together so that the barbs form a triangle
triangle	Snooker	Implement used for setting the red balls at the start of a frame
triple jump	Figure skating	Three complete turns made in the air
troll	Angling	To fish by drawing bait along in the water
try	Rugby	A score made by touching the ball down in the opponents' goal area, behind their goal line
T-stop	Figure skating	To place the free foot at a right angle behind the skating foot so that it scrapes along the ice, bringing the skater to a stop
tsuba	Kendo	The guard of the sword
tsuka	Kendo	The handle of the sword
tsukahara	Gymnastics	Vault consisting of a quarter or half turn on to the pommel horse followed by one and a half somersaults off
turkey	Tenpin bowling	The gaining of three strikes in successive bowls
turnover	Basketball	Loss of possession of the ball by a team before any member has been able to try for a basket
24-second clock	Basketball	A team must attempt a *field goal* within 24 seconds after gaining possession of the ball
twiddle	Cycling	To pedal fast in a gear with no pressure asserted
two-minute period	Basketball	When the game clock shows that two minutes of play remain, the game is considered to be in the two-minute period
up and under	Rugby	Ball kicked upfield high and long to make time for the kicker and attacking players to reach the point where it comes down
uwate-dashi-nage	Sumo	One-handed throw
uwate-nage	Sumo	Hip throw using both hands
veer attack	American football	Offensive formation

MISCELLANEOUS

volley	Volleyball	Two-handed shot that may go over the net or to another team member to *spike*
volo	Bocce	High arcing shot usually thrown with backspin, with the objective of hitting another ball directly or landing very close to the *pallino* with little or no roll. For safety and protection of the court playing surface it is now outlawed
voluntary tackle	Rugby league	Where a player in possession voluntarily stops play and moves on to play the ball when they are not effectively tackled
vorlage	Skiing	Position in which the skier leans forward without lifting the heels from the skis. In plural, also a common name for skiing trousers
vorlaufer	Skiing	Pre-competition skier who tests the safety and degree of difficulty of a ski course (German, lit. 'one who runs ahead')
walk over	Horse racing	Completion of race whereby a single horse has the formality of walking over the finishing line as it is the only entrant in a race
wall pass	Association football	Pass around a defender from one player to another and back (also called a one-two)
warner single wing	American football	Offensive formation
wazari	Judo	Japanese 'almost point'; throw which lands an opponent almost cleanly on their back (scores 7 points in competition)
wazari-ni-chikai-waza	Judo	Partial throw or hold; two make an *ippon* (scores 5 points in competition)
western grip	Table tennis	Traditional method of holding a bat with fingers on the face of the bat
western roll	High jump	Technique, rarely used in modern competition, whereby the front leg is thrown high over the bar and the body and other leg roll over and parallel to the bar
whaxel	Figure skating	Occurs during an *axel* when the skater swings forward the free leg too soon and loses his or her balance as a result
wheelie	Motorcycling	Lifting in the air of the front wheel, caused when a rider applies the power too quickly. Riders often do this deliberately as a way of celebrating victory
wicket maiden	Cricket	Over during which no runs have been scored and a wicket has been taken
wide	Cricket	*Extra* given to the batting side due to the ball being bowled beyond the reach of the batsman
wired	Croquet	To be prevented from taking a particular course by an intervening *hoop* or peg
wishbone	Sailing	Boom composed of two halves that curve outward from the mast on either side of the sail and in again, the clew of the sail between them being attached to the point where they meet aft
wrapped jump	Figure skating	*Jump* that has not been finished because the skater's free leg is wrapped around the landing leg, suggesting that the final revolution has not occurred
yamashita	Gymnastics	Flat handspring over the vaulting horse
yard line	Croquet	Unmarked line a yard inside the boundary on which, after each stroke, any ball which has been sent off court is replaced
yokozuna	Sumo	Grand Champion
yori kiri	Sumo	Strong forward push
yorker	Cricket	Ball bowled at the feet of a batsman whether playing back or forward
yuko	Judo	Hold lasting between 20 and 25 seconds (scores 5 points in competition)
zero tackle	Rugby league	Occurs when possession changes hands after a breach of rules such as a *knock-on*. If the player who picks up the loose ball is then tackled, the tackle does not count to his team's tackles

This is far from being an exhaustive listing of sporting terminology. Dictionaries of terms are available on many individual sports and it would be impossible to catalogue all known terms. I have tried to give a cross-section of technical terms over a range of sports. Some terms will also relate to other sports, e.g. billiard-based sports or running-ball sports.

Sporting Trophies

Name	Sport	Details	First held
Admiral's Cup	Sailing	Biennial international competition for sailing yachts	1957
Air Canada Silver Broom	Curling	Formerly the Scotch Whisky Cup, renamed in 1968	1959
America's Cup	Sailing	Originally called the Hundred Guineas Cup and raced around 1851 the Isle of Wight	
Armada Dish	Equestrianism	Awarded to riders who complete the Badminton Horse Trials five times	1949
Ashes	Cricket	Awarded to the winner of England v Australia Test series (since 1882 called the 'Ashes')	1877
Baron Matsui Inter-Club Cup	Judo	Club competition named after the Japanese ambassador	1928
Bledisloe Cup	Rugby union	New Zealand v Australia	1931
Bologna Trophy	Swimming	England v Scotland v Wales speed swimming contest	1929
Bowring Bowl	Rugby union	Annual Oxbridge varsity match	1872
Brendan Martin Cup	Gaelic football	All-Ireland Ladies' Football Championship	1974
Britannia Cup	Rowing	Club coxed fours race, Henley Regatta	1968
Britannia Cup	Sailing	For small yachts (under 32ft) of any country to challenge the holder	1951
Britannia Shield	Speedway	Inter-club challenge competition	1957
Calcutta Cup	Rugby union	England v Scotland international match	1870
Camanach Cup	Shinty	Shinty championship of Scotland	1896
Canada Cup	Golf	World team pairs championship	1953
Cole Cup	Fencing	Men's sabre competition	1922
Cowdray Park Gold Cup	Polo	see Veuve Clicquot Gold Cup	
Currie Cup	Rugby union	South African provincial championship	1892
Curtis Cup	Golf	Amateur women – USA v Great Britain/Ireland	1932
Davis Cup	Tennis	The International Lawn Tennis Challenge Trophy	1900
Dewar Cup	Rifle shooting	Small-bore shooting competition	1909
Diamond Sculls	Rowing	Blue Riband of single sculling, Henley Regatta	1884
Doggett's Coat & Badge	Rowing	Sculling contest on the Thames between ex-passenger skiffs	1715
Eisenhower Trophy	Golf	Biennial international competition	1958
Espirito Santo Trophy	Golf	Women's amateur international team championship	1908
Federation Cup	Tennis	Women's world amateur team championship	1963
G. Melville Clark National Memorial Trophy	Diving	Awarded to England's most successful diving club	1951
George Hearn Cup	Diving	Awarded to England's most successful diver	1954
Goldberg-Vass Memorial Trophy	Judo	London open competition	1956
Gordon Bennett Trophy	Motor racing	Forerunner of the Grand Prix	1901
Grand Challenge Cup	Rowing	Henley Regatta – eights	1839
Halford Hewitt Cup	Golf	Public schools knockout competition	1924
Hambleton	Harness racing		
Harmsworth Trophy	Powerboat racing	Awarded to fastest endurance monohull	1903
Harry Sunderland Trophy	Rugby league	Man of the Match award in Premiership final; reinstated 2002	1965
Henry Benjamin Trophy	swimming and water polo	Awarded to England's most successful swimming and water polo club	1910
Hopman Cup	Tennis	International mixed-doubles event named after Australian tennis player Harry Hopman	1989
Hurlingham Champion Cup	Polo	International competition discontinued 1939	1876
Iroquois Cup	Lacrosse	English club championship	1890
John Player Cup	Rugby league	see Regal Trophy	
John Player Cup	Rugby league	see Powergen Cup	
James Norris Trophy	Ice hockey	Awarded to National Hockey League Defenceman of the Year	1953
Jules Rimet Trophy	Association football	First World Cup trophy, won outright by Brazil in 1970 for their third tournament win	1930
King George V Gold Cup	Show jumping	Men's international competition at Hickstead, Sussex	1934
Kinnaird Cup	Eton fives	Public schools fives competition	1926
Lance Todd Award	Rugby league	Man of the Match award in the Challenge Cup final	1897
Lapham Trophy	Squash	Canada v USA	1921
Leonard Trophy	Bowls	World team championship	1966
Liam MacCarthy Cup	Hurling	Awarded to the winner of the All-Ireland Senior Hurling Championship	1921

Londonderry Cup	Squash	Public schools old boys' competition	1934
Lonsdale Belt	Boxing	British title – won outright for winning three title fights at the same weight	1909
MacRobertson International Shield	Croquet	International croquet competition	1925
Manuel Avilla Camacho Cup	Polo	Mexico v USA	1941
Marcel Corbillon Cup	Table tennis	Women's world table tennis team championships	1934
Marchant Cup	Rugby fives	London grammar schools' competition	1929
Middleton Cup	Bowls	Inter-county championship	1911
Palma Trophy	Shooting	Long range shooting championships held in Creedmore, USA	1876
Philadelphia Gold Cup	Rowing	Olympic single sculling trophy	1908
Pilkington Cup	Rugby union	see Powergen Cup	1972
Powergen Cup	Rugby union	English club knockout cup (formerly John Player Cup, Pilkington Cup, Tetley's Bitter Cup)	1972
Presidents' Cup	Golf	Men's team competition, USA v Rest of World	1994
Prince of Wales Cup	Sailing	International 14ft dinghy championship	1927
Prince Philip Cup	Rowing	Amateur coxed fours race, Henley Regatta	1963
Prince Philip Cup	Show jumping	Pony club team competition, held at Horse of the Year Show	1957
Prince Rainier Cup	Fencing	Award to the nation with best results in world championships	1950
Princess Elizabeth Challenge Cup	Rowing	Eights for public schools, Henley Regatta	1946
Pura Milk Cup	Cricket	Australian inter-state competition; replaced Shefflield Shield in 1999	1892
Queen Elizabeth II Cup	Show jumping	Women's international competition at Hickstead	1949
Queen's Prize	Rifle shooting	Open competition first held at Wimbledon	1860
Ranfurly Shield	Rugby union	New Zealand rugby trophy for provincial teams	1902
Regal Trophy	Rugby league	League cup formerly John Player Cup, renamed Regal Trophy in 1989	1971
Russell-Cargill Trophy	Rugby union	Awarded to winner of Middlesex Sevens	1951
Ryder Cup	Golf	Men's team competition, USA v Europe (USA v Great Britain/Ireland before 1979)	1927
Sam MacGuire Trophy	Gaelic football	All-Ireland Men's Senior Football Championship	1928
Tennent's Cup	Rugby union	Scottish club knockout cup	1996
Seawanhaka Cup	Sailing	For small yachts (under 25ft) of any country to challenge the holder	1895
Sheffield Shield	Cricket	see Pura Milk Cup	
Silver Goblets/Nickalls Cup	Rowing	Coxless pairs amateur international, Henley Regatta	1845
Sir William Burton Cup	Sailing	National 12ft dinghy championship	1936
Solheim Cup	Golf	Women's team competition – USA v Europe	1990
Stanley Cup	Ice hockey	North American ice hockey championship	1894
Stewards Cup	Rowing	Coxless fours face, Henley Regatta	1841
Strathcona Cup	Curling	Canada v Scotland international competition	1903
Subalterns' Cup	Polo	Inter-services competition	1896
Super 12 Trophy	Rugby union	Southern hemisphere provincial championship (Australia, New Zealand, South Africa)	1995
SWALEC Cup	Rugby union	Welsh club knockout cup (formerly Welsh Cup, Schweppes Cup)	1972
Swaythling Cup	Table tennis	Men's world table tennis team championships	1927
Talbot Handicap	Crown green bowls	Blackpool-based open competition	1882
Tetley's Bitter Cup	Rugby union	see Powergen Cup	1972
Thomas Cup	Badminton	Men's world badminton team championship	1949
Uber Cup	Badminton	Women's world badminton team championship	1957
Val Barker Trophy	Boxing	Awarded to most stylish boxer at an Olympic Games	1904
Veuve Clicquot Gold Cup	Polo	International competition, previously the Cowdray Park Gold Cup	1956
Vince Lombardi Trophy	American football	Awarded to Super Bowl winner, named after Lombardi in 1971	1967
Volvo World Cup	Show jumping	World Championship competition	1979
Walker Cup	Golf	Men's amateur competition – USA v Great Britain/Ireland	1922
Waterloo Cup	Coursing	The 'Derby' of coursing, named after a Liverpool hotel	1836
Waterloo Cup	Crown green bowls	Blackpool-based open competition	1907
Webb Ellis Trophy	Rugby union	Awarded to World Cup winner	1987
Westchester Cup	Polo	Great Britain v USA international match	1886
Wightman Cup	Tennis	USA v Great Britain annual women's team competition, discontinued 1995	1923
Wolfe-Noel Cup	Squash	USA v Great Britain women's match	1933

Worrell Trophy	Cricket	West Indies v Australia Test series	1931
Wyfold Challenge Cup	Rowing	Amateur coxless fours, Henley Regatta	1847
Yeaden Memorial Trophy	Swimming	Awarded by the Amateur Swimming Association to the best-performing English swimmer of the year	1938
Zurich Premiership Trophy	Rugby union	Awarded to the winner of English club league championship competition for top club sides	1987

Sporting Quotations

Age is a question of mind over matter. If you don't mind, age don't matter.
Paige, Leroy 'Satchel' (1906-82), US baseball player

Amateur: one who plays games for the love of the thing. Unlike the professional, he receives no salary, and is contented with presents of clothes, clubs, rackets, cigarettes, cups, cheques, hotel expenses, fares, and so on.
Morton, J.B. (1893-1979), 'Beachcomber' in the *Daily Express*

As no man is born an artist, so no man is born an angler.
Walton, Izaak (1593-1683), author of *The Compleat Angler*

Because it's there.
(When asked why he wanted to climb Mount Everest)
Mallory, George Leigh (1886-1924), British mountaineer

The bigger they come the harder they fall.
Fitzsimmons, Robert (1862-1917), British boxer

Bowler's Holding, the batsman's Willey.
(said during a 1976 England v West Indies Test match)
Johnston, Brian (1913-94), English cricket commentator

The decathlon is nine Mickey Mouse events and the 1500 metres.
Ovett, Steve (1955-), British athlete

The English country gentleman galloping after a fox is the unspeakable in full pursuit of the uneatable.
Wilde, Oscar (1854-1900), Irish poet and dramatist in *A Woman of No Importance*

Float like a butterfly, sting like a bee.
(originally coined by Ali's trainer Drew 'Bundini' Brown)
Ali, Muhammad (1942-), US boxer

For those of you watching in black-and-white, Spurs are in the all-yellow strip.
Motson, John (1945-), British football commentator

For years I thought the club's name was Partick Thistle Nil.
Connolly, Billy (1942-), Scottish comedian

Form is temporary. Class is permanent.
(slogan on a T-shirt worn by Botham in 1990)
Botham, Ian (1955-), English cricketer

Fred Davis, the doyen of snooker, now 67 years of age and too old to get his leg over, prefers to use his left hand.
Lowe, Ted (1920-), British snooker commentator

The goal was scored a little by the hand of God, a little by the head of Maradona.
(explaining his first goal in Argentina's 2-1 defeat of England in the 1986 World Cup)
Maradona, Diego (1960-), Argentinian footballer

Golf is a good walk spoiled.
Twain, Mark (1835-1910), US writer

He can run but he can't hide.
(referring to opponent Billy Conn who was knocked out in the 13th round)
Louis, Joe (1914-81), US boxer

He didn't quite manage to get his leg over.
(referring to Ian Botham's collision with his own wicket)
Agnew, Jonathan (1960-), British cricket commentator

He must have discovered youthanasia [euthanasia]. He never seems to get any older!
Francome, John (1952-), British jockey

He's going for the pink, and for those of you with black-and-white sets, the yellow is behind the blue.
Lowe, Ted (1920-), British snooker commentator

Honey, I forgot to duck!
(to his wife after defeat by Gene Tunney on 23 September 1926)
Dempsey, Jack (1895-1983), US boxer

I'd like to get ten goals this season, but the authorities don't normally let me play a whole season.
Jones, Vinnie (1965-), Welsh footballer

I'm so fast I could hit you before God gets the news.
Ali, Muhammad (1942-), US boxer

I'm so fast that when I turn off the light at night I'm in bed before it gets dark.
Ali, Muhammad (1942-), US boxer

I am the greatest!
(first coined by wrestler Gorgeous George Wagner, 1915-63)
Ali, Muhammad (1942-), US boxer

I can't see who's in the lead but it's either Oxford or Cambridge.
(said during the 1949 Boat Race)
Snagge, John (1904-96), British sports commentator

I got into the ring with Muhammad Ali once and I had him worried for a while. He thought he'd killed me!
Cooper, Tommy (1922-84), British comedian

I had a go at positive thinking, yoga, transcendental meditation, even hypnotism. They only screwed me up, so now I'm back to my normal routine of a couple of lagers.
Rees, Leighton (1940-2003), Welsh darts player

If anyone sees me anywhere near a boat they have permission to shoot me.
(after winning a fourth Olympic gold medal in Atlanta)
Redgrave, Sir Steve (1962-), British rower

If you drink, don't drive. Don't even putt!
Martin, Dean (1917-95), US actor and singer

In my sport the quick are too often listed among the dead.
Stewart, Sir Jackie (1939-), Scottish racing driver

It's an up and under.
Waring, Eddie (1909-86), British rugby commentator

It's funny, but the more I practise, the luckier I become.
Player, Gary (1935-), South African golfer

I was born for soccer, just as Beethoven was born for music.   Pelé (1940-), Brazilian footballer

I would like to thank the press from the heart of my bottom.   Faldo, Nick (1957-), British golfer
(on winning the 1992 Open Championship)

Juantorena opens his legs and shows his class.   Coleman, David (1926-), British athletics commentator
(during the 1976 Olympic 400m final)

Know what I mean, Harry?   Bruno, Frank (1961-), British boxer
(addressing BBC boxing commentator, Harry Carpenter)

Nice guys finish last.   Durocher, Leo (1906-91), US baseball manager
(referring to his baseball team, the New York Dodgers)

No one remembers who came second.   Hagen, Walter (1892-1969), US golfer

Oh, I say!   Maskell, Dan (1908-92), British tennis commentator

Old Trafford is the 'Theatre of Dreams'.   Charlton, Bobby (1937-), English footballer

The Opera ain't over till the fat lady sings   Cook, Dan (1926-), US baseball commentator

Put me back on my bike.   Simpson, Tommy (1938-67), British cyclist
(last words before dying of heart failure during the
1967 Tour de France)

She's about as cuddly as a dead hedgehog. The alsatians   Francome, John (1952-), British jockey
in her yard would go around in pairs for protection.
(referring to his friend, Jenny Pitman)

Some people think football is a matter of life and death. I don't   Shankly, Bill (1919-81), Scottish football manager
like that attitude. I can assure them it is much more
serious than that.

There are people on the pitch, they think it's all over, it is now!   Wolstenholme, Kenneth (1920-2002), football commentator
(on England winning the 1966 World Cup)

There are two things no man will admit he can't do well: Moss, Stirling (1929-), British racing driver
drive and make love.

This was a great game of golf.   Crosby, Bing (1904-77), US singer and actor
(last words before dying of heart failure on the golf course)

We have beaten England. Lord Nelson, Lord Beaverbrook,   Lillelien, Biorge, Norwegian football commentator
Sir Winston Churchill, Sir Anthony Eden, Clement Attlee,
Henry Cooper, Lady Diana. We have beaten them all.
Maggie Thatcher, can you hear me? Maggie Thatcher,
your boys took a helluva beating.
(at the end of a 1981 World Cup tie)

We wuz robbed!   Jacobs, Joe (1896-1940), US boxing manager
(referring to the defeat of Max Schmeling to Jack Sharkey
on 21 June 1932)

When the going gets tough, the tough get going.   Rockne, Knute (1888-1931), American football coach

When the seagulls follow a trawler, it is because they   Cantona, Eric (1966-), French footballer
think sardines will be thrown into the sea.

The wife of the Cambridge President is kissing the cox of the   Carpenter, Harry (1925-), British sports commentator
Oxford crew.

Winning is not everything. It's the only thing   Lombardi, Vince (1913-70), US American football coach

You cannot be serious!   McEnroe, John (1959-), US Tennis player
(catchphrase first coined during the 1981 Wimbledon
tournament)

You're only here for a short visit, so don't hurry, don't worry,   Hagen, Walter (1892-1969), US golfer
and be sure to stop and smell the flowers along the way.

MISCELLANEOUS

Sporting Record 2003

January 2003

1   Arsenal defeated Chelsea 3-2 to open up a five-point lead over Manchester United at the top of the Barclaycard Premiership.

2   Herschelle Gibbs and Graeme Smith shared South Africa's highest Test partnership on the first day of the second and final Test at Newlands, Cape Town. Gibbs, who scored 228, and Smith, with 151, put on 368 for the first wicket.

    Ben Ainslie, the Finn single-handed dinghy world and European champion, was named Yachtsman of the Year by the Yachting Journalists' Association for the third time at the London International Boat Show.

3   Lashings, the star-studded club team based in Maidstone, Kent, signed Australian batsman Mark Waugh for the following season.

5   John Part of Canada ended Phil Taylor's reign as Ladbrokes.com world darts champion, defeating him 7-6 at Purfleet.

6   England beat Australia by 225 runs in the fifth and final Test at the SCG, Sydney, to lose the five-match Test series 4-1.

12   Dutchman Ray Barneveld won the Embassy Darts World Championship at Frimley Green for the third time. Three-times world bowls champion Tony Allcock crashed out of the 2003 championship and immediately announced he would retire after the Welsh Open in February.

13   Ernie Els set a record four-round total at the Mercedes Championship in Kapalua, Hawaii, when he produced a total of 261, 31 under par, to win by eight shots from Rocco Mediate and K.J. Choi.

14   Dagenham & Redbridge defeated Plymouth Argyle 2-0 in their FA Cup third-round replay at Victoria Road to become the second non-league club through to the fourth round for a scheduled meeting with Norwich City.

    England cricket officials defied the Government by voting unanimously to play the World Cup match against Zimbabwe in Harare on 13 February.

19   Alex Marshall of Scotland beat John Price of Wales 10-4, 6-5, to win the World Indoor Bowls Championship at Great Yarmouth.

    Mark Foster of Great Britain won the Dunhill Golf Championship in Johannesburg after a six-man play-off with Paul Lawrie, Trevor Immelman, Anders Hansen, Bradford Vaughan and Doug McGuigan.

    James Male retained the Lacoste World Rackets Championship with a tremendous comeback. After losing the first leg in Philadelphia to Jonathan Larken 4-1, he won the deciding second leg at Queen's Club 15-6, 15-11, 15-3, 15-1.

22   Tatiana Totmianina and Maxim Marinin of Russia won the gold medal in the pairs category at the European Figure Skating Championships in Malmo.

23   Irina Slutskaya of Russia won the gold medal in the women's European Figure Skating Championships in Malmo.

    Andy Roddick of the USA and Younes El Aynaoui of Morocco played the longest final set, in terms of games played, in the history of Grand Slam events since tennis became open in 1968. Victory went to Roddick, 4-6, 7-6, 4-6, 6-4, 21-19.

    Bowlers Lynne Whitehead and Tony Allcock won the inaugural mixed pairs World Matchplay Championship at Potters Leisure Resort, Norfolk, beating Amy Monkhouse and John Price 5-6, 7-4, 2-1, in the final.

25   Big-punching Nicaraguan welterweight Richard Mayorga blasted out previously unbeaten Vernon Forrest in three rounds, then lit up a celebratory cigarette in the ring. Mayorga added Forrest's WBC world crown to his own WBA title.

26   Andre Agassi demolished Rainer Schuttler 6-2, 6-2, 6-1, to win the Australian Open at the Rod Laver Arena, Melbourne Park.

    Snooker player Stephen Hendry defeated Mark Williams 9-5 in the final of the Regal Welsh Open in Cardiff.

    Ernie Els lost his first golf tournament of the season despite being one shot ahead of his playing partner on the 72nd hole. Els bogeyed the hole and Zhang Lianwei of China birdied it to win the Caltex Masters in Singapore by one shot.

    American football's Super Bowl XXXVII resulted in a comprehensive 48-21 win for Tampa Bay Buccaneers over Oakland Raiders.

29   Budge Pountney, 29, the Northampton flanker and former Scottish national captain, announced his retirement from international rugby union.

February 2003

1   Coventry Blaze, champions-elect of the Findus British National Ice-Hockey League, announced they would turn down an invitation to play in the Superleague next season.

2   After three months at no. 2, Nicola Deaton, five times national champion, displaced Katy Parker at the top of the national women's table tennis ranking list.

    Ernie Els won the Heineken Golf Classic at Royal Melbourne by one shot from a rejuvenated Nick Faldo.

    Stephan Eberharter of Austria won the men's super-giant slalom at the World Skiing Championships in St Moritz but the headlines were made by the silver-medal performance of fellow countryman Hermann Maier, after just a few weeks' training.

3   Michaela Dorfmeister of Austria won the women's super-giant slalom at the World Skiing Championships in St Moritz.

6   Richard Caborn, the Minister for Sport, opened a new indoor High Performance Centre at Alexander Stadium,

Perry Barr, Birmingham. One of the features of the complex is a 100m running track at which Mark Lewis-Francis broke the British indoor 100m record, covering the distance in 10.34secs.

8   British and Commonwealth heavyweight boxing champion Danny Williams was stopped in the sixth round of his European title challenge by Sinan Samil, a German-based Turk, in Berlin.
Audley Harrison continued his winning streak as a professional boxer by beating Rob Calloway, who retired with a broken jaw at the end of the fourth round of their heavyweight clash in Brentford.

9   Great Britain were defeated 4-1 by Australia in a Davis Cup tennis tie with Alex Bogdanovic's defeat of Todd Woodbridge the solitary success.

11   Australian master spin bowler Shane Warne bowed out of the cricket World Cup after discovering that a random drugs test taken on 22 January had proved positive for a banned substance which he had taken as a method of extracting fluid from the body.
Her Majesty the Queen enjoyed her first National Hunt win for 53 years when First Love won a minor novice chase at lowly Folkestone. Her last win over fences was Monaveen in October 1949 when she was still Princess Elizabeth.

12   Wayne Rooney of Everton FC, at 17 years and 111 days, became the youngest footballer ever to play for England when he made an appearance in the second half of the 3-1 defeat by Australia at Upton Park, a match in which Sven-Goran Eriksson changed the entire team at half-time.
Brian Kerr made a successful start as manager of the Republic of Ireland with a 2-0 victory over Scotland.
Bode Miller of the USA won the men's giant slalom at the World Skiing Championships in St Moritz, his third medal in total, following a win in the combined event and second place in the super-giant slalom.

13   Former world champion Tony Allcock was appointed as the new chief executive of the English Bowling Association.
Anja Paerson of Sweden dominated both runs to win the giant slalom at the World Skiing Championships.

14   England pulled out of their opening match of the cricket World Cup against Zimbabwe in Harare amid fears for team safety.

15   In the opening RBS Six Nations Championship rugby union matches England defeated France 25-17 and Italy beat Wales 30-22.
Following a 2-0 defeat by Arsenal, the Manchester United manager, Sir Alex Ferguson, kicked a football boot in anger during the post-match discussion and accidentally hit his captain, David Beckham, over the left eye, causing him to need two stitches.

16   In the RBS Six Nations Championship Ireland defeated Scotland 36-6.
Cassie Jackman, who had retired from squash the previous September following a spinal operation, returned to action by winning the British National Championship at Sportcity, Manchester. Peter Nicol beat Lee Beachill in the men's final.
Sheffield Steelers' 3-1 victory over Nottingham Panthers gave them the ice hockey Superleague championship. Muhammad Hafiz Hashim, the Commonwealth champion from Malaysia, won the All-England Badminton Championship. Zhou Mi of China beat her team-mate Xie Xingfang 11-6, 11-5, in the women's final.

19   The shortest game in the history of World Cup cricket was won by Sri Lanka when they took just 4.4 overs to knock off the 37 runs required to beat Canada's record low score of 36.

20   Former world snooker champion Alex Higgins was beaten 5-1 by 16-year-old Darren Dornanby on his comeback match in the unofficial Irish Championship in Londonderry. Higgins's top break was a lowly 23.

22   In the RBS Six Nations Championship England defeated Wales 26-9 at the Millennium Stadium, Cardiff, and Ireland beat Italy 37-13 in Rome.
Mike Tyson knocked out Clifford Etienne after 49 seconds in the first round of their heavyweight clash in Memphis, Tennessee. On the undercard in Memphis, former ice-skating champion, Tonya Harding, was beaten on points by Samantha Browning.

23   Paula Radcliffe broke the 10km world road record in San Juan, Puerto Rico, with a time of 30mins 21secs.
In the RBS Six Nations Championship France beat Scotland 38-3 at the Stade de France, Paris.
Canadian batsman John Davison scored the fastest century in World Cup history when he reached the mark off 67 balls during the pool B match at Centurion Park. A quick-fire 73 off 40 balls by Brian Lara ensured that the West Indies got home by 7 wickets.
Joe Swail beat Fergal O'Brien 10-3 in the final of the Irish Open snooker competition in Londonderry.
Laura Davies of England continued her re-emergence as a leading golfer by winning the ANZ Open in Queensland, Australia.

25   Pakistan cricketer Wasim Akram became the first bowler to take 500 wickets in one-day international matches during his team's 97-run defeat of Holland in the first stage of the World Cup. For the record, his 500th victim was Dutch opener Nick Statham.
Manchester United beat Juventus 3-0 in Turin and, following their subsequent 2-1 home win over the same team, advanced to the quarter-finals of the UEFA Champions League as group winners with two matches still to play.

March 2003

1   Roy Jones jnr defeated John Ruiz to win the WBA Heavyweight Championship, the first boxer since Bob Fitzsimmons to win a middleweight and a heavyweight crown. The 12-round contest in Las Vegas was a one-sided points victory for Jones.

2   Liverpool beat Manchester United 2-0 to win the Worthington Cup final at the Millennium Stadium, Cardiff.
Kelly Fisher, the ladies' world champion snooker player, was beaten by Ronnie O'Sullivan's cousin, Maria Catalano, in the quarter-finals of the East Anglian Ladies' Championships, thus halting a 69-match winning run dating back to her defeat by Sharon Dickson in the last 16 of the 2001 World Championships.
Tiger Woods won the Accenture World Matchplay Championship, defeating fellow countryman David Toms in the final in California.
Britain's Neil Hodgson won the opening two races of the World Superbike Championship in Valencia, Spain.

3   South Africa failed to qualify for the Super Six stage of the cricket World Cup following a rain-affected final match against Sri Lanka which ended in a tie under the Duckworth/Lewis system.
Andre Agassi lost his first tennis match of 2003 when Thomas Enqvist defeated him 6-7, 6-4, 6-1, in the first round of the Scottsdale ATP Franklin Templeton Classic.

4   England failed to qualify for the Super Six stage of the cricket World Cup following a no-result in the final group match between Zimbabwe and Pakistan. Nasser Hussain, the England captain, immediately resigned as skipper of the one-day side.

5   David Felgate was confirmed as the new director of performance at the Lawn Tennis Association.

8   South African fast bowler Allan Donald announced his retirement from international one-day cricket. The 36-year-old, who retired from Test cricket in 2002, took 272 wickets in 164 one-day internationals at an average of 21.78.
In the RBS Six Nations Championship the Ireland rugby union side defeated France 15-12 at Lansdowne Road, Dublin, and Scotland beat Wales 30-22 at Murrayfield.
WBO heavyweight boxing champion, Wladimir Klitschko of the Ukraine, was stopped in the second round by Corrie Sanders of South Africa, not only losing his title but also the chance of fighting Lennox Lewis for a reunification fight.

9   Golfer Robert-Jan Derksen of the Netherlands won the Dubai Desert Classic by one shot from South African, Ernie Els.
In the RBS Six Nations Championship England defeated Italy 40-5 at Twickenham.
David Coulthard won the Australian Formula One Grand Prix, the first of the season and the first under the new scoring system. Coulthard scored 10 points in his McLaren Mercedes while the top eight finishers all scored points.

11   The Smurfit Champion Hurdle was won by Rooster Booster, ridden by Richard Johnson and trained by Philip Hobbs. Other first-day winners at the Cheltenham Festival included Azertyuiop in the Irish Independent Arkle Trophy Chase, ridden by Ruby Walsh and trained by Paul Nicholls (Azertyuiop is named after the top row of a French typewriter).
Tim Henman beat Michael Gambill of the United States 7-5, 6-2, to win his first tennis match for five months.

12   Moscow Flyer, ridden by Barry Geraghty, won the Queen Mother Champion Chase at Cheltenham.
Kenya defeated Zimbabwe by seven wickets in Bloemfontein to ensure a semi-final place in the cricket World Cup.

13   The Cheltenham Tote Gold Cup was won for the second successive year by Best Mate, ridden by Jim Culloty and trained by Henrietta Knight. The François Doumen-trained Baracouda, ridden by his son, Thierry, won the Bonusprint Stayers' Hurdle for the second year in a row.

14   Jason Gardner of Great Britain gained the bronze medal behind Justin Gatlin of the USA in the 60m dash at the World Indoor Athletics Championships in Birmingham, England.
Snooker player Jimmy White pulled off a surprise victory in the televised final of the Poker Million competition.
Great Britain won two gold medals at the World Indoor Athletics Championships via Ashia Hansen in the triple jump and Marlon Devonish in the 200m.

16   Ronnie O'Sullivan defeated Stephen Hendry 9-6 to win the European Open snooker tournament in Torquay, Devon.
Rangers beat Celtic 2-1 in the CIS Cup final at Hampden Park.
Colin Jackson bowed out of international athletics with a fifth place in the World Indoor Athletics Championships.

18   Australia beat Sri Lanka in a rain-affected match to reach the final of the cricket World Cup.
Steve Davis made the final televised stages of the World Snooker Championships at the Crucible Theatre for the first time in three years with a 10-8 victory over Ryan Day in the final qualifying stage.
Finlay Mickel won the men's downhill title at the British Land National Skiing Championships in Tignes, France.

19   Arsenal were beaten 2-1 by Valencia in their last Champions League match and thus failed to qualify for the knockout phase.

20   Peter Reid replaced Terry Venables as manager of Leeds United FC.
Celtic reached the UEFA Cup semi-finals following a 2-0 (3-1 aggregate) defeat of Liverpool at Anfield.
Johnny Moulder-Brown won the men's giant slalom title in the British Land National Skiing Championships in Tignes, France.

22   Pablo, ridden by Michael Hills and trained by his father, Barry Hills, won the Freephone Stanley Lincoln at Doncaster.
In the RBS Six Nations Championship Ireland defeated Wales 25-24 in Cardiff to set up a Grand Slam battle with England, who defeated Scotland 40-9 at Twickenham.
Scott Harrison of Scotland beat Wayne McCullough of Ireland in a one-sided points decision to retain his WBO featherweight title in Glasgow.

23   Australia won the cricket World Cup, defeating India by 125 runs in a one-sided match. Australia scored 359 for two in their 50 overs, Ricky Ponting top-scoring with 140. A spirited 82 by Virander Sehwag gave India brief hope but they were eventually bowled out for 234 runs in Johannesburg.
Despite being physically sick at the second hole, Tiger Woods won the Bay Hill Invitational golf tournament for the fourth consecutive year. Woods dominated from the outset and finished 11 shots clear of the field in the Florida event.
Sam Allardyce, the Bolton Wanderers football manager, was beaten 5-0 by Peter Castle in the first round of the UK Open Darts Championship.
In the RBS Six Nations Championship France defeated Italy 53-27 in Rome.
Kimi Raikkonen of Finland won the Malaysian Grand Prix at Sepang, Kuala Lumpur, in his McLaren-Mercedes.
At the National Long Course Swimming Championships in Sheffield, Katy Sexton, Sarah Price and James Gibson all set new Commonwealth records, which signified that Bill Sweetenham, the Great Britain performance director from Australia, had already improved the national squad considerably since his appointment.

29   Heavyweight boxer Audley Harrison won his tenth successive fight when he outpointed Serbia's Ratko Draskovic at Wembley.

In the RBS Six Nations Championship France defeated Wales 33-5 in Paris.
Oxford beat Cambridge in the women's University Boat Race.
30 Ronnie O'Sullivan defeated John Higgins 10-9 in the final of the Irish Masters Snooker Championship in Dublin.
In the RBS Six Nations Championship England defeated Ireland 42-6 in Dublin to claim the rugby union Grand Slam.
Kenenisa Bekele won the long-course title at the World Cross Country Championships to add to the short-course title he won the day before. He became the first person to retain both titles. Fellow Ethiopian Worknesh Kidane won the senior women's long-course race after being denied the short-course title by Edith Masai of Kenya.
In the second round of the World Superbike Championship in Phillip Island, Australia, Britain's Neil Hodgson claimed his second double victory of the season to lead the Championship with a maximum 100 points.
Julian Snow defeated fellow Briton Spike Willcocks 6-2, 6-1, 6-5, in the final of the British Land Real Tennis Amateur Championship, equalling Howard Angus's record of 16 amateur singles titles.

April 2003

2 England beat Turkey 2-0 at the Stadium of Light, Sunderland, to go to the top of Group Seven of the Euro 2004 Football Championship qualifying competition.
In other group matches Scotland were beaten 1-0 by Lithuania, Northern Ireland 2-0 by Greece and the Republic of Ireland drew 0-0 in Albania.
3 M. Russell of England beat his fellow countryman P. Gilchrist 6-4 to win the world billiards title in Marsascala, Malta.
5 The Martell Grand National was won by Monty's Pass, ridden by Barry Geraghty and trained by J.J. Mangan.
Ricky Hatton of England retained his WBU light-welterweight title in Manchester, defeating American Vince Phillips on points.
6 Oxford won the University Boat Race by the smallest-ever winning margin of one foot.
Kimi Raikkonen won the Brazilian Formula One Grand Prix in a controversial race that was abandoned 16 laps early due to a crash by Mark Webber (Jaguar). Giancarlo Fisichella (Jordan) crossed the finish line first but the race stoppage meant that the leader on the previous lap was declared the winner. David Coulthard was in a clear lead when he made a pit stop three laps before the end of the race. (See 11 April entry.)
10 Steve Waugh became the most-capped player in cricket history when he made his 157th appearance for Australia in the first Test against the West Indies in Guyana.
Phil Tufnell, the Middlesex and England bowler, announced his retirement from first class cricket.
11 Giancarlo Fisichella was awarded the Brazilian Formula One Grand Prix after the FIA announced that a timing error had caused it to miscalculate the leader on the lap before the race was stopped.
13 Canadian golfer Mike Weir won the US Masters in a play-off with American Len Mattiace.
Britain's Paula Radcliffe broke her own world-best time when she won the London Marathon in 2hrs 15mins 25secs. She was the fastest British athlete, male or female.
Serena Williams was defeated 6-3, 6-4, by Justine Henin-Hardenne of Belgium in the final of the WTA event in Charleston, North Carolina. The defeat was Williams' first since another Belgian, Kim Clijsters, beat her in the final of the WTA Tour Championship in Los Angeles in November 2002.
19 Michaela Tabb made history by becoming the first female snooker referee to take charge of an Embassy World Professional Snooker Championship match at the Crucible.
Richard Johnson's win on Quedex in the 2.10 at Stratford made him the eighth jockey to ride 1000 National Hunt winners.
20 Michael Schumacher (Ferrari) won the San Marino Formula One Grand Prix at Imola.
22 Ronnie O'Sullivan made a 147 maximum break in 6mins 30secs during his first-round match in the Embassy World Professional Snooker Championship but was eventually beaten 10-6 by Marco Fu of Hong Kong.
The World Boxing Council, formed in 1963, was declared bankrupt as a result of being ordered to pay $31 million to Graciano Rocchigiani in lost earnings and damages after the WBC failed to recognise the German as its light-heavyweight champion in 1998.
23 Manchester United defeated Real Madrid 4-3 at Old Trafford but failed to make the semi-finals of the UEFA Champions League, losing 6-5 on aggregate.
Nicole Cooke of Great Britain won the Flèche Wallonne women's World Cup cycle race in Huy, Belgium.
26 Bradford Bulls beat Leeds Rhinos 22-20 in the rugby league Challenge Cup Final at the Millennium Stadium, Cardiff.
27 Britain's Neil Hodgson won both races at Sugo, Japan, to make it six wins out of six in the World Superbike Championship.
28 The All-England Lawn Tennis and Croquet Club announced that the custom of bowing and curtseying to royalty would no longer be necessary during Wimbledon fortnight.
30 The 140th edition of *Wisden Cricketers' Almanack* went on sale with a photograph on its cover for the first time. The black and white picture depicted England batsman Michael Vaughan celebrating one of his recent Test hundreds.

May 2003

1 Defending champion Peter Ebdon was beaten 13-12 by Paul Hunter in the quarter-finals of the Embassy World Professional Snooker Championship.
2 Amateur golfer Paul Neilson, 34, claimed Britain's longest hole-in-one on the 394-yard fifth hole at South Winchester Golf Club.
3 Refuse To Bend, ridden by Pat Smullen and trained by Dermot Weld, won the Sagitta 2000 Guineas at Newmarket.
4 Arsenal lost 3-2 at home to Leeds United and thus handed Manchester United the Barclaycard Premiership title.

Michael Schumacher won the Spanish Formula One Grand Prix in Barcelona.
Russian Rhythm, ridden by Kieren Fallon and trained by Sir Michael Stoute, won the Sagitta 1000 Guineas at Newmarket. The Scotland cricket team celebrated their debut in the National League with a victory over Durham.

5 Mark Williams defeated Ken Doherty 18-16 in the final of the Embassy World Professional Snooker Championship.

6 Michael Vaughan was named as the replacement for Nasser Hussain as England's one-day cricket captain.

7 The Lawn Tennis Association announced the cancellation of the National Tennis Championships for financial reasons.

11 Doncaster Rovers beat Dagenham & Redbridge 3-2, on a golden goal decider, at the Britannia Stadium, Stoke, to gain promotion to the Football League.
Marco Fu of Hong Kong defeated world champion Mark Williams 9-5 in the final of the Hasseroder Premier Snooker League.
Golfer Paul Casey of England won the Benson and Hedges International Open at The Belfry.

13 The West Indies cricket team created history by recording the highest total fourth-innings score to win a Test match. Their 418-7 against Australia at St John's, Antigua, eclipsed the 406-4 reached by India at Port of Spain in 1975/76. Despite the victory, West Indies lost the series 3-1.

14 Former England football boss Graham Taylor resigned as manager of Aston Villa Football Club.
Juventus beat Real Madrid 3-1 (4-3 on aggregate) to reach the UEFA Champions League final.

17 In the 122nd FA Cup final, Arsenal defeated Southampton 1-0 at the Millennium Stadium with a goal from Robert Pires.

18 Britain's Neil Hodgson won both races at Monza to maintain his 100 per cent record in the World Superbike Championship.
Michael Schumacher won the Austrian Formula One Grand Prix at the A-1 Ring, Spielberg, despite a fuel-tank fire.

21 FC Porto beat Celtic 3-2 in the 25th minute of extra time, following a 2-2 draw after 90 minutes of the Uefa Cup final in Seville.

23 Annika Sorenstam of Sweden failed to make the cut in the Bank of America Colonial golf tournament at Fort Worth, Texas. Her five-over-par score of 145 was four shots over the cut and 13 shots behind the leader Kenny Perry, but it was a creditable performance by a woman playing in a men's PGA event off the back tees for the first time.
Anthony McGrath, the Yorkshire captain, and James Anderson, the Lancashire pace bowler, made their England Test debuts.

24 Bournemouth beat Lincoln 5-2 in the Nationwide League Division Three play-off final to earn promotion.
Indian Haven, ridden by John Egan and trained by Paul d'Arcy, won the Entenmann's Irish 2000 Guineas at the Curragh.
Werner Schlager of Austria saved four match points before beating Wang Liqin, the defending champion, in the quarter-finals of the men's singles at the World Table Tennis Championships in Paris.

25 England beat Zimbabwe by an innings and 92 runs in the first Test at Lord's with Mark Butcher scoring 137 and taking five wickets, one in the first innings and four in the second.
Ignacio Garrido of Spain won the Volvo PGA Championship at Wentworth after a sudden-death play-off against Trevor Immelman of South Africa. Yesterday, ridden by Mick Kinane and trained by Aidan O'Brien, won the Entenmann's 1000 Guineas at the Curragh.
Werner Schlager of Austria beat Joo Se-Hyuk of South Korea 4-2 to win the World Table Tennis Championship in Paris.

26 Wolverhampton Wanderers defeated Sheffield United 3-0 in the Nationwide League Division One play-off final at the Millennium Stadium, Cardiff, to gain promotion to the Barclaycard Premiership.

27 Greg Rusedski was beaten in straight sets by Russian Nikolay Davydenko in the first round of the French Open, his first competitive match for almost nine months due to injury.

28 AC Milan beat Juventus 3-2 on penalties after a goalless draw in the UEFA Champions League final at Old Trafford.

31 Audley Harrison gained his 11th straight victory as a professional when he stopped Mathew Ellis in the second round at York Hall, Bethnal Green.

June 2003

1 Phil Taylor won the inaugural Skybet UK Open darts championship in Bolton, defeating Shayne Burgess 18-8 in the final.
Juan Pablo Montoya of Colombia won the Monaco Formula One Grand Prix.
James Toseland of Great Britain won the second race at the Oschersleben circuit in Germany to deny Neil Hodgson his tenth straight victory in the World Superbike Championship.
Gilberto Simoni of Italy won the Giro d'Italia cycle race.
Kenny Perry won the Memorial Open Golf Championship, his second US Tour victory on successive weekends.

3 England beat Serbia and Montenegro 2-1 at the Walkers Stadium, Leicester, with Joe Cole scoring the winning goal.

5 Serena Williams was beaten 6-2, 4-6, 7-5, by Belgium's Justine Henin-Hardenne in the French Open semi-finals. The defeat brought to an end Williams' 33-match Grand Slam winning streak.

6 Casual Look, ridden by Martin Dwyer and trained by Andrew Balding, won the Vodafone Oaks at Epsom.
Richard Johnson took six wickets on his England debut in the second Test match against Zimbabwe at Chester-le-Street.

7 Kris Kin, ridden by Kieren Fallon and trained by Sir Michael Stoute, won the vodafone Derby at Epsom.
Justine Henin-Hardenne beat fellow Belgian Kim Clijsters 6-0, 6-4, to win the women's French Open Championships.

8 England beat Zimbabwe by an innings and 69 runs in the second and final Test at Chester-le-Street.
Juan Carlos Ferrero of Spain beat Martin Verkerk of the Netherlands 6-1, 6-3, 6-2, to win the men's French Open title.
Gary Wolstenholme won his second British Amateur Golf Championship at Royal Troon.
Greg Owen of Great Britain won the British Masters Golf Championship at the Forest of Arden.

9 Reading beat the Barcelona-based Real Club De Polo 4-2 on penalties in Brussels, after drawing 1-1 at full time, to become the first English club to win the European Hockey Championship since Slough's triumph in 1980.
Dutch hockey club Den Bosch beat Birmingham-based Olton 7-2 in the final of the women's European Club Championship.

11 England defeated Slovakia 2-1 thanks to a double strike by Michael Owen to maintain second place in qualifying Group Seven of the European Football Championships. Ireland beat Georgia 2-0 to remain in second place in Group Ten.

12 The Houston Astros defeated the New York Yankees 8-0, the first time the Yankees had failed to muster a hit in a game since September 1958, 6980 matches earlier, the longest streak in major league baseball history.

13 A new first class county cricket competition began. The Twenty20 Cup, played over 20 overs per side and split into three divisions of six, the top team in each group plus best runner-up contesting the semi-finals.

15 American Jim Furyk won the US Open Golf Championship at Olympia Fields, Chicago, his first major title.
Michael Schumacher won the Canadian Formula One Grand Prix in Montreal.
Carl Myerscough added 24cm to Geoff Capes' 23-year-old British shot-put record while competing in the National Collegiate Athletic Association Track and Field Championships in Sacramento, California.
Britain's Neil Hodgson continued his dominance of the World Superbike Championship by winning both races at Silverstone.

16 The top seeds at Wimbledon were announced as Lleyton Hewitt and Serena Williams, with Tim Henman seeded no. 10.

18 Manchester United announced that David Beckham would be leaving them to join Real Madrid for the 2003/04 season.

19 Mr Dinos, ridden by Kieren Fallon and trained by Paul Cole, won the Ascot Gold Cup.

20 England fast bowler James Anderson took the last three Pakistan wickets in successive balls, the first hat-trick by an England bowler in 373 one-day internationals. England won the match by seven wickets to draw level (1-1) in the three-match series.

21 Lennox Lewis successfully defended his WBC world heavyweight boxing crown against Vitali Klitschko in Los Angeles; the referee stopped the fight in the sixth round when the Ukrainian suffered a cut eye.
Greg Rusedski landed the 13th title of his career by beating American Mardy Fish to win the Samsung Open at Nottingham.
England beat the Australian Wallabies 25-14 in a rugby union international match in Melbourne.
Australian wonder-horse Choisir, ridden by Johnny Murtagh and trained by Paul 'Champagne' Perry, won the Golden Jubilee Stakes at Royal Ascot to add to his King's Stand Group One win on the first day.

22 England beat Pakistan by four wickets at Lord's to win the NatWest Challenge series 2-1.
Real Madrid secured their 29th Spanish football league title when they beat Athletic Bilbao 3-1 at the Bernabeu Stadium.
Ludger Beerbaum of Germany, riding Goldfever, won the Aachen Equestrian Grand Prix.
Matthew Pinsent and James Cracknell won the Munich World Cup coxless pairs event to avenge their defeat at the hands of the Croatian and South African duos in Milan in May.
Ruben Xaus of Spain won both races in round seven of the World Superbike Championship at the Misano track in San Marino. Neil Hodgson, who had won 11 of the previous 12 races, fell in race one and finished second in race two.
Great Britain, the defending champions, finished third behind France and Germany in the European Cup athletics Super League in Florence. The women's team finished fourth behind Russia, Germany and France.

23 Defending Wimbledon champion Lleyton Hewitt was beaten in the first round by qualifier Ivo Karlovic of Croatia, the first time since 1967 that the defending men's champion had suffered defeat at the first hurdle.

25 Greg Rusedski was fined £1700 for abusive language during his second-round Wimbledon defeat by Andy Roddick. The incident occurred following a call of 'out' from a 29-year-old Lithuanian spectator, Evaldas Zilionis; Rusedski assumed that the call was from a judge, stopped playing the point and then lost the next five games and the match.

26 Marc-Vivien Foe, the former Manchester City and West Ham midfield player, collapsed and died while playing for Cameroon against Colombia in Lyons.

28 Droopy's Hewitt, trained by Andrew Ioannou, won the William Hill Greyhound Derby at Wimbledon after hot favourite Top Savings encountered first-bend crowding and managed only third place. (Droopy's Hewitt was subsequently disqualified.)
Vikram Solanki and Marcus Trescothick shared a record first-wicket stand of 200 during the one-day international victory over South Africa in the NatWest series at The Oval.
Joe Calzaghe retained his WBO super-middleweight title with a second-round stoppage of Byron Mitchell in Cardiff. The American became the first man to knock Calzaghe down during an exciting second round but Calzaghe was stung into action and immediately knocked Mitchell down to give the referee no option but to stop the fight.

29 Ralf Schumacher won the European Formula One Grand Prix at the Nürburgring.
Alamshar, ridden by Johnny Murtagh and trained by John Oxx, beat hot favourite Dalakhani to win the Budweiser Irish Derby.
Luton-based Philip Golding won the French Open golf title at Versailles.

July 2003

1   Ken Bates announced the sale of Chelsea Football Club to 36-year-old Russian businessman, Roman Abramovich. Bates, who bought the club for £1 in 1982, was to remain as chairman.

2   David Beckham was paraded in front of the Real Madrid fans. The new £25-million signing chose the no. 23 shirt for his new club as a tribute to his all-time sporting hero, US basketball legend Michael Jordan.
Vancouver won the right to stage the 2010 Winter Olympic Games.

3   Tim Henman was beaten 6-7, 6-3, 3-6, 4-6, by Sebastien Grosjean of France, in the quarter-finals of the All-England Championship at Wimbledon.

5   Serena Williams defeated her sister Venus 4-6, 6-4, 6-2, in the women's singles final at Wimbledon. The men's doubles title was won by Jonas Bjorkman of Sweden and Todd Woodbridge of Australia who beat Indian Mahesh Bhupathi and Max Mirnyi of Belarus 3-6, 6-3, 7-6, 6-3.
Bradley McGee of Australia won the opening prologue time trial of the Tour de France from an unlucky David Millar. The Scottish rider eventually finished second, beaten by 0.8secs after his chain came off near the finish.

6   Roger Federer of Switzerland beat Mark Philippoussis of Australia 7-6, 6-2, 7-6, to win the men's singles at Wimbledon.
Martina Navratilova equalled Billie-Jean King's record of 20 Wimbledon titles when she and her partner, Leander Paes, won the mixed doubles title beating Andy Ram and Anastassia Rodionova 6-3, 6-3. Kim Clijsters and Ai Sugiyama beat Virginia Ruano Pascual and Paola Suarez 6-4, 6-4, to win the women's doubles.
Ralf Schumacher won the French Formula One Grand Prix at Magny Cours.
Phillip Price of Wales won the Smurfit European Open Golf Championship.
Peter Manley of England defeated John Part of Canada 16-12 in the final of the Las Vegas Desert Darts Classic.

9   Harry Kewell, the Australian forward, was transferred from Leeds to Liverpool for £5 million.

10   The Queen visited the medieval market town of Much Wenlock in Shropshire to witness a demonstration of traditional sports. The Wenlock Olympian Games began in 1850 and the 117th annual event included pig-chasing, tilting the ring, throwing the rock and fencing.

12   Scott Harrison lost his WBO featherweight title on a split points decision to Manuel Medina of Mexico.
England beat South Africa by seven wickets in the final of the NatWest cricket series at Lord's.

13   Valentino Rossi, the Italian MotoGP champion, finished first in the British Grand Prix at Donington but was demoted to third, following a 10-second penalty for overtaking under the yellow flag. The race was won by Max Biaggi.
Vintage Tipple, ridden by Frankie Dettori and trained by Paddy Mullins, won the Darley Irish Oaks at the Curragh.

14   Joseba Beloki of Spain crashed out of the Tour de France while in second place behind leader, Lance Armstrong.
Ian Woosnam qualified for the Open Championship by chipping in on the play-off hole in the qualifying competition.

15   Ed Smith, the exciting Kent batsman, became the first man to score 1000 runs in the season following a double century against Lancashire. In an extraordinary sequence, Smith scored three ducks, four centuries and a double century in the same month.
Cathy Freeman, the Olympic 400m champion, announced her retirement from athletics.

17   World no. 1 golfer Tiger Woods made a disastrous start to the Open Championship at Royal St George's when his opening tee-shot was hit just wide of the fairway but was lost in the rough. He eventually scored a triple-bogey seven.
German golfing star Bernhard Langer was named as the next European Ryder Cup captain.

19   Britain's Mark Roe and Sweden's Jesper Parnevik were disqualified from the Open Championship for failing to exchange scorecards on the first hole.
Surrey Lions won the first Twenty20 Cup, beating Warwickshire Bears by nine wickets in the final at Trent Bridge.
Steve Waugh of Australia became only the second batsman to score centuries against all nine Test opponents, following his innings of 100 not out against Bangladesh. South African Gary Kirsten had been first to the milestone with a century against Bangladesh the previous October.

20   American Ben Curtis, ranked 396th in the world, won the Open Championship at Royal St George's, Sandwich, Kent. The top Briton to finish was Brian Davis in joint-sixth place ahead of Nick Faldo in joint-eighth.
Kate Allenby won the individual bronze medal and helped Great Britain to the team gold at the Modern Pentathlon World Championships in Pesaro, Italy.
Rubens Barrichello of Brazil won the British Formula One Grand Prix at Silverstone despite the appearance of an Irish spectator, running down the Hangar Straight, wearing a red kilt and green waistcoat, during the 11th lap.

21   Tanya Streeter of Great Britain broke the world record for free-diving in an abyss off the Turks and Caicos Islands. The 122m (400ft) dive, in which she had to hold her breath for 3mins 38secs, beat the previous free-diving records for both men and women.
James Gibson of Great Britain gained a bronze medal in the 100m breaststroke at the World Swimming Championships in Barcelona. The gold was won by Kosuke Kitajima of Japan in a world record 59.78secs.

22   Alec Stewart, the Surrey and England Test cricketer, announced his retirement at the end of the 2003 cricket season.
Katy Sexton of Great Britain gained a silver medal in the 100m backstroke at the World Swimming Championships.

23   James Gibson of Great Britain won Britain's first individual gold medal at the World Swimming Championships since 1975. He recorded a time of 27.56secs for the 50m breaststroke, an event which is not included in the Olympics.

24   Herschelle Gibbs and Graeme Smith of South Africa put on 338 runs for the first wicket during the first Test at Edgbaston, a record opening partnership by any team against England.

26   Katy Sexton of Great Britain struck gold in the 200m backstroke at the World Swimming Championships . In a

great day for Britain Mark Foster won silver in the 50m freestyle and Rebecca Cooke won bronze in the 800m freestyle.

Alamshar, ridden by Johnny Murtagh and trained by John Oxx, won the King George VI and Queen Elizabeth Diamond Stakes at Ascot.

27 Lance Armstrong won his fifth consecutive Tour de France.

Zoe Baker of Great Britain won the bronze medal in the 50m breaststroke at the World Swimming Championships.

28 Nasser Hussain resigned as England cricket captain after the rain-affected first Test against South Africa ended in a draw.

30 The reigning British Superbike champion, Steve Hislop, was killed in a helicopter crash in Scotland.

31 Michael Vaughan took over from Nasser Hussain as England cricket captain.

Bradley Wiggins took the gold medal in the men's individual pursuit at cycling's World Track Championships in Stuttgart.

August 2003

1 Graeme Smith of South Africa scored 259 runs in his team's first innings of 682-6 declared, in the second Test at Lord's.

2 Phil Taylor defeated Wayne Mardle 18-12 in the final of the Stan James Darts World Matchplay Championship in Blackpool.

3 Annika Sorenstam of Sweden won the Weetabix British Open Golf Championship at Royal Lytham & St Annes.

Xia Xuanze of China beat Wong Choong Hann of Malaysia 15-6, 13-15, 15-6, in the men's singles final of the badminton World Championships in Birmingham. Zhang Ning of China beat Gong Ruina of China 11-6, 11-3, in the women's final.

South Africa beat England by an innings and 92 runs in the second Test at Lord's despite a stirring 142 by Andrew Flintoff.

Tim Henman defeated Fernando Gonzalez 6-3, 6-4, in the final of the Legg Mason Tennis Classic.

Juan Pablo Montoya of Colombia (Williams) won the German Formula One Grand Prix at Hockenheim.

6 Joe Cole was transferred from West Ham United to Chelsea for £6.6 million.

10 Manchester United defeated Arsenal 4-3 on penalties after the FA Community Shield ended 1-1 after 90 minutes in Cardiff.

Ed Smith, the Kent batsman, who was the first player to score 1000 runs in the 2003 season, was named in the South African squad to face South Africa in the third Test match in Nottingham.

11 Atlanta shortstop Rafael Furcal became only the 12th player in major league baseball history to register an unassisted triple play in the Braves' 3-2 defeat by St Louis. In the fifth inning, Furcal leapt high to snag Woody Williams then stepped on second base to double up catcher Mike Matheny, before jogging a few steps towards first base to tag Orlando Palmeiro.

16 Doug Howlett scored two first-half tries as New Zealand regained the Bledisloe Cup with a 21-17 win over the Australian rugby union team in Auckland.

Northampton beat Newcastle 31-5 in the final of the Middlesex Sevens at Twickenham.

Ireland defeated Wales 35-12 in a rugby union international match.

17 Shaun Micheel of the USA won the US PGA Championship on Oak Hill's East Course in Rochester, New York.

Corrida, ridden by Peter Charles of Ireland, won the Hickstead Jumping Derby for the third successive year.

John White, Scotland's Australian-born world no. 3, won the first Prince English Open Championship at the Crucible Theatre, Sheffield, with a 15-11, 7-15, 15-13, 15-11 defeat of Jonathan Power, Canada's Commonwealth squash champion.

18 England beat South Africa by 70 runs at Trent Bridge to level the Test series 1-1.

Britain's male gymnasts failed to book a place at the 2004 Olympic Games team event when they finished 23rd in the World Championships in Anaheim, California.

22 Great Britain's showjumping team failed to qualify for the Olympic Games in Athens after finishing ninth at the European Championships in Donaueschingen, Germany.

24 Darren Clarke won the NEC International golf tournament at the Firestone Country Club, Akron, Ohio.

Laila Ali knocked out Christy Martin in the fourth round in Biloxi, Mississippi, to retain her world super-middleweight title.

Fernando Alonso of Spain (Renault) won the Hungarian Formula One Grand Prix at the Hungaroring, Budapest, to become, at 22 years and 26 days, the youngest-ever Grand Prix winner in history.

England beat Wales 43-9 in a friendly rugby union international at the Millennium Stadium, Cardiff.

Lima Azimi made history by becoming the first Afghan woman to take part in the World Athletics Championships. Lima's time of 18.37secs failed to take her into the second round of the 100m in Paris.

Glenn Roeder was sacked as manager of West Ham following their 1-0 defeat by Rotherham.

25 South Africa beat England by 191 runs at Headingley to take a 2-1 lead in the Test series.

Darren Campbell won Britain's first medal at the World Athletics Championships in Paris with a bronze in the 100m.

Jonathan Edwards bowed out of international athletics after two disappointing leaps in the triple jump final in Paris.

Shane Byrne, with his tenth victory of the season, clinched the British Superbike title at Cadwell Park.

26 Pete Sampras announced his retirement from professional tennis before the start of the US Open Tennis Championships.

27 Kelli White, the American winner of the sprint double at the World Championships, was involved in controversy when she was found to have tested positive for Modafinil, a substance related to the list of banned medications and stimulants.

28 Kelly Holmes won Britain's second medal at the World Athletics Championships in Paris with a silver in the 800m.

29   Leg-break bowler Alok Kapali claimed Bangladesh's first hat-trick during the second Test against Pakistan.
30   Katherine Grainger and Cath Bishop won gold in the women's pairs at the World Rowing Championships in
     Milan. Tom Kay won a silver in the lightweight single sculls, and the men's coxless fours narrowly missed gold,
     but it was disappointment for Matthew Pinsent and James Cracknell in the coxless pairs final when they only
     managed fourth place behind the Australians.
     Gloucestershire beat Worcestershire in the C&G Trophy final at Lord's.
     England lost their 14-match unbeaten rugby union record when they went down 17-16 to France at Stade
     Vélodrome, Marseilles.
     David Beckham took just 126secs to score on his spanish league debut in Real Madrid's 2-1 win over Real Betis.
31   The Great Britain 4 × 100m squad won a silver medal and Hayley Tullett a bronze on the final day of the World
     Athletics Championships in Paris.
     Julia Warren and Michelle Dollimore won a silver medal in the women's lightweight coxless pairs at the World
     Rowing Championships in Milan. The men's coxed four also won silver and the men's eight claimed a bronze.
     Nicole Cooke of Great Britain won the women's World Cup road-race competition with a fifth place in the
     penultimate round in Germany which meant the cyclist from South Wales could not be caught for the title.
     Lee Westwood of England ended three barren years by winning the BMW International golf event at Nord-
     Eichenrid, Munich.

September 2003

5   Maria Mutola won a $1 million bonus as the outright winner of the Golden League's winner-take-all jackpot for
     winning all six Golden League 800m races. Her last-leg win at the Stade Roi Baudouin, Brussels, was in a time
     of 1min 57.78secs.
6   High Chaparral, ridden by Mick Kinane and trained by Aidan O'Brien, won the Irish Champion Stakes at
     Leopardstown.
7   Great Britain and Ireland's golfers beat USA 12½–11½ to win the Walker Cup at Ganton, Yorkshire, for a third
     successive win.
     Neil Hodgson of Great Britain clinched the World Superbike Championship at Assen with a win and a second-
     place finish.
     Justine Henin-Hardenne beat fellow Belgian Kim Clijsters 7-5, 6-1, to win the women's US Open
     Championship.
     Pippa Funnell won the Burghley Masterfoods International Three-Day Event on Primmore's Pride. Zara
     Phillips, daughter of the Princess Royal, was runner-up on Toytown.
8   England defeated South Africa by nine wickets at the Oval to tie the Test series 2-2 in an extraordinary match
     where South Africa scored 484 runs in their first innings. Andrew Flintoff was named Man of the Series for
     England and Graeme Smith for South Africa.
     Alec Stewart bowed out of international cricket after his 133rd and final Test match for England.
     Andy Roddick of the USA defeated Juan Carlos Ferrero of Spain 6-3, 7-6, 6-3, to win the US Open Championship.
9   Lincolnshire defeated Devon by eight wickets to win the Minor Counties cricket championship.
10   Peter Kenyon resigned as chief executive of Manchester United to take up a similar role at Chelsea FC.
13   Brian Boru, ridden by Jamie Spencer and trained by Aidan O'Brien, won the Sea Biscuit St Leger at Doncaster.
14   Europe defeated the USA 17½–10½ in the Solheim Cup at Barseback, Sweden.
     Paula Radcliffe of Great Britain set a new world-best time of 14mins 51secs for 5000m during the Flora Light
     Challenge in Hyde Park.
     Surrey added to their inaugural Twenty20 Cup victory by winning the National League Division One title.
     Shane Mosley scored a controversial points victory over fellow American Oscar De La Hoya for the WBA and
     WBC light-middleweight titles in Las Vegas. All three judges scored the fight 115-113 to Mosley despite
     ringside pundits scoring heavily in favour of De La Hoya.
     Michael Schumacher won the Italian Formula One Grand Prix at Monza.
     Yetunde Price, the eldest sister of tennis champions Venus and Serena Williams, was shot dead in Compton,
     Los Angeles.
17   Arsenal began their assault on the Champions League with a 3-0 home defeat by Inter Milan.
18   Sussex Cricket Club clinched their first-ever county championship title when they picked up their third batting
     bonus point against Leicestershire at Hove. Worcestershire claimed the second division title.
21   Tottenham Hotspur FC sacked their manager, former England coach Glenn Hoddle, following disappointing
     results.
     Paula Radcliffe won the BUPA Great North Run and set a world-best time of 65mins 40secs for the half-
     marathon distance, although the record was not ratified since the course has a downhill stretch.
     Lancashire Cricket Club clinched the National League Division Two title following a win at Northampton.
22   Former heavyweight boxing champion Frank Bruno was admitted to a mental institution suffering from severe
     depression.
     Greg Rusedski lost the deciding rubber of Britain's Davis Cup tie against Morocco in a controversial match
     against Hicham Arazi, carried over from the previous evening when bad light stopped play with Rusedski
     suffering from extreme exhaustion.
23   Double Olympic medallist Ben Ainslie won his sixth yachting world title when he defended his Finn class crown
     at the Sailing World Championships in Cadiz.
24   Britain's David Millar won the 17th stage of the Tour of Spain cycle race but remained over two hours behind
     race leader Isidro Nozal of Spain.
25   Rio Ferdinand was reported to have refused to take a random drug test on 23 September for UK Sport, the
     agency which tests sportsmen and women. The maximum penalty for this offence is a two-year suspension
     and Ferdinand was automatically set to miss the international against Turkey on 11 October.

28 Michael Schumacher won the US Formula One Grand Prix at Indianapolis to move to within one point of achieving an unprecedented sixth World Drivers' championship.

Roberto Heras of Spain won the Tour of Spain cycle race from fellow countryman Isidro Nozal, who led for 16 days but was overhauled on the penultimate stage, the seven-mile mountain time trial.

Paul Tergat of Kenya broke the world-best time for the marathon by 43 seconds with a time of 2hrs 4mins 55secs in Berlin.

October 2003

3 Cricketer Adam Hollioake set out on a 2000 mile trek to Morocco in memory of his brother and former England player Ben, who was killed in a car crash the previous year. The 32-year-old Surrey captain set off for Tangiers from Edinburgh with plans to complete 21 miles a day, taking 28 days to reach the south coast of England, before sailing from Brighton to Dieppe, cycling to Gibraltar, and rowing to Tangiers. The journey was expected to end on 24 November and Adam was hoping to raise money for sick children.

4 Nicki Pedersen of Denmark won the World Speedway Championship following his second place to Greg Hancock of USA in the Norwegian Grand Prix in Hamar. Jason Crump of Australia was runner-up for the third successive season while defending champion Tony Rickardsson finished the season in third place.

Dalakhani, ridden by Christophe Soumillon and trained by Alain de Royer-Dupre, won the Prix de l'Arc de Triomphe at Longchamp, Europe's premier horse race.

5 Tiger Woods retained his American Express World Championship golf title in Atlanta, Georgia.

6 Denise Lewis, the Olympic heptathlon champion, announced she had dropped her controversial former East German coach, Dr Ekkart Arbeit, and returned to her former coach, Charles van Commence.

7 Robert Miller and his crew aboard the 140ft (42.67m) *Mari Cha IV* broke the world sailing record for 24 hours with a distance of 525 nautical miles (972km).

The Nigerian national team announced that Bryan Robson, the former Middlesbrough manager, would coach them in future.

8 George Best's European Footballer of the Year trophy fetched £167,250 at Bonhams in Chester to become the most expensive piece of sporting memorabilia ever auctioned in Britain.

Towcester racecourse held its first horse-race meeting since deciding to dispense with entrance fees and it was an unmitigated success. The usual average crowd of 1800 was boosted to more than 8000.

A Jockey Club inquiry began into how and why a horse called Trump Card ran instead of a stablemate, Investment Force, at Plumpton 12 days earlier. The trainer, Charlie Mann, had twice previously arrived at British racecourses with the wrong horse.

9 Robert Miller and his crew aboard *Mari Cha IV* broke the world sailing record for crossing the Atlantic by a monohull yacht. Miller, 70, began the crossing from New York on 2 October and arrived off Cornwall six days and 17 hours later.

Cyclist David Millar of Great Britain won the gold medal in the men's time trial at the World Road Championships in Canada.

11 England gained a hard-fought draw against Turkey at the Sukru Saracoglu Stadium, Istanbul, to ensure automatic qualification for the 2004 European Championship finals in Portugal. David Beckham missed a penalty after losing his footing on the run-up but the game was marred by cynical tackling and bad-tempered outbursts by the Turkish players who were condemned to the play-offs. Scotland beat Lithuania 1-0 to make the play-offs, and despite losing at home to Serbia, Wales also made the play-offs. Both Irish teams failed to qualify.

Matthew Hayden of Australia beat Brian Lara's highest-ever Test score of 375 with a score of 380 against Zimbabwe at the WACA in Perth. The Australians eventually declared their first innings on 735-6, Adam Gilchrist ending undefeated on 113.

Britain's Nicole Cook claimed a bronze medal in the women's World Championship cycle road race in Hamilton, Canada. Susanne Ljungskog of Sweden retained her title in a five-way sprint after Jeannie Longo of France was caught 500m from the finish.

12 Michael Schumacher clinched his sixth World Drivers' Championship at Suzuka, Japan. His Ferrari team-mate, Rubens Barrichello, won the race from Kimi Raikkonen but Schumacher's eighth place was enough to pip Raikkonen for the title. Ferrari also clinched the constructors' championship.

Valentino Rossi secured his third consecutive world motorcycling title with victory in the Malaysian 500cc MotoGP. Spain's Daniel Pedrosa clinched the 125cc World Championship with victory in Malaysia.

The first professional ranking tournament of the season, the LG Cup, was won by world champion Mark Williams, 9-5, at the Guild Hall, Preston, even though a maximum 147 break had been achieved by John Higgins.

Germany beat Sweden 2-1 after an extra time golden goal in the fourth women's World Cup final at Carson, California.

13 Australia won the Test against Zimbabwe by an innings and 175 runs at the WACA in Perth.

Rio Ferdinand denied having refused to take a drug test on 23 September, claiming he merely forgot due to the distraction of moving home.

18 Bradford Bulls became the first team to win the rugby league double of Challenge Cup and Super League Grand Final when they defeated Wigan 25-12 at Old Trafford. Stuart Reardon of Bradford won the Harry Sunderland Trophy as Man of the Match.

19 Ernie Els beat Thomas Bjorn 4 & 3 in the final of the HSBC World Matchplay Championship at Wentworth.

Colin Montgomerie extended his record of at least one title win every year since 1992 by capturing the Macau Open.

20 Norman Williamson retired from National Hunt racing having ridden 1268 winners.

22 Scotland flanker Martin Leslie was given a record 12-week ban following his deliberate kneeing of Jason Keyter during Scotland's 39-15 pool B victory over the United States in the rugby union World Cup.

24 Britain's top sprinter, Dwayne Chambers, was reported to have tested positive for tetra-hydro-gestrinone (THG).

25 England beat Bangladesh by seven wickets in the first Test in Dhaka. Steve Harmison took nine wickets in the match.
26 Florida Marlins won the sixth game of baseball's World Series 2-0 against the New York Yankees to take a winning 4-2 lead in the best-of-seven series.
Phil Taylor of England beat John Part of Canada 7-2 in the final of the Paddy Power World Darts Grand Prix.
30 Arsenal FC were severely punished by the Football Association following unseemly scenes at Old Trafford on 21 September when Manchester United's Ruud van Nistelrooy was hounded by several Arsenal players. Lauren Bisan-Etame Mayer was fined £40,000 and suspended for four matches for jostling Van Nistelrooy and kicking out at Quinton Fortune. Martin Keown was fined £20,000 and handed a three-match suspension for his airborne war dance near Van Nistelrooy. Ray Parlour was fined £10,000 and given a one-match ban for his aggressive behaviour towards both Van Nistelrooy and Gary Neville. Patrick Vieira was fined £20,000 and suspended for one match for failing to leave the pitch straight away after being dismissed for kicking out at Van Nistelrooy. Ashley Cole was fined £10,000 for confronting Cristiano Ronaldo. Arsenal FC were fined £175,000. The Football Association was fined £4400 for a tunnel fracas between opposing players during the Euro 2004 qualifying tie in Turkey on 11 October.
The England rugby union team was fined £10,000 and its fitness coach, Dave Reddin, was given a two-match touchline ban for his illegal substitution of Dan Luger resulting in 16 English players being on the field during a World Cup match against Samoa.

November 2003

1 England beat Bangladesh by 326 runs in Chittagong to clinch a 2-0 Test series win.
2 Tony West defeated Raymond Barneveld 7-6 in the Winmau World Masters darts final in Bridlington, Yorkshire.
Sir Ranulph Fiennes succeeded in his challenge to run seven marathons on successive days.
3 The owners of Catford Greyhound Stadium announced its immediate closure.
5 Al-Saadi Gaddafi, the football-playing son of Libyan dictator Muammar Gaddafi, tested positive for the banned steroid nandrolone. Gaddafi had been signed by Serie A side Perugia but had yet to play a game for them.
8 Pat Eddery retired from racing after riding a career-total 4632 winners.
National Hunt jockey Mick Fitzgerald rode his 1000th winner when Orswell Crest won the 2.30 race at Sandown Park.
9 Great Britain & Ireland defeated Continental Europe 15-13 to retain golf's Seve Trophy, at El Saler, Spain.
Petter Solberg of Norway won the World Rally Championship following his victory in the Wales Rally.
11 American Andy Roddick was confirmed as the year-ending world no. 1 tennis player.
12 Dalakhani was named as the Cartier Horse of the Year for winning the French Derby and Prix de l'Arc de Triomphe. Other award winners included Attraction (Top Two-Year-Old Filly), One Cool Cat (Top Two-Year-Old Colt), Falbrav (Top Older Horse), Persian Punch (Top Stayer), Oasis Dream (Top Sprinter) and Russian Rhythm (Top Three-Year-Old Filly).
13 Brian Lara became the leading Test run-scorer in West Indies' history when he scored 191 against Zimbabwe in the second Test at Bulawayo. Lara deposed Viv Richards to stand seventh in the all-time list of run-makers.
14 Neil Cameron resigned as chief executive of the International Badminton Federation.
15 Australia defeated New Zealand 22-10 in Sydney to reach the final of the rugby union World Cup.
Australia beat Great Britain 23-20 in Hull to clinch the rugby league Ashes series 2-0.
16 England defeated France 24-7 in Sydney to reach the final of the rugby union World Cup.
Denmark beat England 3-2 in a friendly football international at Old Trafford.
Stephen Hendry defeated Ronnie O'Sullivan 9-6 to win the British Open snooker title in Brighton.
18 England suffered a ten-wicket defeat by Sri Lanka in a one-day international in Colombo.
19 In the second leg of the European Championship play-offs, Wales were beaten 1-0 by Russia at the Millennium Stadium and Scotland were trounced 6-0 by Holland in Amsterdam, thereby failing to qualify for the finals in 2004. Turkey, who reached the World Cup semi-final in 2002, were beaten 3-2 on aggregate by Latvia, resulting in their elimination.
22 A drop goal by Jonny Wilkinson in the dying seconds of extra time gave England a 20-17 victory over Australia in the final of the rugby union World Cup. The crowd of 82,957 was treated to an exhilarating game with Australia leading 5-0 before an England revival which secured them a 14-5 half-time lead. Australia rallied to end full-time 14-14 before the final drop-kick with only 20 seconds remaining before the sudden-death phase. The try-scorers were Tuqiri for the Wallabies and Robinson for England while both kickers, Flatley and Wilkinson, were successful with four penalties each.
Cheltenham Gold Cup hero Best Mate was beaten by Jair Du Cochet on his seasonal debut at Huntingdon.
Australia beat Great Britain 18-12 in Huddersfield to win the three-match rugby league Test series 3-0.
24 Lancaster City won the National League water polo title for the sixth time in eight years when they defeated Bristol Central, the runners-up, 12-8 at Loughborough University. The Nottinghamshire club, Hucknall, won the second division with Warley claiming top spot in the third.
The former British Open rackets champion, Harry Foster, beat Ally Robinson to win the KBC Peel Hunt National Invitation Championship at Queen's Club, London.
John Daly won the Calloway Golf Pebble Beach Invitational, his second straight win and first in the United States for nine years.
Laura Davies finished as the leading Briton on the LPGA money list at no. 19, two places ahead of Scotland's Catriona Matthew.
25 Arsenal defeated Inter Milan 5-1 to inflict the biggest-ever defeat on a Serie A side in the Champions League in Italy.
26 Steve 'Tugga' Waugh announced he would retire after the final Test against India at home at the Sydney Cricket Ground, scheduled to start on 2 January 2004.

28 World downhill champion Michael Walchhofer won the opening men's World Cup downhill of the season at Lake Louise, Canada.
29 Scott Harrison stopped Manuel Medina in the 11th round to regain his WBO featherweight title at the Braehead Arena, Glasgow.
Leisel Jones of Australia set a short-course world record in the women's 200m breaststroke at the World Cup in Melbourne.
The 50th Scullers' Head of the River Race was cancelled due to gusting winds.
30 Australia defeated Spain 3-1 to win the Davis Cup.
Matthew Stevens beat Stephen Hendry 10-8 in the Travis Perkins UK Snooker Championship final at the Barbican Centre, York.

December 2003

6 England drew the first Test against Sri Lanka, in Galle, with Ashley Giles batting for 111 balls to avoid defeat when England still required 113 runs to win with their last two men at the crease.
7 Sinead and John Kerr, the sister and brother combination from Murrayfield, claimed their first national ice-dance title.
Chemmy Alcott, 21, finished 11th in the super giant slalom at the World Cup meeting in Lake Louise, Canada, the best result by a British woman at a World Cup meeting. The event was won by Renate Gotschl of Austria.
9 The varsity rugby match between Oxford and Cambridge ended in an 11-11 draw at Twickenham.
13 Great Britain ended the European Short Course Swimming Championships with 14 medals. The seven golds were won by Mark Foster (50m butterfly and 50m freestyle), Joanna Jackson (400m freestyle), Alison Sheppard (100m freestyle), Ian Edmond (200m breaststroke), James Gibson (100m breaststroke) and Melanie Marshall (200m freestyle).
Carol Owens of New Zealand beat Britain's Cassie Jackman 3-9, 9-2, 9-7, 9-3, to win the World Squash Open in Hong Kong.
Ricky Hatton, 'The Pride of Manchester', defeated Ghana's Ben Tackie on a unanimous points decision to make an 11th successful defence of his WBU light-welterweight crown. The fight at the MEN Arena, Manchester, was Hatton's 34th unbeaten encounter as a professional.
14 Jonny Wilkinson was named BBC Sports Personality of the Year. Sir Steve Redgrave was voted the Golden Athlete of all the previous winners. The England rugby union side won the team award and Lance Armstrong won Best Overseas Sportsman. A lifetime achievement award was presented to Martina Navratilova.
Georgina Harland of Great Britain won the modern pentathlon World Cup in Athens.
Brian Lara of the West Indies scored 28 runs off a single over to create a new Test match record. Lara hit South African spinner, Robin Peterson, for 4, 6, 6, 4, 4, 4, during the first Test at the Wanderers, Johannesburg.
15 World champion Ivica Kostelic charged to victory in a men's World Cup slalom race in Madonna di Campiglio, Italy. The Croatian, brother of women's World Cup champion Janica, was only sixth after the first run but produced a faultless second run under floodlights to take victory.
17 Richard Callicott was replaced as chief executive of UK Sport by Liz Nicholl, the former chief executive of the All-England Netball Association. UK Sport is the body responsible for elite athletes, hosting major events and carrying out Britain's drug testing.
John White, the Australian squash player who represents Scotland, became world no. 1 on the Professional Squash Association computer rankings.
Justin Wilson's last hope of securing a Formula One drive for the following year was dashed when Minardi offered a contract to Zsolt Baumgartner. Wilson drove for Jaguar in 2003 but was dropped at the end of the season.
18 Seven jockeys were suspended for 19 days after taking the wrong course during a selling hurdle race at Ludlow.
19 Rio Ferdinand, the Manchester United defender, was suspended from playing for eight months for missing a drug test.
20 Lesley McKenna of Scotland took the overall lead in the half-pipe discipline of the Nokia FIS World Cup tour with a hard-won third place in the latest round of the snowboarding World Championship.
21 England were beaten by Sri Lanka by an innings and 215 runs in the third and final Test in Colombo and thereby lost the three-match series 1-0. Muttiah Muralitharan took 26 wickets in the series at 12.3 runs apiece.
Amr Shabana of Egypt, the world no. 11, won the World Open squash title in Lahore to become the first Egyptian and the lowest-ranked player to take the title. Shabana beat the fourth-seeded Thierry Lincou of France 15-14, 9-15, 15-11, 15-7.
The USA beat Europe 11-9 in the Mosconi Cup pool competition in Las Vegas.
22 Pavel Nedved of Juventus and the Czech Republic was named European Footballer of the Year.
26 Edredon Bleu, ridden by Jim Culloty and trained by Henrietta Knight, won the Pertemps King George VI Chase at Kempton.
28 Best Mate, ridden by Jim Culloty and trained by Henrietta Knight, won the Ericsson Chase at Leopardstown in Ireland.
31 England table tennis player Matthew Kenny, 19, was recovering after an operation to repair a shattered eye-socket, damaged during an assault in a public house.

MISCELLANEOUS

Obituaries of Sporting Persons 2003

January 2003

2   Peter Harris, footballer, born 19 December 1925
    Alastair Wood, athlete, born 13 January 1933
3   Sid Gillman, American football coach, born 26 October 1911
10 Pat McCarthy, draughts player, born 31 December 1943
12 Paul Pender, boxer, born 20 June 1930
16 Jeannette Campbell, swimmer, born 8 March 1916
20 Bill Werbeniuk, snooker player, born 14 January 1947
26 Valeriy Brumel, high jumper, born 14 April 1942

February 2003

1   Peter Deakin, rugby administrator, born 1953
4   Johnny Sullivan, boxer, born 19 December 1932
5   Manfred von Brauchitsch, racing driver, born 15 August 1905
13 Kid Gavilan (Gerardo González), boxer (inventor of the bolo punch), born 6 January 1926
14 Nick Duncombe, rugby player, born 21 January 1982
21 Harry Matthews, boxer, born 9 December 1922
27 Charles Knott, cricketer and sports promoter, born 26 November 1914
28 Chris Brasher, athlete and founder of the London Marathon, born 21 August 1928

March 2003

1   Ian Connell, racing driver and engineer, born 15 October 1913
6   Ludek Pachman, chess grandmaster, born 11 May 1924
8   Professor Lim Kok Ann, chess player and bacteriologist, born 27 January 1920
10 Barry Sheene, motorcycle racer, born 11 September 1950
12 Andrei Kivilev, cyclist, born 21 September 1973
16 Major Ronald Ferguson, former polo manager to the Duke of Edinburgh
    and the Prince of Wales
17 Lewis Bernard Cannell, rugby player and radiologist, born 10 June 1926
18 Karl Kling, racing driver, born 16 September 1910

April 2003

22 Louis Shenkin, bridge player and administrator, born 17 January 1917
25 Vernon Pugh, rugby union administrator and barrister, born 5 July 1945
27 Piet Roozenburg, draughts player, born 24 October 1924
29 Sue Sally Hale, polo player, born 1937
    Trevor Ford, footballer, born 1 October 1923
30 Wim Van Est, cyclist, born 25 March 1923

May 2003

10 Milan Vukcevich, chemist and chess problem-setter, born 11 March 1937
11 Ernie Toshack, Australian cricketer, born 8 December 1914
15 Rick Van Steenbergen, Belgian cyclist, born 9 October 1924
16 Mark McCormack, sports promoter and writer, born 6 November 1930
21 Alejandro De Tomaso, car racer and manufacturer, born 10 July 1928

June 2003

1   Sir Peter Yarranton, rugby player and administrator, born 30 September 1924
2   Makoto Kozuru, Japanese baseball player, born 17 December 1922
3   Peter Bromley, racing commentator, born 30 April 1929
7   Olav Ulland, ski jumper, born 23 November 1910
8   Leighton Rees, darts player, born 17 January 1940
18 Larry Doby, baseball player and manager, born 13 December 1923
23 Doug Ring, Australian cricketer, born 14 October 1918
26 Marc-Vivien Foe, footballer, born 1 May 1975
29 Cliff Harrison, rugby union player, born 10 May 1911

July 2003

2   Briggs Cunningham, racing driver and yachtsman, born 19 January 1907
30 Steve Hislop, motorcycle racer, born 11 January 1962

August 2003

2   Alonzo Pettie, rodeo champion, born 18 June 1910
8   Jack Noreiga, West Indian cricketer, born 15 April 1936
9   Trevor Smith, footballer, born 13 April 1936
10 John Banks, bookmaker and racehorse owner, born 19 August 1934
11 Herb Brooks, ice hockey coach, born 5 August 1937
14 Helmut Rahn, German footballer, born 16 August 1929
     Lothar Emmerich, German footballer, born 29 November 1941
19 Robin Hodgkin, mountaineer, born 12 February 1916
24 Kent Walton, television wrestling commentator, born 22 August 1917

September 2003

2   Peter West, television cricket presenter, born 12 August 1920
7   Anton Barichievich, Canadian strongman, born 10 October 1925
8   Gulubhai Ramchand, Indian cricketer, born 26 July 1927
22 Norman Hoffman, pioneer of freefall skydiving, born 24 February 1924
25 George Plimpton, journalist and sports-writer, born 18 March 1927
28 Althea Gibson, tennis player, born 25 August 1927
29 Ernie Fossey, boxing promoter, born 2 September 1930

October 2003

2   Denis Moore, cricketer, born 26 September 1910
6   Joe Baker, footballer, born 17 July 1940
7   John Herring, athlete, born 10 April 1935
12 Bill Shoemaker, jockey, born 19 August 1931
16 Laszlo Papp, boxer, born 25 March 1926

November 2003

23 Paul Grant, Mr Universe 1973, born 26 June 1943
29 Gertrude Ederle, first woman to swim the English Channel, born 23 October 1905

December 2003

5   Antony Rowe, submariner, Olympic rower and book printer, born 4 August 1924
6   Jose Maria Jimenez, racing cyclist, born 6 February 1971

MISCELLANEOUS

Sporting Record 2004

January 2004

1 The IAAF sanctioned Paula Radcliffe's road times over 5km, 10km and the marathon as world records.
2 Robert Croft, the Glamorgan spin-bowler, announced his retirement from International cricket.
4 Phil Taylor beat Kevin Painter 7-6 to become Ladbrokes.com World Darts Champion, at the Circus Tavern, Purfleet.
   Brian Lara became the fastest man to reach 9000 runs in Test cricket during his innings of 115 against South Africa in the Third Test.
5 It was announced that British tennis player Greg Rusedski tested positive for nandrolone last July (see entry for 10 March).
6 Steve Waugh ended his illustrious Test cricket career in Sydney following the drawn Fourth Test against India. The series was drawn with a win each and two draws.
10 Roger Hammond won the senior men's cyclo-cross national championship at Sutton Park, Birmingham
11 Andy Fordham beat Mervyn King 6-3 to win the BDO World Darts Championship.
   Chelsea football star Juan Sebastian Veron was held hostage with his family when a robber forced his way into their London home. The intruder locked the family in a bathroom as he ransacked the property before fleeing with £60,000 of jewellery.
12 Essex Metropolitan, perennial winners of the National Counties Netball League, suffered their first defeat in more than three years when they lost 52-45 to Gloucestershire.
17 Tony McCoy became the first National Hunt jockey to ride 2000 winners when Magical Bailiwick won the 2.50 at Wincanton.
   Martin Johnson, England's World Cup captain, retired from international rugby.
18 Chemmy Alcott, Britain's number one ski racer, announced herself at the elite level by finishing ninth in the World Cup downhill at Cortina d'Ampezzo. It was the best performance by a British woman since Gina Hathorn's similar placing in a slalom at Heavenly Valley in March 1972.
   Alex Marshall of Scotland beat Mark McMahon of Australia 13-3, 9-8, to win the bowls World Indoor Championship in Norfolk.
21 Alex Marshall and Amy Monkhouse beat Andy Thomson and Carol Ashby , 9-10, 11-7, 2-0, to win the bowls World Mixed Pairs Matchplay Indoor Championship at Potters Leisure Resort in Norfolk.
24 Michael Sprott beat Danny Williams on a controversial points decision at the Wembley Conference Centre to become the British and Commonwealth heavyweight champion.
25 Ronnie O'Sullivan defeated Steve Davis 9-8 in the final of snookers' Welsh Open in Cardiff.
   Sebastien Loeb of France won his second-successive Monte Carlo Rally. Ulsterman Kris Meeke was the highest-placed British driver in 14th place.
   Marcel Siem of Germany defeated Frenchman Raphael Jacquelin on the third extra-hole of a sudden-death play-off to win the Dunhill Championship at Houghton Golf Club, Johannesburg.
26 Simon Mason and Kate Walsh were named as UK Players of the Year by the Hockey Writers' Club.
28 Justine Henin-Hardenne once again beat her compatriot Kim Clijsters in a major tennis championship final when she triumphed 6-3, 4-6, 6-3, to add the Australian Open to her French and US titles.
30 Former world champion Michael Nunn was sentenced to 24 years in prison for buying 1kg of cocaine from an undercover agent in Davenport, Iowa, in August 2002. Nunn won 58 of his 62 fights and held the IBF middleweight and WBA super-middleweight titles.
31 Bart Wellens of Belgium won the World Cyclo-Cross Championship at Pontchateau, Brittany. Roger Hammond of Great Britain finished 11th, the best-placing by a Briton since David Baker's ninth place at Leeds in 1992.

February 2004

1 Roger Federer of Switzerland beat Marat Safin of Russia, 7-6 (7-3), 6-4, 6-2, to win the Australian Open tennis title and become the current world number one ranked player.
   The New England Patriots defeated Carolina Panthers 32-29 to win Super Bowl XXXVIII at the Reliant stadium. Adam Vinatieri kicked a field goal four seconds from time to ensure victory and Tom Brady won Most Valuable Player. (Pop singer Janet Jackson created controversy during the half-time duet when Justin Timberlake ripped off her leather bustier and exposed her right breast.)
3 Francis Joyon of France broke the monohull and multihull solo round-the-world records completing his 27,150-mile voyage in 72 days, 22 hours and 54 minutes, aboard his 90ft trimaran *IDEC*.
4 Sir Clive Woodward was announced as the coach of the British and Irish Lions for next year's tour to New Zealand. Former England Grand Slam captain Bill Beaumont was named by the Lions tour committee as manager of the party.
5 Michelle Wei, the 14-year-old golfing sensation, was selected for the American Curtis Cup team and will become the youngest player ever to compete in the match against Great Britain and Ireland.
6 Lennox Lewis, the undisputed heavyweight champion of the world, announced his retirement from boxing.
8 Paul Hunter beat Ronnie O'Sullivan 10-9 in the final of the Masters tournament at Wembley
15 Kristan Bromley of Great Britain won his fourth of the five World Cup bob skeleton events to take the series championship.
   John Daly won the Buick International at Torrey Pines, his first tournament success in the last 190 events he has played.

In the Six-Nations Championship England defeated Italy 50-9 in Rome, France beat Ireland 35-17 in Paris, and Wales beat Scotland 23-10 at the Millennium Stadium, Cardiff.

16   Champion jump jockey Tony McCoy fractured his cheekbone when falling off Polar Red in a novice chase at Plumpton.

20   Tim Henman beat Roger Federer 6-3, 7-6, in the quarter-final of the Rotterdam Open tennis championship. Henman was the last man to beat Federer, the world number one, in October 2003 and has beaten him in all five completed matches they have played.

Kelly Holmes broke the British indoor record over 1000m in Birmingham with a time of 2:32.96. Joe Pavey also broke the British record in the 3000m, her time of 8:34.55 being good enough for third in a world-class field. Kenenisa Bekele of Ethiopia clocked 12:49.61 in the 5000m to eclipse the world record by nearly a second.

21   Joe Calzaghe retained his WBO Super-Middleweight title when he stopped Mger Mkrtchian in the seventh round in Cardiff.

England defeated Scotland 35-13 at Murrayfield in the Six-Nations Championship. France beat Italy 25-0 in the Stade de France.

Tim Henman was beaten 6-3, 6-3, by Lleyton Hewitt in the semi-final of the Rotterdam Open tennis championship.

Glynn Tromans regained the English cross-country title he last won in 2000. Ethiopian-born Birhan Dagne won the women's title.

22   Ireland defeated Wales 36-15 at Lansdowne Road in the Six-Nations Championship.

Jürgen Grobler, the national rowing coach, announced that Matthew Pinsent and James Cracknell would join Steve Williams and Josh West in the coxless four for the forthcoming Olympic Games (see entry for 2 July).

24   British athlete Dwain Chambers was banned for two years by UK Athletics for his positive drug test for the designer drug THG. A British Olympic Association bye-law also prevents him from ever representing Great Britain at an Olympic Games. Chambers' coach, Remi Korchemny, was also charged in California with running an illegal drug distribution operation.

29   Tiger Woods defended his WGC Accenture Matchplay title following a 3 & 2 victory over Davis Love III in California.

Middlesbrough beat Bolton 2-1 at the Millennium Stadium to win the Carling Cup Final.

March 2004

2   Ken Bates, the long-serving Chelsea chairman, resigned his position a year earlier than expected.

5   Jason Gardener of Great Britain won the 60m title at the World Indoor Athletics Championships in Budapest.

World number one Justine Henin-Hardenne was beaten for the first time this year by Svetlana Kuznetsova in the semi-finals of the Qatar Open tennis championship.

6   Stephen Maguire beat Jimmy White 9-3 in the final of the European Snooker Open.

Ireland defeated England 19-13 at Twickenham in the Six-Nations Championship. Italy recorded only their third-ever win in the competition when they beat Scotland 20-14 in Rome.

7   France beat Wales 29-22 at the Millennium Stadium to remain the only unbeaten side in the Six-Nations Championship.

Michael Schumacher won the opening Formula One Grand Prix of the season in Melbourne, Australia.

Michael East finished third in the 1500m at the World Indoor Athletics Championships but was disqualified for impeding another runner, Laban Rotich of Kenya, who was eventually awarded the bronze. Jo Fenn won Britain's second medal of the championships, placing third to Maria Mutola in the 800m in a time of 1:59.50. Stephen Eberharter of Austria won the Men's World Cup Downhill title following his victory in Kvitfjell, Norway.

8   Sebastian Coe resigned as president of the Amateur Athletic Association.

9   Jean Luc van den Heede passed the Creac'h lighthouse on Ushant to slash the westabout, single-handed, non-stop round-the-world record by 29 days. His Adrienn set off on 7 November last year and posted a 122-day, 14-hour, 3-minute voyage on the 'wrong way' route by turning west at Cape Horn. Francis Joyon broke the eastabout record last month.

10   Greg Rusedski was cleared of the drug-taking offence hanging over him since he tested positive for a low level of nandrolone during an ATP tournament in Indianapolis in July 2003.

11   Three Leicester City footballers were released on bail in Cartagena, Spain, accused of sexual assault.

12   Shane Warne became the first spinner in history to reach 500 wickets during Australia's 197-run victory over Sri Lanka in the first Test at Galle.

13   Bode Miller became World Cup Giant slalom champion after the final event was cancelled because of fog. Hermann Maier of Austria won the overall competition. Anja Paerson of Sweden won the women's overall skiing title.

Ronald Wright defeated Shane Mosley to become undisputed light-middleweight champion of the world, in Las Vegas.

14   England beat West Indies by 10 wickets in Kingston, Jamaica, after the home side were bowled out for 47 in their second innings, their lowest-ever Test score.

16   Hardy Eustace, trained by Dessie Hughes and ridden by Conor O'Dwyer, won the Smurfit Champion Hurdle at Cheltenham.

Muttiah Muralitharan became the third bowler in Test history to take 500 wickets, during a Test match against Australia in Kandy, Sri Lanka.

17   Azertyuiop, ridden by Ruby Walsh and trained by Paul Nicholls, won the Queen Mother Champion Chase at Cheltenham.

18   The Cheltenham Gold Cup was won for the third successive year by Best Mate, ridden by Jim Culloty and trained by Henrietta Knight.

20   Audley Harrison knocked out Dutchman Richel Hersisia in the fourth round at Wembley Arena to claim the

lightly-regarded World Boxing Foundation belt.

Benita Johnson became the first Australian to win a world cross-country medal when she won the long-course race in Brussels.

Michael Schumacher won the Malaysian Formula One Grand Prix in Sepang. Jenson Button placed third, his first podium finish.

England defeated Wales 31-21 at Twickenham in the Six-Nations Championship. Ireland beat Italy 19-3 at Lansdowne Road.

21   France beat Scotland 31-0 at Murrayfield in the Six-Nations Championship.

Colin Montgomerie won the Caltex Masters in Singapore, his first European Tour title in 16 months.

27   Andrea Holt clinched her fifth English national women's singles table tennis title, in Sheffield.

Babodana, ridden by Philip Robinson and trained by Mark Tompkins, won the Lincoln Handicap at Doncaster.

28   Cambridge beat Oxford easily in the 150th University Boat Race, after a clash of oars caused Oxford's Chris Kennelly to lose an oar and his seat.

30   British number one Chris Bray was beaten in the real tennis world championship, losing the second leg of the final eliminator to the American Tim Chisholm, the world number two, in New York.

April 2004

2   Manchester United defeated Arsenal 1-0 in the semi-final of the FA Cup.

Heath Streak resigned as captain of the Zimbabwe cricket team and was replaced by wicketkeeper Tatenda Taibu.

3   Amberleigh House, ridden by Graham Lee and trained by Ginger McCain, won the Martell Cognac Grand National.

Matthew Hoggard bowled a hat-trick as England defeated West Indies by eight wickets in the third Test in Barbados.

5   Millionaire businessman Steve Fossett broke the round-the-world sailing record by almost six days aboard his 38-metre maxi catamaran, Cheyenne. Fossett's time of 58 days, 9 hours and 32 minutes beat Frenchman Bruno Peyron's time of 64 days, 8 hours and 37 minutes, set in 2002.

6   Chelsea beat Arsenal 2-1 (3-2 on agg) in the quarter-final of the Champions League.

Monaco defeated Real Madrid 3-1 on away goals (5-5 on agg) in the other quarter-final of the Champions League.

7   Deportivo La Coruna defeated AC Milan 4-0 in La Coruna to win 5-4 on aggregate in the quarter-final of the Champions League. In the remaining quarter final Porto drew 2-2 with Lyons to win 4-2 on aggregate.

11   Jimmy White beat Paul Hunter 9-7 in the final of the Player's Championship in Glasgow. The victory was White's first snooker ranking tournament success for 12 years.

Phil Mickelson of the USA won the US Masters at Augusta with a score of 279, 9 under par.

In the Davis Cup Euro/Africa Group 1, 2nd Round, Great Britain beat Luxembourg 4-1

12   Brian Lara of the West Indies became the first player to score 400 in a Test innings. His 400 not out, scored during the Fourth Test against England in Antigua, eclipsed the 380 scored by Matthew Hayden for Australia against Zimbabwe in 2003. West Indies declared their innings at 751-5, the highest total scored against England in a Test match. The unbroken sixth-wicket stand of 282 between Lara and Ridley Jacobs (107 not out) was also a West Indies record.

Waqar Younis, the great Pakistan fast bowler, announced his retirement from cricket. In his 87 Tests he took 373 wickets at 23.56, second only to his great opening partner Wasim Akram's 414.

14   The Fourth Test match between England and the West Indies ended in a draw.

16   Tricia Heberle resigned as Great Britain and England women's hockey coach following the team's failure to qualify for the Olympic Games in Athens.

17   Grey Abbey, ridden by Graham Lee and trained by Howard Johnson, won the Scottish Grand National at Ayr.

18   Valentino Rossi won the opening MotoGP race in South Africa on a Yahama and thereby created a remarkable record. He won the final race of last season on a Honda to become the first person to take back-to-back successes for different manufacturers.

Tracey Morris finished the London Marathon as leading British woman in a time of 2hrs 33mins 52secs, a personal best time by one hour and six minutes!

21   Ron Atkinson, the ITV football pundit and Guardian columnist, resigned his positions following remarks made during the Champions League semi-final between Chelsea and Monaco. Atkinson's remarks about Marcel Desailly were caught on air by Arabian Radio and Television.

24   Mark Williams the current world snooker champion was beaten in the second round of the 2004 championship by Joe Perry.

25   Michael Schumacher won the San Marino Formula One Grand Prix at Imola. Jenson Button placed second after starting on pole position.

Sweden beat Germany 7-6 to win the men's curling world championship. Canada beat Norway 8-4 in the women's final.

26   Australian swimmer Ian Thorpe was handed a lifeline to compete in the 400m freestyle at this year's Olympics despite being disqualified during the Australian trials after falling from his block at the start of the race. Teammate Craig Stevens withdrew from the eight-length race to accommodate Thorpe.

28   The all-conquering partnership of Tony McCoy and Martin Pipe was ended when McCoy announced he would ride for the Jonjo O'Neill stable in future. On a sadder note, Persian Punch, the most popular flat horse in Britain, had a heart attack and died during the 2-mile Sagaro Stakes at Ascot.

29   Following Dwain Chambers' two-year doping ban, the IAAF announced the disqualification of the Brititsh 4 x 100m team that gained the silver medal at the 2003 World Championships in Paris. The three other athletes to lose their medals are Christian Malcolm, Darren Campbell and Marlon Devonish.

May 2004

1 Haafhd, ridden by Richard Hills and trained by his father Barry, won the 2000 Guineas at Newmarket.
2 Attraction, ridden by Kevin Darley and trained by Mark Johnston, won the 1000 Guineas at Newmarket.
   William Fox-Pitt, riding Tamarillo, won the Mitsubishi Badminton international three-day event.
3 Ronnie O'Sullivan defeated Graeme Dott 18-8 in the final of the Embassy World Snooker Championship in Sheffield.
6 Muttiah Muralitharan of Sri Lanka equalled Courtney Walsh's tally of 519 Test match wickets on the opening day of the first Test against Zimbabwe in Harare. Walsh's record was attained in 132 Test matches.
8 Muttiah Muralitharan of Sri Lanka duly claimed the Test match wicket record on the third day of the first Test against Zimbabwe. His 520th victim was Mluleki Nkala. His 521st wicket was taken with the very next ball. Sri Lanka won the match by an innings and 240 runs. Muralitharan's record was attained in only 89 Test matches.
9 Michael Schumacher won the Spanish Formula One Grand Prix in Barcelona to maintain his 100 per cent success this season.
   Barry Lane of England won the British Masters Golf Championship at the Forest of Arden
10 Yorkshire's Nick Matthew beat world number one squash player, Peter Nicol, on the opening day of the Brit Insurance PSA Super Series at the Broadgate Arena in London.
   In the World Triathlon Championships in Madeira Sheila Taormina of the USA won the women's title and Bevan Docherty of New Zealand won the men's.
15 Arsenal beat Leicester City 2-1 at Highbury to become the first side to finish the season unbeaten in 38 Premier League games.
   South Africa, who narrowly failed to be awarded the 2006 World Cup (losing out to Germany by one vote), were awarded the 2010 finals at the World Trade Centre in Zurich by 14 votes to 10 over Morocco. Nelson Mandela acted as spokesman for his country's bid while Zinedine Zidane (the French footballer of Algerian extraction) was at the forefront of the Moroccan bid.
   Antonio Tarver knocked out Roy Jones Junior in the second round to win the WBC light-heavyweight title.
18 Greg Rusedski was beaten 6-2, 7-6, by local professional Jurgen Melzer in the Raiffeisen Grand Prix in Austria, his first match on the ATP Tour since clearing his name after an alleged doping offence
19 Lord (Sebastian) Coe was appointed chairman of the committee to further London's bid to stage the 2012 Olympic Games.
   Valencia beat Marseilles 2-0 in the UEFA Cup Final in Gothenburg, Sweden.
20 Nick Faldo played his first competitive golf round with the assistance of spectacles. He scored a 75 in the first round of the Deutsche Bank SAP Open in Heidelberg, Germany.
   Manchester United beat Millwall 3-0 to win the FA Cup for the eleventh time. Celtic beat Dunfermline 3-1 in the Scottish Cup final.
   Hednesford beat Canvey Island 3-2 in the FA Trophy final at Villa Park.
   Cyclist Stuart Dangerfield won the National 10-mile Time Trial Championship at Tuxford, Notts, in a course record 18min 40secs.
23 Jarno Trulli of Italy, driving a Renault, won the Monaco Formula One Grand Prix in Monte Carlo after Michael Schumacher crashed out in bizarre fashion behind the safety car. Britain's Jenson Button, driving for BAR, placed second.
   The two elite winners of the Great Manchester Run were Ireland's Sonia O'Sullivan and Craig Mottram of Australia.
   Attraction, ridden by Kevin Darley and trained by Mark Johnston, won the Irish 1000 Guineas, the first horse to complete the double of English and Irish Guineas.
24 Alessandro Petacchi of Italy won his eighth stage of the Tour of Italy to beat the previous record seven stage wins of Belgians Roger de Vlaeminck and Freddy Maertens.
   England beat New Zealand by seven wickets in the First Test at Lords.
27 Nasser Hussain announced his retirement from cricket, three days after his century gave England victory against New Zealand in the First Test.
   Chris Hoy of Great Britain won gold in the 1000m at the World Track Cycling Championships in Melbourne, Australia.
29 Scott Drummond, a Scottish golfer ranked 435th in the world, won the Volvo PGA championship at Wentworth.
   Jamie Staff of Great Britain won gold in the Keirin at the World Track Cycling Championships in Melbourne, Australia.
30 Tim Henman emulated his maternal grandfather, Henry Billington, by reaching the quarter-finals of the French Open.
   Michael Schumacher won the European Formula One Grand Prix at the Nurburgring.
   Damiano Cunego, 23, became the youngest winner of the Tour of Italy for 25 years, as the cycling event ended in Milan with sprinter Alessandro Petacchi winning a post-war record ninth stage.
31 Kenenisa Bekele of Ethiopia broke the 5000m world record in Hengelo, Holland, with a time of 12 min 37.37secs.

June 2004

2 John McGuinness became the fastest rider in the history of the Isle of Man TT races as he covered the 37.73-mile Mountain Course aboard his 1000cc Yamaha in a time of 17min 46.7secs, an average speed of 127.34mph.
   Simply Fabulous, an eight-year-old greyhound beat Tiny Tim, a six-year-old bay gelding, by seven lengths over 2 furlongs of the Kempton Park racecourse. The special race was run as a publicity stunt to advertise the forthcoming derbies on 5 June.

4 Ouija Board, ridden by Kieren Fallon and trained by Ed Dunlop, won the Vodafone Oaks at Epsom.
  Tim Henman was beaten in the semi-finals of the French Open by Guillermo Coria of Argentina, 3-6, 6-4, 6-0, 7-5
5 North Light, ridden by Kieren Fallon and trained by Sir Michael Stoute, won the Vodafone Derby at Epsom.
  Droopys Scholes won the Greyhound Derby at Wimbledon in a time of 28.62 seconds.
  Phil Taylor scored a nine-dart finish during his 8-2 victory over Matt Chapman in the fourth round of the Budweiser UK Open in Bolton
  Anastasia Myskina beat her Russian compatriot Elena Dementieva 6-1, 6-2, in the final of the French Open tennis championship
  England defeated Iceland 6-1 in a friendly football match at the City of Manchester Stadium.
6 John Whitaker, on Buddy Bunn, a horse he had ridden for the first time only the day before, won his fourth DFS British Jumping Derby at Hickstead, beating his 18-year-old niece Ellen, on AK Lacarno, in a jump-off against the clock after they both jumped the only two clear rounds in the competition.
  Gaston Gaudio of Argentina beat Guillermo Coria 0-6, 3-6, 6-4, 6-1, 8-6, in the final of the French Open tennis championships.
  Colin Breeze became the third rider to die in this year's Isle of Man TT Festival following the previous deaths of Serge le Moal and Paul Cowley.
  Cyclist Stuart Dangerfield won the National 25-mile Time Trial Championship in Crawley, West Sussex, in a championship record of 48min 44secs. Michael Hutchinson placed second in 49min 9secs.
  Essex professional golfer Simon Khan won the Wales Open title in a sudden-death play-off against Paul Casey.
  Ernie Els won the Memorial golf tournament in Dublin, Ohio.
  Stuart Wilson became the first Scot to win the Amateur golf championship at St Andrews since Craig Watson defeated Trevor Immelman at Royal St George's in 1997.
  Oscar De La Hoya defeated Felix Sturm of Germany on a controversial points decision to take the WBO middleweight title.
8 Welshman Ian Flanagan, ranked No 866 in the world, defeated last year's Wimbledon finalist Mark Philippoussis, 7-6, 7-6, in the first round of the Stella Artois Championships at Queen's Club.
  American Stacy Dragila and Ethiopian Kenenisa Bekele broke world records in Ostrava. Dragila pole vaulted 4.83m and Bekele ran the 10,000m in 26mins 20.31secs.
11 Elvan Abeylegasse of Turkey broke the seven-year-old women's world 5000m record at the Bergen Golden League meeting in Norway. The Ethiopian-born 21-year-old clocked 14:24.68, beating Bo Jiang of China's mark of 14:28.09.
  Adrian Archibald won the prestigious senior race at the Isle of Man TT.
  Great Britain won the Tri-Nations men's hockey tournament at Nottingham by beating Pakistan for the second time in four days in the final match. The 2-1 victory gave England the first successive victory over Pakistan since the 1952 Olympics.
12 Ricky Hatton celebrated his 36th straight victory with a one-sided points victory over Wilfredo Vilches of Argentina to retain his WBU light-welterweight crown, at the Manchester MEN Arena.
13 Michael Schumacher won the Canadian Formula One Grand Prix in Montreal for the seventh time.
  France defeated England 2-1 in their first Euro 2004 match with two goals in injury time after Frank Lampard gave England a first-half lead.
  England beat New Zealand by four wickets at Trent Bridge to win the three-Test series 3-0
  The United States beat Great Britain and Ireland 10-8 in golf's Curtis Cup played at Formby.
  Labegorce reversed their loss in the final seconds of the Hildon Queen's Cup final last year with a 7-6 triumph over Azzur at Smith's Lawn, Guard's Polo Club, Windsor Great Park.
  American Greg Hancock won the British Speedway GP at the Millennium Stadium, Cardiff.
15 Greg Rusedski defeated Slovakian Karol Kucera 3-6, 7-6, 6-3, at Nottingham, his first victory on the main ATP Tour since early January.
17 England defeated Switzerland 3-0 in their second game in Euro 2004 as the French were held to a 2-2 draw against Croatia.
  The Ascot Gold Cup was won by Papineau, ridden by Frankie Dettori and trained by Saeed bin Suroor.
18 Dual Guineas winner Attraction, ridden by Kevin Darley and trained by Mark Johnston, won the Coronation Stakes at Royal Ascot.
19 Audley Harrison stopped Poland's Tomasz Bonin in the ninth round to retain his World Boxing Foundation belt at Alexandra Palace. Harrison's fights will no longer be sponsored by the BBC.
20 Retief Goosen of South Africa won the US Open golf championship at Shinnecock Hills, Long Island, New York.
  Jan Ullrich of Germany won the Tour of Switzerland by one second.
  Michael Schumacher won the United States Formula One Grand Prix in Indianapolis, his eighth victory from nine races.
  Cyclist Michael Hutchinson won the National 50-mile Time Trial Championship at Bishop's Tawton, Devon, in 1hr 46m 9s.
21 Martina Navratilova beat Catalina Castano of Colombia 6-0, 6-1, in the first round of the ladies' singles at Wimbledon.
  England defeated Croatia 4-2 in Lisbon to qualify for the quarter-finals of Euro 2004.
  Johann Volanthen of Switzerland became the youngest player to score in the history of the European Nations Cup. Wayne Rooney had held this record for four days but Volanthen is three months his junior.
22 Martin Broughton took over as BHB (British Horseracing Board) chairman from Peter Savill.
24 Portugal beat England 6-5 on penalties in the quarter-finals of Euro 2004 after a 2-2 draw after extra time. Swiss referee Urs Meier disallowed an England 'goal' in the dying moments of normal time for a foul on the Portuguese goalkeeper.

26　Nicola Cooke took her fifth British road race cycling crown in six years at the Celtic Manor Resort, Newport.
Robin Reid defeated Ireland's Brian Magee on points to win the International Boxing Organisation super-middleweight crown at Belfast's King's Hall.

27　Roger Hammond retained the British road race cycling crown at the Celtic Manor Resort, Newport.
Grey Swallow, ridden by Pat Smullen and trained by Dermot Weld, won the Budweiser Irish Derby at the Curragh.
Yelena Isinbeyeva of Russia smashed the world record for the women's pole vault in Gateshead with a height of 4.87m.

28　Egyptian Ahmed Nasr won the World Golf Croquet Championship 7-4, 7-3, 7-1, against New Zealander Dennis Bulloch, in Brighton.

30　Tim Henman was beaten in the quarter-finals of the Wimbledon Tennis Championships 7-6, 6-4, 6-2, by Mario Ancic of Croatia.

July 2004

2　Cyclist David Millar, the world time trial champion, admitted taking the banned blood booster EPO at an investigation in France and was immediately sacked by his Cofidis team and suspended from competition.
Alex Partridge, who replaced Josh West in the boat for the coxless four, suffered a collapsed lung and Ed Coode was named as his replacement. The other three members are Steve Williams, James Cracknell and Matthew Pinsent.

3　17-year-old Maria Sharapova of Russia beat American Serena Williams 6-1, 6-4, in the ladies' singles final at Wimbledon.

4　Michael Schumacher won the French Formula One Grand Prix at Magny-Cours, his ninth victory from ten races.
Roger Federer successfully defended his Wimbledon singles title beating American Andy Roddick 4-6, 7-5, 7-6, 6-4. Todd Woodbridge won a ninth men's doubles title at Wimbledon. He and his partner Jonas Bjorkman of Sweden defeated Julian Knowle of Austria and Nenad Zimonjic of Serbia 6-1, 6-4, 4-6, 6-4, to claim their third successive Wimbledon title. Brother and sister pairing Wayne and Cara Black of Zimbabwe beat Todd Woodbridge and Alicia Molik of Australia 3-6, 7-6 6-4, in the mixed double's final. Cara Black and Australian Rennae Stubbs beat Liezel Huber of South Africa and Japan's Ai Sugiyama 6-3, 7-6, to claim the women's doubles title.
Greece beat Portugal 1-0 in the final of Euro 2004 in Lisbon. Angelos Charisteas scored the winner in the 57th minute.
Retief Goosen of South Africa continued his sparkling form by winning the European Open by five strokes in Straffan, Co. Kildare.
Gary Smith of Gillingham and Claire Wright of Bracknell won the men's and women's titles at the British Trampolining Championships in Birmingham.
Meg Mallon of the USA won the US Women's Open Golf Championship at the Orchards Club in South Hadley, Massachusetts.
Svetlana Feofanova of Russia broke the women's pole vault world record in Heraklion, Greece, with a height of 4.88m

5　Graeme Hick scored 116 off 65 balls to equal the highest-ever score in the Twenty20 Cup competition during Worcester's 21-run victory over Northants at Luton.
Soviet Song , ridden by Johnny Murtagh and trained by James Fanshawe, won the Falmouth Stakes at Newmarket and beat the previously unbeaten Attraction in the process.

7　Sir Bobby Charlton holed-in-one at the 147-yard par three 16th at Formby Golf Club in Merseyside but created controversy by accepting a Mercedes A-class valued at about £13,000 for his efforts. Amateur golfers are prevented from accepting prizes in access of £500 and the former Manchester United and England striker will therefore relinquish his amateur status for the next five years. Sir Bobby is expected to auction the car for charity.

9　Brendan Hansen broke the 100m breast-stroke world record at the US Olympic trials in a time of 59.30secs.
Belle Vue's Joe Screen won the British Speedway Championship at Oxford.

10　Australian Leisel Jones broke the women's 200m breast-stroke world record in Brisbane in a time of 2mins 22.96secs.
Beth Tweddle won her fourth successive national all-round gymnastics title at the British Championships in Guildford, Surrey.
Phillip Rabinowitz of South Africa became the fastest 100-year-old in the world when he ran 100m in 30.86secs.
Rabinowitz ran 28.7secs on 4 July but a power failure meant the time could not be ratified.

11　Michael Schumacher won the British Formula One Grand Prix at Silverstone, his tenth victory from eleven races.
Britain's top cyclist Nicole Cooke won the Giro Donne, the 10-day women's Tour of Italy.
Thomas Levet of France won the Scottish Open Golf Championship at Loch Lomond.
Greg Rusedski moved back into the world's top 100 tennis players with victory in the Hall of Fame Championship in Newport, Rhode Island, USA.
Chris White of Great Britain won gold in the men's compound bow at the Field Archery World Championships in Plitvice, Croatia.

18　American Todd Hamilton beat Ernie Els of South Africa in a four-hole playoff for the Open Golf Championship at Royal Troon.
Stuart Wilson of Scotland was the only amateur to make the cut and his score of 296 was 22 shots behind the ten under par winning score but enough to make him leading amateur.
Ouija Board, ridden by Kieren Fallon and trained by Ed Dunlop, won the Darley Irish Oaks at the Curragh.

MISCELLANEOUS

       Carlos Sainz of Spain became the most successful rally driver in history when he captured the Rally of Argentina, his 26th win.

       Azzurra beat Dubai 17-9 to win the Veuve Cliquot Gold Cup, the British Open Polo Championship, at Cowdray Park, Sussex.

       Cyclist Michael Hutchinson won the National 100-mile Time Trial Championship at Attleborough, Norfolk, in 3hr 28m 59s.

22   Andrew Strauss and Robert Key shared a partnership of 291, the highest-ever for the second-wicket at Lord's, on the first day of the first Test against the West Indies.

25   Lance Armstrong made sporting history by winning an unprecedented sixth-consecutive Tour de France.

26   England beat the West Indies by 210 runs at Lord's to take a 1-0 lead in the three-match Npower Test series.

30   Zara Phillips, the Queen's grand-daughter, was knocked unconscious when she fell from her horse, Ardfield Magic Star, at the fourth fence of a cross country trial at Lulworth, Dorset.

       Yelena Isinbayeva broke the women's pole vault world record yet again with a height of 4.90m at Crystal Palace, London.

31   British heavyweight boxer Danny Williams knocked out former world heavyweight champion Mike Tyson in the fourth round of a non-title fight in Louisville, Kentucky.

       Phil Taylor beat Mark Dudbridge of England 18-8 in the final of the World Matchplay darts championship in Blackpool.

August 2004

1   Karen Stupples of England won the women's British Open golf championship at Sunningdale.

       England beat the West Indies by 256 runs at Edgbaston to take a 2-0 lead in the Npower Test series.

       Mark Palios resigned as chief executive of the Football Association.

3   Paul Scholes announced his retirement as an England footballer although he will continue to play for Manchester United.

4   Cyclist David Millar, the world time trial champion, was banned for two years and stripped of his title by the British Cycling Federation after admitting taking the blood-boosting drug Erythropoietin (EPO).

6   Jenson Button announced he is to leave the BAR racing team next year to join Williams.

7   Great Britain were beaten by Sweden 49-48 in the speedway World Cup final at Wimborne Road, Poole, Dorset. The evening ended in controversy amid accusations that Denmark's Hans Andersen who was leading the 25th and final race closed down his throttle to let Sweden's Peter Karlsson overtake while shutting the door on Britain's Scott Nicholls. Britain's Mark Loram scored a record 27 out of a possible maximum 30 points in the heat and final of the competition.

       Australian Steve Glasson beat Alex Marshall of Scotland 21-15 in the final of the men's singles at the World Outdoor Bowls Championships at Ayr Northfield. Scotland regained the world outdoor team title and lifted the Leonard Trophy for the fifth time.

       Leicestershire defeated Surrey by seven wickets in the Twenty20 Cup final at Edgbaston.

8   Arsenal beat Manchester United 3-1 in the FA Community Shield at the Millennium Stadium.

       Ruth Friend riding Two Thyme won the Hunter British Open championship at the Festival of British Eventing at Gatcombe Park.

       Andre Agassi beat Lleyton Hewitt 6-3, 3-6, 6-2, in the final of the Cincinnati Masters tennis tournament.

9   Lee Hughes, a footballer attached to West Bromwich Albion, was jailed for six years for leaving the scene of a car crash.

13   The Athen's Olympic Games opened with controversy after the host nation's two leading sprinters, Ekaterini Thanou and Konstantinos Kenteris, failed to turn up for random dope testing and were withdrawn from the competition by their national team officials.

14   Peter Waterfield and Leon Taylor gained the first British medal of the Athen's Olympics when they won silver in the 10m synchronised platform diving final.

15   Vijay Singh of Fiji won the US PGA championship at Whistling Straits, Wisconsin, in a three-hole playoff against Americans Chris DiMarco and Justin Leonard.

       Michael Schumacher won the Hungarian Formula One Grand Prix at the Hungaroring, Budapest, his seventh-consecutive victory.

16   England beat the West Indies by seven wickets at Old Trafford, their sixth-successive Test victory.

       Hal Sutton, the United States Ryder Cup captain, named Jay Hass and Stewark Cink as his two wild card entries.

17   Stephen Parry of Great Britain won a bronze medal in the 200m Butterfly and broke the British and Commonwealth record in the semi-finals and again in the final.

       Jonny Wilkinson played his first competitive rugby union match since damaging his neck and shoulder last December: Newcastle Falcons beat Connacht 32-9.

18   Alison Williamson of Great Britain won a bronze medal in the 70m archery competition at the Athen's Olympics.

       In a controversial equestrian event in Athens the Great Britain team won a bronze medal and Leslie Law an individual silver although both medals could have been promoted if the original decision to penalise the German gold medal winner Bettina Hoy for cantering through the start twice had been upheld. The team of Pippa Funnell (Primmore's Pride), Mary King (King Solomon), J. Brakewell (Over to You) and Leslie Law (Shear L'Eau) were unfortunate to lose William Fox-Pitt for the final showjumping phase after his horse Tamarillo failed a veterinary check (but see 21 August).

       In yet another unsatisfactory conclusion to an event Britain's Helen Reeves was eventually awarded a bronze medal in the women's K-1 canoe slalom after initially being given fourth place.

19   Shirley Robertson, Sarah Webb and Sarah Ayton gained a gold medal in the Yngling sailing class in Athens.

Nathan Robertson and Gail Emms secured a silver medal in the badminton mixed doubles after losing 15-1, 12-15, 15-12, in the final to the defending champions Ling Gao and Jun Zhang of China.

James Goddard of Great Britain finished fourth in the 200m backstroke but was initially promoted to third following the disqualification of Aaron Peirsol for an illegal turn. The original result stood after an appeal by the American team.

20   Chris Hoy of Great Britain won gold in the 1km cycling time trial in a new Olympic record of 1min 0.711secs. Campbell Walsh of Great Britain gained a silver medal in the men's K-1 canoe slalom. The Scot was originally placed third behind Frenchmen Benoit Peschier and Fabien Lefevre but yet another timing error eventually caused Lefevre to be downgraded.

The men's all-round gymnastics competition also ended in controversy when it was found that the bronze medallist Yang Tae-Young had in fact been docked a tenth of a point in error and should have beaten Paul Hamm and been awarded gold.

21   Britain's men's coxless four of Matthew Pinsent, James Cracknell, Steve Williams and Ed Coode, won an Olympic gold medal in a time of 6min 6.98secs. Pinsent's fourth gold was won in dramatic style beating the Canadians by 8/100th of a second.

Katherine Grainger and Cath Bishop claimed the women's coxless pairs silver and Sarah Winckless and Elise Laverick won bronze in the women's double sculls.

Sailor Ben Ainslie of Great Britain won a hard-fought gold in the Finn class after being disqualified on the first day and fighting back from 19th place to end the class with a comfortable win. Nick Rogers and Joe Glanfield gained a silver medal for Great Britain in the men's 470 class narrowly missing out on gold to the United States duo.

On a momentous day for Great Britain cyclist Bradley Wiggins won gold in the 4000m pursuit and Kelly Sotherton gained a bronze medal in the heptathlon although teammate Denise Lewis pulled out midway through the competition.

David Davies smashed the British and European record when winning bronze in the 1500m freestyle in 14mins 45.90secs.

In another twist to the drama of the Athens Games Bettina Hoy was penalised retrospectively for crossing the start line twice during the equestrian event and Britain's Leslie Law was upgraded to gold medal winner and the team to silver. Pippa Funnell who was originally fourth was promoted to bronze medal position.

South Africa lifted the Tri-Nations trophy defeating the Australian Wallabies 23-19 in the final match in Durban. The Springboks finished on 11 points, one point ahead of Australia and two ahead of New Zealand.

England beat the West Indies by ten wickets at the Oval to win the Test series 4-0 and complete a record-equalling seventh- successive Test victory.

22   Paula Radcliffe, the British favourite for the women's marathon in Athens, pulled out of the event at the 36k mark (22.37 miles) soon after being overtaken for third place.

The women's quadruple scullers, Rebecca Romero, Frances Houghton, Debbie Flood and Alison Mowbray, won silver, beaten by two-thirds of a length by a German crew that included Kathrin Boron, who matched Matthew Pinsent's achievement of four-consecutive gold medals.

Lloyd Smith became only the third person to score a century in the 33-year history of the Village Cup final competition at Lord's. Smith's 113 runs for Welsh side Sully Centurions helped them beat Exhall and Wixford from Warwickshire by 79 runs.

23   Irina Korzhanenko, the Russian gold medallist in the women's shot put competition, tested positive for steroids and was disqualified. Her 21.06m third round put was the only throw by any athlete over 20 metres.

Kelly Holmes of Great Britain won gold in the women's 800m and in cycling the men's 4000m pursuit team won silver.

24   Just half an hour before the medal ceremony for the men's discus, the International Olympic Committee stripped Robert Fazekas, the Hungarian winner, of his gold medal for refusing to give a full urine sample in the routine doping test.

Yelena Isinbayeva broke her own women's pole vault world record with a height of 4.91m after winning the gold medal in Athens. Isinbayeva had two failures, one each at 4.70 and 4.75, before clearing 4.80m on her third attempt to stay in the competition and subsequently win the gold medal.

25   Cyclist Bradley Wiggins gained his third medal at the Athens Games when he claimed bronze with Rob Hayles in the Madison.

Nick Dempsey won his second medal of the Games and Britain's second of the day with bronze in the men's Mistral sailing.

Arsenal broke Nottingham Forest's 26-year-old mark of 42 unbeaten league games with a 3-0 victory over Blackburn Rovers.

26   Britain's Chris Draper and Simon Hiscocks won sailing bronze in the 49er class in Athens.

27   Georgina Harland won a bronze for Great Britain in the Modern Pentathlon following.

Ireland's Cian O'Connor won gold in the men's individual showjumping final.

Xiang Liu of China equalled Colin Jackson's world record of 12.91sec in winning the 110 metres hurdles gold in Athens.

Paula Radcliffe repeated her performance in the marathon by dropping out of the women's 10,000m through exhaustion.

The International Olympic Committee decided to award silver medals to Chris Newton and Bryan Steel for being part of Great Britain's 4000m pursuit squad although neither cyclist rode in the final.

28   On a brilliant night for British athletics Kelly Holmes won the 1500 metres to gain her second gold medal in Athens.

The British 4 x 100m team of Jason Gardener, Darren Campbell, Marlon Devonish and Mark Lewis-Francis beat the crack American team to win an unexpected gold medal to ensure the men's athletics team did not return home medal-less.

Ian Wynne of Great Britain gained bronze in the men's K1 500m kayak final in Athens.

Gloucestershire beat Worcestershire by eight wickets at Lord's to win the Cheltenham & Gloucester Final.

29 The Olympic Games closed in Athens amid another controversy when the final event, the men's marathon, was marred by the same demonstrator who disrupted the British Formula One Grand Prix at Silverstone last year. Irishman Cornelius Horan barged race leader Vanderlei de Lima off the road and held him up for 15 crucial seconds, enabling the chasing runners to close to within a few seconds.

Michael Schumacher won his seventh Formula One world championship despite being beaten into second place by Kimi Raikkonen in the Belgian Grand Prix at Spa.

Europe's Ryder Cup captain Bernhard Langer named Luke Donald and Colin Montgomerie as his wild card selections.

30 Bobby Robson was sacked as manager of Newcastle after picking up just two points from their opening four games.

31 Wayne Rooney was transferred from Everton to Manchester United for £29.85million, a British transfer record, beating the £29.1million transfer of Rio Ferdinand from Leeds to Manchester United (although Ferdinand's transfer is expected to be worth in excess of £30million pounds to Leeds).

September 2004

1 The Tour of Britain cycle race was relaunched with the first stage being a 129-mile route through Lancashire won by Italian rider Stefano Zanini. The race was last held in 1999 but lack of sponsorship and quality fields caused its demise.

England beat India by seven wickets in a one-day international cricket match with Steve Harmison taking a hat-trick and newcomer Alex Wharf being nominated as man-of-the-match.

Several of the horseracing fraternity, including champion flat jockey Kieren Fallon, were arrested and interviewed at Bury St Edmunds police station as part of a long-standing enquiry into race-fixing. No charges were brought against any of the interviewees.

2 Sir Clive Woodward resigned his position of England head coach and his assistant, Andy Robinson, took over the role of caretaker coach.

3 England beat India by 70 runs at the Oval in the second one-day international cricket match for the NatWest Challenge.

Spain and Scotland were drawing 1-1 In a friendly international football match in Valencia when the match was abandoned in the 60th minute after the floodlights failed due to torrential rain.

4 International three-day eventer Caroline Pratt was killed in a tragic accident during the cross-country phase of the Burghley Horse Trials. Caroline, 42, was thrown from her horse Primitive Streak while jumping fence 26 and her horse fell on top of her.

On the first day of the rugby union Zurich Premiership Saracens beat Wasps 13-11 and London Irish beat Harlequins 18-12 both matches being played at Twickenham in front of a record crowd of 51,000. Northampton beat Bath 29-14 at Franklin Gardens in another Premiership opener.

England drew 2-2 with Austria in Vienna in their first World Cup 2006 qualifying match. A goalkeeping error by England keeper David James helped the Austrians equalise midway through the second-half. In other Group 6 qualifiers Wales drew with Azerbaijan 1-1 in Baku and Northern Ireland lost 3-0 to Poland at Windsor Park. In a Group 4 match at Lansdowne Road Ireland beat Cyprus 3-0 despite a depleted team through injuries.

5 Andrew Hoy of Australia riding Moon Fleet claimed his second Burghley Horse Trials victory, 25 years after his first.

Johnny Nelson successfully defended his WBO cruiserweight title with a seventh-round TKO of German Rudiger May in Essen.

The victory was Nelson's 12th defence. Enzo Maccarinelli of Swansea retained his WBU belt by beating Jesper Kristiansen by third-round stoppage and is now on target for a showdown against Nelson.

Mauricio Ardila of Colombia won the Tour of Britain cycle race by 12secs from New Zealand's Julian Dean.

India defeated England by 23 runs at Lord's in the third one-day game of the NatWest Challenge

Obituaries of Sporting Persons 2004

January 2004

2 Geoff Edrich, cricketer, born 13 July 1918
5   Vivian Jenkins, rugby player and journalist, born 2 November 1911
6   Reg Smith, footballer and manager, born 20 January 1912
14   Eric Sturgess, tennis player, born 10 May 1920
19   David Hookes, Australian cricketer, born 3 May 1955
24   Leonidas da Silva, Brazilian footballer, born 6 September 1913
25   Fanny Blankers-Koen, athlete, born 26 April 1918
31   Eleanor Holm, swimmer, born 6 December 1913

February 2004

1   Ally MacLeod, former Scotland football manager, born 26 February 1931
    Bob Stokoe, footballer and manager, born 21 September 1930
6   Sir David Meyrick, Olympic oarsman, born 2 December 1926
21   John Charles, footballer, born 27 December 1931
    Irina Press, athlete, born 10 March 1939
22   Roque Maspoli, Uruguayan goalkeeper, born 12 October 1917
24   Albert Axelrod, foil fencer, born 21 February 1921
25   Jack Flavell, cricketer, born 15 May 1929

March 2004

14   Vic Roberts, rugby player, born 6 August 1924
20   Doug Keller, rugby player, born 18 June 1922
25   Fred Hoyles, Wimbledon tennis referee-in-chief, 1976-82, born 1 October 1923
30   Salvatore Burruni, world champion boxer, born 11 April 1933

April 2004

4   Alberic Schotte, Belgian cyclist, born 7 September 1919
5   Fred Winter, racehorse trainer and champion jockey, born 20 September 1926
7   Robert Sangster, racehorse owner and breeder, born 23 May 1936
12   Ronnie Adams, winner of the 1956 Monte Carlo Rally, born 8 March 1916
    Herbert Barnes, first torchbearer for the Wembley Olympics of 1948, born 2 December 1910
19   Ronnie Simpson, footballer, born 11 October 1930
    George Hardwick, footballer, born 2 February 1920
24   Willie Watson, cricketer and footballer, born 7 March 1920
25   Eddie Hopkinson, goalkeeper, born 29 October 1935
30   Jeff Butterfield, rugby player, born 9 August 1929

May 2004

11   Alf Valentine, West Indian cricketer, born 28 April 1930

June 2004

3   Joe Carr, Irish amateur golfer, born Joseph Benedict Waters, 18 February 1922
6   Jock West, motorcycle racing champion, born 28 February 1909

July 2004

17   Pat Roach, professional wrestler and actor, born 19 May 1937
28   Bob Tisdall, athlete, born 16 May 1907

August 2004

4   Alec Stewart, racehorse trainer, born 21 June 1955
6   Gordon Smith, footballer, born 5 May 1924

Olympic Games: British Gold Medallists

Name		Sport	Event
Abrahams, Harold	1924	Athletics	100m
Ainslie, Ben	2000	Sailing	Laser class
Ainsworth-Davis, Jack	1920	Athletics	4 × 400m relay
Allhusen, Derek	1968	Equestrian	3-day event team
Amoore, Edward	1908	Shooting	small-bore rifle team
Applegarth, Willie	1912	Athletics	4 × 100m relay
Aspin, John	1908	Yachting	12m class
Astor, J.J.	1908	Rackets	men's doubles
Atkin, Charles	1920	Hockey	
Attrill, Louis	2000	Rowing	eights
Bacon, Stanley	1908	Wrestling	middleweight freestyle
Badcock, Felix	1932	Rowing	coxless fours
Bailey, Horace	1908	Football	
Baillon, Louis	1908	Hockey	
Barber, Paul	1988	Hockey	
Barrett, Edward	1908	Tug of war	
Barrett, Frederick	1920	Polo	
Barrett, Roper	1908	Lawn tennis	doubles, indoor men's
Barridge, J.E.	1900	Football	
Bartlett, Charles	1908	Cycling	100km track race
Batchelor, Steve	1988	Hockey	
Beachcroft, Charles	1900	Cricket	
Beesly, Richard	1928	Rowing	coxless fours
Belville, Miles	1936	Yachting	6m class
Bennett, Charles	1900	Athletics	1500m
	1900	Athletics	5000m team
Bennett, John	1920	Hockey	
Bentham, Isaac	1912	Swimming	water polo team
Beresford, Jack	1924	Rowing	single sculls
	1932	Rowing	coxless fours
	1936	Rowing	double sculls
Beresford, John	1900	Polo	
Berry, Arthur	1908	Football	
	1912	Football	
Bevan, Edward	1928	Rowing	coxless fours
Bhaura, Kulbir	1988	Hockey	
Bingley, Norman	1908	Yachting	7m class
Birkett, Arthur	1900	Cricket	
Blackstaffe, Harry	1908	Rowing	single sculls
Boardman, Chris	1936	Yachting	6m class
Boardman, Chris	1992	Cycling	4000m pursuit
Bond, David	1948	Yachting	Swallow class
Bowerman, Alfred	1900	Cricket	
Braithwaite, Bob	1968	Shooting	clay pigeon
Brasher, Chris	1956	Athletics	3000m steeplechase
Brebner, Ron	1912	Football	
Brown, Godfrey	1936	Athletics	4 × 400m relay
Buchanan, John	1908	Yachting	12m class
Buckenham, Claude	1900	Football	
Buckley, George	1900	Cricket	
Bucknall, Henry	1908	Rowing	eights
Budgett, Richard	1984	Rowing	coxed fours
Bugbee, Charlie	1912	Swimming	water polo team
	1920	Swimming	water polo team
Bullen, Jane	1968	Equestrian	3-day event team
Bunten, James	1908	Yachting	12m class
Burchell, Francis	1900	Cricket	
Burgess, Edgar	1912	Rowing	eights
Burghley, Lord David	1928	Athletics	400m hurdles
Burn, Tom	1912	Football	
Burnell, Charles	1908	Rowing	eights
Burnell, Richard	1948	Rowing	double sculls
Bushnell, Bertie	1948	Rowing	double sculls
Butler, Guy	1920	Athletics	4 × 400m relay

Campbell, Charles	1908	Yachting	8m class
Campbell, Colin	1920	Hockey	
Canning, George	1920	Tug of war	
Carnell, Arthur	1908	Shooting	small-bore rifle
Cassels, Harold	1920	Hockey	
Chalk, Alfred	1900	Football	
Chapman, Frederick	1908	Football	
Christian, Fred	1900	Cricket	
Christie, Linford	1992	Athletics	100m
Clift, Robert	1988	Hockey	
Clive, Lewis	1932	Rowing	coxless pairs
Coales, Bill	1908	Athletics	3 miles team
Cochrane, Blair	1908	Yachting	8m class
Coe, Sebastian	1980	Athletics	1500m
	1984	Athletics	1500m
Coe, Tom	1900	Swimming	water polo team
Coleman, Robert	1920	Yachting	7m class
Cook, Stephanie	2000	Modern pentathlon	
Cooke, Harold	1920	Hockey	
Cooper, Charlotte	1900	Lawn tennis	women's singles
	1900	Lawn tennis	mixed doubles
Cooper, Malcolm	1984	Shooting	small-bore rifle, 3 positions
	1988	Shooting	small-bore rifle, 3 positions
Corbett, Walter	1908	Football	
Corner, Harry	1900	Cricket	
Cornet, George	1908	Swimming	water polo team
	1912	Swimming	water polo team
Cracknell, James	2000	Rowing	coxless fours
Crichton, Charles	1908	Yachting	6m class
Crockford, Eric	1920	Hockey	
Cross, Martin	1984	Rowing	coxed fours
Crummack, Rex	1920	Hockey	
Cudmore, Collier	1908	Rowing	coxless fours
Cuming, Fred	1900	Cricket	
Currie, Lorne	1900	Yachting	open class
	1900	Yachting	0.5-1 ton class
Daly, Denis	1900	Polo	
D'Arcy, Vic	1912	Athletics	4 × 100m relay
Davies, Chris	1972	Yachting	Flying Dutchman class
Davies, Lynn	1964	Athletics	long jump
De Relwyskow, George	1908	Wrestling	lightweight freestyle
Deakin, Joe	1908	Athletics	3 miles team
Dean, Billy	1920	Swimming	water polo team
Dennis, Simon	2000	Rowing	eights
Derbyshire, Rob	1900	Swimming	water polo team
	1908	Swimming	4 × 200m freestyle relay
Dines, Joe	1912	Football	
Dixon, Charles	1912	Lawn tennis	doubles, indoor mixed
Dixon, Richard	1908	Yachting	7m class
Dod, William	1908	Archery	York round
(brother of Lottie)			
Dodds, Richard	1988	Hockey	
Doherty, Laurie	1900	Lawn tennis	men's singles
	1900	Lawn tennis	men's doubles
Doherty, Reggie	1900	Lawn tennis	men's doubles
(brother of Laurie Doherty)	1900	Lawn tennis	men's doubles
	1908	Lawn tennis	men's doubles
Donne, William	1900	Cricket	
Douglas, Johnny	1908	Boxing	middleweight
Douglas, Rowley	2000	Rowing	coxed eight
Downes, Arthur	1908	Yachting	12m class
Downes, Henry	1908	Yachting	12m class
(brother of Arthur Downes)			
Dunlop, David	1908	Yachting	12m class
Easte, Philip	1908	Shooting	clay pigeon team
Eastlake-Smith, Gladys	1908	Lawn tennis	singles, indoor women's
Edwards, Jonathan	2000	Athletics	triple jump
Edwards, Jumbo	1932	Rowing	coxless pairs
	1932	Rowing	coxless fours
Eley, Maxwell	1924	Rowing	coxless fours
Elliot, Launceston	1896	Weightlifting	one-handed lift
Ellison, Adrian	1984	Rowing	coxed fours (cox)

Etherington-Smith, Raymond	1908	Rowing	eights
Exshaw, William	1900	Yachting	2-3 ton class
Faulds, Richard	2000	Shooting	double trap
Faulkner, David	1988	Hockey	
Fenning, John	1908	Rowing	coxless pairs
Field-Richards, John	1908	Motor boating	8m class
Finnegan, Chris	1968	Boxing	Middleweight
Fleming, John	1908	Shooting	small-bore rifle, moving target
Fleming, Philip	1912	Rowing	eights
Fletcher, Jennie	1912	Swimming	4 × 100m freestyle relay
Forsyth, Charlie	1908	Swimming	water polo team
Foster, Bill	1908	Swimming	4 × 200m freestyle relay
Foster, Tim	2000	Rowing	coxless fours
Fox, Jim	1976	Modern pentathlon	team event
Freeman, Harry	1908	Hockey	
Garcia, Russell	1988	Hockey	
Garton, Stanley	1912	Rowing	eights
George, Rowland	1932	Rowing	coxless fours
Gillan, Angus	1908	Rowing	coxless fours
	1912	Rowing	eights
Gladstone, Albert	1908	Rowing	eights
Glen-Coats, Thomas	1908	Yachting	12m class
Godfree, Kitty	1920	Lawn tennis	women's doubles
Goodfellow, Fred	1908	Tug of war	
Goodhew, Duncan	1980	Swimming	100m breaststroke
Gordon-Watson, Mary	1972	Equestrian	3-day event team
Gore, Arthur	1908	Lawn tennis	singles, indoor men's
	1908	Lawn tennis	doubles, indoor men's
Gosling, William	1900	Football	
Grace, Fred	1908	Boxing	lightweight
Green, Eric	1908	Hockey	
Green, Tommy	1932	Athletics	50km walk
Gretton, John (serving MP)	1900	Yachting	open class
	1900	Yachting	0.5-1 ton class
Griffiths, Cecil	1920	Athletics	4 × 400m relay
Grimley, Martyn	1988	Hockey	
Grinham, Judy	1956	Swimming	100m backstroke
Grubor, Luka	2000	Rowing	eights
Gunn, Dick	1908	Boxing	featherweight
Gunnell, Sally	1992	Athletics	400m hurdles
Halswelle, Wyndham	1908	Athletics	400m
Hampson, Tommy	1932	Athletics	800m
Hannam, Edith	1912	Lawn tennis	singles, indoor women's
	1912	Lawn tennis	doubles, indoor mixed
Hanney, Ted	1912	Football	
Hardman, Harry	1908	Football	
Harmer, Russell	1936	Yachting	6m class
Harrison, Audley	2000	Boxing	super heavyweight
Haslam, A.	1900	Football	
Haslam, Harry	1920	Hockey	
Hawkes, Robert	1908	Football	
Hemery, David	1968	Athletics	400m hurdles
Herbert, Garry	1992	Rowing	coxed pairs (cox)
Hill, Albert	1920	Athletics	800m
	1920	Athletics	1500m
Hill, Arthur	1912	Swimming	water polo team
Hill, Bertie	1956	Equestrian	3-day event team
Hillyard, George	1908	Lawn tennis	men's doubles
Hirons, Bill	1908	Tug of war	
Hoare, Gordon	1912	Football	
Hodge, Percy	1920	Athletics	3000m steeplechase
Holman, Fred	1908	Swimming	200m breaststroke
Holmes, Andy	1984	Rowing	coxed fours
	1988	Rowing	coxless pairs
Holmes, Fred	1920	Tug of war	
Horsfall, Ewart	1912	Rowing	eights
Humby, Harry	1908	Shooting	small-bore rifle team
Humphreys, Fred	1908	Tug of war	
	1920	Tug of war	
Hunt, Kenneth	1908	Football	
Hunt-Davis, Ben	2000	Rowing	eights
Ireton, Albert	1908	Tug of war	

Jacobs, David	1912	Athletics	4 × 100m relay
Jarvis, John Arthur	1900	Swimming	1000m freestyle
	1900	Swimming	4000m freestyle
Johnson, Victor	1908	Cycling	one-lap race
Johnstone, Banner	1908	Rowing	eights
Jones, Ben	1908	Cycling	5000m track race
	1908	Cycling	3-lap pursuit team
Jones, Ben	1968	Equestrian	3-day event team
Jones, Chris	1920	Swimming	water polo team
Jones, J.H.	1900	Football	
Keene, Foxhall	1900	Polo	
Kelly, Fred	1908	Rowing	eights
Kemp, Peter	1900	Swimming	water polo team
Kerly, Sean	1988	Hockey	
Kingsbury, Clarrie	1908	Cycling	20km track race
	1908	Cycling	3-lap pursuit
Kinnear, Wally	1912	Rowing	single sculls
Kirby, Alister	1912	Rowing	eights
Kirkwood, Jimmy	1988	Hockey	
Knight, Arthur	1912	Football	
Lambert-Chambers, Dolly	1908	Lawn tennis	women's singles
Lance, Tommy	1920	Cycling	2000m tandem
Lander, John	1928	Rowing	coxless fours
Larner, George	1908	Athletics	3500m
	1908	Athletics	10 mile walk
Laurie, Ran	1948	Rowing	coxless pairs
Laws, Gilbert	1908	Yachting	6m class
Leaf, Charles	1936	Yachting	6m class
Leighton, Arthur	1920	Hockey	
Leman, Richard	1988	Hockey	
Lessimore, Edward	1912	Shooting	small-bore rifle team, 50m
Lewis, Denise	2000	Athletics	heptathlon
Liddell, Eric	1924	Athletics	400m
Lindsay, Andrew	2000	Rowing	eights
Lindsay, Robert	1920	Athletics	4 × 400m relay
Lister, Bill	1900	Swimming	water polo team
Littlewort, Henry	1912	Football	
Llewellyn, Sir Harry	1952	Equestrian	Prix des Nations team
Lockett, Vivian	1920	Polo	
Logan, Gerald	1908	Hockey	
Lonsbrough, Anita	1960	Swimming	200m breaststroke
Lowe, Douglas	1924	Athletics	800m
	1928	Athletics	800m
McBryan, Jack	1920	Hockey	
MacDonald-Smith, Iain	1968	Yachting	Flying Dutchman class
McGrath, George	1920	Hockey	
Macintosh, Henry	1920	Athletics	4 × 100m relay
McIntyre, Mike	1988	Yachting	Star class
McKenzie, John	1908	Yachting	12m class
Mackay, Frank (USA born)	1900	Polo	
MacKinnon, Duncan	1908	Rowing	coxless fours
Mackworth-Praed, Cyril	1924	Shooting	running deer (double shot)
MacLagen, Gilchrist	1908	Rowing	eights
McMeekin, Tom	1908	Yachting	6m class
Macnabb, James	1924	Rowing	coxless fours
McNair, Winifred	1920	Lawn tennis	women's doubles
McTaggart, Dick	1956	Boxing	lightweight
McWhirter, Douglas	1912	Football	
Maddison, W.J.	1920	Yachting	7m class
Mallin, Harry	1920	Boxing	middleweight
(retired undefeated after 300 fights)	1924	Boxing	middleweight
Marcon, Sholto	1920	Hockey	
Martin, Albert	1908	Yachting	12m class
Martin, Leonard	1936	Yachting	6m class
Martin, Steve	1988	Hockey	
(played 1 minute)			
Matthews, Ken	1964	Athletics	20km walk
Matthews, M.K.	1908	Shooting	small bore rifle team
Maunder, Alex	1908	Shooting	clay pigeon team
Meade, Richard	1968	Equestrian	3-day event team
	1972	Equestrian	3-day event team
Melvill, Tim	1920	Polo	

Meredith, Leon	1908	Cycling	3-lap pursuit
Merriman, Fred	1908	Tug of war	
Miller, Charles	1908	Polo	
Miller, George	1908	Polo	
(brother of Charles Miller)			
Millner, Jerry	1908	Shooting	free rifle
Mills, Edwin	1908	Tug of war	
	1920	Tug of war	
Mitchell, Harry	1924	Boxing	light heavyweight
Moore, Bella	1912	Swimming	4 × 100m freestyle relay
Moore, F.W.	1908	Shooting	clay pigeon team
Moorhouse, Adrian	1988	Swimming	100m breaststroke
Morris, Stewart	1948	Yachting	swallow class
Morrison, Robert	1924	Rowing	coxless fours
Morton, Lucy	1924	Swimming	200m breaststroke
Murray, Robert	1912	Shooting	small-bore rifle team
Neame, Philip	1924	Shooting	running deer (double shot)
Nevinson, George	1908	Swimming	water polo team
Newall, Queenie	1908	Archery	national round
Nicholas, J.	1900	Football	
Nickalls, Guy	1908	Rowing	eights
Nickalls, Patteson	1908	Polo	
Nightingale, Danny	1976	Modern pentathlon	team event
Noble, Alan	1908	Hockey	
Noel, Evan	1908	Rackets	singles
O'Kelly, Con	1908	Wrestling	heavyweight freestyle
Oldman, Albert	1908	Boxing	heavyweight
Osborn, John	1976	Yachting	Tornado class
Ovett, Steve	1980	Athletics	800m
Packer, Ann	1964	Athletics	800m
Page, Edgar	1908	Hockey	
Palmer, Charles	1908	Shooting	clay pigeon team
Pappin, Veryan	1988	Hockey	
Parker, Adrian	1976	Modern pentathlon	team event
Parker, Bridget	1972	Equestrian	3-day event team
Pattisson, Rodney	1968	Yachting	Flying Dutchman class
	1972	Yachting	Flying Dutchman class
Payne, Ernest	1908	Cycling	3-lap pursuit
Peacock, Bill	1920	Swimming	water polo team
Pennell, Vane	1908	Rackets	men's doubles
Pepe, Joseph	1912	Shooting	small-bore rifle team, 50m
Percy, Ian	2000	Sailing	Finn class
Perry, Herbert	1924	Shooting	running deer (double shot)
Peters, Mary	1972	Athletics	Pentathlon
Phillips, Mark	1972	Equestrian	3-day event team
Pike, J.F.	1908	Shooting	clay pigeon team
Pimm, William	1908	Shooting	small-bore rifle team
	1912	Shooting	small-bore rifle team, 50m
Pinsent, Matthew	1992	Rowing	coxless pairs
	1996	Rowing	coxless pairs
	2000	Rowing	coxless fours
Postans, J.M.	1908	Shooting	clay pigeon team
Potter, Jonathan	1988	Hockey	
Powlesland, Alfred	1900	Cricket	
Pridmore, Reggie	1908	Hockey	
Purcell, Noel	1920	Swimming	water polo team
Purnell, Clyde	1908	Football	
Quash, Bill	1900	Football	
Queally, Jason	2000	Cycling	1km sprint
Radmilovic, Paul	1908	Swimming	water polo team
	1908	Swimming	4 × 200m freestyle relay
	1912	Swimming	water polo team
	1920	Swimming	water polo team
Rampling, Godfrey	1936	Athletics	4 × 400m relay
Rand, Mary	1964	Athletics	long jump
Rawlinson, Alfred	1900	Polo	
Rawson, Ronald	1920	Boxing	heavyweight
Redgrave, Steve	1984	Rowing	coxed fours
	1988	Rowing	coxless pairs
	1992	Rowing	coxless pairs
	1996	Rowing	coxless pairs
	2000	Rowing	coxless fours

Redwood, Bernard	1908	Motor boating	8m class
	1908	Motor boating	under 60ft class
Rees, Percy	1908	Hockey	
Rhodes, John	1908	Yachting	8m class
Rimmer, J.T.	1900	Athletics	4000m steeplechase
	1900	Athletics	5000m team
Ritchie, Major	1908	Lawn tennis	men's singles
Rivett-Carnac, Charles	1908	Yachting	7m class
Rivett-Carnac, Frances	1908	Yachting	7m class
(wife of Charles Rivett-Carnac)			
Roberts, Bill	1936	Athletics	4 × 400m relay
Robertson, Arthur	1908	Athletics	3 miles team
Robertson, Arthur	1900	Swimming	water polo team
Robertson, Shirley	2000	Sailing	Europe dinghy class
Robinson, Eric	1900	Swimming	water polo team
Robinson, John	1908	Hockey	
Robinson, Sidney	1900	Athletics	5000m team
Rook, Laurence	1956	Equestrian	3-day event team
Russell, Arthur	1908	Athletics	3200m steeplechase
Ryan, Harry	1920	Cycling	2000m tandem
Sanders, Terence	1924	Rowing	coxless fours
Sanderson, Ronald	1908	Rowing	eights
Sanderson, Tessa	1984	Athletics	Javelin
Scarlett, Fred	2000	Rowing	eights
Searle, Greg	1992	Rowing	coxed pairs
Searle, Jonny	1992	Rowing	coxed pairs
Sewell, John	1912	Tug of war	
	1920	Tug of war	
Sharpe, Ivan	1912	Football	
Sheen, Gillian	1956	Fencing	individual foil
Shepherd, John	1908	Tug of war	
	1920	Tug of war	
Sherwani, Imran	1988	Hockey	
Shoveller, Stanley	1908	Hockey	
	1920	Hockey	
Smith, Charles	1908	Swimming	water polo team
	1912	Swimming	water polo team
	1920	Swimming	water polo team
Smith, Faulder	1920	Hockey	
Smith, Herbert	1908	Football	
Somers-Smith, John	1908	Rowing	coxless fours
Southwood, Dick	1936	Rowing	double sculls
Spackman, F.G.	1900	Football	
Spiers, Annie	1912	Swimming	4 × 100m freestyle relay
Spinks, Terry	1956	Boxing	flyweight
Stamper, Harry	1912	Football	
Stapley, Henry	1908	Football	
Steer, Irene	1912	Swimming	4 × 100m freestyle relay
Stewart, Douglas	1952	Equestrian	Prix des Nations team
Stiff, Harry	1920	Tug of war	
Strode-Jackson, Arnold	1912	Athletics	1500m
Styles, William	1908	Shooting	small-bore disappearing target
Sutton, Henry	1908	Yachting	8m class
Swann, Sidney	1912	Rowing	eights
Symes, John	1900	Cricket	
Tait, Gerald	1908	Yachting	12m class
Taylor, Henry	1908	Swimming	400m freestyle
	1908	Swimming	1500m freestyle
	1908	Swimming	4 × 200m freestyle relay
Taylor, Ian	1988	Hockey	
Thomas, Harry	1908	Boxing	bantamweight
Thompson, Daley	1980	Athletics	decathlon
	1984	Athletics	decathlon
Thompson, Don	1960	Athletics	50km walk
Thomson, Gordon	1908	Rowing	coxless pairs
Thorne, Ernie	1920	Tug of war	
Thornycroft, Tom	1908	Motor boating	8m class
	1908	Motor boating	under 60ft class
Thould, Tom	1908	Swimming	water polo team
	1912	Swimming	water polo team
Toller, Montague	1900	Cricket	
Trapmore, Steve	2000	Rowing	eights

Turnbull, Noel	1920	Lawn tennis	men's doubles
Turner, R.R.	1900	Football	
Tysoe, Alf	1900	Athletics	800m
	1900	Athletics	5000m team
Vaile, Bryn	1988	Yachting	Star class
Voigt, Emil	1908	Athletics	5 miles
Walden, Harry	1912	Football	
Warriner, Michael	1928	Rowing	coxless fours
Weldon, Frank	1956	Equestrian	3-day event team
Wells, Allan	1980	Athletics	100m
Wells, Henry	1912	Rowing	eights (cox)
West, Kieran	2000	Rowing	eights
White, Reg	1976	Yachting	Tornado class
White, Wilf	1952	Equestrian	Prix des Nations team
Whitlock, Harold	1936	Athletics	50km walk
Whitty, Allen	1924	Shooting	running deer (double shot)
Wilkie, David	1976	Swimming	200m breaststroke
Wilkinson, Cyril	1920	Hockey	
Wilkinson, George	1900	Swimming	water polo team
	1908	Swimming	water polo team
	1912	Swimming	water polo team
Wilson, Herbert	1908	Polo	
Wilson, Jack	1948	Rowing	coxless pairs
Wodehouse, Lord John	1920	Polo	
Wolff, Freddie	1936	Athletics	4 × 400m relay
Wood, Arthur	1908	Yachting	8m class
Wood, Harvey	1908	Hockey	
Woodward, Vivian	1908	Football	
	1912	Football	
Woosnam, Max	1920	Lawn tennis	men's doubles
Wormald, Leslie	1912	Rowing	eights
Wright, Cyril	1920	Yachting	7m class
Wright, Dorothy	1920	Yachting	7m class
(wife of Cyril Wright)			
Wright, Gordon	1912	Football	
Zealey, Jim	1900	Football	

Note: Irish gold medal winners such as Thomas Kiely (1904 decathlon) and Tim Ahearne (1908 triple jump) have been omitted from the above list although when they won their medals Ireland was under British rule.

BBC SPORTS PERSONALITIES OF THE YEAR

1954
1 Chris Chataway (athletics)
2 Roger Bannister (athletics)
3 Pat Smythe (equestrian)

1955
1 Gordon Pirie (athletics)
No record of 2nd and 3rd

1956
1 Jim Laker (cricket)
No record of 2nd and 3rd

1957
1 Dai Rees (golf)
No record of 2nd and 3rd

1958
1 Ian Black (swimming)
2 Bobby Charlton (football)
3 Nat Lofthouse (football)

1959
1 John Surtees (motorcycling)
2 Bobby Charlton (football)
3 Ian Black (swimming)

1960
1 David Broome (showjumping)
2 Don Thompson (athletics)
3 Anita Lonsbrough (swimming)

1961
1 Stirling Moss (motor racing)
2 Billy Walker (boxing)
3 Angela Mortimer (tennis)

1962
1 Anita Lonsbrough (swimming)
2 Dorothy Hyman (athletics)
3 Linda Ludgrove (swimming)

1963
1 Dorothy Hyman (athletics)
2 Bobby McGregor (swimming)
3 Jim Clark (motor racing)

1964
1 Mary Rand (athletics)
2 Barry Briggs (speedway)
3 Ann Packer (athletics)

1965
1 Tommy Simpson (cycling)
2 Jim Clark (motor racing)
3 Marion Coakes (showjumping)

1966
1 Bobby Moore (football)
2 Barry Briggs (speedway)
3 Geoff Hurst (football)

1967
1 Henry Cooper (boxing)
2 Beryl Burton (cycling)
3 Geoff Hurst (football)

1968
1 David Hemery (athletics)
2 Graham Hill (motor racing)
3 Marion Coakes (show jumping)

1969
1 Ann Jones (tennis)
2 Tony Jacklin (golf)
3 George Best (football)

1970
1 Henry Cooper (boxing)
2 Tony Jacklin (golf)
3 Bobby Moore (football)

1971
1 Princess Anne (equestrian)
2 George Best (football)
3 Barry John (rugby union)

1972
1 Mary Peters (athletics)
2 Gordon Banks (football)
3 Richard Meade (equestrian)

1973
1 Jackie Stewart (motor racing)
2 Roger Taylor (tennis)
3 Paddy McMahon (showjumping)

1974
1 Brendan Foster (athletics)
2 John Conteh (boxing)
3 Willie John McBride (rugby union)

1975
1 David Steele (cricket)
2 Alan Pascoe (athletics)
3 David Wilkie (swimming)

1976
1 John Curry (ice skating)
2 James Hunt (motor racing)
3 David Wilkie (swimming)

1977
1 Virginia Wade (tennis)
2 Geoff Boycott (cricket)
3 Barry Sheene (motorcycling)

1978
1 Steve Ovett (athletics)
2 Daley Thompson (athletics)
3 Ian Botham (cricket)

1979
1 Sebastian Coe (athletics)
2 Ian Botham (cricket)
3 Kevin Keegan (football)

1980
1 Robin Cousins (ice skating)
2 Sebastian Coe (athletics)
3 Daley Thompson (athletics)

1981
1 Ian Botham (cricket)
2 Steve Davis (snooker)
3 Sebastian Coe (athletics)

1982
1 Daley Thompson (athletics)
2 Alex Higgins (snooker)
3 Steve Cram (athletics)

1983
1 Steve Cram (athletics)
2 Jayne Torvill/Christopher Dean (ice skating)
3 Daley Thompson (athletics)

1984
1 Jayne Torvill/Christopher Dean (ice skating)
2 Sebastian Coe (athletics)
3 Steve Davis (snooker)

1985
1 Barry McGuigan (boxing)
2 Ian Botham (cricket)
3 Steve Cram (athletics)

1986
1 Nigel Mansell (motor racing)
2 Fatima Whitbread (athletics)
3 Kenny Dalglish (football)

1987
1 Fatima Whitbread (athletics)
2 Steve Davis (snooker)
3 Ian Woosnam (golf)

1988
1 Steve Davis (snooker)
2 Adrian Moorhouse (swimming)
3 Sandy Lyle (golf)

1989
1 Nick Faldo (golf)
2 Frank Bruno (boxing)
3 Steve Davis (snooker)

1990
1 Paul Gascoigne (football)
2 Stephen Hendry (snooker)
3 Graham Gooch (cricket)

1991
1 Liz McColgan (athletics)
2 Will Carling (rugby union)
3 Gary Lineker (football)

1992
1 Nigel Mansell (motor racing)
2 Linford Christie (athletics)
3 Sally Gunnell (athletics)

1993
1 Linford Christie (athletics)
2 Sally Gunnell (athletics)
3 Nigel Mansell (motor racing)

1994
1 Damon Hill (motor racing)
2 Sally Gunnell (athletics)
3 Colin Jackson (athletics)

1995
1 Jonathan Edwards (athletics)
2 Frank Bruno (boxing)
3 Colin McRae (rallying)

1996
1 Damon Hill (motor racing)
2 Steve Redgrave (rowing)
3 Frankie Dettori (horse racing)

1997
1 Greg Rusedski (tennis)
2 Tim Henman (tennis)
3 Steve Redgrave (rowing)

1998
1 Michael Owen (football)
2 Denise Lewis (athletics)
3 Iwan Thomas (athletics)

1999
1 Lennox Lewis (boxing)
2 David Beckham (football)
3 Colin Jackson (athletics)

2000
1 Steve Redgrave (rowing)
2 Denise Lewis (athletics)
3 Tanni Grey-Thompson (wheelchair athletics)

2001
1 David Beckham (football)
2 Ellen MacArthur (sailing)
3 Michael Owen (football)

2002
1 Paula Radcliffe (athletics)
2 David Beckham (football)
3 Tony McCoy (horse racing)

2003
1 Jonny Wilkinson (rugby union)
2 Martin Johnson (rugby union)
3 Paula Radcliffe (athletics)